ENCYCLOPAEDIA JUDAICA

ENCYCLOPAEDIA JUDAICA

SECOND EDITION

VOLUME 1
Aa–Alp

Fred Skolnik, *Editor in Chief*
Michael Berenbaum, *Executive Editor*

MACMILLAN REFERENCE USA
An imprint of Thomson Gale, a part of The Thomson Corporation

IN ASSOCIATION WITH
KETER PUBLISHING HOUSE LTD., JERUSALEM

THOMSON
GALE

Detroit • New York • San Francisco • New Haven, Conn. • Waterville, Maine • London

THOMSON

GALE

ENCYCLOPAEDIA JUDAICA, Second Edition

Fred Skolnik, *Editor in Chief*
Michael Berenbaum, *Executive Editor*
Shlomo S. (Yosh) Gafni, *Editorial Project Manager*
Rachel Gilon, *Editorial Project Planning and Control*

Thomson Gale
Gordon Macomber, *President*
Frank Menchaca, *Senior Vice President and Publisher*
Jay Flynn, *Publisher*
Hélène Potter, *Publishing Director*

Keter Publishing House
Yiphtach Dekel, *Chief Executive Officer*
Peter Tomkins, *Executive Project Director*

Complete staff listings appear on pages 33-36

For more information, contact
Macmillan Reference USA
An imprint of Thomson Gale
27500 Drake Rd.
Farmington Hills, MI 48331-3535
Or you can visit our internet site at
http://www.gale.com

LIBRARY OF CONGRESS CATALOGING-IN-PUBLICATION DATA

Encyclopaedia Judaica / Fred Skolnik, editor-in-chief ; Michael Berenbaum, executive editor. -- 2nd ed.
v. cm.
Includes bibliographical references and index.
Contents: v.1. Aa-Alp.
ISBN 0-02-865928-7 (set hardcover : alk. paper) -- ISBN 0-02-865929-5 (vol. 1 hardcover : alk. paper) -- ISBN 0-02-865930-9 (vol. 2 hardcover : alk. paper) -- ISBN 0-02-865931-7 (vol. 3 hardcover : alk. paper) -- ISBN 0-02-865932-5 (vol. 4 hardcover : alk. paper) -- ISBN 0-02-865933-3 (vol. 5 hardcover : alk. paper) -- ISBN 0-02-865934-1 (vol. 6 hardcover : alk. paper) -- ISBN 0-02-865935-X (vol. 7 hardcover : alk. paper) -- ISBN 0-02-865936-8 (vol. 8 hardcover : alk. paper) -- ISBN 0-02-865937-6 (vol. 9 hardcover : alk. paper) -- ISBN 0-02-865938-4 (vol. 10 hardcover : alk. paper) -- ISBN 0-02-865939-2 (vol. 11 hardcover : alk. paper) -- ISBN 0-02-865940-6 (vol. 12 hardcover : alk. paper) -- ISBN 0-02-865941-4 (vol. 13 hardcover : alk. paper) -- ISBN 0-02-865942-2 (vol. 14 hardcover : alk. paper) -- ISBN 0-02-865943-0 (vol. 15: alk. paper) -- ISBN 0-02-865944-9 (vol. 16: alk. paper) -- ISBN 0-02-865945-7 (vol. 17: alk. paper) -- ISBN 0-02-865946-5 (vol. 18: alk. paper) -- ISBN 0-02-865947-3 (vol. 19: alk. paper) -- ISBN 0-02-865948-1 (vol. 20: alk. paper) -- ISBN 0-02-865949-X (vol. 21: alk. paper) -- ISBN 0-02-865950-3 (vol. 22: alk. paper)
1. Jews -- Encyclopedias. I. Skolnik, Fred. II. Berenbaum, Michael, 1945-
DS102.8.E496 2007
909'.04924 -- dc22

2006020426

ISBN-13:
978-0-02-865928-2 (set)
978-0-02-865929-9 (vol. 1)
978-0-02-865930-5 (vol. 2)
978-0-02-865931-2 (vol. 3)
978-0-02-865932-9 (vol. 4)
978-0-02-865933-6 (vol. 5)
978-0-02-865934-3 (vol. 6)
978-0-02-865935-0 (vol. 7)
978-0-02-865936-7 (vol. 8)
978-0-02-865937-4 (vol. 9)
978-0-02-865938-1 (vol. 10)
978-0-02-865939-8 (vol. 11)
978-0-02-865940-4 (vol. 12)
978-0-02-865941-1 (vol. 13)
978-0-02-865942-8 (vol. 14)
978-0-02-865943-5 (vol. 15)
978-0-02-865944-2 (vol. 16)
978-0-02-865945-9 (vol. 17)
978-0-02-865946-6 (vol. 18)
978-0-02-865947-3 (vol. 19)
978-0-02-865948-0 (vol. 20)
978-0-02-865949-7 (vol. 21)
978-0-02-865950-3 (vol. 22)

This title is also available as an e-book
ISBN-10: 0-02-866097-8
ISBN-13: 978-0-02-866097-4
Contact your Thomson Gale representative for ordering information.
Printed in the United States of America

10 9 8 7 6 5 4 3 2

PREFACE TO THE SECOND EDITION

In the past thirty-five years the *Encyclopaedia Judaica* has come to occupy a rarefied space in the world of Jewish learning. Authoritative, comprehensive, serious yet accessible, it graced the library shelves of scholars and rabbis, of the learned and the studious, and even of the would-be studious, consulted by the curious and the inquisitive, an important starting point for a journey of learning.

It also was that rare work in Jewish life and learning that covered controversy and yet was not controversial. It could not be identified with one school of thought, with one religious, political, or social perspective. Written by Zionists who believed ardently in Jewish peoplehood and the centrality of the land of Israel and the renascent State of Israel for the Jewish future, it also respected the many forms that Jewish life had taken. It performed its task admirably, sharing with the reader what was known and knowable in 1972, the year when it was first published. For a time through Year Books and Decennial volumes, it sought to update its readers on more recent learning, trends, and issues, and for the first time in 1997 it migrated to an electronic version with a wonderful search engine that freed the reader from taking volumes off the shelf and moving from the index to yet another volume.

So we understood as we embarked upon the task of updating the masterful work that much could be lost. We were also confident of what could be gained.

Why a new edition?

The answer is quite simple. Knowledge is dynamic, not static. Much has changed in the last thirty-five years.

Israel of 2006 is quite different from Israel of 1972, when Golda Meir was prime minister. Israel has faced two wars – the war of 1973 (Yom Kippur War) and the war in Lebanon – two Intifadas, the Camp David Accords, the withdrawal from Sinai, the Oslo Accords, the Disengagement, the rise of militant radical Islam, and so much more. Israel has become the home of almost half the world's Jewish population, absorbing Jews from the former Soviet Union, from Ethiopia, Argentina, France, and elsewhere. Soon a majority of the world's Jews will live in Israel, which has become a regional military superpower and a developed country in an increasingly globalized world. Israeli culture has been transformed and its institutions have evolved. Quite simply, the Israel described in 1972 is unrecognizable today.

The Soviet Union is no longer. Lithuania, Latvia, and Estonia have become independent countries; so too have the Ukraine and many of the former Soviet Republics. Jewish life has been transformed by these changes. The Iron Curtain has fallen and thus the Jews of Poland and Hungary, of the Czech Republic and Slovakia live under different conditions; and their world – the possibilities of their world – has changed. East and West Germany have been reunited and the German Jewish community – which once lived with a fascinating past that had been eclipsed by its catastrophic recent history but had no discernible future – is now growing rapidly as it has become home to many Jewish immigrants from the former Soviet Union.

In the United States, Las Vegas and Phoenix are growing most rapidly as Jewish communities as tens of thousands of Jews have moved to these Sun Belt cities and built not only new homes but also new institutions and new environments. Southern Florida has become the third most populated area of Jewish settlement. In the rural South, where Jews had lived for a century or more, synagogues have become museums, thus marking the end of many small communities, while the Jewish population of Atlanta and Jewish life in Atlanta, Dallas, and Houston have expanded dramatically. Once Jewish Day Schools were the province of Orthodox Jews living in major cities. They can now be found wherever there is a significant Jewish population and they serve the entire spectrum of those interested in Jewish learning. In light of such developments, each entry on the fifty states had to be updated; so too the entries on each of the cities in which almost all of American Jews reside.

Religiously, American Jewry has evolved dramatically. Orthodoxy is no longer in danger of extinction but confident and self-sustaining. It is no longer characterized by loss but by gains, and modern Orthodoxy, which once appeared dominant, has been sliding to the right. Chabad has developed as a global presence to be encountered wherever Jews live, wherever Jews travel. It has endured the passing of the Rebbe, centralized charismatic leadership has been replaced by management and by the charisma and dedication of many individual leaders. It has endured a messianic crisis. Liberal forms of Judaism have become more diverse, more creative and more diffuse. New institutions for the training of rabbis have evolved and the neat tripartite division of Jews – Orthodox, Conservative and Reform – has become far more fascinating as multiple forms of Jewish identity and Jewish engagement have become available. Reconstructionist Judaism has created its own institutions; even the anti-institutional world of Renewal Judaism is creating institutions of its own with its own journals, its own publishing house and its own rabbinical and cantorial schools. Non-denominational rabbinical seminaries are flourishing. Rural Jews gather for conferences; Jewish life is alive and flourishing in cyberspace as well as real space, even as a more individualized and less institutionalized Jewish identity takes root.

American Jews live in a world with few barriers, with no glass ceilings. Their Jewishness is not regarded as a handicap but a privilege; highly individualized for many, celebrated or even ignored, it takes a variety of forms and expresses itself in many creative endeavors. The editors of this new edition of the *Encyclopaedia Judaica* are acutely conscious of these changes, both in the choice of individual entries and in the description of various Jewish communities. But along with this extraordinarily positive picture, American Jewry is in the decline numerically; simply put, American Jews are not reproducing, and the rate of intermarriage exceeds even the most alarming predictions of a generation ago. Survivalists are deeply concerned about survival, about the viability of the American Jewish community, in part because of the freedom it enjoys. And with freedom comes the easy freedom not to identify as a Jew, for one is not forced to identify as a Jew. One can embrace any number of other identities, professional and personal, without betrayal.

Yet there is a cross fertilization between Israel and the United States. American Jewish scholars spend sabbatical years in Israel, many have studied in Israel as part of their undergraduate and graduate training, and Israeli scholars spend significant time in the Diaspora. They read each other's work; they publish in each other's journals. Scholarly works initiated in Israel are published in English and American scholarship is read in Israel and often translated into Hebrew.

Thirty-five years ago the women's movement was just beginning and all rabbis were men. Feminist Studies as a discipline was but in its infancy and women were not considered by many an integral part of the Jewish community or the Jewish experience. Much has changed, and this new edition represents a deliberate attempt to include women and the experience of women within its pages; the inclusion was not for inclusion's sake but because we cannot understand Jews or the Jewish experience without understanding the role of Jewish women. Permit a simple example. An earlier entry on "Mikveh" considered Jewish religious teaching on the mikveh and its halakhic requirements. A woman's perspective was not included, which we now understand was a serious omission, one not repeated in this volume.

A new generation has arisen and, with each new generation, new scholarly questions are asked, new methodologies are employed. Thus, even though the giants of the last generation played an important role in editing the *Encyclopaedia Judaica*, extraordinary scholars such as Professors Gershom Scholem, Salo Baron, Menachem Stern, H.L. Ginzburg, and Cecil Roth among others, the fields they developed and in some cases pioneered have moved beyond them; their findings have been built upon, their methodologies refined, enhanced, expanded, and disputed, and the result transforms our understanding even of the fields they illuminated so masterfully a generation ago. We have endeavored to preserve much of their original writing, to add what must be added, to refine where refinement was in order and to change what must be changed with the passage of time. Thus, even while the masterful work of Gershom Scholem has been preserved in its entirety, the intellectual discussion he initiated has gone well beyond his work and his students and their students have begun to ask different questions and reach different conclusions, as is reflected in the second edition addendum to his classic Kabbalah entry. The presentation of the historicity of the Talmud (see below) takes cognizance of the important work of

Jacob Neusner and David Weiss Halivni and others as well as Saul Lieberman and Efraim Urbach.

The generation that created the first edition of the *Encyclopaedia Judaica* was primarily trained in Germany in the great institutions and the extraordinary culture of the Weimar Republic or at the Hebrew University of Jerusalem, perhaps the greatest German university outside of Germany. Alas, that generation has passed. Many of the scholars who wrote for this edition were trained in the United States and, even if trained in Israel, were influenced by the dominance of American culture and American scholarship. Native-born Israel-trained scholars have written with brilliant competence. Historians dominated the first edition; in this new work, the approach of scholars even in the field of Judaic Studies is far more multi-disciplinary.

Entries written for the first edition had to be written differently for the second edition for their fields had evolved in the ensuing decades. Special treatment is accorded to the subject of Jewish Law (Mishpat Ivri) under the direction of Justice Menachem Elon, where it is now possible to examine the principles of Jewish religious law (*halahkah*) as they are reflected in the courts of a sovereign Jewish state. Elon, who had pioneered this field, has expanded his treatment of Jewish law as it has grown in the recent past, confronted new questions and grappled with issues unknown thirty-five years ago.

Certain dramatic changes have occurred within the most classical of fields of studies. As our Bible editor notes:

"Modern critical Bible study as it arose in the 19th century was often couched in terminology affirming that the Old Testament was inferior to the New Testament and that Judaism had been superseded by Christianity. Some notable Christian biblicists were also antisemites. As a result *Wissenschaft des Judentums*, 'the scientific study of Judaism,' neglected the critical study of the Bible. At Reform Judaism's Hebrew Union College and Conservative Judaism's Jewish Theological Seminary it took years before critical study of the Bible was fully embraced. Similarly, the Hebrew University of Jerusalem opened with a chair in biblical exegesis rather than Bible proper. To some extent the first edition of the *Encyclopaedia Judaica* retained this gingerly approach to Bible so that in contrast to most subject areas, apologetic writing was not always discouraged. By the 1990s the American and Israeli Jewish communities had reached a level of self-confidence and maturity that permitted even Orthodox scholars to participate fully in the critical study of the Hebrew Bible. In addition, the 20th century witnessed renewed interest in the great Bible commentators of medieval times. Largely neglected in early modern critical Bible scholarship, these commentaries, which anticipated modern 'discoveries' are regularly studied by contemporary Biblicists, Jewish and Christian." Critical literary studies of the Bible not only dissect the Bible by pointing to the sources of its composition, but consider it as an integrated whole which must be read as one work.

The editors of our Talmud division note that the past thirty years have seen a number of developments in talmudic studies, which required the significant revision of many of the first edition entries dealing with talmudic and midrashic literature. First of all, since the 1970s, we have been witness to a dramatic increase in the study of talmudic literature, not just within the rapidly expanding world of academic Judaic studies, but even more so among the public at large. Many new editions and translations in nearly all branches of talmudic and midrashic literature have been published, often accompanied by reliable and user-friendly commentaries. These in turn have opened up the study of the Mishnah, the Talmud, and other related texts to a wide audience of interested non-professional students. Many of the core entries in the previous edition of the *Encyclopaedia* were written with a pronounced bias toward the agenda of professional scholarship, and it has been one of our concerns both to widen this agenda and to provide the necessary foundation in order to make entries accessible to the public at large (see, for example, Mishnah and Talmud, Babylonian). At the same time two developments in academic scholarship have also had an impact on editorial policy. First of all, the application of modern critical historical methodology to the field of Aggadah and rabbinic biography has brought about no less than a revolution in the attitude toward talmudic and midrashic traditions concerning the lives and deeds of the rabbis (see Aggadah). This profound development has led to the revision of well over a hundred entries describing the lives of greater and lesser rabbinic figures (e.g. Eliezer ben Hyrcanus, Beruryah, Imma Shalom, Johanan ben Zakkai, Meir, Elisha ben Avuyah, Johanan ben Nappaḥa, etc.), while numerous traditional biographies of lesser rabbinic figures who have yet to be critically reexamined have been reproduced intact. Secondly, the increasing sophistication of critical and historical tools for the analysis of talmudic literature as a whole has brought about an equally profound revolution in our understanding of the internal historical development of this literature, and specifically of the relationships between parallel traditions found in the different finished talmudic works (see, for example, Tosefta; Talmud, Babylonian – The Bavli and the Extant Tannaitic Works, The Bavli and the Yerushalmi). The description and dating of the various talmudic compositions – Mishnah, Tosefta, the halakhic and aggadic Midrashim, the Babylonian and Jerusalem Talmudim – included in the earlier edition of the *Encyclopaedia* could not, of course, have taken these new developments into account. As a result, all of the entries dealing with this literature were reviewed, and in many cases (e.g. the Midrashei Halakhah) thoroughly revised.

Judaic Studies in the United States was limited thirty-five years ago. The Association of Jewish Studies had just been founded; its members knew each other. Positions were few. Membership has since then increased a hundredfold, and interest in Jewish Studies is wide throughout the Diaspora, as it has come to be seen as an essential component of Western civilization, though not just of Western civilization. American-trained Judaic Studies academics are on the faculty of every Israeli university, often holding distinguished chairs, so the cross fertilization of Israeli and American scholarship is a daily fact of life in both countries.

My own field of Holocaust Studies was but in its infancy thirty-five years ago. The scholars were mostly survivors or refugees writing of their experience. Many archives were closed, records were unavailable, many survivor memoirs had not yet been written and one could convene a meeting of the significant figures in the field in a conference room large enough for a dozen people. Holocaust Studies as a field could be confined to several paragraphs, a few major works, and an occasional conference. There was no major museum and no Holocaust educational resource centers, no sense of a "Holocaust industry." With the passage of time came the insights of time. There was a more personal intensity to the scholarly battles of the first generation, as many had lived through the events. The works of Bruno Bettelheim, who wrote of the infantalization of the victim; of Hannah Arendt, who condemned Jewish leadership in the Holocaust; and of Raul Hilberg, whose magisterial work minimized the role of Jewish resistance, severely stung. In response, other Jewish scholars fought back angrily, defensively, as if the pride of the living seemingly could be enhanced by a positive depiction of the conduct of the dead. In the past thirty-five years, records were declassified, documents from the former Soviet Union and elsewhere became available as so many archives were opened. Documents and copies of originals could be read in Washington, New York, and Jerusalem and not just Warsaw, Budapest, or Berlin. We have broadened our perspective and sought to come to terms with the dynamics of a growing field of study. And the contributions to this new edition reflect how much more is now known about an event that was in the immediate past thirty-five years ago.

From time to time, as we worked with the vastness of this material, colleagues and friends – especially our children – would ask what place an encyclopedia holds in the world of the web, where access to information is instantaneous and the web so vast. We have endeavored to preserve the sense of authority of the original edition – its reliability. We were mindful of the fact that this work would be consulted for years and years; thus, it is intended to be more than a snapshot of what is known at this time; its insights are meant to withstand the passage of time. Still, in a generation or two, when scholars and students want to know what was known in the first decade of the 21st century, who were the Jews, what they thought, how they lived, they will be able do no better than to consult this work and to understand its ramifications.

The *Encyclopaedia Judaica* grapples with Jews and Judaism, how Jews live, how they perceive themselves, how they encounter the world and shape the world they encounter. From medicine to mysticism, from resurgent Ḥasidism to renewal Judaism, from economics to science, from politics to art, music, theater, and cinema, even cartoons and comedy, sports and entertainment, we have endeavored to be comprehensive and creative.

Keter Publishing House and Macmillan Library Reference (an imprint of Thomson Gale), the publisher and distributor, respectively, of the first edition of the *Encyclopaedia Judaica,* initiated this project. Under the watchful eye of Peter Tomkins, Keter turned to the Jerusalem Publishing House, which has long been known for initiating encyclopedias in many languages all over the world, to organize the project. Frank Menchaca initiated this project for Macmillan, Hélène Potter was assigned to bring it to life. When Menchaca went on to even higher levels of management,

Hélène Potter capably filled the vacuum. Jay Flynn has been entrusted with the all important task of bringing this work to completion.

The scope of a second edition of the *Encyclopaedia* was far too large to be covered by minor revisions and cosmetic updates – too much had changed, too much more had become known. In sum, as the project evolved, half of the original entries had to be changed; more than 2,650 were added.

Over time, it also became clear that an American editor would have to be added to the core staff, to work with Jerusalem-based editor-in-chief Fred Skolnik. Shlomo (Yosh) Gafni, president of the Jerusalem Publishing House (JPH), and his managing editor Rachel Gilon, were a source of guidance and wisdom, with the assistance of Leonardo Szichman, who executed the huge data control. JPH undertook the difficult task of coordinating this project with enormous energy, skill, and dedication. Fred Skolnik was indefatigable and so wonderfully skilled. Associated with the Judaica for 35 years, he was both its champion and the driving force in its enlargement and transformation.

The writers of the *Encyclopaedia* are many. They write with passion and confidence of the fields they know, of the persons, the ideas and the issues they describe. Many could write – and have written – volumes on their subjects. Here they were asked to be concise and precise, to write in a manner that reflected what is known, to avoid polemics, to be scrupulously fair. We have endeavored not only to furnish important details but also to present them in an interesting manner, knowing that, unlike the stuff of journalism, which will not be read tomorrow, this work will be read by many on many tomorrows. It has to endure the test of time.

This edition is a unique partnership. Initiated by Israelis, it brought together Israelis and Americans and scholars from many different countries and many spheres of learning. It took cognizance of the centrality of Israel in the contemporary Jewish world but also of the enduring life, creative vitality, and intensity of the Jewish experience in the Diaspora. It was mindful of the many forms that Jewish life has taken and the diverse ways in which Jews have contributed to their people and the world.

It has been built on a strong foundation; time and again the editors have come to appreciate how comprehensive and authoritative was the work of their predecessors. We have endeavored to take the work of our predecessors forward in the ongoing quest for knowledge and understanding of the Jewish experience.

Michael Berenbaum
Executive Editor

TABLE OF CONTENTS

GENERAL INTRODUCTION

The *Encyclopaedia Judaica*, first published in 1972, has a long history, antedated by a number of predecessors. The English-language *Jewish Encyclopedia*, the first complete work of this nature, appeared in New York at the beginning of the 20th century (its twelfth and final volume was published in 1906). This pioneering work summed up the state of Jewish scholarship and the condition of the Jewish world at the time. It was an extraordinary achievement – especially if one considers the relatively small numbers of the English-speaking and English-reading Jewish population at the time. It was able, however, to call upon the collaboration of Jewish scholars in many countries – in particular the representatives of the Wissenschaft des Judentums, the School of Scientific Jewish Scholarship, then at its height. There were aspects that it tended to overlook or underplay, such as the world of East European Jewry, Kabbalah and Ḥasidism, Yiddish language and literature, and the life and culture of the Jews in Muslim lands, but seen as a whole, it was a monumental work incorporating many entries which became classic statements on their subject. The 16-volume Russian Jewish encyclopedia *Yevreyskaya Entsiklopediya*, which also appeared before World War I, was well conceived and in some respects brilliantly edited. Particularly outstanding was its expertise on East European Jewish subjects. The 10-volume Hebrew *Oẓar Yisrael* (1924), an almost single-handed achievement by J.D. Eisenstein, was on a far smaller scale and had less rigorous standards, although in certain areas its articles presented useful material.

At the time of the revival of Jewish interest and learning in Germany after World War I, Jacob Klatzkin, Ismar Elbogen, and Nahum Goldmann planned a new encyclopedia in the German language. This was intended to incorporate the results of the intervening years of intensive scholarship and research, to reflect the intellectual attitudes which had become established during this period, and to correct certain imbalances found within the *Jewish Encyclopedia*. Klatzkin and Goldmann gathered a galaxy of scholars to produce a new work. This work – called *Encyclopaedia Judaica* – progressed notwithstanding the obstacles and difficulties of those troubled times, until the Nazis rose to power in Germany. Publication had to be suspended after Volume 10 (completing the letter L), leaving incomplete this last monument of the intellectual greatness of German Jewry. Under the same auspices, a Hebrew version – the *Eschkol* encyclopedia – appeared, but only two volumes were issued. Mention should also be made of the five-volume *Juedisches Lexikon*, edited by Georg Herlitz and Bruno Kirschner, published by the Juedischer Verlag in 1927–30. Although more modest in scope than the other works mentioned, it made a useful contribution to Jewish studies and also paid more attention than its predecessors to illustrative material.

In the five first years of World War II the *Universal Jewish Encyclopedia*, edited by Isaac Landman, was issued in the United States in 10 volumes. It was able to reflect the growing importance of U.S. Jewry and to take into account late developments, especially in American Jewish history and biography. It had considerable merits, but was not an ambitious work. Moreover the fact that it was published in a period of major transition in itself set a limit to its utility. It was, however, the *Universal Jewish Encyclopedia* which constituted the basis of the 10-volume Spanish-language *Enciclopedia Judaica Castellana* produced in Mexico between 1948 and 1951. The major contribution of this latter work lay in its original entries dealing with the development of Jewish life in Latin America.

After the establishment of the State of Israel, the Hebrew language *Encyclopaedia Hebraica* began to be published in Jerusalem by the Massada Publishing Company, directed by the Peli family. This was the first large-scale general encyclopedia in the Hebrew language – and naturally it emphasized the Jewish aspects of various subjects, some of them of high scholarly importance and in certain cases even pioneering studies in their field. But though it contains the elements of a Jewish encyclopedia, it was not – nor was it intended to be – a Jewish encyclopedia as such.

The Development of the Encyclopaedia Judaica

For many years, and especially since the cataclysmic events in Jewish history of the 1940s, the need had been felt for an entirely new Jewish encyclopedia, especially in the English language for English-speaking Jewry, who now accounted for about half of the Jews of the world. Furthermore the survivors of the editorial board of the German *Encyclopaedia Judaica* had always been determined that the Nazi attack on their work could not be accepted as a final defeat and that the unfinished publication must be completed. However, they too recognized that now only a relatively small proportion of the Jewish people had access to a work in German and that any new endeavor in this field must be, first and foremost, in English. Dr. Nahum Goldmann, the last active survivor of the original board of editors, had long had this objective.

Initial funding of the project was made possible through an allocation obtained by Dr. Goldmann from the German reparations fund earmarked for cultural purposes. The Rassco Company in Israel also became interested and provided some of the funds during the early stages. In the U.S., the *Encyclopaedia Judaica* Research Foundation was established to raise further support for the project.

During this early period, when the preliminary work was centered in the U.S.,

Prof. Benzion Netanyahu (father of Israeli Prime Minister Binyamin Netanyahu), then editor of the *Encyclopaedia Hebraica*, served as editor in chief. The main editorial offices were established in Philadelphia in 1963.

In 1965 Prof. Netanyahu was compelled through pressure of work to retire from his post, and the editorial center was transferred to Jerusalem. This move was regarded as advisable because Jerusalem had become the unquestioned pivot of Jewish studies in the world, with the greatest concentration of scholars in the subject as well as possessing unrivaled research facilities. Moreover it was now the home of Prof. Cecil Roth, who had been appointed to succeed Prof. Netanyahu as editor in chief.

The publishing responsibility was assumed by the Israel Program for Scientific Translations (at that time an Israel government corporation, later owned by CLAL Israel Investment Company Ltd.). The Israel Program for Scientific Translations had already begun diversifying its publishing program and subsequently set up the Keter Publishing House Ltd. under whose imprint the *Encyclopaedia* appeared. In the U.S. the *Encyclopaedia Judaica* also appeared for a limited time with the imprint of Macmillan under an agreement by which the Macmillan Company would distribute the *Encyclopaedia* in the Western Hemisphere. The financing of the *Encyclopaedia* during the five years of actual work in which it was produced in Israel was made possible initially by a generous loan from the United States government out of counterpart funds available in Israel at a nominal interest. This was supplemented by a considerable investment made by the publisher to bring the project to a successful conclusion.

Work started in earnest in 1967 and a period of five years was allocated for the completion of the entire *Encyclopaedia*. It was decided early on that with well-planned organization and by proper exploitation of technological advances it would be possible to achieve the highly desirable goal of publishing the entire *Encyclopaedia* at one time. This would obviate the time gap inevitable in works that appear gradually, avoid the frustration of having the first volumes of a series but not the continuation to which references are made, and make possible the simultaneous publication of an index volume which the editors saw as basic and indispensable to the whole work.

To complete the *Encyclopaedia* within the given time, it was decided to adopt the principle of maximum subdivision so as to involve the greatest number of editors and contributors. The subject matter was broken down into some 20 divisions and these were again subdivided into departments. Some divisions had only two or three departments, but others included many more – 35 in the history division and more than 70 in the division dealing with the participation of Jews in world culture.

The general flow of an entry was from the contributor to the departmental and divisional editors, then to the central office for translation (where necessary), checking, styling, transliterating and bibliographical verification, approval by the relevant associate editor and by the editors in chief, and then back to the contributor for his approval of the final version (in cases where substantial editorial changes had been inserted). Finally the entry was sent to the index department and then to press.

A number of outstanding scholars served as consulting editors. They advised the *Encyclopaedia* staff in their fields of specialization when requested, but did not bear any editorial responsibility. Nor did any departmental, divisional, or associate editor or deputy editor in chief have any editorial responsibility for the contents of the *Encyclopaedia* apart from those which were his own direct responsibility. The final responsibility for all entries rested with the editors in chief.

Dr. Geoffrey Wigoder was appointed deputy editor in chief and the various divisions were grouped into sections each headed by an associate editor. The associate editors – Prof. Louis Rabinowitz, Prof. Raphael Posner, Dr. Binyamin Eliav, and Mr. Simḥa Katz – together with the editor in chief and his deputy constituted the editorial board. After the death of Prof. Roth in 1970, Dr. Wigoder was appointed editor in chief. The New York office was headed by Dr. Frederick Lachman, who coordinated the departments and divisions whose editors were in North America. Working parallel with those preparing the text was the illustrations and graphics department headed by Mr. Moshe Shalvi. This complex administration was directed by Mrs. Rachel Sabbath. The immensity of the operation can best be illustrated by the fact that apart from the 300 editors and 1,800 contributors with whom contact was maintained, the *Encyclopaedia* employed an internal staff of 150 – not including those who worked on the printing and binding stages. The entire publishing operation was directed by Mr. Yitzhak Rischin, managing director of the Keter Publishing House Ltd.

The Year Books and Decennial Books

It was obvious on the publication of the *Encyclopaedia Judaica* that to maintain its usefulness a mechanism would have to be found to ensure that it remained up to date. The method chosen was the periodic publication of Year Books. These incorporated feature articles on subjects of current interest in the Jewish world as well as extensive photo spreads on relevant topics. Many entries were updated, notably the major countries of Jewish settlement which received special consideration in each volume. Moreover new entries were devoted to personalities, organizations, Jewish studies, and other items that had come into the news or to public attention since the publication of the *Encyclopaedia*.

The Yearbooks continued to be published by Keter Publishing Company and the editors included Rabbi Louis I. Rabinowitz, Professor Pinchas Peli, Dr. Geoffrey Wigoder, and Ms. Fern Seckbach.

In addition, two special Decennial books covering the decades preceding 1982 and 1992 were published, incorporating and supplementing Year Book material.

The CD-ROM Edition

The CD-ROM edition, appearing in 1997, included the complete text of the original 16-volume edition of the *Encyclopaedia Judaica*, as well as the subsequent Year Books and the Decennials published in 1982 and 1992. In the limited time allotted for the *Encyclopaedia Judaica* CD-ROM project, there was no possibility for updating the entire work. Rather, the entire content of the *Encyclopaedia Judaica* was reviewed editorially and items selected for update or expanded coverage, under the supervision of Dr. Geoffrey Wigoder, as editor in chief, together with Fern Seckbach, as deputy editor in chief.

The Second Edition

With the need acutely felt to bring the *Encyclopaedia* into the 21st century, it was now determined to produce a thoroughly revised and updated new edition of the *Encyclopaedia* with the accumulated material in the CD-ROM as its starting point. Accordingly, Thomson Gale signed a licensing agreement with the Keter Publishing House and work on the second edition commenced in August 2003. The project was concluded editorially in the first months of 2006, though last-minute emendations continued to be made until the *Encyclopaedia* went to press in the autumn of 2006. It employed over 50 divisional editors and around 1,200 contributors from all around the world.

To prepare the second edition all entries were systematically reviewed by the divisional editors to select those requiring updating, revision, or rewriting and to propose new entries. Those selected were assigned to the appropriate scholars and writers and the process culminated in the review and editing of all entries received from the contributors. At the end of the process, about half of the original entries had been revised and about 2,650 new entries were produced. In addition, around 30,000 new bibliographical items were added. In all, 4.7 million new words were written for the second edition.

Principles of Selection

An obvious problem in the compilation of any encyclopedia is the decision as to which entries are to be included and which excluded. For the first edition, guidelines were drawn up as a result of which certain subjects were earmarked for definite inclusion while others clearly fell short. But there is always a body of "borderline" entries which potentially could fall in either category. This problem becomes particularly sensitive when dealing with biographies of contemporaries. Which scholars receive entries and which do not? Where is the line to be drawn for rabbis or businessmen or lawyers or scientists?

The Editorial Board laid down general principles, but was fully aware of the potential risk of inconsistency. The Editorial Board considered the entire entry list and paid special attention to the "borderline" entries according to the principles of selection it determined.

Various methods and criteria were established. For example, editors were circumscribed by the word allocation. For example, the editors of the section on Jews in medicine listed many hundreds of Jews who had distinguished themselves in the field. They were asked to subdivide the list into those of major importance of whose inclusion there was no doubt; those who should appear if possible; and those who should at least be mentioned and characterized in the main entry. In this way, the maximum of names appear in the *Encyclopaedia*. But at the same time, it was obvious that along the borderline, different selections would be made by different experts. In certain categories, it is impracticable to talk about objective standards and an element of subjectivity must enter the final selection. This inevitably provides a happy hunting ground for discussion and criticism. However, it must be noted that the editors of this and any such work have no alternative in such instances but to rely on their judgment, formed after consultation with the expert editors and advisers in each field. With contemporary scholars, the tendency was to be more generous with the older generation, whose major work had been completed, and to be more selective with younger scholars who are in the process of producing their major works and where it is therefore more difficult to reach an assessment.

In some subjects, it was possible to fix objective criteria. For example when it came to U.S. Jewish communities, it was decided to include only those numbering more than 4,500 (although here too exceptions had to be made where the community has historical or other social importance). For places in Israel, it was decided that all municipalities would have their own entry as well as kibbutzim and moshavim which were in existence at the time of the establishment of the State in 1948. For those settlements founded subsequently, only those of special interest have their own entry. With regard to the kibbutzim, the process of "privatization" which most have undergone or are undergoing is not noted in each of the many kibbutz entries but rather discussed in general terms in the Kibbutz Movement entry.

In certain biographical entries a problem was to determine who was a Jew. The first principle adopted was that anyone born a Jew qualified for inclusion, even if he or she had subsequently converted or otherwise dissociated himself from Jewish life (where these facts are known, they are stated). The second principle was that a person with one Jewish parent would qualify for inclusion (with the relevant information stated) if he or she were sufficiently distinguished. A person whose Jewish origins were more remote would only be the subject of an entry in very unusual cases. However, a more generous attitude was taken in the case of Marranos, in view of the special circumstances surrounding their history.

A number of non-Jews are also the subject of entries in the *Encyclopaedia*. They have been included because of their relationship to Jewish life or culture (to avoid misunderstanding, the sign ° has been placed before their name at the head of the entry). These have been selected to ensure the completeness of the *Encyclopaedia*, for example in matters of history (e.g., Alexander the Great, Napoleon, Balfour, Stalin), philosophy and thought (e.g., Aristotle, Avicenna, Kant), or literature (e.g., Dante, Shakespeare, Goethe). In these cases, the entry concentrates only on those elements of the subject's life and thought which are of Jewish interest, and for a biography and assessment, the interested reader should refer to a general encyclopedia.

By and large the editors of the second edition have followed the above principles in selecting new subjects for inclusion in the *Encyclopaedia*. At the same time, given the widespread availability of perpetual Jewish calendars on the Internet, it was decided to omit this feature from the new edition. It was thought more beneficial to devote the space to additional text and such new features as the Thematic Outline (see below). On the whole, it has been the explicit aim of the editors to offer entries that the general as well as the specialized reader will expect to find in an encyclopedia of this nature.

Consistency

Notwithstanding all efforts, it has been impossible to maintain perfect consistency in the *Encyclopaedia Judaica*. For one thing, scholars who have written the entries have been allowed a certain latitude in incorporating their own conclusions and this leads occasionally to internal contradictions. For example there are differing views about biblical chronology. It is possible that a scholar writing on a king of ancient Israel may maintain a certain year to have been that of his death; another scholar writing about his successor may be of the view that he began to reign a few years earlier or later; while the author of the general survey of the period may give still different dates. Since the entire subject is a matter of conjecture and all scholars regard their own chronology as well founded, it is impossible to compel them to use dates with which they disagree. Wherever possible, such dates have been coordinated, but the editors are aware of such discrepancies, which must be seen against the differences of opinion among the scholars.

Similarly there can be inconsistencies regarding the transliteration of places and names. The name Leib represents the accepted English version of a Yiddish name; but many with that name who lived in German-speaking countries themselves wrote it Loeb, so that both forms are to be found in the *Encyclopaedia*. Accepted usage is followed in most cases, but there are many problems. In some instances, it is customary in English to anglicize names, such as those of foreign rulers: Empress Catherine – and not Yekaterina or Caterina; Frederick the Great – and not Friedrich; Victor Emmanuel – and not Vittorio Emmanuele. But usage differs in other instances: Christopher (not Cristóbal or Cristoforo) Columbus, but Johann (not John) Sebastian Bach, Leo (not Lev) Tolstoy, but Albrecht (not Albert) Duerer. Just as inconsistency occurs in general usage, so it occurs in specific Jewish contexts. It is common to adapt the better-known names into English and to write Salomon as Solomon or Josef as Joseph, but what about Salomone and Giuseppe? Biblical names have a familiar English form that has been accepted, but it would hardly be appropriate to anglicize Hebrew names in modern Israel and to refer to Moses Dayan.

Whether Slavic names should end with the form -ich, -icz, -itz, or -itch must depend on usage and not logic; and usage is sometimes confusing as, for example, when persons could have spelled their name according to German or Czech usage.

For a number of reasons (in part because of the ambiguity and interchangeability of the forms Aben and Ibn, but mainly because of the sheer weight of numbers) the *Encyclopaedia* has generally entered persons with quasi-surnames beginning with Ibn under the second name – but not in the case of accepted usage such as that of Abraham ibn Ezra who is always referred to as Ibn Ezra. Here too inconsistencies occur.

Problems have also arisen concerning the consistency of place names: the modern Slovakian town of Bratislava, for example, was famous in Jewish life as a center of scholarship as Pressburg, and is frequently referred to as such within a historical context. Both forms will therefore be found in the *Encyclopaedia*. In such instances the Index will prove an invaluable guide in coordinating the various references.

Certain concessions have led to inconsistencies with regard to Hebrew transliteration. Apart from the different systems that have been employed, common English usage has been taken into consideration in some cases. According to *Encyclopaedia* rules, the word for commandment should be transliterated *miẓvah* – but the spelling "bar mitzvah" has in fact passed into the English language as has "kibbutz" (not *kibbuẓ*) and matzah (or matzoh) and it is the accepted usage that has been adopted. Current Anglo-American usage refers, even in legislation, to ritually prepared food as "kosher" but in other contexts the term is transliterated according to Hebrew usage as *kasher*.

There are similar problems regarding the transliteration of terms in modern Hebrew which embody the "mobile *sheva*," which is normally not pronounced in the middle of a word in modern Hebrew. Thus the organization הִסְתַּדְּרוּת should be transliterated in accordance with the rules as *Histadderut*, but it is universally known as Histadrut. And then there are transliterations officially adopted by various bodies – the name of the Religious Zionist movement is Mizrachi by which it appears throughout the world, and so it appears in the *Encyclopaedia* even though according to the rules it should appear as *Mizraḥi*.

Inconsistencies also occur with regard to italicization. Foreign words are generally italicized – but not where they have become part of the English language, or are in German, French, Spanish, or Italian languages. But this too leads to anomalies. Yeshivah is now an English word and is not italicized; but the principal of a yeshivah is a *rosh yeshivah*, which is italicized. Ḥasidim have joyfully entered the English language, but their opponents, the *Mitnaggedim*, remain italicized outsiders.

Cross References and Glossary

The *Encyclopaedia* has been planned as a unit. To avoid unnecessary duplication, cross-references are made to complementary entries and the fullest treatment of any subject will be obtained by consulting both the cross-references given in any entry together with any other references listed under the subject in the Index. However, the *Encyclopaedia* has avoided a plethora of text cross-references which send the reader from volume to volume (such as Ribash see Midrash, Genesis Rabbah, Exodus Rabbah, etc.). Such information will be found by turning to the Index volume which gives all relevant references.

In the text, cross-references are indicated in two ways. The first is by the direct statement "See ..." referring to entries that have directly relevant additional information. The second is by the use of an asterisk (*). The asterisk is placed before the word under which the entry appears. Thus "Abraham *ibn Ezra" indicates that further information related to that entry is to be looked for in the article on Ibn Ezra.

In occasional instances the asterisk has been used to refer the reader to an entry in the Index rather than an article in the text.

Generally speaking, asterisks indicate those further entries which, it is felt, throw additional light on the subject under discussion. For example, in the statement "Benjamin Cardozo was born in New York," there is no cross-reference to New York, both because it is unnecessary and because the entry on New York contains no supplementary information on Cardozo. But the first reference to New York in the entry on "United States" will have a cross-reference because the New York entry in many ways supplements the "United States" entry. Occasional exceptions have been made where some more obscure name or phrase is mentioned, the explanation of which would unduly complicate the text. In most cases, only the first reference to a subject receives a cross-reference, but on occasions it is repeated for special reasons.

It is inevitable in a work of this nature to use a considerable number of Hebrew and technical terms which may not be familiar to the general reader. To explain these on every occasion would make the work far too cumbersome. Therefore, where necessary the cross-reference is given. However, for the convenience of the reader a glossary has been prepared of the most frequently recurring Hebrew terms and specialized names. This glossary is printed at the front of Volume 1, before the start of the entries and at the end of the text in volumes 2 through 21.

Transliteration

For its basic transliteration from the Hebrew, the *Encyclopaedia* has adopted a simplified system. It has been devised with particular regard to the usages of the English-speaking reader. However, certain exceptions have been necessary:

a) The editors of the section dealing with Hebrew and Semitic languages felt that the *Encyclopaedia*'s simplified system could not convey all the nuances required in technical linguistic entries. All entries in this section use the transliteration adopted by the Academy of the Hebrew Language. However, to avoid inconsistencies in proper names, the basic system used in the rest of the *Encyclopaedia* has also been retained for names in these entries.

b) The editors of the Bible section felt the need for a few modifications in the *Encyclopaedia*'s system in order to convey certain nuances. To preserve the maximum unity, these have generally been added in parentheses after the usual transliteration, although in certain cases where it makes no difference to the ordinary reader (use of ṭ in place of t), only one form has been given.

c) Other forms of transliteration will be found in some of the musical notations. This is in accordance with the system that has been developed so as best to print Hebrew transliteration together with music.

d) As already mentioned, in a few instances, Hebrew words have become part of the English language and their spelling standardized. In such cases, the term must be regarded by now as an English word, and the spelling in Webster's New International Dictionary (Third Edition) has been followed.

See accompanying tables regarding transliteration for Hebrew, Arabic, Yiddish, Greek, and Russian.

Furthermore, certain English usages have been taken into account inasmuch as certain words and names have received accepted English forms—for example Koran (rather than Qur'an), Saladin (rather than Salaḥ al-Din). Often, in place of the umlaut in German names an "e" has been added after the accented vowel – thus Koenigsberg, not Königsberg.

Bibliographies

The bibliography available for an entry is integral to the treatment of the subject as a whole. On the basis of these references, the reader who wishes to pursue the subject in greater depth can turn to these basic books and articles.

For the first edition a principle of selectivity had to be adopted in view of the vast amount of material that had accumulated. It had to be be recognized that the German language, in which so much of Jewish research was written, had become inaccessible to most Jewish students. On the other hand, a considerable body of scientific publication on Jewish subjects had now become available in English while the corresponding literature in Hebrew had assumed vast proportions.

Preference was thus given to works in the English language provided they were of an adequate scientific standard. Moreover, where translations were available in English they were listed in some cases in preference to a (generally German) original. However, exceptions were made in some cases where the English translation did not represent the entire original (e.g., in some sections of Graetz's *History of the Jews*). Generally, only the most important and significant works are listed. Full bibliographies can usually be found in the works referred to and where there is a full bibliography on the subject in a work cited, this fact is mentioned.

Many problems were encountered in the course of compiling the bibliography of the first edition, not all of which found an ideal solution. For example, there is the problem of which edition to cite – the first or latest? A book can have its first edition in England in a different form than its first U.S. edition – and even have a different name for each; an article can appear in a periodical and be reprinted as part of a book; many volumes are now being reprinted photographically and are designated as "second editions" although – where no extra material is added – this is inaccurate.

The organization of the bibliographies (basically supplied by the authors) is also not consistent. An attempt was made to give precedence to the major works on the subject and to works in English, while generally speaking, books precede articles. However, in certain cases other arrangements (e.g., chronological) were followed. In the first edition, names of articles in periodicals were usually not listed for reasons of space, but the author and full details of the periodical served to direct the reader to the major studies in such publications. For the bibliographical updates in the second edition of the *Encyclopaedia*, the editors have endeavored to supply full article titles. Bibliographical items added to updated or revised first edition entries are preceded by the heading "Add. Bibliography" in bold face and appear immediately after the old bibliography where one exists, unless the latter is arranged by subtopic. Bibliographies of entries new to the second edition are simply headed "Bibliography."

The standard histories – Graetz, Dubnow, Baron – have not been cited for every article, but only in those cases where they provide material of special significance for the subject in hand. Similarly, regarding individual countries, the standard regional histories have been mentioned only when specially called for and the reader should remember that they must be consulted.

Most of the bibliographical checking for the first edition was done at the Jewish National and University Library, Jerusalem. The unrivaled richness of its collection made possible a thorough investigation of most subjects dealt with and most works cited, but there were cases when certain works or editions were not available and the facts given by the contributor could not be verified.

To make the bibliographies less unwieldy a large number of standard works are quoted by abbreviation. A full list of these abbreviations will be found at the front of Volume 1 of the *Encyclopaedia* and the back of volumes 2 through 21. Such works can be distinguished in the bibliographies by the fact that their titles are not italicized.

Biographical Entries

The title entry for an individual is given according to the name by which he or she was most commonly known. Other names by which a person was known or versions of the name are also in the Index, allowing direct access to the entry, where the alternative names appear in parentheses following the entry title.

Wherever possible, biographical entries are given under the surname if the person had one. Where a combined rendering has become accepted in Europe (e.g., Abenatar) this is followed in the *Encyclopaedia*. In the case of Spanish and Portuguese names (e.g., Texeira de Mattos, Mendes da Costa), accepted usage is followed even though the first component of these names is the basic part.

The place of birth and death are not always given. The reason is that the information given customarily is in many cases conjectural, in others irrelevant. Places of birth are usually mentioned in the text when these have been found to be verifiable. Place of death is not mentioned unless there is a specific reason for giving it. Generally, it can be assumed that a subject died in the place where the person is last mentioned as having resided. To keep the entries within allotted proportions, places of education have generally been omitted as have details concerning awards such as honorary degrees, visiting professorships, prizes (except for major ones such as the Nobel Prize and the Israel Prize), promotion details (e.g., for military figures only the last rank attained is usually given), etc. Though the second edition has been more liberal in this respect, the above principles have generally been followed.

Family Entries

A single entry often covers various members of the same family. This has been especially the case when there are a number of members of the family who are of sufficient interest to warrant a description but where space would not allow individual entries. In such cases the various members are generally treated in chronological order within the entry. It often occurs that in such families there are several members mentioned in the body of the entry but one or two members are of exceptional importance, warranting a separate entry. In this case they are listed with few details in their appropriate chronological context within the family entry, together with an asterisk indicating that they are the subject of separate entries.

In certain instances, two or more members of the same family have been combined into a single entry. There are also examples of composite entries of several people with the same name as in the case, for example, of biblical persons and places where a single entry covers more than one person or place of the same name. In all such cases, each individual subject can be traced through the Index, where an individual listing will be found. If the family name is not repeated in the article following a personal name, it is understood that the name is identical with that of the title entry.

Special Terminology

In a few instances, the *Encyclopaedia* staff had to make decisions regarding the adoption of basic terminology. One such term is "Holocaust" referring to the fate of the Jews resulting from Nazi policies, from 1933 to 1945. Another is "Mishpat Ivri," familiarly called "Jewish Law."

Another is the use of the term Ereẓ Israel. The name Palestine was specifically created by the Romans in order to invalidate the association of the Jewish people with the country they had formerly called Judea. The name Palestine was virtually unknown even when the country was under Muslim (as well as Crusader) rule. The *Encyclopaedia* therefore terms the country by its proper name Ereẓ Israel (literally, the Land of Israel) using the term "Palestine" only in certain contexts (especially with regard to the later Roman period and to the period of the British Mandate when it was the official name of the country). This applies as well to such historical West Bank cities as Hebron, Jericho, and Nablus (Shechem), which are accordingly defined as cities in Ereẓ Israel.

Israel, on the other hand, generally implies in these pages the modern State of Israel. Since the origins of a great part of Israeli institutions and life go back to the 1880s, for certain purposes the term Israel is used retrospectively to this seminal period. For example, the section of the comprehensive entry Israel (by far the largest in the *Encyclopaedia*) headed "State of Israel" covers not only the period from 1948 but also the pre-State period. Though according to official government usage, Israel (and not Israeli) is the adjective relating to Israel and Israeli is a citizen (or permanent resident) of the State of Israel, in most cases "Israeli" has been also used as an adjective in compliance with common usage.

Israel's wars, discussed in the context of Israel's history, are given their Israeli nomenclatures. Thus, for example, Six-Day War for the war of 1967 and Yom Kippur War for the war of 1973.

The *Encyclopaedia* uses the term Jerusalem Talmud rather than Palestinian Talmud because although the latter is more accurate (the work was not written or compiled in Jerusalem) the former conveys the traditional Jewish title *Talmud Yerushalmi.*

Place Names

The basic guide for the form of place names in the first edition was the *Columbia Lippincott Gazetteer of the World* (Columbia University Press, 1966) and where various alternatives are cited there, the preferred form has been adopted. For the sake of consistency the same guidelines have been used for the second edition. Place names occurring in the Bible are given according to *The Holy Scriptures* (according to the Masoretic text; The Jewish Publication Society of America, 1955). Other places in Israel are cited according to the *Encyclopaedia*'s rules of transliteration. This has led to some inconsistencies in cases where ancient and modern places (not always on the same site) have identical names. Thus readers will find that some towns mentioned in the Bible will begin with Beth (e.g., Beth Shean) but others not mentioned there will begin with Bet (Bet She'arim). There will be a similar problem with "En" and "Ein."

Another problem with place names is that in many instances, places had different names at different periods. The usage of the *Encyclopaedia* is that where a place is still in existence, the entry appears under its current name (in a very few cases, an exception has been made where the alternative name is so strong in Jewish tradition that any variant would look bizarre). Variants are given at the beginning of the entry on the place and all these variants are cited in their appropriate places in the Index. When place names occur in the body of entries, it has often been necessary to change the usage according to the period. For example it would be absurd to talk of a person in "Wroclaw" in the first half of the 20th century – he was in Breslau; a book in the 18th century was published in Constantinople, not Istanbul.

A special problem was posed by East European names not to be found in the gazetteer. Many Jews were born or lived in small places which had a reputation in the Jewish world but are not large enough to figure in Western works of reference. Such places were identified in standard atlases and where necessary the *Encyclopaedia*'s regular rules of transliteration for the appropriate language were followed.

A number of major geographical changes have occurred since the original edition of the *Encyclopaedia Judaica* appeared, notably the break-up of the Soviet Union, Yugoslavia, and Czechoslovakia and the reunification of Germany. The reader is advised to look under both the original and former names of these countries. Thus, the major history of many members of the Commonwealth of Independent States (formerly the U.S.S.R.) will be found under Russia and only developments since their independence are under their particular name. Appropriate cross-references will be found in the text.

Proper Names

Some of the problems relating to consistency in the use of proper names have already been mentioned. As noted, the tendency has been to anglicize first names where appropriate. This has been done even though in certain instances the person himself did not use the form. Thus a German Jew would have signed himself (probably in Hebrew letters) as Schlomo or Salomon but – as is customary in standard works of reference in English – these all appear as Solomon.

Every effort has been made to give the spelling of the surname as the person himself spelled it – even if this means that the more usual Berdichevski appears as Berdyczewski and Moshe Glikson appears as Gluecksohn, these being the forms they themselves used. However, problems remain. What about a person who never signed his name, as far as is known, in Latin characters? For example, if such a person's name was רבינוביץ, is it to be transliterated Rabinowitz, Rabbinowitz, Rabbinowicz, Rabbinovich, Rabinovitch, or by any other of the known transliterations, all of which are legitimate? There is no ready-made answer. In some instances, there are precedents to follow; in others, the precedent has to be invented. We are aware that consistency has not always proved possible. Sometimes an apparent inconsistency is deliberate. A man living in a German-speaking country would have written his name Hirsch. But for a man with this name in Eastern Europe there is no reason to use a German form of transliteration; in such instances the rules of Yiddish (or familiar English) transliteration have been followed and the name appears as Hirsh.

Dates

The Hebrew year begins in the fall, three months approximately (in recent centuries) before the Gregorian year. Where the Hebrew year is known (but not the exact date) the probability is that the Gregorian date corresponds to the last nine months rather than the first three months of the Hebrew year. So the *Encyclopaedia* has normally used, e.g., 1298 and not 1297/98 to correspond to the Hebrew year 5058, etc. Where, however, the exact Hebrew date is known, it is possible to be more precise. Where precision is significant the form 1527/28 is used; this implies that the event took place in the Hebrew year 5388 but the period of the year cannot be determined. Before the Gregorian reform of the calendar in 1587 the secular-Christian New Year was considered in most places to have been in March; the Gregorian reform established January 1st but this was adopted only gradually in Europe. The *Encyclopaedia Judaica* assumes, however, in most cases (in accordance with modern historical practice) the beginning of the new year in January, even before the Gregorian reform. To avoid unnecessary complications, account has not been taken of the ten- (to 12- or 13-) day discrepancy between the Gregorian and Julian calendars, which has continued in some areas until our own day. (The 1917 revolutions in Russia are mostly called the February and October Revolutions, although by Western calendars they occurred in March and November.)

Statistics

The whole area of Jewish demography is highly problematical and in many cases precise numbers cannot be determined. Only in recent decades have systematic attempts been made to determine Jewish statistics. Moreover, different criteria have been adopted in different places, and results will vary with such factors as whether any sort of Jewish definition appears in an official census, whether the particular community has been subject to a scientific analysis – and how one defines a Jew! Occasional discrepancies are inevitable. Moreover, in the case of France and the former Soviet Union the problem has proven to be particularly acute. In the former case this derives from the reluctance of community leaders to publicize Jewish population figures. In the latter case, figures vary widely depending on the body producing them and the criteria used. In both cases, other than for the largest communities where current information is available, older figures are often used rather than arbitrary or unsubstantiated later figures. For U.S. communities, the 2001 figures appearing in the *American Jewish Year Book* have been used in the *Encyclopaedia*'s standardized state maps, together with the 2000 U.S. Census figures for the general population, with later figures given in the text where available.

Alphabetization

Entries have been arranged (both in the body of the *Encyclopaedia* and in the Index) in strict alphabetical order – disregarding spaces and hyphens. The criterion is the order of the letters up to the first punctuation sign (comma, period, etc.). This makes for easy reference as well as facilitating the work of the computer.

For example, Ben-Gurion should be sought somewhere after Benghazi and before Benjamin; El Paso will be after Elephantine but before Elul.

The following elements are not considered in alphabetization: definite and indefinite articles; personal titles (e.g., Sir or Baron), with the exception of "Saint"; material that appears in parentheses; the ordinal number of a monarch or pope. In the event of absolutely identical title entries, the following order of precedence prevails: places, people, things. Where persons have identical names, the one who lived earlier comes first. Where the same name is used as a first and family name, entries of the first name precede those of the family name.

For example in looking for an ABRAHAM one would find the order:

ABRAHAM (the patriarch)
ABRAHAM (family name)
ABRAHAM, APOCALYPSE OF (the comma after Abraham acting as a caesura)
ABRAHAM, MAX
ABRAHAM ABELE BEN ABRAHAM SOLOMON (considered as a unit in the absence of a comma)
ABRAHAM A SANCTA CLARA
ABRAHAM BAR HIYYA
ABRAHAM BEN ALEXANDER (note that "bar" and "ben" are considered as spelt in full)
ABRAHAM HAYYIM BEN GEDALIA
ABRAHAMITES
ABRAHAM JOSHUA HESCHEL OF APTA

ABRAHAM (ben Aaron) OF BAGHDAD (note that variants in parentheses are ignored for alphabetization purposes)
ABRAHAM OF SARAGOSSA
ABRAHAMS
ABRAHAMS, ISRAEL
ABRAHAMS, SIR LIONEL (note that titles such as Sir and Lord are ignored for alphabetization purposes)
ABRAHAMS, MOSES
ABRAHAM'S BOSOM
ABRAHAMSEN, DAVID
ABRAHAM ẒEVI BEN ELEAZER

Style

Although basing itself on standard rule of style, the *Encyclopaedia* has in many cases had to establish its own rules to meet its own particular requirements. Spelling was based on Webster's Third International Dictionary, except for a number of specific Jewish and Hebrew words. Italicization is used in the text for non-English words and phrases. (See also section on Consistency.)

Familiar abbreviations of rabbinical authorities (e.g., Rif for Isaac Alfasi or Rashba for Solomon ben Adret) are generally not employed in the text but are used in bibliographical references in articles on rabbinical literature and Jewish law (see section on Abbreviations). The exception here is Rashi (Rabbi Solomon Yiẓḥaki) who is so universally known by his acronym that it would be unnecessarily pedantic to insist on his full name in usual references to him. In other cases, a decision had to be made with regard to the form regularly used; thus the *Encyclopaedia* uses Maimonides rather than Moses ben Maimon or Maimuni and Naḥmanides rather than Moses ben Naḥman. Here again the reader should consult the aliases appearing in the alphabetized Index.

Illustrations

Supplementing the text are over 600 tables, maps, charts, and archaeological plans including a full list of Jewish settlements in Israel and detailed chronologies of Jewish history and of the Holocaust period, as well as an eight-page full-color insert in each volume illustrating all facets of Jewish life in hundreds of photographs. A special section of Holocaust photographs follows the main Holocaust entry.

Signatures and Contributors

Authors' names generally appear at the end of each entry. Where different contributors have written sections of an entry, their names are found at the end of the section they have written. When two (or more) contributions have been merged into a single article a joint signature appears at the end of the entry. Contributions to the second edition are indicated by the words (2nd ed.) after the contributor's name. However, in cases where updates or revisions to a first edition entry are minor, or only new bibliography has been added (see Bibliographies above), the second edition contributor has generally not been cited, lest the mistaken impression be created that the entry was a joint effort. Furthermore, with the removal of the ubiquitous "ED." (for "Editor") signature from first edition entries produced by the EJ editorial staff, such entries are now unsigned, unless the second edition update or revision was significant enough to warrant its attribution to the second edition contributor alone.

Information on the authors (as of the date of writing the entry) can be found in the List of Contributors along with a list of all entries partially or entirely written by each author.

For the first edition the *Encyclopaedia Judaica* received permission to utilize entries appearing in two other encyclopedias in other languages – the German *Encyclopaedia Judaica* and the Hebrew *Encyclopaedia Hebraica*. Where contributors of such entries were living, the English version was sent to them for their approval and where received, the author's initial is given. In a few cases, for one reason or another, the author was not available or not prepared to check the English version; in such cases the entries are merely signed [*Encyclopedia Judaica* (Germany)] or [*Encyclopaedia Hebraica*] to indicate that the source is to be found in these works. For the second edition, permission was received to use material from two other sources: Yad Vashem's *Pinkasei Kehillot* and its English abridgment (*Encyclopedia of Jewish Communities Before and During the Holocaust*) and *The Shorter Jewish Encyclopedia in Russian* (*Kratkoy Evreyskoy Entsiklopedii*). Material from these sources was incorporated into entries written and generally signed by second edition contributors.

Index

One of the highlights of the *Encyclopaedia* is its comprehensive index, originally edited by Prof. Raphael Posner for the first edition. This provides the key which unlocks the *Encyclopaedia* so that each detail becomes readily available for consultation. Ordinarily, an encyclopedia can be consulted only through the alphabetical list of entries. In the case of the *Encyclopaedia Judaica* this would give the reader some 22,000 subjects. With the aid of the Index the option is expanded more than eightfold, and the reader can at once see where information on topics that have not received independent entries but have been treated under other headings can be found. In addition a subject can be followed through all aspects of its treatment in the *Encyclopaedia*. For example, if the reader is interested in Maimonides, he or she will discover not only that there is a major entry on Maimonides but that there are further extensive treatments of Maimonides' thought and work in dozens of other entries – such as the entry *Mishpat Ivri* (Jewish Law), Philosophy, Medicine, Aristotle, Attributes, etc.

The Index is an indispensable tool for the use of the *Encyclopaedia* and the editors recommend that the reader always start by turning to it. Only by consulting the Index will he or she grasp the full treatment of any subject. (Where a person can be referred to under various names or pseudonyms, the Index will guide the reader to the relevant entry.) In planning the *Encyclopaedia*, the editors endeavored to maintain an overview of the complete work and to avoid overlapping, as far as possible. Without the Index, the reader would not be aware of the carefully planned structure of each subject and might conclude that certain important facets had been omitted or overlooked or that in certain cases treatment was inadequate. But by referring to the Index the user will immediately find out under what heading each subject is treated and where the supplementary aspects are dealt with.

It should be noted that the captions to the illustrations have also been indexed. Thus, under Israel, the reader will find page references to all maps and tables in the entry. In this way, the reader has easy access to all the visual material in the *Encyclopaedia*.

For full details on the Index and its use, the reader is referred to the Introduction to the Index in the Index volume.

Thematic Outline

The Thematic Outline, at the front of the Index volume, is an entirely new feature listing all entries in the *Encyclopaedia* under their appropriate subject headings, more or less corresponding to the *Encyclopaedia*'s editorial divisions. Thus, for example, a typical heading of this kind would be "Canada," broken down into Main Entries, General Entries, Community Entries, and Biographical Entries. For the larger divisions (U.S., Israel, Germany, etc.) biographical entries are further subdivided into Public and Economic Life, Academic Life, Popular Culture, Art, Science, etc. Many entries will appear under more than one heading. Scientists, for example, will appear under both the country they are identified with (or more than one country in certain cases) and the Science heading. As definitions are sometimes not clearcut, the existence of an entry can always be checked against the Index.

The aim of the Thematic Outline is to provide at a glance a picture of what is contained in the *Encyclopaedia* as well as to serve as a teaching and research tool showing all the entries available on a given subject.

Conclusion

The preparation of the second edition of the *Encyclopaedia Judaica* was a labor of devotion and dedication on the part of those responsible. It is the product of the diligent work of many hundreds of participants making very special efforts to ensure its successful conclusion. In this, they have been motivated by an awareness of the historic and cultural value of this work and the significant role it can play in Jewish education and culture, in the spread of Jewish knowledge – which is such an urgent priority in the Jewish and non-Jewish world today – and in the closer linking of Israel with Jews as well as non-Jews the world over. The editors are aware that for objective reasons, they have not always attained the desired perfection and that, as is inevitable in any work of comparable size and scope, errors have crept in. But they feel that the final product, seen in its entirety, is indeed a historical contribution to Jewish culture with which they feel privileged to have been associated.

EDITORIAL AND PRODUCTION STAFF (SECOND EDITION)

EDITOR IN CHIEF
Fred Skolnik

EXECUTIVE EDITOR
Michael Berenbaum

EDITORIAL PROJECT MANAGER
Shlomo S. (Yosh) Gafni

EDITORIAL PROJECT PLANNING AND CONTROL
Rachel Gilon

DIVISIONAL EDITORS

ASIA AND AFRICA
Tudor Parfitt
M.A., Dr. Phil.; School of Oriental and African Studies, University of London, U.K.

BIBLE
S. David Sperling
Ph.D.; Rabbi; Professor of Bible, Hebrew Union College, New York

BULGARIA
Emil Kalo
Ph.D.; President of the Organization of the Jews in Bulgaria "Shalom"; Bulgarian Academy of Science, Bulgaria

CANADA
Richard Menkis
Ph.D.; Associate Professor, University of British Columbia, Canada

Harold Troper
Ph.D.; Professor, Department of Theory and Policy Studies, Ontario Institute for Studies in Education, University of Toronto

CHRISTIANITY AND SECOND TEMPLE
Shimon Gibson
Ph.D.; Archaeologist and Senior Research Fellow, W.F. Albright Institute of Archaeological Research, Jerusalem

CZECHOSLOVAKIA
Yeshayahu Jelinek
Ph.D.; Associate Professor Emeritus, Ben-Gurion University of the Negev, Beersheba

ENGLAND
William D. Rubinstein
Ph.D., B.C.; Professor of History, University of Wales-Aberystwyth, U.K.

FRANCE
Sylvie-Anne Goldberg
Ph.D.; Associate Professor, Ecole des Hautes Etudes en Sciences Sociales, France

Ilan Greilsammer
Ph.D.; Professor, Department of Political Science, Bar-Ilan University; Director, Center for European Community Studies, Bar-Ilan University

GERMANY
Michael Brenner
Ph.D.; Professor of Jewish History and Culture, Ludwig-Maximilians-Universität, Munich, Germany

GREECE
Yitzchak Kerem
Professor, Aristotle University, Thessaloniki, Greece; Lecturer and Researcher, Hebrew University of Jerusalem

HEBREW, SEMITIC, AND JEWISH LANGUAGES
Aharon Maman
Ph.D.; Professor of Hebrew, Hebrew University of Jerusalem

HEBREW LITERATURE, MEDIEVAL
Angel Sáenz-Badillos
Ph.D.; Professor of Hebrew Language and Literature, Universidad Complutense, Madrid, Spain

HEBREW LITERATURE, MODERN
Anat Feinberg
Ph.D.; Professor of Jewish and Hebrew Literature, Hochschule für Jüdische Studien, Heidelberg, Germany

HOLOCAUST AND UNITED STATES
Michael Berenbaum
Ph.D.; Professor of Theology (Adjunct), Director, Sigi Ziering Institute, University of Judaism, Los Angeles, CA

ISLAM AND MUSLIM COUNTRIES IN THE MIDDLE EAST AND NORTH AFRICA
Jacob M. Landau
Ph.D.; Professor Emeritus of Political Science, Hebrew University of Jerusalem; winner of the Israel Prize

ISRAEL
Fred Skolnik
Editor in Chief, Encyclopaedia Judaica (2nd edition)

ITALY
Robert Bonfil
Ph.D.; Professor Emeritus of Jewish History, Hebrew University of Jerusalem

JEWISH LAW
Menachem Elon
Ph.D.; Deputy President of the Supreme Court of Israel; Professor of Law, Hebrew University of Jerusalem, School of Law; Visiting Professor of Law, New York and Harvard Universities Schools of Law; winner of the Israel Prize

JEWISH THOUGHT AND PHILOSOPHY
Aviezer Ravitsky
Ph.D.; Professor, Department of Jewish Thought, Hebrew University of Jerusalem; Senior Fellow, Israel Democracy Institute, Jerusalem; winner of the Israel Prize

Raphael Jospe
Ph.D.; Professor; Researcher; Jewish Philosophy Lecturer, Bar-Ilan University

KABBALAH AND ḤASIDISM
Moshe Idel
Ph.D.; Professor of Jewish Thought and Kabbalah, Hebrew University of Jerusalem; Shalom Hartman Institute, Jerusalem; winner of the Israel Prize

KARAITES
Haggai Ben-Shammai
Ph.D.; Professor of Arab Language and Literature, Hebrew University of Jerusalem

LATIN AMERICA
Margalit Bejarano
Ph.D.; Researcher and Teacher, Hebrew University of Jerusalem

Efraim Zadoff
Ph.D.; Historian, Editor, Research Association on Latin American Jews, Jerusalem

MUSIC
Amnon Shiloah
Ph.D.; Professor Emeritus of Musicology, Hebrew University of Jerusalem

NETHERLANDS
Irene Zwiep
Ph.D.; Professor of Hebrew and Jewish Studies, Universiteit van Amsterdam, Holland

Resianne Fontaine
Ph.D.; Lecturer in the Department of Hebrew and Jewish Studies, Universiteit van Amsterdam, Holland

Barend Theodoor Wallet
M.A.; Junior Researcher, Hebrew, Aramaic and Jewish Studies, Universiteit van Amsterdam, Holland

POLAND
Shlomo Netzer
Ph.D.; Modern East European Jewish History, Tel Aviv University

ROMANIA
Leon Volovici
Ph.D.; Senior Researcher, The Vidal Sassoon International Center for the Study of Anti-Semitism, Jerusalem, Hebrew University of Jerusalem

RUSSIA
Shmuel Spector
Ph.D.; Historian, Jerusalem

SCANDINAVIA
Ilya Meyer
B.Ed.; Translator, Transtext Ab, Gothenburg, Sweden

SCIENCE
Bracha Rager
Ph.D.; Professor of Microbiology and Immunology, Faculty of Health Sciences, Ben-Gurion University of the Negev, Beersheba; Ministry of Health

A. Michael Denman
M.D., F.R.C.P.; Emeritus Consultant, Northwick Park Hospital, London, U.K.

Dan Gilon
M.D., F.A.C.C. Professor of Medicine (Cardiology), Director of Non-Invasive Cardiology, Hadassah–Hebrew University Medical Center, Jerusalem

SPAIN, PORTUGAL, AND MARRANOS
Yom Tov Assis
Ph.D.; Department of Jewish History, World Center for Jewish Studies, Hebrew University of Jerusalem

SPORTS
Eli Wohlgelernter
B.A.; Journalist, Jerusalem

SWITZERLAND
Uri Robert Kaufmann
Ph.D.; Historian, Wissenschaftliche Arbeitsgemeinschaft, Leo Baeck Institut, Heidelberg, Germany

TALMUD
Shamma Friedman
Ph.D.; Benjamin and Minna Reeves Professor of Talmud and Rabbinics, Jewish Theological Seminary; Professor, Department of Talmud, Bar-Ilan University

Stephen G. Wald
Ph.D.; Talmud and Rabbinics, Jerusalem

UNITED STATES LITERATURE
Lewis Fried
Ph.D.; Professor of English, Kent State University

WOMEN AND GENDER
Judith R. Baskin
Ph.D.; Knight Professor of Humanities; Director, Harold Schnitzer Family Program in Judaic Studies, University of Oregon

YIDDISH LITERATURE
Jerold C. Frakes
Ph.D.; Professor of German and Comparative Literature, University of Southern California, Los Angeles

YUGOSLAVIA
Zvi Loker
M.A.; Ambassador Retired; Director, Even Tov Archives, Jerusalem

ZIONISM
Isaiah Friedman
Ph.D.; Professor Emeritus of History, Ben-Gurion University of the Negev, Beersheba

CONSULTING EDITORS

ANTISEMITISM
Dina Porat
Ph.D.; Professor, Stephen Roth Institute for the Study of Contemporary Racism and Anti-Semitism, Chaim Rosenberg School of Jewish Studies, Tel Aviv University

ART
Ziva Amishai-Maisels
Ph.D.; Professor of Art History, Hebrew University of Jerusalem; winner of the Israel Prize

Shalom Sabar
Ph.D.; Chair, Dept. of Jewish and Comparative Folklore, Dept. of Art History, Hebrew University of Jerusalem

DEMOGRAPHY
Sergio DellaPergola
Ph.D.; Shlomo Argov Chair in Israel-Diaspora Relations, A. Harman Institute of Contemporary Jewry, Hebrew University of Jerusalem; Senior Fellow, Jewish People Policy Planning Institute

ISRAEL
Gideon Biger
Ph.D.; Professor of Geography, Tel Aviv University

MUSLIM COUNTRIES IN ASIA
Jacob M. Landau
Ph.D.; Professor Emeritus of Political Science, Hebrew University of Jerusalem; winner of the Israel Prize

RABBINICS
Menachem Friedman
Ph.D.; Professor, Dept. of Sociology, Bar-Ilan University

UNITED STATES
Jonathan Sarna
Ph.D.; Joseph H. and Belle R. Braun Professor of American Jewish History, Brandeis University

DEPARTMENTAL EDITORS

Samantha Baskind (U.S. Art)

Ruth Beloff (U.S. General Culture)

Hannah Brown (Israel Film)

Yoel Cohen (Israel Media)

Barry Davis (Israel Popular Music)

Susan Hattis Rolef (Israel Political Life)

Stewart Kampel (U.S. Business, Media, Theater)

Mort Sheinman (U.S. Fashion)

Tom Teicholz (U.S. Film)

Annette Weber (German Art)

ASSISTANT EDITORS

Robert DelBane (U.S. Literature)

Daryl Green (U.S. Literature)

Susan Nashman Fraiman (Ritual Art)

Jonathan S. Milgram (Talmud)

Jeffrey Schooley (U.S. Literature)

STAFF

Assistant Editor in Chief
Fern Seckbach

Macmillan Publishing Director
Hélène Potter

Executive Data Control
Leonardo Szichman

Editorial Secretary
Shoshana Lewis

Translators
Raphael Blumberg; Jonathan Chipman; Nathan Ginsbury; Penina Goldstein; Atar Hadari; Jill Harris; Simon M. Jackson; Dov Lapin; Edward Levin; David Louvish; Michelle Mazel; Michael Prawer; Peretz Rodman; Avinoam Sharon; Penina Tadmor; David Strauss; Shmuel Wozner; Amy Yourman

Copyediting and Proofreading Control and Cross Referencing
Fern Seckbach

Macmillan Project Editors
Jason M. Everett, Scot Peacock

Copyeditors and Proofreaders
Alan D. Abbey; Judith Appleton; Shai Ben Ari; Sheira Cashman; Dahlia Friedman; Aviva Golbert; Rabbi Dr. Shmuel Himelstein; Esther Herskovics; Darlene Jospe; Ronna Katz; Naomi Lehrfeld; Esther Rosenfeld; Mark Elliott Shapiro; Nurit Tomkins; Shachar Yaari; Shirley Zauer

American Manuscript Liaisons
Mark Drouillard, Tosha Petronicolos

Text Reviewers
Randy Bassett; Patti Brecht; Thomas Carson; Justine Ciovacco; Monica M. Hubbard; Gina Misiroglu; Drew Silver; Kathy Wilson

Illustrations Researchers
Rachel Gilon, Fern Seckbach

Color Inserts Permissions Manager
Robyn V. Young

Map Drawing
Manipal Press, India

Charts and Diagrams
Judith Sternberg, Miri Revivo

Manuscript Processing
Raphael Freeman, Chaya Mendelson and Ricky Fleischer

Layout Consultants
Raphael Freeman, Tal Zeidani

Electronic Preparation of the Original Manuscript
n-Cyclop technology developed by VERY Ltd in Israel.

Software and Entry Sorting
Avi Burstein

Typesetting
Raphael Freeman

Page Make-up
Judith Sternberg, Diana Steigler

Scanning
Ami Green

Index Coordinator
Lynne Maday

Indexing
Factiva, a Dow Jones & Reuters Company

Cover Design
Pamela A.E. Galbreath, Brenda S. Grannan

Color Inserts Coordinators
Pamela A.E. Galbreath, Rachel J. Kain

Color Inserts Design
Kathy Krechnyak

Color Inserts Imaging
Randy Bassett, Lezlie Light

Manufacturing Coordinator
Wendy Blurton

EDITORIAL AND PRODUCTION STAFF (FIRST EDITION)

RESEARCH FOUNDATION

Hon. CHAIRMAN, International Board — Ambassador **ARTHUR J. GOLDBERG**

HON. PRESIDENT — Dr. **NAHUM GOLDMANN**

HON. VICE PRESIDENTS — **SAMUEL BRONFMAN** (*deceased*)
JIM NOVY (*deceased*)

PRESIDENT — Dr. **JOSEPH J. SCHWARTZ**

VICE PRESIDENTS — Rabbi **ISADORE BRESLAU**
ABRAHAM FEINBERG
SAMUEL ROTHBERG

TREASURER — **WALTER ARTZT**

SECRETARY — **JOACHIM N. SIMON**

EXECUTIVE VICE PRESIDENT — Dr. **FREDERICK R. LACHMAN**

EXECUTIVE SECRETARY — **MARILYN R. SWIST**

EDITORIAL BOARD

EDITORS IN CHIEF — Prof. **CECIL ROTH**, 1966-1970
Dr. **GEOFFREY WIGODER**, 1971*

DEPUTY EDITORS IN CHIEF — Prof. **RAPHAEL POSNER****
Prof. **LOUIS I. RABINOWITZ*****

ASSOCIATE EDITORS — Dr. **BINYAMIN ELIAV**
Mr. **SIMḤA KATZ**, M.A.

CONSULTING EDITORS — Prof. **ISRAEL ABRAHAMS**, Jerusalem
Prof. **SALO W. BARON**, New York
Prof. **MOSHE DAVIS**, Jerusalem
Prof. **MENAHEM HARAN**, Jerusalem
Prof. **ARTHUR HERTZBERG**, New York
Prof. **ANDRÉ NEHER**, Strasbourg
Prof. **CHAIM M. RABIN**, Jerusalem
Dr. **JACOB ROBINSON**, New York
Prof. **GERSHOM SCHOLEM**, Jerusalem
Prof. **CHONE SHMERUK**, Jerusalem
Prof. **R.J. ZWI WERBLOWSKY**, Jerusalem

ILLUSTRATIONS CONSULTANT — Dr. **BEZALEL NARKISS,** Jerusalem

EXECUTIVE EDITORS — Dr. **FREDERICK R. LACHMAN,** New York
Mr. **ISRAEL SHAMAH**, Jerusalem, Dec. 1965–May 1967

* Deputy Editor in Chief, 1966–June 1970:
Acting Editor in Chief, June 1970–May 1971

** Associate Editor until 1970:
Deputy Editor in Chief until May 1971

*** Associate Editor until 1970

DIVISIONAL AND DEPARTMENTAL EDITORS*

AMERICANA

Divisional Editor
Prof. **Lloyd P. Gartner,** New York

Assistant Divisional Editor
Hillel Halkin, Jerusalem

BIBLE

Divisional Editor
Prof. **Harold Louis Ginsberg,** New York

Associate Divisional Editor
Prof. **Shalom M. Paul,** New York

Departmental Editors
The Ancient Near East (except Egypt)
Prof. **Pinḥas Artzi,** Ramat Gan

Period of the Pentateuch, Desert, Joshua, and Judges
Prof. **Nahum M. Sarna,** Waltham, Massachusetts

Period of the Kingdom
Prof. **Hanoch Reviv,** Jerusalem

Period of the Second Temple
Dr. **Bezalel Porten,** Jerusalem

Biblical Books and Literature; Bible Scholars and Research
Prof. **Menahem Haran,** Jerusalem

Ideas and Religion
Prof. **Shalom M. Paul,** New York

Society and Law
Prof. **Moshe Greenberg,** Jerusalem

Realia
Dr. **Moshe Dothan,** Jerusalem

CANADA

Departmental Editor
Rabbi Dr. **Stuart E. Rosenberg,** Toronto

CONTEMPORARY JEWRY

Divisional Editor
Dr. **Chaim Yahil,** Jerusalem

Departmental Editors

Demography
Dr. **Usiel O. Schmelz,** Jerusalem

Arab and Oriental Countries
Dr. **Hayyim J. Cohen,** Jerusalem

East Europe
Dr. **Binyamin Eliav,** Jerusalem

Latin America
Dr. **Haim Avni,** Jerusalem

EREẒ ISRAEL

Departmental Editors

Historical Geography
Prof. **Yohanan Aharoni,** Tel Aviv
Prof. **Michael Avi-Yonah,** Jerusalem

Flora and Fauna
Prof. **Jehuda Feliks,** Ramat Gan

MODERN EREẒ ISRAEL

Divisional Editor
Dr. **Binyamin Eliav,** Jerusalem

Deputy Divisional Editor
Misha Louvish, Jerusalem

Departmental Editors

Ereẓ Israel from 1880 to 1948
Dr. **Moshe Avidor,** Jerusalem

The State of Israel
Edwin, Viscount **Samuel,** Jerusalem

Personalities in Modern Ereẓ Israel
Benjamin Jaffe, Jerusalem

Places in Modern Ereẓ Israel
Efraim Orni, Jerusalem

HEBREW AND SEMITIC LANGUAGES

Divisional Editor
Prof. **Zeev Ben-Hayyim,** Jerusalem

Assistant Divisional Editor
Dr. **Uzzi Ornan,** Jerusalem

HISTORY

Divisional Editors

General topics: Central and Eastern Europe
Prof. **Haim Hillel Ben-Sasson,** Jerusalem

* Places after the names of editors refer to their academic institutions, where appropriate. For further details see biographical notes in List of Contributors on pages 45–176.

Muslim Countries
Prof. **Haïm Z'ew Hirschberg,** Ramat Gan

Western Europe and Central and East Asia
Prof. **Cecil Roth** *(deceased),* Jerusalem

DEPARTMENTAL EDITORS

General articles on Jewish History
Prof. **Haim Hillel Ben-Sasson,** Jerusalem

Antisemitism
Dr. **Léon Poliakov** (*deceased*), Massy, France

Autonomy and Social Institutions
Prof. **Isaac Levitats,** New York

The Church and the Jews
Dr. **Bernhard Blumenkranz,** Paris

Economic History
Prof. **Haim Hillel Ben-Sasson,** Jerusalem

Ḥasidism
Dr. **Avraham Rubinstein,** Ramat Gan

Islam and Judaism
Prof. **Haïm Z'ew Hirschberg,** Ramat Gan

The Karaites
Dr. **Leon Nemoy,** Philadelphia

The Jewish Labor Movement
Dr. **Moshe Mishkinsky,** Tel Aviv

Marranos
Prof. **Martin A. Cohen,** New York

Period 135–663 C.E.
Prof. **Alan R. Schulman,** New York

The Samaritans
Ayala Loewenstamm, Jerusalem

REGIONS

Arabia
Prof. **Haïm Z'ew Hirschberg,** Ramat Gan

Austria
Meir Lamed *(deceased),* Kibbutz Ne'ot Mordekhai

The Balkan States
Dr. **Simon Marcus,** Jerusalem

The Baltic States
Dr. **Yehuda Slutsky,** Tel Aviv

Bukovina
Dr. **Yehouda Marton,** Jerusalem

The Byzantine Empire
Prof. **Andrew Sharf,** Ramat Gan

China
Dr. **Rudolf Loewenthal,** Los Angeles

Czechoslovakia
Meir Lamed *(deceased),* Kibbutz Ne'ot Mordekhai
Dr. **Oskar K. Rabinowicz** *(deceased),* New York

England
Peter Elman, Jerusalem

Ereẓ Israel (640–1917)
Prof. **Haïm Z'ew Hirschberg,** Ramat Gan

Western Europe (Modern France, Switzerland, Belgium, The Netherlands, Scandinavia)
Dr. **Baruch Mevorah,** Jerusalem

Medieval France
Dr. **Bernhard Blumenkranz,** France

Germany
Prof. **Ze'ev W. Falk,** Jerusalem

Hungary
Prof. **Alexander Scheiber,** Budapest

Hungary: Assistant Departmental Editor
Dr. **Baruch Yaron,** Jerusalem

India and Southeast Asia
Prof. **Walter J. Fischel,** Santa Cruz, California

Italy
Dr. **Attillio Milano** *(deceased),* Hod Ha-Sharon, Israel

Japan
Prof. **Hyman Kublin,** New York

Latin America (Colonial Period)
Prof. **Martin A. Cohen,** New York

The Maghreb
David Corcos, Jerusalem

Asian Regions of the Ottoman Empire (Iraq, Syria, and Turkey)
Aryeh Shmuelevitz, Tel Aviv

Persia and Afghanistan
Prof. **Walter J. Fischel,** Santa Cruz, California

Poland (until 1800) and Lithuania
Prof. **Haim Hillel Ben-Sasson,** Jerusalem

Poland (from 1800)
Moshe Landau, Tel Aviv

Portugal
Prof. **Martin A. Cohen,** New York

Romania
Dr. **Theodor Lavi,** Jerusalem

Russia
Dr. **Yehuda Slutsky,** Tel Aviv

South Africa
Gustav Saron, Johannesburg

Moslem Spain
Prof. **Haïm Z'ew Hirschberg,** Ramat Gan

Christian Spain
Prof. **Haim Beinart,** Jerusalem

Transylvania
Dr. **Yehouda Marton,** Jerusalem

Yemen
Prof. **Haïm Z'ew Hirschberg,** Ramat Gan

CONSULTING EDITOR

Economic History
Dr. **Nachum Gross,** Jerusalem

THE HOLOCAUST

DIVISIONAL EDITORS
Dr. **Shaul Esh** *(deceased),* Jerusalem
Dr. **Jozeph Michman,** Jerusalem

JEWISH LAW

DIVISIONAL EDITOR
Prof. **Menachem Elon,** Jerusalem

DEPARTMENTAL EDITORS

General Articles on Jewish Law; the Legal and Literary Sources of the Law; the Laws of Obligation; Public and Administrative Law; Conflict of Laws
Prof. **Menachem Elon,** Jerusalem

Criminal Law; the Laws of Procedure and Evidence
Justice **Haim H. Cohn,** Jerusalem

The Laws of Property; the Laws of Tort
Prof. **Shalom Albeck,** Ramat Gan

Family Law and Inheritance
Justice Dr. **Ben-Zion (Benno) Schereschewsky,** Jerusalem

Translator, Jewish Law
Julius Kopelowitz, Advocate, B.A., L.L.B. (Rand), Rishon le-Zion

JUDAISM

DIVISIONAL EDITOR
Prof. **R.J. Zwi Werblowsky,** Jerusalem

DEPARTMENTAL EDITORS

Christianity
Dr. **Yona Malachy,** Jerusalem

Education
Dr. **Judah Pilch,** New York

Folklore
Dr. **Dov Noy,** Jerusalem

Judaism, Liturgy
Rabbi Dr. **Raphael Posner,** Jerusalem

CONSULTING EDITOR

Liturgy
Meir Medan, Jerusalem

LITERATURE

MEDIEVAL LITERATURE

DEPARTMENTAL EDITORS

Medieval Hebrew Poetry
Prof. **Abraham M. Haberman,** Tel Aviv

Medieval Hebrew Prose
Prof. **Joseph Dan,** Jerusalem

Translations and Judeo-Arabic Literature
Prof. **Abraham S. Halkin,** Jerusalem

Christian Hebraists
Raphael Loewe, London

MODERN HEBREW LITERATURE

DIVISIONAL EDITOR
Prof. **Ezra Spicehandler,** Jerusalem

DEPARTMENTAL EDITOR
Prof. **Avraham Holtz,** New York

ASSISTANT DEPARTMENTAL EDITOR

Modern Hebrew and Yiddish Literature
Prof. **Curt Leviant,** New Brunswick, New Jersey

RABBINICAL LITERATURE

DIVISIONAL EDITOR
Rabbbi Sir **Israel Brodie,** London

DEPUTY DIVISIONAL EDITOR
Dr. **Yehoshua Horowitz,** Ramat Gan

ASSISTANT DIVISIONAL EDITOR
Dr. **David Tamar,** Jerusalem

MODERN JEWISH SCHOLARSHIP

DIVISIONAL EDITOR
Prof. **Seymour Siegel,** New York

ASSOCIATE DIVISIONAL EDITOR
Dr. **Menahem H. Schmelzer,** New York

PHILOSOPHY, JEWISH

DIVISIONAL EDITOR
Prof. **Arthur Hyman,** New York

SECOND TEMPLE PERIOD

Divisional Editor
Prof. **Abraham Schalit,** Jerusalem

departmental Editors

Apocrypha and Pseudepigrapha
Dr. **Michael E. Stone,** Jerusalem

Dead Sea Scrolls
Prof. **Frederick F. Bruce,** Manchester

Hellenistic Literature
Prof. **Louis H. Feldman,** New York

TALMUD

Divisional Editor
Prof. **Yitzhak Dov Gilat,** Ramat Gan

Departmental Editor

Midrash and Aggadah
Dr. **Joseph Heinemann,** Jerusalem

ZIONISM

Divisional Editor
Getzel Kressel, Ḥolon

THE PARTICIPATION OF JEWS IN WORLD CULTURE

Divisional Editor
Israel Shamah, London

ART

Divisional Editor
Dr. **Alfred Werner,** New York

Departmental Editors

Illuminated Manuscripts
Dr. **Bezalel Narkiss,** Jerusalem

Israel Art
Yona Fischer, Jerusalem

Numismatics
Arie Kindler, Tel Aviv

LITERATURE

Departmental Editors

Balkan Literature
Prof. **Zdenko Löwenthal,** Belgrade

Canadian Literature
Prof. **Miriam D. Waddington,** Toronto

Czechoslovak Literature
Dr. **Avigdor Dagan,** Jeruslaem

Dutch Literature
Gerda Alster-Thau, Ramat Gan

English Literature
Prof. **Harold Fisch,** Ramat Gan

French Literature
Dr. **Denise Goitein,** Tel Aviv

German Literature
Prof. **Sol Liptzin,** Jerusalem

Greek Literature
Prof. **Rachel Dalven,** New York

Hungarian Literature
Dr. **Baruch Yaron,** Jerusalem

Italian Literature
Dr. **Joseph B. Sermoneta,** Jerusalem

Ladino Literature and Jewish Dialects
Prof. **Moshe Lazar,** Jerusalem

Middle Eastern Literature
Dr. **Hayyim J. Cohen,** Jerusalem

Polish Literature
Stanislaw Wygodzki, Givatayim, Israel

Romanian Literature
Abraham Feller, Tel Aviv

Russian Literature
Prof. **Maurice Friedberg,** Bloomington, Indiana

Scandinavian Literature
Dr. **Leni Yahil,** Jerusalem

Spanish and Portuguese Literature
Prof. **Kenneth R. Scholberg,** East Lansing, Michigan

United States Literature
Prof. **Milton Hindus,** Waltham, Massachusetts

Consulting Editors

Polish Literature
Prof. **Moshe Altbauer,** Jerusalem

Romanian Literature
Dora Litani-Littman, Jerusalem

MEDICINE

Departmental Editor
Prof. **Suessmann Muntner,** Jerusalem

Consulting Editor
Dr. **Shabbetai Ginton,** Jerusalem

MUSIC

Divisional Editors
Dr. **Israel Adler,** Jerusalem
Dr. **Bathja Bayer,** Jerusalem

Departmental Editor

Music Illustrations
Avigdor Herzog, Jerusalem

THE SCIENCES

Consulting Editor
Dr. **Harry Zvi Tabor,** Jerusalem

Departmental Editors

Aeronautics, Astronautics, Aviation, Engineering, Invention
Dr. **Samuel A. Miller** *(deceased),* London

Astronomy, Chemistry, Mathematics, Physics, the History and Philosophy of Science
Maurice Goldsmith, London

Biology, Botany, Zoology
Prof. **Mordecai L. Gabriel,** New York

Geology
Prof. **Leo Picard,** Jerusalem

Meteorology
Prof. **Dov Ashbel,** Jerusalem

OTHER DISCIPLINES

Anthropology
Prof. **Ephraim Fischoff,** Eau Claire, Wisconsin

Archaeology
Dr. **Penuel P. Kahane,** Jerusalem

Bridge and Chess
Gerald Abrahams, Liverpool

Criminology
Dr. **Zvi Hermon,** Tel Aviv

Dance
Dr. **Selma J. Cohen,** New York

Economics
Dr. **Joachim O. Ronall,** New York

Education
Prof. **William W. Brickman,** Philadelphia

Geography
Prof. **Moshe Brawer,** Tel Aviv

Historiography
Prof. **Oscar I. Janowsky,** New York

Journalism
Kalman Seigel, New York

Law and Politics
Peter Elman, Jerusalem

Law and Socialism in the United States
Prof. **Milton R. Konvitz,** Ithaca, New York

Linguistics
Prof. **Herbert H. Paper,** Ann Arbor, Michigan

Military Service
Lt. Col. (Res.) **Mordechai M. Kaplan,** Tel Aviv

Jewish Newspapers and Periodicals
Joseph Fraenkel, London

Philosophy
Prof. **Richard H. Popkin,** San Diego, California

Photography
Peter Pollack, New York

Psychiatry
Dr. **Louis Miller,** Jerusalem

Psychology
Prof. **Helmut Adler,** New York

Public Relations
Bernard Postal, New York

Printing and Publishing
John M. Shaftesley, London

Social Welfare
Dr. **Joseph Neipris,** Jerusalem

Socialism and the Labor Movement
Dr. **S. Levenberg,** London

Sociology
Prof. **Werner J. Cahnman,** Newark, New Jersey

Sports
Jesse Silver, Surfside, Florida

Theatre and Film
Stewart Kampel, New York
Stephen Klaidman, Washington D.C.

STAFF

MANAGEMENT

ADMINISTRATIVE MANAGER
Rachel Sabbath

PRODUCTION PLANNING
Moshe Shalvi, B.A.

ASSISTANT
Walter Zanger, M.A.

EDITORIAL STAFF

ASSISTANT EDITORS
Rabbi Morton Mayer Berman, M.H.L.
Rabbi Alexander Carlebach, D.en.D.

STAFF EDITORS
Emanuel Beeri, M.A.
Joan Comay
Arthur Cygielman
Rabbi Michael J. Graetz, M.H.L
Prof. Judith Rosenthal, Ph.D.
Moshe Rosetti
Rabbi Aaron Rothkoff, D.H.L.
Alexander Shapiro, Ph.D.
Godfrey Edmond Silverman, M.A.
Michael Simon, Ph.D.
Lewis Sowden, M.A

RESEARCH EDITOR (HISTORY AND ILLUSTRATIONS)
B. Mordecai Ansbacher, M.A

REVISING EDITOR
Dereck Orlans

WRITERS
Laurentino José Alfonso, B.D.; Essa Cindorf, B.A.; Stuart Cohen M.A.; Jonathan Covan, LL.M.; Abraham David, M.A.; David Goldberg, B.A.; Edward L. Greenstein, B.A., B.H.L.; Yuval Kamrat; Joseph Kaplan, M.A.; Sinai Leichter M.A.; Avital Levy B.A.; Mervyn Lewis M.A.; Aaron Lichentstein, Ph.D.; Ester (Zweig) Liebes, B.A.; David Maisel, M.A.; Rabbi Sefton D. Temkin, Ph.D.; Nechama Unterman, M.A.; Henry Wasserman, B.A.; Adela Wolfe, M.A.; Rabbi Meir Ydit, Ph.D; Moshe Zeidner, B.A.

STYLISTS
Yehuda Ben-Dror (James Marshall), B.A.; Ruth Connell Robertson, LL.B.; Ina Friedman, M.A.; Reva Garmise, B.A.; Yvonne Glikson, B.A.; Avie Goldberg, B.A.; Manya Keller; Judith Krausz, B.A.; Sandra Litt Hai, B.A.; Penina Mellick; Moira Paterson, B.A.; Dip. Ed.; Jack Rosenthal, M.A.; Judith Shalowitz, M.A.; Alice Shalvi, Ph.D.; Claire Sotnick, B.A.

TRANSLATORS
Josephine Bacon; Rabbi Chaim Brovender, Ph.D.; Rivkah Duker, M.A.; Priscilla Fishman; Rabbi David Goldstein, Ph.D.; Rabbi Barnet David Klien, M.A.; Rabbi Israel Hannaniah Levine, Ph.D.; Yael Lotan-Hairston; Anita Matza, M.A.; Fern Seckbach, B.A.; Rabbi Kalman Szulewicz; Leontine Williams

BIBLIOGRAPHERS AND CHECKERS
Shelomo Shunami, Chief Bibliographer (1967–69)
Dina Bachrach, B.A.; Martha Baraz, M.A.; Ruth Berger; Katherine Bloom, B.A.; Rabbi Judah Brumer; Claire Dienstag, M.A.; Daniel Efron, M.A.; Michael J. Frenkel, M.A., Dip. Lib.; Gideon Fuks, B.A.; Daniel Furman; Henri Guttel, B.A.; Abraham Herman; Eva Herman; Giza Kamrat; Eva Kondor; Simcha Kruger, B.S.; Benjamin Lubelski, B.A., Dip. Lib.; Samuel S. Matza, Mag. Jur., M.A.; Mirjam Mundsztuk; David M.L. Olivestone, B.A.; Miriam Prager; Benjamin Richler; Betty-Lou Rosen, M.A.; Janet (Zander) Shvili; Rabbi Andrew Silberfeld, Ph.D.; Rita Sirota, B.A.; Sophie Winston, M.L.S.; Michael Ya'akobi, Dr. jur., Dipl. sc.pol.

TRANSLITERATORS
Hanna Avituv, B.A.; Amikam Cohen B.A.; Uri Davis, B.A.; Leah (Rosen) Teichthal, B.A.

CONTRIBUTORS TO THE ENCYCLOPAEDIA

The following List of Contributors includes contributors to the first and second editions of the Encyclopaedia and all entries entirely or partially written by them. Contributors to the second edition are noted with an asterisk (*). Information about writers applies to the time of submission of the entry. In cases where a writer contributed to both editions the later information is given along with an asterisk. Writers with no entries opposite their names contributed to unsigned entries.

Mahmoud Abassi, B.A.; Writer, Shefaram, Israel: ISRAEL, STATE OF: ARAB POPULATION

Isaac Abraham Abbady, Journalist, Jerusalem: AUSTER, DANIEL

Alan D. Abbey*, M.S.; Journalist, Businessman, Jerusalem: MERCHANT, LARRY; MICHAELS, ALAN RICHARD; ROSE, MAURICE; ROSENBLOOM, CARROLL; ROTHSTEIN, ARNOLD; SEDAKA, NEIL; SIMON, CARLY ELISABETH; SIMON, PAUL FREDERIC; SPECTOR, PHIL

Irving Abella*, B.A., M.A., Ph.D.; Shiff Professor of Canadian Jewish History, York University, Toronto, Canada: CANADIAN JEWISH CONGRESS; GERSHMAN, JOE; HAYES, SAUL

Moses Aberbach, Ph.D.; Baltimore Hebrew College, Maryland: ELDAD AND MEDAD; ELIJAH; EZEKIEL; GOLDEN CALF; ḤOVAH; JACOB; JOSEPH; JUDAH IV; JUDITH; KETI'A BAR SHALOM; MAR BAR RAVINA; NEBUCHADNEZZAR; NICARAGUA; PAPI; PHARAOH; SHEM; SIMEON; YESHEVAV THE SCRIBE; YOSE BEN AKAVYAH

Abraham Abraham, Rabbi; Jerusalem

Gerald Abrahams, M.A.; Barrister at Law, Liverpool: BOLESLAVSKI, ISAAC; BRONSTEIN, DAVID; CARDS AND CARDPLAYING; CHESS; CZERNIAK, MOSHE; FINE, REUBEN; FLOHR, SALO; GOREN, CHARLES HENRY; HOROWITZ, ISRAEL ALBERT; LASKER, EMANUEL; NAJDORF, MIGUEL; NIMZOVITCH, AARON; RESHEVSKY, SAMUEL HERMAN; RÉTI, RICHARD; RUBINSTEIN, AKIVA; STEINITZ, WILHELM; TAL, MIKHAIL; TARRASCH, SIEGBERT

Israel Abrahams, M.A., Rabbi, Emeritus Professor of Hebrew, the University of Cape Town; Former Chief Rabbi of Cape Province, South Africa; Jerusalem: BELIEF; CASSUTO, UMBERTO; GOD; MAN, THE NATURE OF; MOSES; NUMBERS, TYPICAL AND IMPORTANT; PRAYER; TABERNACLE; WORD; WORSHIP

Shlomo Zalman Abramov, Lawyer, former Member of Knesset, chairman of the Editorial Board of the *New Zionist Encyclopaedia*

Stanley Abramovitch, M.A.; Director of the Education Department, American Joint Distribution Committee, Geneva: EDUCATION, JEWISH

Daniel Abrams*, Ph.D.; Senior Lecturer, Philosophy, Bar-Ilan University, Ramat Gan: ASHER BEN DAVID; BAHIR, SEFER HA-; MOPSIK, CHARLES

Jeanne E. Abrams*, Ph.D.; Associate Professor at Penrose Library, University of Denver, and Director of the Rocky Mountain Jewish Historical Society and Beck Archives, University of Denver, Colorado: COLORADO; JACOBS, FRANCES WISEBART; NATIONAL JEWISH CENTER FOR IMMUNOLOGY AND RESPIRATORY MEDICINE

Samuel Abramsky, Ph.D.; Senior Lecturer in Jewish History and in Bible, the University of the Negev, Beersheba: AMALEKITES; BAR KOKHBA; BREAD; ISSACHAR; JERUSALEM; LEVI; MEDES AND MEDIA; MEPHIBOSHETH; MICAIAH; MICHAL; MIDIAN, MIDIANITES; NATHAN; RECHABITES; SOLOMON; WILDERNESS

Claude Abravanel, Lecturer, the Rubin Academy of Music, Jerusalem: ALKAN, CHARLES HENRI-VALENTIN; BONAVENTURA, ENZO JOSEPH; CASTELNUOVO-TEDESCO, MARIO; GOODMAN, BENNY; HELLER, STEPHEN; JUDAH BEN ISAAC; KREIN, ALEXANDER ABRAMOVICH; LANDOWSKA, WANDA; MONTEUX, PIERRE; MOSCHELES, IGNAZ; PEERCE, JAN; TANSMAN, ALEXANDER; TOCH, ERNST; VOGEL, WLADIMIR

Butrus Abu-Manneh*, Ph.D.; Associate Professor, University of Haifa: ABDUL MEJID I; SELIM I; SELIM II

Annalucia Accardo*, Laurea; Associate Professor, University of Rome "La Sapienza", Italy: PALEY, GRACE

Joseph Adar, M.Sc.; Israel Atomic Energy Commission, Ramat Gan

Abraham Addleson, Attorney; Former Mayor of East London, South Africa: EAST LONDON

Howard Tzvi Adelman*, Ph.D.; Associate Professor, Rothberg School, Hebrew University, Jerusalem; Hebrew College: ABRABANEL, BENVENIDA; ASCARELLI, DEVORA; MODENA, FIORETTA; MODENA, LEON; MORPURGO, RACHEL LUZZATTO; SHEḤITAH

Howard L. Adelson, Ph.D.; Professor of Medieval History, City College of the City University of New York: BLOCH, GUSTAVE; COHEN, GUSTAVE; DAVIDSOHN, ROBERT; GROSS, CHARLES; JANOWSKY, OSCAR ISAIAH; LOPEZ, ROBERT SABATINO; SIMSON, BERNHARD VON

Zvi Adiv, M.A.; Assistant in History, the Hebrew University of Jerusalem and Tel Aviv University: DISRAELI, BENJAMIN, EARL OF BEACONSFIELD

Eliyana R. Adler*, Ph.D.; Fellow and Lecturer, University of Maryland: BERLIN, RAYNA BATYA; PROSTITUTION

H.G. Adler, Ph.D.; Historian, London

Helmut E. Adler, Ph.D.; Professor

of Psychology, Yeshiva University, New York: BUHLER, CHARLOTTE; GINOTT, HAIM G.; HEYMANS, GERARDUS F.; LEHRMAN, DANIEL S.; MUENSTERBERG, HUGO; MYERS, CHARLES SAMUEL; PSYCHOLOGY; RAZRAN, GREGORY; RUBIN, EDGAR; SELZ, OTTO; STERN, WILLIAM

Israel Adler, Dr. du 3e cycle; Director of the Center for Research in Jewish Music, the Hebrew University of Jerusalem: ARPA, ABRAMO DALL'; BOLAFFI, MICHELE; CACERES, ABRAHAM; CANTATAS AND CHORAL WORKS, HEBREW; CIVITA, DAVIT; OBADIAH, THE NORMAN PROSELYTE; ORGAN; PADDAN-ARAM

Saul Aaron Adler, D.T.M., F.R.C.P., F.R.S.; Professor of Parasitology, the Hebrew University of Jerusalem: GRUBY, DAVID

Selig Adler, Ph.D.; Professor of American History, the State University of New York, Buffalo: ROOSEVELT, THEODORE; WILSON, WOODROW

Shalom Adler-Rudel, Director of the Leo Baeck Institute, Jerusalem: BERMUDA CONFERENCE; COUNCIL OF JEWS FROM GERMANY; REFUGEES; SALOMON, ALICE; WUNDERLICH, FRIEDA

Evelyn Adunka*, Dr.Phil.; Historian, Vienna, Austria: AUSTRIA; EHRLICH, JACOB; KREISKY, BRUNO; NATIONALRAT; SCHOENERER, GEORG VON; SCHUTZBUND, REPUBLIKANISCHER; VIENNA; VOLKSPARTEI, JUEDISCHE

Laurentino Jose Afonso, B.D.; Jerusalem: NABONIDUS; NETHERWORLD; PROSTITUTION

Irving A. Agus, Ph.D., Rabbi; Professor of Jewish History, Yeshiva University, New York: AVIGDOR BEN ELIJAH HA-KOHEN; MEIR BEN BARUCH OF ROTHENBURG

Jacob Bernard Agus, Ph.D., Rabbi; Adjunct Professor of Modern Jewish Philosophy, Dropsie University; Professor of Rabbinic Judaism, the Reconstructionist Rabbinical College, Philadelphia: GOOD AND EVIL

Abraham Aharoni, Journalist, Tel Aviv: BARATZ, JOSEPH; BAR-YEHUDAH, ISRAEL; BEJERANO; BEN-YEHUDAH, BARUKH; BOGER, ḤAYYIM; BOGHEN, FELICE; CHIZHIK; DAYYAN; HARARI, ḤAYYIM; ISRAELI, BENZION; KRINITZI, AVRAHAM; LEVI, SHABBETAI; METMAN-COHEN, YEHUDAH LEIB; MEYUḤAS, YOSEF BARAN; MOHILEWER, SAMUEL; MOSSINSON, BENZION; NISSAN, AVRAHAM; SHAREF, ZE'EV; SHENKAR, ARIE; SUKENIK, ELIEZER LIPA; SUPRASKY, YEHOSHUA; TABIB, AVRAHAM; ZISLING, AHARON

Yohanan Aharoni, Ph.D.; Professor of Archaeology and of the Historical Geography of Palestine, Tel Aviv University: AHLAB; ALMON-DIBLATHAIM; ANAHARATH; ARAD; BAAL-GAD; BESOR, BROOK OF; BET-CHEREM; BET-SHEMESH; CALEB, CALEBITES; CHINNERETH, CHINNEROTH; DIBON; GEBA; GILEAD; JABIN; JOSHUA; JOSHUA, BOOK OF; KADESH; KENITE; MADON; NABAL

Abba Ahimeir, Ph.D.; Journalist and Writer, Tel Aviv: ANTOKOLSKI, MARK; BATUMI; BRUTZKUS, JULIUS; DERZHAVIN, GABRIEL ROMANOVICH; DIMANSTEIN, SIMON; GUENZBURG, MORDECAI AARON

Ora Ahimeir*, Director General, The Jerusalem Institute for Israel Studies, Jerusalem: JERUSALEM INSTITUTE FOR ISRAEL STUDIES

Shmuel Ahituv, M.A.; Staff, *Biblical Encyclopedia*, Jerusalem: AZAZEL; DIVINATION

Reuben Ainsztein, Writer and journalist, London

Edna Aizenberg, Ph.D.; Instructor in Spanish Literature, Maritime College, New York: SPANISH AND PORTUGUESE LITERATURE

Golda Akhiezer*, M.A.; Doctoral Student of Jewish History; Researcher at the Ben-Zvi Institute and Teacher in the Rothberg School for Overseas Students, the Hebrew University of Jerusalem: ABRAHAM BEN JOSIAH TROKI; ABRAHAM BEN JOSIAH YERUSHALMI; AGA; AZARIAH BEN ELIYAH; BABOVICH, SIMḤAH BEN SOLOMON BEN NAHAMU; BEIM, SOLOMON BEN ABRAHAM; BENJAMIN BEN ELIJAH DUWAN; EZRA BEN NISAN; ISAAC BEN SOLOMON; KAL'I, SAMUEL BEN JOSEPH; KALFA ISAAK BEN JOSEPH; LABANOVICH; LEONOWICZ; LUZKI, SIMḤAH ISAAC BEN MOSES; MOSES BEN ELIJAH HA-LEVI; MOSES BEN ELIJAH PASHA; PIGIT, SAMUEL BEN SHEMARIA; SALMON BEN JEROHAM; SHAPSHAL SERAYA BEN MORDECHAI; SOLOMON BEN AARON; SULTANSKY, MORDECAI BEN JOSEPH; ZEFANIA BEN MORDECHAI; ZERAH BEN NATHAN OF TROKI

Shalom Albeck, Ph.D.; Associate Professor of Talmud and Law, Bar-Ilan University, Ramat Gan: ACQUISITION; ASSIGNMENT; AVOT NEZIKIN; DAMAGES; GERAMA AND GARME; GIFT; HEFKER; LIABILITY; LOST PROPERTY; MARITIME LAW; MAẒRANUT; MISTAKE; NUISANCE; OWNERSHIP; PROPERTY; SALE; SERVITUDES; THEFT AND ROBBERY; TORTS; YE'USH

William Foxwell Albright, Ph.D.; Emeritus Professor of Near Eastern Studies, Johns Hopkins University, Baltimore, Maryland

David Alcalay, Jerusalem: VAJS, ALBERT

Ora Alcalay, B.A., Dip.Lib.; Director of the Library of Yad Vashem, Jerusalem: BELEV, ALEXANDER

Harry J. Alderman, B.A., B.S.; the American Jewish Committee, New York: GOLDSTEIN, FANNY; SCHNEIDERMAN, HARRY

Gabriel Eitan Alexander*, Ph.D.; Head of Keren Kayemeth LeIsrael (JNF), History Research Institute for Zionism and Settlement, Jerusalem: WEISER-VARON, BENNO

Itzhak Alfassi, General Secretary, B'nai B'rith, Tel Aviv: AROLLIA, ISAAC BEN MOSES; ARYEH LEIB OF OŻARÓW; BAMBERG, SAMUEL BEN BARUCH; BARBY, MEIR BEN SAUL; BARDAKI, ISAIAH BEN ISSACHAR BER; BASCHKO, ẒEVI HIRSCH BEN BENJAMIN; BEJERANO, BEKHOR ḤAYYIM BEN MOSES; BELZ; BENGIS, SELIG REUBEN; BERLIN, ISAIAH BEN JUDAH LOEB; BERNSTEIN, ARYEH LEIB; BERNSTEIN, ISSACHAR BERUSH BEN ARYEH LOEB; BEZALEL BEN MOSES HA-KOHEN; BLOCH, JOSEPH LEIB; BOSKOWITZ, ḤAYYIM BEN JACOB; BROIDA, SIMḤAH ZISSEL BEN ISRAEL; CARO, JOSEPH ḤAYYIM BEN ISAAC; CHELM, SOLOMON BEN MOSES; CIECHANOW, ABRAHAM BEN RAPHAEL LANDAU OF; CORONEL, NAḤMAN NATHAN; DEUTSCH, ELIEZER ḤAYYIM BEN ABRAHAM; EGER, SIMḤAH BUNIM BEN MOSES; EISENSTADTER, MEIR BEN JUDAH LEIB; ENGEL, JOSEPH BEN JUDAH; EPHRATI, DAVID TEVELE BEN ABRAHAM;

ETTINGER, MORDECAI ZE'EV BEN ISAAC AARON SEGAL; EULENBURG, ISAAC BEN ABRAHAM MOSES ISRAEL; FINKEL, NATHAN ẒEVI BEN MOSES; GEDALIAH, JUDAH BEN MOSES; GESUNDHEIT, JACOB BEN ISAAC; GRÜNWALD, AMRAM; ḤASIDISM; ḤAYYOT, MENAHEM MANISH BEN ISAAC; HOROWITZ, ISAAC HA-LEVI BEN JACOB JOKEL; ISRAEL, STATE OF: ALIYAH; JACOB BEN AARON OF KARLIN; JACOB BEN EPHRAIM NAPHTALI HIRSCH OF LUBLIN; JENER, ABRAHAM NAPHTALI HIRSCH BEN MORDECAI; JERUSALIMSKI, MOSES NAḤUM BEN BENJAMIN; JUDAH BEN MOSES OF LUBLIN; KAHANA, JACOB BEN ABRAHAM; KAHANOV, MOSES NEHEMIAH; KALLIR, ELEAZAR BEN ELEAZAR; KARFUNKEL, AARON BEN JUDAH LEIB HA-KOHEN; KATZ, REUVEN; KLAUSNER, ẒEVI HIRSCH; KLEIN, SAMUEL SHMELKA; KRENGEL, MENAHEM MENDEL; KRISTIANPOLLER; LANDAU, ELEAZAR BEN ISRAEL; LANDAU, ISRAEL JONAH BEN JOSEPH HA-LEVI; LERNER, MAYER BEN MORDECAI OF ALTONA; LEWIN, AARON BEN NATHAN OF RZESZOW; LIBSCHITZ, BARUCH MORDECAI BEN JACOB; LIPKIN, ISRAEL BEN ZE'EV WOLF; LIPSCHUETZ, HILLEL ARYEH LEIB BEN ZE'EV DOV; LIPSCHUTZ, SOLOMON BEN MORDECAI; MARGOLIOTH, EPHRAIM ZALMAN BEN MENAHEM MANNES; MARLI, SAMUEL BEN MAẒLI'AḤ; MEISELS, DOV BERUSH; MICHAELSON, EZEKIEL ẒEVI BEN ABRAHAM ḤAYYIM; MUSSAFIA, BENJAMIN BEN IMMANUEL; NIEMIROWER, JACOB ISAAC; ORNSTEIN, MORDECAI ZE'EV BEN MOSES; PLOTZKI, MEIR DAN OF OSTROVA; POSNER, SOLOMON ZALMAN BEN JOSEPH; RABINOWITZ-TEOMIM, ELIJAH DAVID BEN BENJAMIN; REICH, KOPPEL; RIVKES, MOSES BEN NAPHTALI HIRSCH; ROSANES, ẒEVI HIRSCH BEN ISSACHAR BERISH; ROSEN, JOSEPH BEN ISAAC; SAFRAN, BEZALEL ZE'EV; SALANT, JOSEPH SUNDEL BEN BENJAMIN BENISH; SCHICK, ABRAHAM BEN ARYEH LOEB; SCHIFF, MEIR BEN JACOB HA-KOHEN; SCHMELKES, GEDALIAH BEN MORDECAI; SCHOR, ALEXANDER SENDER BEN EPHRAIM ZALMAN; SCHOR, EPHRAIM SOLOMON BEN NAPHTALI HIRSCH; SHAPIRA, ELIJAH BEN BENJAMIN WOLF; SOFER, ḤAYYIM BEN MORDECAI EPHRAIM FISCHEL; TAUBES, AARON MOSES BEN JACOB; TEOMIM, ARYEH LEIB; TEOMIM, JOSEPH BEN MEIR; WEINGARTEN, JOAB JOSHUA; WESEL, BARUCH BENDET BEN REUBEN; YOSEF, OVADIAH; ZIRELSON, JUDAH LEIB; ZUENZ, ARYEH LEIB BEN MOSES

David Algaze, M.H.L., Rabbi; New York: GUATEMALA

Uri Algom, Military Historian, former Chief Historian of the Israel Army

Moshe Allon, Jerusalem: ISRAEL, STATE OF: LABOR; SOLEL BONEH

Yigal Allon, Major General (Res.), Israel Defense Forces; Deputy Prime Minister and Minister of Education and Culture, Kibbutz Ginnosar: PALMAḤ; SADEH, YIẒḤAK

Nehemya Allony, Ph.D.; Associate Professor of Hebrew Language and Literature, the University of the Negev, Beersheba: ḤAYYUJ, JUDAH BEN DAVID

Dan Almagor, Ph.D.; Writer, Haifa: BERDYCZEWSKI, MICHA JOSEF; SOMMO, JUDAH LEONE BEN ISAAC

Shlomo Alon*, M.A.; Senior Lecturer, School of Education, the Hebrew University of Jerusalem: DHIMMA, DHIMMI

Yehoshua Alouf, Supervisor of Physical Education, Ministry of Education and Culture, Ramat Gan: A.S.A.; HAPOEL; MACCABI; MACCABI WORLD UNION; SPORTS

Sara Alpern*, Ph.D.; Associate Professor, Texas A. & M. University, Texas: ALBERT, MILDRED ELIZABETH LEVINE; CARNEGIE, HATTIE; HANDLER, RUTH MOSKO; LAUDER, ESTÉE MENTZER; LEIBER, JUDITH MARIA; MALSIN, LANE BRYANT; MARGARETEN, REGINA; PARNIS, MOLLIE; POLYKOFF, SHIRLEY; ROSENBERG, ANNA MARIE LEDERER; ROSENTHAL, IDA

Carl Alpert, Executive Vice Chairman of the Board of Governors, the Technion, Haifa: REINER, MARKUS

Rebecca Alpert*, Ph.D.; Associate Professor of Religion and Women's Studies, Temple University, Philadelphia, Pennsylvania: LESBIANISM; NEWMAN, PAULINE

Paul Awraham Alsberg, Ph.D.; Israel State Archivist; Lecturer in Archival Management, Graduate Library School, the Hebrew University of Jerusalem: ARCHIVES

Gerda Alster-Thau, M.A.; Lecturer in Hebrew and World Literature, Bar-Ilan University, Ramat Gan: DUTCH LITERATURE; LOGGEM, MANUEL VAN; MULISCH, HARRY; VROMAN, LEO

Moshe Altbauer, Ph.D.; Associate Professor of Slavic Linguistics and of Russian Studies, the Hebrew University of Jerusalem: BIEGELEISEN, HENRYK; BRANDSTAETTER, ROMAN; FELDMAN, WILHELM; KLACZKO, JULIAN; PUBLISHING; SLONIMSKI, ANTONI

Harry Alter, Editor, Youngstown, Ohio: YOUNGSTOWN

Avraham Altman, Ph.D.; Lecturer in Japanese Studies, the Hebrew University of Jerusalem

Alexander Altmann, Ph.D., D.H.L., Rabbi; Professor of Jewish Philosophy, Brandeis University, Waltham, Massachusetts: ANGELS AND ANGELOLOGY; ARISTOTLE; ASTROLOGY; BEATITUDE; COMMANDMENTS, REASONS FOR; GOD; ISRAELI, ISAAC BEN SOLOMON; MOSES BEN JOSEPH HA-LEVI; PROVIDENCE; ẒADDIK, JOSEPH BEN JACOB IBN

Mordechai Altschuler, Ph.D.; Associate Professor, Institute for Contemporary Jewry, the Hebrew University of Jerusalem: RUSSIA

Hadas Altwarg, Researcher, Institute of Jewish Affairs, London: ANTISEMITISM

Helen Aminoff*, B.A.; Historian, Beth Israel Congregation; Past-President of Hadassah, Ann Arbor, Michigan: ANN ARBOR

Aharon Amir, Writer and Editor, Tel Aviv

Amihood Amir*, Ph.D.; Professor of Computer Science, Bar-Ilan University, Ramat Gan: COMPUTER SCIENCE

Shimeon Amir, Ph.D.; Senior Lecturer in the Department of Developing Countries, Tel Aviv University; Deputy Director General, Ministry for Foreign Affairs, Jerusalem: PORTUGAL

Yehoshua Amir (Neumark), Dr.Phil., Rabbi; Senior Lecturer in Jewish Philosophy, Tel Aviv University: MACCABEES, FOURTH BOOK OF; MACCABEES, THIRD BOOK OF; OSIANDER, ANDREAS; SIBYL AND

SIBYLLINE ORACLES; SIMON, AKIBA ERNST

Yehoyada Amir*, Professor, Director, Israel Rabbinic Program, Hebrew Union College, Jerusalem: ASCHER, SAUL; BAECK, LEO; BERGMAN, SAMUEL HUGO; BREUER, ISAAC; COHEN, HERMANN; CREATION AND COSMOGONY; GANS, EDUARD; GUTTMANN, JACOB; GUTTMANN, JULIUS; HIRSCH, SAMSON RAPHAEL; PHILO JUDAEUS; SCHWEID, ELIEZER

Ziva Amishai-Maisels*, B.A., M.A., Ph.D.; Professor of Art History, the Hebrew University of Jerusalem: ART: INFLUENCED BY THE HOLOCAUST; ART: MODERN JEWISH ART; BARASCH, MOSHE

Jacob Amit, Editor, Tel Aviv: YAARI, MEIR

Reuven Amitai*, Ph.D.; Associate Professor, Institute of African Studies, the Hebrew University of Jerusalem: AYALON, DAVID; MAMLUKS; MONGOLS; SELJUKS

Shimshon Avraham Amitsur, Ph.D.; Professor of Mathematics, the Hebrew University of Jerusalem: LEVITSKY, JACOB

Moses Bensabat Amzalak, Ph.D.; Honorary Rector and Professor of the Technical University of Lisbon; Former President of the Academy of Sciences of Lisbon: BENARUS, ADOLFO; BENOLIEL, JOSEPH

Jean Ancel*, Ph.D.; Independent Historian, Yad Vashem, Jerusalem: ATAKI; BELGOROD-DNESTROVSKI; BELTSY; BENDERY; BRICEVA; BRICHANY; DOMBROVENI; FALESHTY; KALARASH; KAUSHANY; KHOTIN; KISHINEV; KOTOVSKOYE; LEOVO; LIPKANY; NOVOSELITSA; ORGEYEV; SEKIRYANY; YEDINTSY; ZGURITSA

Pierre Anctil*, Ph.D.; Director, Institute of Canadian Studies, University of Ottawa, Canada: BELKIN, SIMON; BOSCO, MONIQUE; CANADIAN LITERATURE; WISEMAN, SHLOIME

Marc D. Angel*, B.A., B.S., Ph.D., Rabbi; Congregation Shearith Israel, New York: UNION OF SEPHARDIC CONGREGATIONS, THE

Charles Angoff, B.A.; Professor of English, Fairleigh Dickinson University, Rutherford, New Jersey: NATHAN, GEORGE JEAN

B. Mordechai Ansbacher, M.A.; Historian, Jerusalem: ARNDT, ADOLF; ARNHEIM, FISCHEL; BADGE, JEWISH; BEHREND, JACOB FRIEDRICH; BOOKS; BUCER, MARTIN; COINS AND CURRENCY; ELLSTAETTER, MORITZ; FRANKENBURGER, WOLF; JUEDISCHER KULTURBUND; KANTOROWICZ, HERMANN; KEMPNER, ROBERT MAX WASILII; LABAND, PAUL; LUBETKIN, ZIVIA; LUTHER, MARTIN; MALINES; REUTLINGEN; SHUM; SPEYER; TRIER; WALLICH; WIENER GESERA; WITTENBERG, YIẒHAK; ZUCKERMAN, ITZHAK

Heinz L. Ansbacher, Ph.D.; Professor of Psychology, the University of Vermont, Burlington, Vermont: ADLER, ALFRED

Joyce Antler*, Ph.D.; Samuel Lane Professor of American Jewish History and Culture, Brandeis University, Waltham, Massachusetts: ABZUG, BELLA SAVITZKY; LERNER, GERDA KRONSTEIN

J. Aouizerate-Levin*, M.A.; Student, Musicology, the Hebrew University of Jerusalem: SHLONSKY, VERDINA

John J. Appel, Ph.D.; Associate Professor of American Studies, the James Madison College of Michigan State University, East Lansing: CHRISTIAN SCIENCE CHURCH

James L. Apple, Th.D., Rabbi; Great Lakes, Illinois

Raymond Apple, B.A., LL.B., Rabbi; London: MARRIAGE

Shimon Applebaum, D.Phil.; Associate Professor of Classical Archaeology and of Jewish History, Tel Aviv University: DECAPOLIS; HEROD I; LIBYA

Miriam Arad, Literary Critic, Jerusalem: BEN-AMOTZ, DAHN

Shimshon Arad, Israel Diplomat, Jerusalem: WHITE, THEODORE H.

Yitzchak Arad, Librarian and Teacher, Jerusalem: CHAJES, ISAAC BEN ABRAHAM; KIRSCHBRAUN, ELIJAH; MAZUR, ELIYAHU; PERLMUTTER, ABRAHAM ẒEVI

Mordechai Arbell*, M.A.; Former Israel Ambassador to the Caribbean; Ben Zvi Institute, Jerusalem: BARBADOS; CARIBBEANS, SPANISH-PORTUGUESE NATION OF THE: LA NACION; COLOMBIA; CURAÇAO; DELVALLE LEVI MADURO, ERIC ARTURO; DELVALLE, MAX SHALOM; DOMINICAN REPUBLIC; GUIANA; HAITI; MADURO, RICARDO; PANAMA; SURINAME; TUCACAS; VALONA

Archiv Bibliographia Judaica Staff, Johann Wolfgang Goethe-Universitat, Frankfurt, Germany: ISAACSOHN, SIEGFRIED; KELLNER, LEON; KOMPERT, LEOPOLD; KOREFF, DAVID FERDINAND; KRACAUER, ISIDOR; REICHER, EMANUEL; RIESSER, GABRIEL; ROSIN, DAVID; SCHWAB, HERMANN; SPANIER, ARTHUR; STERN-TAEUBLER, SELMA; SUEDFELD, GABRIEL; SULZBACH, ABRAHAM; TAEUBLER, EUGEN; ULLSTEIN; VEIT, MORITZ; YORK-STEINER, HEINRICH ELCHANAN

Morris Ardoin*, M.A.; Director, Communications, Hebrew Immigrant Aid Society, New York: HEBREW IMMIGRANT AID SOCIETY

Moshe-Max Arend, Ph.D.; Lecturer, Bar-Ilan University, Ramat Gan: KARA, JOSEPH

Ramie Arian*: YOUNG JUDAEA

Eliyahu Arieh, M.Sc.; Director of the Seismological Laboratory, Geological Survey of Israel, Jerusalem: EARTHQUAKE; SAMUEL BEN HANANIAH

Nachum Arieli, B.A.; Jerusalem: ABRAHAM BEN DOV OF MEZHIRECH; BARUCH BEN JEHIEL OF MEDZIBEZH

Allan Arkush*, Ph.D.; Judaic Studies, Binghamton University, Binghamton, New York: MENDELSSOHN, MOSES

Abraham Arnold*, L.L.D.; Author, Historian, Journalist; Member Order of Canada, Association for Canadian Jewish Studies, Jewish Heritage Centre of Western Canada, Winnipeg, Canada: CHERNIACK, SAUL MARK; FREEDMAN, SAMUEL; GRAY, MORRIS ABRAHAM;

MANITOBA; ORLIKOW, DAVID; WINNIPEG; ZOLF

Yaakov Arnold*: LIEBER, DAVID

Walter L. Arnstein, Ph.D.; Professor of History, the University of Illinois, Urbana-Champaign: STERN, ALFRED

Wellesley Aron, B.A.; Major (Ret.), British Army; Tel Aviv: IḤUD HABONIM

C.C. Aronsfeld, Researcher, London: GRUEBER, HEINRICH

Shlomo Aronson, Ph.D.; Lecturer in Political Science, the Hebrew University of Jerusalem: ADENAUER, KONRAD; GESTAPO; JAFFA; SS AND SD

Elia Samuele Artom, Dott.in lett., Rabbi; Teacher of Hebrew Language and Literature, Universita degli Studi, Florence; Director and Professor of the Collegio Rabbinico Italiano, Florence and Rome: ABISHAG THE SHUNAMMITE; SEGRE

Menachem E. Artom, Ph.D., Rabbi; Civil Service Commission, Jerusalem: CAPISTRANO, JOHN; MITHRIDATES, FLAVIUS; MORTARA, MARCO; PESARO, ABRAMO; PISA, DA; SARDINIA; SEGRÈ, JOSHUA BENZION; SEGRE, SALVATORE; SIXTUS OF SIENA; TUSCANY; VOLTERRA; VOLTERRA, MESHULLAM BEN MENAHEM, DA

Pinhas Artzi, Ph.D., Rabbi; Associate Professor of Hebrew and Semitic Languages, Bar-Ilan University, Ramat Gan; Associate Professor of Akkadian and Ancient Near Eastern History, Tel Aviv University: CUTH, CUTHAH; DAGON; EUPHRATES; GELB, IGNACE JAY; GOSHEN; GOZAN; KARKAR; MARDUK; PEKOD; PERIZZITES; PICK, ḤAYYIM HERMANN; RESEN; RESHEPH; RODANIM; SIHON; TADMOR

Abraham Arzi, Ph.D., Rabbi; Senior Teacher in Talmud, Bar-Ilan University, Ramat Gan: AL TIKREI; DELITZSCH, FRIEDRICH; DREAMS; ETIQUETTE; KODASHIM; LEKET, SHIKHḤAH, AND PE'AH; MO'ED; RABBAH BAR BAR HANA; RESHUT; TEREFAH; TIKKUN SOFERIM; TOHOROT; ZAKEN MAMRE

Solomon Asch, Ph.D.; Psychologist, Rutgers University, New Jersey: WERTHEIMER, MAX

Dov Ashbel, Dr. Phil.; Emeritus Associate Professor of Meteorology, the Hebrew University of Jerusalem: ATLAS, DAVID; BERSON, ARTHUR JOSEPH STANISLAV; CONRAD, VICTOR; ISRAEL, LAND OF: GEOGRAPHICAL SURVEY; LESS, EMIL; MACHTA, LESTER; MARGULES, MAX; NAMIAS, JEROME; PEPPER, JOSEPH; RUBIN, MORTON JOSEPH; WEXLER, HARRY

Robert Asher, M.A.; Lecturer in History, City College of the City University of New York: FELS; FILENE

Shmuel Ashkenazi, the Rabbi Kook Institute, Jerusalem: AARON BERECHIAH BEN MOSES OF MODENA; DAVID BEN SAMUEL HA-LEVI; EDELS, SAMUEL ELIEZER BEN JUDAH HA-LEVI; EISENSTADT, ABRAHAM ẒEVI HIRSCH BEN JACOB; GOMBINER, ABRAHAM ABELE BEN ḤAYYIM HA-LEVI; IBN ḤAYYIM, AARON; SABA, ABRAHAM BEN JACOB; TYRNAU, ISAAC

Dianne Ashton*, Ph.D.; Professor, Rowan University, Glassboro, New Jersey: GRATZ, REBECCA

Eliyahu Ashtor, Ph.D., Dr. Phil.; Professor of Moslem History and Civilization, the Hebrew University of Jerusalem: ABRAHAM BEN DAVID MAIMUNI; ABRAHAM BEN MAZHIR; ABU AL-MUNAJJĀ SOLOMON BEN SHAYA; ABU 'IMRĀN AL-TIFLĪSĪ; ABU SA'D AL-TUSTARĪ; ALEPPO; ALEXANDRIA; ALMERÍA; AMRAM; BAQŪBA; BAR HEBRAEUS, JOHANAN; BASRA; BEN SIMEON, RAPHAEL AARON; BILBEIS; CAIRO; DAMANHŪR; DAMĪRA; DAVID BEN ABRAHAM MAIMUNI; DAVID BEN DANIEL; DAVID BEN JOSHUA MAIMUNI; DUMUH; EDESSA; EGYPT; EPHRAIM BEN SHEMARIAH; EZRA BEN ABRAHAM BEN MAZHIR; FAIYŪM; FATIMIDS; ḤANOKH BEN MOSES; ḤASSĀN IBN ḤASSĀN; ḤIBAT ALLAH, IBN JUMAY' IBN ZAYN; ḤILLA; ḤISDAI IBN ḤISDAI, ABU AL-FAḌL; ḤISDAI IBN SHAPRUT; IBN AL-BARQŪLĪ; IBN KILLIS, ABU AL-FARAJ YA'QŪB IBN YŪSUF; IBN YASHUSH, ISAAC ABU IBRAHIM; IBRAHIM IBN YA'QŪB OF TORTOSA; IRBIL; JAZIRAT IBN 'UMAR; JEHOSEPH HA-NAGID; JERUSALEM; JESSE BEN HEZEKIAH; JOSHUA BEN ABRAHAM MAIMUNI; JUBAYL; KHARĀJ AND JIZYA; LEBANON; LÉVI-PROVENÇAL, EVARISTE; MAHALLA AL-KUBRA; MAMLUKS; MANN, JACOB; MANSURA; MEVORAKH BEN SAADIAH; MINYAT ZIFTA; MOSES BEN ḤANOKH; NAHRAI BEN NISSIM; NAHRAWĀN; NETHANEL BEN MOSES HA-LEVI; NISIBIS; QAṢR IBN HUBAYRAH; RAḤBAH, AL-; RAQQA; RASHID; SAHLĀN BEN ABRAHAM; SA'ĪD IBN HASAN; SARŪJ; SELJUKS; SHEMARIAH BEN ELHANAN; SHIM'ON, JOSEPH BEN JUDAH IBN; SHOLAL, NATHAN HA-KOHEN; SIDON; SOLOMON BEN ELIJAH HA-KOHEN; SPAIN; SUNBAT; SYRIA; TADEF; TANTA; TRAVELERS AND EXPLORERS; TRIPOLI; TYRE; UKBARĀ; WASIT

Cyril Aslanov*, Ph.D.; Associate Professor, the Hebrew University of Jerusalem: JEWISH LANGUAGES; JUDEO-FRENCH; JUDEO-GREEK; JUDEO-ITALIAN; JUDEO-PROVENÇAL

Simha Assaf, Rabbi; Rector and Professor of Rabbinical and Geonic Literature, the Hebrew University of Jerusalem; Justice of the Supreme Court of Israel: AARON BEN JOSEPH HA-LEVI; ABBAHU; ABIATHAR BEN ELIJAH HA-KOHEN; ABRAHAM BEN ELIJAH OF VILNA; ABRAHAM BEN ISAAC OF NARBONNE; ABRAHAM BEN NATHAN; ADRET, SOLOMON BEN ABRAHAM; AḤA OF SHABḤA; ALFASI, ISAAC BEN JACOB; BUSTANAI BEN ḤANINAI; ELHANAN BEN HUSHIEL; ELHANAN BEN SHEMARIAH; ELIJAH BEN SOLOMON HA-KOHEN; GAON; ISAAC; YESHIVOT

Yom Tov Assis*, Ph.D.; Department of Jewish History, World Center for Jewish Studies, the Hebrew University of Jerusalem: ABOAB, IMMANUEL; ALCONSTANTINI; ALEMÁN, MATEO; ANUSIM; AUTO DA FÉ; ÁVILA; BADAJOZ; BARBASTRO; BARCELONA; BARCELONA, DISPUTATION OF; BARRIOS, DANIEL LEVI DE; BARROS BASTO, ARTURO CARLOS DE; BEJA; BELMONTE; BESALÚ; BRAGANZA; BUITRAGO; BURGOS; BURRIANA; CALAHORRA; CALATAYUD; CANARY ISLANDS; CANTERA BURGOS, FRANCISCO; CARDOZO, ISAAC; CARRION DE LOS CONDES; CASTRO QUESADA, AMERICO; CASTRO SARMENTO, JACOB DE; CASTRO TARTAS, ISAAC DE; CASTRO, PEDRO DE; CERVERA; CHILLÓN; CHUETAS; CIUDAD REAL; CIUDAD RODRIGO; COIMBRA; CUENCA; CURIEL; DAROCA; DUEÑAS; ELCHE; ENRÍQUEZ GÓMEZ, ANTONIO; ESCALONA; ESCUDERO, LORENZO; ESTELLA; FERNANDES VILLAREAL, MANOEL; HUESCA; IBN ZADOK, SOLOMON; INQUISITION; JACA; JAÉN; LEÓN, LUIS DE; LÉRIDA; LIMPIEZA DE SANGRE; MADRID; MAJORCA; MURVIEDRO; OROBIO DE CASTRO, ISAAC; PALENCIA; PAMPLONA; PLASENCIA; SALAMANCA; SANTA COLOMA DE

QUERALT; SARAGOSSA; SEGOVIA; SEVILLE; SORIA; TOLEDO; TUDELA

Alexander Astor, B.A. O.B.E., Rabbi; Auckland, New Zealand: DAMASCUS; DAVIS, SIR ERNEST HYAM; FISHER, SIR WOOLF

Alan Astro*, Ph.D.; Professor, Trinity University, San Antonio, Texas: AYALTI, HANAN J.; BERLINER, ISAAC; BOTOSHANSKY, JACOB; GLANTZ, JACOB; KHALYASTRE; WARSZAWSKI, OSER

Maurice (D.) Atkin, M.A.; Economist, Washington, D.C.: UNITED STATES OF AMERICA

Tsevi Atsmon, M.A.; Rishon le-Zion, Israel: RISHON LE-ZION

Robert Attal, Librarian, the Ben-Zvi Institute and Yad Vashem, Jerusalem: ALGERIA; AYDAN, DAVID; BAḤUẒIM; BEKACHE, SHALOM; CONSTANTINE; GOZLAN, ELIE; HAJJĀJ, DANIEL; LIBYA; SAMAMA, NESSIM; SCIALOM, DAVID DARIO

David Atzmon, M.Jur.; Ministry for Foreign Affairs, Jerusalem

Pierre Aubery, Ph.D.; Professor of French Literature, the State University of New York, Buffalo: LECACHE, BERNARD; MANDEL, ARNOLD

Bernard Auerbach*, L.L.M.; Professor of Law (Retired), University of Maryland: CONTRACT; THEFT AND ROBBERY

Jacob Auerbach, Jerusalem: TEMPLE MOUNT; WESTERN WALL

Rachel Auerbach, Dipl.Hist.Psych.; Historian, Jerusalem: TREBLINKA

Hanoch Avenary, Dr.Phil.; Senior Lecturer in Musicology, Tel Aviv University: ADDIR HU; AKDAMUT MILLIN; ALEINU LE-SHABBE'AḤ; ALGAZI, ISAAC BEN SOLOMON; ALGAZI, LEON; AL-ḤARIZI, JUDAH BEN SOLOMON; ALMAN, SAMUEL; ALTSCHUL, JOSEPH; AMEN; AMIDAH; AVI AVI; AVODAH; BACHMANN, JACOB; BAUER, JACOB; EDIRNE; HAGGADAH, PASSOVER; IBN ABĪ AL-ṢALT; KADDISH; MI-SINAI NIGGUNIM; MOSES BEN JOSEPH HA-LEVI; MUSIC; NUSAḤ; SHTAYGER

Moshe Avidan, Ambassador, Ministry for Foreign Affairs, Jerusalem: FINLAND; POLAND

Moshe Avidor, Ph.D.; Former Ambassador and Director General of the Israel Academy of Sciences and Humanities, Jerusalem: ISRAEL ACADEMY OF SCIENCES AND HUMANITIES; ISRAEL, STATE OF: EDUCATION AND SCIENCE

Nachman Avigad, Ph.D.; Professor of Archaeology, the Hebrew University of Jerusalem: BET SHE'ARIM; JERICHO

Avraham Avi-Hai, Ph.D.; Vice-Provost, School for Overseas Students, Hebrew University of Jerusalem

Gitta (Aszkenazy) Avinor, M.A.; Critic, Haifa: AMIR, AHARON; BARTOV, HANOCH; MEGGED, AHARON; MOSSINSOHN, YIGAL; TAMMUZ, BENJAMIN

Joseph Aviram, M.A.; Director of the Institute of Archaeology, the Hebrew University of Jerusalem

Isaac Avishur, M.A.; Instructor in Bible and Biblical History, the University of the Negev, Beersheba: BIBLE; DAN; EDOM; GEHAZI; ISAIAH; NAOMI; NAPHTALI; SEPHARVAIM

Benad Avital, Ministry for Foreign Affairs, Jerusalem: ISRAEL, STATE OF: HISTORICAL SURVEY

Efrat E. Aviv*, M.A.; Jewish History, Bar-Ilan University, Ramat Gan: IZMIR

Michael Avi-Yonah, Ph.D.; Professor of Archaeology and of the History of Art, the Hebrew University of Jerusalem: ABEL SHITTIM or SHITTIM; ABEL, AVEL; ABEL, LOUIS FELIX; ABEL-BETH-MAACAH; ABEL-MEHOLAH; ABILENE; ACHOR, VALLEY OF; ACHSHAPH; ACHZIB; ACRE; ADAM; ADORAIM; ADULLAM; AGRIPPINA; AI or HA-AI; AKHBAREI/ACCHABARON; ALAMAH; ALBRIGHT, WILLIAM FOXWELL; ALMON or ALEMETH; ALT, ALBRECHT; AMANA; AMMATHA; ANAB; ANATHOTH; ANTHEDON; ANTIPATRIS; ANTONIA; APHEK; APOLLONIA; ARABAH, THE; ARBEL; ARCHELAIS; ARETHUSA; ARGOB; AROER; ASHDOD; ASHKELON; ASHTAROTH, ASHTEROTH-KARNAIM, KARNAIM; ATAROTH; ATHLIT; AVELIM or OVELIM; AZEKAH; AZMON; AZNOTH-TABOR; BAALAH; BAAL-HAZOR; BAAL-MEON; BAAL-PERAZIM; BAAL-ZEPHON; BADE, WILLIAM FREDERIC; BAḤURIM; BANIAS; BASILICA; BEER; BEEROTH; BEERSHEBA; BEN-DOR, IMMANUEL; BENE-BERAK; BENJAMIN OF TIBERIAS; BENZINGER, IMMANUEL; BET AGLAYIM; BET ALFA; BET GUVRIN; BET ḤARODON; BET NETOFAH; BET YERAḤ; BET ZEKHARYAH; BET-ANATH; BET-DAGON; BET-EL; BETHANY; BET-HARAM; BETHBASI; BETHLEHEM; BETHLEPTEPHA; BET-HORON; BETHPHAGE; BETHSAIDA; BETHULIA; BET-MAON; BET-NIMRAH; BET-REHOB; BET-ZUR; BEZEK; BLISS, FREDERICK JONES; BOẒRAH; BURCHARDUS DE MONTE SION; BURCKHARDT, JOHANN LUDWIG; BUTNAH; CABUL; CAESAREA; CAPERNAUM; CAPITOLIAS; CARMEL; CARMEL, MOUNT; CHERITH; CHORAZIN; CLERMONT-GANNEAU, CHARLES; CONDER, CLAUDE REGNIER; COZEBA; CROWFOOT, JOHN WINTER; DAN; DEAD SEA; DEBIR; DEUTSCHER PALAESTINA-VEREIN; DIUM; DOBRATH; DOK; DOTHAN; DURA-EUROPUS; EBEN-EZER; EDREI; EGLON; ELASA; ELATH; ELEALEH; ELTEKEH; ELUSA; EMMAUS; EN-DOR; EN-GANNIM; EN-HAROD; EN-RIMMON; EN-ROGEL; EPHRON; ESHTAOL; ESHTEMOA; ETAM; EUSEBIUS PAMPHILI; FABRI, FELIX; GADARA; GALILEE; GAMLA; GARSTANG, JOHN; GATH; GATH-HEPHER; GATH-RIMMON; GAZA; GEBA; GEDERAH, GEDEROTH; GEDOR; GERASA; GEZER; GIBBETHON; GILGAL; GISCALA; GITTAIM; GOFNAH; GOLAN; GUÉRIN, VICTOR; GUY, PHILIP LANGSTAFFE ORD; HABOR; HADAD; HADID; HADRACH; HALHUL; HAM; HAMMATH; HANNATHON; HAPHARAIM; HAR HA-MELEKH; HAROSHETH-GOIIM; HAURAN; HAVVOTH-JAIR; ḤAẒER, ḤAẒERIM; HAZEROTH; HEBRON; HEPHER; HERMON, MOUNT; HERODIUM; HESHBON; HISTORY: THE AFTERMATH OF THE FIRST ROMAN WAR; HOR; HORMAH; HORONAIM; HUKOK; ḤULEH; HYRCANIA; IBLEAM; IJON; IR-NAHASH; IRON; ISRAEL EXPLORATION SOCIETY; ISRAEL, LAND OF: GEOGRAPHICAL SURVEY; JABBOK; JABESH-GILEAD; JABNEEL; JABNEH; JAHAZ, JAHAZA; JANOAH, JANAH; JAPHIA; JARMUTH; JATTIR, JETHIRA; JAZER; JEHOSHAPHAT, VALLEY OF; JERUSALEM; JEZREEL; JEZREEL, VALLEY OF; JOKNEAM; JORDAN; JOTABAH; JOTAPATA; JOTBATH, JOTHBATAH; JUDEAN DESERT CAVES; KABRITHA; KANAH; KARKAR; KARNAIM; KEDEMOTH; KEFAR AKKO; KEFAR BARAM; KEFAR DAROM; KEFAR GAMALA; KEFAR ḤANANYAH; KEFAR ḤATTIN;

KEFAR KANNA; KEFAR MANDI; KEFAR NEBURAYA; KEFAR OTNAY; KEILAH; KENATH; KENYON, DAME KATHLEEN MARY; KERAK or CHARAX; KIDRON; KINNERET, LAKE; KIR-HARESETH; KIRIATH-JEARIM; KISHON; KLEIN, SAMUEL; LEBANON; LEGIO; LIBNAH; LO-DEBAR; LUZ; LYDDA; MA'ON; MA'ALEH AKRABBIM; MACALISTER, ROBERT ALEXANDER STEWART; MACHAERUS; MADABA, MEDEBA; MAHANAIM; MAIUMAS; MAKKEDAH; MAMPSIS; MAMRE; MARESHAH; MAYER, LEO ARY; MAZAR, BENJAMIN; MEGIDDO; MEROZ; MICHMASH or MICHMAS; MIGDOL; MINNITH; MISREPHOTH-MAIM; MIẒPEH or MIẒPAH; MOAB; MODI'IN; MOLADAH; MORESHETH-GATH; MORIAH; MOUNT OF OLIVES; MOZA; MUSIL, ALOIS; NAARAH; NABLUS; NAHALAL or NAHALOL; NAIN; NARBATA; NAVEH; NAZARETH; NEBO; NEGEV; NETOPHAH; NIẒẒANAH; NOB; ONO; OPHEL; OPHRAH; OSSUARIES and SARCOPHAGI; PALESTINE EXPLORATION FUND; PALMER, EDWARD HENRY; PARAH, PERATH; PARAN; PEKI'IN; PELLA or PAḤAL; PENUEL; PERROT, JEAN MICHAEL; PETRA; PHASAELIS; PHOTIS; PISGAH; POCOCKE, RICHARD; PRESS, YESHAYAHU; PUNON; QUARESMIUS, FRANCISCUS; RABBAH; RABBATH-AMMON; RAFA; RAMAH or HA-RAMAH or HA-RAMATHAIM-ZOPHIM; RAMLEH; RAMOTH; RAMOTH-GILEAD; RED SEA; REHOBOTH; RIMMON-PEREZ; ROBINSON, EDWARD; ROEHRICHT, REINHOLD; RUMA or ARUMAH; SAFED; SALCHAH; SARID; SARṬABA; SAULCY, LOUIS FELICIEN DE JOSEPH CAIGNART; SCHICK, CONRAD; SCHUMACHER, GOTTLIEB; SEETZEN, ULRICH JASPER; SEIR, MOUNT; SENAAH or MIGDAL SENAAH; SENNABRIS; SHAALBIM; SHALEM; SHECHEM; SHEFARAM; SHEPHELAH; SHIḤIN or ASOCHIS; SHIHOR, SHIHOR-LIBNATH; SHILOAH, SILOAM; SHILOH; SHIMRON; SHIVTAH or SOBATA; SHUNEM; SHUSHAN; SICHAR; SIKHNIN or SOGANE; SIN, WILDERNESS OF; SINAI; SMITH, SIR GEORGE ADAM; SOCOH OR SOCO; SODOM AND GOMORRAH; SOREK, VALLEY OF; STARKEY, JOHN LLEWELYN; STEKELIS, MOSHE; SUCCOTH; SUKENIK, ELIEZER LIPA; SUSITA OR HIPPOS; SYNAGOGUE; TAANACH; TABGHA; TABOR, MOUNT; TAMAR; TEKOA; TEMPLE; THEBEZ; THOMSEN, PETER; TIBERIAS; TIMNATH-HERES, TIMNATH-SERAH; TIRZAH; TIVON; TRANSJORDAN; TYRE OF THE TOBIADS; USHA; VINCENT, LOUIS HUGUES; VOGÜÉ, CHARLES EUGENE MELCHIOR, COMTE DE; WADI DĀLIYA; WAR AND WARFARE; WARREN, SIR CHARLES; WATZINGER, CARL; WEIGAND, THEODOR; WILSON, SIR CHARLES WILLIAM; WINCKLER, HUGO; WOOLLEY, SIR CHARLES LEONARD; YARKON; YARMUK; YEIVIN, SHEMUEL; ZANOAH; ZAPHON; ZAREPHATH; ZARETHAN; ZEMARAIM; ZERED; ZEREDAH; ZIKLAG; ZIPH; ẒORAH

Jane (Adashko) Avner*, Ph.D.; Archivist and Consultant, Milwaukee Jewish Historical Society, Milwaukee; Former Associate Curator of Jewish History at the Western Reserve Historical Society, Cleveland: AKRON; CLEVELAND; LAURA AND ALVIN SIEGAL COLLEGE OF JUDAIC STUDIES; LEWIS, PETER B.; OHIO; SAPIRSTEIN-STONE-WEISS FAMILY

Zvi Avneri (Hans Lichtenstein), Dr.Phil.; Senior Lecturer in Jewish History, Haifa University: AARON BEN JOSEPH HA-ROFE; ABNER OF BURGOS; ABOAB, ISAAC II; ABRABANEL, ISAAC BEN JUDAH; ABU 'ĪSĀ, ISAAC BEN JACOB AL-IṢFAHĪNĪ; ABUDARHAM; ABUDARHAM, DAVID BEN JOSEPH; ABULAFIA, SAMUEL BEN MEIR HA-LEVI; ABULAFIA, SAMUEL HA-LEVI; ADLER, NATHAN BEN SIMEON HA-KOHEN; ALBALIA, BARUCH BEN ISAAC; ALBALIA, ISAAC BEN BARUCH; ALDUBI, ABRAHAM BEN MOSES BEN ISMAIL; ALFONSO DE OROPESA; ANDERNACH; ANHALT; ANSBACH; ARONIUS, JULIUS; AUGSBURG; AVELEI ZION; BACHARACH; BARCELONA; BASLE; BAVARIA; BAYONNE; BEAUCAIRE; BEDERSI, ABRAHAM BEN ISAAC; BENVENISTE DE PORTA; BENVENISTE, ABRAHAM; BENVENISTE, SHESHET BEN ISAAC BEN JOSEPH; BERG; BERGHEIM; BERNE; BESANÇON; BÉZIERS; BIELEFELD; BINGEN; BLOIS; BRESSLAU, HARRY; BRUNSWICK; BURGOS; BUXTORF, JOHANNES; DUESSELDORF; DUISBURG; EISENMENGER, JOHANN ANDREAS; EMDEN; EPSTEIN, ABRAHAM; ERFURT; FERRER, VICENTE; GENEVA; HALBERSTADT; HALLE; HAMBURG; HAMELN; HANOVER; HEIDELBERG; HEINEMANN, JEREMIAH; HESSE; HILDESHEIM; IBN ALFAKHAR; IBN SHOSHAN; IBN WAQAR; MEHLSACK, ELIAKIM BEN JUDAH HA-MILZAHGI; OBERMEYER, JACOB; OFFENBACH; OFFENBURG; OLDENBURG; OPPENHEIM; OPPENHEIMER, JOSEPH BEN ISSACHAR SUESSKIND; SHEMARIAH BEN ELIJAH BEN JACOB; VERBAND DER VEREINE FUER JUEDISCHE GESCHICHTE UND LITERATUR; WANDSBECK; WASSERMANN, JAKOB; WESTPHALIA; WOLF, GERSON; WORMS; WUERTTEMBERG

Arie Avnerre, M.A.; Israel Broadcasting Authority, Jerusalem

Haim Avni, Ph.D.; Lecturer in Contemporary Jewry, the Hebrew University of Jerusalem: AGRICULTURE; AMIA; ARGENTINA; CHILE; ENTRE RÍOS; LATIN AMERICA; PORTUGAL; SPAIN

Yitzhak Avni, Director of the Israel Government Coins and Medals Corporation, Jerusalem: MEDALS

Moshe A. Avnimelech, Ph.D.; Emeritus Professor of Geology and Paleontology, the Hebrew University of Jerusalem: BLANCKENHORN, MAX; OPPENHEIM, PAUL LEO

Mindy (Beth) Avrich-Skapinker*, Ph.D.; Member, Immigration and Refugee Board, Toronto, Canada: LASTMAN, MELVIN DOUGLAS; NEWMAN, PETER CHARLES; REISMAN, HEATHER; SCHWARTZ, GERALD

Leila Avrin, Ph.D.; Teaching Fellow, School of Library and Archive Studies, the Hebrew University of Jerusalem: CALLIGRAPHY, MODERN HEBREW; SPITZER, MOSHE

Dov Avron, Ph.D.; Historian, Tel Aviv: GNIEZNO; GREAT POLAND; POZNAN

Benjamin Maria Baader*, Ph.D.; Assistant Professor, University of Manitoba, Canada: DIE DEBORAH

Menachem Babitz, M.A., Ing.; Senior Research Fellow, the Technion Research and Development Foundation, Haifa

Gabriel Bach, LL.B.; State Attorney of the State of Israel, Jerusalem

Gideon Bach*, Professor, Chairman, Department of Human Genetics, Hadassah University Hospital, Jerusalem: GENETIC DISEASES IN JEWS

Roberto Bachi, Ph.D., Dr.Jur.; Professor of Statistics and Demography, the Hebrew University of Jerusalem

Bernard Bachrach, Ph.D.; Assistant Professor of Medieval History, the University of Minnesota, Minneapolis: CLOTAIRE II; RECCARED

Gershon Bacon*, Ph.D.; Associate Professor of Jewish History, Bar-Ilan University, Ramat Gan: IDOLATRY; JUDGES, THE BOOK OF; SCHENIRER, SARAH; SHIMEI; TABEEL, THE SON OF; ZAMZUMMIM; ZEBAH AND ZALMUNNA; ZIMRI; ZIMRI

Yohanan Bader, Dr.Jur.; Member of the Knesset, Ramat Gan: BEGIN, MENAḤEM

Avner Bahat, B.A.; Kefar Masaryk: ZEFIRA, BRACHAH

Dan Bahat*, Ph.D.; Professor, University of St. Michael College, University of Toronto, Canada: WESTERN WALL

Jacob Bahat, Senior Lecturer in Hebrew Language and Literature, Haifa University: HAZAZ, ḤAYYIM

Henry Eli Baker, B.C.L., LL.B.; President of the District Court, Jerusalem; Research Fellow in the Law Faculty, the Hebrew University of Jerusalem: ISRAEL, STATE OF: LEGAL AND JUDICIAL SYSTEM

Zachary M. Baker*, B.A., M.A., M.L.S.; Reinhard Family Curator of Judaica & Hebraica Collections, Stanford University Libraries, Stanford, California: ABRAMOWICZ, DINA

Carol Bakhos*, Ph.D.; Associate Professor of Late Antique Judaism, University of California, Los Angeles: AGGADAH

Avraham Balaban*, Ph.D.; Professor of Modern Hebrew Literature, University of Florida: AVIDAN, DAVID; HOURVITZ, YA'IR; KAHANA-CARMON, AMALIA; OZ, AMOS; ZELDA

Meir Balaban, Dr.Phil.; *Encyclopaedia Judaica* (Germany); Professor of Jewish History, Warsaw: CALAHORA; SAMBOR

Rifat Bali*, Graduate of Sorbonne University, Ecole Pratique Des Hautes Etudes, Istanbul, Turkey: ALATON, ISHAK; ASSEO, DAVID; BENAROYA, AVRAM; CHALOM, MARCEL; FARHI, MORIS; FRANCO, GAD; FRESCO, DAVID; GARIH, ÜZEYIR; GEREZ, JOSEF HABIB; HALEVA, ISAK; HUBEŞ, ROZET; KAMHI, JAK V.; KANETI, SELIM; KARASU, ALBERT; KOHEN, ALBERT; KOHEN, SAMI; LEVI, MARIO; LEYON, AVRAM; MENDA, ELİEZER; VENTURA, MİCHON

Carole B. Balin*, Ph.D.; Associate Professor of History, Hebrew Union College-Jewish Institute of Religion, New York: DUBNOW-ERLICH, SOPHIA; MARKEL-MOSESSOHN, MIRIAM

Ivan Jay Ball, Jr., B.A., B.D.; Foothill Community College, Los Altos Hills, California: ZEPHANIAH

Kurt Jakob Ball-Kaduri, Dr.Jur.; Historian, Tel Aviv: BERLIN; STAHL, HEINRICH

Shlomo Balter, Ph.D., Rabbi; Lecturer in Bible, the City University of New York: EN-DOR, WITCH OF; GERSHON, GERSHONITES; JONATHAN; PUT; ROD OF AARON; ROD OF MOSES; SHAMMAH

Bernard J. Bamberger, D.D., Rabbi; President of the World Union for Progressive Judaism, New York: ANGELS AND ANGELOLOGY; BLANK, SHELDON HAAS; BUTTENWIESER, MOSES; LAUTERBACH, JACOB ZALLEL; MORGENSTERN, JULIAN; NEPHILIM; PARADISE

Arnold J. Band*, Ph.D.; Professor Emeritus of Hebrew, the University of California, Los Angeles: AGNON, SHMUEL YOSEF; ASSOCIATION FOR JEWISH STUDIES; BERDYCZEWSKI, MICHA JOSEF

Menahem Banitt, Ph.D.; Associate Professor of French, Tel Aviv University: BLONDHEIM, DAVID SIMON; JUDEO-FRENCH; LA'AZ

Rivka Irene Banitt, M.A.; Research Assistant in Sociology, the Institute of Criminology, Tel Aviv University: BELGIUM

Judith Barack, M.S.; Writer, New York

Pessah Bar-Adon, Director, Archaeological Expedition in the Judean Desert, Jerusalem: JUDEAN DESERT CAVES

Dan P. Barag, Ph.D.; Professor of Archaeology, the Hebrew University of Jerusalem: GLASS

Oren Barak*, Ph.D.; Lecturer of Political Science and International Relations, the Hebrew University of Jerusalem: BEIRUT; LEBANON; SIDON

Zevi Baras, Jerusalem: LOISY, ALFRED FIRMIN

Jerry Barasch, Department of External Relations, the Hebrew University of Jerusalem: HEBREW UNIVERSITY OF JERUSALEM

Moshe Barasch, Professor of Architecture and Fine Arts, the Hebrew University of Jerusalem

Shalom Bar-Asher*, Ph.D.; Professor of Jewish History, the Hebrew University of Jerusalem: BACRI; CASABLANCA

Jack Barbash, M.A.; Professor of Economics, the University of Wisconsin, Madison: ADVERTISING

Molly Lyons Bar-David, Journalist, Tel Aviv: FOOD; ḤAROSET

Haim Bar-Dayan, Dr. Phil.; Instructor in the History of Music and Art, the Rubin Academy of Music, Jerusalem: BAER, ABRAHAM; BIRNBAUM, EDUARD; ELI ẒIYYON VE-AREHA; GNESIN, MIKHAIL FABIANOVICH; KIPNIS, MENAHEM; MILNER, MOSES MICHAEL; VINAVER, CHEMJO

Elinoar Bareket*, Ph.D.; Senior Lecturer (History of the Jewish People in the Middle Ages), Achva Academic College, Shikmim, Israel: NAGID

Adina Bar-El*, Ph.D.; Researcher, Author, Lecturer, Achva College of Education, Achva, Shikmim, Israel: CHILDREN'S LITERATURE

Naftali Bar-Giora, Jewish Agency, Jerusalem: BENE ISRAEL

Yehoshua Bar-Hillel, Ph.D.; Professor of Logic and the Philosophy of Science, the Hebrew University of Jerusalem: CHOMSKY, NOAM AVRAM

Avraham Barkai*, P.h.D.; Independent Scholar, Leo Baeck Institute, Jerusalem: C. V.-ZEITUNG; CENTRAL-VEREIN DEUTSCHER STAATSBUERGER JUEDISCHEN GLAUBENS

Haim Barkai*, Ph.D.; Economics, Professor Emeritus, the Hebrew University of Jerusalem: ISRAEL, STATE OF: ECONOMIC AFFAIRS

Zeev Barkai, M.A.; Jerusalem: SUGAR INDUSTRY AND TRADE; TEXTILES; TOBACCO TRADE AND INDUSTRIES

Menahem Zvi Barkay, M.A.; Senior Librarian, the Jewish National and University Library, Jerusalem

Isadore Barmash, Journalist, New York: BERNBACH, WILLIAM; RUBINSTEIN, HELENA

Jacob Barnai, M.A.; Assistant in Jewish History, the Hebrew University of Jerusalem: DAVID BEN SHIMEON; RABINOWICH, ELIYAHU AKIVA; ROKEAḤ or ROKAH, ELAZAR BEN SHMELKE; VA'AD HA-PEKIDIM VE-HA-AMARKALIM; VA'AD PEKIDEI EREẒ ISRAEL BE-KUSHTA

Victoria J. Barnett*, M.Div., Union Theological Seminary, New York, Staff Director, Church Relations, U.S. Holocaust Memorial Museum, Washington, D.C.: HOLOCAUST

Hanan Bar-On, Ministry for Foreign Affairs, Jerusalem: ETHIOPIA

Lawrence Baron*, Ph.D.; Nasatir Professor of Modern Jewish History, San Diego State University, San Diego, California: HOLOCAUST

Lori Baron*: FRIEDMAN, HERBERT A.

Salo W. Baron, Ph.D., Rabbi; Emeritus Professor of Jewish History, Literature and Institutions, Columbia University, New York: CALVIN, JOHN; CHAJES, HIRSCH PEREZ; CONFERENCE ON JEWISH SOCIAL STUDIES; ECONOMIC HISTORY; ISRAELITISCH-THEOLOGISCHE LEHRANSTALT; POPULATION

Zvi Avraham Bar-On, Ph.D.; Senior Lecturer in Philosophy, the Hebrew University of Jerusalem

James Barr, D.D., F.B.A.; Professor of Semitic Languages and Literature, the University of Manchester, England: LINGUISTIC LITERATURE, HEBREW

Sylvia J. Barras, Wilkes-Barre and Kingston.

David Bar-Rav-Hay, Advocate; Former Member of the Knesset, Haifa: BLUMENFELD, HERMANN FADEEVICH; GOLDENWEISER, ALEXANDER SOLOMONOVICH; PASSOVER, ALEXANDER

Joel Barromi, Dr.Jur.; Ministry for Foreign Affairs, Jerusalem

Israel Bar Tal, Ph.D.; Lecturer in Jewish History, the Hebrew University of Jerusalem: BAUM, MENAḤEM MENDEL BEN AARON OF KAMENETZ

Yossi (Yosef) Bartov*, Ph.D.; Chief Scientist, Ministry of National Infrastructure, Jerusalem: BENTOR, JACOB

Lois Bar-Yaacov, B.A.; Tel Aviv: HISTADRUT

Elinor Barzacchi-Kommisar, D.E.A.; District Architect of the Jerusalem District, Ministry of Housing, Jerusalem: ISRAEL, STATE OF: CULTURAL LIFE

Hillel Barzel, Ph.D.; Associate Professor of Hebrew and World Literature, Bar-Ilan University, Ramat Gan: KURZWEIL, BARUCH

Joshua Barzilay (Folman), M.A.; Ramat Gan: WESSELY, NAPHTALI HERZ

Eliezer Bashan (Sternberg), M.A.; Instructor in Jewish History, Bar-Ilan University, Ramat Gan: EXILARCH; ḤASAN, ABU ALI JEPHETH IBN BUNDĀR; JOSEPH BEN JACOB BAR SATIA; JOSIAH BEN AARON HE-ḤAVER; JUDAH BEN JOSEPH OF KAIROUAN; KOHEN ẒEDEK OF PUMBEDITA; MAḌMŪN BEN JAPHETH BEN BUNDĀR; NAGID; NEHARDEA; OMAR IBN AL-KHAṬṬĀB; OMAR, COVENANT OF; PUMBEDITA; SOLOMON BEN JUDAH; SURA; UMAYYADS

Judith R. Baskin*, Ph.D.; Knight Professor of Humanities; Director, Harold Schnitzer Family Program in Judaic Studies, University of Oregon: ABLUTION; ABRASS, OSIAS; ADLER, POLLY; ALEXANDER, BEATRICE; AMULET; ARENDT, HANNAH; ASCETICISM; BARRENNESS AND FERTILITY; BARRON, JENNIE LOITMAN; BLOOD; BRINIG, MYRON; CHAGALL, BELLA ROSENFELD; CIRCUMCISION; DULCEA OF WORMS; FESTIVALS; FLORETA CA NOGA; FREHA BAT AVRAHAM; GINSBURG, RUTH JOAN BADER; GREENBLATT, ALIZA WAITZMAN; ḤALLAH; ḤASIDISM; HASKALAH; HEAD, COVERING OF THE; HISTORIOGRAPHY; JEWISH STUDIES; JOB, BOOK OF; JOCHSBERGER, TZIPORA; KARFF, MONA MAY; KRESSYN, MIRIAM; LIEBMANN, ESTHER SCHULHOFF AARON and JOST; MIKVEH; NIDDAH; PETERS, ROBERTA; PIONEER WOMEN; POWDERMAKER, HORTENSE; PRIESAND, SALLY JANE; PULCELINA OF BLOIS; RABBI, RABBINATE; RASHI; REBBETZIN; RESNIK, JUDITH ARLENE; SIMON, KATE; TUSSMAN, MALKA HEIFETZ; WASSERSTEIN, WENDY; WOMAN: EARLY MODERN PERIOD TO 1800 IN EUROPE; WOMAN: ISRAEL; WOMAN: MEDIEVAL, CHRISTIAN WORLD; WOMAN: MODERN PERIOD IN CENTRAL AND WESTERN EUROPE

Samantha Baskind*, Ph.D.; Assistant Professor, Art History, Cleveland State University, Cleveland, Ohio: ADLER, SAMUEL M.; ART: UNITED STATES; BAIZERMAN, SAUL; BARNET, WILL; BASKIN, LEONARD; BENN, BEN; BEN-ZION; BERNSTEIN, THERESA; BLOOM, HYMAN; BLUME, PETER; BOLOTOWSKY, ILYA; BOROFSKY, JONATHAN; CARVALHO, SOLOMON NUNES; CHICAGO, JUDY; DAVIDSON, JO; DINE, JIM; EILSHEMIUS, LOUIS M.; EZEKIEL, MOSES JACOB; FERBER, HERBERT; FRANKENTHALER, HELEN; GOLUB, LEON; GOTTLIEB, ADOLPH; GREENBERG, CLEMENT; GROPPER, WILLIAM; GUSTON, PHILIP; GUTMANN, JOSEPH; HIRSCH, JOSEPH; KATZ, ALEX; KITAJ, R. B.; KRASNER, LEE; KRUGER, BARBARA; LASSAW, IBRAM; LEVINE, JACK; LEWITT, SOL; LICHTENSTEIN, ROY; LIPTON, SEYMOUR; LOUIS, MORRIS; LOZOWICK, LOUIS; MOSLER, HENRY; NEVELSON, LOUISE; OLITSKI, JULES; PEARLSTEIN, PHILIP; RATTNER, ABRAHAM; RIVERS, LARRY; ROTHKO, MARK; SEGAL, GEORGE; SERRA, RICHARD; SOYER, MOSES; SOYER, RAPHAEL; ZORACH, WILLIAM

Jack Bass, B.A.; New York

Yomtov Ludwig Bato, Dr. Phil.; Historian, Ramat Hen, Israel: VIENNA; WERTHEIMER, SAMSON

Geulah Bat Yehuda (Raphael), M.A.; Writer, Jerusalem: ELYASHAR, JACOB SAUL BEN ELIEZER JEROHAM; HAUSDORF, AZRIEL ZELIG; LAPIDOT, ALEXANDER MOSES; LAPIN, ISRAEL MOSES FISCHEL; MEIR, JACOB; PANIGEL, ELIYAHU MOSHE; SALANT, SAMUEL; SPEKTOR, ISAAC ELHANAN

Fritz Bauer, Dr.Jur.; Prosecutor of War Criminals, Frankfurt on the Main: ZENTRALE STELLE DER LANDESJUSTIZVERWALTUNGEN

Yehuda Bauer, Ph.D.; Historian, Professor and Head of the Institute of Contemporary Jewry, the Hebrew University of Jerusalem: BAERWALD, PAUL; BECKELMAN, MOSES W.; BERGEN-BELSEN; BERIḤAH; HOLOCAUST; HOLOCAUST, RESCUE FROM; HYMAN, JOSEPH C.; JORDAN, CHARLES HAROLD; LEAVITT, MOSES A.; ROSEN, JOSEPH A.

Dorothy Bauhoff*, M.A.; Independent Author and Researcher, East Taghkanic, New York: ABRAMS, MEYER H.; AKERLOF, GEORGE A.; DINER, HASIA R.; EISEN, ARNOLD; ELIAS, NORBERT; ENDELMAN, TODD M.; FEINBERG, KENNETH; FELDMAN, LOUIS H.; FISH, STANLEY; FREEDMAN, JAMES O.; FRYMER-KENSKY, TIKVA; GLOCK, CHARLES Y.; GOLB, NORMAN; GOLDBERG, HARVEY E.; GREENBERG, JOSEPH; GUTMANN, AMY; KAUFMAN, IRVING R.; KORMAN, EDWARD R.; KOZINKSI, ALEX; KRAVITCH, PHYLLIS; KUHN, THOMAS S.; LEVIN, RICHARD C.; LEWIS, I. M.; LINGLE, LINDA; MIKVA, ABNER J.; MILGRAM, STANLEY; NOVAK, DAVID; PUTNAM, HILARY; REINHARDT, STEPHEN R.; RODIN, JUDITH; ROSENBERG, HAROLD; ROSKIES, DAVID G.; RUBIN, ROBERT E.; SAHLINS, MARSHALL; SHAPIRO, HAROLD; SMITH, JONATHAN Z.; SOFAER, ABRAHAM; SONNENFELDT, HELMUT; SPERBER, DAN; SPITZER, LEO; SPORKIN, STANLEY; WEINER, ANTHONY; WEINFELD, EDWARD; WEINSTEIN, JACK B.; WISSE, RUTH R.; WOLFE, ALAN S.; WOLFSON, ELLIOT; WOLPE, HOWARD ELIOT

Mark K. Bauman*, Ph.D.; Editor, *Southern Jewish History*; Professor of History (retired), Southern Jewish Historical Society, Ellenwood, Georgia: EPSTEIN, HARRY H.

David Baumgardt, Dr. Phil.; Professor of Philosophy, the University of Berlin; Consultant on Philosophy to the Library of Congress, Washington, D.C.: CASSIRER, ERNST; HERDER, JOHANN GOTTFRIED; LAZARUS, NAHIDA RUTH; LEVI-STRAUSS, CLAUDE

Albert I. Baumgarten, M.A.; Adjunct Lecturer in History, the Herbert H. Lehman College of the City University of New York: SCROLL OF ESTHER

Elisheva Baumgarten*, Ph.D.; Lecturer, Department of Jewish History and Gender Studies Program, Bar-Ilan University, Ramat Gan: BIRTH, GENDER

Jean Baumgarten*, Ph.D.; Professor, Directeur de recherche, Centre National de la Recherche Scientifique (CNRS), Paris, France: BOBE-MAYSE; HARKAVY, ALEXANDER; LIEBERMAN, CHAIM; SHMERUK, CHONE; WEINREICH, MAX; ZINBERG, ISRAEL

Walter Baumgartner, Dr.Phil.; Emeritus Professor of Bible and Oriental Languages, the University of Basle: PRIJS, JOSEPH

Diane Baxter*, Ph.D.; Instructor, Anthropology, The University of Oregon: ANTHROPOLOGY

Steve (Harold Steven) Bayar*, B.A. M.A., Rabbi; Congregation Bnai Israel, Millburn, New Jersey: GRUENEWALD, MAX

Bathja Bayer, Ph.D.; Librarian of the Music Department, the Jewish National and University Library, Jerusalem: ABRAHAM; AGUILAR, EMANUEL ABRAHAM; AUER, LEOPOLD; BEKKER, PAUL; BELSHAZZAR; BEN SIRA, WISDOM OF; BENTWICH; BIBLE; BINDER, ABRAHAM WOLF; CANTILLATION; COSTA, URIEL DA; DA PONTE, LORENZO; DAVID; EL MALE RAḤAMIM; ELIJAH; GERNSHEIM, FRIEDRICH; GERSHWIN, GEORGE; GOLDFADEN, ABRAHAM; GUSIKOW, JOSEPH MICHAEL; HALLELUJAH; HASMONEANS; HA-TIKVAH; HEROD I; HOLLAENDER; ISAIAH; JACOB; JACOB; JEPHTHAH; JEREMIAH; JERUSALEM; JOACHIM, JOSEPH; JOB, BOOK OF; JONAH, BOOK OF; JOSEPH; JOSEPHSON; JOSHUA; JUDITH, BOOK OF; KÁLMÁN, EMMERICH; KARACZEWSKI, ḤANINA; KEDUSHAH; KOL NIDREI; LAMENTATIONS, BOOK OF; LAVRY, MARC; LEKHAH DODI; LEWANDOWSKI, LOUIS; LOVY, ISRAEL; MA'OZ ẒUR; MAQAM; MOSES; MUSIC; NADEL, ARNO; NARDI, NAHUM; NATHAN, ISAAC; NAUMBOURG, SAMUEL; NAVON, ISAAC ELIYAHU; OFFENBACH, ISAAC; ORGAN; PARTOS, OEDOEN; PSALMS, BOOK OF; RACHEL; ROMANOS MELODOS; RÓZSAVÖLGYI, MÁRK; SALMON, KAREL; SALOME; SAMBURSKY, DANIEL; SAMSON; SAUL; SCHMIDT, JOSEPH; SECUNDA, SHOLOM; SEIBER, MÁTYÁS GYÖRGY; SETER, MORDECHAI; SHARETT, YEHUDAH; SHELEM, MATTITYAHU; SHESTAPOL, WOLF; SINGER, JOSEF; SOCIETY FOR JEWISH FOLK MUSIC,; SODOM AND GOMORRAH; SOLOMON; SONG OF SONGS; STERNBERG, ERICH-WALTER; STRAUS, OSCAR; STUTSCHEWSKY, JOACHIM; SUSANNA AND THE ELDERS; TALMUD, MUSICAL RENDITION; THALBERG, SIGISMUND; TOBIT, BOOK OF; WERNER, ERIC; YIGDAL; ZEIRA, MORDECHAI

Steven Bayme*, Ph.D.; National Director, Contemporary Jewish Life Department; American Jewish Committee, Jewish Theological Seminary of America, New York: EDAH

Michael J. Bazyler*, Professor of Law and The "1939" Club Law Scholar in Holocaust and Human Rights Studies, Whittier Law School, Costa Mesa, California: CALABRESI, GUIDO; REPARATIONS, GERMAN; WAR CRIMES TRIALS

Walton Bean, Ph.D.; Professor of History, the University of California, Berkeley: RUEF, ABRAHAM

Elieser Beck, Kibbutz Kefar ha-Maccabi: ZILINA

Arthur Beer, Ph.D., F.R.A.S.; Lately Senior Observer at the Observatories, the University of Cambridge: ABELMANN, ILYA SOLOMOVITCH; ASTRONOMY; BEMPORAD, AZEGLIO; COHN, BERTHOLD; COHN, FRITZ; EPSTEIN, PAUL SOPHUS; FINLAY-FREUNDLICH, ERWIN; GOLDSCHMIDT, HERMANN; IBN SA'ĪD, ISAAC; ISRAELI, ISAAC BEN JOSEPH; LOEW, MORITZ; LOEWY, MAURICE; MĀSHĀ'ALLAH B. ATHAÑ; PRAGER, RICHARD; RUBENSON, ROBERT; SCHLESINGER, FRANK; SCHUSTER, SIR ARTHUR; SCHWARZSCHILD, KARL

Helen Beer*, Dr.Phil.; Lecturer in Yiddish, Hebrew, and Jewish Studies, University College of London, England: MANGER, ITZIK

Moshe Beer, Ph.D.; Associate Professor of Jewish History, Bar-Ilan University, Ramat Gan: ABBA BAR MARTA; ABBA OF AKKO; ABBA OSHAYA OF TIRIAH; ACADEMIES IN BABYLONIA AND EREẒ ISRAEL; ARDAVAN; BE-ḤOZAI; DIMI OF NEHARDEA; ḤABBAR, ḤABBAREI; HAGRONIA; HUẒAL; ISSACHAR; MAḤOZA; MATA MEḤASYA; NARESH; NEḤUTEI;

NISIBIS; PUMBEDITA; RABBAH BEN SHILAH; RAV; RAVA; RAVINA; SAMUEL; SHAPUR; SHEKANZIB; SIMEON BEN LAKISH; TANHUMA BAR ABBA

Emmanuel Beeri, M.A.; Jerusalem: AMENITIES, COMMUNAL; BERTHOLD OF FREIBURG; CALMER, MOSES ELIEZER LIEFMANN; CHATEAUBRIAND, FRANÇOIS RENÉ, VICOMTE DE; CIVILTÀ CATTOLICA, LA; CLERMONT-TONNERRE, COUNT STANISLAS DE; KAHN, LOUIS; LANGALLERIE, PHILIPPE GENTIL DE; LEVEN, NARCISSE; MIRABEAU, HONORE GABRIEL RIQUETI, COMTE DE; MONTI DI PIETA; MORPURGO; MUSSOLINI, BENITO; PREZIOSI, GIOVANNI; ROEDERER, COUNT PIERRE LOUIS; STUDENTS' FRATERNITIES, GERMAN

Doron M. Behar*, M.D., Ph.D.; Physician, Research Scientist, Rambam Medical Center, Haifa: GENETIC ANCESTRY, JEWISH

Arnold Beichman, M.A.; Lecturer in Politics, the University of Massachusetts, Boston: GOLDBERG, ARTHUR JOSEPH

Alexander Bein, Dr. Phil.; Former State Archivist, Former Director of the Central Zionist Archives, Jerusalem: ARCHIVES; BLUMENFELD, KURT YEHUDAH; BODENHEIMER, MAX ISIDOR; ETTINGER, AKIVA JACOB; OLIPHANT, LAURENCE; RUPPIN, ARTHUR

Haim Beinart, Ph.D.; Professor of Medieval Jewish History, the Hebrew University of Jerusalem: ALBARRACÍN; ALCONSTANTINI; ALFONSO DE ESPINA; ALMAGRO; ALMERÍA; BADAJOZ; BALAGUER; BARBASTRO; BARCELONA; BARCELONA, DISPUTATION OF; BESALÚ; BIEL; BRIVIESCA; BUITRAGO; BURRIANA; CÁDIZ; CALAHORRA; CALATAYUD; CALATRAVA; CANARY ISLANDS; CARMONA; CARRION DE LOS CONDES; CARTAJENA; CASTELLÓN DE LA PLANA; CASTROJERIZ; CAVALLERIA, DE LA; CEA; CERVERA; CHILLÓN; CIUDAD REAL; CIUDAD RODRIGO; COCA; CÓRDOBA; CORUNNA; CUENCA; DAROCA; DENIA; DUEÑAS; ÉCIJA; ÉCIJA, JOSEPH; ELCHE; ELVIRA; ESCALONA; ESTELLA; FERRER, VICENTE; FERRIZUEL, JOSEPH HA-NASI; GERONA; GRANADA; GUADALAJARA; GUADALUPE; HARO; HERRERA DE PISUEGRA; HUESCA; HUETE; ILLESCAS; JACA; JAÉN; JÁTIVA; JEREZ DE LA FRONTERA; LA GUARDIA, HOLY CHILD OF; LEA, HENRY CHARLES; LEON; LÉRIDA; LLERENA; LORKI, JOSHUA; LUCENA; MADRID; MAJORCA; MÁLAGA; MAQUEDA; MEDINA DE POMAR; MEDINA DEL CAMPO; MEDINACELI; MÉRIDA; MILLÁS VALLICROSA, JOSÉ MARIÁ; MINORCA; MIRANDA DE EBRO; MONTCLUS; MONTIEL; MONZÓN; MURCIA; MURVIEDRO; NÁJERA; OCAÑA; OLMEDO; ORABUENA; ORENSE; ORIHUELA; PALENCIA; PALMA, LA; PAMPLONA; PERPIGNAN; PLASENCIA; SALAMANCA; SANTA COLOMA DE QUERALT; SARAGOSSA; SEGOVIA; SEPÚLVEDA; SEVILLE; SORIA; TARRAGONA; TOLEDO; TORTOSA; TORTOSA, DISPUTATION OF; TUDELA; VALENCIA

Malachi Beit-Arie, Ph.D.; Research Worker, the Jewish National and University Library, Jerusalem: COLOPHON; PEREK SHIRAH

Michael Beizer, Ph.D.; Director, Centre for the Study and Documentation of East European Jewry, Jerusalem: AZERBAIJAN; BELARUS; GEORGIA; KAZAKHSTAN; KYRGYZSTAN; LATVIA; LITHUANIA; MOLDOVA; PRESS; RUSSIA; TADZHIKISTAN; UKRAINE; UZBEKISTAN

Margalit Bejarano*, Ph.D.; Researcher and Teacher, Hebrew University of Jerusalem: AVNI, HAIM; BACHI, ROBERTO; BLIS, DAVID; COSTA RICA; CUBA; EL SALVADOR; FESELA; GROBART, FABIO; HAVANA; KAPLAN, SENDER MEYER; LATIN AMERICA; LEVY, SION; LIWERANT SZCLAR, DANIEL; SITTEON DABBAH, SHAUL DAVID

Avi Beker: UNITED NATIONS

Judith Belinfante: AN-SKI COLLECTIONS

Randall C. Belinfante*, M.A., M.S., M.A., M.S.L.; Librarian/Archivist, American Sephardic Federation, New York: LEVY, ALBERT J.

David Bellos, Ph.D.; Professor of Literature, University of Manchester: PEREC, GEORGES

Ruth Beloff*, B.A.; Writer, Editor, Jerusalem: ABEL, ELIE; ABELSON, HAROLD HERBERT; ABRAHAMSEN, DAVID; ABRAM, MORRIS BERTHOLD; ABRAMOVITZ, MOSES; ABRAMOWITZ, BINA; ACKERMAN, NATHAN WARD; ADAMS, FRANKLIN PIERCE; ADELSON, HOWARD LAURENCE; ADLER, MORTIMER JEROME; ADLER, SELIG; ALEXANDER, MOSES; ALLEN, WOODY; ALMOND, GABRIEL ABRAHAM; ANTHONY, JOSEPH; APTER, DAVID ERNEST; ARKIN, ALAN W.; ARNSTEIN, WALTER LEONARD; ARONSON, BORIS; ARROW, KENNETH JOSEPH; ASIMOV, ISAAC; ASNER, EDWARD; AUERBACH, CARL A.; AUSUBEL, DAVID PAUL; AXELROD, GEORGE; BACALL, LAUREN; BAILYN, BERNARD; BAKAN, DAVID; BALABAN, BARNEY; BALIN, MARTY; BALINT, MICHAEL; BARA, THEDA; BARR, ROSEANNE; BAZELON, DAVID L.; BEAME, ABRAHAM DAVID; BECKER, GARY STANLEY; BEDACHT, MAX; BELASCO, DAVID; BENARDETE, MAIR JOSÉ; BENDIX, REINHARD; BENNY, JACK; BERG, GERTRUDE; BERGSON, ABRAM; BERLE, MILTON; BERLIN, IRVING; BERMAN, PANDRO S.; BERNARDI, HERSCHEL; BERNBACH, WILLIAM; BETTELHEIM, BRUNO; BIKEL, THEODORE MEIR; BLACK, MAX; BLANK, LEON; BLAU, HERBERT; BLAU, PETER MICHAEL; BLAUSTEIN; BLOCH, HERBERT; BLOOM, BENJAMIN SAMUEL; BLOOM, SOLOMON FRANK; BLOOMINGDALE; BLUM, JEROME; BLUMENTHAL, JOSEPH; BLUMENTHAL, WERNER MICHAEL; BOAS, GEORGE; BONDY, MAX; BOONE, RICHARD; BORAH, WOODROW WILSON; BORGE, VICTOR; BOSKOFF, ALVIN; BOYAR, LOUIS H.; BOZYK, MAX; BRANDEIS-BARDIN INSTITUTE; BRENTANO; BRICE, FANNY; BRODSKY, STANLEY L.; BRONFENBRENNER, MARTIN; BRONFMAN, EDGAR MILES; BROOKS, MEL; BROOKS, RICHARD; BROTHERS, JOYCE; BROUDY, HARRY SAMUEL; BRUSTEIN, ROBERT SANFORD; BUCHWALD, ART; BUHLER, CHARLOTTE; BULOFF, JOSEPH; BUNZEL, RUTH LEAH; BURNS, ARTHUR FRANK; BURNS, GEORGE; BURROWS, ABE; BUTTONS, RED; CAESAR, SID; CANTOR, NORMAN FRANK; CAPLAN, HARRY; CARNOVSKY, MORRIS; CARTER, VICTOR M.; CHEIN, ISIDOR; CHODOROV, EDWARD; CHODOROV, JEROME; CHOMSKY, NOAM AVRAM; CLURMAN, HAROLD; COBB, LEE J.; COHEN, ALEXANDER H.; COHEN, GERSON D.; COHEN, NATHAN EDWARD; COHEN, SAUL BERNARD; COHEN, WILBUR JOSEPH; COMDEN, BETTY; COSER, LEWIS A.; CREMIN, LAWRENCE ARTHUR; CROWN, HENRY; CRYSTAL, BILLY; CURTIS, TONY; DASH, SAMUEL; DASSIN, JULES; DAVIS, MOSHE; DERSHOWITZ, ALAN M.; DIAMOND, I. A. L.; DIAMOND, NEIL; DIAMOND, SIGMUND; DINITZ, SIMON; DONEN, STANLEY; DORFMAN, JOSEPH; DOUGLAS, KIRK; DOUGLAS, MICHAEL; DREYFUSS, RICHARD; DUBERMAN, MARTIN B.; DUBINSKY, DAVID; DUKER, ABRAHAM GORDON; DWORKIN, RONALD; EATON, JOSEPH W.; ECKARDT, ROY A.; EDWARDS, PAUL; EISENSTADT, ABRAHAM

SELDIN; ELAZAR, DANIEL J.; ELLSBERG, EDWARD; EPSTEIN, ALVIN; EPSTEIN, JUDITH; EPSTEIN, JULIUS J. and PHILIP G.; EPSTEIN, MORRIS; ERIKSON, ERIK HOMBERGER; ETHICAL CULTURE; EULAU, HEINZ; EVANS, ELI; EZEKIEL, MORDECAI JOSEPH BRILL; FABRICANT, SOLOMON; FACTOR, MAX; FALK; FALK, PETER; FARBER, MARVIN; FEIFFER, JULES; FEINBERG, ABRAHAM; FEIS, HERBERT; FELDMAN, HERMAN; FELLNER, WILLIAM JOHN; FERKAUF, EUGENE; FERNBERGER, SAMUEL; FEUER, LEWIS SAMUEL; FEUERSTEIN, REUVEN; FILLER, LOUIS; FINE, REUBEN; FINE, SIDNEY; FISHER, EDDIE; FISHER, MAX M.; FISHMAN, JOSHUA AARON; FLEISCHER, MAX; FORD, HARRISON; FOREMAN, CARL; FOX, MARVIN; FOX, WILLIAM; FRANKEL, SAMUEL BENJAMIN; FRANKENHEIMER, JOHN MICHAEL; FRANZBLAU, ABRAHAM NORMAN; FREUND-ROSENTHAL, MIRIAM KOTTLER; FRIED, MORTON HERBERT; FRIEDAN, BETTY; FRIEDLANDER, WALTER; FRIEDMAN, MILTON; FRIENDLY, FRED W.; FULD, STANLEY HOWELLS; GABEL, MAX; GABRIEL, GILBERT W.; GARFIELD, JOHN; GARFUNKEL, ART; GARMENT, LEONARD; GAY, PETER JACK; GEFFEN, DAVID; GERSHOY, LEO; GERSTEN, BERTA; GERTZ, ELMER; GILBERT, FELIX; GILBERT, MILTON; GIMBEL; GINSBERG, EDWARD; GINSBERG, MITCHELL I.; GINSBURG, NORTON SIDNEY; GINZBERG, ELI; GLAZER, NATHAN; GODDARD, PAULETTE; GOLDBERG, BERTRAND; GOLDEN, JOHN; GOLDIN, JUDAH; GOLDSCHMIDT, NEIL EDWARD; GOLDSMITH, RAYMOND WILLIAM; GOLDSMITH, SAMUEL ABRAHAM; GOLDSTEIN, ABRAHAM SAMUEL; GOLDWYN, SAMUEL; GOODMAN, NELSON; GORDON, MAX; GORDON, MICHAEL; GORDON, MILTON M.; GOREN, CHARLES HENRY; GORNICK, VIVIAN; GOULD, MILTON S.; GOULD, SAMUEL BROOKNER; GRANT, LEE; GREEN, ADOLPH; GREENACRE, PHYLLIS; GREENE, LORNE; GREENSPAN, ALAN; GREY, JOEL; GRINKER, ROY RICHARD Sr.; GROSSINGER, JENNIE; GRUNWALD, HENRY ANATOLE; GUTTMAN, LOUIS; HABER, SAMUEL L.; HACKETT, BUDDY; HALLE, MORRIS; HAMEROW, THEODORE STEPHEN; HAMLISCH, MARVIN; HANDLER, MILTON; HANDLIN, OSCAR; HANFMANN, GEORGE MAXIM ANOSSOV; HARBURG, E.Y.; HARRIS, BARBARA; HARRIS, SAM HENRY; HARRIS, ZELLIG SABBETAI; HAUSER, PHILIP MORRIS; HAWN, GOLDIE; HELLINGER, MARK; HENRY, BUCK; HERSHEY, BARBARA; HEXTER, JACK H.; HIMMELSTEIN, LENA; HIRSCH, JUDD; HIRSCHMAN, ALBERT OTTO; HOFFMAN, DUSTIN; HOFFMAN, JEFFREY; HOLLIDAY, JUDY; HOOK, SIDNEY; HOSELITZ, BERTHOLD FRANK; HUROK, SOLOMON; HURWITZ, SAMUEL JUSTIN; HYMAN, HAROLD MELVIN; IAN, JANIS; INKELES, ALEX; IRVING, JULES; ISAACS, EDITH JULIET; JACOBY, OSWALD; JAFFE, SAM; JANOWITZ, MORRIS; JAVITS, JACOB KOPPEL; JESSEL, GEORGE ALBERT; JESSELSON, LUDWIG; JEWISH PUBLICATION SOCIETY OF AMERICA; JOEL, BILLY; JOLSON, AL; JUSTMAN, JOSEPH; KABAKOFF, JACOB; KAHN, ALFRED JOSEPH; KAMPELMAN, MAX M.; KANE, IRVING; KANIN, GARSON; KANTOR, JACOB ROBERT; KAPLAN, LOUIS LIONEL; KARDINER, ABRAM; KASHDAN, ISAAC; KATZ, DANIEL; KATZ, SOLOMON; KATZENBERG, JEFFREY; KATZMAN, SAM; KAUFMAN, BORIS; KAUFMANN, WALTER; KELLER, MORTON; KING, CAROLE; KING, LARRY; KLEIN, JULIUS; KLEIN, LAWRENCE ROBERT; KLUTZNICK, PHILIP MORRIS; KNOPF, ALFRED A.; KNOPFLER, MARK; KOBRIN, SOLOMON; KOCH, EDWARD IRVING; KOLTANOWSKI, GEORGE; KOMAROVSKY, MIRRA; KONVITZ, MILTON RIDVAS; KRAFT, LOUIS; KRAMER, STANLEY E.; KRASNA, NORMAN; KRAUS, MICHAEL; KRIEGER, LEONARD; KRISTELLER, PAUL OSKAR; KROCK, ARTHUR; KROSS, ANNA; KRULEWITCH, MELVIN LEVIN; KUBLIN, HYMAN; KUBRICK, STANLEY; LAHR, BERT; LANDES, DAVID SAUL; LANDES, RUTH; LANG, FRITZ; LASKY, JESSE L.; LASSER, LOUISE; LAURENCE, WILLIAM L.; LAZARSFELD, PAUL F.; LAZEROWITZ, MORRIS; LE ROY, MERVYN; LEAF, HAYIM; LEAR, NORMAN; LEHMAN, ERNEST; LENGYEL, EMIL; LEONTOVICH, EUGENIE; LERNER, ABBA PETACHJA; LERNER, MAX; LESLAU, WOLF; LESLIE, ROBERT L.; LEVENE, SAM; LEVENSON, SAM; LEVI, EDWARD H.; LEVIN, A. LEO; LEVINE, JOSEPH E.; LEVINSON, BARRY; LEVY, LEONARD WILLIAMS; LEVY, MARION JOSEPH, JR.; LEWIS, JERRY; LICHT, FRANK; LIEBERMAN, MYRON; LILIENTHAL, DAVID ELI; LINOWITZ, SOL MYRON; LIPSET, SEYMOUR MARTIN; LITVAK, ANATOLE; LOEW, MARCUS; LOEWENSTEIN, RUDOLPH MAURICE; LOPEZ, ROBERT SABATINO; LORRE, PETER; LOVESTONE, JAY; LOWE, ADOLPH; LUBIN, ISADOR; LUKAS, PAUL; LUMET, SIDNEY; LYONS, LEONARD; MACHLUP, FRITZ; MAHLER, MARGARET; MAIER, JOSEPH; MALACHI, ELIEZER RAPHAEL; MANDEL, MARVIN; MANDELBAUM, DAVID GOODMAN; MANILOW, BARRY; MANKIEWICZ, JOSEPH LEO; MANN, DELBERT; MANN, THEODORE R.; MANUEL, FRANK EDWARD; MARKOWITZ, HARRY M.; MARSCHAK, JACOB; MARTIN, TONY; MARWICK, LAWRENCE; MASSERMAN, JULES HYMEN; MATTHAU, WALTER; MAYER, ARNO JOSEPH; MAZURSKY, PAUL; MELTON, SAMUEL MENDEL; MERTON, ROBERT KING; MIDLER, BETTE; MIDSTREAM; MINOW, NEWTON NORMAN; MINSKY, LOUIS; MIRISCH BROTHERS; MODIGLIANI, FRANCO; MONTOR, HENRY; MOREEL, BEN; MORGENSTERN, OSKAR; MORGENTHAU, HANS JOACHIM; MORRIS, RICHARD BRANDON; MORSE, DAVID ABNER; MORTON, LOUIS C.; MOSES, ROBERT; MOSSE, GEORGE L.; MOSTEL, ZERO; NAGEL, ERNEST; NASATIR, ABRAHAM PHINEAS; NATHAN, ROBERT ROY; NAUMBURG, MARGARET; NEISSER, HANS PHILIPP; NELSON, BENJAMIN; NEMOY, LEON; NEWHOUSE, SAMUEL IRVING; NEWMAN, ARNOLD; NEWMAN, PAUL; NICHOLS, MIKE; NIZER, LOUIS; NOVY, JIM; OCHS; OHRBACH; OPLER, MARVIN KAUFMANN; OPLER, MORRIS EDWARD; PASSOW, AARON HARRY; PASTERNAK, JOSEPH; PATINKIN, MANDY; PERLMAN, ALFRED EDWARD; PERLMAN, HELEN HARRIS; PIPES, RICHARD EDGAR; POLANSKI, ROMAN; POLLACK, SYDNEY; PREMINGER, OTTO LUDWIG; PRINCE, HAROLD; RABB, MAXWELL MILTON; RABINOWICZ, OSKAR K.; RADO, SANDOR; RAINER, LUISE; RAPPAPORT, ARMIN H; RATNER, SIDNEY; REDLICH, FREDERICK C.; REDLICH, NORMAN; REINER, CARL; REINER, ROB; REVSON, CHARLES HASKELL; RIBICOFF, ABRAHAM A.; RIESMAN, DAVID; RIKLIS, MESHULAM; RISCHIN, MOSES; RITZ BROTHERS; ROBINSON, EDWARD G.; RODELL, FRED M.; ROSENTHAL, ERICH; ROSENTHAL, FRANZ; ROSSEN, ROBERT; ROSTOW, WALT WHITMAN; RUBINSTEIN, HELENA; RUBY, JACK; RUKEYSER, MERRYLE STANLEY; RYDER, WINONA; SACHAR, ABRAM LEON; SAFIRE, WILLIAM; SAHL, MORT; SAMUELSON, PAUL ANTHONY; SCHAFER, STEPHEN; SCHAPPES, MORRIS U.; SCHARY, DORE; SCHEFFLER, ISRAEL; SCHISGAL, MURRAY; SCHOTTLAND, CHARLES IRWIN; SCHUSTER, MAX LINCOLN; SCHWAB, JOSEPH J.; SEGAL, GEORGE; SEINFELD, JERRY; SELTZER, LOUIS BENSON; SEMMEL, BERNARD; SEYMOUR, JANE; SHAPIRO, HARRY LIONEL; SHEINKMAN, JACOB; SHORE, DINAH; SHULIM, JOSEPH ISIDORE; SIDNEY, SYLVIA; SILVERMAN, SIME; SILVERS, PHIL; SIMON, HERBERT ALEXANDER; SIMON, NORTON; SINGER, MILTON B; SKLARE, MARSHALL; SMELSER, NEIL JOSEPH; SMITH, MORTON; SOLOW, ROBERT MERTON; SOROS, GEORGE; SOVERN, MICHAEL IRA; SPIEGEL, SAMUEL P.; SPIEGEL, SHALOM; SPIEGELBERG, HERBERT; SPIELBERG, STEVEN; SPIRO, MELFORD ELLIOT; SPOEHR, ALEXANDER; STEIN, HERBERT; STEIN, HERMAN D.; STONE, I.F.; STONE, OLIVER; STRASBERG,

LEE; STRAUS; STRAUSS, LEVI; STREISAND, BARBRA; STRICK, JOSEPH; STROHEIM, ERICH VON; SULZBERGER, ARTHUR HAYS; SUSSKIND, DAVID; SWIG, BENJAMIN HARRISON; SZASZ, THOMAS STEPHEN; SZOLD, ROBERT; TAUBENSCHLAG, RAPHAEL; TAX, SOL; TERKEL, STUDS; THALBERG, IRVING GRANT; TITIEV, MISCHA; TODD, MIKE; TUCKER, SOPHIE; TWERSKY, ISADORE; UNGER, IRWIN; WACHTLER, SOL; WALINSKY; WALLACE, MIKE; WALLACH, ELI; WALTERS, BARBARA; WARNER; WASSERMAN, DALE; WECHSLER, HERBERT; WECHSLER, JAMES ARTHUR; WEINBERG, HARRY; WEINBERG, SAUL S.; WEISBERGER, BERNARD ALLEN; WEISS, PAUL; WELLER, MICHAEL; WESTHEIMER, RUTH; WHITE, MORTON GABRIEL; WIENER, PHILIP PAUL; WILDER, BILLY; WILDER, GENE; WILENTZ, ROBERT N.; WINCHELL, WALTER; WINGER, DEBRA; WINTERS, SHELLEY; WISE, ROBERT EARL; WOLFE, BERTRAM DAVID; WOLPER, DAVID LLOYD; WYLER, WILLIAM; WYNN, ED; WYNN, KEENAN; WYZANSKI, CHARLES EDWARD, JR.; ZEICHNER, OSCAR; ZINNEMANN, FRED; ZUKOR, ADOLPH

Miriam Ben-Aaron, M.A.; Ministry of Health, Haifa: MAHLER, MARGARET

Yehuda Benari, D.en D.; Director of the Jabotinsky Institute, Tel Aviv: JEWISH STATE PARTY

Yehoshoua Ben-Arieh, Ph.D.; Senior Lecturer in Geography, the Hebrew University of Jerusalem: GESHER BENOT YA'AKOV; KINNAROT, VALLEY OF

Schalom Ben-Chorin, Writer and Journalist, Jerusalem: ISRAEL, STATE OF: RELIGIOUS LIFE AND COMMUNITIES

Shmuel Bendor, B.A.; Secretary of the Council for Higher Education, Ministry of Education and Culture, Jerusalem: EDEN, SIR ANTHONY, EARL OF AVON; KOHN, LEO

Yehuda Ben-Dor*, B.A., L.L.B.; Faculty Member, Mandel Leadership Institute, Jerusalem: IZBICA RADZYN; KOTSK, MENAHEM MENDEL OF; LEINER, GERSHON ḤANOKH BEN JACOB; PRZYSUCHA, JACOB ISAAC BEN ASHER; SIMḤAH BUNEM OF PRZYSUCHA

Yehuda Ben-Dror (James Marshall), B.A.; Jerusalem: NEW JERSEY; NEW YORK CITY

Binyamin Zeev Benedikt, Ph.D., Rabbi; Senior Lecturer in Rabbinical Literature and Halakhah, Tel Aviv University: EPHRAIM IBN AVI ALRAGAN; FRIEDMANN, MEIR; MOSES BEN JOSEPH BEN MERWAN LEVI; SAMUEL BEN DAVID

David Ben-Gurion, Former Prime Minister and Minister of Defense of the State of Israel, Sedeh Boker: AḤDUT HA-AVODAH; DECLARATION OF INDEPENDENCE, ISRAEL

Zeev Ben-Hayyim, Ph.D.; Professor of Hebrew Philology, the Hebrew University of Jerusalem; Vice President of the Academy of the Hebrew Language, Jerusalem: BEN-ASHER, AARON BEN MOSES; HEBREW GRAMMAR

Eliashiv Ben-Horin, LL.B.; Ambassador, Ministry for Foreign Affairs, Jerusalem

Meir Ben-Horin, Ph.D.; Professor of Education, Dropsie University, Philadelphia: DROPSIE COLLEGE; HALPER, BENZION; NORDAU, MAX

Ernest Frank Benjamin, Brigadier; Commander of the Jewish Brigade, England

Robert M. Benjamin, M.A., Rabbi; Adjunct Assistant Professor of Humanities, Indiana State University, Terre Haute

Jacov Benmayor, B.A.; Salonika: SALONIKA

Moti Benmelech*, M.A.; Jewish History, the Hebrew University of Jerusalem: BENEVENTO, IMMANUEL BEN JEKUTHIEL; DEL BANCO, ANSELMO; ELIJAH OF LA MASSA; FANO; REUVENI, DAVID

Naphtali Ben-Menahem, Executive Director of the Institute for Hebrew Bibliography, the Hebrew University of Jerusalem: ADLER, SHALOM BEN MENAHEM; BLUM, AMRAM BEN ISAAC JACOB; BRACH, SAUL; BRISZK; DEUTSCH, JUDAH JOEL; EHRENFELD; EHRENREICH, ḤAYYIM JUDAH BEN KALONYMUS; EISENSTADT, MENAHEM ẒEVI; ENGELMANN, GABRIEL; FRENK, BEER; FRIEDBERG, BERNARD; FUCHS, MOSES ẒEVI; FUNK, SOLOMON; GLUECK, ABRAHAM ISAAC; GRUENFELD, JUDAH; GRÜNWALD, AMRAM; GRÜNWALD, JUDAH; GUENZLER, ABRAHAM; HELLER, JUDAH; JOSEPH SOLOMON ZALMAN BEN MEIR; JUNGREIS, ASHER ANSHEL; KAHANA, NAḤMAN; KATTINA, JACOB; LANDSOFER, JONAH BEN ELIJAH; MICHAEL, HEIMANN JOSEPH ḤAYYIM; MODERN, JUDAH; PERLES, ISAAC MOSES; POLLAK, MOSES HA-LEVI; ROSENBAUM, MOSES ḤAYYIM LITS; SCHWARTZ, ABRAHAM JUDAH HA-KOHEN; SCHWARTZ, JOSEPH HA-KOHEN; SCHWARTZ, PHINEHAS SELIG HA-KOHEN; SHAG, ABRAHAM; SILBERSTEIN, DAVID JUDAH LEIB; STERN, GERSHON; STERN, JOSEPH; STERN, MENAHEM; TABAK, SOLOMON LEIB; TENNENBAUM, JACOB; ULMAN, ABRAHAM; WALDEN, AARON BEN ISAIAH NATHAN

Haim Hillel Ben-Sasson, Ph.D.; Professor of Jewish History, the Hebrew University of Jerusalem: AGE AND THE AGED; ANUSIM; APOSTASY; ASHKENAZI, ELIEZER BEN ELIJAH THE PHYSICIAN; ASSIMILATION; AUTONOMISM; BLACK DEATH; BLOOD LIBEL; BUDNY, SZYMON; CHARITY; COMMUNITY; COUNCILS OF THE LANDS; CRAFTS; DAVID BEN ZAKKAI; DISPUTATIONS AND POLEMICS; DOHM, CHRISTIAN WILHELM VON; DUBNOW, SIMON; ELDER; EXPULSIONS; GALUT; GERMANY; GERONDI, ZERAHIAH BEN ISAAC HA-LEVI; GLADIATOR; GOLOMB, ELIYAHU; GRODZINSKI, ḤAYYIM OZER; GRUENBAUM, YIẒḤAK; GUILDS; HADASSI, JUDAH BEN ELIJAH; HAI BEN SHERIRA; HISTORY: FOURTH TO SEVENTH CENTURIES; HISTORY: MODERN TIMES – FROM THE 1880S TO THE EARLY 21ST CENTURY; HISTORY: MODERN TIMES – TO 1880; HISTORY: THE MIDDLE AGES; HOROWITZ, ABRAHAM BEN SHABBETAI SHEFTEL; HOROWITZ, ISAIAH BEN ABRAHAM HA-LEVI; ISRAEL BEN ELIEZER BA'AL SHEM TOV; JACOB OF BELZYCE; JOSEPH BEN ELIJAH OF ZASŁŁAW; KIDDUSH HA-SHEM AND ḤILLUL HA-SHEM; MAGGID; MAIMONIDEAN CONTROVERSY; MESSIANIC MOVEMENTS; MUSAR MOVEMENT; POLAND; SELF-DEFENSE; WIENER NEUSTADT; WINE AND LIQUOR TRADE; ZERAHIAH BEN ISAAC HA-LEVI

Menahem Ben-Sasson*, Ph.D.; Professor, the Hebrew University of Jerusalem, Knesset Member: BEN-ZVI INSTITUTE FOR THE STUDY OF JEWISH COMMUNITIES OF THE EAST; GENIZAH, CAIRO

Haggai Ben-Shammai*, Ph.D.; Professor of Arabic, Department of Arabic Language and Literature, the Hebrew University of Jerusalem: ABU AL-FARAJ HARUN IBN AL-FARAJ; FIRKOVICH, ABRAHAM; JAPHETH BEN ELI HA-LEVI; KALĀM; KARAITES; SAADIAH GAON

Meir Hillel Ben-Shammai, Dr.Phil.; Editor and writer, Jerusalem: ALDABI, MEIR BEN ISAAC; ELIJAH PHINEHAS BEN MEIR; PORTALEONE, ABRAHAM BEN DAVID II

Joseph Ben-Shlomo, Ph.D.; Senior Lecturer in Philosophy, the Hebrew University of Jerusalem: CORDOVERO, MOSES BEN JACOB; SOSKIN, SELIG EUGEN

Daniel Ben-Simhon, Jerusalem: YAD IZHAK BEN-ZVI

Doris Bensimon-Donath, D.esL.; Professor émérite, Institut National Langues et Civilisations, Paris: FRANCE; PARIS

Asher Benson*, Journalist, Dublin: IRELAND; WEINGREEN, JACOB

Yaakov Bentolila*, Ph.D.; Professor Emeritus, Ben-Gurion University of the Negev, Beersheba: ḤAKETÍA

Yakov K. Bentor, Ph.D.; D.es Sc.; Professor of Geology, the Hebrew University of Jerusalem: ANCONA, CESARE D'; BERENDT, GOTTLIEB MICHAEL; GOLDSCHMIDT, VICTOR MORITZ

Haim Bentov, M.A., Rabbi; Lecturer in Talmud, Bar-Ilan University, Ramat Gan: MEKNÈS; RACCAH, MAS'ŪD BEN AARON; SARFATY; SERERO; TOLEDANO; UZIEL

Joseph Bentwich, M.A.; Former Lecturer in Education, the Hebrew University of Jerusalem: BIRAM, ARTHUR

Norman Bentwich, Ph.D.; Emeritus Professor of International Relations, the Hebrew University of Jerusalem: HEBREW UNIVERSITY OF JERUSALEM; JEWISH SUCCESSOR ORGANIZATIONS; UNITED RESTITUTION ORGANIZATION

Aviva Ben-Ur*, Ph.D.; Assistant Professor, University of Massachusetts at Amherst: PHILLIPS, REBECCA MACHADO

Meron Benvenisti, B.A.; Jerusalem: JERUSALEM

Abraham Ben-Yaacob, B.A.; Researcher in Jewish History, Jerusalem: BAGHDAD; DIYALA; EZEKIEL; EZEKIEL BEN REUBEN MANASSEH; EZRA; EZRA; GABBAI; GAGIN, ḤAYYIM ABRAHAM BEN MOSES; HALEVI, EZEKIEL EZRA BEN JOSHUA; HA-LEVI, SASSON BEN ELIJAH BEN MOSES; ḤOẒIN, ẒEDAKAH BEN SAADIAH; ISAAC BAR ISRAEL IBN AL-SHUWAYK; KAẒIN, RAPHAEL BEN ELIJAH; KURDISTAN; MANI; MARDIN; MAṢLI'AḤ ṢĀLIḤ; MA'TUK, SULAYMAN BEN DAVID; MAYMERAN; MEDINI, ḤAYYIM HEZEKIAH BEN RAPHAEL ELIJAH; MOSUL; NAHUM, AARON SASSON BEN ELIJAH; RUWANDIZ; SHINDOOKH, MOSES BEN MORDECAI; SOMEKH, ABDALLAH BEN ABRAHAM; SULEIMANIYA; ZAKHO

Mordecai Ben-Yehezkiel, Writer, Jerusalem: ABRAHAM ḤAYYIM BEN GEDALIAH; ADEL

Aharon Zeev Ben-Yishai, Writer and Critic, Tel Aviv: FRISCHMANN, DAVID; GORDON, JUDAH LEIB; PARODY, HEBREW; SHNEOUR, ZALMAN

Isac Bercovici, Journalist, Bat Yam: CILIBI MOÏSE; GHELERTER, LUDWIG LITMAN; ISER, JOSIF; PAUKER, ANA; PRESS; PSANTIR, JACOB

Michael Berenbaum*, Ph.D.; Professor of Theology (Adjunct), Director, Sigi Ziering Institute, University of Judaism, Los Angeles, California: ABRAHAM EZRA MILLGRAM; ABRAMSON, JERRY EDWIN; ADLER, SAMUEL; AMERICAN COUNCIL FOR JUDAISM; ANIELEWICZ, MORDECAI; ATLAS, JECHEZKIEL; BAAR, HERMAN; BABI YAR; BARSHEFSKY, CHARLENE; BAUM, SHEPARD; BELZEC; BERKOWITZ, HENRY; BERLIN; BERMAN, MORTON MAYER; BERNSTEIN, PHILIP SIDNEY; BESSO, HENRY; BETTAN, ISRAEL; BITBURG CONTROVERSY; BOKSER, BEN ZION; BOLTEN, JOSHUA B.; BORMANN, MARTIN; BRAND, JOEL JENŐ; BRICKNER, BARNETT ROBERT; BUCHENWALD; BULGARIA; CAMPS; CHELMNO; CHURCH COUNCILS; CHURCH, CATHOLIC; COHEN, BOAZ; COHEN, MORTIMER JOSEPH; COLOGNE; COUNCIL OF JEWISH FEDERATIONS AND WELFARE FUNDS; CRESSON, WARDER; CZERNIAKOW, ADAM; DACHAU; DAVIS, SUSAN A.; DENAZIFICATION; DENMARK; DEUTCH, JOHN M.; DORTMUND; DRACHMAN, BERNARD; DRANCY; DROB, MAX; DUISBURG; EISENDRATH, MAURICE NATHAN; ELKES, ELHANAN; ELLSBERG, DANIEL; ENGEL, ELIOT L.; EPSTEIN, CHAIM FISCHEL; EPSTEIN, GILBERT; EUROPA PLAN; EVANS, JANE; EVIAN CONFERENCE; FEINGOLD, RUSSELL; FELDHEIM, PHILIPP; FINEBERG, SOLOMON ANDHIL; FINKELSTEIN, ARTHUR; FINKELSTEIN, LOUIS; FINKELSTEIN, SHIMON; FLEISCHMANN, GISI; FRANK, BARNEY; FRANK, HANS MICHAEL; FRANK, KARL HERMANN; FREIBURG IM BREISGAU; FRIEDMAN, THEODORE; FUERTH; GADOL, MOISE S.; GEFFEN, JOEL; GELB, MAX; GERMANY; GHETTO; GLASER, JOSEPH; GOLDMAN, ISRAEL; GOLDMAN, SOLOMON; GOODBLAT, MORRIS; GORDON, ALBERT I.; GREENBERG, IRVING; GREENBERG, IRVING; GREENBERG, LOUIS; GREENBERG, SIMON; GREENWALD, JEKUTHIEL JUDAH; HAGEN; HALLE; HARLOW, JULIUS; HARRIS, LOUIS; HARRISON, LEON; HEBREW THEOLOGICAL COLLEGE; HELLER; HELLER, BERNARD; HENKIN, JOSEPH ELIJAH; HEYDRICH, REINHARD TRISTAN; HIRSHENSON, HAYIM; HISTADRUT IVRIT OF AMERICA; HOESS, RUDOLF FRANZ FERDINAND; HOLBROKE, RICHARD; HOLOCAUST; HOLOCAUST REMEMBRANCE DAY; HOLOCAUST RESCUERS, JEWISH; HOLOCAUST, THE; HOLOCAUST: AFTERMATH; HOLOCAUST: BEHAVIOR OF THE VICTIMS; HOLOCAUST: SPIRITUAL RESISTANCE IN THE GHETTOS AND CONCENTRATION CAMPS; HOLOCAUST: THE WORLD; HURWITZ, SHMARYA LEIB; INDYK, MARTIN; INTERNATIONAL TRACING SERVICE; ISRAEL, RICHARD J.; ISRAEL, STEVE; JACOBS, GEORGE; JANOWSKI, MAX; JEWISH COUNCIL ON PUBLIC AFFAIRS; JOHN XXIII; JUDENRAT; JUEDISCHER KULTURBUND; JUNG, LEO; K. ZETNIK; KADUSHIN, MAX; KAHN, ROBERT I.; KARP, ABRAHAM J.; KASZTNER, REZSŐ RUDOLF; KELMAN, WOLFE; KIDDUSH HA-ḤAYYIM; KLARSFELD, SERGE; KOHN, EUGENE; KOHN, JACOB; KOLDYCHEVO CAMP; KRISTALLNACHT; KURTZER, DANIEL CHARLES; LANDESMAN, ALTER; LANDMAN, ISAAC; LANGER, LAWRENCE L.; LANTOS, TOM; LAUTENBERG, FRANK R.; LAZARON, MORRIS SAMUEL; LEESER, ISAAC; LEFKOWITZ, LOUIS; LEHRMAN, IRVING; LEVI, PRIMO; LEVIN, CARL; LEVITSKY, LOUIS MOSES; LEW, JACOB; LIEBMAN, JOSHUA LOTH; LUBETKIN, ZIVIA; MAJDANEK; MALINES; MARGOLIS, GARVIEL ZEV; MASSACHUSETTS; MATLIN, MOSHE MEIR; MATT, C. DAVID; MATTUCK, ISRAEL I.; MAYER, SALY; MEED, BENJAMIN; MEMPHIS; MENGELE, JOSEF; MONTANA; MORAIS, SABATO; MUSELMANN; NADICH, JUDAH; NATIONAL SOCIALISM; NAZI MEDICAL EXPERIMENTS; NAZI-DEUTSCH; NEW HAVEN; NEWSPAPERS, HEBREW; NINTH FORT; NORWALK and

WESTPORT; NOVECK, SIMON; OFFNER, STACY; OKLAHOMA; OMAHA; ORANGE COUNTY; OVADIA, NISSIM J.; PARDES, SHMUEL AARON; PARZEN, HERBERT; PITTSBURGH; PITTSBURGH PLATFORM; POHL, OSWALD; POLLARD AFFAIR; PONARY; PREIL, ELAZAR MEIR; PRINZ, JOACHIM; RADEMACHER, FRANZ; REFUGEES; REICHSVEREINIGUNG; REICHSZENTRALE FUER JUEDISCHE AUSWANDERUNG; REINES, ALVIN JAY; RINGELBLUM, EMANUEL; ROSENAU, WILLIAM; ROSENBERG CASE; RSHA; RUBENSTEIN, RICHARD LOWELL; RUDIN, A. JAMES; RUDMAN, WARREN; SACHSENHAUSEN-ORANIENBURG; SAN GABRIEL–POMONA VALLEYS; SANDERS, BERNARD; SAUCKEL, FRITZ; SCHAALMAN, HERMAN E.; SCHACHT PLAN; SCHACHTER, JACOB J.; SCHELLENBERG, WALTER; SCHERMAN, NOSSON; SCHEUER, JAMES H.; SCHIFF, ADAM; SEYSS-INQUART, ARTHUR; SHANKMAN, JACOB K.; SHARLIN, WILLIAM; SIEGEL, MARK; SIEGEL, MORTON K.; SILVERMAN, IRA; SILVERMAN, JOSEPH; SIMON, ABRAM; SINGER, ISRAEL; SIVITZ, MOSHE; SOBIBOR; SOLOVEICHIK MOSHE; SONDERLING, JACOB; SPECTER, ARLEN; SS AND SD; STEINBERG, MILTON; STERNSTEIN, JOSEPH PHILIP; STOLZ, JOSEPH; STREICHER, JULIUS; STROOP, JUERGEN; STUERMER, DER; STUTTHOF; SURVIVORS OF THE SHOAH VISUAL HISTORY FOUNDATION, THE; TENENBAUM, MORDECAI; TISO, JOSEF; TREBLINKA; UNRRA; VOORSANGER, JACOB; VUGHT; WALDHEIM AFFAIR; WALLENBERG, RAOUL; WAR CRIMES TRIALS; WASKOW, ARTHUR; WASSERMAN SCHULTZ, DEBBIE; WEINBERGER, MOSHE; WEINSTEIN, JACOB; WEISSMANDEL, MICHAEL DOV; WESTERBORK; WILLIAM LEHMAN; WIRTH, CHRISTIAN; WISLICENY, DIETER; WITTENBERG, YIẒHAK; WYDEN, RON; YOUNGSTOWN; YUDELOVITZ, ABRAHAM AARON; ZENTRALE STELLE DER LANDE SJUSTIZVERWALTUNGEN; ZLOTOWITZ, MEIR; ZUCKERMAN, ITZHAK; ZUROFF, EFRAIM

Esme E. Berg*: AMERICAN SEPHARDI FEDERATION

Roger Berg, D.Econ.; Editor, Paris: BELFORT; BENFELD; BIARRITZ; BISCHHEIM; UNIVERS ISRAÉLITE

Abraham Berger, M.A.; Former Director, Jewish Division, the New York Public Library; Lecturer in Jewish History, the Academy for Jewish Religion, New York: BLOCH, JOSHUA

Jack S. (Jacob Solomon) Berger*, Ph.D.; Mahwah, New Jersey: ETTINGER, SOLOMON; KOL MEVASSER

Joseph Berger*, M.A.; B.A.; English Literature, Journalism, Senior Reporter for the *New York Times*, New York: DISPLACED PERSONS

Shlomo Z. Berger*: FUKS, LAJB

Joseph Berger-Barzilai, Professor of Political Science, particularly of the Soviet Union, Bar-Ilan University, Ramat Gan: TREPPER, LEOPOLD

Samuel Hugo Bergman, Dr.Phil.; Emeritus Professor of Philosophy, the Hebrew University of Jerusalem: BAUMGARDT, DAVID; BENDAVID, LAZARUS; BENRUBI, ISAAC; BUBER, MARTIN; COHEN, HERMANN; COHEN, MORRIS RAPHAEL; EISLER, RUDOLF; FEIWEL, BERTHOLD; FICHTE, JOHANN GOTTLIEB; FRANK, PHILIPP; GORDON, AHARON DAVID; HEINEMANN, FRITZ; HERZ, MARCUS; HOENIGSWALD, RICHARD; ILNA'E, ELIEZER ISAAC; ITELSON, GREGOR; KRONER, RICHARD; LANDAUER, GUSTAV; LASK, EMIL; NELSON, LEONHARD; SIMMEL, GEORG; SOUL, IMMORTALITY OF; UTITZ, EMIL; WELTSCH, FELIX; WOLF, ABRAHAM

Burton Berinsky, B.A.; Freelance Photographer, New York: ABRAM, MORRIS BERTHOLD

Harvey Berk*, B.A.; Principal and Associates Harvey Berk, Silver Spring, Maryland: B'NAI B'RITH

Eliezer Berkovits, Ph.D., Rabbi; Professor of Jewish Philosophy, the Hebrew Theological College, Skokie, Illinois: TALMUD

Joel Berkowitz*, Ph.D.; Associate Professor and Chair, Judaic Studies, University at Albany, New York: GOLDFADEN, ABRAHAM; GORDIN, JACOB; HIRSCHBEIN, PERETZ; THEATER

Simcha Berkowitz, M.A., M.H.L., Rabbi; the College of Jewish Studies, Detroit: AGUS, IRVING ABRAHAM; GRAYZEL, SOLOMON; SZOLD, ROBERT

Chip Berlet*, Senior Analyst at Political Research Associates, Somerville, Massachusetts: NEO-NAZISM

George L. Berlin*: BALTIMORE HEBREW UNIVERSITY

Jacques Berlinerblau*, Ph.D.; Associate Professor Religious Studies, Hofstra University, New York: BIBLE

Yaffah Berlovitz*, Ph.D.; Professor, Department of Literatures of the Jewish People, Bar-Ilan University, Ramat Gan: HEBREW LITERATURE, MODERN; MICHAEL, SAMI

Harold Berman*, Dr.; Executive Director, Jewish Federation of Greater Springfield, Massachusetts: SPRINGFIELD

Lawrence V. Berman, Ph.D.; Associate Professor of Religious Studies, Stanford University, California: AL-BAṬALYAWSĪ, ABU MUHAMMAD ABDALLAH IBN MUHAMMAD IBN AL-SĪD; AVEMPACE; BRETHREN OF SINCERITY, EPISTLES OF; CAUSE AND EFFECT; EMPEDOCLES; HERMETIC WRITINGS; KALĀM; PLATO AND PLATONISM; STOICISM

Morton Mayer Berman, M.H.L., Rabbi; Honorary Director, Department of English-Speaking Countries, Keren Hayesod United Israel Appeal, Jerusalem: ADLER, MAX; BAMBERGER, LOUIS; BAMBERGER, SIMON; BUCHALTER, LOUIS; DAVIS, EDWARD; EISENBERG, SHOUL; GERTZ, ELMER; LANDAU, EUGEN; MERTON; ROSENBLUM, SIGMUND GEORGIEVICH; SIEGEL, BENJAMIN; WEINSTOCK, SIR ARNOLD, BARON; WERTHEIMER, JOSEPH RITTER VON; WISE, STEPHEN SAMUEL

Moshe Eliahu Berman, M.Eng., F.I.E.E.; Director of Engineering, Ministry of Communications, Tel Aviv: BAGRIT, SIR LEON; PHILANTHROPY

Saul Berman, M.A., M.H.L., Rabbi; Brookline, Massachusetts: LAW AND MORALITY; NOACHIDE LAWS

Isaak Dov Ber Markon, Dr.Phil.; Historian, Ramsgate, England: AARON SELIG BEN MOSES OF ZOLKIEW; BAER, SELIGMAN ISAAC; BALI, ABRAHAM BEN JACOB; BALI, MOSES BEN ABRAHAM; BAṢĪR, JOSEPH BEN ABRAHAM HA-KOHEN HARO'EH AL-; BEGHI; BEIN, ALEXANDER; BIBLE; CARMOLY, ISSACHAR BAER BEN JUDAH LIMA; FĪRŪZ; GIBBOR, JUDAH BEN ELIJAH; IBN ABBAS, JUDAH BEN SAMUEL II; JACOB BEN REUBEN; JAPHETH

BEN DAVID IBN ṢAGHĪR; JOSEPH BEN NOAH; JOSEPH BEN SAMUEL BEN ISAAC HA-MASHBIR; JOSIAH BEN SAUL BEN ANAN; JUDAH HA-PARSI; KAL'I, SAMUEL BEN JOSEPH; KAZAZ, ELIJAH BEN ELIJAH; KIRIMI, ABRAHAM; KUKIZOW; LICHTENSTEIN, HILLEL BEN BARUCH; LUZKI, JOSEPH SOLOMON BEN MOSES; POKI, JUDAH BEN ELIEZER CHELEBI; POTTERY

Leo Bernard, Antiquarian bookseller, Member of the Czech Memorial Scrolls Committee, London: CZECH MEMORIAL SCROLLS, THE

Suzan Berns, Jewish Community Federation of San Francisco

Louis Bernstein, Ph.D., Rabbi; Professor of Jewish History, Yeshiva University, New York: KLAVAN, ISRAEL; LOOKSTEIN, JOSEPH HYMAN; MIZRACHI; POUPKO, BERNARD

Selma Berrol, Ph.D.; Assistant Professor of History, the Bernard Baruch College of the City University of New York: LEIPZIGER, HENRY M.

Mel Berwin*, M.A.; Education Consultant, Jewish Women's Archive, Brookline, Massachusetts: B'NAI B'RITH

Paul Bessemer*, M.A., M.E., C.Phil.; in Middle Eastern History; High School Teacher, Freelance Translator; Eugene, Oregon: JAVID BEY, MEHMED

James D. Besser*, B.A.; Washington Correspondent, *New York Jewish Week*, *Baltimore Jewish Times*, Fairfax, Virginia: KLEIN, MORTON; ZIONIST ORGANIZATION OF AMERICA

Sonja Beyer*, Student for Magister Artium, Hochschule für Jüdische Studien Heidelberg, Heidelberg, Germany: EHRLICH, GEORG; FREUNDLICH, OTTO; KOPF, MAXIM

Rachel Biale, M.A., M.S.W.; Author of *Women and Jewish Law*

Yehuda Leib Bialer, Jerusalem: STEIN, ISAAC

Frank (Franklin) Bialystok*, Ph.D.; Historian, Association of Canadian Jewish Studies, Toronto, Canada: FEDERMAN, MAX; GIVENS, PHILIP; HARRIS, SYDNEY; JEWISH IMMIGRANT AID SERVICES OF CANADA; KAPLAN, ROBERT P.; KAPLANSKY, KALMEN; KAYFETZ, BEN; KUPER, JACK; LANTOS, ROBERT; LENKINSKI, LOUIS; MARMUR, DOV; MARRUS, MICHAEL R.; PHILLIPS, NATHAN; SAMUEL, SIGMUND

Shlomo Bickel, Dr.Jur.; Writer and Critic, New York: ALTMAN, MOISHE; ASHENDORF, ISRAEL; AUERBACH, EPHRAIM; AUSLAENDER, NAHUM; AYALTI, HANAN J.; BAAL-MAKHSHOVES; BOMZE, NAHUM; BOTOSHANSKY, JACOB; CHARNEY, DANIEL; GROSS, NAPHTALI; HALPERN, MOYSHE-LEYB; JUSTMAN, MOSHE BUNEM; LICHT, MICHAEL; LIEBERMAN, CHAIM; LUTZKY, A.; MINKOFF, NAHUM BARUCH; MUKDONI, A.; SHTERN, ISRAEL; YAKNEHAZ

Elias J. Bickerman, Ph.D.; Emeritus Professor of Ancient History, Columbia University, New York: PERSIA

Israel M. Biderman, Ph.D.; Lecturer in Education, New York University; the Jewish Teachers' Seminary, New York: ORLAND, HERSHL

David Bidney, Ph.D.; Professor of Anthropology and Education, Indiana University, Bloomington: ANTHROPOLOGY

Konrad Bieber, Ph.D.; Professor of French and Comparative Literature, the State University of New York, Stony Brook: VERCORS

Rose Bieber, B.A., Lic. en Sc. Comm.; Brussels: ERRERA, PAUL JOSEPH; LIPSKI, ABRAHAM

Erwin Bienenstok, LL.M.; Journalist, London: TELEVISION AND RADIO

Anat Biger*, M.A.; Ph.D. student, Faculty of Arts, Tel Aviv University: ISRAEL, STATE OF: BROADCASTING, FILM, TELEVISION

Gideon Biger*, Ph.D.; Professor of Geography, Tel Aviv University: BANIAS; CARMEL, MOUNT; HYENA; ISRAEL, LAND OF: GEOGRAPHICAL SURVEY; ISRAEL, STATE OF: HISTORICAL SURVEY

Max Bilen, Ph.D.; Lecturer in French Literature, Tel Aviv University: JACOB, MAX; VIGÉE, CLAUDE

Israel Ch. Biletzky, B.A.; Writer, Tel Aviv: EPSTEIN, MELECH; FEINBERG, LEON; GRADE, CHAIM; GROSS-ZIMMERMANN, MOSHE; HERSHELE; KARPINOVITSH, AVROM; LEHRER, LEIBUSH; LEV, ABRAHAM; MENDELSOHN, SHELOMO; MENDELSON, JOSÉ; MENES, ABRAM; NEUMANN, YEḤESKEL MOSHE; OLEVSKI, BUZI; PAPIERNIKOV, JOSEPH; YUD, NAHUM

Frederik Julius Billeskov-Jansen, Ph.D.; Professor of Danish Literature, Copenhagen University: BRANDES, CARL EDVARD; BRANDES, GEORG; GOLDSCHMIDT, MEIR ARON; HERTZ, HENRIK

Frederick M. Binder, Ed.D.; Professor of Educational History, City College of the City University of New York: SACHS, JULIUS

Emanuel Bin-Gorion, Writer and Scholar, Holon, Israel: HORODEZKY, SAMUEL ABBA

Avraham Biran, Ph.D.; Director of the Department of Antiquities and Museums, Ministry of Education and Culture, Jerusalem: ISRAEL MUSEUM; MUSEUMS; ROCKEFELLER MUSEUM

Yoav Biran, B.A; Ministry for Foreign Affairs, Jerusalem: KENYA

Solomon Asher Birnbaum, Dr.Phil.; Former Lecturer in Hebrew Palaeography and Epigraphy, the School of Oriental and African Studies, the University of London: ALPHABET, HEBREW

Maurice Bisgyer, M.A.; Honorary Executive Vice President of B'nai B'rith, Washington, D.C.: KLUTZNICK, PHILIP MORRIS

Eugene C. (Charlton) Black*, Ph.D.; Otillie Springer Professor of Modern European History, Brandeis University, Waltham, Massachusetts: BIGART, JACQUES

Haim Blanc, Ph.D.; Professor of Linguistics, the Hebrew University of Jerusalem: BLOOMFIELD, LEONARD

Simha Blass, Engineer; Former

Director General of Tahal Water Planning for Israel, Tel Aviv

Joseph L. Blau, Ph.D.; Professor of Religion, Columbia University, New York: ADAMS, HANNAH; ETHICAL CULTURE; RECKENDORF, HERMANN SOLOMON; ROTH, LEON

Joshua Blau*, Ph.D.; Professor Emeritus of Arabic Language and Literature, the Hebrew University of Jerusalem: ARABIC LANGUAGE; BARTH, JACOB; HAPAX LEGOMENA; HEBREW LANGUAGE; IBN BAL'AM, JUDAH BEN SAMUEL; IBN BARUN, ABU IBRAHIM ISAAC BEN JOSEPH IBN BENVENISTE; IBN QURAYSH, JUDAH; MENAHEM BEN JACOB IBN SARUQ

Paul Blau, *Encyclopaedia Judaica* (Germany); Vienna: MAKAI, EMIL

Rivkah (Teitz) Blau*, Ph.D.; Author and Lecturer, New York: TEITZ, PINCHAS; UNION COUNTY

Gerald Y. Blidstein*, Ph.D.; Professor of Jewish Thought, the Ben-Gurion University of the Negev, Beersheba: COMMANDMENTS, REASONS FOR; EVEN SHETIYYAH; ISRAEL, KINGDOM OF; NASI; PRIESTS AND PRIESTHOOD

Ruben (Victor) Bloemgarten*, Translator and Unix Systems Engineer, The Netherlands: POLAK, HENRI

Salvador (Edmond) Bloemgarten*, Ph.D.; Historian, Menasseh ben Israel Institute, Amsterdam, The Netherlands: POLAK, HENRI

Douglas M. Bloomfield*, B.A. M.A.; Journalist, Syndicated Columnist, Washington, D.C.: NATIONAL JEWISH DEMOCRATIC COUNCIL; ROSENTHAL, BENJAMIN STANLEY

Richard N. Bluestein, LL.D.; Executive Vice President, the National Jewish Hospital, Denver, Colorado

Harry Bluestone, B.A., A.C.S.W.; Former Executive Director of the Jewish Federation of Delaware, Wilmington

Albert A. Blum, Ph.D.; Professor of Labor History, Michigan State University, East Lansing: GITLOW, BENJAMIN; GOLD, BENJAMIN; LEISERSON, WILLIAM MORRIS

Haim Karl Blum, Dr. Phil.; Historian, Jerusalem: GALATI

Samuel M. Blumenfield, D.H.L., Rabbi; Professor of Hebrew Literature and Culture, Hofstra University, Hempstead, New York: SPERTUS INSTITUTE OF JEWISH STUDIES

Bernhard Blumenkranz, Ph.D., D.es-L.; Maître de Recherches, Centre National de la Recherche Scientifique, Paris: AGDE; AGEN; AIX-EN-PROVENCE; ALBI; ALCUIN; ALÈS; ALFONSUS BONIHOMINIS; ALPHONSE OF POITIERS; ALSACE; AMBROSE; AMMERSCHWIHR; AMULO; ANDREW OF RINN; ANGERS; ANGOULÊME; ANJOU; ANSELM OF CANTERBURY; ANTOINE, NICOLAS; APT; AQUINAS, THOMAS; ARLES; AUVERGNE; AUXERRE; AVIGNON; AVITUS; BADGE, JEWISH; BAIGNEUX-LES-JUIFS; BERNARD OF CLAIRVAUX; BERTHOLD OF REGENSBURG; BIBLE SOCIETIES; BIDACHE; BODIN, JEAN; BORDEAUX; BORROMEO, CARLO; BOSSUET, JACQUES BENIGNE; BOUDIN, JEAN-FRANÇOIS; BOURG-EN-BRESSE; BOURGEOIS, JEAN; BOURGES; BRAY-SUR-SEINE; BRESSE; BRITTANY; BURCHARD OF WORMS; BURGUNDY; CADENET; CAEN; CAPESTANG; CARCASSONNE; CARPENTRAS; CASTELSARRASIN; CAVAILLON; CHÂLONS-SUR-MARNE; CHALON-SUR-SAÔNE; CHAMBÉRY; CHAMPAGNE; CHARLEMAGNE; CHARLES IV; CHARLES V; CHARLES VI; CHARLEVILLE; CHARTRES; CHÂTEAU-LANDON; CHÂTEAU-THIERRY; CHINON; CHURCH FATHERS; CLERMONT-FERRAND; CLUNY; COLBERT, JEAN BAPTISTE; COLMAR; CORBEIL; CRÉMIEU; CRISPIN, GILBERT; DAMIAN, PETER; DAMPIERRE-DE-L'AUBE; DAUPHINÉ; DIGNE; DIJON; DOMINICANS; DRAGUIGNAN; DREUX; ENSISHEIM; EPERNAY; ÉTAMPES; ETTENDORF; EUGENIUS; ÉVREUX; FALAISE; FLORUS OF LYONS; FOIX; FONTAINEBLEAU; FORCALQUIERS; FRANCE; FRANCHE-COMTÉ; FULBERT OF CHARTRES; GASCONY; GELASIUS I; GÉVAUDAN; GRATIAN; GREGORY; GREGORY OF TOURS; GUEBWILLER; HADRIAN I; HAGUENAU; HAVRE, LE; HEGENHEIM; HILDEBERT OF LAVARDIN; HILDUIN; HONORIUS; HRABANUS MAURUS; HYÈRES; INGWILLER; INNOCENT; ISLE-SUR-LA-SORGUE, L'; IVO OF CHARTRES; JACOB OF PONT-SAINTE-MAXENCE; JOHN II; JOHN XXII; JOIGNY; JULIUS III; JUNGHOLZ; LANGUEDOC; LEO; LIMOGES; LIMOUX; LODEVE; LONS-LE-SAUNIER; LOUIS; LUNEL; LYONS; MACHAUT, DENIS DE; MACON; MÂCON; MANESSIER DE VESOUL; MANOSQUE; MANS, LE; MARSEILLES; MELUN; MONTÉLIMAR; MONTEREAU; MONTPELLIER; MORHANGE; MULHOUSE; NANTES; NARBONNE; NEVERS; NICE; NIMES; NÎMES; NYONS; OBERNAI; ODO OF CAMBRAI; ODO OF SULLY; ORANGE; ORLÉANS; PAMIERS; PARIS; PASTOUREAUX; PETER OF BLOIS; PETER OF CLUNY; PEYREHORADE; PHILIP; POITIERS; POITU; PONTOISE; POSQUIÈRES; PROVINS; PUY, LE; RAMERUPT; RAOUL GLABER; RHEIMS; RIBEAUVILLÉ; ROCHELLE, LA; ROSENWILLER; ROSHEIM; ROUEN; ROUFFACH; ROUSSILLON; RUDOLPH; SAINT-DENIS; SAINTES; SAINT-GILES; SAINT-JEAN-DE-LUZ; SAINT-PAUL-TROIS-CHÂTEUX; SAINT-RÉMY-DE-PROVENCE; SAINT-SYMPHORIEN-D'OZON; SAVERNE; SAVOY; SÈLESTAT; SENLIS; SENS; SERRES; SIMON, RICHARD; SISTERON; SOISSONS; SOULTZ; STRASBOURG; TARASCON; TITHES, CHURCH; TOULON; TOULOUSE; TOURAINE; TOURS; TRETS; TRÉVOUX; TROYES; VALENCE; VALRÉAS; VERDUN-SUR-GARONNE; VESOUL; VIBERT OF NOGENT; VIENNE; VILLEFRANCHE-DE-CONFLENT; VITRY

Nachman Blumental, Historian, Jerusalem: BARASH, EPHRAIM; BUEHLER, JOSEF; DACHAU

H. Elchanan Blumenthal, M.A., Rabbi; Jerusalem: HA LAḤMA ANYA; ḤASIDEI UMMOT HA-OLAM; KAVVANAH; NEW MOON, ANNOUNCEMENT OF; NIGHT PRAYER

Henriette Boas, Ph.D.; Journalist, Amsterdam: ELKERBOUT, BEN; FUKS, LAJB; GANS, MOZES HEIMAN; GODEFROI, MICHAEL HENRI; GOUDSMIT, JOEL EMANUEL; HAAN, JACOB ISRAËL DE; HERZBERG, ABEL JACOB; HORODISCH, ABRAHAM; MEIJER, JACOB; MEIJERS, EDUARD MAURITS; MEYER, JONAS DANIEL; MIRANDA, SALOMON RODRIGUES DE; NETHERLANDS, THE; NIEROP, VAN; OPPENHEIM, JACQUES; ORNSTEIN, LEONARD SALOMON; SARPHATI, SAMUEL; SCHUSTER, AARON; VISSER, LODEWIJK ERNST; VORST, LOUIS J.

Charles Boasson, LL.D.; the Truman Center for the Advancement of Peace, the Hebrew University of Jerusalem: ASSER

Mendel Bobe, Engineer, Tel Aviv: COURLAND; LATZKY-BERTHOLDI, JACOB

ZE'EV WOLF; NUROCK, MORDECHAI; YOFFE, ALTER

Y. Michal Bodemann, Ph.D.; Assoc. Professor of Sociology, University of Toronto

Frederick Simon Bodenheimer, Dr. Phil.; Emeritus Professor of General Zoology and Entomology, the Hebrew University of Jerusalem: HA-REUBENI, EPHRAIM

Yohanan Boehm, Music critic, Jerusalem: ZUKERMAN, PINCHAS; DANCE; DA-OZ, RAM; DAUS, AVRAHAM; EDEN-TAMIR; FRIED, MIRIAM; GILBOA, JACOB; GRAZIANI, YITZHAK; HORAH; INBAL DANCE THEATER; INBAL, ELIAHU; ISRAEL PHILHARMONIC ORCHESTRA; JACOBI, HANOCH; JAFFE, ELI; KADMAN, GURIT; KALICHSTEIN, JOSEPH; LAKNER, YEHOSHUA; MAAYANI, AMI; NATRA, SERGIU; ORGAD, BEN ZION; PRESSLER, MENAHEM; RONLY-RIKLIS, SHALOM; SADAI, YIẒḤAK; SCHIDLOWSKY, LEON; SETER, MORDECHAI; SMOIRA-COHN, MICHAL

Harm den Boer*, Ph.D.; Professor, Chair of Spanish Literature, University of Basel, Switzerland: ABENDANA, JACOB BEN JOSEPH; CORREA, ISABEL DE; COSTA, URIEL DA

Gunter Bohm, B.A.; Professor of Jewish Art and Vice Director of the Institute for the Study of Judaism, the University of Chile, Santiago: CHILE; KOSICE, GYULA

Anne Bohnenkamp-Renken*, Ph.D.; Director, Freies Deutsches Hochstift/ Frankfurter Goethe-Museum, Frankfurt University, Germany: GOETHE, JOHANN WOLFGANG VON

Leon Boim, Ph.D.; Associate Professor of Political Science, Tel Aviv University

Willy Bok, M.A.; Acting Director of the Centre National des Hautes Etudes Juives, Brussels: ANTWERP; BRUSSELS; WIENER, ERNEST EDOUARD

Ben Zion Bokser, Ph.D., Rabbi; Adjunct Professor of English, Queens College of the City University of New York: JUSTIN MARTYR; LIFE AND DEATH

Robert G. Boling, Ph.D.; Professor of Old Testament, McCormick Theological Seminary, Chicago: BAAL-BERITH; BOOK OF JASHAR; JOTHAM; SISERA

Sidney Bolkosky*: DETROIT; HOLOCAUST

Shimon Bollag*, Ph.D.; Senior Lecturer, Department of Science Teaching, Jerusalem College of Technology: MATHEMATICS

Ruth Bondi*, Writer and Historian, Ramat Gan: THERESIENSTADT

Robert Bonfil*, Ph.D.; Professor Emeritus of Jewish History, the Hebrew University of Jerusalem: ITALY; PIPERNO BEER, SERGIO

Marlene Booth*, M.F.A.; Documentary Filmmaker and Lecturer, Academy for Creative Media, University of Hawaii, Honolulu, Hawaii: IOWA

Paul Borchardt, *Encyclopaedia Judaica* (Germany); Munich: MOSUL

Poul Borchsenius, M.A., Reverend; Historian, Randers, Denmark: SCANDINAVIAN LITERATURE

Howard Borer*: WORCESTER

Linda J. Borish*, Ph.D.; Associate Professor of History and Women's Studies Program History, Western Michigan University, Kalamazoo, Michigan: COHEN, NATALIE; EPSTEIN, CHARLOTTE; HELDMAN, GLADYS MEDALIE

David Joseph Bornstein, *Encyclopaedia Judaica* (Germany); Berlin: MA'ASEROT; MAKKOT; MAR BAR RAV ASHI; MARI BEN ISSUR; MEREMAR; NAḤMAN BAR RAV HUNA; NAḤMAN BEN ISAAC; NAḤMAN BEN JACOB; NAHUM OF GIMZO; NAHUM THE MEDE; NAKDIMON BEN GURYON; NASHIM; NATHAN DE-ẒUẒITA RESH GALUTA; NATHAN HA-BAVLI; NEGA'IM; NEHORAI; NEZIKIN; NITTAI OF ARBELA; ORLAH

Leah Bornstein-Makovetsky*, Ph.D.; Senior Lecturer in Jewish Studies, College of Judea and Samaria, Ariel, Israel: ADJIMAN; ALEPPO; AMASIYA; ASHKENAZI, BEḤOR; BENVENISTE, MOSES; BURSA; BUSTANAI BEN ḤANINAI; CAPITULATIONS; DAMANHŪR; DAMASCUS; EDESSA; EL-ARISH; FARḤI; GALLIPOLI; HAMON; ISTANBUL; IZMIT; JADĪD AL-ISLĀM; KHARĀJ AND JIZYA; KHAYBAR; KIERA; MAHALLA AL-KUBRA; MANISSA; MANSURA; MENASCE, DE; MOLCHO, DAVID EFFENDI ISAAC PASHA; OTTOMAN EMPIRE; PALTIEL; PORT SAID; RABBI, RABBINATE; RASHID; SAMUEL IBN 'ĀDIYĀ; SAPHIR, JACOB; SARŪJ; SIJILMASSA; SOLAL; SUAREZ; SULEIMAN I; TANTA; TLEMCEN; TOKAT; TRIPOLI; VALENSI

Eugene B. Borowitz, D.H.L., Ed.D., Rabbi; Professor of Jewish Religious Thought and of Education, the Hebrew Union College-Jewish Institute of Religion, New York: FRIENDSHIP; LOVE

Elijah Bortniker, Ph.D.; the Jewish Education Committee, New York: EDUCATION, JEWISH

Jacob Borut*, Ph.D.; Historian, Yad Vashem, Jerusalem: VERBAND DER DEUTSCHEN JUDEN; VERBAND DER VEREINE FUER JUEDISCHE GESCHICHTE UND LITERATUR

Shira Borut, Ph.D.; Research Associate in Parasitology, the Hebrew University-Hadassah Medical School, Jerusalem: RAYSS, TSCHARNA

Alvin Boskoff, Ph.D.; Professor of Sociology, Emory University, Atlanta, Georgia: ARON, RAYMOND; CAHNMAN, WERNER J.; DIAMOND, SIGMUND; GUMPLOWICZ, LUDWIG; GURVITCH, GEORGES

Philippe Boukara*, Doctoral Candidate, Lecturer in History, Institute d'études politiques - Training Department, Mémorial de la Shoah, Paris, France: KAGAN, ELIE; KAHN, ALBERT; KRYGIER, RIVON; LUSTIGER, JEAN-MARIE ARON; SCHWARZ-BART, ANDRÉ; SIRAT, RENE SAMUEL

Alan Keir Bowman, Ph.D.; Assistant Professor of Classics, Rutgers University, New Jersey: PAPYRI

Daniel Boyarin, M.H.L.; New York: MENE, MENE, TEKEL, U-FARSIN; RESURRECTION; TUBAL-CAIN; URIAH; UZ; WATCHERS

Rachel Bracha*, M.A.; Archive Coordinator, World ORT, London, England: ORT

Marshall (A.) Brachman*, M.B.A.; Lobbyist, Washington, D.C.: FROST, MARTIN

Harry M. Bracken, Ph.D.; Professor of Philosophy, McGill University, Montreal

Randolph (L.) Braham*, Ph.D.; Distinguished Professor Emeritus, Graduate Center of the City University of New York: ABONY; ALBERTI-IRSA; ASZÓD; BAIA-MARE; BAJA; BALASSAGYARMAT; BÉKÉSCSABA; BELED; BERETTYÓÚJFALU; BISTRITA; BODROGKERESZTÚR; BONYHÁD; BORSA; BUDAPEST; CLUJ; DEJ

Andreas Brämer*, Dr.Phil.; Associate Director, Institut für die Geschichte der deutschen Juden, Hamburg, Germany: ZUCKERMAN, BENEDICT

Emmanuel Brand, Dipl. Archiv.; Jerusalem: LVOV; MENGELE, JOSEF; WAR CRIMES TRIALS

Jehoshua Brand, Ph.D.; Associate Professor of Talmudic Archaeology, Tel Aviv University: BARON DE HIRSCH FUND; CIRCUSES AND THEATERS; GAON

Paul Anthony Brand*, Dr.Phil.; Senior Research Fellow, All Souls College, Oxford, England: HENRY OF WINCHESTER; ISAAC OF SOUTHWARK

Joseph Brandes, Ph.D.; Professor of History, Paterson State College, Wayne, New Jersey: AGRICULTURE; BACHARACH; JEWISH AGRICULTURAL SOCIETY; SABSOVICH, H. L.; VINELAND

Rainer Brändle*, Dr.Phil.; Assistant, Archiv Bibliographia Judaica, Johann Wolfgang Goethe-Universität, Frankfurt, Germany

Samuel G.F. Brandon, D.D.; Professor of Comparative Religion, the University of Manchester: SICARII

Yehuda Zvi Brandwein, Rabbi; Author, Jerusalem: ASHLAG, YEHUDAH

Joseph Braslavi (Braslavski), Historian, Tel Aviv: JAFFA; KEFAR YASIF; KHAYBAR; MACHPELAH, CAVE OF; MOUNT OF OLIVES; PEKI'IN; RACHEL

Chaya (F.) Brasz*, M.A.; Freelance Historian and Publicist; Former Director of the Center for Research on Dutch Jewry, Jerusalem: AMSTERDAM; GOUDEKET, MAURITS; NETHERLANDS, THE

Alisa Braun*, M.A.; Lecturer, University of California, Davis, California: MANI LEIB

David S. Braun*, Preceptor in Yiddish, Harvard University, Cambridge, Massachusetts: CAHAN, JUDAH LOEB

Eliot Braun*, PH.D.; Archaeologist, Associate Fellow, WF Albright Institute of Archaeological Research, Jerusalem; Associate Researcher, Centre de Recherche Français de Jérusalem: EPSTEIN, CLAIRE

Sidney D. Braun, Ph.D.; Professor of Romance Languages, the Herbert H. Lehman College of the City University of New York: HERTZ, HENRI; MAUROIS, ANDRE; MENDÈS, CATULLE; SUARÈS, ANDRÉ; THARAUD, JÉRÔME and JEAN

Susana Brauner*, M.A.; Senior University Teacher and Investigator, UADE-UBA, Argentina, South America: TEUBAL, EZRA

Susan L. Braunstein*, Ph.D.; Curator of Archaeology and Judaica, The Jewish Museum, New York: ḤANUKKAH LAMP

Zeev Braverman, Elitzur, Tel Aviv: ELITZUR

Sandee Brawarsky*: NEW YORK CITY, UPPER WEST SIDE

Abraham J. Brawer, Dr. Phil.; Geographer and Historian, Tel Aviv: ABU GHOSH; BASHAN; BATUMI; BIELSKO; BIRKENTHAL, DOV BER; BUCHACH; DAMASCUS AFFAIR; GEOGRAPHY; GILBOA; GINNOSAR, PLAIN OF; HOLON; HOROWITZ, ISRAEL ZE'EV; ISRAEL, LAND OF: GEOGRAPHICAL SURVEY; JORDAN; LUNCZ, ABRAHAM MOSES; NAPOLEON BONAPARTE; PALESTINE; SAPIR, ELIYAHU; SCHWARZ, YEHOSEPH; TABOR, MOUNT; TEMPLERS; TIBERIAS; WOLFENBUETTEL; YARMUK

Moshe Brawer, Ph.D.; Associate Professor of Geography, Tel Aviv University: ISRAEL, STATE OF: HISTORICAL SURVEY; PHILIPPSON; RED SEA

Menachem M. Brayer, Ph.D., D.H.L., Rabbi; Clinical Psychologist, Professor of Biblical Literature and Education, Yeshiva University, New York: FROMM, ERICH; LEWIN, KURT ZADEK; MALLER, JULIUS BERNARD; PSYCHOLOGY; ROBACK, ABRAHAM AARON

Jennifer (Stern) Breger*, B.A., M.A.; Silver Springs, Maryland: PRINTING, HEBREW

Marshal Breger*: BUSH, GEORGE HERBERT WALKER; BUSH, GEORGE WALKER

Marc Bregman*: TANḤUMA YELAMMEDENU

Sol Breibart*: CHARLESTON

Shlomo Breiman, Ph.D.; Writer and Scholar, Jerusalem: HELPERN, MICHAEL

Michael Brenner*, Ph.D.; Professor of Jewish History and Culture, Ludwig-Maximilians-Universität, Munich, Germany: AUERBACH, PHILIPP; BECKER, JUREK; BUBIS, IGNATZ; COHN-BENDIT, DANIEL; GALINSKI, HEINZ; GERMANY; HERMLIN, STEPHAN; HOCHHUTH, ROLF; JUEDISCHE VOLKSPARTEI; NACHMANN, WERNER; SPIEGEL, PAUL; STERN, FRITZ RICHARD; ZENTRALRAT DER JUDEN IN DEUTSCHLAND

Marla Brettschneider*, Ph.D.; Professor, Political Philosophy, University of New Hampshire: COHEN, FANNIA; HAUSER, RITA ELEANOR; MESSINGER, RUTH WYLER

Mordechai Breuer, Ph.D.; Educator, Jerusalem: DELITZSCH, FRANZ; FRANKFURT ON THE MAIN; PHILIPPSON; PILPUL; ROSOWSKY, SOLOMON; YESHIVOT

Yochanan Breuer*, Ph.D.; the Hebrew University of Jerusalem: HEBREW LANGUAGE

Herbert Chanan Brichto, Ph.D., Rabbi; Professor of Bible, the Hebrew Union College-Jewish Institute of Religion, Cincinnati: BLASPHEMY; BLESSING AND CURSING; PRIESTLY BLESSING

Ravelle Brickman, B.A.; New York: RACHEL; RUBINSTEIN, IDA

William W. Brickman, Ph.D.;

Professor of Educational History and Comparative Education, the University of Pennsylvania, Philadelphia: EDUCATION; ENGELMANN, SUSANNE CHARLOTTE; FLEXNER, ABRAHAM; GOULD, SAMUEL BROOKNER; KANDEL, ISAAC LEON; KARSEN, FRITZ; PÉREIRE, JACOB RODRIGUES; RICHMAN, JULIA; STERN, ERICH; STERN, WILLIAM; UNIVERSITIES

Bernhard Brilling, Dr. Phil., Rabbi; Lecturer in Jewish History, the University of Muenster, Germany: BADEN; BRESLAU; GOERLITZ; HOMBURG; MINDEN; PADERBORN; SILESIA; SOEST; STETTIN; WARENDORF

David Brinn*, B.Sc.; Editorial Director, Israel 21c, Jerusalem: RAMONE, JOEY; ROTH, DAVID LEE; WEISS, MELVYN I.

Dvora Briskin-Nadiv, B.A., B.Ed.; Assistant in Biblical Studies, the University of the Negev, Beersheba: HABAKKUK

Sir Israel Brodie, B.A., B.Litt., Rabbi; Former Chief Rabbi of the British Commonwealth, London: MILITARY SERVICE

Heinrich Haim Brody, Ph.D.; Scholar of Medieval Hebrew Poetry and former Chief Rabbi of Prague, Jerusalem: AARON SIMEON BEN JACOB ABRAHAM OF COPENHAGEN; AL-AVANI, ISAAC; ANKAWA, ABRAHAM BEN MORDECAI; BANET; CASTELNUOVO, MENAHEM AZARIAH MEIR BEN ELIJAH

Ephraim Broido, Writer and Editor, Jerusalem: SHAKESPEARE, WILLIAM

Abraham Isaac Bromberg, Rabbi; Writer, Jerusalem: SOCHACZEW, ABRAHAM BEN ZE'EV NAHUM BORNSTEIN OF

Maury A. Bromsen, M.A.; Boston, Massachusetts: HARRISSE, HENRY

Fred Bronner, M.A.; Lecturer in Latin American History, the Hebrew University of Jerusalem: ARGENTINA

Lawrence Brook*, B.A.; Publisher, *Deep South Jewish Voice*, Birmingham, Alabama: ALABAMA; BIRMINGHAM

Simcha Shalom Brooks*, B.A., M.A., Ph.D.; Freelance Scholar, London, England: GIBEAH, GEBA; GIBEON

Chaim Brovender, Ph.D., Rabbi; Instructor in Bible, Bar-Ilan University, Ramat Gan: HEBREW LANGUAGE

Hannah Brown*, B.A.; Writer, *Jerusalem Post*, Jerusalem: ALMAGOR, GILA; BAKRI, MOHAMMED; CEDAR, JOSEPH; DAYAN, ASSAF; FOX, EYTAN; GITAI, AMOS; GLOBUS, YORAM; IVGY, MOSHE

Michael Brown*, B.A., M.A., M.H.L., Ph.D., D.D.; Professor Emeritus, York University, Toronto, Canada: JOSEPH; ROSENBERG, STUART E.; SCHEUER, EDMUND

Theodore M. Brown, Ph.D.; Assistant Professor of History, City College of the City University of New York: SINGER, CHARLES JOSEPH

Tracy L. Brown*, M.A., B.A.; Researcher, United States Holocaust Memorial Museum, Washington, D.C.: HOLOCAUST

Rosalind Browne, Art critic, New York

Christopher R. Browning*, Ph.D.; Frank Porter Graham Professor of History University of North Carolina at Chapel Hill, North Carolina: HILBERG, RAUL

Josef Brozek, Ph.D.; Research Professor, Lehigh University, Bethlehem, Pennsylvania: LURIA, ALEXANDER ROMANOVICH; VYGOTSKI, LEV SEMYONOVICH

Frederick Fyvie Bruce, D.D.; Professor of Biblical Criticism and Exegesis, the University of Manchester, England: ASCETICISM; COPPER SCROLL; DAMASCUS, BOOK OF COVENANT OF; DEAD SEA SCROLLS; KITTIM; LIES, MAN OF; LIES, PROPHET OF; LION OF WRATH; MURABBA'AT SCROLLS; PESHER; QUMRAN; SEEKERS AFTER SMOOTH THINGS; SEREKH; SHAPIRA FRAGMENTS; SONS OF LIGHT; TEACHER OF RIGHTEOUSNESS; WAR SCROLL; WICKED PRIEST; YAḤAD; ZADOKITES

Gerald Bubis*: UNITED JEWISH COMMUNITIES

Arthur T. Buch, D.S.Sc., Rabbi; Teacher, New York

Nancy (Nield) Buchwald*, Ph.D.; Independent Scholar, Columbus, Ohio: MANSO, LEO; MARGO, BORIS; MARGOULIES, BERTA; MARIL, HERMAN; MARYAN; MENKES, ZYGMUNT; MOHOLY-NAGY, LÁSZLÓ; MOÏSE, THEODORE SYDNEY; MOPP; NICHOLS, JACK; PANOFSKY, ERWIN; RASKIN, SAUL; REDER, BERNARD; REISS, LIONEL; ROSE, HERMAN; ROSENTHAL, MAX; ROTHSTEIN, IRMA; SCHAMES, SAMSON; SCHANKER, LOUIS; SCHAPIRO, MEYER; SCHOR, ILYA; SCHWARTZ, MANFRED; SIMON, SIDNEY; SPIRO, EUGEN; STERNE, HEDDA; STERNE, MAURICE; TEWI, THEA; TWORKOV, JACK; WILSON, SOL; ZUCKER, JACQUES

Emmanuel Bulz, LL.D., Rabbi; Chief Rabbi of Luxembourg: LUXEMBOURG

Nicolas Burckhardt, Director of the International Tracing Service, Arolsen, Germany: INTERNATIONAL TRACING SERVICE

Yosef Burg, Ph.D., Rabbi; Minister of the Interior, Jerusalem: AVIAD, YESHAYAHU

Israel Burgansky, M.A.; Instructor in Talmud, Bar-Ilan University, Ramat Gan: ḤALLAH; SIMEON BAR YOḤAI; SIMEON BEN ABBA; SIMEON BEN ELEAZAR; SIMEON BEN GAMALIEL I; SIMEON BEN ḤALAFTA; SIMEON BEN JUDAH HA-NASI; SIMEON BEN NANAS; SIMEON BEN NETHANEL; SIMEON HA-PAKULI; SIMEON HA-TIMNI; SIMEON OF MIZPAH

Janet (Handler) Burstein*, Ph.D.; Professor Emeritus of English Literature, Drew University, Madison, New Jersey: HEILBRUN, CAROLYN G.

Giulio Busi*, Ph.D.; Professor of Jewish Studies, Free University Berlin, Germany: BECK, MATTHIAS FRIEDRICH; BOESCHENSTEIN, JOHANN; DI GARA, GIOVANNI; FAGIUS, PAULUS; FORSTER, JOHANN

Mervin Butovsky*, M.A.; Professor of English Literature, Concordia University, Montreal, Canada: LAYTON, IRVING; LEVINE, NORMAN

Gilbert Cahen, Archiviste-Paleographe; Conservateur aux

Archives Departementales de la Moselle, Metz, France: BOULAY; LÉVY, RAPHAËL; LORRAINE; LUNÉVILLE; METZ; NANCY; PHALSBOURG; SARREGUEMINES; THIONVILLE; TOUL; VERDUN

Werner J. Cahnman, Ph.D.; Professor of Sociology, Rutgers University, Newark, New Jersey; Member of the Faculty, New School for Social Research, New York: ADLER, MAX; ARON, RAYMOND; BENDIX, REINHARD; BOSKOFF, ALVIN; DIAMOND, SIGMUND; DRACHSLER, JULIUS; DURKHEIM, ÉMILE; EISENSTADT, SAMUEL NOAH; FRIEDMANN, GEORGES; GINSBERG, MORRIS; GLAZER, NATHAN; GOLDSCHEID, RUDOLF; GORDON, MILTON M.; GUMPLOWICZ, LUDWIG; GUTTMAN, LOUIS; HALPERN, BENJAMIN; HAUSER, PHILIP MORRIS; HORKHEIMER, MAX; INKELES, ALEX; JANOWITZ, MORRIS; JOSEPH, SAMUEL; KRACAUER, SIEGFRIED; LANDSHUT, SIEGFRIED; LAZARSFELD, PAUL F.; LEVY, MARION JOSEPH, JR.; LÉVY-BRUHL, LUCIEN; LIPSET, SEYMOUR MARTIN; MAIER, JOSEPH; MANNHEIM, KARL; MERTON, ROBERT KING; MORENO, JACOB L.; NELSON, BENJAMIN; OPPENHEIMER, FRANZ; RIESMAN, DAVID; ROBISON, SOPHIA; ROSE, ARNOLD MARSHALL; ROSENTHAL, ERICH; SALOMON, ALBERT; SALOMON, GOTTFRIED; SIMMEL, GEORG; SKLARE, MARSHALL; SMELSER, NEIL JOSEPH; SOCIOLOGY; STERN, BERNHARD JOSEPH; SULZBACH, WALTER; TUMIN, MELVIN MARVIN; WIRTH, LOUIS; WORMS, RENÉ

Ivan Caine, M.H.L., Rabbi; Associate Professor of Bible, Reconstructionist Rabbinical College, Philadelphia: NUMBERS, BOOK OF

Justin D. (Daniel) Cammy*, Ph.D.; Assistant Professor of Jewish Studies and Comparative Literature, Smith College, Northampton, Massachusetts: SUTZKEVER, ABRAHAM; WOLF, LEYZER; YUNG-VILNE

Hyman Joseph Campeas, M.A.; Educator, New York: SEPHARDIM

Judith L. (Levine) Cantor*, B.A.; Archivist, Congregation Shaarey Zedek; Jewish Historical Society of Michigan; Past President, former Editor; Historical Society of Michigan, Board of Trustees; Women's Studies Association, Board of Directors, Emeritus, Michigan: MICHIGAN

Kimmy Caplan*, Ph.D.; Senior Lecturer, Bar-Ilan University, Ramat Gan: FRIEDERMAN, ZALMAN JACOB; GORDON, JACOB; SILVERSTONE, GEDALYAH

Richelle Budd Caplan*, M.A.; Director, International Relations, International School for Holocaust Studies, Yad Vashem, Jerusalem: HOLOCAUST

Brenda Cappe*, B.A.; Researcher, OISE/University of Toronto, Canada: LUFTSPRING, SAMMY; RUBENSTEIN, LOUIS; UNGERMAN, IRVING; WEIDER, BEN

Jacob Carciente*, C.E.; Civil Engineer, Professor Universidad Central de Venezuela and Universidad Metropolitana; Former Dean of Engineering, Caracas, Venezuela: BRENER, PYNCHAS; CARACAS; CORO; DE SOLA, JUAN BARTOLOMÉ; VENEZUELA

Michael Hart Cardozo, B.A., LL.B.; Executive Director, Association of American Law Schools, Washington, D.C.: LEHMAN, IRVING; POLLAK, WALTER HEILPRIN

Alexander Carlebach, D.en D., Rabbi; Jerusalem: AARON OF NEUSTADT; AARON OF PESARO; ADASS JESHURUN, ADASS JISROEL; AKADEMIE FUER DIE WISSENSCHAFT DES JUDENTUMS; ARVIT; AUERBACH; BARRENNESS AND FERTILITY; BERLINER, ABRAHAM; BRAUDE, JACOB; CHOTZNER, JOSEPH; COLOGNE; DORTMUND; FERRARA; GOLDSCHMIDT, ERNST DANIEL; HAMBURGER, JACOB; HILDESHEIMER, MEIR; HOLLAENDER, LUDWIG; HOMILETIC LITERATURE; JAFFE, SIR OTTO; KAFAḤ, YOSEF; LEHMANN, EMIL; RABBI, RABBINATE; WAHL, SAUL BEN JUDAH; WEISS, ISAAC JACOB

Ezriel Carlebach, Dr.Jur.; Editor and Writer, Tel Aviv: ALLGEMEINE ZEITUNG DES JUDENTUMS

Alex Carmel, Ph.D.; Instructor in International Relations and History, the Hebrew University of Jerusalem: HAIFA

Ram Carmi, Architect, Tel Aviv

Moshe Carmilly-Weinberger, Ph.D., Rabbi; Professor of Jewish Studies, Yeshiva University, New York: CENSORSHIP; HASKAMAH

Yaacov Caroz, Formerly second in command of the Mossad; Journalist, Tel Aviv

Daniel Carpi, Ph.D.; Associate Professor of Jewish History, Tel Aviv University: BOLZANO; CASALE MONFERRATO; CHIERI; DONATI, ANGELO; FARINACCI, ROBERTO; FOSSANO; FRIULI-VENEZIA GIULIA; ISTRIA; ITALY; LAMPRONTI, ISAAC HEZEKIAH BEN SAMUEL; LATTES, BONET; LATTES, ISAAC BEN JACOB; LATTES, ISAAC JOSHUA; MONCALVO; ROME; SERVI, FLAMINIO

Judy Feld Carr, Mus. M., Mus. Bac.; Musicologist and Music Educator; Chairman, National Task Force for Syrian Jews, CJC; Chairman, Dr. Ronald Feld Fund for Jews in Arab Lands, housed in Beth Tzedec Congregation, Toronto: SYRIA

Hayden Carruth, M.A.; Poet and critic, Johnson, Vermont: REZNIKOFF, CHARLES

Greer Fay Cashman, Journalist, Sydney: MARTIN, DAVID; WATEN, JUDAH

Umberto (Moses David) Cassuto, Litt.Doct., Rabbi; Professor of Bible, the Hebrew University of Jerusalem: ABRAHAM BEN DANIEL; AHITUB BEN ISAAC; AL-BAẒAK, MAẒLI'AḤ BEN ELIJAH IBN; ALEMANNO, JOHANAN BEN ISAAC; ANATOLI, JACOB BEN ABBA MARI BEN SAMSON; APULIA; BENEVENTO, IMMANUEL BEN JEKUTHIEL; BERGAMO; BIBLE; BRESCIA; BRUNETTI, ANGELO; CAGLIARI; CANTARINI, ISAAC VITA HA-KOHEN; CASTELLO, ABRAHAM ISAAC; COMO; CONAT, ABRAHAM BEN SOLOMON; DEL BENE, ELIEZER DAVID BEN ISAAC; FLORENCE; FOLIGNO, HANANEL; FORTI, BARUCH UZZIEL BEN BARUCH; GENNAZANO, ELIJAH ḤAYYIM BEN BENJAMIN OF; GENTILI; ḤALFAN, ELIJAH MENAHEM; IMMANUEL OF ROME; ISAAC BEN JACOB MIN HA-LEVIYYIM; JEDIDIAH BEN MOSES OF RECANATI; JUDAH BEN JEHIEL; KALONYMUS BEN KALONYMUS; LATTES, ABRAHAM BEN ISAAC; LEONE, LEON DI; LEVI, BENEDETTO; LUZZATTO; LUZZATTO, JACOB BEN ISAAC; MANETTI, GIANNOZZO; MARGULIES, SAMUEL HIRSCH; MOROSINI, GIULIO; MOSES OF PAVIA

Calev Castel, M.D.; Kibbutz Netzer Sereni: SERENI, ENZO ḤAYYIM

Moshe Catane, Dr. du 3e cycle, Archiviste Paleographe; Senior Lecturer in French Civilization and Literature, Bar-Ilan University, Ramat Gan; Librarian, the Jewish National and University Library, Jerusalem: ALSACE; ARON, ROBERT; BEER-BING, ISAIAH; BERNARD, TRISTAN; BERR ISAAC BERR DE TURIQUE; BERR, MICHEL; CONSISTORY; DRACH, PAUL-LOUIS-BERNARD; DREYFUS, ALFRED; DRUMONT, EDOUARD-ADOLPHE; GARY, ROMAIN; HALÉVY; HARRY, MYRIAM; HIRSCH, BARON MAURICE DE; JAVAL; KAHN, GUSTAVE; KESSEL, JOSEPH; KLEIN, SALOMON WOLF; LAHARANNE, ERNEST; LEHMANN, JOSEPH; LÉVI ALVARÈS, DAVID; LOEWENSON, JEAN; LUNEL, ARMAND; LYONS; NEHER, ANDRÉ; PORTO-RICHE, GEORGES DE; RABBINOWICZ, ISRAEL MICHEL; SACHS, MAURICE; SINZHEIM, JOSEPH DAVID BEN ISAAC; SPIRE, ANDRÉ

Shulamith Catane, B.A.; Jerusalem: BLOCH, PIERRE; BOKANOWSKI, MAURICE; GOUDCHAUX, MICHEL; GREENSTONE, JULIUS HILLEL; GRUMBACH, SALOMON; KLOTZ, LOUIS-LUCIEN; LYON-CAEN, CHARLES LÉON; MAYER, DANIEL; MAYER, RENÉ; MEYER, LEON; RAYNAL, DAVID; SCHRAMECK, ABRAHAM; STERN, JACQUES; TORRÈS, HENRY

Georges Cattaui, L.en D., Dip. Sc.Pol.; Paris: PROUST, MARCEL

Alberto Cavaglion*, Ph.D.; Teacher, Istituto piemontese per la storia della resistenze e della società contemporanea, Turin, Italy: ALESSANDRIA; CUNEO; GENOA

Henri Cazelles, D.en D.; Professor of Biblical Exegesis and Hebrew, Institut Catholique de Paris: MICAH

Adonella Cedarmas*, Ph.D.; Researcher, University of Udine, Italy: GORIZIA; TRIESTE

David Cesarani*, Ph.D.; Research Professor; Royal Holloway, University of London; London, England: ENGLAND; GILBERT, SIR MARTIN; KINDERTRANSPORT; MAXWELL, ROBERT; RIFKIND, SIR MALCOLM; ROTHSCHILD, NATHANIEL CHARLES JACOB; SACKS, JONATHAN HENRY; TAYLOR, SIR PETER MURRAY

J.H. Chajes*, Ph.D.; Lecturer, Jewish History, University of Haifa: ABERLIN, RACHEL

Scott Chamberlin*, B.A.; Writer and Editor, Los Angeles: KINDERTRANSPORT

Leon Chameides*, M.D.; Emeritus Director of Pediatric Cardiology, Connecticut Children's Medical Center, Clinical Professor University of Connecticut School of Medicine; Member of the Board and Executive Committee of the Jewish Historical Society of Greater Hartford, Connecticut: HARTFORD

Jerome A. Chanes*, Faculty Scholar, Cohen Center for Modern Jewish Studies, Brandeis University, Waltham, Massachusetts: AMERICAN JEWISH COMMITTEE; AMERICAN JEWISH CONGRESS; ANTI-DEFAMATION LEAGUE; ASSIMILATION; CLAL; COMMUNITY; CONFERENCE OF PRESIDENTS OF MAJOR AMERICAN JEWISH ORGANIZATIONS

Zevulun Charlop, Ph.D., Rabbi; Director of RIETS and of Yeshiva Program/Mazer School of Talmudic Studies, Yeshiva University, New York

Yosef Chavit, Researcher, Kiryat Arba: RENASSIA, YOSSEF

Barry Chazan, Ed.D.; former Director, Melton Center for Jewish Education in the Diaspora, the Hebrew University of Jerusalem

Robert Chazan, Ph.D.; Associate Professor of History, Ohio State University, Columbus: NAMES

Mordecai Chenzin, Rabbi; Columbus, Ohio: LEWIN, JUDAH LEIB

Mordecai S. Chertoff, D.H.L.; Director of Public Information, World Zionist Organization – American Section; Executive Director, American Histadrut Cultural Exchange Union, New York: STERNSTEIN, JOSEPH PHILIP

Bryan Cheyette, Ph.D.; Lecturer, Dept. of English, Queen Mary and Westfield College, University of London: FEINSTEIN, ELAINE; JACOBSON, HOWARD; JOSIPOVICI, GABRIEL; RUBENS, BERNICE; STEINER, GEORGE

Arthur A. Chiel, M.A., D.H.L., Rabbi; Woodbridge, Connecticut: NEW HAVEN

Jonathan Chipman, M.A.; Writer and Lecturer, Jerusalem: BA'ALEI TESHUVAH

Dov Chomsky, Poet, General Secretary of the Hebrew Writers' Association, Tel Aviv: WRITERS' ASSOCIATION IN ISRAEL

Noam Chomsky, Ph.D.; Professor of Linguistics, Massachusetts Institute of Technology, Cambridge: HARRIS, ZELLIG SABBETAI

William Chomsky, Ph.D., D.H.L.; Professor of Hebrew and Jewish Education, Dropsie University, Philadelphia

Andre N. Chouraqui, Ph.D.; Historian, Jerusalem: CASSIN, RENÉ SAMUEL

Anatole Chujoy, Dance critic and Historian, New York: HUROK, SOLOMON

Stanley F. Chyet, Ph.D., Rabbi; Professor of American Jewish History, the Hebrew Union College-Jewish Institute of Religion, Cincinnati: HEBREW UNION COLLEGE-JEWISH INSTITUTE OF RELIGION; HENRY, JACOB; JONAS, JOSEPH; LOPEZ, AARON; MARX, ALEXANDER; RIVERA, JACOB RODRIGUEZ; TRADE AND COMMERCE

E.Cindof: HAMMAT GADER

Eli Citonne, Businessman and Photographer, Istanbul: KARAITES

Mordechai Cogan, Ph.D.; Senior Lecturer and Chairman of the Department of Bible, Ben-Gurion University of the Negev, Beersheba

Amnon Cohen*, Ph.D.; Eliahu Elath Professor of History of the Muslim Peoples, the Hebrew University of Jerusalem: SIJILL

Ariel Cohen: LIPPMANN, GABRIEL; LIPSCHITZ, RUDOLF OTTO SIGISMUND

Aryeh Cohen*: PROGRESSIVE JEWISH ALLIANCE

Benjamin Cohen, M.A., Rabbi; Jerusalem: PHINEHAS BEN ḤAMA HA-KOHEN; PHINEHAS BEN JAIR; YANNAI

Beth (B.) Cohen*, Ph.D.; Historian, Chapman University, Los Angeles,

California: ARAD, YITZHAK; BAUMAN, ZYGMUNT; BIELSKI, TUVIA, ASAEL and ZUS; BROWNING, CHRISTOPHER R.; D'AMATO, ALFONSE M.; DICKER-BRANDEIS, FREDERIKE; FORTUNOFF VIDEO ARCHIVE FOR HOLOCAUST TESTIMONY; HARTMAN, GEOFFREY; RAVENSBRUECK

Burton I. Cohen*, Ph.D.; Associate Professor Emeritus of Jewish Education, Jewish Theological Seminary, New York: JEWISH CAMPING

Chaim E. Cohen*, Ph.D.; Senior Lecturer in Hebrew Language, Tel Aviv University: DOTAN, ARON

Chayim Cohen, B.A., B.H.L.; Columbia University, New York: MINOR PROPHETS; POISON; RAHAB; RIGHT AND LEFT; RIMMON; TREASURE, TREASURY; WIDOW

Daniel J. Cohen, Ph.D.; Director of the Central Archives for the History of the Jewish People, Jerusalem: ARCHIVES; LANDJUDENSCHAFT

David Cohen, M.A.; Teacher in Hebrew and Semitic Languages, Bar-Ilan University, Ramat Gan: NEO-ARAMAIC

Elisheva Cohen, Chief Curator of the Israel Museum, Jerusalem: BUDKO, JOSEPH; JESI, SAMUEL; KAPLAN, ANATOLI LVOVICH; KIRSZENBAUM, JESEKIEL DAVID; STRUCK, HERMANN; SZALIT-MARCUS, RACHEL

Evelyn (M.) Cohen*, Ph.D.; Art Historian, Jewish Theological Seminary, New York: ILLUMINATED MANUSCRIPTS, HEBREW

Gerson D. Cohen, Ph.D., Rabbi; President and Professor of Jewish History, the Jewish Theological Seminary of America, New York: HANNAH AND HER SEVEN SONS

Hayyim (Haim) J. Cohen, Ph.D.; Senior Lecturer in Contemporary Jewry, the Hebrew University of Jerusalem: AFGHANISTAN; ALEPPO; ANTIBI; ARABIA; ASHKENAZI, BEḤOR; ATLAS; BATTAT, REUBEN; BAGHDAD; BEIRUT; CAIRO; CASABLANCA; CATTAUI; DAMASCUS; DANIEL, MENAHEM SALIH; DUWAYK; EDIRNE; EGYPT; ELIAS, JOSEPH; FARAJ, MURAD; FARḤI; FEZ; ḤADDAD, EZRA; HARARI; HARARI, SIR VICTOR RAPHAEL; ḤARIRI; ISFAHAN; ISTANBUL; IZMIR; KABĪR, ABRAHAM ṢĀLIḤ AL-; KADOORIE, SASSON; KIRKUK; LIBYA; MEKNÈS; MENASCE, DE; MOROCCO; MOSSERI; MOSUL; MOYAL, ESTHER; NAHOUM, ḤAIM; NISSIM, ABRAHAM ḤAYYIM; PICCIOTTO; PORT SAID; SALÉ-RABAT; SAMRA, DAVID; SASSOON, SIR EZEKIEL; SHAUL, ANWAR; SHIRAZ; TANGIER; TETUÁN; TRIPOLI; ZILKHA, NA'IM

Isaac Cohen, Ph.D., Rabbi; Chief Rabbi of Ireland, Dublin: IRELAND

Israel Cohen, Writer and Editor, Tel Aviv: AHARONOVITCH, YOSEF; AHARONOVITCH, YOSEF; LAUFBAHN, YITSHAK

Jack (Joseph) Cohen*, Ph.D., Rabbi; Retired Director, Hillel Foundation, the Hebrew University of Jerusalem; Retired member of faculty, Reconstructionist Rabbinical College; Founding Member, Kehillat Mevakshei Derech, Jerusalem: KAPLAN, MORDECAI MENAHEM

Judah M. Cohen*, Ph.D.; Assistant Professor, Lou and Sybil Mervis Professor of Jewish Culture, Indiana University, Bloomington, Indiana: CARLEBACH, SHLOMO

Judith Cohen, Ph.D.; Lecturer in Musicology, Tel Aviv University: ADLER, GUIDO; DEUTSCH, OTTO ERICH; EINSTEIN, ALFRED; HERZ, HENRI; HESS, DAME MYRA; HESS, DAME MYRA; LEVI, HERMANN; LEVI, HERMANN; MOTTL, FELIX JOSEF

Julie-Marthe M. Cohen*, M.A.; Curator, Jewish Historical Museum, Amsterdam, the Netherlands: CITROEN, ROELOF PAUL; ELTE, HARRY

Lionel Cohen, M.A.; Instructor in French and Classical Studies, Bar-Ilan University, Ramat Gan: LANGFUS, ANNA; PASCAL, BLAISE

Margot Cohen*: ROCHESTER

Mark R. Cohen*, Ph.D.; Professor of Near Eastern Studies, Princeton University, New Jersey: GOITEIN, SHLOMO DOV; OMAR, COVENANT OF

Martin A. Cohen, Ph.D., Rabbi; Professor of Jewish History, the Hebrew Union College-Jewish Institute of Religion, New York: CARVAJAL; COIMBRA; DIAS, LUIS; ESTE, JOÃO BAPTISTA DE; GRANADA, GABRIEL DE; LATIN AMERICA; MALDONADO DE SILVA, FRANCISCO; MARRANO; MARRANO DIASPORA; NAVARRO; NETANYAHU, BENZION; NEW CHRISTIANS; NORONHA, FERNÃO DE; RIVKIN, ELLIS; VECINHO, JOSEPH

Michael Cohen*: FLEISCHER, CHARLES

Naomi W. Cohen, Ph.D.; Associate Professor of History, Hunter College of the City University of New York: AMERICAN JEWISH COMMITTEE; STRAUS

Nathan Cohen*, Ph.D.; Senior Lecturer in Cultural History, Bar-Ilan University, Ramat Gan: AHARON BEN SAMUEL; ALTMAN, MOISHE; ANSHEL OF CRACOV; BIMKO, FISHEL; BOMZE, NAHUM; BRYKS, RACHMIL; SINGER, ISAAC BASHEVIS

Nilli Cohen*, Director, The Institute for the Translation of Hebrew Literature, Tel Aviv: HEBREW LITERATURE, MODERN

Rachel Cohen, B.A.; Jerusalem: LEBANON; LIBYA

Richard Cohen, B.A.; Associate Director, the American Jewish Congress, New York: SPINGARN

Robert Cohen, B.A.; Jerusalem: CARIBBEANS, SPANISH-PORTUGUESE NATION OF THE: LA NACION

Robert S. Cohen, Ph.D.; Professor of Physics and Philosophy, Boston University, Massachusetts: CHWISTEK, LEON; MEYERSON, EMILE; SCHAFF, ADAM

Selma Jeanne Cohen, Ph.D.; Editor, New York: DANCE; MARCEAU, MARCEL

Tova Cohen*, Ph.D.; Professor, Bar-Ilan University, Ramat Gan: HEBREW LITERATURE, MODERN

Yoel Cohen*, B.Sc., Ph.D.; Senior Lecturer, Netanaya Academic College; Lifshitz Religious Education College Jerusalem; The Holon Institute of Technology; Israel: AL HA-MISHMAR; BAR-ILAN, DAVID; BARNEA, NAHUM; DANKNER, AMNON; DISSENTCHIK, ARYEH; GLOBES; HAARETZ; HA-MODI'A; HA-ẒOFEH; ISRAEL, STATE OF: CULTURAL LIFE; JERUSALEM POST; JERUSALEM REPORT; KIRSCHENBAUM, MORDECHAI; LANDAU,

DAVID; MAARIV; MARGALIT, DAN; MARMORI, HANOKH; MOZES; NIMRODI; PRESS; ROSENBLUM, HERZL; RUBINGER, DAVID; SCHNITZER, SHMUEL; SCHOCKEN; VANUNU AFFAIR; VARDI, MOSHE; YATED NEEMAN; YEDIOTH AHARONOTH; YUDKOVSKY, DOV; ZEMER, HANNAH

Cedric Cohen Skalli*, Ph.D.; Postdoctoral Research, Alumnus Tel Aviv University: ABRABANEL

Yohanan (J.-G.) Cohen-Yashar (Kahn), Ph.D.; Lecturer in Classical Languages and in Philosophy, Bar-Ilan University, Ramat Gan: RENAN, ERNEST

Alexander Cohn, M.Sc.; Municipal Engineer, Bene-Berak: BENE-BERAK

Gabriel H. Cohn, Ph.D.; Lecturer in Bible, Bar-Ilan University, Ramat Gan: JONAH, BOOK OF

Haim Hermann Cohn, Justice of the Supreme Court of Israel, Jerusalem; Associate Professor of Law, the Hebrew University of Jerusalem: ABDUCTION; ADMISSION; ADULTERY; ASSAULT; ATTORNEY; BET DIN AND JUDGES; BLOOD-AVENGER; BRIBERY; CAPITAL PUNISHMENT; CITY OF REFUGE; COMPOUNDING OFFENSES; CONFESSION; CONFISCATION, EXPROPRIATION, FORFEITURE; CONTEMPT OF COURT; CRUCIFIXION; DIVINE PUNISHMENT; EVIDENCE; EXTRAORDINARY REMEDIES; FINES; FLOGGING; FORGERY; FRAUD; GAMBLING; ḤEREM; HOMICIDE; INCEST; INFORMERS; OATH; OPPRESSION; ORDEAL; PENAL LAW; PERJURY; PLEAS; POLICE OFFENSES; PRACTICE AND PROCEDURE; PUNISHMENT; REBELLIOUS SON; SEXUAL OFFENSES; SLANDER; SLAVERY; SORCERY; SUICIDE; TALION; THEFT AND ROBBERY; USURY; WEIGHTS AND MEASURES; WITNESS

Robert A. Cohn*, B.A., J.D., B.S.; Editor-in-Chief Emeritus of the *St. Louis Jewish Light*, St. Louis: SAINT LOUIS

Baruch J. Cohon: IDELSOHN, ABRAHAM ZVI

Margaret L. Coit, Dr. of Letters; Associate Professor of Social Science, Fairleigh Dickinson University, Rutherford, New Jersey: BARUCH

Saul Paul Colbi, Dr.Jur.; Former Director, Department of Christian Communities, the Ministry of Religious Affairs, Jerusalem: HOLY PLACES; JEWISH-CHRISTIAN RELATIONS

Yoseph Colombo, Ph.D.; Lecturer in Jewish Studies, the Luigi Bocconi Commercial University, Milan: PRESS; RASSEGNA MENSILE DI ISRAEL, LA

Vittore Colorni, Ph.D.; Professor of the History of Italian Law, the University of Ferrara, Italy

Michael Comay, B.A., LL.B.; Ambassador, Ministry for Foreign Affairs, Jerusalem: ISRAEL, STATE OF: HISTORICAL SURVEY

Manuela Consonni*, Ph.D.; Lecturer, the Hebrew University of Jerusalem: ALESSANDRIA; ALMANSI; AQUILA; AREZZO; ASTI; CATTANEO, CARLO; MUSSOLINI, BENITO

Alan Cooper*, Ph.D.; Elaine Ravich Professor of Jewish Studies, Jewish Theological Seminary, New York: LAMENTATIONS, BOOK OF

Harvey A. Cooper, B.A.; Journalist, New York: MAYER, LOUIS BURT; PREMINGER, OTTO LUDWIG; THEATER

Jacob H. Copenhagen, Librarian, Jerusalem: HIRSCHEL, LEVIE; ROSENTHAL, LESER

Renee Corcoran*: NEBRASKA; OMAHA

David Corcos, Historian, Jerusalem: AARON BEN BATASH; ABENSUR; ABUDARHAM; ABULKER; ALGERIA; ALGIERS; ARCILA; ATAR; ATLAS; AVILA, DE; AYASH; AẒANCOT; AZEMMOUR; AZEVEDO; BELAIS, ABRAHAM BEN SHALOM; BELISHA; BENCHIMOL; BENGALIL; BENGHAZI; BENIDER; BENOLIEL; BENREMOKH; BENSUSAN; BENWAISH, ABRAHAM; BENZAMERO; BERBERS; BERGEL; BESSIS, ALBERT; BIBAS; BORDJEL; BOUCHARA; BOUGIE; BRUNSCHVIG, ROBERT; BUENO; BUSNACH; CABESSA; CANSINO; CARDOSO; CASABLANCA; CATTAN; CAZES, DAVID; CEUTA; CHOURAQUI; CHOURAQUI, ANDRÉ; CHRIQUI; COHEN, LEVI-ABRAHAM; CONSTANTINE; CORIAT; DAHAN; DARMON; DELMAR; DELOUYA; DJERBA; DRA; DURAN; FEZ; GABÈS; GAGIN, ḤAYYIM; HASSAN; HATCHWELL, SOL; HONEIN; KĀHINA; KAIROUAN; LEVY; LEVY-BACRAT, ABRAHAM BEN SOLOMON; LUMBROSO; MACNIN; MALCA; MOROCCO; NARBONI; OFRAN; OKHLAH VE-OKHLAH; PALACHE; PINTO; QAL'AT ḤAMMĀD; ROSALES, JACOB; ROTE; SEBAG; SEROR; SERUYA; SIJILMASSA; SOLAL; SOUS; TANGIER; TETUÁN; TLEMCEN; TUAT; TUNIS, TUNISIA; UZAN; VALENSI; WAQQĀṢA

David Coren, Member of the Knesset, Kibbutz Gesher ha-Ziv: GADNA

Mort Cornin, B.Litt.; Journalist, Jersey City, New Jersey: HUDSON COUNTY

Maritza Corrales*, M.A.; Researcher, University of Havana, Cuba: WOLF, RICHARD RIEGEL

Alan D. Corre, Ph.D., Rabbi; Professor of Hebrew Studies, the University of Wisconsin, Milwaukee: SEPHARDIM; SOLIS-COHEN

Lewis A. Coser, Ph.D.; Professor of Sociology, the State University of New York, Stony Brook: SCHELER, MAX FERDINAND

Aliza Craimer*, M.A. Phil.; Modern Jewish Studies, University of Oxford, England: ALBERTA; CALGARY; SAFDIE, MOSHE; VEINER, HARRY

Lawrence A. Cremin, Ph.D.; Professor of Education, Columbia University, New York: RICE, JOSEPH MAYER

David (M.) Crowe*, Ph.D.; Professor of History, Elon University, North Carolina: PLASZOW; SCHINDLER, OSKAR

June Cummins*, Ph.D.; Associate Professor, Department of English and Comparative Literature, San Diego State University: TAYLOR, SYDNEY

Louisa Cuomo, Dott. in lett.; Assistant in Italian Language and Literature, the Hebrew University of Jerusalem; Assistant in Judaica, New York University: BAUR, HARRY; FUBINI, MARIO; LEVI, GIULIO AUGUSTO; MOMIGLIANO, ATTILIO; MORPURGO, GIUSEPPE; MUSSAFIA, ADOLFO

Michael Curtis, Ph.D.; Professor of Political Science, Rutgers University, Editor of *Middle East Review*: ANTISEMITISM

Irving Cutler*, Ph.D.; Emeritus Professor of Geography, Chicago State University: CHICAGO

Charles Cutter, M.A., M.L.S.; Hebrew Bibliographer of the Library, Ohio State University, Columbus: BERNSTEIN, IGNATZ; CAHAN, JUDAH LOEB; CASSEL, DAVID

William Cutter*, Ph.D., Rabbi; Steinberg Professor of Human Relations and Professor of Hebrew Literature, Hebrew Union College, Los Angeles: DAVIS, DAVID BRION

Arthur Cygielman, Cand. S.C.; Teacher in Seminar ha-Kibbutzim, Tel Aviv: BOLESLAV V; CRACOW; DABROWA GORNICZA; DAVID-GORODOK; DIVIN; FISHEL; FRANK, MENAHEM MENDEL; GORODENKA; GORODOK; HIRSZOWICZ, ABRAHAM; IVANOVO; IVYE; JEDRZEJOW; JEKELES; JOSKO; JÓZEFOWICZ; KALISZ; KALUSH; KLETS; KOBIELSKI, FRANCISZEK ANTONI; KOBRIN; KOCK; KONIN; KOSOV; KRYNKI; LACHVA; LANCUT; LASK; LECZYCA; LELEWEL, JOACHIM; LEWIN, GERSHON; LEWKO, JORDANIS; LEZAJSK; LOWICZ; MEISEL, MOSES BEN MORDECAI; MEISELS, DAVID DOV; MENAHEM MENDEL BEN ISAAC; MICZYŃSKI, SEBASTIAN; MIEDZYRZEC PODLASK; MIELEC; MIR; MLAWA; MOJECKI, PRZECLAW; NACHMANOVICH; NATANSON, LUDWIK; NOVAYA USHITSA; NOVY DVOR; NOWY DWOR MAZOWIECKI; NOWY SACZ; ORGELBRAND, SAMUEL; OSHMYANY; OSTROW MAZOWIECKA; PARCZEW; PIATTOLI, SCIPIONE; PIOTRKOW; PLOCK; POPPER BOZIAN, WOLF; POTOCKI, VALENTINE; PROHOVNIK, ABRAHAM; PULAWY; PULTUSK; RADOMSKO; RADZIWILLOW; REIẒES; ROZWADOW; SAMBOR; SANDOMIERZ; SIERADZ; SKARGA, PIOTR; SKIERNIEWICE; SOCHACZEW; SOSNOWIEC; SREM; TOMASZOW LUBELSKI; TOMASZOW MAZOWIECKI; VOLCHKO; WEGROW; WEIGEL, CATHERINE; WIELUN; WOLOWSKI; WYSZKOW; ZALCSTEIN, GECL; ZAMBROW; ZDUNSKA WOLA; ZGIERZ

Roney Cytrynowicz*, Ph.D.; Historian, Arquivo Histórico Judaico Brasileiro, São Paulo, Brazil: BAHIA; BRAZIL; KOCH, ADELHEID LUCY; POLITICS; PORTO ALEGRE; RECIFE; RIO DE JANEIRO; SÃO PAULO

Leon Czertok, Dr.Jur.; General Secretary, Centre de Documentation Juive Contemporaine, Paris: SCHNEERSOHN, ISAAC

Moshe M. Czudnowski, Ph.D.; Lecturer in Political Science, the Hebrew University of Jerusalem: ALMOND, GABRIEL ABRAHAM

Larissa (Dämmig) Daemmig*, University Diploma, Librarian, Bet Debora and The Ronald S. Lauder Foundation, Berlin, Germany: FREIBURG IM BREISGAU; FUERTH; FULDA; HAGEN; HALBERSTADT; HALLE; HAMELN; HANOVER; HEIDELBERG; LANDAU; LEIPZIG; LIPPE; LUEBECK; MAGDEBURG; MAINZ; MANNHEIM; MARBURG; MEININGEN; MEMMINGEN; MUEHLHAUSEN; MUNICH; NAUHEIM; NOERDLINGEN; NUREMBERG; OFFENBACH; OFFENBURG; OLDENBURG; OPPENHEIM; OSNABRUECK; PFORZHEIM; RECKLINGHAUSEN; SAXONY; SCHNAITTACH; SPEYER; STRAUBING; STUTTGART; THURINGIA; TRIER; ULM; VILLINGEN; WEINHEIM; WESTPHALIA; WUERTTEMBERG; WUPPERTAL

Avigdor Dagan, Dr.Jur.; Author and former Ambassador, Ministry for Foreign Affairs, Jerusalem: AŠKENAZY, LUDVÍK; BORNFRIEND, JACOB; CZECHOSLOVAK LITERATURE; CZECHOSLOVAKIA; EISNER, PAVEL; FEIGL, BEDRICH; FEUERSTEIN, BEDŘICH; FISCHER, OTOKAR; FRITTA; FUCHS, ALFRED; GELLNER, FRANTIŠEK; GOLDSTUECKER, EDUARD; GOTTLIEB, FRANTIŠEK; GROSMAN, LADISLAV; GROSSMAN, LADISLAV; GUTFREUND, OTTO; GUTTMANN, ROBERT; HAAS, LEO; HOSTOVSKÝ, EGON; JUSTITZ, ALFRED; KAFKA, FRANTIŠEK; KAPPER, SIEGFRIED or VÍTĚZSLAV; KARS, JIŘÍ; KNIEŽA, EMIL; KOHN, JINDŘICH; KOPF, MAXIM; KRAUS, FRANTISEK R.; LANGER, FRANTIŠEK; LANGER, JIŘÍ MORDECHAI; LEDA, EDUARD; LUSTIG, ARNOST; OLBRACHT, IVAN; ORTEN, JIŘÍ; POLÁČEK, KAREL; PRESS; RAKOUS, VOJTĚCH; SCHORSCH, GUSTAV; SIMONE, ANDRÉ; SLÁNSKÝ TRIAL; TRIER, WALTER; VRCHLICKÝ, JAROSLAV; WINTER, GUSTAV; ZELENKA, FRANTIŠEK; ZEYER, JULIUS; ŽÍDEK, PAVEL

Shaul Dagoni, M.D.; Haifa: STAMPS

Rachel Dalven, Ph.D.; Professor of English, Ladycliff College, Highland Falls, New York: CAIMIS, MOISIS; ELIYIA, JOSEPH; GREEK LITERATURE, MODERN; JUDEO-GREEK; MATSAS, NESTORAS; SCHIBY, BARUCH; SCIAKI, JOSEPH

Joseph Dan, Ph.D.; Associate Professor of Hebrew Literature, the Hebrew University of Jerusalem: AARON OF BAGHDAD; ABRAHAM; ALEXANDER THE GREAT; APOCRYPHA AND PSEUDEPIGRAPHA; BEN SIRA, ALPHABET OF; BIOGRAPHIES AND AUTOBIOGRAPHIES; CALAHORA, JOSEPH BEN SOLOMON; CANPANTON, JUDAH BEN SOLOMON; DERASHOT HA-RAN; DEVEKUT; DONNOLO, SHABBETAI; ELEAZAR BEN JUDAH OF WORMS; ELEAZAR BEN MOSES HA-DARSHAN OF WUERZBURG; ELHANAN BEN YAKAR; ELIEZER BEN MANASSEH BEN BARUCH; ETHICAL LITERATURE; EXEMPLA OF THE RABBIS; EXEMPLUM; FICTION, HEBREW; FRANCES, ISAAC; GORDON, JEKUTHIEL BEN LEIB; HAGIOGRAPHY; ḤASIDEI ASHKENAZ; ḤASIDIM, SEFER; ḤEMDAT YAMIM; HOMILETIC LITERATURE; IBN YAḤYA, GEDALIAH BEN JOSEPH; IGGERET HA-KODESH; ISRAEL ḤARIF OF SATANOV; ISRAEL ISSERL BEN ISAAC SEGAL; JABEZ, JOSEPH BEN ḤAYYIM; JACOB KOPPEL BEN MOSES OF MEZHIRECH; JAGEL, ABRAHAM; JOSEPH BEN UZZIEL; JOSEPH DELLA REINA; JUDAH BEN SAMUEL HE-ḤASID; KALONYMUS; LETTERS AND LETTER WRITERS; LUZZATTO, MOSES ḤAYYIM; MAGGID; MAGIC; MANN, ABRAHAM AARON OF POSNAN; MENAHEM ẒIYYONI; MICHAEL AND GABRIEL; MIDRASH ASERET HA-DIBBEROT; MIVḤAR HA-PENINIM; MOSCATO, JUDAH BEN JOSEPH; MOSES, CHRONICLES OF; MUSAR HASKEL; NEVU'AT HA-YELED; ORḤOT ḤAYYIM; POLEMICS AND POLEMICAL LITERATURE; RAZIEL, BOOK OF; SACRIFICE; SAMUEL BEN KALONYMUS HE-ḤASID OF SPEYER; SASPORTAS, JACOB; SEFER HA-ḤAYYIM; SEFER HA-YASHAR; SEFER ḤUKKEI HA-TORAH; SHEKHINAH; TAKU, MOSES BEN ḤISDAI; TISHBY, ISAIAH; TOLEDOT HA-ARI; TOLEDOT YESHU; UZZA AND AZA'EL; VISIONS; WILLS, ETHICAL; ZERUBBABEL, BOOK OF; ẒEVI HIRSCH OF NADWORNA

Robert Dan, Ph.D.; Research Fellow of Orientalia and Librarian, National Szechenyi Library of Hungary, Budapest: KOMÁROMI CSIPKÉS, GYÖRGY

Suzanne Daniel, D.es-L.; Associate Professor of Judeo-Hellenistic Literature, the Hebrew University of Jerusalem: BIBLE

Uriel Dann, Ph.D.; Senior Lecturer in the History of the Modern Middle East, Tel Aviv University: ABDULLAH IBN HUSSEIN; HUSSEIN; JORDAN, HASHEMITE KINGDOM OF

Haim Darin-Drapkin, Ph.D., Scientific Director, International Research Centre for Cooperative Rural Communities, Tel Aviv: ISRAEL, STATE OF: ALIYAH

Joseph J. Darvin, B.S.; Chemist, Spring Valley, New York

Jacob Dash, B.Arch, A.M.T.P.I.; Head of the Planning Department, Ministry of the Interior, Jerusalem: ISRAEL, STATE OF: ALIYAH

Abraham David*, Ph.D.; Senior Researcher, The Jewish National and University Library, the Hebrew University of Jerusalem: ABOAB, SAMUEL BEN ABRAHAM; ABRAHAM BEN N... HA-BAGHDADI; ABRAHAM BEN NATHAN; ABULAFIA, ḤAYYIM NISSIM BEN ISAAC; ALASHKAR, SOLOMON; ALFANDARI, SOLOMON ELIEZER BEN JACOB; ALGAZI, SOLOMON BEN ABRAHAM; ALI BEN ZECHARIAH; ANAU, PHINEHAS ḤAI BEN MENAHEM; ARYEH LEIB BEN ELIJAH; ASHKENAZI, BEZALEL BEN ABRAHAM; ASHKENAZI, JUDAH BEN SIMEON; ASTRUC, SAUL HA-KOHEN; AUERBACH, MEIR BEN ISAAC; AZARIAH BEN SOLOMON; BADHAV, ISAAC BEN MICHAEL; BASOLA, MOSES BEN MORDECAI; BEN-KIKI; BENVENISTE, JOSEPH BEN MOSES DE SEGOVIA; BERAB, JACOB BEN ḤAYYIM; BERLIN, SAUL BEN ẒEVI HIRSCH LEVIN; BERTINORO, OBADIAH BEN ABRAHAM YARE; BLOCH, SAMSON BEN MOSES; BONASTRUC, ISAAC; BRUDO, ABRAHAM BEN ELIJAH; CANPANTON, ISAAC BEN JACOB; CAPSALI, MOSES BEN ELIJAH; CAPUSI, ḤAYYIM; CARO, ISAAC BEN JOSEPH; CASTELLAZZO; CASTRO, ABRAHAM; CASTRO, JACOB BEN ABRAHAM; CORDOVERO, GEDALIAH BEN MOSES; CURIEL, ISRAEL BEN MEIR DI; DANGOOR, EZRA SASSON BEN REUBEN; DANIEL BEN ḤASDAI; DANIEL BEN PERAḤYAH HA-KOHEN; DANIEL BEN SAADIAH HA-BAVLI; DANIEL BEN SAMUEL IBN ABĪ RABĪ'; DAVID BEN ḤAYYIM OF CORFU; DAVID BEN HEZEKIAH; DAVID BEN JUDAH; DAVID BEN SAMUEL; DAYYAN; DEL VECCHIO, SHABBETAI ELHANAN BEN ELISHA; DIENNA, AZRIEL BEN SOLOMON; ELEAZAR BEN ḤALFON HA-KOHEN; ELIJAH BEN BENJAMIN HA-LEVI; EPHRAIM SOLOMON BEN AARON OF LUNTSHITS; EXILARCH; EZEKIEL FEIVEL BEN ZE'EV WOLF; FINN, JAMES; FOUR CAPTIVES, THE; ḤAKAM, AL-; ḤAKIM, SAMUEL BEN MOSES HA-LEVI IBN; ḤALFON BEN NETHANEL HA-LEVI ABU SAʿĪD; ḤASDAI; ḤAVER; ḤAYYIM SHABBETAI; HEZEKIAH BEN DAVID; HEZEKIAH BEN DAVID DA SILVA; IBN ḤABIB, MOSES BEN SHEM TOV; IBN SHUAIB, JOEL; ISAAC; ISAAC BEN ABRAHAM DI MOLINA; ISRAEL BEN SAMUEL HA-KOHEN; ISSACHAR BAER BEN TANḤUM; JACOB BEN ELEAZAR; JACOB BEN ḤAYYIM TALMID; JACOB BEN NETHANEL BEN FAYYŪMĪ; JOSEPH BEN KALONYMUS HA-NAKDAN I; JOSEPH BEN PHINEHAS; JOSEPH DAVID; JOSEPH ḤAYYIM BEN ELIJAH AL-ḤAKAM; JOSIAH BEN JESSE; KARA, AVIGDOR BEN ISAAC; KAẒIN, JUDAH BEN YOM TOV; KHALAẒ, JUDAH BEN ABRAHAM; LANIADO, ABRAHAM BEN ISAAC; LANIADO, RAPHAEL SOLOMON BEN SAMUEL; LANIADO, SAMUEL BEN ABRAHAM; LANIADO, SOLOMON BEN ABRAHAM; LAPAPA, AARON BEN ISAAC; LEON, ISAAC DE; LIPSCHUTZ, ISRAEL BEN GEDALIAH; LONZANO, ABRAHAM BEN RAPHAEL DE; MAHALALEL BEN SHABBETAI HALLELYAH; MALACHI BEN JACOB HA-KOHEN; MARGOLIOT, MOSES BEN SIMEON; MARGOLIOTH, JACOB; MASHĀ'IRĪ, AL; MAẒLI'AḤ BEN SOLOMON HA-KOHEN; MEIR BEN ISAAC SHELI'AḤ ẒIBBUR; MEYUḤAS, ABRAHAM BEN SAMUEL; MEYUḤAS, MOSES JOSEPH MORDECAI BEN RAPHAEL MEYUHAS; MEYUḤAS, RAPHAEL MEYUḤAS BEN SAMUEL; MONZON, ABRAHAM; MORDECAI BEN JUDAH HA-LEVI; MOSES BEN LEVI; MOSES BEN YOM-TOV; MOSES ESRIM VE-ARBA; MOSES KAHANA BEN JACOB; MOSES NATHAN; MOTAL, ABRAHAM BEN JACOB; MUBASHSHIR BEN NISSI HA-LEVI; MUBASHSHIR BEN RAV KIMOI HA-KOHEN; NAJARA; NAJARA, ISRAEL BEN MOSES; NATHAN BEN ABRAHAM I; NATHAN BEN ABRAHAM II; NATHAN BEN ISAAC HA-KOHEN HA-BAVLI; NATHAN BEN JEHIEL OF ROME; NATHAN, MORDECAI; NATRONAI BEN ḤAVIVAI; NAVON, BENJAMIN MORDECAI BEN EPHRAIM; NAVON, EPHRAIM BEN AARON; NAVON, JONAH BEN HANUN; NAVON, JONAH MOSES BEN BENJAMIN; NEHEMIAH BAR KOHEN ẒEDEK; NEHEMIAH HA-KOHEN; NETHANEL BEN MESHULLAM HA-LEVI; NETIRA; NISSI BEN BERECHIAH AL-NAHRAWANI; PALTIEL; PANIGEL, RAPHAEL MEIR BEN JUDAH; PARDO, JOSEPH; PERAḤYAH, AARON BEN ḤAYYIM ABRAHAM HA-KOHEN; PERAḤYAH, ḤASDAI BEN SAMUEL HA-KOHEN; PHINEHAS BEN JOSEPH HA-LEVI; PORTALEONE; PORTO; PORTO, ABRAHAM MENAHEM BEN JACOB HA-KOHEN; PORTO-RAFA, MOSES BEN JEHIEL HAKOHEN; PROVENÇAL, MOSES BEN ABRAHAM; QAZZĀZ, MANASSEH BEN ABRAHAM IBN; REGGIO, ABRAHAM BEN EZRIEL; REGGIO, ABRAHAM BEN EZRIEL; RICHIETTI, JOSEPH SHALLIT BEN ELIEZER; RUNKEL, SOLOMON ZALMAN; SAGIS; SAMEGAH, JOSEPH BEN BENJAMIN; SAMUEL BEN AZARIAH; SAMUEL HA-SHELISHI BEN HOSHANA; SAR SHALOM BEN MOSES HA-LEVI; SARAVAL, JACOB RAPHAEL BEN SIMḤAH JUDAH; SARAVAL, JUDAH LEIB; SCHICK, BARUCH BEN JACOB; SHALOM, ABRAHAM; SHELUḤEI EREẒ ISRAEL; SHOLAL, ISAAC; SHOLAL, NATHAN HA-KOHEN; SID, SAMUEL IBN; SILANO; SIRILLO, SOLOMON BEN JOSEPH; SOLOMON BEN ḤASDAI; SOLOMON SULIMAN BEN AMAR; SONCINO, JOSHUA; STEINHARDT, MENAHEM MENDEL BEN SIMEON; TERNI, DANIEL BEN MOSES DAVID; UKBA, MAR; UZIEL, ISAAC BEN ABRAHAM; WILNA, JACOB BEN BENJAMIN WOLF; YIẒḤAKI, DAVID; ZARKO, JOSEPH BEN JUDAH; ẒAYYAḤ, JOSEPH BEN ABRAHAM IBN; ZE'EVI, ISRAEL BEN AZARIAH; ZECHARIAH MENDEL BEN ARYEH LEIB; ẒEMAḤ ẒEDEK BEN ISAAC; ZUTA

Preston David, M.S.; Executive Director, New York City Human Rights Commission

Yonah David, Ph.D.; Professor Emeritus of Medieval Hebrew Literature, Tel Aviv University: ANAN BEN MARINUS HA-KOHEN; ANAV, BENJAMIN BEN ABRAHAM; FRANCES, IMMANUEL BEN DAVID; JERAHMEEL BEN SOLOMON; MATTATHIAS; MESHULLAM BEN KALONYMUS; MOSES BEN JOAB; OLMO, JACOB DANIEL BEN ABRAHAM; POETRY; REMOS, MOSES BEN ISAAC; RIETI, MOSES BEN ISAAC DA; RIMON, JOSEPH ẒEVI; SHEPHATIAH BEN AMITTAI; YESHURUN, AVOT

David Davidovitch, Eng.; Director of the Museum of Ethnography and Folklore, Tel Aviv: KETUBBAH; SYNAGOGUE; TOMBS AND TOMBSTONES

Esther B. Davidowitz*, B.Sc.; Editor and CommunityActivist Jewish Community Center of Wilkes-Barre; Board of Trustees of the Wilkes University; Kingston, Pa.: WILKES-BARRE AND KINGSTON

Steven Davidowitz*, B.A. M.A., M.B.A.; Registered Representative, Sammons Securities Corp. Kingston, Pennsylvania: WILKES-BARRE AND KINGSTON

Herbert Davidson, Ph.D.; Associate Professor of Philosophy, the University of California, Los

Angeles: SHALOM, ABRAHAM BEN ISAAC BEN JUDAH BEN SAMUEL

Philip (R.) Davies*, M.A., Ph.D.; Emeritus Professor of Biblical Studies, University of Sheffield, England: DEAD SEA SCROLLS; DEAD SEA SECT; ESSENES; YAḤAD

Barry Davis (Yid. Div.)*, B.A.; Senior Lecturer in Jewish History, London Jewish Cultural Center, London, England: TRUNK, YEHIEL YESHAIA

Barry Davis (Isr. Div.)*, B.A.; Journalist, Translator; Jerusalem Post, Downbeat; Moshav Matta: ARTZI, SHLOMO; BANAI; CASPI, MATTI; DAMARI, SHOSHANA; DESHEH, AVRAHAM; EINSTEIN, ARIK; FISHER, DUDU; GAON, YEHORAM; GEFEN, AVIV; HADDAD, SARIT; HA-GASHASH HA-ḤIVER; HANOKH, SHALOM; HITMAN, UZI; NINI, ACHINOAM; POLIKER, YEHUDAH; ZOHAR, URI

Eli Davis, M.D.; Associate Professor of Medicine, the Hebrew University – Hadassah Medical School, Jerusalem: YASSKY, HAIM

Joseph W. Davis, Ramat Ha-Sharon, Israel: DE VRIES, ANDRÉ

Moshe Davis, Ph.D.; Professor, Head of the Institute of Contemporary Jewry of the Hebrew University of Jerusalem

Natalie Zemon Davis*, Ph.D.; Henry Charles Lea Professor of History Emerita, Princeton University, New Jersey: GLUECKEL OF HAMELN

Moshe Dayan, Lieutenant General (Res.), Israel Defense Forces; Minister of Defense, Tel Aviv: WINGATE, ORDE

Alan H. Decherney*, M.D.; Chief Reproductive Biology and Medicine Branch, National Institute of Child Health and Human Development, National Institutes of Health, Bethesda, Maryland: LIEBERMAN, JOSEPH

Robert L. (Louis) DelBane*, B.A.; Research Fellow, Kent State University, Ohio: KAUFMAN, GEORGE SIMON; MAMET, DAVID; MILLER, ARTHUR; PERELMAN, SIDNEY JOSEPH; SIMON, NEIL

Sergio DellaPergola*, Ph.D.; Shlomo Argov Chair in Israel-Diaspora Relations, A. Harman Institute of Contemporary Jewry, the Hebrew University of Jerusalem; Senior Fellow, Jewish People Policy Planning Institute, Jerusalem: BLAYER, PIETRO; CANTONI, RAFFAELE; DEMOGRAPHY; FERRARA; GENOA; ITALY; LEGHORN; MERANO; MIGRATIONS; MILAN; MIXED MARRIAGE, INTERMARRIAGE; NAPLES; PARMA; PIPERNO BEER, SERGIO; PISA; ROME; STATISTICS; TOAFF; VITAL STATISTICS; ZOLLER, ISRAEL

Aaron Demsky, Ph.D., Rabbi; Senior Lecturer in Jewish History, Bar-Ilan University, Ramat Gan: EDUCATION, JEWISH; SCRIBE; SHALMANESER III; SHALMANESER V; TIGLATH-PILESER II; WRITING

Hugh Denman*, B.A., M.A.; Honorary Research Fellow in Yiddish, Hebrew and Jewish Studies, University College, London, England: IMBER, SAMUEL JACOB; KOBRIN, LEON; LEIVIK, H.; MANN, MENDEL; RABOY, ISAAC; REISEN, ABRAHAM; SHALOM ALEICHEM; SHAPIRA, KALONYMOUS KALMAN

Michael Denman*, M.D., F.R.C.P.; Emeritus Consultant, Northwick Park Hospital, London, England: ALFEROV, ZHORES I.; ALTSCHUL, AARON MEYER; ANFINSEN, CHRISTIAN BOEHMER; AVIGAD, GAD; AVIV, HAIM; AXEL, RICHARD; BENACERRAF, BARUJ; BENZER, SEYMOUR; BETHE, HANS ALBRECHT; BLOCH, FELIX; BODMER, SIR WALTER; BOHM, DAVID; BRENNER, SYDNEY; CEDAR, CHAIM; CHARGAFF, ERWIN; COHEN, I. BERNARD; COHEN, PHILIP PACY; COHEN, SIR PHILIP; COHEN, STANLEY N.; COHEN, YIGAL RAHAMIM; COHN, MILDRED; COOPER, LEON N.; CORI, GERTY THERESA; CROHN, BURRILL BERNARD; DASSAULT, MARCEL; DIAMOND, LOUIS KLEIN; DJERASSI, CARL; DRUCKER, DANIEL CHARLES; EDINGER, TILLY; ELION, GERTRUDE BELL; EPHRUSSI, BORIS; FISCHER, EDMOND; FOLKMAN, JUDAH; FRANK, ILYA MIKHAILOVICH; FRISCH, OTTO ROBERT; FURCHGOTT, ROBERT F.; GELFAND, IZRAIL MOISEVICH; GELL-MANN, MURRAY; GILMAN, ALFRED G.; GINZBURG, VITALY LAZAREVICH; GLASER, DONALD ARTHUR; GLAUBER, ROY J.; GOLDBERG, EMANUEL; GOLDSTEIN, JOSEPH LEONARD; GREEN, DAVID EZRA; GREENGARD, PAUL; GROSS, DAVID J.; HAREL, DAVID; HAUPTMAN, HERBERT AARON; HAURWITZ, BERNARD; HERSHKO, AVRAM; HORWITZ, H. ROBERT; JACOB, FRANCOIS; JACOBSON, KURT; JAMMER, MAX; JANOWITZ, HENRY D.; JORTNER, JOSHUA; KALNITSKY, GEORGE; KANDEL, ERIC RICHARD; KANTROWITZ, ADRIAN; KAPLAN, JOSEPH; KARLE, JEROME; KATZ, ISRAEL; KLEIN, GEORGE; KLINE, NATHAN S.; KOGAN, ABRAHAM; KOHN, WALTER; KOLTHOFF, IZAAK MAURITS; KORNBERG, ARTHUR; KORNBERG, SIR HANS LEO; KROTO, SIR HAROLD WALTER; LACHMANN, SIR PETER JULIUS; LANGER, ROBERT S; LEDERER, JEROME F.; LEDERMAN, LEON MAX; LEE, DAVID; LEES, LESTER; LIBAI, AVINOAM; LIFSON, SHNEIOR; LOEWE, FRITZ PHILIPP; LOEWI, OTTO; MASTER, ARTHUR M.; MESELSON, MATTHEW; MOTTELSON, BEN R.; NATHANS, DANIEL; NEUGEBAUER, OTTO; NIRENBERG, MARSHALL WARREN; OLAH, GEORGE A.; OSHEROFF, DOUGLAS DEAN; PAULI, WOLFGANG; PERL, MARTIN LEWIS; PICARD, LEO YEHUDA; PINKEL, BENJAMIN; PNUELI, AMIR; POLANYI, JOHN C.; POLANYI, MICHAEL; POLITZER, H. DAVID; PRESS, FRANK; PRESSMAN, DAVID; PRIGOGINE, ILYA; PRUSINER, STANLEY S.; PTASHNE, MARK STEPHEN; RACKER, EFRAIM; RAHAMIMOFF, RAMI; RAPHAEL, RALPH ALEXANDER; RODBELL, MARTIN; ROSE, IRWIN; ROSEN, FRED SAUL; ROTBLAT, SIR JOSEPH; ROTH, KLAUS FRIEDRICH; SABIN, ALBERT; SALITERNIK, ZVI; SALK, JONAS; SCHALLY, ANDREW VICTOR; SCHAWLOW, ARTHUR L.; SCHWARTZ, LAURENT; SHARON, NATHAN; SHELAH, SAHARON; SILVERMAN, LESLIE; SLEPIAN, JOSEPH; SONDHEIMER, FRANZ; SOSKIN, SELIG EUGEN; SPIEGELMAN, SOL; STEG ADOLPHE; STEIN, YEHEZKIEL; STEINBERG, AVRAHAM; STENT, GUNTHER SIEGMUND; STROMINGER, JACK; SZILARD, LEO; TABOR, DAVID; TABOR, HARRY ZVI; TALMI, IGAL; TAMM, IGOR YEVGENYEVICH; TARSKI, ALFRED; TELLER, EDWARD; TEMIN, HOWARD MARTIN; TEPPER, MORRIS; ULAM, STANISLAW MARCIN; VANE, SIR JOHN R.; VARMUS, HAROLD ELIOT; VOET, ANDRIES; WEINBERG, STEVEN; WEINHOUSE, SIDNEY; WEISSKOPF, VICTOR F.; WESTHEIMER, FRANK HENRY; WIGNER, EUGENE PAUL; WINTROBE, MAXWELL MYER; YALOW, ROSALYN SUSSMAN; YOUNG, ALEC DAVID; ZAIZOV, RINA; ZIFF, MORRIS

Shlomo Derech, Editor, Kibbutz Givat Ḥayyim: KIBBUTZ MOVEMENT

David (Jay) Derovan*, M.A.; Jewish Education, Director, Draitch Adult Jewish Education,

Beit Shemesh, Israel: ABRAHAM BEN DAVID OF POSQUIÈRES; ADLER, NATHAN BEN SIMEON HA-KOHEN; ADRET, SOLOMON BEN ABRAHAM; AḤARONIM; ALSHEKH, MOSES; ASHER BEN JEHIEL; BA'ALEI TESHUVAH; BAKSHI-DORON, ELIAHU; BIBLE CODES; BLAU, AMRAM; BOBOV; BREUER, MORDECHAI; ELIJAH BEN SOLOMON ZALMAN; ELIYAHU, MORDECHAI; FEINSTEIN, MOSES; GAON; GEMATRIA; GERONDI, ZERAHIAH BEN ISAAC HA-LEVI; GERSHOM BEN JUDAH ME'OR HA-GOLAH; HAI BEN SHERIRA; ḤAKHAM BASHI; ḤAYYIM BEN ISAAC "OR ZARU'A"; ḤAYYIM BEN BEZALEL; HELLER, YOM TOV LIPMANN BEN NATHAN HA-LEVI; HERMENEUTICS; HERZOG, ISAAC; HILDESHEIMER, AZRIEL; HOFFMANN, DAVID ẒEVI; ISAAC BEN SHESHET PERFET; ISRAEL MEIR HA-KOHEN; ISSERLES, MOSES BEN ISRAEL; JACOB BEN ASHER; JONAH BEN ABRAHAM GERONDI; KAFAḤ, YOSEF; KAHANEMAN, JOSEPH; KALISCHER, ẒEVI HIRSCH; KARA, JOSEPH; KARELITZ, AVRAHAM YESHAYAHU; LANDAU, EZEKIEL BEN JUDAH; LAU, ISRAEL MEIR; LEIBOWITZ, NEḤAMA; LIPKIN, ISRAEL BEN ZE'EV WOLF; LURIA, SOLOMON BEN JEHIEL; LUZZATTO, SIMONE BEN ISAAC SIMḤAH; MALBIM, MEIR LOEB BEN JEHIEL MICHAEL WEISSER; ME-AM LO'EZ; MEIRI, MENAHEM BEN SOLOMON; SHAPIRA, AVRAHAM ELKANA KAHANA; TA-SHMA, ISRAEL MOSES

Lisa (C.) DeShantz-Cook*, B.A.; Freelance Writer and Editor, Detroit, Michigan: FISCHER, STANLEY; KAHNEMAN, DANIEL; KOHL, HERBERT; NADLER, JERROLD LEWIS; STIGLITZ, JOSEPH E.; WALZER, MICHAEL

Dawn (M.) DesJardins*, B.A.; Freelance Editor and Writer, Westland, Michigan: LEVITT, ARTHUR, SR.; MERTON, ROBERT C.; SCHOLES, MYRON S.

Elisabeth Dessauer*, University Student, University of Munich, Germany: TAUSK, VIKTOR; THIEME, KARL OTTO; URY, ELSE

Nathaniel Deutsch*, Ph.D.; Associate Professor, Swarthmore College, Pennsylvania: LUDOMIR, MAID OF

Shabbetai Devir, Jerusalem: FRANK, ẒEVI PESAḤ

Benjamin De-Vries, Ph.D., Rabbi; Professor of Talmud, Tel Aviv University: HALAKHAH; MAARSEN, ISAAC

Paul Joseph Diamant, Dr.Phil.; Genealogist, Jerusalem

Adam Dickter*: NEW YORK CITY, WILLIAMSBURG

Alain Dieckhoff*, Ph.D.; Research Director, Centre for International Studies and Research, Alumnus of the University of Paris, France: FRANCE

Jacob I. Dienstag, M.A.; Professor of Bibliography, Yeshiva University, New York: MAIMONIDES

Devora Dimant, Ph.D.; Lecturer, Department of Biblical Studies, Haifa University

Yedidya A. Dinari, Ph.D.; Lecturer in Talmud, Bar-Ilan University, Ramat Gan: HILLEL OF ERFURT; ISRAEL OF BAMBERG; ISRAEL OF KREMS; JACOB OF VIENNA; JOSEPH BEN MOSES

Leonard Dinnerstein*, B.S.S., M.A.; Professor Emeritus, University of Arizona, Tucson, Arizona: TUCSON

Yoram Dinstein, Dr.Jur.; Senior Lecturer in Public International Law, Tel Aviv University: UNITED NATIONS

Benzion Dinur (Dinaburg), Emeritus Professor of Jewish History, the Hebrew University of Jerusalem; Former Minister of Education and Culture, Jerusalem: BAER, YITZHAK; BASNAGE, JACQUES CHRISTIAN; BENJACOB, ISAAC; EMANCIPATION; JAWITZ, ZE'EV; ODESSA; TAEUBLER, EUGEN; UKRAINE; WISSENSCHAFT DES JUDENTUMS; YELLIN

David Diringer, Litt. D.; Emeritus Reader in Semitic Epigraphy, the University of Cambridge; Director of the Alphabeth Museum, Tel Aviv: ALPHABET, HEBREW; LIDZBARSKI, MARK

Daniel Dishon, Former Senior Research Associate, Shiloah Center for Middle Eastern and African Studies, Tel Aviv University

Abraham (H.A.) Diskin*, Ph.D.; Associate Professor, Department of Political Science, the Hebrew University of Jerusalem: ISRAEL, STATE OF: HISTORICAL SURVEY

Eial (Yosef) Diskin*, M.B.A.; Tel Aviv University, Tel Aviv: KAPLAN, ABRAHAM

Elliott Dlin*, M.A.; Executive Director, Dallas Holocaust Museum, Dallas, Texas: HOLOCAUST

Eli Dlinn, Yad Vashem, Jerusalem

Shawna Dolansky Overton*, Ph.D.; Adjunct Faculty, University of California, San Diego: PENTATEUCH

Marc Dollinger*, Ph.D.; Richard and Rhoda Goldman Chair in Jewish Studies and Social Responsibility, San Francisco State University, San Franciso: LERNER, MICHAEL; NEW LEFT; TIKKUN

Danuta Dombrowska, M.A.; Historian, Jerusalem: BELCHATOW; BOLEKHOV; BRODY; BRZESC KUJAWSKI; BRZEZINY; BYDGOSZCZ; CIECHANOW; CRACOW; GNIEZNO; GORLICE; GOSTYNIN; INOWROCLAW; KALISZ; KLODAWA; KOLO; KONIN; KROSNO; KROTOSZYN; KUTNO; LASK; LECZYCA; LESZNO; LODZ; LUTOMIERSK; MAJDANEK; NASIELSK; OLESKO; OLKUSZ; OPATOW; OZORKOW; PABIANICE; PLOCK; POZNAN; RUMKOWSKI, CHAIM MORDECHAI; RYPIN; SIERADZ; SOBIBOR; SREM; STOPNICA; STRYKOW; SZCZERCOW; WARSAW; WIELUN; WOLBROM; WRONKI; ZDUNSKA WOLA; ZELOW; ZGIERZ; ZYCHLIN

Stephen G. Donshik, D.S.W.; Director, Israel Office of UJA-Federation of New York, UIA, Jerusalem

Elliot N. Dorf, M.H.L., Ph.D., Rabbi; Provost and Professor of Philosophy, University of Judaism, Los Angeles

David Dori, Kibbutz Ein ha-Ḥoresh: WLOCLAWEK

Yaakov Dori, Dipl. Ing.; Lieutenant General (Res.), Israel Defense Forces and former Chief of Staff; Former President of the Technion, Haifa: TECHNION, ISRAEL INSTITUTE OF TECHNOLOGY

Abraham Doron*, Ph.D.; Professor, Paul Baerwald School of Social Work, the Hebrew University of

Jerusalem: ISRAEL, STATE OF: HEALTH, WELFARE, AND SOCIAL SECURITY

Israel Dostrovsky, Ph.D.; Vice President and Professor of Physical Chemistry, the Weizmann Institute of Science, Reḥovot, Israel

Aron Dotan*, Ph.D.; Professor Emeritus, President, International Organization of Masoretic Studies; Member, Hebrew Language Academy; Head, Cymbalista Jewish Heritage Center, Tel Aviv University: BEN-ASHER, MOSES; MASORAH

Moshe Dothan, Ph.D.; Director of Excavations and Surveys and Deputy Director, Department of Antiquities and Museums, Jerusalem: ASHDOD

Trude Dothan*, Ph.D.; The Philip and Muriel Berman Center for Biblical Archaeology, the Hebrew University of Jerusalem: EKRON

Alan Dowty, Ph.D.; Lecturer in International Relations, the Hebrew University of Jerusalem: MORGENTHAU, HANS JOACHIM

Noah W. Dragoon, M.A.; Jerusalem: HARBIN

Paula Draper*, Ph.D.; Historian, Toronto, Canada: BAYEFSKY, ABA; COHON, GEORGE A.; CRONENBERG, DAVID; DAN, LESLIE L.; RASMINSKY, LOUIS; ROTHSCHILD, KURT; SCHILD, EDWIN; SCHLESINGER, JOE; SPRACHMAN, ABRAHAM AND MANDEL; WOLFE; ZNAIMER, MOSES

Israel Drapkin-Senderey, M.D.; Professor of Criminology and Director of the Institute of Criminology, the Hebrew University of Jerusalem: DELVALLE, MAX SHALOM; TOPOLEVSKY, GREGORIO; WALD, ARNOLD

Daniel Dratwa, DEA Paris X; Curator of Jewish Museum of Belgium, Brussels: BELGIUM

Adina Dreksler, Yad Vashem, Jerusalem: HOLOCAUST: SPIRITUAL RESISTANCE IN THE GHETTOS AND CONCENTRATION CAMPS

Willi Dressen, Public Prosecutor, Zentralle Stalle der Landesjustizver waltungen, Ludwigsburg, Germany: WAR CRIMES TRIALS

A. Stanley Dreyfus, Ph.D., Rabbi; New York: COHEN, HENRY

Jean-Marc Dreyfus*, Ph.D.; Historian, Affiliate Researcher, Institut d'histoire du temps present - CNRS,Paris: UNION GÉNÉRALE DES ISRAÉLITES DE FRANCE; WARSCHAWSKI, MAX; WIEVIORKA, ANNETTE

Walter Driver*, B.A.; Screenwriter, Los Angeles: ABBOTT, BUD; ALDRICH, ROBERT; AVNET, JON; BARRIS, CHUCK; BERGEN, POLLY; BERGMAN, ALAN and MARILYN; BERGMAN, ANDREW; BERMAN, SHELLEY; BERNHARD, SANDRA; BISHOP, JOEY; BLANC, MEL; BRODERICK, MATTHEW; KAHN, MADELINE; KANE, CAROL; KAVNER, JULIE; KAZAN, LAINIE; KEITEL, HARVEY; KLUGMAN, JACK

Yosef Dror*, Ph.D.; Institute of Biochemistry, Food Science and Nutrition, Faculty of Agriculture, the Hebrew University of Jerusalem: BONDI, ARON

Moshe Drori*, LL.B., LL.M.; Judge, Jerusalem District Court, Jerusalem: ABDUCTION; ADULTERY; BET DIN RABBANI; DIVORCE; LEVIRATE MARRIAGE AND ḤALIẒAH; MAINTENANCE; MATRIMONIAL PROPERTY

Alejandro (Daniel) Dubesarsky*, Journalist and Translator for Agencia Judia de Noticias, Buenos Aires, Argentina: NAJNUDEL, LEÓN DAVID; PEKERMAN, JOSÉ NESTOR

Bernard Dubin, M.S.W.; Executive Director of the Jewish Federation of Camden County, New Jersey: CAMDEN

Thomas Dublin*, Ph.D.; Professor, State University of New York, Binghamton, New York: COHEN, ROSE GOLLUP; MALKIEL, THERESA SERBER

Melvyn Dubofsky, Ph.D., Associate Professor of History, the University of Wisconsin, Milwaukee: BRESLAW, JOSEPH; DUBINSKY, DAVID; FEIGENBAUM, BENJAMIN; FEINSTONE, MORRIS; HOCHMAN, JULIUS; NAGLER, ISADORE; ROSENBERG, ABRAHAM; SCHLESINGER, BENJAMIN; SCHLOSSBERG, JOSEPH; SIGMAN, MORRIS

Brother Marcel-Jacques Dubois O.P., Professor, Department of Philosophy, the Hebrew University of Jerusalem: MARITAIN, JACQUES and RAÏSSA

Yael Dunkelman, Toronto: BORNSTEIN, ELI

Douglas Morton Dunlop, M.A.; Professor of History, Columbia University, New York: ATIL; BĀB AL-ABWĀB; BALANJAR; BŪLĀN; JOSEPH; KHAZARS; OBADIAH; OBADIAH; RADANIYA; SAMANDAR; SARKIL

Alexander M. Dushkin, Ph.D.; Emeritus Professor of Education, the Hebrew University of Jerusalem: RIEGER, ELIEZER

Deborah Dwork*, Ph.D.; Rose Professor Holocaust History; Director, Strassler Center for Holocaust and Genocide Studies, Clark University, Worcester, Massachusetts: AUSCHWITZ

Shlomo Dykman, Translator, Jerusalem: TUWIM, JULIAN

Abba Eban, M.A.; Minister for Foreign Affairs, Jerusalem: WEIZMANN, CHAIM

Irene Eber, Ph.D.; Associate Professor in Chinese History, the Hebrew University of Jerusalem: CHINA

Michael H. Ebner, M.A.; Lecturer in American History, the Herbert H. Lehman College of the City University of New York: PASSAIC-CLIFTON

Nathan Eck, Dr.Jur.; Historian, Tel Aviv: HOLOCAUST REMEMBRANCE DAY; MARK, BERNARD; RINGELBLUM, EMANUEL; SOMMERSTEIN, EMIL; TENENBAUM, MORDECAI

A. Roy Eckardt, Ph.D.; Clergyman, United Methodist Church; professor and chairman of the Department of Religious Studies, Lehigh University.

Shuki (Yehoshua) Ecker*, M.A.; Tel Aviv University: ZONANA

Willehad Paul Eckert, Dr.Phil.; Professor of the History of Philosophy, Hochschule der Dominikaner, Walberberg, Germany: CHURCH COUNCILS; CHURCH, CATHOLIC; DANIEL-ROPS,

HENRI; LEO; PAUL VI; PIUS X; PIUS XI; PIUS XII; THIEME, KARL; THIEME, KARL OTTO

Rafael Edelman, Ph.D.; Director of Jewish Studies, Copenhagen University; Head of the Jewish Department, the Royal Library, Copenhagen: ASLAKSSEN, CORT; DENMARK

William B. Edgerton, Ph.D.; Professor of Slavic Languages and Literature, Indiana University, Bloomington: LESKOV, NIKOLAY SEMYONOVICH

Elisha Efrat*, Ph.D.; Professor of Geography, Tel Aviv University: ISRAEL, STATE OF: ALIYAH, POPULATION, HUMAN GEOGRAPHY; JERUSALEM; LACHISH REGION

Natan Efrati, M.A.; Ben Zvi Institute, Jerusalem: ASHKELON; BET-MIDRASH; CAPTIVES, RANSOMING OF; CHORTKOV; CIECHANOW; DAVID BEN MANASSEH DARSHAN; DLUGOSZ, JAN; MA'AMAD or MAHAMAD; PARNAS; PLETTEN; SHULKLAPPER; SICK CARE, COMMUNAL; TANZHAUS

Daniel Efron, M.A.; Jerusalem: LAWRENCE, THOMAS EDWARD; LLOYD GEORGE, DAVID; MANDATE FOR PALESTINE; PALESTINE, INQUIRY COMMISSIONS; PALESTINE, PARTITION AND PARTITION PLANS; SAINT JAMES'S CONFERENCE; SAMUEL, EDWIN; SAMUEL, HERBERT LOUIS; WHITE PAPERS; ZIONIST COMMISSION

Zusia Efron, Director of the Art Museum, Kibbutz En Harod

Yulia Egorova*, Ph.D.; Research Fellow, School of Religious and Theological Studies, Cardiff University, England: BENE ISRAEL; BOMBAY; CHENNAMANGALAM; CRANGANORE; DIVEKAR, SAMUEL EZEKIEL; GANDHI, MOHANDAS KARAMCHAND

Robert M. Ehrenreich*, Dr.Phil.; Director, Academic Programs, Center for Advanced Holocaust Studies, United States Holocaust Memorial Museum, Washington, D.C.: HOLOCAUST

Albert A. Ehrenzweig, J.D., S.J.D., Dr. Utr. Jur.; Professor of Law, the University of California, Berkeley; Honorarprofessor, the University of Vienna: RADIN, MAX

Ariel Ehrlich*, L.L.B.; Lawyer, Ofra, Israel: MILITARY LAW

Carl Stephen Ehrlich*, Dr.Phil.; Bar-Ilan University, Ramat Gan: EDOM

Dror Ehrlich*, Ph.D.; Department of Philosophy, Bar-Ilan University: ALBO, JOSEPH

Uri Ehrlich*, Ph.D.; Jewish Thought, Ben-Gurion University of the Negev, Beersheba: AMIDAH; BIRKAT HA-MINIM

Arnost Zvi Ehrman, Dr.Jur., F.J.C., Rabbi; Talmudic Scholar, Ramat Gan: ANTICHRESIS; ASMAKHTA; CONDITIONS; EDUYYOT; HORAYOT; KELIM; KERITOT; KETUBBOT; KIDDUSHIN; KINNIM; MEGILLAH; ME'ILAH; MENAḤOT; MIDDOT; MIKVA'OT; MO'ED KATAN; SELDEN, JOHN; SHEVI'IT

H. Bruce Ehrmann, M.H.L., Rabbi; Brockton, Massachusetts

David Max Eichhorn, D.H.L., Rabbi; Cape Kennedy, Florida: JEWISH WAR VETERANS OF THE U.S.A.

Shlomo Eidelberg, Ph.D., D.H.L.; Professor of Jewish History, Yeshiva University, New York, and Haifa University: ETTLINGER, JACOB; FALK, JOSHUA BEN ALEXANDER HA-KOHEN; GERSHOM BEN JUDAH ME'OR HA-GOLAH; ḤAYYIM BEN ISAAC "OR ZARU'A"; HESCHEL, ABRAHAM JOSHUA BEN JACOB; KLATZKIN, ELIJAH BEN NAPHTALI HERZ; KOIDONOVER, ẒEVI HIRSCH; LUBLIN, MEIR BEN GEDALIAH; MENAHEM BEN AARON IBN ZERAḤ; MINZ, ABRAHAM BEN JUDAH HA-LEVI; MINZ, JUDAH BEN ELIEZER HA-LEVI; MOSES BEN JACOB OF KIEV; MOSES OF KIEV; RAPOPORT, ABRAHAM BEN ISRAEL JEHIEL HAKOHEN; SHABBETAI BEN MEIR HA-KOHEN; SHALOM SHAKHNA BEN JOSEPH

Amnon Einav, Chief Scientist, Israel Ministry of Energy

Yizhak Einhorn, M.A.; Teacher, Tel Aviv: PEWTER PLATES

Alfred Einstein, Dr. Phil.; Musicologist, Professor of Music, Smith College, Northampton, Massachusetts: MARX, ADOLF BERNHARD

Sydney Eisen, Ph.D.; Professor of History and Humanities, York University, Downsview, Ontario: HEICHELHEIM, FRITZ MORITZ

Esty (Esther) Eisenmann*, Ph.D.; Lecturer, Open University of Israel, Tel Aviv University: KATZ, JOSEPH BEN ELIJAH; MOSES BEN JUDAH, NOGA

Abraham S. Eisenstadt, Ph.D.; Professor of American History, Brooklyn College of the City University of New York: BEER, GEORGE LOUIS; BOORSTIN, DANIEL J.

Ira Eisenstein, Ph.D., Rabbi; Former President of Reconstructionist Rabbinical College, Philadelphia

Yizchak Jacob Eisner, Ph.D.; Ministry of Education and Culture, Jerusalem

Daniel J. Elazar, Ph.D.; Paterson Professor of Intergovernmental Relations, Bar-Ilan University, Ramat Gan, and Chairman, Center for Jewish Community Studies, Jerusalem and Philadelphia: COMMUNITY

Edna Elazary, B.A.; Jerusalem: AGRIPPA I; BASSUS, LUCILIUS; DEMETRIUS; ELIONAEUS, SON OF CANTHERAS; HEROD; HEROD II; HEROD PHILIP I; HEZEKIAH, THE HIGH PRIEST; JACOB BEN SOSAS; JONATHAN SON OF ABSALOM; JOSEPH OF GAMALA; JOSHUA, SON OF SAPPHAS; JUDAH, SON OF ẒIPPORAI; JULIUS ARCHELAUS; KIMḤIT; PHERORAS; PHILIP OF BATHYRA; PHINEHAS BEN SAMUEL; TETRARCH; VALERIUS GRATUS

Jacob Elbaum, M.A.; Assistant in Hebrew Literature, the Hebrew University of Jerusalem: AHITHOPHEL THE GILONITE; ELNATHAN BEN ACHBOR; ESTORI HA-PARHI; GENESIS RABBATI; MIDRASH LEKAḤ TOV; MIDRASH PROVERBS or AGGADAT PROVERBS; MIDRASH SAMUEL; MIDRASH TEHILLIM; TANNA DE-VEI ELIYAHU; YALKUT MAKHIRI; YALKUT SHIMONI

Aliza El-Dror, Public Relations, WIZO, Tel Aviv: WIZO

Yaffa Eliach, M.A.; Lecturer in

Jewish and European History, Brooklyn College of the City University of New York: YSANDER, TORSTEN

E. Elias, Journalist, formerly of Ernakulam, Cochin, India; Haifa, Israel: PAKISTAN

Flower Elias, London: FERRIS, IRIS

Ben-Zion Eliash*, Ph.D., Dr.Jur.; Senior Lecturer, Tel Aviv University School of Law: USURY

Aryeh Eliav, Former Member of Knesset, Tel Aviv: ELIAV, BINYAMIN

Binyamin Eliav, Dr. Phil.; Editor and Official, Ministry for Foreign Affairs, Jerusalem: "CANAANITES"; ANTISEMITISM; ARLOSOROFF, CHAIM; ASSIMILATION; BERGER-BARZILAI, JOSEPH; COMMUNISM; GERSHUNI, GRIGORI ANDREYEVICH; LENIN, VLADIMIR ILYICH; LIFSHITZ, NEHAMAH; LITVINOV, MAXIM MAXIMOVICH; MIKHOELS, SOLOMON; NUMERUS CLAUSUS; POLITICS; RUSSIA

Mordechai Eliav, Ph.D.; Associate Professor of Jewish History and Education, Bar-Ilan University, Ramat Gan: AHLEM; HILDESHEIMER, AZRIEL

Eliezer Eliner, M.A.; Senior Teacher in Talmud, Tel Aviv University: HOSHANOT

Rachel Elior*, Ph.D.; Professor, Cohen Chair of Jewish Philosophy, the Hebrew University of Jerusalem: AARON BEN MOSES HA-LEVI OF STAROSIELCE; CHABAD; FRANK, EVA; JACOB ISAAC HA-ḤOZEH MI-LUBLIN

Yehuda Elitzur, M.A.; Associate Professor of Biblical Historiography, Bar-Ilan University, Ramat Gan: GAD; ISHMAEL; ISHMAEL; PARHON, SALOMON BEN ABRAHAM IBN; ZEBULUN

Yuval Elizur, M.A.; Journalist, Jerusalem

Judith Laikin Elkin*, Ph.D.; Independent Scholar, The University of Michigan, Ann Arbor, Michigan: LAJSA

Gedalyah Elkoshi, Ph.D.; Associate Professor of Hebrew Literature, Tel Aviv University: ALMANZI, JOSEPH; ASEFAT ḤAKHAMIM; BACHER, SIMON; BEILINSON, MOSES ELIEZER; BEN-AVI, ITHAMAR; BEN-ZION, S.; BERSHADSKY, ISAIAH; BICK, JACOB SAMUEL; BLOCH, SAMSON; BRESSELAU, MEYER ISRAEL; BRILL, JEHIEL; BRILL, JOSEPH; CARO, DAVID; COHEN, SHALOM BEN JACOB; DOLITZKI, MENAḤEM MENDEL; EHRENPREIS, MARCUS; ELISHEVA; EPSTEIN, ZALMAN; EUCHEL, ISAAC ABRAHAM; FARMERS' FEDERATION OF ISRAEL; FRAENKEL, FAIWEL; HACOHEN, MORDECAI BEN HILLEL; HALÉVY, ELIE HALFON; HALPERIN, YEḤIEL; HAMEIRI, AVIGDOR; HANKIN, YEHOSHUA; HARZFELD, AVRAHAM; HAYNT; HEILPRIN, PHINEHAS MENAHEM; HERZBERG, WILHELM; HILLELS, SHELOMO; HIRSCHKAHN, ẒVI; ḤISIN, ḤAYYIM; HURWITZ, JUDAH BEN MORDECAI HA-LEVI; LOEWE, LOUIS; SHALKOVICH, ABRAHAM LEIB; SILBERBUSCH, DAVID ISAIAH; SIMḤAH ḤAYYIM WALKOMITZ; SUEDFELD, GABRIEL; TAWIOW, ISRAEL ḤAYYIM; WARSHAWSKY, ISAAC; WAWELBERG, HIPOLIT; WEISSBERG, ISAAC JACOB; WEISSBERG, MEIR; WEITZ, JOSEPH; WERBEL, ELIAHU MORDECAI; WERBER, BARUCH; WETTSTEIN, FEIVEL HIRSCH; WIENER, SAMUEL; ZEID, ALEXANDER; ZHERNENSKY, MOSHE ELIYAHU; ZMORA, YISRAEL; ZMORA, YISRAEL; ZUTA, ḤAYYIM ARYEH

David (H.) Ellenson*, Ph.D., Rabbi; President, Hebrew Union College-Jewish Institute of Religion, New York: RABBINICAL TRAINING, AMERICAN

Richard S. Ellis, Ph.D.; Associate Professor of Near Eastern Archaeology, Yale University, New Haven, Connecticut: ERECH

Peter Elman, Departmental Editor, Law and Politics, *Encyclopaedia Judaica* (1st ed.), Jerusalem: KAHAN COMMISSION

Yaakov Elman*, Ph.D.; Professor of Judaic Studies, Yeshiva University, New York, and Harvard University, Cambridge, Massachusetts: TALMUD AND MIDDLE PERSIAN CULTURE

Menachem Elon*, Ph.D.; Deputy President of the Supreme Court of Israel; Professor of Law, Hebrew University of Jerusalem, School of Law; Visiting Professor of Law, New York and Harvard Universities, Schools of Law: ABORTION; AGUNAH; APOSTASY; ARBITRATION; ASSAULT; AUTHORITY, RABBINICAL; BIGAMY AND POLYGAMY; BRIBERY; BUSINESS ETHICS; CAPITAL PUNISHMENT; CHILD MARRIAGE; CITY OF REFUGE; CODIFICATION OF LAW; COMPROMISE; CONCUBINE; CONDITIONS; CONFESSION; CONFLICT OF LAWS; CONTRACT; DAMAGES; DETENTION; DINA DE-MALKHUTA DINA; DIVINE PUNISHMENT; DOMICILE; DOWRY; EXECUTION; EXTRADITION; EXTRAORDINARY REMEDIES; FINES; HA'ANAKAH; HAFKA'AT SHE'ARIM; HASSAGAT GEVUL; ḤAZAKAH; HEFKER; HEKDESH; HOMICIDE; HUMAN DIGNITY AND FREEDOM; HUSBAND AND WIFE; IMPRISONMENT; IMPRISONMENT FOR DEBT; INFORMERS; INTERPRETATION; KETUBBAH; LABOR LAW; LAW AND MORALITY; LAW OF RETURN; LEGAL PERSON; LEVIRATE MARRIAGE AND ḤALIẒAH; LIEN; LIMITATION OF ACTIONS; MA'ASEH; MAJORITY RULE; MAMZER; MARRIAGE; MARRIAGE, PROHIBITED; MEDICINE AND LAW; MEḤILAH; MINHAG; MISHPAT IVRI; MISTAKE; NOACHIDE LAWS; NUISANCE; OATH; OBLIGATIONS, LAW OF; ONA'AH; ONES; PARTNERSHIP; PENAL LAW; PLEDGE; POLICE OFFENSES; PUBLIC AUTHORITY; PUNISHMENT; RIGHTS, HUMAN; SEVARAH; SEXUAL OFFENSES; SHOMERIM; SLANDER; SUCCESSION; SUICIDE; SURETYSHIP; TAKKANOT; TAKKANOT HA-KAHAL; TAXATION; THEFT AND ROBBERY; VALUES OF THE JEWISH AND DEMOCRATIC STATE; WILLS; WOMAN: AND THE ISRAELI COURTS; YUḤASIN

Aya Elyada*, M.A.; Graduate student for German-Jewish History, Tel Aviv University, Lehrstuhl für jüdische Geschichte und Kultur, Munich, Germany: MUENSTER, SEBASTIAN; OSIANDER, ANDREAS; PELLICANUS, CONRAD; SCHICKARD, WILHELM; SCHUDT, JOHANN JAKOB; WOLF, JOHANN CHRISTOPH

Zeev Elyashiv, M.A.; Ministry of Communications, Jerusalem: MOLODECHNO

Barnett A. Elzas*: POZNANSKI, GUSTAVUS

Frank Emblen, Journalist, New York: ROBINSON, EDWARD G.

Isaac Samuel Emmanuel, Sc.D., Rabbi; Historian, Cincinnati, Ohio: MICHAEL, MOSES

Charles J. Emmerich*: ADAMS, ARLIN MARVIN

Encyclopaedia Hebraica: ABOAB, ISAAC I; ABRAHAM BEN SOLOMON OF TORRUTIEL; ABSALOM; ADONIJAH; AGGADAH; APOLOGETICS; ARENDT, OTTO; ASHER BEN JEHIEL; ASHKENAZ; ÁVILA; AZ ROV NISSIM; BADT, HERMANN; BALFOUR, ARTHUR JAMES, EARL OF; BEN MEIR, AARON; BILHAH; CHAJES, ẒEVI HIRSCH; CHASANOWICH, LEON; DREAMS; EPHRAIM; ESZTERGOM; FREEMASONS; GEMATRIA; GOITEIN, BARUCH BENEDICT; ḤASIDIM; ḤAVER, ḤAVERIM; HILLEL; HOMBERG, NAPHTALI HERZ; HOROVITZ, JOSEF; HOS, DOV; IBN GABIROL, SOLOMON BEN JUDAH; ISRAEL, LAND OF: HISTORY; JERUSALEM; JOEL; JOHANAN BEN ZAKKAI; JOTHAM; JUDAH; JUDAH HA-LEVI; JUDAH HA-NASI; LAMED VAV ẒADDIKIM; LAVI, SHELOMO; LESTSCHINSKY, JACOB; LILIENTHAL, MAX; LILIENTHAL, OTTO; LOEW, ELEAZAR; LOEWENSTEIN - STRASHUNSKY, JOEL DAVID; MEZHIRECH; OSTRACA; PROSELYTES; UNION OF THE RUSSIAN PEOPLE; UR; WAHRMANN, ABRAHAM DAVID BEN ASHER ANSCHEL; WARBURG, OTTO; ZACUTO, ABRAHAM BEN SAMUEL

Encyclopaedia Judaica (Germany): ABELSON, JOSHUA; AKIVA BAER BEN JOSEPH; BENVENISTE, IMMANUEL; CRESCAS, ḤASDAI BEN JUDAH; HERZBERG-FRAENKEL, LEO; ḤIBAT ALLAH, ABU AL-BARAKĀT BEN ALĪ AL-BAGHDĀDĪ; IBN DAUD, ABRAHAM BEN DAVID HALEVI; IBN EZRA, JOSEPH BEN ISAAC; JOEL, MANUEL; JOSEPH MOSES BEN JEKUTHIEL ZALMAN; KAHANA, DAVID; KALLIR, ELEAZAR; KAMENKA-BUGSKAYA; KIRSCHSTEIN, MORITZ; KLODAWA; KORNIK; KOZIENICE; KRZEPICE; KUTY; LECZYCA; LELOW; LESHNEV; LÉVY, SAMUEL; LIDA; LIPNO; LOSICE; LUBARTOW; LUTOMIERSK; LYAKHOVICHI; LYUBOML; MARCUS, AARON; NOTKIN, NATA; OLDENBURG; OPOLE LUBELSKIE; OTWOCK; PRINTING, HEBREW; SCROLL OF ANTIOCHUS

Avraham (Alfred) Engel, Tel Aviv

Paul Engel, M.D.; Professor of Biology, the Central University of Ecuador, Quito

Morton S. Enslin, Th.D.; Professor of Early Christian History and Literature, Dropsie University, Philadelphia: BIBLE

Israel Eph'al, M.A.; Instructor in Biblical History, Tel Aviv University: ISHMAELITES; KEDAR; KETURAH; MEUNITES

Jacob Eliahu Ephrathi, D.H.L.; Senior Lecturer in Talmud, Bar-Ilan University, Ramat Gan: EVEN HA-TOIM; GEBIHA OF BE-KATIL; GEBINI; YOSE BEN DORMASKOS

Ury Eppstein, Ph.D.; Lecturer, Musicology Dept., the Hebrew University of Jerusalem: ABILEAH, ARIE; BERGEL, BERND; BOEHM, YOHANAN; EVEN-OR, MARY; ISRAEL, STATE OF: CULTURAL LIFE

Morris Epstein, Ph.D.; Editor and Professor of English, Stern College for Women, Yeshiva University, New York: MARX, ALEXANDER

Seymour Epstein*, B.S., B.H.L., M.A., Ed.D.; Senior Vice President, Jewish Education and Identity, U.J.A.-Federation, Board of Jewish Education, Toronto, Canada: EDUCATION, JEWISH

Amira Eran*, Ph.D.; the Hebrew University of Jerusalem: GHAZĀLĪ, ABU ḤAMID MUḤAMMAD IBN MUḤAMMAD AL-ṬŪSĪ AL-; KINDĪ, ABU YŪSUF YA'QŪB IBN ISḤAQ AL

Shlomo Erel, Ministry of Defense, Tel Aviv: CHILE; LATIN AMERICA

Patricia Erens, Ph.D.; Department of Communications, Rosary College, River Forest, Illinois

Yehudah Erez, Editor and Writer, Kibbutz Givat Ḥayyim: GOLOMB, ELIYAHU

Abraham Erlik, B.A. (Arch.); Architect, Tel Aviv: BAERWALD, ALEX; KARMI, DOV; KAUFMANN, RICHARD; MANSFELD, ALFRED; MENDELSOHN, ERIC; RECHTER; SHARON, ARYEH

Shimon Ernst, Ph.D.; Librarian, Tel Aviv: HIRSCHENSOHN-LICHTENSTEIN, JEHIEL ẒEVI HERMANN

Lewis John Eron*, Ph.D., Rabbi; Jewish Community Chaplain, Jewish Federation of Southern New Jersey, Cherry Hill, New Jersey: CAMDEN

Shaul Esh, Ph.D.; Senior Lecturer in Contemporary Jewry, the Hebrew University of Jerusalem: ANIELEWICZ, MORDECAI; COHEN, DAVID; DRANCY; FRIEDMAN, PHILIP; GRYNSZPAN, HERSCHEL

Ruth Eshel*, Ph.D.; Dance Critic for Haaretz Daily; Editor of Dance Today, the Dance Magazine of Israel; Lecturer at the University of Haifa; Artistic Director of Beta and Eskesta Dance Troupes-Dance of Ethiopian Jewry, Israel: BATSHEVA AND BAT-DOR DANCE COMPANIES; BE'ER, RAMI; BERTONOFF, DEBORAH; DANCE; NAHARIN, OHAD; SCHUBERT, LIA

Gennady Estraikh*, Dr.Phil.; Associate Professor, New York University, New York: ABTSHUK, AVRAHAM; BEIDER, CHAIM; CHARNEY, DANIEL; DOBRUSHIN, YEKHEZKEL; FEFER, ITZIK; GOLOMB, ABRAHAM; GORDON, SHMUEL; GORSHMAN, SHIRA; HALKIN, SHMUEL; HOFSTEIN, DAVID; JEWISH DAILY FORWARD; KALMANOVITCH, ZELIG; KULTUR-LIGE; KUSHNIROV, AARON; OLEVSKI, BUZI; ORLAND, HERSHL; PERSOV, SHMUEL; RAZUMNY, MARK; REZNIK, LIPE; SFARD, DAVID; SHTIF, NOKHEM; SMOLAR, HERSH; SOVETISH HEYMLAND; TEITSH, MOYSHE; VERGELIS, AARON; WEITER, A.; WENDROFF, ZALMAN; YAKNEHAZ; ZARETZKI, ISAAC

Shmuel Ettinger, Ph.D.; Associate Professor of Jewish History, the Hebrew University of Jerusalem: BERDICHEV; BERSHAD; BERSHADSKI, SERGEY ALEXANDROVICH; BRATSLAV; CHMIELNICKI, BOGDAN; GRAETZ, HEINRICH; HAIDAMACKS,; REUVENI, DAVID; VIENNA, CONGRESS OF; VOLOZHIN; ZIONISM

Yona Ettinger

Jehonatan Etz-Chaim, Instructor in Talmud, Bar-Ilan University, Ramat Gan: DUKHAN; ELEAZAR BEN DAMMA; ELEAZAR BEN JUDAH OF BARTOTA; ELEAZAR BEN PARTA

Yakir Eventov, Haifa: LICHT, ALEXANDER; ZIONISM

Ephraim Evron, Ambassador and Deputy Director General, Ministry for Foreign Affairs, Jerusalem

Yosef Ewen, M.A.; Lecturer in Hebrew Literature, the Hebrew University of Jerusalem and the University of the Negev, Beersheba: BARASH, ASHER

Eli Eytan, Ph.D.; Associate Professor of Hebrew Language, Tel Aviv University; Scientific

Secretary of the Academy of the Hebrew Language, Tel Aviv: HEBREW LANGUAGE

Alexander Ezer, Editor, Jerusalem

Sidra Ezrahi, Ph.D.; Researcher, Jerusalem: HOLOCAUST

Salamon Faber, D.H.L., Rabbi; New York

Emil Ludwig Fackenheim, Ph.D., Rabbi; Professor of Philosophy, the University of Toronto: HEGEL, GEORG WILHELM FRIEDRICH; SCHELLING, FRIEDRICH WILHELM JOSEPH

Karen L. Falk*, M.A., Project Coordinator, Jewish Museum of Maryland, Baltimore, Maryland: MEYERHOFF, HARVEY

Stanley L. Falk, Ph.D.; Associate Professor of National Security Affairs, Industrial College of the Armed Forces, Washington, D.C.: BLOOM, SOL; BLUMENBERG, LEOPOLD; JOHNSON, LYNDON BAINES; MORDECAI, ALFRED; MORDECAI, JACOB; RICKOVER, HYMAN GEORGE

Ze'ev Wilhem Falk, Ph.D., Advocate; Jacob I. Berman Associate Professor of Family Law and Succession, the Hebrew University of Jerusalem; Senior Lecturer in Jewish Law, Tel Aviv University: ALTENSTADT; ASCHAFFENBURG; BAIERSDORF; BAMBERG; BAYREUTH; BONN; BREMEN; BRUNSWICK; CARLEBACH, JOSEPH; CENTRAL-VEREIN DEUTSCHER STAATSBUERGER JUEDISCHEN GLAUBENS; COBURG; DAVID, MARTIN; DE VRIES, BENJAMIN; DUEREN; ELBLAG; FUERTH; HAGEN; HAMELN; HEILBRONN; HILFSVEREIN DER DEUTSCHEN JUDEN; LYCK; RABBINICAL CONFERENCES; WIESBADEN

Kochava Fattal-Binyamin*, Ph.D.; Clinical Instruction and Coordinator of Human Resource Development, Bar-Ilan University, Ramat Gan: ORPAZ AVERBUCH, YITZHAK

Jose Faur, Ph.D.; Associate Professor of Rabbinics, the Jewish Theological Seminary of America, New York: IDOLATRY

Zvi Hermann Federbush, M.A.; Ministry of Education and Culture, Jerusalem: ALPHABET, HEBREW

Nira Feidman, Ph.D.; Research Fellow in Contemporary Jewry, the Hebrew University of Jerusalem: CAMPS

Ricardo Feierstein, Director Editorial Mila, AMIA, Buenos Aires

Julian B. Feigelman, LL.D., Ph.D., Rabbi; New Orleans

Aryeh Feigenbaum, M.D.; Emeritus Professor of Ophthalmology, the Hebrew University of Jerusalem: BENEVENUTUS GRAPHEUS HIEROSOLYMITANUS; HIRSCHBERG, JULIUS

Lawrence H. Feigenbaum, Ph.D.; Lecturer in Education, City College of the City University of New York: DUJOVNE, LEON; KOENIGSBERG, MOSES; LAQUEUR, WALTER ZE'EV; LERNER, MAX; SCHIFF, DOROTHY; SELDES, GEORGE; SONNEMANN, LEOPOLD

Konrad Feilchenfeldt*, Dr.Phil.; Germanist, Ludwig-Maximilians-Universität, Munich, Germany: HEILBORN, ERNST; HEYMANN, WALTHER; HEYSE, PAUL; LEONHARD, RUDOLF; MEYER, RICHARD MORITZ; NEUMANN, ALFRED; WALDEN, HERWARTH

Gil Feiler*, Ph.D.; Senior Researcher, Besa Center, Bar-Ilan University, Ramat Gan: BOYCOTT, ARAB

Isaac M. Fein, Ph.D.; Emeritus Professor of Jewish History, Baltimore Hebrew College: COHEN; ETTING; REHINE, ZALMA

Anat Feinberg*, Ph.D.; Professor, Hochschule für Jüdische Studien, Heidelberg, Germany: ADELMAN, URI; ALMOG, RUTH; ALTERMAN, NATHAN; AMIR, ELI; AVIGUR-ROTEM, GABRIELA; BALLAS, SHIMON; BARTOV, HANOCH; BAR-YOSEF, YEHOSHUA; BE'ER, HAIM; BEJERANO, MAYA; BEN-NER, YITZHAK; BERNSTEIN, ORI; BIRSTEIN, YOSSEL; CASTEL-BLOOM, ORLY; DOR, MOSHE; EYTAN, RACHEL; GELDMAN, MORDECHAI; GUR, BATYA; HAREVEN, SHULAMITH; HEBREW LITERATURE, MODERN; HENDEL, YEHUDIT; HOFFMANN, YOEL; JERUSALEM; KAHANA-CARMON, AMALIA; KANIUK, YORAM; KATZIR, JUDITH; KENAN, AMOS; KENAZ, YEHOSHUA; KERET, ETGAR; LAOR, YITZHAK; LAPID, SHULAMIT; LIEBRECHT, SAVYON; MATALON, RONIT; MEGGED, AHARON; MISHOL, AGI; OREN, RAM; ORLEV, URI; PAGIS, DAN; PINCAS, ISRAEL; RAAB, ESTHER; RAVIKOVITCH, DALIA; REICH, ASHER; SADEH, PINḤAS; SENED, ALEXANDER; SERI, DAN BENAYA; SHABTAI, AHARON; SHAḤAM, NATHAN; SHAḤAR, DAVID; SHALEV, MEIR; SHALEV, ZERUYA; SHIMONI, YOUVAL; SIVAN, ARYEH; SOMECK, RONNY; TAMMUZ, BENJAMIN; TSALKA, DAN; WIESELTIER, MEIR; YONATHAN, NATHAN; ZACH, NATHAN

Lynn Claire Feinberg*, Historian of Religion, Jewish Museum of Oslo, Norway: BENKOW, JO; EITINGER, LEO S.; NORWAY; OSLO; SCANDINAVIAN LITERATURE; WERGELAND, HENRIK ARNOLD

Nathan Feinberg, Dr.Jur.; Emeritus Professor of International Law, the Hebrew University of Jerusalem: BERNHEIM PETITION; BLIOKH, IVAN STANISLAVOVICH; COMITÉ DES DELEGATIONS JUIVES; LEAGUE OF NATIONS; STREICHER, JULIUS; STUERMER, DER

Shmuel Feiner*, Ph.D.; Professor of Modern Jewish History, Bar-Ilan University, Ramat Gan: MENDELSSOHN, MOSES

Henry L. Feingold, Ph.D.; Assistant Professor of Americana and Diplomatica and American Jewish History, the Bernard Baruch College of the City University of New York: McDONALD, JAMES GROVER; NIXON, RICHARD MILHAUS; ROOSEVELT, FRANKLIN DELANO; TRUMAN, HARRY S.

Edward Feinstein*, M. A., Rabbi; Rabbi, Valley Beth Shalom, Encino, California; Instructor, University of Judaism, Los Angeles, California: SCHULWEIS, HAROLD MAURICE

Stephen C. Feinstein*, Ph.D.; Director, Center for Holocaust and Genocide Studies, University of Minnesota: EISENMAN, PETER; HOLOCAUST; MEIER, RICHARD; POLSHEK, JAMES; TIGERMAN, STANLEY

Moshe M. Felber, Ministry of Finance, Jerusalem

Marjorie N. Feld*, Ph.D., Assistant Professor of History, Babson

College, Massachusetts: SETTLEMENT HOUSES

Michael Feldberg*, Ph.D.; Researcher, American Jewish Historical Society, New York: BRESLAU, ISADORE

Meyer S. Feldblum, Ph.D., Rabbi; Associate Professor of Rabbinics, Yeshiva University, New York: WEISS, ABRAHAM

Abraham J. Feldman, B.H.L., Rabbi; Hartford, Connecticut: CONNECTICUT

David M. Feldman, D.H.L., Rabbi; New York: CHASTITY; OMER; ONANISM

Egal Feldman, Ph.D.; Professor of History, Wisconsin State University, Superior, Wisconsin: CHURCH, CATHOLIC; PROTESTANTS

Eliyahu Feldman, Ph.D.; Senior Lecturer in Jewish History, Tel Aviv University: ASTRAKHAN; ATAKI; AZERBAIJAN; BACAU; BAKHCHISARAI; BALLY, DAVICION; BARASCH, JULIUS; BARLAD; BECK, MORITZ; BELGOROD-DNESTROVSKI; BELTSY; BENDERY; BESSARABIA; BOJAN; BOTOSANI; BRAILA; BRICEVA; BRICHANY; BROCINER, JOSEPH; BUCHAREST; BUHUSI; BURDUJENI; BUZAU; DOMBROVENI; EMANUEL; GRUNWALD, MAX; IZMAIL; KALARASH; KAUSHANY; KHOTIN; KILIYA; KOTOVSKOYE; LEOVO; LIPKANY; MARCULESTI; NOVOSELITSA; ORGEYEV; REZINA; RYSHKANY; SEKIRYANY; SOROKI; TELENESHTY; VAD RASHKOV; YEDINTSY; ZGURITSA

Gerald D. Feldman*, Ph.D.; Professor of History, University of California, at Berkeley: GOLDSCHMIDT, JAKOB

Leon A. Feldman, Ph.D., D.H.L., Rabbi; Professor of Hebraic Studies, Rutgers University, New Brunswick, New Jersey: NISSIM BEN REUBEN GERONDI; TAMAKH, ABRAHAM BEN ISAAC HA-LEVI

Louis Harry Feldman, Ph.D.; Professor of Classics, Yeshiva University, New York: ANTIGONUS OF CARYSTUS; BEROSUS; BLOCH, HERBERT; CAPLAN, HARRY; CENSORINUS; HELLADIUS OF ANTINOUPOLIS; HELLENISM; HORACE, QUINTUS HORATIUS FLACCUS; ITINERARIUM ANTONINI; JUVENAL; LEVY, HARRY LOUIS; LOWE, ELIAS AVERY; LUCIAN OF SAMOSATA; MARCUS, RALPH; OROSIUS, PAULUS; THRASYLLUS OF MENDES; TRAUBE, LUDWIG; VIRGIL; VITRUVIUS, POLLO

Mark B. Feldman*, A.B., L.L.B.; Attorney, Garvey Schubert Barer, Washington, D.C.: FEITH, DOUGLAS J.

Myer Feldman, B.A., B.S., LL.B.; Attorney, Washington, D. C.: KENNEDY, JOHN FITZGERALD

Seymour Feldman*, Ph.D.; Professor of Philosophy, Emeritus, Rutgers University, New Jersey: ARISTOTLE; COSMOLOGY; CREATION AND COSMOGONY

Yael S. Feldman*, Ph.D.; Abraham I. Katsch Professor of Hebrew Culture and Professor of Comparative Literature and Gender Studies, New York University, New York: BEN YEHUDA, NETIVA

Jehuda Feliks, Ph.D.; Professor of Botany, Bar-Ilan University, Ramat Gan: AARON BEN SAMUEL; ACACIA; AGRICULTURAL LAND-MANAGEMENT METHODS AND IMPLEMENTS IN ANCIENT EREẒ ISRAEL; AGRICULTURE; ALGUM; ALMOND; ANIMALS OF THE BIBLE AND TALMUD; ANT; ANTELOPE; APE; APPLE; ASS; BALSAM; BARLEY; BAT; BAY TREE; BDELLIUM; BEANS; BEAR; BEE; BEET; BEHEMOTH; BITTERN; BOX; BROOM; BUFFALO; BURNING BUSH; BUZZARD; CABBAGE; CALAMUS, SWEET; CAMEL; CAPER; CAROB; CASTOR-OIL PLANT; CAT; CATTLE; CEDAR; CENTIPEDE; CHAMELEON; CHICKEN; CINNAMON; CORAL; CORIANDER; COTTON; CRANE; CRIMSON WORM; CROCODILE; CUCUMBER; CUMIN; CYPRESS; DEER; DIETARY LAWS; DOG; DOVE; DYE PLANTS; EAGLE; EBONY; ELEPHANT; ETROG; EVOLUTION; FENNEL; FIG; FIVE SPECIES; FLAX; FLEA; FLOWERS; FLY; FODDER; FOX; FRANKINCENSE; FROG; GALBANUM; GARLIC; GAZELLE; GECKO; GNAT; GOAT; GOOSE; GOURD; GRASSHOPPER; GULL; HARE; HAWK; HEMLOCK; HEMP; HENNA; HERBS, MEDICINAL; HOOPOE; HORNET; HORSE; HYENA; HYRAX; HYSSOP; IBEX; INCENSE AND PERFUMES; ISRAEL, LAND OF: FLORAN AND FAUNA; IVY; JACKAL; JUJUBE; JUNIPER; KITE; LAUDANUM; LEECH; LEEK; LEGUMES; LENTIL; LEOPARD; LETTUCE; LEVIATHAN; LION; LIZARD; LOCUST; LOUSE; MALLOW; MANDRAKE; MANNA; MAROR; MELON; MILLET; MIXED SPECIES; MOLE; MONITOR; MOTH; MOUSE; MULBERRY; MULE; MUSHROOMS; MUSTARD; MYRRH; MYRTLE; NIGHTINGALE; NUT; OAK; OLEANDER; OLIVE; ONAGER; ONION; ONYCHA; ORACH; OSTRICH; OWL; PALM; PAPYRUS; PARTRIDGE; PEACH; PEACOCK; PEAR; PELICAN; PEPPER; PHEASANT; PHOENIX; PIG; PINE; PISTACHIO; PLANE TREE; PLUM; POMEGRANATE; POPLAR; QUAIL; QUINCE; RADISH; RAT; RAVEN; REED; RICE; ROCKET; ROSE; SAFFRON; SCORPION; SHEEP; SILK; SKINK; SNAKE; SOAP; SORGHUM; SPARROW; SPICES; SPIDER; SPIKENARD; SQUILL; STORAX; STORK; SUMAC; SWIFT; SYCAMORE; TAḤASH; TAMARISK; TARES; TEKHELET; TEREBINTH; THISTLES AND THORNS; TORTOISE; TRAGACANTH; TURTLE DOVE; VEGETABLES; VINE; VULTURES; WEEDS; WHEAT; WILD BULL; WILLOW; WOLF; WORM; WORMWOOD

Abraham Feller, Journalist, Tel Aviv: BALTAZAR, CAMIL; CĂLUGĂRU, ION; DAN, SERGIU; DORIAN, EMIL; FURTUNĂ, ENRIC; FURTUNĂ, ENRIC; GRAUR, CONSTANTIN; LAVI, THEODOR; LĂZĂREANU, BARBU; LUDO, ISAC IACOVITZ; NEMTEANU, BARBU; PELTZ, ISAC; RELGIS, EUGEN; SAINEANU, LAZAR; STEUERMAN, ADOLF RODION; ZISSU, ABRAHAM LEIB

Abraham Fellman, F.A.C.C.A., C.P.A.; Accountant, Tel Aviv: FREEMASONS

Sarah B. Felsen*, Ph.D. (German Lit.); University of California, at Berkeley: LIESSIN, ABRAHAM; SHOMER

Vivian Felsen*, M.A., L.L.B.; Translator, Toronto, Canada: BERGER, LILI; MEDRES, ISRAEL JONAH; SHULNER, DORA

John Felsteiner, Ph.D.; Professor of English, Stanford University, Stanford, California

Mary Lowenthal Felsteiner, Ph.D.; Professor of History, San Francisco State University, San Francisco: BRUNNER, ALOIS

Paul (B.) Fenton*, Ph.D.; Ambassador (retired), Professor, Director of Jewish Studies, Université de Paris-Sorbonne: ABRAHAM BEN MOSES BEN MAIMON

Bonny V. Fetterman*, B.A., M.A.; Literary Editor, *Reform Judaism Magazine*, New York: WIESEL, ELIE

Bernd Feuchtner*, Dr.Phil.; Publicist, Berlin, Germany: BARSHAI, RUDOLF

Leon I. Feuer, Rabbi; Toledo, Ohio

Robert E. Fierstien*, D.H.L., Rabbi; Temple Beth Or, Brick, New Jersey: RABBINICAL ASSEMBLY

Louis Filler, Ph.D.; Professor of American Civilization, Antioch College, Yellow Springs, Ohio: HOFSTADTER, RICHARD

Leon Fine*, B.A.; Attorney, Tel Aviv: AVI-YITZHAK, DAN; BEINISCH, DORIT; BEN-ISRAEL, RUTH; BERENSON ZVI; COHEN, SHLOMO; ENGLARD, YITZHAK; HESHIN, SHNEUR ZALMAN; MAZUZ, MENI; ZAMIR, ITZHAK

Irving Fineman, B.S.; Author, Shaftsbury, Vermont: ROSTEN, LEO CALVIN

Uzi Finerman, Member of the Knesset, Kefar Yeḥezkel: MOSHAV OR MOSHAV OVEDIM; MOSHAV SHITTUFI

Israel Finestein, M.A., Q.C.; Barrister, London: COHEN, LIONEL LEONARD, BARON; GOODHART, ARTHUR LEHMAN; HEILBRON, DAME ROSE; JESSEL, SIR GEORGE; KARMINSKI, SIR SEYMOUR EDWARD; LAUTERPACHT, SIR HERSCH; SALMON, CYRIL BARNET, BARON

Dan Fink*: IDAHO

Haim Finkelstein*, Ph.D.; Ben-Gurion University of the Negev, Beersheba: ART: MODERN EREZ ISRAEL; ISRAEL, STATE OF: CULTURAL LIFE

Israel Finkelstein*, Ph.D.; Professor, Institute of Archaeology, Tel Aviv University: MEGIDDO

Jacob Finkelstein, Ph.D.; Professor of Assyriology and Babylonian Literature, Yale University, New Haven, Connecticut: MESOPOTAMIA

Norman Finkelstein*, Ph.D.; Professor of English, Xavier University, Cincinnati: OPPEN, GEORGE; REZNIKOFF, CHARLES; UNITED STATES LITERATURE

Gérald Finkielsztejn*, Ph.D.; Senior Archaeologist of the Israel Antiquities Authority, Jerusalem: AGORANOMOS; ASINIUS POLLIO, GAIUS; MARESHAH

Jordan Finkin*, Ph.D.; University of California, Berkeley: LIESSIN, ABRAHAM; SHOMER

Bert Fireman, B.A.; Lecturer in Arizona History, Arizona State University, Tempe: ARIZONA

Harold Harel Fisch, B. Litt.; Professor of English and former Rector, Bar-Ilan University, Ramat Gan: BLAKE, WILLIAM; CHAUCER, GEOFFREY; CUMBERLAND, RICHARD; DICKENS, CHARLES; DISRAELI, BENJAMIN, EARL OF BEACONSFIELD; D'ISRAELI, ISAAC; ELIOT, GEORGE; ENGLISH LITERATURE; HA-TENU'AH LE-MA'AN EREẒ ISRAEL HA-SHELEMAH; HENRIQUES; KOESTLER, ARTHUR; MARLOWE, CHRISTOPHER; MILTON, JOHN; SHAKESPEARE, WILLIAM; SCOTT, SIR WALTER; TARN, NATHANIEL; ZANGWILL, ISRAEL

Solomon Fisch, Ph.D., Rabbi; Leeds: MIDRASH HA-GADOL

Henry Albert Fischel, Ph.D., Rabbi; Professor of Near Eastern Studies, Indiana University, Bloomington: CYNICS AND CYNICISM; EPICUREANISM; GREEK AND LATIN LANGUAGES, RABBINICAL KNOWLEDGE OF; HELLENISM; STOICISM

Walter Joseph Fischel, Professor of Judaic Studies and History, the University of California, Santa Cruz: AARON BEN AMRAM; ABENDANA, ISAAC SARDO; ABRAHAM, SAMUEL; ABRAHÃO, COJE; AFGHANISTAN; AHMADNAGAR; AHWAZ; AKBAR THE GREAT; AKLAR MORDECAI BEN RAPHAEL; ALIBAG; 'AMADIYA; ASHER, ISAIAH BEN MOSES HA-LEVI; AZERBAIJAN; BAHRAIN; BALKH; BENARES; BENE ISRAEL; BOMBAY; BUCHANAN, CLAUDIUS; BURMA; CALCUTTA; CALICUT; CASTRO; CEYLON; CHENNAMANGALAM; CRANGANORE; DAMAVAND; DAVID D'BETH HILLEL; DIVEKAR, SAMUEL EZEKIEL; ELEAZAR BEN JACOB HA-BAVLI; ERNAKULAM; FEINSTEIN, ḤAYYIM JACOB HA-KOHEN; FONSECA, ALVARO DA; GAMA, GASPAR DA; GOA; HACOHEN, RAPHAEL ḤAYYIM; ḤAKHAM, SIMON; HALLEGUA; HORMUZ; ISFAHAN; JADĪD AL-ISLĀM; JOSEPH MAMAN AL-MAGHRIBI; JUDEO-PERSIAN; KASHMIR; KEHIMKAR, ḤAYIM SAMUEL; KHURASAN; KODER, SAMUEL SHABDAI; KORNFELD, JOSEPH SAUL; LAR; LESLAU, WOLF; MADRAS; MELAMED, RAḤAMIM REUVEN; MELAMED, SIMAN TOV; MERV; MOSES, MARCUS; NAJĪB AL-DAWLA; NATHAN, MULLA IBRAHIM; NAVARRO, ABRAHAM; NEUMARK, EPHRAIM; NISHAPUR; ORTA, GARCIA DE; PAIVA, JACQUES; PAKISTAN; PERSIA; POLAK, JACOB EDUARD; POONA; POPPER, WILLIAM; RAHABI, EZEKIEL; RAJPURKAR, JOSEPH EZEKIEL; REINMANN, SALOMON; RIZAIEH; RODRIGUES, BARTHOLOMEW; ROTENBURG; SA'D AL-DAWLA AL-ṢAFĪ IBN HIBBATALLAH; SANANDAJ; SARMAD, MUHAMMAD SA'ID; SASSOON; SHIRAZ; SOLOMON BEN SAMUEL; TABRIZ; TAVUS, JACOB BEN JOSEPH; TEHERAN; TRANSOXIANA; WOLFF, JOSEPH; YAHUDI, YUSUF; YEZD

Jens Malte Fischer*, Ph.D.; Professor, Ludwig-Maximilians-Universität, Munich, Germany: JESSNER, LEOPOLD; KORTNER, FRITZ; PALLENBERG, MAX; SONNENTHAL, ADOLF RITTER VON

Jerome E. Fischer*, M.A.; Executive Director, Jewish Federation of Eastern Connecticut, New London, Connecticut: NEW LONDON

Yona Fischer, Curator of Contemporary Art, the Israel Museum, Jerusalem: ASCHHEIM, ISIDOR; FEIGIN, DOV; HABER, SHAMAI; KRAKAUER, LEOPOLD; LEVANON, MORDECAI; PALDI, ISRAEL; PALOMBO, DAVID; SCULPTURE; SHEMI, MENAHEM; STEMATSKY, AVIGDOR; ZARITSKI, YOSEF

Ephraim Fischoff, D.S.Sc., Rabbi; Professor of Sociology, Wisconsin State University, Eau Claire: BENEDIKT, MORITZ; BIDNEY, DAVID; BOAS, FRANZ; BOGORAZ, VLADIMIR GERMANOVICH; BURCHARDT, HERMANN; ELKIN, ADOLPHUS PETER; FISHBERG, MAURICE; FORTES, MEYER; FRIED, MORTON HERBERT; GLUCKMAN, MAX; GOLDENWEISER, ALEXANDER ALEXANDROVICH; HALBWACHS, MAURICE; HENRY, JULES; JOCHELSON, VLADIMIR; KARDINER, ABRAM; LANDES, RUTH; LEVIN, MAKSIM GRIGORYEVICH; LEVI-STRAUSS, CLAUDE; LÉVY-BRUHL, LUCIEN; LEWIS, OSCAR; LOWIE, ROBERT HARRY; LUSCHAN, FELIX VON; MANDELBAUM, DAVID GOODMAN; MAUSS, MARCEL; MONTAGU, MONTAGUE FRANCIS ASHLEY; MUNKÁCSI, BERNÁT; NADEL, SIEGFRED FERDINAND STEPHAN; OPLER, MARVIN KAUFMANN; OPLER, MORRIS EDWARD; OPPERT, GUSTAV SALOMON; OPPERT, JULES JULIUS; OSCHINSKY,

LAWRENCE; RADIN, PAUL; RÓHEIM, GÉZA; SAPIR, EDWARD; SCHAPERA, ISAAC; SELIGMAN, CHARLES GABRIEL; SHAPIRO, HARRY LIONEL; SINGER, MILTON B; SPIER, LESLIE; SPIRO, MELFORD ELLIOT; SPOEHR, ALEXANDER; STERNBERG, LEV YAKOVLEVICH; SWADESH, MORRIS; TAX, SOL; TITIEV, MISCHA; VAMBERY, ARMINIUS; WEIDENREICH, FRANZ; WEISSENBERG, SAMUEL ABRAMOVICH; ZOLLSCHAN, IGNAZ

Michael Fishbane, M.A.; Instructor in Hebrew and of Biblical Studies, Brandeis University, Waltham, Massachusetts: ARK OF NOAH; COPPER SERPENT, THE; JAVAN; LAMECH; SERAPH

Eugene J. (Joseph) Fisher*, Ph.D.; Associate Director, Secretariat for Ecumenical and Interreligious Affairs, U.S. Conference of Catholic Bishops, Washington, D.C.: JOHN PAUL II

Aleisa Fishman*, Ph.D.; Editorial Coordinator, Academic Publications, United States Holocaust Museum, Washington, D.C.: BRENNER, ROSE; SPIEGEL, DORA

Donna Fishman*, M.A., B H.L.; Executive Director, Gilda's Club Westchester, New York: GILLMAN, NEIL

Robert (J.) Fishman*, M.A., M.S.W.; Executive Director, Jewish Federation Association of Connecticut, Hartford, Connecticut: CONNECTICUT

Sylvia Barack Fishman, Ph.D.; Asst. Prof. of Jewish Studies, Brandeis University, Waltham, Massachusetts: GORNICK, VIVIAN; RICH, ADRIENNE; ROTH, PHILIP MILTON

Artur Fiszer, B.A.; Researcher, Jerusalem: MOMENT, DER; PRESS

Gila Flam*, Ph.D.; Director of Music, National Library, the Hebrew University of Jerusalem: ADLER, ISRAEL; ALDEMA, GIL; ARGOV, ALEXANDER; AVENARY, HANOCH; BARNEA, EZRA; BEREGOVSKI, MOSHE; BOSCOVITCH, ALEXANDER URIYAH; BRAUN, YEHEZKIEL; CHASINS, ABRAHAM; DA-OZ, RAM; GILBOA, JACOB; HERZOG, GEORGE; HESKES, IRENE; IDELSOHN, ABRAHAM ZVI; ISRAEL, STATE OF: CULTURAL LIFE; JACOBI, HANOCH; LACHMANN, ROBERT; MIRON, ISSACHAR; MUSIC; NOY, MEIR; RUBIN, RUTH; SHEMER, NAOMI

Dov Shmuel Flattau (Plato), Dr. Phil., Rabbi; *Encyclopaedia Judaica* (Germany); Teacher and scholar, Tel Aviv: ANGELS AND ANGELOLOGY

Ezra Fleischer, Ph.D.; Senior Lecturer in Hebrew Literature, the Hebrew University of Jerusalem: KRAUSS, FRIEDRICH SALAMO; PHINEHAS BEN JACOB HA-KOHEN; PIYYUT; SCHIRMANN, JEFIM; SIMEON BEN MEGAS HA-KOHEN; SOLOMON BEN JUDAH HA-BAVLI; YOẒEROT

Eugene Jacob Fleischmann, Ph.D.; Maître de Recherche au Centre National de la Recherche Scientifique, Paris: WEIL, ERIC

Lazar Fleishman, Ph.D.; Senior Lecturer, Department of Russian Studies, The Hebrew University of Jerusalem: BELINKOV, ARKADIIVIKTOROVICH

Daniel (E.) Fleming*, Ph.D.; Professor of Assyriology and Hebrew Bible, New York University: EMAR

Heinrich Flesch, Ph.D., Rabbi; *Encyclopaedia Judaica* (Germany); Czechoslovakia: OPPENHEIM; OPPENHEIM, BEER BEN ISAAC; OPPENHEIM, DAVID BEN ABRAHAM

Rachel Floersheim, Ph.D.; New York: KUZNETS, SIMON

David Flusser, Ph.D.; Professor of Comparative Religion, the Hebrew University of Jerusalem: ABRAHAM, TESTAMENT OF; APOCALYPSE; DAVID; ENOCH; GNOSTICISM; ISAIAH, ASCENSION OF; JEROME; JESUS; JOSIPPON; KLAUSNER, JOSEPH GEDALIAH; LEVI, TESTAMENT OF; MASTEMA; MELITO OF SARDIS; MIDRASH VA-YISSA'U; MOSKONI, JUDAH LEON BEN MOSES; NAPHTALI, TESTAMENT OF; PATRIARCHS, TESTAMENTS OF THE TWELVE; PAUL OF TARSUS; REDEMPTION; SEVENTY SHEPHERDS, VISION OF; SMITH, MORTON; SOLOVIEV, VLADIMIR; SON OF MAN; VISIONS; WENDLAND, PAUL

Yeshayahu Foerder, Dr.Phil.; Chairman of the Board of Directors, Bank Leumi le-Israel, Tel Aviv: HOOFIEN, ELIEZER SIGFRIED

Eva Fogelman*, Ph.D.; Social and Personality Psychology, Co-Director Psychotherapy with Generations of the Holocaust and Related Traumas Training Program, Training Institute for Mental Health, New York: HOLOCAUST

Jerome D. Folkman, Ph.D., Rabbi; Adjunct Professor of Sociology, Ohio State University, Columbus

Resianne Fontaine*, Ph.D.; Lecturer in the Department of Hebrew and Jewish Studies, Universiteit van Amsterdam, The Netherlands: IBN DAUD, ABRAHAM BEN DAVID HALEVI; MATKAH, JUDAH BEN SOLOMON HA-KOHEN

Linda (B.) Forgosh*, B.A., M.A.; Curator and Outreach Director, Jewish Historical Society of Metro West, New Jersey: ESSEX COUNTY; MORRIS AND SUSSEX COUNTIES

Morris D. Forkosch, Ph.D., J.S.D.; Professor of Law, Brooklyn Law School; Professor of Economics, New School for Social Research, New York: SOBELOFF, SIMON ERNEST

Ira (N.) Forman*, B.A., M.B.A.; Executive Director, National Jewish Democratic Council, and the Solomon Project, Washington, D.C.: CARTER, JIMMY; CLINTON, WILLIAM JEFFERSON; POLITICS

Umberto Fortis*; Professor, Biblioteca Archivio Renato Maestro Comunità Ebraica di Venezia: VENICE

Everett Fox*, Ph.D.; Allen M. Glick, Professor of Judaic and Biblical Studies, Clark University, Newton, Massachusetts: BIBLE

Marvin Fox, Ph.D., Rabbi; Professor of Philosophy, Ohio State University, Columbus: FREEDOM; GOD; GOD, NAMES OF

Michael V. Fox*, Ph.D., Rabbi; Professor of Hebrew, University of Wisconsin, Milwaukee: AGUR SON OF JAKEH; BOOKS OF THE CHRONICLES OF THE KINGS OF JUDAH AND ISRAEL; ECCLESIASTES or QOHELET; LEMUEL; MOSES, BLESSING OF; NOTH, MARTIN; SEA, SONG OF THE

Nili S. Fox*, Ph.D.; Associate Professor of Bible, Hebrew Union College-Jewish Institute of Religion, Cincinnati, Ohio: NUMBERS, BOOK OF

Abraham H. Foxman, J.D.; Anti-Defamation League of B'nai B'rith, New York: VILNA

Joseph M. Foxman, Research Associate, YIVO Institute for Jewish Research, New York: KOLDYCHEVO CAMP

Abraham Halevy Fraenkel, Dr. Phil.; Emeritus Professor of Mathematics, the Hebrew University of Jerusalem: BORNSTEIN, ḤAYYIM JEHIEL

Carlos Fraenkel*, Ph.D.; Assistant Professor, McGill University, Montreal, Canada: SPINOZA, BARUCH DE

Jona Fraenkel, Ph.D.; Lecturer in Hebrew Literature and in Talmud, the Hebrew University of Jerusalem: RASHI

Josef Fraenkel, Journalist, London: CHAMBERLAIN, JOSEPH; COHEN, ISRAEL; DUGDALE, BLANCHE ELIZABETH CAMPBELL; EHRLICH, JACOB; FRIEDMANN, DESIDER; GOLDBLOOM, JACOB KOPPEL; GOODMAN, PAUL; JEWISH CHRONICLE; JEWISH WORLD; PRESS; SONNENSCHEIN, ROSA; STEINBERG, AARON; STRICKER, ROBERT; WELT, DIE

Vadim (E.) Fraifeld*, M.D., Ph.D.; Senior Research Scientist, Ben-Gurion University of the Negev, Beersheba: FROLKIS, VLADIMIR VENIAMINOVICH

Jerold C. (Coleman) Frakes*, Ph.D.; Professor of German and Comparative Literature, University of Southern California: BOVE-BUKH; BRESCH, JUDAH LOEB BEN MOSES NAPHTALI; BRIYO VE-ZIMRO; BRODERZON, MOYSHE; CAMBRIDGE YIDDISH CODEX; FEINBERG, LEON; GOLDBERG, ABRAHAM; GOLDBERG, BEN ZION; GUTMAN, CHAIM; HAIMOWITZ, MORRIS JONAH; HARSHAV, BENJAMIN; HERMAN, DAVID; JUSTMAN, MOSHE BUNEM; KATZ, ALEPH; KI-BUKH; KRANTZ, PHILIP; LANDAU, ZISHE; LEHRER, LEIBUSH; LEV, ABRAHAM; LITERATURE, JEWISH; MARMOR, KALMAN; MELOKHIM-BUKH; MENDELSON, JOSÉ; ORNSTEIN, LEO; PARIZ UN VIENE; RAVITCH, MELECH; SAPHIRE, SAUL; SCHNAPPER, BER; SHEKHTMAN, ELYE; SHMUEL-BUKH; SIMON, SHLOME; TABACHNIK, ABRAHAM BER; TKATCH, MEIR ZIML; TOLUSH; TSANIN, MORDKHE; VIDVILT; WELNER, PINCHES; YOFFE, MORDECAI

Federica Francesconi*, Ph.D.; History, University of Haifa: ASCOLI, GRAZIADIO ISAIA; BASEVI; BOLOGNA; BOLZANO; BORGHI, LAMBERTO; BOZZOLO; CANTONI, RAFFAELE; CENTO; CONEGLIANO; CREMONA; FAENZA; FINALE EMILIA; FINZI; FORLÌ; FORMIGGINI, ANGELO FORTUNATO; FRIZZI, BENEDETTO; GUASTALLA, ENRICO; IMOLA; LATTES, DANTE; LODI; MANTUA; MODENA; REGGIO EMILIA; VENTURA, RUBINO

Israel Francus, Ph.D., Rabbi; Associate Professor of Rabbinics, the Jewish Theological Seminary of America, New York: ABRAMSON, SHRAGA

Moshe Zvi Frank, B.A.; LL.B.; Journalist, Tel Aviv: BILTMORE PROGRAM

Alex Frankel*: MATLIN, MARLEE

Giza Frankel, Ph.D.; the Ethnological Museum, Haifa: PAPER-CUTS

Jonathan Frankel*, Ph.D.; Professor of Modern Jewish and Russian History, the Hebrew University of Jerusalem: "DOCTORS' PLOT"; DAMASCUS AFFAIR

William Frankel, Former Editor of the *Jewish Chronicle*, London

Norma Franklin*, Ph.D.; Archaeologist, Tel Aviv University: SAMARIA

Harry Freedman, Ph.D., Rabbi; Caulfield, Victoria, Australia: ACADEMY ON HIGH; AKIVA; ARK OF THE COVENANT; BARNACLE GOOSE MYTHS; DEATH, KISS OF; GELMAN, MANUEL; ḤAVER IR; ḤISDA; ISHMAEL BEN JOHANAN BEN BEROKA; JOSIAH; LEVI; LEVI; MANI; MEGILLAT SETARIM; PARAPET; PATRIARCHS, THE; SEA OF THE TALMUD; SINAI, MOUNT; TRIBES, THE TWELVE; YALTA

Shalom Freedman*, Ph.D.; Freelance Writer, Jerusalem: GREENBERG, IRVING; KAPLAN, ARYEH; LAMM, NORMAN; TENDLER, MOSHE

ChaeRan Freeze*, Ph.D.; Associate Professor of East European Jewish History, Brandeis University, Waltham, Massachusetts: SHTETL; WOMAN: EASTERN EUROPE

Harriet Pass Freidenreich*, Ph.D.; Professor of History, Temple University, Philadelphia: COHEN, ELIZABETH D. A. MAGNUS; COSER, ROSE LAUB; DENMARK, FLORENCE LEVIN; FRANKENTHAL, KÄTE; HELLMAN, CLARISSE DORIS; HYDE, IDA HENRIETTA; HYMAN, LIBBIE HENRIETTA; JACOBSON, ANNA; KAUFMAN, JOYCE JACOBSON; KRIM, MATHILDE; LEICHTER, KAETHE PICK; MARCUS, RUTH BARCAN; PEIXOTTO, JESSICA BLANCHE; PEIXOTTO, JUDITH SALZEDO; RICHTER, ELISE; SCHWARTZ, ANNA JACOBSON; WEINBERG, GLADYS DAVIDSON; WOLFF, CHARLOTTE

Jacob Freimann, Dr.Phil., Rabbi; Lecturer in Rabbinics and Jewish History, the Berlin Rabbinical Seminary: ABBA MARI BEN MOSES BEN JOSEPH ASTRUC OF LUNEL; ABRAHAM BEN SAMUEL HE-ḤASID; ISAAC BEN NOAH KOHEN SHAPIRA

Paul Freireich, M.S.; Journalist, New York: KRAMER, STANLEY E.

Gad Freudenthal*: ZAMOSC, ISRAEL BEN MOSES HA-LEVI

Jonathan (G.) Freund*, M.A. Ed.; Program Director, Board of Rabbis of Southern California, Los Angeles: NEUMANN, EMANUEL

Paul A. Freund, S.J.D.; Professor of Law, Harvard University, Cambridge, Massachusetts: BRANDEIS, LOUIS DEMBITZ; FRANKFURTER, FELIX

Richard Freund*, Ph.D.; Director and Professor, Maurice Greenberg Center for Judaic Studies, University of Hartford, Connecticut: SIEGEL, SEYMOUR

George H. Fried, Ph.D.; Associate Professor of Biology, Brooklyn College of the City University of New York: BERNSTEIN, JULIUS; BRONOWSKI, JACOB; COHN, FERDINAND JULIUS; EMBDEN, GUSTAV; HABERLANDT, GOTTLIEB; KATZ, SIR BERNARD; MULLER, HERMAN JOSEPH; PINCUS, GREGORY GOODWIN; SALAMAN; SALAMAN, REDCLIFFE NATHAN; WALD, GEORGE

Lewis (Frederick) Fried*, Ph.D.; Professor, Kent State University, Ohio: AUSTER, PAUL; BUKIET,

MELVIN JULES; CALISHER, HORTENSE; DOCTOROW, EDGAR LAWRENCE; EPSTEIN, LESLIE; FADIMAN, CLIFTON; FAST, HOWARD MELVIN; FELDMAN, IRVING; GOLD, HERBERT; GOLDSTEIN, REBECCA; GOODMAN, ALLEGRA; GREEN, GERALD; GROSSMAN, ALLEN; HARRIS, MARK; HELLER, JOSEPH; HELLMAN, LILLIAN; HOWE, IRVING; IGNATOW, DAVID; KAZIN, ALFRED; KUNITZ, STANLEY JASSPON; LEVIANT, CURT; MAILER, NORMAN; MALAMUD, BERNARD; NEMEROV, HOWARD; NISSENSON, HUGH; PROSE, FRANCINE; RICH, ADRIENNE; ROTH, PHILIP MILTON; SALINGER, JEROME DAVID; SONTAG, SUSAN; STERN, STEVE; UNITED STATES LITERATURE; WALLANT, EDWARD LEWIS; YEZIERSKA, ANZIA

Nathan Fried, Rabbi; Bene-Berak: SUSAN, ISSACHAR BEN MORDECAI

Lillian A. Friedberg, M.A.; Former Executive Director of the Jewish Community Relations Council of Pittsburgh, Pennsylvania: PITTSBURGH

Maurice Friedberg, Ph.D.; Professor of Slavic Languages and Literature and Director of the Russian and East European Institute, Indiana University, Bloomington: ADMONI, VLADIMIR GRIGORYEVICH; AIKHENVALD YULI ISAYEVICH; AIZMAN, DAVID YAKOLEVICH; ALDANOV, MARK; AVERBAKH, LEOPOLD LEONIDOVICH; BABEL, ISAAC EMMANUILOVICH; BAGRITSKI, EDUARD GEORGIYEVICH; BILL-BELOTSERKOVSKI, VLADIMIR NAUMOVICH; BRODSKI, YOSIF; BYADULYA-YASAKAR, ZMITROK; CHERNY, SASHA; DANIEL, YULI MARKOVICH; EHRENBURG, ILYA GRIGORYEVICH; GERSHENZON, MIKHAIL OSIPOVICH; GRANIN, DANIEL ALEKSANDROVICH; GROSSMAN, VASILI SEMYONOVICH; HAGAR; ILF, ILYA; INBER, VERA MIKHAILOVNA; KASSIL, LEV ABRAMOVICH; KAVERIN, BENJAMIN ALEKSANDROVICH; KAZAKEVICH, EMMANUIL GENRIKHOVICH; KHODASEVICH, VLADISLAV FELITSIANOVICH; KIRSANOV, SEMYON ISAAKOVICH; KOROLENKO, VLADIMIR GALAKTIONOVICH; KOZAKOV, MIKHAIL EMMANUILOVICH; LIBEDINSKI, YURI NIKOLAYEVICH; LIDIN, VLADIMIR GERMANOVICH; MARSHAK, SAMUEL YAKOVLEVICH; PASTERNAK, BORIS LEONIDOVICH; RUSSIAN LITERATURE; SELVINSKI, ILYA LVOVICH; SLONIMSKI, MIKHAIL LEONIDOVICH; SLUTSKI, BORIS ABRAMOVICH; TUR BROTHERS; TYNYANOV, YURI NIKOLAYEVICH; UTKIN, JOSEPH PAVLOVICH; WENGEROFF, SEMYON AFANASYEVICH; YEVTUSHENKO, YEVGENI ALEXANDROVICH

Ken Frieden*, Ph.D.; B.G. Rudolph Professor of Judaic Studies, Syracuse University: ABRAMOVITSH, SHOLEM YANKEV; PERETZ, ISAAC LEIB

Daniel M. Friedenberg, B.A.; Curator of Coins and Medals, the Jewish Museum, New York: ARON; FURST, MORITZ; FURST, MORITZ; GRILICHES, AVENIR; JUDIN, SAMUEL; MEDALISTS; MINTMASTERS AND MONEYERS; SIMON, JEAN HENRI; VINCZE, PAUL; WIENER

Eric Lewis Friedland, Ph.D.; Professor of Judaic Studies, Wright State University, Antioch College, University of Dayton, and United Theological Seminary, Dayton, Ohio: PRAYER BOOKS

Henry Friedlander*: EUTHANASIA

Saul Friedlander, Dr.Phil.; Professor of International Relations and Contemporary History, the Hebrew University of Jerusalem

Ellen Friedman, New York: BLUMENTHAL, WERNER MICHAEL; BUNZEL, RUTH LEAH; ELKIND, ARKADI DANIILOVICH; LOMBROSO, CESARE; ZUCKERKANDL, EMIL

Isaiah Friedman*, Ph.D.; Professor Emeritus of History, Ben-Gurion University of the Negev, Beersheba: AARONSOHN; BALFOUR DECLARATION; HERZL, THEODOR; LANGUAGE WAR; MORGENTHAU; OTTOMAN EMPIRE; SYKES, SIR MARK; SYKES-PICOT AGREEMENT; UGANDA SCHEME; ZIONISM

Jeanette Friedman*, B.A.; Editor-in-Chief, *The Wordsmithy*; Editor, *Together, American Gathering of Jewish Holocaust Survivors and Their Descendants*; Chairman, The Brenn Institute, American Jewish Press Association/Folksbiene Yiddish Theater/Second Generation, New Jersey: AARONSOHN, MOSES; ADAMS, THEODORE L.; AISH HATORAH; AMERICAN GATHERING OF JEWISH HOLOCAUST SURVIVORS; ARONOWITZ, BENJAMIN; BARISHANSHKY, RAPHAEL; BAUMOL, JOSHUA; BLEICH, J. DAVID; BLOCH, CHAIM ISAAC; BLUESTONE, JOSEPH ISAAC; BRILL, ISAAC LIPA; BUERGENTHAL, THOMAS; CARDIN, SHOSHANA SHOUBIN; CHARLOP, YECHIEL MICHEL; CHAZAN, ELIYAHU SIMCHA; KAMINETSKY JOSEPH; KENT, ROMAN R.; MENDLOWITZ, SHRAGA FEIVEL; SCHACHTER, HERSCHEL; SINGER, ISRAEL; U.S. ARMY AND THE HOLOCAUST; YOUNG ISRAEL, NATIONAL COUNCIL OF

Judith Friedman Rosen*, Ph.D.; Historian, Graduate Center City University of New York: HOLTZMAN, ELIZABETH J.; KAYE, JUDITH S.; LOWEY, NITA MELNIKOFF; UDIN, SOPHIE A.

Mark Friedman, Mhil.; Director of Cultural Affairs, World Jewish Congress, New York: BRONFMAN, EDGAR MILES

Maurice Friedman, Ph.D.; Professor of Religion, Temple University, Philadelphia: EXISTENTIALISM

Menachem Friedman*, Ph.D.; Professor, Dept. of Sociology, Bar-Ilan University, Ramat Gan: AGUDAT ISRAEL; BLAU, AMRAM; EẒ ḤAYYIM; KAHANA, KALMAN; LEVIN, YIẒḤAK MEIR; MINZ, BENJAMIN; NETUREI KARTA

Mira Friedman, Ph.D.; Department of History of Art, Tel Aviv University; Curator, Tel Aviv Museum: MERZER, ARIEH

Murray Friedman*: COMMENTARY; PODHORETZ, NORMAN

Reena Sigman Friedman*, Ph.D.; Associate Professor of Modern Jewish History, Reconstructionist Rabbinical College, Wyncote, Pennsylvania: ORPHAN, ORPHANAGE

Richard Elliott Friedman*, Th.D.; Katzin Professor of Jewish Civilization, University of California, San Diego: PENTATEUCH

Shamma Friedman*, Ph.D.; Benjamin and Minna Reeves Professor of Talmud and Rabbinics, Jewish Theological Seminary; Professor, Department of Talmud, Bar-Ilan University, Ramat Gan: BAVA BATRA; BAVA KAMMA; BAVA MEẒIA; DIMITROVSKY, CHAIM ZALMAN

Theodore Friedman, Ph.D., Rabbi; Jerusalem: GENTILE; ISAIAH; ISRAEL, STATE OF: RELIGIOUS LIFE AND

COMMUNITIES; JOB, THE BOOK OF; KEDUSHAH; KETUBBAH; LOANZ, ELIJAH BEN MOSES; MAN, THE NATURE OF; MORDECAI BEN ḤAYYIM OF EISENSTADT; STUDY

Carrie Friedman-Cohen*, Lecturer, Department for Yiddish Language and Literature, the Hebrew University of Jerusalem: AUERBAKH, ROKHL; ZYCHLINSKA, RAJZEL

Yohanan Friedmann*, Ph.D.; Professor of Islamic Studies, the Hebrew University of Jerusalem: ISLAM

Avyatar Friesel, Ph.D.; Lecturer in Jewish History, the University of the Negev, Beersheba: OESTERREICHISCHES CENTRAL-ORAGAN FUER BLAUBENSFREIHEIT, CULTUR, GESCHICHTE UND LITERATUR DER JUDEN

Dov I. Frimer*, Ph.D., Rabbi; Professor; Advocate and Attorney at-law, Hebrew University of Jerusalem: CIVIL MARRIAGE

Hillel Frisch*, Ph.D.; Senior Lecturer, Political Science and Middle Eastern History, Bar-Ilan University, Ramat Gan: GAZA STRIP; PALESTINIAN AUTHORITY

Tikva S. Frymer, M.A.; Associate Professor of Near Eastern Languages, Wayne State University, Detroit: ARARAT; ARIEL; ASHERAH; ASHTORETH; AVVIM; GROVES, SACRED; HAZAEL; HONEY; HULDAH; HUSHAI THE ARCHITE; MILK

Aharon Fuerst, Dr. Phil.; Historian, Jerusalem: BURGENLAND; EINHORN, IGNAZ; EISENSTADT, MEIR; EPHRAIM BEN JACOB HA-KOHEN

Alexander Fuks, Ph.D.; Professor of History and Classics, the Hebrew University of Jerusalem: TCHERIKOVER, VICTOR

Daniel Furman, Jerusalem: DUBROVNIK; SPLIT

Ben Furnish*, Ph.D.; Managing Editor, University of Missouri: ADLER, JACOB; PINSKI, DAVID

Abraham M. Fuss*, M.A., J.D., Ph.D.; Attorney, New York: SHETAR

Mordecai L. Gabriel, Ph.D.; Professor of Biology, Brooklyn College of the City University of New York: AHARONI, ISRAEL; ARTOM, CESARE; ASCHERSON, PAUL FRIEDRICH AUGUST; ASKENASY, EUGEN; BODENHEIMER, FREDERICK SIMON; BRESSLAU, ERNST; ENRIQUES, PAOLO; EZEKIEL, MOSES; GOLDSCHMIDT, RICHARD BENEDICT; HAAS, FRITZ; HAAS, GEORG; LEVI, GIUSEPPE; LURIA, SALVADOR EDWARD; LWOFF, ANDRÉ MICHEL; MAGNUS, PAUL WILHELM; METCHNIKOFF, ELIE; RITTENBERG, DAVID; SACHS, JULIUS; SEMON, RICHARD WOLFGANG; SORAUER, PAUL KARL MORITZ; STRASBURGER, EDUARD; WIESNER, JULIUS VON

Edward McGlynn Gaffney Jr.*, Ph.D.; Professor of Law, Valparaiso University School of Law, Valparaiso, Indiana: FRANKEL, MARVIN EARL; GREENE, HAROLD H.; HELLERSTEIN, ALVIN K.

Isaiah Gafni, M.A.; Special Teacher in Jewish History, the Hebrew University of Jerusalem; Assistant in Jewish History, the University of the Negev, Beersheba: ADIABENE; ADMON BEN GADDAI; AGRIPPA, CAIUS JULIUS; AGRIPPA, MARCUS VIPSANIUS; AHASUERUS-XERXES; ALEXANDER THE FALSE; ALEXANDER THE ZEALOT; ALEXANDRIA; ALEXANDRIAN MARTYRS, ACTS OF; ALEXAS; ANANIAS OF ADIABENE; ANANIAS SON OF ZADOK; ANILAEUS AND ASINAEUS; ANTIOCHUS; APAMEA; ARADUS; ARDASHIR; AREIOS; ARISTOBULUS; ARTEMION; ASARAMEL; ASS WORSHIP; ATHRIBIS; ATHRONGES; AUGUSTUS; AURUM CORONARIUM; BACCHIDES; BANUS; BATHYRA; BEN SṬADA; BEN-HADAD; BET GARMU; BET ẒERIFA; CALLISTHENES; CARIA; CASSIUS LONGINUS; CHARES; CILICIA; CLEOPATRA OF JERUSALEM; COELE-SYRIA; COMMAGENE; COSTOBAR; CYRENE; DORIS; DOROTHEUS; DRUSILLA; EDESSA; ELEAZAR; EMPEROR WORSHIP; ETHNARCH; FLAVIUS, CLEMENS; FULVIA; GERUSIA; GLAPHYRA; GORGIAS; GREECE; GYMNASIUM; HASMONEAN BET DIN; HEZEKIAH, THE HIGH PRIEST; HIGH PRIEST; JANUARIUS; JOSEPH BEN ELEM; JOSHUA, SON OF SETH; JOSHUA BEN PHABI; LAMPON AND ISIDOROS; LUCUAS; LYSANIAS; MACEDONIA; MARSUS, C. VIBIUS; MATTATHIAS; MATTATHIAS BEN SIMEON; MENAHEM THE ESSENE; MERCURY; MILETUS; MUCIANUS, CAIUS LICINIUS; NUMENIUS; OBEDAS; OSROENE; PAMPHYLIA; PERGAMUM; PHINEHAS; PHRYGIA; POLEMON II; PTOLEMY; QUADRATUS, UMMIDIUS CAIUS; QUINTILIUS VARUS; SALOME ALEXANDRA; SCHALIT, ABRAHAM CHAIM; SELEUCIA; SELEUCID ERA; SELEUCUS IV PHILOPATOR; SEVERUS, ALEXANDER; SILAS; SOSIUS, GAIUS; SYRIA; THEODOSIUS; TOPARCHY; VENTIDIUS, PUBLIUS; YANNAI, ALEXANDER; ZADOK THE PHARISEE

Bernhard Gajek*, Dr.Phil,; Professor Emeritus, University of Regensburg, Germany: FULDA, LUDWIG

Michael Galchinsky*, Ph.D.; Director of Program in Jewish Studies, Georgia State University, Georgia: GAER, FELICE D.

Israel Gal-Edd, B.A., A.C.I.S.; Senior External Lecturer in International Trade Relations, the Hebrew University of Jerusalem; Former Director General, Ministry of Development, Jerusalem: CHEMICAL CRAFTS AND INDUSTRIES

James S. Galfund*, B.A.; Senior Communications Manager, State of Israel Bonds, Washington, D.C.: BONDS, STATE OF ISRAEL

Israel Galili, Minister without Portfolio, Kibbutz Na'an

Marie Claire Galperine, Ph.D.; Charge de Recherches au Centre National de la Recherche Scientifique, Paris

Eithan Galun*, M.D.; Professor of Medicine, Sam and Ellie Fishman Chair in Gene Therapy; Director, Goldyne Savad Institute of Gene Therapy, the Hebrew University of Jerusalem, Hadassah Hebrew University Hospital: ASCHNER, MANFRED

Riva Gambert*: OAKLAND

Denise Gamzon, Ph.D.; Instructor in French Literature, Tel Aviv University: SCOUTING

Claude Gandelman, M.A.; Jerusalem: IONESCO, EUGÈNE; STAROBINSKI, JEAN

Evelien Gans*, Ph.D.; Professor of Modern Jewish History, University of Amsterdam and Netherlands

Institute for War Documentation, Amsterdam, The Netherlands: GANS, MOZES HEIMAN; KLEEREKOPER, ASSER BENJAMIN; WIJNKOOP, DAVID

Bernard Dov Ganzel, Ph.D.; Historian, New York: LANDSBERG, OTTO; LASKER, EDUARD

Salomon Gaon, Ph.D., Rabbi; Chief Rabbi of the Spanish and Portuguese Associated Congregations of the British Commonwealth, London: PRESS

Joseph Gar, Historian, Jerusalem: KAUNAS; KELME; KRASLAVA; KRUSTPILS; LATVIA; LEVIN-SHATZKES, YIẒḤAK; LIEPAJA; LITHUANIA; MEISEL, NOAH; MEMEL; MINTZ, PAUL; OVCHINSKI, LEVI; PALANGA; PANEVEZYS; RASEINIAI; REZEKNE; RIGA; SAMOGITIA; SCHATZ-ANIN, MAX; VILKAVIŠKIS; ZARASAI

Jonathan Garb*, Ph.D.; Lecturer, the Hebrew University of Jerusalem: IDEL, MOSHE

Irene Garbell, Dr.Phil.; Associate Professor of Semitic Linguistics, the Hebrew University of Jerusalem: DALMAN, GUSTAF HERMANN; DURAN, PROFIAT; GESENIUS, HEINRICH FRIEDRICH WILHELM; GOOR, YEHUDAH

Morris W. Garber, Ph.D.; Assistant Professor of History, Rutgers University, New Brunswick, New Jersey: PATERSON

Zev Garber*, Ph.D.; Professor of Jewish Studies, Los Angeles Valley College: BATE, JULIUS; BAUDISSIN, WOLF WILHELM; BAUMGARTNER, WALTER; BENTZEN, AAGE; BERTHOLET, ALFRED; BLEEK, FRIEDRICH; COOK, STANLEY ARTHUR; COOKE, GEORGE ALBERT; CORNILL, CARL HEINRICH; CORNILL, CARL HEINRICH; DILLMANN, AUGUST; DUPONT-SOMMER, ANDRÉ; EERDMANS, BERNARDUS DIRKS; FISHBANE, MICHAEL; GUNKEL, HERMANN; HAUPT, PAUL; HENGSTENBERG, ERNST WILHELM; HUPFELD, HERMANN CHRISTIAN KARL; JEREMIAS, ALFRED; KATZ, STEVEN T.; KAUTZSCH, EMIL FRIEDRICH; KEIL, KARL FRIEDRICH; KIRKPATRICK, ALEXANDER FRANCIS; KITTEL, RUDOLF; KUGEL, JAMES L.; LEHMANN-HAUPT, CARL FRIEDRICH; LEVENSON, JON D.; MARTI, KARL; MEINHOLD, JOHANNES FRIEDRICH; MEYER, EDUARD; NOWACK, WILHELM GUSTAV HERMANN; ORLINSKY, HARRY MEYER; PARROT, ANDRÉ; PFEIFFER, ROBERT HENRY; ROSENMUELLER, ERNST FRIEDRICH KARL; ROWLEY, HAROLD HENRY; RYSSEL, VICTOR; SCHAEFFER, CLAUDE F. A.; SEGAL, MOSES HIRSCH; SIEVERS, EDUARD; SMEND, RUDOLF; SMITH, JOHN MERLIN POWIS; SMITH, WILLIAM ROBERTSON; STEUERNAGEL, CARL; THEODORE OF MOPSUESTIA; TORREY, CHARLES CUTLER

Yosef Garfinkel*, Professor, Archaeologist, the Hebrew University of Jerusalem: SHA'AR HA-GOLAN

Leib Garfunkel, M.A.; Attorney, Jerusalem: YIDISHE SHTIME

Leah Garrett*, Ph.D.; Associate Professor, University of Denver: AN-SKI, S.; SHAPIRO, LAMED

Isaac Garti, B.A.; Teaching Assistant in Italian Literature, the Hebrew University of Jerusalem: BOCCACCIO, GIOVANNI

Lloyd P. Gartner, Ph.D.; Associate Professor of History, City College of the City University of New York: ADLER, SELIG; ḤASIDISM; HISTORIOGRAPHY; HOROWITZ, AARON JUDAH LOEB; INDUSTRIAL REMOVAL; NEW YORK CITY; PEIXOTTO; SOCIALISM; TRADE AND COMMERCE; UNITED STATES OF AMERICA

John W. Gassner, M.A.; Professor of Drama, Yale University, New Haven, Connecticut: GRUENBERG, LOUIS

Theodor H. Gaster, Ph.D.; Professor of Religion, Barnard College, Columbia University, New York: BEHEMOTH; BELIAL; DEEP, THE; DREAMS; EARTH; HADAS, MOSES; HOST OF HEAVEN

Yehuda Gaulan, Advocate; Ambassador, Ministry for Foreign Affairs, Jerusalem: FINLAND

Daniel Gavron, Writer, Jerusalem: ARAD

Miriam Gay, M.A., M.Sc.; Senior Teacher in Psychology, Bar-Ilan University, Ramat Gan; Ministry of Health, Tel Aviv: EISSLER, KURT R.; REICH, WILHELM

David Geffen*, Ph.D., Rabbi; Director of Information, Gesher Institute, Jerusalem; Researcher and Writer, Jerusalem: ATLANTA; BAḤYA; EVANS, ELI; GEFFEN, TOBIAS; HAMMER, ARMAND; REAGAN, RONALD WILSON; SAFIRE, WILLIAM; SCRANTON; WEINBERG, HARRY

Rela Mintz Geffen*, Ph.D.; President and Professor of Sociology, Hebrew, University Baltimore, Maryland: AUFRUFEN; CANDLES; DIETARY LAWS; FAMILY, AMERICAN JEWISH; HAKKAFOT; ḤAZZAN; MARRIAGE; PASSOVER

Manfred Moshe Geis, Theater Critic, Tel Aviv: GRONEMANN, SAMUEL

Ignace J. Gelb, Ph.D.; Professor of Assyriology, the University of Chicago: HITTITES

Saadia Gelb, M.A., Rabbi; Kibbutz Kefar Blum: IḤUD HABONIM

Nathan Michael Gelber, Dr.Phil.; *Encyclopaedia Judaica* (Germany); Jerusalem: ABRAHAM BEN ISRAEL OF BRODY; ALEKSANDER JAGIELLONCZYK; ALLIANZ, ISRAELITISCHE, ZU WIEN; ASKENAZY, SIMON; AUGUSTOW; AUSTRIA; BARUCH BEN DAVID YAVAN; BEDZIN; BELZ; BELZYCE; BENISCH, ABRAHAM; BERGSON; BERLIN, CONGRESS OF; BIALYSTOK; BOLEKHOV; BORISLAV; BREST-LITOVSK; BRODY; BYDGOSZCZ; BYK, EMIL; DROGOBYCH; EISENBAUM, ANTON; GALICIA; HRUBIESZOW; INOWROCLAW; JASLO; JOSELEWICZ, BEREK; KATZ, ALBERT; OLESKO; OLIPHANT, LAURENCE; OLKUSZ; OPOCZNO; OSTROLEKA; OSTROWIEC; TARNOBRZEG; TARNOGROD; TARNOW; WINNINGER, SOLOMON; WODZISLAW; WOJDA, CAROL FREDERICK

Arden J. Geldman, M.A.; Grants Officer and Projects Administrator, Joint Program for Jewish Education, JAFI and WZO, Jerusalem: FAMILY, AMERICAN JEWISH; UNITED STATES OF AMERICA

Victor Geller*: BESDIN, MORRIS J.

Yaacov Geller, M.A.; Research Assistant in the Institute for Research in the History and Culture of Oriental Jewry, Bar-Ilan University, Ramat Gan: ISTANBUL; OTTOMAN EMPIRE; PALACHE, ḤAYYIM

Edith B. Gelles*, Ph.D.; Senior Scholar, Stanford University, California: FRANKS, BILHAH ABIGAIL LEVY

Dov Genachowski, B.A.; Journalist, Former Senior Economist of the Bank of Israel, Jerusalem: COINS AND CURRENCY; SANBAR, MOSHE

Carol Gendler, M.A.; Instructor in History, College of St. Mary, Omaha, Nebraska: OMAHA; ROSEWATER, EDWARD

Yehuda Gera, Dr.Jur.; Ministry for Foreign Affairs, Jerusalem: GOLDSTEIN, ANGELO; KAFKA, BRUNO ALEXANDER

Daniel E. Gershenson, Ph.D.; Acting Associate Professor of Classics, the University of California, Los Angeles: LOGOS; POSIDONIUS; PYTHAGORAS; THEOPHRASTUS OF ERESOS

Jonathan (M.) Gershoni*, Ph.D.; Professor, Tel Aviv University: FRANKLIN, ROSALIND ELSIE

Gershon K. Gershony, Theater Critic, Jerusalem: GNESSIN, MENAHEM; GRANACH, ALEXANDER; GRANOVSKY, ALEXANDER; SONNENTHAL, ADOLF RITTER VON

Allan Gerson*, J.S.D., J.D., L.L.M.; Attorney, AG International Law, PLLC, Washington, D.C.: REAGAN, RONALD WILSON

Edith Gerson-Kiwi, Dr.Phil.; Associate Professor of Ethnomusicology, Tel Aviv University: KURDISTAN; KESTENBERG, LEO; LACHMANN, ROBERT; VEPRIK, ALEXANDER MOISEYEVITCH; WEINBERG, JACOB; WELLESZ, EGON JOSEPH

Dan Gerstenfeld*, M.A.; Business Editor, Makor Rishon and Israeli Newspapers, Jerusalem: AKIROV, ALFRED; ALEXANDER, KOBI

Zev Gerstl*, Ph.D.; Institute Soil, Water and Environmental Sciences, Agricultural Research Organization – Volcani Center, Beit Dagan, Israel: ENVIRONMENTAL SCIENCES

Elmer Gertz, J.D.; Attorney, Chicago: LOEB-LEOPOLD CASE; ROSENBERG CASE

Devorah Getzler, The Hebrew University of Jerusalem: HEBREW UNIVERSITY OF JERUSALEM

Israel Getzler, Ph.D.; Professor in European History, La Trobe University, Melbourne: MARTOV, JULIUS

Haim M. I. Gevaryahu, Ph.D.; Chairman of the Israel Society for Biblical Research, Jerusalem: KAUFMANN, YEḤEZKEL

Brenda Gevertz*, M.S.S.A.; Executive Director, Jewish Communal Service Association of North America, New York: JEWISH COMMUNAL SERVICE ASSOCIATION OF NORTH AMERICA, THE

Shimon Gibson*, Ph.D.; Archaeologist and Senior Research Fellow, W.F. Albright Institute of Archaeological Research, Jerusalem: ABBA SIKRA; ABSALOM; ABSALOM, MONUMENT OF; ACRA, THE; ACRABA; ACRE; ADASA; AELIA CAPITOLINA; AGATHARCHIDES OF CNIDUS; AGRICULTURAL LAND-MANAGEMENT METHODS AND IMPLEMENTS IN ANCIENT EREẒ ISRAEL; AGRICULTURE; AGRIPPINA; AKHBAREI/ACCHABARON; ALCUIN; ANSELM OF CANTERBURY; ANTIPATRIS; ANTONIA; APHEK; ARAD; ARBEL; ARCHAEOLOGISTS; ARCHAEOLOGY; ARCHELAIS; ARCHITECTURE AND ARCHITECTS; ASHKELON; AUGUSTINE; AVEDAT; AVIGAD, NAḤMAN; AVIRAM, JOSEPH; AVI-YONAH, MICHAEL; BANIAS; BAR KOKHBA; BAR-YOSEF, OFER; BET GUVRIN; BET SHE'ARIM; BET-CHEREM; BETHBASI; BETHPHAGE; BETHSAIDA; BET-NIMRAH; BOẒRAH; CAESAREA; CAIAPHAS, JOSEPH; CANAAN, LAND OF; CAPITOLIAS; CHORAZIN; CIRCUSES AND THEATERS; CISTERN; CITY; COPPER SCROLL; CRUCIFIXION; CULT PLACES, ISRAELITE; CYPROS; DAMASCUS; DAMOCRITUS; DAN; DECAPOLIS; DIBON; DIODORUS OF SICILY; DIOGENES LAERTIUS; DIOS; DIOSCORIDES PEDANIUS; DISCIPLINE, MANUAL OF; DOBRATH; DOK; DOLMENS; DOR; DORIS; DOTHAN, TRUDE; DURA-EUROPOS; EDESSA; EIN KEREM; ELEPHANT; ELUSA; EPHESUS; EUSEBIUS PAMPHILI; GADARA; GAMLA; GAZA; GERASA; GERIZIM, MOUNT; GEZER; GISCALA; GITIN, SEYMOUR; GOFNAH; GOLAN; GOLDMAN, HETTY; GOODENOUGH, ERWIN RAMSDELL; GOPHNA, RAM; HAMMAT GADER; HAR HA-MELEKH; HAZOR; HELENA; HELENA AUGUSTA; HEROD PHILIP I; HERODIUM; HESHBON; HOLOFERNES; JERICHO; JERUSALEM; JEZREEL; JOHN THE BAPTIST; JOTAPATA; JUDEAN DESERT CAVES; KEMPINSKY, AHARON; KENYON, DAME KATHLEEN MARY; LACHISH; LIVY; LUCAN; MA'ON; MACCABEE; MACHAERUS; MACHPELAH, CAVE OF; MADABA, MEDEBA; MAIUMAS; MAMPSIS; MAZAR, AMIHAI; MELITO OF SARDIS; MEMPHIS; MICHMASH or MICHMAS; MIKVEH; MODI'IN; NAARAH; NABLUS; NAIN; NEGEV; NICANOR; NIẒẒANAH; OSSUARIES and SARCOPHAGI; PALESTINE; PELLA or PAḤAL; PETRA; PHOTIS; PONTIUS PILATE; POTTERY; RABAN, AVNER; RABBATH-AMMON; RAMAT HA-GOLAN; REHOBOTH; SALOME; SARṬABA; SHALEM; SHANKS, HERSHEL; SHILOAH, SILOAM; SHILOH; SHILOH, YIGAL; SHIPS AND SAILING; SHIVTAH or SOBATA; SIDON; SILK; SINAI; SINAI, MOUNT; STATIUS, PUBLIUS PAPINIUS; STERN, EPHRAIM; TAMAR; TEKOA; TIBERIAS; TILLICH, PAUL JOHANNES; URMAN, DAN; USSISHKIN, DAVID; VERMES, GEZA

Nahum Tim Gidal, Ph.D.; Photojournalist, Jerusalem

Ludy Giebels*, Ph.D.; Retired Historian, Amsterdam, The Netherlands: DE LIEME, NEHEMIA; HAAN, JACOB ISRAËL DE

Yisrael (Zvi) Gilat*, Senior Lecturer, Law School, Netanya Academic College, Israel: ADOPTION

Yitzhak Dov Gilat, Ph.D.; Associate Professor of Talmud, Bar-Ilan University, Ramat Gan; Senior Lecturer in Talmud, Tel Aviv University: ABBA; ABBA BAR KAHANA; ABBA BAR MEMEL; ABBA BAR ZAVDA; ABBA BENJAMIN; ADDA BAR AHAVAH; ALEXANDRI; AMEIMAR; AMRAM; ARBA AMMOT; ASSI, RAV; AVDIMI OF HAIFA; AVIN; AVIN THE CARPENTER; AVINA; BAR HEDYA; BAR KAPPARA; BARAITA DE-MELEKHET HA-MISHKAN; BEBAI; BEBAI BAR ABBAYE; BEI AVIDAN; BENJAMIN BEN JAPHETH; DESKARTA; DIMI; ELEAZAR BEN MATYA; ELEAZAR BEN YOSE; ELEAZAR BEN YOSE II; ELEAZAR BEN ZADOK; ELEAZAR ḤISMA; ELIEZER BEN HYRCANUS; ELIEZER BEN JACOB; ERUVIN; GITTIN; ḤANINA; ḤULLIN; HUNA BEN NATHAN; ILAI; IMMA SHALOM; ISAAC NAPPAḤA; JACOB; JOSIAH; KALLAH, MONTHS OF; MEGILLAT YUHASIN; NEHARDEA; NEḤUNYA BEN HA-KANAH; RAVINA; SIMEON BEN JEHOZADAK; SIMEON BEN SHETAḤ; SOFERIM; YUDAN

Gad Gilbar*, Ph.D.; Professor, University of Haifa: ṢARRĀF

Shaked Gilboa*, MSc., Ph.D.;

Lecturer in Geography, Tel Aviv University: ABSALON; ABU GHOSH; ACRE; ADULLAM REGION; AFULAH; ALFEI MENASHEH; ALLONEI ABBA; ALLONEI YIẒḤAK; ALLONIM; ALMAGOR; AMIDAR; AMIR, MENAHEM; AMIRIM; ANATHOTH; APELOIG, YITZHAK; APHEK; APOLLONIA; ARABAH, THE; ARAD; ARAD, RON; ARARA; ARIEL; ASHDOD; ASHDOT YA'AKOV; ASHKELON; ATHLIT; AVELIM or OVELIM; AVINERI, SHLOMO; AYALON, AMI; AYANOT; AZOR; BAR-ILAN UNIVERSITY; BARKAI; BASHAN; BAT ḤEFER; BAT YAM; BE'ER YA'AKOV; BE'EROT YIẒḤAK; BEERSHEBA; BEIT JIMĀL; BEN-ARIEH, YEHOSHUA; BENE-BERAK; BENEI AISH; BEN-PORAT, MIRIAM; BEN-SHAKHAR, GERSHON; BET GUVRIN; BET-DAGON; BET-EL; BETHLEHEM; BETH-SHAN; BET-SHEMESH; BINYAMINAH; BLUM, LUDWIG; BOGEN, ALEXANDER; BRAVERMAN, AVISHAY; BRINKER, MENACHEM; CAESAREA; CARMEL, MOSHE; CARMEL, MOUNT; CAROL, ARYEH; CITRUS; COHEN GAN, PINCHAS; CONFINO, MICHAEL; COOPERATIVES; CRIME; DABBŪRIYYA; DAFNAH; DALESKI, HILLEL; DĀLIYAT AL-KARMIL; DALIYYAH; DALTON; DAN; DAVAR; DEAD SEA; DEGANYAH; DIMONAH; DORON, ABRAHAM; DOSTROVSKY, ISRAEL; EILOT; EIN GEV; EIN HA-EMEK; EIN HOD; EIN SHEMER; EIN ZEITIM; EIN ẒURIM; EISENBERG, SHOUL; EL AL; ELAD; ELATH; ELYASHIV; EN-DOR; EN-GEDI; EVEN YEHUDAH; EYDOUX, EMANUEL; FISH, HAREL; FRANKEL, YA'AKOV; GALIL, UZIA; GALON; GAN SHEMU'EL; GAN YAVNEH; GANNEI TIKVAH; GANNEI YEHUDAH; GAT; GAVISON, RUTH; GAZIT; GEDERAH; GELIL YAM; GERSHON, PINCHAS; GE'ULIM; GEVA; GILADI, ALEX; GILBOA; GINNOSAR; GIVAT ADA; GIVAT BRENNER; GIVAT ḤEN; GIVAT SHEMUEL; GIVAT ZE'EV; GIVATAYIM; GROSSMAN, AVRAHAM; GUSH ETZYON; GUSH KATIF; HABIBI, EMIL; HA-BONIM; ḤADERAH; HAGAI, BARUCH; HA-GOSHERIM; HAIFA MUNICIPAL THEATER; HAIFA, UNIVERSITY OF; HA-KIBBUTZ HA-ARẒI HA-SHOMER HA-ẒA'IR; HA-KIBBUTZ HA-DATI; HA-KIBBUTZ HA-ME'UḤAD; ḤAMADYAH; HA-MA'PIL; HA-OGEN; HAPOEL; HAREL; HAREL, MENASHE; HA-SOLELIM; ḤAẒER, ḤAẒERIM; ḤAẒEVAH; ḤAẒOR; ḤAẒOR ASHDOD; HA-ZORE'A; HA-ZORE'IM; HEBREW UNIVERSITY OF JERUSALEM; ḤEFẒI BAH; ḤELEẒ; ḤEREV LE-ET; ḤERUT; HERZLIYYAH; ḤEVRAT HA-OVEDIM; HISTADRUT; HISTADRUT HA-OVEDIM HA-LE'UMMIT; HOD HA-SHARON; ḤOLON; HUKOK; ḤULDAH; HURVITZ, ELI; ILANIYYAH; INBAL DANCE THEATER; ISRAEL MUSEUM; ISRAEL PHILHARMONIC ORCHESTRA; JERICHO; JEZREEL, VALLEY OF; JOKNEAM; KABRI; KALIR, AVRAHAM; KANEV, ISAAC; KARMI, DOV; KARMI'EL; KARNEI SHOMRON; KATZ, ELIHU; KAZIR ḤARISH; KAZRIN; KEFAR AZAR; KEFAR BARAM; KEFAR BARUKH; KEFAR BILU; KEFAR BLUM; KEFAR DAROM; KEFAR HA-ḤORESH; KEFAR HA-MACCABI; KEFAR HA-NASI; KEFAR HA-RO'EH; KEFAR ḤASIDIM; KEFAR HESS; KEFAR MASARYK; KEFAR MENAḤEM; KEFAR NETTER; KEFAR ROSH HA-NIKRAH; KEFAR RUPPIN; KEFAR SAVA; KEFAR SHEMARYAHU; KEFAR TAVOR; KEFAR VERADIM; KEFAR YEḤEZKEL; KEFAR YEHOSHU'A; KEFAR YONAH; KHOURI, MAKRAM; KIBBUTZ MOVEMENT; KINNERET; KINNERET, LAKE; KIRYAT ATA; KIRYAT BIALIK; KIRYAT EKRON; KIRYAT GAT; KIRYAT ḤAROSHET; KIRYAT MALAKHI; KIRYAT MOTZKIN; KIRYAT ONO; KIRYAT SHEMONAH; KIRYAT TIVON; KIRYAT YAM; KLEIN, RALPH; KOKHAV YAIR; KORIAT, ASHER; LACHISH REGION; LAPIDOT, RUTH; LAUTMAN, DOV; LEHAVIM; LEIBOWITZ, KEREN; LEO BAECK INSTITUTE; LEVIEV, LEV; LIBRARY, JEWISH NATIONAL AND UNIVERSITY; LIEBMAN, CHARLES; LIEBMAN, YESHAYAHU; LIPKIN-SHAHAK, AMNON; LOḤAMEI HA-GETTA'OT; LYDDA; MA'ALEH ADUMIM; MA'ALEH HA-ḤAMISHAH; MA'ALOT-TARSHIHA; MA'BAROT; MACCABI; MACCABIAH; MACCABIM-RE'UT; MAGHAR, AL-; MAGIDOR, MENACHEM; MAḤANAYIM; MANHEIM, BILHAH; MAOR, GALIA; MA'OZ ḤAYYIM; MASSADAH; MASSU'OT YIẒḤAK; MA'YAN BARUKH; MA'YAN ẒEVI; MAZKERET BATYAH; MAẒLI'AḤ; MAẒẒUVAH; ME'IR SHEFEYAH; MEITAR; MEKOROT WATER COMPANY; MENAḤEMIYYAH; MERḤAVYAH; MESILLOT; METULLAH; MEVASSERET ZION; MIGDAL; MIGDAL HA-EMEK; MIKVEH ISRAEL; MISGAV AM; MISHMAR HA-NEGEV; MISHMAR HA-SHARON; MISHMAROT; MIẒPAH; MIẒPEH RAMON; MIZRA; MIZRACHI, SHIMON; MO'EẒET HA-PO'ALOT; MOLEDET; MOSHAV OR MOSHAV OVEDIM; MOZA; NA'AN; NAḤAL; NAḤAL OZ; NAHALAL or NAHALOL; NAḤALAT YEHUDAH; NAHARIYYAH; NATIONAL PARKS IN ISRAEL; NATURE RESERVES IN ISRAEL; NAVON, DAVID; NAZARETH; NEGEV; NE'OT MORDEKHAI; NES ẒIYYONAH; NESHER; NETANYAH; NETIV HA-LAMED-HE; NETIVOT; NEVATIM; NEVEH EITAN; NEVEH YAM; NIR AM; NIRIM; NIẒẒANAH; NIẒẒANIM; OFAKIM; OFIR, SHAIKE; OLIVE; OMER; OR AKIVA; OR HA-NER; OR YEHUDAH; ORANIT; OROT; PALESTINE ECONOMIC CORPORATION; PARDES ḤANNAH-KARKUR; PARDESIYYAH; PERI, YA'AKOV; PETAḤ TIKVAH; POLLACK, ISRAEL; PROPPER, DAN; RA'ANANNAH; RABINOVICH, ITAMAR; RĀMA, AL-; RAMALLAH; RAMAT DAVID; RAMAT GAN; RAMAT HA-GOLAN; RAMAT HA-KOVESH; RAMAT HA-SHARON; RAMAT HA-SHOFET; RAMAT RAZIEL; RAMAT YISHAI; RAMLEH; RAMON, ILAN; RAMOT MENASHEH; RAND, YA'AKOV; RECHTER; REGBAH; REḤOVOT; REKHASIM; RISHON LE-ZION; ROSEN, YEHOSHUA; ROSH HA-AYIN; ROSH PINNAH; ROTH-SHACHAMOROV, ESTHER; SA'AD; SAFED; SAFRAI, SHMUEL; SALOMON, GAVRIEL; SAVYON; SEDEH BOKER; SEDEH ELIYAHU; SEDEH NEḤEMYAH; SEDEROT; SHA'AREI TIKVAH; SHA'AR HA-AMAKIM; SHA'AR HA-GOLAN; SHA'AR ḤEFER-BEIT YIẒḤAK; SHACHAR, ARIE; SHADMOT DEVORAH; SHAHAR, SHULAMIT; SHAMGAR, MEIR; SHAMIR; SHARON, ARYEH; SHAVEI ZION; SHE'AR YASHUV; SHEFAYIM; SHELOMI; SHOHAM; SHOHAM, SHLOMO-GIORA; SHOMRAT; SHOVAL; SHUVAL, JUDITH; SHWED, GIL; SIMONSOHN, SHLOMO; TAANACH; TAHAL; TEKUMAH; TEL ADASHIM; TEL AVIV UNIVERSITY; TEL AVIV-JAFFA; TEL KAẒIR; TEL MOND; TEL YOSEF; TIMNA; TIRAT HA-KARMEL; TNUVA; TURNER, YA'AKOV; UDIM; URIM; VAN LEER, LIA; WESTERN WALL; YA'ALON, MOSHE; YAD ḤANNAH; YAD IZHAK BEN-ZVI; YAGUR; YAKUM; YARKON; YARMUK; YAVETS, ZVI; YAVNEH; YEDIDYAH; YEFET, SARAH; YEHUD; YEROḤAM; YESUD HA-MA'ALAH; YIZRE'EL; YOVEL, YIRMIYAHU; ZIKHRON YA'AKOV; ZIM; ẒOFIT; ẒORAH; ẒUR YIGAL

Baruch Gilead, M.A.; Ministry for Foreign Affairs, Jerusalem: TURKEY

Sharon Gillerman*, Ph.D.; Associate Professor of Jewish History, Hebrew Union College-Jewish Institute of Religion, Los Angeles: WRONSKY, SIDDY

Joseph Gillis, Ph.D.; Professor Emeritus, The Rudy Bruner Professor of Science Teaching, Weizmann Institute of Science, Reḥovot: ULAM, STANISLAW MARCIN

Philip Gillon, Journalist, Jerusalem

Neil Gilman, Ph.D.; the Aaron Rabinowitz and Simon H. Rifkind Associate Professor of Jewish Philosophy, the Jewish Theological Seminary of America, author of *Conservative Judaism, The New Century*

Dan Gilon*, M.D., F.A.C.C.; Professor of Medicine (Cardiology), Director of Non-Invasive Cardiology,

Heart Institute, Hadassah–Hebrew University Medical Center, Ein-Kerem Jerusalem: MEDICINE; MIROWSKI, MICHEL

Joseph Ginat, B.A.; Deputy Adviser to the Prime Minister on Arab Affairs, Givatayim, Israel: ISRAEL, STATE OF: ARAB POPULATION

Eyal Ginio*, Ph.D.; Lecturer, the Hebrew University of Jerusalem: EDIRNE

Rosa Ginossar, L.en D., Honorary President of WIZO, Jerusalem: SIEFF, REBECCA; WIZO

Harold Louis Ginsberg, Ph.D.; Professor of Biblical History and Literature, the Jewish Theological Seminary of America, New York: ABOMINATION OF DESOLATION; AHAB; AHASUERUS-XERXES; ANCIENT OF DAYS; ARIOCH; ARTAXERXES; BABEL, TOWER OF; BEN-HADAD; CULT; DANIEL; DANIEL, BOOK OF; ECCLESIASTES; ELIHU; ELIPHAZ; HEART; HIEL; HOSEA, BOOK OF; IMMANUEL; ISAIAH; JEPHTHAH; JOB, THE BOOK OF; KEDEMITES or EASTERNERS; LEMUEL; MAHER SHALAL HASH BAZ; MICHAEL AND GABRIEL; NAMES; PEACE; SHEBA BEN BICHRI; SO

Louis Ginsberg, Petersburg, Virginia

Shabbetai Ginton, M.D.; Ministry of Health, Jerusalem: SHEBA, CHAIM

S. (Seymour) Gitin*, Ph.D.; Dorto Director and Professor of Archaeology, W.F. Albright Institute of Archaeological Research, Jerusalem: EKRON

Marcia Gitlin, B.A.; Jerusalem

Rudolf Glanz, Dr.Jur.; Historian, New York: NEW BEDFORD

Ruth Glasner*, Ph.D.; Professor of History and Philosophy of Science, the Hebrew University of Jerusalem: JEDAIAH BEN ABRAHAM BEDERSI

Nahum N. Glatzer, Ph.D.; Professor of Jewish History, Brandeis University, Waltham, Massachusetts: GANS, EDUARD; MAYBAUM, SIGMUND; MEGILLAT TA'ANIT; MONATSSCHRIFT FUER GESCHICHTE UND WISSENSCHAFT DES JUDENTUMS; ZUNZ, LEOPOLD

Nathan Glazer, Ph.D.; Professor of Education and Social Structure, Harvard University, Cambridge, Massachusetts

William Glicksman, Ph.D.; Lecturer in Jewish History, Gratz College, Philadelphia: CZESTOCHOWA; KIELCE; RADOM

Paul Glikson, B.Sc.; Institute for Contemporary Jewry, the Hebrew University of Jerusalem

Yvonne Glikson, B.A.; Jerusalem: PILGRIMAGE; TALMUD, BURNING OF; WANDERING JEW

Eliezer Gluzberg, Kibbutz Ḥazerim: IḤUD HABONIM

Hans Goedkoop*: HEIJERMANS, HERMAN

Denise R. Goitein, Ph.D.; Senior Lecturer in French Literature, Tel Aviv University: BERNSTEIN, HENRI-LEON; BLOCH, JEAN-RICHARD; BLOY, LÉON; CHALIER, CATHERINE; COHEN, ALBERT; FRENCH LITERATURE; LACRETELLE, JACQUES DE; MIKHAËL, EPHRAÏM; MONTAIGNE, MICHEL DE; SCHWIEFERT, PETER; SCHWOB, MARCEL; TRIOLET, ELSA

Shelomo Dov Goitein, Dr.Phil.; Emeritus Professor of Islamic Studies, the Hebrew University of Jerusalem; Emeritus Professor of Arabic, the University of Pennsylvania, Philadelphia: AARON; ABD AL-MĀLIK IBN MĀRWAN; ABRAHAM; ADEN; ASHTOR, ELIYAHU; BANETH; BILLIG, LEVI

Norman Golb, Ph.D., Professor of Hebrew and Judeo-Arabic Studies, Department of Near Eastern Languages and Civilizations, University of Chicago: ROUEN

Dore Gold*, Ph.D.; Former Israeli Ambassador to the UN; President, Jerusalem Center for Public Affairs, Jerusalem: SAUDI ARABIA

Abraham Goldberg, Ph.D., Rabbi; Senior Lecturer in Talmud, the Hebrew University of Jerusalem: ABBA BAR ZEMINA; ABBA KOHEN BARDELA; ABBA SAUL BEN BATNIT; ABBAYE KASHISHA; OHOLOT

Avie Goldberg, B.A.; Jerusalem: DAVID; JERUSALEM; SFORNO, OBADIAH BEN JACOB

Dara Goldberg*, B.A.; Director, External Affairs, United States Holocaust Memorial Museum, Washington, D.C.: UNITED STATES HOLOCAUST MEMORIAL MUSEUM

Florinda Goldberg*, M.A., Lecturer, Spanish and Latin American Studies, the Hebrew University of Jerusalem: CHOCRÓN, ISAAC; CONSTANTINI, HUMBERTO; DINES, ALBERTO; EICHELBAUM, SAMUEL; ESPINOZA, ENRIQUE; FEIERSTEIN, RICARDO; FUTORANSKY, LUISA; GELMAN, JUAN; GERCHUNOFF, ALBERTO; GLANTZ, JACOBO; GLANTZ, MARGO; GOLDEMBERG, ISAAC; ISAACS, JORGE; ISAACSON, JOSÉ; KOZER, JOSÉ; LIACHO, LÁZARO; LISPECTOR, CLARICE; PIZARNIK, ALEJANDRA; PORZECANSKI, TERESA; RABINOVICH, JOSÉ; ROVINSKY, SAMUEL; SVERDLIK, ODED; TOKER, ELIAHU

Gerald Goldberg, M.A.; Former Lord Mayor of Cork, Ireland

Hillel Goldberg, Ph.D., Rabbi; Jerusalem: HURVITZ, JOSEPH YOZEL

Jacob Goldberg, Ph.D.; Teacher in History, the Hebrew University of Jerusalem: AGRICULTURE; BUTRYMOWICZ, MATEUSZ; CASIMIR III; GDANSK; OLEŚNICKI, ZBIGNIEW; PAWLIKOWSKI, JÓZEF; SIEDLCE; TORUN; WINE AND LIQUOR TRADE; WIŚNIOWIECKI, JEREMI

Lea Goldberg, Dr.Phil.; Author and Associate Professor of Comparative Literature, the Hebrew University of Jerusalem: BEN YIẒḤAK, AVRAHAM; GNESSIN, URI NISSAN

Samuel P. Goldberg, B.S.S., C.S.W., Lecturer in Communal Organization, Columbia University, New York: COUNCIL OF JEWISH FEDERATIONS AND WELFARE FUNDS

Sylvie Anne Goldberg*, Ph.D.; Associate Professor, Ecole des Hautes Etudes en Sciences Sociales; Paris: ḤEVRA KADDISHA; JEWISH STUDIES; MORIN, EDGAR; OUAKNIN, MARC-ALAIN; VIDAL-NAQUET, PIERRE; ZAFRANI, HAIM

Harry Golden, B.A.; Writer and Editor, Charlotte, North Carolina: CONE; FRANK, LEO MAX

David M. Goldenberg*, Ph.D.; Cohon Professor in Jewish Religion and Thought, University of Pennsylvania: DROPSIE COLLEGE

Esther Goldenberg, M.A.; Assistant in Hebrew Language, the Hebrew University of Jerusalem: HEBREW LANGUAGE

Myrna Goldenberg*, Ph.D.; Professor Emerita, Montgomery College, Maryland: KLEPFISZ, IRENA; MEYER, ANNIE NATHAN; SKLAREW, MYRA

Yossi (Yosef) Goldenberg*, Ph.D.; Researcher, Head Librarian, Jerusalem Academy of Music and Dance, the Hebrew University of Jerusalem: HAJDU, ANDRÉ; JADASSOHN, SALOMON; MANOR, EHUD; SCHACHTER, CARL; SCHENKER, HEINRICH; SCHILLINGER, JOSEPH; YARKONI, YAFFA; ZUR, MENACHEM

Samuel Goldfeld, M.D.; Jerusalem

Judah Goldin, D.H.L.; Professor of Classical Judaica, Yale University, New Haven, Connecticut: FINKELSTEIN, LOUIS

Steven Goldleaf*, Ph.D.; Professor, Pace University, New York: NEUGEBOREN, JAY

Alex J. Goldman, LL.B., Rabbi; Stamford, Connecticut

Bernard Goldman, Ph.D.; Professor of Art History, Wayne State University, Detroit: MARIANOS; PORTAL

Cecilia Goldman*, M.A.; Researcher, Jerusalem: GOLDMAN, MARTIN

Israel M. Goldman, M.A., D.H.L., Rabbi; Baltimore: HERFORD, ROBERT TRAVERS; SCHNEEBERGER, HENRY WILLIAM

Jacob Goldman, Rabbi; Jerusalem: HERZOG, ISAAC; KAHANA, SOLOMON DAVID; UNTERMAN, ISSER YEHUDA

Karla Goldman*, Ph.D.; Historian in Residence, Jewish Women's Archive, Brookline Massachusetts: AMERICAN JEWESS; SIMON, CARRIE OBENDORFER; SYNAGOGUE

Michael James Goldman, M. Phil., Minister, Newbury Park, Essex, England: BARAITA DE-NIDDAH

Perry Goldman, Ph.D.; Assistant Professor of History, City College of the City University of New York: LEVIN, LEWIS CHARLES

Robert S. Goldman, M.A.; New York: HARTOGENSIS, BENJAMIN HENRY; RABINOFF, GEORGE W.

Annie Goldmann*, Ph.D. (Sociology).; Research, Ecole des hautes études en sciences sociales, Paris: MOTION PICTURES

Abram Juda Goldrat, Rabbi; Tel Aviv: GORA KALWARIA; ISAAC BEN SAMUEL HA-LEVI; ISAIAH BEN ABRAHAM; ISAIAH MENAHEM BEN ISAAC; JELLIN, ARYEH LOEB BEN SHALOM SHAKHNA; JOEL BEN MOSES GAD; KOPPELMAN, JACOB BEN SAMUEL BUNIM; KRAMER, MOSES BEN DAVID, OF VILNA

Ernst Daniel Goldschmidt, Ph.D.; Scholar and Librarian, Jerusalem: ADDIR HU; AKDAMUT MILLIN; BAKKASHAH; HAGGADAH, PASSOVER; LANDSHUTH, ELIEZER; LITURGY; PRAYER BOOKS; SACHS, MICHAEL; WEINTRAUB, SOLOMON; ZEMIROT

Itzhak Goldshlag, Journalist, Jerusalem: BNEI AKIVA; LANDAU, SHEMUEL ḤAYYIM; MAIMON, JUDAH LEIB; MIZRACHI; NERIAH, MOSHE ẒEVI; NISSIM, ISAAC; OUZIEL, BEN-ZION MEIR HAI; SARNA, EZEKIEL; SHAPIRA, ḤAYYIM MOSHE; SHRAGAI, SHLOMO ZALMAN; SOLOVEICHIK, ISAAC ZE'EV HA-LEVI; SOROTZKIN, ZALMAN BEN BEN-ZION; SUROWIECKI, WAWRZYNIEC; TOLEDANO, JACOB MOSES

Maurice Goldsmith, B.Sc.; Director of the Science Policy Foundation Ltd. and of the Science Information Service, London: BALINT, MICHAEL; BORN, MAX; HOFSTADTER, ROBERT; LANDAU, LEV DAVIDOVICH; LEVY, HYMAN; MEITNER, LISE; MICHELSON, ALBERT ABRAHAM; VEKSLER, VLADIMIR; WEIL, ANDRÉ; WIENER, NORBERT; ZARISKI, OSCAR

Bernard R. Goldstein, Ph.D.; Associate Professor of the History of Science, Yale University, New Haven, Connecticut: BONFILS, IMMANUEL BEN JACOB; LEVI BEN GERSHOM; MAIMONIDES

Eric L. Goldstein*, Ph.D.; Assistant Professor of History and Jewish Studies. Emory University, Atlanta, Georgia: MARYLAND

Israel Goldstein, D.H.L., Rabbi; Former Chairman of the Board of Directors, Keren Hayesod, Jerusalem: KEREN HAYESOD

Marcy Braverman Goldstein*, Ph.D.; History of Religions Scholar, University of Judaism, Los Angeles, California: LEHIGH VALLEY

Michael Goldstein, Professor of Music, Staatliche Hochschule für Musik und Darstellende Kunst, Hamburg: ASHKENAZY, VLADIMIR DAVIDOVICH; BRUSSILOVSKY, YEVGENI GRIGORYEVICH; DAVYDOV, KARL YULYEVICH; GILELS, EMIL GRIGORYEVICH; GLIÈRE, REINHOLD MORITZEVICH; KOGAN, LEONID BORISSOVICH; LAMM, PAVEL ALEKSANDROVICH; OISTRAKH, DAVID FEDOROVICH; RUBINSTEIN, ANTON GRIGORYEVICH; STOLYARSKI, PETER SOLOMONOVICH; TSFASSMAN, ALEXANDER NAUMOVICH; VEINBERG, MOISSEY SAMUILOVICH

Neil (B.) Goldstein*, S.B.; Executive Director, American Jewish Congress, New York: NEW YORK CITY

Raymond Goldstein*, B. Mus.; Musician specializing in Jewish Music; Accompanist, Rubin Academy of Music, Tel Aviv: ARONI, TSVI; BAGLEY, DAVID; DANTO, LOUIS; GANCHOFF, MOSES; GREENBLATT, ELIYAHU; HAINOVITZ, ASHER; HEILMANN, YITZHAK; HERSTIK, NAFTALI; KALIB, SHOLOM; LERER, SHMUEL; LUBIN, ABRAHAM; MALOVANY, JOSEPH; MEISELS, SAUL; MILLER, BEN-ZION; MULLER, BENJAMIN; NULMAN, MACY; RAPPAPORT, JACOB; SCHULHOF, MOSHE; STERN, MOSHE; TAUBE, SAMUEL BARUCH; VIGODA, SAMUEL; WOHLBERG, MOSHE

Sidney Goldstein, Ph.D.; Professor of Sociology and Anthropology, Brown University, Providence, Rhode Island: SPRINGFIELD

Yossi (Jorge) Goldstein*, Ph.D.; Lecturer, Head of Long Term Academic Programs Unit (YAFI), the Hebrew University of Jerusalem and Jewish Agency for Israel: HARKAVI, YITZHAK

Chaim Ivor Goldwater, LL.M.; Ministry of Finance, Jerusalem: GULAK, ASHER; SILBERG, MOSHE

Sharon Goleman*: RAPHAEL, WILLIAM

David Golinkin*, Ph.D., Rabbi; President and Professor of Jewish Law, Jerusalem: CONSERVATIVE JUDAISM; GINZBERG, LOUIS; GOLINKIN, MORDECHAI YA'AKOV; KIEVAL, HAYYIM; KLEIN, ISAAC; LEVI, SAMUEL GERSHON; PERLBERG, ABRAHAM NATHAN; SCHECHTER INSTITUTE OF JEWISH STUDIES, THE

David Goodblatt, M.H.L., Rabbi; Providence, Rhode Island

Erwin Ramsdell Goodenough, Ph.D.; Professor of the History of Religion, Yale University, New Haven, Connecticut: DURA-EUROPUS

Abram Vossen Goodman, Ph.D., Rabbi; President of the American Jewish Historical Society, New York: FEIBELMAN, JULIAN BECK; FELDMAN, ABRAHAM JEHIEL; FINESHRIBER, WILLIAM HOWARD; GITTELSOHN, ROLAND BERTRAM; GOLDENSON, SAMUEL HARRY; NONES, BENJAMIN; PHILLIPS; SOLOMONS, ADOLPHUS SIMEON

Jerry Goodman*, B.A., M.A.; Executive Director, National Committee for Labor Israel, New York: NATIONAL CONFERENCE ON SOVIET JEWRY

Karen Goodman*, M.A.; Independent Scholar, Los Angeles, California: LEWITZKY, BELLA; OVED, MARGALIT

Philip Goodman, Rabbi; Executive Secretary of the Jewish Book Council of America, New York: BOOKPLATES; KRAFT, LOUIS; WEIL, FRANK LEOPOLD

Sheldon (M.) Goodman*, Ph.D.; Clinical Psychologist in private practice, New York Department of Education, New York: FREUD, SIGMUND

George M. Goodwin*: NEWPORT; RHODE ISLAND

Marjanne E. Goozé*, Ph.D.; Associate Professor, Germanic and Slavic Languages, University of Georgia: HERZ, HENRIETTE

Jacob Gordin, Dr.Phil.; *Encyclopaedia Judaica* (Germany): HERRERA, ABRAHAM KOHEN DE

Robert Gordis, Ph.D., Rabbi; Professor of Religion, Temple University, Philadelphia; Professor of Bible, the Jewish Theological Seminary of America, New York: MARGOLIS, MAX LEOPOLD

Bezalel Gordon*, M.A.; Near Eastern Studies, University of Michigan: AMERICAN, SADIE; APPELMAN, HARLENE; BAAR, EMIL N.; BACKMAN, JULES; BARDIN, SHLOMO; BARNSTON, HENRY; BARON, JOSEPH LOUIS; BEERMAN, LEONARD; BENJAMIN, RAPHAEL; BERGER, ELMER; BERMAN, MYRON R.; BERNSTEIN, LOUIS; BETTMANN, BERNHARDT; BLUMENTHAL, AARON H.; BOARD OF DELEGATES OF AMERICAN ISRAELITES; BOHNEN, ELI AARON; BOSNIAK, JACOB; BRICKNER, BALFOUR; BRICKNER, BARNETT ROBERT; BRONSTEIN, HERBERT; BROWNE, LEWIS; CANTOR, BERNARD; CHANOVER, HYMAN; CHIEL, ARTHUR ABRAHAM; CHIEL, SAMUEL; COFFEE, RUDOLPH ISAAC; COHEN, ARMOND E.; COHEN, JACK JOSEPH; COHEN, JACOB XENAB; COHEN, SEYMOUR J.; COOK, SAMUEL; CURRICK, MAX COHEN; DAVIDSON, DAVID; DAVIDSON, MAX DAVID; DONIN, HAYIM HALEVY; DRESNER, SAMUEL HAYIM; DREYFUS, STANLEY A.; EHRENREICH, BERNARD COLONIUS; EICHHORN, DAVID MAX; EICHLER, MENACHEM MAX; ELIASSOF, HERMAN; ETTELSON, HARRY WILLIAM; FALK, JOSHUA; FEUER, LEON ISRAEL; FEUERLICHT, MORRIS MARCUS; FINK, JOSEPH LIONEL; GOLDFEDER, FISHEL; HABERMAN, JOSHUA O.; HAILPERIN, HERMAN; HALPERN, HARRY; HIRSCH, RICHARD; ISRAEL, EDWARD LEOPOLD; ISSERMAN, FERDINAND M.; JACOB, WALTER; KLENICKI, LEON; KOLATCH, ALFRED JACOB; KREITMAN, BENJAMIN ZVI; KUSHNER, HAROLD S.; KUSHNER, LAWRENCE; LELYVELD, ARTHUR JOSEPH; MALEV, WILLIAM S.; MARK, JULIUS; MIELZINER, MOSES; MILLER, ISRAEL; MINDA, ALBERT GREENBERG; MINKIN, JACOB SAMUEL; MOWSHOWITZ, ISRAEL; NEULANDER, ARTHUR H.; NEWFIELD, MORRIS; NEWMAN, LOUIS ISRAEL; NUSSBAUM, MAX; OLAN, LEVI ARTHUR; OLITZKY, KERRY M.; PETUCHOWSKI, JAKOB JOSEF; PILCHIK, ELY EMANUEL; PLAUT, W. GUNTHER; POLISH, DAVID; PRAGER, DENNIS; REGNER, SIDNEY L.; RICE, ABRAHAM JOSEPH; ROSENBAUM, SAMUEL; ROSENBERG, ISRAEL; ROTHSCHILD, JACOB M.; ROUTTENBERG, MAX JONAH; RUDERMAN, DAVID B.; SCHWARTZMAN, SYLVAN DAVID; SEGAL, BERNARD; SHAPIRO, ALEXANDER M.; SILVER, ABBA HILLEL; SILVER, DANIEL JEREMY; SILVERSTEIN, ALAN; SIMON, RALPH; SOBEL, RONALD; SOLOMON, ELIAS LOUIS; STAMPFER, JOSHUA; STEINBERG, PAUL; STERN, CHAIM; STERN, JACK; STERN, MALCOLM HENRY; TEPLITZ, SAUL I.; WASHOFSKY, MARK E.; WAXMAN, MORDECAI; WECHSLER, JUDAH; WEINSTEIN, JACK B.; WOLF, ARNOLD JACOB; ZELIZER, NATHAN; ZIMMERMAN, SHELDON; ZOLA, GARY PHILLIP

Arthur Aryeh Goren, Ph.D.; Lecturer in American History, the Hebrew University of Jerusalem: NEW YORK CITY

Asher Goren, M.A.; Writer, Jerusalem

Haim Goren*, Associate Professor, Tel-Hai Academic College, Israel: GUTHE, HERMANN; SCHICK, CONRAD

Yosef Gorny, Ph.D.; Professor, History of the Jewish People, Tel Aviv University

Shmuel Gorr, B.A.; Rabbi; Jerusalem: BALLARAT; CASSAB, JUDY; KAHAN, LOUIS; SPIELVOGEL, NATHAN; TASMANIA

Peter Gossens*, Dr. Literary Scholar, Westfälische Wilhelms-Universität, Münster, Germany: CELAN, PAUL

Harvey Leonard Gotliffe*, Ph.D.; Professor of Journalism, School of Journalism and Mass Communications, San Jose, California: PRESS

M.J. Gottfarstein: FRANCK, HENRI

Erich Gottgetreu, Journalist, Jerusalem: ADLER, HERMANN; BERENDSOHN, WALTER A.; BORCHARDT, RUDOLF; HEYM, STEFAN; KALÉKO, MASCHA; KRAFT, WERNER; LOEWENSTEIN, KURT; MARGOLIN, JULIJ; STURMANN, MANFRED; WOLFF, THEODOR; ZUKUNFT; ZUKUNFT, DIE

Efraim Gottlieb, Ph.D.; Associate Professor of Jewish Philosophy and

Mysticism, the Hebrew University of Jerusalem: ALCASTIEL, JOSEPH; BAḤYA BEN ASHER BEN ḤLAVA; DATO, MORDECAI BEN JUDAH; EZRA BEN SOLOMON; GERONDI, JACOB BEN SHESHET; ISAAC BEN SAMUEL OF ACRE; MA'AREKHET HA-ELOHUT; MENORAH; NAḤMANIDES; RECANATI, MENAHEM BEN BENJAMIN; RICCHI, RAPHAEL IMMANUEL BEN ABRAHAM ḤAI; SABBATH; SHAPIRA; TEMUNAH, THE BOOK OF

Isaac B. Gottlieb, M.A., Rabbi; Jerusalem: BREUER, JOSEPH

Moshe Gottlieb, Ph.D., Rabbi; Beit Berl, Ẓofit, Israel: BOYCOTT, ANTI-NAZI; LIPSKY, LOUIS; TENENBAUM, JOSEPH L.

Paul Gottlieb, B.A.; Jerusalem: BOMBAY; PAKISTAN

Yemima Gottlieb, B.A.; Jerusalem: GOLINKIN, MORDECAI; PELLEG, FRANK; PELLEG, FRANK

Alfred Gottschalk, Rabbi; President, Hebrew Union College, Cincinnati

Max Gottschalk, Ph.D.; Research Professor of Sociology, the Free University of Brussels: ANTWERP; BELGIUM; BRUSSELS; PHILIPPSON; PHILIPPSON

Norman K. Gottwald, Ph.D.; Professor of Old Testament and of Biblical Theology and Ethics, the Graduate Theological Union, Berkeley, California: AMORITES; JACOB, BLESSING OF; MANASSEH; NOMADISM; SAMUEL, BOOK OF

Percy S. Gourgey, M.B.E.; Journalist, Twickenham, Middlesex, England: KODER, SHABDAI SAMUEL; PRESS

Melissa (J.) de Graaf*, Ph.D.; Lecturer, Brandeis University/ Northeastern University, Boston: BAUER, MARION EUGÉNIE; WERTHEIM, ROSALIE MARIE

Peter Emanuel Gradenwitz, Ph.D.; Lecturer in Musicology, Tel Aviv University: BEN-HAIM, PAUL; DESSAU, PAUL; KORNGOLD, ERICH WOLFGANG; MILHAUD, DARIUS

Michael Graetz, M.A.; Jerusalem: SYMMACHUS BEN JOSEPH; VEREIN FUER KULTUR UND WISSENSCHAFT DES JUDENTUMS

Michael J. Graetz, M.A., Rabbi; Jerusalem: FRIEDLAENDER, DAVID; GOMPERZ; GOOD AND EVIL; LESSING, GOTTHOLD EPHRAIM; MOMMSEN, THEODOR; RAILROADS; REDEMPTION; SABBATH

Naomi Graetz*, M.A.; Senior Teacher, Ben-Gurion University of the Negev, Beersheba: DOMESTIC VIOLENCE

Gil Graff*, Ph.D.; Executive Director, Bureau of Jewish Education of Greater Los Angeles, California.: EDUCATION, JEWISH

Frank D. Grande, M.A.; Lecturer in History, City College of the City University of New York: ERRERA, CARLO; LUMBROSO

Anna Grattarola*: BOLOGNA

Bernhard Grau*, Dr.Phil; Archivist, Staatsarchiv Munich, Munich, Germany: EISNER, KURT

Alyssa M. Gray*, J.D., Ph.D.; Assistant Professor of Codes and Responsa Literature, Hebrew Union College-Jewish Institute of Religion, New York: AMORAIM; JOHANAN BEN NAPPAḤA

John Gray, Ph.D.; Professor of Hebrew and Semitic Languages, the University of Aberdeen, Scotland: KINGS, BOOK OF; SABEA

Solomon Grayzel, Ph.D., Rabbi; Editor Emeritus of the Jewish Publication Society of America; Professor of History, Dropsie University, Philadelphia: ALEXANDER; ANACLETUS II, PETER PIERLEONE; BEA, AUGUSTIN; BENEDICT; BULLS, PAPAL; CALIXTUS; CHURCH COUNCILS; CLEMENT; HUSIK, ISAAC; JEWISH PUBLICATION SOCIETY OF AMERICA; MALTER, HENRY; NEUMAN, ABRAHAM AARON

Bernard Grebanier, Ph.D.; Emeritus Professor of English, Brooklyn College of the City University of New York: BEHRMAN, SAMUEL NATHANIEL; BELASCO, DAVID; HART, MOSS

Arthur Green, Ph.D., Rabbi; President, Reconstructionist Rabbinical College, Wyncote, Pa.

Daryl Thomas Green*, B.A.; English, Kent State University, Ohio

Emanuel Green, Ph.D., Rabbi; Associate Professor of Hebrew and Judaica, Hofstra University, Hempstead, New York: KAUFMANN, YEḤEZKEL

Wm. (William) Scott Green*, Ph.D.; Professor of Religion, University of Miami, Coral Gables, Florida: NEUSNER, JACOB

Aaron Greenbaum, Ph.D., Rabbi; American Joint Distribution Committee, Jerusalem: SAMUEL BEN HOPHNI

Alfred Abraham Greenbaum, Ph.D.; Librarian of the University of Haifa

Avraham Greenbaum, Ph.D.; Senior Lecturer, Modern Jewish History, Haifa; University, and Research Associate, Dinur Institute, the Hebrew University of Jerusalem: JEWISH STUDIES

Fred Greenbaum: CELLER, EMANUEL

Nathan Greenbaum, M.A.; Lecturer in Hebrew Literature and Language, Gratz College; Lecturer in Hebrew, Temple University, Philadelphia: DUSHKIN, ALEXANDER MORDECHAI

Cheryl Greenberg*, Ph.D.; Professor of History, Trinity College, Hartford, Connecticut: BLACK-JEWISH RELATIONS IN THE UNITED STATES

Evelyn Levow Greenberg, Journalist, Washington, D.C.

Joel Greenberg*, B.A., B.Ed.; Professor, University of Waterloo, Canada: DONALDA, PAULINE; HIRSCH, JOHN STEPHEN; RASKY, HENRY; SALTZMAN, HARRY; WAXMAN, AL; WAYNE AND SCHUSTER

Moshe Greenberg, Ph.D., Rabbi; Professor of Bible, the Hebrew University of Jerusalem: AM HA-AREẒ; DECALOGUE; EXODUS, BOOK OF; EZEKIEL; GINSBERG, HAROLD LOUIS; ḤABIRU; ḤEREM; INCEST; LABOR; LEVITICAL CITIES; MOSES; NASH PAPYRUS; OATH; PLAGUES OF EGYPT;

RESURRECTION; SABBATICAL YEAR AND JUBILEE; SEMITES; SPEISER, EPHRAIM AVIGDOR; URIM AND THUMMIM

Daniel Greene*, Ph.D.; Historian, Division of Exhibitions, United States Holocaust Memorial Museum, Washington, D.C.: PHILLIPS, WILLIAM

Jonas C. Greenfield, Ph.D.; Professor of Ancient Semitic Languages, the Hebrew University of Jerusalem: DARIUS; DARIUS THE MEDE; MALKIEL, YAKOV; PHILISTINES; WRITING

Larry (Lawrence) R. Greenfield*, J.D., B.A.; California Director, Republican Jewish Coalition, Los Angeles: REPUBLICAN JEWISH COALITION

Ari Greenspan*, DMD; Efrat, Israel: MATZAH

Charlotte (Joyce) Greenspan*, Ph.D.; Independent Scholar, Alumna of University of California, Berkeley, California: FIELDS, DOROTHY

Leonard J. Greenspoon*, Ph.D.; Professor, Klutznick Chair in Jewish Civilization, Creighton University, Omaha: BIBLE, ANCIENT TRANSLATIONS, SEPTUAGINT

Edward L. Greenstein, B.A., B.H.L.; New York: ALTSCHUL, FRANK; ALTSCHUL, LOUIS; AMTER, ISRAEL; BARRON, JENNIE LOITMAN; BECKER; BEDACHT, MAX; BEHRMAN, MARTIN; BIEN, JULIUS; BITTELMAN, ALEXANDER; BORINSTEIN, LOUIS J.; BRAUDE, MAX A.; BROIDO, LOUIS; BUBLICK, GEDALIAH; DE CORDOVA, JACOB; EISENMAN, CHARLES; HENDRICKS; JAFFA; JOACHIMSEN, PHILIP J.; LOUISIANA; MADISON, JAMES; MELTON, SAMUEL MENDEL; NEW YORK CITY; NEW YORK STATE; PENNSYLVANIA; RATSHESKY, ABRAHAM CAPTAIN; RICE, ISAAC LEOPOLD; ROOSEVELT, FRANKLIN DELANO; ROSENBLATT, SOL ARIEH; STOKES, ROSE PASTOR

Michael Greenstein*, Ph.D.; Professor (retired), Toronto, Canada: CANADIAN LITERATURE

Gideon (M.) Greif*, Ph.D.; Historian, Director, Polish Desk, International School for Holocaust Studies European Department, Yad Vashem, Jerusalem: SONDERKOMMANDO, JEWISH

Ilan Greilsammer*, Ph.D.; Professor of Political Science, Bar-Ilan University, Ramat Gan

Beth (A.) Griech-Polelle*, Ph.D.; Associate Professor of Modern European History, Bowling Green State University, Bowling Green, Ohio: LICHTENBERG, BERNHARD

Zeev Gries, Jerusalem

Tobias Grill*: KAMINKA, ARMAND

Hyman B. Grinstein, Ph.D.; Professor of American Jewish History, Yeshiva University, New York: BLUESTONE, JOSEPH ISAAC; JACKSON, SOLOMON HENRY

Yehoshua M. Grintz, Ph.D.; Professor of Biblical Studies, Tel Aviv University: APOCRYPHA AND PSEUDEPIGRAPHA; ARK OF THE COVENANT; ASHKENAZ; ASHKENZAZ; BALAAM; BARAK; BARUCH; BARUCH, APOCALYPSE OF; BATH-SHEBA; BEL AND THE DRAGON; BENAIAH; BEZALEL; BORSIPPA; ELISHA; ENOCH, ETHIOPIC BOOK OF; EPHOD; GERAR; GERIZIM, MOUNT; GOD; HABAKKUK; HAGGAI; HAMAN; HANANIAH SON OF AZZUR; HANNAH; HEMAN; HEZEKIAH; JAAZANIAH, JAAZANIAHU; JAIR; JAIR; JAMPEL, SIGMUND; JEHOIADA; JEHOIARIB; JEW; JONATHAN BEN UZZIEL; JUBILEES, BOOK OF; JUDITH, BOOK OF; MACCABEES, FIRST BOOK OF; MACCABEES, SECOND BOOK OF; PROVIDENCE; SOLOMON, WISDOM OF; SOUL, IMMORTALITY OF; TEMPLE; TOBIT, BOOK OF; VASHTI; ZECHARIAH (h. pr.); ZECHARIAH (k.); ZECHARIAH (prophet); ZECHARIAH (son of Jeberechiah); ZERAH THE CUSHITE

Alex Grobman*, Ph.D.; President, Institute for Contemporary Jewish Life, Englewood, New Jersey: HOLOCAUST: AFTERMATH; KLAUSNER, ABRAHAM J.

Alfred S. Groh*: WILKES-BARRE AND KINGSTON

David C. Gross*, M.A.; Journalist, New York: PUBLISHING

Jack Gross, Ph.D., M.D.C.M.; Professor of Experimental Medicine and Cancer Research, the Hebrew University-Hadassah Medical School, Jerusalem: BERENBLUM, ISAAC

Walter (Shlomoh) Gross, Dr.Phil.; Journalist, Tel Aviv: WELTSCH, ROBERT

Bernard Grossfeld, Ph.D., Rabbi; Assistant Professor of Hebrew Studies, the University of Wisconsin, Milwaukee: BIBLE

Alan J. Grossman*, Director of Marketing & Communications, UJA Federation of Northern New Jersey: BERGEN COUNTY; HUDSON COUNTY; PATERSON

Avraham Grossman, M.A.; Instructor in History, the University of the Negev, Beersheba: ABRABANEL, ISAAC BEN JUDAH; BEKHOR SHOR, JOSEPH BEN ISAAC; BIBLE; ELIEZER OF BEAUGENCY; KARA, JOSEPH; MENAHEM BEN ḤELBO; RASHI; SAMUEL BEN MEIR

Grace Cohen Grossman*, Senior Curator, Skirball Cultural Center, Los Angeles: MUSEUMS

Lawrence Grossman*, Ph.D.; Editor, *American Jewish Year Book*, New York: YESHIVA CHOVEVEI TORAH; YESHIVA UNIVERSITY

Kurt R. Grossmann, Writer, New York

Mayer Irwin Gruber*, A.B., M.H.L., Ph.D., Litt.H.D.; Professor of Bible and Ancient Near East, Ben-Gurion University of the Negev, Beersheba: HAVILAH; HIVITES; HONOR; JOB, THE BOOK OF; MOURNING; OILS; RED HEIFER; SCEPTER; TIBNI; YEAR

Ruth E. Gruber, B.A.; Journalist, Writer, correspondent for *JTA*, (London) *Jewish Chronicle* and others, photographer specializing on Jewish issues in East-Central Europe, Italy: CZECH REPUBLIC AND SLOVAKIA; CZECHOSLOVAKIA; YUGOSLAVIA

Judy Gruen*, M.S.J.; Writer, Los Angeles: AVRUTICK, ABRAHAM N.; KAMENETSKY, YAAKOV

Kurt Gruenberger, Dr.Jur.; Haifa: MOLLER, HANS

Aaron Gruenhut, M.A.; Librarian, the Jewish National and University

Library, Jerusalem: GURWITSCH, AARON; JOEL, KARL; LIEBERT, ARTHUR

Ithamar Gruenwald, Ph.D.; Lecturer in Jewish Philosophy, Tel Aviv University: MELCHIZEDEK; SONG, ANGELIC

Irene Grumach, Ph.D.; Jerusalem: PERIZZITES; RAMSES; SHISHAK; TIRHAKAH; UZAL

Ralph (E.) Grunewald*, M.A.; Executive Director, National Association of Criminal Defense Lawyers, Washington, D.C.: LERMAN, MILES; OFFICE OF SPECIAL INVESTIGATIONS.; SHER, NEAL

Judith Grunfeld-Rosenbaum, Ph.D.; Educator, London: DEUTSCHLAENDER, LEO

Kurt Grunwald, Dr.rer.Pol.; Economist, Jerusalem: JEWISH COLONIAL TRUST

Inger-Lise Grusd, Oslo: EITINGER, LEO S.

Noe Gruss, Ph.D.; Librarian, Bibliotheque Nationale, Paris: BEUGNOT, AUGUSTE ARTHUR

Regina Grüter (Grueter)*, Ph.D.; Head World War II Research and Archives Unit, Netherlands Red Cross, The Hague, Netherlands: WEINREB, FRIEDRICH

Anne Grynberg*, Ph.D., H.D.R.; Professor of Universities, National Institute of Oriental Languages and Civilizations and Sorbonne, Paris, France: FRENCH LITERATURE

Shlomo Guberman*, M. Jur.; Deputy Attorney-General (Legislation), Retired, Ministry of Justice, Jerusalem: ISRAEL, STATE OF: LEGAL AND JUDICIAL SYSTEM

Alessandro Guetta*, Professor Jewish Thought, Institut National des Langues et Littératures Orientales, Paris: ALATRINI; ALATRINI, ANGELO; BARUCH, JACOB BEN MOSES ḤAYYIM; BASSANI, GIORGIO; BELFORTE, SOLOMON; BENAMOZEGH, ELIJAH BEN ABRAHAM; CALIMANI, SIMONE BEN ABRAHAM; CASTELNUOVO, ENRICO; DA VERONA, GUIDO; DANTE ALIGHIERI; DE BENEDETTI, ALDO; DEBENEDETTI, GIACOMO; FIORENTINO, SALOMONE; FUBINI, MARIO; GORNI; ITALIAN LITERATURE; JEDIDIAH BEN MOSES OF RECANATI; JOHN OF CAPUA; LEGHORN; MOMIGLIANO, ATTILIO; MOMIGLIANO, FELICE; MUSSAFIA, ADOLFO; RIETI

Jacques Yakov Guggenheim, Jerusalem: BARUCH, GREEK APOCALYPSE OF

Florence Guggenheim-Gruenberg, Dr.Sc.Nat.; Historian, Zurich: AARGAU

Terry Guild, Office of Public Affairs, Brandeis University, Waltham, Massachusetts

Yehiel G. Gumpertz, M.D., Jerusalem: BÁRÁNY, ROBERT; JEKUTHIEL BEN JUDAH HA-KOHEN

Herman S. Gundersheimer, Ph.D.; Professor of Art History, Temple University, Philadelphia: ART HISTORIANS AND ART CRITICS

Yosef Guri, M.A.; Senior Teacher in Russian Language, the Hebrew University of Jerusalem: PECHERSKY, ALEXANDER

Aron Gurwitsch, Ph.D.; Professor of Philosophy, the New School for Social Research, New York: HUSSERL, EDMUND GUSTAV ALBRECHT

Hans G. Guterbock, Ph.D.; Professor of Hittitology, the University of Chicago: HITTITES

Simeon L. Guterman, Ph.D.; Professor of History, Yeshiva University, New York: JUSTER, JEAN

Oren Gutfeld*, M.A.; Archaeologist, Institute of Archaeology, the Hebrew University of Jerusalem: HYRCANIA

Itta Gutgluck, B.A.; Jerusalem: BREIDENBACH, WOLF

Israel Gutman, B.A.; Historian, Kibbutz Lehavot ha-Bashan: PARTISANS

Edwin Emanuel Gutmann, Ph.D.; Senior Lecturer in Political Science, the Hebrew University of Jerusalem: EULAU, HEINZ; FINER, HERMAN; HELLER, HERMANN; KIRCHHEIMER, OTTO; KOHN, HANS; LOEWENSTEIN, KARL; ROBSON, WILLIAM ALEXANDER

Joseph Gutmann, Ph.D., Rabbi; Professor of Art History, Wayne State University, Detroit: AGGADAH; HAGGADAH, PASSOVER; JAFFE, MEIR OF ULM

Joshua Gutmann, Emeritus Associate Professor of Jewish History and Jewish Hellenism, the Hebrew University of Jerusalem: ACHISH; AHASUERUS; AHIKAR, BOOK OF; AMAZIAH; ANGARIA; ANGELS AND ANGELOLOGY; ANTISEMITISM; ANTONINUS PIUS; ARISTOBULUS OF PANEAS; ELIJAH; GOD; IDI; OPHIR; URIEL; WARHAFTIG, ZERAH

Linda Gutstein, B.A.; Journalist, New York: BERNHARDT, SARAH; DASSIN, JULES; FOX, WILLIAM

Morris A. Gutstein, Ph.D., D.H.L., Rabbi; Associate Professor of Jewish History and Sociology, the College of Jewish Studies, Chicago: BRITH ABRAHAM; CHICAGO; GREENEBAUM; HORNER, HENRY; MAYER, LEOPOLD; MAYER, LEVY

Henri Guttel, B.A.; Jerusalem: JUDEO-PROVENÇAL; LADINO; ME-AM LO'EZ

Louis (Eliahu) Guttman, Ph.D.; Director, Israel Institute of Applied Research, Jerusalem

Julius Guttmann, Dr.Phil., Rabbi; Professor of Jewish Philosophy, the Hebrew University of Jerusalem: ALEXANDER OF APHRODISIAS

Awni Habash, Ph.D., LL.B.; Lawyer and Sociologist, Bethlehem University: ISRAEL, STATE OF: RELIGIOUS LIFE AND COMMUNITIES

Jacob Haberman, Ph.D., Dr.Jur., Rabbi; Attorney, New York: ABRAHAM BEN MOSES HA-KOHEN HA-SEPHARDI; ASCETICISM; ASHKENAZI, SAUL BEN MOSES HA-KOHEN; BACHARACH, JAIR ḤAYYIM BEN MOSES SAMSON; BACHARACH, MOSES SAMSON BEN ABRAHAM SAMUEL; BELIEF; DASH, SAMUEL; DELMEDIGO, JOSEPH SOLOMON; EGER, AKIVA BEN SIMḤAH BUNIM; EGER, SAMUEL BEN JUDAH LOEB; ELIAKIM GOETZ BEN MEIR; ELIJAH BEN ḤAYYIM; ELIJAH BEN LOEB OF FULDA; GRUENHUT, ELEAZAR; JOSEPH BEN ẒADDIK; JUDAH BEN NISSAN; LICHTENSTADT, BENJAMIN WOLF BEN JUDAH; LICHTSTEIN,

ABRAHAM BEN ELIEZER LIPMAN; LIPSCHUETZ, ISRAEL BEN ELIEZER; LOGIC

Jacob Hirsch Haberman, M.A., Rabbi; Librarian, the Jewish Theological Seminary of America, New York: EHRENTREU, HEINRICH; ENOCH BEN ABRAHAM; FRANKFURTER, MOSES; GEDALIAH, JUDAH; HEILBRONN, JACOB BEN ELHANAN; HELLER, JEHIEL BEN AARON; HELLER, JOSHUA BEN AARON; KAEMPF, SAUL ISAAC; KOERNER, MOSES BEN ELIEZER PHOEBUS; KRONER, THEODOR

Joshua O. Haberman*, D.H.L., Rabbi; Chairman, Foundation for Jewish Studies, Washington, D.C.: HIRSCH, SAMUEL; STEINHEIM, SALOMON LUDWIG

Abraham Meir Habermann, Associate Professor of Medieval Hebrew Literature, Tel Aviv University: AARON ḤAKIMAN; ABI ZIMRA, ISAAC MANDIL BEN ABRAHAM; ABRAHAM BEN ISAAC BEN GARTON; ABUN; ADELKIND, ISRAEL CORNELIUS; ADONIM BEN NISAN HA-LEVI; ALAMANI, AARON HE-ḤAVER BEN YESHU'AH; ALḤADIB, ISAAC BEN SOLOMON BEN ẒADDIK; ALI; ALVAN BEN ABRAHAM; AMITTAI; AMITTAI BEN SHEPHATIAH; AMNON OF MAINZ; ATHIAS, JOSEPH and IMMANUEL; AZHAROT, AZHARAH; BAK; BASS, SHABBETAI BEN JOSEPH; BENJAMIN BEN AZRIEL; BENJAMIN BEN ZERAH; BERECHIAH BEN NATRONAI HA-NAKDAN; BERGMANN, JUDAH; BERLIN; BIBLIOGRAPHY; BIRNBAUM, SOLOMON ASHER; BLOCH; BOMBERG, DANIEL; BOOK TRADE; BRODY, HEINRICH; CARMI, JOSEPH JEDIDIAH; DAVIDSON, ISRAEL; EISENSTEIN, JUDAH DAVID; EPHRAIM BEN ISAAC; EPHRAIM BEN JACOB OF BONN; FRANCES, JACOB BEN DAVID; GANSO, JOSEPH; GENIZAH; GIKATILLA, MOSES BEN SAMUEL HA-KOHEN; ḤĀKIM BI-AMR ALLAH, AL; IBN ALTABBAN, LEVI BEN JACOB; IBN SASSON, SAMUEL BEN JOSEPH; JERUSALEM; KALILA AND DIMNA; KEROVAH; KINAH; LONGO, SAADIAH; MA'ARAVOT; MAQĀMA; MEIR BEN ELIJAH OF NORWICH; PIZMON; POETRY; SAHULA, ISAAC BEN SOLOMON; SAMUEL HA-NAGID; SANTOB DE CARRIÓN; SIMEON BAR ISAAC; SINDABAR; SONCINO; TEHINNAH; TEḤINNAH; TEKI'ATA; WOLF, JOHANN CHRISTOPH; ZARCO, JUDAH

Joseph Hacker, M.A.; Instructor in Jewish History, the Hebrew University of Jerusalem: IBN ḤABIB, JACOB BEN SOLOMON; LERMA, JUDAH BEN SAMUEL; LEVI; LEVI, SOLOMON BEN ISAAC; LEVI, ABRAHAM BEN JOSEPH; LEVI, ISAAC BEN SOLOMON; LEVI, JACOB BEN ISRAEL; LEVI, SOLOMON BEN ISAAC; MEDINA, SAMUEL BEN MOSES DE; MIZRAḤI, ELIJAH; SASSON, AARON BEN JOSEPH

Aviad Hacohen*, Ph.D.; Senior Lecturer and Dean, Sha'arey Mishpat Law College; Faculty of Law, the Hebrew University of Jerusalem: ELON, MENACHEM; PLANNING AND CONSTRUCTION; PUBLIC AUTHORITY; RIGHTS, HUMAN; SEPARATION OF POWERS; TAKKANOT HA-KAHAL

Elisheva Hacohen*, LI.M.; Advocate, Ministry of Justice, Jerusalem: MEDIATION

Mordechai Hacohen, Rabbi; Author, Jerusalem: ABRAMSKY, YEḤEZKEL; AMIEL, MOSHE AVIGDOR; EPSTEIN, BARUCH HA-LEVI; FINKEL, ELIEZER JUDAH; HUTNER, ISAAC; ISRAEL MEIR HA-KOHEN; ISRAEL, STATE OF: RELIGIOUS LIFE AND COMMUNITIES; KAHANEMAN, JOSEPH; KARELITZ, AVRAHAM YESHAYAHU; KASOVSKY, CHAYIM YEHOSHUA; KLUGER, SOLOMON BEN JUDAH AARON; KOTLER, AARON; LEIBOWITZ, BARUCH BER; MAISEL, ELIJAH ḤAYYIM; MEIR SIMḤAH HA-KOHEN OF DVINSK; MELTZER, ISSER ZALMAN; RATH, MESHULLAM; SHAPIRA, MEIR; SHKOP, SIMEON JUDAH; SHVADRON, SHALOM MORDECAI BEN MOSES; SOLOVEICHIK; SOLOVEICHIK, ḤAYYIM; SOLOVEICHIK, JOSEPH BAER, OF VOLOZHIN; TIKTINSKI; WASSERMAN, ELHANAN BUNIM; WEINBERG, JEHIEL JACOB

Shmuel Avidor Hacohen, Rabbi; Writer, Lecturer, Tel Aviv: SCHNEERSOHN, MENAḤEM MENDEL

Jesaia Hadari, Rabbi; Jerusalem

Amnon Hadary, Ph.D.; Writer and Researcher, Jerusalem: JEWISH AGENCY; ZIONIST CONGRESSES

Gershon Hadas, B.A., Rabbi; Kansas City, Missouri: FEDERBUSCH, SIMON; KANSAS CITY

Gideon Hadas*, Ph.D.; Archaeologist, Director of Ein Gedi Oasis Excavations Delegation, Kibbutz Ein Gedi, Israel: EN-GEDI

Pepita Haezrahi, Ph.D.; Senior Lecturer in Philosophy, the Hebrew University of Jerusalem: BERGSON, HENRI LOUIS; BRUNSCHVICG, LEON

Barbara Hahn*, Dr.Phil.; Professor, Vanderbilt University, Nashville, Tennessee: SALONS

Gerlinde Haid*: MAUTNER, KONRAD

Abraham Haim, M.A.; Assistant Lecturer, Department of Middle Eastern Studies, Tel Aviv University: ADJIMAN; AKRA; AMASIYA; ANTIOCH; AYDIN; CAPITULATIONS; CARMONA, BEKHOR ISAAC DAVID; DEHOK; FONSECA, DANIEL DE; HIT; ISTANBUL; IZMIT; JUBAR; KHANAQIN; KUFA; KUFA; MANISSA; MERSIN; SHAKI, ISAAC; SULEIMAN I; TOKAT

Andre Hajdu, M.A., Lecturer in Music, Tel Aviv University and Bar-Ilan University, Ramat Gan: ḤASIDISM; SZABOLCSI, BENCE

Amos Hakham, B.A.; Researcher, Jerusalem: KITTIM

Monika Halbinger*, M.A.; Ph.D. student; Chair for Jewish History and Culture, Ludwig-Maximilians-Universität, Munich, Germany: GROSSMANN, KURT RICHARD; MARX, KARL; ROSENBERG, LUDWIG; ROSENTHAL, PHILIPP; SPRINGER, AXEL CAESAR; WEICHMANN, HERBERT; WEIGEL, HELENE

Elimelech Epstein Halevy, M.A.; Visiting Senior Lecturer in Aggadah, Tel Aviv University: AARON; ADAM; ALEXANDER THE GREAT; AMALEKITES; AMRAM; BEZALEL; CAIN; ELI; HAGAR; ISAIAH; JEROBOAM; JOAB; JONAH, BOOK OF; JONATHAN; JOSHUA; NOAH

David Weiss Halivni, D.H.L., Rabbi; Professor of Rabbinics, the Jewish Theological Seminary of America; Adjunct Professor of Religion, Columbia University, New York: ZUCKER, MOSHE

Abraham Solomon Halkin, Ph.D.; Emeritus Professor of History, the Jewish Theological Seminary of America, Jerusalem: AKNIN, JOSEPH BEN JUDAH BEN JACOB IBN; AMERICAN ACADEMY FOR JEWISH RESEARCH; AVENDAUTH; FINKEL, JOSHUA; IBN BARUN, ABU IBRAHIM ISAAC BEN JOSEPH IBN BENVENISTE; JEDAIAH BEN ABRAHAM BEDERSI; JUDEO-ARABIC LITERATURE; SAADIAH GAON;

SPIEGEL, SHALOM; TRANSLATION AND TRANSLATORS

Hillel Halkin, M.A.; Jerusalem: AM OLAM; ARVEY, JACOB M.; ATRAN, FRANK Z.; BAMBERGER, BERNARD JACOB; ELKUS, ABRAM ISAAC; FALK; FISHER, MAX M.; FREEHOF, SOLOMON BENNETT; GREENBERG, HAYIM; GROSSINGER, JENNIE; HOWE, IRVING; HURWITZ, HENRY; JEWISH DAILY FORWARD; JEWISH DAY; JEWISH MORNING JOURNAL; KAHN, BERNARD; KANE, IRVING; LEHMAN, HERBERT HENRY; LIEBERMAN, ELIAS; MAILER, NORMAN; MENORAH ASSOCIATION AND MENORAH JOURNAL; NEW YORK CITY; NEWSPAPERS, HEBREW; RAYNER, ISIDOR; RICE, JAMES P.; ROSE, ERNESTINE POTOVSKY; ROSENBACH, ABRAHAM SIMON WOLF; SCHULMAN, SAMUEL; SHALOM, ISAAC I.; SOCIALISM; SONNEBORN, RUDOLF GOLDSCHMIDT; STONE, DEWEY D.; SWIG, BENJAMIN HARRISON; TSUKUNFT; UNITED STATES LITERATURE; WOLF; YIDISHER KEMFER

Moshe Hallamish, M.A.; Instructor in Jewish Philosophy, Bar-Ilan University, Ramat Gan: ḤAYYIM ḤAYKL BEN SAMUEL OF AMDUR; JACOB JOSEPH BEN ẒEVI HA-KOHEN KATZ OF POLONNOYE; JEHIEL MICHAEL OF ZLOCZOW; JERUSALEM; JOSEPH BEN SHALOM ASHKENAZI; KORETS, PHINEHAS BEN ABRAHAM ABBA SHAPIRO OF; MOSES ḤAYYIM EPHRAIM OF SUDYLKOW; REUBEN HOESHKE BEN HOESHKE KATZ; ẒEMAḤ, JACOB BEN ḤAYYIM

Morris Halle, Ph.D.; Professor of Modern Languages, Massachusetts Institute of Technology, Cambridge: JAKOBSON, ROMAN

Eileen Hallet Stone*: UTAH

William W. Hallo, Ph.D.; Professor of Assyriology and Curator of the Babylonian Collection, Yale University, New Haven, Connecticut: AKKAD; HARAN; MESOPOTAMIA

Abraham Halperin, Ph.D.; Professor of Physics, the Hebrew University of Jerusalem: NEW BRUNSWICK; NEW JERSEY

Dan Halperin, B.A.; Economist and Journalist, Jerusalem

Liora R. Halperin*, Ph.D.; Student Jewish History, University of California, Los Angeles, California: ROTH, JOEL

Vladimir Seev Halperin, Ph.D.; Director of the World ORT Union, Geneva: ORT; SYNGALOWSKI, ARON

Baruch Halpern*, Ph.D.; Chaiken Family Chair of Jewish Studies; Professor of History; Classics and Ancient Mediterranean Studies, and Religious Studies, Penn State, University Park, Pennsylvania: DAVID

Israel Halpern, M.A.; Professor of Jewish History, the Hebrew University of Jerusalem: ABRAHAM BEN ḤAYYIM; ABRAHAM BEN JOSEPH OF LISSA; CZACKI, TADEUSZ; DEMBITZER, ḤAYYIM NATHAN; FORTIS, ABRAHAM ISAAC; FRENK, EZRIEL NATHAN; HANNOVER, NATHAN NATA; JAROSLAW; LEWIN, LOUIS; MEIR BEN SAMUEL OF SHCHERBRESHIN; SCHIPER, IGNACY

Janice Halpern*, M.D.; Psychiatrist, University of Toronto, Toronto, Canada: FREUD, SIGMUND

Joseph Halpern, M.A., Reverend; Educator and Writer, Ramat Gan, Israel: CHILDREN'S LITERATURE

Lipman Halpern, M.D.; Professor of Neurology, the Hebrew University-Hadassah Medical School, Jerusalem: GOLDSTEIN, KURT

Nikki Halpern*, Institut Charles V, Paris: STEINBARG, ELIEZER

Stanley Halpern*: GARY; SAN DIEGO

Ernest Hamburger, Ph.D.; Political Scientist, New York: ARONS, LEO; BAERWALD, MORITZ; BARTHOLDY, JACOB; ROZIN, JOSEPH

Reuven Hammer, Ph.D., Rabbi; Department of Rabbinics, Jewish Theological Seminary of America; Dean of Jerusalem School and Director of Seminary of Judaic Studies, JTS, Jerusalem

Liz Hamui (Halabe)*, Ph.D.; Professor in Social Science, Universidad Iberoamericana, Mexico City: MEXICO

Samuel (B.) Hand*, Ph.D.; Professor Emeritus, University of Vermont: ROSENMAN, SAMUEL IRVING

Michael Handelsaltz, B.A.; Theater Critic, Book Review Editor, Haaretz, Tel Aviv: ISRAEL, STATE OF: CULTURAL LIFE

Amy Handelsman*, B.A.; Producer, Writer, Los Angeles and New York: RUDNER, RITA; SABAN, HAIM; SANDLER, ADAM RICHARD; SINGER, BRYAN; STAR, DARREN; STILLER, BEN; TOBACK, JAMES; WANAMAKER, SAM

Joëlle Hansel*, Ph.D.; Lecturer, the Hebrew University of Jerusalem: LUZZATTO, MOSES ḤAYYIM

Nelly Hansson*, Ph.D.; Executive Director, Fondation du judaïsme français, Paris, France: KLEIN, THEODORE; LEVY, BERNARD-HENRI; MUSÉE D'ART ET D'HISTOIRE DU JUDAÏSME; VEIL, SIMONE

Menahem Haran, Ph.D.; Associate Professor of Bible, the Hebrew University of Jerusalem: AMOS; HOLINESS CODE; MENORAH; NEHUSHTAN; POOR, PROVISION FOR THE; PRIESTLY VESTMENTS; PRIESTS AND PRIESTHOOD; PROVERB; SHEWBREAD; VATKE, WILHELM; WETTE, DE, WILHELM MARTIN LEBERECHT; WINCKLER, HUGO

Yuval Harari*, Ph.D.; Lecturer, Hebrew Literature - Program of Folklore Studies, Ben-Gurion University of the Negev, Beersheba: MAGIC

Israel Harburg, B.A., Rabbi; Lynn, Massachusetts

Shoshana Hareli, M.A.; Haifa: MO'EẒET HA-PO'ALOT; PIONEER WOMEN

Shulamith Hareven, Writer, Jerusalem: POTOK, CHAIM

Yehoshafat Harkabi, Ph.D.; Major General (Res.), Israel Defense Forces; Senior Lecturer in International Relations and Middle Eastern Studies, the Hebrew University of Jerusalem

Angela Kim Harkins*, Ph.D.; Assistant Professor of Theology, Duquesne University, Pittsburgh, Pennsylvania: BIBLE, ANCIENT TRANSLATIONS, LATIN

Franklin T. Harkins*, Ph.D.; Lilly Fellow and Lecturer in Theology,

Valparaiso University, Indiana: BIBLE, ANCIENT TRANSLATIONS, LATIN

Jules Harlow, Rabbi; Director of Publications, Rabbinical Assembly of America

Isaac Harpaz, Ph.D.; Associate Professor of Agricultural Entomology, the Hebrew University of Jerusalem: AVIDOV, ZVI; HANNOVER, NATHAN NATA

Nisan Harpaz, Chairman, Brit Ivrit Olamit

Jay Harris*: BAND, ARNOLD; BERGER, DAVID; BIALE, DAVID; BOYARIN, DANIEL; CARLEBACH, ELISHEVA; CHAZAN, ROBERT; COHEN, SHAYE J. D.

Lucien Harris, M.A.; Hadassah Medical Organization, Jerusalem: FEIGENBAUM, ARYEH; MICHAELSON, ISAAC CHESAR

Monford Harris, D.H.L.; Professor of Religious Studies, the University of Toronto: HERBERG, WILL

Laszlo Harsanyi, D.L.; Historian, Budapest: BAJA; BALASSAGYARMAT; BODROGKERESZTÚR; KÖSZEG; LIPSHITZ, ISRAEL; MISKOLC; NYIREGYHAZA; PAPA

Michael Harsgor, Ph.D.; Professor, Aranne School of History, Tel Aviv University: PORTUGAL

Judah Harstein*, B.Sc.; Head of Jewish Education, World ORT, London, England: ORT

Alexander Hart*, Ph.D.; Lecturer, University of British Columbia, Vancouver, Canada: MICHAELS, ANNE; STEINFELD, J.J.

David Hartman, Ph.D., Rabbi; Director, Shalom Hartman Institute, Jerusalem

Geoffrey H. Hartman, Ph.D.; Professor of English and Comparative Literature, Yale University, New Haven, Connecticut

Harriet Hartman*, Ph.D.; Professor of Sociology, Rowan University, Glassboro, New Jersey: SOCIOLOGY; STEINEM, GLORIA

Heinz Hartman, M.D.; Physician, Syracuse, New York: SANDMEL, SAMUEL

Louis F. Hartman, L.S.S., L.O.L.; Professor of Semitic and Egyptian Languages and Literatures, the Catholic University of America, Washington, D.C.: ESCHATOLOGY; GOD, NAMES OF

Steven Harvey*, Ph.D.; Professor of Philosophy, Bar-Ilan University, Ramat Gan: AVERROES

Warren Zev Harvey*, Ph.D.; Professor of Jewish Thought, the Hebrew University of Jerusalem: CRESCAS, ḤASDAI BEN JUDAH; IBN SHEM TOV, ISAAC BEN SHEM TOV; IBN SHEM TOV, SHEM TOV; IBN SHEM TOV, SHEM TOV BEN JOSEPH BEN SHEM TOV; PHILOSOPHY, JEWISH

Galit Hasan-Rockem, B.A.; Assistant in Hebrew Literature, the Hebrew University of Jerusalem: FABLE

Wendy Haslem*, Ph.D.; Lecturer, Cinema Studies, University of Melbourne: DEREN, MAYA

Isaac Hasson*, Ph.D.; Associate Professor, the Hebrew University of Jerusalem: JERUSALEM; JIHĀD; UMAYYADS

Shlomo Hasson, B.A.; Jerusalem: AKABA; ḤADERAH; ḤAẒOR; ḤOLON; KIRYAT ONO; LYDDA; MIẒPEH RAMON; NETANYAH; OR AKIVA; PETAḤ TIKVAH; RAMLEH; ROSH HA-AYIN; SHARM EL-SHEIKH, TIRĀN ISLAND, and TIRĀN STRAITS; SHEFARAM; SODOM AND GOMORRAH; ʾUSIFIYYĀ; YEHUD; YEROḤAM

Theodore Hatalgui, M.A.; the Jewish National Fund, Jerusalem: GRANOTT, ABRAHAM; GRANOTT, ABRAHAM

Susan Hattis Rolef*, Ph.D.; Senior Researcher in the Knesset Information Division, The Knesset, Jerusalem: AḤDUT HA-AVODAH-PO'ALEI ZION; ALLON, YIGAL; ALMOGI, YOSEF AHARON; ALONI, SHULAMIT; AMIT, MEIR; ARIDOR, YORAM; AVNERY. URI; BARAK, EHUD; BARAM, MOSHE; BARAM, UZI; BARKAT, REUVEN; BAR-LEV, HAIM; BEGIN, MENAḤEM; BEGIN, ZE'EV BINYAMIN; BEILIN, YOSSI; BEN-AHARON, YITZḤAK; BEN-ELIEZER, BINYAMIN; BEN-GURION, DAVID; BEN-PORAT, MORDEKHAI; BENTOV, MORDEKHAI; BERIT SHALOM; BI-NATIONALISM; BURG, AVRAHAM; BURG, JOSEPH; COHEN, GEULAH; DAYAN, MOSHE; DAYAN, YAEL; DEMOCRATIC MOVEMENT FOR CHANGE; DERI, ARYEH; EHRLICH, SIMḤA; EITAN, RAPHAEL; ELDAD, ISRAEL; ELIAV, ARIE LOVA; ESHKOL, LEVI; GAḤAL; GALILI, ISRAEL; GENERAL ZIONISTS; GRUENBAUM, YIẒḤAK; GUR, MORDECAI; HACOHEN, DAVID; HAMMER, ZEVULUN; ḤAZAN, YA'AKOV; HERUT MOVEMENT; HERZOG, CHAIM; HILLEL, SHLOMO; HURWITZ, YIGAEL; IDELSON, BEBA; INDEPENDENT LIBERAL PARTY; ISRAEL LABOR PARTY; ISRAEL, STATE OF: POLITICAL LIFE AND PARTIES; ITZIK, DALIA; JOSEPH, DOV; KACH; KAPLAN, ELIEZER; KATZAV, MOSHE; KESSAR, ISRAEL; KHOUSHI, ABBA; KNESSET; KOL, MOSHE; KOLLEK, TEDDY; LAHAT, SHLOMO; LAPID, JOSEPH; LAVON AFFAIR, THE; L'AVON, PINHAS; LEVY, DAVID; LIBAI, DAVID; LIKUD; LIVNAT, LIMOR; LOPOLIANSKY, URI; LUZ, KADISH; MAIMON, ADA; MAPAI; MAPAM; MEIR, GOLDA; MERETZ; MERIDOR, DAN; MESHEL, YERUHAM; MILO, RONI; NAMIR, MORDECHAI; NAMIR, ORA; NATIONAL RELIGIOUS PARTY; NAVON, ITZHAK; NE'EMAN, YUVAL; NIR-RAFALKES, NAHUM; NUROCK, MORDECHAI; PA'IL, MEIR; PATT, GIDEON; PERES, SHIMON; PERETZ, AMIR; PO'ALEI AGUDAT YISRAEL; PO'ALEI AGUDAT YISRAEL; PORUSH, MENACHEM; RABIN, YITZHAK; RAMON, HAIM; RAPHAEL, YITZHAK; REMEZ, MOSHE DAVID; RUBINSTEIN, AMNON; SAPIR, PINHAS; SHAHAL, MOSHE; SHALOM, SILVAN; SHAMIR, YITZHAK; SHARANSKY, NATAN; SHARETT, MOSHE; SHARON, ARIEL; SHAS; SHAZAR, SHNEUR ZALMAN; SHEETRIT, MEIR; SHEM-TOV, VICTOR; SHERF, ZE'EV; SHINUI; SHOHAT, AVRAHAM BEIGA; SNEH, MOSHE; SPRINZAK, JOSEPH; TABENKIN, YIẒḤAK; TAMIR, SHMUEL; TSABAN, YA'IR; TSOMET; WEIZMAN, EZER; YA'ACOBI, GAD; YAARI, MEIR; YA'ARI, MEIR; YADIN, YIGAEL; YELLIN-MOR, NATHAN; YESHAYAHU-SHARABI, ISRAEL; ẒADOK, ḤAIM JOSEPH; ZE'EVI, REHAVAM

G. Eric Hauck, B.A.; Journalist, New York: LERNER, ALAN JAY; THALBERG, IRVING GRANT; WYLER, WILLIAM

Yehuda Martin Hausman*, B.A., M.A.; Rabbinic Student, Yeshiva Chovevei Torah, Rabbinic Seminary, Los Angeles: ABRAMS, ELLIOTT; ABRAMS, ROBERT; ARONSON, ARNOLD; BOOKBINDER, HYMAN H.

Meir Havazelet, Ph.D., D.H.L., Rabbi; Professor of Rabbinic Literature and of Bible, Yeshiva University, New York: ABBA; ḤANINA KAHANA BEN HUNA; JACOB HA-KOHEN BAR MORDECAI; JOSEPH BAR ABBA; JOSEPH BAR ḤIYYA; KOHEN-ẒEDEK BAR IVOMAI; MEIR BA'AL HA-NES, TOMB OF; NAHSHON BAR ZADOK; NATRONAI BAR HILAI; NATRONAI BAR NEHEMIAH; PALTOI BAR ABBAYE; RABBAH; SAR SHALOM BEN BOAZ; SHERIRA BEN ḤANINA GAON; ZADOK BAR MAR YISHI; ẒEMAḤ BEN ḤAYYIM; ẒEMAḤ BEN PALTOI

Shlomoh Zalman Havlin, Rabbi; Research Assistant, the Institute for Research in Jewish Law, the Hebrew University of Jerusalem: AARON BEN JACOB HA-KOHEN OF LUNEL; ANAV, JEHIEL BEN JEKUTHIEL BEN BENJAMIN HA-ROFE; ANAV, JUDAH BEN BENJAMIN HA-ROFE; ELISHA BEN ABRAHAM; GERSHOM BEN SOLOMON; HADRAN; HAGGAHOT; HAGGAHOT MAIMUNIYYOT; HA-ḤINNUKH; HANANEL BEN SAMUEL; HEZEKIAH BEN JACOB; ISAAC BEN ABRAHAM; ISAAC BEN ABRAHAM OF NARBONNE; ISAAC BEN ASHER HA-LEVI; ISAAC BEN JACOB HA-LAVAN OF PRAGUE; ISAAC BEN JUDAH OF MAINZ; ISAAC BEN MEIR; ISAAC BEN MERWAN HA-LEVI; ISAAC BEN MORDECAI; ISAAC BEN MOSES OF VIENNA; ISAAC BEN TODROS OF BARCELONA; ISAAC FROM OURVILLE; JACOB BEN NISSIM IBN SHAHIN; JUDAH BEN ISAAC; KOKHAVI, DAVID BEN SAMUEL; KOL BO; LUBETZKY, JUDAH; MANOAH OF NARBONNE; MEIR BEN SIMEON HA-ME'ILI; MESHULLAM BEN JACOB OF LUNEL; PARDO, DAVID SAMUEL BEN JACOB; PERAḤYAH BEN NISSIM; SAMSON BEN ABRAHAM OF SENS; SARDI, SAMUEL BEN ISAAC; SCHLETTSTADT, SAMUEL BEN AARON; SIMḤAH BEN SAMUEL OF SPEYER

Christine (Elizabeth) Hayes*, Ph.D.; Professor of Religious Studies in Classical Judaica, Yale University, New Haven, Connecticut: PURITY AND IMPURITY, RITUAL

Saul Hayes, M.A., Q.C.; Executive Vice President of the Canadian Jewish Congress; Lecturer in Social Work, McGill University, Montreal

Yaakov Arie Hazan, Member of the Knesset; Kibbutz Mishmar ha-Emek: KIBBUTZ MOVEMENT

Aviva Hazaz, M.A.; Jerusalem: HAZAZ, ḤAYYIM

David Hazony*, M.A.; Editor in Chief of the *Journal Azure*, The Shalem Center, Jerusalem: BERKOVITS, ELIEZER

Barth Healey, B.A.; Journalist, New York: FRIENDLY, FRED W.; JESSEL, GEORGE ALBERT

Lee Healey, New York: NICHOLS, MIKE; ROSE, BILLY; SELLERS, PETER; STREISAND, BARBRA; TUCKER, SOPHIE; ZIEGFELD, FLORENZ

Ernest Hearst, Editor, Wiener Library, London: NEO-FASCISM; NEO-NAZISM; NEW LEFT

Jacob Heilbrunn*, M.A.; Editorial Writer, *Los Angeles Times*, Washington, D.C.: BELL, DANIEL; KRISTOL, IRVING; KRISTOL, WILLIAM

Samuel C. Heilman, Ph.D.; Professor, holder of the Harold Proshansky Chair in Jewish Studies Graduate Center of the City University of New York: FEUERSTEIN; ḤAREDIM

Joseph Heinemann, Ph.D.; Senior Lecturer in Hebrew Literature, the Hebrew University of Jerusalem: AMIDAH; ANTISEMITISM; LEVITICUS RABBAH; NAHSHON; PREACHING; RED SEA; ZECHARIAH; ZENTRALE STELLE DER LANDESJUSTIZVERWALTUNGEN

Dirk Heisserer*, Dr. Phil.; Scientist of Literature, LMU, Munich: MANN, THOMAS

Petra Heldt*, Ph.D.; Professor of History of the Church in the East and the Early Writings of the Church, the Hebrew University of Jerusalem: ORIGEN

Leonardo Hellemberg, Managua, Nicaragua: NICARAGUA

Bernard Heller, Ph.D., Rabbi; New York: ADAM

Joseph Elijah Heller, Dr.Phil.; *Encyclopaedia Judaica* (Germany); Lecturer in Hebrew, University College, London: ANDRADE, VELOSINO JACOB DE; BALMES, ABRAHAM BEN MEIR DE; BERLIN, DAVID BEN LOEB; CAMPEN, JOHANNES VAN; CARDOZO, ISAAC; CARVALHO, MORDECAI BARUCH; COHN, LEOPOLD; CUENQUE, ABRAHAM BEN LEVI; DAVID BEN SAUL; DENIS, ALBERTUS; FRANCK, ADOLPHE; FRANKEL, ZACHARIAS; FREUDENTHAL, JACOB; GAFFAREL, JACQUES; GERONDI, MOSES BEN SOLOMON D'ESCOLA; GERONDI, ZERAHIAH BEN ISAAC HA-LEVI; HAAS, SOLOMON BEN JEKUTHIEL KAUFMANN; HESS, MENDEL; HOECHHEIMER, MOSES BEN ḤAYYIM COHEN; ISRAEL BEN BENJAMIN OF BELZEC; ISRAEL BEN JONATHAN FROM LECZYCA; JACOB BEN MORDECAI OF SCHWERIN; KAHANA, ABRAHAM ARYEH LEIB BEN SHALOM SHAKHNA; KARAITES; KARGAU, MENAHEM MENDEL BEN NAPHTALI HIRSCH; KOENIGSBERGER, BERNHARD; LANDAUER, MEYER HEINRICH HIRSCH; LEUSDEN, JOHANN; LUTHER, MARTIN; MOSES BEN MENAHEM GRAF

Kathryn Hellerstein*, Ph.D.; Ruth Meltzer Senior Lecturer in Yiddish and Jewish Studies, Department of Germanic Languages and Literatures, University of Pennsylvania: DROPKIN, CELIA; MARGOLIN, ANNA; MOLODOWSKY, KADIA

Sara O. Heller-Wilensky, Ph.D.; Associate Professor of Jewish Philosophy, Bar-Ilan University, Ramat Gan, Tel Aviv University, and Haifa University: ARAMA, ISAAC BEN MOSES

Yehuda Hellman, Executive Director of the Conference of Presidents of Major American Jewish Organizations; Secretary General of the World Conference of Jewish Organizations, New York: WORLD CONFERENCE OF JEWISH ORGANIZATIONS

Melila Hellner-Eshed*, Ph.D.; Lecturer, Jewish Studies, the Hebrew University of Jerusalem: ZOHAR

Marilyn Henry*, M.P.A., M.A.; Journalist, Teaneck, New Jersey: CONFERENCE ON JEWISH MATERIAL CLAIMS AGAINST GERMANY

Dana Herman*, B.A., M.A.; Doctoral Candidate, McGill University, Montreal, Canada: JEWISH CULTURAL RECONSTRUCTION INC.

Jan Herman, Ph.D.; State Jewish Museum, Prague: BENEŠOV; BOHEMIA; GOLCUV JENIKOV; HERMANUV MESTEC; HROZNETIN; JOSEPH II; KADAN; KASEJOVICE; KLATOVY; KOSOVÁ HORA; LIBEREC; LITOMERICE; LOUNY; MLADA

BOLESLAV; MOST; NOVY BYDZOV; PILSEN; POLNA; PRAGUE; ROUDNICE NAD LABEM; SOBEDRUHY; TABOR; TEPLICE; TURNOV; UDLICE; USTEK; VOTICE; ZATEC

Zvi Herman, Rabbi; Former Member of the Jewish Agency Executive; Former Managing Director of the Zim Israel Navigation Company, Haifa: ZIM

Zvi Hermon, Dr.Phil., Rabbi; Adjunct Professor of Criminology and Corrections, Center for the Study of Crime, Delinquency, and Corrections, Southern Illinois University, Carbondale: ABRAHAMSEN, DAVID; ALEXANDER, FRANZ; CRIME; CRIMINOLOGY; DRAPKIN, ISRAEL; EATON, JOSEPH W.; FRIEDLANDER, KATE; GLUECK, SHELDON; GRUENHUT, MAX; GUNZBURG, NIKO; GUTTMACHER, MANFRED; HENRIQUES; HURWITZ, STEPHAN; KROSS, ANNA; LOMBROSO, CESARE; MANNHEIM, HERMANN; SCHAFER, STEPHEN

Moshe David Herr, Ph.D.; Lecturer in Jewish History, the Hebrew University of Jerusalem: AGE AND THE AGED; AGGADAT BERESHIT; ALBECK; ANTIGONUS OF SOKHO; APTOWITZER, VICTOR; AVODAH ZARAH; BANETH; BAVA MEẒIA; BRUELL; BRUELL, JACOB; CHURCH FATHERS; DAY OF ATONEMENT; DEUTERONOMY RABBAH; ECCLESIASTES RABBAH; EDOM; ESAU; ESTHER RABBAH; EXODUS RABBAH; FASTING AND FAST DAYS; FESTIVALS; GENESIS RABBAH; GUTMANN, JOSHUA; GUTTMANN, MICHAEL; HANANIAH BEN TERADYON; ḤANUKKAH; HOFFMANN, DAVID ẒEVI; HOROVITZ, SAUL; JABNEH; JACOB OF KEFAR SAKHNAYYA; JOSHUA BEN KORḤA; JOSHUA BEN PERAḤYAH; JUDAH BEN BAVA; JUDAH BEN TABBAI; JUDAH BEN TEMA; LAMENTATIONS RABBAH; MIDRASHIM, SMALLER; MIDRESHEI AGGADAH; MINHAG; MONOGAMY; NUMBERS RABBAH; PIRKEI DE-RABBI ELIEZER; PROSTITUTION; ROME; SHAMMAI; TEN MARTYRS, THE; THEODOR, JULIUS; TRAJAN, MARCUS ULPIUS; URBACH, EPHRAIM ELIMELECH; WEISS, ISAAC HIRSCH; YOSE BEN JOEZER OF ZEREDAH; YOSE BEN JOHANAN HA-TANNA OF JERUSALEM; YOSE BEN KISMA; YOSE BEN ZIMRA; ZIEGLER, IGNAZ; ZUCKERMANDEL, MOSES SAMUEL

Eli Herscher*, M.A.H.L., Rabbi; Stephen S. Wise Temple, Los Angeles: ZELDIN, ISAIAH

Lucian-Zeev Herscovici*, M.A.; Historian; Librarian, Jewish National and University Library, Jerusalem: ADAM; ADERCA, FELIX; ARTZI, YITZHAK; AXELRAD, AVRAM; BACAU; BALLY, DAVICION; BALLY, ISAAC DAVID; BALTAZAR, CAMIL; BANUS, MARIA; BARANGA, AUREL; BARASCH, JULIUS; BARLAD; BERLIAND, SHLOMO MEIR; BLANK, MAURICE; BOTOSANI; BRAILA; BRESLASU, MARCEL; BUCHAREST; BUHUSI; BURDUJENI; BUZAU; C.D.E.; CAJAL, NICOALE; CALIN, VERA; CAMPULUNG MOLDOVENESC; CARP, HORIA; CONSTANTA; CRAIOVA; DARABANI; DOMINIC, ALEXANDRU; DORIAN, DOREL; DOROHOI; EGALITATEA; FALTICENI; FERARU, LEON; FOCSANI; GALATI; GASTON-MARIN, GHEORGHE; GERTSA; GHELERTER, LUDWIG LITMAN; GRAUR, CONSTANTIN; GURA-HUMORULUI; HAIMOVICI, MENDEL; HARLAU; HASEFER; HEFTER, ALFRED; HUSI; LAVI, THEODOR; LUCA, B.; ROMANIA

Leo Hershkowitz, Ph.D.; Associate Professor of History, Queens College of the City University of New York: ABRAHAMS, ABRAHAM ISAAC; ABRAHAMS, ISAAC; BARSIMSON, JACOB; BROWN, SAUL PARDO; BUSH, SOLOMON; DE LUCENA; FRANKS, DAVID; FRANKS, DAVID SALISBURY; FRANKS, JACOB; GOMEZ; GRATZ; ISAACS, JOSEPH; JOSEPHSON, MANUEL; KURSHEEDT, ISRAEL BAER; LEVY, AARON; LEVY, ASSER; LEVY, HAYMAN; LEVY, MOSES; MYERS, MORDECAI; NATHAN; NATHAN; NEW YORK CITY; NOAH, MORDECAI MANUEL; PACHECO, RODRIGO BENJAMIN MENDES; PINTO, ISAAC; SALOMON, HAYM; SEIXAS; WAGG, ABRAHAM

Zvi Yehuda Hershlag, Ph.D.; Professor of Economic History and the Economics of Developing Countries, Tel Aviv University: BONNÉ, ALFRED ABRAHAM

Eli Herstein*, Publisher, Yanshuf Publishing, Zur Moshe, Israel: SCIENCE FICTION AND FANTASY, JEWISH

Deborah Hertz*, Ph.D.; Wouk Chair in Modern Jewish Studies, University of California at San Diego: MENDELSSOHN-VEIT-SCHLEGEL, DOROTHEA; VARNHAGEN, RAHEL LEVIN

Arthur Hertzberg, Ph.D., Rabbi; Associate Adjunct Professor of History, Columbia University, New York: ANTISEMITISM; ASSIMILATION; BARON, SALO WITTMAYER; DEISTS; FRENCH REVOLUTION; JEWISH IDENTITY; MONTESQUIEU, CHARLES LOUIS DE SECONDAT, BARON DE LA BREDE ET DE; NUMERUS CLAUSUS; ZIONISM

Abel Jacob Herzberg, Dr.Jur.; Attorney, Amsterdam: VUGHT; WESTERBORK

Avigdor (Yitshaq) Herzog*, M.A.; Lecturer in Jewish Traditional Music, Bar-Ilan University, Ramat Gan: ADON OLAM; AḤOT KETANNAH; INDIA; PSALMS, BOOK OF; SCROLLS, THE FIVE

Chaim Herzog, LL.B.; Major General (Res.), Israel Defense Forces; Military Commentator and Business Executive, Tel Aviv: ISRAEL, STATE OF: DEFENSE FORCES; SIX-DAY WAR; YOM KIPPUR WAR

Abraham Joshua Heschel, Ph.D., Rabbi; Professor of Jewish Ethics and Mysticism, the Jewish Theological Seminary of America, New York

Susannah Heschel*, Ph.D.; Professor Dartmouth College, Hanover, New Hampshire: FEMINISM; GEIGER, ABRAHAM; LILITH

Irene Heskes, Musicologist, New York: RECORDS, PHONOGRAPH

Moshe Hesky, Dr.Jur.; Former Adviser, Philatelic Services, Israel Ministry of Posts; England: STAMPS

Carolyn Hessel*: JEWISH BOOK COUNCIL, THE

R. (Renate) Heuer*, Dr.Phil.; Director, Archiv Bibliographia Judaica, Johann Wolfgang Goethe-Universität, Frankfurt, Germany: REICHER, EMANUEL

Andreas Heusler*, Dr.Phil., M.A.; Senior Scholar, Munich City Archives, Munich, Germany: MERZBACHER, GOTTFRIED; NEUMEYER, ALFRED; NEUMEYER, KARL

Viveka Heyman, M.A.; Teacher in Swedish, Tel Aviv University: JOSEPHSON; SCANDINAVIAN LITERATURE

Michael Heymann, Ph.D.; Director of the Central Zionist Archives,

Jerusalem: HANTKE, ARTHUR; HERLITZ, GEORG

Zalman Heyn, Ministry of Labor, Jerusalem: ISRAEL, STATE OF: LABOR

Eugene B. Hibshman, B.A., B.H., Rabbi; Sioux Falls, South Dakota

Alter Hilewitz, Ph.D., Rabbi; Principal, Hebrew Teachers Training College and Hebrew Training College for Ministers and Rabbis, Johannesburg, South Africa: AḤAI; ELIEZER BEN YOSE HA-GELILI; HOSHAIAH, RAV

Joe Hillaby*, President Elect, Jewish Historical Society of England, Honorary Research Fellow, the Hebrew University of Jerusalem: AARON OF YORK; ARCHA; BRISTOL; BURY ST. EDMUNDS; CANTERBURY; COLCHESTER; ROBERT OF READING; WINCHESTER; WORCESTER

Delbert Roy Hillers, Ph.D.; Professor of Semitic Languages, Johns Hopkins University, Baltimore: BURIAL; DEMONS, DEMONOLOGY

Shmuel Himelstein*, Rabbi, Dr.; Writer, Translator, Editor, Jerusalem: LICHTENSTEIN, AHARON

Maurice Gerschon Hindus, MS.; Writer, New York: FISCHER, LOUIS

Milton Henry Hindus, M.S.; Professor of English, Brandeis University, Waltham, Massachusetts: DAHLBERG, EDWARD; DAVENPORT, MARCIA; FIEDLER, LESLIE AARON; FREEMAN, JOSEPH; GOLDEN, HARRY LEWIS; GOODMAN, PAUL; KAZIN, ALFRED; KRONENBERGER, LOUIS; KUNITZ, STANLEY JASSPON; MALTZ, ALBERT; ORNITZ, SAMUEL BADISCH; ROTH, PHILIP MILTON; SALINGER, JEROME DAVID; UNITED STATES LITERATURE

Edith Hirsch, M.A.; Economist and Teacher, New York: FEILER, ARTHUR; TIETZ; WERTHEIM

Frederik Jacob Hirsch, B.A.; Librarian, Haifa: COHEN, BENJAMIN; HARTOG, LEVIE DE; HILLESUM, JEREMIAS; HOND, MEIJER DE; NEUBAUER, JACOB; ROEST, MEIJER MARCUS; TUNIS, TUNISIA; WAGENAAR, LION

Joseph Hirsch, Ph.D., Chaplain, U.S. Armed Forces, Okinawa: WIERNIK, PETER

Mark D. Hirsch, Ph.D.; Professor of History, Bronx Community College, New York: DUBERMAN, MARTIN B.

Richard Hirsch, Rabbi; Hebrew Union College-Jewish Institute of Religion, Jerusalem: EISENSTEIN, IRA; ISRAEL, STATE OF: RELIGIOUS LIFE AND COMMUNITIES; RECONSTRUCTIONISM; ROSENSTOCK-HUESSY, EUGEN

Alfred Hirschberg, Dr.Jur.; Director of the Confederaçao Israelita de Brasil, National Director of B'nai B'rith of Brazil, São Paulo: KLABIN; LAFER, HORACIO

Eliyahu Hirschberg, M.Jur., M.Ph.; Jerusalem: NAWI; NEHAR PEKOD; NIEGO, JOSEPH

Haïm Z'ew Hirschberg, Ph.D., Rabbi; Professor of Jewish History, Bar-Ilan University, Ramat Gan: AGGADAH; AHL AL-KITĀB; ALAWIDS; ARABIA; ĀSHŪRĀ; AYYUBIDS; BALAAM; BENJAMIN; BIBLE; CANAAN; COMMUNITY; DANIEL; DAVID; ELIJAH; ELISHA; ENOCH; ESCHATOLOGY; EVE; EZEKIEL; EZRA; FRANCOS; GOLIATH; GORNI; ḤABIL; HADITH; ḤAKHAM BASHI; HAMAN; ḤANĪF; ḤIMYAR; HŪD; HUESCA; ISAAC; ISAIAH; ISHMAEL; ISLAM; ISRAEL, LAND OF: HISTORY; ISRAELITE; JACOB; JEREMIAH; JERUSALEM; JETHRO; JIHĀD; JOB, THE BOOK OF; JONAH, BOOK OF; JOSEPH; JOSHUA; KĀKHYA; KAMNIEL, ABU AL-HASAN MEIR IBN; KORAH; LEBANON; LEVI DELLA VIDA, GIORGIO; LIBYA; LOT; MADRID; MAGHREBI-MA'ARAVI; MILLET; MIRIAM; MOCHA; MOSES; MUSTA'RAB, MUSTA'RABS; NEBUCHADNEZZAR; NIMROD; NOAH; OTTOMAN EMPIRE; PALACHE; PHARAOH; POTIPHAR; SALADIN; SAMARITANS; SAMUEL; ṢARRĀF; SETH; SOLOMON; TARAGAN, BEN-ZION; TEHERAN; TERAH; TRIPOLI; TURKEY; UMAYYA IBN ABĪ AL-SALT

Richard S. Hirschhaut*, B.A.; International Relations and Judaic Studies, Project and Executive Director, Illinois Holocaust Museum and Education Center; Former Midwest Director, Anti-Defamation League: FOXMAN, ABRAHAM

Gertrude Hirschler, B.S.; Editor, New York: PIONEER WOMEN

Jehoash Hirshberg*, Ph.D.; Professor of Musicology, the Hebrew University of Jerusalem: ALEXANDER, HAIM; AVNI, TZEVI; BEN-HAIM, PAUL; BUKOFZER, MANFRED; GELBRUN, ARTUR; GRADENWITZ, PETER EMANUEL; HARRAN, DON; HAUSER, EMIL; HOLDHEIM, THEODORE; LOWINSKY, EDWARD ELIAS; MAAYANI, AMI; MUSIC; OLIVERO, BETTY; ORGAD, BEN ZION; SCHIDLOWSKY, LEON; TAL, JOSEF; TISCHLER, HANS; YELLIN-BENTWICH, THELMA

Yair Hirshfeld, Ph.D.; Shiloah Center, University of Tel Aviv

Aron Hirt-Manheimer*, M.A.; Doctor of Jewish Religious Education; Editor *Reform Judaism Magazine*, Union for Reform Judaism, New York: WIESEL, ELIE; YOFFIE, ERIC H.

Philip D. Hobsbaum, L.R.A.M., L.G.S.M., Ph.D.; Lecturer in English Literature, the University of Glasgow: MEYERSTEIN, EDWARD HARRY WILLIAM; PINTER, HAROLD; SHAFFER, SIR PETER; SILKIN, JON; WALEY, ARTHUR; WESKER, ARNOLD; WOLFE, HUMBERT

Jerome (Jerry) Hochbaum*, Ph.D.; Executive Vice President, Memorial Foundation for Jewish Culture, New York: MEMORIAL FOUNDATION FOR JEWISH CULTURE

Nathan Hochberg, M.Sc.; Agronomist, Tel Aviv: WINE AND LIQUOR TRADE

Joseph Hodara, Ph.D.; Lecturer in Latin American History, the National Autonomous University of Mexico, Mexico City: CORDOBA

Sidney B. Hoenig, Ph.D., Rabbi; Professor of Jewish History, Yeshiva University, New York: BELKIN, SAMUEL; REVEL, BERNARD; ZEITLIN, SOLOMON

Miriam Hoexter*, Ph.D.; Associate Professor (retired), the Hebrew University of Jerusalem: IBĀḌĪS

Harold von Hofe, Ph.D.; Professor of German Literature, the University of Southern California, Los Angeles: MARCUSE, LUDWIG

Frederick J. Hoffman, The University of California, Riverside: STEIN, GERTRUDE

Shlomo Hofman, D.Litt.; Lecturer in the History of Music, Tel Aviv University – Rubin Academy of Music: KARAITES; SAMARITANS

Menachem Hofnung*, Ph.D.; Senior Lecturer, Department of Political Science, the Hebrew University of Jerusalem: BARAK, AHARON

S.H. Holland: WELSH, ARTHUR L.

Svend Holm-Nielsen, Dr.Theol.; Professor of Old Testament, Copenhagen University: THANKSGIVING PSALMS

J. Edwin Holmstrom, Ph.D., C.Eng.; Folkestone, England: AYRTON, HERTHA; FRANCK, JAMES; FRENKEL, JACOB ILICH; GABOR, DENNIS; GOLDSTEIN, EUGEN; HECHT, SELIG; HERTZ, GUSTAV; INFELD, LEOPOLD; OPPENHEIMER, J. ROBERT; SEGRÈ, EMILIO GINO; SIMON, SIR FRANCIS EUGENE

Avraham Holtz, D.H.L., Rabbi; Associate Professor of Modern Hebrew Literature, the Jewish Theological Seminary of America, New York: PATTERSON, DAVID

Barry W. Holtz*, Ph.D.; Professor of Jewish Education, Jewish Theological Seminary of America, New York: DORPH, SHELDON; ETTENBERG, SYLVIA CUTLER; MELTON, FLORENCE; RAUCH, EDUARDO

Avner Holtzman, Ph.D.; Lecturer, Department of Hebrew Literature, Tel Aviv University: HEBREW LITERATURE, MODERN

Livnat Holtzman*, Ph.D.; Instructor and Researcher in the Department of Arabic, Bar-Ilan University, Ramat Gan: KALĀM

Ari Hoogenboom, Ph.D.; Professor of History, Brooklyn College of the City University of New York: UNGER, IRWIN

F.J. Hoogewoud*, M.A.; Former Deputy Curator Bibliotheca Rosenthaliana, Amsterdam University Library, The Netherlands: BEEK, MARTINUS ADRIANUS; BOAS, HENRIETTE; PRAAG, SIEGFRIED EMANUEL VAN; PRINS, LIEPMAN PHILIP; SEELIGMANN, ISAC LEO

Bernard Hooker, B.A., Rabbi; Kingston, Jamaica: HART, DANIEL; STERN, PHILIP COHEN

Doreet Hopp*, Ph.D.; Senior Lecturer, State Teachers College-Seminar Hakibbutzim; Tel Aviv University: YEHOSHUA, AVRAHAM B.

Jens Hoppe*, Ph.D.; Historian, Conference of Jewish Material Claims against Germany, Office for Germany, Frankfurt, Germany: FORCED LABOR; FRANKFURT ON THE MAIN

Deborah (C.S.) Hopper*, M. A., B.Sc.; Graduate Student, University of Victoria, Victoria, Canada: GLICK, IRVING SRUL

David Horn, Ph.D.; Professor of Physics, Tel Aviv University

Samuel Abba Horodezky, Ph.D.; Historian, Tel Aviv: ALASHKAR, MOSES BEN ISAAC; ALPHABET, HEBREW, IN MIDRASH, TALMUD, AND KABBALAH; ANGELS AND ANGELOLOGY; BARUCH OF KOSOV; BERECHIAH BERAKH BEN ELIAKIM GETZEL; BLOCH, ISSACHAR BAER BEN SAMSON; CALAHORA, JOSEPH BEN SOLOMON; DAVID BEN AARON IBN ḤASSIN; DELACRUT, MATTATHIAS BEN SOLOMON; ELIJAH; ELIJAH BEN RAPHAEL SOLOMON HA-LEVI; EPSTEIN, ABRAHAM MEIR BEN ARYEH LEIB; EPSTEIN, ARYEH LEIB BEN MORDECAI; EPSTEIN, ISAAC BEN MORDECAI; FORTI RAPHAEL HEZEKIAH BEN ABRAHAM ISRAEL; GENTILI; ḤAZKUNI, ABRAHAM; HEILBUT, ELEAZAR LAZI BEN JOSEPH BEN LAZI; HEILPERN, YOM TOV LIPMAN BEN ISRAEL; HOESCHEL BEN SAUL; HOROWITZ, SHABBETAI SHEFTEL BEN AKIVA; ISAAC BEN ABRAHAM OF POSEN; ISAAC BEN BEZALEL OF VLADIMIR; ISAAC BEN SAMSON HA-KOHEN; ISSACHAR BAER BEN SOLOMON ZALMAN; JACOB BEN BENJAMIN ZE'EV; JACOB DAVID BEN ISRAEL ISSAR; JAFFE, ISRAEL BEN AARON; JEHIEL MICHAEL BEN ELIEZER; JOSEPH BEN ISAAC HA-LEVI; JOSEPH BEN MORDECAI HA-KOHEN; JOSEPH BEN MOSES OF KREMENETS; JOSHUA HOESCHEL BEN JOSEPH OF CRACOW; JUDAH BEN ELIEZER; JUDAH LEIB BEN BARUCH; KLATZKO, MORDECAI BEN ASHER; KOHEN, ELEAZAR BEN ZE'EV WOLF; KREMNITZER, JOHANAN BEN MEIR; LEVY, JUDAH BEN MENAHEM; LEWIN, JOSHUA HESHEL BEN ELIJAH ZE'EV HA-LEVI; LEWINSTEIN, JOSEPH BEN ABRAHAM ABUSH; LIPSCHUETZ; LIPSCHUETZ, BARUCH ISAAC BEN ISRAEL; LIPSCHUTZ, SHABBETAI BEN JACOB ISAAC; LONDON, JACOB BEN MOSES JUDAH; NAHUM, ELIEZER BEN JACOB; OBERNIK, JUDAH; PARNAS, ḤAYYIM NAḤMAN; PERELMANN, JEROHMAN JUDAH LEIB BEN SOLOMON ZALMAN; PESANTE, MOSES BEN ḤAYYIM BEN SHEM TOV; PINTO, JOSIAH BEN JOSEPH; SAMUEL BEN ALI; SHAPIRA, JOSHUA ISAAC BEN JEHIEL

Josef Horovitz, Dr.Phil.; *Encyclopaedia Judaica* (Germany); Professor of Semitic Languages, the University of Frankfurt; Director of the School of Oriental Studies, the Hebrew University of Jerusalem: ABDALLAH IBN SABĀ'; ABDALLAH IBN SALĀM; BABAD; BARUCH BEN SAMUEL OF ALEPPO; BRODA; COHN, MESHULLAM ZALMAN BEN SOLOMON; FRAENKEL-TEOMIM, BARUCH BEN JOSHUA EZEKIEL FEIWEL; HELLER, YOM TOV LIPMANN BEN NATHAN HA-LEVI; ISSAR JUDAH BEN NEHEMIAH OF BRISK; JACOB KOPPEL BEN AARON SASSLOWER; KALISCHER, JUDAH LEIB BEN MOSES; MODAI, ḤAYYIM; MORDECAI BEN NAPHTALI HIRSCH OF KREMSIER; ORNSTEIN, JACOB MESHULLAM BEN MORDECAI ZE'EV; PIRKOI BEN BABOI

David Horowitz, Former Governor of the Bank of Israel, Jerusalem: KAPLAN, ELIEZER

Rivka Horowitz, Ph.D.; Lecturer, Ben-Gurion University of the Negev, Beersheba

Sara Horowitz*: HILLESUM, ETTY; KARMEL, ILONA; KLEIN, GERDA WEISSMAN; OSTRIKER, ALICIA

Yehoshua Horowitz, Dr. Phil.; Educator, Lecturer in Talmud and Rabbinic Literature, Ben-Gurion University of the Negev, Beersheba: AARON BEN MESHULLAM OF LUNEL; AARON SAMUEL BEN NAPHTALI HERZ HA-KOHEN; ABOAB, JACOB BEN SAMUEL; ABRAHAM ABELE BEN ABRAHAM SOLOMON; ABRAHAM BEN AVIGDOR; ABRAHAM BEN BENJAMIN ZE'EV BRISKER; ABRAHAM BEN ISAAC HA-KOHEN OF ZAMOSC; ABRAHAM BEN MORDECAI HA-LEVI; ABRAHAM BEN SOLOMON; ABTERODE, DAVID BEN MOSES ELIAKIM; AḤA OF SHABḤA; ALTARAS; ALTSCHUL; ANATOLI BEN JOSEPH; ANSHEL OF CRACOW; ARCHIVOLTI, SAMUEL; ARDIT; ARDIT, EPHRAIM BEN ABRAHAM; ARḤA, ELIEZER BEN ISAAC; ARYEH JUDAH

LEIB BEN EPHRAIM HA-KOHEN; ARYEH LEIB BEN SAMUEL ẒEVI HIRSCH; ASH; ASHER BEN MESHULLAM HA-KOHEN OF LUNEL; ASHKENAZI, ẒEVI HIRSCH BEN JACOB; AUERBACH; AUERBACH, ISAAC EISIG BEN ISAIAH; BABAD, JOSEPH BEN MOSES; BACHRACH, JUDAH BEN JOSHUA EZEKIEL; BALBO, MICHAEL BEN SHABBETAI COHEN; BASSAN, ABRAHAM HEZEKIAH BEN JACOB; BENJAMIN ZE'EV BEN MATTATHIAS OF ARTA; BERLIN, NOAH ḤAYYIM ẒEVI HIRSCH; BERNAYS; BEZALEL BEN SOLOMON OF KOBRYN; BIALEH, ẒEVI HIRSCH BEN NAPHTALI HERZ; BIALOBLOCKI, SAMUEL SHERAGA; BLOCH, HERMANN; BONAFED, DAVID BEN REUBEN; BOZECCO, BENJAMIN BEN JUDAH; BRESLAU, ARYEH LOEB BEN ḤAYYIM; BRESLAU, JOSEPH MOSES BEN DAVID; BRIEL, JUDAH BEN ELIEZER; BRODA, ABRAHAM BEN SAUL; CASE, JOSEPH BEN ABRAHAM; DAINOW, ẒEVI HIRSCH BEN ZE'EV WOLF; DAVID BEN BOAZ; DAVID BEN NATHAN OF LISSA; DAVIDS, AARON ISSACHAR BEN NAḤMAN; DEMBITZER, ḤAYYIM NATHAN; DEUTSCH, DAVID BEN MENAHEM MENDEL; DISKIN, MOSES JOSHUA JUDAH LEIB; DUSCHAK, MORDECAI; ELIEZER BEN JOEL HA-LEVI OF BONN; ELIEZER BEN SAMUEL OF VERONA; EPSTEIN, JEHIEL MICHAL BEN AARON ISAAC HALEVI; EPSTEIN, JEHIEL MICHAL BEN ABRAHAM HALEV; FALK, JACOB JOSHUA BEN ẒEVI HIRSCH; FISCHELS, MEIR BEN EPHRAIM; FLECKELES, ELEAZAR BEN DAVID; FRAENKEL, DAVID BEN NAPHTALI HIRSCH; FRIEDMANN, DAVID BEN SAMUEL; FULD, AARON BEN MOSES; GATIGNO; GENIZAH, CAIRO; GEONIC LITERATURE; GLOGAU, JEHIEL MICHAEL BEN ASHER LEMMEL HA-LEVI; GRACIAN, SHEALTIEL BEN SOLOMON; HABERMANN, ABRAHAM MEIR; ḤABIBA, JOSEPH; HALAKHOT GEDOLOT; HALBERSTADT, ABRAHAM BEN MENAHEM MENKE; HALBERSTADT, MORDECAI; HALEVI, JOSEPH ẒEVI BEN ABRAHAM; HALEVY, ISAAC; ḤANOKH ZUNDEL BEN JOSEPH; ḤARIF; ḤARIF HA-LEVI; ḤAYYIM BEN ISAAC "OR ZARU'A"; ḤAYYIM BEN JEHIEL ḤEFEẒ ZAHAV; HEILPRIN, SAMUEL HELMANN BEN ISRAEL; HEILPRUN, ELIEZER LEIZER BEN MORDECAI; HILLEL; HILLEL (3rd cen.); HILLEL BEN NAPHTALI ẒEVI; HOLLANDER, ISAIAH BEN AARON; HOROWITZ; HOROWITZ, ABRAHAM BEN ISAIAH; HOROWITZ, ARYEH LEIB BEN ELEAZAR HA-LEVI; HOROWITZ, ARYEH LEIB BEN ISAAC; HOROWITZ, DAVID JOSHUA HOESCHEL BEN ZEVI HIRSCH HA-LEVI; HOROWITZ, ISAAC HA-LEVI BEN JACOB JOKEL; HOROWITZ, ISAIAH BEN JACOB HA-LEVI; HOROWITZ, ISAIAH BEN SHABBETAI SHEFTEL; HOROWITZ, JACOB BEN ABRAHAM; HOROWITZ, JACOB JOKEL BEN MEIR HA-LEVI; HOROWITZ, LAZAR BEN DAVID JOSHUA HOESCHEL; HOROWITZ, MESHULLAM ISSACHAR BEN ARYEH LEIB HA-LEVI; HOROWITZ, PHINEHAS BEN ẒEVI HIRSCH HA-LEVI; HOROWITZ, PHINEHAS BEN ISRAEL HA-LEVI; HOROWITZ, SAMUEL BEN ISAIAH ARYEH LEIB HA-LEVI; HOROWITZ, SAUL ḤAYYIM BEN ABRAHAM HA-LEVI; HOROWITZ, SHRAGA FEIVEL HA-LEVI; HOROWITZ, ẒEVI HIRSCH BEN ḤAYYIM ARYEH LEIBUSH HA-LEVI; HOROWITZ, ẒEVI HIRSCH BEN JOSHUA MOSES AARON HA-LEVI; HOROWITZ, ẒEVI HIRSCH BEN PHINEHAS HALEVI; HOROWITZ, ẒEVI JOSHUA BEN SAMUEL SHMELKE; ḤUSHI'EL BEN ELHANAN; IBN SHOSHAN, DAVID; ISAAC BENJAMIN WOLF BEN ELIEZER LIPMAN; JACOB OF MARVÈGE; JAFFE, SAMUEL BEN ISAAC ASHKENAZI; JEHIEL MICHAEL BEN ABRAHAM MEIR OF CIFER; JEHIEL MICHAEL BEN JUDAH LEIB HE-ḤASID; JESHUA BEN JOSEPH HA-LEVI; JONATHAN BEN JACOB; JOSEPH BEN ISSACHAR BAER OF PRAGUE; JOSEPH BEN JOSHUA MOSES OF FRANKFURT; JOSEPH BEN MORDECAI GERSHON HA-KOHEN OF CRACOW; JOSEPH JOSKE BEN JUDAH JUDEL OF LUBLIN; JOSEPH SAMUEL BEN ẒEVI OF CRACOW; JOSHUA BEN MORDECAI FALK HA-KOHEN; JOSHUA BOAZ BEN SIMON BARUCH; JOSHUA HOESCHEL BEN JACOB; JOSHUA HOESCHEL BEN JOSEPH OF CRACOW; JUDAH ARYEH LEIB BEN DAVID; JUDAH BEN ASHER; JUDAH BEN KALONYMUS BEN MOSES OF MAINZ; JUDAH LEIB BEN ENOCH ZUNDEL; JUDAH LEIB BEN HILLEL OF SCHWERSENZ; KAHANA, JEHIEL ẒEVI BEN JOSEPH MORDECAI; KAMELHAR, JEKUTHIEL ARYEH BEN GERSHON; KAPLAN, ALEXANDER SENDER BEN ZERAH HA-KOHEN; KARA, MENAHEM BEN JACOB; KARMI; KATZ, NAPHTALI BEN ISAAC; KIMḤI, JACOB BEN SAMUEL; KIMḤI, RAPHAEL ISRAEL BEN JOSEPH; KIMḤI, SOLOMON BEN NISSIM JOSEPH DAVID; KOHEN, RAPHAEL BEN JEKUTHIEL SUESSKIND; LANDAU, ISAAC ELIJAH BEN SAMUEL; LARA, DAVID BEN ISAAC COHEN DE; LARA, ḤIYYA KOHEN DE; LEON, MESSER DAVID BEN JUDAH; LEV, JOSEPH BEN DAVID IBN; LICHTSTEIN, ABRAHAM JEKUTHIEL ZALMAN BEN MOSES JOSEPH; LURIA, DAVID BEN JUDAH; MALBIM, MEIR LOEB BEN JEHIEL MICHAEL WEISSER; MASKILEISON, ABRAHAM BEN JUDAH LEIB; MORDECAI BEN HILLEL HA-KOHEN; ONDERWIJZER, ABRAHAM BEN SAMSON HA-KOHEN; PERLES, MOSES MEIR BEN ELEAZAR; PINELES, HIRSCH MENDEL BEN SOLOMON; PROVENÇAL, ABRAHAM BEN DAVID; PROVENÇAL, JACOB BEN DAVID; RAGOLER, ABRAHAM BEN SOLOMON; RAPAPORT, DAVID HA-KOHEN; SAMUEL BEN AVIGDOR; SAMUEL BEN JACOB OF KELMY; SCHICK, MOSES BEN JOSEPH; SHALOM BEN YIẒḤAK OF NEUSTADT; SINZHEIM, JOSEPH DAVID BEN ISAAC; STEINHARDT, JOSEPH BEN MENAHEM; TANḤUM BEN ELIEZER; TEDESCHI, MOSES ISAAC BEN SAMUEL; TREVES; TREVES, JOHANAN BEN JOSEPH; TREVES, JOHANAN BEN MATTATHIAS; VIDAL YOM TOV OF TOLOSA; VITAL, DAVID BEN SOLOMON; WEIL, JACOB BEN JUDAH; WORMS, AARON; WORMS, ASHER ANSHEL; YEHUDAI BEN NAḤMAN; ẒAHALON

Rivka G. Horwitz*, Ph.D.; Professor Emeritus Jewish Philosophy, Ben-Gurion University of the Negev, Beersheba: ROSENZWEIG, FRANZ; RU'AḤ HA-KODESH; SHEKHINAH; THRONE OF GOD

Elaine Hoter, M.A.; Materials developer for the Open University, Tel Aviv: AVINERI, SHLOMO; BEINART, HAIM; BIRAN, AVRAHAM; DAN, JOSEPH; DOTHAN, MOSHE; GREENBERG, MOSHE; GREENFIELD, JONAS CARL; HARAN MENAHEM; MALAMAT, ABRAHAM; NOY, DOV; TADMOR, HAYIM; TALMON, SHEMARYAHU

Louis Hotz, B.A.; Historian, Johannesburg: ALEXANDER, BERNARD; BERGTHEIL, JONAS; BRYER, MONTE; CAPE TOWN; COHEN, SIMON; DURBAN; FRAM, DAVID; GITLIN, JACOB; GLUCKMAN, HENRY; HANSON, NORMAN LEONARD; HARRIS, SIR DAVID; JOHANNESBURG; KANTOROWICH, ROY; KIBEL, WOLF; LANGERMANN, MAX; LE ROITH, HAROLD HIRSCH; MAISELS, ISRAEL AARON; MICHAELIS, SIR MAX; NATHAN, MANFRED; NORDEN; OCHBERG, ISAAC; ORENSTEIN, ALEXANDER JEREMIAH; OUDTSHOORN; SCHLESINGER, ISIDORE WILLIAM; SMUTS, JAN CHRISTIAAN; SOLOMON, BERTHA; SOUTH AFRICAN LITERATURE

Susannah Howland*, B.A.; Law student, Southwestern University School of Law, Los Angeles: KASDAN, LAWRENCE EDWARD; MEYERS, NANCY JANE; MORRIS, ERROL M.; PAKULA, ALAN JAY; PENN, ARTHUR; PERRY, FRANK; RAFELSON, ROBERT; RAPHAELSON, SAMSON; RITT, MARTIN; SHAPIRO, ESTHER JUNE; SHAWN, DICK

Benjamin Hrushovski, Associate Professor of Poetics and

Comparative Literature, Tel Aviv University: PROSODY, HEBREW

John Huehnergard*, Ph.D.; Professor of Semitic Philology, Harvard University: BIBLE, ANCIENT TRANSLATIONS, ETHIOPIC

Alana Hughes*, Director of Administration, Charles and Lynn Schusterman Family Foundation, Tulsa, Oklahoma: SCHUSTERMAN, CHARLES AND LYNN

Horace D. Hummel, Ph.D.; Professor, Department of Exegetical Theology, Concordia Seminary, St. Louis, Missouri: BIBLE

Avi Hurvitz, Ph.D.; Lecturer in Bible and in Hebrew Language, the Hebrew University of Jerusalem: PSALMS, APOCRYPHAL

Elazar Hurvitz, Ph.D., Rabbi; Associate Professor of Bible and Midrash, Yeshiva University, New York: CHAVEL, CHARLES BER

Samuel B. Hurwich, M.D., F.A.A.P.; Jerusalem: ZIONISM

Ariel Hurwitz*: MORESHET

Marshall S. Hurwitz, M.A., Rabbi; Lecturer in Greek and Latin, City College of the City University of New York: EZEKIEL THE POET; HELLENISTIC JEWISH LITERATURE; PSEUDO-PHOCYLIDES

Samuel J. Hurwitz, Ph.D.; Professor of History, Brooklyn College of the City University of New York: RISCHIN, MOSES

Shmuel Hurwitz, Dr. Ag.; Emeritus Professor of Agronomy, the Hebrew University of Jerusalem

Abraham Huss, Ph.D., D.I.C.; Associate Professor of Meteorology, the Hebrew University of Jerusalem: CARMI, T.

Boaz Huss*, Ph.D.; Senior Lecturer, Ben-Gurion University of the Negev, Beersheba: ASHLAG, YEHUDAH

Jehoshua Hutner, Rabbi; Director of the *Encyclopaedia Talmudica* and of Yad Harav Herzog, Jerusalem: ZEVIN, SOLOMON JOSEPH

Arthur Hyman*, Ph.D., Rabbi; Distinguished Service Professor of Philosophy and Dean, Bernard Revel Graduate School of Jewish Studies, Yeshiva University, New York: MAIMONIDES; PHILOSOPHY, JEWISH; WOLFSON, HARRY AUSTRYN

Avi Hyman*, Dr. Education; Director, Research, Academic Technologies, OISE/University of Toronto, Canada: LUFTSPRING, SAMMY; RUBENSTEIN, LOUIS; UNGERMAN, IRVING; WEIDER, BEN

Louis Hyman, M.A.; Historian, Haifa

Semah Cecil Hyman, Former Minister Plenipotentiary, Ministry for Foreign Affairs, Jerusalem: AGRON, GERSHON; JERUSALEM; KISCH, FREDERICK HERMANN; PILGRIMAGE

Moshe Idel*, Ph.D.; Professor of Jewish Thought and Kabbalah, Hebrew University of Jerusalem; Shalom Hartman Institute, Jerusalem: ABRAHAM BEN ALEXANDER OF COLOGNE; ABRAHAM BEN ELIEZER HA-LEVI; ABULAFIA, TODROS BEN JOSEPH HA-LEVI; ALEMANNO, JOHANAN BEN ISAAC; ANTINOMIANISM; CARO, JOSEPH BEN EPHRAIM; DEVEKUT; EIN-SOF; EMANATION; GABBAI, MEIR BEN EZEKIEL IBN; GIKATILLA, JOSEPH BEN ABRAHAM; GOD, NAMES OF; ḤAYYAT, JUDAH BEN JACOB; KABBALAH; KANAH AND PELIYAH, BOOKS OF; LURIA, ISAAC BEN SOLOMON; SCHOLEM, GERSHOM GERHARD

David Ignatow, Adjunct Professor of Writing, Columbia University; Poet-in-Residence, York College of the City University of New York: FEARING, KENNETH; GINSBERG, ALLEN

Shahar Ilan*, Journalist, *Haaretz* Newspaper, Jerusalem: ISRAEL, STATE OF: RELIGIOUS LIFE AND COMMUNITIES

Tal Ilan*, Ph.D.; Professor, Institute for Jewish Studies, Free University, Berlin, Germany: WOMAN: POST-BIBLICAL PERIOD

Shulamit Imber*, M.A.; Pedagogical Director in the International School for Holocaust Studies, Yad Vashem, Jerusalem: HOLOCAUST

Efraim Inbar, Ph.D.; Senior Lecturer, Department of Political Science, Bar-Ilan University

Judith Brin Ingber*, B.A.; Independent Scholar, Dance Historian, University of Minnesota: DANCE; LANG, PEARL

Nahman Ingber, M.A.; Instructor in Poetics and Comparative Literature, Tel Aviv University: MOTION PICTURES

Institute of Jewish Affairs, London

Radu Ioanid*: ARAD

Miriam Isaacs*, Ph.D.; Long-Term Visiting Associate Professor, Yiddish Language and Culture, University of Maryland, College Park: YIDDISH LITERATURE

Benny Isaacson, Tel Aviv

Shirley Berry Isenberg, Anthropologist and Author: BENE ISRAEL

Moshe Ishai, Dr.Juris; Former Ambassador, Tel Aviv: MUSOLINO, BENEDETTO

Benjamin Ish-Shalom*, Ph.D.; Rector, Beit Morasha of Jerusalem: KOOK, ABRAHAM ISAAC

Benjamin J. Israel, Former Secretary of the Bombay Public Service Commission: BENE ISRAEL

Salvator Marco Israel, M.D.; Maître de Recherches Hebraïques, the Bulgarian Academy of Sciences, Sofia: BULGARIAN LITERATURE

Joseph Israeli, Kibbutz Afikim: HA-SHOMER HA-ẒA'IR

Raphael (Rafi) Israeli*, Ph.D.; Professor of Islamic, Chinese, and Middle Eastern History, the Hebrew University of Jerusalem: ISRAEL, STATE OF: ARAB POPULATION; SADAT, MUHAMMAD ANWAR

Stanley Isser, M.A.; Lecturer in History, Queens College of the City University of New York: CHRONOLOGY

Israel (Ignacy) Isserles, M.A., Advocate; Tel Aviv: LACHS, MANFRED;

MUSZKAT, MARION; SAWICKI, JERZY; SZER, SEWERYN

Nissim Itzhak, B.A.; Ministry for Foreign Affairs, Jerusalem: URUGUAY

Norman Itzkowitz, Ph.D.; Associate Professor of Near Eastern Studies, Princeton University, New Jersey: AYALON, DAVID; HEYD, URIEL; LEWIS, BERNARD

Ruth Ivor, Ph.D.; Former Lecturer in the History of Comparative Civilization, the University of Colorado; Siena, Italy: ITALIENER, BRUNO

Alfred L. (Lyon) Ivry*, Ph.D.; Dr.Phil; Professor Emeritus, New York University, New York: ALEXANDER OF APHRODISIAS; ALTMANN, ALEXANDER; BODY AND SOUL; EMOTIONS; FORM AND MATTER; IMAGINATION; INTELLECT; MOSES BEN JOSHUA OF NARBONNE; NATURE; SOUL; THEMISTIUS

Dafna Izraeli, Ph.D.; Professor of Sociology, Bar-Ilan University, Ramat Gan

Edward Jacobs*, Conceptual Designer, Mishkenot Ltd, Jerusalem: RISKIN, SHLOMO

Louis Jacobs, Ph.D., Rabbi; Scholar, London: AKEDAH; HALAKHAH; HALAKHAH LE-MOSHE MI-SINAI; ḤASIDISM; HERMENEUTICS; JUDAISM; MONTEFIORE, CLAUDE JOSEPH GOLDSMID; MOSES; PASSOVER; PEACE; PRAYER; PREACHING; PURIM; RIGHTEOUSNESS; ROSH HA-SHANAH; SABBATH; SHAVUOT; SHEMA, READING OF; SIN; STUDY; SUKKOT; THEOLOGY; TORAH, READING OF

Thorkild Jacobsen, Dr. Phil.; Professor of Assyriology, Harvard University, Cambridge, Massachusetts

Howard Jacobson, Ph.D.; Assistant Professor of Classics, the University of Illinois, Urbana: HERACLES; ITINERARIUM HIEROSOLYMITANUM or ITINERARIUM BURDIGALENSE; TITANS

Joshua Jacobson*, D.M.A.; Professor of Music, Northeastern University, Boston: CHOIRS

David Jacoby, Ph.D.; Associate Professor of History, the Hebrew University of Jerusalem: STARR, JOSHUA

Jonathan Jacoby*: ISRAEL POLICY FORUM

Benjamin Jaffe, M.A., M.Jur.; Writer and official, Jewish Agency, Jerusalem: ALMOG, YEHUDA; ARIEL, DOV; ARLOSOROFF, CHAIM; AVRIEL, EHUD; BARTH, JACOB; BARZILAI,YEHOSHUA; BEN-AMI, OVED; BENTOV, MORDEKHAI; BENTWICH; BERLIGNE, ELIYAHU MEIR; CHELOUCHE; COHN, HAIM; COMAY, MICHAEL SAUL; DANIN, YEḤEZKEL; DOBKIN, ELIYAHU; DULZIN, ARYE LEIB; ELATH, ELIAHU; ELDAD, ISRAEL; FRIENDSHIP LEAGUES WITH ISRAEL; GLUSKA, ZEKHARYAH; GRAJEWSKY, PINCHAS; HACOHEN, DAVID; HARARI, ḤAYYIM; HESHIN, SHNEUR ZALMAN; KHOUSHI, ABBA; LOURIE, ARTHUR; LURIE, ZVI; MAISEL-SHOḤAT, HANNAH; PERSITZ, SHOSHANAH; PINCUS, LOUIS ARIEH; RECANATI; ROKACH, SHIMON; SASSON, ELIYAHU; SCOTT, CHARLES PRESTWICH; SMOIRA, MOSHE; STERN, JOSEPH ZECHARIAH; TOLKOWSKY, SHEMUEL; TSUR, JACOB; VALERO; VILNAY, ZEV

Lee (David) Jaffe*, M.S.; Librarian, University of California, Santa Cruz, California: SANTA CRUZ

Immanuel Jakobovits, Ph.D., Rabbi; Chief Rabbi of the British Commonwealth, London: ARTIFICIAL INSEMINATION; BIRTH CONTROL; CASTRATION; CELIBACY; EUTHANASIA; HOMOSEXUALITY

Oscar Isaiah Janowsky, Ph.D.; Emeritus Professor of History, City College of the City University of New York: GILBERT, FELIX; GOLDMAN, ERIC FREDERICK; KOEBNER, RICHARD; KUBLIN, HYMAN; LANDES, DAVID SAUL; PINSON, KOPPEL S.; SCHAPIRO, JACOB SALWYN

Taeke Jansma, Ph.D.; Professor of Hebrew and Aramaic, the State University of Leiden, the Netherlands

Sara Japhet, M.A.; Instructor in Bible, the Hebrew University of Jerusalem: CHRONICLES, BOOK OF

Jack Jedwab*, Ph.D.; Executive Director, Association for Canadian Studies, Montreal, Quebec: QUEBEC

Yeshayahu (A.) Jelinek*, Associate Professor Retired, Beersheba: BANSKA BYSTRICA; BARDEJOV; BRATISLAVA; CESKE BUDEJOVICE; CHEB; CZECH REPUBLIC AND SLOVAKIA; CZECHOSLOVAKIA; DOLNI KUBIN; DUNAJSKA STREDA; GALANTA; HLOHOVEC; HOLESOV; HRANICE; HUMENNE; HUNCOVCE; KOMARNO; KOSICE; KUGEL, ḤAYYIM; LIBEREC; LIPTOVSKY MIKULAS; LITOMERICE; LOEBL, EUGEN; LOSTICE; LUCENEC; MASARYK, JAN GARRIGUE; MICHALOVCE; MIKULOV; MORAVIA; NITRA; NOVE MESTO NAD VAHOM; NOVE ZAMKY; OSTRAVA; PEZINOK; PIESTANY; POHORELICE; PRAGUE; PRESOV; PROSTEJOV; ROUDNICE NAD LABEM; SLOVAKIA; TABOR; TOPOLCANY; TREBIC; TRENCIN; TRNAVA; TURNOV; UHERSKE HRADISTE; UHERSKY BROD; USOV; USTI NAD LABEM; VOTICE; ŽIDOVSKÁ STRANA; ZILINA; ZNOJMO

Uffa Jensen*: STAHL, FRIEDRICH JULIUS; STOECKER, ADOLF; TREITSCHKE, HEINRICH VON

Jewish Museum Staff*: JEWISH MUSEUM

Leon A. Jick: JEWISH STUDIES

Akira Jindo, Ph.D.; Assistant Editor of "The Weekly Original Gospel" and "The Light of My Life"; Staff Member of Makuya Tokyo Bible Seminary: MAKUYA

Franklin Jonas, Ph.D.; Instructor in History, Long Island University, New York: VLADECK, BARUCH CHARNEY

Faith Jones*, B.A., M.L.I.S.; Head, Literature and Languages, Mid-Manhattan Library, New York: ELBERG, YEHUDA; KACZERGINSKY, SZMERKE; MAZE, IDA; SEGAL, ESTHER; SHUMIATCHER-HIRSCHBEIN, ESTHER; YUDIKA; ZYLBERCWEIG, ZALMAN

Louis de Jong, Litt.D.; Historian and Extraordinary Professor of Contemporary History, the University of Rotterdam; Director of the Netherlands State Institute for War Documentation, Amsterdam

Alfred Joseph, San Salvador: EL SALVADOR

Max Joseph*, B.A.; Screenwriter/Filmmaker, Los Angeles: ARCHERD,

ARMY; BENSON, ROBBY; GUBER, PETER; HALL, MONTY; HALMI, ROBERT; HOWARD, MOE, SHEMP, and CURLY; INSDORF, ANNETTE; IRVING, AMY

Norma Baumel Joseph*, Ph.D.; Associate Professor, Concordia University, Montreal, Canada: BAR MITZVAH, BAT MITZVAH; GOLDSTEIN, ELYSE; ROBACK, LEA

Alfred Jospe, B'nai B'rith Hillel Foundations, Washington, D.C.: MENDELSSOHN, MOSES; STUDENTS' MOVEMENTS, JEWISH; UNIVERSITIES

Raphael Jospe*, Ph.D.; Professor; Researcher; Jewish Philosophy Lecturer, Bar-Ilan University: BIBAGO, ABRAHAM BEN SHEM TOV; FALAQUERA, SHEM TOV BEN JOSEPH IBN; IBN EZRA, ABRAHAM BEN MEIR; JOSPE, ALFRED; KAPLAN, MORDECAI MENAHEM; LOVE; MAIMONIDEAN CONTROVERSY; PEKARSKY, MAURICE BERNARD; PHILOSOPHY, JEWISH; RAVITZKY, AVIEZER; WAGNER, STANLEY M.

Martha Sharp Joukowsky*, Professor Emerita, Brown University, Director, Brown University Petra Great Temple Excavations, Providence, Rhode Island: NABATEANS

Anthony Julius*, M.A., Ph.D.; Solicitor, London: IRVING v. LIPSTADT

Leo Jung, Ph.D., Rabbi; Emeritus Professor of Ethics, Yeshiva University, New York: RABBINER-SEMINAR FUER DAS ORTHODOXE JUDENTUM

Hans Jungmann, M.D.; London, England

David Jutan, Histadrut Ha-Ovedim Ha-Le'ummit, Tel Aviv: HISTADRUT HA-OVEDIM HA-LE'UMMIT

Jacob Kabakoff, B.A., D.H.L., Rabbi; Associate Professor of Hebrew, the Herbert H. Lehman College of the City University of New York: MATZ, ISRAEL

Menahem Zevi Kaddari, Ph.D.; Rector and Professor of Hebrew Language, Bar-Ilan University, Ramat Gan: BEN ZE'EV, JUDAH LEIB; ELIJAH BEN SOLOMON ZALMAN; KOHUT; LOEW, IMMANUEL; NATONEK, JOSEPH; RASHI; WIZEN, MOSHE AHARON

David Kadosh, Ph.D., Rabbi; Assistant Professor of Jewish Philosophy, Yeshiva University, New York: ADAM; CATEGORIES; DECALOGUE; MOSES

Sara Kadosh*, Ph.D.; Director of JDC Archives, American Jewish Joint Distribution Committee, Jerusalem: AMERICAN JEWISH JOINT DISTRIBUTION COMMITTEE

Elieser Kagan, Ph.D.; Lecturer in Hebrew Language and Literature, Haifa University: LEBENSOHN, MICAH JOSEPH; LUZZATTO, EPHRAIM; PAPPENHEIM, SOLOMON; SALKINSON, ISAAC EDWARD

Saul Kagan, New York: COUNCIL OF JEWS FROM GERMANY

Joseph Kage, Canada

Arcadius Kahan, Ph.D.; Professor of Economics, the University of Chicago: ECONOMIC HISTORY; LIBERMAN, YEVSEY GRIGORYEVICH

Menahem I. Kahana*, Ph.D.; Lecturer, the Hebrew University of Jerusalem: MEKHILTA DEUTERONOMY; MEKHILTA OF R. ISHMAEL; MEKHILTA OF R. SIMEON BEN YOḤAI; MIDRESHEI HALAKHAH; SIFRA; SIFRE ZUTA DEUTERONOMY; SIFRE ZUTA NUMBERS; SIFREI; SIFREI NUMBERS

Isaac Ze'ev Kahane, Rabbi; Professor of Talmud and of Jewish History, Bar-Ilan University, Ramat Gan: ASHKENAZI, GERSHON; BOSKOVICE; BRNO; BRUNA, ISRAEL BEN ḤAYYIM; CHEB; EYLENBURG, ISSACHAR BAER BEN ISRAEL LEISER PARNAS; ḤLADIK, ABRAHAM; IVANCICE; UHERSKY BROD

Penuel P. Kahane, Ph.D.; Former Chief Curator of the Samuel Bronfman Biblical and Archaeological Museum, the Israel Museum, Jerusalem: ARCHAEOLOGISTS; BARNETT, LIONEL DAVID; BAUMGARTEL, ELISE J.; BIEBER, MARGARETE; BORCHARDT, LUDWIG; DELOUGAZ, PIERRE PINCHAS; FRANKFURT, HENRI; GHIRSHMAN, ROMAN; GOLDMAN, HETTY; HANFMANN, GEORGE MAXIM ANOSSOV; HIRSCHFELD, GUSTAV; KLEIN, WILHELM; LEHMANN, KARL; LEVI, DORO; LOEWY, EMANUEL; WALSTON, SIR CHARLES; WEINBERG, SAUL S.

Jacqueline Kahanoff, M.A.; Writer, Tel Aviv: MEMMI, ALBERT; PÉGUY, CHARLES-PIERRE

Ezer Kahanov, M.A.; Teacher, Researcher in Jewish History: SEPHARDIM

Moshe Kahanovich, Journalist, Tel Aviv

Ava F. Kahn*, Ph.D.; Historian, California Studies Center, Berkeley, California: CALIFORNIA; FEINSTEIN, DIANNE GOLDMAN; KAHN, FLORENCE PRAG; MAGNIN, MARY ANN COHEN

Benjamin Kahn, M.H.L., Rabbi; International Director of the B'nai B'rith Hillel Foundations, Washington, D.C.: MONSKY, HENRY

Catherine (C.) Kahn*, Archivist, Touro Infirmary Archives, New Orleans: LOUISIANA; NEW ORLEANS

Gilbert N. Kahn*, Ph.D.; Professor, Kean University, Union, New Jersey: HOENLEIN, MALCOLM; LOOKSTEIN, HASKEL; LOOKSTEIN, JOSEPH HYMAN

Leybl Kahn, M.A.; Bibliographer, New York: FISHMAN, JOSHUA AARON; SCHAECHTER, MORDKHE

Lily O. (Okalani) Kahn*, M.A., Ph.D.; Lecturer in Hebrew and Yiddish, University College, London, England: EPSTEIN, MELECH; TENENBAUM, JOSHUA; WARSHAVSKY, YAKIR; YUD, NAHUM

Ludwig W. Kahn, Ph.D.; Professor of German, Columbia University, New York: FRAENKEL, JONAS; STRICH, FRITZ

Sholom Jacob Kahn, Ph.D.; Senior Lecturer in English and American Literature, the Hebrew University of Jerusalem: ANGOFF, CHARLES; MALAMUD, BERNARD

Kathleen Kahrl*: SACRAMENTO

Aryeh-Leib Kalish, Jerusalem: CHELM; JOLLES, JACOB ẒEVI BEN NAPHTALI; ZEMBA, MENAHEM; ZHOLKVA

Frances R. Kallison, B.A.; San Antonio, Texas: SAN ANTONIO

Menachem Kallus*, Ph.D.; Independent Researcher, Writer and

Translator, Alumnus of the Hebrew University of Jerusalem: SHABBETAI BEN TZVI HIRSCH OF RASZKOW

Emil Kalo*, Ph.D.; Philosopher, President of the Organization of the Jews in Bulgaria "Shalom", Bulgaria: BULGARIA; BULGARIAN LITERATURE; KOLAROVGRAD; KYUSTENDIL; NIKOPOL; PETROV, VALERI; PLEVEN; PLOVDIV; RUSE; STARA ZAGORA; VARNA; VIDIN; WAGENSTEIN, ANGEL RAYMOND

Isaac Kalugai, M.Sc.; Emeritus Professor of Chemistry, the Technion, Haifa: JOFFE, ABRAHAM FEODOROVICH

Roger Kamien, Ph.D.; Assistant Professor of Music, Queens College of the City University of New York: SCHENKER, HEINRICH

Stewart Kampel*, B.B.A., M.S.; Freelance Writer, Editor, East Northport, New York; Wellington, Florida: ABRAMS, FLOYD M.; ACE, GOODMAN; ADLER, HARRY CLAY; ADLER, RENATA; ADLER, RICHARD; ADLER, STELLA; ALEXANDER, JASON; ALLEN, PAUL G.; ALTER, ELEANOR B.; ARBUS, DIANE; ARNOLD, EVE; AVEDON, RICHARD; AZENBERG, EMANUEL; BAKSHI, RALPH; BALLMER, STEVE; BANKERS AND BANKING; BEN-AMI, JACOB; BENNETT, MICHAEL; BEN-VENISTE, RICHARD; BERGER, SAMUEL R.; BERNAYS, EDWARD L.; BERNSTEIN, CARL; BERNSTEIN, ELMER; BIALKIN, KENNETH J.; BING, ILSE; BLANK, ARTHUR M.; BLITZER, WOLF; BLOCK, H. & R.; BLOCK, HERBERT LAWRENCE; BLOOMBERG, MICHAEL R.; BLOOMGARDEN, KERMIT; BLUHDORN, CHARLES G.; BOCK, JERRY; BOESKY, IVAN FREDERICK; BOURKE-WHITE, MARGARET; BREITEL, CHARLES; BRIN, SERGEY; BROAD, ELI; BRODER, DAVID SALZER; BRODY, JANE E.; BRUCE, LENNY; BUSCH, CHARLES; CAHN, SAMMY; CAPA, CORNELL; CAPA, ROBERT; CAPP, AL; CARTOONISTS; CHAST, ROZ; CHERTOFF, MICHAEL; CHOPER, JESSE H.; COHEN, H. RODGIN; COLEMAN, CY; COPPERFIELD, DAVID; CRUMB, ROBERT; CULLMAN; CUTLER, BRUCE; DAVID, LARRY; DAVIDSON, WILLIAM; DAVIS, MARVIN H.; DELL, MICHAEL S.; DEPARTMENT STORES; DILLER, BARRY; DOUGLAS, KIRK; DYLAN, BOB; EISENSTAEDT, ALFRED; EISNER, WILL; ELDER, WILL; ELISOFON, ELIOT; ETTLINGER, MARION; FAIN, SAMMY; FAIRSTEIN, LINDA A.; FRANK, ROBERT; FRANKEL, MAX; FREED, ALAN; FRIEDLANDER, LEE; FRIEDMAN, THOMAS L.; FUNT, ALLEN; GABLER, MILTON; GAINES, WILLIAM A.; GELB, ARTHUR; GOLDBERG, RUBE; GOLDIN, DANIEL SAUL; GOLDIN, NAN; GOLDWATER, JOHN L.; GRAHAM, KATHARINE; GRANZ, NORMAN; GREENBERG, MAURICE R.; GROSSFELD, ABRAHAM ISRAEL; GROVE, ANDREW STEPHEN; GURALNIK, DAVID B.; HALSMAN, PHILIPPE; HARNICK, SHELDON; HART, KITTY CARLISLE; HART, LORENZ; HELMSLEY, LEONA; HERMAN, JERRY; HERSH, SEYMOUR; HEWITT, DON; HIRSCHFELD, AL; ICAHN, CARL C.; ISAACS, SUSAN; JACOBI, LOTTE; JACOBS, BERNARD B.; JACOBS, IRWIN M.; JACOBSON, SYDNEY, BARON; JOURNALISM; KAEL, PAULINE; KALB, BERNARD; KALB, MARVIN; KALMAN, MAIRA; KALMAN, TIBOR; KANE, BOB; KANE, GIL; KANN, PETER R.; KARMAZIN, MEL; KAUFMAN, ANDY; KELLERMAN, FAYE; KELLERMAN, JONATHAN; KERTESZ, ANDRE; KING, ALAN; KIRBY, JACK; KISSINGER, HENRY ALFRED; KOPPEL, TED; KOSNER, EDWARD A.; KRANTZ, JUDITH; KURTZMAN, HARVEY; KUSHNER, TONY; LAEMMLE, CARL; LANDESMAN, ROCCO; LASKY, JESSE L.; LAVIN, LINDA; LAWYERS; LAZARUS, MEL; LEE, STAN; LEFRAK, SAMUEL J.; LEIBOVITZ, ANNIE; LELYVELD, JOSEPH; LEVIN, IRA; LEVITT, HELEN; LIMAN, ARTHUR L.; LORTEL, LUCILLE; LOUIS-DREYFUS, JULIA; LUBITSCH, ERNST; MACKLOWE, HARRY; MARCUS, BERNARD; MARCUS, STANLEY; MARKEL, LESTER; MARX BROTHERS; MASON, JACKIE; MENDES, SAM; MERRICK, DAVID; MEYEROWITZ, JOEL; MILKEN, MICHAEL R.; MILSTEIN; NEUWIRTH, BEBE; NEVINS, SHEILA; NEWTON, HELMUT; NOVAK, ROBERT; PALTROW, GWYNETH; PARKER, SARAH JESSICA; PATRICOF, ALAN; PEARLSTINE, NORMAN; PENN, IRVING; PLACHY, SYLVIA; PLAIN, BELVA; POLLACK, MILTON; PRITZKER; PUBLIC RELATIONS; RAGEN, NAOMI; RAND, AYN; RANDALL, TONY; RATNER, BRUCE C.; REINHARDT, MAX; REMNICK, DAVID; RICH, MARC; RICHARDS, MARTIN; RINGL + PIT; ROBBINS, HAROLD; ROBERTS, TONY; ROBINSON, EDWARD G.; RODGERS, MARY; ROSENTHAL, A.M.; ROSS, LILLIAN; ROSS, STEPHEN; RUBIN, GAIL; RUDIN; SAKS, GENE; SAND, LEONARD B.; SCHANBERG, SYDNEY H.; SCHARY, DORE; SCHECK, BARRY; SCHENKER, JOEL W.; SCHNEIDER, IRVING; SCHORR, DANIEL; SCHULTZ, HOWARD; SCHWARTZ, STEPHEN; SCHWIMMER, DAVID; SHAPIRO, IRVING SAUL; SHAPIRO, ROBERT; SHEINDLIN, JUDITH; SHELDON, SIDNEY; SHEVELOVE, BURT; SHUSTER, JOE; SIEBERT, MURIEL; SIEGEL, JERRY; SILVERSTEIN, LARRY; SIMON; SIMONS, JAMES H.; SOKOLOF, PHIL; SPIEGELMAN, ART; SPIELVOGEL, CARL; STEEL, DANIELLE; STEIG, WILLIAM; STEIN, JOSEPH; STEINBERG, SAUL; STEINHARDT, MICHAEL H.; STERN, LEONARD; STERNBERG, JOSEF VON; STIEGLILTZ, ALFRED; STINE, R.L.; STONE, PETER; STRAND, PAUL; STRAUS, ROGER, JR.; STYNE, JULE; SUSANN, JACQUELINE; TAUBMAN, A. ALFRED; TAYMOR, JULIE; THEATER; TISCH; TISHMAN; TRIBE, LAURENCE H.; TRILLIN, CALVIN; TRILLING, DIANA; TUROW, SCOTT; ULLSTEIN; VÉSZI, JOZSEF; VOLCKER, PAUL A.; VORENBERG, JAMES; WALLACE, IRVING; WARNER; WASSER, DENNIS M.; WASSERSTEIN, BRUCE; WEEGEE; WEISS, MELVYN I.; WEISSLER, BARRY and FRAN; WILDER, BILLY; WILPON, FRED; WINKLER, IRWIN; WINOGRAND, GARRY; WYNN, STEVE; ZUCKER, JEFF; ZUCKERMAN, MORTIMER

Mordechai Kamrat, Ph.D.; Educator, Jerusalem: ULPANIM

Yuval Kamrat, Jerusalem: ADRAMMELECH; AHIMELECH; ESAU; GAD; GESHEM, GASHMU; NINEVEH; SHAPHAN; ZADOK

Yosef Kanefsky*, M.S., Rabbi, B'nai David-Judea Congregation, Los Angeles: WEISS, AVI

Izhak Kanev, M.A.; Director of the Social and Economic Research Institute, Tel Aviv: ISRAEL, STATE OF: HEALTH, WELFARE, AND SOCIAL SECURITY

Joshua Kaniel (Mershine), M.A.; Instructor in Jewish History, Bar-Ilan University, Ramat Gan: JERUSALEM; MENAHEM MENDEL OF SHKLOV

Abram Kanof, M.D.; Physician and Art Historian; Professor of Pediatrics, the State University of New York – Downstate Medical Center at Brooklyn; Former President of the American Jewish Historical Society, New York: HAYS, DANIEL PEIXOTTO; HORWITZ, PHINEAS JONATHAN; LEVY, JONAS PHILLIPS; LEVY, URIAH PHILLIPS; PASSOVER; SABBATH; SUKKOT

Arvid S. Kapelrud, Theol.D.; Professor of Biblical Language and Literature, the University of Oslo: MOWINCKEL, SIGMUND OLAF PLYTT

E. Kapitaikin: KALIK, MIKHAIL

Dana Evan Kaplan*, Ph.D., Rabbi; Temple Bnai Israel, Albany: REFORM JUDAISM

Jacob Kaplan, Ph.D.; Director of the Museum of Antiquities of Tel Aviv-Yaffo: CHEMICAL CRAFTS AND INDUSTRIES; METALS AND MINING; SALT TRADE AND INDUSTRY

Joseph Kaplan, M.A., Assistant in Jewish History, the Hebrew University of Jerusalem: ARAGÃO, FERNÃO XIMENES DE; ARBUÉS, PEDRO DE; ARRABY MOOR; CONTRACTORS; FALAQUERA; HIRSCHHORN, SAMUEL; KOLISCHER, HEINRICH; MORTEIRA, SAUL LEVI; NAḤMANIDES; PABLO DE SANTA MARIA; SENEOR, ABRAHAM

Marion Kaplan*, Ph.D.; Skirball Professor of Modern Jewish History, New York University

Mordechai Kaplan, M.Eng.; Lieutenant Colonel (Res.), Israel Defense Forces, Tel Aviv: ASCOLI, ETTORE; BLOCH, CLAUDE; DASSAULT, DARIUS PAUL; KLEIN, JULIUS; KREISER, JACOB GRIGORYEVICH; LAMBERT, AIMÉ; MEKHLIS, LEV ZAKHAROVICH; SCHWEITZER, EDUARD VON; SÉE, LÉOPOLD; SELIGMAN, HERBERT SPENCER; SHMUSHKEVICH, YAACOV; SINGER, JOSEPH; SOMMER, EMIL; VALABRÈGUE, MARDOCHÉE GEORGES

Steve Kaplan, Ph.D.; Harry S. Truman Research Center, The Hebrew University of Jerusalem: BETA ISRAEL; BOGALE, YONA

Yehiel Kaplan*, Dr.Jur.; Senior Lecturer in Law, University of Haifa: PARENT AND CHILD; TAKKANOT; TORTS

Zvi Kaplan, *Encyclopaedia Hebraica*, Jerusalem: ABBA BAR AḤA; ABBA BEN ABBA HA-KOHEN; ABBA YOSE BEN ḤANIN; AḤA BAR ḤANINA; AḤA BEN JACOB; AḤERIM; AIBU; AMMI BAR NATHAN; AMRAM ḤASIDA; ANAN; ANIMALS, CRUELTY TO; ARONSON, SOLOMON; AVDAN; AVDIMI BAR ḤAMA; AVIA; AVIMI; AVIMI BEN ABBAHU; AVIRA; AZARIAH; BAITOS BEN ZONIN; BAR MITZVAH, BAT MITZVAH; BAR-ILAN, MEIR; BATHYRA, SONS OF; BATLANIM; BAVA BEN BUTA; BEBAI; BEN AZZAI, SIMEON; BEN BAG BAG; BEN HE HE; BEN KALBA SAVU'A; BEN PETURA; BEN ẒIẒIT HA-KASAT; BEN ZOMA, SIMEON; BENA'AH; BERECHIAH; BERLIN, NAPHTALI ẒEVI JUDAH; BEẒAH; BLAU, MOSHE; DESSLER, ELIJAH ELIEZER; ERUV; GORDON, ELIEZER; GRAJEWSKI, ARYEH LEIB; ḤALAFTA; ḤALAFTA BEN SAUL; ḤAMA; ḤAMA BAR BISA; HAMNUNA; ḤANA BAR ḤANILAI; ḤANA BEN BIZNA; HANAN THE EGYPTIAN; HANANIAH; HANANIAH BEN ḤAKHINAI; HANANIAH OF SEPPHORIS; ḤANINA BAR ḤAMA; ḤANINA BAR PAPA; ḤANINA BEN ABBAHU; ḤANINA BEN ANTIGONUS; ḤANINA BEN DOSA; ḤANINA BEN GAMALIEL; ḤANINA SEGAN HA-KOHANIM; ḤARLAP, JACOB MOSES BEN ZEBULUN; ḤELBO; HEZEKIAH; ḤIDKA; HIRSCHENSOHN; ḤIYYA; ḤIYYA BAR ABBA; ḤIYYA BAR AVIN; HUNA BEN JOSHUA; HUNA OF SEPPHORIS; ILAI; ISAAC; ISAAC BAR JOSEPH; ISAAC BAR RAV JUDAH; JOHANAN BEN BEROKA; JOHANAN BEN GUDGADA; JOSHUA BEN GAMLA; JOSHUA BEN LEVI; JUDAH BAR EZEKIEL; JUDAH BAR ILAI; JUDAH BAR SHALOM; JUDAH BAR SIMEON; JUDAH BEN ḤIYYA; JUDAH BEN NAḤAMANI; MEIR BEN SAMUEL OF RAMERUPT; SONNENFELD, JOSEPH ḤAYYIM BEN ABRAHAM SOLOMON; TARFON; TEMPLE MOUNT; WERTHEIMER, SOLOMON AARON; ZECHARIAH BEN AVKILUS; ZEEIRA

Charles I. Kapralik, Dr. iur.; London: CENTRAL BRITISH FUND; JEWISH SUCCESSOR ORGANIZATIONS

Israel J. Kapstein, Ph.D.; Emeritus Professor of English Literature, Brown University, Providence, Rhode Island: PERELMAN, SIDNEY JOSEPH

Samuel E. Karff, D.H.L., Rabbi; Lecturer in Jewish Thought and American Culture, Divinity School, the University of Chicago: HIRSCH, EMIL GUSTAVE

Abraham J. Karp, M.H.L., Rabbi; Historian, and Visiting Associate Professor of Jewish History, the Jewish Theological Seminary of America, New York: BURSTEIN, ABRAHAM

Alan Karpas, Jerusalem: STAMPS

Heinrich Karplus, M.D.; Associate Professor of Forensic Medicine, the Hebrew University – Hadassah Medical School, Jerusalem; Director of the Institute of Forensic Medicine, Tel Aviv: EMBALMING

Reuben Kashani, Journalist, Jerusalem: BURIAL; DEATH; MAIMUNA; MARRIAGE

Asa Kasher, Ph.D.; Lecturer in Mathematics and Philosophy, Bar-Ilan University, Ramat Gan: LEIBOWITZ, YESHAYAHU

Hannah Kasher*, Ph.D.; Associate Professor, Bar-Ilan University, Ramat Gan: ABRAHAM; FEAR OF GOD; INCLINATION, GOOD AND EVIL; KASPI, JOSEPH BEN ABBA MARI IBN; LOVE

Aharon Kashtan, Ing., M.A.; Associate Professor of Architecture and Town Planning, the Technion, Haifa: SYNAGOGUE

Alvin Kass, M.A., M.H.L. Rabbi; John Jay College of Criminal Justice of the City University of New York: ADLER, MORRIS; ARZT, MAX; ASHER, JOSEPH MICHAEL; COMMUNITY TOKENS; UNITED SYNAGOGUE OF CONSERVATIVE JUDAISM

Abraham I. Katsh, Ph.D.; President Emeritus of Dropsie University, Philadelphia: KAPLAN, CHAIM ARON

E. (Ethan) Katsh*, J.D.; Professor of Legal Studies, University of Massachusetts at Amherst, Massachusetts: KATSH, ABRAHAM ISAAC

Jacob Katsnelson, Lecturer in Climatology, Tel Aviv University; Director of the Climatology Division, Israel Meteorological Service, Bet Dagan, Israel: DEW; RAIN

Bernard (M.L.) Katz*, M.A., B.L.S.; Librarian, University of Guelph, Toronto, Canada: SAFDIE, SYLVIA

Chava Alkon Katz, Writer, Jerusalem: ZIONISM

Dovid Katz*, B.A., Ph.D.; Professor of Yiddish Language, Literature and Culture; Director of Research, Vilnius University, Lithuania: KATZ, MENKE; KERLER, DOV-BER

Elena (M.) Katz*, Ph.D., Dr.; University College, London, England: SHRAYBMAN, YEKHIEL

Elias Katz, Rabbi; Former Rabbi of Bratislava, Czechoslovakia, Beersheba: BRODY, SOLOMON ZALMAN BEN ISRAEL; ISRAEL MOSES BEN ARYEH

LOEB; JACOB BEN ABRAHAM SOLOMON; JACOB ISAAC BEN SHALOM; JOSEPH BEN MOSES PHINEHAS; JOSEPH BEN ZE'EV WOLF HA-LEVI; JUDAH BEN JACOB HA-KOHEN

Emily Alice Katz*, M. Phil.; The Jewish Theological Seminary of America, Princeton, New Jersey: ABARBANELL, LINA

Harold E. Katz, M.A., A.C.S.W.; Executive Director of the Jewish Community Council, Birmingham, Alabama

Irving I. Katz, B.A., B.B.A., F.T.A.; Detroit, Michigan: BUTZEL; DETROIT; FRANKLIN, LEO MORRIS; FRANKS, JACOB; HERSHMAN, ABRAHAM M.; SOLOMON, EZEKIEL

Israel J. Katz*, Ph.D.; Associate Professor, University of California at Davis: AMERICAN SOCIETY FOR JEWISH MUSIC; GREECE; HEMSI, ALBERTO; IDELSOHN, ABRAHAM ZVI; LADINO; LIST, GEORGE HAROLD; SCHINDLER, KURT; SOLA, ABRAHAM DE; WEISSER, ALBERT; WERNER, ERIC; WINTERNITZ, EMANUEL; YASSER, JOSEPH

Jacob Katz, Dr. Phil.; Rector and Professor of Social Jewish History, the Hebrew University of Jerusalem: ZIONISM

Katriel Katz, Ambassador, Ministry for Foreign Affairs, Jerusalem: SHILOAḤ, REUBEN

Meir Katz, Ph.D.; Musicologist, Jerusalem: WIENIAWSKI, HENRI

Nathan Katz*, Ph.D.; Professor, Dept. of Religious Studies, Florida International University: INDIA; KOCHI; MOTA, NEHEMIA

Simha Katz, M.A.; Associate Editor, *Encyclopaedia Judaica*, and former General Associate Editor, *Encyclopaedia Hebraica*, Jerusalem: AXELROD, PAVEL BORISOVICH; BAAL-MAKHSHOVES; BAKU; BAUSKA; BOGROV, DMITRI; BORISOV; BUSEL, JOSEPH; BYKHOV; ELIJAH BEN ABRAHAM; ENGEL, JOEL; GALICIA; GRUSENBERG, OSCAR OSIPOVICH; GUENZBURG; GUENZBURG; HALICZ; HIRSCH, SAMSON RAPHAEL; ISSERLEIN, ISRAEL BEN PETHAHIAH; OCTOBRISTS; ORSHANSKI, ILYA GRIGORYEVICH; STEINBERG, ISAAC NAHMAN

Steven T. Katz*, Ph.D.; Professor of Religion, Director, Elie Wiesel Center for Judaic Studies, Boston University: AGUS, JACOB B.; HOLOCAUST

Nathaniel Katzburg, Ph.D.; Associate Professor of Jewish History, Bar-Ilan University, Ramat Gan: ḤALUKKAH; HUNGARY; JEREMIAH BEN ISAAC; KITTSEE, ḤAYYIM BEN ISAAC; KITTSEE, JEHIEL MICHAEL BEN SAMUEL; KUNSTADT, ISAAC BEN ELIEZER LIPMAN; ÓNODY, GÉZA; ORTHODOXY; RIVLIN, YOSEF YIẒḤAK

Joy Katzen-Guthrie*, B.F.A., B.A.; Professional Writer and Recording Artist/Composer/Lyricist/Vocalist/Pianist/Speaker/Historian/Heritage Tour Operator: ALASKA

H. Jacob Katzenstein, Ph.D.; Director of the Schocken Library, Jerusalem: HIRAM; JEZEBEL; PHOENICIA, PHOENICIANS; SCHOCKEN INSTITUTE

Gideon Katznelson, M.A.; Lecturer in Modern Hebrew Literature, Tel Aviv University: LAMDAN, YIẒḤAK; SHALOM, SHIN; SHOFMAN, GERSHON

Asher Kaufman*, Ph.D.; Assistant Professor, University of Notre Dame, Indiana: ARAB LEAGUE

Edy Kaufman, Ph.D.; Jerusalem: STUDENTS' MOVEMENTS, JEWISH

Uri (Robert) Kaufmann*, Ph.D.; Historian, Wissenschaftliche Arbeitsgemeinschaft Leo Baeck Institut, Heidelberg, Germany: AARGAU; BASLE; BERNE; BIEL; BLOCH, ROLF; COHN; DREIFUSS, RUTH; DREYFUS; FARBSTEIN, DAVID; FEIGEL, SIGI; FRIBOURG; GENEVA; GOETSCHEL, JULES; GUGGENHEIM, CAMILLE; GUGGENHEIM, PAUL; GUGGENHEIM-GRUENBERG, FLORENCE; HERSCH, JEANNE; LA CHAUX-DE-FONDS; LAUSANNE; LUCERNE; SCHACHNOWITZ, SELIG; SCHAFFHAUSEN; STRECKFUSS, ADOLF FRIEDRICH KARL; SWITZERLAND; TEITLER, SAMUEL; ZURICH

Ben G. Kayfetz, B.A.; Executive Director of National Joint Community Relations Committee, Canadian Jewish Congress and B'nai B'rith, Toronto: BENNETT, ARCHIE; CROLL, DAVID ARNOLD; DAVID; DE SOLA; FEUER, LEWIS SAMUEL; FRANKLIN, SELIM; FREIMAN; GELBER; GRAUBART, JUDAH LEIB; HART, AARON; HART, BENJAMIN; HART, EZEKIEL; HART, SAMUEL; LEWIS, DAVID; RHINEWINE, ABRAHAM; SALSBERG, JOSEPH B.; SASKATCHEWAN

Gad Kaynar*, Dr.; Senior Lecturer, Department of Theater Studies, Tel Aviv University: HEBREW LITERATURE, MODERN; ISRAEL, STATE OF: CULTURAL LIFE

Rudolf Kayser, Dr.Phil.; Assistant Professor of Germanic Language and Literature, Brandeis University, Waltham, Massachusetts: ADLER, PAUL; BAB, JULIUS; BIEBER, HUGO; BRUCKNER, FERDINAND; FRANK, BRUNO; GEIGER, LUDWIG; GERMAN LITERATURE; GUMPERT, MARTIN; HAAS, WILLY; HEILBORN, ERNST; HERMANN, GEORG; HOLITSCHER, ARTHUR; KAHANE, ARTHUR; KASTEIN, JOSEF; KERR, ALFRED; KISCH, EGON ERWIN; KORNFELD, PAUL; LANDSBERGER, ARTHUR; LEONHARD, RUDOLF; MEHRING, WALTER; MEYER, RICHARD MORITZ; NEUMANN, ALFRED; PUBLISHING; REHFISCH, HANS JOSE; ROTH, JOSEPH; RUBINER, LUDWIG; SEGHERS, ANNA; WOLFENSTEIN, ALFRED

Stephen Kayser, Ph.D.; Former Curator of the Jewish Museum, New York; Los Angeles, California

Chaim S. Kazdan, the Jewish Teachers' Seminary, New York: EDUCATION, JEWISH

Hillel Kazovsky*: ABERDAM, ALFRED; ADLER, JANKEL; ADLIVANKIN, SAMUIL; AIZENBERG, NINA; ALTMAN, NATHAN; ANISFELD, BORIS; APPELBAUM, MOSHE; ART: EASTERN EUROPE; AXELROD, MEYER; BARCINSKY, HENRYK; BENN; BERLEWI, HENRYK; BRAUNER, ISAAC; BRAZ, OSIP; BRAZER, ABRAM; BRODSKII, ISAAK; CENTERSZWER, STANISŁAWA

Nissim Kazzaz*, Ph.D.; Retired Academic, Omer, Israel: BAGHDAD; IRAQ; MOSUL; ZAKHO

Batya Kedar, Jerusalem: NETHERWORLD

Benjamin Kedar, Ph.D.; Lecturer in Biblical Studies, Haifa University: BIBLE

Zvi Kedar, M.A.; Ministry for Foreign Affairs, Jerusalem

Martha Keil*, Dr.; Institut für Geschichte der Juden in Österreich, St. Polten, Austria: BANKERS AND

BANKING; ISSERLEIN, ISRAEL BEN PETHAHIAH

Jacob Kelemer, Jerusalem: PARAH; PE'AH

Hermann Kellenbenz, Dr. Phil.; Professor of Economic and Social History, the University of Cologne: BANKERS AND BANKING; COURT JEWS; SPICE TRADE; TRADE AND COMMERCE

Mark Keller, Rutgers University, New Brunswick, New Jersey: DRUNKENNESS

Sharon (Ruth) Keller*, Ph.D.; Assistant Professor, Bible and Ancient Semitic Languages, The Jewish Theological Seminary, New York: EGYPT

Menachem Kellner*, Ph.D.; Professor, University of Haifa: SCHWARZSCHILD, STEVEN SAMUEL

Wolfe Kelman, M.H.L., Rabbi; Executive Vice President, Rabbinical Assembly, New York: LEVY, FELIX ALEXANDER; MORGENSTERN, SOMA; RABBI, RABBINATE

Aaron Kempinski, M.A., Lecturer in Ancient Near Eastern History and Archaeology; Tel Aviv University: LYDIA, LYDIANS

Robert M.W. Kempner, LL.D.; Jurist and Chief Prosecutor, Nuremberg War Crimes Trials; Lansdowne, Pennsylvania: LAWYERS

Isaiah L. Kenen, LL.B.; Executive Director of the American-Israel Public Affairs Committee, Washington, D.C.: UNITED STATES OF AMERICA

Sharon Kenigsberg*: LONG BEACH

Andreas Kennecke*, Dr.Phil.; Research Assistant, University of Potsdam, Germany: SCHLEIERMACHER, FRIEDRICH

Moshe Kerem, M.A.; Lecturer in Education, Haifa University; Kibbutz Gesher ha-Ziv: KIBBUTZ MOVEMENT

Yitzchak Kerem*, Professor, Aristotle University, Thessalonika, Greece; Lecturer and Researcher, Hebrew University of Jerusalem: ALHANATI, DAVID; ANGEL, MARC D.; ARDITI, ALBERT JUDAH; ARTA; ATHENS; BELLELI, LAZARUS MENAHEM; BENSANCHI, MENTESH; CAÏMIS, JULIUS; CANEA; CHIOS; COHEN, JOSEPH ISAAC; CORCOS, DAVID; CORCOS, STELLA; CORFU; CUOMOTINI; DALVEN, RACHEL; DIDYMOTEIKHON; DRAMA; ELAZAR, DANIEL J.; ELAZAR, YA'AKOV; ELIYIA, JOSEPH; FRANCO, AVRAHAM; FRANCO, MOSES; GREECE; GREEK LITERATURE, MODERN; IOANNINA; KASTORIA; KAVALLA; KORETZ, ZVI; KOS; LARISSA; MAESTRO, YAAKOV; MATSAS, JOSEPH; MATSAS, NESTORAS; MOLHO, ISAAC RAPHAEL; NAUPAKTOS; NEHAMA, JOSEPH; NOVITCH, MIRIAM; PATRAS; PHLORINA; RAZON, JACKO; RECANATI, ABRAHAM SAMUEL; RHODES; SALEM, EMMANUEL RAPHAEL; SALONIKA; SCHIBY, BARUCH; SCIAKI, JOSEPH; SEPHARDIM; SERRAI; TRIKKALA; UZIEL, BARUCH; VEROIA; VOLOS; WORLD SEPHARDI FEDERATION; ZANTE

Dov-Ber Kerler*, B.A., Dr.Phil.; Dr. Alice Field Cohn Chair in Yiddish Studies, Borns Jewish Studies Program and Department of Germanic Studies, Indiana University, Bloomington; Director of Indiana University Yiddish Ethnographic Project, Bloomington: KATZ, DOVID; KERLER, YOYSEF

Elton J. Kerness, M.S.W.; Executive Director of the Jewish Community Council of Eastern Union County, New Jersey

Anne J. Kershen, M.Phil.; Barnet Shine Senior Research Fellow and Director, Centre for the Study of Migration, Queen Mary and Westfield College, University of London: LONDON

Solomon Kerstein, Vice President, Bloch Publishing Company, New York: PUBLISHING

Margery (Helen) Kerstine*, M.A.; Archivist, Temple Israel, Memphis: SAMFIELD, MAX

J. Yeshurun Kesheth, Writer and Critic, Jerusalem: CAHAN, YAAKOV

Carole S. Kessner*, Ph.D.; Professor, State University of New York at Stony Brook: EISENSTEIN, JUDITH KAPLAN; LAZARUS, EMMA; SYRKIN, MARIE; WEISS-ROSMARIN, TRUDE

Ruth Kestenberg-Gladstein, Ph.D.; External Teacher in the History of the Jewish People, Haifa University: BASSEVI OF TREUENBERG, JACOB; FAMILIANTS LAWS; HUSSITES

Geoffrey Khan, Ph.D.; Research Assistant, Genizah Unit, Cambridge University Library: GENIZAH, CAIRO

Dan Kharuv, Ph.D.; Editor, *The Shorter Jewish Encyclopaedia in Russian*, Jerusalem: KRIMCHAKS

Herman Kieval, M.H.L., Rabbi; Visiting Associate Professor of Practical Theology; Visiting Assistant Professor of Liturgy, the Jewish Theological Seminary of America, New York: BAREKHU; BARUKH; KOL NIDREI; NE'ILAH; PESUKEI DE-ZIMRA

Andreas Kilcher*, Professor, Universität Tübingen, Deutsches Seminar, Tübingen, Germany: BEN-CHORIN, SCHALOM; BENJAMIN, WALTER; CANETTI, ELIAS; DOEBLIN, ALFRED; EHRENSTEIN, ALBERT; GOLDSTEIN, MORITZ; GUNDOLF, FRIEDRICH; HAAS, WILLY; HESSEL, FRANZ; HILSENRATH, EDGAR; HONIGMANN, BARBARA; KOLMAR, GERTRUD; KORNFELD, PAUL; KROJANKER, GUSTAV; LASKER-SCHUELER, ELSE; LESSING, THEODOR; MARGUL-SPERBER, ALFRED; MAUTHNER, FRITZ; MEHRING, WALTER; MORGENSTERN, SOMA; MYNONA; REICH-RANICKI, MARCEL

Andreas Kilian*, M.A.; Frankfurt, Germany: SONDERKOMMANDO, JEWISH

Joseph Kilinghofer

Israel Kimhi*, M.A.; Geographer and Town Planner, Head of the Research Division on Jerusalem, The Jerusalem Institute for Israel Studies, and the Hebrew University School for Urban and Regional Studies, Jerusalem: JERUSALEM

Arie Kindler, Director of the Kadman Numismatic Museum, Tel Aviv: COINS AND CURRENCY; JUDENPFENNIGE; MERZBACHER; SHEKEL

Stephen D. Kinsey*, M.A.; Middle School Teacher, J.W. Fair Middle School, San Jose, California: SAN JOSE

Mark Kipnis, M.A.; Scientific Editor, Jewish Personalities Division of *The Shorter Jewish*

Encyclopaedia in Russian, Jerusalem: CRIMEAN AFFAIR; GEKHT, SEMEN GRIGOREVICH; GOTS; GRULËV, MIKHAIL VLADIMIROVICH; GUKOVSKY, GRIGORY ALEKSANDROVICH; KIPEN, ALEKSANDR ABRAMOVICH; KNUT, DOVID; KOL'TSOV, MIKHAIL; KOMZET; LOTMAN, YURI MIKHAILOVICH; LOYTER, EFRAIM BARUKHOVICH; ZEMLYACHKA, ROZALIYA SAMOYLOVNA

Aaron Kirschenbaum, Ph.D., Rabbi; Associate Professor of Jewish Law, Tel Aviv University: DOMICILE; LEGAL MAXIMS; LEGAL PERSON; MEḤILAH; ORPHAN, ORPHANAGE; SHI'BUDA DE-RABBI NATHAN

Robert Kirschner*, Ph.D.; Los Angeles, California: HERSCHER, URI DAVID; HOLOCAUST: SPIRITUAL RESISTANCE IN THE GHETTOS AND CONCENTRATION CAMPS; SKIRBALL CULTURAL CENTER

Barbara Kirshenblatt-Gimblett*, Ph.D.; Professor of Performance Studies, and Affiliated Professor of Hebrew and Judaic Studies, New York University, New York: COOKBOOKS, JEWISH

Shimshon Leib Kirshenboim, Ph.D.; Educator, Jerusalem: DZIALOSZYCE; KALUSZYN; KATOWICE; KOLO; KOLOMYYA; KONSKIE; KOVEL; KREMENETS; KROSNO; KROTOSZYN; KUTNO; LESKOW; LESSER POLAND; LIPNO; LODZ; LUBLIN; LUTSK; MINSK MAZOWIECKI; NAROL; NASIELSK; OZORKOW; PABIANICE; PEREMYSHLYANY; PIASECZNO; PLONSK; PODGAITSY; PODKAMEN; PODVOLOCHISK; PRUZHANY; PRZEDBORZ; PRZEMYSL; PRZEWORSK; PRZYSUCHA; RADYMNO; RADZYMIN; RADZYN; ROGATIN; ROPCZYCE; RYMANOW; RYPIN; SASOV; SATANOV; SHARGOROD; SOKOLOW PODLASKI; STASZOW; STOPNICA; STRYKOW; SZCZEBRZESZYN; TYKOCIN; WLODAWA; WOLOMIN; WRONKI; WYSZOGROD; ZAWIERCIE; ZMIGROD NOWY; ZWOLEN; ZYCHLIN

Meir Jacob Kister, Ph.D.; Professor of Arabic Language and Literature, the Hebrew University of Jerusalem: HADITH

Menahem Kister*: AVOT DE-RABBI NATHAN

Melissa (R.) Klapper*, Ph.D.; Assistant Professor of History, Rowan University, Glassboro, New Jersey: HASSENFELD, SYLVIA KAY

Manfred Klarberg, M.A.; Department of Humanities, Footscray College of Technology, Footscray, Victoria, Australia: AARON BEN SAMUEL

Traci M. Klass*, Ph.D.; Visiting Faculty, English, University of Florida, Wellington, Florida: MOSS, CELIA and MARION

Jacob Klatzkin, Dr.Phil.; Philosopher and Editor in Chief of the *Encyclopaedia Judaica* (Germany); Berlin: ARMILUS; AUGUSTINE; INFORMERS

Israel Klausner, Ph.D.; Historian and former Deputy Director of the Central Zionist Archives, Jerusalem: BEN-AMMI, MORDECAI; CAZALET, EDWARD; DEMOCRATIC FRACTION; ELIJAH BEN SOLOMON ZALMAN; FRIEDLAND, NATAN; GLIKIN, MOSHE; GROSSMAN, MEIR; JAFFE, MORDECAI-GIMPEL; KATTOWITZ CONFERENCE; KRAUSE, ELIYAHU; LIPPE, KARPEL; MINSK CONFERENCE; MUYAL, AVRAHAM; NES ẒIYYONAH; NETTER, CHARLES; NEWLINSKI, PHILIPP MICHAEL; ODESSA COMMITTEE; PINELES, SAMUEL; SNEERSOHN, ḤAYYIM ẒEVI; VILNA; WEITZ, NAPHTALI

Joseph Gedaliah Klausner, Dr. Phil. Emeritus Professor of Hebrew Literature and of the Second Temple Period, the Hebrew University of Jerusalem: ALEXANDER SUSSKIND BEN MOSES OF GRODNO; BEN-YEHUDA, ELIEZER; BERNFELD, SIMON; ESCHATOLOGY; MASIE, AARON MEIR; USSISHKIN, ABRAHAM MENAḤEM MENDEL

Yehuda Arye Klausner, Ph.D.; Writer and Scholar, Jerusalem: ACROSTICS; JUNOSZA, KLEMENS; MEZAḤ, JOSHUA HA-LEVI; MICKIEWICZ, ADAM; MULDER, SAMUEL ISRAEL; ORZESZKOWA, ELIZA; PERETZ, ISAAC LEIB

Benjamin J. Klebaner, Ph.D.; Professor of Economics, City College of the City University of New York: LIPSON, EPHRAIM

Claude Klein, Ph.D.; Senior Lecturer in Law, the Hebrew University of Jerusalem: LAWYERS

Hilel Klein, M.D.; Jerusalem: FENICHEL, OTTO

Isaac Klein, Ph.D., Rabbi; Lecturer in Philosophy, the State University of New York at Buffalo: HOSCHANDER, JACOB; HYAMSON, MOSES; MINHAGIM BOOKS; RECANATI; ẒAHALON

Jacqueline Klein*: PASSAIC-CLIFTON

Joseph Klein, M.H.L., Rabbi; Lecturer in Biblical Literature, Clark University, Worcester, Massachusetts: WORCESTER

Nancy (H.) Klein*, M.A.; Retired, Cincinnati: CINCINNATI; FEINBERG, LOUIS; SCHMIDT, SAMUEL MYER

Robert B. Klein*, M.Ed.; English Teacher; Freelance Journalist, Yeshiva High School of Mitzpeh Ramon, Israel: ROTH, MARK; RUDOLPH, MARVIN; SAMPRAS, PETE; SCHAYES, ADOLPH; SCHECKTER, JODY; SCHNEIDER, MATHIEU; SELIG, ALLAN H.; SHERMAN, ALEXANDER; SLUTSKAYA, IRINA; SOLOMON, HAROLD; SPELLMAN, FRANK; STERN, BILL; STILLMAN, LOUIS; STRUG, KERRI; SZEKELY, EVA; TANENBAUM, SIDNEY HAROLD; ZASLOVSKY, MAX

Rudolf Klein*, Ph.D.; Professor of Architecture, Tel Aviv University, The David Azrieli School of Architecture; Saint Steven University, Ybl Miklos Faculty of Architecture, Budapest: BAUMHORN, LIPÓT; SYNAGOGUE

Max M. Kleinbaum, M.A.; American Jewish Congress, Philadelphia: BERGEN COUNTY

Michael L. Klein-Katz, Rabbi; Spiritual Leader, Teacher, and Storyteller, Jerusalem

Heszel Klepfisz, Ph.D., Litt. D., Rabbi; Rector of the Instituto Alberto Einstein; Professor of Judaic Culture, the University of Panama

Jean (C.) Klerman*, B.A., M.L.S.; Principal Librarian, Monmouth County (retired), Co-President, Jewish Heritage Museum of Monmouth County, New Jersey: MONMOUTH COUNTY

Bronia Klibanski, B.A.; Archivist, Jerusalem: BIALYSTOK

Ignacio Klich, Ph.D.; School of Languages, Faculty of Law, Languages and Communication, University of Westminster, London: ARGENTINA

Barnet David Klien, M.A., Rabbi; Jerusalem: BARAITA OF 32 RULES

Sam Kliger*, Ph.D.; Director of Russian Jewish Affairs, The American Jewish Committee, New York: NEW YORK CITY

Jerome Klinkowitz*, Ph.D.; Professor of English, University of Northern Iowa: APPLE, MAX

Alan Klugman*: PALM SPRINGS AND DESERT AREA

Brian Knei-Paz (Knapheis), M.A.; Instructor in Political Science, the Hebrew University of Jerusalem: BELOFF, MAX; BERLIN, SIR ISAIAH

Andrea Knight*, M.A.; Editor, Toronto, Canada: FRUM; GRAFSTEIN, JERAHMIEL S.; MORGENTALER, HENRY; SHARP, ISADOR NATANIEL

Hugo Knoepfmacher, D.Jur.; Government Official, Washington, D.C.: NATIONALRAT; NEUZEIT, DIE; PARLAMENTSKLUB, JUEDISCHER; PICK, ALOIS; SEIPEL, IGNAZ; STEUSS, DAVID; SZÁNTÓ, SIMON; UNION, OESTERREICHISCH-ISRAELITISCHE; VOLKSPARTEI, JUEDISCHE; ZENTRALSTELLE DER FUERSORGE FUER KRIEGSFLUECHTLINGE

Harry Knopf, D.iur.Utr.; Advocate, Tel Aviv: RESTITUTION AND INDEMNIFICATION

Ann-Kristin Koch*, M.A.; Ph.D.; Student, University of Tübingen, Tübingen, Germany: AICHINGER, ILSE; AMÉRY, JEAN; BROCH, HERMANN; ELOESSER, ARTHUR; FRIED, ERICH; GOLL, CLAIRE; GOLL, YVAN; JELINEK, ELFRIEDE; KLEMPERER, VICTOR; LEWALD, FANNY; TABORI, GEORG

Lionel Kochan, Ph.D.; Lecturer in Jewish History, the University of Warwick, Coventry: KRISTALLNACHT

Moshe Kochavi, Ph.D.; Senior Lecturer in Archaeology, Tel Aviv University: EGYPT, BROOK OF; EPHRATH

David Koenigstein*, M.A.T., M.L.S.; Assistant Professor, Librarian, Bronx Community College of the City University of New York: LEVERTOV, DENISE

Barry (Sherman) Kogan*, M.A.H.L., Ph.D.; Efroymson Professor of Philosophy and Jewish Religious Thought, Hebrew Union College-Jewish Institute of Religion, Cincinnati: CAUSE AND EFFECT

Mendel Kohansky, Theater critic, Tel Aviv: BERNSTEIN-COHEN, MIRIAM; HAIFA MUNICIPAL THEATER; HALEVY, MOSHE; MERON, HANNA; MESKIN, AHARON; OHEL; ROVINA, HANNA

Sami Kohen, M.A.; Journalist, Istanbul

Shira Kohn*, Ph.D.; New York University: HILLMAN, BESSIE "BAS SHEVA" ABRAMOWITZ; NATHAN, MAUD

S. Joshua Kohn, D.H.L., Rabbi; Trenton, New Jersey: NAAR, DAVID; TRENTON

Yehudah Pinhas Leo Kohn, LL.D.; Jurist and Diplomat, Jerusalem: BRODETSKY, SELIG; HYDE, THOMAS

Moshe Kol, Minister of Tourism, Jerusalem: HA-OVED HA-ẒIYYONI

Israel Kolatt, Ph.D.; Senior Lecturer in Contemporary Jewry, the Hebrew University of Jerusalem: ISRAEL, STATE OF: LABOR

Yehuda Komlosh, Ph.D., Rabbi; Senior Lecturer in Bible, Bar-Ilan University, Ramat Gan: SELLIN, ERNST; TARGUM SHENI; WIENER, HAROLD MARCUS; ZERAH BEN NATHAN OF TROKI

Eva Kondor, Jerusalem: BAUMGARTEN, SÁNDOR; BÖHM, HENRIK; FREUND, VILMOS; HAJÓS, ALFRÉD; HEGEDÜS, ARMIN; SEBESTYÉN, ARTUR; STERK, IZIDOR; HUNGARIAN LITERATURE; JAKAB, DEZSÖ and KOMOR, MARCELL; KARINTHY, FERENC; KERTÉSZ IMRE; KONRÁD, GYÖRGY; LAJTA, BÉLA; MÁLNAI, BÉLA; QITTNER, ZSIGMOND; SPIRO, GYÖRGY; SZENDE, STEFAN; VÁGÓ, JÓZSEF; VÁGÓ, LÁSZLÓ; VÁNDOR, LAJOS; VAS, ISTVÁN

Milton Ridvas Konvitz, Ph.D.; Professor Emeritus of Industrial and Labor Relations and of Law, Cornell University, New York: AUERBACH, CARL A.; BICKEL, ALEXANDER M.; BOTEIN, BERNARD; DERSHOWITZ, ALAN M.; DWORKIN, RONALD; FEINBERG, ROBERT; FRIENDLY, HENRY JACOB; GOLDMAN, PAUL L.; GOLDMAN, SIDNEY; GOULD, MILTON S.; HELLER, BERNARD; KAMPELMAN, MAX M.; LEVIN, A. LEO; PILCH, JUDAH; SHEINKMAN, JACOB; SILVER, EDWARD S.; WACHTLER, SOL; WILENTZ, ROBERT N.; YANKOWICH, LEON RENE; ZUKERMAN, JACOB T.

Lothar Kopf, Ph.D.; the Jewish National and University Library, Jerusalem: GERSHON BEN SOLOMON OF ARLES; WEIL, GOTTHOLD

Lionel Koppman, M.A.; Director, Public Information and Publications, National Jewish Welfare Board, New York

Nathan Koren, M.D.; Historian, Jerusalem: ALBU, ISIDOR; BALLIN, SAMUEL JACOB; MAGNUS, RUDOLPH

Sharon Faye Koren*, Ph.D.; Assistant Professor of Medieval Jewish Culture, Hebrew Union College-Jewish Institute of Religion, New York: SHEKHINAH

Yedidah Koren*: ARAKHIN; BEKHOROT

William Korey, Ph.D.; Director of the B'nai B'rith United Nations Office, New York: BABI YAR; DISCRIMINATION; EISENMANN, LOUIS; MITIN, MARK BORISOVICH; PIPES, RICHARD EDGAR; YAROSLAVSKY, YEMELYAN; ZINOVIEV, GRIGORI YEVSEYEVICH

Bertram Wallace Korn, D.H.L., Rabbi; Historian, Elkins Park, Pennsylvania: ALABAMA; BENJAMIN, JUDAH PHILIP; BONDI, AUGUST; BONDI, JONAS; BUSH, ISIDOR; CRESSON, WARDER; DAROFF, SAMUEL H.; DROPSIE, MOSES AARON; FLEISHER; GOTTHEIL, GUSTAV; GRANT, ULYSSES SIMPSON; GREENFIELD, ALBERT MONROE; GUTHEIM, JAMES KOPPEL; HART, ABRAHAM; HART, BERNARD; HART, EMANUEL BERNARD; LEVY, MOSES ELIAS; LINCOLN, ABRAHAM; LIT; LOUISIANA; MORWITZ, EDWARD; MOSS, JOHN; PHILADELPHIA; PINNER, MORITZ; SLAVE TRADE; TOURO, JUDAH; UNION OF REFORM JUDAISM

Eli Kornreich*, B.A., M.S., M.A.; President, JCC of Eastern Fairfield County, Bridgeport, CT: BRIDGEPORT

Pawel Korzec, Ph.D.; Research Associate of the Centre National de la Recherche Scientifique, Paris: BOYCOTT, ANTI-JEWISH

David Kotlar, C.E.; Lecturer in Jewish History, Bar-Ilan University, Ramat Gan: MIKVEH

Gideon Kouts, Israeli Correspondent and Journalist, Paris: ATTALI, JACQUES; BADINTER, ROBERT; BENN; BLEUSTEIN-BLANCHET, MARCEL; DANIEL, JEAN; ELKABBACH, JEAN-PIERRE; ELKANN, JEAN-PAUL; FABIUS, LAURENT; FINKIELKRAUT, ALAIN; FITERMAN, CHARLES; KAHN, JEAN; KLEIN, THEODORE; KOUCHNER, BERNARD; KRASUCKI, HENRI; KRIEGEL, ANNIE; LANG, JACK; LANZMANN, CLAUDE; MNOUCHKINE, ALEXANDRE; MOATI, SERGE; MODIANO, PATRICK; OURY, GERARD; ROULEAU, ERIC; SCHWARTZENBERG, ROGER-GERARD; STRAUSS-KAHN, DOMINIQUE; TIM; ZAFRANI, HAIM; ZIONISM

Santiago Ezequiel Kovadloff, Licenciado en Filosofia; Writer, Translator, Professor of Classical Philosophy, Buenos Aires: SPANISH AND PORTUGUESE LITERATURE

Joel Kraemer, Ph.D., Rabbi; Assistant Professor of Arabic and Islamic Studies, Yale University, New Haven, Connecticut: ATOMISM; CAIN; EMANATION; FĀRĀBĪ, ABU NAṢR MUHAMMAD, AL-; HALLO, RUDOLF; MICROCOSM; NEOPLATONISM

Helen Kragness-Romanishan, M.A.; Educator, Wichita, Kansas: KANSAS

Stefan Krakowski, M.A.; Yad Vashem, Jerusalem: AUGUSTOW; BEDZIN; BELZYCE; BIAŁA PODLASKA; BIELSKO; BILGORAJ; BOCHNIA; CHECINY; CHELM; CHMIELNIK; CHORZÓW; CHRYZANOW; CRACOW; CZESTOCHOWA; DABROWA GORNICZA; DZIALOSZYCE; GLIWICE; GORA KALWARIA; GROJEC; HRUBIESZOW; IZBICA LUBELSKA; JANOW LUBELSKI; JASLO; JEDRZEJOW; KALUSZYN; KATOWICE; KIELCE; KONSKIE; KONSKOWOLA; KRASNIK; KROSNO; LODZ; LOWICZ; LUBLIN; MAKOW MAZOWIECKI; MIEDZYRZEC PODLASK; MINSK MAZOWIECKI; NOWY SACZ; OPOCZNO; OPOLE LUBELSKIE; OSTROW MAZOWIECKA; OTWOCK; PARCZEW; POLAND; PRZYTYK; PULAWY; PULTUSK; RADOM; RADOMSKO; RADZYN; RZESZOW; SANDOMIERZ; SANOK; SIEDLCE; SKARZYSKO-KAMIENNA; SKIERNIEWICE; SOKOLOW PODLASKI; SOSNOWIEC; STUTTHOF; SZCZEBRZESZYN; TARNOW; TOMASZOW LUBELSKI; TOMASZOW MAZOWIECKI; WARSAW; WEGROW; WLODAWA; WYSZKOW; ZAMOSC; ZAWIERCIE; ZELECHOW; ZYRARDOW

Shmuel Krakowsky*

Robin Kramer*: WOLF, ALFRED

Samuel Noah Kramer, Ph.D.; Emeritus Research Professor of Assyriology, the University of Pennsylvania, Philadelphia: SUMER, SUMERIANS

William M. Kramer, Ph.D., Rabbi; Emeritus Professor, California State University at Northridge

Rachel Kranson*, Ph.D.; History, Hebrew and Judaic Studies, New York University: INTERNATIONAL LADIES GARMENT WORKERS UNION; SHAVELSON, CLARA LEMLICH

Jonathan Krasner*, Ph.D.; Professor, Hebrew Union College-Jewish Institute of Religion, Cincinnati, Ohio: GAMORAN, MAMIE GOLDSMITH

Elisabeth Kraus*: MOSSE

Naftali Kraus, Journalist, Tel Aviv: HUNGARY; ROMANIA

Adonijahu Krauss, M.A., Rabbi; Jerusalem: KRAUSS, JUDAH HA-KOHEN; KROCH, JACOB LEIB BEN SHEMAIAH

Ernest Krausz, Ph.D.; Lecturer in Sociology, the City University, London: ENGLAND; LONDON

Leonard S. Kravitz, Ph.D., Rabbi; Professor of Midrash and Homiletics, the Hebrew Union College-Jewish Institute of Religion, New York

Yulia Kreinin*, Ph.D.; Senior Lecturer, Department of Musicology, the Hebrew University of Jerusalem: AROM, SIMHA; BABBITT, MILTON; BOTSTEIN, LEON; DORFMAN, JOSEPH; FELDMAN, MORTON; FOSS, LUKAS; GLASS, PHILIP; HAUBENSTOCK-RAMATI, ROMAN; HIRSHBERG, JEHOASH; JAFFE, ELI; KOPYTMAN, MARK RUVIMOVICH; LEIBOWITZ, RENÉ; LIGETI, GYÖRGY; REICH, STEVE; ROCHBERG, GEORGE; ROSEN, CHARLES; SCHNITTKE, ALFRED; SCHOENBERG, ARNOLD; TANSMAN, ALEXANDER; THOMAS, MICHAEL TILSON; VOGEL, WLADIMIR; WEILL, KURT

Howard (Haim) Kreisel*, Ph.D.; Professor of Medieval Jewish Philosophy, Ben-Gurion University of the Negev, Beersheba: NISSIM BEN MOSES OF MARSEILLES; PROPHETS AND PROPHECY; RU'AḤ HA-KODESH

Benjamin Z. Kreitman: EPSTEIN, LOUIS M.

Getzel Kressel, Writer and Bibliographer, Holon, Israel: ABELES, OTTO; AGMON, NATHAN; AḤDUT HA-AVODAH; AKAVYA, AVRAHAM ARYEH LEIB; ALBALA, DAVID; ALKALAI, DAVID; ASHMAN, AHARON; ATLAS, ELEAZAR; AUERBACH, ISRAEL; AVI-SHAUL, MORDEKHAI; BADER, GERSHOM; BAK; BARBASH, SAMUEL; BARNETT, ZERAH; BARUCH, JOSEPH MARCOU; BATO, LUDWIG YOMTOV; BEHAK, JUDAH; BEILIN, ASHER; BEILINSON, MOSHE; BEN ELIEZER, MOSHE; BEN-AMITAI, LEVI; BENEI MOSHE; BEN-YEḤEZKI'EL, MORDEKHAI; BEN-YEHUDA, ḤEMDAH; BEN-ZVI, RAḤEL YANAIT; BEREGI, ÁRMIN BENJAMIN; BERGSTEIN, FANIA; BERTINI, K. AHARON; BIBAS; BIERER, RUBIN; BIKKUREI HA-ITTIM; BILU; BODEK, JACOB; BOSAK, MEIR; BRAUDE, MARKUS; BRILL, JEHIEL; BROIDES, ABRAHAM; BUSTENAI; BUXBAUM, NATHAN; CARMOLY, ELIAKIM; CASTIGLIONI, ḤAYYIM; CHOMSKY, DOV; CHURGIN, YA'AKOV YEHOSHUA; COËN, GRAZIADIO VITA ANANIA; COHEN, ISRAEL; COHN, EMIL MOSES; COWEN, JOSEPH; CREIZENACH, MICHAEL; DAGON, BARUKH; DAVAR; DEEDES, SIR WYNDHAM; DEINARD, EPHRAIM; DELLA TORRE, LELIO; DO'AR HA-YOM; DON-YAḤIA, YEHUDAH LEIB; DUNANT, JEAN HENRI; DYKMAN, SHLOMO; EDER, MONTAGUE DAVID; EICHENBAUM, JACOB; EISLER, EDMUND MENAHEM; ELAZARI-VOLCANI, YIẒḤAK; ELIASBERG, MORDECAI; ESRA; EVEN-SHOSHAN, AVRAHAM; EVER HADANI; FADENHECHT, YEHOSHUA; FAHN, REUBEN; FARBSTEIN, DAVID ẒEVI; FARBSTEIN, JOSHUA HESCHEL; FEDER, TOBIAS; FEITELSON, MENAHEM MENDEL; FELD, ISAAC; FERNHOF, ISAAC; FISCHER, JEAN; FISCHMANN, NAḤMAN ISAAC; FLEISCHER, JUDAH LOEB; FRAENKEL, ISAAC SECKEL; FRANKEL, NAOMI; FREDERICK I; FRIEDEMANN, ADOLF; FRIEDMANN, DAVID ARYEH; GALAI, BINYAMIN; GAMZU, ḤAYYIM;

GAON, MOSES DAVID; GAWLER, GEORGE; GESANG, NATHAN-NACHMAN; GILEAD, ZERUBAVEL; GILYONOT; GLASNER, MOSES SAMUEL; GOLDBERG, ABRAHAM; GOLDENBERG, BAERISH; GOLDENBERG, SAMUEL LEIB; GOLDHAMMER-SAHAWI, LEO; GOLDIN, EZRA; GOLDMAN, YA'AKOV BEN ASHER; GOLDSTEIN, ALEXANDER; GORDON, DAVID; GORDON, SAMUEL LEIB; GOREN, NATAN; GOSLAR, HANS; GOTTLIEB, HIRSCH LEIB; GOTTLIEB, YEHOSHUA; GRAEBER, SCHEALTIEL EISIK; GREENBERG, LEOPOLD JACOB; GROSS, NATHAN; GUEDALLA, HAIM; GUEDEMANN, MORITZ; GUENZIG, EZRIEL; GUTTMACHER, ELIJAH; HA-ASIF; HABAS, BRACHA; HA-BOKER; HAEZRAḤI, YEHUDA; HA-LEVANON; HALPERN, GEORG GAD; HA-MAGGID; HA-MELIẒ; HAMENAḤEM, EZRA; HA-ME'ORER; HA-MIẒPEH; HANNOVER, RAPHAEL LEVI; HAOLAM; HA-PO'EL HA-ẒA'IR; HA-SHILO'AḤ; HA-TEKUFAH; HAUSNER, BERNARD; ḤAVAẒẒELET; HA-YOM; HA-ẒEFIRAH; HA-ẒOFEH; HECHLER, WILLIAM HENRY; HEFER, ḤAYIM; HE-ḤALUTZ; HELLER, JOSEPH ELIJAH; HELLMAN, JACOB; HELSINGFORS PROGRAM; HERBST, KARL; HERRMANN, HUGO; HESS, MOSES; HICKL, MAX; HODESS, JACOB; HOFFMANN, JACOB; HOGA, STANISLAV; HORODISCHTSCH, LEON; HOROWITZ, YA'AKOV; HURWITZ, SAUL ISRAEL; ISH-KISHOR, EPHRAIM; ISRAEL, STATE OF: CULTURAL LIFE; JAFFE, ABRAHAM B.; JANNER, BARNETT, LORD; JARBLUM, MARC; JUEDISCHER VERLAG; K. ZETNIK; KADARI, SHRAGA; KADIMAH; KALEF, YEHOSHUA; KALISCHER, ẒEVI HIRSCH; KAMSON, YA'AKOV DAVID; KANN, JACOBUS HENRICUS; KAPLAN, PESAḤ; KARIV, AVRAHAM YIẒḤAK; KARU, BARUCH; KASHER, MENAHEM; KATZ, BENZION; KATZENELSON, BARUCH; KATZNELSON, RAḤEL; KAZNELSON, SIEGMUND; KELLNER, LEON; KENAANI, DAVID; KEREM ḤEMED; KESHET, YESHURUN; KESSLER, LEOPOLD; KIMḤI, DOV; KINDERFREUND, ARYEH LEIB; KIPNIS, LEVIN; KISHON, EPHRAIM; KLAUSNER, ISRAEL; KLEE, ALFRED; KLEINMANN, MOSHE; KLUMEL, MEIR; KOHELETH MUSSAR; KOHEN-ZEDEK, JOSEPH; KOKESCH, OZER; KORKIS, ABRAHAM ADOLF; KOVNER, ABBA; KROCHMAL, ABRAHAM; KROJANKER, GUSTAV; LANDAU, LEIBUSH MENDEL; LANDAU, MOSES; LANDAU, SAUL RAPHAEL; LAUTERBACH, ASHER ZELIG; LEVI-BIANCHINI, ANGELO; LEVIN, ALTER ISAAC; LEVNER, ISRAEL BENJAMIN; LEWINSKY, YOM-TOV; LEWYSOHN, YEHUDI LEIB LUDWIG; LICHTENBAUM, JOSEPH; LICHTHEIM, RICHARD; LIPSON, MORDEKHAI; LORJE, CHAIM; LUBOSHITZKI, AARON; LUDVIPOL, ABRAHAM; LUIDOR, JOSEPH; MACCOBY, ḤAYYIM ZUNDEL; MAHLER, ARTHUR; MAIMON, ADA; MARGOLIN, ELIEZER; MEHLSACK, ELIAKIM BEN JUDAH HA-MILZAHGI; MEISL, JOSEPH; MEITUS, ELIAHU; MELTZER, SHIMSHON; MENDELSOHN, FRANKFURT MOSES; MICHALI, BINYAMIN YIẒḤAK; MIESES, FABIUS; MIESIS, JUDAH LEIB; MIRSKY, AARON; MOHR, ABRAHAM MENAHEM MENDEL; MOHR, MEIR; MORDELL, PHINEHAS; MORDOVTSEV, DANIIL LUKICH; MOSER, JACOB; NEWSPAPERS AND PERIODICALS, HEBREW; NEWSPAPERS, HEBREW; NISSENBAUM, ISAAC; NOBEL, NEHEMIAH ANTON; NOSSIG, ALFRED; NUSSENBLATH, TULO; OFEK, URIEL; OLSCHWANGER, ISAAC WOLF; OLSVANGER, IMMANUEL; OMER, HILLEL; OPPENHEIM, DAVID; OPPENHEIM, ḤAYYIM; ORLAND, YAAKOV; OTTENSOSSER, DAVID; OTTOLENGHI, MOSES JACOB; OVSAY, JOSHUA; OVSAY, JOSHUA; PAPERNA, ABRAHAM BARUCH; PENN, ALEXANDER; PENUELI, SHEMUEL YESHAYAHU; PERI EẒ-ḤAYYIM; PERLMAN, SAMUEL; PINES, NOAH; POZNANSKY, MENAḤEM; PROBST, MENAHEM MENDEL; PROTESTRABBINER; RABBI BINYAMIN; RABINOVITZ, ALEXANDER SISKIND; RABINOWITZ, YA'AKOV; RABINOWITZ, ẒEVI HA-COHEN; RABINOWITZ, ZINA; RAWNITZKI, YEHOSHUA ḤANA; REINES, ISAAC JACOB; REUVENI, AHARON; RIMON, JACOB; RINGEL, MICHAEL; RIVLIN, ELIEZER; ROKACH, ELEAZAR; ROKEAḤ, DAVID; ROMANO, MARCO; ROSEN, ABRAHAM; ROSENFELD, AHARON; ROTENSTREICH, FISCHEL; ROTHSCHILD, BARON EDMOND JAMES DE; RUBIN, SOLOMON; RUBINSTEIN, ISAAC; RUEBNER, TUVIA; RUELF, ISAAC; SACERDOTI, ANGELO-RAPHAEL CHAIM; SACHER, HARRY; SACHS, SENIOR; SALVENDI, ADOLF; SAN REMO CONFERENCE; SATANOW, ISAAC; SCHACH, FABIUS; SCHACHTEL, HUGO-HILLEL; SCHAECHTER, JOSEPH; SCHALIT, ISIDOR; SCHAPIRA, NOAH; SCHATZ, ZEVI; SCHERLAG, MARK; SCHILLER, SOLOMON; SCHNEIDER, MORDECAI BEZALEL; SCHNIRER, MORITZ TOBIAS; SCHORR, NAPHTALI MENDEL; SCHRENZEL, MOSES; SCHWARZBART, ISAAC IGNACY; SCHWEID, ELIEZER; SELBSTEMANZIPATION; SENED, ALEXANDER; SHAANAN, AVRAHAM; SHALEV, YITZḤAK; SHAMI, YITZḤAK; SHAPIRA, ḤAYYIM NACHMAN; SHAPIRO, ABBA CONSTANTIN; SHOHETMAN, BARUCH; SHREIER, FEIWEL; SHURER, HAIM; SILMAN, KADISH YEHUDA LEIB; SIMON, JULIUS; SIMON, SIR LEON; SLUTZKI, DAVID; SMILANSKY, MEIR; SMOLI, ELIEZER; SOKOLOW, NAHUM; STAVI, MOSES; STEIN, LEONARD; STEINMAN, ELIEZER; STERN, MAX EMANUEL; STRAUSS, ARYEH LUDWIG; STREIT, SHALOM; STRELISKER, MARCUS; SUSSMAN, EZRA; TABIB, MORDEKHAI; TALPIR, GABRIEL JOSEPH; TAUBES, LOEBEL; TCHERNOWITZ, SAMUEL; TCHERNOWITZ-AVIDAR, YEMIMAH; TELLER, ZEVI LAZAR; TEMKIN; TENE, BENJAMIN; TEVET, SHABBETAI; TOCHNER, MESHULLAM; TRIWOSCH, JOSEPH ELIJAH; TRUNK, ISRAEL JOSHUA; UKHMANI, AZRIEL; UNGERFELD, MOSHE; VAN PAASSEN, PIERRE; VITKIN, JOSEPH; WALLACH, MOSHE; WERNER, SIEGMUND; WISSOTZKY, KALONYMUS ZE'EV; WOLFFSOHN, DAVID; WOLFOWSKI, MENAHEM ZALMAN; WOLFSOHN-HALLE, AARON; WORTSMAN, YECHESKIEL CHARLES; YAARI, YEHUDAH; YALAN-STEKELIS, MIRIAM; YEIVIN, YEHOSHUA HESCHEL; ZAMOSC, DAVID; ZAMOSC, ISRAEL BEN MOSES HALEVI; ZARCHI, ISRAEL; ZEITLIN, WILLIAM; ZERUBAVEL, JACOB; ZIONISM; ZIONIST CONGRESSES; ZIPPER, GERSHON; ZLOCISTI, THEODOR

Marie Luise Kreuter*, Dr., Phil.; Freelancer Researcher, Addisabeba, Ethiopia: ECUADOR

Samson Jacob Kreutner, Former Director General, Keren Hayesod – U.I.A., Jerusalem

Max Kreutzberger, Ph.D.; Former Director of the Leo Baeck Institute, New York; Ascona, Switzerland: LEO BAECK INSTITUTE

Conny Kristel*, Ph.D.; Senior Research Fellow, Netherlands Institute for War Documentation, Amsterdam, The Netherlands: JONG, LOUIS DE; PRESSER, JACOB

Jelka (J.) Kröger(-Verhorst)*, M.A.; Art Editor and Researcher, Jewish Historical Museum, Amsterdam, The Netherlands: HAAN, MEIJER DE; HAGUE, THE

Frederic Krome*, Ph.D.; Managing Editor, *The American Jewish Archives Journal* and Adjunct Professor of Judaic Studies and History, American Jewish Archives, Cincinnati, Ohio: AARONSOHN, MICHAEL

Simcha Kruger, B.S.; Librarian,

New York: FREIDUS, ABRAHAM SOLOMON

Mikhail Krutikov*, Ph.D.; Assistant Professor of Jewish-Slavic Cultural Relations, University of Michigan, Ann Arbor: ESTRAIKH, GENNADY; SANDLER, BORIS; WIENER, MEIR

Andreas Kubinyi, Dr. Phil.; Lecturer in History, Eotvos Lorand University, Budapest: MENDEL; PRAEFECTUS JUDAEORUM; SZERENCSÉS, IMRE

Hyman Kublin, Ph.D.; Professor of History, Brooklyn College of the City University of New York: ḤAZZAN; JAPAN; KOBAYASHI, MASAYUKI; KOTSUJI, SETSUZO; RIESS, LUDWIG; TOKYO

Erich Kulka, Historian, Jerusalem: BRATISLAVA; CZECHOSLOVAKIA; KOSICE; LOEBL, EUGEN; LONDON, ARTUR; PRAGUE; SICHER, GUSTAV; UHERSKY BROD

Otto Dov Kulka, Ph.D.; Senior Lecturer in Modern Jewish History, the Hebrew University of Jerusalem: AUSTRIA; ETTINGER, SHMUEL; THERESIENSTADT

Yuri Kulker, Jerusalem: KUSHNER, ALEKSANDER SEMENOVICH

Linda S. Kulp*: ATLANTIC CITY

M. (Muhammed) Mustafa Kulu*, M.A.; Research Assistant, Middle East Technical University, Ankara, Turkey: BAYRAMIC; CANAKKALE; EZINE; KOILA; LAPSEKI; PARIUM

S. (Shirley) Kumove*, Writer and Yiddish Translator, American Literary Translators Association, Texas: PERLE, JOSHUA

Shifra Kuperman*, Lic. Phil., M.A.; University of Basel, Switzerland: BAAL-MAKHSHOVES; EINHORN, DAVID; NOMBERG, HERSH DAVID; OPATOSHU, JOSEPH

Ephraim Kupfer, Research Fellow in Jewish Studies, the Hebrew University of Jerusalem: COMTINO, MORDECAI BEN ELIEZER; ḤAMIẒ, JOSEPH BEN JUDAH; IBN YAḤYA, DAVID BEN SOLOMON; ISSACHAR BERMAN BEN NAPHTALI HA-KOHEN; JACOB BEN ASHER; JAFFE, MORDECAI BEN ABRAHAM; JONAH BEN ABRAHAM GERONDI; JOSEPH HA-KOHEN; JOSEPH ḤAZZAN BEN JUDAH OF TROYES; KASPI, JOSEPH BEN ABBA MARI IBN; LORBEERBAUM, JACOB BEN JACOB MOSES OF LISSA; MANUSCRIPTS, HEBREW; MOELLIN, JACOB BEN MOSES; REISCHER, JACOB BEN JOSEPH; SIKILI, JACOB BEN HANANEL; TAM IBN YAḤYA, JACOB BEN DAVID; TANḤUM BEN JOSEPH YERUSHALMI; TRANI, JOSEPH BEN MOSES; YOM TOV BEN ABRAHAM ISHBILI

Uri K. Kupferschmidt, Ph.D.; Senior Lecturer, Department of Middle Eastern History, University of Haifa

David Kushner*, Ph.D.; Professor of Middle East History, University of Haifa: ANTIOCH; AYDIN; ISKENDERUN; MERSIN

Gilbert Kushner, Ph.D.; Associate Professor of Anthropology, the College at Brockport of the State University of New York

Ernst Kutsch, Dr. Theol.; Professor of Old Testament Theology, Friedrich-Alexander Universität zu Erlangen-Nurnberg, Germany: PASSOVER; SUKKOT

Eduard Yecheskel Kutscher, M.A.; Professor of Hebrew Philology, the Hebrew University of Jerusalem; Professor of Hebrew Language, Bar-Ilan University, Ramat Gan: ARAMAIC; HEBREW LANGUAGE; POLOTSKY, HANS JACOB

Raphael Kutscher, Ph.D.; Lecturer in Mesopotamian Languages and Civilization, Tel Aviv University: EUPHRATES; MARDUK; TAMMUZ

Cecile Esther Kuznitz*, Ph.D.; Assistant Professor of Jewish History, Bard College, Annandale-on-Hudson, New York: YIDDISH LITERATURE; YIVO INSTITUTE FOR JEWISH RESEARCH

Mindaugas Kvietkauskas*, Ph.D.; Research Fellow, Lithuanian Literature, Vilnius University, Lithuania: KATZENELENBOGEN, URIAH; NAIDUS, LEIB

Gail (S.) Labovitz*, Ph.D.; Assistant Professor of Rabbinics, University of Judaism, Los Angeles, California: STUDY

Frederick R. Lachman, Ph.D.; Formerly Executive Editor of the *Encyclopaedia Judaica* and former American Correspondent of *Encyclopaedia Judaica Year Books*, New York: BISGYER, MAURICE; GEORGE, MANFRED; GROSSMANN, KURT RICHARD; LEVIN, THEODORE; SAXON, DAVID STEPHEN; STERN-TAEUBLER, SELMA; THEATER; WALINSKY; ZUCKERMAN, PAUL

Irwin (Jay) Lachoff*, M.A.; Archivist, Xavier University of Louisiana, New Orleans, Louisiana: LOUISIANA; NEW ORLEANS

Josef J. Lador-Lederer, Dr.Jur.; Ministry for Foreign Affairs, Jerusalem: BIENENFELD, FRANZ RUDOLF; ELLENBOGEN, WILHELM; FRIED, ALFRED HERMANN; KELSEN, HANS; KLANG, HEINRICH; KUNZ, JOSEF LAURENZ; LAWYERS; LEMKIN, RAPHAEL; OFNER, JULIUS; POPPER, JOSEF; REDLICH, JOSEPH; RODE, WALTHER; STEINBACH, EMIL; STRISOWER, LEO; VADÁSZ, LIPÓT; VÁZSONYI, VILMOS; WORLD JEWISH ASSOCIATIONS

Gideon Lahav, B.A.; Ministry of Commerce and Industry, Jerusalem: DIAMOND TRADE AND INDUSTRY

Sanford A. Lakoff, Ph.D.; Professor of Political Science, the University of Toronto: RIBICOFF, ABRAHAM A.

Anne Marie Lambert, Ministry for Foreign Affairs, Jerusalem: UNITED NATIONS

Lars Lambrecht*, Ph.D.; Professor of Philosophy and Sociology, University of Hamburg, Germany: MARX, KARL HEINRICH

Ruth Lamdan*, Ph.D.; Lecturer of Jewish History, Tel Aviv University: HANDALI, ESTHER; MALCHI, ESPERANZA

Meir Lamed, Kibbutz Ne'ot Mordekhai: AGUILAR, DIEGO D'; ALTSCHUL, EMIL; ARNSTEIN; AUSPITZ; AUSTRIA; BLOCH, JOSEPH SAMUEL; BOHEMIA; BONDI; ČECHŮ-ŽIDŮ, SVAZ; CHOMUTOV; CHRISTIAN SOCIAL PARTY; COUDENHOVE-KALERGI, HEINRICH VON; CZECH, LUDWIG; DOLNI KOUNICE; ESKELES; FISCHER; FISCHHOFF, ADOLF; GESELLSCHAFT DER JUNGEN HEBRAEER; GRAZ; GUTMANN, WILHELM, RITTER VON; HAINDORF, ALEXANDER; HALFANUS; HAPSBURG MONARCHY; HARDENBERG, KARL AUGUST VON;

HEIMWEHR; HENRY IV; HERMANUS QUONDAM JUDAEUS; HILSNER CASE; HIRSHEL, MEYER; HODONIN; HOFER, ANDREAS; HOHENAU; HOLESOV; HRANICE; HUNCOVCE; JABLONEC NAD NISOU; JAKOBOVITS, TOBIAS; JEITELES; JELLINEK, ADOLF; JEMNICE; JEVICKO; JINDRICHUV HRADEC; JUDENBURG; KHUST; KISCH; KLAGENFURT; KLEMPERER, GUTMANN; KOHN, THEODOR; KOJETIN; KOLLONITSCH, LEOPOLD; KOLODEJE NAD LUZICI; KOMARNO; KORNFELD, AARON BEN MORDECAI BAER; KROCHMAL, MENAHEM MENDEL BEN ABRAHAM; KROMERIZ; KUGEL, ḤAYYIM; KULTUSVEREIN; KURANDA, IGNAZ; KYJOV; LAEMEL, SIMON VON; LANDAU, EZEKIEL BEN JUDAH; LANDESJUDENSCHAFT, BOEHMISCHE; LAZNE KYNZVART; LEATHER INDUSTRY AND TRADE; LEOPOLD I; LICHTENSTADT, ABRAHAM AARON; LIEBEN, SALOMON; LIEBEN, SALOMON HUGO; LITOMERICE; LOEW-BEER; LOSTICE; LUCENEC; MAGNUS, MARCUS; MA'OR KATAN; MARIA THERESA; MARIENBAD; MAXIMILIAN I; MEISEL, MORDECAI BEN SAMUEL; MEYER, PAULUS; MICHALOVCE; MIKULOV; MIROSLAV; MORAVIA; MORAVSKE BUDEJOVICE; MORAVSKY KRUMLOV; NACHOD; NEUDA, ABRAHAM; NITRA; OLOMOUC; OPAVA; OSOBLAHA; OSTRAVA; PERNERSTORFER, ENGELBERT; PETSCHEK; PLACZEK, ABRAHAM; POBEZOVICE NA SUMAVE; POLNA; PŘEMYSL OTTOKAR II; PROSTEJOV; PULKAU; QUETSCH, SOLOMON; RANSCHBURG, BEZALEL BEN JOEL; RUDOLF II; SCHUTZBUND, REPUBLIKANISCHER; SELF-DEFENSE; SHLOM THE MINTMASTER; SONNENFELS, ALOYS VON; SPITZER, KARL HEINRICH; STEINHERZ, SAMUEL; STYRIA; TACHOV; TEKA; TESCHEN; TEWELES, JUDAH; THIEBERGER, FRIEDRICH; TREBIC; TREBITSCH, ABRAHAM; TREST; VEITH, JOHANN EMANUEL; WINKLER, LEO; WOLFSBERG; ZNOJMO

Norman Lamm*, Ph.D., Rabbi; Chancellor, Yeshiva University; Rosh Hayeshiva, Rabbi Isaac Elchanan Theological Seminary, New York: BLASER, ISAAC; KIDDUSH HA-SHEM AND ḤILLUL HA-SHEM; VOLOZHINER, ḤAYYIM BEN ISAAC

Zvi Lamm, Ph.D.; Lecturer in Education, the Hebrew University of Jerusalem: FRANKENSTEIN, CARL

Jacob M. Landau*, Ph.D.; Professor Emeritus of Political Science, Hebrew University of Jerusalem, Jerusalem: BAER, GABRIEL; CARASSO, EMMANUEL; EGYPT; GALANTÉ, ABRAHAM; HEYD, URIEL; IBRĀHĪM PASHA; KEMAL MUSTAFA; LEWIS, BERNARD; MANSURA; MOSSERI; MUBĀRAK, MUHAMMAD HUSNI SA'ID; MUHAMMAD ALI; SANŪ', YA'QUB or JAMES; TEKINALP, MUNIS

Julian J. Landau, M.I.A.; Journalist, Jerusalem: HOFFMAN, PHILIP E.; ISRAEL, STATE OF: ARAB POPULATION

Moshe Landau, M.A.; Educator, Tel Aviv: AGUDDAT AḤIM; BEOBACHTER AN DER WEICHSEL; BERNSTEIN, ARYEH LEIB; BLUMENFELD, EMANUEL; BUCHNER, ABRAHAM; CALMANSON, JACOB; CENTOS; CHWILA; DMOWSKI, ROMAN; ENDECJA; FINKELSTEIN, NOAH; FOLKSPARTEI; GOLDMAN, BERNARD; GRABSKI, STANISLAW; GROSS, ADOLF; HALLER'S ARMY; IZRAELITA; JABLONNA; JELENSKI, JAN; KIRSCHBAUM, ELIEZER SINAI; KOHN, ABRAHAM; KRONENBERG; LOEWENSTEIN, BERNHARD; LOEWENSTEIN, NATHAN; MAYZEL, MAURYCY; MINORITY BLOC; MORGENTHAU COMMISSION; NASZ PRZEGLĄD; NEUFELD, DANIEL; NOWY DZIENNIK; P.P.S.; PRZYTYK; ROSMARYN, HENRYK; ROZWÓJ; SAMUEL COMMISSION; SEJM; SHABAD, ẒEMAḤ; SHOMER ISRAEL; STEIGER TRIAL; STERN, ABRAHAM JACOB; THON, ALBERT; TOZ; UGODA; WALDMANN, ISRAEL; WOLKOWISKI, JEHIEL BER; ZBITKOWER, SAMUEL

Yehuda Landau, Ph.D.; Senior Lecturer in Philosophy, Tel Aviv University

Leo Landman, Ph.D., Rabbi; Assistant Professor of Rabbinical Literature, Dropsie University, Philadelphia: GAMBLING

Hermann Langbein, Vienna: AUSCHWITZ TRIALS

Lucille Lang Day*, A.B., M.A., M.F.A., Ph.D.; Poet and Museum Director, Hall of Health, Hands-on Health Museum, Berkeley, California: FALK, MARCIA

Nicholas de Lange, D.Phil.; Lecturer in Rabbinics, the University of Cambridge: LATERAN COUNCILS III, IV; MARTIN; NICHOLAS; ODO OF CHÂTEAUROUX; SIXTUS IV

Lawrence L. Langer*, Ph.D.; Professor of English, Emeritus, Simmons College, Boston: BAK, SAMUEL

Ruth Langer*, Ph.D.; Associate Professor of Jewish Studies, Boston College: LITURGY

Tzvi Y. Langermann*, Ph.D.; Professor of Arabic, Bar-Ilan University, Ramat Gan

Shaoul Langnas, Ph.D.; Jewish Agency, Tel Aviv: NUMERUS CLAUSUS

Doris Lankin, M.Jur.; Legal Journalist, Jerusalem

Ruth Lapidoth*, Ph.D.; Professor of International Law, the Hebrew University, Jerusalem Institute of Israel Studies: JERUSALEM, LEGAL ASPECTS

Steven Lapidus*, M.A.; Concordia University, Montreal, Canada: GOLDBLOOM

Dvora Lapson, B.A.; Instructor in Dance, the Hebrew Union College School of Education, New York: DANCE

Guiseppe Laras, Dr.Jur., Rabbi; Leghorn, Italy: DEL VECCHIO; MORPURGO, SAMSON BEN JOSHUA MOSES; PAPO, SAMUEL SHEMAIAH; SARAVAL; VITAL

Scott (B.) Lasensky*, Ph.D.; Washington, D.C.: ROSS, DENNIS

Daniel J. Lasker*, Ph.D.; Norbert Blechner Professor of Jewish Values, Ben-Gurion University of the Negev, Beersheba: ISRAELI, ISAAC BEN SOLOMON; JUDAH, HALEVI ; KARAITES; PHILOSOPHY, JEWISH

Michael M. Laskier*, Ph.D.; Professor of Middle Eastern and North African History, Bar-Ilan University, Ramat Gan: AGADIR; AGHLABIDS; ALMORAVIDS; ARAB WORLD; BONE; DEBDOU; DEMNAT; HAFSIDS; MARRAKESH; MEKNÈS; MERINIDS; MOGADOR; MOROCCO; M'ZAB; ORAN; RYVEL; SA'DIS; SAFI; SALÉ-RABAT; TANGIER; TETUÁN; WATTASIDS; ZIRIDS; ZIYANIDS

Egon H.E. Lass*: DOTHAN

Jacob Lassner*, Ph.D., D.H.L.;

Professor of Jewish Civilization, Northwestern University, Evanston, Illinois: ABBASIDS; HALKIN, ABRAHAM SOLOMON

Ted (Theodore) Lauer*, M.A.; Chairman History Department, Touro College, New York: TOURO COLLEGE

Theodor Lavi, Dr. Phil.; Historian, Yad Vashem, Jerusalem: ANTONESCU, ION; ANTONESCU, MIHAI; BACAU; BARLAD; BESSARABIA; BOTOSANI; BRAILA; BUHUSI; BURDUJENI; BUZAU; CHERNOVTSY; CONSTANTA; CRAIOVA; DARABANI; DOROHOI; FALTICENI; FILDERMAN, WILHELM; FOCSANI; GERTSA; HARLAU; HUSI; JASSY; KISHINEV; LECCA, RADÚ; MIHAILENI; MOINESTI; NUMERUS CLAUSUS; PASCANI; PIATRA-NEAMT; PLOESTI; REVISTA CULTULUI MOZAIC; ROMAN; ROMANIA; SCHWARZFELD; SETANESTI; STERN, ADOLPHE; SULITA; TIRGU NEAMT; TIRGU-FRUMOS; TRANSNISTRIA; VASLUI

Anthony Lincoln Lavine, M.A.; Jerusalem: ḤOMA; MARGOLIES, ISAAC BEN ELIJAH; MOSES ZE'EV BEN ELIEZER OF GRODNO; PERLA, JEROHAM FISCHEL BEN ARYEH ẒEVI; SANDZER, ḤAYYIM BEN MENAHEM; SHAPIRO, SAUL BEN DOV

Eric (Jay) Lawee*, Ph.D.; Associate Professor, Humanities, York University, Toronto, Canada: ABRABANEL, ISAAC BEN JUDAH; ABRAHAM BEN JUDAH LEON; ABULRABI, AARON

Mary Lazar*, Ph.D.; Associate Professor, English, Kent State University, Ohio: KOSINSKI, JERZY

Moshe Lazar, Ph.D.; Associate Professor of Romance Philology, the Hebrew University of Jerusalem: LADINO

Gilbert Lazard, D.es L.; Professor of Iranian Language and Civilization, Sorbonne Nouvelle, Paris: AIX-EN-PROVENCE; JUDEO-PERSIAN

Lucien Lazare, Ph.D.; Educator, Jerusalem: GAMZON, ROBERT; KAPLAN, JACOB; LAVAL, PIERRE; LÉVI, SYLVAIN; MANDEL, GEORGES; STRASBOURG; STUDENTS' MOVEMENTS, JEWISH; ZIONISM

Arlene Lazarowitz*, Ph.D.; Associate Professor of History, Director, Jewish Studies Program, California State University, Long Beach: BOXER, BARBARA

Paul Lazarus, Dr.Phil., Rabbi; Historian, Haifa: OPPENHEIM

Hava Lazarus-Yafeh: JUDEO-ARABIC LITERATURE

Hayim Leaf, Ph.D.; Professor of Hebrew Language and Literature, Yeshiva University, New York: CHURGIN, PINKHOS

Abraham Lebanon, M.A.; Teacher in the Hebrew Teachers' College, Jerusalem: DAMASCUS; ELEAZAR BEN JAIR; JEBUS, JEBUSITE; MARIAMNE

Arieh Lebowitz*, B.A.; Communications Director, Jewish Labor Committee, New York: JEWISH LABOR COMMITTEE; JEWISH SOCIALIST VERBAND; MORNING FREIHEIT; WORKMEN'S CIRCLE; YIDISHER KEMFER; YIDISHES TAGEBLAT

Michael Lecker*, Ph.D. Professor, the Hebrew University of Jerusalem: KA'B AL-AḤ BĀR; MUHAMMAD; NAḌIR, BANU l-; QAYNUQĀ', BANŪ; QURAYẒA, BANŪ; WAHB IBN MUNABBIH

Barton G. Lee, M.A., Rabbi; Chicago: FORTAS, ABE; GOLDMAN, MAYER CLARENCE; GREENBAUM, EDWARD SAMUEL

Elaine Leeder*, M.S.W., M.P.H., Ph.D.; Professor of Sociology, Sonoma State University, Rohnert Park, California: PESOTTA, ROSE

Carolyn Leeds*, B.A.; Special Projects Director, Jewish Federation of Greater Indianapolis, Indiana: INDIANAPOLIS

Sidney M. Lefkowitz, Th.D.; Lecturer in Religion, Jacksonville University, Florida

Joseph Leftwich, Editor and Journalist, London: HERMAN, DAVID; KAMINSKI or KAMINSKA; KESSLER, DAVID; MIKHOELS, SOLOMON; MYER, MORRIS; SCHILDKRAUT, RUDOLPH; VILNA TROUPE; WEICHERT, MICHAEL

Israel O. Lehman, D.Phil.; Curator of Manuscripts and Special Collections, the Hebrew Union College – Jewish Institute of Religion, Cincinnati: VILNA

Ruth P. Lehmann, Dipl.O.A.S., F.L.A.; Librarian of Jews' College, London: ABBREVIATIONS; LEVERTOFF, PAUL PHILIP; SIMON, SIR LEON

Grete Leibowitz, Dr.Phil.; Former editorial staff, *Encyclopaedia Hebraica*, Jerusalem: BERLINER, EMILE; JACOBI, KARL GUSTAV JACOB; JACOBI, MORITZ HERMANN

Joshua O. Leibowitz, M.D.; Associate Clinical Professor of the History of Medicine, the Hebrew University-Hadassah Medical School, Jerusalem: AMATUS LUSITANUS; ANATOMY; AUERBACH, LEOPOLD; BARUK, HENRI; BERNHEIM, HIPPOLYTE; BLOODLETTING; BUERGER, LEO; HEIDENHAIN, RUDOLF; HENLE, JACOB; JACOBI, ABRAHAM; ORTA, GARCIA DE; TELLER, ISSACHAR BAER; WEIGERT, CARL; WIDAL, FERNAND; WUNDERBAR, REUBEN JOSEPH; ZACUTUS LUSITANUS

Shnayer Z. Leiman, B.A.; Lecturer in Jewish History and Literature, Yale University, New Haven, Connecticut: BERNFELD, SIEGFRIED; COHN, JONAS; KÁRMÁN, MÓR; LEVI, EDWARD H.; MORGENSTERN, LINA; VAN PRAAGH, WILLIAM

Samuel Leiter, D.H.L., Rabbi; Professor of Modern Hebrew Literature, the Jewish Theological Seminary of America, New York: BIALIK, ḤAYYIM NAḤMAN

André Lemaire*, Ph.D.; Professor in Oriental Studies, École Pratique des Hautes Études, Section des sciences historiques et philologiques, Sorbonne, Paris: CAQUOT, ANDRÉ

Carolyn G. (Gray) LeMaster*, B.A., M.A.; Butler Center Fellow for the Arkansas Jewish History Collection, Butler Center for Arkansas Studies, Central Arkansas Library System, Little Rock, Arkansas: ARKANSAS

Howard M. Lenhoff, Associate Professor of Biochemistry, University of California, Irvine

Aron (di Leone) Leoni*, M.S., Ph.D., M.A.; Former Representative of the Italian paper industries at the European Commission in Brussels.

Consulting Economist (retired). Historian, State University of Padua, Milan: PESARO; PISA, DA

Haim Leor, M.Jur.; Secretary of the Knesset, Jerusalem

Antony Lerman, Researcher, Institute of Jewish Affairs, London

Anne Lapidus Lerner*, Ph.D., M.A., M.H.L., A.B., B.J. Ed.; Director, Program in Jewish Women's Studies; Assistant Professor, Department of Jewish Literature, Jewish Theological Seminary, New York: KNOPF, BLANCHE WOLF

Bialik Myron Lerner, Ph.D.; Instructor in Talmud, Tel Aviv University: ABBA GURYON OF SIDON; ABBA SAUL; AKAVYAH BEN MAHALALEL; ALTAR; ANDROGYNOS; AVTALYON; SHEMAIAH

Harold Lerner, Ph.D.; Political Scientist, New York

Loren Lerner*, Ph.D.; Professor, Concordia University, Montreal, Canada: BORENSTEIN, SAM

Natan Lerner, LL.D.; Executive Director, World Jewish Congress, Tel Aviv: PERLZWEIG, MAURICE L.; TARTAKOWER, ARIEH; WORLD JEWISH CONGRESS

Ralph Lerner, Ph.D.; Associate Professor of Social Sciences, the University of Chicago: PROPHETS AND PROPHECY; STRAUSS, LEO

Benny Leshem*: ISRAEL, STATE OF: HEALTH, WELFARE, AND SOCIAL SECURITY

Donald Daniel Leslie, D.del'U; Fellow in Far Eastern History, Australian National University, Canberra: CHAO; REDEMPTION

Yaacov Lev*, Ph.D.; Professor, Bar-Ilan University, Ramat Gan

Chaim Levanon, Eng. Agr.; Agricultural Engineer and former Mayor of Tel Aviv: GENERAL ZIONISTS

Yehuda Levanon, B.A.; Ministry of Absorption, Jerusalem

Arye Levavi, M.A.; Ambassador, Ministry for Foreign Affairs, Jerusalem

Schneier Zalman Levenberg, Ph.D.; Jewish Agency Representative and Writer, Jerusalem: ADLER, VICTOR; MARX, KARL HEINRICH; NATANSON, MARK; SOCIALISM; ZUNDELEVITCH, AARON

Joseph Levenson, D.H.L., Rabbi; Instructor in Religion, Oklahoma City University, Oklahoma: OKLAHOMA

Marcia (Irene) Leveson*, Ph.D., B.Ed.; Assistant Professor (retired), Honorary Research Fellow, University of the Witwatersrand Johannesburg, South Africa: GORDIMER, NADINE; SOUTH AFRICAN LITERATURE

Martin Levey, Ph.D.; Professor of the History of Science, the State University of New York, Albany: IBN BIKLĀRISH, JUNAS BEN ISAAC

Josef Levi*: FLORENCE

L. Levi*: GREECE

Leo Levi, D.Sc.; Research Fellow in Jewish Musicology, the Hebrew University of Jerusalem: ITALY

Shlomit Levi, Research Associate, Israel Institute of Applied Research, Jerusalem

Yitzhak Levi, Former Managing Director of the Israel Program for Scientific Translations, Jerusalem: INDEPENDENCE DAY, ISRAEL

Curt Leviant, Ph.D.; Associate Professor of Hebraic Studies, Rutgers University, New Brunswick, New Jersey: ARTHURIAN LEGENDS; BURLA, YEHUDA

Dov Levin, Ph.D.; Researcher in the Institute of Contemporary Jewry, the Hebrew University of Jerusalem: KALVARIJA; KEDAINIAI; KRETINGA; KUPISKIS; MARIJAMPOLE; PLUNGE; PONARY; SIAULIAI; VIRBALIS

Norman Levin, Ph.D.; Assistant Professor of Biology, Brooklyn College of the City University of New York: GASSER, HERBERT SPENCER; GURWITSCH, ALEXANDER GAVRILOVICH; SANDGROUND, JACK HENRY; WAKSMAN, SELMAN ABRAHAM

Samuel Levin, Writer, Translator, Givat Savyon

Shalom Levin, M.A.; Member of the Knesset, Tel Aviv: TEACHERS' ASSOCIATION IN ISRAEL

Ze'ev Levin, Former Ambassador, Tel Aviv: KENYA

Baruch A. Levine*, Ph.D.; Skirball Professor Emeritus, New York University: BALAAM; CULT; CULT PLACES, ISRAELITE; FIRST FRUITS; FIRSTBORN; GIBEONITES AND NETHINIM; KEDUSHAH; SOLOMON, SERVANTS OF

Emily Levine*: WARBURG, ABY MORITZ

Jonathan D. Levine*: GREENBERG, SIDNEY

Joyce Levine*, M.A.; Director, Educational Technology, U.J.A. Federation Board of Jewish Education, Toronto, Canada: EDUCATION, JEWISH

Michael Levine, Ph.D.; Lecturer, Dept. of History of Art, the Hebrew University of Jerusalem: ISRAEL, STATE OF: CULTURAL LIFE

Paul (A.) Levine*, Ph.D.; Senior Lecturer in Holocaust History, The Uppsala Programme for Holocaust and Genocide Studies, Uppsala University, Sweden: HOLOCAUST

Stephen Levine*, Ph.D.; Professor, Victoria University of Wellington, New Zealand: NEW ZEALAND

Yael Levine*, Ph.D.; Talmud, Bar-Ilan University, Ramat Gan: ESHET ḤAYIL

Renée Levine Melammed*, Ph.D.; Professor of Jewish History, Schechter Institute of Jewish Studies, Jerusalem: ANUSIM; BARAZANI, ASENATH; BOTON, ABRAHAM BEN MOSES DE; WOMAN: MUSLIM WORLD AND SPAIN; WUHSHA AL-DALLALA

Jacob S. Levinger, Ph.D.; Senior Lecturer in Jewish Philosophy, Tel Aviv University: ASCHER, SAUL; DAVID BEN ARYEH LEIB OF LIDA; DELMEDIGO, ELIJAH BEN MOSES ABBA; DINAH; DUBNO,

SOLOMON BEN JOEL; DUENNER, JOSEPH ẒEVI HIRSCH; DUKES, LEOPOLD; DURAN, PROFIAT; GALIPAPA, ḤAYYIM BEN ABRAHAM; GANZFRIED, SOLOMON BEN JOSEPH; GEIGER, SOLOMON ZALMAN; GERMANY; GORDON, SAMUEL LEIB; GUTTMANN, JULIUS; HAI BEN SHERIRA; HOLDHEIM, SAMUEL

Boris M. Levinson, Ph.D.; Professor of Psychology, Yeshiva University, New York: WECHSLER, DAVID

Robert E. Levinson, Ph.D.; San Francisco: ALEXANDER, MOSES; CALIFORNIA; GERSTLE, LEWIS; HIRSCH, SOLOMON; KAHN, JULIUS; MEARS, OTTO; MEIER, JULIUS; SACRAMENTO; SUTRO, ADOLPH HEINRICH JOSEPH

Seymour Levitan*, B.A., M.A.; Translator of Yiddish Poetry and Fiction, Vancouver, Canada: KORN, RACHEL-HÄRING; SEGAL, JACOB ISAAC

Isaac Levitats, Ph.D.; the Herzliah Hebrew Teachers' Seminary, New York: AUTONOMY; AUTONOMY, JUDICIAL; BET DIN AND JUDGES; BITTUL HA-TAMID; CHARITY; CHIEF RABBI, CHIEF RABBINATE; COMMUNITY; CONFERENCES; CONSISTORY; DAYYAN; EDUCATION, JEWISH; EPISCOPUS JUDAEORUM; FEDERATIONS OF COMMUNITIES, TERRITORIAL; FINANCES, AUTONOMOUS JEWISH; FINES; FRATERNAL SOCIETIES; GABBAI; GEMILUT ḤASADIM; ḤAZAKAH; HEKDESH; ḤEREM BET DIN; ḤEREM HA-IKKUL; ḤEREM HA-YISHUV; ḤEVRAH, ḤAVURAH; MINORITY RIGHTS; NASI; OATH MORE JUDAICO or JURAMENTUM JUDAEORUM; PINKAS; PRESBYTER JUDAEORUM; PUNISHMENT; RABBINICAL CONFERENCES; SEMIKHAH; SHAMMASH; SHEḤITAH; SICK CARE, COMMUNAL; SUMPTUARY LAWS; SYNODS; TAKKANOT HA-KAHAL; TITLES

Lev Levite, Kibbutz En-Harod (Me'uhad): BOROCHOV, BER

Georges Levitte, Writer, Paris: AVIGNON; BAYONNE; BESANÇON; BORDEAUX; CAEN; COLMAR; DIJON; GRENOBLE; LYONS; MULHOUSE; NANCY; NICE; ROUEN; TOULOUSE

Avital Levy, B.A.; Jerusalem: PICA

Richard N. Levy*: CENTRAL CONFERENCE OF AMERICAN RABBIS

Richard S. Levy*, Ph.D.; Professor of History, University of Illinois at Chicago: LAGARDE, PAUL DE; MARR, WILHELM

Louis Lewin, Dr.Phil., Rabbi; *Encyclopaedia Judaica* (Germany); Historian, Breslau: MAGDEBURG; MANNHEIM

Martin Lewin*, M.S.L.S.; Librarian (retired) Buffalo and Eric County Public Library, Buffalo: BUFFALO

Nathan Lewin*, J.D.; Attorney, Columbia Law School Adjunct Faculty, Lewin and Lewin L.L.P., Washington, D.C.: BREYER, STEPHEN GERALD; POSNER, RICHARD ALLEN

Yom-Tov Lewinski, Dr.Phil.; Ethnographer, Tel Aviv: FOOD; GAMES

Tamar Lewinsky*, M.A.; Lecturer, University of Munich, Germany: DEMBLIN, BENJAMIN; FOX, CHAIM-LEIB; FUCHS, ABRAHAM MOSHE; GRYNBERG, BERL; HEILPERIN, FALK; OLITZKY; PERLOV, YITSKHOK; WARSHAWSKI, MARK

Albert L. Lewis, M.H.L., Rabbi; Haddonfield, New Jersey: SHOFAR

Bernard Lewis, Instructor in Films and Filming, New York University School of Continuing Education: WINCHELL, WALTER

Mervyn M. Lewis, M.A.; Jerusalem: DAVIDSON, SAMUEL

Guenter Lewy, Ph.D.; Professor of Government, the University of Massachusetts, Amherst: HOLOCAUST: THE WORLD

Hildegard Lewy, Ph.D.; Visiting Professor, Hebrew Union College, Cincinnati, Ohio

Yohanan (Hans) Lewy, Dr.Phil.; Senior Lecturer in Latin, the Hebrew University of Jerusalem: JOHN CHRYSOSTOM

Bent Lexner*, Rabbinical Diploma, Chief Rabbi, Denmark: BESEKOW, SAMUEL; FEIGENBERG, MEÏR; FOIGHEL, ISI

Gideon Libson*, Ph.D.; Professor of Law, Head of the Institute for Research in Jewish Law, the Hebrew University of Jerusalem: FIQH; ḤEREM SETAM; LAW, JEWISH AND ISLAMIC LAW

Jacob Licht, Ph.D.; Associate Professor of Biblical Studies, Tel Aviv University: ABRAHAM, APOCALYPSE OF; ADAM AND EVE, BOOK OF THE LIFE OF; CALENDAR; DAY OF THE LORD; DEAD SEA SCROLLS; ETHICS; MENAHEM; SOLOMON, ODES OF

Jonathan Licht, B.A., M.F.A.; Writer, Jerusalem: AIMÉE, ANOUK; ALLEN, WOODY; ALPERT, HERB; ARKIN, ALAN W.; BACALL, LAUREN; BALIN, MARTY; BLOOM, CLAIRE; BOONE, RICHARD; BROOKS, MEL; COBB, LEE J.; CUKOR, GEORGE; DA SILVA, HOWARD; DIAMOND, I. A. L.; DIAMOND, NEIL; DOUGLAS, MELVYN; DOUGLAS, MICHAEL; DREYFUSS, RICHARD; EPSTEIN, JULIUS J. and PHILIP G.; FALK, PETER; FOGELBERG, DAN; FORD, HARRISON; FORMAN, MILOS; FRANKENHEIMER, JOHN MICHAEL; FRIEDKIN, WILLIAM; GARFUNKEL, ART; GEFFEN, DAVID; GOLDBLUM, JEFF; GORDON, MICHAEL; GRANT, LEE; HAMLISCH, MARVIN; HARRIS, BARBARA; HAWN, GOLDIE; HENRY, BUCK; HERSHEY, BARBARA; HIRSCH, JUDD; HOFFMAN, DUSTIN; HOUSEMAN, JOHN; IAN, JANIS; KNOPFLER, MARK; LASSER, LOUISE; LEAR, NORMAN; LEHMAN, ERNEST; LELOUCH, CLAUDE; LESTER, RICHARD; LEVINE, JOSEPH E.; LEVINSON, BARRY; LEWIS, JERRY; LOM, HERBERT; LUMET, SIDNEY; MAMET, DAVID; MANILOW, BARRY; MANKIEWICZ, JOSEPH LEO; MATTHAU, WALTER; MAZURSKY, PAUL; MIDLER, BETTE; MILLER, ARTHUR; MIRISCH BROTHERS; MOSTEL, ZERO; NEWMAN, PAUL; NICHOLS, MIKE; PAPP, JOSEPH; PATINKIN, MANDY; POLANSKI, ROMAN; POLLACK, SYDNEY; PRINCE, HAROLD; REINER, CARL; REINER, ROB; RYDER, WINONA; SCHISGAL, MURRAY; SCHLESINGER, JOHN; SEGAL, GEORGE; SELLERS, PETER; SIDNEY, SYLVIA; SIMON, PAUL; SONDHEIM, STEPHEN; SPIEGEL, SAMUEL P.; SPIELBERG, STEVEN; STONE, OLIVER; STREISAND, BARBRA; WALLACH, ELI; WELLER, MICHAEL; WILDER, GENE; WINGER, DEBRA; WINTERS, SHELLEY; WOLPER, DAVID LLOYD

Albert Lichtblau*, Ph.D.; Historian, University Professor, Vice Chair of the Centre for Jewish Cultural History, University Salzburg, Austria: SOMMER, EMIL; SPITZER, KARL HEINRICH; TODESCO, HERMANN; VOGELSANG, KARL VON; WOLF, FRUMET

Aaron Lichtenstein, Ph.D.; Researcher, Baltimore: ASHINSKY, AARON MORDECAI HALEVI; HELLER, THEODOR; HENKIN, JOSEPH ELIJAH; JEFFERSON, THOMAS; JESURUN; LAGOS;

LEÃO, GASPAR DE; NUÑEZ; OPORTO; PAM, HUGO; PORTUGAL; SCHUR, ISSAI; SCHWARZ, SAMUEL; TOMAR; WERNER, HEINZ

Murray (H.) Lichtenstein*, Ph.D., M. Phil., B.A.; Dr. Professor Emeritus, Hunter College, City University of New York: LOTS; PROVERBS, BOOK OF; SHINAR; TERAH

David L. Lieber*, D.H.L., Rabbi; Former President, the University of Judaism; Los Angeles: BANISHMENT; CENSUS; DIVORCE; DORFF, ELLIOT N.; JEALOUSY; PILLAR OF CLOUD AND PILLAR OF FIRE; POVERTY; RANSOM; SABBATICAL YEAR AND JUBILEE; STRANGERS AND GENTILES; VORSPAN, MAX

Esther (Zweig) Liebes, B.A.; Jerusalem: BUNIN, ḤAYYIM ISAAC; DAVID OF MAKOW; DOV BAER OF MEZHIRECH; ELIMELECH OF LYZHANSK; ḤANOKH OF ALEKSANDROW; ISAAC THE BLIND; LOEBEL, ISRAEL; NAḤMAN OF HORODENKA; NAḤMAN OF KOSOV; PRZEDBORZ; RADOSHITSER, ISSACHAR BAER; RAZA RABBA, SEFER; ROPSHITSER, NAPHTALI ẒEVI; RYMANOWER, MENAHEM MENDEL; RYMANOWER, ẒEVI HIRSH; SPINKA, JOSEPH MEIR WEISS OF; WARKA; ZEVI HIRSCH FRIEDMAN OF LESKO

Hans Liebeschutz, Dr. Phil., F.R.Hist.Soc.; Professor Extraord. of Medieval Latin Literature, the University of Hamburg; Emeritus Reader in Medieval History, the University of Liverpool: ABELARD, PETER; ALBERTUS MAGNUS; ALEXANDER OF HALES; AQUINAS, THOMAS; CUSA, NICHOLAS OF; ECKHART, MEISTER; WILLIAM OF AUVERGNE

Charles S. Liebman, Ph.D.; Associate Professor of Political Science, Bar-Ilan University, Ramat Gan: YESHIVA UNIVERSITY

Seymour B. Liebman, M.A., Lecturer in Latin American History, Florida Atlantic University, Boca Raton

Pearl J. Lieff, Ph.D.; Assistant Professor of Sociology, Borough of Manhattan Community College of the City University of New York: COSER, LEWIS A.; EISENSTADT, SAMUEL NOAH

Chaim Lifschitz, Former Inspector, Department of Religious Education, Ministry of Education and Culture, Jerusalem: COHEN, DAVID

Ezekiel Lifschutz, Archivist of the YIVO Institute for Jewish Research, New York: ALTER, VICTOR

B. (Berachyahu) Lifshitz*, Ph.D.; Faculty of Law, the Hebrew University of Jerusalem: ASMAKHTA

David S. Lifson, Ph.D.; Professor of English and of Humanities, Monmouth College, Long Branch, New Jersey: KALICH, BERTHA; THOMASHEFSKY, BORIS

Jacob Jay Lindenthal, Ph.D.; Associate Professor of History, Rutgers University, Newark, New Jersey: BLAU, PETER MICHAEL; ETZIONI, AMITAI WERNER

Edward T. Linenthal*, Ph.D.; Professor of History and Editor, *Journal of American History*, Indiana University, Bloomington, Indiana: BERENBAUM, MICHAEL

Paul Link, M.Sc.; Emeritus Professor of Textiles, Instituto Superior Tecnologico, Buenos Aires; Ḥavazzelet Ha-Sharon, Israel: LAWYERS; LIACHO, LÁZARO; POLITICS; SCHAULSON NUMHAUSER, JACOBO; SPANISH AND PORTUGUESE LITERATURE; STEINBRUCH, AARÃO

Elias Lipiner, B.A.; Journalist, Tel Aviv

Edward Lipinski, D.D., D.Bibl. St.; Professor of Ancient History, of the History of Semitic Religions, and of Comparative Grammar of Semitic Languages, the Catholic University of Louvain, Belgium: ALLEGORY; JEREMIAH; LOVE; MALACHI, BOOK OF; NAHUM; OBADIAH, BOOK OF; REVELATION; SIGNS AND SYMBOLS; SIN

Sonia L. Lipman, B.A.; Writer, London: GERTNER, LEVI and MEIR; MONTEFIORE, JUDITH

Steven (Steve) Lipman*, B.A., M.A.; Staff Writer, *The Jewish Week*, New York: ZLOTOWITZ, BERNARD M.

Vivian David Lipman, C.V.O., Ph.D.; Former Director of Ancient Monuments and Historic Buildings, London: AMES; BASEVI; BEARSTED, MARCUS SAMUEL, FIRST VISCOUNT; BOARD OF DEPUTIES OF BRITISH JEWS; BRODIE, SIR ISRAEL; COHEN; COHEN, ABRAHAM; COHEN, SIR ROBERT WALEY; D'AVIGDOR; DIAMOND, JOHN, BARON; ENGLAND; EXCHEQUER OF THE JEWS; EZRA, DEREK, BARON; FINNISTON, SIR HAROLD MONTAGUE; FRANKLIN; HORE-BELISHA, LESLIE, LORD; JENKINSON, SIR HILARY; JEWS' TEMPORARY SHELTER; JEWS' COLLEGE; JOSCE OF YORK; JOSEPH; KAYE, SIR EMMANUEL; LASKI; LEVER, HAROLD, BARON LEVER OF MANCHESTER; MAGNUS; MANCHESTER; MANCROFT; MEDINA, SIR SOLOMON DE; MELDOLA, RAPHAEL; MENDES; MILITARY SERVICE; MOCATTA; MONTAGU; MONTEFIORE, SIR MOSES; MONTEFIORE, SEBAG-MONTEFIORE; NATHAN; NEWCASTLE-UPON-TYNE; NICHOLAS, EDWARD; NORWICH; NOTTINGHAM; NUÑEZ, HECTOR; PLYMOUTH; POLITICS; PORTER, SIR LESLIE; PORTSMOUTH; RAYNE, SIR MAX, BARON; ROTH, CECIL; ROTHSCHILD; SALOMONS, SIR DAVID; SAMUEL, EDWIN; SAMUEL, HAROLD; SAMUEL, HERBERT LOUIS; SCHIFF, DAVID TEVELE; SCHON, FRANK, BARON; SEGAL, SAMUEL, BARON; SHEFFIELD; SILKIN, LEWIS, FIRST BARON; SILVERMAN, SYDNEY; SINGER, SIMEON; SOUTHAMPTON; STRAUSS, GEORGE RUSSELL, BARON; SUNDERLAND; SWANSEA; TAILORING; TOVEY, D'BLOISSIERS; VEIL, LEWIS COMPIÉGNE DE; WORCESTER; YOUNG, STUART

Walter Lippmann, Demographer, Melbourne: AUSTRALIA

Oded Lipschits*, Ph.D.; Senior Lecturer in Archaeology and Biblical History, Tel Aviv University: RAMAT RAḤEL

Ora Lipschitz, M.A.; Jerusalem: SINAI, MOUNT

Arye Lipshitz, Writer, Jerusalem: BEYTH, HANS; FREIER, RECHA

Deborah E. Lipstadt, Ph.D.; Professor, Modern Jewish History, University of California at Los Angeles: HOLOCAUST

Sol Liptzin, Ph.D.; Emeritus Professor of Comparative Literature, City College of the City University of New York, Jerusalem: ADLER, JACOB; ALTSCHUL, MOSES BEN ḤANOKH; AVÉ-LALLEMANT, FRIEDRICH CHRISTIAN BENEDICT; BASS, HYMAN B.; BECK, KARL ISIDOR; BEER, MICHAEL; BEER-HOFMANN, RICHARD; BEHR, ISSACHAR FALKENSOHN;

BERG, LEO; BERGNER, HERZ; BERMANN, RICHARD ARNOLD; BERNSTEIN, HERMAN; BERNSTEIN, IGNATZ; BICKEL, SOLOMON; BILETZKI, ISRAEL ḤAYYIM; BIMKO, FISHEL; BLUMENTHAL, OSKAR; BOBE-MAYSE; BODENHEIM, MAXWELL; BOERNE, LUDWIG; BOVE-BUKH; BRAUN, FELIX; BROCH, HERMANN; BRODER, BERL; BRYKS, RACHMIL; CALÉ, WALTER; CORALNIK, ABRAHAM; CZERNOWITZ YIDDISH LANGUAGE CONFERENCE; DEUTSCH, BABETTE; DLUZHNOWSKY, MOSHE; DONATH, ADOLPH; EDELSTADT, DAVID; ESSELIN, ALTER; FINEMAN, IRVING; FISHMAN, JACOB; GERMAN LITERATURE; GLANTZ, JACOB; GLANZ-LEYELES, AARON; GODINER, SAMUEL NISSAN; GOETHE, JOHANN WOLFGANG VON; GOLDBERG, BEN ZION; GOLDBERG, ISAAC; GOLDENE KEYT, DI; GOLDFADEN, ABRAHAM; GOLOMB, ABRAHAM; GORDON, MIKHL; GREENBERG, ELIEZER; GROPER, JACOB; GURSHTEIN, AARON; HALKIN, SHMUEL; HALPER, ALBERT; HALPERN, MOYSHE-LEYB; HEILPERIN, FALK; HEIMANN, MORITZ; HEYSE, PAUL; HIRSCHBEIN, PERETZ; HIRSCHFELD, GEORG; HITZIG, JULIUS EDUARD; HOFMANNSTHAL, HUGO VON; HOFSTEIN, DAVID; HURST, FANNIE; ICELAND, REUBEN; IMBER, SAMUEL JACOB; IN-ZIKH; IZBAN, SHMUEL; JUDAH, SAMUEL BENJAMIN HELBERT; KAHAN, SALOMON; KAHLER, ERICH; KALISCH, DAVID; KARPELES, GUSTAV; KATZ, ALEPH; KAUFMANN, FRITZ MORDECAI; KAYSER, RUDOLF; KESTEN, HERMANN; KHALYASTRE; KIPNIS, ITZIK; KLEIN, JULIUS LEOPOLD; KOENIGSBERG, DAVID; KOL MEVASSER; KOMPERT, LEOPOLD; KOREFF, DAVID FERDINAND; KUH, EPHRAIM MOSES; KULBAK, MOYSHE; KURTZ, AARON; LATTEINER, JOSEPH; LEE, MALKE; LESSING, THEODOR; LEVIN, MEYER; LEWISOHN, LUDWIG; LIPINER, SIEGFRIED; LISSAUER, ERNST; LITVAKOV, MOSES; LITVIN, A.; LOCKER, MALKE; LORM, HIERONYMUS; LUBLINSKI, SAMUEL; LUDWIG, EMIL; LUDWIG, REUBEN; LUKÁCS, GEORG; MANGER, ITZIK; MANI LEIB; MANN, THOMAS; MARGOSHES, SAMUEL; MARINOFF, JACOB; MASLIANSKY, ZVI HIRSCH; MAUTHNER, FRITZ; MAYZEL, NACHMAN; MESTEL, JACOB; MIESES, MATTHIAS; MILLER, SHAYE; MOLODOWSKY, KADIA; MOMBERT, ALFRED; MUEHSAM, ERICH; NADEL, ARNO; NADIR, MOYSHE; NEUMANN, ROBERT; NIGER, SHMUEL; NISSENSON, AARON; OLITZKY; OPATOSHU, JOSEPH; OSTROPOLER, HERSHELE; PARKER, DOROTHY; PERSOV, SHMUEL; RABOY, ISAAC; RAVITCH, MELECH; RIVKIN, BORUCH; ROBERT, LUDWIG; ROCHMAN, LEIB; RODENBERG, JULIUS; ROLNICK, JOSEPH; ROSENBLATT, H; ROSSIN, SAMUEL; RUBINSTEIN, JOSEPH; SALTEN, FELIX; SAMUEL, MAURICE; SAPHIR, MORITZ GOTTLIEB; SAPHIRE, SAUL; SARASOHN, KASRIEL HERSCH; SCHNITZLER, ARTHUR; SCHWARTZ, ISRAEL JACOB; SCHWARZ, LEO WALDER; SCHWARZMAN, ASHER; SEGALOWITCH, ZUSMAN; SFARD, DAVID; SHAMRI, ARIE; SIMON, SHLOME; STERNBERG, JACOB; SUSMAN, MARGARETE; TABACHNIK, ABRAHAM BER; TEIF, MOSHE; TEITSH, MOYSHE; TKATCH, MEIR ZIML; TOLLER, ERNST; TORBERG, FRIEDRICH; ULIANOVER, MIRIAM; UNTERMEYER, LOUIS; VARNHAGEN, RAHEL LEVIN; WALDEN, HERWARTH; WALDINGER, ERNST; WEIDMAN, JEROME; WEINPER, ZISHE; WEINREICH, MAX; WEISS, ERNST; WEISSENBERG, ISAAC MEIR; WERFEL, FRANZ; WIENER, LEO; WIHL, LUDWIG; WOLFSKEHL, KARL; YAKNEHAZ; YARMOLINSKY, AVRAHM; YEZIERSKA, ANZIA; YIDDISH LITERATURE; YIVO INSTITUTE FOR JEWISH RESEARCH; YUNGE, DI; YUNG-VILNE; ZUNSER, ELIAKUM; ZWEIG, ARNOLD

Joanna Lisek*, Ph.D.; Lecturer, Wrocław University Polish Philological Institute, Department of Jewish Study; Study for the Animators of Culture and Librarians, Wrocław, Poland: GRADE, CHAIM

Dora Litani-Littman, M.A.; Researcher, Jerusalem: ADERCA, FELIX; BALTAZAR, CAMIL; BANUS, MARIA; BARANGA, AUREL; BLECHER, MARCEL; CHILDREN'S LITERATURE; DOBROGEANU- GHEREA, CONSTANTIN; GALACTION, GALA; GURIAN, SORANA; ODESSA; PANĂ, SAȘA; PORUMBACU, VERONICA; RELGIS, EUGEN; ROMANIAN LITERATURE; ROMAN-RONETTI, MOISE; RUDICH, MAYER; SANIELEVICI, HENRIC; SEBASTIAN, MIHAIL; TZARA, TRISTAN; VORONCA, ILARIE; WALD, HENRI

Stefan Litt*, Ph.D.; Fellow, the Hebrew University of Jerusalem: BOAS

Robert Littman*, Ph.D.; Professor of Classics, University of Hawaii, Honolulu, Hawaii: HAWAII

Meir Litvak, Ph.D.; Department of Middle Eastern History and African Studies, Tel Aviv University

Yosef Litvak, M.A.; Researcher, Ministry of Absorption, Jerusalem: HOLOCAUST, RESCUE FROM; ISRAEL, STATE OF: ALIYAH

Emanuel Litvinoff, Writer and Editor, London: RUSSIA

Jacob Liver, Ph.D.; Professor of Bible, Tel Aviv University: DAVID, DYNASTY OF; DEBORAH; GEDALIAH; GENEALOGY; HOSHEA; JEHOIACHIN; JEHOIAKIM; JERUSALEM; JONATHAN; KING, KINGSHIP; KORAH; MANASSEH; MISHMAROT AND MAAMADOT; SHESHBAZZAR

Linda Livna, Ben-Gurion University, Beersheba: BEN-GURION UNIVERSITY OF THE NEGEV

Eliezer Livneh: VAN VRIESLAND, SIEGFRIED ADOLF

Amira Liwer*, B.A., M.A.; Research student, the Hebrew University of Jerusalem: ZADOK HA-KOHEN RABINOWITZ OF LUBLIN

Darrell B. Lockhart*, Ph.D.; Associate Professor of Spanish, University of Nevada, Reno: GOLOBOFF, GERARDO MARIO; GRÜNBERG, CARLOS MOISÉS; KOVADLOFF, SANTIAGO; MUÑIZ-HUBERMAN, ANGELINA; RAWET, SAMUEL; ROSENCOF, MAURICIO; ROZENMACHER, GERMÁN; SATZ, MARIO; SCLIAR, MOACYR; SHUA, ANA MARÍA; SNEH, SIMJA; STEIMBERG, ALICIA; TIEMPO, CÉSAR; VERBITSKY, BERNARDO; WECHSLER, ELINA

Amanda Lockitch*, B.A., M.A.; Theatre, University of Toronto, Canada: SHERMAN, JASON

Raphael Loewe, M.A.; Lecturer in Hebrew, University College, London: AINSWORTH, HENRY; ANDREW OF SAINT-VICTOR; BACON, ROGER; BECK, MATTHIAS FRIEDRICH; BECK, MICHAEL; BERNARD, EDWARD; BIBLE; BIBLIANDER, THEODOR; BODLEY, SIR THOMAS; BOSHAM, HERBERT DE; BROUGHTON, HUGH; CALLENBERG, JOHANN HEINRICH; CAPITO, WOLFGANG FABRICIUS; CASTELL, EDMUND; COCCEIUS, JOHANNES; COWLEY, SIR ARTHUR ERNEST; CUDWORTH, RALPH; DANBY, HERBERT; EGIDIO DA VITERBO; ERPENIUS, THOMAS; ETHERIDGE, JOHN WESLEY; FOREIRO, FRANCISCO; HEBRAISTS, CHRISTIAN; IMBONATI, CARLO GUISEPPE; NICHOLAS DE LYRE; SCHILLER-SZINESSY, SOLOMON MAYER

Ayala Loewenstamm, M.A.; the Academy of the Hebrew Language, Jerusalem: ABU AL-FAT; ABU AL-ḤASAN OF TYRE; ĀL-ASĀṬĪR; AMRAM DARAH; BABA RABBAH; DUSTAN; MARKAH; PENTATEUCH, SAMARITAN; SAMARITANS

Samuel Ephraim Loewenstamm, Ph.D.; Professor of Bible, the Hebrew University of Jerusalem: ELKANAH; EWALD, HEINRICH GEORG AUGUST; JEDAIAH; JEDUTHUN; JESSE

Kurt Loewenstein, Tel Aviv: FOERDER, YESHAYAHU; LANDAUER, GEORG; MOSES, SIEGFRIED; SENATOR, DAVID WERNER

Rudolf Loewenthal, Ph.D.; Historian, Bethesda, Maryland: AI T'IEN; CANTON; CHINA; HANGCHOW; HARBIN; HONG KONG; KADOORIE; KAIFENG; MONGOLIA; NINGSIA; PEKING; SCHERESCHEWSKY, SAMUEL ISAAC JOSEPH; YANG-CHOU

David Samuel Loewinger, Dr. Phil., Rabbi; Scholar, Former Professor at the Jewish Theological Seminary of Hungary; the Jewish National and University Library, Jerusalem: HELLER, BERNÁT; IBN GAON, SHEM TOV BEN ABRAHAM; LANDAUER, SAMUEL; LONZANO, MENAHEM BEN JUDAH DE; MAGYAR ZSIDÓ SZEMLE; MANUSCRIPTS, HEBREW

Julie Simon Loftsgaarden*, B.A. Print Journalism; Reporter/ Journalist; CBS News Corp.; Austin, Texas: KLEIN, GERDA WEISSMANN and KURT

Zvi Loker*, M.A.; Ambassador (retired); Director, Even Tov Archives, Jerusalem: ALBAHARI, DAVID; DOHANJ, JULIJE; DUBROVNIK; ELDAR, REUVEN; EVENTOV, YAKIR; FREIBERGER, MIROSLAV/ŠALOM; HAJIM, JISRAEL; KADELBURG, LAVOSLAV; KAMHI, LEON; KIŠ, DANILO; LEVI, MORITZ; LIVNI, HILLEL; LJUBLJANA; MADAGASCAR; MANDL, SAADIA; MARIBOR; MAURITIUS; MONASTIR; NIŠ; NOVI SAD; OFNER, FRANCIS-AMIR; OSIJEK; PAVELIĆ, ANTE; PIJADE, MOŠA; RIJEKA; ROTEM, CVI; SARAJEVO; SENTA; SKOPLJE; SOMBOR; SPLIT; SUBOTICA; TIŠMA, ALEKSANDAR; TRAVNIK; VARAŽDIN; YUGOSLAVIA; ZAGREB; ZEMUN; ZENICA; ZRENJANIN

Massimo Longo Adorno*, Ph.D.; Historical Researcher, University of Messina, Italy: AZEGLIO, MASSIMO TAPARELLI, MARCHESSE D'; BACHI, ARMANDO; CARPI, LEONE; DELLA SETA ALESSANDRO; FLORENCE; GUASTALLA, ENRICO; MODENA, ANGELO; OTTOLENGHI, GIUSEPPE; PUGLIESE, EMANUELE; RASSEGNA MENSILE DI ISRAEL, LA; ROMANIN JACUR, LEONE; ROMANIN, SAMUELE; SCHANZER, CARLO; SEGRÈ, ROBERTO; VESSILLO ISRAELITICO; VOLTERRA, VITO; WOLLENBORG, LEONE

Peter Longreich*: HIMMLER, HEINRICH

Haskel Lookstein*, Ph.D., Rabbi; Congregation Jeshurun, Principal, Ramaz School, New York: HOLOCAUST: THE WORLD; MARGOLIES, MOSES ZEVULUN

Max Loppert, B.A.; Music Critic, *Financial Times*, London: ABRAVANEL, MAURICE; ANCONA, MARIO; BABIN, VICTOR; BERGER, ARTHUR VICTOR; BROWNING, JOHN; CHAGRIN, FRANCIS; CHERKASSKY, SHURA; COSTA, SIR MICHAEL; DICHTER, MISHA; DOBROVEN, ISSAY ALEXANDROVICH; DORATI, ANTAL; DU PRÉ, JACQUELINE; DUSHKIN, SAMUEL; FELDMAN, MORTON; FLEISHER, LEON; FRANKEL, BENJAMIN; GOLSCHMANN, VLADIMIR; GRAF, HERBERT; GRAF, HERBERT; GRAFFMAN, GARY; HERRMANN, BERNARD; HORENSTEIN, JASCHA; JACOBS, ARTHUR; KENTNER, LOUIS; KERTESZ, ISTVAN; KIRCHNER, LEON; KOSHETZ, NINA; KURZ, SELMA; LEAR, EVELYN; LEVINE, JAMES; LEWENTHAL, RAYMOND; LONDON, GEORGE; MATZENAUER, MARGARETE; MERRILL, ROBERT; PASTA, GUIDITTA; PAULY, ROSA; PERAHIA, MURRAY; PREVIN, ANDRE; QUELER, EVE; REIZENSTEIN, FRANZ; RESNIK, REGINA; RÉTI, RUDOLF; ROLL, MICHAEL; ROSE, LEONARD; ROSEN, CHARLES; ROSENSTOCK, JOSEPH; ROSENTHAL, HAROLD; ROSENTHAL, MORIZ; RUBINSTEIN, ARTUR; RUDEL, JULIUS; RUDOLF, MAX; SADIE, STANLEY; SANDERLING, KURT; SCHOENE, LOTTE; SILLS, BEVERLY; SOLOMON; SOLTI, SIR GEORG; SPIVAKOVSKY, TOSSY; STEIN, ERWIN; THOMAS, MICHAEL TILSON; WEINSTOCK, HERBERT; WEISSENBERG, ALEXIS; ZUKOFSKY, PAUL

Netanel Lorch, M.A.; Lieutenant Colonel (Res.), Israel Defense Forces; Former Ambassador, Ministry for Foreign Affairs, Jerusalem: BOLIVIA; CUBA; EYTAN, WALTER; FISCHER, JEAN; HOCHSCHILD, MAURICIO; SHALTIEL, DAVID; WAR OF INDEPENDENCE

Giora Lotan, Dr.Jur.; Former Director General of the National Insurance Institute, of the Ministry of Social Welfare, and of the Ministry of Labor, Jerusalem: KARMINSKI, HANNAH; OLLENDORFF, FRIEDRICH

Arthur Lourie, LL.B., M.A.; Deputy Director General of the Ministry for Foreign Affairs, Jerusalem: ENGLAND

Misha Louvish, M.A.; Writer and Journalist, Jerusalem: ALIYAH; CAPITO, WOLFGANG FABRICIUS; GUR, MORDECAI; ISRAEL, STATE OF: ALIYAH; ISRAEL, STATE OF: HISTORICAL SURVEY; ISRAEL, STATE OF: POLITICAL LIFE AND PARTIES; KOLLEK, THEODORE; MA'BARAH; MALBEN; MAPAI; RAFI; STOCKADE AND WATCHTOWER; ZIONIST CONGRESSES

William (Ze'ev) Low, Ph.D.; Professor of Physics, the Hebrew University of Jerusalem; former Director of Jerusalem College of Technology: TECHNOLOGY AND HALAKHAH

Malcolm F. Lowe*, Ecumenical Theological Research Fraternity in Israel: NEW TESTAMENT

Steven (Mark) Lowenstein*, Ph.D.; Levine Professor of Jewish History, University of Judaism, Los Angeles: BREUER, JOSEPH; NEW YORK CITY; SCHWAB, SHIMON

Ernst Gottfried Lowenthal, Dr.rer. Pol.; Berlin and London: PHILO VERLAG; PRESS

Zdenko Lowenthal, M.D.; Professor of the History of Medicine, the University of Belgrade, Yugoslavia: BIHALJI MERIN, OTO; DAVIČO, OSCAR; DEBRECENJI, JOŽEF; ERLICH, VERA STEIN; GLID, NANDOR; GOTTLIEB, HINKO; JUNBRODA, INA; KONFINO, ŽAK; LEBOVIĆ, DJORDJE

Heinz Lubacz, Waltham, Massachusetts: MARCUSE, HERBERT

Benjamin Lubelski: KALLIR, MEIER

Lisa (Jane) Lubick-Daniel*, Masters in Public Policy; McLean, Virginia: EIZENSTAT, STUART

Roy Lubove, Ph.D.; Professor of Social Welfare and History, the University of Pittsburgh: BERNSTEIN,

LUDWIG BEHR; BILLIKOPF, JACOB; BOGEN, BORIS DAVID; EPSTEIN, ABRAHAM; FRANKEL, LEE KAUFER

Steven Luckert*, Ph.D.; Curator of the Permanent Exhibition, United States Holocaust Memorial Museum, Washington, D.C.: VOYAGE OF THE ST. LOUIS

Stefan Lutkiewicz, B.A.; Jerusalem: HIRSZFELD, LUDWIK

Edythe Lutzker, M.A.; Writer, New York: HAFFKINE, WALDEMAR MORDECAI

Jacob Lvavi (Babitzky), Agricultural Engineer, Tel Aviv: BIROBIDZHAN

Klara Maayan, M.A.; Tel Aviv: RZESZOW

Hyam Maccoby, M.A.; Librarian and Lecturer, Leo Baeck College, London

John Macdonald, Ph.D.; Professor of Hebrew and Semitic Languages, the University of Glasgow, Scotland: PENTATEUCH, SAMARITAN; SAMARITANS

Peter Machinist, B.A.; New Haven, Connecticut: LEVIATHAN

Robert B. MacLeod, Ph.D.; Professor of Psychology, Cornell University, Ithaca, New York: KATZ, DAVID

David M. Maeir, M.D.; Director, Shaare Zedek Hospital, Jerusalem

Z. (Ze'ev) A. Maghen*, Ph.D.; Senior Lecturer in Middle East History and Persian Language, Bar-Ilan University, Ramat Gan: HADITH; MEDINA; YAHUD; YAHŪD

Shaul Magid*, Ph.D.; Jay and Jeanie Schottenstein Professor of Modern Judaism, Indiana University, Bloomington, Indiana: SCHACHTER-SHALOMI, ZALMAN

Shulamit S. Magnus*, Ph.D.; Associate Professor in Jewish Studies and History, Chair, Program in Jewish Studies, Oberlin College, Ohio: WENGEROFF, PAULINE EPSTEIN

Raphael Mahler, Dr.Phil.; Emeritus Professor of Jewish History, Tel Aviv University: BALABAN, MEIR; JANOW LUBELSKI; LECZNA; LUBACZOW

Joseph Maier, Ph.D.; Professor of Sociology, Rutgers University, Newark, New Jersey: DURKHEIM, ÉMILE; JOSEPH ISSACHAR BAER BEN ELHANAN

J.F. Maillard, Agrege de l'Universite, Chercheur, Centre National de la Recherche Scientifique, Paris: RAPHAEL, MARK

Jacob Maimon, Jerusalem: ALPHABET, HEBREW

Emmanuelle Main*: PESHER; STERN, MENACHEM; YANNAI, ALEXANDER

Yitzchak Mais*, Historian, Museum Consultant, Jerusalem and New York: ARAD, YITZHAK; MUSEUM OF JEWISH HERITAGE: A LIVING MEMORIAL TO THE HOLOCAUST; STERN, DAVID

David Maisel, M.A.; Jerusalem: COHEN; FEKETE, MICHAEL; SHENHAR, YITZHAK

Jacob J. Maitlis, Dr.Phil.; Scholar, London: MAYSE-BUKH

Donald J. Makovsky, M.A.; Assistant Professor of History, Forest Park Community College, St. Louis, Missouri: MISSOURI

Yona Malachy, D.en D.; Research Fellow, the Institute for Contemporary Jewry, the Hebrew University of Jerusalem: BLACKSTONE, WILLIAM E.; ECKARDT, ROY A.; PROTESTANTS; ZIONISM

Abraham Malamat, Ph.D.; Professor of Ancient Jewish and Biblical History, the Hebrew University of Jerusalem: ARAM, ARAMEANS; ARAM-DAMASCUS; DAMASCUS; EXILE, ASSYRIAN; MARI

Irving Malin, Ph.D.; Associate Professor of English, City College of the City University of New York: SVETLOV, MIKHAIL; TRILLING, LIONEL

Michael Malina*, A.B., L.L.B.; Harvard Law School, Scarsdale, New York: BERMAN, JULIUS

Frances Malino*, Ph.D.; Professor of Jewish Studies and History, Wellesley College, Maryland: ALLIANCE ISRAELITE UNIVERSELLE; HOURWITZ, ZALKIND

Myriam M. Malinovich, Ph.D.; Acting Assistant Professor of Philosophy, San Diego State College, California: KOJÈVE, ALEXANDRE; PERELMAN, BARON CHAIM

Nadia Malinovich*, Ph.D., Adjunct Professor, Institut d'Etudes Politiques de Paris, France: HERSTEIN, LILLIAN; STEIMER, MOLLY

Risa Mallin*, B.A.; Retired Executive Director, Arizona Jewish Historical Society, Phoenix, Arizona: ARIZONA; PHOENIX

Aharon Maman*, Ph.D.; Professor of Hebrew, the Hebrew University of Jerusalem: ABBREVIATIONS; BAR-ASHER, MOSHE; BLAU JOSHUA; ḤAYYUJ, JUDAH BEN DAVID; KADDARI, MENACHEM ZEVI; LINGUISTIC LITERATURE, HEBREW; SARFATTI, GAD B.

Peter (M.) Manasse*, Editor, *20th Century Biographical Encyclopedia of Jews in the Netherlands*, Menasseh ben Israel Institute/University of Amsterdam, the Netherlands: VAN RAALTE, EDUARD ELLIS

Arnold Mandel, L.es L.; Writer and Critic, Paris: ARÉGA, LÉON; BLOCH-MICHEL, JEAN; CRÉMIEUX, BENJAMIN; IKOR, ROGER; SARRAUTE, NATHALIE; SPERBER, MANÈS

Meir Mandel, Ing.Agr., I.A.N.; Kibbutz Kiryat Anavim: GORDONIA

Bernard Mandelbaum, D.H.L., Rabbi; Chancellor, Professor of Homiletics, and Associate Professor of Midrash, the Jewish Theological Seminary of America, New York

Jane Mandelbaum*: PASSAIC-CLIFTON

Charles (H.) Manekin*, Ph.D.; Assistant Professor of Philosophy, University of Maryland: BELIEF; CATEGORIES

Daniel Mann*, B.A., M.A.; Retired Jewish Communal Worker and Educator: FARBAND; LABOR ZIONIST ALLIANCE

Jacob Mann, Ph.D., Rabbi; Professor of Jewish History and Talmud, the Hebrew Union

College-Jewish Institute of Religion, Cincinnati, Ohio: AARON BEN JOSEPH HA-KOHEN SARGADO; ABRAHAM BEN ISAAC HA-KOHEN BEN AL-FURAT

Giora Manor*, Dance Reviewer and Writer; Founder and first editor of the *Israel Dance Review*: AGADATI, BARUCH; MARKOVA, ALICIA; ZEMACH, BENJAMIN

Yohanan Manor, Ph.D.; Head, Information Department, World Zionist Organization, Jerusalem: ANTI-ZIONISM, CONTEMPORARY

Menahem Mansoor, Ph.D.; Professor of Hebrew and Semitic Studies, the University of Wisconsin, Madison: ESSENES; HASSIDEANS

Hugo Mantel, Ph.D., Rabbi; Associate Professor of Jewish History, Bar-Ilan University, Ramat Gan: ODENATHUS AND ZENOBIA; SANHEDRIN

Daniela Mantovan*, Ph.D.; Associate Professor of Yiddish Language and Literature, Hochschule für Jüdische Studien, Heidelberg, Germany: DER NISTER

Haim Maor*, Professor, Artist, Curator and Art Lecturer, Ben-Gurion University of the Negev, Beersheva: ART: MODERN EREZ ISRAEL; ISRAEL, STATE OF: CULTURAL LIFE

Yitzhak Maor, Ph.D.; Historian, Kibbutz Ashdot Ya'akov (Iḥud): AN-SKI, S.; KHARKOV CONFERENCE; KIRSHON, VLADIMIR MIKHAILOVICH; LATVIA; LUNTS, LEV NATANOVICH; MINSKI, NIKOLAI MAXIMOVICH; SOBOL, ANDREY MIKHAILOVICH; VOLYNSKI, AKIM LEVOVICH; ZASLAVSKY, DAVID

Moshe Ma'oz*, Professor Emeritus of Islamic and Middle Eastern Studies, the Hebrew University of Jerusalem: ASAD, HAFEZ AL-; SYRIA

Evasio de Marcellis, M.A.; Teacher in the Department of Ancient Near Eastern Studies, Tel Aviv University: EGYPT; GELB, IGNACE JAY

Frederick J. Marchant*, Ph.D.; Professor of English and Director of Creative Writing and the Poetry Center, Suffolk University, Boston: PINSKY, ROBERT

Julius J. Marcke, J.D.; Professor of Law and Law Librarian, New York University School of Law: CAHN, EDMOND NATHANIEL; CARDOZO, BENJAMIN NATHAN; COHEN, BENJAMIN VICTOR; FRANK, JEROME NEW; FREUND, ERNST; FREUND, PAUL ABRAHAM; FUCHSBERG, JACOB D.; GARMENT, LEONARD; LAWYERS; LEVY, MOSES; PFEFFER, LEO; REDLICH, NORMAN; RODELL, FRED M.; SHULMAN, HARRY; WECHSLER, HERBERT; WYZANSKI, CHARLES EDWARD, JR.

David Marcus*, Ph.D.; Professor of Bible, Jewish Theological Seminary, New York: EZRA AND NEHEMIAH, BOOKS OF

Jacob Rader Marcus, Ph.D., Rabbi; Professor of American Jewish History, the Hebrew Union College-Jewish Institute of Religion, Cincinnati, Ohio: AMERICAN JEWISH ARCHIVES; UNITED STATES OF AMERICA

Joseph Marcus, M.D.; Jerusalem: KANNER, LEO; SPITZ, RENE A.

Marcel Marcus, M.A., Rabbi; Communal Rabbi of Berne, Lecturer at the University of Berne

Simon Marcus, Dr.rer.Pol; Historian, Jerusalem: ALBANIA; ALTARAS, JOSEPH; ARTA; ASAEL, ḤAYYIM BEN BENJAMIN; ATHENS; BEIRUT; BULGARIA; CANEA; CAREGAL, ḤAYYIM MOSES BEN ABRAHAM; CHALCIS; CHIOS; CORFU; CORINTH; CRETE; CYPRUS; DANON, ABRAHAM; DIDYMOTEIKHON; DRAMA; DURAZZO; EDIRNE; FAITUSI, JACOB BEN ABRAHAM; GAGIN, SHALOM MOSES BEN ḤAYYIM ABRAHAM; GALIPAPA, ELIJAH MEVORAKH; GARMISON, SAMUEL; GHERON, YAKKIR MORDECAI BEN ELIAKIM; GHIRON; GOTA, MOSES ZERAHIAH BEN SHNEUR; GRAZIANO, ABRAHAM JOSEPH SOLOMON BEN MORDECAI; GREECE; ḤABIB, ḤAYYIM BEN MOSES BEN SHEM TOV; ḤABIB, MOSES BEN SOLOMON IBN; HABILLO, ELISHA; HAMON; HANDALI, JOSHUA BEN JOSEPH; ḤAYYIM ABRAHAM RAPHAEL BEN ASHER; ḤAYYIM JUDAH BEN ḤAYYIM; ḤAZZAN; ḤAZZAN, ISRAEL MOSES BEN ELIEZER; IBN EZRA, SOLOMON BEN MOSES; IBN JAMIL, ISAAC NISSIM; IBN VERGA, JOSEPH; IOANNINA; ISTRUMSA, ḤAYYIM ABRAHAM; JAVETZ, BARZILLAI BEN BARUCH; KALAI, MORDECAI BEN SOLOMON; KALAI, SAMUEL BEN MOSES; KAPUZATO, MOSES HA-YEVANI; KASABI, JOSEPH BEN NISSIM; KASTORIA; KAVALLA; KOLAROVGRAD; KORONE; KOS; KRISPIN, JOSHUA ABRAHAM; KYUSTENDIL; LARISSA; LEVI BEN ḤABIB; MODON; MUSSAFIA, ḤAYYIM ISAAC; NAUPAKTOS; NIKOPOL; NIŠ; OCHRIDA; PACIFICO, DAVID; PATRAS; PHLORINA; PLEVEN; PLOVDIV; RETHYMNON; ROMANIOTS; RUSE; SAMOKOV; SERRAI; SOFIA; SPARTA; STARA ZAGORA; THEBES; TRIKKALA; VARNA; VEROIA; VIDIN; VOLOS; YUGOSLAVIA; ZANTE

Eliezer Margaliot, Ph.D., Rabbi; Scholar and Teacher, Jerusalem: AḤAI BEN JOSIAH; OSTROGORSKI, MOSES

Mordecai Margaliot, Ph.D.; Professor of Geonic and Midrashic Literature, the Jewish Theological Seminary of America, New York: AḤA; DOSA BEN SAADIAH; HAI BAR RAV DAVID GAON; HAI BEN NAHSHON; HALAKHOT KEẒUVOT; HALAKHOT PESUKOT

David Margalith, M.D.; Former Lecturer in the History of Medicine, Bar-Ilan University, Ramat Gan: COHN, TOBIAS BEN MOSES; FALAQUERA, NATHAN BEN JOEL

Judith Margles*, Executive Director, Oregon Jewish Museum, Portland, Oregon: OREGON; PORTLAND

Jill Margo*: WOLFENSOHN, JAMES DAVID

Julius Margolinsky, Journalist, Copenhagen: ADLER, DAVID BARUCH; BALLIN, JOEL; BRANDES, LUDWIG ISRAEL; COPENHAGEN; DENMARK; GLUECKSTADT, ISAAC HARTVIG; HAMBRO, JOSEPH; HANNOVER, ADOLPH; JACOBSEN, ARNE EMIL; JACOBSON, LUDVIG LEVIN; NATHANSON, MENDEL LEVIN; SALOMONSEN, CARL JULIUS; SIMONSEN, DAVID JACOB

Peter (S.) Margolis*, M.A.; the Hebrew University of Jerusalem; Gratz College, Philadelphia: STRASSFELD, MICHAEL; STRASSFELD, SHARON

Rebecca E. Margolis*, Ph.D.; Professor of History, Humanities and Religious Studies, Vanier College, Montreal, Canada: MIRANSKY, PERETZ; RAVITCH, MELECH; WASSERMAN, DORA AND BRYNA; WILDER, HERTZ EMANUEL; WOLOFSKY, HIRSCH

Yitzhak Margowsky, B.A.; Jerusalem: WAR AND WARFARE

Marin Marian (-Balasa)*, Dr.Phil; Principal Senior Researcher, Musicologist, Writer, Romania Academy of Sciences, Romania: BRAUNER, HARRY; CARP, PAULA; SULIŢEANU, GHISELA; VICOL, ADRIAN

Jonathan Mark*, B.A.; Associate Editor, *The Jewish Week*, New York: SCHNEERSOHN, MENACHEM MENDEL

Zvi Mark*, Ph.D.; Lecturer, Bar-Ilan University, Ramat Gan: NAḤMAN OF BRATSLAV

Shimon Markish, Ph.D.; Senior Lecturer, Geneva University, Geneva, Switzerland: ERASMUS OF ROTTERDAM

Eugene Markovitz, D.H.L., Rabbi; Adjunct Professor of American History, Seton Hall University, South Orange, New Jersey: MENDES

Arthur Marmorstein, Ph.D.; Professor of Bible and Talmud, Jews' College, London: ANGELS AND ANGELOLOGY

José Martinez (Delgado)*, Ph.D.; Associate Professor, Granada University, Spain: GIKATILLA, MOSES BEN SAMUEL HA-KOHEN

Yehuda Marton, Dr. rer Pol.; Journalist, Jerusalem: ALBA IULIA; AMIGO; ARAD; BAIA-MARE; BEZIDUL NOU; BISTRITA; BORSA; BRAŞOV; CAMPULUNG MOLDOVENESC; CAREI; CHERNOVTSY; CLUJ; DARABANI; DEJ; DEUTSCHKREUTZ; DOROHOI; ENDRE, LÁSZLÓ; FAGARAS; FRANKEL, LEO; FRIEDMANN, ABRAHAM; GURA-HUMORULUI; JÁMBOR, FERENC-IOSEF; KASZTNER, REZSŐ RUDOLF; KISTARCSA; KOMOLY, OTTÓ; LÉVAI, JENÖ; LUGOJ; MARGHITA; MARTON, ERNÖ JECHEZKEL; MATTERSDORF, JEREMIAH BEN ISAAC; MUENZ, MOSES BEN ISAAC HA-LEVI; MUKACHEVO; NASAUD; NASNA; ORADEA; ORSOVA; PANET, EZEKIEL BEN JOSEPH; RADAUTI; RAPOPORT, BENJAMIN ZE'EV WOLF HA-KOHEN BEN ISAAC; REBREANU; REGHIN; SADGORA; SALAMON, ERNO; SALONTA; SATU-MARE; SCHUECK, JENÖ; SCHWERIN-GOETZ, ELIAKIM HA-KOHEN; SEINI; SIBIU; SIGHET; SIMLEUL-SILVANIEI; SIRET; SOMREI SABAT; SUCEAVA; SZTÓJAY, DÖME; TALMACIU; TAM, JACOB BEN MEIR; TARGU-MURES; TIMISOARA; TISZAESZLAR; TRANSYLVANIA; TURDA; UJ KELET; VATRA-DORNEI; VISEUL-DE-SUS; WERFEL, FRANZ; WOLF, FRUMET

Martin E. Marty, Ph.D.; Professor of Modern Church History, the University of Chicago: NIEBUHR, REINHOLD; TILLICH, PAUL JOHANNES

Will Maslow, A.B., J.D.; General Counsel, American Jewish Congress, New York: PEKELIS, ALEXANDER HAIM

Daniel M. Master*: DOTHAN

J. Rolando (Roly) Matalon*, M.H.L., Rabbi; Congregation B'nai Jeshurun, New York: MEYER, MARSHALL T.

Lidia Domenica Matassa*, B.A.; School of Religions, Trinity College, Dublin, Ireland: DELOS; ELEPHANTINE; MAGDALA; SAMARITANS

Maritha Mathijsen*, Ph.D.; Professor Dutch Literature, University of Amsterdam, The Netherlands: BRUGGEN, CARRY VAN; MULISCH, HARRY; VROMAN, LEO

Jürgen Matthäus*, Ph.D.; Historian, United States Holocaust Memorial Museum's Center for Advanced Holocaust Studies, Washington, D.C.: FINAL SOLUTION

Amihai Mazar*, Ph.D.; Professor, Eleazar Sukenik Chair in Archaeology, The Hebrew University of Jerusalem: JERUSALEM; REḤOV, TEL

Benjamin Mazar, Dr. Phil.; Pro-Rector, former President and Professor of Archaeology and of Jewish History, the Hebrew University of Jerusalem: EN-GEDI; LEBO-HAMATH

Michel Mazor, Dr.Jur.; Author, Paris: CENTRE DE DOCUMENTATION JUIVE CONTEMPORAINE

Y. (Yaakov) Mazor*, M.A.; Associated Researcher, Jewish Music Research Centre, the Hebrew University of Jerusalem: FEIDMAN, GIORA; ḤASIDISM

David P. McCarthy, Ph.D.; Professor, Hebrew and Semitic Studies, University of Wisconsin

Keren R. McGinity*, Ph.D.; Historian, Brown University, Newton, Massachusetts: ANTIN, MARY; CHESLER, PHYLLIS

Blake McKelvey, Ph.D.; City Historian of Rochester, New York: ROCHESTER

Michael Meckler*, Ph.D.; Permanent Fellow, Center for Epigraphical and Palaeographical Studies, the Ohio State University: COLUMBUS

Meir Medan, M.A.; Chief Scientific Secretary of the Academy of the Hebrew Language, Jerusalem: ABRAHAM HA-BAVLI; ACADEMY OF THE HEBREW LANGUAGE; KLAUSNER, JOSEPH GEDALIAH; LAWAT, ABRAHAM DAVID BEN JUDAH LEIB; LEVITA, ELIJAH

Sheva Medjuck*, Ph.D.; Professor of Sociology, Mount Saint Vincent University, Halifax, Canada: ATLANTIC CANADA

Elliott Hillel Medlov, B.A., Rabbi; Highland Park, New Jersey: SAMUEL HA-KATAN; SIMEON BEN PAZZI

Rafael Medoff*, Ph.D., Director, The David S. Wyman Institute for Holocaust Studies, Gratz College, Melrose Park, Pennsylvania: GOLINKIN, NOAH; KOOK, HILLEL; WAR REFUGEE BOARD

Meron Medzini, Ph.D.; Author, Journalist, Senior Lecturer, School for Overseas Students, The Hebrew University of Jerusalem: HISTADRUT; ISRAEL, STATE OF: ALIYAH; ISRAEL, STATE OF: DEFENSE FORCES; ISRAEL, STATE OF: HISTORICAL SURVEY; KEREN HAYESOD; POLLARD AFFAIR

Moshe Medzini, Journalist and Writer, Jerusalem: NOVOMEYSKY, MOSHE; RUTENBERG, PINḤAS; ZIONISM

Matti Megged, M.A.; Critic and Lecturer in Modern Hebrew Literature, Haifa University and the Hebrew University of Jerusalem: ALONI, NISSIM; ALTERMAN, NATHAN; GOURI, HAIM; YIZHAR, S.

Michal Meidan*, Ph.D.; Candidate, Research Fellow and Lecturer, Asia Centre France, Paris, University of Haifa: CHINA

Levi Meier*, Ph.D., Rabbi; Jewish Chaplain/Clinical Psychologist, Cedars-Sinai Medical Center, Los Angeles: HOSPITALS

Richard Meier, Bach.Arch.; Professor of Architecture, the Cooper Union for the Advancement of Science and Art, New York: SYNAGOGUE

Alexander Meijer, M.D.; Lecturer in Child Psychiatry, the Hebrew University-Hadassah Medical School, Jerusalem: TRAMER, MORITZ

Daphne Meijer(-Sangary)*, M.A.; Journalist, *Nieuw Israelietisch Weekblad*, Amsterdam, The Netherlands: DUTCH LITERATURE

Edmund Meir, Dr. Phil.; Historian, Jerusalem: DARMSTADT; HYMANS, PAUL

Ephraim Meir*, Ph.D.; Professor of Philosophy, Bar-Ilan University, Ramat Gan: BUBER, MARTIN; DERRIDA, JACQUES; EXISTENTIALISM; HESCHEL, ABRAHAM JOSHUA; LEIBOWITZ, YESHAYAHU; LEVINAS, EMMANUEL; LYOTARD, JEAN-FRANÇOIS; ROSENSTOCK-HUESSY, EUGEN; ROSENZWEIG, FRANZ; WITTGENSTEIN, LUDWIG

Isaac Meiseles, Ph.D.; Lecturer in Talmud, Bar-Ilan University, Ramat Gan

Joseph Meisl, Dr.Phil.; *Encyclopaedia Judaica* (Germany); Historian and former Director of the Central Archives for the History of the Jewish People, Jerusalem: BERLIN; DUBNOW, SIMON

Pnina Meislish, B.A.; Ramat Gan: HALBERSTAM; MEISELS, UZZIEL BEN ẒEVI HIRSCH

Abraham Melamed*, Ph.D.; Professor, University of Haifa: ABRABANEL, JUDAH; ASHKENAZI, SAUL BEN MOSES HA-KOHEN; KING, KINGSHIP

Uri Melammed*, Ph.D.; Researcher, The Historical Dictionary Project of the Academy of the Hebrew Language, The Hebrew University of Jerusalem and the Hebrew Language Academy, Jerusalem: TIBBON, IBN

Bent Melchior, Chief Rabbi of Denmark, Copenhagen: DENMARK; FISCHER, JOSEF

Julian Louis Meltzer, Executive Vice Chairman, Yad Chaim Weizmann, Reḥovot, Israel: MARKS, SIMON, BARON; OPPENHEIMER, HILLEL REINHARD; REICHERT, ISRAEL; ROSENHEIM, MAX, BARON; SELA, MICHAEL; THORN, SIR JULES; WOLFSON, SIR ISAAC

Adam (David) Mendelsohn*, B.A., M.A.; Brandeis University, Boston: AARON, ISRAEL; ABRAMOWITZ, DOV BAER; ADLER, JOSEPH; ADLER, LIEBMAN; ALBUM, SIMON HIRSCH; ALPER, MICHAEL; AMATEAU, ALBERT JEAN; BLACK, ALGERNON DAVID; BRUCKMAN, HENRIETTA; COHEN, MARY MATILDA

Ezra Mendelsohn, Ph.D.; Lecturer in Contemporary Jewry and in Russian Studies, the Hebrew University of Jerusalem: LASERSON, MAX; POLAND; SOCIALISM, JEWISH; WOLFE, BERTRAM DAVID

Oskar Mendelsohn, M.A.; Historian, Retired Teacher, Oslo: BENKOW, JO; NORWAY; SCANDINAVIAN LITERATURE; TAU, MAX; WERGELAND, HENRIK ARNOLD

Paul Mendes-Flohr*, Ph.D.; Professor of Modern Jewish Thought, the Franz Rosenzweig Minerva Research Center for German-Jewish Literature and Cultural History, the Hebrew University of Jerusalem: COHEN, ARTHUR A.; ROTENSTREICH, NATHAN

Richard Menkis*, Ph.D.; Associate Professor, University of British Columbia, Canada: ABRAMOWITZ, HERMAN; BECKER, LAVY M.; BELZBERG, SAMUEL; CASS, SAMUEL; DIAMOND, JACK; FEINBERG, ABRAHAM L.; FELDER, GEDALIA; FINESTONE, SHEILA; GORDON, NATHAN; GRAUBART, Y.L.; HOROWITZ; JACOBS, SOLOMON; JOURNALISM; KAHANOVITCH, ISRAEL ISAAC; LAWYERS; ONTARIO; POLITICS; PRESS; PRICE, ABRAHAM A.; RHINEWINE, ABRAHAM; SASKATCHEWAN; SLONIM, REUBEN; STERN, HARRY JOSHUA; TREPMAN, PAUL

Itshak Meraz, M.A.; Jerusalem

Chen Merchavya, Ph.D.; Historian, Jerusalem: RAZIM, SEFER HA

Peretz Merhav, Historian of the Labor Movement, Kibbutz Bet Zera: HA-SHOMER HA-ẒA'IR

Irwin L. Merker, Ph.D.; Associate Professor of History, Rutgers University, Newark, New Jersey: COHEN, ROBERT; EHRENBERG, VICTOR LEOPOLD; FUKS, ALEXANDER; GLOTZ, GUSTAVE; HIRSCHFELD, HEINRICH OTTO; KATZ, SOLOMON; LÉVY, PAUL; POSENER, GEORGES HENRI; SAMTER, ERNST; STEIN, ARTHUR; STEIN, HENRI

Yohanan Meroz, Ministry for Foreign Affairs, Jerusalem: AUSTRIA; BELGIUM; DENMARK; ITALY; NETHERLANDS, THE

Joseph Mersand, Ph.D.; New York: CHAYEFSKY, PADDY; HECHT, BEN; KAUFMAN, GEORGE SIMON; MILLER, ARTHUR; ODETS, CLIFFORD; RICE, ELMER LEOPOLD; SHAW, IRWIN; WOUK, HERMAN

Daniel M. Metz*: SARPHATI, SAMUEL; WERTHEIM, ABRAHAM CAREL

Bruce M. Metzger, Ph.D.; Professor of New Testament Language and Literature, Princeton Theological Seminary, New Jersey: ESTHER, ADDITIONS TO THE BOOK OF; MANASSEH, PRAYER OF; SONG OF THE THREE CHILDREN AND THE PRAYER OF AZARIAH; SUSANNA AND THE ELDERS

Baruch Mevorah, Ph.D.; Senior Lecturer in Jewish History, the Hebrew University of Jerusalem: ASSEMBLY OF JEWISH NOTABLES; BAIL, CHARLES-JOSEPH; CLOOTS, JEAN BAPTISTE DU VAL-DE-GRÂCE, BARON DE; GRÉGOIRE, HENRI BAPTISTE; HOLBACH, PAUL HENRI DIETRICH, BARON D'; NAPOLEON BONAPARTE; SACY, ANTOINE ISAAC SILVESTRE DE

Herrmann M. Z. Meyer, M.A.; Scholar and Advocate, Berlin; Jerusalem: INCUNABULA; JERUSALEM; MAP MAKERS; SONCINO GESELLSCHAFT DER FREUNDE DES JUEDISCHEN BUCHES

Ilya Meyer*, B.Ed.; Translator, Transtext Ab, Gothenburg, Sweden: BRICK, DANIEL; GÖNDÖR, FERENC; JAKUBOWSKI, JACKIE; MALMÖ; NARROWE, MORTON; SCANDINAVIAN LITERATURE; STOCKHOLM; SWEDEN

Isidore S. Meyer, M.A., Rabbi; Historian, New York: ADAMS, JOHN; AMERICAN JEWISH HISTORICAL SOCIETY; FRIEDENBERG, ALBERT MARX; FRIEDMAN, LEE MAX; KOHLER, MAX JAMES; LYONS, JACQUES JUDAH; MONIS,

JUDAH; MONTEFIORE, JOSHUA; SIMSON; WATTERS, LEON LAIZER

Michael A. Meyer*, Ph.D.; Adolph S. Ochs Professor of Jewish History, Hebrew Union College-Jewish Institute of Religion, Cincinnati, Ohio: ADLER, LAZARUS LEVI; BEER, BERNHARD; BRILLING, BERNHARD; GELBER, NATHAN MICHAEL; HEBREW UNION COLLEGE-JEWISH INSTITUTE OF RELIGION; HOCHSCHULE FUER DIE WISSENSCHAFT DES JUDENTUMS; INSTITUTUM JUDAICUM DELITZSCHIANUM; JUEDISCH-LITERARISCHE GESELLSCHAFT; LEBRECHT, FUERCHTEGOTT; LOEWENSTEIN, LEOPOLD; OESTERREICHISCHE NATIONALBIBLIOTHEK; SILBERNER, EDMUND

Thomas Meyer*, Ph.D.; Writer, Rosenzweig Minerva Research Center for German-Jewish Literature and Cultural History, Jerusalem: CASSIRER, ERNST

Torben Meyer, Editor, Copenhagen: BORCHSENIUS, POUL; NATHANSEN, HENRI; WELNER, PINCHES

Carol Meyers*, Ph.D., Mary Grace Wilson Professor, Duke University, Durham, North Carolina: MANDRAKE; WOMAN: BIBLE PERIOD

Eric M. Meyers*, A.B., M.A., Ph.D.; Bernice and Morton Lerner Professor of Judaic Studies; Director for Jewish Studies, President, The American Schools of Oriental Research, Duke University, Durham, North Carolina: MERON; SEPPHORIS

Reuven Michael, M.A.; Kibbutz Afikim: BAUER, BRUNO; CASSEL, PAULUS STEPHANUS; DEUTSCH-ISRAELITISCHER GEMEINDEBUND; FREDERICK II; FREDERICK II OF HOHENSTAUFEN; JACOBY, JOHANN; JUDE, DER; JUEDISCHE FREISCHULE; KATZENELLENBOGEN; KOENIGSBERG; RINDFLEISCH; SAXONY; SCHUDT, JOHANN JAKOB; SIMON, JAMES

Werner Michaelis, Ph.D.; Professor of New Testament History, the University of Berne: MOSES, ASSUMPTION OF

Henry (D.) Michelman*, B.A., M.H.L., Rabbi; New York: GOLDFARB, ISRAEL; SYNAGOGUE COUNCIL OF AMERICA, THE

Dan Michman*, Ph.D.; Professor of Modern Jewish History and Chair, Finkler Institute of Holocaust Research, Bar-Ilan University, Ramat Gan; Chief Historian, Yad Vashem, Jerusalem: AMSTERDAM; ASSCHER, ABRAHAM; COHEN, DAVID; NETHERLANDS, THE

Jozeph Michman (Melkman)*, Ph.D.; Formerly Director-General of Yad Vashem; head of the Department of Culture, Ministry of Education and Culture; Founder and Chairperson of the Institute for Research on Dutch Jewry, Beth Julian, Herzliya, Israel: AMSTERDAM; ASSCHER, ABRAHAM; BERGEN-BELSEN; BERNSTEIN, PEREZ; BOAS; DENAZIFICATION; FELIX LIBERTATE; JUDENRAT; KAPO; LEHREN; LEMANS, MOSES; LEPROSY; MUSSERT, ANTON ADRIAAN; NATIONAL SOCIALISM; NETHERLANDS, THE; SEYSS-INQUART, ARTHUR; SZÁLASI, FERENC; ZACUTO, MOSES BEN MORDECAI

Ed Mickelson*: EDMONTON

Dushan Mihalek*, M.A., Ph.D.; Director of Israeli Music Center, Tel Aviv: BARDANASHVILI, JOSEF; BEN-SHABETAI, ARI; MUSIC; YUGOSLAVIA

Eugene Mihaly, Ph.D.; Rabbi; Professor of Midrash and of Homiletics, the Hebrew Union College-Jewish Institute of Religion, Cincinnati: GUTTMANN, ALEXANDER

Jacques K. Mikliszanski, Ph.D., Rabbi; Professor of Halakhic Literature, the Hebrew College, Boston: ELISHA BA'AL KENAFAYIM; ISSUR GIYYORA; LÉVI, ISRAEL; MASSEKHET; SIMCHONI, JACOB NAFTALI HERTZ; TCHERNOWITZ, CHAIM

Attilio Milano, Ph.D.; Historian, Hod Ha-Sharon, Israel: ABENAFIA, JOSEPH; ABRABANEL; ACQUI; ALGHERO; AMBRON, SHABBETAI ISAAC; ANAU; ANCONA; AQUILA; AQUILEIA; ASCOLI PICENO; ASTI; BARI; BASILEA, SOLOMON AVIAD SAR-SHALOM; BASSANO; BENEVENTO; BERNARDINO DA SIENA; BOLOGNA; BONAVOGLIA, MOSES DE' MEDICI; BONDAVIN, BONJUDAS; BRINDISI; CANTARINI; CAPUA; CASES; CATANIA; CATECHUMENS, HOUSE OF; CESENA; CIVIDALE; COLOGNA, ABRAHAM VITA; CONEGLIANO; CORCOS, HEZEKIAH MANOAH ḤAYYIM THE YOUNGER; COSENZA; CREMONA; DIENCHELELE; FAENZA; FANO; FARAJ BEN SOLOMON DA AGRIGENTO; FERRARA; FINALE EMILIA; FINZI; FORLÌ; GALLICO; GENOA; GORIZIA; ILFA; IMOLA; ITALY; LEGHORN; LOMBARDY; LUCCA; LUGO; MAGINO, MEIR; MANTINO, JACOB BEN SAMUEL; MILAN; PAUL IV; PAVIA; PIACENZA; PIERLEONI; PISA; SAN DANIELE DEL FRIULI; VENOSA; VITERBO

Jonathan Milgram*, Ph.D.; Assistant Professor of Talmud and Rabbinics, Jewish Theological Seminary; New York

Jacob Milgrom, D.H.L., Rabbi; Associate Professor of Near Eastern Languages, the University of California, Berkeley: ABOMINATION; ALTAR; ANOINTING; BLOOD; BLOODGUILT; DESECRATION; 'EGLAH 'ARUFAH; FASTING AND FAST DAYS; FORGIVENESS; ḤALLAH; KIPPER; LEVITICUS, BOOK OF; NAZIRITE

Jose Maria Millas-Vallicrosa, Ph.D.; Professor of Hebrew Studies, the University of Barcelona: RAMON LULL

Rochelle L. Millen*, Ph.D.; Professor of Religion, Wittenberg University, Springfield, Ohio: KADDISH

Irwin (J.) Miller*, Author; Historian and Founding President, The Jewish Historical Society of Lower Fairfield County, Connecticut: STAMFORD

Louis Miller, M.B.; Chief National Psychiatrist, Ministry of Health, Jerusalem: ERIKSON, ERIK HOMBERGER; FEDERN, PAUL; FERENCZI, SÁNDOR; FREUD, ANNA; GREENACRE, PHYLLIS; GRINKER, ROY RICHARD Sr.; HITSCHMANN, EDWARD; HOFF, HANS; HOFFER, WILLI; KARDINER, ABRAM; KLEIN, MELANIE REIZES; KOMAROVSKY, MIRRA; KRIS, ERNST; KUBIE, LAWRENCE; LEWIS, SIR AUBREY JULIAN; MALZBERG, BENJAMIN; MASSERMAN, JULES HYMEN; MENTAL ILLNESS; MINKOWSI, EUGENE; NUNBERG, HERMAN; RADO, SANDOR; RANK, OTTO; REDL, FRITZ; REDLICH, FREDERICK C.; REIK, THEODOR; ROTHSCHILD, FRIEDRICH SALOMON; SACHS, HANNS; SCHILDER, PAUL FERDINAND; STEKEL, WILHELM; STENGEL, ERWIN; TAUSK, VIKTOR; WINNIK, HENRY ZVI; ZILBOORG, GREGORY

Marc Miller*, Ph.D.; Associate

Professor of Jewish Studies, Emory University, Atlanta, Georgia: EDELSTADT, DAVID; ENTIN, JOEL; FALKOWITSCH, JOEL BAERISCH; FEIGENBAUM, BENJAMIN; GINZBURG, ISER; GISER, MOSES DAVID; GLASMAN, BARUCH; GLICK, HIRSH; GODINER, SAMUEL NISSAN; GORIN, BERNARD; GOTTLIEB, JACOB; GROSS, NAPHTALI; GURSHTEIN, AARON; HELLER, BUNIM; HIRSCHKAHN, ẒVI; HORONTCHIK, SIMON; HOROWITZ, BER; ICELAND, REUBEN; JANOVSKY, SAUL JOSEPH; LATTEINER, JOSEPH; LERER, YEHIEL; LIBIN, Z.; LICHT, MICHAEL; LITVINE, M.; LUDWIG, REUBEN; LUTZKY, A.; RABON, ISRAEL; ROSENFELD, MORRIS; SWEATSHOP POETRY; TEPPER, KOLYA; VINCHEVSKY, MORRIS; WEINPER, ZISHE; YUNGE, DI

Samuel Aaron Miller, Ph.D., F.R.I.C.; Chemical Consultant; President of the British Zionist Federation, London: ABEL, EMIL; ABIR, DAVID; ABRAHAM, MAX; AERONAUTICS, AVIATION, AND ASTRONAUTICS; ANDRADE, EDWARD NEVILLE DA COSTA; ASKENASY, PAUL; BACHARACH, ALFRED LOUIS; BAEYER, ADOLF VON; BAMBERGER, EUGEN; BARD, BASIL JOSEPH ASHER; BERGMANN, ERNST DAVID; BERGMANN, MAX; BERLINER, EMILE; BIKERMAN, JACOB JOSEPH; BLAU, FRITZ; BLOCH, KONRAD; BOHR, NIELS HENRIK DAVID; BORSOOK, HENRY; BRAUDE, ERNEST ALEXANDER; CALVIN, MELVIN; CARO, HEINRICH; CARO, NIKODEM; CHAIN, SIR ERNEST BORIS; COHEN, ERNST JULIUS; COHN, EDWIN JOSEPH; COPISAROW, MAURICE; DEUEL, HANS ERWIN; DONATH, EDUARD; DROSDOFF, MATTHEW; DUSHMAN, SAUL; ESTERMANN, IMMANUEL; FAJANS, KASIMIR; FARKAS, LADISLAUS; FEIGL, FRITZ; FLEISCHER, MICHAEL; FODOR, ANDOR; FOX, SIR JOHN JACOB; FRANK, ALBERT RUDOLPH; FREIDLINA, RAKHIL KHATSKELEVNA; FRUMKIN, ALEKSANDR NAUMOVICH; FUNK, CASIMIR; GERHARDT, CHARLES FREDERIC; GOLDBERG, ALEXANDER; GOLDSCHMIDT, GUIDO; GOLDSCHMIDT, HANS; GOLDSTEIN, SIDNEY; GOMBERG, MOSES; GREENBERG, DAVID MORRIS; HABER, FRITZ; HANDLER, PHILIP; HAVURAH; HEIDELBERGER, MICHAEL; HEILBRON, SIR IAN MORRIS; HERZOG, REGINALD OLIVER; HEVESY, GEORGE CHARLES DE; HIRSHBERG, YEHUDAH; ISAACS, JACOB; JACOBSON, PAUL HENRICH; JOLLES, ZVI ENRICO; KAZARNOVSKI, ISAAC ABRAMOVICH; KREBS, SIR HANS ADOLF; LADENBURG, ALBERT; LANDSTEINER, KARL; LEVENE, PHOEBUS AARON THEODOR; LEVI, GIORGIO RENATO; LEVI, MARIO GIACOMO; LIEBEN, ADOLPH; LIEBERMANN, CARL THEODOR; LIPMAN, JACOB GOODALE; LIPMANN, FRITZ ALBERT; LIPPMANN, EDMUND OSKAR VON; LIPPMANN, EDUARD; LOEB, JACQUES; LOEB, MORRIS; LOEWE, LUDWIG and ISIDOR; LONDON, FRITZ; MAGNUS, HEINRICH GUSTAV; MARCKWALD, WILLY; MARCUS, SIEGFRIED; MEYER, VICTOR; MEYERHOF, OTTO; MICHAELIS, LEONOR; MOISSAN, HENRI; NAQUET, ALFRED JOSEPH; NEUBERG, GUSTAV EMBDEN CARL; NEUBERGER, ALBERT; OPPENHEIMER, CARL; PANETH, FRIEDRICH ADOLF; PERUTZ, MAX FERDINAND; PICK, ERNST PETER; RABINOWITCH, EUGENE; ROGINSKI, SIMON ZALMANOVICH; RONA, PETER; ROSENHEIM, OTTO; RUMPLER, EDUARD; SCHOENHEIMER, RUDOLF; SCHWARZ, DAVID; SERBIN, HYMAN; SHAPIRO, ASCHER HERMAN; SILVERSTEIN, ABE; SINGER, JOSEF; STEINMETZ, CHARLES PROTEUS; STERN, KURT GUNTER; SZWARC, MICHAEL; TRAUBE, ISIDOR; WALLACH, OTTO; WARBURG, OTTO HEINRICH; WEIGERT, FRITZ; WEIZMANN, CHAIM; WILLSTAETTER, RICHARD; ZUCROW, MAURICE JOSEPH

Matityahu Minc: MARSHAK, SAMUEL YAKOVLEVICH

Sergio Itzhak Minerbi*, Ph.D.; Former Ambassador to Belgium, Luxembourg and the E.E.C.; Visiting Professor at the University of Haifa: DONATI, ANGELO; EUROPEAN COMMUNITY, THE; HOLOCAUST: THE WORLD; ITALY; ROME; VATICAN

Charles B. Mintzer, Writer, New York: RAISA, ROSA

Victor A. Mirelman*, Ph.D.; Rabbi; Professor of Jewish History, River Forest, Illinois: BENARDETE, MAIR JOSÉ; BRIE, LUIS HARTWIG; BUENOS AIRES; DIEZ MACHO, ALEJANDRO; JOSEPH, HENRY; KAPLAN, ISAAC; LATIN AMERICA; LÉVY, ISIDORE; MIRELMAN; RAPOPORT, SOLOMON JUDAH LEIB; ROMAN, JACOB BEN ISAAC

Irwin Mirkin, B.A.; Communal Worker and Writer, Los Angeles: GOLDIN, HYMAN ELIAS

Dan Miron, Ph.D.; Associate Professor of Modern Hebrew Literature, Tel Aviv University: FEIERBERG, MORDECAI ZE'EV; SADAN, DOV

Aharon Mirsky, Ph.D.; Associate Professor of Hebrew Literature, the Hebrew University of Jerusalem: AL-ḤARIZI, JUDAH BEN SOLOMON

David Mirsky, M.A., Rabbi; Dean and Professor of English and Hebrew Literature, Yeshiva University, New York: HISTADRUT IVRIT OF AMERICA

Samuel Kalman Mirsky, Ph.D., Rabbi; Professor of Rabbinics, Yeshiva University, New York: ELIJAH BEN SOLOMON ZALMAN

Moshe Mishkinsky, Ph.D.; Senior Lecturer in the History of Jewish Labor Movements, the Hebrew University of Jerusalem; Senior Lecturer in Jewish History, Tel Aviv University: ABRAMOWITZ, EMIL; ABRAMOWITZ, GRIGORI; AGUDAT HA-SOẒYALISTIM HA-IVRIM; AMSTERDAM, ABRAHAM MEIR; ARONSON, GRIGORI; BROSS, JACOB; BUND; COMMUNISM; DASHEWSKI, PINḤAS; DOBIN, SHIMON; EINAEUGLER, KAROL; EISENSTADT, ISAIAH; ESTHER; FRUMKIN, BORIS MARKOVICH; GHELERTER, LUDWIG LITMAN; GORDON, ABRAHAM; GOZHANSKY, SAMUEL; GROSSER, BRONISLAW; GUREVICH, MOSHE; HA-EMET; HERSCH, PESACH LIEBMAN; INDEPENDENT JEWISH WORKERS PARTY; JEWISH SOCIAL DEMOCRATIC PARTY; JEWISH SOCIALIST WORKERS' PARTY; KAHAN, BARUCH MORDECAI; KOPELSON, ẒEMAḤ; KREMER, ARKADI; KURSKY, FRANZ; LEKERT, HIRSCH; LESTSCHINSKY, JOSEPH; LIBER, MARC; LIEBERMANN, AARON SAMUEL; LITWAK, A.; LUMINA; LVOVICH, DAVID; MEDEM, VLADIMIR; MIKHALEVICH, BEINISH; MILL, JOSEPH SOLOMON; MUTNIK, ABRAHAM; PAT, JACOB; PESAḤSON, ISAAC MORDECAI; PORTNOY, JEKUTHIEL; RAFES, MOSES; RATNER, MARC BORISOVICH; ROSENTHAL, PAVEL; SHULMAN, VICTOR; TSHEMERISKI, ALEXANDER; UNITED JEWISH SOCIALIST WORKERS' PARTY; VOZROZHDENIYE; WECHSLER, MAX; WEINSTEIN, AARON; ZIONIST SOCIALIST WORKERS' PARTY; ZYGELBOJM, SAMUEL MORDECAI

Richard Mitten, Ph.D.; Historian, Freelance Writer, Vienna: WALDHEIM AFFAIR

Beverly Mizrachi, M.A.; Sociologist, Jerusalem: BEN-DAVID, JOSEPH; BROOKNER, ANITA

Rachel Mizrahi*, Ph.D.; Professor, Universidade de São Paulo, Brazil: SAFRA

Zalmen Mlotek*, M.F.A.; Artistic Director, National Yiddish Theater-Folksbiene, New York: YIDDISH THEATER FOLKSBIENE

Baruch Modan, M.D.; Tel Ha-Shomer, Israel: SICKNESS

H.D. Modlinger: SCHMELKES, ISAAC JUDAH

Arnaldo Dante Momigliano, D.Litt., F.B.A.; Professor of History, University College, London: CLASSICAL SCHOLARSHIP, JEWS IN; HELLENISM

Sidney Monas, Ph.D.; Professor of History and of Slavic Languages, the University of Texas, Austin: SHESTOV, LEV

Shelomo Morag, Ph.D.; Professor of Hebrew Linguistics, the Hebrew University of Jerusalem: PRONUNCIATIONS OF HEBREW

William L. Moran, Ph.D.; Professor of Assyriology, Harvard University, Cambridge, Massachusetts: EL-AMARNA; PHOENICIA, PHOENICIANS

Shmuel Moreh, Ph.D.; Lecturer in Modern Arabic Language and Literature, the Hebrew University of Jerusalem: ALCEH, MATILDE; BAṢRI, MEER; DARWĪSH, SHALOM; IBRAHIM IBN SAHL AL-ANDALUSĪ AL-ISRA'ILI; ISRAEL, STATE OF: ARAB POPULATION; MARḤAB AL-YAHŪDĪ IBN AL-ḤĀRITH; MĪKHĀ'ĪL, MURAD; NOM, IBRAHIM; OBADYA, ABRAHAM; ORIENTAL LITERATURE; PRESS; SAMUEL IBN 'ĀDIYĀ; SHAMOSH, YIẒḤAK; SHASHU, SALIM

Simha Moretzky, Journalist, Bat Yam, Israel: BAT YAM

Michael L. Morgan*, Ph.D.; Chancellor's Professor Philosophy and Jewish Studies, Indiana University, Bloomington, Indiana: FACKENHEIM, EMIL

Susan (Weissglass) Morgan*, B.A.; Public Relations Consultant, Jewish Community Federation of Richmond, Richmond, Virginia: RICHMOND; VIRGINIA

Aryeh Morgenstern, B.A.; Teacher, Netanyah

Goldie Morgentaler*, Ph.D.; Associate Professor of English, University of Lethbridge, Alberta, Canada: ROSENFARB, CHAVA; SHAYEVITSH, SIMKHA-BUNIM

Yehuda Moriel, Ph.D.; Lecturer in Talmud, Bar-Ilan University, Ramat Gan: EDUCATION, JEWISH

Bonnie J. Morris*, Ph.D.; Professor of Women's Studies, George Washington University, Washington, D.C.: ḤASIDISM

Richard B. Morris, Ph.D.; Professor of History, Columbia University, New York: LEVY, LEONARD WILLIAMS

Larry Moses*, B.A., M.A.; M.S.W.; The Wexner Foundation, Ohio: WEXNER, LESLIE H.

Rafael Moses, M.D.; Senior Lecturer in Social Work, the Hebrew University of Jerusalem: HARTMANN, HEINZ; LOEWENSTEIN, RUDOLPH MAURICE

Wolf Moskovitz: KRIMCHAK LANGUAGE

Robert Moskowitz*: PASSAIC-CLIFTON

Andrea Most*, M.A., Ph.D.; Assistant Professor of American Literature, University of Toronto, Canada: SPEWACK, BELLA

Gloria Mound, Researcher, Ibiza: IBIZA and FORMENTERA

Andrew Muchin*, B.A; Freelance Writer and Director of the Wisconsin Small Jewish Communities History Project, Wisconsin Society for Jewish Learning, Milwaukee, Wisconsin: WISCONSIN

Arno Muenster*, Dr.Phil.; Professor of Modern and Contemporary Philosophy, Université de Picardie-Jules Verne, Amiens, France: BLOCH, ERNST

James Muilenburg, Ph.D.; Emeritus Professor of Old Testament, San Francisco Theological Seminary, San Anselmo, California: BUDDE, KARL FERDINAND REINHARD; BUHL, FRANZ PEDER WILLIAM MEYER

Stefan Müller-Doohm*, Dr.Phil.; Professor, University of Oldenburg, Germany: ADORNO, THEODOR W.

Aviva Muller-Lancet, L.es L.; Curator of Jewish Ethnography, the Israel Museum, Jerusalem: BUKHARA

Robert A. Mullins*, Ph.D.; Assistant Professor of Hebrew Bible and Ancient Near Eastern History, Azusa Pacific University, Azusa, California: BETH-SHAN

Lewis Mumford, Professor of Humanities, Stanford University, California; Professor of City and Regional Planning, the University of Pennsylvania, Philadelphia: ROSENFELD, PAUL

Suessmann Muntner, M.D., Visiting Professor of the History of Medicine, the Hebrew University of Jerusalem: ABT, ISAAC ARTHUR; ASAPH HA-ROFE; AVERROES; BAGINSKY, ADOLF ARON; BAMBERGER, HEINRICH VON; BLOCH, IWAN; BUCKY, GUSTAV; COHNHEIM, JULIUS; CYON, ELIE DE; DAMESHEK, WILLIAM; DE LEE, JOSEPH B.; DONNOLO, SHABBETAI; EDINGER, LUDWIG; ERLANGER, JOSEPH; FINKELSTEIN, HEINRICH; FRIEDEMANN, ULRICH; FRIGEIS, LAZARO DE; FROEHLICH, ALFRED; GOLDBERGER, JOSEPH; HAJEK, MARKUS; HERZ, MARCUS; HIRSCH, AUGUST; HIRSCH, RACHEL; JACOB HA-KATAN; JADASSOHN, JOSEF; KAPOSI, MORITZ; KATZENELSON, JUDAH LEIB BENJAMIN; KISCH, BRUNO ZECHARIAS; KOLLER, CARL; KOPLIK, HENRY; KRISTELLER, SAMUEL; KRONECKER, HUGO; LASSAR, OSCAR; LEVINSON, ABRAHAM; LOEB, LEO; MACHT, DAVID I.; MAIMONIDES; MEDICINE; MEYERHOF, MAX; MUNK, HERMANN; PAGEL, JULIUS LEOPOLD; PLAUT, HUGO CARL; POLITZER, ADAM; PREUSS, JULIUS; REMAK; ROMBERG, MORITZ HEINRICH; RUFUS OF SAMARIA; SACHS, BERNARD; SCHICK, BELA; SENATOR, HERMANN; STARKENSTEIN, EMIL; STEINACH, EUGEN; STERN, LINA SOLOMONOVNA; STILLING, BENEDICT; TRAUBE, LUDWIG; UNNA, PAUL GERSON; VALENTIN, GABRIEL GUSTAV; WECHSLER, ISRAEL; ZONDEK

Museum of San Juan Staff*, San Juan, Puerto Rico: PUERTO RICO

Alan E. Musgrave, Ph.D.; Professor of Philosophy, the University of Otago, Dunedin, New Zealand: POPPER, SIR KARL

David N. Myers*, Ph.D.; Professor, University of California, Los Angeles: ELLENSON, DAVID HARRY

Jacob M. Myers, Ph.D.; Professor of Old Testament, the Lutheran Theological Seminary, Gettysburg, Pennsylvania: NEHEMIAH

Jody Myers*, Ph.D.; Professor, Religious Studies, California State University, Northridge: BERG, PHILIP; HAGGADAH, PASSOVER; NEW MOON

Shlomo Na'aman, Ph.D.; Associate Professor of Social History, Tel Aviv University: LASSALLE, FERDINAND

Israel T. Naamani, Ph.D.; Professor of Political Science, the University of Louisville, Kentucky

Jose Luis Nachenson, Ph.D.; Director of Research and Publications, Institute for Cultural Relations Israel-Latin America, Spain, and Portugal, Jerusalem: GRINSPUN, BERNARDO; ISAACSON, JOSÉ; PORTUGAL

Ada Nachmani: IḤUD HABONIM

Amikam Nachmani*, Ph.D.; Professor of International Relations, the Hebrew University of Jerusalem: TURKEY

Jacob Nacht, Dr.Phil.; Scholar, Tel Aviv: ISRU ḤAG

Amos Nadan*, Ph.D., Senior Researcher, The Moshe Dayan Center for Middle Eastern and African Studies, Tel Aviv University: GAZA STRIP

Mordekhai Nadav, Ph.D.; Head of the Department of Manuscripts and Archives, the Jewish National and University Library; Lecturer in Jewish History, the University of the Negev, Beersheba: PINSK; PUKHOVITSER, JUDAH LEIB; TROKI

Pamela S. Nadell*, Ph.D.; Professor of History and Jewish Studies, American University, Washington, D.C.: ASKOWITH, DORA; JONAS, REGINA; NATIONAL FEDERATION OF TEMPLE SISTERHOODS; SCHECHTER, MATHILDE ROTH; SEMIKHAH; WOMAN; WOMEN'S LEAGUE FOR CONSERVATIVE JUDAISM

Ludwig Nadelmann, M.A., Rabbi; Lecturer in the Reconstructionist Rabbinical College, Philadelphia

Judah Nadich, D.H.L., Rabbi; New York: EISENHOWER, DWIGHT DAVID

Micah H. Naftalin*, B.A., J.D.; National Director (CEO), Union of Councils for Jews in the Former Soviet Union, Washington, D.C.: UCSJ

Gerard Nahon, Ph.D.; Charge de Recherches au Centre National de la Recherche Scientifique, Paris: REINACH

Iehiel Nahshon, B.A.; Ministry of Education, Hod ha-Sharon, Israel: SAPHIR, JACOB

Noemi Hervits de Najenson, Ph.D.; Pedagogical Center, No'ar Vehalutz, Jerusalem: GRINSPUN, BERNARDO; ISAACSON, JOSÉ; PORTUGAL

Reuven Nall, LL.B.; Ministry for Foreign Affairs, Jerusalem: PORTUGAL

Uri Naor, Dr.Phil.; Ministry for Foreign Affairs, Jerusalem: SELBSTWEHR

Yaakov Naparstek*, M.D.; Professor and Chairman of Medicine, Hadassah-Hebrew University Medical Center, Jerusalem: MEDICINE

Daniel C. Napolitano*, M.A.; Director, Division of Education, United States Holocaust Memorial Museum, Washington, D.C.: HOLOCAUST

Albert Nar: GREEK LITERATURE, MODERN

Shulamit Nardi, M.A.; Assistant to the President of Israel, Jerusalem: ENGLISH LITERATURE; KOPS, BERNARD; PRESIDENT OF ISRAEL; RAPHAEL, FREDERIC

Bezalel Narkiss, Ph.D.; Senior Lecturer in the History of Art, the Hebrew University of Jerusalem: ARK; BIBLE; DAVID; GOLDSMITHS AND SILVERSMITHS; HAGGADAH, PASSOVER; ILLUMINATED MANUSCRIPTS, HEBREW; ITALIA, SHALOM; JOEL BEN SIMEON; JOSEPH HA-ẒAREFATI; SHIVVITI; TEMPLE

Morton Narrowe, M.H.L., Rabbi; Chief Rabbi of Sweden, Stockholm

Abraham Nasatir, Ph.D.; Professor of History, San Diego State College, California

Yaacov Nash, B.A.; Ministry of Police, Tel Aviv: CRIME

Susan Nashman Fraiman*, M.A.; Lecturer in Art History, Emunah Teacher's College, Jerusalem: SABBATH

Ellis Nassour, M.A.; New York: SELZNICK

John Alfred Nathan, B.A., LL.B.; Tel Aviv: BENSAUDE

Pnina Nave, Ph.D.; Visiting Professor of Jewish Studies, Heidelberg University: BENDEMANN, EDUARD JULIUS FRIEDRICH; BERGNER, ELISABETH

Joseph Naveh, Ph.D.; Research Fellow in West-Semitic Epigraphy, the Hebrew University of Jerusalem; Jerusalem District Archaeologist, Department of Antiquities, Jerusalem: ALEF; ALPHABET, HEBREW; 'AYIN; BET; DALET; GIMMEL; HE; ḤET; KAF; KOF; LACHISH OSTRACA; LAMED; MEM; NUN; PE; RESH; SADE; SAMEKH; SHIN; TAV; TET; VAV; YAVNEH-YAM, LEGAL DOCUMENT FROM; YOD; ZAYIN

Yitzhak Navon, Ministry for Foreign Affairs, Jerusalem: CEYLON

Shmoyl Naydorf*: BORAISHA, MENAHEM

Joseph Nedava, Ph.D.; Associate Professor of Political Science, University of Haifa: BEN-HORIN, ELIAHU; BERIT HA-BIRYONIM; TEHOMI, AVRAHAM; VON WEISL, ZE'EV

Joshua Leib Ne'eman, Lecturer in Bible Cantillation, the Rubin Academy of Music, Jerusalem: BEER, AARON; BIRNBAUM, ABRAHAM BAER; BLINDMAN, YERUḤAM; BLUMENTHAL, NISSAN; DEUTSCH, MORITZ; FRIEDMANN, MORITZ; GEROVICH, ELIEZER MORDECAI BEN ISAAC; GLANZ, LEIB; GOLDSTEIN, JOSEF; HENLE, MORITZ; HERSCHMAN,

MORDECHAI; JAPHET, ISRAEL MEYER; JASSINOWSKY, PINCHAS; KARNIOL, ALTER YEHIEL; KIRSCHNER, EMANUEL; KOHN, MAIER; KOUSSEVITZKY, MOSHE; KWARTIN, ZAVEL; MINKOWSKI, PINCHAS; MOROGOWSKI, JACOB SAMUEL; NOWAKOWSKI, DAVID; SPIVAK, NISSAN

Yuval Ne'eman*, Ph.D.; Founder and Director of the School of Physics and Astronomy at Tel Aviv University; President of Tel Aviv University and director of its Sackler Institute of Advanced Studies; Director of the Center for Particle Theory at the University of Texas, Austin; Founder and Chairman of the Israeli Space Agency; Scientific Director of the Soreq facility, Israel: PHYSICS

Sharon Ne'emani, Magen David Adom, Tel Aviv

Avraham Negev, Ph.D.; Senior Lecturer in Classical Archaeology, the Hebrew University of Jerusalem: AVEDAT

Joseph Nehama, Historian, Salonika: ATHENS; CARASSO, EMMANUEL; SALEM, EMMANUEL RAPHAEL

Andre Neher, Dr. Phil., M.D., Rabbi; Professor of Jewish History and Philosophy, the University of Strasbourg and Tel Aviv University: AMADO LÉVY-VALENSI, ELIANE; ETHICS

Renee Neher-Bernheim, Ph.D.; Research Fellow in Jewish History, University of Strasbourg and Tel Aviv University: GORDIN, JACOB; LOUIS

David Neiman, Ph.D., Rabbi; Associate Professor of Theology, Dean of the Academy for Higher Jewish Learning, Boston: CANAAN, CURSE OF

Joseph Neipris, D.S.W.; Senior Teacher in Social Work, the Hebrew University of Jerusalem: ADLER-RUDEL, SALOMON; CASPARY, EUGEN; COHEN, WILBUR JOSEPH; FRIEDLANDER, WALTER; FUERTH, HENRIETTE; GINSBERG, MITCHELL I.; INTERNATIONAL CONFERENCE OF JEWISH COMMUNAL SERVICE; LEVY, SAM SAADI; PERLMAN, HELEN HARRIS; SCHOTTLAND, CHARLES IRWIN; STEIN, HERMAN D.

Mordkhai Neishtat, Journalist, Tel Aviv: BAAZOV, HERZL; BABALIKASHVILLI, NISSAN; GEORGIA; MAMISTABOLOB, ABRAHAM; MOUNTAIN JEWS; QUNAYṬIRA, AL-

Leon Nemoy, Ph.D.; Scholar in Residence, Dropsie University, Philadelphia: AARON BEN ELIJAH; AARON BEN JUDAH KUSDINI; ANAN BEN DAVID; ASZÓD; BAṢĪR, JOSEPH BEN ABRAHAM HA-KOHEN HARO'EH AL-; CHWOLSON, DANIEL; DAVID BEN HUSSEIN, ABU SULEIMAN; DAVID BEN SOLOMON; ḤASAN BEN MASHI'AḤ; IBN AL-HĪTĪ, DAVID BEN SE'ADEL; ISAIAH BEN UZZIAH HA-KOHEN; ISRAEL HA-DAYYAN HA-MA'ARAVI; JACOB BEN SIMEON; JAPHETH AL-BARQAMANI; JESHUA BEN JUDAH; KARAITES; KIRKISĀNĪ, JACOB AL-; MALIK AL-RAMLĪ; MALINOWSKI, JOSEPH BEN MORDECAI; MENAHEM BEN MICHAEL BEN JOSEPH; MORDECAI BEN NISAN; MOSES BEN SAMUEL OF DAMASCUS; NAH'ĀWENDĪ, BENJAMIN BEN MOSES AL-; PINSKER, SIMḤAH; POSNANSKI; SAHL BEN MAẒLI'AḤ HA-KOHEN ABU AL-SURRĪ; SAHL IBN FAḌL; SALMON BEN JEROHAM; SAMUEL BEN DAVID; SAMUEL BEN MOSES AL-MAGHRIBĪ; SAUL BEN ANAN; TAWRIZI, JUDAH MEIR BEN ABRAHAM

Moshe Nes El*, Ph.D.; Researcher, Freelancer, Amilat, Jerusalem: BERDICHEVSKY SCHER, JOSE; BERMAN BERMAN, NATALIO; CHAMUDES REITICH, MARCOS; CHILE; COHEN GELLERSTEIN, BENJAMIN; COLOMBIA; COSTA RICA; FAIVOVICH HITZCOVICH, ANGEL; HONDURAS; LIBEDINSKY TSCHORNE, MARCOS; SCHAULSON BRODSKY, JORGE; SCHAULSON NUMHAUSER, JACOBO; TEITELBOIM VOLOSKY, VOLODIA

Sara Neshamith, M.A.; Kibbutz Loḥamei ha-Getta'ot: BRZEZINY; POLAND

Amnon Netzer*, Ph.D.; Professor Emeritus of Iranian Studies, the Hebrew University of Jerusalem: ABADAN; ABBAS I; ABBAS II; AHWAZ; AMINA; BABAI BEN FARHAD; BABAI BEN LUTF; BUSHIRE; EMRĀNI; GILĀN; HAMADAN; IRAN; ISFAHAN; JUDAH BEN ELEAZAR; KASHAN; KAZVIN; KERMAN; KHOMEINI; KHURASAN; KURDISTAN; LAR; MĀZANDARĀN; MESHED; MIZRAHI, HANINAH; NĀDER SHAH; NAHĀVAND; PAHLAVI, MOHAMMAD REZA SHAH; PAHLAVI, REZA SHAH; RASHID AL-DIN; RIZAIEH; SA'D AL-DAWLA AL-ṢAFĪ IBN HIBBATALLAH; SHAHIN; SHIRAZ; SHUSHTAR; TABRIZ; TEHERAN; YEZD

Gideon Netzer*, Ph.D.; International Expert in Counter Terrorism and Conflict Crisis Management, National Defense of the I.D.S. College, Israel: ISRAEL, STATE OF: DEFENSE FORCES

Nissan Netzer, M.A.; Former Scientific Secretary, the Academy of the Hebrew Language, Jerusalem: GIKATILLA, ISAAC IBN; MOSES BEN HA-NESI'AH

Shlomo Netzer*, Ph.D.; Modern East European Jewish History, Tel Aviv University: BEDZIN; BIELSK PODLASKI; BRZESC KUJAWSKI; BRZEZINY; HARTGLAS, MAXIMILIAN MEIR APOLINARY; JEWISH HISTORICAL INSTITUTE, WARSAW; LESKOW

Michael J. (John) Neufeld*, B.A., M.A., Ph.D.; Museum Curator, National Air and Space Museum, Smithsonian Institution, Washington, D.C.: AUSCHWITZ, BOMBING CONTROVERSY

Siegbert Neufeld, Ph.D., Rabbi; Ramat Ḥen, Israel: LEWIN, ADOLF; TYKOCINSKI, ḤAYYIM

Jacob Neusner*, Ph.D.; Research Professor of Theology, Bard College, Annandale-on-Hudson, New York: BABYLONIA; BOKSER, BARUCH M.; COHEN, NATHAN EDWARD; KLEIN, PHILIP; LOTAN, GIORA; SELF-HATRED, JEWISH; ZAMARIS; ZURI, JACOB SAMUEL

Gidi (Gideon) Nevo*, Ph.D.; Assistant Professor, The Ben-Gurion Research Institute, Ben-Gurion University of the Negev, Beersheba: MIRON, DAN

Joseph Nevo*, Ph.D.; Professor of Middle East History, University of Haifa: ABDULLAH IBN HUSSEIN; AKABA; HUSSEIN; HUSSEINI, HĀJJ AMIN AL-; JORDAN, HASHEMITE KINGDOM OF; TRANSJORDAN

Dika Newlin, Ph.D.; Professor of Music, North Texas State University, Denton: BLOCH, ERNEST; MAHLER, GUSTAV; MENDELSSOHN, FELIX; MEYERBEER, GIACOMO

Aryeh Newman, M.A.; Lecturer in English, the Hebrew University of Jerusalem: DESECRATION; INDEPENDENCE DAY, ISRAEL; SACRILEGE; YOM HA-ZIKKARON

David Newman, Ph.D.; Senior Lecturer, Department of Geography and Environmental Development, Chairman, Urban Studies Program, Ben-Gurion University of the Negev, Beersheba: GUSH EMUNIM; ISRAEL, STATE OF: ALIYAH; PEACE MOVEMENTS, RELIGIOUS.

Isaac Newman, B.A., Rabbi; London: ESTHER, FAST OF

Sara (Joanne) Newman*, Ph.D.; Associate Professor of English, Kent State University, Ohio: BRONER, ESTHER M.

Hugh Nibley, Ph.D.; Professor of History and Religion, Brigham Young University, Provo, Utah: JERUSALEM

Eliezer Niborski*, M.A.; Editing Collaborator of the *Index to Yiddish Periodicals*, the Hebrew University of Jerusalem: DLUZHNOWSKY, MOSHE; ESSELIN, ALTER; SIEMIATYCKI, CHAIM

Miriam Nick, B.A.; Curator of the Museum of Ethnography and Folklore, Haaretz Museum, Tel Aviv: DRESS

Maren (Ruth) Niehoff*, Dr.; Senior Lecturer, the Hebrew University of Jerusalem: PHILO JUDAEUS

Eduard Nielson, Dr.Theol.; Professor of Theology, Copenhagen University, Denmark: PEDERSEN, JOHANNES

Shemuel Niger (Charney), Writer and Critic, New York: ASCH, SHOLEM; BORAISHA, MENAHEM

Annegret Nippa*, Dr., PD; University Lecturer; Institut für Ethnologie, Universität Leipzig; Leipzig, Germany: DRESDEN

Yeshayahu Nir, Ph.D.; Professor, Institute of Communications, the Hebrew University of Jerusalem: BAR-AM, MICHA; GIDAL, TIM; PHOTOGRAPHY

Nurit Nirel, M.A.; Ministry of Labor, Jerusalem: ISRAEL, STATE OF: LABOR

Mordechai Nisan, Ph.D.; Academic Director, Preparatory Program, Rothberg School for Overseas Students, the Hebrew University of Jerusalem: GULF WAR

David Niv, M.A.; Editor and Historian, Jerusalem: AUSUBEL, NATHAN; BEN-YOSEF, SHELOMO; BETAR; FRIZZI, BENEDETTO; HELPERN, MICHAEL; IRGUN ẒEVA'I LE'UMMI; KATZENELSON, YOSEF; LOḤAMEI ḤERUT ISRAEL; RAZIEL, DAVID; STERN, AVRAHAM

Izhak Noam, Eilat, Israel: ELATH

Mona Nobil, B.A.; Netanyah

Eric Nooter, Ph.D.; AJDC Historian, New York

Anita Norich*, Ph.D.; Associate Professor, University of Michigan: GLANZ-LEYELES, AARON; GREENBERG, ELIEZER; IN-ZIKH; MUKDONI, A.; SINGER, ISRAEL JOSHUA

Abraham Novershtern: YIDDISH LITERATURE

Anita Novinsky, Ph.D.; Lecturer in History, São Paulo University, Brazil

Dov Noy, Ph.D.; Senior Lecturer in Folklore and in Hebrew and Yiddish Literature, the Hebrew University of Jerusalem: ABBREVIATIONS; ABRACADABRA; ABSALOM; ADALBERG, SAMUEL; ADEN; AFGHANISTAN; AFIKOMAN; ALEF; ANGEL OF DEATH; ANIMAL TALES; APOSTASY; ASS; ELIJAH; EVIL EYE; FOLKLORE

Mendel Nun, Kibbutz Ein Gev

Perry E. Nussbaum, D.H.L., Rabbi; Jackson, Mississippi: MISSISSIPPI

David Obadia, Rabbi; Member of the Rabbinical Council of Jerusalem: ABENDANAN; ABI-ḤASIRA; ATTAR, JUDAH BEN JACOB IBN; BEN ZAQEN; BENAIM; BERDUGO; ELBAZ

John M. O'Brien, Ph.D.; Professor of Medieval History, Queens College of the City University of New York: MAXIMUS, MAGNUS CLEMENS

Aryeh Oded, Ph.D.; Department of Middle East and African Studies, Tel Aviv University

Bustanay Oded, Ph.D.; Lecturer in Jewish History, Haifa University: AHAB; AMMON, AMMONITES; ARPAD; BAALIS; BENJAMIN; CANAAN, LAND OF; CAPHTOR; CARCHEMISH; CHEDORLAOMER; CHEMOSH; CUSHAN-RISHATHAIM; CYPRUS; EGLON; EVIL-MERODACH; GEZER CALENDAR; GOLIATH; HEZEKIAH; ISH-BOSHETH; JEHU; JEROBOAM; JOAB; LABAN; MACHIR; MENAHEM; MERODACH-BALADAN; MESHA; MESHA STELE; MOAB; NEBUCHADNEZZAR; OMRI; PEKAH; PEKAHIAH; REHOBOAM; REUBEN; SAUL; SILOAM INSCRIPTION; SIMEON; TOB; TRIBES, THE TWELVE; UZZIAH; ZEDEKIAH

Toni Oelsner, M.A., M.Soc.Sc.; Historian, New York: CHEMNITZ; CONSTANCE; DEPPING, GEORGES-BERNARD; FREIBURG IM BREISGAU; FRIEDBERG; FULDA; KARLSRUHE; KASSEL; KOBLENZ; MEININGEN; MERSEBURG; RAVENSBURG; SLAVE TRADE; STENDAL; STOBBE, OTTO; STOECKER, ADOLF; STRAUBING; STUTTGART; WAGNER, RICHARD

Uriel Ofek, M.A.; Writer and Editor, Tel Aviv

Zvi Ofer, Ministry for Foreign Affairs, Kibbutz Yifat

A. (Adriaan) K. Offenberg*, Ph.D.; Retired Curator of the Bibliotheca Rosenthaliana, University of Amsterdam, The Netherlands: ATHIAS, JOSEPH and IMMANUEL; BENVENISTE, IMMANUEL; CASTRO TARTAS, DAVID DE; MANASSEH BEN ISRAEL; TEMPLO, JACOB JUDAH LEON

Yitzhak Ogen, Writer, Tel Aviv: KARNI, YEHUDA

Ronald E. Ohl, M.A.; Dean of Student Affairs, the Colorado College, Colorado Springs: ABELSON, HAROLD HERBERT; AUSUBEL, DAVID PAUL; GRUENBERG, SIDONIE MATSNER; JUSTMAN, JOSEPH; LIEBERMAN, MYRON

Levi A. Olan, B.A., Rabbi; Dallas, Texas: DALLAS

Evelyne Oliel-Grausz*, Ph.D.; Assistant Professor in Early Modern and Jewish History, Université Paris I Panthéon Sorbonne, Paris, France: NAHON, GERARD

Aryeh Leo Olitzki, Dr. Phil.; Emeritus Professor of Bacteriology, the Hebrew University-Hadassah Medical School, Jerusalem: BESREDKA, ALEXANDER; EHRLICH, PAUL; WASSERMANN, AUGUST VON

Colette Olive*: LÉVY, BENNY

David M. L. Olivestone, B.A.; Jerusalem: KORNITZER, LEON; PUTTERMAN, DAVID; RAVITZ, SHELOMO; RAZUMNI, EPHRAIM ZALMAN; RIVLIN, SHELOMO ZALMAN; ROSENBLATT, JOSEF; SCHORR, BARUCH; SHULSINGER, BEZALEL; SIROTA, GERSHON; WASSERZUG, ḤAYYIM; ZILBERTS, ZAVEL

A'hron Oppenheimer, M.A.; Lecturer in Jewish History and Talmud, Tel Aviv University: ELYASHAR, JACOB BEN ḤAYYIM JOSEPH; HOLY CONGREGATION IN JERUSALEM; KAMẒA and BAR KAMẒA; MEIR; SIKARIKON; TERUMOT AND MA'ASEROT

Deborah Oppenheimer*, D.F.A.; Writer and Producer of *Stories of the Kindertransport*: KINDERTRANSPORT

Vila Orbach, Yad Vashem, Jerusalem: RUSSIA

Nissan Oren, Ph.D.; Lecturer in International Relations, the Hebrew University of Jerusalem: BULGARIA

Shimon Oren, M.A.; Teacher in Education, the Hebrew University of Jerusalem: KRESSEL, GETZEL; LILIENBLUM, MOSES LEIB

Eugene V. Orenstein*, B.A., M.A., Ph.D.; Associate Professor, McGill University, Montreal, Canada: CANADIAN LITERATURE; KIPNIS, ITZIK; RIVKIN, BORUCH; ROLNICK, JOSEPH

Gustav Yaacob Ormann, Ph.D.; Editor, *Kirjath Sepher*, Jerusalem: ABNER

Haim Ormian, Ph.D.; Editor of the *Encyclopaedia of Education* (Hebrew), Jerusalem: LIPMANN, OTTO

Uzzi Ornan, Ph.D.; Senior Lecturer in Hebrew Language, the Hebrew University of Jerusalem: HEBREW GRAMMAR; HEBREW LANGUAGE

Efraim Orni, M.A.; Geographer, Jerusalem: ABU AWEIGILA; ACRE; ADAMIT; ADORAIM; ADULLAM REGION; AFIKIM; AFULAH; ALLONEI ABBA; ALLONEI YIZḤAK; ALLONIM; ALMAGOR; ALMAH; ALUMMOT; AMAẒYAH; AMIR; AMIRIM; AMMI'AD; AMMINADAV; APHEK; ARA; ARABA; ARARA; ARRĀBA; ARṬAS; ASHDOD; ASHDOT YA'AKOV; ASHKELON; ATAROT; ATHLIT; AVIGDOR; AVIḤAYIL; AYANOT; AYYELET HA-SHAḤAR; AZOR; BALFOURIYYAH; BĀQĀ AL-GHARBIYYA; BĀQĀ AL SHARQIYYA; BARKAI; BAT SHELOMO; BE'ER ORAH; BE'ER TOVIYYAH; BE'ER YA'AKOV; BE'ERI; BE'EROT YIZḤAK; BEERSHEBA; BEIT JANN; BEIT JIMĀL; BEN SHEMEN; BENEI DAROM; BENEI DEROR; BENEI ZION; BEROR ḤAYIL; BET ALFA; BET-ARABAH; BET-DAGON; BET ESHEL; BET GUVRIN; BET HA-EMEK; BET HA-LEVI; BET ḤERUT; BET HILLEL; BETHLEHEM; BET IKSA; BET LEḤEM; BET MEIR; BET NEḤEMYAH; BET OREN; BET OVED; BET-SHEAN; BET-SHEMESH; BET-SHITTAH; BET YANNAI; BET YEHOSHU'A; BET YERAḤ; BET YIZḤAK; BET YOSEF; BET ZAYIT; BET ZERA; BINYAMINAH; BIRANIT; BIRIYYAH; BITAN AHARON; BIẒẒARON; BOZRAH; CAESAREA; CARMEL, MOUNT; DABBŪRIYYA; DAFNAH; DĀLIYAT AL-KARMIL; DALIYYAH; DALTON; DAN; DEAD SEA; DEGANYAH; DEIR AL-BALAḤ; DIMONAH; DOBRATH; DOR; DOROT; EILON; EILOT; EIN GEV; EIN HA-EMEK; EIN HA-ḤORESH; EIN HA-MIFRAẒ; EIN HA-NAZIV; EIN HA-SHELOSHAH; EIN HA-SHOFET; EIN HOD; EIN IRON; EIN SHEMER; EIN VERED; EIN YAHAV; EIN ZEITIM; EIN ẒURIM; EL-ARISH; ELYASHIV; EN-DOR; EN-GEDI; EN-HAROD; ESHTAOL; EVEN YIZḤAK; EVRON; EYAL; FASSŪTA; FURAYDIS, AL-; GA'ATON; GALILEE; GALON; GAN ḤAYYIM; GAN SHELOMO; GAN SHEMU'EL; GAN SHOMRON; GAN YAVNEH; GANNEI YEHUDAH; GAT; GAZIT; GEDERAH; GELIL YAM; GESHER; GESHER HA-ZIV; GE'ULEI TEIMAN; GE'ULIM; GEVA; GEVARAM; GEVAT; GEVIM; GEVULOT; GIBBETHON; GINNEGAR; GINNOSAR; GIVAT ADA; GIVAT BRENNER; GIVAT HA-SHELOSHAH; GIVAT ḤAYYIM; GIVAT ḤEN; GIVATAYIM; GOFNAH; HA-BONIM; ḤAFEẒ ḤAYYIM; HA-GOSHERIM; ḤAMADYAH; HA-MA'PIL; HAMMAT GADER; ḤANITAH; HA-OGEN; HA-ON; HAREL; HA-SOLELIM; ḤAẒER, ḤAẒERIM; ḤAẒEVAH; ḤAẒOR ASHDOD; HA-ZORE'A; HA-ZORE'IM; HEBRON; ḤEFER PLAIN; ḤEFẒI BAH; ḤELEẒ; ḤEREV LE-ET; ḤERUT; HERZLIYYAH; ḤIBBAT ZION; HOD HA-SHARON; ḤOGLAH; ḤULATAH; ḤULDAH; ḤULEH VALLEY; ḤURFAYSH; ILANIYYAH; ISRAEL, STATE OF: ALIYAH; ISRAEL, STATE OF: HUMAN GEOGRAPHY; JABNEEL; JENIN; JERICHO; JERUSALEM; JOKNEAM; JOTAPATA; KABRI; KADOORIE; KAFR KAMĀ; KAFR QĀSIM; KARMI'EL; KARMIYYAH; KEFAR AZAR; KEFAR BARUKH; KEFAR BIALIK; KEFAR BILU; KEFAR BLUM; KEFAR EẒYON; KEFAR GIDEON; KEFAR GLICKSON; KEFAR HA-ḤORESH; KEFAR HA-MACCABI; KEFAR HA-NASI; KEFAR HA-RO'EH; KEFAR ḤASIDIM; KEFAR ḤAYYIM; KEFAR HESS; KEFAR ḤITTIM; KEFAR JAWITZ; KEFAR KISCH; KEFAR MALAL; KEFAR MASARYK; KEFAR MENAḤEM; KEFAR MORDEKHAI; KEFAR NETTER; KEFAR PINES; KEFAR ROSH HA-NIKRAH; KEFAR RUPPIN; KEFAR SAVA; KEFAR SHEMARYAHU; KEFAR SYRKIN; KEFAR SZOLD; KEFAR TAVOR; KEFAR TRUMAN; KEFAR URIYYAH; KEFAR VITKIN; KEFAR WARBURG; KEFAR YASIF; KEFAR YEḤEZKEL; KEFAR YEHOSHU'A; KEFAR YONAH; KINNERET (kib.); KINNERET (mosh.); KINNERET, LAKE; KIRYAT ANAVIM; KIRYAT ATA; KIRYAT BIALIK; KIRYAT EKRON; KIRYAT GAT; KIRYAT ḤAROSHET; KIRYAT MALAKHI; KIRYAT MOTZKIN; KIRYAT SHEMONAH; KIRYAT TIVON; KIRYAT YAM; KISSUFIM; LAHAVOT HA-BASHAN; LOḤAMEI HA-GETTA'OT; MA'AGAN MIKHA'EL; MA'ALEH HA-ḤAMISHAH; MA'ALOT-TARSHIHA; MA'ANIT; MA'AS; MA'BAROT; MAGHAR, AL-; MAḤANAYIM; MAJD AL-KURŪM; MANARAH; MA'OZ ḤAYYIM; MASSADAH; MASSU'OT YIZḤAK; MA'YAN BARUKH; MA'YAN ẒEVI; MAZKERET BATYAH; MAẒLI'AḤ; MAẒẒUVAH; MEI AMMI; ME'IR SHEFEYAH; MENAḤEMIYYAH; MERḤAVYAH; MERON; MESILLAT ZION; MESILLOT; METULLAH; MEVASSERET ZION; MIGDAL; MIGDAL HA-EMEK; MI'ILYA; MIKHMORET; MIKVEH ISRAEL; MISGAV AM; MISHMAR HA-EMEK; MISHMAR HA-NEGEV; MISHMAR HA-SHARON; MISHMAR HA-YARDEN; MISHMAROT; MIẒPAH; MIZRA; MODI'IN; MOLEDET; MOZA; NA'AN; NABLUS; NAḤAL OZ; NAHALAL or NAHALOL; NAḤALAT YEHUDAH; NAHARIYYAH; NEGBAH; NEGEV; NEḤALIM; NE'OT MORDEKHAI; NES ẒIYYONAH; NESHER; NETA'IM; NETIV HA-LAMED-HE; NETIVOT; NEVATIM; NEVEH EITAN; NEVEH YAM; NEẒER SERENI; NIR AM; NIRIM; NIẒẒANIM; OFAKIM; OR HA-NER; OR YEHUDAH; OROT; PARDES ḤANNAH-KARKUR; PARDESIYYAH; PORIYYAH; RA'ANANNAH; RAFA; RĀMA, AL-; RAMALLAH; RAMAT DAVID; RAMAT GAN; RAMAT HA-GOLAN; RAMAT HA-KOVESH; RAMAT HA-SHARON; RAMAT HA-SHOFET; RAMAT RAḤEL; RAMAT RAZIEL; RAMAT YISHAI; RAMAT YOḤANAN; RAMAT ẒEVI; RAMOT HA-SHAVIM; RAMOT MENASHEH; RAMOT NAFTALI; REGAVIM; REGBAH; REḤOVOT; REKHASIM; REVADIM; REVIVIM; RĪHĀNIYYA, AL-; RISHPON; ROSH PINNAH; RUḤAMAH; SA'AD; SAFED; SARID; SASA; SAVYON; SEDEH BOKER; SEDEH ELIYAHU; SEDEH NAḤUM; SEDEH NEḤEMYAH; SEDEH WARBURG; SEDEH YA'AKOV; SEDEROT; SHAALBIM; SHA'AR HA-AMAKIM; SHA'AR HA-GOLAN; SHA'AR ḤEFER-BEIT YIZḤAK; SHADMOT DEVORAH; SHAMIR; SHARM

EL-SHEIKH, TIRĀN ISLAND, and TIRĀN STRAITS; SHARONAH; SHAVEI ZION; SHE'AR YASHUV; SHEFAYIM; SHELUḤOT; SHIFTAN, ZE'EV; SHOMRAT; SHOVAL; TAANACH; TAL SHAḤAR; ṬAYYIBA, AL-; TEKOA; TEKUMAH; TEL ḤAI; TEL KAẒIR; TEL MOND; TEL YIẒḤAK; TEL YOSEF; THEBEZ; TIBERIAS; TIMNA; ṬĪRA, AL-; TIRAT ẒEVI; ṬŪL KARM; UDIM; URIM; USHA; YAARI, MENAḤEM; YAD ḤANNAH; YAGUR; YAKUM; YAMMIT REGION; YARDENAH; YARKONAH; YAVNEH; YAVNEH; YEDIDYAH; YESODOT; YESUD HA-MA'ALAH; YIZRE'EL; ẒOFIT; ẒORAH

Michal Oron*, Ph.D.; Deputy Head, Department of Literature, Tel Aviv University: ABULAFIA, ABRAHAM BEN SAMUEL

Asher Oser*, M.A., Rabbi; Congregation Brothers of Joseph, Norwich, Connecticut: RABBINICAL ALLIANCE OF AMERICA; RABBINICAL COUNCIL OF AMERICA; TORAH UMESORAH; UNION OF ORTHODOX JEWISH CONGREGATIONS OF AMERICA; UNION OF ORTHODOX RABBIS OF THE UNITED STATES AND CANADA

Robin Ostow, Ph.D.; Resident Fellow, Centre for Russian and East European Studies, University of Toronto

Jean Ouellette, Ph.D.; Assistant Professor of Semitic Languages, Sir George Williams University, Montreal: INCENSE AND PERFUMES; VAUX, ROLAND DE

Neil Ovadia, M.A.; Lecturer in History, City College of the City University of New York: HART, ISAAC; HART, JOEL; HART, MYER; HAYS; HAYS, ISAAC; LEVY, AARON; LEVY, CHAPMAN; LEVY, NATHAN; MOSES, MYER; SIMON, JOSEPH; ZUNTZ, ALEXANDER

Willard Gurdon Oxtoby, Ph.D.; Associate Professor of Religious Studies, Yale University, New Haven, Connecticut: BABYLONIA

Avraham Oz*

Hilde Pach*, M.A., Ph.D.; Researcher, University of Amsterdam, Department of Hebrew, Aramaic and Jewish Studies, Amsterdam, The Netherlands: LOGGEM, MANUEL VAN; MINCO, MARGA; PRESS

Mordechai Pachter*, Ph.D.; Professor of Jewish Thought, University of Haifa: AZIKRI, ELEAZAR BEN MOSES

Mark Padnos*, M.L.S., M.A.; Assistant Professor, Librarian, Bronx Community College and the City University, New York: BRODY, ALTER; ROSEN, NORMA; ROTH, HENRY

William Pages, Journalist, Newark, New Jersey

Dan Pagis, Ph.D.; Senior Lecturer in Hebrew Literature, the Hebrew University of Jerusalem: POETRY; SCHIRMANN, JEFIM; VOGEL, DAVID

Naomi Paiss*: NEW ISRAEL FUND, THE

Mordecai Paldiel*, Ph.D.; Director for Righteous Among the Nations, Yad Vashem, Jerusalem: BECCARI, ARRIGO; BENOÎT, PIERRE-MARIE; CALMEYER, HANS-GEORG; DOUWES, ARNOLD; FOLEY, FRANCIS; FRY, VARIAN; HAUTVAL, ADELAÏDE; HO FENG-SHAN; KARSKI, JAN; MENDES, ARISTIDES DE SOUSA; NÈVEJEAN, YVONNE; RIGHTEOUS AMONG THE NATIONS; SANDBERG, WILLEM JACOB; SENDLER, IRENA; STEFAN, METROPOLITAN; SUGIHARA CHIUNE-SEMPO; WESTERWEEL, JOHAN

Joanne Palmer* : HERTZBERG, ARTHUR; UNITED SYNAGOGUE OF CONSERVATIVE JUDAISM

Lisa Palmieri-Billig, M.A.; Writer and Journalist, ADL Representative in Italy, Rome: ITALY; MILAN

Eliezer Palmor, M.A.; Ministry for Foreign Affairs, Jerusalem: BULGARIA; HUNGARY; ROMANIA; ROSEN, MOSES; RUSSIA; YUGOSLAVIA

Channah Palti, Jerusalem

David H. Panitz, M.A., Rabbi; Dean of the Academy for Jewish Religion, New York: BARNERT, NATHAN

Esther Panitz, M.A.; Writer, Paterson, New Jersey: WOLF, SIMON

Michael Panitz*, Ph.D., Rabbi; Furman Professor of Judaic Studies, Virginia Wesleyan College, Norfolk, Virginia: COHEN, GERSON D.; CONSERVATIVE JUDAISM; JEWISH THEOLOGICAL SEMINARY; NORFOLK; SCHORSCH, ISMAR

Ruth Panofsky*, Ph.D.; Associate Director, Joint Graduate Programme in Communication and Culture, Ryerson University, Toronto, Canada: BENNETT, AVIE J.; WADDINGTON, MIRIAM; WEINZWEIG, HELEN; WISEMAN, ADELE

Sebastian Panwitz*, Dr.Phil.; Historian, Moses Mendelssohn Zentrum, Potsdam, Germany: GEIGER, LUDWIG

Herbert H. Paper, Ph.D.; Professor of Linguistics, Hebrew Union College-Jewish Institute of Religion, Cincinnati, Ohio: BLOCH, JULES; JUDEO-PERSIAN

Tudor Parfitt*, M.A., Dr.Phil.; School of Oriental and African Studies, University of London, England: BAYUDAYA; BENE EPHRAIM; BENE MENASHE; BENJAMIN, YEHOSHUA; BURMA; EZEKIEL, NISSIM; HOUSE OF ISRAEL COMMUNITY; IBO; JAPAN; KASHMIR; KODER, SHABDAI SAMUEL; MAKUYA; SINGAPORE; TUTSI; ZAKHOR

James W. Parkes, D.Phil; Historian, Blandford, Dorset, England: ALARIC II; HOLY PLACES; PROTESTANTS

Herbert Parzen, M.A., M.H.L., Rabbi; Historian, New York: DE HAAS, JACOB; ZIONIST ORGANIZATION OF AMERICA

Rachel Pasternak*, Ph.D., Senior Lecturer of Behavioral Studies, The College of Management Academic Studies, Tel Aviv: ISRAEL, STATE OF: EDUCATION

Melissa Patack*, J.D.,B.S.; Vice President, State Government Affairs, Motion Picture Association of America, Inc., Encino, California: GLICKMAN, DANIEL ROBERT

David Patterson, Ph.D.; Lecturer in Post-Biblical Hebrew, the University of Oxford; Visiting Professor of Hebrew Studies, Cornell University, Ithaca, New York: BRAUDES, REUBEN ASHER; GOTTLOBER, ABRAHAM BAER; MAPU, ABRAHAM; SMOLENSKIN, PEREZ

Arnold Paucker, M.A.; Director of the Leo Baeck Institute, London: BISCHOFF, ERICH

Benjamin Paul*: HOUSTON; ILLINOIS;

JEWISH WAR VETERANS OF THE U.S.A.; KANSAS; KANSAS CITY; LANCASTER

Shalom M. Paul, Ph.D., Rabbi; Senior Lecturer in Bible, the Hebrew University of Jerusalem and Tel Aviv University: BOOK OF LIFE; BOOK OF THE COVENANT; BOOK OF THE WARS OF THE LORD; CHEBAR; CHERUB; CREATION AND COSMOGONY; ECSTASY; EUPHEMISM AND DYSPHEMISM; PROPHETS AND PROPHECY; SERVANT OF THE LORD; VIRGIN, VIRGINITY

Wolfgang Paulsen, Ph.D.; Professor of German, the University of Massachusetts, Amherst: STERNHEIM, CARL

Moshe Pearlman, B.Sc.; Writer, Jerusalem: WAR OF INDEPENDENCE

Peggy K. Pearlstein*, Ph.D.; Area Specialist, Hebraic Section, Library of Congress, Washington, D.C.: FELDMAN, SANDRA; HARMAN, JANE

Birger A. Pearson, Ph.D.; Associate Professor of Religious Studies, Universities of California, Santa Barbara: NAG HAMMADI CODICES

Abraham J. Peck*, Ph.D., Director, Academic Council for Post Holocaust, Christian, Jewish, and Islamic Studies, University of Southern Maine: ARCHIVES; MAINE

Haviva Pedaya*: NAḤMANIDES

Mark (J.) Pelavin*, J.D.; Associate Director, Religious Action Center of Reform Judaism, Washington, D.C.: SAPERSTEIN, DAVID N.; SAPERSTEIN, HAROLD I.

Moshe Peled, B.A.; Colonel (Res.), Israel Defense Forces; Ministry of Transport, Jerusalem

Natan Peled, Minister of Absorption, Kibbutz Sarid

Kristine Peleg*, Ph.D.; English Lecturer, Century College, Minneapolis, Minnesota: CALOF, RACHEL BELLA KAHN

Gregor Pelger*, Ph.D.; Historian, Salomon Ludwig Steinheim-Institut für deutsch-jüdische Geschichte, Duisburg, Germany: GOLDENTHAL, JACOB; OPPERT, GUSTAV SALOMON; STEINSCHNEIDER, MORITZ; ZEDNER, JOSEPH; ZUNZ, LEOPOLD

Penina Peli, Journalist, Writer, Lecturer; Jerusalem: ADLERBLUM, NIMA

Pinchas Hacohen Peli, Ph.D.; Senior Lecturer in Jewish Philosophy, the University of the Negev, Beersheba; External Teacher in Jewish Studies, the Hebrew University of Jerusalem: ASCETICISM

Frank Pelleg, Pianist and Musicologist, Haifa: OFFENBACH, JACQUES

Rakhmiel Peltz*, Ph.D.; Professor of Sociolinguistics and Director of Judaic Studies, Drexel University, Philadelphia: SPIVAK, ELYE; VEINGER, MORDECAI

Shimon (H.) Pepper*, M.S.W., M.A.; Executive Director, Jewish Federation of Rockland County, Monsey, New York: ROCKLAND COUNTY

Josh Perelman*, Ph.D.; Historian, National Museum of American Jewish History; Post Doctoral Fellow, National Museum of American Jewish History/University of Pennsylvania: NATIONAL MUSEUM OF AMERICAN JEWISH HISTORY

Leon Perez, M.D.; Professor of Social Psychiatry, National University of the Litoral, Santa FM; Professor of Clinical Psychiatry, the University of Buenos Aires: DAIA

Hiram Peri, Dr. Phil.; Professor of Romance Languages, the Hebrew University of Jerusalem: ABRABANEL, JUDAH; ARIAS MONTANO, BENITO; BENDA, JULIEN

Mark Perlgut, M.S.; Journalist, New York: ARONSON, BORIS; KORDA, SIR ALEXANDER; THEATER

Isa Perlis-Kressel, M.A.; Holon, Israel: HERTZKA, THEODOR

Mark Perlman, Ph.D.; Professor of Economics, the University of Pittsburgh, Pennsylvania: GINZBERG, ELI; IDELSON, ABRAHAM; LEVANDA, LEV OSIPOVICH; PERLMAN, SELIG; RABINOVICH, OSIP ARONOVICH; SELEKMAN, BENJAMIN MORRIS; TSCHLENOW, JEHIEL

Shalom Perlman, Ph.D.; Professor of Greek History, Tel Aviv University: SCHWABE, MOSHE

Moshe Perlmann, Ph.D.; Professor of Arabic, the University of California, Los Angeles: APOSTASY; IBN KAMMŪNA, SA'D IBN MANṢŪR; ISLAM; ISRAELSOHN, JACOB IZRAILEVICH; KOKOVTSOV, PAUL KONSTANTINOVICH; SCHREINER, MARTIN; WEIL, GUSTAV

Maurice L. Perlzweig, Ph.D., Rabbi; Head of the International Affairs Department, World Jewish Congress, New York: ROBINSON, JACOB; ROBINSON, NEHEMIAH

Jean Perrot, Directeur de Recherche au Centre National de la Recherche Scientifique, Paris; Director of the Centre de Recherche Prehistorique Français, Jerusalem: AZOR

Jacob Petroff, Ph.D., Rabbi; Senior Lecturer in Classics, Bar-Ilan University, Ramat Gan: ACRO, PSEUDO-; APULEIUS, LUCIUS; ASINIUS POLLIO, GAIUS; CELSUS, AULUS CORNELIUS; CLAUDIAN; CLEMENT OF ALEXANDRIA; EUTROPIUS; EXCERPTA VALESIANA; EZRA, GREEK BOOK OF; FRONTO, MARCUS CORNELIUS; HISTORIA AUGUSTA; HOLOFERNES; JUDAS; JULIUS FLORUS; JUSTIN; LIVY; LUCAN; MACROBIUS, AMBROSIUS; OVID; PERSIUS; PETRONIUS ARBITER, GAIUS; POMPONIUS MELA; QUINTILIAN; ROMAN LITERATURE; RUTILIUS NAMATIANUS; SENECA THE ELDER; SENECA THE YOUNGER; SILIUS ITALICUS, TIBERIUS CATIUS ASCONIUS; SOLINUS, CAIUS JULIUS; SOLOMON, TESTAMENT OF; STATIUS, PUBLIUS PAPINIUS; SULPICIUS SEVERUS; TACITUS; TIBULLUS, ALBIUS; VALERIUS MAXIMUS; VARRO, MARCUS TERENTIUS

Jakob J. Petuchowski, Ph.D., Rabbi; Professor of Rabbinics and of Jewish Theology, the Hebrew Union College-Jewish Institute of Religion, Cincinnati, Ohio: NIETO, DAVID; ORGAN; STEINTHAL, HERMANN HEYMANN; WIENER, MAX

Claire (Ruth) Pfann*, M.A.; Academic Dean; Lecturer in New Testament, University of the Holy Land, Jerusalem: POPES; PROTESTANTS

Stephen (J.) Pfann*, Ph.D.; Professor of Second Temple Period History and Literature, University of the Holy Land, Jerusalem: LOTS; NAZARETH; QUMRAN; SUNDIAL

Anshel Pfeffer*, Journalist, Columnist, Editor and Author, Jerusalem Post, Jerusalem: BARUCH, ADAM; BEN-ZVI, SHLOMO

Israel Philipp, M.A.; Central Zionist Archives, Jerusalem: MACCABEANS, ORDER OF ANCIENT; ROTHSCHILD, JAMES ARMAND DE

Marc Philonenko, Th.D.; Professor of the History of Religions, the University of Strasbourg: JOSEPH AND ASENATH

Leo Picard, Dr.Phil., D.I.C., D.Sc.; Emeritus Professor of Geology, the Hebrew University of Jerusalem: ISRAEL, LAND OF: GEOGRAPHICAL SURVEY; LOEWINSON-LESSING, FRANZ YULYEVICH; ROSENBUSCH, KARL HARRY FERDINAND; SALOMON-CALVI, WILHELM; SUESS, EDUARD

Michele Piccirillo*, Father, Studium Biblicum Franciscanum, Jerusalem: FRANCISCANS

Walter Pinhas Pick, Editor, the *Encyclopaedia Hebraica*, Jerusalem: JERUSALEM; LATRUN

Jacob Picker, Dr.Jur.; Ministry of Finance, Jerusalem

Judah Pilch, Ph.D.; Jewish Teachers' Seminary and Peoples University, New York; Lecturer in Education, Dropsie University, Philadelphia: AMERICAN ASSOCIATION FOR JEWISH EDUCATION; BETH JACOB SCHOOLS; BLAUSTEIN, DAVID; CHARNA, SHALOM YONAH; CHIPKIN, ISRAEL; CHOMSKY, WILLIAM; EDUCATION, JEWISH; KAHNSHTAM, AHARON; KAZDAN, ḤAYYIM SOLOMON; MORRIS, NATHAN

Arieh Pilowsky, B.A.; External Teacher in Foreign Languages, Haifa University: RUBIN, HADASSAH

Shlomo Pines, Dr.Phil.; Professor of General and Jewish Philosophy, the Hebrew University of Jerusalem: AL-MUKAMMIṢ, IBN MARWĀN AL-RĀQI AL-SHIRAZI; AVERROES; AVICENNA; ENOCH, SLAVONIC BOOK OF; FREE WILL; GUTTMANN, JACOB; IBN GABIROL, SOLOMON BEN JUDAH; SOUL, IMMORTALITY OF; SPACE AND PLACE

Benjamin Pinkus, M.A.; Jerusalem: "COSMOPOLITANS"; LOZOVSKI, SOLOMON ABRAMOVICH

Ludwig Pinner, Dr.Phil., Kefar Shemaryahu, Israel: HAAVARA

Judith S. (Shira) Pinnolis*, M.M., M.S.; Reference Librarian, Information Desk Supervisor and Training Coordinator, Brandeis University Libraries, Waltham, Massachusetts: FRIEDMAN, DEBORAH LYNN; FUCHS, LILLIAN; GIDEON, MIRIAM; KREMER, ISA; LIEBLING, ESTELLE; MENDELSOHN HENSEL, FANNY CAECILIE; MLOTEK, CHANA; OSTFELD, BARBARA JEAN; RASKIN, JUDITH; REISENBERG, NADIA; ROSSI, MADAMA EUROPA De'; SCHAECHTER-GOTTESMAN, BELLA; SCHLAMME, MARTHA HAFTEL

Kurt Pinthus, Ph.D.; Writer, New York: HEYMANN, WALTHER

Mordechai Piron, M.A., Rabbi; Brigadier General, Israel Defense Forces; Chief Rabbi of the Israel Defense Forces, Bat Yam: GOREN, SHLOMO

Michael M. Pitkowsky*, M.A., Rabbi; Jewish Theological Seminary, New York

Maurice S. Pitt, M.A.; Educator and Journalist, Wellington, New Zealand: AUCKLAND; BARNETT, SIR LOUIS EDWARD; CHRISTCHURCH; DUNEDIN; HORT, ABRAHAM; LEVIN, NATHANIEL WILLIAM; MYERS, SIR MICHAEL; NATHAN, DAVID; NATHAN, JOSEPH EDWARD; POLACK, JOEL SAMUEL; SELIG, PHINEAS

W. Gunther Plaut, Dr.Jur. Rabbi; Historian, Toronto: FRANKEL, HIRAM D.

Martin Meir Plessner, Ph.D.; Emeritus Professor of Semitics and Islamic Studies, J.W. Goethe-Universität, Frankfurt on the Main; Emeritus Professor of Islamic Civilization, the Hebrew University of Jerusalem: BERGSTRAESSER, GOTTHELF; GALANTÉ, ABRAHAM; GOLDZIHER, IGNAZ; GRUENBAUM, MAX; ORIENTALISTS; ROSENTHAL, FRANZ; YAHUDA, ABRAHAM SHALOM

Milton Plesur, Ph.D.; Associate Professor of History, the State University of New York, Buffalo: BUFFALO; JACOBSON, EDWARD

Hans Pohl, Dr. Phil.; Professor of Constitutional, Social and Economic History, the University of Bonn: SUGAR INDUSTRY AND TRADE

Shmuel Pohoryles, Ph.D.; Professor, Director General, Rural Planning and Development Authority, Israel Ministry of Agriculture, Tel Aviv

Milos Pojar*, Ph.D.; Director, Education and Culture Centre of the Jewish Museum in Prague: GAL, FEDOR; BONDY, RUTH; BONN, HANUŠ; BOR, JOSEF; CZECHOSLOVAK LITERATURE; DAGAN, AVIGDOR; DEMETZ, PETER; DOSTÁL, ZENO; FIRT, JULIUS; FISCHER, OTOKAR; FRÝD, NORBERT; FUCHS, ALFRED; GALSKY, DESIDER; GELLNER, FRANTIŠEK; GOLDFLAM, ARNOST; GOLDSTUECKER, EDUARD; GOTTLIEB, FRANTIŠEK; GROSMAN, LADISLAV; HILSNER CASE; HOSTOVSKÝ, EGON; KLIMA, IVAN; KNIEŽA, EMIL; KRAUS, FRANTISEK R.; KRAUS, IVAN; KRAUS, OTA B.; KULKA, ERICH; LANGER, FRANTIŠEK; LANGER, JIŘÍ MORDECHAI; LAUB, GABRIEL; LEDA, EDUARD; LISTOPAD, FRANTIŠEK; LUSTIG, ARNOST; ORTEN, JIŘÍ; PAVEL, OTA; PICK, JIŘÍ ROBERT; POLÁČEK, KAREL; RAKOUS, VOJTĚCH; ROTTOVÁ, INNA; SIDON, KAROL EFRAIM; SINGER, LUDVIK; ŠPITZER, JURAJ; TIGRID, PAVEL; UHDE, MILAN; VOHRYZEK, JOSEF; WEIL, JIŘI; ZEYER, JULIUS

Arthur Polak, M.D.; Amsterdam: MEDALS

Abraham N. Poliak, Ph.D.; Professor of Islamic History and Research Professor of Khazar Studies, Tel Aviv University: ALROY, DAVID; ARMENIA; CRIMEA; HARKAVY, ALBERT; HESSEN, JULIUS ISIDOROVICH; IGNATYEV, COUNT NIKOLAI PAVLOVICH; UZBEKISTAN; VINAWER, MAXIM; VOZNITSYN, ALEXANDER ARTEMYEVICH; WIELICZKA; WISCHNITZER, MARK

Leon Poliakov, D.es L.; Maître de Recherches au Centre National de la Recherche Scientifique, Paris: ANTISEMITISM; ARGENS, JEAN BAPTISTE DE BOYER; ELDERS OF ZION, PROTOCOLS OF THE LEARNED; FRIES, JAKOB FRIEDRICH; GOBINEAU, JOSEPH ARTHUR, COMTE DE; GORDIN, JACOB; RACE, THEORY OF; ROUSSEAU, JEAN JACQUES; TREITSCHKE, HEINRICH VON; VOLTAIRE

Jean Poliatchek, M.A., Rabbi; Lecturer in French Literature, the Hebrew University of Jerusalem and Bar-Ilan University, Ramat Gan: FLEG, EDMOND

David Polish, Rabbi; Emeritus Rabbi of the Free Synagogue, Evanston, Illinois

Jonathan (Z.S.) Pollack*, Ph.D.; Instructor, History, Madison Area Technical College, Madison, Wisconsin: MADISON

Peter Pollack, Lecturer and Writer on photography, New York: IZIS; LAND, EDWIN H.; NEWMAN, ARNOLD; PHOTOGRAPHY; RAY, MAN; SEYMOUR, DAVID

Hans Jacob Polotsky, Dr.Phil.; Professor of Egyptian and Semitic Linguistics, the Hebrew University of Jerusalem: BAUER, HANS; BENFEY, THEODOR; HALÉVY, JOSEPH

Sidney I. Pomerantz, Ph.D.; Professor of History, City College of the City University of New York: MORRIS, RICHARD BRANDON

Sarah (Elizabeth) Ponichtera*, M.A.; University of S. Texas-Austin: CORALNIK, ABRAHAM; LEE, MALKE; ULIANOVER, MIRIAM

Marvin H. Pope, Ph.D.; Professor of Northwest Semitic Languages, Yale University, New Haven, Connecticut: ADAM; ANATH; BAAL WORSHIP; EVE

Richard H. Popkin, Ph.D.; Professor of Philosophy, the University of California, San Diego; Distinguished Professor of Philosophy, the Herbert H. Lehman College of the City University of New York: ADLER, FELIX; ADLER, MORTIMER JEROME; AIKEN, HENRY DAVID; ARENDT, HANNAH; BOAS, GEORGE; BRUNSWIG, ALFRED; CHERNISS, HAROLD FREDRIK; COHEN, CHAPMAN; COHEN, MORRIS RAPHAEL; COSTA, URIEL DA; DESSAUER, FRIEDRICH; DUBISLAV, WALTER ERNST OTTO; EDMAN, IRWIN; EDWARDS, PAUL; FARBER, MARVIN; FRANK, SEMYON LYUDVIGOVICH; FRAUENSTAEDT, JULIUS; FRIEDLAENDER, OSKAR EWALD; GOLDSTEIN, JULIUS; HALÉVY, ÉLIE; JANKÉLÉVITCH, VLADIMIR; JERUSALEM, KARL WILHELM; JERUSALEM, WILHELM; JONAS, HANS; KAUFMANN, FRITZ; KAUFMANN, WALTER; KOIGEN, DAVID; KOYRÉ, ALEXANDRE; KRISTELLER, PAUL OSKAR; LA BOÉTIE, ETIENNE DE; LA PEYRÈRE, ISAAC; LASSON, ADOLF; LÉON, XAVIER; LIEBMANN, OTTO; MARCK, SIEGFRIED; MARCUS, ERNST; MONDOLFO, RODOLFO; OROBIO DE CASTRO, ISAAC; PALÁGYI, MENYHÉRT; PHILOSOPHY; RAUH, FRÉDÉRIC; REINACH, ADOLF; RICHTER, RAOUL; SANCHES, FRANCISCO; SCHRECKER, PAUL; SCHUHL, PIERRE-MAXIME; SHEFFER, HENRY M.; SPIEGELBERG, HERBERT; SPITZER, HUGO; STEIN, EDITH; STEIN, LUDWIG; STERNBERG, KURT; WAHLE, RICHARD; WALZER, RICHARD RUDOLF; WEININGER, OTTO; WEISS, PAUL; WIENER, PHILIP PAUL

Dina Porat*, Ph.D.; Professor, Head of Stephen Roth Institute for the Study of Contemporary Racism and Anti-Semitism, Chaim Rosenberg School of Jewish Studies, Tel Aviv University: ANTISEMITISM; BLOOD LIBEL

Jonathan D. Porath*, B.A., M.A., M.H.L., Rabbi; Rabbi and Jewish Educator, American Jewish Joint Distribution Committee, Jerusalem: PORATH, ISRAEL

Yehoshua Porath, Ph.D.; Instructor in the History of the Muslim Peoples, the Hebrew University of Jerusalem: ISRAEL, STATE OF: HISTORICAL SURVEY

Bezalel Porten, Ph.D., Rabbi; Teaching Fellow in Jewish History, the Hebrew University of Jerusalem; Senior Lecturer in Biblical Studies, Haifa University: BELTESHAZZAR; BIZTHA; ELIASHIB; EXILE, BABYLONIAN; HAMAN; HISTORY: FROM THE DESTRUCTION TO ALEXANDER; MITHREDATH; MORDECAI; REGEM-MELECH; REHUM; SATRAP; SHADRACH, MESHACH, ABED-NEGO; SHAREZER; SHEALTIEL; TATTENAI; TEMPLE; ZERUBBABEL

Jack Nusan Porter*, Ph.D.; Director, The Spencer Institute for Social Research, Newton, Massachusetts; Newtonville, Mass.: HIRSCHFELD, MAGNUS; NEO-NAZISM; SCHAPPES, MORRIS U.; SONNENSCHEIN, ROSA

Edward Portnoy*, Ph.D.; Adjunct Instructor of History, Jewish Theological Seminary, New York: GILBERT, SHLOMO; MARINOFF, JACOB; NADIR, MOYSHE

Israel Porush, O.B.E., Ph.D., Rabbi; Emeritus Rabbi of the Great Synagogue of Sydney: ADELAIDE; AUSTRALIA; BOAS, ABRAHAM TOBIAS; BRISBANE; DANGLOW, JACOB; DAVIS, ALEXANDER BARNARD; MELBOURNE; MONTEFIORE, JOSEPH BARROW; PERTH; SAMUEL, SIR SAUL; SYDNEY

Akiva Posner, Dr. Phil., Rabbi; Scholar and Librarian, Jerusalem: ALTONA; DRESDEN; EGER, AKIVA BEN MOSES GUENS; EGER, SOLOMON BEN AKIVA; EPPENSTEIN, SIMON; GIESSEN

Marcia Posner, PH.D.; Library Consultant, Children's Literature, New York: CHILDREN'S LITERATURE

Raphael Posner, D.H.L., Rabbi; Assistant Professor of Rabbinics, the Jewish Theological Seminary of America, Jerusalem: ABLUTION; AHAVAH RABBAH, AHAVAT OLAM; AMULET; ANAV, ZEDEKIAH BEN ABRAHAM; ASHREI; CHARITY; HOLY PLACES; JEW; MARRIAGE; SYNAGOGUE

Bernard Postal, Author and Journalist, New York: IOWA; LICHT, FRANK; MANDEL, MARVIN; MASSACHUSETTS; MILITARY SERVICE; MONTANA; NEVADA; PHOENIX; PUBLIC RELATIONS; SHAPIRO, SAMUEL HARVEY

Edward I. J. Poznanski, M.Phil.; Visiting Senior Lecturer in Philosophy, the Hebrew University of Jerusalem: KOTARBIŃSKA, JANINA

Michael Pragai, B.A.; Ministry for Foreign Affairs, Jerusalem: BURMA

Joseph Prager, M.D.; Neurologist and Psychiatrist, Haifa: OPPENHEIM, HERMANN

Leonard Prager*, Ph.D.; Emeritus Professor of English and Yiddish, University of Haifa: ABTSHUK, AVRAHAM; ALFES, BENZION; BOVSHOVER, JOSEPH; BRODER SINGERS; DANIEL, M.; DER NISTER; FEYGENBERG, RAKHEL; FOX, CHAIM-LEIB; FRAM, DAVID; FURMAN, YISROEL; GEBIRTIG, MORDECHAI; GLATSTEIN, JACOB; GOLDENE KEYT, DI; GORDIN, ABBA; GORDIN, JACOB; KOENIG, LEO; KOTIK, YEKHESKL; LURIA, NOAH; MYER, MORRIS; OSHEROWITCH, MENDL; OYVED, MOYSHE; PINES, MEYER ISSER; PREGER, JACOB; RABON, ISRAEL; RASHKIN, LEYB; REZNIK, LIPE; SALKIND, JACOB MEIR; SELIKOVITCH, GEORGE; SHAKESPEARE, WILLIAM; SHATZKY,

JACOB; SHPIGLBLAT, ALEKSANDER; SIEMIATYCKI, CHAIM; SINGER, ISAAC BASHEVIS; SPIEGEL, ISAIAH; STENCL, ABRAHAM NAHUM; TENENBAUM, JOSHUA; TOLUSH; TOPLPUNKT: FERTLYOR-SHRIFT FAR LITERATUR, KUNST UN GEZELSCHAFTLEKHE FRAGES; WEINSTEIN, BERISH; YIDDISH LITERATURE; YUNGMAN, MOSHE; ZYCHLINSKA, RAJZEL

Naftali Prat*, Editor, *Shorter Jewish Encyclopedia in Russian*, Society of Research on Jewish Communities, Jerusalem: ABRAMOVICH, ROMAN ARKADYEVICH; AMUSIN, JOSEPH; BELOV, A.; BERDYANSK; BEREZOVSKY, BORIS ABRAMOVICH; GOMELSKY, ALEXANDER YAKOVLEVICH; GUSINSKY, VLADIMIR ALEXANDROVICH; LIBERALISM AND THE JEWS; NEVZLIN, LEONID BORISOVICH

Jeonathan Prato, Dr.Jur.; Ministry for Foreign Affairs, Jerusalem: RIBEIRO DOS SANTOS, ANTONIO; SPAIN

Leonid Preisman, Ph.D.; Scientific Editor of *The Shorter Jewish Encyclopaedia in Russian*, Jerusalem: MOSCOW

Riv-Ellen Prell*, Ph.D., Professor, University of Minnesota, Minneapolis, Minnesota: MYERHOFF, BARBARA GAY SIEGEL

Tovia Preschel, Rabbi; Professor of Talmud, the Jewish Theological Seminary of America, New York: ALSHEKH, MOSES; ALTSCHULER, DAVID; AMRAM BEN SHESHNA; DANIEL BEN AZARIAH; DANIEL BEN ELEAZAR BEN NETHANEL ḤIBBAT ALLAH; DANIEL BEN ḤASDAI; DAVID BEN DANIEL; DAVID BEN ZAKKAI; HYMAN, AARON; KAHANE, ISAAK; LIEBERMAN, SAUL; MARGALIOT, MORDECAI; MAT, MOSES; MEKLENBURG, JACOB ẒEVI; NAḤMANIDES; PATAI, RAPHAEL; PORTO, ABRAHAM MENAHEM BEN JACOB HA-KOHEN; RABBINOVICZ, RAPHAEL NATHAN NATA; RATNER, DOV BAER; RIVISTA ISRAELITICA; RIVKIND, ISAAC; ROSANES, SOLOMON ABRAHAM; ROSENTHAL, JUDAH; SLATKINE, MENAHEM MENDEL; SUPERCOMMENTARIES ON THE PENTATEUCH; TEMERLS, JACOB BEN ELIEZER; TRAVELERS AND EXPLORERS; ZOMBER, DOV BAER

Walter Preuss, Dr.Phil., D.Econ.; Economist, Tel Aviv: NAFTALI, PEREẒ

Jonathan (J.) Price*, Ph.D.; Professor of Classics and Ancient History, Tel Aviv University: ZEALOTS AND SICARII

Ronald (David) Price*, M.A., Rabbi; Dean of Traditional Judaism; Executive Vice President, Union for Traditional Judaism, Teaneck, New Jersey: INSTITUTE OF TRADITIONAL JUDAISM, THE

Richard (A.) Primus*, Dr.Phil.; Professor of Law, the University of Michigan: STROCHLITZ, SIGMUND

Kevin Proffitt*, M.A., M.S.L.S.; Senior Archivist for Research and Collections, The Jacob Rader Marcus Center of the American Jewish Archives, Cincinnati, Ohio: SCHANFARBER, TOBIAS

Moshe Prywes, M.D.; Associate Professor of Medical Education, the Hebrew University – Hadassah Medical School, Jerusalem; Vice President of the Hebrew University of Jerusalem; President, University of the Negev

Sharon Pucker Rivo*, M.A.; Executive Director of the National Center for Jewish Film, Brandeis Univeristy, Waltham, Massachusetts: KANIN, FAY MITCHELL; LEVIEN, SONYA

Lotte Pulvermacher-Egers, Ph.D.; Lecturer in the History of Art, the Mannes College of Music, New York: ART COLLECTORS AND ART DEALERS

Herbert Pundik, Journalist, Tel Aviv: MAḤAL

Marcus Pyka*, Ph.D., Dr.; Abt. Für Jüdische Geschichte und Kultur Historisches Seminar, Universität Munchen: AGRARIAN LEAGUE; ALLGEMEINE ZEITUNG DES JUDENTUMS; ALTENBERG, PETER; ANDREW OF RINN; ARNDT, ADOLF; ARNDT, ERNST MORITZ; ARNHEIM, FISCHEL; ARNHEIM, HEYMANN; ARONIUS, JULIUS; ASCHAFFENBURG, GUSTAV; AUERBACH, BERTHOLD; AUERNHEIMER, RAOUL; AUSPITZ; BADT, HERMANN; BAMBERGER, LUDWIG; BAMBUS, WILLY; BARNAY, LUDWIG; BECHER, SIEGFRIED; BEER, MICHAEL; BEN-GAVRIEL, MOSHE YA'AKOV; BERGNER, ELISABETH; BERNSTEIN, ARON DAVID; BERNSTEIN, EDUARD; BISMARCK, OTTO VON; BLEICHROEDER; BOERNE, LUDWIG; BRANDT, WILLY; BRESSLAU, HARRY; BURCHARDUS DE MONTE SION; BURG, MENO; CARO, GEORG MARTIN; COHN, EMIL MOSES; DALMAN, GUSTAF HERMANN; FRANKL, VIKTOR EMIL; GRAETZ, HEINRICH; HEGEL, GEORG WILHELM FRIEDRICH; HERDER, JOHANN GOTTFRIED; HIRSCH, BARON MAURICE DE; JOST, ISAAC MARCUS; MASSARY, FRITZI; NIETZSCHE, FRIEDRICH WILHELM

Aldina Quintana (Rodriguez)*, Ph.D.; Post-Doctoral Fellow, the Hebrew University of Jerusalem: LADINO

Uri Ra'anan, M.A.; Professor of International Politics, the Fletcher School of Law and Diplomacy, Tufts University, Medford, Massachusetts: ISRAEL, STATE OF: HISTORICAL SURVEY

Theodore K. Rabb, Ph.D.; Associate Professor of History, Princeton University, New Jersey: ELTON, SIR GEOFFREY RUDOLPH; HEXTER, JACK H.; MOSSE, GEORGE L.

Alfredo Mordechai Rabello*, Dott. giurisp., Professor Emeritus of Law, the Hebrew University of Jerusalem.: ARTOM, ELIA SAMUELE; BERNHEIMER, CARLO; CAMMEO, FEDERICO; CASTELLI, DAVID; CATACOMBS; COLLATIO LEGUM MOSAICARUM ET ROMANARUM; COLLEGIO RABBINICO ITALIANO; COLOMBO, SAMUEL; COLOMBO, YOSEPH; COLORNI, VITTORE; DISEGNI, DARIO; DOMENICO GEROSOLIMITANO; DOMITIAN; HONORIUS FLAVIUS; LAWYERS; MILANO, ATTILIO; MOSCATI, SABATINO; NERVA; NORZI; OSTIA; PACIFICI, ALFONSO; PACIFICI, RICCARDO; PADUA; PARMA; PERREAU, PIETRO; PIEDMONT; POMI, DE'; POMPEII; REGGIO, ISACCO SAMUEL; RIETI; ROMAN EMPERORS; ROVIGO; SALUZZO; SEGRÈ, GINO; SERENI, ANGELO PIERO; SEVERUS, SEPTIMIUS; SIERRA, SERGIO JOSEPH; SOAVE, MOISE; TEDESCHI; THEODOSIUS I; THEODOSIUS II; TURIN; ULPIAN; VERCELLI; VICENZA; VITERBO, CARLO ALBERTO; VITTA, CINO; VITTORIO VENETO; VIVANTE, CESARE; VIVANTI, DAVID ABRAHAM; VOLLI, GEMMA; VOLTERRA, EDOARDO

Wladimir Rabi, M.A.; Judge and Writer, Briançon, France: FONDANE, BENJAMIN; TZARA, TRISTAN

Chaim M. Rabin, D.Phil., Dipl.O.S.; Professor of Hebrew Language, the Hebrew University of Jerusalem:

BEN-NAPHTALI, MOSES BEN DAVID; BOESCHENSTEIN, JOHANN; BUXTORF, JOHANNES; DUNASH BEN LABRAT; HANAU, SOLOMON ZALMAN BEN JUDAH LOEB HA-KOHEN

Dov Rabin, Researcher, Jerusalem: GRODNO; NESVIZH; OSTRYNA; OZON; RADOSHKOVICHI; RADUN; RUZHANY; SIEMIATYCZE; SLONIM; SOKOLKA; SUWALKI

Abraham Rabinovich, B.A.; Journalist, Jerusalem: JERUSALEM

Aviva Rabinovich, M.Sc.; Jerusalem: TRISTRAM, HENRY BAKER

Nachum L. Rabinovitch, B.Sc., Ph.D.; Principal, Jews' College, London

Aron Moshe K. Rabinowicz, Ph.D., M.C.J.; Secretary of the Faculty of Law, the Hebrew University of Jerusalem: POLITISCHE GEMEINDE

Harry Rabinowicz, Ph.D., Rabbi; Historian, London: BEDIKAT ḤAMEẒ; CREMATION; DEATH; DIETARY LAWS; HAKKAFOT; ḤAMEẒ, SALE OF; MELAVVEH MALKAH; SHEḤITAH

Oskar K. Rabinowicz, Dr.Phil.; Historian, New York: AMERY, LEOPOLD CHARLES MAURICE STENNETT; BAMBUS, WILLY; BAR KOCHBA ASSOCIATION; BEREGOVO; BONDY, BOHUMIL; BRANDYS NAD LABEM; BRECLAV; BREZNICE; BUCOVICE; BUDYNĚ NAD OHŘÍ; CESKE BUDEJOVICE; CHURCHILL, SIR WINSTON LEONARD SPENCER; EL-ARISH; FRIEDMANN, PAUL; HERMANN, LEO; JACOBSON, VICTOR; JIHLAVA; KARTELL JUEDISCHER VERBINDUNGEN; KISCH, ALEXANDER; KREMENETZKY, JOHANN; MARGULIES, EMIL; MARMOREK, ALEXANDER; TERRITORIALISM; TREBITSCH, NEHEMIAH; TRIETSCH, DAVIS; USOV; WEINMANN, JACOB; YORK-STEINER, HEINRICH ELCHANAN

Wolf Zeev Rabinowitsch, M.D.; Historian, Haifa: DAVID-GORODOK; ISRAEL BEN PEREZ OF POLOTSK; KARLIN; KOBRIN, MOSES BEN ISRAEL POLIER OF; KOIDANOV; LACHOWICZE, MORDECAI BEN NOAH OF; LYUBESHOV; SLONIM

Abraham Hirsch Rabinowitz, M.A., Rabbi; Senior Chaplain to the Israel Air Force, Jerusalem: ADARBI, ISAAC BEN SAMUEL; ALEGRE, ABRAHAM BEN SOLOMON; AL-MADARI, JUDAH HA-KOHEN BEN ELEAZAR HE-ḤASID; ALMOSNINO, MOSES BEN BARUCH; COLON, JOSEPH BEN SOLOMON; COMMANDMENTS, THE 613; KEẒAẒAH

Chayim Reuven Rabinowitz, B.A., Rabbi; Writer, Jerusalem: FIGO, AZARIAH; LIBOWITZ, SAMUEL NEHEMIAH

Dorothy Rabinowitz, Author, New York: JHABVALA, RUTH PRAWER

Louis Isaac Rabinowitz, Ph.D., Rabbi; Deputy Editor in Chief of the *Encyclopaedia Judaica* (1st ed.); Editor of *Encyclopaedia Judaica Year Books*; Former Chief Rabbi of the Transvaal and former Professor of Hebrew, the University of Witwatersrand, Johannesburg; Former Deputy Mayor of Jerusalem: ABSALOM; AGRICULTURE; AMMON, AMMONITES; ANOINTING; APIKOROS; AUTOPSIES AND DISSECTION; BANISHMENT; BEGGING AND BEGGARS; BIBLE; BLEMISH; BLINDNESS; BLOOD; BOOK OF LIFE; CAPITAL PUNISHMENT; CARO, JOSEPH BEN EPHRAIM; CARTER, JAMES EARL; CHEESE; CHERUB; CONCUBINE; COSMOLOGY; CREATION AND COSMOGONY; CROWNS, DECORATIVE HEADDRESSES, AND WREATHS; DAVID; DAYYAN; DEAF-MUTE; DEMONS, DEMONOLOGY; DERASH; DIVINATION; DRUNKENNESS; EGGS; EGLAH ARUFAH; ENTEBBE RAID; EUPHEMISM AND DYSPHEMISM; FAMILY; FAMINE AND DROUGHT; FEAR OF GOD; FEIGENBAUM, ISAAC HA-KOHEN; FERBER, ẒEVI HIRSCH; FIRE; FLESH; FLOOD, THE; FOUR SPECIES; FREEDOM; GEMILUT ḤASADIM; GERI, JACOB; GOD, NAMES OF; HADRIAN, PUBLIUS AELIUS; HAFTARAH; HAKHEL; ḤAMEẒ; HEART; ḤEDER; ḤEVRA KADDISHA; HONEY; HONOR; HUNTING; IDOLATRY; INGATHERING OF THE EXILES; IR HA-NIDDAḤAT; ISRAEL; KIMBERLEY; KING, KINGSHIP; KUNTERES; LABOR; LEPROSY; LEVITES IN THE HALAKHAH; LION; LOEWENSTAMM; LOTS; LUZ OF THE SPINE; MAIMONIDES; MEAT; MEZUZAH; MNEMONICS or MEMORA TECHNICA; MOSES ISAAC; NAMES; OILS; ONKELOS AND AQUILA; PARABLE; PEACE; PEACE NOW; PENTATEUCH; PERLHEFTER, ISSACHAR BEHR BEN JUDAH MOSES; PESHAT; POVERTY; PROPHETS AND PROPHECY; PROSELYTES; PSALMS, BOOK OF; RABBI, RABBINATE; RABBINICAL SEMINARIES; RIGHT AND LEFT; SALT; SATAN; SCHACH, LEONARD LAZARUS; SEA, SONG OF THE; SEFER HA-MA'ASIM LI-VENEI EREẒ YISRAEL; SEFER TORAH; SELIḤOT; SHULḤAN ARUKH; SON OF MAN; SUICIDE; SYNAGOGUE; TAITAẒAK, JOSEPH; TALMID ḤAKHAM; TALMUD, JERUSALEM; TEN LOST TRIBES; TEXTILES; VIRGIN, VIRGINITY; VOWS AND VOWING; WRITING; YAD; YAHRZEIT; YOKE

Zvi Meir Rabinowitz, Ph.D., Rabbi; Associate Professor of Talmud, Tel Aviv University: AARON OF ZHITOMIR; ALEKSANDROW; ḤAYYIM BEN HANANEL HA-KOHEN; HEILPRIN, JEHIEL BEN SOLOMON; HILLEL BEN ELIAKIM; ISSACHAR DOV BAER BEN ARYEH LEIB OF ZLOCZOW; JEHIEL MEIR OF GOSTYNIN; RADOMSKO, SOLOMON HA-KOHEN RABINOWICH OF; STRELISK, URI BEN PHINEHAS OF; STRELISK, URI BEN PHINEHAS OF; TWERSKY; WEIL, NETHANEL BEN NAPHTALI ẒEVI; WILDMANN, ISAAC EISIK; ZECHARIAH BEN BARACHEL; ZE'EV WOLF OF ZHITOMIR

Mordechai Rabinson, Dr.Phil., Writer, Jerusalem: BRANDSTAEDTER, MORDECAI DAVID

Arnold Rachlis*: ORANGE COUNTY

Sarlota Rachmuth-Gerstl, Ing.; Jerusalem: GALANTA; HUMENNE

Emanuel Rackman, Ph.D., Rabbi; Chancellor, Bar-Ilan University, Ramat Gan: DOMESTIC PEACE

Howard B. Radest, Ph.D.; Associate Professor of Philosophy, Ramapo College, Mahwah, New Jersey: NEUMANN, HENRY

Jihan (Jennifer) Radjai-Ordoubadi*, M.A.; Trainee in Jewish Studies, Heidelberg, Germany: KOLLER-PINELL, BRONCIA; KRESTIN, LAZAR; LEVY, RUDOLF; LILIEN, EPHRAIM MOSES; OPPENHEIMER, JOSEPH; ORLIK. EMIL; OSBORN, MAX; RICHTER, HANS; SALOMON, CHARLOTTE; SEGAL, ARTHUR; WOLF, GUSTAV; WOLLHEIM, GERT H.

Amichai Radzyner*, Ph.D., Lecturer in Jewish Law, Bar-Ilan University, Ramat Gan: APPEAL

Arie Rafaeli-Zenziper, Director of the Russian Zionist Archives, Tel Aviv: PETROGRAD CONFERENCE

Bracha Rager*, Ph.D.; Professor of Microbiology and Immunology, Faculty of Health Sciences, Ben-

Gurion University of the Negev, Beersheba; Ministry of Health, Beersheba: ABIR, DAVID; ADLER, CHARLES; ALTMAN, SIDNEY; ANGRIST, ALFRED ALVIN; ARNON, RUTH; ATLAS, DAVID; BALTIMORE, DAVID; BAUER, SIMON HARVEY; BEN-ABRAHAM, ZVI; BIRK, YEHUDITH; CHET, ILAN; CIECHANOVER, AARON J.; COHEN, PAUL JOSEPH; COHEN-TANNOUDJI CLAUDE; DORFMAN, RALPH ISADORE; DORON, HAIM; DVORETZKY, ARYEH; ELIEL, ERNEST LUDWIG; FAHN, ABRAHAM; FLEISCHER, MICHAEL; FRIEND, CHARLOTTE; GLICK, DAVID; GREENBERG, DAVID MORRIS; GROSSMAN, MORTON IRVIN; GRÜNBAUM, ADOLF; HALPERN, JACK; HARARI, ḤAYYIM; HARRIS, MILTON; HEIDELBERGER, MICHAEL; HELPERN, MILTON; ISRAEL, STATE OF: HEALTH, WELFARE, AND SOCIAL SECURITY; JAFFE, LEONARD; JORTNER, JOSHUA; KARPLUS, HEINRICH; KATZIR, AHARON; KATZIR, EPHRAIM; KEDEM, ORA; LEVITZKI, ALEXANDER; MENDELSSOHN, KURT ALFRED GEORG; NEUFELD, HENRY; PADEH, BARUCH; PENZIAS, ARNO ALLAN; PRYWES, MOSHE; RAGER, ITZHACK; RAM, MOSHE; RAMOT, BRACHA; REVEL, MICHEL; RICHTER, BURTON; SACHS, LEO; SEGRÈ, EMILIO GINO; SHECHTMAN, DAN; SZWARC, MICHAEL; TOBIAS, PHILLIP VALLENTINE; WHITE, ROBERT MAYER; WILLNER, ITAMAR; YONATH, ADA

Sanford Ragins, M.A., Rabbi; Hartsdale, New York: NEBRASKA

Jay (Douglas, Philip) Rahn*, Ph.D., Professor of Music, York University, Toronto, Canada: ADASKIN, MURRAY; ANHALT, ISTVÁN; CHERNEY, BRIAN; FREEDMAN, HARRY; MORAWETZ, OSKAR; WEINZWEIG, JOHN

Rosa Perla Raicher, M.A.; Tel Aviv: URUGUAY; ZIONISM

Mark A. Raider*, Ph.D.; Professor of Jewish History, incumbent of the Jewish Foundation of Cincinnati Endowed Chair in Judaic Studies, and Head of the Department of Judaic Studies at the University of Cincinnati, Ohio: UNITED STATES OF AMERICA

Miriam B. Raider-Roth*, Ed. D.; Assistant Professor of Educational Theory and Practice, University at Albany, State University of New York: GILLIGAN, CAROL FRIEDMAN

Anson Rainey, Ph.D.; Associate Professor of Ancient Middle Eastern Civilization, Tel Aviv University: AHARONI, YOḤANAN; CHALDEA, CHALDEANS; CONCUBINE; FAMILY; SACRIFICE; UGARIT; UGARITIC

Aaron Rakeffet-Rothkoff*, See Aaron Rothkoff

Nahum Rakover, Dr. Jur.; Advisor on Jewish Law, Ministry of Justice, Jerusalem: AGENCY; ECOLOGY; LEASE AND HIRE; SHALISH; SHOMERIM

Hanna Ram, M.A.; History Museum of Tel Aviv: TEL AVIV-JAFFA

Shaul Ramati, M.A.; Lieutenant Colonel (Res.), Israel Defense Forces; Ministry for Foreign Affairs, Jerusalem: THAILAND

Naama Ramot*, M.A.; Musicologist, the Hebrew University of Jerusalem: ADLER, LARRY; ANCERL, KAREL; AX, EMANUEL; BACHAUER, GINA; BARENBOIM, DANIEL; BELL, JOSHUA; BENDIX, OTTO; BERGER, ARTHUR VICTOR; BERTINI, GARY; BRAILOWSKY, ALEXANDER; BRANT, HENRY DREYFUS; BROD, MAX; BRONFMAN, YEFIM; BROWNING, JOHN; COMISSIONA, SERGIU; DICHTER, MISHA; EDEN-TAMIR; FISCHER, ANNIE; FLEISHER, LEON; FRIED, MIRIAM; GOLDBERG, SZYMON; GOTTSCHALK, LOUIS MOREAU; HAENDEL, IDA; HASKIL, CLARA; HINRICHSEN; ISSERLIS, STEVEN; ISTOMIN, EUGENE; KALICHSTEIN, JOSEPH; KATCHEN, JULIUS; KATZ, MINDRU; KENTNER, LOUIS; KLEMPERER, OTTO; KRAUS, LILI; KREISLER, FRITZ; LANDOWSKA, WANDA; LEIGH, ADÈLE; LEVI, YOEL; LOEWE, FREDERICK; MAAZEL, LORIN; MEHTA, ZUBIN; MENUHIN, HEPHZIBAH; MILLER, MITCH; MINTZ, SHLOMO; PERAHIA, MURRAY; PERLMAN, ITZHAK; PISK, PAUL AMADEUS; PRESSLER, MENAHEM; SALZMAN, PNINA; SCHIFF, ANDRÁS; SCHIFRIN, LALO; SERKIN, PETER ADOLF; SHAHAM, GIL; SHMUELI, HERZL; SILBERMANN, ALPHONS; SINGER, GEORGE; SLATKIN, LEONARD; SMOIRA-COHN, MICHAL; SOLTI, SIR GEORG; SONDHEIM, STEPHEN; SPIVAKOVSKY, TOSSY; STERN, ISAAC; STRANSKY, JOSEF; STRAUSS II, JOHANN; SUSSKIND, WALTER; SZELL, GEORGE; SZERYNG, HENRYK; TUGAL, PIERRE; WEISSENBERG, ALEXIS; ZUKERMAN, PINCHAS; ZUKOFSKY, PAUL

Gila Ramras-Rauch*, Ph.D.; Weinstein Professor of Jewish Literature, Hebrew College, Boston: APPELFELD, AHARON

Jo Ranson, Theater Critic, New York: COHN, HARRY; CORWIN, NORMAN LEWIS; FROHMAN; GLASS, MONTAGUE MARSDEN; GOLDWYN, SAMUEL; GREEN, ABEL; GREEN, ABEL; HARBURG, E.Y.; JOLSON, AL

Amia Raphael, London: GOLDSMITHS AND SILVERSMITHS; OFIR, ARIE

Chaim Raphael, Writer, London

Yitzchak Raphael, Ph.D.; Member of the Knesset, Jerusalem: KOWALSKY, JUDAH LEIB; MOSES LEIB OF SASOV; ROZOVSKI, PINḤAS

Nimrod Raphaeli, Ph.D.; Lecturer in Political Science, the Hebrew University of Jerusalem: SIMON, HERBERT ALEXANDER

Nessa Rapoport*, Writer, New York: ROTENBERG, MATTIE LEVI

Solomon Rappaport, Ph.D., Rabbi; Professor of Hebrew, the University of the Witwatersrand, Johannesburg, South Africa: DIO CASSIUS; HERMETIC WRITINGS; HOMER; MARTIAL; PSEUDO-SCYLAX

Uriel Rappaport, Ph.D.; Senior Lecturer in Jewish History, Haifa University: ANANIAS AND HELKIAS; ARCHISYNAGOGOS; BAR GIORA, SIMEON; BOSPHORUS, KINGDOM OF; CARTHAGE; CHALCIS; CICERO, MARCUS TULLIUS; CYRUS; ELEAZAR BEN MATTATHIAS; FLAVIUS, CLEMENS; HADRIAN, PUBLIUS AELIUS; HERODIANS; ḤEVER HA-YEHUDIM; HYRCANUS II; JADDUA; JASON; JASON OF CYRENE; JOHANAN BEN JEHOIADA; JOHANAN THE HASMONEAN; KEFAR SHIḤLAYIM; KOS; LAODICEA; LEONTOPOLIS; LYSIAS; MARCUS AURELIUS ANTONINUS; MENELAUS; MONOBAZ I AND II; NICANOR; NICANOR'S GATE; PHAROS; QUIETUS, LUSIUS; SIMEON SON OF ONIAS I; SIMEON THE HASMONEAN; SIMEON THE JUST; SOLOMON, PSALMS OF; SPARTA; THEOPHILUS; TITUS, ARCH OF; ZENODORUS

Dennis Rapps*, M.A., J.D.; Attorney, General Council, National Jewish Commission on Law and Public Affairs, New York: LEWIN, NATHAN

Ariel Rathaus*, Ph.D.; Translator and Researcher, Jerusalem: FRANCES, JACOB BEN DAVID; SVEVO, ITALO

Annette Levy-Ratkin*, B.A., M.L.S.; Archivist, Jewish Federation of Nashville and Middle Tennessee, Nashville: NASHVILLE

Sidney Ratner, Ph.D.; Professor of History, Rutgers University, New Brunswick, New Jersey: KALLEN, HORACE MEYER

Yohanan Ratner, M.Sc.; Major General (Res.), Israel Defense Forces; Emeritus Professor of Architecture, the Technion, Haifa

Yehuda Ratzaby, M.A.; Senior Lecturer in Medieval Hebrew Literature and in Jewish-Arabic Literature, Bar-Ilan University, Ramat Gan: ABRAHAM BEN ḤALFON; ABYAḌ, YIḤYA BEN SHALOM; ADANI, DAVID BEN AMRAM; ADANI, DAVID BEN YESHA HA-LEVI; ADANI, MIZRAḤI SHALOM; ADANI, SAADIAH BEN DAVID; ALSHEIKH, RAPHAEL BEN SHALOM; BADIḤI, YAḤYA BEN JUDAH; BALIDEH, MOSES; BARUCH BEN SAMUEL; BASHIRI, YAḤYA; DHAMĀRĪ, MANṢUR SULEIMAN; DHAMĀRĪ, SA'ID BEN DAVID; ḤABSHUSH, SHALOM BEN YAḤYA; ḤAMDĪ, LEVI BEN YESHU'AH; IBN ZABARA, JOSEPH BEN MEIR; IRĀQĪ, ELEAZAR BEN AARON HA-KOHEN; IRĀQĪ, SHALOM HA-KOHEN; IRĀQĪ, SHALOM JOSEPH; JIZFĀN, JUDAH BEN JOSEPH; JOSEPH BEN ISRAEL; JOSEPH, SAUL ABDALLAH; KAFAḤ, YIḤYE BEN SOLOMON; KAREH, SOLOMON; KORAḤ, ḤAYYIM BEN JOSEPH; KORAḤ, YAḤYA BEN SHALOM; LAWĀNI, DA'UD; LEVI, SAID BEN SHALOM; MANSURAH, SAADIAH BEN JUDAH; MANSURAH, SHALOM BEN JUDAH; MAWZA'; MIZRAḤI, DAVID BEN SHALOM; NAJRĀN; ṢAADĪ, JUDAH BEN SOLOMON; SAADIAH; ṢALIḤ IBN YAḤYA IBN JOSEPH; ṢĀLIḤ, ABRAHAM; ṢALIḤ, YAḤYA BEN JOSEPH; SĀRŪM, ABRAHAM; ṢEFIRAH, SAADIAH BEN JOSEPH; SHABAZI, SHALEM; SHARABI, SHALOM; WANNEH, ISAAC BEN ABRAHAM; YIḤYE, ISAAC HA-LEVI; ZECHARIAH AL-ḌĀHIRI; ZECHARIAH BEN SOLOMON-ROFE; ZULAY, MENAHEM

Benjamin (C.I.) Ravid*, Ph.D., Professor, Brandeis University: BRIT IVRIT OLAMIT; BONFIL, ROBERT; RAWIDOWICZ, SIMON; VENICE

Melech Ravitch, Writer, Montreal: BERLINER, ISAAC; BIALOSTOTZKY, BENJAMIN JACOB; BICKELS-SPITZER, ZVI; BLUM, ELIEZER; BRODERZON, MOYSHE; BURSZTYN, MICHAL; CHMELNITZKI, MELECH; DILLON, ABRAHAM MOSES; FEFER, ITZIK; FRUG, SHIMON SHMUEL; GEBIRTIG, MORDECHAI; GILBERT, SHLOMO; GISER, MOSES DAVID; GLASMAN, BARUCH; GORDIN, ABBA; GOTTESFELD, CHONE; GOTTLIEB, JACOB; GRYNBERG, BERL; GUTMAN, CHAIM; HOROWITZ, BER; JAFFE, LEIB; KACYZNE, ALTER; KAGANOWSKI, EFRAIM; LANDAU, ZISHE; LAPIN, BERL; LERER, YEHIEL; MALACH, LEIB; MASTBAUM, JOEL; NAIDUS, LEIB; NEUGROESCHEL, MENDEL; NOMBERG, HERSH DAVID; PRYLUCKI, NOAH; SCHNAPPER, BER; TEPPER, KOLYA; WARSHAVSKY, YAKIR; WARSZAWSKI, OSER; YEHOASH; YOFFE, MORDECAI; ẒIVION

Aviezer Ravitzky*, Ph.D.; Professor of Jewish Philosophy, the Hebrew University of Jerusalem: ZERAHIAH BEN ISAAC BEN SHEALTIEL

Norman Ravvin*, Ph.D.; Chair, Canadian Jewish Studies, Concordia University, Montreal, Canada: COHEN, LEONARD; COHEN, MATT; KLEIN, A.M.; KREISEL, HENRY; MANDEL, ELI; RICHLER, MORDECAI

Shoey Raz*, M.A.; Ph.D. Doctoral Student, Department of Philosophy, Bar-Ilan University, Ramat Gan: LATIF, ISAAC B. ABRAHAM IBN

Simha Raz, General Secretary, Brit Ivrit Olamit, Jerusalem: LEVIN, ARYEH

Roberta Rebold, B.A.; Writer and Researcher, Jerusalem: COALITION FOR THE ADVANCEMENT OF JEWISH EDUCATION

Shimon Redlich, Ph.D.; Lecturer in History, the University of the Negev, Beersheba: BIROBIDZHAN; STALIN, JOSEPH VISSARIONOVICH

David (Allen) Rees*, B.A.; Graduate Student (History), Ludwig-Maximilians-Universität, Munich, Germany: MARLÉ, ARNOLD

Uri Regev, L.L.B., Rabbi; Director, The Israel Religious Action Center, Jerusalem

Sidney L. Regner, B.A., Rabbi; Executive Vice President, Central Conference of American Rabbis, New York: SYNAGOGUE COUNCIL OF AMERICA, THE

Ronny Reich, Ph.D.; Director of Documentation, Israel Antiquities Authority, Jerusalem

Harry Reicher*, B.Econ., L.L.B., L.L.M.; Adjunct Professor of Law, University of Pennsylvania Law School; Member, United States Holocaust Memorial Council, Pennsylvania: WAR CRIMES TRIALS

Stefan C. Reif, Ph.D.; Director of Genizah Unit and Head of Oriental Department, Cambridge University Library: GENIZAH, CAIRO

Manfred Reifer, Dr.Phil.; *Encyclopaedia Judaica* (Germany); Tel Aviv: BUKOVINA

Elena Reikher (Temin)*, Ph.D., Musicology, Bar-Ilan University, Ramat Gan: BUKHARA

Jack Reimer, M.H.L., Rabbi; Lecturer, Dept. of Judaic Studies, University of Dayton, Ohio: BETTELHEIM, ALBERT SIEGFRIED; BLUMENTHAL, JOSEPH; BOKSER, BEN ZION; BRAUDE, WILLIAM GORDON; COHEN, MORTIMER JOSEPH; DAYTON; DEMBITZ, LEWIS NAPHTALI; EISENDRATH, MAURICE NATHAN; EISENSTEIN, IRA; FRIEDMAN, THEODORE; GOLDIN, JUDAH; GOLDMAN, SOLOMON; GORDIS, ROBERT; GORDON, ALBERT I.; GORDON, HAROLD; GREENBERG, SIMON; HOFFMAN, CHARLES ISAIAH; JASTROW; KARP, ABRAHAM J.; KOHN, EUGENE; KOHUT; LEESER, ISAAC; LEVITSKY, LOUIS MOSES; MORAIS, SABATO; RAPHALL, MORRIS JACOB

Bob Reinalda*, Ph.D.; Senior Lecturer in International Relations, Radboud University Nijmegen, The Netherlands: MIRANDA, SALOMON RODRIGUES DE

Alvin J. Reines, Ph.D., Rabbi; Professor of Philosophy, the Hebrew Union College-Jewish Institute of Religion, New York: ABRABANEL, ISAAC BEN JUDAH; DIESENDRUCK, ZEVI; METAPHYSICS; NEUMARK, DAVID; REDEMPTION; SKEPTICS AND SKEPTICISM; TIME AND ETERNITY

Jehuda Reinharz, Ph.D.; Assistant Professor of History, the University of Michigan, Ann Arbor: FARBAND; ZIONISM

Shulamit Reinharz*: SZOLD, HENRIETTA

Joel (Ira) Reisman*, B.A.; Healthcare Analyst, Edith Nourse

Rogers Memorial Hospital, Bedford, Massachusetts: ALASKA

Hanns G. Reissner, Ph.D.; Professor of History, New York Institute of Technology, Old Westbury, New York: ABRAHAM; ALTMAN, BENJAMIN; CARO, GEORG MARTIN; DREYFUS; GIMBEL; GOLDMAN; HIRSCH, BARON MAURICE DE; KUHN-LOEB; LAZARD; LAZARUS; LEHMAN; MENDELSSOHN; OPPENHEIM; SAINT-SIMONISM; SERING, MAX; SPEYER; STRAUS; STRAUSS, LEVI; VEIT

Alan Reitman, B.A.; Associate Director of the American Civil Liberties Union, New York: HAYS, ARTHUR GARFIELD

Elie Rekhess*, Ph.D., Senior Research Fellow, Tel Aviv University: ISRAEL, STATE OF: ARAB POPULATION

Joel (E.) Rembaum*, B.A., M.A., Ph.D., Rabbi; Senior Rabbi, Temple Beth Am, Los Angeles: PRESSMAN, JACOB

Gary A. Rendsburg*, Ph.D., Blanche and Irving Laurie Chair in Jewish History, Rutgers University, New Brunswick, New Jersey: EBLA

Yehuda Reshef, LL.B.; Ministry of Justice, Haifa: BORMANN, MARTIN; BUCHENWALD; DARQUIER DE PELLEPOIX, LOUIS; EPPSTEIN, PAUL; FRANK, HANS MICHAEL; FRANK, KARL HERMANN; FRANKFURTER, DAVID; GERSTEIN, KURT; GLOBOCNIK, ODILO; GLUECKS, RICHARD; GOEBBELS, PAUL JOSEF; GOERING, HERMANN WILHELM; HEYDRICH, REINHARD TRISTAN; HIMMLER, HEINRICH; HIRSCH, OTTO; JACOB, BERTHOLD; KALTENBRUNNER, ERNST; KATZMANN, FRIEDRICH; LAMBERT, RAYMOND RAOUL; LUX, STEFAN; MAUTHAUSEN; MUELLER, HEINRICH; MUSELMANN; NATZWEILER-STRUTHOF; POHL, OSWALD; RADEMACHER, FRANZ; RAUTER, HANNS ALBIN; RAVENSBRUECK; REICHSVEREINIGUNG; REICHSZENTRALE FUER JUEDISCHE AUSWANDERUNG; RIBBENTROP, JOACHIM VON; ROSENBERG, ALFRED; RSHA; SACHSENHAUSEN-ORANIENBURG; SAUCKEL, FRITZ; SCHACHT PLAN; SCHELLENBERG, WALTER; STROOP, JUERGEN; VALLAT, XAVIER; WIENER LIBRARY; WIENER, ALFRED; WISLICENY, DIETER

Rosa Perla Resnick*, Ph.D.; University Professor, CUNY, Yeshiva University, Columbia University, New York: RESNICK, SALOMON

Gideon Reuveni*, Ph.D.; Lecturer, University of Melbourne, Australia

Shmuel Dov Revital, Dr.Jur.; State Comptroller's Office, Jerusalem: PARTNERSHIP

Hanoch Reviv, Ph.D.; Lecturer in Jewish History, the Hebrew University of Jerusalem: ABIMELECH; ALALAKH; ARCHIVES; ATHALIAH; BAASHA; CITY; CORVÉE; ELAH; HISTORY: BEGINNING UNTIL THE MONARCHY; HISTORY: KINGDOMS OF JUDAH AND ISRAEL; NABOTH; TRADE AND COMMERCE; ZEDEKIAH

Charles Reznikoff, LL.B.; Author, New York: KONVITZ, MILTON RIDVAS; PANKEN, JACOB

Harold U. Ribalow, B.S.; Writer, New York: FAST, HOWARD MELVIN; FERBER, EDNA; URIS, LEON

Arnold (David) Richards*, M.D.; Psychiatrist, Psychoanalyst, New York University School of Medicine Department of Psychiatry, Psychoanalytic Institute, New York: FREUD, SIGMUND

Elisheva Rigbi*, Ph.D.; Lecturer of Musicology, the Hebrew University of Jerusalem: KATZ, RUTH

Bryan Mark Rigg*, Ph.D.; Private Wealth Manager at Credit Suisse, Dallas: NUREMBERG LAWS

Elimelech Rimalt, Ph.D.; Member of the Knesset, Former Minister of Posts, Ramat Gan: INNSBRUCK

Allie Rimer*: NEW BRUNSWICK

Chanoch Rinott, Ph.D.; Senior Teacher and Director of the Center for Jewish Education in the Diaspora, the Hebrew University of Jerusalem: YOUTH ALIYAH

Moshe Rinott, Ph.D.; Senior Teacher in Education, Haifa University: COHN-REISS, EPHRAIM

Moses Rischin, Ph.D.; Professor of History, San Francisco State College; Director of the Western Jewish History Center, Berkeley, California: CAHAN, ABRAHAM

Yitzhak Rischin, B.A. (Hons.); Managing Director of Keter Publishing House Ltd., Jerusalem: AUSTRALIA; MELBOURNE

Israel Ritov, Journalist, Tel Aviv: HE-ḤALUTZ; Z.S.; ẒE'IREI ZION

Paul Ritterband, M.H.L., Ph.D.; Associate Professor, Departments of Sociology and Jewish Studies, City University of New York

Marina Ritzarev*, Ph.D., Professor, Musicologist, Bar-Ilan University, Ramat Gan: ABELIOVICH, LEV MOYSSEYEVICH; ALSHVANG, ARNOLD ALEKSANDROVICH; ALTSCHULER, MODEST; ARONOVICH, YURI MIKHAYLOVICH; ASHKENAZY, VLADIMIR DAVIDOVICH; AVSHALOMOV, AARON; BABIN, VICTOR; BARMAS, ISSAY; BELY, VICTOR ARKADYEVICH; BLUMENFELD, FELIX MIKHAYLOVICH; BRUSSILOVSKY, YEVGENI GRIGORYEVICH; FEINBERG, SAMUEL YEVGENYEVICH; KROSHNER, MIKHAIL YEFIMOVICH; LEVITSKY, MISCHA; LITINSKI, GENRIKH ILYICH; MAYKAPAR, SAMUIL MOYSEYEVICH; SLONIMSKY, NICOLAS; SLONIMSKY, SERGEI MIKHAILOVICH; STEINBERG, MAXIMILIAN OSSEJEVICH; TARUSKIN, RICHARD; VEINBERG, MOISSEY SAMUILOVICH; WEISSBERG, JULIA LAZAREVNA; ZHITOMIRSKI, ALEXANDER MATVEYEVICH

Benjamin Rivlin, Writer, Jerusalem: DVORZETSKY, MARK MEIR; RIVLIN; RIVLIN, JOSEPH JOEL

Ronald Robboy*, Former Senior Researcher, The Thomashefsky Project; Senior Researcher *Encyclopedia of Yiddish Theater*; Cellist, San Diego Symphony Orchestra, San Diego: THOMASHEFSKY, BESSIE

Marthe Robert, Researcher and Writer, Paris: NÉMIROVSKY, IRÉNE

B.J. Roberts, D.D.; Professor of Hebrew and Biblical Studies, University College of North Wales, Bangor: KAHLE, PAUL ERNST

George Robinson*, B.A., M.F.A.; Film Critic, Music Critic, Author, *Jewish Week*, New York; *Inside Magazine*, Philadelphia: AMRAM,

DAVID; BRECKER BROTHERS; ELMAN, ZIGGY; FEATHER, LEONARD; FLECK, BELA; GETZ, STAN; GIBBS, TERRY; HENTOFF, NAT; KESSEL, BARNEY; KLEIN, MANNIE; KONITZ, LEE; LACY, STEVE; MANN, HERBIE; MANNE, SHELLY; RICH, BUDDY; RODNEY, RED; TORME, MEL

Ira Robinson*, Ph.D., Professor, Concordia University, Montreal, Quebec: COHEN, HIRSH; DENBURG, CHAIM; HERSCHORN, JOSHUA HALEVY; HIRSCHPRUNG, PINHAS; KAGE, JOSEPH; ROSENBERG, YEHUDA YUDEL

Jacob Robinson, Dr.Jur.; Coordinator of Research Activities and Publications on the Holocaust for Yad Vashem and YIVO, New York: HOLOCAUST: BEHAVIOR OF THE VICTIMS; NAZI-DEUTSCH

James T. Robinson*, Ph.D.; Assistant Professor of the History of Judaism, The University of Chicago, The Divinity School, Chicago: TIBBON, IBN

Leye Robinson*: BORAISHA, MENAHEM

Nehemiah Robinson, Dr.Phil.; Director of the Institute of Jewish Affairs, New York: GENOCIDE CONVENTION

Samuele Rocca*, Ph.D., Lecturer in Art History, Wizo College, Haifa: ANCONA; ANCONA; AQUILEIA; ASCOLI, ETTORE; BASSANO; FRIULI–VENEZIA GIULIA; GORIZIA; ISTRIA; LEGIO; LEVI, DORO; LOLLI, EUDE; LOMBROSO, CESARE; LUZZATTO, EPHRAIM; MARGULIES, SAMUEL HIRSCH; MILAN; MOSCATI, SABATINO; NAPLES; OSTIA; POMPEII; RAVENNA; ROME; ROVIGO; SAN DANIELE DEL FRIULI; SERMONETA, JOSEPH BARUCH; TREVISO; TRIESTE; TURIN

Robert Rockaway, Ph.D.; Assistant Professor of American Urban History, the University of Texas, El Paso: BROWN, DAVID ABRAHAM; DETROIT

Stuart Rockoff*, Ph.D.; Director, History Department, Goldring/Woldenberg Institute of Southern Jewish Life, Jackson, Mississippi: GEORGIA; INSTITUTE OF SOUTHERN JEWISH LIFE, GOLDRING / WOLDENBERG; MISSISSIPPI; NUSSBAUM, PERRY

Edouard Roditi, B.A.; Art Critic, Paris: ADLER, JULES; BIHARI, ALEXANDER; PARIS SCHOOL OF ART

Peretz (A.) Rodman*, M.A., Rabbi; Jewish Educator, Independent Scholar, Jerusalem: HAMMER, REUVEN

Ilia (M.) Rodov*, Ph.D.; Lecturer, Bar-Ilan University, Ramat Gan: JERUSALEM

Linda Rodriguez*, M.A.; Former Director, Women's Center, University of Missouri-Kansas City: GLUCK, LOUISE

Nils Roemer*, Ph.D., Senior Lecturer, University of Southampton, England: VEREIN FUER KULTUR UND WISSENSCHAFT DES JUDENTUMS

Leonard (William) Rogoff*, Ph.D., Research Historian, Jewish Heritage Foundation of North Carolina, Chapel Hill, North Carolina: CHARLOTTE; DURHAM; NORTH CAROLINA

Stefan Rohrbacher*, Dr.Phil.; Professor, Heinrich-Heine Universität, Düsseldorf, Germany: AACHEN; AHLEM; ALTENSTADT; ASCHAFFENBURG; AUGSBURG; BADEN; BERLIN; DARMSTADT; DEGGENDORF; DEUTZ; DUESSELDORF; DUISBURG; ERFURT; GERMANY; HAMBURG; JEBENHAUSEN

Emilie Roi*, Writer, Jerusalem: COHN, GEORG

Yaacov Ro'i, M.A.; Visiting Researcher in Middle Eastern Studies, Tel Aviv University: RUSSIA

Betty Roitman, Ph.D.; Associate Professor of French and Comparative Literature, The Hebrew University of Jerusalem

Avshalom Rokach, M.Sc.; Agronomist, Jerusalem: LACHISH REGION

Isaac Rokach, Managing Director of the Pardess Syndicate, Herzliyyah: CITRUS

David Rokeah, Ph.D.; Lecturer in Jewish History, the Hebrew University of Jerusalem: JULIAN THE APOSTATE

Giorgio Romano, LL.D.; Journalist, Tel Aviv: ASCARELLI, TULLIO; BEDARIDA, GUIDO; BEMPORAD, ENRICO; BOLAFFIO, LEONE; CAMERINI, EUGENIO SALOMONE; CAMMEO, FEDERICO; CANTONI, ALBERTO; CANTONI, LELIO; CARNIVAL; CASTELNUOVO, ENRICO; CATTANEO, CARLO; DA VERONA, GUIDO; DE BENEDETTI, ALDO; DEL BANCO, ANSELMO; FALCO, MARIO; FOA; GINZBURG, NATALIA; ITALIAN LITERATURE; LEVI, CARLO; LEVI, EUGENIO; LOPEZ, SABATINO; LUZZATTI, LUIGI; LUZZATTO, GINO; MALVANO, GIACOMO; MANIN, DANIELE; MASSARANI, TULLO; MAYER, SALLY; MICHELSTAEDTER, CARLO; MODIGLIANI, VITTORIO EMANUELE; MORAVIA, ALBERTO; MORPURGO, SALOMONE; MORTARA CASE; MORTARA, LODOVICO; ORVIETO, ANGIOLO; OTTOLENGHI, JOSEPH BEN NATHAN; POLACCO, VITTORIO; PRATO, DAVID; REVERE, GIUSEPPE PROSPERO; ROSSELLI; SABA, UMBERTO; SAN NICANDRO; SONNINO, SIDNEY; TERRACINI, UMBERTO ELIA; TREVES, EMILIO; VITTA, CINO; VIVANTE, CESARE; VIVANTI CHARTRES, ANNIE; VOLTERRA, EDOARDO

Daniel Romanowski, Ph.D.; the Hebrew University of Jerusalem: AZERBAIJAN; BELARUS; KYRGYZSTAN; LATVIA; LITHUANIA; MOLDOVA; PRESS; RUSSIA; UKRAINE

David Rome, M.A.; Librarian, Lecturer in Jewish Studies, Loyola College, Montreal: SHTERN; ZIPPER, YA'AKOV

Joachim O. Ronall, LL.D.; Professor of Economics, Fordham University, New York: ABRAMOVITZ, MOSES; ADLER, GEORG; AFTALION, ALBERT; ALTARAS, JACQUES ISAAC; ALTMAN, OSCAR LOUIS; ANGEL, SHEMAYAHU; BACHE; BACRI; BALLIN, ALBERT; BALOGH, THOMAS, BARON; BAMBERGER, LUDWIG; BECHER, SIEGFRIED; BELMONT, AUGUST; BERGSON, ABRAM; BISCHOFFSHEIM; BLANK, MAURICE; BLEICHROEDER; BLUM, JULIUS; BONN, MORITZ JULIUS; BORCHARDT, LUCY; BRONFENBRENNER, MARTIN; BRUTZKUS, BORIS DOV; BUNZL; BURNS, ARTHUR FRANK; CASSEL, SIR ERNEST JOSEPH; CASTIGLIONI, CAMILLO; CITROËN, ANDRÉ GUSTAVE; COHEN, ARTHUR; COHEN, RUTH LOUISA; COHN, GUSTAV; COLM, GERHARD; DERNBURG; DEVONS, ELY; DORFMAN, JOSEPH; EICHTHAL-SELIGMANN; EINZIG, PAUL; ERLANGER; EZEKIEL, MORDECAI JOSEPH BRILL; FABRICANT, SOLOMON;

FEIS, HERBERT; FELLNER, WILLIAM JOHN; FERKAUF, EUGENE; FRIEDMAN, MILTON; FUERSTENBERG, CARL; GILBERT, MILTON; GOLDENWEISER, EMANUEL ALEXANDROVICH; GOLDSCHMIDT, JAKOB; GOLDSMITH, RAYMOND WILLIAM; GRANT, BARON ALBERT; GREENSPAN, ALAN; GREGORY, SIR THEODORE; GRUENBAUM, HENRY; GUTMANN, EUGEN; HABER; HAHN, ALBERT L.; HALLGARTEN; HEILPERIN, MICHAEL ANGELO; HEINE, SOLOMON; HIMMELSTEIN, LENA; HIRSCHMAN, ALBERT OTTO; HIRSHHORN, JOSEPH HERMAN; HOSELITZ, BERTHOLD FRANK; JASNY, NAUM; JOEL, OTTO J.; KAHN, OTTO HERMANN; KALDOR, NICHOLAS, BARON; KALECKI, MICHAL; KASKEL; KAULLA; KISCH; KOENIGSWARTER; LADEJINSKY, WOLF ISAAC; LÁNCZY, LEÓ; LERNER, ABBA PETACHJA; LINOWITZ, SOL MYRON; LORIA, ACHILLE; LOWE, ADOLPH; LUBIN, ISADOR; MACHLUP, FRITZ; MARGET, ARTHUR W.; MARSCHAK, JACOB; MELCHIOR, CARL; MICHAEL, JAKOB; MIRÈS, JULES ISAAC; MISES, LUDWIG EDLER VON; MORAWITZ, KARL RITTER VON; MORGENSTERN, OSKAR; NADLER, MARCUS; NATHAN, ROBERT ROY; NEISSER, HANS PHILIPP; OHRBACH; OPPENHEIMER, FRANZ; OSTROLENK, BERNHARD; PÉREIRE, ÉMILE and ISAAC; PERLMAN, ALFRED EDWARD; PERLMAN, JACOB; PINNER, FELIX; POLÁNYI, KARL; POSTAN, MICHAEL MOISSEY; PRIBRAM, KARL; RAFFALOVICH, ARTHUR GERMANOVICH; RAISMAN, SIR JEREMY; RICARDO, DAVID; RICH; RIESSER, JACOB; RIKLIS, MESHULAM; ROSTOW, WALT WHITMAN; RUEFF, JACQUES; SAMUEL, RALPH E.; SAMUELSON, PAUL ANTHONY; SCHAEFFER, HANS; SCHLESINGER, KARL; SELIGMAN; SELIGMAN, EDWIN ROBERT ANDERSON; SHARFMAN, ISAIAH LEO; SIMON, NORTON; SOMARY, FELIX; STEIN, HERBERT; STERN, SIR FREDERICK CLAUDE; STIEGLITZ; STROUSBERG, BETHEL HENRY; SUAREZ; SWOPE, GERARD; TAUSSIG, FRANK WILLIAM; URI, PIERRE EMMANUEL; VARGA, YEVGENI SAMOILOVICH; VINER, JACOB; WERTHEIM, MAURICE; WORMSER, OLIVIER BORIS; ZILKHA

Avraham Ronen, Dott. in lett.; Senior Lecturer in the History of Art, Tel Aviv University: WADI AL-NAṬṬŪF

Dan Ronen*, Ph.D.; Director, Division of Culture and Arts Ministry of Education and Culture, Jerusalem: ISRAEL, STATE OF: CULTURAL LIFE, MUSIC, FOLK DANCE

Omri Ronen, Ph.D., Senior Lecturer, Russian and Comparative Literature, Hebrew University, Jerusalem: ALIGER, MARGARITA YOSIFOVNA; BRIK, OSIP MAKSIMOVICH; EICHENBAUM, BORIS MIKHAILOVICH; LIVSHITS, BENEDIKT KONSTANTINOVICH; MANDELSHTAM, OSIP EMILYEVICH; PARNAKH, VALENTIN YAKOVLEVICH; ZHIRMUNSKY, VIKTOR MAKSIMOVICH

Meir Ronnen, B.F.A.; Journalist, Jerusalem

Michael N. Rony*, M.A.; Ph.D. Student, Ben-Gurion University of the Negev, Beersheva: ARAMA, ISAAC BEN MOSES

Emanuel Rose, D.H.L., Rabbi; Portland, Oregon

Or N. Rose*, Ph.D., Rabbi; Associate Dean, The Rabbinical School of Hebrew College, Hebrew College, Boston: GREEN, ARTHUR

Kenneth D. Roseman, Ph.D., Rabbi; Assistant Professor of American Jewish History, the Hebrew Union College-Jewish Institute of Religion, Cincinnati, Ohio: FREIBERG; GOLDSMITH, SAMUEL ABRAHAM; GREENSTEIN, HARRY; SHRODER, WILLIAM J.

Mark Roseman*, Ph.D.; Pat M. Glazer Chair in Jewish Studies, Indiana University: WANNSEE CONFERENCE

Gladys Rosen, Ph.D.; Historical Researcher, New York: DAVIS, MOSHE; EPSTEIN, JUDITH; FREUND-ROSENTHAL, MIRIAM KOTTLER; FRIEDENWALD; HALPRIN, ROSE LURIA; LINDHEIM, IRMA LEVY; MEYER, BARON DE HIRSCH; NAROT, JOSEPH; ROSENSOHN, ETTA LASKER; SATINSKY, SOL; SCHENK, FAYE L.; SELIGSBERG, ALICE LILLIE; STEINBACH, ALEXANDER ALAN; SZOLD, BENJAMIN; TUSKA, SIMON

Janice Rosen*, M.A.; Archives Director, Canadian Jewish Congress, Montreal, Quebec: ROME, DAVID

Moshe Rosen, Jerusalem: ALI IBN SAHL IBN RABBĀN AL-ṬABARĪ

Pinchas Rosen, Former Minister of Justice, Jerusalem: INDEPENDENT LIBERAL PARTY

Michael Rosenak, Ph.D.; Former Director, Melton Center for Jewish Education in the Diaspora, Mandel Associate Professor for Jewish Education, the Hebrew University of Jerusalem

Helen Rosenau, Dr. Phil.; Art Historian, London: ABRAHAM; ADAM; ECCLESIA ET SYNAGOGA; JONAH, BOOK OF

Miriam Rosen-Ayalon, Ph.D.; Associate Professor in Islamic Art and Archaeology; Head of the Department of Islamic Civilization, the Hebrew University of Jerusalem: ETTINGHAUSEN, RICHARD

Fred S. Rosenbaum*, M.A.; History, Founding Director, Lehrhaus Judaica, Berkeley, California: ASHER, JOSEPH; COHN, ELKAN; ECKMAN, JULIUS; MAGNES MUSEUM, JUDAH L.; ROSENMANN-TAUB, DAVID; SAN FRANCISCO BAY AREA

Irving J. Rosenbaum, Rabbi; former President, Hebrew Theological College, Chicago; Davka Corp.

Jonathan Rosenbaum*, Ph.D.; President and Professor of Religion, Gratz College, Melrose Park, Pennsylvania: GRATZ COLLEGE; GRODZINSKY, ZVI HIRSCH

Dan (Daniel) S. Rosenberg*, B.A., M.A., Ph.D.; Rabbi; New York University: FOUNDATIONS

Jennifer Rosenberg*, M.A., M.S.W.; Director of Research, UJA-Federation of New York: NEW YORK CITY

Louis Rosenberg, B.A., B.S.; Research Director, the Canadian Jewish Congress, Montreal, Canada

Pnina Rosenberg*, Ph.D.; Art Curator, Lecturer, Art Historian, specializing in the art of the Holocaust, Ghetto Fighters' House Museum, Tivon, Israel: ART: IN CONCENTRATION CAMPS AND GHETTOES

Shalom Rosenberg, M.A.; Jerusalem

Stephen G. (Gabriel) Rosenberg*, Ph.D., FRIBA; Fellow of Albright Institute of Archaeological Research, Jerusalem, and Honorary Secretary of Anglo-Israel Archaeological Society, London: ONIAS, TEMPLE OF; TOBIADS

Stuart E. Rosenberg, Ph.D., Rabbi; Writer, Toronto: GENIZAH, CAIRO; LAWYERS; POLITICS

Samuel Rosenblatt, Ph.D., Rabbi; Associate Professor of Oriental Languages, Johns Hopkins University, Baltimore: FANO, MENAHEM AZARIAH DA; FREUDEMANN, SIMḤAH; FREUND, SAMUEL BEN ISSACHAR BAER; GALANTE; HAKDAMAH; INCLINATION, GOOD AND EVIL; OLAM HA-BA; PLUTARCH

Alvin H. Rosenfeld*, Ph.D.; Professor of English and Jewish Studies, Director of Institute for Jewish Culture and the Arts, Indiana University: FRANK, ANNE

Gavriel (D.) Rosenfeld*, Ph.D.; Associate Professor, Fairfield, University, Connecticut: FRIEDLAENDER, SAUL

Harry L. Rosenfeld, M.A., Rabbi; rabbi of Congregation Beth Sholom, Anchorage, Alaska

Geraldine Rosenfield, M.A.; the American Jewish Committee, New York: SLAWSON,JOHN

Ariella M. Rosengard*, M.D.: MIROWSKI, MICHEL

Dale Rosengarten*, Ph.D.; Curator and Historian, College of Charleston, South Carolina: SOUTH CAROLINA

Anny Dayan Rosenman*, Ph.D.; Maitre de conférence; Université Paris7 – Denis Diderot. Département de Lettres; Paris, France: JABES, EDMOND; MODIANO, PATRICK

Shabtai Rosenne, Ph.D.; Ambassador, Ministry for Foreign Affairs, Jerusalem: ARMISTICE AGREEMENTS, ISRAEL-ARAB; GROTIUS, HUGO

Menachem (Z.) Rosensaft*, B.A. M.A., J.D.; Attorney, New York: BERGEN-BELSEN

Joseph G. Rosenstein*, Ph.D.; Professor of Mathematics, Rutgers University, Highland Park, New Jersey: NATIONAL HAVURAH COMMITTEE

Morton Rosenstock, Ph.D.; Professor of Social Studies and Librarian, Bronx Community College of the City University of New York: BACKER, GEORGE; BIJUR, NATHAN; BLAUSTEIN; BLOOMINGDALE; BUTTENWIESER; COWEN, PHILIP; CUTLER, HARRY; DEUTSCH, BERNARD SEYMOUR; DITTENHOEFER, ABRAM JESSE; EISNER, MARK; FLEXNER; GUGGENHEIM; HAY, JOHN MILTON; JONAS, NATHAN S.; KRAUS, ADOLF; LEWISOHN; MACK, JULIAN WILLIAM; MARSHALL, LOUIS; MORGENTHAU; ROSENWALD; SAPIRO, AARON; SCHIFF, JACOB HENRY; UNTERMYER, SAMUEL; WARBURG

Erich Rosenthal, Ph.D.; Professor of Sociology, Queens College of the City University of New York: CHICAGO; MIXED MARRIAGE, INTERMARRIAGE

Esther Rosenthal (Schneiderman), Cand. Pedag. Sci.; Jerusalem: CHATZKELS, HELENE

Irving Rosenthal, M.A.; Associate Professor of Journalism, City College of the City University of New York: ADLER, JULIUS OCHS; ANNENBERG, WALTER H.; CARTOONISTS; FORMIGGINI, ANGELO FORTUNATO; KROCK, ARTHUR; LANDAU, JACOB; LAWRENCE, DAVID; LICHTHEIM, RICHARD; LIPPMANN, WALTER; MEYER, EUGENE; NEWHOUSE, SAMUEL IRVING; OCHS; PULITZER, JOSEPH; REUTER, PAUL JULIUS, FREIHERR VON; RICHARDS, BERNARD GERSON; SOUTHWOOD, JULIUS SALTER ELIAS, FIRST VISCOUNT; SULZBERGER, ARTHUR HAYS; SWOPE, HERBERT BAYARD

Judah M. Rosenthal, Ph.D., Rabbi; Former Professor of Biblical Exegesis, the College of Jewish Studies, Chicago; Jerusalem: ABULRABI, AARON; DONIN, NICHOLAS; ḤIWI AL-BALKHI; MESHWI AL-'UKBARĪ; NUSSBAUM, HILARY; OFFICIAL, NATHAN BEN JOSEPH and JOSEPH; PORCHETUS SALVAGUS; PRISCUS; WAGENSEIL, JOHANN CHRISTOPH; YUDGHAN

Moshe Rosetti, Former Clerk of the Knesset, Tel Aviv: BASSIN, MOSES; BEVIN, ERNEST; BLUM, LÉON; CLORE, SIR CHARLES; COHEN, ARTHUR; DEUTSCHER, ISAAC; LASKI, HAROLD JOSEPH; MARSHALL, DAVID SAUL; MEINERTZHAGEN, RICHARD HENRY; MENDES-FRANCE, PIERRE; MOCH, JULES SALVADOR; MOND; WORLD LABOR ZIONIST MOVEMENT; ZEIT, DIE

Gerald Rosin, Central African Jewish Board of Deputies, Harare, Zimbabwe: SLAWSON, JOHN

Fred Rosner, M.D.; Instructor in Medicine, Downstate Medical Center, Brooklyn, New York: ANGRIST, ALFRED ALVIN; BENDER, MORRIS BORIS; DAVIDOFF, LEO MAX; DRESSLER, WILLIAM; FISHBEIN, MORRIS; GARLOCK, JOHN HENRY; GROSSMAN, MORTON IRVIN; GUTMAN, ALEXANDER B.; GUTTMACHER, ALAN F.; HELPERN, MILTON; KAGAN, SOLOMON ROBERT; KLEMPERER, PAUL; LEDERBERG, JOSHUA; LEVINE, PHILIP; TRANSPLANTS

Menahem Rosner, Ph.D.; Professor, Department of Sociology and Anthropology, Haifa University: KIBBUTZ MOVEMENT

Jacob Joshua Ross, Ph.D., Rabbi; Senior Lecturer in Philosophy, Tel Aviv University: FREIMANN, JACOB; REVELATION

Daniel Rossing, M.T.S.; Director, Melitz Center for Christian Encounter with Israel, Jerusalem: ISRAEL, STATE OF: RELIGIOUS LIFE AND COMMUNITIES

Ruth Rossing*, B.A.; Secretary, Translator, Center for the Study of Emerging Diseases, Jerusalem: AHARONOV, YAKIR; BERG, PAUL; BERNSTEIN, HAROLD JOSEPH; BERNSTEIN, JOSEPH; BLOCH, HERMAN SAMUEL; BLOCH, KONRAD; BLUMBERG, BARUCH SAMUEL; BODIAN, DAVID; BOGORAD, LAWRENCE; BOROWITZ, SIDNEY; BROWN, HAROLD; BROWN, HERBERT C.; CALVIN, MELVIN; CHARPAK, GEORGES; DISCHE, ZACHARIAS; DROSDOFF, MATTHEW; EDINGER, LUDWIG; ERLIK, DAVID; FREUDENTHAL, ALFRED MARTIN; FROHLICH, HERBERT; HALEVY, ABRAHAM H.; RAZIN, AHARON; WAHL, ISAAK

Murray Roston, Ph.D.; Professor of English, Bar-Ilan University, Ramat Gan: DAICHES, DAVID; LOWTH, ROBERT

Cvi Rotem, Ph.D.; Journalist, Tel Aviv: GOTTLIEB, HINKO; ROMANO, SAMUEL; YUGOSLAV LITERATURE; YUGOSLAVIA; ZIONISM

Nathan Rotenstreich, Ph.D.; Professor of Philosophy and Former Rector, the Hebrew University of Jerusalem: BERGMAN, SAMUEL HUGO; POZNAŃSKI, EDWARD

Alvin S. Roth, Ph.D., Rabbi; Albany, New York

Cecil Roth, D.Phil., F.R.Hist. Soc.; Reader Emeritus in Jewish Studies, the University of Oxford; Editor in Chief of the *Encyclopaedia Judaica* (1st ed.), Jerusalem: AARON OF LINCOLN; AARON OF YORK; ABBA; ABENAES, SOLOMON; ABENATAR MELO, DAVID; ABENDANA; ABENDANA, ISAAC; ABERDEEN; ABOAB; ABOAB DA FONSECA, ISAAC; ABOAB, IMMANUEL; ABOAB, ISAAC DE MATTATHIAS; ABRABANEL, ABRAVANEL; ABRAHAM BEN SHABBETAI HA-KOHEN; ABRAHAM OF BEJA; ABRAHAMS; ABRAHAMS, ISRAEL; ABRAHAMS, SIR LIONEL; ABSALOM; ABULAFIA; ABULAFIA, EZEKIEL DAVID BEN MORDECAI; ACOSTA, ISAAC; ADLER; ADLER, ELKAN NATHAN; ADLER, HERMANN; ADLER, MICHAEL; ADLER, NATHAN MARCUS; ADOLPHUS; AFFONSO; AFRICA; AGRIGENTO; AGUILAR, GRACE; AGUILAR, MOSES RAPHAEL D'; ALATINO; ALATRINI; ALATRINI, ANGELO; ALESSANDRIA; ALEXANDER; ALEXANDER, MICHAEL SOLOMON; ALFONSO OF ZAMORA; ALMANSI; ALMOSNINO; ALVARES; ANGLO-JEWISH ASSOCIATION; ANTHROPOMORPHISM; ANTONIO; ANTUÑES; ARBIB; ARCHA; ARCHPRESBYTER; AREZZO; ART; ASSUMPÇÃO, DIOGO DA; ATIAS; AUTO DA FÉ; AZEVEDO, MOSES COHEN D'; BAPTISM, FORCED; BARGAS, ABRAHAM DE; BAROU, NOAH; BARRASSA, JACOB; BARROS BASTO, ARTURO CARLOS DE; BARTOLOCCI, GIULIO; BASOLA, MOSES BEN MORDECAI; BASSANI, MORDECAI; BASSANO; BATH; BÉDARRIDES; BEDFORD; BEJA; BELFAST; BELMONTE; BENJAMIN NEHEMIAH BEN ELNATHAN; BENJAMIN OF CAMBRIDGE; BENJAMIN OF TUDELA; BENTWICH; BENVENISTE, ISAAC BEN JOSEPH; BENVENISTE, MOSES; BERNARDINO DA FELTRE; BODLEIAN LIBRARY; BODO; BONJORN, BONET DAVI; BOOK TRADE; BOOKS; BRADFORD; BRAGANZA; BRAHAM, JOHN; BRAMPTON, SIR EDWARD; BRIGHTON; BRISTOL; BROTHERS, RICHARD; BROWNING, ROBERT; BRUDO, MANUEL; BURY ST. EDMUNDS; BUZAGLO; CACERES, SIMON DE; CALLIGRAPHY AND WRITING MASTERS; CAMBRIDGE; CANTERBURY; CAPSALI, ELIJAH; CARDIFF; CARDOZO, AARON NUÑEZ; CARICATURES; CARRASCON, JUAN; CARVAJAL, ABRAHAM ISRAEL; CASSUTO, UMBERTO; CASTRO, DE; CASTRO, JACOB DE; CASTRO, PEDRO DE; CASTRO; CASTRO SARMENTO, JACOB DE; CASTRO TARTAS, DAVID DE; CASTRO TARTAS, ISAAC DE; CEREMONIAL OBJECTS; CHANNEL ISLANDS; CHAPBOOKS; CHATHAM; COLCHESTER; COLUMBUS, CHRISTOPHER; CÓRDOBA, ALONSO FERNANDEZ DE; CORONEL CHACON, SIR AUGUSTIN; CORSICA; COSTA; COSTA, EMANUEL MENDES DA; COSTA ATHIAS, SOLOMON DA; CROMWELL, OLIVER; CROOL, JOSEPH; DAVIN DE CADEROUSSE; DOMUS CONVERSORUM; DORMIDO, DAVID ABRABANEL; DUBLIN; DUSCHINSKY, CHARLES; EDINBURGH; ELIANO, GIOVANNI BATTISTA; ELIAS LE EVESKE; ELIJAH MENAHEM BEN MOSES; EMERY, RICHARD WILDER; ENGLAND; EPITAPHS; ESCUDERO, LORENZO; ESTEVENS, DAVID; EUROPE; EXETER; EZEKIEL, ABRAHAM EZEKIEL; FALK, SAMUEL JACOB ḤAYYIM; FARIA, FRANCISCO DE; FERDINAND, PHILIP; FINCH, SIR HENRY; FORGERIES; FRANCIA, FRANCIS; FRANCO; FRANKS; FRIEDENBERG, SAMUEL; GABBAI IZIDRO, BRAHAM; GAMALIEL BEN PEDAHZUR; GASTER, MOSES; GAUNSE, JOACHIM; GEWITSCH, AARON WOLF; GHIRONDI, MORDECAI SAMUEL BEN BENZION ARYEH; GIBRALTAR; GIDEON, SAMSON; GIOVANNI MARIA; GLOUCESTER; GOLDSMID; GOLDSMID, ALBERT EDWARD WILLIAMSON; GOLDSMITH, LEWIS; GOLLANCZ, SIR HERMANN; GOMPERTZ; GOODMAN, TOBIAS; GORDON, GEORGE, LORD; GREGORY; GUGLIELMO DA PESARO; HAGGADAH, PASSOVER; HART; HART, JACOB; HEREFORD; HERTZ, JOSEPH HERMAN; HIRSCHEL, SOLOMON; HISTORIOGRAPHY; HISTORY: DIASPORA – SECOND TEMPLE PERIOD; HOMEM, ANTONIO; HOST, DESECRATION OF; HUGH OF LINCOLN; HULL; HYAMSON, ALBERT MONTEFIORE; IBN ḤAYYIM, ABRAHAM BEN JUDAH; IBN ḤAYYIM, JOSEPH; IBN YAḤYA, GEDALIAH BEN TAM; INQUISITION; IPSWICH; ITINERARIES OF EREẒ ISRAEL; JACOB BEN JUDAH OF LONDON; JACOBS, JOSEPH; JACOBS, LAZARUS; JESSEY, HENRY; JESUITS; JEWISH CHRONICLE; JEWISH HISTORICAL SOCIETY OF ENGLAND; JOHN THE ESSENE; JUDAIZERS; JURNET OF NORWICH; KAYSERLING, MEYER; KIERA; KING'S LYNN; LAGUNA, DANIEL ISRAEL LOPEZ; LAMEGO; LEE, SIR SIDNEY; LEEDS; LEICESTER; LEIRIA; LEONI, MYER; LEVY, BENJAMIN; LIMERICK; LINCOLN; LINDO; LISBON; LOEWE, HERBERT MARTIN JAMES; LONDON; LOPES; LOPEZ ROSA; LOPEZ, RODERIGO; LUZZATTO, SIMONE BEN ISAAC SIMḤAH; LYONS, ISRAEL; MALTA; MANASSEH BEN ISRAEL; MELDOLA; MENDES, DIOGO; MINHAGIM BOOKS; MODENA, AVTALYON; NASI, GRACIA; NASI, JOSEPH; NATHAN, ABRAHAM; NIETO, ISAAC; NIGER OF PEREA; NORTHAMPTON; NUNES VAIS; ORIA; OXFORD; PACIFICI, ALFONSO; PARKES, JAMES WILLIAM; PASSI, DAVID; PENZANCE; PEREZ BAYER, FRANCISCO; POPES; PORTRAITS OF JEWS; PRINTERS' MARKS; RABINOWICZ, OSKAR K.; RAPHAEL, ALEXANDER; RIBEIRO SANCHEZ, ANTONIO; RIEGER, PAUL; ROBLES, ANTONIO RODRIGUES; ROCHESTER; RODRIGUES, DIONISIUS; ROME; ROSSENA, DANIEL BEN SAMUEL OF; RUBENS, ALFRED; SAMUEL, WILFRED SAMPSON; SCHOMBERG; SCULPTURE; SEPHARDIM; SERMONS TO JEWS; SERVI CAMERAE REGIS; SILVA, JOSHUA DA; ŠINKO, ERVIN; SIPRUTINI, EMANUEL; STAMFORD; SUMBAL, SAMUEL; TAXATION; TEMPLO, JACOB JUDAH LEON; TOLAND, JOHN; TRASKE, JOHN; TREBITSCH, MOSES LOEB BEN WOLF; URBINO; VAEZ, ABRAHAM; VAN OVEN; WARWICK; WINCHESTER; WOLF, LUCIEN; XIMENES, SIR MORRIS; YOM TOV OF JOIGNY; YORK

Ernst Roth, Ph.D., Rabbi; Chief Rabbi of the State of Hesse, Frankfurt on the Main: AACHEN

Lea Roth, M.A.; Jerusalem: ABBA SIKRA; ALBINUS, LUCCEIUS; ANAN BEN SETH; ANAN, SON OF ANAN; AVTINAS; AZIZ; CAESAREA IN CAPPADOCIA; CAIAPHAS, JOSEPH; CAPPADOCIA; CESTIUS GALLUS; CHAEREMON; CLAUDIUS; CLEOPATRA; COPONIUS; CORINTH; CUMANUS VENTIDIUS; CYPROS; CYPRUS; ELEAZAR BEN ANANIAS; ELEAZAR BEN DINAI; EMESA; FADUS, CUSPIUS; FELIX, ANTONIUS; FESTUS, PORCIUS; FLACCUS, AVILLIUS AULUS; GALATIA; GESSIUS FLORUS; HEZIR; HIERAPOLIS; ISHMAEL BEN PHIABI II; JOEZER, SON OF BOETHUS; JOHN OF GISCALA; JONATHAN THE HASMONEAN; JOSEPH; JULIUS SEVERUS; LYDIA, LYDIANS; MENAHEM SON OF JUDAH; PAPPUS AND JULIANUS; PETRONIUS, PUBLIUS; PONTIUS PILATE; POPPAEA, SABINA; PTOLEMY; SABINUS; SILVA, FLAVIUS; SIMEON BEN BOETHUS; TINNEIUS RUFUS; TITUS, FLAVIUS VESPASIANUS

Leon Roth, D.Phil, F.B.A.; Former Rector and Professor of Philosophy, the Hebrew University of Jerusalem: ALEXANDER, SAMUEL

Sol Roth, Ph.D., Rabbi; Lecturer in

Philosophy, Yeshiva University, New York: SLANDER

Sylvia Rothchild, Writer, Brookline, Massachusetts: GOLD, HERBERT

Beno Rothenberg, Ph.D.; Senior Lecturer in Archaeology, Tel Aviv University: EZION-GEBER; TIMNA

Livia Rothkirchen, Ph.D.; Historian, Jerusalem: CZECHOSLOVAKIA; FLEISCHMANN, GISI; FRIEDER, ARMIN; REIK, ḤAVIVAH; SLOVAKIA; SZENES, HANNAH; TISO, JOSEF; TUKA, VOJTECH; VAŠEK, ANTON; WALLENBERG, RAOUL; WEISSMANDEL, MICHAEL DOV

Aaron Rothkoff*, B.A., M.A., M.H.C., D.H.L., Rabbi; Professor of Responsa Literature, Yeshiva University - Gruss Kollel, Jerusalem: ALPHABET, HEBREW, IN MIDRASH, TALMUD, AND KABBALAH; BAT KOL; BERLIN, ḤAYYIM; BET-MIDRASH; DECALOGUE; FINZI-NORSA CONTROVERSY; GOLDEN CALF; GRAJEWSKI, ELIEZER ZALMAN; HAM; HULDAH; ISAAC; JEREMIAH; JETHRO; JUDAH; KALMANOWITZ, ABRAHAM; KEFAR ḤABAD; KIDDUSH; KORAH; KOZIENICE, ISRAEL BEN SHABBETAI HAPSTEIN; MICHAEL AND GABRIEL; MINḤAH; MINOR TRACTATES; MIRIAM; MITZVAH; MOSES; MOURNING; MUSAF; NADAB; NAZIRITE; NEHEMIAH; NEW MOON; PARENTS, HONOR OF; POLACHEK, SOLOMON; PROFANITY; PROSBUL; PUBERTY; RABBAH TOSFA'AH; RACHEL; RACKMAN, EMANUEL; RASHI; RUDERMAN, JACOB ISAAC; RUTH, BOOK OF; SABBATICAL YEAR AND JUBILEE; SACRIFICE; SAMBATYON; SAMSON; SAMUEL; SARAH; SEFER TORAH; SEMIKHAH; SHA'ATNEZ; SHATZKES, MOSES; SHIR HA-YIḤUD; SICK, VISITING THE; SILVER, ELIEZER; SIMḤAT TORAH; SLOBODKA YESHIVAH; SODOM AND GOMORRAH; SOLOMON; SOLOVEICHIK, AARON; SOLOVEITCHIK, JOSEPH BAER; TABERNACLE; TERAH; TITUS, FLAVIUS VESPASIANUS; TOHOROT; TOKHEḤAH; WALKIN, AARON; WIEDENFELD, DOV; WILLOWSKI, JACOB DAVID BEN ZE'EV; YIGDAL; ZADDIK; ZEDEKIAH; ZERUBBABEL; ẒUR MI-SHELLO

Fritz A. Rothschild, D.H.L., Rabbi; Associate Professor of the Philosophy of Religion, the Jewish Theological Seminary of America, New York: HESCHEL, ABRAHAM JOSHUA

Jacob Rothschild, Dr.Phil.; Director of the Graduate Library School, the Hebrew University of Jerusalem: JACOB, BENNO; JACOBSON, ISRAEL; JASTROW; JELLINEK, HERMANN; JOSEPH BEN GERSHON OF ROSHEIM; LEHMANN, MARCUS; LEIPZIG; LESZNO; LEVI, DAVID; LEWY, ISRAEL; LOEWE, HEINRICH; LUEBECK; LURIA; POPPERS, JACOB BEN BENJAMIN HAKOHEN; SALFELD, SIEGMUND; SELIGMANN, CAESAR

Janice Rothschild Blumberg*, B.F.A.; Author, Historian, Independent Scholar, Washington, D.C.: BROWNE, EDWARD B. M.

Jean-Pierre Rothschild*, H.D.R.; Directeur de recherches au C.N.R.S./ Directeur de études à l'Ecole pratique des hautes etudes, Paris, France: REVUE DES ÉTUDES JUIVES; SÉMINAIRE ISRAÉLITE DE FRANCE; SOCIÉTÉ DES ÉTUDES JUIVES; TOUATI, CHARLES; VAJDA, GEORGES

Raphael Rothstein, B.A.; Journalist, New York: BRUSTEIN, ROBERT SANFORD; CANTOR, EDDIE; CLURMAN, HAROLD; MOSTEL, ZERO; SHUBERT; STRASBERG, LEE

Gali Rotstein*: AXELROD, JULIUS; COHEN, MORRIS; HARARI, OVADIAH; HEEGER, ALAN; JUDA, WALTER; MANDELBROT, BENOIT; TOBIAS, PHILLIP VALLENTINE

Yechezkel Rottenberg, M.Jur.; Assistant in Jewish Law, the Hebrew University of Jerusalem: UNJUST ENRICHMENT

Max Jonah Routtenberg, D.H.L., Rabbi; Visiting Professor of Homiletics, the Jewish Theological Seminary of America, New York: SIRKES, JOEL

Robert Rovinsky, Ph.D.; Assistant Professor of Germanic Languages, University of Texas, Austin: COHN, CILLA CYPORA

Marc Rozelaar, Dr.Phil.; Associate Professor of Classical Studies, Tel Aviv University: GOLDMARK, KARL

Marsha L. Rozenblit*, B.A., M.A., Ph.D.; Harvey M. Meyerhoff Professor Jewish History, University of Maryland: HIMMELFARB, GERTRUDE; HISTORIANS; HYMAN, PAULA E.; LEVIN, NORA

Robert Rozette, Researcher and Writer, Jerusalem: BARBIE, NIKOLAUS, TRIAL OF; GRAEBE, HERMANN FRIEDRICH; HIRSCHMANN, IRA ARTHUR; KORCZAK-MARLA, ROZKA; LUTZ, CARL; PLOTNICKA, FRUMKA; WDOWINSKI, DAVID

Alfred Rubens, F.S.A., F.R.Hist. Soc.; Historian of Jewish Art and Costume, London: DRESS; HERALDRY

Betty R. (Rogers) Rubenstein*, Ph.D.; Research Fellow, University of Bridgeport, Connecticut: AGREST, DIANA; ALSCHULER, ALFRED S.; BREUER, MARCEL; BUNSHAFT, GORDON; EIZENBERG, JULIE; FREED, JAMES INGO; GANDELSONAS. MARIO; GEHRY, FRANK OWEN; GORLIN, ALEXANDER; LAPIDUS, MORRIS; LERNER, RALPH; LIBESKIND, DANIEL; SAITOWITZ, STANLEY; SCHWARTZ, FREDERIC; SORKIN, MICHAEL

Harry Rubenstein*: REED, LOU; YARROW, PETER

Joshua Rubenstein*, Northeast Regional Director of Amnesty International and Associate Professor of the Davis Center for Russian and Eurasian Studies, Harvard University: BONNER, ELENA GEORGIEVNA

Richard L. Rubenstein, Ph.D., Rabbi; Professor of Religion, Florida State University, Tallahassee

Adam Rubin*, Ph.D.; Assistant Professor, Hebrew Union College, Los Angeles

Jay L. Rubin*, B.A., M.A.; Executive Vice President, Hillel International, Washington, D.C.: HILLEL; JOEL, RICHARD M.

Lawrence Rubin*, Executive Vice Chairman (retired), Jewish Council for Public Affairs, New York: AMERICAN ISRAEL PUBLIC AFFAIRS COMMITTEE

Uri Rubin*, Ph.D.; Professor of Arabic and Islamic Studies, Tel Aviv University: KORAN

Daniel Benito Rubinstein Novick, National University of Buenos Aires: MENDOZA; SANTA FE

Avraham Rubinstein, Ph.D.; Senior Lecturer in Jewish History, Bar-Ilan

University, Ramat Gan: ABRAHAM JOSHUA HESCHEL OF APTA; ARYEH LEIB SARAHS; CHABAD; DAVID OF TALNA; ḤASIDISM; ḤAYYIM BEN SOLOMON TYRER OF CZERNOWITZ; HOROWITZ, SAMUEL SHMELKE OF NIKOLSBURG; ISRAEL BEN ELIEZER BA'AL SHEM TOV; JACOB ISAAC HA-ḤOZEH MI-LUBLIN; JACOB JOSEPH OF OSTROG; KAZIMIERZ; LEVI ISAAC BEN MEIR OF BERDICHEV; LEVIN, MENAHEM MENDEL; LVOV; MAḤZIKE HADAS; MENAHEM MENDEL OF PEREMYSHLANY; MODZHITZ; RADZYMIN; TEITELBAUM; TWERSKY; WARSAW

Daniel Rubinstein, B.A.; Journalist, Jerusalem: ISRAEL, STATE OF: ARAB POPULATION

Judah Rubinstein, M.A.; Research Associate, Jewish Community Federation of Cleveland: BAKER, EDWARD MAX; BENESCH, ALFRED ABRAHAM; SHAPIRO, EZRA Z.

William D. (David) Rubinstein*, B.A., Ph.D., Professor of History, University of Wales-Aberystwyth, England: ABRAHAMS, GERALD; ABRAHAMS, SIR LIONEL; ABSE, DANNIE; ADELAIDE; ALDERMAN, GEOFFREY; ALIENS ACT; ALVAREZ, ALFRED; AMERY, LEOPOLD CHARLES MAURICE STENNETT; APPLE, RAYMOND; ASHKANASY, MAURICE; ASSIMILATION; AUSTRALIA; BALOGH, THOMAS, BARON; BARNETT, JOEL, BARON; BARON, JOSEPH ALEXANDER; BART, LIONEL; BATTLE OF CABLE STREET; BBAUME, PETER; BELL, SIR FRANCIS HENRY DILLON; BELOFF, MAX; BERMANT, CHAIM ICYK; BLAUBAUM, ELIAS; BLOOM, CLAIRE; BOAS, ABRAHAM TOBIAS; BOAS, FREDERICK SAMUEL; BOGDANOR, VERNON; BOTEACH, SHMUEL; BRÉVAL, LUCIENNE; BRIGHTON; BRITTAN, LEON BARON; BRODIE, SIR ISRAEL; BROOK, PETER STEPHEN PAUL; CARO, SIR ANTHONY; CASS, MOSES HENRY; CASSAB, JUDY; CENTRAL BRITISH FUND; CESERANI, DAVID; COHEN, BARRY; COHEN, HAROLD; COHN, NORMAN; COHN-SHERBOK, DAN; COTTON, JACK; COWEN, ZELMAN; CURRIE, EDWINA; DANBY, MICHAEL; DANGLOW, JACOB; DAVIS, HENRY DAVID; DAVIS, SIR ERNEST HYAM; DELL, EDMUND; DEUTSCH, ANDRE; DISRAELI, BENJAMIN, EARL OF BEACONSFIELD; D'ISRAELI, ISAAC; DUVEEN; EDELMAN, MAURICE; EDEN, SIR ANTHONY, EARL OF AVON; EINFELD, SYDNEY; ELIAS, NORBERT; ELKAN, BENNO; ELKIN, ADOLPHUS PETER; ELLMANN, RICHARD; ELTON, SIR GEOFFREY RUDOLPH; EPSTEIN, BRIAN; FELDMAN, MARTIN; FINESTEIN, ISRAEL; FINK, THEODORE; FINLEY, SIR MOSES; FISHMAN, WILLIAM; FOX, EMANUEL PHILIPS; FRANKAU; GARTNER, LLOYD P.; GAUNSE, JOACHIM; GERSHON, KAREN; GIDEON, SAMSON; GINGOLD, HERMIONE; GOLDHAR, PINCHAS; GOLDSMID-STERN-SALOMONS, SIR DAVID LIONEL; GOLOMBEK, HARRY; GOMBRICH, SIR ERNST HANS; GOODMAN, ARNOLD ABRAHAM, LORD; GOODMAN, MARTIN DAVID; GRADE, LEW, BARON; GRANT, BARON ALBERT; GREEN, PHILIP; GRONER, DOVID YITZCHOK; GROSS, JOHN JACOB; GUNSBERG, ISIDOR; GUTNICK; HAHN, KURT; HAMBURGER, MICHAEL; HAMBURGER, SIR SIDNEY; HAMLYN, PAUL, BARON; HARRIS, SIR PERCY ALFRED; HART, HERBERT LIONEL ADOLPHUS; HATRY, CLARENCE CHARLES; HIMMELWEIT, HILDEGARD; HOBSBAWM, ERIC JOHN; HOWARD, MICHAEL; INSTITUTE OF JEWISH AFFAIRS; ISRAEL, JONATHAN; JACKSON, BERNARD S.; JACOB, NAOMI ELLINGTON; JACOBSON, NATHAN; JAMES, SIDNEY; JANNER, BARNETT, LORD; "JEW BILL" CONTROVERSY, ENGLAND; JEWISH HISTORICAL SOCIETY OF ENGLAND; JOEL, SIR ASHER; JOLOWICZ, HERBERT FELIX; JOURNALISM; KAGAN, JOSEPH, BARON; KALMS, SIR STANLEY, BARON; KATZ, DAVID S.; KATZ, DOVID; KAUFMAN, SIR GERALD; KAYE, SIR EMMANUEL; KISSIN, HARRY, BARON; KOCHAN, LIONEL; KOPELOWITZ, LIONEL; KOSMIN, BARRY; KOSSOFF, DAVID; KUSHNER, TONY; LAKATOS, IMRE; LANDA, ABRAM; LASKI; LAWYERS; LEAVIS, QUEENIE DOROTHY; LEIBLER, ISI JOSEPH; LEITNER, GOTTLIEB WILHEM; LEVENE, SIR PETER, BARON LEVENE OF PORTSOKEN; LEVER, HAROLD, BARON LEVER OF MANCHESTER; LEVI, JOHN SIMON; LEVI, LEONE; LEVIN SMITH, SIR ARCHIBALD; LEVIN, BERNARD; LEVY, AMY; LEVY, BENN WOLFE; LEVY, MICHAEL ABRAHAM, BARON LEVY OF MILL HILL; LEWIS, SAMUEL; LIBERMAN, SERGE; LINCOLN, TREBITSCH; LIPSON, EPHRAIM; LITTMAN, JOSEPH AARON; LOCKSPEISER, SIR BEN; LOWY, FRANK; MACCOBY, HYAM; MAGNUS; MANCHESTER; MANDELSON, PETER; MARRE, SIR ALAN; MAXWELL, ROBERT; MAYER, SIR ROBERT; MELBOURNE; MICHAELIS, SIR ARCHIE; MIESES, JACQUES; MIKARDO, IAN; MILIBAND, RALPH; MILLETT, SIR PETER, BARON; MISHCON, VICTOR, BARON; MOCATTA; MONTAGU; MOONMAN, ERIC; MOSER, SIR CLAUDE, BARON; MOSHINSKY, ELIJAH; NASSAUER, RUDOLF; NEMON, OSCAR; NEWMAN, AUBREY; NICHOLAS, EDWARD; NOVE, ALEC; OPPÉ, ADOLPH PAUL; OPPENHEIM, SALLY, BARONESS OPPENHEIM-BARNES; °SHAKESPEARE, WILLIAM; OXFORD; PACIFICO, DAVID; PARKER, JOHN; PERTH; PHILLIPS, MARION; POLLARD, SIDNEY; PORTER, SIR LESLIE; PRATT, RICHARD; PRAWER, SIEGBERT; PRINGLE, MIA; PROOPS, MARJORIE; PULVERMACHER, OSCAR; PULZER, PETER G.J.; PYE, JAEL HENRIETTA; RABIN, SAM; RACHMAN, PETER; RAJAK, TESSA; RATHBONE, ELEANOR; READING, FANNY; REISZ, KAREL; REITLINGER, GERALD; RENE, ROY; RICARDO, DAVID; RIE, DAME LUCIE; RIFKIND, SIR MALCOLM; RODKER, JOHN; ROMAIN, JONATHAN A.; RUTLAND, SUZANNE; SAATCHI, CHARLES; SACHS, ANDREW; SALOMONS, SIR JULIAN EMANUEL; SAMUDA, JOSEPH D'AGUILAR; SAMUEL, HOWARD; SAMUEL, RAPHAEL; SAMUEL, SIR SAUL; SAMUEL, WILFRED SAMPSON; SAMUELSON, SIR BERNHARD; SASSOON, VIDAL; SAVILLE, VICTOR; SCHAMA, SIMON; SCHAPIRO, LEONARD; SHONFIELD, SIR ANDREW; SHORT, RENEE; SHULMAN, MILTON; SIEFF, ISRAEL MOSES, BARON; SILKIN, LEWIS, FIRST BARON; SINGER, PETER; SLATER, OSCAR; SMORGON; SONNTAG, JACOB; SOSKICE, SIR FRANK, BARON STOW HILL; SOUTHAMPTON; SPEYER, SIR EDGAR; SPIELMAN; SRAFFA, PIERO; STERLING, SIR JEFFREY; STERN; STERNBERG, SIR SIGMUND; STRAUSS, GEORGE RUSSELL, BARON; STUDENTS' MOVEMENTS, JEWISH; SUGAR, SIR ALAN; SUGERMAN, SIR BERNARD; SYDNEY; SYMONDS, SAUL; SYMONS, JULIAN; TASMANIA; TAYLOR, SIR PETER MURRAY; THATCHER, MARGARET, BARONESS; TONNA, CHARLOTTE ELIZABETH; TUCK, RAPHAEL; WAGG; WALSTON, SIR CHARLES; WARBURG, FREDERICK; WARBURG, SIR SIEGMUND; WATEN, JUDAH; WERTHEIMER, ASHER; WILLIAMS, CHARLES; WILSON, HAROLD,; WINSTON, ROBERT, BARON; WISTRICH, ROBERT S.; WOLFENSOHN, JAMES D.; WOLFF, GUSTAV; WOOLF, LEONARD; WOOLF, SIR HARRY, BARON; WYNN, SAMUEL; XIMENES, SIR MORRIS; YARROW, SIR ALFRED, FIRST BARONET; YOUNG, DAVID IVOR, BARON YOUNG OF GRAFFHAM; YUDKIN, JOHN; ZEC, PHILIP; ZELLICK, GRAHAM; ZUKERTORT, JOHANNES

Walter Ruby*, M.A.; Journalist, *New York Jewish Week, New York Daily News*: NEW YORK CITY

David Rudavsky, Ph.D.; Professor of Hebrew Culture and Education, Director of the Institute of Hebrew Studies, New York University: SACHAR, ABRAM LEON

Marcia R. Rudin, M.A.; Author, Lecturer, Expert on religious cults, New York

Arik Rudnitzky*, B.A., M.B.A.; Research Assistant, The Moshe Dayan Center for Middle Eastern and African Studies, Tel Aviv University: ISRAEL, STATE OF: ARAB POPULATION

Bernard G. Rudolph, Historian, Syracuse, New York

Miriam Ruerup (Rürup)*, M.A.; Historian, Zentrum für Antisemitismusforschung, Technische Universtät Berlin/Simon Dubnow Institut, Leipzig, Germany: KARTELL JUEDISCHER VERBINDUNGEN; KARTELL-CONVENT DER VERBINDUNGEN DEUTSCHER STUDENTEN JUEDISCHEN GLAUBENS

Abraham Rutenberg, Engineer; Former Director of the Israel Electric Company, Haifa

Danya Ruttenberg *, B.A., M.A.; Writer, Rabbinical Student at the University of Judaism, Los Angeles: BUTLER, JUDITH

S.J.E.R., see *Shorter Jewish Encyclopaedia in Russian*, Jerusalem

Haim Saadoun*, Ph.D.; The Dean, The Open University of Israel, Tel Aviv: ALAWIDS; ALGERIA; BERBERS; FEZ; GABÈS; TUNIS, TUNISIA

Shalom Sabar*, Ph.D.; Associate Professor, Professor of Jewish Art and Folklore, Hebrew University of Jerusalem: AMULET; ART HISTORIANS AND ART CRITICS; ART: NEW DEVELOPMENTS; HERLINGEN, AARON WOLFF OF GEWITSCH; ICONOGRAPHY; NEW YEAR'S CARDS; SCROLL OF ESTHER; SIMḤAT TORAH

Rachel Sabath-Beit Halachmi*, M.A.; Rabbi; Faculty Member of the Shalom Hartman Institute, Director of Lay Leadership Education, Hebrew Union College-Jewish Institute of Religion, Jerusalem: BOROWITZ, EUGENE B.

Lawrence Sabbath, Art Critic, Montreal

Brad Sabin Hill*, Center for Jewish History

Abram Leon Sachar, Ph.D.; Chancellor, Brandeis University, Waltham, Massachusetts: GLATZER, NAHUM NORBERT

Harry Sacher, M.A.; Attorney, writer, and editor, London: SIEFF, ISRAEL MOSES, BARON

Dov Sadan, Emeritus Professor of Yiddish Literature and of Hebrew Literature, the Hebrew University of Jerusalem: SCHWADRON, ABRAHAM

Benjamin (Wells) Sadock*, M.A.; Graduate Student, Columbia University, New York: BERNSTEIN, IGNATZ; TASHRAK

Monika Saelemaekers*, M.A.; Assistant-Curator, Bibliotheca Rosenthaliana, University of Amsterdam, The Netherlands: BELINFANTE; HERTZVELD-HIJMANS, ESTHELLA; JACOBS, ALETTA HENRIËTTE; NETHERLANDS, THE; SPÄTH, JOHANN PETER

Angel Sáenz-Badillos*, Ph.D.; Professor of Hebrew Language and Literature, Universidad Complutense, Madrid, Spain: ABRAHAM BEN SOLOMON OF TORRUTIEL; ABULAFIA, TODROS BEN JUDAH HA-LEVI; AÇAN, MOSES DE TARREGA; ALEXANDER THE GREAT; ALḤADIB, ISAAC BEN SOLOMON BEN ẒADDIK; AL-ḤARIZI, JUDAH BEN SOLOMON; AVIGDOR, ABRAHAM; BONAFED, SOLOMON BEN REUBEN; DE PIERA, MESHULLAM BEN SOLOMON; DUNASH BEN LABRAT; ELEAZAR BEN JACOB HA-BAVLI; ELIJAH BEN SHEMAIAH; EZOBI, JEHOSEPH BEN HANAN BEN NATHAN; ḤISDAI IBN ḤISDAI, ABU AL-FAḌL; IBN ALTABBAN, LEVI BEN JACOB; IBN BARZEL, JOSEPH; IBN EZRA, ISAAC; IBN GABIROL, SOLOMON BEN JUDAH; IBN GHAYYAT; IBN KAPRON, ISAAC; IBN MAR SAUL, ISAAC BEN LEVI; IBN PAQUDA, DAVID BEN ELEAZAR; IBN SAHL, JOSEPH BEN JACOB; IBN SASSON, SAMUEL BEN JOSEPH; IBN SHUWAYK, ISAAC BEN ISRAEL; IBN ZABARA, JOSEPH BEN MEIR; IBN ZAKBEL, SOLOMON; IBN ZAKBEL, SOLOMON; IMMANUEL OF ROME; INCUNABULA; INSTITUTE FOR THE RESEARCH OF MEDIEVAL HEBREW POETRY; ISAAC BEN ABRAHAM HA-GORNI; ISAAC BEN JUDAH HA-SENIRI; JACOB BEN JUDAH; JOSEPH BEN TANḤUM YERUSHALMI; JOSHUA BEN ELIJAH HA-LEVI; JUDAH BEN ISAAC IBN SHABBETAI; JUDAH HA-LEVI; KALONYMUS BEN KALONYMUS; LETTERS AND LETTER WRITERS; MAGIC; MAQĀMA; MATTATHIAS; PARABLE; PHINEHAS BEN JACOB HA-KOHEN; PIYYUT; POETRY; SAHULA, ISAAC BEN SOLOMON; SANTOB DE CARRIÓN; TRANSLATION AND TRANSLATORS; YEHUDI BEN SHESHET; YOM TOV OF JOIGNY; YOSE BEN YOSE

Shmuel Safrai, Ph.D., Rabbi; Associate Professor of Jewish History, the Hebrew University of Jerusalem: ALLON, GEDALYA; AMORA; AMORAIM; BET HILLEL AND BET SHAMMAI; DOSA BEN HARKINAS; ELEAZAR BEN ARAKH; ELEAZAR BEN AZARIAH; ELEAZAR BEN PEDAT; ELEAZAR BEN SHAMMUA; ELEAZAR BEN SIMEON; ELEAZAR HA-KAPPAR; ELEAZAR OF MODI'IN; HUNA; HUNA BEN AVIN HA-KOHEN; ISAAC; ISAAC BEN AVDIMI; ISAAC BEN ELEAZAR; ISHMAEL BEN ELISHA; ISHMAEL BEN YOSE BEN ḤALAFTA; ISRAEL, LAND OF: HISTORY; JACOB BEN AḤA; JACOB BEN IDI; JACOB BEN KORSHAI; JEREMIAH BEN ABBA; JOHANAN BEN NURI; JOHANAN BEN TORTA; JOHANAN HA-SANDELAR; JONAH; PILGRIMAGE; SABBATICAL YEAR AND JUBILEE; TEMPLE; YOSE BEN ḤALAFTA

Benjamin Sagalowitz, Dr. Jur.; Journalist, Zurich: SWITZERLAND

Avi Sagi*, Professor, Head Program for Hermeneutics; Professor of Philosophy, Bar-Ilan University, Ramat Gan: AKEDAH; GOLDMAN, ELIEZER; HARTMAN, DAVID

David M. Sagiv*, Ph.D.; Researcher, Lexicographer (Hebrew-Arabic/ Arabic Hebrew), the Hebrew University of Jerusalem: BASRA

Rochelle G. Saidel, Ph.D.; Political Scientist, Scientific Researcher, Center for the Study of Women and Gender, University of São Paulo, Brazil

David (Yoram) Saks*, M.A.; Acting National Director South African Jewish Board of Deputies, Johannesburg: AFRICAN JEWISH CONGRESS.; BULAWAYO; CAPE TOWN; CHASKALSON, ARTHUR; EAST LONDON; EDUCATION, JEWISH; GOLDSTONE, RICHARD JOSEPH; HARRIS, CYRIL KITCHENER; JOHANNESBURG; JOURNALISM; KASRILS, RONNIE; KENTRIDGE, SIR SYDNEY; KIMBERLEY; LEON, ANTHONY JAMES; MAURITIUS; PRESS; SCHWARZ, HARRY HEINZ; SHILL,

LOUIS; SLOVO, JOE; SOUTH AFRICA; SUZMAN, HELEN; ZAMBIA; ZIMBABWE

Ida Kay Saks, M.A.; Gary, Indiana: GARY

Zvi Saliternik, Ph.D.; Ministry of Health, Jerusalem: KLIGLER, ISRAEL JACOB

I.M. Salkind, Ph.D.; Scholar, London: AVIGDOR, ABRAHAM

Herman Prins Salomon, Ph.D.; Professor of French Literature, the State University of New York, Albany: RACINE, JEAN

Avrom Saltman, Ph.D., F.R.Hist. Soc.; Professor of History, Bar-Ilan University, Ramat Gan: BLOCH, MARC

Moshe Shraga Samet, Ph.D.; Lecturer in Jewish History and in Sociology, the Hebrew University of Jerusalem: AZULAI, ḤAYYIM JOSEPH DAVID; EMDEN, JACOB; ISHMAEL BEN ABRAHAM ISAAC HA-KOHEN; LANDAU, EZEKIEL BEN JUDAH; NEO-ORTHODOXY; SOFER; SOFER, MOSES

Meyer Samra, B.A., LL.B., Ph.D.; Lawyer, Dept. of Family and Community Services (NSW State Government), Sydney, Australia: AUSTRALIA

Edwin Samuel, Second Viscount Samuel, C.M.G., B.A.; Emeritus Senior Lecturer in British Institutions, the Hebrew University of Jerusalem; Principal of the Israel Institute of Public Administration, Jerusalem: AGRANAT, SHIMON; ALLENBY, EDMUND HENRY HYNMAN, VISCOUNT; EBAN, ABBA SOLOMON; STORRS, SIR RONALD

Rinna Samuel, B.A.; Journalist, Reḥovot, Israel: WEISGAL, MEYER WOLF

Myron Samuelson, Ph.B., LL.B.; Burlington, Vermont

Sheryl Sandberg*, A.B., M.B.A.; Vice President, Global Online Sales and Operation, Google, Mountain View, California: SUMMERS, LAWRENCE H.

Ira E. Sanders, M.A., Rabbi; Little Rock, Arkansas

Samuel Sandmel, Ph.D., D.H.L., Rabbi; Professor of Bible and Hellenistic Literature, the Hebrew Union College-Jewish Institute of Religion, Cincinnati: APOSTLE; FEIGIN, SAMUEL ISAAC

Silviu Sanie*, Ph.D.; Senior Researcher, Head of the Ancient History, Archaeology Institute, Iasi, Romania: SIRET; TIRGU-FRUMOS

David Saperstein*, MHL, JD, Rabbi; Director and Counsel, Religious Action Center for Reform Judaism; Union for Reform Judaism, Georgetown University Law Center, Washington, DC: VORSPAN, AL

Susan Sapiro*, M.A.; Research Associate, DRG, New York: PRAYER: WOMEN AND PRAYER

David Saraph, Tel Aviv: RATOSH, YONATHAN

Jonathan D. Sarna*, Ph.D.; Joseph H. and Belle R. Braun Professor of American Jewish History, Brandeis University: BOSTON; HISTORIOGRAPHY; MARCUS, JACOB RADER

Nahum M. Sarna, Ph.D.; Professor of Biblical Studies, Brandeis University, Waltham, Massachusetts: AARON; AARONIDES; ABIHU; ABIMELECH; ABRAHAM; ACROSTICS; AKEDAH; AMRAPHEL; ASENATH; BIBLE; BOAZ; CAIN; DATHAN AND ABIRAM; DELILAH; ENOCH; GENESIS, BOOK OF; GERSHOM; GIDEON; HALLELUJAH; HUR; ICHABOD; ISAAC; ITHAMAR; JACOB; JAEL; JAPHETH; JEPHTHAH; JETHRO; JOCHEBED; JOSEPH; JOTHAM; NADAB; NIMROD; ORPAH; OTHNIEL; PATRIARCHS, THE; PSALMS, BOOK OF; RACHEL; REBEKAH; SHAMGAR; SHEM; ZIPPORAH

Gustav Saron, LL.B.; General Secretary of the South African Board of Deputies, Johannesburg: BENDER, ALFRED PHILIP; DURBAN; FRAM, DAVID; JOHANNESBURG; SOUTH AFRICA

Jennifer Sartori*, Ph.D.; Academic Specialist, Northeastern University, Boston: COHEN, NAOMI WIENER; DAVIS, NATALIE ZEMON

Louis F. Sas, Ph.D.; Professor of Romance Languages, City College of the City University of New York: GOTTSCHALL, MORTON

Ilana Sasson*, M.Sc., Ph.D.; Jewish Theological Seminary, New York: BIBLE

Menahem Savidor, Lieutenant Colonel (Ret.), Israel Defense Forces; Former General Manager, Israel Railways; Director of the Citrus Products Export Board; National Chairman, Maccabi Sports Organization, Tel Aviv: MACCABI WORLD UNION; MACCABIAH

Rohan Saxena, Writer, Researcher; Jerusalem: ANNENBERG, WALTER H.; ASHKENAZY, VLADIMIR DAVIDOVICH; ASIMOV, ISAAC; BARR, ROSEANNE; BROTHERS, JOYCE; CHAGALL, MARC; CHOMSKY, NOAM AVRAM; DERSHOWITZ, ALAN M.; DOUGLAS, KIRK; DOUGLAS, MICHAEL; DREYFUSS, RICHARD; EITAN, RAPHAEL; FAST, HOWARD MELVIN; FRIEDMAN, MILTON; GEFFEN, DAVID; GINSBERG, ALLEN; GOODMAN, PERCIVAL; GREENSPAN, ALAN; GROSS, CHAIM; GUR, MORDECAI; HABER, WILLIAM; HOFSTADTER, ROBERT; IONESCO, EUGÈNE; JAKOBOVITS, LORD IMMANUEL; JHABVALA, RUTH PRAWER; JONG, ERICA; KATZENBERG, JEFFREY; KING, LARRY; KOCH, EDWARD IRVING; KOLLEK, THEODORE; KRAMER, SAMUEL NOAH; LEIBOWITZ, YESHAYAHU; LURIA, SALVADOR EDWARD; MANDELBROT, BENOIT; PATAI, RAPHAEL; PATTERSON, DAVID; PICON, MOLLY; PINTER, HAROLD; PIPES, RICHARD EDGAR; PREMINGER, OTTO LUDWIG; RABB, MAXWELL MILTON; RAPHAEL, FREDERIC; SEINFELD, JERRY; SONTAG, SUSAN; STERN, ISAAC; STREISAND, BARBRA; SZASZ, THOMAS STEPHEN; WALTERS, BARBARA; WESTHEIMER, RUTH

John H. Scammon, Th.D.; Emeritus Professor of Hebrew and Old Testament, Andover Newton Theological School, Newton Centre, Massachusetts: SAMUEL

Ann Schwartz Schaechner*, B.A.; Retired Nonprofit Executive, El Paso, Texas: EL PASO

Mordkhe Schaechter, Ph.D.; Jewish Teachers' Seminary, New York: HARKAVY, ALEXANDER; JOFFE, JUDAH ACHILLES; LANDAU, ALFRED; LEIBL, DANIEL; LIFSHITS, SHIYE-MORDKHE; MARK, YUDEL; SHTIF, NOKHEM; WEINREICH, MAX; WEINREICH, URIEL; ZARETZKI, ISAAC

Sara Schafler, M.A.; Educator, Lecturer, and Researcher in

Genealogy and Jewish Family History, Chicago: GENEALOGY

Abraham Schalit, Dr. Phil.; Emeritus Professor History, the Hebrew University of Jerusalem: ABSALOM; AGRIPPA II; ALABARCH; ALCIMUS; ALEXANDER; ALEXANDER BALAS; ALEXANDER LYSIMACHUS; ALEXANDER SON OF ARISTOBULUS II; ALEXANDER THE GREAT; ALEXANDRA; ALEXANDRA; ANDRONICUS SON OF MESHULLAM; ANTIGONUS; ANTIGONUS II; ANTIPAS, HEROD; ANTIPATER; ANTIPATER II or ANTIPAS; APION; APOLLONIUS MOLON; ARCHELAUS; ARCHON; ARETAS; ARISTOBULUS I; ARISTOBULUS II; ARISTOBULUS III; ARNONA; ARTAPANUS; ASIA MINOR; BAGOHI; BERENICE; BITHYNIA; BOULE; CTESIPHON; DELOS; DEMETRIUS I SOTER; DEMETRIUS II; DEMETRIUS III EUKARIOS THEOS PHILOPATER SOTER; DIODOTUS-TRYPHON; DIONYSUS, CULT OF; ELEAZAR BEN SIMEON; ELEPHANTINE; EPHESUS; HANAMEL; HELENA; HELIODORUS; HERODIAS; HEZEKIAH; IZATES II; JEREMIAH, EPISTLE OF; JONATHAN BEN ANAN; JOSEPHUS FLAVIUS; JOSHUA BEN DAMNAI; JUDAH MACCABEE; JUDAH THE GALILEAN; JULIAN THE APOSTATE; JUSTUS OF TIBERIAS; SATRAP; VESPASIAN, TITUS FLAVIUS

Lazaro Schallman, Director of the Library of the Jewish Community of Buenos Aires: ROSARIO; SAJAROFF, MIGUEL; YARCHO, NOE

Isaac Schattner, Dr.Phil.; Emeritus Associate Professor of Geography, the Hebrew University of Jerusalem: ISRAEL, LAND OF: GEOGRAPHICAL SURVEY; MAPS OF EREẒ ISRAEL

Josef Schawinski, Author, Tel Aviv: HELLER, BUNIM; MANN, MENDEL

Cathy Schechter*, B.S.; Writer, Consultant, Orchard Communication, Inc., Austin Texas: AUSTIN

Joseph B. Schechtman, Dr. Phil.; Historian and Former Member of the Jewish Agency Executive, New York: JABOTINSKY, VLADIMIR; PASMANIK, DANIEL; RAZSVET; REVISIONISTS, ZIONIST

Jeff Scheckner*, Director of Jewish Community Relations Council, Jewish Federation of Greater Middlesex County, South River, New Jersey: LEAGUE FOR ISRAEL, THE AMERICAN JEWISH; MIDDLESEX COUNTY, NEW JERSEY

Wolfgang Scheffler, Dr.Phil.; Senior Research Fellow in Political Science, the University of Sussex Centre for Research in Collective Psychopathology, London: JUDENREIN

Alexander Scheiber, Dr. Phil., Rabbi; Director and Professor of the Jewish Theological Seminary of Hungary, Budapest: ABONY; ACSÁDY, IGNÁC; AKIVA BEN MENAHEM HA-KOHEN OF OFEN; ALBERTI-IRSA; BALLAGI, MÓR; BÁNÓCZI; BERNSTEIN, BÉLA; BLAU, LUDWIG LAJOS; BRILL, AZRIEL; BUECHLER, ALEXANDER; DEBRECEN; EISLER, MÁTYÁS; GRÜNVALD, PHILIP; GYÖR; HEVESI, SIMON; HIRSCHLER, PÁL; HODMEZOVASARHELY; HUNGARIAN LITERATURE; IZRAELITA MAGYAR IRODALMI TÁRSULAT; KECSKEMET; KECSKEMÉTI, ÁRMIN; KECSKEMÉTI, LIPÓT; KOHN, SAMUEL; LANDESRABBINERSCHULE; LOEW, IMMANUEL; LOEW, LEOPOLD; MAKO; MARCZALI, HENRIK; OBADIAH, THE NORMAN PROSELYTE; POLLAK, MIKSA; RICHTMANN, MÓZES; SPITZER, SOLOMON; SZOLNOK; SZOMBATHELY; VENETIANER, LAJOS

Raymond P. Scheindlin, Ph.D., Rabbi; Assistant Professor of Jewish Studies, McGill University, Montreal: MARCUS, JOSEPH; OBERMANN, JULIAN JOËL

Samuel Scheps, Ph.D.; Economist, Geneva: KLATZKIN, JACOB

Ben-Zion (Benno) Schereschewsky, Dr.Jur.; Judge of the District Court, Jerusalem: AGUNAH; APOTROPOS; BETROTHAL; BIGAMY AND POLYGAMY; CHILD MARRIAGE; CIVIL MARRIAGE; CONCUBINE; DIVORCE; DOWRY; EMBRYO; FIRSTBORN; HUSBAND AND WIFE; KETUBBAH; MAINTENANCE; MAMZER; MARRIAGE; MARRIAGE, PROHIBITED; MIXED MARRIAGE, INTERMARRIAGE; PARENT AND CHILD; RAPE; WIDOW; YUḤASIN

Edward W. Schey*: PASSAIC-CLIFTON

Laura Burd Schiavo*, Ph.D.; Director, Museum Programs, Jewish Historical Society of Greater Washington, D.C.: WASHINGTON, D.C.

Marvin Schick*: BERNSTEIN, ZALMAN CHAIM

Alvin Irwin Schiff, Ph.D.; Executive Vice President, New York Board of Jewish Education

Ellen Schiff*, Ph.D.; Professor Emeritus, Massachusetts College of Liberal Arts, Massachusetts: FRANKEN, ROSE DOROTHY LEWIN

Fritz Schiff, Dr. Phil.; Curator of the Museum of Modern Art, Haifa: BEN-ZVI, ZEEV

Mayer Schiller*, Rabbi; Maggid Shiur, Mashgiach Ruḥani, Yeshiva University High School, New York: LAKEWOOD

Henri Schilli, Chief Rabbi; Lecturer in Midrash and Director of the Séminaire Israélite de France, Paris: SÉMINAIRE ISRAÉLITE DE FRANCE

Ignacy Yizhak Schiper, Dr. Phil.; Lecturer in Jewish Economic History, the Institute of Jewish Studies, Warsaw: AMELANDER, MENAHEM MANN BEN SOLOMON HA-LEVI; BRESCH, JUDAH LOEB BEN MOSES NAPHTALI; HEDEGÅRD, OSKAR DAVID LEONARD

Jefim (Hayyim) Schirmann, Dr.Phil.; Emeritus Professor of Hebrew Literature, the Hebrew University of Jerusalem: ABRAHAM BEN HILLEL OF FOSTAT; ABRAHAM BEN ISAAC; ABRAHAM OF SARTEANO; ABULAFIA, TODROS BEN JUDAH HA-LEVI; AHIMAAZ BEN PALTIEL; ALBARADANI, JOSEPH; BEDERSI, ABRAHAM BEN ISAAC; CARMI, ISAIAH ḤAI BEN JOSEPH; CASPI, SAUL; DAR'Ī, MOSES BEN ABRAHAM; DAVID BEN MESHULLAM OF SPEYER; DE PIERA, MESHULLAM BEN SOLOMON; ELIJAH BEN ELIEZER PHILOSOPH HA-YERUSHALMI; ELIJAH BEN SHEMAIAH; ELIJAH CHELEBI HA-KOHEN OF ANATOLIA; ENSHEIM, MOSES; FALKOWITSCH, JOEL BAERISCH; FARISSOL, JACOB BEN ḤAYYIM; FIOGHI, FABIANO; GALIPAPA, MAIMON; GALLEGO, JOSEPH SHALOM; GAVISON; GERONDI, ISAAC BEN JUDAH; HAMON, AARON BEN ISAAC; ḤARIZI, ABU ISAAC ABRAHAM; IBN ABITUR, JOSEPH BEN ISAAC; IBN AL-TAQANA, MOSES; IBN EZRA, ISAAC; IBN ḤASAN, JEKUTHIEL BEN ISAAC; IBN KAPRON, ISAAC; IBN MAR SAUL, ISAAC BEN LEVI; IBN PAQUDA, DAVID BEN ELEAZAR; IBN SAHL, JOSEPH BEN

JACOB; IBN SHUWAYK, ISAAC BEN ISRAEL; IBN ZAKBEL, SOLOMON; IBN ZAKBEL, SOLOMON; IBN ẒUR, JACOB BEN REUBEN; INSTITUTE FOR THE RESEARCH OF MEDIEVAL HEBREW POETRY; ISAAC BEN ABRAHAM HA-GORNI; ISAAC BEN ḤAYYIM BEN ABRAHAM; ISAAC BEN JUDAH; ISRAEL BEN JOEL; JACOB BEN JUDAH; JACOB BEN NAPHTALI; JOAB THE GREEK; JOHANAN BEN JOSHUA HA-KOHEN; JOSEPH BAR NISSAN; JOSEPH BEN JACOB; JOSEPH BEN SHESHET IBN LATIMI; JOSEPH BEN SOLOMON OF CARCASSONNE; JOSEPH BEN TANḤUM YERUSHALMI; JOSHUA; JOSHUA BEN ELIJAH HA-LEVI; JOSIPHIAH THE PROSELYTE; JUDAH BEN ISAAC IBN SHABBETAI; JUDAH BEN MENAHEM OF ROME; KALAI, JOSEPH B. JACOB; LEVI, JOSHUA JOSEPH BEN DAVID; LUNEL, JACOB DE; MARINI, SHABBETHAI ḤAYYIM; YANNAI; YOSE BEN YOSE

Abraham Schischa, Letchworth, England: BONYHÁD; DUSCHINSKY, JOSEPH ẒEVI BEN ISRAEL; EHRENFELD, SAMUEL BEN DAVID ẒEVI; FRIED, AARON; FRIEDLAENDER, SOLOMON JUDAH; KAUDER, SAMUEL JUDAH BEN DAVID

Benjamin Schlesinger, Ph.D.; Professor of Social Work, the University of Toronto: VIRGIN ISLANDS

Simon S. Schlesinger, Dr.Phil.; Rabbi; Scholar and Educator, Jerusalem: DANZIG, ABRAHAM BEN JEHIEL MICHAL; DEREKH EREẒ

Linda M. Schloff*, Ph.D.; Director Jewish Historical Society of the Upper Midwest, Minneapolis: MINNEAPOLIS-ST. PAUL; MINNESOTA; NORTH DAKOTA; SOUTH DAKOTA

Joachim Schlör*, Dr.Phil.Habil.; Professor of History, University of Southampton, England: GRONEMANN, SAMUEL

Imre Schmelczer, M.A., Rabbi; St. Gallen, Switzerland: WELLESZ, JULIUS

Usiel Oscar Schmelz, Ph.D.; Research Fellow in Contemporary Jewry, the Hebrew University of Jerusalem: DEMOGRAPHY; MIGRATIONS; STATISTICS; VITAL STATISTICS

Menahem Schmelzer, D.H.L.; Librarian and Assistant Professor of Medieval Hebrew Literature, the Jewish Theological Seminary of America, New York: AMZALAK, MOSES BENSABAT; BIBLIOPHILES; EDELMANN, RAPHAEL; FREIMANN, ARON; NEMOY, LEON; STEINSCHNEIDER, MORITZ; TRAVELERS AND EXPLORERS; VEINGER, MORDECAI

Ephraïm Schmidt, Antwerp: ANTWERP

Morris M. Schnitzer, B.S., LL.B.; Lecturer in Law, Rutgers University, New Jersey: FORMAN, PHILLIP; NADAB

Randal F. Schnoor*, Ph.D.; Adjunct Professor, York University, Toronto, Canada: JOSEPH, NORMA BAUMEL; LANDSBERG, MICHELE; MIRVISH

Barbara Schober*, M.A.; Ph.D.; University of British Columbia: BRITISH COLUMBIA; FRANKLIN, SELIM; NATHAN, HENRY; NEMETZ, NATHAN THEODORE; RANKIN, HARRY; SHULTZ, SAMUEL; VANCOUVER; WOSK

Christian Schoelzel*, Dr.Phil.; Managing Director of Culture and More, an Agency for Services in Historical Sciences, Munich and Berlin, Germany: BALLIN, ALBERT; BONN, MORITZ JULIUS; FUERSTENBERG, CARL; MELCHIOR, CARL; RATHENAU, EMIL MORITZ; RATHENAU, WALTHER; RATHENAU, WALTHER; WARBURG, MAX M.

Myron E. Schoen, Union of American Hebrew Congregations, New York: KLEIN, EDWARD E.

Stuart Schoenfeld*, Ph.D.; Professor of Sociology, Glendon College, York University, Canada: TORONTO

William N. Schoenfeld, Ph.D.; Professor of Psychology, Queens College of the City University of New York and Cornell University Medical School, New York: KANTOR, JACOB ROBERT; WEISS, ALBERT PAUL

Kenneth R. Scholberg, Ph.D.; Professor of Romance Languages, Michigan State University, East Lansing: AÇAN, MOSES DE TARREGA; ALBORAYCOS; ALEMÁN, MATEO; ÁLVAREZ GATO, JUAN; AMADOR DE LOS RIOS, JOSE; ARIAS, JOSEPH SEMAH; AUB, MAX; BAENA, JUAN ALFONSO DE; BARRIOS, DANIEL LEVI DE; BELMONTE; BERNAL; BRUSSELS; BUENO; CACERES, FRANCISCO DE; CASTRO QUESADA, AMERICO; CERVANTES SAAVEDRA, MIGUEL DE; CHIRINO; CORREA, ISABEL DE; COTA DE MAGUAQUE, RODRIGO DE; CURIEL; DUJOVNE, LEON; ENRÍQUEZ BASURTO, DIEGO; ENRÍQUEZ GÓMEZ, ANTONIO; ENRÍQUEZ, ISABEL; FERNANDES VILLAREAL, MANOEL; GODÍNEZ, FELIPE; GÓMEZ DE SOSSA, ISAAC; HUARTE DE SAN JUAN, JUAN; ISAACS, JORGE; JEWESS OF TOLEDO; LARA, ISAAC COHEN DE; LEÓN, LUIS DE; MÓNTORO, ANTÓN DE; OLIVER Y FULLANA, NICOLÁS DE; PENSO DE LA VEGA, JOSEPH; PETRUS ALFONSI; PINTO DELGADO, JOÃO; RIBEIRO, BERNADIM; ROJAS, FERNANDO DE; SANTOB DE CARRIÓN; SPANISH AND PORTUGUESE LITERATURE

Gershom Scholem, Dr. Phil.; Emeritus Professor of Jewish Mysticism, the Hebrew University of Jerusalem: ABRAHAM BEN ALEXANDER OF COLOGNE; ABRAHAM BEN ELIEZER HA-LEVI; ABRAHAM BEN ISAAC OF GRANADA; ABRAHAM BEN SIMEON OF WORMS; ACADEMY ON HIGH; ADAM BA'AL SHEM; ADAM KADMON; ANTHROPOMORPHISM; ANTINOMIANISM; AYLLON, SOLOMON BEN JACOB; AẒILUT; AZRIEL OF GERONA; BACHARACH, NAPHTALI BEN JACOB ELHANAN; BARUCH; BENJAMIN BEN ELIEZER HA-KOHEN VITALE OF REGGIO; BENJAMIN, WALTER; BLOCH, MATTATHIAS BEN BENJAMIN ZE'EV ASHKENAZI; BONAFOUX, DANIEL BEN ISRAEL; BOTAREL, MOSES BEN ISAAC; BUZAGLO, SHALOM BEN MOSES; CARDOZO, ABRAHAM MIGUEL; CHIROMANCY; CHOTSH, ẒEVI HIRSH BEN JERAHMEEL; COMMANDMENTS, REASONS FOR; DAVID; DAVID BEN ABRAHAM HA-LAVAN; DAVID BEN JUDAH HE-ḤASID; DEMONS, DEMONOLOGY; DIBBUK; DOENMEH; EIN-SOF; ELIASHOV, SOLOMON BEN ḤAYYIM; ELIEZER FISCHEL BEN ISAAC OF STRZYZOW; ESCHATOLOGY; EYBESCHUETZ, JONATHAN; FRANK, JACOB, AND THE FRANKISTS; GABBAI, MEIR BEN EZEKIEL IBN; GEMATRIA; GIKATILLA, JOSEPH BEN ABRAHAM; GILGUL; GOD; GOLDBERG, OSCAR; GOLEM; GOTTLIEB, EPHRAIM; ḤAYON, NEHEMIAH ḤIYYA BEN MOSES; ḤAYYAT, JUDAH BEN JACOB; ḤAYYIM BEN ABRAHAM HA-KOHEN; HIRSCHFELD, EPHRAIM JOSEPH; ISAAC BEN JACOB HA-KOHEN; JACOB BEN JACOB HA-KOHEN; JELLINEK, ADOLF; JOEL, DAVID HEYMANN; JONAH, MOSES; JOSEPH IBN SHRAGA; JOSEPH IBN ṬABŪL; JUDAH ḤASID, HA-LEVI; KABBALAH; KNORR VON ROSENROTH, CHRISTIAN; LABI, SIMEON; LILITH; LURIA, ISAAC BEN SOLOMON; MAGEN DAVID; MALAKH, ḤAYYIM BEN SOLOMON; MEDITATION; METATRON;

MOLITOR, FRANZ JOSEPH; MOSES BEN SOLOMON BEN SIMEON OF BURGOS; OSTROPOLER, SAMSON BEN PESAḤ; PINHEIRO, MOSES; POPPERS, MEIR BEN JUDAH LOEB HA-KOHEN; PRIMO, SAMUEL; PROSSNITZ, JUDAH LEIB BEN JACOB HOLLESCHAU; PROVIDENCE; QUERIDO, JACOB; RAPHAEL; RAZIEL; REDEMPTION; REUCHLIN, JOHANNES; ROVIGO, ABRAHAM BEN MICHAEL; SAHULA, MEIR BEN SOLOMON ABI; SAMAEL; SANDALFON; SARUG, ISRAEL; SEFIROT; SHABBETAI ẒEVI; SHI'UR KOMAH; SOUL, IMMORTALITY OF; SPIRA, NATHAN NATA BEN SOLOMON; VALLE, MOSES DAVID BEN SAMUEL; VIDAS, ELIJAH BEN MOSES DE; VITAL, ḤAYYIM BEN JOSEPH; VITAL, SAMUEL BEN ḤAYYIM; WORLDS, THE FOUR; WORMSER, SECKEL; YAKHINI, ABRAHAM BEN ELIJAH; YEẒIRAH, SEFER; YOM KIPPUR KATAN; ZACUTO, MOSES BEN MORDECAI; ZOHAR; ZOREF, JOSHUA HESHEL BEN JOSEPH

Julie Schonfeld*, B.A., Rabbi; Director of Rabbinic Development, The Rabbinical Assembly, New York: EILBERG, AMY

Jeffrey Alan Schooley*, M.A.; Research Fellow, Kent State University, Ohio

Julia Schopflin, Researcher, Institute of Jewish Affairs, London

Ismar Schorsch, Ph.D., Rabbi; Assistant in Jewish History, the Jewish Theological Seminary of America, New York: GUEDEMANN, MORITZ

Janos A. Schossberger, M.D.; Psychiatric Director of Kfar Shaul Work Village, Jerusalem: FROMM-REICHMANN, FRIEDA

Keith N. Schoville, Ph.D.; Assistant Professor of Hebrew and Semitic Studies, the University of Wisconsin, Madison: SHULAMMITE, THE; SONG OF SONGS

Heinz Schreckenberg, Dr. Phil.; Department of Classical Antiquity, University of Muenster, Westfalen: SCHÜRER, EMIL

Lynne (Meredith) Schreiber*, M.F.A., B.A.; Writer, Author, Freelance, Southfield, Michigan: SEIGEL, JOSHUA; SILBER, SAUL; TELUSHKIN, NISSAN; WINE, SHERWIN; ZARCHI, ASHER

Theodore Schrire, M.A., M.B., F.R.C.S., F.R.S.S.Af.; Senior Lecturer in Surgery, the University of Cape Town: AMULETS, SAMARITAN

Michael J. Schudrich*, M.A., Rabbi; Chief Rabbi, Jewish Community of Poland, Warsaw, Poland: ANTISEMITISM; BESSER, CHASKEL O.

Alan Richard Schulman, Ph.D.; Associate Professor of Ancient History, Queens College of the City University of New York: AKHENATON; AMENOPHIS III; ANTONINUS PIUS; CUSH; EGYPT; HELIOPOLIS; HOPHRA; HYKSOS; MEMPHIS; MERNEPTAH; MIẒRAYIM; NECO; NILE; PATHROS; PHARAOH; PITHOM; POTIPHAR; POTI-PHERA; RAMSES; SETI I; THEBES; ZOAN

Elias Schulman, Ph.D.; the Jewish Teachers' Seminary, New York: AXELROD, SELIK; AXENFELD, ISRAEL; BOVSHOVER, JOSEPH; DIK, ISAAC MEIR; ENTIN, JOEL; ERIK, MAX; ETTINGER, SOLOMON; FININBERG, EZRA; GINZBURG, ISER; GLICK, HIRSH; GORIN, BERNARD; HAIMOWITZ, MORRIS JONAH; HORONTCHIK, SIMON; HURWITZ, CHAIM; IGNATOFF, DAVID; JANOVSKY, SAUL JOSEPH; KACZERGINSKY, SZMERKE; KALMANOVITCH, ZELIG; KATZENELSON, ITZHAK; KHARIK, IZI; KOBRIN, LEON; KUSHNIROV, AARON; KVITKO, LEIB; LIBIN, Z.; LIESSIN, ABRAHAM; LINETZKY, ISAAC JOEL; MARMOR, KALMAN; NUSINOV, ISAAC; OLGIN, MOSHE J.; SELIKOVITCH, GEORGE; SHUB, DAVID; WARSHAWSKI, MARK; WEITER, A.; ZINBERG, ISRAEL

Iehuda Schuster, Kibbutz Mefalsim: NAḤAL

Nachum Schutz-Adler*, M.A.; Jewish History, Bar-Ilan University, Ramat Gan: MONTEVIDEO; URUGUAY

Paul Schveiger*, Ph.D.; Linguist, Retired, Raanana, Israel: ALBA IULIA; ARAD; BAIA-MARE; BANAT; BEZIDUL NOU; BISTRITA; BRAHAM, RANDOLPH LOUIS; BRAȘOV; BUKOVINA; CARMILLY-WEINBERGER, MOSHE; CILIBI MOÏSE; CLUJ; DEJ; FAGARAS; GRAUR, ALEXANDRU; LUGOJ; MARGHITA; NASAUD; ORADEA; PAUKER, ANA; REGHIN; SALONTA; SATU-MARE; SEINI; SIBIU; SIGHET; TARGU-MURES; TRANSYLVANIA; WALD, HENRI

George Schwab, Ph.D.; Assistant Professor of Modern History, City College of the City University of New York: BEERSHEBA; BERNAYS; HAUSER, HENRI; MARKUS, LUDWIG; PERLBACH, MAX; PRAWER, JOSHUA

Abraham Schwadron (Sharon), Dr. Phil.; Writer and Collector, Jerusalem: AUTOGRAPHS

Ernest Schwarcz, Ph.D.; Professor of Philosophy, Queens College of the City University of New York: BERKSON, ISAAC BAER; BONDY, CURT; BORGHI, LAMBERTO; BROUDY, HARRY SAMUEL; HARTOG, SIR PHILIP JOSEPH; KLAPPER, PAUL; NAUMBURG, MARGARET; RIVLIN, HARRY N.; RUBINSTEIN, SERGEY LEONIDOVICH; SCHEFFLER, ISRAEL

Moshe Schwarcz, Ph.D.; Associate Professor of Philosophy, Bar-Ilan University, Ramat Gan: FORMSTECHER, SOLOMON; KROCHMAL, NACHMAN; LAZARUS, MORITZ

Barry Dov Schwartz, M.H.L., Rabbi; Perth Amboy, New Jersey: MIDDLESEX COUNTY, NEW JERSEY

Carmi Schwartz, M.A., M.S.W.; Associated Jewish Charities and Welfare Fund, Baltimore, Maryland

Casey (Katherine) Schwartz*, B.A.; Student, University of California, Los Angeles: CHOPRA, JOYCE; DEMILLE, CECIL B.; EPHRON, NORA; FRELENG, ISADOR "FRIZ"; HECKERLING, AMY; KATZ, MICKEY; LAMARR, HEDY; LANDAU, MARTIN; LANDON, MICHAEL; LEACHMAN, CLORIS; LEWIS, SHARI; MENKEN, ALAN

Dov Schwartz*, Professor, Dean, Faculty of Humanities, Bar-Ilan University, Ramat Gan: ABBA MARI BEN MOSES BEN JOSEPH ASTRUC OF LUNEL; ABBAS, JUDAH BEN SAMUEL IBN; ANTINOMIANISM; ASCETICISM; LEVI BEN ABRAHAM BEN ḤAYYIM; MAIMONIDEAN CONTROVERSY; SOLOVEITCHIK, JOSEPH BAER; ZARZA, SAMUEL IBN SENEH

Guri Schwartz*: FOSSOLI

Laurel Schwartz*, B.A.; Archives Curator, Jewish Historical Society of San Diego, Archives at San Diego State University, San Diego, California: SAN DIEGO

Marcus Mordecai Schwartz*, M.A., Ph.D., Rabbi; Adjunct Instructor of Talmud, Jewish Theological Seminary of America, New York

Matthew (B.) Schwartz*, Ph.D.; Historian, Wayne State University, Southfield, Michigan: DAVID W. PETEGORSKY; MOSES, ADOLPH

Stan (Stanley) Schwartz*, B.B.A.; President, Jewish Historical Society of San Diego, Archives at San Diego State University, California: SAN DIEGO

Yigal Schwartz*, Ph.D.; Professor, Head of Hebrew Literature Department and Head of Heksherim Research Center, Ben-Gurion University of the Negev: SHAKED, GERSHON

Jan Schwarz*, Ph.D.; Lecturer, University of Chicago: BIOGRAPHIES AND AUTOBIOGRAPHIES; GLATSTEIN, JACOB; ROSENFELD, JONAH

Johannes Valentin Schwarz*, Ph.D., M.A.; Historian, Potsdam University, Germany: ALLGEMEINE ZEITUNG DES JUDENTUMS; BACHER, EDUARD; BAUMGARTEN, EMANUEL MENDEL; BECKER, JULIUS; BEER, MAX; BENEDIKT, MORITZ; BERNHARD, GEORG; FEDER, ERNST; MENORAH; NEUZEIT, DIE; PHILIPPSON; PHILO VERLAG; REUTER, PAUL JULIUS, FREIHERR VON; SIMON, HEINRICH; SIMONE, ANDRÉ; SONNEMANN, LEOPOLD; WELT, DIE; WOLFF, BERNHARD; WOLFF, THEODOR; ZUKUNFT, DIE

Karl Schwarz, Dr.Phil.; Art Historian and Curator of the Tel Aviv Museum: ANTOKOLSKI, MARK

Leo W. Schwarz, B.A., Rabbi; Author, New York: LOWENTHAL, MARVIN

Simon R. Schwarzfuchs, Ph.D., Rabbi; Associate Professor of Jewish History, Bar-Ilan University, Ramat Gan: ALLIANCE ISRAELITE UNIVERSELLE; ANTWERP; BELGIUM; CRÉMIEUX, ISAAC ADOLPHE; CRUSADES; FRANCE; LAUSANNE; LAZARE, BERNARD; LUCERNE; LUXEMBOURG; MALESHERBES, CHRETIEN GUILLAUME DE LAMOIGNON DE; ROTHSCHILD; SPAIN; SWITZERLAND; ZURICH

Steven S. Schwarzschild, D.H.L., Rabbi; Professor of Jewish Philosophy, Washington University, St. Louis, Missouri: ATLAS, SAMUEL; COVETOUSNESS; JUSTICE; NOACHIDE LAWS; SLONIMSKY, HENRY; SUFFERING; TRUTH

Eliezer Schweid, Ph.D.; Senior Lecturer in Jewish Philosophy and Mysticism, the Hebrew University of Jerusalem: AḤAD HA-AM; AVINOAM, REUVEN,; BAVLI, HILLEL; HEINEMANN, YIẒḤAK; TCHERNICHOWSKY, SAUL

Joseph Schweitzer, Ph.D., Rabbi; Chief Rabbi of Pecs; Professor of Jewish History, the Jewish Theological Seminary of Hungary, Budapest: PECS

Hanna Scolnicov*, Ph.D.; Professor, Tel Aviv University: BERGMANN, FELIX ELIEZER

Robert B.Y. Scott, Ph.D.; Emeritus Professor of Religion, Princeton University, New Jersey: BALANCE; PARABLE; PROVERBS, BOOK OF; WISDOM; WISDOM LITERATURE

Mel Scult*, Ph.D.; Professor Emeritus Brooklyn College, C.U.N.Y, New York: KAPLAN, MORDECAI MENAHEM

Fern Lee Seckbach, M.A., C.Phil.; Deputy Editor in Chief, *Encyclopaedia Judaica*, CD-ROM Edition: AHARONOV, YAKIR; EHRLICH, SIMḤA; EITAN, RAPHAEL; FEINBRUN-DOTHAN, NAOMI; FROMAN, IAN; GOLDBLUM, NATAN; GVATI, CHAIM; KATZ, ELIHU; LEVI, MOSHE; LEVITZKI, ALEXANDER; POLLACK, ISRAEL; SPIEGEL, NATHAN; TARIF, AMIN; WEISS, MEIR; WERSES, SAMUEL; YAVETS, ZVI; YEIVIN, ISRAEL

Francois Secret, Directeur d'Etudes a l'Ecole Pratique des Hautes Etudes (Sciences Religieuses), Sorbonne, Paris: BONFRÈRE, JAQUES; GIORGIO, FRANCESCO

Israel Sedaka, Ḥolon, Israel: MEDALS

Ariel Segal*, Ph.D.; Professor, Writer, Historian, International Analyst, University of Miami: IQUITOS

Arthur Segal*, Ph.D.; Professor of Classical Archaeology, University of Haifa: SUSITA OR HIPPOS

Bernard Segal, D.H.L., Rabbi; Executive Vice President, the United Synagogue of America, New York: ABBELL, MAXWELL

Eliezer L. (Lorne) Segal*, Ph.D.; Professor of Religious Studies, University of Calgary, Canada: BERAKHOT; BIKKURIM; DEMAI

Jack Segal, D.H.L., Rabbi; Houston, Texas: HOUSTON

Josef Segal, M.A.; Haifa: AMASA; DOEG; GAD; ISHMAEL; OG; PASHHUR; SHALLUM

Moshe Zevi (Moses Hirsch) Segal, M.A.; Emeritus Professor of Bible, the Hebrew University of Jerusalem: ASTRUC, JEAN; BEN SIRA, SIMEON BEN JESUS; BEN SIRA, WISDOM OF; EICHHORN, JOHANN GOTTFRIED; GRESSMANN, HUGO

Ralph Segalman, Ph.D., A.C.S.W.; Associate Professor of Sociology, San Fernando Valley State College, Northridge, California: EL PASO

Jonathan (Lee) Seidel*, M.A., Ph.D., Rabbi; Adjunct Professor, University of Oregon, Eugene, Oregon: CIRCUMCISION

Oskar Seidlin, Ph.D.; Professor of German Literature, Ohio State University, Columbus: BRAHM, OTTO

Hillel Seidman, Ph.D.; President of the Beth Jacob Teachers' College, New York: STEIN, EDMUND MENAHEM

Kalman Seigel, B.So.Sci.; Journalist, New York: JOURNALISM

Robert A. Seigel, M.A., Rabbi; Chicago: CRONBACH, ABRAHAM

Avraham Sela*, Ph.D.; Senior Lecturer in International Relations, the Hebrew University of Jerusalem: ARAFAT, YASSER; PALESTINE LIBERATION ORGANIZATION; PALESTINIAN AUTHORITY

Michoel A. Seligson*, Rabbi; Lecturer, Otzer Hachasidim Publication House of Lubavitach, Yeshiva Oholei Toraah, Seminary Bais Rivka, New York: DWORKIN, ZALMAN SHIMON

Bernard Semmel, Ph.D.; Professor of History, the State University of New York, Stony Brook: MOMIGLIANO, ARNALDO DANTE

Nora Seni*, Ph.D.; Maître de Conferences, French Institute on Urbanism, University of Paris, France: CAMONDO

Leonardo Senkman*, Ph.D.; Lecturer, Latin American Studies and Researcher at International Center for University Teaching of the Jewish Civilization, the Hebrew University of Jerusalem: AGUINIS, MARCOS; PECAR, SAMUEL; TIMERMAN, JACOBO

Gertrude C. Serata, M.L.S.; Librarian, Honolulu: HAWAII

Joseph Baruch Sermoneta, Ph.D., Dott.in Fil.; Associate Professor of Jewish Philosophy and Mysticism; Senior Lecturer in Italian Language and Literature and in Philosophy, the Hebrew University of Jerusalem: ANCONA; BACHI, RICCARDO; BACHI, ROBERTO; DANTE ALIGHIERI; DEBENEDETTI, GIACOMO; DEL MONTE, CRESCENZO; HALPHEN, LOUIS; HILLEL BEN SAMUEL; ITALIAN LITERATURE; JOHN OF CAPUA; JUDEO-ITALIAN; LEVI, DAVID; LEVI-PEROTTI, GIUSTINA; MOSES OF PALERMO; SULLAM, SARA COPPIO; SVEVO, ITALO

Ronit Seter*, Ph.D.; Adjunct Assistant Professor, George Washington University, Washington, D.C.: FLEISCHER, TSIPPI; SETER, MORDECAI; SHILOAH, AMNON

David Sfard, Ph.D.; Jerusalem: COOPERATIVES; POLAND; PRESS; SMOLAR, HERSH

Bezalel Shachar, M.A.; Lecturer in Adult Education, the Hebrew University of Jerusalem: EDUCATION, JEWISH

Eliyahu Shadmi, Kibbutz Ma'anit

Yosef Shadur, Midreshet Sedeh Boker: SEDEH BOKER

Aaron Shaffer, Ph.D.; Associate Professor of Assyriology, the Hebrew University of Jerusalem: AKKADIAN LANGUAGE; ESARHADDON; FINKELSTEIN, JACOB JOEL; HAMMURAPI; KRAMER, SAMUEL NOAH

William Shaffir*, Ph.D.; Professor of Sociology, McMaster University, Hamilton, Canada: HAMILTON

John M. Shaftesley, O.B.E., B.A., F.R.S.A.; Editor, London: ALKAN, ALPHONSE; BERNSTEIN, SIDNEY LEWIS, BARON; GESTETNER, DAVID; KAHN, RICHARD FERDINAND, LORD; LÉVY; LEVY, SIR ALBERT; SIMON; SPIELMAN; STERN; TYPOGRAPHERS

Natan Shahar*, Ph.D.; Music Department, Beit Berl College, Israel: ALBERSTEIN, HAVA; HAZA, OFRA; HIRSH, NURIT; ISRAEL, STATE OF: CULTURAL LIFE; MEDINA, AVIHU; WILENSKY, MOSHE; ZEHAVI, DAVID

Milton Shain, Ph.D., Associate Professor, Department of Hebrew and Jewish Studies; Director of the Isaac and Jessie Kaplan Centre for Jewish Studies and Research, University of Cape Town: CAPE TOWN; SOUTH AFRICA

Gershon Shaked*, Ph.D.; Professor of Hebrew Literature, the Hebrew University of Jerusalem: BERKOWITZ, YITZḤAK DOV; BRENNER, JOSEPH ḤAYYIM; GROSSMAN, DAVID; HEBREW LITERATURE, MODERN; SHAMIR, MOSHE; SHOHAM, MATTITYAHU MOSHE

Shaul Shaked*, Ph.D.; Professor of Iranian Studies and Comparative Religion, the Hebrew University of Jerusalem: JUDEO-PERSIAN; ZAND, MICHAEL

Yuval Shaked*, Director Jewish Music Center, Composer, Beth Hatefutsoth, Haifa University, Kibbutzim College, Tel Aviv: LEEF, YINAM; RADZYNSKI, JAN; RAN, SHULAMIT; SHERIFF, NOAM; STARER, ROBERT

Aryeh Shalev, Former IDF and Israel Ministry of Defense Spokesman, Former Governor of Judea and Samaria

Mordechai Shalev, M.A.; Ministry for Foreign Affairs, Jerusalem: MARZOUK, MOSHE; TIDHAR, DAVID

Levi Shalit, Editor, Johannesburg

Meir de Shalit, Former Director General Ministry of Tourism, Tel Aviv

Abraham Shaliv, M.A.; Director of the Center for Industrial Planning, Ministry of Commerce and Industry, Jerusalem

Yehudith Shaltiel, Ph.D.; Psychologist, Jerusalem: WOLBERG, LEWIS ROBERT

Alice Shalvi, Ph.D.; Professor, Department of English, the Hebrew University of Jerusalem

Avraham Shapira, Former Editor of *Shedemot*, published by the Kibbutz Movement

Dan (D.Y.) Shapira*, Ph.D.; Professor, Bar-Ilan University, Ramat Gan: JUDEO-TAT

Ilana Shapira, M.A.; Jerusalem: MELCHIZEDEK

Moshe Shapira, B.A.; Research Assistant in the Institute for Research in the History and Culture of Oriental Jewry, Bar-Ilan University, Ramat Gan: HEBRON; RUBIO, MORDECAI

Alexander Shapiro, Ph.D., Rabbi; Lecturer in Jewish History, the University of the Negev, Beersheba: MEISSEN; MERGENTHEIM; MOSBACH; NIEDERSTETTEN; NORDHAUSEN; PADERBORN; ROUSSILLON; SALZBURG; SHUM; SPANDAU; TALHEIM; TRIER; UEBERLINGEN; WETZLAR; ZUELZ

Haim Shapiro, Writer and Journalist, Jerusalem: ISRAEL, STATE OF: RELIGIOUS LIFE AND COMMUNITIES

Harry L. Shapiro, Ph.D.; Emeritus Chairman of the Department of Anthropology, the American Museum of Natural History; Professor of Anthropology, Columbia University, New York

Judah J. Shapiro, D.Ed.; Lecturer in Jewish History and Sociology, School of Jewish Communal Service, the Hebrew Union College – Jewish Institute of Religion, New York

Leon Shapiro, Lecturer in Russian-Jewish History, Rutgers University, New Brunswick, New Jersey: ABRAMOWITZ, RAPHAEL

Marc B. Shapiro*, Ph.D.; Weinberg Chair in Judaic Studies, University of Scranton, Pennsylvania: ANI MA'AMIN; ATLAS, SAMUEL

Yosef Shapiro, Writer, Givatayim, Israel: JOFFE, ELIEZER LIPA; SHOḤAT, ELIEZER

Andrew Sharf, Ph.D.; Associate Professor of History, Bar-Ilan University, Ramat Gan: BASIL I; BYZANTINE EMPIRE; CIRCUS PARTIES; CONSTANTINE VII PORPHYROGENITUS; CONSTANTINOPLE; DANIEL, VISION OF; EPIRUS; HERACLIUS; JUSTINIAN I; LEO III; LEO VI; MANUEL I COMNENUS; MICHAEL II; MICHAEL VIII PALAEOLOGUS; ROMANUS I LECAPENUS; SEVERUS

I. Harold Sharfman, D.H.L., Rabbi; Los Angeles: ILLOWY, BERNARD

Baila Round Shargel*, D.H.L.; Adjunct Assistant Professor, Manhattanville College, Purchase, New York; The Ratner Center, Jewish Theological Seminary, Harrison, New York: FRIEDLAENDER, ISRAEL; WESTCHESTER COUNTY

Rivka Shatz-Uffenheimer, Ph.D.; Senior Lecturer in Jewish Philosophy and Mysticism, the Hebrew University of Jerusalem: ḤASIDISM

Ya'akov Shavit, Ph.D.; Historian, Author, Senior Lecturer, Department of History of the Jewish People, Tel Aviv University: REVISIONISTS, ZIONIST

Zohar Shavit*, Ph.D.; Professor for Culture Research, Tel Aviv University: CHILDREN'S LITERATURE

Rachel (Katznelson) Shazar, B.A.; Wife of the President of Israel, Writer and Editor, Jerusalem: BARON, DEVORAH

Shneur Zalman Shazar, President of the State of Israel, Jerusalem: BEN-ZVI, IZHAK; KATZNELSON, BERL

Mark Shechner*, Ph.D.; Professor of English, University at Buffalo, Amherst, New York: ROSENFELD, ISAAC

Alan Shefman*, B.A., M.A.; Associate, York University, Centre for Practical Ethics; Consultant, The Edge Quality/Communications Consults; City Councillor, Vaughan, Canada: B'NAI B'RITH

Mort Sheinman*, B.A.; Journalism Teacher and Retired Newspaperman, New York: AUERBACH, BEATRICE FOX; CHAIKIN, SOL C.; COLE, KENNETH; DREXLER, MILLARD S.; ELIAS, ELI; FISHER, DONALD; GOODMAN, ANDREW; KARAN, DONNA; KIMMEL, SIDNEY; KLEIN, ANNE; KLEIN, CALVIN RICHARD; KOPELMAN, ARIE LEONARD; LAUREN, RALPH; MARCUS, STANLEY; MAZUR, JAY; NORELL, NORMAN; ORTENBERG, ARTHUR; PERELMAN, RONALD OWEN; POMERANTZ, FRED P.; RAYNOR, BRUCE; ROSEN, CARL; SAKOWITZ, BERNARD; SALTZMAN, MAURICE; SCAASI, ARNOLD; SCHRADER, ABE; SCHWARTZ, DAVID; SHAW, BENJAMIN; SPANEL, ABRAM NATHANIEL; STULBERG, LOUIS; TRAUB, MARVIN S.; TRIGERE, PAULINE; VON FURSTENBERG, DIANE; WACHNER, LINDA JOY; ZUCKERMAN, BEN

Ben-Zion Shek*, B.A., M.A., Ph.D. (University of Toronto); Professor Emeritus, Department of French, University of Toronto: KATTAN, NAIM; ROBIN, RÉGINE

Matityahu Shelem, Composer, Kibbutz Ramat Yohanan: KIBBUTZ FESTIVALS

Richard F. Shepard, Journalist, New York: BUCHWALD, NATHANIEL; BULOFF, JOSEPH; SCHWARTZ, MAURICE

Rona Sheramy*, Ph.D. Executive Director Association for Jewish Studies, New York: TEC, NECHAMA

Arnold Sherman, M.A.; Public Relations Officer, El Al, Lydda Airport: EL AL

Charles Bezalel Sherman, Professor of Sociology, Yeshiva University and the Jewish Teachers' Seminary, New York: CONGRESS FOR JEWISH CULTURE; JEWISH LABOR COMMITTEE; JEWISH SOCIALIST VERBAND; WORKMEN'S CIRCLE

Joseph Sherman*, B.A., M.A., Ph.D., Dr. Oxford University, England: BERGELSON, DAVID; DIK, ISAAC MEIR; SOUTH AFRICAN LITERATURE; WOLPE, DAVID E.

Moshe (D.) Sherman*, Ph.D.; Associate Professor, Touro Graduate School of Jewish Studies, New York: ALPERSTEIN, AVRAHAM ELIEZER BEN YESHAYA; ASH, ABRAHAM JOSEPH; BIRNBAUM, PHILIP

Nancy Sherman*, MFA (Masters in Fine Arts); Executive Vice President; National Yiddish Book Center; Amherst, Massachusetts: NATIONAL YIDDISH BOOK CENTER

Jerome J. Shestack*, L.L.B.; Lawyer; Past President American Bar Association, Philadelphia, Pennsylvania: BECKER, EDWARD ROY

Murray Shiff, M.S.W.; Executive Director (retired), Jewish Federation of Greater Seattle

Margalit Shilo*, Ph.D.; Associate Professor, Bar-Ilan University, Ramat Gan: ḤALUKKAH

Shmuel Shilo, Ph.D., Rabbi; Instructor in Jewish Law, the Hebrew University of Jerusalem: DINA DE-MALKHUTA DINA; LOAN; MAJORITY RULE; ONA'AH; ONES; SUCCESSION; WILLS

Amnon Shiloah*, Ph.D.; Professor Emeritus of Musicology, the Hebrew University of Jerusalem: ABU AL-FAḌL HASDAY; AFRICA, NORTH: MUSICAL TRADITIONS.; AHARON, EZRA; ALEPPO; AL-GHARĪḌ AL-YAHŪDĪ; AL-MANSUR AL-YAHŪDĪ; ARGOV, ZOHAR; ARLEN, HAROLD; AVSHALOMOV, JACOB; BABILÉE, JEAN; BAKKASHAH; BAR, SHLOMO; BAYER, BATHYA; BEN, ZEHAVA; BLOCH, ANDRE; BORIS, RUTHANNA; BOUZAGLO, DAVID; CANTILLATION; CHUJOY, ANATOLE; COHEN, SELMA JEAN; COLONNE, JULES EDOUARD; DANCE; DAVIČO, LUJO; DAVID; DAVID, ERNEST; DUQUE, SIMON DAVID; EMSHEIMER, ERNST; ESPINOSA, EDOUARD; FĀRĀBĪ, ABU NAṢR MUHAMMAD, AL-; FARBER, VIOLA; GASKELL, SONJA; GOLDSTEIN, RAYMOND; HALPRIN, ANN; HAYDEN, MELISSA; IBN ABĪ AL-ṢALT; IRAN, MUSICAL TRADITION; JACOBSTHAL, GUSTAV; JONAS, EMILE; KABBALAH; KATZ, ISRAEL J.; KIDD, MICHAEL; KIRSTEIN, LINCOLN; KUWEITI, SALAH; LÉVY; LÉVY, LAZARE; LOWINSKY, EDWARD ELIAS; MAQAM; MARCEAU, MARCEL; MASLOW, SOPHIE; MIZRAHI, ASHER; MURRAY, ARTHUR; MUSIC; ORENSTEIN, ARBIE; PANOV, VALERY; PLAMENAC, DRAGAN; RINGER, ALEXANDER L.; ROBBINS, JEROME; ROSS, HERBERT; SILLS, BEVERLY; SIMON, PAUL; SPECTOR, JOHANNA; SPIVACKE, HAROLD;

STENN, REBECCA; TEMIANKA, HENRI; VALABREGA, CESARE; WEINSTOCK, HERBERT; WIÉNER, JEAN

Bina Shiloah*, B.Ed.; Dance Coordinator-Rubin Conservatory of Music and Dance, Jerusalem: KRAUS, GERTRUD; LEVI-AGRON, HASSIA; LEVI-TANNAI, SARA; SOKOLOW, ANNA

Zvi Shiloah, B.A.; Journalist, Chairman of the Executive of the Land of Israel Movement, Tel Aviv: GUSH EMUNIM

Gideon Shimoni, Ph.D.; Senior Lecturer, Institute for Contemporary Jewry, Hebrew University of Jerusalem: GANDHI, MOHANDAS KARAMCHAND; KALLENBACH, HERMANN

Yaacov Shimoni, Deputy Director General, Ministry for Foreign Affairs, Jerusalem: HUSSEINI, ḤĀJJ AMIN AL-; ISRAEL, STATE OF: ARAB POPULATION

Felix Eliezer Shinnar, Dr.Jur.; Economist and former Ambassador, Tel Aviv: GERMANY; REPARATIONS, GERMAN.

Chone Shmeruk, Ph.D.; Professor of Yiddish Literature, the Hebrew University of Jerusalem: DER NISTER; DINESON, JACOB; PURIM-SHPIL; SOVETISH HEYMLAND; WIENER, MEIR; YIDDISH LITERATURE

Joshua H. Shmidman, B.A., Rabbi; Instructor in Philosophy, Yeshiva University; New York: HATRED; INSULT; REBUKE AND REPROOF; VENGEANCE; ZEKHUT AVOT

Aryeh Shmuelevitz*, Ph.D.; Professor Emeritus, Moshe Dayan Center for Middle Eastern and African Studies, Tel Aviv University: BAYAZID II; BURSA; EMESA; FARḤI; KIERA

Efraim Shmueli, Ph.D.; Professor of Philosophy; Adjunct Professor of Jewish History and Literature, Cleveland State University: WOYSLAWSKI, ZEVI

Herzl Shmueli, Ph.D.; Senior Lecturer in Musicology, Tel Aviv University: ADMON, YEDIDYAH; AVIDOM, MENAHEM; BOSCOVITCH, ALEXANDER URIYAH

David Shneer*, Ph.D.; Director Center for Judaic Studies, Associate Professor of History, University of Denver: KHARIK, IZI; MARKISH, PERETZ

J. Lee Shneidman, Ph.D.; Associate Professor of History, Adelphi University, Garden City, New York: ABENVIVES

Azriel Shochat, Ph.D.; Associate Professor of the History of the Jewish People, Haifa University: ALAMI, SOLOMON; ELDAD HA-DANI; ERGAS, JOSEPH BEN EMANUEL; ESSEN; HASKALAH; IBN VERGA, SOLOMON; OSNABRUECK; OSTROG

Joseph Shochetman, B.A.; Jerusalem: MOLCHO, SOLOMON

Debby (Deborah Anne Glaser) Shoctor*, B.A., B.J., M.L.I.S.; Archivist, The Jewish Archives and Historical Society of Edmonton and Northern Alberta, Canada: EDMONTON

Baruch Shohetman, M.A.; Bibliographer, Jerusalem: EISMANN, MOSES; GLUECKSOHN, MOSHE; SOCIETY FOR THE ATTAINMENT OF FULL CIVIL RIGHTS FOR THE JEWISH PEOPLE IN RUSSIA; UVAROV, SERGEY SEMYONOVICH

Ana Shomlo-Ninic, M.A.; Writer and Critic, Belgrade: SAMOKOVLIJA, ISAK; YUGOSLAV LITERATURE

Shorter Jewish Encyclopaedia in Russian, Jerusalem: CRIMEAN AFFAIR; DOMALSKY, I.; DONSKOY, MARK SEMENOVICH; GEKHT, SEMEN GRIGOREVICH; GEORGIA; GERY; GOTS; GRULËV, MIKHAIL VLADIMIROVICH; GUKOVSKY, GRIGORY ALEKSANDROVICH; GUREVICH, MIKHAIL IOSIFOVICH; GUSEV, SERGEI IVANOVICH; KALIK, MIKHAIL; KANNEGISER, LEONID AKIMOVICH; KANOVICH, GRIGORY; KAUFMAN, AVRAHAM YOSIFOVICH; KIPEN, ALEKSANDR ABRAMOVICH; KNUT, DOVID; KOL'TSOV, MIKHAIL; KOMZET; KOPYTMAN, MARK RUVIMOVICH; KRIMCHAK LANGUAGE; KRIMCHAKS; LEONIDOV, LEONID MIRONOVICH; LOTMAN, YURI MIKHAILOVICH; LOYTER, EFRAIM BARUKHOVICH; MANEVICH, LEV YEFIMOVICH; MOUNTAIN JEWS; YEVREYSKI KOMISSARIAT; ZELDOVICH, YAKOV BORISOVICH; ZEMLYACHKA, ROZALIYA SAMOYLOVNA

Robert Shosteck, M.A.; Curator of the B'nai B'rith Museum, Washington, D. C.: COHEN, ALFRED MORTON; ELLINGER, MORITZ; SEQUEYRA, JOHN DE

Yehuda Shrenzel, Chess Columnist, Tel Aviv: KASPAROV, GARY

Yisrael Shrenzel, Chess Columnist, Tel Aviv

Shimon Shtober*, Dr.Phil.; Senior Lecturer, Bar-Ilan University, Ramat Gan: SAMBARI, JOSEPH BEN ISAAC

Aaron Shub*, M.A.; Rabbinical Student, University of Judaism, Los Angeles: KOGEN, DAVID

Justin (Benjamin) Shubow*, B.A., M.A.; J.D. Candidate Yale Law School, New Haven, Connecticut: SHUBOW, JOSEPH SHALOM

Malka Hillel Shulewitz, Journalist, Jerusalem: ISRAEL, STATE OF: HEALTH, WELFARE, AND SOCIAL SECURITY

Joseph I. Shulim, Ph.D.; Professor of History, Brooklyn College of the City University of New York: GAY, PETER JACK

David Shulman*, Ph.D.; Professor of India Studies, the Hebrew University of Jerusalem: AKBAR THE GREAT

Nisson E. Shulman, D.H.L., Rabbi; Yonkers, New York: SLONIK, BENJAMIN AARON BEN ABRAHAM

William (L.) Shulman*, Ed.D.; President, Association of Holocaust Organizations, New York: ASSOCIATION OF HOLOCAUST ORGANIZATIONS; HOLOCAUST

Shlomo Shunami, Dip.Lib.; Bibliographer and Librarian, the Jewish National and University Library, Jerusalem: LIBRARY, JEWISH NATIONAL AND UNIVERSITY; WORMANN, CURT

Jonathan Shunary, Ph.D.; Assistant Professor of Hebrew and Biblical Studies, the University of Wisconsin, Madison: ALPHABET, HEBREW

Nili Shupak, B.A.; Jerusalem: JACHIN AND BOAZ; KOHATH AND KOHATHITES; LEAH; OREB AND ZEEB; SHEBNAH; SHEMAIAH

Shifra Shvarts*, Ph.D.; Associate Professor, Chairwoman, Center of Health Policy in the Negev, Ben-Gurion University of the Negev, Beersheva: ISRAEL, STATE OF: HEALTH, WELFARE, AND SOCIAL SECURITY

Rafi Siano*: SAGALOWITZ, BENJAMIN

Albert A. Sicroff, D.del'U; Professor of Romance Languages, Queens College of the City University of New York: LIMPIEZA DE SANGRE

Moshe Sicron, Ph.D.; Government Statistician in the Central Bureau of Statistics; Professor, The Hebrew University of Jerusalem

Bjoern (Björn) Siegel*, M.A., Ph.D. Student, Chair of Jewish History and Culture, Ludwig-Maximilians-Universität, Munich. Germany: BAB, JULIUS; BONDY, CURT; BRAHM, OTTO; CASTIGLIONI, CAMILLO; CHRISTIAN SOCIAL PARTY, GERMAN; CONSERVATIVE PARTY, GERMAN; EPPSTEIN, PAUL; ESRA; FRANKENBURGER, WOLF; FREDERICK I; FRIEDMANN, DESIDER; GELBER, NATHAN MICHAEL; GIEHSE, THERESE; GRANACH, ALEXANDER; GRUEBER, HEINRICH; HEIMWEHR; HERMANN, GEORG; HOROVITZ, JOSEF; JOSEPH II; KAHLE, PAUL ERNST; KAUFMANN, OSKAR; LABAND, PAUL; LADENBURG; LANDAU, EUGEN; LANDSBERG, OTTO; LANDSHUT, SIEGFRIED; LASKER, EDUARD; LASZLO, PHILIP ALEXIUS DE LOMBOS; LAZARUS, MORITZ; LEBRECHT, FUERCHTEGOTT; LEVI, PAUL; LEVISON, WILHELM; LOEWE, LUDWIG and ISIDOR; MARIA THERESA; MARKUS, LUDWIG; MAYER, GUSTAV; MITTWOCH, EUGEN; PAPPENHEIM, BERTHA

Marcia B. Siegel, B.A.; Dance Critic, New York: GASKELL, SONJA; HAYDEN, MELISSA; KAYE, NORA; KIRSTEIN, LINCOLN; LEVINSON, ANDRE; LICHINE, DAVID; ROBBINS, JEROME; RUBINSTEIN, IDA; SAINT-LÉON, ARTHUR MICHEL; SOKOLOW, ANNA; TAMIRIS, HELEN

Mark (A.) Siegel*, M.A., Ph.D.; Vice President, Government Affairs, New Century Financial Corporation; former Deputy Assistant to the President and Liaison to the Jewish Community in the Carter White House; Adjunct Professor of Political Science, Graduate School of Political Management, The George Washington University: STRAUSS, ROBERT SCHWARZ

Richard (A.) Siegel*, M.A.; Executive Director Emeritus, National Foundation for Jewish Culture, Los Angeles: NATIONAL FOUNDATION FOR JEWISH CULTURE

Seymour Siegel, D.H.L., Rabbi; Professor of Theology and of Ethics and Rabbinic Thought, the Jewish Theological Seminary of America, New York: HIGGER, MICHAEL; IMITATION OF GOD; RESURRECTION; WAXMAN, MEYER; WINTER, PAUL

Sergio Joseph Sierra, M.A., Rabbi; Lecturer in Hebrew Language and Literature, the University of Turin: MARSALA; MESSINA; PALERMO; SICILY; SYRACUSE; TRAPANI

Myra J. Siff, M.A.; Instructor in Religion and Bible, Wellesley College, Massachusetts: BABEL, TOWER OF; SAMSON; SARAH

Menahem Binyamin Andrew Silberfeld, Ph.D., Rabbi; Librarian, Jerusalem

David Silberklang*, Ph.D.; Historian; Editor, Yad Vashem Studies; Adjunct Lecturer, the Hebrew University of Jerusalem: BAUER, YEHUDA; GUTMAN, ISRAEL

Lou H. Silberman, D.H.L., Rabbi; Professor of Jewish Literature and Thought, Vanderbilt University, Nashville, Tennessee: CHOSEN PEOPLE; COMPASSION; GOD; JOY; SCHOEPS, HANS JOACHIM

Eisig Silberschlag, Ph.D.; President and Professor of Hebrew Literature, the Hebrew College, Brookline, Massachusetts: BERNSTEIN, ZVI HIRSCH; BLANK, SAMUEL LEIB; BRAININ, REUBEN; EINHORN, MOSES; EPSTEIN, ABRAHAM; EPSTEIN, ABRAHAM; FEINSTEIN, MOSES; FRIEDLAND, ABRAHAM HYMAN; GERSONI, HENRY; GINSBURG, JEKUTHIEL; GINZBURG, SIMON; GOLDMAN, MOSES HA-KOHEN; GREENWALD, JEKUTHIEL JUDAH; HALKIN, SIMON; HEBREW LITERATURE, MODERN; IMBER, NAPHTALI HERZ; KABAKOFF, JACOB; LEAF, HAYIM; LISITZKY, EPHRAIM E.; LOEWISOHN, SOLOMON; MAISELS, MOSES ḤAYYIM; MALACHI, ELIEZER RAPHAEL; MARKSON, AARON DAVID; MAXIMON, SHALOM DOV BER; MIRSKY, SAMUEL KALMAN; PERSKY, DANIEL; PREIL, GABRIEL JOSHUA; RAISIN, JACOB ZALMAN; RAISIN, MAX; REGELSON, ABRAHAM; RESSLER, BENJAMIN; RIBALOW, MENACHEM; ROSENBERG, ABRAHAM ḤAYYIM; ROSENFELD, SAMUEL; ROSENZWEIG, GERSON; SACKLER, HARRY; SCHARFSTEIN, ẒEVI; SCHUR, ZEV WOLF; SCHUR, ZEV WOLF; SCHWARTZ, ABRAHAM SAMUEL; SCHWARZBERG, SAMUEL BENJAMIN; SHMUELI, EPHRAIM; SHULVASS, MOSES AVIGDOR; SILKINER, BENJAMIN NAHUM; SOBEL, JACOB ẒEVI; SOLODAR, ABRAHAM; TOUROFF, NISSAN; TOUROFF, NISSAN; TWERSKY, YOḤANAN; YINNON, MOSHE

Jon Silkin, B.A; Poet, Newcastle-upon-Tyne, England: ABSE, DANNIE; FUCHS, ABRAHAM MOSHE; LITVINOFF, EMANUEL; ROSENBERG, ISAAC; SASSOON, SIEGFRIED LORRAINE

Daniel Jeremy Silver, Ph.D., Rabbi; Adjunct Professor of Religion, Case Western Reserve University, Cleveland: HERESY

David L. Silver, B.A., Rabbi; Harrisburg, Pennsylvania

Drew Silver*, Freelance Editor, New York: BEIT-HALLAHMI, BENJAMIN; BERCOVITCH, SACVAN; BRUNER, JEROME SEYMOUR; DONIGER, WENDY; FEYNMAN, RICHARD PHILLIPS; GELL-MANN, MURRAY; GOFFMAN, ERVING MANUAL; GOULD, STEPHEN JAY; HARRIS, MARVIN; HIRSCH, ERIC DONALD, JR.; LEWIS, ANTHONY; LOWENSTEIN, ALLARD KENNETH; MEYER, MICHAEL A.; MILGROM, JACOB; PERLE, RICHARD NORMAN; REICH, ROBERT BERNARD; REINHARZ, JEHUDA; RENDELL, EDWARD GENE; RIVLIN, ALICE M.; SCHEINDLIN, RAYMOND P.; SCHIFFMAN, LAWRENCE H.; STILLMAN, NORMAN ARTHUR; TIGAY, JEFFREY H; WELLSTONE, PAUL; YOUNG, JAMES E.

Jesse Harold Silver, Sports Writer, Surfside, Florida: HART, CECIL M.; HENSHEL, HARRY D.; MENDOZA, DANIEL; MOSBACHER, EMIL JR.; MYERS, LAWRENCE E.; OLYMPIC GAMES; SEDRAN, BARNEY; SOLOMONS, JACK; SPORTS

Catherine Silverman, Ph.D.; Lecturer in History, City College of the City University of New York: TUCHMAN, BARBARA WERTHEIM

Godfrey Edmond Silverman, M.A.; Jerusalem: BRITISH ISRAELITES; CHILDREN'S LITERATURE; DU BARTAS, GUILLAUME DE SALLUSTE; GALATINUS, PIETRO COLUMNA; GÉNÉBRARD, GILBERT;

GIUSTINIANI, AGOSTINO; GOLLER, IZAK; GUEDALLA, PHILIP; GUIDACERIO, AGACIO; HEINE, HEINRICH; HOCHHUTH, ROLF; LE BÉ, GUILLAUME; LE FÈVRE DE LA BODERIE, GUY; LIGHTFOOT, JOHN; MAES, ANDREAS; MERCIER, JEAN; MUENSTER, SEBASTIAN; NOLA, ELIJAH BEN MENAHEM DA; NOSTRADAMUS; PAGNINI, SANTES; PARAF, PIERRE; PAULI, JOHANNES; PELLICANUS, CONRAD; PISTORIUS, JOHANNES; PLANTAVIT DE LA PAUSE, JEAN; PLANTIN, CHRISTOPHE; POCOCKE, EDWARD; POSTEL, GUILLAUME; PSALMS, BOOK OF; PUBLISHING; RABINOWITZ, SAMUEL JACOB; RAFFALOVICH, ISAIAH; REUCHLIN, JOHANNES; RICIUS, PAULUS; SCALIGER, JOSEPH JUSTUS; SCHICKARD, WILHELM; SLOTKI, ISRAEL WOLF; SOLA, DE; STUDENTS' MOVEMENTS, JEWISH; TREMELLIUS, JOHN IMMANUEL; TRITHEMIUS, JOHANNES; TRITHEMIUS, JOHANNES; TYNDALE, WILLIAM; VELTWYCK, GERARD; VIGENÈRE, BLAISE DE; WAKEFIELD, ROBERT; WIDMANSTETTER, JOHANN ALBRECHT; WOLF, FRIEDRICH; ZUCKMAYER, CARL

Lisa Silverman*, Ph.D.; Assistant Professor of History, University of Wisconsin, Milwaukee: BAUER, OTTO; BEDA; BERMANN, RICHARD ARNOLD; BRAUNTHAL, JULIUS; DONATH, ADOLPH; KRAUS, KARL

Morris Silverman, D.H.L., Rabbi; Hartford, Connecticut: HARTFORD; KOPPLEMANN, HERMAN PAUL

Meir Silverstone, LL.B.; Attorney and former Director General, Ministry of the Interior, Jerusalem

Jakob Naphtali Hertz Simchoni, Dr.Phil.; *Encyclopaedia Judaica* (Germany); Historian, Berlin: AARON SAMUEL BEN MOSES SHALOM OF KREMENETS; ABBA MARI BEN ELIGDOR; ABRAHAM BEN JOSIAH TROKI; ABRAHAM BEN JOSIAH YERUSHALMI; ABRAHAM BEN JUDAH BEN ABRAHAM; ELIJAH BEN AARON BEN MOSES; LUZKI, ABRAHAM BEN JOSEPH SOLOMON

Ernest E. Simke, Honorary Consul-General of Israel, Manila, Philippines: PHILIPPINES

Erica (B.) Simmons*, Ph.D.; Historian, Toronto, Canada: HADASSAH, THE WOMEN'S ZIONIST ORGANIZATION OF AMERICA; JACOBS, ROSE GELL

Akiba Ernst Simon, Dr. Phil.; Emeritus Professor of Education, the Hebrew University of Jerusalem: BAECK, LEO

Aryeh Simon, B.A.; Educator, Youth Village, Ben Shemen, Israel: LEHMANN, SIEGFRIED

Isidore Simon, M.D.; Professor of the History of Hebrew Medicine, Centre Universitaire d'Etudes Juives, Paris: ABRAHAM BEN SOLOMON OF SAINT MAXIMIN; ACOSTA, CHRISTOBAL; ISAAC BEN TODROS; JOSEPH BEN AḤMAD IBN ḤASDAI; NATHAN, MORDECAI

Michael Simon, Dr.Phil.; Former Ambassador, Ministry for Foreign Affairs, Jerusalem: FLAG

Rachel Simon*, Ph.D.; Princeton University, New Jersey: BENGHAZI; DJERBA; LIBYA; TRIPOLI; WOMAN: MODERN PERIOD IN MUSLIM WORLD

Uriel Simon*, Ph.D.; Professor Emeritus of Bible, Bar-Ilan University, Ramat Gan: IBN EZRA, ABRAHAM BEN MEIR; RUDIN, JACOB PHILIP

Perrine Simon-Nahum*: LES COLLOQUES DES INTELLECTUELS JUIFS DE LANGUE FRANÇAISE; SIMON, PIERRE; TRIGANO, SHMUEL

David Jacob Simonsen, Ph.D., Rabbi; Chief Rabbi of Denmark, Copenhagen: BIBLE

Shlomo Simonsohn, Ph.D.; Professor of Jewish History, Tel Aviv University: MANTUA; NEPPI, HANANEL; TRENT; TREVISO; TRIESTE; VERONA

Uriel Simri, Ed.D.; Former Scientific Director of the Wingate Institute for Physical Education and Sport, Netanyah: SPORTS

Yuval Sinai*, Ph.D.; Lecturer, Netanya Academic College, Israel: PRACTICE AND PROCEDURE; WITNESS

Mendel Singer, Writer, Haifa: SCHUSSHEIM, AARON LEIB

Moshe Singer, Moshav Beit Yehoshua: HA-NO'AR HA-IVRI-AKIBA

Sikander Singh*, Dr.Phil.; Lecturer, Heinrich-Heine-Universität, Duesseldorf, Germany: HEINE, HEINRICH

Nancy Sinkoff*, Associate Professor of Jewish Studies and History, Rutgers, The State University of New Jersey: SOCIALISM

Colette Sirat*, Ph.D.; Professor of Hebrew Medieval Paleography and Philosophy, Ecole Pratique des Hautes Etudes, Sorbonne University, Paris, France: AL-CONSTANTINI, ENOCH BEN SOLOMON; BLUMENKRANZ, BERNHARD; JACOB BEN MOSES OF BAGNOLS; LEVI BEN ABRAHAM BEN ḤAYYIM; SCHWAB, MOÏSE; SOCIÉTÉ DES ÉTUDES JUIVES; WOGUE, LAZARE ELIEZER

René Samuel Sirat*, Ph.D., Rabbi; Chief Rabbi of the Central Consistory and Vice Chairperson of the Conference of European Rabbis, Paris, France: DEL MEDICO, HENRI E.; KRASUCKI, HENRI

Magdalena Sitarz*, German and Yiddish Philologist, Institute of German Philology, Jagiellonian University: ASCH, SHOLEM

Harvard Sitkoff, Ph.D.; Assistant Professor of American History, Washington University, Saint Louis, Missouri: JAVITS, JACOB KOPPEL

David Sitton, Chairman of the Executive of the Jerusalem Council of the Sephardi Community, Jerusalem

Gabriel Sivan, Ph.D.; Author, Educator, Former Director, Information and Education Department, South African Zionist Federation, Jerusalem: SCHONFIELD, HUGH JOSEPH

Tracy (Ellen) Sivitz*, M.A., M. Phil., A.B.; Attorney, New York: AMIT; RAKOVSKY, PUAH

Aaron Skaist, Ph.D., Rabbi; Senior Lecturer in Bible and in Semitic Languages, Bar-Ilan University, Ramat Gan: MESOPOTAMIA

Gretchen Skidmore*, M.A.; Director, Civic and Defense Initiatives Education Division, United States Holocaust Memorial Museum, Washington, D.C.: KINDERTRANSPORT

Deborah Skolnick Einhorn*, M.A.; Student, Brandeis University,

Waltham, Massachusetts: PHILANTHROPY

Larry Skolnick*: DAYTON

Nathan Skolnick, M.A.; Bridgeport, Connecticut

Fred Skolnik*, Editor in Chief, *Encyclopaedia Judaica* Second Edition: ASSIMILATION; EDUCATION, JEWISH; ḤAREDIM; HISTORY: MODERN TIMES – FROM THE 1880S TO THE EARLY 21ST CENTURY; ISRAEL, STATE OF: LABOR; JEWISH IDENTITY; PEMBER, PHOEBE YATES; VILNA; YOSEF, OVADIAH; ZIONIST CONGRESSES

Richard Skolnik, Ph.D.; Assistant Professor of History, City College of the City University of New York: CANTOR, JACOB AARON; DICKSTEIN, SAMUEL; FRIEDSAM, MICHAEL; GOLDSTEIN, JUDAH JAMISON; GOLDWATER, SIGMUND SCHULZ; MOSES, ROBERT

Karl Skorecki*, M.D.; Professor of Medicine (Nephrology) and Director of Research, Rappaport Research Institute, Technion - Israel Institute of Technology and Rambam Medical Center, Haifa: GENETIC ANCESTRY, JEWISH

Solomon Leon Skoss, Ph.D.; Professor of Arabic, Dropsie College for Hebrew and Cognate Learning, Philadelphia: ALFASI, DAVID BEN ABRAHAM

Menahem Slae, M.A., Rabbi; The Responsa Project, Bar-Ilan University, Ramat Gan: HALAKHIC PERIODICALS; INSURANCE; RESPONSA

Martin (E.) Sleeper*, Ed.D.; Associate Director, Facing History and Ourselves, Brookline, Massachusetts: FACING HISTORY AND OURSELVES

Nicolas Slonimsky, Musicologist, Los Angeles: BERLIN, IRVING; BERNSTEIN, LEONARD; BLITZSTEIN, MARC; COPLAND, AARON; DIAMOND, DAVID; FOSS, LUKAS; SAMINSKY, LAZARE; WEILL, KURT

Yehuda Slutsky, Ph.D.; Senior Lecturer in the History of the Israel Labor Movement, Tel Aviv University: AARONSOHN; ABKHAZ AUTONOMOUS SOVIET SOCIALIST REPUBLIC; ACOSTA, JOAN D'; AGURSKY, SAMUEL; AMZALAK, ḤAYYIM; ANTEBI, ALBERT; ANTI-FASCIST COMMITTEE, JEWISH; APPEL, JUDAH LEIB; ARAZI, YEHUDA; ARCHANGEL; ARTEMOVSK; ASHKHABAD; AVIGUR, SHAUL; AZERBAIJAN; BAKHCHISARAI; BALTA; BAR; BARANOVICHI; BARATZ, HERMANN; BARNETT, ZERAH; BELAYA TSERKOV; BELKIND; BELKOWSKY, ẒEVI HIRSCH; BELORUSSIA; BEN-GURION, DAVID; BERLIN, ISRAEL; BERMANN, VASILI; BERNSTEIN-KOGAN, JACOB; BIENSTOK, JUDAH LEIB; BIRZAI; BLOOD LIBEL; BOBRUISK; BOGUSLAV; BORISOV; BRANDT, BORIS; BRAUNSTEIN, MENAHEM MENDEL; BRODSKI; BRUCK, GRIGORI; BRYANSK; BUCHBINDER, NAHUM; BUCHMIL, JOSHUA HESHEL; CANDLE TAX; CANTONISTS; CATHERINE II; CAUCASUS; CHERKASSY; CHERNIGOV; CHERNOBYL; CHORNY, JOSEPH JUDAH; CHWOLSON, DANIEL; CRIMEA; DAUGAVPILS; DAYAN, MOSHE; DECEMBRISTS; DENIKIN, ANTON IVANOVICH; DENIKIN, ANTON IVANOVICH; DEPUTIES OF THE JEWISH PEOPLE; DERBENT; DIZENGOFF, MEIR; DIZENGOFF, MEIR; DNEPROPETROVSK; DORI, YA'AKOV; DUBIN, MORDECAI; DUBNO; DUBNOW, ZE'EV; DUBOSSARY; DUBROVNO; DUMA; DUNAYEVTSY; EBNER, MEIR; EISENBERG, AHARON ELIYAHU; ELIASBERG, MORDECAI; ERLANGER, MICHEL; ESTONIA; ETTINGER; EYNIKEYT; FEINBERG; FEODOSIYA; FOLKSPARTEI RUSSIA; FRIEDBERG, ABRAHAM SHALOM; FRIEDLAND; FRIEDMAN, NAPHTALI; FRUMKIN, ISRAEL DOV; FUENN, SAMUEL JOSEPH; GADYACH; GAISIN; GALANT, ELIAHU VLADIMIROVICH; GILADI, ISRAEL; GINSBURG, SAUL; GLUSKIN, ZE'EV; GOLDBERG, BORIS; GOLDBERG, ISAAC LEIB; GOLDSTEIN, SALWIAN; GOLITSYN, COUNT NIKOLAI NIKOLAYEVICH; GOLOVANEVSK; GOMEL; GORKI; GORODOK; GROZNY; GRUNBERG, ABRAHAM; HAGANAH; HA-KARMEL; HA-SHOMER; HASKALAH; ḤAVIV-LUBMAN, AVRAHAM DOV; HE-ḤALUTZ; HE-ḤAVER; ḤISIN, ḤAYYIM; HOROWITZ, ḤAYYIM DOV; IDELOVITCH, DAVID; ILINTSY; ILLEGAL IMMIGRATION; INFORMERS; IRKUTSK; ISAAC OF CHERNIGOV; ISRAEL, STATE OF: DEFENSE FORCES; ISRAEL, STATE OF: HISTORICAL SURVEY; IZYASLAV; JAFFE, BEZALEL; JAFFE, LEIB; JASINOWSKI, ISRAEL ISIDORE; JAUNIJELGAVA; JEKABPILS; JELGAVA; JEWISH SOCIETY FOR HISTORY AND ETHNOGRAPHY; JOFFE, HILLEL; JONAVA; JUDAIZERS; JURBARKAS; KALININDORF; KALINKOVICHI; KAMENETS-PODOLSKI; KAMINER, ISAAC; KANTOR, JUDAH LEIB; KARASUBAZAR; KATKOV, MIKHAIL NIKIFOROVICH; KATZ, BENZION; KATZENELLENBOGEN, ẒEVI HIRSH; KATZENELSON, JUDAH LEIB BENJAMIN; KATZENELSON, NISSAN; KAZAN; KAZATIN; KAZYONNY RAVVIN; KHARKOV; KHERSON; KHOROL; KIEV; KIROVOGRAD; KIRZHNITZ, ABRAHAM; KLINTSY; KOIDANOVO; KOKAND; KONOTOP; KOROBKA; KOROSTEN; KORSUN-SHEVCHENKOVSKI; KOSTOMAROV, NIKOLAI IVANOVICH; KOVNER, ABRAHAM URI; KRASNODAR; KRASNOYE; KREMENCHUG; KRICHEV; KRIVOI ROG; KRIVOYE OZERO; KRUSHEVAN, PAVOLAKI; KUBA; KUIBYSHEV; KULISHER; KUPERNIK, ABRAHAM; KURSK; KYBARTAI; LANDAU, ADOLPH; LANDAU, GREGORY ADOLFOVICH; LEBENSOHN, ABRAHAM DOV; LEKHNO, DAVID; LEONTOVICH, FEDOR; LEPEL; LERNER, ḤAYYIM ẒEVI BEN TODROS; LERNER, JOSEPH JUDAH; LETICHEV; LEVIN, EMANUEL; LEVIN, JUDAH LEIB; LEVIN, SHMARYA; LEVINSOHN, ISAAC BAER; LEVONTIN, JEHIEL JOSEPH; LEVONTIN, ZALMAN DAVID; LEWIN-EPSTEIN, ELIAHU ZE'EV; LEWINSKY, ELHANAN LEIB; LICHTENFELD, GABRIEL JUDAH; LIOZNO; LIPMAN, LEVI; LIPOVETS; LIPSCHITZ, JACOB HA-LEVI; LISHANSKY, YOSEF; LITHUANIA; LITIN; LOZINSKI, SAMUEL; LUBARSKY, ABRAHAM ELIJAH; LUBAVITCH; LUBNY; LUGANSK; LURIA, DAVID BEN JACOB AARON; LURIE, JOSEPH; LUTOSTANSKI, HIPPOLYTE; LYADY; MAGGID, DAVID; MAGGID-STEINSCHNEIDER, HILLEL NOAH; MAKAROV; MANASSEH BEN JOSEPH OF ILYA; MANDELBERG, AVIGDOR; MANDELSTAMM, BENJAMIN; MANDELSTAMM, LEON; MANDELSTAMM, MAX EMMANUEL; MANNE, MORDECAI ẒEVI; MAREK, PESACH; MARGOLIN, MOSES; MARGOLIOTH, JUDAH LOEB; MARGOLIS-KALVARYSKI, HAIM; MAY LAWS,; MAZEH, JACOB; MEDZIBEZH; MEEROVITCH, MENACHÉ; MILEYKOWSKY, NATHAN; MINOR, OSIP S.; MINOR, SOLOMON ZALMAN; MINSK; MOGILEV; MOGILEV-PODOLSKI; MOHILEWER, SAMUEL; MORGULIS, MANASSEH; MOSCOW; MOTZKIN, LEO; MOZYR; MSTISLAVL; MYSH, MICHAEL; NADAV, ẒEVI; NAIDITSCH, ISAAC ASHER; NATHANSON, BERNHARD; NAVON, JOSEPH; NEMIROV; NEVAKHOVICH, JUDAH LEIB; NEW ISRAEL; NEZHIN; NICHOLAS; NIKITIN, VICTOR; NIKOLAYEV; NILI; NISSELOVICH, LEOPOLD; NOVGOROD-SEVERSK; NOVOZYBKOV; NUMERUS CLAUSUS; OLGOPOL; OMSK; ORDZHONIKIDZE; OREL; ORSHA; OSSOWETZKY, O. YEHOSHUA; OVRUCH; PALE OF SETTLEMENT; PAPERNA,

ABRAHAM JACOB; PATTERSON, JOHN HENRY; PAVLOGRAD; PAVOLOCH; PEREFERKOVICH, NEHEMIAH; PERETZ, ABRAHAM; PETLYURA, SIMON; PEVZNER, SAMUEL JOSEPH; PIRYATIN; PLEHVE, VYACHESLAV KONSTANTINOVICH VON; PLUNGIAN, MORDECAI; POBEDONOSTSEV, KONSTANTIN PETROVICH; POCHEP; PODOLIA; POGREBISHCHENSKI; POGROMS; POLONNOYE; POLOTSK; POLTAVA; POLYAKOV; POSENER, SOLOMON; PRILUKI; PROSKUROV; PRYLUCKI, ẒEVI HIRSCH; PUBLISHING; PUKHACHEWSKY, MICHAEL ZALMAN; RAAB, JUDAH; RABBINOWITZ, SAUL PHINEHAS; RABINOVICH, JOSEPH; RABINOVICH, YEHUDAH LEIB; RABINOWITZ, ELIAHU WOLF; RADOMYSHL; RALL, YISRAEL; RALL, YISRAEL; RAPOPORT; RATNER, YOHANAN; RAZSVET; RECHITSA; REICHERSON, MOSES; RODKINSON, MICHAEL LEVI; ROGACHEV; ROKACH, SHIMON; ROKISKIS; ROMM; ROMNY; ROSENBAUM, SEMYON; ROSENTHAL, HERMAN; ROSENTHAL, LEON; ROSTOV; RUSSIA; SAINT PETERSBURG; SAKIAI; SALOMON, JOEL MOSES; SAMARKAND; SAPIR, JOSEPH; SARATOV; SCHAPIRA, HERMANN; SCHEID, ELIE; SCHLESINGER, AKIVA JOSEPH; SCHOENHACK, JOSEPH; SCHUB, MOSHE DAVID; SCHULMAN, KALMAN; SCHULMANN, ELIEZER; SCHWABACHER, SIMEON ARYEH; SEDUVA; SEVASTOPOL; SHAPIRA, ABRAHAM; SHATZKES, MOSES AARON; SHCHEDRIN; SHEFTEL, MIKHAIL; SHEINKIN, MENAHEM; SHEPETOVKA; SHITRIT, BEḤOR SHALOM; SHKLOV; SHOCHAT, ISRAEL; SHOCHAT, MANIA WILBUSHEWITCH; SHPOLA; SIBERIA; SIMFEROPOL; SIMḤONI, ASSAF; SIMḤONI, ASSAF; SKUODAS; SLIOZBERG, HENRY; SLONIMSKI, ḤAYYIM SELIG; SLUCKI, ABRAHAM JACOB; SMILANSKY, MOSHE; SOCIETY FOR THE PROMOTION OF CULTURE AMONG THE JEWS OF RUSSIA; SOLIELI, MORDECAI; SOSIS, ISRAEL; SPEYER, BENJAMIN; STAMPFER, JEHOSHUA; STANISLAVSKY, SIMON JUDAH; STEINBERG, JOSHUA; STEINBERG, JUDAH; STERN, BEZALEL; STRASHUN, MATHIAS; STYBEL, ABRAHAM JOSEPH; SUSSMAN, ABRAHAM; SUWALSKI, ISAAK; SUWALSKI, ISAAK; SYRKIN, JOSHUA; SYRKIN, MOSES NAHUM SOLOMONOVICH; TAMARES, AARON SAMUEL; TARNOPOL, JOACHIM ḤAYYIM; TASHKENT; TAURAGE; TEITEL, JACOB; TELLER, ISRAEL; TELSIAI; TIOMKIN, VLADIMIR; TOMSK; TRUMPELDOR, JOSEPH; TUGENDHOLD, JACOB; UFA; UKMERGE; UTENA; VERKHNEUDINSK; VINNIKOV, ISAAC N.; VLADIVOSTOK; VOLOZHINER, ISAAC BEN ḤAYYIM; VOSKHOD; WAY, LEWIS; WENGEROFF, PAULINE; WILBUSCHEWITZ; WILENSKY, YEHUDAH LEIB NISAN; WITTE, SERGEY YULYEVICH, COUNT; WLOCLAWEK; YEKOPO; YELLIN; YEVSEKTSIYA; ZABLUDOW; ZAGARE; ZAMOSC; ZEDERBAUM, ALEXANDER; ZEITLIN, JOSHUA; ZELECHOW; ZITRON, SAMUEL LEIB; ZLATOPOLSKY, HILLEL; ZUCKERMANN, ELIEZER

Rudolf Smend, Dr. Theol.; Professor of Old Testament, Georg-August-Universität zu Gottingen, Germany: DUHM, BERNHARD; EISSFELDT, OTTO; GEDDES, ALEXANDER; HOELSCHER, GUSTAV; ILGEN, KARL DAVID; JIRKU, ANTON; MICHAELIS, JOHANN DAVID; RAD, GERHARD VON; REUSS, EDUARD; SPINOZA, BARUCH DE; VOLZ, PAUL; WELLHAUSEN, JULIUS; ZIMMERLI, WALTHER

Herbert Allen Smith, M.A.; Director of the Manpower Planning Authority, Jerusalem: ISRAEL, STATE OF: LABOR

Louanna Smith, Concord, New Hampshire

Mark L. Smith*, M.A.; Graduate Student at University of California: FISCHEL, ARNOLD; HOROWITZ, PINCHAS DAVID HA-LEVI; MARTIN, BERNARD; TRUNK, ISAIAH

Morton Smith, Ph.D., Th.D.; Professor of History, Columbia University, New York: BICKERMAN, ELIAS JOSEPH; GOODENOUGH, ERWIN RAMSDELL; MOORE, GEORGE FOOT

Michal Smoira-Cohn, Ph.Lic.; Director of Music, the Israel Broadcasting Authority, Jerusalem

Israel Smotricz, Ph.D.; Tel Aviv: ENDLICH, QUIRIN

Norman Henry Snaith, D.D.; Former Principal, Wesley College, Leeds; Former Lecturer in Hebrew and Old Testament, the University of Leeds: BIBLE

Daniel C. Snell*, Ph.D.; Professor of History, University of Oklahoma: BABYLON; ELAM; NUZI

John M. Snoek, Reverend; Secretary of the World Council of Churches' Committee on the Church and the Jewish People, Geneva: HOLOCAUST: THE WORLD

Leonard V. Snowman, M.A., M.R.C.P.; London: CIRCUMCISION

Bernard Zvi Sobel, Ph.D.; Associate Professor of Sociology, Haifa University

Israel Soifer, B.A.; Jerusalem: ADLER, ELMER; BLUMENTHAL, JOSEPH; DVIR; KNOPF, ALFRED A.; LESLIE, ROBERT L.; PUBLISHING; SCHUSTER, MAX LINCOLN

Alan (M.) Sokobin*, Ph.D., J.D., Rabbi; Lecturer in Law and Associate Professor of History, University of Toledo, Toledo, Ohio: TOLEDO

Moshe Zeev Sole, Dr.Phil., Rabbi; Chief Secretary of the Rabbinical Court, Jerusalem: KLATZKIN, JACOB

Shmuel Soler, General Federation of Labor, Tel Aviv: BECKER, AHARON

David Solomon, M.A.; Researcher in Jewish history, Jerusalem: CAESAR, SEXTUS JULIUS; PHASAEL; POMPEY; PROCURATOR; PTOLEMY; PTOLEMY MACRON

Isidor Solomon, Toorak, Victoria, Australia: ASHKANASY, MAURICE; COWEN, ZELMAN; ISAACS, SIR ISAAC ALFRED; LANDA, ABRAM; LAWYERS; POLITICS; SALOMONS, SIR JULIAN EMANUEL; SOLOMON; STONE, JULIUS

Jeffrey R. Solomon*, Ph.D.; President, The Andrea and Charles Bronfman Philanthropies, New York: FOUNDATIONS

Normon Solomon, Ph.D., Rabbi; Founder-Director of the Centre for the Study of Judaism and Jewish/Christian Relations, Birmingham, England: CONSERVATION; JEWISH-CHRISTIAN RELATIONS

Avraham Soltes, D.H.L., Rabbi; Musicologist, New York: SANDLER, JACOB KOPPEL

Isaiah Sonne: LIBRARIES

Walter Sorell, M.A.; Associate in Dance and Theater History, Columbia University, New York: GUGLIELMO DA PESARO

Yaakov Soroker, Jerusalem Symphony Orchestra: KOPYTMAN, MARK RUVIMOVICH

Arnold Sorsby, M.D., C.B.E., F.R.C.S.; Emeritus Research Professor of Ophthalmology, the Royal College of Surgeons of England, London: BLINDNESS

Henry Sosland, M.H.L., Rabbi; New City, New York: GRUENING, ERNEST HENRY

Edwin N. Soslow, M.A., Rabbi; Lecturer in History and Literature, the Hebrew Union College School of Education, New York: PASSAIC-CLIFTON

Claire Sotnick, B.A.; New York: WOLF

Henry (C.) Soussan*, Ph.D., Rabbi; United States: GESELLSCHAFT ZUR FOERDERUNG DER WISSENSCHAFT DES JUDENTUMS

Dora Leah Sowden, M.A.; Critic and Journalist, Jerusalem: ARBATOVA, MIA; BEIT, SIR ALFRED; BENATZKY, RALPH; BENEDICT, SIR JULIUS; BERGSON, MICHAEL; BERLIJN, ANTON; BRODSKY, ADOLF; BRUELL, IGNAZ; BURSTEIN; COHEN, FRANCIS LYON; CRANKO, JOHN; DAMROSCH; DE PHILIPPE, EDIS; EISLER, HANNS; ELMAN, MISCHA; MOISEIWITSCH, BENNO; ORDMAN, JEANNETTE; SOUTH AFRICAN LITERATURE; TOPOL, CHAIM

Lewis Sowden, M.A.; Writer and Journalist, Jerusalem: ABRAHAMS, ISRAEL; BARNATO, BARNEY; BLOEMFONTEIN; FELDBERG, LEON; GREENBERG, LEOPOLD; HENOCHSBERG, EDGAR SAMUEL; HERBSTEIN, JOSEPH; JOEL, SOLOMON BARNATO; KENTRIDGE, MORRIS; KOTTLER, MOSES; LIPSHITZ, ISRAEL; LOVELL, LEOPOLD; MERRICK, LEONARD; MILLIN, PHILIP; MILLIN, SARAH GERTRUDE; MORRIS, HENRY HARRIS; MOSENTHAL; OPPENHEIMER, SIR ERNEST; ORNSTEIN, ABRAHAM FREDERICK; PORT ELIZABETH; PRESS; RABINOWITZ, JOEL; RABINOWITZ, LOUIS ISAAC; RAMBERT, DAME MARIE; SOLOMON; SOUTH WEST AFRICA; STERN, IRMA; THEATER; ULLMANN, ERNEST; WELENSKY, SIR ROY

Francesco Spagnolo*, Laurea (in Philosophy); Executive Director, American Sephardi Federation, New York: RIVISTA ISRAELITICA

Barry Spain, Ph.D.; Head of the Department of Mathematics, City of London Polytechnic: BESICOVITCH, ABRAM SAMOILOVITCH; BONDI, SIR HERMANN; CANTOR, MORITZ BENEDICT; FEJÉR, LEOPOLD; FUBINI, GUIDO; HADAMARD, JACQUES SALOMON; HAUSDORFF, FELIX; HURWITZ, ADOLF; KÁRMÁN, THEODORE VON; KRONECKER, LEOPOLD; LANDAU, EDMUND; LEVI-CIVITA, TULLIO; MINKOWSKI, HERMANN; MORDELL, LOUIS JOEL; NEUMANN, JOHANN LUDWIG VON; NOETHER; SCHWARZ, KARL HERMANN AMANDUS; SEGRÈ, CORRADO; SYLVESTER, JAMES JOSEPH

Otto Immanuel Spear, Writer on Philosophy, Ramat Gan: ASHER, DAVID; BRUNNER, CONSTANTIN; GOLDSCHMIDT, HENRIETTE; GOMPERZ, THEODOR; LOEWITH, KARL

Heike Specht*, Ph.D.; Editor, Publishing House Munich, Germany: FEUCHTWANGER, LION

Johanna L. Spector, D.H.S.; Professor of Musicology, the Jewish Theological Seminary of America, New York: YEMEN

Shmuel Spector*, M.A.; Historian, Jerusalem: ABKHAZ AUTONOMOUS SOVIET SOCIALIST REPUBLIC; AGURSKY, MIKHAIL; ALEKSANDRIYA; ALEKSANDRIYA; ANANYEV; ANTI-FASCIST COMMITTEE, JEWISH; ARTEMOVSK; ATAKI; AXELROD, LUBOV; BAKHCHISARAI; BALTA; BAUSKA; BELAYA TSERKOV; BELZ; BENDERY; BERDICHEV; BEREGOVO; BERESTECHKO; BEREZA; BEREZINO; BEREZOVKA; BERSHAD; BIRZAI; BIRZULA; BOBROVY KUT; BOBRUISK; BOGUSLAV; BORISOV; BOROVOY, SAUL; BOTVINNIK, MIKHAIL; BRAILOV; BRASLAV; BRATSLAV; BRONSTEIN, DAVID; BYKHOV; CHERKASSY; CHERNOBYL; CHUDNOV; DAUGAVPILS; DEPUTIES OF THE JEWISH PEOPLE; DERAZHNYA; DIMANSTEIN, SIMON; DISKIN, CHAIM; DISNA; DIVIN; DNEPROPETROVSK; DOKSHITSY; DOLGINOVO; DOLINA; DONETSK; DRAGUNSKI, DAVID ABRAMOVICH; DRUYA; DUBNO; DUBOSSARY; DUBROVNO; DYATLOVO; DYMSHYTS, VENIAMIN E.; EFRON, ILYA; EHRENBURG, ILYA GRIGORYEVICH; ESTHER; ESTONIA; EYNIKEYT; FEODOSIYA; FRIEDMAN, NAPHTALI; GADYACH; GAISIN; GALICH, ALEXANDER ARKADYEVICH; GELFOND, ALEXANDER LAZAREVICH; GERSHENZON, MIKHAIL OSIPOVICH; GLUSSK; GOLOVANEVSK; GOMEL; GORODENKA; GORODOK; GORODOK; GRANDE, BENZION MOISEEVICH; GROSSMAN, LEONID PETROVICH; GROSSMAN, VASILI SEMYONOVICH; GUZIK, HANNA; ILYA; ISBAKH, ALEXANDER ABRAMOVICH; IVANOVO; IVYE; IZMAIL; IZYASLAV; JAUNIJELGAVA; JEKABPILS; JELGAVA; JOCHELSON, VLADIMIR; JOFFE, ADOLPH ABRAMOVICH; KAGANOVICH, LAZAR MOISEYEVICH; KALININDORF; KALINKOVICHI; KAMENETS-PODOLSKI; KAMENEV; KANEV; KARASUBAZAR; KAZAN; KAZATIN; KERCH; KHARKOV; KHERSON; KHMELNIK; KHOROL; KIEV; KIROVOGRAD; KLETS; KLINTSY; KOIDANOVO; KOLOMYYA; KONOTOP; KORETS; KOROSTEN; KORSUN-SHEVCHENKOVSKI; KOVEL; KRASLAVA; KRASNODAR; KRASNOYE; KREISER, JACOB GRIGORYEVICH; KREMENCHUG; KREMENETS; KRICHEV; KRIMCHAKS; KRIVOI ROG; KRIVOYE OZERO; KRUSTPILS; KURSK; KUTY; LACHVA; LETICHEV; LIEPAJA; LIOZNO; LIPOVETS; LITIN; LUBNY; LUDZA; LUTSK; MAKAROV; MEDZIBEZH; MEKHLIS, LEV ZAKHAROVICH; MELITOPOL; MEZHIRECH; MOGILEV-PODOLSKI; MOLODECHNO; MOSTISKA; MOZYR; MSTISLAVL; NOVOZYBKOV; ODESSA; OLGOPOL; OLYKA; OREL; ORSHA; OVRUCH; PALANGA; PAVLOGRAD; PAVOLOCH; PEREYASLAV-KHMELNITSKI; POCHEP; RADOMYSHL; RADUN; RECHITSA; REZEKNE; ROGACHEV; ROMNY; ROSTOV; ROVNO; SARNY; SATANOV; SHARGOROD; SHCHEDRIN; SHEPETOVKA; SIMFEROPOL

Charles Samuel Spencer, Art Critic, London: ABRAHAMS, IVOR; BLACK, SIR MISHA; BOMBERG, DAVID; CARO, SIR ANTHONY; COHEN, BERNARD; COHEN, HAROLD; DANIELS, ALFRED; EHRLICH, GEORG; FREEDMAN, BARNETT; GERTLER, MARK; GLUCK, HANNAH; GORDON, WILLY; HALTER, MAREK; HAYDEN, HENRI; HERMAN, JOSEF; HILLMAN, DAVID; INLANDER, HENRY; KANOVITZ, HOWARD; KAY, BARRY; KESTLEMAN, MORRIS; KLEIN, YVES; KLINE, FRANZ; KOPPEL, HEINZ; KORMIS, FRED; KRAMER, JACOB; KRÉMÈGNE, PINCHAS; LE WITT, JAN; LÉVY-DHURMER, LUCIEN; MINTCHINE, ABRAHAM; NEIZVESTNY, ERNST; NEWMAN, BARNETT; OYVED, MOYSHE; RABIN, OSCAR; RABIN, SAM; ROGERS, CLAUDE MAURICE; ROSENBERG, EUGENE; ROSENBERG, LAZAR; ROTHENSTEIN, MICHAEL; ROTHENSTEIN, SIR WILLIAM; SCHOEFFER, NICOLAS; SCHOTTLANDER, BERNARD; SCHOTZ, BENNO; SEROV, VALENTIN; SONNABEND, YOLANDA; STERN, ERNEST; SUTTON, PHILIP; TOPOLSKI, FELIKS; WERNER, MICHAEL; WILSON, "SCOTTIE; ZVIA

Daniel Sperber*, Ph.D., F.R.N.S.; Senior Lecturer in Talmud, Bar-Ilan University, Ramat Gan: ANGARIA; APOSTOMOS; ARNONA; BARAITA DE-NIDDAH; COINS AND CURRENCY; CONFLICT OF OPINION; COSMETICS; DEREKH EREẒ; GENTILE; ḤUNYA OF BETH-HORON; KOI; MIN; MISHMAROT AND MAAMADOT; MONEY CHANGERS; NATIONS, THE SEVENTY; OENOMAUS OF GADARA; PESIKTA RABBATI; SAVORA, SAVORAIM; SIFREI HA-MINIM; SYNAGOGUE, THE GREAT; TABI; TANNA, TANNAIM; TAX GATHERERS; THEODOSIUS OF ROME; TITLES; WEIGHTS AND MEASURES

S. (Shalom) David Sperling*, Ph.D.; Rabbi; Professor of Bible, Hebrew Union College, New York: ABRAHAM; ADRAMMELECH; AKHENATON; AMALEKITES; ARARAT; ASHIMA; BET-REHOB; BIBLE; BOOK OF THE COVENANT; CANAAN, CURSE OF; CHRONICLES, BOOK OF; CROWNS, DECORATIVE HEADDRESSES, AND WREATHS; DAY OF ATONEMENT; DEUTERONOMY; DINAH; ECSTASY; EHRLICH, ARNOLD BOGUMIL; ELIJAH; ELISHA; ENOCH; EPHOD; ETHBAAL; EUNUCH; EVE; EWALD, HEINRICH GEORG AUGUST; EXODUS, BOOK OF; FIRE; FLESH; FLOOD, THE; FRANKFORT, HENRI; GAD; GARDEN OF EDEN; GENESIS, BOOK OF; GERSHON, GERSHONITES; GESHEM, GASHMU; GEVIRTZ, STANLEY; GINSBERG, HAROLD LOUIS; GOD, NAMES OF; GOLIATH; GORDIS, ROBERT; GREENBERG, MOSHE; GRESSMANN, HUGO; HABAKKUK; HADAD; HAGAR; HAGGAI; HALLO, WILLIAM; HAM; HAMAN; HARAN, MENAHEM; HAZAEL; HELD, MOSHE; HENGSTENBERG, ERNST WILHELM; HEZEKIAH; HISTORIOGRAPHY; HISTORY: BEGINNING UNTIL THE MONARCHY; HISTORY: KINGDOMS OF JUDAH AND ISRAEL; HITTITES; HOELSCHER, GUSTAV; HOLINESS CODE; HORSE; HOSHEA; HULDAH; HUNTING; HUPFELD, HERMANN CHRISTIAN KARL; HUR; HYKSOS; IDOLATRY; ILGEN, KARL DAVID; ISAAC; JABIN; JACOB BEN ḤAYYIM BEN ISAAC IBN ADONIJAH; JAEL; JAIR; JAVAN; JEALOUSY; JEBUS, JEBUSITE; JEHOAHAZ; JEHOIADA; JEHOIAKIM; JEHOIARIB; JEREMIAH; JEROBOAM; JEROBOAM II; JESSE; JETHRO; JEZEBEL; JIRKU, ANTON; JOAB; JOASH; JOCHEBED; JOEL; JONAH, BOOK OF; JONATHAN; JONATHAN BEN UZZIEL; JOSHUA; JOSHUA, BOOK OF; JOSIAH; JUDGES, THE BOOK OF; KAUFMANN, YEḤEZKEL; KENITE; KETURAH; KING, KINGSHIP; KINGS, BOOK OF; KITTEL, RUDOLF; KORAH; LEPROSY; LEVINE, BARUCH; LEVITICUS, BOOK OF; LEWY, JULIUS; LION; MALACHI, BOOK OF; MALAMAT, ABRAHAM; MANASSEH; MARTI, KARL; MAZAR, BENJAMIN; MEDES AND MEDIA; MICAH; MIRIAM; MOLOCH, CULT OF; MOSES; MOWINCKEL, SIGMUND OLAF PLYTT; NAHUM; NEHUSHTAN; OBADIAH, BOOK OF; PATRIARCHS, THE; PHILISTINES; PHOENICIA, PHOENICIANS; PROPHETS AND PROPHECY; RAB-SARIS AND RAB-MAG; RAB-SHAKEH; RED HEIFER; REPHAIM; REZIN; RUTH, BOOK OF; SAMUEL; SARAH; SARNA, NAHUM M.; SINAI, MOUNT; SOLOMON; SONG OF SONGS; UGARITIC; WORSHIP; ZECHARIAH; ZEPHANIAH

Ezra Spicehandler, Ph.D., Rabbi; Professor of Hebrew Literature and Director of Jewish Studies, the Hebrew Union College-Jewish Institute of Religion, Jerusalem: BIALIK, ḤAYYIM NAḤMAN; BROIDO, EPHRAIM; GOLDBERG, LEA; GREENBERG, URI ẒEVI; HEBREW LITERATURE, MODERN; RAḤEL; SCHORR, JOSHUA HESCHEL

Renato Spiegel, B.A.; Jerusalem: SARFATI

Howard Spier, Ph.D.; Researcher, Institute of Jewish Affairs, London: ANTISEMITISM

Samuel (J.) Spinner*, M.A., Columbia University, New York: DINESON, JACOB; TSUKUNFT

Judith Spitzer, B.A.; Jerusalem: BEERI, TUVIA; BERNSTEIN, MOSHE; BROWN, AIKA; FRENKEL, ITẒḤAK; HALEVY, YOSEF; LIFSCHITZ, URI; MOREH, MORDECA; NEIMAN, YEHUDAH; WEILL, SHRAGA

Leo Spitzer*, Ph.D.; Kather Tappe Vernon Professor of History, Dartmouth College, Columbia University, New York: BOLIVIA

Maurice Moshe Spitzer, Dr.Phil.; Publisher, Jerusalem

Irving T. Spivack, M.A., M.S.; Margate, New Jersey

Leon H. Spotts, Ph.D.; Executive Director, Atlanta Bureau of Jewish Education, Atlanta, Georgia: BEN-HORIN, MEIR; BLUMENFIELD, SAMUEL; DININ, SAMUEL; DUSHKIN, ALEXANDER MORDECHAI; GAMORAN, EMANUEL; HONOR, LEO L.; HURWICH, LOUIS; KAPLAN, LOUIS LIONEL; SCHOOLMAN, BERTHA S.

Simon Spungin*, Journalist, Haaretz, Tel Aviv: SIMMONS, GENE

Leo Srole, Ph.D.; Professor of Social Sciences, Columbia College of Physicians and Surgeons, New York: SICKNESS

David G. Stahl*, A.B., D.M.D.; Past President, N.H. Historical Society, Retired, New Hampshire Jewish Federation: NEW HAMPSHIRE

Samuel (M.) Stahl*, D.H.L., Rabbi; Rabbi Emeritus, Temple Beth-El, San Antonio, Texas: SAN ANTONIO

Johann Jakob Stamm, Dr.Phil., Dr.Theol.; Professor of Old Testament Studies and Ancient Near Eastern Languages, the University of Berne: NAMES

Shaul Stampfer, Jerusalem: RABINOVICH, ISAAC JACOB

Lena Stanley-Clamp, B.A.; Assistant Director, Institute of Jewish Affairs, London: POLAND

Astrid Starck (-Adler)*, Dr.Phil.; Professor for German and Yiddish, Université de Haute Alsace, France: BASMAN BEN-HAYIM, RIVKE; BERINSKI, LEV; FELZENBAUM, MICHAEL; MAYSE-BUKH; WOOG, MAYER

Moshe Starkman, Writer, New York: DEMBLIN, BENJAMIN; KASSEL, DAVID; PINSKI, DAVID; REJZEN, ZALMAN; ROSENFELD, JONAH; ROSENFELD, MORRIS; SHOMER; SPECTOR, MORDECAI

Arthur F. Starr*, B.A., G,H. L., M.A.H.L.; Rabbi, Hebrew Congregation of St. Thomas, Virgin Islands: VIRGIN ISLANDS

David Benjamin Starr*, Ph.D.; Dean, Hebrew College, Boston: HEBREW COLLEGE

Harry Starr, B.A., LL.B.; President of the Lucius N. Littauer Foundation, New York: LITTAUER, LUCIUS NATHAN

Barbara Staudinger*, Ph.D.; Historian, Institute for the History of Jews in Austria, St. Poelter, Austria: BURGENLAND; CARINTHIA

Martina Steer*, Ph.D.; Historian, University of Vienna, Austria: BADT-STRAUSS, BERTHA

Sidney Steiman, Ph.D., Rabbi; Affiliate Professor of Religion, the Christian Theological Seminary; Lecturer in Sociology, Marian College, Indianapolis, Indiana: INDIANA; INDIANAPOLIS

Hannah Stein, Executive Director of the National Council of Jewish Women, New York: NATIONAL COUNCIL OF JEWISH WOMEN

Israela Stein*, B.A.,; Student, Assistant Librarian, Hebrew University, Jewish National and University Library, Department of Jewish Music, Jerusalem: ABER, ADOLF; ABRAHAM, OTTO; ALPERT, HERB; APEL, WILLI; APPLEBAUM, LOUIS; ATZMON, MOSHE; AVENARY, HANOCH; BACHARACH, BURT; BENDIX, VICTOR EMANUEL; BERLINSKI, HERMAN; BERNSTEIN, LEONARD; BIE, OSCAR; BOSCOVITCH, ALEXANDER URIYAH; BRAUN, YEHEZKIEL; BROOK, BARRY SHELLEY; BUCHWALD, THEO; BURLE MARX, WALTER; CASTELNUOVO-TEDESCO, MARIO; CHASINS, ABRAHAM; CHURGIN, BATHIA; DA-OZ, RAM; DESSAU, PAUL; DIAMOND, DAVID; DUSHKIN, SAMUEL; EHRLICH, ABEL; ERLANGER, CAMILLE; FANO, GUIDO ALBERTO; FIEDLER, ARTHUR; FOGELBERG, DAN; GEDALGE, ANDRE; GEIRINGER, KARL; GILBOA, JACOB; GOULD, MORTON; GRAZIANI, YITZHAK; HENDEL, NEḤAMA; HERRMANN, BERNARD; HERZOG, GEORGE; INBAL, ELIAHU; JACOBI, ERWIN REUBEN; JACOBI, HANOCH; JACOBS, ARTHUR; KIRCHNER, LEON; KRIPS, JOSEF; LAKNER, YEHOSHUA; LEAR, EVELYN; LEFKOWITZ, DAVID; LERT, ERNST; LEVINE, JAMES; LEVY, MARVIN DAVID; LIEBERMANN, ROLF; LIST, EMANUEL; LONDON, GEORGE; MACHABEY, ARMAND; MAJOR, ERVIN; MENDEL, ARTHUR; MENDELSSOHN, ARNOLD; MEZZROW, MILTON; MIRON, ISSACHAR; NATRA, SERGIU; PAULY, ROSA; PERGAMENT, MOSES; POPPER, DAVID; PORGES, HEINRICH; PREVIN, ANDRE; QUELER, EVE; REINER, FRITZ; RESNIK, REGINA; RICARDO, DAVID; RIETI, VITTORIO; RODAN, MENDI; ROLL, MICHAEL; RONLY-RIKLIS, SHALOM; ROSENSTOCK, JOSEPH; ROSENTHAL, HAROLD; ROSENTHAL, MANUEL; RUDEL, JULIUS; RUDOLF, MAX; SADAI, YIẒḤAK; SADIE, STANLEY; SAMUEL, HAROLD; SCHULLER, GUNTHER; SCHWARZ, RUDOLF; SEGAL, URI; SHALLON, DAVID; SHAW, ARTIE

Judith S. Stein, Ph.D.; Assistant Professor of History, City College of the City University of New York: SCHWIMMER, ROSIKA; STEINGUT

Leonard J. Stein, M.A.; Barrister and Historian, London

Siegfried Stein, Ph.D.; Professor of Hebrew, University College, London: MONEYLENDING

Stanley J. Stein, Ph.D.; Professor of History, Princeton University, New Jersey: NASATIR, ABRAHAM PHINEAS

Jonah C. (Chanan) Steinberg*, Ph.D.; Director of Talmudic Studies, Rabbinical School of Hebrew College, Boston: HALIVNI, DAVID WEISS

Lucien Steinberg, M.A.; Research Worker, Centre de Documentation Juive Contemporaine, Paris: BAUM, HERBERT; FRANCE; PARIS

Ronit Steinberg*, Lecturer, Jerusalem: AGAM, YAACOV; ARDON, MORDECAI; ARIKHA, AVIGDOR; AROCH, ARIE; BEZALEL; BEZEM, NAFTALI; CASTEL, MOSHE; DANZIGER, ITZHAK; FIMA, EFRAIM; GERSHUNI, MOSHE; GROSS, MICHAEL; GUTMAN, NAHUM; JANCO, MARCEL; KADISHMAN, MENASHE; KAHANA, AHARON; KARAVAN, DANI; KUPFERMAN, MOSHE; LAVIE, RAFFI; LITVINOVSKY, PINCHAS; OFEK, AVRAHAM; PANN, ABEL; RUBIN, REUVEN; SCHATZ, BORIS; SHEMI, YEHIEL; SIMA, MIRON; STREICHMAN, YEHEZKEL; TAGGER, SIONAH; TEVET, NAHUM; TICHO, ANNA; TUMARKIN, IGAEL; ULLMAN, MICHA

Naomi (M.) Steinberger*, M.A., M.S.; Director of Library Services, Library of the Jewish Theological Seminary, New York: LIBRARIES

Meyer F. Steinglass, B.A.; New York

Chanan Steinitz, Dr. Phil.; Musicologist, Ramot Hashavim, Israel: DUKAS, PAUL

Adin Steinsaltz, Rabbi; Scholar, Jerusalem: AARON BEN MOSES HA-LEVI OF STAROSIELCE; ABRAHAM DOV BAER OF OVRUCH; ABRAHAM GERSHON OF KUTOW; APTA, MEIR; ELIEZER BEN JACOB HA-LEVI+B261 OF TARNOGROD; JACOB SAMSON OF SHEPETOVKA; KALLO, YIẒḤAK ISAAC; KAMENKA, ẒEVI HIRSCH OF; LAWAT, ABRAHAM DAVID BEN JUDAH LEIB; LELOV; MARGOLIOUTH, MEIR OF OSTRAHA; MEIR JEHIEL HA-LEVI OF OSTROWIEC; ROTH, AARON; YESHIVOT; ZHIDACHOV; ZUSYA OF HANIPOLI

Eleanor Sterling-Oppenheimer, Ph.D.; Associate Professor of Political Science, J.W. Goethe-Universität, Frankfurt on the Main: FRANKFURT ON THE MAIN

David Stern*, B.A., Ph.D.; Ruth Meltzer Professor of Classical Hebrew Literature, University of Pennsylvania: COHEN, ARTHUR A.

Ephraim Stern, Ph.D.; Lecturer in Archaeology, Tel Aviv University: HAMOR; MIRIAM; PHINEHAS; WEIGHTS AND MEASURES

Kenneth (S.) Stern*, A.B., J.D.; Specialist on Antisemitism and Extremism; Attorney; Author; American Jewish Committee, New York: HOLOCAUST DENIAL

Malcolm H. Stern, D.H.L., Rabbi; New York: BERNSTEIN, PHILIP SIDNEY; COHEN, JACOB RAPHAEL; HARBY, ISAAC; MINIS; NASSY, DAVID DE ISAAC COHEN; SAVANNAH; SHEFTALL; WASHINGTON, GEORGE

Menahem Stern, Ph.D.; Professor of Jewish History, the Hebrew University of Jerusalem: AGORANOMOS; ALEXANDER POLYHISTOR; AMMIANUS MARCELLINUS; ANANIAS BEN NEDEBEUS; ANTONIUS JULIANUS; ATHENS; CAECILIUS OF CALACTE; CALIGULA, CAIUS CAESAR AUGUSTUS; CAPITO, MARCUS HERENNIUS; CARACALLA, MARCUS AURELIUS ANTONINUS; CELSUS; CRASSUS, MARCUS LICINIUS; DIASPORA; EPICTETUS; FISCUS JUDAICUS; FLACCUS, VALERIUS; GREEK LITERATURE, ANCIENT; HASMONEANS; HISTORY: EREẒ ISRAEL – SECOND TEMPLE; HYRCANUS, JOHN; JANNES and JAMBRES; JERUSALEM; JESHUA; JULIUS CAESAR; MANETHO; MATTHIAS BEN THEOPHILUS; NERO; NICHOLAS OF DAMASCUS; PLINY THE ELDER; POMPEIUS TROGUS; PORPHYRY; PRIESTS AND PRIESTHOOD; QUIRINIUS, P. SULPICIUS; STRABO; SUETONIUS; ZEALOTS AND SICARII; ZENO, PAPYRI OF

Moshe Stern, Jerusalem: ḤIDDUSHIM

Norton B. Stern, O.D.; Editor, Venice, California: ZELLERBACH

Samuel Miklos Stern, D.Phil.; Fellow of All Souls College and Lecturer in the History of Islamic Civilization, the University of Oxford: ABU AL-FARAJ HARUN IBN AL-FARAJ; BANETH; BORISOV, ANDREY YAKOVLEVICH; GERMANY; GOLDENTHAL, JACOB

Walter Stern*: SILVERMAN, MORRIS

Manny Sternlicht, Ph.D.; Associate Professor of Psychology, Yeshiva University, New York: MASLOW, ABRAHAM H.

Bernard Sternsher, Ph.D.; Professor of History, Bowling Green State University, Ohio: LILIENTHAL, DAVID ELI; NILES, DAVID K.

Marie Joseph Stiassny, Lic.Th.; Ratisbonne Monastery, Jerusalem: RATISBONNE BROTHERS

Guy D. Stiebel*, Archaeologist, Institute of Archaeology, the Hebrew University of Jerusalem: MASADA

Ernest Stock, Ph.D.; Lecturer in Politics and Director of the Jacob Hiatt Institute of Brandeis University, Jerusalem: JEWISH AGENCY

Silvio Shalom Stoessl, M.D.; Tel Aviv: CARINTHIA

Jeremy Stolow*, Ph.D.; Associate Professor, McMaster University, Hamilton, Canada: ARTSCROLL

Bryan Edward Stone*, Ph.D.; Associate Professor of History, Del Mar College, Corpus Christi, Texas: TEXAS

Gerald Stone*, M.L.S.; Library and Archives, Ottawa, Canada: OTTAWA

Kurt (Franklin) Stone*, B.A., M.A.H.L., D.D.; Professor, Florida Atlantic University, Boca Raton, Florida: ACKERMAN, GARY; ANSORGE, MARTIN CHARLES; BACHARACH, ISAAC; BEILENSON, ANTHONY CHARLES; BERKLEY, ROCHELLE; BERMAN, HOWARD LAWRENCE; BOSCHWITZ, RUDOLPH ELI; CANTOR, ERIC; CARDIN, BENJAMIN LOUIS; CHUDOFF, EARL; COHEN, JOHN SANFORD; COHEN, WILLIAM S.; COHEN, WILLIAM WOLFE; COPPERSMITH, SAM

Michael E. Stone, Ph.D.; Senior Lecturer in Jewish Hellenism and in Iranian and Armenian Studies, the Hebrew University of Jerusalem: ABEL-MAUL; ABRAHAM, OTHER BOOKS OF; ADAM, OTHER BOOKS OF; AHIKAR, BOOK OF; ANTICHRIST; BARUCH, BOOK OF; BARUCH, REST OF THE WORDS OF; BIBLE; DAMASCUS, BOOK OF COVENANT OF; DANIEL, BOOKS OF; ELIJAH, APOCALYPSE OF; EZEKIEL, APOCRYPHAL BOOKS OF; EZRA, APOCALYPSE OF; HABAKKUK, PROPHECY OF; ISAAC, TESTAMENT OF; ISAIAH, MARTYRDOM OF; JACOB, TESTAMENT OF; LAMECH; LAMECH, BOOK OF; NOAH, BOOKS OF; OIL OF LIFE; PROPHETS, LIVES OF THE; SHADRACH, MESHACH, ABED-NEGO

Heinrich Strauss, Dr. Phil.; Art Historian, Jerusalem: MENORAH

Herbert A. Strauss, Ph.D.; Associate Professor of History, City College of the City University of New York: BÉGIN, EMILE-AUGUSTE; BLOCH, CAMILLE; BUEDINGER, MAX; FRIEDJUNG, HEINRICH; PHILIPPSON; PHILIPPSON; PRIBRAM, ALFRED FRANCIS; SALOMON, JULIUS

Lauren B. Strauss*, Ph.D.; Independent Scholar and Professor, Washington, D.C.: JEWISH WOMAN, THE; GIKOW, RUTH; HARKAVY, MINNA B.

Arie Strikovsky, Ph.D.; Lecturer in Talmud, the Technion, Haifa: RED HEIFER; SIMONA

Avrum Stroll, Ph.D.; Professor of Philosophy, the University of California, San Diego: AL-ḤARIZI, JUDAH BEN SOLOMON; BAR-HILLEL, YEHOSHUA; BLACK, MAX; FEIGL, HERBERT; GOODMAN, NELSON; HART, HERBERT LIONEL ADOLPHUS; HOOK, SIDNEY; KAUFMANN, FELIX; LAZEROWITZ, MORRIS; NAGEL, ERNEST; WAISMANN, FRIEDRICH; WHITE, MORTON GABRIEL

John Strugnell, M.A.; Professor of Christian Origins, Harvard University: PHILO or LIBER ANTIQUITATUM BIBLICARUM

Dirk Jan Struik, Ph.D.; Emeritus Professor of Mathematics, Massachusetts Institute of Technology, Cambridge: KOLMAN, ARNOŠT

Susan Strul, Writer, Jerusalem: ALTER, ROBERT B.; DAWIDOWICZ, LUCY; DOCTOROW, EDGAR LAWRENCE; ELKIN, STANLEY; FEIFFER, JULES; FRIEDAN, BETTY; JONG, ERICA; KAPLAN, JOHANNA; OLSEN, TILLIE; SINCLAIR. CLIVE

Harvey (Joel) Strum*, Ph.D.; Professor of History and Political Science, Sage College of Albany, New York: ALBANY; SCHENECTADY

Bernard Suler, Dr. Phil.; *Encyclopaedia Judaica* (Germany); Berlin: ALCHEMY; AVERROES; BONAFED, SOLOMON BEN REUBEN; KASPI, NETHANEL BEN NEHEMIAH; KELLERMANN, BENZION; LABI, SOLOMON; LEVY, JACOB; MARGARITA, ANTON; MARTINI, RAYMOND

Dror Franck Sullaper*, B.A.; Journalist, Kol Israel, French Language News Department, Jerusalem: ABECASSIS, ELIETTE; ADLER, ALEXANDRE; AMADO LÉVY-VALENSI, ELIANE; ARON, RAYMOND; ASHKENAZI, LEON; ATLAN, HENRI; ATTALI, BERNARD; ATTALI, JACQUES; BACRI, JEAN-PIERRE; BADINTER, ELIZABETH; BADINTER, ROBERT; BARBARA; BARUK, HENRI; BENICHOU, PAUL; BENSOUSSAN, GEORGES; BENVENISTE, EMILE; BERL, EMMANUEL; BERNHEIM, GILLES; BLANCHOT, MAURICE; BOBER, ROBERT; BRENNER,FREDERIC; CALLE, SOPHIE; CHOURAQUI, ANDRÉ; CIXOUS, HÉLÈNE; COPÉ, JEAN-FRANÇOIS; DIDI-HUBERMAN, GEORGES; DRAÏ, RAPHAËL; DRAY, JULIEN; ELKABBACH, JEAN-PIERRE; ELKANN, JEAN-PAUL; FABIUS, LAURENT; FARHI, DANIEL; FARHI, GABRIEL; FINKIELKRAUT, ALAIN; GIROUD, FRANÇOISE; GRAY, MARTIN; GRESH, ALAIN; GRUMBACH, ANTOINE; GRUMBERG, JEAN-CLAUDE; HALTER, MAREK; IONESCO, EUGÈNE

Esther Sulman, New London, Connecticut

Samuel L. Sumberg, Ph.D.; Professor of Germanic and Slavic Languages, City College of the City University of New York: BAUM, VICKI; FULDA, LUDWIG; HOLLAENDER; KINGSLEY, SIDNEY; LOTHAR, ERNST; LOTHAR, RUDOLF; MOSENTHAL, SALOMON HERMANN; ROESSLER, CARL; WARFIELD, DAVID

Frank N. Sundheim, M.A., Rabbi;

Lecturer in Religion, the University of Tampa, Florida: AMERICAN COUNCIL FOR JUDAISM

Monique Susskind Goldberg*, MA., Rabbi; Schechter Institute for Jewish Studies, Jerusalem: GOLINKIN, DAVID

Joanna Sussman*, B.A.; University of Minnesota, Director of Kar-Ben Publishing, Minneapolis: KAR-BEN/LERNER

Sara Sviri*, Ph.D.; Distinguished Visiting Professor, the Hebrew University of Jerusalem: SUFISM

Craig Svonkin*, M.A.; Lecturer, University of California, Riverside: BELLOW, SAUL; BLOOM, HAROLD; CHABON, MICHAEL; GINSBERG, ALLEN; OZICK, CYNTHIA; STEIN, GERTRUDE; TRILLING, LIONEL

Deborah K. Swanson*: CITY OF HOPE NATIONAL MEDICAL CENTER

Manfred Eric Swarsensky, Ph.D., Rabbi; Madison, Wisconsin: TWERSKI, JACOB ISRAEL

Louis J. Swichkow, D.H.L., Rabbi; Historian, Milwaukee, Wisconsin: LEVITAN, SOLOMON; PADWAY, JOSEPH ARTHUR; SCHEINFELD, SOLOMON ISAAC

Donald Sylvan*: JEWISH EDUCATION SERVICE OF NORTH AMERICA

Marie Syrkin, M.A.; Emeritus Professor of English Literature, Brandeis University, Waltham, Massachusetts: ZUCKERMAN, BARUCH

Judith E. Szapor*, Ph.D.; Instructor, York University, Toronto, Canada: GRAY, HERBERT ESER; JACOBS, SAMUEL WILLIAM; KANEE, SOL; STEIN, JANICE GROSS

Yechiel (Sheintukh) Szeintuch*, Ph.D.; Professor of Yiddish Literature and Language; the Hebrew University of Jerusalem: PERLOV, YITSKHOK; STEIMAN, BEYNUSH; STRIGLER, MORDECAI

Leon Aryeh Szeskin, Ph.D.; Director, Department of Economic Survey and Advice, Rural Planning and Development Authority, Israel Ministry of Agriculture, Tel Aviv: COOPERATIVES; EGGED; HAMASHBIR HAMERKAZI; TNUVA

David Szonyi, Program Associate, Department of Community Education, Jewish Theological Seminary of America

Zvi H. Szubin, Ph.D.; Assistant Professor of Classical Languages and Hebrew, City College of the City University of New York: HUMILITY; MERCY; RIGHTEOUSNESS

Robert P. Tabak*, Ph.D.; Rabbi.; Chaplain, Hospital of the University of Pennsylvania, Philadelphia: HOSPITALS; LEVINTHAL; PENNSYLVANIA; PHILADELPHIA; RECONSTRUCTIONIST RABBINICAL COLLEGE; TEUTSCH, DAVID

Joseph Tabory*, Ph.D.; Professor, Dean of Libraries, Bar-Ilan University, Ramat Gan: AFIKOMAN

Gad Tadmor, M.D.; Savyon, Israel: WOOLF, MOSHE

Hayim Tadmor, Ph.D.; Professor of Assyriology, the Hebrew University of Jerusalem: CAMBYSES; ELAM; JEHOAHAZ; JEHOASH; JEHORAM; JOASH; LANDSBERGER, BENNO; LEWY, JULIUS

Emily Taitz*, Ph.D.; Author, Historian, Great Neck, New York: BACHARACH, EVA; CONAT, ABRAHAM BEN SOLOMON; DREYZL, LEAH; ESTERKE; FIRZOGERIN; FISHELS, ROIZL OF CRACOW; GOLDSCHMIDT, JOHANNA SCHWABE; MIRIAM BAT BENAYAH; SARAH OF TURNOVO; STERNBERG, SARAH FRANKEL

Josef Tal, Composer and Senior Lecturer in Musicology, the Hebrew University of Jerusalem: DAVID, FERDINAND; GERSHWIN, GEORGE; HALÉVY, JACQUES FROMENTAL ÉLIE; HILLER, FERDINAND

Shlomo Tal, M.A., M.Jur., Rabbi; Director of the Ze'ev Gold Institute, Jerusalem: CLEVES GET; ISSERLES, MOSES BEN ISRAEL; KATZENELLENBOGEN, MEIR BEN ISAAC; LEVIN, ẒEVI HIRSCH BEN ARYEH LOEB; MINTZ, MOSES BEN ISAAC; POLLACK, JACOB BEN JOSEPH; RESPONSA; SAMUEL BEN DAVID MOSES HA-LEVI

Michael Adin Talbar, B.A.; Ministry of Commerce and Industry, Jerusalem

Cheryl Tallan*, M.A.; Independent Scholar, Toronto, Canada: BRANDEAU, ESTHER; HAVA OF MANOSQUE; KANDLEIN OF REGENSBURG; LAZA OF FRANKFURT; LICORICIA OF WINCHESTER; MERECINA OF GERONA; NATHAN, VENGUESSONE

Frank Talmage, Ph.D.; Assistant Professor of Medieval and Modern Hebrew, the University of Toronto: KIMḤI, DAVID; KIMḤI, JOSEPH; KIMḤI, MOSES; NETHANEL BEN AL-FAYYUMI

Jacob L. Talmon, Ph.D.; Professor of Modern History, the Hebrew University of Jerusalem: NAMIER, SIR LEWIS

David Tamar, Ph.D.; Lecturer in Jewish History, Haifa University: CARO, JOSEPH BEN EPHRAIM; EPSTEIN, MOSES MORDECAI; GALANTE, ABRAHAM BEN MORDECAI; GALANTE, MOSES BEN JONATHAN; GALANTE, MOSES BEN MORDECAI; GALLICO, ELISHA BEN GABRIEL; GEDALIAH HA-LEVI; GERSHON, ISAAC; GRUENHUT, DAVID BEN NATHAN; ḤAGIZ, JACOB; ḤAGIZ, MOSES; ISAIAH ḤASID FROM ZBARAZH; JOSHUA IBN NUN; KLAUSNER, ABRAHAM; KOIDONOVER, AARON SAMUEL BEN ISRAEL; PROVENÇAL, DAVID BEN ABRAHAM

Ittai Joseph Tamari*, Ph.D.; Lecturer, Ludwig-Maximilians-Universität, Munich: AUERBACH, ERICH

Meir Tamari, Ph.D.; Chief Economist, Office of the Governor of the Bank of Israel, Jerusalem: BUSINESS ETHICS

David Tanne, Chairman of the Board of Directors, Tefahot-Mortgage Bank; Former Director General of the Ministry of Housing: AMIDAR; ISRAEL, STATE OF: ALIYAH

Abraham J. Tannenbaum, Ph.D.; Professor of Education, Columbia University, New York: BETTELHEIM, BRUNO; BLOOM, BENJAMIN SAMUEL; CREMIN, LAWRENCE ARTHUR; LORGE, IRVING; PASSOW, AARON HARRY; SCHWAB, JOSEPH J.

Carlos A. Tapiero*, M.A.; Rabbi, Director of Education, Maccabi World Union, Ramat Gan: GUATEMALA

Shimshon Tapuach, Ph.D.; Ministry of Agriculture, Tel Aviv: AGRICULTURE

Judit Targarona (Borrás)*, Ph.D.; Profesora Titular, Universidad Complutense, Madrid, Spain: DE PIERA, SOLOMON BEN MESHULLAM

Noga Tarnopolsky*, A.B.; Journalist, Freelancer, Jerusalem: TARNOPOLSKY, SAMUEL

Esther Tarsi-Gay, Dr.Phil.; the Graduate Library School of the Hebrew University of Jerusalem: CHILDREN'S LITERATURE

Aryeh Tartakower, Ph.D., S.P.D.; Former Lecturer in the Sociology of the Jews, the Hebrew University of Jerusalem; Former Chairman of the Israel Executive of the World Jewish Congress, Jerusalem: BIENENSTOCK, MAX; HITAḤADUT; LEWITE, LEON; REFUGEES; REICH, LEON; STAND, ADOLF; THON, OSIAS

Israel Moses Ta-Shma, M.A., Rabbi; Editorial staff, *Encyclopaedia Hebraica*, Jerusalem: ABRAHAM; ABRAHAM BEN ISAAC OF MONTPELLIER; ABULAFIA, MEIR; AGHMATI, ZECHARIAH BEN JUDAH; AGRAT BAT MAHALATH; ALFASI, ISAAC BEN JACOB; ASHER BEN SAUL; ASHKENAZI, DAN; BABEL, TOWER OF; BARUCH BEN ISAAC OF ALEPPO; BARUCH BEN ISAAC OF WORMS; BARUCH BEN SAMUEL OF MAINZ; BONFILS, JOSEPH BEN SAMUEL; DAVID; DAVID BEN LEVI OF NARBONNE; DAVID BEN SAADIAH; DAY AND NIGHT; DUEREN, ISAAC BEN MEIR; ELHANAN BEN ISAAC OF DAMPIERRE; ELIEZER BEN NATHAN OF MAINZ; ELIEZER BEN SAMUEL OF METZ; ELIEZER OF TOUL; ELIEZER OF TOUQUES; EZRA OF MONTCONTOUR; GABBAI, MOSES BEN SHEM-TOV; GENEALOGY; GERONDI, SAMUEL BEN MESHULLAM; HAGOZER, JACOB AND GERSHOM; HAKDAMAH; HANANEL BEN ḤUSHI'EL; HA-PARNAS, SEFER; HASSAGOT; HAVDALAH; ḤAYYIM BEN SAMUEL BEN DAVID OF TUDELA; ḤAYYIM PALTIEL BEN JACOB; ḤEFEẒ BEN YAẒLI'AḤ; ḤUẒPIT HA-METURGEMAN; IBN MIGASH, JOSEPH BEN MEIR HA-LEVI; IBN PLAT, JOSEPH; IBN SHUAIB, JOSHUA; ISAAC BAR DORBELO; ISAAC BEN ELIEZER; ISAAC BEN JOSEPH OF CORBEIL; ISAAC BEN MENAHEM THE GREAT; ISAAC BEN SAMUEL OF DAMPIERRE; ISAAC OF EVREUX; ISAIAH BEN ELIJAH DI TRANI; ISAIAH BEN MALI DI TRANI; ISRAELI, ISRAEL; ISSUR VE-HETTER; JACOB BEN SAMSON; JACOB BEN YAKAR; JACOB OF CORBEIL; JACOB OF ORLEANS; JAMA, SAMUEL IBN; JEHIEL BEN JOSEPH OF PARIS; JEROHAM BEN MESHULLAM; JOB, THE BOOK OF; JOEL BEN ISAAC HA-LEVI; JONATHAN BEN AMRAM; JONATHAN BEN DAVID HA-KOHEN OF LUNEL; JONATHAN BEN ELEAZAR; JOSEPH BEN BARUCH OF CLISSON; JOSEPH BEN ḤIYYA; JOSEPH BEN JUSTU OF JAÉN; JOSEPH BEN MOSES OF TROYES; JOSEPH ROSH HA-SEDER; JOSHUA HA-GARSI; JUDAH; JUDAH BEN BARZILLAI, AL-BARGELONI; JUDAH BEN KALONYMUS BEN MEIR; JUDAH BEN MOSES HA-DARSHAN; JUDAH BEN NATHAN; JUDAH BEN YAKAR; JUDAH III; KARET; KASHER, MENAHEM; KIMḤI, MORDECAI; LANDAU, JACOB; LATTES, JUDAH; LIMA, MOSES BEN ISAAC JUDAH; LURIA, SOLOMON BEN JEHIEL; MACHIR BEN JUDAH; MAIMON BEN JOSEPH; MASNUT, SAMUEL BEN NISSIM; MEIR BEN BARUCH HA-LEVI; MEIR BEN ISAAC OF TRINQUETAILLE; MEIRI, MENAHEM BEN SOLOMON; MEKIẒE NIRDAMIM; MENAHEM BEN SOLOMON; MENAHEM OF MERSEBURG; MESHULLAM BEN MOSES; MESHULLAM BEN NATHAN OF MELUN; MINHAGIM BOOKS; MORDECAI BEN HILLEL HA-KOHEN; MOSES BEN ABRAHAM OF PONTOISE; MOSES BEN JACOB OF COUCY; MOSES HA-DARSHAN; MOSES OF EVREUX; MUELHAUSEN, YOM TOV LIPMANN; NAḤMANIDES; NAḤMIAS, JOSEPH BEN JOSEPH; NETHANEL BEN ISAIAH; NETHANEL OF CHINON; NIDDAH; NISSIM BEN JACOB BEN NISSIM IBN SHAHIN; PEREZ BEN ELIJAH OF CORBEIL; PETTER BEN JOSEPH; RAGOLER, ELIJAH BEN JACOB; RASHI; RESPONSA; REUBEN BEN ḤAYYIM; RISHONIM; SAADIAH GAON; SAMSON BEN ELIEZER; SAMSON BEN ISAAC OF CHINON; SAMSON BEN JOSEPH OF FALAISE; SAMSON BEN SAMSON OF COUCY; SAMUEL BEN NATRONAI; SAMUEL BEN SOLOMON OF FALAISE; SAMUEL OF EVREUX; SEFER HA-NEYAR; SHEMAIAH OF TROYES; SIMEON BEN MENASYA; SIMEON BEN SAMUEL OF JOINVILLE; SOLOMON BEN JUDAH "OF DREUX"; SOLOMON BEN MEIR; SOLOMON BEN SAMSON; TOSAFOT; VIDAL, CRESCAS; YOSE BEN JUDAH; YOSE BEN KIPPAR; YOSE BEN MESHULLAM; YOSE HA-GELILI

Yitzhak Julius Taub, B.A., M.Jur.; Journalist; Former Secretary General of the Bank of Israel; Director of "The Bialik Institute," Jerusalem: BAR-YOSEF, YEHOSHUA; COINS AND CURRENCY; HOROWITZ, DAVID

Gerald E. Tauber, Ph.D.; Professor of Mathematical Physics, Tel Aviv University: EHRENFEST, PAUL; EINSTEIN, ALBERT; MANDELSHTAM, LEONID ISAAKOVICH

Oded Tavor, B.A.; the Shiloah Center for Middle Eastern and African Studies, Tel Aviv University: SYRIA

Yossi Tavor*, B.Mus.; Journalist, Culture Observer, Voice of Israel, Israeli Broadcasting Authority, Jerusalem: DANCE; EIFMAN, BORIS; PLISETSKAYA, MAYA

Joan E. Taylor*, B.A., B.D., Ph.D.; Adjunct Senior Lecturer, Religious Studies, University of Waikato, Hamilton, New Zealand: EIN FASHKHAH; THERAPEUTAE

Avigdor (Victor) Tcherikover, Ph.D.; Professor of Ancient History, the Hebrew University of Jerusalem: ALEXANDRIA; ARISTEAS, LETTER OF

Guido (Gad) Tedeschi, D.Jur.; Professor of Civil Law, the Hebrew University of Jerusalem: EHRLICH, EUGEN; GLASER, JULIUS ANTON; OPPENHEIM, LASSA FRANCIS LAWRENCE

Tom Teicholz*, J.D., M.S.J.; Film Producer/Journalist, Santa Monica, California: DEMJANJUK, JOHN; MOTION PICTURES

Sheldon Teitelbaum*, B.A.; Writer, *The Jerusalem Report*, Agoura Hills, California: KANTOR, MICHAEL; KRIPKE, SAUL AARON; LAS VEGAS; LOS ANGELES; NEVADA; SCIENCE FICTION AND FANTASY, JEWISH

Sefton D. Temkin, Ph.D.; Rabbi; Professor of Judaic Studies, State University of New York at Albany: COHEN; ADLER, CYRUS; ADLER, SAMUEL; ALTHEIMER, BENJAMIN; AMERICAN HEBREW, THE; AMERICAN ISRAELITE; BENAS, BARON LOUIS; BERKOWITZ, HENRY; BERNHEIM, ISAAC WOLFE; BIRMINGHAM; BOSTON; BRICKNER, BARNETT ROBERT; CEMETERY; COHON, SAMUEL SOLOMON; COURANT, RICHARD; DUKER, ABRAHAM GORDON; ECKMAN, JULIUS; EINHORN, DAVID; FELSENTHAL, BERNHARD; FOUNDATIONS; FRANZBLAU, ABRAHAM NORMAN; FRIEND, HUGO MORRIS; GOLD, HENRY RAPHAEL; HACKENBURG, WILLIAM BOWER; HEIDENHEIM, WOLF; HELLER; HERTZ, EMANUEL; HOCHEIMER, HENRY; JEWISH QUARTERLY REVIEW; KIRSTEIN, LOUIS EDWARD; KOHLER, KAUFMANN; KRAUSKOPF, JOSEPH; LAZARON, MORRIS SAMUEL; LEIPZIGER, EMIL WILLIAM; LEVINTHAL; LIEBMAN, JOSHUA LOTH;

MACAULAY, THOMAS BABINGTON; MENDES; MERZBACHER, LEO; MESSEL; MEYER, MARTIN ABRAHAM; MOSES, ISAAC S.; PHILIPSON, DAVID; ROSENDALE, SIMON WOLFE; SARACHEK, JOSEPH; SCHINDLER, SOLOMON; SCHLOESSINGER, MAX; SHANKMAN, JACOB K.; SHULMAN, CHARLES E.; SINGER, ISIDORE; TRACHTENBERG, JOSHUA; UNITED STATES OF AMERICA; VOORSANGER, JACOB; WALEY; WISE, JONAH BONDI

David Tene, D.del'U; Senior Lecturer in Hebrew Language, the Hebrew University of Jerusalem.: IBN JANĀH, JONAH; LINGUISTIC LITERATURE, HEBREW; YEHUDI BEN SHESHET

Shelly Tenenbaum*, Ph.D.; Associate Professor of Sociology, Clark University, Worcester, Massachusetts: LOW, MINNIE

Philipp Theisohn*, Ph.D.; Research Associate, Eberhard Karls University, Tubingen, Germany: ANDERS, GUENTHER; AUSLAENDER, ROSE; BEER-HOFMANN, RICHARD; EINSTEIN, CARL; FRANZOS, KARL EMIL; HEYM, STEFAN; HILDESHEIMER, WOLFGANG; HOFMANNSTHAL, HUGO VON; HOLITSCHER, ARTHUR; MOMBERT, ALFRED; MOSENTHAL, SALOMON HERMANN; MUEHSAM, ERICH; VAN HODDIS, JAKOB; WINDER, LUDWIG

Pascal Themanlys, Writer, Jerusalem: MILBAUER, JOSEPH

Jeffrey Howard Tigay, M.H.L., Rabbi; Hamden, Connecticut: ABRECH; ADOPTION; ADULTERY; ASENAPPER; BLINDNESS; DRUNKENNESS; EBER; ETHAN; ETHBAAL; LAMENTATIONS, BOOK OF; PARADISE

Jef Tingley*, B.A.; Marketing Director, Jewish Federation of Greater Dallas: DALLAS

Ofra Tirosh-Becker*, Ph.D.; Lecturer, The Center for the Study of Jewish Languages and Literatures, the Hebrew University of Jerusalem: CONSTANTINE

Hava Tirosh-Samuelson*, Ph.D.; Professor of History, Arizona State University, Tucson, Arizona: BEATITUDE; PHILOSOPHY, JEWISH

Ariel Toaff, Ph.D., Rabbi; the Rabbinical College of Italy, Rome: CALABRIA; CATANZARO; DE' ROSSI, GIOVANNI BERNARDO; ELIJAH BEN SHABBETAI BE'ER; ELIJAH OF PESARO; JARÈ; LECCE; MODENA; NAPLES; ORVIETO; OTRANTO; PERUGIA; PESARO; RAVENNA; RECANATI; REGGIO DI CALABRIA; REGGIO EMILIA; RIMINI; SALERNO; SAN MARINO; SENIGALLIA; SFORNO, OBADIAH BEN JACOB; SIENA; SINIGAGLIA; SIPONTO; SPOLETO; TARANTO

Yosef Tobi*, Ph.D.; Professor, University of Haifa: ABDALLAH, YUSEF; ADANI, MAHALAL; ADANI, SAMUEL BEN JOSEPH; ADEN; AMRAN; ARUSI, ABRAHAM BEN MOSES HA-LEVI; BAYHAN; BENAYAH; DHAMĀR; GLASER, EDUARD; ḤABBĀN; ḤAḌRAMAWT; ḤAYDĀN; HIBSHŪSH, ḤAYYIM; ḤIJĀZ; JAMAL SULAYMĀN; KAWKABĀN; KORAḤ, 'AMRAM BEN YIḤYE; KORAḤ, SHALOM BEN YIḤYE; KUḤAYL, SHUKR BEN SĀLIM; MANĀKHAH; MAWZA'; MOCHA; NADDĀF, ABRAHAM ḤAYYIM; NIEBUHR, CARSTEN; QUEEN OF SHEBA; RABĪ' IBN ABI AL-ḤUQAYQ; ṢA'DAH; SA'DĪ, SA'ĪD BEN SOHELOMO; SAN'A; SHAR'AB; SHEIKH, ABRAHAM BEN SHALOM HA-LEVI AL-; SHIBĀM; TAYMA; YEMEN; YŪSUF AS'AR YATH'AR DHŪ NUWĀS

Alexander Tobias, Ph.D.; Librarian, the Jewish Theological Seminary of America, New York: ABRAHAM ABUSCH BEN ẒEVI HIRSCH; BUECHLER, ADOLF; CALENDAR REFORM; HAHN, JOSEPH YUSPA BEN PHINEHAS SELIGMANN; ḤAYYIM BEN BEZALEL; KALMAN OF WORMS; KISCH, BRUNO ZECHARIAS; KUBOVY, ARYEH LEON; LUZZATTO, SAMUEL DAVID; MARGOLIOUTH, MOSES; MARMORSTEIN, ARTHUR; MILLER, LOUIS E.; PINNER, EPHRAIM MOSES BEN ALEXANDER SUSSKIND; ROSENBAUM, MORRIS; ZEDNER, JOSEPH; ZIMMELS, HIRSCH JACOB; ZUCKERMAN, BENEDICT

Henry J. Tobias*, Ph.D.; Professor Emeritus of History, University of Oklahoma: ALBUQUERQUE; KATZ, MOSES; KRANTZ, PHILIP; MAGIDOV, JACOB; NEW MEXICO; VINCHEVSKY, MORRIS

Thomas J. Tobias, B.S.; Charleston, South Carolina: AZUBY, ABRAHAM; COHEN, PHILIP MELVIN; DA COSTA, ISAAC; DE LA MOTTA, JACOB; DE LEON; ELZAS, BARNETT ABRAHAM; MOÏSE, ABRAHAM; MOÏSE, PENINA; MOSES, RAPHAEL J.; SALVADOR; TOBIAS, ABRAHAM; TOBIAS, JOSEPH

Theo Toebosch*, M.A.; Journalist/ Writer, Amsterdam, The Netherlands: JITTA, DANIEL JOSEPHUS

Uri (Erich) Toeplitz, Musician and Teacher, Tel Aviv University – Rubin Academy of Music: ZUKERMAN, PINCHAS; AVNI, TZEVI; BRAUN, YEHEZKIEL; DA-OZ, RAM; DAUS, AVRAHAM; EDEN-TAMIR; FRIED, MIRIAM; GILBOA, JACOB; GRAZIANI, YITZHAK; HEIFETZ, JASCHA; HOROVITZ, VLADIMIR; HUBERMAN, BRONISLAW; INBAL, ELIAHU; JACOBI, HANOCH; JAFFE, ELI; KALICHSTEIN, JOSEPH; KLEMPERER, OTTO; KOUSSEVITZKY, SERGE; LAKNER, YEHOSHUA; MAAYANI, AMI; MENUHIN, SIR YEHUDI; MILSTEIN, NATHAN; NATRA, SERGIU; ORGAD, BEN ZION; PIATIGORSKY, GREGOR; PRESSLER, MENAHEM; RONLY-RIKLIS, SHALOM; RUBINSTEIN, ARTUR; SADAI, YIẒHAK; SCHIDLOWSKY, LEON; SETER, MORDECHAI; SHMUELI, HERZL; SMOIRA-COHN, MICHAL; STERN, ISAAC

Marvin Tokayer, M.A., Rabbi; Former rabbi of Tokyo community; Writer, Jerusalem: HAHN, JOSEPH BEN MOSES; HEILBRONN, JOSEPH BEN DAVID OF ESCHWEGE; JAPAN

Samuel Tolansky, Ph.D., D.Sc., D.I.C., F.R.A.S., F.R.S.; Professor of Physics, Royal Holloway College, the University of London

Bina Toledo Freiwald*, Ph.D.; Associate Professor, Concordia University, Montreal, Canada: MAYNARD, FREDELLE BRUSER

Jerucham Tolkes, Writer, Tel Aviv: CHORIN, AARON; SALKIND, JACOB MEIR; SILBERSCHLAG, EISIG; SONNE, ISAIAH; WALLENROD, REUBEN; WEINBERG, ẒEVI ZEBULUN; WENDROFF, ZALMAN; WUENSCHE, AUGUST KARL; ZHITLOWSKY, CHAIM

William Toll*, Ph.D.; Adjunct Professor, University of Oregon: PISCO, SERAPHINE EPPSTEIN

Haim Toren, M.A.; Writer, Jerusalem: ARICHA, YOSEF

Samuel Totten*, Ph.D.; Professor of Genocide Studies, University of Arkansas, Fayetteville; Member of the Institute on the Holocaust and Genocide, Jerusalem: HOLOCAUST

Charles Touati, Ph.D., Rabbi; Assistant Professor of Jewish Philosophy, Ecole Pratique des

Hautes Etudes, Sorbonne, Paris: LEVI BEN GERSHOM; VAJDA, GEORGES

E.L. Touriel, M.D., Los Angeles: PUGLIESE, UMBERTO

Jacob Toury, Ph.D.; Associate Professor of Jewish History, Tel Aviv University: ANTISEMITISM

Barry (C.) Trachtenberg*, Ph.D.; Professor, University at Albany, New York: ERIK, MAX; NIGER, SHMUEL

Henry Trachtenberg*, B.A., M.A., Ph.D.; Analyst Historian, Historic Resources Branch of Culture, Heritage and Tourism, Manitoba, Canada: HEAPS, ABRAHAM ALBERT; WEIDMAN, HIRAM AND MORDECAI S.

León Trahtemberg*, M.A.; Principal, Leon Pinelo Jewish School, National Council of Education, Lima, Peru: LIMA; PERU

Barbara Trainin Blank*, Writer, President of Blank Page Writing and Editorial Services, Harrisburg, Pennsylvania: HARRISBURG

Hans L. Trefousse, Ph.D.; Professor of History, Brooklyn College of the City University of New York: HANDLIN, OSCAR; JOSEPHSON, MATTHEW; MYERS, GUSTAVUS

Esther Trépanier*, Ph.D.; Professor of Art History, University of Quebec, Montreal: CAISERMAN-ROTH, GHITTA; MUHLSTOCK, LOUIS

Emanuela Trevisan Semi*, Professor in Modern Hebrew and Jewish Studies, Ca' Foscari University, Venice, Italy: BETA ISRAEL; FAÏTLOVITCH, JACQUES

Mirjam Triendl (-Zadoff)*, M.A.; Junior Staff Member, Doctoral Student, for Jewish History of Culture, University of Munich, Germany: BETTAUER, HUGO; BILLROTH, THEODOR; BROD, MAX; BUNZL; FREUD, ANNA; FRIEDELL, EGON; HEIMANN, MORITZ; KADIMAH; KALÉKO, MASCHA; KERR, ALFRED; LUXEMBURG, ROSA; SCHOLEM, WERNER; TORBERG, FRIEDRICH; VEREIN ZUR ABWEHR DES ANTISEMITISMUS; WOLF, GERSON

Harold Troper*, Ph.D.; Professor of History and Education, University of Toronto, Canada: ARNOLD, ABE; ASPER, ISRAEL H.; AZRIELI, DAVID; BARRETT, DAVID; BLANKSTEIN, CECIL; BRONFMAN; CAPLAN, ELINOR; CARR, JUDY FELD; CASS, FRANK; COHEN, NATHAN; COTLER, IRWIN; DIAMOND, JACK; GOTLIEB, ALLAN; HERZOG, SHIRA; JOURNALISM; KOFFLER, MURRAY; LAMBERT, PHYLLIS; LAWYERS; LEWIS, STEPHEN; LITTMAN, SOL; ONTARIO; POLITICS; PRESS; REICHMANN; SEGAL, HUGH; SIEGEL, IDA LEWIS; TANENBAUM; TORONTO

Amram Tropper*: AVOT

Daniel Tropper, Ph.D.; Director, Gesher Foundation, Jerusalem

Isaiah Trunk, Historian, YIVO Institute for Jewish Research, New York: POLAND

Hiller Tryster, Film Critic and Journalist, Jerusalem

Dan Tsalka, Writer and Critic, Tel Aviv: AMICHAI, YEHUDA; GILBOA, AMIR

Tsemah Tsamriyon, Ph.D.; Educator, Haifa: HAME'ASSEF

Benyamim Tsedaka, Writer, Editor Aleph-Bet, Holon, Israel: SAMARITANS

Jacob Tsur, Former Ambassador and former Chairman of the Board of Directors, the Jewish National Fund, Jerusalem: ARIEL, JOSEPH; BLUMEL, ANDRÉ; JEWISH NATIONAL FUND

Tom Tugend*, M.A., Contributing Editor, *Jewish Journal of Greater Los Angeles*, Sherman Oaks, California: HIER, MARVIN; SIMON WIESENTHAL CENTER

Gerald (J.J.) Tulchinsky*, Ph.D.; Emeritus Professor of History, Queens University, Kingston, Canada: ANSELL, DAVID ABRAHAM; BERCOVICH, PETER; CAISERMAN, HANAE MEIER; CANADA; COHEN, LYON; CROLL, DAVID ARNOLD; DAVIS, MORTIMER B.; DUNKELMAN, BENJAMIN; DUNKELMAN, ROSE; PHILLIPS, LAZARUS; ROSE, FRED; ROTHSCHILD, ROBERT PHINEAS

Joseph Turner*: SCHWEID, ELIEZER

Michael Turner*, Ph.D.; Professor, UNESCO Chair for Urban Design and Conservation Studies, Bezalel Academy of Arts and Design, Jerusalem: ENVIRONMENTAL SCIENCES

Chava Turniansky, M.A.; Instructor in Yiddish Language and Literature, the Hebrew University of Jerusalem: TASHRAK; ẒE'ENAH U-RE'ENAH

Naphtali Herz Tur-Sinai (Torczyner), Dr. Phil.; Emeritus Professor of Hebrew Language, the Hebrew University of Jerusalem; President of the Academy of the Hebrew Language, Jerusalem: MUELLER, DAVID HEINRICH

Chasia Turtel, M.A.; Researcher in Jewish History, Jerusalem: BEILIS, MENAHEM MENDEL; BLONDES, DAVID; BOPPARD; CLEVES; COTTBUS; DEUTZ; FRANKFURT ON THE ODER; HANAU; JUELICH; KIEL; KREFELD; KREUZNACH; LANDAU

Shaul Tuval, M.A.; Ministry for Foreign Affairs, Jerusalem: JAPAN; PHILIPPINES

David Twersky*, B.A.; Contributing Editor, *NY Sun*; Director International Relations, American Jewish Congress, West Orange, New Jersey: NEW JERSEY

Isadore Twersky, Ph.D., Rabbi; Professor of Hebrew Literature and Philosophy, Harvard University, Cambridge, Massachusetts: ABRAHAM BEN DAVID OF POSQUIÈRES

Yohanan Twersky, Writer and Editor, Tel Aviv: AMIR, ANDA

Gail Twersky Reimer*, Ph.D.; Founding Director, Jewish Women's Archive, Brookline, Massachusetts: SCHWARTZ, FELICE NIERENBERG

Ida Libert Uchill, B.A.; Denver, Colorado

Jacob B. Ukeles*, Ph.D.; President, Ukeles Associates, New York: NEW YORK CITY

Ellen M. Umansky*, Ph.D.; Carl and Dorothy Professor of Judaic Studies, Fairfield University, Fairfield, Connecticut: ACKERMAN, PAULA HERSKOVITZ; FRANK, RAY; LICHTENSTEIN, TEHILLA; MONTAGU, LILY; STERN, ELIZABETH GERTRUDE LEVIN; THEOLOGY

Rhoda K. Unger*, Ph.D.; Professor, Resident Scholar, Women's Studies Research Center, Brandeis University, Waltham, Massachusetts: JAHODA, MARIE; MEDNICK, MARTHA TAMARA SCHUCH; PSYCHOLOGY; TOBACH, ETHEL

Moshe Unna, Dipl. Agr.; Former Member of the Knesset, Kibbutz Sedeh Eliyahu: HA-PO'EL HA-MIZRACHI; KIBBUTZ MOVEMENT

Alan Unterman, Ph.D.; Jerusalem: FORGIVENESS; LOPIAN, ELIJAH; RU'AḤ HA-KODESH; SHEKHINAH

Morris Unterman, Rabbi; London: SHERMAN, ARCHIE

Ephraim Elimelech Urbach, Dott. in.lett., Rabbi; Professor of Talmud, the Hebrew University of Jerusalem: ABBAYE

Symcha Bunim Urbach, Rabbi; Associate Professor of Jewish Philosophy, Bar-Ilan University, Ramat Gan: ZEITLIN, HILLEL

Ludmilla Uritskaya: AN-SKI COLLECTIONS

Ann Ussishkin, M.A.; Jerusalem: JEWISH COLONIZATION ASSOCIATION; TEMPLERS

David Ussishkin*, Professor of Archaeology, Tel Aviv University, Tel Aviv: MEGIDDO

Baruch Uziel, Former Member of the Knesset; Tel Aviv: ARDITI, ALBERT JUDAH; BEN-AROYA, AVRAHAM

Bela Adalbert Vago, Ph.D.; Senior Lecturer in History, Haifa University and the Hebrew University of Jerusalem: ARROW CROSS PARTY; BAKY, LÁSZLÓ; CODREANU, CORNELIU ZELEA; HUNGARY; IRON GUARD; SIMA, HORIA

Samuel Vaisrub, M.D. M.R.C.P.; Associate Professor, Chicago Medical School; Senior Editor, Journal of the American Medical Association: MEDICINE

Georges Vajda, D.es L.; Professor of Medieval Jewish Thought, Directeur d'Etudes a l'Ecole Pratique des Hautes Etudes, Sorbonne, Paris: ALBALAG, ISAAC; BAḤYA BEN JOSEPH IBN PAQUDA; BIBLIOTHÈQUE NATIONALE; DUNASH IBN TAMIM; IBN MOTOT, SAMUEL BEN SAADIAH; IBN WAQAR, JOSEPH BEN ABRAHAM; MALKAH, JUDAH BEN NISSIM IBN

Heather Valencia*, Ph.D.; Honorary Research Fellow, University of Stirling, Scotland: HALPERN, MOYSHE-LEYB; KARPINOVITSH, AVROM

Hugo Mauritz Valentin, Dr. Phil.; Professor of History, the University of Uppsala, Sweden: BRICK, DANIEL; EHRENPREIS, MARCUS; ELKAN, SOPHIE; FRAENKEL, LOUIS; HECKSCHER, ELI FILIP; ISAAC, AARON; JOSEPHSON; KLEIN, GOTTLIEB; LAMM, MARTIN; LEVERTIN, OSCAR IVAR; MANNHEIMER, THEODOR; SWEDEN; WARBURG, KARL JOHAN; WILHELM, KURT

W.J. (Willem Jan) van Asselt*, Ph.D.; Associate Professor, Church History, Theological Faculty Utrecht University, The Netherlands: COCCEIUS, JOHANNES

Wout (Wouter Jacques) van Bekkum*, Ph.D.; Professor of Semitic Languages and Cultures, Rijksuniversiteit Groningen, Germany: AMSTERDAM; NETHERLANDS, THE

Adam Simon Van Der Woude, M.A.; Professor of Old Testament, the State University of Groningen, the Netherlands: VRIEZEN, THEODORUS CHRISTIAAN

Joris van Eijnatten*, Ph.D.; Senior Lecturer, Early Modern History, VU University Amsterdam, The Netherlands: COSTA, ISAÄC DA

H.F.K. (Hendrik Frans Karel) van Nierop*, Ph.D.; Professor of Early Modern History, University of Amsterdam, The Netherlands: NIEROP, VAN

Robert Jan van Pelt*, Ph.D.; Professor, University of Waterloo, Waterloo, Canada: AUSCHWITZ

Peter van Rooden*, Ph.D.; Chair, Department of Sociology and Anthropology, University of Amsterdam, The Netherlands: EMPEREUR, CONSTANTIJN L'

Edward van Voolen, Ph.D., Rabbi; Curator, Joods Historisch Museum, Amsterdam

Elaine Varady, Israel Museum, Jerusalem: ISRAEL, STATE OF: CULTURAL LIFE

Benjamin (Benno) Varon (Weiser), Abs. Med.; Ambassador, Ministry for Foreign Affairs, Jerusalem: DOMINICAN REPUBLIC; PARAGUAY

Simon Vega, Ben Shemen, Israel: BLANES, JACOB; DARMSTADT, JOSEPH; MYERS, MOSES

Mervin F. Verbit, Ph.D.; Professor of Sociology, Brooklyn College: MIXED MARRIAGE, INTERMARRIAGE

Geza Vermes*, F.B.A.; Professor of Jewish Studies, University of Oxford, Oriental Institute, England: SCHÜRER, EMIL

Saul Viener, M.A.; Richmond, Virginia: CALISCH, EDWARD NATHAN; ELCAN, MARCUS; ISAACS, ISAIAH; JACOBS, SOLOMON; MYERS, SAMUEL

Claude (Andre) Vigée, Ph.D.; Professor of French Literature, the Hebrew University of Jerusalem: CLAUDEL, PAUL; GOLL, YVAN; SCHWARZ-BART, ANDRÉ

David Vinitzky, Givatayim, Israel: BERLIAND, SHLOMO MEIR

Manfred H. Vogel, Ph.D.; Associate Professor of the History and Literature of Religions, Northwestern University, Evanston, Illinois: KANT, IMMANUEL; MONOTHEISM

Samuel Volkman, Rabbi; Charleston, W. Virginia: WEST VIRGINIA

Leon Volovici*, Ph.D.; Senior Researcher, The Vidal Sassoon International Center for the Study of Anti-Semitism, Jerusalem, Hebrew University of Jerusalem: BENADOR, URY; CORNEA, PAUL; COSAȘU, RADU; CROHMĂLNICEANU, OVID S.; DUDA, VIRGIL; ROMANIA

Eva M. von Dassow*, Ph.D.; Assistant Professor, University of Minnesota: HURRIAN

Frauke von Rohden*, Ph.D.; Senior

Lecturer, Freie Universitaet Berlin, Germany: REBECCA BAT MEIR TIKTINER

Albert Vorspan*: SCHINDLER, ALEXANDER M.

Max Vorspan, D.H.L., Rabbi; Vice President, University of Judaism, Los Angeles: BOYAR, LOUIS H.; HELLMAN, ISAIAS WOLF; HOLLZER, HARRY AARON; KOHN, JACOB; LOS ANGELES; MAGNIN, EDGAR FOGEL; NEWMARK; PACHT, ISAAC; SILBERBERG, MENDEL; STROUSE, MYER; WEINSTOCK, HARRIS

Carl Hermann Voss, Ph.D., Reverend; Author and Lecturer, Jacksonville, Florida: WISE, STEPHEN SAMUEL

Simon J. De Vries, Th.D.; Professor of Old Testament, the Methodist Theological School in Ohio, Delaware: KUENEN, ABRAHAM

Ben Zion Wacholder, Ph.D., Rabbi; Professor of Talmud and Rabbinics, the Hebrew Union College-Jewish Institute of Religion, Cincinnati, Ohio: ARISTEAS; BIBLE; CLEODEMUS MALCHUS; DEMETRIUS; EUPOLEMUS; HECATAEUS OF ABDERA; JOB, TESTAMENT OF; PHILO; THALLUS; THEODOTUS

Miriam Dworkin Waddington, M.A., M.S.W.; Associate Professor of English Literature, York University, Toronto

Michael Wade, B.A. (Hons.), Dipl. Ed.; Instructor in English and in African Literature, the Hebrew University of Jerusalem: JACOBSON, DAN

Maurice Wagner, M.A.; General Secretary of the Central African Jewish Board of Deputies, Bulawayo, Rhodesia: BULAWAYO; SALISBURY; ZAMBIA; ZIMBABWE

Stanley M. Wagner*, Ph.D.; D.H.L., Professor Emeritus; Rabbi Emeritus, University of Denver; BHM-BJ Congregation, Denver, Colorado: DENVER; KAUVAR, CHARLES ELIEZER HILLEL; KIRSHBLUM, MORDECAI; MANDELBAUM, BERNARD; RACKMAN, EMANUEL; WURZBURGER, WALTER S.

Felix Bernard Wahle, Tel Aviv

Shalom Salomon Wald*, Ph.D.; The Jewish People Policy Planning Institute, Jerusalem: CHINA

Stephen G. Wald*, Ph.D.; Talmud and Rabbinics, Jerusalem: ABBA ḤILKIAH; AGGADAH; AGRAT BAT MAHALATH; AKIVA; AM HA-AREẒ; ANDROGYNOS; AVOT; BAR KAPPARA; BARAITA DE-MELEKHET HA-MISHKAN; BARAITA, BERAITOT; BAVA MEẒIA; BEN SṬADA; BERURYAH; DAMA, SON OF NETINA; DRUNKENNESS; EDUYYOT; ELEAZAR BEN ARAKH; ELEAZAR BEN HANANIAH BEN HEZEKIAH; ELEAZAR BEN ḤARSOM; ELIEZER BEN HYRCANUS; ELISHA BEN AVUYAH; EZEKIEL; GENESIS RABBAH; ḤAGIGAH; ḤALLAH; HILLEL; IMMA SHALOM; JOHANAN BEN GUDGADA; JOHANAN BEN NAPPAḤA; JOHANAN BEN ZAKKAI; JOHANAN HA-SANDELAR; JOSHUA BEN HANANIAH; JOSHUA BEN KORḤA; JOSHUA BEN PERAḤYAH; JOSHUA HA-GARSI; JUDAH BAR ILAI; JUDAH BEN BATHYRA; JUDAH BEN BAVA; JUDAH BEN DOSOTHEOS; JUDAH BEN GERIM; JUDAH BEN SHAMMUA; JUDAH BEN TABBAI; JUDAH BEN TEMA; JUDAH HA-NASI; KAHANA; KILAYIM; MARTHA; MATTIAH BEN ḤERESH; MEIR; MISHNAH; NAHUM OF GiMZO; NATHAN HA-BAVLI; NEHEMIAH; NEHORAI; NEḤUNYA BEN HA-KANAH; NEZIKIN; OSHAIAH RABBAH; PAPA; RIGHT AND LEFT; SHEMAIAH; SIMEON BAR YOḤAI; SIMEON BEN NETHANEL; SIMEON BEN SHETAḤ; TALMUD; TALMUD, BABYLONIAN; TALMUD, JERUSALEM; TOSEFTA

Solomon H. Waldenberg, M.A, Rabbi; Santurce, Puerto Rico

Miriam Waldman*, Ph.D.; Head of Department, Environmental and Agricultural Research Programs; Israel Ministry of Science and Development; Tel Aviv: ENVIRONMENTAL SCIENCES

James Walker*, Ph.D.; Professor of History; University of Waterloo, Waterloo, Canada: ABELLA, ROSALIE SILBERMAN; BOROVOY, A. ALAN; COHEN, MAXWELL; LASKIN, BORA; MATAS, DAVID

Jehuda Wallach, Ph.D.; Colonel (Res.) Israel Defense Forces; Senior Lecturer in Military History, Tel Aviv University: BEER, ISRAEL; LASKOV, ḤAYYIM; MARCUS, DAVID DANIEL; SINAI CAMPAIGN; ẒUR, ẒEVI

Michael Wallach, B.Sc.; Assistant Editor, *Jewish Chronicle*, London: FISHER, SAMUEL, BARON FISHER OF CAMDEN; GOODMAN, ARNOLD ABRAHAM, LORD; GROSS, JOHN JACOB; GUTTMANN, SIR LUDWIG; KISSIN, HARRY, BARON; TOLANSKY, SAMUEL

Harold M. Waller*, Ph.D.; Professor of Political Science, McGill University, Montreal, Canada: EZRIN, HERSHELL; MONTREAL; STEINBERG

Bart (Barend Theodoor) Wallet*, M.A.; Junior Researcher, Hebrew, Aramaic and Jewish Studies, University of Amsterdam, The Netherlands: AMELANDER, MENAHEM MANN BEN SOLOMON HA-LEVI; AMSTERDAM; ASSER; BERGH, VAN DEN; BREGSTEIN, MARCEL HENRI; COHEN, BENJAMIN; FELIX LIBERTATE; GODEFROI, MICHAEL HENRI; GOUDSMIT, JOEL EMANUEL; MEIJERS, EDUARD MAURITS; MEYER, JONAS DANIEL; NETHERLANDS, THE; OPPENHEIM, JACQUES; POLITICS; VISSER, LODEWIJK ERNST

Kenneth Waltzer, Ph.D.; Teaching Fellow in American History, Harvard University, Cambridge, Massachusetts: LOVESTONE, JAY; PRESSMAN, LEE; ROSE, ALEX; ZARITSKY, MAX

Chaim Wardi, Ph.D.; Senior Lecturer in Christianity in the Middle East and Africa, Tel Aviv University: ISRAEL, STATE OF: RELIGIOUS LIFE AND COMMUNITIES

Itamar Warhaftig*, Ph.D.; Senior Lecturer, Bar-Ilan University, Ramat Gan: CONSUMER PROTECTION; OBLIGATIONS, LAW OF; UNJUST ENRICHMENT; WEIGHTS AND MEASURES

Shillem Warhaftig, Dr.Jur.; Ministry of Justice, Jerusalem: LABOR LAW; NATHANSON, JOSEPH SAUL; STRASHUN, MATHIAS; STRASHUN, SAMUEL BEN JOSEPH

Iris Waskow*, B.A.; Senior Director of Communications, University of Judaism, Los Angeles: UNIVERSITY OF JUDAISM, THE; WEXLER, ROBERT D.

Henry Wasserman, M.A.; Everyman's University, Tel Aviv: BADEN BEI WIEN; BISMARCK, OTTO VON; BROKERS; CONSTRUCTION; DEPARTMENT STORES; DIAMOND TRADE AND INDUSTRY; DOBRUSCHKA-SCHOENFELD; EPHRAIM; FERDINAND; GOLDSMITHS AND SILVERSMITHS; GOMPERZ; GOSLAR;

HEP! HEP!; HOENIGSBERG; JEITELES; KLOSTERNEUBURG; LEIDESDORFER; LINZ; LIVESTOCK, TRADE IN; MARKET DAYS AND FAIRS; MECKLENBURG; MEYER, SELIGMANN; MILITARY SERVICE; MINTMASTERS AND MONEYERS; MUHR, ABRAHAM; NIETZSCHE, FRIEDRICH WILHELM; OETTINGEN; OPPENHEIMER, SAMUEL; OSTRAVA; PALATINATE; PEDDLING; POMERANIA; PRUSSIA; REGENSBURG; ROTHENBURG OB DER TAUBER; ROTHSCHILD; SCHMID, ANTON VON; SCHOENERER, GEORG VON; SCHOTTLAENDER, BENDET; SECONDHAND GOODS AND OLD CLOTHES, TRADE IN; SHIPS AND SAILING; SLAVE TRADE; STOCK EXCHANGES; SUGAR INDUSTRY AND TRADE; TAILORING; TEXTILES; THURINGIA; TOBACCO TRADE AND INDUSTRIES; ULM; VERBAND NATIONALDEUTSCHER JUDEN; VEREIN ZUR ABWEHR DES ANTISEMITISMUS; VORARLBERG; WEBER, KOLOMAN

David J. Wasserstein*, Professor of History and Jewish Studies, Director of the Program in Jewish Studies, Vanderbilt University, Nashville: 'ABD AL-ḤAQQ AL-ISLĀMĪ; CALIPH; MULUK AL-TAWA'IF; SAMAU'AL BEN JUDAH IBN 'ABBAS AL-MAGHRIBI; STERN, SAMUEL MIKLÓS

James F. Watts, Jr., Ph.D.; Assistant Professor of History, City College of the City University of New York: EINSTEIN, LEWIS

Bernard Wax, M.A.; Director of the American Jewish Historical Society, Waltham, Massachusetts: FALL RIVER

James A. Wax, D.H.L., Rabbi; Memphis, Tennessee: MEMPHIS; TENNESSEE

Meyer Waxman, Ph.D., Rabbi; Professor of Jewish Philosophy and Literature, the Hebrew Theological College of Chicago: LITERATURE, JEWISH

Mordecai Waxman, M.H.L., Rabbi; Great Neck, New York: LITERATURE, JEWISH

George Julius Webber, LL.D.; Barrister at Law, Former Reader in English Law, the University of London: LAWYERS

Annette Weber*, Ph.D.; Chair for Jewish Art, Hochschule für Jüdische Studien, Heidelberg, Germany: ART: WESTERN EUROPE; DICKER-BRANDEIS, FRIEDL; HIRSCHFELD-MACK, LUDWIG

Brom Weber, Ph.D.; Professor of English, the University of California, Davis: FRANK, WALDO DAVID; GREENBERG, SAMUEL BERNARD; WEST, NATHANAEL

Harold S. Wechsler, Ph.D.; Assistant Professor of Education, University of Chicago

Fred (Frederick W.) Weidmann*, M.Div., Ph.D.; Director of the Center for Church Life and Professor of Biblical Studies, Auburn Theological Seminary, New York; Adjunct, Union Theological Seminary; Pastoral Associate, Advent Lutheran Church; Society of Biblical Literature; American Academy of Religion; New York: BIBLE

Irwin Weil, Ph.D.; Professor of Russian and Russian Literature, Northwestern University, Evanston, Illinois: GORKI, MAXIM

Shalva Weil, D.Phil.; Senior Researcher, NCJW Research Institute for Innovation in Education, the Hebrew University of Jerusalem

Asher Weill*, Editor and Publisher, Editor, *ARIEL -the Israel Review of Arts and Letters*, Jerusalem: PUBLISHING; WEIDENFELD, GEORGE, BARON

Georges Weill, M.A., Archiviste-Paléographe; Directeur des Services d'Archives des Hauts-de-Seine, France: ANCHEL, ROBERT; ARMLEDER; BAR-LE-DUC; GROSS, HEINRICH; KAHN, LÉON; LÉVY, ALFRED; LIBER, MAURICE; LOEB, ISIDORE; REVUE DES ÉTUDES JUIVES

Abraham Wein, M.A.; Historian, Jerusalem: ARENDA; BERMAN, ADOLF ABRAHAM; BERMAN, JAKUB; DIAMAND, HERMAN; DICKSTEIN, SZYMON; DROBNER, BOLESLAW; JOGICHES, LEON; KATZ-SUCHY, JULIUSZ; LIEBERMAN, HERMAN; MINC, HILARY; SZYR, EUGENIUSZ; WARSKI-WARSZAWSKI, ADOLF; WOHL, HENRYK; ZAMBROWSKI, ROMAN

David Weinberg*, Ph.D.; Professor of History and Director, Cohn-Haddow Center for Judaic Studies, Wayne State University, Detroit: CENTRE DE DOCUMENTATION JUIVE CONTEMPORAINE; COLMAR; FRANCE; GRENOBLE; GURS; LANZMANN, CLAUDE; LILLE; LYONS; MANS, LE; MARSEILLES; METZ; MONTPELLIER; NANTES; NATZWEILER-STRUTHOF; NICE; ROUEN; TOULOUSE; TOURS; VERDUN-SUR-GARONNE

David M. Weinberg, Spokesman, Bar-Ilan University, Ramat Gan: BAR-ILAN UNIVERSITY

Gerhard (L.) Weinberg*, Ph.D.; Professor of History Emeritus, University of North Carolina: HITLER, ADOLF

Jill Weinberg*, M.S.W.; Midwest Director, United States Holocaust Memorial Museum, Highland Park, Illinois: SCHAKOWSKY, JANICE D.

Werner Weinberg, Ph.D.; Professor of Hebrew Language and Literature, the Hebrew Union College-Jewish Institute of Religion, Cincinnati, Ohio: KABAK, AARON ABRAHAM; LETTERIS, MEIR

Deborah (R.) Weiner*, Ph.D.; Research Historian, Jewish Museum of Maryland, Baltimore, Maryland: BALTIMORE

Hanna Weiner, B.A.; Kibbutz Ne'ot Mordekhai: ABIEZER; ADONIRAM; AGAG; AHIMAN, SHESHAI, TALMAI

Hollace Ava Weiner*, M.A.; Writer, Historian, Archivist, Fort Worth, Texas: FRISCH, EPHRAIM; GOLDBERG, JEANNETTE MIRIAM

Miriam Weiner*, B.A.; Genealogist, Author and Historian, President, Routes to Roots Foundation, Inc, Secaucus, New Jersey: INTERNATIONAL ASSOCIATION OF JEWISH GENEALOGICAL SOCIETIES

Morton Weinfeld*, Ph.D.; Professor of Sociology, McGill University, Montreal, Canada: CANADA; ROSENBERG, LOUIS; SPECTOR, NORMAN

Moshe Weinfeld, Ph.D.; Senior Lecturer in Bible, the Hebrew University of Jerusalem: CONGREGATION; COVENANT;

DEUTERONOMY; ELDER; JOSIAH; MOLOCH, CULT OF; ORDEAL OF JEALOUSY; PRESENCE, DIVINE; RUTH, BOOK OF; TITHE

Samuel Weingarten-Hakohen, Jerusalem: BETTELHEIM, SAMUEL; BRATISLAVA; GRISHABER, ISAAC; HELLER, ẒEVI HIRSCH; JAFFE-MARGOLIOT, ISRAEL DAVID; JOAB BEN JEREMIAH; PLAUT, HEZEKIAH FEIVEL; PROSSTITZ, DANIEL; SIDON, SIMEON; SINGER, PESAḤ; STEIN, ELIEZER LIPMAN; UNGAR, JOEL OF RECHNITZ; WEISS, JOSEPH MEIR; WEISZ, MAX

Jacob Weingreen, Ph.D.; Former Professor of Hebrew, University of Dublin: HEBREW GRAMMAR, AN INTRODUCTION TO

Uriel Weinreich, Ph.D.; Professor of Linguistics and of Yiddish Studies, Columbia University, New York: YIDDISH LANGUAGE

Bernard Dov Sucher Weinryb, Emeritus Professor of History and of Economics, Dropsie University, Philadelphia: MAINZ

Donald Weinstein, Ph.D.; Associate Professor of History, Rutgers University, New Brunswick, New Jersey: SEGRÈ, ARTURO

Menachem Weinstein, M.A.; Instructor in the Institute for Research in the History and Culture of Oriental Jewry, Bar-Ilan University, Ramat Gan

Roni Weinstein*, Ph.D.; Research Fellow, Modern and Contemporary Department, Pisa University, Italy: COLUMBUS, CHRISTOPHER

David Weinstock*, M.M., Ph.D.; Assistant Professor, Communication/Journalism, Grand Valley State University, Allendale, Michigan: SAVANNAH; TRENTON; WOLF, ERIC ROBERT

Phyllis Holman Weisbard*, M.A., M.Ed.; Women's Studies Librarian, University of Wisconsin: NEUGARTEN, BERNICE

David B. Weisberg, Ph.D.; Assistant Professor of Bible and Semitic Languages, Hebrew Union College-Jewish Institute of Religion, Cincinnati, Ohio: MURASHU'S SONS

Dvora E. Weisberg*, Ph.D.; Associate Professor of Rabbinics, Hebrew Union College, Los Angeles: AGGADAH

Meyer Wolf Weisgal, Chancellor of the Weizmann Institute of Science, Reḥovot, Israel: WEIZMANN INSTITUTE OF SCIENCE

Aharon Weiss, Ph.D.; Researcher, Jerusalem: BARANOVICHI; BERESTECHKO; BIELSK PODLASKI; BORISLAV; BRASLAV; BUCHACH; BUSK; CHORTKOV; DAVID-GORODOK; DISNA; DOLGINOVO; DROGOBYCH; DRUYA; GLINYANY; GLUBOKOYE; GORODENKA; GORODOK; HOLOCAUST; ILYA; IVYE; JAROSLAW; JUDENRAT; KALUSH; KAMENKA-BUGSKAYA; KLETS; KOBRIN; KOLOMYYA; KOMARNO; KORETS; KOSOV; KOVEL; KREMENETS; KRYNKI; KRZEPICE; KUTY; LACHVA; LANCUT; LESHNEV; LEZAJSK; LIDA; LUBLIN; LUTSK; LYAKHOVICHI; MIR; MONASTYRISKA; NADVORNAYA; NESVIZH; NOVOGRUDOK; OSHMYANY; OSTROG; OSTROLEKA; PEREMYSHLYANY; PINSK; PODGAITSY; PODVOLOCHISK; PRUZHANY; PRZEMYSL; RADZIWILLOW; ROGATIN; ROPCZYCE; ROVNO; ROZWADOW; RUZHANY; RYMANOW; SAMBOR; SANOK; SARNY; SIEMIATYCZE; SLONIM; SOKOLKA; TARTAKOVER, SAVIELLY GRIGORYEVICH; TYKOCIN; ZAMBROW; ZHOLKVA; ZMIGROD NOWY; ZWOLEN

Andrea L. Weiss*, Ph.D.; Assistant Professor of Bible, Hebrew Union College-Jewish Institute of Religion, New York: POETRY

Avi Weiss*, M.A., M.H.L.; Senior Rabbi of the Hebrew Institute of Riverdale,; National President of the AMCHA, Yeshivat Chovevei Torah Rabbinical School, Riverdale, New York: STUDENT STRUGGLE FOR SOVIET JEWRY

Avraham A. Weiss, Dr. Phil.; Senior Clinical Lecturer in Clinical Psychology, the Hebrew University of Jerusalem: RAPAPORT, DAVID

Benjamin Weiss, New York: MISHNAT HA-MIDDOT

Joseph G. Weiss, Ph.D.; Professor of Jewish Studies, London University

Julius Weiss, B.A., LL.B.; New York: PALESTINE ECONOMIC CORPORATION

Raphael Weiss, M.A.; Instructor in Bible, Tel Aviv University: EHRLICH, ARNOLD BOGUMIL

Lee Shai Weissbach*, Ph.D.; Professor of History, University of Louisville, Louisville, Kentucky: KENTUCKY; LOUISVILLE

Rivka Weiss-Blok*, M.A.; General Director (retired), Jewish Historical Museum, Amsterdam, The Netherlands: REMBRANDT VAN RIJN

Chava Weissler*, Ph.D.; Philip and Muriel Berman Professor of Jewish Civilization, Lehigh University, Bethlehem, Pennsylvania: BAS TOVIM, SARAH; HOROWITZ, SARAH REBECCA RACHEL LEAH; SERL BAS JACOB BEN WOLF KRANZ; SHIFRAH OF BRODY; TEHINNAH; TKHINES

Deborah R. Weissman, M.A.; Lecturer, School for Overseas Students and the Melton Center for Jewish Education in the Diaspora, the Hebrew University of Jerusalem

Paul Weissman, Jerusalem: ANTISEMITISM

Joseph Weitz, Writer and Former Head of the Development Authority of the Jewish National Fund, Jerusalem: ISRAEL, STATE OF: ALIYAH

Raanan Weitz, Ph.D.; Member of the World Zionist Executive; Director of the Settlement Study Center, Reḥovot, Israel

Felix Weltsch, Writer and Philosopher, the Jewish National and University Library, Jerusalem: BROD, MAX; KAFKA, FRANZ

Robert Weltsch, Dr.Jur.; Writer and Director of the Leo Baeck Institute, London: ADLER, FRIEDRICH; ALLGEMEINE ZEITUNG DES JUDENTUMS; BAUER, OTTO; BERNSTEIN, ARON DAVID; BERNSTEIN, EDUARD; BRAUNTHAL, JULIUS; GERMANY; HAGGADAH, PASSOVER

Beth S. Wenger*, Ph.D.; Katz Family Term Chair in American Jewish History; Associate Professor of History, University of Pennsylvania: SOLOMON, HANNAH GREENEBAUM

Charles Wengrov, Rabbi; Jerusalem: HALICZ; KOHEN; SHAḤOR

Eugen Werber, Writer, Scholar, Lecturer on Judaica, Belgrade: ALBAHARI, DAVID; KIŠ, DANILO; PAPO, IZIDOR JOSEF

R.J. Zwi Werblowsky, D.es-L.; Professor of Comparative Religion, the Hebrew University of Jerusalem; Former Dean, Faculty of the Humanities: AARON; ANTHROPOMORPHISM; CAIN; CARO, JOSEPH BEN EPHRAIM; CHRISTIANITY; DUALISM; MANICHAEISM; OTTO, RUDOLPH

Preben Wernberg-Moller, D.Phil; Professorial Fellow of St. Peter's College and Reader in Semitic Philology, the University of Oxford: DISCIPLINE, MANUAL OF

Alfred Werner, J.D.; Art Critic and Writer, New York: ARONSON, NAUM LVOVICH; BAKST, LEON; BERENSON, BERNARD; CHAGALL, MARC; EPSTEIN, SIR JACOB; FREUNDLICH, OTTO; GLICENSTEIN, ENRICO; GOTTLIEB, MAURYCY; GROSS, CHAIM; HART, SOLOMON ALEXANDER; HOROVITZ, LEOPOLD; JOSEPHSON; KAUFMANN, ISIDOR; KISLING, MOISE; KOGAN, MOYSE; KOLNIK, ARTHUR; KRAYN, HUGO; LASANSKY, MAURICIO; LEVY, RUDOLF; LIEBERMANN, MAX; LILIEN, EPHRAIM MOSES; LIPCHITZ, JACQUES; LISMANN, HERMANN; LISSITZKY, EL; MANÉ-KATZ; MARCOUSSIS, LOUIS; MODIGLIANI, AMEDEO; MUTER, MELA; MYERS, MYER; NADELMAN, ELIE; OPPENHEIM, MORITZ DANIEL; ORLIK. EMIL; ORLOFF, CHANA; PASCIN, JULES; PASTERNAK, LEONID OSIPOVICH; PEVSNER, ANTON and NAUM NEHEMIA; PICART, BERNARD; PILICHOWSKI, LEOPOLD; PISSARRO, CAMILLE; REMBRANDT VAN RIJN; RYBACK, ISSACHAR; SALOMON, CHARLOTTE; SCULPTURE; SHAHN, BEN; SOLOMON, SIMEON; SOUTINE, CHAIM; SZYK, ARTHUR; URY, LESSER; WALKOWITZ, ABRAHAM; WEBER, MAX; ZADKINE, OSSIP

Samuel Werses, Ph.D.; Associate Professor of Hebrew Literature, the Hebrew University of Jerusalem: ERTER, ISAAC; HEBREW LITERATURE, MODERN; KLAUSNER, JOSEPH GEDALIAH; LACHOWER, YERUḤAM FISHEL; PERL, JOSEPH

Paul G. Werskey, M.A.; Lecturer in Science Policy, the University of Edinburgh: BERNAYS

Benjamin West, Writer, Tel Aviv: KIEV

Robert (David) Wexler*, Ph.D.; President and Colen Distinguished Lecturer, University of Judaism, Los Angeles: WOLPE, DAVID J.

D.H. White, Publisher, Houston: HOUSTON

Libby (K.) White*, M.L.S., M.A.L.S.; Director, Joseph Meyerhoff Library, Hebrew University, Baltimore: AMSTERDAM, BIRDIE; BALABANOFF, ANGELICA; BERNARD, JESSIE; KUNIN, MADELEINE MAY

Stephen J. Whitfield*, Ph.D.; Professor of American Studies, Brandeis University, Watham, Massachusetts: BRANDEIS UNIVERSITY

Sally Whyte, Member, International Association of Art Critics, Conseil International de la Danse (UNESCO), London: BERKOFF, STEVEN; ISAACS, SIR JEREMY; MOSHINSKY, ELIJAH; SHER, SIR ANTHONY; SUZMAN, JANET

Aaron Wiener, M.A.; Engineer, Director General of Tahal, Water Planning for Israel, Tel Aviv: MEKOROT WATER COMPANY; TAHAL

Theodore Wiener, M.H.L., Rabbi; Washington, D.C.: BIOGRAPHIES AND AUTOBIOGRAPHIES; ENCYCLOPEDIAS; FESTSCHRIFTEN

Helene Wieruszowski, Ph.D.; New York: KANTOROWICZ, ERNST HARTWIG; LEVISON, WILHELM; LIEBERMANN, FELIX

Christian Wiese*, Dr. Habil.; Associate Professor for Modern Jewish History and Thought, University of Erfurt, Erfurt, Germany: DELITZSCH, FRANZ; JONAS, HANS

Ephraim Jehudah Wiesenberg, Ph.D., Rabbi; Reader in Hebrew, the University of London: ADAR; AV; CALENDAR; ELUL; IYYAR; KISLEV; MARḤESHVAN; NISAN; SHEVAT; SIVAN; TAMMUZ; TEVET; TISHRI

Geoffrey Wigoder, D. Phil., Editor in Chief of the *Encyclopaedia Judaica* (1st ed.) print and CD-Rom Edition; Director, Oral History Division and Jewish Film Archives, The Hebrew University of Jerusalem; History Consultant, Beth Hatefutsoth, Tel Aviv; Jerusalem: ABRAHAM BAR ḤIYYA; AUSCHWITZ CONVENT; BETH HATEFUTSOTH; CHRISTIANITY; ISRAEL, STATE OF: CULTURAL LIFE; MOTION PICTURES; TERKEL, STUDS

Carsten (L.) Wilke*, Ph.D.; Research Fellow, Salomon Ludwig Steinheim Institute for German Jewish History, University of Duisburg and Essen, Germany: RÉVAH, ISRAEL SALVATOR; SEPHIHA, HAIM VIDAL

Jacqueline (B.) Williams*, Researcher, Writer, Seattle, Washington: SEATTLE; WASHINGTON

H.G.M. Williamson*, B.A., M.A., Ph.D., D.D.; Regius Professor of Hebrew and Student of Christ Church, University of Oxford, England: ANGLO-ISRAEL ARCHAEOLOGICAL SOCIETY

Adam Wills*, Associate Editor, *The Jewish Journal of Greater Los Angeles*, Los Angeles: BENJAMIN, RICHARD; BOGDANOVICH, PETER; BROOKS, ALBERT; BROOKS, JAMES L.; BRUCKHEIMER, JERRY; BURSTYN, MIKE; CAAN, JAMES; CHETWYND, LIONEL; CLAYBURGH, JILL; COEN, JOEL and ETHAN; COOPER, JACKIE; CSUPO, GABOR; CURTIS, JAMIE LEE; CURTIZ, MICHAEL; DANGERFIELD, RODNEY; DAVIS, SAMMY JR.; EISNER, MICHAEL DAMMANN; ELFMAN, DANNY; EVANS, ROBERT; FELDSHUH, TOVAH; FISHER, CARRIE FRANCES; FULLER, SAMUEL MICHAEL; FURIE, SIDNEY J.; GABOR, JOLIE, MAGDA, ZSA ZSA, and EVA; GILBERT, MELISSA ELLEN; GOLAN, MENAHEM; GOLDMAN, WILLIAM; GOODRICH, FRANCES and HACKETT, ALBERT; GORCEY, LEO; GOULD, ELLIOTT; GRAZER BRIAN; GREENE, SHECKY; GUGGENHEIM, CHARLES; HEAD, EDITH; HERSKOVITZ, MARSHALL and ZWICK, EDWARD; HILLER, ARTHUR; JAGLOM, HENRY; KAUFMAN, PHILIP; KEMPNER, AVIVA; KOPPLE, BARBARA; LANSING, SHERRY LEE; LAWRENCE, STEVE and GORME, EDYIE; LEVANT, OSCAR; MALTIN, LEONARD; MANKIEWICZ, HERMAN JACOB; MAY, ELAINE; MAYSLES, ALBERT and DAVID PAUL; MEDVED, MICHAEL; MICHAELS, LORNE; MONROE,

MARILY; MOONVES, LES; MYERSON, BESS; NEWMAN, ALFRED; NEWMAN, RANDY; NIMOY, LEONARD; OVITZ, MICHAEL; PALMER, LILLI; PENN, SEAN; RADNER, GILDA; REDSTONE, SUMNER MURRAY; REISER, PAUL; RICKLES, DON; RIVERS, JOAN; RUDIN, SCOTT; SELDES, MARIAN; SHANDLING, GARRY; SHATNER, WILLIAM; SHEARER, NORMA; SHERMAN, ALLAN; SHILS, EDWARD ALBERT; SIEGEL, BENJAMIN "BUGSY"; SILVER, JOAN MICKLIN; SILVER, RON; SODERBERGH, STEVEN; SONNENFELD, BARRY; SORKIN, AARON; SPELLING, AARON; STEIN, JULES CEASAR; TAYLOR, ELIZABETH; WALETZKY, JOSH; WASSERMAN, LEW; WEBB, JACK; WEINSTEIN, HARVEY and BOB; WEST, MAE; WINKLER, HENRY; WINSTON, STAN; WISEMAN, FREDERICK; YOUNGMAN, HENNY

Renee Winegarten, Ph.D.; Literary Critic, London: GOLDING, LOUIS; GOLLANCZ, SIR ISRAEL; LEVERSON, ADA; WOOLF, LEONARD

Gershon Winer, New York: HERZLIAH HEBREW TEACHERS' INSTITUTE; JEWISH TEACHERS' SEMINARY AND PEOPLE'S UNIVERSITY; MOTKE ḤABAD

Heinrich Zwi Winnik, M.D.; Associate Professor of Psychiatry, the Hebrew University-Talbieh Psychiatric Hospital, Jerusalem: DEUTSCH, FELIX; DEUTSCH, HELENE; EITINGON, MAX; SAKEL, MANFRED JOSHUA

David Winston, Ph.D., Rabbi; Professor of Hellenistic and Judaic Studies, the Graduate Theological Union, Berkeley, California: LYSIMACHUS OF ALEXANDRIA; MOSES

Nathan H. Winter, Ph.D., J.D.; Associate Professor of Hebrew Culture and Education, New York University: ASCOLI; BENDERLY, SAMSON

Chaim Wirszubski, Ph.D.; Professor of Classical Studies, the Hebrew University of Jerusalem: PICO DELLA MIRANDOLA, GIOVANNI

Mark Wischnitzer, Dr.Phil.; Professor of Jewish History, Yeshiva University, New York: CHIEFTAIN; GUILDS; LABANO; OLYKA; OSWIECIM; SANDOMIERZ

Rachel Wischnitzer, M.A., Dipl. Arch.; Emeritus Professor of Fine Arts, Yeshiva University, New York: ARK

Kirk Wisemayer*: VINELAND

Ruth Wisse, Ph.D.; Assistant Professor of Yiddish Literature, McGill University, Montreal: BERGELSON, DAVID; EINHORN, DAVID; ROGOFF, HARRY; SHAPIRO, LAMED

Alfred Witkon, Dr. Jur.; Justice of the Supreme Court, Jerusalem

Rebecca Wittmann*, Ph.D.; Assistant Professor; University of Toronto; Toronto, Canada: WAR CRIMES TRIALS

Aharon Arnold Wiznitzer, Ph.D., D.H.L.; Historian, Los Angeles

Elli Wohlgelernter*, B.A.; Journalist, Jerusalem: ABRAHAMS; ABRAMS, "CAL"; ABRAMSON, JESSE; ADELSTEIN-ROZEANU, ANGELICA; ALBERT, MARV; ALCOTT, AMY; ALLEN, MEL; ARAD, YAEL; ARATON, HARVEY; ARCEL, RAY; ARUM, ROBERT; ATTELL, ABRAHAM WASHINGTON; AUERBACH, "RED"; AXELROD, ALBERT; BAER, MAX; BARNA, VICTOR; BERENSON, SENDA; BERG, JACKIE "KID"; BERG, MORRIS; BERGER, ISAAC; BERGMANN, RICHARD; BERKOW, IRA; BERKOWITZ, MICKEY; BERNSTEIN, SID; BETTMAN, GARY; BIMSTEIN, "WHITEY"; BLUM, WALTER; BOUDREAU, LOU; BRENNER, TEDDY; BUXTON, ANGELA; CHESS, LEONARD; COHEN, SASHA; COHN, LINDA; COPELAND, LILLIAN; COSELL, HOWARD; CUBAN, MARK; DANIEL, DAN; DARMON, PIERRE; DAVIS, AL; DAVIS, AL "BUMMY"; DREYFUSS, BARNEY; ELLIOT, "MAMA" CASS; EPSTEIN, BRIAN SAMUEL; FIELDS, JACKIE; FISCHLER, STAN; FLAM, HERB; FLEISCHER, NATHANIEL STANLEY; FLEISHER, LARRY; FRANKLIN, SIDNEY; FRIDMAN, GAL; FRIEDMAN, BENJAMIN; FRIEDMAN, KINKY; GAYLORD, MITCHELL; GOLDBERG, MARSHALL; GOLDENBERG, CHARLES ROBERT; GOLDSTEIN, RUBY; GOROKHOVSKAYA, MARIA; GOTTLIEB, EDWARD; GRAHAM, BILL; GREEN, SHAWN DAVID; GREENBERG, HENRY BENJAMIN; GREENSPAN, BUD; GRUNFELD, ERNIE; GUZIK, JACOB; HALBERSTAM, DAVID; HARMATZ, WILLIAM; HARRISON, LESTER; HERSHKOWITZ, VICTOR; HOLLANDERSKY, ABRAHAM; HOLMAN, NATHAN; HOLTZMAN, KENNETH DALE; HOLZMAN, WILLIAM; HUGHES, SARAH ELIZABETH; IZENBERG, JERRY; JACOBS, HIRSCH; JACOBS, JAMES LESLIE; JACOBS, JOE; JAFFEE, IRVING W.; JAY, ALLAN LOUIS NEVILLE; KAHN, ROGER; KELETI, AGNES; KOPPETT, LEONARD; KOUFAX, SANDY; KRAFT, ROBERT K.; KRAYZELBURG, LENNY; KRISS, GRIGORI; LANSKY, MEYER; LEBOW, FRED; LEIBER & STOLLER; LEONARD, BENNY; LEVINSKY, BATTLING; LEVY, MARV; LEWIS, TED; LIEBERMAN, NANCY ELIZABETH; LIEBLING, A.J.; LIPSYTE, ROBERT MICHAEL; LITWACK, HARRY; LUCKMAN, SIDNEY; MATZAH; MESSING, SHEP; MILLER, MARVIN JULIAN; MIX, RONALD JACK; MODELL, ARTHUR B.; OCHS, PHILIP DAVID; PATKIN, MAX; PAUL, GABRIEL HOWARD; PIKE, LIPMAN EMANUEL; PODOLOFF, MAURICE; POLLIN, ABE; POMUS, DOC; POVICH, SHIRLEY LEWIS; REESE, JIMMIE; REINSDORF, JERRY; ROSEN, ALBERT LEONARD; ROSENBLOOM, MAX EVERITT; ROSS, BARNEY; SALITA, DMITRIY; SAPERSTEIN, ABRAHAM M.; SAVITT, RICHARD; SCHAAP, RICHARD J.; SCHACHT, ALEXANDER; SCHULTZ, DUTCH; SHAMSKY, ARTHUR LOUIS; SHERRY, LAWRENCE and NORMAN BURT; SPITZ, MARK ANDREW; SPORTS; STARK, ALBERT; STONE, STEVEN MICHAEL

Salomon Wolf, Ph.D.; Jerusalem: KORNIK, MEIR BEN MOSES

Adela Wolfe, M.A.; Jerusalem: ADAM

Ronald Wolfson*: HOFFMAN, LAWRENCE A.

Penny Diane Wolin*, B.F.A.; Photographer, Crazy Woman Creek Press, Sebastopol, California: WYOMING

William Wollheim, Writer, New York

Jeffrey R. Woolf*, Ph.D.; Senior Lecturer, Bar-Ilan University, Ramat Gan: COLON, JOSEPH BEN SOLOMON

Leon Wulman, M.D.; New York: OZE or OSE

Max Wurmbrand, Ramat Gan: FAÏTLOVITCH, JACQUES; HAM; PROSTITUTION; SAALSCHUETZ, JOSEPH LEWIN; SALZ, ABRAHAM ADOLPH; SILBERFARB, MOSES; ZAMENHOF, LUDWIK LAZAR

Uri Shraga Wurzburger, M.Sc.; Managing Director of the Timna Copper Mines, Israel: METALS AND MINING; PRECIOUS STONES AND JEWELRY

Walter S. Wurzburger, Ph.D., Rabbi; Visiting Associate Professor of Philosophy, Yeshiva University, New York: ORTHODOXY; PIETY AND THE PIOUS; PROPHETS AND PROPHECY; REVELATION

Michael Wygoda*, Ph.D.; Senior Director of Jewish Law, Ministry of Justice, Jerusalem: AGENCY; LEASE AND HIRE; LOST PROPERTY

Stanislaw Wygodzki, Writer, Givatayim, Israel: BRANDYS, KAZIMIERZ; HEMAR, MARIAN; JASIEŃSKI, BRUNO; JASTRUN, MIECZYSLAW; LEC, STANISLAW JERZY; LESMIAN, BOLESŁAW; PEIPER, TADEUSZ; RUDNICKI, ADOLF; SCHULZ, BRUNO; SLONIMSKI, ANTONI; STERN, ANATOL; STRYJKOWSKI, JULJAN; WAT, ALEXANDER; WITTLIN, JÓZEF

Veit Wyler, Dr.Jur.; Attorney and Editor, Zurich: GUGGENHEIM, PAUL; PRESS

Edith Wyschogrod, Ph.D.; Assistant Professor of Philosophy, Queens College of the City University of New York

Xun Zhou*, Ph.D.; ESRC Research Fellow, SOAS, University of London, England: CHINA

Avraham Yaari, Writer and bibliographer, Jerusalem: ABRAHAM HA-LEVI; ALEXANDRIA; ALSHEIKH, SHALOM BEN JOSEPH; ASHKENAZI, JONAH BEN JACOB; BAGHDAD; BENJAMIN BEN ELIJAH; BERDICHEV; BERMAN, SIMEON; BING, ISAAC BEN SAMUEL; BULA, RAPHAEL MOSES; CAIRO; CALCUTTA; DAVID BEN JOSHUA; DAYYAN; DISKIN, MORDEKHAI; DIWAN, JUDAH BEN AMRAM; ELIJAH OF LA MASSA; ELISHA ḤAYYIM BEN JACOB ASHKENAZI; FELMAN, AHARON LEIB; GALANTE, JEDIDIAH BEN MOSES; GEDALIAH OF SIEMIATYCZE; GEDILIAH, ABRAHAM BEN SAMUEL; HABILLO, DAVID; ISRAEL; ISRAEL BEN SAMUEL OF SHKLOV; LURIA, JEHIEL BEN ISRAEL ASHKENAZI; MALKHI, EZRA BEN RAPHAEL MORDECAI; MALKHI, MOSES; MALKHI, MOSES BEN RAPHAEL MORDECAI; MEIR BEN ḤIYYA ROFE; NAZIR, MOSES HA-LEVI; PETHAHIAH OF REGENSBURG; PORGES, MOSES BEN ISRAEL NAPHTALI; RAPPAPORT, ISAAC BEN JUDAH HA-KOHEN; SAFED; SAMUEL BEN SAMSON; SHALEM, SAMUEL; SIMḤAH BEN JOSHUA OF ZALOZHTSY; TOLEDO, MOSES DE; URI BEN SIMEON OF BIALA; VOLTERRA, MESHULLAM BEN MENAHEM, DA; YIẒḤAKI, ABRAHAM BEN DAVID; ZOREF, ABRAHAM SOLOMON ZALMAN

Nurith Yaari*, Ph.D.; Senior Lecturer, Tel Aviv University: LEVIN, HANOCH; SOBOL, YEHOSHUA; YERUSHALMI, RINA; YIZRAELY, YOSSI

Hanna (N.) Yablonka*, Ph.D.; Associate Professor, Ben-Gurion University of the Negev, Beersheva: EICHMANN, ADOLF OTTO

Yigael Yadin, Ph.D.; Lieutenant General (Res.), Israel Defense Forces; Professor of Archaeology, the Hebrew University of Jerusalem: HAZOR; TEMPLE; TEMPLE SCROLL

Aharon Yadlin, B.A.; Member of the Knesset; Deputy Minister of Education and Culture, Kibbutz Ḥazerim: ḤEVRAT HA-OVEDIM

Leon J. Yagod, D.H.L., Rabbi; Irvington, New Jersey: TRADITION

Chaim Yahil, Ph.D.; Director General of the Ministry for Foreign Affairs; Chairman of the Israel Broadcasting Authority, Jerusalem: BERLIN; CZECHOSLOVAKIA; EDELSTEIN, JACOB; FINALY CASE; GENEVA; GERMANY; GOLDMANN, NAHUM; ISRAEL, STATE OF: HISTORICAL SURVEY; KAHN, FRANZ; MASARYK, JAN GARRIGUE; MASARYK, THOMAS GARRIGUE; NORWAY; POHORELICE; PRAGUE; RUFEISEN, JOSEPH; SALONIKA; SCHMOLKA, MARIE; SPIEGEL, LUDWIG; STEIN, AUGUST; STEINER, HANNAH; SWEDEN; UHERSKE HRADISTE; UNRRA; VALENTIN, HUGO MAURICE; VAN DAM, HENDRIK GEORGE; WINTER, GUSTAV; ŽDOVSKÁ STRANA; ŽIDOVSKÁ STRANA; ZIONISM

Leni Yahil, Ph.D.; Historian, Jerusalem: BERNADOTTE, FOLKE, EARL OF WISBORG; BRANDES, GEORG; DENMARK; GASSING; MADAGASCAR PLAN; MENDELSSOHN, MOSES; NORWAY; QUISLING, VIDKUN ABRAHAM LAURITZ JONSSØN; RIESSER, GABRIEL; STOCKHOLM; WOLFF, ABRAHAM ALEXANDER

Bracha Yaniv*, Ph.D.; Senior Lecturer, Bar-Ilan University, Ramat Gan: PAROKHET and KAPPORET; TORAH ORNAMENTS

Yaacov Yannai, Commissioner General of the National Parks Authority, Tel Aviv: NATIONAL PARKS IN ISRAEL

Itamar Yaos-Kest, B.A.; Writer and Poet, Tel Aviv: BENJÁMIN, LÁSZLÓ; DÉRY, TIBOR; RADNÓTI, MIKLOS

Edith Yapou-Hoffmann, Ph.D.; Instructor in Art History, Tel Aviv University: ISRAËLS, JOZEF

Jacob Yardeni, D.D.S.; Former Senior Lecturer, the School of Dentistry, the Hebrew University – Hadassah Medical School, Jerusalem: GOTTLIEB, BERNHARD

Galia Yardeni-Agmon, Ph.D.; Writer, Jerusalem: GUTMANN, DAVID MEIR; PINES, YEHIEL MICHAEL

Baruch Yaron, Dr. Phil.; Former Librarian, the Hebrew University of Jerusalem: BARACS, KÁROLY; BIRÓ, LAJOS; BRÓDY, ZSIGMOND; CHILDREN'S LITERATURE; DÉNES, BÉLA; DÓCZY, LAJOS; EGYENLÖSÉG; EMŐD, TAMAS; EÖTVŐS, BARON JÓZSEF; EPPLER, SANDOR; FALK, MIKSA; FALUDY, GYÖRGY; FEJTÖ, FRANÇOIS; FÉNYES, ADOLF; FENYŐ, MIKSA; FISCHER, GYULA; FRANKL, ADOLF; FRIEDMAN, DÉNES; GÁBOR, IGNÁC; GELLÉRI, ANDOR ENDRE; GERÖ, ERNÖ; GISZKALAY, JÁNOS; GYONGYOS; HAJDU, MIKLÓS; HAJNAL, ANNA; HATVANY-DEUTSCH; HELTAI, JENŐ; HEVESI, SANDOR; HODMEZOVASARHELY; HUNGARIAN LITERATURE; IGNOTUS, HUGÓ; JÁSZI, OSZKÁR; KACZÉR, ILLÉS; KAPOSVAR; KARDOS, LÁSZLÓ; KATZ, MENAHEM; KIRJATH SEPHER; KISS, JÓZSEF; KISVARDA; KÓBOR, TAMÁS; KOHLBACH, BERTALAN; KOMLÓS, ALADÁR; KÖRMENDI, FERENC; KRAUSZ, ZSIGMOND; KUNFI, ZSIGMOND; LAKATOS, LÁSZLÓ; LENGYEL, JÓZSEF; LENGYEL, MENYHÉRT; MEZŐFI, VILMOS; MOHÁCSI, JENÖ; MOLNÁR, FERENC; MULT ÉS JÖVŐ; MUNKÁCSI, ERNÖ; NAGYBACZONI-NAGY, VILMOS; NAMÉNYI, ERNEST; NEOLOGY; NUMERUS CLAUSUS; PAKS; PALÁGYI, LAJOS; PAP, KÁROLY; PATAI, JÓZSEF; PESTSZENTERZSEBET; PRESS; PUBLISHING; RÁKOSI, MÁTYÁS; RÉVÉSZ, BÉLA; REVICZKY, IMRE; RICHTMANN, MÓZES; SÁNDOR, PÁL; SATORALJAUJHELY; SCHULHOF, ISAAC; SOMOGYI, BÉLA; SOPRON; SPITZER, SAMUEL; STATUS QUO ANTE; SZABÓ, IMRE; SZABOLCSI, LAJOS; SZABOLCSI, MIKSA; SZEGED; SZEKESFEHERVAR; SZENDE, PÁL; SZENES, BÉLA; SZENES, ERZSI; SZÉP, ERNŐ; SZERB, ANTAL; SZILÁGYI, GÉZA; SZOLNOK; SZOMBATHELY; SZOMORY,

DEZSŐ; TARBIZ; THEBEN, JACOB KOPPEL; TURÓCZI-TROSTLER, JÓZSEF; UJVÁRI, PÉTER; VÁGÓ, JÓZSEF; VÉSZI, JOZSEF; VESZPREM; VIHAR, BELA; WERTHEIMER, EDUARD VON; ZIPSER, MAJER; ZSOLDOS, JENÖ; ZSOLT, BÉLA

Emuna Yaron*, Literary Executor, Shmuel Yosef Agnon Papers and Unpublished Works: AGNON, SHMUEL YOSEF

Reuven Yaron, D.Phil.; Professor of Roman Law and Ancient Near Eastern Law, the Hebrew University of Jerusalem: TAUBENSCHLAG, RAPHAEL

Hanri Yasova, Writer, Istanbul

Meir Ydit, Ph.D.; Dr.rer.Pol., Rabbi; Perth, Australia: AḤOT KETANNAH; ASSI; AV, THE NINTH OF; AVODAH; BADḤAN; BE-MOẒA'EI MENUḤAH; CANDLES; CEMETERY; CHILDREN'S SERVICES; DIRINGER, DAVID; DISINTERMENT; EIN KE-ELOHENU; EL NORA ALILAH; HAZKARAT NESHAMOT; HEAD, COVERING OF THE; HESPED; ḤUKKAT HA-GOI; KABBALAT SHABBAT; LAG BA-OMER; LEKHAH DODI; MEḤIẒAH; MOON, BLESSING OF THE; SE'UDAH; TAḤANUN; TU BI-SHEVAT

Jacob Yehoshua, M.A.; Former Director of the Moslem Department, Ministry of Religious Affairs, Jerusalem: ISRAEL, STATE OF: RELIGIOUS LIFE AND COMMUNITIES

Ze'ev Yeivin, M.A.; Department of Antiquities, Ministry of Education and Culture, Jerusalem: BANNER; BEARD AND SHAVING; BITUMEN; CART AND CHARIOT; COOKING AND BAKING; COSMETICS; CRAFTS; CROWNS, DECORATIVE HEADDRESSES, AND WREATHS; DOOR AND DOORPOST; DRESS; FIRE; FOOD; IVORY; MILLSTONE; PILLAR; SHIPS AND SAILING; THRONE; THUNDER AND LIGHTNING; TOMBS AND TOMBSTONES; WOOD; YOKE

Irwin Yellowitz, Ph.D.; Associate Professor of History, City College of the City University of New York: ABELSON, PAUL; BRESSLER, DAVID MAURICE; DE LEON, DANIEL; DYCHE, JOHN ALEXANDER; GOLDMAN, EMMA; GOMPERS, SAMUEL; HILLQUIT, MORRIS; LONDON, MEYER; POTOFSKY, JACOB SAMUEL; RUBINOW, ISAAC MAX; TAILORING; WALD, LILLIAN

Meir Yoeli, M.Sc., M.D.; Professor of Preventative Medicine, New York University School of Medicine: ADLER, SAUL AARON

Abraham Yoffe, Major General (Res.), Israel Defense Forces; Director of the Israel Nature Reserves Authority, Tel Aviv: LIPSCHUETZ, GEDALIAH BEN SOLOMON ZALMAN; NATURE RESERVES IN ISRAEL

Abraham B. Yoffe, Critic and Editor, Tel Aviv: SHLONSKY, ABRAHAM; ZEMACH, SHLOMO

Gedalia Yogev, Ph.D.; Editor, *The Weizmann Letters*, Jerusalem: DIAMOND TRADE AND INDUSTRY

Mel and Cindy Yoken*, Ph.D.; Chancellor Professor of French, Officer dans l'Ordre des Palmes Academiques, University of Massachusetts, Dartmouth: NEW BEDFORD

Nissim Yosha, M.A.; Center for the Integration of the Heritage of Oriental Jewry, Ministry of Education, Jerusalem

Lillian Youman, Director, Jewish Information and Referral Service, Jewish Federation of Greater Philadelphia, Philadelphia: PHILADELPHIA

David A. Young, Jewish Federation of St. Louis

Dwight Young, Ph.D.; Associate Professor of Ancient Near Eastern Civilization, Brandeis University, Waltham, Massachusetts: FLOOD, THE; NOAH

Toni Young*, B.A., M.A.; Historian, Author, Jewish Historical Society of Delaware, Wilmington, Delaware: DELAWARE; WILMINGTON

William (A.) Younglove*, Ed.D.; Teacher Supervisor, California State University Long Beach, California: CHILDREN'S LITERATURE

Leon I. (Israel) Yudkin*, Ph.D.; Lit. Author and Visiting Professor, Honorary Fellow, University College, London, England: SHABTAI, YAAKOV

Natan Zach, B.A.; Lecturer in Hebrew and Comparative Literature, Tel Aviv University: FICHMAN, JACOB; LENSKI, ḤAYYIM; POMERANTZ, BERL; POMERANTZ, BERL; STEINBERG, JACOB; STERN, NOAH

Efraim Zadoff*, Ph.D.; Historian, Editor, Research on Latin American Jews, Jerusalem: ALPERSOHN, MARCOS; AMIA; ANGEL, AARON; ARGENTINA; BARYLKO, JAIME; BEHAR, LEON; BEIDERMAN, BERNARDO; BENZAQUÉN SAADIA; BERAJA, RUBEN EZRA; BERGER, MEIR; BLEJER, DAVID; BLEJER, MARIO ISRAEL; CHEHEBAR, ISAAC; CONSTANTINER, JAIME; CZENSTOCHOWSKI, WALTER; DAIA; EDUCATION, JEWISH; ELNECAVÉ, DAVID; FASTLICHT, ADOLFO; FELDMAN, SHIMSHON SIMON; FINKELSTEIN, CHAIM; GENEALOGY; GESANG, NATHAN-NACHMAN; GOLDMAN, AHARON HALEVI; GOLDMAN, MOISES; HARF, HANNS; JOURNALISM; KAMENSZAIN, TOBIAS; KITRON, MOSHE; LATIN AMERICA; LERNER, JAIME; LEVY, ROBERT; MILEVSKY, AHARÓN; NAJDORF, MIGUEL; NICARAGUA; PARAGUAY; POLITICS; RAFALIN, DAVID SHLOMÓ; ROSENBERG, MOISHE; SCHLESINGER, GUILLERMO; SEGALL, LASAR; SEROUSSI, ELÍAS; SINGERMAN, BERTA; SOURASKY; TURKOW, MARC; YAGUPSKY, MÁXIMO

Noam Zadoff*, M.A.; Doctoral Student, Richard Koebuer Minerva Center for German History, the University of Jerusalem: ARAKHIN; BEKHOROT; BLUMENFELD, KURT YEHUDAH; BLUMENTHAL, OSKAR; BRUCKNER, FERDINAND; CHRONEGK, LUDWIG; DAWISON, BOGUMIL; DOMIN, HILDE; HEIMANN, MORITZ; KALISCH, DAVID; KASTEIN, JOSEF; KOEBNER, RICHARD; LANDAUER, GUSTAV; OPHUELS, MAX; OPPENHEIMER, FRANZ; POLGAR, ALFRED; ROSENBERG, ARTHUR; SALOMON, ALICE; SATANOW, ISAAC; SCHILDKRAUT, RUDOLPH; SCHMID, ANTON VON; SCHOTTLAENDER, BENDET; VIERTEL, BERTHOLD; WEININGER, OTTO; WEISS, JOSEPH G.

Haim Zafrani, Ph.D., D.es-L.; Charge de Recherche au Centre National de la Recherche Scientifique; Director of the Hebrew Department of the University of Paris-Vincennnes: ABITBOL; ANKAWA, RAPHAEL BEN MORDECAI; ḤAGIZ; JUDEO-ARABIC; SERERO, SAUL

David Zakay, Editor and Journalist, Tel Aviv: ANOKHI, ZALMAN YIẒḤAK

Michael Zand, Ph.D.; Professor of Persian and Tajik Language and Literature, The Hebrew University of Jerusalem; Chief Scientific Consultant to *The Shorter Jewish Encyclopaedia in Russian*, Jerusalem: BUKHARA; GAPONOV, BORIS; GEORGIA; KRIMCHAKS; MOUNTAIN JEWS; WEISSMAN, BARUCH MORDECAI

Walter Zanger, M.A., Rabbi; Jerusalem: EIN KEREM; PHILIPPINES

Melvin S. Zaret*, M.S.W.; Consultant for Jewish Communities, National Agencies and Executives Milwaukee Jewish Federation Executive Vice President, Emeritus and Consultant, Milwaukee: MILWAUKEE

Shaul Zarhi, M.Sc.; Economist, Tel Aviv: COOPERATIVES

Leah Zazulyer*, M.S.; Writer, Translator, School Psychologist Teacher (retired), New York: EMIOT, ISRAEL

Mark Zborowski, Ph.D.; Research Associate in Medicine, Mount Zion Hospital and Medical Center, San Francisco, California: SHTETL

Jekutiel-Zwi Zehawi, Ph.D.; Educator, Tel Aviv: RÓNAI, JÁNOS; SCHOENFELD, JOSEPH

Moshe Zeidner, B.A.; Tel Aviv: MENE, MENE, TEKEL, U-FARSIN

Nadia Zeldes*, Ph.D.; Researcher, Institute of Judaic Studies, the Hebrew University of Jerusalem: AGRIGENTO; ALGHERO; AMALFI; APULIA; BARI; BENEVENTO; BRINDISI; CAGLIARI; CALABRIA; CAPUA; CATANIA; CATANZARO; COSENZA; DIENCHELELE; FREDERICK II OF HOHENSTAUFEN; GAETA; LECCE; MARSALA; MESSINA; MITHRIDATES, FLAVIUS; MOSES OF PALERMO; PALERMO; SALERNO; SAN NICANDRO; TARANTO; TRAPANI; VENOSA

Joyce Zemans*, M.A.; University Professor, York University, Toronto, Canada: ETROG, SOREL; FRENKEL, VERA; ISKOWITZ, GERSHON; PACHTER, CHARLES

Carol Zemel*, Ph.D.; Professor of Art History, York, University, Toronto, Canada: SINGER, YVONNE

Hanna Zemer, B.A.; Editor of *Davar*, Tel Aviv

Marcia Jo Zerivitz*, Founding Executive Director and Chief Curator, Jewish Museum of Florida: BROWARD COUNTY; FLORIDA; JACKSONVILLE; LEE AND CHARLOTTE COUNTIES; MIAMI-DADE COUNTY; NAPLES AND COLLIER COUNTY; ORLANDO; PALM BEACH COUNTY; SAINT PETERSBURG; SARASOTA; TALLAHASSEE; TAMPA

Mordechay Zerkawod, Dr.Phil.; Emeritus Professor of Bible, Bar-Ilan University, Ramat Gan: EHRENKRANZ, BENJAMIN ZEEB

Charles Zibbell, M.S.; Associate Executive Director, Council of Jewish Federations, New York: PHILANTHROPY

David L. Zielonka, M.A.H.L., Rabbi; Professor of Religion, the University of Tampa, Florida

Wendy (Ilene) Zierler*, B.A., M.A., Ph.D.; Assistant Professor, Modern Jewish Literature and Feminist Studies, Hebrew Union College-Jewish Institute of Religion, New York: POGREBIN, LETTY COTTIN; SEID, RUTH

Gershon Zilberberg, Editor of *Olam ha-Defuss*, Tel Aviv: PRINTING, HEBREW

Abraham Zimels, M.A., Rabbi; Senior Lecturer in Bible, the University of the Negev, Beersheba: BIBLE

Hirsch Jacob Zimmels, Ph.D., Rabbi; Former Principal and Lecturer in Jewish History and Rabbinics, Jews' College, London: DAVID BEN SOLOMON IBN ABI ZIMRA; DURAN, PROFIAT; DURAN, SIMEON BEN ẒEMAḤ; DURAN, SOLOMON BEN SIMEON; DURAN, ZEMAḤ BEN SOLOMON; EPSTEIN, ISIDORE; FREIMANN, JACOB; IBN YAḤYA, DAVID BEN JOSEPH; IBN YAḤYA, GEDALIAH BEN DAVID; IBN YAḤYA, JOSEPH BEN DAVID; ISAAC BEN MELCHIZEDEK OF SIPONTO; ISAAC BEN SHESHET PERFET; NORZI, JEDIDIAH SOLOMON RAPHAEL BEN ABRAHAM; TRANI, MOSES BEN JOSEPH; YA'ISH, BARUCH BEN ISAAC IBN

Akiva Zimmerman, Lecturer and Journalist on Ḥazzanut, Tel Aviv: BACON, YIDEL; ACKERMAN, SHABTAI; ALTER, ISRAEL; ARONI, TSVI; BACON, HIRSCH LEIB; BACON, ISRAEL; BACON, SHLOMO REUVEN; BAGLEY, DAVID; BELGRADO, DAVID FERNANDO; BEN-HAIM, YIGAL; BLOCH, CHARLES; BRAUN, ARIE; DANTO, LOUIS; DI-ZAHAV, EPHRAIM; EPHROS, GERSHON; ESHEL, YITZHAK; GANCHOFF, MOSES; GANTMAN, JUDAH LEIB; GERBER, MAYNARD; GREENBLATT, ELIYAHU; HAINOVITZ, ASHER; ḤAZZAN; HEILMANN, YITZHAK; HERSTIK, NAFTALI; KALIB, SHOLOM; KARMON, ISRAEL; KRAUS, MOSHE; LEFKOWITZ, DAVID; LERER, JOSHUA; LERER, SHMUEL; LUBIN, ABRAHAM; MALOVANY, JOSEPH; MANDEL, SHELOMOH; MEISELS, SAUL; MELAMED, NISSAN COHEN; MENDELSON, JACOB BEN-ZION; MENDELSON, SOLOMON; MILLER, BEN-ZION; MULLER, BENJAMIN; POLLAK, ZALMAN; PUTTERMAN, DAVID; RABINOVICZ, HAIM BEN ZION; RABINOVICZ, PINCHAS; RICARDO, DAVID; ROSENFELD, ABRAHAM ISAAC JACOB; SCHULHOF, MOSHE; SOBOL, MORDECHAI; STERN, MOSHE; TALMON, ZVI; TAUBE, MOSHE; TAUBE, SAMUEL BARUCH; UNGAR, BENJAMIN; VIGODA, SAMUEL; WEISGAL, ABBA JOSEPH; WOHLBERG, MOSHE

Oren Zinder, Ph.D.; Jerusalem: LANDAU, LEOPOLD

Zvi Harry Zinder, B.A.; Jerusalem: PUBLIC RELATIONS

Zvi Zinger (Yaron), B.A., Rabbi; the Jewish Agency, Jerusalem:

Avner Ziv, Ph.D.; Professor, Department of Educational Sciences, Tel Aviv University: HUMOR

Ari Z. Zivotofsky*, Rabbinic Ordination, Ph.D.; Lecturer, Bar Ilan University, Ramat Gan: MATZAH

Dov Zlotnick, D.H.L., Rabbi; Associate Professor of Rabbinic Literature, the Jewish Theological Seminary of America, New York

Moshe Nahum Zobel, Dr.Phil.; *Encyclopaedia Judaica* (Germany); Jerusalem: ABRAHAM BEN NATHAN; AFENDOPOLO, CALEB BEN ELIJAH; ALI BEN AMRAM; AL-NAKAWA, ISRAEL BEN JOSEPH; AL-TARĀS, SĪDĪ IBN; APTOWITZER, VICTOR; ASHI; ASSAF, SIMḤA; BACHER, WILHELM; BANET,

MORDECAI BEN ABRAHAM; BANET, NAPHTALI BEN MORDECAI; BARUCH BEN ISAAC OF REGENSBURG; BEN 'ALĀN, JOSHUA; BENVENISTE, ḤAYYIM BEN ISRAEL; BLOCH, MOSES; BLOGG, SOLOMON BEN EPHRAIM; BOSKOWITZ, BENJAMIN ZE'EV HA-LEVI; BREUER, SOLOMON; CONFORTE, DAVID; CRESCAS, ASHER BEN ABRAHAM; GALEN, CLAUDIUS; GOSLAR, NAPHTALI HIRSCH BEN JACOB; GUNZBERG, ARYEH LEIB BEN ASHER; IBN SHEM TOV, JOSEPH BEN SHEM TOV; JONATHAN BEN JOSEPH OF RUZHANY; JOSEPH BEN DAVID HA-YEVANI; KAUFMANN, DAVID; NEW CHRISTIANS

Danah Zohar, M.A.; Jerusalem: BRILL, ABRAHAM ARDEN

Harry Zohn, Ph.D.; Professor of German, Brandeis University, Waltham, Massachusetts: ALTENBERG, PETER; AUERNHEIMER, RAOUL; FEUCHTWANGER, LION; FRIEDELL, EGON; FRISCH, EFRAIM; HOFFMANN, CAMILL; KAUFMANN, FRITZ MORDECAI; KOLMAR, GERTRUD; KRAMER, THEODOR; KRAUS, KARL; PERUTZ, LEO; POLGAR, ALFRED; SACHS, NELLY; SAMPTER, JESSIE ETHEL; TREBITSCH, SIEGFRIED; TUCHOLSKY, KURT; VIERTEL, BERTHOLD; ZWEIG, STEFAN

Gary P. (Phillip) Zola*, Ph.D.; Associate Professor of the American Jewish Experience, Hebrew Union College-Jewish Institute of Religion, Cincinnati, Ohio: AMERICAN JEWISH ARCHIVES; SARNA, JONATHAN DANIEL

Maurice Zolotow, B.A.; Los Angeles: SCHWARTZ, DELMORE

Sharon Zrachya*, Administrative Assistant, Hod Hasharon, Israel: ARNON, DANIEL ISRAEL; AVIDOV, ZVI; COHEN, SEYMOUR STANLEY; FEUER, HENRY; WEIL, JOSEPH

Philipp Zschommler*, M.A.; Jewish Studies, Trainee at the Dai Damascus, Hochschule für Jüdische Studien, Heidelberg, Germany: ADLER, FRIEDRICH; BLAU, TINA; FLECHTHEIM, ALFRED; FREUND, GISÈLE; GRUNDIG, LEA and HANS; HEARTFIELD, JOHN; KAHNWEILER, DANIEL-HENRY; KATZ, HANNS LUDWIG; NUSSBAUM, FELIX; NUSSBAUM, JAKOB; WOLPERT, LUDWIG YEHUDA

Jeno Zsoldos, Ph.D.; Educator, Budapest: ÁGAI, ADOLF; BALÁZS, BÉLA; BANETH, EZEKIEL BEN JACOB; BEN CHANANJA; BERÉNY, RÓBERT; BETTELHEIM; BOKROS-BIRMAN, DEZSÖ; BRÓDY, SÁNDOR; BUDAPEST; GOLDBERGER, IZIDOR; HIRSCH, MARKUS; HIRSCHLER, IGNÁC; HUNGARIAN LITERATURE; ISTÓCZY, GYÖZÖ; KORNFELD, ZSIGMOND; LÁNCZY, GYULA; LEDERER, ABRAHAM; LOEWY, ISAAC; MEZEI, MÓR; MEZEY, FERENC; NAGYKANIZSA; ROSENTHAL, NAPHTALI; SCHEIBER, ALEXANDER; SCHWAB, LÖW; SIMON, JOSEPH; ULLMANN, ADOLPH; WAHRMANN, ISRAEL; WAHRMANN, MORITZ; WEISS, MANFRÉD

Susan Zuccotti*, Ph.D.; Independent Historian (retired), New York: BOLZANO

Louis Zucker, Ph.D.; Emeritus Professor of English, the University of Utah, Salt Lake City: IDAHO

Moshe Zucker, Ph.D., Rabbi; Professor of Biblical Exegesis, the Jewish Theological Seminary of America, New York

Menahem Zulay, Dr.Phil.; Scholar of Medieval Hebrew poetry, Jerusalem: HADUTA BEN ABRAHAM; INSTITUTE FOR THE RESEARCH OF MEDIEVAL HEBREW POETRY; JUDAH HA-LEVI BEI-RABBI HILLEL; ZEBIDAH

Efraim Zuroff*, Ph.D.; Coordinator, Nazi War Crimes Research Institute, Director Israel Office, Simon Wiesenthal Center, Jerusalem: HOLOCAUST, RESCUE FROM; SAR, SAMUEL L.; SARACHEK, BERNARD; VAAD HA-HATZALAH; WIESENTHAL, SIMON

Itay (B.) Zutra*, Ph.D.; Student, The Jewish Theological Seminary of America, New York: FRIEDMAN, JACOB; KULBAK, MOYSHE; SHTERN, ISRAEL; WEINSTEIN, BERISH

Benjamin Zvieli, M.A., Rabbi; Director of Religious Broadcasting, Jerusalem: ISRAEL, STATE OF: RELIGIOUS LIFE AND COMMUNITIES; SYNAGOGUE

Alexander Zvielli, Director, Jerusalem Post Archives, Jerusalem: HUMPHREY, HUBERT H.; LANDAU, MOSHE; SHAMGAR, MEIR; SUSSMAN, YOEL; WITKON, ALFRED

Aharon Zwergbaum, LL.D.; Legal Adviser, World Zionist Organization, Jerusalem: BASLE PROGRAM; MAURITIUS; PALESTINE OFFICE; PATRIA; SHEKEL; ZIONISM

Irene E. Zwiep*, Ph.D.; Professor of Hebrew and Jewish Studies, Universiteit van Amsterdam, The Netherlands: ALTING, JACOBUS; BELINFANTE, ISAAC BEN ELIAH COHEN; CAMPEN, MICHEL HERMAN VAN; CUNAEUS, PETRUS; DOZY, REINHART PIETER ANNE; MULDER, SAMUEL ISRAEL; ROEST, MEIJER MARCUS; SCHULTENS, ALBERT; SEELIGMANN, SIGMUND; SURENHUIS, WILHELM

ABBREVIATIONS

GENERAL ABBREVIATIONS

This list contains abbreviations used in the Encyclopaedia (apart from the standard ones, such as geographical abbreviations, points of compass, etc.). For names of organizations, institutions, etc., in abbreviation, see Index. For bibliographical abbreviations of books and authors in Rabbinical literature, see following lists.

*	Cross reference; i.e., an article is to be found under the word(s) immediately following the asterisk (*).
°	Before the title of an entry, indicates a non-Jew (post-biblical times).
‡	Indicates reconstructed forms.
>	The word following this sign is derived from the preceding one.
<	The word preceding this sign is derived from the following one.
ad loc.	*ad locum*, "at the place"; used in quotations of commentaries.
A.H.	*Anno Hegirae*, "in the year of Hegira," i.e., according to the Muslim calendar.
Akk.	Addadian.
A.M.	*anno mundi*, "in the year (from the creation) of the world."
anon.	anonymous.
Ar.	Arabic.
Aram.	Aramaic.
Ass.	Assyrian.
b.	born; *ben, bar.*
Bab.	Babylonian.
B.C.E.	Before Common Era (= B.C.).
bibl.	bibliography.
Bul.	Bulgarian.
c., ca.	Circa.
C.E.	Common Era (= A.D.).
cf.	*confer*, "compare."
ch., chs.	chapter, chapters.
comp.	compiler, compiled by.
Cz.	Czech.
D	according to the documentary theory, the Deuteronomy document.
d.	died.
Dan.	Danish.
diss., dissert,	dissertation, thesis.
Du.	Dutch.
E.	according to the documentary theory, the Elohist document (i.e., using Elohim as the name of God) of the first five (or six) books of the Bible.
ed.	editor, edited, edition.
eds.	editors.
e.g.	*exempli gratia*, "for example."
Eng.	English.
et al.	*et alibi*, "and elsewhere"; or *et alii*, "and others"; "others."
f., ff.	and following page(s).
fig.	figure.
fl.	flourished.
fol., fols	folio(s).
Fr.	French.
Ger.	German.
Gr.	Greek.
Heb.	Hebrew.
Hg., Hung	Hungarian.
ibid	*Ibidem*, "in the same place."
incl. bibl.	includes bibliography.
introd.	introduction.
It.	Italian.
J	according to the documentary theory, the Jahwist document (i.e., using YHWH as the name of God) of the first five (or six) books of the Bible.
Lat.	Latin.
lit.	literally.
Lith.	Lithuanian.
loc. cit.	*loco citato*, "in the [already] cited place."
Ms., Mss.	Manuscript(s).
n.	note.
n.d.	no date (of publication).
no., nos	number(s).
Nov.	Novellae (Heb. *Ḥiddushim*).
n.p.	place of publication unknown.
op. cit.	*opere citato*, "in the previously mentioned work."
P.	according to the documentary theory, the Priestly document of the first five (or six) books of the Bible.
p., pp.	page(s).
Pers.	Persian.
pl., pls.	plate(s).
Pol.	Polish.
Port.	Potuguese.
pt., pts.	part(s).
publ.	published.
R.	Rabbi or Rav (before names); in Midrash (after an abbreviation) – *Rabbah*.
r.	recto, the first side of a manuscript page.
Resp.	Responsa (Latin "answers," Hebrew *She'elot u-Teshuvot* or *Teshuvot*), collections of rabbinic decisions.
rev.	revised.

Rom.	Romanian.
Rus(s).	Russian.
Slov.	Slovak.
Sp.	Spanish.
s.v.	*sub verbo, sub voce*, "under the (key) word."
Sum	Sumerian.
summ.	Summary.
suppl.	supplement.
Swed.	Swedish.
tr., trans(l).	translator, translated, translation.
Turk.	Turkish.
Ukr.	Ukrainian.
v., vv.	*verso*. The second side of a manuscript page; also verse(s).
Yid.	Yiddish.

ABBREVIATIONS USED IN RABBINICAL LITERATURE

Adderet Eliyahu, Karaite treatise by Elijah b. Moses *Bashyazi.
Admat Kodesh, Resp. by Nissim Ḥayyim Moses b. Joseph Mizraḥi.
Aguddah, Sefer ha-, Nov. by *Alexander Suslin ha-Kohen.
Ahavat Ḥesed, compilation by *Israel Meir ha-Kohen.
Aliyyot de-Rabbenu Yonah, Nov. by *Jonah b. Avraham Gerondi.
Arukh ha-Shulḥan, codification by Jehiel Michel *Epstein.
Asayin (= positive precepts), subdivision of: (1) *Maimonides, *Sefer ha-Mitzvot;* (2) *Moses b. Jacob of Coucy, *Semag.*
Asefat Dinim, subdivision of *Sedei Ḥemed* by Ḥayyim Hezekiah *Medini, an encyclopaedia of precepts and responsa.
Asheri = *Asher b. Jehiel.
Aeret Ḥakhamim, by Baruch *Frankel-Teomim; pt, 1: Resp. to Sh. Ar.; pt2: Nov. to Talmud.
Ateret Zahav, subdivision of the *Levush*, a codification by Mordecai b. Abraham (Levush) *Jaffe; *Ateret Zahav* parallels Tur. YD.
Ateret Ẓevi, Comm. To Sh. Ar. by Ẓevi Hirsch b. Azriel.
Avir Ya'akov, Resp. by Jacob Avigdor.
Avkat Rokhel, Resp. by Joseph b. Ephraim *Caro.
Avnei Millu'im, Comm. to Sh. Ar., EH, by *Aryeh Loeb b. Joseph ha-Kohen.
Avnei Nezer, Resp. on Sh. Ar. by Abraham b. Ze'ev Nahum Bornstein of *Sochaczew.
Avodat Massa, Compilation of Tax Law by Yoasha Abraham Judah.
Azei ha-Levanon, Resp. by Judah Leib *Zirelson.

Ba'al ha-Tanya – *Shneur Zalman of Lyady.
Ba'ei Ḥayyei, Resp. by Ḥayyim b. Israel *Benveniste.
Ba'er Heitev, Comm. To Sh. Ar. The parts on OḤ and EH are by Judah b. Simeon *Ashkenazi, the parts on YD AND ḤM by *Zechariah Mendel b. Aryeh Leib. Printed in most editions of Sh. Ar.
Baḥ = Joel *Sirkes.
Baḥ, usual abbreviation for *Bayit Ḥadash*, a commentary on Tur by Joel *Sirkes; printed in most editions of Tur.
Bayit Ḥadash, see *Baḥ.*
Berab = Jacob Berab, also called Ri Berav.
Bedek ha-Bayit, by Joseph b. Ephraim *Caro, additions to his *Beit Yosef* (a comm. to Tur). Printed sometimes inside *Beit Yosef*, in smaller type. Appears in most editions of Tur.
Be'er ha-Golah, Commentary to Sh. Ar. By Moses b. Naphtali Hirsch *Rivkes; printed in most editions of Sh. Ar.
Be'er Mayim, Resp. by Raphael b. Abraham Manasseh Jacob.
Be'er Mayim Ḥayyim, Resp. by Samuel b. Ḥayyim *Vital.
Be'er Yiẓḥak, Resp. by Isaac Elhanan *Spector.
Beit ha-Beḥirah, Comm. to Talmud by Menahem b. Solomon *Meiri.
Beit Me'ir, Nov. on Sh. Ar. by Meir b. Judah Leib Posner.
Beit Shelomo, Resp. by Solomon b. Aaron Ḥason (the younger).
Beit Shemu'el, Comm. to Sh. Ar., EH, by *Samuel b. Uri Shraga Phoebus.
Beit Ya'akov, by Jacob b. Jacob Moses *Lorberbaum; pt.1: Nov. to Ket.; pt.2: Comm. to EH.
Beit Yisrael, collective name for the commentaries *Derishah*, *Perishah*, and *Be'urim* by Joshua b. Alexander ha-Kohen *Falk. See under the names of the commentaries.
Beit Yiẓḥak, Resp. by Isaac *Schmelkes.
Beit Yosef: (1) Comm. on Tur by Joseph b. Ephraim *Caro; printed in most editions of Tur; (2) Resp. by the same.
Ben Yehudah, Resp. by Abraham b. Judah Litsch (ליטש) Rosenbaum.
Bertinoro, Standard commentary to Mishnah by Obadiah *Bertinoro. Printed in most editions of the Mishnah.
[Be'urei] Ha-Gra, Comm. to Bible, Talmud, and Sh. Ar. By *Elijah b. Solomon Zalmon (Gaon of Vilna); printed in major editions of the mentioned works.
Be'urim, Glosses to Isserles *Darkhei Moshe* (a comm. on Tur) by Joshua b. Alexander ha-Kohen *Falk; printed in many editions of Tur.
Binyamin Ze'ev, Resp. by *Benjamin Ze'ev b. Mattathias of Arta.
Birkei Yosef, Nov. by Ḥayyim Joseph David *Azulai.
Ha-Buẓ ve-ha-Argaman, subdivision of the *Levush* (a codification by Mordecai b. Abraham (Levush) *Jaffe); *Ha-Buẓ ve-ha-Argaman* parallels Tur, EH.

Comm. = Commentary

Da'at Kohen, Resp. by Abraham Isaac ha-Kohen. *Kook.
Darkhei Moshe, Comm. on Tur Moses b. Israel *Isserles; printed in most editions of Tur.
Darkhei No'am, Resp. by *Mordecai b. Judah ha-Levi.
Darkhei Teshuvah, Nov. by Ẓevi *Shapiro; printed in the major editions of Sh. Ar.
De'ah ve-Haskel, Resp. by Obadiah Hadaya (see *Yaskil Avdi).*

Derashot Ran, Sermons by *Nissim b. Reuben Gerondi.
Derekh Ḥayyim, Comm. to *Avot* by *Judah Loew (Lob., Liwa) b. Bezalel (Maharal) of Prague.
Derishah, by Joshua b. Alexander ha-Kohen *Falk; additions to his *Perishah* (comm. on Tur); printed in many editions of Tur.
Derushei ha-Ẓelaḥ, Sermons, by Ezekiel b. Judah Halevi *Landau.
Devar Avraham, Resp. by Abraham *Shapira.
Devar Shemu'el, Resp. by Samuel *Aboab.
Devar Yehoshu'a, Resp. by Joshua Menahem b. Isaac Aryeh Ehrenberg.
Dikdukei Soferim, variae lectiones of the talmudic text by Raphael Nathan*Rabbinowicz.
Divrei Emet, Resp. by Isaac Bekhor David.
Divrei Ge'onim, Digest of responsa by Ḥayyim Aryeh b. Jeḥiel Ẓevi *Kahana.
Divrei Ḥamudot, Comm. on *Piskei ha-Rosh* by Yom Tov Lipmann b. Nathan ha-Levi *Heller; printed in major editions of the Talmud.
Divrei Ḥayyim several works by Ḥayyim *Halberstamm; if quoted alone refers to his Responsa.
Divrei Malkhi'el, Resp. by Malchiel Tenebaum.
Divrei Rivot, Resp. by Isaac b. Samuel *Adarbi.
Divrei Shemu'el, Resp. by Samuel Raphael Arditi.

Edut be-Ya'akov, Resp. by Jacob b. Abraham *Boton.
Edut bi-Yhosef, Resp. by Joseph b. Isaac *Almosnino.
Ein Ya'akov, Digest of talmudic *aggadot* by Jacob (Ibn) *Habib.
Ein Yiẓḥak, Resp. by Isaac Elhanan *Spector.
Ephraim of Lentshitz = Solomon *Luntschitz.
Erekh Leḥem, Nov. and glosses to Sh. Ar. by Jacob b. Abraham *Castro.
Eshkol, Sefer ha-, Digest of *halakhot* by *Abraham b. Isaac of Narbonne.
Et Sofer, Treatise on Law Court documents by Abraham b. Mordecai *Ankawa, in the 2nd vol. of his Resp. *Kerem Ḥamar.*
Etan ha-Ezraḥi, Resp. by Abraham b. Israel Jehiel (Shrenzl) *Rapaport.
Even ha-Ezel, Nov. to Maimonides' *Yad Ḥazakah* by Isser Zalman *Meltzer.
Even ha-Ezer, also called *Raban* of *Ẓafenat Pa'ne'aḥ,* rabbinical work with varied contents by *Eliezer b. Nathan of Mainz; not identical with the subdivision of Tur, Shulḥan Arukh, etc.
Ezrat Yehudah, Resp. by *Isaar Judah b. Nechemiah of Brisk.

Gan Eden, Karaite treatise by *Aaron b. Elijah of Nicomedia.
Gersonides = *Levi b. Gershom, also called Leo Hebraecus, or Ralbag.
Ginnat Veradim, Resp. by *Abraham b. Mordecai ha-Levi.

Haggahot, another name for *Rema.*
Haggahot Asheri, glosses to *Piskei ha-Rosh* by *Israel of Krems; printed in most Talmud editions.
Haggahot Maimuniyyot, Comm,. to Maimonides' Yad Ḥazakah by *Meir ha-Kohen; printed in most eds. of Yad.
Haggahot Mordekhai, glosses to *Mordekhai* by Samuel *Schlettstadt; printed in most editions of the Talmud after *Mordekhai.*
Haggahot ha-Rashash on Tosafot, annotations of Samuel *Strashun on the Tosafot (printed in major editions of the Talmud).
Ha-Gra = *Elijah b. Solomon Zalman (Gaon of Vilna).
Ha-Gra, Commentaries on Bible, Talmud, and Sh. Ar. respectively, by *Elijah b. Solomon Zalman (Gaon of Vilna); printed in major editions of the mentioned works.
Hai Gaon, Comm. = his comm. on Mishnah.
Ḥakham Ẓevi, Resp. by Ẓevi Hirsch b. Jacob *Ashkenazi.
Halakhot = Rif, *Halakhot.* Compilation and abstract of the Talmud by Isaac b. Jacob ha-Kohen *Alfasi; printed in most editions of the Talmud.
Halakhot Gedolot, compilation of *halakhot* from the Geonic period, arranged acc. to the Talmud. Here cited acc. to ed. Warsaw (1874). Author probably *Simeon Kayyara of Basra.
Halakhot Pesukot le-Rav Yehudai Ga'on compilation of *halakhot.*
Halakhot Pesukot min ha-Ge'onim, compilation of *halakhot* from the geonic period by different authors.
Ḥananel, Comm. to Talmud by *Hananel b. Ḥushi'el; printed in some editions of the Talmud.
Harei Besamim, Resp. by Aryeh Leib b. Isaac *Horowitz.
Ḥassidim, Sefer, Ethical maxims by *Judah b. Samuel he-Ḥasid.
Hassagot Rabad on Rif, Glosses on Rif, *Halakhot,* by *Abraham b. David of Posquières.
Hassagot Rabad [on Yad], Glosses on Maimonides, *Yad Ḥazakah,* by *Abraham b. David of Posquières.
Hassagot Ramban, Glosses by Naḥmanides on Maimonides' *Sefer ha-Mitzvot;* usually printed together with *Sefer ha-Mitzvot.*
Ḥatam Sofer = Moses *Sofer.
Ḥavvot Ya'ir, Resp. and varia by Jair Ḥayyim *Bacharach
Ḥayyim Or Zaru'a = *Ḥayyim (Eliezer) b. Isaac.
Ḥazon Ish = Abraham Isaiah *Karelitz.
Ḥazon Ish, Nov. by Abraham Isaiah *Karelitz
Ḥedvat Ya'akov, Resp. by Aryeh Judah Jacob b. David Dov Meisels (article under his father's name).
Heikhal Yiẓḥak, Resp. by Isaac ha-Levi *Herzog.
Ḥelkat Meḥokek, Comm. to Sh. Ar., by Moses b. Isaac Judah *Lima.
Ḥelkat Ya'akov, Resp. by Mordecai Jacob Breisch.
Ḥemdah Genuzah, , Resp. from the geonic period by different authors.
Ḥemdat Shelomo, Resp. by Solomon Zalman *Lipschitz.
Ḥida = Ḥayyim Joseph David *Azulai.
Ḥiddushei Halakhot ve-Aggadot, Nov. by Samuel Eliezer b. Judah ha-Levi *Edels.
Ḥikekei Lev, Resp. by Ḥayyim *Palaggi.
Ḥikrei Lev, Nov. to Sh. Ar. by Joseph Raphael b. Ḥayyim Joseph Ḥazzan (see article *Ḥazzan Family).
Hil. = Hilkhot ... (e.g. *Hilkhot Shabbat).*
Ḥinnukh, Sefer ha-, List and explanation of precepts attributed (probably erroneously) to Aaron ha-Levi of Barcelona (see article *Ha-Ḥinnukh*).
Ḥok Ya'akov, Comm. to Hil. Pesaḥ in Sh. Ar., OḤ, by Jacob b. Joseph *Reicher.
Ḥokhmat Sehlomo (1), Glosses to Talmud, *Rashi* and Tosafot by Solomon b. Jehiel "Maharshal") *Luria; printed in many editions of the Talmud.
Ḥokhmat Sehlomo (2), Glosses and Nov. to Sh. Ar. by Solomon b. Judah Aaron *Kluger printed in many editions of Sh. Ar.
Ḥur, subdivision of the *Levush,* a codification by Mordecai b. Abraham (Levush) *Jaffe; *Hur (or Levush ha-Hur)* parallels Tur, OḤ, 242–697.
Ḥut ha-Meshullash, fourth part of the *Tashbeẓ* (Resp.), by Simeon b. Zemaḥ *Duran.

Ibn Ezra, Comm. to the Bible by Abraham *Ibn Ezra; printed in the major editions of the Bible *("Mikra'ot Gedolot").*
Imrei Yosher, Resp. by Meir b. Aaron Judah *Arik.
Ir Shushan, Subdivision of the *Levush,* a codification by Mordecai b. Abraham (Levush) *Jaffe; *Ir Shushan* parallels Tur, ḤM.
Israel of Bruna = Israel b. Ḥayyim *Bruna.
Ittur. Treatise on precepts by *Isaac b. Abba Mari of Marseilles.

Jacob Be Rab = *Be Rab.
Jacob b. Jacob Moses of Lissa = Jacob b. Jacob Moses *Lorberbaum.
Judah B. Simeon = Judah b. Simeon *Ashkenazi.
Judah Minz = Judah b. Eliezer ha-Levi *Minz.

Kappei Aharon, Resp. by Aaron Azriel.
Kehillat Ya'akov, Talmudic methodology, definitions etc. by Israel Jacob b. Yom Tov *Algazi.
Kelei Ḥemdah, Nov. and *pilpulim* by Meir Dan *Plotzki of Ostrova, arranged acc. to the Torah.
Keli Yakar, Annotations to the Torah by Solomon *Luntschitz.
Keneh Ḥokhmah, Sermons by Judah Loeb *Pochwitzer.
Keneset ha-Gedolah, Digest of *halakhot* by Ḥayyim b. Israel *Benveniste; subdivided into annotations to *Beit Yosef* and annotations to Tur.
Keneset Yisrael, Resp. by Ezekiel b. Abraham Katzenellenbogen (see article *Katzenellenbogen Family).
Kerem Ḥamar, Resp. and varia by Abraham b. Mordecai *Ankawa.
Kerem Shelmo. Resp. by Solomon b. Joseph *Amarillo.
Keritut, [Sefer], Methodology of the Talmud by *Samson b. Isaac of Chinon.
Kesef ha-Kedoshim, Comm. to Sh. Ar., ḤM, by Abraham *Wahrmann; printed in major editions of Sh. Ar.
Kesef Mishneh, Comm. to Maimonides, *Yad Ḥazakah,* by Joseph b. Ephraim *Caro; printed in most editions of *Yad Ḥazakah.*
Keẓot ha-Ḥoshen, Comm. to Sh. Ar., ḤM, by *Aryeh Loeb b. Joseph ha-Kohen; printed in major editions of Sh. Ar.
Kol Bo [Sefer], Anonymous collection of ritual rules; also called *Sefer ha-Likkutim.*
Kol Mevasser, Resp. by Meshullam *Rath.
Korban Aharon, Comm. to *Sifra* by Aaron b. Abraham *Ibn Ḥayyim; pt. 1 is called: *Middot Aharon.*
Korban Edah, Comm. to Jer. Talmud by David *Fraenkel; with additions: *Shiyyurei Korban;* printed in most editions of Jer. Talmud.
Kunteres ha-Kelalim, subdivision of *Sedei Ḥemed,* an encyclopaedia of precepts and responsa by Ḥayyim Hezekiah *Medini.
Kunteres ha-Semikhah, a treatise by *Levi b. Ḥabib; printed at the end of his responsa.
Kunteres Tikkun Olam, part of *Mispat Shalom* (Nov. by Shalom Mordecai b. Moses *Schwadron).

Lavin (negative precepts), subdivision of: (1) *Maimonides, *Sefer ha-Mitzvot;* (2) *Moses b. Jacob of Coucy, *Semag.*
Leḥem Mishneh, Comm. to Maimonides, *Yad Ḥazakah,* by Abraham [Ḥiyya] b. Moses *Boton; printed in most editions of *Yad Ḥazakah.*
Leḥem Rav, Resp. by Abraham [Ḥiyya] b. Moses *Boton.
Leket Yosher, Resp and varia by Israel b. Pethahiah *Isserlein, collected by *Joseph (Joselein) b. Moses.
Leo Hebraeus = *Levi b. Gershom, also called Ralbag or Gersonides.
Levush = Mordecai b. Abraham *Jaffe.
Levush [Malkhut], Codification by Mordecai b. Abraham (Levush) *Jaffe, with subdivisions: *[Levush ha-] Tekhelet* (parallels Tur OḤ 1–241); *[Levush ha-] Ḥur* (parallels Tur OḤ 242–697); *[Levush] Ateret Zahav* (parallels Tur YD); *[Levush ha-Buẓ ve-ha-Argaman* (parallels Tur EH); *[Levush] Ir Shushan* (parallels Tur ḤM); under the name *Levush* the author wrote also other works.
Li-Leshonot ha-Rambam, fifth part (nos. 1374–1700) of Resp. by *David b. Solomon ibn Abi Zimra (Radbaz).
Likkutim, Sefer ha-, another name for *[Sefer] Kol Bo.*

Ma'adanei Yom Tov, Comm. on *Piskei ha-Rosh* by Yom Tov Lipmann b. Nathan ha-Levi *Heller; printed in many editions of the Talmud.
Mabit = Moses b. Joseph *Trani.
Magen Avot, Comm. to *Avot* by Simeon b. Ẓemaḥ *Duran.
Magen Avraham, Comm. to Sh. Ar., OḤ, by Abraham Abele b. Ḥayyim ha-Levi *Gombiner; printed in many editions of Sh. Ar., OḤ.
Maggid Mishneh, Comm. to Maimonides, *Yad Ḥazakah,* by *Vidal Yom Tov of Tolosa; printed in most editions of the *Yad Ḥazakah.*
Maḥaneh Efrayim, Resp. and Nov., arranged acc. to Maimonides' *Yad Ḥazakah ,* by Ephraim b. Aaron *Navon.
Maharai = Israel b. Pethahiah *Isserlein.
Maharal of Prague = *Judah Loew (Lob, Liwa), b. Bezalel.
Maharalbaḥ = *Levi b. Ḥabib.
Maharam Alashkar = Moses b. Isaac *Alashkar.
Maharam Alshekh = Moses b. Ḥayyim *Alashekh.
Maharam Mintz = Moses *Mintz.
Maharam of Lublin = *Meir b. Gedaliah of Lublin.
Maharam of Padua = Meir *Katzenellenbogen.
Maharam of Rothenburg = *Meir b. Baruch of Rothenburg.
Maharam Shik = Moses b. Joseph Schick.
Maharash Engel = Samuel b. Ze'ev Wolf Engel.
Maharashdam = Samuel b. Moses *Medina.
Maharḥash = Ḥayyim (ben) Shabbetai.
Mahari Basan = Jehiel b. Ḥayyim Basan.
Mahari b. Lev = Joseph ibn Lev.
Mahari'az = Jekuthiel Asher Zalman Ensil Zusmir.
Maharibal = *Joseph ibn Lev.
Mahariḥ = Jacob (Israel) *Ḥagiz.
Maharik = Joseph b. Solomon *Colon.
Maharikash = Jacob b. Abraham *Castro.
Maharil = Jacob b. Moses *Moellin.
Maharimat = Joseph b. Moses di Trani (not identical with the Maharit).
Maharit = Joseph b. Moses *Trani.
Maharitaẓ = Yom Tov b. Akiva Ẓahalon. (See article *Ẓahalon Family).
Maharsha = Samuel Eliezer b. Judah ha-Levi *Edels.
Maharshag = Simeon b. Judah Gruenfeld.
Maharshak = Samson b. Isaac of Chinon.
Maharshakh = *Solomon b. Abraham.
Maharshal = Solomon b. Jeḥiel *Luria.
Mahasham = Shalom Mordecai b. Moses *Sschwadron.
Maharyu = Jacob b. Judah *Weil.
Maḥazeh Avraham, Resp. by Abraham Nebagen v. Meir ha-Levi Steinberg.
Maḥazik Berakhah, Nov. by Ḥayyim Joseph David *Azulai.

*Maimonides = Moses b. Maimon, or Rambam.
*Malbim = Meir Loeb b. Jehiel Michael.
Malbim = Malbim's comm. to the Bible; printed in the major editions.
Malbushei Yom Tov, Nov. on *Levush*, OḤ, by Yom Tov Lipmann b. Nathan ha-Levi *Heller.
Mappah, another name for *Rema.*
Mareh ha-Panim, Comm. to Jer. Talmud by Moses b. Simeon *Margolies; printed in most editions of Jer. Talmud.
Margaliyyot ha-Yam, Nov. by Reuben *Margoliot.
Masat Binyamin, Resp. by Benjamin Aaron b. Abraham *Slonik
Mashbir, Ha- = *Joseph Samuel b. Isaac Rodi.
Massa Ḥayyim, Tax *halakhot* by Ḥayyim *Palaggi, with the subdivisions *Missim ve-Arnomiyyot* and *Torat ha-Minhagot.*
Massa Melekh, Compilation of Tax Law by Joseph b. Isaac *Ibn Ezra with concluding part *Ne'ilat She'arim.*
Matteh Asher, Resp. by Asher b. Emanuel Shalem.
Matteh Shimon, Digest of Resp. and Nov. to Tur and *Beit Yosef,* ḤM, by Mordecai Simeon b. Solomon.
Matteh Yosef, Resp. by Joseph b. Moses ha-Levi Nazir (see article under his father's name).
Mayim Amukkim, Resp. by Elijah b. Abraham *Mizraḥi.
Mayim Ḥayyim, Resp. by Ḥayyim b. Dov Beresh Rapaport.
Mayim Rabbim, , Resp. by Raphael *Meldola.
Me-Emek ha-Bakha, , Resp. by Simeon b. Jekuthiel Ephrati.
Me'irat Einayim, usual abbreviation: *Sma* (from: *Sefer Me'irat Einayim*); comm. to Sh. Ar. By Joshua b. Alexander ha-Kohen *Falk; printed in most editions of the Sh. Ar.
Melammed le-Ho'il, Resp. by David Ẓevi *Hoffmann.
Meisharim, [*Sefer*], Rabbinical treatise by *Jeroham b. Meshullam.
Meshiv Davar, Resp. by Naphtali Ẓevi Judah *Berlin.
Mi-Gei ha-Haregah, Resp. by Simeon b. Jekuthiel Ephrati.
Mi-Ma'amakim, Resp. by Ephraim Oshry.
Middot Aharon, first part of *Korban Aharon,* a comm. to *Sifra* by Aaron b. Abraham *Ibn Ḥayyim.
Migdal Oz, Comm. to Maimonides, *Yad Ḥazakah,* by *Ibn Gaon Shem Tov b. Abraham; printed in most editions of the *Yad Ḥazakah.*
Mikhtam le-David, Resp. by David Samuel b. Jacob *Pardo.
Mikkaḥ ve-ha-Mimkar, Sefer ha-, Rabbinical treatise by *Hai Gaon.
Milḥamot ha-Shem, Glosses to Rif, *Halakhot,* by *Naḥmanides.
Minḥat Ḥinnukh, Comm. to *Sefer ha-Ḥinnukh,* by Joseph b. Moses *Babad.
Minḥat Yiẓḥak, Resp. by Isaac Jacob b. Joseph Judah Weiss.
Misgeret ha-Shulḥan, Comm. to Sh. Ar., ḤM, by Benjamin Ze'ev Wolf b. Shabbetai; printed in most editions of Sh. Ar.
Mishkenot ha-Ro'im, Halakhot in alphabetical order by Uzziel Alshekh.
Mishnah Berurah, Comm. to Sh. Ar., OḤ, by *Israel Meir ha-Kohen.
Mishneh le-Melekh, Comm. to Maimonides, *Yad Ḥazakah,* by Judah *Rosanes; printed in most editions of *Yad Ḥazakah.*
Mishpat ha-Kohanim, Nov. to Sh. Ar., ḤM, by Jacob Moses *Lorberbaum, part of his *Netivot ha-Mishpat;* printed in major editions of Sh. Ar.
Mishpat Kohen, Resp. by Abraham Isaac ha-Kohen *Kook.
Mishpat Shalom, Nov. by Shalom Mordecai b. Moses *Schwadron; contains: *Kunteres Tikkun Olam.*
Mishpat u-Ẓedakah be-Ya'akov, Resp. by Jacob b. Reuben *Ibn Ẓur.
Mishpat ha-Urim, Comm. to Sh. Ar., ḤM by Jacob b. Jacob Moses *Lorberbaum, part of his *Netivot ha-Mishpat;* printed in major editons of Sh. Ar.
Mishpat Ẓedek, Resp. by *Melammed Meir b. Shem Tov.
Mishpatim Yesharim, Resp. by Raphael b. Mordecai *Berdugo.
Mishpetei Shemu'el, Resp. by Samuel b. Moses *Kalai (Kal'i).
Mishpetei ha-Tanna'im, Kunteres, Nov on *Levush,* OḤ by Yom Tov Lipmann b. Nathan ha-Levi *Heller.
Mishpetei Uzzi'el (Uziel), Resp. by Ben-Zion Meir Hai *Ouziel.
Missim ve-Arnoniyyot, Tax *halakhot* by Ḥayyim *Palaggi, a subdivision of his work *Massa Ḥayyim* on the same subject.
Mitzvot, Sefer ha-, Elucidation of precepts by *Maimonides; subdivided into *Lavin* (negative precepts) and *Asayin* (positive precepts).
Mitzvot Gadol, Sefer, Elucidation of precepts by *Moses b. Jacob of Coucy, subdivided into *Lavin* (negative precepts) and *Asayin* (positive precepts); the usual abbreviation is *Semag.*
Mitzvot Katan, Sefer, Elucidation of precepts by *Isaac b. Joseph of Corbeil; the usual, abbreviation is *Semak.*
Mo'adim u-Zemannim, Rabbinical treatises by Moses Sternbuch.
Modigliano, Joseph Samuel = *Joseph Samuel b. Isaac, Rodi (Ha-Mashbir).
Mordekhai (Mordecai), halakhic compilation by *Mordecai b. Hillel; printed in most editions of the Talmud after the texts.
Moses b. Maimon = *Maimonides, also called Rambam.
Moses b. Naḥman = Naḥmanides, also called Ramban.
Muram = Isaiah Menahem b. Isaac (from: Morenu R. Mendel).

Naḥal Yiẓḥak, Comm. on Sh. Ar., ḤM, by Isaac Elhanan *Spector.
Naḥalah li-Yhoshu'a, Resp. by Joshua Ẓunẓin.
Naḥalat Shivah, collection of legal forms by *Samuel b. David Moses ha-Levi.
*Naḥmanides = Moses b. Naḥman, also called Ramban.
Naẓiv = Naphtali Ẓevi Judah *Berlin.
Ne'eman Shemu'el, Resp. by Samuel Isaac *Modigilano.
Ne'ilat She'arim, concluding part of *Massa Melekh* (a work on Tax Law) by Joseph b. Isaac *Ibn Ezra, containing an exposition of customary law and subdivided into *Minhagei Issur* and *Minhagei Mamon.*
Ner Ma'aravi, Resp. by Jacob b. Malka.
Netivot ha-Mishpat, by Jacob b. Jacob Moses *Lorberbaum; subdivided into *Mishpat ha-Kohanim,* Nov. to Sh. Ar., ḤM, and *Mishpat ha-Urim,* a comm. on the same; printed in major editions of Sh. Ar.
Netivot Olam, Saying of the Sages by *Judah Loew (Lob, Liwa) b. Bezalel.
Nimmukei Menaḥem of Merseburg, Tax *halakhot* by the same, printed at the end of Resp. Maharyu.
Nimmukei Yosef, Comm. to Rif. *Halakhot,* by Joseph *Ḥabib (Ḥabiba); printed in many editions of the Talmud.
Noda bi-Yhudah, Resp. by Ezekiel b. Judah ha-Levi *Landau; there is a first collection *(Mahadura Kamma)* and a second collection *(Mahadura Tinyana).*
Nov. = Novellae, Ḥiddushim.

Ohel Moshe (1), Notes to Talmud, *Midrash Rabbah,* Yad, *Sifrei* and to several Resp., by Eleazar *Horowitz.

Ohel Moshe (2), Resp. by Moses Jonah Zweig.
Oholei Tam. Resp. by *Tam ibn Yaḥya Jacob b. David; printed in the rabbinical collection *Tummat Yesharim.*
Oholei Ya'akov, Resp. by Jacob de *Castro.
Or ha-Me'ir Resp by Judah Meir b. Jacob Samson Shapiro.
Or Same'aḥ, Comm. to Maimonides, *Yad Ḥazakah,* by *Meir Simḥah ha-Kohen of Dvinsk; printed in many editions of the *Yad Ḥazakah.*
Or Zaru'a [the father] = *Isaac b. Moses of Vienna.
Or Zaru'a [the son] = *Ḥayyim (Eliezer) b. Isaac.
Or Zaru'a, Nov. by *Isaac b. Moses of Vienna.
Orah, Sefer ha-, Compilation of ritual precepts by *Rashi.
Oraḥ la-Ẓaddik, Resp. by Abraham Ḥayyim Rodrigues.
Oẓar ha-Posekim, Digest of Responsa.

Paḥad Yiẓḥak, Rabbinical encyclopaedia by Isaac *Lampronti.
Panim Me'irot, Resp. by Meir b. Isaac *Eisenstadt.
Parashat Mordekhai, Resp. by Mordecai b. Abraham Naphtali *Banet.
Pe'at ha-Sadeh la-Dinim and Pe'at ha-Sadeh la-Kelalim, subdivisions of the *Sedei Ḥemed,* an encyclopaedia of precepts and responsa, by Ḥayyim Hezekaih *Medini.
Penei Moshe (1), Resp. by Moses *Benveniste.
Penei Moshe (2), Comm. to Jer. Talmud by Moses b. Simeon *Margolies; printed in most editions of the Jer. Talmud.
Penei Moshe (3), Comm. on the aggadic passages of 18 treatises of the Bab. and Jer. Talmud, by Moses b. Isaiah Katz.
Penei Yehoshu'a, Nov. by Jacob Joshua b. Ẓevi Hirsch *Falk.
Peri Ḥadash, Comm. on Sh. Ar. By Hezekiah da *Silva.
Perishah, Comm. on Tur by Joshua b. Alexander ha-Kohen *Falk; printed in major edition of Tur; forms together with *Derishah* and *Be'urim* (by the same author) the *Beit Yisrael.*
Pesakim u-Khetavim, 2nd part of the *Terumat ha-Deshen* by Israel b. Pethahiah *Isserlein' also called *Piskei Maharai.*
Pilpula Ḥarifta, Comm. to *Piskei ha-Rosh, Seder Nezikin,* by Yom Tov Lipmann b. Nathan ha-Levi *Heller; printed in major editions of the Talmud.
Piskei Maharai, see *Terumat ha-Deshen,* 2nd part; also called *Pesakim u-Khetavim.*
Piskei ha-Rosh, a compilation of *halakhot,* arranged on the Talmud, by *Asher b. Jehiel (Rosh); printed in major Talmud editions.
Pitḥei Teshuvah, Comm. to Sh. Ar. by Abraham Hirsch b. Jacob *Eisenstadt; printed in major editions of the Sh. Ar.

Rabad = *Abraham b. David of Posquières (Rabad III.).
Raban = *Eliezer b. Nathan of Mainz.
Raban, also called *Ẓafenat Pa'ne'aḥ* or *Even ha-Ezer,* see under the last name.
Rabi Abad = *Abraham b. Isaac of Narbonne.
Radad = David Dov. b. Aryeh Judah Jacob *Meisels.
Radam = Dov Berush b. Isaac Meisels.
Radbaz = *David b Solomon ibn Abi Ziumra.
Radbaz, Comm. to Maimonides, *Yad Ḥazakah,* by *David b. Solomon ibn Abi Zimra.
Ralbag = *Levi b. Gershom, also called Gersonides, or Leo Hebraeus.
Ralbag, Bible comm. by *Levi b. Gershon.
Rama [da Fano] = Menaḥem Azariah *Fano.
Ramah = Meir b. Todros [ha-Levi] *Abulafia.
Ramam = *Menaham of Merseburg.
Rambam = *Maimonides; real name: Moses b. Maimon.
Ramban = *Naḥmanides; real name Moses b. Naḥman.
Ramban, Comm. to Torah by *Naḥmanides; printed in major editions. ("Mikra'ot Gedolot").
Ran = *Nissim b. Reuben Gerondi.
Ran of Rif, Comm. on Rif, *Halakhot,* by Nissim b. Reuben Gerondi.
Ranaḥ = *Elijah b. Ḥayyim.
Rash = *Samson b. Abraham of Sens.
Rash, Comm. to Mishnah, by *Samson b. Abraham of Sens; printed in major Talmud editions.
Rashash = Samuel *Strashun.
Rashba = Solomon b. Abraham *Adret.
Rashba, Resp., see also; *Sefer Teshuvot ha-Rashba ha-Meyuḥasot le-ha-Ramban,* by Solomon b. Abraham *Adret.
Rashbad = Samuel b. David.
Rashbam = *Samuel b. Meir.
Rashbam = Comm. on Bible and Talmud by *Samuel b. Meir; printed in major editions of Bible and most editions of Talmud.
Rashbash = Solomon b. Simeon *Duran.
*Rashi = Solomon b. Isaac of Troyes.
Rashi, Comm. on Bible and Talmud by *Rashi; printed in almost all Bible and Talmud editions.
Raviah = Eliezer b. Joel ha-Levi.
Redak = David *Kimḥi.
Redak, Comm. to Bible by David *Kimḥi.
Redakh = *David b. Ḥayyim ha-Kohen of Corfu.
Re'em = Elijah b. Abraham *Mizraḥi.
Rema = Moses b. Israel *Isserles.
Rema, Glosses to Sh. Ar. by Moses b. Israel *Isserles; printed in almost all editions of the Sh. Ar. inside the text in Rashi type; also called *Mappah* or *Haggahot.*
Remek = Moses Kimḥi.
Remakh = Moses ha-Kohen mi-Lunel.
Reshakh = *Solomon b. Abraham; also called Maharshakh.
Resp. = Responsa, *She'elot u-Teshuvot.*
Ri Berav = *Berab.
Ri Escapa = Joseph b. Saul *Escapa.
Ri Migash = Joseph b. Meir ha-Levi *Ibn Migash.
Riba = Isaac b. Asher ha-Levi; Riba II (Riba ha-Baḥur) = his grandson with the same name.
Ribam = Isaac b. Mordecai (or: Isaac b. Meir).
Ribash = *Isaac b. Sheshet Perfet (or: Barfat).
Rid= *Isaiah b. Mali di Trani the Elder.
Ridbaz = Jacob David b. Ze'ev *Willowski.
Rif = Isaac b. Jacob ha-Kohen *Alfasi.
Rif, *Halakhot,* Compilation and abstract of the Talmud by Isaac b. Jacob ha-Kohen *Alfasi.
Ritba = Yom Tov b. Abraham *Ishbili.
Riẓbam = Isaac b. Mordecai.
Rosh = *Asher b. Jehiel, also called Asheri.
Rosh Mashbir, Resp. by *Joseph Samuel b. Isaac, Rodi.

Sedei Ḥemed, Encyclopaedia of precepts and responsa by Ḥayyim Ḥezekiah *Medini; subdivisions: *Asefat Dinim, Kunteres ha-Kelalim, Pe'at ha-Sadeh la-Dinim, Pe'at ha-Sadeh la-Kelalim.*
Semag, Usual abbreviation of *Sefer Mitzvot Gadol,* elucidation of precepts by *Moses b. Jacob of Coucy; subdivided into *Lavin* (negative precepts) *Asayin* (positive precepts).
Semak, Usual abbreviation of *Sefer Mitzvot Katan,* elucidation of precepts by *Isaac b. Joseph of Corbeil.

Sh. Ar. = *Shulḥan Arukh,* code by Joseph b. Ephraim *Caro.

Sha'ar Mishpat, Comm. to Sh. Ar., ḤM. By Israel Isser b. Ze'ev Wolf.

Sha'arei Shevu'ot, Treatise on the law of oaths by *David b. Saadiah; usually printed together with Rif, *Halakhot;* also called: *She'arim of R. Alfasi.*

Sha'arei Teshuvah, Collection of resp. from Geonic period, by different authors.

Sha'arei Uzzi'el, Rabbinical treatise by Ben-Zion Meir Ha *Ouziel.

Sha'arei Ẓedek, Collection of resp. from Geonic period, by different authors.

Shadal [or Shedal] = Samuel David *Luzzatto.

Shai la-Moreh, Resp. by Shabbetai Jonah.

Shakh, Usual abbreviation of *Siftei Kohen,* a comm. to Sh. Ar., YD and ḤM by *Shabbetai b. Meir ha-Kohen; printed in most editions of Sh. Ar.

Sha'ot-de-Rabbanan, Resp. by *Solomon b. Judah ha-Kohen.

She'arim of R. Alfasi see *Sha'arei Shevu'ot.*

Shedal, see Shadal.

She'elot u-Teshuvot ha-Ge'onim, Collection of resp. by different authors.

She'erit Yisrael, Resp. by Israel Ze'ev Mintzberg.

She'erit Yosef, Resp. by *Joseph b. Mordecai Gershon ha-Kohen.

She'ilat Yavez, Resp. by Jacob *Emden (Yaveẓ).

She'iltot, Compilation arranged acc. to the Torah by *Aḥa (Aḥai) of Shabḥa.

Shem Aryeh, Resp. by Aryeh Leib *Lipschutz.

Shemesh Ẓedakah, Resp. by Samson *Morpurgo.

Shenei ha-Me'orot ha-Gedolim, Resp. by Elijah *Covo.

Shetarot, Sefer ha-, Collection of legal forms by *Judah b. Barzillai al-Bargeloni.

Shevut Ya'akov, Resp. by Jacob b. Joseph Reicher.

Shibbolei ha-Leket Compilation on ritual by Zedekiah b. Avraham *Anav.

Shiltei Gibborim, Comm. to Rif, *Halakhot,* by *Joshua Boaz b. Simeon; printed in major editions of the Talmud.

Shittah Mekubbeẓet, Compilation of talmudical commentaries by Bezalel *Ashkenazi.

Shivat Ẓiyyon, Resp. by Samuel b. Ezekiel *Landau.

Shiyyurei Korban, by David *Fraenkel; additions to his comm. to Jer. Talmud *Korban Edah;* both printed in most editions of Jer. Talmud.

Sho'el u-Meshiv, Resp. by Joseph Saul ha-Levi *Nathanson.

Sh[ulḥan] Ar[ukh] [of Ba'al ha-Tanyal], Code by *Shneur Zalman of Lyady; not identical with the code by Joseph Caro.

Siftei Kohen, Comm. to Sh. Ar., YD and ḤM by *Shabbetai b. Meir ha-Kohen; printed in most editions of Sh. Ar.; usual abbreviation: *Shakh.*

Simḥat Yom Tov, Resp. by Tom Tov b. Jacob *Algazi.

Simlah Ḥadashah, Treatise on *Sheḥitah* by Alexander Sender b. Ephraim Zalman *Schor; see also *Tevu'ot Shor.*

Simeon b. Ẓemaḥ = Simeon b. Ẓemaḥ *Duran.

Sma, Comm. to Sh. Ar. by Joshua b. Alexander ha-Kohen *Falk; the full title is: *Sefer Me'irat Einayim;* printed in most editions of Sh. Ar.

Solomon b. Isaac ha-Levi = Solomon b. Isaac *Levy.

Solomon b. Isaac of Troyes = *Rashi.

Tal Orot, Rabbinical work with various contents, by Joseph ibn Gioia.

Tam, Rabbenu = *Tam Jacob b. Meir.

Tashbaẓ = Samson b. Zadok.

Tashbeẓ = Simeon b. Zemaḥ *Duran, sometimes also abbreviation for Samson b. Zadok, usually known as Tashbaẓ.

Tashbeẓ [*Sefer ha-*], Resp. by Simeon b. Ẓemaḥ *Duran; the fourth part of this work is called: *Ḥut ha-Meshullash.*

Taz, Usual abbreviation of *Turei Zahav,* comm., to Sh. Ar. by *David b. Samnuel ha-Levi; printed in most editions of Sh. Ar.

(Ha)-Tekhelet, subdivision of the *Levush* (a codification by Mordecai b. Abraham (Levush) *Jaffe); *Ha-Tekhelet* parallels Tur, OḤ 1-241.

Terumat ha-Deshen, by Israel b. Pethahiah *Isserlein; subdivided into a part containing responsa, and a second part called *Pesakim u-Khetavim* or *Piskei Maharai.*

Terumot, Sefer ha-, Compilation of *halakhot* by Samuel b. Isaac *Sardi.

Teshuvot Ba'alei ha-Tosafot, Collection of responsa by the Tosafists.

Teshjvot Ge'onei Mizraḥ u-Ma'aav, Collection of responsa.

Teshuvot ha-Geonim, Collection of responsa from Geonic period.

Teshuvot Ḥakhmei Provinzyah, Collection of responsa by different Provencal authors.

Teshuvot Ḥakhmei Ẓarefat ve-Loter, Collection of responsa by different French authors.

Teshuvot Maimuniyyot, Resp. pertaining to Maimonides' *Yad Ḥazakah;* printed in major editions of this work after the text; authorship uncertain.

Tevu'ot Shor, by Alexander Sender b. Ephraim Zalman *Schor, a comm. to his *Simlah Ḥadashah,* a work on *Sheḥitah.*

Tiferet Ẓevi, Resp. by Ẓevi Hirsch of the "AHW" Communities (Altona, Hamburg, Wandsbeck).

Tiktin, Judah b. Simeon = Judah b. Simeon *Ashkenazi.

Toledot Adam ve-Ḥavvah, Codification by *Jeroham b. Meshullam.

Torat Emet, Resp. by Aaron b. Joseph *Sasson.

Torat Ḥayyim, , Resp. by Ḥayyim (ben) Shabbetai.

Torat ha-Minhagot, subdivision of the *Massa Ḥayyim* (a work on tax law) by Ḥayyim *Palaggi, containing an exposition of customary law.

Tosafot Rid, Explanations to the Talmud and decisions by *Isaiah b. Mali di Trani the Elder.

Tosefot Yom Tov, comm. to Mishnah by Yom Tov Lipmann b. Nathan ha-Levi *Heller; printed in most editions of the Mishnah.

Tummim, subdivision of the comm. to Sh. Ar., ḤM, *Urim ve-Tummim* by Jonathan *Eybeschuetz; printed in the major editions of Sh. Ar.

Tur, usual abbreviation for the *Arba'ah Turim* of *Jacob b. Asher.

Turei Zahav, Comm. to Sh. Ar. by *David b. Samuel ha-Levi; printed in most editions of Sh. Ar.; usual abbreviation: *Taz.*

Urim, subdivision of the following.

Urim ve-Tummim, Comm. to Sh. Ar., ḤM, by Jonathan *Eybeschuetz; printed in the major editions of Sh. Ar.; subdivided in places into *Urim* and *Tummim.*

Vikku'aḥ Mayim Ḥayyim, Polemics against Isserles and Caro by Ḥayyim b. Bezalel.

Yad Malakhi, Methodological treatise by *Malachi b. Jacob ha-Kohen.

Yad Ramah, Nov. by Meir b. Todros [ha-Levi] *Abulafia.
Yakhin u-Vo'az, Resp. by Ẓemaḥ b. Solomon *Duran.
Yam ha-Gadol, Resp. by Jacob Moses *Toledano.
Yam shel Shelomo, Compilation arranged acc. to Talmud by Solomon b. Jehiel (Maharshal) *Luria.
Yashar, Sefer ha-, by *Tam, Jacob b. Meir (Rabbenu Tam); 1st pt.: Resp.; 2nd pt.: Nov.
Yaskil Avdi, Resp. by Obadiah Hadaya (printed together with his Resp. *De'ah ve-Haskel).*
Yaveẓ = Jacob *Emden.
Yehudah Ya'aleh, Resp. by Judah b. Israel *Aszod.
Yekar Tiferet, Comm. to Maimonides' *Yad Ḥazakah,*by David b. Solomon ibn Zimra, printed in most editions of *Yad Ḥazakah.*
Yere'im [*ha-Shalem*], [*Sefer*], Treatise on precepts by *Eliezer b. Samuel of Metz.
Yeshu'ot Ya'akov, Resp. by Jacob Meshullam b. Mordecai Ze'ev *Ornstein.
Yiẓhak Rei'aḥ, Resp. by Isaac b. Samuel Abendanan (see article *Abendanam Family).
Ẓafenat Pa'ne'aḥ (1), also called *Raban* or *Even ha-Ezer*, see under the last name.
Ẓafenat Pa'ne'aḥ (2), Resp. by Joseph *Rozin.
Zayit Ra'anan, Resp. by Moses Judah Leib b. Benjamin Auerbach.
Ẓeidah la-Derekh, Codification by *Menahem b. Aaron ibn Zerah.
Ẓedakah u-Mishpat, Resp. by Ẓedakah b. Saadiah Huẓin.
Zekan Aharon, Resp. by Elijah b. Benjamin ha-Levi.
Zekher Ẓaddik, Sermons by Eliezer *Katzenellenbogen.
Ẓemaḥ Ẓedek (1) Resp. by Menaham Mendel Shneersohn (see under *Shneersohn Family).
Zera Avraham, Resp. by Abraham b. David *Yiẓḥaki.
Zera Emet Resp. by *Ishmael b. Abaham Isaac ha-Kohen.
Ẓevi la-Ẓaddik, Resp. by Ẓevi Elimelech b. David Shapira.
Zikhron Yehudah, Resp. by *Judah b. Asher
Zikhron Yosef, Resp. by Joseph b. Menahem *Steinhardt.
Zikhronot, Sefer ha-, Sermons on several precepts by Samuel *Aboab.
Zikkaron la-Rishonim . . ., by Albert (Abraham Elijah) *Harkavy; contains in vol. 1 pt. 4 (1887) a collection of Geonic responsa.
Ẓiẓ Eliezer, Resp. by Eliezer Judah b. Jacob Gedaliah Waldenberg.

BIBLIOGRAPHICAL ABBREVIATIONS

Bibliographies in English and other languages have been extensively updated, with English translations cited where available. In order to help the reader, the language of books or articles is given where not obvious from titles of books or names of periodicals. Titles of books and periodicals in languages with alphabets other than Latin, are given in transliteration, even where there is a title page in English. Titles of articles in periodicals are not given. Names of Hebrew and Yiddish periodicals well known in English-speaking countries or in Israel under their masthead in Latin characters are given in this form, even when contrary to transliteration rules. Names of authors writing in languages with non-Latin alphabets are given in their Latin alphabet form wherever known; otherwise the names are transliterated. Initials are generally not given for authors of articles in periodicals, except to avoid confusion. Non-abbreviated book titles and names of periodicals are printed in *italics*. Abbreviations are given in the list below.

AASOR	*Annual of the American School of Oriental Research* (1919ff.).
AB	*Analecta Biblica* (1952ff.).
Abel, Géog	F.-M. Abel, *Géographie de la Palestine,* 2 vols. (1933-38).
ABR	*Australian Biblical Review* (1951ff.).
Abr.	Philo, *De Abrahamo.*
Abrahams, Companion	I. Abrahams, *Companion to the Authorised Daily Prayer Book* (rev. ed. 1922).
Abramson, Merkazim	S. Abramson, *Ba-Merkazim u-va-Tefuẓot bi-Tekufat ha-Ge'onim* (1965).
Acts	Acts of the Apostles (New Testament).
ACUM	*Who is who in ACUM* [*Aguddat Kompozitorim u-Meḥabbrim*].
ADAJ	*Annual of the Department of Antiquities, Jordan* (1951ff.).
Adam	Adam and Eve (Pseudepigrapha).
ADB	*Allgemeine Deutsche Biographie,* 56 vols. (1875–1912).
Add. Esth.	The Addition to Esther (Apocrypha).
Adler, Prat Mus	1. Adler, *La pratique musicale savante dans quelques communautés juives en Europe au XVIIe et XVIIIe siècles,* 2 vols. (1966).
Adler-Davis	H.M. Adler and A. Davis (ed. and tr.), *Service of the Synagogue, a New Edition of the Festival Prayers with an English Translation in Prose and Verse,* 6 vols. (1905–06).
Aet.	Philo, *De Aeternitate Mundi.*
AFO	*Archiv fuer Orientforschung* (first two volumes under the name *Archiv fuer Keilschriftforschung)* (1923ff.).
Ag. Ber	*Aggadat Bereshit* (ed. Buber, 1902).
Agr.	Philo, *De Agricultura.*
Ag. Sam.	*Aggadat Samuel.*
Ag. Song	*Aggadat Shir ha-Shirim* (Schechter ed., 1896).
Aharoni, Ereẓ	Y. Aharoni, *Ereẓ Yisrael bi-Tekufat ha-Mikra: Geografyah Historit* (1962).
Aharoni, Land	Y. Aharoni, *Land of the Bible* (1966).

Ahikar	Ahikar (Pseudepigrapha).
AI	*Archives Israélites de France* (1840–1936).
AJA	*American Jewish Archives* (1948ff.).
AJHSP	*American Jewish Historical Society – Publications* (after vol. 50 = AJHSQ).
AJHSQ	*American Jewish Historical (*Society) *Quarterly* (before vol. 50 =AJHSP).
AJSLL	*American Journal of Semitic Languages and Literature* (1884–95 under the title *Hebraica*, since 1942 JNES).
AJYB	*American Jewish Year Book* (1899ff.).
AKM	Abhandlungen fuer die Kunde des Morgenlandes (series).
Albright, Arch	W.F. Albright, *Archaeology of Palestine* (rev. ed. 1960).
Albright, Arch Bib	W.F. Albright, *Archaeology of Palestine and the Bible* (1935^{3}).
Albright, Arch Rel	W.F. Albright, *Archaeology and the Religion of Israel* (1953^{3}).
Albright, Stone	W.F. Albright, *From the Stone Age to Christianity* (1957^{2}).
Alon, Meḥkarim	G. Alon, *Meḥkarim be-Toledot Yisrael bi-Ymei Bayit Sheni u-vi-Tekufat ha-Mishnah ve-ha Talmud*, 2 vols. (1957–58).
Alon, Toledot	G. Alon, *Toledot ha-Yehudim be-Ereẓ Yisrael bi-Tekufat ha-Mishnah ve-ha-Talmud*, I (1958^{3}), (1961^{2}).
ALOR	Alter Orient (series).
Alt, Kl Schr	A. Alt, *Kleine Schriften zur Geschichte des Volkes Israel*, 3 vols. (1953–59).
Alt, Landnahme	A. Alt, *Landnahme der Israeliten in Palaestina* (1925); also in Alt, Kl Schr, 1 (1953), 89–125.
Ant.	Josephus, *Jewish Antiquities* (Loeb Classics ed.).
AO	*Acta Orientalia* (1922ff.).
AOR	*Analecta Orientalia* (1931ff.).
AOS	American Oriental Series.
Apion	Josephus, *Against Apion* (Loeb Classics ed.).
Aq.	Aquila's Greek translation of the Bible.
Ar.	*Arakhin* (talmudic tractate).
Artist.	Letter of Aristeas (Pseudepigrapha).
ARN^{1}	*Avot de-Rabbi Nathan*, version (1) ed. Schechter, 1887.
ARN^{2}	*Avot de-Rabbi Nathan*, version (2) ed. Schechter, 1945^{2}.
Aronius, Regesten	I. Aronius, *Regesten zur Geschichte der Juden im fraenkischen und deutschen Reiche bis zum Jahre 1273* (1902).
ARW	*Archiv fuer Religionswissenschaft* (1898–1941/42).
AS	*Assyrological Studies* (1931ff.).
Ashtor, Korot	E. Ashtor (Strauss), *Korot ha-Yehudim bi-Sefarad ha-Muslemit*, 1(1966^{2}), 2(1966).
Ashtor, Toledot	E. Ashtor (Strauss), *Toledot ha-Yehudim be-Miẓrayim ve-Suryah Taḥat Shilton ha-Mamlukim*, 3 vols. (1944–70).
Assaf, Ge'onim	S. Assaf, *Tekufat ha-Ge'onim ve-Sifrutah* (1955).
Assaf, Mekorot	S. Assaf, *Mekorot le-Toledot ha-Ḥinnukh be-Yisrael*, 4 vols. (1925–43).
Ass. Mos.	Assumption of Moses (Pseudepigrapha).
ATA	Alttestamentliche Abhandlungen (series).
ATANT	Abhandlungen zur Theologie des Alten und Neuen Testaments (series).
AUJW	*Allgemeine unabhaengige juedische Wochenzeitung* (till 1966 = AWJD).
AV	Authorized Version of the Bible.
Avad.	*Avadim* (post-talmudic tractate).
Avi-Yonah, Geog	M. Avi-Yonah, *Geografyah Historit shel Ereẓ Yisrael* (1962^{3}).
Avi-Yonah, Land	M. Avi-Yonah, *The Holy Land from the Persian to the Arab conquest (536 B.C. to A.D. 640)* (1960).
Avot	*Avot* (talmudic tractate).
Av. Zar.	*Avodah Zarah* (talmudic tractate).
AWJD	*Allgemeine Wochenzeitung der Juden in Deutschland* (since 1967 = AUJW).
AZDJ	*Allgemeine Zeitung des Judentums.*
Azulai	Ḥ.Y.D. Azulai, *Shem ha-Gedolim*, ed. by I.E. Benjacob, 2 pts. (1852) (and other editions).
BA	*Biblical Archaeologist* (1938ff.).
Bacher, Bab Amor	W. Bacher, *Agada der babylonischen Amoraeer* (1913^{2}).
Bacher, Pal Amor	W. Bacher, *Agada der palaestinensischen Amoraeer* (Heb. ed. *Aggadat Amora'ei Ereẓ Yisrael)*, 2 vols. (1892–99).
Bacher, Tann	W. Bacher, *Agada der Tannaiten* (Heb. ed. *Aggadot ha-Tanna'im*, vol. 1, pt. 1 and 2 (1903); vol. 2 (1890).
Bacher, Trad	W. Bacher, *Tradition und Tradenten in den Schulen Palaestinas und Babyloniens* (1914).
Baer, Spain	Yitzhak (Fritz) Baer, *History of the Jews in Christian Spain*, 2 vols. (1961–66).
Baer, Studien	Yitzhak (Fritz) Baer, *Studien zur Geschichte der Juden im Koenigreich Aragonien waehrend des 13. und 14. Jahrhunderts* (1913).
Baer, Toledot	Yitzhak (Fritz) Baer, *Toledot ha-Yehudim bi-Sefarad ha-Noẓerit mi-Teḥillatan shel ha-Kehillot ad ha-Gerush*, 2 vols. (1959^{2}).
Baer, Urkunden	Yitzhak (Fritz) Baer, *Die Juden im christlichen Spanien*, 2 vols. (1929–36).
Baer S., Seder	S.I. Baer, *Seder Avodat Yisrael* (1868 and reprints).
BAIU	*Bulletin de l'Alliance Israélite Universelle* (1861–1913).
Baker, Biog Dict	*Baker's Biographical Dictionary of Musicians*, revised by N. Slonimsky (1958^{5}; with Supplement 1965).
I Bar.	I Baruch (Apocrypha).
II Bar.	II Baruch (Pseudepigrapha).
III Bar.	III Baruch (Pseudepigrapha).
BAR	*Biblical Archaeology Review.*
Baron, Community	S.W. Baron, *The Jewish Community, its History and Structure to the American Revolution*, 3 vols. (1942).

Baron, Social	S.W. Baron, *Social and Religious History of the Jews,* 3 vols. (1937); enlarged, 1-2(1952^2), 3-14 (1957–69).
Barthélemy-Milik	D. Barthélemy and J.T. Milik, *Dead Sea Scrolls: Discoveries in the Judean Desert,* vol. 1 *Qumram Cave* I (1955).
BASOR	*Bulletin of the American School of Oriental Research.*
Bauer-Leander	H. Bauer and P. Leander, *Grammatik des Biblisch-Aramaeischen* (1927; repr. 1962).
BB	(1) *Bava Batra* (talmudic tractate). (2) *Biblische Beitraege* (1943ff.).
BBB	Bonner biblische Beitraege (series).
BBLA	*Beitraege zur biblischen Landes- und Altertumskunde* (until 1949–ZDPV).
BBSAJ	*Bulletin,* British School of Archaeology, Jerusalem (1922–25; after 1927 included in PEFQS).
BDASI	*Alon* (since 1948) or *Hadashot Arkheʾologiyyot* (since 1961), bulletin of the Department of Antiquities of the State of Israel.
Begrich, Chronologie	J. Begrich, *Chronologie der Koenige von Israel und Juda* (1929).
Bek.	*Bekhorot* (talmudic tractate).
Bel	Bel and the Dragon (Apocrypha).
Benjacob, Oẓar	I.E. Benjacob, *Oẓar ha-Sefarim* (1880; repr. 1956).
Ben Sira	see Ecclus.
Ben-Yehuda, Millon	E. Ben-Yedhuda, *Millon ha-Lashon ha-Ivrit,* 16 vols (1908–59; repr. in 8 vols., 1959).
Benzinger, Archaeologie	I. Benzinger, *Hebraeische Archaeologie* (1927^3).
Ben Zvi, Eretz Israel	I. Ben-Zvi, *Eretz Israel under Ottoman Rule* (1960; offprint from L. Finkelstein (ed.), *The Jews, their History, Culture and Religion* (vol. 1).
Ben Zvi, Ereẓ Israel	I. Ben-Zvi, *Ereẓ Israel bi-Ymei ha-Shilton ha-Ottomani (1955).*
Ber.	*Berakhot* (talmudic tractate).
Beẓah	*Beẓah* (talmudic tractate).
BIES	Bulletin of the Israel Exploration Society, see below BJPES.
Bik.	*Bikkurim* (talmudic tractate).
BJCE	Bibliography of Jewish Communities in Europe, catalog at General Archives for the History of the Jewish People, Jerusalem.
BJPES	Bulletin of the Jewish Palestine Exploration Society – English name of the Hebrew periodical known as: 1. *Yediʿot ha-Ḥevrah ha-Ivrit la-Ḥakirat Ereẓ Yisrael va-Attikoteha* (1933–1954); 2. *Yediʿot ha-Ḥevrah la-Ḥakirat Ereẓ Yisrael va-Attikoteha* (1954–1962); 3. *Yediʿot ba-Ḥakirat Ereẓ Yisrael va-Attikoteha* (1962ff.).
BJRL	*Bulletin of the John Rylands Library* (1914ff.).
BK	*Bava Kamma* (talmudic tractate).

BLBI	*Bulletin of the Leo Baeck Institute* (1957ff.).
BM	(1) *Bava Meẓia* (talmudic tractate). (2) *Beit Mikra* (1955/56ff.). (3) British Museum.
BO	*Bibbia e Oriente* (1959ff.).
Bondy-Dworský	G. Bondy and F. Dworský, *Regesten zur Geschichte der Juden in Boehmen, Maehren und Schlesien von 906 bis 1620,* 2 vols. (1906).
BOR	*Bibliotheca Orientalis* (1943ff.).
Borée, Ortsnamen	W. Borée *Die alten Ortsnamen Palaestinas* (1930).
Bousset, Religion	W. Bousset, *Die Religion des Judentums im neutestamentlichen Zeitalter* (1906^2).
Bousset-Gressmann	W. Bousset, *Die Religion des Judentums im spaethellenistischen Zeitalter* (1966^3).
BR	*Biblical Review* (1916–25).
BRCI	*Bulletin of the Research Council of Israel* (1951/52–1954/55; then divided).
BRE	*Biblical Research* (1956ff.).
BRF	*Bulletin of the Rabinowitz Fund for the Exploration of Ancient Synagogues* (1949ff.).
Briggs, Psalms	Ch. A. and E.G. Briggs, *Critical and Exegetical Commentary on the Book of Psalms,* 2 vols. (ICC, 1906–07).
Bright, Hist	J. Bright, *A History of Israel* (1959).
Brockelmann, Arab Lit	K. Brockelmann, *Geschichte der arabischen Literatur,* 2 vols. 1898–1902), supplement, 3 vols. (1937–42).
Bruell, Jahrbuecher	*Jahrbuecher fuer juedische Geschichte und Litteratur,* ed. by N. Bruell, Frankfurt (1874–90).
Brugmans-Frank	H. Brugmans and A. Frank (eds.), *Geschiedenis der Joden in Nederland* (1940).
BTS	*Bible et Terre Sainte* (1958ff.).
Bull, Index	S. Bull, *Index to Biographies of Contemporary Composers* (1964).
BW	*Biblical World* (1882–1920).
BWANT	*Beitraege zur Wissenschaft vom Alten und Neuen Testament* (1926ff.).
BZ	*Biblische Zeitschrift* (1903ff.).
BZAW	*Beihefte zur Zeitschrift fuer die alttestamentliche Wissenschaft,* supplement to ZAW (1896ff.).
BŻIH	*Biuletyn Zydowskiego Instytutu Historycznego* (1950ff.).
CAB	*Cahiers d'archéologie biblique* (1953ff.).
CAD	*The* [*Chicago*] *Assyrian Dictionary* (1956ff.).
CAH	*Cambridge Ancient History,* 12 vols. (1923–39)
CAH^2	*Cambridge Ancient History,* second edition, 14 vols. (1962–2005).
Calwer, Lexikon	*Calwer, Bibellexikon.*
Cant.	Canticles, usually given as Song (= Song of Songs).

Cantera-Millás, Inscripciones	F. Cantera and J.M. Millás, *Las Inscripciones Hebraicas de España* (1956).
CBQ	*Catholic Biblical Quarterly* (1939ff.).
CCARY	Central Conference of American Rabbis, *Yearbook* (1890/91ff.).
CD	*Damascus Document* from the Cairo *Genizah* (published by S. Schechter, *Fragments of a Zadokite Work*, 1910).
Charles, Apocrypha	R.H. Charles, *Apocrypha and Pseudepigrapha . . .*, 2 vols. (1913; repr. 1963–66).
Cher.	Philo, *De Cherubim.*
I (or II) Chron.	Chronicles, book I and II (Bible).
CIG	*Corpus Inscriptionum Graecarum.*
CIJ	*Corpus Inscriptionum Judaicarum,* 2 vols. (1936–52).
CIL	*Corpus Inscriptionum Latinarum.*
CIS	*Corpus Inscriptionum Semiticarum* (1881ff.).
C.J.	Codex Justinianus.
Clermont-Ganneau, Arch	Ch. Clermont-Ganneau, *Archaeological Researches in Palestine*, 2 vols. (1896–99).
CNFI	*Christian News from Israel* (1949ff.).
Cod. Just.	Codex Justinianus.
Cod. Theod.	Codex Theodosinanus.
Col.	Epistle to the Colosssians (New Testament).
Conder, Survey	Palestine Exploration Fund, *Survey of Eastern Palestine*, vol. 1, pt. I (1889) = C.R. Conder, *Memoirs of the . . . Survey.*
Conder-Kitchener	Palestine Exploration Fund, *Survey of Western Palestine*, vol. 1, pts. 1-3 (1881–83) = C.R. Conder and H.H. Kitchener, *Memoirs.*
Conf.	Philo, *De Confusione Linguarum.*
Conforte, Kore	D. Conforte, *Kore ha-Dorot* (1842^{2}).
Cong.	Philo, *De Congressu Quaerendae Eruditionis Gratia.*
Cont.	Philo, *De Vita Contemplativa.*
I (or II) Cor.	Epistles to the Corinthians (New Testament).
Cowley, Aramic	A. Cowley, *Aramaic Papyri of the Fifth Century B.C.* (1923).
Colwey, Cat	A.E. Cowley, *A Concise Catalogue of the Hebrew Printed Books in the Bodleian Library* (1929).
CRB	*Cahiers de la Revue Biblique* (1964ff.).
Crowfoot-Kenyon	J.W. Crowfoot, K.M. Kenyon and E.L. Sukenik, *Buildings of Samaria* (1942).
C.T.	Codex Theodosianus.
DAB	*Dictionary of American Biography* (1928–58).
Daiches, Jews	S. Daiches, *Jews in Babylonia* (1910).
Dalman, Arbeit	G. Dalman, *Arbeit und Sitte in Palaestina*, 7 vols.in 8 (1928–42 repr. 1964).
Dan	Daniel (Bible).
Davidson, Oẓar	I. Davidson, *Oẓar ha-Shirah ve-ha-Piyyut*, 4 vols. (1924–33); Supplement in: HUCA, 12–13 (1937/38), 715–823.
DB	J. Hastings, *Dictionary of the Bible,* 4 vols. (1963^{2}).
DBI	F.G. Vigoureaux et al. (eds.), *Dictionnaire de la Bible,* 5 vols. in 10 (1912); Supplement, 8 vols. (1928–66)
Decal.	Philo, *De Decalogo.*
Dem.	*Demai* (talmudic tractate).
DER	*Derekh Ereẓ Rabbah* (post-talmudic tractate).
Derenbourg, Hist	J. Derenbourg *Essai sur l'histoire et la géographie de la Palestine* (1867).
Det.	Philo, *Quod deterius potiori insidiari solet.*
Deus	Philo, *Quod Deus immutabilis sit.*
Deut.	Deuteronomy (Bible).
Deut. R.	*Deuteronomy Rabbah.*
DEZ	*Derekh Ereẓ Zuta* (post-talmudic tractate).
DHGE	*Dictionnaire d'histoire et de géographie ecclésiastiques,* ed. by A. Baudrillart et al., 17 vols (1912–68).
Dik. Sof	*Dikdukei Soferim,* variae lections of the talmudic text by Raphael Nathan Rabbinovitz (16 vols., 1867–97).
Dinur, Golah	B. Dinur (Dinaburg), *Yisrael ba-Golah,* 2 vols. in 7 (1959–68) = vols. 5 and 6 of his *Toledot Yisrael,* second series.
Dinur, Haganah	B. Dinur (ed.), *Sefer Toledot ha-Haganah* (1954ff.).
Diringer, Iscr	D. Diringer, *Iscrizioni antico-ebraiche palestinesi* (1934).
Discoveries	*Discoveries in the Judean Desert* (1955ff.).
DNB	*Dictionary of National Biography,* 66 vols. (1921–222) with Supplements.
Dubnow, Divrei	S. Dubnow, *Divrei Yemei Am Olam,* 11 vols (1923–38 and further editions).
Dubnow, Ḥasidut	S. Dubnow, *Toledot ha-Ḥasidut* (1960^{2}).
Dubnow, Hist	S. Dubnow, *History of the Jews* (1967).
Dubnow, Hist Russ	S. Dubnow, *History of the Jews in Russia and Poland,* 3 vols. (1916 20).
Dubnow, Outline	S. Dubnow, *An Outline of Jewish History,* 3 vols. (1925–29).
Dubnow, Weltgesch	S. Dubnow, *Weltgeschichte des juedischen Volkes* 10 vols. (1925–29).
Dukes, Poesie	L. Dukes, *Zur Kenntnis der neuhebraeischen religioesen Poesie* (1842).
Dunlop, Khazars	D. H. Dunlop, *History of the Jewish Khazars* (1954).
EA	El Amarna Letters (edited by J.A. Knudtzon), *Die El-Amarna Tafel,* 2 vols. (1907 14).
EB	*Encyclopaedia Britannica.*
EBI	*Estudios biblicos* (1941ff.).
EBIB	T.K. Cheyne and J.S. Black, *Encyclopaedi Biblica,* 4 vols. (1899–1903).
Ebr.	Philo, *De Ebrietate.*
Eccles.	Ecclesiastes (Bible).
Eccles. R.	*Ecclesiastes Rabbah.*
Ecclus.	Ecclesiasticus or Wisdom of Ben Sira (or Sirach; Apocrypha).
Eduy.	*Eduyyot* (mishanic tractate).

EG — *Enziklopedyah shel Galuyyot* (1953ff.).
EH — *Even ha-Ezer.*
EHA — *Enziklopedyah la-Ḥafirot Arkheologiyyot be-Ereẓ Yisrael,* 2 vols. (1970).
EI — *Enzyklopaedie des Islams,* 4 vols. (1905–14). Supplement vol. (1938).
EIS — *Encyclopaedia of Islam,* 4 vols. (1913–36; repr. 1954–68).
EIS² — *Encyclopaedia of Islam, second edition (1960–2000).*
Eisenstein, Dinim — J.D. Eisenstein, *Oẓar Dinim u-Minhagim* (1917; several reprints).
Eisenstein, Yisrael — J.D. Eisenstein, *Oẓar Yisrael* (10 vols, 1907–13; repr. with several additions 1951).
EIV — *Enẓiklopedyah Ivrit* (1949ff.).
EJ — *Encyclopaedia Judaica* (German, A-L only), 10 vols. (1928–34).
EJC — *Enciclopedia Judaica Castellana,* 10 vols. (1948–51).
Elbogen, Century — I Elbogen, *A Century of Jewish Life* (1960²).
Elbogen, Gottesdienst — I Elbogen, *Der juedische Gottesdienst ...* (1931³, repr. 1962).
Elon, Mafte'aḥ — M. Elon (ed.), *Mafte'aḥ ha-She'elot ve-ha-Teshuvot ha-Rosh* (1965).
EM — *Enẓiklopedyah Mikra'it* (1950ff.).
I (or II) En. — I and II Enoch (Pseudepigrapha).
EncRel — *Encyclopedia of Religion*, 15 vols. (1987, 2005²).
Eph. — Epistle to the Ephesians (New Testament).
Ephros, Cant — G. Ephros, *Cantorial Anthology,* 5 vols. (1929–57).
Ep. Jer. — Epistle of Jeremy (Apocrypha).
Epstein, Amora'im — J N. Epstein, *Mevo'ot le-Sifrut ha-Amora'im* (1962).
Epstein, Marriage — L M. Epstein, *Marriage Laws in the Bible and the Talmud* (1942).
Epstein, Mishnah — J. N. Epstein, *Mavo le-Nusaḥ ha-Mishnah,* 2 vols. (1964²).
Epstein, Tanna'im — J. N. Epstein, *Mavo le-Sifruth ha-Tanna'im.* (1947).
ER — *Ecumenical Review.*
Er. — *Eruvin* (talmudic tractate).
ERE — *Encyclopaedia of Religion and Ethics,* 13 vols. (1908–26); reprinted.
ErIsr — *Eretz-Israel*, Israel Exploration Society.
I Esd. — I Esdras (Apocrypha) (= III Ezra).
II Esd. — II Esdras (Apocrypha) (= IV Ezra).
ESE — *Ephemeris fuer semitische Epigraphik*, ed. by M. Lidzbarski.
ESN — *Encyclopaedia Sefaradica Neerlandica,* 2 pts. (1949).
ESS — *Encyclopaedia of the Social Sciences,* 15 vols. (1930–35); reprinted in 8 vols. (1948–49).
Esth. — Esther (Bible).
Est. R. — *Esther Rabbah.*
ET — *Enẓiklopedyah Talmudit* (1947ff.).
Eusebius, Onom. — E. Klostermann (ed.), *Das Onomastikon* (1904), Greek with Hieronymus' Latin translation.
Ex. — Exodus (Bible).
Ex. R. — *Exodus Rabbah.*
Exs — Philo, *De Exsecrationibus.*
EẒD — *Enẓiklopeday shel ha-Ẓiyyonut ha-Datit* (1951ff.).
Ezek. — Ezekiel (Bible).
Ezra — Ezra (Bible).
III Ezra — III Ezra (Pseudepigrapha).
IV Ezra — IV Ezra (Pseudepigrapha).

Feliks, Ha-Ẓome'aḥ — *J. Feliks, Ha-Ẓome'aḥ ve-ha-Ḥai ba-Mishnah* (1983).
Finkelstein, Middle Ages — L. Finkelstein, *Jewish Self-Government in the Middle Ages* (1924).
Fischel, Islam — W.J. Fischel, *Jews in the Economic and Political Life of Mediaeval Islam* (1937; reprint with introduction "The Court Jew in the Islamic World," 1969).
FJW — *Fuehrer durch die juedische Gemeindeverwaltung und Wohlfahrtspflege in Deutschland* (1927/28).
Frankel, Mevo — Z. Frankel, *Mevo ha-Yerushalmi* (1870; reprint 1967).
Frankel, Mishnah — Z. Frankel, *Darkhei ha-Mishnah* (1959²; reprint 1959²).
Frazer, Folk-Lore — J.G. Frazer, *Folk-Lore in the Old Testament*, 3 vols. (1918–19).
Frey, Corpus — J.-B. Frey, *Corpus Inscriptionum Iudaicarum*, 2 vols. (1936–52).
Friedmann, Lebensbilder — A. Friedmann, *Lebensbilder beruehmter Kantoren*, 3 vols. (1918–27).
FRLT — *Forschungen zur Religion und Literatur des Alten und Neuen Testaments* (series) (1950ff.).
Frumkin-Rivlin — A.L. Frumkin and E. Rivlin, *Toledot Ḥakhmei Yerushalayim*, 3 vols. (1928–30), Supplement vol. (1930).
Fuenn, Keneset — S.J. Fuenn, *Keneset Yisrael,* 4 vols. (1887–90).
Fuerst, Bibliotheca — J. Fuerst, *Bibliotheca Judaica,* 2 vols. (1863; repr. 1960).
Fuerst, Karaeertum — J. Fuerst, *Geschichte des Karaeertums*, 3 vols. (1862–69).
Fug. — Philo, *De Fuga et Inventione.*

Gal. — Epistle to the Galatians (New Testament).
Galling, Reallexikon — K. Galling, *Biblisches Reallexikon* (1937).
Gardiner, Onomastica — A.H. Gardiner, *Ancient Egyptian Onomastica*, 3 vols. (1947).
Geiger, Mikra — A. Geiger, *Ha-Mikra ve-Targumav*, tr. by J.L. Baruch (1949).
Geiger, Urschrift — A. Geiger, *Urschrift und Uebersetzungen der Bibel* 1928²).
Gen. — Genesis (Bible).
Gen. R. — *Genesis Rabbah.*
Ger. — *Gerim* (post-talmudic tractate).
Germ Jud — M. Brann, I. Elbogen, A. Freimann, and H. Tykocinski (eds.), *Germania Judaica,* vol. 1 (1917; repr. 1934 and 1963); vol. 2, in 2 pts. (1917–68), ed. by Z. Avneri.

GHAT	*Goettinger Handkommentar zum Alten Testament* (1917–22).
Ghirondi-Neppi	M.S. Ghirondi and G.H. Neppi, *Toledot Gedolei Yisrael u-Ge'onei Italyah ... u-Ve'urim al Sefer Zekher Ẓaddikim li-Verakhah* . . .(1853), index in ZHB, 17 (1914), 171–83.
Gig.	Philo, *De Gigantibus.*
Ginzberg, Legends	L. Ginzberg, *Legends of the Jews,* 7 vols. (1909–38; and many reprints).
Git.	*Gittin* (talmudic tractate).
Glueck, Explorations	N. Gleuck, *Explorations in Eastern Palestine,* 2 vols. (1951).
Goell, Bibliography	Y. Goell, *Bibliography of Modern Hebrew Literature in English Translation* (1968).
Goodenough, Symbols	E.R. Goodenough, *Jewish Symbols in the Greco-Roman Period,* 13 vols. (1953–68).
Gordon, Textbook	C.H. Gordon, *Ugaritic Textbook* (1965; repr. 1967).
Graetz, Gesch	H. Graetz, *Geschichte der Juden* (last edition 1874–1908).
Graetz, Hist	H. Graetz, *History of the Jews*, 6 vols. (1891–1902).
Graetz, Psalmen	H. Graetz, *Kritischer Commentar zu den Psalmen*, 2 vols. in 1 (1882–83).
Graetz, Rabbinowitz	H. Graetz, *Divrei Yemei Yisrael*, tr. by S.P. Rabbinowitz. (1928 1929^{2}).
Gray, Names	G.B. Gray, *Studies in Hebrew Proper Names* (1896).
Gressmann, Bilder	H. Gressmann, *Altorientalische Bilder zum Alten Testament* (1927^{2}).
Gressmann, Texte	H. Gressmann, *Altorientalische Texte zum Alten Testament* (1926^{2}).
Gross, Gal Jud	H. Gross, *Gallia Judaica* (1897; repr. with add. 1969).
Grove, Dict	*Grove's Dictionary of Music and Musicians,* ed. by E. Blum 9 vols. (1954^{5}) and suppl. (1961^{5}).
Guedemann, Gesch Erz	M. Guedemann, *Geschichte des Erziehungswesens und der Cultur der abendlaendischen Juden*, 3 vols. (1880–88).
Guedemann, Quellenschr	M. Guedemann, *Quellenschriften zur Geschichte des Unterrichts und der Erziehung bei den deutschen Juden* (1873, 1891).
Guide	Maimonides, *Guide of the Perplexed.*
Gulak, Oẓar	A. Gulak, *Oẓar ha-Shetarot ha-Nehugim be-Yisrael* (1926).
Gulak, Yesodei	A. Gulak, *Yesodei ha-Mishpat ha-Ivri, Seder Dinei Mamonot be-Yisrael, al pi Mekorot ha-Talmud ve-ha-Posekim*, 4 vols. (1922; repr. 1967).
Guttmann, Mafte'aḥ	M. Guttmann, *Mafte'aḥ ha-Talmud*, 3 vols. (1906–30).
Guttmann, Philosophies	J. Guttmann, *Philosophies of Judaism* (1964).
Hab.	*Habakkuk* (Bible).
Ḥag.	*Ḥagigah* (talmudic tractate).
Haggai	*Haggai* (Bible).
Ḥal.	*Ḥallah* (talmudic tractate).
Halevy, Dorot	I. Halevy, *Dorot ha-Rishonim,* 6 vols. (1897–1939).
Halpern, Pinkas	I. Halpern (Halperin), *Pinkas Va'ad Arba Araẓot* (1945).
Hananel-Eškenazi	A. Hananel and Eškenazi (eds.), *Fontes Hebraici ad res oeconomicas socialesque terrarum balcanicarum saeculo XVI pertinentes*, 2 vols, (1958–60; in Bulgarian).
HB	*Hebraeische Bibliographie* (1858–82).
Heb.	Epistle to the Hebrews (New Testament).
Heilprin, Dorot	J. Heilprin (Heilperin), *Seder ha-Dorot,* 3 vols. (1882; repr. 1956).
Her.	Philo, *Quis Rerum Divinarum Heres.*
Hertz, Prayer	J.H. Hertz (ed.), *Authorised Daily Prayer Book* (rev. ed. 1948; repr. 1963).
Herzog, Instit	I. Herzog, *The Main Institutions of Jewish Law,* 2 vols. (1936–39; repr. 1967).
Herzog-Hauck	J.J. Herzog and A. Hauch (eds.), *Real encycklopaedie fuer protestantische Theologie* (1896–1913^{3}).
HḤY	*Ha-Ẓofeh le-Ḥokhmat Yisrael* (first four volumes under the title *Ha-Ẓofeh me-Ereẓ Hagar)* (1910/11–13).
Hirschberg, Afrikah	H.Z. Hirschberg, *Toledot ha-Yehudim be-Afrikah ha-Ẓofonit*, 2 vols. (1965).
HJ	*Historia Judaica* (1938–61).
HL	*Das Heilige Land* (1857ff.)
ḤM	*Ḥoshen Mishpat.*
Hommel, Ueberliefer.	F. Hommel, *Die altisraelitische Ueberlieferung in inschriftlicher Beleuchtung* (1897).
Hor.	*Horayot* (talmudic tractate).
Horodezky, Ḥasidut	S.A. Horodezky, *Ha-Ḥasidut ve-ha-Ḥasidim,* 4 vols. (1923).
Horowitz, Ereẓ Yis	I.W. Horowitz, *Ereẓ Yisrael u-Shekhenoteha* (1923).
Hos.	Hosea (Bible).
HTR	*Harvard Theological Review* (1908ff.).
HUCA	*Hebrew Union College Annual* (1904; 1924ff.)
Ḥul.	*Ḥullin* (talmudic tractate).
Husik, Philosophy	I. Husik, *History of Medieval Jewish Philosophy* (1932^{2}).
Hyman, Toledot	A. Hyman, *Toledot Tanna'im ve-Amora'im* (1910; repr. 1964).
Ibn Daud, Tradition	Abraham Ibn Daud, *Sefer ha-Qabbalah – The Book of Tradition,* ed. and tr. By G.D. Cohen (1967).
ICC	International Critical Commentary on the Holy Scriptures of the Old and New Testaments (series, 1908ff.).
IDB	*Interpreter's Dictionary of the Bible,* 4 vols. (1962).
Idelsohn, Litugy	A. Z. Idelsohn, *Jewish Liturgy and its Development* (1932; paperback repr. 1967)
Idelsohn, Melodien	A. Z. Idelsohn, *Hebraeisch-orientalischer Melodienschatz,* 10 vols. (1914 32).
Idelsohn, Music	A. Z. Idelsohn, *Jewish Music in its Historical Development* (1929; paperback repr. 1967).

IEJ	*Israel Exploration Journal* (1950ff.).
IESS	*International Encyclopedia of the Social Sciences* (various eds.).
IG	*Inscriptiones Graecae,* ed. by the Prussian Academy.
IGYB	*Israel Government Year Book* (1949/50ff.).
ILR	*Israel Law Review* (1966ff.).
IMIT	*Izraelita Magyar Irodalmi Társulat Évkönyv* (1895 1948).
IMT	International Military Tribunal.
INB	*Israel Numismatic Bulletin* (1962–63).
INJ	*Israel Numismatic Journal* (1963ff.).
Ios	Philo, *De Iosepho.*
Isa.	Isaiah (Bible).
ITHL	Institute for the Translation of Hebrew Literature.
IZBG	*Internationale Zeitschriftenschau fuer Bibelwissenschaft und Grenzgebiete* (1951ff.).
JA	*Journal asiatique* (1822ff.).
James	Epistle of James (New Testament).
JAOS	*Journal of the American Oriental Society* (c. 1850ff.)
Jastrow, Dict	M. Jastrow, *Dictionary of the Targumim, the Talmud Babli and Yerushalmi, and the Midrashic literature,* 2 vols. (1886 1902 and reprints).
JBA	*Jewish Book Annual* (19242ff.).
JBL	*Journal of Biblical Literature* (1881ff.).
JBR	*Journal of Bible and Religion* (1933ff.).
JC	*Jewish Chronicle* (1841ff.).
JCS	*Journal of Cuneiform Studies* (1947ff.).
JE	*Jewish Encyclopedia,* 12 vols. (1901–05 several reprints).
Jer.	Jeremiah (Bible).
Jeremias, Alte Test	A. Jeremias, *Das Alte Testament im Lichte des alten Orients* 1930^4).
JGGJČ	*Jahrbuch der Gesellschaft fuer Geschichte der Juden in der Čechoslovakischen Republik* (1929–38).
JHSEM	Jewish Historical Society of England, *Miscellanies* (1925ff.).
JHSET	Jewish Historical Society of England, *Transactions* (1893ff.).
JJGL	*Jahrbuch fuer juedische Geschichte und Literatur* (Berlin) (1898–1938).
JJLG	*Jahrbuch derr juedische-literarischen Gesellschaft* (Frankfurt) (1903–32).
JJS	*Journal of Jewish Studies* (1948ff.).
JJSO	*Jewish Journal of Sociology* (1959ff.).
JJV	*Jahrbuch fuer juedische Volkskunde* (1898–1924).
JL	*Juedisches Lexikon,* 5 vols. (1927–30).
JMES	*Journal of the Middle East Society* (1947ff.).
JNES	*Journal of Near Eastern Studies* (continuation of AJSLL) (1942ff.).
J.N.U.L.	Jewish National and University Library.
Job	Job (Bible).
Joel	Joel (Bible).
John	Gospel according to John (New Testament).
I, II and III John	Epistles of John (New Testament).
Jos., Ant	Josephus, *Jewish Antiquities* (Loeb Classics ed.).
Jos. Apion	Josephus, *Against Apion* (Loeb Classics ed.).
Jos., index	*Josephus Works,* Loeb Classics ed., index of names.
Jos., Life	Josephus, *Life* (ed. Loeb Classics).
Jos, Wars	Josephus, *The Jewish Wars* (Loeb Classics ed.).
Josh.	Joshua (Bible).
JPESB	Jewish Palestine Exploration Society Bulletin, see BJPES.
JPESJ	Jewish Palestine Exploration Society Journal – Eng. Title of the Hebrew periodical *Kovez ha-Ḥevrah ha-Ivrit la-Ḥakirat Erez Yisrael va-Attikoteha.*
JPOS	*Journal of the Palestine Oriental Society* (1920–48).
JPS	Jewish Publication Society of America, *The Torah* (1962, 1967^2); *The Holy Scriptures* (1917).
JQR	*Jewish Quarterly Review* (1889ff.).
JR	*Journal of Religion* (1921ff.).
JRAS	*Journal of the Royal Asiatic Society* (1838ff.).
JHR	*Journal of Religious History* (1960/61ff.).
JSOS	*Jewish Social Studies* (1939ff.).
JSS	*Jouranl of Semitic Studies* (1956ff.).
JTS	*Journal of Theological Studies* (1900ff.).
JTSA	Jewish Theological Seminary of America (also abbreviated as JTS).
Jub.	Jubilees (Pseudepigrapha).
Judg.	Judges (Bible).
Judith	Book of Judith (Apocrypha).
Juster, Juifs	J. Juster, *Les Juifs dans l'Empire Romain,* 2 vols. (1914).
JYB	*Jewish Year Book* (1896ff.).
JZWL	*Juedische Zeitschift fuer Wissenschaft und Leben* (1862–75).
Kal.	*Kallah* (post-talmudic tractate).
Kal. R.	*Kallah Rabbati* (post-talmudic tractate).
Katz, England	*The Jews in the History of England, 1485-1850 (1994).*
Kaufmann, Schriften	D. Kaufmann, *Gesammelte Schriften,* 3 vols. (1908 15).
Kaufmann Y., Religion	Y. Kaufmann, *The Religion of Israel* (1960), abridged tr. of his *Toledot.*
Kaufmann Y., Toledot	Y. Kaufmann, *Toledot ha-Emunah ha-Yisre'elit,* 4 vols. (1937 57).
KAWJ	*Korrespondenzblatt des Vereins zur Gruendung und Erhaltung der Akademie fuer die Wissenschaft des Judentums* (1920 30).
Kayserling, Bibl	M. Kayserling, *Biblioteca Española-Portugueza-Judaica* (1880; repr. 1961).
Kelim	*Kelim* (mishnaic tractate).
Ker.	*Keritot* (talmudic tractate).
Ket.	*Ketubbot* (talmudic tractate).

Kid.	*Kiddushim* (talmudic tractate).
Kil.	*Kilayim* (talmudic tractate).
Kin.	*Kinnim* (mishnaic tractate).
Kisch, Germany	G. Kisch, *Jews in Medieval Germany* (1949).
Kittel, Gesch	R. Kittel, *Geschichte des Volkes Israel,* 3 vols. (1922–28).
Klausner, Bayit Sheni	J. Klausner, *Historyah shel ha-Bayit ha-Sheni,* 5 vols. (1950/512).
Klausner, Sifrut	J. Klausner, *Historyah shel haSifrut ha-Ivrit ha-Ḥadashah,* 6 vols. (1952–582).
Klein, corpus	S. Klein (ed.), *Juedisch-palaestinisches Corpus Inscriptionum* (1920).
Koehler-Baumgartner	L. Koehler and W. Baumgartner, *Lexicon in Veteris Testamenti libros* (1953).
Kohut, Arukh	H.J.A. Kohut (ed.), *Sefer he-Arukh ha-Shalem,* by Nathan b. Jehiel of Rome, 8 vols. (1876–92; Supplement by S. Krauss et al., 1936; repr. 1955).
Krauss, Tal Arch	S. Krauss, *Talmudische Archaeologie,* 3 vols. (1910–12; repr. 1966).
Kressel, Leksikon	G. Kressel, *Leksikon ha-Sifrut ha-Ivrit ba-Dorot ha-Aḥaronim,* 2 vols. (1965–67).
KS	*Kirjath Sepher* (1923/4ff.).
Kut.	*Kuttim* (post-talmudic tractate).
LA	Studium Biblicum Franciscanum, *Liber Annuus* (1951ff.).
L.A.	Philo, *Legum allegoriae.*
Lachower, Sifrut	F. Lachower, *Toledot ha-Sifrut ha-Ivrit ha-Ḥadashah,* 4 vols. (1947–48; several reprints).
Lam.	Lamentations (Bible).
Lam. R.	*Lamentations Rabbah.*
Landshuth, Ammudei	L. Landshuth, *Ammudei ha-Avodah* (1857–62; repr. with index, 1965).
Legat.	Philo, *De Legatione ad Caium.*
Lehmann, Nova Bibl	R.P. Lehmann, *Nova Bibliotheca Anglo-Judaica* (1961).
Lev.	Leviticus (Bible).
Lev. R.	*Leviticus Rabbah.*
Levy, Antologia	I. Levy, *Antologia de liturgia judeo-española* (1965ff.).
Levy J., Chald Targ	J. Levy, *Chaldaeisches Woerterbuch ueber die Targumim,* 2 vols. (1967–68; repr. 1959).
Levy J., Nuehebr Tal	J. Levy, *Neuhebraeisches und chaldaeisches Woerterbuch ueber die Talmudim . . .,* 4 vols. (1875–89; repr. 1963).
Lewin, Oẓar	Lewin, *Oẓar ha-Ge'onim,* 12 vols. (1928–43).
Lewysohn, Zool	L. Lewysohn, *Zoologie des Talmuds* (1858).
Lidzbarski, Handbuch	M. Lidzbarski, *Handbuch der nordsemitischen Epigraphik,* 2 vols (1898).
Life	Josephus, *Life* (Loeb Classis ed.).
LNYL	*Leksikon fun der Nayer Yidisher Literatur* (1956ff.).
Loew, Flora	I. Loew, *Die Flora der Juden,* 4 vols. (1924 34; repr. 1967).
LSI	*Laws of the State of Israel* (1948ff.).
Luckenbill, Records	D.D. Luckenbill, *Ancient Records of Assyria and Babylonia,* 2 vols. (1926).
Luke	Gospel according to Luke (New Testament)
LXX	Septuagint (Greek translation of the Bible).
Ma'as.	*Ma'aserot* (talmudic tractate).
Ma'as. Sh.	*Ma'ase Sheni* (talmudic tractate).
I, II, III, and IVMacc.	Maccabees, I, II, III (Apocrypha), IV (Pseudepigrapha).
Maimonides, Guide	Maimonides, *Guide of the Perplexed.*
Maim., Yad	Maimonides, *Mishneh Torah (Yad Ḥazakah).*
Maisler, Untersuchungen	B. Maisler (Mazar), *Untersuchungen zur alten Geschichte und Ethnographie Syriens und Palaestinas,* 1 (1930).
Mak.	*Makkot* (talmudic tractate).
Makhsh.	*Makhshrin* (mishnaic tractate).
Mal.	Malachi (Bible).
Mann, Egypt	J. Mann, *Jews in Egypt in Palestine under the Fatimid Caliphs,* 2 vols. (1920–22).
Mann, Texts	J. Mann, *Texts and Studies,* 2 vols (1931–35).
Mansi	G.D. Mansi, *Sacrorum Conciliorum nova et amplissima collectio,* 53 vols. in 60 (1901–27; repr. 1960).
Margalioth, Gedolei	M. Margalioth, *Enẓiklopedyah le-Toledot Gedolei Yisrael,* 4 vols. (1946–50).
Margalioth, Ḥakhmei	M. Margalioth, *Enẓiklopedyah le-Ḥakhmei ha-Talmud ve-ha-Ge'onim,* 2 vols. (1945).
Margalioth, Cat	G. Margalioth, *Catalogue of the Hebrew and Samaritan Manuscripts in the British Museum,* 4 vols. (1899–1935).
Mark	Gospel according to Mark (New Testament).
Mart. Isa.	Martyrdom of Isaiah (Pseudepigrapha).
Mas.	Masorah.
Matt.	Gospel according to Matthew (New Testameant).
Mayer, Art	L.A. Mayer, *Bibliography of Jewish Art* (1967).
MB	*Wochenzeitung* (formerly *Mitteilungsblatt*) *des Irgun Olej Merkas Europa* (1933ff.).
MEAH	*Miscelánea de estudios drabes y hebraicos* (1952ff.).
Meg.	Megillah (talmudic tractate).
Meg. Ta'an.	*Megillat Ta'anit* (in HUCA, 8 9 (1931–32), 318–51).
Me'il	*Me'ilah* (mishnaic tractate).
MEJ	*Middle East Journal* (1947ff.).
Mehk.	*Mekhilta de-R. Ishmael.*
Mekh. SbY	*Mekhilta de-R. Simeon bar Yoḥai.*
Men.	*Menaḥot* (talmudic tractate).
MER	*Middle East Record* (1960ff.).
Meyer, Gesch	E. Meyer, *Geschichte des Alterums,* 5 vols. in 9 (1925–58).
Meyer, Ursp	E. Meyer, *Urspring und Anfaenge des Christentums* (1921).
Mez.	*Mezuzah* (post-talmudic tractate).
MGADJ	*Mitteilungen des Gesamtarchivs der deutschen Juden* (1909–12).
MGG	*Die Musik in Geschichte und Gegenwart,* 14 vols. (1949–68).

MGG^{2}	*Die Musik in Geschichte und Gegenwart, 2nd edition (1994)*
MGH	*Monumenta Germaniae Historica* (1826ff.).
MGJV	*Mitteilungen der Gesellschaft fuer juedische Volkskunde* (1898–1929); title varies, see also JJV.
MGWJ	*Monatsschrift fuer Geschichte und Wissenschaft des Judentums* (1851–1939).
MHJ	*Momumenta Hungariae Judaica,* 11 vols. (1903–67).
Michael, Or	H.Ḥ. Michael, *Or ha-Ḥayyim: Ḥakhmei Yisrael ve-Sifreihem,* ed. by S.Z. Ḥ. Halberstam and N. Ben-Menahem (1965^{2}).
Mid.	*Middot* (mishnaic tractate).
Mid. Ag.	*Midrash Aggadah.*
Mid. Hag.	*Midrash ha-Gadol.*
Mid. Job.	*Midrash Job.*
Mid. Jonah	*Midrash Jonah.*
Mid. Lek. Tov	*Midrash Lekaḥ Tov.*
Mid. Prov.	*Midrash Proverbs.*
Mid. Ps.	*Midrash Tehillim* (Eng tr. *The Midrash on Psalms* (JPS, 1959).
Mid. Sam.	*Midrash Samuel.*
Mid. Song	*Midrash Shir ha-Shirim.*
Mid. Tan.	*Midrash Tanna'im* on Deuteronomy.
Miége, Maroc	J.L. Miège, *Le Maroc et l'Europe,* 3 vols. (1961 62).
Mig.	Philo, *De Migratione Abrahami.*
Mik.	*Mikva'ot* (mishnaic tractate).
Milano, Bibliotheca	A. Milano, *Bibliotheca Historica Italo-Judaica* (1954); supplement for 1954–63 (1964); supplement for 1964–66 in RMI, 32 (1966).
Milano, Italia	A. Milano, *Storia degli Ebrei in Italia* (1963).
MIO	*Mitteilungen des Instituts fuer Orientforschung* 1953ff.).
Mish.	Mishnah.
MJ	*Le Monde Juif* (1946ff.).
MJC	see Neubauer, Chronicles.
MK	*Mo'ed Katan* (talmudic tractate).
MNDPV	*Mitteilungen und Nachrichten des deutschen Palaestinavereins* (1895–1912).
Mortara, Indice	M. Mortara, *Indice Alfabetico dei Rabbini e Scrittori Israeliti ... in Italia ...* (1886).
Mos	Philo, *De Vita Mosis.*
Moscati, Epig	S, Moscati, *Epigrafia ebaica antica* 1935–1950 (1951).
MT	Masoretic Text of the Bible.
Mueller, Musiker	[E.H. Mueller], *Deutisches Musiker-Lexikon* (1929)
Munk, Mélanges	S. Munk, *Mélanges de philosophie juive et arabe* (1859; repr. 1955).
Mut.	Philo, *De Mutatione Nominum.*
MWJ	*Magazin fuer die Wissenshaft des Judentums* (18745 93).
Nah.	Nahum (Bible).
Naz.	*Nazir* (talmudic tractate).
NDB	*Neue Deutsche Biographie* (1953ff.).
Ned.	*Nedarim* (talmudic tractate).
Neg.	*Nega'im* (mishnaic tractate).
Neh.	Nehemiah (Bible).
NG^{2}	*New Grove Dictionary of Music and Musicians* (2001).
Nuebauer, Cat	A. Neubauer, *Catalogue of the Hebrew Manuscripts in the Bodleian Library ...,* 2 vols. (1886–1906).
Neubauer, Chronicles	A. Neubauer, *Mediaeval Jewish Chronicles,* 2 vols. (Heb., 1887–95; repr. 1965), Eng. title of *Seder ha-Ḥakhamim ve-Korot ha-Yamim.*
Neubauer, Géogr	A. Neubauer, *La géographie du Talmud* (1868).
Neuman, Spain	A.A. Neuman, *The Jews in Spain, their Social, Political, and Cultural Life During the Middle Ages,* 2 vols. (1942).
Neusner, Babylonia	J. Neusner, *History of the Jews in Babylonia,* 5 vols. 1965–70), 2nd revised printing 1969ff.).
Nid.	*Niddah* (talmudic tractate).
Noah	Fragment of Book of Noah (Pseudepigrapha).
Noth, Hist Isr	M. Noth, *History of Israel* (1958).
Noth, Personennamen	M. Noth, *Die israelitischen Personennamen.* ... (1928).
Noth, Ueberlief	M. Noth, *Ueberlieferungsgeschichte des Pentateuchs* (1949).
Noth, Welt	M. Noth, *Die Welt des Alten Testaments* (1957^{3}).
Nowack, Lehrbuch	W. Nowack, *Lehrbuch der hebraeischen Archaeologie,* 2 vols (1894).
NT	New Testament.
Num.	Numbers (Bible).
Num R.	*Numbers Rabbah.*
Obad.	Obadiah (Bible).
ODNB online	*Oxford Dictionary of National Biography.*
OḤ	*Oraḥ Ḥayyim.*
Oho.	*Oholot* (mishnaic tractate).
Olmstead	H.T. Olmstead, *History of Palestine and Syria* (1931; repr. 1965).
OLZ	*Orientalistische Literaturzeitung* (1898ff.)
Onom.	Eusebius, *Onomasticon.*
Op.	Philo, *De Opificio Mundi.*
OPD	*Osef Piskei Din shel ha-Rabbanut ha-Rashit le-Ereẓ Yisrael, Bet ha-Din ha-Gadol le-Irurim* (1950).
Or.	*Orlah* (talmudic tractate).
Or. Sibyll.	Sibylline Oracles (Pseudepigrapha).
OS	*L'Orient Syrien* (1956ff.)
OTS	*Oudtestamentische Studien* (1942ff.).
PAAJR	*Proceedings of the American Academy for Jewish Research* (1930ff.)
Pap 4QS^{e}	A papyrus exemplar of IQS.
Par.	*Parah* (mishnaic tractate).
Pauly-Wissowa	A.F. Pauly, *Realencyklopaedie der klassichen Alertumswissenschaft,* ed. by G. Wissowa et al. (1864ff.)

PD	*Piskei Din shel Bet ha-Mishpat ha-Elyon le-Yisrael* (1948ff.)
PDR	*Piskei Din shel Battei ha-Din ha-Rabbaniyyim be-Yisrael.*
PdRE	*Pirkei de-R. Eliezer* (Eng. tr. 1916. (1965^{2}).
PdRK	*Pesikta de-Rav Kahana.*
Pe'ah	*Pe'ah* (talmudic tractate).
Peake, Commentary	A.J. Peake (ed.), *Commentary on the Bible* (1919; rev. 1962).
Pedersen, Israel	J. Pedersen, *Israel, Its Life and Culture,* 4 vols. in 2 (1926–40).
PEFQS	*Palestine Exploration Fund Quarterly Statement* (1869–1937; since 1938–PEQ).
PEQ	*Palestine Exploration Quarterly* (until 1937 PEFQS; after 1927 includes BBSAJ).
Perles, Beitaege	J. Perles, *Beitraege zur rabbinischen Sprachund Alterthumskunde* (1893).
Pes.	*Pesaḥim* (talmudic tractate).
Pesh.	Peshitta (Syriac translation of the Bible).
Pesher Hab.	Commentary to Habakkuk from Qumran; see 1Qp Hab.
I and II Pet.	Epistles of Peter (New Testament).
Pfeiffer, Introd	R.H. Pfeiffer, *Introduction to the Old Testament* (1948).
PG	J.P. Migne (ed.), *Patrologia Graeca,* 161 vols. (1866–86).
Phil.	Epistle to the Philippians (New Testament).
Philem.	Epistle to the Philemon (New Testament).
PIASH	*Proceedings of the Israel Academy of Sciences and Humanities* (1963/7ff.).
PJB	*Palaestinajahrbuch des deutschen evangelischen Institutes fuer Altertumswissenschaft,* Jerusalem (1905–1933).
PK	*Pinkas ha-Kehillot,* encyclopedia of Jewish communities, published in over 30 volumes by Yad Vashem from 1970 and arranged by countries, regions and localities. For 3-vol. English edition see Spector, *Jewish Life.*
PL	J.P. Migne (ed.), *Patrologia Latina* 221 vols. (1844–64).
Plant	Philo, *De Plantatione.*
PO	R. Graffin and F. Nau (eds.), *Patrologia Orientalis* (1903ff.)
Pool, Prayer	D. de Sola Pool, *Traditional Prayer Book for Sabbath and Festivals* (1960).
Post	Philo, *De Posteritate Caini.*
PR	*Pesikta Rabbati.*
Praem.	Philo, *De Praemiis et Poenis.*
Prawer, Ẓalbanim	J. Prawer, *Toledot Mamlekhet ha-Ẓalbanim be-Ereẓ Yisrael,* 2 vols. (1963).
Press, Ereẓ	I. Press, *Ereẓ-Yisrael, Enẓiklopedyah Topografit-Historit,* 4 vols. (1951–55).
Pritchard, Pictures	J.B. Pritchard (ed.), *Ancient Near East in Pictures* (1954, 1970).
Pritchard, Texts	J.B. Pritchard (ed.), *Ancient Near East Texts* ... (1970^{3}).
Pr. Man.	Prayer of Manasses (Apocrypha).
Prob.	Philo, *Quod Omnis Probus Liber Sit.*
Prov.	Proverbs (Bible).
PS	*Palestinsky Sbornik* (Russ. (1881 1916, 1954ff).
Ps.	Psalms (Bible).
PSBA	*Proceedings of the Society of Biblical Archaeology* (1878–1918).
Ps. of Sol	Psalms of Solomon (Pseudepigrapha).
IQ Apoc	The *Genesis Apocryphon* from Qumran, cave one, ed. by N. Avigad and Y. Yadin (1956).
6QD	*Damascus Document* or *Sefer Berit Dammesk* from Qumran, cave six, ed. by M. Baillet, in RB, 63 (1956), 513–23 (see also CD).
QDAP	*Quarterly of the Department of Antiquities in Palestine* (1932ff.).
4QDeut. 32	Manuscript of Deuteronomy 32 from Qumran, cave four (ed. by P.W. Skehan, in BASOR, 136 (1954), 12–15).
4QEx^{a}	Exodus manuscript in Jewish script from Qumran, cave four.
4QEx$^{\alpha}$	Exodus manuscript in Paleo-Hebrew script from Qumran, cave four (partially ed. by P.W. Skehan, in JBL, 74 (1955), 182–7).
4QFlor	*Florilegium,* a miscellany from Qumran, cave four (ed. by J.M. Allegro, in JBL, 75 (1956), 176–77 and 77 (1958), 350–54).).
QGJD	*Quellen zur Geschichte der Juden in Deutschland* 1888–98).
IQH	*Thanksgiving Psalms* of *Hodayot* from Qumran, cave one (ed. by E.L. Sukenik and N. Avigad, *Oẓar ha-Megillot ha-Genuzot* (1954).
IQIs^{a}	Scroll of Isaiah from Qumran, cave one (ed. by N. Burrows et al., *Dead Sea Scrolls* ..., 1 (1950).
IQIs^{b}	Scroll of Isaiah from Qumran, cave one (ed. E.L. Sukenik and N. Avigad, *Oẓar ha-Megillot ha-Genuzot* (1954).
IQM	The *War Scroll* or *Serekh ha-Milḥamah* (ed. by E.L. Sukenik and N. Avigad, *Oẓar ha-Megillot ha-Genuzot* (1954).
4QpNah	Commentary on Nahum from Qumran, cave four (partially ed. by J.M. Allegro, in JBL, 75 (1956), 89–95).
IQphyl	Phylacteries *(tefillin)* from Qumran, cave one (ed. by Y. Yadin, in *Eretz Israel,* 9 (1969), 60–85).
4Q Prayer of Nabonidus	A document from Qumran, cave four, belonging to a lost Daniel literature (ed. by J.T. Milik, in RB, 63 (1956), 407–15).
IQS	*Manual of Discipline* or *Serekh ha-Yaḥad* from Qumran, cave one (ed. by M. Burrows et al., *Dead Sea Scrolls* ..., 2, pt. 2 (1951).

IQS[a] The *Rule of the Congregation or Serekh ha-Edah* from Qumran, cave one (ed. by Burrows et al., *Dead Sea Scrolls* ..., 1 (1950), under the abbreviation IQ28a).
IQS[b] *Blessings* or *Divrei Berakhot* from Qumran, cave one (ed. by Burrows et al., *Dead Sea Scrolls* ..., 1 (1950), under the abbreviation IQ28b).
4QSam[a] Manuscript of I and II Samuel from Qumran, cave four (partially ed. by F.M. Cross, in BASOR, 132 (1953), 15–26).
4QSam[b] Manuscript of I and II Samuel from Qumran, cave four (partially ed. by F.M. Cross, in JBL, 74 (1955), 147–72).
4QTestimonia Sheet of Testimony from Qumran, cave four (ed. by J.M. Allegro, in JBL, 75 (1956), 174–87).).
4QT.Levi *Testament of Levi* from Qumran, cave four (partially ed. by J.T. Milik, in RB, 62 (1955), 398–406).

Rabinovitz, Dik Sof See Dik Sof.
RB *Revue biblique* (1892ff.)
RBI *Recherches bibliques* (1954ff.)
RCB *Revista de cultura biblica* (São Paulo) (1957ff.)
Régné, Cat J. Régné, *Catalogue des actes . . . des rois d'Aragon, concernant les Juifs* (1213–1327), in: REJ, vols. 60 70, 73, 75–78 (1910–24).
Reinach, Textes T. Reinach, *Textes d'auteurs Grecs et Romains relatifs au Judaïsme* (1895; repr. 1963).
REJ *Revue des études juives* (1880ff.).
Rejzen, Leksikon Z. Rejzen, *Leksikon fun der Yidisher Literature,* 4 vols. (1927–29).
Renan, Ecrivains A. Neubauer and E. Renan, *Les écrivains juifs français* ... (1893).
Renan, Rabbins A. Neubauer and E. Renan, *Les rabbins français* (1877).
RES *Revue des étude sémitiques et Babyloniaca* (1934–45).
Rev. Revelation (New Testament).
RGG[3] *Die Religion in Geschichte und Gegenwart,* 7 vols. (1957–65[3]).
RH *Rosh Ha-Shanah* (talmudic tractate).
RHJE *Revue de l'histoire juive en Egypte* (1947ff.).
RHMH *Revue d'histoire de la médecine hébraïque* (1948ff.).
RHPR *Revue d'histoire et de philosophie religieuses* (1921ff.).
RHR *Revue d'histoire des religions* (1880ff.).
RI *Rivista Israelitica* (1904–12).
Riemann-Einstein *Hugo Riemanns Musiklexikon,* ed. by A. Einstein (1929[11]).
Riemann-Gurlitt *Hugo Riemanns Musiklexikon,* ed. by W. Gurlitt (1959–67[12]), Personenteil.
Rigg-Jenkinson, Exchequer J.M. Rigg, H. Jenkinson and H.G. Richardson (eds.), *Calendar of the Pleas Rolls of the Exchequer of the Jews,* 4 vols. (1905–1970); cf. in each instance also J.M. Rigg (ed.), *Select Pleas* ... (1902).
RMI *Rassegna Mensile di Israel* (1925ff.).
Rom. Epistle to the Romans (New Testament).
Rosanes, Togarmah S.A. Rosanes, *Divrei Yemei Yisrael be-Togarmah,* 6 vols. (1907–45), and in 3 vols. (1930–38[2]).
Rosenbloom, Biogr Dict J.R. Rosenbloom, *Biographical Dictionary of Early American Jews* (1960).
Roth, Art C. Roth, *Jewish Art* (1961).
Roth, Dark Ages C. Roth (ed.), *World History of the Jewish People,* second series, vol. 2, *Dark Ages* (1966).
Roth, England C. Roth, *History of the Jews in England* (1964[3]).
Roth, Italy C. Roth, *History of the Jews in Italy* (1946).
Roth, Mag Bibl C. Roth, *Magna Bibliotheca Anglo-Judaica* (1937).
Roth, Marranos C. Roth, *History of the Marranos* (2nd rev. ed 1959; reprint 1966).
Rowley, Old Test H.H. Rowley, *Old Testament and Modern Study* (1951; repr. 1961).
RS *Revue sémitiques d'épigraphie et d'histoire ancienne* (1893/94ff.).
RSO *Rivista degli studi orientali* (1907ff.).
RSV Revised Standard Version of the Bible.
Rubinstein, Australia I *H.L. Rubinstein, The Jews in Australia, A Thematic History, Vol. I (1991).*
Rubinstein, Australia II *W.D. Rubinstein, The Jews in Australia, A Thematic History, Vol. II (1991).*
Ruth Ruth (Bible).
Ruth R. *Ruth Rabbah.*
RV Revised Version of the Bible.

Sac. Philo, *De Sacrificiis Abelis et Caini.*
Salfeld, Martyrol S. Salfeld, *Martyrologium des Nuernberger Memorbuches* (1898).
I and II Sam. Samuel, book I and II (Bible).
Sanh. *Sanhedrin* (talmudic tractate).
SBA Society of Biblical Archaeology.
SBB *Studies in Bibliography and Booklore* (1953ff.).
SBE *Semana Biblica Española.*
SBT *Studies in Biblical Theology* (1951ff.).
SBU *Svenkst Bibliskt Uppslogsvesk,* 2 vols. (1962–63[2]).
Schirmann, Italyah J.Ḥ. Schirmann, *Ha-Shirah ha-Ivrit be-Italyah* (1934).
Schirmann, Sefarad J.Ḥ. Schirmann, *Ha-Shirah ha-Ivrit bi-Sefarad u-vi-Provence,* 2 vols. (1954–56).
Scholem, Mysticism G. Scholem, *Major Trends in Jewish Mysticism* (rev. ed. 1946; paperback ed. with additional bibliography 1961).
Scholem, Shabbetai Ẓevi G. Scholem, *Shabbetai Ẓevi ve-ha-Tenu'ah ha-Shabbeta'it bi-Ymei Ḥayyav,* 2 vols. (1967).
Schrader, Keilinschr E. Schrader, *Keilinschriften und das Alte Testament* (1903[3]).
Schuerer, Gesch E. Schuerer, *Geschichte des juedischen Volkes im Zeitalter Jesu Christi,* 3 vols. and index-vol. (1901–11[4]).

Schuerer, Hist	E. Schuerer, *History of the Jewish People in the Time of Jesus*, ed. by N.N. Glatzer, abridged paperback edition (1961).
Set. T.	*Sefer Torah* (post-talmudic tractate).
Sem.	*Semaḥot* (post-talmudic tractate).
Sendrey, Music	A. Sendrey, *Bibliography of Jewish Music* (1951).
SER	*Seder Eliyahu Rabbah.*
SEZ	*Seder Eliyahu Zuta.*
Shab	*Shabbat* (talmudic tractate).
Sh. Ar.	J. Caro Shulḥan Arukh. OḤ – *Oraḥ Ḥayyim* YD – *Yoreh De'ah* EH – *Even ha-Ezer* ḤM – *Ḥoshen Mishpat.*
Shek.	*Shekalim* (talmudic tractate).
Shev.	*Shevi'it* (talmudic tractate).
Shevu.	*Shevu'ot* (talmudic tractate).
Shunami, Bibl	S. Shunami, *Bibliography of Jewish Bibliographies* (1965²).
Sif.	*Sifrei Deuteronomy.*
Sif. Num.	*Sifrei Numbers.*
Sifra	*Sifra* on Leviticus.
Sif. Zut.	*Sifrei Zuta.*
SIHM	Sources inédites de l'histoire du Maroc (series).
Silverman, Prayer	M. Silverman (ed.), *Sabbath and Festival Prayer Book* (1946).
Singer, Prayer	S. Singer *Authorised Daily Prayer Book* (1943¹⁷).
Sob.	Philo, *De Sobrietate.*
Sof.	*Soferim* (post-talmudic tractate).
Som.	Philo, *De Somniis.*
Song	Song of Songs (Bible).
Song. Ch.	Song of the Three Children (Apocrypha).
Song R.	*Song of Songs Rabbah.*
SOR	*Seder Olam Rabbah.*
Sot.	*Sotah* (talmudic tractate).
SOZ	*Seder Olam Zuta.*
Spec.	Philo, *De Specialibus Legibus.*
Spector, Jewish Life	*S. Spector (ed.), Encyclopedia of Jewish Life Before and After the Holocaust (2001).*
Steinschneider, Arab lit	M. Steinschneider, *Die arabische Literatur der Juden* (1902).
Steinschneider, Cat Bod	M. Steinschneider, *Catalogus Librorum Hebraeorum in Bibliotheca Bodleiana*, 3 vols. (1852–60; reprints 1931 and 1964).
Steinschneider, Hanbuch	M. Steinschneider, *Bibliographisches Handbuch ueber die . . . Literatur fuer hebraeische Sprachkunde* (1859; repr. with additions 1937).
Steinschneider, Uebersetzungen	M. Steinschneider, *Die hebraeischen Uebersetzungen des Mittelalters* (1893).
Stern, Americans	M.H. Stern, *Americans of Jewish Descent* (1960).
van Straalen, Cat	S. van Straalen, *Catalogue of Hebrew Books in the British Museum Acquired During the Years 1868–1892* (1894).
Suárez Fernández, Docmentos	L. Suárez Fernández, *Documentos acerca de la expulsion de los Judios de España* (1964).
Suk.	*Sukkah* (talmudic tractate).
Sus.	Susanna (Apocrypha).
SY	*Sefer Yeẓirah.*
Sym.	Symmachus' Greek translation of the Bible.
SZNG	*Studien zur neueren Geschichte.*
Ta'an.	*Ta'anit* (talmudic tractate).
Tam.	*Tamid* (mishnaic tractate).
Tanḥ.	*Tanḥuma.*
Tanḥ. B.	*Tanḥuma.* Buber ed (1885).
Targ. Jon	Targum Jonathan (Aramaic version of the Prophets).
Targ. Onk.	Targum Onkelos (Aramaic version of the Pentateuch).
Targ. Yer.	Targum Yerushalmi.
TB	Babylonian Talmud or Talmud Bavli.
Tcherikover, Corpus	V. Tcherikover, A. Fuks, and M. Stern, *Corpus Papyrorum Judaicorum*, 3 vols. (1957–60).
Tef.	*Tefillin* (post-talmudic tractate).
Tem.	*Temurah* (mishnaic tractate).
Ter.	*Terumah* (talmudic tractate).
Test. Patr.	Testament of the Twelve Patriarchs (Pseudepigrapha). Ash. – Asher Ben. – Benjamin Dan – Dan Gad – Gad Iss. – Issachar Joseph – Joseph Judah – Judah Levi – Levi Naph. – Naphtali Reu. – Reuben Sim. – Simeon Zeb. – Zebulun.
I and II	Epistle to the Thessalonians (New Testament).
Thieme-Becker	U. Thieme and F. Becker (eds.), *Allgemeines Lexikon der bildenden Kuenstler von der Antike bis zur Gegenwart*, 37 vols. (1907–50).
Tidhar	D. Tidhar (ed.), *Enẓiklopedyah la-Ḥalutẓei ha-Yishuv u-Vonav* (1947ff.).
I and II Timothy	Epistles to Timothy (New Testament).
Tit.	Epistle to Titus (New Testament).
TJ	Jerusalem Talmud or Talmud Yerushalmi.
Tob.	Tobit (Apocrypha).
Toh.	*Tohorot* (mishnaic tractate).
Torczyner, Bundeslade	H. Torczyner, *Die Bundeslade und die Anfaenge der Religion Israels* (1930³).
Tos.	*Tosafot.*
Tosef.	Tosefta.
Tristram, Nat Hist	H.B. Tristram, *Natural History of the Bible* (1877⁵).
Tristram, Survey	Palestine Exploration Fund, *Survey of Western Palestine*, vol. 4 (1884) = *Fauna and Flora* by H.B. Tristram.
TS	*Terra Santa* (1943ff.).

TSBA	*Transactions of the Society of Biblical Archaeology* (1872–93).
TY	*Tevul Yom* (mishnaic tractate).
UBSB	United Bible Society, *Bulletin.*
UJE	*Universal Jewish Encyclopedia*, 10 vols. (1939–43).
Uk.	*Ukẓin* (mishnaic tractate).
Urbach, Tosafot	E.E. Urbach, *Ba'alei ha-Tosafot* (1957^2).
de Vaux, Anc Isr	R. de Vaux, *Ancient Israel: its Life and Institutions* (1961; paperback 1965).
de Vaux, Instit	R. de Vaux, *Institutions de l'Ancien Testament,* 2 vols. (1958 60).
Virt.	Philo, *De Virtutibus.*
Vogelstein, Chronology	M. Volgelstein, *Biblical Chronology (1944).*
Vogelstein-Rieger	H. Vogelstein and P. Rieger, *Geschichte der Juden in Rom,* 2 vols. (1895–96).
VT	*Vetus Testamentum* (1951ff.).
VTS	*Vetus Testamentum* Supplements (1953ff.).
Vulg.	Vulgate (Latin translation of the Bible).
Wars	Josephus, *The Jewish Wars.*
Watzinger, Denkmaeler	K. Watzinger, *Denkmaeler Palaestinas,* 2 vols. (1933–35).
Waxman, Literature	M. Waxman, *History of Jewish Literature,* 5 vols. (1960^2).
Weiss, Dor	I.H. Weiss, *Dor, Dor ve-Doreshav,* 5 vols. (1904^4).
Wellhausen, Proleg	J. Wellhausen, *Prolegomena zur Geschichte Israels* (1927^6).
WI	*Die Welt des Islams* (1913ff.).
Winniger, Biog	S. Wininger, *Grosse juedische National-Biographie ...,* 7 vols. (1925–36).
Wisd.	Wisdom of Solomon (Apocrypha)
WLB	*Wiener Library Bulletin* (1958ff.).
Wolf, Bibliotheca	J.C. Wolf, *Bibliotheca Hebraea*, 4 vols. (1715–33).
Wright, Bible	G.E. Wright, *Westminster Historical Atlas to the Bible* (1945).
Wright, Atlas	G.E. Wright, *The Bible and the Ancient Near East* (1961).
WWWJ	*Who's Who in the World Jewry* (New York, 1955, 1965^2).
WZJT	*Wissenschaftliche Zeitschrift fuer juedische Theologie* (1835–37).
WZKM	*Wiener Zeitschrift fuer die Kunde des Morgenlandes* (1887ff.).
Yaari, Sheluḥei	A. Yaari, *Sheluḥei Ereẓ Yisrael* (1951).
Yad	Maimonides, *Mishneh Torah (Yad Ḥazakah).*
Yad	*Yadayim* (mishnaic tractate).
Yal.	*Yalkut Shimoni.*
Yal. Mak.	*Yalkut Makhiri.*
Yal. Reub.	*Yalkut Reubeni.*
YD	*Yoreh De'ah.*
YE	*Yevreyskaya Entsiklopediya,* 14 vols. (c. 1910).
Yev.	*Yevamot* (talmudic tractate).
YIVOA	*YIVO Annual of Jewish Social Studies* (1946ff.).
YLBI	*Year Book of the Leo Baeck Institute* (1956ff.).
YMḤEY	See BJPES.
YMḤSI	*Yedi'ot ha-Makhon le-Ḥeker ha-Shirah ha-Ivrit* (1935/36ff.).
YMMY	*Yedi'ot ha-Makhon le-Madda'ei ha-Yahadut* (1924/25ff.).
Yoma	*Yoma* (talmudic tractate).
ZA	*Zeitschrift fuer Assyriologie* (1886/87ff.).
Zav.	*Zavim* (mishnaic tractate).
ZAW	*Zeitschrift fuer die alttestamentliche Wissenschaft und die Kunde des nachbiblishchen Judentums* (1881ff.).
ZAWB	*Beihefte* (supplements) to ZAW.
ZDMG	*Zeitschrift der Deutschen Morgenlaendischen Gesellschaft* (1846ff.).
ZDPV	*Zeitschrift des Deutschen Palaestina-Vereins* (1878–1949; from 1949 = BBLA).
Zech.	Zechariah (Bible).
Zedner, Cat	J. Zedner, *Catalogue of Hebrew Books in the Library of the British Museum* (1867; repr. 1964).
Zeitlin, Bibliotheca	W. Zeitlin, *Bibliotheca Hebraica Post-Mendelssohniana* (1891–95).
Zeph.	Zephaniah (Bible).
Zev.	*Zevaḥim* (talmudic tractate).
ZGGJT	*Zeitschrift der Gesellschaft fuer die Geschichte der Juden in der Tschechoslowakei* (1930–38).
ZGJD	*Zeitschrift fuer die Geschichte der Juden in Deutschland* (1887–92).
ZHB	*Zeitschrift fuer hebraeische Bibliographie* (1896–1920).
Zinberg, Sifrut	I. Zinberg, *Toledot Sifrut Yisrael,* 6 vols. (1955–60).
Ẓiẓ.	*Ẓiẓit* (post-talmudic tractate).
ZNW	*Zeitschrift fuer die neutestamentliche Wissenschaft* (1901ff.).
ZS	*Zeitschrift fuer Semitistik und verwandte Gebiete* (1922ff.).
Zunz, Gesch	L. Zunz, *Zur Geschichte und Literatur* (1845).
Zunz, Gesch	L. Zunz, *Literaturgeschichte der synagogalen Poesie* (1865; Supplement, 1867; repr. 1966).
Zunz, Poesie	L. Zunz, *Synogogale Posie des Mittelalters,* ed. by Freimann (1920^2; repr. 1967).
Zunz, Ritus	L. Zunz, *Ritus des synagogalen Gottesdienstes* (1859; repr. 1967).
Zunz, Schr	L. Zunz, *Gesammelte Schriften,* 3 vols. (1875–76).
Zunz, Vortraege	L. Zunz, *Gottesdienstliche vortraege der Juden ...* 1892^2; repr. 1966).
Zunz-Albeck, Derashot	L. Zunz, *Ha-Derashot be-Yisrael*, Heb. Tr. of Zunz Vortraege by H. Albeck (1954^2).

TRANSLITERATION RULES

HEBREW AND SEMITIC LANGUAGES:

	General	*Scientific*
א	not transliterated[1]	ʾ
בּ	b	b
ב	v	v, ḇ
גּ	g	g
ג		ḡ
דּ	d	d
ד		ḏ
ה	h	h
ו	v – when not a vowel	w
ז	z	z
ח	ḥ	ḥ
ט	t	ṭ, t
י	y – when vowel and at end of words – i	y
כּ	k	k
כ, ך	kh	kh, ḵ
ל	l	ḻ
מ, ם	m	m
נ, ן	n	n
ס	s	s
ע	not transliterated[1]	ʿ
פּ	p	p
פ, ף	f	p, f, ph
צ, ץ	ẓ	ṣ, ẓ
ק	k	q, k
ר	r	r
שׁ	sh[2]	š
שׂ	s	ś, s
תּ	t	t
ת		ṯ
ג׳	dzh, J	ğ
ז׳	zh, J	ž
צ׳	ch	č
◌ָ		å, o, ǒ (short) â, ā (long)
◌ַ	a	a
◌ֲ		a, ^{a}
◌ֵ		e, ẹ, ē
◌ֶ	e	æ, ä, ę
◌ֱ		œ, ĕ, ^{e}
◌ְ	only *sheva na* is transliterated	ə, ĕ, e; only *sheva na* transliterated
◌ִ ◌ִי	i	i
◌ֹ וֹ	o	o, o, o
◌ֻ וּ	u	u, ŭ û, ū
◌ֵי	ei; biblical e	
‡		reconstructed forms of words

1. The letters א and ע are not transliterated.
   An apostrophe (') between vowels indicates that they do not form a diphthong and are to be pronounced separately.
2. *Dagesh ḥazak* (forte) is indicated by doubling of the letter, except for the letter שׁ.
3. Names. Biblical names and biblical place names are rendered according to the Bible translation of the Jewish Publication Society of America. Post-biblical Hebrew names are transliterated; contemporary names are transliterated or rendered as used by the person. Place names are transliterated or rendered by the accepted spelling. Names and some words with an accepted English form are usually not transliterated.

YIDDISH

א	not transliterated
אַ	a
אָ	o
בּ	b
בֿ	v
ג	g
ד	d
ה	h
ו, וּ	u
וו	v
וי	oy
ז	z
זש	zh
ח	kh
ט	t
טש	tsh, ch
י	(consonant) y (vowel) i
יִ	i
יי	ey
ײַ	ay
כּ	k
כ, ך	kh
ל	l
מ, ם	m
נ, ן	n
ס	s
ע	e
פּ	p
פֿ, ף	f
צ, ץ	ts
ק	k
ר	r
שׁ	sh
שׂ	s
תּ	t
ת	s

1. Yiddish transliteration rendered according to U. Weinreich's Modern *English-Yiddish Yiddish-English* Dictionary.
2. Hebrew words in Yiddish are usually transliterated according to standard Yiddish pronunciation, e.g., חזנות = *khazones*.

LADINO

Ladino and Judeo-Spanish words written in Hebrew characters are transliterated phonetically, following the General Rules of Hebrew transliteration (see above) whenever the accepted spelling in Latin characters could not be ascertained.

ARABIC

ء ا	a[1]	ض	ḍ
ب	b	ط	ṭ
ت	t	ظ	ẓ
ث	th	ع	c
ج	j	غ	gh
ح	ḥ	ف	f
خ	kh	ق	q
د	d	ك	k
ذ	dh	ل	l
ر	r	م	m
ز	z	ن	n
س	s	ه	h
ش	sh	و	w
ص	ṣ	ي	y
ـَ	a	ـَا ى	ā
ـِ	i	ـِي	ī
ـُ	u	ـُو	ū
ـَو	aw	ـِيّ	iyy[2]
ـَي	ay	ـُوّ	uww[2]

1. not indicated when initial
2. see note (f)

a) The EJ follows the *Columbia Lippincott Gazetteer* and the *Times Atlas* in transliteration of Arabic place names. Sites that appear in neither are transliterated according to the table above, and subject to the following notes.

b) The EJ follows the *Columbia Encyclopedia* in transliteration of Arabic names. Personal names that do not therein appear are transliterated according to the table above and subject to the following notes (e.g., Ali rather than ʿAlī, Suleiman rather than Sulayman).

c) The EJ follows the *Webster's Third International Dictionary, Unabridged* in transliteration of Arabic terms that have been integrated into the English language.

d) The term "Abu" will thus appear, usually in disregard of inflection.

e) Nunnation (end vowels, *tanwīn*) are dropped in transliteration.

f) Gemination (*tashdīd*) is indicated by the doubling of the geminated letter, unless an end letter, in which case the gemination is dropped.

g) The definitive article *al-* will always be thus transliterated, unless subject to one of the modifying notes (e.g., El-Arish rather than al-ʿArīsh; modification according to note (a)).

h) The Arabic transliteration disregards the Sun Letters (the antero-palatals (*al-Ḥurūf al-Shamsiyya*).

i) The *tā-marbūṭa* (o) is omitted in transliteration, unless in construct-stage (e.g., *Khirba* but *Khirbat Mishmish*).

These modifying notes may lead to various inconsistencies in the Arabic transliteration, but this policy has deliberately been adopted to gain smoother reading of Arabic terms and names.

GREEK

Ancient Greek	*Modern Greek*	*Greek Letters*
a	a	*Α; α; ᾳ*
b	v	*Β; β*
g	gh; g	*Γ; γ*
d	dh	*Δ; δ*
e	e	*Ε; ε*
z	z	*Ζ; ζ*
e; e	i	*Η; η; ῃ*
th	th	*Θ; θ*
i	i	*Ι; ι*
k	k; ky	*Κ; κ*
l	l	*Λ; λ*
m	m	*Μ; μ*
n	n	*Ν; ν*
x	x	*Ξ; ξ*
o	o	*Ο; ο*
p	p	*Π; π*
r; rh	r	*Ρ; ρ; ῥ*
s	s	*Σ; σ; ς*
t	t	*Τ; τ*
u; y	i	*Υ; υ*
ph	f	*Φ; φ*
ch	kh	*Χ; χ*
ps	ps	*Ψ; ψ*
o; ō	o	*Ω; ω; ῳ*
ai	e	*αι*
ei	i	*ει*
oi	i	*οι*
ui	i	*υι*
ou	ou	*ου*
eu	ev	*ευ*
eu; ēu	iv	*ηυ*
–	j	*τζ*
nt	d; nd	*ντ*
mp	b; mb	*μπ*
ngk	g	*γκ*
ng	ng	*γγ*
h	–	‘
–	–	’
w	–	*Ϝ*

RUSSIAN

А	A
Б	B
В	V
Г	G
Д	D
Е	E, Ye[1]
Ё	Yo, O[2]
Ж	Zh
З	Z
И	I
Й	Y[3]
К	K
Л	L
М	M
Н	N
О	O
П	P
Р	R
С	S
Т	T
У	U
Ф	F
Х	Kh
Ц	Ts
Ч	Ch
Ш	Sh
Щ	Shch
Ъ	omitted; see note [1]
Ы	Y
Ь	omitted; see note [1]
Э	E
Ю	Yu
Я	Ya

1. Ye at the beginning of a word; after all vowels except ***Ы***; and after ***Ъ*** and ***Ь***.
2. O after ***Ч***, ***Ш*** and ***Щ***.
3. Omitted after ***Ы***, and in names of people after ***И***.

A. Many first names have an accepted English or quasi-English form which has been preferred to transliteration.
B. Place names have been given according to the *Columbia Lippincott Gazeteer*.
C. Pre-revolutionary spelling has been ignored.
D. Other languages using the Cyrillic alphabet (e.g., Bulgarian, Ukrainian), inasmuch as they appear, have been phonetically transliterated in conformity with the principles of this table.

GLOSSARY

Asterisked terms have separate entries in the Encyclopaedia.

Actions Committee, early name of the Zionist General Council, the supreme institution of the World Zionist Organization in the interim between Congresses. The Zionist Executive's name was then the "Small Actions Committee."

*__Adar__, twelfth month of the Jewish religious year, sixth of the civil, approximating to February–March.

*__Aggadah__, name given to those sections of Talmud and Midrash containing homiletic expositions of the Bible, stories, legends, folklore, anecdotes, or maxims. In contradistinction to **halakhah*.

*__Agunah__, woman unable to remarry according to Jewish law, because of desertion by her husband or inability to accept presumption of death.

*__Aharonim__, later rabbinic authorities. In contradistinction to **rishonim* ("early ones").

Ahavah, liturgical poem inserted in the second benediction of the morning prayer *(*Ahavah Rabbah)* of the festivals and/or special Sabbaths.

Aktion (Ger.), operation involving the mass assembly, deportation, and murder of Jews by the Nazis during the *Holocaust.

*__Aliyah__, (1) being called to Reading of the Law in synagogue; (2) immigration to Ereẓ Israel; (3) one of the waves of immigration to Ereẓ Israel from the early 1880s.

*__Amidah__, main prayer recited at all services; also known as *Shemoneh Esreh* and *Tefillah*.

*__Amora__ (pl. **amoraim**), title given to the Jewish scholars in Ereẓ Israel and Babylonia in the third to sixth centuries who were responsible for the **Gemara*.

Aravah, the *willow; one of the *Four Species used on *Sukkot ("festival of Tabernacles") together with the **etrog, hadas*, and **lulav*.

*__Arvit__, evening prayer.

Asarah be-Tevet, fast on the 10th of Tevet commemorating the commencement of the siege of Jerusalem by Nebuchadnezzar.

Asefat ha-Nivḥarim, representative assembly elected by Jews in Palestine during the period of the British Mandate (1920–48).

*__Ashkenaz__, name applied generally in medieval rabbinical literature to Germany.

*__Ashkenazi__ (pl. **Ashkenazim**), German or West-, Central-, or East-European Jew(s), as contrasted with *Sephardi(m).

*__Av__, fifth month of the Jewish religious year, eleventh of the civil, approximating to July–August.

*__Av bet din__, vice president of the supreme court (*bet din ha-gadol*) in Jerusalem during the Second Temple period; later, title given to communal rabbis as heads of the religious courts (see **bet din*).

*__Badḥan__, jester, particularly at traditional Jewish weddings in Eastern Europe.

*__Bakkashah__ (Heb. "supplication"), type of petitionary prayer, mainly recited in the Sephardi rite on Rosh Ha-Shanah and the Day of Atonement.

Bar, "son of ... "; frequently appearing in personal names.

*__Baraita__ (pl. **beraitot**), statement of **tanna* not found in *Mishnah.

*__Bar mitzvah__, ceremony marking the initiation of a boy at the age of 13 into the Jewish religious community.

Ben, "son of ... ", frequently appearing in personal names.

Berakhah (pl. **berakhot**), *benediction, blessing; formula of praise and thanksgiving.

*__Bet din__ (pl. **battei din**), rabbinic court of law.

*__Bet ha-midrash__, school for higher rabbinic learning; often attached to or serving as a synagogue.

*__Bilu__, first modern movement for pioneering and agricultural settlement in Ereẓ Israel, founded in 1882 at Kharkov, Russia.

*__Bund__, Jewish socialist party founded in Vilna in 1897, supporting Jewish national rights; Yiddishist, and anti-Zionist.

Cohen (pl. **Cohanim**), see Kohen.

*__Conservative Judaism__, trend in Judaism developed in the United States in the 20th century which, while opposing extreme changes in traditional observances, permits certain modifications of *halakhah* in response to the changing needs of the Jewish people.

*__Consistory__ (Fr. *consistoire*), governing body of a Jewish communal district in France and certain other countries.

*__Converso(s)__, term applied in Spain and Portugal to converted Jew(s), and sometimes more loosely to their descendants.

*__Crypto-Jew__, term applied to a person who although observing outwardly Christianity (or some other religion) was at heart a Jew and maintained Jewish observances as far as possible (see Converso; Marrano; Neofiti; New Christian; Jadīd al-Islām).

*__Dayyan__, member of rabbinic court.

Decisor, equivalent to the Hebrew *posek* (pl. **posekim*), the rabbi who gives the decision (*halakhah*) in Jewish law or practice.

*__Devekut__, "devotion"; attachment or adhesion to God; communion with God.

*__Diaspora__, Jews living in the "dispersion" outside Ereẓ Israel; area of Jewish settlement outside Ereẓ Israel.

Din, a law (both secular and religious), legal decision, or lawsuit.

Divan, diwan, collection of poems, especially in Hebrew, Arabic, or Persian.

Dunam, unit of land area (1,000 sq. m., c. ¼ acre), used in Israel.

Einsatzgruppen, mobile units of Nazi S.S. and S.D.; in U.S.S.R. and Serbia, mobile killing units.

*__Ein-Sof__, "without end"; "the infinite"; hidden, impersonal aspect of God; also used as a Divine Name.

*__Elul__, sixth month of the Jewish religious calendar, 12th of the civil, precedes the High Holiday season in the fall.

Endloesung, see *Final Solution.

*__Ereẓ Israel__, Land of Israel; Palestine.

*__Eruv__, technical term for rabbinical provision permitting the alleviation of certain restrictions.

*__Etrog__, citron; one of the *Four Species used on *Sukkot together with the **lulav, hadas*, and *aravah*.

Even ha-Ezer, see Shulḥan Arukh.

*__Exilarch__, lay head of Jewish community in Babylonia (see also *resh galuta*), and elsewhere.

*__Final Solution__ (Ger. *Endloesung*), in Nazi terminology, the Nazi-planned mass murder and total annihilation of the Jews.

*__Gabbai__, official of a Jewish congregation; originally a charity collector.

*__Galut__, "exile"; the condition of the Jewish people in dispersion.

***Gaon** (pl. **geonim**), head of academy in post-talmudic period, especially in Babylonia.
Gaonate, office of *gaon.
***Gemara**, traditions, discussions, and rulings of the *amoraim*, commenting on and supplementing the *Mishnah, and forming part of the Babylonian and Palestinian Talmuds (see Talmud).
***Gematria**, interpretation of Hebrew word according to the numerical value of its letters.
General Government, territory in Poland administered by a German civilian governor-general with headquarters in Cracow after the German occupation in World War II.
***Genizah**, depository for sacred books. The best known was discovered in the synagogue of Fostat (old Cairo).
Get, bill of *divorce.
***Ge'ullah**, hymn inserted after the **Shema* into the benediction of the morning prayer of the festivals and special Sabbaths.
***Gilgul**, metempsychosis; transmigration of souls.
***Golem**, automaton, especially in human form, created by magical means and endowed with life.
***Ḥabad**, initials of *ḥokhmah, binah, da'at*: "wisdom, understanding, knowledge"; ḥasidic movement founded in Belorussia by *Shneur Zalman of Lyady.
Hadas, *myrtle; one of the *Four Species used on Sukkot together with the **etrog*, **lulav*, and *aravah*.
***Haftarah** (pl. **haftarot**), designation of the portion from the prophetical books of the Bible recited after the synagogue reading from the Pentateuch on Sabbaths and holidays.
***Haganah**, clandestine Jewish organization for armed self-defense in Ereẓ Israel under the British Mandate, which eventually evolved into a people's militia and became the basis for the Israel army.
***Haggadah**, ritual recited in the home on *Passover eve at seder table.
Haham, title of chief rabbi of the Spanish and Portuguese congregations in London, England.
***Hakham**, title of rabbi of *Sephardi congregation.
***Hakham bashi**, title in the 15th century and modern times of the chief rabbi in the Ottoman Empire, residing in Constantinople (Istanbul), also applied to principal rabbis in provincial towns.
Hakhsharah ("preparation"), organized training in the Diaspora of pioneers for agricultural settlement in Ereẓ Israel.
***Halakhah** (pl. **halakhot**), an accepted decision in rabbinic law. Also refers to those parts of the *Talmud concerned with legal matters. In contradistinction to **aggadah*.
Ḥaliẓah, biblically prescribed ceremony (Deut. 25:9–10) performed when a man refuses to marry his brother's childless widow, enabling her to remarry.
***Hallel**, term referring to Psalms 113-18 in liturgical use.
***Ḥalukkah**, system of financing the maintenance of Jewish communities in the holy cities of Ereẓ Israel by collections made abroad, mainly in the pre-Zionist era (see *kolel*).
Ḥalutz (pl. **ḥalutzim**), pioneer, especially in agriculture, in Ereẓ Israel.
Ḥalutziyyut, pioneering.
***Ḥanukkah**, eight-day celebration commemorating the victory of *Judah Maccabee over the Syrian king *Antiochus Epiphanes and the subsequent rededication of the Temple.
Ḥasid, adherent of *Ḥasidism.
***Ḥasidei Ashkenaz**, medieval pietist movement among the Jews of Germany.
***Ḥasidism**, (1) religious revivalist movement of popular mysticism among Jews of Germany in the Middle Ages; (2) religious movement founded by *Israel ben Eliezer Ba'al Shem Tov in the first half of the 18th century.
***Haskalah**, "enlightenment"; movement for spreading modern European culture among Jews c. 1750–1880. See *maskil*.
***Havdalah**, ceremony marking the end of Sabbath or festival.
***Ḥazzan**, precentor who intones the liturgy and leads the prayers in synagogue; in earlier times a synagogue official.
***Ḥeder** (lit. "room"), school for teaching children Jewish religious observance.
Heikhalot, "palaces"; tradition in Jewish mysticism centering on mystical journeys through the heavenly spheres and palaces to the Divine Chariot (see Merkabah).
***Ḥerem**, excommunication, imposed by rabbinical authorities for purposes of religious and/or communal discipline; originally, in biblical times, that which is separated from common use either because it was an abomination or because it was consecrated to God.
Ḥeshvan, see Marḥeshvan.
***Ḥevra kaddisha**, title applied to charitable confraternity (**ḥevrah*), now generally limited to associations for burial of the dead.
***Ḥibbat Zion**, see Ḥovevei Zion.
***Histadrut** (abbr. For Heb. **Ha-Histadrut ha-Kelalit shel ha-Ovedim ha-Ivriyyim be-Ereẓ Israel**). Ereẓ Israel Jewish Labor Federation, founded in 1920; subsequently renamed Histadrut ha-Ovedim be-Ereẓ Israel.
***Holocaust**, the organized mass persecution and annihilation of European Jewry by the Nazis (1933–1945).
***Hoshana Rabba**, the seventh day of *Sukkot on which special observances are held.
Ḥoshen Mishpat, see Shulḥan Arukh.
Ḥovevei Zion, federation of *Ḥibbat Zion, early (pre-*Herzl) Zionist movement in Russia.
Illui, outstanding scholar or genius, especially a young prodigy in talmudic learning.
***Iyyar**, second month of the Jewish religious year, eighth of the civil, approximating to April-May.
I.Ẓ.L. (initials of Heb. ***Irgun Ẓeva'i Le'ummi**; "National Military Organization"), underground Jewish organization in Ereẓ Israel founded in 1931, which engaged from 1937 in retaliatory acts against Arab attacks and later against the British mandatory authorities.
***Jadīd al-Islām** (Ar.), a person practicing the Jewish religion in secret although outwardly observing Islām.
***Jewish Legion**, Jewish units in British army during World War I.
***Jihād** (Ar.), in Muslim religious law, holy war waged against infidels.
***Judenrat** (Ger. "Jewish council"), council set up in Jewish communities and ghettos under the Nazis to execute their instructions.
***Judenrein** (Ger. "clean of Jews"), in Nazi terminology the condition of a locality from which all Jews had been eliminated.
***Kabbalah**, the Jewish mystical tradition:
Kabbala iyyunit, speculative Kabbalah;
Kabbala ma'asit, practical Kabbalah;
Kabbala nevu'it, prophetic Kabbalah.
Kabbalist, student of Kabbalah.
***Kaddish**, liturgical doxology.
Kahal, Jewish congregation; among Ashkenazim, *kehillah*.

***Kalām** (Ar.), science of Muslim theology; adherents of the Kalām are called *mutakallimūn*.

***Karaite**, member of a Jewish sect originating in the eighth century which rejected rabbinic (*Rabbanite) Judaism and claimed to accept only Scripture as authoritative.

***Kasher**, ritually permissible food.

Kashrut, Jewish *dietary laws.

***Kavvanah**, "intention"; term denoting the spiritual concentration accompanying prayer and the performance of ritual or of a commandment.

***Kedushah**, main addition to the third blessing in the reader's repetition of the *Amidah* in which the public responds to the precentor's introduction.

Kefar, village; first part of name of many settlements in Israel.

Kehillah, congregation; see *kahal*.

Kelippah (pl. **kelippot**), "husk(s)"; mystical term denoting force(s) of evil.

***Keneset Yisrael**, comprehensive communal organization of the Jews in Palestine during the British Mandate.

Keri, variants in the masoretic (*masorah) text of the Bible between the spelling (*ketiv*) and its pronunciation (*keri*).

***Kerovah** (collective plural (corrupted) from **kerovez̧**), poem(s) incorporated into the **Amidah*.

Ketiv, see *keri*.

***Ketubbah**, marriage contract, stipulating husband's obligations to wife.

Kevuz̧ah, small commune of pioneers constituting an agricultural settlement in Erez̧ Israel (evolved later into *kibbutz).

***Kibbutz** (pl. **kibbutzim**), larger-size commune constituting a settlement in Erez̧ Israel based mainly on agriculture but engaging also in industry.

***Kiddush**, prayer of sanctification, recited over wine or bread on eve of Sabbaths and festivals.

***Kiddush ha-Shem**, term connoting martyrdom or act of strict integrity in support of Judaic principles.

***Kinah** (pl. **kinot**), lamentation dirge(s) for the Ninth of Av and other fast days.

***Kislev**, ninth month of the Jewish religious year, third of the civil, approximating to November-December.

Klaus, name given in Central and Eastern Europe to an institution, usually with synagogue attached, where *Talmud was studied perpetually by adults; applied by Ḥasidim to their synagogue ("*kloyz*").

***Knesset**, parliament of the State of Israel.

K(c)ohen (pl. **K(c)ohanim**), Jew(s) of priestly (Aaronide) descent.

***Kolel**, (1) community in Erez̧ Israel of persons from a particular country or locality, often supported by their fellow countrymen in the Diaspora; (2) institution for higher Torah study.

Kosher, see *kasher*.

***Kristallnacht** (Ger. "crystal night," meaning "night of broken glass"), organized destruction of synagogues, Jewish houses, and shops, accompanied by mass arrests of Jews, which took place in Germany and Austria under the Nazis on the night of Nov. 9–10, 1938.

***Lag ba-Omer**, 33rd (Heb. **lag**) day of the **Omer* period falling on the 18th of *Iyyar; a semi-holiday.

Leḥi (abbr. For Heb. ***Loḥamei Ḥerut Israel**, "Fighters for the Freedom of Israel"), radically anti-British armed underground organization in Palestine, founded in 1940 by dissidents from *I.Z.L.

Levir, husband's brother.

***Levirate marriage** (Heb. *yibbum*), marriage of childless widow (*yevamah*) by brother (*yavam*) of the deceased husband (in accordance with Deut. 25:5); release from such an obligation is effected through *ḥaliz̧ah*.

LHY, see Leḥi.

***Lulav**, palm branch; one of the *Four Species used on *Sukkot together with the **etrog*, *hadas*, and *aravah*.

***Ma'aravot**, hymns inserted into the evening prayer of the three festivals, Passover, Shavuot, and Sukkot.

Ma'ariv, evening prayer; also called **arvit*.

***Ma'barah**, transition camp; temporary settlement for newcomers in Israel during the period of mass immigration following 1948.

***Maftir**, reader of the concluding portion of the Pentateuchal section on Sabbaths and holidays in synagogue; reader of the portion of the prophetical books of the Bible (**haftarah*).

***Maggid**, popular preacher.

***Maḥzor** (pl. **maḥzorim**), festival prayer book.

***Mamzer**, bastard; according to Jewish law, the offspring of an incestuous relationship.

***Mandate, Palestine**, responsibility for the administration of Palestine conferred on Britain by the League of Nations in 1922; mandatory government: the British administration of Palestine.

***Maqāma** (Ar. pl. **maqamāt**), poetic form (rhymed prose) which, in its classical arrangement, has rigid rules of form and content.

***Marḥeshvan**, popularly called Ḥeshvan; eighth month of the Jewish religious year, second of the civil, approximating to October–November.

***Marrano(s)**, descendant(s) of Jew(s) in Spain and Portugal whose ancestors had been converted to Christianity under pressure but who secretly observed Jewish rituals.

Maskil (pl. **maskilim**), adherent of *Haskalah ("Enlightenment") movement.

***Masorah**, body of traditions regarding the correct spelling, writing, and reading of the Hebrew Bible.

Masorete, scholar of the masoretic tradition.

Masoretic, in accordance with the masorah.

Meliz̧ah, in Middle Ages, elegant style; modern usage, florid style using biblical or talmudic phraseology.

Mellah, *Jewish quarter in North African towns.

***Menorah**, candelabrum; seven-branched oil lamp used in the Tabernacle and Temple; also eight-branched candelabrum used on *Ḥanukkah.

Me'orah, hymn inserted into the first benediction of the morning prayer (*Yoz̧er ha-Me'orot*).

***Merkabah**, *merkavah*, "chariot"; mystical discipline associated with Ezekiel's vision of the Divine Throne-Chariot (Ezek. 1).

Meshullaḥ, emissary sent to conduct propaganda or raise funds for rabbinical academies or charitable institutions.

***Mezuzah** (pl. **mezuzot**), parchment scroll with selected Torah verses placed in container and affixed to gates and doorposts of houses occupied by Jews.

***Midrash**, method of interpreting Scripture to elucidate legal points (*Midrash Halakhah*) or to bring out lessons by stories or homiletics (*Midrash Aggadah*). Also the name for a collection of such rabbinic interpretations.

***Mikveh**, ritual bath.

***Minhag** (pl. **minhagim**), ritual custom(s); synagogal rite(s); especially of a specific sector of Jewry.

***Minḥah**, afternoon prayer; originally meal offering in Temple.

***Minyan**, group of ten male adult Jews, the minimum required for communal prayer.

***Mishnah**, earliest codification of Jewish Oral Law.

Mishnah (pl. **mishnayot**), subdivision of tractates of the Mishnah.

Mitnagged (pl. ***Mitnaggedim**), originally, opponents of *Ḥasidism in Eastern Europe.

***Mitzvah**, biblical or rabbinic injunction; applied also to good or charitable deeds.

Mohel, official performing circumcisions.

***Moshav**, smallholders' cooperative agricultural settlement in Israel, see moshav ovedim.

Moshavah, earliest type of Jewish village in modern Ereẓ Israel in which farming is conducted on individual farms mostly on privately owned land.

Moshav ovedim ("workers' moshav"), agricultural village in Israel whose inhabitants possess individual homes and holdings but cooperate in the purchase of equipment, sale of produce, mutual aid, etc.

***Moshav shittufi** ("collective moshav"), agricultural village in Israel whose members possess individual homesteads but where the agriculture and economy are conducted as a collective unit.

Mostegab (Ar.), poem with biblical verse at beginning of each stanza.

***Muqaddam** (Ar., pl. **muqaddamūn**), "leader," "head of the community."

***Musaf**, additional service on Sabbath and festivals; originally the additional sacrifice offered in the Temple.

Musar, traditional ethical literature.

***Musar movement**, ethical movement developing in the latter part of the 19th century among Orthodox Jewish groups in Lithuania; founded by R. Israel *Lipkin (Salanter).

***Nagid** (pl. **negidim**), title applied in Muslim (and some Christian) countries in the Middle Ages to a leader recognized by the state as head of the Jewish community.

Nakdan (pl. **nakdanim**), "punctuator"; scholar of the 9th to 14th centuries who provided biblical manuscripts with masoretic apparatus, vowels, and accents.

***Nasi** (pl. **nesi'im**), talmudic term for president of the Sanhedrin, who was also the spiritual head and later, political representative of the Jewish people; from second century a descendant of Hillel recognized by the Roman authorities as patriarch of the Jews. Now applied to the president of the State of Israel.

***Negev**, the southern, mostly arid, area of Israel.

***Ne'ilah**, concluding service on the *Day of Atonement.

Neofiti, term applied in southern Italy to converts to Christianity from Judaism and their descendants who were suspected of maintaining secret allegiance to Judaism.

***Neology**; **Neolog**; **Neologism**, trend of *Reform Judaism in Hungary forming separate congregations after 1868.

***Nevelah** (lit. "carcass"), meat forbidden by the *dietary laws on account of the absence of, or defect in, the act of **sheḥitah* (ritual slaughter).

***New Christians**, term applied especially in Spain and Portugal to converts from Judaism (and from Islam) and their descendants; "Half New Christian" designated a person one of whose parents was of full Jewish blood.

***Niddah** ("menstruous woman"), woman during the period of menstruation.

***Nisan**, first month of the Jewish religious year, seventh of the civil, approximating to March-April.

Niẓoẓot, "sparks"; mystical term for sparks of the holy light imprisoned in all matter.

Nosaḥ (**nusaḥ**) "version"; (1) textual variant; (2) term applied to distinguish the various prayer rites, e.g., *nosaḥ Ashkenaz*; (3) the accepted tradition of synagogue melody.

***Notarikon**, method of abbreviating Hebrew works or phrases by acronym.

Novella(e) (Heb. **ḥiddush (im)*), commentary on talmudic and later rabbinic subjects that derives new facts or principles from the implications of the text.

***Nuremberg Laws**, Nazi laws excluding Jews from German citizenship, and imposing other restrictions.

Ofan, hymns inserted into a passage of the morning prayer.

***Omer**, first sheaf cut during the barley harvest, offered in the Temple on the second day of Passover.

Omer, Counting of (Heb. *Sefirat ha-Omer*), 49 days counted from the day on which the *omer* was first offered in the Temple (according to the rabbis the 16th of Nisan, i.e., the second day of Passover) until the festival of Shavuot; now a period of semi-mourning.

Oraḥ Ḥayyim, see Shulḥan Arukh.

***Orthodoxy** (Orthodox Judaism), modern term for the strictly traditional sector of Jewry.

***Pale of Settlement**, 25 provinces of czarist Russia where Jews were permitted permanent residence.

***Palmaḥ** (abbr. for Heb. *peluggot maḥaz*; "shock companies"), striking arm of the *Haganah.

***Pardes**, medieval biblical exegesis giving the literal, allegorical, homiletical, and esoteric interpretations.

***Parnas**, chief synagogue functionary, originally vested with both religious and administrative functions; subsequently an elected lay leader.

Partition plan(s), proposals for dividing Ereẓ Israel into autonomous areas.

Paytan, composer of **piyyut* (liturgical poetry).

***Peel Commission**, British Royal Commission appointed by the British government in 1936 to inquire into the Palestine problem and make recommendations for its solution.

Pesaḥ, *Passover.

***Pilpul**, in talmudic and rabbinic literature, a sharp dialectic used particularly by talmudists in Poland from the 16th century.

***Pinkas**, community register or minute-book.

***Piyyut**, (pl. **piyyutim**), Hebrew liturgical poetry.

***Pizmon**, poem with refrain.

Posek (pl. ***posekim**), decisor; codifier or rabbinic scholar who pronounces decisions in disputes and on questions of Jewish law.

***Prosbul**, legal method of overcoming the cancelation of debts with the advent of the *sabbatical year.

***Purim**, festival held on Adar 14 or 15 in commemoration of the delivery of the Jews of Persia in the time of *Esther.

Rabban, honorific title higher than that of rabbi, applied to heads of the *Sanhedrin in mishnaic times.

***Rabbanite**, adherent of rabbinic Judaism. In contradistinction to *Karaite.

Reb, rebbe, Yiddish form for rabbi, applied generally to a teacher or ḥasidic rabbi.

***Reconstructionism**, trend in Jewish thought originating in the United States.

***Reform Judaism**, trend in Judaism advocating modification of *Orthodoxy in conformity with the exigencies of contemporary life and thought.

Resh galuta, lay head of Babylonian Jewry (see exilarch).

Responsum (pl. ***responsa**), written opinion (*teshuvah*) given to question (*she'elah*) on aspects of Jewish law by qualified authorities; pl. collection of such queries and opinions in book form (*she'elot u-teshuvot*).

***Rishonim**, older rabbinical authorities. Distinguished from later authorities (**aḥaronim*).

***Rishon le-Zion**, title given to Sephardi chief rabbi of Ereẓ Israel.

***Rosh Ha-Shanah**, two-day holiday (one day in biblical and early mishnaic times) at the beginning of the month of *Tishri (September–October), traditionally the New Year.

Rosh Hodesh, *New Moon, marking the beginning of the Hebrew month.

Rosh Yeshivah, see *Yeshivah.

***R.S.H.A.** (initials of Ger. *Reichssicherheitshauptamt*: "Reich Security Main Office"), the central security department of the German Reich, formed in 1939, and combining the security police (Gestapo and Kripo) and the S.D.

***Sanhedrin**, the assembly of ordained scholars which functioned both as a supreme court and as a legislature before 70 C.E. In modern times the name was given to the body of representative Jews convoked by Napoleon in 1807.

***Savora** (pl. **savoraim**), name given to the Babylonian scholars of the period between the **amoraim* and the **geonim*, approximately 500–700 C.E.

S.D. (initials of Ger. *Sicherheitsdienst*: "security service"), security service of the *S.S. formed in 1932 as the sole intelligence organization of the Nazi party.

Seder, ceremony observed in the Jewish home on the first night of Passover (outside Ereẓ Israel first two nights), when the *Haggadah is recited.

***Sefer Torah**, manuscript scroll of the Pentateuch for public reading in synagogue.

***Sefirot, the ten**, the ten "Numbers"; mystical term denoting the ten spheres or emanations through which the Divine manifests itself; elements of the world; dimensions, primordial numbers.

Selektion (Ger.), (1) in ghettos and other Jewish settlements, the drawing up by Nazis of lists of deportees; (2) separation of incoming victims to concentration camps into two categories – those destined for immediate killing and those to be sent for forced labor.

Seliḥah (pl. ***seliḥot**), penitential prayer.

***Semikhah**, ordination conferring the title "rabbi" and permission to give decisions in matters of ritual and law.

Sephardi (pl. ***Sephardim**), Jew(s) of Spain and Portugal and their descendants, wherever resident, as contrasted with *Ashkenazi(m).

Shabbatean, adherent of the pseudo-messiah *Shabbetai Ẓevi (17th century).

Shaddai, name of God found frequently in the Bible and commonly translated "Almighty."

***Shaḥarit**, morning service.

Shali'aḥ (pl. **sheliḥim**), in Jewish law, messenger, agent; in modern times, an emissary from Ereẓ Israel to Jewish communities or organizations abroad for the purpose of fund-raising, organizing pioneer immigrants, education, etc.

Shalmonit, poetic meter introduced by the liturgical poet *Solomon ha-Bavli.

***Shammash**, synagogue beadle.

***Shavuot**, Pentecost; Festival of Weeks; second of the three annual pilgrim festivals, commemorating the receiving of the Torah at Mt. Sinai.

***Sheḥitah**, ritual slaughtering of animals.

***Shekhinah**, Divine Presence.

Shelishit, poem with three-line stanzas.

***Sheluḥei Ereẓ Israel** (or **shadarim**), emissaries from Ereẓ Israel.

***Shema** ([Yisrael]; "hear… [O Israel]," Deut. 6:4), Judaism's confession of faith, proclaiming the absolute unity of God.

Shemini Aẓeret, final festal day (in the Diaspora, final two days) at the conclusion of *Sukkot.

Shemittah, *Sabbatical year.

Sheniyyah, poem with two-line stanzas.

***Shephelah**, southern part of the coastal plain of Ereẓ Israel.

***Shevat**, eleventh month of the Jewish religious year, fifth of the civil, approximating to January–February.

***Shi'ur Komah**, Hebrew mystical work (c. eighth century) containing a physical description of God's dimensions; term denoting enormous spacial measurement used in speculations concerning the body of the **Shekhinah*.

Shivah, the "seven days" of *mourning following burial of a relative.

***Shofar**, horn of the ram (or any other ritually clean animal excepting the cow) sounded for the memorial blowing on *Rosh Ha-Shanah, and other occasions.

Shoḥet, person qualified to perform **sheḥitah*.

Shomer, *Ha-Shomer, organization of Jewish workers in Ereẓ Israel founded in 1909 to defend Jewish settlements.

***Shtadlan**, Jewish representative or negotiator with access to dignitaries of state, active at royal courts, etc.

***Shtetl**, Jewish small-town community in Eastern Europe.

***Shulḥan Arukh**, Joseph *Caro's code of Jewish law in four parts:
Oraḥ Ḥayyim, laws relating to prayers, Sabbath, festivals, and fasts;
Yoreh De'ah, dietary laws, etc;
Even ha-Ezer, laws dealing with women, marriage, etc;
Ḥoshen Mishpat, civil, criminal law, court procedure, etc.

Siddur, among Ashkenazim, the volume containing the daily prayers (in distinction to the **maḥzor* containing those for the festivals).

***Simḥat Torah**, holiday marking the completion in the synagogue of the annual cycle of reading the Pentateuch; in Ereẓ Israel observed on Shemini Aẓeret (outside Ereẓ Israel on the following day).

***Sinai Campaign**, brief campaign in October–November 1956 when Israel army reacted to Egyptian terrorist attacks and blockade by occupying the Sinai peninsula.

Sitra aḥra, "the other side" (of God); left side; the demoniac and satanic powers.

***Sivan**, third month of the Jewish religious year, ninth of the civil, approximating to May–June.

***Six-Day War**, rapid war in June 1967 when Israel reacted to Arab threats and blockade by defeating the Egyptian, Jordanian, and Syrian armies.

***S.S.** (initials of Ger. *Schutzstaffel*: "protection detachment"), Nazi formation established in 1925 which later became the "elite" organization of the Nazi Party and carried out central tasks in the "Final Solution."

***Status quo ante** community, community in Hungary retaining the status it had held before the convention of the General Jewish Congress there in 1868 and the resultant split in Hungarian Jewry.

***Sukkah**, booth or tabernacle erected for *Sukkot when, for seven days, religious Jews "dwell" or at least eat in the *sukkah* (Lev. 23:42).

***Sukkot**, festival of Tabernacles; last of the three pilgrim festivals, beginning on the 15th of Tishri.

Sūra (Ar.), chapter of the Koran.

Ta'anit Esther (Fast of *Esther), fast on the 13th of Adar, the day preceding Purim.

Takkanah (pl. ***takkanot**), regulation supplementing the law of the Torah; regulations governing the internal life of communities and congregations.

***Tallit (gadol)**, four-cornered prayer shawl with fringes (*ẓiẓit*) at each corner.

***Tallit katan**, garment with fringes (*ẓiẓit*) appended, worn by observant male Jews under their outer garments.

***Talmud**, "teaching"; compendium of discussion on the Mishnah by generations of scholars and jurists in many academies over a period of several centuries. The Jerusalem (or Palestinian) Talmud mainly contains the discussions of the Palestinian sages. The Babylonian Talmud incorporates the parallel discussion in the Babylonian academies.

Talmud torah, term generally applied to Jewish religious (and ultimately to talmudic) study; also to traditional Jewish religious public schools.

***Tammuz**, fourth month of the Jewish religious year, tenth of the civil, approximating to June-July.

Tanna (pl. ***tannaim**), rabbinic teacher of mishnaic period.

***Targum**, Aramaic translation of the Bible.

***Tefillin**, phylacteries, small leather cases containing passages from Scripture and affixed on the forehead and arm by male Jews during the recital of morning prayers.

Tell (Ar. "mound," "hillock"), ancient mound in the Middle East composed of remains of successive settlements.

***Terefah**, food that is not **kasher*, owing to a defect on the animal.

***Territorialism**, 20th century movement supporting the creation of an autonomous territory for Jewish mass-settlement outside Ereẓ Israel.

***Tevet**, tenth month of the Jewish religious year, fourth of the civil, approximating to December–January.

Tikkun ("restitution," "reintegration"), (1) order of service for certain occasions, mostly recited at night; (2) mystical term denoting restoration of the right order and true unity after the spiritual "catastrophe" which occurred in the cosmos.

Tishah be-Av, Ninth of *Av, fast day commemorating the destruction of the First and Second Temples.

***Tishri**, seventh month of the Jewish religious year, first of the civil, approximating to September–October.

Tokheḥah, reproof sections of the Pentateuch (Lev. 26 and Deut. 28); poem of reproof.

***Torah**, Pentateuch or the Pentateuchal scroll for reading in synagogue; entire body of traditional Jewish teaching and literature.

Tosafist, talmudic glossator, mainly French (12–14th centuries), bringing additions to the commentary by *Rashi.

***Tosafot**, glosses supplied by tosafist.

***Tosefta**, a collection of teachings and traditions of the *tannaim*, closely related to the Mishnah.

Tradent, person who hands down a talmudic statement on the name of his teacher or other earlier authority.

***Tu bi-Shevat**, the 15th day of Shevat, the New Year for Trees; date marking a dividing line for fruit tithing; in modern Israel celebrated as arbor day.

***Uganda Scheme**, plan suggested by the British government in 1903 to establish an autonomous Jewish settlement area in East Africa.

***Va'ad Le'ummi**, national council of the Jewish community in Ereẓ Israel during the period of the British *Mandate.

***Wannsee Conference**, Nazi conference held on Jan. 20, 1942, at which the planned annihilation of European Jewry was endorsed.

Waqf (Ar.), (1) a Muslim charitable pious foundation; (2) state lands and other property passed to the Muslim community for public welfare.

***War of Independence**, war of 1947–49 when the Jews of Israel fought off Arab invading armies and ensured the establishment of the new State.

***White Paper(s)**, report(s) issued by British government, frequently statements of policy, as issued in connection with Palestine during the *Mandate period.

***Wissenschaft des Judentums** (Ger. "Science of Judaism"), movement in Europe beginning in the 19th century for scientific study of Jewish history, religion, and literature.

***Yad Vashem**, Israel official authority for commemorating the *Holocaust in the Nazi era and Jewish resistance and heroism at that time.

Yeshivah (pl. ***yeshivot**), Jewish traditional academy devoted primarily to study of rabbinic literature; *rosh yeshivah*, head of the yeshivah.

YHWH, the letters of the holy name of God, the Tetragrammaton.

Yibbum, see levirate marriage.

Yiḥud, "union"; mystical term for intention which causes the union of God with the **Shekhinah*.

Yishuv, settlement; more specifically, the Jewish community of Ereẓ Israel in the pre-State period. The pre-Zionist community is generally designated the "old yishuv" and the community evolving from 1880, the "new yishuv."

Yom Kippur, Yom ha-Kippurim, *Day of Atonement, solemn fast day observed on the 10th of Tishri.

Yoreh De'ah, see Shulḥan Arukh.

Yoẓer, hymns inserted in the first benediction (*Yoẓer Or*) of the morning **Shema*.

***Ẓaddik**, person outstanding for his faith and piety; especially a ḥasidic rabbi or leader.

Ẓimẓum, "contraction"; mystical term denoting the process whereby God withdraws or contracts within Himself so leaving a primordial vacuum in which creation can take place; primordial exile or self-limitation of God.

***Zionist Commission (1918)**, commission appointed in 1918 by the British government to advise the British military authorities in Palestine on the implementation of the *Balfour Declaration.

Ẓyyonei Zion, the organized opposition to Herzl in connection with the *Uganda Scheme.

***Ẓiẓit**, fringes attached to the **tallit* and **tallit katan*.

***Zohar**, mystical commentary on the Pentateuch; main textbook of *Kabbalah.

Zulat, hymn inserted after the **Shema* in the morning service.

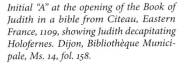

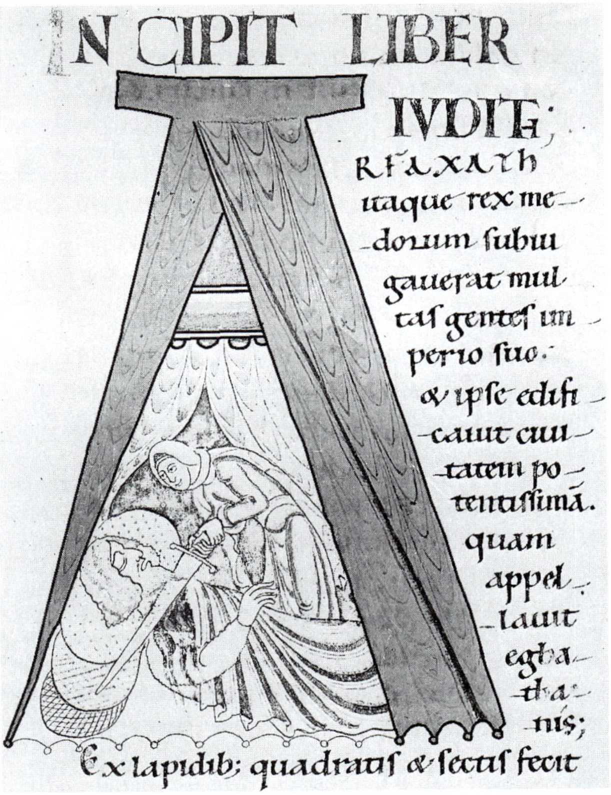

Initial "A" at the opening of the Book of Judith in a bible from Citeau, Eastern France, 1109, showing Judith decapitating Holofernes. Dijon, Bibliothèque Municipale, Ms. 14, fol. 158.

Aa–Alp

AACHEN (**Aix-la-Chapelle**; in Jewish sources: אש, אכא, אייש), city on the German-Belgian border; former capital of the Carolingian Empire. The delegation sent by *Charlemagne to the caliph Harun al-Rashid in 797 included a Jew, Isaac, who probably acted as interpreter or guide, and subsequently reported back to Aachen. Jewish merchants were active in Aachen by about 820. A "Jews' street" is known to have existed from the 11th century. The Aachen community, which paid only 15 marks in tax to the emperor in 1241, cannot have been large. In 1349 the Jews were "given" to the count of Juelich, who received their taxes and authorized Jewish residence in Aachen. The Jews were expelled from Aachen in 1629, most settling in neighboring Burtscheid. However, Jewish moneylenders were again active in Aachen about ten years later. They were included in the municipal jurisdiction in 1777. Prior to the inauguration of a Jewish cemetery in 1823, the Jews of Aachen buried their dead in Vaals across the border in the Netherlands. In 1847 the community was organized under the Prussian Jewish Community Statute. A Jewish elementary school was founded in 1845. The synagogue, built in 1862, was destroyed in the 1938 *Kristallnacht.

The Jewish population had increased from 114 in 1816 to 1,345 by 1933. In 1939, after emigration and arrests, there were 782 Jews living in the city. Others subsequently managed to flee and the rest were deported between March 1942 and September 1944. After the war, there were 62 Jews in Aachen. A new synagogue and communal center were built at the expense of the German government in 1957. In 1966 the Jewish community of Aachen and environs numbered 163. As a result of the immigration of Jews from the former Soviet Union, the number of community members increased from 326 in 1989 to 1,434 in 2003. Another new synagogue and community center were inaugurated in 1995.

BIBLIOGRAPHY: H. Jaulus, *Geschichte der Aachener Juden* (1924). **ADD. BIBLIOGRAPHY:** M. Bierganz, A. Kreutz, *Juden in Aachen* (1988); H. Lepper, *Von der Emanzipation zum Holocaust. Die Israelitische Synagogengemeinde Aachen 1801–1942*, 2 vols. (1994).

[Ernst Roth / Stefan Rohrbacher (2nd ed.)]

AARGAU, canton of northern Switzerland. A few Jewish families are known to have lived there during the Middle Ages. From the 17th to the mid-19th centuries Aargau remained the sole area of permanent Jewish settlement in Switzerland; Jews lived in the two communities of *Endingen and Lengnau, and it was they who waged the struggle for Jewish *emancipation in Switzerland. In the 18th century Aargau Jews obtained rights of residence and movement; these were conferred by special safe conducts and letters of protection against the payment of high imposts, usually granted for a 16-year period. Jewish occupations were restricted to participation in the markets, the cattle and horse trade, peddling, and estate brokerage. Both communities possessed their own synagogues, sharing a cemetery and rabbi. The Jews in Aargau continued to pay the special taxes until their abolition by the Helvetic Republic in 1798. Rights of residence, trade, and ownership of real estate were granted to the Jews by the Helvetic government but were later revoked by the *Judengesetz* (Jews' Law) in 1809. The independent canton of Aargau was founded in 1798/1803. A law regularizing the status of the Jewish communities was passed in 1824 and, in conjunction with the General Education Act of 1835, regulated Jewish life and communal organization on the same principles as those governing similar non-Jewish institutions in the canton. In the 1850s two new synagogues were built, one in Endingen and one in Lengnau, and were later declared cantonal monuments. However, since the Jewish communities were not recognized as communities of local citizens, their members were debarred from canton citizenship. The Great Council of Canton Aargau authorized Jewish emancipation in 1862, but was bitterly opposed by the popular anti-Jewish movement and was subsequently repealed. The Jews of Aargau only obtained full rights of citizenship in 1878 after the Swiss federal parliament had intervened in their favor. Jews began to leave the region for other parts of Switzerland in the middle of the 19th century, their numbers dwindling from 1,562 in 1850 to 990 in 1900 and to 496 in 1950. In 1859 in the town of Baden a Jewish community was founded which built its synagogue in 1913 and erected a cemetery (1879). Between 1900 and the 1940s a small yeshivah was active under Rabbi Akiba Krausz. A Jewish Swiss Home for the Aged was established in Lengnau in 1903. At the turn of the 20th century services were sometimes held in the synagogues on Rosh Ḥodesh and for marriages. Aargau Jewish history came to public attention with the appointment of the first Jewish member of the Swiss governement, Ruth *Dreifuss. In 2000, 342 Jews lived in Aargau.

BIBLIOGRAPHY: E. Haller, *Die rechtliche Stellung der Juden im Kanton Aargau* (1900); A. Steinberg, *Studien zur Geschichte der Juden in der Schweiz waehrend des Mittelalters* (1902); F. Wyler, *Die staatsrechtliche Stellung der israelitischen Religionsgenossenschaften in der Schweiz* (1929); F. Guggenheim-Gruenberg, in: *150 Jahre Kanton Aargau…* (1954); idem, *Die Juden in der Schweiz* (1961); A. Weldler-Steinberg and F. Guggenheim-Gruenberg, *Geschichte der Juden in der Schweiz vom 16. Jahrhundert bis nach der Emanzipation* (1966 and 1970). **ADD. BIBLIOGRAPHY:** W. Frenkel, *Baden, eine jüdische Kleingemeinde. Fragmente aus der Geschichte 1859–1947* (2003).

[Florence Guggenheim-Gruenberg / Uri Kaufmann (2nd ed.)]

AARON (Heb. אַהֲרֹן), brother of *Moses and *Miriam; founder of the priesthood in Israel.

Biblical Information

Aaron belonged to the tribe of *Levi (Ex. 4:14) and was the elder son of *Amram and *Jochebed (*ibid.* 6:20; Num. 26:59; I Chron. 5:29; 23:13). He was senior to Moses by three years (Ex. 7:7), but younger than his sister (as may be inferred from Ex. 2:4). There is no narrative recounting Aaron's birth and nothing is known of his early life and upbringing. He apparently stayed in Egypt all the time Moses was in Midian and became known as an eloquent speaker (4:14). Aaron's marriage to Elisheba, daughter of Amminadab (6:23), allied him with one of the most distinguished families of the important tribe of Judah. His brother-in-law, Nahshon, was a chieftain of that tribe (Num. 1:7; 2:3; 7:12,17; 10:14) and a lineal ancestor of David (Ruth 4:19; I Chron. 2:10). The marital union thus symbolized the religio-political union of the two main hereditary institutions of ancient Israel, the house of David and the house of Aaron. Four sons were born of the marriage, Nadab, Abihu, Eleazar, and Ithamar (Ex. 6:23; 28:1; Num. 3:2; 26:60; I Chron. 5:29; 24:1).

The biblical narrative assigns Aaron a role subordinate to that of Moses. No mention is made of him in the initial theophany (Ex. 3:18; 4:12), and he is introduced into the events of the Exodus only because Moses resists the divine commission (4:14–16). He is to be Moses' spokesman ("prophet") to Israel (4:15–16) and to Pharaoh (7:1–2). He receives a revelation from God to go to meet Moses returning from Midian (4:27), and together the two brothers appear before the people, with Aaron performing his signs in their presence (4:28–30). Later, he performs wonders before Pharaoh. His rod turns into a serpent that swallows the serpent rods of the Egyptian magicians (7:9–12). In the ten plagues that befall the Egyptians, Aaron acts jointly with Moses in the first plague (7:19 ff.), operates alone only in the next two (8:1 ff., 12 ff.), is involved with Moses in the sixth and eighth (9:8 ff.; 10:3 ff.), and does not appear at all in the fifth and ninth (9:1–7; 10:21 ff.). For the rest, he is merely a passive associate of his brother. Although Aaron functions whenever the Egyptian magicians are present, it is significant that even where he plays an active role in performing the marvels, it is not by virtue of any innate ability or individual initiative, but solely by divine command mediated through Moses. Aaron's sons do not inherit either his wondrous powers or his potent rod. The secondary nature of Aaron's activities in the cycle of plagues is further demonstrated by the circumstance that he never speaks to Pharaoh alone and that only Moses actually entreats God to remove the plagues, although Pharaoh frequently addresses his request to both brothers (8:4, 8, 21, 25–26; 9:27 ff., 33; 10:16 ff.).

Strangely, Aaron plays no part at all in the events immediately attending the escape from Egypt, the crossing of the Red Sea, the victory hymns, and the water crisis at Marah (13:17; 16:1). He reappears again in connection with the incident of the manna (16:2–36), and at the battle with the Amalekites when, jointly with Hur, he supports Moses' hands stretched heavenward to ensure victory (17:10–13). Together with the elders of Israel, he participates in Jethro's sacrificial meal (18:12), but plays no role in the subsequent organization of the judicial administration. He does, however, again jointly with Hur, deputize for Moses in his judicial capacity while the latter goes up to the Mount of God to receive the Tablets (24:14). At the revelation at Sinai, Aaron again is a minor participant. He is distinguished from the "priests" and the people in being allowed to ascend the mount (19:24), but has the same status as his two sons, Nadab and Abihu, and the seventy elders of Israel in having to maintain a distance from Moses, although they all "see the God of Israel" and survive (24:1, 9 ff.).

It was during his brother's prolonged absence on the mount that, yielding to popular insistence, he fashioned a golden calf that became a cause of apostasy (ch. 32). On the one hand, the text stresses the grave responsibility of Aaron in this incident. He makes no attempt to dissuade the would-be idolaters, but himself issues instructions, produces the molten image, builds an altar, and proclaims a religious festival (32:2–5). His culpability is thrice emphasized (32:2, 25, 35), and the contrast between his actions and the zealous fidelity of the tribe of Levi is apparent (32:26–29). On the one hand, God wanted to destroy Aaron, but he was saved by virtue of Moses' intercession on his behalf (Deut. 9:20). On the other hand, there is a perceptible tendency to de-emphasize Aaron's share in the episode. The initiative for the idol comes from the people who approach Aaron menacingly (Ex. 32:1). They, not he, identify the calf with a divinity (32:4). He does not participate in the worship and is not mentioned in God's indictment of the people (32:7 ff.); nor is his name mentioned in Moses' intercession (32:11–14, 31–32). The making of the calf is attributed to the people (32:20; cf. Deut. 9:21) and is also described as though the particular bovine form emerged almost accidentally (Ex. 32:24). Despite Aaron's involvement, he was neither punished nor disqualified from the priesthood. The same inclination to play down Aaron's participation in the calf cult is present in the poetic version of the story (Ps. 106:19–22; cf. 106:16; Neh. 9:18).

When it comes to constructing the portable sanctuary, Aaron is conspicuously absent, but he and his sons are appointed priests and are consecrated into that office by Moses (Ex. 28–29; Lev. 8–9). During the ceremonies marking the investiture, his two sons, Nadab and Abihu, died mysteriously, a calamity that he bore in silent resignation (Lev. 10:1–3; Num. 3:4; 26:61; cf. I Chron. 24:2). Aaron's other two sons continued to serve in the priestly office (Num. 3:4; I Chron. 24:2) and Eleazar succeeded his father as high priest (Num. 20:25–28; Deut. 10:6; cf. Josh. 24:33). No reason is given for the selection of Aaron as the archetypal high priest and founder of a hereditary priesthood to the extent that "the house of Aaron" became synonymous with the only legitimate priestly line (see *Aaronides). After his induction as high priest, Aaron is no longer the attendant of Moses, nor does he occupy a position of secular authority, his activities being restricted to the area of the cult. Yet even here, it is Moses, not Aaron, who is the real founder of the cult and who generally receives the divine instructions relative to the priestly duties (cf. Lev. 6:1, 12, 17; et al.). It is to him, too, that the priests are answerable (cf. Lev. 10:16–20). But on one occasion Aaron corrected Moses' understanding of a sacrificial law (*ibid.*).

Nevertheless, Aaron undoubtedly held an outstanding position of leadership, as may be determined by the fact that God often addresses Moses and Aaron jointly (Ex. 9:8–10; 12:1, 43; Lev. 11:1; 13:1; 14:33; 15:1; et al.) and, sometimes, even Aaron alone (Lev. 10:8; Num. 18:1, 8). With Moses, Aaron shares the popular hostility to authority (Ex. 16:2–36; Num. 14:1–45; 16:3; 20:1–13). In the extra-pentateuchal literature his name is coupled with that of his brother as bearers of the divine mission (Josh. 24:5; I Sam. 12:6, 8; Micah 6:4; Ps. 77:21; 105:26; 106:16; cf. 99:6). Significantly, the period of national mourning at his death is the same as that for Moses (Num. 20:29; cf. Deut. 34:8) and throughout biblical literature the name Aaron remains unique to this one personality. A hint of friction between Moses and his brother is apparent from one narrative in which Aaron and his sister were involved in some act of opposition to Moses' prophetic preeminence. Probably because of priestly immunity he escaped divine punishment, but Miriam was stricken. At Aaron's behest, Moses successfully interceded with God on her behalf (Num. 12).

On another occasion, Aaron, together with Moses, was the target of a widespread insurrection against the monopoly of leadership. The exclusive priestly privileges of Aaron and his family against the challenge of Korah and his associates were upheld in a trial by ordeal, which led to the destruction of the rebels (Num. 16). This aroused the indignation of the people which, in turn, brought down upon them divine anger in the form of a plague. Through an incense offering, brought at Moses' directive, Aaron was able to make expiation for the people and to check the outbreak (Num. 17:1–15). This event necessitated a further vindication of Aaron's priestly preeminence. Twelve staffs, one from each tribe and each inscribed with the name of the tribal chieftain, were deposited in the Tent of Meeting. The following day, that of Levi, on which Aaron's name was written, sprouted blossoms and almonds. Henceforth, Aaron's staff lay in the Tent of Meeting as a witness to his unchallengeable priestly supremacy (17:16–26; cf. 20:8 ff.). Further, the subordination of the Levites to Aaron and his sons and their respective duties and privileges in the service of the sanctuary were unequivocally defined (17:18).

Aaron died on the first day of the fifth month at the age of 123 years (33:38–39). The account of his passing is unusually detailed, doubtlessly due to the fact that it involved the all-important matter of priestly succession. The Israelites arrived at Mount Hor from Kadesh and, by divine decree, Aaron ascended the mount accompanied by Moses and Eleazar. The high priest was stripped of the garments of his office and his son was invested in his stead. Aaron then died on the summit of the mount and a 30-day mourning period was held by the entire community (20:22–29; cf. 33:37–38; Deut. 32:50). It should be noted that another tradition has the place of Aaron's death as Moserah (Deut. 10:6), which was seven stages behind Mount Hor in the wilderness wanderings (Num. 33:31–37). Like Moses, Aaron was not permitted to enter the promised land in punishment for disobeying the divine command in connection with the waters of Meribah (20:12, 24; 27:13–14; cf. Deut. 32:50–51), although no clear account of Aaron's role in that incident has been preserved (Num. 20:10). A poetic digest of the narrative mentions only Moses as suffering the consequences of the people's provocation (Ps. 106:32). No explanation for Aaron's death in the wilderness is given in either Numbers 33:37–38 or Deuteronomy 10:6, except that the latter passage follows the story of the golden calf and the sequence may possibly imply a connection between the two events.

Critical View

The difficulty of reconstructing a comprehensive biography and evaluation of Aaron is due to the meager and fragmentary nature of the data available. It is aggravated by the fact that the details are scattered over several originally independent sources which, in the form they have come down to us, represent an interweaving of various traditions. This explains the differences in approach, emphasis, and detail, outlined above. Moreover, consideration has to be given to the possibility that the picture of Aaron, the archetypal high priest, may well be the idealized retrojection of a later period, and that subsequent developments have influenced the narratives in the Pentateuch. While there is no unanimity among scholars of the source critical school as to the proper distribution of many passages among the different pentateuchal sources, especially in regard to those relating to J and E, there is a wide measure of agreement that in the original J and E documents Aaron was neither a priest nor a levite, and that he had no part in the narrative of the ten plagues. In fact, it is regarded as likely that J did not originally mention Aaron. To E is attributed the picture of Aaron as Miriam's brother, as Moses' attendant, as participating in the war with Amalek, Jethro's sacrifice, and the golden calf, as well as acting together with Miriam in opposition to Moses. The redactor who combined JE introduced the story of Aaron as a levite and as Moses' brother and spokesman and, possibly, portrayed him as assisting in the plagues. There is no agreement as to whether D originally mentioned Aaron, or as to the source of the few references to him in that document. To the P source is assigned the exalted image of Aaron as the archetypal and only legitimate levitical high priest, and a leader of the people. Here, too, is the source of the Aaronite genealogies and the notices of his age and his death.

[Nahum M. Sarna]

In the *Aggadah*

The many praises heaped on Aaron in the *aggadah* are due to the desire to minimize his guilt with regard to the sin of the golden calf and to explain why, despite it, he was worthy to be appointed high priest (see: Sif. Deut. 307).

Aaron had great love for Moses. He was completely free of envy and rejoiced in his success. Moses was reluctant to assume his call (Ex. 4:14), because Aaron had for long been the prophet and spokesman of the Jews in Egypt, and Moses was unwilling to supplant him, until God told him to assume the leadership. Far from resenting it, Aaron was glad. For this he was given the reward of wearing the holy breastplate (*Urim* and *Thummim*) upon his heart (Tanḥ. Ex. 27). Aaron is especially praised for his love of peace. Unlike Moses, whose attitude was "let the law bend the mountain" (i.e., the law must be applied), Aaron loved peace and pursued peace.

Aaron never reproached a person by telling him that he had sinned, but employed every stratagem in order to reconcile disputes (ARN[2] 48) especially between man and wife (*ibid.*, emended text p. 50). According to one account this love for peace determined Aaron's attitude toward the golden calf. He could have put to death all those who worshiped it, as Moses did, but his love and compassion for the people prevented him. He regarded peaceful persuasion as the best way of inculcating love of the Torah, and thus Hillel declared: "Be of the disciples of Aaron, loving peace and pursuing peace, loving one's fellow men and bringing them nigh to the Torah" (Avot 1:12). For this behavior Aaron was chosen to be the high priest; God knew that his intentions were honorable (Ex. R. 37:2). According to other accounts Aaron agreed to make the golden calf after procrastinating as much as possible, because his life was threatened, and he feared the same fate as overtook Hur, who according to the Midrash, was assassinated by the people when he opposed them (Ex. R. 41:9; Sanh. 7a). Aaron's rod possessed the same miraculous powers as the staff of Moses and some aggadic sayings make them identical (Yal. Ps. 869). With it, Aaron brought about the first three of the Ten Plagues because the water of the Nile, that shielded Moses as an infant, should not suffer through Moses, by being turned into blood or bringing forth frogs, and the earth that afforded Moses protection when it concealed the slain Egyptian overseer (Ex. 2:12) should not bring forth lice by his action. Both the *aggadah* and Josephus emphasize the great spiritual strength of Aaron at the death of his two sons Nadab and Abihu; he saw his two "chickens" bathed in blood and kept silent (Lev. R. 20:4). "He withstood his ordeal with great courage because his soul was inured to every calamity" (Jos., Ant., 3:208). He did not question God's dealing with him, as Abraham did not when ordered to sacrifice his only son Isaac (Sifra 46a).

Aaron was one of those who died not on account of sin "but through the machinations of the serpent" (Sif. Deut. 338–9). When Aaron died "all the house of Israel" wept for him (Num. 20:29), while after the death of Moses, the stern leader who reprimanded them by harsh words, only part of the people, "the men," bewailed him (Sifra 45d).

[Elimelech Epstein Halevy]

In Christian Tradition

As the ancestor and founder of the one priesthood entitled to offer acceptable sacrifice to God, Aaron was taken as the type of Christ in the New Testament and later Christian tradition: he offers sacrifice, mediates between the people and God, and ministers in the Holy of Holies. The typology is developed especially in the *Epistle to the Hebrews* which stresses the superiority of Jesus' perfect sacrifice to the animal sacrifices of the Aaronic priesthood. Jesus, the high priest of the New Covenant, is foreshadowed by Aaron, the high priest of the Old Covenant, but Christ's priesthood, which is "after the order of

Melchizedek," supersedes and replaces the inferior priesthood of Aaron (see Heb. 5:2–5; 7:11–12; 8:23–27). Influenced by this distinction, the Mormons distinguished in their hierarchy between a lesser, Aaronic priesthood, and the office of high priest which is according to the order of Melchizedek.

[R.J. Zwi Werblowsky]

In the Koran and in Islamic Literature

Like some other biblical figures, Aaron (Arabic: Hārūn) only became known to Muhammad gradually. In the Koran (37:114–20), Moses and Aaron appear together as those who were redeemed (from Egyptian slavery) at the head of their people and to whom the Book was given. In 20:29–30, Moses requests, in a general way, that his brother Aaron be his helper (*wazīr*; cf. also 25:37; see below). In 26:12, he voices his fear that he might be inhibited and unable to speak. Finally, in 28:35 Moses prays to God: "Aaron is more eloquent than I am; send him to strengthen me." Just as the Midrash tries in various ways to exonerate Aaron from all blame in the incident of the golden calf, so the Koran account of that incident assigns him the role of an onlooker and administrator rather than that of chief participant, and attributes the actual making of the golden calf to one Samiri (20:96–7; perhaps meaning "a Samaritan"; see the detailed discussion by H. Speyer, pp. 329–32). The post-koranic Islamic legend describes, in a number of fanciful variations, how Moses demonstrated to the children of Israel that he had not killed his brother, as they suspected, but that he had died a natural death. The relationship of these legends to similar stories in the late Midrash still needs elucidation. An attempt to explain why Mary, the mother of Jesus, is addressed during her pregnancy as "sister of Aaron" (Koran 19:27–29, cf. Ex. 15:20) is made by H. Speyer (p. 243, where further literature is available). The Koran never mentions the fact that Aaron was the father of the priestly tribe of the Kohanim; the ancient biographer of Muhammad, however, was aware of this fact. The two main Jewish tribes in Medina, the Quraiẓa and *Naḍīr, were called *al-Kāhinān*, "the two priestly tribes." When Muhammad's Jewish spouse, Ṣafiyya, was insulted by one of the Prophet's other wives, he allegedly advised her to retort: "My father was Aaron and my uncle Moses." The word *wazīr*, by which Aaron's subordination to Moses is designated in the Koran, became the title "vizier," a kind of prime minister with wide or full powers in Islamic states.

[Shelomo Dov Goitein]

For Aaron in Art, see *Moses.

BIBLIOGRAPHY: Aberbach and Smolar, in: JBL, 86 (1967), 129–40; Albright, Arch Rel, 109–10, 119; Kennett, in: JTS, 6 (1904–05), 161–8; S.E. Loewenstamm, *Masoret Yeẓi'at Miẓrayim be-Hishtalshelutah* (1965), 60–64; Meek, in: AJSL, 45 (1928–29), 144–66; idem,*Hebrew Origins* (1960), 119–47; North, in: ZAW, 66 (1954), 191–9;H. Oort, in: *Theologisch Tijdschrift*, 18 (1884), 235–89; Westphal, in: ZAW, 26 (1906), 201–30. **ADD. BIBLIOGRAPHY:** S. Gevirtz, in: *Biblica*, 65 (1984), 377–81; S.D. Sperling, *The Original Torah* (1998), 103–21. AGGADAH: Ginzberg, Legends, index; Guttmann, Mafte'aḥ, 2 (1917), 37–55. ISLAMIC LITERATURE: J.W. Hirschberg, *Juedische und christliche Lehren im vor- und fruehislamischen Arabien* (1939), 61ff., 129–30; S.D. Goitein, *Studies in Islamic History and Institutions* (1966), 168–96; H. Speyer, *Die biblischen Erzaehlungen im Qoran* (1961), 260ff., 323–6; Schwarzbaum, in: *Fabula*, 5 (1962–63), 185–227.**ADD. BIBLIOGRAPHY:** EIS² III (1971), 231–32, s.v. Hārūn (incl. bibl.).

AARON, ISRAEL (1859–1912), U.S. rabbi. Aaron was born in Lancaster, Pennsylvania, but at the age of 16 moved to Cincinnati to join the first class of students entering the Hebrew Union College. There was little in his background to suggest a rabbinical career. He attended public schools and his parents were immigrants from Hesse-Darmstadt, where his father had served as a junior officer in the military. In 1883, Aaron, together with Henry *Berkowitz, Joseph *Krauskopf, and David *Philipson, formed the first cohort of students to graduate from the new seminary. He later received a doctorate in divinity from the same institution. After graduating, Aaron served the synagogue in Fort Wayne, Indiana, for four years before assuming the pulpit of Temple Beth Zion in Buffalo, New York. Aaron thrived in this latter setting. He was a keen advocate of the reintroduction of congregational singing, seeking to extend the success of his own endeavors in Buffalo to the wider Reform movement. Aaron was also a scholar of medieval Jewry, writing about Muslim-Jewish relations during the Renaissance, and the Iberian Jewish community. As with many of his contemporaries in the Reform rabbinate, he was also active in the civic and cultural life of his city. Aaron was an immensely successful pulpit rabbi, overseeing both the building of a new temple and the enlargement of its membership. This new temple, designed by Edward Kent, an architect who later perished in the *Titanic* disaster, was also ill-omened for Aaron. Barely four days after a celebration organized by his congregation to honor his 25th year of service to Temple Beth Zion, Aaron died at age 52 of an ear infection. David Philipson, a lifelong friend, officiated at both services.

BIBLIOGRAPHY: *American Israelite* (May 16, 1912); *American Jewish Year Book*, 5 (1903–4); CCAR *Yearbook*, 23 (1913); *New York Times* (May 16, 1912); *Universal Jewish Encyclopedia* (1948).

[Adam Mendelsohn (2nd ed.)]

AARON BEN AMRAM (ninth–tenth centuries), court banker in Baghdad. Having built up a position of wealth and influence as private bankers, Aaron and his partner Joseph b. Phinehas were eventually accorded the official position of *jahbadh*, whose functions involved the collecting of state revenues, the issue of bills of exchange on behalf of the government, and long-term loans to the caliph's administration. At the same time, Aaron and his firm acted as private bankers for the vizier and other high officials, who transacted through them their sometimes shady business. The firm attracted the patronage of Jewish merchants, both in Baghdad, where there was a special banking quarter, and from the provinces of the Islamic empire, and beyond. Their banking transactions involved them deeply in international trade. The contributions of Diaspora communities to the upkeep of the talmudical academies in Babylonia were conveyed by letters of credit drawn on such banking houses as that of Aaron b. Amram and his partner. The influence which Aaron and his friends commanded in the Jewish community was commensurate with his position at court and in the economic life of the caliphate. Aaron sided with *Aaron b. Meir, the *gaon* in Ereẓ Israel, in his controversy with *Saadiah b. Joseph, over the supremacy of the Palestinian authorities in proclaiming the religious feasts. His sons and heirs, who inherited his official position and influence, enjoyed the confidence of Saadiah, who made use of their services in dealing with the government.

BIBLIOGRAPHY: A. Harkavy, *Teshuvot ha-Ge'onim*, 4 (1887), nos. 423, 548, 552; L. Ginzberg, *Geonica*, 2 (1909), 87–88; Fischel, Islam, 6–44.

[Walter Joseph Fischel]

AARON BEN BATASH (Ben Senton-Ben Shem Tov; Hārūn al-Yahūdī; d. 1465), vizier in Morocco. Aaron was a member of a family of Spanish origin who settled in *Fez. He served as banker and adviser to ʿAbd al-Ḥaqq, sultan of Morocco, later becoming his vizier. He appointed a relative, Saul b. Batash, intendant of the palace and chief of police. Aaron is mentioned as a scholar and writer. He imposed heavy taxes and was accused of distributing the revenue among his impoverished coreligionists. Anti-Jewish agitation by Muslim divines induced a mob attack on the Jewish quarter in Fez. The sultan and his vizier were assassinated in May 1465. (See *Morocco.)

BIBLIOGRAPHY: R. Brunschvig, *Deux récits de voyage inédits …* (1936), 113–21; A. Cour, *Etablissement des dynasties des Chérifs au Maroc* (1904), 36–38; Hirschberg, Afrikah, 1 (1965), 290–6.

[David Corcos]

AARON BEN DAVID COHEN OF RAGUSA (d. 1656), rabbi and merchant in Ragusa (Dubrovnik). After studying in Venice, Aaron returned to his native city. There he engaged in commerce, his import and export business becoming the most important Jewish commercial house in the city. At the time of the blood accusation against Isaac Jesurun in 1622, Aaron and his father were arrested. In his will, Aaron gave his children guidance for moral behavior and regular study. He also provided for the publication of the *Zekan Aharon* (Venice, 1657), which included his own discourses on the Bible and those of his grandfather (and predecessor in the Ragusa rabbinate), Solomon Ohev (Oef), which were entitled *Shemen ha-Tov*. He appended an account of the blood accusation and a poem of thanksgiving for recital on the annual commemoration of the occurrence. This appendix was reprinted separately under the title *Ma'aseh Nissim* (Venice, 1798). The will, of unique interest for the history of Hebrew publishing, provided for the printing of 800 copies of the work of which 600 were to be exported.

BIBLIOGRAPHY: J. Tadić, *Jevreji u Dubrovniku* (1937), 329–45; 453–4 (French abstract); 431–4 (text of will).

AARON BEN ELIJAH (1328?–1369), Karaite scholar, philosopher, and jurist. Aaron, who lived in Nicomedia (near present-day Izmir, in Turkish Asia Minor), was called Aaron the Younger to distinguish him from Aaron ben Joseph, or Aaron the Elder, who lived a century earlier. Aaron died in an epidemic, apparently in Constantinople.

Aaron's greatest work is a massive Hebrew trilogy of Karaite learning. The trilogy consists of *Eẓ Ḥayyim* ("Tree of Life"), dealing with philosophy of religion, composed in 1346; *Gan Eden* ("Garden of Eden"), dealing with Karaite law, composed in 1354; and *Keter Torah* ("Crown of the Law"), a commentary on the Pentateuch, written in 1362. According to Karaite tradition, Aaron wrote *Eẓ Ḥayyim* when he was 18 years old. This would place his birth in 1328, but it was probably earlier. The trilogy displays fully his great learning in both Karaite and Rabbanite literature. Aaron quotes of course the Karaite authorities, notably the 10th and 11th centuries Jerusalem scholars (his access to their Arabic writings was probably through Hebrew translations and abridgements). But he frequently quotes also the Talmud, Saadia, Rashi, Abraham Ibn Ezra, David Kimḥi, Maimonides, Naḥmanides, the earlier grammarians Judah ibn *Quraysh, Judah Ḥayyuj, Jonah ibn Janaḥ, and others. His Hebrew style, though tinted with arabisms, is clear and fluent.

Legal Teachings

As a jurist, Aaron followed mainly in the footsteps of his Karaite predecessors. He generally opposed any relaxation of the letter of scriptural law, even when it involved great exertion and hardship, except in cases of clear and evident danger to life. Yet on the other hand he accepted Jeshuah ben *Judah's reform of the Karaite law of incest, and rejected the excessive restrictions advocated by Karaite ascetics, such as the prohibition of eating meat in the Diaspora.

Biblical Exegesis

As a biblical commentator, Aaron followed the general Karaite policy of preferring the literal meaning of the biblical text, except where this meaning seemed to lead to conclusions that were blasphemous or illogical. However, this did not prevent him from indulging his philosophical bent by introducing allegorical and metaphorical interpretations where they seemed to him to be more suitable or advisable. His commentary on the Pentateuch has become the standard reference in all Karaite communities.

Philosophy

Aaron's *Eẓ Ḥayyim* was undoubtedly undertaken by him with the aim of creating a Karaite counterpart to *Maimonides' *Guide of the Perplexed*. Unlike Maimonides, Aaron did not venture to cut a new Aristotelian path for Karaite theological-philosophical thought. Instead, he remained attached to the *Muʿtazilite* philosophy (see *Kalam) which dominated his Karaite predecessors, as well as a number of pre-Maimonidean Rabbanite philosophers. Aaron is more orderly, clear, and logical than his Karaite forerunners, but he to a large extent rephrases what the latter had already said. Occasionally he avoids taking a definite stand on some points, and does not refrain from adopting some Aristotelian terminology and argumentation. Accordingly, and under the influence of Aaron b. Joseph, he attempted to forge some sort of reconciliation between traditional Karaite Kalamic positions, regarding it as his duty to stand by the tradition of his predecessors, and more Modern positions.

Although Aaron had to deal with religion in a rational fashion, he begins his philosophical work with a wholesale condemnation of the Greek philosophers and of their brainchild, philosophy, in general. The teachings of the *Mu'tazilite* "investigators" (the term "philosopher" is objectionable to Aaron), on the other hand, are in accord with Scripture (as interpreted by the Karaites), while most Rabbanite thinkers, particularly Maimonides, follow the philosophers and thus often run counter to the true principles of the Torah. Reason is the chief instrument of true knowledge, hence God exists, for His existence was deduced rationally already by the patriarch Abraham. God is one, and is neither corporeal nor characterized by any corporeal qualities. His attributes are both negative and positive – indeed every negation implies a positive assertion – and not exclusively negative, as asserted by Maimonides. His providence and justice extend to all creatures, both human and subhuman. His revelations were given to His prophets for transmission to mankind as a guide to righteous life. The world (i.e., matter) is not eternal (as the Aristotelians taught) but created – this is the chief proof of God's existence – and consequently natural law is not immutable. The universe is made up of indivisible atoms having no magnitude and not eternal, and creation signifies combination of atoms, while dissolution signifies their separation. The atomic theory of matter, rejected by the Aristotelians, is thus reasserted by Aaron. Anthropomorphic descriptions of God in the Bible must be interpreted allegorically. God is all-knowing, but man's will is free, hence no evil can be charged to God; though God foreknows that the wicked will choose evil, the blame is theirs, not God's. Free will necessarily involves retribution according to each man's deserts. Scriptural ordinances are divided into revelational, whose necessity is so sublime that it is beyond rational explanation; and rational, whose necessity is deducible by reason. Good and evil are inherently so, and are not so merely because God approves of the former and condemns the latter. His approval or condemnation simply assists man in recognizing what is good and what is evil. Divine chastisement is not always punishment for antecedent sin: in the case of a righteous person like Job it is a Divine favor intended to increase the sufferer's reward in the world to come. This explains the prosperity of the wicked and the misery of the righteous on earth. Besides, physical bliss is, at best, a base and fleeting enjoyment, hence a more sublime spiritual reward must be postulated in the hereafter. This serves as one of the evidences of the immortality of the soul and the resurrection of the dead. All these philosophical problems are treated with constant reference to, and mostly refutation of, the teachings of the Aristotelians, as set forth by Maimonides.

Aaron also composed a number of poems and hymns, some of which were included in the official Karaite liturgy. *Gan Eden* was published in Eupatoria, 1864 and 1866; Ramle 1972. *Ez Ḥayyim* was edited by Franz Delitzsch (Leipzig, 1841), and was re-edited, with an extensive commentary, by the Karaite scholar Simḥah Isaac Lutzky (Eupatoria, 1847). Extracts from these two works, in English translation, are found in L. Nemoy (ed.), *Karaite Anthology* (New Haven, 1952), 172–95, and most chapters of the latter in two Ph.D. dissertations mentioned below; *Keter Torah* was published in 1867 in Eupatoria; Ramle 1972.

BIBLIOGRAPHY: Husik, Philosophy, 362–87; Guttmann, Philosophies, 81–83; **ADD. BIBLIOGRAPHY:** M. Charner, "Aaron ben Elijah, The tree of life: First half (chapter 1–78) / Translated from the Hebrew with introd. and notes", 1949, Ph.D. Thesis, Columbia University; S.B. Bowman, *The Jews of Byzantium (1204–1453)*, 1985, index; H. Ben-Shammai, "Studies in Karaite Atomism", *Jerusalem Studies in Arabic and Islam*, 6 (1985), pp. 280–285; D. Lasker, in Da'at, 17 (1986) 33–42 (Heb.); D. Frank, "The religious philosophy of the Karaite Aaron ben Elijah: the problem of divine justice", 1991 (Includes English translation of: Sefer Ets Hayyim: chapters seventy-nine through ninety), Ph.D. Thesis, Harvard University; M. Polliack (ed.), *Karaite Judaism: A Guide to Its History and Literary Sources*, (2003), index.

[Leon Nemoy]

AARON (Arnd) BEN ISAAC BENJAMIN WOLF (c. 1670–1721), rabbi in Germany; nephew and son-in-law of the court Jew Jost *Liebmann, who appointed him head of the yeshivah he founded in Berlin. In 1697 Aaron became deputy rabbi and in 1709 rabbi of Berlin. Berlin Jewry was then rent by internal strife in which Aaron supported Liebman's widow in her struggle for leadership of the community against the court Jew Markus Magnus. When in 1713 the Magnus faction prevailed, Aaron left Berlin to become rabbi of Frankfurt on the Oder, which had been detached from the Berlin rabbinate to enable him to officiate there. Aaron was suspected of Shabbatean sympathies. In 1713 he approbated two works by Nehemiah *Hayon.

BIBLIOGRAPHY: Graetz, Gesch, 10 (1896), 322–3, n. 6, 481–510; Graetz, Hist, 5 (1949), 219, 220; Sachs, in: *Juedische Familien-Forschung*, 2 (1928–30), 15–16, 40–41.

AARON BEN JACOB HA-KOHEN OF LUNEL (end of 13th and first half of 14th century), Provençal scholar. Despite his name, he was probably not from Lunel but from Narbonne, where his forefathers lived. In his well-known work *Orḥot Ḥayyim* he makes frequent mention of the customs of Narbonne and often cites the opinions of its scholars. Aaron's grandfather, David, wrote a work on the laws of *terefot* (*Orḥot Ḥayyim*, 2:420), and his great-grandfather, Isaac, was a pupil of *Abraham b. David of Posquières and wrote a commentary on the Jerusalem Talmud (Meiri, *Beit ha-Beḥirah* on *Avot*, ed. by B.Z. Prag (1964), 56). Aaron was among those exiled from France by Philip IV in 1306 and apparently reached Spain, subsequently proceeding to Majorca. *Orḥot Ḥayyim* is for the most part a compilation of *halakhot* taken verbatim from earlier halakhic works sometimes without indicating the source (e.g., extracts from Nathan b. Judah's *Ha-Maḥkim* and David

b. Levi's *Mikhtam*). It is a work of great importance and cites *halakhot* not found in any other source. Halakhic authorities esteemed it greatly, and it was cited by Jeroham b. Meshullam, Isaac b. Sheshet, Simeon Duran, Levi ibn Ḥabib, Joseph Caro, and others. Its sources are extremely varied. Though based on Maimonides, it contains statements of German, French, Provençal, and Spanish scholars. Some (Joseph Caro, Azulai, and others) consider the anonymous work *Kol Bo* (1490) to be an abbreviated version of *Orḥot Ḥayyim*. This view, however, is controverted by a comparison of the two works. Benjacob and S.D. Luzzatto are more correct in maintaining that *Kol Bo* is the *editio princeps* of *Orḥot Ḥayyim*, probably representing an early stage of that book, and antedating the three manuscripts mentioned below.

Part 1 of *Orḥot Hayyim* was first published in Spain before 1492, but no complete copy of it is extant (for part of the missing introduction see A. Freimann, *Thesaurus Typographiae Hebraicae* (1931) B37, 1–2). The existing edition first appeared in Florence in 1750, although the manuscript had already been sent for publication by Elijah Capsali of Candia to Meir of Padua in Venice in the middle of the 16th century (*Responsa Maharam Padua*, no. 77). The order of the *halakhot* is very similar to that of the *Tur, Oraḥ Ḥayyim* of *Jacob b. Asher, Aaron's younger contemporary. The *Tur* quickly gained wide acceptance at the expense of *Orḥot Ḥayyim*. Its second part, dealing with laws of marriage, damages, things ritually prescribed or permitted, and the like was published by M. Schlesinger in Berlin in 1902 from the Warsaw Communal Library Ms. (a copy of the Jerusalem Ms. of 1455) after a rather inadequate comparison with another earlier manuscript, now in the Montefiore Library, London. There are significant differences between these two manuscripts, and between a third (in the Guenzburg Collection, Moscow, copied in 1329) which was not used by Schlesinger and which represents the earliest version of the work, having been written apparently before Aaron went to Majorca, since it omits all the passages (at least 15) referring to that island and to Shem Tov Falkon, the local rabbi. It contains however 12 more chapters than the 73 in the printed version. These deal with faith, philosophy, messianic legends, paradise, hell, the natural sciences, the formulae for documents, and (in a lengthy chapter) the principle of intercalation. The date 1313, given in this chapter, shows that the manuscript was not composed before this date.

BIBLIOGRAPHY: Benjacob, in: *Kerem Ḥemed*, 8 (1854), 167ff.; Benjacob, Oẓar, 51, no. 984, 239, no. 118; S.D. Luzzatto, *Meged Yeraḥim*, 1 (1855), 5–10; idem, *Iggerot Shadal*, 8 (1892), 1232–40, no. 562; Gross, in: MGWJ, 18 (1869), 433–50, 531–41; Gross, Gal Jud, 290, 420; Zunz, Ritus, 31–32, 179–80; M. Schlesinger (ed.), *Sefer Orḥot Ḥayyim*, pt. 2 (1902), introd.; J. Freimann, in: *Ha-Eshkol*, 6 (1919), 107–9.

[Shlomoh Zalman Havlin]

AARON BEN JOSEPH HA-KOHEN SARGADO (also known as **Ḥalaf ibn Sargado**), *gaon* and head of the academy at Pumbedita, 942–60. His antagonist *Saadiah Gaon slanderously altered his Arabic first name, Ḥalaf, to read *Kelev* ("dog") and it appears in this erroneous form in the Hebrew translation of Nathan ha-Bavli's chronicle. No satisfactory explanation has yet been found for the surname Sargado.

The *gaon* Mevasser (916/7–925/6) appointed Aaron *resh kallah* ("head of the *kallah*") although he did not come from a family of scholars. He was the son-in-law of Bishr b. Aaron, one of Baghdad's wealthiest and most respected citizens. According to the tenth-century chronicler Nathan ha-Bavli, who does not seem to have admired Aaron, Aaron was very eloquent and erudite, but Saadiah was a much greater scholar and Aaron envied him for his superior learning. In the campaign against Saadiah, led by the exilarch David b. Zakkai, Aaron took the exilarch's side and attacked Saadiah in a malicious epistle. Upon the death of Gaon Ḥananiah (Ḥanina), the father of *Sherira Gaon, Aaron assumed the direction of the academy, although Amram b. Meswi, Sherira's uncle, who was the *av bet din*, was more deserving of the gaonate. Aaron was a self-righteous and willful person, and his term of office was marked by endless quarrels. Many years later a rival *gaon*, Nehemiah b. Kohen Ẓedek, was nominated, but he was unable to assert himself against Aaron who, according to Sherira, excelled him in scholarship. Sherira's son Hai, who later became *gaon*, was Aaron's pupil in his youth.

Only fragments of Aaron's literary work have been preserved; the *Teshuvot ha-Ge'onim* contain four responsa ascribed to him (*Ḥemdah Genuzah* (1863), no. 37–40, and *Rashi Pardes*, ed. by H.Y. Ehrenreich (1924), 118–22), but only one of these is definitely by Aaron. Another responsum by Aaron was published in *Jeschurun*, 12 (1925), 50–51. Sherira and Hai Gaon mention Aaron's interpretation of a passage in the tractate *Yevamot* in one of their legal opinions (L. Ginzberg, *Geonica*, 2 (1909), 67). Aaron also wrote an Arabic commentary on the Pentateuch, in the same style as that of his rival Saadiah. The few existing fragments are inadequate to judge the character of this work, or its relationship to Saadiah's exegesis. Aaron's commentary on Deuteronomy (beginning with the weekly portion *Shofetim*) is also mentioned. Fragments of his commentary on other parts of the Pentateuch are cited in Abraham Ibn Ezra's commentary on the Pentateuch. Maimonides mentions Aaron among the older Jewish scholars who opposed the view of the Greek philosophers that the universe is eternal.

BIBLIOGRAPHY: H. Malter, *Saadia Gaon* (Eng., 1921), 113–7, 126–82, 428; Neubauer, Chronicles, 1 (1965), 66; (1965), 80ff.; Steinschneider, Arab Lit, 71; B. Lewin (ed.), *Iggeret Sherira Ga'on* (1921), 130–4; Mann, Texts, 1 (1931), index; idem, in: *Tarbiz*, 5 (1933/34), 174–5; idem, in: JQR, 11 (1920/21), 426; A. Harkavy, *Zikhron la-Rishonim*, 1, pt. 5 (1892), 222; S. Poznański, in: JQR, 13 (1922/23), 377–8; idem, in: *Ha-Goren*, 6 (1906), 63.

[Jacob Mann]

AARON BEN JOSEPH HA-LEVI (**HaRAH**, initials of his name **Ha-Rav Aharon ha**-Levi; c. 1235–1300), Spanish rabbi and halakhist. Aaron was a descendant of *Zerahiah b. Isaac ha-Levi. His principal teachers were his brother Phinehas and Moses b. Naḥman (*Naḥmanides). He had many disciples in his native Barcelona; the most famous was Yom Tov b. Abraham of Seville. In 1278 Aaron and Solomon b. Abraham *Adret were designated by Pedro III to settle a dispute in the community of Saragossa. In 1284, on the instructions of the king, he was appointed rabbi of that town for the purpose of ending the continuous dissensions in Saragossa. On Aaron's advice, the community enacted several important ordinances; some were vigorously contested both during his lifetime and in subsequent generations (Isaac b. Sheshet, Responsa, 388). After some time he returned to Barcelona where he apparently engaged in business. In 1286 he went to Toledo and remained there briefly. He returned to Barcelona.

Noted for his originality, Aaron would defer neither to the majority nor to the traditional authorities. At times, both he and Solomon b. Abraham Adret, who had many mutual disciples, were consulted on the same legal question, and answered jointly. Their personalities clashed and they often disagreed. On one occasion they requested French scholars to pronounce a final decision (Yom Tov b. Abraham of Seville, responsa, ed. by Y. Kafaḥ (1959), 79). When Adret published his *Torat ha-Bayit* ("Law of the House") Aaron wrote critical comments called *Bedek ha-Bayit* ("Repair of the House") which were printed together with the former work (Venice, 1608 and in all subsequent editions). His introduction and notes were written in an inoffensive and respectful tone. Adret hastily wrote a sharp rejoinder called *Mishmeret ha-Bayit* ("Guard of the House"), which was issued anonymously. However, Adret admits his authorship in one of his responsa. Most of his attacks were based on statements of the early legal authorities whom Aaron had ignored.

Aaron wrote several independent books. Of his novellae to the Talmud, only those to three tractates have survived – *Ketubbot* (Prague, 1734), *Beẓah* (published in the *Mareh ha-Ofannim* of Jacob Faitusi, Leghorn, 1810), and *Sukkah* (1962); the novellae on *Kiddushin* (1904) are erroneously ascribed to him. A large part of his novellae to *Shabbat* is preserved in the pseudo-R. Nissim commentary to this tractate. Of his commentaries on the *halakhot* of Alfasi, only those on tractates *Berakhot* and *Ta'anit* have survived (*Pekuddat ha-Leviyyim*, 1874; new edition M. Blau, 1957). In his preface Aaron mentioned that he wrote a short commentary on the Talmud called *Nezer ha-Kodesh* in which he gives the *halakhah* without the accompanying discussion. The work is no longer extant. Of his legal decisions, only his *Kelalei Yein Nesekh* on the prohibition of wine prepared by Gentiles (published as an appendix to Adret's *Avodat ha-Kodesh*, (Venice, 1602)), and *Hilkhot Niddah* (1967), have survived. The *Sefer ha-Hinnukh* of Aaron ha-Levi of Barcelona has been wrongly ascribed to him.

BIBLIOGRAPHY: J. Perles, *R. Salomo b. Abraham b. Adereth* (Ger., 1863), 62–63, n. 17; S. and N. Bamberger (eds.), *Pekuddat ha-Leviyyim* (1874), 5–10 (introd.); Michael, Or, no. 293; Graetz, Gesch, 8, pt. 2, 148–9; Gross, Gal Jud, 329–31, no. 20; Baer, Spain, 1 (1961), 224–5, 240, 418 n. 81; Shiloh, in: *Sinai*, 61 (1966/67), 291–7.

[Simha Assaf]

AARON BEN JOSEPH HA-ROFE ("the physician") "the Elder" (c. 1250–1320), *Karaite scholar and writer. Born apparently in Solkhat, Crimea. In 1279 he disputed there with the Rabbanites concerning the method of determining the New Moon of Tishri (see *Calendar). Apparently he also lived in Constantinople. The influence of the Talmud and Rabbanite scholars and philosophers is seen in his writings. His views were based on the Muslim *Kalām philosophical system, but he inclined toward Aristotelianism. In 1293 he completed his commentary on the Pentateuch, *Sefer ha-Mivḥar* (1835), widely used by the Karaites in the 14th and 15th centuries; several supercommentaries were written on it, the last, *Tirat Kesef*, by Joseph Solomon *Luzki. Usually preferring the plain meaning of the Bible, Aaron occasionally also uses aggadic interpretations, taken as a rule from *Rashi. He frequently quotes his Karaite and Rabbanite predecessors, notably *Abraham ibn Ezra. Aaron sometimes interpreted the *halakhah* of his sect leniently, for instance permitting Karaite residents of Jerusalem to eat meat; however this ruling was not accepted. He also disagreed with the "catenary" theory of forbidden marriage (*rikkuv*) which extended the laws against incest to extremely remote relationships, on the ground that it ran counter to the Karaite principle that no addition should be made to biblical injunctions. In these laws, he differed from the Rabbanites only in upholding the Karaite interdict of marrying one's niece. He may have preferred a permanent system of calendation instead the one based on lunar observation. Aaron also wrote commentaries on the Former Prophets and Isaiah 1–59 (*Mivḥar Yesharim*, 1836), and on Psalms 1–71 (several Mss. In Leyden and JTS, New York). He refers to an apparently lost commentary he wrote on Job. An unfinished Hebrew grammar (*Kelil Yofi*, printed Gozlow 1847), recognizably influenced by Jonah ibn *Janaḥ, was completed by Isaac b. Judah Tishbi. His polemics against Rabbanite practices and the *Kabbalah (entitled *Moreh Aharon* and *Sefer Mitzvot*) have not been preserved. Aaron's redaction of the Karaite liturgy remains the official order of Karaite service. He introduced into it *piyyutim* by Solomon ibn *Gabirol, Judah *Halevi, and *Abraham and Moses ibn *Ezra. Aaron himself wrote liturgical poems for Sabbaths and holy days, many of which have been included in the Karaite prayer book, notably those written according to the weekly reading of the Torah. A late commentary on these poems entitled *Tuv Ta'am*, has appeared in a non-critical edition (Ramle 2000). He had a marked influence upon later Karaite writers.

BIBLIOGRAPHY: Fuerst, Karaeertum, 2 (1865), 238–9; Danon, in: *JQR* (1926/27), 165–6, 265–6; Davidson, Oẓar, 4 (1933), 359; Mann, *Texts*, 2 (1935), index; Z. Ankori, *Karaites in Byzantium* (1959), index; **ADD. BIBLIOGRAPHY:** S.B. Bowman, The Jews of Byzantium (1204–1453), 1985, index; J-C. Attias, *Le commentaire biblique: Mordekhai Komtino ou l'hermeneutique du dialogue*, Paris, 1991, index; D.J. Lasker, "Aaron ben Joseph and the transformation of Karaite thought", in: *Torah and Wisdom* (1992) 121–128; G. Brinn, *Beit Mikra*, 47,4 (2002), 305–321 (Heb.); L. Charlap, *Journal of Jewish Studies*, 56,1 (2005) 80–100; idem, *Pe'amim*, 101–102 (2005), 199–220 (Heb.); M.

Polliack (ed.), *Karaite Judaism: A Guide to Its History and Literary Sources*, (2003), index.

[Zvi Avneri]

AARON BEN JUDAH KUSDINI (or **Kosdani**, i.e., "**of Constantinopole**"; end of 12th century), Karaite scholar. Of his works only a responsum addressed to Solomon b. David, the Karaite *nasi* in Cairo, concerning the law of incest is known. In it Aaron reveals himself a zealous partisan of the highly restrictive catenary (*rikkuv*) theory of forbidden marriages favored by the early Karaite authorities. Solomon rejected his views. The responsum is quoted by Karaite writers, who call Aaron *ba'al ha-derashot* ("the author of homilies") but no homilies from his pen have as yet been found.

BIBLIOGRAPHY: A. Neubauer, *Aus der Petersburger Bibliothek* (1866), 55, 117; Mann, Texts, 2 (1935), 140–1, 291.

[Leon Nemoy]

AARON BEN MEIR BRISKER (d. 1807), Polish rabbinical scholar and author. Aaron's father was one of the leaders (*allufim*) of the Brest-Litovsk (Brisk) community and one of the signatories to a letter sent in 1752 to Jonathan Eybeschuetz, whom he supported in the dispute with Jacob *Emden. Aaron studied under Eleazar b. Eleazar Kallir, author of *Or Ḥadash*. He refused to accept a rabbinical position and devoted himself exclusively to his studies. Aaron was delegate to the conference of Jewish notables of Poland which assembled in Warsaw in 1791 to deliberate on the problems of Polish Jewry. He wrote *Minḥat Aharon*, novellae on tractate *Sanhedrin* (Novydvor, 1792) with an appendix entitled *Minḥah Belulah* containing responsa and talmudical treatises. Other responsa (*Anaf Eẓ Avot*) were included in *Mekor Mayim Ḥayyim* (1839) by his grandson Jacob Meir, whose father Ḥayyim had adopted the surname Padua. In his work Aaron shows himself a master of the casuistic method of Talmud study known as *pilpul*.

BIBLIOGRAPHY: D.T. Efrussi, *Toledot Anshei Shem* (1875), 50; A.L. Feinstein, *Ir Tehillah* (1886), 33, 37, 224; M. Wischnitzer, *Istoriya Yevreyskogo Naroda*, 11 (1914), 101; I.T. Eisenstadt and S. Wiener, *Da'at Kedoshim* (1898), 124f.; EG, 2 (1954), 153.

AARON BEN MESHULLAM OF LUNEL (d. c. 1210), one of the leading scholars of Lunel. He was the son of *Meshullam b. Jacob of Lunel. Aaron studied under *Abraham b. David of Posquières, with whom he subsequently corresponded. A book on the laws of *terefot* is attributed to him, but it is likely that this treatise is an extract from his work on the Talmud or on the *halakhot* of Alfasi on tractate *Ḥullin*. *Meshullam b. Moses, son of Aaron's sister, mentions these novellae of his uncle in his *Sefer ha-Hashlamah*. Aaron was expert in astronomy and the computation of the calendar and wrote a booklet comparing the Hebrew and Christian calendars. Judah b. Saul ibn *Tibbon, in his will, urges his son Samuel to study this subject with Aaron and to rely upon him and upon his brother Asher. Aaron was an admirer of Maimonides. In the controversy which arose following the criticism by Meir ha-Levi *Abulafia of Maimonides' views on resurrection, Aaron vigorously defended Maimonides in the name of the "sages of Lunel," lauding him as "Prince (*nasi*) and rabbi, unequaled in East or in West."

BIBLIOGRAPHY: *Sefer ha-Hashlamah le-Seder Nezikin*, ed. by J. Lubetzky, 1 (1885), viii–x; Meir ha-Levi Abulafia, *Kitab al-Rasail*, ed. by J. Brill (1871), 25–40; Benedikt, in: *Sinai*, 33 (1953), 62–74; I. Twersky, *Rabad of Posquières* (1962), 251–3.

[Yehoshua Horowitz]

AARON BEN MOSES HA-LEVI (Horwitz) OF STAROSIELCE (1766–1828), leader of a dissenting group in the *Chabad branch of Lithuanian Ḥasidism. Born in Orshva Aaron was a descendant of the family of Isaiah Leib *Horwitz (Shelah; 1555–1630) and was considered both a brilliant interpreter of ḥasidic teachings and a prominent mystical innovator. He was the most prominent disciple of *Shneur Zalman of Lyady, founder of Chabad Ḥasidism (1745–1813), with whom he remained close friends for 30 years between 1783 and 1813. Personal and subsequently ideological disputes estranged him from Shneur Zalman's elder son and successor Dov Ber (see *Schneersohn, 1773–1827), who assumed Chabad leadership in a period of ensuing conflict. After Shneur Zalman's death in 1813, Aaron headed a major trend of Chabad which was marked and differentiated from the mainstream movement in questions concerning spiritual authority and ecstatic religious expression in prayer. While the importance of the intellectual approach to religious worship (*hitbonenut* in Chabad vocabulary) was accepted by all the followers of Shneur Zalman, the role of mystical rapture and the ecstatic-emotional approach, referring to communion with God known and as *devekut* or *hitpa'alut*, was intensely disputed. Dov Ber maintained a distinction between proper and improper states of ecstasy and stages of mystical rapture, claiming that his perception expressed his father's position. R. Aaron maintained, on the contrary, that he was the true follower of R. Shneur Zalman, who favored unrestricted exaltation in meditation and emotional prayer, which he considered conducive to love and reverence of God, a position which Dov Ber refused to accept. The debate is argued forcefully in the books of R. Aaron detailed below and the two tracts by R. Dov Ber – *Kuntres ha-Hitpa'alut* ("Tract on Ecstasy") and *Kuntres ha-Hitbonenut* ("Tract on Contemplation"). Aaron's most important works are (1) *Sha'arei ha-Yiḥud ve-ha-Emunah* (Shklov, 1820), a commentary completing the second (unfinished) part of the *Tanya*, the main work of Shneur Zalman; (2) *Sha'arei ha-Avodah* (Shklov, 1821) with a forward known as *petaḥ hateshuvah*, explaining and defending his approach, considered the true path set by Shneur Zalman; (3) *Avodat ha-Levi*, a compendium of sermons, letters, and miscellaneous works, published posthumously in 1842 in three volumes (Lemberg ed. and in 1866, Warsaw ed.). The composition of some of the most beautiful Ḥabad melodies is attributed to him. Although one of Aaron's sons attempted to continue his spiritual leadership in his court after his father death, most of his disciples left him to join the main Chabad movement led by Menahem Mendel of Lubavitch or other ḥasidic groups.

BIBLIOGRAPHY: L. Jacobs, *Seeker of Unity* (1966A. Horodezky, Ḥasidut, 3 (1953), 115–25; H.M. Heilman, *Beit Rabbi* (1902), 134–5, 187–190. **ADD. BIBLIOGRAPHY:** R. Elior, *Torat ha-Elohut ba-Dor ha-Sheni shel Ḥasidut Ḥabad* (1982); idem, *The Paradoxical Ascent to God* (1992); R. Elior, *"Ha-Maḥeloket al Moreshet Ḥabad,"* in *Tarbtz*, 49 (1980), 166–86; N. Loewenthal, *Communicating the Infinite* (1990); L. Jacobs, *Tract on Ecstasy* (1963), 9–12.

[Adin Steinsaltz / Rachel Elior (2nd ed.)]

AARON BEN SAMUEL (c. 1620–1701), German rabbinical author. He is best known for his concordance *Beit Aharon* (Frankfurt on the Oder, 1690–91) in which he assembled all biblical passages cited or explained in the Talmud, the midrashim, and the many religious-philosophical, homiletic, and kabbalistic writings, with exact references for each quotation. The *Beit Aharon* is based on such works as *Aaron of Pesaro's *Toledot Aharon* (1581), Simeon b. Isaac ha-Levi's *Masoret ha-Mikra* (1572), and Jacob *Sasportas' *Toledot Ya'akov* (1652). It was published in the Vilna and Grodno edition of the Prophets and Hagiographa in 1780. An enlarged edition by Abraham David Lavat appeared under the title *Beit Aharon ve-Hosafot* (1880). Aaron's other works include *Sisra Torah* (a pun on the Ashkenazi pronunciation of "*Sitrei Torah*"), a homiletic commentary on Judges 4 and 5 (on Sisera and Jael); *Shalo'aḥ Manot*, a short commentary on the Babylonian Talmud; *Megillah* (both lost); and *Ḥibbur Masorah*, a midrashic commentary on the *masorah*. Some excerpts of the latter appeared as an appendix to the *Beit Aharon*. At the request of his wife Aaron translated into Yiddish the *Midrash Petirat Moshe* (Frankfurt on the Oder, 1693), which was popular among women in Poland and Russia. Aaron also wrote a commentary on **Perek Shirah* which appeared as an appendix to the Berlin prayer book (1701).

BIBLIOGRAPHY: Michael, Or, no. 320.

[Jehuda Feliks]

AARON BEN SAMUEL (of Hergerhausen; 1665–c. 1732), author of *Liebliche Tefillah*, a volume of prayers and supplications in Yiddish. Aaron was an orphan supported by charity. Later he was a distiller of brandy for sale in his tavern. He had little schooling, but in 1709 he came to the conclusion that prayers should be recited in the current Jewish vernacular (Yiddish-Taitch) since the public was ignorant of Hebrew, and in pursuit of this aim published (Frankfurt a-M., 1709) his *Liebliche Tefillah* in that language and in his introduction urges that children be taught to pray in that language. It consists of selections from the Prayer Book, Psalms, and a number of personal supplications which include "a beautiful prayer for a servant or maid" and one "…for husband and wife that they live in harmony."

The book was completely forgotten but in 1846 Leopold Stein published an article in which he stated that some 20 years previously thousands of copies had been found in the attics of synagogues and buried. This gave rise to the statement that the book was placed under a ban of the rabbis because it advocated Reform, but despite intensive research no evidence of any such ban has been found and it is probable that the book simply did not take on.

BIBLIOGRAPHY: A. Shohat, *Im Ḥilufei Tekufot* (1960); M. Piekarz, in: *Die Goldene Keyt*, 49 (1964), 168; M. Weinreich, *History of Yiddish* (1973); M. Klarberg, in: *Working Papers*, YIVO (1980) with bibliography. **ADD. BIBLIOGRAPHY:** M. Erik, *Di Geshikhte fun der Yiddisher Literatur fun di Eltste Tsaytn biz der Haskole-Tkufe* (1929), 212–14.

[Manfred Klarberg]

AARON BERECHIAH BEN MOSES OF MODENA (d. 1639), Italian kabbalistic writer and compiler. Aaron was a cousin on his mother's side of Leone *Modena. For the benefit of the pious members of his native Modena, Aaron compiled his *Ma'avar Yabbok* ("The Crossing of the Jabbok" (cf. Gen. 32:22), Venice, 1626, and often reprinted) comprising the readings, laws, and customs relating to the sick, deathbed, burial, and mourning rites. David Savivi of Siena published an abridged version under the title *Magen David* (Venice, 1676), and Samuel David b. Jehiel *Ottolengo, another entitled *Keri'ah Ne'emanah* (*ibid.*, 1715). Aaron also compiled *Ashmoret ha-Boker* ("The Morning Watch," Mantua, 1624; Venice, 1720), containing prayers and supplications for the use of the pious confraternity *Me'irei Shaḥar* in Modena, as well as *Me'il Ẓedakah* and *Bigdei Kodesh* (both Pisa, 1785), containing prayers and passages for study.

[Shmuel Ashkenazi]

AARON ḤAKIMAN (14th century), poet; lived in Baghdad. His prolific works include the incomplete *divan* presently in the Firkovich collection (*Catalog der hebraeischen und samaritanischen Handschriften*, 2 (1875), no. 72) in St. Petersburg; this contains a *kinah* on the persecution of the Jews of Baghdad in 1344 which describes the destruction of the city's synagogues and the desecration of Torah scrolls. Outstanding among the poems of the *divan* are those in honor of *resh galuta* Sar Shalom (b. Phinehas); also included are several brief *maqamas*. His poems demonstrate the author's expert knowledge of classical Spanish poetry and the Bible, but they lack originality.

BIBLIOGRAPHY: J.H. Schirmann, *Shirim Ḥadashim min ha-Genizah* (1966), 139–46.

[Abraham Meir Habermann]

AARONIDES, members of the *priesthood in Israel. The traditional view is that throughout its history the legitimate priesthood comprised only those members of the tribe of *Levi descended directly from *Aaron, the first *high priest. The notion is anticipated in the Pentateuch by the use of such phrases as "for all time" and "throughout the ages" in connection with legislation of concern to "Aaron and his sons" (Ex. 27:21; 28:43; 30:8, 10, 19–21; Lev. 6:11, 15; 7:34ff.; 10:15 et al.). It

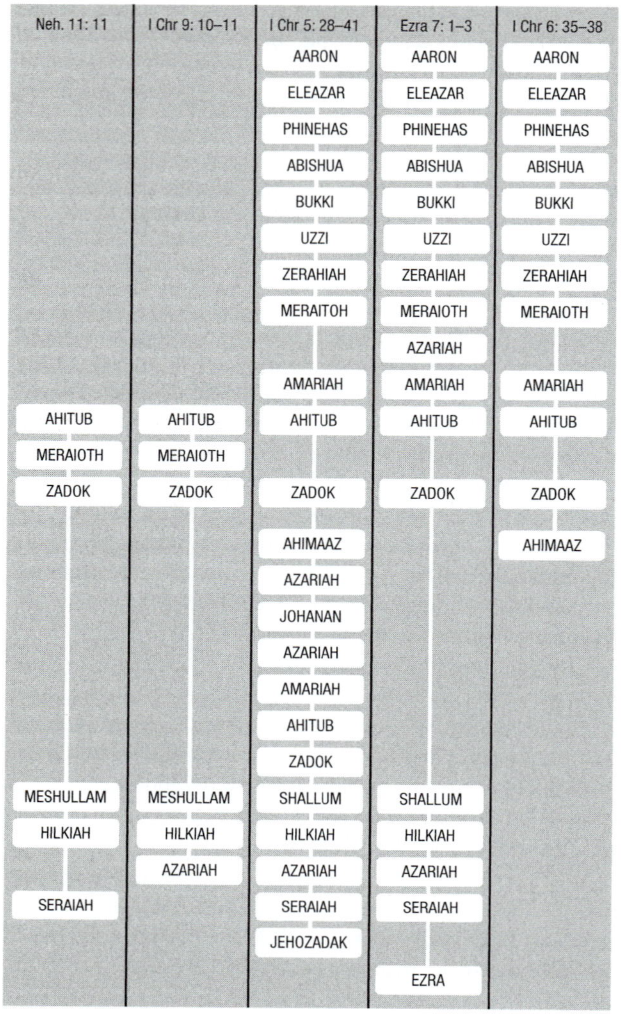

Genealogies of the Aaronides.

is made explicit in the sharp distinction between the Aaronides and the other Levites who are made subordinate to them (Num. 3:10; 17:5; 18:1–7), and it is implicit in the designation of the priesthood in general by such terms as "the son(s) of Aaron" (Josh. 21:4, 10, 13, 19; Neh. 10:39; 12:47; I Chron. 6:39, 42; 12:27; 15:4; 23:28, 32; 24:1; cf. I Chron. 13:9; 26:28; 29:21; 31:19; 35:14), "the House of Aaron" (Ps. 115:10, 12; 118:3; 135:19), and, occasionally, simply "Aaron" (II Chron. 12:27; 27:17; cf. Ps. 133:2). This same situation is assumed by the chronicler in the classification of the priestly clans according to the lines of Eleazar and Ithamar, sons of Aaron (I Chron. 24:1–4). It is also reflected in the various genealogical lists of the high priests (Ezra 7:1–5; I Chron. 5:28–41; 6:35–38).

The Critical View

This picture of the history of the priesthood is regarded as an oversimplification of a very complex situation that can no longer be reconstructed with any degree of confidence. It is possible, however, to isolate the complexities. In the first place, the construction "sons of Aaron," in itself, like the terms "sons of Korah" and "sons of Asaph," may just as well refer to a professional class or guild as to blood kinship. That there were non-Aaronide priests, who were most likely incorporated into the Aaronide guild, may be inferred from the mention of priests prior to the Sinaitic revelation (Ex. 19:22, 24). Further, in the lifetime of Eleazar, son of Aaron, Joshua is said to have allotted 13 Canaanite cities with their pasture lands to the "sons of Aaron, the priests" (Josh. 21:19; cf. 21:4, 10, 13), an impossible situation unless the description "sons of Aaron" is not to be understood literally. Secondly, the exclusive priestly legitimacy of the Aaronides is characteristic of the P document, and is found elsewhere only in the book of Joshua and in the post-Exilic Nehemiah and Chronicles. It is not to be found in D, which seems to confer priestly status and privileges upon the entire tribe of Levi (Deut. 10:8–9, 18:6–7) and to postdate the selection of that tribe to the death of Aaron. Nor are the "sons of Aaron" mentioned in Judges, Samuel, Kings, or the prophets. Ezekiel never refers to them, only to the "levitical priests, the sons of Zadok" (Ezek. 40:46; 43:19; 44:15; cf. 48:11), without ever mentioning their Aaronic ancestry.

As to the clear differentiation between Aaronides and Levites, this may well argue against the historicity of the claim to an original levitical ancestry. One of the strands in the narrative of the revolt of Korah seems to reflect an Aaronide-Levite struggle for priestly prerogatives and to derive from a period before the levitical or Aaronic genealogizing of priests was effected (Num. 16; esp. 1 and 7–10). The same tension between the tribe of Levi and the Aaronides is apparent in the golden calf episode (Ex. 32:26–29). In this connection, it is regarded as significant that Aaron's son Eleazar was buried at Gibeah, a town in the hill country of Ephraim belonging to his son, the high priest Phinehas (Josh. 24:33). It was precisely the bull-cult, with which the name of Aaron was associated, that was a characteristic of the religion of northern Israel (I Kings 12:28–29). This suggests to some the possibility that the Aaronides were close to the Ephraimites and accounted for at least some of the priests of Beth-El (cf. *ibid.* 31; Judg. 20:26ff.). In this case, the description of Moses' brother as "Aaron the Levite" (Ex. 4:14) would be a later insertion into the text, it being in fact superfluous in its present context.

The post-Exilic genealogical lists of the Aaronide high priesthood present numerous problems. Missing entirely are the high priests Amariah (II Chron. 19:11), Jehoiada (II Kings 11:4; 12:10; II Chron. 23:1; 24:20), and Urijah (II Kings 16:10–11, 15). The registers of I Chronicles (5:29–41 and 6:35–38) both list Ahimaaz, but not Azariah, while that of Ezra (7:1–6) records the latter, but omits the former. All three lists, however, have 12 generations between Aaron and the building of Solomon's temple, which suggests schematization to accommodate the 480 years (or 12 40-year generations) supposed to have elapsed between the Exodus and the construction of the sanctuary (I Kings 6:1). Further, I Chronicles (5:36–41) presupposes exactly another 12 generations between Solomon and the first high priest after the Restoration, but the repetition of Amariah, Ahitub, and Zadok (*ibid.* 33–34, 37–38) is suspicious. The genealogy of Ezra from Aaron lists only four high priests between Zadok of Solomon's time and Ezra (Ezra 7:2). The fragmentary lists of I Chronicles (9:10–11) and Nehemiah (11:11) differ slightly from each other, and both vary from the other lists. Completely ignored in these genealogical tables is the line of Ithamar to which the Eli priesthood belonged. It is quite possible that the lists are interested only in the Zadokite high priests. At any rate, they cannot be used uncritically as source material for the history of the Aaronides.

Some scholars believe that the Aaronides constituted a priestly clan that had its origins in Egypt in pre-Mosaic times and very early embraced the new faith of Moses, anticipating in this respect the tribe of Levi. It used its prestige and influence among the people to gain support for Moses. This is regarded as being the real situation behind Exodus 4:14ff., 27–31. Further corroboration of this theory is seen in the fact that in contrast to the justification for the selection of the clan of Phinehas (Num. 25:10–13) and the tribe of Levi (Ex. 32:26–29; Num. 3:12–13, 41, 45; 8:13–17), no reason is given for the choice of Aaron. The priesthood seems to come naturally to him. Another link in the chain of evidence is found in I Sam. 2:27–28, which tells of the selection of the house of Eli, undoubtedly considered Aaronide (I Sam. 22:20; I Chron. 24:3), already in Egypt where it was the recipient of a divine revelation. No mention is made of any wilderness events or of the Levites. It is noted further that Egyptian names figure prominently in the Aaronide priesthood, viz., Hophni (I Sam. 1:3), Phinehas (Ex. 6:25; I Sam. 1:3), Putiel (Ex. 6:25), Pashhur (Jer. 20:1; 21:1; Ezra 2:38), and Hanamel (Jer. 32:7). At some period, and in circumstances that can no longer be determined, the Aaronide priesthood amalgamated with the Levites and became the dominant priestly family. Its great antiquity and prestige ultimately generated the pattern of Aaronic genealogizing.

BIBLIOGRAPHY: Katzenstein, in: JBL, 81 (1962), 377–84; for further bibliography see *Aaron.

[Nahum M. Sarna]

AARON OF BAGHDAD (c. mid-ninth century), Babylonian scholar, described as the son of a certain R. Samuel, who lived in Jewish communities in southern Italy. In the sources he is referred to either as Aaron, or Abu Aaron, or Master Aaron (which might be a corrupted version of Abu Aaron). He met with several scholars in Oria, Lucca, and other communities, and many stories were told about his wisdom as well as his magical powers. His appearance is described in *Megillat *Aḥimaʿaẓ*, which is a literary chronicle of the *Kalonymus family in Italy, and in a document, written by Eliezer ben Judah of Worms in the second or third decade of the 13th century, tracing the history of the tradition of exegesis of prayers used by Eleazar and his teacher, *Judah b. Samuel he-Ḥasid. These two sources agree in attributing to Aaron, who is described by R. Eleazar as *av kol ha-sodot* ("father of all the secrets"), the transmission of certain doctrines and methods from the East to the West, to the Kalonymus family in Italy and Germany. As to the nature of these secrets, it is clear from *Megillat Aḥimaʿaẓ* that before the arrival of Aaron, Jewish scholars in Italy were studying early mystical, eastern works, especially the mysticism of the *Heikhalot* and *Merkabah*. Eleazar's words seem to prove that Aaron contributed to the Ashkenazi ḥasidic tradition of prayer exegesis. The stories in *Megillat Aḥimaʿaẓ* suggest that he may have transmitted some magical formulae, as magic was one of the fields of study (usually secret) of both the Italian and the Ashkenazi scholars. There is no evidence that Aaron contributed anything to the development of theological doctrines or mystical speculations in these areas. Nor is there proof that any known book was written by Aaron or contained a contribution by him. However, in the traditions of the Kalonymus family, Aaron serves as the link connecting its own western culture with the revered centers of learning in Babylonia of the geonic period.

BIBLIOGRAPHY: A. Neubauer, in: REJ, 23 (1891), 230–7; H. Gross, in: MGWJ, 49 (1905), 692–700; Kaufmann, Schriften, 3 (1915), 5–11; Scholem, Mysticism, 41, 84; idem, in: *Tarbiz*, 32 (1962/63), 252–65; Weinstock, *ibid.*, 153–9; J. Dan, in: Roth, Dark Ages, 282–90.

[Joseph Dan]

AARON OF LINCOLN (c. 1123–1186), English financier. Aaron probably went to England from France as an adult. His recorded transactions extended over a great part of England and his clients included bishops, earls, barons, and the king of Scotland. Aaron advanced money to the crown on the security of future county revenues ("ferm of the shires"), as well as to various ecclesiastical foundations, such as the Monastery of St. Alban's, for their ambitious building programs. Nine Cistercian abbeys owed him 6,400 marks for their acquisition of properties upon which he held mortgages. At one time Aaron worked in partnership with a rival Jewish financier, Le Brun of London. After Aaron's death, his vast estate, which might have totaled as much as £100,000, was seized by the king. A special branch of the exchequer, the *Scaccarium Aaronis*, was established and administered the estate until 1191. Some of his debts were later resold to his son Elias. Aaron had no connection with the ancient house in Lincoln which now bears his name.

BIBLIOGRAPHY: J.W.F. Hill, *Medieval Lincoln* (1948), 217–22; H.G. Richardson, *English Jewry under Angevin Kings* (1960), 247–53, passim; Roth, England, 15–17. **ADD. BIBLIOGRAPHY:** ODNB online.

[Cecil Roth]

AARON OF NEUSTADT (**Blumlein**; d. 1421), rabbinical scholar of Krems (Lower Austria). Aaron was a brother-in-law of Abraham *Klausner. He was a student, and then a colleague of Sar Shalom of Vienna (Wiener-Neustadt), and also of Jacob (Jekel) of Eger, rabbi in Vienna. Aaron was rabbi in Wiener-Neustadt and then in Vienna. A halakhic controversy arose between Aaron and Jacob on the question of non-Jews supplying Jewish prisoners with food on the Sabbath, a practice permitted by Aaron (*Leket Yosher,* ed. by J. Freimann, 1 (1903),

64). Aaron's nephew and outstanding pupil was Israel b. Pethahiah *Isserlein, who often quotes his master's biblical and talmudic teachings, in his *Pesakim u-Khetavim* (1519) and in his *Be'urim* (1519). He refers, in particular, to *Hilkhot Niddah,* a halakhic compendium by Aaron. Among Aaron's famous followers were Jacob b. Moses *Moellin (Maharil) and Isaac Tyrnau, author of *Minhagim* (1566), all of whom quote him. During the Vienna persecutions of 1420 Aaron was imprisoned and suffered severe tortures, from which he died.

BIBLIOGRAPHY: Michael, Or, no. 277; J. Freimann (ed.), *Leket Yosher,* 2 (1904), 20–21, no. 14; S. Eidelberg, *Jewish Life in Austria* (1962), index.

AARON OF PESARO (d. 1563), Italian lay scholar and bibliophile. A wealthy businessman of Novellara in northern Italy (not Nicolara, as in some works of reference), he later extended his interests to Gonzaga in the duchy of Mantua, where he was authorized to open a loan-bank in 1557. From a manuscript in his rich library the *Mirkevet ha-Mishneh* of Isaac Abrabanel was published in Sabionetta in 1551, the first Hebrew book printed there. His only known work is *Toledot Aharon*, a concordance of biblical passages cited in the Babylonian Talmud, arranged in the order of the Bible. After his death, his three sons, who succeeded him in his business, sent the manuscript of the work to the wandering Hebrew printer, Israel Ẓifroni, who published it at Freiburg in 1583–84, and Venice in 1591–92. Jacob *Sasportas appended to the work references from the Jerusalem Talmud (*Toledot Ya'akov,* Amsterdam, 1652) while Aaron b. Samuel added references from other rabbinic and kabbalistic works (*Beit Aharon*, Frankfurt on the Oder, 1690–91). *Toledot Aharon* is printed in abbreviated form in most editions of the rabbinic Bible.

BIBLIOGRAPHY: E. Castelli, *Banchi feneratizi ebraici nel Mantovano* (1959), 207; N. Ben-Menahem, *Be-Sha'arei Sefer* (1967), 17; A. Carlebach, in: *Sinai,* 62 (1967/68), 75ff.

[Alexander Carlebach]

AARON OF YORK (1190–1268), English financier, son of *Josce of York. Aaron was one of the wealthiest and most active English Jews living during the reign of Henry III. In 1241 his estate was valued for taxation at £40,000, an incredible sum. He was *Presbyter Judaeorum of English Jewry in 1236–43. During these years, as he complained to the chronicler Matthew Paris, he was compelled to pay the king over 30,000 marks; he relinquished the office and died impoverished. He was styled *nadiv* ("benefactor") in Hebrew, an indication that he was probably a patron of scholarship.

BIBLIOGRAPHY: M. Adler, *Jews of Medieval England* (1939), 127–73; Birnbaum, in: JHSET, 19 (1955–59), 199–205; H.G. Richardson, *English Jewry under Angevin Kings* (1960), passim; Roth, England, 48–49, passim. **ADD. BIBLIOGRAPHY:** ODNB online.

[Cecil Roth]

AARON OF ZHITOMIR (d. 1817), ḥasidic preacher in Zhitomir and other communities in Russia. His homilies on the weekly portions (*parashiyyot*) were recorded by his pupil Levi of Zhitomir and published in *Toledot Aharon* (Berdichev, 1817). In these, Aaron refrains from learned commentary and teaches "morality and pursuit of the service of God." Particular emphasis is given to *devekut* or adhesion to God.

BIBLIOGRAPHY: Horodezky, Ḥasidut, 2 (1953[4]), 194–6; Y. Raphael, *Sefer ha-Ḥasidut* (1955[4]), 221–5.

[Zvi Meir Rabinowitz]

AARON SAMUEL BEN MOSES SHALOM OF KREMENETS (d. c. 1620), rabbi and author. A pupil of *Ephraim Solomon b. Aaron Luntschits when the latter was rabbi at Lemberg, Aaron Samuel was forced to immigrate to Germany as a youth. Toward the end of 1606 he was preaching in Fuerth. In 1611 he was in Eibelstadt (not, as often stated, Eisenstadt), Lower Franconia, where he wrote an ethical treatise entitled *Nishmat Adam*, on the origin and essence of the soul, the purpose of human life, and divine retribution (Hanau, 1611; Wilmersdorf, 1732). In 1615 he became rabbi in Fulda, where he wrote an introduction and notes to a homily on the Decalogue by Baruch Axelrod (Hanau, 1616). In his *Nishmat Adam* he mentions three unpublished works on ethical and religio-philosophical problems (*Be'er Sheva, Or Torah,* and *Ein Mishpat*), as well as novellae to the Talmud, entitled *Kitvei Kodesh.*

BIBLIOGRAPHY: L. Loewenstein, in: JJLG, 6 (1908), 154, n. 1; J.J. Gruenwald, *Ha-Yehudim be-Ungarya* (1912), 18–19 (and A. Freimann's note, p. 14).

[Jakob Naphtali Hertz Simchoni]

AARON SAMUEL BEN NAPHTALI HERZ HA-KOHEN (1740–1814), Polish rabbi. He served as rabbi to the communities of Stefan, Ostrog, Yampol, and Belaya Tserkov. He was an ardent follower of *Dov Baer of Mezhirech and Phinehas Shapira of Korets and was influenced by them in his views on Ḥasidism. He collected extracts from their statements in his books, *Kodesh Hillulim* (Lemberg, 1864). His talmudic novellae and his responsa were destroyed by fire. Only *Kore me-Rosh*, a commentary on the *Midrash Rabbah*, of which a portion only (part of Genesis) has been published (Berdichev, 1811), and *Ve-Ẓivvah ha-Kohen*, an ethical will to his children preceded by an anthology of homiletical and esoteric thoughts (Belaya Tserkov, 1823; Jerusalem, 1953), have survived.

BIBLIOGRAPHY: M.M. Biber, *Mazkeret li-Gedolei Ostraha* (1907), 254–60.

[Yehoshua Horowitz]

AARON SELIG BEN MOSES OF ZOLKIEW (d. 1643), kabbalist. His father, Moses Hillel, was president of the Jewish community in Brest-Litovsk; his brother Samuel was a *parnas* ("delegate") in the Council of the Four Lands. Aaron wrote a compendium of the Zohar entitled *Ammudei Sheva* ("Sevenfold Pillars," Cracow, 1635), in five volumes, with an introduction. The work comprises (1) a commentary, glosses, and explanations of difficult words in the Zohar, based on the works of Meir ibn *Gabbai, Moses *Cordovero, Judah *Ḥayyat, Menahem *Recanati, Elijah de *Vidas, Shabbetai Sheftel *Horowitz, and on the notes to the Zohar by Menahem Tiktin in the margin of his copy; (2) sections from the Mantua edition of the Zohar of 1558–60 which are missing in the Cremona edition of 1558; (3) an index indicating where the various chapters of the Zohar are commented upon by the six authors mentioned above; (4) a similar index for the *Tikkunei Zohar;* (5) a list of 39 parallel passages in the Zohar with their variant readings. The last volume is extremely rare.

BIBLIOGRAPHY: S. Buber, *Kiryah Nisgavah* (1903), 24; A.L. Feinstein, *Ir Tehillah* (1886), 177; G. Scholem, *Bibliographia Kabbalistica* (1933²), 185, no. 4.

[Isaak Dov Ber Markon]

AARON SIMEON BEN JACOB ABRAHAM OF COPENHAGEN (late 18th century), secretary of the Jewish community of Cologne. Aaron is known for his participation in the important controversy known as the *Cleves *get*. Having personal knowledge of the entire case from its inception, Aaron sought to reverse the decision of Tevele Hess of Mannheim and of the Frankfurt rabbinate who had declared the divorce invalid. In conjunction with Israel b. Eliezer Lipschuetz, he appealed to all rabbis of authority in Germany, Holland, and Poland to permit the divorced woman, Leah Gunzhausen, to remarry. The majority expressed agreement with his point of view. He collected expert opinions and published them under the title *Or ha-Yashar* (Amsterdam, 1769; reprinted Lemberg, 1902, with notes by Jekuthiel Zalman Schor entitled *Niẓoẓei Or*). Aaron also wrote *Bekhi Neharot*, a description of the flood at Bonn in 1784 (Amsterdam, 1784).

BIBLIOGRAPHY: C. Brisch, *Geschichte der Juden in Koeln und Umgebung*, 2 (1882), 137–45; M. Horovitz, *Frankfurter Rabbinen*, 3 (1884), 67–78; S. Tal, in: *Sinai*, 24 (1948/49), 152–67, 214–30.

[Heinrich Haim Brody]

AARONSOHN, family of pioneers in Ereẓ Israel. EFRAYIM FISHEL (1849–1939), one of the founders of Zikhron Ya'akov, was the father of the leaders of *Nili, AARON, ALEXANDER, and SARAH. Born in Falticeni, Romania, he went to Ereẓ Israel with his wife Malkah in 1882. He was a gifted farmer, which was an occupation he continued until the end of his long life.

AARON (1876–1919), agronomist, researcher, and founder of the Nili intelligence organization. Born in Romania, he was brought to Ereẓ Israel by his parents at the age of six and grew up in Zikhron Ya'akov. He was an unusual personality whose achievements and service to his people have not been fully appreciated.

His outstanding talents became evident from early childhood, and Baron Edmund de *Rothschild, the colony's patron, generously sponsored his academic education at universities in France, Germany, and the United States.

The experimental station in *Athlit, near Haifa, which Aaronsohn founded on his return to Palestine, was a pioneering venture. It was there that his discovery of the ancestry of the wheat grain established his international reputation as an agricultural scientist.

Aaronsohn's range of interests, however, far transcended his daily research. The social and political problems of his people always competed for his attention, but his greatest passion was for Palestine. His knowledge of the country and those adjacent to it, and of the habits of life of Jew and Arab, was unparalleled.

During World War I and afterwards, when he threw himself into the mainstream of Zionist political activity, this knowledge stood him in good stead, broadening his *Weltanschauung*. But Aaronsohn was not a popular leader. Though endowed with remarkable qualities, which put him head and shoulders above his contemporaries, his individualism operated against him. Temperamental and militant by nature, he was not an easy person to work with.

Aaronsohn's conviction that the Zionist enterprise could flourish best under British protection had matured as early as 1912–13, when he was in New York. He refrained from publishing his views lest they embarrass the Berlin-based Zionist leadership. However, the brutal expulsion of Russian Jews from Jaffa in December 1914 finally shattered his hope that a *modus vivendi* with the Turk was possible.

During 1915–16 Palestine and its adjacent countries were infested with locusts. Djemal Pasha, the commander of the Ottoman Fourth Army, found that the only specialist competent to organize chemical warfare against the plague was Aaronsohn. The latter's forthright manner and skill won the Pasha's confidence but the closer their relationship became, the more concerned Aaronsohn grew about the future of his people.

With the tragedy that had befallen the Armenians at the back of his mind, he feared that at the slightest provocation Djemal would not hesitate to put an end to Zionist colonization. He therefore reached the radical conclusion that unless Palestine was speedily conquered by the British, the prospect for the survival of the *Yishuv* was slender.

It was for this reason that he made his way, by devious means, to England, leaving behind him a well-organized network of espionage. His second objective was to elicit some assurances of British sympathy for Zionist aspirations. On neither count was he successful at this stage, but unwittingly he converted his interlocutors at Military Intelligence to his cause.

Among those who fell under Aaronsohn's spell should be mentioned: Major Walter Gribbon, the officer in charge of Turkish affairs at GHQ; his close assistant, Captain Charles Webster; and Sir Mark Sykes.

Forty years later Sir Charles Webster testified how much his sympathy for the Jewish national ideal had deepened as a result of his admiration for Aaronsohn and his career:

> It was he who gave me my first real contact with one of the Yishuv and I cannot forbear to mention how deep that impression was. It was made not only by the story of his great adventure during the war, but his unexampled knowledge of Palestine and his complete faith that this land could be made to blossom like the rose by Jewish skill and industry.

Such assurances were all the more important at that time because one of the arguments most frequently used was that it was quite impossible for Palestine to accommodate more than a fraction of the numbers which the Zionists claimed could be settled there.

Aaronsohn was equally successful in making converts among British officers both in political and military intelligence in Cairo, which he joined late in 1916. William Orsmsby-Gore, Wyndham Deedes, and Richard Meinerzhagen in particular, proved a source of strength to the Zionists.

Uppermost in Aaronsohn's mind was a swift invasion of Palestine, to crush the Turk and deliver the Yishuv from disaster. It was he who alerted world public opinion to the evacuation of the Jewish population of Jaffa/Tel Aviv in April 1917; a policy which if followed to its conclusion could have resulted in a catastrophe. Exasperated by the sluggish British military advance, Aaronsohn was convinced that if properly handled, a blitz on the Palestinian front was possible.

British Intelligence was faulty and, in spite of all efforts, very little news could be elicited about enemy movements. Even when some information did filter through, it was too stale to be of any use. By contrast, not only did Aaronsohn gather a great deal of information, but by re-establishing contact with his group in Zikhron Ya'akov, he was able to furnish first-hand reports on Turkish troop movements, morale, and conditions behind enemy lines. Moreover, with his well-trained mind, he was able to give useful advice to the British on other matters, including military questions, so much so that it was humorously commented among the General Staff that "Aaronsohn is running the GHQ." A co-author of the *Palestine Handbook*, an indispensable military guide, he was also invited to write for the prestigious *Arab Bulletin*.

It was not before the arrival of General *Allenby that full use was made of Aaronsohn's suggestions. Allenby based his Beersheba operation on exhaustive intelligence data provided by the Aaronsohn group from behind the Turkish lines, which pointed to that sector as the weakest link in the enemy's defenses and one where a British onslaught was least expected. Perhaps the most crucial information was that the wells in the region had been left untouched.

The British won a resounding victory but the Aaronsohn group was less fortunate. Their ring was uncovered by the Turkish authorities at the end of September. Eighteen months later Ormsby-Gore, paying tribute to the Aaronsohn family, wrote:

> They were ... the most valuable nucleus of our intelligence service in Palestine during the war. Aaronsohn's sister was caught by the Turks and tortured to death, and the British Government owes a very deep debt of gratitude to the Aaronsohn family for all they did for us in the war ... Nothing we can do for them ... will repay the work they have done and what they have suffered for us.

General Macdonogh, the director of Military Intelligence, confirmed that Allenby's victory would not have been possible without the information supplied by the Aaronsohn group.

In Brigadier Gribbon's opinion it saved 30,000 British lives in the Palestine campaign. General Clayton considered the group's service "invaluable," while Allenby singled out Aaronsohn as the staff officer chiefly responsible for the formation of Field Intelligence behind the Turkish lines. Sir Mark Sykes acknowledged that it was Aaronsohn's idea of outflanking Gaza and capturing Beersheba by surprise that was the key to Allenby's success.

The Foreign Office, too, had formed a high opinion of him, and his presence in London in autumn 1917, when the Balfour Declaration was still in the balance, assisted in creating a favorable climate of opinion for the Zionist cause.

Aaronsohn made a valuable contribution to the work of the Zionist Commission in Palestine in 1918, and his expertise was eagerly sought by the British and Zionist delegations to the Paris Peace Conference.

On May 15, 1919, Aaronsohn died tragically when a military aircraft taking him from London to Paris crashed in the Channel.

[Isaiah Friedman (2nd ed.)]

ALEXANDER (1888–1948), one of the founders of Nili. In 1913 he founded a short-lived semi-clandestine group for sons of farmers, called Gidonim, in his birthplace Zikhron Ya'akov. A precursor of Nili, the group had as one of its purposes the defense of the settlement. In 1915 he went to Egypt as an emissary of Nili to establish contact with the British Command. From there he went to the U.S., where he was active as an anti-Turkish and pro-Ally propagandist, and wrote *With the Turks in Palestine* (1917), a book on his personal experiences, exposing the evils of Turkish rule. After World War I he founded and for a time headed *Benei Binyamin, an organization of second-generation farmers in Palestine. He contributed to the Jerusalem newspaper *Do'ar ha-Yom* and published his memoirs, as well as booklets on Nili and its members. During World War II he served with the British Intelligence Service in its operations against Germany.

SARAH (1890–1917), martyr heroine of Nili. Born and educated in Zikhron Ya'akov, she married Hayyim Abraham, a Bulgarian Jew, in 1914, and moved to Constantinople. Her married life was unhappy and, in 1915, during World War I, she returned to her family's home. En route, she passed through Anatolia and Syria, and was an eyewitness to the savage persecution of the Armenians by the Turkish authorities. On her return to Zikhron Ya'akov, her brother Aaron enlisted her into Nili's intelligence activities against Turkey. When he left the country, she supervised the agents' operations and relayed information to the British in Egypt. Later, she was responsible for receipt of the gold sent through the Nili organization for help to the *yishuv*. In April 1917 she secretly visited Egypt to consult with her brother Aaron and the British Command. Warning her of the danger that threatened her in Ereẓ Israel, they begged her to remain in Egypt, but she refused, and returned in June. In September, on learning that the espionage network had been uncovered by the Turkish authorities, she ordered its members to disperse, while she remained at home in Zikhron Ya'akov to avoid incriminating rumors, thus facilitating the escape of her fellow members. Arrested in her home on Oct. 1, 1917, she was subjected to brutal torture for four days, but disclosed nothing, and finally put an end to her suffering by shooting herself. In reverence to her memory, pilgrimages are made to her grave in Zikhron Ya'akov on the anniversary of her death.

[Yehuda Slutsky]

BIBLIOGRAPHY: A. Engle, *Nili Spies* (1959); H. Yoffe, *Dor Ma'pilim* (1939), 586–90; A. Aaronsohn (Ḥayyal Pashut, pseud.), *Sarah Shalhevet Nili* (1943^2); M. Smilansky, *Mishpahat ha-Adamah*, 2 (1954^2), 82–88; Dinur, Haganah, 1, pt. 1 (1954), 358–72; pt. 2 (1956), 730–37; 2, pt. 3 (1964^2), index; E. Livneh (ed.), *Nili, Toledoteha shel He'azah Medinit* (1961). AARON: Dinur, Haganah, 1, pt. 2 (1956); 2, pt. 3 (1964^2), index; M.b.H. Hacohen, *Milḥemet Ammim*, 1–5 (1929–30), index; M. Smilansky, *Mishpaḥat ha-Adamah*, 2 (1954^2), 95–98; E. Livneh, *Aaron Aaronsohn* (Heb., 1969). **ADD. BIBLIOGRAPHY:** I. Friedman, *The Question of Palestine, 1914–1918: British-Jewish-Arab Relations* (1992^2), 120–23, 127, 130, 184, 187, 203–5, 207, 272–74, 280, 300.

AARONSOHN, MICHAEL (1896–1976), U.S. rabbi. Born in Baltimore, Aaronsohn attended the University of Cincinnati (B.A., 1923) and was ordained the same year at Hebrew Union College. When the U.S. entered World War I in April 1917, Aaronsohn, who was entitled to a clerical exemption from military service, enlisted the following month. When his parent expressed anxiety over his decision he wrote them that "as good Jews, you should [trust] in God implicitly … without a word of doubt or discouragement." Antisemitism in the U.S. was on the rise during the war and one of the most common accusations was that Jews shirked military service. Aaronsohn, who rose to the rank of battalion sergeant-major (he served with the 147th Infantry Regiment, 39th Division of the AEF), expressed disgust at Jewish draftees who claimed that they were ineligible for overseas duty because they were foreign born, telling his parents that "while I am a Jew and love everything that Judaism stands for, nevertheless I cannot stand for a hypocrite or a low down coward."

While attempting to pull a wounded comrade to safety during the Meuse-Argonne offensive (September 29, 1918), Aaronsohn was blinded by an artillery shell. After eight months at the Red Cross school for the blind he returned to Hebrew Union College and was able to complete his studies when the college hired his sister Dora to be his note taker. During his rabbinic career Aaronsohn promoted a number of causes associated with the mental and physically disabled, for example serving a term as president of the Hamilton County (Ohio) Council for Retarded Children. He was instrumental in founding the Jewish Braille Institute in 1931, which made Jewish texts such as the Bible and Talmud more widely accessible through a free monthly magazine called the *Jewish Braille Review*.

Aaronsohn also served as a chaplain to several organizations, such as the Disabled American Veterans and the Veterans of Foreign Wars. An active member of the Republican Party, he gave the invocation at the Republican National Convention in 1940 and unsuccessfully ran for Cincinnati City Council in 1949, where he campaigned for "a scientific system of taxation." Aaronsohn was the author of numerous articles and three books, including *Broken Lights* (1946), an autobiographical novel.

[Frederic Krome (2nd ed.)]

AARONSOHN, MOSES (1805–1875), preacher, rabbi, and scholar. Born in Salant, Lithuania, Aaronsohn was a preacher (*maggid*) in Eastern Europe (Vishtinetz, Brotski, and Mir) and was recognized for his scholarship by 1836, when he published *Pardes ha-Ḥokhmah*, a book of sermons. He later published *Pardes ha-Binah*, a book of sermons with responsa. Aaronsohn arrived in the United States c. 1860, living on the Lower East Side of Manhattan, where he held services in his home and was known as "The East Broadway Maggid." For four years, he served as a preacher in a number of established synagogues, including Chevrat Vizhaner and the Allen Street Beth Hamedrash, which had split from the Beis Medrash Hagadol. In 1864, he became the rabbi at Congregation Adath Yeshurun in New York City. He continued to write responsa and also included the opinions of those rabbis in Eastern Europe with whom he corresponded regarding contemporary halakhic issues.

Aaronsohn was a strong personality with definite opinions, which eventually erupted into major controversies. He attacked the scholarship and practices of two New York rabbis who were eminent talmudic scholars, Rabbi Abraham Joseph *Ash and Rabbi Judah Mittleman, calling into question divorces written by Rabbi Ash and the *kashrut* of the animals slaughtered under the supervision of Rabbi Mittleman – whom he accused of allowing improper bloodletting before *sheḥitah*. By 1873, when he criticized the *kashrut* of certain California wines, the hostility he created in the clergy caused him to be excommunicated by Ash and Mittleman, and he was forced to leave New York. For a time, he served as an itinerant preacher and finally settled in Chicago, where he died. His book on American responsa, *Matta'ei Mosheh*, was published posthumously in 1878 in Jerusalem.

BIBLIOGRAPHY: Approbations in *Pardes ha-Binah* (1842); Z.H. Bernstein, *Yalkut Ma'aravi 1* (1904), 129–30; J.D. Eisenstein, *Oẓer Yisrael* (1907), 167; idem, *Oẓer Zikhronotai* (1929), 24; Y.Y. Greenwald, *Ha-Shoḥet ve-ha-Sheḥitah ba-Sifrut ha-Rabbanit* (1955), 6–10; M. Sherman, *Orthodox Judaism in America: A Biographical Dictionary and Sourcebook* (1996), 13–14.

[Jeanette Friedman (2nd ed.)]

AARONSON, LAZARUS LEONARD (1894–1966), English poet. A lecturer in economics at London University, Aaronson published several verse collections, including *Poems* (1933) and *The Homeward Journey* (1946). Aaronson dealt at length with his conversion in *Christ in the Synagogue* (1930) but remained preoccupied with his spiritual duality as a Jew and an Englishman in a late poem, "The Jew" (1956).

ADD. BIBLIOGRAPHY: R. Dickson and S. MacDougall, "The Whitechapel Boys," in: *Jewish Quarterly*, 195 (Autumn 2004).

ABADAN, island and seaport located in the province of Khuzistan at the southwest corner of Iran on the left bank of Shatt al-Arab and about 60 km from the Persian Gulf. It grew into a big city because of its oil refinery. During World War II there were about 25,000 refinery employees out of a total population of 100,000. This was a period in which Abadan attracted a relatively large number of Jews from several cities in Iran, mainly from *Isfahan, *Bushire, *Shiraz, and *Kermanshah. According to one source (*Alam-e Yahud*), at this time there were 200 Jewish families (about 800 people) living in Abadan, some of whom were Iraqi Jews. In addition, it has been reported that 300 out of 1,700 foreign professional refinery employees were Palestinian Jews belonging to *Solel Boneh. For this reason, one may say that the post-Reza Shah (1925–41) *He-Ḥalutz movement and Zionist activities in Iran had, to some degree, their roots in the Jewish community of Abadan. Abadan played an important role in rescue missions of the Iraqi Jews during and after the independence of Israel. After the 1979 Islamic revolution, Jews began to leave the city. At the beginning of the 21st century there were few Jewish families living in Abadan, numbering fewer than 20 people.

BIBLIOGRAPHY: "Abadan," in: *Encyclopedia Iranica* (ed. E. Yarshater), 1 (1982), 51–57; *Alam-e Yahud*, 21 (Jan. 8, 1946), 362; Y. Yazdani, *Records on Iranian Jews' Immigration to Palestine, 1921–1951* (1996), 61, 67, 110.

[Amnon Netzer (2nd ed.)]

ABADDON (Heb. אֲבַדּוֹן; "place of destruction"). It is mentioned in the Wisdom literature of the Bible (Job 26:6; 28:22; 31:12; Prov. 15:11; Ps. 88:12); and it occurs also in the New Testament (Rev. 11:11) where, however, it is personified as the angel of the bottomless pit, whose name in Greek is "Apollyon" (Ἀπολλυων, "destroyer"). In the Talmud (Er. 19a) it is given as the second of the seven names of Gehenna (*Gehinnom), the proof verse being Psalms 88:12, while *Midrash Konen* makes it the actual second department of Gehenna.

ABARBANELL, LINA (1879–1963), star of European light opera and Broadway doyenne. Born in Berlin to a prominent Sephardi family active in the professional theater, Abarbanell debuted as Adele in the Berlin Court Opera's production of *Die Fledermaus* in 1904, at the age of 15. As a young woman, she toured European concert halls and theaters, establishing a career as a vocalist and actress. She won especial renown in the world of Viennese operetta, where luminaries of the scene, such as Franz Lehar and Oscar Straus, composed works for her. She spent a season in New York with the Metropolitan Grand Opera in 1905, appearing as Hänsel in the American premiere of Humperdinck's *Hänsel und Gretel*. Abarbanell and her husband, Edward Goldbeck, an editorialist and cultural commentator, and their young daughter settled in Chicago soon after, returning to New York after World War I.

In America, Abarbanell introduced the Viennese light musical repertoire to popular audiences and won fame and critical plaudits with starring roles in Lehar's *The Merry Widow*, among other works. A fashionable, graceful, and vivacious personality, she helped popularize songs and dances of the musicals and light operas in which she appeared. With her husband, she hosted a weekly salon in her Chicago home for European and American artists and writers. Abarbanell essentially supported the family through her theater career, seeing them through bankruptcy in 1921. After the death of her husband in 1934, she transformed herself from performer to producer and director. Her daughter Eva Goldbeck, a fiction writer and reviewer who published in periodicals such as the *New Republic*, died in 1935 at the age of 34. Abarbanell maintained a close relationship with her son-in-law, the composer Marc Blitzstein (*The Cradle Will Rock*), for the rest of her life. She established a successful second career as casting director for Blitzstein and others, in theater (*Porgy and Bess*) and in film (*Carmen Jones*), and remained actively involved in the theater world until her death from heart failure shortly after her 84th birthday.

BIBLIOGRAPHY: E.A. Gordon, *Mark the Music: The Life and Work of Marc Blitzstein* (1989); "Abarbanell, Lina," in: P.E. Hyman and D. Dash Moore (eds.), *Jewish Women in America: An Historical Encyclopedia*, 1 (1997), 3–4; *Variety Obituaries*, vol. 5 (1957–63).

[Emily Alice Katz (2nd ed.)]

ABBA (Heb. אַבָּא), Aramaic equivalent of the Hebrew (*av*, אָב; "father"). The term was in common use from the first century onward (cf. Mark 14:36). In the early centuries of the Christian era it was used in both Jewish and Christian sources in addressing God, and in talmudic times as a prefix to Hebrew names, probably to designate an esteemed scholar (cf. Abba Hilkiah, Abba Saul). K. *Kohler, however, was of the opinion that the title referred specifically to Essenes. Because of its honorable association, it was forbidden to call slaves by this name (Ber. 16b). It often occurs independently, sometimes perhaps as an abbreviation of Abraham. Its fusion with the prefix "*rav*" (for "rabbi") gave rise in Babylonia to the names "Rabbah," "Rava," and to their abbreviated forms, "Ba" and

"Va" in Palestine. It is a common name among Ashkenazi Jews in Eastern Europe and Israel, often used as an agnomen of Abraham. The word survives in European languages as an ecclesiastical designation (Abbas, Abt, Abbot), while in modern Hebrew it has largely displaced the Hebrew *av* as the popular term for "father."

BIBLIOGRAPHY: Klein, in: *Leshonenu*, 1 (1928/29), 326; Kohler, in: JQR, 13 (1900/01), 567–80 (but see Urbach, in: PIASH, 2, pt. 4 (1966), 17–36).

[Cecil Roth]

ABBA (Ba), two *amoraim* are known by this name.

(1) ABBA (late third and early fourth centuries), in his youth probably knew Rav and Samuel, the founders of rabbinic learning in Babylonia. He was, however, primarily a disciple of R. Huna and R. Judah, and frequently is mentioned together with their other disciples. Like R. Zeira, Abba ignored R. Judah's prohibition to leave Babylonia and emigrated to Ereẓ Israel (Ber. 24b). In Ereẓ Israel Abba was a close friend of R. Zeira and other Palestinian scholars. In Tiberias he studied with R. Johanan's chief disciples, R. Eleazar and Resh Lakish. After the death of Eleazar, leadership passed to R. Ammi and R. Assi, but Abba was considered equally great and was referred to in the Babylonian academies as "our teacher in the land of Israel" (Sanh. 17b). Abba dealt in silk (BK 117b) and became very wealthy. This enabled him to honor the Sabbath by buying 13 choice cuts from 13 butchers (Shab. 119a). A very charitable man, he never embarrassed the poor and would put money in his scarf which he would hang behind his back, so that the poor might take the money without him seeing their faces (Ket. 67b). He frequently revisited Babylonia, but always returned to Ereẓ Israel for the festivals. Thus he transmitted Babylonian teaching and traditions to Ereẓ Israel and vice versa (TJ, Shev. 10:2,39c; Ned. 8:1,40d; BM 107a). When the body of his teacher Huna was brought from Babylonia for burial, Abba eulogized him, saying "Our teacher deserved to have the *Shekhinah* rest upon him, were it not that he lived in Babylonia" (MK 25a). Influential in both *halakhah* and *aggadah*, Abba's teachings are found in the Babylonian and Palestinian Talmuds, as well as in the Midrash. (For a critical analysis of the traditions relating to the death and burial of Rav Huna, see S. Friedman, Historical Aggadah, pp. 146 ff.)

(2) ABBA (THE LATER; fourth–fifth centuries), Palestinian *amora*. Abba went to Babylonia, probably during the anti-Jewish reaction following the death of *Julian the Apostate in 363 C.E. Abba is mentioned together with R. Ashi, to whom he transmitted the Palestinian tradition (BK 27b). He is also quoted as saying to R. Ashi: "You have derived teaching from this source, we derive it from a different one, as it is written: 'A land whose stones are iron' [Deut. 8:9], Do not read 'whose stones' [אֲבָנֶיהָ, *avaneha*] but rather 'whose builders' [בּוֹנֶיהָ, *boneha*, i.e., sages]", meaning that a scholar who is not as hard as iron is no scholar (Ta'an. 4a; cf. Bek. 55a). He is not mentioned in the Palestinian Talmud.

BIBLIOGRAPHY: (1) Bacher, Pal Amor; Hyman, Toledot, 3–8. (2) A. Harkavy (ed.), *Teshuvot ha-Ge'onim*, 4 (1887), no. 248; Halevy, Dorot, 2 (1923), 573–6; Hyman, Toledot, 9 ff.

[Yitzhak Dov Gilat]

ABBA (Rava, Rabbah; eighth century), rabbinical scholar; disciple of *Yehudai Gaon and possibly also of *Aḥa of Shabḥa, the author of *She'iltot*. Abba is the author of *Halakhot Pesukot*, a juridical tract in the vein of *She'iltot* from which it apparently quotes. It was published in segments twice – first by S. Schechter and then by J.N. Epstein. A small monograph on the laws of phylacteries (probably part of a larger work), which has been attributed to Abba, was appended by *Asher b. Jehiel – who calls it the work of a *gaon* – to his own laws on the subject, under the title *Shimmusha Rabbah* ("Rabbah's Legal Practice"); it was printed in the Vilna edition of the Talmud in Asher's *Halakhot Ketannot* at the end of tractate *Menaḥot*. *Judah b. Barzillai pointed out that many of its utterances run counter to talmudic regulations, a phenomenon which he attributed to errors by pupils and copyists. Among Abba's best-known pupils was *Pirkoi b. Baboi.

BIBLIOGRAPHY: S. Schechter, in: *Festschrift ... David Hoffmann* (1914), 261–6 (Heb. sect.); Baron, Social^2, 6 (1958), 339–40, n. 43, 356, n. 72; J.N. Epstein, in: *Madda'ei ha-Yahadut*, 2 (1927), 147–63.

[Meir Havazelet]

ABBA BAR AḤA (third century), *amora*. He was born in Ereẓ Israel and emigrated to Babylonia (TJ, Ber. 1:9,3d). Several *halakhot* are quoted by him in the Jerusalem Talmud in the name of "Rabbi" (Judah ha-Nasi) and in the Babylonian in that of "Rabbenu"; therefore he may have been a pupil of Judah ha-Nasi. In the Jerusalem Talmud (*loc. cit.*) Abba b. Aḥa is quoted as saying in the name of Rabbi (according to Ber. 49a, cf. Dik. Sof. 258, in the name of Rabbenu): "If one fails to mention 'covenant' [i.e., the phrase 'for Thy covenant which Thou has sealed in our flesh'] in the Blessing for the Land or 'the kingdom of the House of David' in the blessing 'who rebuildest Jerusalem' [both in the Grace after Meals], it must be repeated correctly." R. Ilai reports decisions in his name (Ber. 49a, et al.). He is the author of the statement, "The nature of this people [Israel] is incomprehensible. Approached on behalf of the golden calf, they contribute; approached on behalf of the tabernacle, they contribute toward it too" (TJ, Shek. 1.145d).

BIBLIOGRAPHY: Hyman, Toledot, 15; Abraham Zacut, *Sefer Yuḥasin ha-Shalem* (1924^2), 99–100.

[Zvi Kaplan]

ABBA BAR AVINA (third century), Palestinian *amora*. He was also called Abba b. Binah, Abba b. Minah, or simply Buna. He was of Babylonian origin and studied there at the academy of *Rav (cf. TJ, Sanh. 3:3,2la) but later immigrated to Ereẓ Israel. Among his pupils were R. *Abba b. Zavda and R. Berechiah. Most of his sayings are quoted in the Jerusalem Talmud and in the Midrash (e.g., Lev. R. 20:12); he is mentioned only once in the Babylonian Talmud (Shab. 60b). Abba

b. Avina was consulted in legal questions (TJ, *ibid.*) and seems to have officiated as a judge (TJ, BM, 5:2,10a). He interpreted I Chronicles 22:14: "Behold in my straits I have prepared for the house of the Lord … etc." to teach that wealth does not matter before the Creator of the universe. A moving confession, composed by him, is quoted at the end of Jerusalem Talmud (Yoma 8:10,45c): "My God, I have sinned and done wicked things. I have persisted in my bad disposition and followed its direction. What I have done I will do no more. May it be Thy will, O Everlasting God, that Thou mayest blot out my iniquities, forgive all my transgressions, and pardon all my sins." The Palestinian *amora*, R. Ḥigrah, was his brother (TJ, Meg. 1:11,71c).

BIBLIOGRAPHY: Bacher, Pal Amor; Hyman, Toledot, 14.

ABBA BAR KAHANA (late third century), Palestinian *amora*. It is possible that he was the son of Kahana the Babylonian, the pupil of Rav who immigrated to Ereẓ Israel. Abba quotes *halakhot* in the name of Ḥanina b. Ḥama and Ḥiyya b. Ashi (Shab. 121b; TJ, Ber. 6:6, 10d), but his talents lay largely in the realm of *aggadah* and, with his contemporary R. Levi, he was regarded as one of its greatest exponents (TJ, Ma'as. 3:10,5 la). Early aggadic traditions of leading *tannaim* such as *Eliezer b. Hyrcanus, *Simeon b. Yoḥai, *Judah b. Ilai, and *Phinehas b. Jair were known to Abba. Among his statements are "Such is the way of the righteous: they say little and do much" (Deut. R. 1:11) and "No serpent ever bites below unless it is incited from above … nor does a government persecute a man unless it is incited from above" (Eccles. R. 10:11). This statement probably reflects the persecutions of the Jews of his time, to which there may also be a reference in the observation "The removal of the ring by Ahasuerus [Esth. 3:10] was more effective than the 48 prophets and seven prophetesses who prophesied to Israel but were unable to lead Israel back to better ways" (Meg. 14a). His homiletical interpretations deal with biblical exegesis; he identifies anonymous biblical personalities (e.g., Dinah was the wife of Job: Gen. R. 19:12, etc.) as well as geographical sites whose location was not clear (Kid. 72a). He embellishes the biblical narrative with tales and *aggadot* (Gen. R. 78:16; Eccles. R. 2:5, etc.). His statements reflect the contemporary hardships and persecutions suffered by the Jews (Lev. R. 15:9). Abba expresses his expectation of redemption in the remark that "if you see the student benches in Ereẓ Israel filled with sectarians [Babylonians], look forward to the approaching steps of the Messiah" (Lam. R. 1:41); *ibid.*, ed. Buber, 39a, however reads "every day" (Heb. בכל יום) instead of "Babylonians" (Heb. בבליים).

BIBLIOGRAPHY: Hyman, Toledot, 48–50; Bacher, Pal Amor; A. Marmorstein, in: *Jeschurun*, 13 (1926), 369ff.

[Yitzhak Dov Gilat]

ABBA BAR MARTA (third and first half fourth centuries), Babylonian *amora*. Some suggest that he was named after his mother because she cured him as a child after he'd been bitten by a mad dog (Yoma 84a). He owed a debt to the exilarch and was seized by his men on a Sabbath. However, the exilarch set him free because he was a scholar (Shab. 121b). In another incident Abba b. Marta managed to outwit the exilarch's men who sought to hold him prisoner because of his debt (Yev. 120a). In another instance Abba b. Marta owed money to Rabbah, the head of the Pumbedita academy. He went to Rabbah with the intention of repaying his debt during the sabbatical year. Rabbah answered in accordance with the *halakhah*. "I cancel it." Abba b. Marta took the money back, instead of saying, as the procedure demanded, "Nevertheless, I insist…." Only after the intervention of Abbaye did he realize that he had not acted properly and repaid the debt (Git. 37b). Another contemporary scholar, Abba b. Menyamin (Menyomi, Benjamin) b. Ḥiyya, who expounded Mishnayot and asked a halakhic question of Huna b. Ḥiyya (Sot. 38b, Ḥul. 80a), is sometimes identified with Abba b. Marta.

BIBLIOGRAPHY: Hyman, Toledot, 53; Bacher, Trad, 243.

[Moshe Beer]

ABBA BAR MEMEL (third and the beginning of the fourth centuries), Palestinian *amora*. Some scholars consider that Memel refers to his place of residence, Mamla or Malaḥ in Lower Galilee. He posed questions to R. Oshaya in Caesarea who may have been his teacher (TJ, BK 2:1, 2d). Eleazar b. Pedat, one of his eminent contemporaries, refers to Abba Memel as his master (Ket. 111a). He discussed halakhic problems with R. Ammi, R. Assi, R. Zeira, and others, and *halakhot* are quoted in his name by many Palestinian sages. He is the author of several principles concerning the interpretation of the biblical text. A *gezerah shavah* ("inference from a similarity of phrases in texts") may be established to confirm but not to invalidate a teaching. One may deduce a *kal va-ḥomer* (inference from minor to major) of one's accord, but not a *gezerah shavah*. An argument may be refuted on the basis of a *kal va-ḥomer*, but not on the basis of a *gezerah shavah* (TJ, Pes. 6:1, 33a). He also stated, "If I had someone who would agree with my view, I would permit … work to be done on the intermediate days of the festival. The reason why work is then prohibited is to enable people to eat and drink and study the Torah; but instead they eat and drink and engage in frivolity …" (TJ, MK 2:3, 81b).

BIBLIOGRAPHY: Frankel, Mevo, 67a-b; Hyman, Toledot, 50–52; Bacher, Pal Amor.

[Yitzhak Dov Gilat]

ABBA BAR ZAVDA (third century), Palestinian *amora*. Abba studied in Babylonia, first under Rav and later under R. Huna. He returned to Ereẓ Israel, where he became one of the leading scholars at the yeshivah of Tiberias. He quotes *halakhot* in the name of the last of the *tannaim*: R. Simeon b. Ḥalafta, R. Judah ha-Nasi, and R. Ḥiyya as well as R. Ḥanina, R. Johanan, and Resh Lakish. After the deaths of R. Johanan and R. Eleazar b. Pedat, Abba b. Zavda became one of the most prominent sages in Ereẓ Israel. At the yeshivah of Tiberias he was given the honor of opening the lecture which Ammi and Assi closed (TJ, Sanh. 1:4, 18c). His humility is stressed by the sages (*ibid.*, 3:5, 21a). His saying, "A Jew, even though he sins, remains a Jew" (Sanh. 44a) is well known. In a sermon delivered on a public fast day, Abba b. Zavda called on those who wished to repent first to mend their evil ways, for "if a man holds an unclean reptile in his hand, he can never become clean, even though he bathes in the waters of Shiloaḥ or in the waters of creation" (TJ, Ta'an. 2:1; in TB, Ta'an. 16a, the statement with slight variations is ascribed to Abba b. Ahavah).

BIBLIOGRAPHY: Hyman, Toledot, 43–44; Frankel, Mevo, 66b.

[Yitzhak Dov Gilat]

ABBA BAR ZEMINA (also **Zimna**, **Zimona**, **Zevina**; fourth century), Palestinian *amora*. His father was probably the Zemina who acted as "elder" of the Jews of Tyre (TJ, Bik. 3:3, 65d). Abba's principal teacher was Zeira. While working as a tailor in Rome, his employer offered him meat which had not been ritually slaughtered and threatened to kill him if he refused to eat it. When Abba chose death, his employer informed him that had he eaten, he would have killed him, saying, "if you are a Jew, be a Jew, if a Roman be a Roman" (TJ, Shev. 4:2, 35a-b). The statement, "if our predecessors were as angels, we are as men; if they were men, we are as donkeys," is quoted by Abba b. Zemina in the name of Zeira (TJ, Dem. 1:3, 21d; in Shabbat 112a, by Zeira in the name of Rabbah b. Zemina).

BIBLIOGRAPHY: Frankel, Mevo, 56b-57; Bacher, Pal Amor; Hyman, Toledot, 44–45.

[Abraham Goldberg]

ABBA BEN ABBA HA-KOHEN (early third century), Babylonian scholar during the transition from the tannaitic to the amoraic period. Abba is overshadowed by his famous son Samuel, and therefore is always referred to in the Babylonian Talmud as "the father of Samuel" (cf. Beẓah 16b). He was a native of Nehardea and decided issues of Jewish law there (Ket. 23a). He subsequently emigrated to Palestine and continued his studies in the academy of R. Judah ha-Nasi (TJ, RH 3:6, 59a; TJ, BM 4:1, 9c). Even after his return to Babylon, he addressed halakhic inquiries to him and maintained contact with his grandson R. Judah Nesia. He was a colleague of R. Levi b. Sisi and their opinions are often cited together (Shab. 108b; MK 26b). Mention is made of a divine revelation granted to the two when they were studying Torah together in the ancient synagogue Shaf ve-Yativ in Nehardea (Meg. 29a). The Jerusalem Talmud (Ber. 2:8, 5c) quotes the funeral oration Abba delivered over his friend. When Rav returned to Babylon, he deferred to Abba by refusing to head the community during the latter's lifetime. Rav engaged in halakhic discussions with Abba, whom he highly respected (Ket. 51b). Abba derived his livelihood from trading in silk and also owned property. Highly charitable, he supported orphans and redeemed captives, and in all his actions attempted to go beyond the mere letter of the law.

BIBLIOGRAPHY: Frankel, Mevo, 56ab; Hyman, Toledot, 11; Epstein, Mishnah, 211.

[Zvi Kaplan]

ABBA BENJAMIN, *tanna* of unknown date. Four aggadic statements are quoted in his name (Ber. 5b–6a). They include: "A person's prayer is heard [by God] only in the synagogue." "If two enter [a synagogue] to pray, and one of them finishes his prayers first, and leaves without waiting for the other, his prayers are torn up before his face." "If the eye had the power to see the demons, no creature would be able to endure them." He has been identified with Benjamin the Righteous who was in charge of a charity fund. Once, when the fund was depleted during a famine, he supported a woman and her seven sons from his own pocket. Later he became gravely ill and was about to die, whereupon the ministering angels addressed the Almighty: "Sovereign of the universe, Thou hast said that he who saves one soul is regarded as having saved the whole world. Shall Benjamin the Righteous who saved a woman and her seven sons die so young?" Immediately the decree against him was annulled and a further twenty-two years were added to his life (BB 11a).

BIBLIOGRAPHY: Hyman, Toledot, s.v.

[Yitzhak Dov Gilat]

ABBA GULISH. Legendary figure mentioned in midrashic literature (Mid. Hag. to Ex. 2:16). Abba Gulish was a priest at a heathen temple in Damascus. However, on one occasion, when in great distress, he supplicated his idol without success. Disappointed with idol worship, he went to Tiberias where he converted to Judaism, zealously observing the precepts. He was there appointed overseer for the poor, but he embezzled the money entrusted to him and was punished by blindness, first of one eye and later of both. An object of contempt, he returned to Damascus where his former friends, regarding his blindness as a punishment for his apostasy, reproached him for his unfaithfulness. He thereupon assembled the people in the shrine for the ostensible purpose of apologizing to the idol, but instead he told them that an idol which is unable to see could not have punished him with blindness; it was the work of the omniscient God. As he descended from the dais, his sight was restored, as a result of which thousands of heathens became proselytes. It is not possible to determine whether there is any historical basis for this legend.

BIBLIOGRAPHY: S. Krauss, in: OLZ, 20 (1917), 110.

ABBA GURYON OF SIDON (second century), talmudic sage. Only two of his statements, both quoted in the name of other sages, have been preserved. One (Kid. 4:14) is "a man should not teach his son the occupation of an ass driver, camel driver, barber, sailor, shepherd, or tavern keeper, these being the trades of robbers." The second is contained in the introduction (ix) to a late Midrash on Esther known as *Midrash Abba Guryon* (ed. by S. Buber, 1886), taken apparently from *Esther Rabbah*. "With the increase of false judges, false witnesses increased; of informers, the wealth of violent men increased; of impudence, respect for human beings ceased; when the beloved children provoked their heavenly Father to anger, He set an arbitrary king over them." The "arbitrary king" is probably Domitian (89–96 C.E.) and the reference to "informers" may be reflected in the coin struck by his successor Nerva to commemorate the abolition of the calumny connected with the Jewish tax.

BIBLIOGRAPHY: S. Klein (ed.), *Sefer ha-Yishuv*, 1 (1939), 129; Hyman, Toledot, 302.

[Bialik Myron Lerner]

ABBA ḤILKIAH, according to the *aggadah* (Ta'an. 23a–b) a saint who lived in the first century C.E. Like many narratives concerning saints in the ancient world, Abba Ḥilkiah was famous for his miraculous ability to bring rain in times of drought (Kalmin, 212). The Talmud describes him not as a learned sage, but rather as a common worker to whom the sages turned in time of need. Once when a pair of scholars came to ask him to pray for rain, he was not at home, and they finally found him hoeing in a field. They greeted him, but he did not return their greeting. Toward evening he gathered wood for his fire, put the wood and his hoe on one shoulder and his cloak on the other. All the way home he wore shoes, but when he passed through water he removed them. When he approached thorns and thistles he raised up his garment. And so the story goes on describing his apparently eccentric behavior, which puzzled the two sages, who nevertheless followed him into his home. Without speaking to the sages he and his wife went up to roof and prayed, and his wife's prayer was answered first. Despite the disclaimers of the humble and saintly man, the sages thanked him for bringing the much needed rain. Before they left, they asked him about his puzzling behavior, and he explained how every element reflected some aspect of practical wisdom or ethical concern. For example his refusal to return their greeting was explained by the fact as a day laborer, he feared to take time off during his work hours lest by so doing he would be defrauding his employer. Similarly, he put the wood and his hoe on one shoulder and the cloak on the other because the cloak was borrowed, and the owner of the cloak had not given him permission to rest wood or a hoe on his cloak, and so on.

The story belongs to a genre of tales of the saints, common in the pagan and Christian world in antiquity. It is somewhat remarkable in the talmudic context because its hero, though not himself a sage, turns out to exemplify many of the most noble values which the sages admired, and was even capable of instructing the sages through his behavior regarding these values (Kalmin, 225–232).

In line with its principle of "creative historiography," the Talmud informs us that this saintly figure, Abba Ḥilkiah, was in fact the grandson (son of the son) of *Ḥoni ha-Me'aggel, the famous "rainmaker" mentioned in Mishnah Ta'an. 3:8. Similarly, the Talmud tells us that Ḥanan ha-Naḥbah, another saintly rainmaker who is the protagonist of the following story in Ta'an. 23b, was also the grandson (son of the daughter!) of Ḥoni.

BIBLIOGRAPHY: Hyman, Toledot, s.v.; R. Kalmin, in: L.I. Levine (ed.), *Continuity and Change* (Hebrew) (2004), 210–232.

[Stephen G. Wald (2nd ed.)]

ABBAHU or **Avahu** (c. 300), usually counted a second generation Palestinian *amora*. He is often presented as the disciple of R. Johanan who purportedly called him "Abbahu my son." He also is said to have studied with Resh Lakish (See *Simeon b. Lakish) and *Eleazar b. Pedat. Abbahu most likely lived in Caesarea, then the center of Roman rule and of Palestinian Christianity. He seems to have been an important halakhic figure and his aggadic sayings are significant in the fields of religion, ethics, and philosophy. Abbahu is presented in rabbinic literature as learned in mathematics, rhetoric, and Greek, which, we are informed, he taught his daughters. Tradition also endows him with good looks and physical strength and great wealth. It is reported that the Romans "showed favor to his generation for his sake," perhaps a token of the great esteem in which they may have held him. His access to government circles may have given him a special position among his colleagues.

The Babylonian Talmud (Sot. 40a) tells us that Abbahu declined academic leadership in favor of *Abba of Acre because the latter was poor and debt ridden. This legend goes on to show Abbahu concealing his true reasons. Various passages also depict him in the following ways: He was a peacemaker even when others gave offense. He judged all men favorably and appreciated even a single merit of a sinner. He had special esteem for the scholars and taught that a scholar who had committed an offense deserving *niddui* ("the minor ban"), should be treated with consideration (TJ, MK 3:4, 81d). He enjoyed a position of honor in the community. He was an ordained judge, entitled to sit in judgment alone, but earned his livelihood in trade. He was apparently head of a group of scholars known as "the rabbis of Caesarea" and trained many outstanding disciples, among them the *amoraim* R. Jeremiah, R. *Jonah, and R. *Yose. He enacted ordinances, issued proclamations, and introduced usages such as the now accepted order of blowing the *shofar* on *Rosh Ha-Shanah* (RH 34a). Because of his position within the Jewish community and his connections with the authorities he made many official trips, both in Ereẓ Israel and abroad. On such occasions he always deferred respect to the customs of the local community.

His aphorisms include: "Where the penitent stand, the wholly righteous cannot reach" (Ber. 34b); "A man should never tyrannize his household" (Git. 7a); "Be among the persecuted rather than persecutors" (BK 93a); "The world endures only on account of the man who utterly abases himself" (Ḥul.

89a). A prayer ascribed to him reflects the times in which he lived: "May it be Thy will ... to save us from the arrogance and harshness of the evil times which threaten to overtake the world" (TJ, Ber. 5:1, 8d).

With regard to Christianity he said, "If a man tells you 'I am God,' he is lying; 'I am the son of man,' he will eventually regret it; 'I shall go up to heaven,' he promises but will not fulfill" (TJ, Ta'an. 2:1,65b). Similarly he explained the verse (Isa. 44:6) "I am the first" means "I have no father"; "I am the last" means "I have no son"; "and beside me there is no God" means "I have no brother" (Ex. R. 29:5). It is stated in his name: "it was ordained [some say, in Usha] that 'Blessed be the name of His glorious kingdom for ever and ever' be recited in a loud voice-to offset any false charges by sectarians" (Pes. 56a; Rashi explains "lest they say that we add something improper in a low voice"). Abbahu isolated the Samaritan priests in his town from the Jewish community and decreed that they should be regarded as Gentiles in all ritual matters. When the Samaritans asked him "Your fathers found our food and wine acceptable, why not you?" he answered, "Your fathers did not corrupt their ways, but you have yours" (TJ, Av. Zar. 5:4, 44d).

BIBLIOGRAPHY: Frankel, Mevo, 58b–60a; Weiss, Dor, 3 (1904[4]), 91–93; Halevy, Dorot, 2 (1923), 350–6; Bacher, Pal Amor, 2; Hyman, Toledot, 62–71; S. Lieberman, *Greek in Jewish Palestine* (1942), 21–33; S. Klein (ed.), *Sefer ha-Yishuv*, 1 (1939), 145–8; Lachs, Samuel Tobias "Rabbi Abbahu and the minim," in: JQR, 60 (1970) 197–212; Perlitz, in: MGWJ, 36 (1887), 60–88; Alon, *Meḥkarim*, 2 (1958), 255–8. L.I. Levine, "R. Abbahu of Caesarea," in: *Smith IV* (1975) 56–76;

[Simha Assaf]

ABBA KOHEN BARDELA (second century), *tanna*. He is not mentioned in the Mishnah but is quoted by Abba Yose b. Ḥanin in the *Sifrei* (Deut. 2). Resh Lakish cites his views on several principles of the laws of acquisition; one is that within a public domain a person may acquire ownership of chattels in a radius of four cubits around him (BM 10a). One of his many aggadic statements is, "Woe to us for the day of judgment. Woe to us for the day of rebuke. Balaam was a wise man of the Gentiles, but could not withstand the rebuke of his ass [cf. Num. 22:30]. Joseph was the youngest of the tribes, but his brothers were unable to bear his rebuke [cf. Gen. 45:3]. When God will rebuke each one of us for what he is, how much less will we be able to bear it" (Gen. R. 93. 10).

BIBLIOGRAPHY: Hyman, Toledot, 56; Bacher, Tann.

[Abraham Goldberg]

ABBA KOLON, legendary person mentioned in midrashic literature as the founder of a city, called "Rome-Babylon." It is related of him (Song R. 1:64): "On the day that Jeroboam, son of Nebat, installed the two golden calves, two huts were built in Rome, yet each time they were erected they collapsed. A wise man, Abba Kolon by name, was present. He told them that unless water from the Euphrates was mixed with the mortar, the buildings would not stand. He volunteered to fetch some and, disguised as a cooper, journeyed afar until he reached his destination. There he drew water from the Euphrates, brought it back and mixed it with the mortar. The huts now remained standing. Henceforth people would say: 'A city without Abba Kolon is unworthy of the name.'" They called this city Rome-Babylon. The moral of this *aggadah* is that Rome was founded as a result of the iniquities of the kings of Israel. According to one opinion the name, Abba Kolon, is derived from Deucalion in Greco-Roman mythology. According to another, he is identified with Ablaccon, a magician in the time of Emperor Tiberius, who is said to have saved the city of Antioch from inundation. It has also been suggested that there is a double allusion in this name: father of "a colony" and "of *kalon*" ("shame").

BIBLIOGRAPHY: S. Krauss, *Griechische und Lateinische Lehnwoerter im Talmud*, 2 (1899), s.v.; N. Bruell, in: *Jeschurun*, 7 (1871), 3 (Ger. section); Ginzberg, Legends, 6 (1959), 280.

ABBA MARI BEN ELIGDOR (Sen Astruc de Noves or **de Sen Negre**; 14th century), French philosopher, astronomer, physicist, talmudist, and exegete. Born in Noves near Avignon, about 1320 he resided in Salon where Samuel b. Judah of Marseilles studied astronomy under him. In 1335 the latter mentions his teacher as still alive and very old. According to the conjecture of Perles and Gross, he is to be identified with Abba Mari of Salon, whom *Kalonymus b. Kalonymus mentions as his teacher and whose refutation of the philosophic views contained in Joseph *Kaspi's *Sefer ha-Sod* is quoted by Kalonymus (Responsa 5, 11, 13). Isaac b. Jacob de Lattes states in his *Sha'arei Ẓiyyon* that Abba Mari wrote commentaries on various tractates of the Talmud "combining interpretation of the text with halakhic decisions," as well as a commentary on the Pentateuch, an exhaustive interpretation of the *Pirkei de-R. Eliezer*, and various treatises on logic, metaphysics, and science. Abba Mari's commentary on Job (and on the story of the Creation), which follows the spirit of the religious-philosophical speculations of Maimonides, is extant (Mss. in Parma, De' Rossi, no. 1372, and Rome, Vatican, no. 244). A philosophical commentary on the Song of Songs (Neubauer, Cat, 1 (1886), 794, no. 2282 and Ms. Cambridge, Schiller-Szinessy, 215) may also be ascribed to Abba Mari. He may also be the author of a commentary to the "Introduction" of Euclid's *Elements* which is to be found at the beginning of the Ms. Munich, no. 91. Graetz's assertion that Abba Mari was arrested in Beaucaire together with Samuel b. Judah of Marseilles is based on a misunderstanding.

BIBLIOGRAPHY: Michael, Or, no. 2, and Berliner's addendum, 610; Renan, Ecrivains, 548–52; Gross, Gal Jud, 380, 389–91, 655, 657; idem, in: REJ, 4 (1882), 207; 9 (1884), 59; idem, in: MGWJ, 28 (1879), 471; HB, 21 (1881/82), 116ff.; Steinschneider, Uebersetzungen, 508, 543ff.; Munk, Mélanges, 489; J. Perles (ed.), *Kalonymos b. Kalonymos, Sendschreiben* ... (1879), 10–11; I. Lattes, *Sha'arei Ẓiyyon*, ed. by S. Buber (1885), 76.

[Jakob Naphtali Hertz Simchoni]

ABBA MARI BEN ISAAC OF ST. GILLES (near Lunel, southern France; c. 1165), bailiff or agent of Count Raymond VI of Toulouse (*pakid ha-shilton Ramon*). He is mentioned by the 12th-century traveler *Benjamin of Tudela, who met him in St. Gilles. Possibly Abba Mari was the father of *Isaac b. Abba Mari, author of the legal codex *Ittur.*

BIBLIOGRAPHY: M.N. Adler (ed.), *Itinerary of Benjamin of Tudela* (1907), 4; Graetz, Hist, 3 (1949), 399; Gross, Gal Jud, 372, 651; Renan, Ecrivains, 520; S. Grayzel, *Church and the Jews* (1933), index.

ABBA MARI BEN MOSES BEN JOSEPH ASTRUC OF LUNEL (c. 1300), writer who opposed extreme rationalism. He especially attacked the spread of philosophical allegorization of Scripture in popular sermons and the use of astral magic for healing. Abba Mari lived in Montpellier where the dispute over Maimonides' *Guide of the Perplexed* had broken out as early as 1232–33 and where the controversy between the philosophical and the traditionalist schools of thought persisted up to the beginning of the 14th century. In order to counteract the rationalistic method of biblical exegesis, which in his view undermined belief, Abba Mari laid down three basic principles of Judaism: the existence, unity, and incorporeality of God; the creation of the world by God; and God's special providence. In his polemical work *Sefer ha-Yare'aḥ* (*yeraḥ* = "moon"; an allusion to his native city Lunel), Abba Mari interprets biblical sayings and stories from the point of view of these three principles. As the leader of the traditionalists in the struggle against their opponents, Abba Mari conducted a vehement propaganda campaign and attempted to induce Solomon b. Abraham *Adret of Barcelona and Kalonymos b. Todros to combine in taking steps against the "corrupters of the holy tradition" (see *Maimonidean controversy). Abba Mari did not succeed, however, in inducing Solomon b. Abraham Adret to oppose publicly the use of astral magic and was barely able to persuade him to join the opposition to allegoristic sermons. Ultimately Adret did join the struggle against rationalism.

After negotiations lasting three years, a 50-year ban was pronounced in the synagogue of Barcelona on the Sabbath before the Ninth of Av, July 1305, against all those who before their 25th birthday engaged in the study of science and of metaphysics. In a special letter to the Provençal communities, this anathema was extended to include those who indulged in rationalistic exegesis and the philosophic interpretation of the *aggadah.* Abba Mari's opponents, led by Jacob b. Machir ibn Tibbon of Montpellier, realizing that this movement was directed against the extreme rationalists, issued a counter-ban. Menahem *Meiri of Perpignan sent Abba Mari a sharp rejoinder, and *Jedaiah ha-Penini Bedersi addressed himself in a like manner to Adret. Abba Mari obtained rabbinic opinions concerning the ban and counter-ban and received many favorable comments on his position, among others from the rabbis of Toledo, headed by *Asher b. Jehiel. This controversy, however, came to an abrupt end when the Jews were expelled from France by Phillip the Fair in 1306. Abba Mari then moved to Arles and after that to Perpignan. His enemies sought to prevent his settling in that city. The leaders of the Jewish community, Samuel b. Asher and his son Moses, however, espoused his cause and befriended him. The letters and pamphlets of this controversy were collected by Abba Mari in his work *Minḥat Kena'ot* (Pressburg, 1838). The halakhic correspondence between Abba Mari and Adret is contained in the responsa of the latter – *She'elot u-Teshuvot ha-Rashba*, 1 (1480; no. 167, 825, in conjunction with no. 413, 424–28; for the correspondence with Asher b. Jehiel, see the latter's *Responsa* no. 24). Abba Mari wrote a *kinah* for the Ninth of Av as well as a commentary on a Purim song in Aramaic, composed by Isaac ibn Ghayyat (Venice, 1632). Presumably, the *piyyut*, published by S.D. Luzzatto in *Kerem Ḥemed* 4 (1839), 30, is also by Abba Mari (cf. Zunz, against this view, Lit Poesie, 537), and similarly the one written entirely in Aramaic, mentioned in *Naḥalat Shadal* 2 (1879), 4, but omitted in Davidson's *Oẓar*. J. *Jabez, at the end of his book *Or ha-Ḥayyim* (1554) includes excerpts from *Sefer ha-Yare'aḥ* without mentioning Abba Mari, but occasionally referring to the author as "one of the disciples of Ben Adret" (*Kerem Ḥemed*, 9 (1856), 47).

A critical edition of *Minḥat Kena'ot* and other pertinent responsa was published by Ḥayyim Zalman Dimitrowsky, in *Teshuvot ha-Rashba* (1990), vol. 2.

BIBLIOGRAPHY: Baer, Spain, 1 (1961), 289ff.; D.J. Silver, *Maimonidean Criticism and the Maimonidean Controversy 1180–1240* (1965), 42–43; J. Sarachek, *Faith and Reason* (1935), 195–264; Zunz, Gesch, 477; Weiss, Dor, 5 (1891), ch. 4; Renan, Rabbins, 647; Gross, in: REJ, 4 (1882), 192–207; Gross, Gal Jud, 286, 331, 461, 466; Davidson, Oẓar 1 (1924), 7, no. 121; 115, no. 2429. **ADD. BIBLIOGRAPHY:** D. Schwartz, "Changing Fronts toward Science in the Medieval Debates over Philosophy," in: *Journal of Jewish Thought and Philosophy* 7 (1997), 61–82; idem, *Faith and Reason: Debates in Medieval Jewish Philosophy* (Heb., 2001); idem, *Studies on Astral Magic in Medieval Jewish Thought* (2005).

[Jacob Freimann / Dov Schwartz (2nd ed.)]

ABBA OF AKKO (**Acre**; third–fourth centuries), Palestinian *amora.* Abba apparently served as a rabbi in Acre. None of his halakhic statements has been preserved. The Midrash (Gen. R. 15:7) quotes a solitary comment to the fact that "the tree of the knowledge of good and evil" (Gen. 2:9) was an *etrog* ("citron"). He was so humble that even when the *amora* (the official interpreter of the lecture) introduced into it his own explanation which differed from his, Abba did not protest (Sot. 40a). Since he was poor, his intimate friend R. Abbahu declined to be nominated as head of the yeshivah and instead proposed Abba for the position in order to provide him with a source of livelihood (*ibid.*, loc. cit.; see Rashi ad loc.).

BIBLIOGRAPHY: Hyman, Toledot, 55–56; Bacher, Pal. Amor.

[Moshe Beer]

ABBA OSHAYA (**Hoshaya**) **OF TIRIAH** (a village in Galilee, near Nazareth), probably lived in Palestine during the fourth century C.E. (Gen. R. 58:2). None of his *halakhot* or *aggadot* has been preserved; but he was remembered for his piety. Abba Oshaya was a launderer who was meticulous in his work. According to the law the launderer could keep the few threads which detached themselves during the wash. Abba Oshaya however refrained from this practice (TJ, BK 10:11, 7c). Another incident tells of a queen who was bathing where Abba Oshaya worked. She lost her jewelry and relinquished all claim to it. Abba Oshaya, however, found it and insisted on returning it to her (TJ, BM 2:5, 8c). Because of his piety he was regarded as being especially beloved of God. The Midrash (Lev. R. 30:1) relates that "When Abba Oshaya died, his bed was seen floating in the air, and the people applied to him the verse 'If a man would give all the substance of his house for love' – the reference being to the love which God bestowed on Abba Oshaya of Tiriah – he would utterly be desposed" (Song 8:7). Abba Oshaya is an example of the influence which some scholars had, not as a result of their teaching, but on account of their exemplary lives. S. Liebermann, however, is of the opinion that Abba Oshaya the launderer is to be identified with the *tanna* "Isaiah of Tarichae" mentioned in *Tosafot* (BK 11:14) as a man of exceptional piety and not with the later *amora* (The Talmud of Caesarea, *Musaf le-Tarbiẓ*, 2 no. 4, p. 85 note 12).

BIBLIOGRAPHY: Hyman, Toledot, 117; S. Klein (ed.), *Sefer ha-Yishuv*, 1 (1939), 73.

[Moshe Beer]

°**ABBAS I** (reigned 1588–1629), regarded as the mightiest king of the Safavid period (1501–1736). In 1598 he transferred his capital from Kazvin to *Isfahan, which he transformed into one of the most magnificent cities in the world by constructing monumental mosques and beautiful avenues and squares. He is mentioned as a great builder of roads and carvanserais, a renowned conqueror, an able organizer of the army, and an austere punisher of his opponents. He was famed for his cruel punishment of disloyal officers and, as a fanatical Muslim, was responsible for the assassination of several Jewish rabbis and for the forced conversion of many Jews in Isfahan and in other cities of Iran. His persecutions of the Jews of Iran are recorded in the Chronicle of Babai ben Lutf of Kashan, according to which there were three waves of forced conversion to Islam between 1613 and 1629, but many of the Jews returned to Judaism afterwards.

BIBLIOGRAPHY: N. Falsafi, *Zendegani-ye Shah Abbas Avval*, 5 vols. (1955–62); A. Netzer, "*Redifot u-Shemadot be-Toledot Yehudei Iran ba-Me'ah ha-17*," in: *Peʿamim* 6 (1980), 32–56; V.B. Moreen, *Iranian Jewry's Hour of Peril and Heroism* (1987); H. Levy, *Comprehensive History of the Jews of Iran* (1999), 302ff.

[Amnon Netzer (2nd ed.)]

°**ABBAS II** (reigned 1642–1666), son of Shah Ṣāfi; regarded, like his great-grandfather *Abbas I, as an able administrator and builder. Abbas II treated any kind of malfeasance with severe punishment. Iranian sources picture him as generally tolerant in religious matters, possibly because he allowed members of the Catholic orders in his empire freedom of action. This tolerance may have to do with his policy of establishing friendly relations with European states in order to win allies against Iran's most formidable enemy, the Ottoman Empire. He died at the age of 36 from alcoholism and syphilis. His cruel treatment of the Jews and forced conversions in many cities of Iran are narrated by *Babai ben Lutf of Kashan, who probably witnessed them. He reported a wave of forced conversions to Islam between 1656 and 1662, after which, however, many Jews returned to Judaism.

BIBLIOGRAPHY: Emad al-Dawla Mirza Mohammad Taher Vahid Qazvini, *'Abbās-Nāmeh* (ed., E. Dehqan, 1950); A. Netzer, "*Redifot u-Shemadot be-Toledot Yehudei Iran ba-Me'ah ha-17*," in: *Peʿamim*, 6 (1980), 32–56; V.B. Moreen, *Iranian Jewry's Hour of Peril and Heroism* (1987); H. Levy, *Comprehensive History of the Jews of Iran* (1999), 302ff.

[Amnon Netzer (2nd ed.)]

ABBAS, JUDAH BEN SAMUEL IBN, moderate rationalist author active sometime between the 13th and 15th centuries. Ibn Abbas' most important contribution was the rationalist-ethical and educational work *Ya'ir Nativ* ("He Will Light the Way"). Ibn Abbas also wrote a short book on ethics, *Mekor Ḥayyim* ("Fountain of Life"), and two other books which have not survived, *Me'ir Einayim* ("Light of the Eyes"), on the reasons for the commandments, and a commentary on Aristotle's *Organon*.

In *Ya'ir Nativ*, Ibn Abbas criticized the extremists on both sides of the controversy over philosophy. On the one hand, he criticized the extreme rationalists for their philosophical *antinomianism and for their laxity in, or even mocking, observance of the commandments. On the other hand, he was critical of the "talmudist" rabbis who studied only Talmud and not philosophy. He was thus a model of the moderate rationalism of the period. Ibn Abbas became famous for the curriculum of studies presented in *Ya'ir Nativ*. The curriculum was printed several times.

BIBLIOGRAPHY: S. Asaf, in: S. Glueck (ed.), *Sources for the History of Education in Israel* (1961), 65–69; D. Schwartz, in: *Tarbiz*, 62 (1993), 585–615.

[Dov Schwartz (2nd ed.)]

ABBAS (Abenabez, Abenavez), MOSES BEN SAMUEL (c. 1350–c. 1420), talmudist, poet, and communal leader in Saragossa, Spain. Moses was born in Tudela and studied under *Solomon b. Ḥasdai, settling in Saragossa after 1370. He was a close friend of the poet Solomon b. Meshullam *da Piera, with whom he corresponded in Hebrew and Spanish, and some of his poems have been included in collections of the latter's works. Moses was repeatedly elected to the office of *muqaddam*, or administrative officer, of the Saragossa community between 1380 and 1420, representing it at court for the first time in 1389. After the massacres of 1391 Moses did much to relieve the survivors. He represented Saragossa at the disputation of *Tortosa (1413–14).

BIBLIOGRAPHY: Baer, Spain, index s.v. *Moses abn Abez;* Baer, Urkunden, index; M. Serrano y Sanz, *Orígenes de la dominación Española en América* (1918), 453 ff.; A. Pacios López, *La Disputa de Tortosa,* 1 (1957), index; S. ben Meshullam Dapiera, *Divan,* ed. by S. Bernstein, 1 (1943), xi, 38–40; S. ibn Verga, *Shevet Yehudah,* ed. by E. Shoḥat (1947), 95; A.M. Habermann, in: *Oẓar Yehudei Sefarad,* 7 (1964), 24–42.

ABBAS, MOSES JUDAH BEN MEIR (c. 1601–1671), talmudist, halakhist, and poet. Abbas came from a Spanish family which, after settling in Salonika, spread throughout Turkey. He himself was born in Salonika. From his youth onward Abbas endured poverty and illness. His rabbis were Mordecai Kalsy, Jonah Adelie, and Solomon (III) b. Isaac (Bet ha-Levi) *Levi. Appointed rabbi in Egypt, he founded a yeshivah and *talmud torah* from which he earned his living. To enlist the necessary financial support he traveled extensively, and wrote appeals to those towns he was unable to visit. In the last years of his life he was a rabbi of Rosetta, where, in about 1669, his house was plundered and he lost all his possessions. Abbas wrote many responsa, most of them in Rosetta, and some during his travels. Two volumes are still extant in manuscript. He wrote *Kisse Kavod* (now at Jews' College, London), a commentary on the minor tractates *Kallah, Soferim,* and *Semaḥot.* While still a youth, Abbas corresponded and exchanged poems with Jewish notables in Turkey. As a poet, he was superior to his contemporaries, but did not reach the heights of the Spanish school. He encouraged young poets, correcting their efforts and couching his replies in verse form. His poems, which employ the meter and language of the Spanish poets, express his sufferings and hopes. According to Conforte, Abbas compiled two volumes of poetry. Some of his secular poems were published by Wallenstein (see bibliography), but hundreds of his scattered poems are still in manuscript. In some of his poems, the name MaShYA (an abbreviation for MoShe Yehudah Abbas) appears as an acrostic.

BIBLIOGRAPHY: M. Benayahu, in: *Zion,* 12 (1946–47), 41–42; M. Wallenstein, in: *Melilah,* 1 (1944), 54–68; 2 (1946), 135–48; 3–4 (1950), 240–54.

ABBA SAUL, mid-second century *tanna.* Quoted frequently in the Mishnah and Tosefta, he was probably a disciple of R. Akiva (in view of the fact that he quotes several *halakhot* in his name; Tosef., Sanh. 12:10). Abba Saul was the colleague of R. Judah b. Ilai and R. Meir (Men. 11:5). He is not usually mentioned with other *tannaim,* nor are *halakhot* transmitted in his name by later *tannaim* (see *Abba Guryon). His terminology often differed from that normally used, not only in relation to burial tools (TJ, Shek. 8:2, 51a) but in other areas as well, so that, for example, one who was commonly called a *shetuki* ("one whose father is not known"), he calls *beduki* ("one requiring examination," Kid. 4:2). He often declared: "The rule is just the opposite" (Git. 5:4) indicating that his version of a tradition differed from that of other *tannaim.* Generally his opinion is quoted as an adjunct to a Mishnah (Sanh. 10:1; et

al.). On the basis of these differences, it has been suggested that there was a different "Mishnah of Abba Saul," which Judah ha-Nasi had used. He transmitted traditions with regard to the pathology and growth of the human embryo (TJ, Nid. 3:3, 50d), and especially with regard to the structure and utensils of the Temple (Mid. 2:5; 5:4; Shek. 4:2; et al.). One of his few aggadic statements is his comment on "This is my God, and I will glorify Him" (Ex. 15:2), which he interpreted as meaning that man should strive to imitate God, endeavoring – like Him – to be gracious and merciful (Shab. 133b; Mekh., Shirah, 3). Later traditions suggest that his father's name may have been Nannos (ARN[1] 29, 87; cf. Nid. 24b, 25b), and his mother's Imma Miriam (Ket. 87a). The Talmud describes him as "the baker for the family of Rabbi [Judah ha-Nasi]" (Pes. 34a), but in another place his occupation was given as a gravedigger (Nid. 24b) and he described prevailing burial customs, reporting how a grave was located in the rock at Beth-Horon (Nid. 61a).

BIBLIOGRAPHY: Frankel, Mishnah, 186–7; I. Lewy, in: *Berichte der Hochschule fuer die Wissenschaft des Judenthums in Berlin* (1876); Hyman, Toledot, s.v.; Epstein, Tanna'im, 160–3.

[Bialik Myron Lerner]

ABBA SAUL BEN BATNIT (first century C.E.), mentioned a number of times in tannaitic sources. According to Beẓah 3:8, Abba Saul was a shopkeeper in Jerusalem who had the custom of filling his measuring vessels with oil and wine before a festival for the convenience of his customers. Praised for his honesty, the Tosefta (*ibid.,* 3:8) reports that he once brought as a gift to the Temple three hundred jars of oil which had accumulated from the drops left in the measuring vessels, to which he had no right. When he was ill and the sages came to visit him, he showed them his right hand, and exclaimed: "See this right hand which always gave honest measure" (TJ, Beẓah 3:9, 62b). His name is associated with a halakhic precedent at the end of Mishnah *Shabbat* (24:5), and Tosefta *Menaḥot* (13:21, Pes. 57a) mentions him in connection with a series of criticisms of the conduct of the high priestly class in the last decades of the Second Temple.

BIBLIOGRAPHY: Hyman, Toledot, s.v.; A. Buechler, *Types of Jewish-Palestinian Piety* (1922), 203.

[Abraham Goldberg]

ABBASI (incorrectly **Akasi** and **Aksai**), **JACOB BEN MOSES IBN** (second half of 13th century), Hebrew translator. Abbasi was born probably in Béziers in southern France, but he lived in *Huesca, Spain. There in 1297–98 he translated Maimonides' commentary on the third order of the Mishnah (*Nashim*) from the original Arabic into Hebrew. As he relates in his introduction, the Jews of Rome had sent an emissary, R. Simḥah, to Spain to obtain a translation of the Mishnah commentary; the emissary was directed to Huesca with recommendations from Solomon b. Abraham *Adret of Barcelona and other Spanish rabbinical authorities. The Huesca community agreed to provide translations of the first three orders of Maimonides' commentary, and commissioned the third to Abbasi with the assistance of Ḥayyim b. Solomon b. Baka, the physician.

In his introduction Abbasi set down his views on the relation of Judaism to philosophy. Citing Ecclesiastes 7:23, "... I said: 'I will get wisdom'; but it was far from me," he declared that the powers of man's mind are limited; neither philosophy nor natural science can reveal the essence of things. The Greek philosophers, whom Abbasi quotes, admitted this. Perfection can be achieved only by the study of the Torah and the observance of its commandments. There are secrets in prophecy that man cannot always penetrate, but the merit of divinely commanded action is evident and leads to deeper knowledge. Abbasi considered men in relation to the Torah in three categories: those who study and observe it, those who study but do not observe it, and those who observe but do not study it. He classified the commandments of the Torah in three categories as well; commandments involving the mind and the soul, commandments pertaining to the body, and commandments dealing with one's possessions. Abbasi continued his discussion describing the importance of the Oral Law as the indispensable and authoritative interpretation of Scripture; he explained the nature of Mishnah, *Gemara*, and certain works codifying the law, and stressed the importance of Maimonides' commentary for the understanding of the Mishnah and establishing *halakhah*. Thus, he praised the Jewish community of Rome for their initiative in commissioning the translation, which he considered of great importance for the future as well.

Abbasi wrote a short preface in which he explained the principles followed in his work, which for the most part are the same as those followed by other contemporary translators. He states that the translation is strictly literal; only rarely did he expand the text for clarity. He corrected obvious mistakes of transcription in the Arabic manuscript according to talmudic sources and Maimonides' other writings, but did not attempt to harmonize this commentary with Maimonides' *Mishneh Torah*. He also wrote a letter to Solomon b. Abraham Adret submitting his translation for approval. Abbasi's translation was included in the first edition of the complete Mishnah commentary (Naples, 1492), and after that often appeared in editions of the Mishnah and Talmud.

BIBLIOGRAPHY: Steinschneider, Uebersetzungen, 924; idem, in: JQR, 11 (1898/99), 333; Vogelstein-Rieger, 420ff.; Gross, Gal Jud, 105.

ABBASIDS, second dynasty in Islam, ruling from 750 to 1258, mostly from their capital of Baghdad. At its height (eighth-ninth centuries) the Abbasid realm extended from Central Asia in the east through North Africa in the west. It thus encompassed virtually all the Jewish communities then known, save those in Europe.

The new dynasts came to power after some 50 years of clandestine revolutionary activity resulted in an open revolt (747–50). The ensuing conflict toppled the Umayyads (661–750), usurpers of the Prophet Muhammad's authority. The change of dynasty has long been regarded as a major watershed in the history of the Islamic state, albeit for different reasons.

Previous generations of Orientalists saw the rise of the Abbasids in the light of 19th century notions of nationalism and race and society. The emergence of the Abbasids was thus depicted as the culmination of a long struggle between the Syria-based "Arab" kingdom of the Umayyads and the conquered people of an Iranian empire that was shattered with the rise of Islam. The conflict was thus seen as being between a ruling institution predicated on the special privilege of a relatively small Arab/Muslim aristocracy and a more broadly defined coalition of forces whose ethnic origins were said to have been in the former Iranian provinces to the east, most especially the great land of *Khurasan. With that, there developed the seductive notion that Islamic government became increasingly Iranized under the Abbasids. In sum, it was believed that the Abbasid triumph heralded the creation of a new political and social order in which a narrowly defined ruling Arab society was replaced by a polity of more universal outlook and composition.

The traditional view has given way to a new consensus. Historians now stress the central role played by Arabs from the eastern provinces, particularly in leading the revolt. It is now believed that the struggle between the rebels and the Umayyads was not to restore an Iranian empire and civilization in Islamized garb, but to restore the pristine Islam of the Prophet's time under caliphs chosen from the House of the Prophet (Hashimites).

In any case, the Abbasid revolution was not a palace coup in which one family displaced another for reasons of personal aggrandizement only to see business continue as usual. A new age had dawned, or so the advocates of the regime claimed in hyperbolic language spiced with apocalyptical symbols. The Abbasid rulers adopted regnal titles suggesting that the messianic age was at hand and they were the chosen instruments of this manifest destiny. The messiah did not arrive but the new rulers altered the political and social landscape dramatically. With unexpected swiftness, the Abbasids redefined an Islamic state that had been founded on Arab privilege and beset by tribal xenophobia. They replaced it with a broadly based polity aspiring to universal outlook and recognition. Viewed as a whole, the deliberate restructuring of Abbasid society seems radical and far reaching. Whether one speaks of new networks of social relationships, a complete overhaul of the military from tribal to regionally based professional units, innovations in provincial administration that allowed for greater representation of non-family affiliates among the governors and sub-governors, or the creation of a highly centralized and massive bureaucracy that employed many non-Arabs, the changes instituted by the new regime represented an ambitious departure in the style and substance of rule hitherto known amongst the Muslims.

To legitimize these dramatic changes, the new ruling order built a magnificent capital at Baghdad in central Iraq. Never before had so grand a city been built. Completed in 766 as a glorified administrative complex, the city eventually grew to an urban area of some 7,000 hectares that was by all accounts densely populated throughout the eighth–tenth centuries. Population estimates vary, but a settlement of well over half a million is certainly possible. With the building of a second imperial center, Samarra, some 55 years later, the Abbasids completely altered the demographic landscape of Iraq, particularly the central region. The vast majority of the inhabitants now lived in major cities and towns, signifying a dramatic shift from agricultural hinterland to urban environment.

Although we lack firm evidence, we can surmise that the increasing urbanization saw a shift in the pattern of Jewish settlement in the region. Babylonian Jews, previously engaged in agriculture and small crafts, must have been attracted, like their Muslim and Christian neighbors, from the declining villages and small towns to the cities where the Abbasid rulers encouraged urban development and expanded commerce and trade. Jews thus became part of the changing economic environment, and eventually played a central role in long-distance trade throughout the Islamic world and beyond. In the ninth century, a group of Jewish merchants called Radhanites after a district in the vicinity of Baghdad traded from China to the Iberian Peninsula. Although business of this sort was not the archetypal Jewish profession, it was a métier to which they readily adapted and with communities of co-religionists dispersed throughout the Islamic world and in Europe, they were able to create an effective business network that included commerce, trade, and also banking.

In the tenth century, a number of Christian and Jewish bankers were employed by various Abbasid functionaries, including the caliphs in Baghdad. Their task was to manage the fortunes of state officials and of the caliph himself. One might ask to what extent the activities of the Jewish bankers in Baghdad had similar parallels elsewhere in the Islamic world. The contemporary Muslim geographer al-Muqaddasi reports that most of the bankers and moneychangers in Egypt were Jews. However, the broad picture of Jewish involvement in the financial transactions of the times has yet to be fully researched.

The Abbasid state could not sustain the political stability of its early decades. Civil war broke out towards the end of the eighth century and military revolts were common in the ninth. By the latter part of the tenth century, the Abbasid empire witnessed the loss of North Africa and Egypt to the *Fatimids, a Shiʿite dynasty that originated in North Africa. To the east, various petty dynasts recognized the suzerainty of the Abbasid caliphs but withheld the tax revenues for themselves. As a result, economic conditions declined throughout the truncated realm. Already in the ninth century, the state, strapped for revenues, confiscated vast wealth from rich Christians (and presumably Jews) and during the reign of the caliph al-Mutawakkil (847–61) went so far as to invoke the discriminatory legislation against the Christians and Jews that had long been Islamic law but was seldom put into effect.

With conditions deteriorating in the Abbasid heartland, many Jews migrated westward to Egypt, North Africa, and more distant lands. Their path was made easier by the relative tolerance they experienced in Egypt and North Africa. Slowly, the center of Jewish commercial activity as well as scholarly enterprise shifted westward. Abbasid Iraq, which had been the home of the *exilarchs and of the *geonim* (see *Gaon), the leading political and scholarly figures of world Jewry, as well as the seat of the great academies of Sura and Pumbedita, was forced to share its preeminence as a Jewish center with rapidly developing communities elsewhere.

Over the centuries the power of the caliphs declined although the empire itself, however truncated, was more or less kept intact. When Baghdad was conquered by the *Mongols in 1258, to all intents and purposes, the Abbasid caliphate came to an end. The Mongol conquest would seem to have created expectations of more relaxed times among Christians and Jews. But the conversion of the Mongols to Islam ended any hopes of dramatic change in the relations among the monotheists.

BIBLIOGRAPHY: J. Lassner, *The Shaping of ʿAbbasid Rule* (1980); idem, *Remembering the Middle East* (2000); S.D. Goitein and P. Sanders, *A Mediterranean Society*, 6 (1993), indices, s.v. Baghdad and Iraq.

[Jacob Lassner (2nd ed.)]

ABBA SIKRA (or **Sakkara**), talmudic name of one of the leaders in the defense of Jerusalem against the Romans in 66–70 C.E. "Abba Sikra" is regarded by some scholars as an epithet meaning "chief of the *Sicarii." Jastrow, however, believes the word *sikra* means "red paint" or the act of "leaping"; Sikr is also recorded as a name for Arabs. In the two parallel accounts of his activities, the Talmud (Git. 56a) calls him Abba Sikra whereas the Midrash (Lam. R. 1:5 no. 31), refers to him as Ben Batiaḥ, but there is no doubt that both refer to the same person. The Talmud calls him "chief of the *biryonim* in Jerusalem," seemingly in a deprecatory sense, since this term is frequently used in connection with robbers and brigands (Sanh. 37a; Ber. 10a). He is linked with two episodes; the burning of the storehouses in Jerusalem, and the smuggling of his uncle, Johanan b. Zakkai, out of the city during the siege. The burning is recorded in connection with a dispute between the sages and the *Zealots. The sages wished to sue for peace, while the latter wished to do battle with the Romans. No conclusion was reached; but Ben Batiaḥ, who was in charge of the storehouses in Jerusalem, burnt them all, to R. Johanan's distress. The resultant famine led R. Johanan to seek the assistance of Abba Sikra in his plan to leave the beleaguered city. Abba Sikra proposed that R. Johanan feign illness and then death. He accompanied the coffin, borne by Eliezer and Joshua, the disciples of R. Johanan, and prevented the guards at the gate from stabbing the body.

BIBLIOGRAPHY: S.J.L. Rapoport, *Erekh Millin*, 1 (1852), 1; Derenbourg, Hist, 280; Guttmann, Mafte'ah, 1 (1906), 115; Klausner, Bayit Sheni, 5 (1951), 229–30; Alon, Meḥkarim, 1 (1957), 249–50. **ADD. BIBLIOGRAPHY:** T. Ilan, *Lexicon of Jewish Names in Late Antiquity. Part 1: Palestine 330 BCE–200 CE* (2002), 397, s.v. Siqra.

[Lea Roth / Shimon Gibson (2nd ed.)]

ABBA UMANA (Heb. אַבָּא אוּמָנָה; fourth century C.E.), Babylonian bloodletter (hence his cognomen). Abba Umana was distinguished for his exceptional piety and, according to legend, daily received a greeting from the Heavenly Academy, a distinction accorded to Abbaye only once a week, and to Rava only once a year. Abbaye, grieved at not being considered as worthy as Abba Umana, was told: "You cannot do what Abba Umana does." In treating women, he conducted himself with the utmost modesty. In order not to put poor patients to shame, he arranged for his fee to be deposited in a place hidden from public view. He never accepted any remuneration from a scholar but instead would give him money to enable him to recuperate. Once Abbaye sent two sages to test him. Abba Umana gave them food and drink, and in the evening prepared mattresses for them. The following morning they took them to the market to sell. On meeting Abba Umana they asked him of what he suspected them. Abba Umana replied that when he missed the mattresses he assumed that they needed money for the redemption of captives. He refused to take the mattresses back, saying that he already devoted them to charity (Ta'an. 21b–22a).

BIBLIOGRAPHY: Hyman, Toledot, 10.

ABBAYE (278–338 C.E.), Babylonian *amora* of the fourth generation; chief of scholars of *Pumbedita. Abbaye was of priestly descent and was reputed to be a descendant of *Eli, the high priest. His father, whose name apparently was Keilil (Zev. 118b), died before, and his mother, at his birth (Kid. 31b). He was raised by his uncle, *Rabbah b. Nahmani, and by a foster mother whom he frequently quoted, calling her "mother." His true name is not known. According to R. Sherira Gaon, he was called "Nahmani" after his paternal grandfather, and Abbaye, then, was a nickname. While he was still a child, his uncle recognized Abbaye's intellectual capacity, and endeavored to educate him appropriately (Ber. 33b). He continued his studies under R. Joseph who apparently succeeded Rabbah as the head of Pumbedita's circle of scholars. There is a legend that Abbaye later helped R. Joseph recall what he had forgotten as the result of illness. Abbaye debated legal points with the leading talmudic scholars of the day, such as Judah and *HISDA (Ta'an. 11b–12a). In his youth he was poor and watered his fields at night to enable him to study by day (Git. 60b), but later he employed tenant farmers (Ket. 60b) and traded in wine (Ber. 56a). Upon Joseph's death (333 C.E.), Abbaye succeeded him as head in Pumbedita and held this position for the rest of his life. Until relatively recently, most modern scholars presumed that his most prominent colleague was *Rava, and that their agreements ("Both Abbaye and Rava say …") and disagreements constituted a major element of the Talmud. Today the predominant view is that direct dialogues between Abbaye and Rava are extremely rare. Nearly all of their presumed dialogues, previously thought to form the backbone of the Babylonian Talmud, are, in fact, discussions between Abbaye and his teacher, Rabbah. This misapprehension resulted from the widespread confusion between the names Rava and Rabbah in the manuscripts and printed editions of the Talmud. Indeed, face-to-face contact between fourth generation Babylonian masters has now been shown to be generally infrequent, leading to the conclusion that they may have studied in disciple circles rather than academies. It seems that the editors of the Talmud in a later period gathered issues of law on which Abbaye and Rava's independently adduced positions contradicted. These contradictions were then hashed out by the anonymous editorial voice of the Talmud. However, actual historically authentic dispute dialogue between Abbaye and Rava is almost nonexistent. In the Talmud's discussions of their contradictory opinions, generally Rava's view was accepted as law; only in six instances did Abbaye's view prevail (BM 22b; etc.). The Talmudic term, "Discussions of Abbaye and Rava" became a general term appellation for the entire system of talmudic dialectics. Abbaye's method of halakhic study combined erudition with keen, logical analysis. Yet, in contrast to his colleague – Rava – he was said to have preferred to rely on transmitted knowledge rather than on independent reasoning (Er. 3a). Discovering similar principles underlying the opinions of various sages, Abbaye would formulate terse general rules and find support for his opinion and that of others in *baraitot*. He also classified difficult passages in earlier sources and included in his studies laws no longer in force (Zev. 44b). He had a large stock of popular sayings, which he prepared with "People say …." Some of his own remarks became popular maxims; among them, "Go outside and see what the people say …," i.e., follow popular tradition. Through his foster-mother he became familiar with remedies and justified their use by the rule that whatever is done for healing is not considered "ways of the Amorites" (i.e., pagan superstition; Shab. 67a). In the field of *aggadah*, Joseph's influence on Abbaye can be seen, but the former sometimes deferred to his pupil's exposition of a different verse. Abbaye was also responsible for reversing Joseph's negative attitude to the book of Ben Sira (Sanh. 100b). He took over *aggadot* and interpretations brought by Dimi from Ereẓ Israel to Babylon (Sanh. 44b). He was the first to discriminate explicitly between the plain contextual meaning of Scripture and its interpretation use for Midrash (Ḥul. 133a). Especially noteworthy is his quotation (from a *baraita*) of an exposition of the verse (Deut. 6:5): "And thou shalt love the Lord, thy God," meaning that "the Name of Heaven should be loved on account of you." One should study Scripture, learn halakhot, be apprenticed to a sage, and deal honorably with one's fellowmen. Then people will say "How pleasant are the ways of this person who has studied Torah, how proper his conduct" (Yoma 86a). In the discussion between the *tannaim* as to whether man should devote his time to the study of Torah to the exclusion of everything else (according to the view of Simeon b. Yoḥai) or whether one should study as well as live a productive life (the opinion of Ishmael), Abbaye concurred with the latter (Ber. 35b). Whenever one of his disciples had completed a tractate he would arrange a feast for scholars, thus showing his appreciation and concern for his students (Shab. 188b–119a). He often stressed the importance of "A soft answer turning away wrath," and of promoting goodwill among men "so that one may be beloved above and well-liked below …" (Ber. 17a). His second wife, Ḥoma, who was the great-granddaughter of R. Judah, was famous for her beauty (Ket. 65a).

BIBLIOGRAPHY: Weiss, *Dor*, 3 (1904[4]), 174ff.; Hyman, *Toledot*, s. v.; Bacher, *Bab Amor*, 107–13. R. Kalmin, in: HUCA, 61 (1990), 125–58; D. Weiss-Halivni, *Midrash, Mishnah, and Gemara: The Jewish Predilection for Justified Law* (1985), 70–78; A. Weiss, *Hithavvut ha-Talmud bi-Shlemuto* (1943), 14–56.

[Ephraim Elimelech Urbach]

ABBAYE KASHISHA ("Abbaye the Elder"; c. 300), Babylonian *amora. He* is called "the elder" in order to differentiate him from the better known *Abbaye of a later generation. He taught and interpreted halakhic *beraitot* (Yev. 24a; Ket. 94a, 96b), but also dealt with aggadic topics (Shab. 56a). He compared dissension and controversy to "the planks of a bridge which at first are loose but ultimately become fixed in place through constant treading" (Sanh. 7a). The later Abbaye quotes a *baraita* transmitted by his namesake (Ket. 94a).

BIBLIOGRAPHY: Hyman, Toledot, s.v.

[Abraham Goldberg]

ABBA YOSE BEN DOSTAI (Dosai; second century C.E.), Palestinian *tanna*. He is not mentioned in the Mishnah, but he transmitted halakhic statements in the names of R. *Eliezer and R. *Yose ha-Gelili (Tosef., Pe'ah 4:2; Ta'an. 2:6; cf. *Tosefta ki-Feshutah*. 1 (1955), 180, 5 (1962), 1080). He was a contemporary of *Yose b. Meshullam, and halakhic remarks are quoted jointly in their names (Tosef., Kelim, BK 6:18; Makhsh. 2:10). *Aggadot* dealing with the reconciliation of contradictory biblical passages are cited in his name by Judah ha-Nasi (Sif. Num. 42).

BIBLIOGRAPHY: Bacher, Tann, 2 (1890), 388–9, 489; Hyman, Toledot, 720–1 Z.K.

ABBA YOSE (Isi) BEN ḤANIN (Hanan, Johanan; second half of first century C.E.), *tanna* who transmitted details of the number and location of the Temple court gates (Mid. 2:6) and the order of the Temple service (Tosef., Suk. 4:15). Several of his statements on *halakhah* have been preserved (Tosef., Er., end; Sif. Num. 8; Sot. 20b). He denounced the priestly families and their corrupt behavior: "Woe is me because of the house of Boethus, woe is me because of their staves! Woe is me because of the house of Kathros, woe is me because of their pens! Woe is me because of the house of Elhanan, woe is me because of their whisperings! Woe is me because of the house of Elisha, woe is me because of their fists! Woe is me because of the house of Ishmael b. Phabi, for they are high priests, and their sons are Temple treasurers, and their sons-in-law trustees, and their servants come and beat us with staves!" (Tosef., Men. 13:21; Pes. 57a). According to some later traditions (DEZ 9, end; cf. Sperber, DEZ, 152), Abba Yose transmitted an *aggadah* conveying the significance of the Temple, in the name of *Samuel ha-Katan: "This world is like the human eyeball. Its white typifies the ocean, which surrounds the world. Its black typifies the world. The pupil of the eye symbolizes Jerusalem. The image in the pupil of the eye symbolizes the Temple, may it speedily be rebuilt."

BIBLIOGRAPHY: Hyman, Toledot, 726; Epstein, Tanna'im, 47.

[Zvi Kaplan]

ABBELL, MAXWELL (1902–1957), U.S. communal worker, lawyer, businessman, and philanthropist. Abbell, who was born in Slonim, Poland, was taken to the U.S. at the age of three by his parents, who settled in Chelsea, Mass. Moving to Chicago, Abbell worked first for the Jewish Social Service Bureau, then as assistant executive director of the Jewish Charities of Chicago (1925–37). In 1937 he established his own accounting firm, and in 1944 he became senior partner of the law firm of Abbell and Schanfeld. He entered the real estate business as well, eventually establishing Abbell Hotels, a large nationwide chain, which he continued to manage until his death. Highly active in local and national Jewish life, Abbell was chairman of the Chicago College of Jewish Studies (1950–54), president of the United Synagogue of America (1950–53), and a founder of the World Council of Synagogues in 1957. His philanthropical activities were devoted mainly to the State of Israel and the Jewish Theological Seminary of America. In 1955 President Eisenhower appointed him chairman of the President's Committee on Government Employment Policy.

[Bernard Segal]

ABBOTT, BUD (William Abbott; 1895–1974), U.S. actor. Famous for playing the straight man in the legendary comedy duo "Abbott and Costello" with longtime partner Lou Costello, Abbott was born to Ringling Brothers' Circus performers in Asbury Park, New Jersey. After dropping out of school in 1909, he began working in carnivals and theaters around the U.S. Eventually he became the manager of the National Theater in Detroit, where he honed his skills playing the straight man alongside vaudeville performers Harry Steepe and Harry Evanson. In 1931, Abbott was working as a cashier at the Brooklyn Theater when he substituted for Lou Costello's usual straight man, who was ill, and what would become one of comedy's most celebrated teams was formed. The duo's first national exposure came in 1938, with an appearance on *The Kate Smith Hour* radio show that led to a contract with Universal the following year. In 1940, Abbott and Costello secured their place in comedic history with their unforgettable supporting role in Universal's *One Night in the Tropics*, in which they performed their signature "Who's on First?" routine. Abbott and Costello's first starring role with Universal came in the comedy *Buck Privates* (1941). The unexpected success of *Buck Privates* led to a string of starring roles in slapstick comedies such as *In the Navy* (1941), *Hold That Ghost* (1941), *Keep 'Em Flying* (1941), *Ride 'Em Cowboy* (1942), *Who Done It?* (1942), *Hit the Ice* (1943), and *In Society* (1944). The duo continued to rely upon their trademark fast-paced, cross-talking formula in more than a dozen other films throughout the latter half of the 1940s and into the early 1950s, when they also began to appear on the television shows *The Colgate Comedy Hour* (1951–54) and *The Abbott and Costello Show* (1952–54). In 1956, Abbott and Costello finally parted ways following an IRS investigation that left both men in dire financial straits. Abbott attempted to revive his career with a new partner, Candy Candido, during the 1960s but found little success. In his final performance, Abbott provided his own voice for the 1966 animated television series, *Abbott and Costello*.

[Walter Driver (2nd ed.)]

ABBREVIATIONS. The abbreviation of words originated in antiquity, probably soon after the alphabet developed from ideographic pictures. While originally rare, their use increased with the general growth in the transmission of ideas by writing. They relieved the shortage of space and precious writing materials, served the convenience of the scribe, and preserved a certain degree of secrecy. An abbreviation also obviated the constant repetition of the full Divine Name. Various methods of abbreviating evolved in the course of time and, when extensively used, they economized in space and materials, although occasionally causing confusion and misunderstandings.

Terminology

The expression *notarikon* (derived from the Greek term for stenography) occurs in the Mishnah (Shab. 12:5) and refers to the use of initial letters, dots, and dashes to indicate abbreviation. It is used in the Talmud to indicate memory devices and is one of the 32 *hermeneutics rules of the *aggadah* (H.G. Enelow (ed.), *Mishnat R. Eliezer* (1933), 39) and one of the most popular and frequently used. By the third century the terms *siman* (Heb. סִימָן; Gr. *sēmeion*) and *alef bet* (אָלֶף בֵּית) were current and applied to mnemonics, as in "Torah can only be acquired with [the aid of] mnemonic signs" (Er. 54b), while the Talmud also refers to *serugin* (סְרוּגִין; Yoma 38a, etc.), a system of abbreviation called trellis-writing, whereby only the initial word or letter is used when quoting a biblical verse. This system has been found in Bible fragments recovered from the Cairo *Genizah. The term *rashei otiyyot* is found only in *Tanḥuma* (B., Ex. 54); *rashei tevot* first in *Tanḥuma Ha'azinu* 5; while the expression *sofei tevot* occurs in the post-talmudic masorah. The grammarian Elijah Levita (1468–1549) speaks of "… abbreviated, broken words, expressions written in *notarikon* and initials…."

History

As the Hebrews wrote at an early stage of their history, the early invention of abbreviations could be assumed. They appear on sixth-century Semitic inscriptions, fifth-century Aramaic documents, and on Samarian jar handles. To mark ownership, for Temple and other sacred purposes, such abbreviations were used well into talmudic times. Although not usually found in official manuscripts of the Bible, abbreviations appear in masoretic writings, Midrash, Mishnah, and Talmud, and they abound in post-tannaitic literature. It has been suggested that the translators of the Septuagint used a Hebrew text with abbreviations. It became one of the main concerns of the masoretic scholars to eliminate ambiguities caused by abbreviations, so that in printed Bibles there are generally no abbreviations; modern Bible commentators, however, while seeking to explain obscure passages, offer emendations suggesting that certain words are actually abbreviations (e.g., J.H. Greenstone in his commentary on Num. 23:3).

Abbreviations appear on Jewish *coins of the Jewish War (66–70) and the Bar Kokhba War (132–135; e.g., שָׁנָה ב' – שב', לְחֵרוּת – לחר); on documents recovered from the Dead Sea Caves and Masada; and on ossuaries of the talmudic period (e.g., יְחֶזְקִיָּה – יחזק). The Mishnah regularly uses them (e.g., רַבִּי – ר'), as does the Talmud (see Pes. 102b–103a) in a discussion on the order of the blessings known as *yaknehaz* (יַקְנְהַ"ז). Rashi, commenting on Numbers 5:11ff. in *Gittin* 60a and *Yoma* 37b–38a, discusses various forms of abbreviations mentioned in the Talmuds. The mnemonic *simanim* were used to group together different *halakhot* with a common denominator such as authorship (e.g., *halakhot*, all by Abbaye, known as יעל קג"ם; BK 73a). Abbreviations were used extensively as formulas of the calendar system (e.g., לא אד"ו ראש, "Rosh Ha-Shanah cannot fall on Sundays, Wednesdays, or Fridays"). In the Middle Ages, the names of frequently quoted scholars and/or their works were abbreviated and made pronounceable, e.g., Rashi (R. Shelomo Yiẓḥaki), Rambam (R. Moses b. Maimon), Rosh (Rabbenu Asher). It was also the practice in the medieval and post-medieval periods to append eulogistic terms in abbreviated forms (e.g., נוחו עֵדֶן – נ"ע, "he rests in paradise") or for martyrs (ה' יִקּוֹם דָּמוֹ – הי"ד, "may God avenge his blood"); among Sephardim ס"ט was used meaning סופו טוב ("may his end be good") and is applied to the living as well, standing for סְפָרַדִּי טָהוֹר, "of pure Sephardi descent." Current also were abbreviated eulogistic phrases in Spanish and Portuguese on tombstones, supplementing or replacing the traditional Hebrew. Abbreviations were also known in the communities of the Marrano Diaspora, e.g., Amsterdam, where there were transliterations into the Latin alphabet of accepted Hebrew abbreviations (e.g., K.K.T.T. – קָהָל קָדוֹשׁ תַּלְמוּד תּוֹרָה, "Holy Congregation Talmud Torah–" as an abbreviation for the Amsterdam Sephardi congregation). The use of abbreviations has continued to grow, particularly in all fields of Jewish scholarship. It has been estimated, for example, that in the *siddur* of Jacob *Emden there are approximately 1,700 abbreviations. Famous personalities continued to be called by an abbreviation such as the Ba'al Shem Tov (Besht, בֶּעשְׁ"ט) and Elijah of Vilna (הַגָּאוֹן ר' אֵלִיָּהוּ – הַגְּרָ"א).

Since the 19th century some authors' initials have almost superseded their actual names (e.g., the poet Judah Leib *Gordon is commonly known as יַלַ"ג). The initials with which the historian and journalist Shneur Zalman Rubashov (later president of the State of Israel) signed his articles eventually became his Hebrew name (שַׁזָ"ר, *Shazar).

Many 19th- and 20th-century Jewish organizations and institutions have become known by their abbreviated titles, e.g., *Alliance Israélite Universelle (כָּל יִשְׂרָאֵל חֲבֵרִים – כִּיַ"ח); or the *Bilu pioneers (בֵּית יַעֲקֹב לְכוּ וְנֵלְכָה for בִּיל"וּ). The Ḥasidic movement emanating from Lubavitch is known by the initials of their motto Ḥabad (חָכְמָה, בִּינָה, דַּעַת – חַבַּ"ד, "wisdom, understanding, knowledge"). Jewish organizations have also taken names from non-Hebrew initials, such as HIAS and *WIZO. The habit of calling international bodies by their initials (e.g., UN, UNESCO, UNSCOP) has found an echo in the Hebrew אוּ"ם for אֻמּוֹת מְאֻחָדוֹת (United Nations). In Israel constant use is made of abbreviations (e.g., *Mapai, מִפְלֶגֶת פּוֹעֲלֵי אֶרֶץ יִשְׂרָאֵל – מַפַּ"י, "the Israel Labor Party"; Ẓahal, צְבָא הֲגַנָּה לְיִשְׂרָאֵל – צַהַ"ל, "Israel Defense Forces"). These groups have adopted abbreviations which have virtually become independent words. Military ranks, units, and equipment are expressed almost exclusively by abbreviations, and so are most public enterprises (e.g., *Tahal, תִּכְנוּן הַמַּיִם לְיִשְׂרָאֵל – תַּהַ"ל, "Water Planning for Israel"). A member of the Israeli parliament is abbreviated חֲבֵר כְּנֶסֶת – חַ"כ; a publisher מוֹצִיא לָאוֹר – מו"ל; Land of Israel, אֶרֶץ יִשְׂרָאֵל – א"י; the rest of the world is חוּץ לָאָרֶץ – חו"ל. Cities with a compound name are often abbreviated (e.g., תֵּל אָבִיב – ת"א, Tel Aviv). Various methods have been used to indicate abbreviations and several types are distinguishable. By the Middle Ages various systems of dots and strokes were known. The modern method uses a single stroke if one word is abbreviated (e.g., מַסֶּכֶת – מס') and double strokes before the final letter of the abbreviation if there are more (e.g., הַקָּדוֹשׁ בָּרוּךְ הוּא – הקב"ה).

Types of Abbreviations

Two types of abbreviations are distinguishable. The first type is when one word is abbreviated: (1) *tevot mogzarot:* the end of the word is dropped (e.g., שֶׁנֶּאֱמַר – שנ'); (2) *tevot nishbarot:* the middle of the word is dropped (e.g., אֶלָּא – אא); (3) *emẓa'ei tevot:* the middle letter represents a word (e.g., ה' for the Tetragrammaton); (4) *sofei tevot:* the beginning of the word is dropped (e.g., אֶבֶן – ן'). The second type is when a group of words is abbreviated: (1) *rashei tevot:* the initial letters are used (e.g., אִם יִרְצֶה הַשֵּׁם – אי"ה); (2) two letters are used of one or several words (e.g., שְׁאֵלוֹת וּתְשׁוּבוֹת – שו"ת; אָדָם הָרִאשׁוֹן – אדה"ר); (3) when one of the words is very short, it is retained (e.g., שְׁוָא נָח – שנ"ח); (4) when an abbreviation is formed of a group of words, it may itself be divided (e.g., בָּרוּךְ אַתָּה ה' אֱלֹהֵינוּ מֶלֶךְ הָעוֹלָם אֲשֶׁר קִדְּשָׁנוּ בְּמִצְוֹתָיו וְצִוָּנוּ – בא"י אמ"ה אקב"ו). Such groups with the addition of vowels have often been rendered pronounceable (e.g., קוֹלִי, רֹאשׁ, עָרוֹב, שָׁשׁ, טוֹב, נִדְבוֹת – קְרַ"ע שָׂטָ"ן, initial letters of verses recited before the *shofar* is blown); (5) such abbreviations are really *acrostics. In large groups, words may be left unrepresented (e.g., in the abbreviation for the Ten Plagues, דְּצַ"ךְ עֲדַ"שׁ בְּאַחַ"ב, the Passover *Haggadah* omits the word מַכַּת before the ב standing for 6) ;(בְּכוֹרוֹת) *sofei tevot:* the abbreviation is formed by a combination of final letters (e.g., בָּרָא אֱלֹהִים לַעֲשׂוֹת – אמ"ת, see also no. 10); (7) *serugin* (trellis-writing): where only the initial word or letter is used when quoting a biblical verse; (8) *ẓeruf:* mystic combination of letters (see below); (9) combination of middle letters (e.g., תְּקִיעָה תְּרוּעָה תְּקִיעָה – קר"ק); (10) initial letters in reverse order (e.g., תְּהִלִּים מִשְׁלֵי אִיּוֹב – אמ"ת); (11) occasionally vernacular proper nouns and other words have been accepted and abbreviated in Hebrew (e.g., *Yahrzeit*, יאָהרצייט – י"צ).

Abbreviation of the Name of God

The name of God is probably the most often abbreviated word, due to its frequent appearance in Jewish writing and the reverence which is accorded it. It was abbreviated in antiquity, mishnaic, and talmudic times as ה' or י'; in Targum Onkelos as ה' and ד'; and in the Middle Ages it was represented by ה' and varying numbers of *yod*'s, *vav*'s, strokes, and dots, from which developed the use of *yod*'s. It has been estimated that there are over 80 substitutes for the Divine Name.

Abbreviation of Names

These are found in connection with euphemisms for the living and eulogies for the dead, in prayers, letters, etc. The Talmud (Git. 36a) reports that the *amoraim* Ḥisda and Hoshaya signed themselves ס' and ע', respectively, and other names were abbreviated in talmudic times (e.g, Resh Lakish for R. Simeon b. Lakish). In medieval times the names of famous rabbis were abbreviated, vowels added, and the resultant abbreviation pronounced (e.g., רַבִּי לֵוִי בֶּן גֵּרְשׁוֹם – רַלְבַּ"ג), a practice also adopted by and for later scholars and their families (e.g., בֶּן רַבִּי יְהוּדָה לֵוִי – בְּרִי"ל; רַבִּי מֹשֶׁה חַיִּים לוּצַטּוֹ – רַמְחַ"ל). The general term for the talmudic sages was חֲכָמֵינוּ זִכְרוֹנָם לִבְרָכָה – חז"ל. In the emancipation period, when the Jews had to adopt surnames, Hebrew abbreviations often formed the basis of "secular" names (e.g., Baeck, בַּעַל קוֹרֵא – ב"ק or בְּנֵי קֹדֶשׁ). Ḥasidic leaders were referred to as אֲדוֹנֵנוּ מוֹרֵנוּ וְרַבֵּנוּ – אַדְמוֹ"ר. The name Katz (כֹּהֵן צֶדֶק – כַּ"ץ) stood for families of priestly descent, and Segal (סְגַן לְוִיָּה – סֶגַ"ל) for those of levite origin. On talmudic ossuaries the letters אָמֵן – א' and שָׁלוֹם – ש' appear after the name of the deceased, while on later tombstones תְּהִי נַפְשׁוֹ צְרוּרָה בִּצְרוֹר הַחַיִּים – תנצב"ה (see I Sam. 25:29), פֹּה נִקְבַּר – פ"נ, and פֹּה טָמוּן – פ"ט (meaning "here lies buried") are common. When referring in letters to deceased persons, it is customary to attach eulogistic abbreviations, such as הֲרֵינִי כַּפָּרַת מִשְׁכָּבוֹ – הכ"מ, used by children during the year of mourning (Kid. 31b; Sh. Ar., YD 240:9); זֵכֶר צַדִּיק לִבְרָכָה – זצ"ל, זִכְרוֹנוֹ לִבְרָכָה – ז"ל (Prov. 10:7); עָלָיו הַשָּׁלוֹם – ע"ה; in correspondence it became usual to prefix *letters and occasionally also printed matter and books with בְּעֶזְרַת ה׳ – בעז״ה, בע״ה, ב״ה ("With the help of God") or שִׁוִּיתִי ה׳ לְנֶגְדִּי תָמִיד – שיל״ת ("I have set the Lord always before me"; Ps. 16:8). The addressee may be greeted with יִשְׁמְרֵהוּ צוּרוֹ וְגוֹאֲלוֹ – יצ״ו or נַטְרֵיהּ רַחֲמָנָא וּפָרְקֵיהּ – נר״ו, both meaning "May God protect him." The formula בְּחֵרֶם דְּרַבֵּנוּ גֵּרְשׁוֹם – בְּחַדְרַ״ג was used to affirm the secrecy of letters. The final greeting in the modern idiom is דְּרִישַׁת שָׁלוֹם – ד״ש and כָּל טוּב – כט״ס or כ״ט or כָּל טוּב סֶלָה.

Names of Towns

The letters יִבָּנֶה עִיר אֱלֹהִים – יע״א ("May God's city be rebuilt," referring to Jerusalem) are appended after the name of any city; after the name of a city in Israel (תִּבָּנֶה וְתִכּוֹנֵן – ת״ו); and after mentioning Jerusalem (עִיר קָדְשֵׁנוּ תִּבָּנֶה וְתִכּוֹנֵן בִּמְהֵרָה בְּיָמֵינוּ אָמֵן – עיקת״ו בב״א or תִּבָּנֶה וְתִכּוֹנֵן בִּמְהֵרָה בְּיָמֵינוּ – תובב״א). The names of Diaspora towns mentioned in Hebrew writing are also abbreviated, e.g., שו״ם for Speyer, Worms, and Mainz; נ״ש for Nikolsburg; פפד״ם for Frankfurt on the Main; and אה״ו for the triple community of Altona-Hamburg-Wandsbeck.

Book Titles

The best-known abbreviations for *book titles are those for the Hebrew Bible, תַּנַ״ךְ, composed of the initial letters of תּוֹרָה נְבִיאִים כְּתוּבִים, and שִׁשָּׁה סְדָרִים – ש״ס for the Babylonian Talmud. Some Jewish classics have become known by the abbreviated form of their titles, thus almost completely obscuring the author's name and book title; thus the שְׁנֵי לוּחוֹת הַבְּרִית of Isaiah b. Abraham *Horowitz is invariably referred to as the שְׁלָ״ה, as is its author. At the beginning of books frequently appear abbreviations such as ה׳ צְבָאוֹת עִמָּנוּ מִשְׂגָּב לָנוּ אֱלֹהֵי יַעֲקֹב סֶלָה – הצעמלאי״ס or עֶזְרִי מֵעִם ה׳ עוֹשֵׂה שָׁמַיִם וָאָרֶץ – עמ״י עש״ו, while the Ashkenazi Jews often end with תַּם וְנִשְׁלַם שֶׁבַח לְאֵל בּוֹרֵא עוֹלָם – תושלב״ע. In the Middle Ages manuscripts were often completed with בָּרוּךְ נוֹתֵן לַיָּעֵף כֹּחַ – בנל״כ, derived from Isa. 40:29 (see *Hebrew Book Titles; *Manuscripts).

In Kabbalah

In medieval kabbalistic literature a combination of letters was termed *ẓeruf otiyyot* (cf. Ber. 55a, etc.), while the term *gilgul* was introduced later. Abbreviations were used for frequently recurring concepts (e.g., אֵשׁ רוּחַ מַיִם עָפָר – ארמ״ע, "fire, wind, water, earth") and the *notarikon* פְּשָׁט רֶמֶז דְּרָשׁ סוֹד – פרד״ס ("plain, symbolic, homiletic, esoteric"), describing the four types of biblical hermeneutics. The spread of mysticism led to an increasing use of abbreviation similar to the talmudic *simanim* (e.g., בָּרָא רָקִיעַ שָׁמַיִם יָם תְּהוֹם – בְּרֵאשִׁית); such terms are considered as possessing particularly profound and secret qualities (see *Magic). Abbreviations also appear on *amulets.

Misunderstandings and Misinterpretations

The increasing and inconsistent use of abbreviations has inevitably led to occasional confusion and made the study of Hebrew texts more difficult, a fact recognized in the 16th century by Solomon Luria (*Yam shel Shelomo*, Hul. 6:6). Misinterpretations have occurred when ambiguous abbreviations were printed in full. In any case, difficulties arise when an abbreviation can be read in more than one way, so that, e.g., in a bibliographical context ד״ו could be read as דְּפוּס וְינִיצְיָאה ("Printed in Venice"), or דְּפוּס וָורְשָׁה ("Printed in Warsaw"), or דְּפוּס וִילְנָה ("Printed in Vilna"), or דְּפוּס וִינָה ("Printed in Vienna"). Because of the risk of misrepresentation, no abbreviations may be used in a bill of divorce (Git. 36a and Sh. Ar., EH 126) or other religious documents. Misrepresentations have also occurred in the work of censors and Christian scholars (e.g., three *yod*'s have been taken to denote the trinity). Hebrew abbreviations have been found on Christian amulets, and Christian writers have used kabbalistic methods, such as regarding a complete word as *notarikon* (e.g., בָּרָא as בֵּן רוּחַ אָב). Because of the many obscurities in Hebrew writings, which Christian scholars were anxious to study, a guide to abbreviations was needed and it was a non-Jew, Johannes *Buxtorf the Elder, who produced the pioneer work *De Abbreviaturis Hebraicis* (1613). The first Jewish work of this kind, by Elijah *Levita, concentrated mainly on the masoretic ambiguities; lists of abbreviations were eventually added to Hebrew works and were followed by independent, comprehensive compilations. Of these, the following are the most important: J. Ezekiel, *Kethonet Yoseph: A Handbook of Hebrew Abbreviations* (Heb.–Eng., 1887); G.H. Haendler, *Erkhei ha-Notarikon* (1897); M. Heilprin, *Ha-Notarikon ...* (1872, 1930); A. Stern, *Sefer Rashei Tevot* (1926); S. Chajes, *Ozar Beduyei ha-Shem* (pseudonyms; 1933); S. Ashkenazi and D. Jarden, *Oẓar Rashei Tevot ...* (1965; 1978); S. Ashkenazi, *Mefa'ne'aḥ Ne'lamim* (1969); A. Steinsalz, *Rashei Tevot ve-Kizzurim be-Sifrut ha-Hasidut ve-ha-Kabbalah* (1968); U. Tadmor, *Ha-Notarikin ba-Ivrit ha-Yisre'elit, Leshonenu La-Am* 39, 225–57; Y. Ben-Tolila, *Ha-Iivrit ha-Medubberet, Leshonenu L-Aam* 40–41 (1990), 266–78.

[Ruth P. Lehmann]

Abbreviations in Jewish Folklore

Many abbreviations were misinterpreted (often quite intentionally) and caused misunderstandings which became part of the Jewish folklore. For example, the *Yaknehaz* abbreviation in the Passover *Haggadah*, denoting the order of the benedictions (*yayin, kiddush, ner, havdalah, zeman)*, was understood as the German *jag'n Has* ("hunt the hare") and pictures of a hare hunt accompany the relevant passage in the printed *Haggadah*. Many folk etymologies are based upon the notion that the obscure word is an abbreviation; so, e.g., the word *afikoman* is explained by the Yemenite *Haggadah* as an abbreviation of *egozim* ("nuts"), *perot* ("fruits"), *yayin* ("wine"), *keliyyot* ("parched grain"), *u-vasar* ("and meat"), *mayim* ("water"), *nerd* ("spices"). The abbreviation of *Akum* for *Oved Kokhavim u-Mazzalot* ("worshiper of the stars and constellations") was interpreted by antisemitic propaganda (Rohling) as *Oved Christum u-Miryam* ("Worshiper of Christ and Mary").

[Dov Noy]

Abbreviations in Learning

Many abbreviations were set up to help students memorize rules such as in Hebrew grammar or in *Halakhah*. Of this type are *bg"d kf"t*, *lmn"r*, in classifying Hebrew characters which show the same phonetic behavior, or *shemelakhto bina* to mark the group of 11 servile letters as against the other 11 letters that only appear as radicals. These are well known. Here and there can be found local acronyms, as in Tetouan (Morocco), where the word *romaḥ* based on "*wayiqqaḥ* ROMAḤ *beyado*" (Num. 25:7) was adapted to summarize the *halakhot* that deal with the conditions under which a *shofar*'s hole can be repaired: *rubbo* (if the greater part of the *shofar* was kept untouched), *mino* (the hole can only be filled with a material of the *shofar*'s type), *hazar* (the original sound of the *shofar* did not change after the repair).

[Aharon Maman (2nd ed.)]

BIBLIOGRAPHY: Simonsen, in: ZHB, 4 (1900), 87–92; Loewenstein, in: *Festschrift … A. Berliner* (1903), 255–64; J.R. Marcus, in: *Jubilee Volume … A. Marx* (Eng. vol., 1950), 447–80; Elijah Levitas, *Masoret ha-Masoret*, ed. by C.D. Ginsburg (1867), 3, 244–68; Steinschneider, in: *Archiv fuer Stenographie* (1887), nos. 466, 467; Neubauer, in: JQR, 7 (1894/95), 361–4; F. Perles, *Analekten …*, 1 (1895), 4–35; S. Schechter and S. Singer (ed.), *Talmudical Fragments in the Bodleian Library* (1896); W. Bacher, *Exegetische Terminologie …*, 1 (1899), 125–8; 2 (1905), 124; G.R. Driver, in: *Textus*, 1 (1960), 112–31; 4 (1964), 76–94; idem, *Judaean Scrolls* (1965), 335–46; *Yeda-Am*, 2, no. 30 (1966), index, 189, s.v. *Notarikon*.

ʿABD AL-ḤAQQ AL-ISLĀMĪ (end of 14th century), Jewish convert to Islam. ʿAbd al-Ḥaqq was apparently a Moroccan Jew (the surname indicates a convert to Islam). We know next to nothing of his identity or his background. Towards the end of the 14th century, at the age of about 40, he converted to Islam. Sixteen years later he wrote a work in Arabic, *The Sword Extended in Refutation of the Rabbis of the Jews*, attacking the Jews and demonstrating the falsity of their beliefs. The text is an unsophisticated manual for disputations with Jews, and uses standard arguments of Islamic anti-Jewish polemic.

ʿAbd al-Haqq claims that the **dhimma*, or contract, between Islam and the Jews has been abrogated by the Jews themselves, as they are no longer genuine monotheists. Mistreatment of the prophets by Jews of biblical times shows this, as does the introduction of post-biblical feasts. The transmission of their Scriptures from early times cannot be trusted, and they have introduced falsifications into the texts, as can be seen from the presence of anthropomorphic passages in the Bible. The books of the Jews, in particular the biblical texts, he asserts, should thus be censored. Nonetheless, like other polemicists (e.g., *Samau'al al-Maghribī), ʿAbd al-Ḥaqq is able to claim authenticity for the biblical text when it agrees with his case, and, making use of knowledge from his Jewish background, he appeals to *gematria* to show that Muhammad and Mecca are referred to in the Bible – thus, in Genesis 12:9, where Abraham is said to have gone "towards the south," *hanegbah* in Hebrew, ʿAbd al-Ḥaqq points out that the numerical value of the letters in this word, 65, is the same as that of the letters in the name of the city of *Mecca. By similar means he shows that king Ahab (in I Kings 20:6 and 22:35) was a believer in Muhammad.

BIBLIOGRAPHY: M. Perlmann, "Abd al-Ḥakk al-Islamī, a Jewish Convert," in: JQR, New Series 31, (1940/41), 171–91; E. Alfonso (ed. and trans., with intro. and notes), *Al-Sayf al-Mamdūd fī al-radd ʿala ahbār al-Yahūd. Espada extendida para refutar a los sabios judios* (1998).

[David J. Wasserstein (2nd ed.)]

ABDALLAH, YUSEF (late 19th–early 20th century), charlatan who revived messianic activity in Yemen in the 1890s. He began his activities no later than 1888 as the herald of the messiah. The leaders of the Jewish community in San'a, led by Ḥayyim *Ḥibshush, actively opposed him until they succeeded in persuading the police chief and the Turkish authorities in San'a to deport him from the city (1895) to the town of Shibām northwest of San'a, where he remained with little influence until his death. Abdallah struggled against his opponents by means of letters and poems. The latter-day discovery and publication of a three-page manuscript of his includes four poems which do not exhibit any extraordinary talent, being in fact trivial in comparison to run-of-the-mill Yemenite poetry. Surprisingly, its content is far from revealing messianic tendencies. It does not offer the slightest suggestion of his supposed status as a messiah, or as the messenger of the messiah. All that appears in the poetry in this respect is a plea for redemption and the hastening of the arrival of the messiah, motifs familiar in Hebrew poetry throughout the generations. What can be found there are complaints about his opponents in the Jewish community and the Turkish and Muslim authorities. As opposed to the negative picture described by Ḥibshush, Koraḥ and most scholars (apart from Nini) find no deviation from the Jewish tradition of messianic expectations and observance of religious law in the poems.

BIBLIOGRAPHY: Y. Kafaḥ, "*Ḥayyim Ḥibshush*," in: *Sefunot*, 2 (1958), 278–79; A. Ya'ari, *Shevut Teiman* (1945), 124–48; Y. Tobi, *Pirkei Shirah*, 4 (2005); Y. Nini, *The Jews of Yemen, 1880–1914* (1991), 145–50; B. Eraqi Klorman, *The Jews of Yemen in the Nineteenth Century* (1993), 158–64; A. Koraḥ, *Sa'arat Teiman*, 53–55; Y. Ratzahbi, *Bo'i Teman* (1967), 204–13.

[Yosef Tobi (2nd ed.)]

ABDALLAH IBN SABĀʾ (also called **Ibn al-Sawdā**; seventh century), supposedly a Jew of south Arabian origin, and regarded as the founder of the Shiʿite sect (one of the two main branches of Islam) shortly after Muhammad's death. The reports by Arab historians concerning his role are contradictory and perhaps reflect the tendency to charge a Jew with partial responsibility for the internal feuds of the Islamic community. Abdallah asserted that Muhammad is the Messiah, who will appear a second time. Meanwhile, ʿAlī, the son-in-law of Muhammad, is his representative. After the assassination of ʿAlī (661), Abdallah allegedly denied that ʿAlī had died, asserting that the slain man was a demon who had taken on ʿAlī's features; ʿAlī himself was hiding among the clouds, and would return to earth later to establish the Kingdom of Justice. The doctrine that not ʿAlī, but someone of similar appearance, had been murdered, has its precedent in the teachings of a Christian sect which denied the crucifixion of Jesus, a belief which persists in the Christology of the *Koran (Sūra 4: 156). But the messianic concepts ascribed to Abdallah show traces of Jewish (two Messiahs) and Christian origin and differ from the messianic concepts which became generally recognized within the Shiʿa. In these, the Messiah (who was identical not with ʿAlī himself, but with one of his descendants) was hiding in a mountain in the vicinity of *Kūfa (in Iraq).

BIBLIOGRAPHY: Friedlaender, in: ZA, 23 (1909), 296–327; 24 (1910), 1–46; Levi della Vida, in: RSO, 6 (1913), 504; C. van Arendonk, *De Opkomst van het Zaidietsche Imamaat.* (1919), 7; Hirschberg, in: *Vienna Jewish Theological Seminary Memorial Volume* (1946), 122–3; EIS², 1 (1960), 51 (includes bibliography).

[Josef Horovitz]

ABDALLAH IBN SALĀM (seventh century C.E.), one of Muhammad's Jewish followers. The name of his father, Salām, was used only among Jews in the Arabia of that time. Abdallah's family is usually regarded as belonging to the Banū *Qaynuqāʿ, one of the Jewish clans of Yathrib (Medina), although some associated it with the typically Arabic clan of the Zayd al-Lāt, which implies that they were under the protection of the latter. Abdallah is said to have been converted by Muhammad soon after the latter's arrival in Medina. When his former coreligionists told Muhammad "He [Abdallah] is our master and the son of our master" Muhammad invited them to follow Abdallah's example. The Jews refused, and only his immediate family, notably his aunt Khālida, embraced Islam. According to other versions, Abdallah's conversion occurred because of the strength of Muhammad's answers to his questions. Another account, which places Abdallah's conversion at a much later date, has more intrinsic plausibility. After Muhammad's death Abdallah was in the entourage of Caliph ʿUthmān and made a vain attempt to prevent his assassination. A year later he warned ʿAli against leaving Medina. If all the obviously legendary and biased accounts about Abdallah are eliminated, not much concrete information remains. His relationship to Ahmad ibn Abdallah ibn Salām, a translator of biblical writings, is unclear. Originally the Jewish scholars of Medina were presented as the questioners of Muhammad, and only later did Abdallah figure. The three questions ascribed to him form the core of the volume entitled *Questions of Abdallah ibn Salām*, first mentioned in 963, which is known in a number of adaptations as *A Thousand Questions.* Outside the context of this work Abdallah is repeatedly mentioned as the source for tales from biblical times. *Genizah* fragments have recently yielded a Jewish version of the Abdallah legend in which he appears as *Absalom.

BIBLIOGRAPHY: Ibn Hishām (ʿAbd al-Malik), *The Life of Muhammad, tr.* by A. Guillaume (1955), 240, 262, 267; Wāqidī, *Kitāb al Maghāzī*, ed. by J. Wellhausen (Ger., 1882), 164, 215; Ibn Saʿd (Muhammad), *Biographien Muhammeds*, 2, pt. 2 (1912), 111; (al-) Ṭabarī (Muhammad ibn Jarīr), *Annales*, 1 (Ar., 1879), index; Balādhurī (Aḥmad ibn Yaḥya), *Ansāb al-Ashrāf*, 5 (Ar., 1936), 74–76, 90; Goitein, in: Zion, 1 (1936), 77–78; Steinschneider, Arab Lit, 8–9; Chapira, in: REJ, 69 (1919), 91; Mann, in: JQR, 12 (1921/22), 127–8; Brockelmann, Arab Lit, 1 (1943), 209; EIS², 1 (1960), 52.

[Josef Horovitz]

°ABD AL-MĀLIK IBN MĀRWAN (ruled 685–705), *Umayyad caliph who restored the unity of the young Arab Empire after years of civil wars. ʿAbd al-Mālik built the Dome of the Rock and the al-Aqṣā Mosque in the Temple area in Jerusalem. The building of the Dome was an act of propaganda for the Muslim faith, partly directed against the still strong Christian community, as is proved by the inscriptions inside the Dome. The restoration of the Temple site to a state of splendor impressed mystically inclined Jewish circles. There is no information about the general situation of the Jews under ʿAbd al-Mālik's rule. According to the majority of sources the armed rising of the Jewish pseudo-messiah Abū ʿIsā of Isfahan was suppressed during his reign. The Jew Sumayr was master of the mint in Iraq during the monetary reforms of ʿAbd al-Mālik.

BIBLIOGRAPHY: S.D. Goitein, *Studies in Islamic History and Institutions* (1966), 135–48; idem, in: *Zion*, 1 (1935), 80–81; Hirschberg, in: *Rocznik Orientalistyczny*, 17 (1951–52), 314–50. **ADD. BIBLIOGRAPHY:** EIS², 1 (1960), 70–71, bibl.

[Shelomo Dov Goitein]

ABDON (Heb. עַבְדּוֹן), a name occurring in the Bible in several different contexts. (1) Abdon the son of Hillel, a minor judge, who came from a town in Ephraim, possibly to be identified with the village Faraʿata southwest of Shechem (Judg. 12:13–15). He "judged" Israel for eight years. The Bible states that "he had 40 sons and 30 grandsons, making 70 descendants who rode on 70 donkeys." This statement may be intended to indicate that Abdon and his descendants had widespread influence and wealth. (2) Abdon the son of Micah (II Chron. 34:20), probably corrupt for *Achbor the son of Micaiah (II Kings 22:12–14). (3) A Benjamite family (I Chron. 8:12, 30; 9:36).

BIBLIOGRAPHY: Y. Kaufmann, *Sefer Shofetim* (1962), 234; M.Z. Segal, *Sifrei Shemu'el* (1964), 88; Noth, Personennamen, index; Hertzberg, in: *Theologische Literaturzeitung*, 79 (1954).

ABDUCTION (or **Manstealing;** Heb. גְּנֵבַת נֶפֶשׁ, *genevat nefesh*), stealing of a human being for capital gain. According to the Bible, abduction is a capital offense. "He who kidnaps a man – whether he has sold him or is still holding him – shall be put to death" (Ex. 21:16); and, "If a man is found to have kidnapped a fellow Israelite, enslaving him or selling him, that kidnapper shall die" (Deut. 24:7). The first passage appears to prohibit the abduction of any person, while the latter is confined to Israelites only; the first appears to outlaw any abduction, however motivated (cf. *Codex Hammurapi*, 14), while the latter requires either enslavement or sale as an essential element to constitute the offense. Talmudic law, in order to reconcile these conflicting scriptural texts or to render prosecution for this capital offense more difficult (or for both purposes), made the detention, the enslavement, and the sale of the abducted person all necessary elements of the offense, giving the Hebrew "and" (which in the translation quoted above is rendered as "or") its cumulative meaning (Sanh. 85b, 86a). Thus, abduction without detention or enslavement or sale, like enslavement or sale or detention without abduction, however morally reprehensible, was not punishable (even by *flogging), because none of these acts was in itself a completed offense. On the other hand, even the slightest, most harmless, and casual use of the abducted person would amount to "enslavement"; and as for the "sale," it does not matter that the sale of any human being (other than a slave) is legally void (BK 68b). In this context, any attempt at selling the person, by delivering him or her into the hands of a purchaser, would suffice. However, the attempted sale has to be proved in addition to the purchaser's custody, because giving away the abducted person as a gift would not be a "sale" even for this purpose (Rashba to BK 78b). The term rendered in the translation quoted above as "kidnap" is *ganov* ("steal"). The injunction of the Decalogue, "Thou shalt not steal" (Ex. 20:13), has been interpreted to refer to the stealing of persons rather than the stealing of chattels. The reason for this is both because the latter is proscribed elsewhere (Lev. 19:11), and because of the context of the command next to the interdictions of murder and adultery, both of which are capital offenses and offenses against the human person (Mekh. Mishpatim 5). It has been said that this interpretation reflects the abhorrence with which the talmudic jurists viewed this particular crime; alternatively, it has been maintained that the reliance on the general words "Thou shalt not steal" made the interdiction of manstealing applicable also to non-Jews and hence amounted to a repudiation of slave trading, which in other legal systems of the period was considered wholly legitimate.

There is no recorded instance of any prosecution for abduction – not, presumably, because no abductions occurred, but because it proved difficult, if not impossible, to find the required groups of *witnesses. These would have been required not only for each of the constituent elements of the offense, but also for the prescribed warnings that first had to be administered to the accused in respect of the abduction, the detention, the enslavement, and the sale, separately. The classical instance of abduction reported in the Bible is Joseph's sale into slavery (Gen. 37; cf. 40:15, "I was kidnapped from the land of the Hebrews"). In the Talmud there is a report from Alexandria that brides were abducted from under the canopy (BM 104a; Tosef. Ket. 4:9), not necessarily for enslavement or sale, but (as it appears from the context) for marriage to the abductors.

[Haim Hermann Cohn]

In Israeli Law

TRAFFICKING IN HUMAN BEINGS TO ENGAGE IN PROSTITUTION. At the beginning of 2000, in the framework of Amendment 56 of the Penal Law, provisions were enacted that prohibited trafficking in human beings for engagement in prostitution. Pursuant to this amendment, section 203A of the Penal Law established a maximum punishment of 16 years' imprisonment for anyone who "sells or purchases a person in order to engage him in prostitution or serving as a middleman in the selling or purchasing of a person for this purpose."

Trafficking in human beings has been prohibited since the very dawn of the history of Jewish Law, in the framework of the commandment of "Thou shall not steal" (Ex. 20:12; Deut. 5:16) and the prohibitions concerning abduction mentioned above. "Joseph's sale by his brothers was an ignominious episode of Jewish history and was regarded as having sealed the fate of the Ten Martyrs" (see Rubinstein). The Knesset's enactment of the aforementioned amendment was in accordance with Basic Law: Human Dignity and Freedom, sec. 2 of which states: "There shall be no violation of the life, body, or dignity of any person as such," while sec. 4 states that "All persons are entitled to protection of their life, body, and dignity."

Jewish Law's prohibition of abduction and the death penalty imposed on the abductor are only applicable upon the satisfaction of four cumulative conditions: an abduction of a human being; the abductee's detention in the abductor's premises; the abductee's enslavement by the abductor; and the abductee's subsequent sale to another (Maim., Yad, *Genevah* 9:2). Some of the *geonim* were lenient regarding the requirement that all four conditions be satisfied and convicted the abductor where he had abducted and sold, or abducted and enslaved (see in detail *Halakhah Berurah*, Sanh. 85b).

The Israeli legislator broadened the prohibition to include serving as a middleman, in addition to the elements of abduction, detention, and sale. Under Israeli Law both the abductor-seller and the buyer are equally culpable and share the same punishment, whereas under Jewish law the abductor is the sole offender. The need for deterrence led the Israeli legislator to broaden the circle of offenders, imposing criminal liability upon the seller, the middleman, and the buyer. With respect to punishment for trading in women, this facilitates punishment even if only some of those involved in the offense are actually caught, and even if the prime actor – the seller – is still at large (occasionally abroad) and hence difficult to capture. The Supreme Court stressed that the prohibition of trading in human beings is intended to prevent violations of human dignity, especially that of women sold for prostitution. Hence, section 203A of the Penal Law should be constructed broadly and applied to any transaction that results in a person being treated as property, be it by way of sale, day-hiring, borrowing, partnership, or any other creation of a proprietary connection to a person (Cr. A 11196/02 *Prodental v. State of Israel*, 57 (6) 40, per Justice Beinish).

CHILD ABDUCTION. The Hague Convention on the Civil Aspects of International Child Abduction was signed in 1980. In 1991, Israel incorporated the Convention's provisions into

Knesset legislation and empowered the Family Courts to enforce them. The goal of the Convention was to secure the prompt return of illegally abducted children to their countries of residence prior to their abduction.

We already find a claim of child abduction in the Bible, where Laban complains about Jacob's flight from Aram Naharaim together with his wives and children (i.e., Laban's daughters and grandchildren). Upon finding Jacob at Mt. Gilead, Laban cries: "What have you done, that you have cheated me, and carried away my daughters like captives of the sword. Why did you flee secretly, and cheat me, and did not tell me, so that I might have sent thee away with mirth and songs, with timbrel and lyre? And why did you not permit me to kiss my sons and my daughters farewell? Now you have done foolishly" (Gen. 31:26–28).

The Convention's point of departure is the provision that abduction is a violation of one of the parent's custodial rights, "under the law of the State in which the child was habitually resident immediately before the removal or the retention" of the child (Article 3(a) of the Convention). Consequently, cardinal importance attaches to the determination of where the minor's habitual place of residence was, prior to the abduction. In one of the judgments given in the Jerusalem District Court, an halakhic principle was invoked in order to determine the minor's customary place of residence. The minor's parents were observant Jews. The father – then resident with his family in Oxford while writing his doctoral thesis – did not observe the Second Day of Festivals ordinarily observed by Jews living outside Israel. His adherence to the Israeli custom in this respect led the Court to infer that the locus of his life had remained in Israel. Consequently, the child's removal to Israel could not be regarded as abduction (F.A. 575/04 (Jer.) *Anon. v. Anon.*). In reaching this conclusion the Court adduced extensive halakhic material, from the Talmud (TB Pes. 51a, 52), Maimonides (Yad, *Yom Tov* 8:2), Shulḥan Arukh (OḤ 493:3), and the responsa (Radbaz, 4:73).

The Convention provides that there may be a justification for not returning the child if "it finds that the child objects to being returned and has attained an age and degree of maturity at which it is appropriate to take account of its views" (Article 13 of Convention, concluding phrase). One of the judgments includes a comprehensive discussion of how to determine whether the child is of an age and level that justifies taking account of his views. The Court noted that "in the State of Israel, as a Jewish state, consideration is accorded to the Jewish heritage, where the matter concerns consideration for the children's wishes and the age at which the law gives effect to the expression of their position" (F.A. (Jer) 621/04 *Anon. v. Anon.*). One of the sources upon which the decision was based was the mishnah in *Niddah* 5:6. This mishnah states that vows made by a girl aged 12 are considered efficacious, while between the ages of 11 and 12 the girl's level of intellectual maturity and comprehension are "examined." In the case of boys, his standing vis-à-vis vows is examined between the ages of 12 and 13, while after age 13 his vows too are fully efficacious, like those of a girl at age 12. The Babylonian Talmud ad loc. states that "the Holy One Blessed be He endowed woman with greater wisdom than the man," in light of the fact that the girl reaches maturity before the boy (cf. *Torah Temimah*, Gen. 2:22, §48). The District Court concluded that in the case in question, two of the four daughters were capable of expressing their position – which was against returning to the United States and in favor of staying in Israel. This position was adopted in consideration of their age, which is the age at which an undertaking for a vow is binding under Jewish Law. As such it is also an age at which the Court can form its impression that their wishes are of a nature that ought to be respected, pursuant to Article 13 of the Convention

The very enactment of the Hague Convention Law in Israel may be viewed as the endorsement of a fundamental principle of Jewish Law, namely, that the child is not an object to be moved from country to country, and abducted by one parent against the wishes of the second parent; but an independent legal entity, vested with both standing and rights (see also *Parent and Child).

[Moshe Drori (2nd ed.)]

BIBLIOGRAPHY: D. Daube, *Studies in Biblical Law* (1947); ET, 5 (1953), 386–93; S. Mendelsohn, *Criminal Jurisprudence of the Ancient Hebrews* (1968²), 52, 126. **ADD. BIBLIOGRAPHY:** E. Rubinstein, *Sakhar be-Venei Adam la-Asok be-Zenut – Sugiyyot be-Mishpat ha-Ẓibburi be-Yisrael* (2003), 360–364; A. Ha-Cohen, "And There Shall You Be Sold to Your Enemies as Bondsman…" in: *Parashat ha-Shavu'a, Ki-Tavo*, vol. 179 (2004) – Ministry of Justice, Department of Jewish Law, and the Center for the Instruction and Research of Jewish Law, Sha'arei Mishpat College.

°ABDULLAH IBN HUSSEIN (1882–1951), first king of the Hashemite Kingdom of *Jordan. Abdullah was born in Mecca, the second son of the *sharīf* Hussein ibn Ali, into the Hashemite family that traced its descent from the prophet Muhammad and had been rulers of Mecca from the 11th century C.E. He grew up in Constantinople, where he received the traditional education of a Muslim gentleman and became, in effect, his father's political secretary. After Hussein had been installed as emir of Mecca in 1908, Abdullah was instrumental in the secret negotiations with the British that resulted in the "Arab Revolt" of 1916 and in the Allies' recognition of Hussein as king of the Hejaz. Toward the end of 1920 Abdullah moved north with a Bedouin army with the avowed intent of restoring his brother Faisal, who had just been evicted by the French, to the throne of Syria. At a meeting in Jerusalem in March 1921, Winston *Churchill, then British colonial secretary, offered Abdullah the administration of Transjordan. Out of this tentative arrangement grew the emirate of Transjordan, with Abdullah as hereditary ruler, under the general terms of the British mandate over Palestine, which comprised Transjordan, but with the clauses pertaining to the Jewish National Home expressly deleted. The police of the emirate, soon styled the "Arab Legion," developed into a field force during World War II under John B. Glubb and took on a Bedouin character more and more. In 1946 a treaty with Britain awarded Abdullah formal independence, and he assumed the royal title forthwith. In 1948 the Arab Legion, with British connivance, occupied the greater part of Samaria and Judea (designated by the UN resolution of Nov. 29, 1947, as part of an independent Arab State). This was secured by Abdullah in the 1949 armistice with Israel, and he incorporated these territories into his kingdom, henceforth called Jordan. On July 20, 1951, Abdullah was assassinated as he left al-Aqṣā Mosque in Jerusalem. His murder was generally ascribed to revenge for his readiness to negotiate with Israel for the partition of Palestine and the annexation of its Arab sections. It was also the culmination of his long-standing feud with the Husseini family and its head Hajj Amīn, the former Mufti of Jerusalem.

Ever since he had arrived in Transjordan Abdullah had been dissatisfied with the barren, desolate piece of land allotted to him by the British and, from the outset, sought to expand his realm. His prime vision was of a multinational Hashemite Greater Syria, but as a pragmatist, he was ready to settle for Palestine or even for its Arab sections alone. Hence, even though Abdullah's published views of the Palestine problem did not deviate from those of Arab nationalists in general, his moderate style when addressing Westerners made them, if anything, more effective. In the Israeli War of Independence, the Arab Legion proved the most dangerous enemy Israel faced in the field. However, for much of the 30-year period of his political activity, Abdullah maintained secret contacts with Jewish leaders, assuring them of his readiness to cooperate on his own terms. The highlights of these contacts were an agreement in 1933 with the *Jewish Agency (subsequently disavowed by Abdullah) to lease about 70,000 dunams of crown land in the Jordan Valley and intermittent talks between Abdullah and certain Jewish leaders (prominent among whom were Golda *Meir and Eliyahu *Sasson) during the War of Independence. All these contacts were without tangible result, with the exception of the modifications in the 1949 armistice line with Jordan. Yet he continued his negotiations with Israel for a peace treaty or for a non-aggression pact until 1950. Abdullah was a confirmed Arab nationalist, but, self-possessed and of an ancient ruling family, he lacked that admixture of frustration and hatred that became a characteristic of the next generation's nationalism. Moreover, even before World War I, Arab nationalism had been welded to his vision of Hashemite aggrandizement, and this twin concept never lost its hold on him. Abdullah is best understood as an opportunistic politician, short-range realist, and dynastic dreamer, also in his dealings with the Jews of Ereẓ Israel. The 1950 annexation of Arab Palestine (the "West Bank") not only led to his eventual murder but also completely changed the nature and the future of Jordan. He wrote *Memoirs of King Abdullah of Transjordan* (English tr., 1950) and *My Memoirs Completed* (English tr., 1954).

BIBLIOGRAPHY: J.B. Glubb, *A Soldier with the Arabs* (1957), index; idem, *Story of the Arab Legion* (1948), index; A. al-Tall, *Kārithat Filastin* (1949) (Hebrew tr. *Zikhronot Abdallah al-Tall*, 1960), passim. **ADD. BIBLIOGRAPHY:** K.T. Nimri, *Abdullah Ibn Hussein, A Study in Arab Political Leadership* (1977); M.C. Wilson, *King Abdullah, Britain and the Making of Jordan* (1987).

[Uriel Dann / Joseph Nevo (2nd ed.)]

°**ABDUL MEJID I** (1823–1861), 31st sultan of the Ottoman Empire; the elder son of Mahmud II and his favorite wife, Bezm-i 'Alem. On November 3, 1839, four months after he ascended the throne, he proclaimed the *Hatt-i Sherif* of Gulhane, which inaugurated the Tanzimat period and in which he pledged the security of life, honor, and property for all the subjects of the empire. Following this, many reforms were undertaken to implement the contents of the edict. During his reign the Crimean War broke out (1853–56). Under the pressure of England and France, his allies in the war, the Porte abolished the poll tax (1855), which had been levied upon Jews and Christians since the Arab conquest. Instead, a tax called *Bedel-i Askeri* (substitute for military service) was levied from non-Muslim conscripts in lieu of military service. The crisis which led to the war brought the rise of a new generation of statesmen at the Porte, led by Ali and Fu'ad Pashas, who were more open toward the west than their predecessors. In February 1856, just before the war ended, the sultan proclaimed a new reform edict (the *Hatti-Humayun*) in which he granted civil and political equality for his non-Muslim subjects in breach of the Muslim Law (the *shari'a*), which aroused much resentment among the Muslim majority. During Abdul Mejid's reign important reforms were undertaken in the army and in education (mainly to prepare government functionaries), in the currency, and above all in the administration of the provinces.

BIBLIOGRAPHY: S.J. Shaw & E.K. Shaw, *History of the Ottoman Empire and Modern Turkey*, 2 (1977), 55ff.; B. Abu-Manneh, *Studies on Islam and the Ottoman Empire in the 19th Century (1826–1876)* (2001), 73–97.

[Butrus Abu-Maneh (2nd ed.)]

ABÉCASSIS, ELIETTE (1969–), French writer. Born in Strasbourg to a Sephardi family of Moroccan origin, Eliette is the daughter of French thinker Armand Abécassis, author of *La pensée juive*. Deeply imbued with the religious atmosphere of her childhood, Eliette Abécassis, after completeing her studies in philosophy and literature at the prestigious Ecole Normale Supérieure, published her first novel in 1996. *Qumran*, a metaphysical and archaeological thriller, whose hero is a young Orthodox Jew and whose plot revolves around the famous Dead Sea Scrolls, was an instant bestseller. Her next two books were centered on the theme of evil and its contagion: *L'or et la cendre* (1997), a novel, and "Petite métaphysique du meurtre" (1998), an essay. To write the screenplay for Amos Gitai's Franco-Israeli film *Kaddosh*, Abécassis immersed herself for six months in the ultra-Orthodox Jerusalem neighborhood of Me'ah She'arim, an experience which, in addition to the screenplay, provided her with the plot of a novel, *La repudiée* (2000). She also directed a short film, *La nuit de noces* (2001).

[Dror Franck Sullaper (2nd ed.)]

ABEL (Heb. הֶבֶל), the second son of Adam and Eve, murdered by Cain, his older brother (Gen. 4:1–9). According to the biblical story, Abel was a shepherd and Cain worked the soil. Each brought an offering to the Lord from fruits of his labor. Abel's sacrifice was accepted by the Lord, but Cain's offering was rejected. Cain, in his jealousy, killed his brother. Explanations of this story are usually sought in a traditional conflict between agriculture and nomadism. Thus the preferential treatment accorded Abel's sacrifice is seen as reflecting a supposed pastoral ideal in Israel. The narrative, however, does not in any way support the existence of such an ideal, nor is there any denigration of farming. On the contrary, working the land seems to be considered man's natural occupation (Gen. 2:15). The antithesis between the brothers is therefore less one of occupations than of qualities of offerings. Whereas Cain's offering is described simply as "of the fruits of the soil," Abel is recorded as having brought "of the choicest of the firstlings of his flock." The story, however, seems to be abbreviated. It lacks any description of the initial motivation and the occasion for the sacrifices and it fails to give the reasons for the rejection of Cain's offering. Neither does it explain how the Lord's response became known to the brothers. The etymology of Abel's name is not clear. There may be some intended connection with *hevel* ("breath, vapor, futility"), symbolizing the tragic brevity of his life (cf., e.g., Eccles. 1:2), though for some reason the derivation of the name is not given, as is the case with Cain. There may also be some relation to the Akkadian *aplu* or *ablu* ("son"), parallel to the usage of the names *Adam and *Enosh.

For Abel in *aggadah*, see *Cain.

BIBLIOGRAPHY: N.M. Sarna, *Understanding Genesis* (1966), 28–32; E.A. Speiser, *Genesis* (1964), 29–33; U. Cassuto, *Mi-Adam ad No'aḥ* (1953), 131–9.

ABEL, AVEL (Heb. אָבֵל). (1) Name, appearing either alone or with the addition of a further indicative place-name, of many places in Ereẓ Israel and Syria. Four cities with this name are mentioned in the lists of Thutmose III. Its meaning is apparently "place of abundant water" (cf. Dan. 8:2–6, "stream"). (2) Avel was a town in ancient Ereẓ Israel which was situated at the origin of the aqueduct of Sepphoris in the mishnaic period (Er. 8:7; Tosef. Er. 9[6]:26). It is the present-day village of al-Rayna, about 3 mi. (5 km.) S.E. of *Sepphoris.

[Michael Avi-Yonah]

ABEL, ELIE (1920–2004), U.S. journalist. Born in Montreal, Canada, Abel received a bachelor's degree from McGill University and a master's degree in journalism from Columbia University (New York) in 1942. He began his career in journalism at the Windsor, Ontario, *Daily Star* and at the *Montreal Gazette*. During World War II he served in the Royal Canadian Air Force. Abel was correspondent in Europe for the North American Newspaper Alliance and also worked for the Overseas News Agency. In 1949, he joined the *New York Times* and served for ten years in Washington, Detroit, Europe, and India. In 1961, he moved into broadcasting, becoming a regular correspondent on the NBC evening news program *The Huntley-Brinkley Report*. During the 1960s, he covered the State Department and served as the network's London bureau chief and chief diplomatic correspondent. After working with the *Detroit News* and NBC, he was named dean of the Graduate School of Journalism at Columbia (1969–79). He then moved to Stanford University (1979–91), serving as chairman of the Communications Department from 1983 to 1986. He also served as Faculty Senate chair (1985–86) and directed the university's program in Washington, D.C. (1993).

Among his many accolades, Abel was awarded the Pulitzer Prize (1958), a Peabody Award (1967), and two Overseas Press Club awards (1969 and 1970). In 1998 he received the Grand Prize for Press Freedom of the Inter-American Press Association for his efforts to fight proposed regulation of journalists.

Abel wrote many books, articles, and reviews. His first book, *Missile Crisis,* appeared in 1966 and was considered the definitive text on the Cuban crisis for decades after its publication. Abel is quoted as saying, "How close we came to Armageddon I did not fully realize until I started researching this book." *Roots of Involvement: The U.S. in Asia 1784–1971*, which he wrote with Marvin *Kalb, was published in 1971. His book about Averell Harriman, *Special Envoy to Churchill and Stalin, 1941–1946*, which he co-authored with Harriman, was published in 1975. Abel's last book, *The Shattered Bloc: Behind the Upheaval in Eastern Europe*, was published in 1990.

[Ruth Beloff (2nd ed.)]

ABEL, EMIL (1875–1958), Austrian physical chemist. He was born in Vienna, where in 1908 he became the first professor of physical chemistry at the Technische Hochschule and head of the Institute attached to the chair, and he established a large and vigorous school. In 1938 he was dismissed under the Nuremberg Laws and found refuge in England, where, until his retirement, he was in charge of the research laboratory of the Ever Ready Co. In an early series of brilliant papers on homogeneous catalysis, he insisted that "it is reactions which catalyse, not substances." Later he contributed many publications on the reactions which occur in the lead chamber process for making sulfuric acid. In England he worked on the basic mechanism of the dry battery cell and wrote on mechanisms based on electron transfer reactions.

BIBLIOGRAPHY: G.M. Schwab, in: *Zeitschrift fuer Elektrochemie*, 59 (1955), 591–2; P. Cross, *ibid.*, 62 (1958), 831–3; *Nature*, 181 (1958), 1765–66.

[Samuel Aaron Miller]

°ABEL, LOUIS FELIX (1878–1953), French archaeologist. Abel was born in Saint-Uze (Drome), France, joined the Dominican Order in 1898, and served as professor at the Ecole Biblique in Jerusalem from 1903 until his death. His principal work was *Géographie de la Palestine*, 2 vols. (1934), the first dealing with physical geography, and the second with political geography and topography. With L.H. *Vincent, he wrote *Jerusalem ancienne et nouvelle* (1912–14), regarded as one of the best monographs on Christian Jerusalem. He also collaborated with Vincent in monographs on Bethlehem, Emmaus, and Hebron. Toward the end of his life, Abel published his *Histoire de la Palestine*, 2 vols. (1952), covering the period from Alexander the Great to the Arab conquest. His other works include studies on the topography of the Hasmonean Wars, an account of travels in the Jordan Valley and in the Dead Sea area, as well as a grammar of the Septuagint and the New Testament.

[Michael Avi-Yonah]

°ABELARD (Abaelard), PETER (1079–1142), French philosopher and theologian. Abelard composed the *Dialogus inter Philosophum. Judaeum et Christianum* (1141; published in PL, 178 (1855), 1611–82). In it a Jew and a Christian, who accept revelation as adequate justification of their creed, are challenged by a philosopher, an Arab by nationality, who accepts only reason and natural law as a basis for the discussion. The dialogue does not offer a final conclusion, but this might possibly reflect the author's emphasis on the method of discussion rather than on its results. In the dialogue the Jew accepts belief in God's revelation as the only norm for faith and conduct; he asks the philosopher, who leads the debate, to prove that such an attitude contradicts reason. In doing so he expresses his people's confidence that God will finally fulfill the biblical promises of a blissful future and compensate them for their depressed position in contemporary society, which he describes in realistic detail. Being forced to pay for survival is an everyday experience for the Jews. In contemporary circumstances they were unable to earn a livelihood from agricultural property; they had to rely on profits from money lending, an occupation which made them more odious to their environment. In his reply the philosopher emphasizes the contrast between this situation and the promise of prosperity in this world, which the Bible holds out for loyal obedience. He concludes that either the Jews have not lived and acted in accordance with divine command or their Law is not the truth. The Christian, according to Abelard's description, although a believer in the authority of revelation, explains his belief in spiritual values as the *summun bonum* in philosophical terms. Abelard used the apologetic writers of the patristic age as his source, wishing to prove that his own attitude as a philosophical interpreter of Christianity corresponded to the classical tradition of the church. The contemporary Jew in his *Dialogus* takes the place of the defender of particular traditions – Jewish or pagan – as depicted in the ancient ecclesiastical treatises adopting philosophical argument; this presentation precludes the possibility that Abelard intended to report a contemporary exchange of arguments. His work is an apology for his own life, and its fictional character is pointed out by the description of the narrative as a dream. On the other hand, the whole design indicates that such conversations with Jews were not unusual in his time. Abelard indeed had some personal contact with Jews and was present when one interpreted the Book of Kings. Abelard's knowledge of Hebrew was restricted to the word lists contained in the biblical studies of St. Jerome. But the educational program of this church father inspired Abelard's recommendation to his former wife Heloise that she and the nuns under her charge learn Hebrew for a genuine understanding of Scripture.

BIBLIOGRAPHY: J.G. Sikes, *Peter Abailard* (*Eng.*, 1932); G. Misch, *Geschichte der Autobiographie*, 3 pt. 2/1 (1959), 523–719; H. Liebeschutz, in: JJS, 12 (1961), 1–18; B. Smalley, *Study of the Bible in the Middle Ages* (1952^2), index; E. Gilson, *History of Christian Philosophy in the Middle Ages* (1955), 153–63.

[Hans Liebeschutz]

ABEL-BETH-MAACAH (Heb. אָבֵל בֵּית־מַעֲכָה), also called **Abel-Maim** (II Chron. 16: 4) or simply **Abel** (II Sam. 20:18). It is the present Tell Abil (Abil al-Qamḥ) northeast of Kefar Giladi and south of Metullah. Pottery found on the surface of the tell dates to the Early Bronze Age and later periods. It may be one of the cities mentioned in the Egyptian Execration Texts (inscribed on figurines) from the early 18th century B.C.E. and is apparently also referred to in the list of cities (no. 92) captured by Thutmose III in Palestine and southern Syria in his first campaign (c. 1469 B.C.E.). In the 12th–11th centuries, it may have passed into the possession of the Danites when they settled in the north of the country, but it subsequently was considered part of (Beth-) Maacah, whose center comprised northern Golan and Bashan. In the days of David, it was a fortified place and "a city and a mother in Israel" (II Sam. 20:19) in which the rebel Sheba, the son of Bichri, was besieged when he fled from Joab's army. It was captured by the Arameans during the reign of Baasa, king of Israel (early ninth century) together with Ijon, Dan, and the rest of the northeastern part of the Israelite kingdom (I Kings 15:20; II Chron. 16:4). In the days of Pekah the son of Remaliah, Tiglath-Pileser III, king of Assyria, conquered all the eastern and northern parts of Israel and the capture of Abel-Beth-Maacah is specifically mentioned (II Kings 15:29). This event is also recorded in Assyrian inscriptions which describe this king's campaign of 733/32 B.C.E. and the annexation of the conquered areas to Assyria (these contain a reference to Abil (m) akka). The city was apparently included in the province of Megiddo. No subsequent mention is made of Abel-Beth-Maacah in ancient sources.

BIBLIOGRAPHY: Horowitz, Ereẓ Yis, 3–4; B. Maisler (Mazar), in: BJPES, 1 (1933), 5; J. Braslavi (Braslavski), in: BJPES, 2 (1935), 43–44; S. Klein, *Ereẓ ha-Galil* (1946); N. Glueck, *River Jordan* (1946); W.F. Albright, in: AASOR, 6 (1926), 19; Abel, Geog, 1 (1933), 249; 2 (1938), 233;

B. Maisler (Mazar), in: *Bulletin des études historiques juives*, 1 (1946), 56; Aharoni, Land, passim.

[Michael Avi-Yonah]

ABELES, OTTO (1879–1945), author and Zionist worker in Austria and Holland. Abeles, who was born in Bruen (Brno), Moravia, was a founder of the Jewish students' organization Veritas. He was also a founder of the Zionist movement in Bohemia and Moravia. After completing his studies at the University of Vienna, he became legal advisor to the Austrian railways. Abeles contributed articles to the Zionist newspaper *Die *Welt* and other Zionist newspapers in German, and was an editor of the organ of the Zionist movement in Austria *Juedische Zeitung*. Together with Robert Stricker he founded the Zionist daily newspaper *Wiener Morgenzeitung*, working on its staff until 1926, when he became an emissary for *Keren Hayesod and traveled through Western Europe as a lecturer. From 1930 he was director of Keren Hayesod in Amsterdam. He was deported to Bergen-Belsen concentration camp, and died immediately after its liberation. Among his works are *Besuch in Eretz Yisrael* (1926), impressions of his first journey to Palestine; *Die Genesung* (1920), a book of poems; and *Zehn Juedinnen* (1931), a book about famous Jewish women. With L. Bato he edited the almanac *Juedischer Nationalkalender* (1915/16–1921/22).

BIBLIOGRAPHY: *Haolam* (Aug. 30, 1945 and Sept. 6, 1945); *Haaretz* (Aug. 24, 1945); *Davar* (Aug. 24, 1945).

[Getzel Kressel]

ABELES, SIMON (**Simele**; 1682–1694), alleged Christian martyr. The Jesuit chronicler John Eder relates that Simon, who was born into a Prague Jewish family, wanted to embrace Christianity at the age of 12. His father Lazar, a glover, was accused of having murdered him. During the investigation Lazar allegedly hanged himself in prison, and a fellow Jew, Loebel Kurtzhandel, was executed as his accomplice. Simon, although not baptized, was buried with honors in the Týn (Thein) church where his grave may still be seen.

BIBLIOGRAPHY: *Processus inquisitorius ... Abeles* (1728); R.A. Novotný, *Staropražské sensace* (1937), 13–15; Polák, in: *Ceskožidovský kalendář* (1912/13).

ABELIOVICH, LEV MOYSSEYEVICH (1912–1985), Belorussian composer. Born in Vilna, Abeliovich studied at the Warsaw Conservatory with Kazimierz Sikorski (composition) in 1935–39, and when the Nazis invaded Poland in 1939, he fled to Minsk and studied composition at the National Conservatory with Vasily Zolotarev, graduating in 1941. After World War II, he devoted himself to composition and was later engaged in the study of Belorussian folk music. His compositions include four symphonies (1962, 1964, 1967, and 1970); *Symphonic Pictures* (1958); *Heroic Poem* (1957); three sonatas and the two-book cycle *Frescoes* (1972) for piano; three sonatas for violin and piano; and chamber music and songs.

BIBLIOGRAPHY: NG^2, s.v.; N. Kalesnikava, *Lev Abeliovich* (1970); T.A. Dubkova, in: *Belarusskaya simfoniya* (1974), 162–87; N. Zarenok et al. (ed.), in: *Vopos kul'tur i iskusstva Belorussii* (1982), 23–8.

[Marina Rizarev (2nd ed.)]

ABELLA, ROSALIE SILBERMAN (1946–), jurist, Canadian Supreme Court justice. Rosalie Abella was born in a *displaced persons camp in Stuttgart, Germany. She migrated to Toronto with her family in 1950. Her father, Jacob Silberman, had been a lawyer in Poland but was admitted to Canada as a garment worker as part of a government labor importation scheme. Many of her family, including an older sibling, were murdered in the Holocaust. She grew up "with a passion for justice," and, as she explains, "As a Jew, I feel that, through the Holocaust, I have lost the right to stand silent in the face of injustice."

She studied classical piano at the Royal Conservatory of Music, remaining an accomplished pianist, and attended the University of Toronto, where she earned a law degree in 1970. She practiced civil and criminal litigation until 1976, when she was appointed to the Ontario Family Court, becoming the youngest, the first female, and the first pregnant Jewish judge in Canadian history. While on the Family Court she served on the Ontario Human Rights Commission (1975–80) and the Premier's Advisory Committee on Confederation (1977–82), chaired the Ontario Labour Relations Board (1984–89), and was sole commissioner for the Royal Commission on Equality in Employment (1983–84) in which she made "employment equity" a strategy for reducing employment barriers unfairly imposed by "race, gender or disability." "Employment equity" was subsequently implemented by the governments of Canada, New Zealand, Northern Ireland, and South Africa.

Leaving the Family Court in 1987, Abella became Boulton Visiting Professor at the McGill Law School (1988–92) and Distinguished Visiting Lecturer at the University of Toronto Law School (1989–92), chaired the Ontario Law Reform Commission (1989–92), and was director of the Institute for Research on Pubic Policy (1987–92). In 1992 she was appointed to the Ontario Court of Appeal, where she gained a reputation as a reform-minded judge and an internationally recognized expert on human rights. Believing that democracy is enhanced by an activist judiciary, Abella championed the Charter of Rights and Freedoms and participated in rulings extending the rights of Metis, racialized minorities, and gays. Sometimes regarded as controversial, she nevertheless finds it "unforgivable" for judges, in her words, "to exchange their independence for state approval" as happened during the Third Reich.

Abella served as a director of the International Commission of Jurists, the Canadian Institute for the Administration of Justice, and the McGill Institute for the Study of Canada, and she was a member of the Hebrew University International Board of Governors and the Committee on Conscience, U.S. Holocaust Memorial Council. She is a frequent and highly engaging speaker on equality issues and a committed promoter of Canadian culture. In 2004 she was elevated to the Supreme Court of Canada. The author or editor of four books and over 70 articles, Abella has received 20 honorary degrees, is a specially elected fellow of the Royal Society of Canada, and has been honored by the Canadian Bar Association, the International Commission of Jurists, and B'nai B'rith. She is married to the distinguished Canadian historian Irving Abella.

[James Walker (2nd ed.)]

ABELMANN, ILYA SOLOMOVITCH (1866–1898), Russian astronomer. Abelmann, who was born in Dvinsk, worked at several Russian observatories, mainly on the complex problems connected with the properties of meteor streams. He was concerned with the calculation of secular orbital perturbations exercised on these streams by the effects of planetary attraction. Abelmann was also well known for his efforts to spread the appreciation of astronomy, which he did through numerous popular articles.

[Arthur Beer]

ABEL-MAUL (Gr. Ἀβελμαωυλ), a city cited in the apocalyptic work the Greek Testament of Levi 2:3, 5 as the place where Levi received a vision of the seven heavens. The name is the Greek form of the Hebrew "Abel-Meholah," mentioned in Judges 7:22 and in I Kings 4:12; 19:16. Abel-Meholah was situated in the mountains of Ephraim, a fact which calls into question the text of Testament of Levi 2:5 which associates it with the Sirion mountain ("the mountain of the shield," a false etymology from Shiryon). In the Dead Sea fragment of Testament of Levi, however, the place where Levi received the vision is Abel-Main, an alternate form of Abel-Maim, the name which replaced the earlier *Abel-Beth-Maacah (cf. I Kings 15:26, II Chron. 16:4). Abel-Maim is in fact situated in the very northern part of Palestine and could easily be connected with the Sirion, the Anti-Lebanon. The confusion in Greek Testament of Levi is evidently the translator's.

BIBLIOGRAPHY: Milik, in: RB, 62 (1955), 398ff.; Charles, Apocrypha, 2 (1913), 304; Press, Ereẓ, 1 (1951), 5; Avi-Yonah, Land, 153, s.v. Abelmea.

[Michael E. Stone]

ABEL-MEHOLAH (Heb. אָבֵל מְחוֹלָה), ancient city in the Jordan Valley that was the birthplace of the prophet *Elisha (I Kings 19:16). Abel-Meholah also appears in the Bible as a place through which the Midianites passed in their flight from *Gideon (Judg. 7:22) and as part of Solomon's fifth administrative district, which comprised the towns of the Jezreel and Beth-Shean valleys (I Kings 4:12). Eusebius identified the place in the Onomasticon with Bethmaela, 10 (Roman) mi. south of Beth-Shean. Accordingly, it is generally accepted that Abel-Meholah lay west of the Jordan at the southern end of the Beth-Shean Valley, apparently in the neighborhood of ʿAyn al-Ḥilwa near the point where the Wadi al-Māliḥ enters the Jordan, perhaps Tell Abu Sifri or Tell Abu Sus. Glueck suggested locating it in Transjordan and to identify it with Tell al-Maqlūb, but this has not been generally accepted.

BIBLIOGRAPHY: N. Glueck, *River Jordan* (1946), 168ff.; idem, in: BASOR, 90 (1943), 9ff.; 91 (1943), 8, 15; idem, in: AASOR, 25–28 (1951), 211ff.; M. Naor, in: BJPES, 13 (1947), 89ff.; A. Alt, in: PJB, 24 (1928), 45, 99; 28 (1932), 39ff.; Abel, Geog, 2 (1938), 234; EM, s.v.; Aharoni, Land, 241, 278; Zobel, in: ZDPV, 82 (1966), 83–108; N. Zori, in: BIES, 31 (1967), 132–5.

[Michael Avi-Yonah]

ABEL SHITTIM or **SHITTIM** (Heb. אָבֵל הַשִּׁטִּים), a town in the plains of Moab where the Israelites camped before crossing the Jordan (Num. 33:49; Josh. 2:1, 3:1). Several noteworthy events are connected with the place and its surroundings. Here Balaam attempted to curse the tribes (Num. 22–24; Micah 6:5) and the Israelites sinned with the daughters of Moab and were punished by a plague (Num. 25). Abel-Shittim is also mentioned in later sources. Zeno (259 B.C.E.) purchased wheat there for his Egyptian master. It was a flourishing town during the period of the Second Temple, renowned for its fertile date groves and grain fields. Josephus mentions a town Abila 60 ris (about 7 mi.) from the Jordan (Jos., Ant., 4:1; 5:1). The early city has been identified by Glueck with Tell al-Hammām at the outlet of Wadi al-Kafrayn which runs from the Mountains of Moab to the Jordan Valley. Chalcolithic and Early Bronze Age I pottery and an abundance of potsherds from the Iron Ages I and II have been found on the tell. In the Hellenistic period, the inhabitants moved to a spot in the Jordan Valley to which they transferred the name of their previous settlement, today Khirbat al-Kafrayn. Captured by the Romans, Abel-Shittim escaped destruction during the Jewish War (66–70) and it was populated at least until the end of the Byzantine period.

BIBLIOGRAPHY: Horowitz, Ereẓ Yis, s.v.; Press, Ereẓ, 1 (1951), 3; N. Glueck, *River Jordan* (1946), passim; idem, in: BASOR, 91 (1943), 13–18; idem, in: AASOR, 25–28 (1951), 371ff.; Abel, Geog, 2 (1938), 234. **ADD. BIBLIOGRAPHY:** K. Prag, in: *Levant* 23 (1991), 55–66.

[Michael Avi-Yonah]

ABELSON, HAROLD HERBERT (1904–2003), U.S. educator. Born in New York, he began his teaching career at City College in 1924, advancing from assistant psychologist in the educational clinic to professor in 1948, and dean of the school of education in 1952. His book *The Art of Educational Research, Its Problems and Procedures* (1933), his articles, and his investigations and interest in personality development reflect his belief that educational research should proceed on the basis of scientific principles. In 1944 he was appointed consultant to the office of the Adjutant General and in 1962 became president of the Interstate Teacher Educational Conference. Other books by Abelson include *The Improvement of Intelligence Testing* (1927) and *Putting Knowledge to Use: Facilitating the Diffusion of Knowledge and the Implementation of Planned*

Change (with E.M. Glaser and K.N. Garrison, 1983). The CCNY School of Education has established the Abelson Award for Excellence in Research, which is given annually for the most creative use of educational measurement in the Graduate Research Project.

[Ronald E. Ohl / Ruth Beloff (2nd ed.)]

ABELSON, JOSHUA (1873–1940), English minister. Born in Merthyr Tydfil (Wales), Abelson was ordained at *Jews' College in London, and occupied pulpits in Cardiff and Bristol. He became principal of the Jewish theological preparatory school Aria College in Portsmouth, after which he was appointed minister to the United Hebrew Congregation of Leeds. Abelson's works include *The Immanence of God in Rabbinical Literature* (1912), in which he examined the theory of the *Shekhinah* in the rabbinic sources, and its connection with the later development of Jewish mysticism. This work was followed by *Jewish Mysticism* (1913), the earliest serious study of the subject in English. He assisted Chief Rabbi Joseph *Hertz in the editing of Hertz's Commentary on the Pentateuch, published in 1929–36.

BIBLIOGRAPHY: JYB (1903–04, 1940); G. Scholem, *Bibliographia Kabbalistica* (1933^2), no. 2; Scholem, Mysticism (1946^2), 55.

[*Encyclopaedia Judaica* (Germany)]

ABELSON, PAUL (1878–1953), U.S. labor arbitrator. Abelson, who was born in Kovno, Lithuania, immigrated to the United States at the age of 14. He studied at the City College of New York and Columbia University and in 1906 published *The Seven Liberal Arts: A Study in Medieval Culture*. Abelson was deeply interested in adult education for immigrants. He lectured in Yiddish for the New York City Board of Education (1902–09), headed programs for adult education at the Educational Alliance, helped establish the Madison House Settlement (1899), and edited the English-Yiddish *Encyclopedic Dictionary* (1915). Abelson's career as a labor arbitrator began in 1910. He was appointed to the staff established by the agreement that settled the New York cloakmakers' strike of that year. The settlement introduced the concept of arbitration into the ladies' garment trade, and a form of impartial adjudication subsequently marked labor-management relations in much of New York City's apparel industry. Abelson later held posts as an arbitrator in the fur, millinery, men's hat, hosiery, Jewish baking, and jewelry trades, among others. After the passage of the National Recovery Act (1933), Abelson was appointed by President Roosevelt as government representative on seven apparel trades boards. He often served as impartial chairman in early stages of arbitration agreements, and his decisions built the precedents and procedures that became the customary law in these industries. His impartiality and mastery of the detailed situation within each industry were instrumental in his success.

[Irwin Yellowitz]

ABENAES, SOLOMON (**Abenaish**, **Abenyaex**, **Aben-Ayesh**; Heb. **Even Yaish**; c. 1520–1603), Marrano statesman. Born as Alvaro Mendes to a Converso family of Tavira, Portugal, Abenaes made a fortune in India by farming the diamond mines of the kingdom of Narsinghgrah. Still ostensibly a Christian, he returned to Europe, becoming a knight of Santiago, and lived successively in Madrid, Florence, Paris, and London. When the Spaniards seized Portugal in 1580, he embraced the cause of the pretender to the Portuguese throne Dom Antonio, prior of Crato, and became one of his most active supporters. In 1585 he settled in Turkey where he reverted to Judaism under the name Solomon Abenaes. Because of his wealth, experience, and connections, he came to be highly regarded at the Turkish court, renewing the position of Joseph *Nasi, who had died in 1579. He farmed the Turkish customs revenue and was created duke of Mytilene, one of the largest Aegean islands. He succeeded in maintaining his position, notwithstanding constant intrigues, for some 20 years. Like Nasi he had an elaborate information service all over Europe which proved highly useful to the Turkish government. Above all, Abenaes devoted himself to the cause of an Anglo-Turkish alliance against Spain, as the support of the claims of Dom Antonio to the Portuguese throne depended on this. For this purpose he maintained close contact with the Marrano group in England, headed by Dr. Hector *Nuñez and the queen's physician Roderigo *Lopez, his relative by marriage. Through them Abenaes was able to bring the Turkish government the first news of the defeat of the Great Armada in 1588. At one time he put forward the audacious plan of establishing Dom Antonio in the Portuguese dominions in India, from where he would be able to sail with strong forces and gain control of Portugal itself. Dom Antonio proved, however, weak and vacillating, and Abenaes accordingly broke with him; Dom Antonio in turn accused him of treachery. In 1591 Abenaes sent a personal representative, Solomon Cormano, to London to present his case before the queen, and in 1592 Judah Ẓarefati (Serfatim), with the same object. The execution of Roderigo Lopez in 1594 on the charge of attempting to poison the queen did not seriously affect Abenaes' position nor did the intrigues against him in Constantinople by David Passy, his Jewish rival, instigated by Dom Antonio and the French ambassador.

Abenaes was one of the architects of the Anglo-Turkish alliance which stemmed the menacing advance of the Spanish power at the close of the 16th century.

Shortly after his arrival in Turkey Abenaes secured the renewal, in his own favor, of the grant of *Tiberias and seven adjoining townships that had originally been made to Nasi. His name is thus associated with this important attempt to reestablish an autonomous Jewish life in Ereẓ Israel. His son JACOB ABENAES (formerly Francisco Mendes) actually settled in Tiberias, but to his father's disappointment, instead of helping in political and administrative organization, spent his time in study.

BIBLIOGRAPHY: C. Roth, *The Duke of Naxos* (1948), 133–4, 205–16, 248–9; Wolf, in: JHSET, 11 (1924–27), 1–91; A. Galante, *Don Solomon Aben-Yaèche, Duc de Mételin* (1936).

[Cecil Roth]

ABENAFIA, JOSEPH (d. 1408), rabbi and physician. Abenafia, who was born in Catalonia, accompanied Martin I of Aragon to Sicily as his personal medical attendant and settled there in 1391. In 1396 he was appointed **dienchelele* (*dayyan kelali*). In 1399 he petitioned the king on behalf of all the Sicilian communities about certain proposed reforms. In 1404 he was nominated examiner of Jewish medical practitioners. Probably because his activities were connected with the king's interests, they encountered opposition within the community and in 1406 the Palermo community asked to be exempted from his authority.

BIBLIOGRAPHY: Roth, Italy, 236–8; Milano, Italia, 176, 482, 624; Baer, Urkunden, 1 (1929), index; B. and G. Lagumina (eds.), *Codice diplomatico dei giudei di Sicilia*, 1 (1884).

[Attilio Milano]

ABENATAR MELO, DAVID (d. c. 1646), Marrano poet. Abenatar was born in the Iberian Peninsula, probably as Antonio Rodriguez Mello. He was arrested by the Inquisition and survived years of imprisonment and torture. After appearing as a penitent at an auto-de-fé, he escaped to Amsterdam and reverted to Judaism. In 1616 he was a founding member of the *talmud torah* (*Ez Ḥayyim*) society there and in the following year subsidized the publication of a prayer book in Spanish (*Orden de Roshasana y Kipur*); in 1622 he similarly printed a Passover *Haggadah*. In 1626 he published a remarkable translation of the Book of Psalms into Spanish verse (*Los CL. Psalmos de David: in lengua española en uarias rimas*) dedicated to "The Blessed God and the Holy Company of Israel and Judah, scattered through the world." The prologue contains an account of his sufferings. The work is more a paraphrase than a translation and contains several allusions to current events and the tyrannies of the Inquisition (cf. Psalm 30, at the end of which he mentions the auto-de-fé at which he himself appeared when 11 Judaizers were burned). He was probably the father of IMMANUEL ABENATAR MELO, *ḥazzan* of the Sephardi community of Rotterdam until 1682 and then of Amsterdam, and grandfather of DAVID ABENATAR MELO, member of the Yesiba de los Pintos and subsequently preacher and *ḥazzan* in Amsterdam. To the same family presumably belonged Diego Henriques Melo who, after trial by the Toledo Inquisition, escaped in 1618 to Amsterdam with his father, sister, and nephew.

BIBLIOGRAPHY: M. Kayserling, *Sephardim* (1859), 169ff.; Kayserling, Bibl, 67–68; Roth, Marranos, 329–30, 397; M. Menéndez y Pelayo, *Historia de los heterodoxos españoles*, 2 (1956), 256–8; H.L. Bloom, *Jews of Amsterdam* (1937), 10; ESN, 8; S. Seeligmann, *Bibliographie en Historie* (Dutch, 1927), 50–57.

[Cecil Roth]

ABENDANA, Sephardi family, with members widely dispersed among the ex-Marrano communities of Northern Europe. The name Abendana is Arabic in origin, commonly written in Hebrew אבן-דנא ,ן'דנא. Various branches of the family became differentiated by the cognomens Osorio, Belmonte, Naḥmias, Mendes (numerous in Hamburg), or, especially, de Brito. Isaac da Costa's statement that they were all descended from Heitor Mendes de Brito, who lived in Lisbon in the second half of the 16th century, is inaccurate. The Hamburg branch was founded by FERNANDO (Abraha) and MANOEL, sons of Manoel Pereira Coutinho of Lisbon whose five daughters were nuns at the convent of La Esperança. The earliest known member of the family in Amsterdam was Francisco Nuñez Pereira or Homem (d. 1625), who is reported to have arrived in Holland with the earliest (legendary) party of Marrano immigrants in 1598. Francisco entered the Jewish community under the name DAVID ABENDANA, after the death of his two sons, considered by his wife Justa (Abigail) to be the outcome of divine punishment for his sin in not having undergone circumcision. He was one of the founding members of the first Amsterdam synagogue. His son, IMMANUEL (1667), became *ḥazzan* of the community.

The family is also found at an early date in America. A DAVID ABENDANA lived in New York in 1681, and a MORDECAI ABENDANA died there in 1690.

BIBLIOGRAPHY: H. Kellenbenz, *Sephardim an der unteren Elbe* (1958), index (genealogical trees, 488ff.); Roth, Marranos, 383; Rosenbloom, Biogr Dict; I. da Costa, *Noble Families among the Sephardic Jews* (1936), 83, 115–6, 144; Kayserling, Bibl., 1, 2; ESN, 8–10.

[Cecil Roth]

ABENDANA, ISAAC (c. 1640–c. 1710), scholar of Marrano origin, younger brother of Jacob b. Joseph *Abendana. In 1662 Isaac went to England, where from 1663 he taught Hebrew at Cambridge and prepared for the university a translation of the Mishnah into Latin, receiving much encouragement from the local scholars. The work was completed in 1671 but remained unpublished; the manuscript, in six quarto volumes, is preserved in the Cambridge University Library. During this time, Isaac had been selling Hebrew books and manuscripts to the Bodleian Library in Oxford, and he moved to that city in 1689, teaching Hebrew at Magdalen College and elsewhere. From 1692 to 1699 he published a series of annual Jewish almanacs for Christian use, with learned supplements which he collected and republished later in a single volume entitled *Discourses on the Ecclesiastical and Civil Policy of the Jews* (Oxford, 1706; 2nd ed., 1709). He was in correspondence with several outstanding English scholars, especially Ralph Cudworth, master of Christ's College and regius professor of Hebrew at Cambridge. There is no authority for the statement that he studied medicine in his youth.

BIBLIOGRAPHY: Roth, Mag Bibl., 157–8, 330, 426.

[Cecil Roth]

ABENDANA, ISAAC SARDO (c. 1662–1709), diamond merchant. Abendana, who was originally from Holland, went to India from London in about 1702. He settled in Pulicat on the Coromandel Coast before moving to Fort St. George (Madras). In the records of the British East India Company there he is referred to as a freeman. As a diamond expert and jeweler his advice was much sought. Thomas Pitt, governor of Fort St. George, with whom he became friendly, also consulted him. Abendana's testament is described in the court records as written in "certain characters and other numerous abbreviations unknown to all of us," probably a reference to Hebrew. It stipulates that his widow was to remarry, if at all, only "in a city where there is a synagogue." She remarried a German Lutheran in 1712, and the ensuing litigation is detailed in the Madras Record Office.

BIBLIOGRAPHY: J.J. Cotton, *List of Inscriptions on Tombstones and Monuments in Madras* (1915), 123; D.A. Lehmann, *Alte Briefe aus Indien* (1965); W.J. Fischel, in: *Journal of Economic and Social History of the Orient*, 3 (1960), 191ff. **ADD. BIBLIOGRAPHY:** M. Arbell, in: *Los Muestros*, 41 (2000), 12–13.

[Walter Joseph Fischel]

ABENDANA, JACOB BEN JOSEPH (1630–1685), biblical commentator and polemist, elder brother of Isaac *Abendana; probably born in Hamburg, of Portuguese parents. Together with Joshua Pardo and Imanuel Abenatar Melo he studied at the Academia de los Pintos in Rotterdam. In 1655 he became principal of the Maskil el Dal fraternity in Amsterdam, where he delivered a memorial address on the inquisitional martyr Abraham Nuñez Bernal. In 1658, after completing his studies, he was appointed *haham* in Amsterdam.

Around 1660 he was in contact with Adam Boreel, the continental Christian Hebraist of the circle dominated by John Dury and Samuel Hartlib, who commissioned him to translate the Mishnah into Spanish. The translation made by Abendana was used by later Christian scholars such as Surenhusius, but was never printed and is now regarded to be lost.

In 1660/1661, Jacob and Isaac published Solomon ibn Melekh's Bible commentary, *Mikhlol Yofi*, with a supercommentary, *Lekket Shikhḥah* (3rd ed., 1965), on the Pentateuch, Joshua, and part of Judges (Vienna, 1818). The work was published with the approbations of Christian scholars, including the celebrated Johannes *Buxtorf of Basel. Jacob Abendana followed up his success with a Spanish translation of Judah Halevi's philosophical work *Kuzari* (published in Amsterdam, 1663, with a dedication to the British merchant-diplomat Sir William Davidson).

By the beginning of 1668, Jacob had joined his brother Isaac in England, and with him set about selling Hebrew books to a devoted clientele that included Henry Oldenburg, Robert Boyle, and Thomas Barlow of the Bodleian Library.

In 1681 Jacob became *haham* of the Spanish and Portuguese synagogue in London (which he had already visited in 1667–68). In that year he was host to Princess Anne, who came to the synagogue during Passover, the first occasion on which a member of the royal family visited the Jews at prayer.

BIBLIOGRAPHY: MGWJ, 9 (1860), 30ff.; Solomons, in: JHSET, 12 (1931), 21–24, 39–40; Samuel, *ibid.*, 14 (1939), 39ff.; ESN, s.v.; P.T. van Rooden and J.W. Wesselius, in: *Quaerendo*, 16 (1986) 110–30; D.S. Katz, in: *Journal of Ecclesiastical History*, 40 (1989), 28–52; idem, in: C.S. Nicholls (ed.), *The Dictionary of National Biography: Missing Persons* (1993), 2.

[Harm den Boer (2nd ed.)]

ABENDANAN (Ibn Danan or Ibn Dannān), Moroccan family of rabbis and scholars. The first known members of the family are ASASE, who emigrated from Morocco to Aragon in 1249, and MAIMON, who was apparently one of the refugees after the anti-Jewish massacres of 1391. Maimon went to Fez with his son MOSES, who became known as the "Rambam of Fez" and wrote many commentaries on the Talmud (which have remained in manuscript). In 1438, Moses was accused of attacking Islam and was sentenced to death; he narrowly escaped this fate, but was compelled to flee the country. It is likely that Maimon II, son of Moses, remained in Fez. His son (or grandson) Saadiah was born there. SAADIAH *IBN DANAN was a physician, halakhist, exegete, grammarian, lexicographer, philosopher, and poet. MAIMON, son of Saadiah, died a martyr's death before 1502 and was buried in Fez. His son SAMUEL (d. after 1566) was rabbi of Constantine (in Algeria), and was instrumental in passing important *takkanot*. According to tradition he was one of the 200 rabbis who ordained Joseph b. Ephraim *Caro. Samuel was the author of responsa and novellae, some of which were published in *Minḥat ha-Omer* (Djerba, 1950). His signature appears on numerous documents between 1526 and 1551, and he was the author of many interesting tales (J.M. Toledano, *Oẓar Genazim*, 1960, 13–16). SAADIAH II, the son (or grandson) of Samuel, participated in passing of *takkanot* between 1550 and 1578 and wrote a commentary on the Bible (still in manuscript). SAMUEL (1542–1621), his son, possessed an extensive knowledge of the local customs of the Jews of Maghreb and of the *takkanot* of Castile. He wrote many legal novellae and rulings as well as a history. SAADIAH III (d. 1680), the son of Samuel, was an *av bet din* and poet. He held discussions with Jacob b. Aaron *Sasportas (*Ohel Ya'akov* (1737), 2 and 3) and issued a number of *takkanot*. Some of his works are extant in manuscript. SAMUEL B. SAUL (1666–c. 1730) was the first editor of the Ibn Danan family chronicles and a history of the Jews of Fez. He is the supposed author of *Ahavat ha-Kadmonim* (edited Jerusalem, 1889), a prayer book according to the custom of Fez. SOLOMON (1848–1929) was an *av bet din*, halakhic authority, preacher, and kabbalist. During the last years of his life he was a member of the supreme *bet din* of appeal of Rabat. He was the author of the responsa *Asher li-Shelomo* (1901) and *Bikkesh Shelomo* (Casablanca, 1935). SAUL (1882– ?), son of Solomon, halakhist and Zionist, founded a Ḥibbat Zion society in Fez in 1910. In 1933 he was appointed *av bet din* of Mogador and

Marrakesh, and in 1949 chief rabbi of Morocco and head of the supreme *bet din* of appeal. In 1965 he resigned and settled in Israel. He published *Hagam Shaul,* responsa (Fez, 1959). From other branches of this family were descended a number of rabbis, among them SOLOMON BEN SAADIAH, 17th-century scholar and physician, and ISAAC (1880–1910), author of *Le-Yiẓḥak Rei'ah* (Leghorn, 1902).

BIBLIOGRAPHY: Azulai, 2 (1852), 35, no. 55; Edelman, in: *Ḥemdah Genuzah*, 1 (1856), xvii–xxi; Neubauer, in: JA, 20 (1862), 256–61; A. Ankawa, in: *Kerem Ḥemed* (1869/71); Bacher, in: REJ, 41 (1900), 268–72; J. Ibn-Ẓur, *Mishpat u-Ẓedakah be-Ya'akov* (1894–1903), nos. 5, 40, 317; S. Ibn-Danan, *Sefer Asher li-Shelomo* (1906), pref.; J.M. Toledano, *Ner ha-Ma'arav* (1911), 44ff., 84ff., 103ff., 134ff.; J. Ben-Naim, *Malkhei Rabbanan* (1931), 83a, 96a, 100b–1b, 111a–b, 114b–5b, 123b–4b; Schirmann, Sefarad, 2 (1956), 665–6; Slouschz, in: *Sura*, 3 (1958), 165–91.

[David Obadia]

ABENMENASSE (also **Abinnaxim**) family of courtiers in Spain. SAMUEL ABENMENASSE, probably born in Valencia, was appointed by Pedro III of Aragon (1276–85) as his *alfaquim*, or physician and secretary for Arabic correspondence (thus being known as "Samuel Alfaquim"). He sometimes acted also as the king's personal emissary. About 1280 he was tax farmer of the *bailía* of *Játiva where he held most of his property. He took part in several expeditions of Pedro, accompanying him to Sicily in 1283, and by royal order was exempted from taxation (1280, 1284) and from the obligation to wear the Jewish *badge (1283). Samuel was subsequently imprisoned for financial offenses and in 1285 was dismissed from all his offices. It is doubtful whether he is the Samuel Alfaquim who went to Granada and Morocco in 1292 and 1294 as Aragonese envoy. Samuel's brother JUDAH (d. c. 1285) was active in affairs concerning the *bailía* of Játiva and vicinity. In 1282 he went to collect the tribute owed by the Muslims in Valencia. He was imprisoned in 1284 on charges of corruption.

BIBLIOGRAPHY: Baer, Spain, 1 (1961), index, s. v. *Samuel Alfaquim;* Romano, in: *Homenaje a Millás-Vallicrosa*, 2 (1956), 251–92.

ABENSUR, family originating in Spain. After the expulsion in 1492 its members are found in Morocco, Italy, Amsterdam, and Hamburg, distinguished as scholars, diplomats, and merchants.

In Spain its members included DON JACOB (c. 1365); SAMUEL (c. 1413), one of the leaders of the community of Valladolid; and ISAAC (c. 1490), a notable of Trujillo.

The branch in Morocco was founded by MOSES (I) known as Abraham [*sic*] the Hebrew, a forced convert to Christianity who returned to Judaism in Fez in 1496. His descendants include ISAAC (d. 1605), a *dayyan* in Fez, murdered as a result of one of his decisions; he collaborated with ABRAHAM and SAMUEL in editing the Castilian communal ordinances. MOSES (II) of Salé (17th century), was author of liturgical poems, elegies, and kabbalistic works including *Me'arat Sedeh ha-Makhpelah* (1910). SHALOM (d. before 1717), Hebrew grammarian, was author of *Shir Ḥadash* (1892) and other works. JACOB REUBEN (b. 1673), born in Fez, was the most celebrated member of the family, also recognized as a rabbinical authority in Europe; he was the author of *Kinot* for the Ninth of Av and responsa, *Mishpat u-Ẓedakah be-Ya'akov* (2 vols., 1894; 1903). Part of his large collection of letters and responsa by writers in Spain and Jerusalem and early Spanish exiles in Morocco were published in *Kerem Ḥemed* (1869–71), and are a valuable source of information on Moroccan Jewry. ISAAC was appointed British consul in Morocco in 1818; SAMUEL (1840) was agent of Emir Abd-el-Kader in Tangiers; AARON (c. 1850) represented Denmark there and his son ISAAC was British delegate to the legislative assembly of Tangiers and for 30 years president of the community. ISAAC LEON (b. Eliezer b. Solomon ha-Sephardi) settled in Ancona, Italy, after 1500. The *bet din* in Rome reversed one of his decisions, and in 1546 published the discussions which followed. He was the author of *Sefer Megillat Ester* (Venice, 1592), a defense of the *Sefer ha-Mitzvot* of *Maimonides against the criticisms raised by *Naḥmanides.

Well known in the Amsterdam community were SOLOMON (d. 1620) and SAMUEL (d. 1665).

The Hamburg branch of the family was descended from the *Marrano Anrique Dias Millão who was burned at an auto-da-fé in Lisbon in 1609. Two of his sons reentered Judaism in Hamburg and took a prominent part in communal life. The elder, Paul de Millão, became known as MOSES, but for safety traded with the Iberian Peninsula under the name of Paul Direchsen. His elder son, JOSHUA (d. 1670), was a leader of the Hamburg community and was a personal acquaintance of Queen Christina of Sweden. The younger, DANIEL (d. 1711), became resident in Hamburg for the Polish crown, followed by his (?) son DAVID. JACOB, younger son of Joshua, was baptized in 1719, Louis XIV being his godfather. After dabbling in international politics and intrigues he became a French agent and assumed the name Louis. The family continued to be known in Hamburg until the 19th century.

BIBLIOGRAPHY: J. Scott, *Travels in Morocco and Algiers* (1842); JHSEM, 6 (1962), 1579; Baer, Urkunden, 2 (1936), 193, 275–7, 509; Hirschberg, Afrikah, 2 (1965), 273, 292; ESN, 183, 185; A.I. Laredo, *Memórias de un viejo Tangerino* (1935), 95, 96; H. Kellebenz, *Sephardim an der unteren Elbe* (1958), 400–17, passim; Z. Szajkowski, *Franco Judaica* (1962), nos. 1462–65.

[David Corcos]

ABENSUR, JACOB (1673–1753), Moroccan rabbi. Born in Fez, Abensur received a sound traditional education under Vidal *Sarfaty and Menahem *Serero, and among his fellow students was Judah ibn *Attar who later became Abensur's colleague on the *bet din* of Fez. He also studied grammar, astronomy and Kabbalah and cultivated poetry and song. In 1693 he was appointed registrar of the *bet din* of Fez, and in 1704 rabbi and head of the *bet din,* serving in this capacity for 30 years, and subsequently at Meknès for 11 years and seven at Tetuán. Abensur was the most illustrious rabbi of Morocco of his time. His extensive knowledge, his modesty, and his passion for justice and equality endeared him both to the intellectual elite and the ordinary people, but he incurred the enmity of some of his colleagues. In his old age, when the Jewish community of Fez was in decline as a result of famine and persecution, Jacob Abensur ordained five rabbis who constituted the "*Bet Din* of Five" and were responsible for the well-being of the community.

Abensur was consulted from far and wide on halakhic questions. Many of his responsa are scattered in the works of Moroccan rabbis; some of them have been collected and published under the title *Mishpat u-Ẓedekah be-Ya'akov* (2 vols., 1894; 1903). His *Et le-khol Ḥefeẓ* (1893), a voluminous collection of liturgical poetry, has been published. His other works have remained in manuscript form.

BIBLIOGRAPHY: H. Zafrani, *Les Juifs du Maroc* (1972).

[Haim Zafrani]

ABENVIVES (Vives), Spanish family, members of which were in the service of the kings of Aragon between 1267 and 1295. The most influential member VIVES BEN JOSEPH IBN VIVES owned estates throughout Aragon and Valencia. An excellent administrator, he brought law and order to the estates under his jurisdiction but became unpopular. In August 1270 several Jews and Muslims proffered complaints against him, alleging that he was a usurer and sodomite, but he was absolved by King James I. In 1271 the king commissioned Vives to suppress a Muslim rising in Valencia. Vives made frequent loans to the king, amounting to at least 45,600 sueldos between 1271 and 1276, and was granted several royal estates as pledges. He was removed from office after James' death in 1276. Other members of the family include ISAAC, who was a tax collector in 1283; SAMUEL, who was granted estates in the area of Alfandech and held several bailiwicks between 1282 and 1295; and JOSEPH, who lent money to the crown and was granted several castles, and held minor administrative posts between 1271 and 1284.

BIBLIOGRAPHY: Toledo, in: *Boletín de la Sociedad Castellonense de Cultura*, 16 (1935), 315ff., 398ff.; Piles, in: *Sefarad*, 20 (1960), 363–5; Baer, Spain, 1 (1961), 411. **ADD. BIBLIOGRAPHY:** A. García, *Els Vives, una família de jueus valencians* (1987).

[J. Lee Shneidman]

ABER, ADOLF (1893–1960), musicologist. Born in Apolda, Thuringia, Aber was assistant at the Institute of Musicology, Berlin, music critic of the *Leipziger Neueste Nachrichten* from 1919 to 1933, and also a partner in the music-publishing firm of Friedrich Hoffmeister. Among his many writings were *Studien zu J.S. Bachs Klavierkonzerten* (1913); *Handbuch der Musikliteratur* (1922); *Die Musik im Schauspiel* (1926); and short biographies of Bach, Beethoven, and Brahms. In 1933, he joined the British publisher Novello & Co. as a musicologist, where he edited the new catalog of the publishing house. Aber edited musical works by German composers and introduced England to the work of Fr. Joede, C. Bresgen, and Willhelm Rettch. In 1958, the German government awarded him for his work in disseminating German music in England and the Commonwealth countries.

BIBLIOGRAPHY: MGG².

[Israela Stein (2nd ed.)]

ABERDAM, ALFRED (1894–1963), painter and graphic artist. Aberdam was born in Krystonopol, East Galicia (now Chervonograd, Ukraine) and received a traditional Jewish education in a *ḥeder* while studying Hebrew with private teachers. In 1905–12 he lived in Lvov, where he finished high school. He decided to become an artist at the age of 14. At this time he came into contact with young Yiddish writers (Melech *Ravitch, Abraham Moshe *Fuks, and others) and with Zionist youth groups in Lvov. He attended their meetings and their lectures on Jewish artists. In 1913 he entered the Academy of Art in Munich, but unsatisfied with the conservative approach to art education there, he left for Paris and studied in private studios. At the beginning of World War I he was drafted into the Austrian army and was wounded and taken prisoner by the Russians. He was sent to Siberia and lived in Irkutsk and Krasnoyarsk, where he became acquainted with David Burliuk and other Russian futurists. In 1917 he was appointed people's commissar for the arts and inspector of the Irkutsk museum and organized an art school there. In 1920 he returned to Lvov. In 1921–22 he visited the Academy of Art in Cracow. In 1922–23 he lived in Berlin and visited the studio of Alexander Archipenko. From the end of 1923 he lived in Paris. In the 1920s and 1930s Aberdam's works were exhibited in salons and in private galleries. In this period he had three one-man shows. He maintained connections with Poland, showed his works in Polish exhibitions, and was a member of the *Plastycy Nowocześni* ("Contemporary Plastic Artists") group. During the Nazi occupation Aberdam had to live underground and could not continue his artistic work. In 1944 he took part in the organization of the Society of the Jewish Artists of Paris. In 1949 and 1952 he visited Israel and had one-man shows. His personal artistic manner reached its maturity in the late 1920s and with time he became one of the most illustrious representatives of the École de Paris. His favorite modes were still-lifes, landscapes, and genre scenes. He devoted a number of his works to the Holocaust (including *Deportation*, 1941–42, Ein Harod Art Museum, Israel).

BIBLIOGRAPHY: C. Aronson, *Scènes et visages de Montparnasse* (1963), 440–45; N. Nieszawer, Marie Boyé, and Paul Fogel, *Peintres Juifs à Paris, 1905–1939. École de Paris* (2000), 39–41.

[Hillel Kozovsky (2nd ed.)]

ABERDEEN, Scottish seaport, northeast of Edinburgh. In 1665 it was reported that a ship with sails of white satin had put into harbor with a large party of Jews, presumably on the way to join the pseudo-Messiah Shabbetai *Ẓevi in the Levant (A New Letter from Aberdeen in Scotland, Sent to a Person of Quality, etc., by R.R., London, 1665). Marischal College in Aberdeen was possibly the earliest British university to give degrees to Jews (Jacob de *Castro Sarmento, 1739, followed by Ralph *Schomberg; perhaps neither professed Judaism at the time). A small community was established in Aberdeen by Polish and Russian Jews in 1893, and in 1966 numbered approximately 85. The Library of Marischal College contains a magnificent Hebrew illuminated Bible manuscript of the Sephardi type, probably originating in Naples. In 2004 approximately 30 Jews resided in Aberdeen. A refurbished community center and synagogue opened in 1983.

BIBLIOGRAPHY: JHSEM, 4 (1942), 107; JYB (1968), 120; C. Roth, *Aberdeen Codex of the Hebrew Bible* (1966). **ADD. BIBLIOGRAPHY:** JYB (2004), 135.

[Cecil Roth]

ABERLIN, RACHEL (2nd quarter of 16th century, Salonika (?)–1st quarter of 17th century, Damascus (?)). Aberlin is described as a mystic in *Sefer ha-Ḥezyonot* ("The Book of Visions"), the memoir of her contemporary R. Hayyim *Vital, the most prominent disciple of the greatest 16th century kabbalist, R. Isaac *Luria. Vital refers to "Rachel Aberlin" and "Rachel ha-Ashkenaziah" frequently in entries that provide rare insight into the mystical religiosity of early modern Jewish women in the period preceding Sabbateanism. He also refers to a "Rachel, sister of R. Judah Mishan," the kabbalist who ratified Vital's authority following Luria's death. Although the connection between Rachel Aberlin and R. Judah Mishan's sister cannot be established with certainty, Vital's references suggest such an identity.

Aberlin settled in Safed in 1564 with her husband, Judah, a wealthy man who led the Ashkenazi community there until his death in 1582. As a wealthy widow, Aberlin became the patron of some of the leading rabbinic figures in her community. We are told by Vital that she established a complex in Safed, where he lived with his family. Vital's references to Aberlin's presence in Jerusalem and Damascus during his years in those cities imply that the two had a close relationship for decades.

Aberlin is portrayed in *Sefer ha-Ḥezyonot* as a woman who regularly experienced mystical visions, from pillars of fire to Elijah the Prophet. She is said to have been "accustomed to seeing visions, demons, souls, and angels," as well as to have had clairvoyant abilities that were acknowledged by Vital, who affirmed that "most everything she says is correct." Aberlin seems to have been an important figure for other women in her community, who regarded her as a spiritual leader. Aberlin's position as the leader of a mystical sisterhood is also suggested by Vital's description of her intervention in a dramatic case of spirit possession involving a young woman in Damascus in 1609. Vital's numerous recollections of Aberlin evince his profound respect for her and her spiritual gifts. In a particularly striking example, Vital relates a dream that Aberlin shared with him in which she saw Vital sitting behind a desk covered with books, while behind him a large heap of straw burned with a radiant fire but was not consumed. Vital explained to Rachel that this vision was a manifestation of Obadiah 1:18, "And the house of Jacob shall be a fire … and the house of Esau for straw." Aberlin, still in her dream, responded, "You tell me the words of the verse as it is written, but I see that the matter is actual, in practice, and completely manifest." This dream demonstrates the distinction between the learned mysticism of the kabbalists and the visionary, ecstatic mysticism of their much less known female counterparts.

BIBLIOGRAPHY: J.H. Chajes, *Between Worlds: Dybbuks, Exorcists, and Early Modern Judaism* (2003); M.M. Faierstein, *Jewish Mystical Autobiographies: Book of Visions and Book of Secrets* (1999).

[J.H. Chajes (2nd ed.)]

ABIATHAR (Heb. אֶבְיָתָר; "the divine father excels"), son of *Ahimelech son of Ahitub of the priestly house of Eli of Shiloh (I Sam. 22:20 ff.). Abiathar was one of David's two chief priests. When the priests of the village of Nob were massacred by order of Saul because they had aided David, Abiathar alone escaped. He then reported the massacre to David, who asked him to join him as his priest. He brought with him an *ephod*, which was used by the priests as an oracle. David twice asked Abiathar to use the *ephod* to ascertain God's command (I Sam. 23:6, 9 ff.; 30:7 ff.). When David became king, Abiathar's line was established as the priestly line of the royal court along with *Zadok's (II Sam. 8:17). It has been suggested, therefore, that the listing of Ahimelech (Abimelech) son of Abiathar as David's priest (II Sam. 8:17; I Chron. 18:16) should be emended to read Abiathar son of Ahimelech, as in the Syriac version. During *Absalom's revolt David was forced to leave Jerusalem, but he sent Abiathar and Zadok there to inform him of the happenings in Absalom's court (II Sam. 15:25, 34 ff.). There they had freedom of movement and thus were able to deliver messages to David about the rebel's intrigues (II Sam. 17:15). Abiathar carried David's message of reconciliation to Amasa and the elders of Judah (II Sam. 19:12) and also served as David's counselor (II Sam. 15:27, 29; 17:15 ff.; 19:12 ff.; I Chron. 27:33–34). During the struggle for succession to David's throne, Abiathar supported *Adonijah (I Kings 1:7); hence Solomon, who was anointed by Zadok, banished Abiathar and his descendants to Anathoth and took away his privileges to act as priest in Jerusalem (I Kings 1:19, 25; 2:22, 26, 35). The prophet Jeremiah was descended from the priests of Anathoth and Jeremiah may have been a descendant of Abiathar (Jer. 1:1).

In the *Aggadah*

Abiathar was indirectly responsible for the continuation of the line of David. Had Abiathar not been saved from the massacre of the priests of Nob, there would have been no *Jehoiada to save the sole survivor of the Davidic line from the massacre instigated by *Athaliah (Sanh. 95b). Abiathar's replacement by Zadok as high priest is explained by the fact that the *Urim* and *Thummim* would not answer him when he consulted them (Sot. 48b). The Zohar (I 63b) illustrates his straitened circumstances thereafter (cf. I Kings 2:26) by the comment: "He who during David's lifetime lived in affluence and wealth, was reduced by Solomon to poverty."

BIBLIOGRAPHY: M. Cogan, *I Kings* [AB] (2000), 177–78.

ABIATHAR BEN ELIJAH HA-KOHEN (c. 1040–1110), last of the Palestinian *geonim*. Abiathar studied under his father ELIJAH B. SOLOMON, president of the Palestinian academy, from 1062 to 1083. A responsum of Elijah addressed to Meshullam b. Moses of Mainz in 1070 was signed also by Abiathar under the title "*ha-Revi'i*" ("the Fourth") implying that he was fourth in rank at the yeshivah. With the capture of Jerusalem by the Seljuks in 1071 and the transfer of the academy to Tyre, Abiathar was appointed "the Third," and later vice president of the academy (*av ha-yeshivah*). In 1081, while his father was still alive, he was appointed *gaon*. Abiathar was involved in a long and bitter controversy with David b. Daniel, the Egyptian exilarch and president of the Fostat (Cairo) Academy, who sought to extend his authority (as had his father *Daniel b. Azariah) over the Palestinian academy and community. Abiathar described this controversy in a "Scroll," published as "*Megillat Abiathar*" by S. Schechter (JQR 1901/02), in which he gave an account of his family's battle against the would-be usurpers. He forcefully defended the special rights of Ereẓ Israel over the Diaspora. "Ereẓ Israel is not called exile; how, then, can an exilarch wield authority over it?" At the beginning of the First Crusade (c. 1095), Abiathar was in Tripoli (Syria). Nothing is known about his last years.

BIBLIOGRAPHY: W. Bacher, in: JQR, 15 (1902/03), 79–96; Mann, Egypt, 1 (1920), 187–95; A. Kahane, *Sifrut ha-Historya ha-Yisre'elit*, 1 (1922), 160–2; Marcus, in: *Horeb*, 6 (1941), 27–40; S. Assaf and L. Meir (eds.), *Sefer ha-Yishuv*, 2 (1944), 39–40 (introd.); S. Goitein, in: KS, 31 (1955/56), 368–70; Braslavi-Braslavsky, in: *Eretz Israel*, 6 (1960), 168–73 (Heb. sect.); idem, in: *Tarbiz*, 32 (1962/63), 174–9.

[Simha Assaf]

°**ABICHT, JOHANN GEORG** (1672–1740), German Lutheran theologian and Hebraist. Abicht studied at Leipzig and at Jena, where he was professor of Hebrew (1702–16). In 1729 he became professor of theology at the University of Wittenberg. His main field of interest was Jewish history and literature and, particularly, rabbinical Bible commentaries, some of which he translated into Latin. His publications are a selection of the Bible commentaries of Rashi, Ibn Ezra, and others, entitled *Selecta Rabbinico-Philologica* (Leipzig, 1705), which included also parts of Maimonides' *Code*; and a Latin translation of Isaiah di Trani's commentary on Joshua (Leipzig, 1712). His interest in the problem of cantillation in the Bible is illustrated by his Latin translation of *Sha'ar ha-Neginot* included as *Porta Accentuum* in Ch. Ziegra's *Accentus Hebraeorum* (1715).

Abicht also wrote a study on the anonymous chronicle *Sefer ha-Yashar* (1732); *Methodus Linguae Sanctae* on Hebrew grammar (1718); studies on Joshua (*Disputationes librum Josuae,* 1714), on the Sabbath (*De lege Sabbathi*, 1731), on Jonah (*De Jona fugiente,* 1702), and on slavery (*De Servorum hebraerorum acquisitione et servitiis*, 1704); a commentary on Zechariah 10:7 (1704), and many other works.

BIBLIOGRAPHY: C.G. Joecher, *Allgemeines Gelehrten-Lexicon,* 1 (1750), 23 and Supplement 1 (1784), 53; NDB, 1 (1953), 19ff.; Steinschneider, Cat Bod, 662; idem, in: ZHB, 1 (1896), 112.

ABIEZER (Heb. אֲבִיעֶזֶר; "my Father [God] is help," or "my Father [God] is hero"; variant **Iezer**, Heb. אִיעֶזֶר, Num. 26:30).

(1) A person and a tribal unit of the tribe of *Manasseh in three genealogical lists in the Bible and a clan in the story of *Gideon.

Iezer and the Iezerites head the list of six eponyms and clans, all sons of *Gilead son of *Machir son of Manasseh (Num. 26:29–33). These are depicted as the "rest" of the sons of Manasseh, including Abiezer, who received ten lots west of the Jordan (Josh. 17:1–6). A different genealogy for Manasseh appears in I Chronicles 7:14–19. Abiezer is represented as a person, not a clan, and is a brother of Ish-Hod and Mahlah, who is daughter of *Zelophehad in other lists. All three are children of Hammolecheth, sister of Gilead, but the text is obscure and there is no certainty as to whose sister she was.

The narrative account of the Book of *Judges attests the existence of the clan of the Abiezrites in the 12th century B.C.E. Joash, the father of Gideon, was surnamed "the Abiezrite" (Judg. 6:11) and his town was "*Ophrah of the Abiezrites" (Judg. 6:24, 8:32). Ophrah, a cultic center, has been located by most scholars at al-Ṭayyiba on the heights of Issachar and north of Beth-Shean. When Gideon blew the horn to gather the people, the clan of Abiezer was the first to answer the call. Evidence from another century for the settlement of the Abiezrites in another region is furnished by the *Samaria Ostraca, which contain names of localities and some districts (nos. 13, 28). The districts, among them Abiezer (אבעזר), are all known from the genealogical lists of Manasseh. Two place names mentioned in several ostraca as being connected with Abiezer are the town of Elmatan at Immātīn and Tetel (?) at al-Tell, which have been identified by W.F. *Albright. Both are south and west of Shechem. The biblical data and the epigraphic data about Abiezer have been regarded as evidence for the organic settlement of an ancient tribal unit in a group of adjoining towns. The tradition of the clan and its eponym were preserved, and the latter became the name of a district. The presence of Abiezer in two different regions may indicate a split of the clan during the process of settlement.

(2) Abiezer the Anathothite (from *Anathoth) was a member of "David's Mighty Men" or "the Thirty" (II Sam. 23:27; I Chron. 11:28). In I Chronicles 27:12 Abiezer the Anathothite is mentioned among the generals of the militia as being in charge of the ninth division for the ninth month.

BIBLIOGRAPHY: (1) Aharoni, Land, 315ff.; EM, 5 (1968), 45ff., s.v. Menasheh; Z. Kallai, *Naḥalot Shivtei Yisrael* (1967), 44, 144ff., 355ff. (2) Y. Yadin, in: J. Liver (ed.), *Historyah Ẓeva'it shel Ereẓ Yisrael…* (1965), 350ff. **ADD. BIBLIOGRAPHY:** (1) S. Ahituv, *Handbook of Ancient Hebrew Inscriptions* (1992), 173, 183.

[Hanna Weiner]

ABIGAIL (Heb. אֲבִיגַיִל), name of two women in the Bible. (1) ABIGAIL wife of Nabal the Carmelite (see *Carmel) and later of David. Abigail is described as both beautiful and sagacious (I Sam. 25:2). In return for "protecting" Nabal's property, David requested a gift of provisions. When Nabal refused, David decided to exact his reward by force. Abigail, apprised of David's approach with armed men, met David with food supplies and apologized for her husband's behavior which she described as the churlish act of a worthless man. David, greatly impressed with Abigail, accepted the food and left in peace. When Nabal died ten days later David wed Abigail. She bore him a son Chileab (I Sam. 3:3), called Daniel in I Chron. 3:1.

In the *Aggadah*

The Midrash is generous in praise of Abigail's beauty, wisdom, and power of prophecy. She is counted among the four women of surpassing beauty in the world (the others are Sarah, Rahab, and Esther), and it is reported that even the memory of her inspired lust (Meg. 15a). Her wisdom was apparent during her first meeting with David when, despite both her own concern for her husband's fate and David's rage, she calmly put a ritual question to him. When David replied that he could not investigate it until the morning, she suggested that the death sentence on her husband be similarly postponed. She met David's protest that Nabal was a rebel, with the retort: "You are not yet king" (*ibid.*). This conversation also revealed her powers of prophecy. The Holy Spirit was upon her when she told David "the soul of my lord shall be bound in the bundle of life" (Lam. R. 21:1); and she foretold David's sin with Bath-Sheba when saying (I Sam. 25:31), "That this shall be no grief unto thee (i.e., but another matter will)" (Meg. *ibid.*). However, her conduct in asking David "to remember thy handmaid" (I Sam. *ibid.*), is said to be unbecoming to a married woman. In the following verse she was therefore addressed by David as "Abigal" (i.e., without the letter *yod*), to indicate that she had shown herself unworthy of the letter with which the name of God begins (Sanh. 2:3).

(2) ABIGAIL daughter of NAHASH, sister of David and Zeruiah, mother of Amasa (II Sam. 17:25; I Chron. 2:16). Her husband was Jether the Ishmaelite (I Chron. 2:17) or Ithra the Jesraelite (II Sam. *ibid.*). (The medieval commentator David Kimḥi surmised that he was known by different names, depending on the area in which he lived.) Concerning her father's name, the Septuagint reads *Jesse instead of Nahash. A talmudic *baraita* also states that Nahash is Jesse (TJ, Yev. 8:3, 9c; Shab. 55). Thus, according to these traditions, Abigail would be David's sister on his father's side. In the Septuagint Abigail is written Abigaia. There is difficulty in explaining the meaning of the name. It is found on a Hebrew seal of the eighth or the seventh century B.C.E.: "To Abigail wife of Asijahu."

BIBLIOGRAPHY: Noth, Personennamen, index; **ADD. BIBLIOGRAPHY:** J. Kessler, in: CBQ, 62 (2000), 409–23; S. Japhet, *I & II Chronicles* (1993), 77.

ABI-ḤASIRA, family of kabbalists and pietists, most of whom lived in Morocco. SAMUEL (16th century), apparently of Moroccan origin, lived in Syria. He was renowned as a scholar of Talmud and practical Kabbalah. The first known member of the family in Morocco is MAKLOUF who lived in Dra. The local scholars wrote a special work (still in manuscript) on his eminence. AYYUSH and his two sons JACOB I and YAḤYA were all kabbalists. JACOB II BEN MASOUD (1807–1880) was a codifier and kabbalist, widely renowned for his great piety; people streamed to him to receive his blessings. Three times he tried to fulfill his dream of going to Ereẓ Israel, but the community and even the government stood in his way. In the end, however, he left despite their protestations. He succeeded in making his way as far as Damanhur, near Alexandria, but there he died and was buried. The anniversary of his death is commemorated in many communities. Jacob's works, almost all of which were published in Jerusalem, include *Doresh Tov* (1884); *Pittuḥei Ḥotam*, on the Torah (1885); *Yoru Mishpatekha*, responsa (1885); *Bigdei ha-Sered*, on the Passover *Haggadah* (1887, and Leghorn, 1890); *Ginzei ha-Melekh*, on Kabbalah (1889, 1961); *Maḥsof ha-Lavan*, on the Torah (1892); *Alef Binah*, on the alphabet (1893); *Ma'gelei Ẓedek* (1893); *Levonah Zakkah*, on the Talmud (1929); *Sha'arei Teshuvah* (1955); and *Yagil Ya'akov*, poems (Algiers, 1908; Jerusalem, 1962). DAVID, a kabbalist, was killed by a cannon shot at the instigation of the local *mukhtar* Mulai Muhammad in 1920. He wrote *Sekhel Tov* (2 vols., 1928) and *Petaḥ ha-Ohel* (3 vols., 1928). His brother ISAAC (1897–1970) emigrated to Israel in 1949, and the same year was appointed chief rabbi of Ramleh and district.

BIBLIOGRAPHY: J. Abi-Hasira, *Doresh Tov* (1884), introd. by A. Abi-Ḥasira; idem, *Ma'gelei Ẓedek* (1893), introd. by A. Abi-Ḥasira; Neubauer, Chronicles, 1 (1887), 152; J.M. Toledano, *Ner ha-Ma'arav* (1911), 211; E. Rivlin, *Rabbi Shemu'el Abi-Ḥasira* (1922); M.D. Gaon, *Yehudei ha-Mizraḥ be-Ereẓ Yisrael*, 2 (1938), 17; J. Ben-Naim, *Malkhei Rabbanan* (1931).

[David Obadia]

ABIHU (Heb. אֲבִיהוּא), second son of Aaron and Elisheba, daughter of Amminadab (Ex. 6:23; Num. 3:2, et al.). He is always mentioned together with his elder brother Nadab. He was anointed and ordained for the priesthood (Num. 3:3; cf. Ex. 28:1; I Chron. 24:1) and participated with his father, brother, Moses, and the elders in the rites accompanying the making of the covenant at the theophany at Sinai, on which occasion they "saw God" and ate a festive meal (Ex. 24:1–10). Although the exact function of Abihu in these rites is not specified, it is clear that the story represents a very ancient tradition, and that Abihu once played a definite, prominent, and positive role in the now lost history of the Israelite priesthood.

The death of Abihu occurred under mysterious circumstances. He was incinerated (although his clothes and those of his brother remained intact) together with Nadab, as the brothers offered "alien fire before the Lord" (Lev. 10:1–3; Num. 3:4; 26:61; cf. I Chron. 24:2). Aaron's cousins, Mishael and

Elẓaphan, were ordered to remove the bodies from the sacred precincts, and the customary mourning rites were suspended (Lev. 10:4–7). The precise nature of the incident is unclear, and neither the locale nor chronology is recorded. Some serious departure from the prescribed cultic ritual seems to be referred to. It has been suggested that they brought incense from outside the sacred area between the altar and the entrance to the Tent of Meeting. It was therefore impure. Abihu and his brother left no sons (Num. 3:4; I Chron. 24:2), and his priestly line was thus discontinued. Some scholars see behind the story of their deaths a forgotten tradition about inter-priestly rivalries and the elimination of two priestly houses. The name Abihu may be variously explained as meaning "the Father [God] is" (i.e., exists), "He [God] is Father," and "Father is He" (a surrogate for God).

For Abihu in Aggadah, see *Nadab.

BIBLIOGRAPHY: Noth, Personennamen, 18, 70, 143; Moehlenbrink, in: ZAW, 52 (1934), 214–5; Y. Kaufmann, Toledot, 1 (1937), 542; de Vaux, Anc Isr, 397. **ADD. BIBLIOGRAPHY:** M. Haran, in: J. Liver (ed.), *Sefer Segal* (1964), 33–41.

[Nahum M. Sarna]

ABIJAH (Heb. אֲבִיָּה; "YHW(H) is my father"), king of Judah c. 914–912 B.C.E.; son of *Rehoboam (on the identity of his mother, see *Asa). In Kings, where he is referred to throughout as Abijam, it is stated only that he followed the sinful ways of his father, and that he was at war with *Jeroboam, king of Israel, throughout his reign. The Book of Chronicles, however, for its own theological reasons, unhistorically depicts him as a pious king who succeeded in wresting a sizable slice of territory from Jeroboam (II Chron. 13:19). According to I Kings 15:19, it is likely that a political alliance existed between Abijah and *Ben-Hadad I, king of Aram-Damascus. Abijah had 14 wives, who bore 22 sons and 16 daughters (II Chron. 13:21). One source of information for the Chronicler on the reign of Abijah was the Midrash of the prophet Iddo (*ibid.* 13:22).

BIBLIOGRAPHY: S. Japhet, *I & II Chronicles* (1993), 697–700.

ABILEAH, ARIE (1885–1985), Israel pianist. Born in Russia, Abileah gave his first concert at the age of six. He studied at the Conservatory of Petersburg under Marie Benoit, Liadov, and Glazounov and completed his artistic training in Geneva with Stavenhagen. He appeared as accompanist of Joseph *Szigeti, Joseph *Achron, and Maurice Maréchal. In 1914 he was appointed chairman of the piano department at the Music Academy in Geneva, a position he held until 1922. He was active in 1922–26 as a piano teacher in Tel Aviv. During 1926–32 Abileah performed at concerts in Paris and New York. In 1932 he settled in Jerusalem where he was appointed professor at the Music Academy and, as chairman of the Musicians' Association, organized chamber music concert series. He made recordings for the Israel Broadcasting Authority.

[Ury Eppstein]

ABILENE, district in Coele-Syria, centered around the city of Abila (modern Suq on the Barada River, 16½ mi. (27 km.) N.W. of Damascus) and extending over the western slopes of Mt. Hermon. Originally part of the Iturean principality, it was held by the tetrarch Lysanias the Younger in the time of Tiberius (Luke 3:1). Gaius Caligula granted it to Agrippa I (Jos., Ant., 18:237) and after the latter's death, the tetrarchy was administered by Roman procurators (44–53 C.E.) until Claudius gave it to Agrippa II (Jos., Ant., 20:138) who ruled it until his death. The local legend connecting Abilene with Abel (al-Nabī Ābil) is spurious.

BIBLIOGRAPHY: Schuerer, Gesch, 1 (1904^4), 716–21; Pauly-Wissowa, 9 (1916), 2379; Bickerman, in: EJ, s.v. *Abila, Abilene.*

[Michael Avi-Yonah]

ABIMELECH (Heb. אֲבִימֶלֶךְ; "the [Divine] Father is King" or "the [Divine] King is Father"), king of *Gerar, who appears in several incidents in connection with Abraham and Isaac. Each of these patriarchs, fearing for his personal safety, represents his wife as his sister. Sarah's honor is saved through a dream theophany in which Abimelech's life is threatened; timely detection of the subterfuge preserves Rebekah's virtue. In both instances the king's integrity is manifest and he is righteously indignant at the deceit (Gen. 20; 26:1–11). Abimelech is also involved with both patriarchs in quarrels over wells (21:25; 26:15–16, 18–21). In both events he is accompanied by Phicol, chief of his troops (21:22, 32; 26:26), and concludes treaties (21:27–32; 26:28–31). Also, Beer-Sheba figures on each occasion (21:31; 26:33). The detailed similarities between the two stories and the resemblances of both to that of Genesis 12:10–20 have generally led critical scholars to assign Genesis 20–21 to the E source and Genesis 12 and 26 to J, regarding all three narratives as variants of a single tradition.

The name is ancient, and attested in the form Abi-milki as the name of the King of Tyre in the 14th century B.C.E., but because the Philistine migrations to Canaan do not antedate 1100 B.C.E., the title "King of the Philistines" (26:1, 8; cf. 18 – not in E) must be viewed as an anachronism.

[Nahum M. Sarna]

In the *Aggadah*

Abimelech was referred to as a righteous Gentile (Mid. Ps. 34). His attempted seizure of Sarah is explained by the fact that he was childless, and that he hoped to be blessed with offspring by marrying such a pious woman (PdRE 26). Among his punishments for his sin were that ruffians entered his house, that boils erupted on his body (Gen. R. 64:9), and that his household became barren (BK 92a). Abimelech, however, clearly did not consider himself to be the only one at fault. According to the aggadic commentary on his words "Behold it is for thee a covering of the eyes" (Gen. 20:16), he said to Abraham "You covered my eyes (i.e., by saying that Sarah was your sister), therefore the son which you will beget will be of covered eyes (i.e., blind)." This prophecy was fulfilled in Isaac's old age (Gen. R. 52:12). The aggadic treatment of Isaac's relations with

Abimelech is briefer. It records that, although he had heard of Rebekah's great beauty, Abimelech remembered his previous punishment, and therefore left her alone (Ag. Ber. 20). However, once Isaac had become so wealthy that people kept saying: "Rather the dung of Isaac's mules, than Abimelech's gold and silver," he became jealous, and claimed that Isaac's wealth was derived from his favors (Gen. R. 64:7).

BIBLIOGRAPHY: J. Skinner, *Genesis* (ICC, 1930²), s.v.; E.A. Speiser, *Genesis* (1964), s.v. **ADD. BIBLIOGRAPHY:** C.S. Ehrlich, *The Philistines in Transition: A History from ca. 1000–730 BCE* (1996); S.D. Sperling, *The Original Torah* (1998), 21–22, 86–90.

ABIMELECH (for meaning, see previous entry), the male offspring of *Gideon the Abiezrite by his Shechemite concubine (Judg. 8:31). During the period of the Judges Abimelech became the ruler of Shechem through the support of his mother's family and the local oligarchy ("the lords of Shechem"; Judg. 9:2–3 et al.) who financed the hiring of a regiment of "worthless and reckless fellows" (9:4). With their aid, Abimelech murdered all but one of the 70 sons of Gideon (see *Jotham) in order to eliminate possible claims to the leadership of Shechem. He had reason for apprehension because of Gideon's special connections with this city. The Bible does not count Abimelech among the *Judges. He is not credited with having "saved" Israel. The placing of his story in the Book of Judges is apparently due to its connection with the traditions about the house of Gideon. At any rate, Abimelech maintained close ties with the Israelites, since he "ruled [not 'judged'] over Israel three years" (9:22). It is probable that the Manassites submitted to him because of his paternal lineage, though it is possible that he attained power solely by means of the support of his hired regiment. It would seem that Abimelech's connection with the Israelites did play a decisive role in contributing to his election as a ruler of Shechem. The preservation of normal relations with Israel was of vital importance to Canaanite Shechem which existed as a foreign enclave within the boundaries of the tribe of Manasseh. According to the narrative, the "lords of Shechem" acclaimed Abimelech "king" over them (9:6). However, all indications point to the fact that the title "king" was used because of the lack of a more appropriate term for the type of ruler that existed in various cities in Syria and Ereẓ Israel who performed the functions and exercised the authority of a king. A ruler of this kind was chosen by the municipal institutions. There is evidence that the ruler was dependent on the city's institutions, which guarded their own status and power. Other non-monarchal rulers governed in Shechem at different times: Hamor the Hivite, ruler of Shechem in the days of Jacob (Gen. 34:2), was "chief of the country"; Lab'ayu, chief of Shechem during the 14th century B.C.E., known from the el-Amarna letters, was another such example. In the course of time a conflict arose between Abimelech and the "lords of Shechem," who had chosen him as their leader (Judg. 9:23). It appears that he wished to increase his power at the expense of the local oligarchy. The appointment of Zebul, who was among Abimelech's most prominent supporters and who protected the latter's interests in Shechem as "the ruler of the city" (9:30), testifies to these aspirations. According to the Bible, the "lords of Shechem" placed "men in ambush against [Abimelech] on the mountain tops" (9:25) in order to prove his incompetence in the delicate area of security and to remove him from power. They even conspired with *Gaal son of Ebed (9:26), a non-local and non-Israelite personage, who headed an army of his own and who seduced the Shechemite population by underscoring the city's descent from Hamor the Hivite, its ancient founder (9:28–29). Possibly this reflects a split within the local population, part supporting Abimelech and part opposing him. Gaal apparently sought and found supporters among the Hivites (Horites) of Shechem, who were almost certainly a significant section of the city's population. It is a fact that Abimelech lost support precisely among the "lords of Shechem."

Since Abimelech had to be informed about the events in Shechem by Zebul's messengers (9:31), it would seem that he was not a permanent resident but lived outside the city proper. Abimelech hastened to Shechem and attacked Gaal and his confederates (9:39–40). Abimelech's supporters in Shechem drove Gaal from the city (9:41). The continuation of the story implies that Abimelech decided to turn the territory of Shechem into his private estate by conquest. He completely destroyed the city, slaughtered its inhabitants, and sowed it with salt (9:45). He then invested Thebez (9:50ff.). During the siege of the tower of Thebez he was mortally wounded by a millstone thrown down on him by a woman (9:53). Badly injured, he asked his armor bearer to slay him rather than let him die disgracefully at the hand of a woman (9:54). Although the story of Abimelech is episodic, it represents a shift in Israelite attitudes leading to the establishment of the monarchy. There is an obvious continuity between the Israelites' request that Gideon be king over them and Abimelech's status as ruler of Israel. Only the period of the consolidation of the monarchal concept in Israel separated Abimelech's rule from the anointing of Saul.

BIBLIOGRAPHY: E. Nielson, *Shechem, a Tradition-Historical Investigation* (1955); E. Taeubler, *Biblische Studien 1: Die Epoche der Richter*, ed. by H.-J. Zobel (1958); Reviv, in: IEJ, 16 (1966), 252–7; G. Dossin, in: *L'Ancien Testament et l'Orient* (1957), 163–7 (*Orientalia et Biblica Lovaniensia*, no. 1); Ehrman, in: *Tarbiz*, 29 (1959), 259; Gevirtz, in: VT, 3 (1953), 192–5 (Eng.); van der Meersch, in: *Verbum Domini*, 31 (1953), 335–43; Milik, in: *Verbum Domini*, 31 (1953), 335–43; Milik, in: RB, 66 (1959), 550–75; Naor, in: BIES, 20 (1950), 16–20; Fensham, in: BA, 24 (1962), 48–50; Gevirtz, in: VT, 13 (1963), 52–62 (Eng.). **ADD. BIBLIOGRAPHY:** J.C. Exum, *Was sagt das Richterbuch den Frauen?* (1997); Y. Amit, *Judges* (1999), 173–80; D. Herr and M. Boyd, in: BAR 28/1 (2002), 34–37, 62.

[Hanoch Reviv]

ABINADAB (Heb. אֲבִינָדָב; "my [or "the"] Divine Father is generous"; the root נדב is a common element in West Semitic names), the father of Eleazar, Aḥio, and Uzzah, who resided in Kiriath-Jearim. The ark was brought to Abinadab's home after its wanderings in the Philistine cities and remained there for a period of 20 years. When David undertook to move the Ark by oxcart to Jerusalem (II Sam. 6:3–4; I Chron. 13:7), Abinadab's son Eleazar was appointed to guard the ark (I Sam. 7:1). Abinadab's two sons, Uzzah (perhaps identical with Eleazar) and Aḥio, marched the one beside or behind and the other in front of it. Josephus relates that Abinadab and his sons were Levites (Ant., 6:18; 7:79), a datum unsupported by other sources.

ABIOB, AARON (1535?–1605?), rabbi, preacher, and biblical commentator. Abiob studied under Samuel *Medina, the greatest halakhic authority of his time. He was appointed rabbi, first in Salonika and subsequently in Constantinople and Usküb. Although a recognized authority in *halakhah*, he would refer cases which he did not wish to decide to his teacher in Salonika. His responsa frequently are quoted in the responsa of Samuel Medina and in those of Solomon b. Abraham Ha-Kohen of Serei. He published *Shemen ha-Mor* (Salonika, 1601), a collection of novellae of other commentators and his own exposition of rabbinic dicta in connection with the Book of Esther. He compiled commentaries on the Pentateuch, called *Korban Aharon*, developed from the discourses he delivered on Sabbaths and festivals. The work was never published and the manuscript is no longer extant. His commentary on Psalms, *Beit Aharon*, was also unpublished. His son Solomon succeeded him as rabbi of Usküb.

BIBLIOGRAPHY: Michael, Or, no. 266; Rosanes, Togarmah, 2 (1938), 127; 3 (1938), 74, 125; M.S. Goodblatt, *Jewish Life in Turkey in the 16th Century* (1952), 26; M. Molcho, in: *Sinai*, 41 (1957), 41.

ABIR (Abramovitz), DAVID (1922–), Israeli aerospace engineer. Abir, who was born in Kaunas, Lithuania, and came to Palestine in 1934, was chief instructor of the Aero clubs of Palestine, which included the aviation unit of the Palmaḥ (1943–46). He served in the Israel Air Force (1949–55) and was head of its engineering department in 1954–55. Abir was at the Haifa Technion from 1955 to 1972, serving as head of the department of mechanics in 1959–61 and then as dean (and professor) of the Faculty of Aeronautical Engineering (1962–64). He was employed at the British Aircraft Corporation, Bristol, U.K. (1964–65) as senior consulting assistant to the chief engineer on the Anglo-French Concorde supersonic aircraft project. Abir also worked (on leave from the Technion) at Israel Aircraft Industries Ltd., Engineering Division, in 1968–71, as director of advanced aircraft studies and chairman of research and development. He joined Tel Aviv University in 1972 as associate dean of the Faculty of Engineering (1972–80). Abir was deputy chairman of the Israel Space Agency, Ministry of Science and Technology (1983–87) and its director general in 1985–87. Abir was chairman of the National Committee for Space Research from 1972 and chairman of the National Committee on Data for Science and Technology from 1988, both at the Israel Academy of Sciences and Humanities. He served as president (1990–94) of the International Committee on Data for Science and Technology (CODATA) of the International Council of Science (ICSU), Paris, France, and was a member of the Council of the International Committee on Space Research (COSPAR) of ICSU from 1972. He was a founding member of the Tel Aviv Academic College of Engineering (from 1996) and served as its deputy president for academic affairs (until 2002). Abir was a fellow of the Royal Aeronautical Society, London, U.K. (from 1965) and a member of the International Academy of Astronautics, Paris, France (from 1972). He contributed papers and articles and wrote and edited books and journals in the fields of aerospace and technology. He was active in the creation of Hebrew terminology in the aviation and related fields, in conjunction with the Israel *Academy of the Hebrew Language and other organizations.

[Samuel Aaron Miller / Bracha Rager (2nd ed.)]

ABISHAG THE SHUNAMMITE (Heb. אֲבִישַׁג; "the [Divine] Father (?)"; meaning unknown; of *Shunem), an unmarried girl who was chosen to serve as *sōkhenet* to King David. The term comes from a root *skn*, "attend to," "take care," and its noun forms can be applied to high officials in Hebrew (Is. 22:15) Abishag's role was of a lower status. She served as bed companion to David in the hope that her fresh beauty would induce some warmth in the old man (I Kings 1:1–4, 15), and as his housekeeper. The notice (1:4) that "the king knew her not" serves less to impute decrepitude to David than to inform the audience that there would be no other claimants to David's throne than Solomon and Adonijah. When Solomon became king, *Adonijah, whose life Solomon had spared although he knew him to be a dangerous rival, asked *Bath-Sheba, Solomon's mother, to intercede on his behalf for permission to marry Abishag. Solomon correctly interpreted this request for the former king's concubine as a bid for the throne (See II Sam 12:8; 16:20–23), and had Adonijah killed (I Kings 2:13–25). Some see in Abishag, who is described as "very fair" (I Kings 1:4), the Shulammite of the Song of Songs (Shulammite being regarded as the same as Shunammite).

In the *Aggadah*

The *aggadah* identifies Abishag as the Shunammite who gave hospitality to Elisha the prophet (PdRE 33). It relates that she was not half as beautiful as Sarah (Sanh. 39b). The fact that David did not make Abishag his legal wife is explained as due to his refusal to exceed the traditional number of wives (18) allowed to a king (Sanh. 22a, and Rashi, *ibid.*). Solomon's action is also vindicated on the grounds that the request made by Adonijah to be permitted to marry Abishag (I Kings 2:13ff.) represented a true threat to Solomon's position, as it is only the king, and not a commoner, who is allowed to make use of the servants of the deceased king (Sanh. 22a).

BIBLIOGRAPHY: Noth, Personennamen, index; Ginzberg, Legends, index. **ADD. BIBLIOGRAPHY:** M. Cogan, *I Kings* (AB; 2000), 156; Z. Kallai, in: Z. Talshir (ed.), *Homage to Shmuel* (2002), 376–81.

[Elia Samuele Artom]

ABISHAI, the son of Zeruiah, brother of *Joab and *Asahel and nephew of David. Abishai was one of David's most loyal military officers. He was one of David's three mighty men and is credited with killing 300 people (II Sam. 23:18). Additionally, he is said to have been the head of this group, and according to some versions he was the head of the thirty heroes (II Sam. 23:18; I Chron. 11:20). Abishai was one of the three generals who defeated Ish-Bosheth, Saul's son, and Abner, the commander of Saul's army. After the battle Abner killed Asahel (II Sam. 2:18ff.). According to II Samuel 3:30, Abishai and his brother Joab eventually avenged their brother's death. However, the Septuagint apparently did not hold them responsible for this murder, reading *'arevu* ("lie in wait") instead of *haregu* ("killed") of the masoretic text. David, nevertheless, certainly thought both of them guilty (II Sam. 3:39). Abishai defeated the Canaanite confederation against David (II Sam. 10), and during Absalom's revolt he commanded one-third of David's forces (II Sam. 18:2). Additionally, he was instrumental in suppressing Sheba, the son of Bichri (II Sam. 20:6–10). He was also one of David's leading generals in other wars with the Philistines (II Sam. 21:15–17) and the Edomites (I Chron. 18:12); he rescued David at Nob from the threats of a Philistine giant, who has been referred to in some sources as Ishbibenob (II Sam. 21:16–17); and he was against the king's policy of making peace with his enemies (II Sam. 16:9–10, 19:23). Abishai's suggestion to kill Saul in his camp was refused by David (I Sam. 26:6ff.).

In the *Aggadah*

Abishai's rescue of David (II Sam. 21:16–17) illustrates his piety and valor. David had been enticed over the Philistine border by Satan and there seized by Ishbibenob, the brother of Goliath. This was miraculously revealed to Abishai while he was bathing in preparation for the Sabbath. He was aided in his search for David by the fact that the earth contracted under him. On his way he encountered and slew Orpah. When Ishbibenob saw him approaching, he planted his spear in the ground and threw David up in the air saying: "Let him fall on it and perish." Abishai, however, pronounced the Divine Name, and David remained suspended in the air until he descended safely in answer to a prayer of Abishai. Abishai and David foiled the final attack of the enraged giant by weakening him with taunts about his mother's death at Abishai's hands (Sanh. 95a). Abishai was equal to 70,000 men of Israel (Mid. Ps. 17:4).

BIBLIOGRAPHY: D. Schley, ABD 1:24–6.

ABITBOL, Moroccan family of rabbis, *dayyanim*, talmudists, and jurists, who led the community of Sefrou. Information about the Abitbol family is found in many Moroccan documents (responsa, collections of letters, etc.), mostly unpublished. The British Museum houses a bulky manuscript (Margoliouth, Cat, 4 (1935), 161, Or. 11, 114), entitled *Sefer Iggerot u-Meliẓot*, containing poems, but mainly the exchange of correspondence between Moroccan rabbis between 1760 and 1810. The manuscript contains valuable information on the history of Moroccan Jewry in general, and the Abitbol family of Sefrou in particular.

(1) SAUL JESHUA BEN ISAAC (c. 1740–1809), called Rav Shisha (the Hebrew initials of his name). Rav Shisha became rabbi and *dayyan* in Sefrou at the age of 18, and served for 50 years. His rabbinical decisions were honored in rabbinical courts in Morocco during and after his lifetime. His responsa were collected by his descendants and published in Jerusalem under the title *Avnei Shayish* (1930[1], 1934[2]). The second volume also contained a collection of biblical and talmudic glosses, sermons, etc., entitled *Avnei Kodesh*, which are not his work, but that of another rabbi of Sefrou, Jekuthiel Michael Elbaz. The poet David Ḥasin composed two *piyyutim* to honor him and his son RAPHAEL (cf. *Tehillah le-David*, 1787). Jacob Berdugo mourned his death in a dirge (cf. *Kol Ya'akov*, 1844).

[Haim Zafrani]

(2) AMOR BEN SOLOMON (1782–1854), Moroccan scholar, codifier, and *dayyan*. Born in Sefrou, Abitbol maintained a yeshivah there at his own expense and supported needy scholars. Many communities turned to him with their halakhic problems. His voluminous library contained many rare manuscripts, among them hundreds of letters addressed to him and to his father from all parts of North Africa, particularly Morocco (Ms. British Museum no. Or. 11. 114; a second group is the Benayahu collection). These contain important information about valuable works and manuscripts. Some of his own and his father's responsa were published as *Minḥat ha-Omer* (1950). This volume includes a collection of his homilies, *Omer Man*, and 26 of his poems and elegies, including one *bakashah* in Arabic. Other responsa by him are scattered throughout the works of his Moroccan contemporaries. Some of his works are still in manuscript. His two sons, Ḥayyim Elijah and Raphael, were also well-known rabbinic scholars.

BIBLIOGRAPHY: J. Ben-Naim, *Malkhei Rabbanan* (1931), 102d; J.M. Toledano, *Ner ha-Ma'arav* (1911), 190; Yaari, Sheluḥei 709; M. Benayahu, in: *Minḥah le-Avraham (Elmaleḥ)* (1959), 30ff.

ABI ZIMRA, ISAAC MANDIL BEN ABRAHAM (16th century), liturgical poet who lived in Algiers. His father Abraham b. Meir Abi Zimra, born in Malaga, author of some poetical compositions, came "from the bitter expulsion of 1492 to the city of Tlemcen" (Abraham Gavison, *Omer ha-Shikhḥah*, 1748, 134a). Abraham Gavison, who knew Isaac, called him "the great poet" (*ibid.*, 122b). Over 60 of Isaac's *piyyutim*, which were strongly influenced by Arabic poetry, are to be found in various manuscripts. Until recently, various communities in North Africa recited his poems. A complete edition of poems was prepared by H.J. Schirmann, but never published.

BIBLIOGRAPHY: Zunz, Lit Poesie, 535–6; Slouschz, in: *Reshumot*, 4 (1926), 25, 27; Zulay, *ibid.*, 5 (1927), 444ff.; Davidson, Oẓar, 4 (1933), 422.

[Abraham Meir Habermann]

ABKHAZIYA (formerly **Abkhaz Autonomous Soviet Socialist Republic**), within Georgia, Transcaucasia, on the eastern shore of the Black Sea. Formerly part of the Ottoman Empire, Abkhaziya became a Russian protectorate in 1810. During the czarist regime, since it lay beyond the *Pale of Settlement, Abkhaziya was barred to Jews from European Russia. In 1846 Jewish artisans were given permission to live temporarily in Sukhum (now Sukhumi), the main city, and by 1897 there were 156 Jews. After the 1917 revolution the number of

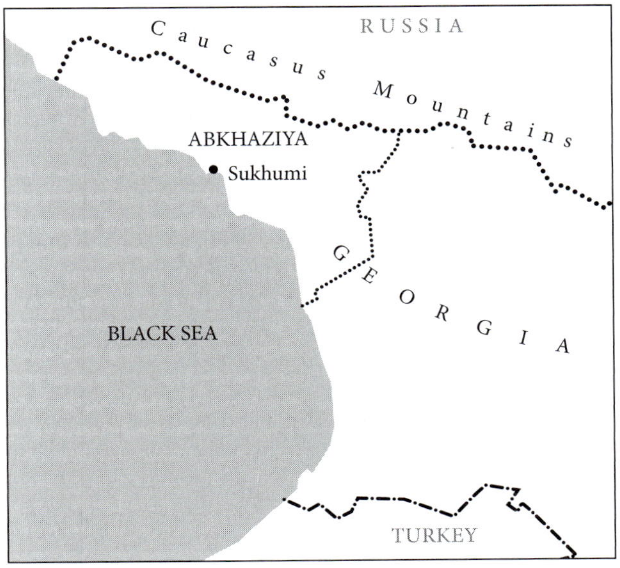

Jews in Abkhaziya increased considerably. The 1959 census recorded 3,332 Jews (0.8% of the total population), 3,124 living in urban settlements and 208 in rural. The majority were concentrated in Sukhumi and most of them were Georgian Jews (see *Georgia). A new synagogue with accommodation for 500 congregants was built in 1960, and a congregation was reported active in 1963. After the dismantling of the Soviet Union in the 1990s, Abkhaziya proclaimed independence and cessation from Georgia, leading to a war in 1993 that ended with the defeat of the Georgian army and Russian troops intervening and separating the belligerents. The war caused the Jews of Abkhaziya to leave, mostly for Israel. Abkhaziya is not recognized by other governments as an independent country. See also *Caucasus.

[Yehuda Slutsky / Shmuel Spector (2nd ed.)]

ABLUTION (Heb. טְבִילָה; "immersion"), act of washing performed to correct a condition of ritual impurity and restore the impure to a state of ritual purity. The ritually impure (or unclean) person is prohibited from performing certain functions and participating in certain rites. Ablution, following a withdrawal period and, in some cases, other special rituals, renders him again "clean" and permitted to perform those acts which his impurity had prevented. Ablution must not be confused with washing for the sake of cleanliness. This is evident from the requirement that the body be entirely clean before ablution (Maim., Yad, Mikva'ot 11:16), but there may nevertheless be some symbolic connection. The ablutions, as well as the impurities which they were deemed to remove, were decreed by biblical law, and understood by the rabbis in religious and not in hygienic or magical terms. This is shown by R. Johanan b. Zakkai's retort to his disciples who had questioned an explanation he gave to a non-Jew about ritual purity: "'The dead do not contaminate and the water does not purify.' It is a command (*gezeirah*) of God and we have no right to question it" (Num. R. 19:4).

Ablution is common to most ancient religions. Shintoists, Buddhists, and Hindus all recognize ablution as part of their ritual practice and there is ample evidence concerning its role in ancient Egypt and Greece (Herodotus, 2:37; Hesiod, *Opera et Dies*, 722). Most ancient peoples held doctrines about ritual impurity and ablution was the most common method of purification. In varying forms ablution is important to Christianity and Islam as well; this is hardly surprising since they are both post-Judaic religions. In Jewish history there have been several sects that have laid great stress on the importance of ablution. The *Essenes (Jos., Wars, 2:129, 149, 150) and the *Qumran community (Zadokite Document, 10:10ff.; 11:18ff. and other DSS texts) both insisted on frequent ablutions as did the Hemerobaptists mentioned by the Church Fathers. The *tovelei shaḥarit* ("morning bathers") mentioned in Tosefta *Yadayim* 2:20 perhaps may be identified with the latter but more likely were an extreme group within the general Pharisaic tradition (Ber. 22a; Rashi, ad loc.).

In the Jewish tradition there are three types of ablution according to the type of impurity involved: complete immersion, immersion of hands and feet, and immersion of hands only.

Complete Immersion

In the first type of ablution the person or article to be purified must undergo total immersion in either *mayim ḥayyim* ("live water"), i.e., a spring, river, or sea, or a **mikveh*, which is a body of water of at least 40 *se'ahs* (approx. 120 gallons) that has been brought together by natural means, not drawn. The person or article must be clean with nothing adhering (*ḥaẓiẓah*) to him or it, and must enter the water in such a manner that the water comes into contact with the entire area of the surface. According to law one such immersion is sufficient, but three have become customary. Total immersion is required for most cases of ritual impurity decreed in the Torah (see *Purity and Impurity, Ritual). Immersions were required especially of the priests since they had to be in a state of purity in order to participate in the Temple service or eat of the "holy" things. The high priest immersed himself five times during the service of the Day of Atonement. Other individuals had to be ritually pure even to enter the Temple. However, it became customary among the Pharisees to maintain a state of purity at all times, a fact from which their Hebrew name *Perushim* ("separated ones") may have developed (L. Finkelstein, *The Pharisees* (1962^3), 76ff.; R.T. Herford, *The Pharisees* (1924), 31ff.).

Total immersion also came to form part of the ceremony of *conversion to Judaism, although there is a difference of opinion concerning whether it is required for males in addition to circumcision, or in lieu of it (Yev. 46a). Since the destruction of the Temple, or shortly thereafter, the laws of impurity have been in abeyance. The reason is that the ashes of the *red heifer, which are indispensible for the purification ritual, are no longer available. Thus, everybody is now considered ritually impure. The only immersions still prescribed are those of the **niddah* and the proselyte, because these do not require the ashes of the red heifer and because the removal of the impurity concerned is necessary also for other than purely sacral purposes (entry into the Temple area, eating of "holy" things). The *niddah* is thereby permitted to have sexual relations and the proselyte is endowed with the full status of the Jew.

In addition to the cases mentioned in the Bible, the rabbis ordained that after any seminal discharge, whether or not resulting from copulation, total immersion is required in order to be ritually pure again for prayer or study of the Torah. Since this was a rabbinical institution, immersion in drawn water or even pouring nine *kav* (approx. 4½ gallons) of water over the body was considered sufficient. The ordinance was attributed to Ezra (BK 82a, b) but it did not find universal acceptance and was later officially abolished (Ber. 21b–22a; Maim., Yad, Keri'at Shema 4:8). Nevertheless, the pious still observe this ordinance. The observant also immerse themselves before the major festivals, particularly the Day of Atonement, and there are ḥasidic sects whose adherents immerse themselves on the eve of the Sabbath as well. The Reform movement, on the other hand, has entirely abolished the practice of ritual ablution. There was a custom in some communities to immerse the body after death in the *mikveh* as a final purification ritual. This practice was strongly discouraged by many rabbis, however, on the grounds that it discouraged women from attending the *mikveh*, when their attendance was required by biblical law. The most widespread custom is to wash the deceased with nine *kav* of water.

The immersion of the *niddah* and the proselyte require **kavvanah* ("intention") and the recitation of a benediction. The proselyte recites the benediction after the immersion because until then he cannot affirm the part which says "… God of our fathers … who has commanded us." Since ablution at its due time is a *mitzvah* it may be performed on the Sabbath, but not, nowadays, on the Ninth of Av or the Day of Atonement. Except for the *niddah* and the woman after childbirth whose immersion should take place after nightfall, all immersions take place during the day.

Vessels to be used for the preparation and consumption of food that are made of metal or glass (there is a difference of opinion concerning china and porcelain) and that are purchased from a non-Jew must be immersed in a *mikveh* before use. This immersion is to remove the "impurity of the Gentiles" (a conception which was introduced, perhaps, to discourage assimilation), and is different from the process of ritual cleansing by which used vessels are cleansed to remove non-kosher food which might have penetrated their walls. This immersion is also accompanied by a benediction.

Washing the Hands and Feet

This second type of ablution was a requirement for the priests before participating in the Temple service (Ex. 30:17ff.).

Washing the Hands

This is by far the most widespread form of ablution. The method of washing is either by immersion up to the wrist or by pouring ¼ *log* (approx. ½ pint) of water over both hands from a receptacle with a wide mouth, the lip of which must be undamaged. The water should be poured over the whole hand up to the wrist, but is effective as long as the fingers are washed up to the second joint. The hands must be clean and without anything adhering to them; rings must be removed so that the water can reach the entire surface area. The water should not be hot or discolored and it is customary to perform the act by pouring water over each hand three times (Sh. Ar., OḤ 159, 1960, 161). The handwashing ritual is commonly known as *netilat yadayim*, a term whose source is not entirely clear. It has been suggested that *netilah* means "taking" and thus the expression would be "taking water to the hands," but the rabbinic interpretation is "lifting of the hands" and is associated with Psalms 134:2.

Washing the hands is a rabbinic ordinance to correct the condition of *tumat yadayim*, the impurity of the hands, which notion itself is of rabbinic origin. Among the biblical laws of purity washing the hands is mentioned only once (Lev. 15:11). According to one tradition "impurity of the hands" (and washing them as a means of purification) was instituted by King Solomon, while another has it that the disciples of Hillel and Shammai were responsible for it (Shab. 14a–b). It seems that the custom spread from the priests, who washed their hands before eating consecrated food, to the pious among the laity and finally became universal. The detailed regulations concerning "impurity of the hands" constitute one of the 18 ordinances adopted in accord with the opinion of the school of Shammai against the school of Hillel, and it met at first with considerable opposition. In order to establish the practice the rabbis warned of dire consequences for those who disregarded it, even going so far as to predict premature death (Shab. 62b; Sot. 4b). R. Akiva, who personally disapproved of the ordinance, nevertheless used the limited water allowed him in prison for this ablution rather than for drinking (Er. 21b). In the New Testament there are several references which suggest that Jesus and his disciples demonstrated their opposition to rabbinic authority by disregarding this ordinance (Mark 7:1; Matt 15:1; Luke 11:37).

The washing of the hands most observed today is that required before eating bread, although according to rabbinic sources washing after the meal before grace is considered at least of equal importance. The reason given for this latter washing is to remove any salt adhering to the fingers which could cause serious injury to the eyes (Er. 17b). It is possible that these washings derive from contemporary Roman table manners, and there is also mention of washing between courses (*mayim emẓa'iyyim*, Ḥul. 105a).

In modern times, priests have their hands washed by the Levites before they perform the ceremony of the Priestly Blessing during public prayer services. The laver thus has become the heraldic symbol for the Levites and often appears on their tombstones. Washing the hands is required on many other occasions, some of which are motivated by hygienic considerations and others by superstitious beliefs. A list of occasions for washing the hands was compiled by Samson b. Zadok in the 13th century: they include immediately on rising from sleep (in order to drive the evil spirits away), before prayer, after leaving the toilet, after touching one's shoes or parts of the body usually covered, and after leaving a cemetery (Tashbaẓ 276; Sh. Ar., OḤ 4:18).

The fact that ablution was so widespread in ancient religions and cultures makes it likely that the Jewish practice was influenced by contemporaneous cults. It is, however, difficult to ascertain the extent of this influence and it is possible that the rabbis were reacting against contemporary practices rather than imitating them. It is clear that, to the rabbis, the main purpose of any ablution was to become "holy" and the system they created was meant to keep the Jew conscious of this obligation. "'(God is the hope [Hebrew "*mikveh*"] of Israel)' (Jer. 17:13); just as the *mikveh* cleanses the impure so will God cleanse Israel" (Yom. 85b).

[Raphael Posner]

Women and Ablution

Immersion for women following menstruation and childbirth is a rabbinic, not a biblical, requirement. The halakhic regulations appear particularly in TB *Niddah*, which discusses the practical consequences for male ritual purity of women's menstrual and non-menstrual discharges. On the eighth "white day," following the cessation of menstrual flow, the wife must immerse in the *mikveh* (ritual bath) before marital relations can resume. Jewish girls were traditionally taught to comply strictly and promptly with the regulations connected with the *niddah* (the menstruating woman). Ablution, which took place only after the body and hair had been thoroughly cleansed, had to be complete. *Halakhah* demanded a single immersion but three became customary. Post-menstrual and post-partum women usually visited the *mikveh* at night, often accompanied by other women.

In the first half of the 20th century, female ritual ablution declined significantly in North America, even among nominally traditional families, despite Orthodox exhortations in sermons and written tracts on the spiritual and medical benefits of *taharat ha-mishpaḥah* (family purity regulations), as these laws came to be called. Factors militating against ritual immersion included disaffection of Americanized children of immigrants with their parents' Old World ways, the success of liberal forms of organized Judaism that did not advocate such ablutions, and the deterrent effect of ill-maintained and unhygienic *mikva'ot*. Many Jewish feminist writers of the late 20th century also condemned *taharat ha-mishpaḥah* regulations as archaic expressions of male anxiety about the biological processes of the female body that reinforced the predominant construction in rabbinic Judaism of women as other and lesser than men.

The 1980s and 1990s saw a resurgence in the numbers of Orthodox Jews and a new sympathy among non-Orthodox denominations for various previously discarded practices of traditional Judaism. In this era, positive new interpretations of ritual ablution developed, accompanied by construction of attractive modern *mikva'ot*. Orthodox advocates of *taharat ha-mishpaḥah* regulations praised the ways in which they enhanced the sanctity of marriage and human sexuality and extolled the feeling of personal renewal and rebirth that followed each immersion.

At the beginning of the 21st century, ritual ablution became a symbolic expression of a new spiritual beginning for both women and men in all branches of North American Jewish practice beyond the domain of *taharat ha-mishpaḥah*. In addition to conversion to Judaism, rituals developed incorporating *mikveh* immersion as part of bar mitzvah and bat mitzvah (coming of age); before Jewish holidays; prior to marriage; in cases of miscarriage, infertility, and illness; and following divorce, sexual assault, or other life-altering events. An indication of the probable long-term impact of this trend was the increased construction of *mikva'ot* by non-Orthodox communities.

[Judith R. Baskin (2nd ed.)]

BIBLIOGRAPHY: Eisenstein, Dinim, 147–8; N. Lamm, *A Hedge of Roses: Jewish Insights into Marriage …* (1966). **ADD. BIBLIOGRAPHY:** R. Adler, "'In Your Blood, Live': Re-Visions of a Theology of Purity," in: D. Orenstein and J.R. Litman (eds.), *Lifecycles* 2 (1997), 197–206; J.R. Baskin, "Women and Ritual Immersion in Medieval Ashkenaz," in: L. Fine (ed.), *Judaism in Practice* (2001), 131–42; Fonrobert, C. *Menstrual Purity* (2000); R. Slonim (ed.), *Total Immersion: A Mikvah Anthology* (1996); R.R. Wasserfall (ed.), *Women and Water* (1999).

ABNER (Heb. אַבְנֵר, אֲבִינֵר), cousin of King *Saul and "captain of his host" (I Sam. 14:50–51); from I Chronicles 8:33 it would appear that Abner was Saul's uncle. At court he occupied the seat of honor next to Jonathan, the crown prince (I Sam. 20:25). In his conflict with Saul, David seems to have suspected Abner of plotting against him (24:10; 26:19). Abner did in fact accompany Saul in his pursuit of David, who taunted him with not guarding his master properly (26:16). After the death of Saul and three of his sons on Mount Gilboa, Abner made Saul's son *Ish-Bosheth king over Israel with his capital at *Mahanaim in Transjordan, while Judah broke away and elected David as their king in Hebron (II Sam. 2:8–11). During the subsequent warfare between Israel and Judah, Abner and his men were routed by David's captain, Joab, at the Pool of Gibeon; Abner killed Joab's younger brother Asahel, but reluctantly and in self-defense. He then made a moving appeal to Joab to stop the fratricidal combat (2:12–32). Abner was reproved by Ish-Bosheth for having lain with Rizpah, the daughter of Aiah, a concubine of King Saul, thus possibly betraying his own aspirations to the kingship (3:7). In his anger Abner communicated with David and conspired with "the Elders of Israel" and Saul's own tribe of Benjamin to offer David the crown of a reunited Israel (3:12ff.). At Hebron he and his son were well received and entertained, while his enemy Joab was away (3:20). Abner promised to rally the entire nation around David. On his return Joab reproached David and warned him against Abner's intrigue. Without the king's knowledge he lured Abner back to Hebron and murdered him at the city's gate (3:30). In this act he also avenged Asahel's death and rid himself of a potential rival, as David had probably promised the chief captaincy to Abner in return for making him king over all Israel. Shocked by this treacherous deed, David cursed Joab and his house. He had Abner buried with full honors; his beautiful dirge and tribute to Abner, "A prince and a great man has fallen this day in Israel," became famous (3:31ff.). On his deathbed David charged his son Solomon to avenge Abner's murder (I Kings 2:5, 32). According to one tradition Abner's tomb is in Hebron near the cave of *Machpelah.

[Gustav Yaacob Ormann]

In the *Aggadah*

Abner, a giant of extraordinary strength (Eccles. R. 9:11) was the son of the Witch of En-Dor (PdRE 33). It was he who refuted Doeg's argument against the admission of Moabite women "in the assembly of the Lord" (see Deut. 23:4) and, supported by Samuel, he established the rule "a Moabite but not a Moabitess," thus enabling David to reign over Israel (Yev. 76b). Abner justified his slaying of Asahel as an action in self-defense, but since he could have merely wounded him, Abner deserved his violent death (Sanh. 49a). Although a pious man (Gen. R. 82:4) and a "lion in the law" (TJ Pe'ah 1:1, 16a) Abner was guilty of many misdeeds which warranted his death. It was in his favor that he had refused to obey Saul's command to kill the priests at Nob; but he should have intervened actively and prevented Saul from executing his bloody design (Sanh. 20a). Even if Abner could not have influenced the king in this matter (*ibid.*), he was guilty of having frustrated a reconciliation between David and Saul and of thinking little of human life (TJ Pe'ah 1:1, 16a). However he was right in espousing the cause of Saul's son Ish-Bosheth against David for he knew from tradition that God had promised two kings to the tribe of Benjamin, and it was therefore his duty to transmit the throne to the son of Saul the Benjaminite (Gen. R. 82:4).

BIBLIOGRAPHY: Noth, Personennamen, 167; Bright, Hist, 169, 175–7; E. Auerbach, *Wueste und gelobtes Land*, 1 (1932), 221–4; Ginzberg, Legends, index, EM, 1 (1965), 59–60.

ABNER OF BURGOS (also **Alfonso of Valladolid** or **of Burgos**; c. 1270–1340), apostate and anti-Jewish polemicist. Abner was practicing as a physician in Burgos in 1295, at the time of the appearance of the false prophet in *Avila. Some of those who had been confused by miraculous portents they had witnessed came to Abner for medical advice. Their reports shook Abner's own faith in Judaism, which was already troubled by doubts. The phenomenon of the sufferings of the Jews in exile and of the righteous had long disturbed him, and he experienced visions which he was unable to interpret. Finding no solution in the Bible or the doctrines of the Jewish and Arab philosophers, he turned to the New Testament and the works of the Christian theologians. Abner wrestled with this problem for 25 years. Jewish scholars tried to restore his faith, but he eventually became converted to Christianity when he was about 50. Some time after his conversion, he sent his disciple, Isaac b. Joseph ibn *Pollegar (Pulgar), a copy of a pamphlet setting forth his messianic theories. Pulgar responded with a work which he circulated among the Jewish communities in Spain. Abner subsequently published a number of books and tracts written in Hebrew and directed to Jews. Some were later translated into Castilian under his supervision. He also engaged in his old age in oral disputes with Jewish scholars, including *Moses b. Joshua of Narbonne. In 1334 he tried to convince the elders of Toledo that they had erred in fixing the date of Passover.

Abner was among the first apostates to formulate an ideological justification for conversion. He rejected the rationalist interpretations of the Torah current in his day and avoided taking a stand on the *Kabbalah, which was known to him. The theological system which he propounded accepts predestination, identified with astrological influences, as well as philosophic determinism. The theories expressed in his *Iggeret ha-Gezerah* ("Epistle on Fate") combine astrology with the doctrine of fatalism of Muslim theologians and the Christology of Paul and Augustine. Abner found the answer to the problem of salvation – individual salvation as well as the salvation of all Christians, who alone truly deserved the name "Israel" – in the doctrines of the Trinity and Incarnation, which he tried to ascribe to Aristotle and the aggadic Midrashim (following Raymond *Martini's *Pugio Fidei).* He proposed harsh measures for dealing with the Jewish question, including conversionist preaching, isolation of the Jews from the Christian population, and stirring up mob violence. These proposals he justified by means of malicious allegations about the Talmud. Following the example of the Karaites, Abner alleged that the Talmud contained an evil "Ten Commandments." He employed Karaite arguments against the Talmud in addition to the criticisms of contemporary rationalists and did not shrink from publishing blatant forgeries. He repeated current slanders that the Jews displayed a hostile and unethical attitude toward Gentiles and gave them a sharper edge.

Some of Abner's works have not yet been published and others have been lost, including his *Milḥamot Adonai* ("Wars of the Lord") which he wrote in Hebrew and translated into

Castilian at the request of the Infanta Doña Blanca. Preserved in Castilian translation are Abner's major work *Moreh Ẓedek* ("Teacher of Righteousness"), under the title *Mostrador de Justicia,* and his tract *Minḥat Kena'ot* ("Offering of Zeal"), directed against Isaac Pulgar. In the original Hebrew are *Sefer Teshuvot li-Meḥaref* ("Refutation of the Blasphemer"), a reply to Pulgar and other minor polemics. Pulgar assembled his arguments against Abner in his *Ezer ha-Dat* ("Aid to Faith"), in which, as customary in the works of other polemicists, he quotes from Abner's writings. Ḥasdai *Crescas, in his *Or Adonai,* quotes whole passages from Abner's works in order to refute them. Subsequently, the apostates *Solomon ha-Levi of Burgos (Pablo de Santa María) and Joshua Lorki (Gerónimo de Santa Fe) drew upon Abner's arguments. In conjunction with the *Pugio Fidei* of Raymond Martini, Abner's writings served as source material for later polemics against Judaism in Spanish Christian literature in general.

BIBLIOGRAPHY: Baer, Spain, index; *Sefarad,* index vols. 1–15, s.v. *Abner de Burgos* and *Valladolid, Alfonso de;* E. Ashkenazi, *Divrei Ḥakhamim* (1849), 37ff.; Graetz-Rabbinowitz, 5 (1896), 396–9; Y. Baer, in: *Minḥah le David* (1935), 198ff.; Baer, Urkunden, 1 pt. 2 (1936), 144, 521; idem, in: *Tarbiz,* 11 (1939/40), 188ff.; idem, in: *Sefer ha-Yovel... G. Scholem* (1958), 152–63 (*Tarbiz,* 27 (1957/58); J. Rosenthal, in: *Meḥkarim... Âbraham A. Neumann* (1962), 1–34 (Hebrew section); idem, in: *Meḥkarim u-Mekorot,* 1 (1967), 324–67: Guttmann, Philosophies, 230–2, 271–2.

[Zvi Avneri]

ABOAB, Spanish family whose descendants remained prominent among the Sephardim of the Mediterranean world as well as in the ex-Marrano communities of Northern Europe. The origin of the name is obscure. The family produced many outstanding Jewish scholars in Spain (see Isaac Aboab, I and II). After the expulsion from Spain, it was found in North Africa, Turkey, Italy (where the form Aboaf became common), and elsewhere. Some members of the family, who fell victims to the forced conversion in Portugal in 1497, preserved the name in secret, resumed it when they reentered Judaism (sometimes with the addition of their baptismal surnames, e.g., Fonseca, Dias, Falleiro) and became outstanding in the communities of the Marrano Diaspora (see Samuel *Aboab, Isaac *Aboab de Fonseca). ABRAHAM, formerly Gonçalo Cardozo, who traded with the Iberian Peninsula under the name of Dionis Genis, was one of the deputies of the Jewish community of Amsterdam in 1638. ELIAS conducted a printing establishment there in 1643–44, and DANIEL SEMAH practiced medicine after graduating at Utrecht in 1667. DAVID, a convert, made his name in England by some pretentious publications, including *Remarks on Dr. Sharpe's Dissertations ... concerning ... Elohim and Berith* (London, 1751). He is possibly identical with the DAVID, born in Italy, who was excommunicated in Curaçao in 1746 after a bitter controversy with the rabbinate. Members of the family resident in Brazil in 1648–54 included MOSES, who later found his way to New York, where he is recorded in 1684. MOSES, formerly of Surinam, conducted learned religious discussions at Leghorn and elsewhere with the Christian scholar Veyssiere de la Croze, who described them in his *Entretiens sur divers sulets ... de critique et religion* (Amsterdam, 1711?).

BIBLIOGRAPHY: Loewenstein, in: MGWJ, 48 (1904), 661–701; 50 (1906), 374–5; M. Eisenbeth, *Les Juifs de l'Afrique du Nord* (1936), 76; ESN, 10–14; Roth, Mag Bibl, 285, nos. 60, 62; 336, no. 4; 409, no. 18; Rosenbloom, Biogr Dict, 2; A. Wiznitzer, *Jews in Colonial Brazil* (1960), 137; F. Secret, in: *Les Nouveaux Cahiers,* 3 (1965), 37–43.

[Cecil Roth]

ABOAB, IMMANUEL (c. 1555–1628), protagonist of Judaism among the Crypto-Jews. The little that is known about his life is derived from his major work *Nomologia,* and from his letters to many Crypto-Jews in Western Europe. He was born in Porto into a New Christian family, his father being Henrique Gomes (Isaac Aboab). After his father's death when he was quite young, he was brought up by his grandfather Duarte Dias (Abraham Aboab, son of Isaac *Aboab II "the last *gaon* of Castile"; see accompanying genealogical tree), who negotiated with the Portuguese authorities for the entrance of the Castilian refugees into the country and was subsequently a victim of the forced conversion of 1497; he mentioned his grandfather quite often. In 1585 Aboab escaped to Italy, where he professed Judaism and studied Hebrew literature. In 1597 he had a religious discussion with an Englishman at Pisa; at the time he was one of the *parnasim* of the community, where his signature appears on some of the ordinances in 1599; subsequently he was in Reggio Emilia (where he was in contact with the kabbalist Menahem Azariah da *Fano) and Ferrara, where he had a debate with a Christian scholar on the translations of the Bible, claiming that the Hebrew version is the authentic one. He then moved to Spoleto, and later to Venice, where he is said to have delivered a discourse on the loyalty of the Jewish people before Doge Marino Grimani and the Grand Council in 1603. Four years later he was at Corfu, where he appeared on important business before the Venetian commander Orazio del Monte, with whom he later carried on a correspondence on the nature of angels. He probably spent some time in North Africa and Amsterdam. In Venice he became the *ḥakham* of the Spanish and Portuguese community until his departure to Israel late in life with a party of 36 relatives to join his daughter Gracia, who maintained two academies, in Safed and Jerusalem, and was in charge of the money collected for the support of the scholars. Aboab was a vigorous defender of Judaism, especially among his fellow Marranos who, while skeptical of Christianity, did not appreciate Jewish tradition. In the last years of his life, he wrote a forceful letter to a Marrano friend in France urging him to return to Judaism. The letter was filled with learned arguments and illustrations from history and was used in manuscript by later scholars. His principal work was his *Nomologia o Discursos legales,* written in Spanish between 1615 and 1625 in Venice, a defense of the validity and divine origin of the Jewish tradition and the Oral Law, published posthumously by his heirs (Amsterdam, 1629; 2nd ed. by I. Lopes, *ibid.,* 1727). The title of the book, *Nomologia* ("The Theory of the Names") refers to the names of scholars from the days of Moses until his own time. The book was published at the persistent request of Sephardi Jews in Western Europe. Aboab claimed that the Written and Oral Laws were inseparable. Displaying a wide knowledge of Talmud and Kabbalah as well as Latin and secular learning, it includes much valuable historical information, especially about scholars who left Spain and Portugal after the expulsion. In chaper 29 Aboab conducted debates with two such Jews who denied the validity of the rabbinic traditions. His letters sent to Converso or ex-Converso acquaintances are a valuable source of information on the religious, theological, and social problems they encountered in Jewish communities where they settled. Aboab strongly criticized those who returned to the Iberian Peninsula after their difficult experience as Jews. His literary and religious projects were interrupted by his death in Jerusalem.

BIBLIOGRAPHY: Loewenstein, in: MGWJ, 48 (1904), 666–8; Sonne, in: JQR, 22 (1931/32), 247–93; C. Roth, *Venice* (1930), 68, 207, 315; idem, in: JQR, 23 (1932/33), 121–62. **ADD. BIBLIOGRAPHY:** M. Orfali, *Imanuel Aboab's "Nomologia o discursos legales"* (Heb., 1997).

[Cecil Roth / Yom Tov Assis (2nd ed.)]

ABOAB, ISAAC I (end of the 14th century), rabbinic author and preacher; probably lived in Spain. His father seems to have been called Abraham and may have been the Abraham Aboab to whom *Judah b. Asher of Toledo (d. 1349) addressed responsa (*Zikhron Yehudah*, 53a and 60a). After devoting most of his life to secular affairs Isaac turned to writing and preaching.

Isaac's fame rests upon his *Menorat ha-Ma'or* ("Candlestick of Light"), one of the most popular works of religious edification among the Jews in the Middle Ages. Written "for the ignorant and the learned, the foolish and the wise, the young and the old, for men and for women," the work has had over 70 editions and printings (1st ed. Constantinople, 1514; Jerusalem, 1961) and has been translated into Spanish, Ladino, Yiddish, and German. Moses b. Simeon Frankfort of Amsterdam, who translated the work into Yiddish and wrote a commentary on it (*Nefesh Yehudah*, Amsterdam, 1701 and many subsequent eds.), also edited a shorter version under the title of *Sheva Petilot* ("Seven Wicks," Amsterdam, 1721; Sudzilkow, 1836). The book became a handbook for preachers and served for public reading in synagogues when no preacher was available.

Isaac wrote his book, apart from its practical aim, to return *aggadah* to its rightful place. Complaining that, because of lack of order in the sources, *aggadah* had been neglected in favor of legal casuistry, he argues that *aggadah* is an essential part of rabbinic tradition, as necessary for man as *halakhah*. According to Isaac, the *aggadah* carried the same authoritative weight as halakhic rabbinic writings. Thus, the reader is expected to believe that the *aggadah* is true, just as the *halakhah* is true. It has been suggested that he wanted to provide a structured compilation of *aggadah*, similar to that which Maimonides, in his *Mishneh Torah*, had provided for the *halakhah*.

Developing the image of the seven-branched candlestick (cf. Num. 4:9), Isaac divides his work into seven *nerot* ("lamps"). These, in turn, are subdivided into main divisions, parts, and chapters. Using the three parts of Psalms 34:15 as general headings, he assigns the seven lamps to them in the following manner: (A) "Depart from evil," (1) guard against envy, lust, ambition; (2) be wary of sins attendant upon speech. (B) "Do good," (3) observance of *mitzvot* such as circumcision, rearing of children, prayer, festivals, honoring parents, founding a family, charity, justice; (4) study of Torah; (5) repentance. (C) "Seek peace and pursue it," (6) peace and love for fellowman; and (7) humility.

Sources

Into this rather loose framework Isaac fitted a wealth of aggadic material, culled from the Talmud and the vast midrashic literature. His use of passages from aggadic works now lost and the variants in the talmudic and midrashic texts he cites make the *Menorat ha-Ma'or* of great importance for establishing the text of the Talmud used in the Spanish-North African academies as distinct from that of the Franco-German school. Isaac is selective in using esoteric texts, and he fights shy of statements that may provoke doubt and heresy. While he agrees with Sherira Gaon that some of the sayings of the rabbis are imaginative exercises, he wants to limit their number. He contends that the great majority of aggadic statements are divinely inspired and, hence, beyond questioning. If they appear strange to us, it is because of our limited understanding. Isaac also quotes from the geonic literature, Alfasi, Rashi, the tosafists, Abraham Ibn Ezra, Maimonides, Abraham ibn Daud, Jacob Anatoli, Jonah of Gerona, Naḥmanides, Isaac ibn Latif, and Solomon b. Abraham Adret, the ritual compilations of Abraham b. Nathan of Lunel (*Ha-Manhig*) and (David) Abudarham, Baḥya's *Ḥovot ha-Levavot*, Joseph Gikatilla's *Sha'arei Orah*, Asher b. Jehiel, and Jacob b. Asher's *Tur*. He often neglects to name the author from whose work he quotes, and his materials are derived many times from secondhand sources.

Thought

The *Menorat ha-Ma'or* is above all an ethical religious treatise. When discussing religious practices such as circumcision or Sabbath and Festival observances, Aboab limits himself to their underlying reasons and general importance. In his speculative views he combines the teachings of Maimonides, whose *Mishneh Torah* and *Guide* he cites constantly, with the ideas of the teachers of Kabbalah, though the complete absence of quotations from the Zohar has puzzled some scholars. In contrast to Maimonides he postulates that God's individual providence for man is unconditional. Isaac recognizes the need for the study of general sciences, of which, according to him, the rabbis of old were masters, and he quotes Plato, Aristotle, and "the physicians who have recently emerged among

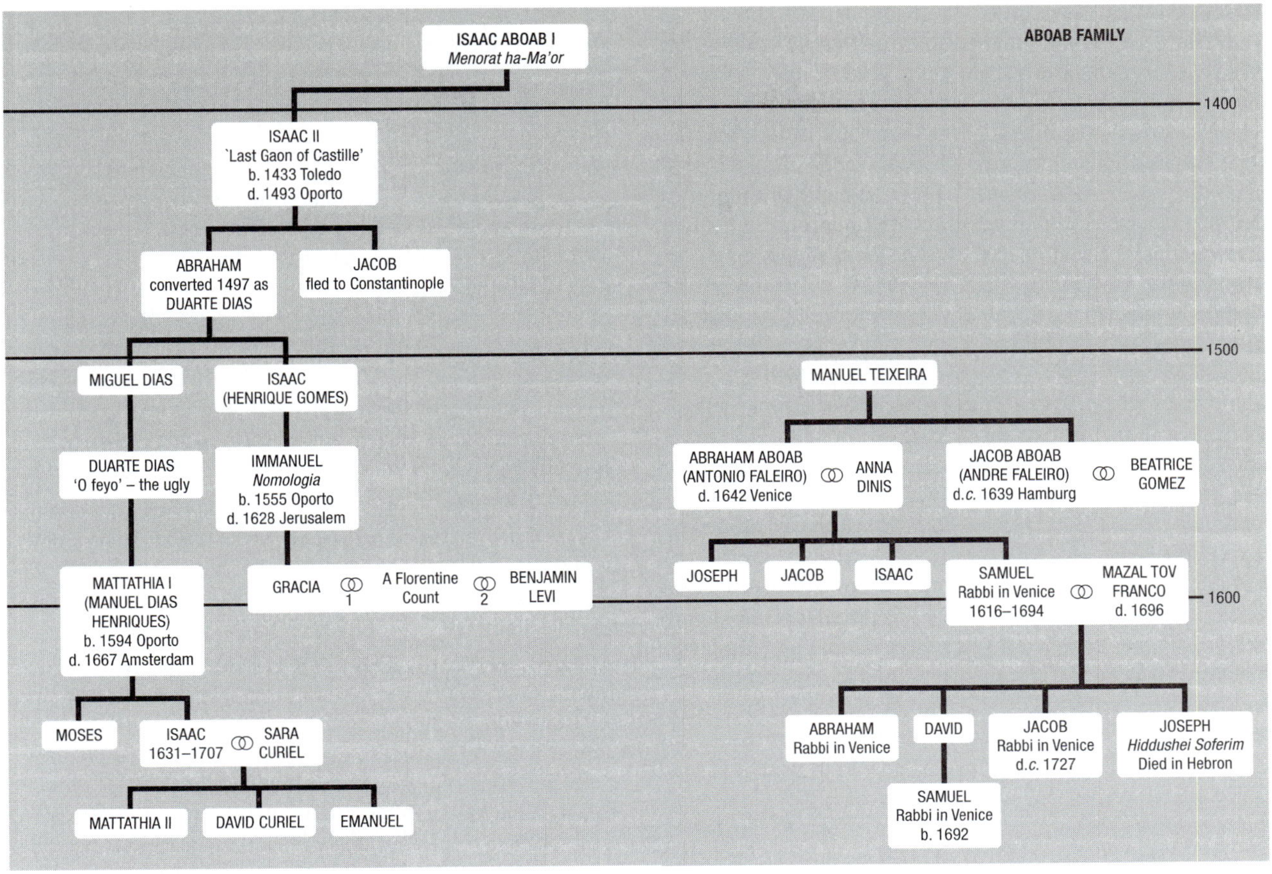

the Gentiles." He also reflects the rabbis' ambivalent attitude to this world and the next: on the one hand, this world is merely a preparation for the next; on the other hand, the Jew must enjoy this world and the life given by God for serving Him and his fellowman.

Al-Nakawa's *Menorat-ha-Ma'or*

Ever since S. Schechter described the *Menorat-ha-Ma'or* of Israel Al-Nakawa (d. 1391; MGWJ, 34 (1885), 114–26, 234–40) and H.G. Enelow published it (1929–34), the relationship between the two books has interested scholars, with most of them inclining toward the dependence of Aboab on Al-Nakawa. Certain scholars contend that this would imply the post-dating of Aboab's work. The subjects discussed under their various headings are strikingly similar in the two works, but their arrangement is hardly more logical in one than in the other. In Aboab's *Menorat ha-Ma'or* the choice of title is justified by the plan, and the need for an ordered presentation of *aggadah* is explained in the "Introduction," whereas Al-Nakawa has nothing to say on this subject. (For the arguments in favor of the precedence of Al-Nakawa's work see Israel b. Joseph *Al-Nakawa.)

Other Works

In the "Introduction" Isaac mentions that he had written two halakhic works: *Aron ha-Edut* ("Ark of Testimony"), whose talmudic materials are arranged according to the Ten Commandments with the opinions of the *geonim* and later commentators in the margin; and *Lehem ha-Panim* ("Showbread"), devoted to prayers and blessings (unique manuscript in Schocken Library, Jerusalem).

The traditional portrait of Isaac Aboab is actually that of Isaac Aboab da Fonseca.

BIBLIOGRAPHY: A bibliography of editions and translations is found in the introduction to *Menorat ha-Ma'or*, ed. by Ben-Menaḥem (1953), 1–14; Zunz, Ritus, 204–10; S.A. Horodezky, in: *Ha-Goren*, 3 (1902), 5–29; H.G. Enelow, *Israel Al-Naqawa's "Menorat ha-Maor"* (1929), 17–22 (introd.); Efros, in: JQR, 9 (1918/19), 337–57; Levitan, *ibid.*, 11 (1920/21), 259–64; Davidson, ibid., 21 (1930/31), 461–8; Higger, *ibid.*, 27 (1936/37), 59–63; Waxman, Literature, 2 (1960²), 282–7; Baer, Spain, index, s.v. *Isaac Abohab*.

[*Encyclopaedia Hebraica*]

ABOAB, ISAAC II (1433–1493), rabbinical scholar. Known as the "last *gaon* of Castile," Aboab was a disciple of Isaac *Canpanton and head of the Toledo Yeshivah. Joseph *Caro refers to him as one of the greatest scholars of his time. During the final years before the expulsion from Spain he headed a yeshivah in Guadalajara, where, in 1491, Isaac *Abrabanel studied with him. When the edict of expulsion was issued against the Jews of Spain in 1492, Aboab and other prominent Jews went to Portugal to negotiate with King João II regarding the admission of a number of Spanish exiles into his country. He and 30 other householders were authorized to settle in Oporto where he died seven months later; a eulogy was delivered by his pupil Abraham Zacuto. He had two sons: JACOB, who ultimately settled in Constantinople where he published in 1538 his father's *Nehar Pishon*, and ABRAHAM, one of the forced converts of 1497 who retained their Jewish loyalties in secret. Abraham adopted the name Duarte Dias, and many of his descendants returned to Judaism (see *Aboab Family). Isaac Aboab's published works include the following: (1) a supercommentary on Naḥmanides' commentary on the Pentateuch (Constantinople, 1525; Venice, 1548, etc.); (2) *Nehar Pishon*, homilies on the Pentateuch and other biblical books, edited by his son Jacob (Constantinople, 1538); (3) talmudic excursuses (*Shitot*) and novellae (those to *Beẓah* were published in the responsa of Moses Galante (Venice, 1608) and *Sefer Shitot ha-Kadmonim* (1959); those to *Bava Meẓia* are quoted by Bezalel Ashkenazi in his *Shitah Mekubbeẓet);* (4) responsa, appended to *Sheva Einayim* (Leghorn, 1745). Oxford and Cambridge manuscripts contain some of his novellae (on *Ketubbot* and *Kiddushin*), as well as homilies. A commentary on Jacob b. Asher's *Arba'ah Turim*, quoted and used by Joseph Caro and later authorities, and a commentary on Rashi (on the Pentateuch), as well as many responsa, are no longer extant.

BIBLIOGRAPHY: Graetz, Gesch, 82 (c. 1900[4]), 218, 330, 348; Weiss, Dor, 5 (1904[4]); Loewenstein, in: MGWJ, 48 (1904), 663–6; Roth, in: JQR, 23 (1932/33), 121–62; A. Marx, *Studies in Jewish History and Booklore* (1944), 80, 85, 88–89, 431–2; idem, in: JQR, 20 (1907/08), 240–71 (add. and corr., *ibid.*, 2 (1911), 237–8).

[Zvi Avneri]

ABOAB, ISAAC DE MATTATHIAS (1631–1707), Dutch Sephardi scholar. His father Manuel Dias Henriques (1594–1667) was born in Oporto into a Marrano family, a descendant of Isaac *Aboab II. After escaping from the Inquisition in Mexico he reverted to Judaism as Mattathias Aboab in Amsterdam in 1626. Isaac was a wealthy East India merchant trading with Spain and Portugal under the assumed name of Dennis Jennis. Although not a rabbi, as generally stated, he patronized rabbinical works and was a prolific writer and copyist. His only published work is a brief handbook of moral conduct, first written for his son in Hebrew but published in Portuguese under the title of *Doutrina Particular* (Amsterdam, 1687, 1691, reprinted by M.B. Amzalak, Lisbon, 1925). He advised his son to read Spanish books from time to time for his entertainment. He also wrote (1685) a morality play (*Comedia*) on the life of Joseph, and compiled a history and genealogy of his own family.

BIBLIOGRAPHY: Revah, in: *Boletim internacional de bibliografia lusobrasileira*, 2 (1961), 276–310 (full list of Aboab's writings); Kayserling, Bibl., 3–45, 55, 81, 110; C. Roth, in: JQR, 23 (1922/33), 122ff.; A. Rubens, *Jewish Iconography* (1954), 65–67; H.I. Bloom, *Jews of Amsterdam* (1937).

[Cecil Roth]

ABOAB, JACOB BEN SAMUEL (d. c. 1725), Venetian rabbi. He was the third son of Samuel Aboab, whom he succeeded as rabbi of Venice and whose biography he wrote (introduction to Samuel Aboab's responsa *Devar Shemu'el* (Venice, 1702)). He studied mathematics and astronomy and enjoyed a high repute for his extensive knowledge. Jacob's halakhic decisions are included in contemporary works. He corresponded with Christian scholars on biographical and bibliographical topics relating to Jewish literature. Among his correspondents were Christian Theophil Unger, a Silesian pastor, and the Frankfurt scholar Ludolf Hiob. An index to *Yalkut Shimoni* and a work on the ingredients of the incense of the sanctuary, both in manuscript, are ascribed to him. His responsum on the chanting of the Priestly Blessing is included in the collection *Meẓiẓ u-Meliẓ* (Venice, 1716), and a poem of his is appended to *Kehunnat Avraham* (Venice, 1719) by Abraham Cohen of Zante.

BIBLIOGRAPHY: Zunz, Gesch, 245; S. Wiener, *Kohelet Moshe*, 2 (1897), 253ff.; Loewenstein, in: MGWJ, 48 (1904), 679–80, 689–701.

[Yehoshua Horowitz]

ABOAB, SAMUEL BEN ABRAHAM (1610–1694), Italian rabbi. Aboab was born in Hamburg, but at the age of 13 he was sent by his father to study in Venice under David Franco, whose daughter he later married. After serving as rabbi in Verona, he was appointed in 1650 to Venice. At the age of 80 he had to leave Venice for some unknown cause and wandered from place to place, until the authorities permitted him to return shortly before his death. Aboab was renowned for both his talmudic and general knowledge and was consulted by the greatest of his contemporaries. He had many disciples. Modest, humble, and of a charitable nature, he devoted himself with particular devotion to communal matters. He was responsible for obtaining financial support from Western Europe for the communities in Ereẓ Israel, and in 1643 collected funds for the ransoming of the Jews of Kremsier taken captive by the Swedes. Aboab was one of the most energetic opponents of the Shabbatean movement. At first he dealt with its followers with restraint, in the hope of avoiding a schism and the possible intervention of the secular authorities. Subsequently, however, he adopted a more rigorous attitude. When *Nathan of Gaza reached Venice in 1668, Samuel was among the rabbis of Venice who interrogated him on his beliefs and activities. His published works include *Devar Shemuel*, responsa (Venice, 1702) published by his son Jacob. It is prefaced by a biography and his ethical will to his sons, and has an appendix called *Zikkaron li-Venei Yisrael* on the investigation of Nathan of Gaza in 1667–68; *Sefer ha-Zikhronot* (Prague, between 1631 and 1651), contains ten principles on the fulfillment of the commandments. Two more of his works, *Mazkeret ha-Gittin* and *Tikkun Soferim*, exist in manuscript. Some of his letters were published by M. Benayahu (see bibliography). Two of his sons, Abraham and Jacob, succeeded him after his death. His other two sons were JOSEPH and DAVID. Joseph had acted as his deputy during his wanderings; eventually he settled in Ereẓ Israel. He wrote halakhic rulings on *Jacob b. Asher's *Arba'ah Turim* and died in Hebron.

BIBLIOGRAPHY: Loewenstein, in: MGWJ, 48 (1904), 674–82; C. Roth, *Venice* (1930), 231–6; Sonne, in: *Ẓion*, 3 (1938), 145–52; Ya'ari, Sheluhei, 65, 277; Scholem, *Shabbatai Sevi* (1973), index; Benayahu, in: *Eretz Israel*, 3 (1954), 244–6 (Hebrew section); idem, in: *Sinai*, 34 (1953/54), 156–202; idem, in: *Yerushalayim*, 5 (1955), 136–86; idem, in: *Sefer Zikkaron ... Solomon Sally Mayer* (1956), 17–47 (Hebrew section); idem, *Dor Eḥad ba-Areẓ* (1988).

[Abraham David]

ABOAB DA FONSECA, ISAAC (1605–1693), Dutch Sephardi rabbi. Aboab was born in Castro Daire, Portugal, of a Marrano family, as Simao da Fonseca, son of Alvaro da Fonseca *alias* David Aboab. He was brought as a child to St. Jean de Luz in France and then to Amsterdam, where he was given a Jewish upbringing; he was considered the outstanding pupil of R. Isaac *Uzziel. At the age of 21, Aboab was appointed *ḥakham* of the congregation Bet Israel. After the three Sephardi congregations in Amsterdam amalgamated in 1639, he was retained by the united community as senior assistant to R. Saul Levi *Morteira. In 1641, following the Dutch conquests in *Brazil, Aboab joined the Amsterdam Jews who established a community at *Recife (Pernambuco) as their *ḥakham*, thus becoming the first American rabbi. He continued for 13 years as the spiritual mainstay of the community. After the repulse of the Portuguese attack on the city in 1646, Aboab composed a thanksgiving narrative hymn describing the past sufferings, *Zekher Asiti le-Nifla'ot El* ("I made record of the mighty deeds of God"), the first known Hebrew composition in the New World that has been preserved. He also wrote here his Hebrew grammar, *Melekhet ha-Dikduk*, still unpublished, and a treatise on the Thirteen Articles of Faith, now untraceable. After the Portuguese victory in 1654, Aboab and other Jews returned to Amsterdam. Morteira having recently died, Aboab was appointed *ḥakham* as well as teacher in the *talmud torah*, principal of the yeshivah, and member of the *bet din*; in this capacity he was one of the signatories of the ban of excommunication issued against *Spinoza in 1656. Aboab became celebrated as a preacher, and some of his sermons and eulogies have been published. The Jesuit Antonio de Vieira, comparing him with his contemporary *Manasseh b. Israel, observed that Aboab knew what he said whereas the other said what he knew. It was a pulpit address delivered by Aboab in 1671 which prompted the construction of the magnificent synagogue of the Sephardi community in Amsterdam; he preached the first sermon in the new building on its dedication four years later. Along with most of the Amsterdam community, Aboab was an ardent supporter of *Shabbetai Ẓevi, and was one of the signatories of a letter of allegiance addressed to him in 1666; he also published *Viddui* ("Confession of Sins," Amsterdam, 1666). Aboab translated from Spanish into Hebrew the works of the kabbalist Abraham Cohen de *Herrera, *Beit Elohim* and *Sha'ar ha-Shamayim* (Amsterdam, 1655). His novellae on tractate *Kiddushin* and a work on reward and punishment entitled *Nishmat Ḥayyim* have not been published. His most ambitious production was a rendering of the Pentateuch in Spanish together with a commentary (*Parafrasis Commentada sobre el Pentateucho*, Amsterdam, 1688). Aboab died at the age of 88 on April 4, 1693. The bereavement of their spiritual guide was so keenly felt by Amsterdam Jewry that for many years the name of Aboab and the date of his death were incorporated in the engraved border of all marriage contracts issued by the community. The breadth of Aboab's interests in non-Hebrew as well as Hebrew literature is illustrated in the sale catalogue of his library which appeared shortly after his death, one of the earliest known in Hebrew bibliography.

BIBLIOGRAPHY: Kayserling, Bibl, 4–5; idem, in: AJHSP, 5 (1897), 125ff.; I. Tishby (ed.), *Sefer Ẓiẓat Novel Ẓevi* (1954), index; Scholem, Shabbetai Ẓevi, index; A. Wiznitzer, *Jews in Colonial Brazil* (1960), index, s.v. *Fonseca, Isaac Aboab da*; idem, *Records of the Earliest Jewish Community in the New World* (1954), index; I.S. Emmanuel, in: AJA, 7 (1955), 24ff.; Silva Rosa, in: *Centraalblad voor Israelieten in Nederland*, 29 (1913); M. Narkiss, in: KS, 15 (1938/39), 489–90; A. Marx, *Studies in Jewish History and Booklore* (1944), 209–11; C. Roth, *Life of Menasseh ben Israel* (1934), index.

[Cecil Roth]

ABOMINATION. Three Hebrew words connote abomination: תּוֹעֵבָה (*to'evah*), שֶׁקֶץ (*shekeẓ, sheqeẓ*) or שִׁקּוּץ (*shikkuẓ, shiqquẓ*), and פִּגּוּל (*piggul*); *to'evah* is the most important of this group. It appears in the Bible 116 times as a noun and 23 times as a verb and has a wide variety of applications, ranging from food prohibitions (Deut. 14:3), idolatrous practices (Deut. 12:31; 13:15), and magic (Deut. 18:12) to sex offenses (Lev. 18:22ff.) and ethical wrongs (Deut. 25:14–16; Prov. 6:16–19). Common to all these usages is the notion of irregularity, that which offends the accepted order, ritual, or moral. It is incorrect to arrange the *to'evah* passages according to an evolutionary scheme and thereby hope to demonstrate that the term took on ethical connotations only in post-Exilic times. For in Proverbs, where the setting is exclusively ethical and universal but never ritual or national, *to'evah* occurs mainly in the oldest, i.e., pre-Exilic, passages of the book (18 times in ch. 10–29; 3 in the remaining chapter). Moreover, Ezekiel, who has no peer in ferreting out cultic sins, uses *to'evah* as a generic term for all aberrations detestable to God, including purely ethical offenses (e.g., 18:12, 13, 24). Indeed, there is evidence that *to'evah* originated not in the cult, and certainly not in prophecy, but in wisdom literature. This is shown not only by its clustering in the oldest levels of Proverbs but also in its earliest biblical occurrence where the expression *to'avat Miẓrayim* (Gen. 43:32; 46:34; Ex. 8:22, ascribed to the J source) refers to specific contraventions of ancient Egyptian norms. Furthermore, Egyptian has a precise equivalent to *to'evah*, and it occurs in similar contexts, e.g., "Thus arose the abomination of the swine for Horus' sake" (for a Canaanite-Phoenician parallel, note *t'bt 'štrt* – Tabnit of Sidon (third century B.C.E.) – in Pritchard, Texts, 505). Thus the sapiential background of the term in the ancient Near East is fully attested. True, *toʿevah* predominates in Deuteronomy (16 times) and Ezekiel (43 times), but both books are known to have borrowed terms from wisdom literature (cf. Deut. 25:13ff., and Prov. 11:1; 20:23) and transformed them to their ideological needs. The noun *sheqeẓ* is found in only four passages where it refers to tabooed animal flesh (e.g., Lev. 11:10–43). However, the verb שקץ, found seven times, is strictly a synonym of תעב (e.g., Deut. 7:26; the noun may also have had a similar range). *Shiqquẓ*, on the other hand, bears a very specific meaning: in each of its 28 occurrences it refers to illicit cult objects. *Piggul* is an even more precise, technical term denoting sacrificial flesh not eaten in the allotted time (Lev. 7:18; 19:7); though in nonlegal passages it seems to have a wider sense (Ezek. 4:14; cf. Isa. 65:4). According to the rabbis (Sifra 7:18, etc.) the flesh of a sacrifice was considered a *piggul* if the sacrificer, at the time of the sacrifice, had the intention of eating the flesh at a time later than the allotted time. Under these circumstances, the sacrifice was not considered accepted by God and even if the sacrificer ate of it in the alloted time he was still liable to the punishment of **karet,* i.e., the flesh was considered *piggul* by virtue of the intention of the sacrificer. This is an extension of the biblical text according to which he would be liable for punishment only if he ate it at the inappropriate time. The rabbis based their interpretation on the biblical passage "It shall not be acceptable" (Lev. 7:18). They reasoned: How could the Lord having already accepted the sacrifice then take back His acceptance after it was later eaten at the wrong time.

BIBLIOGRAPHY: Humbert, in: ZAW, 72 (1960), 217–37.

[Jacob Milgrom]

ABOMINATION OF DESOLATION, literal translation of the Greek Βδέλυγμα ἐρημηώσεως (I Macc. 1:54). This in turn, evidently goes back to a Hebrew or Aramaic expression similar to *shiqquẓ shomen* ("desolate," i.e., horrified – for "horrifying" – "abomination"; Dan. 12:11). Similar, but grammatically difficult, are *ha-shiqquẓ meshomem*, "a horrifying abomination," (disregard the Hebrew definite article?; *ibid.* 11:31); *shiqquẓim meshomem*, "a horrifying abomination", disregarding the ending of the noun? (*ibid.* 9:27); and *ha-peshaʿ shomem*, "the horrifving offense" (*ibid.* 8:13). According to the Maccabees passage, it was something which was constructed (a form of the verb οἰκοδομέω) on the altar (of the Jerusalem sanctuary), at the command of *Antiochus IV Epiphanes, on the 15th day of Kislev (i.e., some time in December) of the year 167 B.C.E.; according to the Daniel passages, it was something that was set (a form of *ntn*) there. It was therefore evidently a divine symbol of some sort (a statue or betyl [sacred stone]), and its designation in Daniel and Maccabees would then seem to be a deliberate cacophemism for its official designation. According to II Maccabees 6:2, Antiochus ordered that the Temple at Jerusalem be renamed for Zeus Olympios – "Olympian Zeus." Since Olympus, the abode of the gods, is equated with heaven, and Zeus with the Syrian god "Lord of Heaven" – Phoenician Bʿal Shamem, Aramaic Beʾel Shemain (see Bickerman) – it was actually Baal Shamem, "the Lord of Heaven," who was worshiped at the Jerusalem sanctuary during the persecution; and of this name, *Shomem*, best rendered "Horrifying Abomination," is a cacophemistic distortion.

BIBLIOGRAPHY: E. Bickerman, *Der Gott der Makkabaeer* (1937), 92–96.

[Harold Louis Ginsberg]

ABONY, town in Pest-Pilis-Solt-Kiskun county, Hungary, located southeast of Budapest. One Jew settled there in 1745; the census of 1767 mentions eight Jews. The Jewish population ranged from 233 in 1784 to 431 in 1930, reaching a peak of 912 in 1840. The Jewish community was organized in 1771 concurrently with the organization of a *Chevra Kadisha*. The community's first synagogue was built in 1775. The members of the community consisted of merchants, shopkeepers, artisans, peddlers and, starting in 1820, tenant farmers. From 1850 onward Jews were able to own land. A magnificent new synagogue was built in 1825 that was mentioned in a responsum by Moses *Sofer. A Jewish teacher was engaged for the community in 1788, and a Jewish school was opened in 1766 and moved to a separate building in 1855. In 1869 a Neolog community was established in town. It was in Abony that the Austro-Hungarian *kolel* of Jerusalem was established in 1863. Among the rabbis of Abony were Jacob Herczog (1837–57), author of *Pert Yaʿakov* (1830); Isaac (Ignác) *Kunstadt (1862–82), author of *Luʾah Eretz*, 1–2 (1886–87); Béla Vajda (1889–1901), author of a history of the local Jewish community; and Naphtali Blumgrund (1901–18). In April 1944, the Neolog community of 275 was led by Izsák Vadász.

According to the census of 1941, Abony had 315 Jewish inhabitants and 16 converts identified as Jews under the racial laws. Early in May 1944, the Jews were placed in a ghetto which also included the Jews from the following neighboring villages in Abony district: Jászkarajenö, Kocsér, Tószeg, Törtel, Újszász, and Zagyvarékas. After a few days, the Jews were transferred to the ghetto of Kecskemét, from where they were deported to Auschwitz in two transports on June 27 and 29. In 1946, Abony had a Jewish population of 56. Most of them left after the Communists took over in 1948 and especially after the Revolution of 1956. By 1959, their number was reduced to 19, and a few years later the community ceased to exist. The synagogue is preserved as a historic monument.

BIBLIOGRAPHY: B. Vajda, *A zsidók története Abonyban és vidékén* (1896). **ADD. BIBLIOGRAPHY:** Braham, Politics; *Zsido Lexikon* (1929), 3–4; PK Hungaryah, 127–28.

[Alexander Scheiber / Randolph Braham (2nd ed.)]

ABORTION. Abortion is defined as the artificial termination of a woman's pregnancy.

In the Biblical Period

A monetary penalty was imposed for causing abortion of a woman's fetus in the course of a quarrel, and the penalty of death if the woman's own death resulted therefrom. "And if men strive together, and hurt a woman with child, so that her fruit depart, and yet no harm follow – he shall be surely fined, according as the woman's husband shall lay upon him; and he shall pay as the judges determine. But if any harm follow – then thou shall give life for life" (Ex. 21:22–23). According to the Septuagint the term "harm" applied to the fetus and not to the woman, and a distinction is drawn between the abortion of a fetus which has not yet assumed complete shape – for which there is the monetary penalty – and the abortion of a fetus which has assumed complete shape – for which the penalty is "life for life." Philo (Spec., 3:108) specifically prescribes the imposition of the death penalty for causing an abortion, and the text is likewise construed in the Samaritan Targum and by a substantial number of Karaite commentators. A. *Geiger deduces from this the existence of an ancient law according to which (contrary to talmudic *halakhah*) the penalty for aborting a fetus of completed shape was death (*Ha-Mikra ve-Targumav*, 280–1, 343–4). The talmudic scholars, however, maintained that the word "harm" refers to the woman and not to the fetus, since the scriptural injunction, "He that smiteth a man so that he dieth, shall surely be put to death" (Ex. 21:12), did not apply to the killing of a fetus (Mekh. SbY, ed. Epstein-Melamed, 126; also Mekh. Mishpatim 8; Targ. Yer., Ex. 21:22–23; BK 42a). Similarly, Josephus states that a person who causes the abortion of a woman's fetus as a result of kicking her shall pay a fine for "diminishing the population," in addition to paying monetary compensation to the husband, and that such a person shall be put to death if the woman dies of the blow (Ant., 4:278). According to the laws of the ancient East (Sumer, Assyria, the Hittites), punishment for inflicting an aborting blow was monetary and sometimes even flagellation, but not death (except for one provision in Assyrian law concerning willful abortion, self-inflicted). In the Code of *Hammurapi (no. 209, 210) there is a parallel to the construction of the two quoted passages: "If a man strikes a woman [with child] causing her fruit to depart, he shall pay ten shekalim for her loss of child. If the woman should die, he who struck the blow shall be put to death."

In the Talmudic Period

In talmudic times, as in ancient *halakhah*, abortion was not considered a transgression unless the fetus was viable (*ben keyama*; Mekh. Mishpatim 4 and see Sanh. 84b and Nid. 44b; see Rashi; *ad loc.*), hence, even if an infant is only one day old, his killer is guilty of murder (Nid. 5:3). In the view of R. Ishmael, only a *Gentile, to whom some of the basic transgressions applied with greater stringency, incurred the death penalty for causing the loss of the fetus (Sanh. 57b). Thus abortion, although prohibited, does not constitute murder (Tos., Sanh. 59a; Ḥul. 33a). The scholars deduced the prohibition against abortion by an a fortiori argument from the laws concerning abstention from procreation, or onanism, or having sexual relations with one's wife when likely to harm the fetus in her womb – the perpetrator whereof being regarded as "a shedder of blood" (Yev. 62b; Nid. 13a and 31a; *Ḥavvat Ya'ir*, no. 31; *She'elat Yavez*, 1:43; *Mishpetei Uziel*, 3:46). This is apparently also the meaning of Josephus' statement that "the Law has commanded to raise all the children and prohibited women from aborting or destroying seed; a woman who does so shall be judged a murderess of children for she has caused a soul to be lost and the family of man to be diminished" (Apion, 2:202).

The Zohar explains that the basis of the prohibition against abortion is that "a person who kills the fetus in his wife's womb desecrates that which was built by the Holy One and His craftsmanship." Israel is praised because notwithstanding the decree, in Egypt, "every son that is born ye shall cast into the river" (Ex. 1:22), "there was found no single person to kill the fetus in the womb of the woman, much less after its birth. By virtue of this Israel went out of bondage" (Zohar, Ex., ed. Warsaw, 3b).

Abortion is permitted if the fetus endangers the mother's life. Thus, "if a woman travails to give birth [and it is feared she may die], one may sever the fetus from her womb and extract it, member by member, for her life takes precedence over his" (Oho. 7:6). This is the case only as long as the fetus has not emerged into the world, when it is not a life at all and "it may be killed and the mother saved" (Rashi and Meiri, Sanh. 72b). But, from the moment that the greater part of the fetus has emerged into the world – either its head only, or its greater part – it may not be touched, even if it endangers the mother's life: "*ein doḥin nefesh mi-penei nefesh*" ("one may not reject one life to save another" – Oho. and Sanh. *ibid.*). Even though one is enjoined to save a person who is being pursued, if necessary by killing the pursuer (see *Penal Law), the law distinguishes between a fetus which has emerged into the world and a "pursuer," since "she [the mother] is pursued from heaven" (Sanh. 72b) and moreover, "such is the way of the world" (Maim., Yad, Roẓe'aḥ 1:9) and "one does not know whether the fetus is pursuing the mother, or the mother the fetus" (TJ Sanh. 8:9, 26c). However, when the mother's life is endangered, she herself may destroy the fetus – even if its greater part has emerged – "for even if in the eyes of others the law of a fetus is not as the law of a pursuer, the mother may yet regard the fetus as pursuing her" (Meiri, *ibid.*).

Contrary to the rule that a person is always fully liable for damage (*mu'ad le-olam*), whether inadvertently or willfully caused (BK 2:6, see *Penal Law, Torts), it was determined with regard to damage caused by abortion, that "he who with the leave of the *bet din* and does injury – is absolved if he does so inadvertently, but is liable if he does so willfully – this being for the good order of the world" (Tosef., Git. 4:7), for "if we do not absolve those who have acted inadvertently, they will refrain from carrying out the abortion and saving the mother" (*Tashbez*, pt. 3, no. 82; Minḥat Bik., Tosef., Git. 4:7).

In the Codes

Some authorities permit abortion only when there is danger to the life of the mother deriving from the fetus "because it is pursuing to kill her" (Maim. *loc. cit.*; Sh. Ar., ḤM 425:2), but permission to "abort the fetus which has not emerged into the world should not be facilitated [in order] to save [the mother] from illness deriving from an inflammation not connected with the pregnancy, or a poisonous fever … in these cases the fetus is not [per se] the cause of her illness" (*Paḥad Yiẓḥak*, s.v. *Nefalim*). Contrary to these opinions, the majority of the later authorities (*aḥaronim*) maintain that abortion should be permitted if it is necessary for the recuperation of the mother, even if there is no mortal danger attaching to the pregnancy and even if the mother's illness has not been directly caused by the fetus (Maharit, Resp. no. 99). Jacob *Emden permitted abortion "as long as the fetus has not emerged from the womb, even if not in order to save the mother's life, but only to save her from the harassment and great pain which the fetus causes her" (*She'elat Yaveẓ*, 1:43). A similar view was adopted by Benzion Meir Ḥai *Ouziel, namely that abortion is prohibited if merely intended for its own sake, but permitted "if intended to serve the mother's needs … even if not vital"; and who accordingly decided that abortion was permissible to save the mother from the deafness which would result, according to medical opinion, from her continued pregnancy (*Mishpetei Uziel, loc. cit.*). In the Kovno ghetto, at the time of the Holocaust, the Germans decreed that every Jewish woman falling pregnant shall be killed together with her fetus. As a result, in 1942 Rabbi Ephraim Oshry decided that an abortion was permissible in order to save a pregnant woman from the consequences of the decree (*Mi-Ma'amakim*, no. 20).

The permissibility of abortion has also been discussed in relation to a pregnancy resulting from a prohibited (i.e., adulterous) union (see *Ḥavvat Ya'ir, ibid.*). Jacob Emden permitted abortion to a married woman made pregnant through her adultery, since the offspring would be a *mamzer* (see **Mamzer*), but not to an unmarried woman who becomes pregnant, since the taint of bastardy does not attach to her offspring (*She'elat Yaveẓ, loc. cit.*, s.v. *Yuḥasin*). In a later responsum it was decided that abortion was prohibited even in the former case (*Leḥem ha-Panim*, last *Kunteres*, no. 19), but this decision was reversed by Ouziel, in deciding that in the case of bastardous offspring abortion was permissible at the hands of the mother herself (*Mishpetei Uziel*, 3, no. 47).

In recent years the question of the permissibility of an abortion has also been raised in cases where there is the fear that birth may be given to a child suffering from a mental or physical defect because of an illness, such as rubeola or measles, contracted by the mother or due to the aftereffects of drugs, such as thalidomide, taken by her. The general tendency is to uphold the prohibition against abortion in such cases, unless justified in the interests of the mother's health, which factor has, however, been deemed to extend to profound emotional or mental disturbance (see: Unterman, Zweig, in bibliography). An important factor in deciding whether or not an abortion should be permitted is the stage of the pregnancy: the shorter this period, the stronger are the considerations in favor of permitting abortion (*Ḥavvat Ya'ir* and *She'elat Yaveẓ, loc. cit.*; *Beit Shelomo*, ḤM 132).

Contemporary Authorities

Contemporary halakhic authorities adopted a strict approach towards the problem of abortion. R. Isser Yehuda *Unterman defined the abortion of a fetus as "tantamount to murder," subject to a biblical prohibition. R. Moses *Feinstein adopted a particularly strict approach. In his view, abortion would only be permitted if the doctors determined that there was a high probability that the mother would die were the pregnancy to be continued. Where the mother's life is not endangered, but the abortion is required for reasons of her health, or where the fetus suffers from Tay-Sachs disease, or Down's syndrome, abortion is prohibited, the prohibition being equal in severity to the prohibition of homicide. This is the case even if bringing the child into the world will cause intense suffering and distress, to both the newborn and his parents. According to R. Feinstein, the prohibition on abortion also applies where the pregnancy was the result of forbidden sexual relations, which would result in the birth of a *mamzer*.

Other halakhic authorities – foremost among them R. Eliezer *Waldenberg – continued the line of the accepted halakhic position whereby the killing of a fetus did not constitute homicide, being a prohibition by virtue of the reasons mentioned above. Moreover, according to the majority of authorities, the prohibition was of rabbinic origin. In the case of a fetus suffering from Tay-Sachs disease R. Waldenberg ruled: "it is permissible … to perform an abortion, even until the seventh month of her pregnancy, immediately upon its becoming absolutely clear that such a child will be born thus." In his ruling he relies inter alia on the responsa of *Maharit* (R. Joseph *Trani) and *She'elat Ya'veẓ* (R. Jacob *Emden), who permit abortion "even if not in order to save the mother's life, but only to save her from the harassment and the great pain that the fetus causes her" (see above). R. Waldenberg adds: "… Consequently, if there is a case in which the *halakhah* would permit abortion for a great need and in order to alleviate pain and distress, this would appear to be a classic one. Whether the suffering is physical or mental is irrelevant, since in many instances mental suffering is greater and more painful than physical distress" (*Ẓiẓ Eliezer*, 13:102). He also permitted the abortion of a fetus suffering from Down's syndrome. Quite frequently, however, the condition of such a child is far better than that of the child suffering from Tay-Sachs, both in terms of his chances of survival and in terms of his physical and mental condition. Accordingly, "From this [i.e., the general license in the case of Tay-Sachs disease] one cannot establish an explicit and general license to conduct an abortion upon discovering a case of Down's syndrome … until the facts pertaining to the results of the examination are known, and the rabbi deciding the case has thoroughly examined the mental condition of the couple" (*ibid.*, 14:101).

In the dispute between Rabbis Feinstein and Waldenberg relating to Maharit's responsum, which contradicts his own conclusion, R. Feinstein writes: "This responsum is to be ignored ... for it is undoubtedly a forgery compiled by an errant disciple and ascribed to him" (p. 466); and regarding the responsum of R. Jacob Emden, which also contradicts his own conclusion, he claims that "... the argument lacks any cogency, even if it was written by as great a person as the *Ya'veẓ*" (p. 468). In concluding his responsum, R. Feinstein writes of "the need to rule strictly in light of the great laxity [in these matters] in the world and in Israel." Indeed, this position is both acceptable and common in the *halakhah*, but in similar cases the tendency has not been to reject the views of earlier authorities, or to rule that they were forged, but rather to rule stringently, beyond the letter of the law, due to the needs of the hour (see Waldenberg, *ibid.*, 14:6).

In the State of Israel

Abortion and attempted abortion were prohibited in the Criminal Law Ordinance of 1936 (based on English law), on pain of imprisonment (sec. 175). An amendment in 1966 to the above ordinance relieved the mother of criminal responsibility for a self-inflicted abortion, formerly also punishable (sec. 176). In this context, causing the death of a person in an attempt to perform an illegal abortion constituted manslaughter, for which the maximum penalty is life imprisonment. An abortion performed in good faith and in order to save the mother's life, or to prevent her suffering serious physical or mental injury, was not a punishable offense. Terms such as "endangerment of life" and "grievous harm or injury" were given a wide and liberal interpretation, even by the prosecution in considering whether or not to put offenders on trial.

The Penal Law Amendment (Termination of Pregnancy) 5737–1977 provided, inter alia, that "a gynecologist shall not bear criminal responsibility for interrupting a woman's pregnancy if the abortion was performed at a recognized medical institution and if, after having obtained the woman's informed consent, advance approval was given by a committee consisting of three members, two of whom are doctors (one of them an expert in gynecology), and the third a social worker." The law enumerates five cases in which the committee is permitted to approve an abortion: (1) the woman is under legally marriageable age (17 years old) or over 40; (2) the pregnancy is the result of prohibited relations or relations outside the framework of marriage; (3) the child is likely to have a physical or a mental defect; (4) continuance of the pregnancy is likely to endanger the woman's life or cause her physical or mental harm; (5) continuance of the pregnancy is likely to cause grave harm to the woman or her children owing to difficult family or social circumstances in which she finds herself and which prevail in her environment (§316). The fifth consideration was the subject of sharp controversy and was rejected inter alia by religious circles. They claimed that the cases in which abortion is halakhically permitted – even according to the most lenient authorities – are all included in the first four reasons. In the Penal Law Amendment adopted by the Knesset in December 1979, the fifth reason was revoked.

The Israeli Supreme Court has also dealt with the question of the husband's legal standing in an application for an abortion filed by his wife; that is, is the committee obliged to allow the husband to present his position regarding his wife's application? The opinions in the judgment were divided. The majority view (Justices Shamgar, Ben-Ito) was that the committee is under no obligation to hear the husband, although it is permitted to do so. According to the minority view (Justice Elon), the husband has the right to present his claims to the committee (other than in exceptional cases, e.g., where the husband is intoxicated and unable to participate in a balanced and intelligent consultation, or where the urgency of the matter precludes summoning the husband). According to this view, the husband's right to be heard by the committee is based on the rules of natural justice, that find expression in the rabbinic dictum: "There are three partners in a person: The Holy One blessed be He, his father and his mother" (Kid. 30b; Nid. 31a; C.A. 413/80 *Anon. v. Anon.*, P.D. 35 [3] 57). Elon further added (p. 89): "It is well known that in Jewish law no 'material' right of any kind was ever conferred upon the parents, even with respect to their own child who had already been born. The parents relation to their natural offspring is akin to a natural bond, and in describing this relationship, notions of legal ownership are both inadequate and offensive" (C.A. 488/97 *Anon. et al. v. Attorney General*, 32 (3), p. 429–30). This partnership is based on the deep and natural involvement of the parents in the fate of the fetus who is the fruit of their loins, and exists even where the parents are not married, and *a fortiori* is present when the parents are a married couple building their home and family. When the question of termination of a pregnancy arises, each of the two parents has a basic right – grounded in natural and elementary justice – to be heard and to express his or her feelings, prior to the adoption of any decision regarding the termination of the pregnancy and the destruction of the fetus.

BIBLIOGRAPHY: J. D. Bleich, *Judaism and Killing* (1981), 96–102; M. Elon, *Jewish Law (Mishpat Ivri): Cases and Materials* (Matthew Bender Casebook Series, 1999), 609–24; J.D. Bleich, "Abortion in Halakhic Literature," in: *Tradition*, 10:2 (1968), 72–120; E.G. Ellinson, "*Ha-Ubar be-Halakhah*," in: *Sinai*, 66 (1970); M. Feinstein, "*Be-Din Harigat Ubar,*" in: *Sefer Zikharon le-Grych Yehezkel Abramsky* (1975); D. Feldman, *Birth Control in Jewish Law* (1968). **ADD. BIBLIOGRAPHY:** D. Frimer, "*Ma'amad shel ha-Av be-Hapalat ha-Ubar be-Mishpat ha-Ivri,*" in: *Gevurot le-Elon* (2005); A. Lichtenstein, *Nispaḥ le-Doḥ ha-Ve'adah al Hapalot Melakhutiot* (1974); D. Maeir, "Abortion and Halakhah: New Issues," in: *Dinei Yisrael*, 7 (1970), 137–150, Eng. section; C. Shalev, "A Man's Right to be Equal: The Abortion Issue," in: *Israel Law Review*, 18 (1983); D. Sinclair, "The Legal Basis for the Prohibition on Abortion in Jewish Law (with Some Comparative References to Canon, Common and Israeli Law)," in: *Shenaton ha-Mishpat ha-Ivri*, 5 (1978), 177–218; idem, *Jewish Biomedical law* (2003), 12–61; A. Steinberg, *Hilkhot Rofim ve-Refu'ah* (1978); I.Y. Unterman, "*Be-Inyan Piku'aḥ Nefesh shel Ubar,*" in: *No'am*, 6 (1963); E.Y. Waldenberg, *Ẓiẓ Eliezer* (1959), 1:14; I. Warhaftig, "*Av u-Veno,*" in *Meḥkarei Mishpat*, 16 (2000), 479ff.; M. Weinfeld, "The Genuine Jewish Attitude Toward Abortion," in: *Zion*, 42 (1977), 129–42, Heb.

[Menachem Elon]

ABRABANEL, family in Italy. After the expulsion of the Jews from Spain, the three brothers, Isaac, Jacob, and Joseph, founders of the Italian family, settled in the kingdom of Naples. The family tree shows the relationships of the Italian Abrabanels. Because of their considerable wealth and capabilities the Abrabanel brothers reached a position of some power both in relation to the Naples authorities and their coreligionists. ISAAC was a financier, philosopher, and exegete; JACOB led the Jewish community in Naples; and JOSEPH dealt in grain and foodstuffs. All three were included among the 200 families exempted by the Spaniards when they expelled the Jews from the kingdom of Naples in 1511. Isaac had three sons, JUDAH (better known as the philosopher Leone Ebreo); JOSEPH, a noted physician who lived first in southern Italy where he treated the famous Spanish general Gonsalvo de Cordoba, then moved to Venice, and later to Ferrara where he died; and SAMUEL, who married his cousin BENVENIDA (See *Abrabanel, Benvenida), a woman of such talent that the Spanish viceroy in Naples, Don Pedro of Toledo, is said to have chosen her to teach his daughter Eleonora. Samuel, who commanded a capital of about 200,000 ducats, was such an able financier that Don Pedro used to seek his advice. When his father-in-law Jacob died, Samuel succeeded him as leader of the Naples community. In 1533, when Don Pedro issued a new edict expelling the Neapolitan Jews, Samuel managed to have the order suspended. However, his efforts were unavailing when the viceroy renewed the edict in 1540, and in the next year all the remaining Jews were compelled to leave the kingdom of Naples. Samuel now moved to Ferrara where he enjoyed the favor of the duke until his death. Benvenida continued her husband's loan-banking business with the support of her pupil Eleonora, now duchess of Tuscany, and extended it to Tuscany. To lighten her burden she took her sons JACOB and JUDAH and ISAAC, Samuel's natural son, into the management of the widespread business. Three years after Samuel's death in 1547, a struggle broke out over the inheritance among the three sons: Jacob and Judah (the recognized sons of Samuel and Benvenida) on the one hand and Isaac (the natural son) on the other. The struggle, which dealt with the legal validity of Samuel's will, involved some of the period's most famous rabbis: R. Meir b. Isaac Katzenellenbogen (Maharam), R. Jacob b. Azriel Diena of Reggio, R. Jacob Israel b. Finzi of Recanati, R. Samuel de Medina, R. Joseph b. David Ibn Lev, and R. Samuel b. Moses Kalai. The conflict was settled apparently by Maharam's arbitration in 1551. One of Benvenida's sons-in-law who became a partner in her business was JACOB, later private banker of Cosimo de' Medici, and his financial representative at Ferrara. Following Jacob's advice, Duke Cosimo invited Jews from the Levant to settle in Tuscany in 1551 to promote trade with the Near East, granting them favorable conditions. Members of the family living in Italy, especially Venice, after this period, Abraham (d. 1618), Joseph (d. 1603), and Veleida (d. 1616), were presumably descended from the Ferrara branch.

BIBLIOGRAPHY: Margulies, in: RI, 3 (1906), 97–107, 147–54; N. Ferorelli, *Gli Ebrei nell'Italia meridionale* (1915), 87–90 and passim; Baer, Spain, 2 (1966), 318, 433, 437; U. Cassuto, *Gli Ebrei a Firenze* (1918), passim; A. Marx, *Studies in Jewish History and Booklore* (1944), index; A. Berliner, *Luḥot Avanim* (1881), index; B. Polacco, in: *Annuariodi Studi Ebraici*, 3 (1963/64), 53–63. **ADD. BIBLIOGRAPHY:** C. Gebhardt, "Regesten zur Lebensgeschichte Leone Ebreo," in: *Leone Ebreo* (1929), 1–66; V. Bonazzoli, "Gli ebrei del Regno di Napoli all'epoca della loro espulsione," in: *Archivio Storico Italiano* 502 (1979), 495–559; 508 (1981), 179–287; C. Colafemmina, *Documenti per la storia degli ebrei in Puglia nell'Archivio di Stato di Napoli* (1990), 206–7, 212, 237, 277–78, 308, 311; H. Tirosh-Rotshschild, *Between Worlds: The Life and Thought of Rabbi ben Judah Messer Leon* (1991), 24–33, 52–54; D. Malkiel, "Jews and Wills in Renaissance Italy: A Case Study in the Jewish-Christian Cultural Encounter," in: *Italia* (1996), 7–69; A. Leone Leoni, "Nuove notize sugli Abravanel," in: *Zakhor*, 1 (1997), 153–206; F. Patroni Griffi, "Documenti inediti sulle attività economiche degli Abravanel in Italia meridionale (1492–1543)," in: *Rassegna Mensile di Israel* (1997), 27–38; R. Segre, "Sephardic Refugees in Ferrara: Two Notable Families," in: B.R. Gampel (ed.), *Crisis and Creativity in the Sephardic World 1391–1648* (1997), 164–85; G. Lacerenza, "Lo spazio dell'Ebreo Insediamenti e cultura ebraica a Napoli (secoli XV–XVI)," in: *Integrazione ed Emarginazione* (2002), 357–427.

[Attilio Milano / Cedric Cohen Skalli (2nd ed.)]

ABRABANEL, ABRAVANEL (Heb. אַבְּרַבַּנְאֵל; inaccurately **Abarbanel**; before 1492 also **Abravaniel** and **Brabanel**), Sephardi family name. The name is apparently a diminutive of Abravan, a form of Abraham not unusual in Spain, where the "h" sound was commonly rendered by "f" or "v." The family, first mentioned about 1300, attained distinction in Spain in the 15th century. After 1492, Spanish exiles brought the name to Italy, North Africa, and Turkey. Members of the family who were baptized in Portugal at the time of the Forced Conversion of 1497 preserved the name in secret and revived it in the 17th century in the Sephardi communities of Amsterdam, London, and the New World. The family was also found in Poland and southern Russia. Of recent years Sephardi immigrants from the eastern Mediterranean area have reintroduced it into western countries. It is also common in Israel.

The first of the family who rose to eminence was JUDAH ABRABANEL of Córdoba (later of Seville), treasurer and tax-collector under Sancho IV (1284–95) and Ferdinand IV (1295–1312). In 1310 he and other Jews guaranteed the loans made to the crown of Castile to finance the siege of Algeciras. It is probable that he was *almoxarife* ("collector of revenues") of Castile. Another eminent member of the family was SAMUEL of Seville, of whom Menahem b. Zerah wrote that he was "intelligent, loved wise men, befriended them, was good to them and was eager to study whenever the stress of time permitted." He had great influence at the court of Castile. In 1388 he served as royal treasurer in Andalusia. During the anti-Jewish riots of 1391 he was converted to Christianity under the name of Juan Sanchez (de Sevilla) and was appointed comptroller in Castile. It is thought that a passage in a poem in the *Cancionero de Baena*, attributed to Alfonso Alvarez de

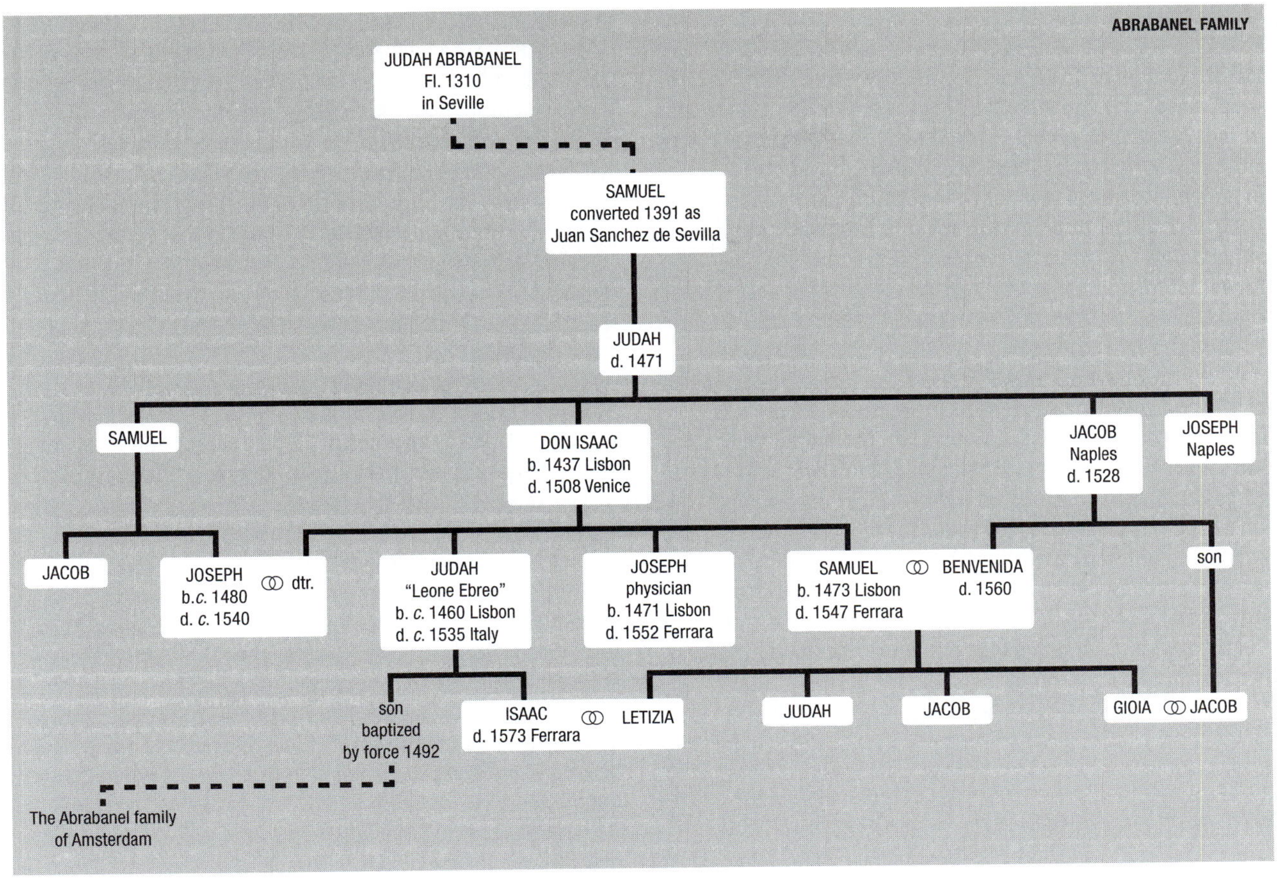

Villasandino, refers to him. He and his family apparently later fled to Portugal, where they reverted to Judaism and filled important governmental posts. His son, JUDAH (d. 1471), was in the financial service of the infante Ferdinand of Portugal, who by his will (1437) ordered the repayment to him of the vast sum of 506,000 reis blancs. Later he was apparently in the service of the duke of Braganza. His export business also brought him into trade relations with Flanders. He was father of Don Isaac *Abrabanel and grandfather of Judah *Abrabanel (Leone Ebreo) and Samuel *Abrabanel.

BIBLIOGRAPHY: M. Kayserling, *Geschichte der Juden in Portugal* (1867), 74ff.; D.S. Blondheim, in: *Mélanges… M. Alfred Jeanroy* (1928), 71–74; C. Roth, *Menasseh ben Israel* (1934), index; B. Netanyahu, *Don Isaac Abravanel* (Eng., 1968²); Baer, Spain, index; J.A. de Baena, *Cancionero…* ed. by J.M. Azaceta (1966), 127. **ADD. BIBLIOGRAPHY:** M.M. Kellner, in: *Journal of Medieval and Renaissance Studies* 6 (1976), 269–96; M.A. Rodrigues, in: *Biblos* (Coimbra), 57 (1981), 527–95; M. Idel, in: M. Dorman and Z. Harvey (ed.), *Filosofyat ha-Ahavah shel Yehudah Abravanel*, (1985), 73–114; M. Awerbuch, *Zwischen Hoffnung und Vernunft*. (1985); S. Regev, in: *Asupot*, 1 (1987), 169–87; C. Alonso Fontela, in: *Sefarad*, 47 (1987), 227–43; G. Weiler, *Jewish Theocracy*, (1988), 69–85; A. Gross, in: *Michael*, 11 (1989), 23–36 (Heb. section); A. Ravitzky, in: L. Landman (ed.), *Scholars and Scholarship* (1990), 67–90; A. Dines, *O Baú de Abravanel* (1992); E. Lipiner, *Two Portuguese Exiles in Castile* (1997).

[Cecil Roth]

ABRABANEL, BENVENIDA (also known as **Benvegnita**, **Bienvenita**; c. 1473–after 1560), one of the most influential and wealthiest Jewish women of early modern Italy. Benvenida was the daughter of Jacob Abrabanel (d. 1528), one of three brothers of Isaac *Abrabanel (1437–1508). She married Isaac's youngest son, Samuel (1473–1547), bringing a very large dowry. By 1492, Benvenida and much of the family had settled in Naples, where her father and then her husband led the Jewish community. Benvenida appears to have raised six children of her own along with an illegitimate son of Samuel's. One of her adult daughters lived in Lisbon, apparently as a Crypto-Jew, and was known for her charity and piety. Eleanora de Toledo (1522–1562), the second daughter of Pedro de Toledo, who became Viceroy of the Spanish rulers of Naples in 1532, was also raised in Benvenida's house. Benvenida was renowned for her religious observance and her generosity; she fasted daily and ransomed at least a thousand captives. In 1524–25, Benvenida became an enthusiastic supporter of the messianic pretender David *Reuveni (d. 1538); she sent him money three times, as well as an ancient silk banner with the Ten Commandments written in gold on both sides, and a Turkish gown of gold. In 1533, Benvenida and several Neapolitan princesses successfully petitioned Emperor Charles v to delay the expulsion of the Jews of Naples for ten years. The Abrabanels left Naples in 1541 when Jews were required to wear a badge, and ultimately settled in Ferrara, a major Sephardi refuge. Doña Gracia (*Nasi) Mendes (c. 1510–1569) settled in Ferrara in 1548; although it is not known if the two women ever met, the interests of their families did not always coincide. In 1555–56, when Doña Gracia attempted to persuade Ottoman Jewish merchants to boycott the papal port of Ancona, the Abrabanel family, particularly Benvenida's son Jacob, took the side of Ancona. Samuel Abrabanel died in 1547 leaving a will filed with and witnessed by Christians in which Benvenida was made general heir to all his movable and immovable property. Samuel's illegitimate son challenged the will on the rabbinic grounds that a woman cannot inherit; from 1550 to 1551, this became a major dispute among the rabbis of Italy and Turkey. Despite this controversy, Benvenida took over Samuel's business affairs, receiving permission from the Florentine authorities to open five banking establishments in Tuscany with her two sons, Jacob and Judah. Later she quarreled with Judah over his marriage and cut him off completely in 1553. Although Benvenida wielded great power, she herself left very few words in the historical record. Beyond a defense of women receiving gifts attributed to her, one folk remedy in her name is found in a British Library manuscript.

BIBLIOGRAPHY: D. Malkiel, "Jews and Wills in Renaissance Italy: A Case Study in the Jewish-Christian Cultural Encounter," in: *Italia*, 12 (1996), 7–69; R. Segre, "Sephardic Refugees in Ferrara: Two Notable Families," in: B.R. Gampel (ed.), *Crisis and Creativity in the Sephardic World, 1391–1649* (1997), 164–85, 327–36.

[Howard Tzvi Adelman (2nd ed.)]

ABRABANEL, ISAAC BEN JUDAH (1437–1508), statesman, biblical exegete, and theologian. Offshoot of a distinguished Ibero-Jewish family, Abrabanel (the family name also appears as **Abravanel**, **Abarbanel**, **Bravanel**, etc.) spent 45 years in Portugal, then passed the nine years immediately prior to Spanish Jewry's 1492 expulsion in Castile. At that time an important figure at the court of Ferdinand and Isabella, he chose Italian exile over conversion to Christianity. He spent his remaining years in various centers in Italy where he composed most of his diverse literary corpus, a combination of prodigious biblical commentaries and involved theological tomes.

Like his father Judah, Abrabanel engaged successfully in both commerce and state finance while in Lisbon. After his father died he succeeded him as a leading financier at the court of King Alfonso v of Portugal. His importance at court was not restricted to his official sphere of activities. Of a loan to the state of 12,000,000 reals raised from both Jews and Christians in 1480, more than one-tenth was contributed by Abrabanel himself. When in 1471, 250 Jewish captives were brought to Portugal after the capture of Arcila and Tangier in North Africa by Alfonso v, Abrabanel was among those who headed the committee which was formed in Lisbon to raise the ransom money.

Abrabanel launched his literary career in Lisbon as well. In addition to a short philosophic essay entitled "The Forms of the Elements" (*Ẓurot ha-Yesodot*), he wrote his first work of biblical exegesis, a commentary on a challenging section in the Book of Exodus (*Ateret Zekenim* ("Crown of the Elders")), and began a commentary on the Book of Deuteronomy (*Mirkevet ha-Mishneh* ("Second Chariot")) as well as a work on prophecy (*Maḥazeh Shaddai* ("Vision of the Almighty")). He was also in touch with cultured Christian circles. His connections with members of the aristocracy were not founded only on business but also on the affinity of humanism. His letter of condolence to the count of Faro on the death of the latter's father, written in Portuguese, provides a striking example of this relationship.

The period of tranquillity in Lisbon ended with the death of Alfonso v in 1481. His heir, João II (1481–1495), was determined to deprive the nobility of their power and to establish a centralized regime. The nobles, led by the king's brother-in-law, the duke of Bragança, and the count of Faro, rebelled against him, but the insurrection failed. Abrabanel was also suspected of conspiracy and forced to escape (1483). Although denying guilt, he was sentenced to death *in absentia* (1485). He evidently managed to transfer a substantial part of his fortune to Castile, and stayed there for a while in the little town of Segura de la Orden near the Portuguese border. Thereafter, Abrabanel quickly established himself as a leading financier and royal servant. By 1485, he had relocated to the Spanish heartland at Alcalá de Henares in order to oversee tax-farming operations for Cardinal Pedro González de Mendoza, the "third king of Spain." The initial total involved was the vast sum of 6,400,000 maravedis, with Abrabanel earning 118,500 maravedis per year as commission. As collateral he put up, without restriction, all that he owned. Abrabanel also supported the campaign of Ferdinand and Isabella against Granada, Islam's last Iberian citadel, offering extensive loans.

Ferdinand's and Isabella's signing of an order of expulsion against Jews in Spain and her possessions took Abrabanel by surprise. After the edict of expulsion had been signed, on March 31, 1492, Abrabanel was among those who tried in vain to obtain its revocation. Abrabanel relinquished his claim to certain sums of money which he had advanced to Ferdinand and Isabella against tax-farming revenues, which he had not yet managed to recover. In return he was allowed to take 1000 gold ducats and various gold and silver valuables out of the country with him (May 31, 1492).

Though occupied with worldly affairs, Abrabanel continued to pursue scholarship and produce works in Spain. Most notably, he composed commentaries on Joshua, Judges, and Samuel soon after arriving in Castile. Among other things, these commentaries attest to Abrabanel's novel approaches to questions concerning the authorship and origins of biblical books, some of which imply the impress of a humanist sense of historicity on his exegesis. Seen from this vantage-point, these commentaries offer perhaps the earliest example of Renaissance stimulus in works of Hebrew literature composed beyond Italy.

After the 1492 expulsion, Abrabanel passed two years

in Naples. Here he completed his commentary on Kings (fall 1493). But he was again prevented from devoting his time to study for long, eventually coming to serve in the court of Alfonso II. Abrabanel tells of wealth recouped in Italy and renewed fame "akin to that of all of the magnates in the land." Abrabanel's fortunes turned again, however, when the French sacked Naples (1494). His library was destroyed. Before departing Naples, Abrabanel managed to complete a work on dogma (*Rosh Amanah* ("Principles of Faith")) structured around Maimonides' enumeration of 13 foundational principles of Judaism. Abrabanel now followed the royal family to Messina, remaining there until 1495. Subsequently he removed to Corfu where he began his commentaries on Isaiah and the Minor Prophets (summer 1495) and then to Monopoli (Apulia), where early in 1496 he completed the commentary on Deuteronomy which he had begun in Lisbon, as well as his commentaries on the Passover *Haggadah* (*Zevaḥ Pesaḥ*), and on *Avot* (*Naḥalat Avot*). Of the same period are his works expressing the hopes for redemption which at times explain contemporary events as messianic tribulations – *Ma'yenei Yeshu'ah, Yeshu'ot Meshiḥo*, and *Mashmi'a Yeshu'ah*. Two other works addressed the problem of the world's createdness, *Shamayim Ḥadashim* ("New Heavens") and *Mifalot Elohim* ("Wonders of the Lord"). In 1503, Abrabanel settled at last in Venice. He was engaged in negotiations between the Venetian senate and the kingdom of Portugal in that year, for a commercial treaty to regulate the spice trade. He now finished commentaries on Jeremiah and Ezekiel, Genesis and Exodus, and Leviticus and Numbers. In a reply to an enquiry from Saul ha-Kohen of Candia, he mentions that he was engaged in composing his book *Ẓedek Olamim*, on recompense and punishment, and *Lahakat ha-Nevi'im*, on prophecy (a new version of *Maḥazeh Shaddai* which had been lost in Naples), and in completing his commentary on Maimonides' *Guide of the Perplexed*. Abrabanel died in Venice and was buried in Padua. Owing to the destruction of the Jewish cemetery there during the wars in 1509, his grave is unknown.

[Zvi Avneri / Eric Lawee (2nd ed.)]

Abrabanel as Biblical Exegete

Though Abrabanel's writings traverse many fields, they mainly comprise works of scriptural interpretation. It was in his role as a biblical interpreter that Abrabanel was most emphatic about his originality as a writer.

In his general prologue to his commentaries on the Former Prophets, Abrabanel spelled out some of his main procedures and aims as an interpreter of Scripture. To ease the task of explaining biblical narratives, Abrabanel would "divide each of the books into pericopes." These would be smaller than the units devised by his 14th century Jewish predecessor, Gersonides, but larger than the ones fashioned by "the scholar Jerome, who translated Holy Writ for the Christians." Before explaining a pericope, he would raise questions or "doubts" about it. Overall, Abrabanel's interpretive aim was twofold: explanation of the verses "in the most satisfactory way possible" and exploration of "the conceptual problems embedded therein to their very end." In short, he would explore both Scripture's exegetical and doctrinal-theological dimensions. Abrabanel warns that such interpretation yields lengthy commentary. In his commentary on the Pentateuch these questions have no fixed number, sometimes amounting to over 40, but in his commentary to the Prophets he limits himself to six. Despite the marked artificiality of this method, Abrabanel states that he chose it as a means of initiating discussion and encouraging investigation.

Abrabanel's exegesis combines a quest for Scripture's contextual sense (*peshat*) with other levels of interpretation. His repeated and emphatic statements about the primacy of *peshat* notwithstanding, Abrabanel incorporates midrashim into his commentaries often and occasionally digresses into detailed explanations of them. At the same time, he says that he describes Rashi's overindulgence in midrashic interpretation as "evil and bitter." Like some *geonim* and Spanish interpreters before him, Abrabanel distinguishes rabbinic dicta that reflect a "received tradition," which he says are indubitably true and hence binding, from midrashim that reflect fallible human reasoning. The latter can be rejected. Abrabanel's criticisms of individual midrashim can be unusually blunt ("very unlikely," "evidently weak," and so forth) even as Abrabanel often uses Midrash as a vehicle to extract maximal insight and meaning from the biblical word.

Abrabanel's commentaries evince a dialogue with a wide variety of earlier commentators. The predecessor who most shaped his exegetical program was *Naḥmanides. Like this earlier Spanish scholar, Abrabanel devotes considerable attention to questions of scripture's literary structure and argues for the biblical text's chronological sequentiality wherever possible.

Abrabanel was ambivalent about philosophically oriented biblical interpretation as practiced by Maimonides and his rationalist successors. He vehemently fought the extreme rationalism of philosophical interpretation (for example in Joshua 10, Second Excursus) as well as interpretations based on philosophical allegory. At the same time he himself had recourse, especially in his commentary on the Pentateuch, to numerous interpretations based on philosophy, as when he interprets the paradise story. Abrabanel refers to kabbalistic interpretation only rarely.

At times, he points to errors and moral failings in the heroes of the Bible. For example, he criticizes certain actions of David and Solomon and points out some stylistic and linguistic defects of Jeremiah and Ezekiel.

Among the innovations in Abrabanel's exegesis are the following:

(1) His comparison of the social structure of society in biblical times with that of the European society in his day (for example, in dealing with the institution of monarchy, 1 Samuel 8). He had wide recourse to historical interpretation, particularly in his commentaries to the Major and Minor Prophets and to the Book of Daniel.

(2) Preoccupation with Christian exegesis. He disputed christological interpretations, but he did not hesitate to borrow from Christian writers when their interpretation seemed correct to him.

(3) His introductions to the books of the prophets, which are much more comprehensive than those of his predecessors. In them he deals with the content of the books, the division of the material, their authors and the time of their compilation, and also draws comparisons between the method and style of the various prophets. His investigations at once reflect the spirit of medieval scholasticism and incipient Renaissance humanism.

Abrabanel's commentaries were closely studied by a wide variety of later Jewish scholars, such as the 19th-century biblical interpreter Meir Loeb ben Jehiel Michael (*Malbim), as well as by many Christian thinkers from the 16th through 18th centuries, some of whom translated excerpts from his biblical commentaries into Latin.

[Avraham Grossman / Eric Lawee (2nd ed.)]

Abrabanel's Thought

The religious thought of Abrabanel appears in no single volume, but is distributed throughout his works. His religious teachings reflect ongoing dialogues with the major figures of earlier medieval Jewish theology, especially Maimonides. Abrabanel typically evaluates earlier views on a given issue, and then sets forth his own teachings. In doing so, he displays considerable philosophic depth and theological erudition. Among Abrabanel's main theological concerns were the world's creation, prophecy, history, politics, and eschatology.

CREATION. God's creation of the world *ex nihilo* stands as the Archimedean point of Abrabanel's religious thought. This view, which alone conforms to the teaching of the Torah, is also sustained by arguments from reason. Abrabanel refutes a number of competing cosmogonies influenced by different streams in ancient and medieval philosophy: the idea of the visible world's eternity, associated in the Middle Ages with Aristotle; the hypothesis of its creation from eternal matter, associated with Plato; and the doctrine of eternal creation. Abrabanel's teaching that God voluntarily created the world from nothing informs his understanding of the universe as a place ruled by God's infinite power in which the miracles of the Bible occurred according to their literal description.

PROPHECY. Prophecy is another cornerstone of Abrabanel's theology. The form in which Abrabanel discusses prophecy is influenced by the Aristotelian-Ptolemaic cosmology and the medieval Jewish philosophers who preceded him, particularly Maimonides. The influence of the latter was largely negative rather than positive, a stimulus that provoked a negative response, but which shaped the character of that response.

Abrabanel vigorously attacked the naturalistic view of prophecy and Judaism advanced by Maimonides, notably in his commentary on the *Guide* (2:32–45). According to this view, prophecy is a natural function of human beings that arises from an individual's achievement of moral, and especially intellectual, perfection. By contrast, Abrabanel argues that prophecy is an essentially supernatural phenomenon in which the prophet is chosen by God. As the miraculous creation of God, prophecy supplies insight that is qualitatively superior to natural or scientific knowledge: the latter is probable and refragable, whereas the former is certain and infallible.

HISTORY. Abrabanel bases his understanding of history upon the Scriptures, which has been established as a perfect source of truth. This is the history of the universe as well as of man. The foundation is the personal God who creates the universe *ex nihilo*. As such, the universe presents no pre-existent nature to limit the absolute power of God. Neither does God relinquish control over the universe to nature, which, intervening between God and man, exercises a mechanical providence over humanity. Abrabanel thus rejects the naturalism of Maimonides and his followers adopted from the Neoplatonized Aristotelianism of medieval science. What befalls man is directly attributable to God, human freedom, or supernatural beings. The major outlines of Abrabanel's theory of history correspond essentially with the rabbinic view. God created the universe according to a grand design which culminates in the salvation of righteous mankind and the vindication of Judaism. Adam was created by God and placed in Eden to realize his spiritual potentialities. Instead, he chose to disobey God by eating of the forbidden tree of knowledge. For this sin, Adam became subject to death and was condemned to live on an inhospitable earth. Ultimately, through Noah, Abraham, and Jacob, the people Israel was developed to continue God's plan of salvation. God exercised a special providence over them, revealing the Torah and giving them the land of Israel, which was perfectly suited for spiritual realization and the reception of prophecy. Yet the Jews sinned against God, and after the destruction of the First Temple were sent into exile, which will continue until the advent of the Messianic Age when the history of this universe will come to an end.

POLITICS. Some of Abrabanel's most trenchant ideas lie in the sphere of politics. The view of Abrabanel on government reflects his religious convictions. The need for the state is temporal, arising with the expulsion of Adam from Eden and ending in the Messianic Age. As a product of spiritual exile, no state is perfect, some are better than others, but none provides salvation. The best possible state serves the spiritual as well as the political needs of its people, as does the state based on the principles of Mosaic law. In his commentaries on Scripture, Abrabanel presents somewhat conflicting views of the optimum society. However, its basic structure along Mosaic lines is presented clearly in his comments upon Deuteronomy 16:18. Two legal systems are provided for, civil and ecclesiastical. The civil system consists of lower courts, a superior court, and the king; the ecclesiastical system consists of levites, priests, and prophets. The officials of the lower courts, which possessed municipal jurisdiction, were chosen by the people. The superior court or Sanhedrin, possessed national jurisdiction, and was appointed by the king, primarily from among the priests and levites. A significant feature of Abrabanel's political convictions generally is seen in this structure: the diffusion of political power. Abrabanel's distrust of concentrated authority is echoed in his intensely negative opinion of monarchy. He considered monarchy a demonstrable curse, and the insistence of ancient Israel upon human kings in place of God's (theocratic) sovereignty, a sin for which it paid dearly. Monarchy's inferiority as a form of government is demonstrable on philosophic and not only on scriptural grounds.

ESCHATOLOGY. Abrabanel produced a substantial eschatological corpus several years after his arrival in Italy. As part of an exhaustive study of the classical (biblical-rabbinic) and medieval Jewish eschatological tradition, he set forth a powerful messianic message that included a specific forecast for the end of days, or for major events anticipating it: the year 1503. Spain's expulsion of her Jews was one significant context for Abrabanel's messianic writings. Christian missionizing based on christological interpretation of biblical and rabbinic sources was another. Just how convinced Abrabanel was by his undeniably vivid apocalyptic rhetoric is hard to say.

Abrabanel's vision of the Messiah and of messianic times differs considerably from Maimonides' naturalistic one. The Messiah will possess superhuman perfection. The days of the Messiah will see miracles in abundance such as unprecedented agricultural fertility. At that time the Jews will be revenged on their enemies in extraordinary ways, the dispersed Jews will return to Israel, the resurrection and judgment will take place, and all Jews will live in Israel under the Messiah, whose rule will extend over all mankind. Though it is often said that Abrabanel's messianic speculations contributed significantly to the powerful messianic movements among the Jews in the 16th and 17th centuries, there is little evidence to support this claim.

[Alvin J. Reines / Eric Lawee (2nd ed.)]

BIBLIOGRAPHY: B. Netanyahu, *Don Isaac Abravanel* (1998[5]); Baer, Spain, index; idem, in: *Tarbiz*, 12 (1940/41), 404–5. **ADD. BIBLIOGRAPHY:** S. Feldman, *Philosophy in a Time of Crisis* (2003); E. Lawee, *Isaac Abarbanel's Stance Toward Tradition* (2001); idem, "Isaac Abarbanel's Intellectual Achievement and Literary Legacy in Modern Scholarship: A Retrospective and Opportunity," in: *Studies in Medieval Jewish History and Literature*, 3 (2000), 213–47.

ABRABANEL, JUDAH (called **Leone Ebreo** or **Leo Hebraeus**; c. 1460–after 1523), physician, poet, and one of the foremost philosophers of the Renaissance. Abrabanel was born in Lisbon, the eldest son of Don Isaac *Abrabanel and was instructed by his father in Jewish studies and in Jewish and Arabic philosophy. He also studied medicine and is mentioned in the register of Lisbon physicians of 1483. When his father was forced to flee from Portugal, in 1483, Judah followed him. At the time of the expulsion of the Jews from Spain (1492), he secretly sent his one-year-old son to Portugal with his nurse, but King John II had the infant seized and baptized. This tragedy weighed heavily on Abrabanel for many years, as is evident from his frequently published poem *"Telunah al ha-Zeman"* ("Complaint against the Time"), composed in 1503. There is, however, reason to believe that the son ultimately returned to the religion of his people and to his family. Abrabanel later settled in Naples where he continued to practice medicine. The physician *Amatus Lusitanus reports that in 1566 he saw in Salonica a philosophical work on the harmony of the heavens which Abrabanel had composed for *Pico della Mirandola (d. 1494). This work is no longer extant. This indicates that he visited Florence (where Pico lived) at that time. His spiritual affinity with the circle of scholars of the Platonic Academy in Florence, particularly with its leading exponents Pico and Marsilio Ficino, may have originated in this visit. Some scholars, however, believe that the person for whom the book was meant was Pico's nephew (d. 1533).

Abrabanel was back in Naples in 1494. When the city was captured by the French in 1495, he went to Genoa, but he returned to Naples and in 1501 was teaching medicine and "astrology" at the university there. From then on, his name occurs in various documents as physician to the Spanish viceroy, Don Gonsalvo de Córdoba. On the title pages of the second (1541) and third (1545) editions of his *Dialoghi di Amore*, he is described as a convert to Christianity. This statement is lacking, however, in the first edition as well as in those subsequent to the third, even in the Latin version of 1564 with its elaborate dedication to a church dignitary. It is very likely, therefore, that it has no foundation in fact, and may have been added merely to stimulate the sale of the work or to emphasize its orthodoxy from the Christian standpoint. There are in fact some passages in the text in which the author speaks of himself as a Jew.

Judah Abrabanel was a skillful versifier, and apart from the elegy on his son's disappearance, he composed three short poems (c. 1504) commending his father's works, and another of 52 stanzas in memory of his father and extolling his commentary on the Latter Prophets (c. 1520). These were included in the printed editions. His reputation rests on his *Dialoghi di Amore*, first published in Rome in 1535. Mariano Lenzi, the editor, claims to have rescued the work "from the obscurity in which it was buried" after the author's death. The precise date of composition is uncertain. According to the author's statement in the text he had reached the middle of the Third Dialogue in 1502, but it is not known when he completed it. The Fourth Dialogue which Abrabanel intended to write never reached Lenzi, and it may never have been written. Almost certainly the book was written in Italian (the conjectures that it was composed in Hebrew or in Spanish are untenable). A Hebrew translation was made after 1660 by Joseph Baruch of Urbino; its style is cumbersome and difficult.

Philosophy

Following Plato's example, Abrabanel presented his ideas in the form of dialogues, of which there are three. The names of the dialogists, Philone and Sophia, who are depicted as platonic lovers, reflect Abrabanel's belief that love elevates to the pinnacle of wisdom. In the character of Sophia we find here the first female in Jewish and non-Jewish literature that is described as an active philosopher. The principal and central theme of the work, from which the discussion branches out in a number of directions, is love, which he regards as the source, the dominating and motivating force, and the loftiest goal of the universe. He investigates and expounds the nature of love and its operation in God, in matter and form, in the four elements, in the spheres, in the constellations, in the terrestrial world and all that it contains from man, his soul, his intellect, and senses, to animals, plants, and inanimate things. Thus, Abrabanel's discourse in the *Dialoghi* rises stage by stage to the bold concept which rounds out his theory, that the goal of love is not "possession," but the pleasure of the lover in his union with the idea of the beautiful and the good, embodied in the beloved. Hence, the sublime end of love, which fills the entire world as a supernal force, is the union of the creation and all creatures with that sublime beauty (which is at the same time sublime goodness and sublime intellect) which exists in God. Such a union, which constitutes an act of both will and intellect, the intellectual love of God (*amore intellettuale di Dio*), is desired and enjoyed also by God. This covenant of mutual love between the universe and its creator forges a mighty "circle of love" which sustains all components of the cosmos, from the outermost sphere to the rock within the earth, in one living, blessed movement, from God and to God. Out of this central theme there flows a remarkable stream of thoughts on many diverse subjects – reflections on religion, metaphysics, mysticism, ethics, aesthetics (especially valuable), logic, psychology, mythology, cosmology, astrology, and astronomy – a vision embracing the spiritual and material universe and its metaphysical goal. Original interpretations of biblical and rabbinic traditions as well as of Greek myths occupy a considerable place in these speculations. Abrabanel always endeavors to reconcile Jewish and Greek teachings, and the revered Plato and his school with Aristotle and his Arab commentators. Among the philosophers by whom he was influenced were *Maimonides and Ibn *Gabirol. The wealth and profundity of the ideas make the *Dialoghi* one of the most important works in metaphysics produced by the European Renaissance. The work had a widespread influence in its time. Twenty-five editions and printings (12 in Italian and 13 in various translations) appeared between 1535 and 1607, and between 1551 and about 1660 it was translated seven times into four languages (French, Latin, Spanish, and Hebrew). In its wake there appeared, especially in 16th century Italy, a large number of essays and dialogues on love, almost all of which borrowed basic ideas from Abrabanel's work. At the same time his unique concept of love permeated the lyrical poetry of the epoch in Italy, France, and Spain. His influence is discernible also in Michelangelo's *Sonnets* and Torquato Tasso's *Minturno*. Among the philosophers who were influenced by Abrabanel, mention should be made of Giordano Bruno and *Spinoza, whose small library contained the *Dialoghi*. But by the end of the 16th century the influence of the work had dwindled. R. Isaac *Alatrini of Modena incorporated various passages in his commentary on the Song of Songs, entitled *Kenaf Renanim*, preserved in manuscript in Oxford and elsewhere. Modern editions include a facsimile edited by C. Gebhardt with elaborate introduction and bibliography (*Bibliotheca Spinozana*, 3, 1929); an edition by Caramella in the series of Italian classics *Scrittori d'Italia* (1929); an anonymous early translation into Hebrew, sometimes ascribed to Leone *Modena (Lyck, 1871); and an English translation by F. Friedeberg-Seeley and Jean H. Barnes (1937). A new Hebrew translation, with an extensive introduction and notes, was published in Jerusalem in 1983 by M. Dorman.

BIBLIOGRAPHY: Y. Klausner, in: *Tarbiz*, 3 (1931/32), 67–98; B. Zimmels, *Leo Hebraeus* (Ger., 1886); H. Pflaum, *Die Idee der Liebe: Leone Ebreo* (1926). **ADD. BIBLIOGRAPHY:** M. Dorman and Z. Levi (eds.), *The Philosophy of Leone Ebreo, Four Lectures* (Heb., 1985); Sh. Pines, in: B.D. Cooperman (ed.), *Jewish Thought in the Sixteenth Century* (1983), 369–98; A. Melamed, in: *Jewish Studies*, 40 (2000), 113–30; B. Gavin, in: *Italia*, 13–15 (2001), 181–210; A. Lesley, in: M. Fishbane (ed.), *The Midrashic Imagination* (1993), 204–25.

[Hiram Peri / Avraham Melamed (2nd ed.)]

ABRACADABRA, magic word or formula used mainly in folk medicine, as an incantation against fevers and inflammations. Several origins for the obscure word have been proposed, most of them regarding it as a derivative of an Aramaic demon-name, now unrecognizable. It occurs first in the writings of Severus Sammonicus, a gnostic physician of the second century C.E. In the same manner as Abracadabra, the name of Shabriri, the demon of blindness, and other magic words were used in Jewish magic, incantations, and amulets. An amulet still in use among some Oriental Jews utilizes a talmudic formula:

(Pes. 112a; Av. Zar. 12b)

SHABRIRI
ABRIRI
RIRI
RI

BIBLIOGRAPHY: J. Trachtenberg, *Jewish Magic and Superstition* (1939), 80 ff., 116 ff.; EJ, 1 (1928), 372 ff.

[Dov Noy]

ABRAHAM (originally **Abram**; Heb. אַבְרָהָם, אַבְרָם), first patriarch of the people of Israel. The form "Abram" occurs in the Bible only in Genesis 11:26–17:5, Nehemiah 9:7, and I Chronicles 1:26. Otherwise, "Abraham" appears invariably, and the name is borne by no one else. No certain extra-biblical parallel exists. *A-ba-am-ra-ma, A-ba-ra-ma, A-ba-am-ra-am* occur in 19th-century B.C.E. Akkadian cuneiform texts. *Abrm* appears in Ugaritic (Gordon, *Ugaritic Textbook* (1965), pp. 286, 348, text 2095, line 4), but is most likely to be read *A-bi-ra-mi* (*Palais Royal d' Ugarit*, 3 (1955), p.20, text 15.63, line 1). There is no evidence that Abram is a shortened form of Abiram. As to the meaning of Abram, the first element is undoubtedly the common Semitic for "father"; the second could be derived from Akkadian *ra'āmu* ("to love") or from West-Semitic *rwm* ("to be high"). "He loved the father" or "father loves" is a far less likely meaning than "he is exalted with respect to father" i.e., he is of distinguished lineage. The meaning "exalted father" or "father is exalted," while less satisfactory, cannot be ruled out. No Hebrew derivation for Abraham exists. In Genesis 17:5 "the father of a multitude [of nations]" is a popular etymology, although it might possibly conceal an obsolete Hebrew cognate of Arabic *ruhâm*, "numerous." More likely, Abraham is a mere dialectic variant of Abram, representing the insertion of *h* in weak verbal stems, a phenomenon known from Aramaic and elsewhere.

The Biblical Data: Genesis 11:26–25:10

The main details of Abraham's life are recorded in Genesis 11:26–25:10. They do not form a continuous narrative but refer to a series of isolated incidents. Son of *Terah, Abraham was the tenth generation from Noah through the line of Shem (Gen. 11:10–26). His two brothers were Nahor and Haran. His wife was Sarai or *Sarah, a paternal half sister (11:29; 20:12). The family migrated from "Ur of the Chaldees" (11:31), the apparent birthplace of Abraham (11:28; 15:7; Neh. 9:7; cf. Josh. 24:2–3), heading for Canaan. It was during the stay at Haran that Abram, then aged 75, received the divine call and promise of nationhood in response to which he proceeded to Canaan together with his wife and nephew *Lot (Gen. 12:1–5). At Shechem he received a further promise of national territory and built an altar before continuing his wanderings in the region between Beth-El and Ai. In this area, too, he built an altar and invoked the divine name, thereafter journeying toward the Negev (12:6–9). (See Map: Abraham's Journeys.)

Driven by famine to Egypt, the patriarch represented his wife as his sister in order to avert personal danger. Sarah was taken to Pharaoh's palace, but released when the deception was uncovered as a result of divine visitations (12:10–20). Abraham returned to Canaan and resumed his peregrinations. At this time, Lot left the clan because of quarrels over pasturelands and departed (13:5–9). This incident was followed by a reiteration of the divine promises of nationhood and possession of the land (13:14–17). Abraham again built an altar, this time in Hebron (13:18). Abraham "the Hebrew" next appears in the role of military chief, described in terms of the ideal "noble warrior," leading a force of 318 retainers against an invading coalition of eastern kings who had captured Lot in plundering *Sodom and Gomorrah. The patriarch rescued his nephew and restored the booty. On his return he was blessed by *Melchizedek, priest-king of Salem, to whom he paid tithes. He refused, however, the offer by the king of Sodom of a share in the recovered spoils (ch. 14). Once again, Abraham received

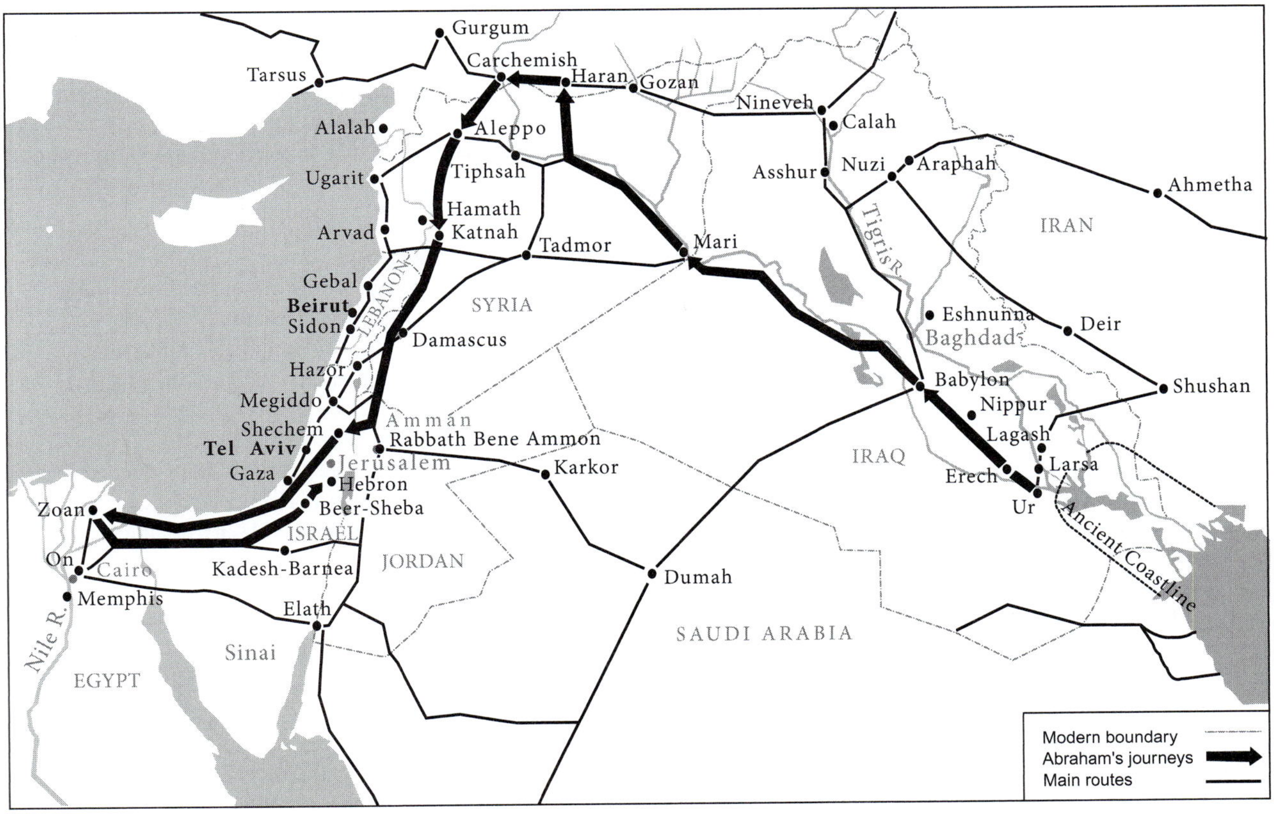

Map showing route of Abraham's wanderings and other main routes of the ancient East.

confirmation of the divine promises, now sealed through an elaborate covenant ceremony (ch. 15).

Ten years had now elapsed since the first promise of abundant offspring, but Sarah remained childless. She therefore presented her maidservant *Hagar to her husband as a second wife. *Ishmael was born of the union, Abraham being then 86 years old (16:1ff.). The Bible is silent about the next 13 years. Then Scripture reports that God reaffirmed and strengthened the promise of a rich posterity. Abraham and Sarah were to beget "a multitude of nations" and kings would issue from them (17:1–8). It is at this point that their names were changed from Abram and Sarai to Abraham and Sarah, respectively (17:5, 15). In addition, the institution of *circumcision was ordained as an ineradicable token of the immutability of God's covenant with Abraham and his posterity (17:9–14). Sarah was explicitly promised a son to be called *Isaac, through whom the covenant would be maintained (17:16–19, 21). Abraham then performed circumcision on himself and on Ishmael, as well as upon all males in his household (17:23–27).

Alongside the terebinths of Mamre three messengers appeared to the patriarch who entertained them hospitably and learned from them of the impending birth of his son and heir (18:1–10). Sarah was amused by these tidings as had been Abraham earlier (18:12; cf. 17:17), but the Lord Himself confirmed their truth (18:14). He also revealed His decision to destroy Sodom and Gomorrah. Abraham pleaded for revocation of the sentence for the sake of an innocent nucleus that might be found therein. None such could apparently be found, although Lot was saved from the subsequent destruction through the merit of Abraham (18:16–19:29). The patriarch journeyed to the Negev area and settled between Kadesh and Shur. While in Gerar, he again passed off his wife as his sister. King *Abimelech took Sarah into his palace, but released her unharmed after being rebuked in a dream theophany (ch. 20). The time of fulfillment of the divine promise was now at hand. Sarah, aged 90 (17:17), bore the 100-year-old Abraham a son who was named Isaac (21:1–3, 5). This event, however, proved to be a cause of domestic disharmony. Sarah demanded the expulsion of Hagar and Ishmael. It was only divine intervention in favor of Sarah that persuaded the distressed Abraham to agree (21:9–21). At this time, at Abimelech's initiative, the patriarch concluded a pact of non-aggression, which also regulated the watering rights in the Beer-Sheba area. He subsequently spent considerable time in the land of the Philistines (21:22–34).

The climax of Abraham's life was the divine command to sacrifice Isaac in the land of Moriah (see **Akedah*). Abraham obeyed unhesitatingly and his hand was stayed only at the last moment by an angel. Having passed the supreme test of faith, the patriarch now received, for the last time, the divine blessing – the promise that his descendants would be as numerous as the stars of heaven and the sands on the seashore; they would seize the gates of their foes; all the nations of the earth would bless themselves by his progeny (22:1–19). Abraham's subsequent acts were concerned with winding up his affairs. The death of Sarah in Kiriath-Arba (Hebron) was the occasion for acquiring the cave of *Machpelah, as a family sepulcher, from Ephron the Hittite (ch. 23). Then, Abraham commissioned his senior servant to travel to Haran to find a wife for Isaac, the idea of a local Canaanite daughter-in-law being thoroughly repugnant to him (ch. 24). After Isaac's marriage to Rebekah, Abraham himself remarried. Several children were born of this marriage to Keturah, like Isaac and Ishmael the eponyms of nations. Thus was fulfilled the promise (Gen 17:4) that Abraham would be the father of many nations. However, he willed all his possessions to Isaac, gave his other sons gifts and sent them away to the land of the East. Abraham died at the age of 175 and was buried in the cave of Machpelah by Isaac and Ishmael (25:1–11).

The Biblical Data: In the Rest of the Bible

Mention of Abraham in the rest of the Bible is overwhelmingly in connection with the divine promises, and usually there is simultaneous reference to all three patriarchs. The few points of contact with the Abrahamic biography are mainly confined to the Book of Genesis (26:1; 35:27; 49:31), though the exodus from Ur and the change of name are mentioned in the late books (Neh. 9:7; cf. Josh. 24:2–3; I Chron. 1:26). A cryptic reference to Abraham's idolatrous ancestry is to be found in Joshua 24:2, while Isaiah (29:22) seems to cite some widely known tradition not otherwise recorded in the Bible. Abraham is called God's "servant" (Gen. 26:24; Ps. 105:6, 42) and "friend" (Isa. 41:8; II Chron. 20:7), and though the patriarch is not an ethnographic figure, Israel is called "the offspring of Abraham" (Isa. 41:8; Jer. 33:26; Ps. 105:6; II Chron. 20:7) and "the people of the God of Abraham" (Ps. 47:10). Surprisingly, "God of Abraham" as a generalized divine epithet appears only this once. Otherwise, Abraham is invariably associated with the other patriarchs in divine appellations.

The Image of Abraham

The picture that emerges from the biblical texts suggests a wealthy head of a large establishment, a semi-nomadic tent dweller (Gen. 12:8; et al.), whose peregrinations are confined mainly to the central hill country of Palestine and the Negev and who clings to the periphery of a few great urban centers. He possesses flocks, silver and gold, slaves (*ibid.* 12:5, 16, et al.), and a private army (14:14). He makes military alliances (14:13), has dealings with kings (12:15ff.; 14:18ff.; 17:22ff.; 21:22–32), and negotiates the purchase of land with city notables (23:2–20). Abraham is peace loving (13:8–9), magnanimous and principled in victory (14:22ff.), hospitable to strangers (18:1ff.), concerned for his fellowmen (18:23–33), obedient to God and his laws (26:5), and committed to transmitting to his posterity the ideals of justice and righteousness that he espouses (18:19). He is the very symbol of the God-fearing man (22:12) and the man of supreme faith (15:6; 22; Neh. 9:8). He is privy to divine decisions (Gen. 18:17; cf. Amos 3:7) and is also termed "a prophet" (Gen. 20:7) in that he can intercede with God on another's behalf (cf. Deut. 9:20; Jer. 7:16).

The Critical View

The disconnected and fragmentary nature of the narrative, as well as stylistic considerations, seem to point to a composition based on various oral traditions and written sources. Among followers of the documentary theory, there is a broad measure of agreement in respect of source division among JE and P, but little consensus as to the age and historic value of the material used by these sources. No external records have been found as yet that refer by name to Abraham or to any personage directly connected with him. In the absence of such synchronistic controls, and in the light of the difficulties of the biblical chronological data (see *Chronology), the place of the patriarch in the framework of history cannot be precisely determined. The attempts in the mid-20th century to marshal sociological and onomastic evidence from archeological discoveries at Nuzi, Mari, and elsewhere to provide a historical setting for Abraham in the second millennium B.C.E. have not withstood the test of time. Most alleged parallels between the Abrahamic stories have been shown to be faulty (e.g., wife-sister marriage), or not to be confined to a specific period in the second millennium (e.g., surrogate motherhood). Contemporary scholarship tends to see Abraham as a fictitious symbolic model of faith, as a figure who legitimates the claims of Israel to its land, and whose actions foreshadow the deeds of his children. Some of the tales of Abraham foreshadow the actions of Israelite kings, notably David (see *Patriarchs).

Whatever the age and source of the individual units, it is quite clear that in its present form the cycle of Abrahamic traditions is a unified and symmetrical historiographic composition. These traditions are encased within a framework of genealogies – the first listing the patriarch's ancestors (Gen. 11:10–32) and the second his descendants (25:1–18). The action opens and closes in a Mesopotamian setting (12:1–4; 24:4ff.). The first utterance of Abraham to God is an expression of doubt (15:2–8); his last is one of supreme confidence in the workings of divine providence (24:7). Finally, both the first and last communications from God to Abraham involve agonizing decisions and tests of faith, and they are cast in a strikingly similar literary mold: almost identical language is used in the case of both calls (12:1; 22:2); the exact destination is withheld in both cases; the motif of father parting with son is shared by each narrative; the tension of the drama is heightened by the accumulation of descriptive epithets (*ibid.*); in each instance Abraham builds an altar (12:8; 22:9); and in each he receives divine blessings of similar content (12:2–3; 22:17–18).

[Nahum M. Sarna / S. David Sperling (2nd ed.)]

In the *Aggadah*

In aggadic literature Abraham is regarded as having observed all the commandments (Yoma 28b; Kid. 4:14; et al.) even though they had not yet been revealed. He acted in strict conformity with the Oral Law: "No one occupied himself so much with the divine commandments as did Abraham" (Ned. 32a). He even muzzled his animals that they should not graze in the fields of others (Gen. R. 41:6). Abraham instituted the morning prayer (Ber. 26b), and the precepts of the **ẓiẓit* and **tefillin* originate from him (Mid. Hag. to Gen. 14:23). These statements probably constitute a polemic against Christian *antinomianism which was prevalent toward the end of the first century C.E. and which later maintained that the commandments of the Torah were a punishment inflicted upon Israel. Abraham's principal virtue was that he was the first to recognize God, which is variously stated to have taken place when he was one, three, ten, or 48 years old (Gen. R. 95:2; 64:4). His recognition of God sprang from the notion that every citadel must have a leader (*ibid.* 39:1). Abraham waged a strenuous battle in the cause of spreading the idea of monotheism and won over many converts. When he smashed the idols of his father, an idol manufacturer, King *Nimrod had him thrown into a fiery furnace from which he was delivered by the angel Gabriel (Pes. 118a).

Abraham became a priest (Gen. R. 55:6), after the priesthood was taken from Melchizedek and given to him (Ned. 32b; Gen. R. 46:5; et al.). He was one of the great prophets, with whom God spoke not in dreams or visions but while he was in full possession of his normal cognitive faculties. "God omitted no blessing in the world with which He did not bless him" (SER 6). Through coins bearing his image Abraham's fame spread (Gen. R. 39:11). Around his neck was hung a precious stone which brought masses flocking to him, for whoever looked on it was healed (BB 16b, et al.). He was granted the privilege of blessing others (Tanḥ. Lekh Lekha 5), and his blessing spread upon all who came into contact with him (Gen. R. 39:12). Renowned for his hospitality to strangers, he had open doors to his house on all four sides (Gen. R. 48:9) and himself waited on his guests, and taught them the Grace after Meals, thus bringing them to believe in God (*ibid.* 54:6). Because of his proselytizing activities, he is regarded as the father of all proselytes, who are given the patronymic Abraham.

Abraham was circumcised on the Day of Atonement by Shem the son of Noah, "and every year the Holy One, blessed be He, looks upon the blood of the covenant of our patriarch Abraham's circumcision and forgives all our sins" (PdRE 29). Circumcision was one of the ten trials wherewith Abraham was tried (see later) and by virtue of it he sits at the gate of hell and does not permit the circumcised to enter (Gen. R. 48:8). The phrase, "entry into the covenant of Abraham our father," used to this day for the ceremony of circumcision, is already found in the Damascus Document 12:11 (ed. Ch. Rabin, *Zadokite Documents* (1958[2]), 60–61). According to an early tradition Abraham underwent ten trials (Avot 5:3) of which different lists are given in the Midrashim (ARN 33:2; Mid. Ps. to 18:25; 98; PdRE 26). In answer to the sectarians who sought thus to prove the weakness of Abraham's faith, the sages emphasized that it is only the righteous, who are certain to pass the test, who are tried (Gen. R. 55:1–2). "Lovingkindness is spread abroad" (Gen. R. 60:2) and the world and all therein are preserved because of Abraham's merit. The manna (Tanḥ. Buber, Ex. 34), victory in war (Gen. R. 39:16; Esth. R. 7:13), and general forgiveness of Israel's sins (Song R. 4:6) are ascribed to his merit. The dramatic description of Abraham's appeal to save the people of Sodom (Gen. 18:23–33) is given a new dimension in the Midrash, which compares his arguments with God to those of Job (Gen. R. 49:9). According to this Abraham employed a "cleaner" language than did Job (*ibid.*).

In this connection the Midrash emphasizes the extreme contrast between the basic hospitality of Abraham and the spurious "hospitality" of the people of Sodom (Ag. Ber. 25). It is of interest to note that the Akedah is regarded as more of a trial of Abraham than of Isaac. In a desire to compare the trial of Abraham with that of Job, the *aggadah* assigns to Satan a role in the drama of Abraham as well (Sanh. 89b). The disciples of Abraham have "a benign eye, a humble spirit and a lowly soul" (Avot 5:19). Abraham however is not regarded as beyond criticism. The Talmud states that "Abraham our father was punished and his descendants enslaved in Egypt" because he pressed scholars into military service (based on Gen. 14:14), went too far in testing God, and prevented men from "entering beneath the wings of the Divine Presence" (based on Gen. 14:21; Ned. 32a). Moreover, Abraham hesitated to circumcise himself, whereupon Mamre rebuked and encouraged him (Gen. R. 42:8). In a biting comment, Rava denied Abraham the right to intercede on behalf of his people: In time to come Israel will ask of God: "To whom shall we go – to Abraham to whom Thou didst say, 'Know of a surety that thy seed be a stranger in a land that is not theirs, and shall serve them; and they shall afflict them...' and yet he did not plead for mercy for us?" (Shab. 89b).

The prevailing Hellenistic outlook influenced the description of Abraham in the Apocrypha. He is the founder of a city and a legislator, the two principal functions of a great leader according to the Hellenistic concept, and his wisdom is described in extravagant terms. According to the Apocrypha his recognition of God stemmed from his knowledge of astronomy which he taught to the great men of his generation. Hence there developed the idea that Abraham was an expert in many and varied spheres. The Book of Jubilees even declares that he instructed men in the art of improved plowing, so as to conceal the seeds from the ravens (11: 18–24). His Babylonian origin is emphasized in conformity with the contemporary outlook which regarded that country as the cradle of mysticism. On the basis of Genesis 17:5 Abraham was deemed to be the progenitor of the Spartans too (I Macc. 12:20–22; II Macc. 5:9). The Testament of *Abraham and the Apocalypse of *Abraham are devoted to him. Philo deals with him in his *De Migratione Abrahami*, while extracts from Hellenistic Jewish writers about him have been preserved by Eusebius. In IV Macc. 14:20; 15:28 Abraham typifies the ability to withstand oppression. The background of this description of Abraham was the persecution of the Jews of Alexandria at that time.

[Israel Moses Ta-Shma]

In Jewish Philosophy

Over the generations, Jewish thinkers, from Philo Judaeus of Alexandia to Joseph *Soloveitchik and Yeshayahu *Leibowitz, have regarded Abraham as the archetypal believer, in accordance with the image of Abraham in the Hebrew Bible and Midrash: his origins in pagan environs (Josh. 24:2); the testimony of Genesis 15:6 that Abraham "believed in the Lord", and Abraham's absolute obedience to divine commandments, beginning with his leaving his homeland (Gen. 12:1) and culminating in his binding of his son Isaac (Gen. 22:2; see *Akedah*). In addition to this biblical image of Abraham, Jewish philosophers found in rabbinic Midrashim views of Abraham according to which he smashed the prevalent idols and came to believe in the one God (Gen. R. 38); Genesis 12:5 ("and the persons he had acquired in Haran") was interpreted to mean people Abraham converted (Gen. R. 39:14; cf. Targum Onkelos and Rashi to Gen. 12:5); and Genesis 34:12 ("He took him outside and said: Look at the sky") was understood as meaning that Abraham no longer had anything to do with astrology.

Eventually two paradigms evolved, in which the image of Abraham came to reflect two basic approaches to Jewish philosophy. According to the first school of thought, in which religion was understood rationally, Abraham was seen as a philosopher whose faith in God was the conclusion of scientific reasoning. According to the other school of thought, Abraham was seen as a believer whose faith and experience of divine revelation transcended his earlier philosophical or scientific speculation.

The first view of Abraham as a philosopher is found in Hellenistic Jewish literature. *Philo Judaeus of Alexandria described Abraham as an autodidact philosopher who concluded that God exists. Philo interpreted Abraham's wanderings and wars allegorically as a process of coming to know God (*De Abrahamo* 68). Philo's younger contemporary, the historian *Josephus Flavius, similarly attributed to Abraham the spreading of monotheism after he had rationally deduced the existence of God who cares providentially for human welfare (*Antiquities* I, 7:155–56) and who had instructed the Egyptians in the ancient Chaldean sciences, such as arithmetic and astronomy, which were later transmitted to the Greeks (*Antiquities*, 167–68).

This view of Abraham as a philosopher is also found in medieval Jewish thought. *Maimonides characterized Abraham as a natural philosopher who independently articulated the Aristotelian cosmological proof of an incorporeal unmoved mover of the heavenly sphere. Paradoxically, for Maimonides, in *Judah Halevi's famous phrase, the "God of Abraham" effectively was identified with the "God of Aristotle." During his wanderings from Mesopotamia to Canaan, Abraham then spread his concept of a transcendent God (Yad, Avodah Zarah 1:3; *Guide of the Perplexed* 3:29), and became "the father of the whole world by teaching them faith" (*Responsa*, ed. Blau, 293). Only Moses, "the father of all prophets" (Commentary on Mishnah Avot 4:4; *Guide of the Perplexed* 3:54) was of a higher rank than Abraham (Guide 2:45). It should be noted that, in Maimonides' view, prophecy itself was understood to be a thoroughly rational phenomenon (Commentary on Mishnah, Introduction to Sanhedrin ch. 10, sixth principle; see *Prophecy). Nevertheless, Maimonides states that Abraham and Moses prophetically grasped the supranatural understanding of creation *ex nihilo* and thus differed from the Aristotelian philosophic belief in the world's eternity (Guide 2:13, 17, 23).

The Hellenistic and medieval Jewish view of Abraham as philosopher is also found in modern Jewish thought. Nachman *Krochmal's *Guide of the Perplexed of the Time* pictures Abraham as a philosopher who deduced the teleological proof from design of God's existence and as the first monotheist who affirmed the "Absolute Spirit."

The other school of thought, which identifies Abraham as the first believer, is most clearly enunciated by *Judah Halevi, whose *Kuzari* (4:16) juxtaposes "the God of Abraham" (identified with the *Tetragrammaton) with "the God of Aristotle" (identified with the name *elohim*). "The God of Abraham" is the personal God of the Bible, who is loved and known through the direct experience called "taste" (Arab. *dhauq*; Heb. *ta'am*), whereas the impersonal "God of Aristotle," who is indifferent to the world and to human affairs, is known through rational speculation (Arab. *qiyas*; Heb. *hekesh, hakashah*). In Halevi's view, Abraham himself underwent a radical transformation in his life: after composing the *Sefer *Yeẓirah* in his early years as a philosopher, Abraham merited divine revelation and true faith, as a consequence of which he was prepared to obey any divine commandment (*Kuzari* 4:24–27). Halevi thus partially accepts the rationalist view of Abraham as a philosopher, but it was as a prophet, receiving divine revelation, and not as a natural philosopher, that Abraham attained his spiritual greatness.

Following Halevi, Isaac *Arama argued that philosophy and faith are unrelated. Philosophers know what can be demonstrated and deny whatever cannot be demonstrated, but reject the concept of "faith" (*Ḥazut Kashah* 3). Arama's works describe in detail the gradual progression of Abraham's faith, beginning with his transition from idolatry to a scientific-philosophic conclusion regarding the existence of one God (*Akedat Yiẓḥak* 16), which in turn led to practical application in loving *imitatio Dei*. Abraham's spiritual progression culminated in his religious faith in reward and punishment and in his fear of God, which were realized in his binding of his son Isaac as an expression of his absolute obedience to God (*Ḥazut Kashah* 3).

In the 20th century, Joseph Soloveitchik's *Lonely Man of Faith* (1965) presents a view of Abraham as dissatisfied with his early Mesopotamian contemplation of remote and alienating skies, which had led him to conclude that there is one God. As he progressed, Abraham needed personal revelation. In contrast with the view of Halevi and Arama, according to which Abraham passed from an earlier philosophic or scientific contemplative stage to prophetic receiving of divine revelation, or Soloveitchik's understanding of Abraham as undergoing a personal experience of revelation, Yeshayahu Leibowitz describes Abraham as reaching his faith as a result of a voluntary, religious decision and not as the conclusion of rational contemplation. Abraham, in Leibowitz's view, represents "faith for its own sake," namely an unreasoned obedience to the divine commandment, without any human benefit or expectation of reward.

Several Jewish thinkers have also dealt with Abraham's personality, including judging his questionable behavior in Egypt (Gen. 12) and Gerar (Gen. 20), when, fearing that he might be killed, he presented his wife Sarah as his sister. *Saadiah Gaon's *Book of Beliefs and Opinions* deals with the charge that Abraham lied, and justifies his behavior by suggesting that Abraham phrased his statement ambivalently, since "sister" could mean any relative, thus permitting his words to be interpreted as if they were true. Conversely, *Naḥmanides did not hesitate to criticize Abraham's behavior, not so much for his misleading words but for thereby leading the people to great sin and for causing his "righteous wife" to stumble (Commentary to Gen. 12:10, 20:12). Abraham's sin resulted from his insufficient trust in God's assistance. Isaac Arama's presentation (discussed above) of Abraham's gradual spiritual progress and the development of his personality attributed his behavior in these incidents to an early stage, when Abraham had not yet attained perfect faith in divine providence and utter trust in divine assistance (*Binding of Isaac* 16).

[Hannah Kasher (2nd ed.)]

In Christian Tradition

Next to Moses, Abraham is the Old Testament figure most frequently referred to in the New Testament, being mentioned 72 times. The Evangelists emphasize the physical descent of Jesus, from Abraham through David (Matt. 1:1, 2–17; Luke 3:34), but Christian tradition considers Abraham essentially in the spiritual sense as the father of all believers destined to inherit the divine promises. According to Paul (Rom. 4; Gal. 3:7–9), to the authors of the Epistle of James (2:21–23) and the Epistle to the Hebrews (11:8–10), Abraham, because of his "faith" (cf. Gen. 15:6, and see above), became the repository of the divine promises through whose seed all nations of the earth would ultimately be blessed (cf. Gen. 12:2–4). Hence all Christians, through their faith in the Messiah, are the children of Abraham to the extent that Abraham's righteousness because of his faith (and not because of his belief in the Law) is imparted to all believers in Jesus (Rom. 4:13–25). The *Church Fathers interpret the figure of Abraham in moral and typological terms. They emphasize his obedience to God in leaving his homeland (Ambrose), thus prefiguring the Apostles' following of Jesus (Augustine). His submission to God's will in all trials, even to the point of being prepared to sacrifice his son (see *Akedah*) has been taken as a prefiguration of the death of Jesus. The New Testament mentions once "*Abraham's bosom" (Luke 16:22) – a rabbinic term referring to the place of repose of the righteous in the hereafter. In the writings of *Luther and of the 19th-century philosopher S. Kierkegaard, Abraham figures as the paradigm of the man of faith whose total commitment to God is based not on reason but on pure faith.

In Islamic Tradition

"The [book] leaves of Abraham" are mentioned, together with those of Moses, in two of the older suras (87:19; 53:37) of the Koran. This indicates that Abraham was known to Muhammad as one of the fathers of the monotheistic belief from the beginning of the latter's career; however, Muhammad must have learned that Abraham did not promulgate a book. When Muhammad began to fill his suras with stories of the prophets, Abraham received a large share, mainly on the basis of material drawn from talmudic legends. Abraham, by his own reasoning, recognized that his Creator was God and not a shining star, the moon, or the sun. He smashed the idols of his father, was thrown into a furnace, was miraculously saved, and migrated to the Holy Land. Though long childless, he believed in God's promise of a son and, when a son was born to him, he was prepared to sacrifice him at God's command. It is remarkable that Ishmael, later so prominent in the Koran, does not appear in any connection with his father during the middle Meccan period, e.g., Sura 29:26, "We [God] gave him [Abraham] Isaac and Jacob, and bestowed on his posterity the gift of prophecy and the book." Also, 11:24, "We brought her [Sarah] the good tidings of Isaac and, after Isaac, Jacob" (cf. similar statements in 37:112–3 and 21:72). During this period, Ishmael is not treated as an individual in a story, but is merely mentioned as a name in a series of prophets and saints, together with such biblical personalities as Aaron, Job, or Elisha, i.e., far removed from Abraham. Just as there is no connection between Abraham and Ishmael, so there is none between Abraham and the building of the Kaaba, the sanctuary of Muhammad's native city, until late in Muhammad's prophetic career (e.g., Sura 2:118 ff.).

There is also little doubt that, in one form or another, he heard the story of Abraham as the founder of the Holy Temple of Jerusalem, as told in the Book of Jubilees (22:23–4). The story goes back to II Chronicles 3:1, according to which Solomon built the Temple on the same Mount of Moriah on which Abraham was to sacrifice Isaac (Gen. 22:2). The Book of Jubilees elaborates the story and lets Abraham say that he has built this house in order to put his name on it in the country which God has given to him and to his posterity, and that it will be given to him (Jacob) and to his posterity forever. With the aid of the new material Muhammad constructed the ingenious theory that Abraham built the Kaaba together with his son Ishmael (2:121), father of the Arabs, and thus founded the religion of Islam, which he, Muhammad, promulgated among his own people. The very word Islam and the idea contained in it, namely that of complete dedication to God, is connected with the story of Abraham, e.g., Sura 2:125, "When God said to him [Abraham], 'dedicate yourself to God [*aslim*],' he said, 'I dedicate myself to the Lord of the Worlds.'" Or (22:77): "This is the religion of your father Abraham. He called you *muslimīn*," i.e., those who dedicate themselves to God. This expression goes back to Genesis 17:1 in the version of Targum *Onkelos, where Abraham is admonished by God to become *shelīm*, and the subsequent definition of a proselyte as one who dedicates himself to his Creator (*hishlīm aẓmo la-bore*; cf. Goldziher, in: M. Steinschneider, *Polemische und apologetische Literatur in arabischer Sprache* (1877), 266, n. 56). Muhammad emphatically states that Abraham was neither a Jew nor a Christian (Sura 2:140/134; 3:6760); this new knowledge did not lead him back to his original primitive universalism, but, on the contrary, made Islam, the religion of Abraham, father of the Arabs, exclusive, the "best religion" (3:110/106), prior in time, and therefore in quality, to all others.

The koranic story of Abraham, which contains many rabbinical legends, is fully covered by H. Speyer in *Die biblischen Erzaehlungen im Qoran* (1961, pp. 120–86; see also Moubarac in bibl.). The enormous expansion of these stories in Islamic religious, historical, and narrative literature has been researched by four generations of Jewish scholars, beginning with A. *Geiger (*Was hat Mohammed aus dem Judenthume aufgenommen*, 1833) up to B. Heller (especially in EJ, and in EIS², s.v. *Ibrāhīm*). These researches show that the legends had been spread in Arabia in very early times. *Umayya ibn Abī al-Salt, Muhammad's contemporary and rival, also knew the tales about Abraham.

[Shelomo Dov Goitein]

In Medieval Hebrew Literature

The various legends about Abraham scattered in midrashic literature formed the basis from which medieval Hebrew writers tried to construct a coherent story of his birth, his youth, and his recognition of the one God. The medieval story was written in a few versions. Three stories, published by A. *Jellinek in his *Beit ha-Midrash* (one long and detailed version and two short legends, see bibliography), are replete with motifs and elements which are not midrashic, but probably originated with the medieval authors. Abraham's recognition of the existence of only one God, which made him the first monotheist, and Abraham as a martyr, are the two principal recurring motifs. In the narratives centered around the first motif, Abraham was left in a cave immediately after birth because Nimrod, the god-king of Babylonia, who had had an astrological warning that a child would be born that year who would dethrone him, decreed that all male children be killed. In the cave the angel *Gabriel nursed Abraham, who within a few days could already walk and talk. Upon his return to his father's house, he began to spread monotheistic belief.

In the medieval work *Sefer ha-Yashar*, which renders the biblical stories in a medieval style (see *Fiction: The Retelling of Bible Stories), the story of Abraham, told in detail, is based both upon midrashic and medieval literatures, to which the anonymous author added details of his own. In one of the stories about Abraham known in the Middle Ages (the earliest version is found in 12th-century sources), Abraham in his youth went to study with Shem, the son of Noah. Together they made a *golem*, that is, a person out of earth and water who miraculously came to life. Such stories were later told about the prophet *Jeremiah and *Ben Sira, who claimed to be his grandson. This *golem* story is undoubtedly connected with another medieval belief about Abraham, mainly that he was the author of *Sefer Yeẓirah* ("Book of Creation"), one of the first cosmological writings in Hebrew, which was extensively used by Jewish mystics who saw it as a revelation of the mystical way in which the heavenly and earthly worlds were created. It was believed that proper use of the knowledge in *Sefer Yeẓirah* would also enable the mystics to create a *golem*, and that the work contained the process of reasoning that Abraham followed to establish the unity of God. To medieval philosophers and mystics, Abraham had been not only a person, but also a symbol. In the controversy that raged around the study of philosophy in Spain and in Provence at the beginning of the 14th century, the philosophers were accused of interpreting the story of Abraham and Sarah allegorically, through seeing the figures of Abraham and Sarah as personifications of the relationship between matter and form (according to Aristotelian philosophy). The kabbalists on the other hand, saw Abraham as a personification of *Ḥesed* ("loving-kindness"), the fourth of the Ten **Sefirot* (see *Kabbalah).

[Joseph Dan]

In the Arts

Early literary treatment of episodes in the life of Abraham in addition to the sacrifice of Isaac (see **Akedah*) have been found in medieval English miracle plays, such as the *Histories of Lot and Abraham*, and in the 15th-century French *Mistere du Viel Testament*, which deals with Abraham's complete life. The outstanding Renaissance work on the theme is one of a series of Italian religious dramas, the *Rappresentazione de Abram e di Sara sua moglie* (1556). The episode involving Hagar has also inspired some plays, notably *Hagar dans le desert* (1781) by the French Comtesse de Genlis, and a Dutch drama *Hagar* (1848) by the convert Isaac *da Costa, who saw in Hagar's return to Abraham's tent Islam's ultimate reconciliation with Christianity. The outstanding Jewish work of fiction based on the theme is *Yesod Olam* ("Foundation of the World") by Moses ben Mordecai *Zacuto. Based on midrashic sources, this play, dramatically insubstantial though it is, is significant by reason of its being one of the earliest plays to be written in Hebrew.

The story of Abraham has inspired greater creative endeavor in the pictorial arts. Scenes from the patriarch's life have been illustrated in paintings, sculpture, manuscript illuminations, and mosaics. Usually represented as a white-bearded old man, armed with a knife, Abraham was a favorite subject not only for Christian artists (as a prefiguration of Jesus), but also for Moslems. Two rare examples of cyclic treatment are the 12th-century mosaics in the cathedral of San Marco, Venice, and a set of 16th-century Flemish tapestries by Bernard van Orley. Varying combinations of important episodes are found in fifth-century mosaics in the church of Santa Maria Maggiore, Rome; in the sixth-century manuscript known as the Vienna Genesis; in the sixth-century mosaics in Ravenna; in the bronze doors of San Zeno, Verona, the altar of Verdun, and the frescoes of Saint-Savin, Poitou (all 12th century); and in Ghiberti's bronze doors at the Florence baptistry (15th century).

Episodes particularly favored by Christian artists were Abraham's encounter with Melchizedek, the visit of the three angels, and the *Akedah*. In the first, stress was laid on the dual significance of the scene, Abraham's offering of tithes to the priest-king symbolizing the presentation of gifts to the infant Jesus by the three Magi, and Melchizedek's offering of bread and wine to Abraham prefiguring the Eucharist. The Melchizedek episode appears in the works at Rome, Ravenna, and Poitou referred to above and in the 13th-century portal of Amiens cathedral, and it inspired Tintoretto's painting for the Scuola di San Rocco, Venice (16th century). Melchizedek is usually depicted wearing a crown and bearing a chalice, while Abraham is often shown as a knight in armor. The visit of the angels has been variously interpreted by Christian artists. In the eastern church the angels were seen as a prediction of the Trinity and there are many icons on this theme, notably the delicate painting by Andrei Rublev (1422), now in Moscow. In western countries, their announcement of the impending birth of Isaac was thought to prefigure the Annunciation, and this traditional medieval reading inspires the Rome mosaics, the Verdun altar, the doors of San Zeno, and the 12th-century Psalter of Saint Louis (Paris). From the 17th century onward this incident was taken as the archetype of hospitality, inspiring such post-Renaissance paintings as those of *Rembrandt (1636, now in Leningrad), Murillo, and the Tiepolos. The dismissal of Hagar – whom the Church took to prefigure the superseded "Old Law," Sarah symbolizing the New – was popular in the 17th century particularly with Dutch artists, mainly because it offered opportunities for domestic and emotionally dramatic scenes. The episode was thus exploited by Rubens, Rembrandt, Nicolaes Maes, and Jan Steen. A French artist of a later period who treated the same subject was Corot. A parable in the Gospel of Luke (16:22) was responsible for a quaint treatment of Abraham in representations of the Last Judgment on Gothic cathedrals such as Paris, Rheims, Bourges, and Bamberg. Here the saved souls are shown being gathered into "Abraham's bosom." Among modern Jewish artists, Chagall, who was particularly fascinated by the life of Abraham, painted many scenes from the patriarch's life story, including the circumcision of Isaac.

The most popular representation of Abraham in Jewish art was that showing the *Akedah*. This appears on the western wall of the *Dura-Europos synagogue of the third century C.E. This theme lent itself to representations in the continuous or narrative style, in which a sequence of events is represented without frame or formal interruptions, as in the mosaic floor of the *Bet Alfa (sixth century C.E.) synagogue. Other popular themes were the appearance of the three angels to Abraham and his condemnation to death through fire by Nimrod. An outstanding example of the latter is found in a British Museum illuminated manuscript (Ms. Add. 27210) where Abraham is rescued by two figures, not found in other illustrations. An elderly bearded male with outstretched arms is seen in the foreground, while in the background is an angel with clearly defined wings. It is improbable that both these figures represent angels as they appear of different age and complexion. The older figure may therefore represent God, a fact which would suggest a Christian illuminator.

[Helen Rosenau]

The story of Abraham provided the basis for several musical compositions from the late 18th century onward. The Hagar and Ishmael episode was the theme of oratorios, notably Scarlatti's *Agar et Ismaele esiliati* (1683) and Giovanni Battista Vitali's *Agar* (1671). Of the few works on the sojourn in Egypt, the oratorio *Sara in Egitto* (1708) probably holds the record among "pasticcios" – works in which several composers collaborated or were used – since the setting of the libretto was entrusted to no fewer than 24 composers. Schubert's first song, written in March 1811, was "*Hagars Klage.*" The only opera on this subtheme, *Agar au désert* (1806) by Etienne Nicolas Méhul, was never performed. Michael *Gnessin wrote an opera on Abraham's youth, during his visit to Ereẓ Israel in 1922. Prominent among the more specifically Jewish compositions are the Ladino (Judeo-Spanish) romances, *Cuando el Rey Nimrod, Abram Abinu*, and *En primero alabaremos,* which reflect the legend of Abraham's birth found in the *Sefer ha-Yashar*; some also mention the *Akedah*. The romanza *El Dios de cielo de Abraham* used to be sung in Tetuan, Morocco.

[Bathja Bayer]

BIBLIOGRAPHY: Noth, Personennamen, 52, 145. **ADD. BIBLIOGRAPHY:** R. Clements, *Abraham and David* (1967); T.L. Thompson, *The Historicity of the Patriarchal Narratives* (1973); J. van Seters, *Abraham in History and Tradition* (1974); Y. Muffs, in: JJS, 33 (1982), 81–107; A.E. Knauf, in: BZ, 29 (1985), 97–103; N.M. Sarna, *The JPS Torah Commentary Genesis* (1989); A. Millard, "Abraham," in: ABD, 1:35–41; S.D. Sperling, *The Original Torah* (1998), 75–90. IN THE AGGADAH: Ginzberg, Legends, 1 (1942), 185ff.; 5 (1947), 207ff.; Schwarzbaum, in: *Yeda Am*, 9 (1963/64), 38–46; E.E. Halevy, *Sha'arei ha-Aggadah* (1963), 72–82; G.H. Box, *Apocrypha of Abraham* (1918); A. Marmorstein, *The Doctrine of Merits in Old Rabbinical Literature* (1920), index; Sandmel, in: HUCA, 26 (1955), 151–332; J.J. Petuchowski, *ibid.*, 28 (1957), 127–36; Wacholder, *ibid.*, 34 (1963), 83–113; G. Vermes, *Scripture and Tradition in Judaism* (1961), 67–126. IN JEWISH PHILOSOPHY: **ADD. BIBLIOGRAPHY:** M. Hallamish, H. Kasher, and Y. Silman (eds.), *The Faith of Abraham* (Heb., 2002); D.J. Lasker, "The Prophecy of Abraham in Karaite Thought," in: *Jerusalem Studies in Jewish Thought*, 14 (*J.B. Sermoneta Memorial Volume*, 1998). IN CHRISTIAN TRADITION: Cahiers Sioniens, 5, no. 2 (1951), 93ff.; G. Kittel, *Theological Dictionary of the New Testament*, 1 (1964), 9; J. Hastings (ed.), *Dictionary of the Bible*, 1 (1911), 16–17; *Dictionnaire de théologie catholique*, 1 (1902), 99–111. IN ISLAM: A. Sprenger, *Leben und Lehre des Mohammad*, 2 (1869), 276ff.; C. Snouk Hurgronje, *Het Mekkaansche Feest* (1880), 30ff.; B. Heller, in: REJ, 85 (1928), 117, 126; 98 (1934), 1–18; J.W. Hirschberg, *Der Diwan des as-Samau'al ibn 'Adi'* (1931), 63–64; idem, *Juedische und christliche Lehren im vor- und fruehislamischen Arabien* (1939), 124–9; J. Ankel, in: HUCA, 12–13 (1938), 387–409; Y. Moubarac, *Abraham dans le Coran* (1958), includes bibliography; S.D. Goitein, *Ha-Islam shel Muḥammad* (1956), 180–6. **ADD. BIBLIOGRAPHY:** I. al-Khalil, in EIS^2, 3, s.v. (incl. bibl.). MEDIEVAL HEBREW LITERATURE: A. Jellinek, *Beit ha-Midrash*, 1 (1938^2), 18–19; 5 (1938^2), 40–41; G. Scholem, *Kabbalah and its Mysticism* (1965), 168–79. IN ART: L. Réau, *Iconographie de l'art chrétien*, 2, pt. 2 (1956), 125–38; T. Ehrenstein, *Das Alte Testament im Bilde* (1923), 135–54; *The Bible in Art* (1956), plates 39–48; J. Leveen, *The Hebrew Bible in Art* (1944), index.

ABRAHAM, family of U.S. merchants. ABRAHAM ABRAHAM (1843–1911), son of a Bavarian immigrant, and Joseph Wechsler, himself an immigrant, established a dry goods store in Brooklyn, New York, in 1865. It became Brooklyn's largest department store, with six branches in metropolitan New York. On Wechsler's retirement in 1893 Abraham and the brothers Isidore and Nathan *Straus took over the firm, which they named Abraham & Straus. However, the *Straus' main interest remained focused on Macy's. Abraham's son-in-law, SIMON F. ROTHSCHILD (1861–1936), succeeded to the presidency of A. & S. in 1925, and from 1930 to 1936 was chairman of its board. Another son-in-law, CHARLES EDUARD BLUM (1863–1946), was president from 1930 to 1937 and board chairman from 1937 to 1946. In 1937 WALTER N. ROTHSCHILD (1892–1960), a grandson of Abraham Abraham and son of Simon F. Rothschild, became A. & S. president and served as board chairman from 1955 to 1960. Subsequently A. & S. became a unit in the chain known as Federated Department Stores, Inc. Abraham's great-grandson, and son of Walter N. Rothschild, WALTER N. ROTHSCHILD JR. (1920–2003), was president of A. & S. from 1963 to 1969. He served as chairman of the New York Urban Coalition from 1970 to 1973 and as chairman of the National Urban Coalition from 1973 to 1977. The family participated actively through all the generations in general and Jewish philanthropies but became remote from Jewish life.

[Hanns G. Reissner]

ABRAHAM, APOCALYPSE OF, a work of the second century C.E., extant only in the Slavonic version of a Greek translation of a presumably Hebrew original. Several variant forms of the Slavonic exist, including reworked versions in the medieval Eastern church sacred histories known as the *Palaiai*. The late Christian editing gives it a flavor which is strange to the Jewish reader. But only one interpolation can be identified as Christian and that not with certainty. Although translations of the book have been accessible to western scholars for 50 years, it is little known.

The book opens with a legend of Abraham's discovery of God (ch. 1–8), a theme well known from the *aggadah* and early Christian literature. This tells of Abraham's tragicomic adventures as an assistant in his father's business of making and selling idols, and culminates in his realization and recognition of the Creator. The legend concludes with a voice urging Abraham to leave his father's house, which is immediately destroyed by lightning.

A further heavenly call commands him to fast for 40 days and to offer the sacrifice described in Genesis 15:9. This leads to the main visionary section of the book. The angel Iaoel (Mss. Ioal, Iloel, etc.) appears (ch. 10–11) and leads him to the place of the sacrifice; the victims appear miraculously (ch. 12). The vulture (Gen. 15:11), later unmasked as Azazel, tells Abraham to flee the "holy heights" and to leave the angel (ch. 13). At the angel's bidding, Abraham refuses to listen to Azazel (ch. 14). The furnace (Gen. 15:17) appears, and angels carry up the sacrificial victims while the wings of the undivided dove serve to carry Abraham and his angelic guide to heaven (ch. 15).

Trembling, Abraham sees the Divine Glory (ch. 16), praises God, and prays for instruction (ch. 17). He is then enabled to contemplate the four-faced cherubim (ch. 18) and bidden to look down on the several lower heavens, which open under him. He observes the angels of the seventh and sixth heavens, and the stars in the fifth (ch. 19–20). The lower heavens remain undescribed, for he next sees an overall picture of the world (ch. 21). He also sees a great multitude of people, some on the right and some on the left. This is "the Creation." Those on the left are all the generations of mankind, those on the right, the chosen people (ch. 22). Next he is shown several scenes such as the Fall, the Temple, and its destruction (ch. 23–27), which form a condensed history of the world. As these are explained to him, he dares to ask some questions, such as "Why does God will (or permit) evil?" and "How long shall the suffering of the elect people last?" The rather obscure answers appear to contain an assertion of human free will (ch. 24). A computation of "eons" and "hours" is briefly sketched (ch. 28).

Finally (ch. 29) "a man" appears. He is worshipped by the heathen of the left side: from the right some revile him, others worship him. Azazel, who is contradictorily described both as coming from the left side and as a descendant of Abraham, also worships him. The "man's" function is "the remission for (?) the heathen in the last days," at which time the chosen people shall be tried by him. Although his description is followed by an eschatological prediction, he does not seem to be an instrument of the final deliverance. Abraham's vision ends with a statement about the "eon of righteousness" (ch. 29).

Back on earth he prays for further instruction, which he receives in the form of another prediction of the last things, including ten chastisements prepared for the heathen (ch. 30) and the salvation of the people at the hands of the elect one (ch. 31). There follows a short prediction of the Egyptian servitude and the deliverance – a paraphrase of Genesis 15:13–14 (ch. 32). This serves as the conclusion of the book, which thus fits neatly into the framework of a Midrash on Genesis 15.

The Jewish origin of the book cannot be doubted. The author's main concern, the nation's destiny, is discernible even in the peculiar passage about "the man." The most obvious and perhaps the correct explanation of this passage is to declare it a late Christian interpolation, yet "the man" does not fit the medieval Christian concept of Jesus. His function is not clearly messianic. This problematic passage therefore may have originated in some Judeo-Christian sect, which saw Jesus as precursor of the Messiah, or it may be Jewish, badly rewritten by an early Christian editor. Perhaps it reflects a Jewish view of Jesus as an apostle to the heathen, an explanation which would make it unique, and indeed startling.

The Apocalypse of Abraham is perhaps the last important product of the Apocalyptic movement. Possibly influenced by IV *Ezra, it reflects the plight of the Jews as the "people despised by the nations." However, the destruction of the Temple is not fresh in the author's memory. The characteristic, elaborate pseudepigraphic framework is missing and not all the extant recensions present it as a first-person account by Abraham. Within the tight framework of a simple version, the book successfully presents several important apocalyptic themes, including speculation about a transcendent God presiding over the heavens, a view of history as a sequence of periods, and an attempt to "compute the date of the end." Dualistic and deterministic tendencies are clearly present, but not strongly developed. There is, indeed, no special emphasis on any point of doctrine. The author, aiming at a restatement of ideas developed by his predecessors, is not too eager to break fresh ground. This impression, however, must be qualified by the possibility that the book has been abbreviated or badly edited, although it has survived as a remarkably complete literary unit.

BIBLIOGRAPHY: G.N. Bowetsch, *Apokalypse Abrahams* (1897); G.H. Box, *Apocalypse of Abraham* (1918); P. Riessler, *Altjuedisches Schrifttum…* (1928), 13–39; J. Kaufmann, in: EJ, 1 (1928), 548–53; Rubinstein, in: JJS, 8 (1957), 45–50; Schuerer, Gesch, 3 (1909^4), 336–9.

[Jacob Licht]

ABRAHAM, DAVID (1909–), Indian motion picture actor. Born in Bombay of a Bene Israel family, he used David as his professional name. Though trained in law, he took up acting in 1937 and subsequently appeared in over 100 Hindustani films, becoming widely known for his comedy roles. He toured the U.S. in 1952 as member of the Indian Film Delegation. Also active in the Indian Olympic Association, he was weight-lifting referee at the Olympic Games, Helsinki, 1952, and Fourth Maccabiah, Israel, 1953.

ABRAHAM, GERALD (1904–1988), British musicologist. Abraham was born in Newport, Isle of Wight. Although largely self-taught in the field, he became a highly respected authority on Russian music, learning Russian and Slavonic languages in the course of his work; he published three books devoted to Russian music. He also wrote *A Hundred Years of Music* (1938) and *Chopin's Musical Style* (1939), a small, serious scholarly work. He was employed by the BBC in various capacities, including assistant controller of music during 1935–47 and 1962–67.

Abraham was the first professor of music at Liverpool University, teaching there from 1947 to 1962, exposing his students to Russian music on an academic level. He was president of the Royal Music Association from 1969 to 1974, becoming a Commander of the Order of the British Empire in the latter year.

Among his publications were a collection of his essays, *Slavonic and Romantic Music* (1968), and the *Concise Oxford History of Music* (1979), in which the broad range of his interests was fully displayed. He edited monographs or symposia on Schubert, Schumann, Sibelius, Handel, Tchaikovsky, Borodin, and others, as well as the *New Oxford History of Music* (1955–86); he also served as chairman of the editorial board of the *New Grove Dictionary of Music and Musicians.*

ABRAHAM, KARL (1877–1925), German psychoanalyst. Born in Bremen to religious parents, Abraham was Germany's first psychoanalyst and a major figure in both the organizational and scientific development of psychoanalysis. Abraham received his early clinical experience at a mental hospital in Dalldorf. He became acquainted with Freud's work through Bleuler and Jung in Zurich, and first met Freud in 1907. A deep friendship and professional alliance bound the two men until Abraham's death. Abraham's work covered almost every field of psychoanalysis, but his most significant contributions through pioneering studies were in the fields of libidinal development, character formation, the psychoses, and addiction. He investigated the effects of infantile sexuality and family relationships on the child's mental development, and drew a correlation between characteristic mental disorders and the problems at different stages of the child's mental development. Toward the end of his life, Abraham concentrated almost exclusively on manic-depressive psychosis, where he paralleled and deepened Freud's work. This work is written up in his paper of 1911 translated in 1927 as "Notes on the Psychoanalytic Investigation and Treatment of Manic-Depressive Insanity and Allied Conditions." Abraham related melancholia to regression to the oral level and to the loss of love and its patterning after mourning. Schizophrenia, too, is a regression from a traumatic situation to an early infantile level of development. Abraham was president of the Berlin Psychoanalytical Society from its founding until his death. He was also secretary (1922–24), and then president (1924–25), of the International Psychoanalytical Association. Most of his research work appears in his *Clinical Papers and Essays on Psychoanalysis* (1955) and his published correspondence with Freud in *A Psychoanalytic Dialogue* (1965).

BIBLIOGRAPHY: E. Jones, in: *International Journal of Psycho-Analysis*, 7 (1926), 155–81 (includes bibliography); E. Glover, in: L. Eidelberg (ed.), *Encyclopedia of Psychoanalysis* (1968), 1–8 and index; M. Grotjahn, in: F. Alexander et al. (eds.), *Psychoanalytic Pioneers* (1966), 142–59. **ADD. BIBLIOGRAPHY:** H. Abraham, *Karl Abraham. Sein Leben fuer die Psychoanalyse* (1976).

ABRAHAM, MAX (1875–1922), German theoretical electrophysicist. Born in Danzig, Abraham was an assistant to the physicist Max Planck. He worked in turn at Goettingen (1900), Cambridge (England), and in the U.S. In 1909 he became professor of mechanics in Milan, but in 1915 was expelled as an enemy alien. He then served in the German army. In 1919 he was appointed professor of physics at the Technische Hochschule Stuttgart. Abraham studied the dynamics of electrons, and his two-volume *Theorie der Elektrizitaet* went through eight editions between 1904 and 1930.

BIBLIOGRAPHY: *Physikalische Zeitschrift*, 24 (1923), 49–53; *Elektrotechnische Zeitschrift*, 44 (1923), 20; NDB, 1 (1952), 23–24.

[Samuel Aaron Miller]

ABRAHAM, OTHER BOOKS OF. In addition to the Apocalypse of Abraham, extant in Slavonic, and the Testament of Abraham, preserved in a number of versions, there are several references in the literature of the first centuries of this era to works attributed to Abraham. Among the apocryphal works included in the early Christian lists attributed to Pseudo-Athanasius and Nicephorus, there is a book entitled *Abraham.* Its length is given as 300 stichoi. Similar, unclear references may be found in Apostolic Constitution 6:16 and elsewhere. More significant is Epiphanius' account (Adversus Haereses 38:5) of the Sethian Gnostic sect as "composing certain books in the name of great men… of Abraham, which they say to be an apocalypse and is full of all sorts of wickedness." Origen refers to a book relating a contest between good and evil angels over the salvation or perdition of Abraham's soul (Homilies on Lk. 35). It has been suggested that this incident may be related to the weighing of the soul, whose good and evil deeds are of equal measure, as described in *Testamentum Abraham* (A, 12f.). Yet, it must be noted that these two stories are far from identical, and Origen is probably drawing on a different Abraham book. An Arabic *Life of Abraham* is mentioned by James (*Apoc. Anecd.* 2, 81). Armenian works called *The Story of Abraham, Isaac and Mambres, The Ten Temptations of Abraham, History of Abraham, Memorial of the Patriarchs Abraham, Isaac, and Jacob* and others exist in manuscripts (e.g., Erevan 569, 717, 1425 et al.), but have never been studied.

BIBLIOGRAPHY: M.R. James, *Lost Apocrypha of the Old Testament* (1920), 16ff.; idem, *Testament of Abraham* (1892), 7–29.

[Michael E. Stone]

ABRAHAM, OTTO (1872–1926), ethnomusicologist. Born in Berlin, Abraham graduated in medicine at Berlin University in 1894 and thereafter dedicated himself to psychoacoustics and the physiology of music. From 1896 to 1905 he was assistant to Carl Stumpf (1868–1936) at the Berlin Institute of Psychology, and collaborated with E.M. von *Hornbostel in the establishment of the "Phonogrammarchiv" in 1900 which is known for its unique historical collections of music of the world. Abraham's work on tone perception was one of the pioneer studies in the psychology of music. His studies, mostly with Hornbostel, on the non-Western musical traditions and his suggested methods for transcribing this music put him among the founders of modern systematic ethnomusicology. Abraham introduced the first German attempt to record non-Western music. He recorded on wax cylinders a visiting Siamese court orchestra, music from South Africa and Japan, Armenian and Muslim songs, and Indian and Amerindian music. Between 1903 and 1906, Abraham and Hornbostel published important studies based on their tonometric measurements and transcriptions of those recorded examples. Among his articles are "Wahrnehmung kürzester Töne und Geräusche" (1898), "Studien Ueber das Tonsystem und die Musik der Japaner" (1902–3), "Phonographierte Tuerkische Melodien" (1904), "Phonographierte Indianermelodien aus Britisch-Colombia" (1906), "Zur Akustik des Knalles" (1919), and "Zur Psychologie der Tondistanz" (1926).

BIBLIOGRAPHY: Grove online; MGG²; J. Ellis et al., *Abhandlungen zur vergleichenden Musikwissenschaft, von A.J. Ellis, J.P.N. Land, C. Stumpf, O. Abraham und E.M. von Hornbostel, aus den Jahren 1885–1908* (1922)

[Israela Stein (2nd ed.)]

ABRAHAM, SAMUEL (d. 1792), merchant in Cochin. Abraham, who was probably of Polish birth, arrived in Cochin in about 1757 and served both the Dutch and English East India Companies. Abraham chiefly traded in timber for shipbuilding and to a lesser extent in paper, rice, pepper, and iron. He advanced large loans to the Dutch and English companies. With other leading Jewish merchants, he was entrusted with confidential diplomatic missions by the Dutch governor. His house was a meeting place for local princes, dignitaries, and merchants. Abraham established the first known contact between the Jews of Cochin and those of the Western Hemisphere with a Hebrew letter to the Jewish congregation of New York (c. 1790). It was accompanied by an outline history of the Jews in Malabar.

BIBLIOGRAPHY: W.J. Fischel, in: *Harry Austryn Wolfson Jubilee Volume* (1965), 255–74.

[Walter Joseph Fischel]

ABRAHAM, TESTAMENT OF, apocryphal story of the death of Abraham. It is preserved in two Greek versions, the longer one being the more original. There are also Arabic, Coptic, Ethiopic, and Romanian versions. The book is part of an extensive literature of testaments and, in addition to the Testament of Abraham, there exist Testaments of Adam, Isaac, Jacob, the Twelve Patriarchs (sons of Jacob), Job, etc. The dependence of the book upon Jewish aggadic sources and the absence of Christian motifs with the exception of a possible influence of New Testament phraseology upon the actual wording show that the Testament of Abraham was composed by a Jew, writing in Greek, and was possibly based on a Hebrew (or Aramaic) original. The exact date of its composition is unknown. The book utilizes both Midrashim about Abraham and the *aggadah* about the death of Moses (see Assumption of *Moses). Thus, the reluctance of Abraham to accept his death from the hand of the archangel Michael is founded upon the narrative of Moses' death in Jewish sources. Finally Abraham is prepared to accept God's decision, if the angel will show him the whole universe. This wish is fulfilled and the author includes in his book interesting apocalyptic material. The heavenly judge is Abel, the son of Adam, because God wants humanity to be judged by a man (see *Son of Man). At the end, Abraham is killed by deception on the part of the Angel of Death.

BIBLIOGRAPHY: M.R. James, *Testament of Abraham* (1892); G.H. Box, *Testament of Abraham* (1927); P. Riessler, *Altjuedisches Schrifttum…* (1928), 1091–1103; Ginzberg, Legends, 229–306.

[David Flusser]

ABRAHAM ABELE BEN ABRAHAM SOLOMON (1764–1836), talmudic scholar in Lithuania. Abraham, who was known as Abele Poswoler, was a pupil of Solomon of Wilkomir. In his youth he became rabbi in Poswol (near Kovno) and in 1802 was appointed head of the Vilna *bet din*, a position which he held for 30 years. In 1835 he intervened in the dispute between the publishers of the Romm Talmud and those of the Slavuta Talmud. The Slavuta publishers had started their enterprise first and claimed that the Romm family had intruded on their domain. When the Jewry of Ereẓ Israel was in financial straits in 1822, Abraham appealed to the wealthy Jews of Poland and Lithuania to aid the *yishuv* but the appeal was of limited success. Abraham did not publish many responsa and talmudic novellae, but some were preserved in the works of his contemporaries. Of particular interest is the fact that Abraham, although a devout Jew, gave his approbation to the *Te'udah be-Yisrael* by Isaac Baer Levinsohn, one of the leading Russian *maskilim*.

His novellae and responsa appeared in a book called *Be'er Abraham* from a manuscript with the *Be'er ba-Sadeh* commentary by Rabbi Shmuel David Movshowitz (Jerusalem Institute, Jerusalem, 1980). The book contains a commentary on tractate *Berakhot*, novellae and halakhic rulings (from different books), and 112 responsa on different subjects in the four parts of the Shulḥan Arukh.

BIBLIOGRAPHY: S.J. Fuenn, *Kiryah Ne'emanah* (1915²), 244–5; H.N. Maggid-Steinschneider, *Ir Vilna*, 1 (1900), 19–29; A.M. Luncz (ed.), *Yerushalayim*, 5 (1898), 222; 9 (1911), 7–8; H.N. Dembitzer, *Meginnei Ereẓ Yisrael* (1904²), 4–5; I. Klausner, in: *Arim ve-Immahot be-Yisrael*, 1 (1946), 168; *Yahadut Lita* (1959), 87, 271–3, 298; S.D. Movshowitz, Introduction to *Be'er Abraham*, 11–19; D. Zaritzki, *Be'er Abraham*, 21–30.

[Yehoshua Horowitz]

ABRAHAM ABUSCH BEN ẒEVI HIRSCH (1700–1769), German rabbi and halakhist. He was also called Abraham Abusch Lissa and also Abusch Frankfurter, from the towns Lissa and Frankfurt where he served as rabbi, after having been rabbi of Mezhirech. After the interregnum brought about by the departure of Jacob Joshua *Falk, the community of Frankfurt approached him to become its rabbi. The community of Lissa was reluctant to part with him and only did so after much persuasion on the part of the communal leaders of Frankfurt. His pious and meek disposition and the stories of his charitable deeds became legendary. The name of Abraham Abusch is associated with a *cause célèbre,* "the *Cleves *get*" (divorce; see *Lipschuetz, Israel). Although several renowned rabbis approved the divorce Abraham persisted in his opinion that it was invalid. The members of his community supported him by enacting a regulation barring from the Frankfurt rabbinate anyone who had approved the divorce. For some time, he also held the important position of *parnas* or president of the "*Councils of the Lands." Although he was renowned as a talmudic scholar, few of his writings have survived. Several of his works appeared under the title *Birkat Avraham:* (1) novellae on five tractates of *Seder Mo'ed* (1881); (2) commentary on the Passover *Haggadah* (1887), with a supplement, *Maḥazeh Avraham* (1908); (3) a volume also known as *Kaneh Avraham* (1884), kabbalistic commentary on Genesis; (4) a commentary on *Berakhot* (1930); and (5) on Ruth (1934). He also wrote *Darkhei ha-Ḥayyim*, on remedies, medicines, and charms (1912). His ethical will was also published (1806).

BIBLIOGRAPHY: M. Horovitz, *Frankfurter Rabbinen*, 3 (1884), 65ff.; L. Lewin, *Geschichte der Juden in Lissa* (1904), 185ff.

[Alexander Tobias]

°**ABRAHAM A SANCTA CLARA** (c. 1644–1709), Augustinian friar and anti-Jewish propagandist; court preacher in Vienna from 1677. His numerous sermons and tracts violently attacked the Jews along the traditional lines of popular anti-Jewish hatemongering. He charged the Jews with causing the plague by witchcraft, denounced them along with the devil as Christianity's worst enemy, and gave currency to the *host desecration libel. The coarse language and style of his sermons and tracts influenced the Viennese brand of *antisemitism (and its disseminators such as S. *Brunner, J. *Deckert, and K. *Lueger) and of *National Socialism.

BIBLIOGRAPHY: R.A. Kann, *A Study in Austrian Intellectual History* (1960), 50–115 (bibliography 306–9); O. Frankl, *Der Jude in den deutschen Dichtungen des 15., 16., und 17. Jahrhunderts* (1905), index. **ADD. BIBLIOGRAPHY:** F. Schillinger, *Abraham a Sancta Clara: pastorale et discours politique dans l'Autriche du XVIIe siècle* (1993).

ABRAHAM BAR ḤIYYA (**Ḥayya**; d. c. 1136), Spanish philosopher, mathematician, astronomer, and translator. Little is known about Abraham's life apart from the fact that he lived in Barcelona. Two titles by which he was known provide clues to his public activity. One was *Savasorda*, a corruption of the Arabic *ṣāḥib-al-shurṭa*, originally meaning "captain of the bodyguard," but by Abraham's time denoting a functionary whose duties were both judiciary and civil, the exact scope of which can only be surmised. A court position was not unique for a Jew in Christian Spain at that time, and Abraham would have been useful for his mathematical and astronomical knowledge, his skill in surveying, and his linguistic abilities (he states in his writings that from his early youth he "gained honor before princes and royalty"). The other title, *nasi*, was not uncommon in Spanish Jewry and although in this instance also the exact significance is undetermined, it appears to denote an office within the Jewish community exercising a judiciary function with the power of imposing punishments and regulating communal taxation.

The only incident known from his life is a clash with his distinguished contemporary in Barcelona, *Judah b. Barzillai al-Bargeloni. This occurred at a wedding which Abraham insisted on postponing because the stars were not propitious, whereas Judah wished to proceed with the ceremony as he held astrological beliefs to be "a custom of the Chaldeans." At some period of his life Abraham visited France – perhaps Provence – which at that time was ruled by the count of Barcelona. It appears that this visit was connected with the problems of land surveying.

The dates and places of his birth and death are unknown. A manuscript dated 1136 refers to him as "of blessed memory" but this could be a later interpolation. However, Plato of Tivoli, who cites him as a collaborator in his translations up to 1136, does not mention Abraham in connection with a translation in 1138. As there is no evidence of his having lived subsequently, it has been assumed that he died c. 1136.

Philosophy

Concentrating on cosmogony, Abraham held that all things were first created in potentiality where they could be divided into matter, form, and not-being. In order to actualize them, God removed the not-being and joined form to matter. Matter is divided into pure matter and the dregs of matter, while form is divided into closed form and open form. The first stage in the process of creation is the emanation of a light from the closed form. This closed form is too pure to combine with matter and is identified with the form of angels, souls, etc. The light shines on the open form, qualifying it to combine with matter; one part of the open form combines with the pure matter and from this juncture the firmaments are created; the other part joins the dregs, thereby creating the four elements and the beings of the corporeal world. A further emanation of light over the firmament causes that form already attached to matter to change its place – and this brings about the creation of the moving stars; while a further emanation of light touches that matter which can change its form, and from this are formed all that fly, swim, and go. Man is the summit of creation, distinguished by his rational faculty. He has free will and can choose between the right way and sinning; if he sins, he still has the possibility of repentance. The way to repentance is always open, but the reward of eternal life is only for the God-fearing and God-acknowledging. All aspects of this world are transient and the important consideration is the world to come. The saintly individual lives an ascetic life in this world in order to be rewarded in the next. By observing the Torah, Israel obtains the reward of the world to come. Just as time had a beginning, so it must have an end and this will usher in the era of salvation when the wicked will be destroyed and only Israel and any others who accept the Torah will survive. Only Israel will be resurrected – the righteous to eternal life, the wicked to eternal justice.

Although points of similarity with other medieval thinkers are frequently discernible in Abraham's philosophical work, his writings contain an original admixture of Neoplatonic, Aristotelian, and rabbinic ideas, with original interpretations. He was sufficiently independent to reject philosophical for rabbinical theories when he deemed necessary, and his philosophy falls into no ready-made categories. He was one of the very first to write on scientific and philosophic subjects in Hebrew and many of the terms coined by him have passed into accepted Hebrew usage. His Hebrew is simple and lucid, similar in style to the later Midrashim.

Mathematical Works

Abraham was the author of the first encyclopedic work in Hebrew, *Yesodei ha-Tevunah u-Migdal ha-Emunah* ("Foundations of Understanding and Tower of Faith"). This was probably based on translations from the Arabic (it was published by Steinschneider in *Hebraetsche Bibliographie*, vol. 7, Sp. tr. by J.M. Millás Vallicrosa, 1952). Only sections have been preserved and these deal with geometry, arithmetic, optics, and music. He also wrote about mathematics in his *Ḥibbur ha-Meshiḥah ve-ha-Tishboret* ("Treatise on Mensuration and Calculation"; Sp. tr. by J.M. Millás Vallicrosa, 1931), the original object of which was to help French Jews in the measurement of their fields. This is the first Hebrew work to show that the area of a circle is πr^2 and is the first known work – after an Egyptian papyrus of the 18th century B.C.E. – to give the formula of a truncated pyramid. It was published by M. Guttmann (2 pts., 1912–13). Plato of Tivoli translated the work into Latin in 1145 as *Liber Embadorum* ("The Book of Areas") and this introduced Arabic trigonometry to the West. It was the chief source for the writings of the celebrated mathematician, Leonardo Fibonacci of Pisa.

Astronomical Works

Abraham's main astronomical work, known as *Ḥokhmat ha-Ḥizzayon*, consisted of two parts. The first part, *Ẓurat ha-Areẓ ve-Tavnit Kaddurei ha-Raki'a* ("Form of the Earth and Figure of the Celestial Spheres"), is a geography – "a short review of lands according to the seven climates" – which long remained the chief source of geographical knowledge among Jews (it was published by M. Jaffe and Jonathan b. Joseph in Offenbach, 1720; Sp. tr. by J.M. Millás Vallicrosa, 1956). The second part, *Ḥeshbon Mahalekhot ha-Kokhavim* ("Calculation of the Courses of the Stars"; with Sp. tr. by J.M. Millás Vallicrosa, 1959), was often quoted; it incorporates a complete section on intercalation. The whole work is probably the first exposition of the Ptolemaic system in Hebrew and was the first complete textbook on astronomy in that language.

Abraham further considered problems of intercalation in his *Sefer* (or *Sod*) *ha-Ibbur* ("Book of Intercalation"), which was written in 1122 "to enable the Jews to observe the festivals on the correct dates." This work explains the principles of intercalation and shows how to calculate the Hebrew and Arabic years (publ. by H. Filipowski, London, 1851). It was often quoted by later authorities and was accepted as authoritative. Mention should also be made of the astronomical and astrological tables compiled by Abraham which were also often quoted, although never published. They include reckonings for year-cycles, the New Moon, the Egyptian, Arabic, Roman, and Alexandrian years, etc.

Astrology and Eschatology

Another of Abraham's smaller compositions was his letter to Judah b. Barzillai al-Bargeloni, defending astrology in connection with the above-mentioned incident at the Barcelona wedding (publ. by Z. Schwarz, 1917). However, the main source of knowledge of Abraham's astrological views is to be found in *Megillat ha-Megalleh* ("Scroll of the Revealer"; publ. by A. Posnanski, 1924; Sp. tr. by J.M. Millás Vallicrosa, 1929). This is an eschatological book, the first by a European rabbi, written with the object of determining the end of time. After working out a correspondence between the seven days of Creation with seven eras of world history, Abraham came to the conclusion that redemption would come to the world in the year 1383 C.E. and resurrection in 1448. He adduces proofs from both the Bible and astrology. This work was of considerable influence, for example, on *Judah Halevi, whose theory of the transmission of the prophetic spirit derives from it, and on the kabbalists, particularly those of the German school. Most of *Abrabanel's astrological knowledge was derived from this work, parts of which were translated into Latin and French.

Knowledge of Abraham's philosophy is partly derived from this work but even more from his *Hegyon ha-Nefesh ha-Aẓuvah* (publ. by E. Freimann, Leipzig, 1860; Eng. tr. by G. Wigoder, "Meditation of the Sad Soul," 1969). This deals with creation, repentance, good and evil, and the saintly life. The emphasis is ethical, the approach is generally homiletical – based on the exposition of biblical passages – and it may have been designed for reading during the Ten Days of Penitence. It is less frequently quoted than Abraham's other works. A so-called "lost work" called *Geder Adam* is probably identical with *Hegyon ha-Nefesh*. Apart from his original compositions, Abraham collaborated in several of the translations made by Plato of Tivoli from Arabic to Latin. These played an important role in the transmission of Arabic scientific knowledge to Europe. There is also a translation of *De Horarum Electionibus*, a work on algebra by Ali ibn Aḥmad al-Imrānī made by Abraham; it is not known whether he did this on his own or in collaboration with Plato of Tivoli.

BIBLIOGRAPHY: L.D. Stitskin, *Judaism as a Philosophy: The Philosophy of Abraham bar Hiyya* (1960); G. Wigoder, *Meditation of the Sad Soul* (1969), introd.; W. Bacher, *Bibelexegese der juedischen Religionsphilosophen des Mittelalters vor Maimûni* (1892); Baer, Spain, 1 (1961), index; I. Efros, *Problem of Space in Jewish Mediaeval Philosophy* (1917); idem, in: JQR, 17 (1926/27), 129ff.; 20 (1929/30), 113–38; J. Guttmann, in: MGWJ, 47 (1903), 446–68, 545–69; M. Guttmann, in: *Ha-Ẓofeh me-Ereẓ Hagar*, 1 (1911), 1–30; Husik, Philosophy, index; D. Neumark, *Geschichte der juedischen Philosophie des Mittelalters* (1907); Rabin, in: *Meẓudah*, 3 (1945), 158–70 (repr. in M. Bar Asher and B. Dan (eds.), *Ḥikrei Lashon* (1999), 309–23 (Heb.)); Scholem, in: MGWJ, 75 (1931), 172–91; Baron, Social², index; J.M. Millás Vallicrosa,

Estúdios sobre la história de la ciencia española (1949), 219–26; Levey, in: Isis, 43 (1952), 257–64; idem, in: *Osiris*, 11 (1954), 50–64. **ADD. BIBLIOGRAPHY:** S. Klein-Braslavy, "The Creation of Man and the Story of the Garden of Eden in the Thought of Abraham Bar Hiyya," in: I. Orpaz, N. Govrin, A. Kasher, B.Y. Michali, and Z. Malachi (eds.), *Professor Israel Efros – Poet and Philosopher* (1981), 203–29 (Heb.); T. Lévy, "Les débuts de la littérature mathématique hébraïque: la géométrie d'Abraham bar Hiyya (XIe–XIIes.)," in: *Micrologus*, 9 (2001); *Gli Ebrei e le Scienze. The Jews and the Sciences* (2001), 35–64; M. Rubio, "The First Hebrew Encyclopedia of Science: Abraham Bar Hiyya's *Yesodei ha-Tevunah u-Migdal ha-Emunah*," in: S. Harvey (ed.), *The Medieval Hebrew Encyclopedias of Science and Philosophy* (2001), 140–53.

[Geoffrey Wigoder]

ABRAHAM BAR JACOB (c. 1669–1730), convert to Judaism who worked as a copper engraver in Amsterdam. Born in Germany, Abraham b. Jacob had been a Christian pastor in the Rhineland before converting to Judaism. He was particularly celebrated for his collaboration in the Amsterdam *Haggadah* of 1695 to which he contributed a series of engravings partly copied from the *Icones Biblicae* of Mattheus Merian of Basle and a map of Palestine with Hebrew lettering. This work set a new fashion in *Haggadot* and served as a model for more than 200 years. Abraham b. Jacob's other works include the title pages to Joseph b. Ephraim *Caro's Shulḥan Arukh (1697–98), Isaiah b. Abraham *Horowitz's *Shenei Luḥot ha-Berit* (1698), and Joseph b. Ḥayyim Sarfati's *Yad Yosef* (1700); an amulet for women in childbirth; and a wall calendar for 130 years with baroque illustrations. The engraving of a portrait of *ḥakham* Isaac *Aboab da Fonseca of Amsterdam, painted by Joseph b. Abraham, is also ascribed to him.

BIBLIOGRAPHY: Wolf, Bibliotheca, 3 (1727), 39; Roth, Art, 444, 445, 521. **ADD. BIBLIOGRAPHY:** A. Yaari, *Meḥkarei Sefer* (1958), 250–51; H. Brodsky, in *Jewish Art*, 19 (1993/4), 148–57; idem, in: *Journal of the Israel Map Collectors Society*, 13 (1996) 37–43.

ABRAHAM BEN ALEXANDER KATZ OF KALISK (Kalisz; 1741–1810), ḥasidic leader in Poland and Ereẓ Israel. He was a disciple of *Dov Baer of Mezhirech. According to ḥasidic tradition he first studied under *Elijah b. Solomon, the Gaon of Vilna. He joined the *Talk*, an ḥasidic conventicle whose precise nature is unknown. Abraham gave expression to the ḥasidic principle of serving God with fervor in a bizarre fashion, "turning somersaults in the streets and marketplaces" and ridiculing talmudic scholars. These exaggerated practices were among the reasons for the excommunication pronounced on the Ḥasidim by the rabbinical court of Vilna in 1772.

In 1777 Abraham immigrated to Ereẓ Israel with the group of Ḥasidim led by *Menahem Mendel of Vitebsk. He first settled in Safed and later in Tiberias, where he spent his last years. After the death of Menahem Mendel, Abraham succeeded him as head of the ḥasidic groups in Ereẓ Israel. His cordial relations with the founder of the Ḥabad movement, *Shneur Zalman, came to an end after the latter published his *Tanya* in 1796; Abraham expressed his disillusionment with Shneur Zalman's philosophical system, and Shneur Zalman, who was also treasurer of the fund in Russia, retaliated by stopping the flow of contributions. Abraham emphasized the importance of the ḥasidic group, independent of the authority of a *ẓaddik*. He believed in *dibbuk ḥaverim*, a close association between comrades who through contemplation and self-abnegation arrive together at a state of mystical ecstasy. His sayings and letters are collected in *Ḥesed le-Avraham* (1851) and *Iggerot Kodesh* (1927).

BIBLIOGRAPHY: Brawer, in: KS, 1 (1924/25), 142–50, 226–38; I. Halpern, *Ha-Aliyyot ha-Rishonot shel ha-Ḥasidim le-Ereẓ Yisrael* (1946), 65–79, passim; Horodezky, Ḥasidut, 2 (1953^4^), 39–46; Dubnow, Ḥasidut, 111f., 335–7, 483; Weiss, in: JJS, 6 (1955), 87–99; Scholem, Mysticism, 334–5; Schatz, in: *Molad*, 20 (1962), 514–5.

ABRAHAM BEN ALEXANDER (Axelrad) OF COLOGNE (13th century), kabbalist. A disciple of R. *Eleazar b. Judah of Worms, he immigrated to Spain where he probably studied with the kabbalist R. Ezra. Solomon b. Abraham *Adret knew him personally in his youth, and tells of his extraordinary oratorical gifts, and the interesting material in his sermons (Responsa no. 548). Abraham wrote a treatise concerning the Tetragrammaton, *Keter Shem Tov*, in which he tried to achieve a synthesis between the mysticism of the Jewish pietists (Ḥasidim) in Germany based on combinations of letters and numbers, and the Kabbalah of the **Sefirot* (with which he had become acquainted in Provence or in Spain). His text is composed of a short summary of his system and represents a kind of cosmological symbolism that relies on the conclusion provided by Abraham *Ibn Ezra in his *Sefer ha-Shem*, as well as on the statements of the kabbalists R. Ezra and R. Azriel. The work, which is extant in numerous manuscripts, was first published independently in Amsterdam in 1810. It also appeared under the title *Ma'amar Peloni Almoni* in the collection of writings *Likkutim me-Rav Hai Gaon* (1798). A new edition was published by Jellinek (1853). In Samson b. Eliezer's work *Barukh she-Amar* (1795), *Keter Shem Tov* is attributed to Menahem Ashkenazi, another disciple of Eleazar of Worms. Benjacob is wrong in stating that there is another work entitled *Keter Shem Tov* by Abraham consisting of a mystic commentary to Psalms, Joshua, and Judges.

[Gershom Scholem]

In one of the manuscripts found in Jerusalem, *Keter Shem Tov* is entitled *Ma'amar be-Kabbalah Nevu'it*, a "Treatise on Prophetic Kabbalah," and this title indicates the role played by this Ashkenazi figure in transmitting certain Ashkenazi modes of thought to Barcelona, where Abraham *Abulafia's prophetic Kabbalah made its first step.

[Moshe Idel (2nd ed.)]

BIBLIOGRAPHY: A. Jellinek, *Auswahl kabbalistischer Mystik*, 1 (1853), 9 (Ger. pt.); idem, in: MGWJ, 2 (1853), 78; M. Steinschneider, in: HB, 6 (1863), 126; 8 (1865), 147; idem, in: Jeschurun, 6 (1869), 169; Graetz, Gesch, 7 (1904^3^), 74, n. 2.

ABRAHAM BEN AVIGDOR (d. 1542), rabbi and author. For 20 years, Abraham served as the rabbi of Prague. One of his pupils was Abraham Jaffe, the father of Mordecai *Jaffe. In 1534 Abraham and the famous *shtadlan* Joseph (Joselmann) of Rosheim framed 23 *takkanot* designed to adjudicate an inter-communal dispute in Bohemia and to restore harmony in the community. After the expulsion of the Jews from Bohemia in 1541, Abraham composed the *seliḥah* beginning *"Anna Elohei Avraham,"* recited in the Polish ritual on Yom Kippur. According to David *Gans, Abraham had a knowledge of "all the seven sciences." His works included (1) glosses on the *Tur Oraḥ Ḥayyim* by Jacob b. Asher, published in Prague and Augsburg both in 1540; (2) a supercommentary on Rashi's Bible commentary, quoted in the *Devek Tov* of Simeon Ossenburg, and in *Minḥat Yehudah* by Judah Leib b. Obadiah Eilenburg (1609); (3) decisions, quoted by Moses Isserles and Joel Sirkes.

BIBLIOGRAPHY: Zunz, Lit Poesie, 390; Zunz, Poesie, 57; Michael, Or, no. 31–32; K. Lieben, *Gal Ed* (1856), no. 121 (Heb. section 64–65; Ger. section 57–58); Landshuth, Ammudei, 2; Kracauer, in: REJ, 16 (1888), 92; S. Hock, *Familien Prags* (1892), 396, n. 2; Davidson, Oẓar, 1 (1924), 279, no. 6111.

[Yehoshua Horowitz]

ABRAHAM BEN AZRIEL (13th century), liturgical commentator, one of the "Elders of Bohemia." Abraham was a disciple of the great German pietists, *Judah b. Samuel he-Ḥasid and *Eleazar b. Judah of Worms (Rokeah) as well as of *Baruch b. Isaac of Regensburg, the latter two being his chief teachers. *Isaac b. Moses Or Zaru'a was his disciple. About 1234 he wrote *Arugat ha-Bosem* ("Spice Garden"), a commentary on liturgical poems (edited by E.E. Urbach with commentary, 1939). The work reveals a comprehensive knowledge of every branch of Jewish learning: masoretic text and vocalization, exegesis and grammar, the halakhic and aggadic Midrashim, the two Talmuds and their early expositors, and philosophical and kabbalistic literature. All obscure references in the *piyyutim* are explained in great detail. As a result of its prolixity, the book did not have a wide circulation and is only rarely quoted in later literature. However, after Abraham *Berliner discovered the manuscript in the Vatican library, scholars realized its importance. Abraham's main sources are: Abraham Ibn Ezra, Eleazar Rokeaḥ, Judah Ḥayyuj, Judah b. Samuel he-Ḥasid, Joseph Kara, Jacob Tam, Moses of Taku, Rashi, Solomon Parḥon, Samuel b. Meir, Nathan b. Jehiel of Rome, and Maimonides. He was the first of the French and German scholars to make full use of the whole of Maimonides' work. The quotations in the book give an insight into the nature and character of many books no longer extant, by authorities such as Samuel b. Meir and Eleazar Rokeaḥ (who is mentioned by name more than 170 times) and by scholars whose names were previously unknown. Abraham was known for his critical insight and independence and did not hesitate to contradict his teacher, Eleazar Rokeaḥ. His quotations from the halakhic and aggadic literature, the *Tosefta*, and the Babylonian and Palestinian Talmuds are valuable, for there are many differences between his texts and those appearing in the printed editions.

BIBLIOGRAPHY: Steinschneider, in: HB, 9 (1869), 174; MWJ, 1 (1874), 2–3, 5; Perles, in: MGWJ, 26 (1877), 360–73; Kaufmann, *ibid.*, 31 (1882), 316–24, 360–70, 410–22; E.E. Urbach (ed.), *Arugat ha-Bosem* (1967), introduction.

ABRAHAM BEN BENJAMIN ZE'EV BRISKER (d. 1700), Lithuanian author and preacher. After the decree of expulsion from Lithuania in 1655 Abraham went to Vienna, where he became a pupil of R. Shabbetai Sheftel *Horowitz. After the expulsion of the Jews from Vienna in 1670 Abraham returned to Brest Litovsk and continued his studies under R. Mordecai Guenzburg and R. Ẓevi Hirsch. At the end of his preface to *Zera Avraham* he described his tribulations: "Most of my days were spent in sorrow, and I studied under difficulties and in wandering." He mentions his intention "to immigrate to the Holy Land" which, however, he did not fulfill. He signed himself *"Alluf* Abraham" as one of the representatives of Brest Litovsk at the meeting of the *Council of the Lands in Lublin in 1683. Abraham is the author of *Asarah Ma'amarot*, a commentary on *Avot*, chapter 6 (Frankfurt on the Oder, 1680); *Zera Avraham,* which includes sermons on "the connection between the weekly portions, and other verses, Midrashim and commentaries according to a literal interpretation" (Sulzbach, 1685); and *Perush al Eser Atarot* – a kabbalistic work (Frankfurt on the Oder, 1968). In the preface to *Asarah Ma'amarot* he refers to his unpublished works *Berit Avraham* (a brief summary of the decisions of Shabbetai b. Meir ha-Kohen and *David b. Samuel ha-Levi on *Yoreh De'ah*) and *Ḥesed Avraham*, a kabbalistic commentary on the weekly scriptural portions.

BIBLIOGRAPHY: A.L. Feinstein, *Ir Tehillah* (1886), 32, 158, 191; D. Kaufmann, *Die letzte Vertreibung der Juden aus Wien…* (1889), 223–4; EG, 2 (1954), 53–54, 153.

[Yehoshua Horowitz]

ABRAHAM BEN DANIEL (1511–1578), Italian rabbi and poet. Abraham, who was born in Modena, was employed as tutor by Jewish families in various Italian cities from 1530. Later, he became rabbi and preacher in Ferrara. He composed numerous religious and liturgical poems. According to his statement these numbered more than 5,000. Some poems deal with autobiographical occasions; others celebrate historical events (e.g., the false accusation against the Jews in Rome, 1555). Several are dedicated to his family and friends, or written as prayers for them. The poems which include elegies and **azharot* are almost all written in Hebrew, a few, in Aramaic. In 1553 he collected his liturgical and religious poems under the title, *Sefer ha-Yashar.* Later he prepared a second, larger collection in two volumes, now lost, entitled *Sefer ha-Yalkut* (this might, however, be the title of another work of his). A third collection (unless it is part of *Sefer ha-Yalkut*) is in the Montefiore Collection.

BIBLIOGRAPHY: L. Zunz, in: *Ha-Palit* (1850), 25; Zunz, Lit Poesie, 535; Neubauer, Cat, 1 (1886), 381; H. Hirschfeld, in: JQR, 14

(1901/02), 633; idem, *Descriptive Catalogue of the Hebrew Manuscripts of the Montefiore Library* (1904), 82; Fuenn, Keneset, 38; Davidson, Oẓar, 4 (1933), 357; Schirmann, Italyah, 243.

[Umberto (Moses David) Cassuto]

ABRAHAM BEN DAVID MAIMUNI (c. 1246–c. 1316), *nagid* of Egyptian Jewry. Abraham was the eldest son of R. David, the grandson of Maimonides. During his father's old age he shared the position of *nagid* with him for ten years. After his father's death he remained *nagid* and was successful in 1313 in convincing a large group of Karaites, among whom were some wealthy men and intellectuals, to return to Rabbanite Judaism.

BIBLIOGRAPHY: S. Assaf, *Be-Oholei Ya'akov* (1943), 184; Ashtor, Toledot, 1 (1944), 228–32; Goitein, in: *Tarbiz*, 34 (1964/65), 253–5; Eshtori ha-Farḥi, *Kaftor va-Feraḥ*, ed. by H.Edelmann (1852), 13b.

[Eliyahu Ashtor]

ABRAHAM BEN DAVID OF POSQUIÈRES (known as **Rabad**, i.e., **R**abbi **A**braham **B**en **D**avid; c. 1125–1198); talmudic authority in Provence. Abraham was born in Narbonne, and died in Posquières, a small city near Nîmes famous for the yeshivah he established there. He lived during a remarkable period of remarkable development of intellectual activity in southern France. His father-in-law, Abraham b. Isaac, who headed the rabbinical court in Narbonne, exerted considerable influence on Abraham ben David, whose brilliance he fully appreciated. Abraham studied with Moses b. Joseph and *Meshullam b. Jacob of Lunel, two of the most respected and influential scholars of the time. Meshullam encouraged the methodical transmission of the philosophic, scientific, and halakhic learning of Spanish Jews to French Jewry, and his influence on Abraham in this respect was great. It also seems safe to assume that the enlightened atmosphere of his circle widened the scope of Abraham's learning so that he developed into a keen and resourceful halakhist, undisputed master in his own field, and highly knowledgeable in developments in related areas (philosophy and philology). He encouraged Judah ibn Tibbon, who had translated the first chapter of Baḥya ibn Paquda's *Ḥovot ha-Levavot* at the request of Meshullam of Lunel, to complete the translation. Meshullam stimulated Abraham's literary creativity by having him compose a treatise (*Issur Mashehu*, in: S. Assaf, *Sifran shel Rishonim* (Jerusalem, 1935, 185–98; M. Hershler, Jerusalem, 1963)) on an important problem of Jewish ritual law.

A mature scholar, prominent in Montpellier and Nîmes, and a man of great wealth (it has been suggested that he dealt in textiles), he settled permanently in Posquières, except for a short period (1172–73) when he fled to Narbonne and Carcassonne as a result of hostility on the part of the local feudal lord. He founded and directed a school to which advanced students from all parts of Europe flocked and he provided for all the needs of indigent students out of his own pocket. Some of his students and close followers, *Abraham b. Nathan ha-Yarḥi, Isaac ha-Kohen, *Meir b. Isaac, *Jonathan b. David ha-Kohen of Lunel, Asher b. Saul of Lunel, and his own son *Isaac the Blind (of Posquières) became distinguished rabbis and authors in the principal Jewish communities of Provence, thus extending Abraham's influence and contributing to significant literary developments at the end of the 12th and the beginning of the 13th centuries. He himself asserted that his word was law in all Provence (*Temim De'im* (Lvov, 1812), 12a–b, no. 113). Scholars from Franco-Germany, Spain, North Africa, Italy, Palestine, and Slavic countries knew, studied, and respected him. *Naḥmanides describes his erudition and piety with great awe and Solomon b. Abraham *Adret says that Abraham revealed unfathomed depths of the law "as if from the mouth of Moses, and explained that which is difficult" (*Torat ha-Bayit, Beit ha-Nashim*, introduction).

Rabad's literary activity was original and many sided. His works may be classified under the headings of codes of rabbinic law, commentaries on various types of talmudic literature, responsa, homiletic discourses, and critical annotations and glosses (*hassagot*) on standard works of rabbinic literature. His writings are characterized by precision in textual study, persistence in tracing statements back to their original source, discovery of later interpolations, and logical analysis of problems. He was one of the most skillful practitioners of the critico-conceptual method of talmudic study – probing into the inner strata of talmudic logic, defining fundamental concepts, and formulating disparities as well as similarities among various passages in the light of conceptual analysis. As a result, abstract, complex concepts, which were discussed fragmentarily in numerous, unrelated sections of the Talmud, are for the first time defined with great vigor and precision. This critical methodology was the first clean break from the geonic method of Talmud study. By doing so, Rabad approached each rabbinic subject unaided by the wisdom of the previous generations. On the one hand, he viewed each subject as part of the greater talmudic whole; yet on the other hand, he only commented on what interested him. Thus, his commentaries may be described as annotatory rather than cursory, that is, closer to the tosafistic method of textual elucidation and analysis than the method of complete, terse textual commentary associated with Rashi or R. Hananel. Many of his theories and insights were endorsed and transmitted by subsequent generations of talmudists and incorporated into standard works of Jewish law up to the Shulḥan Arukh and its later commentaries. Indeed, his talmudic commentaries had an enormous impact on the next generation of talmudic scholars, notably *Naḥmanides and his disciple, Solomon ben Abraham *Adret. Even though they continued to quote him frequently, the scholarship and reputation of these and other scholars of the succeeding generations overshadowed Rabad's work. Rabad's talmudic commentaries firmly established his position among Jewish scholars. With the first publication of Rabad's *hassagot* alongside Maimonides' text of the *Mishneh Torah* in the early 16th century, Rabad's reputation shifted from that of commentator on the Talmud to commentator on the *Mishneh Torah*.

Some medieval writers, notably Ḥasdai Crescas (*Or Ado-*

nai, introduction) assert that Abraham wrote a commentary on the entire Talmud and Menahem b. Solomon *Meiri described him as "one of the greatest of the commentators" (*Beit ha-Beḥirah*, passim). Only sections of this imposing undertaking have been preserved and only two complete commentaries on *Bava Kamma* (Kaidan, 1940; Jerusalem, 1963[2]) and *Avodah Zarah* (New York, 1960) have been published; sizable extracts are to be found in the *Shitah Mekubbeẓet* of Bezalel Ashkenazi and citations from it are quoted in the writings of the *rishonim*. His commentary and *tosafot* to the first two chapters of *Kiddushin* have been published by Wacholder, in: HUCA 37 (1966), Heb. sect. 65–90.

The most important of his codes, which included *Hilkhot Lulav, Ḥibbur Harsha'ot* (on power of attorney), and *Perush Yadayim*, is the *Ba'alei ha-Nefesh* (first edition Venice, 1602). A complete and better edition was published by Y. Kafaḥ (1964). In seven, close-knit chapters, Abraham formulated and discussed in great detail the laws relating to women. The last chapter of the work entitled *Sha'ar ha-Kedushah* ("the gate of holiness") describes the moral norms and pious dispositions which enable man to achieve self-control in sexual matters and to attain purity of heart and action. The common denominator of all his codes is their preoccupation with practical matters, unlike Maimonides, whose theoretical concept of codification necessitated the inclusion of all laws, even those of no practical value. Abraham's codes are predicated on exposition and commentary and provide complete source references.

Abraham wrote commentaries on the Mishnah, which had gradually become subservient to and assimilated in the Talmud as a unit of study, with the result that as late as the 12th century, commentaries on the Mishnah were rare and fragmentary. Abraham's full-fledged commentaries on *Eduyyot* and *Kinnim* (both published in the standard editions of the Talmud), two abstruse, academic treatises, were original and also very influential. (The commentary on *Tamid*, ascribed to Abraham, is not his.) At the beginning of the *Eduyyot* commentary he himself declared: "In all these matters I have nothing to fall back upon, neither a rabbi nor a teacher. I beseech the Creator to guide me correctly in this matter." Unlike Maimonides, who strove to distill the quintessence from intricate discussions, in order to render the Mishnah an independent subject of study, Abraham was interested primarily in interpreting those obscure sections of the Mishnah which had no further explanation in the Talmud, passing over those passages satisfactorily explained in the Talmud, merely giving cross references.

His commentaries on the tannaitic Midrashim are of special historic importance, because he was probably the first medieval scholar (but see *Hillel b. Eliakim of Greece) to have written exhaustive commentaries on these texts. While his commentaries on the *Mekhilta* and *Sifrei* are quoted, only the commentary on *Sifra* is extant (first edition Constantinople, 1523; scientifically edited by I.H. Weiss, Vienna, 1862). The commentary, which pays considerable attention to the nature and method of the *Sifra* and, therefore, to problems of talmudic hermeneutics, begins with an emphatic prologue on the necessity of tradition "in order to harass the opinions of the heretics (*minim*) who refuse to obey and believe."

The *hassagot*, critical scholia, with which his name is inextricably linked, were his last works. He composed copious *hassagot* on the *halakhot* of Alfasi, on the *Sefer ha-Maor* of *Zerahiah b. Isaac ha-Levi, and the *Mishneh Torah* of Maimonides. As the Hebrew term *hassagah* denotes, these glosses are both criticism and commentary, dissent and elaboration, stricture and supplement; they are not exclusively polemical, although the polemical emphasis varies in intensity and acuity from one to the other. The critique on Alfasi is mild and objective; that on Maimonides may be described as moderate, marred by occasional outbursts of intemperate invective; while that on Zerahiah ha-Levi is caustic and personal. Abraham began by reviewing Alfasi and taking exception to some of his halakhic interpretations and normative conclusions. In answer to his criticisms Naḥmanides wrote his *Sefer ha-Zekhut*. When the *Sefer ha-Maor* appeared, Abraham felt that Zerahiah ha-Levi had carried the criticism of Alfasi to unjustified lengths and that often Zerahiah was captious and carping for no good reason. Anticipating the more comprehensive refutation of Naḥmanides in *Milḥamot*, Abraham penned a sharp answer to the strictures of Zerahiah. He accused him, inter alia, of plagiarism, amateurishness, excessive reliance on Rashi and the French school, and general incompetence. The book, called *Katuv Sham*, was published in full for the first time in Jerusalem (1960–2). Extracts from it had been published previously in the Romm edition of the Talmud, and elsewhere. This work climaxes a lifetime process of mutual criticism and attack – the acrimonious exchange in *Divrei ha-Rivot* and Zerahiah's criticism of Abraham's *Ba'alei ha-Nefesh and Kinnim* commentary (*Sela ha-Maḥaloket*, latest edition, ed. Kafaḥ, 1964). Abraham's critique of Maimonides, written in cryptic and in a style often difficult to understand, became a standard companion of Maimonides' text (from the Constantinople edition, 1509). These *hassagot* are highly personal and unsystematic. Rabad does not comment on every aspect of each section of the entire *Mishneh Torah*. However, his glosses are very wide ranging, containing every conceivable form of annotation: criticism concerning interpretive matters, textual problems, local customs and the like, and many forms of commentary, listing the source, reconstructing Maimonides' explanation of a text, showing the derivative process followed by Maimonides in the formulation of a law, warding off possible criticism, and the like. Abraham claimed that Maimonides "intended to improve but did not improve, for he forsook the way of all authors and his cut and dried codification, without explanations and without references, approximated *ex cathedra* legislation too closely." Rabad's *hassagot* are not limited to points of law; he was quick to take Maimonides to task for his philosophical opinions as well. For instance, contrary to Maimonides' assertion that God is incorporeal and that to think of God as having a body makes one a heretic, Rabad claims that there "were many who were greater and better than him who followed this path due to what they saw in verses, and even more due to rabbinic homilies that confuse the mind" (see *Mishneh Torah*, Laws of Repentance 3:7). Later generations did not view this statement as disagreeing with Maimonides, but as recognition of the need to think of God in anthropomorphic terms.

Abraham wrote many responsa, some of them printed in *Tummat Yesharim* (Venice, 1622). A more complete compendium was issued by Y. Kafaḥ (1964). He wrote a few homilies, as testified by many *rishonim*, but only his homily on Rosh Ha-Shanah has been printed (London, 1955).

One type of literature, the kabbalistic, which came into prominence during his lifetime, is not represented in his writings. It is known, however, that he exerted formative influence upon it through his children, who, having learned mystical teachings from him, became literary leaders and guides in the emergent Kabbalah. Later kabbalistic writers such as Isaac of Acre, Shem Tov b. Gaon, and Menahem Recanati claimed Abraham as one of their own, worthy of receiving special revelation.

BIBLIOGRAPHY: I. Twersky, *Rabad of Posquières* (1962), includes complete bibliography; S. Abramson, in: *Tarbiz*, 36 (1967), 158–79. **ADD. BIBLIOGRAPHY:** Y. Gellman, in: *New Scholasticism*, 58:2 (1984), 145–69; H. Soloveitchik, in: *Jewish History*, 5:1 (1991), 75–124; idem, in: *Studies in the History of Jewish Society in the Middles Ages and in the Modern Period* (1980); J. Cohen, in: *The Frank Talmage Memorial Volume*, 2 (1992), 65–78; N. Samuelson, in: *Kerem, Creative Explorations in Judaism*, 1 (1992–93), 65–74.

[Isadore Twersky / David Derovan (2nd ed.)]

ABRAHAM BEN DOV OF MEZHIRECH (known as *ha-Malakh* ("the Angel"); 1741–1776), ḥasidic sage. A contemporary who watched Abraham on the Ninth of *Av bewail the destruction of the Temple, remarked: "Then I understood that it was not in vain that he was named by all 'the Angel,' for no man born of woman could have such power." A solitary ascetic who mainly concentrated on study of Kabbalah, Abraham did not emulate the tradition of popular aspects of Ḥasidism instituted by the Ba'al Shem Tov and by his father, considering them "too earthly." His ideal of the **ẓaddik* was directly opposed to the usual type of such ḥasidic leaders, being "one who is incapable of leading his contemporaries, one whom they would not tolerate because he is immersed in learning and unable to descend 'to the lowest grade' in order to lift up his generation." In his youth Abraham was a friend of *Shneur Zalman of Lyady with whom he studied Talmud and Kabbalah in Mezhirech. He was the author of a commentary on the Pentateuch *Ḥesed le-Avraham* (Czernowitz, 1851). His son, Shalom Shraga (1766–1803) of Prohobist, was the father of Israel of *Ruzhyn (Ryshyn), the first of the Ruzhyn dynasty.

BIBLIOGRAPHY: A. Zak, *Kerem Yisrael* (1931); Horodezky, Ḥasidut, 2 (1953⁴), 49ff.; Dubnow, Ḥasidut (1932), 213–4; M. Buber, *Tales of the Ḥasidim*, 1 (1968), 113–7.

[Nachum Arieli]

ABRAHAM BEN ELIEZER HA-LEVI (called ha-Zaken; c. 1460–after 1528), kabbalist. Born in Spain, Abraham was a pupil of Isaac Gakon (in Toledo?). While still in Spain he wrote several kabbalistic treatises of which his *Masoret ha-Hokhmah* ("Tradition of Wisdom"), on the principles of the Kabbalah, has been preserved (KS, 2 (1925), 125–30; 7 (1931), 449–56). After the expulsion of the Jews from Spain in 1492, Abraham wandered through Italy, Greece, Turkey, and Egypt until about 1514 when he moved to Jerusalem with the school of the Egyptian *nagid*, R. Isaac ha-Kohen *Sholal. In Jerusalem, he was one of the most respected scholars of the yeshivah and became widely known through his literary and religious activities. A letter of his from the year 1528 deals with Beta Israel (*Kovez al Yad*, 4 (1888), 24). He presumably died soon afterward; in 1535, R. *David b. Solomon ibn Abi Zimra mentions him as someone long dead.

The expulsion of the Jews from Spain shocked Abraham deeply. His activities as an apocalyptic kabbalist probably date from the time of this national disaster. Like many of his contemporaries, such as Abraham *Zacuto, Isaac *Abrabanel, and others, he believed that the year 1524 would be the beginning of the messianic era, and that the Messiah himself would appear in 1530–31. He devoted himself to elaborating his conviction. He searched for proof in the Bible and the Talmud as well as in kabbalistic literature, and he tried to arouse the Jewish people to prepare for the coming deliverance through penitence. Abraham is one of the best stylists in kabbalistic literature. In 1508 in Greece he wrote the treatise *Mashreh Kitrin* ("Untier of Knots," 1510), with explanations of the Book of Daniel. This book, like all other works of Abraham, was ably written in the apocalyptic prophetic vein. Later he wrote *Ma'amar Perek Ḥelek*, an explanation of the talmudic statements on the messianic redemption at the end of the tractate *Sanhedrin*. In 1517, in Jerusalem, Abraham wrote his extensive commentary on the *Nevu'at ha-Yeled* ("The Child's Prophecy") in the same vein (still in manuscript). It is unlikely that Abraham was the author of the *Nevu'at ha-Yeled* itself. His commentary contains an apocalyptic survey of Jewish history, from the fall of the Second Temple to his own day. In 1521 he wrote *Iggeret Sod ha-Ge'ullah* ("The Epistle of the Mystery of Redemption") in which, following his views, he interpreted the statements of the *Zohar on redemption (also in manuscript). Abraham issued many calls to penitence, in one of which (1525) he expressed himself in detail on the appearance of Martin *Luther. Thus, he prepared the way for the coming activities of Solomon *Molcho. Various other kabbalistic writings of Abraham have been preserved: *Ma'amar ha-Yiḥud* ("Essay on the Unity of God"); *Megillat Amrafel* ("Scroll of Amraphel"), published in part in KS, 7 (1930–31), probably identical with his commentary on the Song of Songs; *Tiferet Adam* ("Glory of Man"); and *Livyat Ḥen* ("Chaplet of Grace"; the latter two not extant). His instructions (*hora'ah*) on the recitation of the prayer *Makhnisei Raḥamim* have been published as have his penitential prayers seeking the intercession of angels (*Kerem Ḥemed*, 9 (1856), 141ff.). Abraham is in no way to be linked with the kabbalistic work *Gallei Rezayya* nor is he the author of the apology of the Kabbalah, *Ohel Mo'ed* ("Tent of Meeting"). He has often been confused with other scholars of the same name, among them *Abraham b. Eliezer ha-Levi Berukhim.

[Gershom Scholem]

The writings and activity of this kabbalist have drawn substantial attention in scholarship in the last generation. Some of Abraham ha-Levi's kabbalistic views are close to theories found in the circle of kabbalists who produced the literature known as *Sefer ha-Meshiv*, and he preserved the earliest version of the famous legend about R. *Joseph della Reina's abortive attempt to bring about the advent of the Messiah. It seems that his messianic and magical concerns are also related to the tenor of this vast kabbalistic literature.

[Moshe Idel (2nd ed.)]

BIBLIOGRAPHY: Steinschneider, in: *Oẓar Neḥmad*, 2 (1857), 146–57; G. Scholem, in: KS, 1 (1924/25), 163f.; 2 (1925/26), 101–41, 269–73; 7 (1930/31), 440–56. **ADD. BIBLIOGRAPHY:** A. David, "A Jerusalemite Epistle from the Beginning of the Ottoman Rule in the Land of Israel," in: *Chapters in the History of Jerusalem at the Beginning of the Ottoman Period* (Heb., 1979); M. Idel, "Inquiries in the Doctrine of *Sefer Ha-Meshiv*," in: J. Hacker (ed.), *Sefunot*, 17 (1983), 185–66 (Heb.); idem, "Magic and Kabbalah in the Book of the Responding Entity," in: M. Gruber (ed.), *The Solomon Goldman Lectures*, 6 (1993), 125–38; I. Robinson, "Two Letters of Abraham ben Eliezer Halevi," in: I. Twersky (ed.), *Studies in Medieval Jewish History and Literature* (1984), 403–22; G. Scholem, "The Maggid of Rabbi Joseph Taitatchek and the Revelations Attributed to Him," in: *Sefunot*, 11 (1971–78), 69–112; G. Scholem and M. Bet Arieh, "Abraham ben Eliezer ha-Levi," in: *Ma'amar Mesharei Qitrin* (1977).

ABRAHAM BEN ELIEZER HA-LEVI BERUKHIM (c. 1515–1593), pious ascetic and Safed kabbalist. Born in Morocco, he immigrated to Palestine probably before 1565. In Safed he joined Moses *Cordovero's circle and became a friend of Elijah de *Vidas. When Isaac *Luria went to Safed (late 1569), Abraham joined his school and was a member of its "fourth group." Ḥayyim *Vital had a great affection for him and in several places quotes kabbalistic sayings of Isaac Luria which he had heard from Abraham. Vital quotes Luria as saying that in the "origins of the souls of the Safed kabbalists," Abraham derived from the patriarch Jacob. Abraham was a visionary and ascetic, who preached piety and morality, and called for repentance. He was called the "great patron of the Sabbath" and he went out on Friday mornings to the markets and streets to urge the householders to hurry with the preparations for the Sabbath meals and close their shops early so that they would have time to purify themselves for the Sabbath. Almost nothing is known about his life. Many legends have been preserved about his piety and about Luria's affection for him. His *Tikkunei Shabbat* were printed at the end of *Reshit Hokhmah ha-Kaẓar* (Venice, 1600) and thereafter in numerous editions as a separate book. On the other hand, his *Ḥasidut*, containing the rules of pious behavior which he established for his group in Safed, circulated in manuscript even in the Diaspora, and was published by Solomon Schechter (*Studies in Judaism*, 2nd Series (1908), 297–9). He was the first editor and collector of articles of the *Zohar which had not been included in the Mantua edition of 1558–60; these were afterward published under the title *Zohar Ḥadash*. It is not clear whether he was the author of *Gallei Rezayya*, parts of which were published in his name (1812). It is probable that Tobiah ha-Levi, author of *Ḥen Tov*, was his son.

BIBLIOGRAPHY: Ḥ. Vital, *Sefer ha-Ḥezyonot* (1954); S. Shlimel, *Shivḥei ha-Ari* (1609); M. Benayahu, *Sefer Toledot ha-Ari* (1967).

ABRAHAM BEN ELIJAH OF VILNA (1750–1808), talmudic and midrashic scholar. Abraham received most of his education from his father *Elijah b. Solomon Zalman, "the Vilna Gaon." He acquired complete command of rabbinic literature and much general knowledge. He had a strikingly critical approach to history and literature. Even before *Zunz, Abraham investigated the nature and development of the Midrashim and had written a valuable introduction to his edition of *Midrash Aggadat Bereshit* (Vilna, 1802). His work *Rav Pe'alim* (1894), an alphabetical index of all the midrashic works known to him, contains critical observations on 130 Midrashim. Abraham wrote a universal geography, *Gevulot Ereẓ* ("The Earth's Boundaries," published anonymously, Berlin, 1821). He composed commentaries on several tractates of the Talmud and on *Midrash Rabbah*, glosses and notes to the Jerusalem Talmud, a book on weights and measures in the Talmud, another on place-names mentioned in Talmud and Midrash, and several other works, some unpublished. Abraham was active in communal affairs and was one of the *parnasim* of the Vilna Jewish community. Together with his brother, Judah Loeb, he published several of his father's works, and incorporated in them explanatory material from his father's oral teaching.

BIBLIOGRAPHY: J.H. Lewin, *Aliyyot Eliyahu* (1861^2), 94ff.; Yaveẓ, in: *Kenesset Yisrael*, 1 (1886), 132–3; Kaufmann, in: MGWJ, 39 (1895), 136–9; S. Buber, *Yeri'ot Shelomo* (1896), 3–4 (introd.); S.J. Fuenn, *Kiryah Ne'emanah* (1915^2), 210–2; J.L. Maimon (ed.), *Sefer ha-Gra*, 1 (1953), 108–10.

[Simha Assaf]

ABRAHAM BEN ḤALFON (15th or 16th century), Hebrew poet in Yemen. His verse follows the genre of Spanish poetry in its meter, style, and content. Y. Tovi published his poems in 1991. Their subjects include moral and ethical exhortations, songs for weddings and circumcisions, religious verse, and hymns for special occasions and festivals. If he is identical with the person of the same name mentioned in the *Sefer ha-Musar* (pp. 46, 84, 151) of Zechariah Al-Dahri, he must have flourished in the 16th century, not in the 15th as was formerly believed.

BIBLIOGRAPHY: I. Davidson, in: *Ẓiyyunim* (*J.N. Simḥoni Memorial Volume*, 1929), 58–81; idem, in: *Minḥah le-David* (*D. Yellin Jubilee Volume*, 1935), 187–96; Ish-Shalom, in: *Tarbiz*, 18 (1947), 187–93.

ADD. BIBLIOGRAPHY: *Shirei Avraham ibn Halfon*, ed. Y. Tovi (1991); R. Halevi (ed.), *Shirat Yisra'el be-Teiman*, 1 (1998), 355–71.

[Yehuda Ratzaby]

ABRAHAM BEN ḤAYYIM (Heilprin; d. 1762), leader of the Jewish community in Lublin city and province, Poland. Abraham b. Ḥayyim at times represented the Lublin community in the assemblies of the Council of Four Lands. From 1753 to 1757 he acted as *parnas* of the Council, an office previously held by his grandfather, Abraham Abele b. Israel Isser, and his son's father-in-law, the physician Abraham Isaac *Fortis (Ḥazak). During Abraham b. Ḥayyim's tenure, one of his sons, Moses Phinehas, acted as the *ne'eman* ("treasurer") of the Council of the Four Lands. Other members of his family served in several communities as rabbis or communal leaders. In the controversy that arose over the connection of Jonathan *Eybeshuetz with the *Shabbatean movement, Abraham and his son Jacob Ḥayyim of Lublin strongly supported Eybeshuetz. Abraham was described by contemporaries as "princely and munificent," but nothing is now known of his occupation. He died in Lublin at an advanced age. The Bet ha-Midrash de-Parnas Academy, which he founded, existed in Lublin until the destruction of the community during World War II.

ADD. BIBLIOGRAPHY: Halpern, Pinkas; M. Balaban, *Die Judenstadt von Lublin* (1919).

[Israel Halpern]

ABRAHAM BEN ḤAYYIM, THE DYER (Dei Tintori; 15th century), Italian pioneer of Hebrew printing from Pesaro. Though Abraham may have been active in Hebrew typecasting and printing by 1473, his name as a printer appeared for the first time in two books printed in *Ferrara in 1477 – Levi b. Gershom's commentary of Job and Jacob b. Asher's *Tur* (*Yoreh De'ah*), using the first 40 pages which Abraham *Conat had printed in *Mantua in 1476.

Five years later (1482) at *Bologna, Abraham printed a Pentateuch with Targum Onkelos and Rashi's commentary, probably the first printed book with vocalization and cantillation. In the colophon, the proofreader Joseph Ḥayyim praises Abraham as "unequaled in the realm of Hebrew printing and celebrated everywhere."

Israel Nathan *Soncino and his son Joshua Solomon secured Abraham's services for the work on the first printed Hebrew Bible – with vocalization and cantillation – which left the press at Soncino in February 1488. The edition of the Psalms, with R. David Kimḥi's commentary of 1477, and the Five Scrolls, with Rashi and with Abraham Ibn Ezra's commentary on Esther (1482–83?), may also have been printed by Abraham (see *Incunabula).

BIBLIOGRAPHY: D.W. Amram, *Makers of Hebrew Books in Italy* (1909), index; M. Steinschneider and D. Cassel, *Juedische Typographie* (1938^2), 14–15; H.D. Friedberg, *Toledot ha-Defus ha-Ivri bi-Medinot Italyah…* (1956^2), index. **ADD. BIBLIOGRAPHY:** P. Tishbi, in: *Kiryat Sefer*, 60 (1986), 908–18.

ABRAHAM BEN HILLEL (Ben Nissim) OF FOSTAT (Egypt; d. 1223), scholar, poet, and physician. Abraham is probably identical with Abraham the Pious (he-Ḥasid or he-Ḥaver) referred to frequently by his friend Abraham b. Moses b. *Maimon in his writings. In 1167 Abraham b. Hillel, Maimonides, and other rabbis signed a *takkanah* to safeguard the observance of the laws of family purity in Egypt (Maimonides, *Teshuvot* (Responsa), ed. by A.H. Freimann (1934), 91–94). In 1196 Abraham wrote *Megillat Zuta*, describing satirically the exploits of an adventurer called *Zuta (and his son) who imposed himself repeatedly on the Jewish community of Egypt. *Megillat Zuta* is written in rhymed prose with a prologue and epilogue in metered verse. The number of manuscripts extant seems to attest the popularity of the work, which was first published by Neubauer (JQR, 8 (1896), 543ff.). Abraham and Josiah b. Moses verified a responsum by Jehiel (?) b. Eliakim Fostat, which deals with the controversy concerning the reference, in legal documents and during prayers, to the person of the reigning *nagid*. After Abraham's death his collection of books was put up for sale in the Palestinian synagogue of Fostat under the auspices of Abraham b. Moses b. Maimon. The library contained 75 medical works, about 30 Hebrew books, among them biblical books, works on Hebrew grammar, a copy of the Mishnah, part of a talmudic tractate, Maimonides' *Book of Precepts* and *Guide*, as well as several copies of Saadiah's *Siddur*.

BIBLIOGRAPHY: A. Wertheimer, *Ginzei Yerushalayim*, 1 (1896), 37ff.; Kahane, in: *Ha-Shilo'aḥ*, 15 (1905), 175ff.; Eppenstein, in: *Festschrift… I. Lewy* (Heb., 1911), 53; idem, in: *Festschrift… D. Hoffmann* (Heb., 1914), 131, 135ff.; Mann, Egypt, 1 (1920), 234–6; 2 (1928), 303ff., 327; Abrahams, in: *Jews College Jubilee Volume* (1906), 101ff.; A. Marx, *Studies in Jewish History and Booklore* (1944), 201–2; Goitein, in: *Tarbiz*, 32 (1962/63), 191–2.

[Jefim (Hayyim) Schirmann]

ABRAHAM BEN ISAAC (Gerondi; mid-13th century), *ḥazzan*, kabbalist, and *paytan* in Gerona (Spain). One of the greatest kabbalists of his time, he was a pupil of *Isaac the Blind from whom he learned the mystical intentions of the prayers according to the Kabbalah. Gerondi later enlarged on this teaching and introduced it into his own order of the prayers. Although his work *Kabbalah me-Inyan ha-Tefillah le-Rabbi Avraham* ("Tradition Concerning Prayer, According to R. Abraham") was not published until 1948 (see Scholem in bibl.), his contemporaries quote various ideas on the subject of prayer from it. *Naḥmanides held him in great esteem and tradition has it that he eulogized Abraham and offered a prayer in kabbalistic style by his grave. Abraham's hymn for the eve of Rosh Ha-Shanah, **Aḥot Ketannah* ("Little Sister"), which describes the sufferings of the Jewish people in exile, has become well known. It is as yet unclear whether other hymns signed Abraham b. Isaac Ḥazzan are wholly or in part his work, or whether they were composed by another writer of the same name.

BIBLIOGRAPHY: G. Scholem, *Reshit ha-Kabbalah* (1948), 128, 243–8; Schirmann, Sefarad, 2 (1956), 291–4, 692; Zunz, Poesie, 311, 410; Davidson, Oẓar, 4 (1933), 355.

[Jefim (Hayyim) Schirmann]

ABRAHAM BEN ISAAC BEN GARTON, first known Hebrew printer. He produced Rashi's commentary on the Pentateuch, completed at *Reggio Calabria on Feb. 17, 1475. Although this book bears the earliest date, it was not necessarily the first Hebrew book (see *Incunabula) printed, as it may have been preceded by others which have disappeared, or bear no date of publication. The only extant copy of the book, in the De' Rossi Collection in the Palatine Library, Parma, Italy, is slightly defective; it is in folio and contains 116 pages of 37 lines each. The text of this edition is significantly different from later ones. De' Rossi formerly owned another copy which was lost in transit. Abraham's country of origin is unknown, but it is conjectured that he came from Spain. No other book that came from his press is known.

BIBLIOGRAPHY: A.M. Habermann, *Toledot ha-Sefer ha-Ivri* (1945), 33, and illustration 9; D.W. Amram, *Makers of Hebrew Books in Italy* (1909), 24; C. Roth, *Jews in the Renaissance* (1959), 169–73; Pavoncello, in: *Klearchos* (Reggio di Calabria), 21–22 (1964), 53–57. **ADD. BIBLIOGRAPHY:** P. Tishbi, in: *Kiryat Sefer*, 60 (1986), 865–69.

[Abraham Meir Habermann]

ABRAHAM BEN ISAAC HA-KOHEN BEN AL-FURAT (11th century), Egyptian physician and philanthropist. His father Isaac ha-Kohen b. al-Furat was a highly respected physician in Fostat (Old *Cairo) and his uncle Solomon ha-Kohen b. Joseph was the *gaon* in Palestine. Abraham held a high position in the government and was probably one of the court physicians. He may also have been president of the Jewish community; hence his honorary title ("prince of the community"). Apart from his general scholarship, Abraham also appears to have been learned in the Talmud. His erudition, nobility of character, and philanthropy are lauded in several poems and letters found in the Cairo *Genizah*.

BIBLIOGRAPHY: Mann, Egypt, 1 (1920), 28, 83ff.; 2 (1922), 26, 54ff., 81ff., index; Mann, Texts, 2 (1935), 151; Goitein, in: HUCA, 34 (1963), 179.

[Jacob Mann]

ABRAHAM BEN ISAAC HA-KOHEN OF ZAMOŚĆ (18th century), Polish rabbi and author. Abraham served for a short period as head of the *bet din* in Tarlow, but, as he was extremely wealthy, he was able to resign his position and in 1754 returned to Zamość, his birthplace. There he occupied himself with both religious and secular studies. He knew German, Polish, and Latin. In 1753 he was a member of the Zamość delegation to the central committee session of the *Councils of the Lands, held at Jaroslav. In 1754 he participated in the conference held at Constantinov where he was a signatory to the ban passed there on the printers of the Sulzbach Talmud. From this time, he played an active role in Polish Jewish life and became widely known. In the *Emden-*Eybeschuetz dispute he opposed the official line of the Council of Four Lands which supported Eybeschuetz and he defended Jacob Emden (with whom he corresponded in 1759–60). He strove zealously against any mystical messianic and Shabbatean revival and signed the 1753/54 letters of protest against the Shabbateans. *Beit Abraham*, his book of responsa and talmudic novellae, was printed in 1753; the book contained also the novellae of his father Isaac b. Abraham ha-Kohen, as well as his own halakhic novellae, in an appendix called *Minḥah Belulah*.

BIBLIOGRAPHY: Preface to *Beit Abraham* (1753); J. Emden, *Sefer ha-Shimmush* (1758), 81a; Z. Horowitz, *Kitvei ha-Ge'onim* (1928), 138, no. 2; M. Tamari (ed.), *Zamość bi-Ge'onah u-ve-Shivrah* (1953), 41, 48–49; Halpern, Pinkas, index.

[Yehoshua Horowitz]

ABRAHAM BEN ISAAC OF GRANADA, Spanish kabbalist, putative author of *Berit Menuḥah* ("The Covenant of Rest"), one of the main works of the *Kabbalah. Nothing is known of his life or of the era to which he belongs. In the introduction to his commentary on *Sefer *Yeẓirah*, Moses *Botarel gives a long quotation from *Sefer ha-Berit* ("The Book of the Covenant") written by a scholar called Abraham b. Isaac of Granada. But both language and contents prove that this book was not written by the author of *Berit Menuḥah*, which was without doubt composed in Spain during the 14th century. It explains the innermost meaning of the vocalization of God's name in 26 different ways. However, only the first ten ways were printed, and this only in a very corrupt form (Amsterdam, 1648): Ḥ.J.D. *Azulai saw more than twice this number in a manuscript. The actual content of this work is very enigmatic as, in many respects, its symbolism and mysticism do not correspond with the conventional Kabbalah. The influence of Abraham *Abulafia's Kabbalah is recognizable but the language-and-letter-mysticism of Abulafia is combined with a complicated light-mysticism. Moreover, the book's aim was to provide a systematic basis for the so-called Practical Kabbalah. The few clear passages reveal the author as a profound thinker and visionary. In eight places, he quotes his own thought process as the words of "the learned Rabbi *Simeon bar Yoḥai," mostly in Aramaic. But these quotations are not to be found in the *Zohar, and in view of their style and contents do not belong there. The work was highly regarded by later kabbalists, especially by Moses *Cordovero and Isaac *Luria, who read their own thinking into Abraham's symbolism. Cordovero wrote a lengthy commentary on part of the book. Abraham quotes two more of his own works, *Megalleh ha-Ta'alumot* ("Revealing Hidden Things") and *Sefer ha-Gevurah* ("The Book of Power"), on the names of God and Practical Kabbalah. His *Ḥokhmat ha-Ẓeruf* ("Science of Letter Combinations"), 12 chapters in the spirit of Abulafia, is preserved in manuscript form (Margoliouth, Cat, no. 749, vi), but he is not the author of the *Sefer ha-Ḥeshek* ("The Book of Desire," *ibid.*, 748); Aaron *Marcus endeavored to prove that Abraham was identical with Abraham b. Isaac of Narbonne, author of *Eshkol*, and in doing so he tried to date the *Berit Menuḥah* two centuries earlier, however, his argument is not tenable.

BIBLIOGRAPHY: Margoliouth, Cat, 3 (1935), 24–27; Jacob ha-Levi, *Kunteres She'elot u-Teshuvot min ha-Shamayim*, with commentary *Keset ha-Sofer* by A. Marcus (1895), 18–26; G. Scholem, in: *Soncino Blaetter (Festschrift Aron Freimann)* (1935), 54–55.

[Gershom Scholem]

ABRAHAM BEN ISAAC OF MONTPELLIER (d. c. 1315), talmudist of Provence, a contemporary of Menahem b. Solomon ha-*Meiri. Little is known of his life. He was born in Montpellier about 1250, and toward the end of his life settled in Carpentras. Abraham b. Isaac was known for his liberal outlook. When *Abba Mari Astruc wrote to him concerning the Maimonidean controversy and the proposed prohibition of the study of philosophy to anyone under 25 years old Abraham urged Abba Mari to desist from the controversy because freedom of thought and opinion should not be suppressed (*Minḥat Kena'ot*, 92). Abraham wrote a commentary on most of the Talmud, based principally on the views of Maimonides. He gives a brief commentary on the text in the style of Rashi; at the end of each topic he gives the practical *halakhah* derived from it. Only a minor part of this commentary has been published, including his commentary on *Kiddushin* appearing in the Romm 1880 edition of the Talmud (wrongly ascribed to Isaac of Dampierre) and those on *Yevamot, Nedarim*, and *Nazir* (New York, 1962). His commentaries to many other tractates were familiar to later scholars such as Moses *Alashkar and Menahem de *Lonzano, but they were not generally known. *David b. Ḥayyim ha-Kohen of Corfu wrote: "I have hitherto heard nothing of him as an authority" (Responsa, Bayit 5, Ḥeder 1), but at the end of that same responsum he added that he had come across the commentary "and I rejoiced greatly … he was an outstanding scholar." Some of Abraham's responsa are extant. In addition to those which appear at the end of his commentary to *Nazir* there are those which appear in *Teshuvot Ḥakhmei Provinẓyah* (1967), ed. by A. Sofer. There is no evidence that he was related to *Solomon b. Abraham of Montpellier. It is strange that he does not mention in his works the names of any scholars after Moses b. Naḥman.

BIBLIOGRAPHY: Avraham min ha-Har, *Perush al Massekhet Yevamot Nedarim ve-Nazir*, ed. by M.J. Blau (1962), preface; I. Lévi, in: REJ, 38 (1899), 102–22; Shatzmiler, in: Sefunot, 10 (1966), 17–18.

[Israel Moses Ta-Shma]

ABRAHAM BEN ISAAC OF NARBONNE (known as **Rabi Abad**; c. 1110–1179), talmudist and spiritual leader of Provence; author of *Sefer ha-Eshkol*, the first work of codification of the halakhic commentary of southern France, which served as a model for all subsequent compilations. Abraham was a student of *Isaac b. Merwan ha-Levi and *Meshullam b. Jacob of Lunel. It is probable that Joseph *Ibn Plat, too, was one of his teachers. Abraham aparently spent some time in Barcelona where, it seems, he also studied with *Judah b. Barzillai al-Bargeloni. He was *av bet din* in his native Narbonne, and his prestige was such that he was cited by the early scholars simply as "the Rabbi, *Av Bet Din*." *Benjamin of Tudela speaks of him as "principal of the yeshivah" in Narbonne. Among his renowned students were *Zerahiah ha-Levi and *Abraham b. David of Posquieres, who became his son-in-law. Abraham's halakhic compendium *Sefer ha-Eshkol* is an abridged version of the *Sefer ha-Ittim*, by Judah b. Barzillai al-Bargeloni, with additions from Rashi, R. Tam and his contemporaries, and Abraham himself. In the main, he omitted the geonic responsa and those of Alfasi. As most of the *Ittim* was lost, the *Eshkol* took on additional significance, in that it rescued a part, at least, of the extensive source material in the *Sefer ha-Ittim*. The very ambitious enterprise of excerpting Judah b. Barzillai al-Bargeloni's book was carried out with the support and under the inspiration of his teacher, Meshullam b. Jacob, who encouraged the introduction of Spanish *halakhah* and tradition into Narbonne. The *Eshkol* was first published by Ẓevi Benjamin *Auerbach (1869) with an introduction and commentary, but doubts about the authenticity of at least parts of Auerbach's manuscript were expressed by Shalom *Albeck. The ensuing controversy was inconclusive. Auerbach's manuscript is rich in additions, the exact origin of which is not clear. Although there are no grounds for accusing Auerbach of willfully tampering with the manuscript, the version of the *Eshkol* that Albeck had in hand is undoubtedly the authentic one. Albeck himself published part of the *Sefer ha-Eshkol* (with introductions and notes) and his son Hanokh *Albeck completed this edition (1935–38). Abraham played a vital role as the principal channel through which the Spanish traditions passed into Provence and from there to northern France. At the same time, he emphasized the local traditions of the "Elders of Narbonne," of which he also made great use. His eclecticism is clear from the fact that he also gave due consideration to north-French halakhic traditions, using his personal authority to decide between the various traditions. Abraham was the recipient of numerous queries. A collection of his responsa has been published (ed. Kafaḥ, Jerusalem, 1962) and another is extant in the Guenzburg Collection. Several of the responsa were published by S. Assaf in *Sifran shel Rishonim* (1935), and in *Sinai*, 11 (1947). He also wrote commentaries to the entire Talmud (except for the Order of *Kodashim*) which were quoted by his contemporaries and by later scholars, such as Zerahiah ha-Levi, *Naḥmanides, Solomon b. Abraham *Adret, and others, but only his commentary on the second half of the tractate *Bava Batra* is extant (in a Munich manuscript, a fragment of which was published in *Oẓar ha-Ḥayyim*, 12, 1936). The commentary resembles that of *Samuel b. Meir (Rashbam), which served, in a way, as a transition from Rashi's commentary to the novellae of the tosafists, except that Abraham makes greater use of the earlier commentators and quotes them verbatim. He also excerpted Judah b. Barzillai's *Sefer ha-Din*.

BIBLIOGRAPHY: Gross, in: MGWJ, 17 (1868), 241–55, 281–94; Assaf, in: *Madda'ei ha-Yahadut*, 2 (1926/27), 17; Benedikt, in: *Tarbiz*, 22 (1950/51), 101–5; I. Twersky, *Rabad of Posquières* (1962), 7–10.

[Simha Assaf]

ABRAHAM BEN ISRAEL OF BRODY (1749–1836), Italian kabbalist. He resided in Leghorn and Trieste but finally settled in Ferrara where he remained 30 years. He was known as an ascetic who frequently fasted an entire week and studied six days and nights consecutively. He would purchase rabbinic works and distribute them to needy scholars. It was believed in Ferrara that his profound piety more than once saved the Jewish community from disaster. Among his publications are *Likkutei Amarim* ("Gleanings," Zolkiev, 1802), which include a commentary on the *Pirkei Shirah* and extracts from kabbalistic works, and *Devar ha-Melekh* (Leghorn, 1805–08) on the 613 commandments.

BIBLIOGRAPHY: Ghirondi-Neppi, 15; Fuenn, Keneset, 15.

[Nathan Michael Gelber]

ABRAHAM BEN JEHIEL MICHAL HA-KOHEN of Lask, Poland (d. c. 1800), kabbalist and rabbinical emissary. Abraham was renowned for his asceticism, fasting during the week and eating only on the Sabbath. He settled in Jerusalem shortly after 1770. Ten years later he returned to Europe as an emissary to collect funds on behalf of the rabbis of Jerusalem, and was then involved in a number of disputes with them regarding these collections. He traveled extensively and is known to have been in Nice for four years, in Ferrara (where he met Graziadio Neppi), Glogau, Berlin, and Warsaw. Wherever he went, he exhorted the Jewish community to repentance and good deeds and encouraged more intensive communal activity, including the building of synagogues. On his return to Jerusalem (1790) he was arrested and held ransom for the failure of the Jewish community to pay taxes. He died in prison, probably as a result of maltreatment. The best known of his kabbalistic works are *Ve-Ḥashav lo ha-Kohen* (1884), *Ve-Shav ha-Kohen* (Leghorn, 1788), *Beit Ya'akov* (Leghorn, 1792), *Ayin Panim ba-Torah* (Warsaw, 1797).

BIBLIOGRAPHY: Yaari, Sheluḥei, 550, 553–6.

ABRAHAM BEN JOSEPH (Yoske) OF LISSA (Leszno; d. 1777), communal leader in Poland. Abraham, son of the rabbi of Zlotow, was apparently wealthy and engaged in trade. In the 1730s he represented *Great Poland on the *Councils of the Lands. He presided over the Council as *parnas* in 1739–43 and 1751–53. He also served as *ne'eman* ("treasurer") of the Council during his last term as *parnas* and later in the 1750s and 1760s. While *parnas*, Abraham attempted to arbitrate the dispute between Jonathan *Eybeschuetz and Jacob *Emden (to whom he was related by marriage). The Council of the Four Lands was drawn into this controversy which stirred the Jewish world. Abraham, who was then serving his second term as *parnas* of the Council, tried to settle the dispute without taking a definite side. His brothers, especially Moses, lived in Lissa and also took part in the leadership of the community. The family was renowned for its wealth, its strong principles, and its charitableness. The sources do not indicate their means of livelihood but it is likely that they were merchants.

ADD. BIBLIOGRAPHY: Halpern, Pinkas; Y. Trunk, "*Leberur Emdato shel Abraham ben Yoske, Parnas Va'ad Arba Araẓot, be-Maḥloket bein Yonatan Eybeschuetz ve-Ya'akov Emden,*" in: *Zion*, 33 (1968), 174–79.

[Israel Halpern]

ABRAHAM BEN JOSIAH TROKI (1636–1687), Karaite poet and mystic; son of the physician Josiah b. Judah b. Aaron of Troki, Lithuania, who was a disciple of the famous Jewish scholar and kabbalist, Joseph Solomon *Delmedigo from Candia. According to A. *Firkovich, Abraham was the personal physician of King Jan III Sobieski of Poland and of Grand Duke Sigismund II. Abraham was one of the leaders of the Karaite communities of Lithuania and one of the signatories to the decisions of their assemblies.

His writings include (1) *Beit Avraham*, a collection of mystical treatises; (2) *Beit ha-Oẓar*, a medical work completed in 1672 (manuscript in St. Petersburg, Evr. I 733); (3) *Massa ha-Am*, seven treatises whose content is uncertain (according to J. *Fürst, they describe the condition of the Jews and Judaism); Firkovich reports that Abraham personally translated this work into Latin and sold it to the Dominican Order in Vilna; (4) *Pas Yed'a*, miscellaneous treatises (perhaps a 17th-century anti-Christian Rabbanite treatise *Pas Yed'a Katava*, written by Yehudah Briel, which Abraham owned or copied); (5) *Sefer Refu'ot* (manuscript in St. Petersburg, Evr. I 732), a medical work, also containing information on the history of the Jews in Lithuania; S. *Poznanski identifies this with a collection of medical prescriptions in Latin mentioned by Fürst and Firkovich; (6) three liturgical poems, one appearing in a Karaite prayer book (ed. Vilna, vol. 4, p. 102) and two in manuscript. Abraham is not to be confused with *Abraham b. Josiah Yerushalmi.

BIBLIOGRAPHY: E. Carmoly, *Histoire des médecins juifs* (1844), 187; I.M. Jost, *Geschichte der Israeliten*, 2 (1820), 371; A.B. Gottlober, *Bikkoret le-Toledot ha-Kara'im* (1865), 151–4; Finn, Keneset, 29; A. Neubauer, *Aus der Petersburger Bibliothek* (1866), 72, 128, 130; Fuerst, Karaeertum, 3 (1869), 30, 94, 168; Mann, Texts, 2 (1935), index, 1529.

[Jakob Naphtali Hertz Simchoni / Golda Akhiezer (2nd ed.)]

ABRAHAM BEN JOSIAH YERUSHALMI (c. 1685–after 1734), Karaite scholar, one of the most important authors in the Crimea, *ḥazzan* and teacher of Torah, from *Chufut-Kaleh. The agnomen Yerushalmi probably indicates that his father, Josiah, made the pilgrimage to Jerusalem. His religious philosophical treatise *Emunah Omen*, written in 1712 (pub. Eupatoria, 1846), dealt with the following subjects: the divine origin and eternity of the Torah; which religion is the true one, the Karaite or the Rabbanite?; does tradition permit Jews to study the secular sciences? Abraham defended the Karaite conception of the Torah, arguing that the differences between the rabbinic and Karaite views about fulfillment of the commandments are insignificant. He shows respect for the talmudic authorities and later Rabbanite scholars with whose work he was well acquainted. Although opposed to the study of secular sciences (except in the service of the Torah), Abraham was familiar with both Karaite and Rabbanite philosophical and scientific literature. Abraham's numerous other works include homiletical discourses, liturgical poetry incorporated in the Karaite prayer book, and *Sha'ol Sha'al* (Ms. St. Petersburg, Evr. II A 322), a treatise on the laws of ritual slaughter. Abraham was the grandfather of Benjamin b. Samuel *Aga.

BIBLIOGRAPHY: Fuerst, Karaeertum, 3 (1869), 68–73; A. Geiger, *Nachgelassene Schriften*, 2 (1875), 351–7 (analysis of *Emunah Omen*); S. Poznański, in: *Ha-Goren*, 8 (1912), 58–75; Mann, Texts, 2 (1935), 1277–78. **ADD. BIBLIOGRAPHY:** S. Poznanski, *Ha-Kara'i Avraham ben Yoshiyahu Yerushalmi* (1894).

[Jakob Naphtali Hertz Simchoni / Golda Akhiezer (2nd ed.)]

ABRAHAM BEN JUDAH BEN ABRAHAM (15th century), the "Elder," Karaite biblical exegete and liturgical poet of Constantinople. In his main work *Yesod Mikra*, a commentary of the Bible, Abraham quotes Rabbanite as well as Karaite authorities and refrains from polemics against the Rabbanites. It is preserved in two manuscripts (Jewish Theological Seminary and Leyden) both transcribed by his grandson Judah b. Elijah Tishbi (in 1511 and 1518, respectively). Fifteen liturgical poems by Abraham are included in the Karaite prayer book.

BIBLIOGRAPHY: M. Steinschneider, *Catalogue Leyden* (1858), nos. 1–5; Mann, Texts, 2 (1935), 1420–21; S. Poznański, in: *Yevreyskaya Entsiklopediya*, 1 (c. 1910), 291–2.

[Jakob Naphtali Hertz Simchoni]

ABRAHAM BEN JUDAH LEON (second half of 14th century), disciple of Ḥasdai *Crescas. Abraham came to Spain from his native Candia (Crete) sometime after 1375, the year in which he completed a Hebrew translation of Euclid's *Elements*. In 1378, he finished his quadripartite theological tome entitled *Even Shetiyyah* ("Foundation Stone") "in the house of my master … Don Ḥasdai Crescas." The nature of the relationship between this work and Crescas' teachings remains a matter of debate, though the two contain many similarities. Abraham's work is often called *Arba'ah Turim* ("Four Columns") on the basis of the title page of the lone manuscript in which it survives.

BIBLIOGRAPHY: Sh. Rosenberg, "The *Arba'ah Turim* of Abraham bar Judah, Disciple of Don Ḥasdai Crescas" (Heb.), in: *Jerusalem Studies in Jewish Thought*, 3 (1983–84), 525–621; E. Lawee, "The Path to Felicity: Teachings and Tensions in *Even Shetiyyah* of Abraham ben Judah, Disciple of Hasdai Crescas," in: *Mediaeval Studies*, 59 (1997), 183–223.

[Eric Lawee (2nd ed.)]

ABRAHAM BEN MAZHIR (first half of the 12th century), head of the Damascus yeshivah. Abraham, the son of a prominent Damascus Jew, married into the family of Gaon Solomon ha-Kohen b. Elijah, founder of the Damascus yeshivah, a continuation of the Palestinian yeshivah. When Solomon ha-Kohen's son Maẓli'aḥ settled in Fostat, Abraham became the head of the yeshivah, and served in this capacity during the 1130s and 1140s.

BIBLIOGRAPHY: Mann, Egypt, 1 (1920), 224ff.; Mann, Texts, 1 (1931), 250ff.

[Eliyahu Ashtor]

ABRAHAM BEN MORDECAI HA-LEVI (late 17th century), Egyptian rabbi and author. In 1684 Abraham succeeded his father as head of the Egyptian rabbinate. His son-in-law, the physician Ḥayyim b. Moses Tawil, published a collection of Abraham's responsa (arranged in the order of the four *Turim*) and a treatise on divorce entitled *Ginnat Veradim* (Constantinople, 1716–17) and *Ya'ir Netiv* (1718), respectively. In Venice, Abraham printed his father's responsa *Darkhei No'am* (1697–98), adding to it his own treatise on circumcision which involved him in a halakhic controversy with his contemporaries. He annulled the ban on reading *Peri Hadash* by *Hezekiah Da Silva – imposed by Egyptian rabbis in the previous generation. A collection of brief decisions and rules entitled *Gan ha-Melekh* was printed at the end of *Ginnat Veradim*. His remaining works, consisting of Bible commentaries, sermons, and eulogies, have remained in manuscript.

BIBLIOGRAPHY: Michael, Or, no. 177; S.M. Chones, *Toledot ha-Posekim* (1929), 141; S. Rosanes, *Divrei Yemei Yisrael be-Togarmah*, 4 (1935), 379–81; Heilperin, in *Zion*, 1 (1936), 84, n. 2; Sonne, *ibid.*, 252–5.

[Yehoshua Horowitz]

ABRAHAM BEN MOSES BEN MAIMON (1186–1237), theologian, exegete, communal leader, mystical pietist, and physician. Little was known about him prior to the discovery of the Cairo *Genizah, which has preserved many of his writings, in part autographic. Born in Fustat, Egypt, on the Sabbath eve, the 28th of Sivan/June 1186, he was the only son of the great Jewish philosopher Moses *Maimonides (1135/8–1204). His mother was the sister of Ibn Almali, a royal secretary who had married Maimonides' only sister. He was an exceptionally gifted child as his father himself testifies:

> Of the affairs of this world I have no consolation, save in two things: preoccupation with my studies and the fact that God has bestowed upon my son Abraham, grace and blessings similar to those he gave to him whose name he bears [i.e. the Patriarch Abraham] … for, in addition to his being meek and humble towards his fellow men, he is endowed with excellent virtues, sharp intelligence and a kind nature. With the help of God, he will certainly gain renown amongst the great (Maimonides' letter to Joseph ben Judah, *Epistulae*, ed. D. Baneth, p.96).

He studied rabbinics, and possibly philosophy and medicine,

with his father, who groomed him from childhood by having him attend his audience chamber. At his father's death in 1204, Abraham became leader of Egyptian Jewry at the tender age of 18. The mystical testament Maimonides supposedly addressed him is spurious. It was not until 1213 that he was appointed *nagid*, an office which became his descendants' privilege for almost two centuries. Following his appointment, a temporary controversy erupted among the Jews of Egypt over the practice of evoking his name in public prayer. As representative of the Jewish community to the Ayyubid government, he enjoyed personal relations with the Muslim authorities and men of letters, especially after he became court physician to the Ayyubid Sultan al-Malik al-Kamil (reg. 1218–38), Saladin's brother. His acquaintances include the Arab historian Ibn Abi Usaybi'a, who described him and his professional skills:

> Abu-l-Muna Ibrahim, son of the *ra'is* Musa ibn Maymun was born in Fostat, Egypt. A celebrated physician, learned in the art of medicine, and excellent in its practice, he was employed in the service of al-Malik al-Kamil Muhammad b. Abu Bakr b. Ayyub. He also came frequently from the palace to treat the sick in the al-Nasiri hospital in Cairo, where I met him in the year 631/1234 or 632/1235 while I was practicing there. I found him to be a tall sage, lean in body, of pleasant manners, refined speech, and distinguished in medicine. Ibrahîm, son of the *ra'is* Musa died in the year (…) and thirty and six hundred (*History of Physicians*, ed. Mueller, p. 118).

Despite the temporal and spiritual turmoil of the period, he proved to be an able administrator, a charismatic teacher, and an independant and influential scholar. Although he recognized the incompatibility of leadership and spiritual perfection, he was dedicated to his political vocation as a means of reversing religious decline. Abundant letters in the Genizah give witness to the multiple social and administrative chores to which he attended with the humility of a pietist and the determination of a leader. Hampered, as was his father, by pastoral responsibilities, he nonetheless produced notable works in six main areas: 1) responsa, 2) polemics, 3) exegesis, 4) theology, 5) *halakhah*, and 6) ethics. Despite their originality, his writings have survived in a fragmentary state. A unique letter, addressed in 1232 to R. Isaac b. Israel Ibn Shuwaykh, head of the Baghdad Academy, has preserved an autobiographical account of his literary activity:

> I have not yet had the leisure to complete the compositions begun after my father's demise, [namely] a detailed commentary on the Talmud and a work explaining the principles of the *Ḥibbur* [i.e. Maimonides' *Code*]. However, the Lord has assisted me in completing one work in the Arabic tongue, based on the principles of fear and love (of God), entitled *Compendium for the Servants of the Lord*. I have revised and almost entirely copied it, and part of it has been broadcast to distant lands. True enough I have begun the Torah commentary of which thou hast heard, and which I would have completed within a year or so were I to find relief from the sultan's service and other tasks. However, I can only devote to it short hours on odd days, for I have not yet finished revising the first composition stated to be almost complete, a small part remaining to be finished with Heaven's help. On this account I have covered only close to half the book of Genesis of the Torah commentary I am composing. When I shall have concluded the revision of [my] composition, of which the greater part is [already] finished, I shall endeavor with all my might to complete the Torah commentary and subsequently also a commentary on the Prophets and the Hagiographa, Heaven, willing. But 'the work is long' and the day and the workers are as described by Rabbi Tarfon (Avot 2: 15), and "there are many thoughts in a man's heart but the counsel of the Lord that shall stand" (Prov. 19:21) (Rosenblatt, 1:124–5)

Responsa

Numerous items have been discovered in the Genizah since the single manuscript of his responsa was published by A. Freimann, Jerusalem, 1937. As head of the Cairo Rabbinical Court, he corresponded on legal matters with countries as far flung as Yemen (Cf. Responsa, p. 107–36), Byzance (p. 93), and Provence (p. 1). These responsa afford an opportunity of assessing his important communal rôle. Their content discusses, among other things, problematic passages in his father's halakhic and philosophical writings, ritual matters and customs, exegetical remarks, and apostates, a concern in his time. Besides certain social ordinances (*takkanot*) he introduced, of special historical interest are his responsa concerning the burning of the *Guide for the Perplexed*, and specific pietist practices. Questioners include prominent scholars such as R. Solomon b. Asher of Provence, Me'ir b. Barukh, disciple of R. Abraham b. David of Posquières, and Joseph b. Gershom and R. Anatoli b. Joseph, both *dayyanim* from France who had settled in Alexandria.

Polemics

Some lenghtier responsa reply to the halakhic and philosophical detractors of his father's works, thereby strengthening Abraham's own prestige. In 1213 he composed in Arabic replies to Daniel Ibn al-Mashita's strictures on his father's *Book of Precepts* and *Code*, published as *Birkhat Avraham* (Lyck, 1865) and *Ma'aseh Nissim* (Paris, 1867). Later, Abraham declined when requested by his father's disciple Joseph Ibn Shimon to excommunicate Ibn al-Mashita for his discourteous remarks about Maimonides in his *Taqwim al-adyan* ('Redress of Religion') and his commentary on Ecclesiastes. Abraham's *Milḥamot ha-Shem* ("Wars of the Lord," ed. princeps Vilnius, 1821), written in Hebrew after 1235, in which he defends his father's eschatology, immaterial conception of the Godhead, rationalizing methods, and metaphorical interpretations, was singularly directed against the criticism of the rabbis of Provence, whom he accuses of a pagan anthropomorphism influenced by their Christian environment (see *Maimonidean Controversy). Interestingly, the text was interpretated mystically in the 16th century by Eliezer Eilenberg of the kabbalistic school of Abulafia.

Exegesis

Though Maimonides' philosophical writings set out to determine a proper understanding of problematic scriptural passages, his unfulfilled ambition to compose a complete biblical commentary was to be taken up by Abraham in Arabic. Of his proposed Bible commentary only that on Genesis and Exodus, completed in 1232, has survived. A disciple of the Andalusian rationalist school, he generally prefers literal meaning, though he is not adverse to *midrash*. He quotes the geonic and Spanish exegetes, especially Abraham Ibn Ezra, and even adduces the opinions of Rashi. Particularly noteworthy are comments cited in the names of his grandfather Maimun b. Joseph, and father, Moses Maimonides. He does admit moderate philosophical interpretation, adopting some of his father's doctrines, especially in connection with prophetic visions, which he calls "mysteries." The latter term he applies too to his own pietistic interpretations inspired by Sufi concepts and practices projected back into the patriarchal past. "His explications of the Bible and the Talmud are so graceful, so lucid, so persuasive that one is almost convinced that his *derash* is *peshat*, that his moralistic and pietist interpretation constitutes the literal meaning of the text" (S.D. Goitein). Despite its pleasant style, the commentary did not attain wide recognition, probably because it was not rendered into Hebrew, and has survived in a single manuscript, published, with a modern Hebrew translation, by E. Wiesenberg (London, 1958). Like his father, Abraham also applied metaphorical interpretations to the *midrash*. His *Ma'amar al Odot Derashot Ḥazal* (ed. Margaliot), twice translated into Hebrew, is an extract from his *Kifaya*.

Theology and Halakhah

Abraham's magnum opus *The Compendium for the Servants of the Lord* (in Arabic: *Kifayat al-abidin*; in Hebrew: *Ha-Maspik le-Ovedei ha-Shem*), completed *circa* 1232, is a sum of theology, *halakhah*, and ethics. Of the 10 original volumes unfortunately only a small, nonetheless substantial, portion has been preserved in various libraries. This loss deprives us of a definitive assessment of his approach to legal and ethical issues. Written in a lively and attractive Arabic, but at times repetitive and digressive, it circulated widely, reaching Provence in the West, and was read at least into the 18th century in the East. Abraham had been the first to institute as a central textbook of rabbinic study his father's *Mishneh Torah*, of which his own codified program of Jewish law and ethics, likewise referred to as the *Ḥibbur*, has been called an Arabic version. Although relying heavily upon it, both halakhically and structurally, the *Kifaya* is an independent work betraying a very definite shift in emphasis. Departing from his father's prescriptive mode, Abraham stresses, in a descriptive tone, the spiritual significance of the traditional Jewish precepts (*mitzvot*, divine commandments) and the "mysteries" they conceal, in much the same manner as al-Ghazali did in his classical Islamic summa, *Ihya ulum ad-din* ("Revival of the Religious Sciences"). While sharing his father's dedication to strict adherence to the intricacies of religious ritual, he is sometimes at variance with his father's rulings. After one such discrepancy, he writes:

> Had my father heard [my explanation], he would have admitted it just as he had ordained to admit the truth. Indeed, we always observed that he would agree even with his slightest pupil with what was right, despite the breadth of his knowledge, which never belied the breadth of his religious integrity (Dana, p. 71).

Following his father's distinction between the elite and the masses, he devotes its initial sections to the "common way," i.e. religious obligations incumbent upon the community as a whole, whereas the last sections, of a markedly pietistic tendency, expound the "special way," reserved for the elect few. Of particular interest are his ritual reforms set out in the chapters on prayer, which include such Islamic-influenced practices as ablution of the feet before worship, standing in ordered rows during prayer, kneeling and bowing, and raising the hands in supplication. Some of these had existed in Temple times but had been abandoned in reaction to Christian worship. Indeed, Abraham justified the adoption of Muslim customs and symbols as restorations of lost Jewish traditions, which, having fallen into oblivion, had been preserved by the Sufis. Using his prerogative as *nagid*, he endeavored to enforce these far-reaching measures. Although intended to improve the spiritual decorum of the synagogue, they were not to go unchallenged by the Egyptian establishment. Despite his office and family prestige, which considerably furthered the pietists' aims, his opponents, headed by the Nathanel and Sar Shalom families, who had presided over the Fostat Academy, even protested to the Sultan al-Malik al-Adil, accusing the Jewish pietists of "unlawful changes." Abraham retaliated with a memorandum signed by 200 of his followers, in which he states that his pietist practices were carried out solely in his private synagogue. He further replied to charges of "false ideas" and "gentile customs" in a special tract in defense of the pietists, whom he considers spiritually "superior to the scholars." His commentary on the Talmud and the work explaining the principles of the *Ḥibbur* (i.e., Maimonides' *Code*) have not survived.

Ethics

A large portion of the ethical chapters was published together with an English translation by S. Rosenblatt under the title *High Ways to Perfection*. Though in many respects he conducted himself – and indeed was considered – as the continuator and interpreter of Maimonides' doctrine, his personal style was markedly different. Though he repeatedly states that he lived according to his father's principles, he transferred the latter's elite intellectualist system to the ethical plane, molding it into a pietistic way of life rather than a philosophical one. In fact, Abraham expressed reservations about philosophy in his *Milḥamot ha-Shem*:

> Fools have imagined in their silliness that whoever engages in science is a heretic denying the Torah, and whoever studies philosophy follows their creed concerning the principles of the faith. Now we oppose their opinion that the world is preexistant with the belief of the Torah, refuting them with replies and proofs to clarify the creed of the Torah that the world is ad-

> ventitious and created ... as our Sages enjoined us: "Be eager to learn Torah; know what answer to give to the unbeliever" (Avot 2:19). We act likewise towards all their opinions which contradict the faith of the Torah. But, for all that, we are not to contradict their belief in the unity of the Creator (p. 59).

While recognizing the superiority of scientific speculation over the passive performance of the Law, Abraham considers the esoteric accomplishment of the precepts to be superior to philosophy. Indeed, in the *Kifaya*, he states with a note of opposition, reminiscent of Juda Halevi:

> God has enabled [the true adherents of the Law who have grasped its secret meaning] to understand by means of His Law what the scientists and philosophers do not understand, and He has established for them, by means of His signs and miracles, proof for what the latter deny ...

The pivotal difference being not one of theory but of practice, Abraham's foremost goal was to become a *ḥasid* rather than a *ḥakham*. While recognizing the importance of strict observance of religious law and of intellectual accomplishment, he insists more heavily on man's ethical achievements. In his day, the great spread of Islamic Sufi brotherhoods in Egypt constituted an immediate spiritual model. Under its sway, he tried to promote a form of pietism which earned him the epithet by which he is often referred to in later literature, Abraham *he-ḥasid* ("the Pious"). The *Kifaya* preaches an extreme form of Sufi-like ascetism, whereas Maimonides, though acknowledging in his *Commentary on Avot* the merit of self-mortification, rejects it in favor of the golden mean of temperance. The fourth and final section, presents the ethical stages of the "special way," modeled on the well- known stations (*maqamat*) of classical Sufi manuals: sincerity, mercy, generosity, gentleness humility, faith, contentedness, abstinence, mortification and solitude, whose mystical goal, *wusul* ("arrival"), culminated in the encounter with God and the certitude of his light. Entrance to the "path" is subject to an initiatory ritual such as the bestowal of a mantle, as Elijah did:

> By casting his cloak over [Elisha], Elijah hinted to him... that Elijah's spiritual perfection would be transferred to him and that he [Elisha] would attain the degree which he himself had attained. Thou art aware of the ways of the ancient saints [*awliya'*] of Israel, which are not or but little practised among our contemporaries, that have now become the practice of the Sufis of Islam, "on account of the iniquities of Israel", namely that the master invests the novice [*murid*] with a cloak [*khirqah*] as the latter is about to enter upon the mystical path [*tariq*]. "They have taken up thine own words" (Deuteronomy 33:3). This is why we moreover take over from them and emulate them in the wearing of sleeveless tunics and the like (Rosenblatt, 2: 266).

Abraham openly admires the Muslim Sufis, whose practices, he claims, ultimately derive from ancient Israelite custom. After having stated that the true dress of the ancient prophets of Israel was similar to the ragged garments (*muraqqa'at*) of the Sufis, he declares:

> Do not regard as unseemly our comparison of that [the true dress of the prophets] to the conduct of the Sufis, for the latter imitate the prophets [of Israel] and walk in their footsteps, not the prophets in theirs. (Rosenblatt, 2: 320).

He finds biblical counterparts for Sufi ascetic exercises such as combating sleep, solitary retreats in dark places, weeping, nightly vigils and daily fasts, as in the following passage:

> We see the Sufis of Islam also profess the discipline of mortification by combatting sleep. Perhaps such a practice is derived from the statement of David: 'I will not give sleep to mine eyes, nor slumber to mine eyelids' (Ps. 132:4) ... Observe then these wonderful traditions and sigh with regret over how they have been transferred from us and appeared amongst a nation other than ours whereas they have disappeared in our midst. My soul shall weep in secret ... because of the pride of Israel that was taken from them and bestowed upon the nations of the world (Rosenblatt, 2:322).

One of the most typical aspects of the Sufi path is the necessity of the spiritual guidance of an experienced teacher who has traversed all the stages of the path in order to initiate the spiritual wayfarer into its intricacies. Abraham sees the origin of this principle in the discipline of the ancient prophets:

> Know that generally in order for the Way to attain successfully its true goal [*wusul*], it must be pursued under the guidance [*taslik*] of a person who has already attained this goal, as it is said in the tradition: "Acquire a master" (Avot 1:6). The biblical accounts concerning masters and their disciples are well known; Joshua the servant of Moses was one of his disciples, who, having attained the goal, succeeded him. The prophets adopted the same conduct. Samuel's guide [*musallik*] was Eli, Elijah was that of Elisha, and Jeremiah that of Barukh son of Neriah. Moreover the "disciples of the prophets" were thus called because the prophets were their spiritual guides. This practice was adopted by other nations (the Sufis), who instituted in imitation of Jewish custom the relation between *shaykh* and servant, master and disciple ... If the wayfarer is capable and remains faithful to instructions, he will attain his goal through the guidance of an accomplished master (Rosenblatt, 2: 422).

The denomination "the disciples of the prophets" is a key to the process of recovering from the Sufis the lost "prophetic discipline." Its restoration was a prerequisite to the return of prophecy itself, whose imminence was predicted by Maimonides. The absence of the final chapter of the *Kifaya* which dealt with the attainment of the ultimate goal (*wusul*), is an irretrievable loss.

Other Works

Abraham refers to other compositions now lost, such as a treatise on truth, and an explanation of the 26 premises of the introduction to the second part of the *Guide*. It has been shown that the *Kitab al-hawd* and the *Taj al-'arifin*, ascribed to him by the 17th century chronicler Sambari, probably belong to other authors. Some manuscripts erroneously attribute to him the *Sodot ha-Moreh* ("Secrets of the Guide"), in fact by Abraham *Abulafiia. His authorship of the folktale *Ma'aseh Yerushalmî* (Jerusalem, 1946), is unlikely.

Influence

Abraham was at the hub of a pietistic circle of a sectarian nature whose adepts were dissatisfied with formal religion. Partly inspired by Abraham Abu ar-Rabia (d. 1223), also known as *he-ḥasid*, whom he calls "our Master in the Way," this circle included Abraham Maimonides' father-in-law, Hananel ben Samuel, and his own son Ovadiah (1228–1265) author of the mystical *al-Maqala al-Hawdiyya* ("Treatise of the Pool"). Despite an enormous literary output, the movement did not engender a widespread community of ascetics similar to Sufism, probably because of the vehement opposition to Abraham's ritual reforms. Indeed, this opposition, as well as the movement's own elitist character seriously impeded its spread. With the general decline of Oriental Jewry, his Sufi-type Jewish pietism sank into oblivion, though some of its mystical elements were possibly absorbed into the nascent Kabbalah. However, the exegetical and ethical writings of several of his direct descendants perpetuated his tendency to temper Maimonides' spiritual ideology with Sufi mysticism. Later authorities, such as the 13th cent. Karaite Yefet b. Za'ir, *Sefer ha-Ḥinnukh*, Aaron ha-Yarḥi, R. *David ibn Abi Zimra, Moses al-Ashkar, Joseph *Caro, Abraham Ibn Migash, and Mas'ud *Rakah, utilize his works, which were still being read in the 18th century. Abraham Maimonides passed away on Monday, 18 Kislev, 1237. Eliezer b. Jacob ha-Bavli (*Diwan*, no. 199) composed an elegy for him in which he wrote:

> Who believed wholeheartedly in his Lord,
> Counted to him as righteousness?
> Who arose and, with the hand of reason, overthrew the idols of ignorance,
> Reducing its image to shivers?
> Who established in Memphis [= Egypt] an inn, opening its gates to wayfarers?
> Who bound upon the altar of understanding, like young lambs, the offspring of thought?
> With whom did his Lord make a covenant between the pieces, with flaming torches?
> 'Twas Abraham, who, the day of his demise, rent our hearts and inner parts.

Although his father's blessing of greatness had been fullfiled, Abraham's renown may have been greater still had he not been overshadowed by Maimonides' towering figure.

BIBLIOGRAPHY: WORKS: N. Dana (ed.), *Sefer ha-Maspik le-Ovedei ha-Shem* (1989); A.H. Freimann (ed.), *Abraham Maimuni, Responsa* (1937); R. Margaliot (ed.), R. Abraham Maimuni, *Milhamot ha-Shem* (1953); S. Rosenblatt (ed.), *The High Ways to Perfection of Abraham Maimonides*, 2 vols. (1927–38); E. Wiesenberg (ed.), *Abraham Maimonides Commentary on Genesis and Exodus* (1958). GENERAL: G. Cohen, "The Soteriology of Abraham Maimuni," in: *Studies in the Variety of Rabbinic Cultures* (1991); S. Eppenstein, *Abraham Maimuni: sein Leben und seine Schriften* (1914); P. Fenton, "Abraham Maimonides (1187–1237): Founding a Mystical Dynasty," in: M. Idel and M. Ostow (eds.), *Jewish Mystical Leaders and Leadership in the 13th Century* (2000), 127–154; idem, *Deux traités de mystique juive* (1987); S.D. Goitein, "Abraham Maimonides and his Pietist Circle," in: A. Altmann (ed.), *Jewish Medieval and Renaissance Studies* (1967), 145–164; N. Wieder, *Islamic Influences on the Jewish Worship* (1948).

[Paul Fenton (2nd ed.)]

ABRAHAM BEN MOSES HA-KOHEN HA-SEPHARDI (late 15th and early 16th centuries), Italian rabbi. A scion of a prominent priestly family in the Spanish city of Cuenca, Abraham went to Italy at about the age of 20 in the wake of the expulsion from Spain. He resided first in Ferrara, then moved to Bologna, where he was appointed rabbi. He became involved in the controversy concerning the litigation between Abraham Raphael Finzi of Bologna and Immanuel di Norzi of Ferrara. The former did not wish the case to be tried in Ferrara, because of Norzi's strong influence there. When R. Abraham *Minz insisted that the Ferrara court had jurisdiction, a controversy ensued. The rabbinical opinions expressed on both sides were published under the title *Piskei ha-Ga'on R. Liva mi-Ferrara ve-Rav Avraham Minz* (Venice, 1519), and included that of Abraham b. Moses. The dispute was brought before the rabbinical authorities of Poland, who agreed with Abraham b. Moses. His learning won particular praise from R. Jacob *Pollak, the father of Polish talmudic scholarship, and from R. Moses *Isserles (in his supplements to the *Sefer Yuḥasin*). Attacked by Minz as a "contentious priest" (cf. Hos. 4:4) and a "smooth-talking Sephardi," Abraham countered by deeming the abusive epithets titles of honor and stating at the same time that he had never previously had a dispute with anyone. The rest of his responsa, his commentary on the *She'iltot*, sermons, and comments on Rashi's commentary on the Pentateuch, remain unpublished. He published an edition of the *Sefer Ḥasidim* ("Book of the Pious") with an introduction and an index (Venice, 1538). His son-in-law, the husband of his daughter Paloma, was the historian Joseph ha-Kohen.

BIBLIOGRAPHY: A. Marx, in: *Abhandlungen ... H.P. Chajes* (1933), 149–93, especially 172–3; Sonne, in: HUCA, 16 (1941), 48–50, 53–55, 81–84 (Hebrew section).

[Jacob Haberman]

ABRAHAM BEN NATHAN (end 11th–beginning 12th century), talmudic scholar and *dayyan* in Fostat, where he was active in the first quarter of the 12th century. His father Nathan was the *av bet din* of the Palestinian academy (probably at Tyre). Abraham also lived in Ereẓ Israel toward the end of the 11th century and his signature is affixed to a document issued at Ramleh. In 1102, however, he was in Fostat, and his signature appears as the first on an attestation document. In a *genizah* document dated from 1116 Abraham is described as the "great, distinguished rabbi," and in letters he is addressed as "foundation stone and leader of the yeshivah" and "pride of the judges and support of the *nasi*"; he is also designated as *reish bei rabbanan* and *rosh ha-seder* (head of the academy). It is assumed that Abraham held the officially recognized office of *dayyan al-Yahud* ("judge of the Jews"), regarded by the authorities as the representative dignitary of the Jews second to the *nagid*.

BIBLIOGRAPHY: Mann, Egypt, 1 (1920), 194, 267; 2 (1922), index.

[Moshe Nahum Zobel]

ABRAHAM BEN NATHAN (Abu Isḥāq Ibrahim ibn ʿAṭāʾ; c. 1025), first *nagid* of the Jewish community of Kairouan. He was court physician to Badis, the viceroy of Tunisia, and to al-Muʿizz his son and successor, who became independent ruler. Abraham did much for the Jewish communities of North Africa. Two poems praising the *nagid* for his communal activities are extant. Isḥāq ibn Khalfon, the court poet, dedicated several of his poems to his benefactor. He was honored in a song of praise by R. *Hai Gaon. Abraham exchanged responsa with R. *Samuel b. Hophni, the *gaon* of Sura. The latter's son, R. Israel, dedicated a book on liturgical laws to him.

BIBLIOGRAPHY: Poznański, in: *Festschrift Harkavy* (1908), 175–220; Brody, in: YMḤSL, 3 (1936), 27–31; Goitein, in: *Zion*, 27 (1962), 11–23, 156–65; idem, in: *Tarbiz*, 34 (1965), 164–9. **ADD. BIBLIOGRAPHY:** Hirschberg, Afrikah 1, (1974), 112–13, 211–13; M. Ben-Sasson, *Qayrawan*, 348–62.

[Simha Assaf / Abraham David (2nd ed.)]

ABRAHAM BEN NATHAN HA-YARHI (c. 1155–1215), Provençal talmudic scholar. His name "Ha-Yarḥi" is the Hebrew translation for "of Lunel" where he spent many years. He was born at Avignon and was related to *Isaac b. Abba Mari. He studied with the scholars of Lunel, with Abraham b. David of Posquières, and in Dampierre in northern France, under the tosafist Isaac the Elder, and other scholars of his circle. Abraham wandered through many countries, and visited Toledo, Spain, in 1194. Later he settled there and apparently became a member of the rabbinical court (before 1204). He left Toledo again, went to France, and returned to Spain in 1211.

During his travels Abraham made a point of "observing the customs of every country and every city" and noted that "they [the Jews] varied in their religious practices and that they were divided into 70 languages." He recorded various customs, particularly concerning prayer and other synagogue usages, in a book which he called *Manhig Olam* known popularly as *Sefer ha-Manhig* (Constantinople, 1519; republished by A.N. Goldberg, Berlin, 1855). This work has come down in a corrupt form. Chapters and paragraphs are omitted and the printed text contains many mistakes. Various attempts have been made (by Freimann, Toledano, and Raphael) to correct it and fill some of the lacunae. The correct text however has been preserved in the manuscripts. In this book he describes the customs of both southern and northern France, of Germany, England, and Spain. His literary sources include the Talmuds and the Midrashim, the works and responsa of the *Geonim* and the writings of French, Spanish, and other scholars. This work is the first book of *minhagim* (local customs) written in Europe. Its explicit purpose was to show that there is a halakhic basis for every *minhag*. The need for such a compilation was mainly the result of the spread of the halakhic works of the Spanish authorities in Provence, which took place at that time and caused confusion and misunderstanding at both places (see Asher b. Saul). Abraham also wrote a commentary to *Massekhet Kallah Rabbati* (Tiberias [Jerusalem], 1906; JQR, 24 [see bibliography]) and *Maḥazik ha-Bedek* on the laws of ritual slaughtering and forbidden foods (lost). Some of Abraham's responsa are preserved (S.A. Wertheimer, *Ginzei Yerushalayim*, 1 (1896), 19–32).

BIBLIOGRAPHY: J. Reifmann, in: *Ha-Meliẓ*, 1 (1860/61), 63–64, 99–101; idem, in: MWJ, 5 (1878), 60–67; B. Toledano (ed.), *Perush Massekhet Kallah Rabbati* (1906), introd.; Higger, in: JQR, 24 (1933/34), 331–48; A.H. Freimann, in: *Festschrift … J. Freimann* (1937), 105–15 (Heb. pt.); B. Toledano, in: *Sinai*, 41 (1958), 75–80; I. Twersky, *Robad of Posquières* (1962), 240–4; Raphael, in: *Sefer Yovel … H. Albeck* (1963), 443–64; S. Abramson, *Rav Nissim Gaʾon* (1965), 566 (index); Cassel, in: *Jubelschrift … L. Zunz* (1884), 122–37.

ABRAHAM BEN N… HA-BAGHDADI (10th century), communal leader in Babylonia. Information on Abraham is to be found in the poems of praise dedicated to him by one Abraham ha-Kohen, who seems to have been his secretary. He held a military command under the caliph and was a protector of the Jewish community. The reopening of the yeshivah of *Sura about 988 is attributed to him. He also maintained friendly relations with *Hai Gaon. There is reason to believe that Abraham ha-Baghdadi was a member of the *Netira family; he was possibly the son of Netira II and the grandson of Sahl, who was the son of Netira I. One of his sons was named Sahl, probably after his great-grandfather.

BIBLIOGRAPHY: Scheiber, in: *Zion*, 30 (1965), 123–27. **ADD. BIBLIOGRAPHY:** Scheiber, in: *Zion*, 18 (1953), 6–13; Mann, in JQR, 9 (1918/19), 153–60; *Tarbiz*, 5 (1933/34), 177–78.

[Abraham David (2nd ed.)]

ABRAHAM BEN SAMUEL HE-ḤASID (of Speyer; 12th century), rabbi and liturgical poet, the brother of R. *Judah b. Samuel he-Ḥasid. Abraham b. Samuel and *Judah b. Kalonymus, together with R. Shemariah b. Mordecai, later constituted the *bet din* of *Speyer, and are referred to as "the wise men of Speyer." *Eliezer b. Nathan of Mainz describes Abraham as "the sun of our orphaned age." Abraham's retort to a baptized Jew is recorded in the *Sefer Niẓẓaḥon*. In contrast to his father and brother, who were both famous for their mysticism and pietism, Abraham was known for his exoteric teachings and only slight traces of esoteric ideas can be found in his writings. Abraham wrote four elegies in which he described Jewish suffering during the first two Crusades (1096 and 1147).

BIBLIOGRAPHY: Urbach, Tosafot, 577 (index); Davidson, Oẓar, 4 (1933), 358, s.v. *Avraham mi-Speyer (ben Shemuʾel)*; Abraham b. Azriel, *Arugat ha-Bosem*, ed. by E.E. Urbach, 4 (1963), 90–91; V. Aptowitzer, *Mavo le-Sefer Ravyah* (1938), 307–8; Germ Jud, 342, and index.

[Jacob Freimann]

ABRAHAM BEN SAMUEL OF DREUX (second half of 13th century), rabbinical scholar in northwestern France. Abraham was the chief spokesman in a religious disputation in Paris with Paul, a Spanish "cordelier" (conceivably to be identified with Pablo *Christiani) under the reign of Philip the Bold (1270–85). He evidently wrote a commentary on the Book of Daniel, from which was derived an explanation of Daniel 9:24 mentioned in the record of the controversy. It was formerly thought he came from Dreux.

BIBLIOGRAPHY: Neubauer, in: JQR, 5 (1892/93), 713ff.; J. Rosenthal, in: *Aresheth*, 2 (1960), 145.

ABRAHAM BEN SHABBETAI HA-KOHEN (1670–1729), poet, physician, artist, and philosopher. Born in Crete when the island was under Venetian rule, he studied medicine and philosophy at the University of Padua and then practiced on the island of Zante. He was the author of *Kehunnat Avraham* (Venice, 1719), a paraphrase of portions of Psalms in rhymed verse in various meters, to which was appended *Benei Keturah*, a similar paraphrase of *Pirkei Shirah*. The title page of the book is followed by an engraved self-portrait of the author, who was also probably responsible for other engravings in the book. He also published a volume of homilies on the Pentateuch, *Kevod Ḥakhamim* (Venice, 1700).

BIBLIOGRAPHY: Ghirondi-Neppi, 32, no. 76; A. Rubens, *Jewish Iconography* (1954), no. 2006.

[Cecil Roth]

ABRAHAM BEN SIMEON OF WORMS (15th century), pseudonym of the unknown author of a supposedly comprehensive guide to "the divine magic" according to the Kabbalah, especially the conjuration of the Guardian Angel who presides over every man's spiritual life. The author tells at length the story of his life and describes his wanderings that began in the year 1409 and lasted for decades. He lists the heroic deeds which he accomplished with magic devices. The author alleges that he wrote the book for his young son Lamech. The book is found in numerous German, French, and English manuscripts, dating from the 16th to the 18th centuries. Part of it was translated (c. 1700) into Hebrew under the name *Segullat Melakhim* ("Treasure of Kings"). The book was no doubt written originally in German, although the author claims it to be a translation from Hebrew. The question of its authorship, whether Jewish or Christian, is a matter of dispute. The general style of the book shows the author's knowledge of Hebrew. The work may well have been written by a Jew, with the passages with clearly Christian content added later. It may also have been written by a Christian kabbalist who had read the writings of *Pico della Mirandola and Johannes *Reuchlin. The German version was printed at the beginning of the 19th century, bearing, however, the date 1725. The book has had great influence among those interested in the occult in England and France since the end of the 19th century. In its English version (1898) it is attributed to Abra Melin "The Mage," which is but a corruption of the name Abramelin, mentioned as the main teacher of the author. Abramelin seems to be taken from Abraham Elymas, the latter being the name of a magician mentioned in the Acts of the Apostles. The magic material in the book is essentially of Jewish origin, and constitutes one of the main channels of Jewish influence on late Christian magic. The German and the French–English versions differ considerably.

BIBLIOGRAPHY: Michael, Or, no. 257; Steinschneider, Uebersetzungen, 907ff.; Benjacob, Ozar, s.v. *Segullat Melakhim;* G. Scholem, *Bibliographia Kabbalistica* (1927), 2.

[Gershom Scholem]

ABRAHAM BEN SOLOMON (c. 1400), Oriental biblical exegete, possibly from Yemen. His commentary on the Bible is written in Arabic, but contains some Hebrew excerpts. He makes use of very early midrashic sources, some otherwise unknown, quotes "Simeon b. Yoḥai in the Zohar," and draws upon authorities who preceded him, primarily Saadiah Gaon, Jonah ibn Janaḥ, Nathan b. Jehiel, Tanhum b. Joseph Yerushalmi, and David Kimḥi. In his commentary, Abraham draws linguistic parallels between Arabic, Aramaic, and Hebrew, and includes details of the life of Jews and Arabs in the Orient. Parts of his commentary, known as *Midrash Alẓi'ani*, written about 1422, are extant in various Yemenite manuscripts in Jerusalem, Oxford, and London. The British Museum manuscript, copied in 1513, contains his commentary on the Early Prophets, while a Bodleian manuscript, comprising three volumes, includes that on the Early Prophets, Jeremiah, and Ezekiel.

BIBLIOGRAPHY: M. Steinschneider, in: HB, 19 (1879), 131–6; 20 (1880), 7–12, 39–40, 61–65; Steinschneider, Arab Lit, 248; G. Karpeles, *Geschichte der juedischen Literatur*, 2 (1886), 771; J. Ratzaby, in: KS, 28 (1952/53), 267; S. Greidi, in: KS, 33 (1957/58), 112.

[Yehoshua Horowitz]

ABRAHAM BEN SOLOMON OF SAINT MAXIMIN (15th century), French physician. César Nostradamus praises Abraham as a scholar, philosopher, and physician of Provence (*Histoire et Chronologie de Provence* (1624), 618). It was probably Abraham and other Jewish physicians who drew the attention of René of Anjou, count of Provence (1409–1480), to the deplorable situation of the Jews in his kingdom. René issued a decree in 1454, which lessened the hardships brought about by the proclamation of Charles II forcing all Jews to wear the wheel-shaped badge. It also confirmed the right of Jews to practice medicine. René set an example by making Abraham his personal physician and exempting him from all taxes levied on Jews. It has been suggested that Abraham may be identical with Abraham Avigdor II (1433–1488) of Marseilles (REJ, 6–7 (1883), 294). Gottheil (EJ, 1 (1928), 120) adds that Abraham might be the son of Solomon b. Abraham Avigdor I, the translator.

BIBLIOGRAPHY: Steinschneider, Uebersetzungen, 643; G.B. Depping, *Les Juifs dans le Moyen-Age* (1839), 206, 335; Hildefinger, in: REJ, 47 (1903), 232; 48 (1904), 70–75, 265; Kahn, *ibid.*, 39 (1899), 95–112; E. Wickersheimer, *Dictionnaire Biographique des Médecins en France au Moyen-Age* (1936), 5–6; H. Friedenwald, *Jews and Medicine*, 2 (1944), 689.

[Isidore Simon]

ABRAHAM BEN SOLOMON OF TORRUTIEL (b. 1482), chronicler. Born in Spain, after the Expulsion of 1492 he was brought to Fez by his 70-year-old father, Solomon of Torrutiel, an expert in Talmud and a pupil of R. Isaac *Canpanton. In Fez he participated actively in the life of the Jewish community. In 1510 he wrote his Hebrew chronicle, probably not preserved in its entirety. As he indicates in the introduction, his plan was to continue the *Sefer ha-Kabbalah* of Abraham *Ibn Daud. In the first part of his book he gives additions to that work, including some Jewish sages not enumerated by Ibn Daud. In the second part he continues the history of Jewish scholars and scholarship up to 1463, in his own time. The third section is a chronicle of Spanish kings seen from a Jewish perspective, followed by the history of the expulsion of the Jews from Spain and their establishment first in Portugal and later on in Fez, until 1510.

In his introduction he speaks of his intention to include in his book the prognostications of Abraham *Zacuto. From this and other indications it has been concluded that Abraham used for his chronicle the works of Abraham Zacuto (*Sefer Yuḥasin*) and Joseph b. *Ẓaddik of Arévalo. Detailed analysis of the three works shows all used the same Hebrew source, consisting of a chronology of Jewish scholars and a scanty summary of a well-known Spanish world chronicle. Abraham also mentions traditions which are not found in the works of the other two authors. Particularly valuable are his notes on the fate of the Spanish exiles, based on his personal eyewitness observations. The work, first published in Neubauer's Chronicles (V. 101ff.), has appeared in a Spanish translation by J. Bages (Granada, 1921). He seems to be also the author of a kabbalistic work, *Avnei Zikkaron*, translated into Spanish by F. Cantera (1928).

BIBLIOGRAPHY: F. Baer, *Untersuchungen ueber Quellen und Kompositionen des Schebet Jehuda* (1936), 28; Roth, in: *Sefarad*, 9 (1949), 450. **ADD. BIBLIOGRAPHY:** A. David, *Shetei Khronikot Ivriyot mi-Dor Gerush Sefarad* (1979), for Joseph b. Ẓaddik of Arévalo; *El libro de la cábala de Abraham ben Salomon de Torrutiel*, tr. F. Cantera (1928); Y. Moreno (tr.), *Dos crónicas hispanohebreas del siglo XV* (1992).

[*Encyclopaedia Hebraica* / Angel Saenz-Badillos (2nd ed.)]

ABRAHAM DOV BAER OF OVRUCH (d. 1840), rabbi and ḥasidic leader in the Ukraine. Abraham succeeded his father David as rabbi of Khmelnik. He subsequently became rabbi in Ovruch and Zhitomir. He was a devoted disciple of Nahum of Chernobyl, and after Nahum's death kept in contact with his son Mordecai. Abraham Dov went to Ereẓ Israel in 1831, settling in Safed, where he became leader of the Ḥasidim. During the calamities which struck Safed at that time, caused by Druze attacks and an earthquake, Abraham organized relief and encouraged the people to remain. His teachings are recorded in his book *Bat Avin* (Jerusalem, 1847).

[Adin Steinsaltz]

ABRAHAM EL-BARCHILON, fiscal agent of Sancho IV of Castile, 1284–95. Abraham was born in Toledo. His close connection with Don Lope de Haro, a grandee of Sancho's court, helped to augment his influence. After holding various fiscal offices, Sancho leased him his principal state revenues, including the prerogative to mint gold coins, the collection of the debts of Jewish creditors, receipts from fines and penalties imposed for fiscal offenses, export duties, and the arrears of all the taxes farmed during the reign of Sancho's father, Alfonso X. Abraham was also authorized to regain for the Crown all alienated estates. A series of documents of 1287–88 dealing with this matter bears his signature in Hebrew. Abraham continued in office even after Lope de Haro's execution in 1289, now working in partnership with the poet Todros Halevi.

BIBLIOGRAPHY: Baer, Spain, 1 (1961), 131–3; Baer, Urkunden, 1, pt. 2 (1936), 72–77, 89ff.; Neuman, Spain, 2 (1942), 245ff., 338.

ABRAHAM GAON (tenth century), head of the Palestinian yeshivah. Abraham was a great-grandson of the *gaon* *Aaron b. Meir who was involved with *Saadiah in the calendar controversy of 921–22. The view that Abraham was the founder of the Palestinian gaonate has been shown to be untenable, since this gaonate existed at least a century before Abraham and its supremacy was then recognized by its Babylonian counterpart. Manuscripts of genealogical tables mentioning Abraham refer to four of his sons. One of them, Aaron, became the successor to his father's successor, Josiah, *av bet din*. Isaac was "third man" (i.e., next in rank to the *av bet din*) under Abraham's immediate successor, Joseph ha-Kohen, i.e., while Meir was head of the academy (*rosh ha-seder*), probably in Egypt.

BIBLIOGRAPHY: S. Poznański, *Babylonische Geonim…* (1914), 4–5, 84, 97; Mann, Egypt, 1 (1920), 71, no. 6; S. Assaf and L.A. Mayer (eds.), *Sefer ha-Yishuv*, 2 (1944), 89, 127; Abramson, Merkazim, 31, 32.

ABRAHAM GERSHON OF KUTOW (d. c. 1760), ḥasid, talmudic scholar, and kabbalist. He was probably born in Kutow (Kuty), Ukraine, where his father was rabbi. He was the brother-in-law of *Israel b. Eliezer Ba'al Shem Tov. As a youth, he moved to Brody where he continued to study at a *klaus*. According to ḥasidic tradition, Abraham resented his sister's marriage to the Ba'al Shem Tov and at first slighted him, but later became one of his most ardent disciples. In 1747 he went to Ereẓ Israel, intending to spread the teachings of Ḥasidism there, settling first in Hebron and later in Jerusalem. He formed especially close ties with the Sephardi scholars in Jerusalem and in other countries. The correspondence between him and Israel Ba'al Shem Tov is an important source of information for the beginnings of the ḥasidic movement. According to a tradition transmitted by R. Israel of Kuznitz,

R. Abraham Gershon told the Besht how ideal prayer is connected to a divestment of corporeality and the speech of the *Shekhinah* from the throat of the person who prays.

BIBLIOGRAPHY: Horodezky, Ḥasidut, index.

[Adin Steinsaltz / Moshe Idel (2nd ed.)]

ABRAHAM HA-BAVLI (apparently early 11th century), grammarian. Abraham ha-Bavli is mentioned by Abraham Ibn Ezra and Jacob b. Meir (Rabbenu Tam). His *Sefer ha-Shorashim* ("Book of Roots"), only part of which has been published (1863), deals with roots of one to four letters, interchanges in the order of the root letters, homonymic roots, and an elision or interchange of one of the root letters for another letter. Some scholars mistakenly identify him with the Karaite grammarian David b. Abraham *Alfasi.

BIBLIOGRAPHY: A. Neubauer, in: *Journal Asiatique*, 2 (1863), 195. **ADD. BIBLIOGRAPHY:** A. Maman, *Comparative Semitic Philology in the Middle Ages from Saadia Gaon to Ibn Barun (10th–12th cent.)* (2004).

[Meir Medan]

ABRAHAM HA-LEVI (15th century), leader of the Jerusalem community. Abraham went on a mission to the Mediterranean islands and Italy in 1455, two years after the Turkish capture of Constantinople. The capture had aroused many messianic hopes among Jews in Jerusalem. These hopes were strengthened by the tales told by pilgrims from Babylonia, Persia, and Yemen. They told of a war in Ethiopia against the Christians, an earthquake in Jerusalem which uncovered remains of the First Temple, the expulsion of the Franciscans from Mount Zion, and the dream of an aged Babylonian kabbalist to the effect that the "Prince" (Guardian Angel) of Israel would overcome the "Prince" of Edom (Rome). Abraham also appealed for help in maintaining the holy places of Jerusalem. In the course of his mission he arrived at Corfu, then under Venetian rule. There he was denounced to the authorities, who destroyed his credentials. Abraham's letters are an important source for the history of the Jewish community in Jerusalem in the 15th century.

BIBLIOGRAPHY: A. Neubauer, in: *Kobez al Jad*, 4 (1888), 45–50; A. Yaari, *Iggerot Ereẓ Yisrael* (1943), 88–89; Yaari, Sheluḥei, 211–2.

[Avraham Yaari]

ABRAHAM ḤAYYIM BEN GEDALIAH (1750–1816), Galician rabbi. Abraham studied under his father Gedaliah b. Benjamin Wolf, who was *av bet din* in Zloczow. He was a disciple of *Dov Baer the "Maggid of Mezhirech," *Jacob Joseph of Polonnoye, and *Jehiel Michel of Zloczow. He was also a pupil of the two brothers: Samuel Shmelka Horowitz of Nikolsburg and Phinehas Levi Horowitz, his first father-in-law. When Issachar Baer (his father-in-law by his second marriage) immigrated to Ereẓ Israel, Abraham Ḥayyim succeeded him as *av bet din* of Zloczow. He was a brilliant exegete and facile writer, possessed of an easy, graceful style, and is referred to as a "learned exponent of ḥasidic thought." His *Oraḥ Ḥayyim* (Zolkiew, 1817) on the Bible is a treasury of thoughts and sayings of the ḥasidic rabbis. It was published posthumously by his stepson, Joseph Azriel b. Ḥayyim Aryeh Leibush, with an introduction by Ephraim Zalman Margolioth, who praises his piety and charity and gives biographical details. Abraham Ḥayyim wrote a commentary on *Pirkei Avot*, *Peri Ḥayyim* (1873), and a commentary on the *Haggadah*, under the same name (1873).

BIBLIOGRAPHY: A. Walden, *Shem ha-Gedolim he-Ḥadash*, 2 (1864), 4a, no. 73; S. Buber, *Kiryah Nisgavah* (1903), 20–21, s.v. *Gedaliah;* Y. Raphael, *Sefer ha-Ḥasidut* (1947), 67.

[Mordecai Ben-Yehezkiel]

ABRAHAMITES (also "**Nový Bydžov-Israelites**"), Bohemian judaizing sect, a product of the Counter-Reformation. They revered the Old Testament, rejected the Trinity, abstained from pork, and rested on Saturday; some members practiced circumcision. The existence of the sect became known to the authorities in 1747 in the region of *Nový Bydžov. A commission of inquiry was then appointed and proceedings were instituted against 60 Abrahamites, which lasted until 1748, when the leader, Jan Pita, a tailor, and three others were executed. As Pita admitted to having had contact with Nový Bydžov Jews, one of them, R. Mendel, was burnt at the stake (1750) after separate proceedings; others of the accused Jews adopted Catholicism. The sect continued clandestinely until the patent of toleration of non-Catholics was issued in 1781, when the Abrahamites came into the open. However, since they refused to comply with an official injunction to declare themselves either Christian or Jewish, they were deported to garrisons on the Hungarian border and the men forced into military service. The sect subsequently disintegrated.

BIBLIOGRAPHY: Prokěs, in JGGJČ, 8 (1936), 147–308; *Dr. Blochs Wochenschrift* (1903), 476–7, 509–11; J. Moštik, *Sekta tak zvaných israelitů severovýchodních čechách* (1938).

ABRAHAM JOSHUA HESCHEL OF APTA (Opatow; d. 1825), Polish ḥasidic **ẓaddik*, known as "the Rabbi of Apta." He was the disciple of *Elimelech of Lyzhansk (Lezhaisk) and possibly also of the *maggid* *Jehiel Michel of Zloczow (Zolocher). He served as rabbi of the communities of Kolbuszowa Apta (Opatow) from 1809 to 1813 and Jassy (Moldavia), in 1813–14 settling in Medzibozh (Podolia), where he lived until his death. Abraham strongly opposed the *maskilim* in Brody for disseminating what he considered heretical ideas among Russian Jewry. Following the discriminatory legislation passed by Czar *Alexander I, depriving Jewish contractors (arendars) and taverners of their livelihood, Abraham and Isaac of Radzivilow ordered a public fast. As president of the Volhynian *kolel*, he was active in fundraising for the community in Ereẓ Israel. Acknowledged as an authority by many *ẓaddikim* in his old age, Abraham was called upon to excommunicate deviationists in the controversy between the Bratslav and

*Przysucha (Pshiskha) Ḥasidim, and did his best to promote unity and peace in the ḥasidic camp.

Abraham left instructions that his sole epitaph should be *Ohev Yisrael* (a lover of Israel), a description by which he is remembered among the Ḥasidim. The problems of Jewish leadership and care for his people exercised his imagination, and he would recount fantastic "reminiscences" about the events he said that he had witnessed in former incarnations as high priest, a king of Israel, *nasi*, and exilarch. His revelations were regarded by the Hasidim as mysteries of the type experienced by *Rabbah b. Bar Ḥana. A religious ecstatic, he delivered homilies on Sabbaths and festivals emphasizing love of the Creator and the importance of cleaving (**devekut*) to Him. He exerted a wide popular influence. His adherents believed that the violent gestures with which he accompanied the sermons denoted *hitpashetut ha-gashmiyyut* (the shedding of bodily existence). One of Abraham Joshua Heschel's contemporaries recounts that "in the midst of the meal, when the spirit was upon him, he cried out in a loud and dolorous voice and gesticulated; his head fell back almost to his heels, and all the people who sat round the sacred table… trembled and feared… and he started to relate secrets of the Torah and hidden mysteries; he opened his saintly mouth and spoke with great fervor; his face was [like] a torch, he raised his voice in ecstasy." Nevertheless, Abraham Joshua Heschel concentrated on the system of practical Ẓaddikism and held that the *ẓaddik* "through his wisdom lifts up Israel to bind them to heaven and to bring prosperity, blessing, and life from the source of blessings." His works include *Torat Emet* (Lemberg, 1854) and *Ohev Yisrael* (Zhitomir, 1863).

Abraham's son ISAAC MEIR (d. 1855) succeeded his father as *ẓaddik* of Medzibozh, later moving to nearby Zinkov. His grandson MESHULLAM ZUSSIA (d. 1886) was also *ẓaddik* in Zinkov; he edited his grandfather's sermons, *Ohev Yisrael*. His descendants continued to be revered as *ẓaddikim* in various places in Podolia (Krolevets, Kopycznce, Ternopol).

BIBLIOGRAPHY: L.I. Newman, *Hasidic Anthology* (1934), index, s.v. *Apter*: M. Buber, *Tales of the Hasidim*, 2 (1948), 107–22; A. Berger, *Eser Orot* (1910), 102–25; M. Guttmann, *Mi-Gibborei ha-Ḥasidut*, 1 (1953), 172, 232; Dubnow, Ḥasidut, 1 (1930), 314–5; Horodezky, Ḥasidut, 2 (1923), 177–88; idem, in: *Tarbiz*, 27 (1957/58), 372–9; Haberman, in: YIVO *Bletter*, 39 (1955), 278–83.

[Avraham Rubinstein]

ABRAHAM JUDAEUS BOHEMUS (Abraham of Bohemia; d. 1533), banker and tax collector. Abraham first served as banker to Ladislas II, king of Hungary and Bohemia. He emigrated to Poland in about 1495 and settled in *Cracow. Armed with recommendations from Ladislas and Maximilian I of Germany, he soon became banker to the Polish king Alexander Jagellonski and later to Sigismund I. In 1512 Sigismund appointed him collector of the taxes paid by the Jews in Greater Poland and Masovia, and in 1514 the office was extended to include the Jews throughout Poland. The king warned the Jews, and especially the rabbis, to cooperate with him and not to interfere with him by excommunicating him, or in any other way. Abraham was several times acknowledged to be under the sole jurisdiction of the king. Abraham used his influence to act as **shtadlan* at the royal court for his fellow Jews. Sigismund had to remind the Jews of Cracow to pay the promised 200 florins to Abraham "for defending them against accusations brought up against them." In 1518 Abraham was granted freedom of commerce and banking in all Poland. According to tradition he was the father (or grandfather) of Mordecai *Jaffe.

BIBLIOGRAPHY: M. Balaban, *Dzieje Żydów Krakowie i na Kazimierzu (1304–1808)*, 1 (1912), 61–65, 353; M. Bersohn, *Dyplomataryusz 1388–1782* (1910), nos. 492, 493.

ABRAHAM OF BEJA (second half of 15th century), Portuguese traveler and linguist. He was apparently also a Hebrew scholar and styled "rabbi" for that reason. In 1485 King João II of Portugal sent João Perez of Covilhão across Africa to investigate the country of the mythical Christian king Prester John, and to discover the land route to India. Impressed by Abraham's knowledge of languages, King João sent him across the Mediterranean to join up with the expedition together with another Jew, Joseph Capatiero, who already had travel experience in the East. In due course he linked up with Perez in Egypt and continued with him as far as Ormuz in India. At that point he was left to return westward by the caravan route, via Damascus and Aleppo.

BIBLIOGRAPHY: F. da Ficalho, *Viagens de Pedro Covilhan* (1898); H.H. Hart, *Sea Road to the Indies* (1952), 43–78; J. Mendes dos Remedios, *Os Judeus em Portugal*, 1 (1895), 248–9.

[Cecil Roth]

ABRAHAM OF SARAGOSSA (early ninth century), merchant in Muslim Spain who traded mostly with the Franks and eventually settled in the Frankish kingdom. There he received (around 835) a *privilegium* from Louis the Pious, one of the three extant privileges granted to Jewish merchants by a Carolingian monarch. It became the standard for succeeding privileges, including the following aspects: court oaths and trial procedures, services and representation, right to trade, and imperial protection. According to this privilege, Abraham entrusted himself to the emperor in a manner similar to a royal vassal.

BIBLIOGRAPHY: Roth, Dark Ages, index; Ashtor, Korot, 1 (1966²), 188; Baron, Social², 4 (1957), 48–50; MGH, *Formulae Merowingici et Karolini Aevi* (1882), 325, no. 52.

ABRAHAM OF SARTEANO (late 15th century), Italian Hebrew poet. Abraham was born in Sarteano, Tuscany. He wrote a poem of 50 tercets entitled *"Sone ha-Nashim"* ("The Woman Hater") in which he denounces women, drawing examples from the Bible, from rabbinic legends, and from Greek and Roman history and mythology. The poem aroused a spirited literary controversy over the merit of women which continued into the 16th century. Abraham's remarks were challenged by Avigdor Fano in *Ozer Nashim* and by Elijah *Genazzano in *Meliẓot.*

BIBLIOGRAPHY: H.J. Schirmann, *Ha-Maḥazeh ha-Ivri ha-Rishon* (1965²), 122ff.; Schirmann, Italyah, 210–5; Neubauer, in: *Israelietische Letterbode*, 10 (1884–85), 98–101; Steinschneider, *ibid.*, 12 (1886–87), 55–56; Davidson, Oẓar, 1 (1924), 184, n. 1825.

[Jefim (Hayyim) Schirmann]

ABRAHAMS, family of English rabbis and scholars. ABRAHAM SUZMAN (c. 1801–1880) migrated from Poland to England in 1837, becoming principal *shoḥet* in London in 1839. He spent the end of his life in Palestine. He wrote an autobiography *Zekhor le-Avraham* (1860). His son BARNETT (1831–1863) was the *dayyan* of the Sephardi community in London (although himself an Ashkenazi) and was appointed principal of Jews' College in 1856. A graduate of |University College, London, he was the first English rabbi to hold a British university degree. He died at the age of only 32 of acute rheumatism. Barnett's three sons, Joseph, Moses, and Israel, devoted their lives to serving the Jewish community. JOSEPH (1855–1938) was rabbi in Melhourne, Australia, from 1883 to 1923 and rabbi emeritus from 1924 until his death. He helped found the United Jewish Education Board of Victoria and was its president (1896–1901). He wrote a number of monographs on Jewish subjects, the most important one being *The Sources of Midrash Echah Rabba* (Berlin, 1883). MOSES (1860–1919) was the minister of the Jewish community of Leeds. He was the author of *Aquila's Greek Version of the Hebrew Bible* (1919). Israel *Abrahams was a noted scholar.

BIBLIOGRAPHY: P. Abrahams, in: JHSET, 21 (1962–67), 243–60 (on Abraham). **ADD. BIBLIOGRAPHY:** ODNB online; H.L. Rubinstein, Australia I, index.

[Cecil Roth]

ABRAHAMS, family of English athletes. SIR ADOLPHE ABRAHAMS (1883–1967), physician and author, studied at Cambridge, where he was sculling champion (1904–05). During World War I he was a major in the Royal Medical Corps and subsequently held several important medical posts in London hospitals. He was also medical officer in charge of the British Olympic teams from 1912 until 1948, president of the British Association of Sports and Medicine, and a fellow of the Royal Society of Medicine. His many publications included: *The Photography of Moving Objects* (1910); *Indigestion* (1920); *Woman – Man's Equal?* (1954); and two books written with his brother, Harold: *Training for Athletes* (1928) and *Training for Health and Athletics* (1936).

SIR SIDNEY ("SOLLY") ABRAHAMS (1885–1957), British colonial official, brother of Adolphe and Harold. Born in Birmingham, he studied at Cambridge and entered the British Colonial Service, becoming town magistrate in Zanzibar (1915), advocate general, Baghdad (1920), attorney general of Zanzibar (1922), chief justice of Uganda (1933–34), Tanganyika (1934–36), and Ceylon (1936–39). A noted athlete, he represented Cambridge in the long jump (1904–06) and the 100-yard dash (1906), and competed for Great Britain in the 100-meter race and long jump in the 1906 Olympics, finishing fifth in the long jump with a leap of 6.21 meters. He also competed in the long jump at the 1912 Olympics, finishing in 11th place with a jump of 6.72 meters, just shy of 22-feet. Sidney was elected president in 1947 of Britain's oldest athletic club, the London Athletic Club, becoming the first Jew to hold the post.

HAROLD MAURICE ABRAHAMS (1899–1978), athlete and lawyer who became the first European to win an Olympic sprint title when he won the 100-meter dash in 1924. Born in Bedford, he began racing at the age of eight following his brother Solly, and at the age of 12 won his first 100-yard race in 14.0 seconds. He won the English public schools' 100-yard dash and long jump titles in 1918. He studied at Cambridge, where he won eight victories against Oxford in the 100-yard, 440-yard, and long jump from 1920 to 1923. Harold was also the president of the university's Athletic Club.

At the 1920 Antwerp Olympics, Harold was a member of the sixth place 4 × 100-meter team, but failed to advance past the preliminary heats in the sprints or long jump. In 1924 Harold established a British long jump record of 24 feet, 2½ inches, a record that stood for the next 32 years. Six months before the 1924 Games, Harold hired a personal coach, Sam Mussabini, thus becoming the first British amateur to pay for a personal trainer. At the 1924 Olympics, he won a silver medal in the 4 × 100-meter (41.2), and finished in sixth place in the 200-meter finals. For the 100-meter final, his key British rival, Eric Liddell, withdrew from the competition because it was held on Sunday and Liddell was a devout Christian. Facing his main competition against Americans Jackson Scholz and Charles Paddock – the 1920 gold medallist and world-record holder – Harold surprised everyone by winning the gold medal in 10.6 seconds.

Soon after his Olympic triumph of 1924, he suffered an injury while long jumping and retired from international athletics. He remained a prominent figure in the athletics world however, and was captain of the British Olympic team (1928) and chairman of the British Amateur Athletic Board from 1968 to 1975. He also reported on athletics for English press and radio. During World War II, he served in the Ministry of Economic Warfare, was head of the statistics section (1941–42), and in 1946 became an assistant secretary at the Ministry of Town Planning. He became one of the most famous Olympic athletes in history with the release of the film *Chariots of Fire* in 1981, which told of the struggles of Harold, Liddell, and Mussabini.

Philip Noel-Baker, Britain's 1912 Olympic captain and a Nobel Prize winner, wrote of Harold in 1948: "I have always believed that Harold Abrahams was the only European sprinter who could have run with Jesse Owens, Ralph Metcalfe, and the other great sprinters from the U.S. He was in their class, not only because of natural gifts – his magnificent physique, his splendid racing temperament, his flair for the big occasion – but because he understood athletics, and had given more brainpower and more willpower to the subject than any other runner of his day."

Harold wrote several books, including *Sprinting* (1925), *Athletics* (1926), *The Olympic Games, 1896–1952*, and *The Rome Olympiad* (1960).

[Elli Wohlgelernter (2nd ed.)]

ABRAHAMS, ABRAHAM (also known as **Abraham ben Naphtali Tang**; d. 1792), English scholar; grandson of the Prague *dayyan* Abraham Taussig Neu-Greschel (d. 1699) and like his grandfather signed himself with the Hebrew initials טנ"ג (TNG) and therefore generally known as Tang. Apparently born and brought up in London, Abrahams was well-grounded in Jewish and secular studies. In 1772 under the pseudonym "A Primitive Hebrew" he published an English translation of the mishnaic tractate *Avot* including *Maimonides' commentary and observations of his own. He also wrote two parallel mystical commentaries in Hebrew on Ecclesiastes (1773, unpublished), which include a concise account of classical mythology, with quotations from Ovid, Vergil, and Seneca. A Hebrew treatise (unpublished) attempts to establish the politico-historical setting of the talmudic reference to the "sages of Athens" (Bek. 8b). Abrahams also translated into Hebrew William Congreve's *Mourning Bride* (1768, Ms. in Jews' College, London). He had some ability as a scribe and copied and illuminated a Passover *Haggadah* (now in the Jewish Museum, London). He was a pronounced English patriot and a political radical.

Another ABRAHAM ABRAHAMS (d. 1813) criticized the tax system in Hampstead in the *Book of Assessment* (1811), the earliest work of this type by an English Jew.

BIBLIOGRAPHY: C. Roth, in: *Essays... I. Brodie* (Eng. vol., 1967), 368–72; Schirmann, in: *Scripta Hierosolymitana*, 19 (1967), 3–15; JC (Dec. 19, 1884); Neubauer, Cat, nos. 7, 9, 32, 35. Dan Ruderman, *Jewish Enlightenment in an English Key: Anglo-Jewry's Construction of Modern Jewish Thought* (2000), index. **ADD. BIBLIOGRAPHY:** ODNB online.

[Cecil Roth]

ABRAHAMS, ABRAHAM (1897–1955), English author, editor, and Zionist leader. Abrahams was head of the Jewish Telegraphic Agency's New York Bureau in 1933 and editor of *The Jewish Standard* from 1940 to 1948, after which he took an increasingly active part in the strengthening of the Zionist Revisionist Movement. For a time he was political secretary of the Revisionist Party in England. Abrahams published *Poems* (1932) and *Background of Unrest* (1945); his wife, Rachael Beth-Zion Abrahams, was also a writer and journalist.

ADD. BIBLIOGRAPHY: J.B. Schectman, *Fighter and Prophet: The Jabotinsky Story – The Last Years* (1961), index.

ABRAHAMS, ABRAHAM ISAAC (1720–1796), religious official and merchant, who was known throughout the American Colonies as a *mohel* and Hebrew teacher. He spent most of his life in New York City. The Congregation Shearith Israel directed him to "keep a publick school in the *ḥebra* [community hall] to teach the Hebrew language, and translate the same into English, also to teach English Reading, Writing and Cyphering." He was "rabbi" of the congregation from 1761 and *ḥazzan* from 1766. In addition to his religious duties, he was a distiller, snuff maker, tobacconist, and merchant, and was elected a constable in New York City in 1753.

BIBLIOGRAPHY: J.R. Marcus, *American Jewry, Documents, 18th Century* (1959), index; Rosenbloom, Biogr Dict, s.v.

[Leo Hershkowitz]

ABRAHAMS, GERALD (1907–1980), British lawyer, chess master, and writer on chess. Abrahams was born in Liverpool. At 18 he developed the "Abrahams Defense" adopted by many noted players. He won several championships in Britain and prizes in international master tournaments. His books include *Teach Yourself Chess* (1948); *The Chess Mind* (1951); *Technique in Chess* (1961); and *Let's Look at Israel* (1966). Abrahams also wrote several original works on Jewish identity, including *The Jewish Mind* (1961), and many works on law.

[William D. Rubinstein (2nd ed.)]

ABRAHAMS, ISAAC (1756–1832?), physician. He was the first Jewish graduate of Columbia (Kings) College, receiving an A.B. degree from that institution in 1774. At commencement he delivered a Latin oration "On Concord." After 1786 Abrahams took up permanent residence in New York where he became involved in the affairs of the synagogue, as he previously had done in Philadelphia and Baltimore. He served as president of the Congregation Shearith Israel in 1801. There is some difficulty in an exact identification since there was at least one other contemporary of the same name.

BIBLIOGRAPHY: H. Morrison, *Early Jewish Physicians in America* (1928), index; Rosenbloom, Biogr, Dict.

[Leo Hershkowitz]

ABRAHAMS, ISRAEL (1858–1925), English scholar. In 1902 he was appointed reader in rabbinic and talmudic literature at Cambridge, succeeding Solomon *Schechter. He played a considerable role in the university, both personal and scholastic, and had some distinguished non-Jewish pupils. For many years his home was the focus of university Jewish life. His influence was greater, however, as a writer than as a teacher, and over many years he was the chief exponent of Jewish scholarship in England. Although in some respects a popularizer, even his most ephemeral writings were nevertheless distinguished by their scholarship, just as his most learned writings did not lack charm. He was also one of the founders of and most devoted workers for the *Jewish Historical Society of England and similar bodies. In religion, he favored extreme reform and was the intellectual bulwark of the Jewish Religious Union when it was established in 1902, and of the Liberal Jewish Synagogue which developed out of it. Though not ordained as rabbi or minister, he was a frequent lay preacher. His most important works were his *Jewish Life in the Middle Ages* (1896; 2nd ed. by C. Roth based on author's materials, 1932); *Studies in Pharisaism and the Gospels* (2 vols., 1917–24); *Hebrew Ethical Wills* (2 vols., 1926); notes to the *Authorized Daily Prayer Book* edited by his father-in-law, S. Singer (1914); and numerous collections of essays on Jewish literature. His weekly literary causeries and reviews over the signature I.A. were for many years a feature of the **Jewish Chronicle,* and when in 1919 the anti-Zionist *Jewish Guardian* was founded, he was among its literary mainstays. Nevertheless, he was an ardent advocate of the establishment of a Jewish university in Jerusalem, even as early as 1908 when he visited Ereẓ Israel (cf. *Jewish Chronicle*, Feb. 28, 1908). He edited the **Jewish Quarterly Review*, from its establishment in 1888 down to 1908, in association with his friend, collaborator, and supporter Claude G. *Montefiore. Abrahams was an ardent champion of Britain, viewing it as more favorable to its Jews than any other European country.

BIBLIOGRAPHY: *Jewish Studies in Memory of Israel Abrahams* (1927), incl. bibl.; A.M. Hyamson, *Israel Abrahams: a Memoir* (1940); idem, *Jew's College: 1855–1955* (1955), 27–28, 31–32, 43–44, 70–71; H.M.J. Loewe, *Israel Abrahams… a Biographical Sketch* (1944); idem, in: AJYB, 28 (1926/27), 219–34; Montefiore, in: JHSET, 11 (1924–27), 239–46; S. Levy, in: JHSEM, 3 (1937), 41ff. (bibl.).

[Cecil Roth]

ABRAHAMS, ISRAEL (1903–1973), South African rabbi and scholar. Born in Vilna and educated at Jews' College and London University, he was rabbi in London and Manchester before going to South Africa in 1937 as chief rabbi of the Cape Town Hebrew Congregation. In 1951 he became chief rabbi of the United Council of Hebrew Congregations of the Cape. From 1938 he held the chair of Hebrew at Cape Town University. He retired in 1967 and settled in Israel. An eloquent speaker, he held high office in all important communal institutions in Cape Town and was especially active in promoting the Zionist movement and Jewish education. He was a consulting editor to the *Encyclopaedia Judaica*. His major scholarly work was his translation into English of *Cassuto's Hebrew commentaries: *Documentary Hypothesis* (1961); *The Book of Genesis*, 2 pts: *From Adam to Noah* (1961) and *From Noah to Abraham* (1964); *Exodus* (1967); and *The Goddess Anath* (1970); he also translated tractate *Hagigah* for the *Soncino Talmud* (1938). His other writings include: a history of Cape Jewry, *The Birth of a Community* (1955); *Pathways in Judaism* (1968); and *Living Waters* (1968).

[Lewis Sowden]

ABRAHAMS, IVOR (1935–), British sculptor. Abrahams was born in Wigan, England, and studied in London. He was later apprenticed to a bronze foundry and worked as a display artist before becoming a teacher of sculpture in 1960; between 1960 and 1970 he lectured at a number of British art schools. His sculpture was always informal, using unusual, non-sculptural materials. His first one-man exhibition was in 1962, but it was not until 1970 that he established his reputation when he held his first exhibition in New York. He subsequently exhibited his work regularly in America, London, and Europe. His three-dimensional prints, incorporating collage techniques, won him international fame. Abrahams is represented in the Victoria and Albert Museum, London, Bibliotheque Nationale, Paris, Boymans Museum, Rotterdam, and other public collections throughout the world. In 1991 he was elected to the Royal Academy.

[Charles Samuel Spencer]

ABRAHAMS, SIR LIONEL (1869–1919), English civil servant and Anglo-Jewish historian, nephew of Israel *Abrahams. A graduate of Balliol College, Oxford, in 1902 Abrahams became financial secretary for India, in which capacity he successfully reorganized the Indian currency. In 1912 he was appointed assistant undersecretary of state for India. As an Oxford student, he wrote *The Expulsion of the Jews from England in 1290* (1895). He contributed a number of important studies on the medieval period to the Transactions of the Jewish Historical Society of England. He was president of the society from 1916 to 1918. In 1912 he became involved in what became known as the "Indian Silver Case," in which accusations were made that a Jewish merchant bank in London had improperly suggested that an order for silver required by the Indian government be placed with its firm. As a result, antisemitic innuendos about Abrahams and others were made in sections of Britain's press, but those named were cleared of any wrongdoing by a House of Commons Select Committee.

BIBLIOGRAPHY: P.H. Emden, *Jews of Britain* (1943), 145–6; JHSET, index; *The Times* (Dec. 1, 1919); JC (Dec. 12, 1919). **ADD. BIBLIOGRAPHY:** ODNB online.

[Cecil Roth / William D. Rubinstein (2nd ed.)]

ABRAHAMS, NICOLAI CHRISTIAN LEVIN (1798–1870), Danish author and literary scholar. After graduating from the University of Copenhagen, Abrahams taught there from 1829 and became professor of French literature after his baptism in 1832. Abrahams, who helped to popularize French culture in Denmark, published a *Description des manuscrits français du Moyen-Age de la Bibliothèque Royale de Copenhague* (1844). His autobiography, *Meddelelser af mit liv* (1876), appeared posthumously.

ABRAHAM'S BOSOM, designation in the New Testament (Luke 16:22–31) of the abode of the blessed souls of the pious and poor in the other world (compare IV Macc. 13:17; Matt. 8:11, where all three patriarchs, Abraham, Isaac, and Jacob, are enumerated as those in whose company the pious souls dwell). The Hebrew expression *be-ḥeiko shel Avraham* ("in Abraham's bosom") is mentioned in aggadic literature (e.g., PR 43:180b) dealing with the martyrdom of Miriam (*Hannah) and her seven sons. She urges her youngest child to die for the sanctification of God's name, saying: "O my son, do you wish that all thy brethren sit in Abraham's bosom, except you?" Abraham's bosom is mentioned also in *Midrash ha-Gadol* to Genesis (ed. Margulies (1947), 206) and in the Talmud (Kid. 72b) where it probably refers to the covenant of Abraham (see also PdRK (1868), 25b, S. Buber's emendation). In Christian mythology, Abraham's bosom stands also for the abode in the netherworld of the unbaptized children and for purgatory, from where, after punishment, Abraham conducts the purified souls into paradise. This notion is hinted at in the talmudic passage (Er. 19a) which describes Abraham as shielding from punishment in hell all those who have not effaced the sign of circumcision (compare also, Gen. R. 48:8). Whether Abraham's bosom is the abode of bliss, or, on the contrary, a place in Gehenna, it expresses the popular Jewish belief about Abraham as the warden in paradise and protector of the meritorious souls in the other world.

BIBLIOGRAPHY: H.L. Strack and P. Billerbeck, *Kommentar zum Neuen Testament aus Talmud und Midrash*, 2 (1924), 225–7.

ABRAHAMSEN, DAVID (1903–2002), U.S. criminologist and psychiatrist. Born in Trondheim, Norway, Abrahamsen worked in Oslo and London. In 1940 he moved to the United States, where from 1948 to 1952 he served as director of scientific research at Sing Sing Prison. He was research associate at Columbia University's College of Physicians and Surgeons from 1944 to 1953 and founded the university's Forum for the Study and Prevention of Crime. In 1966 he was appointed medical and psychiatric director of the Foundation for the Prevention of Addictive Diseases. Abrahamsen taught at Columbia University, Yale Law School, the New York School of Social Work, and the New School for Social Research, New York.

While he wrote several books on psychological themes – *Men Mind and Power* (1945); *The Road to Emotional Maturity* (1958); *The Emotional Care of Your Child* (1969) – Abrahamsen's works are principally devoted to criminological subjects. They include *Crime and the Human Mind* (1944); *Study of 102 Sex Offenders at Sing Sing Prison* (1950); *Who Are the Guilty? – A Study of Education and Crime* (1952); *The Psychology of Crime* (1960); "Study of Lee Harvey Oswald: Psychological Capability of Murder," in: *New York Academy of Medicine Bulletin*, 43 (1967), 861–88; *Our Violent Society* (1970); *The Murdering Mind* (1973); *The Mind of the Accused: A Psychiatrist in the Courtroom* (1983); *Confessions of Son of Sam* (1985); *Murder and Madness: The Secret Life of Jack the Ripper* (1992); and *Nixon vs. Nixon: An Emotional Tragedy* (1997). Abrahamsen's interest in Jewish life is seen in *Jeger Jode* ("I Am a Jew," 1935), a cultural and humanitarian document about the life of Jews and their contribution to culture.

In 1982 he donated a large collection of his papers to Columbia University's Rare Book and Manuscript Library, dating from 1902 to 1981. The papers relate primarily to the research and interviews he conducted while writing *Nixon vs. Nixon* and to his close relationship and correspondence with convicted multiple murderer David Berkowitz. There are more than 140 letters to Abrahamsen from Berkowitz, aka "Son of Sam," who murdered a succession of young people in New York City in the mid-1970s. The papers also reflect Abrahamsen's interest in other famous crimes, such as the Leopold/Loeb kidnapping and murder of Bobby Franks, and in politics (particularly Adlai Stevenson's 1952 campaign).

[Zvi Hermon / Ruth Beloff (2nd ed.)]

ABRAHAM ẒEVI BEN ELEAZAR (1780–1828), rabbi and *posek* in Poland. In his youth he lived in Piotrkow near Lodz, where he studied under his grandfather, Solomon b. Jehiel Michel, and Moses, the *av bet din*. In 1800 he served as rabbi of Pilica, and later, before 1819, as *av bet din* of Piotrkow. In formulating his rulings Abraham Ẓevi utilized the *pilpul* method employed in the *Urim ve-Tummim* of Jonathan *Eybeschuetz, the *Noda bi-Yhudah* of Ezekiel *Landau, and the *Hafla'ah* of Phinehas *Horowitz. He gave his rabbinical works the general title *Efod Zahav*, but designated each by a special name. The only two that have been published are *Berit Avraham* (Dyhernfurth, 1819), responsa on sections of the Shulḥan Arukh, and *Gufei Halakhot* (pt. 1, Lodz, 1911), novellae to the tractates *Shabbat, Pesaḥim*, and *Ketubbot*. Remaining in manuscript form are *Ma'alot Yuḥasin*, novellae to the *Even ha-Ezer; Halva'at Ḥen*, novellae on the *halakhot* concerning usury; pt. 2 of his *Gufei Halakhot* containing novellae on the rulings of the great *posekim;* and *Pa'amonei Zahav*, his sermons.

ABRAHÃO, COJE (16th century), agent and diplomat in the service of the Portuguese viceroys in *Goa, India, from 1575 to 1594; Abrahão's full name and personal background are unknown. That he played a leading role in the affairs of Portuguese India is attested to by numerous letters preserved in the Portuguese historical archives in Goa. These letters praise him for his trustworthiness and reliability, and the continual reference to him as "Coje Abrahão Judeo" shows his Jewish identity. Abrahão was entrusted with important diplomatic missions to the rulers of the kingdom of Bijapur, and accompanied the ambassador of Shah Yusuf Ali Adil of Bijapur on a diplomatic mission to Portugal in 1575. As a reward for his services, King Sebastian of Portugal granted Abrahão a pension in 1576. In 1582, on behalf of Portugal, he was attestor to a peace treaty with the shah.

BIBLIOGRAPHY: Fischel, in: JQR, 47 (1956/57), 37ff.; P. Pissurlencar (ed.), *Agentes da diplomacia portuguêsa na lndia* (1952), 551–6.

[Walter Joseph Fischel]

ABRAM, MORRIS BERTHOLD (1918–2000), U.S. attorney, civic leader, second president of Brandeis University. Abram was born in Fitzgerald, Ga. Following service as a major in Air

Force Intelligence during World War II, Abram was counsel in the U.S. prosecution staff at the Nuremberg Trials (1946), then assistant to the director for the Marshall Plan (1948). As counsel for the Anti-Defamation League in the South (from 1955), as well as member of several civic committees, Abram led a prolonged fight against the Georgia county unit election system, which culminated in a 1963 Supreme Court ruling known as the one-man one-vote principle. Abram was appointed the first general counsel of the Peace Corps by President Kennedy, later serving in several positions in the United Nations, to which he was appointed by Presidents Kennedy and Johnson. He was an appointee of three additional presidents – Jimmy *Carter, Ronald *Reagan, and George H.W. *Bush. He led U.S. delegations to numerous international meetings, including the United Nations Commission on Human Rights and the former Conference on Security and Cooperation in Europe, and was a former vice chair of the U.S. Commission on Civil Rights.

As president of the American Jewish Committee, 1963 to 1968, Abram led talks on Catholic-Jewish relations with Pope Paul. He was president of Brandeis University from 1968 to 1970. He served as chairman of the National Conference on Soviet Jewry (NCSJ) from 1983 until 1988, at the peak of the movement to free Soviet Jews. During that period, he also served for three years as chairman of the Conference of Presidents of Major American Jewish Organizations. Under President Bush, he served as U.S. Ambassador to the United Nations in Geneva and founded United Nations Watch following his term as ambassador. He was a president of the American Jewish Committee, chairman of the United Negro College Fund, and chairman of the board of Cardozo Law School.

For many years he was a senior partner at the law firm of Paul, Weiss, Rifkind, Wharton & Garrison. Abram published *The Day Is Short* in 1982, in which he reviewed his career and his battle with an acute form of leukemia.

[Burton Berinsky / Ruth Beloff (2nd ed.)]

ABRAMOVICH, ROMAN ARKADYEVICH (1966–), Russian billionaire of Jewish origin. Abramovich was born in Saratov of a non-Jewish mother who died soon after giving birth to him, and later defined himself as "Ukrainian." His father, Arkady Nahimovich, who worked at the Siktivkar economic council (*sovnarkhoz*), died in an accident when he was four years old. Abramovich was then adopted by his uncle Abram and lived with the family in Moscow, where he finished his secondary schooling. According to Abramovich, he graduated later from the Gubkin Institute of Oil and Gas. After the fall of Communism, Abramovich became active in business, taking over control of the Sibneft (Siberian oil) company after his mentor Boris *Berezovsky, who brought him into Yeltsin's inner circle, fled the country in the wake of a criminal investigation. Abramovich also owned 50% of Rusal (Russia's biggest aluminum company) and 26% of Aeroflot. In December 1999 he was elected deputy of the State Duma from the Chukotsk Autonomous Region. In December 2000 he was elected governor of the region.

In 2003 Abramovich bought London's Chelsea soccer club. He also owned the Russian Avangard Omsk ice hockey team. In 2003 he was included in *Fortune* magazine's list of the world's richest men under 40, with his personal wealth estimated at $8.3 billion. In the same year *Forbes* also included Abramovich in its list of billionaires, placing his wealth at $5.7 billion.

[Naftali Prat (2nd ed.)]

ABRAMOVITSH, SHOLEM YANKEV (**Jacob**, also **Mendele Moykher Sforim**; 1835 or 1836–1917), Hebrew and Yiddish writer, often called the "grandfather" of modern Judaic literature. Abramovitsh was born in Kapulia (Kopyl), near Minsk; he lived in Berdichev from 1858 to 1869 and subsequently in Zhitomir. In 1881 he was appointed principal of the *talmud torah* in Odessa, a position he held until 1916 – except for two years spent in Geneva, Switzerland, following his traumatic experience of the 1905 pogroms. Abramovitsh's long life spanned several periods in the development of Jewish society in Eastern Europe: the *Haskalah and the period of reform under Czar *Alexander II, the aftermath of the 1881 pogroms, *Ḥibbat Zion, the Socialism of the *Bund, and Zionism.

Abramovitsh began his literary career as a Hebrew essayist and fiction writer but soon turned to Yiddish. With five short novels written between 1864 and 1878, he laid the foundation for modern Yiddish fiction. In 1886, he returned to Hebrew with a series of short stories that literary historians have often viewed as a seminal contribution to the revival of modern Hebrew literature. He also expanded his early Yiddish works and translated them into Hebrew. As an integral member of the Jewish intelligentsia in Odessa, Abramovitsh was in contact with the Yiddish writer *Sholem Aleichem, with the historian Simon *Dubnow, and with Hebrew writers such as Ḥ.N. *Bialik, Y.Ḥ. *Rawnitzki, and *Aḥad Ha-Am.

Readers and critics have often referred to Abramovitsh as "Mendele Moykher Sforim" ("Mendele the Book Peddler"), yet Dan Miron showed in *A Traveler Disguised* (1973; 1996) that this is misleading. First appearing in 1864 and evolving in Yiddish and Hebrew over the next half century, Mendele is a character or persona in Abramovitsh's works. Hence it is inaccurate to use the designation as if it were simply the author's pen name. Abramovitsh seems to have created the Mendele persona as a way of reaching a broad readership. Instead of speaking from above, as did many Hebrew *maskilim*, he uses the folksy Mendele as his mouthpiece. Sometimes the enlightened Abramovitsh employs irony at the expense of the more naïve Mendele. The Jubilee editions of his complete works, in both Hebrew (1909–12) and Yiddish (1911–13), try to circumvent this problem by having it both ways, using a title followed by a parenthesis: *Ale verk fun Mendele Moykher Sforim (S.Y. Abramovitsh)*.

Abramovitsh was the son of Ḥayyim Moyshe Broyde, a prosperous and respected man who was one of the outstanding talmudic scholars in the small town of Kapulia. Situated in the Minsk province of Czarist Russia (now Belarus), this *shtetl* was culturally associated with Jewish Lithuania ("Lita"). Hence Abramovitsh was schooled in the prevailing Lithuanian rabbinic style, with emphasis on the Hebrew Bible, its Aramaic translation, and the Talmud. He received an unusually rigorous *ḥeder* education from a talented *melammed* (teacher) named Yose Rubens; according to Abramovitsh's own account, during his years at *ḥeder* he memorized most of the Hebrew Bible. Instructed by Rubens until the age of 11, Abramovitsh was impressed by his artistic abilities as a wood carver. Following the death of his father in about 1849, Abramovitsh studied at yeshivot in Timkovitz, Slutsk, and Vilna. After two years in Slutsk he returned to live with his mother, now remarried and living in the picturesque village of Mielnik, which was surrounded by a forest. His experiences there may be reflected in his story "*Dos Tosefos-Yontev Kelbl*" ("The Calf," 1911), in which a yeshivah boy returns home and becomes engrossed by the world of nature. At about the age of 17, Abramovitsh wrote his first Hebrew poetry, consisting of odes to nature in the neo-Biblical style known as *meliẓah*.

Abramovitsh later traveled south with an aunt in an effort to find her husband, who had fled his creditors when his business failed. Their resourceful guide, Avreml Khromoi (Abraham the Lame), regaled them with stories about the better life that awaited them in Volhynia. Avreml did not travel by the shortest route but made as many stops as possible to collect charity. The difficult experiences during these circuitous travels became the impetus for Abramovitsh's greatest Yiddish novel, *Fishke der Krumer* ("Fishke the Lame," 1869/1888). At the end of their journeys Abramovitsh settled in Kamenets-Podolski, where he was briefly married to a mentally ill woman. There he also met the maskilic author Avraham-Ber Gottlober, probably his model for the impoverished writer Herr Gutmann in *Dos Kleyne Mentshele* ("The Little Man," 1864). Although Gottlober was not impressed by the juvenile Hebrew verses that the young Abramovitsh showed him, he recognized his talent. As a teacher at the government school for Jewish boys, Gottlober was able to direct Abramovitsh's studies and introduce him to the wider world of literature, mathematics, and science. With the assistance of Gottlober's daughters, Abramovitsh learned German and Russian, passed a teacher's examination, and taught at the Kamenets-Podolski government school in 1856–58. During that time education became the subject of his first publication, "*Mikhtav al Devar ha-Ḥinukh*" ("A Letter on Education," 1857), published with Gottlober's help in the Hebrew journal *Ha-Maggid*.

Abramovitsh married Pessie Levin in 1858 and moved with her to Berdichev, supported by his father-in-law, while he continued his autodidactic education and literary activities. Berdichev was heavily populated by ḥasidim, which led Abramovitsh into conflict with a form of Jewish life that he had seldom encountered in the north, except during his studies in Timkovitz. His fiction, in which a town resembling Berdichev is called "Glupsk" (= a town of fools), expressed his hostility toward the Jewish community leaders. In *Dos Vintshfingerl* ("The Wishing-Ring"), he mocked ḥasidic resistance to modernization: "The ḥasidim were not pleased, because Gutmann dressed like a German. And when the floor of the school was washed, they became furious. 'What's the meaning of this? To do such a thing in a school! What's this, washing off the mud that our ancestors left behind?!'" (1865, p. 7).

In 1860 Abramovitsh published his first book, a collection of Hebrew essays entitled *Mishpat Shalom* ("The Judgment of Peace," alluding to the author's name), which included a translated article on whether corporeal punishment of children is permissible. A cause of much subsequent debate was his lead essay, "*Kilkul ha-Minim*" ("The Confusion of Gender"), which critiqued a work by Eliezer Zweifel. He occupied himself with natural sciences and began to translate Harald Othmar Lenz's *Gemeinnützige Naturgeschichte* ("Natural History for General Use," 1835–39), which appeared in Hebrew as *Sefer Toledot ha-Teva* ("The Book of Natural History," 3 vols., 1862–73). This project reflected his concern that Jews were not sufficiently educated in matters of science and nature, yet it achieved limited results because the audience for secular Hebrew writing was small. Abramovitsh's first Hebrew novel, *Limdu Heitev* ("Learn to Do Well") was published in Warsaw in 1862. The Russian title page calls it "a novel in the pure Hebrew language," which shows Abramovitsh's early adherence to the literary principles of the Berlin Enlightenment, including a strong preference for the supposedly "pure language" (*leshon ẓaḥ*) of the biblical prophets. Because he emulated that allusive, ornamental style, his early Hebrew writings were derivative and aesthetically unremarkable. He revised his short novel and published it under the new title *Ha-Avot ve-ha-Banim* ("Fathers and Children," 1868), alluding to the 1862 novel of the same title by Ivan Turgenev.

Prospects for advances in the Jews' material conditions and educational privileges improved in the 1860s under Alexander II. At that time, Abramovitsh followed the maskilic bent in the didactic goals of his fiction: according to his 1889 autobiographical account in Nahum *Sokolow's *Sefer Zikkaron*, "I said to myself, here I am observing the ways of our people and seeking to give them stories from a Jewish source in the Holy Tongue, yet most of them do not even know this language and speak Yiddish. What good does a writer do with all of his toil and ideas if he is not useful to his people? This question – for whom do I toil? – gave me no rest and brought me into great confusion."

In November 1864, serialization of Abramovitsh's *Dos Kleyne Mentshele* ("The Little Man"), to which many scholars trace the beginning of modern Yiddish literature, began in *Kol Mevasser* ("A Heralding Voice" – the Yiddish supplement to *Ha-Meliẓ*, edited by Alexander Tsederboym (*Zederbaum)). The book was reprinted in 1865 with the subtitle: *Oder a Lebensbashraybung fun Yitzhok Avrom Takif* ("Or, a Life-description by the Powerful Man Isaac Abraham"). While no author's name appeared on the title page, Abramovitsh hinted at his identity by attributing the book to "a man" (*ish*, Aleph-Yod-

Shin, Abramovitsh's initials in reverse). Such anonymity was a common stratagem among Yiddish authors, both because their political views often drew censure and because Yiddish writing was held in low esteem.

Abramovitsh raged against the complacent rich who, as he wrote in a letter to Lev Binshtok, "rest in the shadow of money." His own financial circumstances were especially difficult around 1866, when he published his second collection of Hebrew essays, *Ein Mishpat* ("Fountain of Judgment") and the second volume of *Sefer Toledot ha-Teva*, for which he drew terminology from talmudic sources and in this respect influenced modern Hebrew usage. Some critics believe that his descriptions of nature and animal behavior anticipate his later fiction.

At a time when modern Yiddish theater was still in its infancy, Abramovitsh wrote the play *Di Takse* ("The Tax," 1869; it bore the ironic subtitle: *Oder di Bande Shtot Baley Toyves*, "Or, the Gang of City Benefactors"). Written in order to advance his reformist goals, it is more successful as social criticism than as drama. He had encountered widespread corruption among the community leaders of Berdichev and depicted the wrongdoings of these false benefactors in a transparent satire. According to one account, the powerful men of Berdichev forced Abramovitsh to leave the town after his satiric portrayal was published. Abramovitsh then moved to Zhitomir, where he studied at the Rabbinical Institute. Since this school educated many young Jewish men seeking higher education, and not only would-be rabbis, it was not unusual that Abramovitsh ended his studies there without receiving a degree.

In the 1870s, Abramovitsh experimented with writing Yiddish verse, favoring outmoded tetrameter and pentameter couplets. His poetic efforts ranged from an allegorical poem about the Jewish people, "Yudl" (1875), to traditional Judaic literature. He wrote Yiddish translations of Sabbath songs called *Zmires Yisroel* ("Songs of Israel," 1875) and compiled nature hymns in a Yiddish adaptation of the ḥasidic *Perek Shirah* (1875). He planned to translate the prayer book and the Psalms into Yiddish, but this project remained unfinished and only fragments are extant. In contrast to the German *maskilim*, Abramovitsh (like Mendel Lefin) recognized the importance of reaching common Yiddish readers in their mother tongue while also combating the influence of the *Tsene-Rene* with its archaic language and heavy reliance on midrashic elaborations.

One of Abramovitsh's most widely read books was his allegorical novel, *Di Klyatshe; Oder Tsar Baley Khayim* ("The Nag; or, Cruelty to Animals," 1873). Its epigraph quotes from Song of Songs 1:9, which Abramovitsh expands in Yiddish: "To my mare among Pharaoh's chariots I compare you – People of Israel." During the period of reform between 1856 and 1881, the number of Jews at Russian high schools and universities increased from about 1% to over 10% of the total population of students. Yet Isrolik, a typical boy who has received a traditional Jewish education, runs into difficulties because of his unfamiliarity with subjects such as history and Slavic folklore. As he becomes mentally imbalanced, Isrolik hallucinates about meeting a talking horse and trying to improve her lot. Her sufferings are "as old as the Jewish exile," because she represents the fate of the Jewish people.

Unlike most of Abramovitsh's fiction, which concentrates on Jewish life in the impoverished *shtetlekh* in the Pale of Settlement, *Di Klyatshe* presents a wider panorama of Czarist Russia, with special attention to relations among antisemites and Jews; hooligans who torment the nag obviously represent antisemites. There is even a critique of the well-intentioned *maskilim*, when Isrolik reads aloud his letter to a benevolent society – an oblique representation of the Society for the Spread of Enlightenment (OPE). The nag refers to the ornamental, pseudo-biblical Hebrew style when she responds bitterly: "*Melitza, melitza, melitza!*" She rightly doubts whether any practical results will ensue from Isrolik's highfalutin rhetoric. Yet *Di Klyatshe* was a bold political allegory: in one of his nightmarish fantasies, for instance, Ashmodai – the King of the Demons – seems to represent the Czar.

Kitser Masoes Binyomen Hashlishi ("The Brief Travels of Benjamin the Third," 1878) centers on a pair of hapless, would-be explorers, Benjamin and Senderl, who somewhat resemble Cervantes' Don Quixote and Sancho Panza. Instead of depicting a petty nobleman who has read too many chivalric romances and acts as if he inhabits one, Abramovitsh portrays Benjamin as a Jew who has read too many narratives about travel to the Holy Land. Abramovitsh attacks the impracticality and worldly ignorance of Benjamin and his sidekick Senderl, because they are stereotypical traditional Jews whose life experience consists almost exclusively of Torah study. Benjamin's provisions for travel consist of little more than his prayer book, prayer shawl, and *tefillin*; only Senderl has the sense to bring food. Their wives are market women who eke out a meager living and dominate their families. Toward the end of the book, Abramovitsh takes aim at the horrific phenomenon of *khappers* (press-gangs) who kidnap Jews for induction into the Czar's army; in this comic account, however, Benjamin and Senderl are discharged because they prove to be more trouble than they are worth.

A reprint of *Dos Kleyne Mentshele* (1879) brought to a close the most productive period of Abramovitsh's Yiddish writing. The comparatively optimistic period of reform begun in 1855 by Alexander II, the so-called "Liberator Czar," had ended abruptly with his assassination in 1881 – followed by anti-Jewish pogroms and a period of reaction during which the conditions for Yiddish publishing also changed. During the same period Abramovitsh experienced personal and family troubles. His daughter Rashel, a talented art student, died in St. Petersburg, while his son Meir (Mikhail), a Russian poet, was exiled for political activism and later converted to Christianity. Abramovitsh described his malaise in a letter to Lev Binshtok on January 16, 1880: "As soon as I take up the pen, I feel an overwhelming heaviness: my hands are bound as if by magical chains" (see *Dos Mendele Bukh*, 107). On June 5, 1884, he wrote to another friend that "the misfortunes of the recent period have turned my heart into stone, so that my tongue has not allowed me to speak and my hands have not allowed me to write a word" (*ibid.*, 128). For several years he produced no major works in Yiddish. Subsequently, in 1886–1896, as part of the movement to revive Hebrew, he devoted much of his creative energy to writing Hebrew short fiction.

In 1888, Sholem Aleichem sought out Abramovitsh, hoping to include his writings in the anthology he was editing, *Di Folksbibliotek* ("The Jewish Popular Library"). Their correspondence quickly assumed an intimate tone, with Sholem Aleichem referring to Abramovitsh as "Grandfather," while Abramovitsh referred to Sholem Aleichem as "Grandson" – although their difference in age was only 23 years. At first Abramovitsh was evasive, complaining of insufficient time because of his work as principal of the Odessa Talmud Torah, but he did contribute the first two parts of the expanded and quite altered version of *Dos Vintshfingerl* ("The Wishing-Ring," 1888–89). This narrative of Hershele's impoverished childhood in Kabtsansk ("Beggarsville"), replete with irony and satire, still shows traces of nostalgia for *shtetl* life.

Although Abramovitsh had continued publishing sporadically in Hebrew throughout the 1870s, he devoted this decade mainly to writing in Yiddish. He returned to Hebrew with the story, "*Be-Seter Ra'am*" ("In the Secret Place of Thunder," 1886–87), his first Hebrew belletristic work since 1868. Hebrew became Abramovitsh's literary focus in the 1890s, when in addition to publishing Hebrew short fiction he began translating his Yiddish novels. One of his most successful Hebrew stories is "*Shem ve-Yefet ba-Aggalah*" ("Shem and Japheth on the Train," 1890), in which Mendele the Book Peddler abandons his horse and carriage and travels in a third-class train compartment. There he meets Moyshe the Tailor, a latter-day Moses who has no Torah to offer beyond stratagems for the survival of the oppressed.

Following a decade in which Abramovitsh printed his Hebrew short fiction, 1896–97 saw the publication of Hebrew versions of *Masa'ot Benyamin ha-Shlishi* ("Travels of Benjamin the Third") and *Be-Emek ha-Bakhah* ("In the Vale of Tears"). A few years later, Ḥ.N. Bialik translated the first eight chapters of *Fishke der krumer* ("Fishke the Lame") as *Sefer ha-Kabeẓanim: Nun Kefufah* ("The Book of Beggars: A Crooked Letter *Nun*," 1901), but Abramovitsh was not satisfied. For the most part Abramovitsh translated or adapted his own works into Hebrew. In the late novel *Shloyme, Reb Khayims* ("Solomon, Ḥayyim's Son") – or, in Hebrew, *Ba-Yamim ha-Hem* ("In Those Days") – Abramovitsh is less satiric than in his early works.

Critical Assessment

Abramovitsh records the plight of Russian Jewry suffering tyranny and hate from without and exploitation by the Jewish upper classes from within. In some works Abramovitsh continues the Haskalah tradition of satirizing folk beliefs (e.g., in *Fishke der Krumer* and *Kitser Masoes Binyomin ha-Shlishi*). Elsewhere he evokes the intimate experiences of Jewish childhood, as in works such as the late verion of *Dos Vintshfingerl* and the autobiographical novel *Shloyme, Reb Khayims*. Many of his characters are drawn from Jewish life in the towns and cities of Belorussia and Lithuania, where he spent his childhood, while other works portray characters from Volhynia and southern Russia, with the action taking place in Berdichev, Zhitomir, Odessa, and other towns in the Jewish Pale of Settlement. Following a Russian tradition, Abramovitsh uses fictitious place names that satirically describe the qualities of their inhabitants – such as "Glupsk," the town of fools modeled on Berdichev; "Tsviatshits," a town of hypocrisy; "Tuneyadevka," suggesting parasitism; and "Kabtsansk," or Paupersville. Although Abramovitsh was immersed in Judaic traditions, he also was influenced by European fiction, as reflected in his parody of *Don Quixote* (in *Kitser Masoes Binyomin ha-Shlishi*). His *Dos Kleyne Mentshele* ("The Little Man") and *Fishke der Krumer* ("Fishke the Lame") reflect the Russian satiric tradition of Gogol and Saltykov-Shchedrin as well as the picaresque novel of authors such as Henry Fielding. He adopted some typical patterns of the sentimental adventure story in *Fishke der Krumer*, in which surprising coincidences occur. Based on that novel, Chaver-Paver wrote a screenplay and Edgar Ulmer directed the powerful Yiddish film *Fishke der Krumer* (known in English as "The Light Ahead," 1939).

Although Abramovitsh began writing in Yiddish for the practical purpose of reaching a larger reading public, he eventually came to regard his work in Yiddish to be of intrinsic artistic value in its own right. Abramovitsh's style is an effective instrument for satire and irony, especially when it is deliberately incongruous: phrases originally expressing the sacred are applied to the profane, and the reverse. In a 1907 letter to Y.Ḥ. Rawnitzki, for example, Abramovitsh alluded to the Creation story when he recalled his original goal: "Let us create a Hebrew style that will be lively, speaking clearly and precisely, the way people do in our time and place, and let its soul be Jewish." In many of the prefaces to his novels, Mendele Moykher Sforim uses mock prayers that begin, "Praised be the Creator…," and then turn into attacks on corruption. Abramovitsh's traditional narrators – such as Mendele Moykher Sforim, Isaac Abraham Takif, or Alter Yaknoz – provide Abramovitsh with many opportunities for ironic play and enable him to achieve artistic distance from his story.

Abramovitsh's Hebrew style went through a number of stages. In the 1860s he was still under the influence of Abraham *Mapu's neo-biblical rhetoric, particularly in his early Hebrew stories. Abramovitsh carried on the tradition of expanding the Hebrew language, as introduced by Haskalah writers such as Isaac *Satanow, Menahem Mendel (Lefin) Levin, and Joseph *Perl, whose style absorbed elements of Mishnaic Hebrew, medieval philosophical literature, and ḥasidic literature influenced by spoken Yiddish. Abramovitsh's process of creating a synthetic Hebrew style composed of many historical layers reached its peak after 1886. On the occasion of Abramovitsh's 75th birthday, in 1910–11, Ḥ.N. Bialik asserted that Abramovitsh was the "creator of the *nusaḥ*," which he described as a new synthesis drawing from many historical layers of Hebrew. According to Bialik, Abramovitsh's *nusaḥ* had already become the dominant style in Hebrew literature. Many 20th century critics accepted Bialik's view, although some writers such as Y.Ḥ. *Brenner countered with a kind of anti-*nusaḥ*. In any event, Abramovitsh contributed to greater fluidity in Hebrew style by moving beyond the more rigid biblical *meliẓah* of his predecessors.

Abramovitsh wrote in both Yiddish and Hebrew throughout his career, which led to a productive interaction between his writings in these languages. Simon Dubnow made an important observation on Abramovitsh's bilingual creativity: when he "had the Yiddish original of the first parts of *Dos Vintshfingerl* in front of him, he made the Hebrew translation – or more precisely, the reworking – masterfully and without any difficulties. When it came to writing more without the Yiddish original, however, he sensed that it would not go smoothly. One cannot create content and language at the same time, but only one after the other; one must create the content first, in the language of the life that is portrayed in the artwork. On this foundation, then, he could build the style of the revived Hebrew language (*Fun "Zhargon" tsu Yidish* ("From 'Jargon' to Yiddish"), 1929, p. 46). In his striving for artistic perfection, Abramovitsh continually reworked his novels and stories, enlarging and polishing them. The later versions of his works, and particularly the Jubilee Edition, moderated his satiric stance; he also diminished the pro-Enlightenment propaganda that was present in early works such as *Dos Vinshfingerl*. During the process of bilingual recreation, in later adaptations of his works, Abramovitsh introduced important variations in content and style. He did not merely translate his works from Yiddish into Hebrew but rather reinvented them.

Abramovitsh is rightly remembered for his descriptions of nature, his trenchant satire, and his sympathetic portrayals of the poor. The lack of natural descriptions in Judaic literature prior to Abramovitsh is legendary. Abramovitsh's narrator Mendele, however, pays great attention to the natural world. Satire had been a common literary device among the *maskilim* writing in German and Hebrew, and Abramovitsh became the most powerful satiric author in Yiddish letters. Because his basic ideology was that of the Jewish Enlightenment, Abramovitsh continued writing in a satiric vein even after the political setbacks of 1881. Later in life, in part because of his position at the *talmud torah* in Odessa, Abramovitsh tempered his critiques. Beyond his satiric impulses, Abramovitsh shows ample sympathy toward the underclass and unusual sensitivity to the plight of poor Jewish boys.

Abramovitsh's Yiddish and Hebrew writings attracted attention from the start, but critical interest in them grew especially in the 1880s, after he had published his major Yiddish works. This interest increased early in the 20th century as Abramovitsh's Hebrew fiction won admiration, on the one hand, and drew reserved and even negative reaction on the other. From an ideological point of view, critics have been interested in his attitude toward the Ḥibbat Zion movement and his stand on the social problems of the oppressed multitudes in Russia. Readers have sometimes seen Abramovitsh as a preacher, loyal to his people and calling for a radical change in Diaspora life. Other critics such as David Frishman stressed the documentary character of Abramovitsh's descriptions of the *shtetl*, which might someday serve as a historical testimony to the Jewish way of life in the 19th century. Some other critics have thought that his harsh portrayals of *shtetl* life give a distorted image of Jewish existence there. While critics have admired his descriptions of nature and his epic achievement in recreating Jewish *shtetl* types, they have occasionally argued that – because he uses exaggeration and grotesque caricature – Abramovitsh inadequately represents the lives of individuals.

A unique source of information about Abramovitsh's formative years is an essay in the Russian-Jewish journal *Voskhod* ("Sunrise," 1884), by his childhood friend Yehuda-Leyb (Lev) Binshtok. Also essential are Abramovitsh's essay "*Reshimot le-Toledotai*" ("My Life Story," in Nahum Sokolov's *Sefer Zikkaron*, 1889) and his many letters contained in *Dos Mendele Bukh* ("The Mendele Book," ed. Nakhman Mayzel, 1959). A fictionalized account of Abramovitsh's childhood may be found in his autobiographical novel *Shloyme Reb Khayims*, which appeared serially in Yiddish starting in 1899 (printed in book form, 1911); in Hebrew, the autobiographical novel appeared as *Ba-Yamim ha-Hem* ("In Those Days," starting with the *Petikhtah*, 1894; printed in book form, 1911).

On the occasion of Abramovitsh's 75th birthday and in celebration of his wide popularity based on 50 years of writing, the Jubilee editions of his works were published in 1909–11 (Hebrew, in three volumes) and in 1911–13 (Yiddish, in 16 volumes). Some important studies of Abramovitsh are by Shmuel Niger (1936), Meir Viner (1946), Gershon Shaked (1965), and Dan Miron (1973). In English, Ken Frieden (1995) gives an overview of his life and work and interprets his major fiction in relation to the other classic Yiddish writers – Sholem Aleichem and I.L. Peretz. In a new vein, Naomi Seidman (1997) discusses gender issues in Abramovitsh's writing.

BIBLIOGRAPHY: *Ale Verk fun Mendele Moykher Sforim (S.Y. Abramovitsh)* (1911–13), standard ed. of Yiddish works; *Kol Kitvei Mendele Moykher Sforim (S.Y. Abramovitsh)* (1909–12) and *Kol Kitvei Mendele Mokher Sfarim* (1966), Hebrew works; *Tales of Mendele the Book Peddler*, ed. D. Miron and K. Frieden (1996); *Classic Yiddish Stories Stories of S.Y. Abramovitsh, Sholem Aleichem, and I.L. Peretz*, ed. and trans. K. Frieden et al. (2004); Sh. Niger, *Mendele Moykher Sforim: Zayn Lebn, Zayne Gezelshaftlekhe un Literarishe Oyftuungen* (1936); M. Viner, *Tsu der Geshikhte fun der Yidisher Literatur in 19-tn Yorhundert* (1946); Y. Klausner, in: *Sifrut*, 6 (1950), 353–516; Rejzen, in: *Leksikon*, 6 (1965), 48–72; G. Shaked, *Bein Ẓeḥok le-Dema: Iyyunim be-Yiẓirato shel Mendele Mokher-Sfarim* (1965); D. Miron, *A Traveler Disguised: A Study in the Rise of Modern Yiddish Fiction in the Nineteenth Century* (1973; 1996); Sh. Werses, *Mi-Mendele ad Hazaz: Sugi'ot be-Hitpatḥhut ha-Sipporet ha-Ivrit* (1987); K. Frieden, *Classic Yiddish Fiction: Abramovitsh, Sholem Aleichem, and Peretz* (1995); N. Seidman, *A Marriage Made in Heaven: The Sexual Politics of Hebrew and Yiddish* (1997).

[Ken Frieden (2nd ed.)]

ABRAMOVITZ, MAX (1908–2004), U.S. architect, born in Chicago. From 1947 to 1952 Abramovitz was deputy director of the Planning Office of the United Nations. He was partner in the firm of Harrison & Abramovitz, which built the United Nations Secretariat, New York (1950). The design incorporated the ideas of an international panel of architects that included Le Corbusier and Oscar Niemeyer. This construction, the east and west sides of which were faced almost entirely with glass, proved a prototype of later buildings. His firm specialized in office buildings such as the Alcoa Building, Pittsburgh (1953), and the Socony Mobil Building, New York (1956), in which story-high metal units were used for the curtain walls. He also worked on projects of Jewish interest. These include Temple Beth-Zion, Buffalo, N.Y., and the Hillel Foundations on the campuses of the University of Illinois (1951) and of Northwestern University (1952). His three chapels (Protestant, Catholic, Jewish) at Brandeis University (1954) expressed the harmony and equality of the three faiths as represented on the campus, while at the same time respecting their differences. The chapels were similar structures placed around a pool. In 1963 Abramovitz built the new Philharmonic Hall, New York. The facade features two superimposed rows of concrete shafts softened with flattened vaults. It has been regarded as an example of American "neoclassicism." In 1973 Philharmonic Hall was renamed Avery Fisher Hall. Located at the northern end of the Lincoln Center Plaza, the concert hall is home to the New York Philharmonic Orchestra and can seat an audience of more than 2,700. The Plaza, built in 1964–65 by Harrison & Abramovitz, was rebuilt in 1984–85 by Lew Davis and renamed Paul Milstein Plaza in 1997. Abramovitz's auditorium of the University of Illinois at Urbana (1964) is a vast saucer dome surrounded by a circulation gallery that can accommodate more than 18,000 spectators.

The Empire State Plaza in Albany, N.Y., considered one of the most ambitious urban renewal projects in modern U.S. history, was designed by Harrison & Abramovitz and built between 1965 and 1979. The government complex consists of ten buildings set on a six-story platform, which forms the plaza.

ABRAMOVITZ, MOSES (1912–2000), U.S. economist. Born in New York City, he was an instructor at Harvard (1936–38) and from 1938 to 1940 a member of the staff of the National Bureau of Economic Research. In 1940 he began teaching at Columbia but interrupted his work during World War II to serve as the principal economist of the War Production Board and the Office of Strategic Services. He spent the final year of the war as a lieutenant in the U.S. Army, and with the close of the conflict was appointed economic adviser to the U.S. representative on the Allied Commission on Reparations. In 1946 he resumed his teaching at Columbia but left in 1948 for Stanford University. He taught at Stanford for almost 30 years, taking leave only during 1962–63 to work as economic adviser to the secretary-general of the Organization for Economic Cooperation and Development in Paris. He served as chair from 1963 to 1965 and from 1971 to 1974. During his tenure at Stanford and after his retirement, he gained international admiration and renown for his fundamental insights and pioneering contributions to the study of long-term economic growth. His main fields of interest were economic history and development and business cycles.

Abramovitz served as president of the American Economic Association (1979–80), the Western Economic Association (1988–89), and the Economic History Association (1992–93). His publications include *An Approach to a Price Theory for a Changing Economy* (1939); *Inventories and Business Cycles* (1950); with Vera Eliasberg, *The Growth of Public Employment in Great Britain* (1957); *Evidences of Long Swings in Aggregate Construction since the Civil War* (1964); and *Thinking About Growth and Other Essays* (1989). Abramovitz's article "Catching Up, Forging Ahead, and Falling Behind" (1986) is one of the most frequently cited papers ever published by the *Journal of Economic History*.

[Joachim O. Ronall / Ruth Beloff (2nd ed.)]

ABRAMOWICZ, DINA (1909–2000), librarian and specialist on Yiddish studies and on Jewish history and culture in Eastern Europe. Born in Vilna, she was raised in a Russian-speaking home with strong family ties to the Haskalah, the Yiddish-speaking intelligentsia, and the Bund. Abramowicz was educated in Yiddish and Polish schools, including a Polish gymnasium, and she received an M.A. in philosophy and Polish literature from Stefan Batory University in Vilna (1936). From 1939 to 1941 she was assistant to the head librarian of the Jewish Central Children's Library of Vilna, and during the Nazi occupation she worked in the Vilna Ghetto Library. Most of the library's books had previously belonged to the Hevrah Mefitse Haskalah, in whose former building it was housed. Abramowicz escaped the ghetto before its liquidation and from 1943 until liberation in 1944 she served in a Jewish partisan unit. Abramowicz immigrated to the United States in 1946, where she was reunited with her father, who had been there since 1939. Her mother perished in Treblinka in 1943, and her younger sister survived the war in France. In America, Abramowicz resumed her career as a librarian at the *YIVO Institute for Jewish Research, where she served as assistant librarian (1947–62), head librarian (1962–87), and senior reference librarian (1987–2000). Under Abramowicz's leadership the YIVO Library grew into one of the largest and most important repositories of printed Judaica, especially in her areas of specialization: Yiddish language and literature (including children's literature), Jewish history and culture in Eastern Europe, and the Holocaust. Abramowicz was assiduous in her efforts to acquire new and unusual publications for the library. She supervised the absorption of much of the prewar Vilna YIVO library after it was recovered in Europe and brought to New York. In addition, she published book reviews, topical articles, annual lists of new Yiddish books, and bibliographies of translations from Yiddish into English, and she co-edited a collection of essays on 19th- and early 20th-century Lithuanian Jewry, *Profiles of a Lost World: Memoirs of East European Jewish Life before World War II* (1999) with her father Hirsz Abramowicz. Abramowicz's contributions as reference librarian and cultural gatekeeper were particularly noteworthy, and she received awards from several national library associations and Jewish organizations. Over the years she provided in-depth consultations to thousands of researchers, including novelists, scholars, filmmakers, journalists, and genealogists. Through her personal experiences, professional training, intellectual engagement, and longevity, Abramowicz came to personify the legacy of Eastern European Jewish civilization. She died in New York City.

BIBLIOGRAPHY: D. Abramowicz, "The World of My Parents: Reminiscences," in: *YIVO Annual*, 23 (1996), 105–57; idem, *Guardians of a Tragic Heritage: Reminiscences and Observations of an Eyewitness* (1998); J. Sharlet, "Keeper of a Civilization," in: *The Book Peddler / Der Pakn-treger*, 21 (1996), 9–21.

[Zachary M. Baker (2nd ed.)]

ABRAMOWITZ, BINA (**Fuchs**; 1865–1953), Yiddish actress. At the age of 14, Bina Fuchs joined the chorus of Mogulesko's company in Odessa and later acted with Naphtali Goldfaden's troupe, being typecast in "mother" roles. After her marriage to Max Abramowitz, the couple toured Russia giving concerts, and in 1886 accompanied Mogulesko to the U.S. In New York she played with various Yiddish companies, including Maurice Schwartz's at the Jewish Art Theater. She created many roles in Jacob Gordin's plays. Abramowitz also appeared in films made in the U.S. They include the silent movie *Broken Hearts* (1926), directed by Maurice Schwartz, and the Yiddish-language films *The Unfortunate Bride* (1932) and *Yiskor* (1933).

[Ruth Beloff (2nd ed.)]

ABRAMOWITZ, DOV BAER (1860–1926), U.S. rabbi, religious Zionist leader, and founding member of the Union of Orthodox Rabbis of America. Abramowitz was born in Lithuania but made *aliyah* together with his parents as a young boy. He was educated at the Eẓ Ḥayyim yeshivah in Jerusalem and appointed as a district rabbi in the city after receiving ordination in 1885. Abramowitz left Israel for America in 1894, moving first to Philadelphia, and later to New York City, where he served as the rabbi of Congregation Mishkan Israel. He quickly became a prominent figure in the Orthodox community, admired for both his scholarship and his leadership abilities. While in New York, he published a text on the Jewish marriage code, a collection of sermons, and a multi-volume study of Jewish law as well as editing a short-lived scholarly journal. He also joined with Moses Matlin and Judah Bernstein to push for the establishment of a seminary to train English-speaking rabbis to serve American pulpits. The Rabbi Isaac Elchanan Yeshiva, the product of their combined labors, was founded in 1897. Five years later, he joined with a group of other immigrant rabbis who had received their ordination at yeshivot in Europe and Palestine to form the Union of Orthodox Rabbis of America (Agudat ha-Rabbonim). Abramowitz moved to St. Louis, Missouri, in 1906 after accepting an offer to become head of the city's *bet din*. This position provided Abramowitz with the status and time to pursue a variety of initiatives close to his heart. A passionate proponent of religious Zionism, Abramowitz campaigned on behalf of the Mizrachi movement, starting its first American office in 1910 and encouraging its expansion. Abramowitz was appointed as the president of the American Mizrachi at its founding in 1914. During World War I his focus shifted to easing the plight of the embattled Jewish communities of Eastern Europe. Abramowitz collected money for the Central Relief Committee, the organization established to rally the often fractious American Jewish community on behalf of their beleaguered brethren caught between opposing armies on the Eastern Front. Following the war, Abramowitz returned to his Zionist activities, founding an organization to support emissaries who visited America to raise funds for Palestine. After over 25 years in America, Abramowitz returned to settle in Palestine in 1921. Among his writings are *Dat Yisrael* (1897–1905), *Ketav ha-Dat* (1900), and *Kuntres Sefer Ketubbah* (1900).

BIBLIOGRAPHY: M. Sherman, *Orthodox Judaism in America: A Biographical Dictionary and Sourcebook* (1996); *Universal Jewish Encyclopedia* (1948).

[Adam Mendelsohn (2nd ed.)]

ABRAMOWITZ, EMIL (1864–1922), physician, one of the first Social Democrats in Russia. Abramowitz was born in Grodno and studied in France. He was active in the movement in Minsk and Kiev in the 1880s. His wide education, personal warmth, and persuasiveness as an exponent of socialism enabled him to influence numerous workers. The program he drew up for workers' circles was followed for a long time in the Jewish labor movement. Abramowitz was imprisoned for his political activities and spent many years in exile in Siberia, where he gained a reputation for his cultural activities and dedication to the medical profession. During World War I he served as an army doctor; in 1919 he was again imprisoned, as a Menshevik. The letters he wrote between 1914 and 1917 reveal concern over the fate of Russian Jewry and pessimism as to its future.

BIBLIOGRAPHY: *Deyateli Revolyutsionnogo Dvizheniya v Rossii (Bio-Bibliograficheskiy slovar)*, s.v.; E. Tcherikower, *Historishe Shriftn*, 3 (1939), 410ff.

[Moshe Mishkinsky]

ABRAMOWITZ, GRIGORI (pseudonyms: **Ẓevi Abrahami**, **W. Farbman**, and **Michael Farbman**; 1880?–1933), Zionist socialist, publisher, and journalist. Born in Odessa, Russia, Abramowitz studied in Munich and Zurich where he became an active Zionist. At first sharing the ideology of the *Democratic Fraction, he later joined the Zionist socialist group

"Ḥerut" in Zurich. As a supporter of the project for Jewish colonization in *Uganda, Abramowitz wrote a series of articles on "Zionism and the Uganda question" in the Zionist organ *Yevreyskaya* (Zhizn, 1905). For the *Zionist Socialist Workers Party he wrote on Jewish emigration and the economy. After withdrawing from public activities, Abramowitz founded a book-publishing firm. He lived in England from 1915 and while there contributed to English and American journals as an expert on Soviet affairs. His books include *After Lenin* (1924) and *Five-Year Plan* (1931). He founded the *European Year Book* in 1926.

BIBLIOGRAPHY: JC (June 2, 1933).

[Moshe Mishkinsky]

ABRAMOWITZ, HERMAN (1880–1947), Canadian rabbi. Born in Lithuania, Abramowitz moved to New York City with his family in 1890. He received a B.A. from the City College of New York (CCNY) in 1900 and was ordained at the *Jewish Theological Seminary (JTS) two years later. He was appointed rabbi at Montreal's Shaar Hashomayim synagogue in 1902, where he served until his death 44 years later. In 1907 he was also the first student to earn a D.H.L. at JTS.

Although Abramowitz initially felt some discomfort about being outside the United States (and later reminisced that his departure from New York for Montreal "was like pioneering on distant foreign fields") he grew to embrace his congregation and Canadian Jewry. He was regarded an effective, dignified, and caring spiritual leader. Many of his sermons were reprinted in the English-language Canadian Jewish press. He encouraged the congregational Sunday school and lay involvement in the synagogue. Abramowitz was also involved in Jewish communal life outside the synagogue. In his first decade in Montreal, he visited western farm colonies in Quebec and western Canada as a representative of the *Jewish Colonization Association. He was instrumental in raising funds for TB patients at Montreal's Mount Sinai Hospital, and in 1913 he was an expert witness on the Talmud in a law suit against the Quebec notary and journalist Plamondon, who delivered a speech (subsequently printed) accusing Jews of the *blood libel.

With the outbreak of WWI, Abramowitz served as chaplain to the Jewish soldiers in Canada. He held the rank of captain. In the interwar period, he was on the board of the Federation of Jewish Philanthropies of Montreal, the Montreal Talmud Torah, and the Montreal General Hospital. During WWII, although suffering from failing health, he chaired the Religious Welfare Committee of Canadian Jewish Congress. Abramowitz also left his mark on Conservative Judaism. In 1926 he was elected president of the *United Synagogue of America, the first person from outside the United States.

During Abramowitz's tenure, Shaar Hashomayim became the congregation of Montreal's "uptown" elite. His congregants included the wealthiest members of the community, including factory owners at odds with their Jewish workers. This may have led to suspicion of Abramowitz by the Jewish masses. Over time, however, he seems to have earned the respect of many of the "downtown" Jews and the Yiddish journalist B.G. *Sack wrote a heartfelt obituary in the Yiddish daily, the *Kanader Adler*.

[Richard Menkis (2nd ed.)]

ABRAMOWITZ (Rein), RAPHAEL (1880–1963), socialist leader and writer. He was born in Dvinsk, Latvia, and from 1899 took part in the activities of the illegal student movement in Riga, where he joined the *Bund in 1901. An outstanding speaker, prolific writer, and energetic organizer, he was speedily recognized as one of the chief spokesmen of the second generation of Bund leaders. In 1903–04, he was active in the "colonies" of the Russian students in Liège and Zurich. In 1905 he was elected a member of the central committee of the Bund and in 1906 became a member of the central committee of the Russian Social Democratic Workers' Party. During the Russian Revolution of 1905, Abramowitz was the Bund candidate for the second Russian *Duma. He was arrested several times for his socialist activities and exiled to Siberia in 1910 but in 1911 succeeded in escaping abroad. Abramowitz returned to Russia in 1917, and played a leading role as a Menshevik representative, notably in the All-Russian Central Executive Committee of the Soviet. After the October Revolution, he and Julius *Martov were included in the Menshevik faction which for a while believed that gradual democratization of the Bolshevik regime was possible. He opposed a contemplated merger of the Bund with the Communist Party and was among the founders of a separate "Social-Democratic Bund" (April 1920). At the end of 1920 Abramowitz went to Berlin, where the following year he and Martov founded the Menshevist organ *Sotsialistitcheskiy Vestnik*, which he continued to edit until shortly before his death. Between 1923 and 1929 he was a leading member of the executive of the Socialist International. Abramowitz moved to Paris in 1939 and in 1940 succeeded in reaching New York.

Abramowitz was a contributor to the Yiddish Socialist *Jewish Daily Forward* and the monthly *Zukunft*, and a founder and editor of the Yiddish *Algemayne Entsiklopedye* (1934–50), and of *The Jewish People, Past and Present* (1946–55). He edited the laborite *Modern Review* (New York, 1947–50). His books include *Lerbukh tsu der Geshikhte fun Yisroel* (in collaboration with A. Menes, 1923); *Der Teror gegen di Sotsialisten in Rusland un in Gruzye* (in collaboration with Tsereteli and Sukhomolin, Yiddish, 1925; translated into French, German, and Dutch); two volumes of memoirs, *In Tsvay Revolutsyes* (1944) and *The Soviet Revolution, 1917–1939* (1962).

BIBLIOGRAPHY: LNYL, 1 (1956), 12–16; *Sotsialistitcheskiy Vestnik*, 43 (1963), nos. 3–4, 26–28.

[Leon Shapiro]

ABRAMS, "CAL" (**Calvin Ross**; 1924–1997), U.S. baseball player, lifetime .269 hitter over eight seasons, with 433 hits,

32 home runs, 257 runs, and 138 RBIs. Born in Philadelphia to Russian immigrant parents, he moved with his family to Brooklyn when he was a child. Having grown up in Brooklyn in the shadow of Ebbets Field, Abrams fulfilled a life-long dream when he signed with the Brooklyn Dodgers after graduating from James Madison High School. But after two weeks in the minor leagues he was drafted into the army, where he served four years. Abrams spent three years in the minor leagues, winning the Southern Association championship with Mobile in 1947 while hitting .336. Abrams, who batted and threw left-handed, played for the Brooklyn Dodgers (1949–52), Cincinnati Reds (1952), Pittsburgh Pirates (1953–54), Baltimore Orioles (1954–55), and Chicago White Sox (1955), and had a perfect fielding percentage in three different seasons, 1950, 1952, and 1956. Abrams is best remembered for one of the most famous plays in Dodger franchise history. In the final game of the 1950 season, with the Dodgers one game behind the Philadelphia Phillies in the pennant race, Abrams tried to score from second with two out in the bottom of the ninth of a 1–1 game on a hit by Duke Snider, but Abrams, who had been waved home by third base coach Milt Stock, was thrown out by the Phillies' Richie Ashburn. Had Cal scored, the Dodgers would have won the game and forced a playoff with the Phillies for the pennant. Dick Sisler hit a three-run home run in the top of the tenth to win the game – and the pennant – for Philadelphia. It was the closest Abrams ever got to the postseason. Dodgers fans vilified Abrams for years but he was defended by both Ashburn and Phillies pitcher Robin Roberts for the play, who agreed with many others who said Abrams should not have been sent home by Stock.

[Elli Wohlgelernter (2nd ed.)]

ABRAMS, CHARLES (1901–1970), U.S. housing and urban planning expert, lawyer, and author. Abrams, who was born in Vilna, was taken to the U.S. in 1904. Admitted to the New York bar in 1923, Abrams became involved in housing and urban development both as a property owner and lawyer during the 1920s and 1930s when he campaigned for the preservation of Greenwich Village's historic streets and buildings. He laid the groundwork for U.S. public housing laws and, in the course of his career, held housing posts on the city, state, national, and international levels. These included counsel to the New York City Housing Authority (1934–37), and leader of, and adviser to, several UN housing missions, mostly to underdeveloped countries. Abrams was a state vice chairman of the New York State Liberal Party in the 1940s. From 1955 to 1959 Abrams was chairman of the New York State Commission Against Discrimination and a member of Governor Harriman's cabinet. In 1965 he chaired the committee whose recommendations led to the creation of the New York City Housing and Development Administration.

Abrams lectured in housing and economics at the New School for Social Research (1936–60), and chaired both Columbia University's city planning department (1965) and its division of urban planning (1965–68).

As housing columnist for the *New York Post* (1947–49), Abrams vigorously exposed real estate abuses and inadequacies in city, state, and federal housing policies. His books include: *Revolution in Land* (1937); *Future of Housing* (1946); *Forbidden Neighbors* (1955); and *Man's Struggle for Shelter* (1964).

ABRAMS, ELLIOTT (1948–), U.S. neoconservative political figure. After graduating from Harvard Law School in 1973, Abrams worked in corporate law but quickly decided to pursue a career in politics and public service instead. Abrams volunteered in Senator Henry "Scoop" Jackson's 1972 bid for the Democratic Party's presidential nomination, and in 1975, when Abrams was looking to get into politics, Jackson offered him a campaign staff position.

After Jackson lost the presidential nomination to Jimmy Carter, Abrams remained in Washington, D.C., where he became chief legal counsel to newly elected Senator Daniel P. Moynihan (Dem., N.Y.), another outspoken advocate of U.S. interventionism, and eventually became Moynihan's chief of staff.

During these years, the Democratic Party, under the auspices of President Carter, softened its stance on the Soviet Union. Carter was accused by hawks of "giving up too much" in arms control negotiations with the Soviet Union. A minor *coup d'etat* ensued among several Jewish Democrats who had worked for Senator Jackson: Elliott *Abrams, Richard *Perle, Doug Feith, and Paul Wolfowitz switched to the Republican Party, supported Ronald Reagan in 1980, and began to espouse a political-intellectual ideology known as neoconservatism.

Abrams was assistant undersecretary of inter-American affairs at the time of the Contras affair involving the illicit sale of weapons to Iran and the channeling of the receipts to the Contras. When he was called to testify before Congress, he claimed to have had no knowledge of any illegal activities. A later Independent Counsel investigation alleged that he had lied to Congress. He pleaded guilty to two counts of withholding information from Congress. On November 15, 1991, the presiding judge, Aubrey E. Robinson, sentenced Abrams to two years probation and 100 hours of community service. On December 24, 1992, outgoing President George H.W. Bush granted Abrams a full pardon amid much controversy.

From 1989 to 2002, Abrams wrote and worked for a number of research and public policy organizations. He was a senior fellow at the Hudson Institute, a member of the Council on Foreign Relations, and a member of the National Advisory Council of the American Jewish Committee. He also served as president of the Ethics and Public Policy Center. In 2002, Abrams returned to public life. The younger President George W. Bush appointed Abrams to the post of senior director of the National Security Council, with responsibilities for the Middle East, a position that did not require the Senate confirmation that he was unlikely to get.

Abrams was also the author of three books: *Undue Process* (1993), a scathing critique of the Office of Independent Counsel; *Security and Sacrifice* (1995), which urges an aggressive U.S. foreign policy; and *Faith or Fear: How Jews Can Survive in Christian America* (1997), which argues that American Jewry would fare far better if it adopted conservative values and alliances, particularly with the Christian right. It was written with a grant from a prominent Conservative Foundation.

[Yehuda Martin Hausman (2nd ed.)]

ABRAMS, FLOYD M. (1936–), U.S. lawyer. Abrams, who was born in New York, graduated from Cornell University and Yale Law School and achieved fame as the nation's most prominent defender of the rights of the press under the First Amendment, arguing many important cases before the United States Supreme Court. At the law firm of Cahill, Gordon & Reindel, he argued more First Amendment and media cases before the Supreme Court than any lawyer in United States history. Perhaps his most important case involved the *New York Times*, which acquired a secret history of the United States policy in Vietnam from the administrations of Harry S. Truman through Lyndon B. Johnson in 1967, and begin printing it on June 13, 1971 (the war in Vietnam was still going on at the time). Abrams was co-counsel for the *Times* as the administration of Richard M. Nixon sought to enjoin the *Times* from printing the archive on grounds of national security. In a lower court decision, the government was able to bar the paper from printing the stories. The *Times* agreed to suspend publication while it awaited a decision in the Supreme Court. It was the first time in American history that the government exercised a prior restraint on the press. But the *Times* eventually prevailed. The case reached the Supreme Court, which decided by a 6–3 vote that the government's case against releasing the material was not compelling and allowed the series to be printed. Over the years Abrams represented virtually every major media organization in First Amendment-related cases: CNN, ABC, NBC, CBS, *Time, Business Week, The Nation*, and *Reader's Digest*, among others. Abrams was also counsel to the Brooklyn Museum in its legal battle with Mayor Rudolph Giuliani, who sought to close an art exhibition he considered blasphemous and in poor taste. In addition to his legal representation, Abrams was chairman of several American Bar Association committees on freedom of speech and of the press. He served as a visiting lecturer at Yale Law School and William J. Brennan Jr. Visiting Professor of First Amendment Law at the Columbia University Graduate School of Journalism.

[Stewart Kampel (2nd ed.)]

ABRAMS, MEYER H. (1912–), U.S. literary critic and scholar. Born in Long Branch, New Jersey, Abrams was educated at Harvard University, where he earned his bachelor's and master's degrees and, in 1940, his doctorate. He also studied at Cambridge University in 1934 and 1935 with I.A. Richards, author of *Coleridge on Imagination* (1934). Regarded as one of the most influential critics of Romantic literature, Abrams first established his reputation with his 1953 work *The Mirror and the Lamp: Romantic Theory and the Critical Tradition*. Here Abrams defines Romanticism in terms of its "expressive orientation." He characterizes 18th-century literature as a mirror, or "reflector," which seeks to faithfully reflect the exterior world; 19th-century literature, on the other hand, is a lamp, or "projector," which seeks to illuminate and express the inner life of the artist. With this metaphor, Abrams is considered to have created a significant definition of English Romanticism, one that profoundly affected subsequent studies.

In his later work, *Natural Supernaturalism: Tradition and Revolution in Romantic Literature* (1971), Abrams links English and German Romanticism to a Judeo-Christian conception of man's fall, redemption, and return to paradise, and he uses Wordsworth's "The Recluse" as the exemplar of his theory. Critical reception to *Natural Supernaturalism* was mixed, with Deconstructionists and New Historicists challenging its authority. Abrams's 1989 work, *Doing Things with Texts: Essays in Criticism and Critical Theory*, which includes previously published essays, addresses these critiques and further elaborates his literary theory.

During his long career at Cornell University, beginning in 1938, Meyer Abrams established a reputation as an esteemed Jewish scholar in a field previously dominated by non-Jewish academics. Professor emeritus at Cornell from 1983, Abrams is the recipient of numerous honors and awards, including a Ford Foundation fellowship in 1953, Guggenheim fellowships in 1958 and 1960, the James Russell Lowell Prize from the Modern Language Association of America in 1972 for *Natural Supernaturalism*, and the Award for Literature from the American Academy and Institute of Arts and Letters in 1990. He served as general editor of *The Norton Anthology of English Literature* (1962 and subsequent editions; founding editor emeritus of the 2005 edition) and was named a fellow of the American Academy of Arts and Sciences and the American Philosophical Society.

[Dorothy Bauhoff (2nd ed.)]

ABRAMS, ROBERT (1938–), U.S. politician, attorney general of New York. Abrams received his B.A. from Columbia College in 1960 and graduated from New York University School of Law in 1963. In 1965, he was elected at the age of 27 to the first of three terms in the New York State Assembly. In 1978, he ran a successful campaign for attorney general of New York State, becoming the first Democrat to hold the position in 40 years. As attorney general, he commanded one of the largest law offices in the nation, overseeing 1,200 employees, including 475 attorneys in 14 different locations throughout the State of New York. Abrams remained attorney general for 15 years. He is credited with altering New York's abortion law, prosecuting organized crime figures, implementing environmental protection laws, and protecting victims' rights (particularly abused children).

A leader among U.S. attorney generals, Abrams served as president of the National Association of Attorney Generals. His colleagues also awarded him the Wyman Award as an outstanding attorney general. In 1992, Abrams ran against incumbent Senator Alphonse D'amato, losing by 1.2 percentage points. Married to an observant Jewish woman, he would not campaign or work on Friday evening or Sabbath morning, and considered it a professional requirement to be more lax Saturday afternoon. Subsequently he worked as an attorney for the law firm Strook & Strook & Lavan LLP in New York.

[Yehuda Martin Hausman (2nd ed.)]

ABRAMSKY, YEḤEZKEL (1886–1976), talmudic scholar. Abramsky was born in Lithuania. He studied at the yeshivot of Telz, Mir, and Slobodka as well as under Ḥayyim *Soloveichik of Brisk. He achieved a reputation as a profound talmudic scholar and active communal worker. During World War I and the Russian Revolution he wandered in Russia and applied himself to learning, lecturing, and strengthening religious life. He was appointed rabbi of Slutsk and Smolensk. In 1928 Abramsky and S.J. Zevin published *Yagdil Torah*, a periodical dedicated to strengthening Torah study in the unfavorable conditions of the Soviet Union. It was probably the last Jewish religious periodical published in the Soviet Union for nearly 60 years. In 1930 he was arrested as a "counter-revolutionary." Abramsky was sentenced to hard labor in Siberia, but, after two years, his wife and friends succeeded in obtaining his release. He went to London, where he was appointed rabbi of the Machzike Hadath congregation, and subsequently became *dayyan* of the London *bet din*. He became a British subject in 1937. In London, his strong personality was largely responsible for the influence of traditional Orthodoxy in the official community. He was appointed a member of the Moeẓet Gedolei ha-Torah of *Agudat Israel. In 1951 he retired and took up residence in Jerusalem, where he became a significant figure in the yeshivah world. Abramsky wrote *Divrei Mamonot* (1939) and *Erez Yisrael* (1945), but his scholarly fame rests on his *Ḥazon Yeḥezkel*, a 24-volume commentary on the Tosefta, with his novellae (first volume, 1925). In 1955 he was awarded the Israel Prize. Several of his responsa were published in London (1937). In Israel he was recognized as a rabbi of great stature, and his funeral in Jerusalem was attended by an estimated 40,000 mourners.

ADD. BIBLIOGRAPHY: ODNB online.

[Mordechai Hacohen]

ABRAMSON, 18th–19th century family of German medalists and engravers.

JACOB ABRAHAM (1723–1800), born in Poland, worked in the mints of Berlin, Stettin, Koenigsberg, and Dresden. In 1752, Frederick II of Prussia appointed him medalist at the Berlin mint. Abraham struck 33 commemorative medals, among them one in memory of Moses *Mendelssohn. His son, ABRAHAM (1754–1811), studied with his father and with Tassaert at the Berlin Kunstakademie. Working at first with his father but after 1784 on his own, he produced a series of medals depicting German scholars. The first medal, of Moses Mendelssohn, which he did with his father, was followed by many others including Lessing and Kant. He worked as his father's assistant from 1771, but was appointed royal medalist in 1782 and in this function cut mainly mint dies and worked at portrait medals in wax; after 1786 he exhibited them at the Kunstakademie. Aided by a government grant, he made a tour of Vienna, Venice, and Rome from 1788 to 1792. Beside his work for the mint Abraham received government commissions for commemorative medals and wax portraits. He also executed work for Russia and several German states, among them a medal to celebrate Jewish emancipation in Westphalia in 1808. Abraham also did private work, such as medals of Markus *Herz (1803), and Daniel *Itzig (1793). His signature was Abr, A/S, N, or sometimes just A. Of his lapidary work only a carnelian with the portrait of Frederick William II is known. In 1792 Abramson was member of the Berlin Akademie der Kuenste and of other similar bodies.

His brother, MICHAEL JACOB (1750–1825), was also an engraver. He exhibited after 1787 at the Berlin Kunstakademie but apparently later emigrated to Scandinavia. His works include a copper-plate engraving of Ẓevi Hirsch *Levin, chief rabbi of Berlin (1798). It is suspected but unconfirmed that he was baptized. HIRSCH (d. 1800), another son of Jacob, also worked as an engraver at the Berlin mint.

BIBLIOGRAPHY: C.T. Hoffman, *Jacob Abraham und Abraham Abramson, 55 Jahre Berliner Medallienkunst: 1755–1810* (1927); A. Kirchstein, *Juedische Graphiker: 1625–1825* (1918); D.M. Friedenberg (ed.), *Great Jewish Portraits in Metal* (1963).

ABRAMSON, JERRY EDWIN (1946–), U.S. politician. Born in Louisville, Kentucky, Abramson graduated from Indiana University (1968). After having served in the U.S. Army between 1969 and 1971, for which he received a medal for meritorious service, he returned to law school and was graduated from Georgetown School of Law in 1973. He then entered private practice with Greenbaum, Doll, and McDonald, where he became a partner and immediately became active in Democratic politics, first as a member of the Board of Alderman and later as general counsel to Kentucky Governor John Y. Brown. He was elected mayor of Louisville in 1986, a position he held for 12 years. A national leader, he was president of the U.S. Conference of Mayors in 1993–94 and vice chair of the Democratic Platform Committee when his fellow southerner Bill Clinton ran for president in 1992. He chaired the Clinton reelection efforts for Kentucky. After being barred for reelection by term limits, Abramson became mayor once again after the government of Louisville had been regionalized, serving from 2003 as Louisville metro mayor.

[Michael Berenbaum (2nd ed.)]

ABRAMSON, JESSE (1904–1979), U.S. sportswriter. Known as the leading track and field writer in the U.S., Abramson was the first person from the media to be elected to the National Track & Field Hall of Fame, in 1981. He witnessed every Olympics from 1928 until 1976, as a reporter for the *New*

York Herald Tribune, for the *International Herald-Tribune* in 1972, and as foreign press liaison at the 1968 and 1976 Games. His obituary in the *New York Times* noted: "Colleagues called him 'The Brain,' in recognition of his profound knowledge of track and his phenomenal memory for detail." Abramson was honored with the Grantland Rice Award of the Sportsmen Brotherhood, the James J. Walker Award for service to boxing, and the career achievement award from the New York Track Writers Association. He was a founder and long-time president of the N.Y. Track Writers Association, which presents the annual Jesse Abramson Award to the outstanding athlete of the year. Abramson also reported on football and boxing, serving as president of the New York Football Writers Association, and was awarded the Boxing Writers' Association of America Nat Fleischer Memorial Award for Excellence in Boxing Journalism in 1976.

[Elli Wohlgelernter (2nd ed.)]

ABRAMSON, SHRAGA (1915–1996), rabbinic scholar. Born in Ciechanowiec, in the district of Bialystok, Poland, he received rabbinic ordination in 1936, in which year he immigrated to Ereẓ Israel where he continued his education in various yeshivot and at the Hebrew University. He served on the faculty of the Jewish Theological Seminary in New York from 1952 until 1958, the final year as associate professor. From 1958 he was professor of Talmud, Geonica, and *rishonim* at the Hebrew University in Jerusalem. His scholarly contributions are to be found in the areas of Talmud, Geonica, rabbinic Hebrew, biblical exegesis and interpretation in the Middle Ages, medieval Hebrew poetry and literature, and medieval Hebrew philology. They are noteworthy for their erudition in talmudic and rabbinic literature and their disciplined scientific research methods. His main field, however, is Geonica to which he has made important contributions. He was awarded the Israel Prize for Jewish studies in 1974.

His most important published work was *R. Nissim Ga'on* (Heb., 1965). Among his earlier works are critical editions of R. Samuel ha-Nagid, *Ben Mishlei* (1948) and *Ben Kohelet* (1953). His other published works include *Massekhet Avodah Zarah* (1957), a publication of a manuscript of the tractate *Avodah Zarah* of the Babylonian Talmud; *Massekhet Bava Batra* (1958), a Hebrew translation of the tractate *Bava Batra* of the Babylonian Talmud; *Ba-Merkazim u-va-Tefuẓot bi-Tekufat ha-Ge'onim* (1965), on the geonic period; *Bi-Leshon Kodemim* (1965), a study in medieval Hebrew poetry; and *Sheloshah Sefarim shel R. Yehudah ibn Bala'am*.

[Israel Francus]

ABRASS, OSIAS (**Joshua**; 1829–1883), Russian *ḥazzan* and synagogue composer. He was born in Berdichev and became known as "Pitshe Odesser" ("The Mite from Odessa") when as a boy he gained fame for his soprano solos in the choir of his teacher, Bezalel Shulsinger in Odessa. Abrass also studied with *Sulzer in Vienna. He was *ḥazzan* and choir leader in Tarnopol in 1840 and in Lvov in 1842. In 1858 he became chief *ḥazzan* in the Odessa synagogue, the largest in Russia. Abrass' phenomenal vocal performance as well as his contributions to synagogal choir music enhanced the fame of this synagogue and set new standards in Eastern European liturgical singing. His sole printed work was *Simrat-Joh; Gottesdienstliehe Gesaenge der Israeliten* (1874) for cantor and choir. His virtuosity in coloratura was compared with that of Adelina Patti, the great soprano, as exemplified by his "Simrat-Joh" No. 27, or the following "ornamental extension" of the note E-flat (*ibid.* No. 32):

Abrass' 39 published compositions may be judged best as a further attempt to connect the traditional *meshorerim* style with Western choral music. He uses chordal harmony, effects learned from Rossini (No. 10), and even fugato technique (No. 18) only to embellish a basically monodic melody. See also G. Ephros, *Cantorial Anthology*, 1 (1919), no. 51.

BIBLIOGRAPHY: Friedmann, Lebensbilder, 2 (1921), 73–79; Idelsohn, in: *Ha-Toren*, 11 (1924), 138–54; E. Zaludkowski, *Kulturtreger fun der Yidisher Liturgie* (1930), 67–71; Sendrey, Music, index; A. Rosen (ed.), *Geshikhte fun Khazones* (1924).

[Hanoch Avenary]

ABRAVANEL, MAURICE (**de**) (1903–1993), conductor. Born in Salonika, Abravanel studied at Lausanne University, and in Zurich and Berlin. He began his career in 1924 as conductor at the Zwickau Municipal Theater. Before leaving Germany in 1933, he had already conducted at the Berlin Opera, and subsequently he conducted ballet performances in Paris, London, and at the Rome Opera. He toured Australia with the British National Opera Company before moving to the United States in 1936, where he conducted at the Metropolitan (1936) and in Chicago (1940–41). In 1946, he conducted musicals such as *Weill's *Lady in the Dark* for a season on Broadway. In 1947, he became conductor of the Utah State Symphony Orchestra at Salt Lake City, which he made into one of the most adventurous and remarkable musical bodies in the United States based in a small city. Abravanel was also a professor at the University of Utah.

[Max Loppert (2nd ed.)]

ABRECH (or **Abrek**; Heb. אַבְרֵךְ, *avrekh*), probably a command or a title. After deputizing Joseph, Pharaoh "had him ride in the chariot of his second-in-command, and they cried before him, 'Abrek!'" (Gen. 41:43; cf. the Persian ceremony in Esth. 6:11). The exact meaning of the word is uncertain. One view equates the word with Egyptian *'ib-r.k*, "attention!" or "have a care." A difficulty according to this view is that the singular suffix *k* appears where one would expect the plural suffix *tn.* Another view (reminiscent of the ancient Jewish derivation from *brk* ("kneel")) notes that *brk* (borrowed from Semitic) means "render homage" in Egyptian and that the initial *alef* of *Abrek* may possibly be equated with the Egyptian imperative prefix ʾ; proponents of this interpretation therefore translate "kneel!" or "render homage!" This command is similar to the later Egyptian command of homage "to the ground! to the ground!" Both kneeling and complete prostration as acts of homage are represented in Egyptian art. Others take the word as a title, citing the Akkadian *abarakku*, "chief steward of a private or royal household" (I.J. Gelb et al., *The Chicago Assyrian Dictionary*, vol. 1, pt. 1, pp. 32–5); note Gen. 41:40a: "You shall be in charge of my house…." None of these views is free of difficulty, and the question remains open.

BIBLIOGRAPHY: T. Lambdin, in: JAOS, 73 (1953), 146; J. Vergote, *Joseph en Egypte* (1959), 135ff., 151.

[Jeffrey Howard Tigay]

ABSABAN, SOLOMON (d. 1592), scholar of Safed and disciple of Isaac *Luria. Solomon was a friend and contemporary of Moses *Alshekh and studied under Joseph *Caro. It is probable that, like Alshekh, he was among those ordained by Caro. From 1562 his signature appeared on letters and decisions together with those of Joseph Caro and Moses di *Trani. In 1571 he joined them in excommunicating the physician Daoud, an opponent of Joseph *Nasi. In a manuscript responsum (Oxford, 832, n. 23) his signature appears at the head of the list of leading rabbis of Safed. Absaban taught in the talmudic academies of Safed, where Jacob *Abulafia was among his students. In 1582 he served as *av bet din* of Safed. Absaban associated with the mystics there, and was a friend of Eleazar b. Moses *Azikri, who referred to him as distinguished in wisdom, piety, and holiness. Ultimately he settled in Damascus where he presided over the yeshivah until his death.

BIBLIOGRAPHY: Conforte, Kore, 39a, 40a, 41b, 43a; Neubauer, Chronicles, 1 (1887), 151.

ABSALOM (Heb. אַבְשָׁלוֹם, אַבְשָׁלֹם, אֲבִישָׁלוֹם), third son of *David, born during his reign in Hebron, probably about 1007/06 B.C.E.

In the Bible

Absalom was the son of Maacah, the daughter of King Talmai of Geshur. When his half brother Amnon dishonored his full sister Tamar (II Sam. 13:1–20), he considered himself the avenger of her honor and ordered Amnon killed at a shearing feast on his estate, to which he had invited all the king's sons (*ibid.* 13:23–29). Fearing David's wrath, he took refuge at the court of his grandfather, probably a vassal-king of David by that time (c. 987 B.C.E.). Meanwhile, *Joab took up his cause with the king and obtained David's permission for Absalom to return to Jerusalem without fear of punishment; later a full reconciliation was effected between the two (*ibid.* 14:33; c. 983 B.C.E.).

Probably David's second son, Chileab (II Sam. 3:3) or Daniel (I Chron. 3:1), either died young or was mentally or physically handicapped, because it was Absalom, the next oldest son of David, who was the most obvious candidate for the succession. He was a handsome man of prepossessing appearance, a glib tongue, and winning manners (II Sam. 14:25; 15:2–6), and seems to have gained a great deal of popularity among the common people as well. Though strong headed and willful, he knew how to bide his time in order to achieve his desires (cf. *ibid.* 13:20) and how to work for that end (cf. *ibid.* 14:28–30).

Considering these qualities, it is difficult to understand what induced him to plot a revolt against his father (c. 979 B.C.E.); but since there was no strict law that David's successor must be his oldest living son, perhaps Absalom was worried by the influence of David's favorite wife Bath-Sheba and the possibility that David might, as he eventually did, proclaim his oldest son by her his successor.

Be that as it may, the plot was carefully planned at Hebron (cf. II Sam. 15:7). The revolt seems to have enjoyed wide support in Judah, which was perhaps offended by the old king's refusal to show any palpable preference for his own tribesmen, as well as among other Israelite tribes, who were dissatisfied with the gradual bureaucratization of the kingdom and the curtailment of tribal rights.

David retreated with his immediate entourage – bodyguards (the *gibborim*), foreign mercenaries (the Cherethites and Pelethites), 600 Gittites, and some of the people who remained loyal to him – to Transjordan. At the same time, he took care to leave a "fifth columnist" in Jerusalem in the person of *Hushai the Archite, and with him two intelligence messengers, *Ahimaaz and Jonathan, the sons of the two high priests. Hushai succeeded in persuading Absalom to reject his adviser *Ahithophel's sensible proposal to pursue the old king and defeat him before he could find further support. In the subsequent battle in Transjordan (in the forest of Ephraim) Absalom's tribal levees proved no match for David's veteran mercenaries under Ittai the Gittite, who was supported by the loyal Israelites under Joab and Abishai. Absalom was caught by his head in a thick tree and killed on Joab's orders, which contravened the express command of David to spare his life (II Sam. 18:9). The king's mourning for his son almost cost him the support of his loyal troops (*ibid.* 19:1–9).

Absalom had no son, which prompted him to erect a memorial monument for himself (*ibid.* 18:18; cf. however *ibid.* 14:27); he apparently had a daughter, Maacah, who was named for his mother and who later married her cousin *Rehoboam and became the latter's favorite queen and mother of the heir-apparent *Abijam.

[*Encyclopaedia Hebraica*]

In the *Aggadah*

Although the Bible stated that it was by his head and not specifically by his hair that Absalom was caught, the rabbis assume that it was by his hair and make of his death a homily on false ambition, unfilial conduct, and poetic justice. Of the perfect physical qualities ascribed to Adam, Absalom is regarded as having inherited his hair (*Pirkei Rabbenu ha-Kadosh*, in L. Grueenhut, *Likkutim*, 3 (1899), 72). It grew so luxuriantly that although he had taken the Nazirite vow prohibiting the cutting of the hair, he was permitted to trim it from time to time (Nazir 5a). It was his hair, in which he gloried, which brought about his death (Sotah 1:8). He was caught "in the heart of a tree" (II Sam. 18:14). "But did one ever hear of a tree having a heart. This turn of phrase teaches that when a man becomes so heartless as to make war on his own father, nature takes on a heart to avenge the deed" (Mekh. Shirata 6). So unforgivable was his conduct that he is enumerated among those who have no share in the world to come (Sanh. 103b). In *Exodus Rabbah* 1:1 he is cited as one of the exemplars of "spare the rod and spoil the child." His abode is in hell where he is in charge of ten heathen nations (A. Jellinek, *Beit ha-Midrash*, 2 (1938), 50) but David's lament saved him from the extreme penalties of hell (Sot. 10b).

[Louis Isaac Rabinowitz]

In Folklore

In Jewish folk sayings and in Palestinian legends clustered around the Pillar of Absalom (Yad Avshalom) in the Kidron Valley of Jerusalem, rebellious Absalom serves as an example of punishments inflicted upon sons transgressing the Fifth Commandment. According to the report from Jerusalem (1666) of a French Christian pilgrim (Bernardin Surius), the inhabitants of Jerusalem used to bring their children to the tomb of Absalom to shout and throw stones at it, stressing the end of wicked children who did not revere their parents.

[Dov Noy]

In the Arts

In Western literature Absalom has been regarded as a symbol of manly beauty. The subject inspired a medieval mystery play and several Elizabethan dramas. George Peele's *The Love of King David and Fair Bethsabe* (1599) deals at length with Absalom's rebellion, which is blamed on David's illicit love affair with Bath-Sheba, and in tune with the bloodthirsty taste of the era shows the unfortunate prince, suspended by his hair from a tree, being done to death by Joab. John Dryden's *Absalom and Achithophel* (1681), a political satire in verse, presents Charles II as David, Charles' illegitimate son the Duke of Monmouth as Absalom, and Lord Shaftesbury as the false counselor Ahithophel. Some 20th-century works based on this theme are *Absalom* (1920), a translation of a Japanese play by Torahiko Kōri; Howard Spring's novel *O Absalom* (1938; later reissued in the U.S.A. as *My Son, My Son*); and William Faulkner's novel *Absalom, Absalom* (1936).

Some artists in the late Middle Ages interpreted Absalom's death as a prefiguration of the Crucifixion. Parts of the story occasionally appear in illuminated manuscripts, such as the Winchester Bible, a French *Bible moralisée* (1250) now in Toledo, and the 14th-century Anglo-Norman Queen Mary's Psalter (British Museum), which illustrates most of the biblical narrative. Absalom's end also appears in an Italian 15th-century pavement mosaic in Siena Cathedral. *The Reconciliation of David and Absalom* (1642) was painted by *Rembrandt. The Pillar of Absalom (Yad Avshalom), which stands on the traditional site of Absalom's burial place, is one of several sepulchral monuments in the Kidron Valley, Jerusalem, that date from the Second Temple and Roman periods. The monument is executed in the late Hellenistic style, however, and its link with Absalom does not predate the 16th century.

David's lament for Absalom has inspired a number of composers, notably Heinrich Schuetz, whose motet for bass solo and trombone quartet *Fili mi Absalon* (in *Symphoniae Sacrae* vol. 1 (1629), no. 13) is a masterly work. No less poignant is *Lugebat David Absalon: Absalon fili mi*, a four-voice motet by Josquin des Prés, written a century earlier. In the 16th century Jacob Hand (Gallus) arranged a notable setting of the lament. A number of oratorios, mainly of the 18th century, describe Absalom's rebellion and death. A recent composition is *David Weeps for Absalom* (1947), a work for voice and piano by David *Diamond. The Judeo-Spanish song "Triste estaba el Rey David" (arranged for choir by Joaquín Rodrigo, 1950), tells the story of Absalom's rebellion in romantic form.

BIBLIOGRAPHY: BIBLE: S. Yeivin, *Meḥkarim be-Toledot Yisrael ve-Arẓo* (1960), 196–7, 236–9; Tadmor, in: *Journal of World History*, 11 (1968), 49–57; Bright, Hist, 187–90; E.Auerbach, *Wueste und gelobtes Land*, 1 (1932), 201–2, 232–6, 273; Noth, Hist Isr, 199–200, 219–220; Alt, *Essays on Old Testament History and Religion* (1967), 318, 329; 297ff. **ADD. BIBLIOGRAPHY:** A Rofé, in: E. Blum (ed), *Mincha: Festgabe fuer Rolf Rendtdorff zum 75. Geburtstag* (2000), 217–28. AGGADAH: Ginzberg, Legends, 4 (1947), 94–5, 104–7; 6 (1946), 266ff. FOLKLORE: Z. Vilnay, *Legends of Palestine* (1932), 107–9. ARTS: L. Réau, *Iconographie de l'art chrétien*, 2, pt. 1 (1956), 125–38; T. Ehrenstein, *Das Alte Testament im Bilde* (1923), 577–601; *The Bible in Art* (1956), 173; EM, 1 (1965), 68–69.

ABSALOM (1) Judah Maccabaeus' ambassador in 164 B.C.E. (II Macc. 11:17). (2) The father of Mattathias and Jonathan, who both held high commands during the Maccabean wars (I Macc. 11:70 and 13:11; Jos., Ant., 13:161, 202). (3) The younger son of John Hyrcanus I. Upon the death of his father, Absalom was imprisoned by his brother Aristobulus I and released when Alexander Yannai ascended the throne. He played a prominent part in the defense of Jerusalem against Pompey, but was captured by him (Jos., Ant., 14:71; cf. Wars, 1:154). (4) Jewish partisan leader at the beginning of the Roman War. He was associated with the Sicarii leader *Menahem b. Judah, and called by Josephus "his most eminent supporter in his tyranny." When *Eleazar son of Ananias, the captain of the

Temple, turned against Menahem and assassinated him, Absalom shared his fate (Jos., Wars, 2:448). Because of his views regarding the Zealots and Qumran, Cecil *Roth identified him with the Absalom mentioned in the *Pesher* ("Commentary") on Habakkuk found at Qumran (1 QpHab), but few scholars would accept this. (5) The name Absalom appears on an ossuary from Givat ha-Mivtar and in a tomb inscription from Silwan, both dated to before 70 C.E. The name "abshi," perhaps an abbreviation of Absalom, appears in a deed on papyrus of 131 C.E. from Wadi Muraba'at. (6) A Late Hellenistic tomb monument named after Absalom, David's rebellious son (II Sam. 3:3), is situated in the Kidron Valley, west of the Temple Mount, in Jerusalem. The style of the tomb, which shows Orientalizing architectural influences, suggests a first century B.C.E. date for the time it was hewn. Recent work on this monument by J. Zias and E. Puech has brought to light a Byzantine inscription in Greek next to the entrance to the tomb which refers not to Absalom but to the father of John the Baptist. It reads: "This is the tomb of Zachariah, martyr, very pious priest, father of John."

BIBLIOGRAPHY: C. Roth, *The Dead Sea Scrolls: A New Historical Approach* (1965^2), 13–14, 74ff. **ADD. BIBLIOGRAPHY:** T. Ilan, *Lexicon of Jewish Names in Late Antiquity. Part I: Palestine 330 B.C.E–200 C.E.* (2002).

[Abraham Schalit and Cecil Roth / Shimon Gibson (2nd ed.)]

ABSALOM, MONUMENT OF. Situated in the Kidron Valley, close to the Temple Mount in Jerusalem, are a number of monumental rock-hewn tombs of which one has been attributed by tradition to Absalom in reference to II Samuel 18:18, where it is stated that Absalom set up for himself a "pillar" in the King's Valley. In Arabic it is known as "Tantour Firaoun" (pharaoh's crown). This monument is a prominent feature in the topography of Jerusalem and was frequently commented upon by travelers and pilgrims since medieval times. The monument is freestanding and the lower part was rock-cut, whereas the upper part – hat-like in appearance – was built out of finely carved ashlars in a local architectural style utilizing Hellenistic features. The monument has been studied by many scholars since the 19th century: C. Clermont-Ganneau dug there, H. Vincent made a detailed study, and a substantial study of this and the other funerary monuments in the Kidron Valley was made by N. Avigad in the 1950s. Excavations around the foot of the monument were made by E. Oren in the 1970s, but the results remain unpublished. Probably the best short descriptions appear in guidebooks published by K. Prag and J. Murphy-O'Connor. Access to the entrance to the inner tomb chamber is from the south. The entrance led to a rock-hewn chamber which was originally square with a bench within an *arcosolium* on the west side, with a ceiling with a sunken panel decorated with a central wreath and four circles in relief, and with a fine carved cornice along the junction between ceiling and walls. The style of the monument suggests a date late in the Early Roman period, i.e., the first century C.E., contrary to some scholars who have suggested a date in the first century B.C.E. The internal chamber underwent major changes in the Byzantine period, 4th–6th centuries C.E., and it was probably converted into a reclusive cell for a Byzantine monk. Above the entrance to the tomb are faint Greek inscriptions which were first recorded by J. Zias in 2000. According to Emile Puech, one of these inscriptions is of Byzantine age and mentions Zacharias, father of John the Baptist: "This is the tomb of Zachariah, martyr, very pious priest, father of John." The adjacent complex of tomb chambers associated with the monument contained a chapel and was held to mark the graves of St. Zacharias, St. Simeon, and St. James (the first bishop of Jerusalem) in the 12th century. Traces of medieval wall paintings are visible on some of the chamber walls. Within the interior chamber of the monument itself is a late medieval three-line Hebrew inscription ("Shamsi ben … [unclear]" – incorrectly read by Dalman in 1914) which was probably incised by a Jewish traveler to Jerusalem. In the 19th century a bridge for a road crossing over the Kidron Valley existed in front of the funerary monument and is evident in old photographs (e.g., F. Bedford, 1862).

BIBLIOGRAPHY: N. Slousch, "The Excavations Around the Monument of Absalom," in: *Proceedings of the Jewish Palestine Exploration Society*, 1 (1925), 7–30; G. Dalman, "Inschriften aus Palästina," in: ZDPV, 37:6 (1914), 137–38; N. Avigad, *Ancient Monuments in the Kidron Valley* (1954); K. Prag, *Jerusalem* (Blue Guide) (1989); J.M. O'Connor, *The Holy Land* (1992).

[Shimon Gibson (2nd ed.)]

ABSALON (1964–1993), Israeli sculptor. Absalon was born in Ashdod as Meir Eshel and adopted the name Absalon when he arrived in Paris in the late 1980s. He won his reputation as an artist from the 1:1 scale architectural models that he constructed of idealized living units. These wooden models, painted white, demonstrate an obsession with order, arrangement, and containment, and have associations both of protective shelters and monastic cells. His sculptures are reminiscent of the works of the Russian constructivists, the Dutch De Stijl, and Le Corbusier. His last exhibition was of *Six Cellules* in Paris in 1993. Absalon died of AIDS at the age of 28.

[Shaked Gilboa (2nd ed.)]

ABSE, DANNIE (1923–), English poet. Abse was born in Cardiff. After four years in the Royal Air Force in World War II he qualified as a doctor. From 1947 to 1954 he edited and published the magazine *Poetry and Poverty.* Although his work included fiction and drama, he was primarily a poet. Abse has thought deeply about the Holocaust, and his challenge to God to explain Himself to man (in "The Abandoned") is in the Hebraic tradition. His verse collections include *After Every Green Thing* (1949); *Walking Under Water* (1952); *Tenants of the House* (1957); *Poems. Golders Green* (1962); *Selected Poems* (1963); and *Small Desperation* (1968). He wrote two novels, *Ash on a Young Man's Sleeve* (1954) and *Some Corner of an English Field* (1956); and two dramas, *Fire in Heaven* (1956) and *Three Questor Plays* (1967). Abse's *White Coat; Purple Coat: Col-*

lected Poems 1948–1988 appeared in 1991. He has also written two volumes of autobiography, published in 1974 and 2001. His brother LEO ABSE (1917–) was a Labour member of the British Parliament for a Welsh seat from 1958 until 1997. He introduced bills liberalizing legislation governing homosexuality (1967) and divorce (1968). A solicitor, Leo Abse wrote "psychobiographies" of British politicians Margaret Thatcher and Tony Blair.

[Jon Silkin / William D. Rubinstein (2nd ed.)]

ABT, ISAAC ARTHUR (1867–1955), U.S. pediatrician. Abt, who was born in Wilmington, Illinois, served as professor of pediatrics at Northwestern University (1897–1902), Rush Medical College (1902–08), and again at Northwestern from 1908. He was the first president of the American Academy of Pediatrics (1931). Abt wrote prolifically on clinical, social, and experimental subjects in the field of pediatrics and wrote an encyclopedic eight-volume work *Pediatrics* (1923–36). The section dealing with nutritional disturbances in infancy is of particular significance. He was the first American pediatrician to use protein milk in the treatment of diarrhea in infants. His work *The Baby's Food* was published in 1917.

BIBLIOGRAPHY: S.R. Kagan, *Jewish Contributions to Medicine in America* (1939), 147–50; idem, *Jewish Medicine* (1952), 364; *Journal of the American Medical Association*, 159 (1955), 1785; Parmelee, in: B.S. Veeder (ed.), *Pediatric Profiles* (1957), 109–16.

[Suessmann Muntner]

ABTERODE (Abedroth, Aptrod), DAVID BEN MOSES ELIAKIM (d. 1728), rabbinic author. Apparently he was born at Abterode near Frankfurt where he served as *dayyan*. He wrote a commentary on *Sefer Ḥasidim* and glosses on liturgical poems. All his manuscripts were destroyed in the great fire of Frankfurt in 1711. His son Solomon (Zalman) rewrote from memory the commentary on *Sefer Ḥasidim* and published it together with the text (1724); other editions contain an abridged version of the commentary only. Jacob Emden criticized the commentary (*She'elot Ya'veẓ*, 1:160), which Joseph David *Sinzheim, the author's great-grandson, defended in his book *Yad David* (1799), 28d (on Shab. 81a).

BIBLIOGRAPHY: Michael, Or, no. 768; M. Horovitz, *Frankfurter Rabbinen*, 2 (1883), 73; idem, *Avnei Zikkaron* (1901), 202–3, no. 1938; J. Freimann, in: J. Wistinetzki (ed.), *Sefer Ḥasidim* (1924), 9; R. Margaliot (ed.), *Sefer Ḥasidim* (1957), 7 (introd.).

[Yehoshua Horowitz]

ABTSHUK, AVRAHAM (Avrom; 1897–1937), Soviet Yiddish writer and critic. Born in Lutsk, Volhynia, he lived in Kiev after 1921. In the late 1920s and 1930s he was associated with the Jewish Research Institute of the Ukrainian Academy of Science in Kiev. In 1926 he began contributing short stories to the Kharkov-based literary journal *Di Royte Velt* and is best known for *Hershl Shamay* (1929; part 2, 1934), an occasionally humorous narrative which deals with the industrialization of Jewish workers under the Soviets. Abtshuk's *Etyudn un Materyaln tsu der Geshikhte fun der Yidisher Literatur-Bavegung in F.S.R.R.* ("Studies and Materials for the History of the Yiddish Literature Movement in Soviet Russia," 1934) is important both as a document and as a source of documents; it contains minutes, letters, and resolutions of Yiddish literary groups in Kiev, Moscow, Kharkov, and Minsk. Abtshuk was associate editor of the proletarian writers' periodical *Prolit* (1928–32) and its successor *Farmest* (1933–37). Accused of Trotskyist tendencies and Jewish nationalism, allegedly evident in *Hershl Shamay*, he perished during the Stalinist "purges."

BIBLIOGRAPHY: A.Pomerantz, *Di Sovetishe Harugey Malkhes* (1962), 44–51, 428–9; LNYL, 1 (1956), 2–3. **ADD. BIBLIOGRAPHY:** G. Estraikh, in: *Slovo*, 7 (1994), 1–12.

[Leonard Prager / Gennady Estraikh (2nd ed.)]

ABU, Arabic word meaning "father of" used in personal names. Jews living in Islamic countries followed the Arab custom, and addressed one another by their *kunya* (Arabic, "nickname"). Originally, the *kunya* contained the word *abu*, and the name of a son of the person concerned, normally that of the eldest, e.g., a man whose son's name was Zayd, was called Abu Zayd. If there was no son in the family, this could not apply but, nonetheless, imaginary *kunyas* developed, and these predominated among Jews. Thus, persons called Abraham were often addressed as *Abu Isḥāq* ("Father of Isaac") or Jacob was known as *Abu Yūsuf* (Joseph) instead of Jacob. The reverse procedure was even more common. Since it was customary to call a child after his grandfather, the *kunya* often contained the names of the father of the biblical or other historical personality after whom the man was named. As the father of Moses was Amram (Arabic *ʿImrān*), as *Abu ʿImrān*. The word *abu* also denotes "possessor," especially of a certain quality. Well-known examples of this use are *Abu-al-ʿĀfiya* ("possessor of health") from which the family name *Abulafia is derived. The honorifics preferred by Jews were generally those expressive of abstract notions, both in the singular and plural, e.g., *Abu al-Saʿd* ("happiness") and *Abu al-Barakāt* ("blessings"). This might be compared to the Hebrew equivalents *Avi-Musar* (father of ethics, moral, moralist) and *Aḥi-Musar* (brother of ethics) used in Hebrew poetry. Sometimes two *kunyas* were given, one at birth and another added on some special occasion, such as recovery from a dangerous illness. Biblical and talmudic names were connected with *kunyas* believed to be of the same or similar meaning.

BIBLIOGRAPHY: EIS, 1 (1913), 73–74.

ABU AL-FAḌL HASDAY (late tenth century), Spanish scholar. According to the 13th-century Arab biographer Ibn Abī Uṣaybiʿa, Abu al-Faḍl, who lived in Saragossa, was a member of a distinguished Andalusian Jewish family of priestly descent. He was competent in medicine, philosophy, arithmetic, and music. He had a good knowledge of both Arabic and Hebrew. Moses ibn Ezra refers to Abu al-Faḍl as one who "acquired knowledge in all branches of science, was accomplished in philosophy, and well versed in Hebrew and Arabic poetry and prose."

BIBLIOGRAPHY: H.G. Farmer, *History of Arabian Music to the 13th Century* (1929), 221; M. Ibn Ezra, *Shirat Yisrael*, ed. by B. Halper (1924), 69; Ibn Abī Uṣaybiʿa, *ʿUyūn al-Anbāʾ fī Ṭabaqāt al-Aṭibbāʾ*, ed. by A. Mueller, 2 (Ar., 1884), 50.

[Amnon Shiloah]

ABU AL-FARAJ HARUN IBN AL-FARAJ (Heb. **Aaron b. Jeshuʿa**; Jerusalem, first half of 11th century), Karaite grammarian, lexicographer and exegete. Abu al-Faraj accepted the Greek theory (which reached him through Arabic channels) that language is an artificial product of human convention and is governed by the laws of logic. His method and terminology draw heavily on Arab linguists. He held that all forms of the Hebrew verb are based on the infinitive, and made a detailed study of the particle. He also pioneered the investigation of biblical Aramaic grammar in its relationship to Hebrew, as well as comparative treatment of Hebrew, Aramaic, and Arabic. He followed strictly the principle of bi-literal roots. The works of Abu al-Faraj became well known among Rabbanite scholars of Spain, who refer to him at times simply as "the Jerusalemite Grammarian." All his writings are in Judeo-Arabic. They include *Al-Kitāb al-Mushtamil*, on the roots and formations of the Hebrew language (mss. in St. Petersburg; among them the copy made in 1112 for the *gaon* Elijah b. Abiathar) of which chapter 8 treats Aramaic grammar; *Al-Kitāb al-Kāfī*, a digest of the former, published by G. Khan, M. Angeles Gallego, and J. Olszowy-Schlanger as *The Karaite tradition of Hebrew Grammatical Thought in Its Classical Form: A Critical Edition and English Translation of al-Kitāb al- kāfī fī al-luga al-'Ibrāniyya by Abu al-Faraj Hārūn ibn al-Faraj*, Leiden 2003; *Sharḥ al-Alfāẓ*, an Arabic translation of selected verses or clauses in the Bible, with explanatory notes, arranged in the order of the Bible; and a commentary on the Pentateuch in Arabic, said to be an abridgement (*talkhīṣ*) of that of *Joseph b. Noah, who was his teacher. Even though an abridgement, it is quite extensive; most of it survived in several fragmentary mss. in St. Petersburg. Another important contribution was his work on the phonetics of biblical Hebrew according to the Tiberian tradition and the rules of cantillation of the biblical text, entitled *Hidāyat al-Qāri* ("The Guide of the Reader"). Until quite recently it was ascribed to various other authors. The importance of the work lies in its uniqueness as a source for the living tradition in 11th-century Ereẓ Israel. The work was written in a long and short version. Of the former only short fragments have survived, while most of the latter was published in a critical annotated edition by I. Eldar (Jerusalem 1994). Various Hebrew and Judeo-Arabic adaptations had been circulating in the Middle Ages in Europe and the Near East, one of them a paraphrase by the Byzantine Karaite Joseph ha-Qustandini (11th century?), entitled *Adat Devorim*.

BIBLIOGRAPHY: Steinschneider, Arab Lit, no. 48; W. Bacher, *Die Anfaenge der hebraeischen Grammatik* (1895), 155ff.; H. Hirschfeld, *Literary History of Hebrew Grammarians and Lexicographers* (1926), 50ff.; Bacher, in: REJ, 30 (1895), 232–56; Poznański, *ibid.*, 33 (1896), 24–39, 197–218; 46 (1908), 42–69; idem, in: JQR, 18 (1927/28), 11; S.L. Skoss, *Arabic Commentary of Ali ben Suleiman on Genesis* (1928), 11–27. **ADD. BIBLIOGRAPHY:** G. Khan, in: M. Polliack (ed.), *Karaite Judaism: A Guide to Its History and Literary Sources* (2003), 291–318; A. Maman, *Comparative Semitic Philology in the Middle Ages: From Sa'adiah Gaon to Ibn Barun (10th–12th c.)* (2004), 375–80 and passim.

[Samuel Miklos Stern / Haggai Ben-Shammai (2nd ed.)]

ABU AL-FAT (Samaritan **Abi-Afeta Ban Ab-Ḥisdah**; 14th century), author of a Samaritan chronicle in Arabic, *Kitāb al-Tarīkh* ("Annals"). Born in Damascus of the Danati family, which was renowned for its scholars and scribes, Abu al-Fat went on a pilgrimage to Nablus in 1352. He was invited by the high priest Phinehas b. Joseph to write the history of his people from the creation of the world to his own time. Only in 1355, on a second visit to Nablus, was he able to start this undertaking. He brought with him three fragmentary chronicles in Hebrew and a *Silsila* (chain), i.e., a genealogical list of the Samaritan high priests beginning with *Aaron (Moses' brother) that came from the home of the high priest in Damascus; this was presumably the *Tolidah* (see *Samaritans, Language and Literature). The high priest in Nablus put at his disposal a number of chronicles in Hebrew and Arabic, among which was the still extant Samaritan *Book of Joshu* in Arabic. Another work in the otherwise unknown chronicle of Ẓadakah was rejected by Abu al-Fat as unreliable.

The 14th century was a time of revival for the Samaritan community in Nablus, and Abu al-Fat sought to make use of the scanty and dispersed source material still existing in his time before it might be lost. Like all medieval chronicles, his work contains much legendary material. The dating is not always accurate. Abu al-Fat wrote in Middle Arabic, and his language is colored by many Hebraisms, showing his dependence on the Pentateuch and in some places on other Hebrew scriptures. The occasional use of elegant Arabic rhetorical figures reveals that he was also versed in Arabic literature. Abu al-Fat's *Annals* end at the time of Muhammad, but, in accordance with Samaritan practice, various manuscripts were extended by later scribes. R. Payne-Smith began to edit the Arabic text together with a literal English translation (in M. Heidenheim's *Deutsche Vierteljahrschrift fuer englisch-theologische Forschung und Kritik* (1863), 303–35, 431–59), but discontinued his work with the appearance of E. Vilmar's scholarly edition *Abulfathi Annales Samaritani* (Gotha, 1865). Vilmar added a detailed introduction and short notes in Latin.

BIBLIOGRAPHY: A.E. Cowley, *Samaritan Liturgy*, 2 (1909), xix; J.A. Montgomery, *Samaritans* (1907, repr. 1968), 305–7; M. Gaster, *Samaritans…* (1925), 3, 99, 156–7; I. Ben-Zvi, *Sefer ha-Shomeronim* (1935), Samaritans (1964), 46.

[Ayala Loewenstamm]

ABU AL-ḤASAN OF TYRE (Samaritan **Ab-Ḥisda Aẓẓuri**; c. 11th century), Samaritan halakhist, exegete, and liturgical writer of priestly origin. His surname Aẓẓuri may designate his origin from either the Syrian town Ẓor (Tyre) or the village Zorta near Nablus. The first translation of the Samaritan Pentateuch into Arabic is ascribed to him; it was revised two centuries later by Abu Saʿīd (see *Samaritans, Language and Literature). His chief work, written in Arabic and called *Kitāb al-Tabbākh* ("Book of the Cook" or "Book of the Druggist," and called by the Samaritans themselves "Book of the Meat") is a compendium of oral law dealing with many aspects of Samaritan practice and belief. It includes many polemical passages against the Jews – *Rabbanites and Karaites alike – and against some Christian and Muslim tenets. His halakhic decisions are still valid in the Samaritan community.

Three of Abu al-Ḥasan's exegetical treatises in Arabic are extant: *Sharḥ Ašrat Addēbārem*, a commentary on the Ten Commandments (John Rylands Library, Manchester, Gaster Collection, Ms. 1929); a commentary on "*Ha'azinu*" (Deut. 32), known also as *al-Khuṭba al-Jāmiʿa* ("The General Sermon," *ibid.*, Gaster Collection, Ms. 1813); and *Kitāb al-Maʿād* ("Book of Resurrection"; Bodeleian Library, Oxford, Ms. Hunt. 350). In the last he adduces proofs from the Pentateuch for the Samaritan belief in the day of vengeance and recompense (Deut. 32:35) and for the rising of the dead from the dust of their graves. Verses from "*Ha'azinu*" form an important part of these proofs. As the above manuscripts are included in some copies of *Kitāb al-Ṭabbākh*, as parts of the entire compendium, it remains questionable whether they originally belonged to the compendium and later became independent works under the influence of copyists and scribes, or vice versa. Abu al-Ḥasan also became known as a liturgical writer. His hymns are composed in Hebrew and in 11th-century Aramaic.

BIBLIOGRAPHY: J.A. Montgomery, *Samaritans* (1907, repr. 1968), 293, 298; A.E. Cowley, *Samaritan Liturgy* (1909), 70, 79–81; 2 (1909), 869, 875; J. MacDonald, *Theology of the Samaritans* (1964), index; P.R. Weis in: BJRL, 30 (1946–47), 144–56; 33 (1950–51), 131–7; M. Gaster in: EIS, 4 (1934), 3–5 (Supplement); idem, *Samaritans…* (1925), 151–2; Z. Ben-Ḥayyim, *Ivrit ve-Aramit Nusaḥ Shomeron*, 1 (1957), 35 (introd.); 3, pt. 2 (1967), 17, 277–80; A.S. Halkin, in: *Leshonenu*, 32 (1968), 208–46.

[Ayala Loewenstamm]

ABU AL-MUNAJJĀ SOLOMON BEN SHAYA (12th century), government official in Egypt. His Hebrew name was Solomon b. Shaya and he was also known as *Sanīʿ al Dawla* ("The Noble [exalted] of the State"). Abu al-Munajjā was responsible for the administration of several districts in eastern Egypt and became famous for digging an irrigation canal (1113–18) which greatly benefited agriculture. The vizier al-Afḍal, the regent, was jealous of him because the canal was called *Baḥr Abu al-Munajjā* (the canal of Abu al-Munajjā) and the regent wanted it to bear his name. The enemies of the Jews defamed him with the result that he was exiled to Alexandria and imprisoned without a trial. After several years he freed himself by a ruse. Among the *genizah* fragments were found poems in his honor which recount the story of his case until he was finally reinstated. He is described as a benefactor of the Jews. According to Arab authors, Abu al-Munajjā was the ancestor of a family of physicians, Banu al-Safīr, mostly converts to Islam who served as the court physicians of the Egyptian rulers.

BIBLIOGRAPHY: A. al-Maqrīzī, *Khiṭaṭ 1*, 71ff., 487ff.; Ibn Doukmak, *Description de l'Egypte* (1893), 47; Mann, Egypt, 1 (1920), 215–7; 2 (1922), 264–9; Fischel, Islam, 87–88, n.4.

[Eliyahu Ashtor]

ABU AWEIGILA (Ar. **Abu ʿAweiqila**), strategic position in eastern Sinai, about 19 road mi. (30 road km.) W. of *Niẓanah. Situated near the course of Wadi el-Arish, at a road fork connected with el-Arish in the northwest and with Ismailiya in the west, it was a battlefield in the 1948, 1956, and 1967 wars. In one of the last battles of the War of Independence Israeli forces drove the Egyptians from ʿAslūj (near *Revivim) through Niẓana to Abu Aweigila, and from there moved on in the direction of el-Arish. During the Sinai Campaign the capture of the stronghold ultimately decided the outcome of the war. Before the Six-Day War (June 1967) the Egyptians extended their fortifications for many kilometers to all sides of Abu Aweigila and stationed a division in the area. The capture of the position enabled the Israeli Army to break through to the entire Sinai Peninsula.

[Efraim Orni]

ABUDARHAM (Heb. אבודרהם; also **Abudarhan**, **Abudarhen**, **Abudaram**, **Abudaran**; Ar. "father of coins" meaning "the rich man"), Spanish family. DAVID BEN SOLOMON ABUDARHAM constructed in the 13th century the synagogue of Almaliquin in Toledo, apparently identical with the Abudarham synagogue destroyed in the riots of 1391. He was probably the grandfather of the liturgical scholar David b. Joseph *Abudarham. Another DAVID ABUDARHAM in the same period was a tax farmer in Toledo: when tax assessment was assigned to the Jewish communities of Castile in 1290, it was decided that in case of dispute David was to render final decision. After the expulsion from Spain in 1492 the family was scattered throughout Italy and North Africa. MOSES and ISAAC ABUDARHAM gave hospitality to David *Reuveni in Rome in 1524. JUDAH ABUDARHAM, a fugitive from the Inquisition, became purveyor to the Portuguese in Agadir. After 1541 the family settled in Tetuan where it long provided the community with spiritual and political leaders. Another JUDAH ABUDARHAM was among the founders of the Gibraltar community; one of the Gibraltar synagogues, founded in 1820, still bears the family name. A third JUDAH ABUDARHAM represented France in Tetuan for 30 years.

BIBLIOGRAPHY: Baer, Spain, 1 (1961), 214; Baer, Urkunden, index; Roth, in: JQR, 39 (1948/49), 132; Steinschneider, *ibid.*, 10 (1897/98), 130; Kaufmann, in: REJ, 38 (1899), 254; I.Benwalid, *Va-Yomer Yiẓḥak*

(1855), 182a–187a; J.M.Toledano, *Ner ha-Ma'arav* (1911), 158, 192, 200; Miège, Maroc, 2 (1961), 107, 174, 547; Millás Vallicrosa, in: A. González Palencia, *Los mozárabes de Toledo en los siglos XII y XIII*, 3 (1928), 563–95.

[Zvi Avneri and David Corcos]

ABUDARHAM, DAVID BEN JOSEPH (14th century), liturgical commentator in Spain, author of *Sefer Abudarham*, written in 1340 in Seville. Abudarham came from a distinguished family, and apparently an earlier namesake was a communal leader in Toledo. Abudarham was moved to write his book, like *Asher b. Saul of Lunel before him, because "the customs connected with prayer have become varied from one country to another, and most of the people do not understand the words of the prayers, nor do they know the correct ritual procedures and the reasons for them." The book is based on the Talmud and the decisions of the *geonim*, and on the early and later commentators. It abounds in source material of Spanish, Provencal, French, and Ashkenazi origins, not all of which has otherwise survived. Abudarham made extensive use of the prayer book of Saadiah Gaon, and it seems he was the last to see and use an original of this book. He also utilized the *Manhig* of *Abraham b. Nathan ha-Yarḥi of Lunel and the *Minhagot* of Asher b. Saul, the legal dicta of *Asher b. Jehiel, and the *Turim*. Some scholars think he was a disciple of *Jacob b. Asher, author of the *Turim*. Abudarham commented upon the prayers in great detail and traced the variations in custom in different countries. He included a commentary on the Passover *Haggadah*, rules of intercalation, the order of weekly pentateuchal readings and *haftarot* for the entire year, and calendrical and astronomical tables. Abudarham appended to his book rules governing benedictions, dividing them into nine sections, along with their interpretation and explanation. His book was first published in Lisbon in 1490 and has since been republished frequently. H.J. Ehrenreich began an edition of it in Klausenberg in 1927, based upon a different manuscript together with an extensive commentary, but did not complete it. An edition, known as *Abudarham ha-Shalem* with variant readings, according to the same manuscript, introduction, and supercommentary, by S.A. Wertheimer, was published in Jerusalem (1959, 1963) by his grandson. However, a comprehensive critical edition of this book is still lacking. Abudarham also wrote a commentary on liturgy for the Day of Atonement ascribed to *Yose b. Yose, as well as on other liturgical poems (published under the title of *Tashlum Abudarham*).

BIBLIOGRAPHY: Michael, Or, no. 729; A.L. Prinz (ed.), *Tashlum Abudarham* (1900), introd.; Ḥ. Tchernowitz, *Toledot ha-Posekim*, 2 (1947), 247–50; A.J. Wertheimer (ed.), *Abudarham ha-Shalem* (1963²), introd., 393–6.

[Zvi Avneri]

ABU GHOSH, Israeli Arab village in the Judean Hills 8 mi. (13 km.) W. of Jerusalem. Its area consists of 1 sq. mi. (2.5 sq. km.). In 1968 Abu Ghosh had a population of 1,710, 98% of them Muslims, and the rest Christians. In 2003 the population was 5,200. In 1992 the village received municipal council status. The village's agricultural economy was based on grain and vegetables, vines, olives, and deciduous fruit. Income levels were about half the national average in 2004.

Biblical *Kiriath-Jearim lies within its boundaries. Its name from the Arab conquest (seventh century) was Qaryat al-ʿInab ("Borough of the Grapevine"). The name Abu Ghosh stems from a high-handed 17th-century sheikh of Circassian origin, who controlled the region and whose heirs imposed a toll on every traveler to and from Jerusalem, until an end was put to the extortions at the time of the Egyptian governor Ibrahim Pasha, around 1835. After the establishment of the nearby kibbutzim *Kiryat Anavim (1920) and *Ma'aleh ha-Ḥamishah (1938), relations between the villagers and Jews were friendly and remained so in the Israeli War of Independence. Some of the villagers cooperated with the *Haganah and with *Loḥamei Ḥerut Israel. Abu Ghosh has a Catholic monastery and a convent. The village includes a well-preserved crusader church built at the spot around 1142 because the site was then held to be *Emmaus of the New Testament. The church was partially destroyed in 1187 and rebuilt by the French government in 1899. It is under the guardianship of the Lazarist Fathers. A stone inserted in its wall bears the imprint of the Roman Tenth Legion (*Fretensis*), apparently stationed here in the first century C.E. The Josephine Convent of the Ark, built in 1924, stands supposedly on the site of the house of *Abinadab (II Sam. 6). From 1957, an annual music festival was held in the village. Nearby is Aqua Bella (Heb. Ein Ḥemed), a partially destroyed 12th-century crusader monastery, which has been made into a national park.

[Abraham J. Brawer / Shaked Gilboa (2nd ed.)]

ABU ʿIMRĀN AL-TIFLĪSĪ (**Abu ʿImram Mūsā al-Ẓafārānī**), founder of a Jewish religious sect in the ninth century. He emigrated from Iraq to *Tiflis, in Georgia, hence the designation al-Tiflīsī. Information about him is to be found in the writings of his Karaite opponents, among them, al-Kirkisānī. Al-Tiflīsī developed his own *halakhah*. While agreeing with accepted Karaite views, such as the Karaite dating of the Feast of Weeks and the prohibitions of the marriage of first cousins and eating the tail fat of sheep, he devised his own method of determining the occurrence of *Rosh Ḥodesh* ("New Moon"). According to *Japheth b. Ali ha-Levi, a tenth-century Karaite, al-Tiflīsī rejected the doctrine of resurrection. This, however, is doubtful, for his other opponents would have attacked al-Tiflīsī for such a deviation. The sect of Tiflisites survived several generations after the death of its founder, as evidenced by Judah Hadassi's 12th-century *Eshkol ha-Kofer*.

BIBLIOGRAPHY: Nemoy, in: HUCA, 7 (1930), 389; S. Pinsker, *Likkutei Kadmoniyyot*, 1 (1860), 26; Z. Ankori, *Karaites in Byzantium* (1959), 369–71.

[Eliyahu Ashtor]

ABU ʿĪSĀ, ISAAC BEN JACOB AL-IṢFAHĪNĪ, founder of a Jewish sect in Persia, the first to be formed after the destruction of the Second Temple. Abu ʿĪsā was also called Obadiah, evidently an honorific bestowed on him by his admirers. According to the Karaite scholar al-*Kirkisānī, Abu ʿĪsā lived during the reign of Caliph ʿAbd al-Malik ibn *Marwān (685–705); the Arabic historian Shahrastāni places him during the reigns of the Umayyad caliph Marwān ibn Muhammad (744–50) and al-Mansur (754–75). The latter period seems correct because the religious and political ferment in the Islamic world during the eighth century forms the suitable background for the establishment of the sect. Abu ʿĪsā proclaimed himself a prophet and herald of the Messiah. He led a revolt against the Muslims, and many Persian Jews rallied behind him. After several years the rebellion was suppressed. His army was defeated by the Muslims near the ancient city of Rhagae (present-day Rai) southeast of Teheran, and Abu ʿĪsā himself was killed. His followers did not believe that he was dead but rather that he had entered a cave and disappeared. According to another tradition, he placed his followers in a circle which he drew with a myrtle branch and they remained beyond reach of the enemy. Only Abu ʿĪsā rode out of the area and dealt the Muslims a mighty blow single-handedly. He afterward went to the "Sons of Moses" beyond the desert to prophesy to them. The sect which Abu ʿĪsā founded, known as the Isunians or Isfahanians, still existed in the time of al-Kirkisānī (c. 930), who found about 20 adherents in Damascus. The movement launched by his disciple *Yudghan and the early activities of *Anan b. David reflect the influence of Abu ʿĪsā's teachings. His followers maintained that Abu ʿĪsā had been an illiterate tailor who wrote his books through prophetic inspiration. He taught that five prophets, among them Jesus and Muhammad, preceded the coming of the Messiah and that he himself was the final harbinger. Basing himself on Psalm 119:164 ("Seven times daily do I praise Thee"), he ordained seven daily prayers for his followers, but did not reject recitation of the **Shema* and the *Amidah* or observance of the holy days as practiced by *Rabbanites. The latter regarded the Isunians as legitimate Jews in all respects. That the Isunians tended to be stringent is evidenced in their prohibition of meat and wine and their ban on divorce.

BIBLIOGRAPHY: Friedlaender, in: JQR, 1 (1910/11), 203ff.; 2 (1911/12), 481ff.; Nemoy, in: HUCA, 7 (1930), 328, 382–3; Poznański, in: *Reshumot*, 1 (1925), 209–13; A.Z. Aešcoly, *Ha-Tenuʿot ha-Meshiḥiyyot be-Yisrael*, 1 (1956), 100–2, 117–26; Dinur, Golah, 228–31.

[Zvi Avneri]

ABUKARA, ABRAHAM BEN MOSES (d. 1879), Tunisian rabbi. Abukara was probably the grandson of Abraham Abukara (d. 1817), one of the scholars of Tunis, who in 1803 signed a regulation introducing uniformity in various religious practices. A profound scholar, Abraham wrote a commentary and novellae on the Shulḥan Arukh, *Yoreh De'ah*, in four parts. The first part, *Beit ha-Safek* (on the laws in case of "doubt"), was published by his relative Jacob b. Elijah Abukara, who added an introduction under the title *Ben Avraham* (Leghorn, 1882). The other parts were lost. Jacob also published the *Issur ve-Hetter* of *Jeroham b. Meshullam from a manuscript in the collection of Abraham, together with *Ben Avraham*.

BIBLIOGRAPHY: D. Cazès, *Notes bibliographiques sur la littérature juive-tunisienne* (1893), 29–32; B. Wachstein, *Mafte'aḥ ha-Hespedim*, 1 (1922), 3; Hirschberg, Afrikah, 2 (1965), 135; Ta-Shema, in: *Sinai*, 64 (1969).

ABULAFIA (Heb. אַבּוּלְעָפִיָה; Arabic for "father of health"; also **Abulaffia**, **Abulefia**, **Abualefia**, **Abu Alafia**, etc.), widespread and influential family, members of which were rabbis, poets, statesmen, and communal leaders in Spain. After the expulsion of the Jews from Spain the name became common in some Oriental countries. A distinguished rabbinical family was established in Palestine and Syria after Ḥayyim ben Moses (?) Abulafia moved from Smyrna to Tiberias. The most important Spanish branch, centered in Toledo from the 12th century, were levites and generally called Levi (Arabic Al-lavi) Abulafia, etc. The epitaphs of many members of the family, sometimes obsequiously phrased, are preserved; they included (beside those subsequently mentioned in individual articles) the physician Moses ben Meir (1255); Joseph ben Meir, rabbi in Seville, perhaps his grandson (1341); the communal leaders and royal officials Meir ben Joseph, Samuel, and Meir ben Solomon (victims of the Black Death, 1349–50); and Samuel ben Meir (1380). Samuel Abolafia of Almeria was in charge of the commissariat for the Catholic monarchs during the campaign against Granada in 1484. The New Christian magistrate Juan Fernandez Abolafia participated in the plot against the *Inquisition in Seville and was a victim of the first *auto-da-fé there in 1481. Joseph David Abulafia (I) (d. 1823), was *av bet din* in Tiberias before 1798 and later rabbi in Damascus. He signed letters of introduction for the emissaries of Tiberias as did his grandson Joseph David Abulafia (II) (d. 1898), who was also rabbi in Tiberias. Moses and Jacob Abulafia were among the Jews arrested in Damascus in 1840 in connection with the *Damascus blood libel: the former, designated as a rabbi, informed against his coreligionists. Isaac Abulafia was rabbi in Damascus (1876–88). In Italy in modern times the name was rendered as Bolaffio, Bolaffi, etc. It is said that the first Jew to settle in Spain in the modern period was an Abulafia from Tunis.

BIBLIOGRAPHY: Baer, Spain, index; Baer, Urkunden, index; *Sefarad* (1957), index volume; Cantera-Millás, Inscripciones, index. **ADD. BIBLIOGRAPHY:** J.C. Gómez Menor, in: *I Congreso internacional "Encuentro de las tres culturas"* (1983), 185–93.

[Cecil Roth]

ABULAFIA, ABRAHAM BEN SAMUEL (1240–after 1291), founder of the prophetic Kabbalah. Born in Saragossa, Spain, Abulafia moved to Tudela in his childhood and studied with his father until the latter's death in 1258. In 1260 he left Spain for the Land of Israel in search for the legendary *Sambatyon river. However, the war between the Mongols and Mamluks in 1260 caused his return to Europe, via Greece. He studied in the early 1260s in Capua with R. Hillel of Verona, concentrating basically the *Guide of the Perplexed*, and then returned to Spain. In 1270 he began to study a particular kind of Kabbalah in Barcelona, whose most important representative was Barukh Togarmi, and received a revelation with messianic overtones. He soon left for Castile, where he disseminated his prophetic Kabbalah among figures like R. *Moses of Burgos and R. Joseph *Gikatilla. Some time around 1275 he taught the *Guide of the Perplexed* and his Kabbalah in a few cities in Greece and in 1279 he made his way through Trani to Capua, where he taught four young students. In the summer of 1280 he arrived in Rome and attempted to see the Pope Nicholas III in order to discuss his vision of Judaism as a mystical religion. This meeting was part of a messianic scheme. However, the pope died suddenly and Abulafia was imprisoned for some weeks and then left for Messina, Sicily. There he was active for a decade (1281–91) and had several students as well as some in Palermo. Around 1285 a polemic commenced between him and R. Solomon ben Abraham ibn *Adret of Barcelona concerning Abulafia's claims that he was a prophet and messiah. This controversy was one of the principal reasons for the exclusion of Abulafia's Kabbalah from the Spanish schools.

Abulafia's literary activity spans the years 1271–91 and consists of several dozen books, treatises on grammar, and poems. He wrote many commentaries: three on the *Guide of the Perplexed* – *Sefer ha-Ge'ulah* (1273), *Sefer Ḥayyei ha-Nefesh*, and *Sefer Sitrei Torah* (1280); on *Sefer Yeẓirah*: – *Oẓar Eden Ganuz*, (1285/6), *Gan Na`ul*, and a third untitled; and a commentary on the Pentateuch – *Sefer-MafteḥOt ha-Torah* (1289). More influential are his handbooks, teaching how to achieve the prophectic experience: *Ḥayyei ha-Olam ha-Ba* (1280), *Or ha-Sekhel*, *Sefer ha-Ḥeshek*, and *Imrei Shefer* (1291). Of special importance for understanding his messianology are his "prophetic books" written between 1279 (Patras) and 1288 (Messina), where revelations including apocalyptic imagery and scenes are interpreted as pointing to spiritual processes of inner redemption. The spiritualized understanding of the concepts of messianism and redemption as an intellectual development represents a major contribution of the messianic ideas in Judaism. As part of his messianic propensity, Abulafia become an intense disseminator of his Kabbalah, orally and in written form, trying to convince both Jews and Christians.

In his first treatises, *Get ha-Shemot* and *Mafte'aḥ ha-Re`ayon*, Abulafia describes a linguistic type of Kabbalah similar to the early writings of R. Joseph Gikatilla. In his later writings, the founder of prophetic Kabbalah produces a synthesis between Maimonides' Neoaristotelian understanding of prophecy as the result of the transformation of the intellectual influx into a linguistic message and techniques to reach such experiences by means of combinations of letters and their pronunciation, breathing exercises, contemplation of parts of the body, movements of the head and hands, and concentration exercises. Some of the elements of those techniques stem from commentaries on *Sefer Yeẓirah* of Ashkenazi origin, while others reflect influences of Yoga, Sufism, and hesychasm. He called his Kabbalah "the Kabbalah of names," that is, of divine names, being a way to reach what he called the prophetic experience, or "prophetic Kabbalah," as the ultimate aims of his way: unitive and revelatory experiences. In his writings expressions of what is known as the *unio mystica* of the human and the supernal intellects may be discerned. Much less concerned with the theosophy of his contemporary kabbalists, who were interested in theories of ten hypostatic *sefirot*, some of which he described as worse than the Christian belief in the trinity, Abulafia depicted the supernal realm, especially the cosmic Agent Intellect, in linguistic terms, as speech and letters.

In his later books, Abulafia repeatedly elaborated upon a system of seven paths of interpretation, which he used sometimes in his commentary on the Pentateuch, which starts with the plain sense, includes also allegorical interpretation, and culminates in interpretations of the discrete letters, the latter conceived of as the path to prophecy. Abulafia developed a sophisticated theory of language, which assumes that Hebrew represents not so much the language as written or spoken as the principles of all languages, namely the ideal sounds and the combinations between them. Thus, Hebrew as an ideal language emcompasses all the other languages. This theory of language might have influenced *Dante Alighieri. In his writings Abulafia uses Greek, Latin, Italian, Arabic, Tatar, and Basconian words for purpose of gematria.

Abulafia's Kabbalah inspired a series of writings which can be described as part of his prophetic Kabbalah, namely, as striving to attain extreme forms of mystical experiences. The most important among them are the anonymous *Sefer ha-Ẓeruf* (translated into Latin for *Pico), *Sefer Ner Elohim*, and *Sefer Sha`arei Ẓedek* by R. Nathan ben Saadiah Harar, who influenced the Kabbalah of R. *Isaac of Acre. The impact of Abulafia is evident in an anonymous epistle attributed to Maimonides; R. Reuven Ẓarfati, a kabbalist active in 14th century Italy; Abraham *Shalom, Johanan *Alemanno, Judah *Albotini, and Joseph ibn Zagyah; Moses *Cordovero and Ḥayyim *Vital's influential *Sha`arei Kedushah*; *Shabbetai Ẓevi, Joseph *Hamiẓ, Phinehas Elijah Horowitz, and *Menahem Mendel of Shklov.

Extant in many manuscripts, Abulafia's writings were not printed by kabbalists, most of whom banned his brand of Kabbalah, and only by chance introduced in their writings a few short and anonymous fragments. Scholarship started with an analysis of his manuscript writings by M.H. Landauer, who attributed the book of the *Zohar* to him. A. Jellinek refuted this attribution and compiled the first comprehensive list of Abulafia's writings, publishing three of Abulafia's shorter treatises (two epistles, printed in 1853/4, and *Sefer ha-Ot* in 1887), while Amnon Gross, published 13 volumes, which include most of Abulafia's book and those of his students' books (Jerusalem, 1999–2004). Major contributions to the analysis of Abulafia's thought and that of his school have been made by Gershom Scholem and Chaim Wirszubski. Some of Abulafia's treatises were translated into Latin and Italian in the circle of Pico della Mirandola, mostly by Flavius Mithridates, and Pico's vision of Kabbalah was significantly influenced by his views. This is the case also with Francesco Giogio Veneto's *De Harmonia Mundi*. Abulafia's life inspired a series of literary works such poems by Ivan Goll, Moses Feinstein, and Nathaniel Tarn; Umberto Eco's novel *Foucault's Pendulum*; and a George-Elie Bereby's play; in art, Abraham Pincas's paintings and Bruriah Finkel's sculptures; and several musical pieces.

BIBLIOGRAPHY: A. Berger, in: *Essays … S.W. Baron* (1959), 55–61, U. Eco, *The Search for the Perfect Language* (1995); M. Idel, *The Mystical Experience in Abraham Abulafia* (1988); idem, *Language, Torah and Hermeneutics in Abraham Abulafia* (1989); idem, *Studies in Ecstatic Kabbalah* (1988); idem, *Messianic Mystics* (1998), ch. 2; *Natan ben Sa'adyah Har'ar, Le Porte della Giustizia*, a Cura di Moshe Idel (2001); R. Kiener, "From *Ba'al ha-Zohar* to Prophet to Ecstatic: The Vicissitudes of Abulafia in Contemporary Scholarship," in: P. Schaefer and J. Dan (eds.), *Gershom Scholem's Major Trends in Jewish Mysticism, 50 Years After* (1993), 117–44; M.H. Landauer, in: *Literaturblatt des Orients*, 6 (1845), 322ff.; Scholem, Mysticism, ch. 4;. Ch. Wirszubski, *Pico della Mirandola's Encounter with Jewish Mysticism* (1988); E.R. Wolfson, *Abraham Abulafia: Hermeneutics, Theosophy, and Theurgy* (2000).

[Moshe Idel (2nd ed.)]

ABULAFIA (Bolaffi), EZEKIEL (Hezekiah) DAVID BEN MORDECAI (18th century), Italian scholar and poet. His family originated in Aquileia, but he himself lived first in Leghorn and then in Trieste, where he married the daughter of R. Isaac Formiggini. He began to write at the age of 13, but his early compositions (including an elegy on the victims of the disaster in the Mantua ghetto in 1776) were lost. His only published work was *Ben Zekunim* (1793). The first part, entitled *Yesod Olam*, is an introduction to the Talmud for young people, based on the *Halikhot Olam* of *Jeshua b. Joseph ha-Levi. The final section quotes commendatory statements on the Talmud by gentile scholars such as *Galatinus and *Basnage. The second part, *Mizmor le-David*, contains miscellaneous poems and elegies, revealing a fair knowledge of classical mythology and literature, and closes with patriotic poems, e.g., on the educational reforms of Emperor Joseph II. The preface embodies a vigorous vindication of the Hebrew language. An early work on Psalms, *Shiggayon le-David*, has been lost.

BIBLIOGRAPHY: Schirmann, Italyah, 461–2; A.M. Habermann, *Mivḥar ha-Shirah ha-Ivrit*, 2 (1965), 148–50.

[Cecil Roth]

ABULAFIA, ḤAYYIM BEN DAVID (c. 1700–1775), rabbi and codifier. Abulafia, a grandson of Ḥayyim ben Jacob Abulafia, was born either in Jerusalem or in Smyrna. He studied under Isaac *Rappaport, author of *Battei Kehunnah*. About 1740 he was appointed rabbi of Larissa (Greece). Among his many pupils was Joseph Naḥmoli, author of *Ashdot ha-Pisgah*. In 1755, as a result of tribulations suffered by the community, he left for Salonika, where he apparently remained, acting as *av bet din*, until 1761. In that year the Sephardi rabbi of Amsterdam, Isaac ibn Dana de Brito, died and Abulafia was invited to succeed him. But Jacob Saul, the rabbi of Smyrna, died at the same time and, when Abulafia was invited to fill his position, he accepted the invitation. Many of Abulafia's halakhic decisions are found in the works of Turkish scholars, who often sought his approbation for their works. Most of his own works were destroyed in the great fire of Smyrna of 1772 – including the major part of a large work on the *Sefer Mitzvot Gadol* of Moses of Coucy. Part of it was published posthumously together with his responsa *Nishmat Ḥayyim* (Salonika, 1806). Parts of his works were printed with the above-mentioned *Ashdot ha-Pisgah* (1790). Ḥayyim *Modai, his successor in the Smyrna rabbinate, was his pupil.

BIBLIOGRAPHY: M. Benayahu, in: *Horeb*, 10 (1947/48), 27–34; I.S. Emmanuel, *Maẓẓevot Saloniki*, 1 (1963).

ABULAFIA, ḤAYYIM BEN JACOB (I) (1580–1668), Palestinian talmudist, known as the First. After studying in Safed, Abulafia was ordained by his father in about 1618. In 1628 Abulafia settled in Jerusalem and later moved to Hebron, where despite his advanced age he directed the yeshivah. He was one of the leading rabbis of his era. In 1651–52 Abulafia was a central figure in the controversy over the election of a new rabbi of the Hebron community and went to Cairo to enlist the support of the influential Raphael Joseph, head of Egyptian Jewry, and arrange a compromise. When Nathan of Gaza began his propaganda in support of Shabbetai Zevi, Abulafia adopted a negative attitude similar to that of his father toward the visions of Ḥayyim *Vital. Although he was skeptical, he wished to avoid open conflict, and did not threaten excommunication as did his father in the case of the latter. In 1666 he was one of the delegation of four who went to Gaza on behalf of the Constantinople community to investigate the authenticity of Nathan's prophecies, and about this time he returned to live in Jerusalem. His grandson was Ḥayyim ben Jacob *Abulafia (II), who renewed Jewish settlement in Tiberias in 1740.

BIBLIOGRAPHY: M. Benayahu, *Rabbi Ḥayyim Yosef David Azulai* (1959), 293–302; Ben-Zvi, Eretz; Scholem, Shabbetai Ẓevi, 221, 228, 511. **ADD. BIBLIOGRAPHY:** M.D. Gaon, *Yehudei ha-Mizraḥ be-Ereẓ Yisrael*, 2 (1938), 7.

ABULAFIA, ḤAYYIM BEN JACOB (II) (c. 1660–1744), rabbi, known as the Second. He is grandson of Hayyim ben Jacob *Abulafia the First. About 1666 the Abulafia family moved from Hebron to Jerusalem, where Hayyim studied with Moses Galante and others. In 1699 he went on a mission to Salonika, and in 1712 he served as rabbi in Smyrna and in 1718 in Safed where he remained until 1721, when he was reappointed rabbi of Smyrna, living there for almost 20 years.

Abulafia believed in the imminence of the messianic era and considered the restoration of *Tiberias, which had been in ruins for almost 70 years, a necessary prerequisite to it. Sheikh Dahir al-'Amr, the ruler of Galilee, invited him to "come up and take possession of the land." In 1740 he moved from Smyrna to Tiberias. Despite his advanced age, Abulafia began rebuilding the city, and he sent his sons and sons-in-law abroad to enlist aid for the restoration. According to diverse legends, he planted gardens, vineyards, and fields, and built a glorious synagogue and *bet midrash*, a bathhouse, a press for sesame oil, stores for market day, established the Rabbi Meir Baal Haness Fund, and sent his two sons on missions abroad to collect money; he also built houses and courtyards for his fellow Jews.

In 1742–43 war broke out between Suleiman, pasha of Damascus, and Dahir. Abulafia encouraged the Jews to remain in Tiberias and gave full support to the sheikh. In the two campaigns, which ensued – the first of which ended on the 4th of Kislev 1743 and the second ending with the death of Suleiman on the 5th of Elul – the sheikh was victorious. Abulafia declared these two dates as holidays, which the Jews of Tiberias continued to observe annually. He died in Tiberias on the 16th of Nisan 5504.

Abulafia was a prolific author, but only those of his works which he published while in Smyrna have appeared in print: (1) *Yashresh Ya'akov* (1729), on the *Ein Ya'akov*; (2) *Mikra'ei Kodesh* (1729), on the laws of Passover, on Esther, homilies, and novellae on the Talmud and Maimonides; (3) *Eẓ ha-Hayyim* (1729), on the weekly portions; (4) *Yosef Lekaḥ*, pt. one on Genesis and Exodus; pt. two on Leviticus (1730); pt. three on Numbers and Deuteronomy (1732); (5) *Shevut Ya'akov* (1734), on the *Ein Ya'akov*; (6) *Ḥanan Elohim* (1737), on the Pentateuch, appended to *Hayyim va-Ḥesed*, by his grandfather, Isaac Nissim b. Gamil.

BIBLIOGRAPHY: L. Kopf, in: KS, 39 (1964), 273–9; Ben Zvi, Eretz Israel, index; M. Benayahu, ed. *Zimrat ha-Areẓ* (1946), intro. **ADD. BIBLIOGRAPHY:** M.D. Gaon, *Yehudei ha-Mizraḥ be-Ereẓ Yisrael*, 2 (1938), 7.

ABULAFIA, ḤAYYIM NISSIM BEN ISAAC (1775–1861), rabbi and communal worker, known also, from the initial letters of his name, as "Ḥana." Born in Tiberias, he succeeded his father as the head of the Jews of Tiberias. He was for a short time rabbi of Damascus. After the defeat of the Egyptian commander *Ibrahim Pasha by the Turks (1840), when some of the Arab sheikhs began to seize control of the villages and towns abandoned by the Egyptians and oppressed and maltreated their Jewish inhabitants, Abulafia asked the commander of the Turkish forces in Sidon (Saida) and Tripoli to take action to stop these acts. The latter immediately had instructions dispatched to the governor of Safed forbidding persecution of the Jews. Toward the end of his life Abulafia moved to Jerusalem and, in 1854, he was elected *rishon le-Zion* succeeding Isaac *Covo. In Jerusalem he supported Ludwig August *Frankl in the founding of the Laemel school. His writings have remained in manuscript, except for individual responsa published in the works of his contemporaries.

BIBLIOGRAPHY: Frumkin-Rivlin, 3 (1929), 279–81; M.D. Gaon, *Yehudei ha-Mizraḥ be-Ereẓ Yisrael*, 2 (1937), 7–8; Yaari, Sheluḥei, index, s.v.; J.M. Toledano, *Oẓar Genazim* (1960), index; I. Ben Zvi, *Meḥkarim u-Mekorot* (1966), index (*Ketavim*, vol. 3).

[Abraham David]

ABULAFIA, ISAAC (d. 1764), talmudist and emissary for Ereẓ Israel. Abulafia was the son of Ḥayyim ben Moses (?) Abulafia. He immigrated with his father to Tiberias in 1740. Active in the rebuilding of Tiberias, he went in 1743 as an emissary for this purpose to Damascus and probably to other places as well. He was appointed by his father to succeed him as rabbi and as leader of the community of Tiberias, and held these offices for 20 years. In 1764 he was appointed by the leaders of the Jerusalem community as a member of a delegation that went to Constantinople to have Raḥamim ha-Kohen removed from office as representative of "Pekidei Ereẓ Israel be-Kushta" ("The Representatives of the Land of Israel in Constantinople"). On hearing that Raḥamim had already been officially appointed, some of the delegates thought it useless to proceed with the journey. Isaac, however, went to Constantinople and argued the case before Jacob Zonana, head of the "Pekidei Ereẓ Israel," but Zonana justified the appointment. Isaac was the author of *Paḥad Yiẓḥak* (Moscow Ms. Guenzburg, 29), a comprehensive commentary on the *Sefer Yere'im* of *Eliezer b. Samuel of Metz. One of his responsa was published in the *Neḥpeh be-Khesef* (1768) of Jonah Navon (pt. 1, ḤM, 81a).

BIBLIOGRAPHY: M. Benayahu, *Rabbi Ḥ.Y.D. Azulai* (Heb., 1959), 389–90.

ABULAFIA, ISAAC BEN MOSES (1824–1910), rabbi and halakhist. Abulafia, who was born in Tiberias, was rabbi of Damascus from c. 1877. His authoritarian attitude and his habit of making independent halakhic decisions roused the opposition of the other rabbis and of the communal leaders of Damascus, who united in an attempt to remove him from his position. In 1896 they turned to Moses ha-Levi, the *ḥakham bashi*, in Constantinople, who acceded to their request by appointing Solomon Eliezer Alfandari rabbi of Damascus. The two rabbis did not at first cooperate with each other. Later, however, Alfandari brought Abulafia into the sphere of his activities. Toward the end of his life Abulafia acted as rabbi in Tyre. From there he moved to Jerusalem, and finally to Tiberias, where he died. An outstanding halakhic scholar, his responsa *Penei Yiẓḥak* were published in six volumes (1871–1906). Some scholars, especially Shalom Ḥai Gagin of Jerusalem, were critical of the first volume, and Abulafia wrote *Lev Nishbar* (1878) in reply to his critics.

BIBLIOGRAPHY: Ben-Zvi, in: *Oẓar Yehudei Sefarad*, 6 (1963), 7–16.

ABULAFIA, JACOB BEN SOLOMON (1550?–1622?), Damascus rabbi. Abulafia, the grandson of Jacob b. Moses *Berab, studied under Solomon *Absaban and under Moses Besodo – apparently in Damascus – together with Yom Tov *Ẓahalon. There is evidence that he may have been friendly with Isaac *Luria. It is known that he was in Safed in 1589. In 1593 he was serving as rabbi of the Spanish congregation in Damascus. About 1599 he received ordination (*semikhah*) – together with seven other great scholars of Safed – from Jacob (II) *Berab; Abulafia was definitely in Safed in the summer of 1599. He again visited there in the summer of 1609, returning to Damascus that same year. He ordained his closest pupil Josiah *Pinto about 1617, apparently in Safed. His relationship with Ḥayyim *Vital was extremely strained. Abulafia had no faith in Vital's visions, and mocked his approach to Kabbalah. The tension between them reached its peak in 1609. Abulafia was primarily a halakhist, but he also wrote expository homilies on the Pentateuch. Some of his responsa and novellae on the Pentateuch appear in the works of his contemporaries. Ḥ.Y.D. *Azulai saw a large manuscript volume of his responsa.

BIBLIOGRAPHY: Azulai, 1 (1852), 85, no. 202; Judah Aryeh di Modena, *Ari Nohem*, ed. by N.S. Leibovitz (1929), 80; Ḥ. Vital, *Sefer ha-Ḥezyonot*, ed. by A.Z. Aescoly (1954), 24ff., 91–129; M. Benayahu, in: *Sefer Yovel … Y. Baer* (1960), 253, 257, 260–1, 266–7.

ABULAFIA, MEIR (1170?–1244), talmudic commentator, thinker, and poet; the most renowned Spanish rabbi of the first half of the 13th century. His only son Judah died in 1226, but his grandchildren and great-grandchildren through his daughters lived in Toledo about a century after his death. Meir himself and his family carried the title *nasi*, and the whole family was connected by marriage with the foremost families of Toledo. In his youth, Abulafia went from Burgos to Toledo where he spent the rest of his life. It seems that as early as 1204 he was a member of the Toledo *bet din*, together with Meir ibn Migash and *Abraham b. Nathan ha-Yarḥi. He played an important part in the organization of the communities in Spain, especially that of Toledo, where he instituted many religious regulations.

Abulafia's literary activity spans four general areas: *halakhah*, masorah, the controversy over Maimonides' opinion on the subject of resurrection, and Hebrew poetry. His greatest though least known work is his extensive commentary, which covered about half the Talmud. This commentary, unique both in quantity and in quality, may be considered the summation and the conclusion of the talmudic school of the Spanish rabbis, and Abulafia its last representative (his younger contemporary and countryman *Naḥmanides brought an end to the local traditional method by his introduction of the tosafists' method of study from Germany and France). In his book, originally named *Sefer Peratei Peratin* ("Book of Minute Details"), Abulafia goes into the smallest details of each subject, attempting to extract from his explanations the maximum of practical rules. Its rapid disappearance may be attributed to its relative verbosity, as well as to the preference shown for the books of Naḥmanides. The work is written entirely in Aramaic, in the style of the *geonim* and Isaac *Alfasi, and all decisions are presented with confidence. Abulafia never mentions his teachers and rarely his predecessors by name, but he does draw upon and even quote (though anonymously) the early Spanish rabbis. Most of Abulafia's specific references are to the *geonim*, especially to *Hai and *Sherira, and he refers as well to Alfasi, *Hananel, Joseph *Ibn Migash, *Rashi, *Maimonides, and Jacob *Tam. His knowledge of the teachings of the French and German talmudists is evidently limited.

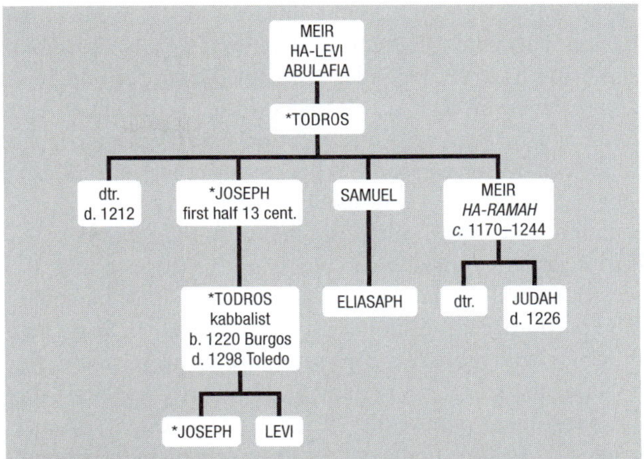

After H. *Brody, in YMHSI, 2(1936), 6

His work presents many old Spanish versions of the Talmud which are of special importance. Only two parts have hitherto been published (under the name *Yad Ramah*) – those dealing with the tractates *Bava Batra* and *Sanhedrin* (Salonika, 1790–98). However, manuscripts of his commentaries to many other tractates (none of which is extant) were known to the rabbis in earlier generations. Thus a great part of his commentary on the tractate *Horayot* is included in *Azulai's *Sha'ar Yosef* on the tractate *Avot*, in Samuel Uceda's *Midrash Shemu'el* (1579), and on the tractates of *Nezikin*, in Bezalel *Ashkenazi's *Shitah Mekubbeẓet*. He is quoted a great deal anonymously in Menahem ha-Meiri's commentaries on the Talmud.

Even from his own time, the study of Abulafia's work was limited because of the penetration into Spain of the tosafists' method of learning. Surprisingly, however, *Asher b. Jehiel of Toledo, a scholar of German origin, considered Abulafia the decisive local authority and he, his pupils (among them Jehoram and Abraham ibn Ismael), and his sons, especially *Jacob b. Asher, author of the *Turim*, studied his teachings, a great part of the *Turim* being based upon them. There were two editions of Abulafia's work, one longer than the other. The shorter edition came first, and not the reverse, as is generally held. Examples of both editions are extant. The existing commentary to *Bava Batra* is from the longer edition and that to *Sanhedrin* from the shorter one. In the longer edition Abulafia first explains all the Mishnayot, and only then the talmudic discussion. Of the hundreds of responsa which Abulafia wrote, only an incomplete collection of about 70 paragraphs is available. They are included in the *Or Ẓaddikim* (Salonika, 1799). Many of his responsa are scattered in the literature of the *rishonim* and others were inserted in the *Turim*. Other collections of responsa attributed to him in the rabbinical literature are not his.

His work *Masoret Seyag la-Torah* (Florence, 1750) dealt with research, based on old manuscripts, into the traditional text of the Scriptures, and, for a long time, influenced laws governing the writing of scrolls of the Torah. Menahem ha-

Meiri's *Kiryat Sefer* on the same subject is based on Abulafia's version. For many generations there existed in Spain scrolls of the Torah which were allegedly copied from the one Abulafia wrote for his own use. Abulafia wrote a scroll of the *Sefer Torah* as a master copy (mastercodex) and it achieved great fame both in Germany and in the countries of North Africa. "A great and outstanding rabbi, distinguished in wisdom," R. Samuel ben Jacob came especially from Germany to Toledo in order to make a copy of this scroll in 1250 and another copy was made in 1273 in Burgos by R. Isaac ben Solomon of Morocco. Additional copies were made in Spain and Provence from the earlier copies until 1410. The *Masoret Seyag la-Torah* also attained a remarkable popularity and Abraham ibn Ḥassan, one of the exiles of Spain, related that R. Isaac de Leon, who was one of the outstanding *posekim* in the generation before the Expulsion, issued instructions that all scrolls of the Torah in Spain were to be corrected according to the rules laid down in the *Masoret.*

The great importance of this work was equally recognized in later generations, and such distinguished scholars as Menahem ben Judah de *Lonzano in his *Or Torah*, Jedidiah Solomon *Norzi in his *Minhat Shai*, and Solomon ben Joseph *Ganzfried in his *Keset Ha-Sofer* laid down that the defective and *plene* spellings in a *Sefer Torah* were to be in accordance with this copy of Abulafia.

Nevertheless the extant copy, the first work of Abulafia to be published (Florence, 1750), is faulty and incomplete and also includes later additions. For instance, the *Likkutei ha-Masoret* and the *Tikkunei Soferim* as well as the list of *Petuḥot* and *Setumot* in the Torah, which are printed at the end of the volume, are not by Abulafia. They represent Ashkenazi traditions which were compiled according to the *Tikkun Sefer Torah* of Yom Tov Lipmann *Muelhausen which was recently discovered in manuscript and subsequently published. These traditions were added to the *Masoret* during the 16th century. On the other hand, the original book included references to the Talmud and halakhic discussions which were omitted from many of the manuscripts, and from the published edition. These changes explain the numerous discrepancies between the existing *Masoret* and the masoretic views of Abulafia as reflected in the *Kiryat Sefer* of Ha-Meiri, which are based on Abulafia's master copy. Abulafia also took special pains to explain the correct way of writing the scriptural portion of *Ha'azinu*, as set forth in an authenticated manuscript of Maimonides' *Yad ha-Ḥazakah*, which he received from Samuel ibn *Tibbon. His comments in this regard are important for establishing the authenticity of the manuscript copy of the Bible known as the Aleppo Codex.

Abulafia is best known for his controversy with Maimonides over the doctrine of resurrection. Maimonides' views on this subject seemed heretical to him. Abulafia, in spite of his youth, publicly denounced them, and was the first in Europe to do so during Maimonides' lifetime. His accusations were mainly in the form of letters to the rabbis of southern France, especially the "sages of Lunel," who held Maimonides in great esteem and strongly defended his views. The whole correspondence, which also included an exchange of letters with the rabbis of northern France, did not bring the hoped for result and was a great disappointment to Abulafia. Thirty years later, when the controversy was renewed, he was asked by Naḥmanides to take part in it again, but remembering his earlier failure, he refused. Much of the correspondence, edited by Abulafia, was published as *Kitāb al-Rasa'il* (Paris, 1871). Abulafia's conception of resurrection, far from being an abstract philosophy, is based upon the traditional belief, according to which the words of the rabbis on the subject are taken in their literal sense. Notwithstanding this (and contrary to Graetz's opinion), Abulafia possessed a wide knowledge of the Hebrew and Arabic philosophy of his time. In his work are mentioned the *ḥakhmei ha-tushiyyah* ("philosophers") and their opinions concerning the creation of man, the nature of the "heavenly host" (angels), and the like (see his instructive words on Sanh. 38b concerning "Adam was a heretic"). Those of his pupils who are known by name are principally philosophers and translators of works on astronomy and natural sciences from Arabic into Hebrew. Among them are Isaac Israeli (II), author of *Yesod Olam*, and Judah b. Solomon, author of *Midrashei ha-Ḥokhmah* (Ms.). In his correspondence with the rabbis of Provence, Abulafia objected to many of the decisions rendered by Maimonides in his *Yad ha-Ḥazakah.* Some of his *hassagot* ("criticisms"), like those of Abraham b. David, were printed at the side of Maimonides' text. A collection of these, on the tractate *Sanhedrin*, was published by Y. Ha-Levy Lipshitz in *Sanhedrei Gedolah* (1968), but there are many errors in his introduction. Although Abulafia opposed many of Maimonides' opinions and beliefs and resented the exaggerated respect which the rabbis of Provence accorded him, he held Maimonides in great esteem. In his work on *Sanhedrin*, which (in chapter *Ḥelek*) contains quotations from *Kitāb al-Rasā'il*, Maimonides is one of the few rabbis mentioned by name. After Maimonides' death Abulafia wrote a long elegy on him (published together with his *piyyutim*). A collection of Abulafia's letters (and a small number of his poems), published by Brody in 1936, reveals Abulafia to have been acquainted with the poetry of earlier Spanish Jews and to have been influenced by Moses Ibn Ezra in his meter, rhyme, and construction.

BIBLIOGRAPHY: Graetz, Gesch, 7 (c. 1900[4]), 30–32, 45–47, 52, 86; Yellin, in: KS, 6 (1929/30), 139–44; Brody, in: *Tarbiz*, 6 (1934/35), 242–53; idem, in: YMḤSI, 2 (1936), 2–90; Benedikt, in: *Sinai*, 33 (1952/53), 63–64, n. 3; Goshen-Gottstein, in: *Kitvei Mifal ha-Mikra*, 1 (1960), 21–31; Albeck, in: *Zion*, 25 (1959/60), 85–121; J.L. Maimon, *Sinai* 45 (1959), 12–16; H. Lieberman, idem, 68 (1971), 182–184; Albeck, in: *Mazkeret… Rav Herzog* (1961/62), 385–91; Baer, Spain, 1 (1961), 100, 106ff., 397ff.; Ta-Shema, in: KS, 43–45 (1967/69). **ADD. BIBLIOGRAPHY:** B. Septimus, *Hispano-Jewish Culture in Transition: The Career and Controversies of Ramah* (1982); N. Vogelman-Goldfeld, *Moses Maimonides' Treatise on Resurrection: An Inquiry into Its Authenticity* (1986).

[Israel Moses Ta-Shma]

ABULAFIA, SAMUEL BEN MEIR HA-LEVI (c. 1320–1361), Spanish financier, communal leader, and philanthropist. Abulafia's generosity provided a number of Jewish communities in Castile with synagogues, including the magnificent one still standing in Toledo (later the Church of El Tránsito) with florid Hebrew inscriptions in his honor. The synagogue was built by his order in 1357. This splendid synagogue was the best illustration of the status of Castilian Jewry in general, and of his prestigious position in particular. He was versatile in the Torah and was known as an observant Jew. At first steward of the estates of the king's tutor Don Juan Alfonso de Albuquerque, Abulafia later became treasurer and adviser of Pedro the Cruel of Castile. Many royal documents are signed by him in Hebrew with his seal, containing a castle, the emblem of Castile. During the revolt of the grandees in 1354 he was one of Pedro's principal supporters. Abulafia did much to reinforce the power of the monarchy in its struggle against the nobility by improving the financial state of the kingdom. He ordered an inquiry into the activities of the tax farmers and appointed in their place reliable persons, who were often his own relatives or other Jews; in addition he confiscated the property of the rebel nobles and amassed considerable wealth in two of the royal fortresses. He also served as a diplomat, being sent in 1358 to Portugal to negotiate a political agreement between the two kingdoms. In 1360 Pedro suddenly ordered Abulafia's arrest, whereupon he was brought to Seville and there tortured to death. His enormous fortune was confiscated, as well as that of his relatives. Samuel's imposing residence in Toledo, which still stands, is today the El Greco museum.

BIBLIOGRAPHY: Baer, *Urkunden*, II, Nos 187; 171, 205, 223, 180; Neuman, Spain, index; F. Cantera Burgos, *Sinagogas Españolas* (1955), 56–149; Cantera-Millás, Inscripciones, 336ff., 367–8; C. Roth, in: *Sefarad*, 8 (1948), 3–22. **ADD. BIBLIOGRAPHY:** P. León Tello, *Judíos de Toledo* (1979), 1, 137ff.; 2, 1399–44.

[Zvi Avneri]

ABULAFIA, SAMUEL HA-LEVI (13th century), scientist and engineer employed by King Alfonso x of Castile (1252–84). Abulafia constructed a water clock for Alfonso and translated for him from the Arabic a manual on the manufacture and uses of the candle clock, *Fábrica y usos del Relox de la Candela*. He also perfected hoisting devices and wrote a treatise about them, still extant in manuscript.

BIBLIOGRAPHY: G. Sarton, *Introduction to the History of Science*, 2 (1931), 843; Baer, Spain, index, s.v. *Samuel Halevi of Toledo;* Millás, in: G.S. Métraux and F. Grouzet, *The Evolution of Science* (1963), 160–2.

[Zvi Avneri]

ABULAFIA, TODROS BEN JOSEPH HA-LEVI (c. 1220–1298), Spanish rabbi and kabbalist. Rabbi Todros ben Joseph ha-Levi was born in Burgos, Spain, and died in Toledo. The Abulafia family was famous and respected in Spain. His uncle, Rabbi Meir ha-Levi *Abulafia, was the "exilarch" of Spanish Jewry and widely known for his war against the Rambam (*Maimonides) and his writings. Todros, who lived during the reign of Fernando III and Alphonso x, owed his great prominence to his wisdom and wealth, and like his uncle became the head of Castilian Jewry.

The sources portray Todros, on the one hand, as a public figure and a national-religious leader, a person of wide horizons, well versed in halakhic and midrashic literature and an occasional poet. On the other hand, he is also seen as an experienced courtier who found his way to the hearts of the king and queen. He is thought to be one of the first kabbalists in Spain, and one can learn from his writings how the basic concepts of the Kabbalah were formed. Above all, he was a model to his generation of modesty and purity. His life symbolized the absolute negation of his generation's penchant for the ways of the knight and the promiscuity of the king's court.

He spent his youth in Burgos. There he became friendly with Rabbi Moses ben Simeon, who was the disciple of the brother rabbis Jacob and Isaac of Soraya, and it would seem that Todros heard from his friend some of what Rabbi Moses had learned from Kabbalah teachers.

During his days in Toledo, Todros rose to a lofty position. King Alfonso x welcomed him to his court and made him one of his retinue on his voyage to France in 1275. Todros stayed with the queen in Perpignan, where he met the poet Abraham Badrashi (Bedersi). The meeting produced an exchange of rhymed letters and messages. (Some of the poems were published in the book *Segulot Melakhim*, Amsterdam, 1768; others are in manuscript form, British Museum ADD 27,168 930; Vienna manuscript 111).

In Toledo, Todros began his period of creativity. He wrote on halakhic and moral issues related to life and the affairs of his day. He did his utmost to free Jews who had been arrested on the king's orders (1281). At the same time he reacted furiously to serious violations of religious commandments and morality in Jewish society, threatening with imprisonment and excommunication those who would break the laws. (His sermon on changing evil ways is incorporated in his book *Zikkaron Li-Yehudah*, 1846). Apart from his public activity, the kabbalistic writings of Todros reveal him as a mystic, a kabbalist who preserves traditions and ideas and attempts, by fusing the various schools of Kabbalah (Gerona Kabbalah and Castilian Kabbalah), to bridge the gaps between the kabbalists of his day. His first book, *Sha'ar ha-Razim* (edition of M. Kushnir Oron, Jerusalem, 1989) is a kabbalistic interpretation of verse 19 of Psalms. In this book one perceives the hesitancy of the author, who is afraid of divulging secrets. The book was written as a letter replying to his friend Rabbi Moses of Burgos. In fact, the book may be viewed as an interpretative work, a kind of summing-up of the various traditions in Kabbalah as known by Todros, who attempts to fuse them through his interpretation

His second book, *Ozar ha-Kavod* (Warsaw, 1879), written late in his life, is an interpretation of talmudic legends. As in *Sha'ar ha-Razim*, in this book too the author's personality shines through. He gathers together different traditions and fuses them through the style of his writing, fusing mainly the writings of the Ḥasidei Ashkenaz, the letters of the *Ḥug ha-Iyyun*, and the Ismaili-Gnostic tradition with the traditions of the Gerona and the Castilian kabbalists. In both books one finds echoes of the concepts, themes, and ideas of the secret teachings that a generation later became the foundations of Kabbalah. Todros is thus important as a preserver of traditions who passed them on to the next generation. Thanks to his writings, it is often possible to understand the secrets hinted at in the writings of his teachers, the Castillian kabbalists, as well the mystical tradition in Spain and its crystallization during its early generations. (In addition to these two books, he may have written an interpretation of Chapter 1 of Ezekiel, which is mentioned in the writings of kabbalists but has not been found.)

Todros belongs to that circle of kabbalists called by Gershom *Scholem "the Gnostic kabbalists." Rabbi Todros emphasizes in his writings the uniqueness of that circle and its method in the wide frame of Kabbalah and kabbalists of his day.

Todros was considered a uniquely exemplary figure, who may have served, as Y. Libbes believes (*Keiẓad Nitḥabber Sefer ha-Zohar*), as a model for the depiction of Rabbi *Simeon Bar Yokhai in *Sefer ha-Zohar*. References to him may be found in the poems of Todros ben Judah (the kabbalist's nephew) and in the writings of Isaac ben Latif, Abraham Badrashi, and Isaac Albalag (in his book *Tikkun ha-De'ot*, p. 101).

His son Joseph was a friend of the kabbalist *Moses de Leon, who was thought to be the author of *Sefer ha-Zohar*, an attribution rejected by present-day scholars, who see him as just one its authors. Joseph received from de Leon copies of parts of *Sefer ha-Zohar*.

[Michal Oron (2nd ed.)]

ABULAFIA, TODROS BEN JUDAH HA-LEVI (1247–after 1298), Hebrew poet. He was born in Toledo and spent most of his life there. Todros was a member of a well-known family of the city, although his kinships with other Abulafias, such as Meir *Abulafia, or with "the Rav," Todros ben Joseph *Abulafia, are not completely clear. The branch of his own family was probably not very rich, and he had to search for a job serving the richest members of the Jewish community. He accompanied Don Isaac b. Don Solomon Zadok (Don Çaq de la Maleha; see *Ibn Zadok) on his travels, collecting taxes. He shared in his diversions and, apparently through his influence, was brought in touch with the royal court. In his presentation before the royal court, he offered to King Alfonso the Wise a goblet with an engraved Hebrew poem.

In his youth Abulafia composed numerous poems in honor of Jewish notables close to the court of Alfonso x of Castile and later Sancho iv, Solomon Ibn Zadok and his son Isaac, the rabbi Todros ben Joseph Abulafia and his son Joseph, etc., and even to persons of the royal family. He divided his time between poetry and finance and succeeded at both. In common with others of his class at that period, his morals were lax and he had many liaisons with non-Jewish women. He was among the Jews of Castile arrested by royal order in January 1281, in connection with the revolts of Don Sancho, the son of the King, which had as a consequence the sentence of death for Don Çaq de la Maleha. In prison he wrote many poems which seem to indicate a change in outlook, although none of them expresses contrition for his past behavior. After the release of the prisoners, with the impact of their misfortune still fresh in their minds, the rabbi Todros ben Joseph Abulafia called upon his kinsmen to repent and demanded that all those who continued to consort with Muslim or Christian women be excommunicated. The poet himself, however, did not alter his own conduct nor did he see in it any contradiction of his religious views.

After great effort Abulafia succeeded in regaining his status at court; in 1289 he is mentioned among the men of affairs in the service of Sancho iv, and some years later headed a group of Jewish financiers who received important monopolies. The last certain date mentioned in his poems is 1298.

Abulafia was a prolific writer. His *Gan ha-Meshalim ve-ha-Ḥidot* ("Garden of Apologues and Saws," the *diwan* collected by himself, adding Arabic headings) contains more than 1,000 poems; it was published by M. Gaster in 1926 (as a facsimile of the manuscript), and in three volumes by D. Yellin (1934–37): an extensive selection appears in Schirmann's anthology *Ha-Shirah ha-Ivrit bi-Sefarad u-vi-Provence*, 2 (1956), 413–48, 694. There are very different opinions on his virtues as a poet and on the value of his literary production. Although the themes, technique, and genres of his poems continue the classical traditions of Andalusian Hebrew literature, he lived in a post-classical period with clear signs of mannerism and a tendency to virtuosity. His poetry can be called epigonal in its search for surprising elements, plays on words, trivia, vulgar language, etc. For some scholars, most of Abulafia's poems seem repetitive and superficial, although they are valuable for the historical material they contain and for the interesting relation to the general literature of the times that is revealed, for example, polemical verses, poems on spiritual love, etc. Without denying the interest of these poems as historical documents, many with an autobiographical character, they also show clear signs of the high literary qualities of their author. In some poems he appears wholly familiar with Andalusian conventions, trying to overcome them in a very sophisticated way. Writing in a different environment, and in accordance with the sociological and cultural changes of the Jewish communities in Castile, Todros imitated the Andalusian models, genres, motifs, and conventions, adapting them to the new tendencies of the time not only in Hebrew but also in Romance literature. Renouncing Hebrew-Arabic formalism, and being in contact with the life of the Castilian Court and its literary preferences, Abulafia followed the realistic tendencies of his time.

It is true that some of his poems may be seen as a low variety of literary texts in comparison with high literary compositions. Few of the Judeo-Spanish poets wrote about themselves as candidly as Abulafia, even on matters which were likely to arouse the resentment of his readers. The poet was able to deride even the physical defects of his opponents using an equivocal language. Following Romance patterns, like that of the *tensones*, Todros discusses with other poets, like Pinḥas, in a tone varying between the festive and the serious, which of them is better qualified to write poetry. It is a display of skill in the use of language and verse, trying to show subtleness in praising the speaker's own poetry and ridiculing the adversary with the kind of invectives that sometimes clearly enter the realm of obscenity. The tone is not of bitterness nor has it any tragic greatness; the poets are just mocking each other and trying to overcome the adversary with a sophisticated play on words. On other occasions, he maintained literary correspondence at a higher level with other poets of his time. Todros dedicated long series of poems to notable Jewish courtiers of his time, like "the Rav," or Solomon Ibn Zadok; the series are divided into sections, on different Andalusian topics, preceded by Arabic and Hebrew introductions, showing the ability of the poet to adapt the classical genres to the praise of the distinguished courtiers.

His "girdle" poems (47 *muwashshahāt*) are very interesting, particularly due to the *kharajāt* preserved in them, in old Spanish, Hebrew, and Arabic.

BIBLIOGRAPHY: H. Brody, in: YMḤSI, 1 (1933), 2–93; Y. Baer, in: *Zion*, 2 (1937), 19–55; Baer, Spain, 1 (1961), 123ff., 133–7, 237–40; B. Chapira, in: REJ, 106 (1941–45), 1–33; Davidson, Oẓar, 4 (1933), 383–6; Lewin, in: *Oẓar Yehudei Sefarad*, 10 (1968), 48–66. **ADD. BIBLIOGRAPHY:** J. Targarona, in: *Helmantica*, 36 (1985), 195–210; A. Doron, *Meshorer ba-Ḥatsar ha-Melekh: Todros ha-Levi Abulafyah: Shirah Ivrit bi-Sefarad ha-Noẓrit* (1989); F. Márquez Villanueva, *El concepto cultural Alfonsí* (1994); Schirmann-Fleischer, 2, 366–424; A. Sáenz-Badillos, in: C. Carrete (ed.), *Actas del IV Congreso Internacional "Encuentro de las tres culturas" (Toledo, 30 de septiembre–2 octubre 1985)* (1988), 135–46; *Prooftexts*, 16 (1996), 49–73; *Jewish Studies at the Turn of the 20th Century. Proceedings of the 6th EAJS Congress, Toledo 1998*, 1 (1999), 504–12.

[Jefim (Hayyim) Schirmann / Angel Saenz-Badillos (2nd ed.)]

ABULKER (Aboulker = Abu I-Khayr), Algerian family, whose members attained rabbinical and communal distinction. ISSAC BEN SAMUEL (I) (late 15th–early 16th centuries), scholar, astronomer, and translator. Expelled from Spain in 1492, Abulker settled in Padua, Italy, where in 1496 he completed his Hebrew commentary on the "Extracts of the Almagest" of al-Farghani. According to some modern authors this commentary is actually only a copy of the work of an earlier Jewish astronomer, Moses Ḥandali. Some time later Abulker translated from Latin into Hebrew under the title of *Sefer ha-Moladot* the *Liber de Nativitatibus*, originally written in Arabic by al-Ḥasibi (on the appearance of the new moon). He also translated into Hebrew the *Liber Completus*, a Latin translation (Venice, 1485) by Petrus of Reggio of *Ahkām al-Nujum* by the famous 12th-century Tunisian astronomer Ali ibn Abi al-Rijal (Abenragel). When ISAAC BEN SAMUEL ABULKER (II), the rabbi of Algiers, denounced the abuses of Joseph Bacri, the latter depicted Abulker as a troublemaker and the bey had Abulker and six other Jewish notables beheaded in 1815. His son SAMUEL and his grandson ISAAC (III) were leaders of Algerian Jewry in the 19th century. The son of the latter, HENRI-SAMUEL (1876–1957), professor of medicine and head of Algerian Jewry, formed and presided over the Algerian Zionist Federation and worked vigorously for organizations which fought antisemitism. As head of the wartime Resistance, he secretly collaborated with the Allies to assist the American landing in Algiers on Nov. 7–8, 1942. His son JOSÉ (b. 1920), a professor of neurosurgery in Paris, was the leader of the Resistance forces which occupied Algiers, thus facilitating the landing.

BIBLIOGRAPHY: Steinschneider, Uebersetzungen, 546, 557–80; M.Haddey, *Livre d'Or des Israélites Algériens* (1872), 73, 83; I. Bloch, *Inscriptions Tumulaires* (1888), 124–7; M. Ansky, *Juifs d'Algérie* (1950), index; Hirschberg, Afrikah, index.

[David Corcos]

ABULRABI (Abu al Rabi), AARON (also called **Aldabi** or **Alrabi**; first half of the 15th century), Sicilian-born biblical exegete, theologian, and polemicist. Born in Catania in Aragonese Sicily, Abulrabi became an itinerant scholar whose travels took him to Italy, Turkey, Alexandria, Damascus, Jerusalem, and Kaffa on the Black Sea. Along the way he engaged in intra- and interreligious discussion and dispute. He describes an exchange with an unnamed pope and his cardinals in Rome in which he refuted the Christian curialists' suggestion that the tabernacle cherubs reflected "the craft of talismans," thereby breaching biblical prohibitions on "other gods" and the manufacture of "graven images." He also reports debates with a Karaite scholar in Jerusalem and various Christian interlocutors.

The only witness to Abulrabi's life and thought is a tome that combines Torah commentary with supercommentary on Rashi's *Commentary on the Torah*. The work postdates 1446 in the version that has come down. At its outset, Abulrabi states that he will focus on Rashi's words inasmuch as they were "mostly hewn from the eminent [rabbinic] oaks of old." At times, Abulrabi issues sharp criticisms of Midrashim in a forthright manner almost without precedent in Rabbanite literature. Abulrabi's work was printed together with the supercommentaries on Rashi of Samuel Almosnino, Jacob Canizal, and Moses *Albelda under the title *Perushim le-Rashi* (Constantinople, 1525). In his commentary, Abulrabi mentions that he wrote the following other works: *Sefer ha-Meyasher*, on Hebrew grammar; *Sefer Matteh Aharon*, a polemical work; and three apparently theological studies: *Nezer ha-Kodesh; Sefer ha-Nefesh*; and *Sefer Peraḥ ha-Elohut*. In the course of his commentary, he quotes philosophic and kabbalistic sources, though rarely by name. He also quotes his father, learned brothers Shalom, Baruch, Moses, Jacob, and his father-in-law Moses *Gabbai, who, like Abulrabi, composed a supercommentary on Rashi's *Commentary on the Torah*.

BIBLIOGRAPHY: Perles, in: REJ, 21 (1890), 246–69. **ADD. BIBLIOGRAPHY:** E. Lawee, "Graven Images, Astromagical Cherubs, Mosaic Miracles: A Fifteenth-Century Curial-Rabbinic Exchange," in: *Speculum*, 81 (2006); J. Hacker, "*Ha-Megidut bi-Ẓefon Afrikah be-Sof ha-Me'ah ha-Ḥamesh Esrei*," in: *Zion* 45 (1980–81), 127, n. 34; Schorr, in: *Zion*, 1 (1840), 166–68, 193–96.

[Judah M. Rosenthal / Eric Lawee (2nd ed.)]

ABUN (also **Abuna**, **Bun**), a variation of the Aramaic name "Abba," common in Palestine, France, and Spain. Several scholars and poets by this name were known in the Middle Ages, but there is little information available about them. (1) The father of a Palestinian liturgical poet, Eleazar, whose style and method are similar to those of Kallir, was called both Abun and Bun. (2) The grandfather of the Franco-German liturgical poet Simeon b. Isaac bore the name Abun, also Abuna. A native of Le Mans, France (it is conceivable that (Le) Mans is in fact a corruption of Mainz), who lived at the end of the ninth century, he may be the one to whom Solomon *Luria refers in his responsum 29 (Lublin, 1575): "R. Abun who excels in Torah, wisdom, wealth, and in all the innermost secrets, expounding every letter in 49 different ways." Some scholars identify him with Abun, a physician who was head of a school for medicine in Narbonne, some of whose disciples taught medicine in Montpellier. (3) A Spanish poet by the name Abun b. Sharada lived around the 11th century, first in Lucena and then in Seville. His poems were praised by his contemporaries as well as by later writers. Solomon ibn *Gabirol mentions him in his poems alongside *Menahem b. Saruk, *Dunash b. Labrat, and *Samuel ha-Nagid (*Shirei Shelomo ibn Gabirol*, ed. by Ḥ.N. Bialik and Y.H. Ravnitzky, 1 (1928^2), 65, no. 28). He is also mentioned in Moses *Ibn Ezra's *Shirat Yisrael* (ed. by B. Halper (1924), 69) and in Judah *Al-Ḥarizi's *Taḥkemoni* (ed. by A. Kaminka (1899), 40). From Moses Ibn Ezra it can be gathered that the poems of Abun were no longer current in his day and it seems evident that even he did not see them. (4) A Spanish scholar and philanthropist of the 12th century, to whom Moses Ibn Ezra addressed many poems and about whom he composed several lamentations on his death, calling him "*Rabbana Abun*," "*Ha-Gevir*" ("the Magnate"), and "Abun, the words of whose mouth were like a watercourse in a dry land." (5) A Spanish liturgical poet known from five poems written in the spirit and style of early *paytanim* of Spain. He may be the Abun b. R. Saul also known as "the pious R. Abun of Majorca."

BIBLIOGRAPHY: Spiegel, in: YMḤSI, 5 (1939), 269–91; Davidson, Oẓar, 4 (1933), 347.

[Abraham Meir Habermann]

ABU SAʿD AL-TUSTARĪ (d. 1048), Egyptian financier and courtier. Muslim sources refer to him as Abū Saʿd b. Sahl al-Tustari (i.e., from Tustar (Shustar) in southwestern Persia). In Jewish sources he appears as Abraham b. Yashar. Abū Saʿd was primarily a dealer in precious objects and jewels, while his brother Abū Naṣr Fadl (*Ḥesed* in Hebrew) was a banker. Abū Saʿd sold to the Caliph al-Ẓāhir (1021–36) a female black slave, who gave birth to the later Caliph al-Mustanṣir. When at the age of seven the boy succeeded his father, his mother exercised great influence in the affairs of state, and Abū Saʿd was one of her advisers. He utilized his position at court to help the Jews of Egypt and Syria, then under the rule of the Fatimid caliphs. Rabbanites as well as Karaites turned to him for help. Hence, scholars disputed to which community he belonged. Abū Saʿd was murdered in 1048 by hired assassins of Ṣadaka b. Yūsuf al-Falāḥī, a Jewish convert to Islam, who had been appointed vizier on Abū Saʿd's recommendations. Abū Saʿd's brother Abū Naṣr, court financier and community representative, was also assassinated.

BIBLIOGRAPHY: Mann, Egypt, 1 (1920), 73, 76ff., 108, 112, 119, 128ff.; 2 (1922), 75ff., 376ff.; Poznański, in: REJ, 72 (1921), 202ff.; Goitein, in: JQR, 45 (1954/55), 36–37; Fischel, Islam, 68ff.

[Eliyahu Ashtor]

ABYAḌ, YIḤYA BEN SHALOM (1873–1935), student friend of R. Yiḥya *Kāfaḥ; among the heads of the Dor De'ah ("generation of wisdom") movement in Yemen. Abyaḍ was renowned as a biblical scholar and as an expert in astronomy and natural medicine. His medical treatment acquired popular acclaim and many sick people, both Jews and Muslims, came to him for help, and he was noted for treating people free of charge. Abyaḍ was head of the Maswari synagogue in San'a and taught Torah to the Jewish public; nonetheless, he earned his livelihood as a silver- and goldsmith. His ornaments were distinguished by their artistic delicacy. After the death of the chief rabbi, Yiḥya Isaac, in 1932, the community heads appointed him successor. However dissident groups and violent factions prevailed, and the rabbi's health was soon undermined.

BIBLIOGRAPHY: A. Koraḥ, *Saʿarat Teiman* (1954), 76–77.

[Yehuda Ratzaby]

ABZARDIEL (Abazardiel, Abenzardel, Azardel), MOSES (d. c. 1354), secretary to King Alfonso XI of Castile. A learned rabbinical scholar, Moses served for some time as *dayyan* in *Toledo. His signature appears in Latin characters in royal documents dealing with finance and taxes between 1331 and 1339. Its absence from later royal records may be related to the anti-Jewish reaction in Castile. Presumably he is the "R. Moses, the chief scribe of the king" mentioned by Ibn Verga in his *Shevet Yehudah* (ed. by Shochat (1947), 53ff.). He is probably identical with the Moses b. Joseph Abi Zardil commemorated on an elaborate tombstone in Toledo.

BIBLIOGRAPHY: Baer, Urkunden, 1, pt. 2 (1963), 142–4, 159; Baer, Spain, 1 (1961), 327, 356, 358ff.; Cantera-Millás, Inscripciones, 54–58; Zelson, in: JQR, 19 (1928/29), 145ff.

ABZUG, BELLA SAVITZKY (1920–1998), U.S. social activist, politician, and advocate for women's rights. Abzug was born in the Bronx, New York, to a religious, immigrant family. Her father, Emanuel Savitzky, a butcher, then salesman, died when Bella was 13, and her mother, Esther, became the family breadwinner. Abzug attended Walton High, an all-girls public school. Active as a teenager in the Labor Zionist group Ha-Shomer ha-Ẓa'ir, she studied Hebrew at the Florence Marshall Hebrew High, continuing her studies at the Jewish Theological Seminary. She taught Hebrew and Jewish history at a Bronx Jewish Center. In 1938, Abzug enrolled in Hunter College, where she led demonstrations against fascism. Graduating in 1942, she worked for a defense contractor, then entered Columbia University Law School on scholarship. One of only a few women in her class, she became an editor of the *Columbia Law Review*. Midway through law school, she married Martin Abzug; the couple had two daughters. Following graduation, Abzug opened her own law firm, specializing in labor union and civil liberties work.

In 1961, Abzug helped found Women's Strike for Peace and served as its national legislative and political director. An early opponent of the Vietnam War, she founded the Coalition for a Democratic Alternative and helped to organize the Dump-Johnson campaign. She won election to Congress from Manhattan's 19th Congressional District in 1970, becoming one of 12 women in the House, the first elected on a woman's rights/peace platform. In 1971, she co-founded the National Women's Political Caucus. Returned to the House twice more, Abzug's major legislation included the Equal Credit Act, Social Security for homemakers, family planning, abortion rights, Title IX regulations, the Freedom of Information Act, the Right to Privacy Act, the "Government in the Sunshine" Law, and the Water Pollution Act. The first to call for President Nixon's impeachment during the Watergate scandal, she conducted inquiries into covert and illegal activities of the CIA and FBI. Abzug also sponsored pioneering legislation to permit the free emigration of Soviet Jewry, and was a leading supporter of economic and military aid to Israel. In 1975, she led the fight to condemn the UN General Assembly's resolution equating Zionism with racism, and played a leading role in condemning anti-Zionist and anti-Jewish attacks at international feminist conferences in Mexico and Copenhagen.

In 1976, Abzug left the House to run for the Senate from New York but lost to Daniel Patrick Moynihan in a four-way race. In 1977, she presided over the first National Women's Conference in Houston. With colleagues in 1980, she established WOMEN USA; a decade later she co-founded and co-chaired the Women's Economic Development Organization (WEDO), an international advocacy group supporting women's empowerment, economic development, and environmental security. Her books included *Bella Abzug's Guide to Political Power for Women* (1984), written with Mim Kelber.

BIBLIOGRAPHY: J. Antler, *The Journey Home: How Jewish Women Shaped Modern America* (1997); J. Nies, *Nine Women: Portraits from an American Radical Tradition* (2002).

[Joyce Antler (2nd ed.)]

ACACIA (Heb. שִׁטָּה, *shittah*), a tree of Israel considered to be identical to the *shittah* tree. In the past it was extensively used for construction. Today it is planted to beautify the arid regions of Israel. Acacia-wood is mentioned repeatedly (Ex. 25–27) as the sole wood used in the construction of the Tabernacle. The word also appears as several biblical place names: Shittim near Gilgal (Num. 25:1; etc.); "And all the brooks of Judah … shall water the valley of Shittim" (Joel 4:18); and Beth-Shittah near Beisan (Judg. 7:22). According to Isaiah, acacia trees would line the path of the returning exiles, and would make the wasteland bloom at the time of redemption (Isa. 4:19). There is almost universal agreement that the *shittah* is to be identified with the acacia. Several species of the tree grow in Israel, mostly in the wadis of the Judean desert and in the southern Negev. It is thorny and has leaves compounded of small leaflets. The yellow flowers are small and grow in globular clusters. It is not tall; its trunk is thin and generally bent sideways. It is therefore somewhat difficult to identify this tree with the *shittah* from which the Tabernacle boards "a cubit and a half the breadth of each" (Ex. 26:16) were cut. Noting this difficulty, the Midrash already asked the question: Where in the desert were our forefathers able to find acacia-wood? One solution suggests that the trees were brought from Migdal Ẓevo'aya in the Jordan Valley near the mouth of the Yarmuk and that a small forest existed there (Gen. R. 94:4). Regarded as holy, its trees were not cut down by the local inhabitants. At present, a small grove of *Acacia albida*, tall trees with thick trunks, which, in contrast to the other species in Israel, grows only in non-desert regions, stands there. This species must have been the "acacia-wood standing up," i.e., with an erect trunk, which provided the wood for the Tabernacle and its accessories. This tropical tree, too, would transform the desert, according to Isaiah, in contrast to the other varieties of acacia which had always grown in the dry regions. This wood is very hard, but light. It does not absorb moisture and so its volume remains constant. It is, therefore, most suitable for construction and was used in shipbuilding.

BIBLIOGRAPHY: J. Feliks, *Olam ha-Ẓome'aḥ ha-Mikra'i* (1968²); Loew, Flora, 2 (1924), 377ff; Dalman, Arbeit, 7 (1942), 32ff.

[Jehuda Feliks]

ACADEMIES IN BABYLONIA AND EREẒ ISRAEL.

Designations

The talmudic term for an academy, yeshivah (lit., "sitting"), derives from the fixed order of seating assigned to the sages and their pupils who regularly participated in the activities of the academy. Occasionally the term meant not an academy but the private activity of studying the Torah (Nid. 70b). There are several synonyms for yeshivah, such as *bet ha-midrash* (lit., "the house of study"), *bet din* (lit. "the house of law"), *bet din gadol* (lit. "the great house of law"), and *metivta* (or *motva*) *rabba* (lit. "the great session"; Bek. 5b). In Babylonia the expression *metivta*, the literal Aramaic rendering of yeshivah, was used.

As for *bet va'ad* (lit. "meeting place"), this refers specifically to the yeshivah (*bet din*) of the *nasi* in Ereẓ Israel.

History of the Academy in the Second Temple Period

According to the *aggadah*, the biblical patriarchs and their sons studied in a yeshivah. There was one in existence, too, during the Egyptian bondage, as also during the forty years of wandering in the wilderness (Yoma 28b; et al.). But the first reference to "yeshivah" as a place of study occurs apparently in the appendix to Ecclesiasticus 51:29: "Let my soul rejoice in my sitting (yeshivah), and be ye not ashamed with my song." The expression "in my sitting," in parallelism with "my song," would seem to point to the ethical and wise maxims which Ben Sira taught in his school, and not to halakhic subjects. But since Ben Sira declares in the same chapter (verse 23), "Turn unto me, ye unlearned, and dwell in my house of learning" (*bet ha-midrash*), it is very probable that yeshivah and *bet ha-midrash* are synonyms for a school. More than a century later, Hillel the Elder said: "The more Torah, the more life; the more yeshivah, the more wisdom" (Avot 2, 7). There is no detailed information extant on the academies of Hillel and Shammai, nor on the arrangements relating to the discussions and studies prevailing in them. There is, however, information on the discussions of these two sages and their pupils on halakhic subjects. For example, "When grapes are being vintaged for the vat (i.e., for making wine), Shammai holds that they are susceptible of becoming unclean, while Hillel maintains that they are not.... A sword was planted in the *bet ha-midrash* and it was proclaimed: 'He who would enter, let him enter, but he who would depart, let him not depart' (so as to be present when a vote was taken). And on that day Hillel sat in submission before Shammai, like one of the pupils" (Shab. 17a). There were extremely bitter controversies on *halakhah* between the pupils of Hillel and those of Shammai which, on one occasion, ended in bloodshed (TJ, Shab. 1:7, 3c). There were halakhic discussions in the *bet ha-midrash* that continued inconclusively for years (Er. 13b). On one occasion the *halakhah* was decided in accordance with Hillel's view, outside the academy, in the courtyard of the Temple Mount (Tosef., Ḥag. 2:11; TJ, Beẓah 2:4, 61c). Generally, however, the *halakhah* was decided within the academy, after thorough consideration and discussion, by finally "taking a vote and deciding" according to the opinion of the majority.

The *tannaim* regarded the Great Sanhedrin, which had its seat in the Chamber of Hewn Stone, as a yeshivah (Mid. 5:4; Sanh. 32b) "from which Torah goes forth to all Israel" (Sif. Deut. 152). R. Ishmael relates "when a man brings the tithe of the poor to the Temple, he enters the Chamber of Hewn Stone and sees the sages and their pupils sitting and engaging in the study of the Torah, whereupon his heart prompts him to study the Torah" (Mid. Tan. to 14:22). In a like manner, Yose b. Ḥalafta (of Sepphoris, who flourished in the middle of the second century C.E.) described the functions, procedures, and religious authority of this central institution: "... The *bet din* in the Chamber of Hewn Stone, though comprised of 71 members, may function with as few as 23. If one must go out, and sees that there are not 23, he remains. There they sit from the time of the daily burnt-offering of the morning until the time of the daily burnt-offering of the afternoon. On Sabbaths and festivals they enter the *bet ha-midrash* on the Temple Mount only. If a question was asked, and they had heard (the answer), they gave it; if not, they took a vote. If the majority held it to be levitically unclean, they declared it unclean; if the majority held it to be levitically clean, they declared it clean. From there the *halakhah* goes forth and spreads in Israel.... And from there they send and examine whoever is a sage and humble, pious, of unblemished reputation, and one in whom the spirit of his fellow-men takes delight, and make him a **dayyan* in his town. After he has been made a *dayyan* in his town, they promote him and give him a seat in the *Ḥel* ("a place within the Temple area"), and from there they promote him and give him a seat in the Chamber of Hewn Stone. And there they sit and examine the pedigree of the priesthood and the pedigree of the levites" (Tosef., Sanh. 7:1). Although the participation of pupils in the debates was a characteristic feature of the academies, when it came to arriving at a decision, only their teachers, and not they, voted (*ibid.*, 7:2).

The question has been raised as to whether an institution similar to the academy of the Pharisaic sages existed among other sects. C. Rabin (*Qumran Studies* (1957), 103ff.) regards the term *moshav* ("session") or *moshav ha-rabbim* ("the public session") in the Dead Sea Scrolls as referring to an academic-juridical institution, analogous to the academy mentioned in rabbinic literature, which met from time to time.

The Pupils at the Academies in the Second Temple Period

In rabbinic literature, information about the pupils who studied in the academies is extremely sparse. One *aggadah* relates of Hillel in his student days that "once, when he found nothing from which he could earn some money, the guard of the *bet ha-midrash* (who usually received half of what Hillel earned) would not allow him to enter. He climbed up and sat upon the skylight to hear the words of God from Shemaiah and Avtalyon" (Yoma 35b). It is further related that "Shammai and Hillel did not teach the Torah for remuneration" (Mid. Ps. to 15:6). In the appendix to Ecclesiasticus 51:23–25 it is stated: "Turn unto me, ye unlearned, and dwell in my house of learning.... Buy wisdom for yourselves without money." Hillel, of whom it is said that "he drew his fellow-men near to the Torah" (Avot 1:12), had 80 pupils and "the least among all of them was Johanan b. Zakkai" (BB 134a). On the subject of accepting pupils there was a divergence of opinion between Hillel and Shammai: "Bet Shammai maintain that one should only teach a person who is wise and humble, of a good pedigree, and rich (some read "worthy"), and Bet Hillel declare that one should teach every person, for there were many sinners in Israel who were attracted by the study of the Torah and from whom there came forth righteous, pious, and worthy men" (ARN[1] 3, 14).

There is no information extant on academies for the study of the Torah outside of Jerusalem, except for an account of Johanan b. Zakkai, who spent some time in Galilee, where scarcely any pupils or householders sought instruction from him (TJ, Shab. 16:8, 15d). One who wished to study had to leave his home and go to Jerusalem, and this naturally imposed a burden on the poor, who for years had to live away from their homes in order to spend the major part of the day in the company of their teachers, listening to their halakhic discussions, to their decisions, and to what took place in the academy, this being the accepted manner of the study of the Torah, known as "attendance on scholars." It is recorded of Eliezer b. Hyrcanus, that he left his father's home, went to Jerusalem, where he studied under Johanan b. Zakkai, and suffered from hunger, as he received no support from his father (ARN[1] 6; ARN[2] 13, 30–1). Pupils also went from abroad to study the Torah in Jerusalem. They included Nehemiah of Bet Deli, who went from Babylonia and studied under Gamaliel the Elder (Yev. 16:7), and Saul of Tarsus, i.e., Paul, who went from Cilicia in Asia Minor (Acts 22:3). There were no written halakhic works available, for in general the principle was observed that "words which are transmitted orally are not permitted to be recited from writing" (Git. 60b).

From the Destruction of the Second Temple to the Close of the Mishnah

After the destruction of the Second Temple, several academies were established simultaneously. This is attested by a *baraita* (Sanh. 32b) which enumerates the academies and their heads, as follows: Johanan b. Zakkai at Beror Ḥayil, Gamaliel at Jabneh, Eliezer at Lydda, and Joshua at Peki'in. In the next generation there were Akiva at Bene-Berak, and Ḥanina b. Teradyon at Siknin, and these were followed by Yose at Sepphoris, Mattiah b. Ḥeresh in Rome, Judah b. Bathyra at Nisibis (in Mesopotamia), and Hananiah, the nephew of R. Joshua b. Hananiah, in Babylonia. The list, though incomplete, testifies to the founding of academies both in and outside Ereẓ Israel during the second century C.E. (See Map: Main Academies.) It concludes with a reference to the academy at Bet She'arim, headed by Judah ha-Nasi, which, because of the unique nature of his position and of the religious authority with which he was invested, was apparently the only one in his day, although after his death, academies were again established simultaneously at Tiberias, Caesarea, and Lydda.

The Function and Authority of the Academies

On the assembly of the sages at Jabneh after the destruction of the Second Temple there is the following statement: "When the sages assembled at the academy of Johanan b. Zakkai at Jabneh, they said: 'A time will come when a man will seek one of the laws of the Torah and not find it, one of the rabbinic laws and not find it.'... They said: 'Let us begin from Hillel and Shammai ...'" (Tosef., Eduy. 1:). Hence, the sages began to receive "testimonies" from those who had survived the war against the Romans. They scrutinized these, arrived at a decision, and laid down the *halakhah*. At that time the arrangement of halakhic collections according to subject matter received renewed and fruitful impetus. The center of religious authority was the Great Academy, in whose activities the **nasi* took part and over which he presided when not engaged in public affairs. In this *bet din* the new moon was proclaimed, as was the intercalation of the year (RH 2:8–9; Eduy. 7:7), the fixing of a uniform *calendar for Ereẓ Israel and the Diaspora contributing greatly to the preservation of national unity. Here, too, matters relating to the liturgy (Ber. 28b), and religious questions which were of public concern and on which no general agreement had hitherto been reached, were finally decided. In this central institution, 71 sages sat (Sanh. 1:6) when it was necessary to decide on basic halakhic matters affecting the people of Ereẓ Israel as a whole – matters such as the levitical uncleanness of hands through touching sacred scrolls, etc. (Yad. 3:5; 4:2). The following description of the proceedings of the Sanhedrin may well have applied to the central academy at Jabneh: "The Sanhedrin sat in a semicircle so that its members might see one another, and two judges' scribes stood before them, one on the right and one on the left, and wrote down the arguments of those in favor of acquittal and of those in favor of conviction.... In front of them sat three rows of scholars, each of whom knew his proper place. If they needed to ordain another judge, they ordained one from the first row, whereupon one from the second row moved up to the first, and one from the third row to the second. A member of the public was chosen and given a seat in the third row. He did not occupy the seat of the first scholar but one suitable for him" (Sanh. 4:3–4). The discussions in the Sanhedrin were thus conducted in public in the presence of pupils and of members of the community. In this way the pupils had learned the Torah in the days of the Second Temple. Both in Ereẓ Israel and in Babylonia, a *bet din* was always an integral part of an academy. The order of discussion was as follows: If several matters of law came up, only one would be dealt with on one day (Tosef., Sanh. 7:2). "No vote is taken on two matters simultaneously, but votes are taken separately and questions put separately" (Tosef., Neg. 1:11). At the end of the discussions a vote was taken, where necessary, such as in cases where "one prohibits and one permits, one declares levitically unclean and one clean, and all say: We have not heard a tradition concerning this – in such instances a vote is taken" (Tosef., Sanh. 7:2). The Tosefta also describes procedural details and ceremonial arrangements customary in the academies in Ereẓ Israel in tannaitic times.

Information on the academies in Ereẓ Israel and Babylonia in the Days of the Amoraim is more detailed than on the preceding period, Generally, the *amoraim* adopted the arrangements and methods of instruction of their academies from the *tannaim*.

The Rosh Yeshivah and his Assistants

The *rosh yeshivah* – the head of the academy – would "sit and expound" and convey his remarks to the *meturgeman* ("inter-

Map showing the main academies in Babylonia and Ereẓ Israel.

preter"; Ber. 27b), also called an **amora*. Where the audience was large, the *rosh yeshivah* would be assisted by numerous *amoraim* (Ket. 106a). Since all the pupils did not immediately grasp what was said, the outstanding pupils would repeat and explain the lesson (BK 117a, and Rashi, *ibid.*; Ta'an. 8a, Rashi). After they understood it, the pupils would repeat the lesson orally (Er. 54b). It is possible that the sages permanently attached to an academy prepared the pupils for the *rosh yeshivah*'s forthcoming lecture by teaching them the Mishnayot (see Meg. 28b; cf. Hor. 12a: Mesharsheya's statement). The *rosh yeshivah* gave his lectures, at least in the large academies, in the morning and in the evening (Shab. 136b), the pupils spending the rest of the day in reviewing the lecture and perhaps also in preparing for the next one. These outstanding pupils were called *reishei kallah* ("the leaders of the rows"), possibly because of the permanent seating arrangements at the academy. Mention is made of seven rows of pupils, graded according to their knowledge, the first row being occupied by the outstanding pupils (BK 117a) and so on, There is also a reference to 24 rows of pupils (Meg. 28b), the youngest pupils occupying seats behind the fixed rows (Ḥul. 137b).

The *rosh yeshivah* was also assisted by a *tanna*, distinguished by his exceptional knowledge of the "Mishnah of the *Tannaim*" and of the Oral Law in general, which he memorized by constant repetition, the Oral Law generally not having been written down (Git. 60b). The services of the *tanna* were often required in the academy for the quoting of tannaitic statements, his remarks being cited in the Babylonian Talmud, usually after the introductory formula: "A *tanna* taught before rabbi so-and-so." In general the *tanna*'s knowledge was mechanical and not rooted in an especially profound understanding of the material; in consequence the sages, especially in Babylonia (Meg. 28b), did not have a particularly high opinion of them.

The Election of a Rosh Yeshivah

A *rosh yeshivah* was generally appointed by the sages of the academy both in Ereẓ Israel (Sot. 40a) and in Babylonia (Ber. 64a). Sometimes several candidates would compete for the position, the ability to make an irrefutable statement serving as the criterion for election (Hor. 14a).

The Academies in Babylonia in the Days of the Amoraim

The beginnings of the central academies in Babylonia are associated with Rav at *Sura and Samuel at *Nehardea. Each headed a famous school which possessed central religious authority in the Babylonian Diaspora. The academy at Sura flourished almost 800 years; that at Nehardea was destroyed at the end of the '50s of the third century C.E. and was succeeded by a number of academies, finally settling in *Pumbedita, where it survived, with intermissions, until about the middle of the 11th century C.E. (See Map: Main Academies). The principal innovation of the Babylonian academies was the institution of the *yarḥei kallah* (months of *kallah), the assembly of the Babylonian sages at one of the leading academies in the months of Adar and Elul, when they discussed a prescribed tractate which they had studied during the preceding five months. A detailed description of the arrangements of study during the *yarḥei kallah* is given by R. Nathan ha-Bavli in *Seder Olam Zuta* (ed. Neubauer, 87–88). Although this account relates to the middle of the tenth century C.E. similar arrangements were presumably already in vogue in the days of the *amoraim*.

The Aim of the Studies in the Academies

The studies in the academies were designed to produce scholars who would be conversant in all fields of the Oral Law and who could derive from the existing *halakhah* laws applicable to new situations (see Rav's statement and the discussion in Ḥul. 9a).

The Method of Study

The pupils participated actively in the *rosh yeshivah*'s lectures, as well as in the halakhic discussions in the formulation of the law, the students' religious responsibility in this connection being duly stressed (Sanh. 7b). It was the duty of the pupils to raise objections when they believed their teacher to have erred in judgment (Shevu. 31a) and students even contested legal decisions of the *rosh yeshivah* (Ket. 51a). The *rosh yeshivah* often called in his students when deciding in cases of ritual law (Ḥul. 45b), when examining a slaughterer's knife (*ibid.*, 17b), or when dealing with questions concerning the ritual fitness of an animal (*ibid.*, 44a–b), and similar questions. From time to time the *rosh yeshivah* would test his pupils in their knowledge and understanding of the *halakhah* (Er. 76a; Ḥul. 113a).

BIBLIOGRAPHY: Schwarz, in: JJGL, 2 (1899), 83–106; Bacher, Trad, 255–6 (on the function of the *tanna*); H. Zucker, *Studien zur juedischen Selbstverwaltung im Altertum* (1936), 126–47; Halevy, Dorot, 2 (1923); Alon, Toledot, 1 (1953), 114–92; Assaf, Ge'onim, 42–52; Epstein, Mishnah 488 (on *bet va'ad* as an academy); 673–81 (on the *tanna*); Beer, in: *Bar-Ilan Annual* (Heb., 1964), 134–62; idem, in: *Papers of the Fourth World Congress of Jewish Studies*, 1 (1966), 99–101 (Heb.).

[Moshe Beer]

ACADEMY OF THE HEBREW LANGUAGE, Israeli institution that is the supreme authority on the Hebrew language. Established by the Knesset in accordance with the "Law for the Supreme Institute for the Hebrew Language, 1953," it succeeded the Hebrew Language Committee (*Va'ad ha-Lashon ha-Ivrit*) inaugurated in Jerusalem in 1890. In 1889 a group calling itself "Safah Berurah" had been formed, with the object of "spreading the Hebrew language and speech among people in all walks of life." This group elected the Committee, the first members of which were Eliezer *Ben-Yehuda, David *Yellin, R. Ḥayyim *Hirschenson, and A.M. *Luncz. Initially the Committee devoted itself to establishing Hebrew terms needed for daily use and to creating a uniform pronunciation for Hebrew speech to replace the then current variety of pronunciations. After only one year of existence, organizational problems disrupted the Committee's activities, but in 1903 at the Teachers' Conference in Zikhron Ya'akov, it was reconvened with an enlarged membership, and thereafter held regular monthly meetings.

In *Principles of the Committee's Activities*, drafted by Ben-Yehuda, its purpose was declared to be: (1) "To prepare the Hebrew language for use as a spoken language in all facets of life – in the home, school, public life, business, industry, fine arts, and in the sciences." (2) "To preserve the Oriental qualities of the language and its distinctive form, in the pronunciation of the consonants, in word structure and in style, and to add the flexibility necessary to enable it fully to express contemporary human thought."

The sources used by the Committee were Hebrew literary vocabulary of all periods; Aramaic, provided it was given Hebrew forms; Hebrew roots from which new forms could develop; and Semitic roots, especially Arabic. Non-Semitic words found in the sources were used only if they already had a Hebrew form or had been absorbed into the language and were in common use.

Scientific problems of linguistic principle were discussed in the *Zikhronot* ("Records of the Committee on Language"). In 1912, the Committee was recognized by the Teachers' Organization and the Committee for the Propagation of Hebrew as "the final authority in authorizing and choosing new words." In a lecture given at the convention of the Organization for Hebrew Language and Culture in Vienna in 1913 (published in *Zikhronot*, 4 (1914)), David Yellin defined the Committee as not merely a factory for new words, as its opponents alleged, but the highest authority for all matters of language, encouraging the coordinated work of all Hebrew linguists and writers. At the 11th Zionist Congress (1913), M. *Ussishkin proposed a resolution authorizing the Committee "to serve as the center of the renaissance and development of the Hebrew language" and urging the Zionist General Council to give it the necessary moral aid and material assistance. After World War I, the beginning of the British Mandate and the Jewish National Home, Hebrew became an official language in Palestine. The Committee, which had been largely inactive during the war, now felt an obligation to expand the program of the Language Committee far beyond its previous range. Practical linguistics and the supply of new words were to be increased, and it engaged in language research, intended to lay the scientific foundations for the practical work.

With an increased membership, the Committee met frequently, establishing and publishing professional terminology. To prepare for the establishment of the Haifa Technion and the Hebrew University, as well as to facilitate the development of trade and industry, work in the various subjects was divided among subcommittees, consisting of members of the Committee and experts in the particular field. These met in Jerusalem, Tel Aviv, and Haifa, referring their findings to other specialists in the field as well as to all members of the Language Committee. After final approval, lists were published in the Hebrew Language Committee's quarterly, *Leshonenu*, or in a special dictionary.

The Sephardi pronunciation was established as the standard for spoken Hebrew and instruction in the schools. Rules of spelling were established: grammatical when the writing was vocalized and "full" (*plene*) in unvocalized writing. Rules of punctuation were determined, and doubtful matters of grammar clarified. While developments in technology and the sciences forced the committees on terminology to include many non-Semitic words in the Hebrew dictionary, the formation of verbs from foreign words was deliberately restricted because, while nouns are easily assimilated into Hebrew, verbs are not. Nevertheless, the formation of verbs such as טִלְפֵּן (*talpen*, "telephone") and גִּלְוֵן (*galven*, "galvanize") proved unavoidable. Grammatical nouns encountered certain scholarly and practical obstacles: the establishment of spelling rules was long delayed by disputes between adherents of biblical spelling and those of the "full" spelling current in post-biblical literature.

The law adopted by the Knesset in 1953 established the Academy and defined its function as the "development of Hebrew, based on the study of the language in its various periods and branches." The maximum number of members is 23. Well-known scholars in various fields of Jewish and Hebrew studies were appointed as members of the Academy, together with practicing writers, and a number of advisory and honorary members were invited to join them. N.H. *Tur-Sinai was chosen to be president of the Academy, a position he held until 1973. Subsequent presidents were Ze'ev Ben *Ḥayyim (1973–1981), Joshua *Blau (1981–1988), and Moshe Bar-Asher (1988–).

The supreme body within the Academy is the plenum, to which linguistic problems discussed in the various committees are referred for final discussion and approval. The plenum meets five or six times a year. The committees on terminology hold weekly or biweekly meetings attended by at least two members from the Academy as well as by specialists in the areas under discussion. Scientific secretaries assemble the available linguistic material in each area, which is then checked against literary sources and decisions already taken in other areas. After discussion, the secretary collates the material and transmits it to all Academy members and to further specialists in the field, who are entitled to comment on, or take issue with, the committee's findings. The material is finally presented to the plenum for discussion, authorization, and publication, either in the *Zikhronot ha-Akademyah* or in the series of technical dictionaries, originally instituted by the Hebrew Language Committee. Among dictionaries published in recent years are those on electronics, chemistry, molecular biology, psychology, library science, diplomacy, medicine, and home economics. Committees on terminology are at work in the fields of banking, law, sociology, nomenclature of plants, and artificial intelligence. The Haifa office for technical terminology is a joint body of the Academy and the Technion. Committees on grammar and spelling follow a similar work pattern, but since the problems in this area are complex, there are usually greater differences of opinion and theory, centering, as a rule, on the conflict between the dictates of historical grammar and those of living speech and practical teaching. Language forms created outside the Academy, whether originating in foreign influence, in slang, or in the language of children, also demand a clear decision by the Academy.

A practical problem over which the Academy, in common with its predecessor, has labored for many years, is the determining of Hebrew spelling. Hebrew writing is mostly consonantal, the vowels being represented by vocalization signs. This spelling, inadequate in the past, is even more so in the present, since the vowels are rarely indicated either in script or in print. The spelling used in the past generations, which substitutes *matres lectionis* for vowels, is incomplete (although it is called "full"), lacks uniformity, and is not universally accepted. The rules for unvocalized spelling, established by the Hebrew Language Committee, were never generally accepted and various systems have been retained. In 1968, after prolonged debate, the Academy decided to maintain two modes of spelling: one vocalized according to all the established grammatical rules, the other an unvocalized spelling in accordance with the rules of the Hebrew Language Committee. A related question is how to transliterate Hebrew into Latin letters in such a way that the non-Hebrew reader is able to pronounce the name as it is said in Hebrew, and after much discussion, a system was approved. In addition, rules have been determined for the transliteration of foreign names into Hebrew as well as for transliteration from Arabic into Hebrew. Rules have also been established for vocalization of foreign words. New rules for Hebrew punctuation were approved in 1993. The Academy assists public bodies requiring linguistic guidance, such as the National Committee on Names, scientific projects, the state broadcasting system, etc.

Academy decisions are published either as technical dictionaries, in lists of terms, or as collections of rules in the annual *Zikhronot ha-Akademyah la-Lashon ha-Ivrit.* A special project of the Academy is the *Historical Dictionary of the Hebrew Language*, begun in 1954 by an editorial board headed by Z. Ben-Ḥayyim, planned to include all Hebrew words and their uses from the earliest sources until the present. Preparatory work on material from tannaitic literature, the Talmud, and Midrash has been completed. Work continues on readying ancient *piyyut*, geonic, Karaite, and North African literature, and modern Hebrew literature (dating from 1750). The historical dictionary project is fully computerized and applies programs especially adapted to the dictionary's requirements. In 1994 the Academy established the "Masie Institute" to bring the Academy closer to the public and for research into the history of the revival of Hebrew in Israel and the Diaspora from its earliest stages to the establishment of the State of Israel. The publications of the Committee and of the Academy are *Zikhronot* for the years 1920–28, vol. 5 edited by J. Klausner, vol. 6 by S. Ben-Zion, D. Yellin, and A. Ẓifroni. Afterwards the committee decisions were published in *Leshonenu* (see below) up to 1954. Then, when the Academy was established, a new series of *Zikhronot* was commenced under the name of

Bronze figurines of bulls dating from the 12th–10th c. B.C.E., Judea. *Photo: Z. Radovan, Jerusalem.*

There are hundreds of animals mentioned throughout the Bible, ranging from the fantastic, such as the great fish that swallows Jonah, to the everyday, such as rams and calves. The fauna of Israel and the surrounding area where the stories of the Bible took place is extremely varied, as is its flora, because Israel enjoys four climate zones. The images here show a few of these animals represented in sculpture, drawing, and other art forms.

ANIMALS OF THE BIBLE

Detail of the mosaic floor of the 4th c. C.E. Gaza synagogue depicting a lioness and her cub. *Photo: Z. Radovan, Jerusalem.*

ABOVE: **Illustration of Jonah being swallowed by the great fish from a Hebrew Bible, 1299.** *© Visual Arts Library (London)/Alamy.*

LEFT: **Cast of Hebrew seal (9th–8th c. B.C.E.) inscribed "Shema, servant of Jeroboam," found in Megiddo.** *Photo: Z. Radovan, Jerusalem.*

Ram caught in a bush, detail of the mosaic floor of the 6th c. C.E. synagogue at Bet Alfa. *Photo: Z. Radovan, Jerusalem.*

Ivory calf, from Megiddo, Israel, Israelite period (c. 1200–600 B.C.E.). Bronze Age. *Erich Lessing/Art Resource, NY.*

RIGHT: Bronze monkey from Megiddo, Israelite period (c. 1200–600 B.C.E.). *Photo: Z. Radovan, Jerusalem.*

BELOW: From one of the wall paintings of the Dura Europos synagogue: The consecration of the tabernacle, showing the ark of the covenant, the *menorah,* and sacrificial animals. *Photo: Z. Radovan, Jerusalem.*

Hamat Tiberias synagogue mosaic floor. Detail from the zodiac panel depicting the sign of Taurus. *Photo: Z. Radovan, Jerusalem.*

Leopard detail, ca. 6th c. C.E., from the mosaic in the pavement at the synagogue of Maon at Nirim, Israel. *Erich Lessing/Art Resource, NY.*

Zikhronot ha-Akademia la-Lashon ha-Ivrit: vols. 1–2 (1954–55), 3–4 (1956–57), 5 (1958), 6 (1959), 7–8 (1960–61), 9 (1962), 10–11 (1963–64), 12 (1965), 13 (1966), 14 (1967), 15 (1968), 16 (1969), 17 (1970), 18 (1971), 19–20 (1972–73), and 21–24 (1974–77) of the new series were probably edited by Meir Medan, but no name of an editor is specified; vols. 25–27 (1978–80), 28–30 (1981–83) and 31–34 (1984–87) were edited by Y. Yannai; 35–37 (1988–90) by Y. Yannai and J. Ofer; 38–40 (1991–93) and 41–43 (1994–96) by J. Ofer; and vol. 44–46 (1997–99) by D. Barak. *Leshonenu*, a quarterly, was edited by A. Ẓifroni (1929–34, five volumes) and N.H. Torczyner (*Tur-Sinai) from 1934 to 1954. These continued under the auspices of the Academy and were edited by Z. Ben-Ḥayyim from 1955 to 1965, by E. Kutscher from 1965 to 1971, by S. Abramson from 1972 to 1980, by Y. Blau from 1981 to 1999, and from 2000 by M. Bar-Asher. *Leshonenu la-Am*, popular pamphlets on matters of language, consist of six pamphlets edited by A. Avrunin, M. Ezraḥi, and I. Pereẓ (and more regularly from 1949 to date, a few pamphlets a year). There is also a series of technical dictionaries. The Academy's lexical innovations used to be disseminated among the public through *Lemad Leshonkha* ("Learn Your Language") pages published bimonthly, and since 1989 in the framework of a regular newsletter called *Aqaddem*. Among the most important recent publications are the *Ma'agarim* CD which includes all the sources of the ancient period, the critical edition of the *Talmud Yerushalmi* according to the Leiden MS, and the second part of *Sefer ha-Mekorot* (the Book of Sources) for the North African Hebrew literature from 1391 to date (1,941 pages).

BIBLIOGRAPHY: Ben-Ḥayyim, in: *Ariel*, 13 (1966), 14–20 (Eng.); *Zikhronot Va'ad ha-Lashon (ha-Ivrit)*, 1–3 (1912–13; second printing in one volume, 1929); 4 (1914); 5 (1921); 6 (1928); Yellin, in: *Leshonenu*, 10 (1940), 269–77; Klausner, *ibid.*, 278–89; 16 (1949), 250–67; 18 (1953), 227–38; *Zikhronot ha-Akademyah la-Lashon ha-Ivrit*, 46 vols. (1954–99); S. Eisenstadt, *Sefatenu ha-Ivrit ha-Ḥayyah* (1967); Ben-Ḥayyim, in: *Leshonenu*, 23 (1959), 102–23; for bibliography see *Leshonenu*, index vol. for vols. 1–25 (1967), 70–72.

[Meir Medan]

ACADEMY ON HIGH. In rabbinic tradition, a heavenly body of scholars. Post-mishnaic (talmudic and midrashic) literature speaks of an Academy on High, for which two terms are used: "*Yeshivah shel Ma'lah*" ("Academy on High") and "*Metivta de-Raki'a*" ("Academy of the Sky"). It is clear from *Bava Mezia* 86a that the two terms are identical. Generally speaking, the Academy on High has the same features as an earthly academy. Scholars continue their studies and debates there; therefore the death of a sage is expressed as a summons to the Academy on High (BM 86a). Very daringly, the Almighty Himself is made to participate in its debates and is not even an absolute authority. One of His rulings is contested by all the other scholars, and a human, Rabbah b. Nahamani, is especially summoned from earth (i.e., to die) for a final decision, which he gives before he dies. Although his ruling concurs with that of the Almighty, it is given independently.

Every day God gives a new interpretation of the Torah (Gen. R. 49:2), and He cites the opinions of various scholars (Ḥag. 15b). He also instructs young children who died before they could study (Av. Zar. 3b; however, the Academy on High is not mentioned there). The most surprising of all students is *Asmodeus, the king of the demons, who is depicted as studying daily in both the heavenly and the earthly academies (Git. 68a). Admission to the Academy on High is automatic for scholars (Eccl. R. 5:11, no. 5), although it may be denied for certain reasons (Ber. 18b). Others may enjoy the privilege for particularly meritorious deeds. These include teaching Torah to a neighbor's son (BM 85a) and assisting scholars to study by promoting their commercial ventures (Pes. 53b).

Greetings were sent from this Academy to people who were still alive. Abbaye received these once a week on the eve of the Sabbath. Rava, his contemporary, was greeted once a year, on the eve of the Day of Atonement. However, a certain *Abba Umana ("the bloodletter") was privileged to receive greetings daily because of the due proprieties which he observed when bleeding women patients. Scholars have their definite places there, according to rank. The great *amora* Johanan was not deemed worthy of sitting next to Ḥiyya (BM 85b). They sit in a semi-circle, like the Sanhedrin on earth (Eccles. R. 1:11, no. 1). Nothing suggests that this academy is identical with paradise. On the Day of Atonement, before *Kol Nidrei*, the permission of the Academy on High is invoked to hold the Service together with "transgressors." It is also invoked in the prayer recited before changing the name of a sick person, see *Seder Berakhot* (Amsterdam, 1687), 259ff.

[Harry Freedman]

In Kabbalah

The Zohar makes a clear distinction between the two terms "Academy of Heaven" and "Academy on High." The former is headed by *Metatron and the latter by God Himself (II, 273b; III, 163a, 192a, 197b, 241b, etc.). Promotion from one academy to the other is mentioned, as are some academy heads in certain departments of the heavenly academy, e.g., "the Academy of Moses", "the Academy of Aaron." A long section in the portion *Shelaḥ Lekha* (III, 162ff.) is devoted to a description of the imaginary wanderings of *Simeon b. Yoḥai in these academies and his meeting with the head of the Academy of Heaven. The place of Metatron in the Zohar is taken in the Testament of Rabbi Eliezer the Great, composed by the author of the Zohar himself, by Rav Gaddiel Na'ar, who forms the subject of a special legend (Seder Gan Eden, *Beit Midrash* of Jellinek, III, 136). In order to distinguish between the two academies, *Midrash ha-Ne'lam* on Ruth (Zohar Ḥadash, 84a) changed the term "Academy of Heaven" which occurs in the Talmud (Ber. 12b) to "Academy on High." Legendary motifs concerning the Heavenly Academy which occur in the Talmud were completely remolded in the Zohar, especially in the story of R. Ḥiyya's ascent to the Academy of Heaven (Zohar I, 4a). The *Messiah seems also to come into this academy at certain times so as to study the Torah with the sages of the academy.

[Gershom Scholem]

BIBLIOGRAPHY: Ginzberg, Legends, index s.v. *Academy*, and *Heavenly Academy;* G. Scholem, in: *Le-Agnon Shai* (1959), 290–305.

AÇAN, MOSES DE TARREGA (**Zaragua**?; c. 1300), Catalan poet. Moses Açan, whose true name was probably Moses Nathan (Naçan), is known for his verse treatise in Catalan on chess. The introduction begins with an account of the Creation, stressing man's obligation to worship God the Creator. It ends with an explanation of the rules of chess and a condemnation of other games, especially card playing. The work was translated into Castilian by a Jew or Jewish convert in 1350; a manuscript copy was preserved in El Escorial. He seems to be also the author of a collection of 58 short poems of ethical content, *Toẓa'ot Ḥayyim*, published by Menahem ben Yehuda de Lonzano in 1618. Their originality and literary value are not very high. In the acrostic he calls himself Moses Ben-Netanel Bar-Solomon. He could also be identical with one of the notable Jews of the Crown of Aragon who signed the *takkanot* in Barcelona on 1354.

The author has been also identified with the Moses b. Joseph Açan who at Cuenca in 1271 warned King Alfonso x of a conspiracy of the Castilian nobles led by the Infante Felipe, but this identification is unfounded.

BIBLIOGRAPHY: J. Amador de los Ríos, *Estudios sobre los Judíos de España* (1848), 289ff.; Kayserling, Bibl, 8. **ADD. BIBLIOGRAPHY:** F. Baer, *Die Juden in christlichen Spanien* (1929), 306, 339, 359; Schirmann, Sefarad, 541–43; Schirmann-Fleischer, *The History of Hebrew Poetry in Christian Spain and Southern France* (1997), 569–70; V. Keats, *Chess among the Jews*, 3 (1995), 65–70.

[Kenneth R. Scholberg / Angel Saenz-Badillos (2nd ed.)]

ACE, GOODMAN (1899–1982), U.S. humorist. Born in Kansas City, Mo., as Goodman Aiskowitz, he was an actor, comedian, and writer who supplied dozens of performers with funny things to say but also became well known for the malapropisms he provided for his wife on a nationally heard radio program that ran from 1930 to 1945. At his peak Ace was probably the highest-paid writer in television. The son of a haberdasher, he got his first job as a hat salesman. He shifted quickly to newspaper writing and became a columnist on the *Journal Post*. Seeking to supplement his salary as a columnist and theater and film reviewer, he did extra work commenting on films for a radio station. After he finished a 15-minute program, the station manager asked him and his wife Jane, who happened to be at the station, to stay on the air because the performers for the next segment had not yet shown up. The ad-lib show proved so popular that the Aces were hired to do two programs a week. By 1931 they had moved to the CBS network. Over the air the quips and bon mots seemed to flow effortlessly, but Ace had carefully composed each misused expression for Jane Ace. She died in 1974. Ace wrote for performers as diverse as Danny *Kaye, Perry Como, Sid *Caesar, Milton *Berle, and Bob Newhart.

[Stewart Kampel (2nd ed.)]

ACHAN (Heb. עָכָן), sacrilegious transgressor from the tribe of Judah, son of Carmi, son of Zabdi, son of Zerah. In the time of Joshua, Achan violated the **ḥerem* imposed on Jericho and was subsequently executed (Josh. 7). Despite the ban on spoils from Jericho, Achan misappropriated a fine *shinar* mantle, 200 shekels of silver, and a wedge (lit. "tongue") of 50 shekels' weight and buried them in the ground under his tent. The Israelites were defeated in an attempt to take *Ai because of the trespass of the *ḥerem*. Lots were cast to determine who was responsible and Achan was indicated. On the principle of collective responsibility the people had been punished for the transgression of this one man, since Achan's sin was ascribed to all of Israel (Josh. 7:1, 11). Achan confessed his sin publicly before God and Israel (Josh. 7:20–21). Another example of collective responsibility is that he was stoned with all his family in the valley of *Achor ("troubling"), where the articles he had taken were burned and a great mound of stones was raised over him. The word *achor* is a play on the name Achan. In I Chronicles 2:7 he is actually called "Achar, the troubler of Israel."

The story of Achan may be an amalgam from two different sources. The first half of Joshua 7:25 reads "and they stoned him," while the second half says "and they stoned them," which is not only a duplication but employs a different Hebrew verb for "to stone." The story is widely regarded as an independent, Judean, etiological narrative, explaining the origin of the name valley of Achor and the presence there of a big pile of stones (Josh. 7:26). According to Y. Kaufmann, however, it belongs to a class of biblical legal literature which illustrated rulings by example. These were actual cases decided on the spot and the story preserved the result of the case (e.g., Lev. 10:1–7, 12–20; 24:10–23; Num. 9:6–44; 27:1–11; 36:1–12; I Sam. 30:22–25).

In the *Aggadah*

Achan was a hardened criminal whose sins (previous to stealing the spoil from Jericho) included desecration of the Sabbath, obliterating the signs of his circumcision, and adultery (Sanh. 44a). Nevertheless, he is one of the three men who, by their confessions, lost this world, and gained the world to come (ARN version B, 4–5:3). When his fellow tribesmen were willing to espouse his cause to the extent of slaying one group after another in Israel, Achan said to himself: "Any man who preserves one life in Israel is as though he had preserved the entire world… It is better that I should confess than be responsible for a calamity" (Num. R. 23:6). His confession was a victory over his evil inclinations. "The Lord shall trouble thee this day" (Josh. 7:25), implied: "This day thou art troubled, but thou wilt not be troubled in the world to come" (Lev. E. 9:1 and Sanh. 6:2).

BIBLIOGRAPHY: de Vaux, Anc. Isr., index, s.v. *Akan* and *Ḥerem*; Y. Kaufmann, *Sefer Yehoshu'a* (1959), 116–7; Malamat, in: *Sefer ha-Yovel… Y. Kaufmann* (1960), 149ff. **ADD. BIBLIOGRAPHY:** S. Stern, *The Biblical Herem* (1991); S. Ahituv, *Joshua* (1995), 121–29.

ACHBOR (Heb. עַכְבּוֹר), the name of two biblical figures. (1) Achbor was the father of Baal-Hanan, king of Edom (Gen. 36:38–39; I Chron. 1:49). Some scholars maintain that the father's name is not Achbor, but a duplication of Beor (Gen. 36:32), because the king's native city is not given (as in all the other cases, rather than their father's name). Nonetheless, there is no doubt that the name existed. It can denote a mouse (*akhbar*), as it is normal for biblical persons to bear animal names. Furthermore, there may also be a cultic connotation for this name, as is proved by the discovery of sacrificial mice (cf. also the golden mice in I Sam. 6:4, 5, 11), and the reference in Isaiah 66:17 to a non-Yahwistic cultic practice in which mice were eaten. This is in addition to the preservation of a tradition by Maimonides that the Horites sacrificed mice. It is further interesting to note that a seal bearing the words "Hananyahu ben Akhbor" was found in Jerusalem.

(2) Achbor, the son of Micaiah, was one of the men sent by King Josiah to consult the prophetess *Huldah (II Kings 22:12–14; in II Chron. 34:20, he is called *Abdon, probably a corruption of Achbor). On the mission he is believed to have represented the pro-Egyptian families, who were influential in the last days of the Kingdom of Judah (see *Ahikam). His son, *Elnathan, was one of the ministers in the time of Jehoiakim (Jer. 26:22; 36:12). Possibly "*K-[-]iahu* son of Elnathan," an army officer mentioned in one o f the Lachish ostraca (no. 3, 1.15), was Achbor's grandson in the time of Zedekiah.

BIBLIOGRAPHY: Albright, in: JBL, 51 (1932), 79–80; Yeivin, in: *Tarbiz*, 12 (1940/41), 253, 255.

ACHISH (Heb. אָכִישׁ), *Philistine king of *Gath, mentioned at the end of Saul's reign. In I Samuel 27:2, his father's name is given as Maoch. Achish's realm was extensive and included the city of Ziklag and its environs (I Sam. 27:6). Fugitives from Judah often sought shelter in his land because of its proximity to Judah (I Kings 2:39–40). At first Achish refused *David permission to stay in his territory, possibly to avoid becoming embroiled in a political conflict with Saul (I Sam. 21:11ff.). After a company of several hundred men, however, had gathered around David, Achish welcomed him and even allocated to him the Ziklag region (I Sam. 27). It is possible that David took his first steps in royal administration when he was in the kingdom of Gath.

In the Septuagint Achish is called Akchous, Agchous, Agchis. If the late readings reflect some early tradition, it would seem almost certain that the original form of the name was Achush or Akkush, which corresponds or is related to Ikusu, the name of one of the kings of Ekron in the days of Esarhaddon and Ashurbanipal, now attested to in a monumental inscription from Ekron. The name Achish is not Semitic in form, and some scholars have related it to Agchioses, the name of a king in the neighborhood of Troy who lived around the time of the Trojan War (*Iliad*, 2:819; 20:239; et al.). The fact that the form *Agchisis* is not Greek supports the theory that Achish and *Agchisis* may have had a common origin. Since the name *Akhshan* is found in an Egyptian list as the name of a son of Kaphtor (*Keftiu*), it is plausible to assume that the form "Achish" stems from the same group of peoples to which the Philistines belonged. But it is also conceivable that the name is Horite, because the combination of sounds in "Achish" is possible in Horite. J. Naveh has argued that Achish was an appellative employed as a throne name.

A king of Gath called Achish is also referred to in the fourth year of Solomon's rule; he is called "Achish son of Maacah" (I Kings 2:39). Perhaps there were two kings by this name; Achish son of Maoch, the predecessor, and Achish son of Maacah, the successor of an intermediate king called Maacah.

BIBLIOGRAPHY: Mazar, in: PIASH, vol. 1, no. 7 (1964), 1ff. **ADD. BIBLIOGRAPHY:** V. Sasson, in: UF 29 (1997), 627–39; J. Naveh, in: BASOR 310 (1998), 35–37; A. Demsky, in: BAR 24, 5 (1998), 53–58.

[Joshua Gutmann]

ACHOR, VALLEY OF (Heb. עֵמֶק עָכוֹר), site near Jericho where *Achan was stoned to death for helping himself to some of the forbidden booty taken from Jericho (Josh. 7:24–26). Achor is mentioned in Joshua (15:7) as being located on the border of Judah and Benjamin, between Debir and Adummim. Both Hosea (2:17) and Isaiah (65:10) predicted that in time to come this valley would cease to be a desert. Achor figures in the *Copper Scroll from the Dead Sea as the site of vast hidden treasures. Eusebius (Onom. 18:17–20) located it north of Jericho in the direction of Galgala, and it has been placed by most scholars in or near Wadi el-Qelt, or farther north at the large Wadi Nuwei'imeh. A more recent suggestion is al-Buqei'ah, a large plain in the Judean Desert southwest of Jericho.

BIBLIOGRAPHY: Abel, Geog, 2 (1938), 48; Milik, in: RB, 66 (1959), 331–2; Noth, in: ZDPV, 71 (1955), 1–59; M. Baillet et al., *Discoveries in the Judaean Desert*, 3 (1962), 262ff.; J.M. Allegro, *Treasure of the Copper Scroll* (1960), 64–68; Wolff, in: ZDPV, 70 (1954), 76–81; Muilenburg, in: BASOR, 140 (1955), 11–19.

[Michael Avi-Yonah]

ACHRON, JOSEPH (1886–1943), composer and violinist. Achron made his debut at the age of eight, touring Russia as a prodigy violinist. He studied with *Auer and Liadow at St. Petersburg, and later taught at the Kharkov Conservatory (1913–18). Achron began his composing career by writing light music. His association in St. Petersburg with the group of Jewish writers and musicians who founded the Society for Jewish Folk Music brought about a change in musical interests, and manifested itself in his *Hebrew Melody* (1911). After attempting to settle in Berlin (1918–22) and Palestine (1924), he went to New York in 1925. There he wrote music for Yiddish plays and was commissioned to compose *Evening Service for the Sabbath* for Temple Emanu-El (1932). In 1934 he moved to Hollywood, wrote film music, but continued serious composition. Achron's work shows the stresses resulting from his double role as a performing musician and a composer. He composed more than 80 works, including violin sonatas and concertos, *Symphonic Variations and Sonata on the Folk Song "El Yivneh ha-Galil"* (1915), *Concerto for Piano Alone* (1941), *Golem Suite* (1932), *Sextet for Woodwinds* (1942), and incidental music to plays by *Goldfaden, *Shalom Aleichem, Peretz, and Sholem *Asch. The bulk of his manuscripts is preserved in the National and University Library, Jerusalem.

ISIDOR (1892–1948), brother of Joseph, born in Warsaw, was a pianist and composer. He studied in St. Petersburg and toured Europe and the U.S., where he settled in 1922.

BIBLIOGRAPHY: A. Weisser, *Modern Renaissance of Jewish Music* (1954), 81–91; P. Gradenwitz, *Musikgeschichte Israels* (1961), 160; J. Stutschewsky, *Mein Weg zur juedischen Musik* (1935), 24ff.; Sendrey, Music, index; P. Moddel, *Joseph Achron* (Eng., 1966).

ACHSAH (Heb. עַכְסָה; probably "anklet," cf. Isa. 3:18), the daughter of *Caleb, the son of Jephunneh. Achsah's father announced that he would give her in marriage to the man who would capture Kiriath-Sepher (later called *Debir; modern Tell Beit Mirsim). *Othniel, son of Kenaz, the latter apparently a younger brother of Caleb (Caleb and Kenaz both being the sons of the Kenizzite Jephunneh), took Kiriath-Sepher and married Achsah (Jos. 15:16–17; Judg. 1:12–13). Apparently because Othniel desired a dowry in addition to the girl (whom her father had "given away as Negeb Land" [i.e., without dowry], see Kaufmann ad loc.), she asked her father for a piece of property known as Upper and Lower Springs and Caleb acceded to her request (Jos. 15:18–19; Judg. 1:14–15). This story is told in connection with the apportionment of land to the families of the tribe of Judah (Josh. *ibid.*; Judg. *ibid.*). Caleb, according to the critical view, represents a tribe or group of families (cf. I Sam. 25:2–3) that was incorporated into Judah. The detailed story intended to describe the settlement of Othniel and the families of Kenaz in a Calebite region. Furthermore, the story brings to light the relations between the families of Caleb and that of Kenaz (probably both Hurrians).

The name Achsah is derived from the root עכס (cf. Isa. 3:18; Prov. 7:22), meaning to reverse, tie backward, hence anklet, bangle.

BIBLIOGRAPHY: Noth, Personennamen, 223. **ADD. BIBLIOGRAPHY:** J. Stamm, in, SVT16 ת (FS Baumgartmerl 1967), 328; Y. Amit, *Judges* (1999), 35–36.

ACHSHAPH (**Akhshaf**; Heb. אַכְשָׁף), ancient Canaanite town, usually mentioned together with Acre in Egyptian documents from the Middle and New Kingdoms (cf. the Execration Texts of early 18th century B.C.E.), the list of cities conquered by Thutmosis III (c. 1469 B.C.E.), the El-Amarna letters (14th century B.C.E.), and the Papyrus Anastasi (13th century B.C.E.). It was in the territory allotted to Asher in the period of the Israelite conquest (Josh. 19:25). The king of Achshaph is listed among the 31 kings who fought Joshua (*ibid.* 12:20); he participated in the battle at the Waters of Merom (*ibid.* 11:1). The various sources indicate a location in the southern part of the Plain of Acre, perhaps one of the more prominent of its many ancient tells: Tell Kisan 6 mi. (10 km.) S.E. of Acre, or Khirbet al-Harbaj, E. of Haifa near Kefar Ḥasidim.

BIBLIOGRAPHY: Maisler (Mazar), in: BJPES, 6 (1939), 151–7; Alt, in: PJB, 20 (1924), 26; 24 (1928), 60; J. Garstang, *Joshua, Judges* (1931), 98–99, 354; Albright, in: BASOR, 61 (1936), 24; 81 (1941), 19; 83 (1941), 33; EM, s.v.; Press, Ereẓ, 1 (1946), 19.

[Michael Avi-Yonah]

ACHZIB (Heb. אַכְזִיב). The name may mean "charming," "delightful." (1) Ancient Canaanite harbor town north of Acre near the cliff called "the ladder of Tyre." North of the village is a tell in which potsherds dating from and after the Early Bronze Age have been found. According to Joshua 19:29 and Judges 1:31, Achzib belonged to the tribe of Asher, but it did not come under the effective control of the Israelites, as the Canaanites continued to occupy it. A large number of tombs from the period of the Israelite monarchy have been discovered south and east of the tell. *Sennacherib captured Achzib from the king of Tyre in 701 B.C.E. In the period of the Second Temple, Achzib is mentioned (in the Greek form Ekdippa) as a road station, 9 Roman mi. north of Ptolemais (Acre., Jos., Wars, 1:257; Pliny, 19). A Roman milestone has been found on the site, on the Acre–Antioch road, in addition to many Roman tombs. In the mishnaic period, Achzib, then called also Kheziv (Gesiv in the Palestinian Talmud), was considered a part of Erez Israel and its inhabitants were bound by all the biblical laws pertaining to the sabbatical and jubilee years, priestly dues, and tithes (Shev. 6:1; 4:6; Hal. 4:8; 2:6; Tosef. Oho. 18:14). Achzib occupied an important position as a base-camp for the Crusader armies and was known as Casal Imbert after the knight who held it. The Arab geographers of the Middle Ages (Ibn Jubayr, 307; Yaqut, 2:964; Idrisi, 2) refer to it as al-Zib, a fortified village. Until 1948 the site was occupied by the Arab village of al-Zib, 9 mi. (15 km.) north of Acre. Nearby is the kibbutz *Gesher ha-Ziv whose name was partly inspired by the ancient city. In excavations conducted in 1941–44 and 1959–64, fortifications and occupational levels were discovered beginning with the Middle Bronze Age II (first half of the second millennium B.C.E.) to the Roman period and also from the Crusader period and Middle Ages. Most of the tombs investigated were Phoenician (tenth to seventh centuries B.C.E.); others were from the Persian and Roman periods. The tombs were rock-hewn and also contained pottery, figurines, scarabs, and bronze and silver jewelry. Four tombstones were especially significant, being engraved with the name of the deceased; and in one instance, with his occupation (metal worker). A Phoenician inscription on the shoulder of a jar mentions Adonimelekh.

(2) A city of the biblical period in the Shephelah of Judah, between Keilah and Mareshah (Josh. 15:44; Micah 1:14–15) also called Chezib (Gen. 38:5). It is mentioned by Eusebius (Onom. 172:6) as Chasbi near Adullam, a reference which would confirm its proposed identification with Tell al-Bayḍā (today Lavnin) west of Adullam.

BIBLIOGRAPHY: (1) Saarisalo, in: JPOS, 9 (1929), 38ff.; Abel, Geog, 2 (1938), 237; Prawer, Ẓalbanim, index; EM s.v.; Press, Ereẓ, 1 (1946), 18; Prausnitz, in: IEJ, 15 (1965), 256–8. **ADD. BIBLIOGRAPHY:** idem, in: IEJ, 25 (1975), 202–10; J. Dearman, in: JNSL, 22 (1996), 59–71. (2) Saarisalo, in: JPOS, 11 (1931), 98; Elliger, in: ZDPV, 57 (1934), 121–4.

[Michael Avi-Yonah]

ACKERMAN, GARY (1942–), U.S. congressman. Ackerman was born in Brooklyn and raised in Queens, New York. His parents, Max and Eva (Barnett) Ackerman, were the children of East European immigrants. Ackerman was educated in the New York public school system and graduated from Queens College. Following his graduation, Ackerman spent four years teaching junior high school. In 1970, when his wife gave birth to the first of their three daughters, Ackerman petitioned the New York Board of Education for an unpaid leave of absence. He was turned down; under the then existing policy, maternity leave was solely for women. In what was to become a forerunner of the Federal Family Leave Act, Ackerman successfully sued the Board of Education in a landmark case, which established the right of either parent to claim such leave.

At the end of his unpaid leave, Ackerman left teaching in order to start a weekly newspaper, the *Flushing Tribune*, eventually renamed the *Queen's Tribune*. Ackerman was elected as a Democrat to the New York State Senate in 1978 and to the United States Congress in a special election held in 1983 to fill the unexpired term of the late Benjamin Rosenthal. During his more than 20 years in Congress, Ackerman has been a forthright supporter of Israel. As a member of the House Committee on International Relations, Ackerman has traveled the globe extensively. He was one of the first members of Congress to draw attention to the rescue of Soviet and Ethiopian Jews. He has long made it a practice to go to synagogue in every country he visits.

A celebrated character on Capitol Hill, who always wears a white carnation in his lapel and lives on a houseboat docked in the Potomac River, Ackerman is perhaps best known for being the co-founder (along with New York Senator Charles *Schumer) of an informal group known as "The Congressional Minyan." Ackerman's *minyan* is a group of Jewish legislators and staff members who gather several times a month in the Congressman's office to study Torah and Talmud with a rabbi he flies in from New York City. Once a year, Ackerman also hosts an annual "Taste of New York" gathering on Capitol Hill, which features Jewish food and waiters imported from New York. Widely popular with his largely Jewish constituency, Ackerman has been reelected every two years since 1984 by wide margins.

BIBLIOGRAPHY: K.F. Stone, *The Congressional Minyan: The Jews of Capitol Hill* (2000) 4–7.

[Kurt Stone (2nd ed.)]

ACKERMAN, NATHAN WARD (1908–1971), U.S. psychiatrist, born in Russia. Ackerman joined the Menninger Clinic in Topeka, Kansas, and became the chief psychiatrist of the Child Guidance Clinic in 1937. In 1957 he established the Family Mental Health Clinic in New York City and began teaching at Columbia University. He was a clinical professor of psychiatry at Columbia, chief psychiatrist of the Child Guidance Institute of the Jewish Board of Guardians, and supervising psychiatrist of the Family Mental Health Clinic of the Jewish Family Service, New York.

Ackerman held that the family unit is the crucial link between individual personality and the social and cultural milieu, that psychiatric abnormality in a child is at times an expression of disturbed emotional relations in the entire family, and that cure requires therapy of the conflicts and relations of the family group as such. His astute ability to understand the overall organization of families enabled him to look beyond the behavioral interactions of families and into the hearts and minds of each family member. He used his strong will and provocative style of intervening to uncover the family's defenses and allow their feelings, hopes, and desires to surface. Committed to sharing his ideas and theoretical approach with other professionals in the field, he published *The Unity of the Family* and *Family Diagnosis: An Approach to the Preschool Child* (1938), both of which inspired the family therapy movement. Together with Don Jackson, he founded the first family therapy journal, *Family Process* (1960), which is still a leading journal of ideas in the field today.

Ackerman opened the Family Institute in New York City in 1960, which was later renamed The Ackerman Institute for Family Therapy. A nonprofit institution, its twofold mission was to develop innovative and effective models of treatment for families in trouble and to train clinicians to implement these models.

On behalf of the American Jewish Committee, Ackerman was coauthor of *Anti-Semitism and Emotional Disorder* (1950). On family therapy he wrote numerous articles in professional journals; the books *The Psychodynamics of Family Life* (1958), *Treating the Troubled Family* (1966), *Expanding Theory and Practice in Family Therapy* (1967), and *Family Process* (1970); and edited several anthologies, such as *Family Therapy in Transition* (1971). He also coauthored with Marie Jahoda *Anti-Semitism and Emotional Disorder, a Psychoanalytic Interpretation* (1950). His selected papers were published in *The Strength of Family Therapy* (1982).

[Ruth Beloff (2nd ed.)]

ACKERMAN, PAULA HERSKOVITZ (1893–1989), first woman to assume spiritual leadership of a U.S. mainstream Jewish congregation. Born in Pensacola, Florida, Ackerman was active in the Reform movement throughout her life. Graduating as high school valedictorian in 1911, she received a scholarship to Sophie Newcomb College, which she declined for personal and family reasons. To supplement her family's income, she became a private music instructor and high school math and Latin teacher. She also taught at Temple Beth-El, the Reform congregation to which her family belonged, leading its congregational choir as well. In 1919 she married Dr. William Ackerman, the rabbi of Temple Beth-El; the couple left Pensacola for a better-paying rabbinic position in Natchez, Mississippi, and in 1922 moved on with their 15-month-old son, Billy, to Meridian, Mississippi. During her husband's tenure as rabbi of Temple Beth Israel in Meridian, Ackerman taught preconfirmation classes and led worship services when her husband was ill or out of town. Initially hesitant when the congregation invited her to succeed her husband as rabbi following his death in 1950, she accepted the position when the congregation received informal permission from Maurice *Eisendrath, president of the Union of American Hebrew Congregations. Ackerman viewed this invitation as a divine call to service and an opportunity "to plant a seed for enlarged activity for the Jewish woman." Soon after, Eisendrath withdrew his approval, maintaining that he had become convinced that congregational leaders unqualified to discharge full rabbinical duties would create more problems than they would solve. However, the synagogue's leadership upheld the appointment, declaring that "practically all of the members of our congregation believe she is qualified, and we want her." Paula Ackerman served as Temple Beth Israel's spiritual leader from January 1951 through the fall of 1953; she conducted services, preached, taught, and officiated at weddings, funerals, and conversions. Attracting international attention from the press, she erroneously was labeled "America's first Lady Rabbi." After retirement, she remained active on city, state, and national religious and cultural boards and traveled throughout the U.S., lecturing on religious themes. In 1962, she briefly served as spiritual leader of Temple Beth-El in Pensacola until a new rabbi could be found. In 1986 the Union of American Hebrew Congregations formally recognized her pioneering contribution to Jewish communal life at a special ceremony held at The Temple in Atlanta.

BIBLIOGRAPHY: P. Ackerman, Papers, American Jewish Archives, Cincinnati, Ohio; idem, Sermons (1915–53), private possession of Dr. William Ackerman; K.M. Olitzky, L. Sussman, and M. Stern (eds.), *Reform Judaism in America: A Biographical Dictionary* (1993), 1–2; E.M. Umansky and D. Ashton (eds.), *Four Centuries of Jewish Women's Spirituality: A Sourcebook* (1992), 184–86.

[Ellen M. Umansky (2nd ed.)]

ACKERMAN, SHABTAI (1914–), *ḥazzan*. Ackerman was born in Kishinev (Bessarabia). He sang in synagogue choirs from his childhood on. He studied cantorial liturgy under David Roitman, David Moshe Steinberg, and Abraham Kalechnik, and led the services at the Kishinev synagogue. Wounded by the Nazis in World War II, he nevertheless succeeded in escaping to Russia. In 1945 he conducted services in the Great Synagogue in Moscow and then returned to Romania, where he was cantor in the Baron Rothschild synagogue and Ahavat Achim in Bucharest. In 1950 he moved to Israel and served in the Beth El synagogue, Tel Aviv, and from 1952 to 1954 he was chief cantor in the Great Synagogue of Tel Aviv. At the same time he was chairman of the Israel Cantors' Association. From 1955 to 1982 he was cantor of the Beth Abraham Hillel Moses synagogue in Detroit. From 1983 he was cantor of Temple Beth Israel in Deerfield Beach, Florida. The Shabtai Ackerman Scholarship Fund was established in his name. In 1985 he became chairman of the Florida Cantors Association. His recordings include *Songs of the Ages – Cantorial Masterpieces.*

[Akiva Zimmerman]

ACKORD, ELIAS (d. 1811), physician, born in Mogilev (White Russia). Ackord, who studied medicine in Berlin, received his medical diploma in 1788 in St. Petersburg. From 1789 he served as an army doctor in Kiev and in Wasilkov, and subsequently practiced as a civilian. Interested in the reform of Jewish conditions in Poland, Ackord translated an anonymous pamphlet, *Die Juden oder die nothwendige Reformation der Juden in der Republik Polen* (1786), from Polish into German, urging the necessity of improving the status of Polish Jewry. Ackord recorded with satisfaction that he, a native of Poland, was able to translate the work into German. He attacked and amended several of the writer's conclusions, stating that they were insulting to the Jews. He denied the author's assertion that Jews opposed secular learning, adding that they had been prevented from receiving a higher education. His arguments reflect the influence of the school of Moses Mendelssohn and the scholars of the Haskalah.

ACOSTA, CHRISTOBAL (1515–1580), Marrano physician and botanist. Acosta's father, probably born a Jew and a victim of the Forced Conversion in Portugal in 1497, emigrated first to one of the Portuguese fortresses in North Africa and then to Mozambique, where Acosta was born. He studied in Portugal, qualified as a physician, and in this capacity accompanied the Portuguese viceroy Luis de Ataïde in 1568 to India, where he spent many years in medical practice. In 1569–71 he was a physician at the Royal Hospital in Cochin. Later he undertook many long and arduous journeys, suffering shipwreck, captivity, and many hardships in Persia, China, Arabia, and North Africa. The trips were for the purpose of studying natural history. On his return he settled down in Burgos (Spain) where he spent the rest of his life. Acosta's main interest in his travels was the study of the medicinal plants of the East Indies. His great work on the subject was *Tractado de las drogas y medicinas de las Indias Orientales con sus Plantas debuscadas al vivo.* This treatise was originally published in Burgos in 1578, and describes 69 plants and other sources of medicines, with illustrations of 46 plants and their roots. Acosta was undoubtedly influenced by Garcia da *Orta, whom he knew in India, but he revealed originality in his reproduction of certain plants from nature. Acosta's *Tractado de las drogas* was translated into Latin, Italian, and French. There is no evidence that Acosta had any Jewish leanings, despite his ancestry; and indeed he wrote two works which breathe a spirit of Catholic piety: *Tractado en contra y pro de la vida solitaria*, and *Tractado en loor de las mujeres de la caridad* (both Venice, 1592). In the latter work, Acosta describes himself as "Cristobal Acosta Affricano."

BIBLIOGRAPHY: H. Friedenwald, *Jews and Medicine* (1944), 445–7; E.H.F. Meyer, *Geschichte der Botanik*, 4 (1857), 408; S. Kagan, *Jewish Medicine* (1952), 120; C. Markham, *Colloquies on the Simples and Drugs of India by Garcia de Orta* (1913), xiv–xv (introd.); Glésinger, in: RHMH (March 1955), 21; D.J. Olmedilla y Puig, *Estudio histórico de la vida y escritos del sabio médico…* (1899). **ADD. BIBLIOGRAPHY:** L. Priner, in: *New York State Journal of Medicine*, 70 (Feb. 15, 1970), 581–84; R.N. Kapil and A.K. Bhatnagar, in: *Isis*, 67 (1976), 449–52.

[Isidore Simon]

ACOSTA, ISAAC (**Yhsak**; d. 1728), French Sephardi rabbi. Probably a native of Amsterdam, Acosta became *ḥazzan* of the Jewish community of Peyrehorade, near Bayonne, formed by Marrano fugitives from the Iberian Peninsula. His *Historia Sacra Real* (1691), dedicated to the wardens of the community, is one of the earliest manifestations of Judaism in this place. Later (apparently after an interlude in Biarritz) he succeeded R. Ḥayyim de Mercado as *ḥakham* at Bayonne, where he composed his handbook for the administration of the last rites to the dying, *Vía de Salvación* (1709; reprinted by M. Kaplan, Bayonne, 1874), and his major work, *Conjeturas Sagradas* (Leyden, 1722), a commentary in Spanish on the Early Prophets, based on the classical Hebrew commentators and the Midrash.

BIBLIOGRAPHY: Kayserling, Bibl, 8 (and Da Silva Rosa's additions, 4); M. Schwab, *Inscriptions Hébraïques de la France* (1904), 375–7; Gross, Gal Jud, 93; Loeb, in: REJ, 22 (1891), 111.

[Cecil Roth]

ACOSTA, JOAN D' (17th–18th centuries), court jester of Czar Peter I of Russia, descended from a Portuguese Marrano family. After prolonged wanderings in Western Europe, he settled in Hamburg as a broker and from there reached the new Russian capital, St. Petersburg. His quick wit and command of many European languages brought him to court, and in 1714 he was appointed court jester. At the time this was a position of some importance, since it was the jester's function to ridicule the customs of the old Russian society, in order to facilitate transition to a western European mode of life. D'Acosta had a wide knowledge of the Scriptures and the Czar enjoyed conversing with him on theological subjects. D'Acosta reached an old age and also served as jester at the court of the czarina Anna.

BIBLIOGRAPHY: J. Doran, *History of Court Jesters* (1858), 305; Dubnow, in YE, 1 (1908), 653; S. Ginsburg, *Amolike Peterburg* (1944), 14–15.

[Yehuda Slutsky]

ACQUI, town in Piedmont, Italy. Jews began to settle in Acqui, then in the independent marquisate of Montferrat, during the 15th century. The Gonzaga dynasty, which ruled from 1536, was at first kindly disposed toward the Jews, failing to comply with the Papal order to confiscate the Talmud in 1553, and in 1562 protecting them from mob violence. Later its attitude became influenced by Counter-Reformation trends and in 1570 the Jews in Acqui were ordered to wear the Jewish *badge and live apart from Christians. Both the war fought in 1612–31 and the plague of 1630 were disastrous for the Jews of Acqui. The only loan bank then allowed failed in 1614. In 1630 Jewish property was pillaged. Conditions improved under the Gonzaga-Nevers dynasty. However, from 1708, under the rule of the House of Savoy, conditions again deteriorated. In 1731, the 41 Jewish families were restricted to living in a ghetto, although they were permitted to maintain loanbanks. A further source of livelihood was the textile industry, some Jews in Acqui owning silk or cotton mills. The ghetto became heavily overcrowded when the Jews of Monastero had to move there in 1737. By the end of the 18th century, their position had improved markedly, although as late as 1789 Jews were debarred from appearing in public on feast days. When the French Republican armies entered Acqui in 1796, Abraham Azariah (Bonaiut) Ottolenghi, later the rabbi, zealously took up the revolutionary cause. Disorders followed the French retreat, however, and the Ottolenghi family in particular suffered. Jews were excluded from attending public schools in Acqui for some time after they had been permitted to do so in most of Piedmont. At the beginning of the 19th century the Jewish population numbered about 700. In 1848 the Jews were emancipated and the ghetto abolished. The Jewish population, which numbered only 500 in 1870, decreased to 200 by 1899, and 50 a generation later. By the late 1960s there were no Jews living in Acqui. Rabbis of Acqui include Joshua Ben-Zion *Segré (18th century) and several members of the Ottolenghi family. The old synagogue was demolished, together with the ghetto, in 1881, and a new one constructed in the Via Jona Ottolenghi, which still stands.

BIBLIOGRAPHY: S. Foà, *Gli ebrei nel Monferrato nei secoli xvi e xvii* (1914); Levi, in: RMI, 9 (1934–5), 511–34; S. Foà, *ibid.*, 19 (1953), 163f., 206f.; Milano, Italia, index; Roth, Italy, index.

[Attilio Milano]

ACQUISITION (Heb. קִנְיָן; **kinyan**) the act whereby a person voluntarily obtains legal rights. In Jewish law almost all kinds of rights, whether proprietary (*jus in rem*) or contractual (*jus in personam*; see *Obligations), can be voluntarily acquired only by way of *kinyan*. Acquisition of rights by way of *kinyan* can be divided into three groups:

(1) Acquiring ownership over ownerless property (*hefker*) such as animals, fish in river or ocean, and lost property which the owner has abandoned hope of finding; (2) rights over property which has an owner, acquisition being by way of sale or gift. Acquisition of ownerless property (original acquisition) is called in the Talmud, *ein da'at aḥeret maknah* (literally "when no other mind conveys title") and acquisition

from a previous owner (derivative acquisition) is called *da'at aḥeret maknah* ("another mind conveys title"). In this latter group are also included lesser rights than ownership (*jura in re aliena*) such as a lease or an easement; (3) contractual or personal rights such as debts, or the hiring of workmen, the acquisition of which also depends upon "another mind conveying the right."

In the case of original acquisition the formalities of acquiring title are to demonstrate that the property is in unrestricted possession of the person acquiring it, meaning that he has the ability and intent to use it whenever he wishes to do so, which includes the power to prevent others from interfering with that use. The *halakhah* enumerates, according to objective tests, the acts by which people would usually recognize that the property is in the possession of the acquirer. Consequently, the list of recognized forms of original acquisition is a closed one.

With regard to derivative acquisition, however, the function of *kinyan* is not to demonstrate that it has passed into the possession of the person acquiring it, but that the alienator and the acquirer had determined to conclude the transaction. In fact, the party acquiring title performs the *kinyan*, and the alienator expresses his approval orally. The sole reason for a formal *kinyan* is that a mere oral agreement may not be taken seriously and might enable the parties to withdraw from the proposed transaction. For this reason derivative acquisition can be effected in a greater variety of ways than original acquisition; when the parties derive mutual benefit from the transaction showing that they have wholeheartedly reached an agreement to conclude it, no formal *kinyan* is even required (R. Johanan, BM 94a). For the same reason an acquisition is valid if done in a mode customary among local merchants even though different from the talmudic *kinyanim* (Sh. Ar., ḤM 201:2). Since in the case of derivative acquisition the *kinyan* serves not to show possession but to indicate that the parties made up their minds to conclude the transaction, it can also be used for creation of contractual rights, such as a duty to sell something which is not yet in existence (*davar she-lo ba la-olam*) – even though one cannot effect transfer of a non-existent object (see *Assignment; Sh. Ar., ḤM 60:6). The acquisition of rights requires "intention" on the part of the acquirer. The statement in the Talmud (BM 11a) that "a person's premises acquire for him without his knowledge" (see below) must therefore be taken to refer to the acquisition of such an object as the owner of the premises would have desired to acquire had he known of its presence there, and it must, by the same token, be property which is usually found there (Tos. to BB 54a).

There are general modes of *kinyan* which apply to both original and derivative acquisition, and others which apply only to derivative acquisition by way of sale and gift. Under the first class come:

(1) Kinyan Ḥaẓer

("Acquisition through one's courtyard"). A person's premises "acquire" for him such movable property as comes into it. Since, as stated, the property must be within his possession and control, such premises, in order to "acquire" on his behalf, must be fenced in, or "he stands at the side thereof" guarding what is in it (BM 11a), or that others keep away from the premises for any other reason (*ibid.* 102a). Consequently a shopkeeper does not acquire property lost in his shop, if it is in a place to which customers have access, but only if it is in a place to which he alone has access (Maim. Yad, Gezelah, 16:4). Nor does a person acquire anything in premises to which the public has access (Novellae Rashba to BM 25b). Similarly, a man's premises do not acquire fledglings because they can fly away (BM 11a) or chattels which may be blown away (Git. 79a). Similarly, treasure hidden in the ground, even of guarded premises, belongs to the finder (BM 25b) and not to the owner of the ground because the owner is not likely to find it because it is hidden, and therefore he has no control of it. The *ḥaẓer* need not necessarily be immovable property; the same rule applied to utensils if their owner had the right to leave them in a certain place where they would not be removed (BB 85a). It follows that a person's animal cannot acquire for him since it is a "moving courtyard" (Git. 21a) and may wander beyond its owner's care, On the other hand, a boat would "acquire" for its owner fish which leap into it (BM 9b) since it is property guarded by its owner. With regard to derivative acquisition, since there is no need to demonstrate that the property is in the possession of its acquirer, even an unguarded *ḥaẓer* can acquire according to one opinion (BM 11b).

(2) Arba Ammot

("Four cubits"). The area round a person having a radius of four cubits is regarded as having the same properties as a *ḥaẓer*, providing that he is in a place where he has control over the article (BM 10b). There seems to be a difference between the Babylonian and the Jerusalem Talmuds with regard to *kinyan* by *arba ammot*. According to the former it acquires even without an express formula on the individual's part, unless he has clearly stated or indicated that he does not wish to acquire and the Talmud refers to it as applying only to original acquisitions. The Jerusalem Talmud, on the other hand, requires an express declaration on his part that his *arba ammot* shall acquire the article for him (Elijah of Vilna to TJ, Pe'ah 4:2) and makes this rule apply also to derivative acquisition. Opinions differ as to the capacity of minors to acquire by *kinyan ḥaẓer* or *arba ammot* (BM 11a).

(3) Hagbahah ("lifting"), Meshikhah ("pulling") and Mesirah ("transfer")

Movable objects are acquired by *hagbahah* in the case of articles which can be lifted without difficulty; where they are too heavy, or can be raised only with difficulty, *meshikhah* takes its place (BB 86a). Both serve to demonstrate that the article thereby comes into the acquirer's possession, and is guarded for him as in his *ḥaẓer.* The article may be raised merely by the force of his body (Tos. to BK 98a). There is a difference of opinion as to whether it must be lifted one handsbreadth or three (Tos. to Kid., 26a). *Meshikhah*, applying to an animal, can be effected by striking or calling it so that it comes to one (BB 75a) or by leading or riding it (BM 8b). The prevailing opinion is that *meshikhah* applies only in premises owned by both parties or in a side street (BB 76b), but not in a public place. According to one opinion, however, it is effective in a public thoroughfare as well (TJ, Kid. 1:4, Tos. to BK 79a). The above-mentioned methods of *kinyan* apply both to original and derivative acquisition, but in cases of derivative acquisition the express permission of the alienator to the acquirer to perform *kinyan* is an indispensable element in the *kinyan* (BK 52a; BB 53a). These methods of *kinyan* apply also to personal obligations, such as those of a bailee (Tos. to BK 79a) or an artisan for his work (BM 48a; see *Labor Law). *Mesirah* consists of grasping at the object to be acquired (BB 75b) and the term *mesirah* indicates that it is done at the behest of the transferor (Tos. to *ibid.*) Since it does not demonstrate intention to control the subject matter which is a necessary element of possession, it applies only to derivative acquisition. It is employed where *meshikhah* is ineffective, i.e., in a public place or in an *ḥaẓer* not belonging to either party.

(4) Ḥazakah

Whereas all the foregoing modes of acquisition apply to movables only, in the case of immovable property acquisition is by an act of *ḥazakah* (Kid. 26a) which consists of any act usually done by an owner, such as fencing, opening a gateway or locking the premises (BB 42a), or weeding or hoeing (*ibid.*, 54a), or putting down a mattress to sleep there (*ibid.*, 53b). In general, any improvement of the land is regarded as an act usually done by the owner (Maim. Yad, Mekhirah, 1:8). Such an act as preventing floodwaters from inundating a field, however, would not constitute a *ḥazakah* as it could be regarded simply as a voluntary neighborly act (BB 53a). There is a difference of opinion as to whether merely traversing the land is acquiring as it constitutes an act usually done by the owner (BB 100a). With regard to a sale or gift, the land acquired by the *ḥazakah* includes everything stipulated by the parties (Sh. Ar, ḤM 192:12); with regard to ownerless property, it includes only such part as is patently seen to be in his possession (*ibid.* 275:3–9). As with *meshikhah*, in the case of derivative acquisition the alienator must specifically instruct the acquirer to take possession, or otherwise indicate his consent (BK 52a; BB 53a). There are forms of acquisition by *ḥazakah* which apply either to original or to derivative acquisition, but not to both (Sh. Ar., ḤM 275:12–13). (For the *ḥazakah* established by three years' possession which is a method of proof and does not come within the category of *kinyan*, see *Ḥazakah*).

The following methods of *kinyan* apply to derivative acquisitions only because they do not demonstrate possession but rather the intention of the parties to conclude the transaction:

(5) Kinyan Kesef

("Acquisition by money"). The transfer by the purchaser to the seller of the agreed monetary price of the article. R. Johanan is of the view that in strict law this mode of *kinyan* applies both to movables and immovables, and with regard to derivative acquisition the *kinyan* was done by paying money only and not by *hagbahaḥ* and *meshikhah*. But it was enacted that instead of paying money *meshikhah* should be necessary, since if the object remains in the possession of the transferor he may not guard it against being destroyed by fire or other dangers (BM 47a). Similarly, the need for a deed (*shetar*) was added in the case of immovables (Kid. 26a). The Jerusalem Talmud (Kid. 1:5) indicates other modes of *kinyan* with regard to immovables, one based on the removal of a shoe as mentioned in Ruth 4:7, and the other being *keẓaẓah*, without any indication of the period when those modes were practiced. But *kesef, shetar*, and *ḥazakah* alone remained. However, even though, since tannaitic times, neither movables nor immovables were acquired solely by *kinyan kesef*, the sale of immovables was not regarded as completed until the money had passed, though it could be paid to a third party according to the seller's instructions (Kid. 7a). Where only part of the purchase money is paid, the balance being postponed by the transferor in the form of a loan, even if only implicitly and without the loan being expressly stated, the part payment concludes the transaction, unless it is clear from the conduct of the transferor that this part payment did not complete the transaction, even if *kinyan* took place (BM 77b). *Kinyan kesef* is already mentioned in the Bible (Gen. 23; Jer. 32:6–15).

(6) Kinyan Shetar

("Acquisition by deed"). In *kinyan shetar* the deed is not just evidence of the act of acquisition but constitutes the act of acquisition itself (*shetar kinyan*, Sh. Ar., ḤM 191:2). The vendor writes on paper or other material "my field is given (or sold) to you" and the receipt of that deed by the purchaser establishes his title even in the absence of witnesses (*ibid.*, l). Movables cannot be acquired by *shetar. Kinyan shetar* is already mentioned in the Bible (Jer. 32).

(7) Ḥalifin ("barter"), Kinyan Sudar ("Kinyan of the Kerchief")

The exchange of property is as effective as the payment of money in establishing acquisition, even if the two objects exchanged are not of equal value. Thus, if the alienator draws to him an article owned by the acquirer the transaction is affected. *Ḥalifin* cannot however be effected by current coinage since this would constitute *kinyan kesef*, which depends upon the monetary value (see BM 45b). Out of this there developed the act of acquisition called *kinyan sudar*, which is therefore also called *kinyan ḥalifin* (Kid, 6b; et al.). The kerchief (*sudar*) is merely pulled by the acquirer and can then be returned to the owner (*ibid.*, Ned. 48b). This mode of acquisition being very easy to perform in all kinds of situations, it became so prevalent that it is referred to simply as *kinyan* (cf. Git. 14a;

BM 94a; BB 3a). The origin of *kinyan sudar* may be traced to Ruth 4:7. Throughout the tannaitic period it is never expressly mentioned. It is first mentioned at the beginning of the amoraic period in the dispute as to whether, as in the case of barter proper, the *sudar* must belong to the acquirer, or to the alienator (BM 47a); the former view prevailed. Apparently, because of the simplicity of this mode of acquisition, this *kinyan* is not regarded as completed even after the ceremony, as long as the parties are still talking about the deal (BB 114a).

(8) Aggav Karka

("The acquisition of movables incidental to land.") Movables may be acquired as an adjunct to land, the act of *kinyan* being performed only with regard to the land (Kid. 26a). It probably originated in the acquisition of a courtyard with everything contained therein (cf. Tosef., BB 2:13) or similar cases as field, olive press, etc. subsequently being extended to apply to everything belonging to them (cf. BB 78a), even if not actually there at the time of the transaction, and finally to all movables of unlimited amount being sold incidentally to any immovable property, even if they do not have any connection whatever with it (Kid. 26b). Thus the movables did not have to be assembled (*ibid.* 26a–b) except in the case of slaves (BK 12a). The final development was to acquire movables as an adjunct to an unspecified piece of land (Sh. Ar., ḤM 202:7 gloss) and the land could be acquired by sale and the movables as a gift, and conversely. As a facile mode of acquiring movables, not necessitating the presence of the parties on the site, it was in operation for long periods, In the geonic period the "four cubits in Ereẓ Israel" which every Jew theoretically owns, was made the basis of a practice whereby an agent could be appointed to recover a deposit or a debt, *aggav karka*, of these four cubits (Maim. Yad, Sheluḥin, 3:7).

(9) Usage and Custom

Generally speaking, any custom adopted by the local merchants as a mode of acquisition is valid according to Jewish law (Sh. Ar., ḤM 201:2), since it fulfills the principle that the purpose of the *kinyan* is to bring about the decision of the parties to conclude the transaction. Conversely, when a once accepted mode of acquisition fell into desuetude it could no longer be employed (cf. C. Albeck, *Shishah Sidrei Mishnah, Seder Nashim* (1958), 410–12; addenda to Kid. 1:4–5). The Babylonian Talmud mentions the custom of wine-merchants marking the barrels they had purchased (BM 74a), and in post-talmudic times three such customs prevalent among Christians were adopted since they fulfilled the same function as "affixing a mark" (Sh. Ar., ḤM 201:2). They are (a) the handshake (*Teki'at kaf*) mentioned in Proverbs 6:1 as a form of giving surety (*Piskei ha-Rosh*, BM 74a in the name of "R.H.," probably the tosafist Ḥayyim Cohen and not R. Hananel, who expressed a contrary view; see *Or Zaru'a*, BM 231). Some authorities even regarded a handshake as the equivalent of an oath (*Mordekhai* to Shevu. 757) but others regarded it as an act of acquisition (for the parallel among Christians see *Palmata, Handschlag*); (b) the handing over of a coin by the purchaser to the vendor, which was originally a medieval Christian custom (Arrha, earnest money); and (c) handing over a key – the vendor hands to the purchaser the key of the premises where the merchandise is housed. Handing over a key is mentioned in the Babylonian Talmud (BK 52a; Tos. to *ibid.*), but only as the authorization by the alienator for the acquirer to make the *kinyan ḥazakah* and in the Jerusalem Talmud as a mode of derivative acquisition of the building (*Mareh ha-Panim* to Kid. 1:4). As a mode of acquiring movables it was a Christian custom (*Traditio clavium*; see B. Cohen, *Jewish and Roman Law*, 2 (1966), 538–56), Present day rabbinical courts have applied the principle of regarding local custom as valid; thus the transfer of immovable property through registration in the Land Registry is a valid *kinyan* in Jewish Law (PDR, 1:283).

(10) Acquisition with No Formal Act

Where it is clear that the parties concerned decide a transaction to their mutual benefit and satisfaction a formal *kinyan* is not essential (see Ket. 102b; Git. 14a; BM 94a; BB 176b; cf. Maim. Yad, Mekhirah, 5:11). This rule obtains generally with regard to personal obligations but can include rights in *rem* (see BB 106b and *Haggahot ha-Rashash* on Tos. Bek. 18b). This principle was extended in the post-talmudic period (Hai Gaon, in *Ḥemdah Genuzah*, no. 135; responsa Meir of Rothenburg, ed. Prague, 941; responsa Ribash 476; Sh. Ar., ḤM 176:4). For other modes of acquisition see *Admission, *Assignment, *Confiscation and Expropriation, **Hefker*, **Hekdesh*, *Succession, *Theft, and Robbery.

In the state of Israel, sale is governed by the Law of Sale, 1968, based on the uniform international draft (Hague, 1964); gift is governed by the Law of Gift, 1968; and the acquisition of immovables by the Land Law, 1969. Ownership, in the case of sale, passes by way of offer and acceptance and, in case of gift, by delivery of the property. Transfer of title to land becomes valid only on registration in the Land Registry. Contractual obligations are created by agreement between the parties in any manner whatever. Legislation vests ownership of all unowned property in the state, which cannot therefore be originally acquired.

[Shalom Albeck]

Legal Acts Which Do Not Require a Kinyan

Further to the above discussion regarding the requirement of a *kinyan* in order to give force to a legal act, it should be noted that as of the 13th century, we find the legal principle that any legal transaction undertaken by the public is valid even in the absence of a formal *kinyan*, "Any thing that is done by the public does not require a *kinyan*, [even] in a situation in which an individual would require a *kinyan*" (Responsa Maharam of Rothenburg, cited in *Mordekhai, Bava Meẓia*, #457–458). This new principle was applied to various categories of legal transactions, such as employer-employee relations, guarantees and gifts, and other legal matters to which the public is a party (see Responsa Maharam b. Reb Barukh (Prague), 38;

Responsa Ribash, §476; Sh. Ar., ḤM 163. 6 (Rema); 204.9; Responsa *Mayim Amukkim*; Responsa *Ra'anah* – Rabbi Eliahu b. Rabbi Hayyim, §63). The established and accepted rule was that "whatever the leaders of the community agree to do has validity without a *kinyan*" (Responsa Rosh, Kelal 6.19, 21). This distinction between the *kinyan* of an individual and the *kinyan* of the public or its representatives also affected the application of other basic requirements normally applying to the *kinyan*. Thus, a public authority has full authority to acquire or transfer something not yet in existence; despite the general rule of Jewish law that "*asmakhta* does not convey title" (see *Asmakhta), the acts of a public authority are valid even where performed by way of *asmakhta* (Responsa *Mayim Amukim*, op cit.; Responsa *Mabit* 3. 228; see *Contract, Law of Obligations").

The above-cited sources served as a basis for the Supreme Court's ruling, given by Justice Elon, regarding the heightened requirement of good faith imposed on the public authority in its actions performed within the realm of the law (HC 376/81, *Lugassi v. Minister of Communications*, 36(2) PD 449). Additional sources are cited further on in the decision (pp. 465–471; see *Public Authority and Administrative Law).

An additional category in which there is no need for a *kinyan* in order to give force to a legal act is the area of wills (see *Succession). Generally speaking, a will must be accompanied by a *kinyan* in order to prove the finality of the decision and to give it legal force. However, in the case of a will made on a deathbed (the will of a *shekhiv me-ra*) – that is, one made by a person who is ill and in danger of dying, or a healthy person in a situation causing him to regard himself as facing death – the will is valid even without a *kinyan*, because we assume that, due to the unique circumstances involved in its making, it was performed as a final decision (Maimonides, Yad, Zekhiyah u-matanah 8.2, 4, 24, 26.)

In an Israeli Supreme Court decision in the *Koenig* case (FH 80/40 *Koenig v. Cohen*, 36(3) PD 701), Justice Menahem Elon held that this halakhic rule should determine the interpretation of Section 23 of the Succession Law, 5725–1964. Section 23 utilizes the Talmudic term "*shekhiv me-ra*" (Lit: moribund] in referring to a person making a will when on the point of death:

> A person who is a *shekhiv me-ra* or who under the circumstances reasonably regards himself as facing death may make an oral will before two witnesses who understand his language.

Justice Elon ruled that Section 23's use of the Talmudic term *shekhiv me-ra* indicates the origin of the law in the Jewish law regarding a deathbed will, and hence the applicability of the Jewish Law regarding the deathbed will *(= ẓava'at shekhiv me-ra)*. The decision in the Koenig case dealt with a case in which a woman left a will made on a piece of paper without a date and signature just before she killed herself. The justices disagreed regarding the legal validity of the will, and Justice Elon contended that the will should be seen as a deathbed will and hence should be considered valid, notwithstanding its deficiencies and flaws (*ibid*, pp. 733–38.)

Alternative Explanation of the Essence of Kinyan Sudar

According to another view, *kinyan sudar* is not a derivative of *kinyan halifin* (barter), i.e., the exchange of property, but derives rather from the institution of surety (see *Suretyship). The transaction takes effect when the conveyor of title, or the obligatee, undertakes to bind himself (*meshabed nafsho*) (BM 47a). In other words: he places himself in the "position" of a purchaser, conveyor of title, debtor, worker, etc., in accordance with the legal action for purpose of which *kinyan sudar* is performed.

[Menachem Elon (2nd ed.)]

BIBLIOGRAPHY: Maim. Yad, Mekhirah, 1–9; Sh. Ar., ḤM 189–203; Gulak, Yesodei, 1 (1922), 102–27; 2 (1922), 32–57; Gulak, *Le-Ḥeker Toledot ha-Mishpat ha-Ivri*, 1 (1929), (41–86); Herzog, Instit, 1 (1936), 137–200; S. Albeck, *Sinai*, 62 (1967/68), 229–61; ET. s.v. *Aggav. Arba Ammot, Da'at Aḥeret Maknah, Hagbahah, Hitḥayyevut.* **ADD. BIBLIOGRAPHY:** Maimonides, *Yad, Mekhirah*, 1–9; Sh. Ar., ḤM 189–203; Gulak, *Yesodei*, 1 (1922), 102–27; 2 (1922), 32–57; Gulak, *Le-Ḥeker Toledot ha-Mishpat ha-Ivri*, 1 (1929), 41–86; Herzog, *Institutions*, 1 (1936), 137–200; S. Albeck, in: *Sinai*, 62 (1967/68), 229–61; M. Elon, *Ha-Mishpat ha-Ivri* (1988), 1:101–2, 196, 476–482, 516, 533f, 741f; 2:835–7; idem, *Jewish Law* (1994), 1:113–4, 220–1; 2:580–5,628–29,649f, 913f; 3:1022–24; B. Lifshitz, *Mishpat u-Pe'ulah* (2002); M. Elon and B. Lifshitz, *Mafte'aḥ ha-She'elot ve-ha-Teshuvot shel Ḥakhmei Sefarad u-Ẓefon Afrikah* (1986), 2:425–40; B. Lifshitz and E. Shochetman, *Mafte'aḥ ha-She'elot ve-ha-Teshuvot shel Ḥakhmei Ashkenaz, Ẓarefat ve-Italyah* (1997), 291–98; B. Lifshitz, *Obligation and Acquisition in Jewish Law* (1988); I. Warhaftig, *Ha-Hitḥayvut* (2001), 375–83.

ACRA, THE (from the Greek *akros*, "high"), fortress established in Jerusalem on a site in close proximity to the Jewish Temple in 167 B.C.E. by Antiochus Epiphanes in order to keep the Jewish population of the city in subjection. It seems to have replaced another Hellenistic citadel (*acropolis*) used as the administrative center for the *eparchos*, who was responsible for maintaining public order and collecting revenues from the inhabitants, but little information about this place is known except that it was the place to which Menelaus fled when the fortifications of the city were breached by Jason (II Macc. 4:27, 5:5). It was also mentioned in the Letter of Aristeas (2nd century B.C.E.) as situated "in a very lofty spot and [it] is fortified with many towers, which have been built up to the very top with immense stones, with the object, as we were informed, of guarding the Temple precincts …" The exact topographical situation of the subsequent Seleucid Acra is also unclear. It was built in 167 B.C.E. following the destruction of the city by Antiochus IV and was in use until it was dismantled by Simon or Jonathan at the time of the construction of the "First Wall" fortifications of Jerusalem c. 140 B.C.E. During the Maccabean revolt the Acra was regarded as a symbol of wickedness and inequity overshadowing the Temple of the pious. Various attempts were made by Judah Maccabee and the Hasmonean Jonathan to oust the Greeks from their stronghold, with success eventually falling to Simon (1 Macc. 13:49–50) on the 23 Iyyar of 142 (Meg. Ta'an., 2) and it was he who subsequently had it leveled. Josephus Flavius in his writings (Ant., 12:252, 13:215; Wars, 1:39, 5:138, 253, 6:392) pointed to the Acra as situated in the Lower City, i.e., in the area of the southeastern hill (the "City of David"), at the same time indicating that it was higher than the adjacent Temple Mount which therefore allowed the Greek garrison to control the activities in the area of the Temple. Scholars regarded the situation of the Acra as suggested by Josephus unsustainable on both topographical and archaeological grounds, since the Lower City area had always been substantially lower than the uppermost part of the Temple Mount area, and also because excavations in the City of David area had not brought to light remains of a separate Hellenistic fortress. Hence, alternative locations for the Seleucid Acra were sought by scholars – on the Ophel, at the southeast corner of the Temple Mount, north of the Temple Mount, and at various places on the Western Hill – none of which could be proven archaeologically. Of these the Ophel seems to be the most likely location since it was situated within the area of the northern extension of the "City of David" in the Lower City and also because it was a topographical prominence which could very well have supported a building or tower that easily might have reached the level of the adjacent Temple Mount, i.e., a height of 60–100 ft. (20–30 m.).

BIBLIOGRAPHY: L.-H, Vincent, "Acra," in: *Revue Biblique*, 43 (1934), 205–236; W.A. Shotwell, "The Problem of the Syrian Akra," in: BASOR, 176 (1964), 10–19; Y. Tsafrir, "The Location of the Seleucid Akra," in: RB, 82 (1975), 501–21; idem, in: Y. Yadin (ed.), *Jerusalem Revealed* (1975), 85–86; M.Ben-Dov, "The Selecuid Akra – South of the Temple," in: *Cathedra*, 18 (1981), 22–35 (Heb.); B. Mazar, "The Temple Mount, in: *Biblical Archaeology Today* (1985), 463–68; L. Dequeker, "The City of David and the Seleucid Acra in Jerusalem," in: E. Lipinski (ed.), *The Land of Israel: Cross-Roads of Civilizations* (1985), 193–210; G.J. Wightman, "Temple Fortresses in Jerusalem. Part I: The Ptolemaic and Seleucid Akras," in: *Bulletin of the Anglo-Israel Archaeological Societies*, 9 (1989–90), 29–40; G. Finkielsztejn, "Hellenistic Jerusalem: the Evidence of the Rhodian Stamped Handles," in: *New Studies on Jerusalem*, 5 (1999), 21–36.

[Shimon Gibson (2nd ed.)]

ACRABA, place on the edge of the desert in the eastern Samaria mountains. Acraba is a site with archaeological remains from the Roman and Byzantine periods. The site has not been excavated but surveys conducted there in the 19th century by V. Guérin, C.F. Tyrwhitt-Drake, and C. Clermont-Ganneau revealed the remains of numerous ancient buildings, including a church, Greek inscriptions, cisterns, an open reservoir (*birkeh*), and a number of burial caves. The site was inhabited during the Late Hellenistic period by Idumeans, Samaritans, and Jews. The site was apparently part of a toparchy that was established in the area during the Hellenistic period. First mentioned in 1 Macc. 5:3 and Judith 7:18, the town was later conquered by Hyrcanus and added to the territory of Judea. It was a Jewish village during the First and Second Jewish Revolts and was subsequently transferred to the dominion of the city of Neapolis [= Shechem]. Acrabbeim was mentioned by Eusebius (*Onom.* 14) as situated on the "boundary of Judea toward the east, belonging to the tribe of Judah. There is a town by this name nine miles (15 km.) from Neapolis to the east heading down toward the Jordan, on the way to Jericho across the toparchy called Acrabattene." The site appears on the Madaba map of the mid-sixth century C.E. with the Greek inscription: "Akrabim, now Akrabittine." Two Monophysite monasteries may have existed at the site according to a sixth century C.E. epistle, one was dedicated to St. Stephen and the other was founded by a certain Abbot Titus. The village still exists today ('Aqraba) and is inhabited by Moslems – the mosque is apparently situated above the remains of a church.

BIBLIOGRAPHY: J. Wilkinson, *Jerusalem Pilgrims Before the Crusades* (1977), 149; B. Bagatti, *Ancient Christian Villages of Samaria.* (2002), 55–56; Y. Tsafrir, L. Di Segni, and J. Green, *Tabula Imperii Romani. Iudaea Palaestina: Eretz Israel in the Hellenistic, Roman and Byzantine Periods. Maps and Gazetteer* (1994), 56–57; G.S.P. Freeman-Grenville, R.L. Chapman, and J.E. Taylor, *Palestine in the Fourth Century. The Onomasticon by Eusebius of Caesarea* (2003),108; M. Piccirillo and E. Alliata (eds.), *The Madaba Map Centenary 1897–1997* (1999), 62.

[Shimon Gibson (2nd ed.)]

ACRE (Heb. עַכּוֹ, **Acco, Akko**; Ar. عَكّا *'Akkā*; Ptolemais; **St. Jean d'Acre**) coastal city in northern Israel situated on a promontory at the northern end of the Bay of Haifa, 14 mi. (23 km.) north of Haifa, in the Acre Coastal Plain.

Ancient Acre

Ancient Acre is first mentioned in the Egyptian Execration Texts (c. 1800 B.C.E.) and it appears after the battle of Megiddo in the list of cities conquered by Thutmose III (c. 1468 B.C.E.). In the El-Amarna letters, the king of Acre, Zurata, and later his son, Zutana, appear as rivals of Megiddo and together with the king of Achshaph, as allies of Jerusalem. Acre is also mentioned in the lists of Seti I and Rameses II. The Greeks later derived the name Acre – a Semitic word – from the Greek *akē* ("healing") and connected it with the legend of Heracles. During the reign of Ptolemy II, the name of the city was changed to Ptolemais, by which it was known until the Arab conquest.

The geographic position of Acre made its occupation vital to every army waging campaign in Syria and Ereẓ Israel. It was allotted to the tribe of Asher which, however, could not subdue it (Judg. 1:31) and it remained an independent Phoenician city. It submitted to the Assyrian king Sennacherib (701 B.C.E.) but revolted against Ashurbanipal who took revenge on the city in about 650 B.C.E.

Under Persian rule Acre served as an important military and naval base in the campaigns against Egypt. Coinage of Tyrian *staters* began there in 350 B.C.E. Alexander's conquest of Syria and the fall of Tyre in 332 B.C.E. enhanced Acre's position as is evidenced by the gold and silver coins struck there. In 312 B.C.E. Ptolemy I razed its fortifications during his retreat from Antigonus but he reoccupied the city 11 years later. An association of loyal "Antiochenes" was founded in Acre when the city became Seleucid. The city was hostile to the neighboring Jews in Galilee, and Simeon the Hasmonean had to beat off its attacks (164 B.C.E.). His brother Jonathan was treacherously taken prisoner in Acre by the usurper Tryphon in 143 B.C.E. After the overthrow of the latter five years later, the town was held by Antiochus VII Sidetes, who bestowed upon it the titles "holy and inviolable" and was in turn honored by it in inscriptions. After his death Acre became virtually independent, although it acknowledged the nominal suzerainty of various Ptolemaic rulers. It resisted all attacks of Alexander Yannai (Jos., Ant. 13:2), although it lost the Carmel region to him. From Cleopatra Selene, Acre passed to Tigranes, king of Armenia (until 71 B.C.E.) and became Roman with Pompey's occupation of the country, Caesar landed there in 48–47 B.C.E. and his visit marked a new era for the city. Herod later made it his base for the conquest of his kingdom (39 B.C.E.). At the outbreak of the Jewish War in 66 C.E. the inhabitants massacred 2,000 of the Jewish population. The following year Acre became Vespasian's base of operations against Galilee. Nero then settled veterans of four legions (3rd, 5th, 10th, 12th) there and made it a Roman colony: Colonia Claudia Ptolemais Germanica. As a harbor, Acre was by now overshadowed by Herod's new port of *Caesarea. Its rights were augmented by the emperor Heliogabalus and its independent coinage continued until 268 C.E. A Christian community lived in Acre from the time of the apostle Paul (Acts 21:7).

The Roman city of Ptolemais which stretched far beyond the present Old City, extended around Tell al-Fukhar, which was the site of Phoenician Acre up to the Hellenistic period. Excavations were conducted at Tell al-Fukhar by M. Dothan between 1973 and 1979. Early Bronze I remains were found on bedrock and were fairly sparse, with wall remnants, floors, and several pits. It is possible that at the end of this period the sea level rose and the site was temporarily inundated. Substantial fortifications were uncovered dating from the Middle Bronze Age II A–B, including a 60 ft. (18 m.) stretch of rampart of solid clay and earth surmounted by a wall. Remains of a two-story brick citadel were also exposed. These defenses surrounded the mound on all sides, save the south where it was protected by the swamps of the nearby Naaman River. A gate was uncovered to the southwest, with three chambers and three pairs of asymmetrical pilasters. The citadel was destroyed towards the end of the 18th century B.C.E. Large buildings and numerous finds (including bronze *Reshef* figurines) were discovered at the site dating from the Late Bronze I–II indicating that it was a well-planned city, even though it apparently lacked defenses. Although there are some signs of occupation at the site circa 1200 B.C.E., perhaps by some of the "Sea Peoples," very little was found that could be associated with the subsequent 11th–9th centuries B.C.E. Based on the archaeological finds, the city evidently revived and flourished during the eighth and seventh centuries B.C.E., and evidence of public buildings built of ashlars was unearthed at the site. One of these buildings was destroyed apparently by Sennacherib towards the end of the eighth century B.C.E. A cache of small silver ingots belongs to this level. The Persian period was one of the most important phases in the development of Acre as an administrative and commercial center, probably from the time of Cambyses onwards. Subsequently, Acre became an important naval center of importance to both Egypt and Persia. Among the finds from this period on the tell were cultic figurines in a pit and two ostraca bearing Phoenician inscriptions, and many Greek artifacts including Attic wares, suggesting that Greek merchants and Phoenicians lived side by side in this specific part of Acre.

Acre had two harbors, one northwest of the present port, with the other south of it. The center of Hellenistic Akke/Ptolemais moved towards the harbors and away from the tell. Numerous buildings and fortifications have been unearthed. Finds include large quantities of stamped amphora handles, indicating that wine was imported from Rhodes, Cos, and Thasos. In later Roman times, the Jewish and Samaritan quarters were also situated near the Old Port. Despite the fact that the town was considered as being strictly outside the halakhic boundaries of the Holy Land (cf. Git. 2a), the Jews re-established their community there after the war against Rome because it was the most convenient port for Galilee (although they buried their dead outside the city and within the halakhic boundaries of Ereẓ Israel at the foot of Mt. Carmel and later in Kefar Yasif up to the 19th century). It served as a port of embarkation for the Patriarchs (and other rabbis) traveling to Rome and as a home port for their commercial fleet. Rabbi *Gamaliel II visited a bath dedicated to Aphrodite in Acre (Av. Zar. 3:4). Its fair was one of the three most famous in Ereẓ Israel (TJ, Av. Zar. 1:4, 39d) and its fisheries gave rise to the saying "to bring fish to Acre" as an equivalent of the modern "bringing coals to Newcastle." According to both Josephus and Pliny, glass was discovered in its vicinity, in the sands of the Belus River (Na'aman) which were used for glass manufacture throughout antiquity. In Byzantine times Acre was the seat of a bishopric in the archdiocese of Tyre and had a large Samaritan community. In 614 C.E. it was taken, according to one source, by Jews allied with the Persian invaders of the Byzantine Empire; the Persians evacuated it 14 years later and Byzantine rule was restored. Shortly thereafter, however, in 636 C.E., it fell to the Arabs and resumed its original name, which had been preserved by the Jews, as can be seen from Talmudic sources.

[Michael Avi-Yonah / Shimon Gibson (2nd ed.)]

Medieval Period

Letters in the Cairo *Genizah* refer to *kehal Akko* ("the congregation of Acre") and *rasheha* ("its leaders"). In the second half of the 11th century R. Moses ibn Kashkil, known as a scholar in many fields, arrived in Acre from Mahdiah, N. Africa. In 1104 Acre was captured by Baldwin I, Crusader king of Jerusalem. It was lost by the Crusaders in 1187 and recaptured in 1191 when the city became the Crusader capital. In 1165 *Maimonides had paid a short visit to the town and later corresponded with the local *dayyan*, Japheth b. Elijah. In 1170 *Ben-

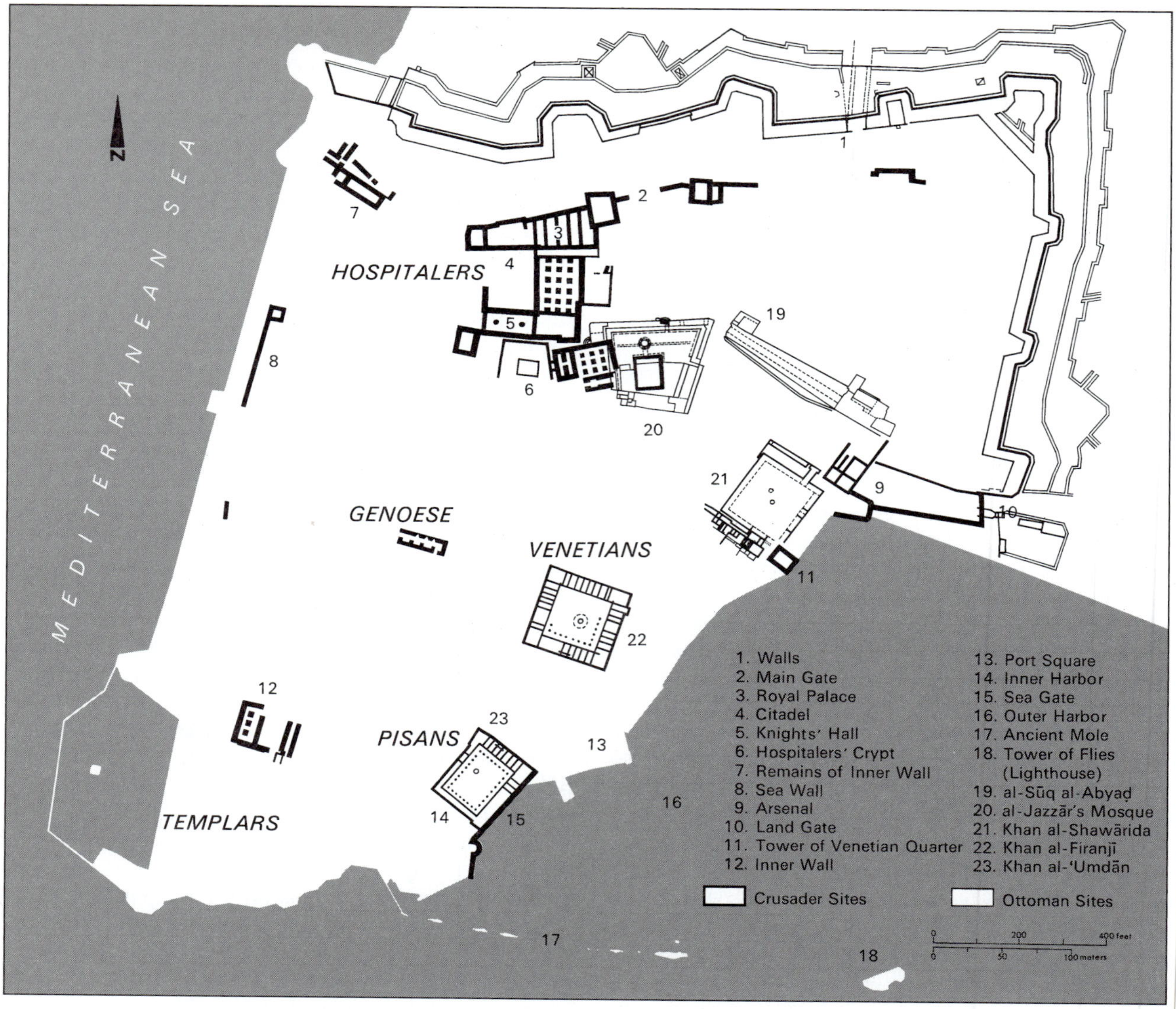

Plan of Acre showing Crusader and Ottoman sites.

jamin of Tudela found 200 Jews in Acre and lists the names of the leading scholars, R. Zadok, R. Japheth, and R. Jonah. *Pethahiah of Regensburg (c. 1175) also mentions in a short sentence Jews in the town. During this period Acre served as the port of disembarkation for both pilgrims and immigrants to Palestine. The Jewish community presumably received an impetus with the arrival of 300 rabbis from France and England in 1211. Among those who settled in the town were the scholars *Samuel b. Samson and his son, R. Jacob ha-Katan, Jonathan b. Jacob ha-Kohen of Lunel, and *Samson b. Abraham of Sens. Another event that stimulated both the quantitative and qualitative development of the community was the arrival in 1260 of R. *Jehiel b. Joseph of Paris, his son, and 300 of his pupils. Upon their arrival he founded a yeshivah, known as Midrash ha-Gadol de Paris, where he taught many pupils. There is also information that at about this time the scholars of Ereẓ Israel and Babylon addressed their questions on religious matters to "the scholars of Acre." The town became a center of study and attracted many scholars. R. Abraham *Abulafia lived there for a while and *Naḥmanides, who first settled in Jerusalem, moved to Acre, where he died in 1270. In the late 13th century, R. Solomon Petit taught in a yeshivah in Acre. In 1291 the town was conquered and destroyed by the Mamluks, led by al-Malik al-Ashraf who massacred Christian and Jewish inhabitants. Only a few managed to escape. After the Ottoman conquest in 1516 Acre again regained its importance as a port, and Jews gradually began to return. However, the settlement in Acre in the mid-16th century was small and impoverished. It may be assumed that Acre Jewry served as a link between the Jews of Galilee and the Mediterranean countries, and traded with Sidon, Aleppo, and Jerusalem. A letter dated 1741 states that there were over 100 Jewish householders. Moses Ḥayyim *Luzzatto died there of the plague in 1747. The revival of Acre as an important administrative and economic center was connected with the activities of the pashas Ẓahir al-ʿAmr and Aḥmad al-Jazzār. In 1750 Acre fell into the hands of al-ʿAmr, and in 1775 it became the capital of the *vilayet* of Sidon under Aḥmad al-Jazzār. *Simḥah of Zalozhtsy (1764–65) notes that the Jewish settlement was small and poor. Abbé Giovanni Mariti (1767) records that the Jews had a synagogue but were not allowed to enlarge it. Al-Jazzār fortified the town, using large numbers of forced laborers, and built markets, inns (*khān*), and a water supply. He developed Acre into a political and military center strong enough to deter Napoleon, who in 1799 unsuccessfully besieged Acre. The British fleet under Sir Sidney Smith helped al-Jazzār to defend the city and Napoleon's failure here marked the collapse of his Middle Eastern expeditions. In 1816 the traveler J.S. Buckingham stated that the Jews of Acre constituted a quarter of the population, had two synagogues, and were led by Ḥayyim *Farḥi. Farḥi was highly respected by the authorities; his influence was decisive in Acre, and extended down as far as the Jaffa region. He was killed by Abdallah, the ruler of Acre. The census of 1839, requested by Sir Moses *Montefiore, listed 233 Jews; and the 1849 census, 181 Jews. Most were poor and lived in the eastern and northern parts of the town. In 1856 there were only 120 Jews, and in 1886, 140. In the mid-19th century the Jews of Acre worked as peddlers and artisans, but many were without means of support.

[Natan Efrati]

Modern Acre

Acre stagnated and its shallow harbor was unfit for modern shipping. In the first decade of the 20th century, however, the Turks lifted the prohibition on building outside the Old City walls, and a new city quarter came into being on the north side, laid out with straight, and sometimes broad, roads. Although its population reached its lowest ebb before World War I, the town slowly started growing after its occupation by British forces (September 1918). There was always a Jewish population in Acre, residing alongside the Arab-Muslim, Christian, and Bahai inhabitants.

The Jewish residents, who numbered 350 in 1936, abandoned the town when the Arab riots broke out that year. During the British Mandate the fortress of al-Jazzār served as a prison in which political prisoners were also held (members of the Jerusalem *Haganah, with Vladimir *Jabotinsky, in 1920; members of the Haganah and other underground organizations in 1936–39; a group of Haganah commanders, with Moshe *Carmel and Moshe *Dayan in 1939–41). Jewish underground fighters, among them Shelomo *Ben-Yosef, and Arab rioters were executed there. This fortress was attacked by the *Irgun Ẓeva'i Le'umi in 1947.

During the early months of the War of Independence (1948), Acre served as an Arab base for operations against Jewish settlements further north and for a planned attack on Haifa. On May 13, 1948, however, Acre was stormed by Haganah forces and was included in the State of Israel, together with all of Western Galilee. Those of its Arab inhabitants who remained were, from the end of 1948, joined by Jewish immigrants. Acre's population grew from 12,000 between 1953 and 1955 to 32,800 (including 8,450 non-Jews) in 1967 and 45,800 in 2002 (76% Jews, 22% Muslims, 2% Christians). At the beginning of the 21st century, most of the Arab residents lived in the Old City, while the Jewish population was concentrated to the north and east of it. The quarter east of the Old City (and of the Nahariyyah highway) was built shortly after 1948. The expansion to the north and northeast took place later, while an industrial zone took shape on the dunes south of Acre, with the installations of the industrial company called "Steel City" at its southern extremity on the Haifa Bay beach. Acre itself became an industrial center. The Steel City factories closed down during the 1990s but were replaced by others, including the Tambour paint factory and a pipe plant. The municipal area now extended over 4 sq. mi. (10 sq. km.).

Acre serves most of Western Galilee in trade and administration matters, being the center of the Acre sub-district as it had been during the British Mandate. Included in its municipal area are a government Experimental Agricultural Station (founded under the British Mandate) and the Berit Aḥim (Kefar Philadelphia) youth village. Acre is an important Muslim center, its al-Jazzār Mosque being the largest within Israel's pre-1967 borders. Together with Haifa, it is also the world center of the *Bahai faith. There are churches of several denominations (Roman Catholic, Maronite, Melkite), and a considerable number of synagogues.

Efforts were made to preserve the Oriental character of the Old City and to excavate and repair its remains. The crypt of the citadel (the refectorium of the order of St. John) was cleared, and a municipal museum, with Crusader and Arab antiquities, was established in the old Turkish bath. Excavations outside the city wall have uncovered extensive Hellenistic and Roman cemeteries and the remains of a temple with a dedication to Antiochus VII. The ancient remains in the Old City date mainly from the Ottoman period. These include the double wall of the city, the citadel, two caravanserais – the Khān alʿUmdān and Khān al Firanji – and the mosque and bath built by al-Jazzār. A few remains of the Crusader period are still visible in the Burj al-Sultan and the sea wall. The Old City of Acre is a major tourist attraction, and in 2002 UNESCO declared it a world cultural preservation site. Since the 1980s a fringe theater festival has been held in the Old City every Sukkot.

[Efraim Orni / Shaked Gilboa (2nd ed.)]

BIBLIOGRAPHY: Abel, Land, 2 (1938), 235–7; Press, Ereẓ, 4 (1955), 725–9; L. Kadman, *Coins of Akko-Ptolemais* (1961); Avi-Yonah, in: IEJ, 9 (1959), 1–12; Applebaum, *ibid.*, 9 (1959), 274; Landau, *ibid.*, 11 (1961), 118–26; Prawer et al., *Ma'aravo shel ha-Galil* (1965); S. Klein (ed.), *Sefer ha-Yishuv*, 1 (1939), s.v.; Z. Vilnay, *Akko* (Heb., 1967), includes bibliography; A. Yaari, *Masot Ereẓ-Yisrael* (1946), 397; M. Ish-Shalom, *Masei Noẓerim…* (1965), index; Alḥarizi, *Taḥkemoni*, ed. by A. Kaminka (1899), 353–4; Prawer, Ẓalbanim, index; Ben Zvi, Ereẓ-

Yisrael, index; Moses of Trani, resp. 151; Mann, in: *Tarbiz*, 7 (1936), 92; M.N. Adler (ed.), *Itinerary of Benjamin of Tudela* (1907), 21; Kook, in: *Zion*, 5 (1933), 97–107; Ashtor, Toledot, 1 (1944), 131–3; A. Aharonson *Akko* (Heb. 1925). **ADD. BIBLIOGRAPHY:** M. Dothan, "Accho" (short reports appearing at intervals in "Notes and News"), in: *Israel Exploration Journal*, 23–34 (1973–84); idem, "A Phoenician Inscription from 'Akko," in: *Israel Exploration Journal*, 35 (1985), 81–94.

°**ACRO, PSEUDO-**, a scholium to Horace which from the 16th century was ascribed to Acro, a second-century commentator. The actual author is unknown. The Jewish interest in the work is contained in a note on *Horace's *Satires* I, 9, 70, which states that since Moses was born circumcised, he wanted all the Jews to follow suit so that he would not be unique.

[Jacob Petroff]

ACROSTICS (and Alphabetizing Compositions). A literary style in which successive or alternating verses, or clusters of verses, begin with the letters of the alphabet in sequence.

Bible

Biblical literature has preserved, in complete or truncated form, 14 alphabetizing compositions. Except for one (Nah. 1), they are restricted to the Hagiographa (Ps. 9–10, 25, 34, 37, 111, 112, 119, 145; Prov. 31:10–31; Lam. 1–4). Complete acrostics occur in the conventional order in Psalms 111, 112, 119; Proverbs 31:10–31; and Lamentations 1, as well as, with a curious but unexplained variant transposition of *ayin* and *pe*, in Lamentations 2:16–17, 3:46–51, 4:16–17. While the possibility of textual dislocation cannot be entirely ruled out here, the successive repetition of the irregularity makes it a less likely solution, particularly in view of the identical phenomenon behind the Greek version of Proverbs 31:25–26, and apparently in the original forms of Psalms 34:16–17 (*ẓa'aku*, v. 18 now has a remote subject) and Psalms 10:7–8c (cf. also Hebrew Ecclus. 51:23–25). In the case of four psalms the acrostic arrangement is impaired. Psalm 25 omits *vav* and *kof*, duplicates *resh*, and adds an extra *pe* at the end. Psalm 34, too, lacks *vav* and has supernumerary *pe*. The *ayin* is missing in Psalm 37, and the *nun* in Psalms 9–10 (originally a unity) and Nahum 1 are unmistakable torsos of originally alphabetic compositions, but are too mutilated to permit reconstruction in full.

The types of alphabetic structure vary. By far the most frequent is when the initial successive letters head each full verse (Ps. 25, 34, 115; Prov. 31:10–31; Lam. 1, 2, 4). Sometimes they begin alternate verses (Ps. 9–10 [?], 37) and sometimes each half verse (Ps. 111; 112; Nah. 1 [?]). The most sophisticated and elaborate arrangement appears in Psalm 119 and Lamentations 3 in which each stanza comprises eight verses in the former and three verses in the latter, all commencing with the same letter. The impact of the acrostic principle is also present in Lamentations 5 with its 22 verses, even though no abecedary is used. Whatever the age of the individual alphabetic compositions, it is clear that the phenomenon cannot be used as a criterion for the dating of biblical texts. The word and sentence acrostic is found in at least five works in Akkadian literature. Although the only two dated examples come from the seventh and sixth centuries B.C.E., there is no reason to doubt that the principle was not in vogue in Mesopotamia much earlier. Moreover, since the traditional order of the alphabetic signs is now known to have been fixed no later than the 14th century B.C.E., there is every likelihood of its early employment in Israel in literary compositions.

It is not possible to decide what considerations influenced the choice of this particular device. Sometimes it seems to provide a connecting link between variations upon a single theme. At other times it apparently serves to impose an external order and system upon material that lacks inner coherence or logical development. Frequently, it must have been used as a mnemonic aid in a pedagogic or didactic context as well as in a cultic-liturgical situation. For instance, it would be particularly suited to the rote recitation of moralistic instruction, divine attributes, and hymns of praise and thanksgiving. A magical or mystical purpose can be ruled out in the biblical period, but purely aesthetic considerations might occasionally have been at work. Finally, it is not at all improbable that the arrangement of literary material in alphabetic sequence from beginning to end would signify the striving for comprehensiveness in the expression of an emotion or idea.

[Nahum M. Sarna]

Post-Biblical

In later usage the letters, syllables, or words are arranged in such a way that their combinations have meaning independent of their meaning in the general context (and not necessarily alphabetically). There are three main types of acrostics: *Akrostikhon* – in the narrowest meaning of the word, when the letters (or syllables or words) that are to be joined are consistently found at the beginning of each line, verse, sentence, or paragraph; *Telestikhon* – when they are at the end; *Mezostikhon* – when they are in the middle. With regard to content there are two types of acrostic. One is alphabetic when the first letters (or last in *telestikhon*, etc.) of each line (or verse, etc.) combine to produce the alphabet or the alphabet in reverse (in Hebrew called *tashrak* תשר"ק) or regular and reverse in turn (*atbash*, אתב"ש; *atbaḥ* אטב"ח; *tashab* תאש"ב) and the like. There are also variations, e.g., entire works in which every word begins with the same letter. The other is an acrostic of words, in which the combinations produce a word or complete sentence.

Originally, the acrostic fulfilled several important functions. It simplified learning by heart and prevented mistakes, deletions, and additions. Furthermore, it preserved the name of the author, which often appeared as an acrostic. One Midrash (PR 46) attributes an acrostic to Moses: "And Moses came and they began (Psalm 92) with the letters of his name מִזְמוֹר שִׁיר [לְיוֹם] הַשַּׁבָּת." According to another Midrash (Song R. 1:7), Solomon composed an alphabetic acrostic. On the other hand, the view (appearing in the *Pesikta Rabbati*) that the Bible also contains acrostics of words is doubtful. Following the model of the Bible are the acrostics in The Wisdom of Ben Sira (li, 36–54; although somewhat corrupted).

It is not known whether there was a special Hebrew name for the acrostic. In a later period it was called a *siman* ("sign"), and then a *ḥatimah* ("signature"). Alphabetic acrostics had names which were derived from the Greek ἀλφαβητάρια (e.g., Eccles. R. 7:7, 18; in the parallel in Ruth R. 6:6 mistakenly *Alfanterin* (אַלְפַנְתְּרִין), and especially: Alfa Beta, Alfabeta, etc.). Under Arabic influence alphabetic acrostics began to be called *fibetim* (singular: *fibeta*), dropping the first syllable which was thought to be the (Arabic) definite article (al-). These foreign names may indicate that the acrostics in prayers and *piyyutim* were not a direct continuation of biblical acrostics but were influenced by those which had become part of Roman, Byzantine, Syrian, and Arabic literature (though in certain aspects it was the Hebrew *piyyut* that influenced the Syrian and Byzantine and not the reverse). In any event the acrostic in its different forms is often found in the prayers and *piyyutim*. An alphabetic prayer is found in the tractate *Soferim* (19:9). Other examples are the prayers: "אֵל בָּרוּךְ גְּדוֹל דֵּעָה" (Alphabet), and "תִּכַּנְתָּ [or: תִּקַּנְתָּ] שַׁבָּת רָצִיתָ קָרְבְּנוֹתֶיהָ..." (*Tashrak*) and others. The *paytanim*, beginning with Yose b. Yose, Yannai, Kallir, R. Saadiah Gaon, and others, employed acrostics, which became increasingly longer and more complicated. The letters of the alphabet were repeated in differing and unusual combinations. The names of the *paytanim*, their fathers, place of residence, pseudonyms, often combined with blessings, verses from the Bible, etc., were woven into the *piyyut* in acrostic form. The poets of Spain, Solomon ibn Gabirol, Judah Halevi, Abraham Ibn Ezra, and others, followed the *paytanim* in this, especially in their liturgical poetry. The acrostic found its way into prose writing, especially rhymed prose, letters, introductions to various works, etc. An example is the beginning of the famous letter of Ḥisdai ibn Shaprut to the king of the Khazars which was written at his behest by Menahem b. Saruk. The introduction of R. Shabbetai Donnolo to his *Sefer Ḥakhmoni* includes the acrostic "שַׁבְּתַי בַּר אַבְרָהָם, חֲזַק הוּא דוֹנוֹלוֹ הַנּוֹלַד מֵאוֹרַס [i.e., Oria]". In the Middle Ages, and even later, entire works were composed in which every word began with the same letter. The most famous of these is "*Elef Alfin*" ("A thousand *alefs*"), attributed to Abraham Bedersi. A common form of acrostic is when the initial letters of the first few words of a work spell the name of God. Kabbalistic literature considered acrostics, like all combinations of letters and syllables, to be important. The use of acrostics, already criticized by R. Isaac Arama in the 15th century, has continued to the present but only as a diversion.

BIBLIOGRAPHY: BIBLE: Loehr, in: ZAW, 25 (1905), 173–98; S.R. Driver, *Introduction to the Literature of the Old Testament* (1913[9]), 337, 367f., 456f., 459; F. Dornseiff, *Das Alphabet in Mystic und Magie* (1925[2]); Munch, in: ZDMG, 90 (1936), 703–10; Marcus, in: JNES, 6 (1947), 109–15; G.R. Driver, *Semitic Writing* (1948), 181, 200–8; N.K. Gottwald, *Studies in the Book of Lamentations* (1954), 23–32; W.G. Lambert, *Babylonian Wisdom Literature* (1960), 63, 66 ff. POSTBIBLICAL: M. Steinschneider, *Jewish Literature* (1965[2]), 149–51; Elbogen, Gottesdienst, 78, 86, 207, 209, 285, 291 ff., 309; A.M. Habermann, *Ha-Piyyut* (1946), 8 ff.; I. Heinemann, *Ha-Tefillah bi-Tekufat ha-Tanna'im ve-ha-Amo-ra'im* (1966[2]), 88–91, 148, 152f., 168f; S. Lieberman, *Hellenism in Jewish Palestine* (1950), 79–82; Zunz-Albeck, Derashot, 9, 47, 180, 183, 185 and notes; I. Davidson, in: *Lu'aḥ Aḥi'ever*, 1 (1918), 91–95. **ADD. BIBLIOGRAPHY:** E. Fleischer, *Shirat ha-Kodesh ha'ivrit bimei ha-Benayim* (1975), 512, index.

[Yehuda Arye Klausner]

ACSÁDY, IGNÁC (1845–1906), Hungarian historian and writer. Born in Nagy-Károly, Acsády took his doctorate of philosophy in Budapest. He wrote many novels and plays and was a regular contributor to the Hungarian press. His main importance lies, however, in the field of historiography. Acsády's work as an historian is marked by his anti-feudal and progressive views. In his novel *Fridényi bankja* ("Fridenyi's Bank," 1882; new edition: 1968) he criticized the dominant role of money in the contemporary world. His liberal outlook is also stressed in his *A magyar birodalom története* ("History of the Hungarian Empire"), and especially in his most important work *A magyar jobbágyság története* ("History of Hungarian Serfhood"), which was translated into Slovakian and Russian. Acsády's main interests were economic conditions in the 16th and 17th centuries and the fate of the common people. He advised the Jews to unite with the peasants against the antisemitism of the lower and middle classes, and he fought constantly for equal rights for the Jews of Hungary. In 1883 he published *Jewish and Non-Jewish Hungarians after the Emancipation*, and in 1894 he helped to found the Hungarian Jewish Literary Society. After World War II a street in Budapest was named after him and a plaque dedicated in his memory.

BIBLIOGRAPHY: P. Gunst, *Acsády Ignác történetirása* (1961).

[Alexander Scheiber]

ACTION FRANÇAISE, French royalist and antisemitic movement formed after the *Dreyfus affair, mainly active between 1896 and 1939. The doctrine of its principal theorist Charles *Maurras, termed "integral nationalism," was the radical expression of the conception of organic national unity. Prominent among its leaders were the writer Léon *Daudet, and the historian Jacques Bainville. The party organ, also named *L'Action française*, was established as a daily in 1908. The Action Française took pride in having reactivated antisemitism in France, alleging that the Jews were one of the principal agents of national disintegration and economic and moral corruption. They were part of an evil plot hatched by a would-be "confederation of the Four Estates," which, beside the Jews, included Protestants, Freemasons, and foreigners in general. These were allegedly using the slogans of liberty and revolution to mask mercenary interests and the political fragmentation of national life by the parties. The Action Française waged scurrilous campaigns against economic enterprises. It hence attacked *métèques* ("foreigners") according to Maurras' formula "not to divide, but to define." The Semite in particular was singled out as basically barbarian; to combat him was a proof of incorruptibility and concern with national interests. Even so, the Action Française rejected the idea of racist antisemitism as absurd.

The importance of the Action Française lies in the respectability of some of its leaders and the influence they exercised on certain circles of French officers between the two world wars. The antisemitic legislation enacted by the Vichy government after the fall of France in World War II was directly inspired by ideas of the Action Française and its program of excluding the Jew from French society and politics. The last issue of *L'Action française* appeared in Lyons in August 1944. Its spirit has been kept alive by Fascist-inclined and racist publications, such as the weeklies *Aspect de la France, Rivarol*, and *La Nation française*.

BIBLIOGRAPHY: S.M. Osgood, *French Royalism under the Third and Fourth Republics* (1960), includes bibliography; E.R. Tannenbaum, *Action Française: Die-Hard Reactionaries in Twentieth-Century France* (1962); E.J. Weber, *Action Française: Royalism and Reaction in Twentieth-Century France* (1962), with bibliography.

ACZÉL, TAMÁS (1921–1994), Hungarian author and journalist. Aczél wrote the prizewinning novel *A szabadság árnyékában* ("In the Shadow of Freedom," 1948). A member of the circle of Imre Nagy, he fled to Paris after the suppression of the 1956 revolution and edited the radical emigrant periodical *Irodalmi Ujság*.

ADA, townlet in Vojvodina, Serbia, until 1920 in (Austro-) Hungary. Jews came there from German-speaking areas; they also spoke Yiddish and later Hungarian. They were allowed to settle in the late 17th century in order to repopulate the southern provinces devastated during the Turkish wars, but were forbidden to use Hebrew or Yiddish in official documents, testaments, and *pinkasim*. The first rabbis were Aaron Acker (d. 1837) and Jacob Heilprin. During the 1848–49 troubles, when Serbia sent volunteers to help the Slav populations in Hungary, a Serbian troop occupied Ada and took 60 Jews – including Rabbi Heilprin – to Senta where they were all murdered. Ada remained one of the dozen or so Orthodox communities along the Thissa River following the split between the Neologist majority and Orthodox minority in 1868/69. They maintained *talmud torah* schools and formed an Association of Orthodox Communities that worked in close cooperation with the Neologist Federation of Jewish Communties in Belgrade. The synagogue was built in 1896. In 1925 there were 452 Jews in Ada, but many left for bigger towns. During World War II Ada was occupied by Hungary and a concentration camp was established there. Of its 350 Jews in 1940, only 59 remained after the war, when the community was temporarily reestablished. Most subsequently left for Israel.

[Zvi Loker (2nd ed.)]

ADADI, ABRAHAM ḤAYYIM BEN MASOUD ḤAI (1801–1874), halakhic authority and kabbalist. Born in Tripoli and orphaned at an early age, Abraham was raised by his grandfather, Nathan Adadi, an outstanding scholar. In 1818 the family emigrated to Safed, where Adadi studied and was occasionally required to travel abroad as an emissary of the community. While in Leghorn in 1837 he heard of the great earthquake in Safed, and therefore changed his plans and returned to Tripoli, where he served as rabbi and *dayyan* and maintained a *bet midrash*. Some time after 1865, Adadi returned to Safed, remaining there for the rest of his life. Adadi paid particular attention to the local *minhagim* ("customs"), especially of Tripoli and Safed, and also of places he visited. His books incorporate much historical information, particularly about Tripoli. In this he was doubtless influenced by Abraham *Ḥalfon, his greatest Tripolitanian contemporary. Adadi's works include: *Ha-Shomer Emet* (Leghorn, 1849), primarily *halakhot* and customs concerning Torah scrolls; *Va-Yikra Avraham* (Leghorn, 1865), responsa, etc.; *Zeh ha-Kelal* on talmudic methodology; and *Makom she-Nahagu*, customs omitted from *Ha-Shomer Emet*. The rest of his works, including talmudic novellae and sermons, are still in manuscript (Ben-Zvi Institute, Jerusalem). An original poem in praise of Safed appears at the beginning of his *Ha-Shomer Emet*.

BIBLIOGRAPHY: N. Slouschz, *Massa'ai be-Ereẓ Luv*, 1 (1935), 24ff.; Yaari, Sheluḥei, 675ff.; Farija Zu'areẓ et al. (eds.), *Yahadut Luv* (1960), 71; Franco, *Histoire des Israélites de L'Empire Ottoman*, 121.

ADAH (Heb. עָדָה; "ornament" or [according to the Arabic] "morning"; cf. Heb. personal names: Adaiah, Adiel), name of wife of *Lamech and wife of *Esau. Adah was one of the two wives of Lamech (Gen. 4:19–20). To her and to his other wife Zillah, Lamech recited his song (Gen. 4:23ff.). Her children, *Jabal and *Jubal, were the first to practice, respectively, pastoral pursuits and music, thus inaugurating a new stage of human progress. Her importance for the genealogy in Genesis 4 is derived from this fact, because Lamech's wives are the only women mentioned there. In the account in Genesis 5:28ff. there is no mention of Adah, Zillah, and their children. Noah, the firstborn of Lamech, appears instead, together with other sons and daughters, whose names are not mentioned.

Adah was the wife of Esau (Gen. 36:2) and the daughter of Elon (but cf. Gen. 26:34, where the daughter of Elon, who married Esau, is Basemath). Esau, who is also called *Edom (*ibid.* 36:1), and was probably the patriarch of Edom, married Adah, a Hittite, who was a native of Canaan. This account provides information on a Hittite element in Edom, a fact unknown from other sources, except in connection with other wives of Esau (Judith and Basemath, Gen. 26:34; cf. 28:9). Nonetheless, this information is difficult to fit in. On the other hand, Adah's Canaanite origin is probable, due to the wide range of nationalities included in the term Canaan. Adah was the mother of Eliphaz and his children, who were *allufim and counted as her descendants (Gen. 36:11–12, 15–16) rather than those of Lamech.

ADD. BIBLIOGRAPHY: U. Hübner, ABD, 1, 60.

ADALBERG, SAMUEL (1868–1939), Polish literary historian and folklorist. Born in Warsaw, Adalberg studied in a number of European capitals. His main work, a compendium of Polish proverbs, sayings, and proverbial phrases, *Księg przysłów, przypowieści i wyrażeń przysłówiowych polskich* (1889–94), remains the most extensive collection ever made in this field. Its 40,000 entries include both folk proverbs and quotations from major Polish writers of the 16th to 18th centuries that have become proverbs. For this work Adalberg was rewarded with membership of the philological section of the Cracow Academy of Science. He also translated and annotated 580 Yiddish proverbs drawn from the collection of Ignatz *Bernstein. This was published in the Polish ethnographical journal *Wisła* (vol. 4, 1890) and was also issued as a separate booklet. From 1918 Adalberg was an adviser on Jewish matters to the Polish Ministry of Education and Religious Affairs, and was thus able to do much for Jewish communal and educational institutions. He committed suicide when the Nazis occupied Warsaw.

BIBLIOGRAPHY: J. Krzyżanowski, *Mądrej głowie dość dwie słowie*, 2 (1960), index. **ADD. BIBLIOGRAPHY:** Y. Gruenbaum, *Penei ha-Dor*, 1 (1958), 363–66; S. Netzer, *Ma'avak Yehudei Polin al Zekhuyoteihem ha-Ezraḥiyot ve-ha-Lu'umiyyot* (1980), 48.

[Dov Noy]

ADAM (אָדָם), the first man and progenitor of the human race. The Documentary Hypothesis distinguishes two conflicting stories about the making of man in Scripture (for a contrary view, see U. Cassuto, *From Adam to Noah*, pp. 71ff.). In the first account of Creation in the Bible (attributed by critics to the Priestly narration; Gen. 1) Adam was created in God's image (verse 27), as the climax of a series of Divine creative acts, and was given dominion over the rest of creation (verses 28–30). In the second story (attributed by critics to the J or Yahwist strand; Gen. 2–3), after the completion of heaven and earth, God fashioned "the man" (*ha-adam*) from dust of the ground (*ha-adamah*), breathed life into his nostrils, and placed him in the Garden of Eden to be caretaker. Permission was given to eat freely from any tree of the Garden except, under penalty of death, from the Tree of Knowledge of Good and Bad. In order that the man might not be alone but would have appropriate aid, God formed the various animals and had the man determine what they should be called. The man gave names to all the animals, but found among them no suitable help. God then put the man to sleep, extracted one of his ribs, and fashioned it into a woman, and presented her to the man who found her eminently satisfactory and congenial. The naked pair had no feeling of shame until the serpent seduced the woman to eat the fruit of the forbidden tree. The woman shared the fruit with her husband with the result that they became aware of their nakedness and hid from God. As punishment for this transgression, the serpent was condemned to crawl on its belly and eat dust. The woman was sentenced to the pangs of childbirth, a craving for her man, and subjection to him. The man, for his part, for listening to his wife and for violating the prohibition, was destined to toil and sweat in order to wrest a bare living from an accursed and hostile soil until his return to the dust whence he came. Perpetual enmity was established between snake and man. God then made skin tunics (better: "tunics for the skin") and clothed the man and woman. The man had now become like one of the divine beings "knowing good and bad" (Gen. 3:22, i.e., everything; cf. Gen. 31:24; Lev. 5:4; II Sam. 13:22; Isa. 41:23). To keep the man from taking and eating of the Tree of Life and thereby acquiring the other quality that distinguished the divine beings, immortality, God expelled him from the Garden of Eden and barred access to the Tree of Life by means of the *cherubim and the flaming sword. Next one reads that "the man" had experience of his wife *Eve, who bore him *Cain and later *Abel (Gen. 4:1–2), and further on that "Adam," at the age of 130 years, sired *Seth by his wife (4:25; 5:3), after which he lived on for another eight centuries without report of further events, except that he "begot sons and daughters" and died at the age of 930 (5:4–5).

The presence of the article before the word *adam* in Genesis 2:7–4:1 militates against construing it as a proper name. However, in 4:25, and also in 5:1–5, the article is dropped and the word becomes Adam. The masorah takes advantage of the ambiguity of the consonantal spelling (*l'dm*) which can mean "to/for the man" or "to/for Adam," depending on the vocalization, to introduce the proper name Adam into Genesis 2:20 and 3:17, 21, contrary to the import of the passage. Similarly, the Septuagint and Vulgate begin at Genesis 2:19 to translate *ha-adam* as the proper name Adam.

The only further mention of Adam in the Bible occurs in the genealogical table of I Chronicles 1:1. It is moot whether *adam* in *ke-adam* of Hosea 6:7 and Job 31:33, and *benei adam* of Deuteronomy 32:8, is to be taken as the proper name. In the apocryphal books, however, there are several probable allusions to Adam and the creation story (Ecclus. 17:1; 49:16; Tob. 8:6; Wisd. Sol. 2:23; 9:2; 10:1).

The etymology of the word *adam* is ambiguous. The feminine form *adamah* designates the ground or soil, and the play on the two forms *adam* and *adamah* in Genesis 2:7 suggests for *adam* the meaning "earthling." The root אדם (*'dm*) is also connected with the color "red," which might apply to the color of the soil from which man was formed. The word *adamu* is used in Akkadian for "blood," *adamatu* for "black blood" in pathological conditions, and the plural *adamātu* for "dark, red earth [used as dye]." The word *admu/atmu* ("child") probably has no relation to *adam* but is rather to be connected with a root *wtm* and related to Hebrew *yatom* ("orphan"). In Old South Arabic *'dm* has the meaning "serf." The occurrence of *'dm* as the apparent theophorous element in few personal names such as *'bd 'dm* ("servant of *'dm*"; MT, Obed-Edom, II Sam. 6:10ff.), suggests a deity *'dm*, but there is little additional direct evidence for this. In an Akkadian synonym list the word *adamu* is equivalent to an "important, noble person." The personal names *A-da-mu, A-dam-u* also appear in Old Akkadian and Old Babylonian (*Chicago Assyrian Dictionary*, 1, part 1 (1964), 95, s.v. adamu B; cf. also W. von Soden, *Akkadisches Handwoerterbuch*, 1 (1965), 10).

[Marvin H. Pope]

In the *Aggadah*

Adam was formed from a mixture of water and earth, as is implied in Genesis 2:7. According to Greek mythology too, Prometheus formed men from water and earth (Apollodorus, 1:7, 1); and Hesiod (*Opera et Dies*, 61) relates that Hephaestus kneaded earth and water and made woman. The ancient Egyptians also believed that "man was formed from miry and swampy land" (Diodorus 1:43, 2).

There is no reference in the existing texts of the Septuagint to the statement of the *aggadah* (Mekh. 60:14) that the translators of the Bible changed Genesis 1:26 from the plural "Let us make man in our image, after *our* likeness," to "I will make man in my likeness and image" in order to remove any suggestion of anthropomorphic polytheism. The aggadists were actually more concerned with possible polytheistic interpretations than with the suggestion of anthropomorphism, the belief in anthropomorphism being widespread in both Hellenistic and philosophical works (e.g., among the Epicureans). In any event, many of the aggadists attempted to remove these anthropomorphisms. Some of them explain, "in His image" as meaning "with the dignity of his Maker" (see Tanh. Pekudei 2; Gen. R. 11:2).

In the creation of the universe, whatever was created later had dominion over what preceded it, and Adam and Eve were "created after everything in order to have dominion over everything" (Gen. R. 19:4). They were "created last in order that they should rule over all creation… and that all creatures should fear them and be under their control" (Num. R. 12:4). The subjection of the creatures is also greatly stressed in Adam 37–39; *Apocalypsis Mosis*, 10–12. Another reason for man's being created last was "that he should immediately enter the banqueting hall (everything having already been prepared for him). The matter may be likened to an emperor's building a palace, consecrating it, preparing the feast, and only then inviting the guests" (Tosef. Sanh. 8:9). On the other hand, Adam was created last, so that "should he become conceited, he could be told, 'The gnat was created before you'" (*ibid.* 8:8). Adam alone, of all living things, was created "to stand upright like the ministering angels" (Gen. R. 8:11; cf. Ḥag. 16a). Both Adam and Eve were created "fully developed… Adam and Eve were created as adults 20 years of age" (Gen. R. 14:7). In fact, everything created, "the sun and the moon, the stars and the planets, all were created fully developed, all the works of creation being brought into existence in their completed state" (Num. R. 12:8). The same opinion was held by Philo and by a number of Greek and Roman scholars (Dion Chrysostomus, 36:59).

Thales, "father of philosophers," used to say, "Every thing that exists is very beautiful, being the work of God" (Diogenes Laertius, 1:35). In the same vein, Philo maintained (Op., 47:136–41) that Adam was a perfect creature. The aggadists exalt the beauty of Adam, saying, "The ball of Adam's heel outshone the glory of the sun: how much more so the brightness of his face" for "Adam was created for the service of the Holy One, and the orb of the sun for the service of mankind" (PdRK 101).

The rabbis interpret Genesis 1:27 to mean that Adam was created as a hermaphrodite (Er. 18a; Gen. R. 8:1; cf. also Jub. 2:14; 3:8). He was created on New Year's Day, the first of Tishri, and all that is related of him occurred on that very day. In the first hour his dust was assembled; in the second he was roughhewn; in the third his limbs were articulated; in the fourth the soul was breathed into him; in the fifth he stood erect; in the sixth he gave names to all creatures; in the seventh Eve was brought to him; in the eighth they begot Cain and Abel; in the ninth they were forbidden to eat of the tree of the knowledge of good and evil; in the tenth they sinned; in the eleventh sentence was passed; and in the twelfth they were driven out of Eden (Sanh. 38b; cf. also Lev. R. 29:1).

When Adam was to be created, the angels were consulted. Some favored his creation for the love and mercy he would show; others were opposed to it because of the falsehood and strife he would stir up. In the end, the Holy One decided to create man (Gen. R. 8:5; Mid. Ps. to 1:22). The angels were filled with such awe at his creation that they wished to worship him, whereupon Adam pointed upward (PdRE 10; Tanh. Pekudei 3), or, according to another version, God caused a deep sleep to fall upon him and the angels realized his limitations (Gen. R. 8:10). All the angels were ordered to bow down to him and they did so, all except *Satan, who was hurled into the abyss and conceived a lasting hatred for Adam (PdRE 13). This myth of Satan's fall is to be found in the Apocryphal books, e.g., Adam 12–17.

It is characteristic of the book of Genesis that it gives the history of its principals up to a certain stage in their lives and then leaves them, taking up the story of their successors. Likewise, in the case of Adam, the Bible gives his story up to his expulsion from the Garden of Eden, and then deals with the succeeding generations, though Adam lived on for many years. No account is given of how Adam familiarized himself with the strange new world, which lacked those ideal conditions to which he had been accustomed. The *aggadah*, to some extent, attempts to fill the gap. It relates that "when the sun set (after he was driven out) darkness began to fall. Adam was terrified… thinking, 'The serpent will come to bite me.' The Holy One made available for him two flints (or, two stones) which he struck, one against the other, producing light" (Pes. 54a; Gen. R. 11:2). This subject is also dealt with by *Adam and Eve* 2:1, which relates that "the Lord God sent diverse seeds by Michael the archangel and gave them to Adam and showed him how to work and till the ground that they might have fruit, by which they and their generations might live." This is greatly developed in the Christian Adam books, the *Cave of Treasures* and the *Conflict of Adam and Eve*. This *aggadah* also hints at the answer to another question, how human civilization developed. This theme, especially the origin of light, the catalyst of all human development, greatly occupied Greek scholars. According to other *aggadot*, darkness itself and the seasonal change to winter terrified Adam until he became familiar with the order of the universe – sunset and sunrise, long days and short days (Av. Zar. 8a).

When Adam sinned, he lost his splendor. As a result of his sin, all things lost their perfection "though they had been created in their fullness," (Gen. R. 11:2; 12:6). Like Philo, the aggadists held that the beauty of the generations was slowly diminishing. All other people "compared to Sarah, are like apes compared to a man; Sarah compared with Eve, is like an ape compared to man, as was Eve compared to Adam" (BB 58a).

Satan selected the serpent as his tool because of its being the most subtle of beasts and the nearest to man in form, having been endowed with hands and feet (Gen. R. 19:1; 20:5). With regard to the identification of the tree of good and evil, the vine, the wheat, the citron, and the fig are suggested. According to this last view, it was because the fig tree had served as the source of Adam's sin that it subsequently provided him with the leaves to cover his nakedness, the consciousness of which was the direct result of that sin (Ber. 40a; Gen. R. 15:7; compare the Syriac *Apocalypse of Adam* (ed., Renan; 1853), 32). Adam was sent forth from the Garden of Eden in this world; whether he was also sent forth from the Eden of the next world is disputed (Gen. R. 21:7). With Adam's sin, the divine presence withdrew from this world, returning only with the building of the Tabernacle (PdRK 1). Adam learnt of the power of repentance from Cain. When Cain said to him, "I repented and have been forgiven," Adam beat his face and cried out, "So great is the power of repentance and I knew it not." Whereupon he sang the 90th Psalm, the Midrash interpreting its second verse as, "It is good to make confession to the Lord" (Gen. R. 22:13). In the *Life of Adam and Eve*, however, Adam and Eve's repentance after the expulsion from the garden is described at length (Adam 1–11). Adam was given the Noachian Laws (Sanh. 56b) and was enjoined to observe the Sabbath (Mid. Ps. to 92:6). He would have been given the whole Torah if he had not sinned (Gen. R. 24:5; 21:7). He was the first to pray for rain (Ḥul. 60b) and to offer sacrifice (Av. Zar. 8a). During the time he was separated from his wife, before he begot Seth, he gave birth to demons (Er. 18b; Gen. R. 20:11). The Zohar (7:34; 3:19) states that *Lilith, a demon, was the wife of Adam before the creation of Eve.

[Elimelech Epstein Halevy]

Medieval Jewish Philosophy

In Hellenistic and medieval Jewish philosophy Adam is often regarded as a prototype of mankind, and Genesis 2:8–3:24, interpreted as an allegory on the human condition. In spite of their predominant interest in the allegorical interpretation of the creation of Adam and his stay in the Garden of Eden, most Jewish philosophers appear to accept the historicity of the biblical account. For them the biblical story of Adam has both a literal and allegorical meaning.

Philo, following a Platonic model, sees in the twofold account of the creation of Adam a description of the creation of two distinct men, the heavenly man, created in the image of God (Gen. 1:27), and the earthly man, formed out of the dust of the earth (Gen. 2:7). The heavenly man is incorporeal. The earthly man is a composite of corporeal and incorporeal elements, of body and mind (Philo, I L.A. 12). Philo maintains that it is the mind of man and not his body which is in the image of God (Philo, Op. 23). The earthly Adam excelled all subsequent men both in intellectual ability and physical appearance, and attained the "very limit of human happiness" (Philo, Op. 3). But Adam did not remain forever at this level. Through eating from the forbidden tree of the knowledge of good and evil he brought upon himself a "life of mortality and wretchedness in lieu of that of immortality and bliss" (Philo, Op. 53). Philo interprets the eating from the forbidden tree allegorically as the indulgence in physical pleasures. Because Adam succumbed to his physical passions, his understanding descended from the higher level of knowledge to the lower level of opinion. While Philo at times does accept the literal interpretation of certain elements in the story, he generally rejects the literal meaning entirely and interprets all the elements of the story allegorically. Adam becomes the symbolic representation of mind; Eve, the representation of sense-perception; the serpent, the representation of passion; and the tree of knowledge, the representation of prudence or opinion. Though Philo did not exert any direct influence upon the medieval Jewish philosophers, there are many similarities between his conception of *Adam ha-Rishon* and that of medieval Jewish philosophy. The similarities in the descriptions of the perfections of the first man may have their origin in the midrashic descriptions of Adam, while the similarities in the interpretation of his sin probably result from the philosophic concerns common to Philo and the medievals.

*Judah Halevi maintains that Adam was perfect in body and mind. In addition to the loftiest intellect ever possessed by a human being, Adam was endowed with the "divine power" (*ha-ko'aḥ ha-Elohi*), that special faculty which, according to Halevi, enables man to achieve communion with God. This "divine power," passed down through various descendants of Adam to the people of Israel, is that which distinguishes the people of Israel from all other peoples (*Kuzari*, 1:95).

*Maimonides explains that when the Bible records that Adam was created "in the image of God" it refers to the creation of the human intellect, man's defining characteristic, which resembles the divine intellect, rather than to the creation of the body. Unlike Halevi, Maimonides believes that communion with God can be achieved through the development of the intellect, and that no special faculty is necessary. Thus, Maimonides emphasizes the intellectual perfection of Adam. Before the sin Adam's intellect was developed to its fullest capacity, and he devoted himself entirely to the contemplation of the truths of physics and metaphysics. Adam's sin consisted in his turning away from contemplation to indulge in physical pleasures to which he was drawn by his imagination and desires. As a result of his sin, Adam became occupied with controlling his appetites, and consequently his capacity for contemplation was impaired. His practical reason which before the sin had lain dormant was now activated, and he began to acquire practical rather than theoretical knowledge, a knowledge of values rather than of facts, of good and evil rather than of truth and falsehood, and of ethics and politics rather than of physics and metaphysics. It is clear that for Maimonides practical wisdom is inferior to theoretical wisdom, and that, therefore, the activation of Adam's practical reason at the expense of his theoretical reason was a punishment (*Guide*, 1:2).

Maimonides interprets various Midrashim on the story of Adam and the Garden of Eden allegorically in accordance with his interpretation of Adam's sin as the succumbing to physical passion. The Midrash describes the serpent as a camel ridden by Samael. According to Maimonides the serpent represents the imaginative faculty, while Samael, or the evil inclination, represents the appetitive faculty. Maimonides suggests that in the midrashic description of the tree of life in *Genesis Rabbah* 15:6 the tree represents physics and its branches metaphysics. The tree of knowledge, on the other hand, represents ethics or practical wisdom rather than physics and metaphysics. Instead of eating from the tree of life, i.e., devoting himself to the study of physics and metaphysics which would have enabled him to attain immortality, Adam ate from the forbidden tree; he followed his imagination and succumbed to his passions, thereby impairing his capacity for the contemplation of truth, and acquiring the capacity for the acquisition of a knowledge of ethics (*Guide*, 2:30).

Joseph *Albo maintains that Adam, as the prototype of mankind, is the choicest of all the creatures of the sublunar world and the purpose of the creation because he is the only creature that has a knowledge of God. All other creatures exist for his sake, and he has a dominion over them. Albo, too, interprets the story of the Garden of Eden allegorically, regarding it as a "symbolic allusion to man's fortune in the world" (*Sefer ha-Ikkarim*, 1:11). In his interpretation Adam represents mankind; the Garden of Eden, the world; the tree of life, the Torah; and the serpent, the evil inclination. The placing of Adam in the garden, in the midst of which stands the tree of life, symbolizes the fact that man is placed in the world in order to observe the commandments of the Torah. In the banishment of Adam from the Garden of Eden after he ate from the forbidden tree Albo sees an allusion to the punishment that will befall man if he disobeys the Divine commandments.

[David Kadosh / Adela Wolfe]

In Christian Tradition

Adam as the progenitor of the human race and as the type of humanity as such, plays a far greater role in Christian theological thought than in classical Judaism, since the former uses the account in Genesis 1–2 (and especially the story of Adam's sin and expulsion from Paradise) as a basis for its doctrine of man and his relation to God. Endowed with many extraordinary qualities as the crown of God's creation (e.g., perfect righteousness, sanctifying grace, absence of concupiscence, viz. evil inclination, immortality, etc.), he lost these at his fall ("original sin") and transmitted his fallen and corrupted nature to all his posterity. Only by the coming of Jesus, the "Second Adam," was humanity restored to its original grandeur and perfection "for as in Adam all die, even so in Christ shall all be made alive" (I Cor. 15:22). As the heavenly Adam succeeded the earthly Adam, so humanity of the flesh will become a spiritual humanity (I Cor. 15:44–49). The teaching of Paul greatly influenced Augustine and later Calvin in their formulations of the doctrine on original sin, implying as it does the innate corruption of human nature.

According to one Christian tradition, Adam is buried not in the Machpelah cave at Hebron but under the Calvary in the Holy Sepulcher, Jerusalem, so that the redemptive blood of Jesus shed at the crucifixion, flowed on his grave. In the Greek Orthodox Church a feast in honor of the parents of humanity, Adam and Eve, is kept on the Sunday preceding Christmas.

In Islamic Legend

Adam is more favorably presented in the Koran than in the Bible. The Adamic legend, as Muhammad related it, is as follows: Allah created Adam to become his regent (caliph) on earth (Sura 2:28) and made a covenant with him (Sura 20:114; cf. Hos. 6:7 and Sanh. 38b). At first the angels opposed it, fearing that man would evoke evil and bloodshed. However, Allah endowed Adam with the knowledge of the names of all things. The angels, who do not know these names, recognize Adam's superiority and pay him homage. Only Iblīs (Gr. *diábolos*, the Devil) revolts, claiming that he who is born of fire should not bow before one who is born of dust, whereupon Allah expels Iblīs from Paradise. Adam and Eve are forbidden to eat the fruit of a tree, but *Šayṭān* (Satan) appears and whispers in their ears: Allah has forbidden this tree to you, so that you will not live eternally like the angels (Sura 7:19). They eat from the tree, become aware of their nakedness, and cover themselves with the leaves of Eden. Allah proclaims eternal enmity between Man and Satan. Then Adam repents for his sin.

*Geiger recognized that the concept that God had consulted the angels and that voices had been raised against the creation of man belongs to an old *aggadah* (Sanh. 38a–b; Gen. R. 8:1). The fact that the Koran knew nothing of the serpent but placed Satan in its place points perhaps to Christian influence. Umayya ibn Abi'l-Salt, Muhammad's contemporary, knew of the serpent in connection with Adam's disobedience, but not the Satan.

Later Muslim interpreters and collectors of legends completed the story of the Koran from the Bible, *aggadah*, and their own poetic elaboration: Allah sent his angels, Gabriel and Michael, down to Earth in order to fetch dust for the creation of man; but the Earth rejected them and the Angel of Death forcibly took dust from the surface (surface of the earth in Arabic, *Adīm*, thus Adam). Adam was created from red, white, and black dust – hence the various skin colorings of mankind. The dust for the head came from the Ḥaram in Mecca; the chest, the sanctuary in Jerusalem; the loins, Yemen; the feet, Ḥejāz; the right hand, the East; and the left hand, the West. For a long time the body was lifeless and without a soul. Suddenly the spirit penetrated the body, Adam sneezed and exclaimed with the angels, "Praise be to Allah."

The notion of the homogeneity of the human race, as expressed in the legend which says that dust was gathered from the whole Earth to create Adam's body, is found in the Talmud (Sanh. 38a). Rav, however, suggested the following: dust was taken for the body from Babylon; the head, Ereẓ Israel; and the remaining limbs, the rest of the countries (Sanh. 38b). The idea that in the beginning Adam lay still as a figure of clay without a soul (golem), also originates from an *aggadah* (bibliography and interpretation in Bacher, Pal Amor, 2 (1896), 50–51; in addition, Mid. Hag. to Gen. 2:7). The *aggadah* and the Islamic legend both share the belief that God was the first couple's "best man," and that the forbidden fruit was wheat. This is the reason why Gabriel taught Adam agriculture: wheat banished man from Paradise, but wheat also introduced him to the earthly world. The *aggadah* is interested in calculating just how the hours of Adam's first day were spent (Sanh. 38b). That Adam did not stay an entire day in Paradise is derived from Psalms 49:13: "But man abides ["spends the night"] not in honor." According to the Islamic legend, Adam foresaw the future generations and their prophets. In the *aggadah* there is also a most impressive description of how one generation after the other – with its great men and sages – file past Adam (Sanh. 38b; Av. Zar. 5a; ARN 31:91; Gen. R. 24:2; PR 23:115).

Nor is there any doubt as to the reciprocity between the Islamic legend and the late Midrash. Thus, for instance, the specific statement that Adam was formed from red, white, and black earth – hence the differences in the complexion of mankind – is a further development of both the late *aggadah* (Targ. Yer., Gen. 2:7; PdRE 11) and the Islamic legend. The Koran (2:28–32) recognizes Adam's superior status in that he knew the names of the creatures and things. Familiar is the Islamic oath: "By Allah who taught the names to Adam" (see Gen. R. 17:4). *Pirkei de-R. Eliezer* 16 says – under Islamic influence – that Samael came to Eden riding on the serpent; what the serpent said, all came from Samael (similar, Mid. Hag. to Gen. 3:1–5). The following example appears to be significant concerning the mutual influence of *aggadah* and Islamic legend: *Genesis Rabbah* 19:8 cites Genesis 2:17: "On the day on which you eat from it, you will die," in connection with Psalms 90:10: "The number of our years is seventy," and thus interprets: "One Lord's Day, that is, 1,000 years [Ps. 90:4] was allotted to Adam, but he only lived 930 years and gave 70 years to each of his descendants." *Pirkei de-R. Eliezer* 19 relates that Adam gave 70 years of his life to David. According to Tabari (1:156), Adam let David have 40 of his own years.

[Bernard Heller]

Illuminated Manuscripts

Adam and Eve often appear in illuminated manuscripts, especially in the scenes of the Temptation and the period after the Fall. Among them is the Hebrew manuscript (British Museum Add. 11639), where the serpent is shown with a human face. This indicates the influence of the Jewish legend, which relates that before the Temptation of Eve, the serpent had wings, hands, and feet and was the size of a camel. Other illustrations are more conventional in examples such as the British Museum *Haggadah* (Ms. Or. 2884) and the *Haggadah* of Sarajevo, but it is interesting to note that the non-Jewish manuscripts such as Octateuch in Istanbul (Serail, Codex 8), a Bible Moralisée in the British Museum (Add. 15248), and Hugo van der Goes' diptych in Vienna are influenced by this Jewish legendary approach.

[Helen Rosenau]

In the Arts

The story of Adam and Eve is frequently exploited in Western literature because of its theological association with the Christian doctrine of Original Sin. The oldest surviving treatment is the 12th-century Anglo-Norman *Jeu d'Adam*. In medieval English, French, and Spanish miracle plays Adam is represented as a precursor of Jesus. An early Protestant interpretation was *Der farend Schueler im Paradeiss* (1550), a comedy by the German dramatist and poet Hans Sachs. The drama *L'Adamo* (1613), by the Italian actor-playwright Giambattista Andreini, probably influenced the English Puritan John *Milton, whose *Paradise Lost* (1667) depicts Adam as a free agent overcome by Satan, but sustained by his belief in ultimate redemption. This post-medieval conception of the first man also permeates two Dutch works, the *Adamus Exul* (1601) of Hugo Grotius (Hugo de Groot) and *Adam in Ballingschap* ("Adam in Exile," 1664) by Joost van den Vondel. Milton's epic poem was dramatized by John Dryden as *The State of Innocence, and Fall of Man* (1677), while a Rousseauesque yearning for an imagined Golden Age appears in the drama *Der Tod Adams* (1757) by the German poet F.G. Klopstock.

Some later plays on this theme are *Az ember tragédiája* ("The Tragedy of Man," 1862) by the Hungarian writer Imre Madách; *Adam Stvořitel* ("Adam the Creator," 1927) by the Czech authors Josef and Karel Čapek; *Nobodaddy* (1925) by the American writer Archibald Macleish; and the first part of G.B. Shaw's *Back to Methuselah* (1921). The English writer C.M. Doughty based his "sacred drama" *Adam Cast Forth* (1908) on a Judeo-Arabian legend; while Arno *Nadel wrote his play *Adam* (1917) on the basis of a fragment by S. *An-ski.

In the sphere of art there are early treatments of the Adam and Eve theme in second-century frescoes at Naples and in the Christian chapel at *Dura-Europos in Syria, as well as on Roman sarcophagi. There are also representations in medieval mosaics and in metal and in both Christian manuscripts and Jewish *Haggadot of the Middle Ages. Scenes from the creation of Adam to the expulsion from Eden were much favored by medieval artists and early sculptures include the reclining Eve by the 12th-century French sculptor Gislebertus, and a pair of gaunt figures at Bamberg Cathedral in Germany (c. 1235).

In the 15th century the reawakening feeling for the beauty of the human body gave artists an opportunity to depict the nude within the framework of religious art, particularly in Renaissance Italy. Masaccio's fresco in the Brancacci Chapel in Santa Maria del Carmine in Florence (1427) shows Adam and Eve leaving the Garden of Eden with their faces buried in their hands in a striking gesture of despair. In the best-known representation of the theme, Michelangelo's *The Creation of Adam* (1511) in the Sistine Chapel in the Vatican, the newly created man reclines on a rock while the Creator sweeps by with the heavenly host. Other treatments are those of Raphael and Tintoretto, and Titian's robustly sensual *Fall* (1570) in the Prado, Madrid. Adam and Eve were also represented by various masters of the Flemish, Dutch, and German schools, notably the brothers Van Eyck, Albrecht Duerer, Hieronymus Bosch, Lucas Cranach, and Hugo van der Goes. In the painting *The Spring* by the French artist Nicolas Poussin (1660–64), Adam and Eve are seen in a peaceful landscape resembling a vast park (in the Louvre, Paris). A century later the theme inspired a watercolor by William *Blake, while Marc *Chagall painted a *Creation*, a *Paradise*, and an *Expulsion from Eden*, all remarkable for their iridescent colors. Two modern examples are Rodin's *Eve* (1881) for his *Gates of Hell*, and Jacob *Epstein's heroic and deliberately primitive *Adam* (1938).

The earliest musical work of any distinction based on the Bible story is the opera by the German composer, J.A. Theile, *Der erschaffene, gefallene und wieder aufgerichtete Mensch* (1678). There have been many librettos based on Milton's *Paradise Lost* and on its Continental imitations, notably Klopstock's *Der Tod Adams*, which was set to music as *La Mort d'Adam* (1809) by the French composer J.-F. Lesueur. Anton *Rubinstein's first oratorio, *Das verlorene Paradies* (1858), and E. Bossi's Italian *"poema sinfonico-vocale," Il paradiso perduto* (1903), were both based on Milton's epic. Two interesting French compositions were F. David's *L'Eden* (1848) and Jules Massenet's stage music for the *"mystère" Ève* (1875). The American composer Everett Helm's *Adam and Eve* (1951) is a modern adaptation of a 12th-century mystery play.

See also: *Creation in the Arts.

BIBLIOGRAPHY: BIBLE: Amsler, in: *Revue de Théologie et de Philosophie*, 2 (1958), 107–12; N. Sarna, *Understanding Genesis* (1966), 1–36. AGGADAH: Guttmann, Mafte'aḥ, 1 (1906), 621–48; Ginzberg, Legends, 1 (1942), 49–102; 5 (1947), 63–131; Altmann, in: JQR, 35 (1944/45), 371–91; J. Jervell, *Imago Dei* (1960); Smith, in: BJRL, 40 (1957/58), 473–512; idem, in: *E.R. Goodenough Memorial Volume* (1968), 315–26.; M. Stone, *History of the Literature of Adam and Eve* (1992); G. Anderson, *The Genesis of Perfection* (2001); P. van der Horst, DDD: 5–6. PHILOSOPHY: Guttmann, Philosophies, 289; D. Kaufmann, *Meḥkarim ba-Sifrut ha-Ivrit shel Yemei ha-Beinayim* (1962), 126–35; Talmage, in: HUCA, 39 (1968), 177–218; H.A. Wolfson, *Philo*, 2 (1947), index. **ADD. BIBLIOGRAPHY:** D. Steinmetz, in: JBL, 13 (1984), 193–207; J. Barr, *Garden of Eden* (1992); D. Carr, in, ZAW, 110 (1998), 327–47; E. Pagels, *Adam, Eve, and the Serpent* (1998); N. Sarna, *Genesis the JPS Torah Commentary* (1989), 16–30. CHRISTIAN TRADITION: Driscoll, in: *Catholic Encyclopedia*, 1 (1907), 131–2; *Dictionaire de Théologie Catholique*, 1 (1929), 368–86; J. Daniélou, *Sacramentum Futuri* (1950), 3–52 (Fr.); Jeremias, in: G. Kittel (ed.), *Theological Dictionary of the New Testament*, 1 (1964), 141–3. ISLAM: J.W. Hirschberg, *Juedische und christliche Lehren im vor und fruehislamischen Arabien* (1939), 47–53, 105–114; A.I. Katsch, *Judaism in Islam* (1954), index. **ADD. BIBLIOGRAPHY:** Adam, in: EIS², 1, s.v. (incl. bibl.). IN THE ARTS: T. Ehrenstein, *Das Alte Testament im Bilde* (1923), 1–78; *The Bible in Art* (1956), 5–17; Weitzmann, in: *Muenchner Jahrbuch fuer bildende Kunst*, 3–4 (1952–53), 96ff.; *Reallexikon zur deutschen Kunstgeschichte*, 1 (1937), 126–67 (with illustrations).

ADAM (Heb. אָדָם), city on the eastern bank of the Jordan River mentioned in Joshua 3:16 as the place where the Jordan ceased flowing at the time of the Israelite crossing. It also appears in the inscriptions of Pharaoh Shishak (10th century B.C.E.). King Solomon's foundries were in the vicinity of Adam (I Kings 7:46; II Chron. 4:17). The place is perhaps also mentioned in Hosea 6:7 and Psalms 68:19, 78:60, and 83:11 as an ancient site of worship.

The ford that was situated during ancient times at Adam is marked on the *Madaba Map and is still found at a place the Arabs call Damiyeh on the road from Shechem to Gilead and Moab. It is south of the confluence of the Jabbok and the Jordan on the one side and north of the mouth of Wadi Fariah on the other. On the small Tell el-Damiyeh near the ford, potsherds from the Canaanite and Israelite periods (Late Bronze to Iron Age I–II) as well as from the Roman and Byzantine periods have been found.

BIBLIOGRAPHY: Kutscher, in: BJPES, 2 (1935), 42; Torczyner, *ibid.*, 11 (1944–5), 9ff.; Goitein, *ibid.*, 13 (1947), 86–88; Albright, in: AASOR, 6 (1926), 47ff.; idem, in: BASOR, 19 (1925), 19; J. Garstang, *Joshua-Judges* (1931), 355; Noth, in: ZDPV, 61 (1938), 288; Glueck, in: BASOR, 90 (1943), 5; idem, in: AASOR, 25–28 (1951), 329–34; Aharoni, Land, index.

[Michael Avi-Yonah]

ADAM, Jewish monthly literary journal in the Romanian language. The first number of *Adam* was published in Bucharest on April 15, 1929. The journal was subsequently published for 12 years, until July 1940, in book form. Its founder and director was the writer and publicist I. *Ludo (Isac Iacovitz). He edited the review until 1936, when he left Romania temporarily and sold it to Miron Grindea and Idov Cohn. They continued publication until their emigration from Romania, Miron Grindea to England (where he published a new review under the same name in London in English) and Idov Cohn (Cohen) to Palestine. *Adam* was a successful publication, reflecting the personality of its editor, Ludo, who wrote most of the articles.

He succeeded in attracting various contributors, intellectuals with various outlooks, among them Felix *Aderca, Ury *Benador, F. Brunea-Fox, Ion Calugaru, Avraham *Feller, Benjamin Fundoianu, Jacob Gropper, Rabbi M.A. Halevy, Michael *Landau, Theodor Loewenstein, Marius *Mircu, Chief Rabbi Jacob Niemirower, Eugen *Relgis, and A.L. *Zissu. Some of them (as well as others) served their literary apprenticeship at *Adam*. It was a review that refused to surrender to the ghetto mentality and also attracted non-Jewish contributors, among whom the best known were Tudor Arghezi, Gala Galaction, Eugen Lovinescu, and N.D. Cocea. *Adam* also featured many illustrations, including work by Victor *Brauner, Marcel *Jancu, M.H. *Maxy, Jules *Perachim, and Reuven *Rubin. *Adam* also engaged in polemics. Its basic idea was that Jewish-Romanian writers, before they could be Romanian writers, must be Jewish writers. In 1939, *Adam* published a yearbook on the occasion of its tenth anniversary.

BIBLIOGRAPHY: *Adam* (1929–40); *Almanahul Adam* (1939); A. Mirodan, *Dictionar neconventional*, 1 (1986), 18–21; M. Mircu, *Povestea presei evreiesti din Romania* (2003), 320–58; H. Kuller, *Presa evreiasca bucuresteana* (1996), 116–19.

[Lucian-Zeev Herscovici (2nd ed.)]

ADAM, LAJOS (**Louis**; 1879–1946), Hungarian physician. His appointment in 1927 as assistant professor at the University of Budapest aroused violent opposition in antisemitic circles, but in 1930 he was appointed full professor and director of the surgical clinic. In 1946 he became *Rector Magnificus*. His contribution to the technique of local anesthesia was of great importance. Among other books he wrote *A heli érzéstelenités kéMzikoenyve* ("The Handbook of Local Anesthesia").

ADAM, OTHER BOOKS OF, apocryphal books which contain Christian reworkings of the Jewish Adam legend, some of which include valuable ancient traditions. These books are in addition to the *Life of Adam and Eve* (see *Book of the Life of *Adam and Eve*). In early lists several works, presumably in Greek, are mentioned. The most prominent of these are *Apocalypse, Penitence, Testament*, and *Life*. The *Apocalypse*, quoted in *Epistle of Barnabas* 2:10, deals with Adam's penitence. A horarium and some other texts, also connected with repentance and cited by Georgius Cedrenus (*Historiarum compendium* 1:18), appear in a second Greek form, as well as in Syriac (R. Graffin (ed.), *Patrologia Syriaca*, 2, pt. 1 (1907), 1319–37), where they are quoted as being from the *Testament*. This Syriac version mentions the *Cave of Treasures*, connecting it with various Eastern books. A long passage attributed to the *Life of Adam* is preserved by Georgius Syncellus (ed. Dundorff, p. 5ff.). This passage is related to material found in Jubilees 3:1–11. The *Cave of Treasures*, a Syriac work, also deals with the story of Adam. A central feature of this work is a cave of treasures, in which Adam lived and was buried, and from which he was taken into the Ark by Noah to be reburied at Golgotha. The book also exists in Arabic (D.M. Gibson, *Apocrypha Arabica* (1901), Eng. and Arab.).

The Ethiopic *Book of Adam and Eve* is also a Christian composition, having much in common with the *Cave of Treasures*, including the burial tradition. Armenian books connected with the Adam story include *The Death of Adam, History of Adam's Expulsion from Paradise, History of Cain and Abel, Adam's Sons*, and *Concerning the Good Tidings of Seth*. Other unpublished Adam books also exist. These writings are certainly not Gnostic, as Preuschen maintained. They are early although it is impossible to give a precise date. There are Georgian translations of the *Cave of Treasures*, the *Life*, and other Adam books. There are also some texts in Arabic, including an Arabic version of the Ethiopic Adam book. Epiphanius (*Panarion* 26) quotes a Gnostic composition, and a Gnostic Coptic Adam Apocalypse is found among the Nag Hammadi texts.

BIBLIOGRAPHY: IDB, 1 (1962), 44f.; M.R. James, *Lost Apocrypha of the Old Testament* (1920), 1–8; Charles, Apocrypha, 2 (1913), 127ff.; C. Bezold, *Die Schatzhoehle* (1883); Buttenwieser, in: UJE, s.v.; S.C. Malan, *Book of Adam and Eve* (1882), from the Ethiopic; Luedtke, in: ZAW, 38 (1919–20), 155–68 (Ger. about Georgian text); J. Issaverdens, *Uncanonical Writings of the Old Testament* (1900), 85–89; Preuschen, in: *Festgruss… B. Stade* (1900), 165–252; Stone, in: HTR, 59 (1966), 283–91 (Eng. about Armenian text); P. Prigent, *L'Epître de Barnabé…* (1961), 43ff.; A. Dillmann, *Das christliche Adambuch des Morgenlandes* (1853); Cardona, in: U. Bianchi (ed.), *Le Origini dello Gnosticismo* (1962), 645–8; A. Boehlig and P. Labb, *Koptisch-Gnostische Apokalypsen* (1963).

[Michael E. Stone]

ADAM AND EVE, BOOK OF THE LIFE OF, apocryphal work dealing with Adam's life and death. It has been preserved in Greek, Latin, and Slavonic versions differing considerably from one another. General considerations point to composition in Palestine between 100 B.C.E. and 200 C.E.

The Greek version, known erroneously as the *Apocalypsis Moysis*, begins with the expulsion from Paradise, and relates the story of the death of Abel, the birth of Seth, Adam's illness, and the journey of Eve and Seth to Paradise in search of oil from the tree of life to ease Adam's suffering. Adam dies and he is buried in the third heaven by the angels. Six days later Eve dies and Seth is instructed regarding burial and mourning.

The Latin version is known as the *Vita Adae et Evae*. Its main part roughly corresponds to the Greek text, but there are some omissions and additions. The most extensive and important addition precedes the material found in the Greek version. It tells how Adam and Eve, finding life outside Paradise difficult, decide to entreat God for nourishment and propose to do penance by standing in water; Eve in the Tigris for 37 days and Adam in the Jordan for 40. By a trick, the Devil induces Eve to end her penance before the designated time.

The Slavonic version follows the Greek closely, although it shortens some passages. It also includes the main addition of the Latin in a different form and not at the beginning of the book, but as a part of Eve's account of the Fall. According to the Slavonic version, Adam and Eve, expelled from Paradise, beg God for nourishment and are given the seventh part of Paradise. Adam begins plowing, but the Devil prevents him from continuing until Adam acknowledges his lordship over Adam and the earth. To trick the Devil, Adam writes: "I and my children belong to whoever is Lord of the earth." There follows the story of the penance of Adam and Eve, as found in the Latin, but with the significant difference that Eve withstands the Devil's blandishments and completes her penance. The rest of the addition is missing.

The religious spirit expressed in the *Book of Adam and Eve* is somber and somewhat pessimistic. It illuminates many minor points of theological interest, but presents no clear and central doctrine. Only the resurrection and final judgment are taught repeatedly and emphatically. Angels are represented as important, but there is no speculation about them and none about the End of Days. The simpler Greek version, which is mildly dualistic, also teaches a distinction of body and soul. There is no doctrine of original sin in the Christian (or Qumranic) sense. Adam is considered perfect; Eve is morally weak, but not wicked. She loves and obeys Adam and repeatedly deplores her own shortcomings. There is also a mild halakhic interest in the matter of burial. The additional material contained in the Latin version stresses Eve's weakness and the wickedness of the Devil, and actually teaches that there was a second temptation, which Adam withstood. This part is more speculative, and is concerned with man's struggle against the Devil and with the origin of evil. The penance by water shows a marked tendency toward asceticism, which might be a modification of an earlier tendency, emphasizing the importance of purity.

The work cannot be assigned to any known or definable sector or movement in Judaism. There are similarities both with apocalyptic writing (Enoch, Jubilees) and with the rabbinic *aggadah*, but none of these is sufficiently close or precise to indicate identity of teaching. The simpler Greek version is closer to the mainstream of Judaism. The story of Adam and Eve's penance and second temptation displays a unique development of ancient Jewish thought. A book of Adam (*Sifra de-Adam ha-Rishon*) is mentioned in *Bava Meẓia* 85b; but this work must have been different from the *Book of Adam and Eve.*

BIBLIOGRAPHY: Charles, Apocrypha, 2 (1913), 123–54; for further bibliography see O. Eissfeldt, *Old Testament, An Introduction* (1965), 636.

[Jacob Licht]

ADAM BA'AL SHEM, a legendary figure about whom various tales have been collected in small Yiddish pamphlets published in Prague and in Amsterdam in the 17th century. They relate the miracles performed before Emperor Maximilian II by a kabbalist, whose historical existence has not been verified. According to these tales, Adam Ba'al Shem was born and was buried in Bingen near Worms; however his permanent place of residence was Prague. The stories about him were popular and used by the compiler of *Shivḥei ha-Besht* (Berdichev, 1815) who transformed Adam Ba'al Shem into an esoteric kabbalist in Poland who died close to the birth or in the childhood of *Israel b. Eliezer Ba'al Shem Tov, the founder of Ḥasidism. Ḥasidic legend attributed to him writings on the mystery of Kabbalah which he commanded his son to give to Israel Ba'al Shem Tov. Apparently, the earlier figure of a German Jewish folktale (Adam Ba'al Shem) was combined in ḥasidic legend with that of the Shabbatean prophet Heshel Ẓoref, who died in Cracow around the time of Israel Ba'al Shem Tov's birth. Heshel's work, *Sefer ha-Ẓoref*, on the mysteries of Shabbatean Kabbalah, undoubtedly reached the Ba'al Shem Tov who ordered them to be copied by his disciple Shabbetai of Raschkow. Copies of the copy were preserved in the courts of several *ẓaddikim*. The Ḥasidim were not aware of the Shabbatean character of these works, but several legends spread about their contents. The author of *Shivḥei ha-Besht* or the creators of the legends about the Ba'al Shem Tov modified the character of these writings and attributed them to Adam Ba'al Shem. An unfounded assumption seeks to identify Adam Ba'al Shem with a Russian Christian of German origin, called Adam Zerneikov, who supposedly had contact with the father of Israel Ba'al Shem Tov.

BIBLIOGRAPHY: W. Rabinowicz, in: Ẓion, 5 (1940), 125–32; G. Scholem, *ibid.*, 6 (1941), 89–93; 7 (1942), 28; idem, in: I. Halpern, *Beit Yisrael be-Folin*, 2 (1954), 48-53; R. Margaliot, *Ba-Mishor* (1941), 14–15; Ch. Shmeruk, in: *Zion*, 28 (1963), 86–105; Y. Elhiach, in: PAAJR, 36 (1968), 66–70.

[Gershom Scholem]

ADAMIT (Heb. אֲדָמִית), kibbutz in northern Israel, on the Lebanese border. Adamit, affiliated with Kibbutz Arẓi (Ha-Shomer ha-Ẓa'ir), was founded in 1958, following completion of a serpentine road to secure the access to its small mountain plateau. Most of the settlers were Israel-born and the economy was based on orchards, vineyards, and livestock. In 2004 its population was 106. The name "Adamit" derives from the Arabic "Idmith", but is also reminiscent of the biblical town of Adami (Josh. 19:33), assumed to have been located in the vicinity.

[Efraim Orni]

ADAM KADMON (Primordial Man), kabbalistic concept. The Gnostics inferred from the verse "Let us make man in our image" (Gen. 1:26) that the physical Adam was created in the image of a spiritual entity also called Adam. The early *Kabbalah speaks of *adam elyon* ("supreme man"; in the Zohar the corresponding Aramaic is *adam di-l'ela* or *adam ila'ah*). The term sometimes represents the totality of the Divine emanation in the ten **Sefirot* ("spheres") and sometimes in a single *Sefirah* such as *Keter* ("crown"), *Ḥokhmah* ("wisdom"), or *Tiferet* ("beauty"). The term "*Adam Kadmon*" is first found in *Sod Yedi'at ha-Meẓi'ut*, an early 13th-century kabbalistic treatise. In the *Tikkunei Zohar*, the Divine Wisdom is called *Adam ha-*

Gadol ("The Great Man"). The spiritual man is hinted at in the verse "a likeness as the appearance of a man" (Ezek. 1:26) which the prophet Ezekiel saw in the vision of the divine chariot. The letters of the Tetragrammaton (see Names of *God) when spelled out in full have the numerical value of 45, as do the letters of the word Adam. In this fact support was found for the revelation of God in the form of a spiritual man (*Midrash Ruth Ne'elam* in the Zohar). In contrast to the First Man Adam, this spiritual man is called in the Zohar proper the *adam kadma'ah ila'ah* ("primordial supreme man"), and in *Tikkunei Zohar* he is called *Adam Kadmon* ("primordial man") or *Adam Kadmon le-khol ha-kedumim* ("prototype of primordial man"). In the Kabbalah of Isaac *Luria, great importance and new significance is given to *Adam Kadmon*. There *Adam Kadmon* signifies the worlds of light which, after the retraction of the light of **Ein-Sof* ("The Infinite"), emanated into primeval space. This *Adam Kadmon* is the most sublime manifestation of the Deity that is to some extent accessible to human meditation. It ranks higher in this system than all four worlds: *Aẓilut* ("emanation"), *Beri'ah* ("creation"), *Yeẓirah* ("formation"), and *Asiyyah* ("making"). The portrayal of this *Adam Kadmon* and his mysteries, and in particular the description of the lights which flow from his ears, mouth, nose, and eyes plays an important role in Ḥayyim *Vital's *Eẓ Ḥayyim* and in other kabbalistic works of the Lurianic school. Through this theory the mystical anthropomorphism of the school becomes crystallized. This anthropomorphic figure recurs in all the stages and in all the worlds. Consequently there is an *adam de-veriah* ("man of creation"), *adam di-yzirah* ("man of formation"), and an *adam de-asiyyah* ("man of making"). In contrast to *Adam Kadmon*, who is from the holy emanation, stands Satan, from the world of iniquity. In the *Tikkunei Zohar*, and subsequently in the Lurianic Kabbalah, Satan is called *adam beliyya'al* ("evil man"). In the Lurianic Kabbalah, there is no relationship between *Adam Kadmon*, which is the light which transcends all other lights, and the *Messiah. Such a connection was made only in the system of the extreme Shabbateans, who believed in the divinity of the Messiah and regarded *Shabbetai Ẓevi as the incarnation of *Adam Kadmon*. (He figures as such in a number of poems of the sect of the *Doenmeh.)

BIBLIOGRAPHY: S.A. Horodezky, in: *Ha-Goren*, 10 (1928), 95ff.

[Gershom Scholem]

ADAMS, ARLIN MARVIN (1921–), U.S. jurist, public servant, and legal educator. Born in Philadelphia, Pennsylvania, Adams worked for a produce distributor during the Depression to pay for college at Temple University. When he graduated first in his class in 1941, the chair of the political science department took him by trolley to the University of Pennsylvania, where he obtained a full scholarship for the young man by declaring to the law school registrar: "He is the best that we've ever had."

A day after Pearl Harbor, Adams volunteered for the Navy, received a commission, and in 1942 was sent to the north Pacific. After the war, he resumed his studies at Penn, where he served as editor-in-chief of the law review and graduated second in his class in 1947. He completed a clerkship with Horace Stern, probably Pennsylvania's greatest chief justice, and then joined Philadelphia's premier law firm, Schnader, Harrison, Segal and Lewis. Adams earned a reputation as a brilliant, yet humble attorney, and after only three years he became the youngest associate in the firm's history to make partner. At this time, he also earned an M.A. in economics from Temple and Penn.

In 1963, Adams joined Governor William Scranton's cabinet. As Pennsylvania's secretary of public welfare (1963–66), he instituted a medical program for indigents that anticipated Medicaid and developed educational training for poor children that became the prototype for the federal Head Start program. Scranton described Adams as "the ablest and most effective secretary of welfare that this Commonwealth has ever known."

When President Nixon nominated Adams for a seat on the United States Court of Appeals for the Third Circuit, the Senate unanimously approved the selection without holding any hearings. Adams served 18 years on the court (1969–87), earning the highest praise and ensuring himself a place alongside scholar-judges such as Learned Hand and Benjamin *Cardozo. As with Hand, appointment to the United States Supreme Court eluded Adams, although he was three times on the short list for selection to the High Court. While Adams wrote landmark opinions in several areas, his most enduring legacy came in decisions involving the First Amendment religion clauses. His erudite, careful opinions possessed a Burkian quality, striking a balance between the nation's commitment to institutional separation between church and state and recognition of a vital role for religion in public life. In a concurring opinion in *Malnak v. Yogi* (1979), Adams led the way in defining "religion" for constitutional purposes, fashioning a three-part test that widely influenced courts in America and in other nations.

In 1987, the indefatigable Adams returned to the Schnader firm, where he continued to accept major public duties, most notably as independent counsel (1990–95) to investigate irregularities in President Reagan's Department of Housing and Urban Development and as trustee in the New Era proceedings (1995), then the largest non-profit bankruptcy case in U.S. history. Adams achieved unparalleled results in both cases, securing 16 criminal convictions or guilty pleas in the HUD scandal and obtaining a collection rate of over 90 percent in New Era, thereby saving numerous charities from financial ruin.

Throughout his life, Adams faithfully served academia, the community, and his religion. He held positions as chairman of Penn Law School's Board of Overseers (1985–92); president of the American Philosophical Society (1993–96), founded in 1743 by Benjamin Franklin; and president of Knesseth Israel, one of Philadelphia's oldest synagogues. For almost three decades, Adams taught a Freedom of Religion seminar at Penn Law School. The course inspired Adams to write numerous articles and *A Nation Dedicated to Religious Liberty*, a groundbreaking book that resurrected William Penn as a champion of religious freedom and asserted that the core value of the religion clauses was religious liberty, not separation of church and state.

In 2004, Penn Law School recognized "a lifetime of dedicated public service" by endowing a chair in constitutional law in his name. When he received the esteemed Philadelphia Award in 1997, Justice Sandra Day O'Connor said: "[Adams] has accomplished more in his lifetime than a hundred ordinary heroes combined. … He saw that the rule of law had to be administered with a spirit of compassion and a caring for those in need."

BIBLIOGRAPHY: A.M. Adams and C.J. Emmerich, *A Nation Dedicated to Religious Liberty: The Constitutional Heritage of the Religion Clauses* (1990).

[Charles J. Emmerich (2nd ed.)]

ADAMS, FRANKLIN PIERCE (1881–1960), U.S. newspaper columnist known by his byline "F.P.A." and noted for his wit and erudition. Born in Chicago, he started his daily column "The Conning Tower" in the New York *Tribune* in 1914. It appeared successively in the *World*, the *Herald-Tribune*, and the *Post*.

A member of the illustrious Algonquin Round Table, Adams lunched every day in the 1920s and 1930s at a round table at New York City's Algonquin Hotel with a group of some of the most brilliant writers of that period. They traded quips and critiques, many of them still repeated today. The group was formed at the suggestion of Dorothy *Parker, who was living in the Algonquin Hotel at the time. There was no formal membership, so people came and went, but the primary early members included Parker, Adams, Robert Benchley, Alexander Woollcott, George S. *Kaufman, Edna *Ferber, and Harpo *Marx. Others visited as well, including actors and entertainers such as Douglas Fairbanks, George *Gershwin, Irving *Berlin, Jascha *Heifitz, Moss *Hart, Budd *Schulberg, and Oscar *Hammerstein. But most of the Round Table members were critics. Outspoken and outrageous, they would exchange ideas and gossip, which found their way into Adams' "Conning Tower" column in the *Tribune* the next day. Though society columns referred to them as the Algonquin Round Table, they called themselves the Vicious Circle. "By force of character," observed drama critic Brooks Atkinson, "they changed the nature of American comedy and established the tastes of a new period in the arts and theater."

Adams' epigrams, verse, and parodies were reprinted extensively, and his weekly *Diary of Our Own Samuel Pepys* is regarded as historical source material. His appearances on *Information Please* on radio and TV (1939–52) had a large following.

[Ruth Beloff (2nd ed.)]

°**ADAMS, HANNAH** (1755–1831), considered the first American woman professional writer. Hannah Adams' early interest in religion led to her *Dictionary of All Religions and Religious Denominations* (1817^4), a superficial compilation, but significant for the sympathetic tone of the article on Jews. In a later, more careful work, *History of the Jews from the Destruction of Jerusalem to the Present Time* (1812), she relied on contemporary historical and demographic information prepared by Jewish correspondents. The chapter concerning the Jews in the New World is of particular interest, and has been reprinted and translated into German and Hebrew.

BIBLIOGRAPHY: H. Stark, in: DAB, 1 (1928), 60–61; J.L. Blau and S.W. Baron, *Jews of the United States, 1790–1840*, 1 (1963), 87–93.

[Joseph L. Blau]

°**ADAMS, JOHN** (1735–1826), first vice president (1789–97) and second president (1797–1801) of the United States. Adams, a champion of religious freedom and separation of church and state, was also a fervent admirer of the Old Testament in the tradition of his New England ancestors, and a Judeophile. In a letter written to Mordecai Manuel *Noah in 1818 he remarked: "I wish your nation may be admitted to all the privileges of citizens in every country of the world. This country has done much. I wish it may do more, and annul every narrow idea in religion, government and commerce." In the course of his lengthy correspondence with Thomas Jefferson during the last two decades of his life, Adams exhibited a steady interest in the religious philosophy of the Jews. He advocated that Hebraic studies become part of a classical education, and in a codicil to his will four years before his death he bequeathed land for the erection of a school in which he expressed the hope that Hebrew would be taught together with Latin and Greek. In a characteristic attack on Voltaire's derogatory attitude toward the Bible and the Jewish people, he wrote to his friend Judge Francis Adrian van der Kemp in 1808: "How is it possible this old fellow should represent the Hebrews in such a contemptible light? They are the most glorious Nation that ever inhabited this Earth. The Romans and their Empire were but a Bauble in comparison of the Jews. They have given Religion to three quarters of the Globe and have influenced the affairs of Mankind more, and more happily than any other Nation, ancient or modern."

BIBLIOGRAPHY: I.S. Meyer, in: AJHSP, 37 (1947), 185–201; 45 (1955), 58–60.

[Isidore S. Meyer]

ADAMS, THEODORE L. (1915–1984), U.S. rabbi. Adams was the epitome of the emerging modern Orthodox rabbis in America during much of the 20th century. Born in Bangor, Maine, he was the son of the town *shoḥet*. His pious immigrant parents sent their son to New York for a proper Jewish education. After studying at Yeshiva Torah Vodaath, he went to Yeshiva College (B.A., 1936) and continued for *semikhah* at

Yeshiva's Rabbi Isaac Elchanan Theological Seminary (1938). He occupied pulpits in Congregation Mt. Sinai in Jersey City and Congregation Ohab Zedek in Manhattan. In these he transformed the congregations from their old-style European immigrant milieu into modern Orthodoxy.

With a commanding presence dressed in self-confidence, he attracted the attention of many Jewish causes. His rabbinic colleagues elected him to the presidencies of the *Rabbinical Council of America and the interdenominational *Synagogue Council of America. In his later years, he earned a Ph.D. in Jewish education and joined the staff of *Touro College.

[Jeanette Friedman (2nd ed.)]

ADANI, DAVID BEN AMRAM (13th or 14th century), Yemenite rabbi and scholar. An ancient source calls him "David b. Amram, the *nagid* from the city of Aden." It is not clear whether the title referred to David or his father. **Nagid*, however, was a title borne by the leader of the Jewish community of Aden from the 12th century. Adani was a renowned scribe whose copies of the Pentateuch were much sought after because of their exactness. He is the compiler of the **Midrash ha-Gadol*.

BIBLIOGRAPHY: HB, 20 (1880), 135ff.; Steinschneider, Arab Lit, no. 205, n. 2.

[Yehuda Ratzaby]

ADANI, DAVID BEN YESHA HA-LEVI (15th century), Yemenite commentator on Maimonides. His works include Arabic glossaries which explain difficult phrases in Maimonides' *Mishneh Torah* and a commentary on the Mishnah.

BIBLIOGRAPHY: Y. Ratzaby, in: KS, 28 (1952/53), 276.

[Yehuda Ratzaby]

ADANI, MAHALAL (originally **Mahallal ben Shalom ben Jacob**; 1883–1950), Yemenite scholar and industrialist. His wife, Hannah, was the daughter of Judah Moses, president of the Aden Jewish community (1922–24). Mahalal was a singular figure in the Aden Jewish community, being both learned and an entrepreneur. He obtained his general and Jewish education auto-didactically and set up factories for cigarettes and ice. Mahalal visited Ereẓ Israel in 1895 and 1903, and after fulfilling a central role in strengthening the community's connections with the Zionist movement and in establishing a modern educational system, he finally immigrated to Ereẓ Israel in 1930. Adani continued his business activities in Ereẓ Israel but devoted most of his time to the study of religious, philosophical, and historical texts. He left behind dozens of handwritten essays, including commentaries on most of the biblical books; an interpretation of Rabbi *Kook's *Orot ha-Kodesh*; and a philosophical novel entitled *Rayon Ru'aḥ*. During his lifetime he published only two books: *Or ha-Ḥozer* (1940) on Ecclesiastes and *Bein Aden ve-Teiman* ("Between Aden and Yemen," 1947, 1988²), which was edited by D. Sadan. From 1988 his books were brought to press by Y. Tobi. These include his commentaries: *Job* (1993); *Song of Songs, Proverbs, and Ecclesiastes* (1997); *Psalms, Pirkei Avot, Ruth, Lamentations, and Esther* (1998); *Ha-Nefesh ha-Ḥayyah* and *Ru'aḥ ha-Kodesh* (2001); and *Pirkei Mikra* (2004).

BIBLIOGRAPHY: Y. Tobi, in: Mahalal ha-Adani, *Bein Aden ve-Teiman*, II, 357–424, 479–513.

[Yosef Tobi (2nd ed.)]

ADANI, MIZRAḤI SHALOM (second half of 19th century), kabbalist and scholar. The appellation Mizraḥi was given to Adani because of his eastern Yemenite origin. In manhood he immigrated to Jerusalem where he joined the kabbalistic circle of the *bet ha-midrash* Bet El. He wrote *Sukkat Shalom* ("Tabernacle of Peace," 1891), novellae on the tractate *Bava Kamma*, the introduction to which contains a description of his adventures on his way to Ereẓ Israel; and *Shelom Yerushalayim* ("The Peace of Jerusalem," 1899), novellae on the *Eẓ Ḥayyim* of R. Ḥayyim *Vital, as well as some others on the kabbalistic writings of R. Shalom *Sharabi. He used a wealth of sources, the Babylonian and Jerusalem Talmuds, the halakhic authorities, and the responsa literature.

BIBLIOGRAPHY: Y. Ratzaby, in: KS, 28 (1952/53), 269, no. 81, 398, no. 193.

[Yehuda Ratzaby]

ADANI, SAADIAH BEN DAVID (**Saʿid ibn Daud**, known also as **al-Yamanī al-Rabbānī**; 15th century), talmudist. Adani lived in Damascus, Aleppo, and Safed. His works, written in Judeo-Arabic, deal with subjects studied in the Yemenite communities: Midrash, *halakhah*, and lunar intercalation. *Najāt al-Ghāriqīn* ("The Salvation of the Drowning") and *Zafenat Paneʿaḥ* ("Deciphering Mysteries") are aggadic and halakhic commentaries on the Pentateuch and the Sabbath readings from the Prophets. At the request of students Saadiah wrote a commentary on Maimonides' *Mishneh Torah*. Adani used the form of catechism popular among the Jews of Yemen. He prepared an Arabic calendar entitled *al-Jādwalavn* which contains a philosophic poem. In his writings, he shows familiarity with the practices of Yemenite Jewry, although he did not live there. It is noteworthy that this 15th century Yemenite scholar could state: "Thank God the belief in *shedim* ('demons and devils') has ceased, like other superstitions and magical practices. I have enlarged on this matter only because most European Jews and some also in these countries still cling to many preposterous beliefs."

BIBLIOGRAPHY: Steinschneider, Arab Lit, 202; S. Assaf, in: KS, 22 (1945/46), 240–4.

[Yehuda Ratzaby]

ADANI, SAMUEL BEN JOSEPH (**Yeshua**; 1863–?), author. Adani's grandfather, R. Yeshua, was the head of the Jewish rabbinical court in Aden and his mother's grandfather, R. Shilo, was a member of it. In 1878 he married the granddaughter of Menaḥem Mansur, then head of the Jewish court. Adani was a great scholar and studied the Kabbalah with Aden's rabbis. He visited Ereẓ Israel in 1899 and 1902. His book *Naḥalat Yosef* (Jerusalem, 1906) is the most important work of Adenese scholarship. This work is to some extent an encyclopedia in two parts: (a) General instruction in Jewish tradition – Hebrew grammar, *halakhah,* angelology, paradise, astronomy, etc. Though the author asserts that enlightenment does not threaten tradition, he takes a definite position against the Jewish philosophers and educators in the new age, who prefer the conclusions of research and Aristotelian views to Jewish tradition (1, 14, 70a–77b). On the other hand, he opposes those who presume to be too strict with the laws of Judaism (1, 15, 77a–85b). (b) The traditions of Adenese Jewry during the year and the life cycle, an account of his family, a description of his visits to Ereẓ Israel, and riddles and jokes as well as his poetry. The chapter about his family is the main source on the Aden community in the 19th century.

BIBLIOGRAPHY: R. Ahroni, *Yehudei Aden* (1991), 188–95; idem, *The Jews of the British Crown Colony of Aden* (1994), 170–72.

[Yosef Tobi (2nd ed.)]

ADAR (Heb. אֲדָר), the post-Exilic name (of Assyrian origin) of the 12th month in the Jewish year. Occurring in Assyrian inscriptions and also in Hebrew and Aramaic biblical records (Esth. 3:7 with seven parallels; Ezra 6:15), it is held to be identical with the first element in the compound proper name *Adrammelech of a patricidal son of *Sennacherib (II Kings 19:37; Isa. 37:38) and of the Molech-like idol worshiped by the Sepharvite ancestors of the Samaritans (II Kings 17:31). The zodiacal sign of this month is Pisces. In some years an extra month is added to the year (see *Calendar) which is called Adar *Sheni* ("Second Adar" or *ve*-Adar – so vocalized against a firm rule in Hebrew vocalization). In such years the original month is called Adar *Rishon* ("First Adar"). The addition of a second Adar raises problems with regard to the celebration of *bar mitzvah and the observance of **Yahrzeit* and the recitation of **Kaddish*. The law is as follows: A boy born in Adar of a regular year but whose 13th year is a leap year celebrates his bar mitzvah in Adar II (Sh. Ar., OḤ 55:10). For a person deceased in Adar of a regular year, the *Yahrzeit* in a leap year is observed in Adar I; there are, however, conflicting opinions in this and it is suggested that *Kaddish* be recited also in Adar II (*ibid.* 568:7). In the present fixed Jewish calendar, the month consists of 29 days in regular years while in leap years Adar I consists of 30 days and Adar II of 29 days. The first day of Adar (of Adar II in a leap year) never falls on Sunday, Tuesday, or Thursday. In the 20th century Adar in its earliest occurrence extends from February 12 to March 11 or 12 and in its latest from March 2 to 30 while the 59 days of Adar I with Adar II extend from February 2 to March 31 or April 1 at the earliest and from February 11 to April 9 or 10 at the latest.

Memorable days in Adar (Adar II in leap years) comprise: (a) The Four Special Sabbaths (*Shekalim* may be read on the Sabbath before Adar I and *ha-Ḥodesh* on Nisan 1, but invariably Sabbaths *Zakhor* and *Parah* fall in Adar). (b) The seventh of Adar, the anniversary of the death of Moses as calculated from Deuteronomy 34:8 and Joshua 1:11; 3:2; and 4:19, observed as a fast (Meg. Ta'an. 13, ed. Neubauer). According to tradition Adar 7 was also the date of Moses' birth (see *Adar, the Seventh of). (c, d) Adar 9 and 24 once observed as fasts (*ibid.*) commemorating the fateful controversies between the Schools of Shammai and Hillel (Shab. 17a) and the leprosy which befell King Uzziah (II Kings 15:5; II Chron. 26:19–21). (e) Nicanor Day on Adar 13 at first observed as a feast commemorating the Hasmonean victory over the Syrian general Nicanor (I Macc. 7:49; II Macc. 15:36; Meg. Ta'an. 12) and subsequently observed as the Fast of *Esther preliminary to Purim (*Piskei ha-Rosh*, Meg. 1:1). (f, g) *Purim and Shushan Purim on Adar 14–15. (h) The 16th of Adar was not to be a day of mourning for on that day they commenced to build the walls of Jerusalem (Meg. Ta'an. 12); by order of Nehemiah or perhaps under the Maccabees. (i) The 17th was a feast commemorating the miraculous escape of the Sages of Israel from their Herodian or Roman enemies. (j) The 20th was a feast day because on that day Onias (*Ḥoni ha-Me'aggel) effected deliverance from a drought (*ibid.*). These invest the whole month with a joyful character, hence the talmudic ruling "When Adar comes in, gladness is increased" (Ta'an. 29a).

[Ephraim Jehudah Wiesenberg]

ADAR, THE SEVENTH OF, anniversary of both the birth and death of Moses according to talmudic tradition (Meg. 13b; Kid. 38a, etc.). The date is derived from a comparison of biblical dates (Deut. 34:8; Josh. 1:11; 3:3; 4:19; Jos., Ant., 4:327, gives the first day of Adar as the day of Moses' death). In Oriental communities it became a day of fasting and commemoration for the pious because of the belief that a spark of the soul of Moses is found in every righteous person. In medieval Egypt the date signaled a central event in the life of the community. During the preceding Hanukkah, messengers were sent to all Jews in the area to invite them to come to celebrations at the ancient synagogue in the village of *Dumuh near Cairo which, according to tradition, was erected 40 years before the destruction of the First Temple on the spot where Moses had prayed before going to Pharaoh. The seventh of Adar was a day of prayer and supplication. The eighth was a day of celebration, apparently of a "carnival" nature. To insure the serious aspect of the festivities, the rabbis of Egypt enacted certain prohibitions. Women must be accompanied by their husband, brother, or grown son; men and women were separated in seating; dancing, singing, and the putting on of plays or "shadow shows" (a sort of puppet show) were forbidden. While this observance was later discontinued, Sephardi Jews still light candles for the "ascension of the souls of the righteous" on the seventh of Adar. Some communities recite special *piyyutim* on this date and also on Simḥat Torah, when the biblical account of Moses' death is read in the synagogue. Among these are "Cry! O Jochebed, with a bitter, hard voice!

Sinai, Sinai, where is Moses?!" (Davidson, Oẓar, 4 (1933), 371); "Be graceful to us, O Lord because of the merit of Moses" (*ibid.*, 3 (1930), 416); and "Happy art thou, O Mount Abarim, over all the high mountains" (*ibid.*, 1 (1924), 8446). In 17th-century Turkey and Italy (and later also in Northern Egypt) it became customary in some circles to observe this date as a fast day, and to recite portions from a special *tikkun* (selected passages from Scripture, Mishnah, and Zohar), compiled by Samuel *Aboab of Venice. In Eastern and Central Europe, as well as in the United States, this day was observed by the members of the *ḥevra kaddisha* as a fast day which was terminated by a special banquet at which new members were admitted and a new board elected. After the *Minḥah* service in the synagogue, the rabbis used to eulogize Moses and all famous rabbis and Jewish scholars who had passed away during the preceding year. The day is still widely celebrated in Orthodox communities. In Israel, it has been officially designated as the day for commemorating the death of Israeli soldiers whose last resting place is unknown.

BIBLIOGRAPHY: M. Hakohen, *Seder Zayin Adar, Mekorot, Minhagot Seliḥot u-Tefillot* (1961); Ashtor, Toledot, 2 (1951), 385.

ADAR, ZVI (1917–1991), Israel educator. Adar was born in Petaḥ Tikvah and became a teacher at the Bet ha-Kerem teachers' seminary in Jerusalem (1938–53). He subsequently taught at the School of Education at the Hebrew University where he became a professor. He interested himself in the speculative aspects involved with Jewish identity in the past and its meaning in the present, transmitting his thoughts to the younger generation through the medium of education. He wrote extensively, his most important work being *Ha-Arakhim ha-Ḥinnukhiyyim shel ha-Tanakh* (1954; *Humanistic Values in the Bible*, 1968). In this work Adar attempted to use literary analysis to reveal the educational values in the biblical narrative. As the Bible was one of the main subjects of instruction in the Israel educational system Adar tried to show how the Bible could be used as a means for character education. He also wrote *The Book of Genesis: An Introduction to the Biblical Word* (1990). He was one of the editors of the *Enẓiklopedyah Ḥinnukhit* (1961–69). He also wrote *Ha-Mikẓo ot ha-Humanistim ba-Ḥinnukh ha-Tikhon* (1969), and on Jewish education in Israel and the U.S. in his book *Ha-Ḥinnukh ha-Yehudi be-Yisrael u-ve-Arẓot ha-Berit* (1970; *Jewish Education in Israel and the United States*, 1977). In 1969 he was appointed dean of the faculty of humanities at the Hebrew University.

ADARBI, ISAAC BEN SAMUEL (1510?–1584?), rabbi and halakhic authority. Adarbi was preacher of the congregation of Lisbon Jews in Salonika and later rabbi of the Congregation Shalom, Salonika (before 1554). He was a disciple of Joseph *Taitaẓak (whose novellae he published as an appendix to his own work) and was a colleague of Samuel b. Moses de Medina. His efforts to unite the various Salonikan communities were reflected in his *Divrei Shalom* (Salonika, 1580), a collection of 30 of his sermons. He appended homiletic comments to the Pentateuch, some chapters of which (on Exodus) are preserved in the Guenzburg Manuscripts (Moscow) No. 158. Four hundred and thirty of his responsa were published in *Divrei Rivot* (Salonika, 1581; republished Venice, 1587; Sudzilkon, 1833). These responsa show that he was a halakhist of distinction, fearless in his judgments, and often differing in his decisions from Samuel de Medina, who in his turn attributed hostile personal motives to Adarbi (Responsa Maharashdam, ḤM No. 40). Nevertheless, they approved each other's halakhic rulings.

BIBLIOGRAPHY: Benjacob, Oẓar, 106, no. 121, 130; Rosanes, Togarmah, 2 (1938), 102; I.S. Emmanuel, *Histoire des Israélites de Salonique*, 1 (1936), 184–5; idem, *Mazzevot Saloniki*, 1 (1963), 159–60; M.S. Goodblatt, *Jewish Life in Turkey in the 16th Century* (1952), 18, passim.

[Abraham Hirsch Rabinowitz]

ADASA (Heb. חֲדָשָׁה, *Ḥadashah*). (1) A village on a small hill strategically overlooking the Beth-Horon road close to the place of Judah Maccabee's final victory over Nicanor. Nicanor fell in the battle and his army fled toward Gazera/Gezer (I Macc. 7:39–40, 45; cf. Elasa which is probably a scribal error for Adasa in II Macc. 14:6). The town is mentioned in the Mishnah as a place with 50 inhabitants, or with three courtyards and two households (Er. 5:6). It is the present-day Khirbet 'Adasa, a little more than 5 mi. (9 km.) north of Jerusalem. The site has not been excavated, but visible archaeological remains include the remains of a settlement with scattered Herodian, Roman, and Byzantine pottery, rock-hewn caves, and agricultural features round about. This site is not to be confused with another Khirbet 'Adasa north of Jerusalem, situated immediately to the northeast of Tell el-Ful, mentioned by some scholars, which has remains that only date back to Mamluk times. Yet another Khirbet 'Adasa is situated west of Gibeon (el-Jib), but the remains there are primarily of the Byzantine period. (2) Ḥadashah/Adasa is also the name of a town in the Shephelah of Judah. It is mentioned in Joshua 15:37 and located close to Migdal-Gad and Zenan. Since Lachish and Eglon are referred to in the same district, Adasa's location should probably be sought in southwest Judah. However, no convincing suggestion has thus far been proposed for the site. Eusebius (26:1) situated Adasa of Joshua 15:37 at a totally different location, close to Gophna (Jifna), but Jerome (27:1) rightly expressed his doubts about this identification.

BIBLIOGRAPHY: B. Bagatti, *Ancient Christian Villages of Samaria* (2002), 20–21; B. Bar-Kochva, *Judas Maccabaeus* (1989), 349ff.; M. Fischer, B. Isaac, and I. Roll, *Roman Roads in Judaea. II: The Jaffa-Jerusalem Roads* (1996), 120–22; G.S.P. Freeman-Grenville, R.L. Chapman, and J.E. Taylor, *The Onomasticon by Eusebius of Caesarea* (2003), 22–105; A. Kloner, *Survey of Jerusalem: The Northeastern Sector* (2001), 21; Y. Tsafrir, L. Di Segni, and J. Green, *Tabula Imperii Romani. Iudea, Palaestina. Maps and Gazetteer* (1994), 57.

[Shimon Gibson (2nd ed.)]

ADASKIN, MURRAY (1905–2002), Canadian violinist, conductor, composer, teacher. Adaskin was born in Toronto of Russian immigrant parents. He studied music in Toronto and while still in his teens became a violinist with the Toronto Symphony Orchestra (1923–36). He played with the Banff Springs Trio (1932–41) and Toronto Trio (1938–52). Adaskin was a major figure in the decentralization of Canadian concert music. From the 1930s to 1950s, he toured the country with his wife, Frances James, Canada's leading soprano, and both were pioneers in disseminating contemporary music by radio broadcasting.

After studying composition with John Weinzweig (1944) and, in Santa Barbara and Aspen with Charles Jones (1949–51) and Darius Milhaud (1949–53), Adaskin was appointed to the University of Saskatchewan (1952–72). There he served as head of music and composer-in-residence and conducted the Saskatoon Symphony Orchestra (SSO). In 1973, he moved to Victoria, where he continued to compose and teach violin and composition.

A leader in postwar cultural nationalism, Adaskin insisted that the SSO commission Canadian works annually and based many of his own pieces on Canada's landscape and early history as well as its First Nations' traditions. A conservative modernist, Adaskin's neo-classic works also include music on Jewish themes. His *T'filat Shalom* (1973) was commissioned by the father of Adaskin's violin student Jeff Krolik who premiered the piece in Jerusalem.

A founding member of the Canadian League of Composers, Adaskin served on the Canada Council (1966–69) and was named an Officer of the Order of Canada (1980).

BIBLIOGRAPHY: G. Lazarevich, *The Musical World of Frances James and Murray Adaskin* (1988).

[Jay Rahn (2nd ed.)]

ADASS JESHURUN, ADASS JISROEL, originally the breakaway (*Austritt*) minority of Orthodox congregations in Germany in the mid-19th century (see *Neo-Orthodoxy). These congregations dissociated themselves on religious grounds from the unitary congregations established by state law in which the majority tended toward *Reform Judaism. Their main aim was to safeguard strict adherence to Jewish law. The Hebrew terms *Adass* (or *Adat, Adath*) *Jeshurun* and *Adass Jisroel*, meaning "congregation of Jeshurun" and "congregation of Israel," were chosen by these congregations to express their conviction that, even if in the minority, they were the "true Israel." The names were cherished for their socioreligious connotations by Orthodox groups in the West where Reform Judaism was widespread. The Israelitische Religionsgesellschaft of Frankfurt on the Main, with Samson Raphael *Hirsch as rabbi, called itself Adass Jeshurun from 1851, as did a similar community in Cologne from 1867. The congregation founded in Berlin in 1869, the first rabbi of which was Azriel *Hildesheimer, and one in Koenigsberg in 1913, chose the name Adass Jisroel. The Berlin Adass Jisroel established its own educational network. Between 1890 and 1903 there was an Adass Jeshurun congregation in Belfast, composed of immigrants from Russia. In England, the strictly Orthodox congregation which grew out of the north London *bet ha-midrash* (1909) was called Adath Yisroel. After 1933, immigrants from Germany, loyal to the concept of Adass Jisroel, formed a congregation in northwest London; Manchester has both an Adass Jeshurun and an Adass Jisroel synagogue. Such communities have also been formed in various places in the United States, the best-known in Washington Heights, New York City. Others exist in Canada, Australia, South Africa, and Israel. The names have also been used by other groups, e.g., by the Reform Adass Jeshurun in Amsterdam in 1796. The synagogue of an Adas Israel congregation in Louisville, Ky., was consecrated in 1849.

BIBLIOGRAPHY: H. Schwab, *History of Orthodox Jewry in Germany* (1950); A. Carlebach, *Adath Yeshurun of Cologne* (1964); M. Sinasohn, *Adass Yisroel Berlin* (1966).

[Alexander Carlebach]

ADDA BAR AHAVAH (Aḥavah).

(1) Babylonian *amora* of the third century. He was born on the day R. Judah ha-Nasi died (Kid. 72a–b; Gen. R. 58:2). A distinguished pupil of Rav, he twice rent his garments in mourning for Rav's death; the second time, when he realized that there was now no authority to consult on halakhic matters (Ber. 42b–43a). His main interest centered on *halakhah*, which is reported in his name by the leading sages of his day. He was extremely pious and reputed to work miracles; his contemporaries were convinced that in his company no hurt would befall them (Ta'an. 20b). During a drought his prayers for rain were answered immediately (TJ, Ta'an. 3:13, 67a). When asked by the sages how he had attained a ripe old age, he replied: "No one ever came to synagogue before me, or remained behind when I left. I have not walked four cubits without meditating on the Torah, and never in an unclean place. I have not indulged in regular sleep. I have not disturbed my colleagues at the academy, nor called any of them by a nickname. I have not rejoiced at a colleague's misfortune, nor gone to sleep with an angry thought against a colleague. I have not gone in the market place to anyone who owed me money, nor ever lost my temper at home" (TJ, Ta'an. 3:13, 67a; cf. Ta'an. 20b). Another dictum is: "One who has sinned and confesses his sin but is unrepentant is to be compared to a person who holds in his hand an unclean insect. Even though he immerses himself in all the waters of the world, nothing avails him" (Ta'an. 16a). In TJ, Ta'anit 2:1, 65a this statement with slight variations is ascribed to Abba b. Zavda. A work entitled *Baraita (Tekufah) de-Rav Adda* dealing with the principles of intercalation is ascribed to Adda. It is no longer extant, but it was still known in the 14th century (Zunz-Albeck, Derashot 274).

(2) Babylonian *amora* of the fourth century. A favorite pupil of Rava who called him "my son," he esteemed his teacher so highly that he said to his colleagues: "Instead of

gnawing bones under Abbaye, you should rather eat fat meat under Rava" (BB 22a), Many of the rabbis blamed themselves for his premature death because of their treatment of him (*ibid.*).

BIBLIOGRAPHY: Hyman, Toledot, 102–3; Frankel, Mevo, 61b.

[Yitzhak Dov Gilat]

ADDIR BI-MELUKHAH (Heb. אַדִּיר בִּמְלוּכָה; "Mighty in Kingship"), acrostical hymn recited toward the close of the Passover *seder* in the Ashkenazi and some other rites. It enumerates various attributes of God in the first two lines of each strophe, followed by a list of the various types of angels and the praises which they voice.

The hymn is first found in German manuscripts of the early 13th century and was probably written in Germany about that time.

In the *Ez Ḥayyim* of the 13th-century Jacob Ḥazzan of London (edited by I. Brodie, 1 (1960), 332), an additional stanza gives the acrostic Jacob, and conceivably this author wrote the poem.

BIBLIOGRAPHY: *Responsa Meir of Rothenburg*, ed. by Y.Z. Kahana, 1 (1957), 279, no. 462; Zunz, Vortraege, 133; Kaufmann, in: JQR, 4 (1892), 32, 560–1; Davidson, Oẓar, 2 (1929), s.v. *Ki Lo Na'eh;* E.D. Goldschmidt, *Pessach-Haggada* (Heb., Ger., 1937), 100–2; idem, *Haggadah shel Pesaḥ* (1947), 74–75; idem, *Haggadah shel Pesaḥ* (1960), 97.

ADDIR HU (Heb. אַדִּיר הוּא; "Mighty is He"), a hymn in the form of an alphabetic acrostic enumerating the qualities of God (mighty, blessed, great), and imploring Him to rebuild the Temple, a prayer which is repeated in the refrain:

"Speedily, speedily/In our days, and soon to come;/ Build, O God! Build, O God/ Build Thy house speedily."

Addir Hu is one of several hymns added to the Passover **Haggadah* in the Middle Ages to be chanted after the conclusion of the formal part of the **seder* service according to the Ashkenazi rite. Since the 16th century *Addir Hu* appears in printed texts. A Judeo-German version recited by Ashkenazi Jews was first printed in Gershom b. Solomon ha-Kohen's *Haggadah* (Prague, 1527). Because of the refrain in that version (*Bau dein Tempel shire*) the Jews of southern and western Germany called the *seder* night "*Baunacht*" and the celebrating of the *seder* "*bauen,*" i.e., to build. In the Avignon *Maḥzor* (1775) it is recited on all festivals.

[Ernst Daniel Goldschmidt]

Music

Only in the Ashkenazi tradition is *Addir Hu* given greater prominence than the other *Haggadah* songs. It is sung to basically the same tune in all Jewish homes, and this is used in the synagogue as a musical motif of the festival. The music appeared in print as early as 1644 but may be even older, since one of its variants is in a Shtayger scale with a diminished seventh. In the 18th century it was often quoted in cantorial Passover compositions. In the synagogue, the tune is used in various parts of the service, including the **Hallel*, the **Kaddish* over the Scroll of the Law, and the Priestly Benediction. The domestic versions introduce many variations, abbreviations, and distortions characteristic of folk music.

[Hanoch Avenary]

BIBLIOGRAPHY: E.D. Goldschmidt, *Haggadah shel Pesaḥ* (1960), 75; Davidson, Oẓar, 1 (1924), 52, no. 1086; E. Pauer, *Traditional Hebrew Melodies* (1896); Selig, in: *Der Jude*, 3 (1769), 385–7 (see facsimile). MUSIC: Idelsohn, Melodien, 6, pt. 1 (1932), 63, no. 155; 68–69, nos. 164, 165, 167; 72, no. 171; 83, no. 199; 184, no. 200; Idelsohn, Music, index (18th-cent. works); F.J. Fétis, *Histoire générale de la Musique*, 1 (1869), 467 (earliest Oriental version).

ADEL (Hodel), only daughter of *Israel b. Eliezer Ba'al Shem Tov. Ḥasidim recall her name with veneration and she figures in many ḥasidic legends. She cared for her father on his sickbed. Her husband Jehiel Ashkenazi was honored by contemporary Ḥasidim and by his father-in-law. The couple earned their living from the store which she supervised. She was the mother of the *ẓaddikim* *Moses Ḥayyim Ephraim of Sudylkow and *Baruch of Medzibezh. Her daughter, Feige, the wife of Simhah b. Nahman of Gorodenka (Horodenca), was the mother of *Naḥman of Bratslav who said of his grandmother that "all the *ẓaddikim* believed her to be endowed with Divine Inspiration, and a woman of great perception."

BIBLIOGRAPHY: *Shivḥei ha-Besht* (1931), 108–9, 180–1; *Ma'asiyyot me-ha-Gedolim ve-ha-Ẓaddikim* (1909), 33–38.

[Mordecai Ben-Yehezkiel]

ADELAIDE, capital of South Australia, established in 1836. Among its first settlers were a number of Jews engaged in commerce and sheep farming. Joseph Barrow Montefiore, a cousin of Sir Moses *Montefiore, who became in 1832 the first president of the Sydney Synagogue, lived in Adelaide at the time of the founding of the synagogue there. Local Jewish life was stimulated after 1838 by Emanuel Solomon from Sydney, who organized religious services on the New Year and the Day of Atonement and in 1845 successfully applied to the government for land for a cemetery. In 1847 Eliezer Levi Montefiore sought state support for Jewish religious institutions. In 1848 there were 58 Jews living in Adelaide, and the first congregation was organized with Judah Moss Solomon as its president. J.B. Montefiore gave addresses in English during the High Holidays. The first synagogue, used also as a schoolroom, was opened in 1850 and the present one, adjoining it, in 1870, when the community numbered 435. A.T. *Boas was invited to act as minister in 1870 and served for nearly half a century. Vabian Louis *Solomon, son of Judah Moss Solomon, was premier of the colony for a brief period in 1898. The community declined considerably in numbers after World War I, but there was a subsequent increase, especially with the emigration of Jews from Egypt after the mid-1950s. Since the 1960s the Jewish population of Adelaide has numbered about 1,200, although, unlike most other Jewish communities in Australia, there has been a decline in population in recent years. In 2001, according to the Australian census, 979 persons declared themselves to be Jewish by religion. An Orthodox and a Liberal synagogue operated. There were no other organized Jewish communities in South Australia apart from Adelaide, where the South Australian Board of Deputies had its headquarters.

BIBLIOGRAPHY: H. Munz, *Jews in South Australia* (1936); Saphir (trans. by Falk), in: *Journal of the Australian Jewish Historical Society*, 1 (1948), 192–4; Goldman, *ibid.*, 4 (1958), 351, 376; Apple, *ibid.*, 6 (1968), 206–7, 209–10. **ADD. BIBLIOGRAPHY:** H.L. Rubinstein, in: JA I, index, and W.D. Rubinstein, in: JA II, index; B.K. Hyams, *Surviving: A History of the Institutions and Organisations of the Adelaide Jewish Community* (1998).

[Israel Porush / William D. Rubinstein (2nd ed.)]

ADELANTADOS (singular **Adelantado** or **Adelantatus**), one of the designations applied in documents of Christian *Spain to the *parnasim*, elective members of the Jewish community board who were invested with executive authority. They are sometimes referred to in Castile as *viejos* (Heb. *zekenim;* "elders") or *muquddāmin*, in Catalonia as *fideles* (Heb. *ne'manin*; "trustees"), and in Aragon and Navarre both as *muqaddāmin* and as *jurados*.

BIBLIOGRAPHY: Neuman, Spain, index s.v. *mukkadmin*.

ADELKIND, ISRAEL CORNELIUS (16th century), Italian printer. Adelkind was the son of a German immigrant who settled in Padua. He worked in the publishing house of Daniel *Bomberg in Venice from the time of its establishment, except for intervals at other Venetian publishers, such as Dei Farri (1544; where one of his brothers and later his son Daniel also worked) and Giustiniani (1549–52). Adelkind greatly admired the Bomberg family, adding the name of Daniel Bomberg's father, Cornelius, to his own, and named his son after Daniel himself.

Adelkind supervised the publication of the first editions of the two Talmuds (1520–23), which Bomberg printed, and the *Midrash Rabbah* (1554) printed jointly by Bomberg and Giustiniani. In 1553 the printer Tobias Foa invited Adelkind to manage a printing press in Sabbioneta and, in particular, to supervise the publication of the Talmud. However, a ban was imposed on the Talmud in 1553 after only a few tractates had appeared. Nevertheless, he remained with the firm until 1555 and took part in the publication of other works. He also printed books in Judeo-German, e.g., Elijah Levita's translation of the Psalms (1545). The statement of a Christian contemporary that Adelkind was converted to Christianity is questionable.

BIBLIOGRAPHY: D.W. Amram, *Makers of Hebrew Books in Italy* (1909), 176, 180ff.; J. Bloch, *Venetian Printers of Hebrew Books* (1932), 12ff., 22ff.; Sonne, in: KS, 4 (1927/28), 57; 5 (1928/29), 176, 278; 6 (1929/30), 145; Perles, *Beitraege zur Geschichte der hebraeischen und aramaeischen Studien* (1884), 209ff.; British Museum, *Catalogue of Italian Books 1465–1600* (1958), 758–9.

[Abraham Meir Habermann]

ADELMAN, URI (1958–2004), Israeli writer. Adelman studied and later taught musicology at Tel Aviv University, wrote for the stage and for television, and published four books on computers. His reputation rests on four thrillers, all of them bestsellers, which combine wit, erudition, and suspense. The first, "Concerto for Spy and Orchestra" (1993), intertwines espionage and musicology within the confines of the Pravoslav church in Jerusalem. "Lost and Found" (1998) was followed by "Tropic of Venus" (2000), a story of love and mysterious identities which won Israel's Golden Book Prize. Adelman's last novel, published shortly before his sudden death, is entitled *Sha'ot Metot* ("Dead Hours"), a thriller played out against the background of the Intifada, in which a young surgeon who wishes to save lives finds himself accused of homicide.

WEBSITE: www.ithl.org.il.

[Anat Feinberg (2nd ed.)]

ADELSON, HOWARD LAURENCE (1925–2003), U.S. medieval historian. Born in New York, Adelson taught at Princeton, served with the U.S. Air Force in the Korean War, and then joined the faculty of City College, New York. He began teaching economic history, early medieval history, and ancient and medieval numismatics in 1954 and remained there for nearly 50 years. He developed the Ph.D. program in medieval history at the Graduate Center at City University of New York (1969). He was also an officer of the National Committee on American Foreign Policy.

An ardent Zionist active in Jewish affairs, he served, from 1994, as co-chair of American Academics for Israel's Future; was on the Board of Governors of the Hebrew University of Jerusalem; chaired the Academic Affairs Committee of the University's Rothenberg International School; and, in the last ten years of his life, was chairman of the Anna Sobel Levy Foundation, which supports junior U.S. military officers studying Israel. For more than 20 years he wrote a weekly column for the *Jewish Press* that had a large following. Adelson was active as well in the American Numismatic Society and did research in medieval economic history and political thought. Among his achievements was the discovery, by analyzing the movement of coins, that there had been trade between the eastern and western halves of the Byzantine Empire. Adelson's books include: *Light Weight Solidi and Byzantine Trade during the Sixth and Seventh Centuries* (1957); *The American Numismatic Society 1858–1958* (1958); and *Medieval Commerce* (1962).

[Ruth Beloff (2nd ed.)]

ADELSTEIN-ROZEANU, ANGELICA (1921–2006), Romanian table tennis player; considered the greatest female table tennis player in history, winning 18 world titles, including six straight singles championships from 1950 to 1955. Born in Bucharest, Romania, Adelstein-Rozeanu was the first Romanian woman to win a world title in any sport. She began playing at the age of nine and won her first title in competitive play at the age of 12. She won the Romanian National Women's Championship in 1936 at age 15 and won it every year until 1957 excluding the war years. In addition to her run of individual world titles, she picked up seven gold medals in women's and mixed doubles between 1950 and 1956 and helped Romania win the team championship in 1950, 1951, 1953, 1955, and 1956. Adelstein-Rozeanu served as president of the Romanian Table Tennis Commission from 1950 to 1960, and in 1954 was awarded the Merited Master of Sport, the highest sports distinction in Romania. She also received four Order of Work honors from her government. Adelstein-Rozeanu moved to Israel in 1960, where she won the Maccabiah Games Table Tennis Championship in 1961 and the Israeli national championship in 1960–1962.

[Elli Wohlgelernter (2nd ed.)]

ADEN, port and city in S.W. Arabia, now part of the Federation of South Arabia, possibly identical with the Eden referred to in Ezekiel 27:23. Aden had a medieval Jewish community of great importance for the history of Jewish letters. It reached its peak during the 12th century. About 150 letters and documents written in, sent to, or concerning Aden were found in the Cairo *Genizah*. In addition, Yemenite Jews of that period communicated with other Jewish communities via Aden. By the end of the 11th century there was a "representative of the merchants" in Aden, Abu Ali Hasan (Heb. Japheth) ibn Bundar (probably a name of Persian origin). He bore the Hebrew title *sar ha-kehillot* ("chief of the congregations"), which indicates that he was head of the Jewish communities of both Aden and *Yemen. His son, *Maḍmūn, was "*nagid* of the Land of Yemen."

In addition to business and family ties, there were communal and religious relations between the Jews of Aden and practically all the Jewish communities of the Islamic empire. "Aden and India" formed one juridical diocese: the Jewish merchants and craftsmen of about 20 different ports of India and Ceylon were under the jurisdiction of the rabbinical court of Aden. In Yemen itself the authority of the court of Aden extended as far as Saʿda, the northernmost important Jewish community of the country. In turn, the rabbinical court of Aden regarded itself subordinate to that of the Egyptian capital, which had been instituted by the head of the Palestinian academy. In a letter addressed in 1153 to Old Cairo, the rabbis of Aden describe themselves as authorized by their exilarch and their *nagid*, but add that they acknowledge their "masters in Egypt" as an authority higher than themselves (see Strauss (Ashtor), in *Zion*, 4 (1939), 226, 231).

Conflict of Religious Authority

Because of relations with both Iraq and Palestine-Egypt, the Jewish community of Aden was drawn into the rivalry between the respective Jewish authorities. The dissensions of the Old Cairo community were transmitted to Aden, where they erupted in the spring of 1134. On the Sabbath before Passover that year, a scholarly Jew from Saʿda was asked to lead the community in prayer. Following his home custom and the written instructions of the *nagid* Maḍmūn, he mentioned both the exilarch and the Palestinian *gaon* in his sermon. However, the Old Cairo opponents of Maẓli'aḥ, who happened to be present, objected; and a cousin of the exilarch, recognized as his representative, forced the scholar from Saʿda to recant his error publicly. After Passover the merchants from North Africa and Egypt who went to Aden – most of them ardent followers of the Palestinian *gaon* – gathered around Ḥalfon b. Nethanel Dimyati, known in Hebrew literature as an intimate friend of the poet Judah Halevi. The followers of Maẓli'aḥ even threatened to apply to the Fatimid authorities to settle the dispute, but did not carry out the threat.

It is known that at the end of the 11th or the beginning of the 12th century the Jews of Aden contributed regularly to the upkeep of the academies of Iraq (see Goitein, in *Tarbiz*, 31 (1961/62), 363). Maḍmūn and other well-to-do merchants of Aden also sent regular contributions consisting partly of money and partly of precious Oriental spices and clothes to the *gaon* and members of the rabbinical court in Old Cairo.

The Jews of Aden and Yemen submitted religious queries to the scholars of Egypt even before the time of Maimonides. For example, Maḍmūn once sent *gaon* Maẓli'aḥ a set of translucent Chinese porcelain accompanied by the religious query, often repeated in later sources, whether china should be regarded ritually as glass or pottery. Isaac b. Samuel ha-Sephardi, one of the two chief judges of Old Cairo between 1095–1127, sent responsa to Yemen, which, like Maimonides' letters to Yemen, were certainly sent via Aden. (See the article on **nagid* for the later *negidim* of Aden and Yemen.)

The Aden tradition of contributing to the academies of Iraq and Palestine was extended to that of *Maimonides. A very large donation for it is indicated in a letter sent from Aden. Abraham, Maimonides' son and successor, answered queries addressed to him by the scholars of Aden.

Adani and Yemenite Jews

The impressive number of chiefs of congregations and *negidim* of Aden in the 11th and 12th centuries and later may be misleading: these notables did not exercise authority over the Jews of Yemen throughout the whole period. Despite the close connection between the Jews of Aden and those of inner Yemen, there were tangible differences between them, and they were referred to as "Adani" and "Yemeni," respectively, when traveling abroad. In the 12th century Adanis were found in Egypt and as far west as Mamsa in Morocco (cf. DIT, no. 109 (= manuscript Cambridge, T.-S., 12. 1905), Yosef al-ʿAdanī al-Mamsāwī).

There were also Karaites in Aden. They tried to gain adherents to their beliefs, and the poems of Abraham Yiju in honor of Maḍmūn b. Japheth credit him with crushing their efforts. Disputations with Karaites are reflected in Yemenite writings of that period.

The Importance of Aden for Hebrew Literature

The Jews of Aden were ardent collectors of books. Maḍmūn b.

David in his letter of July 1202 asked to have the medical treatises of Maimonides and other useful books sent to him; he specifically requested copies written on good paper and in a clear hand. The Jews of Aden were such avid bibliophiles that the Egyptian India traveler Ḥalfon b. Nethanel went there for books that he could not get elsewhere (DIT, no. 246). Many of the most important literary creations written in Hebrew, such as the poems of Judah Halevi and Moses ibn Ezra, have been preserved in manuscripts found in Yemen. The *Midrash ha-Gadol* of David *Adani shows that he possessed an exceptionally rich, specialized library, containing works that have not yet been found in their entirety elsewhere.

Most of the letters from Aden, consisting predominantly of business correspondence, are in Arabic, which was in those days the *lingua franca* of commerce throughout the Islamic world and beyond. However, the often very long Hebrew poems appended to these letters, as well as the personal letters written in Hebrew, prove that their writers were well versed in Hebrew literature and inclined toward the midrashic style and the *piyyut*.

Jewish Tombstones

A great many tombstones with Hebrew inscriptions were found in Aden. Some are preserved in the British Museum and many more in museums in Aden, but most of them have become known through rubbings and photographs made of tombs still *in situ*. The oldest inscriptions are from the 12th century; and those referring to persons mentioned also in the *genizah* documents are of particular interest. There are others from the 13th and 14th centuries and a great number from the 16th through the 18th. The wording in the older inscriptions is extremely modest and concise, while the later ones are occasionally more elaborate. In the tombstones of women, as a rule, the names of their fathers, but not those of their husbands, are indicated, even when the woman concerned was described as an *ishah ḥashuvah* ("an important lady"). (The comprehensive study of the subject by H.P. Chajes in the *Sitzungsberichte* of the Viennese Academy of Sciences, 147 (1904), no. 3, was complemented by additional material published by I. Ben-Zvi, in *Tarbiz*, 22 (1952/53), 198ff.; E. Subar, in JQR, 49 (1959), 301ff.; S.A. Birnbaum, in JSS, 6 (1961), 95ff.; and by the critical survey by S.D. Goitein, in JSS, 7 (1962), 81–84.)

Aden remained a busy port and its Jewish community prospered well into the 16th century. Despite a decline in Jewish participation in the India trade, Jewish Mediterranean merchants continued to frequent Aden, and scholars called Adani and known to have lived in Aden made considerable contributions. The replacement of a local dynasty by the Ottoman Turks in 1538 did not adversely affect the fortunes of the Jews of Aden. A Muslim book of legal opinions from the beginning of the Ottoman period gives the number of Jewish male taxpayers as 7,000. Since taxes customarily were paid for boys at the age of nine approximately, this number of taxpayers indicates the existence of about 3,000 Jewish families in Aden. In the 18th century, when the India trade was at its lowest ebb and the tribal sultan of Laḥj ruled it, Aden fell into utter decay.

[Shelomo Dov Goitein]

Modern Period

A new chapter in the history of Aden Jewry, as part of the political and economic changes in Aden itself, began with the conquest of the port and city from the Sultan of Laḥj by the British captain S.B. Haines in 1839, supposedly in response to the aggressive action of the sultan against a British ship anchored next to Aden. In fact, the conquest of the port was intended to assure a safe place to anchor and fuel for British ships arriving from the Mediterranean basin via the Red Sea and Aden on their way to India. In 1839 the population of Aden was only 600, 250 of them Jewish and 50 Banyans (Indians). Soon after the British had occupied Aden, the governor abrogated the Jews' status as a protected community (*dhimmī) and restored discriminatory laws in accordance with Islamic tradition (*Ghiyār*). This was done despite the sultan's explicit orders. Haines' reports describe the delighted reaction of the Jews to the British conquest as do the later accounts of the Jewish sources: Y. Sappir, S.D. Karasso, and M. ha-Adani. As a result of the occupation, the economic development of Aden took wing, especially after the opening of the Suez Canal in 1869. As a consequence, a profound transformation occurred in the economic structure of Aden's Jewry from traditional handcrafts to various kinds of commerce. Particularly prominent was the Moses (Messa) family, whose head, Menahem Moses (d. 1864), was the president of the community. This family became very wealthy, especially as suppliers to the British army and its administration in Aden, which trusted the Jewish merchants more than the Muslim ones. The Moses family continued to be the social and economic leaders of Aden Jewry in the next two generations, particularly Menahem Moses' son, Banin (d. 1922), who succeeded his father as the head of the family and president of the community.

Because of the equal rights enjoyed by the Jews and the access to the outside world, Aden became attractive to Yemenite Jews. Many Jews emigrated to Aden as refugees escaping Yemen and the deteriorating political situation that particularly affected Jews and merchants. Jewish ship passengers and emissaries stopped at Aden and some decided to settle there. The number of Jews in Aden in 1860 was 1,500 and, by 1945, 4,500 Jews inhabited the city. In this way the Aden community took on a somewhat "international" character somewhat different from that of Yemen Jewry. Aden became the entry port to Yemen. Leaders of the local community, such as Moses Hanoch ha-Levi from the Caucasus and Banin Moses looked out for the well-being of Yemenite Jews and the refugees passing through Aden on their way to Ereẓ Israel. Banin Moses even supported educational and outreach institutions of various Diaspora communities in Jerusalem and many of the emissaries from Ereẓ Israel used to apply to him for contributions.

The profound political and economic changes did not result in social and cultural change. The Moses family, and especially Banin Moses, who held the economic reins of the community, virtually controlled single-handedly the social and religious administration of the community. He stymied all innovation, such as the establishment of modern schools and cooperation with the Zionist movement. As a result, a professional class of Jews did not come into being in Aden. Only after the death in 1924 of Judah Moses, the third family president, did a new family president, Selim (1924–38), another son of Menahem Moses, establish a modern educational system for girls and boys and strengthen the connections with the Zionist movement in Ereẓ Israel. His partner in these activities was Mahalal *Adani. In this way the young generation – women as well as men – acquired a modern Zionist Hebrew education; however, none continued on to higher education. Neither did the small Hebrew printing press established in Aden in 1891 become a milestone in the cultural development of the community, as only a small number of religious books were printed there for the needs of religious life: various liturgical books and rules for ritual slaughter.

The abrogation of the status of the Jews as a protected community led to a deterioration in relations with the Muslim majority, heightened by the conflict with the Arabs in Ereẓ Israel. Even though the Jewish community in Aden grew in numbers, the growth of the Muslim community was incomparably larger. As opposed to their relative size at the start of the British occupation in 1839, when they constituted approximately half the population, at this stage they became just a small religious minority. Apart from individual Muslim attacks against Jews, a large-scale attack on the Jewish quarter occurred in 1932 and continued for a few days. The Jewish stores were pillaged, many Jews were beaten, and the "Farḥi" synagogue was desecrated. The British police showed its indifference by doing little to punish the attackers. Following these incidents, Aden Jewry no longer felt safe and immigration to Ereẓ Israel became an alternative. Simultaneously, the Islamic nationalist movement began to develop in Aden, seeking to end the British occupation. The situation of the Jews further deteriorated after the riots in Ereẓ Israel in 1936–39. However, Yemenite and Aden Jews faced difficulties in immigrating to Israel because of British Mandate policy, which limited the number of certificates to Palestine.

In contrast to the declining political and economic situation, educational and social activities increased among the young generation in Aden thanks to the numerous emissaries arriving from Ereẓ Israel. These emissaries included Yemenite and Aden Jews who had already moved to Israel such as Yosef ben David, Ovadia Tuvia, Binyamin Ratzabi, and Shimon Sha'er (Avizemer). These activities were not approved of by the traditional Jewish religious authorities, which caused tension between them and the younger rebellious generation. But social change was nipped in the bud as Arab violence was stepped up following the UN decision to establish a Jewish state in Palestine. In the new pogroms, which continued for three days with no British intervention, nearly a hundred Jews were killed in Aden and the nearby city of Sheikh 'Uthmān. Others were injured, two Jewish schools were burned down, and most Jewish stores and small businesses were pillaged. The Jewish community lost all at once its economic underpinning and its faith in the British government. An investigating committee initiated by the British government did little to improve the financial and mental state of the Jews. Most of them preferred to immigrate to Israel with the founding of the Jewish state. Out of a population of 4,500, only 1,100 remained in 1946. In the mid-1950s, 830 lived there, a small minority among the 135,000 members of the Muslim community. The number of Jews diminished further in the course of the following years when their political situation worsened due to the tension between Israel and the Arab states and the radicalism of the Islamic nationalist Arab movement in Aden and its struggle against the British occupation. The 1958 incidents are an example of this trend: Jews were attacked in their synagogues, cars were destroyed, and an attempt was made to burn the Jewish school. With Britain's departure after the Six-Day War in June 1967, many of the Jews who still lived in Aden left. In the following November an independent state was established in Aden. The remnants of the Jewish community arrived partly in Israel and partly in London, leaving their belongings and institutions behind them. The Jews who immigrated to London as British citizens joined the members of the community who had moved there several years earlier. This strengthened the Aden community in London, which still retains its religious traditions.

[Yosef Tobi (2nd ed.)]

Folklore

The folklore of the Jews of Aden was strongly influenced and dominated by that of the Jews of *Yemen. This was especially evident in their narrative lore. Among the unrelated local customs: The *tallit* ("mandīl") was worn with green silk edges; a goat was slaughtered and placed under the bed of a mother in childbirth; on the first day of the seven-day wedding celebration a heifer was slaughtered. These animal sacrifices were also practiced by neighboring non-Jewish tribes, and it is doubtful whether they stem directly from ancient Jewish traditions.

[Dov Noy]

BIBLIOGRAPHY: R.B. Serjeant, *Portuguese off the South Arabian Coast* (1963), 139–40; J. Saphir, *Even Sappir*, 2 (1874); H. von Maltzan, *Reise nach Suedarabien*, 1 (1873), 172–81; Mahalal ha-Adani, *Bein Aden le-Teiman* (1947); Y. Sémach, *Une Mission d'Alliance au Yémen* (1910); S. Yavnieli, *Massa le-Teiman* (1952); Great Britain, Admiralty, *Handbook of Arabia* (1920); Colonial Office, *Report of the Commission of Enquiry into Disturbances in Aden in December 1947* (1948), no. 233; Histadrut ha-Ovdim, *Ẓeror Iggerot al ha-Sho'ah be-Aden* (1948); Bentwich, in: *Jewish Monthly* (April 1948); Yesha'ya, in: *Yalkut ha-Mizraḥ ha-Tikhon* (Feb. 1949); Jewish Agency, *Dappei Aliyah* (1949–50); Samuel b. Joseph Yeshua Adani, *Naḥalat Yosef* (1907); E. Brauer, *Ethnologie der jemenitischen Juden* (1934); S. Assaf, *Mekorot u-Meḥkarim be-Toledot Yisrael* (1946); A. Yaari, *Ha-Defus ha-Ivri be-Arẓot ha-Mizraḥ*, 1 (1937), 86ff.; idem, in: KS, 24 (1947/48), 70. **ADD. BIBLIOGRAPHY:** R. Aharoni, *Yehudei Aden* (1991); idem, *The Jews of the British Crown Colony of Aden* (1994); J. Tobi, *West of Aden: A Survey of the Aden Jewish Community* (1994).

°**ADENAUER, KONRAD** (1876–1967), first chancellor of the postwar German Federal Republic. Son of a Catholic official in the Cologne law courts, Adenauer was elected in 1906 to the city council of Cologne on behalf of the Center (Catholic) Party, and in 1917 became mayor of the city, a post which he held until he was dismissed by the Nazis in March 1933. Jewish friends helped him financially during the Nazi period. Adenauer was twice arrested by the Gestapo and escaped from a Nazi prison shortly before the Rhineland was occupied by the Allies. In 1949 Adenauer emerged as leader of the new party, the Christian Democratic Union, and was elected chancellor of the Federal Republic. He was instrumental in gaining its full sovereignty in 1955. Prompted not only by political motives but also by his own deep feelings, Adenauer tried to open lines of communication with the Jewish people and the State of Israel. His offer of financial assistance coincided with the initiative of the Israel government and of Jewish organizations which, immediately after the war, demanded restitution and compensation from the Allies and later from both the East and West German governments. In 1952, after the *Reparation Agreements with Israel and the Jewish organizations were signed in Luxembourg, Adenauer proposed to establish full diplomatic relations with Israel, but was refused. Despite the opposition to the financial commitment in reparations and compensation by influential groups both in his own party and outside, Adenauer realized both its moral importance and its political advantage for Germany. In 1960 he met with the Israeli prime minister David *Ben-Gurion in New York and promised to continue financial aid to Israel after the end of the reparation commitment. Later, he declared himself ready to supply arms to Israel. He changed his mind on the establishment of diplomatic relations, however, because he feared that it might result in Arab recognition of East Germany. (See Israel Relations with *Germany.) In 1966, three years after his resignation from the post of chancellor, Adenauer visited Israel as a guest of the Israeli government. He devoted a chapter in his memoirs (*Erinnerungen*, 3 vols., 1965–67; in English *Memoirs*, 1, 1966) to his relationship with Israel and with world Jewry.

ADD. BIBLIOGRAPHY: H.P. Schwarz, *Adenauer* (1986–91); H. Koehler, *Adenauer, Eine politische Biographie* (1997); Y.A. Jelinek, in: *Orient*, 43 (2002), 4157.

[Shlomo Aronson]

ADENI, SOLOMON BAR JOSHUA (1567–1625?), commentator on the Mishnah. In 1571 he immigrated with his father, a *ḥakham* in San'a, Yemen, and his family to Safed, where he studied under David Amarillo. In 1577–78 Adeni's father moved to Jerusalem. After his father's death (1582) Adeni, then in difficult circumstances, was cared for and supported by R. Moses b. Jacob Alḥāmi. Alḥāmi continued, until his death, to support Solomon, who arranged Adeni's marriage in 1590. In about 1582 Adeni entered the yeshivah of the kabbalist Ḥayyim *Vital, but later studied under others as well, among them Bezalel *Ashkenazi, who came to Jerusalem. Studying in seclusion, he wrote annotations in the margins of the Mishnah, and as these increased, he abbreviated them. It was apparently after the death of Bezalel Ashkenazi that Adeni settled in Hebron, where he earned a meager living as a schoolteacher. His wife, daughter, and two sons died in 1600, apparently from a plague. His eight children from a second marriage all died in childhood from epidemics and diseases.

Adeni's commentary on the Mishnah, *Melekhet Shelomo*, was intended to encompass the entire Torah, explain the Talmuds, and to concentrate their commentaries and halakhic discussions in one place. The importance of the work is twofold: (1) to determine the clearest text of the Mishnah; and (2) to explain the Mishnah according to primary sources by his own method.

Adeni made use of many manuscripts of the Mishnah and the foremost rabbinic authorities then available in Ereẓ Israel. Adeni's method is remarkably accurate. He checked his quotations from primary sources. If the original text was not available, he noted from whom he copied his citation. His commentaries are the closest to the literal meaning of the Mishnah. He comments on the biographies of rabbis and he illustrates the orders *Zera'im* and *Tohorot* with many illustrations, and corrects the classical mishnaic commentators. He opened his comments with the words "the compiler states" and when he differed with a scholar, he modestly wrote, "And to me, a layman, it seems my humble opinion…"

Because of these attributes his work became an indispensable commentary for study of the Mishnah. In addition, it is an important source for philologists. Yom Tov Heller's commentary on the Mishnah, *Tosafot Yom Tov* (Prague, 1585–87) appeared after Adeni had finished his work. However, praising Heller's work highly, Adeni included selections from it when his book was published. Despite its importance the commentary was printed for the first time only in 1905. Adeni also produced some of Bezalel Ashkenazi's glosses and commentaries on the Mishnah and the Talmud in a work called *Binyan Shelomo le-Ḥokhmat Beẓalel.*

Another work equally important, but less famous because it was lost in manuscript, is *Divrei Emet*, glosses on the Bible. Ḥ.J.D. *Azulai saw this manuscript in Jerusalem and used it extensively in his work on the Bible, *Ḥomat Anakh.*

Little is known about Adeni's later life. The last information about him dates from 1625.

BIBLIOGRAPHY: Azulai, 1 (1878), 120, no. 57; 2 (1878), 20, no. 7; A. Marx, in: JQR, 2 (1911/12), 266–70; Epstein, Mishnah, 2 (1948), 1290; E.Z. Melamed, in: *Sinai*, 44 (1959), 346–63; M. Benayahu, *ibid.*, 30 (1952), 66–68; idem, *Rabbi Ḥ.Y.D. Azulai* (1959), 134.

ADERCA, FELIX (**Froim Zeilig**; 1891–1962), Romanian novelist and journalist. Born in Puiesti (near Vaslui) and educated in Craiova, Aderca made his literary debut with volumes of poetry. The titles of the first two reflect his early preoccupation with feeling and harmony: *Motive și simfonii* ("Motifs and Symphonies," 1910) and *Fragmente și romanțe* ("Fragments and Romances," 1912). Then came the cold, cerebral period of *Reverii sculptate* ("Sculptured Reveries," 1912) and *Prin lentile* *negre* ("Through Black Lenses," 1912), finally emerging into the sensuality of *Stihuri venerice* ("Erotic Poems," 1915). Eroticism was to become the keynote of Aderca's first novels. *Moartea unei republici roșii* ("The Death of a Red Republic," 1924) gave expression to his deep humanitarianism and pacificism. The reconstruction of the tragic atmosphere in Romania in World War I in *1916* represents not only Aderca's outstanding work but is regarded as one of the best war books ever written. Two of his novels are distinctly Kafkaesque in form: *Aventurile domnului Ionel Lăcustă Termidor* ("The Adventures of Mr. Ionel Lacusta Termidor," 1932) and *Revolte*. The latter, written in 1938 but only published in 1945, is a series of sketches lampooning legal procedures.

Ebullient and argumentative, Aderca was a prolific journalist. His interviews with men of ideas, collected in *Mărturia unei generatii* ("Testimony of a Generation," 1929), introduced a new genre into Romanian literature. In his youth, Aderca contributed to various Romanian Jewish publications (*Ha-Tikvah, Lumea evree,* and *Adam*) and showed some attachment to Judaism and Zionism. He also published hundreds of articles about antisemitism. Aderca translated into Romanian books dealing with Jewish themes, among them the trilogy of Sholem Asch. Aderca believed in the idea of symbiosis between his Judaism and the Romanian language and culture. Persecuted during the Holocaust period (1938–44), he worked as a librarian in the Jewish community of Bucharest. He was unpopular with the Communist regime after World War II and from 1947 was allowed to publish virtually nothing but instructional literature for young people. One of his last works was a monograph on Constantin Dobrogeanu-Gherea (1948), the Russian-Jewish refugee literary critic and sociologist who promoted socialist theories in Romania. Some of Aderca's literary works were republished in the "liberalization" period (after 1965), but most of them were republished only after the collapse of the Communist regime in Romania (1989). Fragments of his works were translated into Hebrew in Israel.

BIBLIOGRAPHY: G. Calinescu, *Istoria literaturii romane* (1941), 705–8; T. Teodorescu-Braniste, *Oameni și Cărți* (1923), 71; E. Lovinescu, *Evoluția Poeziei Lirice* (1927), 366–8; C. Baltazar, *Scriitor și Om* (1946), 11–14. **ADD. BIBLIOGRAPHY:** A. Mirodan, *Dictionar neconventional,* 1 (1986), 25–35, 438–9; M. Aderca, *F. Aderca si problema evreiasca* (1999).

[Dora Litani-Littman / Lucian-Zeev Herscovici (2nd ed.)]

ADIABENE, district in the upper Tigris region. During most of the Hellenistic period Adiabene was a vassal kingdom within the Parthian Empire. From 36 to 60 C.E. Adiabene was ruled by Izates, son of King *Monobaz and Queen *Helena. By that time the small kingdom had attained a measure of power and influence within the Parthian Empire, and it was Izates who restored the deposed Parthian king Artabanus III to his throne. For this, Izates was granted the extensive territory of Nisibis and its surroundings, and proceeded to play an important part in the dynastic struggles within Parthia after the death of Artabanus III.

Before he became king, both Izates and his mother Helena had been converted to Judaism. As a youth, Izates had been sent to Charax Spasinu (capital of the kingdom of Charakene, between the Tigris and the Euphrates) and it was there that he came under the influence of a Jewish merchant named *Ananias. At the same time, Helena had been converted by another Jew, and when Izates returned to Adiabene he was determined to complete his own conversion by undergoing circumcision. Against the wishes of Helena and Ananias the rite was performed, for Izates had been convinced by another Jew, a Galilean named Eleazar, that failure to do so would be considered "the greatest offense against the law and thereby against God." This story, as it appears in Josephus (Ant., 20:34ff.), bears an interesting resemblance to the account given in the Midrash (Gen. R. 46:11). Monobaz and Izates were sitting and reading the book of Genesis; when they came to the verse "ye shall be circumcised," they began to weep, and secretly had themselves circumcised. "When their mother learned of this she went and told their father: 'A sore has broken out on our sons' flesh, and the physician has ordered circumcision.'" The king then gave his consent to what had already been performed.

After their conversion the Adiabenian rulers were quick to establish strong ties with the Jews of Palestine. Appreciation of their generosity toward the population and the Temple is expressed in a variety of talmudic sources. "King Monobaz (older brother and successor to Izates) made of gold all the handles for the vessels used on the Day of Atonement. His mother Helena set a golden candlestick over the door of the Sanctuary. He also donated a golden tablet on which the paragraph of the Suspected Adulteress was written" (Yoma 3:10; cf. Tosef. *ibid.* 2:3; TJ *ibid.* 3:8, 41a; TB *ibid.* 37a–b). Josephus reports that when Queen Helena visited Jerusalem (c. 46 C.E.) the journey greatly benefited the inhabitants, who were suffering from severe famine. Helena sent her attendants to Alexandria and Cyprus to procure grain and dried figs, which were distributed forthwith to the needy. "She left a very great name that will be famous forever among all our people for her benefaction. When her son Izates learned of the famine, he likewise sent a great sum of money to leaders of the Jerusalemites" (Jos., Ant., 20:49ff.). The Mishnah (Naz. 3:6) connects Helena's pilgrimage to Palestine with a Nazarite vow she took. With regard to the famine, the Talmud relates that King Monobaz dissipated all his treasures and those of his ancestors in years of scarcity. When reproached by members of the court for squandering his money, Monobaz replied: "My fathers stored up below and I am storing up above," i.e., in heaven (BB 11a; see also Tosef. Pe'ah 4:18; TJ *ibid.* 1:1, 15b). This piety is praised in other sources as well. Although there is no need to affix a *mezuzah* to a temporary abode, "the house of King Monobaz used to do so when staying at a hostel, merely in remembrance of the *mezuzah*" (Tosef. Meg. 4:30; Men. 32b). While in Judea, Helena erected a large *sukkah* in Lydda for the Feast of Tabernacles, and it was frequented by the rabbis (Tosef. Suk. 1:1).

The allegiance of the Adiabenians to the Jewish State was again proved during the Roman War of 66–70 in which the royal family took an active part. Josephus comments that "in the Jewish ranks the most distinguished for valor were Monobaz and Cenedaeus, kinsmen of Monobaz, king of Adiabene" (Jos., Wars, 2:520).

By the late second century C.E., Judaism must have been firmly established in Adiabene. Christianity, which usually spread in existing Jewish communities, was accepted in Adiabene without difficulty.

BIBLIOGRAPHY: Jos., index; selected bibliography in *Josephus Works* (Loeb Classics edition), 9 (1965), 586; see also Neusner, Babylonia, 1 (1965), 58–64; Schalit, in: ASTI, 4 (1965), 171ff.

[Isaiah Gafni]

ADJIMAN, family in Constantinople. Some members held important positions at the court of Ottoman sultans in the 18th and early 19th centuries. Some Adjimans were purveyors and treasurers of the Janissaries and therefore were called by the titles *Ocak Bazergani* ("Merchant to the Corps") or *Ocak Sarrafi* ("Banker to the Corps"). The bazergans must have ranked among the most prominent figures in the Istanbul markets, conducting large-scale transactions. They were also known as philanthropists.

BARUCH ADJIMAN was the first rich man of the family in Istanbul. He settled in Jerusalem and died there in 1744. His two sons, Yeshaya Adjiman (d. 1751–2) and Eliya Adjiman, remained in Istanbul. His daughter was married to David Zonana.

ELIYA ADJIMAN was one of the wealthiest persons in the Jewish community and a philanthropist who helped Rabbi Ezra *Malkhi during his visit to Istanbul in 1755. His sons were Baruch, Abraham, and David Adjiman. He was *ocak bazergani* in 1770.

YESHAYA ADJIMAN died in 1751 or 1752 and like his brother was one of the wealthiest Jews in Istanbul. His sons were Baruch (first mentioned in 1755 and last information from 1791/2 or 1803) and Jacob, who is mentioned in the years 1755 and 1769/70.

BARUCH ADJIMAN was *ocak bazergani* from 1766–68 to 1782. It is not clear if he was the son of Eliya or of Yeshaya, as each had sons named Baruch. He was a wealthy man and a philanthropist in Istanbul. Jewish and Ottoman sources tell about his financial difficulties during the war between the Ottoman Empire and Russia (1768–74) and also in 1777. He left many debts. There is also a document from the year 1791/2 in which Baruch, son of Yeshaya Adjiman, signed his name as *Pakid Ereẓ Israel* in Istanbul.

Another YESHAYA ADJIMAN signed his name as *Pakid Yerushalayim* in Istanbul. There are documents which deal with his assistance in 1820 in building a hotel in Jaffa for pilgrims to the Jewish festivals. He was the last Jewish *ocak bazergani*, serving from c. 1820 until he was executed with Bekhor Isaac *Carmona in 1826. An elegy was written in their memory.

ABRAHAM ADJIMAN was appointed a member of parliament in Istanbul in 1877–78. He served as the head of the Jewish community in Istanbul in 1880 but, following a dispute in which he was involved, he ceased to occupy his office. The dispute was between Adjiman and Nissim bar Nathan, who declared that Adjiman had wished to do harm to the rabbis, wishing to control the meat tax, which the rabbis opposed. In response Adjiman did not pay the chief rabbi his salary.

BIBLIOGRAPHY: M. Franco, *Essai sur l'histoire des Israélites de l'Empire Ottoman* (1897), 134; A. Galanté, *Histoire des Juifs d'Istanbul*, 2 (1942), 58; *Yehudei ha-Mizraḥ be Ereẓ Yisrael*, 2 (1938), 28–29; Ben-Zvi, Ereẓ Yisrael, 677. **ADD. BIBLIOGRAPHY:** Rosanes, Togarmah, 5, 141–43, 416–17; Yaari, Sheluḥei, 663; H. Kayali, in: A. Levy (ed.), *The Jews of the Ottoman Empire* (1994), 509–17; A. Levy, in: *ibid.*, 427–28; idem, in: M. Rozen (ed.), *Yemei ha-Sahar* (1994), 257–61.

[Abraham Haim / Leah Bornstein-Makovetsky (2nd ed.)]

ADLER, family originally from *Frankfurt. There are different theories as to the origin of the family name. According to one, the early members of the family lived in a house bearing the sign of an eagle (Ger. *Adler*). The main branch, whose members were kohanim, i.e., of priestly stock, traced its descent to Simeon Kayyara (see **Halakhot Gedolot*), the presumed author of the *Yalkut Shimoni*. The first outstanding member of the family was the kabbalist Nathan B. Simeon *Adler (1741–1800), whose pedigree may be traced back to an earlier Nathan Adler of the beginning of the 18th century. MARCUS (MORDECHAI; d. 1843), served as *dayyan* in Frankfurt and subsequently for 25 years as rabbi of Hanover. He had six children, most noted of whom was Nathan Marcus *Adler (1803–1890) who became the chief rabbi of the Ashkenazi congregations of Great Britain in 1848. He was succeeded by his second son, Hermann Naphtali *Adler (1839–1911). Nathan Marcus' eldest son, MARCUS NATHAN ADLER (1837–1911), mathematician and educator, was active in England in Jewish communal life and published a critical edition and translation of the *Travels of Benjamin of Tudela* (1907, reprinted 1964); a half-brother Elkan Nathan *Adler (1861–1946), Nathan's youngest son, was an outstanding Hebrew bibliophile. Marcus Nathan's son HERBERT MARCUS (b. 1876), a lawyer, was director of Jewish education in London. Hermann's daughter NETTIE (1869–1950), a social worker and educator, wrote articles on child welfare.

A second Adler family, unconnected with the Frankfurt family (above), originated in Worms. The first known, ISAAC ADLER (d. 1823), served as rabbi in Worms from 1810. One of his sons, Samuel *Adler (1809–1891), was rabbi in New York. Samuel's son, Felix *Adler (1851–1933), was founder of the *Ethical Culture movement.

[Cecil Roth]

ADLER, U.S. theatrical family. The founder was JACOB ADLER (1855–1926), one of the leading Jewish actor-managers of his time, and a reformer of the early Yiddish theater. Born in Odessa, he first acted with amateurs, and in 1879 joined one

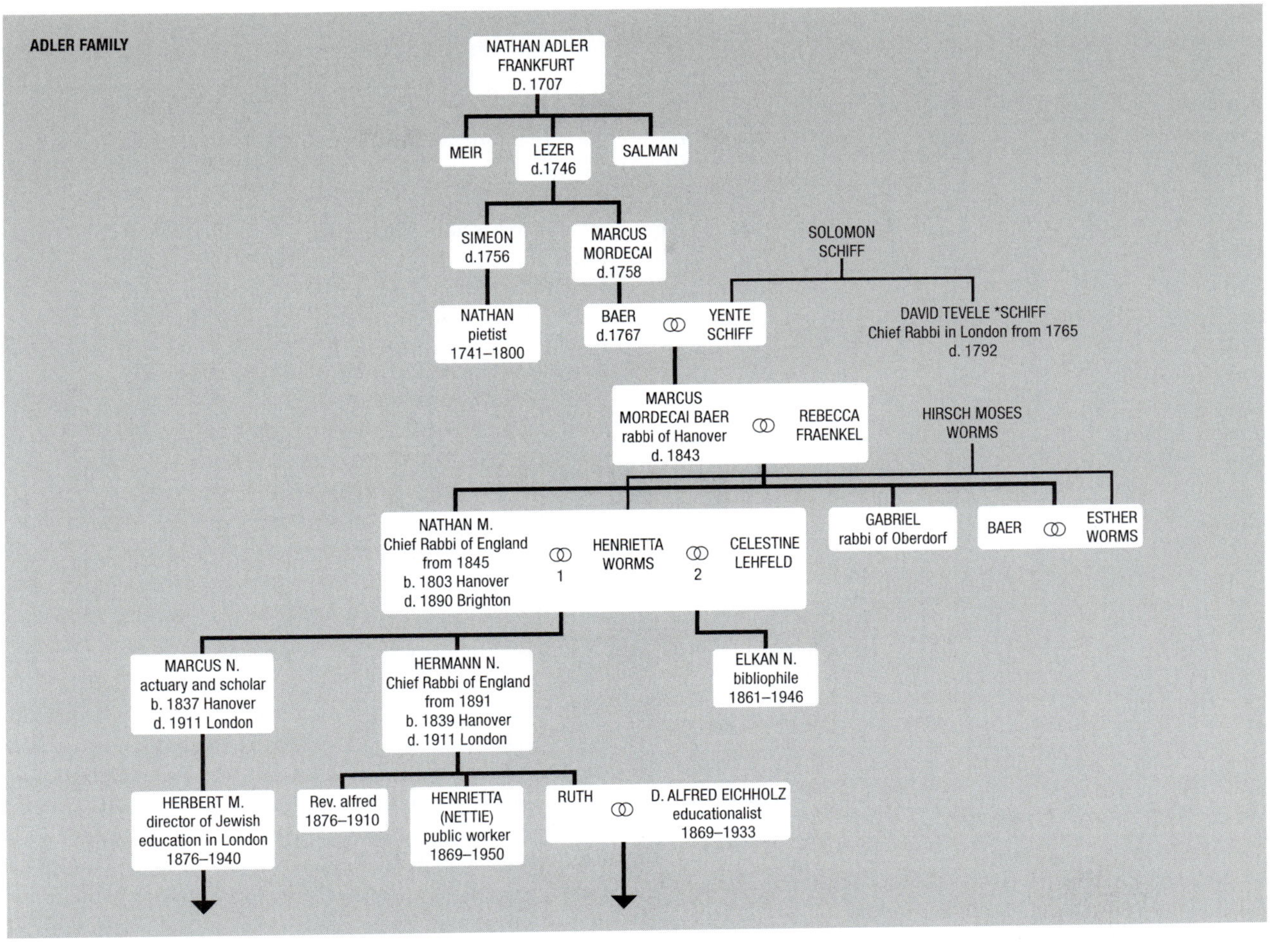

of Abraham *Goldfaden's touring companies. Good looks assured him early success in young-lover roles and he continued touring until the Czarist prohibition of Yiddish theater in 1883 forced him to leave Russia. In London, he appeared with his second wife, Dinah Lipna, in melodramas and in Gutzkow's *Uriel Acosta*. Success brought him invitations from New York, but he remained in London until disaster struck the Jewish Theater at the Prince's Club in January 1887 when a false cry of "Fire" caused a stampede and the death of 17 people. Arriving in the U.S., he found himself crowded out of New York and he could play only in Chicago. He returned to Europe on a tour which included Warsaw, Lodz, Lemberg, and London, and which made his reputation as a dynamic actor of striking personality. Returning to New York in 1890, he opened at Poole's Theater with a play that failed, but he quickly followed it with *Moshele Soldat* ("Soldier Moshele") which was an immediate success and made him an idol of the Yiddish theater.

As an actor, Adler was often criticized as stagy, but he could always captivate an audience and he displayed remarkable power in heroic roles. He was dissatisfied with the melodramas and operettas then in vogue, and looked for plays that gave him dramatic scope. He found them in the work of Jacob *Gordin, a serious writer whose plays other actors had rejected. The two produced Gordin's *Siberia* (1891) and inaugurated what has been called the "golden epoch" of the Yiddish theater. They followed this success with Gordin's *The Great Socialist, Der Yidisher King Lear,* and *Der Vilder Mensh*. In these productions, Adler achieved a triumph which was capped by his appearance as Shylock in Shakespeare's *The Merchant of Venice*, 1893, playing in Yiddish while the rest of the cast played in English.

In ensuing years, Adler controlled various theaters such as The People's and the Grand, where his children often performed with him. He interspersed serious plays with melodramas. After World War I, now almost a legendary figure, he went on brief tours, appeared in the film *Michael Strogoff*, and was portrayed in a Broadway play, *Cafe Crown*, which satirized his flamboyant way of life and his large family. Illness made his later appearances infrequent, but he never lost his glamour for the Jewish public. His memoirs, serialized in Yiddish in *Die Varheit*, mostly between 1916 and 1919, appeared for the first time in English in 1999 as *A Life on the Stage*. In it he describes his tempestuous actor's life in the Ukraine and the pogroms he barely escaped.

SARA ADLER (LEVITSKY; c. 1858–1953), Adler's third wife, played opposite her husband and became associated with his pioneering work. She appeared in hundreds of plays, most notably as Katusha Maslova in Gordin's adaptation of Leo Tolstoy's *Resurrection*, which established her reputation as a great star of the Yiddish stage. Her autobiography, *My Life*, was serialized in the Yiddish daily *Forward* (New York, 1937–39).

CELIA (1889–1979), daughter of Jacob Adler and Dinah Lipna, appeared at the age of nine with her father in *Der Yidisher King Lear*. In 1919 she joined Maurice *Schwartz's Yiddish Art Theater, directed her own repertory company, 1925–1926, with Samuel Goldenberg, and in 1937 appeared in the Yiddish film, *Vu iz Mayn Kind?* Of the children of Jacob and Sara Adler, FRANCES (1892–1964) toured America in Yiddish repertory. JULIA (1899–1995) played Jessica to her father's Shylock, following this with roles in Jacob Gordin's plays. Stella *Adler (1902–1992) acted on the English-speaking stage and became a founding member of the New York Group Theater and a renowned acting teacher. LUTHER (1903–1985) was a noted actor on the New York and London stage and in motion pictures. His successes included Ben Hecht's drama of Israel *A Flag is Born*, Clifford Odets' *Golden Boy*, and Arthur Miller's *A View From the Bridge*. He also played Tevye in *Fiddler on the Roof*, the musical based on stories by *Shalom Aleichem.

BIBLIOGRAPHY: B. Gorin, *Geshikhte fun Yidishen Teater*, 1 (1918); L. Kobrin, *Erinerungenfun a Yidishen Dramaturg*, 2 (1925). **ADD. BIBLIOGRAPHY:** L. Rosenfeld, *Bright Star of Exile: Jacob Adler and the Yiddish Theater* (1977, 1988^2).

ADLER, ALEXANDRE (1950–), French historian and journalist. After completing his studies in history, he specialized in the former Soviet Union and the Middle East and quickly became one of the most eminent French experts in geopolitics. A professor in higher military education on behalf of the French Ministry of Defense, Adler is mainly known for his contributions to newspapers, news magazines, and radio and television. He was the editorial director of the weekly *Courrier International* and a regular columnist for the conservative daily *Le Figaro*. In addition, he helped found *Proche-Orient Info*, a website devoted to Middle East affairs and committed to the fight against new forms of racism and antisemitism, and was appointed adviser to the chairman of the Representative Council of Jewish Institutions of France (CRIF). Adler published several books, among them *J'ai vu finir le monde ancien* (2002), an essay on the consequences of the terror attacks on the World Trade Center, and *L'Odyssée Américaine* (2004), a reflection on the evolution of American behavior in international affairs.

[Dror Franck Sullaper (2nd ed.)]

ADLER, ALFRED (1870–1937), Austrian psychiatrist. He was the founder of individual psychology, a theory of personality and method of psychotherapy based on the concepts of unity, self-determination, and future-orientation of man. His views were opposed to the elementaristic and mechanistic views of man which prevailed at that time. Born in Vienna, Adler qualified at the university there in 1895. After his marriage he adopted Protestantism, a small minority denomination in Austria at that time, considering it the most liberal religion. Adler's theories were set forth in such a manner as to be understandable and useful to a wide audience, including especially teachers and counselors. He himself established many child-guidance clinics. In 1902 Freud invited Adler to participate in his discussion group which had weekly meetings in Vienna. In 1910 Adler was elected the president of the Vienna Psychoanalytic Society, which grew out of the informal discussion group. In 1911 he resigned from the society as a consequence of his new theoretical views and established his own society and journal. From 1926 on Adler visited the United States regularly and eventually settled in New York where he was professor of medical psychology at the Long Island Medical College. He died while on a lecture tour in Scotland.

Primary in Adler's system is the conception that the organism, growing from a single cell, remains biologically and psychologically a unit. All partial processes such as drives, perception, memory, and dreaming are subordinated to the whole. Adler called this unitary process the individual's style of life. A unitary concept of man requires one overall motivating force. For Adler it is a striving to overcome and compensate for inferiorities directed toward a goal of superiority or success, which the individual creates quite uniquely. Though the goal may take on strange forms, it always includes maintenance of self-esteem. The individual, however, cannot be considered apart from society. The three important life problems, occupational, social, and sexual, are all actually social and require a well developed "social interest" for a successful solution. Thus the individual's goals will include social usefulness corresponding to the ideals of the community. Neurotic, psychotic, sociopathic, addictive, suicidal, and sexually deviant personalities are all failures in life because of an underdeveloped social interest and strong inferiority feelings. The role of the psychotherapist is to raise the patient's self-esteem through encouragement, illuminate his mistakes in lifestyle, and strengthen his social interest. In this way a cognitive reorganization is produced and the patient directed toward more socially useful behavior. Birth order (among siblings), dreams, and early recollections are used by the therapist in diagnosing the patient's lifestyle.

Interest in Adler's psychology increased with the gain in the humanistic conception of man, which he pioneered. Adlerian societies exist in numerous European countries, in the United States, where the *Journal of Individual Psychology* is published, and in Israel. A government supported Adlerian institute was established in Tel Aviv to train school psychologists, counselors, and teachers.

BIBLIOGRAPHY: H. and R. Ansbacher (eds.), *Individual Psychology of Alfred Adler; A Systematic Presentation in Selections from his Writings* (1956; paperback, 1964), including extensive bibliographies and indices. **ADD. BIBLIOGRAPHY:** T. Weiss-Rosmarin, in: *Individual Psychology*, 46 (1990), 108–18.

[Heinz L. Ansbacher]

ADLER, CHARLES (1899–1980), U.S engineer and inventor. A life-long resident of Baltimore, Maryland, Adler began his career as an inventor at 14, receiving a patent on an electric automotive brake. After attending Johns Hopkins University, he served briefly in the army during World War I and in 1919 became associated with the Maryland and Pennsylvania Railroad. In 1928 he developed and installed the first traffic-actuated signal light (actuated by the sound of a car horn). In 1937 he became a consultant to the Baltimore and Ohio Railroad, continuing to invent safety and signal devices for automobiles, trains, and aircraft. He was granted over 60 U.S. patents for devices in general use. He was a member of the Maryland Traffic Safety Commission from 1952 until his death.

[Bracha Rager (2nd ed.)]

ADLER, CYRUS (1863–1940), U.S. Jewish scholar and public worker. Adler was born in Van Buren, Arkansas, son of a cotton planter. In 1867, upon his father's death, Adler and his family moved to Philadelphia, where they lived with Mrs. Adler's brother, David Sulzberger. They were members of the Sephardi Congregation Mikveh Israel, and its atmosphere, together with the influence of Adler's uncle and his cousin, Mayer *Sulzberger, did much to shape Cyrus Adler's religious traditionalism and devotion to scholarship. Graduating from the University of Pennsylvania in 1883, Adler thereafter studied Assyriology under Paul *Haupt at Johns Hopkins University. He taught Semitics at the university, becoming assistant professor in 1890. Meanwhile, he had joined the Smithsonian Institution, and became librarian there in 1892. Two years before, he had been sent to the Orient as special commissioner of the Columbian Exposition.

Adler took part in the founding of the *Jewish Publication Society of America (1888), serving as chairman of its various committees throughout his life. He was responsible for the establishment of the Society's Hebrew press. Adler was also a founder of the *American Jewish Historical Society (1892), and its president for more than 20 years. He edited the first seven volumes of the *American Jewish Yearbook* (1899–1905; the last two vols. with H. Szold) and was a departmental editor of *The Jewish Encyclopedia* (1901–06).

Adler played an active role in reorganizing the *Jewish Theological Seminary of America under the presidency of Solomon *Schechter. He was president of the Board of Trustees from 1902 to 1905, dividing his time between the Seminary and the Smithsonian. When Schechter died, he became acting president (1915), taking office permanently in 1924. Adler maintained the academic standards set by Schechter, and was responsible for erecting the Seminary's new buildings. He was one of the founders of the *United Synagogue of America (1913) and served as its president. In 1908 Adler was elected president of *Dropsie College, conducting its affairs and those of the Seminary simultaneously. Together with Schechter he had taken over the editorship of the **Jewish Quarterly Review* (1910) on behalf of Dropsie College, and after Schechter's death served as sole editor (1916–40).

Adler was one of the founders of the *American Jewish Committee (1906). He became chairman of its executive board in 1915 and in 1919 represented the Committee at the Paris Peace Conference. Appointed president of the Committee in 1929, Adler, by then aging, had to face the bitterness of the economic depression, followed by the rise of Nazism. Adler frequently found himself in opposition to the leaders of American Zionism, but he took part in the *Jewish Agency for Palestine.

Adler's success lay in his ability to bridge worlds which early in the 20th century had little common ground. An observant Jew, knowledgeable in the field of Jewish scholarship, he was also familiar and respected in the world of American government and scholarship. Adler was a tireless worker and a scrupulous and constructive administrator. He was able to interpret the needs of traditional-minded Jews to the men of wealth in American Jewry. His style allowed little scope for public display of emotion, and this, combined with his aloofness from Zionism, limited his relations to those with whom he was closest in his observance of Judaism.

He wrote a *Descriptive Catalogue of a Collection of Objects of Jewish Ceremonial Deposited in the U.S. National Museum by Hadji Ephraim Benguiat* (1901), with index, *I Have Considered the Days* (1941), and *Lectures, Selected Papers, Addresses* (1933), which contains a bibliography of his writings and addresses.

BIBLIOGRAPHY: A.A. Neuman, in: AJYB, 42 (1940–41), 23–144; H. Stern, *The Spiritual Values of Life* (1953), 88–105; L. Lipsky, *A Gallery of Zionist Profiles* (1956), 208–13; H. Parzen, *Architect of Conservative Judaism* (1964), 79–127; Ben-Horin, in: AJHSQ, 46 (1966), 208–31.

[Sefton D. Temkin]

ADLER, DANKMAR (1844–1900), U.S. architect and engineer. Adler was born in Stadtlengsfeld, Germany, the son of Rabbi Liebmann Adler (1812–1892). He was taken to the U.S. at an early age and was trained at American universities. During the Civil War he practiced as an engineer and later built up a successful architectural practice in Chicago. In 1879 Louis Sullivan (1856–1924) joined the firm and in 1881 became a partner. Adler and Sullivan are credited with introducing a completely new concept of office architecture and this found its expression in the steel-framed skyscraper. Their first framed building (Chicago, 1887) was a commercial building called the Auditorium and was later acquired by Roosevelt University. Together they designed more than a hundred structures, including the transportation building at the Chicago Columbian Exposition in 1893, and two impressive skyscrapers: the Wainwright Building in St. Louis, Missouri, and the Prudential

Building in Buffalo, New York. They were responsible for the Kehillath Anshe Maariv in Chicago, where Adler's father had become rabbi in 1861. Here, too, they broke with tradition. Believing that form follows function, they made the facade of this synagogue secondary to the tall roof that covered the main body of the hall. The Adler-Sullivan partnership was dissolved in 1895 and neither architect did any distinguished work after that. It was in their office that Frank Lloyd Wright (1869–1959), one of America's greatest architects, was trained.

BIBLIOGRAPHY: H. Morrison, *Louis Sullivan* (1962²), 283–93; Roth, Art, 749–50.

ADLER, DAVID BARUCH (1826–1878), Danish banker and politician. The banking firm of D.B. Adler and Co., which Adler founded in 1850, promoted the establishment of an independent modern credit system in Denmark. He was among the founders of the Privatbank (1857), remaining a director until 1866, and helped to launch the Kjøbenhavns Handelsbank in 1873. He negotiated foreign loans on behalf of the government, and was a founder member of the Copenhagen Chamber of Commerce. Adler entered politics as a Liberal and Free Trader, and became a member of parliament, city councilor, and member of the Board of Representatives (*Repraesentantskabet*) of the Jewish community. He encouraged Danish art and industry, and gave generously to charity. One of his daughters was the educationalist Hanna Adler, and another, Ellen, was the mother of Niels *Bohr.

BIBLIOGRAPHY: *Dansk biografisk leksikon*, 1 (1933).

[Julius Margolinsky]

ADLER, ELKAN NATHAN (1861–1946), Anglo-Jewish bibliophile, collector, and author. Adler, the son of Chief Rabbi Nathan Marcus *Adler, was a lawyer by profession and had unusual opportunities to travel under favorable conditions and to build up a remarkable library. He was among the first persons to realize the importance of the Cairo *Genizah*. He visited Egypt in 1888 and 1895–96 and brought back approximately 25,000 fragments from the *Genizah*. His library ultimately included about 4,500 manuscripts of which he published a summary *Catalogue of Hebrew Manuscripts in the Collection of E.N. Adler* (1921). He also had a collection of some 30,000 printed books in Judaica and in general fields. In order to make good the embezzlements of a business associate he sold his library in 1923 to the Jewish Theological Seminary of America in New York and the duplicates of the printed books (including many incunabula) to the Hebrew Union College in Cincinnati, thus helping to raise both of these libraries to positions of significance. By an agreement made at that time, the manuscripts that he subsequently collected passed after his death to the Jewish Theological Seminary. Adler's published writings were mainly based on his travels and on materials in his own collection. Among them are *About Hebrew Manuscripts* (1905), a collection of bibliographical essays; *A Gazetteer of Hebrew Printing* (1917); *Jews in Many Lands* (1905); *Auto de Fé and Jew* (1908); *History of the Jews of London* (1930); *Jewish Travellers* (1930, repr. 1966); and articles on the Samaritans and on the Egyptian and Persian Jews. Adler played an active role in English-Jewish communal affairs, especially as regards educational and overseas matters, and was an early member of the Hovevei Zion in England. His personal archives are at the library of the Jewish Theological Seminary of America.

BIBLIOGRAPHY: *Essays… E.N. Adler* (JHSEM, 4–5 (1942–48), includes his bibliography); *Register of the Jewish Theological Seminary of America* (1923); JC (May 4, 1923, Sept. 20, 1946); *United Synagogue Recorder*, 3 (1923); E.C.R. Marmorstein, *Scholarly Life of E.N. Adler* (1962); M. Ettinghausen, *Rare Books and Royal Collections* (1966).

[Cecil Roth]

ADLER, ELMER (1884–1962), U.S. publisher and bibliophile. In 1922 Adler established Pynson Printers in New York City and began to produce books noted for excellent design and craftsmanship. A cofounder of Random House, he printed its first publication, a limited edition of Voltaire's *Candide* with illustrations by Rockwell Kent.

From 1930 to World War II, he published and edited the *Colophon*, a quarterly in book form for bibliophiles. A few issues appeared in 1948 as the *New Colophon*.

In 1940 Adler dissolved the Pynson Printers, presented his magnificent library of printing and printing history to Princeton University, joined its library staff, and organized a department of graphic arts. He retired from Princeton in 1952 and moved to San Juan, Puerto Rico. Here he built up another outstanding printing arts library and museum for the university.

[Israel Soifer]

ADLER, EMANUEL PHILIP (1872–1949), U.S. newspaper publisher, born in Chicago. He began his career in Iowa and rose to be president of Lee Syndicate Newspapers, controlling ten dailies in Iowa, Illinois, Nebraska, Missouri, and Wisconsin. He founded the Tri-City Federated Jewish Charities in 1921 and organized the Jewish Community Office to act for Jewish organizations in Davenport, Des Moines, and Sioux City, Iowa. His son, Philip David Adler, later publisher of the *Davenport Times*, issued a book about him (1932) written by A.M. Brayton.

ADLER, FELIX (1851–1933), U.S. philosopher and educator. Adler was born in Germany, the son of the Reform rabbi Samuel *Adler. He studied at Columbia University and preached as a rabbi at Temple Emanu-el in New York, but was too rationalistic to accept Judaism in any traditional sense. In 1874 he accepted a professorship in Hebrew and Oriental literature established at Cornell. Two years later he founded the Society for Ethical Culture, which advocated an ethic apart from any religion or dogma. The Society gained support mainly among intellectuals in America and abroad. Adler worked for various social causes such as maternal and child welfare, vocational training schools, medical care for the poor, labor problems, and civic reform. In 1883 he founded the first U.S. group for child study. Adler was appointed professor of social ethics at Columbia in 1902. His main writings include *Creed and Deed* (1877); *Moral Instruction of Children* (1892); *Prayer and Worship* (1894); *An Ethical Philosophy of Life* (1918), which is partly autobiographical; and *The Reconstruction of the Spiritual Ideal* (1924; The Hibbert Lectures). He was an editor of the *International Journal of Ethics.*

BIBLIOGRAPHY: H. Simonhoff, *Saga of American Jewry from 1865–1914* (1959), 178–85; H. Cohen, *They Builded Better Than They Knew* (1946), 32–40; H. Neumann, *Spokesmen for Ethical Religion* (1951), 3–62.

[Richard H. Popkin]

ADLER, FRIEDRICH (1878–1942), German designer of arts and crafts. Born in Laupheim, Southern Germany, Adler went to Munich to study at the Royal School for Applied Arts at the age of 16. In the world of Munich art nouveau Adler was especially influenced by the artist Hermann Obrist. In order to break with Wilhelminian traditions, Obrist propagated a reform concept of cultural policy and art related to the art nouveau movement. In 1902 Adler continued his studies at the newly founded Debschitz School in Munich, where he became a teacher in 1903. The aim of the school was to intensify the contact between artists and manufacturers in the applied arts. Adler taught the technique of working in stucco and of edifice sculpture. From 1907 to 1933 he taught at the Hamburg School for Applied Arts, where he was appointed professor in 1927. When he lost his position after the National Socialist takeover in 1933, Adler continued to offer private lessons to Jewish students. From 1935 he took an active part in the Hamburg Jewish Cultural Union (*Juedischer Kulturbund*). In July 1942 he was deported to Auschwitz and apparently murdered there in the same year. Adler's work was multifaceted and his creations and designs were shown in several exhibitions such as the International Exhibition for Modern and Decorative Arts in Turin (1902) and the world exposition in Brussels (1910). His principal fields of activity were handcrafted work and the design of furniture and metal objects especially made of tin. During the exhibition of the German *Werkbund* in Cologne in 1914 he met with universal approval for his concept of a synagogue building and for his Jewish ceremonial objects. The latter were fine silver objects in the style of art nouveau and were manufactured by the famous Heilbronn company for silverware Peter Bruckmann & Sons. Only a few of these ritual objects have survived, such as a magnificent Passover set made of silver, ivory, and glass from 1913/14 and an Eternal Light from the same year (both in the Spertus Museum, Chicago).

BIBLIOGRAPHY: *Spurensuche: Friedrich Adler zwischen Jugendstil und Art Déco* (Muenchner Stadtmuseum (Catalogue, 1994).

[Philipp Zschommler (2nd ed.)]

ADLER, FRIEDRICH (1879–1960), prominent figure in the Austrian labor movement and secretary of the Socialist International. The son of Victor *Adler, he was born in Vienna, studied physics in Switzerland, and lectured at Zurich University. Adler, who was baptized at the age of seven and later renounced Christianity, had no religion. Adler returned to Austria at the age of 32 and entered active political life. During World War I he attacked the policy of the Austrian government and criticized his own Socialist party for supporting it. In order to awaken the public conscience against the horrors of war he shot and killed Count Sturgkh, the prime minister, in a Vienna restaurant on October 21, 1916, and was sentenced to death. His sentence was commuted to 18 years imprisonment, and, under the amnesty which followed the fall of the monarchy in 1918, he was released. Adler was one of the founders of the left-wing International Working Union of Socialist Parties in 1921. From 1923 to 1939 he acted as secretary of the Labor and Socialist International. During World War II he lived in the United States but returned to Europe after the defeat of Germany. While he had many contacts with Zionist Socialists and although he had a Jewish marriage, he believed in assimilation and opposed Jewish national aspirations.

BIBLIOGRAPHY: J. Braunthal, *Victor und Friedrich Adler* (1965). **ADD. BIBLIOGRAPHY:** *Biographisches Handbuch der deutschsprachigen Emigration*, 1 (1980), 6–7, incl. bibl.; R. Ardelt, *Friedrich Adler. Probleme einer Persönlichkeitsentwicklung um die Jahrhundertwende* (1984).

[Robert Weltsch]

ADLER, GEORG (1863–1908), German economist and economic historian. Born in Posen, Adler taught at the universities of Berlin, Basle, and Kiel, and became professor of political economy at Freiburg. While in Basle, in 1894, he drafted the first law on workmen's unemployment insurance at the request of the Swiss government. He nevertheless considered the labor movement as necessary for social reform. A follower of the German historical school of economists, he advocated moderate socialism and bitterly opposed the revolutionary socialism of Karl *Marx. He remained a protagonist of social insurance and of international legislation for the protection of labor. His works include *Die Geschichte der ersten sozial-politischen Arbeiterbewegung in Deutschland* (1885); *Die Grundlagen der Karl Marx'schen Kritik der bestehenden Volkswirtschaft* (1887); and *Geschichte des Sozialismus und Kommunismus* (1899).

BIBLIOGRAPHY: NDB, 1 (1953), 69.

[Joachim O. Ronall]

ADLER, GUIDO (1855–1941), Austrian musicologist; one of the founders of modern musicology. Born at Eibenschitz (Moravia), he was appointed lecturer in musicology at Vienna University in 1881. He was a founder and editor of the *Vierteljahrsschrift fuer Musikwissenschaft* (1884–94) and in 1898 succeeded his former teacher, Eduard Hanslick, as professor of music history at Vienna, a position he held until his retirement in 1927. Adler made Vienna one of the leading centers of musicological training and research. The International Society of Musicology, founded upon his initiative, elected him its honorary president in 1927. He was editor-in-chief of *Denkmaeler der Tonkunst in Oesterreich*, which he had founded in 1894, but was removed from this position by the Nazis in 1938. He remained in Vienna until his death. His work contributed much to the development of musicological discipline. Important publications are his *Richard Wagner* (1904), *Gustav Mahler* (1916), and the *Handbuch der Musikgeschichte* (1924), which he edited.

BIBLIOGRAPHY: MGG, s.v.; P. Nettl, in: *Musica*, 15 (1961), 97, Ger.; *Guido Adler... Festschrift* (1930); Sendrey, Music, index.

[Judith Cohen]

ADLER, HARRY CLAY (1865–1940), U.S. newspaper executive. Adler was born in Philadelphia. He was chairman of the board and general manager of the *Chattanooga Times* from 1901, a paper owned by his brother-in-law, Adolph S. *Ochs, who later became publisher of the *New York Times*. When Ochs went to New York, Adler, already an executive on the paper, was appointed general manager, a position he held for 30 years. He served as chairman of the southern division of the Associated Press from 1917 to 1922, and was considered the "father" of Chattanooga's commission form of government. Adler used the editorial columns of his newspaper, and the Citizens' League which he organized, to campaign against the policies of the entrenched political machine until it was overthrown. He was active in charities and for three years was a president of the Mizpah Congregation in Chattanooga.

[Stewart Kampel (2nd ed.)]

ADLER, HERMANN (**Naphtali**; 1839–1911), British chief rabbi, son of Nathan Marcus *Adler. Born in Hanover, Hermann Adler was taken to London as a child, when his father became British chief rabbi, and was educated at University College School and at University College, London, where he graduated with a B.A. in 1854. Adler was thus one of the first British rabbis to receive a middle-class secular education in England. He continued his studies in Prague under Rabbi S.J. *Rappaport, where he was ordained as a rabbi in 1862. Adler went on to receive a doctoral degree from Leipzig University, his thesis being on (of all things) Druidism. In 1863 he became principal of *Jews' College, and in 1864 minister of Bayswater Synagogue in the West End of London. After 1879 he deputized as delegate chief rabbi for his father who was ill and was elected to succeed him in 1891. Adler followed and developed the tradition set by his father, combining Orthodoxy with organizational ability, as well as having a firm feeling for the dignity of his office. He was largely instrumental in securing general recognition of the chief rabbi as the main representative of English Jewry, taking his place alongside the heads of other religious communities on public occasions. Opposed to the ideas of Theodor *Herzl, in 1897 Adler termed political Zionism an "egregious blunder," although he had previously visited Palestine and been active in the Ḥovevei Zion movement. His period of office coincided with the great Russo-Jewish influx into the British Isles. This created a large "foreign" element in the community, whose confidence he did not gain. Despite periods of friction, Adler succeeded in maintaining his position as chief rabbi of Anglo-Jewry as a whole, the *Reform and *Sephardi communities being satisfied to be formally represented by him on public occasions. In the relatively small Anglo-Jewish community of the second half of the 19th century, with its integration into non-Jewish society and its painfully achieved balance, Adler saw a sort of self-contained "National Jewish Church," led on the lay side by the head of the Rothschild family and on the ecclesiastical by the Adlers, as the Jewish equivalent of the Anglican or Catholic hierarchy; Hermann Adler even imitated the Anglican episcopal garb. Hence they were seriously perturbed by the influx of Eastern European refugee immigrants from 1882 onward, which disturbed the delicate balance of the community. In politics, Adler was an avowed Tory and supported the Boer War. Adler published historical and other studies and numerous sermons, as well as preliminary studies for an edition of the *Eẓ Ḥayyim* by the 13th century scholar *Jacob b. Judah Ḥazzan of London. A selection of his sermons was published under the title *Anglo-Jewish Memories* (London, 1909). Adler's career is evidence of how comprehensively the acculturated section of Anglo-Jewry had adapted to Britain and had been accepted by its "Establishment."

BIBLIOGRAPHY: C. Roth, in: L. Jung (ed.), *Jewish Leaders, 1750–1940* (1953), 475–90; L.P. Gartner, *Jewish Immigrant in England, 1870–1914* (1960), 114–6, 209–10; Schischa, in: J.M. Shaftesley (ed.), *Remember the Days* (1966), 241–77; Roth, Mag Bibl, index; H.A. Simons, in: *Judaism*, 18 (1969), 223–31. **ADD. BIBLIOGRAPHY:** ODNB online; G. Alderman, *Modern British Jewry* (1992), index.

[Cecil Roth]

ADLER, HERMANN (pseudonym **Ẓevi Nesher**; 1911–), German-language poet, essayist, and playwright. Adler was born in Deutsch-Diószeg, near Pressburg (Bratislava), but grew up in Nuremberg and after graduating from a teachers' seminary at Wuerzburg taught in Landeshut (Kamienna Gora), Silesia. He returned to Czechoslovakia in 1934 and enlisted in 1939 in the Czechoslovak Legion in Poland. During World War II, he joined the Jewish resistance movement in Lithuania and Poland, playing an active part in the ghetto uprisings in Vilna and Warsaw. He escaped to Budapest, but was later deported to Bergen-Belsen, from which he was subsequently released, taking up residence in Switzerland, where he remained. His experiences of Nazi brutality on the one hand and of human dignity and heroism on the other were reflected in several gripping books, partly factual reporting, partly poetic crystallization, such as *Ostra Brama, Legende aus der Zeit des grossen Untergangs* (1945), Ostra Brama being the name of a Catholic monastery near Vilna where a number of Jews were hidden and rescued; *Gesänge aus der Stadt des Todes* (1945); *Ballade der Gekreuzigten, Auferstandenen, Verachteten* (1945).

Among other books which Adler wrote on the fate of the Jews during the Holocaust, and religious poetry, are *Fieberworte von Verdammnis und Erloesung* (1948) and *Bilder nach dem Buche der Verheissung* (1950). He frequently chose the medium of radio and television. One of his TV plays (which won a prize from the Zweites Deutsches Fernsehen) was *Feldwebel Anton Schmidt*, the story of a German sergeant who during the occupation of Vilna had helped Adler to organize the escape of Jews who joined up with the Jewish resistance movement elsewhere. Schmidt, who was subsequently arrested and sentenced to death by the Nazis, is also referred to in his *Ostra Brama*. The significance of Adler's descriptions of the Holocaust for Christian readers was stressed by the Swiss-Catholic historian and theologian Karl *Thieme in his epilogue to his selection from Adler's writings (*Vater … vergib! Gedichte aus dem Ghetto*, 1950).

Writing more often on psychological themes in later years, Adler published *Judentum und Psychotherapie* (1958) and *Handbuch der tiefenpsychologischen Symbolik: Ein Lexikon der Symbolik mit Lesetexten und Index* (1968). He also translated Itzhak *Katzenelson's Warsaw Ghetto epic *Dos Lid fun Oysgehargetn Yidishn Folk* from Yiddish into German (*Das Lied vom letzten Juden*, 1951). Of his own works, *Gesaenge aus der Stadt des Todes* appeared in Hebrew and Dutch translations.

BIBLIOGRAPHY: *Israelitisches Wochenblattfuer die Schweiz* (Oct. 8, 1971); D. Stern, *Werke jüdischer Autoren deutscher Sprache* (1967).

[Erich Gottgetreu]

ADLER, HUGO CHAIM (1894–1955), cantor and composer. Born in Antwerp, Adler served as a chorister to Yossele *Rosenblatt in Hamburg. He officiated as cantor in Mannheim, 1921–39, studied composition with Ernst *Toch, and was strongly influenced by the modern musical idiom. The *Juedisches Lehrhaus* of Franz *Rosenzweig in Frankfurt helped to shape his thoughts and he set to music some of Rosenzweig's Hebrew hymns. Adler adopted the idea of the musical *Lehrstueck*, an ethical-political cantata first realized by Brecht and Hindemith, and composed a Maccabean cantata *Licht und Volk* (performed in 1931) and *Balak und Bileam* (1934). The performance of his *Akedah* was prevented by the Kristallnacht pogrom of November 1938. After his escape to the U.S. he was appointed cantor in Worcester, Massachusetts. There he reshaped the music of the service and composed music for complete liturgies as well as many short pieces and the cantatas *Parable of Persecution* (1946), *Behold the Jew*, and *Jona* (1943). Adler's importance rests upon his skill in replacing 19th-century additions to synagogue song by a lucid contemporary idiom and striving, in his cantatas, for a collective musical expression of Jewish consciousness.

BIBLIOGRAPHY: Sendrey, Music, indexes; *American Hazan*, 2, no. 1 (1956); Fromm, in: *Jewish Music Notes* (Fall 1956), 3–4.

[Hanoch Avenary]

ADLER, ISRAEL (1925–), Israeli musicologist and librarian. Born in Berlin, Adler immigrated to Palestine in 1937 and studied at yeshivot. From 1949 to 1963 he studied in Paris with Solange Corbin at the Ecole Pratique des Hautes Etudes and J. Chailley at the Institut de Musicologie. In 1963 he took a doctorat de 3ème cycle with a dissertation on the music of Jewish communities in 17th- and 18th-century Europe. He was the head of the Hebraic Judaic Section of the Bibliothèque Nationale from 1950 to 1963. He returned to Israel in 1963, and became head of the music department of the Jewish National and University Library in Jerusalem. He founded and was director of the Jewish music research center at the Hebrew University from 1963 to 1969 and 1971 to 1994, and was chief editor of *Yuval*, the record of its studies. In 1964 he founded the National Sound Archives as part of the music department of the National Library and in 1967 he founded the Israel Musicological Society. From 1969 to 1971 Adler was director of the Jewish National and University Library. In 1971 he was appointed associate professor at Tel Aviv University and in 1973 he joined the Department of Musicology at the Hebrew University of Jerusalem. From 1967 he was a member of the RISM committee and vice president of the Association Internationale des Bibliothèques Musicales (1974–77). He was a guest lecturer at numerous European and North and South American universities. Among his publications are *La pratique musicale savante dans quelques communautés juives en Europe aux XVIIe et XVIIIe siècles*, 2 vols. (1966); *Musical Life and Traditions of the Portuguese Jewish Community of Amsterdam in the XVIIIth Century* (Jerusalem, 1974); *Hebrew Writings Concerning Music in Manuscripts and Printed Books from Geonic Times up to 1800*, RISM, B/IX/2 (1975); "Three Musical Ceremonies for Hoshana Rabba at Casale Monferrato (1732–1733, 1735)," in: *Yuval*, 5 (1986), 51–137; *Hebrew Notated Manuscript Sources up to circa 1840: A Descriptive and Thematic Catalogue, With a Checklist of Printed Sources* (Munich, 1989); *The Study of Jewish Music: A Bibliographical Guide* (Jerusalem, 1995).

BIBLIOGRAPHY: Grove online; MGG².

[Gila Flam (2nd ed.)]

ADLER, JACOB (1872?–1974), Yiddish poet and humorist, often writing as **B. Kovner**. Adler was born in Dinov, Austria-Hungary (now Dynow, Poland), but in 1894 immigrated to the United States where he worked in sweatshops, agitated for socialism, and wrote nostalgic poems about the "old country" for various journals, especially his mentor David Pinski's *Der Arbeter*. These poems were collected in his first volume, *Zikhroynes fun Mayn Haym* ("Memories of My Home," 1907), with an introduction by Pinski. They are full of nostalgia for the Jewish milieu of his childhood, which he views as carefree and idyllic, despite its poverty: the festive Sabbaths and holidays, spent in the sweet comfort of the synagogue; the pure yearnings of first love; the final, sad parting from family and birthplace. The volume ends with a lament for himself, sick and weak though young, his life ebbing away in an alien land. He sought relief from the misery of existence in sardonic humor, contributing under various pseudonyms to the popular humorous periodicals *Der Groyse Kundes* and *Der Kibetser*, and co-editing *Der Yidisher Gazlen* with Moyshe Nadir. In 1911, Abraham Cahan, editor of *Forverts*, invited him to join his staff and assigned him the pseudonym of B. Kovner, thus enabling him to exchange a former pseudonym "Der Galitsiyaner" for a new identity as a "Litvak." Kovner's humorous feuilletons immediately became a success and his characters, such as the shrewish busybody Yente Telebende, her henpecked husband Mendl, Moyshe Kapoyer, and Peyshe the Farmer soon became household names in American Yiddish homes. His anecdotes and witticisms circulated widely. His characters inspired many songs and stage routines. Many of Adler's humorous sketches were collected in six Yiddish volumes between 1914 and 1933 and two in English translation (*Laugh, Jew, Laugh*, 1936, and *Cheerful Moments*, 1940). His *Lider* ("Poems," 2 vols., 1924), which appeared at the height of his fame, revealed the sadness and loneliness of the humorist. These poems were grouped into cycles with such titles as "Alone" and "Between Gray Walls." Even the few poems designated as humorous were bitterly satiric. He continued to write prolifically until his late nineties.

BIBLIOGRAPHY: Rejzen, *Leksikon*, 1 (1928), 42–44; LNYL, 1 (1956), 24f.; M. Nadir, *Teg fun Mayne Teg* (1935), 220–273; H. Rogoff, *Der Gayst fun "Forverts"* (1954), 257–259.

[Sol Liptzin / Ben Furnish (2nd ed.)]

ADLER, JANKEL (**Jacob**; 1895–1949), painter, graphic artist, and art critic. Adler was born in Tuszyn, near Łodz. As a child, he received a traditional Jewish education. In 1912, living with his uncle in Belgrade, he worked in the post office and studied to become an etcher. In 1913, he moved to Germany and settled in Barmen (now Wuppertal), where he was employed as a textile worker and shop assistant. From 1916, he attended the local school of applied arts (Kunstgewerbschule), where his tutor was Gustav Wiethuechter. In 1917–18, Adler got to know many young German intellectuals, writers, and modernist artists and became close to the "Das Junge Rheinland" artistic group, who were seeking ways for a renewal of German art. While interested in modernist trends in European culture and establishing ties within the German artistic community, Adler never lost touch with his national roots. His works, starting from the earliest ones, always treated Jewish themes quite distinctly. By way of example, his still-lifes of this period incorporate images of Jewish ritual objects bearing symbolic significance. In 1918, Adler returned to Poland. Together with other young Jewish artists, he took part in the exhibition arranged by the Artistic Society of Łodz. His desire to express national self-awareness in contemporary art forms brought him close to young Jewish artists in Łodz who were pursuing the same goal. This circle formed "Yung Yiddish," a group that brought together Yiddish writers and modernist artists. Adler was among its founders; he took an active part in its performances and published his poems and etchings in its anthologies. In 1919, he displayed his works at the Jewish Kultur-Liga exhibition in Białystok. His works of this period are executed in an expressionist style incorporating elements of cubism and are characterized by ecstatic pathos and use of Jewish mystic symbols (as in *My Parents*, 1919; Muzeum Sztuki, Łodz). In 1920, Adler returned to Germany and for some time resided in Berlin, where he established close contacts both with German radical avant-garde artists and Jewish artistic circles, among them Marc *Chagall, Elsa Lasker-Schueler, and Henryk *Berlewi, with whom he collaborated. Later, Adler returned to Barmen and in 1920–21 participated in events organized by Dadaist and other avant-garde groups from Duesseldorf and Cologne. He continued maintaining close contacts with Poland and the Jewish modernist artistic movement there. He illustrated two collections of Yiddish poetry published in Łodz in 1921, one of them being *Peril oifn brik* by Moshe *Broderzon, the founder and artistic standard-bearer of the "Yung Yiddish" group. At the International Artistic Exhibition in Duesseldorf, he represented Polish artists. Together with Berlewi, he represented East European Jewish artists and was active in organizing the Congress of the Union of Progressive International Artists (Duesseldorf, May 29–31, 1922) and signing the Union's manifesto. He showed his works at the International Exhibition of Revolutionary Artists in Berlin. In 1922, Adler joined the "Das Junge Rheinland" group and from 1923 participated in "Novembergruppe" exhibitions. After "Das Junge Rheinland" split, Adler became the leader of the "Rheinland" group. In 1924, he took part in the First General German Art Exhibition in the U.S.S.R. He executed monumental murals for the Duesseldorf Planetarium in 1925–26. In the late 1920s, Adler frequently visited Poland, where several of his solo exhibitions took place. Being a prominent figure in German avant-garde art, he unambiguously called himself a "Jewish artist" in his interviews to the Polish and German press. In his publications and statements of the 1920s and 1930s, Adler formulated his own idea of "contemporary Jewish art," which, in his view, should express the striving for "creating new forms" which he believed to be inherent in Judaism and connected to ḥasidic humanistic mysticism. During the 1920s and the early 1930s, his individual artistic manner crystallized, organically combining elements of cubism, primitivism, expressionism, and "Neue Sachlichkeit." At the same time, he often incorporated images of Jews, Jewish inscriptions, and kabbalistic symbols into his compositions. In 1933, when the Nazis came to power in Germany, Adler moved to France. In 1935–37 he lived in Poland and had two solo exhibitions in Warsaw and Łodz. In 1937, Adler's works were withdrawn from German museums as embodiments of "degenerate art." Several of them were shown at "Entartete Kunst" and "Der ewige Jude." In 1937, Adler moved to France; when the country was occupied by Germans in 1940, he fled to the south where he joined the Polish Army. After the Battle of Dunkirk, he was evacuated together with other Polish soldiers to Glasgow, Scotland, and was discharged due to poor health. From 1941, he lived in London, where he was among the initiators of artistic events presenting artists who had fled continental Europe. In addition, he was active in the Ohel club in London, where Jewish intellectuals and artists congregated. Adler's works from the mid-1930s and especially in the 1940s are characterized by a complete rejection of figurative manner and transition to symbolic abstraction. A number of his works created in this period treated "Jewish themes" and reflect his understanding of the Holocaust (as in *Two Rabbis*, 1942; Museum of Modern Art, New York). In 1946–47, Adler's solo exhibitions were on display in London, Dublin, Paris, an d New York.

BIBLIOGRAPHY: S.W. Hayter, *Jankel Adler* (1948); Y. Sandel, *Plastishe kunst bei Poilishe Yiden* (1964), 146–55; A. Klapheck, *Jankel Adler* (1966); *Jankel Adler 1895–1949*, Catalogue (Koeln, 1985); J. Malinowski, *Grupa "Jung Idysz" i żidowskie środowisko "Nowej Sztuki" w Polsce. 1918–1923* (1987); idem, *Malarstwo i rzeźba Żydow Polskich w XIX i XX wieku* (2000), 159–62, 164–68, 170–72, 175–80.

[Hillel Kozovsky (2nd ed.)]

ADLER, JOSEPH (1878–1938), U.S. rabbi, scholar, and educationist. Adler was born in Kletzk, Lithuania, and immigrated to America in 1909 after failing in the wood-product industry. His extensive religious education – including stints in yeshivot in Nesvizh, Minsk, Mir, Slobodka, Kovno, and Aishishok as well as rabbinical ordination – probably provided him with little preparation for the cutthroat lumber business, but served him well in the New World. His studies were not confined solely to religious subjects, as he also acquired a familiarity with Russian and Hebrew literature. After arriving in New York City, Adler served as rabbi in a succession of Orthodox synagogues. He joined the Agudat ha-Rabbonim, an organization whose membership was limited to European-trained rabbis. Adler was also active in the religious Zionist movement, directing the Downtown Keren ha-Yesod and becoming an office bearer in the Mizrachi Organization of America. Concerned with the religious laxity of many of his fellow immigrants, he became one of the organizers of the Jewish Sabbath Alliance, an initiative aimed at fostering Sabbath observance within the New York Jewish community. Similar motives most likely inspired his participation in the development of the system of Orthodox religious education. Adler was appointed in 1923 by Shraga Feivel *Mendlowitz, a pioneer of religious day school education in America, as a Talmud teacher at Yeshivah Torah ve-Da'at in Brooklyn. While the school and its later imitators maintained a traditional focus and approach to textual study, Mendlowitz sought to produce a generation of religiously educated American Jews, not train future religious functionaries. In 1931, Adler became the Talmud teacher and principal of Mesivta Tipheret Jerusalem, a yeshivah on the Lower East Side for young men who wanted to combine yeshivah studies during the daytime with evening university classes. This yeshivah was part of an expanding network of religious schools that were established in the interwar and postwar periods by a resurgent Orthodox movement. He held this position until his death.

BIBLIOGRAPHY: *American Jewish Year Book*, 41 (1939–1940); J. Sarna, *American Judaism: A History* (2004); M. Sherman, *Orthodox Judaism in America: A Biographical Dictionary and Sourcebook* (1996); *Who's Who in American Jewry* (1926).

[Adam Mendelsohn (2nd ed.)]

ADLER, JULES (1865–1952), French artist. A prolific painter of landscapes, Adler was better known for his urban and industrial scenes such as *The Strike*, *The Factory Interior*, and *Towing the Barge*. These works reveal his socialist outlook and his keen interest in social problems. Adler was regarded as a leading member of the realist school of painting. His son Jean (1899–1944), a painter of promise and integrity, was killed by the Nazis.

BIBLIOGRAPHY: Roth, Art, 581–2.

[Edouard Roditi]

ADLER, JULIUS OCHS (1892–1955), U.S. newspaperman and soldier. Adler was born in Chattanooga, Tenn. He graduated from Princeton University and then joined the staff of the *New York Times*, published by his uncle, Adolph *Ochs. At the same time he enrolled as a citizen-soldier. Before World War I he was in the cavalry, but he transferred to the infantry on the outbreak of war. Adler was gassed while commanding a battalion on the Western Front. During World War II he commanded the 77th Infantry Division which was responsible for the defense of the Hawaiian Islands from 1941 to 1944. In 1948 he was promoted to major-general in the reserve. Meanwhile, Adler became vice president of the *New York Times*, and after a number of years he became the paper's general manager (1935). He was also publisher of the *Chattanooga Times*. In 1945 Adler was one of 17 newspaper executives invited by General Eisenhower to visit the liberated concentration camps and he wrote a series of moving and dramatic articles on them for the *New York Times*. In 1954 he was appointed chairman of the National Security Training Commission, and later headed a commission supervising the building of a combat-ready reserve through a modified form of universal military training.

BIBLIOGRAPHY: E. Rubin, *140 Jewish Marshals, Generals and Admirals* (1952), 287; J. Ben Hirsch, *Jewish General Officers*, 1 (1967), 91; *New York Times* (Oct. 4–7, 1955).

[Irving Rosenthal]

ADLER, LARRY (1914–2001), harmonica (mouth organ) player. Born in Baltimore, Adler won the Maryland Harmonica Championship at the age of 13. He first performed in revues and films, developing the technique of the 12-hole chromatic harmonica. He worked in England from 1934 to 1939, with many prominent jazz musicians. In 1939 he made his debut as a concert soloist with the Sydney Symphony Orchestra. In 1940, determined to read music, he studied with Ernst Toch.

During World War II Adler joined the dancer Paul Draper touring for U.S. organizations abroad. On his return to the U.S. in 1959, he embarked on a career as a concert performer appearing as a soloist with leading symphony orchestras. Adler was acknowledged as the first harmonica player who elevated the instrument to concert status. His repertoire included arrangements of classical works, and famous composers wrote for him such as Darius *Milhaud, R. Vaughan Williams, Gordon Jacob, and Malcolm Arnold. Adler toured extensively and broadcast frequently on radio and television. He appeared in films and composed scores for the cinema, such as *Genevieve* and *A High Wind in Jamaica.*

In 1988 Adler was made a fellow of Yale University. His CD *The Glory of Gershwin* earned him a place in the Guinness Book of Records as the oldest artist to reach the British pop charts. He also recorded as a pianist and singer and published several books, including *How I Play* (1936), *Harmonica Favorites* (1944), the autobiography *It Ain't Necessarily So* (1984), and *Have I Ever Told You* (2001).

BIBLIOGRAPHY: Grove online, s.v.; *Baker's Biographical Dictionary* (1997).

[Naama Ramot (2nd ed.)]

ADLER, LAZARUS LEVI (1810–1886), German rabbi and pedagogue. Adler's education included intensive Talmud study in Gelnhausen (Hesse-Nassau) and Wuerzburg and secular studies culminating in a doctorate from the University of Erlangen in 1833. In 1852 Adler became district rabbi of the province of Hesse-Kassel and retained this post until his retirement to Wiesbaden in 1883. Adler represented the more conservative branch of the Reform movement in Germany. While a consistent advocate of religious and educational progress, he opposed measures, such as the abolition of circumcision, which he felt would create an unbridgeable gulf between factions of the Jewish community. He was president of the Kassel rabbinical conference (1868) and an important participant in the German-Jewish synods of Leipzig (1869) and Augsburg (1871). From 1837 to 1839 Adler published *Die Synagoge*, a periodical containing sermons, popular historical studies, and essays dealing with contemporary Jewish issues. His final religious position is presented in *Hillel und Schamai* (1878).

BIBLIOGRAPHY: M. Kayserling (ed.), *Bibliothek juedischer Kanzelredner*, 2 (1870), 222–5.

[Michael A. Meyer]

ADLER, LIEBMAN (1812–1892), U.S. rabbi. Born in the town of Lengsfeld in the Grand Duchy of Saxe-Weimar, Adler received his education at the Jewish high school in Frankfurt and later trained at the teachers' seminary in Weimar. He taught at the synagogue school in Lengsfeld until 1854, immigrating to America in his early forties. Adler served as rabbi at Temple Bethel in Detroit before assuming the pulpit of Kehillath Anshe Maarabh in Chicago in 1861. His arrival coincided with a period of dissension within the German congregation over the introduction of liturgical reforms. A self-styled "orthodox reformer," Adler proved to be a perfect fit for the divided congregation, able to act as a mediator between the younger reform-minded generation and older traditionalist immigrants. Under his stewardship, the synagogue gradually adopted reformist innovations. Adler served the congregation for over 20 years, earning the adoration of its membership. He delivered sermons in German until 1872, when the congregation hired a minister able to preach in English. During the Civil War, he spoke out forcefully against slavery. Adler was a regular contributor to the German-language Jewish press in America. He also published three volumes of sermons in German. The Jewish Publication Society printed a collection of his sermons in translation in 1893.

BIBLIOGRAPHY: L. Adler, *Sabbath Hours* (1893); CCAR *Yearbook* (1912), 293–95; M. Gutstein, *A Priceless Heritage: The Epic Growth of Nineteenth Century Chicago Jewry* (1953), 101–4; B. Felsenthal and H. Eliassof, *History of Kehillath Anshe Maarabh* (1897), 40–45; J. Sarna, *JPS: The Americanization of Jewish Culture, 1888–1988* (1989), 43.

[Adam Mendelsohn (2nd ed.)]

ADLER, MAX (1866–1952), U.S. merchant-executive, musician, and philanthropist, who provided the money for America's first planetarium. Born in Elgin, Illinois, Adler as a child revealed remarkable talent for the violin. After receiving instruction in Elgin and Chicago, he was sent in 1884 to study at the Royal Conservatory in Berlin. Upon his return to the United States in 1888, he joined Boston's Mendelssohn Quintet as violinist and manager. In 1897, in response to the invitation of his brother-in-law, Julius *Rosenwald, president of Sears, Roebuck and Company, Adler left the concert platform to supervise the firm's music department. He rose rapidly to a vice presidency and membership on the board of directors. His enthusiasm for music never waned, and among his many philanthropic acts was the assistance he gave promising young musicians. His principal philanthropy was his gift to Chicago in 1930 of the Adler Planetarium and Astronomical Museum.

BIBLIOGRAPHY: P.D. Bregstone, *Chicago and its Jews* (1933); H.J. Smith, *Chicago's Great Century, 1833–1933* (1933).

[Morton Mayer Berman]

ADLER, MAX (1873–1937), Austrian socialist theoretician. Adler studied law at the university of his native Vienna, where he was professor of sociology from 1920. He joined the socialist movement in his youth and was a Social-Democratic deputy in the Austrian parliament for more than twenty years.

In his first major work, *Kausalitaet und Teleologie im Streite um die Wissenschaft* (1904), as well as in such later writings as *Das Soziologische in Kants Erkenntnis-Kritik* (1924) and *Kant und der Marxismus* (1925), he considers society and social phenomena not only as products of social interaction, but also as *a priori* concepts of the human mind. The social nature of consciousness brings about actual sociation and societal development. Using this theory as a basis, he formulated a dynamic proletarian (as opposed to a static bourgeois) sociology, and epistemologically clarified the materialistic conception of history. He attempted to fortify the dialectic elements in Marxism with the principles of idealistic philosophy. These ideas are worked out in *Marxistische Probleme* (1913), *Wegweiser-Studien zur Geistegeschichte des Sozialismus* (1914), *Die Staalsauffassung des Marxismus* (1922), *Marx als Denker* (2nd ed. 1925), *Lehrbuch der materialistisehen Geschichtsauffassung* (1930–32), and *Das Raetsel der Gesellschaft* (1936). His book *Neue Menschen* (1926) was translated into Hebrew under the title *Anshei ha-Maḥteret* (1931).

Adler's combination of philosophical idealism and socioeconomic realism led him to a deterministic interpretation of Marxism and to revisionism in socialist politics. He warned that the ruling classes would be likely to abandon parliamentary democracy as soon as class antagonisms became intensified and that a revolutionary posture of the unified Socialist movement was therefore necessary. This position is clarified in his book *Politische oder soziale Demokratie* (1926).

BIBLIOGRAPHY: Blum, in: *Archiv fuer die Geschichte des Sozialismus und der Arbeiterbewegung*, 8 (1919), 177–247; Hort, in: *Archiv fuer Geschichte der Philosophie und Soziologie*. 38 (1928), 243–58; Fogarasi, in: *Unter dem Banner des Marxismus*, 6 (1932), 214–31; Braunthal, in: *Der Kampf* (Wien), 26 (1933), 7–13; Franzel, in: *Der Kampf* (Prag), 4 (1937), 291–7; NDB, 1 (1953), 71–2.

[Werner J. Cahnman]

ADLER, MICHAEL (1868–1944), English minister and historian. Born into an immigrant Russian-Jewish family, he later adopted the name Adler. In 1890 he was appointed minister of the newly founded Hammersmith Synagogue in London and was for many years minister of the Central Synagogue. In World War I he served as senior Jewish chaplain to the armed forces, receiving a medal for his efforts. He was also chairman of the Jewish Central Lads' Brigade. He published, mainly in the *Transactions of the Jewish Historical Society of England* (of which he was president, 1934–36), a number of fundamental essays on the history of the Jews in England in the Middle Ages, based largely on documentary sources. Many of these were republished in his *The Jews of Medieval England* (1939). He also published two Hebrew grammars and edited *British Jewry, Book of Honour* (1922) on the service of the English Jews in World War I.

BIBLIOGRAPHY: JHSET, 15 (1946), 191–4; M. Adler, *History of the Hammersmith Synagogue* (1950), 9–13 (memoir by A. Barnett); *The Times* (Oct. 2, 1944); JC (Oct. 6, 1944).

[Cecil Roth]

ADLER, MORITZ (1826–1902), Hungarian painter. Born in Budapest, Adler studied in Munich and in Paris. On his return to Hungary, he settled in Budapest. Adler's reputation was created with his painting *Memento Mori* (1852). A meticulous artist, he was popular as a painter of genre and still life, and made portraits of many eminent Hungarians of his time. His *Apotheosis of Baron Joseph Eötvös* pays tribute to this champion of the emancipation of Hungary's Jews.

ADLER, MORRIS (1906–1966), U.S. Conservative rabbi. Adler, son of a rabbi, was born in Slutzk, Russia, and was brought to the U.S. in 1913. After serving in Buffalo, N.Y., Rabbi Adler accepted the pulpit of Shaare Zedek in Detroit, Mich. (1938), where, except for his chaplaincy (1943–46), he remained for the rest of his life. Under Rabbi Adler's leadership the congregation grew into one of the largest in the world, and he was considered by many to be the leading spokesman of the Detroit Jewish community. He was especially devoted to the field of adult Jewish education, on which he lectured and wrote extensively. A friend of labor leader Walter Reuther, Rabbi Adler served as chairman of the Public Review Board of the United Auto Workers (1957–66) and was a member of the Michigan Fair Election Practices Commission and the Labor-Management Citizens' Committee. He was a member of the Governor's Commission on Higher Education (1963–66). Positions he held in the Jewish world included chairmanship of the B'nai B'rith Adult Jewish Education Commission (1963–66) and various offices in the Rabbinical Assembly. He wrote *Great Passages from the Torah* (1947) for adult Jewish study, and *World of the Talmud* (1958). He also edited the *Jewish Heritage Reader* (with Lily Edelman, 1965).

He was killed during Sabbath services in his synagogue by a mentally ill youth. The day of his funeral was declared by Governor George Romney a day of mourning in the state of Michigan. A collection of his writings, compiled by his widow Goldie Adler and Lily Edelman, *May I Have a Word With You*, appeared in 1967. A second posthumous volume, *The Voice Still Speaks: Message of Torah for Contemporary Man* (ed. Jacob Chinitz), appeared in 1969.

[Alvin Kass]

ADLER, MORTIMER JEROME (1902–2001), U.S. philosopher and educator. Born in New York, Adler studied and later taught psychology at Columbia. From 1927 to 1929 he was assistant director of the People's Institute in New York. In 1930, he was appointed associate professor of philosophy of law at the University of Chicago (full professor in 1942), where he was active in curriculum reform. In 1952 he became director of the Institute for Philosophical Research in Chicago. Adler opposed John Dewey's influence in education, and advocated studying the great books of the Western tradition. While he continued his educational reforms on a more conservative basis, the concept of seminars on "great books" and "great ideas" continued to become integrated into programs at other educational institutions. In 1952, his work in this area culminated in the publication of the *Great Books of the Western World* by the Encyclopaedia Britannica company in 54 volumes (1945–52), with R.M. Hutchins.

Adler helped found the Institute for Philosophical Research and the Aspen Institute. He taught business leaders the classics at the Aspen Institute for more than 40 years. He was also on the board of the Ford Foundation and the Board of Editors of the *Encyclopaedia Britannica*, where his influence was clearly felt in its policies and programs. He was also the co-founder, along with Max Weismann, of the Center for the Study of Great Ideas.

In 1977, Adler published an autobiography entitled *Philosopher at Large*, which was later followed by another account entitled *A Second Look in the Rearview Mirror: Further Autobiographical Reflections of a Philosopher at Large* (1992). He spent a lifetime making philosophy's greatest texts accessible to everyone. Throughout his teaching career, he remained devoted to helping those outside academia educate themselves further. According to Adler, no one, no matter how old, should stop learning. He wrote more than 20 books after the age of 70, and at the age of 95 was working on his 60th, *The New Technology: Servant or Master?*

Adler's main works include *Art and Prudence* (1937); *St. Thomas and the Gentiles* (1938); *How to Read a Book* (1940); *A Dialectic of Morals* (1941); *The Capitalist Manifesto* (with L. Kelso, 1958); *Great Ideas from the Great Books* (1961); *The Conditions of Philosophy* (1966); *The Difference of Man and the Difference It Makes* (1968); *Reforming Education: The Opening of the American Mind* (1977); *The Time of Our Lives: Ethics of Common Sense* (1970); *Aristotle for Everybody: Difficult Thought Made Easy* (1980); *The Paideia Proposal: An Educational Manifesto* (1982); *The Angels and Us* (1982); *Six Great Ideas* (1984); *A Vision of the Future: Twelve Ideas for a Better Life and a Better Society* (1984); *Ten Philosophical Mistakes* (1985); *How to Speak / How to Listen* (1985); *A Guidebook to Learning: For a Lifelong Pursuit of Wisdom* (1986); *Truth in Religion: The Plurality of Religions and the Unity of Truth* (1990); *How to Think about God: A Guide for the 20th-Century Pagan* (1991); *Desires, Right & Wrong: The Ethics of Enough* (1991); and *Adler's Philosophical Dictionary: 125 Key Terms for the Philosopher's Lexicon* (1995).

A self-described pagan for most of his life, Adler converted to Christianity in 1984 and was baptized by an Episcopalian priest. In 1999, he converted to Roman Catholicism.

[Richard H. Popkin / Ruth Beloff (2nd ed.)]

ADLER, NATHAN BEN SIMEON HA-KOHEN (1741–1800), German rabbi. Born into a distinguished family in Frankfurt, Adler was a student of Tevele David *Schiff, and became known as an "*illui*" (an extraordinarily talented student of Talmud). In addition to talmudic subjects, he studied the natural sciences and Hebrew and Aramaic grammar. At the age of 20 he had achieved a reputation for his scholarship and piety. He founded a yeshivah which drew students from many cities. His students included Seckel Loeb *Wormser, Mendel *Kargau, and Moses *Sofer. Adler was especially attracted to practical Kabbalah. He gathered a congregation in his home and conducted the services from the prayer book of Isaac *Luria, employing the Sephardi pronunciation he had learned from R. Ḥayyim Modai of Jerusalem who had been his houseguest for several years. Adler even had the priestly blessing recited daily, and departed from accepted practices in other particulars. He was especially stringent in regard to laws relating to ritual slaughter and the dietary laws. Although he was careful not to cite the Zohar or to canvass disciples for his views, there was considerable friction between his followers and the community leaders. Nevertheless, his profound learning and impeccable conduct were universally acknowledged. In 1779, his followers excommunicated one of the members of the Frankfurt community. Adler was summoned to the *bet din* to account for this presumptuous act. He refused to appear, and in consequence a resolution was passed and proclaimed in the synagogues, forbidding him to conduct services in his house, forbidding any member of the community from participating in these services, and threatening transgressors with excommunication. Adler ignored the order, whereupon a statement was issued by the rabbis and communal leaders of Frankfurt, signed by Phinehas *Horowitz. It threatened to place Adler under a ban which would prevent him from fulfilling any rabbinic functions and withdraw his right to decide on religious matters. The decision was referred to the civil authorities and approved by them, and Adler was obliged to submit. A temporary truce resulted when Adler was invited to accept the post of rabbi of Boskowitz in Moravia (1782). His devoted follower, Moses Sofer, decided not to abandon his master, and Adler encouraged him to accompany him. Eighteen years later, in his eulogy on Adler, Sofer declared, "I ran after him for 100 miles, forsaking my mother's house, and the home in which I was born." On their way, they passed through Prague where they were received with great honor by Ezekiel *Landau. Adler, however, was not happy in Boskowitz, and after three years a dispute broke out between him and the community as a result of his attempt to introduce regulations regarding *terefot* which were more stringent than those hitherto in use. As a result he was obliged to leave the city. He and Sofer reached Vienna in the spring of 1785, but eventually Adler returned to Frankfurt, while Sofer settled in Prossnitz. In Frankfurt Adler reopened his yeshivah and reconvened his congregation. No action was taken by the community, but, in 1789, two of his students were punished by the communal leaders for alarming the community with accounts of their dreams. Adler and his disciples placed great significance on heavenly signs, miracles, and especially dreams. Adler himself was well-known for his dreams. As part of his kabbalistic life style, he was in constant search of divine revelation and prophetic visions. The excommunication pronounced ten years earlier against Adler and his *dayyan*, R. Lazer Wallase (the maternal grandfather of Abraham *Geiger), was renewed. About that time an anonymous polemical pamphlet entitled *Ma'asei Ta'atu'im* (1790) appeared in Frankfurt, describing the practices of the Ḥasidim who were attracted to Adler. The author of the brochure, a certain Loeb Wetzler, who wrote in the style of the early Haskalah, claimed that the Ḥasidim had devised new laws. Adler's community did deviate from common practice in the areas of prayer, asceticism, and wearing two sets of *tefillin* instead of the usual one, all based on their study of Kabbalah. The added strictures of law, the asceticism, and the life style based on Kabbalah were very close to similar practices of the nascent ḥasidic communities developing in Eastern Europe during the same period. To a certain extent the opposition to these "deviant" practices was motivated by a resurgence of interest in the Shabbatean movement that occurred at the same time. The excommunication on Adler was removed on the 11th of Elul 1800, only three weeks before his death. The eulogy was delivered by R. Phinehas Horowitz, *av bet din* of Frankfurt. Adler left no writings except some brief notes, based on explanations he had heard from Tevele David Schiff. He wrote these in the margins of his copy of the Mishnah. Some, on *Berakhot* and tractates of the order *Zera'im*, were published by R. Ẓevi Benjamin Auerbach under the title *Mishnat Rabbi Nathan* (1862). Some of Adler's views on *halakhah* and *aggadah* and his *minhagim* were published in Moses Sofer's *Ḥatam Sofer* and *Torat Moshe* (1906[2]). Adler's method in teaching the Oral Law was original. He took the Mishnah as his starting point, gave the results of the discussion of the *Gemara* on it, and then pointed out the various stages in the development of the *halakhah* as it appears in the works of the early codifiers, particularly Maimonides and Alfasi.

BIBLIOGRAPHY: Z.B. Auerbach, *Mishnat R. Nathan* (1862), introd.; A. Geiger, in: HB, 5 (1862), 77–79; M. Horovitz, *Frankfurter Rabbinen*, 4 (1885), 38–51; idem, *Avnei Zikkaron* (1901), liii, no. 4478; L. Loew, *Gesammelte Schriften*, 2 (1890), 91–95; A.Y. Schwarz, *Derekh ha-Nesher* (1928); Dubnow, Ḥasidut, 2 (1930), 434–41; J. Unna, in: *Guardians of Our Heritage*, ed. by L. Jung (1958), 167–85; O. Feuchtwanger, *Righteous Lives* (1965), 69–71; Y. Katz, in: *Studies in Mysticism and Religion* (1967), 119–22 (Hebrew section). **ADD. BIBLIOGRAPHY:** R. Elior, in: *Zion*, 59 (1994); idem, in: *Mysticism, Magic and Kabbalah in Ashkenazi Judaism: International Symposium Held in Frankfurt a.M.* (1995), 223–42.

[Zvi Avneri / David Derovan (2nd ed.)]

ADLER, NATHAN MARCUS (1803–1890), British chief rabbi. Nathan Adler was born in Hanover, then under the British crown, and was educated in Germany. He became rabbi of Oldenburg in 1829 and succeeded his father, Marcus Baer Adler, at Hanover the following year. In 1844 he was elected chief rabbi of the United Hebrew Congregations of the British Empire in succession to Solomon *Hirschel. He was chosen by a representative gathering of national delegates, and not, as with his predecessors, by the London Great Synagogue alone. S.R. *Hirsch was among the other candidates. During his 45 years of office the Anglo-Jewish community developed its modern features, which Adler did much to shape. His firm but enlightened orthodoxy was coupled with a strong and attractive personality. Adler was largely responsible for the failure of the *Reform movement, established in England shortly before his arrival, to make much headway there. His wide-ranging and ambitious conception of his office was made clear in his *Laws and Regulations for all the Ashkenazi Synagogues in the British Empire*, issued in 1847. He was mainly responsible for the establishment of *Jews' College in 1855 and was a moving spirit in the organization of the Jewish Board of Guardians in 1859. In 1866 he took the first steps toward the creation of the *United Synagogue. His pastoral tours and visits to provincial communities made his influence felt throughout the country, and he was also able to secure recognition of his authority in the British colonies. Adler regarded Anglo-Orthodoxy as lax compared with the Continent and therefore in need of central direction. Outside the community he was regarded as the official representative and public spokesman for Judaism. Ill health curtailed his activity after 1879, when his son Hermann *Adler was appointed delegate chief rabbi. His principal literary work is *Netinah la-Ger*, a Hebrew commentary on the Targum *Onkelos (Vilna, 1875; published in numerous editions). His *Ahavat Yonatan*, a commentary on the Targum Jonathan, remains in manuscript (JTSA, Ms. Adler, 1173). Adler enjoyed an international reputation for his scholarship. He greatly strengthened the position of the chief rabbi.

BIBLIOGRAPHY: C. Roth, in: L. Jung (ed.), *Jewish Leaders 1750–1940* (1953), 477–90; Friedlaender, in JQR, 2 (1890), 369–85; Schmidt, in: YLBI, 7 (1962), 289–311; JC (Jan. 24, 1890); C. Roth, *History of the Great Synagogue…* (1950), 266ff.; L.P. Gartner, *Jewish Immigrant in England 1870–1914* (1960), index. **ADD. BIBLIOGRAPHY:** ODNB online; G. Alderman, *Modern British Jewry* (1992), index.

[Cecil Roth]

ADLER, PAUL (1878–1946), German author. Adler studied law in his native Prague and served for a short time as a judge. He moved to France and Italy and finally settled in Hellerau, an artists' community near Dresden. He joined the "Hellerau Circle," inspired by the publisher Jacob Hegner, who gathered about him neoromantic and expressionist authors, the exponents of an esoteric, religious mysticism. Adler was coeditor of *Neue Blaetter*, the circle's periodical. In 1933, he returned to Czechoslovakia and survived the Nazi occupation in hiding. Adler's best known legendary tales, collected in *Elohim* (1914), teem with fantastic characters, and anticipate those of Franz *Kafka. *Elohim's* giants, angels, and titans combine the symbolism of the Talmud, of Christianity, and of paganism. Adler's two major novels were *Naemlich* (1915) and *Die Zauberfloete* (1916); here he interpreted creation as a work of destruction. In later years he became interested in Japanese literature and collaborated in a monograph, *Japanische Literatur* (1925).

ADD. BIBLIOGRAPHY: A. Herzog, in: *Aschkenas*, 9 (1999), 483–502; D. Hoffmann, in: A. Kilcher (ed.), *Metzler Lexikon der deutsch-juedischen Literatur* (2000), 6f.; D. Hoffmann, in: *Trumah*, 13 (2003), 209–26.

[Rudolf Kayser]

ADLER, POLLY (**Pearl**; 1900–1962), U.S. author and owner of bordellos. The eldest of nine children of Gertrude Koval and Morris Adler, a tailor, Pearl Adler hoped to complete gymnasium studies in her native Belorussia. However, her father sent her to America to prepare the way for the immigration of the rest of the family. On her own in New York, she was raped at 17 by a sweatshop foreman and resorted to an abortion. Alienated from relatives, she learned to support herself in the sex industry, a survival necessity followed by a significant number of Jewish female immigrants from Eastern Europe. Unsuccessful in legitimate undertakings, Adler became a madam, operating a series of increasingly upscale brothels catering to gangsters and the fashionable upper classes. She retired in 1943 to Burbank, California, where she completed high school and enrolled in college courses. Her notoriety as the classic American madam, "a feisty, albeit disreputable, victor over adversity," was sealed by the publication of her popular memoir, *A House Is Not a Home* (1953) and its film version (1964).

BIBLIOGRAPHY: A.M. Millin, "Adler, Polly," in: P.E. Hyman and D. Dash Moore (eds.), *Jewish Women in America*, 1 (1997), 16–17.

[Judith R. Baskin (2nd ed.)]

ADLER, RENATA (1938–), U.S. journalist, novelist, and film critic. Born in Milan, Italy, Adler graduated from Bryn Mawr College in 1959; the Sorbonne in 1961; Harvard University in 1962; and Yale University Law School. Trained as a journalist, Adler worked intermittently for 20 years at the *New Yorker* magazine. Hired in her twenties by the legendary editor William *Shawn, she reported from Vietnam; from Selma, Ala., a civil rights hot spot; and from the Middle East. Her first two books were collections of essays and reviews written on assignment for that magazine and for the *New York Times,* where she worked, still in her twenties, for 18 months as a film critic, at a time when film became a serious intellectual, artistic, and political pursuit. Her generally negative reviews so angered the movie-making industry that in 1968 United Artists took out a full-page ad in the *New York Times* denouncing her. Strom Thurmond attacked her on the floor of the Senate for her critique of the John Wayne film *The Green Berets*.

She returned to the *New Yorker* and was promptly sent to report on the civil war in Biafra. Then she went to Washington, where she was hired by the House Committee investigating the Watergate scandal to write speeches for the chairman, Representative Peter Rodino. In 1969, she turned to writing short stories. Her early work surfaced in the *New Yorker,* and she eventually collected and reshaped much of this short fiction into an award-winning first novel, *Speedboat*, a collection of short paragraphs offering snippets of narrative, sometimes presented randomly. Essentially Adler was creating a disturbing portrait of urban life. The critics, however, were unimpressed. The literary controversy was rekindled in 1983 with her second novel, *Pitch Dark*, an autobiographical story about a young woman running from her relationship with a married man. It was similar in style to her first novel, with a skeletal plot and observations arranged haphazardly.

Her legal training was reflected in her 1986 book, an exhaustive investigation into shoddy news reporting practices, *Reckless Disregard: Westmoreland v. CBS et al.; Sharon v. Time.* It dealt with Ariel Sharon's libel suit against *Time* for its reporting of the Sabra and Shatila massacre in Lebanon and Westmoreland's suit against CBS for accusing him of deception in estimating North Vietnamese troop strengths. Adler accused the defendants of refusing to acknowledge even the possibility of error and their lawyers with having displayed "a concerted disregard for the fundamental goals of truth and accuracy." CBS tried to get the book suppressed; the network was unsuccessful and the manuscript was published without change.

In the late 1980s, Adler became a single mother by adopting a baby and wrote little. Her critique of the venerated *New Yorker* film critic Pauline *Kael, published in the *New York Review of Books*, was particularly noteworthy for the viciousness of her attack. In 1999, she published *Gone: The Last Days of the New Yorker,* a critique of the magazine after it changed ownership and editors. In 2001 came *Canaries in the Mineshaft: Essays on Politics and Media.* She also contributed articles and short stories, sometimes under the pseudonym Brett Daniels, to the magazines *National Review, Vanity Fair, Harper's Bazaar, Commentary*, and *Atlantic*. She was a member of the editorial board of *American Scholar* from 1969 to 1975. She was a Guggenheim Fellow in 1973–74, won first prize in the O. Henry Short Story Awards in 1974, won the American Academy and Institute of Arts and Letters Award in 1976, and the Ernest Hemingway Prize in 1976 for the best first novel. She taught at several universities and was a member of PEN and the National Academy of Arts and Letters.

[Stewart Kampel (2nd ed.)]

ADLER, RICHARD (1921–), U.S. composer, lyricist. Bronx-born Adler, the son of a classical pianist-teacher, Clarence Adler, graduated from the University of North Carolina and served as a lieutenant (JG.) in the U.S. Navy during World War II before concentrating on composing. He began collaborating with Jerry Ross, also Bronx-born and Jewish, in 1950 and had a popular success with the song "Rags to Riches." But their first Broadway musical, *The Pajama Game,* in 1954, brought them recognition for the way the songs worked with the plot and for their integration of American speech idioms. The show, about a labor-union conflict and the threat of a strike in a pajama factory, was directed by the venerable George Abbott and also launched the career of Harold *Prince as a producer and established Bob Fosse as a major choreographer. Jerome *Robbins was hired as a backup in case Fosse did not work out. The show had hit songs like "Hernando's Hideaway," "Hey There," and "Steam Heat." The next year Adler and Ross gave Broadway *Damn Yankees*, a musical comedy version of the Faust story, with such songs as "Whatever Lola Wants" and "(You Gotta Have) Heart." But Ross died that year, at the age of 29, of a bronchial infection and Adler began to work alone.

Adler had little commercial success with Broadway musicals in the 1960s and 1970s but his symphonic works, including "Yellowstone Overture"; "Wilderness Suite," commissioned by the Interior Department for full orchestra to celebrate the wilderness park lands; and "The Lady Remembers," commissioned by the Statue of Liberty / Ellis Island Foundation to celebrate the statue's centennial, also for full orchestra; and his ballets were performed widely and won awards. He also achieved success at composing musical commercials ("Let Hertz Put You in the Driver's Seat") and earned himself the sobriquet "king of the jingles." Adler was also called on to produce shows to mark celebrations and stage entertainments for inaugural galas. Perhaps his most celebrated show was produced on May 19, 1962, when Marilyn *Monroe sang "Happy Birthday" to President John F. Kennedy during a birthday salute at Madison Square Garden. Adler won two Tony (theater) awards and four Pulitzer Prize nominations; he was a member of the Songwriter's Hall of Fame.

In later years, Adler turned to a form of meditation called Siddha Yoga, which he said helped him deal with the grief when his son died of cancer at the age of 30 and when he himself battled throat cancer.

[Stewart Kampel (2nd ed.)]

ADLER, SAMUEL (1809–1891), rabbi and pioneer of the Reform movement. Adler, born in Worms, was the son of Rabbi Isaac Adler, who gave him his early education. He received a traditional education at the Frankfurt Yeshivah and studied privately with Rabbi Jacob Bamberger. He also received a secular education at the University of Bonn and Giessen, where he studied philosophy and especially Hegel under Joseph Hillebrand. He officiated as preacher and assistant rabbi at Worms, and in 1842 was appointed rabbi of the Alzey (Rhenish Hesse) district. Adler was one of the early protagonists of Reform and took part in the rabbinical conferences of 1844–46 (see *Reform Judaism). He worked strenuously for the improvement of Jewish education and the removal of legal disabilities affecting Jews. He believed that rituals had to be changed to fit contemporary circumstance and worked on improving the status of women in Jewish education and in prayer. In 1857 Adler went to America as rabbi of Congregation Emanu-el in New York, succeeding Leo *Merzbacher. A classic reformer, he rejected supernatural revelation and the authority of the law. He omitted references to the return to Zion in the prayer book and during the parts of the service that were not devotional, head covering was removed at Emanu-El. He published a revised edition of its prayer book in 1860, and in 1865 helped form a theological seminary under the auspices of his congregation. He was also one of the founders of the Hebrew Orphan Asylum. Adler's interests were scholarly, and he appears to have exercised little influence on the community. In 1874 his congregation resolved on his retirement and appointed him rabbi emeritus. When the Central Conference of American Rabbis was established (1889), Adler was made honorary president. Among his publications are *A Guide to Instruction in Israelite Religion* (1864) and a selection of his writings, *Kobez al Jad*, was published privately (1886). An English translation of Adler's memoirs was published privately by A.G. Sanborn (1967). His son Felix was presumed to be his successor but left the rabbinate to found the Ethical Culture Society and therefore take his father's ideas to the next stage of their evolution where the particularity of Jews and Judaism are no longer necessary.

ADD. BIBLIOGRAPHY: M. Berenbaum: "The Dimension of Samuel Adler's Religious View of the World," in *Hebrew Union College Annual*, 46 (1975), 377–412; K.M. Olitzsky, L.J. Sussman, and M.H. Stern, *Reform Judaism in America: A Biographical Dictionary and Sourcebook* (1993), 4–6.

[Sefton D. Temkin / Michael Berenbaum (2nd ed.)]

ADLER, SAMUEL M. (1898–1979), U.S. painter. Born in New York City, Adler began drawing as a child. His parents saw the life of an artist as a challenge and thus did not encourage his interest. Nonetheless, at the age of 13 – several years earlier than typical admissions – Adler began artistic training at the National Academy of Design in New York. A talented violinist as well, he supported himself by playing in various venues, from weddings to symphonies. Before graduation Adler left the Academy, dedicating himself to music full time.

In 1933 Adler returned to painting. His first one-man show was not until mid life, when he had a 1948 exhibition at the Joseph Luyber Galleries in New York. This exhibition showed only his current work as two years previously he had destroyed all but two of his paintings. Overnight, critics lauded Adler as an important contemporary artist. Within the year he was teaching art at New York University and from this period on his works were displayed at, and acquired by, various venues in New York and elsewhere.

While Adler grew up with little religious training, he turned to depictions of the Jewish experience when he entered the art world. He created dozens of paintings of rabbis, including *White Rabbi* (1951), which shows a young rabbi in a *tallit* and *kippah* standing in front of Sabbath candles. In this work, and others, one can see the influence of Amadeo *Modigliani's simplified, symmetrical approach to the human figure. Adler always kept the human form at the center of his art, even as he moved away from representational painting to more abstract collages.

Adler discussed his view of Jewish art in a 1964 public lecture: "I believe in a dimension in every work of art that lies beyond the measurables, an inexplicable, a quality of life we call presence, that cannot be construed as either Jewish or Christian."

BIBLIOGRAPHY: "Jewish Art Explained by Prof. Adler," in: *The News-Gazette* (Champaign, Illinois, March 8, 1964), 16; E. Grossman, *Art and Tradition* (1967); S. Adler, *Samuel M. Adler: 25 Years of the Image of Man '47–'72* (1972).

[Samantha Baskind (2nd ed.)]

ADLER, SAUL AARON (1895–1966), Israeli physician and parasitologist. Adler was born in Karelitz, Russia, but was taken to England as a child of five. He studied medicine at Leeds University and specialized in tropical medicine at the University of Liverpool. During World War I he served as a doctor and pathologist with the British armies on the Iraqi front. Between 1921 and 1924 he did research on malaria in Sierra Leone. In 1924 he made his home in Jerusalem and joined the staff of the Hebrew University Medical School. Four years later he was appointed professor and director of the Parasitological Institute of the university. Adler translated Darwin's *Origin of Species* into Hebrew.

Under the auspices of the British Royal Society, he organized a number of scientific expeditions in the countries and islands of the Mediterranean. He specialized in the etiology and pathology of tropical diseases, the ways in which parasites pathogenic to man and animals are spread, and the immunology of protozoan infections. Adler introduced the Syrian golden hamster (brought to the Hebrew University from Aleppo by Israel *Aharoni) into experimental medicine. His work on malaria, cattle fever, leprosy, and dysentery, and his pioneer research into the Leishmania diseases (the Jericho and kala-azar groups) and their carriers, the sandflies, won him an international reputation. In 1933 Adler was awarded the Chalmers Gold Medal of the Royal Society of Tropical Medicine and Hygiene for his work on the transmission of kala-azar by the sandfly. In 1957 he was made a Fellow of the Royal Society.

[Meir Yoeli]

ADLER, SELIG (1909–1984), U.S. historian. Born in Baltimore, Maryland, Adler graduated from the University of Buffalo in 1931. He was appointed to the history faculty of the University of Buffalo in 1938 and subsequently named Samuel Paul Capen Professor of American History at the State University of New York at Buffalo in 1959. He specialized in American diplomatic and American Jewish history. His *Isolationist Impulse* (1957) is a study of isolationist thinking in the United States between the two World Wars. *American Foreign Policy Between the Wars* (1965) is a judicious, widely accepted account of that contentious subject. *From Ararat to Suburbia: A History of the Jewish Community of Buffalo* (with Thomas E. Connolly; 1960) is one of the most extensive and exact histories of any Jewish community. He was also the archivist for the Buffalo Jewish community archives that bear his name, which are located in the Butler Library at Buffalo State College. Active in Jewish communal and cultural affairs, Adler was a member of the New York Kosher Law Advisory Board and of the executive board of the American Jewish Historical Society.

[Lloyd P. Gartner / Ruth Beloff (2nd ed.)]

ADLER, SHALOM BEN MENAHEM (1847–1899), rabbi and author. Adler was educated in the home of his uncle R. Hillel *Lichtenstein. In 1869 Adler was appointed rabbi of Szerednye (now Sered, Slovakia), a position he occupied for 30 years until his death. His *Rav Shalom*, published posthumously by his son-in-law Elijah Sternhell (1902), is distinguished for its inspiring homilies and beautiful style. His unpublished works include novellae on the Talmud and responsa. His three sons were all rabbis: Menahem Judah, his successor; Phinehas, the rabbi of Radvancz; and Joab, the rabbi of Tapoly-Hanusfalva, who was born in 1880 and killed by the Nazis.

BIBLIOGRAPHY: P.Z. Schwartz, *Shem ha-Gedolim me-Ereẓ Hagar*, 2 (1913), 36a; A. Stern, *Meliẓei Esh*, 3 (1962); *Kislev*, 16, no. 42; B. Eisenstadt, *Dor, Rabbanav ve-Soferav*, 6 (1965), 10; O.Z. Rand and A.M. Grynblatt, *Toledot Anshei Shem*, 1 (1950), 1.

[Naphtali Ben-Menahem]

ADLER, STELLA (1901–1992), U.S. actress and acting teacher. An exponent of Method acting and probably the leading American teacher of her craft, Adler was born into a celebrated acting family rooted in the Yiddish theater (see *Adler). She made her stage debut at four, appeared in nearly 200 plays, and occasionally directed productions. She also shaped the careers of thousands of performers at the Stella Adler Conservatory of Acting, which she founded in Manhattan in 1949 and where she taught for decades.

Born in Manhattan, the youngest daughter of Jacob Adler and the former Sara Levitzky, Russian immigrants who led the Independent Yiddish Art Company, Stella had five siblings, and they all became actors, notably Luther. Her parents were the leading classical Yiddish stage tragedians in the United States. Stella started on the stage in 1905 at the Grand Street Theater on the Lower East Side in Manhattan. She played both girls' and boys' roles and then ingénues in a variety of classical and contemporary plays over ten years in the United States, Europe, and South America, performing in vaudeville and the Yiddish theater. She won acclaim as the leading lady of Maurice *Schwartz, but she sought more versatility. Her work schedule allowed little time for formal schooling.

She was introduced to the Method theories of Konstantin Stanislavsky, the legendary Moscow Art Theater actor and director, in 1925 when she took courses at the American Laboratory Theater school, founded by Richard Boleslavski and Maria Ouspenskaya, former members of the Moscow troupe. Adler's most frenetic years were with the Group Theater, a cooperative ensemble dedicated to reinvigorating the theater with plays about important contemporary topics. The Group, founded by Harold *Clurman (whom she married in 1943), Lee *Strasberg and Cheryl Crawford, also believed in a theater that would probe the depths of the soul. Both aspects appealed to her and she joined in 1931. She won high praise for performances in such realistic dramas as *Success Story* by John Howard Lawson and two seminal Clifford *Odets plays, *Awake and Sing!* and *Paradise Lost*. She was also hailed for directing the touring company of Odets' *Golden Boy*. Recalling her years with the company, she deplored a dearth of good roles for women in "a man's theater aimed at plays for men." But she credited the company with evoking in her an idealism that shaped her later career. "I knew that I had it in me to be more creative, had much more to give to people," she said. "It was the Group Theater that gave me my life."

Before the Method revolutionized American theater, classical acting instruction had focused on developing external talents. Method acting was the first systematized training that also developed internal abilities, sensory, psychological, and emotional. Strasberg, who headed the Actors Studio until his death in 1982, rooted his view on what Stanislavsky stressed in his early career. Adler went to Paris and studied intensively with Stanislavsky for five weeks in 1934. She found he had revised his theories to stress that the actor should create by imagination rather than by memory and that the key to success was "truth, truth in the circumstances of the play." She instructed: "Your talent is your imagination. The rest is lice." She was a stern taskmaster, believing that a teacher's job is to agitate as well as inspire. She demanded craftsmanship and self-awareness, calling it the key to an actor's sense of fulfillment. When students failed to understand roles, she acted them out, insisting: "You can't be boring. Life is boring. The weather is boring. Actors must not be boring."

She appeared in three films: *Love on Toast* (1938), *Shadow of the Thin Man,* and *My Girl Tisa* (1948). Her later stage roles included a fiery lion tamer in a 1946 revival of *He Who Gets Slapped* and in London an eccentric mother in a black comedy, *Oh Dad, Poor Dad, Mama's Hung You in the Closet and I'm Feeling So Sad,* in 1961. She restated her theories in *Stella Adler on Acting,* published by Bantam Books in 1988. For her students, who included Marlon Brando, Robert De Niro, Warren Beatty, and Candice Bergen, she was both the toughest critic and the most profound inspiration, saying: "You act with your soul. That's why you all want to be actors, because your souls are not used up by life."

[Stewart Kampel (2nd ed.)]

ADLER, VICTOR (1852–1918), pioneer and leader of the Austrian Social-Democratic party and a prominent figure in the international labor movement. Born in Prague, Adler was taken as a child to Vienna where his father became a rich man and, two years before his death, embraced Catholicism. A physician by profession, Adler devoted his life to the cause of the working class. His greatest political victory was the granting of universal suffrage by the Imperial Government in 1905. He was a member of the Austrian parliament from 1905 to 1918 and foreign minister in the Socialist government of 1918. Adler was a victim of antisemitic agitation and suffered from the ambivalent attitude to Jews on the part of his colleagues at school and university. After his marriage he converted to Christianity "to save his children from embarrassment." During his long political life he was always conscious of his origin but avoided taking a clear stand on Jewish issues. He opposed a debate on antisemitism at a congress of the Socialist International in Brussels in 1891. In later life, free from any religious affiliations, Adler refused to acknowledge the specific problems of the Jewish proletariat and opposed the idea of Jewish nationhood.

BIBLIOGRAPHY: E. Silberner, *Western European Socialism and the Jewish Problem (1800–1918)* (1955). **ADD. BIBLIOGRAPHY:** L. Meysels, *Victor Adler* (1997).

[Schneier Zalman Levenberg]

ADLERBLUM, NIMA (1881–1974), author and philosopher. Adlerblum, a daughter of Ḥayyim *Hirschensohn, was born in Jerusalem but left the city with her parents when she was about 11, moving to Turkey and later to the United States. She studied in Paris and subsequently at Columbia University, where she became closely associated with John Dewey. Her doctoral thesis, *A Study of Gersonides in His Proper Perspective* (Columbia University Press, 1926), was actually a call for a new approach to Jewish philosophy, which she felt was wrongly assessed by being viewed in its relation to other contemporary philosophies, maintaining that its true main thrust could be detected only when it was examined within its own environment. This conception, she argued, was best expressed by *Judah Halevi (1075–1145) who, in his *Kuzari,* maintained that Judaism had its own spiritual ideas and ideals, which were intimately bound with the historic experience of the Jewish people. Her attitude coincided with John Dewey's philosophical theory that the value of abstract thinking depended on its concern with living experience and its fruitful application to life, but her views were challenged and criticized by many scholars.

In her *A Perspective of Jewish Life Through Its Festivals* (1930) she further expounded her philosophical theory of Judaism, and in her *Elan Vital of the Jewish Woman* (1934) she stressed that woman's sensitivity in certain areas was vital and would enrich Jewish scholarship when it was opened up to them. She also published philosophical treatises on medieval Jewish thinkers. Adlerblum served on the international committee for spreading the teaching of John Dewey (outside America), was a member of the American Philosophical Association, and a life fellow of the International Institute of Arts and Letters. She was active in Hadassah from its inception, serving on its National Board from 1922 to 1935.

After an absence of 80 years she returned to Israel. A number of her articles on the vivid impact of her childhood in Jerusalem on her thinking were included in *The Jewish Heritage Series* edited by Rabbi Leo Jung (New York).

[Penina Peli (2nd ed.)]

ADLER-RUDEL, SALOMON (1894–1975), social worker. He was born in Czernowitz, Austro-Hungary (now Ukraine). Adler-Rudel was director of the Welfare Organization of Eastern Jews in Berlin (1919–30) and was active in developing welfare services for Jewish migrants from Eastern Europe. As director of the Berlin Jewish community's department of productive welfare from 1930 to 1934, he contributed to programs to reduce dependence and to increase self-support among welfare cases. From 1926 to 1929 he served as editor of the *Juedische Arbeits – und Wanderfuersorge.* When the Nazis came to power, he moved to London where he was administrator of the *Central British Fund (1936–45). During World War II, he was prominent in rescue activities of Jews from Europe. After the war he settled in Ereẓ Israel and was director of the Jewish Agency's department of international relations. In this capacity, he prepared agreements with the International Refugee Organization and other international migration bodies for the transfer to Israel of the "hard-core" cases in the European Displaced Persons Camps. From 1958 he was director of the *Leo Baeck Institute for German Jews in Jerusalem. In 1959 he published *Ostjuden in Deutschland 1880–1940*.

[Jacob Neusner]

ADLIVANKIN, SAMUIL (1897–1966), painter and graphic artist. Adlivankin was born in Tatarsk, Mogilev province, Russia. As a child, he received a traditional Jewish education. In 1912–17, he studied at the Odessa Art School. In 1916, he became a member of the Odessa Association of Independent Artists and participated in their exhibitions. In 1918–19, Adlivankin studied at the Moscow Free Art Workshops, where his tutor was V. Tatlin (1885–1953). In the constructivist works created by Adlivankin in 1919–20, Tatlin's influence is clearly manifested. In 1921–23 he joined the New Painters' Society (NOZH) and showed his work at its 1921 exhibition in Moscow. His works of this period feature scenes of everyday Soviet life, treated ironically or satirically and executed in the expressionist manner, sometimes incorporating elements of primitivism. In 1923–28, Adlivankin drew caricatures for various magazines and worked on political posters together with V. Mayakovsky. In the late 1920s he worked for a number of film studios and made set designs for several productions. In the early 1930s, he made several trips to Jewish agricultural communities in the Crimea and Ukraine that inspired several works portraying the life of Jewish kolkhozes and showed them at the exhibition dedicated specifically to this theme, which took place in Moscow in 1936. In the notorious, overtly antisemitic campaign launched in 1949 against "cosmopolitism," Adlivankin, together with other Soviet culture figures who happened to be ethnic Jews, was subjected to severe criticism and distanced from public cultural life until the mid-1950s: his works were not accepted for exhibits, he received no commissions, etc. The first and only one-man exhibition in his lifetime was held in 1961 in Moscow.

BIBLIOGRAPHY: *The Great Utopia. Russian and Soviet Avant-Garde-Art 1915–1932.* Exh. Cat. Moscow (1993), 748 (Rus.).

[Hillel Kazovsky (2nd ed.)]

ADLOYADA (Heb. עַדְלָיָדַע; Aramaic עַד דְּלָא יָדַע), Purim carnival. The name is derived from the rabbinic saying (Meg. 7b) that one should revel on Purim until one no longer knows (*ad de-lo yada*) the difference between "Blessed be Mordecai" and "Cursed be Haman." The first *Adloyada* was held in Tel Aviv (1912) and spread to other communities in Israel. It is celebrated by carnival processions with decorated floats through the main streets, accompanied by bands.

BIBLIOGRAPHY: J.T. Lewinski (ed.), *Sefer ha-Mo'adim*, 6 (1956), 277–296.

ADMISSION, legal concept applying both to debts and facts. Formal admission by a defendant is regarded as equal to "the evidence of a hundred witnesses" (BM 3b). This admission had to be a formal one, before duly appointed witnesses, or before the court, or in writing. When the denial of having received a loan is proved to be false, this is regarded as tantamount to an admission that it has not been repaid. Admissions were originally regarded as irrevocable, but in order to alleviate hardships caused by hasty admissions, the Talmud evolved two causes for their revocation; a plea that the person making the admission had not been serious, or that he had had a special reason for making the admission. When partial admission has been made, the admission is accepted and he is bound to take an oath with regard to the remainder. Admissions can also apply to procedural matters; e.g., on the part of a party to an action that he has no witnesses, in which case he cannot subsequently call one.

The formal admission of a debt, or of facts from which any liability may be inferred, is in civil cases the best evidence of such liability (Git. 40b, 64a; Kid. 65b). The requirements of formality may be met: (1) by making the admission before two competent witnesses, expressly requested to hear and witness the admission (Sanh. 29a); (2) by way of pleading before the court, whether as plaintiff or defendant (Sh. Ar., ḤM 81:22); (3) in writing (*ibid.*, 17); (4) through any of the recognized modes of *kinyan* ("*acquisition" *ibid.*); (5) on oath or the "symbolic shaking of hands by the two parties… which is the equivalent of an oath" (*ibid.*, 28; Herzog, Instit, 2 (1939), 103).

While generally the admission must be explicit, in an action for the recovery of a loan, the denial of the loan would amount to an admission of nonpayment which is implicit in the denial (BB 6a; Shevu. 38b); on proof of the loan, the defendant will then be bound by his admission that he has not repaid it. Conversely, where a plaintiff claims that the defendant owes him a certain species of goods without reserving his right to claim also some other species, he is deemed to have admitted that the defendant owes him only the species claimed and no other, and any admission by the defendant that he does owe another species than that claimed, will not avail the plaintiff (BK 35b). The general rule in a conflict between two contradictory admissions is that the explicit prevails over the implicit and the negative (e.g., "I have not acquired property"") over the positive (e.g., "I have transferred my property"; Tosef., BB 10:1; Git. 40b), but an admission presumed to stem from the knowledge of the relevant facts prevails over one possibly made in ignorance of those facts (cf. BB 149a).

As formal admissions were originally irrevocable, they were widely used as a means of creating new liabilities, as distinguished from the mere acknowledgment of already existing ones. Even though recognized as factually false admissions, they were held to bind the person making them (BB 149a), whether by way of gratuitously incurring a new and enforceable obligation (Ket. 101a–102b; Maim. Yad, Mekhirah, 11:15), or by way of transfer (*kinyan*). The property concerned thus passes from the owner to the person now admitted by him to have acquired it from him, the concurrence of the beneficiary not being required as he was only benefiting by the admission (Git. 40b; Maim. Yad, Zekhiyyah, 4:12). Admissions of this nonprocedural variety are also termed *udita* or *odaita*.

With a view to alleviating hardships caused by precipitate admissions, talmudic jurists evolved two *pleas for having them revoked: the plea of feigning (*hashta'ah*) and the plea of satiation (*hasba'ah*). Where a man, not of his own accord but in reply to a question or demand, made an admission, and on being sued maintained that he had not been serious about it and that the admission was not true, an oath would be administered to him to the effect that he had not intended to admit the debt and that he did not in fact owe it (Sanh. 29b). Similarly, a statement of a person that he had admitted debts owed by him, only for the purpose of ostensibly reducing his assets so as not to appear rich was accepted (Sanh. 29b). Neither plea is valid against admissions made in court, or in writing, or by *kinyan*, or on oath (Sh. Ar., ḤM 81). As to admissions made in writing, some scholars hold that so long as the deed has not been delivered to the creditor, the admittor may plead that he was not serious or that he wrote it in order to appear poor (Sh. Ar., ḤM 65:22 and Isserles to Sh. Ar., ḤM 81:17). A dying man is presumed not to be frivolous on his deathbed, and his admissions are irrevocable (Sanh. 29b), so are admissions made by his debtors in his favor and presence while he is dying (Isserles *ibid.*, 81:2). The public (the community) must be presumed neither to make rash admissions nor to be interested in appearing without means, hence none of the pleas is available against admissions made by or on behalf of the public (Isserles *ibid.*, 81:1). Where only part of a claim is admitted, the admittor will be adjudged to the extent of his admission and be required to take the oath that he does not owe the remainder (Shevu. 7:1). This rule is based on the presumption that no debtor has the temerity to deny his debt falsely in the face of his creditor (Shev. 42b; BM 3a), a presumption which, curiously enough, does not necessarily apply to a debtor denying the whole (as distinguished from a part) of the debt. Where the whole is denied, the oath is administered to the defendant upon the presumption that a plaintiff will not normally abuse the process of the court (Shev. 40b). Where the defendant satisfies the admitted portion of the claim without adjudication, the claim is deemed to be for the nonadmitted portion only and to be denied in whole (BM 4a, 4b). While a part admission must fit the subject matter of the claim (Shev. 38b), it need not necessarily fit the cause of action; thus, the admission of a deposit might fit the claim on a loan (Sh. Ar., Ḥ.M. 88:19). The claim of the whole must precede the admission of the part, the admittor who is not yet a defendant being regarded as a volunteer returning a lost object (Sh. Ar., ḤM 75:3). An admission is not allowed to prejudice the admittor's creditors: the holder of a bill may not be heard to admit that he has no claim on it, or the possessor of chattel that they belong to somebody else, so as to deprive his creditors of an attachable asset (Kid. 65b; Ket. 19a). Admissions need not relate to substantive liabilities, but may be procedural in nature: thus a party may admit that he has no witnesses to prove a particular fact, and he will not then be allowed to call a witness to prove it, lest the witness be suborned (Sanh. 31a); or, having once admitted a particular witness to be untrustworthy, he will not later be able to rely on his testimony (Ket. 44a). Admissions could be accepted for one purpose and rejected for another, e.g., the admission of a wrongful act would be inadmissible as a *confession in criminal or quasi-criminal proceedings, but could afford the basis for awarding damages in a civil suit. This rule is found to have been applied to larceny (BM 37a; see *Theft and Robbery), to the seduction of women (Ket. 41a; see *Rape), to arson (Solomon b. Abraham Adret, resp. 2:231), to *usury (*ibid.*), to embezzlement (see *Theft and Robbery), and to breach of trust (Isserles to Sh. Ar., ḤM 388:8; Yom Tov b. Abraham Ishbili, Ket. 72a); a wife admitting her adultery was held to lose, on the strength of her admission, any claim to maintenance or other monetary benefits, but not her status as a married woman, thus incurring no liability to be divorced or punished (Maim. Yad, Ishut, 24:18). An early authority posed the question whether the injunction, "you shall have one standard of law" (Lev. 24:22), should not be read to prohibit any distinction between civil and criminal law with regard to admissions; the answer is in the negative, because in civil causes it is said: "He shall pay"; but in criminal cases it is said: "He shall die" (Tosef. Shevu. 3:8).

BIBLIOGRAPHY: Z. Frankel, *Der gerichtliche Beweis nach mosaisch-talmudischem Rechte* (1846), 127–30, 336–58; M. Bloch, *Die Civilprocess-Ordnung nach mosaisch-rabbinischem Rechte* (1882), 41–43; Gulak, Yesodei, 2 (1922), 44–47; 4 (1922), 78–84; Gulak, Oẓar, 211–3; Karl, in: *Ha-Mishpat ha-Ivri*, 3 (1927/28), 95–98; Herzog, Instit, 1 (1936), 196–200, 268; 2 (1939), 42, 44, 94–97; ET, 1 (1951³), 116–7, 253–4, 267–8; 8 (1957), 404–31; J.J. Rabinowitz, *Jewish Law* (1956), 257–63. **ADD. BIBLIOGRAPHY:** B. Lifshitz, *Obligation and Acquisition in Jewish Law* (1988).

[Haim Hermann Cohn]

ADMON (Gorochov), YEDIDYAH (1897–1982), Israeli composer. Admon, who was born in Yekaterinoslav, Ukraine, went to Ereẓ Israel in 1906. From 1923 to 1927 he studied theory of music and composition in the U.S. In 1927 he returned to Palestine and in the same year published his first songs, among them the popular "Gamal Gemali" (Camel Driver's Song). In 1930 he went to Paris to study with Nadia Boulanger, the French music teacher. For several years Admon was director of the Israeli Performing Rights Society (ACUM). After spending 13 years in America, he returned to Israel in 1968. Admon was a pioneer in the field of Israeli song. He was one of the first Israeli composers, and one of the earliest to create a new style which served, often subconsciously, as a model for other composers. This style blends four elements: the music of the Oriental Jewish communities, especially the Yemenite and Persian; Arab music; ḥasidic music; and Bible cantillation. The result is an absolute organic unity. The rhythm of the Hebrew language is also an important factor in Admon's music. He was awarded the Israel Prize for the arts in 1974. His work includes music for the theater – *Bar Kokhba; Michal, Daughter of Saul*; and *Jeremiah* – for piano and violin, and a symphonic poem, *The Song of Deborah.*

BIBLIOGRAPHY: P. Gradenwitz, *Music and Musicians in Israel* (1959²), index.

[Herzl Shmueli]

ADMON BEN GADDAI, one of the few civil law judges in Jerusalem whose name is mentioned in talmudic literature (Ket. 13:1–9; TB, Ket. 105a). Admon probably lived in the latter days of the Second Temple, as three of the seven *halakhot* in his name are supported in the Mishnah by R. *Gamaliel the Elder. Admon and his colleagues received a salary of 99 maneh (1 maneh = 100 denarii) from the Temple treasury. However, due to early variants in mishnaic tradition regarding Admon's title, his precise judicial function is not clear. He is referred to as either one of the *dayyanei gezerot* (דַּיָּנֵי גְזֵרוֹת "decree judges") or one of the *dayyanei gezelot* (דַּיָּנֵי גְזֵלוֹת "robbery judges"). On this and similar changes of the Hebrew letters ר and ל see Epstein, *Tarbiz*, 1 (1930), n. 3, 131–2.

BIBLIOGRAPHY: Frankel, Mishnah, 63–65; Weiss, Dor, 1 (1904[4]), 181ff.; A. Buechler, *Das grosse Synhedrion in Jerusalem* (1902), 111–4.

[Isaiah Gafni]

ADMONI, VLADIMIR GRIGORYEVICH (1909–1993), Soviet Russian literary and linguistic scholar. A professor at the Pedagogical Institute of Leningrad, he specialized in Germanic and Norwegian languages and literature and in the theory of literary translation. He wrote monographs on Ibsen (1956) and Thomas Mann (1960; in collaboration with T.I. Silman) and on problems of German syntax (1955). He also translated and edited the standard Russian version of the works of Ibsen (4 vols., 1956–58). During the 1964 trial of the young Leningrad Jewish poet Yosif *Brodski, Admoni, who testified for the defense, was ridiculed by the presiding Soviet judge for his "strange-sounding" (i.e., Jewish) name.

BIBLIOGRAPHY: Y. Brodski, *Stikhotvoreniya i poemy* (1965); *Kratkaya literaturnaya entsiklopediya*, 1 (1962), 88.

[Maurice Friedberg]

ADMOR (Heb. אדמו"ר; plur., *Admorim*), the title by which ḥasidic rabbis are known. The term is an abbreviation of the Hebrew words *Adonenu, Morenu, ve-Rabenu* ("our lord, teacher, and master").

ADOLPHUS, English family, known in the synagogue as Bira. Its members included JACOB ADOLPHUS, stockholder in the Bank of England (late 17th century), founder member of the London Ashkenazi Synagogue. Among his sons were: SIMON, a physician, who was admitted to the University of Halle at the request of Frederick William I of Prussia on condition that he did not practice there, and MOSES (b. c. 1690), who married Abigail, daughter of Benjamin *Levy, founder of the London Ashkenazi community. In his 56th year he matriculated at the University of Leiden, Holland, in philosophy and literature, along with his son SIMHAH (Joy, 1714–1760), who graduated in medicine and subsequently practiced in Cleves, Germany (1748–56) where he headed the Jewish community. Joy Adolphus published *Histoire des Diables Modernes* (London, 1763; Cleves, 1770, 1771), satirizing the political and social scene, and dedicated the book to Frederick the Great, whom he is said to have served as personal physician. Another son of Moses was MICHAEL or MEIR (died 1785), prominent in London communal life, and as warden of the Great Synagogue, one of the original members of the *Board of Deputies of British Jews. JOHN (1768–1845), historian and lawyer, grandson of Joy, was author of *History of England from the Accession of King George III to the Conclusion of Peace in 1783* (3 vols., London, 1802). His mother was Christian and he was out of touch with the Jewish community. However, he was caricatured by Cruikshank as a Jew. Originally a solicitor, he became a barrister in 1807 and achieved notable success at the bar. His son, JOHN LEYCESTER ADOLPHUS (1794–1862), educated at Oxford, was a barrister and literary critic. He became a close friend of Sir Walter Scott. There was also an Adolphus family in America in the colonial period, founded by ISAAC (died 1774) who came to New York from Bonn, Germany, about 1750. Another family of this name was established in Jamaica not later than 1733, its most eminent member being Major General Sir JACOB ADOLPHUS (1775–1845), inspector general of army hospitals.

BIBLIOGRAPHY: P. Emden, *Jews of Britain* (1943), 62; C. Roth, *History of the Great Synagogue* (1950), 160–3; Roth, Mag Bibl, index; E. Henderson, *Recollections of John Adolphus* (1871); F. Baer, *Protokollbuch der Land udenschaft des Herzogtums Kleve* (1922), 63, 122; Stern, Americans, 5; J.P. Andrade, *Record of Jews in Jamaica* (1941), 148–9, 207–8; Rubens, in: JHSET, 19 (1955–59), 25; Roth, in: JHSEM, 4 (1942), 106–7; A. Rubens, *Anglo-Jewish Portraits* (1935), 2–4. **ADD. BIBLIOGRAPHY:** ODNB online.

[Cecil Roth]

ADONAI, ADONAI, EL RAḤUM VE-ḤANNUN (Heb. יְהוָה, יְהוָה, אֵל רַחוּם וְחַנּוּן; "The Lord, The Lord, God, merciful and gracious"; Ex. 34:6–7), initial words of the Thirteen Attributes of God. Based upon a talmudic saying that God Himself revealed this formula to Moses as being effective for obtaining Divine Pardon (RH 17b), it is recited on the following occasions:

(1) in the *Seliḥot* of the month of Elul, during the *Ten Days of Penitence, and on fast days including the Day of Atonement when it is preceded by the *piyyutim* "*El Melekh Yoshev*" or "*El Erekh Appayim*";

(2) before removing the Torah scrolls from the Ark on Rosh Ha-Shanah, the Day of Atonement, and the three Pilgrim festivals (Ashkenazi rite);

(3) at the opening of the *piyyut* attributed to *Amittai (II) which is recited on the fifth day of *Seliḥot*, on the Day of Atonement, and on Mondays and Thursdays (Ashkenazi rite);

(4) at the morning and afternoon prayers before *Taḥanun* (mostly Sephardi rite);

(5) during prayers in an emergency situation, e.g., for a critically ill person. In the liturgical recital of the Thirteen Attributes the final words *lo yenakkeh* ("He does not remit all punishment"; Ex. 34:7) are omitted.

BIBLIOGRAPHY: Zunz, Ritus, 408; Elbogen, Gottesdienst, 222; Davidson, Oẓar, 1 (1929), 31, no. 629.

ADONI-BEZEK (Heb. אֲדוֹנִי בֶזֶק; "the lord [of the city] of Bezek"), Canaanite ruler in the early stages of the Hebrew conquest of Canaan (Judg. 1:1–7) and probably leader of an anti-Israelite coalition formed by "the Canaanites and the Perizzites." The allies gathered at *Bezek and forced the tribe of Judah, together with Simeon, to take defensive action. The coalition was defeated at Bezek and retreated eastward towards Jerusalem. The tribe of Judah pursued and captured Adoni-Bezek and mutilated him. He was brought to Jerusalem where he died.

Adoni-Bezek is most likely a title since, as a personal name, the second element would refer to a place or a god. However, a city as a component in biblical proper names is without analogy and a deity Bezek is not otherwise attested. The name is most likely a corruption of *Adoni-Zedek (cf. Josh. 10:1ff.).

BIBLIOGRAPHY: Y. Amit, *Judges* (1999), 32.

ADONIJAH (Heb. אֲדֹנִיָּה, אֲדֹנִיָּהוּ; "YHWH is my lord"), fourth son of King David by his wife Haggith of Hebron (II Sam. 3:2ff.; I Chron. 3:1ff.). I Kings 1:5–6 notes that his father had not disciplined him. After the death of his brothers Amnon, Absalom, and, presumably, Chileab, Adonijah conducted himself as heir apparent (I Kings 1:5–6). When David was on his deathbed, Adonijah attempted to seize power in order to forestall succession by *Solomon. In this he was supported by such veteran courtiers of David as *Joab and *Abiathar, and by many members of the royal family and the courtiers of the tribe of Judah (*ibid.* 7). Zadok the priest, Nathan the prophet, and others who had risen to prominence more recently, sided with Solomon (*ibid.* 8). Under Nathan's influence, David ordered that Solomon should be anointed king in his own lifetime, in accordance with his promise to Bath-Sheba (*ibid.* 10ff.). At first Solomon took no action against his brother (*ibid.* 50–53), but after David's death, when Adonijah wished to marry *Abishag the Shunammite, his father's concubine, Solomon correctly interpreted this as a bid for the throne and had him executed (*ibid.* 2:13ff.).

Other biblical figures of the same name were Adonijah a Levite who, with other Levites, priests, and princes, taught in the cities of Judah during the reign of Jehoshaphat (II Chron. 17:8); and Adonijah, one of the leaders who signed the covenant in the days of Nehemiah (Neh. 10:17).

[*Encyclopaedia Hebraica*]

In the *Aggadah*

Adonijah was one of those who "set their eyes upon that which was not proper for them; what they sought was not granted to them; and what they possessed was taken from them" (Sot. 9b). The biblical verse "and he [Adonijah] was born after Absalom" (I Kings 1:6) is interpreted to mean that, although the two were of different mothers, they are mentioned together since Adonijah acted in the same way as Absalom in rebelling against the king (BB 109b). The extent of his rebellion is illustrated in the aggadic tradition that he even tried the crown on his head (Sanh. 21b) and according to Rashi (loc. cit.), it would not fit. The importance and danger of Adonijah's rebellion is emphasized by the teaching that, although Solomon succeeded to the throne by the law of inheritance, he was ceremoniously anointed in order to counteract Adonijah's claim (Mid. Tan. 106).

ADD. BIBLIOGRAPHY: M. Cogan, *I Kings* (2000), 164–68.

ADONIM BEN NISAN HA-LEVI (c. 1000), *paytan* and rabbi. Adonim, who served as a rabbi in Fez, Morocco, was among the first to use Arabic-Spanish metrics in his writings. Only a few of his *piyyutim* have survived, among them the lamentation "*Bekhu, Immi Benei Immi*"; the *reshut* to *Parshat ha-Ḥodesh* (see Special *Sabbaths) "*Areshet Sefatenu Petaḥ Hodayot*"; and the *seliḥot* "*Eli Hashiveni me-Anaḥah u-Mehumah*" and "*Ro'eh Yisrael Ezon Enkat Ẓonekha.*" His *piyyutim* excel in their fine poetic language and their originality. Several philosophical concepts which were discussed in intellectual circles in his days find expression in his works.

BIBLIOGRAPHY: S. Pinsker, *Likkutei Kadmoniyyot* (1860), 56–57, 105–7; Fuenn, Keneset, 72; Scheiber, in: *A. Marx Jubilee Volume* (1950), 539–42; Zulay, in: *Sinai*, 29 (1951), 24–34.

[Abraham Meir Habermann]

ADONIRAM (or **Adoram**, **Hadoram**; Heb. אֲדֹנִירָם, אֲדֹרָם, הֲדֹרָם; "the Lord / my Lord is exalted"), son of Abda. Adoniram is described in a list of King David's officials from the later years of David's reign (II Sam. 20:24) as the minister "in charge of forced labor." He continued in the same office during Solomon's reign (I Kings 4:6) and was in charge of the levy of all Israel sent to *Lebanon to cut lumber (I Kings 5:27–28). During the first year of *Rehoboam, Adoniram was sent to face the discontented and revolting assembly at Shechem (12:1–19). The people, for whom he no doubt personified the detested corvée, stoned him to death (12:18). B. Mazar (Maisler) has suggested that Adoniram was of foreign origin, as the institution of forced labor was adopted by the Israelite monarchy from Canaanite patterns, and that it was only natural to appoint a Canaanite official as its head. The names of Adoniram and his father support the view of his Canaanite origin, since *ad* is synonymous with *ab* (*av* – father – in West-Semitic languages), while "Abda" is an abbreviated theophorical name found in Phoenician inscriptions. Some scholars believe that the lengthly tenure assigned by the Bible to Adoniram's office is due to chronological confusion.

BIBLIOGRAPHY: Mendelsohn, in: BASOR, no. 85 (1942), 14ff.; Maisler (Mazar), in: *Leshonenu*, 15 (1947), 38–39; idem, in: BJPES, 13 (1947), 108; de Vaux, Anc Isr, 128–9, 144ff.; EM, 1 (1965), 116–7. **ADD. BIBLIOGRAPHY:** M. Cogan, *I Kings* (2000), 204.

[Hanna Weiner]

ADONI-ZEDEK (Heb. אֲדֹנִי צֶדֶק; "[the god] Zedek [the god of justice] is lord" or, "my Lord is righteousness"), king of *Jerusalem at the time of the Israelite conquest of Canaan (Josh. 10:1–3). Adoni-Zedek was the leader of a coalition together with four of the neighboring *Amorite cities – Hebron, Jarmuth, Lachish, and Eglon. The coalition was formed as a reaction to the conclusion of a covenant between the Israelites and the *Gibeonites as well as to the conquest of *Ai by the Israelites, who threatened the region and the sovereignty of the city-states over this area. The members of the coalition attacked Gibeon. The Gibeonites, however, solicited the aid of Joshua, who preferred to fight against the Amorites in an open area. The Amorites were defeated at Gibeon, and, finding no alternative route of escape, retreated to Beth-Horon where their pursuers routed them with the help of a hailstorm; the five allied kings hid in a cave at Makkedah but were found and killed. Nothing is said about the capture of Jerusalem, although its king had lost his life; a reduction of Jerusalem's influence, however, did result from the war.

It is apparent that Jerusalem was an important city-state at the time, as is clear not only from this biblical passage but also from the *El-Amarna letters (14th century B.C.E.). Six of these letters, sent by the king of Jerusalem (Abdi-Ḥepa) to the pharaoh of Egypt, warrant the conclusion that Jerusalem (and Shechem) controlled the hill country of Judah and Ephraim and ruled over "the land of Jerusalem" (Pritchard, Texts, 487–9). Adoni-Zedek is unknown from other sources, but he fits well into the above picture of pre-Israelite Jerusalem. Some identify him with *Adoni-Bezek (Judg. 1:5–7), because the Septuagint reads Adoni-Bezek in place of the masoretic Adoni-Zedek.

BIBLIOGRAPHY: Noth, Personennamen, 114, 161ff.; idem, in: PJB, 33 (1937), 23–26; idem, *Das Buch Josua* (1953²), 60–63; Yeivin, in: *Ma'arakhot*, 26–27 (1945), 63; Albright, in: JBL, 54 (1935), 193, n. 66; Levy, in: HUCA, 18 (1943–44), 435. **ADD. BIBLIOGRAPHY:** B. Batto, in: DDD, 929–34.

ADON OLAM (Heb. אֲדוֹן עוֹלָם; "Lord of the World"), rhymed liturgical hymn in 12 verses (in the Ashkenazi rite) extolling the eternity and unity of God and expressing man's absolute trust in His providence. The Sephardi rite has 16 verses. The author is unknown, though it has been attributed to Solomon ibn *Gabirol (11th century). It may, however, be much older and stem from Babylonia. The hymn has appeared as part of the liturgy since the 14th century in the German rite and has spread to almost every rite and community. It was incorporated into the initial section of the *Shaharit* Service, but it has been suggested on the basis of the penultimate line that it originally formed the conclusion of the Night Prayers where it also still appears. Its main place now is at the conclusion of the Sabbath and festival *Musaf* Service (with the Sephardim even on the Day of Atonement) and of the **Kol Nidrei* Service. *Adon Olam* has become a popular hymn. In Morocco it serves as a wedding song and it is also recited by those present at a deathbed. The hymn has been translated several times into English verse, among others by George Borrow in his *Lavengro* (reprinted in Hertz, Prayer, p. 1005) and by Israel Zangwill (reprinted *ibid.*, 7, 9), and into other European languages.

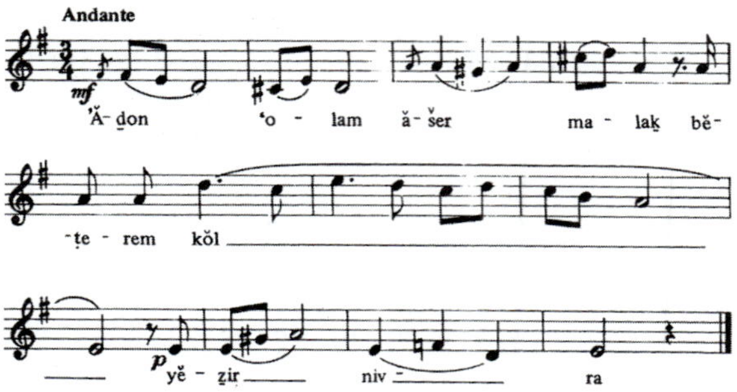

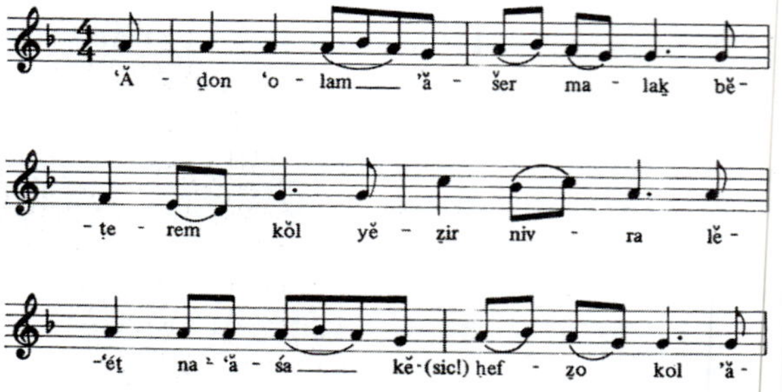

Music

Adon Olam is generally sung by the congregation. In the Ashkenazi tradition it is also sometimes rendered by the cantor on certain festive occasions, and then the melody is adapted to the *nosaḥ* of the section of the prayer into which it is incorporated. The great number of melodies for *Adon Olam* includes both individual settings, and borrowings from Jewish and Gentile sources. Ex. 3, from Djerba, is a North African "general" melody for *piyyutim*. Two versions from Germany in Idelsohn (Melodien, 7 (1932), nos. 59 and 336) both borrow the western Ashkenazi melody of *Omnam Ken*, while no. 346a is a German folk tune. A melody from Tangiers (I. Levy, *Antologia*, 1 (1965), no. 96) is the tune of the Romance *Esta Rahel la estimoza*. The composed or adapted tunes are mostly based upon a strict measure of four or three beats, both equally suitable for conforming to the *ḥazak*-meter of the text – one short and three longs. The melody is sung in many schools in Israel at the end of the pupils' morning prayer (in 4/4 measure; cf. the same, in 3/4 measure, YE, vol. 1, p. 514). Salamone de' *Rossi included an eight-voice composition of *Adon Olam* in his *Ha-Shirim Asher li-Shelomo* (Venice, 1622/23).

[Avigdor Herzog]

BIBLIOGRAPHY: Elbogen, Gottesdienst, 88; Abrahams, Companion, vii–ix; Davidson, Oẓar, 1 (1924), 29, no. 575; C. Roth, *Essays and Portraits* (1962), 295ff.; Baer S., Seder, 35; idem, *Toẓe'ot Ḥayyim* (1871), 57. MUSIC: Sendrey, Music, indexes.

ADOPTION, taking another's child as one's own.

Alleged Cases of Adoption in the Bible

The evidence for adoption in the Bible is so equivocal that some have denied it was practiced in the biblical period.

(A) GENESIS 15:2–3. Being childless, Abram complains that *Eliezer, his servant, will be his heir. Since in the ancient Near East only relatives, normally sons, could inherit, Abram had probably adopted, or contemplated adopting, Eliezer. This passage is illuminated by the ancient Near Eastern practice of childless couples adopting a son, sometimes a slave, to serve them in their lifetime and bury and mourn them when they die, in return for which the adopted son is designated their heir. If a natural child should subsequently be born to the couple, he would be chief heir and the adopted son would be second to him.

(B) GENESIS 16:2 and 30:3. Because of their barrenness, Sarai and Rachel give their servant girls to Abram and Jacob as concubines, hoping to "have children" (lit. "be built up") through the concubines. These words are taken as an expression of intention to adopt the children born of the husbands and concubines. Rachel's subsequent statement, "God… has given me a son" (30:6) seems to favor this view. A marriage contract from *Nuzi stipulates that in a similar case the mistress "shall have authority over the offspring." That the sons of Jacob's concubines share in his estate is said to presuppose their adoption. Bilhah's giving birth on (or perhaps "onto") Rachel's knees (30:3; cf. 50:23) is believed to be an adoption ceremony similar to one practiced by ancient European and Asiatic peoples among whom placing a child on a man's knees signified variously acknowledgment, legitimation, and adoption. Such an adoption by a mistress of the offspring of her husband and her slave-girl would not be unparalleled in the ancient Near East (see J. van Seters, JBL, 87 (1968), 404–7), but other considerations argue that this did not, in fact, take place in the episodes under consideration. Elsewhere in the Bible the sons of Bilhah and Zilpah are viewed only as the sons of these concubines, never of the mistresses (e.g., 21:10, 13; 33:2, 6–7; 35:23–26). Rachel's statement "God… has given me a son" reflects not necessarily adoption but Rachel's ownership of the child's mother, Bilhah (cf. Ex. 21:4, and especially the later Aramaic usage in Pritchard, Texts^3, 548a plus n. 5). The concubines' sons sharing in Jacob's estate does not presuppose adoption by Rachel and Leah because the sons are Jacob's by blood and require only his recognition to inherit (cf. *The Code of Hammurapi*, 170–1). Finally the alleged adoption ceremony must be interpreted otherwise. Placing a child on the knees is known from elsewhere in the ancient Near East (see I.J. Gelb et al., *The Chicago Assyrian Dictionary*, vol. 2 (1965), 256, s.v. *birku*; H. Hoffner, JNES, 27 (1968), 199–201). Outside of cases which signify divine protection and/or nursing, but not adoption (cf. T. Jacobsen, JNES, 2 (1943), 119–21), the knees upon which the child is placed are almost always those of its natural parent or grandparent. It seems to signify nothing more than affectionate play or welcoming into the family, sometimes combined with naming. (Only once, in the Hurrian Tale of the Cow and the Fisherman (J. Friedrich, *Zeitschrift fuer Assyriologie*, 49 (1950), 232–3 ll. 38ff.), does placing on the lap occur in an apparently adoptive context, but even there it is not clear that the ceremony is part of the adoption.) Some construe the ceremony as an act of legitimation, but no legal significance of any sort is immediately apparent. Significantly, the one unequivocal adoption ceremony in the Bible (Gen. 48:5–6) does not involve placing the child on the knees (Gen. 48:12 is from a different document and simply reflects the children's position during Jacob's embrace, between, not on, his knees). Furthermore, Genesis 30:3 speaks not of placing but of giving birth on Rachel's knees. This more likely reflects the position taken in antiquity by a woman during childbirth, straddling the knees of an attendant (another woman or at times her own husband) upon whose knees the emerging child was received (cf. perhaps Job 3:12). Perhaps Rachel attended Bilhah herself in order to cure, in a sympathetic-magical way, her own infertility (cf. 30:18, which may imply that Rachel, too, had been aiming ultimately at her own fertility), much like the practice of barren Arab women in modern times of being present at other women's deliveries. Genesis 50:23 (see below) must imply Joseph's assistance at his great-grandchildren's birth; or, if taken to mean simply that the children were placed upon his knees immediately after birth, it would imply a sort of welcoming or naming ceremony.

(C) GENESIS 29–31. It is widely held that Jacob was adopted by the originally sonless Laban, on the analogy of a Nuzi contract in which a sonless man adopts a son, makes him his heir, and gives him his daughter as a wife. This in itself is not compelling, but the document adds that, unless sons are later born to the adopter, the adopted son will also inherit his household gods. This passage, it is argued, illuminates Rachel's theft of Laban's household gods (31:19), and herein lies the strength of the adoption theory. But M. Greenberg (JBL, 81 (1962), 239–48) cast doubt upon the supposed explanation of Rachel's theft, thus depriving the adoption theory of its most convincing feature. In addition, the Bible itself not only fails to speak of adoption but pictures Jacob as Laban's employee.

(D) GENESIS 48:5–6. Near the end of his life Jacob, recalling God's promise of Canaan for his descendants, announces to Joseph: "Your two sons who were born to you ... before I came to you in Egypt, shall be mine; Ephraim and Manasseh shall be mine, as Reuben and Simeon are"; subsequent sons of Joseph will (according to the most common interpretation of the difficult v. 6), for the purposes of inheritance, be reckoned as sons of Ephraim and Manasseh. In view of the context – note particularly that grandsons, not outsiders, are involved – many believe that this adoption involves inheritance alone, and is not an adoption in the full sense. (M. David compares the classical *adoptio mortis causa.*) This belief is strengthened by the almost unanimous view that this episode is intended etiologically to explain why the descendants of Joseph held, in historical times, two tribal allotments, the territories of Ephraim and Manasseh.

(E) GENESIS 50:23. "The children of Machir son of Manasseh were likewise born on Joseph's knees" is said to reflect an adoption ceremony. To the objections listed above (b), it may be added that unlike (d), Joseph's adoption of Machir's children would explain nothing in Israel's later history and would be etiologically pointless.

(F) EXODUS 2:10. "Moses became her [= Pharaoh's daughter's] son." Some, however, interpret this as fosterage.

(G) LEVITICUS 18:9. A "sister... born outside the household" could mean an adopted sister, but most commentators interpret it as an illegitimate sister or one born of another marriage of the mother.

(H) JUDGES 11:1ff. S. Feigin argued that Gilead must have adopted Jephthah or else the question of his inheriting could never have arisen. But since Jephthah was already Gilead's son, the passage implies, at most, legitimation, not adoption.

(I) RUTH 4:16–17. Naomi's placing of the child of Ruth and Boaz in her bosom and the neighbors' declaration "a son is born to Naomi" are said to imply adoption by Naomi. But the very purpose of Ruth's marriage to Boaz was, from the legal viewpoint, to engender a son who would be accounted to Ruth's dead husband (see Deut. 25:6 and Gen. 38:8–9) and bear his name (Ruth 4:10). Adoption by Naomi, even though she was the deceased's mother, would frustrate that purpose. The text says that Naomi became the child's nurse, not his mother. The child is legally Naomi's grandson and the neighbors' words are best taken as referring to this.

(J) ESTHER 2:7, 15. Mordecai adopted his orphaned cousin Hadassah. (This case, too, is taken by some as rather one of fosterage.) This possible case of adoption among Jews living under Persian rule is paralleled by a case among the Jews living in the Persian military garrison at Elephantine, Egypt, in the fifth century C.E. (E. Kraeling, *The Brooklyn Museum Aramaic Papyri* (1953), no. 8).

(K) EZRA 2:61 (= Nehemiah 7:63). One or more priests married descendants of Barzillai the Gileadite and "were called by their name." This may imply adoption into the family of Barzillai.

(L) EZRA 10:44. Several Israelites married foreign women. The second half of the verse, unintelligible as it stands, ends with "and they placed/established children." S. Feigin, on the basis of similar Greek expressions and textual emendation, viewed this as a case of adoption. Since the passage is obviously corrupt (the Greek text of Esdras reads differently), no conclusions can be drawn from it, though Feigin's interpretation is not necessarily ruled out.

(M) I CHRONICLES 2:35–41. Since the slave Jarha (approximately a contemporary of David according to the genealogy) married his master's daughter, he was certainly manumitted and, quite likely, was adopted by his master; otherwise, his descendants would not have been listed in the Judahite genealogy.

(N) In addition to the above possible cases, one might see a sort of posthumous adoption in the ascription of the first son born of the levirate marriage (Gen. 38:8–9; Deut. 25:6; Ruth 4) to the dead brother. The child is possibly to be called "A son of B [the deceased]"; in this way he preserves the deceased's name (Deut. 25:6–7; Ruth 4:5) and presumably inherits his property.

SUMMARY. Of the most plausible cases above, two (A, D) are from the Patriarchal period, one reflects Egyptian practice (F), and another the practice of Persian Jews of the Exilic or post-Exilic period (J). From the pre-Exilic period there is a possible case alleged by the Chronicler to have taken place in the time of David (M), one or two other remotely possible cases (G) and (K), the latter from the late pre-Exilic or Exilic period) and the "posthumous adoption" involved in levirate marriage (N). The evidence for adoption in the pre-Exilic period is thus meager. The possibility that adoption was practiced in this period cannot be excluded, especially since contemporary legal documents are lacking. Nevertheless, it seems that if adoption played any role at all in Israelite family institutions, it was an insignificant one. It may be that the tribal consciousness of the Israelites did not favor the creation of artificial family ties and that the practice of polygamy obviated some of the need for adoption. For the post-Exilic per-iod in Palestine there is no reliable evidence for adoption at all.

Adoption as a Metaphor

(A) GOD AND ISRAEL. The relationship between God and Israel is often likened to that of father and son (Ex. 4:22; Deut. 8:5; 14:1). Usually there is no indication that this is meant in an adoptive sense, but this may be the sense of Jeremiah 3:19; 31:8; and Hosea 11:1. (B) IN KINGSHIP. The idea that the king is the son of a god occurs in Canaanite (Pritchard, Texts, 147–8) and other ancient Near Eastern sources. In Israel – which borrowed the very institution of kingship from its neighbors (I Sam. 8:5, 20) – this idea could not be accepted literally; biblical references to the king as God's son therefore seem intended in an adoptive sense. Several are reminiscent of ancient Near Eastern adoption contracts. Thus, Psalms 2:7–8 contains a declaration, "You are my son," a typical date formula "this day" (the next phrase, "I have born you," may reflect the conception of adoption as a new birth), and a promise of inheritance (an empire); II Samuel 17:7 contains a promise of inheritance (an enduring dynasty), a declaration of adoption, and a statement of the father's right to discipline the adoptive son (cf. Ps. 89:27ff.; I Chron. 17:13; 22:10; 28:6).

Since the divine adoption of kings was not known in the ancient Near East, and the very institution of adoption was rare – if at all existent – in Israel, the question arises as to where the model for these metaphors was found. According to M. Weinfeld (JAOS, 90 (1970)) the answer is found in the covenants made by God with David and Israel. These are essentially covenants of grant, a legal form which is widespread in the ancient Near East. In some of these a donor adopts the donee and the grant takes the form of an inheritance. Thus in the biblical metaphor God's adoption of David serves as the legal basis for the grant of the dynasty and empire, and God's adoption of Israel underlies the grant of a land (Jer. 3:19; also noted by S. Paul). According to Y. Muffs, the pattern of the covenant in the Priestly Document (P) is modeled on adoption by redemption from slavery (cf. Ex. 6:6–8). In later times adoption was used metaphorically in the Pauline epistles to refer variously to Israel's election (Rom. 9:4), to the believers who were redeemed from spiritual bondage by Jesus (Rom. 8:15; Eph. 1:5; Gal. 4:5), and to the final eschatological redemption from bondage (Rom. 8:21–23). Whether Paul modeled the metaphor on biblical or post-biblical, ancient Near Eastern, or Roman legal sources is debated.

[Jeffrey Howard Tigay]

Later Jewish Law

Adoption is not known as a legal institution in Jewish law. According to *halakhah* the personal status of parent and child is based on the natural family relationship only and there is no recognized way of creating this status artificially by a legal act or fiction. However, Jewish law does provide for consequences essentially similar to those caused by adoption to be created by legal means. These consequences are the right and obligation of a person to assume responsibility for (a) a child's physical and mental welfare and (b) his financial position, including matters of inheritance and maintenance. The legal means of achieving this result are (1) by the appointment of the adopter as a "guardian" (see **Apotropos*) of the child, with exclusive authority to care for the latter's personal welfare, including his upbringing, education, and determination of his place of abode; and (2) by entrusting the administration of the child's property to the adopter. The latter undertaking to be accountable to the child and, at his own expense and without any right of recourse, would assume all such financial obligations as are imposed by law on natural parents vis-à-vis their children. Thus, the child is for all practical purposes placed in the same position toward his adoptors as he would otherwise be toward his natural parents, since all matters of education, maintenance, upbringing, and financial administration are taken care of (Ket. 101b; Maim., Yad, Ishut, 23:17–18; and Sh. Ar., EH 114 and Tur *ibid.*, Sh. Ar., ḤM 60:2–5; 207:20–21; PDR, 3 (n.d.), 109–125). On the death of the adopter, his heirs would be obliged to continue to maintain the "adopted" child out of the former's estate, the said undertaking having created a legal debt to be satisfied as any other debt (Sh. Ar., ḤM 60:4).

Indeed, in principle neither the rights of the child toward his natural parents, nor their obligations toward him are in any way affected by the method of "adoption" described above; but in fact, the result approximated very closely to what is generally understood as adoption in the full sense of the word. The primary question in matters of adoption is the extent to which the natural parents are to be deprived of, and the adoptive parents vested with, the rights and obligations to look after the child's welfare. This is in accordance with the rule that determined that in all matters concerning a child, his welfare and interests are the overriding considerations always to be regarded as decisive (Responsa Rashba, attributed to Naḥmanides, 38; Responsa Radbaz, 1:123; Responsa Samuel di Modena, EH 123; Sh. Ar., EH 82, *Pitḥei Teshuvah* 7).

Even without private adoption, the court, as the "father of all orphans," has the power to order the removal of a child from his parents' custody, if this is considered necessary for his welfare (see **Apotropos*). So far as his pecuniary rights are concerned, the child, by virtue of his adopters' legal undertakings toward him, acquires an additional debtor, since his natural parents are not released from their own obligations imposed on them by law, i.e., until the age of six. Furthermore, the natural parents continue to be liable for the basic needs of their child from the age of six, to the extent that such needs are not or cannot be satisfied by the adopter; the continuation of this liability is based on *Dinei Ẓedakah* – the duty to give charity (see *Parent & Child; PDR, 3 (n.d.), 170–6; 4 (n.d.), 3–8).

With regard to right of inheritance, which according to *halakhah* is recognized as existing between a child and his natural parents only, the matter can be dealt with by means of testamentary disposition, whereby the adopter makes provision in his will for such portion of his estate to devolve on the child as the latter would have gotten by law had the former been his natural parent (see Civil Case 85/49, in: *Pesakim shel Beit ha-Mishpat ha-Elyon u-Vattei ha-Mishpat ha-Meḥoziyyim be-Yisrael*, 1 (1948/49), 343–8). In accordance with the rule that "Scripture looks upon one who brings up an orphan as if he had begotten him" (Sanh. 19b; Meg. 13a), there is no halakhic objection to the adopter calling the "adopted" child his son and the latter calling the former his father (Sanh. *ibid.*, based on II Sam. 21:8). Hence, provisions in documents in which these appellations are used by either party, where the adopter has no natural children and/or the child has no natural parent, may be taken as intended by the one to favor the other, according to the general tenor of the document (Sh. Ar., EH 19, *Pitḥei Teshuvah*, 3; ḤM 42:15; Responsa Ḥatam Sofer, EH 76). Since the legal acts mentioned above bring about no actual change in personal status, they do not affect the laws of marriage and divorce, so far as they might concern any of the parties involved.

In Israel

In the State of Israel, until 1981, adoption was governed by the Adoption of Children Law, 5720/1960, which empowered the district court and, with the consent of all the parties concerned, the rabbinical court, to grant an adoption order in respect of any person under the age of 18 years, provided that the prospective adopter was at least 18 years older than the prospective adoptee and the court were satisfied that the matter was in the best interests of the adoptee. Such an order had the effect of severing all family ties between the child and his natural parents. On the other hand, such a court order created new family ties between the adopter and the child to the same extent as are legally recognized as existing between natural parents and their child – unless the order was restricted or conditional in some respect. Thus, an adoption order would generally confer rights of intestate succession on the adoptee, who would henceforth also bear his adopter's name. However, the order did not affect the consequences of the blood relationship between the adoptee and his natural parents, so that the prohibitions and permissions of marriage and divorce continued to apply. On the other hand, adoption as such does not create such new prohibitions or permissions between the adopted and the adoptive family. There was no legal adoption of persons over the age of 18 years.

[Ben-Zion (Benno) Schereschewsky]

In 1981 the Knesset repealed the Adoption of Children Law, 5720/1960 and enacted in its stead the Adoption of Children Law, 5741/1981 (hereinafter – the Law), empowering the Family Court to issue adoption orders. The Law and its subsequent amendments provide for two substantively different modes of adoption. The first is local adoption, in which the Child Welfare Authority – a branch of the Welfare Ministry – functions as an adoption agency: it determines the adoptive parents' eligibility and even initiates adoption proceedings of the minor in the court, by way of special welfare officers for adoption. Proceedings to declare a minor adoptable can only be initiated by these welfare officers. The Child Welfare Authority is similarly responsible for the removal of a child from the custody of his natural parents against their wishes, for purposes of adoption. Occasionally, and under special circumstances, even prior to the child being declared adoptable the Authority may hand over the child "to a person who has agreed to receive him into his house with a view to adopting him" (§12 (c) of the Law). The second mode is that of "intercountry" (i.e., international) adoption, in which the adoption is undertaken by non-profit organizations under the supervision of a "central authority," i.e., the Child Welfare Authority.

The difference between the two kinds of adoption is as follows: local adoption also involves numerous cases in which the biological parents do not consent to hand their child over for adoption, in which case, quite naturally, the identity of the adoptive parents is withheld (closed adoption) to protect the adopted child from potential harm at the hands of his natural parents. In international adoption, the adoption is the product of negotiations between the prospective adoptive parents and the natural family. Under the Law, the rabbinical court is also permitted to issue adoption orders with the consent of all the parties, i.e., the parents (or adoptive parents, respectively) and the minor (when the case concerns a minor above the age of nine) or with the consent of the attorney general (in cases of a minor below nine). Even in those cases in which the rabbinical court has jurisdiction pursuant to the parties' consent, it is nevertheless obliged to comply with all the provisions of the law (§27).

The arrangements for international adoption were transformed when the law was amended in 1996, in accordance with the format of the Hague Convention on Protection of Children and Co-operation in Respect of Intercountry Adoption, which Israel ratified in 1993. Together with the incorporation of the Convention's provisions in the Law, the legislature also addressed a particular problem, unique to the State of Israel by virtue of its Jewish character. Under section 5 of the Law: "The adopter shall be of the same religion as the adoptee." How then can a Jewish family receive an adoption order for a non-Jewish child, brought to Israel from abroad? The legislature resolved this problem by amending section 13A of the Capacity and Guardianship Law, 5722/1962, which now provides that the court may give an instruction for the minor's religious conversion "to the religion of the person who provided for the minor with the intention of adopting him, during the six months that preceded the filing of the application for conversion."

In addition to the court's authorization, the minor who is a candidate for adoption must undergo a conversion process; according to the *halakhah*, a minor who is to be converted must be ritually immersed for conversion through the authority of the *bet din*. This is so, "because it [the conversion] is a benefit to him" (Ketubot 11a). The Israeli rabbinical courts have avoided converting minors who are candidates for adoption when the prospective adoptive parents will not provide him/her with an education based upon religious observance.

The case law of the Israel Supreme Court on adoption (given by Deputy President Menachem *Elon) emphasized the extensive impact of Jewish law on actual adoption procedures. The Law provides that "the adoption shall not affect any legal prohibition or permission as to marriage or divorce" (§16(c)); accordingly, the Adoption Register may be inspected by a marriage registrar in the course of carrying out his official function (§30 (2)). In doing so he raises the legal "veil" separating the adopted child from his natural family in order to establish the "legitimacy of his pedigree"; in other words, to prevent marriages between a brother and sister, etc. Furthermore, an adoption performed "for the benefit of the adoptee" does not represent the optimal solution, and preference should be given to the other arrangements, which do not sever the child from his natural family, despite their defective parental capacity. "Adoption is not intended as a punishment for the natural parents… we punish by confiscating property; we punish by denying freedom, but we do not punish by taking children away" (C.A. 3063/90 P.D. 45 (5) 837, 848), save for cases in which there is unequivocal, objective proof that the parents are incapable of raising their children.

As a rule, there is no discussion of the "child's best interests" until after examination as to whether there is any statutory ground for "removing the child from the natural guardianship of his parents and placing him in the home of the adopters" (H.C. 243/88 *Konsols v. Turgeman*, 45 (5) P.D. 837, 848). For the same reason, all possible efforts should be made to avoid ordering that the adoption of the minor be a "closed" adoption, which separates the minor from his natural identity. Indeed, in its capacity as the "father of minors," the court is commanded to "ensure the welfare and the future of the minor" and order that he be severed from his natural family – but this, only done when the court is convinced that leaving the minor with his family, or placing him with a foster family or in an "open adoption" will cause him terrible suffering due to his parents' incompetence (Elon, in the following judgments: C.A. 310/82, 37 (4) P.D. 421; C.A. 3763/92, 47 (1) P.D. 869). Similarly, the court will order the Child Welfare Service to seriously consider a request from the natural family that their child be given to "a family belonging to their own religious community, that maintains a religious lifestyle" (C.A. 3063/90 45 (3) 837) and, in exceptional circumstances, consider assenting to the parents' request that their child be adopted by their relatives who have no children of their own. This is in accordance with the prevalent custom in a number of Jewish communities whereby "when a couple belonging to the extended family is childless, another couple in the family, blessed with children, gives one of them to the couple that was denied their own offspring, and the latter can adopt and raise the child, as if he was their own child" (C.A. 568/80 35 (3) 701, 702).

Where the question arose of severing an adoptee minor from the religion of his natural parents, Justice Elon raised another consideration for withholding authorization of an adoption performed against the natural parents' wishes, or with their coerced consent: "We remember the battles fought by Jewish families and institutions in order to restore Jewish children to their families and religion. Prior to being sent to the death camps and gas chambers these families placed their children with Christians to care for them and raise them. It is befitting that we emulate their conduct in similar situations, when the tables are turned and the context is no longer the death camps but rather gangs of avaricious criminals" (the case of the "Brazilian girl" who was abducted from her natural mother; H.C. 243/88, 45 (2) P.D. 652).

In describing the character of the institution of adoption, its interpretation and implementation by the Israeli judiciary, Justice Elon further stated:

> I wholeheartedly agree that we must not hinder the development of the institution of adoption, having regard primarily for its crucial importance in locating a warm and secure home and a loving, devoted family for children who have suffered at the hands of fate. In pursuing this important goal we must also ensure the totality of the adoptive parents' rights and obligations in their relations with the adopted child. However, we must not ignore our principal and basic obligation, which is to maintain, promote and preserve the earliest and most fundamental social unit in human history: the natural family, its descendants, offshoots and progeny, the unit which always has, does, and always will continue to guarantee the survival of human society. This is certainly the case when dealing with the history of the Jewish family, in which the family unit, in both the immediate and extended sense, was the central pillar that guaranteed Jewish survival and continuity. This principle applies *a fortiori* in our times, in which the institution of the natural family has encountered tumultuous upheavals and frequent crises, which have weakened its capacity to function. (C.A. 488/77, 32 (3) P.D. 421 434)

And, in another decision:

> Tearing a child away from his biological parents is more difficult than splitting the Red Sea. The same applies to all decisions concerning a minor's adoption; all the more so in a case such as the one confronting us, in which the children are no longer infants and know their parents and their siblings. But as a court that is the "father of all minors," it is our responsibility to ensure their welfare and their best interests. It is incumbent upon us to find them a home in which they will merit love and warmth, physical well-being and spiritual tranquility, and all of the basic, elementary needs that they are not receiving in the home of their biological parents. (C.A. 658/88, 43 (4) P.D. 468, p. 477)

[Yisrael Gilat (2nd ed.)]

BIBLIOGRAPHY: BIBLE COMMENTARIES: J. Skinner, *The Book of Genesis* (ICC, 1930²); E. Speiser, *Genesis* (1964); N.M. Sarna, *Understanding Genesis* (1966); W. Rudolph, *Ruth* (1962); M.J. Dahood, *Psalms*, vol. 1 (1966). GENERAL: T.H. Gaster, *Myth… in the Old Testament* (1969), 448–9, 741–2; de Vaux, Anc Isr, 51–54, 111–3 (bibl. 523); S. Feigin, in: JBL, 50 (1931), 186–200; idem, *Mi-Sitrei he-Avar* (1943), 15–24, 50–53; H. Granqvist, *Birth and Childhood Among the Arabs* (1947), 60, 114, 252–9; M. David, *Adoptie in het Oude Israel* (Dutch, 1955); Z. Falk, *Hebrew Law in Biblical Times* (1964), 162–4; F. Lyall, in JBL, 88 (1969), 458–66; H. Donner, in: *Oriens Antiquus*, 8 (1969), 87–119; H.E. Baker, *Legal System of Israel* (1968), index. SPECIAL STUDIES: B. Stade, in: ZAW, 6 (1886), 143–56; G. Cooke, *ibid.*, 73 (1961), 202–25; C. Gordon, in: BA, 3 (1940), 2–7; H.H. Rowley, *The Servant of the Lord…* (1952), 163–86 (= HTR, 40 (1947), 77–99); I. Mendelsohn, in: IEJ, 9 (1959), 180–3; R. Patai, *Sex and Family in the Bible and the Middle East* (1959), 42, 78–79, 92–98, 205, 224; W.F. Albright, in: BASOR, 163 (1961), 47; H. Hoffner, in: JNES, 27 (1968), 198–203; J. Preuss, *Biblisch-Talmudische Medizin* (1923), 460–1; S. Kardimon, in: JSS, 3 (1958), 123–6; J. van Seters, in: JBL, 87 (1968), 401–8; Z. Falk, in: *Iura*, 17 (1966), 170–1. JEWISH LAW: J. Kister, *Sekirah al Immuẓ Yeladim…* (1953); G. Felder, Hakohen, in: *Sinai*, 48 (1961), 204ff.; Findling, in: *No'am*, 4 (1961), 65ff.; Ezraḥi, *ibid.*, 94ff.; Rudner, *ibid.*, 61ff.; B. Schereschewsky, *Dinei Mishpaḥah* (1967²), 395ff. **ADD. BIBLIOGRAPHY:** M. Elon, *Jewish Law – History, Sources Principles* (1994), 827, 1763–1765; idem, *Jewish Law (Mishpat Ivri): Cases and Materials* (Mathew Bender Case Books, 1999), 313–22; A. Abraham, "*Imuẓ Yeladim*," in: *Hama'ayan* (1994), 29; "Sample of Adoption Order given by the Rabbinical Court for a Minor, in accordance with the *Halakhah*," in: *Shurat ha-Din* (2000), 475; A.J. Goldman, *Judaism Confronts Contemporary Issues* (1978), 63–73; Y. Rosen, "*Giyyur Ketinim ha-Me'umazim be-Mishpaḥah Ḥillonit*," in *Teḥumin*, 20 (2000), 245; M. Steinberg, *Responsum on Problems of Adoption in Jewish Law* (1969); I. Warhaftig, *Av u-Veno, Mehkarei Mishpat*, 16 (2000), 479; R. Yaron, "Variations on Adoption," in: *Journal of Juristic Papyrology*, 15 (1965), 171–83.

ADORAIM (Heb. אֲדוֹרַיִם), ancient city of Judah, southwest of Hebron. It appears in the Bible only in the list of cities fortified by Solomon's son, *Rehoboam (II Chron. 11:9). Adoraim (Adoram) is also mentioned in the Book of Jubilees 38:8–9. In the Hellenistic period, when it was known as Adora, it was one of the chief cities of Idumea; the Ptolemaic official Zeno visited it in 259 B.C.E. (Zeno papyri, 76). The city is also mentioned in I Maccabees 13:20 in connection with the campaigns of the Hasmonean *Jonathan and his adversary Tryphon in 143 B.C.E. It was later captured by John Hyrcanus together with Marisa and the whole of Idumea (Jos., Wars, 1:63; Ant., 13:257). The Roman proconsul Gabinius (d. 48/7 B.C.E.) chose it as the seat of one of his *synhedria* ("councils"; Jos., Ant., 14:91) and it retained its Jewish character until the end of the Bar Kokhba War (135 C.E.). The site is occupied by the twin villages of Dūrā al-ʾArajān, 5 mi. (8 km.) south west of Hebron, situated on a plateau overlooking the coastal plain, with a population of 10,000.

[Michael Avi-Yonah]

Modern Period

The name Adoraim also describes a ridge of the Hebron Hills. Most of the ridge, including the site of ancient Adoraim, remained until 1967 on the Jordanian side of the 1949 armistice lines. However, the name Adoraim was given in the middle 1950s to a specially planned region in the Judean Foothills under Israel control between the Bet Guvrin–Hebron road and Kibbutz.

[Efraim Orni]

BIBLIOGRAPHY: EM 1 (1965), 103–4; Abel, in: RB, 35 (1926), 531; 36 (1927), 145; Abel, Geog, 2 (1938), 239; W.F. Albright, in: BASOR, 89 (1943), 14 no. 37; Albright, Stone, 347 D. Kallner (Amiram), in: BJPES, 14 (1948–49), 30–37; Kanael, in: IEJ, 7 (1957), 98–106.

ADORNO, THEODOR W. (1903–1969), German philosopher, sociologist, composer. As a sociologist (in conjunction with Max *Horkheimer et al.) he developed the Critical Theory of society (the so-called Frankfurt School project) and published treatises in the fields of literary and cultural criticism. As a composer he produced over 30 musical works in various genres.

After completing his academic studies in philosophy, psychology, sociology, and musical sciences in Frankfurt/Main in 1925, Adorno took composition lessons with Alban Berg in Vienna – an education he had begun (with Bernhard Sekles) when he was still a high school student. Alongside his studies with Berg he also published numerous musical reviews. In 1931 he qualified as a university professor in philosophy and took up a chair in philosophy at the Johann Wolfgang Goethe Universität of Frankfurt/Main. During this time Adorno was most strongly influenced by Walter *Benjamin and particularly by his notion that language preserves historical truth. When the National Socialists came to power, he was deprived of his chair. Adorno had always considered his Jewish descent (his father was Jewish and Adorno's last name was Wiesengrund-Adorno until his mid-forties) to be unimportant but the race laws introduced by the Nazis made him into an outsider. This turning point in his life and his personal experience of having an outsider status in society generated a politically accentuated intellectualism. In the period 1934–49 he lived as an emigré – initially in England (Oxford) and then in the United States (New York and Los Angeles). During this period he wrote major philosophical and sociological works, most of which were published after his return to Germany (October 1949): *The Philosophy of Modern Music* (1949), *Dialectic of Enlightenment* (1947), *The Authoritarian Personality* (1950), *Minima Moralia* (1951), and *Against Epistemology: Meta-Critique – Studies in Husserl and the Phenomenological Antinomics* (1956).

Teaching philosophy and sociology in the 1960s, Adorno made a name for himself not only as an extremely successful university lecturer and public intellectual but also as the director of the Institute of Social Research in Frankfurt, gaining fame for such publications as *What Does It Mean: Working Up the Past* (1959) and *Education after Auschwitz* (1967).

Adorno's critical stance towards the world and the negativism of his social criticism resulted from his personal experience of sustained horror: Exposure to the monstrous cruelty of the Nazi genocide was the guiding moral force behind his philosophical theory of society and its ultimate source. His intellectuality resided in his ability to maintain the tension between opposing phenomena instead of synthesizing or harmonizing the differences. The individual experience of acknowledging the uniqueness of the Other crystallized into a fundamental concept which Adorno brought to bear in seeking a decent social order: "living one's difference without fear."

In the 1960s Adorno published a volume on Gustav Mahler (1960), three volumes of *Notes on Literature* (1965–68), and his main philosophical opus, *Negative Dialectics* (1968). During this decade he was given the German Critics' Award for Literature and for his 60th birthday the city of Frankfurt/Main bestowed the Goethe Medal on him. His *Aesthetic Theory* was published posthumously. In addition to a large number of letters he exchanged with contemporaries, his *Complete Works* comprise his musical compositions, 20 volumes of collected writings, and the equally comprehensive posthumous writings (Suhrkamp Verlag).

BIBLIOGRAPHY: M. Jay, *Adorno* (1984); S. Müller-Doohm, *Adorno. A Biography*, trans. R.Livingstone (2005).

[Stefan Müller-Doohm (2nd ed.)]

ADRAMMELECH (Heb. אַדְרַמֶּלֶךְ). (1) A deity named Adrammelech was worshiped, together with *Anammelech, by the people of *Sepharvaim (II Kings 17:31), possibly Assyrian Saparrê, who settled in Samaria after its destruction in 722 B.C.E. No Assyrian or Babylonian deity is known by the name Adrammelech. Inscriptions from Gozan (Tell Ḥalaf on the Khabur, beginning of the ninth century B.C.E.) were once thought to attest the name of a god Adad-Milki. Accordingly, it was suggested to correct Adrammelech to Adadmelech assuming the common graphic confusion of *dalet* and *resh*. But the reading Adad-Milki in the Gozan inscriptions themselves now seems questionable. The element *melech* in the name is probably the Hebrew word for king, so Addir-Melech, "the glorious one is king," is a possibility. At the same time Addir-Molech, "glorious is (the god) Molech" (see *Moloch), cannot be ruled out.

(2) According to the received Hebrew text, Adrammelech was the name of a son of *Sennacherib, king of Assyria (II Kings 19:37; Isa. 37:38). Together with his brother *Sharezer, Adrammelech murdered his father in the temple of Nisroch and escaped to the land of *Ararat (cf. II Chron. 32:21). Abydenus (Eusebius, *Armenia Chronicle*, ed. Schoene, 1:35) gives the name of the murderer as Adramelus. That reading is now confirmed by cuneiform evidence that gives the regicide's name as Arda-Mulissi, "servant of Mulissu," Mulissu being the neo-Assyrian name of the goddess Ninlil. In turn we may correct the Hebrew to ארדמלס.

The biblical description of Sennacherib's murder is given in relation to the Assyrian defeat near Jerusalem (II Kings 19:36–37; Isa. 37:37–38; cf. II Chron. 32:21). In point of fact, many years elapsed between Sennacherib's campaign in Phoenicia and Ereẓ Israel (c. 701 B.C.E.) and his death (681 B.C.E.), but the Bible telescopes these events to show that the prophecy of Isaiah about Sennacherib (II Kings 19:7; Isa. 37:7) was fulfilled.

ADD. BIBLIOGRAPHY: (1) S. Kaufman, in: JNES, 37 (1978), 101–9; A. Millard, in: DDD, 10–11; G. Heider, in: DDD, 581–85. (2) S. Parpola, in: *Mesopotamia*, 8 (1980), 171–82.

[Yuval Kamrat / S. David Sperling (2nd ed.)]

ADRET, MOSES IBN (d. 1772), rabbinic scholar of Smyrna. Ḥ.J.D. *Azulai described Adret as an eminent and saintly scholar with extensive knowledge in rabbinic literature, endowed with a keen intellect and a phenomenal memory. Adret often took an independent and critical stand against older authorities. Twelve of his works, listed by Azulai, include novellae on the major part of the Talmud, notes on the Mishnah, *Maimonides' code, *Asher b. Jehiel's compendium, and *Jacob b. Asher's *Arba'ah Turim*, as well as responsa, and Bible commentaries. Only *Berakh Moshe*, novellae on various Talmud tractates, has been published (Salonika, 1802). His *Torat Moshe* (commentary on the Mishnah) was supposed to have appeared in Leghorn, but has not survived. Responsa by Adret were incorporated in E. Malki's collection *Ein Mishpat* (Constantinople, 1770, YD, nos. 7, 8, 9, 10). In responsum no. 10 Adret boasted of his complete mastery of the whole range of talmudic sources and the various halakhic works he had composed to justify his stand in his protracted dispute with Malki, who speaks sarcastically of Adret's vaunted piety and modesty (*ibid.*, no. 11).

BIBLIOGRAPHY: Azulai, 1 (1852), 130, no. 95, s.v. *Moshe Adret.*

ADRET, SOLOMON BEN ABRAHAM (known from his initials as **RaShBa**, **R**av **Sh**lomo **B**en **A**braham; c. 1235–c. 1310), Spanish rabbi and one of the foremost Jewish scholars of his time, whose influence has remained to this day. Adret belonged to a well-to-do family of Barcelona where he lived all his life. His principal teacher was Jonah b. Abraham *Gerondi and Adret always refers to him as "my teacher." He also studied under Naḥmanides, being considered one of his outstanding students and principal exponent of his "school" in the interpretation of the Talmud.

While still young, Adret engaged extensively in financial transactions, and the king of Aragon was among his debtors. After a few years he withdrew from business and accepted the position of rabbi in Barcelona, which he held for more than 40 years. Adret was recognized as the leading figure in Spanish Jewry before he was 40 and his opinions carried weight far beyond the frontiers of Spain. He was a man of great accomplishments, strong character, and incorruptible judgment. Not long after he entered upon his office as rabbi, he vigorously defended an orphan against leading court Jews and the powerful Christian nobles who supported them. Yet, he was a humble man, with a warm, sensitive heart. Pedro III of Aragon submitted to him for adjudication of a number of complicated cases that had arisen between Jews of different communities. Against his will, the case of an informer belonging to an aristocratic family was assigned to him for trial by order of the king: he sentenced the man to death. Three years later the relatives of the condemned man appealed the verdict. Adret referred the case to *Meir b. Baruch of Rothenburg, the foremost rabbinic authority in Germany, who sustained the verdict.

Questions were addressed to Adret from all parts of the Jewish world including Germany, France, Bohemia, Sicily, Crete, Morocco, Algiers, Palestine, and Portugal. The communities gathered his responsa into special collections and kept them as a source of guidance. He explained the most abstruse matters in clear and simple terms. Many of his responsa deal with the clarification of problematic biblical passages, and some of them touch on questions of philosophy and the fundamentals of religion. Altogether Adret wrote thousands of responsa (3,500 have been printed). One responsum, written a few days before his death, is signed by his son. Adret's responsa constitute a primary source of information for the history of the Jews of his period and, to some extent, also for general history. When Maimonides' grandson David was denounced to the Sultan of Egypt, Adret collected 25,000 dinars from the Spanish community to secure his release. Similarly when the Rome community wished to translate Maimonides' commentary on the Mishnah into Hebrew, Adret secured the necessary manuscripts and translators, one of whom testified, "It is because of the awe with which our master inspires us, that we have persisted in our undertaking."

Adret acquired a considerable knowledge of Roman law and local Spanish legal practice. He played a vital role in providing the legal basis for the structure of the Jewish community and its institutions, and many of his responsa are devoted to communal matters and to the activities of rabbinic courts. He defended the rights of the Jewish communities and opposed all attempts at arbitrary control and recourse to non-Jewish tribunals. That Adret was considered by his contemporaries to be one of the outstanding authorities of the generation is obvious from the efforts that Abba Mari *Astruc made to enlist his support in the campaign for the preservation of the traditional way of study and traditional values against the philosophical school. These efforts ultimately culminated in a ban (see below). The correspondence on the subject was included by Astruc in his *Minḥat Kenaot* (Pressburg, 1838).

Adret had a considerable knowledge of philosophy and was well-versed in the scientific literature of his day, although he headed the movement against the spreading of these subjects among the masses. To an opponent of a ban on secular studies he wrote: "You seem to think that we have no share in (secular) wisdom... This is not the case... for we know these lofty sciences and we are aware of their nature" (Abba Mari b. Moses of Lunel, *Minḥat Kena'ot* (1838), 43). He defended Maimonides in the second attack directed against his writings in France and in Palestine. He opposed both the allegorical method of interpreting the Bible that was then prevalent among the rationalists in southern France and in Spain, and the extreme mystical tendency which was making headway in Spain, and he strongly attacked the activities of Abraham *Abulafia. He also took precautions against those who denied the Divine origin of the Torah and forsook its study for that of the sciences. In the bitter conflict which flared up in the communities of southern France, Adret was on the side of the traditionalists. There were extremists who wished to prohibit the study of the sciences completely; in the text of the ban which they suggested to Adret they proposed that such studies be prohibited until the age of 30. However, Adret, in the famous ban he proclaimed in Barcelona in 1305, adopted a middle course. He permitted the study of physics and metaphysics from the age of 25, put no restriction at all on the study of astronomy and medicine, and sanctioned the reading of Maimonides' works. In the end the communities in southern France resisted Adret's ban. In part, their resistance stemmed from the efforts of Philip the Fair (1285–1314) to unite all of France. Since rabbinic bans required authorization from the State, the acceptance of a ban originating in Spain might have been viewed as treason by the French crown.

Adret took up arms also, both in oral and written disputes, against detractors of Judaism, such as Raymond *Martini and his work *Pugio fidei*. Adret replied to this in a special work in which he defended the eternity of the Torah and the value of its practical commandments. In his responsa (4, 187) he gave details of a disputation he had with a leading Christian scholar. He wrote a book refuting the attacks of the 11th-century Mohammedan scholar, Aḥmad ibn Ḥazm (published by Perles, 1863). A variety of reasons have been suggested as to why Adret wrote his attack on ibn Ḥazm. They include the fact that Christian polemicists drew many of their arguments from ibn Ḥazm's tract, that Adret's book served to bolster the communities of Jews under Muslim rule, and that Adret was fearful that ibn Ḥazm's biblical criticisms might be accepted.

Collections of the responsa of Adret are extant today. They pose a difficult literary problem. The first collection was printed in Rome before 1480 and the second, of which only a few copies remain, in Constantinople in 1516. In 1908 (on the front page incorrectly 1868) these two collections were reprinted in Warsaw, and the editor called them "Part 7" of the responsa of Adret. An additional collection, containing 1255 responsa, was printed in Bologna in 1539. It is this which is referred to as the Responsa of Adret "Part 1." The so-called "Part 2" containing 405 responsa, called *Toledot Adam*, was published in Leghorn in 1657, and "Part 3" with 488 responsa, also in Leghorn, in 1788. "Part 4" was published in Salonika in 1803 and "Part 5" in Leghorn in 1825. "Part 6" was published together with the 1908 Warsaw edition previously mentioned. Many of the responsa are not the work of Adret, but of other scholars whose responsa the copyists collected together with his. On the other hand, most of the responsa in the collection attributed to Naḥmanides (Venice, 1519) are the work of Adret. These collections, amounting to a few thousand responsa, contain many responsa identical in wording and context. A critical edition of Adret's responsa, which should facilitate identification and determine authorship, is a primary scholastic need and is still lacking.

Adret headed a yeshivah to which students flocked, even from Germany (Responsa 1,395) and other countries. Among his distinguished students were *Yom Tov b. Abraham of Seville, Shem Tov *Ibn Gaon, and *Bahya b. Asher. According to Adret, his academy housed valuable manuscripts of the Talmud brought from the Babylonian academies or which had been checked in the academies of Kairouan. It appears that he composed his famous novellae to the Talmud in connection with his lectures to his students. His novellae to 17 tractates of the Talmud have been published: *Berakhot* (Venice, 1523); *Shabbat* (Constantinople, 1720); *Eruvin* (Warsaw, 1895); *Beẓah* (Lemberg, 1847); *Rosh Ha-Shanah* (in part, Constantinople, 1720, and in a complete, critical edition, 1961); *Megillah* (Constantinople, 1720; complete edition, 1956); *Yevamot* (Constantinople, 1720); *Gittin* (Venice, 1523); *Kiddushin* (Constantinople, 1717); *Nedarim* (*ibid.*, 1720); *Bava Kamma* (*ibid.*, 1720); *Bava Mezia* (in part, Jerusalem, 1931); *Bava Batra* (*ibid.*, 1957);

Shevu'ot (Salonika, 1729, and in full, Jerusalem, 1965); *Avodah Zarah* (in part in Jerusalem, 1966); *Hullin* (Venice, 1523); *Niddah* (Altona, 1797 and a complete edition, Jerusalem, 1938). The novellae to *Menahot* are not his, and the novellae to *Ketubbot* ascribed to him are actually by Naḥmanides. *Ketubbot* and *Nazir* are still in manuscript. In his novellae, Adret was greatly influenced by Naḥmanides' method, a synthesis of the methods of French scholars and of the early Spanish authorities such as Joseph *Ibn Migash and his colleagues. He carried, however, Nahmanides' methods to their extreme, establishing the French school in Spain, though there exist strong literal ties between the two methods. The novellae enjoyed a wide circulation; they have gone through many editions and are still extensively consulted by students of the Talmud.

Adret also devoted much time to commenting on the *aggadot* in the Talmud and wrote a special work on the subject (*Ḥiddushei Aggadot ha-Shas*, Tel Aviv, 1966). In his commentaries, Adret followed the methods of inquiry of the moderate Spanish scholars; the influence of Maimonides' Guide is also evident. It is evident from many places in his works that Adret interested himself in Kabbalah and even acquired great knowledge of it. In this he resembled his teacher Naḥmanides. On the other hand it appears that he did his best to conceal his opinions on the subject. However it is significant that most of his pupils wrote commentaries to the mystical part of Naḥmanides' commentary on the Pentateuch, many of them still in manuscript.

Beside his responsa and novellae, Adret wrote two legal manuals. The more important, *Torat ha-Bayit*, deals with most of the ritual observances, such as ritual slaughter, forbidden foods, gentile wine, and the laws of *niddah* (Venice, 1607), together with *Sha'ar ha-Mayim* – laws of *mikveh* (first published in Budapest, 1930, and again in Jerusalem, 1963). The book is divided into seven parts, is written with great profundity and perception, and embodies detailed halakhic discussions. He reviews the methods of his predecessors, raises and meets objections, refutes and corroborates, decides among opposing views, and advances his own opinion. For practical purposes of guidance, he wrote a compendium of the larger work, *Torat ha-Bayit ha-Kaẓer* (Cremona, 1566). Aaron ha-Levi of Barcelona (see **Ha-Ḥinnukh*), a fellow townsman and old friend of the author, wrote many critical notes on this book in his *Bedek ha-Bayit*. Although Aaron ha-Levi in his introduction and criticisms wrote in a respectful tone, Adret felt offended and wrote in reply his *Mishmeret ha-Bayit* (all included in the 1608 Venice edition) which was issued anonymously and contained no clue to the author's identity. It purports to have been written by a scholar solicitous of Adret's honor. However, in one of his responsa Adret revealed that he was the author. Adret's refutations are written in a pungent style reminiscent of *Abraham b. David of Posquières' strictures on Maimonides, and in this book he reveals himself as a doughty polemicist.

Adret's *Avodat ha-Kodesh* on the laws of the Sabbath and the festivals is also extant. It appeared in two versions, one complete and the other abridged. The former has not yet been published, while the latter was published in Venice in 1602. He also wrote *Piskei Ḥallah* (Constantinople, 1516) on the laws relating to **Ḥallah.*

The changes in rabbinic study in Spain started by Naḥmanides were finally effected by Adret. His responsa have at all times been highly influential and were a major source of the Shulḥan Arukh.

BIBLIOGRAPHY: Baer, Spain, index, s.v. *Solomon b. Abraham ibn Adret (Rashba)*; J. Perles, *R. Salomo b. Abraham b. Adereth* (Breslau, 1863); I. Epstein, *The "Responsa" of R. Solomon ben Adreth of Barcelona* (1962); A. Rosenthal, in: KS, 42 (1966/67); A.S. Halkin, in: *Perakim* (1968), 35–57; Havlin, in: *Moriah*, 1 (1968), 58–67; L.A. Feldman, in: *Sinai*, 33 (1969), 243–7. **ADD. BIBLIOGRAPHY:** C. Adang, in: *Judios y Musulmanes en al-Andalus y el Magreb* (2002), 179–209; S. Klein-Braslavy in: *"Encuentros" and "Desencuentros": Spanish Jewish Cultural Interaction throughout History* (2000), 105–29; M. Saperstein, in: *Jewish History*, 1:2 (1986), 27–38; L. Feldman, in: *Rabbi Joseph H. Lookstein Memorial Volume* (1980), 119–24; D. Horwitz, in: *Torah u-Madda Journal*, 3 (1991–92) 52–81.

[Simha Assaf / David Derovan (2nd ed.)]

ADRIEL (Heb. אַדְרִיאֵל; "God is my help"), son of Barzillai the Meholathite; the husband of *Merab, the daughter of Saul (I Sam. 18:19). Saul pledged his daughter Merab to David; however, when the time came to fulfill his promise, he gave her to Adriel. Critics have suggested that the name Michal in II Samuel 21:8 is an error for Merab (which is read by the Lucianic recension of the Septuagint and by the Peshitta). David handed over the five sons of Adriel and Merab to the Gibeonites for impalement (II Sam. 21:8–10).

ADULLAM (Heb. עֲדֻלָּם), city in Judah in biblical times. It was originally a Canaanite town, the seat of Hirah the Adullamite (friend and father-in-law of Judah (Gen. 38:1, 12, 20)). Adullam's king was defeated by Joshua and the city is mentioned together with 13 others as belonging to the second district of Judah (Josh. 12:15; 5:35). This region contained many caves which could offer refuge to outlaws. In one of these, David hid after fleeing from Saul, and it served as his headquarters for a time during his war with the Philistines (I Sam. 22:1). It was there that the three "mighty men" brought David water from the well at Beth-Lehem (II Sam. 23:13; I Chron. 11:15ff.; Jos., Ant., 6:247). Rehoboam included Adullam in his line of fortifications beside Soco in the valley of Elah (II Chron. 11:7). After the return from Babylonian exile it is mentioned in Nehemiah 11:30 among the places inhabited by Jews. It remained a Jewish town in Hasmonean times (II Macc. 12:38, cf. I Macc. 5:59–60); Judah the Maccabee withdrew to Adullam after his battle against Gorgias near Marissa (Mareshah) in 163 B.C.E. Eusebius (Onom., 24:21) describes fourth-century Adullam as a large village, 10 Roman mi. east of Eleutheropolis (Bet Guvrin). It has been identified with al-Sheikh Madhkūr, 9 mi. (15 km.) northeast of Bet Guvrin. The name Adulam may have survived in Khirbat ʾId al-Māʾ (or Miyeh) in the vicinity of that tell.

BIBLIOGRAPHY: Clermont-Ganneau, Arch, 2 (1899), 429ff.; Dalman, in: PJB, 9 (1913), 33ff.; Albright, in: BASOR, 15 (1924), 3ff.; Abel, in: RB, 33 (1924), 22; Beyer, in: ZDPV, 54 (1931), 115; Abel, Geog, 2 (1938), 239; Press, Ereẓ, 4 (1955), 686; Aharoni, Land, index. **ADD. BIBLIOGRAPHY:** S. Japhet, *I & II Chronicles* (1993), 665–66.

[Michael Avi-Yonah]

ADULLAM REGION (Heb. חֶבֶל עֲדֻלָּם), settlement region in southern Israel, N.W. and W. of the Hebron Hills, comprising over 100,000 dunams (25,000 acres). Geographically, it belongs partly to the Judean Hills and partly to the Shephelah. The name was chosen because the assumed site of ancient *Adullam lies in the center of this region. After the principle of comprehensive regional planning had been adopted by the relevant authorities in the mid-1950s, the area was first included in the *Lachish Region (which eventually became the prototype of all such planning). After 1957, however, the Adullam Region was treated as a separate area, as conditions there were much more difficult and land reclamation had to precede all settlement activity. The Jewish National Fund, therefore, assumed responsibility for the first stage of the urgent development of this border region. In the project, three clusters of villages were arranged around the "rural centers" of Ẓur Hadassah in the northeast, Neveh Mikha'el in the center, and Li-On (later renamed Sarigim) in the southwest. New villages were founded in the framework of the regional plan (e.g., Avi'ezer, Roglit (later united with Neveh Mikha'el), Adderet, Givat Yeshayahu, Ẓafririm), and earlier settlements in adjoining areas (e.g., Netiv ha-Lamed He, Bet Guvrin, Mevo Beitar, Matta, Bar Giora, and Neḥushah) were included in the project. Farming land was reclaimed by terracing and stone clearing, and by drainage of soil in small valleys. The water supply was greatly improved by drilling of deep wells in and near the region. The actual development of villages and their farming branches was carried out by the Jewish Agency's Agricultural Settlement Department. In the higher northeastern part of the region with its limestone rocks, terra rossa soils, and its cool and relatively wet climate, deciduous fruit and grapevines became important factors in the local economy, and poultry breeding constituted a main source of income. In the lower southwest parts with their broader valleys and deeper rendzina or alluvial soils, the economy was based on field crops (wheat, cotton, sunflowers, sorghum, etc.) as well as tobacco, vegetables, sheep, and cattle. In 1968 a road was built connecting Neveh Mikha'el with the reestablished *Gush Eẓyon bloc. At the beginning of the 21st century the region included 16 moshavim, a kibbutz, and two rural communities, reaching a population of approximately 8,000. The economy of the region developed to include wine and olive oil production, citrus groves, fruit orchards, cotton, and flowers. In addition to farming, many of the settlers earned their livelihoods in the tourist industry.

[Efraim Orni / Shaked Gilboa (2nd ed.)]

ADULTERY (Heb. נִאוּף, *ni'uf*; sometimes, loosely, זְנוּת, *zenut*; זְנוּנִים, *zenunim*; lit. "fornication, whoredom"). Voluntary sexual intercourse between a married woman, or one engaged by payment of the brideprice, and a man other than her husband.

Biblical Period

The extramarital intercourse of a married man is not *per se* a crime in biblical or later Jewish law. This distinction stems from the economic aspect of Israelite marriage: the wife was the husband's possession (of a special sort, see *Marriage), and adultery constituted a violation of the husband's exclusive right to her; the wife, as the husband's possession, had no such right to him. Adultery is prohibited in the Decalogue (Ex. 20:13; Deut. 5:17), where it is listed between murder and theft (cf. Jer. 7:9; Ezek. 16:38; Hos. 4:2; Ps. 50:18; Prov. 6:30ff.; Job 24:14–15) among offenses against one's fellow. Like all sexual wrongs, it defiles those who commit it (Lev. 18:20; Num. 5:13). It is termed "(the) great sin" in Genesis 20:9 and in Egyptian and Ugaritic texts (cf. *[ha]-ʿAverah*, "[the] transgression," for sexual crimes in rabbinic texts, e.g., Av. Zar. 3a). Its gravity is underscored by its being punishable by the death penalty for both the man and the woman (Lev. 20:10; Deut. 22:22). Stoning by the public, a procedure often prescribed for crimes felt to threaten the well-being of the nation as a whole, among which were sexual crimes (Lev. 18:24–27; 20:22; Deut. 24:4; cf. Jer. 3:1–2), is mentioned in Deuteronomy 22:24; cf. Ezekiel 16:40; 23:46–47 (cf. John 8:3–7). Other punishments are reflected in non-legal texts. Burning is mentioned in Gen. 38:24 (cf. Lev. 21:9). Stripping, known in ancient Near Eastern divorce procedure, is reflected in the metaphor of Hos. 2:5 and mentioned in Ezekiel 16:37, 39; 23:26. The mutilation mentioned in Ezekiel 16:39; 23:25 does not seem to reflect Israelite practice, but rather the legal traditions of Mesopotamia, where Ezekiel lived (cf. 23:24: "[the nations] shall judge you according to their laws," and, cf. *The Middle Assyrian Laws*, 15 in Pritchard, Texts, 181; the same punishment for adulteresses in Egypt is attested by Diodorus Siculus, *Bibliotheca*, 1:18, according to G.A. Cooke, *The Book of Ezekiel*, 254).

Other ancient Near Eastern law collections also prescribe the death penalty for adulterers, but, treating adultery as an offense against the husband alone, permit the aggrieved husband to waive or mitigate the punishment (*The Code of Hammurapi*, 129, in: Pritchard, Texts, 171; *The Middle Assyrian Laws,* 14–16, in: Pritchard, Texts, 181; The *Hittite Laws*, 197–98, in: Pritchard, Texts, 196). Biblical law allows no such mitigation. Because the marriage bond is divinely sanctioned (cf. Mal. 2:14; Prov. 2:17) and the prohibition of adultery is of divine origin, God as well as the husband is offended by adultery (cf. Gen. 20:6; 39:8–9; Ps. 51:6), and an offense against God cannot be pardoned by man. Mesopotamian religious literature also views adultery as offensive to the gods, but, unlike the situation in Israel, this religious conception is not reflected in Mesopotamian legal literature.

Whether the severe provisions of the law were actually carried out in biblical times cannot be ascertained. Proverbs 6:23–35, warning of the harm and disgrace which will befall the adulterer, and Job. 31:11, which terms adultery "an assessable transgression" (E.A. Speiser, JBL, 82 (1963), pp. 301–306) seem to assume that the crime could be composed monetarily at the husband's discretion. But whether passages from the wisdom literature, with its strong international literary ties, reflect actual practice in Israel is a moot question.

As in other cases (see M. Greenberg, IDB, 1 (1962), 739), here too, biblical law distinguishes between intentional and unintentional acts. In the Priestly Code, the final clause in Numbers 5:13 (lit. "she was not caught"; cf. the use of the word in Deut. 22:28) may mean that a woman who has had extramarital intercourse is guilty only if she was not forced. In the Deuteronomic Code (Deuteronomy 22:23–27), the presumption of consent on the part of the engaged girl is treated: If in the open country where no help would be available in response to a cry from the girl, she is presumed to have been forced and only her attacker is executed; if the crime occurred in the city, where help would presumably have been afforded her had she cried out, she is presumed to have consented, and is stoned with her paramour. No such presumptive distinction is made in this passage regarding the married woman: she and her lover must die in any case (Deut. 22:22; unlike *The Hittite Laws*, 197, in: Pritchard, Texts, 196, which makes this very distinction for married women). According to J.J. Finkelstein (JAOS, 86 (1966), 366ff.; JCS, 22 (1968–9), 13), the absence of such a distinction may reflect reality: the experience of daily life may have shown that married women who had had extramarital intercourse were likely to have been seeking sexual experience. While payment of a brideprice established a marriage tie constitutive of adultery, the "designation" of a slave woman to marry a man (free women are engaged by brideprice while slave women are designated for marriage by their masters; cf. Ex. 21:8) does not establish such a tie before the woman has been redeemed or freed. Hence a designated slave woman and her paramour are not executed, but the paramour must pay an indemnity and bring a guilt offering (Lev. 19:20–22). The question of the slave woman's consent is not raised in the law, presumably because she is not a legal person and her consent is legally immaterial.

Evidence for prosecution of adultery is scant in the Bible. Some passages suggest the husband's initiative in prosecuting (Num. 5:11–31; cf. Prov. 6:32–35), while another might be construed as reflecting public initiative (Deut. 22:22; cf. Sus. 28–41, 60ff.). None of these passages is decisive. If a husband in a fit of jealousy but without evidence suspects his wife of adultery, the case is turned over to God (by means of the "ritual for cases of jealousy," Num. 5:11–31; see *Ordeal of Jealousy) for decision and, where the wife is guilty, for punishment.

IN NARRATIVE, PROPHETIC, AND WISDOM LITERATURE. The theme of adultery appears in several biblical narratives. Abraham's and Isaac's wives were taken or nearly taken by foreigners who believed them to be the patriarchs' sisters (Gen. 12:10–20; 20:2ff.; 26:6–11), but Genesis 20:4 and 26:10 deny that any sexual contact took place. It is noteworthy that these passages seem to assume that these foreigners would sooner commit murder than adultery, "the great sin." Tamar's fornication (Gen. 38) might be viewed as technically adulterous, since she had already been assigned for Shelah. Potiphar's wife attempted to seduce Joseph, who refused to sin against his master and against God (Gen. 39:7–12). David committed adultery with Bath-Sheba, wife of Uriah the Hittite (II Sam. 11). The narrative about Hosea's marriage (Hos. 1) describes Hosea's wife as adulterous, but this is probably a legendary motif of the sort typical in third-person prophetic narratives (see *Hosea).

Adultery is one of the crimes with which the prophets, particularly Hosea (4:2; etc.) and Jeremiah (7:9; 23:10, 14; etc.), charged Israel. The adultery and ravishing of wives is mentioned among threatened punishments (Deut. 28:30; Amos 7:17).

The book of Proverbs warns extensively against the seductions of the adulterous woman (2:16–19; 5:1–14; 6:24–35; 7:5–27; cf. 30:20). She is a gadabout (a frequent description of promiscuous women in the ancient Near East: cf. Gen. 34:1; *The Code of Hammurapi*, 141, 143, in: Pritchard, Texts, 172; J.J. Finkelstein, JAOS, 86 (1966), 363, with nn. 28–29), rarely found in her own home (Prov. 7:11–12). She uses a smooth tongue to lure the foolish – like oxen to the slaughter – to her bed (2:16; 5:3; 6:24; 7:13ff.). Adulterers seek the protection of darkness (7:9; cf. Job 24:15; Eccles. 23:18). The adulterer is more foolish than a thief, who will at least escape with his life (Prov. 6:30ff.). Wisdom warns (6:20ff.; 7:4ff.) that traffic with the adulterous woman leads inevitably to loss of wealth (5:9–10) and life (2:18–19; 5:5; 6:32–35; 7:22–23, 26–27). One ought to "drink water from his own cistern" (5:15) and not from another's.

AS A METAPHOR FOR IDOLATRY. The exclusive loyalty which Israel must give God is analagous to the exclusive fidelity a wife owes her husband. Thus, Israelite religion seized upon the metaphor of marriage to express Israel's relationship with God and already in early texts employed language from the sphere of adultery to describe worship of other gods: Israel "goes a-whoring" (*zanah*) after other gods (Ex. 34:16; Num. 15:39–40) and YHWH, the "impassioned" or "jealous" (*qanna*) God, becomes "wrought up," or "jealous" (*qanna*) over Israel (Ex. 20:5; 34:14; Deut. 5:9; cf. Num. 5:14); idolatry, like adultery, was described as "great sin" (Ex. 32:21, 30–31; II Kings 17:21). Later prophets, especially the author of Hosea 1–3 and after him Jeremiah (2:23; 3:1ff.) and Ezekiel (16:1ff.; 23:1ff.), gave the metaphor full and explicit expression.

[Jeffrey Howard Tigay]

In Jewish Law

It appears that originally it was the husband's right to punish his adulterous wife himself (cf. the story of Judah – ordering even his daughter-in-law to be burned: Gen. 38:24) and that he could take the law into his own hands even against the adulterer (cf. Prov 6:34). It was only when adultery was elevated to the rank of a grave offense against God as well that the husband was required to resort to the priests or to the courts. Yet, so far as the adulterer was concerned, it is probable that he could always buy himself off by paying to the husband a sum of money by way of compensation: *compounding was not prohibited for adultery (cf. Prov. 6:35) as it was for murder (Num. 35:31). Where sufficient evidence was available both of the act of adultery (Mak. 7a) and of the adulterer and the adulteress having first each been duly warned (Sanh. 41a), both would be liable to the death penalty. The trial reported in the apocryphal book of *Susannah (37–41) was held without any evidence being adduced of a previous warning having been administered, either because the book predates the mishnaic law to this effect, or because the warning appeared irrelevant to the point of the story. No particular mode of execution is prescribed in the Bible, but talmudical law (Sifra 9:11) prescribed strangulation as being the most humane mode of *capital punishment (Sanh. 52b et al.). An older tradition appears to be that the punishment for adultery was stoning: the lighter offenses of the unvirginal bride (Deut. 22:21) and of the betrothed woman and her adulterer (Deut. 22:24) were punished by stoning, and the severer offense of adultery would certainly not have carried a lighter punishment. Stoning of adulteresses is moreover vouched for in prophetic allegories (e.g., Ezek. 6:38–40) and is described in the New Testament as commanded by the Law of Moses (John 8:5). In the aggravated case of adultery by a priest's daughter, the adulteress was burned (Lev. 21:9), while the adulterer remained liable to strangulation (Sif. 5:19). Burning is provided for another similar offense (Lev. 20:14) and is also found in prophetic allegory (e.g., Ezek. 23:25; Nah. 3:15). Where the woman was a slave "designated" for another man, the punishment was not death (Lev. 19:20), but he had to bring a sacrifice (*ibid.* 21:7), while she was flogged (Ker. 11a). Where insufficient evidence was available (the nature of the offense being such as usually took place in secret: cf. Job 24:15), a husband was entitled to have his wife, whom he suspected of adultery, subjected to the *ordeal of the waters of bitterness (Num 5:12–31). If found guilty, her punishment was a kind of talio, she being made to suffer with those organs of her body with which she had sinned (Sot. 1:7). One of the features of the ordeal was that the woman's hair was "loosened" (Num. 5:18), that is, disarranged (except, according to R. Judah, if her hair was very beautiful: Sot. 1:5). This disarrangement of the hair (usually covered and concealed) may be the origin of the later punishment of shaving a woman's head – more particularly in cases where lesser misconduct, and not the act of adultery, could be proved against her. Other punishments meted out to adulteresses in post-talmudic times included death, both by strangulation (hanging) and by burning, imprisonment, and, commonly, public flogging.

[Haim Hermann Cohn]

Maimonides rules that "if a woman has, while married to her husband, committed adultery unwittingly or under duress, she is permitted to him…" (Yad *Ishut* 24:19). Adultery committed under duress is rape, and is dealt with at length in the relevant entry (see *Rape). The question is what defines "inadvertent adultery" in this context and how it is adapted to the modern legal categories of mistake of law and mistake of fact.

ADULTERY DUE TO MISTAKE OF FACT. In a situation where a woman thought that the man with whom she engaged in sexual relations was her husband, but was in fact another man, the *halakhah* regards the act as "inadvertent" or, in contemporary terminology – a mistake of fact. The Mishnah (Yeb. 3:10) deals with a case in which two men betrothed two women and, at the time of marriage, they exchanged the women between themselves. The Mishnah rules that in such a case, where the parties acted unwittingly and unintentionally (see TB Yeb. 33b where it explains that the term "[they were] exchanged" indicates that the exchange was inadvertent), all four parties involved must bring sin offerings, because they unwittingly violated the prohibition against relations with a married woman. However, the original couples are permitted to continue living together as man and wife (following an initial separation of three months in order to enable determination of the biological father in the event of pregnancy). The halakhic ruling is that "at all events they are permitted to one another after three months, for they are considered to have acted under duress because they were mistakenly exchanged" (*Yam shel Shlomo,* to Yebamot, ch.3, §17).

Another source dealing with adultery as the result of a mistake of fact was based on an actual case, recorded in TB *Nedarim* 91a–b. A woman informed her husband that they had conducted sexual relations on the previous night. The husband expressed astonishment; denying that this had taken place. The woman responded that apparently she had sexual relations with one of the spice sellers, mistakenly assuming that it was her husband. R. Naḥman rules that the woman was not to be believed, for "perhaps she set her eyes on another" and made up the story, so that she could receive a divorce from her husband. He explains that this case concerned the wife of a kohen (priest) who would be forbidden to her husband even in the event of rape. Had the case involved the wife of an Israelite "since even according to her words she believed he was her husband, then there is no greater duress than that – and when there was duress regarding one of Israelite descent, she is permitted."

What follows from these sources is that adultery resulting from mistake of fact is governed by the law of duress, and therefore the law of adultery, including the prohibition of the woman to her husband, does not apply.

ADULTERY RESULTING FROM IGNORANCE OF THE LAW. The responsa literature contains a number of responsa discussing the question of how to view adultery when it resulted from a mistake in the law (i.e., ignorance of the law). One case dealt with by Rashba concerned a woman who had accepted a ring from a man to whom she had been introduced during a meal, and a few years later she married another man. Rashba ruled that she is considered an adulteress, and is prohibited to both of them. In his responsum, he discusses the claim that the woman was unaware that she was married to the first man, and that the adultery was therefore the result of a mistake. He wrote as follows: "Should it be claimed that she was under duress because she did not know that she was forbidden to marry – this is incorrect, for she ought to have verified the matter, and in any case where she did not examine, she is prohibited to both of them … But what kind of duress was there that she could rely upon in order to marry? For if so [were we to accept this claim], we would permit all women who had committed adultery, by saying: she believed that she had not become prohibited by this action. And the matter is clear" (Resp. *Rashba*, 1:1189).

When R. Joseph Colon (Maharik) was asked how to judge a woman "who had intentionally committed adultery while married to her husband, and did not know whether the act was forbidden: should it be regarded as an unintentional act?" His response was: "In my humble opinion, she cannot be permitted to her husband under the law applying to one who acted inadvertently, because she intended to betray her husband, and committed adultery while still married to him" (Resp. *Maharik*, 168). He based his position on Numbers 5:12: "If any man's wife go aside and commit a trespass against him" – in other words: the trespass is against the husband and not against the law (or, in Maharik's language, against God). There is no requirement that the woman actually intend to commit the sin of adultery; it is sufficient that she betrays her husband. Maharik offers the following explanation of the aforementioned passage from Maimonides – that the woman who commits adultery inadvertently is permitted to her husband – "this is only applicable where the mistake relates to the act of adultery, and was not a mistake regarding the prohibition itself, for the reason that her adultery is not considered to have been inadvertent is that she intended to commit adultery, but was unaware of the prohibition. What case would be deemed as inadvertent adultery? One in which she thought that it was her husband, as in the case mentioned in *Nedarim* 91."

These responsa were codified in later halakhic literature (see *Beit Yosef* on *Tur* EH 115, s.v. *u-mishum hakhi; Rema*, to *Sh. Ar.* EH 178.3; *Yam shel Shlomo*, Yeb. 3:17). The subject was the source of further discussion in subsequent responsa literature (see *Leḥem Yehudah* of R. Judah Eish, *Hilkhot Ishut* 24; Hida, *Ḥayyim She'al*, 2: 48).

In a judgment given in Israel, by the Ashkelon Regional Rabbinical Court (8 PDR 184) the aforementioned conception was accepted: namely, the distinction between a mistake of fact, which constitutes a defense with respect to adultery, and a legal-halakhic mistake – ignorance of the *halakhah* – which cannot exempt the woman from the consequences of the act of adultery. In the case in question, the Rabbinical Court ruled that the parties must divorce, and a few months later the *get* was given. It was proven to the court that the woman and another man had engaged in sexual relations after a divorce judgment had been given, believing that once a divorce judgment had been issued there was no longer any prohibition involved, even though they knew that the *get* had not yet been given. The Rabbinical Court based its ruling on the aforementioned responsa of Rashba and Maharik (as well as additional halakhic sources). The woman and the man, with whom she had become pregnant during the intermediate period between the divorce ruling and the *get*, were forbidden to marry each other, in accordance with the law that an adulterous woman is forbidden both to her husband and to her lover.

Summing up the position of Jewish law – which is also the positive law of the State of Israel in this area – adultery under duress is not considered adultery. As for adultery resulting from a mistake, a distinction is drawn between a mistake in fact, which is regarded as a case of duress, and hence not in the category of adultery, and a legal-halakhic mistake – i.e., ignorance of the prohibition on adultery, or of the law that only a *get* terminates the marriage; neither of the variants of the latter category will be regarded as duress. A woman engaging in sexual relations with another man under such circumstances is deemed an adulteress, and as such forbidden both to her husband and to her lover.

[Moshe Drori (2nd ed.)]

Family Aspects

See *Mamzer; *Divorce; *Husband and Wife.

BIBLIOGRAPHY: BIBLE: M. Greenberg, in: *Sefer Y. Kaufmann* (1960), 5–28; idem. in: IDB, 1 (1962), 739; de Vaux, Anc Isr, 36–37; S. Loewenstamm, in: BM, 13 (1962), 55–59; 18–19 (1964), 77–78; M. Weinfeld, *ibid.*, 17 (1964), 58–63; E. Neufeld, *Ancient Hebrew Marriage Laws* (1944), 163–75; L. Epstein, *Sex Laws and Customs in Judaism* (1948), 194–215; G. Cohen, in: *The Samuel Freedland Lectures* (1966), 1–21; H.L. Ginsberg, in: *Sefer Y. Kaufmann* (1960), 58–65; J.J. Finkelstein, in: JAOS, 86 (1966), 355–72. JEWISH LAW: Buechler, in: MGWJ, 5 (1911), 196–219; idem, in: WZKM, 19 (1905), 91–138; V. Aptowitzer, in: JQR, 15 (1924/25), 79–82; ET, 2 (1942), 290–3; 4 (1952), 759–64; Sh. M. Paul, *Studies in the Book of the Covenant in the Light of Cuneiform and Biblical Law* (Leiden, 1970), 96–98. **ADD. BIBLIOGRAPHY:** M. Drori: "Inadvertent Adultery (*Shegagah*) in Jewish Law: Mistake of Law and Mistake of Fact," in: H. Ben-Menahem and N.S. Hect (eds.), *Authority, Process, and Method – Studies in Jewish Law* (1998), 231–67; A. Enker: "The Claim of Ignorance of the Law in Jewish Criminal Law," in: *Mishpatim*, 25 (1995), 87–128 (Heb.); idem, "Mistake of Law and Ignorance of Law in Jewish Criminal Law," in: *Jewish Law Association Studies*, 7 (1994), 41–50.

ADVERTISING. In few modern industries have Jews had greater influence than in advertising, and this applies particularly in America. It has even been suggested that Jewish advertising men are responsible for the wide scope and shape of the modern advertising agency. Though the use of advertising began after the Civil War of 1865, until the beginning of the 20th century, business concerns wishing to promote the sale of their goods or services developed their own programs and even wrote their own copy. The existing agencies were thus brokers in media space. This was the pattern when Albert D. Lasker, often called the father of modern advertising, joined the Chicago agency of Lord and Thomas in 1898. He soon realized that by providing first-rate copywriters, who were creative, imaginative artists, the agency could be of far greater help to the client than by just offering the service of selling him space for his advertisements. In 1904, when only 24 years of age, he became a partner in the firm and by 1912, Lasker became the sole owner of Lord and Thomas. He built it in three decades into one of the best known and most respected advertising agencies in America.

Milton H. Biow may be regarded as the man who molded the advertising agency into a form which would meet the requirements of modern business. He began in 1918 with a one-man business and in the four decades of its existence, it became one of the largest and best known agencies both in the United States and abroad. Biow's agency was credited with being the first to use radio and television "spots" for short advertisements. This era saw the development of the partnership agencies. One of these, Grey Advertising, was founded in 1917 by 18-year-old Lawrence Valenstein. Later he formed a three-man partnership with two men he had taken into his employment, Arthur C. Fatt and Herbert D. Strauss. Each of the three was successively president of the company. All three believed advertising to be an important ingredient in the wider activity of marketing, and the firm played a leading part in developing the system of creating a demand for a product before introducing it to the market. In 1936 the agency started Grey Matter, a newsletter of merchandising comment and interpretation, which was widely read both by the advertising industry and by business generally. By the late 1960s the agency was one of the most successful with branches in Canada, Japan, and a number of European countries.

Two former directors of Grey Advertising, William *Bernbach and a non-Jew, Ned Doyle, joined with Maxwell Dane in 1949 to form another three-man partnership, Doyle, Dane, Bernbach, which developed rapidly. Bernbach may well be regarded as the successor to Lasker, Biow, and the Grey partners, becoming the leader of the "creative revolution" that was sweeping across Madison Avenue, the New York center of American advertising. Bernbach began to use copy in which advertisers spoke to the public in low-keyed, even self-deprecating terms. This new approach of intelligent subtlety was quickly and widely emulated. In 1955 Norman B. Norman and a number of his associates in the agency firm of William H. Weintraub and Co. bought control of the agency and changed its name to Norman, Craig, and Kummel. They soon expanded its business by the use of the "empathy" formula, which Norman described as "emotional advertising" aimed at having the reader find himself inside the advertisement.

Other Jews who have made important contributions to advertising are Julian Koenig and Frederic S. Papert (1926) who founded Papert, Koenig, and Lois; Maxwell B. Sackheim (d. 1982), an expert in mail order advertising; David Altman, of Altman, Stoller, and Chalk, specialist in fashion advertising; Ernest Dichter, a psychologist who founded the Institute for Motivational Research; Stanley Arnold, sales promotion consultant; and Monroe Green, an advertising vice president of the *New York Times*. Green was largely responsible for building the *New York Times Sunday Magazine* into a powerful combination of trade and consumer publication. In the 1920s and 1930s Jews in advertising were mainly relegated to media or market research jobs, and had no part in front office, account-management, or contact functions. But the skill and accomplishments of many of them opened the gates to Jews and other members of minorities, in a profession that had been restricted to gentiles for decades. Among the Jews who rose to prominence in the American advertising industry in more recent years were Carl *Spielvogel, who later became United States ambassador to Slovakia; Donny Deutsch, who sold his agency for many millions and began a career in television; and Linda Kaplan Thaler, whose creativity started with advertising jingles and expanded into a flourishing, multifaceted agency.

It was not until the 20th century after World War II, that Jews rose to prominence in advertising in Britain. The multiplicity of media used in modern advertising called for creative ability and Jews found outlets for their skills in this profession. Jewish agencies include Caplan's Advertising, Progress Advertising, and Richard Cope and Partners. Probably the best-known contemporary British advertising agency is Saatchi & Saatchi, founded by the two *Saatchi brothers. In general, however, Jews play only a limited role in British advertising.

On the continent of Europe advertising developed slowly until after World War I when the growth of methods of communication was rapid, but Jewish participation was brought to an abrupt close by the Nazi Holocaust. Since World War II expanding American agencies and to some degree British agencies have extended their operations to the continent to compete with their European counterparts and it is here that Jews have begun to play a creative role.

In Israel

There was little organized advertising in Mandatory Palestine. The first advertising agency was set up in Jerusalem in 1922 by Benjamin Levinson, who was followed by a handful of others. Several more modern agencies were established by newcomers from Germany in 1933–39. Large-scale advertising started only with the rapid development of industry and the creation of a growing consumers' market in Israel, especially after the Sinai Campaign (1956). Today, Israeli advertising is indistinguishable in its methods and pervasiveness from advertising in any other Western-style consumer society.

The favorite medium is still the daily press: In 2003 Israel's newspapers received 53% of advertising revenues ($293 million). Next came television with 33% and radio with 7%. Internet advertising, the new frontier, had a modest 2%. The Israel Advertising Association, established in 1934, has 60 agencies as members.

BIBLIOGRAPHY: B.B. Elliott, *A History of English Advertising* (1962); J. Gunther, *Taken at the Flood: The Story of Albert D. Lasker* (1960); M. Mayer, *Madison Avenue, USA* (1958); M.H. Biow, *Butting In: An Adman Speaks Out* (1964). IN ISRAEL: *Sefer ha-Shanah shel ha-Ittonaim* (1965), 353–70.

[Jack Barbash]

AELIA CAPITOLINA, name given to the rebuilt city of Jerusalem by the Romans in 135 C.E. Following the destruction of Jerusalem by the Romans in 70 C.E. the city remained in ruins except for the camp (*castrum*) of the Tenth Legion (Fretensis), which was situated in the area of the Upper City and within the ruins of the Praetorium (the old palace of Herod the Great), protected, according to the first-century historian Josephus (War, 7, 1:1) by remnants of the city wall and towers on the northwest edge of the city. Although Jews were banished from the city (except apparently during the Ninth of *Av), some Jewish peasants still lived in the countryside, and remains of houses (with stone vessels) have been found immediately north of Jerusalem (close to Tell el-Ful). Following the disastrous *Bar Kokhba Revolt, the emperor *Hadrian began rebuilding Jerusalem, from 135 C.E., naming it after himself (Aelius Hadrianus) and the god Jupiter Capitolinus. Some scholars believe that an impetus for the breakout of the Bar Kokhba revolt was the pagan construction activities in the city, but archaeological finds would appear to indicate that most of the principal building activities there (including those on the Temple Mount) took place only after the revolt had been quashed and when a colony was already established there. Jews were no longer allowed access to the city and it was populated by foreigners and settled Roman veterans. Aelia (approximately 120 acres in size) rapidly took on the character of a pagan city with special gates, civic centers (*demosia*), bathhouses, latrines, sanctuaries, and shrines, and pagan equestrian statues were even set up on the Temple Mount. The whereabouts of the Capitoline Temple is debated, with some scholars placing it in the area of the present Church of the Holy Sepulcher, while others suggest situating it in the area of the destroyed *Antonia Fortress on the north side of the Temple Mount. Shrines to Aphrodite and Serapis are also known. Most of the building activities took place in the northern sectors of the Old City of today (in the Christian and Moslem Quarters), and around the southwestern foot of the Temple Mount. The city remained unfortified until after the Tenth Legion had been transferred to Aila (Eloth), with a fortification wall built in the third century around the northern part of the city only. The name Aelia was perpetuated in the Early Islamic period as *Ilia*.

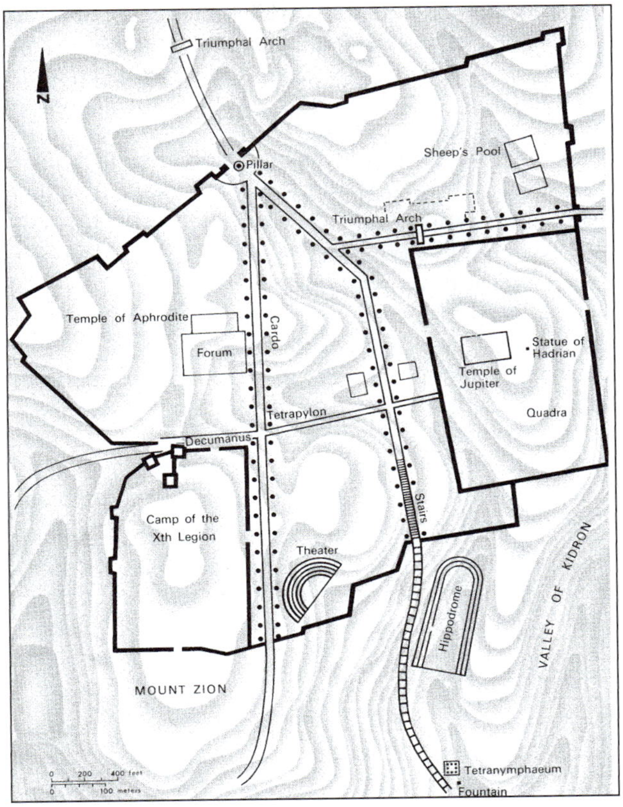

Aelia Capitolina.

BIBLIOGRAPHY: B. Issac, "Roman Colonies in Judaea: the Foundation of Aelia Capitolina," in: *The Near East under Roman Rule* (1998), 87–111; F. Millar, "The Roman *Coloniae* of the Near East: A Study of Cultural Relations," in: H. Solin and M. Kajava (eds.), *Roman Eastern Policy and Other Studies in Roman History* (1990), 28–30; D. Bar, "Aelia Capitolina and the Location of the Camp of the Tenth Legion," in: *Palestine Exploration Quarterly*, 130 (1998), 8–19; G.D. Stiebel, "The Whereabouts of the x Legion and the Boundaries of Aelia Capitolina," in: A. Faust and E. Baruch (eds.), *New Studies in Jerusalem* (1999), 68–103.

[Shimon Gibson (2nd ed.)]

°**AELIAN** (**Claudius Aelianus**; c. 170–235 C.E.), Greek sophist. Aelian mentions the Jews in several places. In *Varia Historia*, 12, 35, he includes the Jewish Sibyls (see *Apocalypse) in a list of *Sibylline oracles. In his *De Natura Animalium*, 6, 17, he tells of a snake enamored of a girl in Judea during the reign of Herod. He also mentions the deer on Mount Carmel.

AERONAUTICS, AVIATION, AND ASTRONAUTICS. An early contribution by a Jew to aviation was the cigar-shaped airship with an aluminum framework designed in 1892 by the Zagreb timber merchant David *Schwarz. His designs were sold to Count Zeppelin, who carried them through to produce the airship known as the "Zeppelin." Another pioneer of flight-theory was Josef *Popper (1838–1921), who as early as 1888 considered the problems of flight-theory in his *Flugtechnik*. The development of French aviation was furthered by Henri *Deutsch de la Meurthe (1846–1919), who donated the first prize won by the Brazilian Santos-Dumont in October 1901 for flying an airship around the Eiffel Tower. After establishing an experimental aeronautics station at Sartrouville, Deutsch founded the Aeronautic Institute at Saint-Cyr in 1909. His daughter Suzanne (1892–1937) continued his work. In 1901 Arthur *Berson, director of the Prussian Aeronautical Observatory and a major personality in contemporary investigations of the upper atmosphere, navigated a balloon to what was then a record height of 35,100 feet (10,700 meters), and in 1908 he made a flight over the equator in East Africa at great heights. Other Jewish aviation pioneers were Emile *Berliner, the first man to make lightweight revolving-cylinder internal-combustion engines and to equip airplanes with them; Eduard *Rumpler, whose "*Rumplertaube*" was used by Germany in World War I; August Goldschmidt of Vienna, an inventor of a novel type of balloon in 1911; the Russian pilot Vseuolod Abramovich, who held the world record in 1912; Fred Melchior of Sweden, an expert pilot who won many awards; Arthur L. *Welsh, U.S. aviation instructor and test pilot, who died in 1912 while testing a new load-carrying military biplane; Ellis Dunitz (1888–1913), chief instructor in the German Naval Air Service; Victor Betman, winner in 1914 of the speed flight between Vienna and Budapest; Arthur Landmann of Germany, holder of the world endurance record for 1914; and Leonino Da Zara, the father of Italian aeronautics.

Interwar Period

Marcel Bloch (later *Dassault) became a major aircraft manufacturer in France from the period between the two world wars. Harry F. Guggenheim (see *Guggenheim Family) was a U.S. pilot in World War I, and later a lieutenant-commander in the U.S. Navy (and U.S. ambassador to Cuba). His father, Daniel Guggenheim, established the Guggenheim Foundation, at that time the leading private organization in the aeronautics field, and in 1925 he created a pioneer school of aeronautics at New York University. Still active after World War I, Emile Berliner, with the help of his son Henry Adler *Berliner, designed and built three different kinds of helicopters (1919–26). Karl Arnstein was chief construction engineer with the Zeppelin Company; in 1924 one of his airships flew the Atlantic. With the coming of the Nazis he left Germany for America, and from 1934 was employed by the Goodyear-Zeppelin Corporation as chief engineer and vice president. Among the many airships he designed were the dirigibles "Los Angeles" and "Akron," which were used by the U.S. Navy. America's first civilian superintendent of airmail was Captain Benjamin B. Lipsner, and Harold Zinn of Savannah was the first flying mail carrier in North and South Carolina. Sergeant Benjamin Roth was the mechanic in the aeronautic squad in the Byrd expedition to the Antarctic in the 1920s. Professor Aldo Pontremoli, head of the department of physics at the University of Milan, was in charge of meteorological research in the 1928 Italian expedition to the North Pole, an expedition which cost him his life. Charles A. Levine (1897–1991) was the first flight passenger over the Atlantic. In 1927 he traveled 3,903 mi. (6,295 km. – a world record at the time) from New York to Eisleben, Germany. Levine himself financed this pioneer flight. In 1930 the Viennese Robert Kronfeld created a world record by gliding 93 mi. (150 km.) and in 1931 he won the London *Daily Mail* prize by gliding over the English Channel. Jewish women pilots included Mildred Kauffman of Kansas City, Peggy Salaman of England (winner of the third prize in the King's Cup Race in 1931 who established a record in the same year by her flight from England to Cape Town with Gordon Score), and Lena Bernstein of France. A number of Jews were also academic authorities on aerodynamics.

Postwar Aeronautics

Sir Ben *Lockspeiser was deputy director at the British Ministry of Aircraft Production in the critical years of the war from 1941. In France, René Bloch was director of aviation in the French Navy and later in the Ministry of Defense. Erich Schatzki was a pilot and then chief engineer of Lufthansa in pre-Nazi days, and an early general manager of Israel's El Al. Benedict Cohn was head aerodynamicist for the Boeing Company, and Benjamin Pinkel headed the Rand Corporation's aero-astronautical department. Richard Shevell (1920–2000) helped design the DC-10 at Douglas Aircraft and taught aeronautics at Stanford.

Astronautics

Jews were involved in the activities of the National Advisory Council for Aeronautics in the U.S.A., and many are concerned with some aspect or other of its successor organization, the National Aeronautics and Space Administration (NASA), which operates the U.S. astronautical program. Three directors of large divisions of NASA were Abe *Silverstein (Lewis Research Center), Abraham Hyatt (program planning and evaluation), and Leonard Jaffe (Communications Systems of Satellites). Daniel Saul *Goldin was the longest-serving director of NASA (1992–2001). Astronaut Jeffrey *Hoffman (1944–) participated in five space missions in the 1980s and 1990s. Two Jewish astronauts who met tragic ends were Judith *Resnik, who died on January 28, 1986, on a space shuttle mission when her Challenger spacecraft blew up on launch, and the Israeli Ilan *Ramon, lost on re-entry in the Columbia mission of January 16–February 1, 2003.

Little is known of the personalities involved in the technical management of the Soviet space program. While it is quite likely that some of them are of Jewish origin, this cannot actually be proved. However, the Soviet cosmonaut Lieutenant-Colonel Boris Volynov, commander of spaceship "Soyuz-5" which in January 1969 performed the first link-up in space with a transfer of cosmonauts from one spaceship to another, was reported to be Jewish.

[Samuel Aaron Miller]

AESCOLY (Weintraub), AARON ZE'EV (1901–1948), Hebrew writer, historian, and ethnologist. Aescoly studied in

Berlin, Liège, and Paris, where for a short time he taught at the Ecole Nationale des Langues Orientales Vivantes. In 1925 he immigrated to Palestine, although he did scholarly research in Paris from 1925 to 1930 and from 1937 to 1939. From 1939 he directed the I. Epstein Training College for kindergarten teachers which he had founded. During World War II he served in the British Army and, as chaplain, in the Jewish Brigade. Aescoly's contributions to Jewish scholarship cover a wide field. In the introduction to his critical edition of *Sippur David Reuveni* ("Story of David Reuveni," 1940), and in a number of other studies, he dealt with messianic movements. His edition of Ḥayyim Vital's *Sefer ha-Ḥezyonot* (1954) and his *Ha-Tenuot ha-Meshiḥiyyot be-Yisrael* ("Messianic Movements in Israel," 1956) were both published posthumously. His ethnological writings include *Geza ha-Adam* ("The Human Race," 1956²), *Yisrael* (1953²), and a number of studies on the *Beta Israel (*Sefer ha-Falashim*, 1943; *Ḥabash*, 1936; *Recueil de textes falashas*, 1951). Aescoly's historical studies include *Ha-Emanzipazyah ha-Yehudit, Ha-Mahpekhah ha-Ẓarefatit u-Malkhut Napoleon* ("Jewish Emancipation, the French Revolution and the Reign of Napoleon," 1952); a history of his native community of Lodz (1948); and an edition of S. Luzzatto's book on the Jews of Venice (published with D. Lattes' translation, 1951). On literature he wrote *Ma'amar ha-Sifrut* (1941) and translated writings of Lao-Tse (1937). He also edited S.D. Luzzatto's *Yesodei ha-Torah* (1947).

BIBLIOGRAPHY: Kressel, Leksikon, 1 (1956), 161.

AFENDOPOLO, CALEB BEN ELIJAH (1464?–1525), Karaite scholar and poet. Born probably in Adrianople, he lived most of his life in the village of Kramariya near *Constantinople, and ultimately in *Belgrade where he died. A pupil of his brother-in-law, Elijah *Bashyazi, Afendopolo remained an Orthodox Karaite of the school of *Aaron b. Elijah of Nicomedia, although he was on friendly terms with several Rabbanite scholars. He acquired much of his knowledge of arithmetic, geometry, astronomy, and Greek-Arabic philosophy, including the works of Maimonides, from the Rabbanite Mordecai *Comtino, and learned modern languages, such as Italian, Greek, and Arabic. Maimonides' views on the messianic era and on the purpose of the commandments proved a formative influence. Afendopolo taught and wrote on a variety of subjects. Most of his numerous treatises remain in manuscript, now in various collections, and often treat diverse unrelated topics.

While surpassing his Karaite contemporaries in the depth and breadth of his scientific studies, Afendopolo lacked originality. A talented eclectic, he mastered the wealth of past and contemporary scholarly material at his disposal, and his writings are a valuable source of reference concerning scholars and works whose existence would otherwise remain unknown. He owned an extensive library of original manuscripts as well as copies he made himself. His works include (1) an unfinished supplement to *Adderet Eliyahu* by Elijah Bashyazi (1532); (2) *Iggeret ha-Maspeket*, on dietary and other laws; (3) *Patshegen Ketav ha-Dat*, on the reading of the Pentateuch and *haftarot;* (4) *Asarah Ma'amarot*, sermons reflecting his religious views (fragments are included in *Dod Mordekhai* by *Mordecai b. Nisan ha-Zaken, Hamburg, 1714); (5) indices to *Ez Ḥayyim* by Aaron b. Elijah and to *Eshkol ha-Kofer* by Judah b. Elijah *Hadassi; (6) *Avner ben Ner*, a discourse on ethics in the style of the Arabic *maqāmāt;* (7) *Gan ha-Melekh*, poetry and prose, containing autobiographical and historical details as well as two elegies on the expulsion of the Jews from Lithuania in 1495; (8) *Mikhlal Yofi*, on the principles of astronomy, withrelation to the calculation of the calendar (9) liturgical poems, included in the Karaite prayer book; (10) a commentary on the Nicomachean arithmetic; (11) *Gal Einai*, on astronomy (known only by the title); and (12) *Iggeret Maspeket*, mainly a glossary of astronomical terminology.

BIBLIOGRAPHY: S. Bernstein, in: *Horeb*, 11 (1951), 53–84; Mann, Texts, 2 (1935), index. **ADD. BIBLIOGRAPHY:** M. Steinschneider, *Gesammelte Schriften* (1925), 184–96; M. Malachi, in: *Shay le-Heiman* (1977), 343–62; H. Ha-Levi, *Hagut Ivrit be-Arẓot ha-Islam* (1982), 167–72; S.B. Bowman, *The Jews of Byzantium (1204–1453)*, 1985, index; Z. Malachi, in *Masoret ha-Piyyut*, 3 (2002), 31–44; M. Polliack (ed.), *Karaite Judaism: A Guide to Its History and Literary Sources*, (2003), index.

[Moshe Nahum Zobel]

°AFFONSO. Name of several kings of Portugal. AFFONSO HENRIQUES (1139–1185), the first king of Portugal, continued the relatively tolerant policy to the Jews of his Castilian forebears, giving the Jews autonomy in civil as well as criminal cases. His *almoxarife* or treasurer was Yaḥia ibn Ya'ish, to whom he granted considerable privileges. His grandson, AFFONSO II (1211–1223), also had Jews in his employment in responsible offices, though he confirmed the anti-Jewish provisions of the *Lateran Council of 1215 and endorsed the resolutions passed by the Cortes at Coimbra encouraging baptisms. AFFONSO III (1245/8–1279) on the other hand, almost systematically disregarding many ecclesiastical restrictions against the Jews, employed them widely in the financial administration, and reorganized the internal affairs of the Jews of the kingdom. He was responsible, among other matters, for the organization of the office of chief rabbi (*Arraby moor) of Portugal, with its far-reaching powers. AFFONSO IV (1325–1357) was unfavorably disposed toward the Jews, enforced the wearing of the Jewish *badge, and restricted the right of emigration for any person of property. AFFONSO V (1438–1481) relaxed the enforcement of the anti-Jewish regulations. He is memorable for having in his service Isaac *Abrabanel and Joseph ibn Yaḥia, with whom he is said to have had learned discussions on science and philosophy. He attempted with only qualified success to suppress the anti-Jewish riots of 1449 and punish the ringleaders. In his compilation of laws, collected under the title *Ordenações Affonsinas*, the regulations concerning the Jews occupy a prominent place (book 2). In an edict of 1468, while renewing the restriction of the Jews to their judíarias, he permitted them to do business at the fairs elsewhere.

BIBLIOGRAPHY: Mendes dos Remedios, *Judeus em Portugal* (1895), passim; M. Kayserling, *Geschichte der Juden in Portugal* (1867), passim; M.B. Amzalak, *Uma carta de lei... de D. Afonso v* (1926); Roth, Marranos, index.

[Cecil Roth]

AFGHANISTAN, Muslim state in central Asia (**Khorasan** or **Khurasan** in medieval Muslim and Hebrew sources).

History

Early Karaite and Rabbanite biblical commentators regarded Khorasan as a location of the lost *Ten Tribes. Afghanistan annals also trace the Hebrew origin of some of the Afghan tribes, in particular the Durrani, the Yussafzai, and the Afridi, to King *Saul (Talut). This belief appears in the 17th-century Afghan chronicle *Makhzan-i-Afghān,* and some British travelers in the 19th century spread the tradition. Because of its remoteness from the Jewish center in Babylonia, persons unwanted by the Jewish leadership, such as counter-candidates for the exilarchate (see *Exilarch), often went to live in or were exiled to Afghanistan.

Medieval sources mention several Jewish centers in Afghanistan, of which *Balkh was the most important. A Jewish community in Ghazni is recorded in Muslim sources, indicating that Jews were living there in the tenth and eleventh centuries. A Jew named Isaac, an agent of Sultan Mahmud (ruled 998–1030), was assigned to administer the sultan's lead mines and to melt ore for him. According to Hebrew sources, vast numbers of Jews lived in Ghazni but while their figures are not reliable, Moses *Ibn Ezra (1080) mentions over 40,000 Jews paying tribute in Ghazni and *Benjamin of Tudela (c. 1170) describes "Ghazni the great city on the River Gozan, where there are about 80,000 [8,000 in a variant manuscript] Jews…." In Hebrew literature the River Gozan was identified with Ghazni in Khorasan from the assertion of Judah *Ibn Bal'am that "the River of Gozan is that river flowing through the city of Ghazni which is today the capital of Khorasan."

A Jewish community in Firoz Koh, capital of the medieval rulers of Ghūr or Ghuristan, situated halfway between Herat and Kabul, is mentioned in *Tabaqāt-i-Nāṣirī,* a chronicle written in Persian (completed around 1260) by al-Jūzjānī. This is the first literary reference to Jews in the capital of the Ghūrids. About 20 recently discovered stone tablets, with Persian and Hebrew inscriptions dating from 1115 to 1215, confirm the existence of a Jewish community there. The Mongol invasion in 1222 annihilated Firoz Koh and its Jewish community.

Arab geographers of the tenth century (Ibn Ḥawqal, Iṣṭakhrī) also refer to Kabul and Kandahar as Jewish settlements. An inscription on a tombstone from the vicinity of Kabul dated 1365, erected in memory of a Moses b. Ephraim Bezalel, apparently a high official, indicates the continuous existence of a Jewish settlement there.

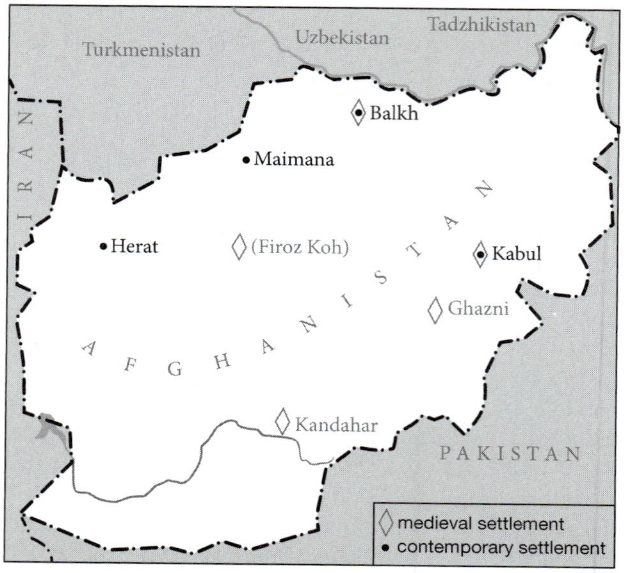

Map of Afghanistan showing places of Jewish settlement in the Middle Ages and modern times.

The Mongol invasion, epidemics, and continuous warfare made inroads into Jewish communities in Afghanistan throughout the centuries, and little is known about them until the 19th century when they are mentioned in connection with the flight of the **anusim* of Meshed after the forced conversions in 1839. Many of the refugees fled to Afghanistan, Turkestan, and Bokhara, settling in Herat, Maimana, Kabul, and other places with Jewish communities, where they helped to enrich the stagnating cultural life. Nineteenth-century travelers (*Wolff, *Vámbery, *Neumark, and others) state that the Jewish communities of Afghanistan were largely composed of these Meshed Jews. Mattathias Garji of Herat confirmed: "Our forefathers used to live in Meshed under Persian rule but in consequence of the persecutions to which they were subjected came to Herat to live under Afghan rule." The language spoken by Afghan Jews is not the Pushtu of their surroundings but a *Judeo-Persian dialect in which they have produced fine liturgical and religious poetry. Their literary merit was recognized when Afghan Jews moved to Ereẓ Israel toward the end of the 19th century. Scholars of Afghanistan families such as Garji and Shaul of Herat published Judeo-Persian commentaries on the Bible, Psalms, *piyyutim*, and other works, at the Judeo-Persian printing press established in Jerusalem at the beginning of the 20th century. The Jews of Afghanistan did not benefit from the activities of European Jewish organizations. Economically, their situation in the last century was not unfavorable; they traded in skins, carpets, and antiquities.

[Walter Joseph Fischel]

Recent Years

Approximately 5,000 Jews were living in Afghanistan in 1948. Of these, about 300 remained in 1969. They were concentrated in Kabul, Balkh, and mainly Herat. (See Map: Jews in Afghanistan.) Jews were banished from other towns after the assassination of King Nādir Shāh in 1933. Though not forced to live in separate quarters, Jews did so and in Balkh they even closed the ghetto gates at night. A campaign against Jews began in 1933. They were forbidden to leave a town without a permit. They had to pay a yearly poll tax and from 1952, when the Military Service Law ceased to apply to Jews, they had to pay ransoms for exemptions from the service (called *ḥarbiyya*). Government service and government schools were closed to Jews, and certain livelihoods forbidden to them. Consequently, most Jews only received a *ḥeder* education. There were only a few wealthy families, the rest being poverty-stricken and mostly employed as tailors and shoemakers. Until 1950 Afghan Jews were forbidden to leave the country. However, between June 1948 and June 1950, 459 Afghan Jews went to Israel. Most of them had fled the country in 1944, and lived in Iran or India until the establishment of the State of Israel. Jews were only allowed to emigrate from Afghanistan from the end of 1951. By 1967, 4,000 had gone to Israel. No Zionist activity was permitted, and no emissaries from Israel could reach Afghanistan. There was a *ḥevrah* ("community council") in each of the three towns in which Jews lived. The *ḥevrah* was composed of the heads of families; it cared for the needy, and dealt with burials. The *ḥevrah* sometimes meted out punishments, including excommunication. The head of the community (called *kalāntar*) represented the community in dealings with the authorities, and was responsible for the payment of taxes.

According to the *New York Times*, one Jew remained in Afghanistan in 2005.

[Haim J. Cohen]

Folklore

A survey of local Jewish-Afghan folk tales and customs reveals the influence of both Meshed (Jewish-Persian) and local non-Jewish traditions. This is especially true of customs relating to the year cycle and life cycle. The existence of several unique customs, such as the presence of "Elijah's rod" at childbirth, and several folk cures and charms are to be similarly explained. Jewish-Afghan folk tales have been collected from local narrators in Israel and are preserved in the Israel Folk Tale Archives. A sample selection of 12 tales from the repertoire of an outstanding narrator, Raphael Yehoshua, was published in 1969, accompanied by extensive notes and a rich bibliography.

[Dov Noy]

BIBLIOGRAPHY: Nimat Allah, *History of the Afghans* (London, 1829), tr. by B. Dorn; Holdich, in: *Journal of the Royal Society of Arts*, 45 (1917), 191–205; H.W. Bellew, *Races of Afghanistan* (1880); I. Ben-Zvi, *The Exiled and the Redeemed* (1961), index; Fischel, in: HJ, 7 (1945), 29–50; idem, in: JAOS, 85, no. 2 (1965), 148–53; idem, in: JC, Supplement (March 26, 1937); idem, in: L. Finkelstein (ed.), *Jews, their History, Culture and Religion*, 2 (1960³), 1149–90; G. Gnoli, *Le iscrizioni giudeo-Persiane del Gur (Afghanistan)* (1964), includes bibliography; E.L. Rapp, *Die Juedisch-Persisch Hebraeischen Inschriften aus Afghanistan* (1965); Brauer, in: JSOS, 4 (1942), 121–38; R. Klass, *Land of the High Flags* (1965); N. Robinson, in: J. Freid (ed.), *Jews in Modern World*, 1 (1962), 50–90. **ADD. BIBLIOGRAPHY:** B. Yehoshua-Raz, *Mi-Nidḥei Yisrael be-Afganistan le-Anusei Mashhad be-Iran* (1992); *Peʿamim*, 79 (1999); A. Netzer, "*Yehudei Afganistan*," in: G. Allon (ed.), *Ha-Tziyyonut le-Ezoreiha* (2005).

AFIA, AARON (16th century), Sephardi physician and philosopher in practice in Salonika. With wide linguistic and scientific knowledge, he collaborated in the Hebrew translation by *Daniel b. Perahyah of the "Perpetual Almanac" of Abraham *Zacuto (Salonika, 1543), and in Moses *Almosnino's still unpublished version of the "Treatise on the Sphere" by Johannes de Sacrobosco and other works. His own treatise on the nature of the soul (*Opiniones sacadas de los philosophos sobre la alma…*) was appended to *Los dialogos de Amor* (Venice, 1568), the Spanish translation of Judah *Abrabanel's (Leone Ebreo) "Dialogues of Love." Afia was friendly with the great physician *Amatus Lusitanus, who records (Centuria 7, 24th cure) how they discussed together with a colleague recently arrived from Portugal the source of laughter, which Afia, following Aristotle, placed in the heart. Afia is a remarkable exemplification of the fashion in which European culture in its broadest sense continued to flourish for a time among the descendants of the exiles from Spain.

BIBLIOGRAPHY: Steinschneider, Uebersetzungen, 645; Neubauer, Cat, 1 (1886), 699; Rosanes, Togarmah, 2 (1938), 105–7; H. Friedenwald, *Jews and Medicine*, 2 (1944), 707; J. Nehama, *Histoire des Israélites de Salonique*, 4 (1936), 159.

AFIKE JEHUDA (Heb. אֲפִּיקֵי יְהוּדָה), society for the "advancement of study of Judaism and of religious consciousness," founded in Prague in 1869 on the initiative of Samuel Freund, and named in memory of Judah Teweles. It supported the *talmud torah* (until taken over by the community in 1879), and Teweles' yeshivah. The society organized lectures (to which women were admitted from 1879) by outstanding scholars and published them, mainly in the two anniversary volumes, *Afike Jehuda Festschrift* (1909 and 1930). A project initiated in 1919 by the society to publish a Jewish biographical lexicon did not materialize. The society continued to exist until the German occupation of Prague in 1939.

BIBLIOGRAPHY: A. Deutsch, in: *Zeitschrift fuer Geschichte der Juden in der Tschechoslowakei*, 1 (1931), 174–9.

AFIKIM (Heb. אֲפִּיקִים; "stream courses," referring to the Jordan and the Yarmuk Rivers), kibbutz in the central Jordan Valley, in Israel. Afikim, affiliated with Iḥud ha-Kevuzot ve-ha-Kibbutzim, was founded in 1932 by pioneer youth from Soviet Russia, who were among the last organized groups able to leave that country in the 1920s. In 1967 Afikim had 1,290 inhabitants from many countries, making it one of the largest communal settlements in Israel. In 2002 its population was 1,030. In addition to engaging in intensive farming (irrigated field crops, fodder, milch cattle, poultry, carp ponds, bananas, dates, grapefruit), the kibbutz economy was based on a large plywood factory, producing principally for export. It also became a partner in the nearby factory for cellotex and similar materials. The prehistoric site of al-'Ubaydiyya is situated near the kibbutz.

[Efraim Orni]

AFIKOMAN (Heb. אֲפִיקוֹמָן), name of a portion of *mazzah* (unleavened bread) eaten at the conclusion of the Passover evening meal. In most traditions, early in the evening, the person conducting the *seder* breaks the middle of the three *mazzot* into two pieces, putting away the larger portion, designated as *afikoman*, for consumption at the conclusion of the meal. Some Yemenites, who use only two *mazzot*, break off a part of the lower *mazzah* just at the beginning of the meal. The word *afikoman*, of Greek origin but uncertain etymology, probably refers to the aftermeal songs and entertainment (cf. TJ, Pes. 10:8, 37d), accompanied by drinking, which was common after festive meals in ancient times. The Mishnah states: "One may not add *afikoman* after the paschal meal" (Pes. 10:8), for the paschal meal was not to be followed by customary revelry (Pes. 119b–120a). This ruling was later understood to mean that the paschal lamb should be the last food eaten during the evening and, after the cessation of the paschal sacrifice, *mazzah* replaced it as the last food eaten during the evening. This *mazzah* is first referred to as *afikoman* in medieval times (cf. *Mahzor Vitry*). This *afikoman* has become a symbolic reminder of the paschal sacrifice.

In many Ashkenazi communities it is customary for the children present to attempt to "steal" the *afikoman* from the person leading the *seder* (who therefore tries to "hide" it from them). A favorite time for such a "theft" is while the leader is washing his hands before the meal, and the "ransom" is usually the promise of presents. The custom encourages the children to keep awake during the *seder* (see Pes. 109a). This practice of stealing the *afikoman* is, however, nearly unknown in Sephardi Jewish communities.

It became a folk custom to preserve a piece of the *afikoman* as a protection against either harm or the "evil eye," or as an aid to longevity. The power attributed to this piece of *mazzah* is based on the assumption, in the realm of folklore rather than law, that its importance during the *seder* endows it with a special sanctity. Thus, Jews from Iran, Afghanistan, Salonika, Kurdistan, and Bukhara keep a portion of the *afikoman* in their pockets or houses throughout the year for good luck. In some places, pregnant women carry it together with salt and coral pieces, while during their delivery they hold some of the *afikoman* in their hand. Another belief is that this special *mazzah*, if kept for seven years, can stop a flood if thrown into the turbulent river, and the use of the *afikoman* together with a certain biblical verse is even thought capable of quieting the sea. At the *seder* Kurdi Jews tie this *mazzah* to the arm of one of their sons with this blessing: "May you so tie the *ketubbah* to the arm of your bride." Sephardi Jews in Hebron had a similar practice. In Baghdad someone with the *afikoman* used to leave the *seder* and return disguised as a traveler. The leader would ask him, "Where are you from?" to which he would answer, "Egypt," and "Where are you going?" to which he would reply, "Jerusalem." In Djerba, the person conducting the *seder* used to give the *afikoman* to one of the family, who tied it on his shoulder and went to visit relatives and neighbors to forecast the coming of the Messiah.

BIBLIOGRAPHY: Maim. Yad, *Hamez u-Mazzah*, 6:2; 8:9; Sh. Ar., OH 473:6; 477:1–7; 418:1–2; Moshe Veingarten, Haseder He'arukh (1990), 554–562; E. Brauer, *Yehudei Kurdistan* (1947), 235–6; J. Kafih, *Halikhot Teiman* (1961), 22; M. Mani, *Hevron ve-Gibboreiha* (1963), 69–70; M. Zadoc, *Yehudei Teiman* (1967), 181–2; D. Benveniste, in: *Saloniki Ir va-Em be-Yisrael* (1967). 151. **ADD. BIBLIOGRAPHY:** J. Tabory, *The Passover Ritual Throughout the Generations* (Hebrew; 1996), 23 n. 49; 65–66; 318–24; I.J. Yuval, *"Two Nations in Your Womb": Perceptions of Jews and Christians* (Hebrew; 2000), 249–58.

[Dov Noy / Joseph Tabory (2nd ed.)]

AFRICA. The propinquity of the land of Israel to the African continent profoundly influenced the history of the Jewish people. Two of the patriarchs went down to *Egypt; the sojourn of the children of Israel in that land left an indelible impression on the history of their descendants; and the Exodus from Egypt and the theophany at Sinai, in the desert between Africa and Asia, marked the beginning of the specific history of the Hebrew people. Later, in the time of the judges and the monarchy, Palestine was periodically occupied by the Egyptian pharaohs, especially after Thutmose III, in their attempts to extend their influence northward. Important Egyptian archaeological remains have been found throughout Erez Israel, testifying to indubitable Egyptian influences in the background, literature, and language of the Bible. After the destruction of the First Temple in 586 B.C.E. some of the survivors took refuge in Egypt and the Jewish military colony at *Elephantine; ample records which survive from the Persian period seem to have originated at about this time. This settlement at Elephantine marked the beginning of the extension of Jewish influences toward the interior of the continent, and in all probability it was not the only colony of its kind.

Intensive Jewish settlement in Africa began after the conquests of Alexander the Great in the fourth century B.C.E. For the next hundred years or more, Erez Israel was intermittently under the rule of the Egyptian Ptolemies, alternating with the Syrian Seleucids; the country naturally gravitated toward Africa economically as well as politically. Moreover, in the course of their periodic campaigns north of the Sinai Peninsula the Ptolemies deported some elements of the local population to the central provinces of their empire, or brought there prisoners of war as slaves. According to ancient tradition, Alexander had specifically invited Jews to settle in his newly founded city of *Alexandria, and it is certain that early in its history they formed a considerable proportion of its population. Before long, Alexandria became a great center of Jewish

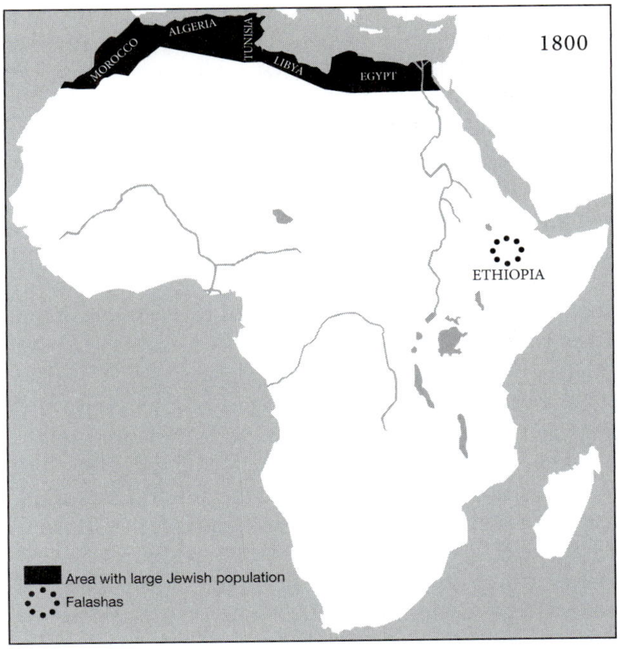

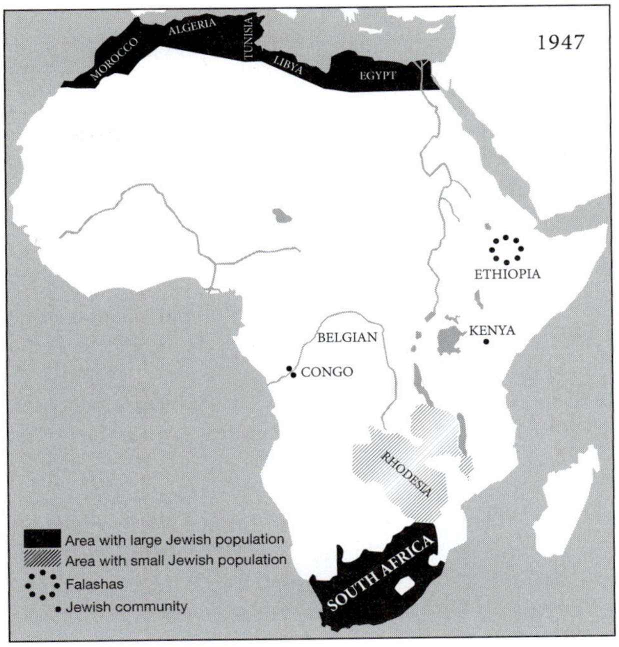

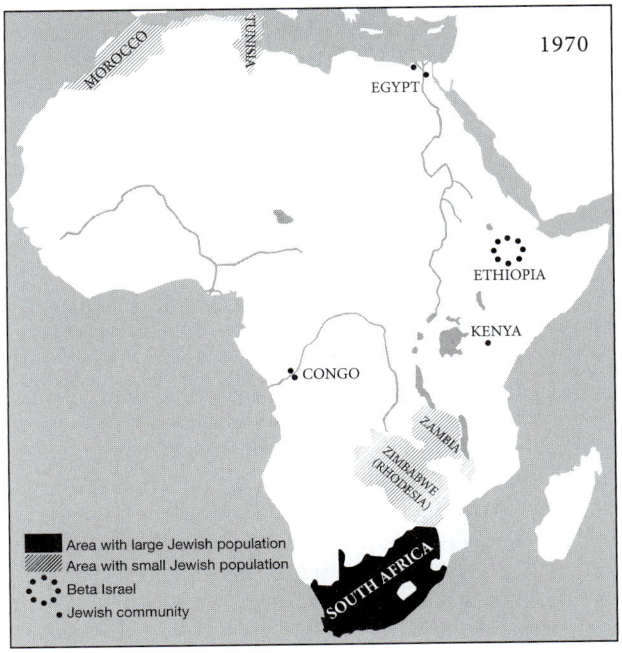

Main concentrations of Jewish population on the African continent at different periods.

culture expressed in the Greek language and largely in terms of Greek civilization culminating in the *Septuagint translation of the Bible and in the allegorical writings of *Philo. It is significant that inscriptions found near Alexandria provide the earliest positive evidence of the existence of the synagogue as an institution. From Egypt the Jewish settlement spread westward along the North African coast reaching *Cyrene at least as early as the second century B.C.E. According to some scholars, Palestinian Hebrews had reached further west long before this, as early as the days of the First Temple, accompanying and helping the *Phoenicians in their expeditions and playing an important role in the establishment of the Punic colonies, including *Carthage itself. It is further suggested that these settlers had a considerable influence in the interior of Africa and were ultimately responsible for the vaguely Jewish ideas and practices that may still be discerned in certain areas. In any case, in the Roman imperial period there were Jewish settlements throughout the Roman provinces as far west as the Strait of Gibraltar. In some areas the Jewish colonies were of great numerical importance and were able to play an independent political role. In Egypt the friction between the Alexandrian Jewish colony and its neighbors was so marked that it developed into a perpetual problem and seems almost to have anticipated the 19th-century antisemitic movement. After the fall of Jerusalem in 70 C.E, *Zealot or Sicarii fugitives from the Palestinian campaigns fled to Egypt, where they instigated a widespread revolt among the Jewish population. The rebels succeeded in dominating large stretches of the countryside, though they were unable to capture the fortified cities. A similar revolt on a smaller scale, about which less information has survived, seems to have occurred simultaneously in Cyrene.

Although swiftly subdued by the Romans, these outbursts were soon followed by the Great Revolt of 115–7 all along the North African coast, at least as far as Cyrene, as well as in Cyprus and Mesopotamia. This revolt, organized apparently by some directing spirit of real genius, momentarily achieved sweeping success, with the insurgents dominating Cyrene and large tracts of the Egyptian countryside. It was, however, bloodily suppressed, and the Jewish settlements in the area of revolt never fully recovered from this blow. When Christianity was adopted as the official religion of the Roman Empire, Judaism was at a further disadvantage. Force as well as blandishment was exerted against the Jews; there were bloody anti-Jewish riots in Alexandria, and the significance of North African Jewry for a time waned almost to vanishing point. When in the sixth century the Byzantines reoccupied the former Roman provinces of North Africa, organized Jewish life was systematically suppressed. On the other hand, Jewish influence during the preceding period had not been restricted to the coastal strip, or to persons of Jewish birth. There is some evidence that suggests conscious proselytizing efforts by the Jews in the African interior, or at least extensive imitation of Jewish rites and beliefs there. Traditions of Jewish origin and traces of Jewish practice are to be found among Berber tribes and black peoples well into the continent and it may well be that the *Beta Israel of Ethiopia survive as testimony to a proselytizing activity that once attained considerable proportions. The curious tales told in the ninth century by the Jewish traveler *Eldad ha-Dani of independent Jewish tribes apparently in the African interior, may be a romanticization of what he had actually seen and experienced. The Arab invasions of the seventh century seem to have found only very small scattered Jewish communities along the African coast. The story of the "Jewish" Berber queen Dahiya al-Kahina seems to be largely legendary although it may be that at that time a woman ruled over a Judaizing Berber tribe. After the Arab conquest these communities were revived and probably reinforced by new immigrants, mainly from Asia, who accompanied the Arab conquerors, or who came to take advantage of the new economic opportunities. The new communities were completely Arabized in language and social life; hardly an echo or trace of the previous Greco-Roman Jewish culture can be discerned among them. The newly founded city of Fostat (Old *Cairo) became the largest Jewish center in Egypt; further west *Kairouan in *Tunisia was of primary importance and, indeed, from the eighth to the 11th centuries was perhaps the greatest center of rabbinic culture outside Babylonia. The documents found in the Cairo *Genizah* make possible a reconstruction of the economic, social, and religious life of the Jews throughout this area in graphic detail. It is significant that in the ninth century *Saadiah Gaon, who may be credited with the revitalization of Jewish scholarship in Mesopotamia, was born, and apparently educated, in the Fayyum district of Egypt. The work of the physician and philosopher Isaac *Israeli, who lived in Kairouan, typified the contribution that the Jews of this area made to contemporary science.The condition of the Jews in Africa under Muslim rule was generally favorable, subject to the usual discriminatory provisions of the Islamic code, which were sporadically enforced; there was a surge of violent persecution in Egypt in the early 11th century, but it was an isolated episode. The triumph of the fanatical, unitarian *Almohad rulers in the 12th century proved disastrous to the Jews; the practice of Judaism was prohibited in *Morocco and the neighboring lands, and they were forcibly converted to Islam. The result was that for a long time Judaism could be observed only in clandestine circumstances. A considerable number of Jews, including the family of Moses *Maimonides, migrated east, making Egypt a major center of Jewish cultural life. After the Almohad domination ended, Jewish life in northwest Africa recovered slowly, but on a restricted and culturally retrograde scale. The wave of massacres and expulsions in Spain and the Balearic Islands in 1391 resulted in a large migration across the Strait of Gibraltar; first there were refugees from these onslaughts and later, on a larger scale, those who had been baptized by force and now desired to revert to Judaism. Thus, especially in the coastal towns of what was later called *Algeria, alongside the old established, quasi-native "Berber" communities, fresh "Spanish" colonies with their own rites and traditions and of a far higher cultural standard arose. The number of Spanish (and later Portuguese) fugitives reaching Africa, primarily Morocco, again increased after the expulsion from Spain in 1492. Their sufferings at the hands of marauders and rapacious local rulers were sometimes appalling. However, in the end they were able to adjust themselves, and henceforth a well-organized Spanish-speaking community, observing the religious regulations provided by "**takkanot* of Castile," dominated Jewish life as far east as Algiers. Further along the Mediterranean coast and in the interior (exceptin the largest towns), the Spanish element was less significant.

The Jews generally continued to live under the universal Muslim code, in many places compulsorily confined to the Jewish quarter, their lives hemmed in by discriminatory regulations. They were often compelled to wear a distinctive garb, they had to show respect to Muslims in the street, and they were excluded from certain occupations. On the other hand they were at least allowed to reside at will, except in one or two "holy" cities such as Kairouan, and the periodic Christian incursions on the coastal towns frequently entailed disaster for them. In the ports especially, the Jews played an economic role of great importance, and, with their linguistic versatility, were the principal intermediaries for transactions with European merchants. Occasionally, Jews were dispatched as ambassadors or envoys to the European powers. Sometimes, a person of outstanding ability would become minister of finance or even vizier, wielding much influence until the disastrous fall which was generally in store for him, sometimes involving his coreligionists as a body.

This description characterizes the history of the Jews almost throughout the Barbary States from the 16th century until well into the 19th. Conditions were somewhat but not conspicuously better in the areas farther east, particularly in Egypt, especially after the establishment of Turkish rule at the beginning of the 16th century. It was only with the introduction of European influences, beginning in Algeria in 1830 and culminating in Morocco and Tripolitania after 1912, that the North African Jews were relieved to a great extent of their medieval status. Nevertheless, except in Egypt and some coastal towns, the process of modernization within the communities was slow. On the other hand, in the upper classes the outward occidentalization of the Jews in language and social life became very marked, while the French administration in Algeria formally recognized the Jews as a European element, the *Crémieux decree in 1870 giving Algerian Jews French nationality.

Meanwhile occidental Jews had established themselves in areas of European settlement at the southernmost tip of the African continent. Isolated settlers are recorded here in the early 19th century; a community largely of English origin was founded in *Cape Town in 1841, spreading from there to other places. The Kimberley diamond field, which opened in the 1860s, was a considerable stimulus to new settlement. With the discovery of gold in Transvaal in the 1880s many Jews emigrated there from Eastern Europe, founding important communities in and around *Johannesburg. After World War I, immigration, especially from Lithuania, assumed relatively large proportions, and the *South African Jewish community of some 100,000 was among the most affluent in the world. From South Africa the Jewish settlement spread northward into Rhodesia (*Zimbabwe), as soon as that territory was opened up in the 1890s. During the period between World War I and World War II there was a Sephardi influx as well, mainly from Rhodes, which spread to the Belgian *Congo. There were also small European Jewish colonies in the British East African territories, joined by immigrants from Egypt and even Yemen.

The Vichy regime in France during World War II brought a temporary setback in Jewish status in the French-dominated areas of North Africa and the revocation of the Crémieux decree. The subsequent Nazi military occupation had distressing, although not enduring, consequences. The European withdrawal from Africa after World War II, coupled with economic changes in that continent, profoundly affected the Jewish communities, all the more so with the wave of anti-Jewish feeling that spread throughout the Arab world after the foundation of the State of Israel. A large portion of the Jewish community of Tunis and almost the whole Jewish community of Algeria left (mostly for France) when the French period of domination ended. The changed circumstances resulted in the migration also of the Jews of Egypt and Cyrenaica, in great part to Israel. *Aliyah* to Israel, immigration to France, and other countries also reduced the Jewish settlement in Morocco, numerically the largest in Africa, to one-fifth of its former number, approximately 50,000 in 1969; political conditions there did not deteriorate formally. The only part of the continent in which the Jewish communities did not initially diminish was South Africa, although gradually with the end of apartheid the community dropped significantly in numbers. By 2005 the community had fallen to about 75,000 with some 1,800 Jews a year emigrating to other countries largely because of the dramatic rise in violent crime.

The most remarkable example of Black Judaizing movements is to be found in South Africa and Zimbabwe among the *Lemba tribe, and there are similar movements throughout the continent which range from movements which depend on perceived shared origins – sometimes invoking the myth of the *Ten Lost Tribes of Israel – to movements of conversion such as the *Bayudaya in Uganda.

The establishment of the State of Israel brought a renewal of the movement to bring the *Beta Israel of Ethiopia into closer relations with world Jewry. The State of Israel also established cordial relations with the emergent African states, entering into diplomatic relations with them and sending economic, military, and agricultural experts to assist them in solving their problems (see *Israel, Historical Survey, Internal Aid and Cooperation). However, under pressure from the Arabs after the Yom Kippur War of 1973, 29 African countries broke off diplomatic relations with Israel, though in the course of the years, starting with the Democratic Republic of the Congo (formerly Zaire) in 1982, most reestablished relations.

BIBLIOGRAPHY: Bibliographies will be found under the individual countries. The following general works will be found useful: A. Cahen, *Les Juifs dans l'Afrique septentrionale* (1867); D. Cazès, *Essai sur l'histoire des Israélites de Tunisie* (1888); J. Chalom, *Les Israélites de la Tunisie* (1908); S. Mendelssohn, *Jews of Africa* (1920); N. Slouschz, *Judéo-Hélénes et Judéo-Berbéres* (1909); idem, *Travels in North Africa* (1927); G. Saron and L. Hotz, *Jews in South Africa* (1955); L. Herrmann, *History of the Jews in South Africa* (1930); J.J. Williams, *Hebrewisms of West Africa: From Nile to Niger with the Jews* (1930); M. Eisenbeth, *Les Juifs de l'Afrique du Nord* (1936); idem, *Les Juifs au Maroc* (1948); C. Martin, *Les Israèlites Algériens de 1830 à 1902* (1936); A.N. Chouraqui, *Between East and West* (1968); Institut far Yidishe Inyonim, *Di Yidishe Yeshuvim in di Arabishe Lender* (1957); H.Z. Hirschberg, *Me-Ereẓ Mevo ha-Shemesh* (1957); Hirschberg, Afrikah, 2 vols. (1965); idem, in: *Journal of African History*, 4 (1963), 313–39; M. Simon, *Recherches d'histoire Judéo-Chrétienne* (1962), 30–100; Monteil, in: *Hesperis*, 38 (1951), 265–98; M. Krein in, *Israel and Africa: A Study in Technical Co-operation* (1964); S.W. Baron, et al., in: JSOS, 24 (1962), 67–107. **ADD. BIBLIOGRAPHY:** T. Parfitt, *The Lost Tribes of Israel: The History of a Myth* (2002); idem, *Journey to the Vanished City – The Search for a Lost Tribe of Israel* (1999).

[Cecil Roth]

AFRICA, NORTH: MUSICAL TRADITIONS. Geographically, North Africa (the countries of the Maghreb, i.e., Morocco, Tunisia, Algeria, and Libya) belongs to Africa, but culturally it is a part of the Islamic world. Some scholars have set up a twofold division of the entire area: the musical culture of the coastal region and that of the interior, roughly corresponding to "urban" and "rural," or "Andalusian" (i.e., Spanish-influenced) and "Berber" (i.e., autochthonous) music. Neither of these areas however, is homogeneous, and there are sometimes considerable differences in musical style between one coastal or interior district and another. North Africa is therefore a musical crossways of many traditions: old Mediterranean, Berber, Bedouin, Near Eastern (including Turkish, and recently Egyptian), Andalusian (or "Moorish"), and Saharan. Not all of these are present at the same place and time, and often one is faced with stylistic blends, which are difficult to define.

The Jews, historically among the oldest elements of the population, have taken an active part in each stage of the area's musical history. They have also preserved more elements from older traditions, with the conservation typical of "fringe cultures," and, in addition, have absorbed still other outside influences through factors in their own history. Both before and after the appearance of Islam there was close and permanent contact with Palestinian, Babylonian, and Egyptian Jewry. During the *reconquista* and after the expulsion of the Jews from Spain, Spanish, Portuguese, and later also Italian Jews settled in North Africa. The musical usages of the immigrants were influenced by the local ones and influenced them in return. This blending of styles and openness to influence has remained typical of North African Jewish music.

Thus, the musical traditions and practices of the North African Jews represent a conglomerate of a variety of old and new, sacred and secular, folk and art, local and shared musical styles. One can also add the advent of recent innovative stylistic blends representing the attempt to modernize the old tradition. Interestingly, talented Jewish musicians in all four countries were intimately involved in the creation and promotion of the new styles. As a rule, one can state that the musical traditions and practices of the North African Jews are interconnected in various ways with those of the non-Jewish environment. However, comparisons between the Jewish and non-Jewish musical styles are particularly difficult to make, since each is in itself a complex of historical and cultural entities, not to mention the serious obstacles characterizing any other oral tradition – the lack of musical documents and the lack of accuracy in oral transmission. This makes it impossible to state what derives from a Jewish and what from an Arab source. Nevertheless, one can speak of certain specific traits.

It seems nevertheless that the distinguishing traits should be essentially sought in the linguistic, thematic, and functional particularities. First and foremost are the musical rendering of biblical readings and prayers, and the singing of liturgical Hebrew poems, *piyyuṭim*, written by the most famous poets of the Jewish people as well as by locally distinguished ones. These include hymns of praise, supplications, lamentations, and the celebration of holidays. The French specialist in Moroccan music, Alexis Chottin, mentions the remarkable fact that when Hebrew texts are adapted to replace the original, they maintain the Arab metric and prosody, which, he points out, is not translation. In addition to the setting of the borrowed melodies to Hebrew texts, this type of arrangement usually leads to melodic and rhythmical changes, so their functional use in Jewish-specific circumstances may be considered as factor highlighting their Jewishness. A special category of bilingual poetry called *maṭrūz* (combined Hebrew and Arab verses and strophes) should also be noted. The question of Jewishness in the Oriental music appeared in connection with the intriguing phenomenon which arose from the broad-based ethnic movement of the 1980s in Israel. Challenging the widely held belief that Oriental musical traditions have a folk and indigenous background, representatives of the latter responded by arguing that the erudite mystical-religious ceremonial music known as *bakkashot*, should be placed on the same level as western classical music.

The singing of *bakkashot* and *piyyuṭim* always refers to North African classical music, which, itself, is identified with the Andalusian compound and multi-sectional form of the *nūba* in all of the African centers. Established in Spain, the basic components and characteristics of the Andalusian *nūba* have survived in the major traditions of Fez, Tlemcen, Algier, and Tunis where they are called respectively: *āla, gharnāṭī, ṣanʿa,* and *ma'lūf.* Some differences notwithstanding, they are very similar in spirit and structure. The individual *nūba* is named after the mode or *ṭab*ʿ (nature or temperament); for example *nūba dīl, nūba raṣd,* etc. The overall physiognomy of the *nūba* in all centers is more or less alike: it comprises an instrumental prelude or preludes and a series of pre-composed vocal pieces that represent autonomous phases of the *nūba*, each having its own set of poetic texts as well as melodic and rhythmic characteristics. Most of the poems sung in this repertory consist of *muwashshaḥāt* and free-measured pieces that intersperse the various phases. The overall structure as well as the individual phases are governed not only by modal unity but also by rhythmic acceleration that reaches its peak toward the end of the *nūba*.

Morocco

Travelers who record their impressions usually display exceptional intellectual curiosity and their observations can supply important evidence. By an extraordinary coincidence, three different travelers recorded their impressions of wedding ceremonies held in the same community of Tangier: the Jewish Italian writer Samuel *Romanelli in 1787; the French painter Delacroix in 1832; and the French author Alexandre Dumas in 1832. All three travelers describe Jewish women dancing, and the traditional group of three musicians, which accompanies the dancing and singing: the *ʿūd* (the classical Arab short-necked lute), the *kamanja* (short-necked bowed lute) or the modern violin which has come to be its substitute, the *darbūka* (pottery vessel-drum) or the *ṭār* (frame drum). The *kamanja* or violin is played in the medieval fashion, with the body of the instrument resting on the knee. Delacroix, who also recorded in his journal that the Jewish musicians of Mogador were the best in all Morocco, depicted this traditional ensemble along with a dancer. Romanelli records that the instrumentalists, poet-singers, and preachers were remunerated in two ways. In the synagogue, the intended payment was only announced out loud, but outside the synagogue the coins were immediately put on the instrument or on the performer's breast.

Jewish musicians also distinguished themselves as entertainers in local gentile society, either in company with Muslim musicians or as special "Jewish bands." One folktale tells how such a Jewish ensemble was commanded to give a concert before the sultan on the Ninth of Av (see *Av, Ninth of). Since they could not refuse to appear, they played the melodies of the traditional **kinot,* and henceforth were known as "The Singers of Woe."

The art of the *payṭan* (religious poet, and by extension, singer of religious poetry) is also rooted strongly in the Andalusian tradition. In almost every synagogue there is a *payṭan* in addition to the *ḥazzan*. His principal task is to sing prayers such as *Nishmat* and **Kedushah*, and all the *piyyuṭim*. A *payṭan* may take part in the performance of the *bakkashot*, but not every *payṭan* possesses the necessary knowledge for this special art, so that a vocally and musically gifted layman will often function as the "leader" there. Since the *bakkashot* were performed early on Sabbath mornings, the instrumental part is completely avoided. As a result, the singers evolved the habit of adding passages sung to the syllables *na na na* in which the role of the accompanying instrument is thus imitated. These syllables and the wealth of vocalizes (textless ornamented phrases) is in fact a remarkable feature of the North African art of singing. When the *bakkashot* and *piyyuṭim* are sung on a weekday, they are usually accompanied by the traditional instrumental ensemble.

In the realm of folk music one should mention the folk tradition of group performance, especially in the Atlas Mountain regions, often in the form of women's ensembles. Their music and dances are not different from those of the Berber tribes.

Music plays an important role in the pilgrimage festivals at the numerous *hillulot* (sing. **hillula*). It marks and enhances the celebration of a revered public figure and the mass pilgrimage to the site of his burial, which, in some cases, is venerated by both Jews and Muslims. The ritual of sainthood is deeply entrenched in all strata of the people.

A special Moroccan custom is the *taḥdīd*, a ceremony conducted the night before circumcision when it is believed that the newborn, subject, prior to circumcision, to harm by evil forces, is at the highest vulnerability. In this event a sword is used to banish the evil spirits while a selection of appropriate biblical verses is chanted.

Another well-known celebration marked by singing and dancing is the **Maimuna* (which has been transferred to Israel). At these gatherings many original creations of the *qaṣīda* type can be heard. The *qaṣīda*, a popular song in Hebrew or in the vernacular, is sung both by the educated and the lower classes. Some *qaṣīda* songs are anonymous and well-known poets created others. In the framework of the *bakkashot* were introduced dozens of *qaṣīdas* composed by local poets borrowing their tunes from Arab *qaṣīdas*. Their texts include praises of the saints, ethical and religious subjects, and comments on historical and present or recent events. They are sung with or without accompaniment, and the tunes are mostly adaptations of well-known melodies. Such *qaṣīda* songs are found in all North African countries. One of the most talented poets of this genre was David Elkayim (1851–1940), and among the most celebrated *payṭanim* were David Ḥasin (1727–1792), David Iflah, and David *Buzaglo (1903–1975).

Tunisia

The first and earliest documents focusing on the eternal debate concerning the permissibility of music are the two responsa of *Hai Gaon to questions addressed by representatives of Tunisian Jewry. One of them, perhaps addressed to the community of *Kairouan, forbids the *ḥazzanim* to sing poems in the "language of the Ishmaelites," even at banquets. Another one, often quoted in later literature, is addressed to the community of *Gabès, and discusses whether the traditional prohibition (Git. 7:1) against singing with instrumental accompaniment and which restricts all secular songs in memory of the destruction of the Temple also applies to wedding celebrations. Hai Gaon approved of singing pious hymns of praise on such occasions, but secular Arab love songs were strictly forbidden, even without accompaniment; "and so to what you have mentioned ... that women play the drums and dance [at such festivities], if this is done in public there is nothing more grave; and even if they ... only sing, this is most unseemly and forbidden." The free and unsegregated participation of women singers in wedding festivities, family rejoicings, pilgrimages to saints' tombs, and their prominence as professional mourners, were probably related to similar usages in Berber society and have survived until the present.

The Tunisian term *laʿb* (lit. amusement but used for dancing) is mentioned in two **Genizah* documents: in one, the birth of a boy in Fostat, Egypt, is celebrated with *laʿb* by his family at Mahdia in Tunisia; in another, a poor Tunisian teacher alludes, surprisingly, to *laʿb* at the burial of his son.

In proximity to Gabès lay the famous Island of *Djerba, home to a quite old Jewish community. It was there that in 1929 Robert *Lachmann carried on important fieldwork research with the hope of disclosing in their liturgical cantillation older stratum of Jewish music. His important analytical study of this tradition was published after his premature death (see Bibl.).

The output of *piyyuṭim* and songs the Jewish poets wrote in Hebrew and Judeo-Arabic is considerable and played an important educative and socio-cultural role. They cover numerous song genres and themes related to Jewish life.

Toward the end of the 19th century and during the first decades of the 20th Jewish musicians played an essential role in the indigenous cultural reform movement as well as in the crystallization of a new musical style. They were involved in the growth of the cinematographic and record industries and the introduction of the modern Egyptian musical style, and distinguished by the remarkable involvement of numerous talented female musicians. Some of those female musicians established their own café-concert halls, which attracted numerous Jewish and non-Jewish music fans. Leila Sfez, who owned a popular café-concert hall, was the aunt of the legendary actress and singer Ḥbiba Msika, whose tragic premature death was the subject of a film produced by the Tunisian Slama Bachar. Interestingly, the first records of Tunisian music, published in 1908, included the interpretations of the Jewish female musicians: Louisa the Tunisian, and the sisters Semama, Fritna, and Ḥbiba Darmon.

In an article dedicated to Jewish musicians published in 1960, the Tunisian author ʿAlī Jandubī warmly extolled the valuable contribution they made to Tunisian music and musical life. He mentions the special skills of many famous

Jewish female and male musicians, including a few of Libyan origin. Among the famous singers and instrumentalists he mentions are Isaac, Abraham Tibshi, Khaylu al-Sghir, Mridakh Slama and his son Sousou, Gaston Bsiri, Ḥbiba Msika, and Raoul Journo.

In 1928, the Jerusalemite cantor, *payṭan*, and composer Asher Mizraḥi arrived in Tunis, staying until 1967, the year of his return to Israel. He soon became a dominant figure, particularly in the realm of synagogal and paraliturgical music, thus enriching the musical life of the community.

Algeria

Following the riots against the Jews in Spain in 1391, a wave of refugees found shelter in Algeria. Among the newcomers was the rabbinic authority, philosopher, and kabbalist Simeon ben Tzemah *Duran (b. Majorca, 1361), who was elected chief rabbi of Algeria in 1408 and died in 1444. Duran was the author of a comprehensive book, *Magen Avot*, which deals with religious philosophy and diverse sciences, including an important section on the science of music. In addition to generalities he wrote on music, its nature and influence, the bulk of his exposition concerns the biblical accents, which are "genera of melodies," extolling their importance for the understanding of biblical texts and their rhetoric-musical meanings. Regarding the melodies used for the *piyyuṭim*, he tends to admit that they were adopted from other nations.

We find years later interesting and unique evidence of the involvement of Jewish musicians in indigenous music. It occurs in the book of a young Russian pianist, Alexandre Christianowitch (1835–1874): *Esquisse historique de la musique arabe*, published in 1863. The author, an officer in the czar's navy, was compelled, for reasons of health, to stay in Algiers. For two years he did research on the local classical music. He reports that his first encounter with indigenous music took place in a Moorish café-concert hall where he heard a group of Jewish musicians, and that later on his Muslim mentor was critical concerning the authenticity of the classical music played by the Jews. This is, however, not the case in recent Muslim sources, which, on the contrary, warmly extol the role played by Jewish musicians such as Maalem Benfarachou, Laho Seror, and Mouzinou in the preservation of the old classical Andalusian tradition. This approach characterizes in particular the book of Algerian musicologist Nadya Buzar-Kasbadji: *L'Émergence artistique algérienne au* XX*e siècle* (published in 1988). The first chapter of this book is, to a large extent, dedicated to the Jewish musician Edmond Nathan Yafil. The author describes him as "an outstanding personage who has been the pivotal actor in an artistic Renaissance movement wherein Arab-Andalusian music constituted the leaven." She adds that Yafil remained faithful to the Arab-Andalusian tradition, which connected Jews and Arabs, endowing them with a feeling of common identity. Yafil also founded in 1911 the al-Moutribiyya music society, most of whose members were Jewish musicians.

Like their Moroccan, Tunisian, and Libyan Jewish colleagues who immigrated to France, Jewish Algerian musicians pursued a successful career in their new environment, often in close collaboration with non-Jews. This is, for instance, the case with the blind female singer and *'ud* player Sultana Da'ud, alias "Reinette l'Oranaise," who, after she achieved remarkable success in Algeria, continued to be admired by her numerous fans in France for her expressive and poignant art. Samples of her repertory were issued in several cassettes and CDs. Another example is the recent comeback of the popular singer Enrico Massias to the classical music of Algeria. This occurred after the assassination of his master and father-in-law, the celebrated Jewish musician Raymond Leiris.

BIBLIOGRAPHY: A.Z. Idelsohn, *Melodien*, 5 (1928), devoted to Morocco; R. Lachmann, *Jewish Cantillation* (1940); A. Mizrahi, *Ma'adanei melekh* (1945); A. Herzog, *The Intonation of the Pentateuch in the Heder of Tunis* (1963); Sh. Romanelli, *Ketavim nivḥarim* (1969), 29, 54–56; I. Ben-Ami, "*Nagganim ve-lahaqot*," in: *Tazlil*, 10 (1970); E. Gerson-Kiwi, "*Robert Lachmann*," in: *Yuval*, 3 (1974), 100–108; idem (ed.), *R. Lachmann: Gesange der Juden auf der Insel Djerba* (1978 – Yuval Monograph Series, 7); idem, *Migrations and Mutations of the Music in East and West* (1980), 130–136; A. Chottin, *Tableau de la musique marocaine*, ed. P. Geuthner (n.d.), 149–53; I. Ben-Ami, in: *Tazlil*, 10 (1970), 54–58; Levy, *Antología*, passim; A. Amzalag, *Shir yedidot*, in: *Pe'amim*, 32 (1982), R.F. Davis, "Some Relations between Three Piyyutim from Djerba and Three Arabic Songs," in: *The Maghreb Review*, 5–6 (1984/85), 134–144; A. Shiloah, "The Language of the Heart," in: *Ariel*, 105 (1997), 15–28; idem, "Rencontres et ententes," in: *Perspectives* 9 (2002), 170–183; idem, in: H. Sa'adoun (ed.), *Kehillot Yisrael – Morocco* (2003), 205–212; idem, in: S. Fellous (ed.), *Juifs et Musulmans en Tunisie* (2003), 309–316.

[Amnon Shiloah (2nd ed.)]

AFRICAN JEWISH CONGRESS. The African Jewish Congress was founded in 1992 as a representative coordinating body for the Jewish communities in Sub-Saharan African countries. Its main aims are (a) to enable smaller Jewish communities to establish and maintain contact with larger Jewish communities, which in turn provide them with access to various facilities, and (b) to give Africa and African Jews a voice in international Jewry through a properly constituted forum. The establishment of the AJC was made possible by the demise of white minority rule in South Africa, which ended South Africa's isolation on the international stage and enabled its large Jewish community to take the lead in setting up a representative body for African Jewry. The AJC has its head offices in *Johannesburg, *South Africa, located within the administrative structure of the South African Jewish Board of Deputies (SAJBD) and is affiliated to the *World Jewish Congress. The main professional officer of the AJC is its spiritual leader, who regularly travels to the affiliated countries to, amongst other things, officiate at religious services and life-cycle events, visit individual Jews living in isolated areas, and oversee the maintenance of Jewish cemeteries. Rabbi Moshe Silberhaft has fulfilled this role since the organization's creation while founder-member Mervyn Smith, a former national president of the SAJBD, has served as its president and represented the organization at the World Jewish Congress. The AJC holds annual meetings on a rotational basis in the various affiliate countries. These include Botswana, Democratic Republic of the *Congo (Zaire), *Kenya, Lesotho, *Madagascar, Malawi, *Mauritius, Mozambique, Namibia, South Africa, Swaziland, Tanzania, *Uganda, *Zambia, and *Zimbabwe.

[David Saks (2nd ed.)]

AFTALION, ALBERT (1874–1956), economist, born in Bulgaria. Aftalion acquired distinction through his work on the theory of crises, which he attributed to cyclic trends in economic growth. His teaching at the universities of Lille and Paris reflected the influence of the economic theories of the Viennese school. His work represents an analysis of the events of the interwar period, an examination of French inflation from 1919 to 1924, and the movements of gold and international currency in relation to the balance of payments. Aftalion's writings include *Les crises périodiques de surproduction* (1913), *La valeur de la monnaie dans l'économie contemporaine* (1948³), *L'or et sa distribution mondiae* (1932), *L'équilibre dans les relations economiques internationales* (1937), and *L'or et la monnaie, leur valeur. Les mouvements de l'or* (1938).

[Joachim O. Ronall]

AFTERLIFE. Judaism has always maintained a belief in an afterlife, but the forms which this belief has assumed and the modes in which it has been expressed have varied greatly and differed from period to period. Thus even today several distinct conceptions about the fate of man after death, relating to the immortality of the soul, the resurrection of the dead, and the nature of the world to come after the messianic redemption, exist side by side within Judaism. Though these conceptions are interwoven no generally accepted theological system exists concerning their interrelationship.

In the Bible

The Bible is comparatively inexplicit on the fate of the individual after death. It would seem that the dead go down to *Sheol, a kind of Hades, where they live an ethereal, shadowy existence (Num. 16:33; Ps. 6:6; Isa. 38:18). It is also said that Enoch "walked with God, and he was not; for God took him" (Gen. 5:24); and that Elijah is carried heavenward in a chariot of fire (II Kings 2:11). Even the fullest passage on the subject, the necromantic incident concerning the dead prophet Samuel at En-Dor, where his spirit is raised from the dead by a witch at the behest of Saul, does little to throw light on the matter (I Sam. 28:8ff.). The one point which does emerge clearly from the above passages is that there existed a belief in an afterlife of one form or another. (For a full discussion see Pedersen, *Israel*, 1–2 (1926), 460ff. A more critical view may be found in G. von Rad, *Old Testament Theology*, 2 vols., 1962.) Though the talmudic rabbis claimed there were many allusions to the subject in the Bible (cf. Sanh. 90b–91a), the first explicit biblical formulation of the doctrine of the resurrection of the dead occurs in the book of Daniel, in the following passage:

"Many of them that sleep in the dust of the earth shall awake, some to everlasting life, and some to reproaches and everlasting abhorrence" (Dan. 12:2; see also Isa. 26:19; Ezek. 37:1ff.).

In Second Temple Literature

In the eschatology of the apocryphal literature of the Second Temple period, the idea of heavenly immortality, either vouchsafed for all Israel or for the righteous alone, vies with the resurrection of the dead as the dominant theme. Thus IV Maccabees, for instance, though on the whole tending toward Pharisaism in its theology, promises everlasting life with God to those Jewish martyrs who preferred death to the violation of His Torah, but is silent on the subject of resurrection. II Maccabees, on the other hand, figures the latter prominently (cf. II Macc. 7:14, 23; IV Macc. 9:8; 17:5, 18). The doctrine was, however, stressed by sectarian groups and is vividly expressed in the New Testament. For Philo the doctrine of the resurrection is subservient to that of the immortality of the soul and is seen by him as a figurative way of referring to the latter. The individual soul, which is imprisoned in the body here on earth, returns, if it is the soul of a righteous man, to its home in God; the wicked suffer eternal death (see H.A. Wolfson, *Philo*, 2 vols. (1947–48); index, s.v. *Soul, Resurrection).*

In Talmud and Midrash

When a man dies his soul leaves his body, but for the first 12 months it retains a temporary relationship to it, coming and going until the body has disintegrated. Thus the prophet Samuel was able to be raised from the dead within the first year of his demise. This year remains a purgatorial period for the soul, or according to another view only for the wicked soul, after which the righteous go to paradise, *Gan Eden*, and the wicked to hell, *Geihinnom* (Gehinnom; Shab. 152b–153a; Tanh. Va-Yikra 8). The actual condition of the soul after death is unclear. Some descriptions imply that it is quiescent, the souls of the righteous are "hidden under the Throne of Glory" (Shab. 152b), while others seem to ascribe to the dead full consciousness (Ex. R. 52:3; Tanh. Ki Tissa 33; Ket. 77h, 104a; Ber. 18b–19a). The Midrash even says, "The only difference between the living and the dead is the power of speech" (PR 12:46). There is also a whole series of disputes about how much the dead know of the world they leave behind (Ber. 18b).

In the days of the messianic redemption the soul returns to the dust, which is subsequently reconstituted as this body when the individual is resurrected. It is somewhat unclear whether the resurrection is for the righteous alone, or whether the wicked too will be temporarily resurrected only to be judged and destroyed, their souls' ashes being scattered under the feet of the righteous. A view supporting the doctrine of eternal damnation is found, but this is disputed by the claim, "There will be no Gehinnom in future times" (RH 17a; Tos. to RH 16b; BM 58b; Ned. 8b and Ran, *ibid.*; Av. Zar. 3b). The doctrine of the *resurrection is a cornerstone of rabbinic eschatology, and separated the Pharisee from his Sadducean opponent. The Talmud goes to considerable lengths to show how the resurrection is hinted at in various biblical passages, and excludes those who deny this doctrine from any portion in the world to come (Sanh. 10:1; Sanh. 90b–91a; Jos., Wars, 2:162 ff.). The messianic reign is conceived of as a political and physical Utopia, though there is considerable dispute about this matter (Ber. 34b; Shab. 63a; and the glosses of Rashi). At its end will be the world to come (*olam ha-ba*), when the righteous will sit in glory and enjoy the splendor of the Divine Presence in a world of purely spiritual bliss (Ber. 17a). About this eschatological culminating point the rabbis are somewhat reticent, and content themselves with the verse "Eye hath not seen, O God, beside Thee" (Isa. 64:3; Ber. 34b), i.e., none but God can have a conception of the matter. In the world to come the Divine Presence itself will illuminate the world. (For a general discussion see "The Doctrine of the Resurrection of the Dead in Rabbinic Theology" by A. Marmorstein in *Studies in Jewish Theology,* 1950.)

In Medieval Jewish Philosophy

The medieval Jewish philosophers brought conceptual and systematic thought to bear on the more imagist rabbinic eschatology, and one major problem they faced was to integrate the notions of immortality and resurrection. *Saadiah Gaon was perhaps the most successful among them, since he conceived of the state of the reunited soul and body after the resurrection as one of spiritual bliss (*Book of Beliefs and Opinions,* 9:5). Due to the nature of Greek psychology, however, the emphasis among the other Jewish philosophers, both Platonist and Aristotelian, is on the soul's immortality – the resurrection being added only because of doctrinal considerations. It is clear in the case of *Maimonides, for instance, that the immortality of the soul is paramount (*Guide*, 2:27; 3:54). Though he makes the belief in the resurrection, rather than in the immortality of the disembodied soul, one of his fundamental principles of Jewish faith (cf. Mishnah, Sanhedrin, introd. to Helek), it is only the latter which has meaning in terms of his philosophical system. Indeed the resurrection does not figure in the *Guide of the Perplexed* at all.

In general the neoplatonists saw the soul's journey as an ascent toward the Godhead, and its beatitude as a purely spiritual bliss involving knowledge of God and spiritual beings and some form of communion with them. Their negative attitude toward the flesh, in favor of the spirit, left no room for a resurrection theology of any substance. The Jewish Aristotelians, who thought of the acquired intellect as the immortal part of man, saw immortality in terms of the intellectual contemplation of God. Some of the Jewish Aristotelians held that in their immortal state the souls of all men are one; while others maintained that immortality is individual. This emphasis on salvation through intellectual attainment was the subject of considerable criticism. Crescas, for example, claimed that it was the love of God, rather than knowledge of Him, which was of primary soteriological import (*Or Adonai*, 3:3).

In Kabbalistic Literature

Kabbalistic eschatology, more systematic than its rabbinic predecessor, is, if anything, more complex in structure and varied as between the several kabbalistic subsystems. The soul is conceived of as divided into several parts, whose origin is in Divine Emanation, and is incarnated here on earth with a specific task to fulfill. The soul of the wicked, i.e., of he who has failed in his assigned task, is punished and purified in hell or is reincarnated again (*gilgul*) to complete its unfinished work. In certain cases, however, the wicked soul is denied even hell or reincarnation and is exiled without the possibility of finding rest. Much of the literature is devoted to detailing the various stages of ascent and descent of the soul and its parts. (For a discussion of the various kabbalistic systems, and the variety of views held, see G. Scholem, *Major Trends in Jewish Mysticism*, particularly ch. 6.)

In Modern Jewish Thought

Orthodox Judaism has, throughout, maintained both a belief in the future resurrection of the dead as part of the messianic redemption, and also a belief in some form of immortality of the soul after death. The former figures in the liturgy at a number of points, including the morning prayer (Hertz, Prayer, 18), expressing the believer's trust that God will return his soul to his body in time to come. It is also a central motif of the second benediction of the *Amidah* (*ibid.*, 134). The belief in the soul's survival after death is implicit in the various prayers said in memory of the dead and in the mourner's custom of reciting the *Kaddish* (*ibid.*, 1106–09, and 212, 269–71). Reform Judaism has, however, given up any literal belief in the future resurrection of the dead. Reform theology concerns itself solely with the belief in a spiritual life after death and has modified the relevant liturgical passages accordingly.

AFULAH (Heb. עֲפוּלָה; עִיר יִזְרְעֶאל, **Ir Yizre'el**), city in the Jezreel Valley, Israel. It lies at the foot of both the southwestern and northwestern slopes of Givat ha-Moreh and received municipal status in 1972. Afulah was founded in 1925 by the American Zion Commonwealth, which planned to make the town the urban center of the Jewish settlements in the Jezreel Valley. Old Afulah's location on a highway and railroad crossroads (N. and N.W. to Nazareth and to Haifa, N.E. to Tiberias, S.E. to Beth-Shean, S. to Jenin and Nablus, S.W. to Megiddo and Haderah) was seen as a promising asset. The hopes attached to Afulah, however, only materialized to a small degree, because the kibbutzim and moshavim of the valley rarely used its facilities, except for the regional hospital of Kuppat Ḥolim (the first in the country). Instead they developed their own services or preferred to use those of Haifa. In addition, the speculative sale of building plots to absentee, mostly overseas, proprietors hampered the town's development. In 1948 Afulah had a population of 2,500.

After the establishment of the State of Israel, however, many immigrants were housed in Afulah, and a new section, Afulah Illit (Upper Afulah), was laid out at a distance of 1.8–3.1 mi. (3–5 km.) from the older part of the town on Givat ha-Moreh, climbing to about 984 ft. (300 m.) above sea level. Industries – principally textile as well as a sugar refinery and a plastics factory – were opened in the city, which became the seat of the Jezreel subdistrict, its territory extending over 11 sq. mi. (28.6 sq. km.). The population of Afulah grew to approximately 17,000 in the late 1960s and 38,500 in 2002. Among the city's residents are recent immigrants from the former Soviet Union, Latin America, and Ethiopia.

The name Afulah, preserved by a small Arab village al-'Afula (which lay at the site until World War I), may come from the Canaanite-Hebrew root *ofel* ("fortress tower"), possibly mentioned in the list of Thutmose III. In excavations carried out at the ancient tell of Afulah, remnants of the Middle and Late Canaanite and Early Israelite periods were discovered. A settlement of the transition period from the Chalcolithic to the Early Bronze Ages (c. 32nd century B.C.E.) was discovered in the vicinity. Near the site of the present-day town Napoleon's army defeated the Turks in 1799. The place became a station on the narrow-gauge railway built in 1905, from Haifa to Damascus, and a second railway was laid from Afulah to Jenin and Nablus in 1913. The former ceased operating in 1948, and the latter in 1936.

[Efraim Orni / Shaked Gilboa (2nd ed.)]

AGA, family name of Crimean Karaites, originating in the title given to the holder of an important office (Turk.). The first person to go under this name was Samuel ben Abraham (1717–1770), the son of *Abraham ben Josiah Yerushalmi, the prominent Karaite scholar of the Crimea. Samuel lived in Chufut-Kale and was the leader of its community, also known by the title *rosh ha-golah* (exilarch). He was a "court Jew" in the court of Tatar Khan Qirim Giray, who appointed Samuel to mint coins for the Khanate in 1768. Samuel protected the interests of his community before the officials. He wrote a number of liturgical poems and some of them were included in the Karaite *siddurs*. Unknown persons murdered him on his way from Bakhchisarai, the capital of the Khanate, near Chufut-Kale. He had three sons: Eliezer, Benjamin, and Simḥah.

His son BENJAMIN AGA (d. 1824) was a leader and intercessor for the community of Chufut-Kale. He also was appointed to mint coins for the Khanate in the court by the new Khan, Shahin Giray. In 1781 Benjamin leased the custom duties on the sale of wine. He became one of the Khan's unofficial court advisers. Like his father, he protected his community's interests. In 1777 he succeeded in annulling a harmful decree of Devlet Giray, the pretender to the Khan's throne, who falsely accused the Karaites of stealing the Khan's money. Benjamin corresponded with Karaite leaders of Poland, Lithuania, Constantinople, and Jerusalem and financially supported their communities in times of distress. Following the Russian annexation of the Crimea he continued to serve as the official head of the community and to represent it before the Russian authorities. In 1795 Benjamin was chosen together with two other community leaders of the Crimean Karaites to travel to St. Petersburg on a special mission to the government. Their delegation won exemption for Crimean Karaites from the double taxation imposed on all the Jews of the Russian Empire, and to secure other rights, such as the purchase of immovable property. In 1806 Benjamin reestablished, together with his brother Simḥah, a publishing house in Chufut-Kale. Benjamin was an expert in Karaite *halakhah* and an authority on the Karaite calendar.

BIBLIOGRAPHY: G. Akhiezer, in: M.Polliack (ed.), *Karaite Judaism* (2003), 737–39; F.E. Miller and J.S. Luzki, *Iggeret Teshu'at Yisrael* (1993); S. Poznanski, *Ha-Kara'i Avraham ben Yoshiyahu Yerushalmi* (1894), 5; S. Pigit, *Iggeret Nidhḥei Shemuel* (1894), 6–10; Mann, Texts, 2 (1935), 1535, 1582, index.

[Golda Akhiezer (2nd ed.)]

AGADATI (Kaushanski), BARUCH (1895–1975), dancer, visual artist, filmmaker, and cultural animateur. Agadati was born in Bessarabia (Russia). As a teenager, he arrived in Jerusalem and enrolled in the Bezalel Academy for Fine Arts, founded and run by the sculptor Boris *Shatz. He was then one of many students from abroad (mainly Russia) who enrolled before World War I in Bezalel or in the Herzliyyah Gymnasium in Tel Aviv. In the summer of 1914 when WWI broke out, Agadati was visiting his parents abroad and could not return for the next term.

In Odessa he studied visual arts as well as ballet. At the age of 18 he became soloist of the ballet company of the municipal theater there. He was interested in Jewish culture and prepared a series of cartoon portraits of types of men of the *shtetl* which he performed with great success.

Agadati returned to Ereẓ Israel in 1919. After a few months he began to perform what he called concerts, dancing solos with the accompaniment of a piano. He was deeply influenced by the "constructivist" abstract painting style prevalent in Russia at the time, making his movements slow but powerful, sculptural, and cubistic, and designing his own costumes in abstract forms. He soon added new "portraits in movement" to his *shtetl* characters, such as an effeminate Arab dandy from Jaffe and a Yemenite agricultural worker from Petaḥ Tikvah.

In the mid-1920s he published a book on "The Hebrew Dance," calligraphically handwritten in a limited edition of only 100 copies, with many photos and illustrations. He also began organizing Purim balls, which developed into the Tel Aviv *Adloyada* – a procession of floats and much dancing.

Every year Agadati would tour in Europe, to great critical acclaim. His attitude to the musical accompaniment was radically new: sometimes he would let his accompanist play the music and only after the end of the music would he dance in silence – to the music he had just heard. In 1929 he decided to go a step further and composed a dance to be performed in total silence – an approach used many decades later by Jerome *Robbins (in *Moves*) and Merce Cunningham. In 1929, however, the audience was unprepared for such a radical experimental approach and after Agadati finished the performance there was no applause. Agadati felt he had lost contact with his audience and decided to stop dancing altogether.

He turned to films and directed and produced (with others) the first Hebrew-speaking movie. He also returned to painting. His wooden shack in Tel Aviv became the unofficial center of modernist artists active in Ereẓ Israel in the 1930s and 1940s. "Agadati's Shack" was later torn down by small-minded municipal officials.

BIBLIOGRAPHY: G. Manor, *Agadati – The Pioneer of Modern Dance in Israel* (1986).

[Giora Manor (2nd ed.)]

AGADIR, Atlantic seaport and important tourist resort in southwestern Morocco; the site of the ancient Roman Portus Risadir. It lies near the Haha province and the Sous, the latter region having served in past centuries as an important marketplace (*suq*) on the fringes of the Sahara Desert. Because Agadir was strategically located on both the Atlantic seaboard and near the Sous Valley, it became a vital trade depot for European and local merchants. Important caravans passed through Agadir into the Sous from the earliest times to the 19th century. They brought African slaves, gold dust from western Sudan, and ostrich feathers from the southern Sahara Desert. Textile products and leatherwork from *Marrakesh also found their way to the Sous through Agadir, as did European medicines and guns.

In the latter half of the 15th and early 16th centuries the Portuguese penetrated Morocco – then ruled by the Wattasid dynasty – and took control of the coastal areas. In 1505, they occupied Agadir and held on to it until 1541, when the new Saʿdian kings of the Sous, who then founded the Moroccan Sharifian Saʿdi dynasty, liberated the city. Under the Portuguese occupation and subsequently, Agadir and the Sous attracted Genoese merchants who traded in Sudanese gold and in local products like wax, hides, gum, and indigo.

Agadir's importance as a trade/transit route reached its zenith in the 1760s. Until then the trade activities of the local merchants, many of whom were Jews, gained considerable support in Moroccan ruling circles. In 1764, however, that city lost out to the new port of Essaouira (*Mogador), which was constructed by the Sharifian Alawite sultanate with the aim of replacing Agadir as the outlet for the Sous trade. Essaouira then became the most important port in Morocco until the end of the 19th century.

To attract merchants from different parts of Morocco to Essaouira, including Jewish entrepreneurs, known as *tujjar al-sulṭān* ("Sultan's merchants"), the *makhzan* (governmental administration) built, or allowed the merchants to build, houses, extended credit, and lowered customs duties for the new arrivals. Not only did prominent Jewish merchants from Agadir relocate to Essaouira, moving their businesses to the new town, other members of the Jewish community settled there permanently.

Agadir captured the attention of European diplomacy during the colonial period, as Morocco was about to be divided into French and Spanish protectorates. At the time, local Moroccan opposition culminated in revolts against the French. France responded by sending an occupation force to *Fez in May 1911. Germany, which then regarded itself as a serious contender for influence inside Morocco, saw in French aggression an effort to curtail Moroccan independence and sought to challenge it. In a veritable show of force and under the pretext of "protecting our interests and the safety of our citizens," the Germans dispatched the gunboat *Panther* to the shores of Agadir (July 1911). It was done with the clear intent of pressuring France to reduce her territorial aspirations in Morocco to a minimum. In November, a Franco-German accord was signed. The agreement stipulated that the Germans would not oppose the imposition of a French protectorate over Morocco in return for some French sub-Saharan territories to be ceded to Germany. Two years later the French were in full control over Agadir.

Under the French Protectorate (1912–56), growth in Agadir began with the construction of a major port (1914), the development of the Sous plain, and exploitation of inland mineral resources as well as the fishing and fishing-canning industries. After the 1930s, the French turned Agadir into an attractive tourist resort and encouraged extensive urbanization, laying the groundwork for modern infrastructures.

Agadir has also known tragedies. Early in March 1960 two earthquakes, killing 12,000 people, destroyed the city. Among those killed were several hundred persons belonging to Agadir's 2000-strong Jewish community, buried under the rubble of the collapsed buildings. As many as 800 Jewish survivors were lodged temporarily at an army base on the outskirts of *Casablanca. After prolonged negotiations with the authorities, the Casablanca Jewish community took many refugees into their homes. Orphans whose parents were killed in the earthquake were adopted by Casablanca's leading families. A new central city, including an international airport, was built in the 1960s to the south of the old town, linked by road with *Safi and *Marrakesh. As many as 110,000 people subsequently lived in Agadir; few among them were Jews.

BIBLIOGRAPHY: J.M. Abun-Nasr, *A History of the Maghrib in the Islamic Period* (1987); E. Burke III, *Prelude to the Protectorate of Morocco: 1860–1912* (1976); P. Guillen, *L'Allemagne et le Maroc* (1967); C.-A. Julien, *A History of North Africa: Tunisia, Algeria, Morocco from the Arab Conquest to 1830* (ed. and rev. by R. Le Tourneau, 1970); C.R. Pennell, *Morocco since 1830: A History* (2000); D.J. Schroeter, *Merchants of Essaouria: Urban Society and Imperialism in Southwestern Morocco, 1844–1886* (1988).

[Michael M. Laskier (2nd ed.)]

AGAG (Heb. אֲגָג), the name of an *Amalekite king who was captured by *Saul (I Sam. 15). By sparing Agag's life Saul disobeyed *Samuel's order to annihilate the Amalekites. This occasioned the final break between Samuel and Saul. Later Samuel killed Agag at Gilgal "before the Lord" (*ibid.* 33).

One of Balaam's oracles sets Israel's king "higher than Agag" (Num. 24:7). The Septuagint adds "Agag" as the subject of another short oracle (*ibid.* 23). The name may have served as a recurrent designation for Amalekite chieftains or a clan.

Agagite (Heb. אֲגָגִי) is the gentilic name of *Haman, in the *Scroll of Esther (3:1; 10:8, 5, etc.). It connects the archenemy of the Jews in Persia with the Amalekites. It has been suggested that designation of Haman as an Agagite sounds legendary. It may represent a nickname, applied to this persecutor of the Jews because the Amalekites are denounced as the archenemy of Israel in the Torah (Deut. 25:17–19). Some scholars prefer the Septuagint's reading: Βουγαιος ("Bugaean" instead of "Agagite"), a Persian gentile name, *baga*, meaning "God."

[Hanna Weiner]

In the *Aggadah*

Agag's death came too late. Had he been killed by Saul during the course of the battle, a later generation of Jews would have been spared the troubles caused by Haman. It is taught that in the short span of time between the war and the execution of Agag, he became the ancestor of Haman (SER 20). The delay is attributed to the powers of persuasion of Doeg the Edomite over Saul. He argued that the law prohibits the slaying of an animal and its young on the same day. How much less permissible was it to destroy old and young at one time (Mid. Ps. 52:4).

When Agag was eventually sentenced to death, it was according to heathen, and not Jewish, law. Thus, there were no witnesses to his crime, and he was given no warning of his punishment (PdRK 3:6).

BIBLIOGRAPHY: AGAG: Albright, in: JBL, 63 (1944), 218ff. AGAGITE: J. Hoschander, *The Book of Esther in the Light of History* (1923), 21ff.

ÁGAI, ADOLF (A. Rosenzweig; 1836–1916), Hungarian novelist, editor, and physician. Born in Jánoshalma, Ágai was the son of a prominent physician. After studying medicine in Vienna, he accepted a hospital appointment in Budapest. He also turned to writing, and his features in Budapest dailies, written under the pen-name "Porzó," were extremely popular. In 1868 Ágai abandoned medicine when he began the publication of a successful satirical weekly, *Borsszem Jankó.* Three years later he launched and became editor of the first long-lived Hungarian children's newspaper, *Kis Lap* ("Little Paper"), which appeared until 1904. Although he was opposed to Zionism, Ágai contributed to Herzl's Zionist journal, *Die Welt.* In his essays, he frequently depicts scenes from provincial Jewish life, based on memories of his childhood. Collections of his feuilletons are included in *Porzó tarcalevelei* ("Porzo's Feuilletons," 1876) and *Utazás Peströl Budapestre* ("Trip from Pest to Budapest," 1908). His collected novels appeared under the title *Igaz történet* ("True Story," 1893).

BIBLIOGRAPHY: *Irodalmi Lexikon* (1927); *Magyar Zsidó Lexikon* (1929); L. Steiner, *Adolf Ágai* (Hung., 1933).

[Jeno Zsoldos]

AGAM, YAACOV (1928–), Israeli painter and sculptor. Born Ya'akov Gibstein in Rishon le-Zion to an Orthodox Jewish family. His father, a rabbi, sent him to religious schools. Agam was arrested in 1945 by the British on suspicion of being a member of the Jewish underground and kept in prison for 18 months. He received his professional training at the Bezalel Academy of Arts and Design in Jerusalem under the influence of his modernist teacher Mordecai *Ardon. Agam continued his art studies in Zurich with Johannes Itten and at the Atelier d'Art Abstrait in Paris. In 1953 he had his first one-man show at the Galerie Craven, in Paris, where he presented his preliminary Kinetic Art. These works went under the general title of "Transformable Pictures" and characterized his style during the 1970s (*Pace of Time*, 1970, Tel Aviv Museum of Art). The works featured parallel triangles painted with abstract forms. Through the movement of the spectator the views changed and the kinetic quality of the work came to the fore. Agam said that his interest in concepts of time derived from Jewish spirituality, in which the world is seen as involved in a perpetual dynamism.

With his kinetic sculpture the spectator was required to be more active, to touch and move the sculpture's components. More than once Agam referred to these works in the terminology of the world of games. The images appearing in them were mostly derived from Jewish symbolism (*The Hundred Gates*, 1972, President's Residence, Jerusalem). Over the years, Agam enlarged his repertoire of works. His involvement with the environment was expressed through his decoration of building facades and interiors. His famous kinetic fountain combining water, fire, and music altogether, is a very impressive and complex piece of art (*Fire and Water*, 1986, Dizengoff Square, Tel Aviv).

In 1996 Agam was awarded the UNESCO Prize for Education on his didactic plan for combining art and science.

BIBLIOGRAPHY: F. Popper, *Agam* (1990); S. Aragaki, *Agam – Beyond the Visible* (1997).

[Ronit Steinberg (2nd ed.)]

°**AGATHARCHIDES OF CNIDUS** (second century B.C.E.), Hellenistic historian and scholar. A native of Cnidus, Agatharchides lived in Egypt (Alexandria) during the reigns of Ptolemy VI Philomater (181–145) and Ptolemy VII Euergetes (145–116). His principal works are a history of Asia in ten books and a history of Europe in 49 books, neither of which is extant. There is no evidence that he referred to Jews very much in his work, except for a passage quoted twice by Josephus (Apion, 1:205–11; Ant. Jud., 12:5–6) referring to the "superstition" of the Jewish defenders of Jerusalem which prevented them from fighting on the Sabbath: "The people known as Jews ... have a custom of abstaining from work every seventh day; on those occasions they neither bear arms nor take any agricultural operations in hand, nor engage in any other form of public service, but pray with outstretched hands in the temples until the evening."

BIBLIOGRAPHY: M. Stern, *Greek and Latin Authors on Jews and Judaism.* Volume I: *From Herodotus to Plutarch* (1974), 104–9.

[Shimon Gibson (2nd ed.)]

AGDE (Heb. אקדי or אגדי), town 13 mi. (20 km.) E. of *Béziers in southern France. Jews are mentioned in Canon 40 promulgated by the Council of Agde held by the church there in 506. By the middle of the 13th century Jews had settled permanently in Agde under the jurisdiction of the bishop. The majority of these became liable to the crown tax in 1278. The Jews of Agde buried their dead in the cemetery of nearby Béziers. After the general expulsion of the Jews from the Kingdom of France in 1306, some of the Agde community found refuge in Perpignan and *Carpentras, then not under French suzerainty. At the beginning of World War II about 2,000 Jewish refugees from Austria and Germany were sent to a forced labor camp near Agde, the number increasing to 3,000 after the Franco-German armistice in June 1940. Most of them were deported on Aug. 24, 1942.

BIBLIOGRAPHY: Gross, Gal Jud, 21ff.; G. Saige, *Juifs du Languedoc* (1881), 5, 34, 39, 225, 309; B. Blumenkranz, in: *Mélanges le Bras* (1965), 1055; Z. Szajkowski, *Analytical Franco-Jewish Gazetteer, 1939–5* (1966), 198.

[Bernhard Blumenkranz]

AGE AND THE AGED.

Old Age

IN THE BIBLE. Extreme longevity is attributed to the Fathers of Mankind (e.g., Methusaleh, 969 years) and the Fathers of the Israelite People (Abraham, 175; Isaac, 180; Jacob, 147; Moses, 120). By some, Genesis 6:3 is taken to mean that God has set a limit of 120 years to human life (Ḥizzekuni, cf. Ibn Ezra); in accord with this notion is the popular Jewish reckoning of a long life. However, sober reality is reflected in Psalms 90:10: "The days of our years are 70 years, and if by reason of strength, 80 years." The Bible regards longevity (Isa. 65:20; Zech. 8:4; Ps. 92:15), a long life followed by death at "a good old age" (Gen. 15:15; et al.), as a blessing; whereas the opposite is regarded as a curse (I Sam. 2:31–32). Long life is promised as a reward for observing certain commandments (Ex. 20:12; Deut. 22:7; 25:15), or for obeying the Law as a whole (Deut. 6:2). But there are also some grim descriptions of old age (II Sam. 19:33–38). Especially instructive are the descriptions of old age in Ecclesiastes (12:1–7) in which old age is "the calamitous days" in which a man takes no pleasures. It may be noted that a similar view of old age can be found in the Epic of Gilgamesh (See *Flood). A realistic observation prompted the moving prayer: "Do not throw me away in the time of old age; when my strength is failing me, do not forsake me" (Ps. 71:9).

The experience of the aged caused the belief that old age and wisdom went together (Job. 12:12; cf. ibid., 20). Nevertheless, the Book of Job also stresses that there are young men who are wiser than old men (Job 32:6ff.; Eccles. 4:13). The Bible enjoins respect for the aged: "You shall rise before the aged and show deference to the old" (Lev. 19:32). This was probably the custom throughout the whole ancient Middle East (Ahikar 2:61). Consideration for old age and its disabilities is mentioned frequently in the Bible. Disrespect for the aged was regarded as a sign of a corrupt generation (Isa. 3:5). Ruthlessness toward the aged is a manifestation of extreme harshness by an enemy: "… who will show the old no regard" (Deut. 28:50); "Upon the old man you made your yoke very heavy" (Isa. 47:6); and "He has shown no favor to the elders" (Lam. 4:16; cf. 5:12). The actual chronological age of a man was not an absolute factor in regard to the disabilities of old age; thus, Samuel says of himself "I have grown old and gray" (I Sam. 12:2) when he is only 52. And King David is described as "very old" (I Kings 1:15) when he was 70. There are few descriptions of the physical signs of old age in the Bible: that of Isaac when his eyes were dim (Gen. 27); that of the manner of Eli's fall, "because the man was old and heavy" (I Sam. 4:18); and Barzillai's deafness (II Sam. 14:33–38). By contrast with these descriptions, there are idyllic descriptions of old age: "There shall yet be old men and women in the public squares of Jerusalem" alongside "boys and girls playing in her public squares" (Zech. 8:4). The biological process of aging is seen as the depletion of the body's "natural heat" as, for instance, in the case of King David. ("King David was now old, advanced in years; and though they covered him with bedclothes, he did not feel warm" (I Kings 1:1)). This view was a basic premise with Galen and was accepted by preceding generations almost until modern times.

Ecclesiastes (12:1–6) gives an outstanding description of old age. Later geriatric literature was based on this section. Many Jewish commentators found biological symbolism in its details and in the 16th to 18th centuries John Smith and others also explained these verses in medical terms. In its crisp and concentrated metaphorical style, Ecclesiastes contains one of the most striking descriptions in world literature of the infirmities of old age. It appears to be entirely expressive of the state of mind and view of life of an aging or old man, and it was thus interpreted by the sages. King Solomon, who in his youth is supposed to have written The Song of Songs, in his maturity Proverbs, and in his old age Ecclesiastes, was regarded by them as a symbol of the changes which take place in the being and in the experiences of a man in the course of his life: "When a man is young, he quotes poetry; when he matures, he quotes proverbs; when he grows old he speaks of futilities …" (Song R. 1:10). Similarly, A. Schopenhauer states, "Only in his 70th year does a man understand the full meaning of the [second] verse of Ecclesiastes." In the Second Temple era old age was regarded as a blessing and the aged as worthy of respect (Eccles. 8:9; II Macc. 6:23, 27; IV Macc. 5:4ff.; 7:13–15). Yet it was stressed, that not the number of years was important but wisdom and honesty (Wisdom of Solomon 4:8–9, 16). Ben Sira (30:24) recognized that anxiety ages a man, while in the Book of Jubilees (23:11) premature aging accompanied by mental confusion is caused by sin. That is why in the Dead Sea Sect nobody above 60 years of age could act as judge (Damascus Covenant X:7–10); yet in general the Sect and the Essenes respected old men (Manual of Discipline VI:8; Philo, Prob. 81, 87; Josephus, Wars, 2:9–10).

RABBINIC PERIOD. According to the Talmud, old age (*ziknah*) begins at 60, ripe old age (*seivah*, "grey hairs") at 70 (Avot 5:21), though oldness may appear prematurely (Shab. 152a; Eruv. 56a; Tanḥ., Ḥayyei Sarah 2). Like Ecclesiastes, the rabbis viewed the later years of life as unattractive (Shab. 151b); the old resemble apes (Lam. R. 1:2), they cannot reason (Shab. 89b). The afflictions of the old are described, as in Ecclesiastes, metaphorically: "The rocks have grown tall, the near have become [too] distant [to visit], two [legs] have become three [with a cane], and the peacemaker of the house has ceased [to function as such]." So it is said, "Youth is a crown of roses; old age a crown of [heavy] willow rods" (Shab. 152a). A man must pray that in his later years "his eyes may see, his mouth eat, his legs walk, for in old age all powers fail" (Tanḥ, Mi-Keẓ 10).

There are some rare instances of praise for oldness itself. R. Simeon b. Eleazar valued the advice of the old: "If the old say 'tear down' and the children 'build' – tear down, for the 'destruction' of the old is construction; the 'construction' of the young, destruction" (Meg. 31b). According to R. Johanan, only elders sat in the Sanhedrin (Sanh. 17a). These statements reflect the ancient view that age, with its experience, is a guarantee of wisdom, and without age there is no understanding. The general opinion, however, is that with age comes loss of intellectual capacity. Elisha b. Avuyah said, "What does learning when old resemble? It is like writing on blotted-out paper" (Avot 4:20). Oldness itself is not a virtue – wisdom and knowledge of Torah determine its value (Kin. 3:15). Even the opinions of the old were not universally preferred to those of the young. When R. Abbahu claimed authority in a given dispute due to his age, R. Jeremiah answered, "Is the matter decided by age? – It is decided by reason" (BB 102b). Targum Onkelos also reflected this view when translating "You shall rise before the aged" (Lev. 19:32) as "Arise before those knowledgeable in Torah." The rabbis held that even a young scholar is called *zaken* ("elder") and should be honored, while no honor is due the ignorant or sinful, though old (Sifra, Kedoshim, 7:12). However, Isi b. Judah differed: "'You shall rise before the aged' – all the aged"; R. Johanan agreed, even concerning gentile elders; but R. Naḥman and Rav did not act in this manner (Kid. 32b–33a). According to Maimonides, one must honor the exceedingly old, even if they are not wise, by rising (Yad, Talmud Torah 6:9).

An age limit existed, past which one was not to hold a responsible position. Already in biblical times, the levites' service in the Tabernacle was limited: "At the age of 50, they shall retire from the work force and serve no more" (Lev. 8:25–26). The retired could do less strenuous work, either assisting their fellows, or guarding. In talmudic times, it was forbidden – for psychological reasons – to have the very old serve as Sanhedrin members (Sanh. 36b. Maim., Yad, Sanhedrin 2:3). In kabbalistic literature and tradition, those well-versed in mystic knowledge are represented as aged; many of the names in the Zohar are followed by "elder" (*saba*).

[Moshe David Herr]

Care of the Aged

In the society of ancient Israel the aged and elderly were highly respected, and accorded a central position in family life and the tribal structure. This continued after a national organization based on kingship was adopted. This attitude is essentially linked with the biblical precept enjoining fear and honor of, and obedience to father and mother (*kibbud av va-em*, cf. Lev. 19:3, 32). Barbarism in an alien nation is described by denouncing it as one "that shall not regard the person of the old" (Deut. 28:50). A state of anarchy in Israel is characterized by the fact that "the child shall behave insolently against the aged" (Isa. 3:5; 47:6). The term "elders" appears throughout the Bible, Mishnah, and Talmud as a synonym or designation for judges, leaders, or sages. The Jewish image of the aged was therefore originally one denoting leadership and rule. Of course, physical facts asserted themselves and horror of weakness and senility was frequently acknowledged. In talmudic times the problem of earning a livelihood in old age was faced: "Every profession in the world is of help to a man only in his youth, but in his old age he is exposed to hunger" (Kid. 82b). Respect alone was of little assistance to the aged in the changed circumstances of late antiquity and the transformation which society had undergone. However, no attempt was made to issue specific regulations or create institutions to help the aged or care for them as such. If not living among the family, as was customary, destitute aged people were treated as part of the general social problem created by poverty and weakness and the precepts concerning *charity and alms giving (*ẓedakah*) applied to them. Thus, although old age was originally invested with strength and majesty, people of the lower strata of society who had lost the support and care provided by the family underwent much suffering, if not humiliation, in their old age. The transition from the position of the powerful elder to that of an aged pauper requiring special assistance outside the frame of the family is an outcome of the heritage of Judaic-Muslim-Christian civilization.

IN THE MIDDLE AGES. The aged are singled out in medieval Jewish ethical works and general halakhic regulations (*takkanot*) as worthy objects for special charity and tender treatment. In the 11th century *Rashi defined the age requiring assistance as "when I shall be 60 or 70" (commentary to Ps. 71:17). Persecutions and massacres in the Middle Ages led to the breakup of families, and large-scale migrations brought additional suffering for the aged. A resolution passed at the Council of Lithuania (see *Council of the Lands) in 1650, after the *Chmielnicki massacres, stressed the duty to support "… in any case married and unmarried women and old persons" and reflects the breakup of the family under catastrophe. About the same date, the Jewish community in Rome introduced care of the aged as one of the four divisions of its charitable activity. A home for the aged was founded in Amsterdam by the Sephardi community in 1749.

EIGHTEENTH TO NINETEENTH CENTURIES. From the second half of the 18th century the need for introducing special treatment and care of the aged was felt more strongly in Jewish societies which were beginning to experience the breakup of the traditional family cohesion. These were more prepared to view old age as a social problem separate from poverty. In this period the time-honored concept of respect for the aged began to combine with new feelings of estrangement between the generations together with compassion and understanding for the weakness of the old as part of social responsibility. Thus an increasing number of Jewish foundations to care for the aged were established. The *Mishenet Zekenim* ("Support of the Aged") society, established in Hamburg in 1796, made weekly provision for the needy aged. An old-age home was founded in Berlin in 1829, and in 1839 the Hamburg community set aside a building for old men and women where they received lodging, support, and clothing. The Frankfurt community founded a home in 1844 for men and women aged over 60 without means of support. A Viennese family donated several houses for accommodating aged Jews of the community. The number of Jewish homes for the aged increased from the middle of the 19th century, as social care of the aged developed. By the present century most large communities in Europe included a home for the aged (often called *Moshav Zekenim*) among their welfare institutions. In 1938, there were in Germany 67 homes for the aged with 3,568 beds.

The revolutionary changes in society affecting the general attitude toward the aged and provisions for their welfare which began at the end of the 19th century are deepening and becoming increasingly pronounced and complicated. Among general factors responsible for this change are the modern appreciation of youth and understanding of its specific psychological and social needs, coupled with a corresponding understanding of the needs of the old, their psychology and social requirements; the demographic changes, first throughout the western world and later in other countries, resulting from birth control on the one hand and the prolongation of life expectancy on the other; and the introduction of pension laws and schemes as the problems of the aged emerge as a political factor in appealing to electorates with an increasing percentage of aged persons.

CONTEMPORARY PERIOD. In addition, factors specific to Jewish society are the huge emigration from Europe from the end of the 19th century, the Nazi Holocaust, and forced emigration from Arab countries in the Near East and North Africa after the creation of the State of Israel. The impact of these general changes is most clearly seen in the main Jewish centers of today, and in the experiments currently being attempted to solve the problems to which they have given rise.

U.S. CARE FOR AGED. In the United States, the cultural and social estrangement that developed between "second-" or "third-generation" Jews and their "first-generation" immigrant parents and grandparents inevitably strained the close, tightly knit Jewish family life that was a legacy of Europe. The first homes of the aged, therefore, often tended to be institutions of "last resort." Care of the aged in America was also originally hindered by a resistance to paid social workers. Similarly, family agencies displayed a reluctance to deal with the aged. Over the years this pattern has significantly altered so that care for the aged is largely in professional hands. Family agencies served about 20,000 persons aged 60 and over in their homes in 1966.

The general tendency in the United States is to avoid employing terms or arrangements traditionally linked with old age and care for the aged; aged persons are referred to as "senior citizens," for whom "towns" and "resorts" have been established. Emphasis has been placed on providing services to enable the aged to remain in their communities where they can retain the satisfactions of normal community life. At the same time experiments to meet the specific needs and inclinations of the aged are made while attempting to provide them with accommodation apart from the family. This trend is gaining ground in Jewish society. The concept of institutional care for the aged has changed from one of a permanent retreat to a resource to be used as needed.

IN ISRAEL. Two basically different traditional patterns of family life are encountered: the Oriental in families from the Near East and North Africa, and the European in families from Europe and the United States. The Oriental family has retained much more of the traditional veneration for the aged and is much less influenced by the modern attitude toward youth than the western family. However, the mass exodus from the Arab countries created a problem of care for the aged in families who have been broken up by forced migration. Thus, the traditional Oriental family also encountered modern problems concerning its old people in Israel. Provision also had to be made for the survivors of the Nazi Holocaust and concentration camps. The combined problems of abandonment, physical weakness, illness, premature aging, and old age were dealt with by the *Malben organization, founded and maintained by the *American Jewish Joint Distribution Committee and its institutions. In addition, a new social phenomenon in Israel was that of family life in the kibbutz, which had specific problems concerning aging and the relationship between the generations. Although the kibbutz provided collective support and care of the individual member irrespective of his family status, health, or psychological problems, the strain on the aged and the aging was particularly great since it was a society originally created by the senior members themselves, founded on the ideal of physical labor and appreciation of the supreme and eternal value of youth.

In this framework the spiritual and psychological side of aging is present in its "pure form," i.e., separate from the usual physical and material problems.

In Israel in 1964, 5.5% of the male population and 5.9% of the female population were aged over 65 (the age of retirement). The majority were living within the family or independently. About 7,500 old persons were in special institutions. These consisted of the traditional old-age homes (*moshav zekenim*) and the more modern living centers for the aged, of which there are different forms. By the early 2000s, 10% of Israel's population was aged over 65, with 250,000 Israelis aged over 75. The consequence has been a great strain on public facilities and a proliferation of upscale retirement homes and the fashion of employing live-in Filipino caretakers among the well-to-do. The care of the aged in 21st century Israel therefore fully reflected the economic imbalances that prevailed in the country. The poor among the aged have become a marginal group barely able to survive.

[Haim Hillel Ben-Sasson]

BIBLIOGRAPHY: L. Loew, *Die Lebensalter in der juedischen Literatur* (1875), 253–75; J. Preuss, *Biblisch-talmudische Medizin* (1911), 515; H. Rolleston, *Aspects of Age, Life and Disease* (1928), 31–34; G. Weil, *Maimonides ueber die Lebensdauer* (1953); Plessner, in: *Jerusalem Post* (Jan. 9, 1953); Leibowitz, in: *Journal of the History of Medicine*, 18 (1963); idem, *Al Oraḥ ha-Ḥayyim le-ha-Rambam* (1953); Habermann, in: *Haaretz* (Jan. 16, 1953); idem (ed.), *Kitvei R. Avraham Epstein*, 2 (1957), 34–37; I. Bergman, *Ha-Ẓedakah be-Yisrael* (1944); Council of Jewish Federations and Welfare Funds, Inc., N.Y., *Administration of Homes for the Aged* (1951); idem, *Council Reports* (1949–); Central Atlantic Regional Conference on Services to the Aged, *Disturbed and Disturbing Aged Person* (1955); Symposium on Research and Welfare Policies for the Elderly (Jerusalem, November 1968), *Family Life, Social Relationships, and the Need of the Aged* (1968); Israel, Central Bureau of Statistics, *Special Publication No. 199* (1966); AJYB, 57 (1956), 3–98 passim.

AGEN, capital of the Lot-et-Garonne department, southwestern France. A charter of 1263 specifies the charges imposed on Jewish residents in Agen for all articles brought into the city, in addition to dues they owed to the bishop. In 1309 (not 1250, as stated by U. Robert) the seneschal of Agen was directed to seize copies of the Talmud and other Jewish works, probably left behind after the general expulsion of the Jews in 1306. A number of Jews returned to Agen in 1315 and perished in the *Pastoureaux massacres of 1320. The "Rue des Juifs," first documented in 1342, certainly existed earlier. Remains of the synagogue were still visible in the 16th century. In 1968 the Jewish community in Agen, which consisted of approximately 500 persons, mostly immigrants from North Africa, had a synagogue and community center.

BIBLIOGRAPHY: Gross, Gal Jud, 44; Ibn Verga, *Shevet Yehudah* (1947), ed. by A. Schochat and Y. Baer, 22; *Revue de l'Agenais* (1917), 218–9; A. Ducom, *La Commune d'Agen* (1892), 162, 284–5; U. Robert, in: REJ, 3 (1881), 214.

[Bernhard Blumenkranz]

AGENCY, legal concept whereby the lawful acts of someone authorized by, and acting on behalf of, another are as effective as if performed by the principal; recognized in Jewish law from ancient times. A basic concept in the Talmud is that "a man's agent is as himself," i.e., that a man is bound by the acts of his duly constituted agent as if he himself had acted. Throughout the ages Jewish law developed a complex and sophisticated civil law of commerce and finance in which the law of agency played an important part, being the subject of many talmudic discussions and halakhic rulings. For example, the contrary principle was enacted that there can be no agency to do a wrongful act; the sender is not held accountable for the deeds of his agents. The law also laid down rules governing the manner of constituting an agency, its limitations, its mode of execution, and its revocation or termination. The appointment, competence, and powers of an agent are also dealt with. Because of their contractual aspects, agency was also recognized in matters of marriage and divorce, whereby an agent could legally acquire a wife for his principal or effectively deliver to her a bill of divorce on his principal's behalf. Generally the Jewish law of agency was developed to meet the social and commercial needs of the community as it constantly changed from age to age; therefore it was inclined to be more flexible and adaptable than some other legal subjects, which, consequently, did not always enjoy the same degree of contemporary relevance. In the State of Israel agency is a matter of civil law and is governed by a principal statute of 1965.

Details

As a result of agency, the possible field of legal activity is extended beyond the normal physical and other limitations.

The concept of agency was not recognized in ancient legal systems. Only in the later stages of Roman law did agency achieve a limited form of recognition – a phenomenon ascribed to the powerful status of the Roman *pater-familias* ("family head") on whose behalf all acquisitions by his kinsmen or servants were made in any event, thus obviating any urgent need for developing a doctrine of agency. In Jewish law the principle of agency was, however, already recognized in ancient times. While there is no express scriptural provision for it, the *tannaim* applied the doctrine of agency in various halakhic fields, i.e., to the laws of *mamonot* ("commercial law"), *terumah* ("heave offering"), sacrifices, divorce, and betrothal, and established the rule that "a man's agent is as himself" (*Sheliḥo shel adam kemoto*). According to the Tosefta (Kid. 4:1), Bet Shammai and Bet Hillel agreed that a person appointed to carry out a specific mandate is disqualified from acting as a witness in a case involving such mandate, whereas amoraic sources quote a tannaitic tradition to the opposite effect (Kid. 43a) and the talmudic *halakhah* was decided accordingly. The agent is not regarded as the principal, in the full sense of the term "as himself," since the agent is competent to testify with regard to the subject matter of his mandate in circumstances where the principal is disqualified from being a witness.

CRIMINAL LAW. In this field a contrary rule was laid down, namely, that "there can be no agent to do a wrong" (*Ein shali'aḥ li-devar averah;* Kid. 42b). The reasoning behind the rule is derived in answer to the hypothetical question: "Whose words does one obey? Those of the master" (i.e., the Almighty) "or of the pupil" (i.e., the mandator)? The legal import of the rule is that the agent himself is the transgressor, and liable, whereas the principal is exempt in respect of any transgression committed by the agent in execution of the former's mandate. There is, on the other hand, a tradition that a person who says to his agent, "Go forth and kill that soul!" (Kid. 43a), is personally liable, but the *halakhah* was decided to the effect that "in all matters a person's agent is 'as himself' except with regard to wrongdoing ..." (Isserles to Sh. Ar., ḤM 182:1). However, the scholars laid down that in three fields the doctrine of agency applied also to transgression: (1) misappropriation of a deposit (*sheliḥut yad*); (2) slaughtering and selling (of stolen animals – see *Theft and Robbery); and (3) conversion of consecrated property (see **Hekdesh*) to profane use (*me'ilah*).

In addition to these three specifically excepted cases, there are also a number of general exceptions to the rule that there can be no agent to do a wrongful act. According to the *amora* Ravina, the rule does not apply if the prohibition does not extend to the agent himself, e.g., where a priest commissions an Israelite to celebrate *kiddushin* with a divorcee on the priest's behalf (a marriage prohibited to a priest). Similarly, the *amora* Samma is of the opinion that an agency is constituted when the agent, in committing transgression, fails to act of his own free will; e.g., when he is unaware that his act amounts to a transgression (BM 10b; Isserles to Sh. Ar., ḤM 182:1 and 348:8). Furthermore, an agency to do a wrong is constituted whenever an agent delegated to commit a wrong must be presumed likely to execute his assignment because he is known to commit such wrongs (Sh. Ar., ḤM 388:15, gloss; see also Siftei Kohen, *ibid.*, 67 for a contrary opinion). Whenever the law recognizes agency in the commission of a wrong, the agent himself will be liable (Siftei Kohen sub. sec. 4 to Sh. Ar., ḤM 292; see also Netivot ha-Mishpat to Sh. Ar., ḤM 348:4).

LIMITATIONS. The rabbis of the Talmud, relying on the scriptural text, excluded the operation of the maxim that a person's agent is as himself in certain instances (TJ, Kid. 2:1; Yev. 101b). Some of the *posekim* exclude agency when the mandate cannot be carried out at the time of the agent's appointment (Darkhei Moshe to Tur, ḤM 182:1, based on Naz. 12b); but others differ (Responsa Maharit 2:23; Arukh ha-Shulḥan to Sh. Ar., ḤM *ibid.*). On the question of the husband's competence to annul the vows of his wife on the day of hearing them (Num. 30:9), the rabbis decided that it would not be the same if the vows were heard by an agent, and that the latter was not competent to annul them since "the appointment of an agent is not appropriate to a passive act" (*be-midi de-mi-meila;* Ned. 72b). Similarly, there can be no agency with regard to a precept (*mitzvah*) which one is personally obliged to perform, such as laying *tefillin* or sitting in a **sukkah* (Tos. to Kid. 42b). So, too, the rabbinical enactment permitting *assignment of debt by way of *ma'amad sheloshtan*, has been interpreted as requiring the participation of the parties themselves and the assignor could not appoint an agent for this purpose (Sh. Ar., ḤM 126:20). Some scholars hold that an agent can not deliver an oath on behalf of his principal (Responsa, *Noda bi-Yhudah*, first series, YD 67 and last series YD 147).

It is not a requirement of agency that the manner of carrying out the mandate should be specifically detailed; the principal may grant his agent a degree of discretion, e.g., in celebrating *kiddushin* on his principal's behalf, an agent may be authorized to treat either with a specific woman or with one of a larger group (Maim., Yad, *Ishut* 3:14). Or, the principal can instruct his agent, "Go and purchase for me a field which you consider suitable," in which case the choice of the field is left to the full discretion of the agent. To be properly constituted, agency requires that the parties thereto are both legally competent and it was laid down that *einam benei da'at* ("persons who lack proper understanding," i.e., *Ḥeresh, shoteh, ve-katan* ("deaf-mutes, idiots, and minors")) were disqualified from acting as either principal or agent (Git. 23a; Sh. Ar., ḤM 188:2).

APPOINTMENT AND POWERS. It appears from tannaitic and amoraic sources, neither of which specifically discuss the manner of appointing an agent, that such appointment may be done orally. The *halakhah* was so decided, it being held that there was no need for a formal *kinyan* (see Modes of *Acquisition). In various places it nevertheless became the practice to assign by way of a formal *kinyan.* This was partly due to the influence of an analogous procedure in certain matters where an act of *kinyan* was required by law, such as the appointment of an agent in a lawsuit or for the purposes of agency in divorce – although the *kinyan* is not essential to the underlying agency itself but rather for the purpose of *bittul moda'ah* (see **Ones*). It was also due in part to the desire of the parties to express in a formal act that the decision to conclude an agency was a serious one, and not one undertaken irresponsibly (Maim., Mekhirah 1, 12–12).

The agent is required to act strictly within the scope of his mandate, and if he exceeds his authority, all his actions are rendered null and void. The same result follows if the agent errs in any detail of his mandate, since the latter is appointed "to uphold and not to depart from the mandate" (Maim., Yad, *Sheluḥin* 1:3, Sh. Ar., ḤM 182:2). The possible consequences of a complete nullification can, however, be averted by especially stipulating for such a contingency (Maim. and Sh. Ar., *ibid.*). Thus it became the practice for a condition of this kind to be inserted in written instruments (see Hai Gaon, *Sefer ha-Shetarot*, 65–67).

Some authorities went so far as to hold that even in the absence of such a condition, there was a presumption – if the mandate were carried out – that the principal had authorized the agent to "uphold and to depart from the mandate," unless the contrary could be proved by the principal (Sh. Ar., ḤM 182:4). An agent who departs from the terms of his mandate and deals with a third party without disclosing that he is acting as an agent, will be liable for his actions (Maim., *Sheluḥin* 2:4; Sh. Ar., 182:2 and 6).

REVOCATION. The mandate of the agent may be revoked by the principal. The Talmud records a dispute between the Palestinian *amoraim*, Johanan and Resh Lakish, as to whether or not revocation can be done orally (TJ, Ter. 3:4, 42a and Git 4:1, 45c; see also Kid. 59a), and the *halakhah* was decided in favor of such revocation. Where a formal *kinyan* accompanies the agent's appointment, some take the view that the "act" of *kinyan* cannot be revoked orally, but the general opinion is in favor of it. In order to prevent the principal from withdrawing his agent's mandate, it became customary to submit the former to an oath to this effect. This procedure normally served as an effective deterrent, but if, despite the oath, the principal revoked it, the revocation is effective. Agency is also terminated upon the death of the principal.

It was recognized that a revocable mandate could prejudice a third party who was unaware of it, e.g., a debtor who paid his debt to the creditor's agent would continue to be indebted to the creditor or his heirs if it subsequently transpired that the agent's mandate had previously been revoked. It was determined, on various grounds, that in such circumstances the debtor would be released from his obligation. Isaac b. Abba Mari expressed the opinion that a defendent who received a deed of authorization from the agent, would suffer no damage even if it later transpired that the mandate had been revoked (*Sefer ha-Ittur, harsha'ah*). Abraham b. David of Posquières justified the debtors release on the ground that the creditor's revocation of the mandate was tantamount to negligence. Later the above rule was justified on the further ground that, even if by the laws of agency the defendant had dealt with a person who was no agent, the transaction was nevertheless afforded legal validity by virtue of the laws of suretyship (Arukh ha-Shulḥan to Sh. Ar., ḤM 122:2).

BROKERAGE. On the question of the agent's failure to observe the terms of his mandate, Jewish law distinguishes between an agent who acts in a voluntary capacity (*shali'a*) and one who does so for payment called a *sarsur* ("broker" or "factor,") e.g., one who receives property for the purposes of sale, the latter being required to make good any consequent loss to the principal. Maimonides adds that in a case where the broker sells property at less than the authorized price, the purchaser must restore the goods to the owner if he knows that it was being sold by a broker on behalf of the true owner (*ibid.*, 2:6; and see Sh. Ar., ḤM 185:1). Similarly, in case of theft or loss the liability of the broker is equal to that of a bailee for reward (Maim. and Sh. Ar., *ibid.*). An agent may not purchase for himself the property which he has been authorized to sell, even at the authorized selling price (Sh. Ar., *ibid*).

NON-PERFORMANCE OR IMPROPER PERFORMANCE BY THE AGENT. The principal has no claim for pecuniary compensation against an agent who relinquishes his appointment without fulfilling his mandate (Sh. Ar., *ibid.*, 183:1). However, one opinion says that the principal has a claim for "loss of profits" against an agent who acts for payment, e.g., for the profits likely to have been earned by the principal had the mandate been properly carried out (Netivot ha-Mishpat to Sh. Ar., *ibid., Be'urim*, 1).

When the agent is given money by his principal in order to purchase property, and such property is purchased by the agent for himself with his own money the transaction is valid, "although the agent is a rascal," but the transaction will be for the benefit of the principal if the agent purchased for himself with the money of the principal (Sh. Ar., *ibid.*, and Isserles).

AGENCY FOR THE RECOVERY OF DEBTS. (See *Attorney). The appointment of an agent for the recovery at law of a debt owing to a claimant, is the subject of particular problems. The rabbis of *Nehardea decided (BK 70a) that the claimant's representative must be equipped with an "instrument of permission" (*ketav harsha'ah*, "power of attorney"), bearing the following written instruction by the claimant: "Go and take legal action to acquire title and secure for yourself." Unless this is done the defendant may plead that the representative has no standing in the matter. The possibility of a plea of this nature arises from the talmudic principle that a creditor's representative cannot seize property in settlement of a debt owing to his principal, if there are additional creditors (Ket. 84b). This principle was construed at the commencement of the geonic period as applying whether the action of the agent is likely to prejudice other creditors, or merely the debtor or himself (She'iltot *de-Rav Aḥai Ga'on*, 150). Another explanation offered for the aforesaid plea is the possible suspicion that the mandate was no longer in force, because of the principal's death or because it had been revoked by him. The aforesaid wording of the authorizing instrument rendered the agent a party to the legal proceedings, which in turn gave rise to the fear that the agent would keep whatever he recovered for himself. It therefore became customary at first to supplement the authorization with a further formality such as the principal's declaration before witnesses that he was appointing the agent as his representative (Hal. Gedolot, BK 88, col. 3), and in other ways. Gradually these additional measures were abandoned, and the instrument of authorization itself was accepted – without further formality – as constituting the agent a party, along with the defendant, to the proceedings and at the same time as safeguarding the rights of the principal (Temim De'im, 61; Or Zaru'a, BK 4:300). Since, according to the abovementioned wording of the authorization, or power of attorney, the principal in effect assigned (*hakna'ah*) to the agent the subject matter of the power of attorney, it was impossible – according to talmudic *halakhah* – for such power of attorney to relate to matters which could not validly be assigned. Thus the rabbis of Nehardea decided that no power of attorney could be written relating to movables, in respect of which the defendant denied the claim. In the post-talmudic period these restrictions were removed – by way of interpretation, custom and rabbinical enactment – and Jacob b. *Asher records the practice of giving a power of attorney unrestricted as to subject matter (Tur., ḤM 123:2). A convenient act of *kinyan* employed to accompany the authorization, was assignment of the subject matter of the claim *aggav karka* (incidental to land; see Modes of *Acquisition).

In the geonic period, when most Jews had ceased to be landowners, it became necessary to find ways of employing the method of *kinyan aggav karka*, making it applicable to those who possessed no landed property. Thus arose the custom of assignment by way of **arba ammot be-Ereẓ Israel* ("four cubits of land" which every Jew was considered to own in Ereẓ Israel; Responsum Nahshon Gaon, Responsa Geonica, ed. 1929, p. 31; see Modes of *Acquisition). In post-geonic times, diminishing reliance was placed on this method, and Maimonides was of the opinion that an assignment (i.e., power of attorney) so effected was not binding on the debtor (Yad, Sheluḥin 3:7). In Germany and France it became customary to rely on *hoda'ah* (i.e., an admission by the principal that he owned land; see *Admission; Modes of *Acquisition). Naḥmanides suggested *kinyan* or assignment incidental to a synagogue seat or a place in the cemetery, common to all (Novellae to BB 44b) and further modes of assignment are discussed by other scholars.

ACQUISITION OF PROPERTY THROUGH A THIRD PARTY OTHER THAN AN APPOINTED AGENT. This may arise through an application of the rule that "a benefit may be conferred on a person in his absence" (Eruv. 7:11). Thus A may acquire property from B on behalf of C without the latter's knowledge, if this is to his benefit – for instance, a gift. C becomes the owner of the property as soon as A's acquisition thereof is complete, unless C, upon hearing of the matter, rejects such ownership, in which event the transaction is void ab initio (Maim., Yad, Zekhiyyah, 3:2; Sh. Ar., ḤM 243:1; see also Modes of *Acquisition).

In the State of Israel the laws of agency are governed by the "Agency Law, 5725–1965," which confirms the doctrine that "a man's agent is as himself" and further provides that the actions of the agent, including his knowledge and intention, are binding on and benefit the principal – as the case may be (sec. 2).

[Nahum Rakover]

Legal Acts that Are Not a Subject for Agency

There are certain acts that by definition cannot be an object of agency and others in which it is the law that proscribes their performance by way of an agent.

AN ACT WHICH BY DEFINITION REQUIRES PERSONAL PERFORMANCE. In principle, any legal or religious act can be performed by way of an agent, provided that performance of the act is not also its purpose. This is the case, for example, with the betrothal of a woman, in which giving the money is not the goal as such, but is rather a means for altering the woman's status from that of an unmarried woman to that of a married woman. However, when the actual performance of the act is also the goal, such as donning *tefillin* or dwelling in the *sukkah*, such an act cannot be an object of agency (Responsa, *Iggerot Moshe*, EH. 1 #156).

AN ACT WHICH BY LAW REQUIRES PERSONAL PERFORMANCE. By way of example, the law does not permit the agent to act on the principal's behalf when his act involves the violation of third party rights (Ket. 84b; Piskei ha-Rosh, Gittin, 1:13). There are certain acts regarding which opinions are divided as to whether the law permits their performance by way of an agent, such as the abandonment of an asset (Bet Yosef, OH. 434:4; cf. Commentary of Gra (Vilna Gaon) *ibid*); an undertaking (Netivot ha-Mishpat, 45:2. cf. *Kezot ha-Ḥoshen, ibid.* 2); admission (Resp. Ribash, 392, cf. Resp. Maharshdam, HM, 439); oath (summary of positions in Resp. Maharsham, 5:26).

"THERE IS NO AGENCY FOR [THE COMMISSION OF] AN OFFENSE." The codifiers disputed the legal import of this rule. According to some, this rule is exclusively relevant in the criminal realm. In other words: One does not punish a person for an offence committed by another person operating as his agent, despite the fact that in the civil sense the legal consequences of the act are the same as they would have been had the principal performed it himself (*Netivot ha-Mishpat* 182:1). On the other hand, there is a view that extends this rule to the civil dimension too, arguing that a prohibited action performed by an agent also lacks any legal effect on the civil level too, because by definition the act was not a subject of agency (Resp. *Nodah bi-Yehudah*, 1st ed., EH, 64, 75).

The halakhic authorities disputed the applicatory scope of the rule "there is no agency for [the commission of] an offence". According to Rabbina, there can be agency for an offence wherever the agent "does not incur liability" ("*eino bar hiuva*") (BM 10b). In reliance on this view, there are authorities who rule that there can be agency for an offence wherever the agent does not hesitate over whether to obey the teacher (= God) or the student (the principal) and the principal can rely on him to perform the agency, as in the case in which the agent acts on the basis of a mistake (*shogeg*) (Rema, ḤM, 182:1, and 348; and see Sema, *ibid.*).

According to R.Sama, the possibility of agency for an offense is restricted to cases in which the agent does not exercise free will or discretion regarding whether or not to commit the act. In reliance on this view, other authorities ruled that can be agency for the commission of an offence in cases in which the agent acted under duress. However, other authorities dispute this view too, and in their opinion the denial of agency for an offence even applies where an act is committed under duress, because the agent's act itself is nonetheless volitional, hence the principal will not incur liability. On the other hand, the agent too is exempted from liability for the same act by force of the rule in Jewish Law, that a person acting under duress is exempt from liability (Resp. *Nodah bi-Yehudah*, 1st ed., EH, 75; *ibid.*, 80:16).

LEGAL CAPACITY. Apart from the disqualification of the deaf, the mute, and minor from serving as an agent or a principal, there is also a requirement that the agent and his principal be of the same religious identity, even for the performance of a legal action which is not of a religious character, such as purchasing and selling. As such, one who is not Jewish (*ben brit*) is disqualified from serving as the agent of another Jewish person, or as his principal (Bavli, Kiddushin 41a). However, these restrictions were only established in relation to agency for the performance of a legal act, but where it concerns the performance of a material act (*nuntius*), even if that act has legal ramifications, such as the paying of debt, nothing prevents its performance by one who is not Jewish (Resp. Ḥattam Sofer, OḤ 201).

DIGRESSION FROM AUTHORIZATION AND DAMAGE TO THE PRINCIPAL'S INTERESTS. If the agent fundamentally digresses from the terms of his authorization, his action is invalid *ab initio* (Maim, Yad. Hilkhot Sheluḥin ve-Shutafim, 1:2). If he discharged his agency in a manner that harms the economic interests of the principal, his agency can be annulled by the principal, who may claim "I sent you to repair and not to damage" (Maim, Yad. Hilkhot Sheluḥin ve-Shutafim, 1:2–3; Sh. Ar. ḤM, 182:2–3, 6). As a rule, regardless of whether the agency was invalidated *ab initio* or annulled by the principal, the third party must restore to the situation to what it was initially.

On the other hand, there are cases in which even if the agent digressed from his authorization, or harmed the principal's interests, it is impossible to invalidate his actions in respect of a third party or to return to the original situation. In these cases the agent must indemnify the principal for the damage he caused. For example: Where the agent did not present himself as an agent in his dealings with a third party, in other words, where the agency was hidden (Maim, Yad. Hilkhot Sheluḥin ve-Shutafim, 2:4; Sh. Ar. ḤM, 182:2); where the principal does not succeed in proving that the agency was only for the purpose of repairing and not to damage (Sh. Ar. ḤM, 182:6, and Sema *ibid.*, s.10); and according to some authorities, where the agent intentionally mislead the third party into thinking that he was acting under authorization (*Shitah Mekubeẓet*, BM 74b, in the name of the Ra'abad).

In this context, the liability of an unpaid agent does not differ from that of a paid agent (a middelman) (Sema., ḤM 185:1: "For even when not paid, the agent is liable when he digresses"), however, if the agent has possession of the principal's asset, then the liability imposed on him is that of a paid bailee, if he was a paid agent; and of an unpaid *bailee if he was an unpaid agent.

Secondary Agency

An agent can appoint a secondary agent, whose action will directly credit and obligate the principal (Kid. 41a), provided that the principal himself has no opposition (to the appointment) and the agency itself is not defined as 'words' (*mili*). There is a dispute regarding the precise definition of the concept '*mili*', but all agree that an action defined as *mili* is one that does not achieve a legally valid result. For example, an agent for the writing of a *get* (divorce bill) cannot appoint a secondary agent, because the actual writing of a *get* has no legal consequences (Mordechai, Gittin, 420)

The death of the principle agent does not annul the secondary agency (Git. 29b). From this it may be inferred that the secondary agent operates as the extended arm of the principal. Even so, it is still disputed whether the main principal can annul the agency of the secondary agent (Taz, EH 26, and on the other hand, Keẓot ha-Ḥoshen, 188:2)

The Decisions of the Israel Supreme Court

The provisions of Jewish law regarding agency served as a basis for the decision of the Israel Supreme Court in the case of *Moverman* (CA 604/77 *Moverman v. Segal*, PD 32(3) 85). In that case the Court was required to make a determination regarding the validity of an agreement that the executor of an estate made with a woman who was designated as a beneficiary of the estate. The agreement provided for a waiver of the woman's rights under the will in exchange for the receipt of a fixed monthly payment from the executor of the estate. The Court found that the agreement contained a number of legal flaws, such as a suspicion that the executor of the estate exerted undue influence on the woman prior to her signing the agreement. The Court (Justice Menachem Elon) did not rely on that suspicion as the only reason for invalidating the agreement, and ruled that according to Jewish law, a transaction that the executor of an estate carries out regarding the estate for his personal needs, requires prior approval by the court, and if the executor did not take steps to obtain such approval prior to carrying out the transaction, the court must engage in a "thorough examination of the reasonableness and fairness of the transaction, *vis-à-vis* the estate and the beneficiary (*ibid.*, p. 97). The Court ruled on the question from the perspective of the laws of agency:

> The question of invalidating a legal transaction because of a suspicion of conflict of interest has been dealt with thoroughly in Jewish law … regarding the sale of the object of the agency … 'an agent cannot buy it for himself even for the price at which the owner has authorized him to sell it' (Sh. Ar., ḤM, 185:2).

According to the view of some of the sages … the reason is one of suspicion, in other words, a conflict of interest between his acting on behalf of the principal and his acting on his own behalf (see, *e.g.*, Beit Yosef on the Tur, ḤM. ibid.; Prisha on the Tur, ḤM 175:30, and Bach. *ibid*; *Sema*, Sh. Ar. ḤM 175:26).

According to the view of other sages, the flaw inherent in an agent buying for himself is rooted in the fact that in such a case there has been no transfer from one domain to another:

'For an agent cannot buy for himself, even at the price that the owner has authorized him to sell it, inasmuch as he was made an agent to sell the land to a client, but he cannot authorize himself to buy it for himself, for a man cannot sell to himself; for the definition of a sale is the transfer of the object from one domain to another, and this hasn't left his domain insofar as he is acting in place of the owner' (Tur, ḤM, 185.3, in the name of *Rashba*)" (*Ibid*, p. 98).

In accordance with the above, in addition to a similar conclusion that is arrived at from the perspective of the laws of inheritance and guardianship in Jewish Law (see under Apotropos), Justice Elon rules that the validity of the transaction that the executor has carried out for himself with regard the estate that he is administering is contingent upon the prior approval of the court. Because no such approval was given, the transaction is subject to judicial review and the court must "examine the nature and the essence of the transaction from the perspective of what is in the best interests of the beneficiary" (*ibid*, p. 101).

[Michael Wygoda (2nd ed.)]

BIBLIOGRAPHY: Simmons, in; JQR, 8 (1896), 614–31; M. Cohn, in: *Zeitschrift fuer eergleiehemde fzechtswissenschaft*, 36 (1920), 124–13, 354–460; Gulak, *Yesodei*, 1 (1922), 42–50; 2 (1922), 198–9; 4 (1922), 54–60; Gulak, *Ozar*, 191–2, 272–9; t. H. Levinthal, *Jewish Law of Agency* (1923); Herzog, *Institutions*, 2 (1939), 141–53; ET, 1 (1951'), 338–42; 12 (1967), 135–98; Rakover, *Ha-Shelihut ve-ha-Harsha'ah ba-Mishpat ha-Ivri* (1972); idem; *Sinai*, 63 (1968), 56–80; idem, H.E. Baker, *Legal System of Israel* (1968), 118–21; 65 (1969), 117–38. **ADD. BIBLIOGRAPHY:** M. Elon, *Ha-Mishpat ha-Ivri* (1988), 1:100, 255, 288, 337f, 462–4, 526, 533–4, 573, 813; 2:1136, 1259; 3:1345, 1362, 1464, 1628. idem, Jewish Law (1994), 1:112, 298, 342f, 404f; 2:564–6, 641f., 649–51, 706, 996; 3:1364–65, 1505; 4:1606, 1625; 1739; 1939; idem, *Jewish Law: Cases and Materials* (1999), 14–15; M. Elon and B. Lifshitz, *Mafte'aḥ ha-She'elot ve-ha-Teshuvot shel Ḥakhmei Sefarad u-Ẓefon Afrikah* (1986), (2), 525–530; B. Lifshitz and E. Shochetman, *Mafte'aḥ ha-She'elot ve-ha-Teshuvot shel Ḥakhmei Ashkenaz, Ẓarefat ve-Italyah* (1997), 532–55; A. Kirshenbaum, *Iyyunim bi-Sheliḥut li-Devar Averah* (1), *Dinei Israel* (4) 1973, 55; idem, "*Ha-Kelal Milei Lo Mimseran le-Shali'aḥ: Nitu'aḥ Te'oreti*," in: *Shenaton ha-Mishpat ha-Ivri*, 5 (1978), 243; idem, "*Ha-Kelal Milei Lo Mimseran le-Shali'aḥ: Halakhah le-Ma'aseh*" in: *Shenaton ha-Mishpat ha-Ivri*, 6–7 (1979–1980), 271; S. Shilo, *She-elot Yesod be-Sugyat ha-Sheliḥut ba-Mishpat ha-Ivri be-Hashva'ah le-Ḥok ha-Sheliḥut*, in: *Dinei Israel*, 9 (1978–1980),120; D. Frimer, *He'arot le-Sugyat Mahut ha-Sheliḥut*, in: *Shenaton ha-Mishpat ha-Ivri*, 10–11 (1982–1983) 113; D. Sinclair, *Pasluto shel Goy be-Dinei ha-Sheliḥut*, in: *ibid*., 95; S. Etinger, *Pirkei Sheliḥut ba-Mishpat ha-Ivri* (1999); M. Wygoda, "On the Relationship Between the Capacity to Perform a Legal Task and the Capacity to Appoint an Agent to Perform It," in: *Jewish Law Annual*, 14:315–30.

AGGADAH or **HAGGADAH** (Heb. הַגָּדָה, אַגָּדָה; "narrative"), one of the two primary components of rabbinic tradition, the other being *halakhah*, usually translated as "Jewish Law" (see: Kadushin, *The Rabbinic Mind*, 59f.). The term *aggadah* itself is notoriously difficult to define, and it has become the custom among scholars to define *aggadah* by means of negation – as the non-halakhic component of rabbinic tradition (Fraenkel, *Midrash and Aggadah*, 20). While fair enough, one must be careful in adopting this approach not to define the parallel term *halakhah* too narrowly. The *halakhah* of the rabbinic tradition can be described in part as a system of laws, but not infrequently it also has the character of a personal moral and spiritual discipline. It can be expressed in the form of concrete judgments about specific cases, but also in rules involving varying degrees of abstraction and generality. Talmudic tradition often uses stories to express a *halakhah*. This is obviously so when the story reports an explicit legal precedent. But it may also be true when a story merely describes the behavior of a notable sage, if it is understood that this behavior is worthy of imitation. Despite the varied forms in which the *halakhah* is expressed, the rules, judgments and precedents included in talmudic literature all have one thing in common: they all categorize specific forms of behavior and well defined areas of experience in line with formal dichotomies, such as "permissible" or "forbidden," "pure" or "impure," "holy" and "profane," etc. *Aggadah*, on the other hand, investigates and interprets the *meaning*, the *values*, and the *ideas* which underlie the specific distinctions which govern religious life. In line with the accepted tendency to define *aggadah* as "that which is not *halakhah*," one could say that the relation between *aggadah* and *halakhah* is similar to the relation between theory and practice, between idea and application, and, in the area of ethics, between character and behavior.

[Stephen G. Wald (2nd ed.)]

The aggadah is first and foremost the creation of Palestinian Jewry, from the time of the Second Temple to the end of the talmudic period. Throughout that time, Palestine was the meeting ground of different religions and cultures as well as the field of violent political clashes. Its Jewry, confronted incessantly by bitter struggles with a variety of foes from within and without, evolved in the *aggadah* an ingenious instrument for deriving guidance from the Torah, for educating the people, strengthening their faith, and bolstering their pride and courage. Though much aggadic material has been preserved in the Babylonian Talmud, it, too, is predominantly of Palestinian origin, as are all the older Midrashim. The contribution of Babylonian Jewry in the field of *aggadah*, although often reworking earlier Palestinian aggadic themes, often achieves new levels of imagination and originality, frequently striking, engaging, and earthy. Sometimes a "mere" linguistic clarification can be the occasion for developing and elaborating a fragmentary tradition in new and unexpected directions (see: Friedman, BT *Bava Meẓi'a* VI, *Commentary*, 148).

According to Bacher the word *haggadah* is derived from the expression *higgid* (or *maggid*) *ha-katuv*, "Scripture related [or relates]," with which an aggadic discourse often opened. However, the *aggadah* did not always derive from biblical exegesis, but often arose independently of it. The word *aggadah* is rather to be understood as meaning simply "relating," i.e., events which have occurred, and in *Sotah* 7b *"devarim shel aggadah"* is used in this sense (cf. B. Lifshitz, *The Jewish Law Yearbook*, 22, 233–328, and the debate between Lifshitz and J. Fraenkel in *Netuim*, 11–12 (2004), 63–91). The important consideration here is the "telling," the narration, the wording, the style. The "telling," in this instance *aggadah*, however, is designed to touch the human heart (Yoma 75a), "so that one should recognize Him who created the world, and so cling to His ways" (Sif. Deut. 49). Its purpose is "to bring Heaven down to earth and to elevate man to Heaven" (Zunz).

Content and Form

The *aggadah* comprehends a great variety of forms and content. It includes narrative, legends, doctrines, admonitions to ethical conduct and good behavior, words of encouragement and comfort, and expressions of hope for future redemption. Its forms and modes of expression are as rich and colorful as its content. Parables and allegories, metaphors and terse maxims; lyrics, dirges, and prayers, biting satire and fierce polemic, idyllic tales and tense dramatic dialogues, hyperboles and plays on words, permutations of letters, calculations of their arithmetical values (*gematria*) or their employment as initials of other words (*notarikon*) – all are found in the *aggadah*. "Whatever the imagination can invent is found in the *aggadah*, with one exception: 'mockery and frivolity'" (Zunz), the purpose always being to teach man the ways of God. The *aggadah*'s variegated contents and multiplicity of forms can be accounted for by a consideration of its sources and its manner of growth.

The Folkloristic Aggadah

Although the aggadic literature as known is an expression of the ideas and feelings of the *tannaim* and *amoraim*, in many instances it merely adapted ancient material to its needs. Ready at hand were myths dating back to biblical times, popular legends of national heroes – patriarchs, prophets, and kings – and fanciful stories, some the product of the Jewish imagination and "wisdom," and others remnants of the folklore treasury of nearby and faraway peoples, which had become judaized in the course of time. The sages, however, were interested in establishing a connection between the current, popular *aggadah* and the Bible. Many *aggadot* seem to stem solely from Bible exegesis or a penetrating examination of the text; yet modern scholarship has been able to determine the place and time of their origin and so to separate the original layers from the later additions of the sages. The study of the epic literature of the ancient Orient, the apocrypha, and the legends of other peoples has helped greatly in this regard, as the following instances show. "R. Judah stated in the name of *Rav: 'When the Holy One blessed be He sought to build the world, He said to the Prince of the Sea "Open your mouth and swallow all the waters in the world." He said to Him "Master of the World, it is enough that I should retain my own." Immediately He struck him with his foot and he died, as it is said: "He breaks the sea with His power; with His understanding He smites through *Rahab"'" (BB 74b). Similar statements (Ginzberg, Legends Jews, 5 (1925), 17–18, 26–27) are merely the traditional myths of the revolt of the sea which were preserved in popular memory, and which parallel, fundamentally, the Mesopotamian myth of the war of the god creator against Tiamat, and Canaanite legends recorded in the Ugaritic inscriptions (Cassuto, in: *Keneset*, 8 (1943), 141–2).

It is related in a *baraita* that when an accused adulteress was being summoned to confess, she was reminded of biblical parallels for confession, as when not only *Judah but *Reuben too, "confessed and were not ashamed" (Sot. 7b; Sif. Deut. 35:5). With regard to Reuben this is not evident from the biblical narrative itself, but in the Talmud it is derived from the text by homiletical exegesis, by comparing it with the passage, "May Reuben live and not die.... And this he said for Judah" (Deut. 33:6–7; Sot. *ibid.*). The details of the story, however, appear in the apocryphal Testaments of the Twelve Patriarchs (Reu. 3). The influence of universal folklore on the *aggadah* is especially evident in the proverbs and fables. Late talmudic and post-talmudic sources ascribe to *Hillel the knowledge of the "conversations of trees and clouds, and of the beasts and animals" (Sof. 16:9), an element common to the folklore of all peoples. Another relatively late tradition (Suk. 28a) states that his pupil, Johanan b. Zakkai, knew the parables of laundrymen and fox fables. The *amora*, Johanan, related that R. Meir had known 300 fox fables. On the other hand, there is no confirmation from tannaitic sources for this claim, and it seems that the real "hero" of this tradition is the early *amora*, Bar Kappara, whose talents in this field may have been transferred to the earlier figure R. Meir by the *aggadah* (see: Friedman, The Talmudic Parable, 28). For his own part Johanan states that he himself knew only three such fables (concerning which he quotes only three biblical verses): "The fathers have eaten sour grapes, and the children's teeth are set on edge" (Ezek. 18:2); "Just balances, just weights" (Lev. 19:36); "The righteous is delivered out of trouble" (Prov. 11:8). The Talmud (Sanh. 38b–39a) takes it for granted that the fables to which these verses correspond were known to all. When *Hai Gaon was asked to expatiate upon Johanan's statement, he said: "Know that these fables contain moral lessons which are presented as if they emanated from the mouths of the beasts of the fields, like the writings of the Hindus which are called *Kitab Kalila wa-Dimna* and which contain moral lessons, wise sayings, and metaphors in the forms of animal fables. As for these fables of R. Meir, each was attached to a biblical verse which expressed a similar idea. So the story would be told: 'It happened that a lion caught a fox and wanted to eat it. The fox said to him: What do I possess that can appease your appetite ...'" (B.M. Levin, *Oẓar ha-Ge'onim*, 6, pt. 2, on *Sukkah* (1934), 31–32).

A more Jewish version of the fable is quoted by Rashi (in Sanh. 39a). Sometimes only the proverb or moral teaching is given, the story itself being known from Aesop or from Indian fables. At other times only the title of the story is mentioned: "Said R. Ammi: 'Come and see how great are the men of faith. From what is this derived? – from the incident of the weasel and the well. If it is so with one who trusts a weasel and a well, how much more so with one who trusts in God'" (Ta'an. 8a and Rashi *ibid.*). Yet other stories which were widely known among all peoples have no known earlier source than the *aggadah*. Although these are recorded as incidents in the lives of the sages, they have a folk origin (PdRK 7 – the story about R. Simeon b. Yohai – this tale of the wise farmer's daughter has spread among the Germanic, Slavic, and Romanian peoples). "The Jews may well be described as the great disseminators of folklore. Many a legend that originated in Egypt or Babylonia was appropriated by the European peoples, and many a European fairy tale found its way to Asia through the medium of the Jews, who on their long wanderings from the East to the West, and back from the West to the East, brought the products of Oriental fancies to the occidental nations, and the creations of occidental imagination to the Oriental peoples" (Ginzberg, Legends Jews, 5 (1925), vii).

The Discourse

From the earliest times the public reading from the Torah and the prophetic books occupied a prominent place in the synagogue service (BK 82a; TJ, Meg. 1:1, 70b). "They read in the book, in the Law of God, distinctly; and they gave the sense and caused them to understand the reading" (Neh. 8:8). At the conclusion of the reading, an exposition adapted to the level of the listeners would be delivered. This exposition contained the seeds of the *derashah* or discourse, which may be regarded as a continuation of the activities of the prophets "who reproved in the gates" (Isa. 29:21; Amos 5:10). The ordinance requiring the appropriate exposition to be delivered before the festivals was regarded as of the greatest antiquity, the sages asserting: "Moses ordained that Israel should enquire and expound concerning the Festivals" (Sif. Num. 66). Philo mentions the discourse many times (*De Somniis* 2:127; *Apologia* 7:12). On the Sabbath that Paul came to Antioch, after the Torah and *haftarah* reading, the congregants turned to him and asked him whether he wished to preach (Acts 13:14–15). Gamaliel, Joshua, Eleazar b. Azariah, and Akiva delivered discourses in Rome (Ex. R. 30:9). There is also an account of Akiva's address in the town of Ginzak in Media (Gen. R. 33:5). These discourses were delivered to the common people, in some instances gentiles being present in the audience. "At the time the elder sits and discourses, many strangers become proselytes" (Song R. 4:2). The "words of admonition" spoken on fast days were none other than a *derashah* (Ta'an. 2:1; Tosef., Ta'an. 1:8). Addresses were also delivered on the occasion of family joys and sorrows (Ket. 8b). People flocked to these addresses (Sot. 40a), and enjoyed listening to them. It was accurately said: "'The delights of the sons of man' – these are the *aggadot*, which are Scripture's delight" (Eccl. R. 2:8). The *aggadah* eventually became the core of the discourse, the preacher utilizing the occasion to point to the virtues and faults of his audience, to voice their feelings and aspirations, to scrutinize the events of the time, and to judge their deeds and those of their enemies. Whatever he had to say would be linked to the portion of Scripture they had just heard. At times it is difficult to determine whether the biblical exegesis is the source of the aggadic idea or whether the idea was read into the Scriptural passage. This, however, is immaterial. The spirit of the Bible pulsates in these *derashot*. Only individuals permeated with this spirit, in whom the words of the Bible had become alive, could relate their thoughts and feelings so closely to the text as to emerge with an exegesis and aggadic idea which seem, at times, to have arisen simultaneously. This total involvement with Scripture also explains why, despite the wide differences in the form, style and content of aggadic literature, and the vast distances in time and often in space which it spanned, no radical differences in its essential nature are perceivable.

In addition to its role in the public address, *aggadah* was studied and taught in the academies. Periods of instruction and study would be enlivened by aggadic interludes. When R. Zeira, on one occasion, was not up to delivering a halakhic discourse, he was besought, "Let the Master deliver an aggadic exposition," the latter requiring less exertion (Ta'an. 7a). The exegesis of some word in the course of a halakhic investigation would often lead to an aggadic discourse (BB 78b). The wording of a *halakhah* would sometimes recall a popular maxim (BK 92b). Obviously the aggadic expositions of the sages in the academies were subsequently made use of by popular preachers, just as those of the public sermons found their way back to the academies. The *aggadah* is a fusion of both.

Aggadic Methods

The freedom of interpretation allowed to the *aggadah* is given expression in the 32 hermeneutical principles included in the *Baraita of the Thirty-two Rules attributed to Eliezer b. Yose the Galilean (appearing in the printed editions of the Babylonian Talmud after the tractate *Berakhot* and in *Mishnat Rabbi Eliezer* (ed. by H.G. Enelow (1933), 10ff.)), but probably post-talmudic in its present formulation. Some of these principles are the same as those used in halakhic exposition, such as the seven principles of Hillel and the thirteen of R. Ishmael. Others are either exclusively or generally intended for the *aggadah*. Not invented by the sages, they closely resemble the exegetical methods used by the Greek orators and the grammarians of the ancient world (see: Lieberman, Hellenism). The talmudic sages employed these principles in finding scriptural allusions to and support for their ideas and in holding the attention and interest of their audiences. To personify the relationship between God and the people of Israel, the talmudic sages like the interpreters of Homer, from Anaxagoras onward, and like Philo of Alexandria, used parables as allegories. The *aggadah* knows of no conflict between literal and figurative explanations. The verb "*pashat*" is used both in reference to the plain or literal meaning (*peshat*) and to interpretations which are obviously homiletic (*derash*). Only toward the end of the amoraic period does the rule appear: "A verse cannot depart from its plain meaning" (Shab. 63a; Yev. 11b; cf. Bacher, *Exegetische Terminologie der Juedischen Traditions literatur*, 2 (1905),

170–3; R. Loewe in: *Papers of the Institute of Jewish Studies, London* (1964), 140–85) and a distinction was thus established between the two. (See also *Midrash.)

The Structure and Style of the Discourse

The *derashot* or discourses of the *tannaim* and *amoraim* have rarely come down in their original form. Ideas that were once coherent are now separated and scattered. In the extant Talmuds they are fragmented, joined with other elements, and removed from their original order. To the words of the early expositors the remarks of the later sages on the same topic have been added. Most evidence on the arrangement of the addresses dates back to amoraic times. The Talmud states that R. Meir would devote one third of his discourse to *halakhah*, one third to *aggadah*, and the rest to parables (Sanh. 38b). Since the discourses were based primarily on the weekly Torah and *haftarah* readings, some preachers would link elements from both. Indeed, the linking together of verses from all three divisions of the Bible and the exposition of Torah verses through verses in the other books was an integral part of the discourse. The Midrash relates that "R. Eliezer and R. Joshua … sat and occupied themselves with Torah … and they linked (the correct reading is *horzin*) words of the Torah to the Prophets, and of the Prophets to the Hagiographa …" (TJ, Hag. 2:1, 77b; cf. Lev. R. 16:4).

A striking feature of most extant Midrashim is the proem or introduction (*petiḥah*). A verse from a remote source, usually the Hagiographa or the later Prophets, is adduced. This verse is then interpreted and eventually associated with the section to be expounded, at which point the preacher concludes by repeating the original verse. In some aggadic Midrashim, a series of proems (*petiḥot*) serve as introductions to the systematic exposition of an entire portion of the Torah. Although it seems that each *petiḥah* served as the introduction to a specific sermon, some were, very likely, complete sermons in themselves (Heinemann, in: *Fourth World Congress of Jewish Studies*, 1968). Vestiges of such sermons as delivered by the *tannaim* have been preserved. The *petiḥah*, though primarily an expository instrument, also served the purpose of emphasizing the unity of the Bible.

It was customary to conclude aggadic discourses with words of comfort. The sages took note that "all the prophets began with words of reproof and ended with words of comfort" (PdRK ed. Mandelbaum, 238). Sometimes the conclusion of the discourse flowed naturally from the content of the discourse; sometimes it was a deliberate addition. There are many stylistic resemblances between the *derashah* and the stoic and cynic diatribe, both being rich in dramatic description, anecdote, and antithesis. In these discourses, dialogues are created within the context of biblical events, e.g., "The Egyptians said, 'Let us flee from the face of Israel.' The wicked and foolish among them said: 'Shall we flee from before the afflicted and degraded people? Shall we flee from before Israel?' The wise among them replied: 'Let us indeed flee from the face of Israel'" (Mekh., Be-Shalaḥ, 8).

The aggadic expositors focused their attention upon topics of everyday life, not hesitating to color their remarks with popular maxims, some translated from Greek to Aramaic while others were retained in the original. Aggadic homilies, often faithful reflections of actual customs and institutions of the Roman Empire, are rich in analogy: "This may be compared to a king …" "To a prince …" and the like.

Two styles may be discerned in the *aggadah*, one simple and the other ornate. In the first, the folklore basis is clearly evident. There is no striving after refinement; no embellishment is added and the language itself is sharp, and even coarse. In the second, the refined and the pleasant, the arresting and the attractive, are consciously sought after. In most aggadic works both styles are indiscriminately represented. Points of contact between the *heikhalot* literature and rabbinic sources may occasionally be detected in the Talmuds and Midrashim (see: G. Scholem, *Jewish Gnosticism, Merkabah Mysticism and Talmudic Tradition* (1962), 23–27), as well as rudiments of poetry (Mirsky in: YMHSI, 7 (1958), 1–129). The tannaitic homilies may be seen as representing the first stirring of the **piyyut* style, the later *amoraim* refining and polishing until the *piyyut* form was finally assumed (see: Mirsky, *ibid.*, passim).

Historical Aggadah

This category consists of additions and supplements to the Bible narrative and ancient *aggadot* preserved among the people, some dating back to Bible times themselves. Incidents and deeds only hinted at in Scripture serve as the kernels of dramatic accounts. Minor biblical figures become leading heroes. Biblical heroes become prototypes, for instance Abraham is the archetype of all proselytizers, Esau the fashioner of violence and deceit. In aggadic history, the limitations of space and time are transcended and anachronisms abound. Shem and Eber, for example, founded academies (*battei midrash*) where Jacob studied Torah (Gen. R. 63:9). Biblical heroes and their deeds are freed from the restraining bonds of time, the aggadic authors striving to discover in them meaning for their own and for their subsequent generations. The verse: "The voice is the voice of Jacob but the hands are the hands of Esau" is seen as the contrast not only between Jacob and Esau but also between their descendants, Israel and Rome, for "the deeds of the fathers are a sign to the children." In the *aggadah* can be found side by side a tendency to clear national heroes of all guilt, to exalt and glorify the nation and its past, and harsh criticism of even the patriarchs and the prophets. What is more, these two attitudes do not necessarily represent opposing views of different sages, but may even appear in the dicta of the same rabbi. Yet there is no contradiction or lack of consistency. For when they spoke of the past, their eyes were fixed on the present. Just as they desired to comfort and encourage by their words of praise, so were their critical observations intended to reprove and chastise. Yet their attitude to the present did not always determine their outlook on the past (see: Urbach, in: *Molad* (1961), 368–74). Aggadic literature even preserved stories and legends which were "foreign growths in the vineyards of Israel." Some of these had traveled far before reaching the Jewish people; others were the creations of propagandizing sects and parties now extinct. Later generations, while still maintaining their fierce hatred of the sects, accepted vestiges of their doctrines without being aware of their origins. Parallels in the apocryphal literature, in Philo and Josephus, and in the early Church Fathers attest to the antiquity of *aggadot* of this type. In the course of time the historical *aggadah* was expanded. To the portrayal of the history of Israel in the distant past, was added a description of the sufferings and disasters and the gratifications and consolations of the present. Alongside the stories of Bible heroes, biographical details of the *tannaim* and *amoraim*, their deeds, virtues, conduct, and manners, were introduced. With the obvious pleasure taken by the aggadists in the actual telling of a story, it must not be forgotten that their principal motive was not to create works of art, but to aid man, to instruct him "to know how to fear God and walk in His ways."

Doctrines

Systematic philosophies or theological doctrines are not to be found in the *aggadah* (see: Kadushin, *The Rabbinic Mind*, 280–81). Nevertheless, numerous attempts are made to provide well considered, if fragmentary, answers to questions concerning God, His attributes, the secret of Divine Providence, His rule over man and creation, the nature of idolatry, the source, character, and purpose of human existence, the relationship of man to God and to the world, the problem of the righteous and the wicked, reward and punishment, the position of the Jews among the gentile nations, the mission of the Jews, the Messianic era, and the world-to-come. It is true that the esoteric doctrine of "what is above and below; what came before and will come afterward" only concerned the elect, who were bold enough to enter the world of mysticism and to occupy themselves with the "Creation" and "Chariot" chapters of the Bible (Gen. 1 and Ezek. 1), but many esoteric teachings became part and parcel of the *aggadah*. The older works of the *aggadah* are also the most ancient sources of Jewish mysticism (Urbach, in: *Studies in Mysticism and Religion Presented to G. Scholem* (1967), Heb. sect. 1–28).

On all other topics most of the *tannaim* and *amoraim* expressed their views freely. There is hardly a generation which did not submit contradictory solutions to the problems mentioned above. To mention a few examples: Bet Shammai and Bet Hillel differed on whether the heavens or the earth were created first. Four generations later, R. Simeon delivered his opinion: both were created simultaneously, like a pot and its lid (Gen. R. 1:15). The *amora*, Resh Lakish, differs and offers a compromise: "When they were created, He created heaven first and afterward the earth; when He stretched them forth, He stretched forth the earth first and afterward the heaven" (Hag. 12a).

Again, in respect to proselytes, the Talmud contrasts Shammai's impatience with them to the well known patience of Hillel (Shab. 31a). These opposing attitudes are ascribed to *amoraim* as well. R. Eleazar, in the third century, declared: "God dispersed the Jews among the nations only that proselytes should join them" (Pes. 87b). R. Ḥelbo, a generation later, made the biting remark: "Proselytes are as hard for Israel to endure as a scab (*sappaḥat*), as it is written (Isa. 14:1): 'And the stranger shall join himself with them, and they shall cleave (*nispaḥ*) to the house of Jacob'" (Yev. 47b).

The verse, "This book of the law shall not depart out of thy mouth all the days of thy life" (Josh. 1:8) was interpreted by R. Ishmael to mean "Make them follow the way of the world" i.e., engage in normal occupations. Simeon b. Yoḥai objected: "Is it possible that man should plow in the proper season, sow in the proper season, reap in the harvest season? What will happen to the Torah? But when Israel obeys the will of the All-Present, its chores are performed by others." On this, the *amora* Abbaye commented: "Many followed the advice of Ishmael and it worked well, of Simeon b. Yoḥai and failed." Abbaye's colleague, Rava, forbade the sages to gather at the academy during the harvest seasons (Ber. 35b).

R. Eliezer and R. Joshua disagreed as to whether the redemption of Israel is conditional upon its repentance, the controversy reappearing in a different version several generations later, between Rav and Samuel. "Rav said: 'All predestined dates have passed. Everything now depends on repentance and good deeds.' Samuel said: 'It is sufficient for the mourner to keep his period of mourning'" (i.e., they will be redeemed even without repentance; Sanh. 97b). Special emphasis was given to those *derashot* dealing with the Messiah, the world to come, resurrection, the redemption of Israel and of the world. Here too, controversies abound, some sages adopting the apocalyptic trend and others a more realistic approach. All, however, share a common conviction – the eventual triumph of the Jewish people over all their sufferings, and the ultimate victory of Judaism over all the world's evils and abominations. All that has been said in this regard revolves around two poles: the nation and its land, on the one hand, and the universal, the perfection of the world on the other. It would be surprising if aggadic literature, which grew over a period of over 1,000 years in lands of different religions and cultures, did not bear the imprint of time and place. Foreign languages (Greek in Ereẓ Israel, Persian in Babylonia) enriched the Hebrew and Aramaic vocabularies; elements of Platonic, Stoic, and Pythagorean philosophies, and concepts which had gained currency in the prevalent Hellenistic culture infiltrated into the *aggadah*. Political and religious events also influenced trends of beliefs and doctrines in certain areas of the *aggadah*. On certain issues of religious thought, there were many-sided polemics which persisted for many generations. The later sages revived the discussions of the problems from the changed perspective of their own times (Urbach, in: *Y. Kaufmann Jubilee Volume* (1960), Heb. sect., 122–48) with even greater vigor and boldness. The editors of the *aggadah* collected the various views pro and con, and left them side by side, since in their opinion all were "the words of the living God." The ethical doctrines in the *aggadah*, the teaching and preaching of virtuous conduct to the public, clearly reflect not only the views and opinions of the sages who strove for human betterment, but also the political, social, and cultural environment of the generations to whom they addressed themselves. They brought all classes, without prejudice, under critical review. Even the sages themselves were not spared. The spiritual trends and the various sects, whether they remained within the Jewish fold or abandoned it, left their impress on the *aggadah*. Stories, interpretations of verses, and many dicta are eminently polemics against Sadducean, Gnostic, Christian, and especially Judeo-Christian sects. The aggadic sages rebut the charges of emperors, various heretics, and even philosophers against the Torah – and then go over to the attack.

Whatever the Jewish people, including its sages, scribes, teachers, and preachers, thought or felt during a period of more than 1,000 years is reflected in the *aggadah*. Later generations found in this great treasury the expression of their own deepest feelings. On the one hand they derived support and proofs for their views and concepts, and on the other, they were able, when necessary, to declare that the aggadic view contrary to their own was not binding, or that it constituted a foreign addition. The attitudes of scholars and rabbis toward the *aggadah* – its literary or free interpretation, its evaluation as binding doctrine or as imaginative, literary creation – differed widely at various periods in history. Even after the *aggadah* had ceased to grow and other modes of creative expression had replaced it (i.e., *piyyut*, philosophy, Kabbalah), it remained a perennial source of inspiration and insight.

The Aggadists

Although most of the masters of the *aggadah* excelled in *halakhah* as well, there were sages, *tannaim*, and *amoraim*, who specialized in *aggadah*. Although it was said of Akiva that he "composed halakhic and aggadic interpretations" (TJ, Shek. 5:1, 48c), the Talmud ascribes to one of his contemporaries, Eleazar b. Azariah, a negative evaluation of his expertise in *aggadah*: "Akiva, what have you to do with the *aggadah*? Cease your talk, and turn to the laws of *Nega'im* and *Oholot*" (Hag. 14a). R. Tarfon is reported to have said of R. Ishmael: "He is a great scholar and expert in homiletic exposition" (MK 28b). R. Johanan stated in the name of R. Eleazar b. R. Simeon, "Wherever you find the words of R. Eleazar b. R. Yose the Galilean, shape your ear like a funnel" (Hul. 89a). Among the Palestinian *amoraim* were many masters of the *aggadah*; R. Jonathan, R. Samuel b. Naḥman, R. Isaac Nappaḥa, R. Levi, R. Abba b. Kahana, R. Berechiah, and R. Tanḥuma are especially famous as aggadists. Some of them apparently, are referred to by the collective name, *rabbanan de-aggadeta* ("the rabbis of the *aggadah*," TJ, Ma'as. 1:2, 48d; TJ, Yev. 4:2, 5c). They were not immune to criticism, however. It is told of R. Ze'ira that he used to rebuke the aggadic expositors, calling them "magician scribes" and characterizing their interpretations as turning over and over and conveying nothing (TJ, Ma'as. 3:9, 51a). R. Johanan's thrust, "There is a tradition transmitted by my fathers not to teach *aggadah* to a Babylonian or a southerner since they are uncouth and not learned in Torah" (TJ, Pes. 5:3, 32a; Pes. 62b), is no more than a rejoinder to remarks such as those expressed by R. Ze'ira.

[*Encyclopaedia Hebraica*]

Women in Aggadah

The many aggadic images of females and the feminine offer a complex, nuanced portrait of women. Through midrashic expansions of biblical narratives and rounding out of biblical characters, biblical women are given a voice, albeit a voice filtered through the minds of men. In *aggadah*, one hears Sarah protesting her imprisonment in the house of Pharaoh (Gen. Rab. 41:2), Leah praying that her last child will be a daughter (b. Ber. 60a), and Rachel describing how she assisted her father in his deception of Jacob in order to protect her sister from embarrassment (Lam. Rab. Proem 24). Biblical women, like their male counterparts, are constructed in *aggadah* as paradigms and models for all Jews; thus Tamar's willingness to be burnt unless Judah identified his seal, staff and cord serves to teach that "it is better that a person throw himself into a fiery furnace than shame his fellow in public" (b. Ber. 43b). The range of *aggadah* illustrates that there is no monolithic rabbinic view of women; classical *aggadah* includes both accolades and sharp critiques. While the women of the generation of the Exodus are praised for their faith and devotion (*Midrash Tanhuma* Pinhas 7), Eve is blamed for "corrupting Adam" and "extinguishing his soul" (Gen. Rab. 17:8). Just as there are *aggadot* that praise the good qualities of the matriarchs, so too there are *aggadot* that highlight their shortcomings. In many *aggadot* that describe some aspect of the relationship between God and the people Israel, Israel is portrayed in the feminine. When God is compared in parables to a "flesh and blood king," Israel may be portrayed as the king's consort or his daughter. These parables are used to describe the divine-human relationship as one marked by love, anger, betrayal and reunion. The use of the feminine to symbolize Israel is inconsistent; parables are equally likely to characterize Israel as God's son. It would be incorrect to read the emotional turmoil of the king-parables as an indication of rabbinic dislike of women or as a critique on family life among the ancient rabbis. Instead, these *aggadot* demonstrate the rabbis' willingness to identify, as part of collective Israel, with the feminine. Scholars who have attempted to compare or contrast attitudes toward women in *halakhah* and *aggadah* have drawn no clear-cut conclusions. At times, aggadic traditions attempt to explain or justify women's legal status and obligations. Some discussions of the three commandments especially associated with women (separation of dough, separation during menstruation, and lighting the Sabbath lights) describe these responsibilities as punishment or atonement for the shortcomings of Eve (Gen. Rab. 17:8). In other cases, *aggadah* may serve to soften or critique a law that touches on the lives of women, as in the case of divorce (Gittin 35a).

[Dvora E. Weisberg (2nd ed.)]

WOMEN'S OTHERNESS. Although aggadic views about women vary, they are generally based on the conviction of women's essential alterity from men. "Women are a separate people" (Shabbat 62a) asserts the predominant supposition that the physical characteristics, innate capacities, and social functions of females are inherently dissimilar and generally less valued than those of males. Niddah 31b points out that males are welcomed at birth because of their physical potential for generativity and because they enter the covenant through circumcision. Females, on the other hand, are not a cause for celebration; they are empty wombs requiring male insemination, their birth delays their parents' resumption of sexual relations by an additional week, and their menstruation requires them to be separated from their husbands for almost half of each month. Woman's otherness is said to originate in the secondary nature of her creation. The final segment of Niddah 31b suggests that the preferred position for sexual intercourse is that in which the man, on top, looks towards his origins in the earth (i.e., to the cosmic substance from which God created him) while the woman, facing upward, looks toward the man from whose body she was created. The assumption that the initial human creation was a solitary male from whose body a woman was subsequently built is the view that most commonly appears in the rabbinic *aggadah* (e.g., Ketubbot 8a; Gen. Rab. 18:2). Several extended aggadic narratives catalog and justify a series of female disabilities as consequences of the lesser nature of female creation and the first woman's subsequent deleterious moral choices (Gen. Rab. 17:8; ARN B 9; Eruvin 100b). Aggadic passages reflect anxiety regarding women's sexual unreliability; unaccompanied women in the public sphere are suspect and may be divorced (Ketubbot 7:6; Gittin 90b); women gathering in groups are connected with witchcraft (Pesaḥim 8:7; Avot 2:7; Pesaḥim 110a, 111a). Having to wear a veil outside of the domestic sphere (Sotah 3:8) is seen as a female burden connected with guilt and shame (Gen. Rab. 17:8; Eruvin 100b); ARN B 9 comments: "In the same way Eve disgraced herself and caused her daughters to cover their heads." A woman who remains veiled even within the home is truly pious and will be rewarded (Yoma 47a). Foreign women, like Hagar (Gen. 16–21) and Cozbi (Num. 25), are usually understood to exemplify unrestrained sexuality and ill will towards Israel and are represented with particular hostility in aggadic sources (*Gen. Rab.* 53:13–14; Me'ilah 17b; b. Sanhedrin 82a; Num. Rab. 21:3). Rahab, the noble harlot of Joshua 2 and 5:25, and Ruth, the Moabite ancestress of King David, are among the few women from outside the Israelite community who are praised, essentially because each is understood to have joined herself to the community of Israel through faith and marriage (Zevahim 116a–b; Megillah 14b; Sifre Num. 78; Ruth Rab. 2:1).

[Judith R. Baskin (2nd ed.)]

The Aggadah in Modern Scholarship

Leopold *Zunz's classic work, *Die Gottesdienstlichen Vortraege der Juden* (1832), marks the beginning of modern research in the field of *aggadah*. Ever since then, scholars, prominent among them Nachman *Krochmal, S. *Rapoport, S. *Buber, A.H. *Weiss, A. *Epstein M. *Friedmann, J. *Theodor, W. *Bacher, H. *Albeck, and I. *Heinemann, have concentrated on three tasks: (1) to publish critical and corrected editions and also such material as was still in manuscript, (2) to compile the aggadic treasury in some systematic form; and (3) to examine the contents, ideas, and methods of the midrashim and thus to determine the dates of the various works. An especially significant and original contribution was made by Bacher, who gathered and arranged in chronological order, the aggadic material of all the *tannaim* and *amoraim*, thus making the aggadic creation of each sage accessible, and enabling us to assess his particular approach and "world of ideas." Bacher's works: *Die Agadah der Tannaiten* (1878) and *Die Agadah der Palaestinensischen Amoraeer* (1892–99) were published in German and translated into Hebrew. Louis *Ginzberg, in his *Legends of the Jews* (1909–38), arranged the *aggadot* around a chronology of biblical personalities and events. His collection is extraordinarily rich and broad in scope, and his notes and explanations are a gold mine of information on the history of the *aggadah*, especially in its relation to the Apocrypha and Patristic Literature. The *Sefer ha-Aggadah* of *Bialik and *Rawnitzki is a popular work which has achieved a very wide circulation. It includes most of the important branches of the *aggadah*, (in Hebrew translation, where the sources are in Aramaic). The first section is arranged in chronological order, the second, according to topics. The compilers found it necessary to graft versions to one another, and also to omit material offensive to the modern reader. A subject index is appended to the work. First published in 1910, the *Sefer ha-Aggadah* has gone through eighteen impressions, including an enlarged edition published in 1936.

[*Encyclopaedia Hebraica*]

Later Studies

Since the 1970s, when literary theory emerged as a burgeoning field of interest, intersecting with other areas of inquiry, studies in *aggadah* have been marked by an increasing awareness of its literary features. Scholars, primarily in North America, but also in Israel, have come to pay less attention to the historical veracity of aggadic texts, and to focus their attention more on the "literariness" of classical rabbinic texts. Underlying this new trend in the study of *aggadah* is the notion that rabbinic stories not only reflect beliefs, values, and customs, but also possess the earmarks of literature and should thus be examined in light literary motifs, themes, and structure. Many contemporary scholars are thus no longer interested, for example, in how a story about a certain rabbi may be utilized in constructing his historical biography. Instead, rabbinic narratives are analyzed in terms of their literary quality. At the same time, however, they are regarded as artifacts that function as conveyors and mediators of rabbinic culture. The historical import of narratives is therefore undiminished to the extent that they yield insight into the milieu of those who recorded, transmitted and lived by them.

The following is a précis of some of the many works that have affected contemporary studies of *aggadah*.

Neusner's *The Development of a Legend* has proven to be a turning point in the field of rabbinics. Here he methodically demonstrates how stories depicting the life of Rabbi Johanan Ben Zakkai evolved into what is considered the "normative tradition," and how they tell us more about those who produced the narratives or deemed them authoritative than about the actual personage. Rather than viewing the corpus of rabbinic literature as monolithic, Neusner's source and form-critical analyses highlighted the importance of the diachronic, as well as structural aspects of rabbinic texts. More fundamentally, his work called attention to the need to explore basic assumptions about the nature of rabbinic literature. Neusner's underlying assumptions, shared by his compatriots in biblical studies – Hebrew Scriptures and New Testament – provided the basis for much future study in rabbinics.

Advancements in literary studies and theory attracted such scholars as Boyarin and Stern, whose work exemplify the interdisciplinary approach to *aggadah* and Midrash that broadly speaking characterizes the general trend in North American research into rabbinics today. Boyarin's *Intertextuality and the Reading of Midrash*, dealing primarily and explicitly with Midrash through a postmodern critical lens, is a significant contribution to the field of academic rabbinic research. Here Boyarin discusses rabbinic interpretation as discourse that is historically and ideologically situated. Through a study of the *Mekhilta* and its use of quotations, he illustrates how rabbinic interpretation is both the continuation and disruption of tradition. Although the work does not deal with *aggadah* per se, it provides a methodological framework for analyzing rabbinic narratives, and as such it has been regarded by many scholars as groundbreaking. Stern's *Parables in Midrash* is an in-depth analysis of the function of the *mashal* (parable) in rabbinic literature that explores its compositional and exegetical techniques, its rhetoric and role in midrashic discourse. Stern draws the conclusion that parables about kings constitute the preeminent form of narrative in rabbinic texts. Although he emphasizes the *mashal*, Stern also examines other literary forms such as the *petiḥta* (the proem of the homiletic Midrash), and the *ma'aseh* (reportage). Stern's later work, *Midrash and Theory*, investigates rabbinic texts theoretically and deals squarely with the impact of literary criticism on rabbinic exegesis. Kugel's *In Potiphar's House* examines a series of stories that elaborate on the Joseph narrative in Genesis. Here he traces the development of *aggadah vis-a-vis* traditions found in sources as diverse as early Christian writing, *piyyut*, and the Qur'an, in light of the manner by which exegetical motifs are created and evolve. In addition to examining the historical development of rabbinic narratives, in the final chapter of his book, "Nine Theses," he reflects on several aspects of Midrash and *aggadah*, and formulates general conclusions about the workings of early biblical exegesis. Kugel's *The Bible as it Was*, an expansive collection of biblical interpretation, also contributes significantly to the study of rabbinic narratives in so far as it offers erudite commentary on the ancient interpretive traditions, and elucidates how they in turn gave rise to crucial transformations in the meaning of a biblical story.

Talmudic scholars, such as Kalmin and Rubenstein, have focused on the study of *aggadah* in the Talmud. In *The Sage in Jewish Society of Late Antiquity*, Kalmin compares stories produced more or less at the same time but in different locations. By doing so, he demonstrates how the differences between Babylonian and Palestinian rabbinic social structures help explain distinctions between depictions of biblical heroes in aggadic texts. In the same vein of attempting to read narratives for their cultural significance, in *Talmudic Stories: Narrative Art, Composition and Culture*, Rubenstein closely examines six talmudic stories with an eye toward both literary aspects and cultural contexts.

Israeli scholarship has also contributed to the study of *aggadah* from a literary and interdisciplinary perspective. First and foremost, the comprehensive works of Isaac Heinemann (*Darkhei Ha-Aggadah*) and Jonah Fraenkel (*Darkhei Ha-Aggadah ve-Ha-Midrash* and *Midrash ve-Aggadah*) have shaped the ways in which generations of Israeli scholars and students have approached and understood the aggadic literature (see below). Dov Noy, whose folkloristic approach in general, and his listing of rabbinic folkloric motifs, *Motif Index of Talmudic-Midrashic Literature*, in particular, signaled a serious shift in the study of *aggadah*. These scholars in turn paved the way for a new generation of scholars whose are deeply engaged in aggadic studies. Noteworthy Israeli contributors to literary analysis of *aggadah* include Ofra Meir, who examines the relationship between rabbinic biblical exegesis and narrative from a literary perspective, Avigdor Shinan, who engages the nexus between *aggadah* and *targum*, Galit Hasan-Rokem, who approaches the study of rabbinic folktales from a cultural poetics perspective, and Joshua Levinson, who examines rabbinic narrative expansion and reformulation of biblical stories in the light of contemporary critical literary theory.

[Carol Bakhos (2nd ed.)]

The tendency toward interdisciplinary methodology and theoretical generalization described above has for the past two decades been accompanied by a parallel and probably related tendency toward the erosion of accepted and authoritative cultural canons in both literary and religious studies. While primarily characteristic of North American scholarship, these trends have also had their followers in Israel (see above). Nevertheless, it would be fair to say that in many Israeli circles the classical literature of the *aggadah* has largely retained its canonical status as well as much of its cultural and (for some) its religious authority. As a result, the fundamental assumption underlying much study and research into the aggadic literature in Israel (and similar Hebrew language research outside of Israel) is that the study of aggadic texts in their original languages (Hebrew and Aramaic) and the detailed explication of the form and content of these texts are fully justified for their own sake, and are of interest to a wide audience of professional and non-professional students. This assumption has shaped much of the direction and focus of recent Israeli studies of the *aggadah*.

By the early 1970s Israeli scholarship had already produced a number of seminal works in the field of *aggadah*. First of all, Zunz's *Gottesdienstlichen Vortraege* had been translated into Hebrew, and richly annotated and updated by Hanoch Albeck (1946) thus placing a fairly comprehensive, reliable and accessible introduction to aggadic literature in the hand of every student. Second, Isaac Heineman published in 1950 (second edition 1954) his revolutionary typology of the rabbinic *aggadah*, *Darkhei ha-Aggadah*, which provided a detailed description of the methods of rabbinic aggadic under two general headings: "creative historiography" and "creative philology". The significance of this work lay in focusing the reader's attention for the first time on the ways in which the rabbis actually interpreted biblical texts and narratives, thus largely replacing the age-old polemical and apologetic discussions of how the rabbis "should have" interpreted the scripture. Thirdly, Ephraim Urbach published in 1969 his monumental work, *Ḥazal* (translated: *The Sages: Their Concepts and Beliefs*, 1987), which restated the entire theological, ethical, and eschatological content of the world of the *aggadah* in a modern format easily accessible to student and scholar alike. By 1970 the student of *aggadah* also possessed, in addition to the classic critical edition of *Genesis Rabbah*, begun by Theodor and finished by Albeck, critical editions of Levitcus Rabbah (M. Margulies) and *Pesikta de-Rav Kahana* (B. Mandelbaum), comprising, together with *aggadah* in the Talmudim, the basic corpus of the classical amoraic aggadic literature. Viewing aggadic literature as an integral part of talmudic rabbinic literature as a whole, the work of J.N. Epstein, H. Albeck, and S. Lieberman was seen to have laid firm foundations for the historical and philological analysis of the textual traditions in which the literature of the *aggadah* was preserved.

Without a doubt, the most important Israeli figure in the study of *aggadah* for most of the last three decades has been Jonah Fraenkel. One cannot overestimate the profound and pervasive impact of Fraenkel's work, both as a scholar and as a teacher. His influence is in some ways even stronger today, despite the fact that many of his former students have moved in new and different directions. This is due to the publication of his two comprehensive and synthetic works, *Darkhei ha-Aggadah ve-ha-Midrash* (1996) and *Midrash ve-Aggadah* (1996), which have appealed to a wide audience, and are not limited to a small circle of professional scholars. Similarly the recent publication of *Sippur ha-Aggadah – Aḥdut shel Tokhen ve-Ẓurah* (2001) has made many of his classic studies, along with a number of new articles, easily accessible to the general public. Aside from popularizing the fruits of modern research into the *aggadah*, Fraenkel's own contribution lies in two areas. First of all, building upon the work of Isaac Heinemann, Fraenkel further developed and elaborated the typology of the *aggadah* viewed from the perspective of the isolated act of rabbinic scriptural interpretation. More importantly, however, Fraenkel described and analyzed the macro-forms in which these interpretations are imbedded: the expanded biblical narrative, narratives relating to the talmudic sages themselves, the parable, the aggadic *memra* (amoraic statement), etc. Moreover, he shows the articulation and explication of these forms, understood in the light of modern literary theory, to be essential to the appreciation of the ideational content of the *aggadah* itself, thus continuing the work of his teacher, Ephraim Urbach. In one respect, however, Fraenkel made a clear break with Urbach's methodolology, a point which he has repeatedly emphasized. Urbach tended to compare and contrast parallel versions of a given tradition, and after philological and higher-critical analysis to posit a reconstructed original, which he then used as the basis for his analysis. Fraenkel's insistence on the unity of form and content in each and every version of a tradition led him to reject Urbach's approach and to refrain from conflating – and even from comparing – alternative versions of a tradition, basing his exposition on a detailed and exhaustive analysis of data present in a given talmudic text.

At the same time the scholarly tradition of Epstein, Albeck, and Lieberman has not been ignored. Scholars such as Jacob Elbaum, Menahem Kister, Chaim Milikowsky, Avigdor Shinan, Menachem Hirshman, Joseph Tabory, Paul Mandel, Menachem Kahana, M.B. Lerner, and Hananel Mack have written hundreds of studies both analyzing particular passages and addressing broader critical and methodological issues. Most of these scholars are also deeply involved in long term projects of preparing the next generation of critical editions and commentaries on the classical and post classical aggadic works. Shamma Friedman's work on the historical *aggadah* of the Bablylonian Talmud is noteworthy, because, on the one hand, it provides a radical alternative to one of Fraenkel's most fundamental notions, and, on the other hand, it may also be seen as complementary to Fraenkel's approach as a whole.

Friedman has produced a series of studies concerning a wide range of topics within the field of talmudic research, treating both *halakhah* and *aggadah*, and frequently of the reciprocal relation between them. One theme runs through all these studies: the notion of "development" or "evolution" – that later talmudic scholars often self-consciously reinterpreted and reformulated earlier versions of a given tradition. Applying the results of these studies to the historical *aggadot* of the Babylonian Talmud, Friedman has shown that the elaborate and colorful descriptions of events in the lives of both the *tannaim* and the more significant *amoraim* do not reflect ancient and independent traditions, but rather are the product of a synthetic literary process of deliberate and considered editorial revision. While Jacob Neusner deserves credit as a pioneer in this field of research, Friedman's exacting philological and higher-critical studies allow one to go beyond the largely negative conclusions of Neusner and his school, and to proceed to the positive task of reconstructing the substantial and formal considerations which went into this elaborate process of editorial revision. Stories originally told of one sage are transferred to another. Several independent and fragmentary traditions are combined into an extended and integrated whole, whose narrative and ideational aims far transcend the relatively limited scope of the original sources.

On the one hand Friedman's method contrasts with Fraenkel's emphasis on viewing each text as an integral whole – and studying it in isolation from other parallel versions of the tradition. On the other hand Friedman's comparative and developmental analysis of parallel traditions also represents an equally explicit rejection of conflating parallel texts, in that it demands a rigorous distinction and demarking of the boundaries between parallel traditions, in order to determine the causal and interpretive links which hold between them.

[Stephen G. Wald (2nd ed.)]

In Islam

Aggadic Bible tales and views were disseminated in pre-Islamic *Arabia by Jews. A. *Geiger first showed in his pioneering treatise *Was hat Mohammed aus dem Judenthume aufgenommen?* (1833) that the *aggadah* had an important bearing on the shaping of ideas about Allah and the history of mankind held by *Muhammad and the hanifs, his monotheistic-minded contemporaries (cf. e.g., Koran 22, 32; 30, 79; 98, 4). In the *Koran Muhammad preferred to use vague expressions, often avoiding the mention of names of biblical personalities or even changing them. The earliest commentators endeavored to explain such passages and tales, which they did with the help of the *aggadah*. Muslim authors prepared special books called *Qiṣaṣ Al-Anbiya* ("Legends of the Prophets"), something similar to later *Midrashim, in which aggadic tales from the Bible – which also for the Muslim includes the New Testament – have been gathered. (For further information see: *Bible (in Islam); *Koran; and sections on biblical personalities (such as Abraham) in Islam.)

[Haïm Z'ew Hirschberg]

Aggadah in Illuminated Manuscripts

Recent investigations have revealed that many aggadic motifs appear in the illuminations of Christian Old Testaments, such as the sixth-century *Vienna Genesis*, the seventh-century *Ashburnham Pentateuch*, and the 11th/12th-century Byzantine *Octateuchs*. These manuscripts are all assumed to be based on lost earlier models. The appearance of these aggadic motifs has led some scholars to put forward the theory that an ancient illustrated Jewish manuscript tradition served as inspirations for the Christian manuscripts. This theory is not conclusive, as no illustrated Jewish manuscripts are known before the ninth century. In addition, knowledge of early Christian biblical illuminations is very limited, since the earliest preserved Christian Old Testament manuscripts date from the sixth century. Furthermore, the writings of the Church Fathers incorporated many aggadic motifs which may have inspired the Christian aggadic illustrations.

Aggadic motifs in the *Vienna Genesis* include the accounts of how Joseph encounters the angel Gabriel on his way to find his brethren, Potiphar's wife visits Joseph in prison; and Asenath, Joseph's wife, is present at Jacob's blessing.

In the *Ashburnham Pentateuch* Adam and Eve build a hut after their expulsion; the giants drown during the flood; Rebekah inquires at the academy of Shem and Eber; Joseph and his brothers dine together at the same table in Egypt; and The Angel of Death slays the Egyptian firstborn. In the Octateuchs, the serpent walks upright in the Garden of Eden; Lamech kills Cain and Tubal-Cain; the raven sent out by Noah feeds on human carcass: and God, Himself, intervenes in the sacrifice of Isaac. Some other legends appearing in manuscripts are: Nimrod casting Abraham into the fiery furnace; Pharaoh's daughter, bathing in the nude, finds Moses; the test of Moses, Moses' imprisonment, and his wedding to Zipporah; Pharaoh bathing in the blood of Jewish children; Mount Sinai hovering over the children of Israel; the legendary throne of Solomon; and Mordecai stepping on Haman's back and Haman's daughter emptying a chamberpot on her father. C.O. Nordström has pointed out many Jewish legends in Byzantine, Spanish, and French art, mainly in the life of Moses, and his miracles. In his book on the Alba Bible he refers to many aggadic motifs in this very important manuscript. For a critical analysis of this book, see *The Art Bulletin*, 51 (1969), 91–96.

[Joseph Gutmann]

BIBLIOGRAPHY: AGGADAH: Zunz, Vortraege, Zunz-Albeck, Derashot; Bacher, Bab Amor; Bacher, Tann; Bacher, Pal Amor; Ginzberg, Legends, L. Ginzberg, *Die Haggada bei den Kirchenvaetern und in der apokryphischen Literatur* (1900); H.L. Strack, *Introduction to the Talmud and Midrash* (1931), 201–34, Graetz, in: MGWJ, 3 (1854), 311–9, 352–5, 381–92, 482–31, 4 (1855), 186–92; Guedemann, in: *Jubelschrift… L. Zunz* (1884), 111–21; V. Aptowitzer, *Kain und Abel in der Agada…* (1922), Marmorstein, in: HUCA, 6 (1929), 141–204; Heller, in: J. Bolte and G. Polivka (eds.), *Anmerkungen zu den Kinder und Hausmaerchen der Brueder Grimm*, 4 (1930), 315–418, Stein, in: HUCA, 8–9 (1931–32), 353–71, I. Heinemann, *Altjuedische Allegoristik* (1935); idem, *Darkhei ha-Aggadah* (1954), H.N. Bialik, *Halakhah and Aggadah* (1944), S. Lieberman, *Greek in Jewish Palestine* (1942), 144–60, idem, *Hellenism in Jewish Palestine* (1950), 47–82; Seeligmann, in: VT, Suppl., (1953), 150–81 (Ger.), *Zeitschrift fuer Theologie und Kirche*, 52 (1955), 129–61; B. Gerhardsson, *Memory and Manuscript* (1961); G. Vermes, *Scripture and Tradition in Judaism* (1961); A.J. Heschel *Torah min ha-Shamayim be-Aspaklaryah shel ha-Dorot*, 2 vols. (1962–65), vol. 3 (1995); E.E. Halevi, *Sha'arei ha-Aggadah* (1963). **ADD. BIBLIOGRAPHY:** M. Kadushin, *Organic Thinking* (1938); idem, *The Rabbinic Mind* (1952); J. Heinemann, *Aggadot Ve-Toldotehen* (1974); J. Fraenkel, in: J.W. Welch (ed.), *Chiasmus in Antiquity: Structures, Analyses, Exegesis* (1981) 183–97; idem, *Iyyunim be-Olamo ha-Ruḥani shel Sippur ha-Aggadah* (1981); idem, *Darkhei ha-Aggadah ve-Hamidrash* (Hebrew; 1996); idem, *Midrash ve-Aggadah* (1996); idem, *Sippur ha-Aggadah – Aḥdut shel Tokhen ve-Ẓurah* (2001); S. Friedman, BT *Bava Meẓi'a VI, Commentary* (1990); idem, "The Talmudic Parable in its Cultural Setting," in: JSIJ, 2 (2003), 25–82; idem, "The Historical Aggadah of the Babylonian Talmud" (Hebrew), in: S. Friedmand (ed.), *Saul Lieberman*

Memorial Volume (1993),119–64; Idem, "A Good Story Deserves Retelling – The Unfolding of the Akiva Legend," in: JSIJ, 3 (2004), 1–39; idem, "The Further Adventures of Rav Kahana – Between Babylonia and Palestine," in: P. Schäfer (ed.), *The Talmud Yerushalmi and Graeco-Roman Culture*, 3 (2002), 247–71; idem, "History and Aggadah: The Enigma of Dama Ben Netina" (Hebrew), in: *Jonah Fraenkel Festschrift* (forthcoming); idem, "The Aggadah of Rav Kahana and Rabbi Yohanan (Bava Qamma 117a-b) and the Hamburg-Geniza Recension" (Hebrew), in: *Meyer S. Feldblum Memorial Volume* (forthcoming); S. Wald, BT *Pesahim III* (2000), 211–39, 253–68; A. Kosman, in: Hebrew Union College Annual, 73 (2002) 157–90; M.A. Friedman & M.B. Lerner (eds.), *Te'uda XI – Studies in the Aggadic Midrashim, in Memory of Zvi Meir Rabinowitz* (1996); M. Kister, in: *Tarbiz*, 67 (1998), 483–529. WOMEN IN AGGADAH: J.R. Baskin, *Midrashic Women: Formations of the Feminine in Rabbinic Literature* (2002); M.A. Friedman, "Tamar, a Symbol of Life: The 'Killer Wife' Superstition in the Bible and Jewish Tradition," in: *AJS Review*, 15 (1990), 23–61; D.M. Goodblatt. "The Beruriah Traditions;" in: *Persons and Institutions in Early Rabbinic Judaism* (1977); D.E. Weisberg, "Men Imagining Women Imagining God: Gender Issues in Classical Midrash," in: *Agendas for the Study of Midrash in the Twenty-First Century* (1999); T. Ilan, *Mine and Yours are Hers: Retrieving Women's History from Rabbinic Literature* (1997). LITERARY AND INTERDISCIPLINARY STUDIES: D. Boyarin, *Intertextuality and the Reading of Midrash* (1990); M. Fishbane, *Biblical Myth and Rabbinic Mythmaking* (2003); A. Goshen-Gottstein, *The Sinner and the Amnesiac: The Rabbinic Invention of Elisha Ben Abuya and Eleazar Ben Arach* (2000); G.H. Hartman and S. Budick (eds.), *Midrash and Literature* (1986); G. Hasan-Rokem, *Web of Life: Folklore and Midrash in Rabbinic Literature*, tr. Batya Stein (2000); idem, *Tales of the Neighborhood: Jewish Narrative Dialogues in Late Antiquity* (2003); J. Kugel, in: *Midrash and Literature*, G. Hartman and S. Budick (eds.) (1986); idem, *In Potiphar's House: The Interpretive Life of Biblical Texts* (1990); idem, *The Bible as It Was* (1997); J. Levinson, "Literary Approaches to Midrash," in: C. Bakhos (ed.), *Current Trends in the Study of Midrash* (2006); idem, *The Untold Story – Art of the Expanded Biblical Narrative in Rabbinic Midrash* (Heb., 2005); H. Mack, *The Aggadic Midrash Literature* (1989); O. Meir, *Ha-Sippur ha-Darshani* (1987); D. Noy, "Motif Index of Talmudic-Midrashic Literature" (Doctoral diss., Indiana University. Bloomington, 1954); idem, *Mavo le-sifrut ammamit* (1966); J. Neusner, *Development of a Legend: Studies on the Traditions Concerning Yohanan Ben Zakkai* (*Studia Post-Biblica*, vol. 16) (1970); J. Rubenstein, *Talmudic Stories: Narrative Art, Composition, and Culture* (1999); idem. *The Culture of the Babylonian Talmud* (2003); R. Sarason, in: *Studies in Aggadah, Targum and Jewish Liturgy in Memory of Joseph Heinemann*, Ezra Fleischer and Jacob Petuchowski (eds.), (1981); A. Shinan, *Targum va-Aggadah Bo* (1992); D. Stern, in: *Prooftexts*, 1 (1981), 261–91; idem, *Parables in Midrash* (1991); idem, *Midrash and Theory: Ancient Jewish Exegesis and Contemporary Literary Studies* (1996); D. Stein, *Memra, Magyah, Mitos: Pirke de Rabbi Eliezer le-Or Meḥkar ha-Sifrut ha-Amamit* (2004). AGGADAH IN ILLUMINATED MANUSCRIPTS: Mayer, Art, nos. 1809–1901, C.O. Nordström, *The Duke of Alba's Castilian Bible* (1967), Gutmann, in: *Gesta*, 5 (1966), 39–44, H.G. Enelow, *Significance of the Agada* (1914), I. Heinemann, *Darkhei ha-Aggadah* (1954^{2}) L. Ginzberg, *On Jewish Law and Lore* (1955); S. Spiegel, in: L. Ginzberg, *Legends of the Bible* (1956), introduction, O. Camhy, in: *Judaism*, 8 (1959), 68–72, S.M. Lehrman, *World of the Midrash* (1961); G. Vermes, *Scripture and Tradition in Judaism* (1961), J. Neusner, *History and Torah* (1965), 17–29 (repr. from *Judaism*, 9 (1960), 47–54).

AGGADAT BERESHIT (Heb. אַגָּדַת בְּרֵאשִׁית), an *aggadic* Midrash to the Book of Genesis. In the Oxford manuscript (see below) the book is called *Seder Eliyahu Rabbah*, while in the Middle Ages it was cited under the names *Tanna devei Eliyahu* and *Ḥuppat Eliyahu*; the name *Aggadat Bereshit* first appearing in the first printed edition. *Aggadat Bereshit* is a homiletical Midrash constructed in a unique manner. It consists of 83 (or 84) sections in cycles of three, the first interpreting a verse from Genesis, the second a verse from the Prophets, and the third a verse from Psalms. The verse from Genesis is in general the beginning of the weekly scriptural reading according to the triennial cycle which was in vogue in Ereẓ Israel in early times. The verse from the Prophets is usually from the *haftarah* and that from Psalms also has a relevance to the portion of the Law and the *haftarah* (some scholars think it was taken from a chapter of Psalms read on that particular Sabbath). Both the beginning of the Midrash (which in its present state starts in Gen. 6:5) and its end (the last section of the Psalms) are missing. Each section has a proem of the classical type which begins: "This is what Scripture tells us," i.e., opening with a verse not of the portion expounded and finally connected with the verse at the beginning of the portion expounded. However, the introduction, like the Midrash proper, shows signs of relatively late composition. The sections on the Pentateuch are longer than those on the Prophets, and the sections on Psalms the shortest of all, consisting, in general, only of the introduction. The language of the Midrash is late mishnaic Hebrew; there are some Greek words. *Aggadat Bereshit* is a collection of homilies from different sources. The editor made use of early Midrashim of the *amoraim* and also of many Midrashim of the **Tanhuma-Yelammedenu* type. This factor – together with its Aramaic-free Hebrew, pseudographic sayings, signs of late style and terminology, and an explicit polemic against Christianity (27 and 31) – would appear to place its date of editing at about the tenth century. *Aggadat Bereshit* was first published at the end of the *Shetei Yadot* (Venice, 1618) of Menahem di *Lonzano. After this it was republished in Vilna, 1802, by *Abraham b. Elijah of Vilna, and frequently thereafter. In 1903 S. Buber collated the first printed edition with an Oxford manuscript and published a critical edition with introduction and notes.

BIBLIOGRAPHY: Zunz-Albeck, Derashot, 124, 394; J. Mann, *The Bible as Read and Preached in the Old Synagogue*, 1 (1940), passim.

[Moshe David Herr]

AGHLABIDS (known as **Banū al-Aghlab**), Arab Muslim dynasty that ruled Ifriqiyya (modern-day *Tunisia and eastern *Algeria) from 800 to 909. Its rulers were princes commonly referred to as *amīrs*. It was subject to the *Abbasid caliphs of Baghdad but was in fact independent. The capital city was *Kairouan (al-Qayrawān) in Tunisia. During the ninth century Kairouan civilization flourished, its capital becoming one of the largest Maghrebi commercial centers. The *amīrs* invested funds in public works to conserve and distribute water, contributing to the prosperity of their country. Their fleet was supreme in parts of the Mediterranean and their corsairs captured ships at sea. Captured persons and property were subsequently redeemed for profit. The Aghlabids also gained temporary control over Sicily, Malta, and Corsica.

The data on the Jews of this principality are scant. It is known, however, that the Jews of Kairouan began to expand and prosper under the Aghlabid *amīrs*. They fostered and preserved intimate and strong bonds with the Babylonian *geonim* and the Jewish communities of Palestine and Egypt. A medical school existed in Kairouan. One of its noted teachers was Isaac *Israeli, the physician to the last Aghlabid *amīr* Ziyādat Allah III.

BIBLIOGRAPHY: P.K. Hitti, *History of the Arabs* (1958); Nissim b. Jacob, *Ḥibbur Yafeh min ha-Yeshuʿah*, ed. H.Z. Hirschberg (1954); I.M. Lapidus, *A History of Islamic Societies* (2002).

[Michael M. Laskier (2nd ed.)]

AGHMATI, ZECHARIAH BEN JUDAH (late 12th and early 13th centuries), North African talmudist. He apparently came from Agmat in southern Morocco. His name has only recently become known, and there are hardly any data on his life and work. Aghmati wrote a comprehensive work, *Sefer ha-Ner*, on the *halakhot* of *Alfasi. He uses geonic material extensively and quotes statements of *Baruch b. Samuel of Aleppo, *Hananel, Isaac *Ibn Ghayyat and Joseph *Ibn Migash, for which *Sefer ha-Ner* is sometimes the sole source. The book also quotes from other early scholars, among them Ashkenazi luminaries, such as Rashi and *Gershom b. Judah. The variant versions of the Talmud quoted by Aghmati are of great importance. The author himself seldom introduces his own opinion. His commentaries on the tractates *Berakhot* (Jerusalem, 1958), *Bava Kamma, Bava Meẓia*, and *Bava Batra* (London, 1961, facsimile edition) have been published, while those on *Shabbat* and *Eruvin* are still in manuscript. His book was probably completed between 1188 and 1190.

BIBLIOGRAPHY: M.D. Ben-Shem (ed.), *Sefer ha-Ner li-Verakhot* (1958), introd.; J. Leveen (ed.), *Digest … compiled by Zechariah b. Judah Aghmati* (1961), introd.

[Israel Moses Ta-Shma]

AGMON (Bistritski), NATHAN (1896–1980), Israeli dramatist and publicist. He began his literary career while still in Russia, publishing articles of literary criticism in Hebrew journals. In 1920 he arrived in Palestine, and from 1922 until his retirement in 1952 worked in the central office of the Jewish National Fund in Jerusalem, directing its Youth and Information Departments. His early writings in Palestine described life in collective agricultural settlements. Among the first original Hebrew dramatists to be presented on the Palestinian stage, his first play *Yehudah Ish-Keriyyot* ("Judas Iscariot") was published in 1930. In 1931 he wrote *Shabbetai Ẓevi*, which was produced by the Ohel Theater in 1936. Messianism, which he considers a symbol of humanity's struggle to achieve a just society, is the central motif in his dramas, especially the two above-mentioned plays. He also published articles and books on South American Jewry and on Zionism. His collected plays appeared in 1960 in three volumes. In 1964 Agmon published a philosophical work, *Ḥazon Adam* ("Human Vision"); his autobiography, *Be-Sod ha-Mitos* ("Knowing the Secret of the Myth"), appeared in 1980.

BIBLIOGRAPHY: G. Yardeni, *Siḥot im Soferim* (1961), 83–92. **ADD. BIBLIOGRAPHY:** G. Shaked, *Ha-Sipporet ha-Ivrit*, 3 (1988), 70–76; T. Hess, *Shi'ur Komah shel Marvad Nashiyut ba-Koveẓ Kehilateynu u-va-Roman Yamim ve-Leylot me-et Natan Bistritski* (1995).

[Getzel Kressel]

AGMON, SHMUEL (1922–), Israeli mathematician. Born in Tel Aviv, Agmon is the son of writer Nathan *Agmon (Bistritski). He received his doctorate from the University of Paris in 1949. His work focused on the theory of partial differential equations of elliptic type and on spectral and scattering theory of Schrodinger operations. He was a member of the Israel Academy of Sciences and Humanities from 1964 and received the Rothschild Prize in mathematics in 1959 and the Israel Prize in exact sciences in 1991.

AGNON, SHMUEL YOSEF (Czaczkes, Samuel Josef; 1888–1970), Hebrew writer; Nobel Laureate in literature. One of the central figures in modern Hebrew fiction, his works deal with major contemporary spiritual concerns: the disintegration of traditional ways of life, the loss of faith, and the subsequent loss of identity. His many tales about pious Jews are an artistic attempt to recapture a waning tradition. He was born in Buczacz, Galicia, where his father, an erudite follower of the Ḥasidic *rebbe* of Chortkov, was a fur merchant. Rabbinic and Ḥasidic traditions as well as general European culture influenced the home. Agnon's education was mainly private and irregular. He studied the Talmud and the works of Maimonides with his father; read much of the literature of the Galician *maskilim;* and studied Ḥasidic literature in the synagogue of the Chortkov Ḥasidim. He learned German from Mendelssohn's translation of the Pentateuch (the *Biur*) as well as from a tutor and read books from his mother's small German library, where he also found German translations of Scandinavian writers. He began writing at the age of eight in Hebrew and in Yiddish. In 1903 he published his first work, a Yiddish poem on Joseph Della Reina and a rhymed "*haskamah*" (preface) in Hebrew to Ẓevi Judah Gelbard's *Minḥat Yehudah*. In 1904 he began to publish regularly, first poetry and then prose, in *Ha-Mizpeh*, edited in Cracow by S.M. Laser, who continually encouraged him. In 1906 and 1907, he also contributed several poems and stories in Yiddish, primarily to *Der Juedische Wecker*, which appeared in his own town. Up to his departure from Buczacz he published some 70 pieces in both languages – poems, stories, essays, addresses, etc., that were occasionally signed Czaczkes but more often appeared under a pseudonym. His most comprehensive Yiddish work of that period, *Toytn-Tants* (1911), attests to the development of his literary talent and to a definite affinity with German neo-romanticism. But once he left Buczacz, he no longer wrote in Yiddish.

When Agnon left for Ereẓ Israel, in 1908, he was already a well-known young author. His emigration removed him from *shtetl* life, which no longer answered his spiritual needs and placed him in the midst of a new and evolving creative Hebrew literary center. However, he was atypical of the pioneers of the Second Aliyah; those who espoused the "conquest of labor" considered him bourgeois, while the Russian Jews scorned him as a Galician. He supported himself by tutoring and occasional literary efforts. He also worked intermittently in a number of clerical positions and resided in both Jaffa and in Jerusalem. While he abandoned his religious practices during these years, he was not completely identified with the modernism of the new settlers. On the contrary, he was charmed by the old *yishuv* and was drawn more and more to Jerusalem, where the Jewish historical milieu nurtured his creative imagination. In "*Agunot*" ("Forsaken Wives"), his first story published in Palestine during the Jaffa period (*Ha-Omer,* Fall 1908), he first used the pseudonym "Agnon"; and in 1924 it became his official family name. Many other stories followed (appearing mostly in *Ha-Poel ha-Ẓa'ir*). Although most of his works from this period are unknown, those few that were later republished, such as "*Agunot,*" were radically reedited by Agnon. One of his stories, "*Ve-Hayah he-Akov le-Mishor,*" was republished separately by J.H. Brenner (1912) and became his first book. Like many of his youthful contemporaries, Agnon was drawn to Germany. Arriving in midsummer of 1912, he remained there until the fall of 1924. His presence in Germany during those years was a major influence on Zionist youth, who found in him a change from the accepted circle of Hebrew writers in Germany, who were contemptuous of Agnon and his style. During his first years in Germany he supported himself by tutoring and by editing for the *Juedischer Verlag* with Aaron Eliasberg. Finally he met the wealthy businessman S. *Schocken who became his admirer, supporter, and publisher. In Berlin and Leipzig he associated with Jewish scholars and Zionist officials. He read widely in German and French (in German translation) literature and expanded his knowledge of Judaica. He also began to acquire and collect valuable and rare Hebrew books. Some of his stories, in the German translation of M. Strauss, appeared in Martin Buber's journal, *Der Jude,* and spread his fame among German Jews. The most productive of Agnon's creative years in Germany were spent in Wiesbaden and Bad Homburg near Frankfurt. He was unburdened by the quest for livelihood: during the inflationary years he lived quite comfortably, as did other Hebrew writers of that day, due to the support of A. Stybel. In Homburg he was a member of a circle of Hebrew writers. He also began to prepare with M. Buber a collection of Ḥasidic stories and lore. However, this radiant period ended in 1924, when fire swept his home and destroyed most of his books and manuscripts, including *Bi-Ẓeror ha-Ḥayyim* ("In the Bond of Life," whose imminent publication by Stybel had already been announced), a long novel depicting the flow of modern Jewish history against an autobiographical background. The destruction by fire of his writings makes it difficult to assess the scope of his creativity in this crucial period. However, a scrutiny of the other published works of that time and of some published subsequently reveals several basic facts: (1) Most of the stories are set in Poland in the world of pious Jews (new versions of stories of the Jaffa-Jerusalem period appear, as do other distinctive works such as "*Bi-Ne'areinu u-vi-Zekeneinu,*" "*Ovadyah Ba'al Mum,*" and "*Bi-Demi Yameha*"). (2) In most stories of this period Agnon's characteristic style approximates that of the world depicted: the Hebrew of the pietistic books of the last centuries whose linguistic structure is influenced by Yiddish. (3) Because of the suspension of many Hebrew publishing ventures in Europe during World War I, Agnon published no Hebrew stories during the early war years, although some appeared at that time in German translation. (4) He had already acquired a circle of readers who eagerly read three collections of his stories: *Sippurei Ma'asiyyot* (1921), *Be-Sod Yesharim* (1921), and *Al Kappot ha-Manul* (1922).

In 1924, Agnon returned to Palestine and settled in Jerusalem. In the riots of 1929, his home in the Talpiyyot suburb was plundered and many books and rare manuscripts dealing with the history of the Jewish settlement in Palestine were destroyed.

The first edition of Agnon's collected works in four volumes (1931) included selected stories published until mid-1929, as well as the second version of *Hakhnasat Kallah* (*The Bridal Canopy,* 1937), which had been lengthened to a novel. This folk-epic was recognized as one of the cornerstones of modern Hebrew literature, and the entire collection established Agnon as one of its central figures. The impression of Agnon as a pietistic writer was enhanced by the collection of stories *Be-Shuvah va-Naḥat* (1935) and strengthened by two non-fiction collections: *Yamim Noraim* (1938; *Days of Awe,* 1948), an anthology of High Holiday traditions; and *Sefer, Sofer ve-Sippur* (1938), about books and writers. Even the novel *Sippur Pashut* (1935; *A Simple Story*, 1985), which is set at the close of the previous century and depicts the clash between the older and younger generations, did not openly convey to the readers the profound tension which underlies Agnon's "serenity." A cycle of five stories called *Sefer ha-Ma'asim* was published in 1932, followed a year later by *Pat Shelemah* (*A Whole Loaf,* 1956). Readers were astounded by the nightmarish environment of these short works of fiction which artistically articulated the confusion of the author standing on the threshold between the new world and the old. The eradication of boundaries between fantasy and reality, the inner monologue, and the perplexing environment exist also in "*Panim Aḥerot*"(1933), "*Afar Ereẓ Yisrael,*" and "*Ba-Ya'ar u-va-Ir.*" These stories were collected only in 1941 in *Ellu ve-Ellu.* In addition, in the 1930s three narratives appeared which subsequently became the nucleus of *Temol Shilshom* (*"Rabbi Geronim Yekum Purkan"* in 1931; *"Tehillato shel Yiẓḥak"* in 1934; *"Balak"* in 1935). In spite of this evidence of the darker side of Agnon, the critics and readers were not attuned to this new mode until the early 1940s. Agnon rose to a new level of artistic creativity in his book *Ore'aḥ Natah Lalun*, which was originally published in serial form in *Haaretz* (Oct. 18, 1938, to April 7, 1939) and then appeared in his collected works (1939; *A Guest for the Night*, 1968). In this novel an anonymous narrator visits his town in Galicia after an absence of many years and witnesses its desolation. Although the factual core of the story was Agnon's short visit to Buczacz in 1930, the novel mirrors the hopelessness and spiritual desolation of the Jewish world in that decade in Europe and in Palestine. A grotesquely nightmarish scene of the city is presented: its synagogues are empty; its people are shattered; and its society, generally, is moribund. Although Agnon was directly motivated to write this novel by the events of the 1930s, it is noteworthy that even in his youthful writings he envisioned his town as a "city of the dead." At times the narrative technique of *Ore'aḥ Natah Lalun* is similar to that of *Sefer ha-Ma'asim* where the despair is often recorded by shocking portrayals. Thus, at the onset of the 1940s, the readers learned to react not only to Agnon's story of the lives of the pious but also to a wide variety of subjects and narrative techniques. Critics such as G. Krojanker, B. *Kurzweil, and Dov *Sadan began to give Agnon the interpretation he merited. They demonstrated that, however indirectly, his works were concerned with the deep psychological and philosophical problems of the generation. His greatest novel, *Temol Shilshom*, made its appearance in 1945 (*Only Yesterday*, 2000). The setting and time of this work are in Palestine in the days of the Second Aliyah, but its spirit parallels the period in which it was written, the years of the Holocaust. The novel focuses upon an unsophisticated pioneer, who returns to the ways of his forebears, but after being bitten by a mad dog, dies a meaningless death. The complex situations and interlocking motifs of his novel, as well as its moral concern, marked a new peak in Hebrew fiction.

Agnon collected some of his stories in two volumes, *Samukh ve-Nireh* (1951) and *Ad Hennah* (1952); re-edited *Hakhnasat Kallah, Ore'aḥ Natah Lalun*, and *Temol Shilshom*; and, in 1953, published the second edition of his collected works in seven volumes (an eighth volume, *Ha-Esh ve-ha-Eẓim,* was published in 1962). However many stories were omitted, including *Shirah*, a novel set in the academic community in Jerusalem (see below). With the publication of this last edition, the scope of his writings could be evaluated for the first time: novels, folktales, and "existentialist" stories. Following the appearance of the 1953 edition, Agnon published about half a dozen new short works every year, mainly in the Israeli newspaper *Haaretz*, the majority of them dealing with Buczacz. As separate books he published *Attem Re'item*, a collection of rabbinic commentaries related to the revelation at Sinai (1959), and *Sifreihem shel Ẓaddikim*, tales of the Ba'al Shem Tov and his disciples (1961). The modern nightmarish theme is evidenced during these years, by the stories *"Ad Olam"* (1954; "Forevermore," 1961), *"Hadom ve-Kisse"* (1958), *"Ha-Neshikah ha-Rishonah"* (1963), and *"Le-Aḥar ha-Se'udah"* (1963). Agnon received many awards including the Israel Prize (in 1954 and 1958). The crowning honor was the Nobel Prize for literature (1966), the first granted to a Hebrew writer.

[Arnold J. Band]

Posthumous Publications and Works on Agnon

Since Agnon's death many volumes of his literary remains, prepared for publication by his daughter, Emunah Yaron, have appeared. These volumes include stories which appeared during Agnon's lifetime, but which were not included in editions of his collected writings.

Shirah (1971; *Shira*, 1989) is a novel about Manfred Herbst, a lecturer in Byzantine history at the Hebrew University in Jerusalem. Approaching middle age, and the father of two grown daughters, Herbst is torn between his affection and loyalty to his devoted wife, who has just borne him a third daughter, and his passion for the nurse Shirah. The novel unfolds in Jerusalem of the 1930s and 1940s.

Ir u-Melo'ah ("The City and the Fullness Thereof," 1973) is a collection of tales about Buczacz, Agnon's native city. The stories cover 600 years of life in the city and are, in effect, the history of Poland and its Jews.

Ba-Ḥanuto shel Mar Lublin ("In Mr. Lublin's Shop," 1974) is an account of Agnon's years in Leipzig during World War I. A rich gallery of personalities from all strata of the population, both Jewish and German, passes before our eyes.

Lifnim min ha-Ḥomah ("Within the City's Wall," 1975) comprises four major stories. The first, the title story, demonstrates in poetic style Agnon's deep attachment to Jerusalem; the second, *Kisui ha-Dam* ("The Blood Screen"), is replete with incidents that occur within and beyond the land of Israel; the third, *Hadom ve-Kisse* ("The Footstool and the Chair"), is a mythological account of the author's birth and his previous life; the last story in the volume, *Le-Aḥar ha-Se'udah* ("After the Feast"), in which Agnon describes his own departure from the world, represents the apex of his writings.

Me-Aẓmi el Aẓmi ("By Myself for Myself," 1976) is a collection of Agnon's articles, speeches, and sundry other matters, while *Pitḥei Devarim* ("Opening Remarks," 1977) is a volume of stories, most of which were previously unpublished. *Sefer, Sofer, ve-Sippur* ("The Book, the Writer, the Tale," 1978) is an expanded version of the 1938 edition with new material.

In 1977 the Hebrew University issued a volume of stories and poems of juvenilia written by Agnon in Yiddish, entitled *Shmuel Yosef Agnon, Yiddish Work.* It consists of stories and poems that appeared in various periodicals from 1903 to 1912, i.e., from when he was 15 years old until he settled in Ereẓ Israel, and it contains an extensive introductory chapter in Yiddish by Dov Sadan.

Korot Bateinu ("History of Our Families," 1979) contains two stories, one about Jewish family life in Galicia and the other tracing the history of Agnon's own family beginning with the Middle Ages, interweaving imagination and historical truth. *Esterlein Yekirati* ("Estherle My Dear," 1983) contains the correspondence between Agnon and his wife, Esther, in the years 1924–1931. *Sefer ha-Otiyyot* (*Agnon's Alef Bet*, 1998) is an abecedary in verse written in 1919 at the behest of the Culture Committee of the Zionist Organization and for some reason never published. The manuscript was a late discovery.

Takhrikh shel Sippurim ("A Shroud of Stories," 1984) contains stories published in periodicals in Agnon's lifetime as well as some found among his literary remains, mostly about the life of the Jews in Poland and Ereẓ Israel. Another two, about the Jews of Germany, were added for the 1989 printing: "*Gabriella*" and "*Leregel Iskav*" ("For Business Reasons").

Sippurei ha-Besht ("Tales of the Ba'al Shem Tov," 1987) was part of the Codex Ḥasidicum planned by Agnon and Buber when Agnon was still in Germany. It was ready for press in 1924 but was destroyed in the fire in Agnon's Bad Homburg home. The present volume was put together by Emuna Yaron and her husband from material in the literary remains.

S.Y. Agnon – S.Z. Schocken, Ḥillufei Iggerot 1916–1959 (1991) is the correspondence between Agnon and his publisher. *Attem Re'item* (*Present at Sinai*, 1994) adds new material to the 1959 edition. *Mi-Sod Ḥakhamim* ("From the Circles of the Wise," 2002) contains the correspondence of Agnon with Brenner, Y. *Lachower, Sadan, and Berl Katznelson.

Also appearing were two volumes of *Kovetz Agnon*, edited by Reuven Mirkin, Dan Laor, Rafael Weiser, and Emuna Yaron and containing, among other writings, unpublished chapters of *Shirah*, a 1909 story called "*Be'erah shel Miriam o Keta'im mi-Ḥayyei Enosh*" ("Miriam's Well, or Chapters from Human Life"), and chapters from *Sefer Ma'asim* not included in the original edition. In addition, there are letters to Martin Buber from the years 1909–24 and correspondence between Agnon and Hanokh *Yalon as well as essays on Agnon.

Dramatizations of Agnon's work have proliferated. Habimah presented *Hakhnasat Kallah* (*The Bridal Canopy*); the Cameri Theater performed *Ve-Hayah he-Akov le-Mishor* ("And the Crooked Shall Be Made Straight"); and the Khan Theater of Jerusalem staged *Ha-Rofe u-Gerushato* ("The Doctor and His Divorcee"), *Panim Aḥerot* ("Metamorphosis"), and *Bi-Demi Yameha* ("In the Prime of Life").

In 1980 Habimah Theater produced *Sippur Pashut* and Orna Porat's Youth and Children's Theater adapted five of Agnon's stories for the stage. *Shirah* and *Esterlein Yekirati* have also been put on stage, a number of stories have been adapted for the screen ("*Farnheim*," "*Ma'aseh ha-Oz*," etc.), and two films have been made about Agnon's life.

After Agnon's death the author's family donated his private archives to the Hebrew University. They include manuscripts and drafts of most of his works, his published writings in all existing editions, and translations of his works into numerous languages. The archives also contain everything that has been written about Agnon: books, essays, and articles as well as letters written by and to Agnon, and a collection of photographs and photocopies. The material is kept up-to-date and an annual evening of study of Agnon's work has been held. It also issued a book: *Anthology of Shai Agnon, Research and Documents on His Work* edited by Gershon Shaked and Raphael Weiser (1978). In 1982, the Jerusalem Municipality opened Agnon's Talpiyyot home to the public. The library was catalogued and researchers can consult the books. Various activities focusing on Agnon and his work are held in the house for schoolchildren and adults.

A complete bibliography of Agnon's works was published by Yohanan Arnon in 1971 as well as a comprehensive bibliography of books and articles on his works by Dr. Yonah David (1972). After Agnon's death, critical studies of his work gained new momentum, taking a new turn. Arnold Band, in his book *Nostalgia and Nightmare*, opened new vistas in analyzing Agnon's work by examining his stories in their various versions, although Dov Sadan previously used this method of analysis on some of the stories. The bibliography at the end of Band's book contributed greatly to the study of Agnon in that it was the first comprehensive bibliography of Agnon's work from its early beginning up to 1967. Agnon has been translated into 34 languages, including Persian, Chinese, and Mongolian, and written about critically in dozens of books and well over a thousand articles and essays. In 1996, the Institute for the Translation of Hebrew Literature issued a bibliography of his work in translation, including selected publications about Agnon and his writing.

[Emuna Yaron (2nd ed.)]

BIBLIOGRAPHY: A.J. Band, *Nostalgia and Nightmare* (1968), 497–521 (includes list of works, translations, and bibliography); B. Kurzweil, *Massot al Sippurav shel Shai Agnon* (1963); idem (ed.), *Yuval Shai* (1958); D. Sadan and E. Urbach (eds.), *Le-Agnon Shai* (1959); M. Tochner, *Pesher Agnon* (1968); Goell, Bibliography, index; Y. Elstein, *Iggulim ve-Yosher* (1970); D. Canaani, *Agnon be'al Peh* (1971); M.Y. Herzl, *Shai Olamot, Mekorot le-Agnon, Hakhnassat Kalah* (1973); H. Barzel, *Bein Agnon le-Kafka, Meḥkar Mashveh* (1972), *Sippurei ha-Ahavah shel Agnon* (1975), and Agnon, *Mivḥar Ma'amarim al Yeẓirato* (with introduction) (1982); G. Shaked, *Iyyunim be-Sippurei Agnon* (1973); R. Lee, *Masa el Rega ha-Ḥesed, Iyyunim be-Yeẓirato shel Agnon ve-Ḥ. Hazaz* (1978); D. Sadan, Al S.Y. Agnon, *Masot U-Ma'amarim* (1978); E. Aphek, *Ma'arakhot Milim, Iyyunim be-Signono shel S.Y. Agnon* (1979); A. Bar-Adon, *S.Y. Agnon u-Teḥiyyat ha-Lashon ha-Ivrit* (1977); M.Z. Kaddari, *S.Y. Agnon Rav Signon* (1980); Y. Mazor, *Ha-Dinamikah shel Motivim be-Yeẓirot S.Y. Agnon* (1979); *Yediot Genazim S.Y. Agnon z"l* (1970); *Yediot Genazim, S.Y. Agnon* (1981); H. Weiss, *Parshanut le-Ḥamishah mi-Sippurei S.Y. Agnon* (1974), *Agunot, Bein Galui le-Samui, Revadim be-Sippur ha-Ivri ha-Kaẓar* (1979), and *Agunot, Ido ve-Einam, Mekorot Mivnim Mashmauyot* (1981); B. Hochman, *The Fiction of S.Y. Agnon* (1970); H. Fisch, *S.Y. Agnon* (1975). **ADD. BIBLIOGRAPHY:** D. Aberbach, *At the Handles of the Lock: Themes in the Fiction of S.J. Agnon* (1984); B. Arpali, *Rav-Roman: Ḥamishah Ma'amarim al Temol Shilshom* (1988); G. Shaked, *Shmuel Yosef Agnon: A Revolutionary Traditionalist* (1989); A. Hoffman, *Between Exile and Return, S.Y. Agnon and the Drama of Writing* (1993); N. Ben-Dov, *Agnon's Art of Indirection: Uncovering Latent Content in the Fiction of S.Y. Agnon* (1993); D. Schreibaum, *Pesher ha-Ḥalomot bi-Yeẓirato shel Sh. Y. Agnon* (1993); Y. Friedlander, *Al Ve-Haya he-Akov le-Mishor* (1993); H. Barzel and H. Weiss (eds.), *Ḥikrei Agnon:*

Iyyunim u-Meḥkarim bi-Yeẓirat Agnon (1994); D. Laor, *Shai Agnon: Hebetim Ḥadashim* (1995); A. Holz, *Marot u-Mekomot: Hakhnasat Kalah* (1995); W. Bargad, *From Agnon to Oz: Studies in Modern Hebrew Literature* (1996); N. Ben-Dov, *Ahavot lo Me'usharot: Tiskul Eroti, Omanut u-Mavet bi-Yeẓirat Agnon* (1997); D. Laor, *Ḥayyei Agnon* (1998); S. Katz, *The Centrifugal Novel: S.Y. Agnon's Poetics of Composition* (1999); A. Oz, *The Silence of Heaven: Agnon's Fear of God* (2000); Sh. Werses, *Shai Agnon ki-Feshuto* (2000); M. Shaked, *Ha-Kemet she-be-Or ha-Raki'a: Kishrei Kesharim bi-Yeẓirat Agnon* (2000); Sh. M. Green, *Not a Simple Story: Love and Politics in a Modern Hebrew Novel* (2001); D.M. Harduf, *Mikhlol ha-Shemot be-Kitvei Shmuel Yosef Agnon* (2002); R. Katsman, *The Time of Cruel Miracles: Mythopoesis in Dostoevsky and Agnon* (2002). **WEBSITE:** www.ithl.org.il.

°**AGOBARD** (779–840), archbishop of Lyons from 814. Agobard, who was born in Spain, was canonized by the Catholic Church. His metropolitan province included some of the most important Jewish settlements in Western Europe. A prolific writer and active church leader, he sharply opposed the Jews, both in his deeds and in his writings, out of religious, political, and social motives. Six of Agobard's pamphlets are devoted to the Jewish question: (1) *Epistula de baptizandis Hebraeis* ("On the Baptism [of the children] of Jews"); (2) *De baptismo judaicorum mancipiorum* ("On the Baptism of Jewish-owned Slaves"); (3) *Contra praeceptum impium de baptismo judaicorum mancipiorum* ("Against an Impious Precept Concerning the Baptism of Jewish-owned Slaves"); (4) *De insolentia Judaeorum* ("On the Insolence of the Jews"); (5) *De judaicis superstitionibus* ("On the Superstitions of the Jews"); (6) De *eavendo convictu et societate judaica* ("On the Necessity of Avoiding Association with Jews"). His writings are of interest not only as the earliest outspoken anti-Jewish document of the Carolingian period, but even more because of the comprehensive nature of his attacks on the various aspects of Jewish life. In 820 Agobard attempted to convert by force Jewish children in Lyons as well as in Chalon, Macon, and Vienne. From his letter to Emperor Louis the Pious in justification of his efforts, it appears that the imperial authorities had previously protected Jews against this design. The problem of the religious adherence of pagan slaves owned by Jewish merchants was raised by Agobard. He complained that the way to the Christian faith was closed to them because, in contrast to the principles of canon law regarding Christian slaves, the church was not given jurisdiction over pagan slaves. His attempt to exert ecclesiastical influence in such cases, however, was frustrated by the intervention of the *missi dominici* (plenipotentiary emissaries of the emperor). Agobard also attempted to preach a trade boycott of staples of wine and meat brought to market by Jewish landowners. His writings contain information about the influence that Jewish preachers had over some Christians. To counterbalance intellectual sympathy with the religious activities of the synagogue, Agobard took up the theme of Jewish superstition as a topic of controversy. He maintained that the Jews were falsifying their own tradition by mythological interpretations of the Bible and urged the severance of existing social contacts between Christians and Jews. His pupil Amulo continued his anti-Jewish policy and propaganda.

BIBLIOGRAPHY: B. Blumenkranz, *Les auteurs chrétiens latins du moyen âge sur les Juifs et le Judaïsme* (1963), 152–70 (full bibliographical data in notes); A. Bressolles, *Saint Agobard, évêque de Lyon* (1949); H. Reuter, *Geschichte der religioesen Aufklaerung im Mittelalter* (1875), 24–41; A. Kleinclaus, *L'Empire Carolingien* (1902), 268–76; J.A. Cabaniss, *Agobard of Lyons* (1953).

AGORANOMOS, inspector of market transactions in Greek cities. This office was imported into Ereẓ Israel during the Hellenistic period and existed during the whole Roman period. The *agoranomos* supervised the making of weights and measures, the quality of goods and the transactions between buyers and sellers. The sources give no indication as to whether he regulated matters between employee and employer, as was the case in Hellenistic cities. Several inscribed lead and stone weights (from Maresha, Scythopolis, Ashdod, Tiberias, Gaza, and Jerusalem), as well as a standard of measures for liquids (from Maresha), are the material evidence of the responsibility of this office in regard to weights and measures during the Hellenistic, Herodian, and Roman periods. In Jerusalem, the controversy between Onias, the high priest, and Simeon in regard to the office of the *agoranomia* was one of the causes of the civil war in the early 70s of the second century B.C.E. (II Macc. 3:4ff.). This episode may refer to the responsibility of the *agoranomos* levying the taxes of the Temple. The authority to appoint the *agoranomos* was apparently vested in the high priest, and later in the king: the known weights of the Herodian period are dated according to the regnal years of Herod the Great, Herod Antipas, Agrippas I, and Agrippas II. According to Josephus the tetrarch Herod Antipas appointed Agrippa I as *agoranomos* of Tiberias before he was appointed king by Caius Caligula in order to provide him with an income (Ant., 18:149). Josephus also refers to the *agora* in Jerusalem, where the *agoranomos* probably sat (Ant., 14:335; Wars, 1:251). There are several rabbinic sources that provide evidence about the office of the *agoranomos*. However, the word was variously altered: *agronimon, agardemis/agardemin, hagronimos, igranamin,* and so on. Interestingly, although the Old Testament refers to the obligation of using accurate weights and measures, nothing is known about how this law was enforced, or about the persons responsible for it, before the Hellenistic period. In Jerusalem, before 70 C.E., the holder of this office had authority only over measures, but in Babylon he could also fix the prices of commodities (Tosef., BM 6:14; BB 89a; TJ, *ibid.* 5:11). In Babylon the appointment of this official in the cities, where commerce was concentrated in Jewish hands, was a function of the exilarch. For some time Rav filled this role. The *agoranomos* had authority to inspect merchandise such as wine or bread in order to evaluate its quality. When the *agoranomos* appeared in the marketplace, merchants would sometimes hide and the shopkeepers would lock their doors for fear of punishment. The importance of the *agoranomos* is attested by a passage (Lev. R. 1:8) which notes that a king, on visiting a province, would first discuss matters with the *agoranomos*. The name of the office seems to have been translated from the third century C.E. on as *ba'al ha-shuk*, and also assimilated with the office of *logistes* (accountant), itself translated as *khashban*. Other offices related to the management of the supply on the market of Greek cities are evidenced in rabbinic sources: the *astynome*, a parallel to the *agoranome* (TJ, Ma'aser Sheni 5:2, *istononsin*), and the *sitones*, supplying the grain (*ibid.* 4:1, *khatonaya/sitonaya*).

BIBLIOGRAPHY: Krauss, in: Tal Arch, 2 (1911) 372ff. **ADD. BIBLIOGRAPHY:** G. Finkielsztejn, "Administration du Levant sous les Séleucides. Remarques préliminaires," in: M. Sartre, *La Syrie hellénistique, Topoi Suppl.*, 4, (2003), 465–84; D. Sperber, in: ZDMG, 127 (1977), 227–43; idem, "On the Office of the *Agoranomos* in Roman Palestine," in: *Zeitschrift der Deutschen Morgenlandischen Gesellschaft*, 127 (1977), 227–43.

[Menahem Stern / Gérald Finkielsztejn (2nd ed.)]

AGRAMUNT, town in northeast Spain, belonging to the former county of Urgel. Jews living in Agramunt in the 13th century were liable to the same fiscal duties as the Christian townspeople but were also obliged to pay taxes to the count of Urgel and the king of Aragon. In 1272 Solomon b. Abraham *Adret was appointed arbitrator of a disagreement between the Agramunt and *Lérida communities. The infant Alfonso received permission to settle 40 Jewish families in Agramunt in 1316. Agramunt was a cultural center. Ezra b. Solomon b. Gatiño (see *Gatigno) completed his glosses on Abraham *Ibn Ezra's biblical commentary there in 1372. In the early 15th century Solomon *Bonafed corresponded with friends in Agramunt. Shealtiel Isaac Bonafos practiced as a physician there toward the end of the 1420s. A tombstone with a Hebrew inscription, probably of the 13th century, is preserved in Agramunt. In the 1980s one of the streets traditionally known as the medieval Jewish quarter was renamed carrer del Call.

BIBLIOGRAPHY: Regné, Cat, no. 550; *Colección de documentos inéditos del archivo general de la Corona de Aragón*, vol. 10, p. 276, Neubauer, Cat, nos. 230, 232, 1426, 1984 A, 38; Baer, Urkunden, 1 (1929), 148, 861f., 1070; Cantera-Millás, Inscripciones, 280–3, Piles Ros, in: *Sefarad*, 10 (1950), 179, Millás, *ibid.*, 14 (1954), 387–8.

AGRANAT, SHIMON (1906–1992), third president of the Supreme Court of Israel. Agranat, who was born in Louisville, Kentucky, went to Palestine in 1930, and settled in Haifa, where he entered private law practice. He was appointed a magistrate in 1940 and president of the Haifa District Court in 1948. In 1950 Agranat was appointed justice of the Supreme Court, becoming its deputy president in 1960 and president in 1965, retiring from the position in 1976. From 1954 until 1960 he was visiting professor of criminal law at the Hebrew University in Jerusalem, and, from 1960 to 1966, president of the court of the World Zionist Organization. He wrote *Dinei Oneshin* ("Penal Law," 1960). Agranat was awarded the Israel Prize in 1968. In November 1973 he was appointed chairman of a commission (named the Agranat Commision) to investigate and report on the civil and military aspects of the *Yom Kippur War. Its findings led to the resignation of Chief of Staff David *Elazar, and though it exonerated government leaders for the country's lack of preparedness, Prime Minister Golda *Meir subsequently resigned as well.

BIBLIOGRAPHY: Tidhar, 14 (1965), 4534.

[Edwin Samuel, Second Viscount Samuel]

AGRARIAN LEAGUE (in German "**Bund der Landwirte**"), extreme conservative German organization for the defense of agrarian interests, formed in 1893. Its membership included most of the Protestant farmers and farm laborers in the period of the German *Kaiserreich*. Ideologically, the League constituted a bridge between the tenets of Christian German nationalism ("Das Christliche Deutschtum") and romantic and racialist tendencies. It was outspokenly antisemitic, although in a religious rather than a racialist sense. This did not prevent it from cooperating with the racialist antisemites of the Berlin Movement (Berliner Bewegung, see *Antisemitism). Non-Christians were explicitly excluded from the League by its program. The League waged a campaign against what it considered the three enemies of the "true Germany: the Liberals, the Social Democrats, and the Jews." In 1921, the Agrarian League was united with other agrarian associations in the Reichslandbund, which took part in the "national opposition" against the Weimar Republic. From 1931 on, the Reichslandbund supported Hitler's National Socialist Party.

BIBLIOGRAPHY: H.-P. Pulzer, *The Rise of Political Anti-Semitism in Germany and Austria* (1988²); H.-P. Mueller, in: *Zeitschrift fuer wuerttembergische Landesgeschichte*, 53 (1994), 263–300; H.-U. Wehler, in: *Deutsche Gesellschaftsgeschichte*, 4 (2003), 91–93, 382–84.

[Marcus Pyka (2nd ed.)]

AGRAT BAT MAHALATH, "Queen of the Demons" in talmudic legend. It was taught that "a person should not go out alone at night, on Wednesdays and Sabbaths, because Agrat bat Mahalath and 180,000 destroying angels go forth, and each has permission to wreak destruction independently." Ḥanina b. Dosa limited her power to these nights; Abbaye further reduced it (Pes. 112b). Another authority states that the following sentence, whispered repeatedly, is effective against witchcraft: "Agrat bat Mahalath came and caused the death, by arrows, of [two other female demons,] Asya and Belusia" (Pes. 111a; see *Ein Ya'akov* version). According to *Numbers Rabbah* 12:3: "Thou shalt not be afraid of the terror by night" (Ps. 91:5), refers to Agrat bat Mahalath and her chariot. Some scholars hold that Agrat bat Mahalath is identical with *Lilith. The view that the name "Agrat" is derived from the Persian "A(n)gra," meaning enemy or demon, and Mahalath from the root *mḥl* (מחל; "dance") meaning therefore "the dancing witch," has been shown to be without foundation. The kabbalists identify Mahalath with the daughter of Ishmael (Gen. 28:9), who gave birth to demons and evil spirits. The midrashic source for this is now lost (cf. Maharsha Pes. 112b).

For recent views of the meaning of the name "Agrat," see Sokoloff (*Dictionary of Jewish Babylonian Aramaic*), pp. 110a and 233b. The name also occurs in Jewish magic amulets; see Shaked and Naveh, pp. 78–81. For Agrat bat Mahalath in the Zohar, see Margaliot, p. 205.

BIBLIOGRAPHY: A. Kohut, *Ueber die juedische Angelologie und Daemonologie* (1866), 88; Ginzberg, Legends, 5 (1955), 39; *He-Arukh ha-Shalem* (1937), s.v. **ADD. BIBLIOGRAPHY:** J. Naveh and S. Shaked, *Amulets and Magic Bowls* (1987^2); R. Margaliot, *Malakhei Elyon* (1988).

[Israel Moses Ta-Shma / Stephen Wald (2nd ed.)]

AGREST, DIANA (1945–), architect. Agrest was born in Buenos Aires and received her degree in architecture from the University of Buenos Aires in 1967. She studied in France with Roland Barthes, known for his work in semiotics. Agrest and Mario *Gandelsonas, her husband, together designed a trio of apartment houses in Buenos Aires (1977) that responded to modern tradition but also explored issues such as scale, typology, and material within the classical traditions and contemporary conditions within the city. Agrest came to New York in 1971, where she became a fellow of the Institute of Architecture and Urban Studies (1972–84). She taught at Cooper Union for the Advancement of Science and Architecture, New York, where she was an adjunct professor from 1976, and at Columbia University. She was a worldwide lecturer and also taught at Princeton and Yale universities. Her theoretical ideas are expressed in a wide variety of publications such as *Skyline* and *Oppositions*. Her books include: *Architecture from Without, Theoretical Framing for a Critical Practice* (1991), and *The Sex of Architecture* (1996). These volumes explore the symbolic performance of architecture in relation to the urban condition, the formal and ideological development of building types, the relationship between architecture and other visual discourses, including film, and, most uniquely, the position of gender and body in Western architecture. In 1980 she went into partnership with Mario Gandelsonas to form the firm A & G Development Consultants, Inc. The firm became a leader in a field which refines late modernism with semiotics and Freudian theories. A & G also designed office and apartment interiors, including furniture. A Park Avenue apartment interior (c. 1990) used materials such as pink marble, granite, and exotic woods combined in a geometric severe design. The firm built an unusual house, *Villa Amore*, in Sagaponack, Long Island, New York. It is made up of a cluster of buildings designed to reflect farmland that is fast becoming tracts for housing. The 8,000-sq. ft. home, completed in 1991, built partly on stilts, connects by walkways to other components. The master bath is a glass cylinder and there is a waterfall and a pool. In 2000, the firm completed the Melrose Community Center in a low-income neighborhood in the Bronx, New York. It was designed to accommodate the 3,000 youngsters who live in neighboring housing projects. The main low building is oval-shaped and the exterior is silver and red. These colors continue in the interior of the building. The 14,000-sq.ft. building took six years to complete and contains a full-size basketball court, a dark room, a restaurant-style kitchen, and a computer lab.

BIBLIOGRAPHY: D. Agrest, S. Allen, and S. Ostrow, *Architecture, Technique and Representation (Critical Voices in Art, Theory, and Culture)* (2000).

[Betty R. Rubenstein (2nd ed.)]

AGRICULTURAL LAND-MANAGEMENT METHODS AND IMPLEMENTS IN ANCIENT EREẒ ISRAEL. Ereẓ Israel is a small country with a topographically fragmented territory, each geographical region having a distinctive character of its own. These regions include: the coastal plain, the lowlands, the hilly country, the inland valleys, the north-south rift valley, and the arid and desert areas. The whole of the country, excluding the desert regions, has an area of a little over 10,000 sq. miles (26,000 sq. km.) and it has been estimated that of this only 2,500 sq. miles (6,544 sq. km.) are capable of cultivation. The country's semi-tropical climate, with a hot and dry season (between April and October) and a cold season with an unpredictable rainfall (between November and March), its varying altitudes, terrain, and soils, all imposed limitations on the type of land management which could be undertaken in the different parts of the country. There were very few springs of water, so dry farming was practiced in most parts. Agriculture in semi-arid regions, for instance the Negev, depended entirely on run-off irrigation. As a result, certain regions were suited for the cultivation of grain crops, others for fruits and vegetables, and some for animal husbandry. The writer of Deuteronomy was under no illusion regarding the restricted agricultural potential of the land. Speaking to the People of Israel before the entrance to Canaan, Moses said: "For the land, whither thou goest in to possess it, is not as the Land of Egypt, from whence ye came out, where thou sowest thy seed, and wateredst it with thy foot, as a garden of herbs. But the land, whither ye go to possess it, is a land of hills and valleys, and drinketh of the rain of heaven" (Deut. 11:10–11).

While the geographical fragmentation of the country would seem to encourage political and cultural regionalism, the diversity of the economic pursuits within the country resulted inevitably in heightened commercial interaction between people from one part of the country and the other, rather than isolationism. During the Bronze and Iron ages, more than 50 percent of the population in Ereẓ Israel were agriculturalists living in the countryside. The rest lived in towns or small cities and dealt primarily with administrative and commercial and industrial activities. Almost all farmers lived in small villages or hamlets, since the isolated farmstead was not known until the eighth century B.C.E. In the vicinity of these settlements they established fields and grew their crops and orchards. Numerous agricultural land-management techniques and implements were used over the millennia. By the Byzantine period (sixth to seventh centuries C.E.) crop yields appear to have reached levels that have only been approached in modern times.

Topographical

In ancient times the rural countryside was divided into vineyards and olive groves, arable fields, orchard plantations, vegetable gardens, and areas of public land given over to pasture and industrial activities (e.g., lime and charcoal burning, and stone quarrying). Topographically, the vineyards and olive groves were more suited to sloping ground or to the highlands. Vines are unable to grow with ease above 2750 ft. (900 m.) above sea level. Olives are also said to be difficult to grow above 2450 ft. (800 m.) or below 1225 ft. (400 m.). However, olive presses have been found on Mount Hermon at sites with elevations up to 3,300 ft. (1000 m), as at Kafr Dura. Olive trees could even be grown in areas with an annual rainfall of only c. 200–300 mm., as in northern Africa. Grain was best adapted to the plains, the broad valleys, and some of the internal valleys. Vegetables and certain types of fruit trees were grown in areas with access to permanent sources of water, springs, wells, or cisterns.

The location of many fields reflect traditional answers to the problems of the natural environment. Hence, field boundary walls were established along the same lines as those built thousands of years earlier, simply because they were the most topographically convenient. North-facing slopes were particularly favored for the establishment of new fields and this is because they were less exposed to the sun and their soils were able to retain moisture for longer. The size and shape of fields was usually affected by the steepness of the ground, with smaller and narrower fields on extremely steep slopes. The appearance of the field could also be dictated by the rockiness of the terrain. In Samaria and in the Modi'in foothills, for example, vines and olive trees were cultivated in "boxlike" pockets of deep soil scattered in certain areas of rocky outcrops. Whether or not the field was used for arable purposes or for fruit trees would very much depend on the type of soil available, the rockiness of the ground, aspect, drainage, and so forth. The position of natural sources of water used for irrigation, whether a spring or well, would have an effect on the location, shape and function of nearby fields.

Land Management

Agricultural fields and their crops are mentioned in a number of ancient written sources, principally the Bible and the early Jewish writings from the Roman period. Information about fields may also be found in some of the Classical sources, but these are usually not directly relevant to Ereẓ Israel. A smaller amount of information may also be derived from ancient inscriptions and various other epigraphic materials.

The Bible contains a wealth of information about agricultural practices and the landscapes of the country during the Iron Age II period, although some of the passages may contain strands of information relating to earlier periods. Each town and village had its own surrounding territory of fields and common land. Most of the agricultural land was in private ownership and the family inheritance was referred to as the *naḥalah* or *aḥuzah*. Royal estates also existed and *oẓarot* ("storehouses") were built in the fields (I Chron. 27:25). Landmarks were set up between the various plots of land. The general term for cultivated land was *sadeh* (Lev. 27:16). The word was used to designate cultivated pieces of land next to the towns as well as open areas used for pasturage. The area of land which could be plowed with a pair or team of oxen during the course of a single day was referred to as the *ẓemed sadeh* (I Kings 19:19). A *ma'anah* was half of that area (I Sam. 14:4). The *kerem* referred to vineyards and olive groves (*kerem zayit*, Judg. 15:5). Mixed fruit trees were grown in the *gan* or *ginnah*, usually next to the houses (Song 5:1; 6:2; 14:12), or in the *pardes* (Song 14:13). Plantations of fruit trees (the *mattah*) were grown further afield and were sometimes irrigated (Ezek. 31:4).

Isaiah 5:1–8 has a description of terraced fields being prepared for a vineyard: the vegetation was uprooted (*'zq*), stones were cleared (*sql*) and then stone fences and an observation tower were built: "My well-beloved hath a vineyard in a very fruitful hill. And he fenced it, and gathered out the stones thereof, and planted it with the choicest vine, and built a tower in the midst of it, and also made a winepress therein: and he looked that it should bring forth grapes…" (Isa. 5:1–2). A subsequent verse (5:5) implies that the stone fence (*gader*) surrounding the terraced unit was surmounted by a thorny hedge. This was used to protect the grapes from animals and also from people walking along the *mishol ha-keramim*, the "path between the vineyards" (Num. 22:24). Some of the terraced slopes were not plowed but dug with hoes (Isa. 12:11). The heaps of stone visible in the terraced areas are referred to in Hosea 12:11 as the *gallim* ("heaps") "in the furrows of the fields" and in Micah 1:6 as the *ai* ("pile") in the field.

It has been suggested that one of the terms used in the Bible for terraces (especially for vineyards but also for orchards) is *sadmot* (II Kings 23:4; Jer. 31:40; Deut. 32:32; Isa. 16:8). Hence, Habakkuk 3:17 should perhaps now be read as follows: "The fig tree does not blossom/ There is no produce on the vines/ The yield of the olive fails/ The *shadmot* ("terraces") do not produce food." The *shdmt* are also mentioned in two Late Bronze Age Ugaritic texts. The first, CTA 23: 8–11, is rendered: "Let them fell him [the god Mot] on the terrace like a vine." The second, CTA 2.1.43, is a damaged text and the context is not as clear. Another suggestion that has been made is that *gbi* (Jer. 39:10; 52:16) was an alternative word for "terrace" and that *yogevim* referred to the workers/owners of irrigated terraces. This seems unlikely and the reference is probably to the vats of winepresses located in vineyards (cf. King 1993, 159). Additional references to terraces in the Bible include the *meromei sadeh* mentioned in the premonarchic Song of Deborah (Judg. 5:18) and the *sadeh teromot* in David's Elegy for Saul and Jonathan (II Sam. 1:21), both of which seem to refer to "built fields" on hillslopes. Terraces are more commonly referred to as *madregot*, and in Ezekiel 38:20 it is written: "…and the mountains shall be thrown down, and the *madregot* ('terraces') shall fall, and every wall shall fall to the ground." (cf. sing. *madregah* mentioned in Song of Songs 2:14).

The surfaces of fields were fertilized with manure, household rubbish, and ashes. Strict laws existed about fallowing land on the seventh year (Ex. 23:11). Roads are mentioned passing next to vineyards and fields of wheat (Deut. 19:14; Num. 22:30). Fields were sometimes expropriated and given by the ruler as presents to his supporters (I Sam. 8:14; 22:7). The process of buying a field was described in Jeremiah 32:44: "Men shall buy fields for money and subscribe evidences, and seal them, and take witnesses in the land of Benjamin, and in the places about Jerusalem…" Recent archaeological evidence indicates that during the Iron II period, specifically from the eighth century B.C.E., there was an unprecedented expansion of agricultural territory with extensive terracing in the highlands. Terracing later spread into the Negev and Judean Deserts. Similarly, various biblical passages indicate a hunger for land during the course of the Divided Monarchy with the break-up of family inheritances and the creation of large estates owned by rich landlords. These landlords were cursed in Isaiah 5:8, where it is said that "woe unto them that join house to house, that lay field (*sadeh*) to field, till there be no place (left)…." Micah 2:2 spoke out against those who "…covet fields, and take them by violence…."

Fields were frequently mentioned in early Jewish sources from the Roman period. Fields were of different sizes, from the small plot known as the *beit roba* (approximately 336 sq. ft. 32 sq. m.) to the *bet se'ah* which had an area of 940 sq. yds. (784 sq. m.). The agricultural holding, the *bet kor,* was about 23.5 dunam in size, but most peasants probably had holdings of a much greater size than this. Boundaries for fields were sometimes indicated by a road, a path, a *wadi* – bed, an expanse of water, or even a water channel (Pe'ah 2:1–3). Much information is provided in these sources about the surface treatment of fields (plowing, manuring, and fallowing) and their yields. The depth of plowing achieved during this period was mentioned in *Bava Kamma* (2:5) as 3 *tephaḥim* (about 11 in., or 27 cm.) which is far greater than the maximum depth of 8 in. (20 cm.) known from recent traditional farming. This indicates that either a heavier form of plow was used or that the line of the furrows was plowed twice over to achieve the required depth. An area plowed during one day with a yoke of animals was known as *bet hafarash.* Fields with different types of soils were known by different names, for example *sadeh madrin* and *sadeh kaskasin.* Fields were even established on the summit of hills where the soil was so thin that "the oxen cannot pass over with the plow" and they had to be cultivated with mattocks (Pe'ah 2:2). The yield of a field was frequently estimated while the crop was still standing. The land of an orchard could belong to one person and the trees to another (see Pe'ah 3:4), a practice which still existed at the beginning of the 20th century. A distinction was made between fields used for dry-farming (*bet ba'al*) and for irrigation (*bet selaḥin*).

There were two kinds of gardens in Ereẓ Israel during antiquity: the horticultural garden and the decorative garden. There is no evidence that a combination of the two ever existed. Vegetable gardens were usually located near a source of water, a spring or a cistern. Important archaeological evidence for irrigated garden plots has come to light during the investigation of Byzantine monasteries in the Judean Desert and elsewhere. Decorative gardens and groves of trees probably existed adjacent to temples and palaces from very early times, but direct archaeological evidence is still lacking. For the later periods, remains of decorative gardens have been discovered at the Herodian palace complex at Jericho. Plants and bushes were planted in ceramic pots with holes in their sides. Similar pots were found in the first-century gardens at Pompeii and in the second-century gardens at Hadrian's villa at Tivoli. Planting pots with holes in their sides are mentioned in Demai 5:10 and in connection with a vineyard in Kilayim 7:8. Cucumbers are said to have been grown in planting pots made of cattle-dung and unfired clay. The latter also had round holes in their sides, the size of which is debated in Ukẓin 2:9–10, "How great should be the hole?" the answer being, "such that a small root can come out."

Very few ancient epigraphic finds have been made concerning agricultural land management in Ereẓ Israel. Most of the inscriptions and documents which have been found deal with matters of economic administration and only very indirectly with work in agricultural fields. However, some evidence does exist and a number of examples will be given. The Gezer calendar is probably one of the earliest and most interesting of the documents preserved relating to agricultural activities. It lists information about the activities which needed to be undertaken at different points during the agricultural year. The text was clearly written by an inexperienced hand, perhaps by an apprentice scribe, and can be dated to the end of the 10th century B.C.E. Information on fields exist in a number of other Iron Age inscriptions. For example, the Tel Siran inscription from Jordan, dated to c. 600 B.C.E. which mentions a vineyard (*krm*) and gardens (*gnt*).

A larger amount of material exists for the Roman and Byzantine periods. Interesting information on agricultural plots in the lower Dead Sea region has emerged from the Babatha archive, deposited in c. 132 C.E. in a cave in the Judean Desert. The largest of the plots owned by Babatha measured 20 *bet seahs* or 12.5 dunam. One of the Greek papyri (BB 21) deals with the sale of a date crop and indicates the names of three orchards in the area of Maoza from which the dates came: the Pherora orchard, the Nikarkos orchard, and the Molkhaios orchard. Another document (BB 16) is the land registration for four other groves of palm trees owned by Babatha at Maoza. Two of them are described as extending down towards the Dead Sea. For each grove an identifying name was given, the size of the grove, the taxes paid on it and the names of lands or features abutting the groves.

An important batch of non-literary papyri dating from the sixth and seventh centuries C.E. came to light during the Colt expedition to Auja Hafir (Nessana) in the central Negev.

They include a vast amount of information on the agricultural lands belonging to the settlement, on sown land, vineyards, gardens, reservoirs, water channels, rights to water, and data on crops of wheat, barley, *aracus*, olives, and dates.

Terracing

Very little is known about the earliest forms of agricultural terracing in the highlands of Ereẓ Israel. It seems reasonable to assume that the technology of creating flat areas on hillsides by building walls and leveling fills was invented by various rural groups acting in cooperation at a local level, in different parts of the Levant and at different times. Hence, various centers of origin for terrace construction may have existed, with Ereẓ Israel being one of them. Incipient forms of terracing, such as soil held in place by logs of wood, by rows of wooden stakes, or piled rocks, would be very difficult to detect in the archaeological record. It was probably recognized early on that obstructions placed across a stream channel would eventually help towards stopping the movement of eroded soils and would induce a process of alluviation. Early slope terracing may have taken place initially in the lower parts of hills with newer terraces later being built further up the slopes. Another suggestion which has been made is that the natural steplike appearance of many of the slopes in the highlands, with thin layers of chalky marl interposed between limestone or dolomite strata, may have prompted man's first attempts at terracing. However, no evidence supports the assumption made by some investigators that the earliest terraces with stone walls must have been crudely executed, low in height, and built on relatively slight slopes. Indeed, the earliest terrace found at Sataf, which is of Early Bronze Age date (late fourth millennium B.C.E.), was relatively well constructed and was built on a very steep slope. It has also been suggested that the origins of terracing should be sought in the marginal semi-arid regions of the Near East. The suggestion is that the "channel-bottom, weir terrace" type was possibly the earliest form of terrace. However, terracing in the Negev and in the Judean Desert cannot be shown to be older than the Iron Age II (seventh century B.C.E.), even though flood farming itself existed in the Negev from as early as the Chalcolithic or Early Bronze Age. Studies of New World terracing have also shown that the earliest terraced sites must have been in the *less* arid areas first.

Another important point which needs to be taken into account is that the idea of creating leveled areas on hillslopes for agricultural purposes is not dissimilar from the basic technology of architectural terracing or slope stabilization. At settlement sites in Ereẓ Israel, architectural terracing can be traced back to as early as the Natufian period. A system of four architectural terraces supporting 13 hut dwellings, are known from the Natufian site of Nahal Oren. These terraces were 80 ft. (24 m.) in length and 6–17 ft. (2–5 m.) in breadth, and their retaining walls were built of field stones. At many Early Bronze Age sites, architectural terracing supported houses and other structures on the slopes of hills. Examples of EB architectural terracing are known from Tel Yarmut, Tell el-'Umeiri, and sites in the Wadi el-Hasa. Architectural terracing continued to be used throughout the rest of the Bronze Age. At Jerusalem, a remarkable series of architectural terraces were unearthed by Kenyon on the east slopes of the City of David, probably dating from the very beginning of the Iron Age. Since the technology of architectural terracing in Ereẓ Israel can be traced back to late prehistoric times, it is possible to assume that terracing for agricultural purposes likewise had a similar antiquity in the hilly areas of the country.

Archaeological evidence indicates that terracing was introduced into the highlands of Ereẓ Israel at the beginning of the Early Bronze Age. It is not surprising that the earliest known use of terracing in the highlands should coincide with the introduction of plow agriculture in that area. However, terracing was clearly only practiced on a limited scale during the Early Bronze Age and as late as the eighth century B.C.E. No evidence supports the theory that the early Israelites (or Proto-Israelites) were responsible for inventing or introducing terracing into the highlands during the early Iron Age. They simply made use of an existing technology without any special adaptations or innovations. This refutes the stand taken by some scholars who have suggested, without any supporting evidence, that terracing prior to the early Iron Age was "unsystematic." Archaeological work has shown that the major expansion of terracing in the highlands took place at a number of times over a period spanning some 1600 years, from the Iron Age II (eighth century B.C.E.) to the *Abbasid period, with cycles of contraction operating in the landscape at intervals of between 250 and 350 years. A decline in the use of the terraced areas appears to have set in around 750 C.E. and apart from some signs of renewed terracing activities during the *Mamluk and *Ottoman periods, especially in areas of irrigated terraces, this decline continued until the present century.

Demarcation of Agricultural Territory

The demarcation of agricultural territory was quite frequently referred to in biblical passages. The boundary, or territory, was referred to as *gevulah*. In Deuteronomy 19:14 the injunction is that "thou shalt not remove thy neighbour's *gevul* (landmark), which they of old time have set in thine inheritance…" (see also Prov. 22:28). The practice of tampering with landmarks, especially with those in the "fields of the fatherless" – abandoned fields – was apparently prevalent during the Iron Age, and if caught the perpetrator was cursed and punished (Deut. 27:17; Job 24:2; Prov. 23:10). The physical appearance of these "landmarks" is unknown but they were probably permanent and immovable. A boundary stone at the edge of a field of grain is depicted in a New Kingdom tomb painting from Egypt. These boundary markers were often swept away by the inundations of the Nile and had to be replaced by reference to documented cadastration. This problem did not exist in Ereẓ Israel, but markers could be moved during disputes between neighboring farmers. There is no evidence, however, to suggest that the exact locations of the markers were documented in any way. Josephus, writing in the late first century

C.E., warned: "Let it not be permitted to displace boundary marks, whether of your own land or of the land of others with whom you are at peace; beware of uprooting as it were a stone by God's decree laid firm before eternity." (Ant. IV, 8:18).

Very little archaeological evidence exists for the demarcation of territory in Ereẓ Israel during ancient times. Hence, there are difficulties in defining the extent of cultivation and pastureland belonging to a settlement at any given period. But some evidence does exist. The lands of *Gezer, for example, were marked out during the late second or early first century B.C.E. with inscribed boundary stones. Some of these markers also refer to the adjoining estates of Alkios, Alexa, and Archelaus. Boundary stones are known to have been set up to delimit taxable properties between cities, towns, and villages in the Roman provinces. Inscribed boundary stones delimiting agricultural territories, dating from the time of Diocletian (late third century), have been found in the Hauran, the western Golan, and in the Huleh Valley.

Less information exists on the use of stones or markers to demarcate the ownership over lands of a specific farm or individual plots of land. The more permanent type probably took the form of prominent natural rocks, ancient trees, large piles of stones, posts, fences, or walls (see Or. 16:5). Boundary markers in the form of monoliths were found along roads bordering areas of fields in Samaria and Modi'in and dated to the Hellenistic and Roman periods. In *Bava Batra* (4:8) it is stated that "if a man sold a field he has sold also the [boundary] stones that are necessary to it."

Temporary markers made of piles of stones were the easiest to create and they can be seen all over areas of ancient and traditional field systems. In the highlands near Jerusalem such landmarks were known in Arabic as *rassem* or *hejar et-tuhm*. The latter term was also used for the pile of stones located at both ends of a cultivation strip in the plains. One commentator of the 19th century noted that the lands of the Sharon were marked out with small lumps of stone. Mark Twain in his description of agriculture in the Lebanon (1869) wrote that he saw "rude piles of stones standing near the roadside at intervals, and recognized the custom of marking boundaries which obtained in Jacob's time. There were no walls, no fences, no hedges – nothing to secure a man's possessions but these random heaps of stones." Wilson in 1906 reports that to mark off two plots a double furrow was driven between them and piles of stones were set up at short intervals within the furrow. These piles were usually quite small.

Care has to be taken not to identify all stone piles seen in the fields as markers delimiting ownership. Many of the larger piles in the fields are clearance heaps of surplus stones (see Shev. 2:3; 4:1). Others covered the ruins of ancient structures and this was referred to in Oho. 15:7. The remains of numerous structures were found beneath piles of stones during archaeological surveys around Jerusalem. Some of these may have been memorial heaps, for example the large stone pile (*gal avanim*) mentioned as having been erected over the place where Achan was stoned and set on fire (Josh. 7:26). A group of large stone piles investigated in southwestern Jerusalem, dating from the Iron II, may have been memorials of this sort, or perhaps they were connected with harvest rites since agricultural installations, including a wine press, are known in their immediate vicinity. Many piles of stones on the top of hills were perhaps connected with peasant rituals, and Rabbi *Akiba (second century C.E.) warned that "wheresoever thou findest a high mountain or a lofty hill and a green tree, know that an idol is there!" (Av. Zar. 3:5). Aborted fetuses were sometimes buried within cairns (Oho. 16:12). At the beginning of this century, stone cairns (*rujm*) were being set up at sites where murders had taken place. A stone heap of this kind was known in Arabic as *meshad*, i.e., a "witness."

All individual fields were originally marked out in one way or another, even if only in a very rudimentary fashion. It was only then that the clearing and plowing of the land could begin. All agricultural work carried out with plows or with hoes produce scarps or banks of soil along the edges of the plots being prepared for cultivation. Loose stones from the surface of the field, which are a hindrance to plowing procedures, would have been thrown to the edges of the plots, thus creating boundary lines of low piled stones. In areas where there was very little competition for the land, this way of marking out the plot was clearly sufficient. Alternatively the plot of land could be marked out with a ditch (which had to be at least 3 ft. (0.93 m.) deep and about 1 ft. (0.37 m.) wide according to Kilayim 4:1). Ridged or dug-out boundaries of this sort may be detectable on the ground but field boundaries made out of perishable materials, such as piled logs of wood or reeds, will usually not be archaeologically evident.

In areas where there was pressure on the land or where there was a possibility of disputes between neighboring farmers, a proper system of field boundaries became necessary. Such fences tended to be built of stone where rocky outcrops were available to the farmer. In areas where stone was not freely available, especially in the plains and in the broad valleys, the field boundary was probably defined by a furrow in the ground, a wooden fence, a row of fruit trees (see Or. 1:1), or a thorny hedge. Archaeological evidence for such boundaries is rarely found. Stone fences, however, survive quite well and traces can still be seen in many parts of the country, as well as in the arid areas of the Negev and Judean Deserts.

Thorny hedges are referred to in various biblical passages. In the Parable of Jotham there is mention of plots of fruit trees edged by the *atad* bush which, if unattended, would easily grow wild (Judg. 9:15). It has been suggested that this was the thorny bush (*Lycium europaeum*) which still grows in the Kisuphim area where it originally was used during the Byzantine period as a hedge around fields. The *mesukat hedek* (identified as *Solanum incanum L.*) is another type of thorny hedge, sometimes mentioned in association with stone walls (Isa. 5:5; Prov. 15:19; Hos. 2:6). Hedges surrounding fields were also mentioned in the Mishnah (BK 3:2). The hedge was referred to as the *hasav* in TB, BB 55a. The thorny bush *Sarcopeteria spinosum* is presently used by traditional farmers as a hedge around cultivated fields. The practice of surrounding fields with cactus bushes (Arabic *sabreh*) dates back only to the Ottoman period when the cactus was first introduced into Ereẓ Israel. In the 19th century, rectangular fields were cleared within the woodland of northern Golan, leaving rows of oak trees standing as boundaries between the various plots.

Stone fences were usually built to a height of about 3 ft. (1 m. and with an average width of over 2 ft. (0.75 m.). This wall (known in Arabic as *jedar*) was built without the use of mortar. It has been estimated that a modern builder could construct a dry-stone wall around 15 ft. (4.5 to 5 m.) in length, 1.5 ft. (0.50 m.) thick and 4 ft. (1.4 m.) high (using 115 cu. ft. – 3.3 cu. m.) of stone) in the space of one working day. Principally the walls served to keep animals (dogs, foxes, and jackals) away from the crops. Frequently the tops of such walls were reinforced with a thorny bush (*netsh* in Arabic; usually this was the *Poterium spinosum* in the central highlands). The bush would project a few inches beyond the upper edge of the wall and was kept in place with the weight of a few stones. Repairs to these walls were always made in time for the period leading up to the vintage. In the Bible, the stone fence around a vineyard is referred to as the *gader avanim* (Prov. 24: 31; cf. Isa. 5:5; Ps. 62:4). Special builders known as *goderim* were employed for the task of building stone fences (cf. Ezek. 22:30).

The stone fence was also known as a *gader* among Jewish farmers in the Roman and Byzantine periods (Matt. 21:33; Pe'ah 2:3; Oho. 17:3). The *hayis* apparently referred to the secondary partition wall in the field systems and the *gader* to the main enclosure wall. The boundary path between two plots of land was referred to as the *mesar* (TJ, Kid. 1:5). It was apparently not customary to build stone fences in the flat lands of wide valleys (BB 1:2). The minimum measurements that this fence had to have according to the Mishnah, was a height of 3 ft. (0.93 m.) and a width of 1 ft. (0.37 m.) (Kil. 2:8). If it was less than this height then it could be regarded as a "quarry" and its stones dismantled and taken away. However, its foundations (to a height of about 4 in. (10 cm.) always had to be left intact (see Shev. 3:6). The boundary markers were set up outside the line of the fence so that if the wall collapsed the farmer still could claim ownership over the place and the fallen stones. However, in the case of two separately owned plots of land, the boundary stones were set up on either side and if the wall collapsed then the stones belonged to both of the farmers (BB 1:2). Ditches were sometimes dug along the foot of the fences (BB 7:4) and in a vineyard a border 7.35 ft. (2.24 m.) wide was left uncultivated between the fence and the vines (Kil. 6:1).

The use of stone fences around fields has been found dating back to the period of the Iron Age II. The fact that they have not yet been found does not mean, however, that stone fences were not built during earlier periods as well. Iron Age stone fences have been documented at sites in the Judean Hills, but fewer in Samaria. A possibility to consider is that stone fences around fields may originally have been derived from the type of stone walls used to surround animal pens, for example those from the Iron Age I which are known from Mount Ebal and Giloh.

Roads can be most useful in outlining the borders of agricultural lands or in separating one group of fields from another, particularly in defining the extent of fields which were not in any other way demarcated with stone fences. Three types of roads are known from the rural countryside of Ereẓ Israel: highways, regional roads, and local rural roads. A border of about 25 ft. (8 m.) was left uncultivated on either side of the highway, which was of no prescribed width (BK 6:4). The local roads were the access routes which linked the farms and villages with their fields and areas of pasture. They also gave farmers access to the regional roads leading to the market settlements. Produce would have been conveyed to market using beasts of burden. Wheeled transport was rarely used as roads were too narrow and stony. Most local roads extended between sites with prominent water sources (such as springs) and served as "corridors" between blocks of fields. Cisterns and wells are frequently found alongside both types of roads. High walls built of stone were erected on either side of roads, to separate the public space from the agricultural land. They prevented animals from entering unattended fields and damaging crops, especially the flocks of sheep and goats which were shepherded along these roads from the animal pens next to the settlement to the area given over to pasture which was usually located some distance away. The walls also served to discourage passing travelers from entering the fields and picking fruit during the harvest seasons.

Natural "gates," or private roads, led from the local roads into the field systems. Local roads were either for public use or were under private ownership and a clear distinction was made between the two during Roman times (see Pe'ah 2:1 and Kil. 4:7). A private road (*derekh ha-yaḥid*) was prescribed as having a width of about 6.5 ft. (2 m.) and a public road (*derekh ha-rabbim*) a width of about 25 ft (8 m.) (BB 6:7). A road ending at a cistern, lime kiln, cave, or wine press was usually a private road (Toh. 6:6). In some cases blocks of fields may be observed laid out within a pre-existing network of local roads. When such roads can be dated, they can then provide a *terminus ante quem* date for the field systems. Datable roads when encroached on by field systems will provide a *terminus post quem* date. Bowen (1961) wrote that the "integration of fields with any trackway leading into a settlement seems the best assurance of contemporary relationship, or at least in some phase, though the individual fields might of course have suffered considerable subsequent alteration and not necessary be characteristic of the period of the settlement."

Shape and Size of Fields

Agricultural fields in Ereẓ Israel were usually very small and approximately rectangular. There were, of course, exceptions to the rule as well as regional and local variations. The fields in the flat areas of the plains and broad valleys were on the whole proportionally larger and more rectangular than the fields located on sloping ground. Fields in extremely rocky terrain were even smaller in size. The shape of an individual field on sloping ground was quite often determined by topographical and lithological factors. The edges of the fields were either defined by natural features (such as a *wadi*, a gully, rocky outcrops, etc.) or by man-made boundaries (such as stone markers, stone fences, or terrace walls). The size of the fields also depended on the type of farming technology available to the farmer. Plowed land was always larger than land cultivated only with hoes. This was also true of the digging and clearing equipment which were essential in the highlands for clearing stones, breaking up the ground, and flattening the field surfaces. Different sized fields are to be found in the areas around the villages. Some of this may be the result of the fragmentation of land owing to the division of property at different times. The fields associated with farms, however, appear to have been much more uniform in size and were sometimes part of integral systems that were quite well defined. Compared to the fields used for dry farming, irrigated plots of land tended to be smaller and extremely regulated, with flatter surfaces and well-defined boundaries.

Fields also tended to be of rectangular shape because they were easier to measure for the purpose of estimating surface area or the quantity of crops grown in them. Measuring lines (*kavei ha-middah*) or cords (*ḥevelim*) are mentioned in a number of biblical passages referring to the measuring of lands and fields for the purpose of division (II Sam. 8:2; Isa. 34:17; Jer. 31:39; Micah 2:4–5; Amos 7:17; Ezek. 47:3; Ps. 16:6). The "line" or "cord" had knots at specified intervals along its length. The measurement of the distance between the knots of the biblical cord is unknown. Perhaps it was the length of the *kaneh* ("measuring reed") mentioned in Ezekiel 40, which was used for measuring small areas and expanses. A tax assessor who is seen measuring standing crops with a knotted cord to determine the yield was skillfully depicted in a painting on the wall of a New Kingdom tomb in Egypt. The knotted cord is shown extended horizontally across the top of the crops and held between the assessor and his assistant. A roll of additional cord is shown slung across the assessor's left shoulder.

In Roman Ereẓ Israel, land which was to be sold had first to be "measured by the line" (BB 7:2–3; see also the methods of measuring differently shaped fields as explained by Columella V, 1,13–2, 10). It is reported that the farmers of Beth Namer "used to reap their crops by measuring-line and leave *pe'ah* (gleanings) from every furrow" (Pe'ah 4:5). The division of agricultural land by surveying is mentioned in one of the Nessana papyri (*P. Ness.* 58) dating from the late seventh century. Measuring cords are also mentioned in a passage from *Pirkei de-Rabbi Eliezer,* dated to between the eighth and early ninth century, which deals with the Muslim conquest of Ereẓ Israel in the seventh century C.E. It says that the conquerors will "measure the land with ropes, and make the cemetery into a dunghill where the flock rests, and they will measure them and from them unto the tops of the mountains …." The knotted cord during the Roman and Byzantine periods was probably marked out with a measuring rod of a standard size used in Ereẓ Israel (cf. Kel. 7:6), perhaps identical to the *orgua* or *kalamos* measures. An iron measuring rod, five cubits in length and dating to the seventh century, has been discovered during excavations at an ecclesiastical farm at Shelomi in Western Galilee. This rod may have been a *kalamos* measure of 11 *spithamai*, 8.5 ft. (257.4 cm.) Long cords for the purpose of measuring village lands for taxation purposes were still used by the Ottomans in the 19th century. In Southern Ereẓ Israel, lands were divided up with a measuring line (*ḥavaleh*) before plowing. This line was made of goat's hair and was a little more than one centimeter thick.

The earliest archaeological evidence for the general appearance of the layout of field systems in Ereẓ Israel dates from the Iron Age II. This may have been the period during which widespread field systems were first laid out as blocks of rectangular-shaped plots on high ground and along the valleys. In some areas, it would appear that these blocks of fields developed piecemeal, but in the highlands and in the semi-arid regions a number of these systems appear to have been planned in advance. However, it is only during the Roman and Byzantine periods that fields were laid out in a specific pattern in different parts of Ereẓ Israel and Syria. Some even follow Roman land-partition principals.

The size of the individual field used for arable purposes during antiquity was usually the area of land which could be plowed with a yoke of oxen during the course of one day's work. According to Bava Batra (1:6) the practical size of sown ground in dry farming was an area of 11,000 sq. ft. (1,176 sq. m.) (but according to R. Judah – 2nd century C.E. – this could be reduced to as little as 5,500 sq. ft. (588 sq. m.). The size of plots used as vegetable gardens and vineyards were even smaller. The size of plots were apparently progressively reduced in the course of the third and fourth centuries. In Samaria, at Khirbet Buraq most individual plots were between 1 and 7.5 dunam in size, with the largest not exceeding 15 dunam. The size of individual plots is in fact not helpful in an attempt to reconstruct the area of smallholdings, since most families in the Roman period would have owned more than several plots and these could very easily have been scattered. Furthermore, a family could also have controlled areas of pasture and woodland outside the field system.

Various suggestions have been put forward regarding the size of the lands cultivated by the individual peasant smallholder in Roman and Byzantine Ereẓ Israel. As a result of his archaeological surveys in Samaria, Dar has estimated the size of the typical family holding around a number of Byzantine village sites at between 25 and 45 dunam (note that four dunam are the equivalent to one acre). At Khirbet Buraq the holdings were estimated at 25 dunam each and around Qarawat bene Hassan at between 39.7 and 45.6 dunam in size. These figures do not take into account the possibility of the scattered ownership of land. At sites in the Galilee, holdings averaged between 6 and 11 dunam and around Nablus between 15 and 18 dunam (compare these figures with the average of

16 dunam for a block of enclosed fields noted by some scholars for the Galilee).

In a study of the economy of Roman Ereẓ Israel, Safrai proposed that an average family of four individuals, practicing subsistence agriculture, would have required lands covering an area of approximately 11 dunam (or 13.7 dunam for a family of five). However, with the burden of taxes and the need for outside purchases a minimum of 20 dunam seemed to him to be a far more realistic figure. Safrai's figures are based on calculations regarding the possible harvest yields of plots used for the cultivation of wheat, olives, figs, grapes, and legumes. However, such yields could have varied quite substantially from one part of the country to another, depending on the type of soils available, location and precipitation levels.

Broshi in another study has suggested that a family of five needed an area of 50 dunam for subsistence, a figure which seems quite reasonable compared to estimates of the sizes of traditional holdings during recent times. This also fits well with the estimated minimum requirement of 20 iugera (= 50 dunam) for a farm in Roman Italy which cultivated land with the plow and kept animals. However, Broshi does not believe that manuring was carried out in the sown areas and so in antiquity the smaller areas did not produce yields which were any greater than those of traditional agriculture of the 19th century.

A number of ancient sources exist dealing with the question of the size of the peasant holding in antiquity (note the following equivalents are used here: 25 dunam = 2.5 hectare = 10 iugera = 20 plethra). In his *Historia Ecclesiastica* (III, 20:1), Eusebius mentions Judas's nephews cultivating an area of 39 plethra (= 48.7 dunam). Thus each farmer would have had a holding of about 24 dunam. Talmudic sources also contribute much information, but more about the quantity of yields and the measurement of individual plots of land than about the size of the individual holding. Additional figures are available regarding the sizes of holdings in other ancient Mediterranean countries and Egypt. Apparently the smallest and largest allocation of land in Roman Italy was from 2 iugera (= 2.5 dunam) to 200 iugera (= 5,000 dunam) or more. Since 2 iugera was clearly insufficient to support a family even on a subsistence level, this allotment must have been additional to areas used for pasturage. In 133 B.C.E., allotments for the poor in Italy measured between 10–30 iugera (= 25–75 dunam). In Greece, in the Metaponto area, plots varied between 48 and 530 dunam, with 50 percent of these totaling about 138 dunam in size. In Egypt, the average property size varied during the mid-fourth century: 76 iugera (190 dunam) at Hermopolis and 37 iugera (92.5 dunam) at Antinoöpolis).

The above figures make it quite clear that there are many difficulties in estimating the size of the average small peasant holding in antiquity, prior to the Abassid period when there was a general decline in the agricultural productivity of the land lasting until modern times. However, the size of a holding will have differed considerably from one type of environment to another, with larger holdings in the more rugged environments having poorer soils, and smaller allotments in the flat fertile plains and internal valleys where there was much more pressure on the land. At times when there was a serious fragmentation of holdings, with lands being absorbed by larger estates, such as during the 3rd–4th centuries C.E., there would have been pressure on privately owned ancestral holdings and these would naturally become smaller with individual fields being sold off piecemeal. The size of the holding also depended on the type of agricultural regime being practiced and whether or not it included the replenishment of soil fertility with proper manuring and fallowing procedures. The lack of such procedures could well have restricted the size of the areas being cultivated. Finally, the minimum size of a subsistence holding will differ considerably between one which had to support a family and one which supported an extended family. Furthermore, a peasant farmer could have held more than one holding. The attempts made by Dar and Safrai to divide up the fields surrounding ancient villages into holdings of theoretical sizes, seems to be fundamentally flawed when one considers the evidence regarding the lands owned by Rabbi Yohanan in the 3rd century, whose fields were not concentrated at one location at all but scattered at different locations in the countryside between Tiberias and Sepphoris.

However, the existence of such problems should not mean that scholars should abandon the attempt to delimit the minimum size of peasant holdings in Ereẓ Israel during the different periods. The maximum cultivable land in Ereẓ Israel in 1931 amounted to 6.54 million dunam which, subdivided by the population number of 600,000 for that general period, provides an average of 11 dunam of land per inhabitant. This figure can be compared favorably with Broshi's suggested 10 dunam of land per individual in antiquity. However, two facts need to be taken into consideration regarding the 1931 figure: first, not all the population at that time were involved in agriculture and, secondly, a large percentage of the available cultivable land was not necessarily being cultivated. For example, records show that up to 55 percent of the hills around Nablus-Tulkarm had neglected terraces in the Mandate period. Hence, a more realistic minimum of 5 dunam per individual seems likely. A family of five would therefore have had a holding of approximately 25 dunam or more. Hence, the suggested size of a peasant holding in Ereẓ Israel during the time preceding the Abassid period, i.e., before 750 C.E., probably varied considerably between 25 and 50 dunam.

It is interesting to compare these figures with information known about the size of the average smallholding in different parts of the Near East during more recent times. An average of 50 dunam per peasant family has been estimated according to figures taken from an Ottoman census of 1909, for the lands in the three sanjaqs of Jerusalem, Nablus and Acre; 85 percent of landowners from Hebron cultivated areas ranging between 1–20 dunam. The sizes of average holdings in three present-day agricultural villages in the Zarqa River basin in Jordan range between 19 and 68 dunam. In Syria, however, a peasant holding in an area of dry farming was much larger, averaging 50–70 dunam. At Episkopi in Cyprus, the village was estimated to have had a total of 10,000 dunam of land and a maximum population of 700 individuals; thus a holding for a family of five would have averaged at about 71.5 dunam. At Ashvan in Anatolia the total landholding per family averaged 122 dunam but 40 dunam of this was used for pasturage.

The systematic study of field systems during archaeological work, combined with a critical examination of evidence gathered from a variety of sources, provides very important information on the history of rural land management in different parts of Ereẓ Israel. One of the major problems in establishing a typology of field systems for Ereẓ Israel is that the best evidence comes from hilly areas and from the marginal semi-arid areas, and it is questionable whether these patterns were also the same in areas of flat land. While the tenurial organization of land cannot be worked out solely from the archaeological remains of the fields themselves, the archaeological work is able to provide historians with empirical data on the appearance and extent of ancient field systems of different periods. In some field systems the evidence points to continuity, with the position of boundaries being respected and retained from period to period. In some cases substantial changes have occurred and this may have been the result of the dispossession of lands, new property relationships, or new forms of exploitation.

Dating fields is still an acute problem for archaeologists. One scholar wrote in 1984 in a pessimistic vein that in his opinion "it is very rarely possible to attribute an ancient agricultural field or system of old terraces to a specific period." Research in the 1990s and early 2000s shows that this is no longer the case and methods of landscape archaeology enable scholars to disentangle field systems belonging to several periods. The first step, of course, is to evaluate the degree of association between a system of fields and adjacent villages and farms, and the network of communications (paths, roads, etc.). Field boundaries and their relationships with earlier features, from dolmens to earlier fields, must be examined. Some of these earlier features may have been respected or dismantled. The extent of a field system also needs to be determined. It is not always an easy task to establish where one system stops and another starts. Attempts should also be made to examine patterns of field boundaries and the stages of construction of stone fences defined through structural analysis. Some field systems are of an aggregate pattern and others may have a planned parcelation arrangement with a more rectilinear design. Some systems are responsive to the local terrain, others are not. Ancient boundaries are frequently "fossilized" in modern boundaries. A comprehensive study subsequently needs to be made of sherd scatters located next to the settlements, around cisterns, wine and oil presses, alongside the edges of fields and across the field surfaces. Many of these sherd scatters may turn out to be the result of ancient manuring practices. This will provide the surveyor with a general idea as to the date of the fields which are being examined. The excavation of test pits within the settlement and next to the various features seen within the area of the fields, can serve as a "control" over the results from the survey. The overall results will show whether or not there has been cultural continuity or discontinuity within a given landscape of agricultural fields.

Recent work has shown that a variety of ancient land-management systems were operating in different parts of Ereẓ Israel in antiquity. These reflect the many different ways that the rural population responded to environmental and climatic constraints. The quality of these responses depended on the level of social and economic organization achieved by the different farming communities and on the level of farming technologies available to them. The tactics of village communities differed considerably from those of individual farmers, and this had a clear effect on the general layout of fields in a landscape. The earliest known evidence for the imposition of a regular and widespread cultivation pattern in Ereẓ Israel can be dated to the Iron II period. The parcelation of land was consolidated during the Hellenistic to Roman periods. Thereafter, areas of field systems expanded and in time, particularly during the Byzantine and Umayyad periods, became much more complex and fragmented than before.

Today, the shape and character of fields in Ereẓ Israel have changed dramatically. Mechanized equipment now allows for the cultivation of extremely large tracts in areas of flat land. Terraces can be cut into the slopes of hills with bulldozers and soil can be transported by truck from one place to another. The use of artificial fertilizers has meant that fields no longer need to lie fallow and yields can be constantly high. A wide variety of weeds, however, are thus being banished to the margins of fields and complete wildlife habitats are being destroyed. Large areas of fields in the traditional landscape have already been eradicated. Their boundaries and fences have now been erased forever and can only be seen in aerial photographs. The morphology of the agricultural landscape is no longer the same and the growing of cash crops has replaced the economic variability of ancient times. While it is sad to observe the rapidly disappearing traditional landscapes, harvests in Israel, the West Bank, and Jordan are now much greater and more plentiful than they ever were in antiquity and this can only be to the advantage of the local farmers of today.

Manuring Procedures

In ancient Ereẓ Israel, an enormous amount of effort was dedicated to the proper organic fertilization of fields and periodic fallowing. The archaeological evidence for ancient manuring is represented by the very large quantities of sherds which can be found scattered in the fields all over the country. In many cases they represent frequent farming procedures undertaken to improve the fertility of the soil, especially in areas where frequent cropping was undertaken with very little fallowing. The fertilizers and manure had to have the right composition of potassium, phosphorus, lime, magnesium and nitrogen, allowing for the proper growth of the crops in the fields.

Fertilizers and manure of all sorts were extremely valued in antiquity as soil-improving agents. The most frequently-used manure was the dung of cattle, sheep and goats which was collected from the mangers and animal pens and distributed in the fields with household rubbish. The term *domen* was used in the Bible when referring to manure left in the field as an organic fertilizer (II Kings 9:37; Ps. 83:11; Jer. 9:21). When animal dung was mixed wet with straw, it was known as *madmena* (Isa. 25:10). Household rubbish and sherds were probably added to the dung while wet and this would have helped break down the dung before being scattered in the fields. Human excrement was not apparently used and was clearly forbidden by Jewish custom, unlike in China where human faeces, diluted and fermented, was one of the principal manuring agents used in the fields. However, ashes (*efer*: cf. Ezek. 28:18) and burnt ashes from animal sacrifices (*deshen*: cf. Isa. 34:7) were probably used. This was certainly the case during the Roman period when ashes of a sacrificed animal were "sold to gardeners as manure" (Yoma 5:6). A dove-raising industry existed in Ereẓ Israel in the Hellenistic and Roman periods and is represented by the discovery of numerous *columbaria* caves and structures. The dove droppings from these *columbaria* were highly sought after especially for fertilizing valuable garden plants. The rule was that *columbaria* had to be located at a distance of 25 m. from the farm or village (BB 2:5). Organic waste materials such as the cakes resulting from the pressing of olives, were pulverized and then added to the compost heaps which were then later scattered on the orchards and gardens. In Roman times, an importance was attributed to fertilization procedures with organic materials and compost produced from organic waste (BK 3:3; Shev. 2:14, etc.). The importance of fertilizer is shown by the comparison of dung to precious stones (Sanh. 59b). Blood (Yoma 5:6), ash, and fine sand (Tosef., Shab. 8:9) were all used. Sheep droppings were applied by enclosing the flock in a temporary fold ("*sahar*"). The enclosure would be set up for some time and then be moved from place to place in the field (Tosef., Shev. 2:15, 19).

Manure was used in orchards, gardens, and sown fields. The best time to manure the fields was after the first rains in time for the winter crops and in the spring for the summer crops. The rains softened the ground as well as the manure itself. In irrigated areas, manuring was continued throughout the year. Manure was distributed to the fields in special baskets (known in Latin as *sirpeas*; cf. Kel. 19:10; 24:9) which were loaded on beasts of burden. It has been estimated that 235 cu. ft. (6.7 cu. m.) of manure were used per dunam of land. The manure was first deposited in heaps in the field and was then scattered by a process of plowing or hoeing (cf. Shev. 3:1–4). Seeds from weeds could sometimes get into the soil of a field through animal dung and this was something which concerned Jewish farmers during the Roman period (Kil. 5:7). A field that had undergone manuring was known as a *bet ha-zevalim*. Movable enclosures were sometimes set up in the fields to help localize the dung of grazing animals. In dry soil, manures could effect the movement of water between the surface of the ground and the subsoil, and so manures had to be only lightly covered. But care had to be taken to make sure that the manure was dug in properly, since unrotted manure could burn crops (White 1970: 129). Manure was heaped around individual trees and then dug in. In Luke 13:8 reference is made to the manuring of a fig tree so that it should bear fruit.

Broshi has suggested that manure was mainly used in orchards and gardens during the Roman and Byzantine periods and not at all in the fields that were used for the growing of grain. The claim has also been made that because of pressure on the land only one third of it was actually allowed to lie fallow during that period, but this would have been contrary to the Jewish rulings of the time (BM 9:7). The true extent of the manuring practices at that time is clearly demonstrated by the enormous distribution of sherd scatters in areas used for the growing of grain across the country. Manuring at a distance of more than a mile (1.5 to 2 km.) from the village would probably have been uneconomical without the use of carts.

The phenomenon of sherd scatters representing manuring regimes is known from ancient fields investigated in many of the Mediterranean lands, from Spain to Greece, and as well as in other parts of the world. Various methods have now been developed for the study of the distribution of sherd scatters within agricultural lands and around settlements. In Ereẓ Israel, organic household, and courtyard rubbish was gathered and used as a fertilizer for the fields, and this rubbish frequently included broken pottery. Household refuse was sometimes mixed with animal manure to make it easier to scatter in the fields. In Samaria, sherds have been found in the fields around Qarawat bene Hassan, up to 2–3 km. from the village center, as well as around Khirbet Buraq and in other fields. Sherd distributions have also been studied in the fields around agricultural settlements in the Golan. Soil was sometimes taken from the ruins of ancient sites and scattered on the fields as a fertilizing agent. Archaeologically, this is known only from sites with plots used for irrigation purposes, as at Sataf west of Jerusalem.

In the Ottoman period sown fields were very rarely manured and in many areas this eventually resulted in the substantial exhaustion of the land during the 19th century and the early part of the 20th century. Manure was mainly kept for use in vegetable gardens and some orchards, or dried and used for fuel. However, Baldensperger in 1907 does mention the manuring not just of orchards but also of sown ground. Karmon and Shmueli have also pointed out that unlike other parts of the country, the regular manuring of terraced plots was being carried out around Hebron until the 1970s. Reifenberg in 1947 complained that organic manure was often very badly handled in Ereẓ Israel: "the heaps being exposed not only to the intense sun but also to the torrential winter rains. The dung is very often left for weeks in small heaps on the field instead of being plowed in as quickly as possible."

Irrigation

Although Ereẓ Israel was described as possessing "brooks of water, of foundations and depths, springing forth in valleys and hills" (Deut. 8:7), the reality is that there were very few permanent sources of water that could be used for agricultural purposes, namely a number of perennial rivers, and springs and wells, and mostly what local farmers could rely on was winter rainwater (Deut. 11.10–11); otherwise their lands would remain dry (forlorn like "the garden that hath no water," Isa. 1:30). The few permanent sources of water that did exist were therefore exploited to the fullest and the danger of drought was always present (Deut. 11:17). Water rights and ownership of access to water led to serious disputes in antiquity (e.g., the disputes with the Philistines regarding wells of water, Gen. 21:25; 26:15–22). Rabbinic legislation covered many aspects of the distribution of water among those who shared in water rights. "Water turns" were assigned (MK 11b) to those entitled to use the supply. Some individuals were compelled to buy or lease seasonal rights (TJ, MK 1:2, 80b). Many biblical passages make use of the well, spring, and river as symbols of abundance and security (Isa. 58:11; Jer. 31:11). Orchards, too, grow better when partially irrigated. Hence the comparison made between the person who puts his trust in God to "a tree planted by streams of water" (Jer. 14:8; Ps. 1:3).

Irrigation methods were many and diverse. In those parts rich in rivers and springs, as in the Jordan and Ḥuleh valleys, water flowed into the fields by gravitation and was directed through channels dug with shovels or pressed down by foot (cf. Deut. 11:10). Trees were similarly irrigated (Ezek. 17:7; Song 5:13): a shallow pit dug around a tree was filled with water, which would sink deep into the ground and moisten the roots (Kal. R. 3:52, 4). However, mechanical means were sometimes needed to lift water into the fields. The most simple of containers was the *deli* ("pitcher") of earthenware or metal attached to a rope or chain (Shab. 15:2; Kel. 14:3). A similar utensil was the *ḥavit* or jug, which was also used for water drawing (Mak, 2:1). A larger device for lifting water was the *kilon* of mishnaic times (Makhsh.. 4:9, etc.), which was also frequently depicted in ancient Egyptian and Babylonian representations; it has survived up to the present time in the traditional agricultural practices of Egypt (known there in Arabic as the *shaduf*). It consists of a vertical pillar on which a long horizontal bar is placed. To the one extremity of the bar, a jug is attached by rope or pole, while the other extremity is weighted down by a stone to balance and facilitate the raising of the full container. Herodotus described the Egyptian use of this device (Gr. κηλωνήιον, "keloneion"; cf. *History* 1:139). The bucket wheel was used at wells for irrigation and was turned by a horse, mule, or ox. Water was conveyed to the fields by conduits on high stone walls, sometimes arched. Examples of waterwheels used to raise water from rivers and wells of the "Persian" type with ceramic jars attached to them (*antila*), are known in Ereẓ Israel dating back to the Roman period. The *antila* is essentially a vertical wheel to which earthenware pitchers or wooden containers are attached. An animal rotates a shaft whose attached, wooden-toothed gear in turn engages the wheel to which the drawing pails are tied. According to the *halakhah*, water drawn by an *antila* invalidates a *mikveh*, since the waters are separated from their source during the process. The Tosefta (Makhsh. 3:4; Mik. 4:2) designates another vessel, the "*kevulin*" or "*keḥulin*" whose use does not invalidate the *mikveh*, since the water is not detached from its source during the operation. This *keḥulin* (Lat. *cochlea*, "snail") consists of an Archimedean screw in a pipe. The screw, turned by an animal, forces the water to rise. Strabo (17:807) reported that water for the Roman camps was drawn from the Nile by means of κοχλίαι.The *galgal* or *gullah* described in Ecclesiastes (12:6), with a wheel turning an axle to which a pail or two were attached by rope or chain, may have been an earlier type of *antila* device. Such a device was frequently mentioned as μηχανή ἀντλοῦσα (i.e., "drawing machine") in Hellenistic Egyptian papyri. Evidence of its use has been found in the south of Israel in a Byzantine Greek inscription that reads: "This excellence too of μηχανή, the glorious father Helarion invented." The horizontal waterwheel may have been developed in the Upper Galilee during the second century B.C.E., but clear archaeological evidence for this is still lacking. The large upright wheel operated by water power (*na'urah* in Arabic) was first developed in Syria, the most famous examples being those at Hama. It was later introduced into Ereẓ Israel, where it was used to draw water from some of the perennial rivers and is referred to in the *halakhah* as a device with "self-drawn water from the sea or river" (Tosef., Mik. 4:2, so in correct texts). The Jerusalem Talmud designates this instrument by the name "*agatargatkaya*" (TJ, MK 1:2, 80b), which is related to the Greek term καταρράκτης, "cataract" or "waterfall." It refers to the cataract effect created by the water-driven wheel. In addition to these water wheels, underground *Qanat* systems were constructed to exploit the shallow groundwater in the arid basins of the Arabah and the lower Jordan Valley. Examples of these systems have been surveyed by Porath, who has suggested, on the basis of his fieldwork, that the knowledge of *qanat* construction may have been introduced into the region from Iran either during the late fourth century B.C.E. or (and this seems much more likely) during the Umayyad period in the seventh century C.E. However, the use of these chain wells did not last beyond the Abassid period.

The most important source of water in the hilly regions are the springs, and an estimated 800 exist in Ereẓ Israel. In ancient times the lands adjacent to the springs were mainly used for irrigation purposes. Only a handful of these springs, namely the Dan, Yarkon, and Na'aman springs, have a flow of more than one cubic meter of water per second. A little more than 40 produce a volume of between 100,000 and 1,000 liters per second. The rest produce much smaller amounts of water, sometimes as little as one liter per minute. Irrigated plots of land tended to be located fairly close to routes giving ease of access for those conveying their produce (such as vegetables) to the markets or back to the village or farm. Irrigated plots tended to be fairly close to the settlement for security reasons.

Most springs in the hills of Ereẓ Israel had various installations attached to them, including flow tunnels and large water-storage pools. The irrigated fields were located below the pools and water was conveyed to the fields along channels by a process of gravitation (it would "leave higher ground and go to the lower," Ta'an. 7a). Each terrace area received water once every cycle of specified number of days, according to the size of the terraces owned. Spring-irrigated lands have been investigated during archaeological surveys in Samaria and in the Judean Hills. Spring-irrigated system of terraces have been investigated at Ain Yael, Sataf, and Suba.

Artificially watered or irrigated fields were frequently mentioned in the Mishnah. Irrigated land was known as *bet ha-selahin* to distinguish it from the areas of rain-fed land known as *bet ba'al*. The smallest irrigated allotment was between 350 and 700 sq. ft (32.5 and 65 sq. m.) (BB). It is interesting to compare this with the allotment of 1 dunam of irrigated terraced land which every family farms in present-day Battir. Title over irrigated lands was given to anyone who could prove three years undisputed possession (BB 3:1). The surface of the irrigated field was divided up into square plots of about 5 × 5 sq. ft. (0.56 × 0.56 m.), separated one from the other by an earthen border (*gubal*) about 4 in. (10 cm) in height (Kil. 3:1). Irrigated plots were heavily manured and the frequent manuring of beds of cucumbers and other vegetables was mentioned in Shevi'it 2:2. Soil taken from ancient ruined sites was frequently used to top-up and fertilize irrigated fields. The furrow or channel which brought water to these plots had a width and depth of about 10 cm wide and 10 cm deep (Kil. 3:2). Channels led from tree to tree (MK 1:3). In large areas of irrigated lands, small plastered tanks were frequently built at the end of the main irrigation channels. Because of evaporation rates, these small tanks were the first to be filled with water: "The cistern nearest to a water-channel is filled first – in the interests of peace" (Git. 5:8). It was only then that the plots between the spring and the tanks could be directly irrigated from the main channel. Springs in areas of irrigated fields were known to suddenly dry up (BM 9:2). A distinction was made in *Mo'ed Katan* 1:1 between old springs and "newly flowing springs."

Irrigation plots were frequently established next to aqueducts leading from the springs. Plots of land irrigated in this fashion existed next to the aqueduct which led water to the settlement of Na'aran in the Golan. An interesting Greek inscription of Justinianic date was found near the principal aqueduct leading to Jerusalem. It prohibited the use of the land on either side of it, up to 15 ft. (4.6 m.), for cultivation purposes. This was to prevent water from being siphoning off for irrigation. This prohibition reminds one of the ban in Roman Ereẓ Israel regarding the cultivation of plots of land on either side of highways.

Cistern irrigation was also practiced in Ereẓ Israel and dates back at least to the Iron Age (e.g., Isa. 27:3). Vines watered by irrigation are mentioned in a field with furrows (*arugot*) in Ezekiel 17:5–7. Cistern-irrigated plots are mentioned in Jewish sources of the Roman period (see MK 1:1;) and in Pe'ah 5:3 a field was irrigated "with a pitcher." Cistern-irrigated plots of land have been investigated by Dar at a number of sites in Samaria (1986a, 200–2). A cistern in an orchard is mentioned in one of the Nessana papyri (Kraemer 1958).

Traditional irrigation in Ereẓ Israel clearly perpetuates ancient practices as Dalman was able to show in his publications. Many of the Arabic toponyms in Ereẓ Israel are linked to the word *ain* ("spring") indicating the importance of the spring even when it was located a few kilometers away from the settlement. Descriptions of traditional spring-irrigated plots and watering procedures were frequently published by 19th and early 20th century travelers. Water was divided up for irrigation either by degrees or by hours. General research on irrigation has been carried out by Avitsur and at springs in the terraced Judean Hills by Ron. The irrigated areas investigated by Ron comprised only 0.6 percent of the total of the terraced areas west of Jerusalem. This percentage is probably true for all of the terraced areas of the hills of Ereẓ Israel.

Installations and Implements

Associated with each system of ancient agricultural fields, in addition to the villages and farms, are the remains of solitary structures, towers, caves, cisterns, *columbaria*, wine and oil presses, threshing floors, and animal pens. Pools for steeping flax and fig-drying installations are also mentioned in the sources. Many of these features were linked by roads and paths. Near them were lime kilns and quarries.

The existence of rural towers in areas of terraced fields has been frequently commented on by travelers and scholars since the 19th century. A detailed study of these structures was carried out by Ron in the terraced zones of the Judean Hills. Approximately 50 percent of these stone towers were associated with vineyards and 39 percent with orchards. In general terms, the layout of the tower resembled the organized space of the traditional village house, with the lower area serving for storage and the upper part for habitation. Towers were usually located at a distance of 500 meters and up to a kilometer from the village or according to Wilson writing in 1906 up to 6 or 8 km. from the village. The interior was perfect for the cool storage of agricultural produce, since its temperature was 8 to 13 degrees cooler than outside it. Water cisterns and wine presses were frequently found next to the towers. Ron believes that these towers indicate private family ownership of land with cultivation taking place in small plots, thus reflecting a traditional subsistence economy. A detailed study of towers associated with fields in Samaria dating from Hellenistic and Roman times was made by Dar. Similar structures have been examined in terraced areas around Jerusalem, some of them dating back to the Iron Age II. Additional tower-like structures in areas of terracing, also dating from the Iron Age II, have been examined in the Tell el-'Umeiri area in Jordan, to the southwest of Amman. This kind of structure should perhaps be identified with the stone-tower (*migdal*) mentioned in Isaiah 5:2. Additional structures located in fields are mentioned in the Mishnah, including "cone-shaped huts, watch booths, and summer huts" (Ma'as. 3:7; cf. Kil. 5:3). The sale of a field also meant the sale of the watchman's hut and its stones, unless it was made of perishable materials and "if it was not fastened down with clay" (BB 4:9). The differences between these ancient structures and the more recent ones are not as outstanding as Dar believes. Dar argues that these structures differ architecturally, with the ancient examples built of hewn stone without built stairs and with the recent examples built of surplus stone cleared from the fields. The ancient towers, however, could easily have been supplied with wooden ladders and this would have given them a much better defensive edge than having built stairs. Furthermore, surveys around Jerusalem have shown that many of the traditional towers were in fact built of stone supplied from quarries and not cleared from fields at all. The similarities between the ancient and traditional towers are much greater: both sets of towers were located in fields at a distance from the settlement, they had cool interiors suitable for storing agricultural produce and they could have been used as watchtowers during the harvest seasons. In antiquity, the social standing of the farmer was probably indicated by the size and appearance of the tower. Even some of the more recent towers can be quite imposing. Extremely flimsy structures could also be erected in the fields during harvest times, such as the traditional structures in the fields near Beth Shean (Dalman 1932, Pls. 12–13). The Bible refers to temporary structures of this sort; the *melunah* in an irrigated plot of cucumbers and the *sukkah* in a vineyard (Isa. 1:8; 4:6; 24:20).

Fenced-off animal pens are frequently found adjacent to field systems, since arable farmers in Ereẓ Israel usually also kept stock. These were grazed on the common lands and on arable fields when fallow. At harvest the crops were protected by tethering animals or keeping them within fenced enclosures. The study of animal pens is instructive in regard to the relationship in antiquity between livestock to arable activity in a given landscape.

The excavation of rural sites, such as farms and villages, has brought to light the remains of agricultural installations, farming equipment, and food-processing equipment. These provide information on the level of technology and farming methods available to the farmers at different periods. Indirectly they also provide information on what was grown in some of the surrounding fields. Agricultural installations may include wine and oil presses, and large flour mills. The dating of a specific type of installation within a settlement can help towards dating similar installations found associated with the fields outside a settlement. Important studies of wine and oil presses have been undertaken in recent years by various scholars, notably by Frankel. Examples of farming equipment may include digging sticks, plows, mattocks, hoes, sickles, pruning knives, and so forth. These may be compared with traditional farming equipment used in Ereẓ Israel (see, for instance, the work of Avitzur and more recently by Ayalon). Examples of food-processing equipment may include pestles and mortars, querns, rotary mills, and so forth.

[Shimon Gibson (2nd ed.)]

Plowing

The light plow (or ard) was one of the most important farming implements used in the fields of Ereẓ Israel for the breaking up of ground and preparing it for cultivation. The introduction of this implement into Ereẓ Israel at the end of the fourth millennium BCE. probably had a revolutionary effect on the appearance of the earliest fields and the size of the average plot probably increased considerably (the earliest evidence for plowing in the Near East are the plow marks dating to the fourth millennium B.C.E. which were found at Susa A, and the Uruk pictograms of plows which date from the late fourth millennium B.C.E.).

Traditional plowing helps to understand the ancient procedures. Proper plowing ensured a successful harvest. Before plowing was commenced, especially in a mountainous area, the plots were cleared of stone with the use of a hoe or mattock (in a process known in Arabic as *naqb*). The manner in which the plot of land was plowed has been described by a number of different authorities, among them Wilson, Turkowski, and Avitzur. This operation had to be undertaken properly to ensure a successful harvest, otherwise the crop could be ruined (Job 4:8). Continuous plowing of the entire field was never attempted. Instead, the area was divided into separate plots (each plot known in Arabic as a *ma'anah*) usually one-third or one-fourth of a *faddan* and with a length of between 90 and 120 ft. (27 and 36 m.). According to Wilson, a furrow (Arabic *tilm*) was first run on the ground "and others plowed parallel to this, until a piece of ground of that length and about half the breadth is finished; then a similar piece is plowed next; and so on until the whole is completed." Not only the type of plow but also the type of draft animal used for the plowing could affect the overall depth of the resulting furrows. The maximum depth of plow in modern times was 8 in. (20 cm.) according to Dalman. In antiquity the plowpoint penetrated the soil to a depth of three handbreadths (Gen. R. 31; BB 12:2), i.e., 27 cm., and this helped to maintain the overall fertility of the land (TJ, Ta'an. 4:8, 68b).

The relatively small area plowed by the farmer per day in antiquity has been estimated by Feliks (see *Agriculture) to be about 1,170 sq. m. (cf. Tosef., BM 11:9), which is about one third of what is usually covered using traditional Arab methods of plowing. The prophet Isaiah noted that the soil had to be plowed twice before it was sown: the first time to expose the soil to the penetration of rainwater, and the second to level the ground for the planting (Isa. 28:24). The Mishnah, however, enumerates four separate plowings: one in the summer, after the harvest, in the form of broad lines or plots that were set far apart (referred to as the "furrows of *pati'aḥ*" in the language of the Mishnah; Kil. 2:6). The second plowing took place after the first rains, and then, too, the furrows were not placed close together. Spaces were left intentionally between the furrows to prevent torrential downpours from eroding the soil. In this way each field would have the appearance of alternate furrows and ridges (*"gedudim"* in the Bible). Rain leveled the ground and was soaked into it. The Psalmist (45:11) prayed for a good year in which rain would soak into the soil and level the *"gedudim"* in the ground. Following this, the main deep plowing was commenced in which the furrows were placed close together (the *"shiddud"* of the Bible) and in this way the soil was ready for sowing. Finally, the fourth plowing was undertaken in order to cover the seed itself (Tosef., Kil. 1:15).

To preserve the fertility of the soil, a rotation system was practiced in which land was sown and left to fallow alternately. In the fallow year, the field was plowed five to seven times to rid it of noxious weeds and to restore its fertility. These plowings were called *"tiyyuv"* or *"nir"* (Tosef., Shev. 3:10; Men. 85a). A well-plowed field attracted attention owing to its cleanness (Avot 3:7). It was not easy for the farmer to adapt himself to this cycle, since it meant he was only able to plant his field during three years out of seven, the seventh (*shevi'it*) being the Sabbatical year (Mekh. de-Kaspa 20), but he knew that this was the only way to ensure continuous, abundant harvests. Only artificially-fertilized fields may be plowed year after year with fairly good results.

The plow used in antiquity was not essentially different from that used in traditional Arab farming, except that the earlier implement was sturdier and was capable of penetrating deeper into the soil. The main parts of the plow were made of wood with the plowshare (biblical *"et"*; talmudic *"yated"* or *"kankan"*) made of metal (bronze in earlier times; later of iron). Numerous examples of such implements have been uncovered in archaeological excavations in Israel. The metal part was funnel-shaped, ending in a sharp point. The plowshare was attached to the sharp wooden tailpiece (*"ḥerev"*) which in turn was joined to the "knee" (*"borekh"*) and was tied to the handle, a long pole (*"yaẓul"*) attached to the yoke (see Kelim 21:2).

The plowman depressed the handle with one hand. In the other he held a long staff or goad (*"malmad ha-bakar"*), one end of which held a nail and was used to goad the oxen and hold them in line, while the other end was shaped like a shovel and served to clean the plow (*"maḥareshet"* in the Bible; *"ḥarḥur"* in talmudic literature; see I Sam. 13:21; Kelim 13:3). The oxen were tied to the plow by the yoke, which was a pole (the biblical *"motaḥ"*) placed on the neck of the ox or cow. To yoke a pair of oxen, an additional pole was drawn under their necks while pegs (*"simyonim"*) joined the two poles together and thereby enclosed the heads of the oxen in frames. A broken pole could not be repaired, and the animal would have to be released. Hence breaking the yoke symbolized liberation (Jer. 2:20, etc.). Generally the yoke was made of wood; only in exceptional cases was it made of metal, so accordingly an "iron yoke" represented abnormal or tyrannical oppression (Deut. 28:48). A single ox was tied to his yoke by ropes (*"moserot," "aguddot motah"*). The snapping of these bonds, too, became a metaphor for liberation (Jer. 2:20; Isa. 68:6).

A sturdy strain of oxen capable of bearing a double-poled yoke was used for plowing. Evidence points to the Zebu oxen, capable of sustained exertion, as being in common use in Talmudic times. The Torah regards the ox and the donkey as plowing animals (Deut. 22:10), and Isaiah mentions the use of donkeys for tilling the soil (30:24). Rabbinic literature, however, names only the ox and the cow as plowing animals.

Sowing and Planting

The main crops were the winter grains, which were planted at various times prior to the rains, and especially following the first rain. Usually the farmer spaced his sowing activities at intervals over the winter season as a protective measure (cf. Eccles. 11:6), for if he planted all his crops together, a single adverse natural phenomenon could ruin them all at one blow. The normal planting season lasted from Tishri (October) to the end of Tevet (December; Tosef., Ta'an. 1:7). In some instances, planting also took place in Shevat (January), as was the practice with the barley for the *Omer* offering (Men. 8:2).

A distinguishing feature of local agriculture in Roman times was the small quantity of seed sown per unit of land, approximately 4–8 kg. of grain per 1,000 sq. m. (Tosef., Kil. 1:16). This is much less than the average amount planted in traditional Arab farming. This probably explains the meaning of the saying: "Thou shalt carry out much seed into the field and shalt gather little in" (Deut. 28:38). The yield of an Arab farmer is 3–4 times the amount of seed, while the Jewish farmer during Roman times reaped 30 or 40 fold, sometimes even obtaining a harvest of "a hundred measures" (BM 105b; Pes. 87b; see also Matt. 13:8; Varro, Rerum *Rusticarum Libri*, 1:44). These high yields were a result of rational and intensive methods of cultivation.

Hoeing and Weeding

The usual cycle in crop cultivation was plowing, planting, hoeing (TJ, Shek. 68:4), with the last activity designed to remove noxious weeds. The main implement involved, the *"ma'ader,"* is somewhat different from the modern hoe. It consisted of two sticks tied together by a cord (Tosef., Kelim, BB 1:8) to form an acute angle. At the end of the shorter stick, a metal "tooth" was inserted (Kelim 13:2). Such hoes frequently appear in Egyptian drawings. For deeper plowing and hoeing, the *kardom* (Peah, 6:4; Kelim 29:7; cf. *ibid.*, 13:3) was used. An implement resembling the modern hoe, the *magrefah*, served for moving earth or fruit (Gen. R. 16; Kelim 13:4). The *ma'ader* was used for digging in mountain areas which could not be successfully plowed (Isa. 7:25; Peah 2:2). The process of deep digging to prepare the earth for saplings was known as *"izzuk"* (Isa. 5:2; cf. Sif. Deut. 355).

Harvesting

No special importance was ascribed to summer planting in ancient times. *Kaẓir* applied to winter crops. There were two such harvests: first, the early ripening of the grain, the various types of *barley; later, the *wheat and rice-wheat harvest

(Ex. 9:31). At Passover, the *Omer* of barley was offered (Lev. 23:10; cf. II Sam. 21:9; II Kings 4:42). The Gezer calendar also lists the barley as the first of the cereal harvests. Before the *Omer* was offered, the new season's grain was not to be eaten (Lev. 23:14). Only in the Jericho Valley, was harvesting permitted before Passover (Men.10:8). Seven weeks later, the wheat harvest began with the offering of "the two loaves of bread" (Lev. 23:17).

At harvest time, the climate in Israel is hot and dry. More than once the reaper was felled by sunstroke (cf. II Kings 4:18–20; Judith 8:2–3). He rose early to take advantage of the cool, morning hours (Prov. 10:6), and he had to work quickly to avoid plunder, pests and the scattering of the grains. He sought, in addition to his family, to employ hired hands. The division of labor is depicted in the Book of Ruth. A supervisor would watch the workers. Girls were occupied with gleaning and also in making sheaves. The owner supplied part of the food to his workers, namely bread dipped in vinegar. Only the wicked who exploited their workers failed to provide food (Job 24:10–11).

Even though the work was backbreaking, it was performed to the accompaniment of joyous shouts (Ps. 126:5–6; Isa. 9:2). The poor, who gathered their gifts, also contributed to the festive atmosphere. Sometimes, joy would be absent and especially when the land was afflicted by drought (Deut. 11:17, etc.) or when an enemy had attacked the reapers and pillaged the harvest (Isa. 16:7).

Various implements were used during the harvesting procedures. The "*Ḥermesh*" (Deut. 16:9) and "*maggal*" (Jer. 2:16) are two such implements mentioned in the Bible. The latter is the usual term appearing in rabbinic literature, and it is almost certain that the two names signify the same object, the sickle. The scythe, the long handle of which was grasped with both hands, was not known in ancient Ereẓ Israel. The sickle had a short handle, in which there was inserted a curved blade with its short teeth bent backward. (Ḥul. 7:2). Archaeological excavations in Israel have uncovered flint, bone, bronze and iron sickles. Some sickles extend back in time to the Natufian and Neolithic periods. When harvesting, the reaper grasped the stalks in his left hand. In his right he held the sickle, which he would "send out" (Joel 4:14) and pull back, so severing the stalk (Isa. 17:5; Ps. 129:7). When his left hand was full, he would lay the grain on the ground in united bundles ("*ẓavitim*"; Ruth 2:16) or else tie them together with a straw ("*kerikhiot*"; Men. 10:9). The small heaps (*ẓevatim* or *kerikhot*) laid along the harvested rows would be gathered up by the sheaf-binder and held in his bosom ("*Ḥoẓen*"; Ps. 129:7). They were then put together in larger bundles, which had no fixed size, fluctuating between three and 30 pints (½ and 17 liters) of kernels (Pe'ah 6:6). The bundles were left lying on the ground or else tied together in sheaves (Gen. 37:7–8; BM 22a). The next step, which took place once the grain was dry, consisted of collecting the grain in a large stack ("*gadish*"). An alternative practice was to heap the grain in various types of stacks to hasten or retard the drying process as desired (Pe'ah 5:8). This stacking was the final destination of the grain prior to its being transported to the *goren* or threshing floor.

The *goren* stood close to the city or village (I Kings 22:10). To prevent the chaff from being blown into houses, the rabbis ruled that the threshing floor should not be nearer than 50 cubits (i.e., approximately 25 metres) from the city (BB 2:8). The location could neither be on high ground nor exposed to strong winds which would scatter the grains during winnowing (Ruth R. 5). Usually, the threshing floor was in a broad public place. It was surrounded by a fence of thornbushes (Sot. 13a). Trampling (Jer. 51:35) and sprinkling water hardened and leveled the floor. Then the grain was brought and spread out in a circle. During the threshing, the straw and ears were pounded to separate the kernels from the husks. This could be accomplished in several ways. A wooden board, about 0.70 m. wide and 1.20 m. or more long, was used. Its underside was set with stones, mainly of basalt (sometimes of flint), so that when dragged by a pair of oxen, the board would separate the grain. The device, the *morag*, is still used in traditional Arab farming (Arabic "*norg*"). Since this tool was only adopted much later in Greece and Rome, some scholars have suggested that it might have been an invention of the farmer in Ereẓ Israel. This assumption may explain the exclamation of Isaiah (end of ch. 28): "This also cometh from the Lord of hosts; wonderful is His counsel and great His wisdom," for in the preceding verses the prophet enumerates the threshing tools then in use: the *ḥaruẓ*, i.e., the *morag ḥaruẓ* (*ibid.* 41:15), the normal *morag* with saw-like strips of iron in addition to the stones set in it. Isaiah also referred to the "*ofan agalah*" and "*galgal agalah*" ("cartwheels") which were stone wheels or iron discs sharpened like saws, examples of which are still extant among the Arab farmers of today. The last type of tool was introduced into Hellenistic Egypt and Rome. The chronicler of Roman agriculture called it "*plostellum poenicum*" (Varro, *Rerum Rusticarum Libri*, 1:52). In contrast to mechanical means, another threshing method was the running of several oxen tied together ("*revekah*"; Tosef., Par. 2:3) over the grains. Seemingly other animals were also used in this type of threshing, for the rabbis interpreted the Pentateuchal prohibition against muzzling an ox while threshing (Deut. 25:4) to include other animals as well (BK 5:7). The heavy implements described above were suitable for wheat and legumes. More delicate grains were normally threshed with a stick (Isa. *ibid.*) as were smaller quantities of wheat (Judg. 6:11; Ruth 2:17). While the threshing was in progress, additional quantities of grain would constantly be thrown in the path of the threshers by means of a wooden-pronged implement resembling a pitchfork ("*eter*"; Tosef., Uk. 1:5).

Winnowing

Threshing separated the three components of the grain: kernels, chopped straw, and chaff. Winnowing, which consisted of throwing the threshed substances into the wind, caused the lighter elements to be carried away while the heavier kernels fell into a heap. The implement used for this process, the *mizreh* (Isa. 30:24), resembled a pitchfork with broad prongs. Following this the kernels would be thrown up by means of a shovel-like implement, the *raḥat* (cf. Tanh. to Isa. *ibid.*). Once this operation was over, the stack was considered to be complete. The farmer would measure its size (Haggai 2:16) and stand guard over it until it was transferred to the barn (Ruth 3:7).

The chopped straw left over from the winnowing was kept as livestock feed or compost, or was used as an additive in mortar. The chaff was useless except for making fire (Gen. R. 83:3). Yet even after the final winnowing, the kernel heaps still retained waste matter. The grains would then be shaken horizontally in a sieve (*"kevarah"*), a round device, to whose bottom a fiber net was attached. The heavier waste would fall through the threads, and the lighter material gathered on top of the kernels. The top waste would constantly be removed, until only the clean kernels remained within the sieve (cf. Amos 9:9; Ma'as 15:6). The kernels were then milled or crushed, and further cleaned with the aid of sieves with perforations of various sizes, depending on the required size of the finished product (Avot 5:15).

[Jehuda Feliks / Shimon Gibson (2nd ed.)]

ADD. BIBLIOGRAPHY: S. Avitzur, *Man and His Work: Historical Atlas of Tools and Workshops in the Holy Land* (1976); E. Ayalon, Review, in: *Israel Exploration Journal*, 55 (2005), 116–20; O. Borowski, *Agriculture in Iron Age Israel* (1987); M. Broshi, "The Diet of Palestine in the Roman Period – Introductory Notes," in: *The Israel Museum Journal*, 5 (1986), 41–56; M. Broshi, "Agriculture and Economy in Roman Palestine: Seven Notes on Babatha's Archive,"in: *Israel Exploration Journal*, 42 (1992), 230–40; G. Dalman, *Arbeit und Sitte in Palastina*, vols. 1–7 (1928–42); S. Dar, *Landscape and Pattern: An Archaeological Survey of Samaria, 800 B.C.E.–636 C.E.* BAR International Series 308 (1986); C. Dauphin, "Man Makes His Landscape," in: *Bulletin of the Anglo-Israel Archaeological Society*, 11 (1991–92), 22–28; J. Feliks, *Agriculture in Eretz-Israel in the Period of the Bible and Talmud* (1990); R. Frankel, *Wine and Oil Production in Antiquity in Israel and Other Mediterranean Countries* (1999); R. Frankel, S. Avitsur, and E. Ayalon, *History and Technology of Olive Oil in the Holy Land* (1994); C.H.J. de Geus, "The Importance of Archaeological Research into the Palestinian Agricultural Terraces, with an Excursus on the Hebrew Word *gbi*," in: *Palestine Exploration Quarterly*, 107 (1975), 65–74; S. Gibson and G. Edelstein, "Investigating Jerusalem's Rural Landscape," in: *Levant*, 17 (1985), 139–55; idem, "Agricultural Terraces and Settlement Expansion in the Highlands of Early Iron Age Palestine: Is there Any Correlation Between the Two?" in: A. Mazar (ed.), *Studies in the Archaeology of the Iron Age in Israel and Jordan* (2001); D.C. Hopkins, *The Highlands of Canaan: Agricultural Life in the Early Iron Age* (1985); A. Kasher, A. Oppenheimer, and U. Rappaport (eds.), *Man and Land in Eretz-Israel in Antiquity* (1986); A.M. Maier, S.Dar, and Z. Safrai, *The Rural Landscape of Ancient Israel.* (2003); Z.Y.D. Ron, "Agricultural Terraces in the Judaean Mountains," *IEJ*, 16 (1966), 33–49, 111–22; idem, "Development and Management of Irrigation Systems in Mountain Regions of the Holy Land," in: *Transactions of the Institute of British Geographers*, N.S. 10 (1985), 149–69; Z. Safrai, *The Economy of Roman Palestine.* (1994); D. Sperber, *Roman Palestine 200–400: The Land. Crisis and Change in Agrarian Society as Reflected in Rabbinic Sources.* (1978); L.E. Stager, "The Archaeology of the Family in Ancient Israel," in: BASOR, 260 (1985), 1–35; G. Stanhill, "The Fellah's Farm: An Autarkic Agro System," *Agro-Ecosystems*, 4 (1978), 438.

AGRICULTURE. This entry is arranged according to the following outline:

IN THE LAND OF ISRAEL

The study of the history of ancient agriculture in the Land of Israel has been the focus of a great amount of research in recent decades. Much more data is now available as a result of an intensification of data-collection and the use of new methodologies during archaeological excavations and surveys, especially in regard to the development of rural settlements (villages, hamlets and farms) and their landscapes (fields, terraces, access routes to markets), and the technology of agricultural implements (digging tools, ground stone objects) and installations (wine and oil presses). The intensive gathering of plant and wood remains at sites using flotation procedures has helped to enlarge knowledge about the variety of cultivations and fruits trees available during different archaeological periods. Botanical remains are frequently found on the floors of houses and storage buildings, on the surfaces of courtyards, in fire-pits and in silos. Inventories of crops are thus produced and this helps towards a reconstruction of agrarian practices and dietary patterns. Further insights into the history of agriculture have also emerged as a result of inter-disciplinary work with geomorphologists, agronomists, and botanists. The analysis of Phytoliths – fossilized mineral particles produced biogenetically within plants – under microscope, has been found to be useful in the study of cultivated cereals. Palynological studies have also contributed to the investigation of landscape changes and the overall effect humans have on their environment, though usually only on a regional scale. Pollen studies are less helpful in elucidating changes on a micro-environmental level. Pollen cores have hitherto been taken from the Dead Sea and from the Sea of Galilee.

For a survey of agricultural methods and the conclusions of recent archaeological research, see preceding entry.

[Shimon Gibson (2nd ed.)]

In Prehistory

Some archaeologists date the beginnings of agriculture in Palestine to the Mesolithic period, when the Natufian culture made its appearance with its bone and flint artifacts, some of which have survived to the present day. In the Kabara caves on Mt. Carmel, a flint sickle with its handle shaped to represent a fawn's head has been found. To that same period belong the sickles, mortars, and pestles which have been discovered in other localities in Palestine. According to these scholars, all these artifacts indicate the cultivation of cereals. According to others, however, these utensils were used merely to reap and mill wild grain. Archaeological finds testifying to soil cultivation and cattle raising become more numerous in the Neolithic Age, the period of caves and huts, agricultural implements, and cleaving tools. All these are evidence of settled communities which produced and stored food. To this period, likewise, belong excavated, prehistoric locations such as the Abu Uzbah cave on Mt. Carmel, the Neolithic cave near Sha'ar ha-Golan in the Jordan Valley and the lower strata of Jericho. In the Chalcolithic period, the transition between the Neolithic and the Bronze Age (4000 B.C.E.), agricultural settlements in the valleys, especially in the proximity of water sources, increased. Settlements were established in the plains of Moab (N.E. of the Dead Sea) where the Telleilat el-Asul (Ghassul) were found – mounds covering simple buildings, grain storages, agricultural implements, and artisans' tools made of calcareous or flint stone. By the later Chalcolithic period copper vessels like those found in Tel Abu-Matar near Beersheba appeared. In this area and at nearby Khirbet al-Bitar, excavations have unearthed ricewheat (*Triticum dicoccum*), einkorn (*Triticum monococcum*), two-rowed barley (*Hordeum distichum*), and lentils (*Lens esculenta Moench*). Elsewhere, olive and date kernels, grape seeds, and pomegranate rinds have been discovered.

From the Beginning of the Bronze Age to the Conquest of Joshua

This period includes the early (3000 B.C.E.), middle (until 1550 B.C.E.), and part of the late Bronze Age. The earliest literary evidence of local agricultural activity is provided by an inscription on the grave of the Egyptian officer Weni, who conducted a military expedition in Palestine during the reign of Pepi I (beginning of 24th century B.C.E.) "The army returned in peace after smiting the country of the sand dwellers [the inhabitants of the coastal plain]... after he had cut down its figs and vines." At that time the King's Highway running along the coastal plain and through the Jezreel and Jordan valleys became increasingly important, and many settlements were established along its length. Settlements were also founded in the south of the Judean mountains, for example at Tell Beit-Mirsim, apparently the biblical Debir. The Sanehat Scroll (20th century B.C.E.) described the travels in Palestine of this Egyptian officer and the document proves that, in the southern regions of the country, there were settlements which supported themselves by farming and cattle raising. Evidence of many settlements during the 18th century B.C.E. is furnished by the Egyptian "Execration Texts." During the Hyksos occupation, the Habiru, apparently the Hebrew tribes of the patriarchal era, are first mentioned. They were nomads who did not establish any permanent settlements. Some occupied the marginal grasslands and occasionally sowed there. Thus Isaac planted in the Naḥal Gerar region "in that year," and, as a result of plentiful rain fall, reaped a "hundredfold" harvest (Gen. 26:12). Other scriptural references suggest that the land was closely settled and highly valued at this time. Abraham's and Lot's shepherds quarreled with each other while the "Canaanite and Perizzite dwelt then in the land" (Gen. 13:7). For a burial plot he wanted to purchase, Abraham had to pay Ephron, the Hittite, the full price (*ibid.*, ch. 23), and Jacob similarly had to pay a large sum for the section of the field in Shechem where he pitched his tents (*ibid.*, 33:19). The depiction at the Temple of Amon of Thutmose's expeditions in Palestine (c. 1478 B.C.E.) and his famous victory at Megiddo includes reliefs of the plants he brought from Palestine (the Karnak "Botanical Garden"). An inscription states that "the amount of harvest brought... from the Maket [plain of Jezreel] was 280,000 heqt of corn [150,000 bushels] beside what was reaped and taken by the king's soldiers."

Early Israelite

In contrast to scriptural references, external evidence on the state of local agriculture just before and after the Israelite conquest is rather meager. Yet from all sources, the incontrovertible fact emerges that no radical climatic changes occurred. Huntington's theory of the country becoming increasingly arid from the biblical time until today must, therefore, be rejected. It is not supported by any examination of the sources or archaeological discovery. These indicate that the areas sown and planted then coincide with the regions watered by rain or irrigation today. An intensively farmed, settled area existed in the irrigated regions of the Jordan Valley and another along the Mediterranean coast (where the annual precipitation exceeds 300 mm.), but there were no stable agricultural settlements in the northern Negev. The land there was cultivated once in several years, when plentiful rainfall would yield abundant harvests. The southern Negev and Arabah were waste, except for desert oases and irrigation projects where waters flowing down from the mountains were collected in dams. Such projects were limited during the kingdom, but increased in the Nabatean era (see below). The condition of afforestation was no different then than at the beginning of Jewish colonization in modern times. Forest and woods spread over the hill and rocky regions which were difficult to cultivate and in areas where the lack of security made soil cultivation and the erection of agricultural installations too hazardous. The "vines and figs" of the regions bordering the routes of the traversing armies were pillaged. This explains the presence of woods in the Naḥal Iron (Wadi ʿArah) district mentioned in the expedition of Thutmose III (and later the "large forest" on the Sharon Plain mentioned by Strabo). Broad forests also extended along the north and northeast boundaries of the country – in Gilead, Bashan, and the Lebanon. There, in the vegetation along the Jordan and in the deserts, lurked wild beasts (see Fauna of *Israel). During the intervals when the land lay desolate, animals would invade the ruins where forests had begun to grow. Several times the scriptural warning against the danger of a too rapid military conquest had been issued "thou mayest not consume them too quickly, lest the beasts of the field increase upon thee" (Deut. 7:22; Ex. 23:29; Num. 26:12). Having wandered in the desert for many years, the children of Israel were unfamiliar with local conditions and could hardly have been expected to succeed in mastering the intensive farming which obtained, for the most part, in the newly conquered territory. Furthermore, the neglect caused by wars and conquest had temporarily devastated large farming tracts, and these had been overrun by natural forests – a condition later recalled in Isaiah 18:9. Scrub and woods became widespread, and farmland degenerated into pasture (cf. *ibid.*, 7:28).

During the transition period, the children of Israel, presumably, were primarily engaged in tending flocks, as in patriarchal days. The Song of Deborah yields no trace of extensive occupation with agriculture, even though the soil was tilled. The tribe of Reuben is described as living "among the sheepfolds, to hear the pipings of the flocks" (Judg. 5:16). Scripture also testifies to the existence of broad grazing lands in Gilead, and Bashan in Transjordan, the areas settled by the tribes of Reuben and Gad and half the tribe of Manasseh, all of whom owned much livestock (Num. 32; Deut. 3:19; Josh. 1:14). Although the Bible does portray the land of Canaan as "flowing with milk and honey" (date syrup), no conclusions can be drawn from this expression as to the relative importance of grazing land ("milk") as opposed to soil cultivation ("honey"). Livestock was raised to a limited extent in the border grassland regions and deserts, or was fed on the stubble of the grain fields and the stalks of the vegetable gardens. During the period of the conquest, sheep and cattle were also grazed in the forests which had covered the farm lands. The talmudic sages undoubtedly relied on an ancient tradition when they included, among the ordinances enacted by *Joshua, one permitting the grazing of flocks in the wooded areas (BK 81a).

The agricultural prosperity of Israel, however, is determined by the rainfall. This fact is emphasized already in the Bible which praises the country as a land that "drinketh water as the rain of heaven cometh down" (Deut. 11:10–11), in contrast to Egypt which was irrigated. This blessing, however, also entails the danger, repeated several times in the Bible and rabbinical literature, that, on account of sin, rainfall could be withheld, with drought and famine resulting. Although the country is described as "a land of brooks of water, of fountains and depths springing forth in valleys and hills" (*ibid.*, 8:7), there is no evidence that in ancient times there were more than the hundreds of small springs and the few moderate and large fountains which now exist. Scripture praises the plain of the Jordan as "well watered," and so it is, even today (Gen. 14:10).

Either through experience or by borrowing the agricultural skills of the indigenous population, the Israelites gradually mastered the cultivation of the soil. The Talmud describes their predecessors as "well versed in the cultivation of the land," saying, "Fill this amount with olives; fill this amount with vines," and interprets their names accordingly: "Hori they that smelled the earth; Hivi they that tasted the earth like a serpent" (Shab. 85a). Even the spies admitted that Israel was a land "flowing with milk and honey and this is its fruit" (Num. 13). The Pentateuch states that the conquerors would enter a land with a highly developed agriculture, fertile soil, and established agricultural installations (Deut. 6:11). Special reference is made to hill cultivation where terraced fields were planted with vines and fruit trees and contained water cisterns, oil and wine presses, and tanks. Since the Canaanites had not yet been ousted from the fertile valleys, the wheat fields were not available to the Israelites (Judg. 1:19, 27–36).

Hill cultivation is intensive by nature; land holdings are small, and knowledge and experience are needed for such farming to yield a livelihood. These conditions apparently explain why the descendants of Joseph (Ephraim and half the tribe of Manasseh) complained to Joshua that the mountain of Ephraim was too small to maintain them. Joshua advised them to go to the forests of Gilead and Bashan (the land of the Perizzites and Rephaim), fell the trees, and settle there; upon the assumption that in securing the dominating heights, they would succeed in dislodging the Canaanites from the valleys (Josh. 17:14–18). Clearing the forests was by no means easy, and was not yet completed in the reign of David, for this region included the "Forest of Ephraim" where the armies of David and Absalom fought each other (II Sam. 18:6–8). The Israelites did gradually succeed not only in mastering agricultural skills but also in organizing permanent town and village settlements. The nomads, enemies of the Israelites from the desert period, now envied the successful Israelite colonization. Together with their flocks, they raided Israelite territory and plundered the fields. Between each wave, the Israelites harvested their fields in haste and stored the produce in hidden receptacles (Judg. 6:2). Rather than use an exposed threshing floor, Gideon was forced to thresh his harvested wheat in a barn where fleeces were dried (*ibid.*, 6:37–40). He was a well-to-do farmer, owning cattle and sheep, vines, and wheat fields. The ordinary Israelite farmer, however, seems to have been poor. His main diet consisted of barley, and consequently the children of Israel were contemptuously represented in the Midianite soldier's dream as a "cake of barley bread" baked on coals (*ibid.*, 7:13).

The state of agriculture at this time may be deduced from the laws of land inheritance in the Pentateuch, and the descriptions of the settlement of the tribes, the divisions of parcels of land among the various families, and the procedure of redeeming estates recounted in the Book of Ruth. These sources reveal Hebrew agriculture as based on the small single family holding. It depicts an idyllic prosperous village life, although workers were only hired at harvest time, and even the wealthy Boaz personally supervised the stacking of the grain after the winnowing. In the course of time, however, a poor, landless class arose – as Scripture itself had foreseen: "the poor shall never cease out of the land" (Deut. 25:11). The unfortunates were the recipients of the gifts to the poor: the gleanings, the forgotten sheaves, the corners of the fields, the poor tithe. To the priests and levites, the heave offerings and tithes were given. The Book of Ruth reflects this, as well as the redeeming of fields to insure the continuity of family ties with the land. This almost sacred bond tying the Hebrew farmer to his inherited land was characteristic of Israel agriculture in every period. Here, too, is a reason for the speedy recovery of the local agriculture after every period of desolation. It should also be noted that the Israelite farmer always maintained a distinctly high cultural level. This fact is attested to by the "*Gezer Calendar", which gives a succinct but comprehensive account of the annual cycle of seasonal agricultural occupations. If the conjecture is correct that this calendar was a lesson transcribed by a boy, it is evidence that formal instruction in agriculture was imparted during the period of the Judges. The Hebrews also acquired agricultural techniques from their neighbors, as may be deduced from Shamgar the son of Anath's smiting the Philistines with an ox goad (Judg. 3:31) – not the primitive implement made entirely of wood, but one with a metal nail knocked through one end, and a metal spade attached to the other. In later sources, the *dorban* (also an ox goad) is mentioned as one of the few metal implements the Hebrews were allowed to take to the Philistines to be repaired and sharpened, metal work being prohibited to the Israelites lest they fashion arms to war upon their Philistine overlords (I Sam. 13:19–22). It appears that the children of Israel adopted agricultural skills and the use of the new types of implements brought by the Philistines who invaded the country in the 13th century from the Aegean islands, and who settled in the southern coastal region and the lowlands of Judah. Their main gainful occupation was farming. Although they were the enemies of the Hebrews, they nevertheless refrained from attacking the farms on the hills and in the valleys. A period of agricultural stability ensued. This period provides the background for the Book of Ruth.

The Period of the First Temple

Israelite agriculture was based, as has been shown, on the autarchic family farm. With the rise of the monarchy, this order was threatened with collapse. Samuel warned the assembled people: "He (the king) will take your fields and your vineyards, and your olive yards, even the best of them, and give them to his servants" (I Sam. 8–14), but it is doubtful if the prediction came true. Although David owned royal estates over which he appointed officials (I Chron. 27:26–29), they were apparently conquered and annexed territories, or else previously unworked areas which were developed by royal initiative. In the days of Solomon, boundaries were extended, and officials "who provided victuals for the king and his household" (I Kings 4:7) administered the royal estates. Agriculture prospered, and the memory of that condition was perpetuated in Scripture: "Judah and Israel dwelt safely, every man under his vine and fig tree from Dan to Beer-Sheba…" (*ibid.*, 5:5). Uzziah, king of Judah, is called "lover of husbandry," and was noted for owning fields and vineyards, and for building "towers in the wilderness and hewing out many cisterns" (II Chron. 26:10). Evidence corroborating this statement has been found in recent times through the excavation in the Negev hill region of an agricultural settlement, irrigated by an accumulation of rain water flowing down from the mountains. Settlements of this type were, apparently, guard posts and supply stations along the Negev caravan routes. In those days agriculture and agronomy reached their peak and were described by Isaiah as wisdom emanating from God, Who had taught the sons of man excellent methods of plowing and reaping (Isa. 28:23–29). It is noteworthy that these verses mention threshing implements which appeared only many generations later in Egypt and Rome. After the death of Uzziah security deteriorated and a decline set in among the Hebrew settlements in the lowlands. Against this background, Isaiah prophesied better days to come, when settlements would extend through the lowlands, when the farmer would sow his irrigated fields near the springs, and the shepherd tend his flocks without interference (*ibid.*, 32:19–20).

The story of Naboth's vineyard, which was coveted by King Ahab, who wished to convert it into a vegetable garden, reflects agricultural conditions in the Northern Kingdom. Whereas the Jewish king respected the sanctity of a paternal inheritance to an Israel farmer, Queen Jezebel, a Sidonian princess, could not appreciate it (I Kings 21). With the passage of time, apparently, the poor and its widows and orphans were, in increasing numbers, likewise evicted from their holdings, and the prophet denounced those "who join house to house, that lay field to field" (Isa. 5:68). Nevertheless, in the main, the right of inheritance to patriarchal estates was upheld. When Jerusalem was actually under siege, Jeremiah, exercising his right of redemption, bought a plot of land (32:7–12). The remarkable agricultural prosperity of the land of Israel during the First Temple period is indicated in Ezekiel 27:17, which lists the exports of Judah and Israel to the market of Tyre as wheat of Minnith (probably a place in Transjordan), "pannag" (which cannot be clearly identified), honey, oil, and balm. With the destruction of the Kingdom of Israel at the end of the eighth century B.C.E. Samaria was denuded of its Israelite population, and repopulated by the nations the King of Assyria transported from other districts of his empire. The new inhabitants – later called Samaritans and in the Talmud, "Kutim" – failed to farm their land properly. Perhaps the lions that attacked them (II Kings 17:25–27) had found a lair in the forests which encroached on neglected farms. There is no further information on conditions in Galilee. Some Israelites must have remained, since Hezekiah communicated with them (II Chron. 30), and Josiah extended his domain over them (*ibid.*, 34:6). A few biblical passages point to persisting desolation, and a prophecy predicted the restoration of cultivation in Samaria (Jer. 31:5).

The Period of the Return and the Second Temple

Having destroyed the Temple, Nebuzaradan left "the poorest of the land to be vinedressers and husbandmen" (II Kings 25:12), apparently tenant farmers or hired workers of the royal estates. He may also have left behind those familiar with local methods in order to prevent the further deterioration of the farms by unskilled and inexperienced labor. The impoverished Jews and the foreigners who settled in abandoned Jewish territory could not, however, maintain the terraced hill farms and orchards. When the exiles returned, they found the land forsaken and desolate. They proceeded to repair the terraces, to restore the agricultural installations and to plant vines and fruit trees. Yet, due to their ignorance of how to exploit the rain water for hill cultivation, they failed to establish viable farms. Somewhat later, conditions improved. Farming prospered, and the prophet Malachi regarded the changed situation as a manifestation of God's love for His people. Desolate Edom is contrasted with prospering Judah (1:2–3). From the books of Ezra and Nehemiah it appears, however, that this optimism was premature, particularly in view of the ensuing moral degeneration. Poor farmers were evicted from their lands by the rich, and a new landowning class emerged. The new conditions loosened the bonds of devotion tying the farmer to his patrimony, and Jewish agriculture suffered. Now the foreigners, who had been forced to restore the lands seized from the Israelites, began to raise their heads. They obtained employment from the new owners and were often able to buy back the lands they had forfeited. Fields, vineyards, and orchards were neglected, and the woods again spread. From these trees, the Jews were enjoined to cut branches and build tabernacles (Neh. 8:15). As a result of the social and agrarian reforms instituted by Ezra and Nehemiah the Jewish population became more securely settled. Although a significant portion of the land still belonged to the king of Persia, the Jewish settlement broke through its boundaries by extending northward toward Galilee. The meager historical source material for the period includes the Book of Judith, assigned to the early fourth century (the period of Artaxerxes II, 404–359 B.C.E.). The setting of the hook is the hills overlooking Jezreel, and the Jewish settlements mentioned as existing in the vicinity (Judith 7:3–13) apparently formed the link between the inhabited areas of Judea and the colonies that flourished in Galilee in later generations.

The level of Jewish agriculture in the Hellenistic period is not altogether clear. The author of the *Letter of *Aristeas* (pars. 112–118: early third century B.C.E.) praised the agricultural productivity of the country and the great "diligence of its farmers. The country is plentifully wooded with numerous olive trees and rich in cereals and vegetables and also in vines and honey. Date palms and other fruit trees are beyond reckoning among them." He apparently exaggerated the extent of the irrigated areas and the importance of the Jordan River as a water source. He similarly referred to large parcels of land – "each a holder of one hundred auroura lots" – about 275,000 square meters. Perhaps he wanted to draw an analogy between the Nile and the Jordan, comparing the small lots of Judah with the large holdings of Egypt. Had Ereẓ Israel been as densely populated as he claimed, the landholding of each family must have been much smaller than he estimated. His assertion might, however, indicate the growth of the landowning class on the one hand and a landless class on the other, conditions that arose soon after the return of the Babylonian exiles. The book of Ben Sira stresses such a contrast between the classes. In the *Zeno papyri (259 B.C.E.), Syria and Palestine are described as exporters of agricultural produce: grain, oil, and wine.

The Hasmonean Period

A period of further consolidation and expansion of Jewish settlement. The Hasmonean revolt relied mainly on the farmers, who received their just reward once the war had been won when many Gentile holdings fell into their hands. The farmers adhered closely to the Torah, especially to the precepts pertaining to the land, such as the year of release. Josephus relates (Wars, 1:54–66) that John Hyrcanus was forced to raise his siege of Ptolemy's stronghold because of the scarcity of food occasioned by the sabbatical year. During the reign of Alexander Yannai the Hasmonean kingdom reached the peak of its expansion, Jewish colonization of Galilee increased, and it became the largest center of Jewish population outside of Judea.

The Mishnaic and Talmudic Period

Began a generation before the destruction of the Temple and ends at the time of the division of the Roman empire. Josephus describes an abundance and fertility in the land at the end of the Second Temple period. He lavishes praise on Galilee in particular where "the land is so rich in soil and pasturage and produces such a variety of trees, that even the most indolent are tempted by these facilities to devote themselves to agriculture. In fact every inch of soil has been cultivated by the inhabitants; there is not a parcel of wasteland. The towns, too, are thickly distributed and even the villages, thanks to the fertility of the soil, are all so densely populated that the smallest of them contains above fifteen thousand inhabitants" (Jos., Wars, 3:42–43). The last number is an obvious exaggeration, especially in view of the number of villages in Galilee, which he elsewhere puts at 204 (Jos., Life, 235). He also describes Samaria and Judea: "Both regions consist of hills and plains, yield a light and fertile soil for agriculture, are well wooded, and abound in fruits, both wild and cultivated... But the surest testimony to the virtues and thriving conditions of the two countries is that both have a dense population"; but he is less enthusiastic about Transjordan which "is for the most part desert and rugged and too wild to bring tender fruits to maturity." Yet, he continues, even there, there were "tracts of finer soil which are productive of every species of crop, country watered by torrents descending from mountains and springs" (Wars 3:44–50). He praises the valley of Gennasereth where "there is not a plant which its fertile soil refuses to produce" – both those "which delight in the most wintry climate" and those which "thrive on heat," and concludes that "Nature had taken pride in this assembly, by a tour de force of the most discordant species in a single spot" (*ibid.*, 3:517–18). With equal enthusiasm Josephus regarded the valley of Jericho and the plentiful spring of Elisha which waters it. There grow "the most charming and luxuriant parks. Of the date palms watered by it there are numerous varieties differing in flavor ... here too grow the juicy balsam, the most precious of all local products, the henna shrubs and myrrh trees so that it would be no misnomer to describe this place as divine" (*ibid.*, 4:468 ff.). Similar praise of the date palms of Jericho are found in the nature studies of Pliny, who gives the names and characteristics of the varieties of dates which were export items (*Historia Naturalis*, 13:9). He also mentions the balsam groves of Jericho and En-Gedi, and writes parenthetically: "But to all the other odors that of balsam is considered preferable, a plant that has only been bestowed by Nature upon the land of Judea. In former times it was cultivated in two gardens only, both of which belonged to kings of that country.... The Jews vented their rage upon this shrub just as they were in the habit of doing against their own lives, while, on the other hand, the Romans protected it; indeed combats have taken place before now in defense of a shrub ... the fifth year after the conquest of Judea, these cuttings with the suckers were sold for the price of 800,000 sesterces" (*ibid.*, 12:25, 24).

On account of the density of the population, holdings were quite small. The typical size may be estimated from Eusebius's account (*Historiae Eccleseastiea*, 3:20, 1 ff.) of the two grandsons of Judah, brother of Jesus, who declared to the Roman government that they derived their sustenance from an area of 39 plethra (34,000 m^2.) which they cultivated with their own hands, from which it follows that the average family derived its livelihood from 17,000 m^2. Several passages in talmudic literature refer to the unit *bet kor* or 30 *se'ah* (about 23,000 m^2 in area) as a large field and a substantial inheritance (e.g., Mekh., *Be-Shallaḥ*, 87–88). On the other hand, some individuals at the close of the Second Temple period possessed immense fortunes. Among them was the almost legendary R. Eleazar b. Ḥarsum (Kid. 49b), a high priest, "of whom it was said that his father had left him 1,000 cities, yet he would wander from place to place to study Torah" (Yoma 35b). These cities were razed during the Bar Kokhba War (TJ, Ta'an. 4:8, 69a)

In those times, the state of agriculture fluctuated constantly in accordance with the policies of the Roman conquerors. Josephus relates that, after the destruction, Titus issued a decree expropriating Jewish landholdings which he ordered sold or leased out (Wars, 5:421). At first these lands were acquired mainly by Gentiles who leased the plots to the former Jewish owners, and these later tried to buy back their land. To assure the restoration of the lands to their former Jewish owners, the talmudic sages enacted ordinances forbidding competition and speculation in land (BB 9:4; TJ, Ket. 2:1, 26b; Git. 52a, et al.). On the other hand, a class of extremely wealthy landowners emerged at that time like the *nasi* dynasty, R. Eliezer b. Azariah, and others, who had acquired heirless estates from the Roman government. Asked what constituted a wealthy person, their contemporary R. Tarfon answered: "Whoever owns 100 vineyards, 100 fields, and 100 slaves to work them" (Shab. 25b). The response, it should be noted, is one of the isolated instances in rabbinic literature which refers to the employment of slave labor in agriculture (see also TJ, Yev. 8:1, 8d). Gentile (there were no Jewish) slaves were chiefly employed in housework and urban domestic services, whereas agriculture was the province of farmers, tenants, lessors, and hired workers. In the first years following the destruction, Gentiles still possessed and also worked many former Jewish farms. Rabbinic literature alludes to this situation in the gloomy *baraita:* "For seven years the Gentiles held vintage in the vineyards soaked with Israel's blood without fertilizing" (Git. 57a). With the passage of time, however, the Jewish population resettled on the farms and regained ownership. Natural increase forced the size of each family's holding to decrease, the average now being four-five *bet se'ah*, i.e., 3,000–3,500 m^2. of field crops, the area known as *bet ha-peras* (Oho. 17:2 – in Latin: *forus).* Plots of this size are mentioned in deeds of sale dating from the time of Bar Kokhba, found in Wadi Murabba'at in the desert of Judah (Benoit, Milik, de Vaux, *Les grottes de Murabaat, pp.* 155 ff.). These documents speak of the sale of "an area where five *se'ah* of wheat can be sown." Presumably an area of 3,500 m^2 sufficed to supply the cereal needs of a family. In addition the farmer owned vines and orchards. Executed during Bar Kokhba's rebellion, these deeds prove that even in the thick of war, Jews continued to buy and sell land.

The rebellion and its aftermath seriously affected Jewish agriculture. Certain localities were utterly devastated, "since Hadrian had come and destroyed the country" (TJ, Pe'ah 7:1, 20a). Especially in Judea, where the Roman government took possession of the lands of the thousands of war dead, the desolation was great. In the words of the *aggadah*: "Hadrian owned a large vineyard, 18 *mil* square, and he surrounded it with a fence of the slain of Bethar" (Lam. R. 2:2, no. 4). Galilee, too, sustained heavy damage. Before "the times became troubled," the area had been so densely populated that R. Simeon b. Yoḥai found a way of measuring the distances between the villages so that not one was beyond the Sabbath range (2,000 cubits) of its nearest neighbor (TJ, Er. 5:1, 22b–c). Its olive groves had previously been so numerous that one "dipped one's feet in oil" there, yet later "olives [were] not normally found there" (TJ, Pe'ah, 7:1, 20a). Oppressive decrees and heavy taxes jeopardized the existence, both physical and spiritual, of the farmer. Before the revolt, Simeon b. Yoḥai, the disciple of Akiva, was particularly interested in the religious precepts applying to land; after it, he complained: "Is that possible? If a person plows in the plowing season and reaps in the reaping season… what is to become of the Torah?" (Ber. 35a). The suggested solution was employment in trade and in crafts in the city. Yet once again, agriculture recovered. Jewish settlement expanded and even penetrated to the northern coastal regions (Tosef., Kil. 2:16).

Further increases in population led to further decrease in the size of family holdings. In the next generation there is a conflict of opinion as to what constituted the minimum size of land divisible among heirs. The majority of sages held it to be a plot large enough to provide each heir with one and a half *bet se'ah* (1,176 m^2.) while Judah regarded a field even half that size as divisible among heirs (BB 7:6; Tosef., BM 11:9). Normally a single owner would have several fields of this size, yet there were cases where an individual farmer had to subsist on an even smaller plot of land. A certain Samaritan reportedly drew his sustenance from a field a *bet se'ah* in area (784 m^2; Ket. 112a).

The period from the disciples of Akiva until the third amoraic generation (middle of second century to end of third century C.E.), was both spiritually and physically one of the most productive periods of all times. It saw an unprecedented progress in agriculture. Highly cultured, the Jewish farmer did not allow himself to stagnate and he was always ready to adopt new techniques and to experiment with new strains (see *Agricultural Methods). Many *aggadot* celebrate the abundance and fertility of the land of Israel at the time, and mention grape clusters as large as oxen; mustard as tall as fig trees; two radishes being a full load for a camel; turnips large enough to constitute a fox's den; a peach large enough to feed a man and his animal to satiety, etc. Certain localities were designated as the referent in "the land of milk and honey," as for instance, sixteen *mil* around Sepphoris in Galilee and the vicinities of Lydda and Ono (see Meg. 6a; Ket. 111b; TJ, Pe'ah 7:4, 20a–b).

Depression set in at the end of R. Johanan's lifetime. "In his days, the world changed" (TJ, Pe'ah 7:4, 20a), either through natural causes (BM 105h) or else through Roman taxation. In any event the lot of the farmer became progressively worse. Farmers had, in earlier times, most strictly observed the prescriptions of the sabbatical year; now they became more lax (Sanh. 26a). Previously "one was not supposed to raise sheep and goats" in the land of Israel; now Johanan advocated sheep raising (Ḥul. 84a). It had obviously become increasingly difficult for the Jewish farmer to be self-supporting. In principle, R. Eliezer, who had previously laid down that whoever did not own land was no man, now came to the cruel realization that there was no occupation less distinguished than agriculture. Only those farmers close to the rulers could maintain themselves, and he therefore concluded: "Land was only given to the powerful" (Yev. 63a; Sanh. 58b).

An exodus from village to city ensued in which the process of the displacement of the Jewish farmer began. Gentiles replaced them to such an extent, that the question arose as to whether most of the land of Palestine was in Gentile or Jewish hands. The new owners neither felt an attachment to the land nor possessed the skills of their predecessors. Especially in the hill regions, lands were now abandoned or turned into pastures, and once more the forests began to encroach on the deserted farms.

The Byzantine-Muslim Period

Under Byzantine rule, the situation hardly improved. However there is evidence, even for that time, of the existence of Jewish settlements in the Valley of Jezreel and in the Negev, as well, where remains of exquisite ancient synagogues are visible (Bet Alfa, Nirim, etc.). The Nabatean agriculture which flourished in the Negev mountain area is also noteworthy. This people had developed a highly perfected system of gathering runoff water and so irrigating arid, desolate regions. With the Moslem conquest, many Byzantine lands were laid waste, the owners fleeing or killed. These lands became state property and were leased out to tenant farmers. The Muhammadan rulers were totally ignorant of agriculture and their heavy taxes drove the owners from the land. Here and there, especially in Galilee, some Jewish settlements persevered. Later, there was an improvement. By the 11th century Ramleh figs had become an important export item, and cotton, sugar cane, and indigo plants were cultivated.

The Crusader conquest wreaked further damage on local agriculture. The Franks, who took possession, farmed large tracts extensively, using a combination of European and local techniques. The village population became serfs indentured to the land. There is almost no information available on Judea at that time. It is known, however, that Jews suffered less than the Muslim population at the hands of the crusaders. There is mention of Jewish settlements in Galilee (Gischala (Gush Ḥalav), Alma, Kefar Baram, etc.) where the population engaged mainly in handicrafts and trade. Little is known of Jews in Palestine in the time of the Mamluks. At the end of the 14th century, Jews expelled from France settled in Ereẓ Israel, among them Estori Parḥi, whose work *Kaftor va-Feraḥ* describes the country and its agriculture. The author made his home in Beth-Shean, an area where Jews were living, as they did too, in Safed, Gischala, Lydda, Ramleh, and Gaza.

A marked improvement in agriculture and an increase in population occurred under Ottoman rule, at the end of the 16th century. Jews were engaged in the manufacture of finished products from agricultural raw materials: wine, textiles, and dyeing. They lived in Ein Zeitim, Biriyyah, Peki'in, Kefar Kanna, and elsewhere. In the 17th century the Jews in the villages were harassed by both Bedouin tribes and government soldiers; the population there consequently declined. Dahir al-Amr who ruled over Galilee in the 1740s encouraged the settlement of fallahin, and Jews also came to live in the region, in villages like Kefar Yasif and Shefaram. After his death, another period of decline ensued. Only at the end of the 19th century was there noticeable improvement. The Jewish population increased, and Sir Moses Montefiore among others formulated plans for settling Jews on the land. The Mikveh Israel agricultural school was founded in 1870 and a little later the first Jewish colonies, Moẓa and Petaḥ Tikvah sprang up. In 1881, the American consul in Jerusalem noted that 1,000 Jewish families were earning their livelihood from agriculture. Colonization gained new strength from the First Aliyah in 1882, and from then and until today the extent of Jewish agricultural settlement has been constantly expanding (see *Israel, State of: Agriculture).

[Jehuda Feliks]

IN BABYLON

The Jews in Babylonia enjoyed a considerable measure of internal autonomy under the rule of the *Exilarch, who was almost a tributary monarch; consequently the agricultural customs and usages appertaining to the land of Israel obtained in Jewish Babylonia and it is specifically stated that the ten enactments traditionally attributed to Joshua to protect the sometimes conflicting rights of cattle owners, farmers, and the ordinary public, obtained also in Babylon (BK 81b). On the other hand it was clearly laid down that when the civil law conflicted with Jewish law in these matters the former prevailed (cf. BB 55a). During the whole of the period of the *amoraim* and their successors the **savoraim*, i.e., from the third to the eighth centuries, the economy of Babylonia was essentially an agricultural one. From the end of the fifth century onward however, that agricultural economy gradually changed to a money one, and by the eighth century the latter prevailed. This important change is reflected in the **takkanah* enacted by R. Huna ha-Levi b. Isaac and R. Manasseh b. Joseph, the *geonim* of Pumbedita, together with their colleague Bebai of Sura, between 785 and 788 C.E. whereby the previous law that a widow could claim her *ketubbah* only on the landed property of her husband was changed to enable her to claim on his movable property also. Generally speaking the agricultural conditions in Babylonia were similar to those of Ereẓ Israel, with the result that the Babylonian *amoraim* found little difficulty in applying the rules laid down in the Mishnah, which reflects conditions in Ereẓ Israel, to those of their own country. Nevertheless, there were distinct differences, some of which are herewith noted. The land was more fertile than that of Ereẓ Israel. Situated between the Euphrates and the Tigris, and intersected with numerous tributaries and man-made canals, there was an abundant water supply which was largely independent of rain, and on the verse of Jeremiah 51:13 "thou that dwellest upon many waters, abundant in treasures" the Palestinian *amora* *Hoshaiah commented "Why are the granaries of Babylonia always filled with grain? Because there is an abundance of water," while the Babylonian Rav commented, "Babylonia is rich, because the harvest is gathered even when there is no rain" (Ta'an. 10a). Where in Ereẓ Israel prayers for the relief of drought were characteristic, in Babylonia public prayers were offered against the peril of floods, and were even offered up on their behalf by their coreligionists in Ereẓ Israel (Ta'an. 22b). The climate was also distinctly better than in Ereẓ Israel (RH 20a). As a result Jewish Babylonia enjoyed exceptional fertility and the Euphrates is made to say "I cause plants to grow in 30 days and vegetables in three days" (Gen. R. 16:3). The date palm was the most characteristic of the trees of Babylonia. It grew luxuriously and extensively. Rav stated that their abundance enabled the Jews of Babylonia to find an easy livelihood there (Ta'an. 29b) and Ulla, of Ereẓ Israel on a visit to Babylon, remarked that "the reason God exiled the Jews to Babylonia was that, having plentiful dates for food, they could devote themselves to the study of Torah" (Pes. 87b). At the time of the emperor Julian (361–63 C.E.) the whole of Mesene as far as the Persian Gulf was like one huge palm grove. The olive, which was one of the staple commodities of Ereẓ Israel, did not flourish to any large extent in Babylonia. From a non-talmudic source it is learnt that it began to be more extensively cultivated in the fourth century but in the early period its place, both for lighting and for food, was taken by sesame oil. Thus when R. Tarfon wished to limit the oil for the Sabbath lamp to olive oil (Shab. 2:2) Johanan b. Nuri protested, "If so, what shall the Babylonians do, who have only sesame oil" (Shab. 26a), and so characteristic was this difference that whereas "oil" without any qualification was taken in Ereẓ Israel to refer to olive oil, in Babylonia it was taken to refer to sesame (Ned. 53a). Cotton seed oil was also in common use (Shab. 21a). Hemp, which had to be imported into Ereẓ Israel (Kil. 9:7), at least in mishnaic times (in the amoraic period it seems to have been successfully cultivated; cf. TJ, Kil. 32d) was grown extensively in Babylonia and cloth made from it was common and cheaper than linen (BM 51a). It was also used for ropes (Ket. 67a). A plant unique in Babylonia, as compared with Israel, was the cuscuta from which beer was manufactured. In some parts of the country it was regarded as the national drink as wine was in Ereẓ Israel (Pes. 8a); R. Papa was a brewer (Pes. 113a). Where pepper was regarded as the most exotic of plants in Ereẓ Israel (cf. Suk. 35a), it was freely grown in Babylonia, as was ginger (Ber. 36b; Shab. 141a).

Livestock

Despite the agricultural fertility of Babylonia, it would appear that the rearing and breeding of "small cattle"; sheep and goats, was even more profitable in Babylonia. Thus it is given as good counsel that one should sell one's fields to invest the proceeds in flocks, but not vice versa, and R. Ḥisda refers to the wealth this occupation brings to those who engage in it (Ḥul. 84a–b). From a statement that one should clothe himself with the wool of his own sheep and drink the milk of his own sheep and goats (*ibid.*), it would appear that every householder had a few, and there is other evidence that the tendency was for small individual flocks. Cows and oxen were bred both for plowing and for slaughter (Naz. 31b). The ass was used for riding and the mule for transport (BM 97a). Horses were apparently used only for military purposes (Av. Zar. 16a; Rashi to Pes. 113a). Camels were also used for travel and the dromedary, the "flying camel," is mentioned as a means of rapid transport (Mak. 5a). All the common domestic birds, chicken, ducks, and geese were extensively raised (cf. Beẓ. 24a) as was the breeding of pigeons (BB 23b), and the Jews of Babylonia were skilled agriculturists (BB 80a). Fish were abundant in the rivers and lakes of Babylonia and there is extensive reference to the various methods of catching them (see Newman, pp. 136–40).

[Louis Isaac Rabinowitz]

IN THE MIDDLE AGES

Ideals

The transition of the Jews in the Diaspora to an urban population mainly constituted of merchants and artisans began from about the end of the eighth century. Yet Jews continued to regard agriculture as the ideal and most important Jewish occupation, the basis of the way of life and social ethics emerging from the Bible and permeating the whole of talmudic literature. In 13th-century Germany the Jewish moralist *Eleazar b. Judah b. Kalonymus of Worms, in describing the primary, divinely ordained state of society, relates that God "created the world so that all shall live in pleasantness, that all shall be equal, that one shall not lord it over the other, that all shall cultivate the land …" However, "when warriors multiplied, and every man relied on his might, when they left off cultivating the land and turned to robbery, He brought down on them the Flood" (*Ḥokhmat ha-Nefesh*, 22b). The utopian agricultural society is here described as being destroyed by knightly feudal behavior which brought divine retribution on the world. Ideals of this kind continued to persist and have inspired the return to the soil in Zionism and related attempts at Jewish colonization in modern times.

History

The place of agriculture in Jewish economic and social life steadily diminished from the fourth century. Increasingly severe edicts were issued by Christian emperors prohibiting Jews from keeping slaves, first applying to Christian slaves only and then to all slaves. These restrictions obviated any large-scale Jewish agricultural undertakings by depriving them of workers. The church also developed the conception that Jews should be denied any positions of authority or honor. This attitude later automatically excluded Jews from the feudal structure based on land ownership and the social structure which it combined. In these conditions, Jews were only fit for the lowest rank of serfs, but the religious and moral aspects of such a position made this impossible for all practical purposes.

Under Islamic administrations, both Jewish and Christian farmers bore the additional burden of a special land tax, the *Kharaj*, and suffered from a policy by which the produce delivered in land taxes was excessively undervalued. In Iraq, where there was a large concentration of Jews engaged in agriculture, they suffered from the general neglect of irrigation in the first two generations of Muslim rule. On the other hand, urban life and trading as an occupation were respected in Islamic society; they were a powerful attraction in the Caliphate, in particular to the Jew who wanted to escape oppressive discrimination in the villages. From the second half of the ninth century, the cultural milieux of the great Muslim cities like Baghdad drew increasing numbers of the population. The expansion of the Caliphate and the diversification of its economy provided growing opportunities for Jews in urban occupations. Additionally, the requirements of organized religion formed a further incentive to urbanization for the majority of Jews.

Thus from the end of the eighth century agriculture became a marginal Jewish occupation in both Christian and Muslim lands. However, Jews continued as farmers wherever legal and social conditions permitted. Large groups of Jewish farmers are known in North Africa in the ninth century. They are mentioned in connection with irrigation, gardening, viticulture, and the commercial production of cheese (which is known to have been stamped with the word *berakhah*, "blessing"). Livestock breeding was apparently an unimportant branch in Jewish agriculture. In Egypt in the 12th century Jews entrusted cattle or sheep to non-Jews to be raised for meat. Similarly, they frequently handed over fields, vineyards, orchards, and gardens to Gentile sharecroppers, although Jewish *bustāni* (gardeners) are mentioned in documents of the Cairo *Genizah*. They perhaps worked in "the orchard of the synagogue of the Palestinians" in Old Cairo (Fostat). While cheese making and beekeeping by Jews have a large place in the *Genizah* records, they are overshadowed by the production of wine. Naturally "pressers" of grapes are mentioned, although these probably worked only on a seasonal basis. Another agricultural specialist frequently mentioned in the *Genizah* from the 11th to the 13th centuries was the *sukkari*, the manufacturer and seller of sugar, which was produced mostly from cane but sometimes from raisins or dates. In western North Africa (the Maghreb) Jews owned cultivated land in the villages and city outskirts. Some of the tales of R. *Nissim b. Jacob of Kairouan (first half of the 11th century) have a rural or semirural setting and are probably located in North Africa (cf. Hirschberg in bibliography).

After the Muslim conquest of Spain in 711, Jews there gradually entered the agrarian sphere taking advantage of changes such as the apportionment of land, liquidation sales, or the expropriation of rebels. Andalusia attracted a stream of immigrants from North Africa, including numerous Jews who were often skilled farmers. These possibly constituted the majority of Jewish landowners and peasants mentioned there in tenth-century records. Problems concerning cornfields and orchards are dealt with at length in the Spanish rabbinical responsa of the period, which also mention technical innovations, for instance pumping methods. The Jewish *karram* (winegrower) had to see to every aspect of viticulture, from amelioration of the soil to grape pressing. After the Spanish territories passed to Christian rule, Jews continued to engage in agriculture. In Leon and Castile, Aragon and Catalonia, Jews are often recorded as settlers and developers of newly occupied areas, frequently in collaboration with the monasteries. Jews owned large tracts of land, in particular near the towns, since many members of the Jewish upper strata participated in the parcellation and recolonization of lands captured from the Muslims during the Christian Reconquest from the 12th century on. Some Jewish smallholders cultivated their own plots: fields and pastures, orchards and gardens are mentioned. Jews also employed hired labor. Some dealt in livestock and agricultural products, or engaged in crafts based on agricultural materials, such as hides and fibers. It is not known whether the raw material for the important Spanish-Jewish silk industry was produced locally or bought from Sicilian Jews.

In Italy, Jewish economic activity was not subjected to legal restrictions until the 16th century, but the majority of Jews there lived in the cities. However, their (probably uninterrupted) presence in rural areas, particularly in central and southern Italy, is evidenced. Jews were among the first to cultivate the mulberry in Italy, and the flourishing silk industry was largely controlled by Jews. In Sicily Jews owned and cultivated vineyards and olive groves. Some excelled in cultivating the date palm; Frederick II gave certain Jews the stewardship of his private grove. Beside these farmers there were Jewish fishermen. Sicilian Jews also owned land or herds which were looked after by non-Jews on a sharecropping basis. Many Jews in Sicily in the 13th and 14th centuries were engaged in commerce or crafts based on agriculture.

In southern France, especially in Provence, conditions were similar to those in Spain and Italy. Great Jewish *allodia* are mentioned in the early Middle Ages, some near Narbonne are recalled in a legendary context. In the greater part of medieval France and Germany, however, the Jews who engaged in agriculture were the exception rather than the rule. In the time of Charlemagne (eighth–ninth centuries), some Jews still farmed large tracts of land. In suitable regions Jews are found specializing in viticulture, fruit growing, and dairy farming. These capital intensive and semi urban branches of agriculture could be combined with commercial activities. In addition, while vineyards or orchards required expert supervision, they did not demand continual labor, so that even scholars like *Rashi and Jacob *Tam could grow grapes for a living while devoting time to study.

In the Balkans and Greece, *Benjamin of Tudela (mid-12th century) found a Jewish community of 200 (families?) in Crissa, engaged in agriculture, and another near Mount Parnassus. Further east, Jewish farmers were already found in the tenth century. On the northern shores of the Black Sea they introduced advanced techniques of plowing and perhaps also new irrigation methods, and rice growing. Rice was in fact widely grown in the Volga region under the *Khazars, but was discontinued after their downfall.

In Eastern Europe, Jews turned to the countryside more frequently from the 14th century. When expelled from many of the cities, they settled on the estates of the nobility and in villages. The transition was also due to their increasing connection with the growing and sale of wine (see *Wine and Liquor Trade). In Lithuania, Jewish settlement in the towns was early combined with agricultural activity. Thus Grand Duke Witold granted the Jews of Grodno in 1389 the right to "use the sown pasture land which they hold now or may acquire in the future, paying to our treasury the same as the gentile citizens." With the development of the **arenda* ("leasehold") system and trade in agricultural products, the Jews in Poland-Lithuania became increasingly involved in agriculture as leaseholders of agricultural assets, for instance of distilleries or mills, or as administrators of the rural estates; they also dealt in everything pertaining to agriculture and supplied the needs of both peasants and landlords. The Jewish leaseholder (*arendar*) of agricultural assets on a large scale gradually developed into a kind of capitalist farmer, entering agriculture by providing capital and business management. The large number of small-scale *arendars* also became increasingly involved in village life and affairs. Not only the many Jews living near or in the villages, but also those in the small Jewish townships that became characteristic of Polish and Lithuanian Jewry owned vegetable gardens and orchards near their houses. Their livelihood and way of life was closely bound up with peasant life and activities. However, the number of Jews who may be classified as belonging to the agricultural sector at any given time in the period remains a moot point. These connections to a certain degree enabled the renewal of Jewish agriculture in modern times. It is safe to generalize that the greater part of Eastern European Jewry was conditioned by semirural environment until well into the 19th century.

TRADE IN AGRICULTURAL PRODUCTS: MIDDLE AGES AND MODERN TIMES. In the early Middle Ages Jewish international trade mainly consisted of commerce in agricultural products from the Far and Middle East destined for luxury consumption in Western Europe. Jewish merchants traded in *spices at least from the sixth century (see *Radanites), and also in dyestuffs (see *Dyeing). Conducted on a large scale, this trade was naturally based on the contacts established by Jews in the Orient with local producers and merchants. Information from the end of the tenth century shows extensive activity in this sphere by Jewish merchants from Egypt, Tunisia, and Syria. During the 11th and 12th centuries trading in agricultural products was carried on by Jews in all the Mediterranean countries, either as individual enterprises or, when on a larger scale, frequently in partnerships, which sometimes also included Muslim merchants. The trade included sugar exported from Egypt, and dried fruits, especially from Syria, as well as condiments, dyes, oil, cheese, and wines throughout the area.

The small Jewish merchants at that time included peddlers who acted as intermediaries between the rural producers and the city. In the Near East as well as in the more backward European countries they traded their goods for agricultural products which they sold at the urban markets. Jews living in the Aegean islands of Byzantium sometimes leased the state revenues from the trade in grain and wines. Attempts to oust Jews from dealing in wines, grain, and other foodstuffs were made in France and Germany in the eighth and ninth centuries, for instance by the Synod of Frankfurt in 794. Bishop *Agobard complained that the Jews of Lyons in his day dealt in wines and meat. Jews owned vineyards and dealt in wines in France up to the 12th century. In England, the *Statutum de judeismo* of 1275, after forbidding the Jews to engage in moneylending, authorized them to practice trades and crafts. A large number of wealthy Jews therefore turned to trade in grain and wool. While the Jewish merchants of Bristol, Canterbury, Exeter, and Hereford mainly dealt in grain, those of Lincoln, Norwich, and Oxford were wool merchants. In the states of Christian Spain, the Jewish trade in agricultural products was widely developed, and in some places ordinances regulating this trade were issued by the local communities. In Portugal in the 14th century the authorities restricted the activities of Jewish peddlers and traders who bought honey, oil, and wax from the mountain villages and sold these commodities in the cities.

Even when moneylending became the paramount Jewish economic activity in Western Europe the Jews in the West continued to deal in agricultural products, in particular in wines, wool, and grain, frequently in combination with their loan activities. This is attested in the responsa literature of the period. In the 15th century many Jews in the southeastern parts of the German Empire acted as middlemen in buying the products of the villages and landed estates (*Gut*) and selling them to the towns. Buying up, and especially horse-trading, became the specialties of Jews in *Bavaria and Franconia, in which they continued to engage well into modern times. The Jewish peddler later found in the United States was continuing a traditional Jewish occupation in Germany and Eastern Europe. However, the anti-Jewish enactments passed by the church frequently succeeded in preventing Jews from trading in agricultural products. The bull issued by Pope Paul IV in 1555 included a provision prohibiting Jews from dealing in grain. In Venice the *ricondotta* of 1777 prohibited Jews from trading in grain and foodstuffs. With the economic development of Western Europe after the great geographical discoveries of the 15th and 16th centuries, *Poland-*Lithuania became the chief supplier of agricultural products, cattle, and forest produce to the West. Up to the time of the partitions of Poland at the end of the 18th century Jews took a considerable part in the extraction and sale of the agricultural produce on which the arenda system was based, and thus became associated with the export trade to the West, using both the river and land routes. In the late 17th and during the 18th centuries the role of the *Court Jews as victuallers to the armies of the Hapsburg Empire and princes of Germany was largely facilitated by their contacts with Jews in Poland-Lithuania who provided the necessary supplies. The financial success of Jews in this field often became the basis for the accumulation of large capital, as instanced by the career of S. *Zbitkower. Trade in cattle, and especially oxen, was one of the most important branches of the export trade in which Jews took part from the 16th century. It entailed the driving of cattle from Eastern Europe to the West, then the best way of transporting meat. The major part of the herd was bought in Moldavia; the cattle were fattened for a time in the Ukraine, and with the additions bought there were driven to Silesia, West Germany, and France. Jewish dealers sold part of their cattle at the large fairs in Brzeg on the Oder. After the partitions of Poland and up to the present century, the traditional Jewish trade in agricultural products continued, despite attempts by the Russian authorities to expel the Jews from the villages. In the **shtetls* of the *Pale of Settlement in *Belorussia, *Volhynia, and the *Ukraine the small-scale Jewish trader would buy goods from the peasants on market days, or through itinerant peddlers and dealers, and sell the village products in bulk to the larger Jewish merchants, who then exported them to Germany. In consequence, trade in essential agricultural products used in industry, such as bristles, flax, and hemp, was almost a Jewish monopoly in this area during the period. Identical in structure was the grain trade in Galicia and Poland in the 19th century, in which the *Dorfgaenger* or *Dorfgeher* were engaged. The Jewish traders traveled from village to village, visiting markets and fairs in the small towns where they bought grain and also cattle, despite official attempts to prohibit them from doing so.

The grain trade of Poland became almost exclusively a Jewish preserve during the 19th century. Many Jewish firms dealt in grain, and Jews also acted as the agents for German and French firms, some also in Jewish ownership. There were 36,907 Jews occupied in the grain trade in Poland in 1897, i.e., 6.9% of the Jewish merchants living in this area. Of the 224 grain merchants in business in Warsaw in 1867, 214 were Jews. In 1873, five Jews became members of the constituent committee of the Corn Exchange in Warsaw. Jewish grain dealers were also prominent during the establishment of the state grain stores in Prussia, Silesia, and Galicia in the 18th century. Jewish contractors undertook to provide approximately 74% of the grain during the shortage in Galicia in 1785–86. Several communities in East Prussia and Latvia, such as those of Koenigsberg and Riga, owe their origin and development to the expansion of Jewish interests in the grain trade. In the 18th century the bulk of the grain exported by the land route from Poland to Silesia was concentrated in Jewish hands. In Lithuania, Jews who exported grain to Silesia bought colonial goods in Breslau, which they supplied to the Lithuanian towns. A large part of the wine export trade of Hungary, which in the 18th and 19th centuries went largely to Poland, Ukraine, and Czechoslovakia, was in Jewish hands. The wine merchants sometimes organized armed caravans to defend the transports from marauders. Between the two world wars a large number of Jews in Poland and the Baltic States continued to engage in the trade in agricultural products, from peddling to large-scale export business, although attempts were made on a governmental level to oust the Jews from this economic sector and, through the creation of state-subsidized agricultural cooperatives, to all but eliminate Jews from trading with the local agriculturists. Thus from the end of the Middle Ages Jews played an important role – and, in many regions, a pioneering one – in the development of trade between manor and village on the one hand and the city on the other, an essential factor in the rise of modern economy.

[Jacob Goldberg]

IN MODERN EUROPE

In the modern period, Jews in Europe developed direct contact with agriculture in various ways. Jewish businessmen in Western Europe entered the agricultural sphere as part of their share in the development of capitalist economy. Many of the merchants owning plantations in the West Indies, especially of sugar cane, were Jews. In continental Europe from the late 18th century Jewish merchant bankers frequently branched out into mining and industry, and also into forestry and capitalist farming. This type of activity, chiefly financial and commercial at least in origin, for example sugar beet growing, was developed by a significant number of Jews in southern Germany in the first half of the 19th century and in Russia in the second half of the century. The number of such pioneer businessmen who were actively involved in farm management by the end of the 19th century cannot be ascertained. Apparently at least in Galicia, Slovakia, and Romania, the class of Jewish capitalist owners or tenants of agricultural lands or assets had become quite large by 1900, and was directly concerned with farming.

It was in Eastern Europe that the movement to settle numbers of Jews on the land took place. From the middle of the 19th century the rapid growth of population and deteriorating economic conditions in Russia forced many of the Jews there out of their traditional occupations. A large minority turned to agriculture, chiefly the suburban type of dairy and truck farming. By doing so, the small-scale Jewish farmer could remain in the same locality, avoid the difficulties of obtaining larger areas of land, and concentrate on intensive cultivation of commercial crops.

Already from the 18th century the population increase and economic impoverishment combined with new ideologies which envisioned a more "natural" mode of existence for the Jews to press for changes in Jewish social life. The theoreticians proposed alterations in the Jewish occupational structure with the aim of achieving a more balanced Jewish social stratification. This, they considered, would make Jews less open to the attacks of antisemites who condemned Jews for their pursuit of "non-productive" economic activities (see *History, Jewish Medieval and Modern; *Haskalah, *Antisemitism; *Zionism). Various schemes were proposed on both governmental and private initiative for the "productivization" of the Jewish masses and included plans for Jewish agricultural settlement. These were either confined to the country concerned, or combined programs for emigration and colonization with broader social and political issues. Among these the most notable are the Zionist movement and the projects of Baron *Hirsch, as well as the *Birobidzhan scheme.

Jewish researchers estimate that the number of Jewish agriculturalists of all types in Eastern Europe reached a maximum of between 400,000 and 500,000 in the early 1930s, i.e., forming up to 6% of the total Jewish population there. They varied both in the form of agricultural organization and the type of farming undertaken. They included the Jewish shepherds in the Carpathian mountains, beekeepers, owners of milch cows, or vegetable growers in the small Galician and Bessarabian towns, and the mixed farming colonists in Ukraine. Although the Jewish output was insignificant in the total agricultural sector, Jews took an important part and even predominated in certain branches. In northern Poland, Jewish farmers predominated in vegetable growing, including hotbed crops, notably cucumbers. In certain districts in Poland and Bessarabia, tobacco was practically a Jewish speciality.

The recent development of a Jewish agricultural sector has undergone many vicissitudes both in direction and scope, through ideological and political changes, both within Jewish society and in the attitudes of the environing societies and states. These are revealed in the history of the Zionist movement in Ereẓ Israel and of the settlements in *Crimea and Birobidzhan. The greatest interruptions were caused by the Russian revolution of 1917 and the British Mandate in Palestine.

Ukraine

Although proposals for Jewish agricultural colonization were aired in Austria and Prussia at the end of the 18th century, the first substantial attempts to carry out such a scheme were initiated by the czarist government in 1807. They were commenced in the governments of Kherson and Yekaterinoslav as part of renewed efforts by the government to colonize the steppe and at the same time to assimilate the Jews, to remove them from the villages and townships of the Ukraine Pale of Settlement, and to make them less "parasitical." A total of 38 villages, each with 100 to 300 family farms were founded in these areas. Some were given Hebrew names, such as Nahar-Tov and Sedei Menuḥah. According to Russian official data, these 38 villages included almost 7,000 farms with 42,000 inhabitants in 1913. The average area of the holding was 11.8 *desyatines* (about 32 acres).

The Jewish settlements in the Ukraine suffered severely after World War I during the revolution and the civil war, but most were reconstructed with aid from Jewish organizations such as ORT and ICA. In 1924 additional villages, now with Yiddish names such as Blumenfeld and Frayland, were founded, partly by younger members of the old settlements. In 1927 there were 35,000 Jews living in 48 villages in the Ukraine, farming a total of about 250,000 acres.

At first confined to grain production, the colonies in the Ukraine later diversified their output by introducing livestock and fodder, vegetables, and fruits. After the war the production of irrigated crops, notably grapes, was much increased, and cooperative dairies were set up. Loans and instructors supplied by ICA and ORT assisted these developments, which resulted in well established prosperous communities of a pronounced Jewish and rural character. In the late 1920s the Soviet government allocated additional land for Jewish settlements. Around the existing core there developed three administrative districts with a majority of Jewish farmers: Kalinindorf, Nay-Zlatopol, and Stalindorf. The Ukraine thus harbored the largest concentration of Jewish agriculturalists in Europe, who had their own schools, a newspaper (*Der Stalindorfer Emes*), and a Yiddish theater. The new villages, numbering over 50, were based on mechanized cooperative farming, with more livestock and acreage per family than previously. Machinery and instruction were supplied partly by the government and partly by ICA. Two further sections of Jewish settlement developed in the Ukraine in the 1920s, in the vicinity of Odessa and in the district of Pervomaysk. After economic changes villages and agricultural suburbs comprising several thousands of Jewish families grew up in these two districts. The movement of Jews to the soil in the southern Ukraine received a renewed impetus in 1928–30 with the Soviet drive for collectivization.

Belorussia

The czarist regulations of 1835 provided a legal basis for Jewish colonies within the Pale of Settlement. These western Russian provinces, which then included Lithuania and Volhynia, provided many of the settlers of the Ukraine and also saw the growth of a similar Jewish agricultural sector themselves. However the climate and soil in the west were much less favorable. Settlement was more scattered and land tenure less uniform. At the beginning of the 20th century there were 258 Jewish settlements in the western provinces, with almost 6,000 farms and 36,000 inhabitants. These villages each had a maximum of 40 family units, farming an average of 18 acres. On government land a unit might comprise 30 acres, but on land privately leased or purchased they ranged from 5 to 13 acres. This compelled intensification (an average of two cows per unit was high for these regions) and search for supplementary employment. Tillage remained according to local technique on a three-year rotation. Technical and living standards improved from the beginning of the 20th century, due to the aid furnished by ORT and ICA. In these conditions, the settlers in the area who overcame the initial hardships never reached prosperity, but developed a specific Jewish rural way of life in which they took pride.

After the war most of these villages remained in the USSR. All had suffered severely from the years of fighting in World War I and the revolution of 1917. In the early 1920s thousands of Belorussians, including Jews, were driven by hunger to become farmers. The Jews tended to prefer suburban lots, but collectives received higher land quotas. In the collective, it was also easier to maintain Jewish cohesion and cling to some vestiges of Jewish religious life. Thus, about 40% of the 2,300 families who settled on the land before 1925 were members of collective groups. The movement, encouraged by allocation of public land, continued until 1929. There was then a total of 9,100 Jewish farmer families in Belorussia, with 58,500 members and 170,000 acres. Most of these specialized in dairy farming, preferring fodder crops to grains, and many kept orchards and gardens. The introduction of tractors facilitated the replacement of draft horses by dairy cattle. In the Mogilev and Bobruisk districts the majority of Jewish agriculturalists were individual farmers living on the fringes of the small towns, receiving aid from ORT. Collectives predominated in the Minsk district; they received government assistance and later became kolkhozes. Many of the Jewish kolkhozes eventually merged with non-Jewish ones and lost their Jewish identity (see also *Birobidzhan and *Crimea).

Poland

The dissolution of the state toward the end of the 18th century, combined with efforts to reform Polish society and political life, invested the attempts to turn Jews to agriculture with an importance and attention far beyond their real scope. Even so, there were considerable achievements, for which the initiative came from various sources, including the upper circles of Jewish society, enlightened members of the Polish gentry, and Russian governmental circles. They succeeded in bringing the movement for settling Jews on the land to public attention, and in developing Jewish village life. By the middle of the 19th century there were about 30,000 Jews living from agriculture in the central districts of Poland. Ten Jewish villages were considered models for the surrounding areas.

After World War I, Poland inherited the Lithuanian and Volhynian areas of Belorussia, where there were 1,400 Jewish farms. About half were in the northern section, only one-third of the farms had less than 15 acres each; in the more fertile south the majority were small-scale units. Especially in the early 1920s, additional Jewish families turned to farming in northern Poland, settling in areas adjacent to established units as well as in new locations. The new settlers were all tenants, and in this respect were worse off economically than their forerunners. They concentrated in the small towns and city suburbs rather than in the villages, specializing in truck farming, notably of cucumbers; from the suburbs of Vilna and other cities they marketed hotbed vegetables as far as Warsaw. Near Grodno, Jews specialized in tobacco growing. In the mid-1930s there were close to 2,900 Jewish farm units in 142 locations in northeastern Poland, with approximately 60,000 acres. In Volhynia, 940 units in 20-odd locations farmed an additional 11,000 acres.

In Galicia, entirely different conditions had prevailed under Austrian rule. Here the Jewish agricultural sector comprised three classes: large landlords; tenants and agents; farm hands and smallholders. According to Austrian data of 1902, out of 2,430 large land- and forest-owners, 438 Jews owned a total of over 750,000 acres. Generally these were absentee owners: merchants, bankers, and industrialists, but some were actively concerned with farm management, and a few made a name for themselves as proficient farmers. Below the two upper classes, a stratum of Jewish subagents and even farm hands had developed. However, the majority of East Galician Jewish agriculturists were village shopkeepers, who also each owned a small plot. On part he grew vegetables and fodder; the rest he let to his non-Jewish neighbor. With the development of rural cooperative stores, however, many such shopkeepers were forced toward the end of the 19th century to turn to these plots as their chief source of livelihood. The agricultural society of Jewish landlords: as well as Baron Hirsch's foundation, supported the movement to agriculture and encouraged marketing and dairy cooperatives. The 1921 census records 48,000 Jewish earners as at least partially subsisting on agriculture.

Developments in the interwar period, particularly after 1929, caused a renewed movement of Galician Jews to agriculture. In 1932 ICA opened a central agency in Lvov, and at the same time grass root initiative culminated in the foundation of YILAG ("Yidishe Landvirtshaftlikhe Gezelshaft": Jewish Agricultural Society). The credit facilities, education, and instruction provided by these two organizations encouraged modernization and cooperation. YILAG published the monthly *Der Yidisher Landvirt* from 1933 to 1939. In 1933 there were already eight Jewish farming cooperatives and 12 cooperative dairies in Galicia, with a total membership of 1,400. The dairies processed 4½ million liters of milk annually. Dairy farming was quite profitable in the hill regions, where natural pasture enabled a family to keep up to five milch cows if the problems of marketing could be solved. The cooperatives therefore developed transportation as well as processing facilities, and branched out into retailing. Eventually six shops (four in Lvov alone) for dairy and poultry products under the name "Ḥemah" ("butter" in Hebrew) became very popular with the Jewish urban customer.

After World War II, Jewish survivors of the Holocaust, of whom some had been farmers before the war, settled in villages in the districts formerly in Germany. ORT renewed its activity in Poland and undertook the vocational guidance of the new farmers. Various educational projects were started. However, the whole movement was short-lived, and most participants soon left the soil (and the country).

Romania

The various sections of Romania differ greatly in their geography and history. In Bukovina, Austrian rule created social and political conditions similar to those of Galicia, with an accordingly similar structure of the Jewish agricultural sector. Of the small-scale farmers, who numbered 2,000 families before 1914, many owned their holdings, which averaged five to 25 acres. However, only approximately 500 families survived on the land after World War I, and these were completely impoverished. In the 1930s their reconstruction was planned and financed by ICA, based on dairy or sugar-beet farming. In Bessarabia, early settlements had been part of the czarist projects, especially from 1850. Additional villages and scattered farms brought the number of Jewish farmers up to perhaps 5,500 families in the late 1920s. Of special interest in this region were the tobacco growers, who worked diminutive plots with effort and skill. Although well known for the high yield of their land and the quality of the leaves they produced, the Jewish tobacco growers could still barely subsist because of high rents and fluctuating prices. Before 1914, over 90% of the tobacco growers in Bessarabia had been Jews; they continued to predominate in the inter-war period. There were also many Jewish winegrowers in Bessarabia working under similar conditions, and with like success. Mixed farming, with much maize, was also represented in the Jewish sector. In the Carpathian Maramures, part of which belonged to Romania and part to Czechoslovakia in the inter-war period, numerous extremely poor Jews, perhaps numbering up to 60,000, gained a subsistence from cattle and sheep, with some supplementary orchards and beehives. Dairies were set up there by ICA in the 1930s.

The process of the return of Jews in Europe to the countryside and villages from the towns is in part due to an intensification of the historical and economic trends which began in the later Middle Ages. However, the driving forces both from within Jewry itself and outside it have been mainly ideological and political.

[Shimshon Tapuach]

IN THE UNITED STATES

As indicated in colonial records, there were individual Jewish landowners and farmers early in the 18th century. The first attempt to establish a Jewish farm community, however, dates back to the 1820s, when Mordecai Manuel *Noah received permission to found his model community of Ararat in the Niagara River region of New York. During the same period, Moses Elias *Levy settled Jews on a Florida tract, and by 1837, 13 families launched the Sholem farm colony in Wawarsing, New York. Within five years the last were forced to disperse, partly because of depressed economic conditions. There were other isolated instances of Jewish farmers, including some in California, throughout the century.

By 1881, however, with the beginning of massive Jewish immigration from Eastern Europe, group settlement received a major impetus. Many of the newcomers were imbued with the agrarian idealism of the *Am Olam, stressing the nobility of farm labor as the most honest of occupations; a few had experience as agriculturalists in Russia. At the same time, the relatively small American Jewish community hoped to develop among the immigrants a healthy yeoman class, away from the cities; it became increasingly sensitive also to anti-immigration sentiment stemming not only from nativist elements, but also from the new urban working class. In a rural setting, philanthropy would combine with self help to absorb the newcomers. Such settlement efforts were aided by the *Alliance Israélite Universelle, and a number of new American organizations: at first the Hebrew Emigrant Aid Society (1882–83), then the Baron de Hirsch *Fund (1891–) and its subsidiary, the *Jewish Agricultural Society (1900–). A score of colonies were established in areas ranging from the swampy bayous of Louisiana to the dry prairies of Kansas and the Dakotas, as far northwest as Oregon; within a few years all failed for such reasons as poor site selection, floods, droughts, factionalism, insect blight, and always inadequate experience and financing. In the East, however, the settlements ringing *Vineland, N.J. (1882), and the all-Jewish town of Woodbine, N.J. (1891), survived into the 20th century. Their staples were vegetables, especially sweet potatoes and small fruits.

Early in the 20th century, both Vineland and Woodbine unfurled the banner of "Chickenville," joined later by Jewish farm communities in Toms River and Farmingdale, N.J. Thereby, the poultry industry was able to absorb Jewish immigrants in the 1930s, and beyond World War II, with new centers in the Lakewood, N.J. area, Colchester, Manchester, and Danielson, Conn., and Petaluma, Calif. (north of San Francisco). New York's Jewish farmers, especially throughout Sullivan and Ulster counties, have been well represented since the turn of the century in the poultry industry, dairying, vegetables, and resort facilities. In Connecticut, Jewish farmers specialized in dairying also, as well as tobacco and potatoes; others pioneered in the famed potato industry of Aroostook County, Maine.

Some notable contributions stand out: in the area of education, the Baron de Hirsch Agricultural School (Woodbine, N.J.) and the National Farm School (Doylestown, P.A.), both pioneering institutions. Also, Jewish farmers founded cooperatives for joint marketing, especially of poultry and eggs, purchase of feed and fertilizer, insurance, and comprehensive community service programs.

At the end of World War II, there were about 20,000 Jewish farm families with perhaps fewer than half that number by the late 1960s, mainly because of trends which led to a decline of American agriculture generally down to only five percent of the total population. Jews continued to be represented in all branches of American agriculture, whether citrus in Florida or vegetables in California's Imperial Valley, but the number of Jews in agriculture continued to decline in the last third of the 20th century as the overall number of Americans engaged in agriculture dropped further to fewer than 2.5 percent.

[Joseph Brandes]

IN CANADA

Canada's vast and underpopulated expanses of fertile land were hardly known to the Jews in czarist Russia and other countries who were seeking asylum. Thus, despite Canada's favorable attitude to immigration, only a small segment of the Jewish emigrants from Europe went to Canada. The first attempt to establish Jewish agricultural settlement in Canada was made in 1884 (after a two year delay mainly due to the government's refusal to assign land for the Jews when they first arrived) when a small group tried to farm 560 acres mear Moosomin, Saskatchewan. Their experiment ended in failure after five years of struggle. A few years later, the Young Men's Hebrew Benevolent Society of Montreal approached Baron de Hirsch to assist Jewish immigrants in Canada, as he did the immigrants in the U.S.A., and soon afterward the *Jewish Colonization Association (ICA) established a special Canadian committee for the promotion of agricultural settlement among the Jewish immigrants. With the beginning of large-scale Jewish immigration to Canada in the 1880s some Jews wished to become farmers under the government's homestead policy. Because of the belief that Jews would not make good farmers the government tended to discourage Jewish group-land settlement. Nevertheless between 1884 and 1910 some 17 Jewish farm settlements were started, mostly in western Canada with the help of the Jewish Colonization Association. Among the best known are Oxbow and Wapella (1888), Hirsch (1892), Lipton (1901), Edinbridge and Sonnenfeld (1906), and Rumsey (1908). Five or six of these settlements lasted for half a century or longer.

By 1920 the population in those settlements reached 3,500, while their annual produce totaled over $1,000,000 It has been estimated that Jewish farmers in Canada produced enough wheat in the 1930s to feed the entire population of Canada. Some 200,000 acres were allocated for grain and the farmers' assets were valued at $7,000,000. The Jewish settlers, new arrivals from Ukraine, Romania, or Lithuania, had almost no training in agriculture, nor any knowledge of the environment, so that their achievement was considerable. Despite the extremely difficult climatic conditions in the prairies, which are covered with snow for eight or nine months of the year, the small and isolated communities maintained strong Jewish cultural activity, often using their last means to bring over itinerant Hebrew teachers for the homesteads. Sometimes a teacher would stay with one family for a whole winter. The younger generation went to study at the colleges of the prairie cities of Winnipeg, Regina, Saskatoon, Edmonton, and Calgary. In time, they became doctors, lawyers, agronomists, and businessmen and settled in town. When the government imposed immigration quotas, the settlements began to suffer manpower shortages and the aging parents, no longer able to carry the burden of isolation, loneliness, and hard work, gradually joined their children in the cities. Some farmsteads fell into decay and were sold; others are still owned by the descendants of the original settlers. Only individual Jewish families have remained on farms, especially those in the proximity of the cities.

IN LATIN AMERICA

Jewish agriculture in Latin America was concentrated in three separate regions during various periods. The first region, the plantation area, was located in the northeast of the continent and in the Caribbean Islands. From the beginning of the 16th century – only a few years after the discovery of *Brazil – *New Christians were engaged in exploiting the resources of the Brazil tree and exporting its products to Europe. The same group most probably brought the cultivation of sugar from Madeira to Brazil. From that time on, Marranos played a leading role in the development of the sugar cane and sugar refinery industries at Engenhos. In the middle of the 17th century, after the Dutch rule ended and the Portuguese took over, Jews engaged in the cultivation of sugarcane (and possibly other branches of agriculture) in the Caribbean Islands, especially in the areas of the Guiana that remained under Dutch rule. In Surinam, the memory of this period of Jewish agricultural settlement has been preserved in the name of a village, Joden Savanne.

In the wake of mass immigration by Russian Jews toward the end of the 19th century, new and large agricultural settlements were established in the grain and beef areas of southeastern Latin America. The widespread development of agriculture in the Argentinean *pampas* and the large-scale immigration campaign that the government conducted in Europe brought the settlement project of Baron de Hirsch to Argentina. Even though the Hirsch project did not fulfill the expectations of its founder, i.e., to concentrate hundreds of thousands of Jewish settlers in a compact and autonomous area, the total area of the project's agricultural land amounted during its peak period (1925) to 617,468 hectares (1,525,146 acres). The total Jewish agricultural population in the five provinces reached 33,135, of whom 20,382 were farmers and their families and the rest were hired laborers and artisans etc. in 1925 (see *Argentina, Agricultural Settlement).

In 1903 the Jewish Colonization Association (ICA) began to develop additional agricultural settlements in Rio Grande do Sul, southern Brazil. One hundred thousand hectares (247,000 acres) were acquired and two settlements were established that encompassed several agricultural centers. This Brazilian project was never consolidated (see *Brazil, Agricultural Settlement). Attempts at agricultural settlement in Uruguay on government-owned land in 1914 and on private land in 1938–39 were also unsuccessful (see *Uruguay).

The persecution of the Jews in Germany during the 1930s and the limitations imposed upon immigration by the governments of Argentina and Brazil led to additional experiments in Jewish agricultural settlement in other geographical areas, mainly in the Andes. Of all these attempts only one, the settlement of Sosua, which was established with the support of the *American Jewish Joint Distribution Committee in the Dominican Republic, partially succeeded.

[Haim Avni]

BIBLIOGRAPHY: EREẒ ISRAEL: J. Schwarz, *Tevu'ot ha-Areẓ* (1900[3]); M. Zagorodsky, *Avodat Avoteinu* (1949); B. Cizik, *Oẓar ha-Ẓemaḥim* (1952); Alon, Toledot; S.D. Jaffe, *Ha-Ḥakla'ut ha-Ivrit ha-Kedumah be-Ereẓ Yisrael* (1959); S. Hurwitz, *Torat ha-Sadeh*, 3 (1959); Y. Feliks, *Olam ha-Zome'aḥ ha-Mikra'i* (1968); idem, *Ha-Ḥakla'ut be-Ereẓ Yisrael bi-Tekufat ha-Mishnah ve-ha-Talmud* (1963), incl. bibl.; idem, *Kilei Zera'im ve-Harkavah* (1967); idem, in: *Sefer ha-Emek* (1957), 123–33; Aharoni, *ibid.*, 107–14; Yeivin, *ibid.*, 115–22; H. Vogelstein, *Die Landwirtschaft in der Zeit der Mischna* (1894); Krauss, Tal Arch 2 (1911); Loew, Flora; Dalman, Arbeit; A.L.E. Moldenke, *Plants of the Bible* (1952). **ADD.BIBLIOGRAPHY**: A. Horowitz, "Pollen: Key to Negev Climate in Prehistoric Times," in: ILN, 4 (1978–79), 62–63; A. Horowitz, *The Quaternary of Israel.* (1979); U. Baruch, "The Late Holocene Vegetational History of Lake Kinneret (Sea of Galilee), Israel," in: *Paleorient,* 12 (1986), 37–48; R. Gophna, N. Liphshitz, and S. Lev-Yadun, "Man's Impact on the Natural Vegetation of the Central Coastal Plain of Israel during the Chalcolithic Period and the Bronze Age," in: *Tel Aviv,* 13–14 (1986–87), 71–84; Y. Weisel, N. Liphschitz, and S. Lev-Yadun, "Flora in Ancient Eretz-Israel," in: A. Kasher et al. (eds.), *Man and Land in Eretz – Israel in Antiquity.* (1986); A. Rosen, "Environmental Change and Settlement at Tel Lachish, Israel," in: BASOR, 263 (1986), 55–60; A. Rosen, *Cities of Clay: The Geoarchaeology of Tells.* (1986); idem, "Phytolith Studies at Shiqmim," in: T.E. Levi (ed.), *Shiqmim I: Studies Concerning Chalcolithic Societies in the Northern Negev Desert, Israel (1982–1984).* BAR International Series (1987), 243–49; D. Zohary and M. Hopf, *Domestication of Plants in the Old World* (1988); I. Drori and A. Horowitz, "Tel Lachish: Environment and Subsistence During the Middle Bronze, Late Bronze and Iron Age," *Tel Aviv,* 15–16 (1988–89), 206–11; I. Rovner, "Fine-Tuning Floral History with Plant Poal Phytolith Analysis," in: W.M. Kelso and R. Most (eds.), *Earth Patterns: Essays in Landscape Archaeology* (1990), 297–308; U. Baruch, "Palynological Evidence for Human Impact Upon the Flora of the Land of Israel in Antiquity," *Qadmoniot,* 27 (1994), 47–63. BABYLON: J. Newman, *Agricultural Life of the Jews in Babylonia* (1933), 136–40. MIDDLE AGES: S.D. Goitein, *A Mediterranean Society,* 1 (1967), 116–27, 425–30; G. Caro, *Sozialund Wirtschaftsgeschichte der Juden im Mittelalter und der Neuzeit*, 2 vols. (1920–24); Ashtor, Korot; Baer, Spain; Baron, Social; B. Blumenkranz, *Juifs et Chretiens dans le monde occidental* (1960); H.Z. Hirschberg, *Yisrael be-Arav* (1946); Hirschberg, Afrikah; A. Milano, *Vicende economiche degli Ebret nell Italia meridionale ed insulare durante il Medioevo* (1954); Neuman, Spain; S. Saige, *Les Juifs du Languedoc* (1881); O. Stobbe, *Die Juden in Deutschland* (1866). TRADE IN AGRICULTURAL PRODUCTS: Baer, Spain, index, s.v. *Commerce;* G. Caro, *Sozial-und Wirtschaftsgeschichte der Juden im Mittelalter und in der Neuzeit*, 2 vols. (1908–20); Kosover, in: YIVO Bleter, 12 (1937), 533–45; I. Schipper (ed.), *Dziee handlu żydowskiego na ziemiach polskich* (1938); Roth, England, 73, 115; H.G. Richardson, *English Jewry under Angevin Kings* (1960), index, s.v. *Corn dealing:* S.D. Goitein, *A Mediterranean Society* (1967), 116–26, 265. MODERN EUROPE: V. Niktin, *Yevreyskiya poseleniya severo i yugozapadnogo kraya* (1894); Yevreyskoye kolonizatsionnoye obshchestvo, *Sbornik ob ekonomicheskom polozheniyu Yevreyev v Rossii* (1904); S.Y. Borovoi, *Yevreyskaya zemledelcheskaya kolonizatsiya v staroy Rossii* (1928); B. Brutzkus, *Di Yidishe Landvirtshaft in Mizrakh-Erope* (1926); Jewish Agricultural Society, *Der Yidisher Landvirt* (1932–39); S. Tapuach, in: *YIVO Bleter,* 10 (1936), 19–25; idem, in: *Przeglǎd Socjologiczny;* 5 (1937); I. Schipper et al. (eds.), *Żydzi w Polsce odrodzone*, 2 vols. (1932–33), index; J. Babicki, *Yidishe Landvirtshaft in Stanislaver Voyevodshaft* (1948[2]); idem, in: *Yidishe Ekonomik*, 1–3 (1937–39); L. Babicki, in: *Sprawy Narodowościowe*, no. 4–5 (1932); Bartis, in: *Zion.* 32 (1967), 46–75; A. Tartakower, *Megillat ha-Hityashevut* (1958); Kh. Schmeruk, *Ha-Kibbutz ha-Yehudi ve-ha-Hityashevut ha-Ḥakla'it be-Byelorusyah ha-Sovyetit 1918–32* (1961); *Ḥakla'im Yehudim be-Arvot Rusyah* (1965). UNITED STATES: H.J. Levine and B. Miller, *American Jewish Farmer in Changing Times* (1966); E. Lifshutz, in: AJHSQ, 56 (1966), 151–62. CANADA: Belkin, in: A.D. Hart (ed.), *Jew in Canada* (1926); Sack, *ibid.;* A. Rhinewine, *Looking Back a Century* (1932); L. Rosenberg, Agriculture in Western Canada (1932); idem, *Canada's Jews* (1939); A.A. Chiel, *Jewish Experiences in Early Manitoba* (1955); idem, *Jews in Manitoba* (1961).

AGRIGENTO (Girgenti), town in Sicily. The Jewish community of Agrigento dates to classical antiquity, as attested by a tombstone found there, perhaps of the fifth century. In 598, during the pontificate of *Gregory the Great, a number of Jews were converted to Christianity. The community continued to exist throughout the period of Muslim domination and Girgenti is mentioned in a letter from the Cairo **Genizah* c. 1060. The Jewish community is recorded in 1254 when the revenues from the Jews were taxed in favor of the church. *Faraj da Agrigento was one of the most active translators employed by Charles of Anjou in Naples. In 1397 the Jews of Agrigento had to equip a force of 200 foot soldiers for one of King Martin I of Aragon's military expeditions. In 1426 the citizens of Agrigento petitioned unsuccessfully for royal permission to enforce anti-Jewish measures. In 1476 King John II ordered that the money bequeathed by Solomon Anello to promote Hebrew learning in Agrigento be given instead to Guglielmo Raimondo Moncada (alias Flavius Mithridates), a Sicilian Jewish convert to Christianity. Among the reasons cited was the accusation that Jewish schools in the city taught calumnies against the Christian faith, alluding to the spread of a certain Hebrew book among Sicilian Jews. This book is thought to have been *Toledot Yeshu* ("The Life of Jesus"), a medieval pseudo-history of the life of Jesus. Anello's heirs contested the decision but in the end the school was closed down and the revenues were assigned to Moncada. In 1477 a compromise was reached and the Jews of Agrigento were ordered to provide Moncada a house in Palermo instead of the school building in their city. That same year the heirs of Solomon Anello finally succeeded in repossessing some of the books and estate. At the time of the expulsion of the Jews from territory under Spanish rule in 1492 the municipal treasurer was imprisoned for speculation at Jewish expense.

BIBLIOGRAPHY: G. Di Giovanni, *L'ebraismo della Sicilia* (1748), 289–98; B. and G. Lagumina, *Codice diplomatico dei giudei di Sicilia*, 1 (1884), 6, 21, 182, 388; 2 (1895), 184; 3 (1909), 116; Roth, Italy, index; Milano, Italía, index; C. Roth, in: JQR, 47 (1956/57), 329–30 (= idem, *Gleanings* (1967), 74–75). **ADD. BIBLIOGRAPHY:** S. Simonsohn, "Some Well-Known Jewish Converts during the Renaissance," REJ, 148 (1989), 17–52; idem, *The Jews in Sicily*, 6 vols. (1997–2004); H. Bresc, *Arabes de langue, juifs de religion. L'évolution du judaïsme sicilien dans l'environment latin, XIIe–XVe siècles* (2001).

[Cecil Roth / Nadia Zeldes (2nd ed.)]

AGRIPPA I (10 B.C.E.–44 C.E.), tetrarch of Batanea (the Bashan) and Galilee, 37–41 C.E., and king of Judea, 41–44 C.E.; grandson of *Herod and *Mariamne the Hasmonean, and son of *Aristobulus and *Berenice. Agrippa was educated in Rome with other princes at court, and became friendly with Drusus, son of the emperor Tiberius. After a period of dissipation

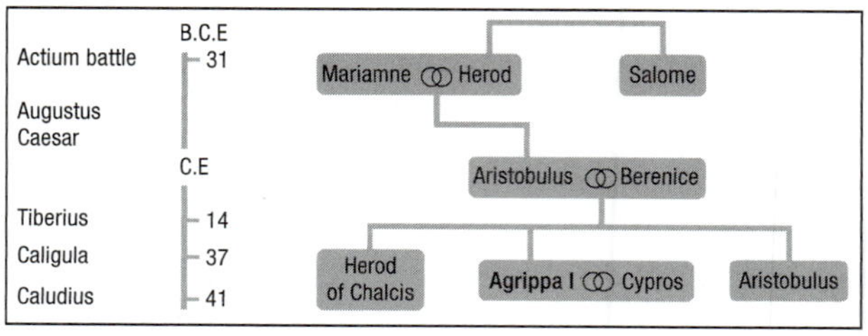

he became saddled with debts, and in 23 C.E. had to return home and he stayed on the family estates in Idumea. He was subsequently appointed *agoranomos* ("market overseer") in Tiberias by his brother-in-law, the tetrarch Herod *Antipas. After a quarrel with Antipas, he went to Syria, where he again became involved in debts, and to escape from his creditors went to Rome where he became friendly with Gaius, later the emperor Caligula. While drunk, however, he was caught off guard expressing a wish that Caligula were emperor instead of Tiberius, and was sent to prison for his indiscretion. Caligula on his accession released Agrippa and appointed him to the tetrarchies of *Herod Phillipus and Lysanias consisting of Bashan-Trachonitis, Gaulanitis, Argob, and Abel, with the title of king. In 39 C.E. he was granted the tetrarchy of Herod Antipas, who had been exiled by Caligula, consisting of Galilee, Tiberias, Sepphoris, and Perea. During this period Agrippa used his connections in Rome to intercede with Caligula on behalf of the Jews. They wished Caligula to retract an order to erect his statue in the Temple in Jerusalem. Shortly afterward Caligula was murdered. Agrippa, who was in Rome at the time, was among those who supported the succession of Claudius. He was rewarded in 41 C.E. by the addition of Samaria and Judea to the area under his rule. The event was celebrated with great ceremony, and an official covenant of friendship was concluded between Agrippa and Claudius, the deed of the covenant being placed in the Capitol. With the acquisition of these territories, Agrippa now reigned over the whole area of his grandfather Herod's kingdom and the procuratorship of Judea was temporarily suspended.

There was little to differentiate Agrippa's foreign policy as a client king of Rome from that of other Hellenistic monarchs. Agrippa gave financial help to foreign cities, and built several public buildings, including a theater and amphitheater in Berytus (Beirut). Because of his connections with Rome, Agrippa was regarded as the leading vassal king of the East, and once managed to bring several other kings together in Tiberias. The meeting was broken up by Marsus, the governor of Syria, possibly because he suspected a conspiracy with the king of Parthia.

The three years of Agrippa's reign were a period of relief and benefit for the Jewish people of Judea. The residents of Jerusalem were exempted from the impost on houses. Agrippa also made an attempt to fortify the walls of the city, until prevented by Marsus. He omitted the patronymic "Herod" from coins minted for him and followed a markedly pro-Jewish policy when he was required to arbitrate disputes between Jews and non-Jews, as in a dispute with the citizens of Dor (Dora). He was also mindful of the welfare of Jews in the Diaspora. His most important achievement was the attainment of an edict of privileges for the Jews of Alexandria from Claudius.

Agrippa made frequent changes in the appointment of the high priest. He was highly sympathetic to the *Pharisees and was careful to observe Jewish precepts. He married his daughters to Jewish notables, and withdrew his consent to the wedding of one daughter to Antiochus, king of Commagene, when the latter refused to be circumcised. His close association with the Pharisees is attested in the statement of Josephus that "his permanent residence was Jerusalem, where he enjoyed living, and he scrupulously observed the ancestral laws." Apparently, it is Agrippa I who is referred to in the Mishnah which points out that when celebrating the festival of the first fruits, "even King Agrippa carried the basket [of fruits] on his shoulder" (Bik. 3:4). He is also apparently mentioned in *Sotah* 7:8 which states that contemporary rabbinical sages accorded him particular regard when he made a special point of standing up to read the Torah, even though it was permissible for a king to do so while seated. When he reached the passage, "one from among thy brethren shalt thou set a king over thee; thou mayest not put a foreigner over thee," his eyes filled with tears, since he was not of pure Jewish descent. The sages, however, called out, "Agrippa, you are our brother! You are our brother!" Agrippa died suddenly when in Caesarea, possibly as a result of poisoning by the Romans who feared his popularity with the population. After his death, Judea reverted to the status of a Roman procuratorship.

BIBLIOGRAPHY: Jos., Wars, 1:552; 2:178–83; 11:206–20; Ant., 18:142–204, 228–55, 289–301; 19:278–361; Sehuerer, Gesch, 1 (1901^{4}), 549–64; Klausner, Bayit Sheni, 4 (1950^{2}), 287–305; Dubnow, Hist, 1 (1967), 728–57.

[Edna Elazary]

AGRIPPA II (**Marcus Julius** or **Herod Agrippa II**; 28–92 C.E.), last king of the Herodian line; son of Agrippa I. Like his father he was educated in Rome and he was there when he learnt of his father's death. The emperor Claudius refused to let him succeed on account of his youth. His uncle, *Herod II of Chalcis, died in the year 48 and Agrippa received this small kingdom two years later. Agrippa's coins indicate that he reckoned his reign from the year 50. During his reign he was accorded the title "king" although at no time was he king of Judea as his father had been. Claudius entrusted to him the supervision of the Temple in Jerusalem and gave him the right to appoint the high priest. In 54 his rule over Chalcis was brought to an end; he was compensated with the tetrarchy of Lysanias which consisted of Bashan-Trachonitis and Gaulanitis and with the administration of the province of Varus. From then on he was one of the most important rulers in the eastern part of the Roman Empire. During Nero's reign his borders were extended once again. In 61 he received parts of Galilee including Tiberias and two towns in Transjordan. The dates of these

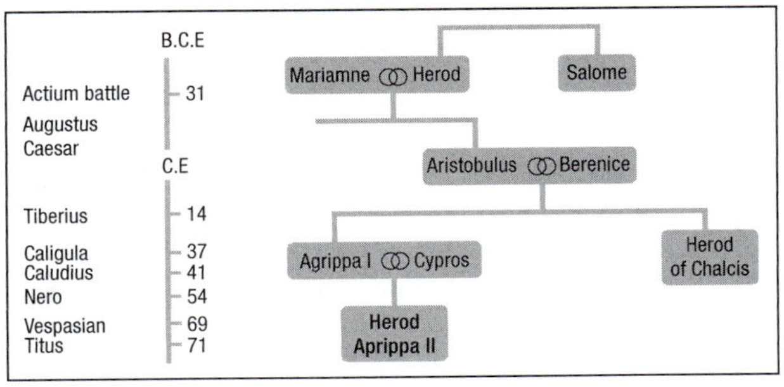

events are recorded on the king's coins, which, in his non-Jewish territories, bore his likeness. At the Jewish revolt against Rome in 66, Agrippa was in Alexandria. He hurried back to Jerusalem to try to convince the people of their helplessness against the power of Rome. His mission failed and he supported Rome in the war that ensued. He fought in Vespasian's campaign and was slightly wounded in an engagement near Gamala. In 68, on receiving the news of Nero's death, he set sail with Titus for Rome. On the way they heard of the murder of the new emperor Galba. Titus immediately returned to his father while Agrippa journeyed on to Rome. When Vespasian was proclaimed emperor, he sent word to Agrippa, who left Rome furtively and offered his services to the new emperor. Vespasian granted him new estates which appear to have been in the north. Agrippa's kingdom was populated mostly by non-Jews, but his attitude toward Judaism was different from that of his forefathers. At least while he was in Judea he showed a superficial respect for Jewish religious practices; some scholars even claim that he was the Agrippa whose attachment to Judaism was praised by the rabbis. According to the New Testament he showed an indifferent attitude toward the spread of Christianity (Acts 25–26). His promotion of Hellenistic culture is attested by a number of inscriptions. There were rumors that Agrippa had incestuous relations with his sister *Berenice (cf. Juvenal, Satires, 6:156), but this may have been merely Roman gossip based on the fact that Berenice lived for some years in her brother's house.

BIBLIOGRAPHY: Schuerer, Gesch, 1 (1904^{4}); A.H.M. Jones, *The Herods of Judaea* (1938), 217–22, 231–5, 237–42, 249–59, passim.

[Abraham Schalit]

AGRIPPA, CAIUS JULIUS, governor of the Roman province of Asia (late first century C.E.). Agrippa's father, a King Alexander, is possibly the Alexander referred to by Josephus (Ant., 18:139 ff.) as a great-grandson of Herod and Mariamne. This Alexander married Jotape, daughter of Antiochus of Commagene, and was appointed king of Cetis(?) (ησιοδος, amended by A. Wilhelm (*Archaeologisch-Epigraphische Mittheilungen…*, 17 (1894), 5) into κητιδος) in Cilicia by Vespasian. His offspring, apparently including Agrippa, "abandoned from birth the observance of Judaism and adopted the Greek way of life" (Greek inscriptions in the British Museum, 3, sect. 2,187).

BIBLIOGRAPHY: B. Curtius (T. Mommsen), in: *Hermes*, 4 (Ger., 1870), 190; Schuerer. Gesch, 1 (1901[4]), 561, n. 41.

[Isaiah Gafni]

°**AGRIPPA, MARCUS VIPSANIUS** (63–12 B.C.E.), Roman general and statesman, devoted friend and son-in-law of the emperor Augustus. Agrippa was appointed governor of the eastern provinces, which he ruled (until 21 B.C.E.) from Mytilene, on the island of Lesbos. During his stay there, Agrippa was visited by Herod; this was the beginning of a long friendship between the two men. Agrippa was eventually named heir to Augustus. When Agrippa returned to Asia Minor in 16 B.C.E., Herod invited him to visit his kingdom, and the next year the Roman general was received with great enthusiasm in Jerusalem. In the spring of 14 B.C.E. Herod, who was in command of a fleet, offered assistance to Agrippa in his planned expedition to the Bosphorus. This expedition did not take place, however, and instead the two allies traveled together through a great part of Asia Minor. When, in the course of this journey, the Jews of Ionia complained to Agrippa regarding an attempt by the Greeks to infringe their civic and religious rights, the Roman regent, probably under Herod's influence, upheld them. Their relationship was summed up by Josephus: "He [Herod] stood in Caesar's affection next after Agrippa, and in Agrippa's, next after Caesar." In 13 B.C.E. Herod sent his son Antipater to Rome, entrusting him to Agrippa so that he might gain Caesar's friendship. The following year, however, Agrippa died.

BIBLIOGRAPHY: Jos., Wars, 1:400, 416; Jos., Ant., 12:125–7; 15:318, 350–61; 16:12–62, 86, 141, 157, 167–73; 17:229; Philo, *De Legatione ad Gaium*, 291; Schuerer, Gesch, index; M. Reinhold, *Marcus Agrippa* (Eng., 1933); Pauly-Wissowa, 2nd series, 16 (1961), 1226–75.

[Isaiah Gafni]

AGRIPPINA, station in the line of beacons kindled during the period of the Second Temple, northward from the Mount of Olives to announce the time for reciting blessings during the *New Moon period: "… from Sarteba to Agrippina and from Agrippina to Hauran…" (RH 2:4). Gropina, the usual reading found in the Mishnah, is a corruption of the name. It is probable that Agrippina was included in the network of fortifications erected by Josephus in 66–67 C.E. Dalman suggested identifying Agrippina with the ruins of Kawkab al-Hawā' (now Kokhav ha-Yarden, the Crusader Belvoir) in the Beth-Shean district, 975 ft. (297 m.) high. Impressive ruins of the Crusader castle of Belvoir, built in the 12th century by the order of Knights Hospitallers and captured by Saladin in 1189, have been restored by the Israel Parks Authority. Stones used for the construction of the fortress were taken from various sources, including dismantled ancient buildings from the Byzantine period. One of these stones probably came from a synagogue and it has a carved depiction of a seven-branched *menorah* between two arches (*aediculae*) and an Aramaic dedicatory inscription.

BIBLIOGRAPHY: Conder-Kitchener, 2 (1882), 117; Dalman, in PJB, 18–19 (1923), 43ff.; Avi-Yonah, in: I-EJ. 3 (1953), 95; J. Schwartz, *Tevu'ot ha-Areẓ* (1900[3]). **ADD. BIBLIOGRAPHY:** Y. Tsafrir, L. Di Segni, and J. Green, *Tabula Imperii Romani. Iudaea – Palaestina. Maps and Gazetteer.* (1994), 168–69.

[Michael Avi-Yonah / Shimon Gibson (2nd ed.)]

AGRON (Agronsky), GERSHON (1894–1959), Israeli journalist and mayor of Jerusalem. Agron was born in Mena, Ukraine, and was brought to the United States as a child. During World War I he served with the *Jewish Legion in Palestine. In 1920–21 he was employed by the Zionist Commission press bureau. From 1921 to 1924 Agron was editor of the Jewish Telegraphic Agency and correspondent for international press agencies, for the London *Times*, and for the *Manchester Guardian*. In 1932 he founded the English-language daily *Palestine Post* (from 1950 *The *Jerusalem Post*), which served to convey Zionist aspirations to the British in Palestine and provided the local population with news from outside Palestine, especially from the Middle East. An emissary for the Zionist Organization on several occasions, Agron was a member of the Jewish Agency delegation to the UN conference at San Francisco in 1945. He was director of the Israel Government Information Services from 1949 to 1951. As mayor of Jerusalem from 1955 to 1959, Agron was instrumental in the expansion and development of the new city. His diaries and letters appear in *Asir ha-Ne'emanut* ("Prisoner of Trustworthiness," 1964), published by S. Shapiro.

BIBLIOGRAPHY: Tidhar, 2 (1947), 960f.; H.M. Sachar, *Aliyah: The Peoples of Israel* (1961), 39–70.

[Semah Cecil Hyman]

AGUD(D)AT HA-SOẒYALISTIM HA-IVRIM ("Hebrew Socialist Union"), first Jewish socialist workers' organization; founded in London, England, functioning from May to December 1876. Its 38 members were workers, mainly tailors and cabinetmakers, mostly from Russia. The leading founder and secretary of the union was A.S. *Liebermann. His closest associate was V. Smirnov, secretary of the revolutionary Russian periodical *Vpered* ("Forward"). Lazarus Goldenberg was an active member. The minutes book was written in Yiddish, the statutes also in Hebrew. The aim of the Union was to spread socialist ideas among Jewish workers, to organize them to fight "oppressors," and to establish contact with other workers' organizations. The Union's attempts to establish Jewish trade unions failed. Some of its members with cosmopolitan leanings questioned the existence of the Union as a specifically Jewish organization, while others, such as Liebermann and L. Weiner, from the socialist circles of Vilna, believed in the right of Jewish workers to appear as Jews independently. In their opinion, the purpose of the London Union was to encourage similar organizations in all the Diaspora. The Union met with opposition from the leaders of the London Jewish community, and the *Jewish Chronicle* even accused it of missionary intent. This pressure and internal dissension led to its dissolution. Some of its members later became active in the Jewish workers' movement in England.

BIBLIOGRAPHY: E. Tcherikower, in: YIVO, *Historishe Shriftn*, (1929), 468–594; L. Gartner, *Jewish Immigrant in England* (1960), 103–6; Sapir, in: *International Review of Social History*, 10, pt. 3 (1935), 1–17; Elman, in: JHSET, 17 (1951–52), 57–58, passim; Mishkinsky, in: *Journal of World History*, 11, nos. 1–2 (1968), 284–6. **ADD. BIBLIOGRAPHY:** G. Alderman, *Modern British Jewry* (1992), 169–72.

[Moshe Mishkinsky]

AGUDAT ISRAEL (Heb. אֲגֻדַּת יִשְׂרָאֵל; "Union" or "Association" of Israel), world Jewish movement and political party seeking to preserve *Orthodoxy by adherence to **halakhah* as the principle governing Jewish life and society. The ideal on which Jewish life should be modeled, in the view of Agudat Israel, is embodied in the social and religious institutions, the way of life and mores, that obtained in the Diaspora centers in Eastern and Central Europe in the 19th century. Its geographical and linguistic orientation made it automatically a purely Ashkenazi movement. The formation of an organized movement and political party to achieve these aims was itself an innovation. It was deemed necessary to present a viable counterforce to the advances made by assimilation and *Reform trends, and by *Zionism, the *Bund, and autonomism in Jewry. The establishment of a movement was discussed in 1909 by members of the German *neo-Orthodox group, but internal dissension in the Orthodox camp delayed it for three years. The final impetus was given when the tenth Zionist Congress decided to include cultural activities in its program, thereby recognizing a secular Jewish culture coexistent with the religious. Some members of the *Mizrachi party left the Zionist movement and joined the founders of Agudat Israel in an assembly held in May 1912 at Kattowitz in Upper Silesia.

Agudat Israel was constituted of three groups reflecting German neo-Orthodoxy, Hungarian Orthodoxy, and the Orthodox Jewries in Poland and Lithuania. These differed in political and social outlook, and in their opinions on cultural and organizational matters. A major divergence was the attitude to general European culture, society, and mores, which German Orthodoxy accepted. They also disagreed about whether to remain part of the main Jewish communal unit or to form separate Orthodox communities, and whether Jews should adopt the language of the state or adhere to *Yiddish. Their attitude toward Zionism was also a moot point.

Branches of Agudat Israel were established throughout the Ashkenazi world. Later it developed a youth movement (Ẓe'irei Agudat Israel) and a women's movement (Neshei Agudat Israel) in several countries. In Germany the "Ezra" youth movement was affiliated with it. The labor movement that formed within Agudat Israel separated from the parent body after disagreement on national, social, and religious issues (see *Po'alei Agudat Israel).

Within its ranks, Agudat Israel presented a spectrum of the attitudes which had influenced its creation. Particularly acute was the question of secular education. Some of the initiators of the Kattowitz conference tried to achieve a synthesis by formulating the principle: "The East shall give of its Torah learning to the West, and the West of its culture to the East," Western culture referring to the Western European, German-style, middle class type. This program was contested sharply by the Eastern European sector of Agudat Israel, who claimed that the only plausible basis for unity was maintenance of the status quo; each group should retain its way of life without change. This solution was contained in 18 clauses presented by Ḥayyim *Soloveichik, rabbi of Brest-Litovsk, as a condition of the participation of Polish and Lithuanian rabbis in the movement.

In regard to Zionism, Agudat Israel was created partly by groups who consistently opposed any attempt to revive Jewish nationhood in Ereẓ Israel through human agency. This they compared with a rebellious attempt by a disbanded regiment to resume its identity and hoist its banner without the express permission of its commander. The secularist elements in the nascent Hebrew culture added to Agudist resentment of Zionism. The **ẓaddikim* of Eastern Europe (*Ḥasidism) regarded the influence of Zionism on the youth, and its negative revolutionary view of Diaspora existence (see **Galut*), as religiously and socially destructive. Agudat Israel, therefore, maintained an ambivalent attitude toward renewed settlement in Ereẓ Israel, mainly because of its opposition to the Zionist movement. The Agudists resented the cooperation of religious with non-religious Jews within the Zionist movement on the basis of national unity, and unequivocally resisted the creation of a secular Jewish society in the Holy Land. Most Agudists considered that the way of life and culture gradually taking shape in the modern settlements in Ereẓ Israel, and propagated by Zionist educational and cultural activities, were subverting and destroying the only true Jewish way of life, upheld by religious families and communities in the Diaspora. The revival of Hebrew as a secular language seemed a sacrilege. With regard to sponsoring independent settlement in Ereẓ Israel, Agudists were already divided at the Kattowitz conference. Gradually, however, there emerged an opinion which after the *Holocaust apparently became the ideological basis of the organization in Israel. Ereẓ Israel should figure at the center of their program, which should, according to the Agudist leader Isaac *Breuer, aim at "uniting all the people of Israel under the rule of the Torah, in all aspects of political, economic, and spiritual life of the People of Israel in the Land of Israel."

The constituents of Agudat Israel were united in their aim to reestablish the authority of the prominent rabbis as the supreme institution of Jewry. This was a basic ideal, even if views were divided on the qualifications for leadership. German members considered secular academic qualifications acceptable, while Eastern European members demanded exclusively rabbinical qualifications. However, the agreement on the overall objective, to give expression to rabbinical authority on all matters, was reflected in the structure and central institutions of the new party, providing them with a unique pattern. The Agudat Israel central institutions as eventually established are, in order of formal importance:

(1) The *Mo'ezet Gedolei ha-Torah* ("Council of Torah Sages") in 1964 numbered 15 rabbis, all halakhic authorities, chosen on the basis of preeminence in talmudic learning. There are no defined criteria whereby its members are appointed. The number of members of the council is not predetermined. The council ensures, at least, in theory, that no activity will be undertaken by Agudat Israel without the consent of representatives of halakhic authority. The decisions of the Council of Torah Sages are accepted as legal verdicts, and the details of their consultations are secret. In 1964 the party declared officially: "The absolute obedience to the Council of Torah Sages gave Agudat Israel its specific character; even its opponents cannot avoid seeing that it is the only movement obedient absolutely to a supreme spiritual-Torah authority."

(2) *Kenesiyyah ha-Gedolah* ("Great Assembly"), "the highest (political) authority of the association," is composed of representatives of the local branches of Agudat Israel. Each 200 members may elect a representative to the Great Assembly. The first two Great Assemblies were held in Vienna in 1923 and 1929.

(3) *Central World Council*, or Presidium, is elected by the Great Assembly.

(4) *The World Executive Committee.* Before World War II the strongest numerically and most active politically of the branches of Agudat Israel was in Poland. This was partly because of the support given to the movement by the ḥasidic *ẓaddikim*, in particular by the dynasty of Gur. Its local political aims and strength were reflected in the Jewish representation in the Polish *Sejm* (parliament) and the Agudist achievements in the elections. In 1919 Agudat Israel presented an independent slate, obtaining 92,293 votes, and returning two deputies to the *Sejm*. In 1922 it joined the "*Minorities bloc" with the Zionists (see *Gruenbaum, Yizḥak), returning six deputies (to the *Sejm*) and two senators. In 1928 it formed jointly with the *Folkspartei* and the merchants' organization the list of the "general Jewish national bloc"; this list, affiliated to the government list, obtained 183,998 votes, but no seat; the sole Agudat Israel deputy was returned from the government list. In 1930, on the same affiliation, it obtained 155,403 votes and one seat; an additional deputy was returned from the government list and one senator. In 1935 one deputy was returned and one appointed by the president of the state; in 1938 two deputies were returned. From 1933 onward some leaders, in particular J. Rosenheim in Germany and Harry Goodman in England, spoke in the name of Agudat Israel on many political issues.

The educational activities of Agudat Israel, conducted in many countries, concerned Orthodox schools and educational institutions. In Eastern Europe and Ereẓ Israel these were mainly *talmud torah* institutions and yeshivot. Later, it maintained the Bet Ya'akov network of elementary and high schools for girls. From 1953 the Agudat Israel party in Israel supervised schools of the "independent educational network," mainly *talmud torah* schools, which refused to be included in the general educational state network (see *Israel, Education). The educational enterprises of Agudat Israel are supported by the *Keren ha-Torah* ("Torah Fund"), founded by the movement.

After the rise to power of the Nazis in Germany the policy of Agudat Israel to Zionist settlement in Palestine changed fundamentally. The third Great Assembly, held at Marienbad in September 1937, was influenced by the pressure of political events in Palestine and the Diaspora. It discussed anew its attitude toward the eventual creation of a Jewish state and cooperation with the Zionists. Ideologically the strict stand prevailed: "A Jewish State can only be founded on the law of the Torah being recognized according to the Torah. A Jewish State not founded on and governed by Torah principles… cannot possibly call itself a Jewish state." But Agudat Israel took part in the St. James Palace Conference convened by the British government early in 1939. The Agudists coordinated their policies there with those of the Zionist Organization.

The numerical strength of Agudat Israel was seriously impaired by the Holocaust. By the end of World War II the movement in Eastern Europe was all but annihilated. Most of its members were living in Ereẓ Israel, although some eventually immigrated to the United States and Western Europe. At the meeting of the Central World Council at Marienbad in August 1947, three centers for the movement were established: in Jerusalem, New York, and London.

Agudat Israel cooperated with the Zionist Organization in extending help to Diaspora Jewry. In practice it completely identified itself with the Zionist demand for the establishment of a Jewish state. Faithful to its basic principles, Agudat Israel, nevertheless, hesitated to recognize a secular Jewish state. However, on the strength of assurances given in a letter from the *Jewish Agency in June 1947 that the status quo in matters of religion would be observed, Agudat Israel was prepared to join the provisional council of the State of Israel. The fourth Great Assembly, held in Jerusalem in 1954, slightly altered the structure of the leadership, adding a World Executive. The next Great Assembly was also held in Israel in 1964. By that time Israeli representatives predominated in the Agudat Israel central institutions.

Agudat Israel in Ereẓ Israel

In Ereẓ Israel Agudat Israel was founded in 1912, but was inactive in public life until July 1919, when it was refounded in Jerusalem by members of the extreme Orthodox faction who were fanatically opposed to Zionism.

From 1919 until 1935, under the leadership of Moshe *Blau, Agudat Israel was completely identified with the ultra-Orthodox community. The principle guiding its activities was the achievement of complete social and political separation from the community organized under the auspices of the Zionist Movement. Agudat Israel fought bitterly to avoid being included in the officially recognized framework of the Jewish population of Palestine (**Keneset Yisrael*) and obtained the right for those who so wished to cease to belong to it. They established separate rabbinical institutions, under the leadership of R. Hayyim Yosef *Sonnenfeld, which operated alongside the chief rabbinate headed by R. Abraham Isaac *Kook. Under the leadership of Jacob Israel de Haan (1922–24), Agudat Israel in Palestine attempted to achieve a *modus vivendi* with the Arab nationalists. However, this policy was discontinued after de Haan's assassination by the *Haganah, for subversive activities (1924). The relentless personal attack carried on by Agudat Israel against Rabbi Kook violently antagonized most of the growing *yishuv*. Other Agudist leaders, notably Isaac Breuer and Pinḥas *Kohn, managed through political action with the British authorities and the *League of Nations to prevent the unification of the Jewish community in Palestine within a single organizational framework. They thus obtained official recognition of the separation of the settlers of the "old *yishuv*," from the *Keneset Yisrael*, or organized Jewish community, and the competence of the *Va'ad Le'ummi ("National Council of the Jews for Palestine"). An attempt made by Agudat Israel to establish an agricultural settlement, Maḥaneh Israel, failed, mainly through lack of funds.

In 1935 the waves of emigration from Poland and Germany brought with them a different type of Agudat Israel member, who wanted to integrate economically and, to a certain extent, even politically into the new *yishuv*. This brought about a fundamental change in the structure, aims, and political activities of Agudat Israel in Palestine. In February 1935 a delegation arrived from the movement's headquarters in Poland, which reorganized the Agudat Israel administration in Palestine and established an agency to deal with matters of immigration and absorption and to negotiate with outside bodies. This agency represented immigrants from Poland and Germany, the members of the Orthodox workers' organization Po'alei Agudat Israel, and members from the old *yishuv*. The latter lost its dominance in the party, and the ultra-Orthodox community separated from Agudat Israel (see **Neturei Karta*). Even before this, however (in the late 1920s), Agudat Israel had begun to cooperate with the official *yishuv* institutions, particularly in the municipalities. This tendency was now increased, mainly among Po'alei Agudat Israel.

The Peel Commission recommendations on the establishment of a Jewish state in part of Palestine (July 1937) caused a heated debate in Agudat Israel in Palestine. In principle, all rejected the idea of a secular Jewish state, but opinions were divided as to whether, in view of the existing plight of European Jewry, the idea should be rejected entirely, or whether, should such a state be established, its inhabitants might not return to the religious fold. Almost all the representatives of the old *yishuv* in Agudat Israel rejected the idea of a Jewish state. The representatives of the immigrants from Germany were divided in their opinions. The immigrants from Poland and Po'alei Agudat Israel tended to accept the idea of a Jewish State.

From 1940 to 1947 Agudat Israel cooperated with the national Jewish institutions, and also had a special committee to coordinate policies regarding the British authorities. In April 1940, the leader of Agudat Israel in Poland, the ḥasidic rabbi of the Gur dynasty (the "Gerer *Rebbe*"), and his son-in-law, Yiẓḥak Meir Levin, arrived in Palestine, and a new drive was launched for active participation in the life of the *yishuv*. The influence of the Polish immigrants in Agudat Israel greatly increased.

When Agudat Israel joined those who demanded a Jewish state, it received representation in the Provisional Council of State (Mo'eẓet ha-Medinah) which signed the Declaration of Independence.

Agudat Israel became a political party when the State of Israel was founded in 1948 and has been represented in all national and municipal bodies. Its leader, Rabbi Y.M. Levin, was minister of social welfare from 1949 to 1952. In all these institutions Agudat Israel fought for the observance of the *halakhah* in public life. Its principal campaigns have been in the field of education and, in 1953, after the educational "trends" were abolished and a unified school system established under the law of compulsory free education, Agudat Israel organized an independent school system of its own. It has also achieved the exemption of "religious" girls and of yeshivah students from military service.

Immigration after the establishment of the State of Israel resulted in increased power for the "Hungarian element" in Agudat Israel, and the "Polish hegemony" was somewhat weakened. About the time of the establishment of the State, friction increased between Agudat Israel and Po'alei Agudat Israel; at the elections to the Second Knesset the two parties submitted separate lists of candidates, and separated com-

Agudat Israel in the Knesset

	Votes	Percentage	Seats
2nd Knesset, 1951	13,999	2.01	3
3rd Knesset, 1955[1]	39,836	4.67	6
4th Knesset, 1959[1]	45,559	4.70	6
5th Knesset, 1961	37,178	3.69	4
6th Knesset, 1965	39,795	3.30	4
7th Knesset, 1969	44,002	3.22	4
8th Knesset, 1973[2]	60,012	3.80	15
9th Knesset, 1977	58,652	3.30	4
10th Knesset, 1981	72,132	3.73	4
11th Knesset, 1984	36,079	1.70	2
12th Knesset, 1988	102,714	4.50	5
13th Knesset, 1992[3]	86,167	3.30	4
14th Knesset, 1996[3]	98,657	3.30	4
15th Knesset, 1999[3]	125,741	3.70	5
16th Knesset, 2003[3]	133,087	4.30	5

1 Together with Po'alei Agudat Israel in Torah Religious Front.
2 Together with NRP.
3 Together with Degel ha-Torah in Yahadut ha-Torah.

pletely in 1960, when Po'alei Agudat Israel joined the government.

In the elections to the First *Knesset in 1949, Agudat Israel and Po'alei Agudat Israel joined with the *Mizrachi and *Ha-Po'el ha-Mizrachi parties to form a "Religious Front." This front gained third place in the distribution of seats in the Knesset. For subsequent elections, see Table: Agudat Israel.

[Menachem Friedman]

In the United States

The world organization attempted to establish an American branch in 1922 but without success, though it did establish a youth section. Agudat Israel of America was actually founded in 1939. It received considerable impetus from the arrival in the U.S. in 1941 of R. Aaron *Kotler, who was a member of the supreme rabbinical council of the world organization. He enjoyed a preeminent position among Orthodox rabbis and was devoted to the ideal of establishing institutions for exclusively Orthodox interests. Agudat Israel also drew support from the well-organized Adath Jeshurun (Breuer) community of Washington Heights, N.Y., which transplanted the traditions of German "Austritt-Orthodoxie," and from certain ḥasidic rabbis. Agudat Israel of America was active in rescue work among the Jews of Europe during and after World War II. It opposed the participation of other Orthodox bodies in roof organizations which include non-Orthodox elements. It supported federal aid to parochial education. Agudat Israel has divisions for children, girls, and youth, including camps serving thousands of youngsters. It also has a job training program called COPE, a job placement division, and a housing program, is an active lobbyist at all levels of government, and maintains full-time regional offices, including one in Washington. In 1952 it began the publication of a monthly *Dos Yidishe Vort*, and in 1963 of an English monthly, the *Jewish Observer.*

BIBLIOGRAPHY: Agudas Jisroel, *Berichte und Materialien* (1912); I. Breuer, 25 *Jahre Aguda* (1937); idem, *Am ha-Torah ha-Me'urgan* (1944); idem, *Moriyyah: Yesodot ha-Ḥinnukh ha-Le'ummi ha-Torati* (1954^2); idem, *Le-Kivvun ha-Tenu'ah* (1936); J. Rosenheim, *Agudist World Problems* (1941); Y.L. Orlian, *La-Seve'im ve-la-Re'evim* (1955^2); N. Krauss (ed.), *Ha-Shenaton ha-Dati ha-Enẓiklopedi* (1962), 186–97; L.J. Fein, *Politics in Israel* (1967), 93–95, 127, 167, 175; M.H. Bernstein, *Politics in Israel* (1957), 48, 57, 71–74; *Jewish People and Palestine: Statement ... to the Anglo-American Committee of Enquiry...* (1947); Liebman, in: AJYB, 66 (1965), 21. PUBLICATIONS: *Jewish Observer* (New York, 1963–), monthly; *Agudist Information Service* (London, 1950–56); *Beit Ya'akov* (Tel Aviv, monthly); *Ha-Modi'a* (1950–), daily.

AGUDDAT AḤIM (Heb. אֲגֻדַּת אַחִים; "The Brotherhood"), assimilationist organization formed in *Galicia in 1880. They were one of two opposite trends of orientation among Jews advocating assimilation in Galicia, then under Austrian administration and torn by national conflicts. One group, represented by the Shomer Israel, established in 1869, favored Jewish adoption of German culture; the members of the Aguddat Aḥim were motivated by feelings of Polish patriotism and desired to assimilate into Polish social and cultural life. In 1880 a group of Jewish intelligentsia and students established Aguddat Aḥim to promote Polish assimilation, and expressed its views in a new Polish-language newspaper, *Ojczyzna* ("Homeland"), edited by Nathan *Loewenstein with Alfred *Nossig among its first contributors. Aguddat Aḥim was active in the political and journalistic spheres and also among the Jewish youth in schools and universities. By 1884, however, the hopes that Jews would be accepted in Polish national life were shaken by an increase in antisemitism among the Poles and reports of pogroms in Warsaw. The counsel of despair now voiced in *Ojczyzna* stated that for Jews the only alternatives were conversion to Christianity or migration to Ereẓ Israel. A number of active members of Aguddat Aḥim abandoned all thoughts of assimilation, rallied to *Zionism, and the organization was dissolved.

BIBLIOGRAPHY: N.M. Gelber, *Toledot ha-Tenu'ah ha-Ẓiyyonit be-Galiẓyah* (1958), 83–157; I. Schiper, in: A. Tartakower and A. Hafftka (eds.), *Zydzi w Polsce Odrodzonej*, 1 (1932), 393–4; J. Tennenbaum, *Galitsye, Mayn Alte Heym* (1952), 72–74.

[Moshe Landau]

AGUILAR, DIEGO D' (**Moses Lopez Pereira**; c. 1699–1759), Marrano financier. D'Aguilar, born in Portugal, where his father held the tobacco monopoly, went in 1722 via London to Vienna, where he reverted to Judaism. In Austria he reorganized the state tobacco monopoly, which he held from 1723 until 1739 for an annual payment of seven million florins. In 1726 d'Aguilar was made a baron and subsequently privy councillor. He helped to raise large loans for the Imperial treasury – the amount for 1732 was ten million florins – and advanced the empress 300,000 florins for rebuilding Schoenbrunn Castle. D'Aguilar used his influence at court to assist the Jews. In 1742, in conjunction with Issachar Berush *Eskeles, he succeeded in preventing the expulsion of the Jews from *Moravia. He was also at the center of the negotiations to prevent their expulsion from *Prague in 1744. He helped the Mantua community in 1752, organized relief for the Belgrade community after a destructive fire, and collected funds for Ereẓ Israel. He is said to have prevented the expulsion of the Jews from Vienna by contacting the sultan. D'Aguilar founded the "Turkish (i.e., Sephardi) congregations in Vienna and *Timisoara.

When the Spanish government asked for his extradition for trial by the Inquisition as a Judaizer, Aguilar moved in 1757 with his 14 children to London. There he took an active part in the life of the Sephardi community. His eldest son, EPHRAIM LOPEZ PEREIRA (1739–1802), second Baron D'Aguilar, was also active for a time in London Jewish communal life. Later he became notorious as an eccentric and miser, and proprietor of what became known as "Starvation Farm." Another son, JOSEPH (d. 1774), severed his connection with Judaism, entered the army, and was progenitor of an important English military family, including General Sir GEORGE CHARLES (1784–1855), who commanded in the Chinese War (1841–42), and General Sir CHARLES LAWRENCE (1821–1912).

BIBLIOGRAPHY: N.M. Gelber, in: JSOS, 10 (1948), 360–2 (includes bibliography); J. Fraenkel, *Jews of Austria* (1967), 327–9; Roth, England, 288–9; J. Picciotto, *Sketches of Anglo-Jewish History* (1956^2), 91–93, 457–8; Ben-Zvi, in: *Sefunot*, 2 (1958), 192–3; Mevoraḥ, in: *Zion*, 28 (1963), 128ff.; S. Simonsohn, *Toledot ha-Yehudim be-Dukkasut Mantovah*, 1 (1962), 357–9; idem, in: *Sefer Yovel… N.M. Gelber* (1963), 145–9; H. Schnee, *Hoffinanz und der moderne Staat*, 3 (1955), 247; 4 (1963), 316–7; Hyamson, *Sephardim of England* (1951^2), index; Roth, Marranos, 308–10; Roth, England, index; N.M. Gelber, in: REJ, 97 (1934), 115ff.

[Meir Lamed]

AGUILAR, EMANUEL ABRAHAM (1824–1904), British pianist and composer. Born in London, he was the brother of the novelist, Grace *Aguilar. Aguilar received his musical education at Frankfurt, and his early compositions were performed there with success. In 1848 he gave a concert with the Gewandhaus Orchestra of Leipzig, and then returned to London, where he devoted himself to teaching. He gave annual piano recitals of classical works, especially those of Beethoven. His own compositions include two operas, three symphonies, three cantatas, chamber and piano music, and a set of preparatory pieces for Bach's "Well Tempered Clavier." Aguilar noted down the melodies of the Amsterdam Sephardi tradition as sung by David Aaron De *Sola, and arranged the harmonizations for De Sola's *Ancient Melodies of the Liturgy of the Spanish and Portuguese Jews* (London, 1857, 1931^2).

BIBLIOGRAPHY: F.-J. Fétis, *Biographie universelle des musiciens*, 1 (1873^2), 37–38; Baker, Biog Dict, s.v.; Riemann-Gurlitt, s.v.

[Bathja Bayer]

AGUILAR, GRACE (1816–1847), English author of Portuguese Marrano extraction, who wrote a number of novels on Jewish themes and some religious works addressed primarily to Jewish women. Her first book was a volume of poems, *The Magic Wreath*, which she published anonymously when she was only 19. Her truly creative period, however, began in 1842, and in the five years until her death at the age of 31 her literary output was remarkable, particularly because at the same time, although very ill, she was helping her mother run a private school at Hackney (outside London). Most of Grace Aguilar's books were not published until after her death. Her novel *Home Influence* (1847), "a tale for mothers and daughters," and its sequel, *Mother's Recompense* (1851), had considerable success, but it was *The Days of Bruce* (1852), a romance set in 14th-century Scotland, that made her famous. The best known of her Jewish novels was *The Vale of Cedars* (1850), a romantic, highly idealized picture of the Marranos in Spain. Twice translated into German and twice into Hebrew, it long retained popularity. She also wrote stories and sketches based on Jewish life and family traditions. In a more serious vein, she translated from French the apologetic work of the ex-Marrano, *Orobio de Castro, *Israel Defended* (1838). She herself wrote *The Spirit of Judaism: In Defense of Her Faith and Its Professors* (1842), and *The Jewish Faith* (1846). The latter took the form of letters addressed to a friend wavering in her religious conviction. Her *Women of Israel* (1845) was a series of biographical sketches of biblical characters, intended to arouse the pride of young Jews in their heritage. Grace Aguilar was one of the first English Jews to attempt to write a history of the Jews in England; it appeared in *Chambers' Miscellany* (1847). She died while on a visit to Germany. Her collected works, in eight volumes, appeared in 1861. In recent years there has been a considerable revival of interest in Aguilar, who wrote from the unusual, marginal position of a female Jewish intellectual in Victorian Britain. A collection of her selected writings was published in 2003, edited by Michael Galchinsky.

BIBLIOGRAPHY: A.S. Isaacs, *Young Champion, One Year in Grace Aguilar's Girlhood* (1933); Abrahams, in: JHSET, 16 (1945–51), 137–48; *JC Supplement* (July 27, 1930); F. Modder, *Jew in the Literature of England* (1939), 182–7; DNB, s.v. S.Aguilar, "Memoir," prefixed to *Home Influence* (1849). **ADD. BIBLIOGRAPHY:** M. Galchinsky, *The Origins of the Modern Jewish Woman Writer: Romance and Reform in Victorian England* (1996); idem. (ed.), *Grace Aguilar: Selected Writings* (2003); ODNB.

[Cecil Roth]

AGUILAR, MOSES RAPHAEL D' (d. 1679), Dutch rabbi and scholar. He went to Brazil from Amsterdam in 1641 with other members of his family (including his nephew, the martyr Isaac de *Castro Tartas) and became rabbi-*ḥazzan*, probably in the Magen Avraham congregation of Mauricia (adjoining Recife). On his return to Amsterdam he opened a private school, and was subsequently (1659) engaged to fill Manasseh ben Israel's place in the Etz Hayyim seminary. He wrote some 20 books, but only two were published in his lifetime – a Hebrew grammar for school use (*Epitome da Grammatica hebrayca*, Leiden, 1660; Amsterdam, 1661^2), and *Dinim de Sechitá y Bedicá* (Amsterdam, 1681). His work on the immortality of the soul, *Tratado da Immortalidade da Alma*, was published by M. de Jong (Coimbra, 1935). The auction catalogue of his rich library (Amsterdam, 1680) is one of the earliest known in Jewish bibliography.

BIBLIOGRAPHY: Imanuel, in: AJA, 14 (1962), 59–61; A. Wiznitzer, *Jews in Colonial Brazil* (1960), 171; ESN, 22–23; C. Gebhardt, *Uriel da Costa* (1922), 250–3.

[Cecil Roth]

AGUILAR DE CAMPÓO, fortress-town in Castile, district of Palencia, northern Spain. The earliest evidence of a Jewish settlement is furnished in the lease of a flour mill in 1187 witnessed by 17 Jews, including two blacksmiths. In the 13th century it was a medium-sized community, with 15 families or about 70 Jews. The farming and other revenues in the districts were in the hands of Don Çaq de la Maleha (*Ibn Ẓadok) and his associates. The taxes paid by the Jewish community in 1290 amounted to 10,718 maravedis. In 1311 the Infant Pedro confirmed the rights of the convent of Santa Maria to tithes and the dues of porteria paid by the Jews; these were reconfirmed in 1370, although the Jewish community had been decimated by English soldiery during the civil war in 1367. The community in Aguilar apparently continued to exist until the expulsion of the Jews from Spain in 1492. Over one of the gates of the city, Puerta de Reinosa, there is a long inscription in Judeo-Castilian (i.e., Spanish in Hebrew characters, almost unique among the Spanish Jewish inscriptions) testifying that the tower was constructed by Don Çaq (Isaac) son of Solomon ibn Malak(e) and his wife Bellida in 1380. The inscription is unique from the historical and linguistic points of view. Fourteenth-century documents speak of the location of the Jewish quarter. It seems very likely that the *juderia* was in what is now known as Tobalina Street. A new Jewish quarter was established towards the end of the 15th century.

BIBLIOGRAPHY: Baer, Urkunden, 2 (1936), index; I. Huidobro and Cantera, in: *Sefarad*, 14 (1954), 335–52; L. Huidobro Serna, *Breve historia y descripción de la muy leal villa de Aguilar* (1954); Cantera-Millás, Inscripciones, 329–31; P. León Tello, *Los judíos de Palencia* (1966); L. Suárez Fernández, *Documents acerca de la expulsion de los judíos* (1964), index. **ADD. BIBLIOGRAPHY:** G. Ruiz, *La Cascajera*, no. 6 (Oct. 1982), 24, 29.

AGUINIS, MARCOS (1935–), Argentinean writer. Born in Cordoba, Argentina, Aguinis received a Ph.D. in neurosurgery, studied psychoanalysis, and worked as a therapist while devoting himself to literature. Following the democratization process in Argentina (1983), Aguinis became a highly regarded intellectual engaged in public affairs as well as in the local Jewish community. During the first government after the military regime, he was elected undersecretary of culture; two years later he was appointed personal counselor to President Alfonsin, with a rank equivalent to undersecretary of state. For many years Aguinis was also a councilor in the *DAIA.

Aguinis' books deal with Jewish themes: Crypto Jews, the Holocaust, antisemitism, Christianity, and the struggle for democracy and cultural pluralism in Argentina. His most famous historical novel, *La Gesta del Marrano* (1992), deals with Francisco Maldonado de Silva, a Converso physician who lived in Concepción (Chile) and was burned at the stake in Lima in 1639. The book was conceived as a paean on freedom, reaching a broad audience because it dealt with the common fate of Jews, converts, blacks, and indigenous people in the Spanish Catholic Colonial America.

Drawing on historical events of the Nazi era, the novel *La matriz del infierno* (1997) ranges from the rise of National Socialism in Germany to the nationalist and authoritarian political culture of Argentina during the 1930s. It emphasizes the cultural and spiritual contradiction between Nazism and the Jewish outlook as well as the attitude of the Christian Church to the Holocaust. While in his early novel *La Cruz Invertida* (1970) Aguinis contrasted sharply the position of the progressive priests affiliated to the Latin American liberation theology movement and the conservatism of the Church hierarchy, in *La matriz del infierno* almost all the Argentinean priests are silent about Hitler's crimes. This novel contributed to the critical debate among Christians and members of other creeds on the hypocrisy and contradictory attitude of the ecclesiastic hierarchy.

Aguinis' later novel *Los Iluminados* (2000) deals with globalization and U.S. fundamentalist groups and their connection to international drug trafficking.

Other literary works of Aguinis deal with central contemporary issues in Latin America, such as the problem of violence and Argentine authoritarianism. *La conspiracion de los idiotas* (1979) is an incisive criticism of the Argentinean military mind and its obsession with conspiracy theories. Written towards the end of the last military dictatorship, it tells the story of an allegedly subversive colony of handicapped and Downs Syndrome patients, alluding to the paranoid prejudices of the authoritarian figure who believes in imaginary enemies.

Aguinis wrote two courageous letters addressed to an unnamed general in essay form: *Carta esperanzada a un General* (1983) after the Falkland War and *Nueva carta esperanzada a un General* (1996). Both books analyze the circumstances in which Argentineans made their transition to democracy. Among other books that focused on Argentina's plight are *Cantata de los diablos* (1972), *Un pais de novela. Viaje hacia la mentalidad de los argentinos* (1988), and *Elogio de la culpa* (1993).

Aguinis' fiction and essays attempt to demythologize history and memory; surprisingly his first novel, *Refugiados* (1969), conceived before the Six-Day War, gave early and keen insight into the Israel-Palestine conflict; on the other hand, the characters of his short stories collected in *Operativo Siesta* (1978) and *Importancia por contacto* (1983) move through biblical tales and Jewish history in search of identity.

Aguinis fiction and essays, based primarily on ideas, address a broad audience by exploring the emotions, sensibilities, and behavior of Jews and non-Jews alike. In many cases, the most compelling characters in his literary oeuvre symbolize the plight of Argentina and of the Jews in its midst.

[Leonardo Senkman (2nd ed.)]

AGUNAH (Heb. עֲגוּנָה; lit. "tied," cf. Ruth 1:13), married woman who for whatsoever reason is separated from her husband and cannot remarry, either because she cannot obtain a divorce from him (see *Divorce), or because it is unknown whether he is still alive. The term is also applied to a *yevamah* ("a levirate widow"; see *Levirate Marriage), if she cannot obtain *ḥaliẓah* from the levir or if it is unknown whether he is still alive (Git. 26b, 33a; Yev. 94a; and *Posekim*). The problem of the *agunah* is one of the most complex in halakhic discussions and is treated in great detail in halakhic literature (no less than six volumes of *Oẓar ha-Posekim* are devoted to it – see bibliography).

Essence of the Problem

The *halakhah* prescribes that a marriage can only be dissolved by divorce or the death of either spouse. According to Jewish law, divorce is effected not by decree of the court, but by the parties themselves, i.e., by the husband's delivery of a *get* ("bill of divorce") to his wife (see *Divorce). Hence the absence of the husband or his willful refusal to deliver the *get* precludes any possibility of a divorce. Similarly the mere disappearance of the husband, where there is no proof of his death, is not sufficient for a declaration by the court to the effect that a wife is a widow and her marriage thus dissolved. The husband, on the other hand, is unaffected by *aginut*, i.e., by his wife's refusal to accept the *get* or her disappearance without trace, since in such a case under certain conditions the law affords him the possibility of receiving *hetter nissu'in* ("permission to contract an additional marriage"; see *Bigamy). In most cases of *agunot* the question is whether or not the husband is still alive. Such cases result, for instance, from uncertainty about the husband's fate caused by conditions of war or persecution – particularly in recent times as a result of the Nazi Holocaust, but the problem can also arise, for example, if the husband suffers from chronic mental illness making him legally incapable of giving a *get* or simply if he willfully refuses to do so.

Rabbinical scholars have permitted many relaxations in the general laws of evidence in order to relieve the hardships suffered by the *agunah*. On the other hand great care was always taken to avoid the risk that permission may inadvertently be given for a married woman to contract a second marriage that would be adulterous and result in any children from such a second marriage being *mamzerim* (see **Mamzer*). Achieving both these ends, i.e., to enable the *agunah* to remarry while ensuring that an adulterous union does not result, is the object of intensive discussion in the laws of the *agunah*.

Mode of Proof (of the Husband's Death)

It is a basic rule of *halakhah* that facts are to be determined on the testimony of two witnesses (see *Evidence). However, the Mishnah already attributes to R. Gamaliel the Elder the *takkanah* that when a husband is missing because of war, and his fate is unknown, the wife may be permitted to remarry on the testimony of only one witness to his death (Yev. 16:7). Although somewhat later R. Eliezer and R. Joshua disagreed with this ruling, at the time of R. Gamaliel of Jabneh it was again determined (*ibid.*) not only that one witness was sufficient but also that hearsay evidence might be admitted, as well as the evidence of a woman, a slave, a handmaiden, or a relative (which classes were otherwise legally incompetent as witnesses). The legal explanation given for these far-reaching rules is that it is to be presumed that a person will not give false testimony on a matter which is likely to come to light, since the husband, if still alive, will undoubtedly reappear sooner or later (Yev. 93b; Maim., Yad, Gerushin 12:15). Moreover, it may be assumed that the wife herself will endeavor to make sure of her husband's death before remarrying, since she will become prohibited to both men if it later transpires that her first husband is still alive, and her other rights, especially pecuniary ones, will be affected too (v. infra; Yev. 87b; Sh. Ar., EH 17:3, 56). Another reason given is that a relaxation of the law is appropriate in times of danger, the possibility that a woman may remain an *agunah* being deemed to be such a time of danger (Yev. 88a, 122a and Rashi *ibid.*; see also **Takkanot*).

An *agunah* may also be permitted to remarry on the strength of her testimony alone as to her husband's death, when she is known to have lived in harmony with her first husband and his absence is not due to war conditions, for the reason, already mentioned, that certainly she has made careful inquiries herself before seeking to contract another marriage (Yev. 93b, 114b–116, and *Posekim*). On the other hand, five categories of women are incompetent to testify as to the husband's death, including his mother and his daughter by another marriage, since it is feared, in view of their customary hatred of the wife, that they are likely to deliver false evidence, so that she should remarry and thus become prohibited to her first husband if it should later transpire that he is still alive (Yev. 117a and *Posekim*).

Similarly, an *agunah* may be relieved of her disability on the unsolicited statement of an apostate Jew (see *Apostasy) or a non-Jew, as to her husband's death; for instance, if during a casual conversation they happened to say, "it is a pity that so and so is dead, he was a fine man," or, "as we were walking together, he suddenly dropped dead," or the like (Yev. 121b–122a; Maim.; *ibid.* 13:11; Sh. Ar., EH 17:14). For the purpose of permitting an *agunah* to remarry it is sufficient if written documents exist that testify to the husband's death (Sh. Ar., EH 17:11). The *halakhah* originally considered documents emanating from non-Jewish authorities as insufficient to permit an *agunah* to remarry (Maim., Yad, Gerushin 13:28; Sh. Ar., EH 17:14), but according to the opinion of most *posekim*, this *halakhah* does not apply to present-day non-Jewish authorities, whose documents, such as death certificates, etc., may be relied on (see, e.g., Ḥatam Sofer, responsa EH 1:43).

Subject-Matter of the Proof

The *halakhah*, while striving to be lenient as possible in the method of proving the husband's death, imposes strict requirements concerning the nature of the evidence with regard to the husband's death, lest a woman still married may thus be permitted to marry another man (Maim. *ibid.* 15: Sh. Ar., EH 17:29). The identity must be established of the person whose death it is sought to determine and there exist most detailed rules in order to establish it with the maximum amount of certainty under the circumstances. Thus evidence as to circumstances from which death would be likely to result in a majority of cases is not considered as sufficient proof of death itself since it may be merely the opinion of the witness that the husband is dead, but not testimony as to the fact of death. Hence, the wife will not be permitted to remarry on the strength of evidence to the effect that her husband was seen to fall into the sea and drown in "water having no end" (i.e., where one can see only the sea but not its surroundings) when his death was not actually seen to have taken place, since he may have been rescued. If, however, the witness testifies that he was later present at the funeral of the husband or some other clear evidence of death, for example, that an identifiable limb was found at the place of drowning, it is accepted as evidence of death. On the other hand the death of the husband will be accepted as having been sufficiently proved and the *agunah* will be permitted to remarry on the strength thereof if there is evidence that he drowned in water "having an end" (i.e., that one can see its surroundings); and the witness stayed long enough at the scene "for the victim's life to depart," without seeing him rise to the surface (Yev. 120–121; Maim. *ibid.* 15–27; Sh. Ar., EH 17–42, esp. 32).

Agunah in the Case of a Civil Marriage

A deserted wife who, practically speaking, has no prospects of obtaining a *get* from her husband, but was married in a civil ceremony only (see Civil *Marriage), may in certain circumstances be declared by the court to have never entered a marriage and thus be permitted to marry another man without need of a *get* from her first husband. The court will reach this conclusion particularly if the wife is able to prove that her first husband expressly refused to marry her in a religious ceremony, declaring thus by implication that he did not wish to create the status of a marriage according to Jewish law (Resp. *Melammed Leho'il*, EH 20).

***Mitzvah* to Permit *Agunot* to Remarry**

Finding a way for permitting an *agunah* to remarry is deemed a great *mitzvah* (Responsa Asheri, 51:2). Indeed, an onerous application of the law, without justification, and in cases where there is no suspicion of deception, is regarded not only as a failure to perform a *mitzvah*, but even as a transgression (Responsa Maimonides, ed. Freiman, 159; Sh. Ar., EH 17:21, Isserles). However, in view of the danger of legalizing a possibly adulterous union, it is customary for an *agunah* to be permitted to remarry only after consultation with, and consent having been obtained from, other leading scholars (Sh. Ar. *ibid.* 34; Isserles and other commentators).

Consequences of Remarriage

An *agunah* who remarries, after permission is granted by the court, is generally entitled to the payment of her **ketubbah* (Yev. 116b; 117a; Maim., Yad, Ishut 16:31; Sh. Ar., *ibid.* 43, 44). If an *agunah* remarries after permission has been given, and then her first husband reappears, her legal position is that of an *eshet ish* "a married woman" who has married another man, thus becoming prohibited to both men (see *Adultery). Accordingly, she requires a *get* from both, and any children born to her of her second husband will be *mamzerim* according to biblical law. Any children born to her from a union with her first husband, after he takes her back but prior to her having received a *get* from her second husband, will also be *mamzerim*, but only according to rabbinical law. In such event she is not entitled to her *ketubbah* from either husband (Yev. 87b; Maim., Yad, Gerushin 10:5, 7; Sh. Ar., EH 17:56).

Proposals for Precautions to Avoid a Woman's Becoming an *Agunah*

In view of the unhappy straits in which an *agunah* is likely to find herself, ways were sought already in early times of taking precautions against such an eventuality. Thus it was customary for anyone "going to wars of the House of David, to write a bill of divorce for his wife" (Ket. 9b and Rashi and Tos. *ibid.*). This *get* was a conditional one, i.e., becoming effective only should the husband not return from war until a specified date, whereupon the wife would become a divorcee and be entitled to marry another man without having to undergo a levirate marriage or *Ḥalizah* (Sh. Ar., EH 143). In certain countries this practice is adopted even in present times by those going to war, but complications may ensue; since the rules and the consequences of a *get* of this nature are beset with halakhic problems (Sh. Ar., *ibid.*), particularly when the husband is a *kohen*, since his wife will be a divorcee if he fails to return by the specified date, and by law he must not thereafter remarry her (See *Marriages, Prohibited). One of the solutions suggested was for the husband to grant his wife an unconditional divorce, save that each promises to remarry the other upon the husband's return from war. This, however, would not avail a *kohen* for the reasons mentioned. Furthermore, in the event of the wife's refusal to keep her promise upon her husband's return, the question may arise whether on the strength of the *get* she is free to marry another man, because of the reasonable possibility that the husband intended that the *get* be conditional, i.e., to be of effect only in the event of his failure to return from the war (see above). On this question there is a wide difference of opinion on the part of the authorities without any unanimity being reached (see S.J. Zevin, in bibliography). Another solution proposed, has been the stipulation of a condition at the time of the marriage to the effect that in certain circumstances the marriage should be considered retroactively void, for instance if the husband should fail, without his wife's permission, to return to her after a long absence of specified duration and should refuse, despite her demand, to grant her a *get*; or if he should die childless, leaving a brother who refuses to fulfill the obligations of a levir, etc. (see, for instance, *Ḥatam Sofer*, EH 1:111). This approach also presents formidable halakhic difficulties and was not generally accepted by the majority of the *posekim* (see Freimann, Kahana, and Berkovits, in bibliography). A wife who is on bad terms with her husband and can prove the likelihood of her becoming an *agunah*, may possibly obtain an injunction from the court restraining her husband from traveling abroad without granting her a conditional *get*, as mentioned above.

It was also sought to avoid the disability of an *agunah* by the enactment of a *takkanah* by halakhic scholars to the effect that the *kiddushin* should be deemed annulled retroactively upon the happening or non-fulfillment of certain specified conditions, such as the husband being missing or his willful refusal to grant a *get*. But this *takkanah*, based on the rule that "a man takes a woman under the conditions laid down by the rabbis… and the rabbis may annul his marriage" (Git. 33a), has rarely been employed since the 14th century. In recent times it has been suggested that halakhic scholars should adopt one or other of these procedures in order to solve certain problems relating to *agunah* (see Freimann, Silberg (in the court decision cited in bibliography), and Elon, in bibliography).

In the State of Israel

The question of permitting an *agunah* to remarry, being a matter of marriage and divorce, falls under the exclusive jurisdiction of the rabbinical courts with regard to Jews who are nationals or residents of the State, in terms of the Rabbinical Courts Jurisdiction (Marriage and Divorce) Law, 5713/1953 (sec. 1), which courts deal with the matter in accordance with the *halakhah*. The provisions of the Declaration of Death Law, 5712/1952 (enacted to meet consequences of the Nazi Holocaust), empowering the Jerusalem District Court under certain conditions to make a declaration as to a person's death, has no bearing on the problem of an *agunah*, since "a declaration of death constituting evidence by virtue of this Law, shall not affect the provisions of law as to the dissolution of marriage" (see *ibid.*, 17).

[Ben-Zion (Benno) Schereschewsky]

A New Approach

Numerous approaches have been suggested in an effort to find a suitable solution to the problem of the *agunah*, based on the enormous range of materials and sources in which even the experienced scholar may find it difficult to orient himself.

Discussion of the issue of *agunot* first appears during the tannaitic period, but has continued until today. This issue is a classic example of how the world of *halakhah* operates: an interplay of innovation and tradition in legal decisions, the existence of truths that in one sense are absolute, and in another sense contingent upon exigencies of time and place, and the fine balance between the law and the judge. Hence, it is highly instructive as an indicator of the way in which social and historical realities integrate in the formulation of *halakhah*, underscoring the reflections, doubts, and debates, the application of far-reaching and far-sighted solutions on the one hand and the search for direction toward such solutions on the other.

According to Jewish law, just as the marital bond is created by the actions of the two individuals involved, so too divorce can only be effected by their complementary and reciprocal actions, namely by the husband giving, and the wife accepting, the *get* (bill of divorce). And just as *kiddushin* is a voluntary act performed by the two spouses, so too the act of divorce (at least since the *ḥerem* issued by Rabbenu Gershom at the end of the tenth century) must be performed voluntarily by both spouses. Thus, according to *halakhah*, a couple is not actually divorced by virtue of the decision of a court that decides on their divorce. When the court (*bet din*), in response to irrevocable discord between the couple, rules that they must divorce, it merely declares that the couple must carry out the act of divorce, by giving and receiving a *get*; the decision of the court itself does not effect the divorce. In other words, the decision is not *constitutive*, as it is in most contemporary legal systems, but rather *declarative*, informing the couple of their obligation to divorce.

This fundamental difference between divorce in Jewish law and in other legal systems has certain advantages. For example, in Jewish law the divorce can be the product of a mutual agreement, with neither of the spouses being required to show any grounds for divorce, as was the case in most legal systems, and as is still the case in some until today. However, this difference also creates difficulties, as when one of the couple is not able, in the sense of legal capacity, or not willing, to take part in the giving and receiving of the *get*: not able – when one of the spouses suffers from a mental illness that renders him legally incompetent, or when the husband is absent (whether voluntarily or not); not willing – when he (or she) is capable of giving or receiving the *get*, yet refuses to do so, whether in order to extort money from the spouse, or to otherwise abuse her or to take revenge upon her. In all these instances it is the wife who is worse off, since she becomes an *agunah* (a chained woman), unable to remarry so long as the death of her husband has not been proven (should he have disappeared), or until he gives her a *get* (where he is alive, but is either mentally incapacitated or has refused to give the *get*). Should she marry or have sexual relations, any children born to her will be *mamzerim* (misbegotten), who are unable to marry other Jews. These severe consequences do not ensue in the case of a husband whose wife is unable or unwilling to accept the *get*, neither in terms of the status of his children (born to him from another woman while he is still married) nor in terms of his potential marriage to another woman. Indeed, permission may be granted for him to remarry, should his wife unlawfully refuse to accept the *get*.

In terms of solutions to the problem of *agunot*, a distinction must be drawn between the various circumstances that can lead to the woman's becoming an *agunah*. The cases in which the husband is missing as a result of war, natural disaster, or other similar circumstances, are usually solved by halakhic authorities and scholars within a reasonable amount of time. Their solutions are based on the principle that "in the case of *agunot* [i.e., in order to prevent a woman from becoming or remaining an *agunah*] the Sages were lenient." In accordance with this principle, for example, the Sages significantly relaxed the level of proof required to ascertain the husband's death. Testimony that would otherwise be unacceptable – whether emanating from a heavenly voice, hearsay, or the like – could be utilized by the court to free a woman from the shackles of being an *agunah*. Relying upon this principle, all the *agunot* from Israel's wars in recent decades were permitted to remarry, as were the wives of the sailors who disappeared when the Israeli submarine *Dakar* sank without a trace in 1967, in accordance with a halakhic decision of late Chief Rabbi Shelomo *Goren. In this latter case, there was almost no evidence available to indicate the fate of the crew; nonetheless, within a very short time none of these women was left an *agunah*.

ISSUES THAT ARE DIFFICULT TO RESOLVE. Difficulties arise in regard to those cases where there is no doubt that the husband is alive, but in which he is incapable or refuses to give the *get*. Cases in which the husband refuses to give the *get*, in order to extort money or take revenge, etc., are both the most difficult and the most numerous. These problems are particularly widespread and serious in countries outside Israel, where there is a legal option for civil marriage and divorce. A civil court may rule that the couple is divorced, but from the halakhic perspective, the woman may not remarry unless her husband gives her a *get*, and husbands often exploit this situation in order to extort money or other concessions from their wives. Again, from the halakhic perspective, there is no parallel limitation on the husband who wishes to remarry. In an attempt to solve this problem, a number of solutions have been proposed. In the United States, for example, proposals were made for the addition of an appropriate clause in the standard *ketubbah* (marriage settlement document), or the introduction of state legislation which prevents the husband from marrying another woman so long as he has not removed any obstacle to the remarriage of his wife, from who he is already civilly divorced.

The principal method proposed by halakhic authorities to relieve the problem of *agunot* was that of *annulment* of the marriage. This approach was first discussed at the time of the *tannaim*, on the basis of the principle that "anyone who betroths [a woman] does so subject to the conditions laid down by the rabbis, and the rabbis have the power to annul the betrothal," if it "was effected improperly" or "in deviation from the conditions laid down by the rabbis." This approach was initially widely used, but later its use decreased significantly, particularly as a result of historical changes in Jewish life – the dispersion of Jews throughout the Diaspora and, in certain countries, among various Jewish centers, as well as the ideological and cultural schisms that arose with the onset of the Emancipation.

Before discussing the particulars of this subject, mention should be made of an additional approach, which has not been given sufficient consideration: namely, *kiddushei ta'ut* ("erroneous betrothal"). There is a difference between solving the problem of *agunot* by annulling the marriage – that is, in which the marriage is itself binding, but the *bet din* annuls it and permits the couple to marry – and solving the problem of *agunot* by utilizing the principle of "*kiddushei ta'ut*," meaning that the marriage itself was never in effect, thereby obviating the need for its annulment. This distinction may be of value in the search for a speedier solution for the distress of contemporary *agunot*. Examples of use of the principle of *kiddushei ta'ut* to permit *agunot* to remarry can be found in the responsa of R. Simḥah of Speyer, one of the outstanding sages of Ashkenazi Jewry at the end of 12th century; of R. Simeon b. Ẓemah *Duran (Algiers, 14th century); in the reasoning of R. Joseph Dov *Soloveichik, one of the leading scholars of 19th century Lithuanian Jewry; and in the responsa of R. Moses *Feinstein, a leading halakhic authority of our own generation. (For research regarding this approach see Hacohen, *The Tears of the Oppressed*, in the bibliography. This approach may provide a partial solution to the problem of *agunot*.)

As stated above, the main overall solution to the problem of *agunot*, particularly in view of contemporary needs, is that of annulment of marriage. Of particular importance in this context are the reasons that led to the almost total rejection of this solution; on the basis of a close analysis of these reasons, and in light of the establishment of the State of Israel, it may now be possible to return to this solution.

ANNULMENT OF MARRIAGE – PROBLEMS AND ANALYSIS. From the 12th century we have the report of R. Eliezer b. Nathan of Mainz concerning an incident involving a fraudulent marriage. No explicit enactment regulating the manner of effecting a marriage was applicable to the case and the halakhic authorities disagreed as to whether it was possible to invalidate the marriage (*Rabban*, EH 3, fol. 47b). The authorities of Worms and Speyer sought to annul the marriage of the first husband in reliance on the talmudic statement "that it was effected improperly." However, this was not the view of the halakhic authorities of Mainz, who argued that since the completion of the Talmud, the post-talmudic authorities do not have a power to annul such a marriage. This was also the view of one of their contemporaries – Rabbenu Tam – who argued that even the *geonim* lacked the authority to annul such marriages (*Sefer ha-Yashar,* R. Tam, Responsa Section, Rosenthal ed., §24).

In the 13th century, Asheri and Rashba made an important distinction in regard to annulment of marriages (*Rosh*, 35.1; 35.2; *Rashba*, 1 §§1026, 1162, 1185). Under this distinction, the post-talmudic halakhic authorities do not have the general power to annul a marriage on the grounds that "it was effected improperly" or that it was entered into "subject to the conditions laid down by the rabbis"; but if an enactment explicitly states that a marriage in violation of its provisions will be annulled, then the marriage is invalid.

> If the communities, or each individual community, should wish to erect a legislative safeguard against these unfortunate occurrences, let them all jointly adopt an enactment fully confiscating, whether permanently or for a fixed period, any money given [to effect a marriage] to any woman of their community(ies), unless the woman willingly accepts it with the consent of her father or in the presence of whomever they wish.
>
> Every enactment – whether by a particular community or a group of communities – that expropriates the money given to effect a marriage is thus fully valid; and consequently a marriage that does not fulfill the conditions set forth in the enactment is void.

Rabbenu Jeroham (14th century, France) also held this view:

> Every community has the power to adopt an enactment and to agree that any marriage effected in the presence of fewer than ten persons is invalid; and it may also establish other similar conditions that all who marry do so subject to the conditions established by the residents of the community" (*Toledot Adam ve-Ḥavvah*, Sec. *Ḥavvah*, XXII, 4).

In the 14th century, a substantial change occurred in the attitude adopted by the halakhic authorities regarding the actual exercise of legislative power to annul a marriage. We have already noted a certain reluctance on the part of Rashba, who initially ruled that the matter required further consideration but subsequently gave a definitive ruling permitting an enactment for the annulment of marriages. Some time later, even graver doubts were raised by R. *Isaac b. Sheshet Perfet (Ribash), who made his consent to validate such an enactment conditional upon "the approbation of all the halakhic authorities of the region," as a means of dividing the responsibility for the decision among as many halakhic authorities as possible (*Ribash* §399).

Furthermore, according to Ribash the principle that "all who marry do so subject to the conditions laid down by the rabbis" can be broadened and applied to conditions laid down by the community:

> In addition, even if we had to resort to the rationale that "all who marry do so subject to the conditions laid down by the rabbis" to justify every annulment of marriage, we may also state that all who marry do so subject to the conditions laid down by the community in its enactments, given that we have already accepted that all those who marry without any express stipulations as to the terms of marriage do so in accordance with the customs of the town.... Thus, we reach the conclusion that the community may adopt such an enactment, and a marriage that contravenes a communal enactment is invalid, and no divorce is necessary."

This was Ribash's rendition of the law in theory. "However, as to its practical application, I tend to view the matter strictly; and I would not rely on my own opinion (i.e., in view of the gravity of the matter) to declare that she needs no divorce to be free [to remarry], unless all the halakhic authorities of the region concurred, so that only a 'chip of the beam' should reach me [i.e., that I do not take upon myself the full responsibility, but only part of it]."

Ribash did not yet make an absolute distinction between the theoretical authority to adopt an enactment annulling a marriage, and the practical exercise of that authority. The qualification introduced by Ribash was only that such legislation requires the approval of all the halakhic authorities of the region. However, the position expressed by his younger contemporary, Rashbaz (Simeon b. Ẓemaḥ Duran), was far more adamant – namely, that an enactment nullifying a marriage should never be applied in practice. His ultimate justification for the strict ruling was "the gravity of sexual matters" (*Tashbez*, 2 §5).

Rashbaz states unequivocally that in terms of the "essence" of the *halakhah*, the existing authority to annul a marriage derives from the principle of *hefker bet din hefker* [the bet din's authority to expropriate money] and he emphasizes that the authority to annul a marriage rests in every competent court and in every generation. But this is only on a theoretical level. On a practical level a strict approach should be adopted regarding marriage because of the gravity of improper sexual unions, and hence this authority should not be exercised (see also *Tashbez*, 1, §133).

This same view and rationale are echoed in a responsum by Rashbaz's grandson, the second Rashbash (R. Simeon b. Solomon *Duran), at the end of the 15th and the beginning of the 16th centuries (*Yakhin u-Bo'az* 2, §20).

During the same period (towards the turn of the 16th century) we also hear of the first detailed explanation for the phenomenon of the growing inclination to abstain from exercising regulative power to annul marriages that are halakhically valid. This trend was explained by R. Moses *Alashkar, who was active at that time in Spain, in Egypt, and later on in the Land of Israel. First, he made it quite clear that the halakhic authorities and the community have the power to adopt an enactment by which a marriage entered into in violation of their regulations is void. However, he further ruled that, as opposed to enactments in other areas of Jewish Law, where there is nothing to prevent each community from fully exercising the legislative authority vested in them, the adoption of far-reaching enactments with regard to the annulment of marriage are not permitted – mainly for reasons of general legal policy – unless the enactments are adopted by all or at least most of the communities in a particular country. Maharam Alashkar pointed out that in this ruling he was following in the footsteps of Ribash, who also required that the enactment be adopted by all of the communities in the region. However, Maharam Alashkar explained this requirement within the particular context of marriage and divorce law (*Maharam Alashkar,* §48).

The fact that an enactment was only adopted by a particular community and not by all the communities – or at least a majority of them – prevented Maharam Alashkar from approving the enactment and declaring it valid. While Jewish Law confers legislative authority to a local community, and even to a tradesmen's association, it is not proper to "take a lenient approach" to marriages "valid according to the Torah" purely on the basis of one community's enactment. This is so, because local legislation in matters of marriage and divorce creates a serious danger of degeneracy and of making a mockery of the entire institution of marriage. An enactment of one community clearly does not bind a member of any other community. Consequently, if a member of another community marries a woman in violation of the enactment, the marriage will be valid (since we apply the law of the husband's community), while if a member of the community that adopted the enactment marries a woman in violation of the enactment, the woman will not be married, and is permitted to marry someone else without a divorce. This kind of situation is intolerable in terms of the integrity and stability of the institutions of marriage and family!

An interesting example of this significant change in the legislative trend regarding enactments dealing with annulment of marriages is the difference between two enactments, adopted approximately 100 years apart in the very same location – the community of the Castilian exiles in *Fez. The first enactment, adopted in 1494, reads as follows (*Kerem Ḥemer,* 2, *Takkanah* §1; for the Fez enactments, see *Ha-Mishpat ha-Ivri,* p. 652):

> No Jewish man shall betroth any Jewish woman other than in the presence of ten persons among whom there is either a scholar of the community (who receives his wages from the community treasury) or a local judge; the same applies to their entering under the *ḥuppah.* If it is done in any other manner, the marriage is void *ab initio.*

One hundred years later, a new enactment was adopted in Fez, similarly requiring that a betrothal take place in the presence of ten persons. However, this enactment contained a substantial change in the sanction imposed on the violator of the enactment; while he is subject to punishment and fines, the marriage itself is considered valid and is not annulled. Instead, the husband is compelled to give a divorce (*Kerememer, Takkanah* §34; the latter enactment was adopted in 1592).

In reality, in the 16th and even in the 17th century enactments were still being adopted in various communities in Italy and elsewhere prohibiting the celebration of marriages in the presence of fewer than ten persons and explicitly stating that a marriage in violation of the enactment is void *ab initio* (see for example the Casalli enactment of 1571; a similar enactment was adopted in Corfu in 1652). However, the overwhelming majority of halakhic authorities refused to endorse the practice of annulment of marriages and it appears that these particular enactments were never actually applied (*Naḥalat Ya'akov* §57; the responsum was written in 1615).

It is highly noteworthy that as late as the 18th and 19th centuries, legislation was enacted in the Jewish centers of the Eastern countries, requiring marriages to be celebrated in the presence of ten persons and a rabbi, and providing for annulment as a sanction for violation.

In the middle of the 18th century in Damascus, Syria, an enactment of this kind was adopted by the halakhic authorities together with the communal leaders, led by R. Mordecai Galante. The full text of the *takkanah* was preserved (*Berekh Moshe* by Moses Galante, the son of Mordecai Galante, §33). It states that "in order to remove the stumbling blocks placed by deceivers" they enacted that:

> No Jewish man marry any woman, except in the presence of ten Jewish persons, including the rabbi who is the teacher of Torah and who the community recognize as judges ... and two individuals from among the communal leaders and officials are also to be included among these ten persons. This, our enactment and decree, shall be in effect from this day forward until the day of the coming of the Righteous Teacher, the Messiah of the God of Jacob ... and if any man shall intentionally marry in secret in the presence of two witnesses and not in the presence of ten Jewish persons, as mentioned above ... his marriage will have no effect and we annul his marriage by way of absolute expropriation like the court of Ravina and R. Ashi, which had the power to expropriate a person's property.

In the middle of the 19th century this enactment was reaffirmed and fortified by the scholars and leaders of the Damascus community, led by Isaac *Abulafia (in his *Penei Yiẓḥak,* EH, §16; p. 94d).

> In our community there is an earlier enactment ... that no man marry in the presence of two witnesses, unless the rabbi or his representative consents and ten persons are present, two of whom must be communal leaders ... and that if any man shall intentionally marry in secret in the presence of two witnesses ... not only shall he be labeled a transgressor, but his marriage is annulled by the rabbis and the money given to effect the *Kiddushin* is completely expropriated under principle of *hefker bet din hefker* like the court of Ravina and R. Ashi, which had the power to expropriate property ... In as much as an incident occurred within the past three years, we have reenacted this legislation and proclaimed it publicly with full force and effect, with all transgressors being made subject to excommunication and ban as is known.

There were disputes among the halakhic authorities regarding the interpretation, validity, and applicability of this enactment (see Freimann, *Seder Kiddushin ve-Nissu'in,* 286ff.). As a fundamental ruling regarding the manner of establishing the *halakhah* and adopting enactments, it was sharply criticized by R. Shalom Moses Hai Gagin, of Jerusalem:

> This is an astounding opinion in which the author states that he saw in the code books that it is permissible to adopt an enactment at variance with the rulings of R. Joseph Caro, even to the point of leniency concerning a prohibition contained in the Torah; to date he has not revealed the identity of this authority to us. This is nothing more than his own view, and his own unsupported opinion. It cannot possibly be contended that the world's great scholars ever gathered together and agreed to rule contrary to R. Joseph Caro, the author of the Shulḥan Arukh, even in a single particular (*Yismaḥ Lev,* EH, §15).

According to R. Gagin, the enactment was only intended to annul a marriage in rare and exceptional cases (e.g., in which there were additional defects, or in special cases in which there was a problem of *iggun*).

In his responsum relating this matter, R. Isaac Abulafia strongly defended his position regarding the power to adopt such an enactment:

> What should I say in response to that author who is wise in his own eyes... who compares those who have studied and gained wisdom to ignorant reed cutters? [i.e., who compare people who have studied extensively to ignorant reed cutters; see Sanh. 33a] For the fundamental question, namely, whether a court and a community may enact legislation to annul a marriage that is valid according to the Torah, has been extensively discussed by the *rishonim,* i.e., Ribash and Rashbez, and by other leading authorities, who proved directly on the basis of several talmudic passages that enactments annulling a marriage regarded by the Torah as valid can be adopted on the basis of two sound and fully articulated reasons: (1) that all who marry do so subject to the conditions laid down by the rabbis, and the rabbis annul this marriage; and (2) that pursuant to the principle of *hefker bet din hefker,* the court has sufficient authority to exercise the power of expropriation....

> This being so, there is here an a *fortiori* inference: since they have the power to annul a marriage that is completely and clearly valid under the law of the Torah, as stated above, then *a fortiori,* in order to erect a safeguard, they may also adopt an enactment that is contrary to R. Joseph Caro on this particular point, and may instead follow the authorities who disagree with him. If they possess the power to annul and dissolve a marriage that is valid according to the Torah, they must certainly have the authority to adopt an enactment that contravenes the strict view of R. Joseph Caro, for otherwise, what have the halakhic authorities accomplished with their enactment? The matter is simple and clear and beyond all doubt (*Lev Nishbar* §3, 15a).

It should be emphasized that many of the leading halakhic scholars in the Eastern countries shared this view and ruled accordingly, that the halakhic authorities have the power to annul marriages by way of an enactment (in another context, see Elon, "The Uniqueness of Halakhah," in the bibliography):

> The question arose again in its full gravity, during the second half of the 19th century, when it was determined in Algerian law that it was obligatory to conduct a civil marriage ceremony prior to conducting *ḥuppah* and *kiddushin,* and that in the absence of the civil ceremony the couple would not be considered married in accordance with the laws of the State. This change carried tremendous potential for abuse by which the husband could cause his wife to become an *agunah*; for if they had been married under religious law without the marriage having been preceded by a civil ceremony, then he could then legally marry another woman. Alternatively, if the woman who had the status of a married woman, went and married another person, she would thereby blemish the status of her children from the second husband. In order to prevent mishaps of this nature and the like, the Algerian rabbis turned to one of the great halakhic authorities of Turkey, R. Chaim Palagi, from Ismir, who proposed, in view of the increasing numbers of cases in which woman were chained to the marital bond and the attendant danger of *mamzerut,* that they adopt a enactment for the annulment of marriages effected without there having been a prior civil marriage ceremony. Some time later, a similar enactment for the annulment of marriages was adopted in Algeria by R. Elijah Ḥazan, and he was supported by the halakhic authorities of Tunis and Constantine and others too. There were other authorities who did not approve of the annulment of marriages, and refused to adopt this kind of enactment in their own locations. Among these was R. David Moeati, one of the Algerian rabbis. The dispute continued between other halakhic authorities as well. R. Ḥayyim Bleich, an eminent rabbi from Tlemcen, Algeria, wrote a special treatise supporting the idea of annulment of marriages under these circumstances, even after the consummation of marriage (see Freimann, *Seder Kiddushin ve-Nissu'in,* 334–37). It would appear that the majority of the halakhic authorities supported the adoption of this enactment and ruled accordingly, and it served as the basis for annulment of marriages in the Egyptian communities (Freimann, 337–44; see further in Elon, *ibid.*, 34–35, *infra*).

Our discussion shows that in Ashkenazi Jewry, following the period of R. Moses *Isserles, one of the leading halakhic authorities of the 16th century, enactments were no longer made for the annulment of marriages as a solution for the problem of *agunot.* The position accepted by the Ashkenazi authorities was that they did not have the power to adopt enactments for the annulment of marriages, in view of the considerations dealt with above. Among Oriental Jewry, on the other hand, this practice continued, alongside intensified discussion of the need and the possibility of annulling marriages by appropriate enactments. In a number of locations in the Oriental Diaspora these enactments were actually put into practice, surviving until this very day. The phenomenon has invariably been the subject of incisive and often stormy discussions, and has remained on the public agenda, and some of the halakhic authorities did not recoil from adopting the enactments which in their view were both necessary and appropriate.

THE CENTRALITY OF THE LAND OF ISRAEL AND THE STATE OF ISRAEL – THE KEY TO THE SOLUTION OF THE PROBLEM OF AGUNOT. It would appear that the great historic transformation of the condition of the Jewish people wrought by the restoration of Jewish sovereignty (a transformation unparalleled in its magnitude in the entire course of Jewish history) could and should lead to a change in the trend of refraining from the exercise of halakhic legislative authority. The reasons for this were the fragmentation and dispersal of local communal legislation, and the absence of a central authority for the Jewish people in its entirety. Accordingly, the new reality of ingathering and unification should serve as an impetus for the renewed resumption and exercise of legislative authority and for the emergence of a central authority, which can adopt legislation applicable to the Jewish people in its entirety. The halakhic center in the State of Israel should be the main Jewish center, exercising halakhic hegemony over the entire Jewish dispersion. In that capacity, it is authorized to reassume the authority to adopt enactments which, from the time of their adoption or over time, would become the legacy of the Jewish people wherever it be. The new historical reality ought to give rise to a new halakhic reality, the central innovation of which will lie in the restoration of the "crown" to its ancient glory. This new situation both warrants and demands the renewal of the full scope of creative legislative activity in all branches of Jewish law, including marital law, in order to strive to perfect the world of *halakhah* and the world of the Jewish people. (A proposal in this spirit for a solution of the problem of *agunot* was made by Prof. Abraham Chaim Freimann, *Seder Kiddushin ve-Nissu'in,* 397).

In the State of Israel, as the center of the Jewish world, marriages and divorces of all Jewish men and women are effected, pursuant to the State Law, in accordance with the conditions stipulated by its halakhic authorities and scholars.

Our discussion until now indicates that the dearth of practical application of enactments for *agunot* and for annulments of marriage in the larger portion of Jewish communities in the Jewish dispersion is rooted in the historical phenomenon of the fragmentation into numerous centers and different communities, a phenomenon that gave rise to a multiplicity of halakhic practices. We find more and more cases in which the enactment was accepted and practiced in one particular center, or even in one particular community. As the fragmentation increased, it increasingly precluded any possibility of annulment of marriages. The situation was one in which there could be two couples, one belonging to a community that had adopted an enactment for the annulment of marriage and the other to a community which had not adopted that enactment. As a result, one could no longer claim that marriage was effected in accordance with the conditions stipulated by the rabbis, because there was no single set of conditions of the rabbis: rather there were two different systems, which alternated from center to center and from community to community. This point was made and reiterated in the responsa of the halakhic authorities just examined.

Needless to say, these enactments ought to be made by the rabbis and scholars of the State of Israel, the center of the Jewish world. However, such enactments need to be adopted in consultation and coordination with Jewish scholars and halakhic authorities from the entire Jewish world. Consequently, anyone who marries would be doing so in accordance with the enactments made by the authorities of the Land of Israel, in the State of Israel. There would thus be one enactment for the entire Jewish people. The factor of centrality thus both accommodates and compels the renewed adoption of an enactment for *agunot* that would unshackle Jewish women both in the State of Israel and in all the centers the world over.

PEACE AS A CONSIDERATION IN JEWISH LAW. In our discussion of an enactment for the annulment of marriages as a solution for the plight of *agunot*, the consideration of *peace* was one of the considerations that periodically arose, either as a compelling reason for finding a solution or as the means for finding such a solution. Indeed, it plays a unique function in the discussions of the halakhic authorities in the context of enactments for *agunot*.

Halakhic authorities derived this principle from the verse in Proverbs 3:17: "Her ways are ways of pleasantness and all her paths are peace." This verse describes the virtues of wisdom, and in the Jewish tradition it serves to extol the Torah and those who study it. It was further established as a general guideline for the manner of interpretation of the rules of Jewish Law in all its various fields, and as the purpose and goal of the entire world of Jewish Law. In the world of the halakhic authorities, "the ways of pleasantness" and the "paths of peace" were integrated into a single principle, each aspect complementing the other, with the emphasis alternately placed on either "pleasantness" or "peace." This integrated principle was the source of a variety of rulings in all areas of *halakhah*, chief among them being family law. (See *Maharsha*, end of Yeb. 122b; Maim., Yad, *Megillah ve-Hannukah* 4:12–14.)

A SIGNIFICANT THOUGH PARTIAL SOLUTION: A MODERN APPLICATION OF RABBENU TAM'S *HARḤAKOT*. We concluded our above discussion of the subject of *agunot* with the expectation that the resolution of this difficult and painful problem would be found by resorting to the creative utilization of the tool of annulment of marriage, which would be examined, discussed, and applied from the center of the Jewish people in the Land of Israel in the State of Israel. It is interesting to note that the first steps towards a solution to the problem of *agunot* have already been taken. We refer here to the efficient, variegated, and specific use of a special law, in a manner that induces the husband to immediately comply with the decisions and judgments that obligate him to release his wife from the chains of her *agginut*.

As we observed, the predominant view in the vast majority of Jewish centers was the proscription of physical coercion as a means of forcing the husband to give his wife a *get*, except for certain exceptional cases: "We should be strict in not using coercion by way of physical coercion, so that the *get* does not become a '*coerced get*' [one given under physical compulsion, against the husband's will and thus invalid]" (*Rama* Sh. Ar., EH 154.21). On the topic of physical coercion as a means of forcing the husband to give a *get*, see the entry *Divorce and its conclusion: "Enforcement of Divorce in the State of Israel." This strict ruling frequently gave rise to problems of *agginut* and the halakhic authorities searched for halakhic and social remedies to this serious problem.

The method proposed by Rabbenu Tam (one of the leading 12th century Tosafists) was based on ostracizing the recalcitrant husband who refused to give the *get* to his wife, cutting him off from communal life and severing all contact with him. In other words: "they are not permitted to talk to him, do business with him, host him, feed him, provide him with drink, accompany him and visit him when he is ill … we will separate from him" (*Sefer ha-Yashar* §24). Physical coercion or other kinds of harm (such as imprisonment, etc.) are forbidden, because in those cases the husband's consent to give a *get* may stem from his inability to withstand the physical pressure and not because he has consented to give a *get*. The social sanctions, by prohibiting any contact with him, are insufficient as a means of forcing him to grant a *get*, for from a physical perspective he is capable of bearing the pressures of denial of contact with him. Accordingly, if he deigns to give his wife the *get*, it may be presumed that he does so willingly.

Notably, resort to this kind of sanction in the judgments of rabbinical courts in the State of Israel has been extremely rare. Two factors may explain this. Firstly, the "fear of instruction" of the halakhic authorities echoes the view of a number of *posekim* who ruled that these sanctions constitute coercion and are therefore only permitted in the rare cases in which coercion is permitted. The second factor is that the sanctions referred to in the aforementioned sources were utilized primarily in order to ostracize and exclude the husband from communal religious life, limiting its effectiveness to those cases in which the husband belonged to that particular community.

Moreover, the economic aspect of abstaining from any financial and commercial dealings with the husband would be unlikely to be particularly effective in the contemporary reality. It would therefore seem that the idea and the principle of the sanctions, as they should be applied in the current reality, require application and execution by the authorities of the State, exercising its legally conferred power over its entire citizenry.

Sanctions (Exclusionary Measures) in Legislation of the Knesset

This method has in fact been proposed by researchers and various judicial and governmental circles. A halakhic dialogue has begun regarding the possibility of utilizing tools wielded by the State authorities, and whether the use of such tools does not constitute "coercion," if only because the exclusion from participation in communal life and the possibility of coercion is only permitted in certain exceptional cases, as stated above. The proposals became memorandums, discussions, draft laws, and culminated in the formulation of a list of "exclusionary (shunning) measures" which received expression in the Knesset legislation under the Rabbinical Courts Law (Upholding Divorce Rulings), 5755–1995. Since its adoption a number of amendments have been introduced on an almost annual basis.

Under this law (§1) if a certain period of time has passed since the decision of the Rabbinical Court ruling that the husband must give a *get* to his wife, and the husband has not upheld the judgment:

The Rabbinical Court may, in a restrictive order, impinge on the rights enumerated below, in full or in part, for such period and under such conditions as it may prescribe:

(1) To leave the country;

(2) To receive an Israeli passport or *laissez passer* pursuant to the Passports Law, 5712–1952, to hold them or extend their validity, provided that they retain their validity for purposes of returning to Israel;

(3) To receive, hold or renew a driver's license;

(4) To be appointed, elected or to serve in a statutory position or a position in an inspected body within the meaning of the State Comptroller Law 5718–1958 [Consolidated Version];

(5) To deal in a profession the occupation in which is regulated by Law, or to operate an enterprise which requires a legal license or permit;

(6) To open, or hold a bank account or to draw checks on a bank account, by determining that he is a restricted customer within the meaning of the Checks Without Cover Law, 5741–1981.

While the historical source of these provisions lies in the "Sanctions (*harḥakot*) of Rabbeinu Tam," their ramifications extend far further afield. The order issued is a "restrictive order" affecting the possibility of leaving the country, receiving a passport, driver's license, appointment to official positions, occupation in a profession, opening and maintaining a bank account, and being imprisoned in solitary confinement for a prescribed number of days. Restrictions of this nature may for the most part be regarded as violations of the basic rights in accordance with the Basic Laws: Human Dignity and Freedom, and Freedom of Occupation (e.g., freedom of movement, freedom of occupation, right to property). At the same time, they are of tremendous importance in the promotion of a solution to the problem of *agunot* in the world of *halakhah* and as part of the world of *halakhah*. The restrictions imposed here by the legislator, whose values are those of a Jewish and democratic state, are a continuation of the exclusionary measures, established in the halakhah of the 12th century, and named after one of its most eminent leaders and authorities, the noted Tosafist, Rabbenu Tam. Mention should be made here of an interesting correspondence relating to the application of this Law, cited in the Report of the State Comptroller, Justice Eliezer Goldberg (Annual Report 54B, 2003, and accounts for fiscal year of 2002, pp. 515–23), under the heading "Rabbinical Courts." In the response submitted by the director of the Rabbinical Courts to the State Comptroller's Office, it states that "a *mesurevet get* (wife whose husband has refused to give a *get*) is defined by the Rabbinical Court as a wife whose husband was obligated to give her a *get*, and has still not given it to her after 30 days." In accordance with this definition, there are only 200 *mesuravot get*. This led to a proposal of the State Comptroller that the Rabbinical Court should initiate the issue of a restrictive order even if the judgment itself did not stipulate that the husband was obligated to give his wife a *get*, but only stipulated that the Rabbinical Court recommends or suggests that the husband give his wife a *get*. This is in accordance with the Law itself which states (section 1 (b)): "For purposes of this section, it is immaterial if the judgment used the wording of coercion, obligation, *mitzvah* (positive precept), suggestion, or any other wording"; and this would result in a decrease in the numbers of *agunot*. The president of the Rabbinical Court replied that "should it be necessary," the Rabbinical Court would adopt this kind of initiative (*ibid.*, 521–23).

We are once again confronted by the social role filled by the State of Israel, as an esteemed, venerable, and sovereign legislative authority, in both the development of *halakhah* and the resolution of halakhic problems that arise in its framework.

This law contributed significantly to a solution of the *agunot* problem. For further details regarding its provisions, see the entry on Divorce, especially the concluding section, "Enforcement of Divorce in the State of Israel." Admittedly, the problem remains to be completely and satisfactorily resolved – for the Jews in the State of Israel, and certainly for Jews living in the countries of the Diaspora, to whom the provisions of the law dealing with compliance with judgments do not apply. Nonetheless, the partial promotion of a solution, as embodied in the provisions of the law, is still of great significance in the anchoring of the values of the State of Israel as a Jewish and democratic state, in accordance with the provisions of the purpose section of the Basic Laws.

As stated, the Law of the Knesset is just a beginning, albeit an important one, for the solution of the problem of *agu-*

not. The need exists, and it is incumbent upon us to aspire to a complete resolution of the *agunot* problem. Such a solution exists in the form of annulment of marriages, which could be effected by the adoption of an enactment in the center of the Jewish world in the Land of Israel, with the cooperation and assistance of halakhic authorities from Jewish communities all over the world. To be sure, the halakhic world is divided regarding the issue of the authority of the rabbis to annul marriages in this manner, but this has always been the case. Moreover, this was the situation in the period immediately preceding our period, in a location quite close to ours. I refer here to the dispute between the two great halakhic authorities, R.I. Abulafia and R.C. Ganin, during the 19th century in the Jewish center of Damascus, in Syria, the neighbor of Israel (see *supra*). Accordingly, if there was a dispute regarding the enactment that originated in Damascus in Syria, then an enactment issuing from Jerusalem, in the Land of Israel in the State of Israel, which constitute the center of the Jewish world, should certainly be proposed, accepted, and applied in practice in order to free Jewish women from the chains and suffering of being *agunot*.

In conclusion, it should be noted that the issue of a wife's *agginut* occasionally arises in judicial deliberations, not in relation to the *agginut* per se, but rather in the context of adjudication of other legal matters, such as the amount of damages owing to a widow whose husband died through his employer's negligence, the issue of an extradition order against a husband for a crime committed in another country, and the like. (See Elon, C.A. 110/80 *Gabbai v. Willis*, 36 (1) P.D. 449; C.A. *Aloni v. Minister of Justice*, 41 (2) P.D. 1; H.C. 644/79 *Guttman v. Tel-Aviv Jaffa Regional Rabbinical Court*, 34 (1) P.D. p. 443–50; H.C. 822/88 *Rozensweig v. Attorney General*, 42 (4) P.D. p. 761–59.)

[Menachem Elon (2nd ed.)]

BIBLIOGRAPHY: Bernstein, in: *Festschrift… Schwarz* (1917), 557–70; Blau, *ibid.*, 193–209; Gulak, Yesodei, 3 (1922), 24; Zevin, in: *Sinai*, 10 (1942), 21–35; A. Ch. Freimann, *Seder Kiddushin ve-Nissu'in* (1945), 385–97; Uziel, in: *Talpioth*, 4 (1950), 692–711; ET, 3 (1951), 161; 6 (1954), 706ff.; 9 (1959), 101–2; I.Z. Kahana, *Sefer ha-Agunot* (1954); Weinberg, in: *No'am*, 1 (1958), 1–51; Roth, in: *Sefer Zikkaron Goldziher*, 2 (1958), 59–82; Benedict, in: *No'am*, 3 (1960), 241–58; Goren, in: *Mazkeret… Herzog* (1962), 162–94; Unterman, *ibid.*, 68–73; E. Berkovits, *Tenai be-Nissu'in u-ve-Get* (1967); B. Scheresehewsky, *Dinei Mishpaḥah* (1967²), 64–65, 89, 93; PD, 22, pt. 1 (1968), 29–52 (Civil Appeals nos. 164–7 and 220–67); M. Elon, *Ḥakikah Datit…* (1968), 182–4; G. Horowitz, *Spirit of Jewish Law…* (1953), 95–96, 292–4; L.M. Epstein, *Marriage Laws in the Bible and the Talmud* (1942), index; *Mishpetei Ouziel, She'elot u-Teshuvot be-Dinei Even ha-Ezer* (1964), 33–49; *Oẓar ha-Posekim*, 3–8 (1954–63); S. Greenberg, in: *Conservative Judaism*, 24:3 (Spring, 1970), 73–141. **ADD. BIBLIOGRAPHY:** M. Elon, *Jewish Law: History, Sources, Principles* (1994) 402–3, 522–30, 803, 830–31, 834–35, 846–79, 1754–56; idem, "The Uniqueness of *Halakhah* and Society in North African Jewry, from the Expulsion of Spain to the Present," in: *Halakhah u-Petiḥut: Hakhmei Maroko ke-Posekim le-Dorenu* (1985), 15–38, Heb.; idem, *Ma'amad ha-Ishah: Mishpat ve-Shipput, Masoret, u-Temurah; Arakheha shel Medinah Yehudit ve-Demokratit* (2005), 297–372, 384–451; J.D. Bleich, "A Proposal for Solution to the Problem of the Husband who Refuses to Grant Get," in: *Torah she-be-al Peh*, 31 (1990), 124–39, Heb.; Z. Falk, "The Power of Permissiveness" (Heb.), in: Z. Falk, *Halakhah u-Ma'aseh be-Medinat Yisrael* (1962), 48–49; idem, *Dinei Nissu'in* (1983); idem, *Takkanot be-Nissu'in ve-Gerushin* (1993); A.H. Freimann, *Seder Kiddushin ve-Nissu'in Aḥarei Ḥatimat ha-Talmud; Mehkar Histori–Dogmati be-Dinei Yisrael* (1945); T. Gretner, "The Law of *Mezonot* for the Divorcée and the non- Divorcée – for the Benefit of *Agunot*," in: *Moriah*, 16:183–84 (1988), 66–81, Heb.; A. Hacohen, *The Tears of the Oppressed* (2004), foreword by M. Elon; Y.I. Herzog, *Kitvei ha-Rav Herzog*; A. Rosen-Zvi, *Dinei ha-Mishpaḥah be-Yisrael – Bein Kodesh le-Ḥol* (1990–91), 255–60; D. Novak, *Halakhah in a Theological Dimension* (1985); E. Shochetman, "Annulment of Marriage – A Possible Way of Solving the Problem of Refusal to Provide a *Get*" (Heb.), in: *Shenaton ha-Mishpat ha-Ivri*, 20 (1998), 349–97; M. Shawa, *Ha-Din ha-Ishi be-Yisrael*, (1992³); P. Shifman, *Safek Kiddushin be-Mishpat ha-Yisraeli* (1975); idem, *Mi Mefaḥed mi-Nissu'in Ezraḥi'im* (1995); B. Teomim-Rabinovitz, "Coercion in Divorce," in: *No'am*, 1 (1950), 287–312, Heb.

AGURSKY, MIKHAIL (1933–1991), Russian historian and activist. Agursky was born in Moscow, the son of Shmuel Agursky, a noted Soviet party activist and historian of the revolutionary movement who was arrested in 1938 and exiled to Kazakhstan for five years. Mikhail received his Ph.D. in the field of cybernetics in 1969. He took part in the civil rights movements in the U.S.S.R. and in Samizdat (self-publishing), contributing to the anthology *Iz pod glyb* ("From the Underground"). In 1975 he emigrated to Israel and worked at the Hebrew University of Jerusalem. In 1979 he received a doctorate from the University of Paris for his thesis "The National-Bolshevist Ideology," which was published in Paris in Russian in 1980. He also wrote "The Soviet Golem" (Russ., 1983), *Third Rome: National Bolshevism in the U.S.S.R.* (1987), "Trade Relations between the Soviet Union and the Countries of the Middle East" (Heb., 1990), and with Margaret Shklovski the anthology "Literary Heritage; Gorky and the Jewish Question" (Russ., 1986).

[Shmuel Spector (2nd ed.)]

AGURSKY, SAMUEL (1884–c. 1948), Communist author. Agursky, who was born in Grodno, joined the Bund and fled Russia in 1905 because of his involvement in revolutionary activities. He eventually went to the United States and contributed to the Jewish anarchist press. He returned to Russia in 1917 and helped found the Jewish section of the Communist Party *Yevsektsiya. In 1919, when deputizing for S. *Dimanstein, the commissar for Jewish affairs, Agursky issued an order closing the Jewish communal institutions. He wrote on the history of the Jewish labor movement and edited collections of historical and literary works. He disappeared at the time of the 1948 anti-Jewish purges. Agursky's writings include *Der Yidisher Arbeter in der Komunistisher Bavegung, 1917–1925* ("The Jewish Worker in the Communist Movement, 1917–25," 1926); *Di Yidishe Komisaryaten un di Yidishe Komu-*

nistishe Sektsies, 1918–1921 ("The Jewish Commissariats and the Jewish Communist Sections, 1918–21," 1928).

[Yehuda Slutsky]

AGUR SON OF JAKEH (Heb. אָגוּר בִּן־יָקֶה), an otherwise unknown figure mentioned in the enigmatic title to Proverbs 30:1–33. Possibly the title refers only to the first 14 verses since the Septuagint separates these two sections, placing the first between Proverbs 24:22 and 23 and the second following Proverbs 24:33. It was already pointed out by Rabbenu *Tam (Jacob b. Meir) that the *aluqah* (לַעֲלוּקָה; "*leech*") in Proverbs 30:15 may refer to a different sage with the name Alukah (in the category of names such as Nahash ("serpent"), Parosh ("flea"), etc.); hence the second section is to be attributed to another sage, Alukah. This assumption is borne out by the marked difference in content between the two sections, the first being in the nature of an ethical admonitory disquisition (in the spirit of Job 42:2), while the second consists mainly of numerical aphorisms. It has been suggested that ha-Massa (המשא) in Proverbs 30:1 should be amended to ha-Massa'i (המשאי; "the Massaite"), since Proverbs 31:1ff. is attributed to the mother of a king of Massa (cf. Gen. 25:14; I Chron. 1:30), one of the *Kenite peoples whose wisdom the Israelites admired.

BIBLIOGRAPHY: Albright, in: *Studi Orieetalistici in onore di Giorgio Levi della Vida*, 1 (1956), 1–14 (Eng.); Torrey, in: JBL, 73 (1954), 93–96; G. Sauer, *Die Sprueche Agurs* (1963); Grintz, in: *Tarbiz*, 28 (1959), 135–7.

[Michael V. Fox]

AGUS, IRVING ABRAHAM (1910–1984), U.S. educator and scholar; brother of Jacob *Agus. Agus was born in Swislocz, Poland, and studied at the Hebrew University in Jerusalem (1926–27), and at Dropsie College (1937). He served as educational director in Memphis, Tenn. (1939–45), dean of the Harry Fischel Research School in Talmud (Jerusalem, 1947–49), and principal of the Akiba Academy in Philadelphia (1949–51). From 1951 he was professor of Jewish history at Yeshiva University. Using responsa literature as a primary historical source, Agus wrote extensively on Jewish life in the Middle Ages. Among his works are *Rabbi Meir of Rothenburg* (2 vols., 1947), describing Jewish life in 13th-century Germany, and *Teshuvot Ba'alei ha-Tosafot*, an edition of previously unpublished responsa by the Tosafists (1954). His later writings concentrated on Jewish communal life in pre-Crusade Europe, showing that the Franco-German Jews, though a small group, were able to preserve talmudic traditions by their great devotion to study and observance of Judaism. In *Urban Civilization in Pre-Crusade Europe* (2 vols., 1965) Agus credits these Ashkenazi Jewish communities, which excelled in commercial ventures, with providing the prototype of town life and organization in Catholic Europe.

BIBLIOGRAPHY: A.A. Neuman and S. Zeitlin (eds.), *Seventy-Fifth Anniversary Volume of the Jewish Quarterly Review* (1967), 69–79.

[Simcha Berkowitz]

AGUS, JACOB B. (1911–1986), U.S. rabbi and philosopher. Agus (Agushewitz) was born into a distinguished rabbinical family in the *shtetl* of Sislevitch (Swislocz), situated in the Grodno Dubornik region of Poland. After receiving tutoring at home and in the local *ḥeder*, he joined his older brothers as a student at the Mizrachi-linked Takhemoni yeshivah in Bialystok.

In 1925 the Agushewitzes migrated to Palestine. Unfortunately, the economic conditions and the religious life of the *yishuv* were not favorable and in 1927 the Agushewitz family moved again, this time to America, where Jacob's father, R. Judah Leib, had relocated a year earlier to fill the position of rabbi in an East Side New York synagogue.

The family settled in Boro Park (Brooklyn) and Jacob attended the high school connected with Yeshiva University. After completing high school, he continued both his rabbinical and secular studies at the newly established Yeshiva University. He received his rabbinical ordination (**semikhah*) in 1933. After two further years of intensive rabbinical study, he received the traditional *yoreh yoreh yaddin yaddin semikhah* in 1935.

In 1935 Agus took his first full-time rabbinical position in Norfolk, Virginia. One year later he left Norfolk for Harvard University, where he enrolled in the graduate program in philosophy. At Harvard, his two main teachers were Professor Harry A. Wolfson and Professor Ernest Hocking. Agus' doctoral dissertation was published in 1940 under the title *Modern Philosophies of Judaism*. It critically examined the thought of the influential German triumvirate of Hermann *Cohen, Franz *Rosenzweig, and Martin *Buber, as well as the work of Mordecai *Kaplan, who in 1934 had published the classic *Judaism as a Civilization*.

While in the Boston area, Agus paid his way by taking on a rabbinical position in Cambridge and he continued his rabbinical learning with R. Joseph *Soloveitchik.

At Harvard, for the first time in his life, Agus encountered serious, even intense, criticism of traditional Judaism. In response, he decided to devote much of his energy for the rest of his life to explicating, disseminating, and defending the ethical and humanistic values embodied in the Jewish tradition, and in particular, how these values were interpreted by its intellectual and philosophical elites.

After receiving his doctorate from Harvard, Agus accepted the post of rabbi at the Agudas Achim Congregation in Chicago. Though the congregation permitted mixed seating, it was still considered an Orthodox synagogue. In this freer midwestern environment, removed from the yeshivah world of his student days, the orthodoxy of Yeshiva University, and the intensity of Jewish Boston, Agus began to have doubts about the intellectual claims and dogmatic premises of Orthodox Judaism. In particular, he began to redefine the meaning of *halakhah* and its relationship to reason and independent ethical norms.

In 1943, disenchanted with his Chicago pulpit, Agus accepted a call to Dayton, Ohio. During this period he also attempted to gather support for an agenda of change and halakhic reform at the Orthodox Rabbinical Council of America (RCA) convention in 1944 and 1945. When this failed he decided to break decisively with the organized Orthodox community and its institutions. He officially broke with the RCA in 1946–47 and joined instead the Conservative movement's Rabbinical Assembly. In this new context he became a powerful presence and an agent of change, serving on the Committee on Jewish Law and Standards for nearly 40 years, until his death.

In 1950, R. Agus accepted the position of rabbi at the newly formed Conservative congregation Beth El in Baltimore. A small congregation of some 50 families when he arrived, it grew over his three decades as its rabbi into a major congregation. During this period Agus also continued his scholarly work. He was a regular contributor to a variety of Jewish periodicals, such as the *Menorah Journal, Judaism, Midstream,* and *The Reconstructionist,* and he served on several of their editorial boards. He also occasionally published in Hebrew journals. At the same time, he began to teach at Johns Hopkins University in an adjunct capacity, to lecture at B'nai B'rith institutes, and to speak at colleges and seminaries around the country. In 1959 he published his well-known study *The Evolution of Jewish Thought,* an outgrowth of his lectures.

Beginning in 1968 Agus, while continuing his rabbinical duties in Baltimore, accepted a joint appointment as professor of rabbinic civilization at the new Reconstructionist Rabbinical College in Philadelphia and at Temple University. In addition, he worked with the American Jewish Committee at both the local and the national level on various communal issues, with the Synagogue Council of America on Jewish-Christian issues, with a host of Jewish communal agencies, and he was active in Jewish-Christian dialogue in the hope of reducing antisemitism and helping to restructure the Christian understanding of Jews and Judaism.

Among Agus' writings are *Modern Philosophies of Judaism* (1941); *Banner of Jerusalem* (1946), a study of the life and thought of R. Abraham Isaac *Kook; *Guideposts in Modern Judaism* (1954); *The Meaning of Jewish History* (2 vols., 1963); *The Vision and the Way* (1966); *Dialogue and Tradition* (1969); and *The Jewish Quest* (1983). Agus also published a volume on Judaism as part of the Catholic Theological Encyclopedia and served as a consultant to Arnold Toynbee on Jewish matters. Some of his letters to Toynbee are printed in Toynbee's "*Reconsiderations,*" the 12th volume of his *Study of History.*

BIBLIOGRAPHY: S.T. Katz (ed.), *American Rabbi: The Life and Thought of Jacob B. Agus* (1996).

[Steven T. Katz (2nd ed.)]

AḤA (Aḥai; fourth century), Palestinian *amora.* Born in Lydda, Aḥa studied *halakhah* under R. *Yose b. Hanina and *aggadah* under R. *Tanḥum b. Ḥiyya, and transmitted the teachings of most of the contemporary Palestinian authorities. He is extensively quoted in the Jerusalem Talmud, but seldom in the Babylonian. His younger colleagues called him "the Light of Israel" (TJ, Shab. 6:9, 8c). His statement that "the Temple will be rebuilt before the reestablishment of the Davidic dynasty" possibly refers to his hopes for the rebuilding of the Temple by the Emperor *Julian the Apostate. Aḥa declared that "The Divine Presence (*Shekhinah*) never departed from the Western Wall of the Temple." An anti-Christian polemical note can be detected in some of his discourses, of which a typical example is: "'There is one that is alone; there is none other…' (Eccles. 4:8)… this refers to God, as it is written, 'The Lord is our God, the Lord is One,' 'there is none other' – i.e., He has no partner in His world; nor does He have a son or a brother." After the *Musaf* sermon on the Day of Atonement he would announce that whoever had children should go and give them food and drink (TJ, Yoma 6:4, 43d). He furthermore declared that anyone who inflicted excessive corporal punishment on a pupil should be excommunicated (TJ, MK 3:1, 81d). It is related that on the day of his death stars were visible at noontime (TJ, Av. Zar. 3:1, 42c).

BIBLIOGRAPHY: Bacher, Pal Amor; Hyman, Toledot, s.v.

[Mordecai Margaliot]

AHAB (Heb. אַחְאָב; "paternal uncle"), son of *Omri and king of Israel (I Kings 16:29–22:40). Ahab reigned over the Israelite kingdom in Samaria for 22 years (c. 874–852 B.C.E.).

Foreign Affairs

Ahab continued his father's policy in the cultivation of peaceful and friendly relations with the kingdom of Judah in the south and with that of Phoenicia in the north. The pact with Judah was sealed with the marriage of *Athaliah, who was either Ahab's sister or his daughter, and *Jehoram son of King Jehoshaphat of Judah (II Kings 8:18; II Chron. 18:1). The alliance between the Israelite kingdom and Tyre was also a continuation of the policy initiated by his father Omri. From the economic viewpoint the two states were complementary. The economy of Tyre and Sidon was based on trade and manufacture, whereas Israel owed her wealth to agricultural produce. Thus, Tyre supplied Israel with the products of her industries and with technical skills, chiefly in the spheres of building and skilled craftsmanship (see *Samaria). In return Israel supplied agricultural products (cf. I Kings 5:21–25; 9:10–11; Ezek. 27:17).

The triangular alliance among Judah, Israel, and Tyre had important economic implications, since these three states constituted a geographic unit extending from the Mediterranean in the northwest, to the desert and the Red Sea in the southeast. Tyre marketed her produce on the main trade routes, which passed through Israel and Judah, to the Arabian Peninsula and Egypt. Israel and Judah benefited from the levying of customs tolls on the caravans that made their way from the Arabian Peninsula northward to Philistia and Phoenicia, and vice versa. This alliance did not have the power to alleviate the political and military pressure exerted on Israel by Da-

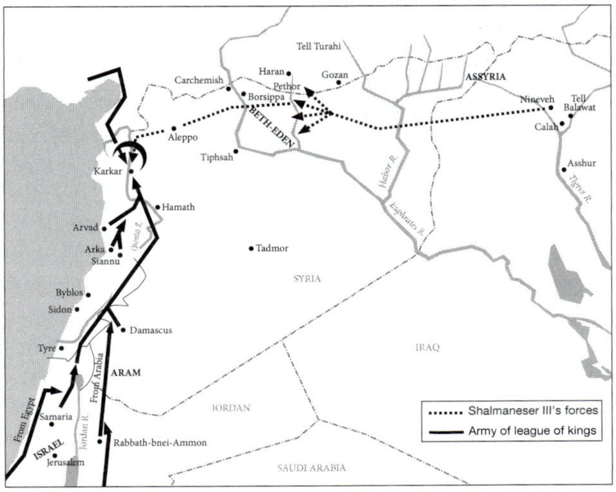

The Battle of Karkar, 853 B.C.E., to which Ahab contributed 2,000 chariots and 10,000 infantry.

mascus, which had already been her most formidable enemy in the time of *Asa. The threat from Damascus had increased greatly in the period of the house of Omri. *Ben-Hadad, king of Damascus, was neither satisfied with the conquest of areas in north Transjordan nor prepared to make do with the bazaars of the Damascus merchants in Samaria, but aimed at imposing his rule on the whole kingdom, intending to make its king one of the several vassal rulers who owed him fealty (I Kings 20:1–6).

In the biblical account three wars are mentioned between Ahab and the Arameans, although it is not precisely clear when the first two took place. In the first confrontation (20:1–22), Ben-Hadad succeeded, together with 32 vassal kings, in penetrating into the heart of the Israelite kingdom, and even laid siege to Samaria. It is conceivable that the serious economic plight of the kingdom (17:1–16), which was the result of a period of severe drought and scarcity, facilitated Ben-Hadad's speedy penetration into the very heart of Israelite territory. However, he did not succeed in conquering Samaria. Ben-Hadad's insulting demand from the Israelite king (20:3–6) and his arrogant attitude to the people and their king (20:10) caused the unification of the people under Ahab's rule and a surge of national enthusiasm which was shared by the prophets (20:13–14, 28). The defeat inflicted on Ben-Hadad in this confrontation by Ahab warded off the immediate danger but did not remove the long-term threat to Samaria's security. Thus, one year later (20:22, 26), Ben-Hadad once again prepared his troops for battle, assembling them on this occasion at *Aphek. Ahab's second victory drastically altered the power equilibrium between the two states. Ben-Hadad not only restored the Israelite cities which had previously fallen into his possession but even granted Israelite merchants monopolistic trading rights in Damascus (20:34).

According to the biblical evidence, the third and final war was preceded by a three-year period during which there was no friction between Aram and Israel (22:1). Certain scholars connect this period of calm in the relations between the two states with what is related in the inscription of Shalmaneser III, king of Assyria, concerning his battle at Karkar in Syria in the sixth year of his reign (853 B.C.E.) against an alliance of 12 kings of Syria and Israel. Hadadezer, king of Aram, Irḫuleni, king of Hamath, and Ahab, king of Israel (Akk. *A-ḫa-ab-bu māt Sir-'i-la-a-ia*) stood at the head of the alliance. The greater Assyrian threat forced the states of Syria and Israel to lay aside their internal feuds and unite in a political and military alliance capable of combating the danger of Assyrian aggression. Ahab's status among the allies and his part in the war was prominent. He was given third place in the list of allies, immediately after Hadadezer and Irḫuleni, and he himself is said to have provided 2,000 chariots, more than half the total number. In addition, Ahab contributed 10,000 infantry to the battle array. Shalmaneser III claimed that he defeated these allies, but the evidence indicates that if the Assyrian king was not defeated, then, at the very least, the battle ended in a stalemate. With the removal of the Assyrian threat from Israel there was a considerable increase in the internal conflicts among the local powers. The Aramean-Israelite conflict caused the revolt of Mesha, king of Moab (see *Mesha Stele), a vassal who paid an annual tribute to the king of Israel. However, it is not certain whether Mesha had already freed himself of Israelite rule in Ahab's lifetime, or whether he succeeded in doing so only after his death (Mesha Stele, 7–8; II Kings 1:1; 3:4–5).

Damascus and Samaria did not reach an agreement concerning the disputed area in north Transjordan. Ahab, with the support of King *Jehoshaphat of Judah, set out for Ramoth-Gilead with the intention of restoring it to Israelite rule. Ahab, for some unknown reason, on this occasion chose to disguise himself as a soldier in the ranks. It is hard to believe that this action was prompted merely by fear, since Ahab's behavior, from the moment he was lethally wounded by an arrow to his death later in the evening of the same day, demonstrated his courage and his hope that the battle would not end in defeat for Israel (I Kings 22). The description of Ahab's death in battle in I Kings 22:34–38 is inconsistent with the notice in v. 40 (*ibid.*) that he "slept with his ancestors," which is otherwise used only of peaceful death, and points to originally separate accounts.

Internal Affairs

Ahab's foreign policy brought about vast changes in the economy of the Israelite kingdom, both in helping to strengthen the administration and in increasing the state's military potential. Ahab completed the building of the city Samaria, including the acropolis and the royal palace within it, and surrounded the city with a strong, high wall. In the same way, Ahab saw to the fortification of additional cities, such as Jericho (I Kings 16:34). Archaeological evidence shows that other cities, such as Hazor, Shechem, and Megiddo, expanded in the reign of Ahab and their outer, defensive walls were reinforced. It would seem that the "stables" excavated at Megiddo served Ahab's chariot troops. In the various regions ("provinces") he appointed army officers (20:14–15) who were responsible for the security of the province and for the farming of taxes. The widespread fortification of cities, beautiful palaces with ivory ornamentation (22:39), the "Samarian" pottery, easily distinguishable for its high quality craftsmanship and artistic level, and the imported luxury goods, all indicate a period of economic prosperity. Ahab's chariots, mentioned in the inscription of Shalmaneser III, and also the stables which were excavated at Megiddo, suggest that the kingdom of Israel benefited not only from the Arabian trade conducted along the main arteries of the trade routes which crossed the territories of Judah and Israel but also from the chariot and horse trading between Egypt and Anatolia (cf. 10:28–29). However, the judgment of the author of the Books of Kings on Ahab is very harsh, because of the affair of *Naboth the Jezreelite (I Kings 21) and because of the establishment of the cult of the Tyrian Baal in Samaria. Ahab coveted the vineyard of Naboth the Jezreelite and offered to buy it or to exchange it for another (21:1–2), but Naboth was unwilling to give up his family inheritance (cf. Lev. 25:14–28). According to the biblical account Ahab accepted Naboth's refusal, but his wife *Jezebel arranged to have Naboth accused falsely of insulting God and Naboth was tried and executed and his property was confiscated by the king's treasury. The Naboth episode was symptomatic of the internal frictions under the rule of the house of Omri. It illustrates the ruthless conduct of the ruling class and the frequently cruel eviction of the small farmer from his land.

The wars with Aram and the years of drought which beset the country obviously caused great hardship to the small farmers, who were reduced to debt and were later compelled to give up their land or even to sell their children into slavery for want of funds to clear their obligations (cf. II Kings 4:1). On the other hand, economic prosperity brought great wealth to the nobility and to the rich merchants who engaged in barter with the traders from Tyre. The introduction of a chariot force created a new military aristocracy, structurally opposed to the framework of a patriarchal tribal society. By entrusting authority to the army commanders in the "provinces," Ahab dealt a hard blow to the clan leaders ("the elders of Israel"). Sooner or later an effective opposition was bound to rise against the ruling class, an opposition which would be composed naturally of all those elements which had suffered from and had been embittered by Ahab's rule. This opposition movement was championed by the prophets, led by the prophet *Elijah from Gilead.

Just as the deception in the Naboth incident was contrived by Jezebel, who represents the Phoenician element in the house of Omri, so the cult of Baal from Tyre penetrated into Samaria as a result of Jezebel's efforts to implant Phoenician culture in Israel. From reading the biblical account one has the impression that the worship of Baal and Asherah constituted a grave danger to the Israelite cult (I Kings 16:31–33). A sanctuary was built to Baal in the center of Samaria. Some 450 priests of Baal and 400 prophets of Asherah enjoyed royal protection and ate at Jezebel's table (I Kings 18:19; II Kings 10:21). Mt. Carmel, lying on the border between Israel and Phoenicia, was the site of the impressive altar of Baal, whereas the altar of the Lord was destroyed (I Kings 18:30). The cult of Baal involved the persecution of the faithful followers of God and his prophets (18:4, 13), among whom was Elijah, who symbolized the uncompromising fighter against tyrannical rule and its crimes on the one hand, and the cult of Baal on the other (18:17–41; 19:10–14; 21:17–24). Ahab himself was not a zealous follower of Baal (his children bore Yahwistic names) and did not deny all the ancient Israelite traditions. On the one hand, he believed in what the Israelite prophets said, consulted with them before military campaigns, and even showed submission and repented after the prophet's rebuke concerning the murder of Naboth (18:46; 20:13–14, 28; 21:27–29; 22:16–18). But, on the other hand, Ahab granted freedom of action and unlimited authority to Jezebel in all administrative spheres. The biblical historiographer, who culled most of his information concerning Ahab's reign from the biographical literature on the prophets and the miracles they performed (cf. II Kings 8:4), condemned Ahab for not showing any resistance to Jezebel's incitement (I Kings 21:25), and because, in his opinion, Ahab bore the responsibility for his wife's deeds. It also must be observed that then, as now, political opposition may be couched in religious terms, and vice versa.

[Bustanay Oded]

In the *Aggadah*

Ahab was one of the three or four kings who have no portion in the world to come (Sanh. 10:2). Over the gates of Samaria, he placed the inscription, "Ahab denies the God of Israel." Influenced by Jezebel, he became such an enthusiastic idolater that he left no hilltop in Israel without an idol before which he bowed, and he substituted the names of idols for the Divine Name in the Torah. Nevertheless, Ahab possessed some redeeming features. He was generous in support of scholars and revered the Torah (Sanh. 102b). As a reward for the honor he gave to the Torah, written in the 22 letters of the alphabet, Ahab was permitted to reign for 22 years (*ibid.*). According to R. Levi (TJ Ta'an. 4:2, 68a; Gen. R. 98:8), a genealogical table of Jerusalem mentioned that Ben Kovesin (or Bet Koveshin) was one of the descendants of Ahab. Although it is difficult to determine the trustworthiness of this tradition, it does indicate that the attitude of the rabbis toward Ahab was not completely unfavorable.

Ahab was so wealthy that each of his 70 (or 140) children had both summer and winter palaces (Esth. R. 1:12). He is said to have ruled over the whole world and his dominion extended over 252 (or 232; SER 9) kingdoms (Esth. R. 1:5). His merits might have outweighed his sins, had it not been for the killing of Naboth. On his death, 36,000 mourning warriors marched before his bier (BK 17a).

[Harold Louis Ginsberg]

BIBLIOGRAPHY: M.F. Unger, *Israel and the Aramaeans of Damascus* (1957), 62–69; A. Parrot, *Samaria, Capital of Israel* (1956); Morgenstern, in: HUCA, 15 (1940), 134–6; Anderson, in: JBL, 85 (1966), 46–57; Miller, *ibid.*, 441–54; idem, in: VT, 17 (1967), 307–24; Whitley, *ibid.*, 2 (1952), 137–52; Napier, *ibid.*, 9 (1959), 366–78. **ADD. BIBLIOGRAPHY:** M.A. Cohen, in: ErIsr, 12 (1975), 87–94; M. Cogan, I *Kings* (2000), 496.

AHAB (Heb. אַחְאָב), son of Kolaiah, a false prophet in Babylon. He was among the persons exiled from Judah to Babylonia by Nebuchadnezzar together with King Joiachin. He and Zedekiah son of Maaseiah purported to be prophets and stirred up unrest among the exiles (Jer. 29:21ff.). Jeremiah asserts that they were also guilty of adultery, a phenomenon not unknown among fanatics in his (23:14) and other ages. Jeremiah predicted that their death by burning at Nebuchadnezzar's command would become a standard by which people would curse (29:22).

[Harold Louis Ginsberg]

AḤA BAR ḤANINA (c. 300 C.E.), Palestinian teacher. He came from the "south," i.e., Lydda, and when he moved to Galilee, he took with him much of the halakhic tradition which he had acquired there from R. *Joshua b. Levi (Suk. 54a). In Tiberias he studied under R. Assi from whom he received the tradition of R. Johanan (Sanh. 42a) and also received instruction from Abbahu. The Aḥa mentioned in the Talmud without patronymic is often Aḥa b. Ḥanina. R. Naḥman, one of the great Babylonian teachers, relies on Aḥa b. Ḥanina, and often takes his opinion into account (Er. 64a). Despite his Palestinian origin, his teachings are found mostly in the Babylonian Talmud. Some scholars maintain that he visited Babylonia and studied under R. Huna. An aggadist, he particularly inveighed against slander (Ar. 15b). Aḥa attached great importance to the study of the Torah even under difficult economic circumstances such as he himself experienced (Sot. 49a). He emphasized the importance of congregational prayer and of performing good deeds, especially visiting the sick (Ber. 8a), and he said "he who visits the sick removes one-sixtieth of their suffering" (Ber. 8a; Ned. 39b).

BIBLIOGRAPHY: Hyman, Toledot, s.v.; Bacher, Pal Amor.

[Zvi Kaplan]

AḤA BAR RAV (end fourth century and beginning fifth century C.E.), Babylonian *amora*. He was a pupil of Ravina I. Many of his opinions were reported by his grandson R. Mesharіyya, who belonged to the school of the *savoraim. The quotations in the Talmud reveal the wide gamut of halakhic problems in which Aḥa was interested. He disputed with Ravina with regard to ritual slaughter (Ḥul. 33a), about liability for damages (Sanh. 76b), and concerning the right of a firstborn to a double portion of the inheritance, including loans due to the deceased (BB 124b).

BIBLIOGRAPHY: Hyman, Toledot, s.v.

AḤA BEN JACOB (c. 300 C.E.), Babylonian *amora*. He was a disciple of Huna and older contemporary of Abbaye and Rava. He taught in the city of Paphunia (Epiphania), near Pumbedita (Kid. 35a). Aḥa held discussions with R. *Naḥman, and although the latter was unable to answer his questions (cf. BK 40a), he often cites Naḥman as his authority (BB 52a). He also held discussions with Abbaye and Rava (Hor. 6b; Ḥul. 10b) and took issue with Ḥisda (cf. Beẓah 33b). His differences of opinion with Rava extended also to the *aggadah* (Shab. 87b). Nevertheless, Rava had great respect for him and praised him as "a great man" (BK 40a). On one occasion Aḥa asserted that "Satan and Peninnah had as their true intent the service of God." At this point, the talmudic story continues, Satan appeared and in gratitude kissed Aḥa's feet (BB 16a). Several other talmudic stories concerning Aḥa also involve Satan (cf. TJ, Shab. 2:3, 5b; Suk. 38a; Men. 62a). A tendency toward mysticism can be detected in several of his statements (Ḥag. 13a; 13b, etc.).

In addition to his reputation as a scholar he was famous for his piety. Miracles are attributed to him and a story is told of his exorcising a demon (Kid. 29b). Miraculous events are also related regarding his death (BB 14a). His son (Kid. 29b) and grandson (Sot. 49a), both named Jacob, were also scholars.

BIBLIOGRAPHY: Hyman, Toledot, s.v.; Bacher, Bab Amor.

[Zvi Kaplan]

AḤAD HA-AM (**Asher Hirsch Ginsberg**; 1856–1927), Hebrew essayist, thinker, and leader of *Ḥibbat Zion movement. Aḥad Ha-Am was born in Skvira, Kiev Province in Russia. He received a traditional Jewish education in the home of his father, a Ḥasid who was a wealthy village merchant. He studied Talmud and medieval philosophy with a private teacher, and was deeply influenced by Maimonides' *Guide to the Perplexed*. He read the literature of the Haskalah, and studied Russian, German, French, English, and Latin – independently. After his marriage in 1873, he continued his studies, particularly philosophy and science, at home. He tried several times to enter a university, but family obligations and his unwillingness to meet certain formal requirements disrupted his academic plans and he remained self-taught. As a result of powerful rationalist tendencies he first gave up Ḥasidism and then abandoned all religious faith.

In 1884 he settled in Odessa, an important center of Hebrew literature and Ḥibbat Zion. He remained there, with brief intervals, until 1907, coming into contact with its foremost authors and communal figures. In Odessa he was drawn into public affairs as a member of the Ḥovevei Zion Committee under Leon *Pinsker's leadership. His first important article, *Lo Zeh ha-Derekh* (1889, *The Wrong Way*, 1962), vigorously criticized the Ḥovevei Zion's policy of immediate settlement in Ereẓ Israel and advocated instead educational work as the groundwork for more dedicated and purposeful settlement. Written under the pseudonym Aḥad Ha-Am ("One of the

People"), the controversial essay made its author famous and unintentionally propelled him into intensive literary activity. His articles, most of which were published in *Ha-Meliẓ*, all dealt with subjects connected with Judaism, the settlement of Ereẓ Israel, and Ḥibbat Ẓion. At this time, the secret order of *Benei Moshe, which sought to realize the ideas expressed in his first article, was founded with Aḥad Ha-Am as its spiritual leader. The order existed for eight years, during which his literary activity was directly or indirectly connected with its work (*Nissayon she-Lo Hiẓli'aḥ;* "An Unsuccessful Attempt").

In 1891 Aḥad Ha-Am visited Ereẓ Israel and summed up his impressions in *Emet me-Ereẓ Yisrael* ("Truth from Ereẓ Israel"), a strongly critical survey of the economic, social, and spiritual aspects of the Jewish settlements. In 1893 he paid a second visit, and published similar criticisms. To foster the educational work which he considered a prior condition for settlement, he planned an encyclopedia on Jews and Judaism (*Oẓar ha-Yahadut*) which he hoped would encourage Jewish studies and revitalize Jewish thought. Although this effort failed, he acquired great influence as manager of the Aḥi'asaf publishing house and editor of the monthly *Ha-Shilo'aḥ* – posts which he assumed in 1896. *Ha-Shilo'aḥ*, the most important organ of Zionism and Hebrew literature in Eastern Europe, served a broad Jewish readership, contributed to the development of modern Hebrew literature, and provided Aḥad Ha-Am with a platform for a series of historic controversies. Immediately after the magazine was founded, a debate broke out between himself and "the young men" (M.J. *Berdyczewski, O. *Thon, and M. *Ehrenpreis), who sought to encourage the writing of Hebrew literature in all phases of life, and bring about a transformation of values in Jewish culture. Aḥad Ha-Am, however, feared that writing that was not specifically Jewish was premature and might lead to the severance of Jewish cultural continuity. He instead advocated concentration on Jewish problems and Jewish scholarship (*Li-She'elat ha-Sifrut ha-Ivrit;* "On the Question of Hebrew Literature").

This controversy – characteristic then of the clashing tendencies in Hebrew literature – was followed by the great debate on the political Zionism of *Herzl and *Nordau, in the wake of the First Zionist Congress at Basel. The realistic and pessimistic Aḥad Ha-Am was wary lest an extensive and premature campaign would end in failure and disappointment. He had no faith in the efficacy of Herzlian diplomacy and was troubled by the estrangement of Herzl and Nordau from Jewish values and culture. He accused them of neglecting cultural work which he regarded as paramount, and through which he hoped to prepare the people for Zionism and protect them against cultural sterility and assimilation (*Ha-Ẓiyyonut ha-Medinit;* "Political Zionism"). In 1900, after visiting Ereẓ Israel again, he took part in the Ḥovevei Zion delegation to Baron Edmond de *Rothschild in Paris. His articles severely criticized the Baron's officials in Palestine, their dictatorial attitude, the ensuing degeneration among the settlers, and the neglect of national values in the education system of the *Alliance Israélite Universelle (*Battei ha-Sefer be-Yafo* ("The Schools in Jaffa") and *Ha-Yishuv ve-Epitropsav* ("The Yishuv and its Patrons")). The question of Hebrew national education and assimilation in the West also occupied much of his attention at the time.

In 1903 Aḥad Ha-Am retired from the time-consuming editorship of *Ha-Shilo'aḥ* and took up a post with the Wissotzky tea firm, intending to devote himself to his neglected literary pursuits. However, he continued his public activities. Following the Kishinev pogroms, he encouraged Jewish self-defense and after the Sixth Zionist Congress, intervened vigorously in the debate on the Uganda Plan, which he regarded as a natural consequence of the detachment of political Zionism from Jewish values. At the conclusion of this debate he devoted himself to writing on subjects not directly connected with current events. He apparently hoped to expound his theories in a comprehensive and systematic form, and wrote a number of essays on these lines (*Moshe, Basar va-Ruaḥ, Shilton ha-Sekhel;* Eng. ed. 1962), but failing health and perhaps inner obstacles prevented him from achieving his aim.

In 1907, after a private visit to Ereẓ Israel, he moved to London where he continued his public activity. He played a role in obtaining the *Balfour Declaration, yet was not overwhelmed by the Zionist movement's enthusiasm following the Declaration. Aḥad Ha-Am perceived its limitations, especially in connection with the Arab question (see, on the Arabs, the Introduction to the 1905 edition of *Al Parashat Derakhim*), and evidently had a better appreciation of its true significance than his colleagues. During this period, his literary work was much diminished.

In 1922 he settled in Ereẓ Israel, where he remained until his death. He completed his four-volume collected essays started in 1895, *Al Parashat Derakhim*, dictated several chapters of memoirs, and edited his letters (6 vols. (1923–25), and in a more comprehensive edition, edited by L. Simon and Y. Pogravinsky (1957–60)).

A self-confessed stranger to literature, Aḥad Ha-Am entered it by chance; in time, however, he developed a carefully chiseled, lucid, and precise style, a desire for consistency, and a profound sense of responsibility. His failure to systemize his teachings in a comprehensive work may have been the result of lack of time, or of his reluctance to undertake a great task. His natural skepticism and his lack of confidence, governed to a considerable extent by the limitations of education and character, also led him to recoil in the face of the audacity of the "young authors" and the daring of political Zionism. His estimation of himself, then, as an occasional writer, was correct. His articles, including even those based on an all-embracing world outlook, are basically the responsible reactions to contemporary problems of a pragmatic thinker, deeply devoted to his aims, but considerably influenced in his arguments by varying conditions and circumstances. This was largely the consequence of the fact that Aḥad Ha-Am owed his ideas to incompatible sources: positivism and idealism, but never succeeded in working out systematically the relation between the two. Nevertheless, they are historically significant and express the self-questioning of the generation that brought about a momentous change of direction in Jewish history. Aḥad Ha-Am's reservations concerning political Zionism, the immediate settlement of Ereẓ Israel, and the Zionist movement's elation regarding the Balfour Declaration were primarily based upon his misgivings about the tendency to haste which is characteristic of every mass messianic awakening. Aḥad Ha-Am feared that Zionism might have the same end as other such movements in Jewish history that led to despair and disastrous disintegration (*Ha-Bokhim;* "They Who Weep"). He may never have believed wholeheartedly in the reality of the Zionist solution, even on the limited scale of his own definition. He clearly saw the political and economic problems and felt that they could not be overcome.

In his very first article *Lo Zeh ha-Derekh* he ascribed the difficulties of Jewish settlement in Ereẓ Israel to the weakness of the national consciousness among the Jews. A great enterprise demands a readiness on the part of the masses to sacrifice their private advantage for the sake of the community, but as a result of dispersion and the distress of exile, the Jews had not grown accustomed to such altruism. When they came to the homeland, they expected rapid economic success and immediately gave way to despair when this was not forthcoming. Hence, he believed, the pace of settlement should be slowed down, and be preceded by intensive education to prepare the people for self-sacrifice and to strengthen its national consciousness. In other words, the decisive test should be postponed indefinitely, on the implied assumption that the work of preparation for the realization of the aim would in itself constitute a partial solution. It would not, indeed, solve what Aḥad Ha-Am defined as "the question of the Jews," namely, the economic, social, and political problems of the Jewish masses. In any case, he felt that Zionism would not solve these problems. On the other hand, it could solve what he defined as "the question of Judaism"; that is, it could create a new type of Jew, proud of his Jewishness and deeply rooted in it, thus ensuring the continuation of the spiritual creativity of Judaism and the Jews' devotion to their people.

These pragmatic considerations are the starting-point for a first theoretical analysis of the question: What is the nature and the source of the national consciousness? How is it weakened and how can it be strengthened? It is characteristic, again, of Aḥad Ha-Am's pragmatic method that, despite his sensitivity to the weak national consciousness among the Jews, he did not study the cultural and historical bases for such national consciousness, but assumed its existence as a natural fact. When the Jews of Germany, France, and Britain asked "Why do we have to remain Jews?" Aḥad Ha-Am replied that the question was not legitimate. Just as a man does not ask why he has to be a particular individual, so the Jew cannot ask why he must remain a Jew; this is a given fact that cannot be changed by volition. On the assumption that nationality is naturally acquired, he builds a characteristic analogy between the "individual ego" and the "national ego," which represents the nation's collective identity and embraces all individuals throughout the generations. He did not systematically explain this concept, but his intention is suggested in his distinction between a person's attitude toward his people and toward humanity. The latter is "abstract;" a person rationally understands the unity of all men, recognizes his bonds with them, and his moral duty toward them. But this abstraction is not sufficient to arouse his love for the individual as such. The attitude to the nation is "tangible," that is, emotional. It is not derived from thought, but from a natural, biological impulse. Every individual carries from birth a sense of belonging to the group into which he was born; the family, tribe, or nationality, which is the foundation of his existence (*Ha-Adam ba-Ohel;* "Man in his Tent"). The "national ego" is, therefore, anchored in the "individual ego."

This leads to a second analogy, found in many of Aḥad Ha-Am's essays (*Ḥeshbon ha-Nefesh* (*Summa Summartum*, 1962)). The individual acts, as Darwin taught, in obedience to the "will to live." This is an elemental impulse that needs no justification; it is a given fact. The nation also acts through its own "will to live." However, this means that each individual aspires to exist with his nation and to maintain its existence; in this sense the "national will to live" is an outcome of the individual will to live." Moreover, under natural conditions the individual regards the survival of the nation as taking precedence over his own survival, because the nation is his biological base and will continue to exist even after the death of the individual. Hence, the individual naturally regards himself as an ephemeral cell in an organism that existed before him and will continue to exist after he is gone. In his desire to survive, he wishes to perpetuate his people, and through the same impulse he will be prepared, in time of need, to sacrifice his personal survival for that of the nation.

Aḥad Ha-Am asked how this natural feeling has been weakened among the Jews. How have they arrived at a situation in which they prefer their personal survival to the survival of their people? And he responded that this is a result of the unnatural conditions of exile. On the one hand, it is apparently caused by social, political, and economic distress, factors not deeply probed by Aḥad Ha-Am, no doubt because he did not regard Zionism as a solution for such problems. On the other hand, he analyzed the spiritual situation of Judaism in modern times, which he presented without enquiry or proof, as an independent cause of the weakening of the Jews' national consciousness. This weakening he ascribed to two causes: first, the paralysis of the spiritual creative powers of traditional Judaism in the Diaspora, which had become enslaved to the written word (*Ha-Torah she-ba-Lev;* "Torah of the Heart") and, second, the tremendous force of Europe's vibrant and creative culture. While the educated young Jew admired and identified with European culture, he despised the heritage of his fathers and could not identify with it. If Jews wished to halt this process, they must revive the creative power of traditional Judaism and combat the Jewish intellectual's self-deprecation in the face of European culture, in order to revive his identification with his pride in his heritage (*Ha-Musar ha-Le'ummi;* "National Morality").

Aḥad Ha-Am did not probe why such an effort should be made. He assumed the existence of the national feeling, if only in a weak and distorted form, both in the souls of the zealots of a petrified tradition and also in those of the assimilationists. In denying this national feeling, or its obligations, he felt that assimilationists denied themselves and were living in "slavery in the midst of freedom," as well as in moral and spiritual distress. Only when they returned to a complete life in the midst of their people would they return to themselves (*Avdut be-Tokh Ḥerut;* "Slavery in Freedom," 1962). But what was it that really bound the Jewish intellectual to his heritage? Aḥad Ha-Am tried to discover this bond in the primary impulse of "the national will to existence." This will not only demands loyalty to the heritage of Judaism but directly molds its specific content. Thus, Aḥad Ha-Am thought he could arouse the devotees of tradition to adapt it to the new conditions, as a duty derived from these values themselves, and persuade those Jews who had assimilationist tendencies to recognize the vital bond between themselves and their people's heritage. In general he argued (as in *Avar ve-Atid;* "Past and Future," 1962) that since the "ego" is a combination of past and future, and the suppression of one of these dimensions suppresses the "ego," therefore every Jew, if he is loyal to himself, must keep faith with the past but adapt its values to the needs of survival in the future. He tried to show in detail (in *Mukdam u-Me'uḥar ba-Ḥayyim*; "Precession and Succession in Life") that even the specific values of the Jewish faith, such as monotheism or the messianic vision, are only functions of the national will to existence, for they can be cherished in an existential attachment to the past and concurrently adapted to the thoughtways of an adherent of modern European culture, in an attempt to perpetuate the national existence.

In this way, Aḥad Ha-Am expressed his ambivalent attitude to tradition, an attitude characteristic of the generation that received a traditional education in childhood but discarded tradition upon reaching maturity. He identified himself with the tradition as an inseparable part of his cultural personality; that is, his memories. But he could no longer define his world outlook and his way of life in its terms. He therefore exchanged the belief that certain values were absolute imperatives for an emotional attachment to such values, and sought in them a reflection of his attitude to them. At the same time, Aḥad Ha-Am did not ignore the difficulties caused by this ambivalence. Asserting that certain values are part of the ancient heritage which maintained the nation in the past, he realized, was insufficient to ensure a positive attitude to them in the present. If we seek to guarantee the nation's survival in the future, we must identify ourselves with the values of its heritage for their own sake. Thus, Aḥad Ha-Am sought those values with which the Jewish intellectual could directly identify himself. While in some essays he based the national bond on the "will to live" of the "national ego" in terms drawn from positivism, in others (such as *Moshe* and *Ha-Musar ha-Le'ummi*), he based the national bond with Judaism on a specific ideal in terms drawn from idealist philosophy. The ideal of Judaism is the ideal of absolute justice, which is "the quest for truth in action," and which was revealed in prophecy. The inner content of the Jewish faith is pure morality, which Judaism bequeathed to European culture and to which it remained faithful in all its historical metamorphoses.

The contradiction between this concept and the previous one is obvious, and they have only one common denominator, the pragmatic considerations which underlie both. Aḥad Ha-Am's purpose in these essays was not to define the essence of Judaism in general, but to seek those values with which the Jewish intellectual could identify and of which he could be proud. He was therefore able, as it were, to go back on his own statements and in several essays (such as *Al Shetei ha-Se'ipim*; "Two Domains") declare that the essence of Judaism is absolute monotheism, and not undiluted morality. He adopted this attitude during his dispute with Liberal Judaism, which displayed tendencies to assimilation on the assumption of an identity between the ethical ideal of Judaism and that of modern European humanism. To the extent that this identity did not lead to the preservation of the national uniqueness but blurred its identity, he repudiated it and made a new start in his search for the characteristic values of Judaism.

The same degree of ambivalence is revealed in Aḥad Ha-Am's attitude to the *halakhah*. For pragmatic reasons he found it convenient not to deal with this question, but his general statements about the petrified tradition aroused strong reactions even from rabbis who were favorable to Ḥibbat Zion. He therefore had to consider the question of *halakhah* in the hope of maintaining a *modus vivendi* between the religious and secular wings of Judaism (*Divrei Shalom;* "Words of Peace"). This *modus vivendi* was based, of course, on the assumption that both sides were concerned for the continued existence of the Jewish people as a people with a distinct spiritual identity, and regarded the return to Zion as the solution. On this basis the debate on the content of Judaism could be postponed to the distant future. But it was clear that the secular and religious wings had certain expectations of each other. Aḥad Ha-Am's problem was to formulate these expectations without immediately destroying the basis common to both wings. Hence, he rejected Reform by an unqualified acceptance of the Orthodox view, without examining the arguments of the reformers on their merits, arguing that the words of the Torah could not be taken as divine commands and then corrected according to human understanding; the correction undermined the fundamental assumption of religion and thus made itself superfluous. On the other hand, however, Aḥad Ha-Am could not abandon his demand for changes in the *halakhah* in order to adapt it to the way of life of the modern Jew; nor could he conceal the fact that changes in the *halakhah* had indeed taken place in the past. He found the solution in a historical formula: religion is subject not to reform but to development. In other words those who introduce changes in it do not do so deliberately, as reformers. Instead, after their world view has changed and under the influence of contemporary conditions, they interpret tradition as if they had planned to uphold those things they consider true and obligatory. Aḥad Ha-Am therefore believed that the influence of life in Ereẓ Israel would lead to the development of religion, and there would no longer be any need to directly demand changes in the *halakhah*.

In their new framework Jewish social and cultural life would be enriched and broadened and the very existence of the Jews as members of one nation would not be endangered.

There were several foundations for Aḥad Ha-Am's version of practical Zionism: his distrust of an impetuous and premature attempt to carry out a great enterprise; his disbelief in the reality of the Zionist program as a solution to the Jewish problem; and the aspiration to solve the problem of Judaism by reviving its unfettered spiritual creativity and strengthening the Jews' identification with their reinvigorated heritage (*Dr. Pinsker u-Maḥbarto*; "Pinsker and his Brochure" in: *Federation of American Zionists*, 1911, and *Teḥiyyat ha-Ru'aḥ*; "The Spiritual Revival," 1962). He did not present the vision of the ingathering of the exiles in Ereẓ Israel even as an ultimate long-term goal. Most of the Jewish people would continue to exist in exile, on the assumption that its social and economic situation would ultimately improve and it would achieve equality of civic rights. In any case, the solution to the "question of the Jews" should be sought, in his view, in the lands of the Diaspora. Those who were troubled by "the question of Judaism" would settle in Ereẓ Israel, where they would maintain a Jewish State which would serve as a "spiritual center" for the Diaspora. Its independent society, which would be entirely Jewish, would constitute a focus of emotional identification with Judaism, and the spiritual values that would be created in Ereẓ Israel would nourish all parts of the people and ensure its continued existence and unity. After the Balfour Declaration, Aḥad Ha-Am presented another argument for his limited program; consideration for the national rights of the Palestine Arabs.

Aḥad Ha-Am's works not only influenced his disciples and admirers, but also prompted debates and criticism which fertilized modern Jewish thought to the extent that every stream in Zionism has been influenced by the challenge of his writings. After the establishment of the State of Israel, his doctrines, both political and theoretical, were submitted to renewed criticism, but his essays are still studied and are an influential factor in Jewish thought both in the Diaspora and Israel. One of the most influential authors and thinkers of his generation, his articles and essays constitute one of the major achievements of modern Hebrew literature.

BIBLIOGRAPHY: L. Simon (tr. and ed.), *Aḥad Ha-Am, Essays, Letters, Memoirs* (1946); idem, *Aḥad Ha-Am Asher Ginzberg; a Biography* (1960), idem, *Aḥad Ha-Am, the Lover of Zion* (1961); idem (tr. and ed.), *Selected Essays by Aḥad Ha-Am* (1962), N. Bentwich, *Aḥad Ha-Am and his Philosophy* (1927); A. (Leon) Simon and J.A. Heller, *Aḥad Ha-Am, ha-Ish. Po'olo ve-Torato* (1955); Kressel, Leksikon, 1 (1956), 60–71; J. Fraenkel, *Dubnow, Herzl, and Aḥad Ha-Am* (1963).

[Eliezer Schweid]

AḤAI (**Aḥa**; late fifth and early sixth century), Babylonian scholar of the period of transition between the *amoraim* and the *savoraim*, at the time of the final redaction of the Talmud. Since most of his statements aim at resolving problems or clarifying matters in their more or less final form, they are generally prefaced by such distinctive formulae as פריך ("he raised an objection") and פשית ("he explained"). He is mentioned together with other *savoraim* (Ḥul. 59b; Ta'an. 18b). Sages of Ereẓ Israel wrote to their colleagues in Babylonia, "Give heed to the opinion of R. Aḥai, for he enlightens the eyes of the Diaspora" (Ḥul., loc. cit.). *The Epistle of *Sherira Gaon* (ed. Lewin, 38) refers to three *savoraim* named Aḥai or Aḥa: Aḥa of Bei Ḥattim (a place near Nehardea), Aḥai b. Huna who died in 505 C.E., and Aḥa the son of Rabbah b. Abbuha who died on the Day of Atonement in 510 C.E. Aḥai without a cognomen is probably Aḥai b. Huna.

BIBLIOGRAPHY: Halevy, Dorot (1923), 56–60; Z.W. Rabinowitz, *Sha'arei Torat Bavel* (1961), 344, 528; Hyman, Toledot. s.v.

[Alter Hilewitz]

AḤAI BEN JOSIAH (end of second century), Babylonian halakhist at the close of the tannaitic period. His father Josiah was a pupil of R. Ishmael. Aḥai's statements are quoted several times in the halakhic Midrashim of the school of Ishmael, the *Mekhilta* on Exodus and the *Sifre* on Numbers. Toward the end of Judah ha-Nasi's life Aḥai placed the inhabitants of a certain town in Babylonia under the ban because they had desecrated the Sabbath (Kid. 72a). Among Aḥai's adages are "He who gazes at a woman is bound to come to sin, and he who looks even at a woman's heel will have unworthy children" (Ned. 20a); "He who buys grain in the market is like an infant whose mother has died and who is taken from one wet nurse to another, but is never satisfied… But he who eats of his own produce is like an infant raised at his mother's breast" (ARN[1], 31). He applied the verse "Thou shalt not deliver unto his master a bondman" (Deut. 23:16) to a slave who escaped from another land to Ereẓ Israel (Git. 45a). It is assumed that he established the yeshivah in Ḥuzal in Babylonia, known after his death as "the school of Aḥai," which was famous in the early third century and became the nucleus of Rav's yeshivah (TJ, Av. Zar. 4:1, 43d; Ma'as. 4:6, 51c)

BIBLIOGRAPHY: Hyman, Toledot, 136; Bacher, Tann; Epstein, Tanna'im, 571–2; Halevy, Dorot, 2 (1923), 182–4.

[Eliezer Margaliot]

AḤA (**Aḥai**) **OF SHABḤA** (680–752), scholar of the Pumbedita yeshivah in the geonic period and author of *She'iltot* ("Questions"). He came from Shabḥa, which is adjacent to Basra. When a vacancy occurred in the geonate of Pumbedita a few years before the death of Aḥa, the exilarch Solomon b. Ḥasdai appointed Natronai Kahana b. Emunah of Baghdad, a pupil of Aḥa, as *gaon* (748). Incensed at this slight, Aḥa left Babylonia (c. 750) and settled in Palestine. His departure deeply affected his contemporaries and many followed him.

By the next generation a considerable number of Babylonian Jews were settled in Palestine. In many places they even built separate synagogues following the Babylonian ritual. The *She'iltot* (always so called, and not by the more correct name *She'elata*), was the first book written after the close of the Talmud to be attributed to its author. Much of its subject matter is very old, even antedating the final redaction of the Talmud. There are statements in the *She'iltot* that do not appear in the Talmud or which are there in a different version. It also contains "reversed discussions" (i.e., where the statements of the disputants are reversed, contradictory, or different from those in the standard texts). Other portions belong to the period of the *savoraim* and of the first *geonim*. A number of decisions cited by the *geonim* as the tradition of "many generations" or which refer to "earliest authorities" are verbally reproduced in the *She'iltot*. Even the legal terminology is identical with that of the legal decisions of the *savoraim* as transmitted by the *geonim*. Nevertheless, apart from his quotation of the decisions of other authorities, it can be assumed that some of the halakhic decisions are his own.

Both in content and in form, *She'iltot* is unique in Jewish literature. It is unlike midrashic literature since its halakhic elements exceed its aggadic. However, it has some similarity to *Midrash Yelammedenu* in that both deal with *halakhah* derived from Scripture. It is also without parallel in the literature of the Codes, being arranged neither according to subject matter nor according to the sequence of the sections in which the Pentateuch is divided. Aḥa's method is to connect decisions of the Oral Law with the Written Law. The connections are often original and even surprising, though sometimes unconvincing. Often he bases a legal decision not upon its halakhic source in the Torah but on its narrative portion. The laws of theft and robbery, for example, are based on Genesis 6:13: "And the earth is filled of violence because of them." For the laws of the study of the Torah he finds a passage in the section of *Lekh Lekha*. In the section *Va-Yiggash*, which tells of the famine in Egypt, the author launches a remarkable attack on hoarders and profiteers: "And he who acts thus shall obtain no forgiveness." *She'iltot* thus concerns itself not only with the ritual commandments but also with the "duties of the heart," the ethical obligations required of man. Time and again he denounces unethical conduct and praises high moral standards; some of the *she'iltot* are elevating ethical discourses. The book is written in Aramaic; had it been translated into good Hebrew, it would doubtless have enjoyed wide popularity. Various scholars agree that the *She'iltot* consists of sermons delivered during ordinary Sabbaths as well as on the *Shabbta de-Rigla* (the first Sabbath of the academic term, a month before Sukkot) and during the Sabbaths of the *kallah months. It was almost certainly the custom during the geonic era to give the *she'ilta* form of sermon in the synagogue of the yeshivah. Some assert that both types of lecture (the *metivta* and the *perek*) delivered at the Babylonian academies remained in the archives of the academy and only during the geonic period were they copied and edited. (See *Academies in Babylonia and Palestine.) The chapters included in *She'iltot* are those on which discourses were delivered by the *amoraim* before the close of the Talmud and during the early geonic period. According to this opinion the *She'iltot* contain such discourses which were assembled and edited by Aḥa (Mirsky).

Each *she'ilta* is divided into four parts. The first serves as a general introduction to the subject, speaks of the value and significance of the particular commandments, and serves as a preparation for the question that is to be discussed. The second part is always introduced with the words: "but it is necessary that you learn," or in an abridged form: "but it is necessary," followed by the question. Then comes the third part, the homiletical part, which begins: "Praised be the Lord, who has given us the Torah and the commandments through our teacher Moses to instruct the people of Israel," after which the preacher proceeds from subject to subject. The fourth part is introduced by the formula: "With respect to the question I have set before you…," and then answers the question propounded in the second part. Some assume that the lecture was called "*she'ilta*" because its most important part is the question and its solution. However, not all the *she'iltot* have come down in their complete form: in most of them the third part is missing. One *she'ilta* is to be found in the Talmud itself (Shab. 30a) and it appears that this pattern of public sermon is ancient.

Many scholars have dealt with the question of whether Aḥa wrote the book of *She'iltot* while he was still in Babylonia or after his immigration to Palestine. Some are of the opinion that Aḥa began it in Babylonia and completed it in Palestine. There are indications which point to its having been written in both countries. According to Weiss, Graetz, and Poznanski, the *She'iltot* was compiled in Babylonia. L. Ginzberg, basing himself upon linguistic evidence, thought that the book was compiled in Palestine. On the other hand, J.N. Epstein concluded that its language is the Aramaic of the Talmud with the special nuances of the Aramaic of the *geonim*, and that therefore it was probably compiled in Babylonia. One problem still inadequately investigated is the extent to which the *She'iltot* makes use of the Jerusalem Talmud. Some scholars (Ratner and Reifmann) maintain that this is a major source. Poznański, on the other hand, points to only seven passages definitely taken from the Jerusalem Talmud. Ginzberg and Kaminka refute much of the evidence supporting the view that the *She'iltot* made use of the Jerusalem Talmud.

The *She'iltot* has come down in a fragmentary and defective form. In its extant state it contains 171 *she'iltot*, some repeated twice or even three times, some fragmentary. Tchernowitz has endeavored to explain the unusual repetitions on the assumption that the *She'iltot* was directed against the Karaites who were making considerable progress at that time. Aḥa's sermons deal particularly with those commandments which the Karaites disregarded, particularly those of rabbinic provenance. In various manuscripts, especially in the Cairo *Genizah*, there are *she'iltot* and parts of *she'iltot* not to be found in the extant editions. Excerpts of *she'iltot* are to be found also in the *Halakhot Gedolot* and in several other sources. Some scholars think that *Halakhot Gedolot* was composed before the *She'iltot*, whereas others maintain the opposite view, holding that *Halakhot Gedolot* drew upon the *She'iltot*. *Halakhot Pesukot* is also considered to be later than the *She'iltot*. It seems probable that after the publication of *She'iltot*, the *geonim* continued to preach *she'iltot* orally and that these formed the basis of the *Halakhot Pesukot* which were later compiled by the disciples of Yehudai Gaon. Special mention should be made of the book *Ve-Hizhir*, apparently written in Palestine in the tenth century, which contains a large number of *she'iltot*. A whole literature of *she'iltot* then grew up which used Aḥa's book as a prototype. The *rishonim* also made great use of the *She'iltot*.

She'iltot was first published in Venice in 1566. Other editions worthy of mention are (1) *She'iltot* with the commentaries *She'ilat Shalom* and *Rishon le-Ẓiyyon*, by Isaiah Berlin Pick (1786); (2) with the commentary *To'afot Re'em* of Isaac Pardo (1811); (3) with *Ha'amek She'elah* of Naphtali Ẓevi Judah *Berlin, considered the most complete commentary (1861–67; 2nd edition, with additions and supplements, 1947–52); (4) with the commentary *Rekaḥ Mordekhai* of Eliezer Mordecai Keneg (1940); (5) a new edition with a voluminous introduction, commentary, and *variae lectiones*, published by S.K. Mirsky (*Genesis and Exodus*, in 3 vols., 1959–63). Mirsky mentions 11 manuscripts of *She'iltot* and 4 commentaries which have never been published.

BIBLIOGRAPHY: J. Reifmann, in: *Beit Talmud*, 3 (1882), 26–29, 52–59, 71–79, 108–17, 144–8; L. Ginzberg, *Geonica*, 1 (1909), 75–79; A. Kaminka, in: *Sinai*, 6 (1940), 179–92; J.N. Epstein, in: JQR, 12 (1921/22), 299–390; idem, in: *Tarbiz*, 6 (1934/35), 460–97; 7 (1935/36), 1–30; 8 (1936/37), 5–54; 10 (1938/39), 283–308; 13 (1941/42), 25–36; V. Aptowitzer, in: HUCA, 8–9 (1931–32), 373–95; S.K. Mirsky, *She'iltot*, 1 (1959), 1–41; Baron, Social², 6 (1958²), 37–40, 336–9. **ADD. BIBLIOGRAPHY:** R. Brody, *The Textual History of the She'iltot* (1991); E. Itzchaky, in: *Moreshet Yaakov*, 5 (1991), 128–32.

[Simha Assaf / Yehoshua Horowitz]

AHARON, EZRA (1903–1995), composer, *'ud* player, and singer. Aharon was born in Baghdad, where he acquired a sound reputation as a versatile musician and a leading virtuoso and composer. The His Master's Voice and Baidaphon companies recorded many of his compositions. He was selected by the Iraqi authorities to head a group of musicians to represent his country at the First International Congress of Arab Music held in Cairo in 1932. The delegation comprised six Jewish instrumentalists plus a vocalist who was a Muslim. The participants in the Congress, including the composers Bartok and Hindemith and the musicologists Robert *Lachmann, Curt *Sachs, and H.G. Farmer, chose Aharon as the best musician present. He came to Palestine in 1934 and settled in Jerusalem, where a year later a group of notables, including Professor David *Yellin, future second president of Israel Izhak *Ben-Zvi, the renowned educator David Avisar, his great supporter Robert Lachmann, and others, established in his honor a special society for the promotion of Israeli Oriental song. When the first radio station was established in Jerusalem in 1936 by the British Mandatory government, he was selected by composer Karl *Salomon to head a special section of Jewish Oriental music. After the establishment of the state, Aharon founded and directed an Oriental ensemble at *Kol Israel*. He composed 270 Hebrew songs including synagogal *piyyutim*, melodies set to poems of famous medieval and contemporary Hebrew poets, such as *Bialik, *Tchernichowsky, *Shimoni, and Sh. *Shalom, as well as about 200 instrumental and vocal Arabic pieces, which represent a landmark in the history of Palestinian and Judeo-Arabic music. In the performance of his Hebrew compositions he appeared together with Western and Oriental musicians; Arabs and Jewish Oriental musicians played and sang his Arabic compositions. Written scores exist for a great portion of his works.

BIBLIOGRAPHY: A. Shiloah, in: Y. Ben-Arieh (ed.), *Yerushalayim bi-tekufat ha-mandat* (2003), 449–72.

[Amnon Shiloah (2nd ed.)]

AHARONI, ISRAEL (1882–1946), Ereẓ Israel naturalist and zoologist. Aharoni was born in Vidzy, near Vilna, and studied at the University of Prague. In 1904 he settled in Jerusalem, where he taught French and German in a Sephardi *talmud torah*, and later, Hebrew in the newly founded *Bezalel School of Art. Aharoni's interest in zoology led him to begin a natural history museum and he was among the first settlers in Ereẓ Israel to study the local fauna. His zoological explorations extended over all of Palestine, parts of Syria, and the Arabian Peninsula. In 1924 Aharoni became a staff member of the new Institute of Natural History of Palestine. In the following years he wrote extensively on local birds and made a survey of the mammals of Palestine. Over 30 new species of mammals, birds, and insects were named in his honor. In 1930 he made an expedition to Syria, from which he returned with a pregnant female golden hamster. From the progeny of this single animal a colony was established at the Hebrew University of Jerusalem. The golden hamster proved to be a useful subject for biological and medical research and thousands of hamsters, all offspring of Aharoni's original animal, were provided to laboratories all over the world. Aharoni was custodian of the Zoological Museum and taught at the Hebrew University. He influenced the development of biology in Palestine through his pioneering fieldwork, his university teaching, and his textbook, *Torat ha-Ḥai* ("Animal Life," 1930).

[Mordecai L. Gabriel]

AHARONI, YOḤANAN (1919–1976), Israeli archaeologist. Aharoni, born in Germany, settled in Palestine in 1933 and was a member of kibbutz Allonim from 1938 to 1947. From 1948 to 1950 he served in the Israeli Army. He was inspector in Galilee for the Department of Antiquities from 1950 to 1955. An archaeological survey conducted by him in Upper Galilee shed new light on the early Israelite settlement during the Early Iron Age. Among his activities during that period were the first explorations in the caves of the Judean Desert, a preliminary archaeological survey of *Masada, and excavations at Kedesh in Galilee and Tel Ḥarashim near Peki'in in Upper Galilee. Aharoni served for four seasons as a staff archaeologist on the *Hazor expedition. He became a research fellow at the Hebrew University and rose to the rank of associate professor (1966). At *Ramat Raḥel he uncovered the remains of an impressive Judean citadel. Aharoni also participated in two seasons of intensive exploration of the caves in the Judean Desert (1960–61). From 1963 to 1967 he conducted five seasons of excavation on the Iron Age fortress at Tel *Arad. Subsequently, Aharoni investigated the small temple at *Lachish for comparisons with that at Arad and found there an older Israelite shrine. In 1968 he became chairman of the department of ancient Near Eastern studies at Tel Aviv University and director of the Institute for Archaeology. In 1969 he commenced the excavation of Tel Be'er Sheva (Tell el-Sabi'), the site of the biblical *Beer-Sheba. Besides his numerous articles in the field of historical geography, he wrote *Hitnaḥalut Shivtei Yisrael ba-Galil ha-Elyon* (1967) on the settlement of Israelite tribes in Upper Galilee, and the comprehensive study *Ereẓ Yisrael bi-Tekufat ha-Mikra* (1962; *The Land of the Bible*, 1967). His Hebrew work, *Atlas Karta bi-Tekufat ha-Mikra* (Jerusalem, 1964), was combined with a complementary work by M. Avi-Yonah to form *The Macmillan Bible Atlas* (New York, 1968). Aharoni was joint editor of the *Encyclopaedia Judaica*'s department on the historical geography of Ereẓ Israel.

[Anson Rainey]

AḤARONIM (Heb. אַחֲרוֹנִים; lit. "the later" [authorities]), a term used to designate the later rabbinic authorities, in contrast to the **rishonim*, the earlier authorities. Although scholars differ as to the exact chronological dividing line between the two, some antedating it to as early as the period of the *tosafists (12–13th century) and others to the appearance of the *Sha'arei Dura* of Isaac ben Meir *Dueren (beginning of 14th century), the general consensus of opinion is that the period of the *rishonim* ends with the death of Israel *Isserlein (1460) and that of the *aḥaronim* begins with the appearance of the *Shulḥan Arukh of Joseph *Caro with the additions of Moses *Isserles (1525–1572). Caro in his monumental work *Beit Yosef*, of which the Shulḥan Arukh is a codified digest, had taken into consideration the works of all his predecessors, but had tended to ignore the decisions of the Ashkenazi *posekim* of Germany and Poland since the appearance of the *Arba'ah Turim* of *Jacob b. Asher, and this omission was filled by Isserles. It is therefore a fitting point at which to commence the later period.

As a result of the introduction of the method of **pilpul* by R. Jacob *Pollack (d. 1530) and the increasing study of Torah in Poland, the desire to discover new interpretations and to raise problems in the Talmud and resolve them by means of *pilpul* became particularly vigorous in that country, and the second half of the 16th century saw the appearance of some of the greatest *aḥaronim* and commentators of the Talmud and gave a powerful impetus to the study of Torah in Poland.

R. Solomon b. Jehiel *Luria (the Maharshal; 1510–1573) opposed the *Beit Yosef* and the Shulḥan Arukh on the same grounds as Isserles. Relying on the Talmud itself as the only source for halakhic ruling he established in each case the *halakhah* of the Talmud and after comparing the different views of all the *posekim* decided the *halakhah* only as it reflected the statement of the Talmud itself. In his *Yam shel Shelomo*, he took care to determine the correct version of the talmudic text; his *Ḥokhmat Shelomo* comprises annotations on the Talmud, Rashi, and the *tosafot*. To the same era belong R. Abraham b. Moses di *Boton (1545–1588), author of the *Leḥem Mishneh*, and R. Bezalel *Ashkenazi (d. 1592), author of the *Shitah Mekubbeẓet*, covering most tractates of the Talmud and giving the explanations of the *rishonim* to the topics of the Talmud. He also compiled responsa. Others are R. Solomon b. Abraham ha-Kohen (the Maharshakh; d. 1602), one of the greatest rabbis of Turkey and author of four volumes of responsa, to the first of which is appended explanations of and novellae to Maimonides' *Yad*; R. Jacob b. Abraham *Castro (the Maharikas; 1525–1610), author of *Erekh Leḥem* on the four parts of the Shulḥan Arukh, regarded as the basis for halakhic decision by the rabbis of Ereẓ Israel and Egypt; and R. Elijah b. *Ḥayyim (Maharanaḥ; 1530–1610), author of *Teshuvot ha-Ranah*.

17th Century

The opposition to the Shulḥan Arukh was continued by R. Mordecai *Jaffe (1530–1612), author of the *Levushim* (issued 1590–1599), which summarizes the *halakhah*, explaining the reasons, sources, and grounds for deciding between the divergent views of different *posekim*, but taking a stand against the prolixity of the *Beit Yosef* on the one hand and the exceptional brevity of the Shulḥan Arukh on the other. He, too, relies in the main upon the views of the Ashkenazi and Polish scholars, and in this respect also opposes Caro's tendency to decide in favor of the view of the Sephardim; R. Joseph b. Moses *Trani (Maharit; 1568–1639), who compiled commentaries to most tractates of the Talmud, to Maimonides' *Yad*, and to the *Turim*; also R. Joshua *Falk b. Alexander ha-Kohen (the Sema; d. 1614), author of the *Derishah u-Perishah* and the *Sefer Me'irat Einayim* (Sema), endeavored to explain the *Tur* and the Shulḥan Arukh at length and to supplement those laws whose sources and reasons are not given in the Shulḥan Arukh, attempting at the same time to compromise between Caro and Isserles. The method of R. Meir b. Gedaliah *Lublin (Maharam of Lublin; 1558–1616) was to penetrate deeply into the meaning of the Talmud and the *tosafot*, the final decision being based on examination of the talmudic sources and the early *posekim*, which caused him to oppose basing halakhic decisions upon the Shulḥan Arukh. His best-known book, *Me'ir Einei Ḥakhamim*, consists of novellae and interpretations of the Talmud. R. Benjamin Aaron *Slonik (d. 1620), a distinguished pupil of Isserles and the colleague of the "Sema," the "Levush," and Meir of Lublin, compiled the responsa *Masat Binyamin* (1633) and was regarded in his generation as an outstanding *posek*. Another contemporary of the Maharam, Samuel Eliezer b. Judah *Edels (the Maharsha; 1555–1631), penetrated deeply into the plain meaning of the Talmud and the *tosafot*. His opposition to the Shulḥan Arukh is not so obvious, since he does not deal with halakhic rulings. Despite this he complains about those "who give halakhic rulings from the Shulḥan Arukh without knowing the reason for each matter." He compiled *Ḥiddushei Halakhot* (2 pts.; 1612–1621) and *Ḥiddushei Aggadot* (2 pts.; 1627–1631). This latter work makes the Maharsha's commentaries different from most others. Maharsha endeavors to understand the often cryptic *aggadot* through allegorical and symbolic interpretations. The *Shenei Luḥot ha-Berit* of R. Isaiah b. Abraham ha-Levi *Horowitz (the Shelah; 1560–1632) contains laws following the order of the festivals, an enumeration of the 613 commandments (see *Commandments, the 613), and their reasons. *Halakhah* is only a small portion of the *Shenei Luḥot ha-Berit*. This encyclopedic work includes philosophy, Kabbalah, biblical and talmudic interpretations as well as ethics (*musar*) and discussions of talmudic methodology. His son, R. Shabbetai Sheftel (1590–1660), was the author of the *Sefer Vavei ha-Ammudim*, appended to his father's work. R. Nathan Nata b. Solomon *Spira (1585–1633) published novellae to the *Hilkhot ha-Rif* entitled *Ḥiddushei Anshei Shem* (1720). R. Meir b. Jacob ha-Kohen *Schiff (Maharam Schiff; 1608–1644) compiled novellae to the whole Talmud and the *Turim*, of which only those to five tractates were published under the title *Ḥiddushei Halakhot* (1741; 1747). R. Joel b. Samuel *Sirkes (the Baḥ; d. 1640) was aware, as was the Sema, that the *Beit Yosef* could not explain the *Tur* in a sufficiently satisfactory manner because its main purpose was to arrive at halakhic decisions and, in consequence, in his *Bayit Ḥadash* wrote "an extensive commentary on the *Tur* having at the same time the aim of restoring it to its former authority and glory in *halakhah* in order thereby to diminish" the value of the Shulḥan Arukh. One of the greatest scholars of Salonika, a great *posek* and one of the greatest responders, was R. *Ḥayyim Shabbetai (Maharḥash; 1557–1647). R. *Joshua Hoeschel b. Joseph of Cracow (d. 1648) endeavored in his *Meginnei Shelomo* (1715) to defend the views of Rashi against the criticism of the tosafists. A colleague of the Baḥ, R. Eliezer b. Samuel Ḥasid Ashkenazi, who was one of the rabbis of the Council of Four Lands, wrote halakhic *pilpulim* into his *Dammesek Eliezer* (1646), which were utilized by Ḥayyim *Benveniste in his *Keneset ha-Gedolah*. R. Yom Tov Lipmann *Heller (1579–1654), author of the *Tosafot Yom Tov*, also opposed the Shulḥan Arukh, his aim being to make the Mishnah the basis for authoritative *halakhah*, taking into consideration the early and later commentators and *posekim*. He compiled an extensive commentary in two parts on the Rosh: (1) *Ma'adanei Melekh* and (2) *Leḥem Ḥamudot*. R. Moses b. Isaac Judah *Lima (d. 1658) made a summary in his commentary *Ḥelkat Meḥokek* on the Shulḥan Arukh, *Even ha-Ezer*, which is based upon a comparison of talmudic sources and the views of the *rishonim* with the Shulḥan Arukh, while emphasizing the method of *pilpul*. There are extant from R. *Joshua Hoeschel b. Jacob, known popularly as the "Rebbi Reb Hoeschel" (d. 1663), halakhic novellae to tractate *Bava Kamma* and novellae on the *Sefer Mitzvot Gadol*. Two commentators on the Shulḥan Arukh, known from their works as the Taz and the Shakh, through whom the Shulḥan Arukh attained its most developed state and widespread acceptance, were active during the period of the *Chmielnicki pogroms of 1648: R. *David b. Samuel ha-Levi (the Taz; 1586–1667) intended through his commentary *Turei Zahav* to restore authoritative decision to its proper place, arriving at the definitive *halakhah* through comparing the different views in order to arrive at a final decision, yet in his eyes the Shulḥan Arukh was the decisive halakhic ruling. In 1978, C. Chavel published a definitive edition of the Taz's novellae on Rashi's commentary on the Pentateuch. R. *Shabetai b. Meir ha-Kohen (Shakh; 1621–1663) in his *Siftei Kohen* explains the Shulḥan Arukh and decides between its author and Isserles, striving at the same time to harmonize their views. In the *Siftei Kohen* on the *Ḥoshen Mishpat* he summarizes the views of all the *rishonim* and *aḥaronim*, trenchantly criticizing and negating the existing views and laying down new legal principles. R. Menahem Mendel b. Abraham *Krochmal (1600–1661), a disciple of both the Baḥ and the Taz, is the author of the noted responsa *Ẓemaḥ Ẓedek* (1675) on the four parts of the Shulḥan Arukh.

In the generation of the Shakh there was in Poland-Lithuania, particularly in Vilna, a concentration of outstanding Torah scholars. R. *Hillel b. Naphtali Ẓevi (1615–1690) compiled the novellae *Beit Hillel* (1691) on the Shulḥan Arukh, *Yoreh De'ah* and *Even ha-Ezer*. R. Moses b. Naphtali Hirsch *Rivkes of Vilna (second half of the 17th century) compiled the *Be'er ha-Golah* (1662), giving the talmudic sources of the laws of the Shulḥan Arukh, in Maimonides' *Yad*, and in the works of the *rishonim*. R. *Ephraim b. Jacob ha-Kohen (1616–1678) wrote the well-known responsa *Sha'ar Efrayim*. R. Aaron Samuel b. Israel *Koidonover (Maharshak; 1624–1676) wrote the novellae *Birkat ha-Ẓevaḥ* (1669). R. *Samuel b. Uri Shraga Phoebus (mid 17th cen.) was the author of the commentary *Beit Shemu'el* (1689) to the *Even ha-Ezer*. R. Ḥayyim b. Israel Benveniste (1603–1673) in his *Keneset ha-Gedolah* gave a digest of the particulars of all new decisions cited in the responsa of outstanding *aḥaronim* from the time of Joseph Caro to his own time. This work, the first after the Shulḥan Arukh to assemble an anthology of responsa, was accepted in Sephardi and Ashkenazi rabbinical circles as an authoritative work that could be relied upon for practical rulings. Of other responsa anthologies mention must be made of the *Panim Ḥadashot* (1651) of Isaac b. Abraham Hayyim *Jesurun (d. 1655) and the *Leket ha-Kemaḥ* of R. Moses *Ḥagiz (1672–1751). R. Aaron *Alfandari (1690?–1774) in his *Yad Aharon* supplements the *Keneset ha-Gedolah* from works not in the possession of Benveniste. He also wrote *Mirkevet ha-Mishneh*, novellae to Maimonides' *Yad*.

The following authoritative commentaries to the *Oraḥ Ḥayyim* should be noted: the *Olat ha-Tamid* (1681) of Samuel b. Joseph of Cracow, and especially the *Magen Abraham* (1692) of Abraham Abele b. Ḥayyim ha-Levi *Gombiner (1637–1683), who endeavored to arrive at a compromise between Caro's rulings and the amendments of Isserles, and in whose eyes the Shulḥan Arukh was the final authority; Gershon b. Isaac *Ashkenazi (Ulif; d. 1693), compiler of the responsa *Avodat ha-Gershuni* (1699) and *Ḥiddushei ha-Gershuni* (1710), notes and novellae to the Shulḥan Arukh, is known for his strictness in laws of marriage; Jair Ḥayyim Bacharach (1638–1701), whose reputation rests on his responsa *Havvat Ya'ir* (1699) and was opposed to *pilpul*; Aryeh Leib *Gunzberg (1640–1718), author of the responsa *Sha'agat Aryeh, Sha'agat Aryeh ha-Ḥadashot*, and novellae to tractates of the Talmud. Among the rabbis of Jerusalem in that generation were: Moses b. Jonathan *Galante (1620–1689), author of *Ẓevaḥ ha-Shelamim* (1698) and *Korban Ḥagigah* (1709); Moses b. Solomon ibn *Ḥabib (1654–1696), author of novellae to tractates of the Talmud and of *Get Pashut* (1719). *Peri Ḥadash* (1692), a commentary compiled by *Hezekiah b. David Da Silva (1659–1698), added to the Shulḥan Arukh and contains pungent criticism of the *posekim*, including Caro himself. Abraham b. Saul *Broda (1650–1717) wrote novellae on talmudic tractates entitled *Eshel Avraham* and *Toledot Avraham*. Elijah b. Benjamin Wolf *Shapira (1660–1712) was the author of *Eliyahu Rabbah*, novellae on the *Sefer ha-Levush*. Ẓevi Hirsch b. Jacob *Ashkenazi (Ḥakham Ẓevi; 1600–1718) published in 1712 his responsa, novellae, and comments. His son, Jacob *Emden (1698–1776), compiled *Mor u-Kezi'ah*, comments and novellae to the *Oraḥ Ḥayyim*. Jacob Emden also wrote an extensive commentary on the prayer book as well as various philosophical works. Samuel b. Joseph Shattin ha-Kohen (Maharshashakh; d. 1719), an outstanding German scholar, published *Kos ha-Yeshu'ot* (1711), novellae to the tractates of the order *Nezikin*. Judah *Rosanes (d. 1727), one of the greatest Turkish scholars, achieved fame with his *Mishneh la-Melekh* (1731), novellae on the *Yad*, and *Al Parashat Derakhim* (1728). Jacob b. Joseph *Reischer (d. 1733) compiled the commentaries *Minḥat Ya'akov, Shevut Ya'akov*, and *Ḥok le-Ya'akov* on the Shulḥan Arukh. Most of the halakhic works, novellae, and responsa of David *Oppenheim (1664–1736), famed for his large library, remain in manuscript. Alexander Sender b. Ephraim Zalman *Schor (d. 1737) was the author of *Simlah Ḥadashah* (1733), rulings in the laws of *sheḥitah* and *terefot* together with a pilpulistic commentary *Tevu'ot Shor* that became an authoritative source on matters pertaining to *sheḥitah*. Elazar Rokeaḥ of Brody (d. 1741) compiled *Arba Turei Even* (1789), novellae to the *Yad* and the *Tur*. A contemporary of the *Peri Ḥadash*, Hayyim b. Moses *Attar (1696–1743), author of the Or *ha-Ḥayyim* on the Pentateuch, wrote *Peri To'ar*, a commentary on the *Yoreh De'ah*, in which he defends the *Tur, Beit Yosef*, and all *rishonim* from the criticisms of the *Peri Ḥadash*.

18th Century

Among outstanding *aḥaronim* in the 18th century are Meir b. Isaac *Eisenstadt (Maharam Esh; 1670–1744), author of *Panim Me'irot* (3 pts.; 1710–1738); and Isaac Hezekiah b. Samuel *Lampronti (1679–1756), author of the halakhic encyclopaedia *Paḥad Yiẓḥak*. The *Yad Malakhi* (1767) of his contemporary *Malachi b. Jacob ha-Kohen is a methodology of the Talmud and *posekim* in three parts. Jacob Joshua b. Ẓevi Hirsch *Falk (1680–1756) achieved fame with his extensive talmudic work *Penei Yehoshuah* (4 pts.). Nethanel b. Naphtali Ẓevi *Weil (1687–1769) was the author of *Korban Netanel* (1755), a commentary of the *Rosh* of Asher b. Jehiel to the orders *Mo'ed* and *Nashim*, and of *Netiv Ḥayyim*, notes to the *Oraḥ Ḥayyim*. Aryeh Loeb b. Saul *Loewenstamm (1690–1755) of Amsterdam republished the responsa of Moses Isserles (1711), adding to it *Kunteres Aḥaron*, parallels from the responsa of the Maharshal. Jonathan *Eybeschuetz (1690–1764) wrote the pilpulistic and acute commentaries *Kereti u-Peleti* (1763) to the *Yoreh De'ah* and *Urim ve-Tummin* (1775) to the *Ḥoshen Mishpat*. Ẓedakah b.Saadiah *Ḥoẓin of Baghdad (1699–1773) published novellae to all four parts of the Shulḥan Arukh. Among the works of Judah b. Isaac *Ayash (1700–1760), an Algerian scholar who settled in Ereẓ Israel during his last years, known also to German and Polish scholars, are *Leḥem Yehudah* on Maimonides' *Yad* and the responsa *Beit Yehudah*. Eliezer b. Samuel De *Avila (1714–1761), a great Moroccan scholar, compiled *Magen Gibborim*, novellae to talmudic tractates, and *Milḥemet Mitzvah* (1805) on the sources of *halakhot* in the Talmud and *posekim*.

Exceptional prominence was achieved by Ezekiel b. Judah ha-Levi *Landau (1713–1793), the author of the *Noda bi-Yehudah*, who in his novellae established new halakhic rulings. Solomon b. Moses *Chelm (1717–1781) became known through his *Mirkevet ha-Mishneh* in which he defends Maimonides from the strictures of *Abraham b. David of Posquieres (the Rabad), at the same time explaining the views of Maimonides and the commentators on the *Yad*. David Samuel b. Jacob *Pardo (1718–1790) is known through his *Shoshannim le-David* on the Mishnah and *Hasdei David* on the Tosefta. Meir *Margoliouth's (d. 1790) responsa *Me'ir Netivim* reflect the precarious basis of Jewish life in Poland and Lithuania.

Samuel b. Nathan ha-Levi of Kalin's (1720–1806) *Maḥaẓit ha-Shekel* (1807) is a commentary on the *Magen Avraham* to the *Oraḥ Ḥayyim* and on the *Shakh* to *Yoreh De'ah Hilkhot Meliḥah*. One of the most prominent personalities among *aḥaronim* in the 18th century is *Elijah b. Solomon Zalman, the Gaon of Vilna (ha-Gera; 1720–1797). In his commentary on the Shulḥan Arukh he stresses the connection between its decisions and the primary sources in the two Talmuds; when explaining the talmudic view the Gaon indicates his sources at the same time as he examines the different versions and determines the talmudic text. Noted for its terse style, the Gaon's commentary on the Shulḥan Arukh reflects his outstanding scholarship and genius. Ḥayyim Joseph David *Azulai (the Ḥida; 1724–1806) wrote halakhic laws and responsa, as well as the *Shem ha-Gedolim*, a comprehensive compilation of Jewish authors and their works up to that time. In 1771, about a century after the publication of the Shakh and the Taz, Joseph *Teomim (1727–1792) published his commentary *Peri*

Megadim, whose main purpose was to comment on them, adding new laws he had collected and laying down halakhic principles. Another well-known commentary is the *Levushei Serad* to *Oraḥ Ḥayyim* and *Yoreh De'ah* of David Solomon Eibeschutz of Soroki (Safed, 1809). Pinḥas ha-Levi *Horowitz of Frankfurt on Main (1730–1805) became known from his *Sefer Hafla'ah* and *Sefer ha-Makneh*. In his well-known commentary *Keẓot ha-Ḥoshen* on *Ḥoshen ha-Mishpat*, Aryeh Leib b. Joseph ha-Kohen *Heller (1745–1813) used the method of *pilpul*, at the same time stressing the need for rational understanding. Particular note should be taken of *Shneur Zalman of Lyady (1747–1812), the founder of Ḥabad Ḥasidism and author of the *Tanya*, who prepared for his ḥasidic followers a new Shulḥan Arukh which was issued in five parts in 1864. Abraham b. Samuel *Alkalai (1749–1811) wrote *Zekhor le-Avraham* on the *Turim*, which was relied on by halakhic authorities in Ereẓ Israel. Ḥayyim b. Isaac *Volozhiner (1749–1821), the distinguished disciple of the Gaon of Vilna and founder of the Volozhin Yeshivah, continued the latter's method of shunning *pilpul* and stressing the literal and straightforward meaning in *halakhah*. The vast majority of his writings were destroyed by fire at the end of his life, leaving us with only a small number of responsa and his philosophical work, *Nefesh ha-Ḥayyim*. Meshullam *Igra (1752–1802), an outstanding Galician and Hungarian scholar, compiled *Igra Ramah* on the orders of *Mo'ed* and *Nashim*, and responsa. Mordecai b. Abraham *Banet (1753–1829) wrote *Be'ur Mordekhai*, novellae on the *Sefer ha-Mitzvot* of the *Mordekhai*, as well as other novellae. Jacob *Lorbeerbaum of Lissa (1760–1832), in his commentary *Netivot ha-Mishpat* on the *Ḥoshen ha-Mishpat*, summarized the sources of the *halakhah*, while his *Ḥavvat Da'at* to the *Yoreh De'ah* is of decisive importance for halakhic ruling. The following Yemenite rabbis living in the second half of the 18th century should be noted: Yaḥya b. Joseph *Saliḥ, *av bet din* in San'a and author of the responsa *Pe'ullat Ẓaddik* dealing with the practical problem of Yemenite Jews; David b. Shalom *Mizraḥi (1696–1771) and his son Yiḥya (1734–1809) in San'a wrote the responsa *Revid ha-Zahav* (1955) on *Oraḥ Ḥayyim* and *Yoreh De'ah* on the customs of Yemenite Jews.

19th Century

Of the most notable 19th century scholars, the following deserve mention: Joshua Heschel b. Isaac *Babad (1754–1838), author of the responsa *Sefer Yehoshua* (1829); Baruch b. Joshua Ezekiel Feiwel *Fraenkel-Teomim (1760–1828), known from his *Barukh Ta'am*; one of the greatest *aḥaronim* in this period was Akiva b. Moses *Eger (1761–1837), famous for his novellae, his *Gilyon ha-Shas*, and responsa; Moses b. Samuel *Sofer (Ḥatam Sofer; 1762–1839), known by his responsa, novellae on the Talmud, and Pentateuch commentary; Abraham Samuel Benjamin *Sofer, author of *Ketav Sofer*, son of the Ḥatam Sofer, and his son Simḥah Bunem, author of *Shevet Sofer*; *Israel b. Samuel Ashkenazi of Shklov (d. 1839), author of *Pe'at ha-Shulḥan* on laws connected with Ereẓ Israel that were not dealt with by Caro in his Shulḥan Arukh; Ephraim Zalman *Margolioth (1760–1828), author of *Beit Efrayim* on all four parts of the Shulḥan Arukh, *Sha'arei Teshuvah*, and *Pitḥei Teshuvah*; Abraham b. Gedaliah *Tiktin (1764–1821), author of *Petaḥ ha-Bayit* on the Talmud and Shulḥan Arukh; Jacob Meshullam *Ornstein (1775–1839), author of *Yeshu'ot Ya'akov*; Israel b. Gedaliah *Lipschutz (1782–1861), famous for his *Tiferet Yisrael* commentary on the Mishnah; Solomon b. Judah Aaron *Kluger (Maharshak; 1783–1869) wrote novellae on the Shulḥan Arukh and compiled works on *halakhah* and *aggadah*; Menahem Mendel Schneersohn of Lubavitch (1789–1866), author of the responsa *Ẓemaḥ Ẓedek*; Ḥayyim b. Leibush *Halberstam, the ḥasidic rabbi of Zanz (1793–1876), author of the responsa *Divrei Ḥayyim*, characterized by its blending of scholarship and Ḥasidism; Judah b. Israel *Aszod (1794–1866), outstanding Hungarian rabbi, became widely known through his *She'elot u-Teshuvot Maharia* and *Ḥiddushei Maharia*; Jacob b. Aaron *Ettlinger (1798–1871), known from responsa *Binyan Ẓiyyon* (1868), his *Arukh la-Ner*, novellae to tractates of the Talmud, and his *Bikkurei Ya'akov*; Isaac Meir Alter of Gur (1799–1866), known for his *Ḥiddushei ha-Rim* and *She'elot u-Teshuvot ha-Rim*; Samuel b. Joseph *Strashun (1794–1872) wrote *haggahot* (notes) to the Talmud; Joseph *Babad (1800–1875) became famous through his *Minḥat Ḥinnukh* (1869), extensively used especially among yeshivah students, its main aim being not to determine the *halakhah* but to stimulate further study by raising new problems. The *Minḥat Ḥinnukh* is an extensive commentary of the medieval work, *Sefer ha-Ḥinnukh*. Mention must be made of the abridgments of the Shulḥan Arukh by Abraham *Danzig (1748–1820) in his *Ḥayyei Adam* and *Ḥokhmat Adam* and by Solomon *Ganzfried (1804–1886) in his *Kitzur Shulḥan Arukh*; Zevi Hirsch b. Meir *Chajes (1805–1855) wrote the *Darkhei Hora'ah* and *Mevo ha-Talmud* (1845) on talmudic methodology, the responsa *Maharaz* (1849), and notes and novellae on most tractates of the Talmud; Moses b. Joseph *Schick (Maharam Schick; 1807–1879), a Hungarian *posek*, author of about 1,000 responsa; Joseph Saul *Nathanson of Lemberg (1810–1875), the *posek* of his generation, who opposed *pilpul;* David Dov *Meisels (1814–1876), known from his responsa *Ha-Radad* on *Oraḥ Ḥayyim* and *Even ha-Ezer* (1903); Naphtali Ẓevi Judah *Berlin (the Neẓiv; 1817–1893) of Volozhin, author of *Ha'amek Davar* on the Pentateuch and *Ha'amek She'elah* on the *She'iltot* of R. Aḥai; Moses Joshua Judah Leib *Diskin (Maharil Diskin; 1817–1898), the rabbi of Brest-Litovsk, who served as rabbi of Jerusalem from 1877, compiled *Torat Ohel Moshe* and responsa; Jacob Saul b. Eliezer Jeroham *Elyashar (1817–1906), Sephardi chief rabbi of Ereẓ Israel wrote thousands of responsa in answer to inquiries; Isaac Elhanan b. Israel *Spektor of Kovno (1817–1896), author of the responsa *Be'er Yizḥak*, *Naḥal Yizḥak* on the *Ḥoshen ha-Mishpat*, and the responsa *Ein Yizḥak*; Joseph Baer *Soloveichik of Volozhin (1820–1892) wrote the novellae *Beit ha-Levi* and responsa with the same title; Shalom b. Yaḥya *Ḥabshush (1825–1905), *dayyan* and head of a yeshivah in San'a, published novellae and comments on the laws of *sheḥitah* and *terefot*; Isaac Judah b. Hayyim Samuel

*Schmelkes (1828–1906) of Lemberg is known for his responsa *Beit Yiẓḥak* in six volumes; Jehiel Michael *Epstein's (1829–1908) *Arukh ha-Shulḥan* aims at bringing some of the rulings of the Shulḥan Arukh up to date; he also wrote *Arukh ha-Shulḥan le-Atid*; Shalom Mordecai b. Moses *Shvadron (1835–1911), known as Maharsham, whose genius is reflected in the seven volumes of his responsa; Abraham Bornstein of *Sochaczew (1839–1910), author of the responsa *Avnei Nezer* on the Shulḥan Arukh; Isaac Jacob *Reines (1839–1915), who in his *Ḥotam Tokhnit* and *Urim Gedolim* eschewed *pilpul* and introduced a purely logical approach to *halakhah*. Of noted commentators on the Jerusalem Talmud in the 18th–19th centuries, mention must be made of *Elijah b. Loeb of Fulda (Raf; d. 1725); David b. Naphtali Hirsch *Fraenkel (1707–1762), author of the *Korban ha-Edah*; Moses b. Simeon *Margoliot (1710–1781), author of the commentary *Penei Moshe*; Jacob David b. Ze'ev *Willowski (Ridbaz; 1845–1913), who settled in Safed in his last years and whose commentary on the Jerusalem Talmud and his responsa are regarded as classics.

Among Oriental *aḥaronim* the following are worthy of note: Hayyim *Palache (1788–1869) of Smyrna, author of 26 books, including the responsa *Lev Ḥayyim* and comments on the Shulḥan Arukh; *Joseph Ḥayyim b. Elijah Al-Ḥakam (1833–1909) of Baghdad, a great *posek* known from his Ben *Yehoyaddah* and *Ben Ish Ḥai,* which embrace *halakhah, aggadah,* and homiletics.

20th Century

Until 1933 the study of Torah was centered in the great and famous yeshivot of Eastern Europe – Poland, Lithuania, Hungary, and Czechoslovakia. During that period centers of Torah also began to be established in the United States. From 1933 on, and following World War II, as a consequence of the liquidation of these centers, the center of spiritual life passed to the United States and Israel, and some scholars immigrated to these new centers during the latter part of their lives: *Meir Simḥah ha-Kohen of Dvinsk (1843–1926), author of the *Or Same'aḥ* on Maimonides' *Yad* and *Meshekh Ḥokhmah* on the Pentateuch; Zevi Hirsch *Shapira of Munkacz (1850–1913), author of *Darkhei Teshuvah* on the Shulḥan Arukh, and his son Ḥayyim Eleazar (1872–1937), author of the responsa *Minhat Elazar*; Elijah b. Naphtali Herz *Klatzkin (1852–1932); Hayyim b. Joseph Dov *Soloveichik (Ḥayyim Brisker; 1853–1918), who wrote novellae on tractates of the Talmud and the *Yad* and devised a new system of talmudic dialectics, and his son Isaac Ze'ev (1886–1960); Joseph *Rozin ("the Rogachover"; 1858–1936), known from his responsa *Zafenat Pa'ne'aḥ* and commentary on the Pentateuch with the same title; *Israel Meir ha-Kohen (Ḥafez Ḥayyim; 1853–1933), author of the *Ḥafez Ḥayyim*, dealing with the laws of slander and gossip, and *Mishnah Berurah* on the first section of the Shulḥan Arukh. The *Mishnah Berurah* rapidly became the most widely accepted work of *halakhah* among Ashkenazi Jewry since the publication of the Shulḥan Arukh. Moses Samuel *Glasner (1856–1924), who compiled *Dor Revi'i* and *Shevivei Esh* on the Pentateuch; Joseph b. Judah *Engel (1859–1920), whose works on *halakhah, aggadah,* and Kabbalah are arranged in an encyclopedic manner, in most cases alphabetically; Judah Leib *Zirelson (1860–1941) of Kishinev, author of the responsa *Aẓei Levanon, Gevul Yehudah, Lev Yehudah*; Ḥayyim Ozer *Grodzinski (1863–1940), author of the responsa *Avi'ezer* (3 pts.); Abraham Isaac ha-Kohen *Kook (1865–1935), author of the novellae and responsa *Mishpat Kohen* and *Iggerot ha-Re'ayah*; the Galician rabbi Menahem Munish b. Joshua Heschel *Babad (1865–1938), author of the responsa *Ḥavaẓẓelet ha-Sharon*; Zalman b. Ben-Zion *Sorotzkin (1881–1966), author of the responsa *Moznayim le-Mishpat* and *Oznayim la-Torah* on the Pentateuch; Ben Zion Meir Ḥai *Ouziel (1880–1953), Sephardi chief rabbi (*rishon le-Zion*) and author of the responsa *Mishpetei Ouziel, Sha'arei Ouziel, Mikhmannei Ouziel*; Isaac ha-Levi b. Joel *Herzog (1888–1959), Ashkenazi chief rabbi of Israel, wrote *Divrei Yiẓḥak* (1921), *Torat ha-Ohel* (1948) on Maimonides' *Hilkhot Sanhedrin*, and the responsa *Heikhal Yiẓḥak* (1960; 1967) on *Even ha-Ezer,* in which he also discusses problems arising from the Holocaust and the establishment of the State of Israel; Dov Berish b. Jacob *Wiedenfeld (1881–1965) of Trzebinia, Galicia, author of the responsa *Dover Meisharim* (2 pts.; 1958); Moshe Avigdor *Amiel (1883–1946), chief rabbi of Tel Aviv, published *Darkhei Moshe, Ha-Middot le- Ḥeker ha-Halakhah*; Menahem Zemba (1883–1943), outstanding Polish talmudist of the last generation whose works reflect a blending of acumen and erudition combined with logic and profundity, was the author of the responsa *Zera Avraham* (1920), *Oẓar ha-Sifrei* (1929), *Oẓar ha-Sifra* (1960); Jehiel Jacob *Weinberg (1885–1966), author of the responsa *Seridei Esh* (4 vols.; 1961–1969) on practical problems arising in recent generations; Moses Mordecai *Epstein (1866–1934), author of *Levushei Mordekhai*, novellae and expositions on topics in tractates *Zevaḥim* and *Menaḥot*; Baruch Ber *Leibowitz (1866–1939), author of *Birkat Shemu'el* on tractates of the Talmud; Isser Zalman *Meltzer (1870–1954), author of *Even ha-Ezel* in eight parts; Ẓevi Pesaḥ *Frank (1873–1960), chief rabbi of Jerusalem, who followed the methods of Isaac Elhanan Spektor and Samuel Salant; Elḥanan Bunim *Wasserman (1875–1941), who followed a middle path between *pilpul* and erudition, stressing the decisions of the *rishonim*; Meshullam *Rath (1875–1963), a member of the Israel chief rabbinate council, author of the responsa *Kol Mevasser*; Avraham Yeshayahu *Karelitz (Ḥazon Ish; 1879–1954) published 23 volumes entitled *Ḥazon Ish* (the first in 1911); his novellae and *halakhot* embrace the whole Talmud and all four parts of the Shulḥan Arukh. Karelitz had an enormous impact on the *halakhah* of the latter half of the 20th century, especially in Israel. Reuven *Katz (1880–1963), rabbi of Petaḥ Tikvah, author of the responsa *Degel Re'uven* and *Duda'ei Re'uven;* Isser Yehuda *Unterman (1886–1976), who, with the object of consolidating practical *halakhah*, established a methodological theory of talmudic research, wrote *Shevet Yehudah* on halakhic problems; Ovadiah Hadayah (1893–1969) wrote *Yaskil Avdi* in six parts; Moses *Feinstein (d. 1986) of the U.S., author of the responsa

Iggerot Moshe and the accepted *posek* of Orthodox American Jewry during the second half of the 20th century; Isaac *Nissim (d. 1981), chief rabbi of Israel and *rishon le-Zion*, published his responsa in his *Yein ha-Tov*; Eliezer Judah b. Jacob Gedaliah Waldenberg (b. 1917), *dayyan* in Jerusalem, is the author of *Ẓiẓ Eli'ezer*; Shlomo Goren (d. 1994), chief rabbi of Israel, published, among others, *Yerushalmi ha-Meforash* (1961), and *Torat ha-Mo'adim* (1964); Ovadiah *Yosef (b. 1920), Sephardi chief rabbi of Israel, is the author of the volumes *Yabbi'a Omer* published in Jerusalem between 1954 and 1969.

The *aḥaronim* laid down many rules for *halakhah*. The fundamental principle is to take care to act in accordance with the decisions of the Shulḥan Arukh. Some have insisted that those giving authoritative rulings from the Shulḥan Arukh must know their sources in the Talmud (Maharsha to Sot. 22a, s.v. *ary*). On the other hand the author of the *Pitḥei Teshuvah* holds that after the addition of the well-known commentaries such as the *Taz, Shakh*, and *Magen Avraham* it is permitted to rule from the Shulḥan Arukh itself (*Yoreh De'ah* 242:8). In the view of many *aḥaronim* the authoritative works are to be regarded as "our teachers" and anyone failing to take them into consideration in deciding the *halakhah* is regarded as guilty of "giving a (different) halakhic decision in the presence of his teacher" (*Peri Megadim*, beginning OH, section 3).

There is a well-known rule that *halakhah* may not be learned from the *aggadah* and the Midrashim (*Tosefot Yom Tov*, Ber. 5:4; *Noda bi-Yhudah*, 2nd ed., *Yoreh De'ah*, no. 161), but one may derive from them a custom being practiced by Jews (*Noda bi-Yhuda*, ibid.). On the other hand, several *aḥaronim* hold that where the *aggadot* and Midrashim do not contradict the Talmud but merely add to it they may be relied upon (*Mayim Ḥayyim* of the *Peri Ḥadash*, no. 128; *Shevut Ya'akov*, pt. 2, no. 178).

The novellae of the *aḥaronim* reflect a tendency to *pilpul* and to expand the subjects under discussion with the object of arriving at new halakhic rulings. The conclusions arrived at by outstanding *aḥaronim* are accepted as new halakhic rulings.

The responsa of *aḥaronim* discuss a variety of different problems occasioned by the times. These topics reflect local and temporal conditions: World War I, the condition of Jews in the world after it, World War II, the Holocaust, the establishment of the State of Israel – all these raised problems which are dealt with by the great *aḥaronim* with the object of finding solutions in conformity with the *halakhah*. Indeed, their contribution to our understanding of the Babylonian and Jerusalem Talmuds cannot be underestimated. Throughout the last five centuries the *aḥaronim* advanced our knowledge and comprehension of Jewish law, while constantly and rigorously applying it to everyday life. The decision process in Jewish law in the 21st century is not complete without careful consultation with all previous sources, including those of the *aḥaronim*.

BIBLIOGRAPHY: S.M. Chones, *Toledot ha-Posekim* (1921²); C. Tchernowitz, *Toledot ha-Posekim*, 1 (1946), 14–17; 3 (1947); S.J. Zevin, *Ishim ve-Shitot* (1952); idem, *Soferim u-Sefarim* (1959); B. Katz, *Rabbanut, Ḥasidut, Haskalah*, 1 (1956), 3–200; 2 (1958), 9–116, 178–80; Waxman, Literature, 2 (1960²), 144–96; 3 (1962), 51–58, 705–34; I. Zinberg, *Toledot Sifrut Yisrael*, 3 (1957), 167–225, 226–41, 275–98; 5 (1959), 199–215. **ADD. BIBLIOGRAPHY:** M. Elon, *Mishpat Ivri*, 3 (1981).

[Yehoshua Horowitz / David Derovan (2nd ed.)]

AHARONOV, YAKIR (1932–), Israeli physicist. Aharonov was born in the Haifa suburb of Kiryat Ḥayyim and received his B.Sc. from the Haifa Technion (1956). While working under Professor Boehm on his doctorate at Bristol University in England in 1959, Aharonov discovered the Aharonov-Boehm Effect, essential to quantum theory and of far-reaching impact on modern physics. After receiving his Ph.D. from Bristol University (1960), he taught at Brandeis University (1960–61) and Yeshiva University (1964–67) in the U.S. From 1973 he held a joint position as professor of theoretical physics at Tel Aviv University and at the University of South Carolina. Aharonov is a fellow of the American Physical Society, a member of the Israel National Academy of Science, and a member of the U.S. National Academy of Sciences. Prizes and awards include the Rothschild Prize in physics (1984), the Elliot Cresson Medal (1991), and the Wolf Prize in physics (1998). In 1989 he was awarded the Israel Prize in physics.

[Fern Lee Seckbach and Ruth Rossing (2nd ed.)]

AHARONOVITCH, YOSEF (1877–1937), writer, editor, and Palestinian labor leader. Aharonovitch, who was born in Kirovka, in the Ukraine, acquired his general education in Odessa. On his way to Ereẓ Israel, he was a Hebrew teacher in Brody, Galicia, where he also established a youth movement, Ḥalutzei Zion. He arrived in Ereẓ Israel in 1906, and worked as a laborer and watchman in the Nes Ẓiyyonah and Reḥovot orange groves. A year later he became editor of *Ha-Po'el ha-Ẓa'ir*, the first journal of the Palestinian labor movement. During World War I Aharonovitch was exiled to Egypt, where he edited the anthology *Ba-Nekhar* ("On Foreign Soil") in Alexandria in 1918. After the war he returned to his editorial work in Palestine and to public life. Aharonovitch retired from *Ha-Po'el ha-Ẓa'ir* in 1922 to become director of Bank ha-Po'alim ("The Workers' Bank") in Tel Aviv. A leader of the Jewish community in Palestine, the Zionist movement, the Ha-Po'el ha-Ẓa'ir Party, and later Mapai, he helped to formulate the ideology and practical character of the Palestinian labor movement through his articles, speeches, and personal example. Aharonovitch believed in adapting to a dynamic new reality without being chained to dogmas and beliefs. He proposed that practical agricultural and industrial work should be carried out by Jews, and that the concerted efforts of pioneers were needed to prepare the ground for mass immigration. He crusaded for integrity in public life and efficiency in the country's social and economic institutions. His articles appeared in numerous newspapers and journals, including *Ma'barot, Davar, Moznayim, Ha-Olam, Ha-Yom, Ha-Ḥinnukh*, and *Haaretz*.

His pseudonyms included Temidi, Y.A., and Ben Sarah. In the last two years of his life he was chairman of the Hebrew Writers' Association. Two volumes of his selected articles, *Kitvei Yosef Aharonovitch*, were published in 1941 by his wife, the novelist Devorah *Baron, and Eliezer Shoḥat.

BIBLIOGRAPHY: Kressel, Leksikon, s.v.; Ḥ. Shurer, *Yosef Aharonovitch* (1962), S. Jawnieli, *Ketavim* (1962), 503–13; I. Cohen, *Gesharim* (1955), 36–44; D. Sadan, *Avnei Zikkaron* (1954), 43–67; J. Fichmann, *Be-Terem Aviv* (1959), 377–90; M. Smilansky, *Mishpaḥat ha-Adamah*, 4 (1953), 65–84.

[Israel Cohen]

AHASUERUS (Heb. אֲחַשְׁוֵרוֹשׁ), king of Persia, who according to the Book of Esther ruled from India to Ethiopia (see Book of *Esther; *Artaxerxes).

In the Aggadah

Ahasuerus generally is portrayed as vacillating, lacking in character, and easily swayed. But the positive aspects of his personality are also emphasized. He is depicted as one of the few kings in history who ruled over the entire earth (Meg. 11a; Targ. Sheni to Esth. 1:2). Before his death Nebuchadnezzar had placed all the treasures of the world he had looted in a ship, and sunk it in the Euphrates to prevent anyone finding them. God, however, had revealed their location to Cyrus when He gave orders that the Temple was to be rebuilt. Ahasuerus' great wealth derived from this treasure. But he neither succeeded in sitting on Solomon's throne nor in erecting a similar one (*Midrash Abba Guryon*). It was through Esther's influence that he appointed *Mordecai as his counselor, for she told Ahasuerus that whereas his predecessors, Nebuchadnezzar and Belshazzar, had consulted prophets, he invariably turned for advice to ordinary mortals. Ahasuerus is said to have desecrated the Temple vessels and priestly robes at the feast he made for all the provinces of his kingdom even though he knew what had happened to Belshazzar for such conduct (Meg. 11b). Other *aggadot* declare that his hatred of Israel exceeded Haman's but he feared he might suffer a fate similar to that of the other enemies of the Jews.

BIBLIOGRAPHY: Guttmann, Mafte'aḥ; Ginzberg, Legends, index.

[Joshua Gutmann]

AHASUERUS-XERXES (Heb. אחשורש; Aram. Papyri חשי(א)רש; Dura Synagogue חשורש; Old Persian *Xšayāršā*; Gr. Ξερξης). If one ignores the vowels, the biblical consonantal text is a close approximation of the king's name. The Persian king known to the Greeks as Xerxes I (reigned 486–465 B.C.E.) was the son of *Darius I. As soon as he ascended the throne, Xerxes was confronted by a revolt in Egypt. At the same time, the enemies of Judah apparently tried to incite him against its inhabitants (Ezra 4:6). After reducing Egypt "to a worse state of servitude than it was in under Darius" and crushing another revolt in Babylon, he attempted a more ambitious undertaking, the subjugation of Greece. After the disastrous outcome of this adventure, which took place between the third and seventh years of his reign, Xerxes settled down to a life of self-indulgence, reflected in the account of Ahasuerus in the *Scroll of Esther, which agrees with the Greek authors in its conception, or even caricature, of life at the Persian court. Ahasuerus is represented in the Book of Daniel as the father of *Darius the Mede (Dan. 9:1) and, in one recension of the Book of Tobit, as allied with Nebuchadnezzar at the capture of Nineveh (Tob. 14:15). Since Nineveh was actually captured (in 612 B.C.E.) by kings Cyaxares of Media and Nabopolassar of Babylon, it is natural to surmise that later generations confused Cyaxares with Ahasuerus-Xerxes just as they confused Nabopolassar with Nebuchadnezzar. The Book of Esther does not mention the death of Xerxes in a bloody court coup.

BIBLIOGRAPHY: H.T. Olmstead, *History of the Persian Empire* (1948), 214ff.; R.N. Frye, *The Heritage of Persia* (1962), index; R.G. Kent, *Old Persian* (1953^2), 147–53. **ADD. BIBLIOGRAPHY:** P. Briant, *From Cyrus to Alexander* (2002), 515–68.

[Isaiah Gafni / Harold Louis Ginsberg]

AHAVAH RABBAH (Heb. אַהֲבָה רַבָּה; "With great love"); **AHAVAT OLAM** (Heb. אַהֲבַת עוֹלָם; "Everlasting love"), two versions of the second of the two benedictions preceding the recitation of the *Shema* in the morning and evening services. In the Talmud there is a difference of opinion as to which is the correct version (Ber. 11b) and a *baraita* is quoted which definitely favors *Ahavah Rabbah.* This controversy continued even into medieval times (see Levin, Oẓar, vol. 1, p. 29; ET, vol. 4, p. 391). As a compromise decision *Ahavah Rabbah* was adopted for the morning service and the other for the evening (Tos., MG Ber.). The Sephardi and Italian rites, however, only have *Ahavat Olam.* It is not clear whether the difference between the two versions was limited to the opening formula or whether it extended to the content. From the prayer book of *Saadiah Gaon it would appear that the former is the case. In their present form the two prayers have the same basic theme, but they differ considerably in presentation, and *Ahavah Rabbah* is much the longer and the more complex of the two. Both benedictions tell of God's love as the explanation for Israel's receiving the Torah. The prayers introduce the *Shema* which is basically a Torah reading – and promise, in consequence, continual preoccupation with its study and observance. In both, God is besought to continue bestowing His love on His people, but in *Ahavah Rabbah* the idea of the election of Israel is stressed. *Ahavat Olam* ends, "Blessed art Thou, O Lord, Who lovest His people Israel," whereas *Ahavah Rabbah* closes with "Who has chosen His people Israel in love." The Mishnah (Tam. 5:1), as interpreted in the *Gemara* (Ber. 11b–12a), records that *Ahavah Rabbah* was the benediction with which the priestly prayer service in the Temple commenced. According to the *halakhah* (Sh. Ar., OḤ 47:7) either of the two can serve as a substitute for the **Birkat ha-Torah*, the blessing to be recited before study.

In the Middle Ages various *piyyutim* were composed for insertion into *Ahavah Rabbah* and *Ahavat Olam* on festivals. Those for the latter are still recited in some synagogues. Both benedictions appear with minor textual variations in the different rites; *Ahavat Olam* much less, however, than *Ahavah Rabbah*. The Reform ritual has retained the traditional text of the former but has abbreviated the latter considerably, omitting the messianic passages. *Ahavat Olam* has been set to music by Mombach and others, and forms part of the repertoire of most synagogue choirs.

BIBLIOGRAPHY: Elbogen, Gottesdienst, 20–21, 25, 100–1; Abrahams, Companion, xlviiiff., cx; J. Heinemann, *Ha-Te'fillah bi-Tekufat ha-Tanna'im ve ha-Amora'im* (1964), 43, n. 34; 106; E. Munk, *World of Prayer* (1954), 107.

[Raphael Posner]

AHAZ (Heb. אָחָז, a diminutive of יְהוֹאָחָז, as shown by the reference to him as *Ya-u-ha-zi* in cuneiform (the inscription of Tiglath-Pileser III), meaning "YHWH holds fast"), king of Judah (743–727 B.C.E.), son of *Jotham and father of *Hezekiah. Ahaz succeeded to the throne at the age of 20 and ruled for 16 years. It seems, however, that he ruled alone for seven years only, sharing the first nine years with his father as regent for his grandfather *Uzziah (785–733 B.C.E.), who was incapacitated by a terrible skin disease. Ahaz apparently refused to join the anti-Assyrian alliance of Aram, northern Israel, the Philistines, and others, no doubt believing Assyrian power to be irresistible. This refusal led to the "Syro-Ephraimite war" of 733, when Israel and Aram invaded Judah (II Kings 15:37; II Chron. 28:5ff.), carried off many captives, and planned to conquer Judah and to set up, under a certain Ben Tabeel, a regime favorable to an anti-Assyrian alliance (for a different motivation, see H.L. Ginsberg in Bibliography). In the course of the war Ahaz lost control over the Negev and the western slopes of the Judean hills to the Philistines (II Chron. 28:18), and of Elath to the Edomites (II Kings 16:6).

Ahaz turned for help to the Assyrian Tiglath-Pileser III whose suzerainty he, or Uzziah, had probably recognized one or more years previously. Tiglath-Pileser thereupon advanced against Aram and Israel. Ahaz went to Damascus to pay homage to the victor; from there he sent instructions to the high priest Uriah to introduce Aramean (Assyrian?) cults into the Temple in Jerusalem and, in particular, to build an altar modeled on an (Assyrian type?) altar he had seen in Damascus. Later, he himself made sacrifices on this altar (II Kings 16:7ff.). Ahaz made other far-reaching changes in the Temple and, besides despoiling the Temple treasury and his own, melted down some of the Temple vessels for his tribute to the Assyrian king. He also installed a sundial in the Temple (II Kings 20:11). Of his ministers, the names of Shebna, the steward (?; Isa. 22:15), and Eshna, "servant of Ahaz," are known, the latter from a recently discovered seal (see: EM, 1 (1950), 207). More recently, a seal impression reading "belonging to Ahaz (son of) Yehotam, King of Judah" was published.

Ahaz, accused of practicing ancient Canaanite cults, such as the Moloch fire rite, is one of the kings who did evil in the eyes of the Lord (II Kings 16:3–4). According to II Kings, Ahaz was buried in the royal vault in the City of David, but according to II Chronicles, merely in Jerusalem. In the Talmud (Pes. 56a) his son Hezekiah is commended for giving Ahaz a pauper's funeral as an atonement for Ahaz' sins and in order to disassociate himself from his father's religious policies. Although Ahaz' own record was tarnished, the rabbis credited him with having been the son and father of righteous kings as well as having accepted Uzziah's reproof, which secured him a share in the world to come (Sanh. 104a).

BIBLIOGRAPHY: H.L. Ginsberg, in: *Fourth World Congress of Jewish Studies. Papers*, 1 (1967), 91ff.; W. Rudolph, *Chronikbücher* (1955), 289–90; Y. Liver (ed.), *Historyah Ẓeva'it shel Ereẓ Yisrael…* (1964), index, incl. bibl.; EM, 1 (1965), 206–9, incl. bibl.; A. Reifenberg, *Ancient Hebrew Arts* (1950), 34; Ginzberg, Legends, index. **ADD. BIBLIOGRAPHY:** N. Na'aman, in: VT, 48 (1998), 333–49; R. Deutsch, *Messages from the Past* (1999), 205.

AHAZIAH (Heb. אֲחַזְיָה, אֲחַזְיָהוּ; "YHWH holds firm"), the name of two biblical kings.

(1) Son of *Ahab, king of Israel (c. 853–852 B.C.E.). The biblical account of his two-year reign (I Kings 22:52–II Kings 1:18) faults Ahaziah for following his father and mother in sponsoring the cult of the Tyrian Baal, inquiring of Baal-Zebub of Philistine Ekron in addition to his maintenance of the calf-cult initiated by Jeroboam I. The defeat of the army of Israel and the death of Ahab in the war with the Arameans (853 B.C.E.) encouraged *Mesha, king of Moab, to free himself from Israelite suzerainty and to engage in war with Ahaziah. Apparently the Ammonites also gained their freedom at that time (II Chron. 20:1). The traditional alliance between the house of Omri and Judah suffered when *Jehoshaphat, king of Judah, refused partnership in the maritime commercial venture organized at the port of Ezion-Geber which was proposed by the king of Israel (I Kings 22:49–50; see, however, II Chron. 20:35–37). In the second year of his reign Ahaziah was severely injured in a fall from the window of an upper story of his palace and sent to ask for an oracle of Baal-Zebub, god of Ekron. *Elijah reproved him for this act and prophesied that he would die (II Kings 1:2ff.). Given the fantastic elements in the chapter, i.e., repeated fire from heaven called down by the prophet, we might do well to explain the account of Ahaziah's deeds as a theological justification for his brief reign and premature death. Ahaziah left no sons and was succeeded on the throne by his brother Jehoram.

(2) The son of *Jehoram, king of Judah, and *Athaliah, daughter (or sister) of Ahab, king of Israel. Ahaziah ascended the throne at the age of 22 and reigned for one year over Judah (c. 842–841 B.C.E.; II Kings 8:25ff.). His name is misspelled "Johoahaz" in II Chronicles 21:16–17 and "Azariah" in II Chronicles 22:6. He followed his mother Athaliah in all matters relating to the cult. The political alliance with the dynasty of Omri was revived and he and his uncle or cousin King Jehoram of Israel went to war against Ḥazael, king of Aram (II Kings 8:28–29; II Chron. 22:5–6). Jehoram was wounded in

the battle, and Ahaziah visited him in Jezreel. Because of this kinship and friendship, *Jehu killed him as well as Jehoram (II Kings 9:27–28; II Chron. 22:9).

BIBLIOGRAPHY: Bright, Hist, 223ff., 232–4; Yeivin, in: JQR, 50 (1959/60), 219ff.; EM, 1 (1965), 210–1. **ADD. BIBLIOGRAPHY:** M. Cogan and H. Tadmor, *II Kings* (AB; 1988), 21–28, 98–100; W. Thiel, in: ABD, 1, 107–9.

AḤDUT HA-AVODAH, Zionist Socialist Labor Party in Palestine founded in 1919. First steps toward its formation were taken in 1918 by soldiers of the *Jewish Legion at Tell el Kabir, Egypt, where many Palestinian Jewish workers and members of *Po'alei Zion from America were serving as volunteers in the Jewish battalions of the British Army. The majority of the volunteers belonged to an influential non-party group, led by Berl *Katznelson and Shemuel *Yavneeli, and to Po'alei Zion, led by Izhak *Ben-Zvi and David *Ben-Gurion. There were also a few volunteers who were leading members of the other Labor Party, *Ha-Po'el ha-Ẓa'ir, among them Levi Shkolnik (*Eshkol) and Abraham Haft, although their party objected to participation in the Legion. In February 1919, a conference of Po'alei Zion unanimously called for unity, but a Ha-Po'el ha-Ẓa'ir conference rejected the proposal. Immediately afterward, at Petaḥ Tikvah, a conference of the Agricultural Workers' Union, which included members of both parties, voted 48 to 12 for the establishment of a workers' federation to be responsible for all political, economic, and cultural activities, and for settlement on the land. Most Ha-Po'el ha-Ẓa'ir members did not join, but established separate labor exchanges and a separate agricultural settlement center. A founding conference resulting from the agricultural workers' decision was elected by 1,871 workers, with 47 rural delegates, 15 urban, and 19 representing the legionnaires from abroad. It met shortly afterward and decided to establish the Zionist Socialist Federation of the Workers of Ereẓ Israel, Aḥdut ha-Avodah, as an autonomous body, comprising all workers and members of the professions living solely from their labor without exploiting others. It was to participate in the World Zionist Organization and the Socialist International; to organize the provision of work, cooperative supplies, vocational training, and general education; to protect the workers' dignity and interests; and to enhance the creative capacity of the working class. Aḥdut ha-Avodah aspired, through organized mass immigration, to mold the life of the Jewish people in Ereẓ Israel as a commonwealth of free and equal workers living on its labor, controlling its property, and arranging its distribution of work, its economy, and its culture. Only a minority of Ha-Po'el ha-Ẓa'ir members joined, and, in order to avoid competition in labor matters, both groups agreed to establish the General Federation of Jewish Workers in Ereẓ Israel (*Histadrut), which was founded in December 1920. Aḥdut ha-Avodah became dominant in the Histadrut, of which Ben-Gurion was elected secretary-general. It also became dominant in the Elected Assembly of the *yishuv*, but continued to aim at complete workers' unity. After prolonged negotiations, Aḥdut ha-Avodah and Ha-Po'el ha-Ẓa'ir merged in 1930 to form Mifleget Po'alei Ereẓ Israel (*Mapai).

[David Ben-Gurion]

A study of Aḥdut ha-Avodah, *Aḥdut ha-Avodah ha-Historit,* by Jonathan Shapiro (1975) traces the consolidation of the party out of various factions and how the veteran leadership from the Second Aliyah period kept the reins of power in their hands. Shapiro attributes the party's organizational strength to its social and ideological roots going back to the Jewish experience in Russia.

BIBLIOGRAPHY: G. Kressel, *Mafte'aḥ la-Kunteres, 1919–1945* (1945).

AḤDUT HA-AVODAH, the name of several publications issued by the different labor movements in Ereẓ Israel at various times. (1) The first such periodical was published in 1919, a few months prior to the formation of the Aḥdut ha-Avodah Party, under the editorship of B. *Katznelson. It dealt with the ideology of the new party, labor questions, and contemporary problems of the *yishuv*. (2) After the Aḥdut ha-Avodah Party merged with *Ha-Po'el ha-Ẓa'ir in 1930 to form *Mapai, an anthology was published under the title *Aḥdut ha-Avodah* (2 vols., 1929–32). It contained articles on all aspects of Jewish life in Ereẓ Israel and in the Diaspora – political, economic, and social – by different leaders of the Aḥdut ha-Avodah Party. The editors were B. Katznelson, Shaul *Avigur, and Mordecai Senir. (3) A new social literary monthly, *Aḥdut ha-Avodah*, was established in 1930 and edited by C. *Arlosoroff. It continued until 1932. (4) A number of works, collections of articles, published by Mapai appeared under the same name between 1943 and 1946. (5) When Aḥdut ha-Avodah left Mapai to form a separate party in 1944, it published the weekly *Ha-Tenu'ah le-Aḥdut ha-Avodah* (abbreviated to *Le-Aḥdut ha-Avodah*). It ceased to exist on Jan. 22, 1946, when Aḥdut ha-Avodah merged with *Ha-Shomer ha-Ẓa'ir to form Mifleget ha-Po'alim ha-Me'uḥedet (*Mapam).

[Getzel Kressel]

AḤDUT HA-AVODAH–PO'ALEI ZION ("Unity of Labor–Workers of Zion"), Zionist Socialist Party established in 1946. *Aḥdut ha-Avodah emerged as an independent party in 1944 after a faction in Mapai calling itself *Si'ah Bet* (B Faction) seceded from it because of its objections to the policies of the *Histadrut leadership. In 1946 it united with the left-wing Po'alei Zion, assuming the name Aḥdut ha-Avodah–Po'alei Zion. In 1948 the new party joined with Ha-Shomer ha-Ẓa'ir to form *Mapam and ran within its framework in the elections to the First and Second Knessets. In August 1954, due to ideological differences set against the background of antisemitic "show trials" in Moscow and Prague, it resumed its independence. Aḥdut ha-Avodah–Po'alei Zion ran independently in the elections to the Third, Fourth, and Fifth Knessets, winning ten, seven, and eight seats, respectively. In the elections to the Sixth Knesset it ran on a single list – the Alignment – with *Mapai, and in 1968 it united with Mapai and *Rafi to form the *Israel Labor Party.

The core group of the party membership was made up of members of Ha-Kibbutz ha-Me'uḥad (see *Kibbutz), and among its best-known leaders were Yitzḥak *Tabenkin, Yigal *Allon, Yisrael *Galili, and Yitzḥak *Ben-Aharon. Throughout its independent existence the party was radical in its Zionist and social outlook, advocating a Jewish state with full rights for the Arab minority within what later came to be known as "Greater Israel." It opposed the various partition plans and, during the *War of Independence, demanded that the IDF occupy the whole territory of Eretz Israel within the boundaries of the British Mandate. Both in 1949 and again in 1957, following the *Sinai Campaign, it opposed the withdrawal of the IDF from the Sinai Peninsula, unless the Arab states accepted a peace settlement.

During World War II Aḥdut ha-Avodah–Po'alei Zion favored not only participation of Jewish youth in the British Army, but also the establishment of an underground military force under the sole authority of the *Haganah. Its members played an important role in the foundation and leadership of the *Palmaḥ. It advocated a comprehensive struggle against the British Mandatory regime, the organization of large-scale clandestine immigration, settlement in areas forbidden to Jewish settlement, and, after the war, sabotage operations against British installations in Palestine. However, it objected to acts of personal terror, such as those practiced by the two dissident underground organizations I.Ẓ.L. (*Irgun Ẓeva'i Le'ummi) and Leḥi (*Loḥamei Ḥerut Israel), though it objected to cooperation between the Haganah and the Mandatory police in the apprehension of members of these organizations, advocating instead their detention in Haganah undercover prisons.

The party adopted the philosophy of "scientific socialism," containing distinctly Marxist elements, but advocated "Zionist socialism" unfettered by any international, ideological, or organizational authority. Although sympathetic to the social experiment in the Soviet Union, it rejected the dictatorial regime in that country, and criticized manifestations of violence and persecution in it as well as its policy toward the Jews and Zionism. At the same time it maintained ties with other left-wing socialist movements and groups around the world. Aḥdut ha-Avodah opposed David *Ben-Gurion's policy of rapprochement with West Germany.

From 1959 until 1965 Aḥdut ha-Avodah–Po'alei Zion was a member of governments led by Ben-Gurion and Levi *Eshkol. It was also an active member of the Histadrut leadership, advocating the preservation of the Histadrut's independence, and the maintenance of full ideological and organizational democracy within it. After the establishment of the Labor Party, one of its leaders, Yitzḥak Ben-Aharon, served as secretary general of the Histadrut in the years 1969–73. In 1954 it started publishing a Hebrew daily, *Lamerhav*, that survived until 1971, and for a while after 1967 it published a Yiddish weekly, *Folksblat*.

[Susan Hattis Rolef (2nd ed.)]

AḤERIM (Heb. אֲחֵרִים; lit. "others"), a pseudonym for sages whose teachings are quoted anonymously in the tannaitic literature. According to the Talmud (Hor. 13b, 14a), *aḥerim* was used as a pseudonym for R. *Meir so that his teachings would not be propounded under his name in the *bet ha-midrash* – this, in punishment for his attempt, together with R. *Nathan, to assail the dignity and authority of the *nasi*, *Simeon b. Gamaliel II, and to remove him from office. The punishment, however, did not remain in force very long, the Talmud continuing that on one occasion Judah ha-Nasi, son of Simeon b. Gamaliel II, was teaching a certain Mishnah to his son Simeon with the words, "*aḥerim* say," whereupon Simeon said to his father, "Who are they whose waters we drink but whose names we do not mention?" at which Judah deferred to his son's opinion and in place of "*aḥerim* say" stated explicitly, "On Rabbi Meir's behalf it is said" (*ibid.*). In point of fact, in the Mishnah, which Judah edited, the expression "*aḥerim* say" does not occur. The tosafists, however, have pointed out the difficulty in the identification of "*aḥerim*" with Meir, for in many passages the words "*aḥerim* say" occur in opposition to Meir's view. One tosafist suggested that only those teachings which Meir received from his teacher, *Elisha b. Avuyah, later called *Aḥer*, were introduced under this pseudonym. The tosafists themselves, however, found this explanation unsatisfactory, and suggested instead that those opinions which he changed after he was punished and referred to as *aḥerim* are cited under this pseudonym, while his earlier views appear under his own name (Tos., Sot. 12a).

BIBLIOGRAPHY: Hyman, Toledot, 138.

[Zvi Kaplan]

AHIJAH (Heb. אֲחִיָּה; "my [or the] brother is YHWH"), son of *Ahitub, priest of the house of Eli (I Sam. 14:3). Ahijah was apparently the chief priest in Shiloh during the reign of Saul (cf. Jos., Ant., 4:107), although his name does not appear in the list of chief priests in I Chronicles 6:50–55 and in Ezra 7:2–5. Several scholars identify Ahijah with *Ahimelech, son of Ahitub, who served as priest of Nob in Saul's days, assuming that the name Ahijah is the short form of Ahimelech or that the element *melekh* ("King") in his name was replaced by the divine name.

When Saul fought against the Philistines at Michmas, Ahijah wore an ephod (I Sam. 14:3). According to I Samuel 14:18, Ahijah served before the Ark of God; however, according to the same chapter, verse 3 (and also according to the LXX; *Baraita di-Melekhet ha-Mishkan*, 6 [and cf. Ish Shalom's ed., p. 44]; Ibn Ezra's commentary to Ex. 28:6 – all referring to I Sam. 14:18), "ephod" is to be read (instead of "ark"). Furthermore, only the ephod (and not the ark) is mentioned in the Bible as having been used for consulting the divine will (cf. the consultation by means of the ephod in I Sam. 23:9; 30:7). Ahijah may also have been the priest who inquired of God first whether to advance against the Philistines and then, upon failing to obtain a response, provoked God's displeasure (I Sam. 14:36ff.).

AHIJAH THE SHILONITE (Heb. אֲחִיָּה הַשִּׁלֹנִי), Israelite prophet during the latter part of Solomon's reign and during the concurrent reigns of *Rehoboam and *Jeroboam. Jeroboam son of Nebat of Zeredah (which, according to the Septuagint, I Kings 12:24, was near Shiloh), enjoyed the support of Ahijah, whose main antagonism against Solomon was due to the tolerance shown by the king to foreign cults. At a secret meeting with Jeroboam outside Jerusalem he tore Jeroboam's new garment (or his own – the text is ambiguous) into 12 pieces as a symbol of the 12 tribes and gave him ten. The kingdom of Israel would be divided; only one other tribe (Benjamin), beside Judah, would remain loyal to the House of David (*ibid.* 11:29–39). Not improbably, Ahijah expected Jeroboam to restore the ancient central sanctuary of his native Shiloh. When Jeroboam, instead, set up golden calves in sanctuaries at Beth-El and Dan, the estrangement between him and Ahijah became inevitable. When Jeroboam's son Abijah fell ill, the king who no longer dared to face the old seer, by now almost blind, sent his wife in disguise to inquire about the child's fate. He not only foretold her son's death but predicted a dire end for the House of Jeroboam (*ibid.* 14:1–18).

In II Chronicles 9:29 Ahijah, in accordance with the Chronicler's practice, is cited, along with the other two prophets who were active in the reign of Solomon, as an author of the books of Kings' account of Solomon's reign.

In rabbinic tradition, Ahijah was a Levite at Shiloh. He was the sixth of seven men whose lifetimes following one another encompass all time (BB 121b) and is given a life span of more than 500 years. (On this basis Maimonides, in the introduction to his Code, makes him an important link in the early tradition of the Oral Law.) Ahijah was reputed to be a great master of the secret lore (Kabbalah), and ḥasidic legend makes him a teacher of *Israel Ba'al Shem Tov. He is said to have died a martyr's death at the hands of Abijah, son of Rehoboam and king of Judah.

BIBLIOGRAPHY: Bright, Hist, 208ff.; Kaufmann, Religion, 270ff.; J. Morgenstern, *Amos Studies*, 1 (1941), 202ff.; E. Auerbach, *Wueste und gelobtes Land*, 2 (1936), index; Yeivin, in: *Sefer Dinaburg* (1949), 30ff.; Caquot, in: *Semitica*, 11 (1961), 17–27 (Fr.); Ginzberg, Legends, 4 (1913), 180.

AHIKAM (Heb. אֲחִיקָם; "the divine kinsman has risen [for battle]"), son of *Shaphan and father of *Gedaliah, a high royal official. Ahikam was one of the men sent by King Josiah to the prophetess *Huldah (II Kings 22:12, 14; II Chron. 34:20). Later, during the reign of Jehoiakim, when Jeremiah prophesied the destruction of Jerusalem, Ahikam used his influence to protect Jeremiah from death (Jer. 26:24).

Ahikam was a member of one of the most influential pro-Babylonian families in the last days of the Judean Kingdom. Shaphan, his father, was the scribe of Josiah (II Kings 22:3ff. et al.); his brother Elasah was one of the men sent to Babylon by Zedekiah who brought the letter written by Jeremiah to the elders in exile (Jer. 29:1–3); his brother *Jaazaniah is mentioned in Ezekiel 8:11 among the elders of Jerusalem; and his son Gedaliah was appointed governor of Judah after the destruction of Jerusalem (Jer. 40:5–6). A seal impression published recently appears to bear his name.

BIBLIOGRAPHY: K.L. Tallqvist, *Assyrian Personal Names* (1914), 16; C.H. Gordon, *Ugaritic Grammar* (1940), 41; Virolleaud, in: *Revue d'assyrologie*, 15–16 (1940), 30, 34; Cassuto, in: *Orientalia*, 16 (1941), 473 (It.); Yeivin, in: *Tarbiz*, 12 (1940/41), 255. **ADD. BIBLIOGRAPHY:** R. Deutsch, *Messages from the Past* (1999), no. 25.

AHIKAR, BOOK OF, a folk work, apparently already widespread in Aramaic-speaking lands during the period of Assyrian rule. It was evidently well-known among the Jewish colonists in southern Egypt during the fifth century B.C.E. and at the beginning of the twentieth century the major part of an Aramaic text of the work was discovered among the documents of the Jewish community of *Elephantine. Greek writers were likewise acquainted with its contents. The book has survived in several versions: Syriac, Arabic, Ethiopic, Armenian, Turkish, and Slavonic. These texts bear a fundamental similarity to the ancient Elephantine version. It may be subdivided into two parts: (1) the life of *Ahikar; (2) the sayings uttered for the benefit of Nadan, his adopted son.

Ahikar the Wise, the hero of the work, is mentioned in the apocryphal book of Tobit as one of the exiles of the Ten Tribes. He purportedly attained high rank, being appointed chief cupbearer, keeper of the royal signet, and chief administrator during the reigns of Sennacherib and Esarhaddon. In his later years, realizing that he would leave no offspring, he adopted his sister's son Nadan and groomed him for a high office at court. Ahikar's instructions to Nadan in preparation for this position are couched in the form of epigrams. Ahikar, however, ultimately convinced that his protegé was not equal to the task, disowned him. Nadan thereupon slandered Ahikar before the king. When this accusation was proved false, Nadan was handed over to Ahikar who imprisoned him near the gateway to his home. Thereafter, whenever Ahikar passed by this place, he uttered words of reproof to his former adopted son. These remarks, presented as aphorisms, comprise the last section of the Book of Ahikar. Both the contents and aim of the work indicate its Aramean-Assyrian milieu. In

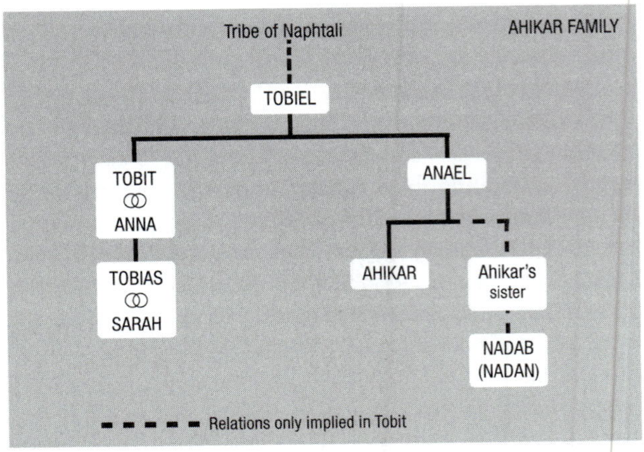

textual format, it resembles Job, which also contains not only wisdom sayings, but also events associated with the hero of the tale. Also similar to Ahikar is Proverbs 31:1: "The words of King Lemuel"; which, though presently comprising only the apothegmatic section, may well originally have contained biographical data concerning Lemuel. Works along these lines were not unknown among the peoples of antiquity and in Israel too, the Wisdom literature did not fail to take ideas from non-Israelite sources. However, the Book of Ahikar, despite its dissemination and popularity among the Jews, left no imprint upon Hebrew literature. The reason may be that its many pagan features remain unblurred, even in late editions belonging to the Christian era. A profounder cause, however, is the fact that a spirit of total submissiveness to and awe of human rulers pervades the work to such an extent that their edicts and promulgations are regarded as inviolable law. This note of self-negation before a king of flesh and blood, which is of the very essence of the work, was entirely alien to the Jewish spirit.

[Joshua Gutmann]

Ahikar

Although the Book of Ahikar did not exert any direct influence on Jewish literature, Ahikar himself was assimilated in Jewish sources. Chapter 14:10 states that Ahikar raised Nadab (i.e., Nadan) and refers to the slander story described in the Book. According to 1:21–22, Ahikar is Tobias' cousin, son of Tobit's brother Anael. Chapter 11:18 raises textual problems, but the reading of the Codex Sinaiticus (Nadab), which makes both Ahikar and Nadab cousins of Tobias, is not impossible. Strictly speaking Nadab would be his second cousin.

The Jews made this hero of the pagan Wisdom tale into a pious Jew of the tribe of Naphtali, an instance of how they adopted and reused international Wisdom traditions. The transformation of Ahikar into an exiled Israelite was accompanied, in Tobit 14:10, by emphasis on the vindication of righteousness in the relationship between Ahikar and Nadab. Ahikar was also mentioned in Hellenistic literature and in a variety of later sources. Ahikar is now known from Babylonian sources as the court sage in the time of King Sennacherib.

[Michael E. Stone]

BIBLIOGRAPHY: A. Yellin, *Sefer Aḥikar he-Ḥakham* (1938); R.Harris, et al., *Story of Ahikar from Syriac, Arabic, Armenian, etc.* (1898); Cowley, Aramaic, 204–48; Charles, Apocrypha, 2 (1913), 715–84; J.B. Pritchard (ed.), *The Ancient Near East* (1958), 245–49.

AHIMAAZ (Heb. אֲחִימַעַץ; "the [or my] brother is counselor[?]"), name of three biblical personalities.

(1) Father-in-law of King Saul (I Sam. 14:50).

(2) Son of the priest *Zadok. When David fled Jerusalem because of the revolt of *Absalom, Ahimaaz, together with Jonathan, the son of David's other priest Abiathar, remained just outside the city. A messenger of their fathers delivered information about the rebels' plans to them, which they conveyed to David (II Sam. 15:27–36; 17:15–22). Later, being a swift runner, he overtook and passed the messenger who was to report the outcome of the battle with Absalom to David. He thus reported the defeat of the rebels, but left to the messenger the unenviable task of informing the king that Absalom had been killed (*ibid.* 18:19–32).

(3) A son-in-law of Solomon, his prefect over the district of Naphtali (I Kings 4:15). Some identify him with Ahimaaz the son of Zadok (above). If that conjecture is correct, it is likely that his prefectship was bestowed on him because he was debarred from the priesthood, possibly because of a defect acquired in combat. According to I Chronicles 5:34–36, Azariah the great-grandson of Ahimaaz succeeded Zadok as a priest in Solomon's Temple, but it seems that the verses are corrupt and this Azariah is Ahimaaz' son. The name Ahimaaz probably also appears on a signet ring discovered at Tell Zakariyeh (ancient Azekah). It has not been satisfactorily explained. The name Maaz occurs in I Chronicles 2:27.

BIBLIOGRAPHY: M.Z. Segal, *Sifrei Shemu'el* (1956), index, s.v.; Katzenstein, in: JBL, 31 (1962), 311ff.; Diringer, Iscrizioni, 120–1. **ADD. BIBLIOGRAPHY:** H. Tawil, in: Beit Mikra, 44 (1999), 372–84.

AHIMAAZ BEN PALTIEL (b. 1017), chronicler and poet of Capua, south Italy. In 1054 when he removed to Oria, the place of origin of his family, he compiled *Megillat Yuḥasin* ("The Scroll of Genealogies"), also known as *Megillat Aḥima'az* ("The Ahimaaz Scroll" or the "Chronicle of Ahimaaz"). It describes in rhymed prose the genealogy of his family from the ninth century to his own time. The Ahimaaz family counted among its members prominent personalities, who had been

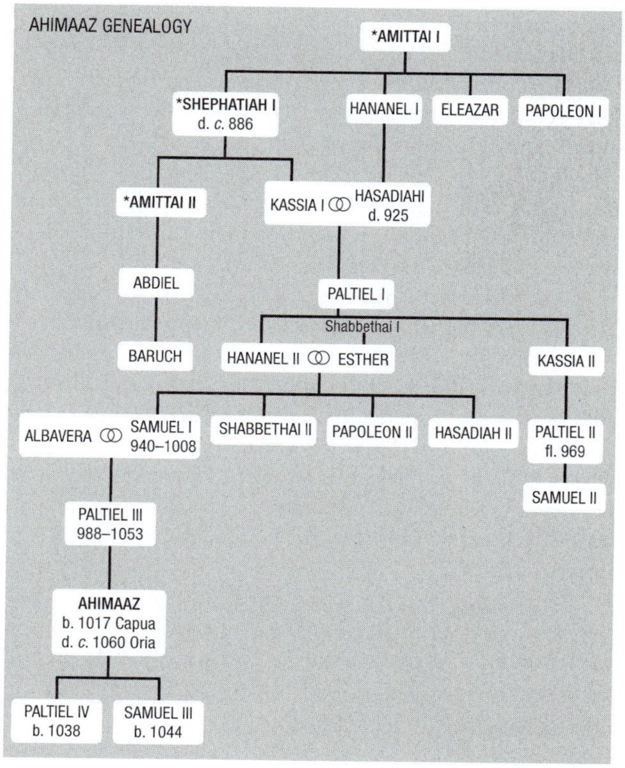

leaders of their generations in the different communities of Italy, as well as in North Africa, e.g., Shephatiah, Amittai b. Shephatiah, Paltiel. They actively participated in some of the most important events in these countries. *Megillat Aḥimaʿaz* is consequently a significant Jewish historical source covering several periods and countries. Apart from historical data, it includes legends and fantastic tales and, despite some inaccuracies, it is a reliable historical document. The one known manuscript is in the library of Toledo Cathedral, where it was discovered by A. Neubauer in 1895. It has since been edited several times; the edition by B. Klar appeared in 1944 (second edition, M. Spitzer, 1974). Ahimaaz also composed a poem in honor of the *nagid* *Paltiel (included in the Scroll) and a number of *piyyutim*. A photograph of the manuscript was published in 1964 in Jerusalem. In 1965, the text of the manuscript was published with a concordance: *Megillat Aḥimaʿaz Meʾubbedet u-Muggeshet ke-Ḥomer le-Millon*, edited by R. Mirkin with the assistance of I. Yeivin and G.B. Tsarfati. There is an English translation by M. Salzman (1924, 1966) and an Italian one by C. Colafemmina (2001).

BIBLIOGRAPHY: B. Klar (ed.), *Megillat Aḥimaʿaz* (1944), 139–56, postscript; Klar, in: *Sinai*, 22 (1947/48), 243–8; Kaufmann, Schriften, 3 (1915), 1–55 (appeared in MGWJ, 40 (1896), 462ff.); Waxman, Literature, 1 (1960), 425–7; Roth, Dark Ages, 104, 251; Neubauer, Chronicles, index. s.v. *Aḥimaʿaz*. **ADD. BIBLIOGRAPHY:** Bonfil, *Tra due Mondi* (1996), 67–133.

[Jefim (Hayyim) Schirmann]

AHIMAN, SHESHAI, TALMAI, the sons of *Anak, who were said to have inhabited *Hebron when the spies sent by Moses reconnoitered Canaan (Num. 13:22). Their names have not been identified with certainty. Ahiman may be Semitic, while Kempinsky and Hess regard Sheshai and Talmai as Hurrian. The sons of Anak are described as *Nephilim (*ibid.* 13:33), a term probably indicating extraordinary stature and power (cf. Gen. 6:4). In Deuteronomy 2:21 (cf. Deut. 1:28) the Anakim are described as "great, numerous, and tall." Traditions about an ancient giant race were apparently current in Israel, Amon, and Moab (see *Og, *Rephaim).

According to Joshua 15:13–14, *Caleb attacked Ahiman, Sheshai, and Talmai and dispossessed them (cf. Judg. 1:20). Another passage credits the tribe of Judah with the victory over the three brothers (Judg. 1:10). Finally, according to Joshua 11:21–22, Joshua annihilated the Anakites. The name Ahiman occurs as well in I Chronicles 9:17 and in three epigraphs: a jug from *Elephantine, one seal from Megiddo, and another of unknown provenance. Talmai is also the name of a king of Geshur in northern Transjordan who was a contemporary of David.

BIBLIOGRAPHY: C.F. Burney, *The Book of Judges* (1920), 9–10; Mazar, in: *Sefer Dinaburg* (1949), 321; EM, 1 (1965), 218–9 (incl. bibl.). **ADD. BIBLIOGRAPHY:** A. Kempinsky, in: EM, 8, 575–76; R. Hess, in: CBQ, 58 (1996), 205–14; B. Levine, *Numbers 1–20* (AB; 1993), 355.

[Hanna Weiner]

AḤIMEIR, ABBA (pseud. of **Abba Shaul Heisinovitch**; 1898–1962), journalist and writer, Revisionist leader in Palestine. Aḥimeir was born in Dolgi near Bobruisk, Belorussia, studied at the Herzlia High School in Tel Aviv (1912–14) and returned to Russia where he became a member of *Ẓeʾirei Zion. After World War I he studied history at the universities of Liège and Vienna. On his return to Palestine in 1924, he joined *Ha-Poʿel ha-Ẓaʿir, but his views gradually underwent a change to extreme opposition to both communism and socialism. In 1928 he joined the *Revisionists and advocated active opposition to the Mandatory government. He was the first to organize illegal public action in Palestine, and as a result was arrested several times from 1930 onward. When Chaim *Arlosoroff was murdered in June 1933, Aḥimeir was accused of plotting the murder, an accusation which he vehemently denied. After spending a year in prison, he was cleared by a court of appeals before defense witnesses had been called. He was nevertheless detained in prison, charged with organizing Berit ha-Biryonim, an underground group formed for the purpose of fighting British policy in Palestine, and sentenced to a further 18 months' imprisonment. Aḥimeir's views contributed to the ideological basis of the *Irgun Ẓevaʾi Leʾummi and *Loḥamei Ḥerut Israel underground movements. He wrote numerous articles, many of them violently polemical. His impressions of prison life appeared as a book, with the punning title *Reportazhah shel Baḥur "Yeshivah"* ("Report by an Inmate," 1946). His views on the problems of Judaism and Zionism are set down in *Im Keriʾat ha-Gever* ("When the Cock Crows," 1958) and *Judaica* (Heb., 1961). After Aḥimeir's death a committee was formed to publish his works under the title *Ketavim Nivḥarim* ("Selected Works").

AHIMELECH (Heb. אֲחִימֶלֶךְ; "[the divine] brother is king" or "the Melech [deity] is my brother"), name of three biblical figures.

(1) Ahimelech, son of Ahitub, was a member of the priestly family of *Eli, who served in the Temple of *Nob (I Sam. 21–22). Ahimelech has been identified with *Ahijah, son of Ahitub, who is also mentioned in the time of Saul and who acted as a priest in Saul's war with the Philistines (14:3, 18). Ahimelech probably founded the Temple of Nob after the destruction of *Shiloh by the Philistines in the time of Samuel. He served as the high priest in Nob, and "85 persons that wear linen ephods" were under his charge (22:16–18).

When David escaped from Saul, he first came to Nob where Ahimelech provided him with bread and with the sword of Goliath, which was kept in the Temple (21:1–10, 22:10–15). *Doeg the Edomite informed Saul about it and stated that Ahimelech "inquired of the Lord" for David (22:10), for which Ahimelech (22:15) excused himself by pointing out that it was not the first time, for he had always understood that David was Saul's trusted revenger. Saul, however, put to death Ahimelech and the rest of the priests of Nob. One son of Ahimelech, *Abiathar, escaped and joined David.

(2) Ahimelech, son of Abiathar, was probably the grandson of the former. He is mentioned as a priest, together with Ẓadok, son of Ahitub, in one of the lists of David's officials (II Sam. 8:17). In a parallel list he is called Abimelech (I Chron. 18:16; possibly a scribal error, as testified by some Mss. of the MT, as well as by the Vulg.). In the lists of David's officials in II Samuel 20:25, and I Chronicles 26:24, as well as in the historical narratives, only Abiathar and Zadok are mentioned as high priests. Therefore, scholars doubted the historicity of Ahimelech and emended the text in II Samuel 8:17 to read "Ẓadok and Abiathar son of Ahimelech son of Ahitub."

(3) Ahimelech the Hittite was one of the men who joined David when David fled from Saul (I Sam. 26:6). He was probably one of David's warriors, as he is mentioned with *Abishai b. Zeruiah. Ahimelech was only one of many foreigners who attached themselves to David, although most of the others joined David after he was made king.

[Yuval Kamrat]

In the *Aggadah*

Ahimelech would not allow David to partake of the sanctified shewbread, until David pleaded that he was in danger of starvation (Men. 95b). The dispute between Ahimelech and Saul (I Sam. 22:12–19) was based on Ahimelech's action in consulting the Urim and Thummim on David's behalf. Saul maintained that it was a capital offense, since it was a privilege reserved for the king, while Ahimelech maintained that, when affairs of state were involved, the privilege was a universal one, and certainly applied to David, in his position as a general of the army. Abner and Amasa supported Ahimelech's argument, but Doeg did not, and Saul therefore placed upon him the task of killing Ahimelech (Yal. 131).

BIBLIOGRAPHY: (1) Yeivin, in: *Sefer Dinaburg* (1949), 30ff.; W.W.S. von Baudissin, *Kyrios als ottesname*, 3 (1929), 97ff.; Albright, Arch Rel, 202; (2) Moehlenbrink, in: ZAW, 52 (1934), 204–5; Rowley, in: JBL, 58 (1939), 113ff.; (3) Maisler, Untersuchungen, 78.

AHITHOPHEL (Heb. אֲחִיתֹפֶל) **THE GILONITE** (i.e., of the Judean town of Giloh), adviser of King *David (II Sam. 15:12; I Chron. 27:33–34): "Now, in those days, advice from Ahithophel was like an oracle from God" (II Sam. 16:23). Ahithophel was the only one of David's inner council who joined *Absalom in his revolt against his father (15:12). His defection was a source of great anxiety to David (15:31), and prompted him to charge *Hushai the Archite with counteracting Ahithophel's counsel (15:34; 16:15ff.). On Ahithophel's advice Absalom took possession of David's concubines, thus demonstrating that the breach between him and his father was final (16:21). Ahithophel further proposed that he himself should pick 12,000 men and pursue David so as to overwhelm him at the nadir of his strength (17:1–3). Hushai, however, persuaded Absalom to muster a vast army before attempting to battle with such formidable adversaries as David and his professional warriors. Ahithophel, realizing that the respite afforded to David would be fatal to Absalom and his supporters, returned home and committed suicide (17:23).

A juxtaposition of II Samuel 11:3 and 23:34 suggests that Bath-Sheba, the wife of Uriah, whom David debauched, was a granddaughter of Ahithophel. This act of David could thus be the motive for Ahithophel's defection (cf. Sanh. 101b).

The meaning of the name is doubtful. It may be a theophoric combination, the *ophel* ("folly") being a pejorative substitute for the name of a Canaanite god (see *Euphemism); but in Deuteronomy 1:1, it is the name of a place (Tophel).

[Jacob Elbaum]

In the *Aggadah*

The rabbis rank Ahithophel and Balaam as the two greatest sages, the former of Israel and the latter of the Gentiles. Both, however, died in dishonor because of their lack of humility and of gratitude to God for the divine gift of wisdom (Num. R. 22:7). Ahithophel's inciting of Absalom to rebel against his father, King David, was in order to gain the throne himself, since he mistakenly regarded prophecies of royal destiny concerning his granddaughter, Bath-Sheba, to apply to himself (Sanh. 101b). The name of "Ahithophel" is interpreted as "brother of prayer" (Heb. *aḥi tefillah*), referring to the fact that he composed three new prayers daily (TJ Ber. 4:3, 8a). Socrates was said to have been his disciple (Moses Isserles, *Torat ha-Olah* 1:11, quoting an old source). He was 33 years old when he took his life, and he was one of those who have no share in the world to come (Sanh. 10:2).

BIBLIOGRAPHY: S. Yeivin, *Meḥkarim be-Toledot Yisrael ve-Arẓo* (1950), 201–2; Noth, Personennamen, index; Bright, Hist, 188; Ginzberg, Legends, 4 (1913), 94–97. **ADD. BIBLIOGRAPHY:** D. Daube, in: VT, 48 (1998), 315–25.

AHITUB (Heb. אֲחִיטוּב, אֲחִטוּב; "the [my] (divine) brother is good"), priest, son of Phinehas, the son of *Eli; brother of Ichabod and father of Ahimelech and Ahijah, who lived during Saul's reign (I Sam. 14:3; 22:9, 11–12, 20). The Bible gives no details about Ahitub, and it is not clear whether he survived the destruction of Shiloh and continued to officiate as priest or died together with his family in the war against the Philistines (cf. Ps. 78:64). Some scholars assume that Ahitub settled in Nob, made it a priestly town, and officiated there over 85 priests (I Sam. 22:18) until his son *Ahimelech succeeded him. In II Samuel 8:17 and I Chronicles 18:16 he is named as father of *Zadok, but this may be an attempt to link the priestly Zadokite line with the legitimate Aaronide line of Shiloh (cf. I Chron. 5:33–34; 6:37–38). It is doubtful, however, whether the Ahitub mentioned in the line of priests (*ibid.* 5:37–38; 9:11) refers to the same man. In the last cited verse he is called "the ruler [*nagid*] of the House of God."

The name Aḥtb is found in an ancient Egyptian inscription (12–18 dynasties); Aḫūṭāb and Aḫūṭābū appear in Akkadian; and Ahūṭab on an Elephantine ostracon.

BIBLIOGRAPHY: de Vaux, Anc Isr, 127–8, 372–5; Yeivin, in: *Sefer Dinaburg* (1949), 45ff.; EM, 1 (1965), 215–6 (incl. bibl.). **ADD. BIBLIOGRAPHY:** S. Japhet, *I & II Chronicles* (1993), 351–52.

AHITUB BEN ISAAC (late 13th century), rabbi and physician in Palermo. Ahitub's father was a rabbi and physician; his brother David was a physician. He became known while still a young man for his philosophic and scientific learning. When the kabbalist Abraham *Abulafia went to Sicily to win adherents for his teaching, Solomon b. Abraham *Adret of Barcelona communicated with Ahitub in order to enlist his support in his controversy against Abulafia.

Ahitub was the author of *Maḥberet ha-Tene*, a poem resembling the *Maḥberet ha-Tofet ve ha-Eden* of *Immanuel of Rome. In this allegorical work he describes his journey to Paradise where he went to discover the right way of life. There he enjoyed the food of the blessed, and when he returned to earth he brought with him some of the waters of Paradise. These he used to water his garden which then yielded delicious fruits. The first of these he placed in a basket (*tene*), consecrated them to God, and then offered the fruits to anyone who wished to taste them. The number of these fruits was 13, representing the 13 *Articles of Faith. Ahitub's work was incorporated in the *Sefer ha-Tadir* of Moses b. Jekuthiel de Rossi who added a *piyyut* on the articles of faith. This *piyyut* was published twice (A. Freimann, in ZHB, 10 (1906), 172; Hirschfeld, in JQR, 5 (1914/15), 540).

Ahitub also translated Maimonides' *Treatise on Logic* from the Arabic into Hebrew. This translation was still known in the 16th century, and its variant readings were recorded in the margins of some copies of the first edition of another Hebrew translation of the work, this one by Moses ibn *Tibbon. Ahitub's translation was forgotten until a manuscript of it was found and published by Chamizer. An edition of the translation appears in Maimonides' *Treatise on Logic* (ed. by I. Efros (1938), 67–100; cf. Eng. section, 8–9ff.).

BIBLIOGRAPHY: Zunz, Gesch, 515–6; Guedemann, Gesch Erz, 2 (1888), 202–3; Kaufmann, Schriften, 2 (1915), 236; ZHB, 10 (1906), 95, 171–5; 11 (1907), 159; Margoliouth, Cat, 3 (1965), 394; Chamizer, in: *Judaica, Festschrift zu Hermann Cohens 70 Geburtstag* (1912), 423–56; JQR, 5 (1914/15), 532–3, 540; 7 (1916/17), 128; 11 (1920/21), 309–11; Schirmann, in: YMḤSI, 1 (1933), 123–47; J. Klatzkin, *Oẓar ha-Munaḥim…*, 1 (1926), 107–8.

[Umberto (Moses David) Cassuto]

AHLAB (Heb. אַחְלָב), Canaanite city allotted to the tribe of Asher, which, however, was unable to conquer it at the beginning of the Israelite settlement (Judg. 1:31). This is apparently the same city of Asher which appears in the form *me-Ḥevel* (מֵחֶבֶל; "from Hebel"; Josh. 19:29). According to the Septuagint, this form is an error for Meheleb and it is mentioned as Maḥalliba in Sennacherib's account of his campaign in 701 B.C.E. between Zarephath (Zaribtu) and Ushu (mainland Tyre). Ahlab is identified with Khirbet el-Maḥalib, on the Lebanese coast, 3½ mi. (6 km.) north of Tyre and approximately 1 mi. (2 km.) south of the mouth of the Litani River.

BIBLIOGRAPHY: EM, s.v.; Abel, Geog, 2 (1938), 67, 384; Pritchard, Texts, 287; Aharoni, Land, index.

[Yohanan Aharoni]

AHL AL-KITĀB (Ar. "The People of the Book"), name of the Jews, Christians, and Sabeans (al Ṣābdʾa) in the Koran (Sura 3:110; 4:152; et al.) because they possess a *kitāb*, i.e., a holy book containing a revelation of God's word. Pre-Islamic Arabic poetry refers to Jewish and Christian Scripture. It especially dwells on the *Zabūr*, a holy book – whose origin is from the word *mizmor* ("psalm") – which Muhammad knew as given to David (Sura 17:15), i.e., the Book of Psalms. Muhammad frequently mentions the *tawrā* (the Torah, possibly the entire Bible) revealed to the Israelites (e.g., Sura 3:58, 87; 48:29) which contains clear allusions to Muhammad's appearance (Sura 7:156; 33:44; 48:4). He also is acquainted with the *Injīl* (Evangelium, the Gospels), a term which covers the entire New Testament. Muhammad emphasizes that the *Injīl* confirms the statements of the Torah (Sura 5:50; cf. 48:29; 57:27). He does not specify the holy book of the Sabeans although he mentions them three times in the Koran (Sura 2:59; 5:72; 22:17), along with the Jews and the Christians, and promises them their part in salvation. According to the Arabs, Muhammad meant the Mandeans, a Judeo-Christian sect whose believers lived in Babylonia. In the early period of his mission, Muhammad related positively to the *Ahl al-Kitāb* and their teachings. But his attitude changed as a result of the disappointment in his hope of persuading them to accept his faith. Then Muhammad accused them of intentionally falsifying the Torah or at least distorting its interpretation (Sura 2:70; 3:64, 72, 73; cf. 5:16; 6:91). Despite this, Muhammad determined that the *Ahl al-Kitāb*, as the authors of holy books, deserve special treatment, and because they had agreed to pay the *jizya* ("poll tax"), the command to fight against them was not enforced (Sura 9:29). Since the *Ahl al-Kitāb* fulfilled this condition, they became the *Ahl al-Dhimma* ("protected people"; see *Dhimmī). In a later period this position caused the *Ḥarrān* ("star worshipers") who called themselves Sabeans and the Persians, who believed in Zoroastrianism and relied on their holy book, to merit inclusion in the term *Ahl al-Kitāb*.

As a result of their belief in the books of divine revelation, the *Ahl al-Kitāb* enjoyed a favored status in Islam. A Muslim is permitted to intermarry with their women and to eat what they have slaughtered. On the other hand, the accusations of Muhammad as to falsifications of Scripture and distorted interpretations caused the creation of an extensive polemical literature and disputations which at times actually poisoned the relations between the adherents of the different religions.

BIBLIOGRAPHY: M. Steinschneider, *Polemische und apologetische Literatur in Arabischer Sprache* (1877), 320–9; M. Perlmann, in: JQR, 37 (1940/41), 171–91; H. Lammens, *L'Islam, croyances et institutions* (1941), 28–31; H.Z. Hirschberg, *Yisrael ba-Arav* (1946), 114–5; E. Strauss, in: *Sefer ha-Zikaron le-Veit ha-Midrash le-Rabbanim be-Vina* (1946), 182–97; P.K. Hitti, *History of the Arabs* (1960), 143–4, 233. **ADD. BIBLIOGRAPHY:** G. Vajda, in: EIS², 1, 264–66 (incl. bibl.).

[Haim Z'ew Hirschberg]

AHLEM, village near Hanover, known for its Jewish horticultural school, the first of its type in Germany. The school was founded in 1893 by the Jewish philanthropist Moritz Alexander Simon and was open to all suitable Jewish applicants, regardless of ideological affiliation. It trained hundreds of Jewish youths as agriculturalists and skilled workers. The three-year curriculum included agricultural subjects, especially horticulture, in addition to general subjects taught in secondary schools. On its foundation boys from the age of 14 were admitted; from 1903 to the 1920s girls over 16 were accepted for vocational training and home economics, and subsequently horticulture. A boarding school and elementary school for children between the ages of eight and 13 were added. In 1933 the number of pupils totaled approximately 50, but increased to 120 between 1936 and 1938. The school was authorized by the Nazis as a center for vocational training for Jewish youth intending to emigrate and was permitted to issue graduation certificates. Between 1933 and 1939 about 300 pupils graduated from Ahlem, and some of them emigrated to Ereẓ Israel. Even before the closure of the school in July 1942, Ahlem was made an assembly point for the deportation of Jews by the Gestapo. Between December 1941 and February 1945, more than 2,400 Jews of the Hanover and Halberstadt region were deported from Ahlem to Riga, Theresienstadt, Warsaw, and Auschwitz. For a short time, the tradition of the *Gartenbauschule* was revived and a kibbutz was established by Holocaust survivors in Ahlem in 1945.

ADD. BIBLIOGRAPHY: F. Homeyer, *Beitrag zur Geschichte der Gartenbauschule Ahlem 1893–1979* (1980).

[Mordechai Eliav / Stefan Rohrbacher (2nd ed.)]

°**AHLWARDT, HERMANN** (1846–1914), German publicist and antisemitic politician. In 1893, when headmaster of a primary school in Berlin, Ahlwardt was dismissed for embezzling money collected from the pupils. He made antisemitism his profession and used it as a political springboard. His first work, *Der Verzweiflungskampf der arischen Voelker mit dem Judentum* ("The Last Stand of the Aryan Peoples against Judaism," 1890–92), described an alleged Jewish world conspiracy. Its second part, "The Oath of a Jew" (*Der Eid eines Judens*), included slander against G. von *Bleichroeder, a leading Jewish banker. Prosecution followed and Ahlwardt was sentenced to four months' imprisonment. He was hardly out of prison when he published another defamatory leaflet *Judenflinten* ("Jewish Rifles"), claiming that the guns supplied to the German Army by a Jewish manufacturer were defective. However, Ahlwardt was saved from serving a second sentence by parliamentary immunity, as he had been elected in 1892 to the Reichstag as member for Arnswalde-Friedeberg (Brandenburg) on the platform propounded to the peasants there that their misery was due to "the Jews and the Junkers." His pamphlets (no less than ten of which appeared in 1892) were assisted by the press and Roman Catholic clergy, with the result that antisemitic rioting, the burning of the synagogue at Neustettin, and the revival of ritual murder accusations ensued. To the embarrassment of his own party, the Conservatives, Ahlwardt occupied the time of the Reichstag with his slanderous "revelations" about the Jews. He continued to hold his seat there until the Reichstag was dissolved in 1893 when he was immediately imprisoned for libel. In spite of this and the opposition of the Conservatives he was reelected by the same constituencies and held his seat until 1902. He was sentenced for blackmail in 1909 and died unnoticed.

ADD. BIBLIOGRAPHY: P. Pulzer, *The Rise of Political Anti-Semitism in Germany and Austria* (1988²); C. Jahr, in: LBIYB, 48 (2003), 67–85.

AHMADNAGAR, capital of the former kingdom of the Niẓām Shah dynasty on the west coast of India. Under Burhān Niẓām Shah I (1510–53), a Shi'a Muslim, it became a center of Hindu-Muslim culture and learning. Among the scholars attracted to his court and enjoying its atmosphere of complete religious tolerance were some Marranos from Portugal, including Sancho Pirez, who became a favorite of the king and was a friend of Garcia *d'Orta. Garcia refers in his *Colloquia* (no. 26) to "Jews in the territory of Nizamuluco [Niẓām Shah]." A Jewish settlement also existed in the port of the kingdom, Chaul (now Revanda).

BIBLIOGRAPHY: R. Shyam, *Kingdom of Ahmadnagar* (1966).

[Walter Joseph Fischel]

AḤOT KETANNAH (Heb. אָחוֹת קְטַנָּה; "Little Sister"), name of a hymn for Rosh Ha-Shanah. It was composed by Abraham Ḥazzan Gerondi, a writer of devotional hymns, who flourished about the middle of the 13th century in southern France. The poem consists of eight metrical stanzas of four to five lines, each ending with the refrain *Tikhleh shanah ve-kileloteha* ("May this year with its curses end"). The last stanza ends *Taḥel shanah u-virekhoteha* ("May the year and its blessings begin"). The acrostic gives the name of the author "Abram Ḥazzan." The opening words of the hymn are taken from Song of Songs 8:8 "We have a little sister" and refer to the traditional allegorical interpretation of the Song of Songs. The poem evokes Israel's sufferings in exile and implores God's mercy "to fortify the song of the daughter and to strengthen her longing to be close to her lover." At first adopted into the Sephardi ritual, where it is recited before the evening prayer of Rosh Ha-Shanah, the poem was subsequently adopted in the Ashkenazi and Yemenite rites, especially in kabbalistic circles.

[Meir Ydit]

Music

Aḥot Ketannah is sung either by the entire congregation, or by the cantor alone with the congregation joining in the refrain. The melody is uniform throughout the Sephardi Diaspora, with only slight local variations, and may therefore belong to the common pre-expulsion stock. Notated examples may be found in Idelsohn, Melodien, 1, no. 93; 2, no. 48 (mus. ex. 1); 3, nos. 43, 46, 175; 4, nos. 185, 186 (mus. ex. 2), 187, 192; 5, no. 159; Levy, Antologia, 2, nos. 93–101; F. Consolo, *Sefer Shirei Yis-*

rael (1890), 125; E. Aguilar and D.A. de Sola, *Sephardi Melodies* (1857, 1931), no. 26; O. Camhy, *Liturgie Sepharadie* (1959), nos. 63, 64; Cremieu, J.S. and M., *Chants hébraïques... de l'ancien Comtat Venaissin* (1885), no. 1.

[Avigdor Herzog]

BIBLIOGRAPHY: Zunz, Lit Poesie, 140.

AHRWEILER (Heb. ארווילרא), small German town near Bonn. There was a considerable Jewish community in Ahrweiler in the 13th century, some of its members owning houses in Cologne. In the 14th century the Jews of Ahrweiler dealt in salt and wine. The community suffered during the *Black Death massacres of 1348. The physician and exegete Baruch b. Samson ("Meister Bendel") lived in Ahrweiler in the 15th century. Among the rabbis of Ahrweiler were Ḥayyim b. Johanan Treves (d. 1598), who also officiated as **Landrabbiner* for the territory of the Electorate of Cologne, and his son-in-law Isaac b. Ḥayyim. A notable family which adopted the name "Ahrweiler" included among its members the Frankfurt *dayyan* Hirz Ahrweiler (d. 1679) and his son Mattathias, rabbi of Heidelberg (d. 1729). The small Ahrweiler community of modern times numbered only 4 Jews in 1808; 28 in 1849; 65 in 1900 (1% of the total population); and 31 in 1933. It maintained a cemetery and synagogue built in 1894. The synagogue was burned and desecrated on **Kristallnacht* (Nov. 9–10, 1938); the last Jews were deported from Ahrweiler in July 1942.

BIBLIOGRAPHY: Salfeld, Martyrol, 273, 287; Germ Jud, 2 (1968), 3–4. **ADD. BIBLIOGRAPHY:** H. Warnecke, *Die Ahrweiler Synagoge. Ein Beispiel jüdisch-deutscher Geschichte im 19. und 20. Jahrhundert* (1983); B. Klein, in: F.G. Zehnder (ed.), *Hirt und Herde. Religiosität und Frömmigkeit im Rheinland des 18. Jahrhunderts* (2000), 251–78.

AHWAZ, capital of the Persian province of Khuzistan. Ahwaz was called Be-Ḥozai in the Talmud (Ta'an. 23; Pes. 50; Gitt. 89; Ḥull 95). Several *amoraim* originated from the city, including R. Aḥa, R. Ḥanina, and R. Avram Ḥoza'ah. As a junction between Babylonia and Persia, Ahwaz was an important medieval center for the eastern trade, with a flourishing Jewish population. Two Jews in the service of Caliph al-Muqtadir, Joseph b. Phinehas and Aaron b. Amram, were tax farmers for the province, owning real estate and a bazaar there which yielded a considerable income. They rose to the position of court bankers. The revenue from Ahwaz province is mentioned as security for a large loan they advanced to the government. Ahwaz remained a center of Jewish commercial activities throughout the Middle Ages, as attested by correspondence between Jewish merchants in Ahwaz with associates in *Fez and *Cairo. One of the earliest indications that Jewish merchants in Khuzistan used the Persian language is a Judeo-Persian law report, dated around 1021, found near Ahwaz.

As in *Abadan, Ahwaz became one of the first centers of Zionist activitiy in Iran beginning with the occupation of the southern region by the British Army (Sept. 1941). During this period there were 300 Jews in Ahwaz, constituting 70 families, many of them immigrants from Iraq and from other cities like *Isfahan, *Shiraz, *Kashan, Arak, and *Kermanshah. The majority were merchants, mainly in the textile trade. There were five wealthy families in Ahwaz; the rest belonged to the middle class. There were two synagogues, one belonging to Jews of Iraqi origin and the other to Persian-speaking Jews. After 1948, many Jews immigrated to Israel and to *Teheran. The majority of the Jews of Ahwaz left the city after the Islamic Revolution (1979). At the beginning of the 21st century, there were fewer than five families living there.

BIBLIOGRAPHY: Fischel, Islam, index; S.D. Goitein, *A Mediterranean Society*, 1 (1967), index. **ADD. BIBLIOGRAPHY:** *Alam-e Yahud*, 16 (Nov. 20, 1945), 285; ibid., 22 (Jan. 15, 1946), 379; B.-Z. Eshel, *Yishuvei ha-Yehudim be-Babel be-Tekufat ha-Talmud* (1979), 58–59; A. Netzer, "*Yahudiyānei Iran dar avāset-e qarn-e bistom*," in: *Shofar*, 244 (June 2001), 23.

[Walter Joseph Fischel / Amnon Netzer (2nd ed.)]

AI or **HA-AI** (עַי, הָעַי; in the Samaritan version of Gen. 12:15 called Ayna; in Jos., Ant. 5:35 – Naian), place in Ereẓ Israel. It is mentioned together with Beth-El as near the site where Abraham pitched his tent (Gen. 12:8; 13:3). In Joshua 7:2, it is located beside Beth-Aven, east of Beth-El. Ai was the second Canaanite city which Joshua attacked (Josh. 7–8). After the first attempt to capture the city had miscarried because of the sin of *Achan, the king of Ai and his army were defeated in an ambush and the city was left in ruins (see also Josh. 12:9). Although the old site of Ai remained abandoned, an Israelite city with a similar name arose nearby. Isaiah mentioned Aiath (עַיָּת – Isa. 10:28) as the first of the cities occupied by the Assyrians in their march on Jerusalem, before Michmas and Geba. In the post-Exilic period, returnees from Ai are mentioned together with people from Beth-El (Ezra 2:28; Neh. 7:32) and Aijah (עַיָּה) appears as a city of Benjamin (Neh. 11:31). Most scholars identify the ancient city with et-Tell near Deir Dibwan, c. 1 mi. (2 km.) southwest of Beth-El. Excavations at the site carried out in 1933–35 by Judith Marquet-Krause were renewed in 1964 by J.A. Callaway. The city was found to have been inhabited in the Early Bronze Age from c. 3000 B.C.E. Several massive stone walls were discovered as well as a sanctuary containing sacrificial objects and a palace with a large hall, the roof of which was supported by wooden pillars on stone bases. The city was destroyed not later than in the 24th century B.C.E. and remained in ruins until the 13th or 12th century B.C.E. when a small short-lived Israelite village was established there. This discovery indicates that in the time of Joshua, the site was a waste (also implied by the name Ai, literally, "ruin"). Scholars explain the discrepancy in various ways. Some consider the narrative of the conquest of Ai contained in the book of Joshua an etiological story that developed in order to explain the ancient ruins of the city and its fortifications. Others assume that the story of Ai was confused with that of nearby Beth-El which evidently was captured during the 13th century. Others dispute the identification without, however, being able to propose another suitable site. Khirbet Ḥaiyan,

c. 1 mi. (2 km.) south of et-Tell, has been suggested as the site of the later city; the only pottery found there, however, dates from the Roman and later periods.

BIBLIOGRAPHY: J. Marquet-Krause, *Les fouilles de'Ay (et-Tell)* (1949); Vincent, in: RB, 46 (1937), 231ff.; Albright, in: AASOR, 4 (1924), 141–9; idem, in: BASOR, 74 (1939), 15ff.; Abel, Geog, 2 (1938), 239–40; Aharoni, Land index; U. Cassuto, *Commentary on the Book of Genesis*, 2 (1964), 331–2; M. Noth, in: PJB, 31 (1935), 7–29; J.M. Grintz, in: *Sinai*, 21 (1947), 219ff.; J.A. Callaway, in: BASOR, 178 (1965), 13–40; J.A. Callaway and H.B. Nicol, *ibid.*, 183 (1966), 12–19. **ADD. BIBLIOGRAPHY:** A. Ben-Tor (ed.), *The Archaeology of Ancient Israel* (1992), index.

[Michael Avi-Yonah]

AIBU

(1) Babylonian sage who flourished in the transitional period from the *tannaim* to the *amoraim* (late second – early third century C.E.). The father of *Rav and the brother of Ḥiyya (Pes. 4a; Sanh. 5a), he studied in Ereẓ Israel, where he frequently visited Eleazar b. Zadok, whose customs and halakhic decisions he quotes (Suk. 44b).

(2) The son of Rav, who told him "I have labored with you in *halakhah*, but without success. Come and I will teach you worldly wisdom" (Pes. 113a).

(3) The grandson of Rav (Suk. 44b), and a frequent visitor to his home.

(4) *Amora* and prominent aggadist (late third – early fourth century C.E.). While he transmitted some halakhic statements in the name of Yannai (Ket. 54b; Kid. 19a; et al.), he was mainly interested in *aggadah*, quoting the aggadic interpretations of *tannaim* and *amoraim* such as R. Meir (Mid. Ps. 101, end), R. Eliezer b. R. Yose ha-Gelili (Tanḥ. B., No'aḥ, 24, 53), and R. Johanan (Gen. R. 82, 5). His aggadic comments, popular among homilists, were frequently quoted by them, especially by R. Yudan b. Simeon (*ibid.*, 73:3; Mid. Ps. 24:11; et al.), R. Huna, R. Phinehas, and R. Berechiah. One of his aggadic maxims is "No man departs from this world with half his desires realized. If he has a hundred, he wants two hundred, and if he has two hundred, he wants four hundred" (Eccl. R. 1:13).

BIBLIOGRAPHY: Bacher, Pal Amor; Hyman, Toledot, 138.

[Zvi Kaplan]

AICHINGER, ILSE (1921–), Austrian writer and lyricist, and author of radio plays. One of twin daughters born to a Jewish physician and a teacher, Aichinger spent her childhood in Linz and after the early divorce of her parents moved to Vienna. There she and her maternal relatives were confronted with the persecution of the Nazi regime. In her first publication, *Aufruf zum Mißtrauen* (1946), she cautioned against what she perceived to be a new and dangerous self-confidence in Austria after the collapse of Nazi rule. At an early age, she had expressed an interest in studying medicine, but she was unable to do so because of the Nuremberg Laws. At the end of World War II, she was able to pursue her interest in medicine, but dropped out of university in 1948 to complete her first novel, *Die groessere Hoffnung* (1948). The novel explores the angst and suffering of both the Jews and their pursuers during the Third Reich. The text reflects Aichinger's commitment to the weak and skepticism about the German language. After 1950, she was employed as a reader at the S. Fischer publishing house. In 1953 she married Guenter Eich, whom she had met at a conference of the "Gruppe 47," where she received an award for her *Spiegelgeschichte*. This is a piece of literary prose that narrates a reversed life with the attempt to unlearn everything including language and thus postulating silence. Aichinger's collection of narratives *Rede unter dem Galgen* was also published in 1953. In these narratives she examines a range of human emotions, including angst, alienation, paradox, and ambivalence. Aichingers lyric and narrative texts increasingly show the reduction of linguistic means focusing on subjectivity, thereby blending reality and dream, inner and outer world. Examples of these themes can be found in *Eliza Eliza* (1965), *Schlechte Woerter* (1976), *Verschenkter Rat* (1978) or *Kleist, Moos, Fasane* (1984). Aichinger also published a number of radio plays, including *Knoepfe* (1953), *Besuch im Pfarrhaus* (1962), *Auckland* (1970), and the radio dialog *Belvedere* (1995). These radio plays illustrate existential borderline experiences between assimilation and resistance. A later publication is *Film und Verhaengnis: Blitzlichter auf ein Leben* (2001), notes on films and photography which turn a spotlight on the cultural life of Vienna between 1921 and 1945.

Aichinger's awards over the years include the Nelly Sachs-Preis, the Georg Trakl-Preis, the Franz Kafka-Preis, and the Joseph-Breitbach-Preis. She was a member of the Deutsche Akademie fuerr Sprache und Dichtung, the Akademie der Kuenste Berlin, and the Bayerische Akademie der Schoenen Künste.

BIBLIOGRAPHY: B. Thums, *"Den Ankuenften nicht glauben wahr sind die Abschiede": Mythos, Gedaechtnis und Mystik in der Prosa Ilse Aichingers* (2000); K. Bartsch, *Ilse Aichinger* (1993); S. Moser, *Ilse Aichinger. Leben und Werk* (1990); G. Lindemann, *Ilse Aichinger* (1988); D. Lorenz, *Ilse Aichinger* (1981).

[Ann-Kristin Koch (2nd ed.)]

AIJALON (Ayyalon) (Heb. אַיָּלוֹן; "place of deer"). (1) City situated in a broad valley (valley of Aijalon) which is one of the approaches to the Judean Hills. Volcanic activity occurring in the area in the latest geological period left some basalt traces and the hot springs found at *Emmaus in ancient times. Potsherds found on a large tell, about 3 mi. (5 km.) north of Bab-al-Wad, show continuous occupation from the Late Bronze Age onward. The village of Yalu is built on the tell.

The El-Amarna letters indicate that the region was included within the kingdom of Gezer in the 15th and 14th centuries, B.C.E. This kingdom was on hostile terms with Jerusalem, whose ruler Puti-Hepa complained that his caravans were being robbed in the valley of Aijalon ("Yaluna," EA, 287). In a letter to Amenhotep IV (EA, 273), the queen of the city of Zaphon (?) reports that the Habiru attacked the two sons of Milkilu, king of Gezer, in Ayaluna (Aijalon) and in Ṣarha

(Zorah). Joshua referred to the valley of Aijalon in connection with his defeat of the Amorites. Joshua asked for a miracle to prevent the sun from setting so that the Israelites could avenge themselves on the Amorites. Joshua said: "Sun, stand thou still upon Gibeon; and thou, Moon, in the valley of Aijalon" (Josh. 10:12). The city is included in the tribal area of Dan (Josh. 19:42) and in the list of levitical cities (Josh. 21:24; I Chron. 6:54), but the Danites were unable to subject the Amorites, and later the region came under the influence of the "house of Joseph" (Ephraim; Judg. 1:34–35). The valley became a field of battle between the tribes of Dan, Ephraim, Judah, and Benjamin on the one side and the Amorites and Philistines on the other (I Chron. 7:21; 8:6). The region was finally conquered by the Israelites under David. Aijalon is included in Solomon's second administrative district under "the son of Deker" (I Kings 4:9). With the division of the kingdom, the valley remained within the kingdom of Judah, in the territory of Benjamin, and Rehoboam fortified it as part of his defense system of Jerusalem (II Chron. 11:10). It is mentioned in the list of cities (no. 26) captured by Shishak, king of Egypt, in about 924 B.C.E. and the Philistines also captured it during the reign of Ahaz but held it only briefly (II Chron. 28:18). There is no reference to Aijalon during the Second Temple period. The valley was located on the route taken by Cestius Gallus, the governor of Syria, in his campaign against Jerusalem in 66 C.E. (Jos., Wars, 2:513–6). In Byzantine times, Aijalon is mentioned as *Ialo,* a name which is preserved in the present-day Arab village of Yalu.

In 637 C.E., Aijalon was the headquarters of the Arab armies which suffered heavily at Emmaus. The region was badly damaged in an 11th-century earthquake. During the Crusades it was once again a battlefield and a fort was built there by the Crusaders (today *Latrun). It was also a scene of fighting during Allenby's campaign in 1917 and in the War of Independence (1948) a prolonged battle was fought in the region over the roads leading to Jerusalem. After the War of Independence, a few Israeli settlements were established in the region. These were considered border settlements, and during the 1950s they were under terrorist attack. In 1967 the whole area was occupied by the Israel Defense Forces, and the Arab inhabitants fled to Ramallah. In 1976 a large park was established on the deserted land of the Arab villages.

(2) Town in the territory of Zebulun where the judge, Elon, was buried (Judg. 12:12). Its location is unknown.

BIBLIOGRAPHY: G.A. Smith, *Historical Geography of the Holy Land* (1931[25]), 210–14, 250ff.; Abel, Geog, 1 (1933), 399; 2 (1938), 240ff.; Aharoni, Land, index; EM, S.V.

AIKEN, HENRY DAVID (1912–1982), U.S. philosopher. Aiken was born in Portland, Oregon, and taught at the universities of Columbia, Washington, Harvard (1946–65), and Brandeis (1965–80), specializing in ethics, esthetics, and the history of philosophy. He was influenced by the British analytic movement, by the American naturalists – especially Santayana, and by David Hume's moral and political writings, some of which he edited. Among the works he wrote are *The Age of Ideology* (1957), selections including a commentary on 19th-century thought; *Reason and Conduct* (1962), a collection of essays in moral philosophy; and *Predicament of the University* (1971).

[Richard H. Popkin]

AIKHENVALD YULI ISAYEVICH (1872–1928), Russian literary critic and essayist. An opponent of the dominant school of social criticism, he made his name as a major exponent of the subjective, impressionist approach. His works include *Pushkin* (1908), *Etyudy O zapadnykh pisatelyakh* ("Studies of Western Writers," 1910), *Siluety russkikh pisateley* ("Outlines of Russian Writers," 3 vols. (1906–1910)), and *Spor o Belinskom* ("The Belinski Controversy," 1914), an appraisal of Vissarion Belinski, the first Russian to view literary criticism as a molder of public opinion. In 1922 Aikhenvald and a number of other non-communist intellectuals were expelled from the U.S.S.R. He was killed in a streetcar accident in Berlin.

BIBLIOGRAPHY: *Istoriya russkoy kritiki,* 2 (1958), 424–5; G. Struve, *Russkaya literatura v izgnanii* (1956).

[Maurice Friedberg]

AIMÉE, ANOUK (**Françoise Dreyfus**; 1932–), French actress. Starting her film career as a teenager and the daughter of actress Geneviève Sorya, the Paris-born Aimée gained the attention of the French public in 1957 in the film *Les Mauvaises Rencontres*. In Federico Fellini's *La Dolce Vita* (1960), and *8½* (1963), she was cast in roles reflecting modern boredom and world-weariness. She was nominated for an Academy Award as best actress for her part in Lelouch's *A Man and a Woman* (1966). Among her more than 80 films are *Justine* (1969), *The Appointment* (1970), *Salto nel Vuoto* (Cannes Award for Best Actress, 1980), *Un Homme et une Femme: 20 Ans deja* (1986), *Il y a des jours…et des lunes* (1990), and Robert Altman's *Ready to Wear* (1994). She was married to the actor Albert Finney from 1970 to 1978.

[Jonathan Licht]

°**AINSWORTH, HENRY** (1569–1622), English Bible scholar. Ainsworth was educated at Cambridge and already knew Hebrew when, as an adherent of the Brownist sect (later called Congregationalists), he went into exile in Amsterdam. He served there as a teacher (1596–1610) in the independent English Church, and subsequently as its minister. Through Jewish contacts in Amsterdam he improved his Hebrew knowledge, the considerable extent of which is reflected in his writings. These include *Silk or Wool in the High Priest's Ephod…* (London, 1605); an English version, with annotations, of Psalms (Amsterdam, 1612), which was adopted by the Puritans of New England until they produced their own in 1640; and *Annotations* to the Pentateuch, with Psalms and Song of Songs (1616–27). This work, which includes rabbinic material, was translated into Dutch in 1690 and into German in 1692; Song of Songs in English meter in 1623. Ainsworth's *Annotations* were used two and a half centuries later by the revisers of the English Bible. He was considered one of the finest English Hebraists of his time.

ADD. BIBLIOGRAPHY: ODNB online.

[Raphael Loewe]

AISH HATORAH, outreach organization based in Jerusalem, Israel, and housed in a building facing the Western Wall, directly above the plaza. It was founded by American-born rabbi Noah Weinberger in 1974. Weinberger had grown up on Manhattan's Lower East Side, where he was raised in an Orthodox home and was proud of his mother's involvement in the establishment of the Esther Schoenfeld Beth Jacob School for Girls. He saw his mission as fighting assimilation and answering the question, "Why be Jewish?" His strategy involved the use of high technology and powerful and media-savvy business executives and celebrities to help send out his institution's message. It operates 26 full-time branches and offers programs in 80 cities, representing 17 countries on five continents and attended by 100,000 people annually in addition to the 4,500 students who study at Aish Jerusalem every year. Over 175 people have graduated from the rabbinic program and have gone to North America to do outreach work.

Aish Programs

DISCOVERY. A one-day program that explores the rational basis for Jewish belief and practice. More than 100,000 people worldwide have attended the Discovery program. Guest hosts for these seminars have included American entertainers Ed *Asner, Kirk *Douglas, Elliot *Gould, Joel *Grey, and Jason *Alexander. Aish instructors conduct hundreds of related seminars in cities around the world, including Johannesburg, London, Sydney, Melbourne, Santiago, and Jerusalem, as well as in 45 U.S. cities for university campuses, Jewish community centers, and Reform, Conservative, and Orthodox synagogues.

THE EXECUTIVE LEARNING PROGRAM. Successful men and women of all ages participate in individually designed personal study programs in their homes and offices. With limited free time, and often with limited background in Judaism, hundreds of busy executives find a way to fit Torah study into their active lives. Among those who participate are Robert Hormats, vice chairman of Goldman-Sachs International, and Michael Goldstein, CEO of Toys R Us.

THE ISRAEL EXPERIENCE. The 4,500 people participating in Aish Jerusalem programs in Israel attend the Discovery Seminar; the one-month Essentials for men or JEWEL for women; introductory programs; and the Jerusalem Fellowships. The latter was founded in 1985 by senators Daniel Patrick Moynihan and Arlen Spector. The program combines touring Israel, studying Judaism, and meeting Israel's top leadership from across the political spectrum.

EYAHT COLLEGE OF JEWISH STUDIES FOR WOMEN. Rebbetzin Denah Weinberg founded the school in 1990 to empower Jewish women.

THE RUSSIAN PROGRAM. This reaches over 50,000 people in the Former Soviet Union (FSU), plus another 3.5 million viewers through its popular television series. In Moscow, Aish runs the Intellectual Cafe, a bimonthly seminar teaching Talmud to beginners through a logic game. Aish-FSU has four permanent branches, including one accredited college.

In Israel, Aish created a social action organization, AVIV, which provides legal, medical, and social services to aid Russian Jews after they make *aliyah*. Aish has also created a series for Radio Reka, the immigrant radio station that has 200,000 listeners in Israel and one million in Russia.

HIGH TECH AND JERUSALEM FUND MISSIONS TO ISRAEL. The Albert Einstein High Tech Mission brings leaders of hitech industry to Israel to meet their peers and explore potential investments, strategic partnerships, and spirituality in the Holy Land. Companies who have participated include the founders, CEOs, or presidents of AOL, Infospace, Ness, National Semiconductor, Computer Associates, IDT, Drugstore.com, ZDNet, StarTek, Net2Phone, The Red Herring, Draper Fisher Jurvetson, Scient, Disney Internet, Akamai, and ATT.com.

THE THEODOR HERZL MISSION. Co-sponsored with the mayor of Jerusalem, it brings world leaders from across the world to Israel for one week. Participants have included Lady Margaret Thatcher, U.S. senators John Kerry, Harry Reid, and Joseph Biden, former House speaker Newt Gingrich, former U.S. Ambassador to the UN Jeanne Kirkpatrick, Congressman Peter Deutsch, Governors Tom Ridge (PA) and Christine Whitman (NJ), philanthropist Carroll Petrie, Elie Wiesel, Alan Dershowitz, Barry Sternlicht, chairman of Starwood Hotels, the world's largest hotel company, Starbuck's Howard Schultz, and Accuweather president Joel Meyer.

THE CAPITAL CAMPAIGN. Aish HaTorah is building a hitech Jewish education center incorporating state of the art Internet, video, computer, and satellite hook-ups. The Kirk Douglas Theater, dedicated by the Hollywood legend, will present a film about the Jewish contribution to humanity. Aish also acquired several sites in the Old City, projected for use as classrooms, dormitories, and offices.

AISH.COM. With its 1,000,000 hits a year, the site is user-friendly, hi-speed, and full of information and contact numbers about all of its programs.

[Jeanette Friedman (2nd ed.)]

AI T'IEN (b. c. 1545), Chinese Jew through whom detailed knowledge of Chinese Jewry first reached the Western world at the beginning of the 17th century. Ai T'ien was born in *Kaifeng, Honan province, and obtained his licentiate in Chinese classics as a minor school official (*chü-jên*) in 1573. In 1605 he went to Peking to seek employment, which led to his eventual appointment at Yangchow. While in Peking, in June 1605, he visited the Italian Jesuit missionary, Matteo Ricci. Ai gave Ricci a detailed account of his own family and the status of the Jewish community in Kaifeng, as well as the relationship of the Jews with the local Muslims and Nestorian Christians. Ricci came to the conclusion that the community in Kaifeng were of Jewish descent and sent this information in a letter dated July 26, 1605, to the general of the Jesuit order in Rome. This was the first report to reach Europe concerning the existence of Jews in China, and a document of primary importance for Chinese Jewish history.

BIBLIOGRAPHY: W.C. White, Chinese Jews (1966[2]), pt. 1, 11, 31–37; pt. 2, 144; pt. 3, 110–2.

[Rudolf Loewenthal]

AIX-EN-PROVENCE (Heb. אייגש or אייגייש), town in the Bouches-du-Rhône department, southern France. The first reference to the presence of Jews in Aix-en-Provence dates from about 1283. They then owned a synagogue and a cemetery situated at Bourg St.-Saveur, which was under the jurisdiction of the archbishop. In 1299 they contributed to the annual tax paid to the count by the Jews of Provence. The Jewish population in 1341 numbered 1,205 (about 1/11 of the total), occupying 203 houses, mainly on the Rue Verrerie (called Rue de la Juiverie until 1811); not far from there the du Puits-Juif still exists (probably the public well in this street gave rise to the legend that the Jews owned a medicinal spring). A synagogue was situated on the corner of the Rue Vivaut and Rue Verrerie, and another (1354) in the lower town. In 1341 King Robert of Anjou attempted to set up a compulsory Jewish quarter, but notwithstanding repeated injunctions it had evidently failed to materialize by 1403. The community in Aix was administered by at least two syndics. The Jews did not have to pay taxes to the municipality since they contributed to the annual tax paid by the Jews of Provence to the crown. The contributions of Aix Jewry amounted to 16% of the total in 1420, and to over 25% in 1446.

By letters patent of Sept. 25, 1435, Jews were prohibited from practicing brokerage, and were obliged to wear the Jewish *badge. These restrictions followed the anti-Jewish riots, which had taken place in 1430, when nine Jews were killed, many were injured and 74 were forcefully baptized. A general amnesty was subsequently granted to the inhabitants of Aix. The position of the Jews in Aix was ameliorated when, in 1454 King René of Anjou allowed them to employ Christian servants, reduced the size of the badge, and exempted Jews from wearing it while traveling.

When in 1481 Provence passed to France, Louis XI confirmed the privileges formerly enjoyed by the Jews of Aix and Marseilles. Aix Jewry again suffered disaster, however, when on May 10, 1484, they were attacked by bands of marauders from the Dauphiné and Auvergne and the highlands of Provence. The raids were repeated intermittently until 1486. In that year, the Aix municipality asked Charles VIII to expel the Jews. The general decree of expulsion, issued in 1498, became effective in 1501. The Parliament of Provence reissued the prohibition on Jews settling in Aix in 1760, 1768, and 1787.

In cultural matters, the Aix community took a prominent part in the *Maimonidean controversy that divided Jewish scholars. The Jews of Aix were mentioned by the Provencal poet Isaac b. Abraham ha-Gorni who criticized them for their inhospitable attitude toward strangers.

Shortly after 1789 nine Jewish families from Avignon settled in Aix-en-Provence. The Jewish population numbered 169 in 1809 and 258 in 1872 (out of a total population of 29,000), dwindling to 214 in 1900. In the mid-19th century Aix was the center in which the former traditions of the *Comtat Venaissin communities were most faithfully preserved, largely through the activities of members of the *Milhaud and *Crémieux families. In 1829, the Hebrew book by Moses Crémieux *Ho'il Moshe Be'er* was printed in Aix by François Gigia.

The census conducted by the Vichy government in May 1941 recorded 33 Jewish families living in Aix. When the Germans entered the unoccupied zone in November 1942, 2,000 Jewish refugees from Germany and Eastern Europe were sent to Aix. Most of them were quartered in the nearby camp of Milles. In May 1943, following the roundup of Jews by the Germans in southern France, almost all the Jews in Aix were arrested and interned at *Drancy. They were subsequently deported to Germany and most perished in the Holocaust.

[Bernhard Blumenkranz]

Modern Times

The community practically disappeared during the years immediately following World War II. All the archives of the community disappeared during World War II. As the synagogue that was inaugurated in 1840 was no longer used for worship, it was sold in 1952 and became a Protestant church. The prayer books were distributed among several neighboring communities. The synagogue's centenary could not be celebrated in 1940, but Darius *Milhaud, a native of Aix and great-grandson of the community's president when the synagogue was built, composed a cantata for the occasion, *Crown of Glory*, based on three poems by Ibn *Gabirol and on prayers from the *Comtat Venaissin. The arrival of North African Jews after 1956 created a new community. In 1967 there were about 1,000 Jews living in Aix-en-Provence. As of 1987, the population was said to be 3,000. The rabbi and the rite of the synagogue are North African. The community is administered by a council called the Association Culturelle Israélite, which is affiliated with the Consistoire Centrale de France. An attempt was made to torch the synagogue on the afternoon of Yom Kippur, October 9, 2000.

[Gilbert Lazard]

BIBLIOGRAPHY: Z. Szajkowski (Frydman), *Franco-Judaica* (1963), index; idem, in: JSS, 6 (1944), 31–54; idem, *Analytical Franco-Jewish Gazetteer* (1966), 166, 168; E.Baratier, *Demographie provençale* (1961), 59–60, 216–211; Gross, Gal Jud, 46–48; J. Lubetzki, *La condition des Juifs en France sous l'occupation allemande* (1945), index; Shirmann, in: *Lettres Romanes*, 3 (1949), 175–200; *Guide des Communautès Juives de France*. 7 (1966), index.

AIZENBERG, NINA (1902–1974), Russian painter, graphic artist, and stage designer. Aizenberg was born in Moscow. In 1918–24, she studied in Moscow at the High Arts and Technical Workshops (VHUTEMAS). From 1924, she worked as a stage designer for several Moscow theaters. In 1926, Aizenberg became the principal stage-designer for the Blue Robe (*Sinyaa Bluza*), a propaganda-variety theater, where she developed a novel approach to designing sets and costumes. This approach, based on constructivist theater techniques, made possible quick in set and costume changes through the artful use of basic components in various combinations. In 1928–30, Aizenberg was a member of the Association of Decorative Artists, in 1930–32 she joined October group, which united artists working in the constructivist manner and adherents of "industrial art." In the early 1930s, she was active in the festive design of Moscow's streets on holidays marking the events of the Revolution. From the mid-1920s through the 1930s, she regularly showed her work at set design and decorative art exhibits in Moscow and Leningrad. In 1938–41, she executed designs for sports parades and rallies. In 1940–50, Aizenberg worked as a set designer for various theaters in Russia and other Soviet republics. She executed a series of landscape paintings in the 1950s. The first and only solo exhibition in her lifetime took place in 1964 in Moscow.

BIBLIOGRAPHY: *Nina Aizenberg: 40 Years in Theatre.* Exh. Cat. Moscow (1964) (Rus.); *Nina Aizenberg: Transformations. Russian Avant-Garde Costume and Stage Design* (Jerusalem, 1991); N. Van Norman Baer (ed.), *Theatre in Revolution. Russian Avant-Garde Stage Design 1913–193,* Fine Arts Museums of San Francisco (1992), 74, 191; J.E. Bowlt, *The Artists of Russian Theatre: 1880–1930* (Moscow, 1994), 13–16 (Rus.).

[Hillel Kazovsky (2nd ed.)]

AIZMAN, DAVID YAKOLEVICH (1869–1922), Russian writer. He studied painting in Odessa and Paris, but in his early thirties turned to literature. Aizman wrote a great deal about the Jewish poor, in a style reminiscent of Maxim *Gorki. In such short stories as "Ob odnom zlodeyanii" ("About a Crime," 1902), "Zemlyaki" ("Fellow-countrymen," 1903), and "Savan" ("The Shroud," 1903) as well as in the play *Ternovy kust* ("The Blackthorn Bush," 1907), Aizman portrayed revolutionary-minded Jewish intellectuals and their persecution by the Czarist police. His later work bears the imprint of Russian Symbolist prose, e.g., the short story "Utro Anchla" (1906), the novella "Krovavy razliv" ("Bloody Deluge," 1908), and the fantastic dream "Svetly bog" ("The Radiant God," 1914). Although he was very popular in his day – an eight-volume edition of his works was published in Russia in 1911–1919 – Aizman's stories last appeared in the U.S.S.R. in 1926, and by the second half of the century his name was almost totally forgotten.

BIBLIOGRAPHY: *Kratkaya literaturnaya entsiklopediya*, 1 (1962), 108–9.

[Maurice Friedberg]

AKABA, Jordanian port on the northeastern corner of the Gulf of Eilat. Due to freshwater wells in the vicinity, it has constituted, since antiquity, an oasis in an otherwise hot desert devoid of life. Under Roman rule it was called Aelana, and an army post was stationed there. In the early Arab period, the town had an important Jewish community. In the tenth century, Akaba was a large port, and the Crusaders made it a key position in their outer defense line. In the 12th century, however, the town began to decline and remained little more than a wayfarers' station on the pilgrims' road to Mecca. A change came in 1906 when the border between Egypt and the Ottoman Empire was demarked along the Rafah-Taba line (following a British-Ottoman encounter known as the "Akaba Incident"). Once again Akaba became the focus of international interest in World War I when the Hashemite Arab Army under Amir Feisal and T.E. *Lawrence conquered it from the Turks on July 7, 1917. They made it their headquarters from which raids into Transjordan and Syria were organized. Akaba was also the meeting place of Amir Feisal with Chaim *Weizmann in June 1918. Administratively Akaba belonged to the Ottoman province of Hijaz and, after WWI, to the Hashemite Kingdom of Hijaz. When the Saudis ousted the Hashemites in 1925, the British annexed Akaba (and its neighboring district of Maʿān) to the Emirate of Transjordan. Under the Mandate the British built a harbor there, but the place remained of minor importance until the end of Israel's *War of Independence (1948) when it became Jordan's only outlet to the sea. In the 1950s, the port was enlarged and the highway to Maʿān and ʿAmmān improved. In 1961 a deepwater port was inaugurated, and installations for the storing and loading of phosphates and for the discharge of oil were built. The port's annual capacity was increased to 600,000 tons, the number of ships calling rose from 173 in 1954 to 667 in 1966, and the tonnage of goods handled rose from 92,000 to 1,200,000. In 1965 following a Jordanian-Saudi territorial-exchange agreement, Jordan was given a 25-km.-long coastline south of Akaba which contributed to the development of the town and of its harbor. In 1972 an international airport was opened and a railroad later connected Akaba with the north. During the Iran-Iraq War (1980–88) and the Iranian blockade of Iraq's seaports, Akaba became the main lifeline of the Iraqi economy and war machine and most of the country's imports and exports went through its harbor (18,000 out of the 30,000 containers passed through Akaba in 1982 originating in or destined for Iraq). During the 1980s the harbor was greatly expanded with Iraqi financial aid, reaching an annual capacity of over six million tons. In 2002 the town numbered 70,000 inhabitants (as opposed to 11,000 in 1967). Its economy was based on port services, foreign and internal tourism, fishing, and some farming. Following the Jordanian-Israeli peace accord of 1994, the Akaba Special Economic Zone (ASEZ) was founded to offer economic incentives and business opportunities to encourage job-creating foreign investments.

BIBLIOGRAPHY: T.E. Lawrence, *Seven Pillars of Wisdom* (1935), index. **ADD. BIBLIOGRAPHY:** R. Wilson (ed.), *Politics and Economy in Jordan* (1991).

[Shlomo Hasson / Joseph Nevo (2nd ed.)]

AKADEMIE FUER DIE WISSENSCHAFT DES JUDENTUMS, academy founded in Berlin in 1919 for the furtherance of Jewish scholarship and the encouragement of young scholars and the publication of their work. The idea of such an academy had been mooted by Franz *Rosenzweig in his seminal open letter ("Zeit ist's," 1917; "It is time" in *On Jewish Learning* (1965)) to his teacher Hermann *Cohen, who took it up enthusiastically. The academy was to be in two parts: an academy in the accepted sense, with members and corresponding members, and a research institute which, by giving grants to younger scholars, would enable them to pursue their work in the various divisions of study, such as Talmud, history, Hebrew literature and language, philosophy, Kabbalah, economics, etc. From the original plan, only the research institute materialized; its first director was E. *Taeubler, who was succeeded by Julius *Guttmann. The academy made itself responsible for a number of publications, such as the continuation of Theodor and Albeck's edition of *Genesis Rabbah* (1912–32, repr. 1965), Hermann Cohen's *Juedische Schriften* (3 vols., 1924) and his philosophical writings (2 vols., 1928), and a bicentenary edition of the works of Moses *Mendelssohn, which was planned for 16 volumes, but only seven appeared (1929–38). The academy's *Korrespondenzblatt* with annual reports appeared from 1919 to 1930. For some time the academy also shared responsibility for the *Zeitschrift fuer Demographie und Statistik der Juden*. A *Festschrift* was published in 1929 to celebrate its tenth anniversary. Its work came to an end in 1934.

BIBLIOGRAPHY: Guttmann, in: *Festgabe zum zehnjaehrigen Bestehen der Akademie...* (1929), 3ff. **ADD. BIBLIOGRAPHY:** D. Myers, in: HUCA, 63 (1992), 107–44; M. Brenner, *The Renaissance of Jewish Culture in Weimar Germany* (1996).

[Alexander Carlebach]

AKAVYA (Yakobovits), AVRAHAM ARYEH LEIB (1882–1964), Polish-born Hebrew and Yiddish writer and editor. After the publication of his first story in David Frischmann's *Ha-Dor* (1901), Akavya became a steady contributor to the Hebrew press and literary periodicals. He also wrote stories and novels in Yiddish, and translated from Yiddish to Hebrew. Akavya edited several Yiddish weeklies, the Hebrew daily *Ha-Boker* (with D. Frischmann (1909)), the biweekly for youth *Shibbolim*, and (after World War I) *Ha-Ẓefirah* and *Ha-Yom*. He went to Palestine in 1935 and was an editor of the short *Massadah* encyclopedia and later the chief editor of the *Yizre'el* encyclopedia. He devoted many years of research to the Hebrew calendar and published various books on the subject.

BIBLIOGRAPHY: Kressel, Leksikon, 2 (1967), 562–5.

[Getzel Kressel]

AKAVYAH BEN MAHALALEL (first century C.E.), member of the Sanhedrin. He engaged in a dispute with *Ḥanina Segan ha-Kohanim and *Dosa b. Harkinas (Neg. 1:4) and the three are mentioned consecutively in *Avot de-Rabbi Nathan* (Version A, 19–21). Akavyah was offered the position of *av bet din* on condition that he renounce four of his decisions in which he disagreed with the majority but he declined, declaring: "It is better for me to be called a fool all my days than that I should become even for one hour a wicked man in the sight of God; and that men should say, 'He withdrew his opinions for the sake of getting power'" (Eduy. 5:6). Three of these dissenting opinions appear in the Mishnah (Neg. 5:3; Nid. 2:6; Bek. 3:4). A fourth, concerning the administration of the water of bitterness to a proselyte or emancipated slave suspected of infidelity to her spouse, indirectly resulted in Akavyah's excommunication. After testimony had been adduced in the name of Shemaiah and Avtalyon, he scornfully remarked, '*Degma hishkuha*,' i.e., "they made her drink in simulation only," or, as explained by others, "men who were like her (i.e., proselytes or descendants of proselytes) made her drink" Eduy., *ibid.*). Although he did not retract his statements before his death, Akavyah admonished his son to accept the opinion of the majority. His son's entreaty, "Commend me to your colleagues," elicited the reply: "Your own deeds will bring your commendation or your rejection" (Eduy. 5:7). According to the Mishnah Akavyah died while still under the ban of excommunication, and the *bet din* stoned his coffin (*ibid.*, 6). R. Kahana considered him a "rebellious elder," but he was not executed because he based his opinions on tradition (Sanh. 88a). Judah b. Ilai (Eduy., *ibid.*) and Judah b. Bathyra (Sif. Num. 105), however, denied that Akavyah was put under a ban. The former declared, "God forbid that (we would think that) Akavyah was excommunicated, for the Temple court was never closed in the face of any man in Israel so great in wisdom and in fear of sin as Akavyah b. Mahalalel." Akvayah's maxim, "Reflect upon three things and you will not come within the power of sin: know whence you came, whither you are going, and before whom you are destined to give account" (Avot 3:1; cf. ARN[1], 29), illustrates his own stress on ethical conduct.

BIBLIOGRAPHY: Mendelsohn, in: REJ, 41 (1900), 31–44; Marmorstein, *ibid.*, 81 (1925), 181–7; Hoenig, in: *Studies and Essays in Honor of A.Neuman* (1962), 291–8; Alon, *Meḥkarim*. 1 (1957), 115–20; J. Brand, in: *Minḥah li-Yhudah* (Zlotnick) (1950), 5–9, 19.

[Bialik Myron Lerner]

°**AKBAR THE GREAT (Akbar Abū al-Fatḥ Jalāl al-Dīn Muhammad**; 1542–1605), Moghul emperor in India. Akbar's subjects were permitted a remarkable degree of religious tolerance and freedom. The emperor tried to build a bridge of understanding between Hindus and Muslims and to create a new eclectic religion of pure theism ("tauḥīd Ilāhū" or "Dīn Ilāhī"). He collected translations of the holy books of all faiths, and held regular religious disputations in his palace at Fatehpur Sikri, near Agra. The participants also included Jews, probably from Persia, Afghanistan, or Khurasan, as well as Hindus, Jains, Zoroastrians, and Jesuits. The presence of Jews is reliably reported by Moghul court historians, by the Jesuit traveler A. Monserrate, and by the author of the *Dabistan*. A synagogue (*kenisa*) also existed in the Moghul realm according to the English traveler, Sir Thomas Roe (1616). Akbar's interest in the translation of holy books brought the famous Florentine traveler and scholar Giambattista Vecchietti to Agra. Vecchietti had collected many ancient *Judeo-Persian biblical translations during his journeys in Persia, and while a guest of Akbar, he transliterated the Judeo-Persian manuscript of the Psalms into Persian script.

BIBLIOGRAPHY: Fischel, in: PAAJR, 17 (1949), 137–77; idem, in: HTR, 45 (1952), 3–45. **ADD. BIBLIOGRAPHY:** I. Alam Khan, "The Nobility under Akbar and the Development of his Religious Policy, 1560–1580," in: *Journal of the Royal Asiatic Society* (1968), 29–36: J.F. Richards, "The Formation of Imperial Authority under Akbar and Jahangir," in: M. Alam and S. Subrahnayan (eds.), *The Mughal State 1526–1750* (1988), 126–167.

[Walter Joseph Fischel / David Shulman (2nd ed.)]

AKDAMUT MILLIN (Heb. אַקְדָּמוּת מִלִּין; "Introduction"), opening words of an Aramaic poem by R. Meir b. Isaac Nehorai. The poem was recited in the synagogue on Shavuot as an introduction to the Aramaic translation (*targum*) of Exodus 19–20 (the theophany at Mount Sinai). Exodus 19:1 was read aloud in Hebrew, "*Akdamut Millin*" was then read, followed by the next few verses in the Hebrew, and after that the same verses in Aramaic. The remainder of the reading was finished in the same sequence: two to three verses of the Hebrew text followed by the Aramaic translation of the preceding verses. The recitation of "*Akdamut Millin*" now generally precedes the Reading of the Torah, in deference to the objections of later halakhic authorities against interrupting the Reading of the Torah (cf. *Magen David* to Sh. Ar., OḤ 494), particularly since it is no longer customary to read the Aramaic translation. The poem consists of 90 acrostic lines forming a double alphabet followed by the author's name. It praises God as creator and lawgiver, expatiates on Israel's fidelity to God despite all sufferings and temptations, and ends with a description of the apocalyptic events at the end of days and the future glory of Israel. The poem is recited in the Ashkenazi rite only. A similar work by the same author, introducing the reading of the Aramaic version of the Song of Moses (Ex. 15:1–10) on the seventh day of Passover, is found in some medieval manuscripts. "*Akdamut Millin*" has been translated into English in various prayer books, notably by Joseph Marcus (Silverman, Prayer, 185–8) and Raphael Loewe (*Service of the Synagogue*, London, 1954, 210). There are also several versions of the "*Akdamut*" in Hebrew (see *Sefer ha-Mo'adim*, 3 (1950), 141–4). A similar poem, "*Yeẓiv Pitgam*," is recited on the second day of Shavuot before the reading of the *haftarah*. In East European folk tradition the origin of the poem is connected with the widespread legend that R. Meir b. Isaac saved the Jewish community of Worms by invoking the help of a miraculous emissary of the Ten Lost Tribes from across the *Sambatyon. In many versions of the legend, extant in manuscripts and still alive in oral tradition, the hero is identified with R. *Meir Ba'al ha-Nes, and the "*Akdamut*" *piyyut* celebrates a victory over the Jew-baiters.

[Ernst Daniel Goldschmidt]

Music

The poem has been given two musical settings which have become well-known in Ashkenazi synagogues. One of these can claim great antiquity by its psalmodic style of recitation; the simple but expressive declamation suits the narrative character of the poem. Its identity in the Western and Eastern branches of the Ashkenazi rite, and its use for the *Kiddush* and other prayers, indicates its age. Another melody is found only in the West, and apparently is of a later date, although its motives were already incorporated in cantorial works of 1744 and 1796. Moreover, this second tune serves as a motto theme of the Feast of Weeks and is applied in the **Hallel*, the *Priestly Blessing, and other prayer texts.

[Hanoch Avenary]

BIBLIOGRAPHY: Davidson, Oẓar, 1 (1924), no. 7314; Elbogen, Gottesdienst, 191; Idelsohn, Music, 156; Fishman, in: *Ha-Tor*, 3, no. 25–26 (1923), 11; Zunz-Albeck, Derashot; Zunz, Lit Poesie, 151; J.-T. Lewinski, *Sefer ha-Mo'adim*, 3 (1950), 135–60; ZDMG, 54 (1900), 118; Rivkind, in: *Yivo Filologische Schriftn*, 3 (1929), 1–42, 599–605; M. Kosover and A.G. Duker, *Minḥah le-Yiẓḥak* (New York, 1949), no. 59. MUSIC: A. Friedmann, *Der synagogale Gesang* (1908), 80; Idelsohn, Melodien, 6, pt. 1 (1932), nos. 236, 247, 250, 255–7; EJ.

AKEDAH (**'Aqedah**; Heb. עֲקֵדָה, lit. "binding (of Isaac)"), the Pentateuchal narrative (Gen. 22:1–19) describing God's command to *Abraham to offer *Isaac, the son of his old age, as a sacrifice. Obedient to the command, Abraham takes Isaac to the place of sacrifice and binds him (*va-ya'akod*, Gen. 22:9, a word found nowhere else in the Bible in the active, conjugative form) on the altar. The angel of the Lord then bids Abraham to stay his hand and a ram is offered in Isaac's stead. The *Akedah* became in Jewish thought the supreme example of self-sacrifice in obedience to God's will and the symbol of Jewish martyrdom throughout the ages.

Critical View

The *Akedah* narrative is generally attributed to source E (which uses *'Elohim* as the Divine Name) with glosses by the Redactor (R, hence also the use of the Tetragrammaton); or to source J (in which the Divine Name is the Tetragrammaton) which may have made use of E material (Peake's *Commentary on the Bible* (1962), 193). The original intent of the narrative has been understood by the critics either as an etiological legend explaining why the custom of child sacrifice was modified in a certain sanctuary by the substitution of a ram (Gunkel), or as a protest against human sacrifice (Skinner, *Genesis* (1910), 331–2). The name Moriah ("land of Moriah," Gen. 22:2) occurs elsewhere (II Chron. 3:1) as the name of the Temple site; hence the Jewish tradition that the Temple was built on the spot at which the *Akedah* took place. There is no further reference to the *Akedah* in the Bible.

The *Akedah* influenced both Christian and Islamic thought. In early Christian doctrine, the sacrifice of Isaac is used as a type for the sacrifice of Jesus (see Tertullian, *Adversus Marcionem*, 3:18; Clement of Alexandria, *Paedogogica*, 1:5,

1; Schoeps, in: JBL, 65 (1946), 385–92). In Islam, the *Akedah* is held up for admiration (Koran 37:97–111), but the more accepted opinion is that it was Ishmael, Abraham's other son and the progenitor of the Arabs, who was bound on the altar and that the whole episode took place before Isaac's birth. The *Akedah* has been a favorite theme in religious art for centuries.

In Jewish Life and Literature

In the early rabbinic period, reference was made to Abraham's sacrifice in prayers of intercession. The Mishnah (Ta'an. 2:4) records that on public fast days the reader recited: "May He that answered Abraham our father on Mount Moriah answer you and hearken to the voice of your crying this day." The Mishnah also states (Ta'an. 2:1) that on fast days, ashes were placed on the Ark and on the heads of the *nasi* and the *av bet din;* a later teacher explained (Ta'an. 16a) that this was a reminder of the "ashes of Isaac." In the *Zikhronot* ("Remembrance") prayers of Rosh Ha-Shanah, there is an appeal to God to remember the *Akedah:* "Remember unto us, O Lord our God, the covenant and the lovingkindness and the oath which Thou swore unto Abraham our father on Mount Moriah: and consider the binding with which Abraham our father bound his son Isaac on the altar, how he suppressed his compassion in order to perform Thy will with a perfect heart. So may Thy compassion overbear Thine anger against us; in Thy great goodness may Thy great wrath turn aside from Thy people, Thy city, and Thine inheritance." One of the explanations given for the sounding of the *shofar* ("ram's horn") on Rosh Ha-Shanah is as a reminder of the ram substituted for Isaac (RH 16a). The story of the *Akedah* is the Pentateuchal reading on the second day of Rosh Ha-Shanah (Meg. 31a). During the Middle Ages, a number of penitential hymns took the *Akedah* for their theme and indeed a whole style of *piyyut* is known by this name. Pious Jews recited the *Akedah* passage daily (Tur., OḤ. 1) and, following this custom, the passage is printed in many prayer books as part of the early morning service.

In Rabbinic Literature

The *Akedah* was spoken of as the last of the ten trials to which Abraham was subjected (Avot 5:3; Ginzberg, Legends, 5 (1925), 218, note 52) and was considered as the prototype of the readiness for martyrdom. "Support me with fires" (homiletical interpretation of Song 2:5) is said to refer to the fire of Abraham and that of Hananiah, Mishael, and Azariah (Dan. 3:12–23; PdRK 101b); this particular association is probably due to the fact that both cases illustrate not actual martyrdom but the readiness for it. On the other hand, numerous instances of real martyrdom were also compared to the *Akedah*, sometimes to the disadvantage of the latter. Thus in the story of the "Woman and her Seven Sons," every one of whom suffered death by torture rather than bow to the idol, the widow enjoins her sons: "Go and tell Father Abraham: Let not your heart swell with pride! You built one altar, but I have built seven altars and on them have offered up my seven sons. What is more: Yours was a trial; mine was an accomplished fact!" (Yal. Deut. 26). In the parallel passage in the Babylonian Talmud (Git. 57b), the widow's admonition is softened through the omission of the second half of the first sentence and the last sentence.

In legal literature, the *Akedah* served as a paradigm for the right of a prophet to demand the temporal suspension of a law. Isaac obeyed his father and made ready to become the victim of what would normally have been considered a murder, but Abraham, as an established prophet, could be relied upon that this was really God's will (Sanh. 89b). The opinion is found in the Midrash (Gen. R. 56:8) that Isaac was 37 years old at the time of the *Akedah.* Abraham *Ibn Ezra (commentary on Gen. 22:4) rejects this as contrary to the plain meaning of the narrative in which Isaac is old enough to carry the wood but young enough to be docile. Ibn Ezra (commentary on Gen. 22:19) also quotes an opinion that Abraham actually did kill Isaac (hence there is no reference to Isaac returning home with his father), and he was later resurrected from the dead. Ibn Ezra rejects this as completely contrary to the biblical text. Shalom *Spiegel has demonstrated, however, that such views enjoyed a wide circulation and occasionally found expression in medieval writings, possibly in order to deny that the sacrifice of Isaac was in any way less than that of Jesus; or as a reflection of actual conditions in the Middle Ages when the real martyrdom of Jewish communities demanded a more tragic model than that of a mere intended sacrifice. It was known in those days for parents to kill their children, and then themselves, when threatened by the Crusaders. Geiger (JZWL, 10 (1872), 166ff.) suggests that interpretations of Isaac's sacrifice as a means of atonement for his descendants were influenced by Christian doctrine. In rabbinic literature, tensions can be generally observed between the need to emphasize the significance of the *Akedah* and, at the same time, to preserve the prophetic protest against human sacrifice. Thus, on Jeremiah 19:5 the comment is made: "which I commanded not" – this refers to the sacrifice of the son of Mesha, the king of Moab (II Kings 3:27); "nor spake it" – this refers to the daughter of Jephthah (Judg. 11:31); "neither came it to my mind" – this refers to the sacrifice of Isaac, the son of Abraham (Ta'an. 4a).

In Religious Thought

A theme of such dramatic power as the *Akedah* has attracted a rich variety of comment. Philo (*De Abrahamo*, 177–99) defends the greatness of Abraham against hostile criticism that would belittle his achievement. These critics point out that many others in the history of mankind have offered themselves and their children for a cause in which they believed – the barbarians, for instance, whose Moloch worship was explicitly forbidden by Moses, and Indian women who gladly practice Suttee. Philo argues, however, that Abraham's sacrifice was unprecedented in that he was not governed by motives of custom, honor, or fear, but solely by the love of God. Philo (*ibid.*, 200–7) also gives an allegorical interpretation of the incident: Isaac means "laughter"; and the devout soul feels a duty to offer up its joy which belongs to God. God, however, in His mercy, refuses to allow the surrender to be complete and allows the soul to retain its joy. Worship is the most perfect expression of that joy.

Medieval thinkers were disturbed at the idea of God's testing Abraham, as if the purpose of the *Akedah* were to provide God with information He did not previously possess. According to Maimonides (Guide 3:24), the words "God tested Abraham" do not mean that God put him through a test but that He made the example of Abraham serve as a test case of the extreme limits of the love and fear of God. "For now I know that you fear God" (Gen. 22:12) means that God has made known to all men how far man is obliged to go in fearing Him. According to Naḥmanides (ed. by C.B. Chavel, 1 (1959), 125–6), the *Akedah* focuses on the problem of reconciling God's foreknowledge with human free will. God knew how Abraham would behave, but from Abraham's point of view, the test was real since he had to be rewarded not only for his potential willingness to obey, but for actually complying. *Sforno's elaboration of this thought (commentary to Gen. 22:1) is that Abraham had to transcend his own love of God by converting it from the potential to the actual, in order to resemble God whose goodness is always actual, the aim of creation being that man imitates his Creator.

The mystics add their own ideas to the *Akedah* theme. In the Zohar (Gen. 119b), the patriarchs on earth represent the various potencies (*sefirot*) in the divine realm: Abraham the Divine Lovingkindness, Isaac the Divine Power, and Jacob the Harmonizing Principle. Abraham is obliged to display severity in being willing to sacrifice his son, contrary to his own special nature as the "pillar of lovingkindness," and thus set in motion the process by which fire is united with water, mercy with judgment, so that the way can be paved for the emergence of complete harmony between the two in Jacob. This mirrors the processes in the divine realm by which God's mercy is united with His judgment so that the world can endure. The Ḥasidim read various subtleties of their own into the ancient story. One version states that Abraham and Isaac knew, in their heart of hearts, that the actual sacrifice would not be demanded but they went through the motions to demonstrate that they would have obeyed had it been God's will (*Elimelech of Lyzhansk, *No'am Elimelech* on Gen. 22:7). The true lover of God carries out even those religious obligations which are personally pleasant to him solely out of the love of God. Abraham obeyed the second command not to kill Isaac solely for this and for no other reason (Levi Isaac b. Meir, *Kedushat Levi* on Gen. 22:6). Another version is that when God wishes to test a man, He must first remove from him the light of full comprehension of the Divine, otherwise the trial will be incomplete. Abraham was ready to obey even in this state of "dryness of soul" (Israel b. Shabbetai of Kozienice, *Avodat Yisrael* on Gen. 22:14). The lesser Divine Name Elohim is, therefore, used at the beginning of the narrative, and not the Tetragrammaton, to denote that the vision in which the command was given was lacking in clarity. Abraham's greatness consisted in his refusal to allow his natural love for his son to permit him to interpret the ambiguous command as other than a command to sacrifice (Mordecai Joseph b. Jacob Leiner of Izbica, *Mei ha-Shilo'aḥ* on Gen. 22:7).

To the moralists (*ba'alei ha-musar*) the *Akedah* was a fertile text for the inculcation of religious and ethical values. For Isaiah *Horowitz (*Shenei Luḥot ha-Berit, Va-Yera*, end), the *Akedah* teaches that everything must be sacrificed to God, if needs be; how much more, then, must man be willing to give up his lusts for God. Moreover, whenever man has an opportunity of doing good, or refraining from evil, he should reflect that perhaps God is testing him at that moment as He tested Abraham.

The best-known treatment of the *Akedah* theme in general literature is that of Søren Kierkegaard (*Fear and Trembling*). Kierkegaard sees Abraham as the "knight of faith" who differs from the "ethical man"; for the latter the moral law is universal and it has a categorical claim to obedience; the "knight of faith," however, knows also of the higher obligation laid upon him as a free individual in his relationship to his God and this may involve him in a "teleological suspension of the ethical." Abraham is called upon to renounce for God all that he holds precious, including the ethical ideal to which he subscribes and which he has constantly taught. Consequently, Abraham did not know what duty had been imposed on him: to obey God's command or his ethical obligation? According to Kierkegaard, this tension between these two conflicting obligations is what characterized Abraham as a "knight of faith." Kierkegaard was the first thinker to posit the believer's doubts as the characteristic of religious life itself. Kierkegaard's position has been criticized by various Jewish thinkers.

Milton *Steinberg (*Anatomy of Faith* (1960), 147), rejected Kierkegaard's view as "unmitigated sacrilege. Which indeed is the true point of the *Akedah*, missed so perversely by Kierkegaard. While it was a merit in Abraham to be willing to sacrifice his only son to his God, it was God's nature and merit that He would not accept an immoral tribute. And it was His purpose, among other things, to establish that truth." Other thinkers such as J.B. Soloveitchik have found the Kierkegaardian insights fully compatible with Judaism. Ernst Simon (in *Conservative Judaism*, 12 (spring 1958), 15–19) believes that a middle position between the two is possible. Judaism is an ethical religion and would never in fact demand a teleological suspension of the ethical. Abraham is, therefore, ordered to stay his hand. The original command to sacrifice Isaac is a warning against too complete an identification of religion with naturalistic ethics.

Y. *Leibowitz went further than Kierkegaard by suggesting that the believer has the obligation to overcome his ethical duty and unconditionally obey the divine command. Leibowitz thus regarded the *Akedah* as a paradigm of religious life, a position unusual in Jewish thought, which generally maintains that the divine command is not opposed to ethical duty.

Kalonymus Shapira, the rabbi of Piaseczno, maintained that the meaning of the *Akedah* is that the divine command itself determines morality, thus adopting the "divine command morality" prevalent in Christian literature. He wrote:

> The nations of the world, even the best of them, think that the truth is a thing in itself, and that God commanded truth because the truth is intrinsically True.... Not so Israel, who say "You God are truth"... and we have no truth beside Him, and all the truth found in the world is there only because God wished it and commanded it...Stealing is forbidden because the God of truth has commanded it... When God ordered Abraham to sacrifice his son Isaac, it was true to sacrifice him and, had God not said later "neither do anything to him" it would have been true to slaughter him. (K. Shapira, *Esh Kodesh*, Jerusalem, 1960, 68)

Shapira's unusual position is an attempt to deal with the problem of theodicy in light of the horrors of the *Shoah. His exceptional treatment of the *Akedah* thus demonstrates that Jewish thought generally did not incorporate the theory of "divine command morality." The *Akedah* thus became a basis for justifying sacrifice and devotion, but because of the centrality of morality to Jewish tradition in general, and specifically to halakhah, it was only with Soloveitchik and Leibowitz that the *Akedah* became a paradigm of religious life itself.

[Louis Jacobs / Avi Sagi (2nd ed.)]

In Israeli Culture

The *akedah* myth is used by Israeli society to understand itself. Moshe Shamir, a leading writer from the founders' generation called the *akedah* "the story of our generation" (*Be-Kulmus Mahir* ("Quick Notes"), 1960, p. 332). Changes in the attitudes to this myth point to shifts in the ways Israeli society approaches the meaning of its existence.

Two basic attitudes can be discerned in relation to the *akedah*. Whereas the first views the *akedah* as the deepest symbol of modern Israeli existence, epitomizing the Zionist revolution and the sacrifices it exacted, the second rejects both the myth and its implications.

The *akedah* myth has been sanctified by many Israeli writers. Uri Zevi Greenberg writes: "Let that day come.../ when my father will rise from his grave with the resurrection of the dead/ and God will command him as the people commanded Abraham./ To bind his only son: to be an offering – /... let that day come in my life! I believe it will."(Uri Zevi Greenberg, "*Korban Shaharit*" ("Morning Offering"), in: *Sulam* 1972 (13), pp. 145–147).

When speaking of the Zionist experience, Abraham Shlonsky writes, "Father/ take off your *tallit* and *tefillin* today/... and take your son on a distant lane/ to mount Moriah" ("*Hulin*" ("Worldliness"), in: A. Shlonsky, *Ketavim* [Writings], vol. 2, (1954), p. 136). Hayyim Gouri writes of Isaac's descendants being "born with a knife in their hearts." (H. Gouri, "*Yerushah*" ("Heritage"), in: *Shoshanat Ha-Ruhot* ("Compass-Rose"), 1966). The relationship between Abraham and Isaac is also transformed in modern Hebrew literature. Contrary to the passive figure of the biblical story, the Isaac of Israeli literature is an active hero who initiates the *akedah*. Modern literature also lays greater emphasis than the biblical text on intergenerational cooperation, as if no rift divided the fathers offering the sacrifice from their sons. Isaac becomes the paradigmatic Zionist pioneer, representing an entire generation: rather than being passive victims, the modern Isaacs assume responsibility for their destiny and sacrifice themselves on the altar of national renaissance.

In the 1967 Six-Day War, when for the first time the generation of founders were too old to fight, and the post-independence generation of their children fought in their place, the *akedah* remained a powerful symbol, at least for some. The post-war collection of interviews, *The Seventh Day: Soldiers Talk About the Six-Day War* (Hebrew: *Siaḥ Loḥamim*, 1967; English, 1970) records a father who said: "We do knowingly bring our boys up to volunteer for combat units.... These are moments when a man is given a greater insight into Isaac's sacrifice. Kierkegaard asked what Abraham did that night. What did he think about? ... He had a whole night to think.... It's a question that touches on the very meaning of human existence. The Bible says nothing about it... For us, that night lasted six days" (p. 202).

Conversely, doubts about the *akedah* myth already began to surface soon after independence. In the central work about the War of Independence, by S. Yizhar, we read: "There is no evading the *akedah*... I hate our father Abraham, who binds Isaac. What right does he have over Isaac? Let him bind himself. I hate the God who sent him and closed all paths, leaving only that of the *akedah*. I hate the fact that Isaac serves merely as a test between Abraham and his God... (S. Yizhar, *Yemei Ziklag* ("The Days of Ziklag"), 1958, vol. 2, p. 804).

After the Six-Day War, a gradual change in attitude towards the *akedah* evolved. In 1968, about 10 years after the publication of Yizhar's novel, Habimah Theater staged a play by Yigal Mossinsohn where Shimshon, a blinded officer, thinks of his life in terms of an *akedah* (Yigal Mossinsohn, *Shimshon Katsin be-Ẓahal, O Requiem le-Ereẓ Pelishtim* ("Samson the IDF officer, or Requiem to the Land of the Philistines)). Mossinsohn states his wish to be released from this "grand" myth. In his view, fathers and sons are jointly responsible for the *akedah*, which must end. In its place, Mossinsohn-Shimshon expects to lead a normal life when "my children... will no longer know war."

In May 1970, Habimah Theater staged a play by Hanoch Levin. ("*Malkat Ha-Ambatyah*" ("Queen of the Bath"), in: H. Levin, *Mah Ikhpat la-Ẓippor* ("What Does it Matter to the Bird?"), 1987). The play deals with the sons' profound contempt for their parents and, in a passage called "*Akedah*," Abraham and Isaac engage in a rather mundane and sarcastic dialogue, conveying deep disdain for the parents who believe that they, rather than their sons, are the victims of the sacrifice. In the poem "Dear father, when you stand on my grave," which follows the "*Akedah*" dialogue, Levin writes, "And do not say that you've brought a sacrifice,/ because I was the one who brought the sacrifice,/... dear father, when you stand on my grave/ old and weary and very lonesome,/ and when you see how they lay my body to rest – / ask for my forgiveness, father" (p. 92).

The weariness and pain of the *akedah* come to the fore after the Yom Kippur war. Thus, for instance, Menahem Heyd writes: "And there was no ram – / and Isaac in the thicket.// And the angel did not say lay not/ and we – / our son, our only son, Isaac." ("*Yiẓhak Halakh le-Har Moriah*" ("Isaac Went to Mount Moriah"), *Yedi'oth Aharonot*, December 28, 1973.) The pain is particularly intense because no ram came to replace Isaac. Many poets report this feeling – the miracle failed.

In Yariv Ben Aharon's roman à clef – *Peleg* (1993) about the sons' generation, the *akedah* becomes the litmus test of the relations between fathers and sons: the fathers will not be satisfied with less than the sons' sacrifice (p. 116). The covenant of secular Zionists with their land forced the actual sacrifice of their children, and the *akedah* no longer symbolized an act of faith but an expression of the deep bond with the land. Ben Aharon blames the parents for the secular distortion of the religious symbol and desires to restore its religious connotations. He thereby seeks to bring about a quasi-religious renaissance, in the tradition of A.D. Gordon, and rejects the prevalent secular overtones of Zionist culture, where the *akedah* served to justify the death of the sons.

Protests against the *akedah* myth gained strength after the Lebanon War. Yehudah Amihai speaks of a plot to sacrifice the sons: "The true hero of the *akedah* was the ram" (Y. Amihai, "*Ha-Gibor ha-Amiti shel Ha-Akedah*" ("The True Hero of the Sacrifice"), in: *She'at Hesed* [("The Hour of Grace") 1983). Replacing the two heroic figures, Abraham and Isaac, with an antihero – the ram – is part of a trend seeking to moderate the dramatic overtones characteristic of Israeli life. The hero is not the one involved in purposeful action, but rather the one confronted with a tragic situation and unable to understand the forces that have led to it.

A poem by Yitzhak Laor offers the most poignant expression of this protest: "To pity the offering?… To trust a father like that? Let him kill him first. Let him slam his father/ his only father Abraham/ in jail in the poorhouse in the cellar of the house just so/ he will not slay./ Remember what your father did to your brother Ishmael (Y. Laor, "*Ha-Metumtam ha-Zeh Yiẓhak*" ("This Fool, Isaac"), in: *Rak ha-Guf Zokher* ("Only the Body Remembers"; 1985), p. 70).

Yizhar had adopted the *akedah* story but had pointed an accusing finger at the fathers, while Mossinsohn longed for release from its oppressive weight. Laor now blames the sons' compliance, their willingness to die rather than refuse. He rejects the narrative: the sons should have remembered the cruelty of the founding fathers, father Abraham, and their immoral behavior toward Ishmael, the Arabs. This poem exposes a deep breach between fathers and sons, between founders and followers. To a large extent, it also entails a rejection of the entire Zionist ethos.

[Avi Sagi (2nd ed.)]

In the Arts

Among Christian writers and artists the biblical account of Abraham's readiness to sacrifice Isaac was interpreted as a foretelling of the crucifixion of Jesus. A parallel was drawn between the two stories: Abraham was God the Father sacrificing his "only begotten son"; Isaac himself carrying the wood to the altar was Jesus bearing his cross; while the ram actually sacrificed represented the crucified savior. In Western literature the episode occurs from the Middle Ages onward in various dramatic forms and in different countries. It figures in all the important English miracle play cycles and in an early work of the Eastern Church, the Cretan *Sacrifice of Abraham* (1159), where God's design is revealed, but the ram escapes slaughter. An example of the Italian *sacre rappresentazioni* is Feo Belcari's *Abramo e Isacco* (1449), while there is a more austere treatment in the 16th-century Spanish *Auto del sacrificio de Abraham.* The theme enjoyed special popularity among Protestants. Théodore de Bèza (Beza), the French humanist and reformer who was a close associate of Calvin in Geneva, gave his drama *Abraham sacrifiant* (1550) the conventional form of a mystery. It was notable for some revolutionary undertones, however, Abraham appearing as a stern Huguenot, humanized by love for his son. This play was widely translated and often reprinted. In the 17th century, the German dramatist Christian Weise wrote the play *Die Opferung Isaacs* (1680). Among the strict Protestants of the 18th century there were two Swiss German authors who dealt with the episode. Johann Jacob Bodmer wrote *Abraham* (1778), and Johann Kaspar Lavater the religious drama *Abraham und Isaak* (1776). Adele Wiseman's *The Sacrifice* (1956) transposes the story to a modern Canadian setting.

Jewish artists portrayed the *Akedah* in some synagogues of the early centuries of the current era, notably at *Dura-Europos (third century) and *Bet Alfa (sixth century). In both cases the hand of God was depicted as stretching forth to restrain Abraham from sacrificing his son. This is in direct conflict with the biblical text (Gen. 22:11), which states that he was restrained by the voice of an angel. Later Jewish sources are French and German Hebrew Bibles of the late 13th century, the 14th-century Spanish Sarajevo *Haggadah,* and a 15th-century Italian *mahzor,* which contains pictures illustrating the Aramaic *piyyutim* on the Ten Commandments recited on the festival of Shavuot. The illustration of the sacrifice of Isaac accompanies the fifth Commandment, and Isaac's willingness to follow his father is seen as an example of filial piety. There are early Christian representations of the story in the third-century Roman catacomb of Priscilla, in the Vatican grottos, and in glass, ivory, and jewels. Later examples have been found in the cathedrals of Chartres and Verona, and in churches elsewhere. During the early Renaissance, Donatello and Ghiberti produced work on the theme, as did Andrea del Sarto, Sodoma, Titian, Beccafumi, and Cranach later in the 16th century. Caravaggio gave it emotionally realistic treatment, and *Rembrandt depicted the angel's intervention in a painting of 1635 and in an etching in which the angel grips Abraham's arm with one hand and protects Isaac's face with the other. Guardi and Tiepolo treated the subject with the 18th-century lightness.

The melody of the Judeo-German *Akedah* poem, which was used for liturgical, religious, and historical songs in both Hebrew and German, is shown by the indication *be-niggun Akedah* (i.e., to be sung "to the *Akedah* tune"). The melody is first mentioned by Jacob *Moellin (*Sefer Maharil,* 49b). Another similar indication – *be-niggun "Juedischer Stamm"* – refers to the same tune. No notation of this time has been found so far, but A.Z. Idelsohn suggested that it was identical with the liturgical *Akedot* of the old west-Ashkenazi tradition. In European music there are at least 50 works on the sacrifice of Isaac, mostly oratorios. As in literature and art, the *Akedah* is often linked with the Crucifixion, Metastasio have stated this explicitly in the textbook title of his libretto *Isacco, figura del Redentore* (1740). The Viennese court oratorio owes its inception and style to the Emperor Leopold I's "sepolcro" *Il sacrificio d'Abramo* (1660), which was performed in the court church during Passion Week. Many eminent 18th-century musicians composed settings for Metastasio's libretto which was originally written for the Viennese court. Popular German oratorios include J.H. Rolle's *Abraham auf Moria* (1776) and M. Blumner's *Abraham* (1859–60). In Poland the biblical story inspired an opera by Chopin's teacher, Ks. J. Elsner (1827), and an oratorio by W. Sowński (1805–1880). In Abraham *Goldfaden's Yiddish "biblical operetta" *Akeydas Yitskhok* (1897), the *Akedah* itself figures only near the end of the work. Hugo Adler wrote an *Akedah* (1938), based on the Buber-Rosenzweig German translation of the Bible and on selections from the Midrash and *Akedot piyyutim,* which was modeled on the classical oratorio. Igor Stravinsky's *Akedat Yizhak* (Abraham and Isaac), a "sacred ballad" for baritone and chamber orchestra set to a Hebrew text, was first performed in Jerusalem in 1964.

See also: *Abraham in the Arts and, *Isaac in the Arts.

BIBLIOGRAPHY: S.J. Zewin, *Le-Or ha-Halakhah* (19643), 165–75; S. Spiegel, *The Last Trial* (1969). IN THE ARTS: T. Ehrenstein, *Das Alte Testament im Bilde* (1923), 181–202; Idelsohn, Music, table XXV no. 7 and pp. 170, 380–1, 383; Idelsohn, Melodien, 7 (1932), XLIV nos. 256, 312a; N.H. Katz and L. Waldbott, *Die traditionellen Synagogen-Gesaenge*, pt. 2 (1868), 73–74; A. Baer, *Ba'al Te'fillah* (1883), no. 1320; S. Scheuermann, *Gottesdienstliche Gesaenge der Israeliten...* (1912), 49; A. de Bèze, in: N.J.E. Rothschild, *Le Mistère du Viel Testament*, 2 (1879), xlix–lxii (bibliography). **ADD. BIBLIOGRAPHY:** A. Sagi, "The Meaning of the *Akedah* in Israeli Culture and Jewish Tradition," in: *Israel Studies* 3:1 (1998), 45–60. A. Sagi and D. Statman, *Religon and Morality* (1995); A. Sagi, *Kierkegaard, Religion and Existence (*2000); A. Sagi and D. Statman, "Divine Command Morality and Jewish Tradition," in: *Journal of Religious Ethics,* 23:1 (1995), 39–68.

AKERLOF, GEORGE A. (1940–), U.S. economist, Nobel Prize laureate. Born in New Haven, Connecticut, where his father was a member of the Yale faculty, Akerlof earned his bachelor's degree from Yale University in 1962 and his doctorate from the Massachusetts Institute of Technology in 1966. Akerlof's father, who was born in Sweden, was a chemist; his mother's family was of German-Jewish descent. His maternal grandfather established the first clinic in cardiology in the United States at Johns Hopkins, though he was later denied tenure there, according to Akerlof, because of his Jewish identity.

After receiving his doctorate, Akerlof joined the Economics Department of the University of California, Berkeley, where he began work on his landmark study "The Market for 'Lemons,'" for which he would later win the Nobel Prize for economics (in 2001), though it was initially rejected for publication by academic journals. In 1967 and 1968 he was a visiting professor at the Indian Statistical Institute in New Delhi, and then returned to Berkeley. From 1978 to 1980 he was Cassel Professor of Economics with Respect to Money and Banking at the London School of Economics. He subsequently served as Koshland Professor of Economics at Berkeley.

"The Market for 'Lemons': Quality Uncertainty and the Market Mechanism" was published in the *Quarterly Journal of Economics* in 1970. In this study of the role of asymmetric information in the market, Akerlof demonstrates how markets malfunction when buyers and sellers operate under different information, as in the example of used cars commonly called "lemons." The work had applications in other areas, such as health insurance, employment contracts, and financial markets. In *Efficiency Wage Models of the Labor Market (1986),* coauthored with his wife, Janet Yellen, Akerlof and Yellen propose rationales for the efficiency wage hypothesis, in which employers pay more than the market-clearing wage, contradicting neoclassical economic theory. Yellen later served as chair of the U.S. Council of Economic Advisors under President Bill Clinton.

Akerlof served as senior staff economist with the Council of Economic Advisors in 1973 and 1974 and was visiting research economist for the Federal Reserve System Board of Governors from 1977 to 1978. A member of the board of editors of the *Quarterly Journal of Economics* in 1983 and of the *American Economic Review* from 1983 to 1990, he was named a senior fellow of the Brookings Institution in 1994 and served on the board of directors of the National Bureau of Economic Research in 1997. In 2001 Akerlof shared the Nobel Prize for economics with A. Michael Spence and Joseph E. Stiglitz for their contributions to analyses of markets with asymmetric information.

[Dorothy Bauhoff (2nd ed.)]

AKHBAREI/ACCHABARON (Heb. עַכְבְּרֵי; modern Akbara), village in Upper Galilee possibly mentioned in the inscriptions relating to the campaigns of Tiglath-pilesar III (eighth century B.C.E.) near the line of fortifications erected by Josephus in 66 C.E. (Jos., Wars, 2:573; idem, Life, 37, 188). Eleazar, son of Simeon b. Yoḥai, died there, and when the people of Biri proposed removing his body to Meron, the inhabitants of Akhbarei objected (BM 84b). The *amoraim* Hananiah b. Akbari and Yose b. Avin lived there and Rabbi Yannai established a *bet midrash* with his pupils supporting themselves from agriculture. According to tradition the burial places of Yannai, Nehorai, and Dostai were pointed out at the site (*Kaftor va-Feraḥ*, 11, 47a). According to one source (Eccles. R. 2:8) pheasants were raised there. A Jewish community still existed in Akhbarei in the 11th century, but in 1522 the Jewish traveler Moses Bassola found its synagogue – referred to in Arabic by the locals as *"el-kenisah"* – in ruins. The remains of the synagogue were identified by Z. Ilan and subsequently partly excavated by E. Damati in 1988. Walls of houses, tombs, cisterns, and oil presses are also known from the site. It is identified with the Arab village of Akbara (now deserted), situated on a high cliff 3 mi. (5 km.) south of Safed, which used to cultivate olives, fruit, and tobacco.

BIBLIOGRAPHY: S. Klein (ed.), *Sefer ha-Yishuv*, 1 (1939), 117; Abel, Geog, 2 (1938), 235; Press, Ereẓ, 4 (1955), 724f.; G. Dalman, *Sacred Sites and Ways* (1935), index; B. Maisler (Mazar), in: BJPES, 1 (1933), 1–6; Neubauer, Géogr, 226f. **ADD. BIBLIOGRAPHY:** Z. Ilan, *Ancient Synagogues in Israel* (1991), 51; Y. Tsafrir, L. Di Segni, and J. Green, *Tabula Imperii Romani. Iudaea – Palaestina. Maps and Gazetteer.* (1994), 56.

[Michael Avi-Yonah / Shimon Gibson (2nd ed.)]

AKHENATON or **AKHENATEN** (**Amenophis IV**; c. 1367–1350 B.C.E. or 1350–1334), Egyptian pharaoh. Son of *Amenophis III and one of the most controversial figures in Egyptian history, Akhenaton has been credited, with justification, as the earliest monotheist in history. When Akhenaton came to the throne, after the wars of the 18th-dynasty kings in Asia had ceased, the most important and most powerful deity in Egypt was Amun-Re, and his was the most powerful priesthood. Second to Amun was the cult of the sun god Re in his various manifestations. Amun-Re had given victory to Egypt's pharaohs. They, in turn, showed their gratitude with wealth and endowments to the Amun-Re priesthood. Fostering the cult of a minor manifestation of the sun god Aton, Akhenaton made a complete break with the Amun cult, eventually going so far as to ban it and persecute its adherents. He abandoned his given name Amenophis, "Amun-is-satisfied," for Akhenaton, "He-who-is-useful to the sun-disc," or "Glorified-spirit-of-the-sun-disk." Although the king's actions had social and economic ramifications, and clearly weakened the Amun-Re priestshood as well as the priesthoods and cults of the other gods, it would be inaccurate to see his religious revolution as a pretext. Akhenaton broke sharply with the past, suppressed the cults of all the ancient gods, and championed a dehistoricized god of light and time. His solar deity was the creator of what would later be called "the universe," its sustainer and the mirror image of pharaonic monarchy. Akhenaton's iconoclasm extended beyond the elimination of images of deity and ridding the cult of myth. He even had the hieroglyphic script purged of its anthropomorphisms and theriomorphisms (images of gods in animal form) and did away with the world of The Beyond. Akhenaton's iconography reduced the sun to a solar disk, the Aton/Aten. Some scholars point to the fact that only Akhenaton and his wife worshipped the Aton, while the king himself was worshipped by the people, as proof that that the teachings of the king did not amount to true monotheism. But it might be more productive to compare Akhenaton's role to that of Jesus as the door to the Father in Christianity (Ephesians 3:4) and to a lesser extent, to that of the *Ẓaddik* as the mediator between God and humanity in Ḥasidism. As the army sided with the king, Akhenaton's revolution temporarily succeeded. The capital was transferred from Thebes to Akhetaton (modern El-Amarna), Amun-Re was suppressed, and the Aton became the paramount deity of Egypt. After Akhenaton's death, the old religious order triumphed and Atonism was vigorously stamped out.

Akhenaton's capital at Amarna was not only the center of a vigorous naturalistic art that broke with tradition in subject matter, though not in form or canon, but was also the site where the Amarna tablets, some 380 cuneiform texts, mostly letters, representing a portion of the foreign archives of the Egyptian court, were found. When first studied, these texts, the most important contemporary sources for Egypt's foreign policy toward Palestine and Syria, presented a picture of the empire's decline due to Akhenaton's indolence and pacificism. The threat of a Hittite invasion, the raids of *Habiru nomads, and treason on the part of the Egyptian vassals all seemed to be ignored by the Egyptian court. This was not the case, however. Egypt's main interest was to keep the trade routes to Mesopotamia open, and only incidentally to keep the tenuous peace. When Egyptian interests were really threatened, action was taken. There is even evidence in the Amarna Letters that Akhenaton was planning a campaign in Asia at the time of his death (see also *Tell el-Amarna). Forty years later the only mention of him in an Egyptian text is as "that criminal of Akhenaton."

BIBLIOGRAPHY: J.A. Wilson, *Culture of Ancient Egypt* (1958), 208–9, 215–28, 230–3; A.R. Schulman, in: *Journal of the American Research Center in Egypt*, 3 (1964), 51–69; C. Aldred, *Akhenaten* (1968); A. Weigall, *The Life of Akhnaton* (1922^2); D.B. Redford, *History and Chronology of the Eighteenth Dynasty of Egypt* (1967), 88–182. **ADD. BIBLIOGRAPHY:** Idem, *Akhenaten, the Heretic King* (1984); idem, ABD, 1, 135–37; idem, *Egypt, Canaan, and Israel in Ancient Times* (1992), 377–82; J. Assmann, in: *Bibel und Kirche*, 49 (1994), 78–82.

[Alan Richard Schulman / S. David Sperling (2nd ed.)]

AKIROV, ALFRED (1941–), Israeli entrpreneur. Akirov built a business empire ranging from real estate and hotels to high-tech, securing his position as one of the country's leading businessman, known for his determination and sound business instincts. He was born in Iraq in 1941 and immigrated in his childhood to Israel with his parents. He started working in construction in the family business and then struck out on his own. After a couple of business ventures, including participation in the acquisition of the Arkia Airline and a textile company, he set up his own holding company, Elrov, in 1978.

The company, which was listed on the Tel Aviv Stock Exchange in 1983, was active in two core businesses: real estate and technology and communication. Akirov demonstrated his expertise in the property business by building some of Israel's best-known development projects, including the Europe Building and the Opera Tower in Tel Aviv. The company also built and owns several large shopping malls in Israel's central area.

As the Israeli economy entered its worst economic recession in 2000, Elrov shifted part of its focus to overseas activity and the company acquired commercial centers in Switzerland, England, France, and the United States.

Akirov won fame with the building of the David Citadel, Jerusalem's most luxurious hotel, overlooking the walls of the capital's Old City. Plans to develop a nearby $150 million project, known as the Mamilla project, which included an upscale residential and business area, ran into difficulties after a long dispute with the municipality of Jerusalem.

Elrov also invested, through its Technorov subsidiary, in some of Israel's most promising high-tech start-ups and venture capital funds. However, the burst of the high-tech bubble in 2000 forced the company to write off much of its investment.

[Dan Gerstenfeld (2nd ed.)]

AKIVA (c. 50–135 C.E.), one of the most outstanding *tannaim*, probably the foremost scholar of his age. A teacher and martyr, he exercised a decisive influence in the development of the *halakhah*. A history of Akiva's scholarly activities – his relations to his teachers, R. Eliezer b. Hyrcanus, R. Joshua b. Hananiah, Rabban Gamaliel II, and to his disciples, R. *Meir, R. *Simeon b. Yoḥai, R. *Yose b. Ḥalafta, R. *Eleazar b. Shammua, and R. *Nehemiah – would be virtually identical to a history of tannaitic literature itself. The content of Akiva's teaching is preserved for us in the many traditions transmitted and interpreted by his students, which make up the vast majority of the material included in the Mishnah, the Tosefta, and the *Midreshei Halakhah*. Later tradition regarded Akiva as "one of the fathers of the world" (TJ, Shek. 3:1, 47b), and credited him with systematizing the *halakhot* and the *aggadot* (TJ, Shek. 5:1, 48c).

In the eyes of later storytellers, the period of the *tannaim* was a heroic age, and even the slightest scrap of information about the least of the *tannaim* can develop in the later *aggadah* into a tale of epic proportions. In the case of truly significant and heroic figures, like R. Akiva, this process of literary expansion and elaboration is inevitable. The resulting legends relating to Akiva's life and death are well known (see bibliography below), and we will summarize a few of them in outline here:

The Bavli tells that in his early years Akiva was not only unlearned, an *am ha-areẓ*, but also a bitter enemy of scholars: "When I was an *am ha-areẓ* I said, 'Had I a scholar in my power, I would maul him like an ass'" (Pes. 49b). Of relatively humble parentage (Ber. 27b), Akiva was employed as a shepherd in his early years by (Bar) Kalba Savu'a, one of the wealthiest men in Jerusalem (Ned. 50a; Ket. 62b). The latter's opposition to his daughter Rachel's marriage to Akiva led him to cut them both off. Abandoned to extreme poverty, Rachel once even sold her hair for food. Rachel made her marriage to Akiva conditional upon his devoting himself to Torah study. Leaving his wife behind, Akiva was away from home for 12 years (according to *Avot de-Rabbi Nathan* – 13 years). The Talmud relates that when Akiva, accompanied by 12,000 students, returned home after an absence of 12 years he overheard his wife telling a neighbor that she would willingly wait another 12 years if within that time he could increase his learning twofold. Hearing this, he left without revealing himself to her, and returned 12 years later with 24,000 students. Later in his career, Akiva was imprisoned by the Romans for openly teaching the Torah in defiance of their edict (Sanh. 12a). When Pappos b. Judah urged him to desist from studying and teaching in view of the Roman decree making it a capital offense, he answered with the parable of the fox which urged a fish to come up on dry land to escape the fisherman's net. The fish answered "'If we are afraid in the element in which we live, how much more should we be afraid when we are out of that element. We should then surely die.' So it is with us with regard to the study of the Torah, which is 'thy life and the length of thy days'" (Ber. 61b). He was not immediately executed and was reportedly allowed visitors (Pes. 112a; but cf. TJ, Yev. 12:5, 12d). Akiva was subsequently tortured to death by the Romans by having his flesh torn from his body with "iron combs." He bore his sufferings with fortitude, welcoming his martyrdom as a unique opportunity of fulfilling the precept, "Thou shalt love the Lord thy God with all thy heart and with all thy soul … even if you must pay for it with your life" (Ber. 61b).

Akiva also played a significant role in narratives which centered on the other great figures of his time. When R. Eliezer b. Hyrcanus was excommunicated, it was Akiva who was chosen to break the news to him (BM 59b). In the controversy between Rabban Gamaliel II and R. Joshua, Akiva attempted to effect a reconciliation between them (Ber. 27b–28c; cf. RH 2:9).

Granting the literary and religious power of these legends, the modern critical reader must approach them with care. Take, for example, the tradition, brought above, which ascribes to Akiva in his early years a bitter hatred and antagonism toward rabbinic scholars. This tradition appears in the Bavli as part of an extended collection of similar traditions (Pes. 49a–b), ascribed to various rabbinic scholars from the Land of Israel in the 2nd and 3rd centuries. S. Wald has shown (Pesaḥim III, 211–239) that this entire talmudic passage is a product of late tendentious revision of earlier sources, reflecting the antagonism between later Babylonian sages and their real or imagined interlocutors – *ame ha-areẓ* in their terminology. With regard to R. Akiva himself, this source must be viewed as pseudoepigraphic at best, and can neither be ascribed to him in any historical sense, nor can it be reconciled with other traditional accounts of his early life. For example, in the Talmud Yerushalmi (Naz. 7:1, 66a) we hear a very different story: "R. Akiva said: This is how I became a disciple of the sages. Once I was walking by the way and I came across a dead body [*met mitzvah*]. I carried it for four miles until I came to a cemetery and buried it. When I came to R. Yehoshua and R. Eliezer I told them what I had done. They told me: 'For every step you took, it is as if you spilled blood.' I said: 'If in a case where I intended to do good, I was found guilty, in a case where I did not intend to do good, I most certainly will be found guilty!' From that moment on, I became a disciple of the sages." The fact that Akiva in this story, while still an *am ha-areẓ,* both sought and expected the approval of the two sages who would in the future be his closest teachers, clearly contradicts the notion that at this stage in his life he both hated and held the sages in contempt.

Admittedly, we have no clear and compelling reason to accept the Yerushalmi's version of events as historically accurate. Nevertheless the very fact that it gives us an alternative version of how Akiva "became a disciple of the sages" raises questions – at the very least – about the historical reliability of the Bavli's story about Kalba Savu'a and his daughter. These traditions have themselves been the subject of intense study, most recently by S. Friedman, who traced the evolution of these stories within the Babylonian rabbinic tradition. Given the number and complexity of the traditions surrounding the figure of R. Akiva, it will in all likelihood be some time before it will be possible to evaluate their relative historical value and the religious, social, and literary tendencies imbedded in them.

Among the early traditions ascribed to Akiva in the Mishnah, we find him affirming the ideas of free will and God's omniscience, "Everything is foreseen, and free will is given" (Avot 3:15). He taught that a sinner achieves atonement by immersion in God's mercy, just as impurity is removed by the immersion in the waters of a *mikveh* (Yoma 8:9). Akiva is reported to have said: "Beloved is a man in that he was created in the image [of God]" (Avot 3:18), and held that "Thou shalt love thy neighbor as thyself" is the most fundamental principle of the Torah (Sifra, Kedoshim, Ch. 4:13). Akiva's insistence that the Song of Songs be regarded as an integral part of the canon – "All the Writings are holy; but the Song of Songs is Holy of Holies" (Yad, 3:5) – may be related to his mystical interests (Lieberman, *Mishnat Shir ha-Shirim*). According to Tosefta *Hagigah* (2:2), Akiva received instruction in the mystical traditions concerning the divine *merkavah* from R. Joshua, who himself received these traditions from R. Johanan b. Zakkai. In addition, R. Akiva is counted as one of the four sages who "entered the *pardes*," and was the only one of the four who "ascended in peace and descended in peace," i.e., participated in this mystical experience and emerged unharmed. As a result of these traditions, R. Akiva became the protagonist of *Heikhalot Zuṭarti*, one of the earlier works of the *heikhalot* literature, imparting instructions to the initiate concerning the dangers involved in ascending to heaven and concerning the techniques necessary for evading these dangers.

For Akiva's method of midrashic interpretation of scripture, and the school of *Midrash Halakhah* which bears his name, **Midrashei Halkhah.*

See also *Bar Kochba.

BIBLIOGRAPHY: L. Finkelstein, *Akiva, Scholar, Saint and Martyr* (1936, 1962²); Bacher, Tann, 1 (1903); Weiss, Dor, 2 (1904), 97–106; Frankel, Mishnah (1923²), 118–30; Halevi, Dorot, 7 (1923), 455–67, 620–9, 659–64; Derenbourg, Hist, 329ff., 395ff., 418ff.; Hyman, Toledot, 988–1008; J.S. Zuri, *Rabbi Akiva* (Heb., 1924); Alon, Toledot, 1 (1958), index; I. Konovitz, *Rabbi Akiva* (Heb., 1965²). **ADD. BIBLIOGRAPHY:** S. Lieberman, in: *Jewish Gnosticism, Merkabah Mysticism, and Talmudic Tradition* (1960), 118–126; S. Friedman, in: *Saul Lieberman Memorial Volume* (Heb., 1988), 119–164; S. Friedman, in: JSIJ, 3 (2004), 1–39; D. Boyarin, *Carnal Israel* (1993); T. Ilan, in: *Jewish Women in Greco-Roman Palestine* (1995); idem, in: *AJS Review,* 22:1 (1997), 1–17; S. Wald, *Pesaḥim III* (Heb., 2000), 211–239.

[Harry Freedman / Stephen G. Wald (2nd ed.)]

AKIVA BAER BEN JOSEPH (**Simeon Akiva Baer**; 17th century), talmudist and kabbalist. Akiva was among the Jews who were expelled from Vienna in 1670. He thereafter wandered through the whole of Bohemia and parts of Germany, earning his living by teaching Talmud and delivering lectures in the synagogue on the Sabbath. He interrupted his travels when he was elected rabbi of Burgpreppach, in Bavaria. There Akiva wrote a kabbalistic commentary on daily prayers entitled *Avodat ha-Bore* ("The Worship of the Creator," 1688), comprised of five parts, each beginning with one of the letters of his name (A.K.I.B.A.). This work met with success and was published three times. A new commentary for the Sabbath and holidays was added to the third edition. Akiva interrupted his travels a second time to become rabbi of Zeckendorf, near Bamberg. There he met the leader of the community, Seligman Levi Meir, with whom he composed a short encyclopedia to *Midrash Rabbah*, which was published under the title *Pi Shenayim* ("A Double Share," 1702). He remained in Zeckendorf six years. From there Akiva was called to Schnaitach, which at that time had a large Jewish community. There he was imprisoned during a riot. After his release, Akiva became rabbi of Gunzenhausen and, finally, second rabbi of Ansbach. He was the author of two works in Yiddish, which had even a wider circulation than his Hebrew works, namely: *Abbir Ya'akov* ("The Mighty [God] of Jacob," 1700), a collection of legends from the Zohar and from the *Midrash ha-Ne'elam* about the patriarchs, based on the first 47 chapters of Genesis; "*Ma'asei Adonai*" ("The Deeds of the Lord"), a collection of wondrous stories from the Zohar, from the works of Isaac Luria, and from other kabbalistic books.

BIBLIOGRAPHY: Steinschneider, Cat Bod, 2612, no. 7210; Benjacob, Oẓar, 2, no. 22; 427, no. 12; 457, no. 69.

[*Encyclopaedia Judaica* (Germany)]

AKIVA BEN MENAHEM HA-KOHEN OF OFEN (Buda; second half of 15th century), Hungarian financial expert and scholar in Buda. After Jacob *Mendel, Akiva was the most influential Jew at the court of King Matthias I of Hungary (1458–90). Epitaphs of members of the family (in Prague) refer to him as *nasi* and "head of the entire Diaspora." In 1496 Akiva was still living in Buda. Later forced to leave Hungary as a result of the slanderous allegations of jealous Hungarian magnates, he settled in Prague where he established a yeshivah. Akiva had 12 sons and 13 daughters, 12 of whom married *kohanim* (priests). When on holidays 25 members of his family pronounced the priestly blessing, they were considered to fulfill an interpretation of Numbers 6:23: "Thus (Heb. *koh* the numerical equivalent of the letters being 25) shall ye bless…"

BIBLIOGRAPHY: S. Kohn, *A zsidók története Magyarországon* (1884), 227–8; S. Bűchler, *A zsidók története Budapesten* (1901), 57–58; idem, in: *Magyar-Zsidó Szemle*, 27 (1910), 82–83; B. Mandl, in: *Mult és Jövő*, 25 (1935), 316; MHJ, 2 (1937), 537–8; A. Schreiber, *Hebraeische Kodexueberreste in ungarlaendischen Einbandstafeln* (1969), 122.

[Alexander Scheiber]

AKKAD (Heb. אַכַּד), one of the capital cities of *Nimrod in Shinar (Sumer), according to the "table of nations" (Gen. 10:9–10). In the cuneiform sources, Akkad (Sumerian Agade or Aggide) refers to both a city and a country in northern Babylonia which first flourished as the seat of the "(Old) Akkadian" kings in the Sargonic period (c. 3380–3200 B.C.E.). The city's exact location is still unknown, but it must have been situated on the (ancient) Euphrates, upstream from Nippur and not far from Babylon. According to tradition, it was founded by Sargon, a Semite who began his career at the court of the city of Kish. He assumed a name characteristic of a usurper (Sargon literally: "the king is legitimate") and the title "king of Kish." In this he was followed by his sons Rimush and Manishtusu. His grandson Naram-Sin assumed new titles and dignities and seems to have brought the Akkadian Empire to new heights, but in so doing he overreached himself. By the end of his reign, the rapid decline of the empire had begun. Later Sumerian tradition attributed this to Naram-Sin's sins against the Temple of Enlil at Nippur, but modern scholarship tends to attribute it to the increasing inroads of the barbarian Gutians from the eastern highlands. Under Naram-Sin's son, Shar-kali-sharri, Akkadian rule was progressively restricted, as the more modest title of "King of Akkad" attests. The decline and fall of the dynasty left a deep impression on the country: Naram-Sin was turned into a stereotype of the unfortunate ruler in later literature, and the "end of Agade" became not only a fixed point for subsequent chronology but also a type-case for omens and prophecies.

While the destruction of the city of Akkad was complete, the name of the country survived into later periods. The geographical expression "[land of] Sumer and [land of] Akkad" came to designate the central axis of Sumero-Akkadian political hegemony; i.e., the areas lying respectively northwest and southeast of Nippur. The kings who held that religious and cultural capital therefore assumed the title "king of Sumer and Akkad." They tended to replace it, or from Hammurapi on even to supplement it, with the loftier title of "king of the four quarters [of the world]" when to these two central lands they added the rule of the western and eastern lands, Amurru and Elam (see *Sumerians). From Middle Babylonian times

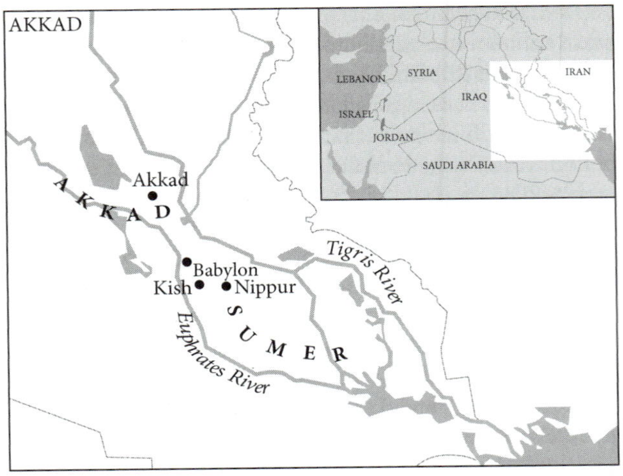

on (1500–1000), the noun Akkad was used in the cuneiform sources as a virtual synonym for Babylonia.

The adjective "Akkadian" was used in various senses by the ancients: originally it designated the Semitic speakers and speech of Mesopotamia as distinguished from the Sumerian, then the older Semitic stratum as distinguished from the more recent Semitic arrivals of *Amorite speech, and finally Babylonian as distinguished from Assyrian. In modern terminology, *Akkadian is used as a collective term for all the East Semitic dialects of Mesopotamia.

Which of these meanings best applies to the "Akkad" of Genesis 10:10 can only be answered in the context of the entire Nimrod pericope (Gen. 10:8–12) and of the identification of Nimrod. Probably the figure of Nimrod combines features pertaining to several heroic kings of the Mesopotamian historic tradition, from Gilgamesh of Uruk to Tukulti-Ninurta I of Assur (see E.A. Speiser). However, the reference to Akkad as one of his first or capital cities points to the Old Akkadian period, and to its two principal monarchs, Sargon and Naram-Sin. Both were central figures of Mesopotamian historiography, and Naram-Sin in particular introduced the title of "mighty [man]" into the Mesopotamian titulary. Genesis 10:8 may reflect this innovation.

BIBLIOGRAPHY: I.J. Gelb, *Old Akkadian Writing and Grammar* (1961[2]); W.W. Hallo, *Early Mesopotamian Royal Titles* (1957); Speiser, in: *Eretz Israel*, 5 (1959), 34–36 (Eng. section); Finkelstein, in: *Proceedings of the American Philosophical Society*, 107 (1963), 461–72.

[William W. Hallo]

AKKADIAN LANGUAGE. Akkadian is the designation for a group of closely related East Semitic dialects current in Mesopotamia from the early third millennium until the Christian era. Closely connected to it is Eblaite, the language found at Tell Maradikh (ancient Ebla) in northern Syria.

The name is derived from *akkadūm*, the relative adjective of *a.ga.dé* = *Akkad (biblical אַכַּד), the capital of the Sargonic Empire (c. 2400 B.C.E.). It is not known what the speakers of

East Semitic in Mesopotamia called themselves or their speech prior to this period. The available textual evidence does not show any marked dialectical discontinuity between the pre-Sargonic and the Sargonic periods. The earliest textual occurrence is from the first dynasty of Ur (c. 2600 B.C.E.) and the latest from the first century C.E. The dialectical history of Akkadian can be schematically represented as follows:

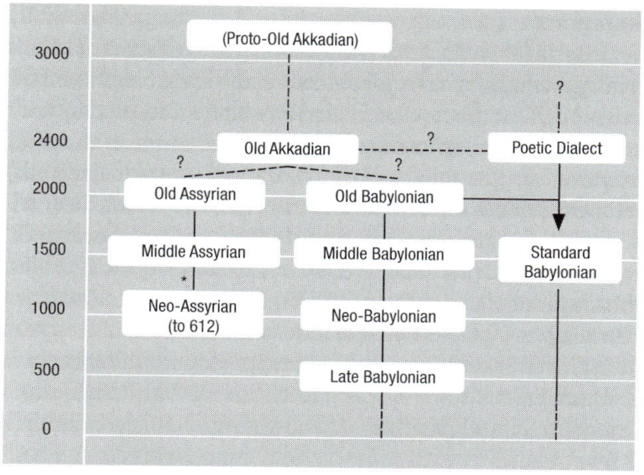

* Linear development uncertain

The Old Akkadian corpus consists of royal inscriptions, economic documents, letters, and the occasional literary text from the pre-Sargonic, Sargonic, and Ur III periods (to c. 2000 B.C.E.). These texts, in particular the royal inscriptions, are in large measure known from Old Babylonian copies, products of the Nippur scribal school in southern Babylonia. Most of the other original material also comes from this region, but texts have been found further afield: in *Elam, northern Syria, and eastern Anatolia (Asia *Minor). It is not clear whether Old Akkadian is the parent of the later Akkadian dialects. While some obvious phonologic and morphologic isoglosses would seem to indicate that Old Assyrian is the descendant of Old Akkadian, the latter in other, more basic aspects, has much in common with Old Babylonian. However, both Old Assyrian and Old Babylonian may have evolved from other unknown and undocumented dialects. (On this point see M. Hilgert, "New Perspectives in the Study of Third Millennium Akkadian," *Cuneiform Digital Library Journal*, 4 (2003), 1–14.)

Assyrian

Old Assyrian is mainly known from letters and economic documents excavated in eastern Anatolia, chiefly in the lower city at Kultepe (ancient Kaniš) where an Assyrian mercantile colony (*kārum*) was located at the beginning of the second millennium. The corpus includes a small number of royal inscriptions and about a dozen literary texts, including some incantations; a few of the texts originated in *Assur and other north Mesopotamian sites, such as Nuzi.

The best known Middle Assyrian document is the so-called "Middle Assyrian laws" from Assur, dating from the middle and second half of the second millennium B.C.E. Economic and legal documents and letters are also attested.

Neo-Assyrian texts consist for the most part of letters and economic documents with a few literary texts. Documents written in this dialect come to an abrupt end with the destruction of Nineveh and other cities in 612 B.C.E. and the complete collapse of the Assyrian Empire shortly thereafter. It should be noted that the Neo-Assyrian royal inscriptions are written in Standard Babylonian, as are the inscriptions of the dynasties ruling southern Babylonia in the first millennium B.C.E. The relative absence of legal material from the private sector seems to be due to an increasing use of Aramaic.

Babylonian

Old Babylonian is richly documented in large numbers of letters, economic records, state and legal documents, including the Code of Hammurapi, royal inscriptions, and a sizable corpus of literary texts consisting of hymns and various types of lyric and epic poetry. Several dialects, some showing substrate influence, can be discerned: a southern and northern dialect in Babylonia, a northeast dialect centered in the *Diyalah region, and provincial dialects such as those from Susa and *Mari. Literary texts are generally written in a poetic register (formally called "dialect") which exhibits archaic forms and syntax. This poetic dialect, the so-called "hymnic-epic dialect," could be either a survival of an earlier stage of the language or an older dialect with close affinities to Old Akkadian in a restricted stereotyped use. Post-Old Babylonian Akkadian literature from all centers is usually written in a linguistic register which is an artificial literary offshoot of Old Babylonian, and is influenced by archaic forms current in the older poetic dialect, called Standard Babylonian. Standard Babylonian was cultivated by the scribes for literary purposes from the middle of the second millennium and through the first millennium B.C.E. until Akkadian ceased to be used. Standard Babylonian suppressed literary creativity in local dialects, e.g., Assyrian, but it tends to show a strong influence of the locally spoken tongue.

Middle Babylonian is attested in letters, economic and official documents, and a few literary documents. While the size of the corpus of Middle Babylonian texts found in Mesopotamia proper is moderate, geographically this dialect (and variations of it) is the most widely spread and was used all over western Asia during the second millennium B.C.E. The Akkadian material from the archives of Bogazköy and Ras Shamra (*Ugarit) are written in local forms of Middle Babylonian, as are the letters of El *Amarna found in Egypt, which, however, originated in Anatolia, Syria, Palestine, and Mesopotamia. The wide diffusion of Akkadian during the period was due to its use as a diplomatic language.

Neo-Babylonian is likewise represented mainly by a large corpus of non-literary sources, especially letters and economic documents. The use of the last surviving "living" dialect, Late Babylonian, petered out completely during the Seleucid period. Standard Babylonian continued to be in use in the temple scriptoria, in the transmission of canonical compositions, and in the compilation of astronomical texts which are the last remnant of the Mesopotamian tradition. The latest datable text so far recognized is an astronomical almanac written in 385 Seleucid era (74/75 C.E.).

Phonology

Akkadian is written with signs which apparently were originally devised for Sumerian. The application of the Sumerian system to Akkadian resulted in a mixed method of writing: on the one hand with logograms and, on the other, with syllables of the type *vC, Cv*, or *CvC* (*C* = consonant; *v* = vowel). The phonemic system and structure of Sumerian is radically different from that of Akkadian and the writing system consequently presented inadequacies which were only partially overcome during the long history of writing Akkadian. A phonological interpretation is likewise hindered due to a tendency toward historic writing.

VOWELS. The vocalic phonemes represented are the long and short *a, i, u, e. E* does not seem to be original but is derived from *a* or *i*; e.g., *ilqaʾ* > *ilqe* ("he took"), while *i* tends to become *e*, especially in Assyrian, and the etymologically long *ī* became *ē* already in Old Babylonian times. Rare mixed writings, e.g., *ma-ru-iṣ* (Old Babylonian; "is sick"), have been used in attempts to demonstrate other vowel qualities, in this case the *u-i* sequence being taken as representing ʉ. Greek transcriptions from the Seleucid period which reflect the pronunciation of Late Babylonian represent *u* by *o*, e.g., οζον = *uzun* ("ear of"), and *ū* by *ω*, e.g., νωρ = *nūr* ("light of"). Diphthongs are monophthongized, e.g., ‡*ayn-* > *īn-* ("eye"), ‡*mawt-* > *mūt* ("death"). (The double dagger, ‡, indicates the reconstructed form.) Pseudo-diphthongs, such as Old Babylonian *nawrum* ("bright"), probably represent *nawirum*. A basic characteristic of the Assyrian dialects is the vowel harmony operative with short unaccented *a* in an open syllable which assimilates progressively, e.g., *awutum* (nominative singular), *awitim* (genitive singular), *awatam* (accusative singular; "word"); in Babylonian: *awatum, awatim, awatam*. Vowel length is phonemic, e.g., *šarratum* ("queen"), *šarrātum* ("queens").

CONSONANTS. The considerable reduction in consonants characteristic of Akkadian (and of later forms of other Semitic languages, such as Hebrew and Aramaic), as compared to the theoretically reconstructed consonant phonemes of Proto-Semitic, or those of other Semitic languages such as Ugaritic or Arabic, is already evident in Old Akkadian. By the time of the earliest written Akkadian, the dentals *ḏ, ṭ* and *ḍ* had shifted to *z, ṣ*, and *ṣ* respectively, while *ṯ* was on its way to *š̱* but in Old Akkadian is distinguished graphically from etymological *š* and *ś*.

The laryngeals for the most part merged with ʾ or disappeared (Sumerian substrate influence?), compensating with the lengthening of the vowel and apophony, e.g., ‡*baʿlum* > *bēlum* ("lord"), although in Assyrian and some Babylonian dialects this process is not complete. In Old Akkadian ʾ and *ḥ* are at least partially distinct as shown by such writings as *ra-si-im* = *raʾšim*, later *rēšim* (genitive singular of "head") and the special use of the sign *É* as in *il-qa- É* = ‡*ilqaḥ* ("he took," cf. Sumerian É.GAL > Akkadian *ekallum* > Hebrew היכל). The influence of intrusive West Semitic dialects is reflected in doublets, e.g., Old Babylonian *ḫadannum* for *adannum* ("fixed time," *ʿdn*), Neo-Assyrian *ḫannū* for *annū* ("this," *hn-*). (On laryngals see L. Kogan, "*g in Akkadian," UF, 33 (2001), 263–98.)

Of the various phonological changes affecting consonants as a result of environmental conditioning two should be mentioned. In the nominal patterns *mapras* and *mupras* (except in certain nominal forms, e.g., the participle of the verb of the derived themes; see below) of roots containing a labial phoneme, *m* dissimilates to *n* (Barth's Law), e.g., ‡*markabtum* > *narkabtum* ("chariot"). Likewise, in any given root one of two emphatics dissimilate, viz, ṣ > s (very rare), q > k, ṭ > t – in this order of stability (Geers' Law), e.g., ‡*ṣabātuṃ* >*ṣabātum* ("to seize"), ‡*qaṣābu* > *kaṣābu* ("to cut away").

Initial *w* disappeared already in Old Babylonian, e.g., *warḫu* (Old Babylonian), *arḫu* (post-Old Babylonian; "month"). In Assyrian, *wa-* > *(wu >) u*, e.g., *warḫum* > *urḫum*. Babylonian intervocalic *-w-* > *-m-*, e.g., *awīlum* > *amīlum* ("man"). In Assyrian, *wa-* > *wu* > *u*, e.g., *warhum* > *urhum*. Babylonian *dēq* ("is good"). On the other hand, intervocalic *-m-* in Late Babylonian > *w* or ʾ, e.g., *Šamaš* > ‡*Š(a)w(a)š* ("the sun god" (from Aramaic transcriptions); cf. CAYH for *šamē* ("of heaven") in Seleucid Greek transcriptions; cf. Hebrew סיון (< *Simānu*). Survival of the *y* is limited.

Morphology

PRONOUNS. Akkadian shows a rich range of bound and unbound pronominal forms, especially personal pronouns. In the third person, the distinctive element is *š*, where West Semitic, for example, has *h*, e.g., *šu* ("he"), *ši* ("she"). Unbound pronominal forms distinguish three case forms: nominative, genitive/accusative, dative, e.g., *anāku, yāti, yāši* ("I"), respectively, and in bound forms genitive, dative, and accusative, e.g., *bēlī* ("my lord"), *išpur-šunūšim* ("he sent to them"), *išpur-šunūti* ("he sent them"), respectively where it can be seen that in the plural at least *-š-* is characteristic of the dative and *-t-* of the accusative. The dative pronouns are a strong isogloss between Old Akkadian and Old Babylonian. They are restricted in Old Assyrian where the genitive-accusative forms function as datives; dative forms appear regularly from Middle Assyrian on. There is also a possessive pronominal adjective, e.g., *yāʾum* ("mine"). Of the various *deixis* forms, *annūm* ("this") and *ullum* ("that") can be cited, but many dialect words and forms for the near and far *deixis* also occur. In addition, the third person unbound pronoun can be used anaphorically, e.g., *awīlum šu* ("that man"). Interrogatives include *mannum* ("who") and *mīnum* ("what"), *ayyum* ("which [one]") and *mā* ("what") in older dialects. The indefinite pronoun is *mamman* (< ‡*man-man*). A true relative pronoun is found only in Old Akkadian: *šu, ši, ša*, fem. *šat*, plural *šūt, šāt*. Old Assyrian has some of these forms in personal names but in later dialects they occur residually in stereotyped phrases, mostly literary. The particle *ša* serves as an all-purpose relative, in both nominal and verbal phrases, e.g., *bitum ša rēdim* ("the soldiers house") and *ša īpušu* ("which he made"). (On this see G. Deutscher, "The Akkadian Relative Clauses in Cross-Linguistic Perspective," ZA, 92 (2002), 86–105.)

NOUNS AND ADJECTIVES. Nouns and adjectives show structural patterning as in other Semitic languages, e.g., *parrāsum* as an "occupational" pattern, e.g., *dayyānum* ("judge") or *qarrādum* ("warrior"); and *maprasum* indicating instrument or place, e.g., *maškanum* ("depot"; cf. Barth's Law above).

Formally, there are two genders, masculine (zero marker) and feminine (*at* marker). There are three numbers: singular, plural, and dual. Mimation in the singular of both genders and in the plural feminine, and nunation in the dual are regular until the end of the Old Babylonian and Old Assyrian periods. The singular is triptotically declined forming a nominative, accusative, and genitive in the earlier periods, yielding later to a binary opposition of nominative/accusative and genitive. The plural and dual are diptotic. Traces of a productive dual, nominal, and verbal, are evident in Old Akkadian but by post-Old Akkadian times it has become virtually vestigial, surviving mostly in set words and phrases.

The vocative is expressed by a stressed form with zero ending in the singular, e.g., *eṭel* (< ‡*eṭel*, "O, youth"), *kalab* (< ‡*kalb*, "O, dog"). Plural vocatives seem to coincide with the nominative forms. The morphology of the adjective differs from that of the noun uniquely in that the masculine plural exhibits the morphemes *-ūtu(m)* for the nominative and *-ūti(m)* for the oblique cases, e.g., *šarrū rabūtum* ("the great kings"). The construct case of the noun is a short form with the case markers removed or reduced, e.g., *bēl bītim* ("the householder"), *ilšu* ("his god"), *mārat awīlim* ("man's daughter"), *ilū mātim* ("the gods of the land"). The noun or adjective, used as a predicate, can be declined with the bound suffix personal forms, those of the first and second person showing affinity to the personal pronouns, e.g., *šarrāku* ("I am king"), *lū awīlāt* ("be a man!"), while the third person shows gender and plural affixes only, e.g., *libbašu ṭāb* ("he is satisfied"), *Ištar rigmam ṭābat* ("Ištar, sweet of voice"). Feminine nouns are declined in the stative without the feminine marker, e.g., *gašrāte malkāti (< malkatum) šumūki ṣirū* ("You [Ištar] are powerful, you are a princess, your names are majestic").

PREPOSITIONS AND CONJUNCTIONS. Prepositions govern the genitive ease of nouns, e.g, *alpam kīma alpim* ("[he will replace] ox for ox"), and most prepositions can also function as conjunctions in which case the verb appears in the subjunctive, e.g., *kīma ērubu* ("when/as soon as he entered"). It should be noted that *ina* ("in"), *ana* ("to") and *ištu* ("from") suppleted the common Semitic prepositions *b,(ʾ)l,* and *mn* respectively at a preliterate stage of Akkadian.

OTHER PARTICLES. Common negations are *lā* and *ul*, e.g., *lā iddinūšum* ("they did not give him"), *ul aššat* ("she is not a wife"), *lā kittum* ("untruth"). Conjunctives are *u*, "and," "or," e.g., *bēl šamē u erṣetim* ("Lord of heaven and earth"), and the enclitic *-ma* used post-verbally as a sentence conjunctive, e.g., *ul itārma... ul uššab* ("he shall not return and take his seat [as judge]"). After nominal or pronominal forms, it forms a stressed predicate (cleft sentence), e.g., *adi máti* ("until when"), *adi matīma* ("until when is it that – ?"), *umma Ḫammurapīma* ("thus Hammurapi," introductory formula in letters), *šūma ilikšu illak* ("it is he who will perform the [feudal] service").

Umma, with or without the enclitic *-mi*, or in the Assyrian dialects *mā*, introduces direct speech. A strong interrogative tone can be indicated by vowel lengthening, e.g., *ina bītika mannum biri anākū bariākū* ("who in your household goes hungry? Should I go hungry?"). Unreal statements are indicated by the enclitic *-man*. Conditional sentences are introduced by *šumma* (or *šumma-man* for unreal conditions) with the verb in the indicative.

ADVERBIAL CONSTRUCTIONS. In adverbial constructions the accusative is often used, e.g., *imittam* ("to the right"). Among the adverbial formatives are the locative-adverbial in *-um/ū* which with nouns functions sequentially as a case, *libbu/libbum* = *ina libbim, libbuššu* < *-umšu* ("in it"), and is used as an adverbial formative, e.g., *balum* ("without"). The locative terminative affixes *-iš* in the meaning "to," e.g., *ašriš* ("to the place") and adverbially as in *elīš* ("above," "upward").

VERBS. BASIC PATTERNS. All tenses of the verb are prefixed forms: *iprus* ("he cut") preterite, *iparras* ("he cuts") present-future with characteristic doubling of the middle root radical, and, unique to Akkadian, *iptaras* ("he has cut / will have cut") perfect, a syntactically conditioned stressed or consequential form, e.g., *dayyānum dīnam idīn... warkānumma dīnšu īteni* ("the judge passed judgment but afterward changed his verdict") or as a future perfect, e.g., *inūma issanqūnikkum* ("When they will have reached you..."). The imperative can be derived from the preterite base, e.g., *pursus* (< ‡*prus*), imperative singular (cf. below). The precative is formed by the proclitic particle *lu* + preterite for the third person singular and plural and *i* + preterite for the first person plural, e.g., *lipuš* < *lu* + *ipuš* ("let him do"), *lubluṭ* <*lu*+*abluṭ* ("may I stay alive"), *i nillik* ("let us go"). Contracted forms in Assyrian differ. Other moods include the indicative in main or independent clauses having gender and plural suffixes, the subjunctive in *-u* (Assyrian also in *-ni*, also affixed to non-verbal forms) in subordinated clauses, e.g., *ša īpušu* ("which he did"). In Babylonia affixes of the subjunctive and ventive are mutually exclusive. Unique to Akkadian, and of a different character, is the *ventive*, or *allative*, indicating motion toward the speaker or focus of action, e.g., *illik* ("he came"), *illikam* ("he came here"). The base form participle is patterned *pārisum* (cf. Hebrew *qal* active participle), while other themes (~ Hebrew *binyanim*) have *mu-* prefix forms. There is no passive participle, but the verbal adjective of each theme is a partial semantic surrogate. The verbal adjective, used in the predicative form, is declined (the stative) with bound suffix pronominal forms, as with the predicative state of nouns (cf. above). In form, then, the stative bears great resemblance to the West Semitic perfect and the old perfective in Egyptian. In meaning the stative generally indicates the resultant state indicated by the action of the verb in its finite forms, e.g., *maška labiš* ("he is/was clothed in a skin").

Various pronominal morphemes are prefixed to the finite forms of the verb to indicate the person. The plural number is indicated in the second and third person by suffixes. Old Akkadian, Assyrian, and, less commonly, the poetic dialect distinguish the third person feminine singular while in Babylonian the masculine form serves both.

THEMES (~ HEBREW *BINYANIM*). In common with other Semitic languages, semantic nuances can be given to the verb by a system of themes or forms exhibiting characteristic structures. The basic forms are commonly four in number, though rarer types can also be demonstrated. The basic verb theme is termed *G* (~ Hebrew *qal*) and contains verbs with both stative, e.g., *(w)arāqum* ("to be/become pale") and fientive (transitive) meaning, e.g., *ṣabātum* ("to seize"). Verbs show various tense vowels between the second and third root radicals in the present-future and preterite: *a – u, a – a, i – i,* and *u – u*. The characteristic vowel of the perfect is the same as that of the present, thus *iparras* ("he cuts"), *iptaras* ("he has cut"), *iprus* ("he cut").

The *D* theme (~ Hebrew *piʿel*) is characterized by the doubling of the middle root radical and, in common with the *Š* theme, it employs a different set of pronominal prefixes than *G*, and shows a characteristic *a – i* alternation between the tense vowel of the present and preterite. The perfect here goes with the preterite in the choice of tense vowel, thus *uparras, uptarris, uparris*. In meaning the *D* can be factitive, especially with stative verbs, e.g., *dummuqum* ("to make good"; *damāqum*, "to be good"); causative, e.g., *lummudu* ("to teach"; *lamādu*, "to learn"); estimative, e.g., *q/gullulu* ("to treat disparagingly"; *qalālu*, "to be/become insufficient"); iterative, e.g, *sullūm* ("to pray"), *quʾʾum* ("to wait"). The *D* also serves as a denominating theme, e.g., *ṣullulu* ("to roof over"; *ṣulūlu*, "roof") and more rarely indicates plurality of object, or subject.

The *Š* theme (Hebrew *hiphʿil*) is so termed after the *-š(a)-* morpheme placed before the first root radical. Thus, *ušapras, uštapris, ušapris* have the same tense vowel alternation as in *D* and of the nuances conveyed by this theme the main one is causative, e.g., *šūṣūm* ("to bring out"; *waṣūm*, "to go out"). An internal *Š* indicates entry into a state or condition of some duration, e.g., *šulburum* ("to grow old"), *šumšūm* ("to spend the night").

In the *N* theme, an *n(a)* morpheme is placed before the first root radical. Like in the *G* theme, various tense vowels are shown, and these can be correlated with those of the *G*. For *parāsum*, the forms are *ipparras* (< ‡*inparras), ittapras* (< ‡*intapras*), *ipparis* (< ‡*inparis*). The *N* theme is commonly a passive to the *G*, e.g., *napšurum* ("to be untied, absolved, explained"). Other nuances are reflexive, e.g., *nalbušum* ("to get dressed") and related middle meanings, e.g., *naplusum* ("to look [benignly] upon"). Stative verbs take on an ingressive meaning, e.g., *nabšūm* ("to come into being"; *bašūm*, "to be").

Within each theme occur forms with *-ta* and *tan/tana-* infixes. The *t* forms (*Gt, Dt, Št, Nt*) with the *-ta-* infixes give a reciprocal or separative meaning, e.g., *imtalkū* (["the judges] consulted together"), *ittalak* ("he went off"). Some *t* forms coincide with perfect forms making the latter difficult to recognize. The *tn* forms (*Gtn, Dtn, Štn, Ntn*) with a *-tan/tana-* infix give a durative or iterative force, e.g., *ittanallak* ("he walks around/back and forth"), *imtanaqqutū* ("[the stars] fall down [from heaven]").

Akkadian lacks a developed series of parallel passive themes. The *G* theme shows no trace of such related forms. Here the *N* theme serves as passive. In the *D* theme, some *t* forms, identical with other *t* forms of the *D* theme, have a passive or middle nuance, e.g., *utellulum* ("to become clean, cleanse oneself"; *elēlum*, "to be clean"; *ullulum*, "to cleanse"), *eleppam uṭṭebbe uša libbiša uḫtalliq* ("he subsequently sank the boat and thereby caused the loss of its cargo") as against *mātī... uḫtalliq* ("my country has been destroyed"). Likewise, in the *Š* theme, *t* forms can have a passive or middle meaning. Compare *šeʾam kī maṣi tuštaddin* (perfect; "how much grain have you brought in?") and *šeʾum ša uštaddinu* ("grain which was brought in"). These *t* forms are termed *Št1* in distinction to a rarer non-passive *t* form, *Št2*, which has a unique present, e.g., *lā tuštallapat* ("you are not to touch").

WEAK VERBS. There are several classes of "weak" verbs. *Primae Aleph* has two groups, those without apophony, e.g., *akālum* ("to eat"), and those with, e.g, *epēšum* ("to do"). The vowel coloring is generally a function of the underlying laryngeal, although some forms show a strong *aleph*. The basic phonological change here is that *vʾ* > *v¯*; thus, ‡*iʾpuš* preterite (pattern *iprus*) > *īpuš* ("he made"), and similarly throughout the paradigm. *Mediae Aleph* also have "*a*" and "e" classes. They further differentiate in a strong *aleph* group, e.g., *išʾal* ("he asked") and a *ā/ē* group which decline like vocalic roots (see below), but crossovers are not uncommon. *Primae Nun* is characterized by the assimilation of the *N* root element to a following consonant, e.g., *iddin* < ‡*indin* ("he gave"). In *Primae Waw* initial or intervocalic *w* goes to ʾ or *m* in post-Old Babylonian times, e.g., *walādum* > *alādum* ("to give birth"). In fientive verbs *vw* > *uw* > *ū*, e.g., ‡*iwsib* > *uwsib* > *ūšib* ("he sat"). Statives behave like *Primae Yod*, e.g., *īqer* (not *ūqer* < ‡*iwqer*; note that the occurrence of the initial or final *y* is very restricted in historic Akkadian and these verbs generally behave like *Primae Aleph* with the apophony of *a* >*e*). Both fientive and stative verbs have *Primae Yod* type *Š* forms, e.g., *ušēšib* ("he seated" as if < ‡*usayšib*), *ušūšib* type forms (< *ušawšib*) occurring only rarely in poetic dialect (but note Neo-Assyrian *ittušib*, Babylonian *ittašab* ("he sat")).

Vocalic roots ("hollow verbs" *Mediae Waw/Yod*) are of the pattern *CvC*, where the middle radical has to be considered as a long vowel: *ū, i, ā*, or *ē* (secondary). In the *G* present-future and in the present-future and preterite of the *D*, the suffixing of vocalic morphemes induces reduction of the theme vowel – middle root radical and gemination of the third root radical, e.g., *ikān* ("he is upright"), *ikunnū* ("they are upright"). In Assyrian uncontracted forms are usual, thus *ikūan*. The last major division of weak verbs is the *Tertiae Infirmae*. These are final *-u*, e.g., *iḫdu* ("he was happy"); final *-i, iqbi* ("he spoke"); final *-a, ikla* ("he withheld"); and final *-e, išme* ("he heard"). These vowels are *anceps* and are long when followed by bound morphemes, e.g., *iqbi*, but *iqbīšum* ("he told him"). Two main groups of quadrilateral verbs occur of the type $C^1 C^2 C^3 C^4$ in the *Š* and *N* themes, e.g., *nabalkutum* ("to jump over"), *šubalkutum* ("to cause to jump over, overturn"), including a weak class, e.g, *naparkū* ("to be idle, unemployed"). A third type is of the pattern $Š\ C^1\ C^2\ C^2$ where C^2 is *l* or *r*, e.g., *šuḫarrurum* ("to be deathly still").

It should be noted that the normal position of the Akkadian verb in the sentence is at the end (unlike its nearest Semitic relatives) and this is most likely due to the influence of Sumerian, where the verb is similarly placed.

BIBLIOGRAPHY: A. Ungnad, *Grammatik des Akkadischen*, ed. by L. Matouš (1969⁵); K.K. Riemschneider, *Lehrbuch des Akkadischen* (1969); E. Reiner, *A Linguistic Analysis of Akkadian* (1966), includes bibliography; W. von Soden, *Grundriss der Akkadischen Grammatik* (1952); E.A. Speiser (ed.), *World History of the Jewish People*, 1 (1964), 112–20; G. Bergstraesser, *Einfuehrung in die semitischen Sprachen* (1963²), 20–36; B. Meissner, *Die Keilschrift*, ed. by K. Oberhuber (1967³). **ADD. BIBLIOGRAPHY:** J. Huehnergard, *A Grammar of Akkadian* (= Harvard Semitic Museum Studies, 45), 1997; idem, "Semitic Languages," in: J.M. Sasson (ed.), *Civilization of the Ancient Near East* (1995), 2117–134.

[Aaron Shaffer]

AKKUM (Heb. עכו"ם), abbreviation consisting of the initial letters of עֲבוֹדַת כּוֹכָבִים וּמַזָּלוֹת ("worship of stars and planets") or עוֹבְדֵי כּוֹכָבִים וּמַזָּלוֹת ("worshipers of stars and planets"). It was originally applied to the Chaldean star worshipers but it was later extended to apply to all idolaters and forms of idolatry. This word is not found at all in the oldest editions of the Mishnah, Talmud, the Yad of Maimonides, or the Shulḥan Arukh. Most editions of these works have a note to the effect that the laws against *Akkum* refer only to ancient idolaters and not to Christians.

BIBLIOGRAPHY: J.S. Bloch, *Israel and the Nations* (1927), 65–75, 85–86, 100; D. Hoffmann, *Der Schulchan Aruch* (1894), 129–50, 160–78; H.L. Strack, *Introduction to the Talmud and Midrash* (1931), 262, n.66.

AKLAR MORDECAI BEN RAPHAEL (1856–1936), rabbi and author; member of the Persian **anusim* community who professed Judaism in secret. Aklar, who was born in *Meshed, Persia, was known as a Muslim by the name of "Mulla Murad." Aklar succeeded his father as the secret rabbi of the *anusim* community in Meshed. He immigrated to Jerusalem in 1927 and there continued to serve as the spiritual leader of the Meshed and Bukharian communities. His Judeo-Persian renderings of liturgical works, translated in Jerusalem, are a major contribution to this literature. They include *Avodat ha-Tamid* (1908), *Olat Shabbat* (1910), *Seliḥot* (1927), *Piyyutim for the Holidays* (1928), and the Passover *Haggadah* (1930). In his Judeo-Persian prayer book he incorporated a Hebrew poem by Solomon b. Mashi'aḥ, describing the tragic events which led to the forced conversion of the community in Meshed in 1839. His unfinished manuscripts include translations from the writings of Maimonides, and Saadiah Gaon, of the *azharot* of Solomon ibn Gabirol, parts of the Koran, and memoirs.

BIBLIOGRAPHY: Fischel, in: MGWJ, 77 (1933), 119; M.D. Gaon, *Yehudei ha-Mizraḥ be-Ereẓ Yisrael*, 2 (1938), 116; 706.

[Walter Joseph Fischel]

AKNIN, JOSEPH BEN JUDAH BEN JACOB IBN (c. 1150–1220), philosopher and poet. Aknin was born in Barcelona, Spain. Probably as a result of the Almohad persecutions, he, or perhaps his father, moved to North Africa, presumably Fez, Morocco. He remained there until his death, not withstanding his ardent wish to go elsewhere so that he could practice Judaism openly. That he felt guilty about living as a Crypto-Jew is evident from a discussion in which he passed harsh judgment on forced converts. He and Maimonides met each other during the latter's sojourn in Fez and Aknin wrote a sad couplet on the sage's departure for Egypt. However, he must not be identified or confused with Joseph b. Judah ibn *Shim'on, a disciple of Maimonides, who eventually was wrongly called "ibn Aknin." Little else is known of Aknin's life. He may have been a physician by profession – he certainly was adept in the subject. Nothing is known of his family life or descendants.

Aknin is the author of a number of works:

(1) *Sefer Ḥukkim u-Mishpatim*, no longer extant, was a book of laws divided into treatises, the first of which dealt with doctrines and beliefs. It may have been modeled on Maimonides' *Mishneh Torah*, although, unlike this work, it limited itself to laws still practiced by the Jews of the time. He spoke of it as "my major work."

(2) *Risālat al-ibānah fi uṣūl al-diyānah* ("Clarification of the Fundamentals of Faith") is also no longer extant. Nevertheless, it is known from a passage cited in another work that this work engaged in a discussion of man's freedom.

(3) *Ma'amar al ha-Middot ve-ha-Mishkalot* is an anonymous medieval Hebrew translation of an Arabic work by Aknin, entitled *maqāla le-Rabbenu Yehosef ben Aknin Zal fima'ri fat Kammiyyāb al-maqādīr al-madhkūrafi Torah she-bi-khetav ve-Torah she-be'al peh.* The Arabic original is extant in manuscript in the Bodleian Library (Ms. Poc. 186; cf. Steinschneider, Arab Lit, 230–1); the Hebrew translation of

the work was published in *Ginzei Nistarot* (ed. by J. Kobak, 3 (1872), 185–200). The introduction states: "It is my purpose to gather all that is scattered in [the] Mishnah and Talmud on coins, weights, measurements, boundaries, and time, and compare it with present-day standards."

(4) *Mevo ha-Talmud*, written in Hebrew and divided into 12 chapters, concerns "principles which a person must know if he desires to become skilled in talmudic lore." It was published under the title *Einleitung in den Talmud* with an introduction by H. Graetz in *Festschrift... Zacharias *Frankel* (Breslau, 1871; repr. 1967).

(5) *Ṭibb al-Nufūs al-Salīma wa-Muʿālajat al-Nufūs al-Alīma* ("The Hygiene of Healthy Souls and the Therapy of Ailing Souls") is an ethical compilation written in Arabic. After a lengthy introductory chapter, in which Aknin offers his views on the composition of the soul and the functions of its three parts, and in which he explains his beliefs regarding the afterlife of both the righteous and the wicked, he turns to an examination of such themes as speech and silence, keeping a secret, filial piety, food and drink, the true goods in life, and so forth. He urges moderation in all areas with a clear suggestion of the futility of material self-indulgence and the gain of spiritual and religious pursuit. Every section opens with a statement of the right course, supported by rabbinic references and followed in many instances by epigrams and sayings culled from classical and Arabic studies. Chapter 26, which deals with "the trials and tribulations which afflict us," reviews the oppressive laws of Abu Yūsuf Yaʿqūb al-Mansūr, one of the Almohad rulers (cf. Halkin in bibl.). Chapter 27, on "the disciplines of teacher and student," lists the |necessary qualification of the instructor, the conditions required of a good student, and the curriculum of study. Until the age of 30, the student should be concerned with traditional Jewish lore, which he should master to such a degree that he will be able to hold his ground when apparent difficulties and challenges seem to impugn the validity of tradition. The rest of his life should be devoted to the cultivation of logic, music, mathematics, mechanics, and metaphysics. This chapter was published in its Arabic original and a German translation by M. Guedemann, in his *Das judische Unterrichtswesen waehrend der spanisch arabischen Periode* (1873, pp. 43–138, and appendix pp. 1–57); and in Hebrew by S. Epstein, in: *Sefer ha-Yovel... N. Sokolow* (1904, pp. 371–88).

(6) *Sefer ha-Musar*, written in Hebrew, is a commentary on the mishnaic tractate *Pirkei Avot*. In it Aknin follows Maimonides' commentary on this tract, and although he does not follow it slavishly, the latter's influence is obvious. Interested in psychology and ethics, he dwells particularly on statements that deal with conduct, beliefs, and dispositions. He often develops as part of his exposition lengthy discussions on the constitution of the soul, man's responsibility for his actions, miracles in a world governed by natural laws, creation, and other metaphysical issues. The work was edited by W. Bacher as *Sefer Musar* (1910).

(7) *Inkishāf al-asrār wa-ṭuhūr al-anwār* ("The Divulgence of Mysteries and the Appearance of Lights") is a commentary in Arabic on the Song of Songs. The work starts from the premise that it would be preposterous to believe that the wise King Solomon would compose a love story or indulge in erotic banter: the book bears such an external character simply as a pedagogic expedient to attract the young. According to his interpretation, the Song of Songs is a description of the mutual craving of the rational soul and the active intellect and the obstacles in the path of their union. Aknin boasts that no one preceded him in this approach to an interpretation of the Song of Songs. In fact, although Maimonides plainly offered a general explanation of the book along these lines, Aknin was the first to work out the theme in detail in a complete commentary. In his commentary he offers a tripartite explanation of each verse: first, what he calls the exoteric sense, that is, an explanation of the grammatical forms and of the plain meaning, but he avoids the introduction of the erotic aspect; second, what he calls the rabbinic interpretation, an explanation concerned with the fate of Israel, its tragedy, and its hopes (this is the most widely accepted allegorical interpretation, which is drawn from various literary compilations, mainly Midrashim on the Song of Songs); and third, the endowment of each word in the verse under discussion with implications of physiology, psychology, logic, and philosophy, which Aknin consistently opens with the phrase "and according to my conception." This work was edited and translated into Hebrew by A.S. Halkin as *Hitgallut ha-Sodot ve-Hofaʿat ha-Meʾorot* (1964).

Aknin is typical of a group of intellectuals in the Jewish community under Islam that was impressed with the learning and doctrines of Greek and Hindu origin cultivated by Muslim intellectuals. However, he saw no conflict between his religious and secular learning. He was certain of the validity of his Jewish beliefs and way of life, and he was convinced that the ultimate goals of his Jewish and secular learning were identical. Aknin did not leave a mark on his peers in his or later generations, and his influence, evidently, was very limited.

BIBLIOGRAPHY: A.S. Halkin, in: PAAJR, 14 (1944), 25–147; idem, in: *Alexander Marx Jubilee Volume* (1950), 389–424; idem, in: *Joshua Starr Memorial Volume* (1953), 101–10; idem, in: *Sefer ha-Yovel... Ẓevi Wolfson* (1965), 93–111; Guttmann, Philosophies, 188–90.

[Abraham Solomon Halkin]

AKRA, town in Iraqi Kurdistan, known as Ekron among Jews. There was an ancient Jewish community in Akra. In the 19th century between 300 and 500 Jews seem to have been living there. According to the official census of 1930, about 1,000 persons of a total population of approximately 19,000 were Jews. They spoke Aramaic-Jebelic and were engaged in agriculture, whitewashing, goldsmithery, the perfume trade, and in commerce generally. Many of the orchards of the district belonged to Jews. The community was centered around its synagogue. In 1950 the Jews were attacked by their Kurdish neighbors and many of them were injured; after this incident they immigrated to Israel.

BIBLIOGRAPHY: A. Ben-Jacob, *Kehillot Yehudei Kurdistan* (1961), 81–84; A. Brawer, *Avak Derakhim*, 1 (1944), 269.

[Abraham Haim]

AKRISH, ISAAC BEN ABRAHAM (b. 1530), talmudic scholar, traveler, and publisher. Son of a Spanish exile, who went to Salonika after having lived in Naples, Akrish, despite his lameness, traveled extensively throughout his life. His special interest was in manuscripts which he attempted to save from destruction. Arriving in Egypt about 1548, he was engaged by *David b. Solomon ibn Abi Zimra, the head of Egyptian Jewry, to teach his grandchildren. Whatever he earned he spent in purchasing manuscripts, and devoted his time to copying those in Ibn Zimra's library. In 1554, on his way to Candia, his books were confiscated by the Venetian authorities in the wake of the recent edict against the Talmud. Succeeding in rescuing his books, he apparently traveled to Constantinople and then in 1562 back to Egypt. Later he returned to Constantinople where patrons such as Don Joseph *Nasi and Esther *Kiera helped him to engage scribes to copy manuscripts. In 1569 a fire destroyed most of his books. He left Constantinople for Kastoria where he lived for four years in poverty.

Akrish then began publishing books and documents he had collected during his travels. Three such collections, which are of great importance, were published in Constantinople between 1575 and 1578 without title pages or specific titles. The first (republ. as *Kovez̧ Vikkuḥim*, 1844) contained *Iggeret Ogeret*, a collection of polemical writings, including Profiat *Duran's famous letter, *Al Tehi ka-Avotekha*, the polemical letter of Shem Tov ibn *Falaquera, and *Kunteres Ḥibbut ha-Kever* by Akrish himself. The second collection (1607[3]) contains several important items about the Ten Lost Tribes, the letter of *Hisdai ibn Shaprut to the king of the *Khazars, and *Ma'aseh Beit David bi-Ymei Malkhut Paras*, which is the story of *Bustanai. The Khazar correspondence was published by Akrish to "strengthen the people in order that they should believe firmly that the Jews have a kingdom and dominion."

The third collection of three commentaries on the Song of Songs by *Saadiah, Joseph ibn Caspi, and an unknown author, possibly Jacob Provençal, were annotated and corrected by Akrish himself. He also wrote *Ḥeshbon ha-Adam im Kono* (published with *Kunteres Ḥibbut ha-Kever* in *Sar Shalom* by Shalom b. Shemariah ha-Sephardi, Mantua, 1560?).

BIBLIOGRAPHY: Steinschneider, Cat Bod, 1084, 1521; Graetz, Gesch, 9 (1891[3]), index; Bruell, in: *Jahrbuecher fuer Juedische Geschichte und Literatur*, 8 (1887), 53ff.; I. Davidson, *Sefer Sha'ashu'im* (1914), 88; (1925), 67ff.; Rosanes, Togarmah, 2 (1951), 461; C. Roth, *House of Nasi: Duke of Naxos* (1948), 173ff.; A. Yaari, *Meḥkerei Sefer* (1958), 212–13, 235ff., 279; idem, *Ha-Defus ha-Ivri be-Kushta* (1967), 118ff.; Dunlop, Khazars, 128ff.; Benayahu, in: *Sefunot*, 6 (1962), 134.

AKRON, industrial city in northeast Ohio. Akron is Ohio's fifth largest city, with a population of 217,074 (2000 census). German Jewish merchants settled in Akron prior to the Civil War, but the first congregation, the American Hebrew Association – known today as Temple Israel (Reform) – was founded in 1865. The community grew slowly until it received an influx of settlers from Eastern Europe in the 1880s. Engaging in the clothing business, cigar making, and other small businesses, the Jewish population reached a peak of 7,500 in the 1930s. In 2005, there were approximately 3,500 Jews in Akron and its suburbs with five congregations: Anshe Sfard/Revere Road (Orthodox, founded 1915), Chabad of Akron (Orthodox, 1986), Beth El Congregation (Conservative, 1946), Temple Beth Shalom (Reform, 1977), and Temple Israel (Reform, 1965). The Jewish Community Board of Akron, founded in 1935 as the Federation of Jewish Charities, announced in 2004 that its director would also lead the Jewish Federation of Canton, Ohio, a neighboring city with a Jewish population of approximately 1,200. The Jewish Community Board offers support to the Shaw Jewish Community Center, the Jewish Family Service, the Jerome Lippman Day School, and the *Akron Jewish News*. It also provides funding for campus services to Kent State University, the University of Akron, and Hiram College. Noted Akron residents were Judith A. *Resnik (1949–1986), a NASA astronaut who perished in the explosion of the orbiter *Challenger*, and Jerome Lippman (1913–2005) who invented a heavy-duty waterless hand soap during World War II.

BIBLIOGRAPHY: J.A. Avner, "Judaism," in: T.S. Butalia and D.P. Small (eds.), *Religion in Ohio* (2004); H. Kaplan, "Century of Adjustment: A History of the Akron Jewish Community, 1865–1975," unpublished dissertation, Kent State University (1978). **WEBSITE:** www.jewishakron.org.

[Jane Avner (2nd ed.)]

AKZIN, BENJAMIN (1904–1985), constitutional lawyer and political scientist. Akzin was born in Riga, Latvia, received doctorates from the universities of Vienna and Paris, lectured in various American universities, and was a Library of Congress expert on matters of law and international relations. He went to Israel in 1949 and joined the faculty of the Hebrew University as professor of constitutional law and political science and served as dean of the law faculty in 1951–54, 1956–58, and 1961–63. Akzin was an early supporter of the Revisionist Party and from 1936–41 was head of the political division of the New Zionist Organization. From 1945 to 1947 he served as political advisor and then as secretary of the Zionist Emergency Committee in the United States. Akzin wrote numerous political and scholarly articles as well as the following books: *Problémes fondamentaux du droit international publique* (1929); *New States and International Organizations* (1955); *Torat ha-Mishtarim* (1963); *State and Nation* (1964); *Sugyot be-Mishpat u-ve-Medina'ut* (1966). Akzin was founder and first editor of the *Israel Law Review*. He was awarded the Israel Prize in law for 1967.

Akzin served as rector and acting president of the Haifa University from 1969 to 1972. He was elected honorary president of the World Federation of UN Associations, and of the Political Science Association of Israel, and was president of the Council of Friendship Associations between Israel and foreign countries.

In 1975 his *Be-Ayin Boḥenet* ("Looking at the Passing Scene") was published.

ALABAMA, state in the southeastern region of the United States. In 2005 its population was estimated at 4,447,100, with a Jewish population of about 9,000. The largest Jewish communities were *Birmingham, with approximately 5,300 Jews; Montgomery, the state capital, with approximately 1,300; and Mobile, with 1,100. There were four Jewish federations in the state, and one periodical, the twice-monthly *Deep South Jewish Voice*.

While Jewish traders are known to have been active in Alabama as early as 1757, and a number of Jews lived in Mobile in the 1760s under British rule, it was not until the 1820s that the first permanent Alabama Jewish community was established in Mobile. Abram (Abraham) Mordecai, a Pennsylvania-born Jew who had settled in central Alabama by 1785 and established the state's first cotton gin near Montgomery, was made a key character in Albert James Pickett's *History of Alabama* (1851), and became a legend in Southern folklore.

The largest antebellum Jewish settlement was in Mobile, where sufficient Jews established themselves to purchase a cemetery in 1841. Previous Jewish graves dating back to 1829 are suitably marked in the oldest, non-sectarian Protestant graveyard in town. Congregation Shaarai Shomayim u-Maskil el Dol was chartered on Jan. 25, 1844. Israel I. Jones (1810–1877), a London Jew who arrived early in the 1830s, was president of the congregation for most of his life; one of his daughters married the well-known New Orleans rabbi, James Koppel Gutheim (1817–1886). An auctioneer and tobacco merchant, Jones was active in politics, served as an alderman, was president of the Mobile Musical Association, and introduced streetcars to Mobile.

A welfare society, the Chevra Mevaker Cholim, was organized in Montgomery on Nov. 17, 1846, by 12 German Jewish immigrants including Emanuel *Lehman, uncle of Herbert H. *Lehman. The society conducted services, purchased a cemetery, and on June 3, 1849, with 30 members transformed itself into Congregation Kahl Montgomery. The mobility of immigrant Jews and the tentativeness of their settlement is indicated by the constitutional provision of Kahl Montgomery that "four members shall be sufficient to continue the Society, but should there be only three members, the Society shall be dissolved." The congregation is now called Temple Beth Or, and its first building, built in 1862 with seed money from Judah Touro, is the oldest synagogue building in the state. It now houses a church.

Other communities were established where trails met rivers, such as at Claiborne. That community was defunct by the 1870s, after it was bypassed by the railroad.

During the Civil War more than 130 Alabama Jews served in the Confederate Army, and in 1861, when 13 of them enlisted as a group in the Twelfth Alabama Regiment, Mobile Jews held a special service. James K. Gutheim, however, went to Montgomery as an exile rather than take the oath of allegiance to the United States after New Orleans' occupation by federal forces. He served in Montgomery and in nearby towns until the end of the Civil War. Judah P. *Benjamin lived in Montgomery during his tenure as attorney general of the Confederacy, and the last soldier killed in the defense of Mobile was a Jew from South Carolina. The congregations in Mobile and Montgomery, like virtually all of the older Southern congregations, turned to Reform following the Civil War, joined the Union of American Hebrew Congregations after its creation in 1873, and were served by graduates of the Hebrew Union College.

Eastern European immigrants began to arrive in Alabama towns early in the 1870s. They were treated with a combination of philanthropic generosity and social aloofness, which persisted longer in tradition-conscious southern communities than in the northern communities. These immigrants created their own Orthodox congregations in Mobile, Montgomery, and Birmingham, most of which joined the Conservative movement following World War II.

Jewish merchants were found in most Alabama towns of any size, with synagogues springing up in small mining towns like West Blocton and Bessemer, and larger cities like Selma. Immigrants often began selling house to house, saving enough money to buy a cart, then rent a storefront.

The town of Sheffield was founded in 1884 by a land company that included the Moses brothers of Montgomery. Falkville was named for Louis Faulk, who was the first merchant and postmaster, and Saks was established for area tenant farmers by Joseph Saks, founder of a clothing store in Anniston.

Before World War II, many Alabama communities faced shrinking populations, intermarriage on the part of the children and grandchildren of the older settlers, gradual acculturation by the children of the new immigrants, and slow disintegration of traditional Jewish loyalties. But European antisemitism in the 1930s and the sudden influx of Jewish soldiers to many southern towns during World War II, when great camps and air bases were established in the area, brought a return of Jewish consciousness to many disappearing communities. Many northern Jews also came to places like the University of Alabama after finding themselves shut out of northern universities by Jewish quotas. Many Jewish scholars who fled Nazi Germany were similarly shunned by prestigious northern universities and found employment in southern historically black colleges in places like Tuskegee. Scorned in Nazi Germany because they were Jews, they found themselves comparatively well treated in the South because they were white and yet they worked with disadvantaged and persecuted

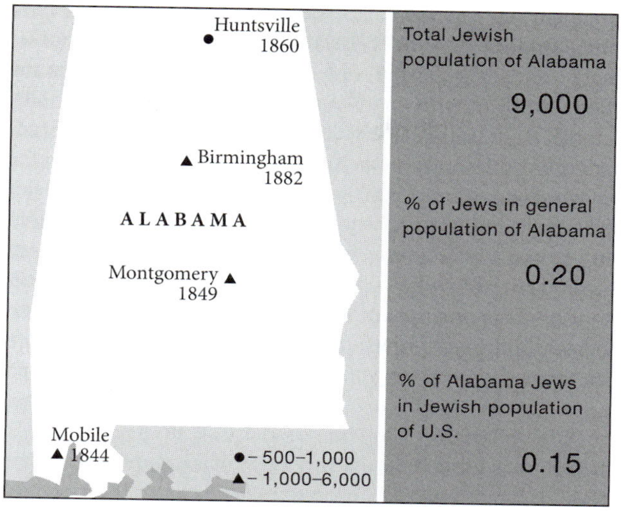

Jewish communities in Alabama and dates of establishment. Population figures 2001.

black students for whom their race rather than religion was the defining identity. In the post-World War II period, new synagogues were built in the suburbs in Mobile, Montgomery, and elsewhere, and Jewish community life revived with the younger generation of Jews.

In 1943, the Alabama Legislature became the first American governmental body to pass a resolution supporting the establishment of a Jewish state in Palestine.

During the 1950s and 1960s, while there was a significant revival of interest in Judaism, there was also a recurrence of antisemitic attacks on Jews, including the firebombing of Beth Israel in Gadsden and the attempted 1958 bombing of Birmingham's Beth-El. Segregationist politicians called integration a "Communist-Jewish conspiracy," leading many in the Jewish community who were sympathetic to the civil rights movement to work behind the scenes so the movement would not lose legitimacy in the eyes of whites. An overwhelming percentage of northern whites who came to the region to work for civil rights were Jews, causing resentment by southern Jews who were trying to balance a delicate situation and who had to live with any backlash provoked by their northern co-religionists.

Many northern Jews were among the Freedom Riders who were attacked by white supremacists in Anniston and Birmingham, and Rabbi Abraham Joshua *Heschel was among the Jewish figures who marched with Dr. Martin Luther King in Montgomery in 1965.

By the 1960s, smaller Jewish communities in the state began to die out as children and grandchildren of the original Jewish immigrants went off to college, became professionals, and chose not to return to their family businesses. Congregations in places like Demopolis and Jasper closed as the Jewish population aged and shrank.

Larger communities, and those connected to university towns, continued to have a stable population. The days of the Jewish country club were gone, but the 1990s saw Mobile's Conservative Ahavas Chesed move to the suburbs, and a new congregation in Auburn. Almost all of Birmingham's Jewish institutions also expanded greatly or were rebuilt in the 1990s. The state's Gulf Coast is now also seen as a prime destination for retirees who do not want to go to South Florida.

While for many outside the region, the 1960s painted a picture of the South as being a hostile home for Jews, overt antisemitic incidents were rare. The 1990s saw some bruising church-state battles, but in general Jews were respected as "God's chosen people" by the largely evangelical population of the state. In 1995, Governor Fob James paid tribute to Israel in his inauguration, with the singing of "*Hatikvah*" and the blowing of the *shofar* by a Jerusalem rabbi. In 1999, Don Siegelman, a Catholic, was elected governor, making his wife, Lori, the state's first Jewish First Lady. The University of Alabama has a well-endowed and well respected Judaic Studies program and the University of Alabama Press has an impressive list of Judaic publications, including the first English translation of Franz Rosenzweig's *The Star of Redemption* and Arthur D. Green's *Tormented Master.*

[Bertram Wallace Korn / Lawrence Brook (2nd ed.)]

ALABARCH (Gr. ἀλαβάρχης), title designating office-holders appointed to the fiscal administration in Egypt and other countries in the Roman and Byzantine periods. Since reference is made to the office being held by two wealthy Jewish notables of Alexandria (*Alexander Lysimachus and *Demetrius, the second husband of Princess Mariamne, daughter of Agrippa I, cf. Jos., Ant., 20:147), some historians have identified it as that of the head of the Jewish community (*ethnarch). The title is mentioned, however, in several sources without any Jewish connection.

Many scholars regard this office as identical with the arabarchs (cf. Cicero, *Adversus Atticum* 2:17; Juvenal, *Saturae* 1:130), the letters "i" and "r" (λ, ρ) being interchanged through dissimilation. These arabarchs were Roman officials who were responsible for the collection of imposts from incoming and outgoing vessels from the eastern ("Arabian") bank of the Nile; Wilcken (*Griechische Ostraka,* 1 (1899), 350–1) and Dittenberger quote a document which includes a tariff of the contractors who farmed the harbor dues paid to the arabarchs. Josephus (Apion, 2:64) mentions that the Jews received from Ptolemy (?) the "wardship of the river," and it is therefore possible that Alexander Lysimachus and Demetrius held this office.

According to a less acceptable opinion, the word is a hybrid of the Greek *archō* and the Semitic root *ʿarab* (ערב) meaning "to barter" (cf. Ezek. 27:9) and the title therefore designates an official of the mercantile tax administration (V. Burr, *Tiberius Julius Alexander*, Ger., 1955, 16, n.4, 87ff.).

The suggestion of Rostovtzeff that the alabarch was responsible for the collection of specific Jewish taxes is untenable, since such taxes were not imposed until the time of Vespasian (69–70 C.E.) and until then, they paid ordinary taxation to the usual tax collectors.

It seems that the alabarch exercised different functions in different localities and periods and there is no definite information as to their precise functions.

The title does not occur in the Talmud but it has been suggested that the variant reading אפרכוס found in some texts to explain the "*Avrekh*" of Genesis 41:43 (Sifrei Deut. 1:1; Yalkut Shimoni 1:792) is a corruption of "Abarchus = Alabarchus" (see Mid. Tan. to 1:1).

BIBLIOGRAPHY: Schuerer, Gesch, 3 (1907^4), 132, no. 42; W. Dittenberger, *Orientis Graeci Inscriptiones Selectae*, 2 (1905), 255f., 258, no. 570, 413–9, no. 674; M. Rostovtzeff, in: *Yale Classical Studies*, 2 (1931), 49ff.; Graetz, Gesch, 3 (1905^3), 631–51; idem, in: MGWJ, 25 (1876), 209–24, 308–20; Lesquier, in: *Revue Archéologique*, 6 (1917), 94ff.; idem, *L'armée romaine d'Egypte* (1918), 432ff.; Baron, Social, 1 (1952^2), 409–10, no. 16; Tcherikover, Corpus, 1 (1957), 49, n.4.

[Abraham Schalit]

ALAGÓN, town near Saragossa, northeastern Spain. There is evidence that Jews were living in Alagón while the area was still under Muslim rule. Shortly after the reconquest in 1119 Christians began to buy land from the Jewish residents. In her testament of 1208 Queen Sancha of Aragon bequeathed a number of Alagón Jews to the convent of Sigena. The expulsion of six butchers from the town by the community board resulted in a *cause célèbre* in the 1280s. In 1283 the infante Alfonso ordered that a representative gathering for the allocation of the annual tax in the *collecta* of *Saragossa should be held each year in Alagón. Its proximity to Saragossa apparently saved Alagón during the massacres throughout Spain in 1391. A list of accounts from 1403 to 1408 includes the names of Jewish notables, and charitable societies (*cofraías*) as well as *Conversos. The community ceased to exist with the expulsion of Spanish Jewry in 1492.

BIBLIOGRAPHY: Baer, Spain, 1 (1961), 140, 430; Baer, Urkunden, 1 (1929), index; Ashtor, Korot, 2 (1966), 165–6; Cacigas, in: *Sefarad*, 6 (1946), 74–78; Piles, *ibid.*, 10 (1950), 87–89, 367; J. Ma. Lacarra, *Documentos para el estudio de la Reconquista del Valle del Ebro* (second series, 1949), index.

ALALAKH (Alalach, Alalah), ancient city situated south of Lake Antiochia, near the bend of the Orontes River in Turkey; now Tell Atshana. The site was excavated by the English archaeologist Sir Leonard Woolley in 1937–39 and in 1946–49. Mesopotamian documents mentioning Alalakh and its kings and archaeological finds have added greatly to the understanding of the history of this city and its importance in the area west of the Euphrates during the first half of the second millennium B.C.E. Alalakh sheds indirect light on the Syro-Palestinian context of biblical *realia*. The most important finds for ancient Near Eastern studies are the 450 clay tablets written in Akkadian. These tablets are from the royal archives of the city and are with minor exceptions from two periods: an early archive from Stratum VII dating from the 18th century B.C.E. and a later archive from Stratum IV from the 15th century. The archives contain a few international treaties and many administrative, economic, and legal documents. They throw light upon the history of Alalakh, its royal and administrative organization, social strata, mode of life, and ethnic origins, and on the economic activity of its inhabitants during these two periods. Of special importance to scholarship is the possibility of tracing the development of a city-state and of understanding the political, ethnic, economic, and social development of Alalakh from the 18th to the 15th centuries B.C.E. In addition to the documents, a statue of a king inscribed with the history of Idrimi (who ruled in Alalakh approximately at the end of the first half of the second millenium B.C.E.) was found. The inscription consists of a narrative which differs in tone and content from the ordinary run of *res gestae* in the ancient Near East, though it closely resembles biblical narratives. Some of its details are reminiscent of the history of David during his premonarchial period, a fact that indicates the widespread prevalence of certain literary motifs in the biographical style of the books of Samuel. These epigraphic finds are part of the ever-growing corpus of documents from the Fertile Crescent that shed light on linguistic, economic, social, and ethnic conditions in pre-Israelite Palestine and on the ancient Near Eastern origins of Israel's institutions (law, customs, government) and spiritual culture. Thus Alalakh furnishes fresh evidence added to that of *Nuzi and *Ugarit for the right of a father to determine which of his sons should be considered the eldest, disregarding the custom of primogeniture. According to this right, Abraham could prefer Isaac over Ishmael (Gen. 21:10ff.), and Ephraim could be elected in the place of Manasseh, Joseph's elder son (*ibid.* 48:13ff.). Jacob's seven additional years of work to earn the right to marry Rachel (*ibid.* 29:18, 27) may also find its parallel in marriage contracts from Alalakh. One of the conditions of such contracts is the option given to a husband to marry a second wife if the first fails to bear children for seven years. In other spheres, mention should be made of the contribution of the international treaties from Alalakh regulating, inter alia, the extradition of escapees from one country to another. This may contribute to the understanding of the extradition of the two servants of *Shimei by Achish, king of Gath (I Kings 2:39ff.), suggesting the possibility of a similar treaty between Solomon and Achish (but cf. Deut. 23:16–17). There is also an illustration from another document of the manner in which Jezebel acquired for Ahab the property of Naboth the Jezereelite (I Kings 21:8ff.). It is clear from the document in question, that the king had the right to confiscate the property of a rebel or a person guilty of a crime against the king and executed for this reason.

BIBLIOGRAPHY: D.J. Wiseman, *The Alalakh Tablets* (1953); idem, in: D. Winton Thomas (ed.), *Archaeology and Old Testament Study* (1967), 119–35; S. Smith, *The Statue of Idri-mi* (1949); C. Fensham, in: JBL, 79 (1960), 59–60; G. Buccellati, in: BO, 4 (1962), 95–96; W.F. Albright, in: BASOR, 118 (1950), 14–15; I. Mendelsohn, *ibid.*, 156 (1959), 38ff.; S. Loewenstamm, in: IEJ, 6 (1956), 225; M. Tsevat, in: HUCA, 29 (1959), 125ff. **ADD. BIBLIOGRAPHY:** M. Astour, in: ABD, 2, 42–45.

[Hanoch Reviv]

ALAMAH (Helam), city in Gilead in which Jews were besieged at the beginning of the Hasmonean revolt (I Macc. 5:26). It is generally identified with 'Alama, on the banks of Wādi al-Ghār, 40 mi. (60 km.) east of the Sea of Galilee, but archaeological investigations have not yet been undertaken there.

BIBLIOGRAPHY: Abel, Geog, 2 (1938), 241. **ADD. BIBLIOGRAPHY:** M. Avi-Yonah, *Gazetteer of Roman Palestine* (1976), 64; R. Dussaud, *Topographie historique de la Syrie antique et médiévale* (1927), 334, 384.

[Michael Avi-Yonah]

ALAMANI, AARON HE-ḤAVER BEN YESHU'AH (commonly known as "Ben Zion" and also "Alluf-Zion"; 12th century), rabbinical judge, physician, and poet. He was born probably in Jerusalem, at the end of the 11th century, and lived for many years in Alexandria, Egypt. When *Judah Halevi went to Alexandria in 1140, he stayed at Alamani's house and became friendly with him. Judah Halevi respected him greatly, composed songs of friendship to him and his children, and continued his relations with the family after leaving Alexandria. Apparently Aaron's name as a poet had been known to Judah Halevi even before he left Spain. More than 30 of his liturgical hymns and poems are now known, all influenced by Hebrew poetry in Spain. It is also possible that certain *piyyutim* where only the name Aaron appears were composed by him. His sons, Yeshu'ah and Zadok, were also poets.

BIBLIOGRAPHY: Zunz, Lit Poesie, 328f., 537; Fuenn, Keneset, 83; Brody, in: ZHB, 6 (1902), 18–24; Schirmann, in: YMḤSI, 6 (1945), 265–88; Abramson, in: YMḤSI, 7 (1958), 165, 168, 179–80; Davidson, Oẓar, 4 (1933), 359f.

[Abraham Meir Habermann]

ALAMI, SOLOMON (c. 1370–1420), Spanish moralist. Alami's family name was apparently Ibn Laḥmish (or Naḥish); possibly he was called Alami because he was blind (the meaning of the word in Arabic). He fled from Spain to Portugal during the persecutions of 1391. There he composed in 1415 his *Iggeret ha-Musar,* also published under the title *Iggeret ha-Tokhaḥah ve-ha-Emunah* ("Epistle of Reproof and Faith"), which has gone through 18 editions (the last ed. by A.M. Habermann, 1946). It is written in rhyming prose and is divided into five sections, corresponding to the five senses. Alami was inspired to write it by the "perplexity which has plagued me these 24 years: Why does God seek to destroy us each generation?" and by his final conviction that "we ourselves have dug the pit into which we have fallen." He criticizes acidly the various classes of Spanish Jewry, exposing the moral shortcomings of the court Jews, tax farmers, philosophers, and rabbis as well as the common people. Alami believed that the upper classes were mainly responsible for the catastrophe that had befallen Spanish Jewry. The court Jews had betrayed the office which they had attained by the will of Providence; "their eyes and their hearts were turned only to selfish gain, to inherit dwellings that were not theirs in the lands of their enemies… to shift the burden of taxation from themselves to the poor… By their evil ways they became obnoxious to their enemies… and they were driven from the courts of kings and princes… and later not a single Jew remained who had access to the king to seek the good of his people and speak on their behalf." The rabbis "showed favoritism in the law and did not reprimand the people for base conduct." They prided themselves on their empty interpretations and boasted of their secular knowledge. The common people were dishonest in their dealings with the Gentiles: "We dealt with them falsely and dishonestly, and we robbed them through unjust practices, until they despised us and held us to be thieves and liars, fornicators and a gang of traitors, so that every vile and shameful occupation is identified with the Jews." Alami contrasted the lack of decorum in synagogues with the behavior of Christians at prayer. He advocated physical labor, personal cleanliness, and modesty. Concerning forced conversions, he urged the Jews to abandon their homes rather than abjure their faith: "When pagans rise up against you to force you to desert God, to drive you from His inheritance, leave the land of your birth and your father's house for any land you may find where you may observe His law."

BIBLIOGRAPHY: Baer, Spain, 2 (1966), 239–42, 484, n. 55; Steinschneider, in: JQR, 11 (1898/99), 456; Zunz, Schr, 2 (1876), 177–82.

[Azriel Shochat]

°ALARIC II (485–507), Visigothic king. Alaric II was a strong and prudent ruler of the Visigoths, who had established themselves in Spain and southern France on the breakdown of the western Roman Empire. The Visigoths had adopted Arian Christianity, a form which their orthodox Roman subjects hated as heretical. Probably because of this the rulers were inclined to favor their Jewish subjects, though the only known details are what can be culled from the Visigothic laws. In 506 Alaric issued a shortened compendium of the Roman *Codex Theodosianus* of the middle of the fifth century, known as the *Breviarium Alariciense.* In this the laws affecting Jews were reduced from over 50 to 10, omitting many which were contradictory. Those forbidding violence against Jews were also omitted, not from anti-Jewish feeling, but as unnecessary. Jews were still basically Roman citizens, but the exceptions to their equality with other citizens remained though no new restrictions were added. The only privilege allowed them was freedom from court action on their holy days. They were excluded from honors, but had to bear all the burdens of public life. They were refused any authority over Christians or the purchase of Christian slaves, and those they inherited they were not allowed to circumcise. They were punished if they molested a Jew who sought baptism, and their clergy enjoyed no immunities.

BIBLIOGRAPHY: J. Parkes, *Conflict of the Church and the Synagogue* (1934), 317ff., 351ff.

[James W. Parkes]

ĀL-ASĀṬĪR (Ar. الاساطير), Samaritan work in Aramaic of unknown authorship, date, and provenance ascribed by the Samaritans themselves to Moses. Written in the form of a chronicle, the work is a legendary account of 26 generations from Adam to Moses. The story is focused on the four patriarchs – Adam, Noah, Abraham, and Moses – the "Fundamentals of the World." The book is divided into 12 chapters. The first ten, from Adam to Israel's victory over the Midianites, span a period of 2,800 years according to Samaritan chronology. The first half of the 11th chapter contains a description of the borders of the Holy Land that has still not been satisfactorily explained. The last part consists of prophecies about the future of the world until the advent of the *taheb* ("the restorer"; see Religion of *Samaritans). The composition of the book gives the impression that it was written by one hand without interpolations. In some places its genealogical lists and chronological data conflict with those found in the Pentateuch or in other Samaritan chronicles, but these discrepancies may well have been caused by the inaccuracy of copyists. The title of the work, *al-Asāṭīr,* is Arabic and means legends or tales, as in the Koranic expression *asāṭīr al-Awwalīn* ("the Legends of the Ancients"). This fact in itself is not proof of the late origin of the book, as the title may have been a later addition. No express mention of *al-Asāṭīr* is found in the list of source material enumerated by *Abu al-Fatḥ in the introduction to his *Annal*, but it might be included in the summarizing expression "some histories." The language of the book, influenced by the Arabic language and Muslim terminology, is difficult to understand. Although the narrative may contain many old midrashic motifs, it could not have been composed before the end of the tenth–the beginning of the 11th century C.E., when Aramaic was still used in the Samaritan community but Arabic had already begun to supersede it. The author seems familiar with the geography of northern Ereẓ Israel and Syria and probably lived in this region, where large Samaritan communities then flourished in Acre, Tyre, and Damascus. Ismāʿīl al-Rumayḥī was the first to attribute the composition of *al-Asāṭīr* to Moses in his *Molad Moshe* (beginning of the 16th century). The work is often cited in the Bible commentary of Muslim al-Danāfi (who attributes it once to Adam) and Ibrahim al-Ayya (17th, 18th centuries, respectively). The book is not highly esteemed by the modern Samaritan community. There exist a translation into Arabic and one into Samaritan modern Hebrew (see Language and Literature of *Samaritans) called *Pitron*. M. Gaster edited the book together with the *Pitron*. He translated it into English, and appended a commentary (*The Asatir, The Samaritan Book of the Secrets of Moses*, 1927). An edition with Hebrew translation and commentary was published by Z. Ben-Ḥayyim (*Tarbiz*, 14 (1942/43), 104–25, 174–90; 15 (1943/44) 71–87).

BIBLIOGRAPHY: J. Macdonald, *Theology of the Samaritans* (1964), 44.

[Ayala Loewenstamm]

ALASHKAR, JOSEPH BEN MOSES (c. 1500), rabbinical author and Hebrew poet. A victim of the expulsion from Spain in 1492, Alashkar settled in Tlemcen (Algeria) where he became the head of a yeshivah. He was a fertile writer, but none of his works was published. They include (1) *Avrekh*, commentaries on Rashi; (2) *Edut bi-Yhosef*, commentary on the laws of ritual slaughter in Maimonides' *Code;* (3) *Mirkevet ha-Mishneh*, on *Pirkei Avot*; (4) *Refu'at ha-Nefesh*, religious ethics.

In addition, he wrote poems and books in verse form, among them a paraphrase of the tractate *Avot*, verses on the 70 kinds of *terefah*, two poems in honor of his contemporary and fellow countryman, Solomon b. Simeon *Duran, as well as several religious odes and hymns.

BIBLIOGRAPHY: Carmoly, in: *Oẓar Neḥmad*, 3 (1860), 105–10; Fuenn, Keneset, 456; Davidson, Oẓar, 4 (1933), 400.

ALASHKAR, MOSES BEN ISAAC (1466–1542), talmudist and liturgical poet. Alashkar, who was born in Spain, studied in his youth with R. Samuel Valensi in Zamora. In 1492, when the Jews were expelled from Spain, Alashkar sailed to North Africa. On board he was kept below deck with other Jewish refugees, and nearly drowned when the ship foundered. He wrote a poem, "*Be-Mah Akaddem*," inspired by this experience. Alashkar settled in Tunisia, but when the Spaniards landed in North Africa in 1510 and part of the Jewish population made prisoner, Alashkar fled. He resettled in Patras, Greece, where he established a yeshivah. Alashkar later immigrated to Egypt, and in 1522 became *dayyan* in Cairo, where he distinguished himself as a talmudist. His halakhic decisions were widely cited; he also corresponded with most of the outstanding rabbis, e.g., Elijah *Capsali, *Levi b. Ḥabib, and Jacob *Berab. Alashkar was involved in halakhic disputes with Samuel b. *Sid and Jacob Berab. In a poem and in a letter to Levi b. Ḥabib, Alashkar complained about the hostility toward him in Cairo. The dissensions eventually led to his departure to Jerusalem, where he died.

Alashkar was well versed in Arabic, and studied the responsa written by earlier scholars, especially Maimonides. He also studied Abraham b. Moses b. Maimon's *al-Kifāya* and Samuel b. Hophni ha-Kohen Gaon's *al-Aḥkām.* That Alashkar knew Kabbalah is apparent from his kabbalistic explanations cited by Samuel Uceda in his *Midrash Shemu'el*, and in several of Alashkar's liturgical poems. Alashkar, however, was opposed to the diffusion of secret lore and mysticism.

Though generally conciliatory and moderate in polemics, occasionally Alashkar severely criticized halakhic statements that seemed untenable to him. Once he even accused his close friend, Levi b. Ḥabib, of making a statement contrary to common sense (Responsa, no. 41). Similarly, he rejected opinions by Joseph *Colon, *Jacob b. Asher, and Joseph *Albo. The editors of Alashkar's responsa mitigated or deleted several statements directed against Berab. Alashkar's responsa, 121 in number, were first published in Venice in 1554. Appended to the responsa are five liturgical poems by Alashkar, printed also with two others in Y. Zarki's anthology *Yefeh Nof* (Sabionetta, 1575).

BIBLIOGRAPHY: Graetz, Hist, 4 (1949), 391; 5 (1949), 392; Landshuth, Ammudei, 21ff.; S.A. Horodezky, *Le-Korot ha-Rabbanut* (1914), 57–70; Frumkin-Rivlin, 1 (1928), 57–59; Davidson, Oẓar, 4 (1933), 443; Rosanes, Togarmah, 1 (1930), 196f.

[Samuel Abba Horodezky]

ALASHKAR, SOLOMON (16th century), leader *(çelebi)* of Egyptian Jewry, who was also known by his title *muʿallim* ("master"). Alashkar was a wealthy trader and philanthropist who supported scholars and yeshivot in Ereẓ Israel and Egypt. In the 1560s a fierce feud broke out between him and R. Jacob ibn Tibbon, one of the foremost Egyptian rabbis, who insulted Alashkar. Rabbis Joseph *Caro, Moses di *Trani, and Israel de *Curiel, all of Safed, were asked to make peace between them, but failed. Alashkar was one of those who helped to subsidize publication of the Shulḥan Arukh (Venice, 1565). When his fortunes changed and he was unable to meet his debts to the governor of Egypt, Hussein Pasha, the latter ordered Alashkar's execution (1583?); but he was saved because the governor himself was killed and, according to Joseph *Sambari, Alashkar recovered financially.

BIBLIOGRAPHY: A. Scheiber and M. Benayahu, in: *Sefunot*, 6 (1962), 127–134. **ADD. BIBLIOGRAPHY:** J. Sambari, *Divrei Yosef* (ed. S. Shtober, 1994), 417–18; A. David, *To Come To the Land* (1999), 46–47, 83, 195.

[Abraham David]

ALASKA, state of the U.S. located in far northwest North America. Jews first came to Alaska in sizable numbers during the Gold Rush of the late 1890s, when they set up general merchandise stores, law offices and mining operations. After the Gold Rush subsided, some Jews remained in the cities. From the 1940s to the 1970s, most of the Jewish population consisted of military personnel. Due to construction of the Alaskan Pipeline in the mid-1970s and the resultant growth of the oil industry, the population grew. Subsequently, Alaska attracted Jews seeking a quieter lifestyle. From 1970 to 2001, the population increased dramatically, going from 190 to 3,400. Today, over three-quarters of the Jewish population resides in the three largest cities. Anchorage, Fairbanks and Juneau had populations of 1,600, 500 and 300, respectively, in 1994. Smaller communities exist in Sitka, Homer, Ketchikan, Soldotna, Kenai, Haines and Bethel.

The first Jews came to Alaska with the Russian explorer Vitus Bering. In the period of Russian rule, the Jews of Alaska were trappers and traders. In the 1850s and 1860s, San Francisco Jews developed extensive commercial ties with the Russian-American Company in Alaska, and many Jewish fur traders visited regularly. Shortly after the United States purchased Alaska from Russia in 1867, Jewish traders, miners, fur dealers, and merchants arrived from San Francisco to probe the new territory.

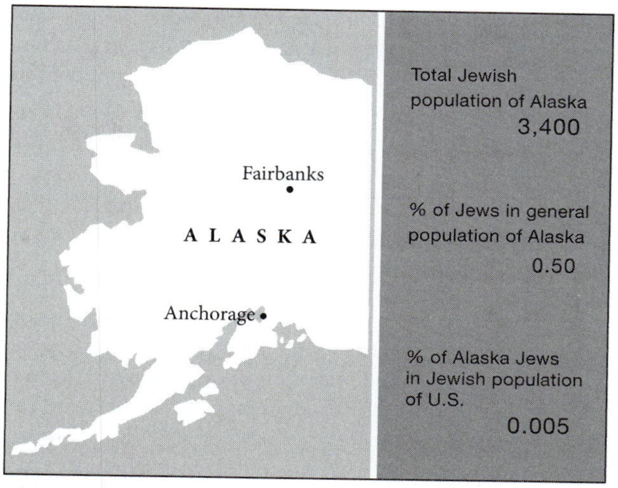

Jewish population 2001.

Lewis Gerstle and Louis Sloss, San Francisco merchants, founded the Alaska Commercial Company in 1868. The company developed steamboat transportation and financed some of Alaska's first mining ventures.

As many as 200 Jews lived in the Klondike at the height of the gold rush. Dawson City, in the Yukon Territory, was site of the region's first Jewish services (1898). The small Jewish section of Klondike's cemetery Bet Chaim was established 1902 and later restored in 1998 through the efforts of the Jewish Historical Society of the Yukon. During the Nome gold boom of 1900, a Jewish congregation was initiated when some sixty Jews attended Rosh Ha-Shanah services. In 1901, the congregation established the state's first Jewish organization, the Hebrew Benevolent Society. The isolated community declined after WWI.

Polish immigrant Solomon Ripinsky arrived in 1884. His various occupations echo those of other Jewish pioneers: law clerk, teacher, trading post operator, postmaster, notary, lawyer, elected convention delegate, and U.S. Commissioner. Mt. Ripinsky in Haines is named for him.

The first Jewish settlers of Juneau were Robert Gottstein and his wife (1885). Their son Jacob came to Anchorage at its founding in 1915. He established a trading and warehouse business, the J.B. Gottstein Company, that later combined with Carr's Grocery to form Carr-Gottstein, Inc., at one time the largest private employer in Alaska.

In 1904, a group of fortune hunters and businessmen in Fairbanks organized a congregation and a year later acquired a cemetery that is still the only Jewish burial ground in Alaska. The congregation became Congregation Bikkur Cholim in 1908, holding services at the home of Lithuanian Jew Robert Bloom, a congregation founder who had arrived in the Klondike in 1898 and served as the Yukon's first lay rabbi for nearly half a century. He was chairman of Alaska's Jewish Welfare Board, instrumental in the establishment of an Air Force base in Alaska, a founder of the University of Alaska (1918) and a charter member of its Board of Regents. Jessie Spiro Bloom established the Fairbanks kindergarten and first Alaskan Girl Scout chapter (1925). The First Jewish Congregation of Fairbanks was established in 1980 at the Army post chapel. Renamed Or HaTzafon (Light of the North), the congregation is affiliated with the Reform movement.

Around Anchorage, Orthodox, Conservative, and Reform Jewish chaplains at Elmendorf Air Force Base rotated tours of duty from the early 1940s to mid 1980s. Reform Congregation Beth Sholom was established in 1958 and its current synagogue built in 1982. From 1984 to 2000, Rabbi Harry L. Rosenfeld was Beth Sholom's rabbi. Alaska's first Chabad Center and only Orthodox congregation, Shomrei Ohr, was established in 1991 by Chabad emissaries Rabbi Yossi and Esty Greenberg.

In Juneau, the Reform Juneau Jewish Community (JJC) operates in public locations and members' homes. In 2004, the congregation purchased a former community center to serve as the home for a future synagogue and Jewish school.

From the time Jews first settled in Alaska, they have been prominent in political life. The first mayor of Anchorage was Leopold David; several years later Zachary Loussac served in the same capacity. In 1958, when Alaska was approved for statehood, Ernest *Gruening, a former territorial governor, was elected as a United States senator. From 1965 to 1997, Jay A. Rabinowitz was a justice on the Alaska Supreme Court, serving four terms as Chief Justice. Avrum M. Gross served as Attorney General from 1974 to 1980. Jews currently make up 5% of the State Legislature and the Anchorage Municipal Assembly.

The television drama "Northern Exposure" (1990–1995) featured a Jewish doctor, Joel Fleischman, among the inhabitants of a fictitious Alaskan town.

BIBLIOGRAPHY: J.S. Bloom, "The Jews of Alaska," in: American Jewish Archives, 15:2 (1963), 97–116. R. Glanz, *The Jews in American Alaska, 1867–1880* (1953); R. Gruber *Inside of Time: My Journey From Alaska to Israel* (2002); J. Katzen-Guthrie, "A Thriving Jewish Life on the Northern Frontier" (2004), at: www.joyfulnoise.net/JoyAlaska5.html; T.T. Kizzia, "Sanctuary: Alaska, the Nazis, and the Jews," in: *Anchorage Daily News* (May 16–19, 1999), at: www.adn.com/adn/sanctuary/stories/; B. Reisman and J.I. Reisman, *Life on the Frontier: The Jews of Alaska* (1995); S. Steinacher and K.J. Graham, "Jewish History in Nome," in: *The Nome Nugget* (2000), at: www.yukonalaska.com/Special/baylestorah.htm.

[Joy Katzen-Gutherie and Joel Reisman (2nd ed.)]

ALATINO (Alatini), Italian family of physicians and scholars from Spoleto (Umbria). JEHIEL REHABIYAH (VITALE) ALATINO was physician to Pope Julius III (1550–55) and to the cardinal of Urbino. His half-brother, MOSES AMRAM (d. 1605), a celebrated physician, translated into Latin the paraphrase by Themistius of Aristotle's lost work *De Coelo* (Venice, 1574) from a Hebrew manuscript, and Galen's commentary on Hippocrates' *De aere, aquis et locis* from Hebrew into Latin (anonymously, Paris, 1679). When the Jews were expelled from the minor centers of the papal states in 1569, Moses left Spoleto. He settled in Ferrara, and then in Venice, where he died. Moses' son AZRIEL PETHAHIAH (BONAIUTO), also a physician, assisted his father in his later translation. In 1617 Azriel, who had remained in Ferrara after his father's departure, was compelled to conduct a public disputation there with the Jesuit Alfonso Caracciolo, in the presence of 2,000 persons. He defended the Jewish view concerning the eternity of the Jewish Law, and argued that Jesus did not fulfill the essential prerequisites of the Messiah. Azriel's account of the disputation, *Vikku'aḥ al Niẓḥiyyut ha-Torah* ("Debate on the Eternity of the Law"), was first published by Jarè (1875). In 1624 he was a member of a delegation sent to the papal legate in a futile attempt to prevent the establishment of a ghetto at Ferrara. He wrote *Torat ha-Mukẓeh* (unpublished). His views were liberal; he supported Leone *Modena's argument permitting Jews to go bareheaded. Recently, it has been suggested by scholars that Angelo Alatini, the author of the pastoral drama *I Trionfi,* published in Venice in 1611, was probably a member of this family, and should not be confused with the almost homonymous Angelo Alatrini, whose Italian verse translation of Hebrew liturgical texts was published in the book *L'Angelica Tromba* (Venice, 1628).

BIBLIOGRAPHY: C. Roth, *Jews in the Renaissance* (1959), 82–85, 223; H. Friedenwald, *Jews and Medicine* (1944), index; Margulies, in: *Festschrift… A. Berliner* (1903). **ADD. BIBLIOGRAPHY:** M.S. Shulvass, *The Jews in the World of the Renaissance* (1973), 208, 291n, 319n; R.C. Melzi, "Una Commedia Rinascimentale di Angelo Alatini: I Trionfi," in: *Italia*, 13-15 (2001), 344–45.

[Cecil Roth]

ALATON, ISHAK (1927–), industrialist. Born in Istanbul, Alaton graduated from Lycée Saint-Michel in 1946. After his military service he worked in Sweden in 1951–53 as an engineering trainee. In 1954 he founded the Alarko Company together with his associate Üzeyir *Garih. Over a period spanning some 50 years Alarko Holdings has grown into a group of 22 independent companies working in the fields of contracting in Turkey and abroad, building and operating hydroelectric and thermal power plants and airconditioning equipment, as well as operating in the fields of tourism and real estate development. Alaton was honored by the King of Sweden in 1993 with the Nordstjaernan (North Star) first degree. He is the vice chairman of the board of TESEV (Turkish Economic and Social Studies Foundation), a non-government organization, and honorary consul of the Republic of South Africa. His *Görüş ve Öneriler* was published in 2000.

[Rifat Bali (2nd ed.)]

ALATRI, SAMUEL (1805–1889), Italian politician and communal leader. Born in Rome, he joined the council of the Jewish community in 1828 and served on it throughout his life, eventually becoming president. On his many missions abroad he met leading Jews, especially in England and France, who encouraged him to conduct a struggle for the rights of his fellow Jews in Rome, in which he was to persevere for many decades. He took a keen interest in education, studying foreign institutions and applying the experience he gained for the benefit of Jewish institutions of learning in Rome. Alatri was chosen as spokesman of the annual deputation of the Rome community permitted to wait on Pope Gregory XVI. A gifted orator, he impressed the reactionary pope and gained enough influence with him to effect remedies in individual cases of distress. With the accession of Pius IX, who at first showed liberal tendencies, Alatri also entered general public life and was appointed a director of the papal bank. In 1849, when Rome was declared a republic and was besieged by French troops, Alatri was a member of the city's defense committee. In 1870, when King Victor Emmanuel put an end to the pope's temporal power and a plebiscite was held in Rome which advocated the incorporation of the city into the kingdom of Italy, Alatri was a member of the commission which handed the king the favorable results. The new status of the city also brought about the long-hoped-for change in the situation of the Jews there. Alatri was later elected to parliament and was appointed to regularize the state budget. Many of his speeches appeared in print, among them the outstanding address he delivered to mark the opening of the rabbinical seminary in Rome (1887).

BIBLIOGRAPHY: A. Berliner, *Geschichte der Juden in Rom*, 2 (1893), 209–12; Vogelstein-Rieger, index; *Vessillo Israelitico*, 37 (1889), 180–5, 212–3, 260–1, 295–7, 367–70. **ADD. BIBLIOGRAPHY:** M. Alatri, *Cenni biografici di Samuele Alatri scritti da suo figlio Marco: l'8 Gennaio 1890* (1929); A. Tagliacozzo, "Samuele Alatri; figura dominante nell'Ebraismo romano del secolo scorso," in: *Rassegna Mensile di Israel* 39 (1973), 278–96.

ALATRINI (or **Alatrino**), Italian family originating in Alatri in central Italy and later dispersed throughout the country. Its members were known from the 14th century as copyists of Hebrew manuscripts, and from the 15th century as authors.

MATTATHIAS BEN ABRAHAM ALATRINI (16th century), of Città di Castello, was author of a commentary (unpublished) on the *Beḥinat Olam* of *Jedaiah ha-Penini, completed in 1562–63. ISAAC BEN ABRAHAM (16th–17th century), grandson of Mattathias, was active in Cingoli and Modena, where in 1621 he was authorized by the duke to teach Hebrew to Christians. He wrote *Kenaf Renanim*, a commentary on the Song of Songs in five parts (unpublished), in which he quotes passages from the *Dialoghi di Amore* of Leone Ebreo (Judah *Abrabanel). There also exists a Hebrew dictionary of philosophical terms with Italian translations, either composed by him or compiled from his works. JOHANAN JUDAH BEN SALOMON (fl. 2nd half of 16th century) was an early Jewish author in Italian and a poet in Hebrew. He wrote *L'angelica tromba* (Ferrara, 1589), an Italian version in "*terza rima*" (the poetic meter of Dante's *Divina Commedia*) of three *seliḥot*, to which he added some "Sonetti spirituali" (spiritual sonnets). The book was translated into Hebrew by Alatrini's grandson Natan Jedidiah of Orvieto, with the title *Barekhi nafshi* (1628). His Hebrew poems belong to the genre of *tokheḥah* and praise of friends (Abraham Yagel, Barukh ha-Cohen). One *tokheḥah* is translated by the author into Italian. He is perhaps identical with Angelo Alatrini (c. 1534–before 1611), of Città di Castello, early Jewish author in Italian. He wrote *I Trionfi* (Venice, 1611), a pastoral fable, completed in Ferrara in 1575 and seen through the press by Leon *Modena, who added a sonnet in Petrarchian style. *I Trionfi* follows an arcadian model, with moral purposes and characters drawn from Latin mythology; but it also contains sections written in a more popular style, with obscene allusions.

BIBLIOGRAPHY: C. Roth, *Jews in the Renaissance* (1959), 135, 269–70; Schirmann, Italyah, 256–60; Mortara, Indice. **ADD. BIBLIOGRAPHY:** U. Cassuto, *Encycl. Judaica*, vol. 2 (1971), 101; D. Pagis, *Ḥidush u-Masoret* (1976), 284–85; M.R. Cohen, *The Autobiography of a Seventeenth-Century Venetian Rabbi. Leone Modena's Life of Judah* (1988), 235; D. Bregman, *Ẓeror Ẓehubim* (1998), 111; H.E. Adelman and B.C.I. Ravid, "Historical Notes" to M.R. Cohen, *The Autobiography of a Seventeenth-Century Rabbi* (1988), 235; R.C. Melzi, "Una commedia rinascimentale di Angelo Alatini: *I Trionfi*," in: Italia 13 (2001), 343–56.

[Cecil Roth / Alessandro Guetta (2nd ed.)

AL-AVANI, ISAAC (early 13th century), poet who lived in Baghdad. The satirist Al-Ḥarizi called Al-Avani a rich man whose poetry was poor, and who paid heavily to be made head of the academy. He wrote that Al-Avani (literally "vessel") had no value: "his song is bare, crude earthenware," and the answer to any inquiry about Al-Avani's poetry should be, "Behold it is hidden among the vessels" (I Sam. 10:22). Al-Ḥarizi's harsh judgment was unjust. Al-Avani's only extant poem, a *muwashshaḥ* ("girdle poem") on friendship, *Aḥar ha-Ẓevi Zanu Ra'yonai*, compares favorably with the best of its genre. In view of Al-Ḥarizi's unfair appraisal of Al-Avani's poetry, the statement concerning the purchase of his position must also be questioned.

BIBLIOGRAPHY: Al-Ḥarizi, *Taḥkemoni*, ed. by A. Kaminka (1899), 190; Brody, in: ZHB, 2 (1897), 157–9; Kaufmann, *ibid.*, 188ff.; S. Poznanski, *Babylonische Geonim im nachgeonaeischen Zeitalter* (1914). **ADD. BIBLIOGRAPHY:** D. Segal, *The Book of Tahkemoni* (2001), 188.

[Heinrich Haim Brody]

ALAWIDS (Ar. **ʿAlawiyyūn**), dynasty of sharifs, i.e., noble descendants of the prophet Muhammad, by his daughter Fāṭima and her husband, Ali ibn Abu Ṭālib, his cousin. It rose to power in *Morocco in the middle of the 17th century and continues to reign there. The dynasty claims to be descended from Hasan, the elder son of Muhammad, and it is therefore called Alawids of the Hasan branch. These sharifs came from Arab countries and settled in the Tāfīlālt region, in southeastern Morocco, as early as the 13th century; thus, they are also called Filālī (or Hilālī). The rise of the Alawids to power in the 17th century was connected with riots and uprisings which broke out in the country at the end of the reign of the

Saÿdis, about whom much is also related in Jewish chronicles. These chronicles, *Divrei ha-Yamim*, based on the family of Ibn Danān, *Kisse ha-Melakhim* by Raphael Moses Elbaz, and *Yaḥas Fas* by Abner Zarfaty, devote ample space to the events of the time and to a description of the sharifs. Historians consider al-Rashīd (1660–72) as the true founder of the dynasty; one of the famous Alawids was the sharif Ismail (1672–1727), a controversial figure. Arabic sources view him as the one who established the dynasty, an energetic ruler who succeeded in uniting and consolidating the state and introducing order and security. In contrast, the contemporary European sources emphasize Ismail's cruelty to his subjects and to Christian captives. According to them, no one in the history of the Maghreb spilled innocent blood as he did. Jewish courtiers and officials such as Daniel Toledano, Joseph Maymeran, Moses Abenatar, Abraham b. Quiqui, and others (see *Morocco) surrounded Ismail. European diplomatic reports and contemporary travelogues supply rich material which stresses the great part of these Jews in the relations with European countries. After Ismail's death there were 30 years of riots and uprisings in the country (1727–57) when the sons of Ismail fought each other over the distribution of the inheritance and rule over Meknes, the capital. The entire population suffered and only with the accession of Muhammad ibn ʿAbdallah (1757–90) was the country pacified. However, immediately after his death, the reign of terror of his son Yazīd (1790–92) began. The latter vented his anger on Jews and Christians, particularly on Spaniards, and maintained friendly relations only with the British, as his mother (or her mother) was English. Disunity prevailed and his brothers proclaimed themselves kings, one in the southwest, and the other in the southeast. The situation of the Jews during that time is described by S. *Romanelli in *Massa be-Arav*.

In the 19th century a certain relaxation in the relations between the rulers and the population took place, while in contrast, tension mounted with the neighbors across the border, the French ruling in Algeria and the Spaniards who for hundreds of years held a series of cities on the Mediterranean coast of Morocco (Ceuta, Mellila) and hoped to expand their authority in the north. As is usual during times of troubles and wars, the Jews were the major victims, both during the Franco-Moroccan war (1844–45) and the Spanish-Moroccan war (1859–60). Indeed, in 1864 the sharif Moulay Muhammad (1859–73) gave Sir Moses *Montefiore an audience and promised him that his government would be concerned with the civil rights and protection of the Jews. He even issued a royal edict, Ẓahīr, in that spirit whose proclamations and instructions were in effect only on paper. In 1863 the *capitulations treaty was signed between France and Morocco. Belgium, Sardinia, the United States, England, and Sweden were also party to this agreement which influenced the improvement of the situation of the Jews in Morocco who had succeeded in various ways to be included in its framework. The Madrid Convention in 1880 expanded the application of the capitulations to additional countries and decided on lengthy and comprehensive commentaries to its items (chapters). This clearly contained the reduction of Moroccan independence and sovereignty.

From 1873 to 1912 the Alawid sharifs made desperate attempts to preserve the integrity of their kingdom and protect it from imperialist aspirations of the European countries, particularly France who sought to annex Morocco to its overseas empire after it had extended its protection over Tunisia in 1881. The reign of Hasan (1873–94) and ʿAbd al-ʿAzīz constituted an unceasing decline of sharif rule. The sharif ʿAbd al-Ḥāfiẓ (1909–13) was compelled to sign a treaty with France on March 30, 1912, according to which France received most of Morocco as its protectorate. A similar treaty was signed at the end of the same year with Spain, whose share of the loot included the northern region of Morocco extending along the Mediterranean coast. ʿAbd al-Ḥāfiẓ relinquished the throne and his brother Moulay Yusuf (1913–26), who was prepared to cooperate with the authorities of the protectorate powers, ruled in his stead. His son Muhammad v (1926–61) became king at the age of 18. He possessed a great deal of diplomatic talent and helped France during the difficult period of World War II. In addition, he opposed the racist policy of the Vichy government and announced his personal protection of the Jews in his country. He was removed in 1953, apparently by political opponents in his country who enthroned one of his relatives, Sīdī Muhammad ibn ʿArafa. Muhammad spent two years in exile and was returned to his country with great honor in 1955 and continued to rule. After his death his son Hasan (1961–1999) became king.

King Hasan's regime was characterized by the tightening of internal control and a military buildup. He oppressed his political opponents and tried to unify the country. He also fought against the Polisario resistance in southern Morocco. King Hasan's attitude toward Moroccan Jews was favorable. Under his regime most Jews left the country during the "Yachin Operation" (1961–64). Jews who remained in Morocco lived safely and could practice their religion and continue their economic activity. The Israeli secret services helped King Hasan to build his own secret services. In addition, Hasan headed the Jerusalem committee of the Arab League. His contribution to the peace process in the Middle East was of great importance. Moroccan Jews in Israel, France, and Morocco also helped Israeli leaders make contact with the palace.

King Mohamed VI, Hasan's son, took over at a very young age. He quickly began to introduce some reforms with regard to democratic processes and women's rights. Thus, he released political prisoners and authorized expatriates, such as Abraham Zarfaty, a Moroccan Jewish communist and syndicalist, to return to Morocco. The country was open to Israeli tourists but diplomatic relations were broken off because of the Intifada. Mohamed VI found in Morocco a small Jewish community of not over 7,000 people, most of them in Casablanca and enjoying Jewish communal life.

BIBLIOGRAPHY: EI[2]; H. Terrasse, *Histoire du Maroc*, 2 (1950), 239–408; N. Babour, *A Survey of North West Africa* (1962), 75–188, 329–86; Budgett Meakin, *The Moorish Empire* (1899), 136–216; G. Vajda, *Un recueil de textes historiques judéo-marocains* (1951); Hirschberg, Afrikah, 2 (1965), 245–54, 260–305. **ADD. BIBLIOGRAPHY:** R. Assaraf, *Mohammed v et les Juifs du Maroc à l'époque de Vichy* (1997); idem, *Une certaine histoire des Juifs du Maroc, 1860–1999*, (2005); M. Kenbib, *Juifs et Musulmans au Maroc 1859–1948: Contribution à l'histoire des relations inter-communautaires en terre d'Islam* (1994); M.M. Laskier & Eliezer Bashan, "Morocco," in: R. Simon et al., *The Jews of the Middle East and North Africa in Modern Times* (2003), 471–504; M.M. Laskier, *Israel and the Maghreb, from statehood to Oslo*, (2004); E. Bashan, *Yahadut Maroco, Avara ve-tarbuta*, (2000), 298–87; H. Saadoun, *Ha-Yehudim be-Maroco ha-Aẓma'it*, in: H. Saadoun (ed.), *Yehudei ha-Mizraḥ ba-Me'ot ha-Tesha-Esre ve-ha-Esrim, Marocco*, (1994), pp.97–92; Yaron Zur, *Kehillah Keru'ah, Yehudei Marocco ve-ha-Le'ummiyyut 1943–1954* (2002).

[Haïm Z'ew Hirschberg / Haim Saadoun (2nd ed.)]

ALBA, JACOB DI (late 16th–early 17th century), preacher and rabbi in Florence. *Toledot Ya'akov* (Venice, 1609) is a collection of his sermons. In the introduction, he gives details of his life, mentioning that he had traveled for many years and lived for a long time in Constantinople, before being appointed preacher of the Jewish community of Florence. The structural basis of his homilies is to begin with a biblical verse, then to quote a passage from the Talmud or the Midrash which often is only slightly connected to the verse, the exordium to the body of the homily in which he raises a number of rhetorical questions regarding the talmudic passage, and the main part of the sermon in which the questions are answered. His method is in the tradition of R. Moses *Alshekh, the famous preacher of Safed. The book is arranged according to the weekly pentateuchal readings and includes references to the various festivals in relation to the nearest Sabbath; there are no special sermons for the holy days. Some of the readings are discussed in two different sermons. Though Jacob availed himself of certain philosophical terms in his sermons, he was not oriented toward philosophical preaching; nor was he influenced by the Kabbalah. His sermons usually are in the regular rabbinic tradition.

ALBA DE TORMES, city in the province of Salamanca, Spain. A charter, granted by Alfonso VII of Castile in 1140, takes into detailed consideration the relation of Jews to Christians. Both population groups were made equal in civil juridical matters; litigation between Christians and Jews was to take place in the synagogue; less indemnity was to be paid for the murder of a Jew, while a Jewish murderer of a Christian was to be put to death and his goods confiscated. The charter of Alba is one of the oldest Spanish *fueros* to fix the rate of interest on Jewish loans. A Hebrew chronicle records persecutions in the kingdom of Leon in 1230 in which Alba Jewry also suffered. The testament of Don Judah, a wealthy Jew of Alba (1410), indicates the existence of local usages governing the laws of inheritance, in addition to the Jewish laws. A satirical play in verse was written in the 15th century by the *bachilmer* Juan de Trasmiera about the members of the Jewish community in Alba, who brought a suit against a dog which bit them. It mentions the names of various Jews and their occupations, as well as of Conversos who were called as witnesses to the dog's attacks, and employs vivacious expressions which were in current use. The dog was sentenced to be hanged, but freed itself from the gallows and bit the onlookers, while the Jews stayed away from Alba until the dog had died. The satire reflects the popular prejudices of the period. The community existed until 1492.

BIBLIOGRAPHY: Baer, Urkunden, 2 (1936), index; A. Castro and F. de Onis (eds.), *Fueros Leoneses* (1916), 297, 308ff.; M. Gaibrois de Ballesteros, *Historia del reinado de Sancho IV* (1922), 115, 151, 168, 177; *Revista de archivos, bibliotecas y museos, Madrid*, 30 (1926), 409–16; J. Amador de los Ríos, *Historia... de los Judios de España* (1960[2]), 549, 963–5.

ALBAHARI, DAVID (1948–), Yugoslav author and translator. Born in Pec, Albahari graduated from Teachers College in Belgrade and settled in Zemun as a freelance writer of short stories and novels. His prose interweaves abstraction and reality, the lyric and the fantastic. He has edited literary magazines and translated literature from English, and is a member of the PEN club, the writers' union of Serbia, and the president of the Federation of Jewish Communities of Yugoslavia. His books include the collected short stories *Family Time* (1973), *Ordinary Tales* (1978), *Description of Death* (1982), and *Simplicity* (1988); the novels *The Judge Dimitrievich* (1982), *Shock in the Shed* (1984), and *Zinc;* and the anthology *Contemporary World Short Stories* (1982), in two volumes. Some of his stories and novels have been translated into Hebrew, English, Hungarian, and other languages. In 1993 he was elected president of the Federation of Jewish Communities in Belgrade, but in 1994 he resigned and immigrated to Canada. He settled in Calgary, continuing to produce new books in the Serbo-Croat language, among them *Enticement* (1996), *The Snowman* (1997), and *Goetz and Meyer* (1999).

[Eugen Werber / Zvi Loker (2nd ed.)]

ALBA IULIA (in the Roman period **Apulum**; Hung. **Gyulafehérvár**; medieval Latin **Alba Carolina**; Ger. **Karlsburg**, also **Weyssenburg**; referred to in Yiddish and Hebrew sources by the German name **Karlsburg**; in Ladino sources **Carlosburg**), city in Transylvania. Alba Iulia was the seat of residence of the princes of Transylvania in the 16th and 17th centuries; for several centuries it was administered by Hungary but was incorporated into Romania after World War I. The Jews there, originally Sephardim, benefited from the patronage of the princes of Transylvania. A Hebrew document of 1591 mentions a *bet din* there. In 1623 Prince Bethlen Gábor granted the Jews of Alba Iulia a liberal charter of residential and commercial privileges, framed at the insistence of Abraham Szasza, a Jewish physician from Constantinople, who had been invited to settle there. The privileges were endorsed by the National Assembly in 1627. However in the code *Approbatae Constitutiones* passed by the National Assembly in 1653, Jewish residence in Transylvania remained restricted to Alba Iulia. Prince Apaffi Mihñly I reaffirmed Jewish privileges in 1673 after anti-Jewish outbreaks had occurred. The charter was renewed a number of times. The Christian Hebraist, János Apáczai Csere (1625–1659), was active in Alba Iulia and recommended the inclusion of Hebrew in the senior school curriculum. Data in a census of 1735 show that the Jews then living in Alba Iulia originated from Poland, Turkey, Moldavia, Wallachia, Hungary, Moravia, and Belgrade. But during the 18th century the number of Jews living there decreased very sharply as a result of Rakoczi's rebellion; only after the return of the region to peaceful conditions did the number of Jews begin to increase again. From that period the Ashkenazi element became increasingly predominant. Alba Iulia was regarded as the Jewish "capital" of Transylvania. The *shofet* (judge) of the community was styled the "head of the Jewish people of the region." Between 1754 and 1868 the rabbi of the congregation held the title "rabbi of Karlsburg and chief rabbi of the state." The first known chief rabbi was the Sephardi *ḥakham* Abraham Isaac Russo (d. 1738). Best known was Ezekiel *Panet, who officiated in Alba Iulia between 1823 and 1845. The last chief rabbi to officiate was Abraham Friedman (1879). Until the emancipation of the Jews in Austria-Hungary in 1867 their entire religious life developed under the strict control and censorship of the Roman-Catholic bishop of the region. After the religious schism in Hungarian Jewry in 1867 the Alba Iulia congregation remained within the *status quo ante faction. An Orthodox congregation was formed in 1908, and in 1932 it was joined by the original congregation of Alba Iulia, which had until then adhered to its status quo position. The *pinkas* (minute book) of the community for the period 1736–1835, written in a mixture of Hebrew, Yiddish, Judeo-Spanish, German, Hungarian, and Romanian, has been preserved. The *Neolog rite of the Hungarian Jews was almost entirely absent in this city. A Jewish newspaper, the *Siebenbuerger Israelit*, was published in 1883 for a short time. In the 17th century there were about 100 Jews living in Alba Iulia; in 1754, 54 taxpayers; in 1891, 1,357 persons; in 1910, 1,586 (out of a total population of 11,616); in 1920, 1,770 (out of 9,645); and in 1930, 1,558 (out of 12,282). As the area became a hotbed of the antisemitic *Iron Guard, conditions for Jews became difficult. In 1938 a bomb exploded in one of the synagogues. All the property of the community was confiscated in 1941, and the men were seized for forced labor. The Jewish population of Alba Iulia increased during World War II, however, as Jews were sent there from the surrounding areas by the authorities. Heavy fighting in 1944 caused an additional influx. The maximum figure was 2,070 in 1947. This was considerably diminished by emigration in the 1960s. At the outset of the 21st century the number of Jews living in Alba Iulia was very small, as it was in all of Transylvania and Romania.

BIBLIOGRAPHY: S. Kohn, *Héber kútforrások és adatok Magyarország történetéhez* (1881), 104; Eisler, in: IMIT (1900), 316–32; (1901), 221–44; idem, *Az erdélyi zsidók multjából* (1901); idem, in: *Sinai* (Bucharest), 1 (1928); 2 (1929); 3 (1931); Krausz, in: *Erdélyi Zsidó Évkönyv*, 6 (1940–41), 78–84; MHJ, 2 (1937); 5, pt. 1 (1959); 5, pt. 2 (1960); 8 (1965); 10 (1967), index; M. Carp, *Cartea Neagră*, 1 (1946); PK Romanyah, 277–9.

[Yehouda Marton / Paul Schveiger (2nd ed.)]

ALBALA, DAVID (1886–1942), Jewish and Zionist leader in Serbia and Yugoslavia. Albala was born in Belgrade, studied medicine at the University of Vienna, and practiced in Belgrade. In 1903 he founded Gideon, the first Zionist youth association in Belgrade. In 1917 he served on the Serbian delegation to the U.S. that attempted to gain support for the country, which had been conquered by the armies of the Austro-Hungarian Empire. While in the U.S. he advocated enlistment of Jews into the *Jewish Legion, and obtained an official letter of sympathy and support for the political aims of Zionism from the Serbian foreign minister in the U.S. (Dec. 27, 1917). After World War I he was a leading figure of Yugoslav Jewry and its Zionist movement. In 1935 he visited Palestine and established a forest in memory of King Alexander of Yugoslavia. At the outbreak of World War II he was sent to Washington on behalf of the Yugoslav government.

BIBLIOGRAPHY: AJYB, 44 (1942/43), 348; *Davar* (Aug. 7, 1941); N.M. Gelber, *Hazharat Balfour ve-Toledoteha* (1939), 302; N. Agmon (Bistritski; ed.), *Megillat ha-Adamah*, 2 (1951), 231–2.

[Getzel Kressel]

ALBALAG, ISAAC (13th century), translator and philosopher. Albalag probably lived in Catalonia. In 1292, Albalag composed the only work of his which has come down, a Hebrew version of al-*Ghazālī's *Magāsidal-Falāsifa* (Hebrew, *Kavvanot* or *De'ot ha-Filosofim*), with a prologue and 75 more or less elaborate notes to which he gave the special title *Tikkun ha-De'ot*. In this independent addition to his translation, Albalag sought not so much to elucidate the basic text as to subject it to a critical evaluation, for the real purpose of his annotated translation was to determine the respective roles of revelation and philosophy in the speculations of the intellectual Jew.

According to Albalag, philosophy is identical with Aristotle's teachings as interpreted by *Averroes. This affirmation necessarily placed him in direct opposition to *Avicenna and to *Maimonides, an opposition to which he often gives expression. Yet, although he is closely dependent upon Averroes, he does not follow him blindly, or in all matters. According to Albalag, four fundamental beliefs are common to revelation (Torah) and to philosophy: the existence of God, reward and punishment, the soul's survival of physical death, and Providence. (It should be noted that rejection of the eternity of the universe is not listed among these beliefs.) Revelation addresses itself to the mass of believers in terms which are within their power of comprehension. An appropriate allegorical exegesis can always extract philosophical truths from the Torah; thus, Albalag interprets the first two chapters of Genesis (*Ma'aseh Bereshit*) in the sense of eternal *creation, though he does say that such exegesis does not yield absolute certitude. Albalag does not deny that the Torah, which is above all a "political" book, a guide for life designed to ensure good order in human society, contains truths inaccessible to human reason. However, those truths, described as "prophetic," are of as little interest to the common man, whose welfare is assured by obedience to the letter of the Law, as to the intellectual who is capable of attaining through philosophy the truths necessary for the beatitude of his immortal soul. Albalag seems to acknowledge some sort of individual immortality (see Immortality of *Soul); at any rate, he does not follow Averroes in the latter's radical doctrine of the total fusion of the disembodied rational souls with the Active *Intellect. As for the vaunted "tradition" of the esoterics, it has, according to Albalag, no serious claims to authenticity. Even though he speaks in respectful terms of three contemporary kabbalists (*Isaac b. Jacob ha-Kohen, Todros b. Joseph *Abulafia, and *Moses b. Solomon b. Simeon of Burgos), it is precisely the demonology which was so dear to them that he discards. In those cases where allegorical exegesis fails to resolve the contradiction between the indisputable facts of scriptural faith and the results of philosophic speculation, there is no alternative but to acknowledge each in its own sphere, namely, the truth laid down by the revealed text and the contrary truth irrefutably established by rational demonstration. Albalag's line of thought and his vocabulary (truth imposed by way of nature, truth believed by way of miracle) indicate with great plausibility the influence of contemporary Latin Averroists who were accused of professing the theory of the "double truth." In the final analysis it is, however, doubtful whether Albalag would have granted full validity to a truth which was not exclusively rational, at least in the case of any man who was not a prophet. One of Albalag's notes on the part of al-Ghazālī *Magāsid* devoted to logic, which is in some of the manuscripts, was borrowed from a certain Abner, who could only have been *Abner of Burgos.

Although later Jewish philosophers and theologians made frequent use of Albalag's translation of al-Ghazālī, *Tikkun ha-De'ot* brought him, except for the praises of his younger contemporary Isaac b. Joseph ibn Pollegar, nothing but censure and abuse on the part of the kabbalists, such as Shem Tov *Ibn Shem Tov, and the fideist opponents of Aristotelian philosophy in the 15th century, such as Abraham *Shalom and Isaac *Abrabanel. Nevertheless, his work was eagerly copied and undoubtedly read with interest in the Jewish intellectual circles of southern Italy and Greece during the same century. Beginning with the 16th century, however, his name and work were almost forgotten. They owe their emergence in the history of Jewish thought to the researches of J.H. *Schorr who published extracts of the *Tikkun ha-De'ot.*

BIBLIOGRAPHY: G. Vajda, *Isaac Albalag* (1960; contains an almost complete French translation of Albalag's notes and a bibliography of works on Albalag); J.A. Schorr, in: *He-Ḥalutz*, 4 (1859), 83ff.; 6 (1861), 85ff.; 7 (1865), 157ff.; Steinschneider, Uebersetzungen, 299–306; Guttmann, Philosophies, 200–3, 205, 245, 259; Touati, in: REJ, 2 (1962), 35–47.

[Georges Vajda]

ALBALIA, BARUCH BEN ISAAC (1077–1126), Spanish judge and head of a yeshivah in Córdoba; son of Isaac *Albalia. Born in Seville, he went to Lucena after his father's death (when he was 17 years old) in fulfillment of his father's express wish, in order to get R. Isaac *Alfasi to drop the hostility he had long harbored toward his father, and to be accepted as a student in Alfasi's academy. He studied there nine years, together with Joseph *Ibn Migash. After the death of Alfasi, Albalia became judge and head of the yeshivah in Córdoba. Among his many disciples was his nephew Abraham *Ibn Daud. Albalia was well versed in Greco-Arabic philosophy. Among his friends, he counted *Judah Halevi, and Moses Ibn Ezra. There is a play on words in one of Halevi's poems (*Divan*, ed. by H. Brody, 1 (1935), 120): "His name is 'Baruch' [blessed], and he, like his name, is blessed, and all who bless themselves with his name, are, in turn, blessed," apparently alluding to Albalia and testifying to his influence on Spanish Jewish intellectuals. On his death Moses Ibn Ezra eulogized him in a poem beginning with the verse: "*Einot Tehom Hemmah ve-lo-Einayim*" (*Shirei ha-Ḥol.*, ed. by H. Brody (1935), 92) and Judah Halevi did the same in a poem beginning "*Mar la-Am Yikre'u Aẓarah*" (*Selected Poems*, ed. Brody (1946), with English translation, 82).

BIBLIOGRAPHY: Schirmann, in: *Tarbiz*, 9 (1937/38), 49f.; Daud, Tradition, 86.

[Zvi Avneri]

ALBALIA, ISAAC BEN BARUCH (1035–1094), Spanish astronomer and talmudist. Isaac was born in Córdoba. According to *Ibn Daud, in his youth he had a great Jewish scholar, R. Perigors from France, as a teacher. He was also close to R. Samuel ben Joseph ha-Nagid, and later to the latter's son *Jehoseph ben Samuel ha-Nagid, to whom in 1065 he dedicated his calendrical work *Maḥberet Sod ha-Ibbur* ("The Secret of Intercalation"). After the disastrous death of Jehoseph ha-Nagid (1066), R. Isaac spent great sums of money in reassembling the family library which had been scattered. In 1069 al-Muʿtamid, king of Seville, appointed him to his retinue as court astrologer, and also as rabbi and **nasi* over the Jews in his realm. R. Isaac used his influence at court to improve the status of the Jews of the kingdom. Isaac was renowned for his great erudition, both in general and in Jewish studies. At the age of 30, he began to write his *Kuppat ha-Rokhelim* ("Spice-Peddlers' Basket"), a commentary on difficult passages in the Talmud, but did not complete it. R. Moses *Ibn Ezra refers to him as a "poet and grand stylist" (*Shirat Yis-*

rael, ed. by B.Z. Halper (1924), 72). Two of Albalia's responsa have been preserved: one on the laws of *ẓiẓit* in *Abraham b. David of Posquières' *Temim De'im*, no. 224, and one in Arabic in *Toratam shel Rishonim* (ed. by Ch. M. Horowitz, 2 (1881), 36–38). He died in Granada.

BIBLIOGRAPHY: Ibn Daud, Tradition, 78–81; Ashtor, Korot, 2 (1966), 290 ff.

[Zvi Avneri]

ALBANIA, Balkan state (bordering Serbia and Montenegro (formerly Republic of Yugoslavia), Macedonia, and Greece) on the eastern shores of the Adriatic Sea; from 1478 to 1913 under the sovereignty of Turkey.

*Benjamin of Tudela heard of people living in the region, evidently Wallachians, toward the end of the 12th century: "They are not strong in the faith of the Nazarenes and call each other by Jewish names, and some say that they are Jews." Jewish settlements were founded at the beginning of the 16th century in the Albanian seaports by exiles from Spain, who were joined by refugees from other areas. There were sizeable trading communities at Berat, Durazzo, Elbassan, and Valona: here there were Castilian, Catalonian, Sicilian, Portuguese, and Apulian synagogues.

In 1673 Shabbetai Ẓevi was exiled by the sultan to Albania, dying in Dulcigno. In 1685, during the Turkish-Venetian War, members of the Valona community fled to Berat. Those who remained were taken prisoner, including Nehemiah *Ḥayon. Between 1788 and 1822 Jews suffered from the extortions of Ali Pasha. The Jewish minorities were accused of collaborating to suppress the rebels during the Albanian revolt in 1911.

After World War I only a small number of Jews were living in Albania, in Koritsa (1927). According to a 1930 census, there were 204 Jewish inhabitants in Albania. The Albanian community was granted official recognition on April 2, 1937. In 1939, some families from Austria and Germany took refuge in Tirana and Durazzo.

[Simon Marcus]

The Holocaust Period

In July 1940 all Jews were ordered to transfer to Berat, Lushnje, and Fier. Nine months later, during the battle between Greece and Italy in April 1941, when part of Yugoslavia was annexed to Albania, an additional 120 Jewish refugees from Serbia, Croatia, and Macedonia arrived there. In addition, 350 Jewish prisoners of war were brought in from Montenegro. Jewish refugees were well treated by the native population. The local community in Kavaje assisted 200 Jewish refugees. In 1942 refugees from Pristina were transferred to Berat and protected there.

In September 1943 after the change in the Italian government and the German domination of Italy, Albania came under German control and the situation of the Jews deteriorated dramatically. Some Jews fled to the partisans. Others obtained false papers. Albanian bureaucrats gave identity papers to many Jews of Kavaje so they could go to Tirana and hide there and in 1944 the governors of Albania refused to cooperate in submitting a list to the Germans of all the Jews.

Cities in Albania known to have had Jewish inhabitants.

In all, 600 Jews were saved from the Holocaust. Only six Jews from Shkoder were arrested and sent to a camp in Pristina. No Jews were turned over to the Germans.

Modern Period

After World War II until the collapse of Communism in 1990, the community, numbering 200–300, was completely cut off from the Jewish world. All religion was strictly outlawed and there was no communal life, no rabbi, and no Jewish educational facilities. In 1991 almost the entire community was airlifted to Israel. Relations between Albania and Israel were subsequently normalized, with an agricultural cooperation agreement signed in 1999 and Israeli aid accepted for the Kosavar refugees there. Efforts were made by the Joint to revive community life among the few dozen remaining Jews, nearly all in the capital, Tirana. A synagogue still existed in Valona (Vlore) but was no longer in use.

BIBLIOGRAPHY: G. Scholem, in: *Zion*, 17 (1952), 79–83; Scholem, *Shabbetai Ẓevi*, 2 (1957), 787–90; Bernstein, in: *Jewish Daily Bulletin* (April 17–18, 1934); A. Milano, *Storia degli Ebrei italiani nel Levante* (1949), 63–66; J. Starr, *Romania…* (Eng., 1949), 65, 81–83. **ADD. BIBLIOGRAPHY:** PK; M. Arbell, "The Jewish Community of Vlor–Valona–Avilona and Its Role in the Adriatic," in: *Los Muestros*, 50 (2003), 16–20.

ALBANY, capital of the state of New York, 150 miles north of New York City; population, 95,000 (2004); estimated Jewish population, 12,000–13,000 with half living in suburbs but members of Albany congregations. Public records indicate the presence of Jews as early as 1658. Asser Levy owned property, obtained burgher's rights, and lived in Albany in the 1650s. Other early Jewish merchants and traders who resided in Albany included Jacob Lucena, Hayman Levy, Jonas Phillips, Asher Levy, Levi Solomons and Levi Solomons (II). The second Solomons, who lived with his family in Albany in the early 19th century, started a chocolate and snuff business and belonged to New York's Shearith Israel.

A Jewish community emerged in the 1830s as immigrants from Bavaria and Posen arrived in Albany. German-speaking Jews organized Congregation Beth El in 1838. By 1841, the congregation had bought a burial ground and purchased its first synagogue building. Divisions over language and ritual led to the founding of Beth El Jacob in 1841 by Jews of Polish origin. After acquiring property for a synagogue and separate burial grounds, the congregation built a new synagogue in 1847. Prominent Gentiles including Mayor William Parmalee attended the dedication of Beth El Jacob on April 28, 1848. Isaac Mayer *Wise arrived in the United States from Bohemia and became Albany's first rabbi when he took over leadership of Beth El in 1846. He was the teacher at the congregation's Hebrew school, then one of only four in the United States. Wise's advocacy of changes in ritual split the congregation with the famous confrontation at the Rosh Ha-Shanah service on September 7, 1850. Synagogue officers prevented him from taking out the Torah scrolls, a fight ensued, and Wise and members of the congregation were arrested. By October 11, 1850, Wise and 77 supporters had organized Anshe Emeth, the fourth Reform congregation in the United States. Members of all three congregations were poor and worked as peddlers, tinsmiths, tailors, or middlemen. About 800 Jews lived in Albany in 1860.

By the 1880s, the arrival of Jews from the Russian Empire expanded the Jewish population to 3,000. Further immigration of Russian- and Polish-speaking Jews increased the community to 4,000 in 1900 and 10,000 in the 1920s. Assimilation and Americanization led to the merger of Beth El and Anshe Emeth in 1885 to form Beth Emeth, the only Reform congregation in Albany. Rabbi Wise returned to Albany in 1889 to dedicate the synagogue for the combined congregation. Recent immigrants, while Orthodox, did not feel comfortable in Beth El Jacob and formed a separate congregation, Sons of Abraham, in 1882. In 1902 another group of Russian Jews split off and established the United Brethren Society, as a separate congregation that followed a ḥasidic prayer book, and the congregation incorporated in 1905.

From the 1830s to about 1950, the South End, especially the area around South Pearl Street, remained a Jewish neighborhood with kosher meat markets, restaurants, Jewish-owned businesses, synagogues, and communal institutions. As Albany expanded in the early 1900s Jewish residents moved "up the hill" and started new congregations in the Pine Hills and Delaware neighborhoods. Ohav Shalom, the first Conservative congregation, began in 1911, and purchased property for a synagogue in 1922. Another group of Jews in Pine Hills began to meet at Schwartz's Mansion and became Tifereth Israel in 1936. Sons of Israel, a third Conservative congregation, began in the 1930s, and constructed a synagogue in 1935.

The passing of the immigrant generation, Americanization, and suburbanization led to a relocation and reorganization of the synagogues. The Orthodox synagogues merged with the United Brethren Society, joining Beth El Jacob in 1959, and Beth El Jacob merged with Sons of Abraham in 1974 to form Beth Abraham-Jacob. The combined congregation dedicated a new synagogue in 1991. A small group of Orthodox Jews sought to create an informal religious community, and established a *shtibl*, a small house of prayer, Shomray Torah, in 1965. Reform Congregation Beth Emeth built a new synagogue in 1957. A split within the congregation created a new Reform congregation, Bnai Sholom, in 1971, and the new congregation dedicated its own synagogue in 1979. Two Conservative congregations merged in 1949 as Tifereth Israel, and Sons of Israel joined to build a new synagogue, dedicated as Temple Israel in 1956, which was led for a generation by Rabbi Herman Kieval and produced rabbis and scholars. A Hebrew-speaking day camp, Camp Givah, was perhaps the only one in the United States at the time. Ohav Shalom remained separate and dedicated a new building in 1964. Starting in November 1991 Jews seeking an informal and egalitarian community created the Havurah Minyan of the Capital District, following Conservative ritual. In 1995, Ohav Shalom voted to become equalitarian in worship and ritual life. While the Jewish community increasingly resides in the suburbs, synagogues and the Albany Jewish Community Center remain in the city. This led ḥasidic Jews to establish Chabad houses in Albany, Delmar, Guilderland, and, in December 2004, in Colonie.

Jewish residents organized social, fraternal, mutual aid, and self-defense institutions. In 1843 the Society for Brotherly Love became the first mutual aid and burial society. Congregations started burial societies and in 1855 merged their mutual aid groups into the Hebrew Benevolent Society. Merger with the Jewish Home Society led to the Albany Jewish Social Service in 1931, now Jewish Family Services. It aided Jewish refugees in the 1930s, Holocaust survivors in the 1940s and 1950s, and from 1988 it resettled 1,300 Soviet Jews, the latest Jewish immigrants to the Albany area. State government workers and scholars working at the local universities including State University of New York at Albany are a distinct component of the current Jewish community.

B'nai B'rith opened a German-speaking chapter in 1853, but an English-language chapter, the Gideon Lodge, began in 1870 and replaced the German language branch by 1910. A women's organization, United Order of True Sisters, started a chapter in 1857, and is still active. Concern for the elderly poor led to the Jewish Home Society in 1875, which merged with Daughters of Sarah in 1941, and in the 1970s they built a new facility in Albany. Gideon Lodge joined with the Albany

Jewish Community Council to build senior citizen housing, Bnai Brith Parkview Apartments, which opened in 1973, and Congregation Ohav Shalom built senior citizen housing next to their synagogue in 1974.

In the early 2000s Jewish educational institutions included the Orthodox Maimonides Hebrew Day School. Combining Jewish and secular education is Bet Shraga Hebrew Academy, which is named after a Jewish educator and not a prominent donor – the brilliant and dynamic Jewish educator Philip "Shraga" Arian, who served as the educational director at Temple Israel, opened in 1963. Responding to the antisemitism of the 1930s and activities of the German-American Bund, local veterans formed the Jewish War Veterans in 1935, and it remains a local veterans organization concerned with patriotism, education, and antisemitism. Starting in 1938 local Jewish groups created the Albany Jewish Community Council, now the Jewish Federation of Northeastern New York, to combat antisemitism, coordinate among Jewish organizations, and represent the community. The Holocaust Survivors and Friends Education Center raises public awareness of the Holocaust, especially in public schools. Starting out in the Hebrew Institute in 1915, the YMHA and YWHA merged into the Jewish Community Center in 1925. Formally incorporated in 1926, the JCC gradually replaced the Hebrew Institute as a meeting place for Jewish groups and as a center for recreational activities. The JCC built its current headquarters and recreational center in 1960. The variety of Jewish institutions peaked in about 1915, when there were anarchist, socialist, Zionist, and Yiddish-language benevolent societies in Albany. Today's synagogues and organizations reflect the ongoing tensions between assimilation and retention of Jewish identity and religious practice. While probably half of Albany's Jewish community actually resides in suburbs, synagogues have not followed the pattern in other Jewish communities and relocated to the suburbs. All the congregations have relocated but remain within the city of Albany. Finally, the resettlement of 1,300 Soviet Jews in the Capital District since 1988 represents the most significant Jewish immigration into the Albany area since the early 1920s.

BIBLIOGRAPHY: S.W. Rosendale, in: AJHSP, 3 (1895), 61–71; I.M. Wise, *Reminiscences* (1945); L. Silver, in: YIVOA, 9 (1954), 212–46; N. Rubinger, "Albany Jewry in the Nineteenth Century" (Ph.D. diss., Yeshiva University, 1971); M. Gerber, *Pictorial History of Albany's Jewish Community* (1986); H. Strum, in: *Jewish History and Community in Albany, NY* (Exhibition Catalogue, Opalka Gallery of the Sage Colleges, 2003), 1–37; D. Ornstein, *ibid.*, 37–41; D. Cashman, in: A. Roberts and M. Cockrell, *Historic Albany: Its Churches and Synagogues* (1986), 120–40.

[Harvey Strum (2nd ed.)]

ALBARADANI, JOSEPH (tenth century), liturgical poet and chief *ḥazzan* in the Great Synagogue of Baghdad. The surname is derived from a suburb of Baghdad called Baradan. The fact that his liturgical poems were composed to correspond with the annual Torah reading cycle (and not with the triennial one current at the time in Ereẓ Israel) supports the view that he was of Babylonian origin. Many of Joseph's poems are preserved in all the large *genizah* collections but only a few specimens have appeared in print. Beside the *kerovot* for the Torah readings, Joseph composed several short *masdar* poems (introductions, at a later period called *reshuyyot*). Strangely enough, some of these were included in the Sicilian liturgical collection, *Ḥizzunim*. He was succeeded as *ḥazzan* by his son Nahum ha-Ḥazzan, who was a friend of the *geonim* *Sherira, *Hai b. Sherira, and *Samuel b. Hophni. In 999 he went on an official mission to Kairouan from where he was to continue on his way to Spain. However, Hai Gaon ordered him back in 1006 in order to take over the post of his late father. He, too, was the author of liturgical poems. Nahum was in turn succeeded by his son Solomon al-Baradani as *ḥazzan* and *paytan*.

BIBLIOGRAPHY: I. Davidson, in: *Livre d'hommage… S. Poznanski* (1927), 62, passim (Heb. part); idem (ed.), *Genizah Studies*, 3 (1930), 92, 95–105, 116, 128–37; Marcus, in: JQR, 21 (1930/31), 85–88; Mann, *ibid.*, 9 (1918/19), 150–2, 154ff; idem, in: AJSLL, 46 (1929–30), 277ff.; Mann, Texts, 1 (1931), 113, 122, 151–3; Goldziher, in: REJ, 50 (1905), 182–8; Zulay, in: YMHSI, 2 (1936), 388; 5 (1939), 158, 160, 162, 172; Spiegel, *ibid.*, 272; A.M. Habermann, *Be-Ron Yaḥad* (1945), 33–34; idem, in: *Haaretz* (April 11, 1960); idem, *Ateret Renanim* (1967), 105, 137–9; Bernstein, in: *Tarbiz*, 13 (1941/42), 150–64.

[Jefim (Hayyim) Schirmann]

AL-BARGELONI (i.e. "of Barcelona"), **ISAAC BEN REUBEN** (b. 1043), Spanish talmudist and liturgical poet. In a *genizah* fragment Al-Bargeloni is described as a pupil of *Ḥanokh b. Moses and must, therefore, have studied for some time in Córdoba. His permanent residence was the coastal city of Denia, where he was presumably active as a *dayyan* until his death. *Naḥmanides was one of his descendants. Abraham *Ibn Daud extols his learning, including him among the four distinguished contemporaries of Isaac Alfasi, also called Isaac. Moses *Ibn Ezra and *Al-Ḥarizi praise his poetical talent, especially his ingenuity in interpolating biblical verses into his poems. This skill is particularly manifest in Isaac's *azharot*, in which all 145 strophes end with a biblical quotation. The *azharot* have been included in most North African rites published since 1655 and have been frequently published, both alone and together with those of Solomon ibn *Gabirol. Of Isaac's other poems there are extant two introductions to the *azharot*, two *tokheḥot* (one unpublished), two *mi-khamokha*, and an *ahavah*. His halakhic works consist of commentaries to single tractates of the Talmud (not preserved), and a translation from Arabic to Hebrew of *Hai Gaon's *Sefer ha-Mikkaḥ ve-ha-Mimkar* made in 1078. According to Simeon b. Ẓemaḥ *Duran (Responsa 1:15), *Judah b. Barzillai al-Bargeloni was Isaac's pupil.

BIBLIOGRAPHY: Rapoport, in: *Bikkurei ha-Ittim*, 10 (1829), 191; Mann, in: REJ, 74 (1922), 157–9; Davidson, Oẓar, 4 (1933), 418; J.H. Schirmann, *Shirim Ḥadashim min ha-Genizah* (1966), 196–200; Ibn Daud, Tradition, index.

ALBARRACÍN, Spanish city near Teruel in Aragon. Jews were living there in the 12th century. The *fuero* (charter), granted to Albarracín by the local overlord about 1220, includes regulations governing the legal status and economic activities of the Jews. In 1391 the municipal council attempted to compel the Jews to submit to its legislation, but the king opposed this move. The Jews of Albarracín suffered in the anti-Jewish riots in *Spain that year; in 1392 the gate of the Jewish quarter was broken down and several of the inhabitants were massacred. There is evidence that the Jews in Albarracín maintained their communal organization, social identity, and economic activities until the expulsion. Albarracín was among the communities which requested of Juan II in 1458 to ratify new communal regulations. The community was permitted to levy a *cisa* tax on foodstuffs and was released from a series of other taxes; the procedure regarding oaths was changed. Between 1484 and 1486 an Inquisitional tribunal operated in Albarracín, but for the most part the trials of the local Conversos took place in Teruel. The expulsion of the Jews from Albarracín, among other communities, was ordered in May 1486. The Jews were granted three months in which to comply; in July the king advised *Torquemada to grant them an additional six months. At the time of the general expulsion from Spain in 1492, however, some Jews were still apparently living in Albarracín and the aged rabbi Solomon urged his congregation to accept exile rather than conversion to Christianity.

BIBLIOGRAPHY: Baer, Spain, 2 (1966), index; Baer, Urkunden, 1 (1929), index; González Palencia, *Anuario de la historia del derecho español*, 8 (1931), 479ff; Piles Ros, in: *Sefarad*, 7 (1947), 355ff; 10 (1950), 89.

[Haim Beinart]

ALBAZ, MOSES BEN MAIMON (16th century), Moroccan kabbalist. Albaz, who lived in Tarrodant, was the author of *Heikhal Kodesh*, which he began writing in 1575. It is an interpretation of the prayers in the kabbalistic idiom, based mainly on the Zohar and Menahem *Recanati's works. The manuscript was owned by R. Jacob *Sasportas, who published it with the annotations of R. Aaron ha-Sab'uni of Salé (1653). His work *Sod Kaf-Bet Otiyyot* is preserved in the copy by R. Joseph b. Solomon ibn Mussa (London, Jews' College, Montefiore Ms. 335).

BIBLIOGRAPHY: Azulai, 2 (1852), no. 55, s.v. *Heikhal Kodesh;* G. Scholem, in: KS, 6 (1929/30), 276, 457; J. Ben-Naim, *Malkhei Rabbanan* (1931), 95b.

AL-BAẒAK, MAẒLI'AḤ BEN ELIJAH IBN (11th century), *dayyan* in Sicily. Maẓli'aḥ was a pupil of *Hai Gaon in Pumbedita and later he apparently migrated to Sicily where he was appointed *dayyan*. *Nathan b. Jehiel, author of the *Arukh*, was his pupil and it is quite likely that the explanations of Arabic and Persian terms appearing in Nathan's work were derived from his teacher. Maẓli'aḥ wrote a letter in Arabic to Samuel ha-Nagid, concerning Hai Gaon, of which fragments only are extant. One fragment has a commentary by Hai Gaon to Psalms 103:5, and in another it is stated that Hai Gaon, with a view to seeking a correct interpretation of Psalms 141:5, sent Maẓli'aḥ to the Nestorian patriarch, who showed him the Syriac version. On a journey to Europe – or on some other occasion – Maẓli'aḥ stopped over in Ereẓ Israel, when he acted as a judge in a civil dispute in Ramleh.

BIBLIOGRAPHY: Steinschneider, Arab Lit, 132; idem, *Gesammelte Schriften*, 1 (1925), 67, n. 87; Mann, in: JQR, 9 (1918/19), 151; Vogelstein-Rieger, 1 (1896), 358; Neubauer, in: *Israelitische Letterbode*, 2 (1876–77), 177; Lewin, in: *Ginzei Kedem*, 3 (1925), 67–68; Assaf, in: KS, 2 (1925/26), 184; Krauss, in: HHY, 11 (1927), 204–5.

[Umberto (Moses David) Cassuto]

ALBECK, family of talmudic scholars.

SHALOM (1858–1920), talmudic and rabbinic scholar, born and educated in Warsaw. Though he earned his living in business, Albeck gained distinction as an astute scholar. His *Mishpeḥot Soferim* (pt. 1, 1903), a biographical encyclopedia of the *tannaim* and *amoraim*, only covered a small part of the letter *alef.* Albeck also began to publish the *Even ha-Ezer* of *Eliezer b. Nathan, together with an introduction and commentary (pt. 1, 1904); and the *Sefer ha-Eshkol* of *Abraham b. Isaac of Narbonne, with an introduction and notes (pt. 1, 1910), completed by his son Ḥanokh (1935–8). Albeck's questioning of the authenticity of the earlier edition of this work by Z.B. *Auerbach gave rise to a keen literary polemic. Albeck also planned to publish the Babylonian Talmud with variant readings on the basis of manuscripts and with a modern commentary, but only a specimen was published, *Moda'ah Talmud Bavli* (1913). A critical study of the writings of *Judah b. Barzillai al-Bargeloni appeared in *Festschrift... Israel Lewy* (1911).

His son ḤANOKH (Chanokh; 1890–1972), talmudic scholar, studied at the Theological Seminary and the University of Vienna, became research scholar at the *Akademie fuer die Wissenschaft des Judentums in Berlin (1920) and lecturer in Talmud at the *Hochschule fuer die Wissenschaft des Judentums (1926). In 1936 he immigrated to Ereẓ Israel and was professor of Talmud at the Hebrew University, until 1956. Albeck's work covers almost all areas of talmudic research. In his studies on tannaitic literature, he came to the conclusion that the editors (not only of tannaitic literature, but also of the Talmud) compiled their materials without adapting, abridging, or reworking them, as their only objective was to collect scattered materials. This first attempt to offer a comprehensive solution to the various problems arising out of the study of talmudic literature provoked a keen controversy, not yet settled. In Albeck's opinion, as opposed to that of David *Hoffmann, the principal differences between the two types of halakhic Midrashim stem from divergent redactions. Albeck even set out to prove that both the *Tosefta and the halakhic Midrashim, as they are known, were unknown to the two Talmuds. In his work on the *halakhah* in the Book of Jubilees Albeck argued that it does not stem from any of the three known sects (Pharisees, Sadducees, or Essenes), but that it originated in the circles of another sect, the "Circle of

*Enoch," and shows affinity to the *halakhah* of the *Damascus Covenant. These conclusions have assumed special importance since the discovery of the *Dead Sea Scrolls. After the death of J. *Theodor, Albeck completed the publication of the latter's monumental critical edition of *Genesis Rabbah* and he wrote the comprehensive introduction as well. This work is a striking example of an extremely accurate critical edition. Albeck also edited the Hebrew translation of Zunz's *Gottesdienstliche Vortraege*, adding a great amount of new material. His major works are an edition of *Meiri's *Beit ha-Beḥirah* on *Yevamot* (1922); *Untersuchungen ueber die Redaktion der Mischna* (1923); *Genesis Rabbah* (1926–36); *Untersuchungen ueber die halakischen Midrashim* (1927); *Das Buch der Jubilaeen und die Halacha* (1930); *Ha-Eshkol* by Abraham b. Isaac, 1-2 (1935–38); *Bereshit Rabbati* (1940); *Meḥkarim bi-Veraita ve-Tosefta* (1944); *Ha-Derashot be-Yisrael*, Zunz's work (1947); *The Mishnah* (with introductions, commentary, and notes; 1952–59); *Mavo la-Mishnah* (1959); *Mavo la-Talmudim*, 1 (1969). Beside his major works, he also wrote many scholarly essays in Hebrew and German.

BIBLIOGRAPHY: Ch. Tchernowitz (Rav Ẓa'ir), in: *Ha-Tekufah*, 8 (1920), 491–4; A.M. Habermann, in: S.K. Mirsky (ed.), *Ishim u-Demuyyot be-Ḥokhmat Yisrael be-Eiropah ha-Mizraḥit* (1959), 319–23; *Sefer ha-Yovel le-… Ḥanokh Albeck* (1963).

[Moshe David Herr]

ALBELDA, MOSES BEN JACOB (1500–before 1583), rabbi and philosopher. It is likely that Moses Albelda was born in Spain, and that he was the grandson of a Moses Albelda who settled in Salonika. He lived a life of hardship and wandering. He states that he acted as both *dayyan* and *rosh yeshivah*. He was rabbi of Arta (Greece) in 1534, and later of Valona (Albania). His sons, Judah and Abraham, went to considerable trouble to publish their father's works. These are characterized by a distinctive style and are eminently readable. His commentary and biblical expositions are mainly philosophical. His sermonic works are *Reshit Da'at* (Venice, 1583), discourses on philosophical themes and rabbinical dicta; *Sha'arei Dimah (ibid.*, 1586), on such varied themes as Providence, the vicissitudes of the times, the death of the righteous, and the destruction of the Temple. His biblical works are in two parts, the first, *Olat Tamid* (*ibid.*, 1601), exegetical, and the second, *Darash Moshe* (*ibid.*, 1603) homiletical. These works mention a number of others that he wrote, including commentaries on Joshua, Esther, and Samuel, and on Maimonides' *Guide* and *Sefer ha-Mitzvot*.

BIBLIOGRAPHY: Steinschneider, Cat Bod, 1768, no. 6427; JE, 1 (1901), 332.

ALBERSTEIN, HAVA (1946–), Israeli singer and composer. Born in Stettin (Poland), Alberstein came to Israel with her parents in 1951. She started singing and accompanying herself on the guitar while still at school. During her military service she performed as soloist in army bases throughout the country. Upon completion of her military service she began performing in concerts and for several years played the guitar while singing, but in 1971 she started appearing with a small ensemble and without her guitar, thus demonstrating her dramatic ability on stage. She then began writing her own lyrics. The songs in her 1986 album *The Immigrants* incorporated autobiographic elements and a measure of criticism of Israeli society. She expressed her political views in such songs as "The Magician," "Ḥad Gadya," and others. In "Ḥad Gadya" she changed the words of the traditional song to liken Israeli soldiers to devouring animals during the Intifada, which led to a storm of protest and a radio ban on the song. In 1988 she began composing her own music as well and produced the album *The Need for a Word, the Need for Silence*. In 1992 she recorded her first album in English, *The Man I Love*, following it by a number of others, notably one with the Klezmatics Band in 1998. With over 50 albums to her credit, Alberstein frequently performed abroad and is considered a major Israeli singer. She is notable in the field of children's songs and is considered one of the greatest singers of Yiddish songs, with some ten albums. She received the Kinnor David Prize several times as well as the Manger Prize.

[Nathan Shahar (2nd ed.)]

ALBERT, MARV (**Marv Philip Aufrichtig**; 1941–), U.S. television and radio sportscaster, member of the Basketball Hall of Fame. Albert was born in Manhattan Beach, Brooklyn, New York, the son of a grocer, and grew up there with his brothers, Al and Steve, both of whom also became professional broadcasters. The three brothers started practicing in their youth, staging a "contest" between the two family hamsters and doing the play-by-play of the Hamster Olympics. Albert worked on Howard *Cosell's national radio show as a teenager and then with Marty *Glickman at WCBS Radio when he was in college. Albert attended Syracuse University from 1960 to 1962 and graduated from New York University in 1965. Glickman gave Albert his start in broadcasting, allowing him to broadcast his first New York Knicks basketball game on radio on January 27, 1963, at age 22. He broadcast the Knicks full time on radio from the 1967–68 season through the 1985–86 season. He also broadcast the Knicks on television, but was dismissed after he criticized the team's poor play on-air in 2004.

Albert was the radio voice of the New York Rangers hockey team, beginning with his first game on March 13, 1963, and full time from 1965–66 to 1996–97. He later broadcast NBA basketball, NFL football, college basketball, boxing, NHL all-star games, and baseball studio and pre-game shows for the NBC network from 1979 to 1998. He also broadcast basketball for the TNT network and was the voice of Monday Night Football on Westwood One Radio/CBS Radio Sports. Prior to joining NBC, Albert was the radio voice of the New York Giants football team from 1973 to 1976, and for 13 years was the sports anchor for Ch. 4/WNBC-TV.

Albert became the focus of a media frenzy in 1997 when he pleaded guilty to a misdemeanor assault charge amid embarrassing allegations about his sex life. As a consequence he was forced to leave broadcasting, but was rehired by the MSG and Turner networks in 1998 and NBC in 1999. He was hired in 2005 to handle play-by-play duties for the New Jersey Nets beginning in the 2005–6 season. Albert, whose iconic catchphrase is an emphatic "Yes!" punctuating a jump shot in basketball, has won six Cable Ace Awards for Outstanding Play-By-Play Announcer, three New York Emmy awards as Outstanding On-Camera Personality, and was named New York State Sportscaster of the Year an unprecedented 20 times. In 1997 he was awarded the Curt Gowdy Media Award by the Naismith Memorial Basketball Hall of Fame.

Albert played himself in a number of films and is the author of *Krazy about the Knicks* (1971), *Ranger Fever* (1973), *Marv Albert's Sports Quiz Book* (1976), *Yesss!: Marv Albert On Sportscasting* (1979), and *I'd Love To But I Have a Game* (1993).

[Elli Wohlgelernter (2nd ed.)]

ALBERT, MILDRED ELIZABETH LEVINE (1905–1991), international fashion consultant, educator, lecturer, columnist, and radio and television personality. Albert was the youngest of four children of Thomas Levine and Elizabeth Sugarman. Born in Russia, she emigrated with her family, who settled in Roxbury, Massachusetts. While a student at the Sargent School of Physical Education (now part of Boston University), Mildred Levine met her future husband, James Albert. The couple married in 1928 and had three children. A teacher of art, dance, and literature at Florence Street Settlement House in the South End of Boston, Albert also taught posture at Massachusetts General Hospital and was sought out to give private lessons in good posture and proper etiquette to daughters of prominent Boston families. In the 1930s she established the Academie Moderne, a finishing school for young women that combined lessons on poise, grace, and good speaking skills with exposure to museums and cultural events. In 1944, Albert co-founded the Hart Model Agency and Promotions, Inc. with Muriel Williams Hart and her husband, Francis Hart; during those years she began covering major designer fashion shows as Boston's "First Lady of Fashion." Albert sold the school and the agency in 1981, but remained dean emeritus to the school and consultant to the agency. From the 1930s through the 1970s, Albert hosted weekly radio programs on fashion and beauty. She continued fashion show coverage on the CBS *Good Day Show* into the 1980s, and late in life as a reporter for the *Tab* newspapers. Although not religiously observant, Albert identified strongly with Jewish history and culture. She shared her name and money as a generous philanthropist, co-coordinating fashion shows for various charities; she served on the board of the Hebrew Teachers College in Boston in the 1920s and 1930s. Albert was the recipient of numerous awards, including the State of Israel Bonds 35th Anniversary Award in 1983; in 1990 Boston's Mayor Flynn declared "Mildred Albert Day" to honor the city's "official Grande Dame." Albert's papers are located at the Schlesinger Library of Radcliffe College.

BIBLIOGRAPHY: S. Alpern, "Mildred (Levine) Albert," in: *Jewish Women in America* (P.E. Hyman and D.D. Moore, eds.), vol. 1 (1997), 32–33.

[Sara Alpern (2nd ed.)]

ALBERTA, province in Western Canada. Alberta boasts Canada's fourth largest provincial population, with over 3.2 million people (July 2004). Its two major cities are Edmonton, the provincial capital, with approximately 5,500 Jews, and Calgary, home of the Canadian oil industry, with 8,200 Jews.

Although the province's nearly 15,400 Jews live primarily in the main cities of Edmonton and Calgary, the Jewish presence in Alberta was not always so overwhelmingly urban. Prior to the creation of Alberta in 1905, Jews were found in villages, towns, and on farms around the region. The earliest record of a Jew in Alberta was that of a gold prospector in Fort Edmund. The Hudson Bay factor's journal reads: "September 15, 1869 – Mr. Silverman (a Jew) and a party of four Americans and a Negro started for Fort Benton today." Other Jewish traders and merchants also visited the region from Montana Territory.

Permanent settlement in the region did not take place until the 1880s when two significant historical developments coincided: the extension of the Canadian Pacific Railway into Western Canada (it reached Calgary in 1883) and the terrible pogroms against East European Jews following *Alexander III's ascension to the throne in 1881. In 1882, around 150 Russian Jews worked on the CPR's railway gang, laying 100 miles of track to Medicine Hat. It was reported that they kept the Sabbath, ate kosher food, had a Torah scroll for services, and were directed by a Yiddish-speaking foreman.

The first permanent Jewish residents, in what became Alberta, were brothers, Jacob Lyon Diamond and William Diamond. In 1888, Jacob Diamond moved to Calgary and worked as a pawnbroker and traded liquor and hides. Although historical sources differ slightly over the timetable of William's arrival in Calgary and Edmonton, it seems that he opened a tailor shop in Calgary in 1892. The brothers initiated the first formal Jewish service for the High Holidays in 1894 and founded many of the Calgary community's institutions, such as its cemetery in 1904. Jacob Diamond established Calgary's first synagogue, Beth Jacob, in 1911. In Edmonton, Abe Cristall opened a liquor store soon after his arrival to the city in 1893. William Diamond was instrumental in establishing the first Jewish religious council in Alberta in 1906, a year after his move to Edmonton. Hyman Goldstick, the province's first full-time Jewish religious leader, moved to Edmonton from Toronto in 1906 and served Calgary, Edmonton, and smaller surrounding Jewish communities.

Recognizing the need to populate the West, Canada's high commissioner in London, Sir Alexander Galt, convinced the prime minister, Sir John A. Macdonald, that the Russian Jewish refugees could serve a useful purpose, colonizing the West as farmers. Alberta's first Jewish farming settlements developed in 1893 at Pine Lake and near Fort Macleod. The Jewish community at Pine Lake, numbering 70, was the largest in the region at the time. By 1895, the difficult conditions, inexperience, and lack of Jewish communal institutions contributed to the decline of this settlement and a smaller settlement near Fort Macleod. In 1901, there were 242 Jews in the region.

A decade passed before there was another serious attempt made at Jewish agricultural settlement. Settlements were established at Trochu, Rumsey, and Sibbald in 1905, 1906, and 1911, respectively. Living conditions improved after the arrival of the Canadian Northern Railway in 1910 and families joined the male settlers and opened businesses in the railway villages. In Rumsey, Jews occupied important positions within the wider community as justices of the peace and school trustees. The *Jewish Colonization Association, an international organization supported by Jewish philanthropists like Moses *Montefiore, provided settlers with loans for reuniting farm families and financial support for communal essentials like kosher food, religious services, and education. The Canadian government provided little, if any, support to the Jewish settlers. During the heyday of Jewish farming in Alberta, up to 70 Jewish families were operating farms around Rumsey and Sibbald. In 1914, the 100-person Jewish community of the Montefiore colony near Sibbald built a synagogue and hired a rabbi. As was the case everywhere, the Depression in the 1930s had a devastating effect on the Jewish colonists and by World War II few Jewish farmers remained at Rumsey or Sibbald. By the war's end, the Jewish presence in rural Alberta was virtually non-existent.

But for all the efforts at agricultural settlement, Jews tended to concentrate in urban areas where there were economic opportunities as merchants, traders, and peddlers. By 1911, there were 1,207 Jews in the province, with more than half of them in the two major cities (604 in Calgary and 171 in Edmonton). Aside from Edmonton and Calgary, larger Jewish communities were also established in Lethbridge (home to the third largest Jewish community in Alberta) and Medicine Hat. As it took many years for these communities to acquire a synagogue building, services were conducted for years in people's homes. In the small town of Vegreville, Jews lived harmoniously with the town's Ukrainian and French Canadian residents and were active in municipal life. The Jewish presence in small towns and cities in Alberta, however, gradually disappeared due to the richer Jewish communal life and better economic opportunities available in Edmonton and Calgary.

After World War I, Canada briefly opened its doors to immigration. In 1921, the Canadian census found 3,186 Jews in Alberta. By 1930, however, the number of Jews admitted to the country was in decline as a result of growing immigration restriction. Nevertheless, the number of Jews in the province grew by almost 15 percent between 1921 and 1931, largely due to migration of Jews from Manitoba and Saskatchewan. In 1931, 92 percent of Alberta's 3,700 Jews lived in urban settings.

Alberta's Jewish population grew slowly through the war years and into the postwar era but prosperity in the 1970s led to a significant increase in the number of Jews in the province, primarily in Edmonton and Calgary. With that growth came the development of large Jewish community centers and Reform temples in both cities. Serving Calgary and Edmonton, the *Jewish Star* was published between 1980 and 1990. Since then, the *Jewish Free Press* serves the Calgary Jewish community and *Edmonton Jewish Life* and *Edmonton Jewish News* serve Edmonton. Jews in both cities also established community day schools.

Although the early Jewish community in Alberta faced antisemitism, and antisemitism was a fact of life in the Canadian government's immigration policy until after World War II, it has not been very pronounced in the major cities of Alberta. Jews in Alberta did not face enrollment quotas in professional schools as did Jews in Manitoba, Ontario, and Quebec. Discrimination was not blatant and organized in Alberta but existed at an informal level, for instance with social clubs. There was the exception of the Social Credit Party which took power in 1935. The victory gave antisemitic politicians a platform from which to spout their views and appeal to their largely rural support base. Major Douglas, the party's founder, blamed the Jews for Alberta's hard times during the 1930s and while Premier William Aberhardt publicly spoke against antisemitism, his personal writings and social circle, including Henry Ford, belied an ambivalent, if not, negative attitude.

A case that received wide attention was that of James Keegstra, a high school teacher in the town of Eckville, Alberta. In 1984, Keegstra was charged with unlawfully promoting hatred against an identifiable group, in violation of the Canadian Criminal Code, through his anti-Jewish statements, e.g., calling Jews "barbaric," "manipulative," and "sadistic," and claiming that Jews "created the Holocaust to gain sympathy." His defense lawyer, known for defending neo-Nazis and Holocaust deniers like Ernst Zundel, argued that the Criminal Code violated Keegstra's Charter right to freedom of expression. The case went all the way to the Supreme Court, which in a 4–3 decision ruled against Keegstra and maintained that Criminal Code Section 319(2) constituted a reasonable limit on freedom of expression, noting "there is obviously a rational connection between restricting hate propaganda and fostering harmonious social relations between Canadians."

Despite the infamy of the Keegstra case in Alberta, Alberta's Jewish population has found the province to be a secure and prosperous home. Jews in Alberta have risen to prominence in important and prestigious leadership roles in the larger community. Sheldon Chumir, a well-known Calgary lawyer, Rhodes scholar, and Liberal politician, was twice elected to the Alberta Legislature. Calgary was also home to Canada's first female chief of police, Christine Silverberg. In September 2001 a Jew was appointed president and vice chancellor of the University of Calgary, and, in October 2004 Edmonton elected a Jewish mayor, Stephen Mandel. The Edmonton Symphony was founded by Abe Fratkin and the Canadian Football League's Edmonton Eskimos was also founded by Jews. Jews have played a vital role in the arts in Alberta – Shoctor founding the Citadel Theatre in Edmonton and contributing significantly to Calgary's Centre for the Performing Arts.

As with many other North American communities, in the final decades of the 20th century, two newer Jewish groups have joined the primarily Ashkenazi established Jewish community in Alberta, Israelis and Russians. Reform, Conservative, Orthodox, and Ḥabad denominations of Judaism all have a presence in Alberta, although the majority of Alberta's Jews are non-Orthodox.

BIBLIOGRAPHY: M. Rubin, "Alberta's Jews: The Long Journey," in: H. and T. Palmer (eds.), *Peoples of Alberta: Portraits of Cultural Diversity* (1985), 329–47; H.M. Sanders, "Jews of Alberta," in: *Alberta History*, 47 (1999), 20–26.

[Aliza Craimer (2nd ed.)]

ALBERTI-IRSA (also known as **Albertirsa**), twin cities in the Monor district of Pest-Pilis-Solt Kiskun county, Hungary. Jews first settled there in 1746. In 1770 there were 13 Jewish residents in Alberti and 95 in Irsa, mainly occupied as merchants, tailors, tavern owners, distillers, and bookbinders. The communal regulations (*takkanot*) date from 1772. The *chevra kadisha* was organized by Rabbi Abraham Pressburger in 1784. A synagogue was built in 1809, and a *talmud torah* in 1804; a Jewish elementary school was opened in 1851. The participation of the community in the Hungarian struggle for independence in 1848–49 cost it an indemnity of 1,200 gulden, levied by the Austrian authorities. Many of the Jewish residents left Alberti-Irsa after 1850, when Hungarian Jews were permitted freedom of movement. The community constituted itself as a Status Quo community in February 1881, although a number of Jews organized themselves as an Orthodox congregation. The two were consolidated in 1889 by Rabbi Zsigmond Büchler. In 1929 the congregation had 250 members, including those of the other communities in the district. The rabbis of Alberti-Irsa include Abraham Pressburger, author of *Even ha-Ot* (Prague, 1793); Amram Rosenbaum (1814–26); Hayyim Kittsee (1829–40), head of a large yeshivah and author of the responsa, *Ozar Hayyim* (1913); Jónás Bernfeld (1853–72); and Zsigmond Büchler (1886–1941).

According to the census of 1941, Irsa had a Jewish population of 124 (1.7% of the total), and Alberti of 21 (0.5%). In addition the twin towns had one and six converts, respectively, who were identified as Jews under the racial laws. The status quo congregation of the twin cities, led by Rabbi Imre Blau, had 92 members in 1941. After Blau was drafted into a forced labor service company in 1942, the community came under the leadership of Rabbi István Székely. After the German occupation of Hungary on March 19, 1944, Rabbi Székely was appointed head of the local Jewish Council. The 149 Jews of the twin cities were first concentrated in a local ghetto that was established in the so-called Fodor lumber yard and in the "Singer building." They were later transferred to the ghetto of Monor from where they were deported to Auschwitz in early July 1944. The community numbered 14 in 1968, but ceased to exist a few years later.

BIBLIOGRAPHY: S. Buechler, *Az alberti-irsai izraelita hitközség története* (1909); MHJ, 7 (1963), 744; *Zsidó Lexikon* (1929), 22. **ADD. BIBLIOGRAPHY:** PK Hungaria, 153–155.

[Alexander Scheiber / Randolph Braham (2nd ed.)]

°**ALBERTUS MAGNUS** (about 1200–1280), German scholastic philosopher and theologian. He was a key figure at the rising University of Paris and in the schools of the Dominican Order, especially in Cologne. Among his students was Thomas *Aquinas. Although he belonged to the group of scholars that witnessed the condemnation of the Talmud in 1248, he was interested in Jewish literature and never attempted to hide his reliance on *Maimonides as a mediator between philosophy and Bible. Occasionally, he referred to Maimonides and Isaac *Israeli, the compiler of neo-Platonic doctrines, as men who frivolously adapted philosophy to Jewish law. However, "Rabbi Moyses'" ("Maimonides") discussions on the limits within which peripatetic cosmology may be accepted by a believer in divine creation as described in Genesis had a very positive meaning for a Dominican who was introducing the whole of Aristotle's system into the orbit of ecclesiastical learning. For his own attempt at synthesis Albertus was inclined to combine Aristotelianism with neo-Platonic ideas; therefore Avencebrol's (Ibn *Gabirol's) *Fons vitae* was an important text for him. He did not know, however, that this author was a Jew of great renown.

During the latter half of the 13th century friars began using information from Maimonides' *Dux neutrorum* (*Guide of the Perplexed*) for their exegetical work. Albertus shared this trend, following Maimonides in his interpretation of the Book of Job as a philosophical treatise on the relation of divine providence and human suffering. Parts of Albertus' works were known to late medieval Jewish philosophers through Hebrew translations.

BIBLIOGRAPHY: Steinschneider, *Uebersetzungen*, 456–66, 494–5, 776–7. **ADD. BIBLIOGRAPHY:** G. Binding and P. Dilg, in: *Lexikon des Mittelalters*, 1 (1980), 294–299; J. Mueller, *Natuerliche Moral und philosophische Ethik bei Albertus Magnus* (2001); I.M. Resnick, *Albert the Great* (2004), incl. ann. bibl.

[Hans Liebeschutz]

ALBI, town in France. The church council held at Albi in 1254 issued a number of canons (63–70) embodying anti-Jewish restrictive measures. One or two Jewish families resided in Albi toward the end of the 13th century. A few settled there after 1315 without authorization from the local authorities. In 1320 several were massacred by the *Pastoureaux. Subsequently Jews were only permitted to enter Albi in transit on payment of a toll of 12 deniers. In 1967 there were approximately 70 Jews in Albi, mainly of North African origin.

BIBLIOGRAPHY: S. Grayzel, *The Church and the Jews in the Thirteenth Century* (1966), index; Nahon, in: REJ, 121 (1962), 63.

[Bernhard Blumenkranz]

ALBIGENSES, generic name, deriving from the city of Albi, loosely applied to a number of Christian heretical sects which developed in Provence and south France in the 12th century, the term being used especially in connection with Cathari. Knowledge of their precise doctrines is vague, being derived mainly from the vilifications of their Roman Catholic opponents, now partly reinforced by the information embodied in Inquisitional trials. The Roman Catholic Church suspected that some of these heresies were deliberately stimulated by the Jews. This is out of the question, especially as in most cases the sectarian doctrines embodied dualistic elements which were even further removed from Judaism than those of normative Christianity. On the other hand, some of the allied bodies, such as the "Passagi" and "Circumcisi," had an Old Testament basis and can be characterized as Judaizing sects (see *Judaizers). Some of the other sectaries also apparently studied Hebrew in order to have a better understanding of the Old Testament, and personal relations between Albigenses and Jews seem to have been relatively cordial, this fact itself adding to the suspicions and animosities of the church. The Cathari accused the Roman Catholic Church of corruption, ritualistic pomp, and superficiality. Seeing them as a challenge to its power, the Church in return condemned them as Manicheans and Church Judaizers. However, though the Cathari rejected image worship, maintained certain prohibitions on the consumption of meat, and denied that Jesus was God, their theology and ritual contained a variety of contradictory elements. In fact, their attitude toward Judaism and the Old Testament was clearly hostile, as is borne out by the records of the Inquisition and the contemporary chronicles which cannot be suspected of a Catharistic bias. Jewish law was rejected by the Cathari as evil, because the "devil in the shape of a calf" (*diabolus in forma vituli*) had given it to them. Judaism as a whole was held to be an emanation of the material, visible, and consequently evil God.

Catharist hostility toward Judaism on the theological level, however, was not reflected on the social and cultural plane. Jews were held in high esteem in the French Midi, where their status was probably the best in Europe. Cities like Albi, Béziers, Carcassonne, Toulouse, Lunel, Montpellier, Marseilles, Beaucaire, and Nîmes, which were most affected by the heresy, also had large Jewish populations. Concomitantly, rulers of the Midi openly favored both Albigenses and Jews, whom they appointed to important functions in the fiscal administration. Roger II, of Béziers, probably a Cathar himself, intermittently appointed Jews to the office of bailiff (*bailli*), a tradition apparently carried on by his son Raymond-Roger. Count Raymond VI of Toulouse, patron of Provençal poetry and tolerant of Catharism, generally favored Jews and employed Abba Mari b. Isaac of St. Gilles as one of his officials. In granting privileges to the Jews, the princes were motivated by reasons more powerful than mere sympathy. Owing to their commercial activity Jews often were a considerable source of revenue and some princes were in debt to them. More generally, the degree of independence of thought in Provence and the good will displayed to one another by Christians and Jews are probably explained by the fact that the whole region was then exposed to a wide range of outside influences which made it an island of civilization and tolerance, far removed from medieval obscurantism.

The situation which thus obtained in Provence Jewish prosperity expanding in the midst of heresy was doubly intolerable to the established church. In 1195, at the Council of Montpellier it was decreed that anyone who allowed Jews (or Muslims) to exercise public office would be excommunicated. In 1209, Pope *Innocent III (1198–1216) ordered the Cistercians to preach a crusade against the Albigenses (January 1209). An army of monks, fanatics, and nobles marched into southern France. It was headed by Arnold of Citeaux, Cardinal Bertrand, and the rapacious Simon de Montfort, King Philip II of France having refused to lead the enterprise. The first stage of the operation ended with the capitulation of Raymond VI of Toulouse. In June 1209, at Montélimar, he and his nobles pledged themselves by oath "to forever removing the Jews from all administration and office, not ever to restore them, nor to accept other Jews for any office… nor use their council against Christians, nor… to permit them to employ Christians, men or women, in their homes as servants." Next the Crusaders took Béziers and Carcassone (July/August 1209), defended by young Raymond-Roger. Twenty thousand Christians and 200 Jews were massacred at Béziers. Many others were carried away as captives. In September 1209 the Council of Avignon decreed that "the Jews should be restrained from the exaction of usury by excommunicating those Christians who enter into commercial relations with them… and that the Jews be compelled to remit what they had gained through usury. We also prohibit them… to presume to work in public on the Sundays or festivals. Nor shall they eat meat on days of abstinence." Seven years later the wife of Simon de Montfort emulated her consort by having all the Jews of Toulouse arrested. Children under age were promptly baptized, but the adults resisted conversion and were eventually set free.

The Albigensian Crusade came to an end in 1229 with the Treaty of Paris, which destroyed the power of the princes in the south. The remaining adherents of Catharism were left to the care of the Inquisition, which dealt them a final blow by setting up a collective stake at Montségur (1245).

BIBLIOGRAPHY: S. Grayzel, *The Church and the Jews in the Thirteenth Century* (1959), index; L.I. Newman, *Jewish Influence on Christian Reform Movements* (1925), index; G. Saige, *Les Juifs de Languedoc* (1881); Graetz, Gesch, 7 (c. 1900[4]), 8ff., 53; A. Borst, *Die Katharer* (1953); C. Schmidt, *Histoire et doctrine de la secte des*

Cathares ou Albigeois (1849); H.C. Lea, *History of Inquisition in the Middle Ages* (1958); J.M. O'Brien, in: *Comparative Studies in Society and History*, 10 (1967/68), 215–20.

°**ALBINUS, LUCCEIUS**, Roman procurator of Judea, 62–64 C.E. During the brief interval between the death of his predecessor Festus and his arrival, the high priest *Anan son of Anan summoned the Sanhedrin and sentenced James, the brother of Jesus, to death. Thereupon delegations were sent to Agrippa II and even to Albinus, then on his way from Alexandria, to protest against Anan's illegal act, since he had no authority to convene the Sanhedrin without the procurator's consent (Jos., Ant., 20:197–203). Josephus depicts Albinus as unusually rapacious. He increased the burden of taxes and released prisoners only on payment of a ransom (Jos., Wars, 2:272–3). Under Albinus the *Sicarii intensified their activities and when they were unable to ransom their followers they would seize some of the leading citizens and make their release dependent upon that of their members held prisoner by Albinus. Thus Ananias, the high priest, was constrained to persuade Albinus to release ten Sicarii in exchange for his son, Eleazar's secretary, kidnapped by them (Jos., Ant., 20:208–9). Josephus relates that several years before the destruction of the Second Temple, portents foretold its approaching doom. Among them was a farmer, Jesus, the son of Ananias, who day and night proclaimed the coming destruction by crying out: "A voice from the east, a voice from the west, a voice from the four winds, a voice against Jerusalem and the sanctuary, a voice against the bridegroom and the bride, a voice against all the people." Brought before Albinus, Jesus unceasingly repeated his dirge, even under torture. Albinus concluded that he was mad and sent him away (Jos., Wars, 6:300–5). Signs of the imminent outbreak of hostilities were probably evident in the days of Albinus, who, in 64 C.E., was succeeded by Florus, the last procurator of Judea.

BIBLIOGRAPHY: Pauly-Wissowa, 26 (1927), 1559–61, no. 11; Schuerer, Gesch., 1 (1901^{4}), 583–5; H.G. Pflaum, *Les carriéres procuratoriennes équestres sous le Haut-Empire Romain*, 1 (1960), 75–77, no. 33.

[Lea Roth]

ALBO, JOSEPH (15th century), Jewish philosopher in Christian Spain. Albo participated in the famous Jewish-Christian disputation at *Tortosa and San-Mateo (1413–14) as a representative of the Jewish community of Daroca and wrote a theological-philosophical treatise by the name of *Book of Principles* (Heb. *Sefer ha-Ikkarim*). Albo's *Ikkarim* has become one of the most famous compositions of medieval Jewish thought and was translated into Latin, English, German, Russian, and Italian (part A only).

Little is known about Albo's life. The general opinion regarding the dates of his birth and death (1380–1444) is based on assumptions rather than on historical documents or facts. Albo was born, presumably, in the Crown of Aragon, where he studied with Ḥasdai *Crescas of Saragossa, to whom he refers in his book as his teacher (*Ikkarim*, 1, 26; 3, 16; cf. *Book of Principles*, 1, ed. Husik, Philadelphia, 1929, vol. 1, p. 200, 1, 18; vol. 3, p. 148, 1, 9). According to Albo's own words, he moved to Soria in the Crown of Castile, very possibly following the destruction of his community at Daroca (1415), and there he completed his major treatise (*Ikkarim*, intro.; cf. *Principles*, vol. 1, p. 37, 2, 1–2). Historical documents indicate that Albo was a social as well as a religious leader in both Daroca and Soria. His judgment was requested, for instance, in matters of family quarrels as well as in halakhic questions. It also seems that he was a physician and that he understood, apart from the Hebrew language in which he wrote his philosophical treatise, both Spanish and Latin. Whether or not he could read Arabic is an unresolved question.

A survey of Albo's written work shows, quite interestingly, that the *Ikkarim* was not his sole publication. Several researchers claim that Albo also wrote a polemical treatise in Spanish by the name of *The One* (Heb. *Ha-Eḥad*). Others attribute to Albo a composition called *One Hundred Pages* (Heb. *Me'ah Dapin*) that deals with the dogmas of faith. Finally, two other short compositions attributed to Albo are still available only in manuscripts: (a) Commentary to Maimonides' *Treatise on Logic*; (b) notes on Maimonides' Thirteen Principles.

Sefer ha-Ikkarim

CHRONOLOGICAL AND HISTORICAL BACKGROUND. Nevertheless, Albo's major contribution to the history of Jewish philosophy lies in his *Sefer ha-Ikkarim*. Another aspect of the uncertainty surrounding Albo's biography is the difference of opinions regarding the exact year in which he completed the writing of this book (e. g. 1424, 1425, 1428, and a more cautious opinion stating only that it could not have been before 1415). The prevailing opinion among scholars seems to be, however, that it was completed by the year 1425.

Important chronological information concerning the composition process of the *Ikkarim* can be drawn from Albo's retrospective comment at the end of part A of his book. Albo notes that his initial intention was to discuss exclusively the doctrine of religious dogmas, an aim that was fulfilled in the course of part A alone. However, later on, at the request of a group of people who presumably had read his original work, he decided to expand his discussion of these matters and, consequently, to add three more parts to the first (*Ikkarim*, 1, 26; cf. *Principles*, vol. 1, p. 203, 2, 1–9). In light of this remark several scholars have concluded that part A of the *Ikkarim* was, and henceforth should be treated as, a work Albo had written independently of the final version of the whole book. The question as to the year in which part A of the *Ikkarim* was actually written in its first version remains open. Scholars addressing this issue are mainly divided with regard to the question of whether it was written before Albo's immigration from Aragon to Castile and before the Tortosa disputation, namely, many years before the completion of the entire composition, or not, namely, a relatively short period of time before the book's completion. Differences between part A and parts B–D of the book with regard to both style and content can be considered to favor the former point of view.

After considering the narrow chronological aspect of the composition stages of the *Ikkarim*, the broader historical one should also be taken into account. Two historical-cultural circumstances can be pointed to as sources of influence on Albo's theoretical activity: (1) Massive, rapidly growing, and multidimensional pressure exerted by the Christian church upon the Jews in northern Spain to encourage them to convert to Christianity. (2) Internal dissension within the Jewish theological camp between rationalistic thinkers on the one hand and conservative and kabbalistic thinkers on the other hand. It should be noted that these motifs have been highlighted in the research that has been conducted on Jewish thought in 15th-century Spain in general.

CONTENTS AND CHARACTERISTICS. As indicated above, the *Ikkarim* is divided into four parts. Part A presents Albo's dogmatic system, namely the system of the main beliefs in what he calls "Divine Law." That system is divided into three hierarchic categories: (a) fundamental principles (Heb. *Ikkarim*), (b) derivative principles (Heb. *Shorashim*), and (c) obligatory dogmas (Heb. *Anafim*). Denying one of the fundamental or the derivative principles, Albo claims, is equivalent to heresy, but not the denial of one of the obligatory dogmas, which is considered by him merely a religious sin.

According to Albo there are three fundamental principles of "Divine Law": (1) the existence of God, (2) divine revelation, and (3) reward and punishment. The remaining three parts of the *Ikkarim* (parts B–D) address these principles, respectively.

Part B discusses the first fundamental principle in Albo's list, namely the existence of God, and its four derivative principles which are God's unity, incorporeality, independence of time, and absence of defects. The main theme of part B is the doctrine of the divine attributes, yet attention should also be drawn to Albo's interesting critical discussion of Maimonides' philosophical proofs for the existence of God (*Ikkarim*, 2, 4–5; cf. *Principles*, vol. 2, pp. 26–35).

Part C discusses the second fundamental principle, namely divine revelation, and its two derivative principles, which are prophecy and the authenticity of the messenger of "Divine Law." Other important issues discussed in the framework of part C are the question of ultimate human felicity, the Law of Moses and its commandments, and finally the religious duties of fear and love of God.

Part D discusses the third fundamental principle, namely reward and punishment, and its two derivative principles, which are God's knowledge and providence. In the course of this part Albo addresses the problem of evil and offers interesting analyses of two major religious phenomena, prayer and repentance. In the sequel Albo discusses extensively the doctrines of reward and punishment in the hereafter, resurrection of the dead, and the messiah.

Thus, the *Ikkarim* offers a systematic, detailed, and broad examination of the cornerstones of religious philosophy in general, and of Jewish thought in particular. To be precise, this book offers a summation of medieval Jewish thought as it appears from the abundance and divergence of its philosophical and theological sources. The Jewish thinkers who seem to have had the greatest influence on Albo's thought are *Maimonides, *Naḥmanides, *Nissim of Gerona, Ḥasdai Crescas, and Simeon ben Ẓemaḥ *Duran. Albo was also familiar with kabbalistic sources and views on the one hand and with works of non-Jewish philosophers, such as *Aristotle, *Avicenna, *Averroës, and Thomas *Aquinas, on the other.

These qualities of the *Ikkarim*, in addition to its plain language, have contributed to its popularity within divergent Jewish and non-Jewish circles. The *Ikkarim* was one of the first philosophical treatises to be printed (1485), and in the following two centuries it was twice commented on, first by Jacob Koppelmann (*Ohel Ya'akov*, 1584), then by Gedaliah Lipschuetz (*Ez Shatul*, 1618). Moreover, Albo's name is mentioned in the works of later Jewish philosophers, medieval as well as modern, and references to his book can be found in their writings. Such thinkers are, for example, Isaac *Arama, Isaac *Abrabanel, *Spinoza, and Moses *Mendelssohn. Lastly, Christian theologians in the 16th and 17th centuries used the *Ikkarim* in order to promote their polemical purposes.

A last remark should be made in regard to the research conducted on Albo's thought during the last 150 years. This research has taken three main courses: (1) an exposure of the philosophical sources of the *Ikkarim*, (2) a discussion of the historical circumstances in which Albo's theoretical activity took place, and (3) an examination of Albo's theological opinions.

Until recently researchers shared the general agreement that Albo was not an original thinker, but rather an eclectic one. Correspondingly, the *Ikkarim* was mainly considered a popular homiletic and encyclopedic treatise that lacked originality and philosophic profundity. This approach to Albo's work emphasized especially his polemical and apologetic interests in the light of the massive Christian spiritual as well as physical attacks on the Jews of his time and place.

An alternative approach to Albo's work wishes to supplement the analysis of his philosophy as such with an analysis of his philosophical "art of writing." In other words, it views the *Ikkarim* as not merely a compendium of views randomly put together but as a composition that was written purposefully and meticulously as an esoteric work, very much like Maimonides' in his *Guide for the Perplexed*. Albo intentionally expresses certain points of view on the exoteric, outer level, of the book and conceals other, opposing ones on its esoteric, inner level. It should be mentioned that this approach to Albo's thought is primarily supported by his opening remarks in part b of the *Ikkarim*, where he indicated that the book contains deliberate contradictions and therefore should be carefully read (*Ikkarim*, 2, opening; cf. *Principles*, vol. 2, pp. 1–4).

Albo's treatise indeed hardly displays any significant theoretical novelty. However, researchers of both camps point to one discussion that reflects some originality, that is, the discussion of the different kinds of "Law," namely "Divine," "Human," and "Natural" (*Ikkarim*, 1, 5–8; cf. *Principles*, vol. 1, pp. 70–92). They assert that Albo was probably the first Jewish thinker to use the political concept of "Natural Law" in his book, possibly under the influence of Thomas Aquinas. Another discussion that points to an original approach to a familiar subject is the one regarding the meaning of human love of God (*Ikkarim*, 3, 35–37; cf. *Principles*, vol. 3, pp. 316–51). This discussion has influenced several later Jewish thinkers who addressed the issue.

BIBLIOGRAPHY: S. Back, *Joseph Albo's Bedeutung in der Geschichte der jüdischen Religionsphilosophie: Ein Beitrag zur genauern Kenntniss der Tendenz des Buches "ikkarim"* (1869); Y. Baer, Spain, 2, ch. 11 (1966); D. Ehrlich, *"Filosofyah ve-Omanut ha-Ketiva be-Sefer ha-Ikkarim le-Rabbi Yosef Albo,"* dissertation, Bar-Ilan University (2004); H. Graetz, *History of the Jews*, 4 (1894), 239–44; J. Guttmann, *"Le-Ḥeker ha-Mekorot shel Sefer ha-Ikkarim,"* in: S.H. Bergman and N. Rotenstreich (eds.), *Dat u-Madda: Kovez̤ Ma'amarim ve-Harẓa'ot* (1955), 169–91; idem, *Philosophies of Judaism: The History of Jewish Philosophy from Biblical times to Franz Rosenzweig* (1964), 247–51; W.Z. Harvey, "Albo's Discussion of Time," in: JQR, 70 (1979–80), 210–38; I. Husik, *A History of Mediaeval Jewish Philosophy* (1916), 406–27; M. Kellner, *Dogma in Medieval Jewish Thought From Maimonides to Abravanel* (1986),140–56; H. Kreisel, *Prophecy: The History of an Idea in Medieval Jewish Philosophy* (2001), 486–543; D.J. Lasker, *"Torat ha-Immut be-Mishnato ha-Filosofit shel Yosef Albo,"* in: *Da'at*, 5 (1980), 5–12; R. Lerner, "Natural Law in Albo's *Book of Roots*," in: J. Cropsey (ed.), *Ancients and Moderns: Essays on the Tradition of Political Philosophy in Honor of Leo Strauss* (1964), 132–47; S. Rauschenbach, *Josef Albo: Juedische Philosophie und christliche Kontroverstheologie in der Frühen Neuzeit* (Studies in European Judaism, 3) (2002); D. Schwartz, *Setirah ve-Hastarah ba-Hagut ha-Yehudit Bi-Yemei ha-Beinayim* (2002), 182–96; E. Schweid, *"Bein Mishnat ha-Ikkarim shel R. Yosef Albo le-Mishnat ha-Ikkarim shel ha-Rambam,"* in: *Tarbiz*, 33 (1963), 74–84; idem, *"Ha-Nevua'h be-Mishnato shel R. Yosef Albo,"* in:*Tarbiz*, 35 (1965), 48–60; idem, *"Ha-Pulmus neged ha-Naẓrut ke-Gorem Me'aẓev be-Mishnat ha-R.Y. Albo,"* in: PWCJS, 4 (1968), 309–12; C. Sirat, *A History of Jewish Philosophy in the Middle Ages* (1985), 374–81; A. Taenzer, *Die Religionsphilosophie Josef Albo's nach seinem werke "Ikkarim": Systematisch Dragestellt und Erläutert* (1896); S.B. Urbach, *Amudei ha-Maḥshavah ha-Yisra'elit*, v. 2 (1972), 519–656.

[Dror Ehrlich (2nd ed.)]

ALBORAYCOS. One of the insulting names applied to converted Jews in Spain in the 15th century. An anti-Converso work, the *Libro del Alborayque*, apparently from the north of Spain (c. 1488), derives the term from the name of the marvelous mount of Muhammad, al-Burāq. Just as the steed was neither horse nor mule, male nor female, so the insincere converts were not Jews, Muslims, or Christians. The work specifies 20 characteristics of al-Burāq and applies each of them to the Conversos.

BIBLIOGRAPHY: S. Resnick, in: *Hispania*, 9:34 (Sp., 1949), 58; N. López Martínez, *Los judaizantes castellanos y la Inquisición* (1954), 53–54, 391–404 (text of the *Libro llamado el Alboraique*); Loeb, in: REJ, 18 (1889), 238–42; J. Caro Baroja, *Los Judíos en la España moderna…*, 1 (1962), 174–5; J.E. Longhurst, *The Age of Torquemada* (1964²), 91–95.

[Kenneth R. Scholberg]

ALBOTINI (Albutaini), JUDAH BEN MOSES (d. 1519), kabbalist and commentator on *Maimonides' writings. His father was a scholar in Lisbon. Albotini was one of the "Members of the Yeshivah of Jerusalem" and, in 1509, signed with them an ordinance to exempt scholars from taxes. He succeeded Jacob of Triel as head of the Jerusalem yeshivah, and as such was also head of the Jerusalem rabbis. Albotini was the author of several halakhic and kabbalistic books, all of which have remained in manuscript. His main work is the *Yesod Mishneh Torah* on Maimonides. The book includes the notation and explanation of the sources which preceded Maimonides. It discusses the foundation of every *halakhah* and the manner in which it was substantiated by Maimonides. Albotini held that the critics of Maimonides made strange and superfluous suppositions because Maimonides' sources were not accessible to them. He, however, had several sources and manuscripts which were not available to them. Of special interest in his work are the introductions (*derushim*) which encompass subjects treated by Maimonides. He discusses these extensively in the place where they are first mentioned, analyzes the problems, explains the practical issues, and sums up the subject matter. In addition to the manuscripts of homiletical commentaries on *halakhah* and *aggadah* and the ancient authors, he also possessed the correct manuscripts of the *Mishneh Torah* and chose, according to them, the correct version. In 1518–19, he completed his commentary on Maimonides' *Sefer ha-Madda, Sefer Ahavah*, and *Sefer Zemannim* (British Museum, Ms. Add. 19.783). However, from *Sefer Nashim*, Albotini explained only the laws of marriage and a number of chapters from the laws of divorce (Ms. Deinard 398, J.T.S., Schechter collection, New York). Three additional books on Maimonides, now lost, are (1) *Moreh ha-Mishnah*, which proposed to explain the veracity of his commentary on the Mishnah; (2) *Sefer Yeshu'ot*, on *Seder Nezikin*; Albotini intended to include rulings on money matters by R. Isaac *Alfasi, Maimonides, *Sefer Mitzvot Gadol*, and *Tur Ḥoshen Mishpat*; (3) a commentary on Maimonides' commentary on the *Mishnah*, or more precisely, on the division of the *Tumot* (uncleannesses) in the introduction to *Seder Tohorot* (order of cleannesses). Albotini wrote this book in Jerusalem in 1501. *Sullam ha-Aliyyah* ("The Ladder of Ascent"), a manual for contemplative mystics, is his only known kabbalistic work. Albotini was attracted by Abraham *Abulafia's prophetic kabbalism and by his doctrine of combinations (*ẓeruf*).

Another work called *Mar'ot Elohim* ("Visions of God"), which probably dealt with *Ma'aseh Bereshit* (esoteric doctrine of the creation) and with *Ma'aseh Merkavah* (mystic speculations on the celestial chariot) is mentioned in *Yesod Mishneh Torah*. At the beginning of the latter there are also some chapters dealing with kabbalistic subjects: *Derush ha-Havayah, Derush Hishtalshelut ha-Nimẓa'im*, and *Derush ha-Nefesh*, which constitute an introduction to *Hilkhot Yesodei ha-Torah*.

Albotini's book reflects the cumulative impact of the various layers of ecstatic Kabbalah: Abulafia's *Or ha-Sekhel*, R. Nathan ben Saadiah's *Sha'arei Ẓedek*, and R. Isaac of Acre. *Sullam ha-Aliyyah* was printed by E.Y. Porush in Jerusalem, 1989.

BIBLIOGRAPHY: G. Scholem, in: KS, 2 (1925/26), 107, 138–41; idem, *Kitvei Yad be-Kabbalah* (1930), no. 6, 32, 225–30; M. Benayahu, in: *Sinai*, 36 (1955), 240–74.

°**ALBRIGHT, WILLIAM FOXWELL** (1891–1971), U.S. biblical archaeologist and Semitics scholar. The son of Methodist missionaries, Albright studied at Johns Hopkins University, earning his doctorate under Paul Haupt. In 1929, he became professor of Semitic languages at Hopkins. He directed the American School of Oriental Research in Jerusalem, 1920–29 and 1933–36. Albright's excavations in Ereẓ Israel include Gibeath-Shaul (Tell al-Fūl), 1922–23, 1933; Adar and Bāb al-Dhrāʿ in Moab in 1924 and 1933; *Beth-El in 1927 and 1934; and Petra in 1935. His main achievement in field work was the excavation of Tell Beit Mirsim (the biblical Debir?), which he directed in 1926, 1928, 1930, and 1932. He also participated in the University of California expedition to Sinai (1947–48) and was chief archaeologist of expeditions of the American Foundation for the Study of Man at Wadi Bayḥān (Beihan), Hajar Bin Humayd, and Timnaʿ in Arabia (1950–51). His main publications (apart from over 1,500 articles) are *From the Stone Age to Christianity* (1940; 1946[2]); *Archaeology and the Religion of Israel* (1942); *The Archaeology of Palestine* (1949); and *The Excavation of Tell Beit Mirsim* (1932–43). In this last work, Albright laid the foundations for the scientific ceramic chronology of the Canaanite and Israelite periods in Ereẓ Israel: his philological and topographical studies solved some of the most difficult problems in Egyptian and Semitic philology and in the identification of places. In his approach to biblical history (*The Biblical Period from Abram to Ezra* (1949), New *Horizons in Biblical Research* (1966), and *Archaeology, Historical Analogy, and Early Biblical Tradition* (1966)), Albright was a theologically conservative scholar, dating the Patriarchs to the first half of the second millennium on the basis of his intensive study of the Near Eastern background of the period; similarly he assigned the composition of the historical books of the Bible known as the "Former Prophets" to the 13th–10th centuries B.C.E. and most of the Psalms to the pre-Exilic period. Albright was one of the first scholars to authenticate the *Dead Sea Scrolls. His students include most of the prominent archaeologists of the later 20th and early 21st century in the United States and Israel, among them G.E. Wright, N. Glueck, and B. Maisler (Mazar). He also trained such eminent biblicists and Semiticists as J. Bright, F.M. Cross, D.N. Freedman, and W. Moran. Albright was the foremost biblical archaeologist of modern times, combining a devotion to evangelical Christianity with a scientific approach to the problems of archaeology and the Bible. While many of his broad syntheses of the Bible with archaeology came under criticism beginning in the 1970s, Albright must be credited for providing the very framework within which such criticism could occur. Likewise, his work on many aspects of Semitic philology remains invaluable.

BIBLIOGRAPHY: H.M. Orlinsky, *An Indexed Bibliography of the Writings of William Foxwell Albright* (1941); L. Finkelstein (ed.), *American Spiritual Autobiographies* (1948), 156–81; G.E. Wright (ed.), *The Bible and the Ancient Near East* (1961), includes bibliography up to 1958; A. Malamat (ed.), in: *Eretz Israel*, 9 (1969). **ADD. BIBLIOGRAPHY:** L.G. Running, in: DBI 1, 22–23.

[Michael Avi-Yonah]

ALBU, SIR GEORGE (1857–1935), South African mining magnate and financier. Born in Berlin, Albu in 1876 joined his brother Leopold as a diamond broker in South Africa and became prominent in Kimberley and later on in the Johannesburg goldfields. He opposed Kruger's restrictive policies but denounced the Jameson Raid of 1895, aimed at the overthrow of the administration. In 1887 he formed the company of G. and L. Albu which, reorganized as the General Mining and Finance Corporation in 1895, controlled some of the largest gold-producing properties on the Rand. Albu introduced innovations in goldmining techniques. He supported Jewish institutions, including the Johannesburg Hebrew High School. In 1912 he was made a baronet. His daughter, Margaret, married Bishop Wilfrid Parker of Pretoria in 1933.

BIBLIOGRAPHY: W. Macdonald, *The Romance of the Golden Rand* (1933). **ADD. BIBLIOGRAPHY:** G. Wheatcroft, *The Randlords* (1985), index.

ALBU, ISIDOR (1837–1903), German physician and public health specialist. Albu was born in Berlin and graduated from Berlin University in 1864. His work was devoted primarily to problems of social hygiene, medical statistics, and epidemiology, and his writings included *Mortality in Berlin, Studies on Cholera, Typhoid and Smallpox in Berlin*, and *Typhus und Grundwassergang in Berlin* (1877). His major work was the authorized summary of the rules laid down by Riant in *Leçons d'Hygiène* (1874). This work became a widely used handbook of general, personal, and public hygiene. Albu was responsible for the establishment of eye clinics in Berlin and other cities of Germany. In 1882 he went to Iran where he became professor of medicine at the University of Teheran and personal physician to the shah, Nāṣir al-Dīn.

BIBLIOGRAPHY: Wininger, Biog, 1 (1925), 94–95; *Biographisches Lexikon der hervorragenden Aerzte*, 1 (1929[2]), 77.

[Nathan Koren]

ALBUM, SIMON HIRSCH (1849–1921), U.S. rabbi. Album was born in Tazitz, Lithuania, and studied at the Volozhin yeshivah where he received his ordination. After spending much of his early career working as a rabbi in Russia, Album immigrated to America in 1891. He settled in Chicago and assumed the pulpit of the new Mishna Ugemoro Synagogue, which served the substantial immigrant community. He held this pulpit until his death, overseeing the growth of the congregation and the opening of a second satellite synagogue. Despite his successes as a scholar, communal leader, and congregational rabbi, Album's tenure was not entirely untroubled. His involvement in a number of intra-communal squabbles suggests a difficult personality and penchant for feuding. The most serious of these confrontations occurred in 1903 after Jacob David *Willowski was invited to Chicago to serve as the chief rabbi of a collection of allied synagogues. Willowski quickly set out to establish oversight and control of the *kashrut* supervision of Chicago's vast abattoirs. This move angered Album, who shortly before had secured an arrangement to act as the sole supervisor for the *shoḥatim* working at the major packing plants that supplied much of America's centrally slaughtered meat. Bridling at this perceived affront, and probably resentful of his rival's status, Album published a polemic that vilified Willowsky. The ugly public dispute that followed created friction and divisions within the immigrant community, eventually degenerating into a violent confrontation in a synagogue between supporters of the two men. The bickering subsided when Jacob Willowski resigned his post and left Chicago for Palestine. Among Album's writings are *Divrei Emet* (1904–12), *Meḥa'ah Geluyah* (1910), and *Teshuvah al Ḥanutat ha-Metim* (1916).

BIBLIOGRAPHY: *American Jewish Year Book*, 24 (1923); H. Gastwirt, *Fraud, Corruption and Holiness: The Controversy over the Supervision of Jewish Dietary Practice in New York, 1881–1940* (1974); H. Meites, *History of the Jews of Chicago* (1924); *New York Times* (June 13, 1921).

[Adam Mendelsohn (2nd ed.)]

ALBUQUERQUE, city in New Mexico. Available documentation dates a village of Alburquerque (the first "r" was later dropped) from 1706. The comparatively lush land adjacent to the Rio Grande River to the west of the Sandia Mountains in central New Mexico and 60 miles south of Santa Fe proved to be an attractive point for settlement for Spanish newcomers from Mexico. A number of Indian pueblos already existed there. American military occupation after 1846 and the territorial status accorded New Mexico in the United States allowed Americans to join the existing Hispanic and Indian population.

Jews were among the early American traders to the area. As early as 1852 Simon Rosenstein was operating a store on the plaza – now called Old Town – and possessed real estate in 1850. He married a Hispanic woman and may have been the first Jew divorced in New Mexico in 1866.

In 1880 the Atcheson, Topeka and Santa Fe railroad created a railroad depot and yards over a mile from the old plaza, which became a focal point for New Albuquerque and New Mexico. By 1883, some 25 Jewish males formed the first Jewish organization in Albuquerque and New Mexico, a chapter of B'nai B'rith. They were young, mostly single, and all were merchants or clerks. By 1896 their number had nearly tripled; and the group, although still young, showed maturation through marriage and the creation of families. As a result, Albuquerque's Jews created a congregation in 1897, the second in the Territory after Congregation Montefore in Las Vegas. It was named Congregation Albert, the name acquired through auction to the highest bidder by Alfred Grunsfeld in honor of his father. It adhered to Reform practice. This Congregation is now the oldest in the state. In 1921 a more traditional Conservative congregation formed under the name B'nai Israel.

Although Albuquerque was the largest city in the state before World War II, the Cold War provided great impetus to its further growth. As a result of the whole area's isolation and open spaces Albuquerque became a center for atomic research and attendant industries and the site for numerous military bases. With a population of 35,000 in 1940 the city grew to 200,000 by 1960. By 2000 it had 448,000.

The increase of Jewish population in Albuquerque outmatched the city's general growth. In 1940 the estimate of Jewish numbers was 450 – over one-third of the state's total Jewish persons. In 2000 the estimate was 7,500, perhaps 70 percent of the state's Jews.

The social character of the Jewish population changed dramatically after World War II. Scientists, doctors, attorneys, and faculty became quite common, gradually matching shopkeepers. A survey carried out in 1977 counted more than 100 Jewish faculty members at the University of New Mexico in the city. In the last decades of the 20th century Jewish women joined the ranks of professions in rapidly increasing numbers. However, Jewish-owned businesses – new and old – continued to exist and prosper.

Jewish residents have long participated in the political life of the community. The first mayor of an incorporated Albuquerque in 1885 was Henry N. Jaffa. Mike Mandell followed him in 1890. Jews continued to serve on various local commissions after World War II. In the late 1980s, Steve Schiff, a former district attorney and a Republican, was elected to the United States House of Representatives and served until his death in 1998.

Their increasingly varied social character gave witness to Jews assuming an ever-broadening range of important roles. Home builder Sam Hoffman constructed large housing developments in the early postwar era until his death in 1959. Architect Max Flatow, who arrived in 1947, contributed some of the city's tallest modern structures and the College of Education complex at the University of New Mexico. From 1985 to 1992 Neil Stulberg conducted the New Mexico Symphony Orchestra in the city.

In the latter decades of the 20th century all dimensions of activity broadened. In religious organization Chavurat Hamidbar was formed in 1973 and Nahalat Shalom (Renewal Independent) came into existence under Rabbi Lynn Gottlieb in 1983. In the early 1990s Chabad made its presence known.

In addition, secular organizations grew up after World War II with an eye to aiding Jewish refugees and supporting Israel as well as seeking to aid a growing number of elderly and to educate Jewish children. By the end of the century a well-developed Jewish Community Council and a splendid campus placed Albuquerque in the category of middle-sized Jewish communities in the United States.

BIBLIOGRAPHY: M. Simmons, *Albuquerque: A Narrative History* (1982); H.J. Tobias, *A History of the Jews in New Mexico* (1990).

[Henry J. Tobias (2nd ed.)]

ALCALÁ DE HENARES (Heb. אלקלעא), city in Castile, central Spain. Under Muslim rule Jews lived in Alcalá. After Alcalá was captured from the Moors in 1118, the Jews were granted equal municipal rights with Christians regarding residence, evidence, and criminal compensation. At the end of the 13th century the community was rather small. It grew immensely, as the Jews' taxes indicate. The annual tax paid by the Jews of Alcalá to the Crown, amounting to 8,000 *maravedis*, was granted by Henry II in 1366 to the archbishop. It seems that during the 1391 massacres the Jews there did not suffer persecution. In 1395, 19 Jews protested in the synagogue against the nomination of the archbishop's physician Maestre Pedro, a convert from Judaism, as judge of appeals for the Jews of the archdiocese. The Jews of Alcalá were derided in a late 14th-century satire by the *Converso Pedro Ferrús, entitled *Cancionero de Baena*, depicting a wanderer who entered the synagogue seeking lodging for the night and was scared out of his wits by the inhospitable congregation. The community dwindled after the wave of massacres which swept Spain in 1391, but was later renewed. In the course of the 15th century the community grew constantly to become one of the largest in central Castile. In the 1474 distribution of taxes Alcalá was the third highest paying community in the district of Toledo. There were about 200 Jewish families then. For a short while, Isaac Abravanel lived there. Conversos continued to visit the city's synagogues, as suggested by the Marrano poet Pedro Ferrús; many were tried by the *Inquisition. Hebrew studies at the University of Alcalá were encouraged by Cardinal Francisco *Ximenes de Cisneros in the early 16th century, and the "Complutensian Polyglot" edition of the Bible was compiled under his patronage. Some important Hebraists, such as the Converso Alfonso de Zamora, worked there.

The location of the Jewish quarter of Alcalá de Henares is well known. It was within the area defined by the streets Mayor, Santiago, Imagen, and Cervantes. In Mayor Street it extended in both directions. We know also about two synagogues in Alcalá: the Mayor was at the back of No 10 in Carmen Calzado Street. The other synagogue was in Santiago Street.

BIBLIOGRAPHY: G. Sanchez, *Fueros castellanos* (1919), 305; Rios, *Historia… de los judíos de España* (1960²), index; R. Santa Maria, in: *Boletín de la Real Academia de la Historia*, 17 (1890), 184–5; F. Pérez Castro, *El manuscrito apologético de Alfonso de Zamora* (1950), xix–xxviii; Suárez Fernández, Documentos, index; J.M. Azáceta (ed.), *Cancionero de Juan Alfonso de Baena*, 2 (1966), 654–6; Y. Baer, *History of the Jews in Christian Spain*, index. **ADD. BIBLIOGRAPHY:** J.L. Lacave, *Juderías y sinagogas españolas* (1992), 276–9.

ALCALAY (Alkalaj), ISAAC (1882–1978), rabbi. Born in Sofia, he studied at the Vienna Rabbinical Seminary and in 1909 was appointed chief rabbi of Serbia. While occupying this post he served as emissary of the Serbian government (1915–18), visiting the U.S. in 1918 on a mission on behalf of Serbian Jewry (which he described in the *American Jewish Year Book*, vol. 20, pp. 75–87; later published separately). In 1923 he founded the Rabbinical Federation of Yugoslavia and became its first president, helping to edit its annual *Jevrejski Almanah* (cf. volumes for 1920–30). In 1923 he was elected chief rabbi of Yugoslavia by King Alexander, a position of political importance at the time (see *Yugoslavia). He continued his activities abroad, attending the first Sephardi Congress (held at Vienna in 1925), where he was elected vice president of the World Sephardi Federation. When King Alexander made him a senator, Alcalay was the only Jew to sit in the Yugoslavian Upper House (1930–38). Until the Holocaust, Chief Rabbi Alcalay was a central figure and a unifying force for Yugoslav Jewry. He fled the country when the Germans occupied Yugoslavia in 1941 and, after a short stay in Palestine, settled in the U.S. in 1942, where he served as rabbi of the Sephardi community of New York. He later unified and organized the Sephardi communities there and became the chief rabbi of the Central Sephardic Jewish Community of America in 1943. He published a study on travels of Jews through the Balkans at the end of the 18th and beginning of the 19th centuries (1928). In 1970, Alcalay was awarded a medal by Yeshiva University of New York. In 1971, on the occasion of his 90th birthday, the Association of Yugoslav Jews in the U.S. issued a souvenir journal in his honor.

ALCALAY, REUVEN (1907–1976), Hebrew lexicographer and translator. Alcalay was born in Jerusalem and graduated from the Hebrew Teachers' College there. He entered government service during the Mandatory period and was translator-in-chief and superintendent of the Government Press Office from 1920 to 1948. On the establishment of the State, he served as deputy-director of the Government Information Office and from 1948 to 1951 was editor of the *Israel Government Year Book*. Alcalay translated many books from English into Hebrew, but his major achievement was in the field of lexicography, where his publications include the *Complete Hebrew–English Dictionary*, 4 vols. (1958); the *Complete English–Hebrew Dictionary*, 4 vols. (1963); the *Complete Hebrew Dictionary*, 3 vols. (1968–71), which contains hundreds of words coined by him for modern concepts; and *Words of the Wise* (1968), an anthology of Hebrew (and Yiddish) proverbs.

ALCAN, ALKAN, name of several French families, possibly deriving from Elkanah:

Alphonse *Alkan (1809–1889), Parisian printer, bibliographer, and author of works on printing and illustration.

MICHEL ALCAN (1811–1877), politician, engineer, and author of works on textile technology. He was born in Donnelay and afterward lived in Paris. He took an active part in the 1830 and 1848 revolutions in France, and was elected to the National Assembly, where he sided with the left wing (the Mountain).

MOŸSE ALCAN (1817–1869), publisher and poet. He lived in Metz, where he was a member of the Jewish consistory. FÉLIX (1841–1925), Moÿse's son, was a publisher and scholar. He lectured on mathematics before entering the publishing business of his father in Metz. He later founded his own firm in Paris, which from 1880 specialized in producing textbooks, mainly on philosophy.

ALCAÑIZ, city in Aragon, Spain, subject to the Order of *Calatrava. The jurisdiction of the order also extended to the 30 Jewish families living in Alcañiz. Several families, formerly scattered in the surrounding villages, joined the community in 1380. In 1383 Pedro IV exempted the Jews of Alcañiz from having to attend missionary disputations with apostates. During the massacres of 1391, the infant Martín ordered that the Jews in Alcañiz should be protected. At the beginning of the 15th century the Jews of Alcañiz achieved some prosperity and a certain level of Jewish leaning. *Astruc ha-Levi of Alcañiz was a protagonist in the disputation of *Tortosa, 1413–14. Alcañiz was also the home of Joshua Halorki, a learned Jew who became Jerónimo de Santa Fe and the instigator of the disputation of Tortosa, which proved disastrous to the Jewish community. Most of its members converted to Christianity. After this only 15 families in Alcañiz and its environs adhered to Judaism, and probably fewer at the time of the expulsion of 1492. In the 15th century the Jewish quarter was enclosed and its gates locked at night.

BIBLIOGRAPHY: Uhagón: *Boletín de la Real Academia de la historia, Madrid* 35 (1899), 51ff.; J. Jacobs, *Inquiry into the Sources of the History of the Jews in Spain* (1894), index; Baer, Studien, 146; Baer, Spain, index; Baer, Urkunden, 1 pt. 1 (1929), index: Vendrell, in: *Sefarad*, 3 (1943), 128, 149; 13 (1953), 87–104; Vidiella, in: *La Zuda*, 12 (1924), 114–19. **ADD. BIBLIOGRAPHY:** C. Laliena Corbera, in: *Destierros aragoneses* (1988), 115–26.

ALCASTIEL, JOSEPH, Spanish kabbalist, who lived in Játiva, Aragon, at the time of the expulsion of the Jews in 1492. While there is no evidence that Alcastiel was among the exiles he is indeed mentioned by R. Isaac ha-Kohen of Játiva, an expellee from Valencia. A recently published treatise contains Alcastiel's responsa to 18 questions purportedly asked by Judah *Ḥayyat, although it is not known that Alcastiel ever lived in Italy or knew Ḥayyat: Ḥayyat does not mention him in his writings nor do his writings show the influence of Alcastiel's work. On the other hand, Alcastiel's ideas, distinguished by their originality and insight, influenced other important kabbalists in the generation after the expulsion from Spain, such as Meir ibn *Gabbai, Solomon ha-Levi *Alkabeẓ, Moses *Cordovero, and, almost certainly, Isaac *Luria. According to one account, these responsa were written at Játiva in 1482. The treatise entitled *Ma'amar Mufla al ha-Tanninim* ("Wondrous Treatise on the Sea Monsters"; Ambrosian Library, Milan, Ms. 62/12) is ascribed to *Ha-Ḥakham ha-Elohi Alcastilo* ("the divine scholar Alcastilo"). Judging by its content and style, the author of this was Joseph Alcastiel and not Joseph b. Samuel of Catalonia as suggested in the catalog.

BIBLIOGRAPHY: Scholem, in: *Tarbiz*, 24 (1954/55), 167–206. **ADD. BIBLIOGRAPHY:** M. Idel, "Chronicle of an Exile: R. Isaac ben Hayim Ha-Kohen of Jativa," in: Y. Assis and Y. Kaplan (eds.), *Jews and Conversos at the Time of the Expulsion* (1999), 259–71 (Heb.).

[Efraim Gottlieb]

ALCEH, MATILDE (1923–1967), Turkish poet. Born in Istanbul, she contributed poems to various periodicals, including the daily *Cumhuriyet*, and also published some translations. The collection *Mart* ("The Gull," 1953) contained some of her characteristic lyrical verse. The only Turkish woman poet of Jewish birth, she married a Muslim and died in a car accident in Yugoslavia.

[Shmuel Moreh]

ALCHEMY, ancient art that was the origin of chemistry. The Jewish association with alchemy dates from ancient times. Zosimos, a fifth-century Greek historian, states that the Jews acquired the secrets of the "sacred craft" of the Egyptians and the knowledge of the "power of gold" which derives from it by dishonest means, and they imparted the knowledge of alchemy to the rest of the world. In ancient Greek manuscripts, which contain lists of writings on alchemy, a number of alchemic and magic writings are attributed to Moses; one work is ascribed to *Hoshea, king of Israel. *Bezalel was also considered a proficient alchemist on the basis of Exodus 31:1–5. The author of the above-mentioned writings was, most probably, Moses of Alexandria, a famous alchemist, which would explain why they were later ascribed to Moses the Lawgiver; in any case it seems certain that the author was a Jew since his writings show traces of Jewish monotheism and other Jewish beliefs.

Toward the end of the Middle Ages, and later, the connection between alchemy and the Bible and Prophets was strengthened in the view of Christian alchemists who despaired of finding the philosopher's stone by natural means and sought to attain it by the grace of God who reveals His secret only to His faithful. The alchemists believed, therefore, that the patriarchs, the prophets, and the kings of Israel possessed the secret of the "stone." Gerhard Dorn (end of 16th century) contended that the whole art of alchemy was contained in the verse, "God made the firmament" (Gen. 1:7). Michael

Maier, the physician of Rudolf II, and chief exponent of the Rosicrucian order in Germany in the 17th century, found its basis in the verse, "the spirit of God hovered over the face of the waters" (Gen. 1:2), "the waters" being mercury. Aegidius Guthmann of Augsburg wrote a lengthy "alchemical" interpretation of the first verses of Genesis. Tubal-Cain, who lived before the Flood, was considered the father of alchemy since it was said of him that he was "the forger of every cutting instrument of brass and iron" (Gen. 4:22). These alchemists particularly singled out the name Mehetabel, the daughter of Matred, the daughter of Me-Zahab (Gen. 36:39). The name Me-Zahab ("waters of gold") was interpreted to mean that he knew how to produce drinkable gold (*aurum potabile*); and Mehetabel possibly reminded them of the Greek *metabole* (μεταβολή), "transmutation." Abraham *Ibn Ezra heard this interpretation of Me-Zahab and remarked in his commentary: "Others say it refers to those said to make gold out of brass, but this is nonsense."

The first men mentioned in Genesis would not have, according to the alchemists, reached such old age, had they not made use of the *elixir vitae*. They also contended that "Abram was very rich in cattle, in silver, and in gold" (Gen. 13:2) because he learned the secret of alchemy from Hermes in Egypt. All the patriarchs, as well as Judah, wore the philosopher's stone on their bodies. Moses was, however, according to them, the first and foremost among the biblical experts. As late as the 18th century, an alchemist wrote a book: *Urim und Tumim von Moses, Handleitung vom grossen Propheten und Feldherrn zum Weisenstein* ("Oracles of Moses, a Guide to the Philosopher's Stone by the Great Prophet and General," Nuremberg, 1737). King David was considered an expert alchemist, since he could only have raised "a hundred thousand talents of gold, and a thousand talents of silver" for the building of the "house of the Lord" (I Chron. 22:14) by alchemical means. Further support for this assumption was adduced from the fact that David bequeathed to his son, Solomon, *millu'im avnei-pukh* ("stones to be set, glistening stones," *ibid.* 29:2) which are the philosopher's stones. Solomon learned the secret from his father, and was, therefore, able to provide "silver and gold to be in Jerusalem as stones" (II Chron. 1:15). According to the story quoted by Johanan Alemanno (in his *Sefer ha-Likkutim* ("Collectanea"; from the Arab alchemist Abu Aflaḥ of Syracuse)), supposedly originally found in the esoteric *Sefer ha-Mazpun*, ascribed to King Solomon, the "precious stone" with which the Queen of Sheba presented Solomon (I Kings 10:2) was none other than the philosopher's stone which she had inherited from her first husband, Sman (who was a great Nabatean sage). The Queen of Sheba's aim was to test King Solomon's wisdom, but he already knew the secret and recognized the stone immediately (cf. I.S. *Reggio, in *Kerem Ḥemed*, 2 (1836), 48–50).

The prophet Elijah, also considered a great expert in alchemy, is frequently mentioned by the Christian alchemists, and some of their writings bear his name. Jewish influence is evident from the fact that they too contend that Elijah would, on his return to earth, provide the answer to all the unsolved problems. The prophet Isaiah was also considered to have been an expert, on the basis of the verses: "I will set thy stones in fair colors [*pukh*] and lay thy foundations with sapphires" (Isa. 54:11) and "For brass I will bring gold, and for iron I will bring silver" (Isa. 60:17). The adepts also include the prophets Elisha, Ezekiel, Zechariah, Malachi (the first verses in chapter three of the book of Malachi were interpreted in an alchemic and Christological manner), Daniel, and Ezra. The names of Job's three daughters, Jemimah, Keziah, and Keren-Happuch were also interpreted in a religious and alchemic spirit.

Alchemy and Kabbalah

Alchemy and the *Kabbalah were closely linked in the Middle Ages. A kabbalistic outline is found in the early alchemist manuscript of Saint Mark (11th century) called *Solomon's Labyrinth*. The wandering German alchemist, Salomon Trismosin, boasted that he drew his knowledge from kabbalistic writings which had been translated into Arabic. His great disciple, Paracelsus, maintained that expert knowledge of Kabbalah was an essential prerequisite for studying alchemy. However, neither he nor his master had more than a superficial knowledge of the Kabbalah, if any at all, although both talked about it a great deal. Paracelsus even based his strange theories on it, i.e., that of the creation of a *golem, a homunculus, through alchemy. The lesser Christian alchemists, especially the religious ones, following his example, also tended to make use of the Kabbalah for their purposes, though most had no knowledge of it. When, at the beginning of the 17th century, alchemy took a religious, mystical turn (in particular with the rise of the Rosicrucians), the prestige and influence of the Kabbalah became even more widespread; alchemy and Kabbalah became synonymous among Christians. This identification was generally speaking groundless. While many kabbalists undoubtedly accepted alchemy as a fact, the interests and symbol systems of Kabbalah and alchemy respectively were utterly different. Nevertheless occasional – albeit relatively insignifican – mutual influences are evident, and traces of alchemical lore are to be found in the *Zohar. The saying "through the gaze of the sun and its power, dust evolves and grows gold" (Zohar, 1:249–50) agrees with Artephius' theory that the metals grow like plants, but whereas the plants are composed of water and dust, the metals are composed of sulphur and mercury; the heat of the sun's rays penetrates the earth and combines with these elements to form gold, the metal of the sun. Simeon *Labi, the commentator on the Zohar, interprets this saying in his *Ketem Paz* in a definitely alchemical manner and states that the kabbalists call gold, "sun," and silver, "moon." The following saying (Zohar, 2:148a), bears an even stronger alchemical influence: "The heavenly gold is bright and shines in the eyes … and whoever clings to it when it descends into the lower world, conceals it within himself and for this reason it is also closed gold (*zahav sagur*), for it is not seen by the eye which does not possess it; but the gold of the earth is 'lower gold' and is easier to discover." The alchemical theory is even clearer in the passage following the one just quoted: "…. when silver thus reaches its fulfillment it becomes gold; we find, then, that silver transforms itself into gold and when this happens, it attains the stage of perfection." Hence, it is clear that the author of the Zohar not only believed in the transmutation of metals, but that he also adopted the alchemical theory of perfect and imperfect metals, as well as the belief that when silver is transformed into gold it reaches a higher grade of perfection.

*Moses b. Shem Tov de Leon, in his *Shekel ha-Kodesh* (London (1911), 118–22), also uses the language of the alchemists: "Copper is red and this generates the nature [*teva*, or *ẓeva*, "color"] of both, for those who know the craft [*melakhah*] make out of it the nature [color] of gold and silver." According to the alchemical teachings, copper too has the faculty of direct transformation into gold (without having to go through the intermediary stage of silver). It is true that the Zohar does not include mercury in the list of metals for the *Merkabah (*merkavah;* "divine chariot"; Zohar, 2:423–4), which has the greatest importance in alchemy, but this is possibly because, in common with Jābir (eighth century alchemist and physician), the Zohar did not consider mercury to be a metal at all but a spirit (*pneuma*). Ḥayyim *Vital, who at an earlier stage in his career took a lively interest in alchemy, lists mercury among the seven metals. Abraham b. Mordecai *Azulai (1570–1643) quotes Vital in the last part of *Ḥesed le-Avraham* (1863) that the seven metals correspond to the seven *Sefirot* ("degrees of divine emanation"), from *Ḥesed* to *Malkhut*, "hence, mercury corresponds to the seventh planet *kokhav* ['Mercury']… and it is already known to you that *Yesod* [one of the *Sefirot*] is also called *El Ḥai* ['the Living God'] and it corresponds to *Kesef Ḥai* ['Quick-Silver']." Mercury is allocated to *Sefirah Yesod*, because it is the basic element in all metals and in its ideal form is the basic element in the philosopher's stone, just as *El Ḥai* is the foundation of the universe. Ḥayyim Vital studied alchemy. This is shown in the following passage in *Shivḥei Rabbi Ḥayyim Vital* (1826): "He [Isaac *Luria] also told me that he saw inscribed on my forehead the verse: 'And to devise skillful works, to work in gold and in silver and in brass' [Ex. 35:32], an allusion to the two-and-a-half years during which I forsook the study of the Torah and pursued alchemy." Ḥ.J.D. *Azulai speaks of the philosopher's stone in his *Midbar Kedemot* (Lemberg, 1869, fol. 19), and calls it *esev* ("weed") as it was also called by the alchemists (and as it is called in other kabbalistic writings as well as in Hebrew manuscripts dealing with alchemy). Numerous prescriptions for the making of gold are found in books of practical Kabbalah (*Nifla'im Ma'asekha*, Leghorn (1881), s.v. *zahav*); these were probably taken from the writings of Jewish as well as gentile alchemists.

The influence of the Kabbalah on alchemy was greater than that of alchemy on Kabbalah, especially after the latter was diffused in Christian circles by *Pico della Mirandola, *Reuchlin, *Galatinus, and others. Some of the Christian alchemists adopted the theory of the ten *Sefirot* as well as the doctrine of the secrets of letters obtained by *ẓerufim* ("combinations") and *gematriot* and made them a basis for the Work of Holiness. Some used to inscribe on the melting-pot Hebrew and Syriac words copied from kabbalistic writings or words obtained by the above-mentioned methods. (The combination of letters was supposed to bring about the combination of metals.) The use of kabbalistic methods is also found in the book *Ars Magna*, attributed to Raymond Lull. Christian *Knorr von Rosenroth was one of the alchemists who had a real knowledge of Kabbalah. His *Cabbala denudata* (1677) contains translations of passages from the Zohar as well as lengthy quotations from *Esh Meẓaref*, a book on alchemy written in a kabbalistic spirit, which is probably a translation of a Hebrew manuscript. The author of *Esh Meẓaref* explains the relation of the metals to the *Sefirot* and quotes extensively from the Zohar; he too relates mercury to the *Sefirah Yesod.* He also quotes from another Jewish alchemist, Mordecai, who found a way to produce artificial silver by means of a four-month-long process. It is probable that this alchemist was Mordecai the son of Leone *Modena who transformed lead into silver and died as a result of his experiments (*Ḥayyei Yehudah* (Kiev, 1912), 33). Under the influence of Knorr von Rosenroth's work, a whole literature of kabbalistic alchemy was created. The book *Or Nogah* is particularly noteworthy. It was written in Hebrew and German and printed in Vienna, 1747. Its author, Aloisius Wiener, a nobleman of the Sonnenfels family, was a baptized Jew and an expert in Kabbalah, called "Lipmann Berlin" before his conversion.

The number of Jews who practiced the art of alchemy was apparently relatively small; however, the state of knowledge on this point is incomplete. It seems that the Jews of Egypt, particularly Alexandria, many of whom were gold- and silversmiths, during the Greek and Roman periods, were devotees of alchemy, magic, and *demonology (Suk. 51b). Zosimos testified that the "true teachings about the Great Art" were to be found only in "the writings and books of the Jews." However, the conclusion at which De Pauw arrived 150 years ago, namely that the Jews were the creators of alchemy, is incorrect. Alchemy is neither a Jewish science nor a Jewish art. The Jews were engaged in it in the same measure as they were engaged in other secular trades and fields of knowledge. However, the fact that in 1545 Martin *Luther warned Archduke Joachim II of Brandenburg against alchemy with which the Jews dealt indicates that he shared the general belief concerning the close connection between alchemy and Judaism.

In some alchemic writings the philosopher's stone is symbolized as a circle enclosing a hexagonal star ("the star of David"): the circle alludes to the kabbalistic **Ein-Sof* ("Infinite"); the triangle which points upward represents the element fire; and the one which points downward the element water. Fire and water together constitute heaven (*shamayim* = *esh* + *mayim*). From the 17th century, this was used by alchemists to symbolize the primeval matter out of which the main element of the philosopher's stone, philosophic mercury, the "quintessence," is extracted.

Jewish Personalities in Alchemy

In the Egyptian-Greek period one of the greatest alchemists was a woman known as "Mary the Jewess" (Maria Hebraea). According to Lippmann, she lived in the first century C.E. Her name and works are often mentioned in alchemic literature. According to Zosimos she was greatly skilled in alchemy and invented numerous ovens and boiling and distilling devices out of metal, clay, and glass. She even taught how to plaster them with the "philosopher's clay." The most important among her ovens, the *kerotakis* (also called "Mary's oven"), served to liquefy solids and to separate, through sublimation, the evaporable parts from the non-evaporable ones. Its main use, however, was for the preparation of the so-called "divine water" (a combination of sulfuric acid used to "bleach" metals). Mary also discovered the water, sand, and oil baths, vessels which even today are indispensable in any chemical laboratory. Mary is also the first to mention hydrochloric acid and one may therefore assume that she discovered it. The following esoteric saying, paralleled in kabbalistic writings, is ascribed to her: "Two are one, three and four are one, one will become two, two will become three." Another strange saying which excludes non-Jews from dealing with alchemy is also attributed to her: "Do not touch [the philosopher's stone with your hands]; you are not of our stock, you are not of Abraham's bosom." There is no doubt that she really existed and was famous in her time. Zosimos identified her with Miriam the prophetess, the sister of Moses; the Christian alchemists, who were eager to add the luster of biblical sanctity to their art, called her by this very name: "Maria Prophetissa, Moysis Soror."

Khalid b. Jasikhi (Calid Hebraeus) was an Arabian Jew and writer. He was revered by the Arab alchemists, who considered him to be the first alchemist of the Arabic period. Steinschneider, however, believes that he was an Arab. Artephius, the great alchemist of the 12th century, "before whom there lived no other expert equal to him" was a baptized Jew according to the author of *Keren ha-Pukh.* Artephius is said to have brought the creation of the philosopher's stone to perfection. He wrote three books on alchemy "whose importance is invaluable." In one of them, he relates that he wrote his work at the age of 1,025 years (thus supporting the belief that the philosopher's stone brings long life). Some scholars believe that Artephius was an Arab. However, the fact that he did not write anything in Arabic (all his works are written in Latin), seems to belie this contention.

At the beginning of the Christian period in alchemy (13th century), Jacobus Aranicus, a Jewish alchemist living in France, taught alchemy to the Christian scholar Vincent de Beauvais. Later (in the 15th century; according to Lippmann, the 17th century), two Dutch Jews became famed as alchemists: Isaac and his son John Isaac, both called "Hollandus," since their family name was unknown. The father was a diamond cutter and his son a physician. They led solitary lives and became famous only posthumously, through the works which they left behind; some authors consider them equal to Basilius Valentinus. They knew how to prepare "royal water" out of nitrate and sea-salt, as well as the "spirit of urine" (ammonia), and produced artificial gems. In the first quarter of the 18th century, a strange Jewish adept named Benjamin Jesse lived in Hamburg. His name became known only after his death, when a complete laboratory was discovered in a locked room of his house.

It is most probable that there were other Jewish alchemists in the Middle Ages as well as in the later period, particularly among the physicians and naturalists of the Spanish and Renaissance periods. It is certain that more books on alchemy have been written than have survived, partly because they were lost and partly because their authors hid behind the names of famous predecessors. It seems that among kabbalists, too, there were quite a number of alchemists, beside those already mentioned. The Jews of Morocco were particularly assiduous in their study and practice of alchemy, even into recent times. According to G. Scholem's testimony, a Jewish kabbalist from Morocco who was also an alchemist still lived in Jerusalem early in the 20th century. Baruch *Spinoza, though not a practitioner of alchemy, was nevertheless keenly interested in it.

While alchemic literature runs into thousands of volumes, there is no original work in this field in Hebrew literature. It seems, therefore, that Jewish adepts did not write their works in Hebrew. However, information on alchemy is scattered in the Hebrew works of several medieval and later authors. Hebrew authors referred to alchemy (*alkimiyyah*) as *melakhah* ("craft"), or *ḥokhmat ha-ẓerifah* ("the art of refining"). Among the Jewish scholars who in one way or another had some relation to alchemy, one should add the following: *Baḥya b. Joseph ibn Paquda, who in his *Ḥovot ha-Levavot* (beginning of chapter *Bittaḥon*) describes the ways of life and work of the alchemists, and apparently had no doubt about the truth of alchemy. Abraham Ibn Ezra also believed in alchemy as may be inferred from his commentary on the burning of the golden calf (Ex. 32:20): "for there is a thing which, when thrown into the fire together with the gold, it burns and becomes black and it will never become gold again; and this has been tried and it is true." *Maimonides knew some of the writings of Hermes (*Guide of the Perplexed*, ed. by S. Pines (1963), 521) but considered them to be nonsense. He does not even mention alchemy. Nevertheless, *Iggeret ha-Sodot* was later attributed to him; in this he allegedly explains to his disciple Joseph ibn *Aknin the secrets of alchemy in *Sha'ar ha-Shamayim* (Venice, 1547, section 2). Johanan Alemanno, who introduced Pico della Mirandola (who was interested in alchemy) to the Kabbalah, believed in alchemy, and mentioned it in *Sefer ha-Likkutim* and in *Ḥeshek Shelomo* (Leghorn, 1790). Abraham b. David Portaleone wrote a book in which alchemy is discussed, called *De aurodialogi tres* (Venice, 1584). Judah Loew b. Bezalel of Prague, a devotee of alchemy, was summoned to the alchemist King Rudolf II. According to the stories which circulated, they discussed the mysteries of alchemy.

Leone Modena recounts in his book *Ḥayyei Yehudah* that he and his son Mordecai dealt in alchemy for a profit. According to Modena, they began to do so on the advice of the physician, Abraham di Cammeo, who was rabbi in Rome, and himself an alchemist. Shemaiah, the uncle of Modena, was killed as a result of his alchemic activities. Modena's disciple, Joseph Solomon *Delmedigo, considered alchemy a very superior art (*Maẓref la-Ḥokhmah* (Warsaw, 1890), 49; see below). In 1640 Benjamin Mussafia, the author of *Musaf he-Arukh* and physician at the Danish court, published a Latin letter on alchemy, entitled *Mei Zahav*, in which he brings examples from the Talmud and Midrash (Yoma 44b; Ex. R. 35; and Song R. 3, etc.) to prove both the truth of alchemy, and the fact that the sages of the Talmud and Midrash practiced this craft. The majority of his quotations do not really prove anything. However, the saying by the disciples of Judah on "refined gold" (*zahav mezukkak*) that "it is buried for seven years in dung and it comes out refined" (Song R. 3:17) reminds one of the methods employed by the alchemists; similarly, the expression "gold that bears fruit" (*zahav she-oseh perot, ibid.*) most likely is derived from alchemy.

Among the great scholars of modern times, Jonathan *Eybeschuetz believed in alchemy (*Ya'arot Devash*, 1 (1779), passim); his opponent, Jacob *Emden, doubted it. "I wish to know whether that science [i.e., alchemy] is still thriving and whether those things have been proved beyond doubt" (*She'ilat Ya'veẓ* (Altona, 1739), 1, note 41).

Among the Jewish scholars who deny the truth of alchemy, one should cite *Judah Halevi who mentions alchemy disparagingly in *Kuzari.* Judah b. Solomon ha-Kohen ibn Matka, in his encyclopedia, *Midrash Ḥokhmah*, says that alchemy is "empty talk" and refers to alchemists by quoting the verse: "he that keepeth company with harlots wasteth his substance" (Prov. 29:3). Simeon b. Ẓemaḥ *Duran states in *Magen Avot* (pt. 2 (Leghorn, 1785), 10, 71) that "the craft of alchemy" is an error; "many got involved in it and wasted their lives but none ever succeeded in it." An important Hebrew manuscript on alchemy is preserved in the Berlin Staatsbibliothek; judging by its contents it cannot be earlier than the 17th century and its author is possibly Joseph Solomon Delmedigo. A second important Hebrew manuscript on alchemy, which includes a catalogue of alchemic literature, is found in the Gaster Library, now in the British Museum; it probably dates from the second half of the 15th century.

BIBLIOGRAPHY: Rubin, in: *Ha-Shaḥar*, 6 (1875), 1–96 (third pagination); Scholem, in: MGWJ, 69 (1925), 13–30, 95–110; M. Berthelot, *Origines de l'alchemie* (1885); idem, *Chimie au moyen-âge* (1893); E.O. von Lippmann, *Entstehung und Ausbreitung der Alchemie* (1919); Steinschneider, in: MGWJ, 38 (1894), 39–48; Eisler, *ibid.*, 69 (1925), 364–71; E.J. Holmyard, *Alchemy* (1957), 45–47, index.

[Bernard Suler]

ALCIMUS (Hellenized form of the Hebrew name **Jakim** or **Eliakim**), high priest 162–160 (or 159) B.C.E. Alcimus was a member of a high-priestly family and was the nephew of *Yose b. Joezer of Zeredah. When Demetrius I Soter ascended the Seleucid throne, Alcimus came to him to complain of the persecution of the Hellenists by Judah Maccabee and his followers, and he suggested that the king appoint him high priest, promising to be faithful to the Seleucids and to oppose Judah and his faction. Demetrius appointed him and sent him back to Judea, accompanied by Syrian troops under the command of Bacchides. At first, the *Hassideans supported him because he was of high-priestly stock, while Judah's faction opposed him because he had arrived with foreign troops. Alcimus had barely secured his position in Judea, when he arrested 60 Hassideans and put them to death. This act aroused popular indignation, and when Bacchides and his soldiers left Judea, Alcimus was driven from Jerusalem by Judah and his supporters. He returned to Demetrius, and once more asked for military support. The king sent a new army against Judah Maccabee, this time under the command of *Nicanor. Judah defeated Nicanor in battle twice, Nicanor being killed in the second battle. Demetrius again sent Bacchides against Judah, and this time the Jewish leader was defeated and killed. Alcimus returned to Judea and ruled with Syrian help. He broke into the *soreg* (one of the approaches to the Temple) in order to remove the wall which non-Jews were forbidden to pass. The *soreg* was breached in 13 places, and the Hassideans were infuriated. Alcimus' sudden death was interpreted by the people as an act of divine retribution.

BIBLIOGRAPHY: I Macc. 7:5–25; 9:1–2, 54–57; Jos., Ant., 12:385–6, 391–7, 413; 20:235; Middot, 2:3; Gen R. 55:22; Klausner, Bayit Sheni, index, s.v. *Yakim*; Graetz, Hist, 1 (1949), 482–508; Schuerer, Hist, 39 ff., 44 ff.

[Abraham Schalit]

ALCOLEA (Heb. אלקוליא) **De Cinca**, town in Aragon. In 1320 the infante Alfonso gave special privileges to Jews settling there. They were exempt from taxation other than a substantial house tax. Problems regarding the communal taxes are discussed (c. 1380) in the responsa of R. *Isaac b. Sheshet. Isaac, son of R. Vidal de Tolosa, who lived in Alcolea, disputed the assessment and was denounced to the countess. The community broke up in 1414 in the aftermath of the disputation of *Tortosa.

BIBLIOGRAPHY: Baer, Spain, 2 (1966), 83; Baer, Studien, 146, 189 ff.; del Arco, in: *Sefarad*, 7 (1947), 281.

ALCONIÈRE, THEODORE (**Herman Cohn**; 1797–1865), Hungarian painter. Alconière received his training in Vienna and then spent some years in Rome, where he acquired his dramatic romantic style. While in Italy he was appointed court portraitist to the duke of Parma. In 1848 he moved to Hungary, where he painted many equestrian portraits of the nobility and scenes from everyday life. After 1850 he lived mainly in Vienna. Impoverished, he began supporting himself by the production of humorous lithographs and even took to counterfeiting banknotes. However, his conscience troubled him and instead of circulating the money, he handed himself over to the police. He died two years later in a Vienna hospital. Alconière was the most distinguished Jewish painter among the first generation of Hungarian nationalists.

BIBLIOGRAPHY: Roth, Art, 555–6.

ALCONSTANTINI, family of Jewish courtiers in 13th-century Aragon probably originating from Constantine, North Africa. Naḥmanides refers to them disapprovingly as "the Ishmaelites of the court." Many members of the family were hated by the ordinary Jews for their arrogance and lack of sensitivity to the social problems of their community. The first members to attain importance were the brothers BAḤYA (Baḥi'el, Bafi'el) and SOLOMON of Saragossa. By 1229 the two brothers were already in receipt of crown grants from James I of Aragon – the revenues from the local dyeing vats and two pounds of mutton daily from the Jewish slaughterhouse. In the same year Baḥya, who was Arabic interpreter to the court, was sent to Majorca with the count of Roussillon to conduct negotiations for the surrender of the Muslims. Baḥya also took part in Jewish communal affairs and in 1232 signed the counterban against the group who had banned the study of *Maimonides. The overweening ambitions of the two brothers to attain the position of supreme judicial authority (*dayyan*) in Aragonese Jewry were frustrated by Judah de la Cavallería, the royal *baile*. *Naḥmanides also opposed the claims of the family to have one of its members appointed as rabbi and judge of Aragonese Jewry. However, Baḥya continued his diplomatic activities. During the distribution of the lands of the conquered territories in the 1260s he received grants of large estates. In 1240 Solomon held a village and fortress near Tarragona and the revenues from some Catalonian knights.

Of Baḥya's two sons, MOSES and SOLOMON, the former was by far the more active and important. The two brothers appear in the sources from 1264. Moses was appointed *baile* of Saragossa from 1276 until the end of 1278; he succeeded the late Judah de la Cavallería, of a family that was Alconstantini's staunchest opponent. As *baile* of Saragossa he was much involved in the collection of the salt tax in Aragon. In the years 1280–81 Moses was the *baile* of the city of Valencia. Even before his campaign for the conquest of Sicily had begun, Pedro III gave in to the growing anti-Jewish pressure of the clergy and the nobility. Moses was the last Jew in the royal service to be dismissed from office. He was thrown into prison and brought to trial, in which he almost lost his life. The trial was the result of unpaid debts which he incurred during his work for the king. He was greatly disliked by Jews and Christians for his unscrupulous conduct.

Moses was also deeply involved in the affairs of the Jewish community. Members of the Alconstantini family were at constant odds with the community and its leading members, first and foremost Judah de la Cavallería. Solomon Alconstantini was appointed one of the three magistrates (*berurim*) of the Saragossa community in 1271. Moses was implicated, with Meir b. Eleazar, in beating up R. *Yom Tov Ishbili for having delivered a legal opinion to the royal clerk on the feuds of the local great families.

The Alconstantini family was still aspiring to the office of chief justice and "crown rabbi" of the kingdom in 1294, and the queen of Castile applied to James II of Aragon with the request that Solomon Alconstantini be confirmed in this office. James, however, refused, on the ground that the privileges granted to the family had lapsed during the reigns of his predecessors: "for great damage and destruction has been suffered by all the Jews in our kingdom, and it would be unreasonable that for the sake of one Jew we should thereby lose all the others."

In the 14th century the Alconstantini family declined from its former eminence. Some physicians of this name are mentioned as living in Aragon. SOLOMON (early 14th century), probably a descendant of the family, was the author of *Megalleh Amukot*. Enoch B. Solomon *Al-Constantini was the author of philosophical works. An Alconstantini represented the *Huesca community in the disputation of *Tortosa (1413–14). After the expulsion from Spain, members of the Alconstantini family are found in Turkey. Later, they moved to Ancona, where the name assumed the Italian form, Constantini. Some of them were rabbis and community leaders in Ancona during the 17th and 18th centuries. When the French conquered Ancona (1797) SANSONE was one of the three Jews elected to the city council.

BIBLIOGRAPHY: Baer, Spain, index; Baer, Urkunden, 1 (1929), index; idem, in: *Dvir*, 2 (1924), 316; Miret and Schwab, in: REJ, 68 (1914), 179; Ibn Verga, *Shevet Yehudah*, ed. by A. Shochat (1947), 95. **ADD. BIBLIOGRAPHY:** D. Romano, *Judíos al sevicio de Pedro el Grande de Aragón* (1983), 87–112

[Haim Beinart / Yom Tov Assis (2nd ed.)]

AL-CONSTANTINI, ENOCH BEN SOLOMON (c. 1370), physician and philosopher. His work *Mar'ot Elohim* ("Divine Visions") is extant in almost 30 manuscripts (described in the edition by C. Sirat in *Eshel Be'er-Sheva* (1976), 120–99).

The book is divided into three chapters, preceded by an introduction. The first chapter interprets Isaiah 1:1–6; the second Ezekiel 1:1–20; the third, Zechariah 10. The exegesis is entirely philosophical and deals with the separate intelligences, the spheres, and the human intellect. Al-Constantini was influenced by Maimonides, Al-Fārābī, Avicenna, Averroes, Samuel ibn Tibbon, Moses of Narbonne, Levi b. Abraham, and Solomon ibn Gabirol (in the abridged version of Gabirol's *Mekor Ḥayyim*, the *Likkutim* by Shem Tov ibn Falquera). A Bodleian manuscript (Opp. 585) of Al-Constantini's work contains glosses by Menahem Kara.

BIBLIOGRAPHY: L. Gruenhut, in: *Festschrift … A. Harkavy* (1908), 403–430; C. Sirat, in: REJ, 121 (1962), 247–354.

[Colette Sirat (2nd ed.)]

ALCORSONO (אלכרסאני, כרסאנו, כראסאנו), **JUDAH BEN JOSEPH** (14th century), Moroccan theological scholar. For unknown reasons he was put in prison where he wrote *Aron ha-Edut* ("Ark of Testimony") on such subjects as *Ma'aseh Bereshit* and *Ma'aseh Merkavah*, the story of the Garden of Eden, providence, prophecy, and Satan's dispute with God (Job, chs. 1 and 2). The work is divided into 22 chapters corresponding to the number of letters in the Hebrew alphabet.

Manuscripts of the work are preserved in several libraries; one has been annotated by Moses *Ḥagiz. In Saadiah b. Maimun *Ibn Danan's *Ma'amar al Seder ha-Dorot*, Alcorsono is mentioned as an astrologer (Z.H. Edelman (ed.), *Ḥemdah Genuzah*, (1855), 30).

BIBLIOGRAPHY: Ghirondi-Neppi, 196; Michael, Or, no. 1007; Benjacob, Oẓar, 49, no. 963.

ALCOTT, AMY (1956–), professional golfer, member of the LPGA and World Golf Hall of Fame. Born in Kansas City, Missouri, Alcott grew up in Los Angeles, where she began playing golf as an eight year old putting toward sprinkler heads. She won the United States Golf Association juniors championship in 1973, two years before joining the Ladies Professional Golf Association (LPGA) shortly after her 19th birthday. Alcott proceeded to win the third professional tournament she entered, the 1975 Orange Blossom Classic, which set a record for the fastest career win, and was subsequently named the tour's rookie of the year. She went on to win 29 professional tournaments, including five majors: the Peter Jackson Classic in 1979, the U.S. Women's Open in 1980, and the Nabisco Dinah Shore in 1983, 1988, and 1991. Alcott set a one-round tournament record of 65 when she won the 1984 Lady Keystone Open and tied the tour record of winning at least one tournament in 12 straight years. She shot her fifth career hole-in-one in 2001. Alcott was named Golf Magazine's Player of the Year in 1980 and was awarded the LPGA's Founders Cup in 1986, designed to recognize altruistic contributions to the betterment of society by a member. She wrote *Guide to Women's Golf* (1991) and produced the instruction video *Winning at Golf with Amy Alcott* (1991).

[Elli Wohlgelernter (2nd ed.)]

°**ALCUIN** (**Albinus Flaccus**; c. 735–804), educator and tutor of Charlemagne from 781. Born in York, he was educated in a school where one of his teachers had been a student of Bede. Author of several books and educational manuals, Alcuin's exegetical works make frequent reference to commentaries on scripture by Jewish scholars; his knowledge of them derives from the works of *Jerome. He was present at a religious disputation between a Christian scholar and a Jew in Pavia, Italy, held between 750 and 760.

BIBLIOGRAPHY: B. Blumenkranz, *Auteurs chrùtiens… sur les juifs* (1963), 144ff.; Roth, Dark Ages, 113. **ADD. BIBLIOGRAPHY:** L.Wallach, *Alcuin and Charlemagne* (1959).

[Bernhard Blumenkranz / Shimon Gibson (2nd ed.)]

ALDABI, MEIR BEN ISAAC (c. 1310–c. 1360), religious philosopher, with strong leanings toward the Kabbalah. Aldabi was a grandson of *Asher b. Jehiel. As a young man he received a comprehensive education in biblical and rabbinic literature, and afterward he turned to philosophical and scientific studies. In 1348 he apparently left his native Toledo and settled in Jerusalem, where, in 1360, he finished his long contemplated work, *Shevilei Emunah* ("Paths of Faith"). It was first published in Riva di Trento, 1518.

Aldabi was moved to write his book by the belief, prevalent in the Middle Ages, that the Greek philosophers (especially Plato and Aristotle) derived the essentials of their knowledge from Jewish sources. He determined to assemble the fragments of ancient Jewish wisdom scattered throughout the various works of the philosophers and natural scientists and to trace them back to their original sources. Actually, as stated in the introduction, the book is merely a compilation of subjects and theories, some of them translated by him from foreign languages, and culled from different works. The various subjects are not arranged systematically but are presented in random sequence. He borrowed mainly from Hebrew literature and to some extent, particularly in the fields of medicine and astronomy, from Arabic literature. His philosophy is based largely on that of *Maimonides, his ethics on that of *Baḥya b. Joseph ibn Paquda, and his theology on that of *Naḥmanides and his circle. The influence of the last is particularly evident in Aldabi's predilection for Kabbalah which he ties in with his rationalist philosophy. He relies on the encyclopedic *Sha'ar ha-Shamayim* of his predecessor Gershon b. Solomon of Arles, and for his psychological theories he uses the views of Joseph ibn *Ẓaddik and *Hillel b. Samuel of Verona. Aldabi's book is divided into ten "paths" (*netivot*) in which he treats (1) the existence and unity of God, His names, and divine attributes both from a philosophic and a kabbalistic point of view; (2) the creation of the world, geography and astronomy, and the elements; (3) the creation of man and family life (part of this section is taken, without acknowledgment, from the *Iggeret ha-Kodesh* of Naḥmanides); (4) embryology, anatomy, and human physiology (a digest of the accepted theories on anatomy and physiology in medieval medicine, presented on the basis of the comparison between the microcosm and macrocosm); (5) rules for physical and "spiritual" hygiene (on the nature of anger, joy, and the like); (6) the nature and the faculties of the soul; (7) religious observances as defined by the Torah and rabbinic tradition; (8) the uninterrupted chain of the Oral Law from Moses to the Talmud; (9) reward and punishment and metempsychosis; and finally (10) the redemption of Israel, resurrection, and the world to come.

The last two chapters are based largely on the opinions of Naḥmanides and Solomon b. Abraham *Adret.

BIBLIOGRAPHY: Weiss, Dor, 5 (1891), 117, 141, 214; Steinschneider, Cat, 1690; Steinschneider, Uebersetzungen, 9–27; Bruell, *Jahrbuecher*, 2 (1874), 166–8; Zinberg, Sifrut, 2 (1956), 136–40, 396; G. Sarton, *Introduction to the History of Science*, 3 (1948), index; D. Kaufmann, *Die Sinne* (1884), index; Waxman, Literature, 2 (1960^2), 318–9.

[Meir Hillel Ben-Shammai]

ALDANOV, MARK (pseudonym of **Mark Aleksandrovich Landau**; 1889–1957), Russian novelist. Aldanov was born in Kiev and trained as a chemist and lawyer. He left Russia in 1919 and settled in France. During World War II he lived in the United States, but eventually returned to Europe and died in Nice. A writer of exceptional erudition and sophistication, Aldanov excelled in the historical novel – a genre in which he had few peers in Russian literature. He also wrote other prose works including several treatises on the philosophy of history. He is best remembered for his tetralogy *Myslitel* ("The Thinker"), a work set in Russia and Western Europe during the Napoleonic era. Aldanov's novel *Desyataya simfoniya* (1931; *The Tenth Symphony*, 1948) is based on the life of Beethoven; and *Nachalo kontsa* (1936–42; *The Fifth Seal*, 1943) depicts Europe on the eve of World War II. Aldanov was singularly successful in blending historical and fictitious characters and events, but unlike so many other Russian novelists – especially Tolstoy in *War and Peace* – he erected his historical scaffolding merely as a support for the fictional structure. This did not, however, discourage his tendency to devote more time to historical research than to pruning his own work. Aldanov also differed from Tolstoy in believing that the fate of men and nations was shaped not by laws but by historical accident. His writing shows a partiality for paradox and a fondness for a pose of ironic detachment. His novels were translated into many languages but, unlike those of some of his émigré colleagues, were unobtainable in the U.S.S.R. A staunch anti-Communist, Aldanov remained a liberal Russian intellectual, retaining only tenuous links with his Jewish heritage.

BIBLIOGRAPHY: G. Struve, *Russkaya literatura v izgnanii*, (1956).

[Maurice Friedberg]

ALDEMA, GIL (1928–), Israeli musician and composer. Aldema's father, Abraham Eisenstein (Aldema), was active in the early Israeli satirical theater. Gil Aldema studied piano and violin. Among his teachers were Menashe Rabina and Paul *Ben-Haim. During his army service he was wounded. Later he studied at the Jerusalem Music Academy and directed folk singing activities. In 1952 he became a music teacher and composed his early songs. In 1957 he went to the U.S. to study music and worked as a music arranger for the Carmon Dance Company. From the 1960s to the 1980s he worked at Kol Israel (Israel Broadcasting Authority) as a musical director of light music. Aldema is known for his work and arrangements for choirs such as Rinat, Cameran, and others. He composed many songs, such as *"Ana Halakh Dodekh," "Ashirah li-Yediday," "Zemer Ikkarim," "Maḥol Dayyagim,"* and more, which were published in *Ẓiyyunei ha-Derekh* (1979), *Maḥberet Mezameret* (1981), *Shir le-Elef Arisot* (1983), and *Menifah Kolit* (2000). Among his awards are the AKUM Prize for his contribution to Israeli folk music (1984) and the Israel Prize for Israeli folk songs (2004).

[Gila Flam (2nd ed.)]

ALDERMAN, GEOFFREY (1944–), British historian. An Oxford graduate, Geoffrey Alderman was professor of politics and contemporary history at Middlesex University in London and later vice president of American Intercontinental University in London. One of the best-known historians of the Jewish community in Britain, Alderman is the author of *Modern British Jewry* (1992), a sophisticated and deeply researched history of the Anglo-Jewish community since 1858; *The Jewish Community in British Politics* (1983); *London Jewry and London Politics, 1889–1986* (1989); a history of the right-wing Orthodox, *Federation of Synagogues, 1887–1987* (1987); and other works. In recent years he has written an often controversial weekly column in the *Jewish Chronicle* newspaper, which generally reflects his Orthodox Zionist viewpoint.

[William D. Rubinstein (2nd ed.)]

°**ALDO MANUZIO** (1449–1515). Italian humanist, Hebraist, and printer. In 1494 he set up a printing press in Venice which soon became famous. Printing Greek and Latin grammatical works, he appended to several of them the first printed Hebrew grammar for Christian students (*Introductio perbrevis in linguam hebraicam*, date of foreword 1501). This was reprinted separately eight times by Aldo himself under a slightly different title (a facsimile reprint was published in 1927). Aldo also printed Leone Ebreo's (Judah *Abrabanel) *Dialoghi di Amore* (1544, 1545) calling him a convert to Christianity. The type is very similar to that used by Gershom *Soncino. This led to a rather acrimonious competition between the two great printers.

BIBLIOGRAPHY: Dukes, in: REJ, 1 (1880), 150ff.; C. Roth, *Jews in the Renaissance* (1959), 142, 181, 224; A. Marx, *Studies in Jewish History and Booklore* (1944), index, s.v. *Aldus Manucius;* M. Marx, in: HUCA, 11 (1936), 445–6.

ALDRICH, ROBERT (1918–1983), U.S. director, producer. Born in Cranston, Rhode Island, to a prominent East Coast family, Aldrich departed from family tradition to become one of Hollywood's most provocative filmmakers. After attending the University of Virginia, where he played football and studied economics, Aldrich began his film career as a production clerk for RKO at the onset of WWII. Aldrich quickly became an assistant director and spent the rest of the decade learning from esteemed directors such as Lewis Milestone, Joseph Losey, Abraham Polonsky, and Charlie Chaplin. Aldrich made his directorial feature film debut in 1953 with *The Big Leaguer.* The following year, he made his directorial breakthrough with the western *Apache* featuring Burt Lancaster as a pacifist Native American warrior in a film that presaged Aldrich's career-long exploration of violence and morality. Aldrich solidified his reputation as a director with *Vera Cruz* (1954), another western starring Lancaster, this time opposite Gary Cooper, as the two men vied for gold in Mexico. Aldrich's distinctive style continued to crystallize in two provocative film-noir features, *Kiss Me Deadly* (1955) and *The Big Knife* (1955), both of which earned him critical acclaim in Europe. After a series of disappointing films in the late 1950s, Aldrich rejuvenated his career with *What Ever Happened to Baby Jane?* (1962), for which Bette Davis won the Academy Award for Best Actress. Aldrich's turbulent career was marked by two more highlights, *The Dirty Dozen*, the highest grossing film of 1967, and the popular prison film *The Longest Yard* (1974), starring Burt Reynolds. Aldrich served as president of the Director's Guild of America from 1975 to 1979, during which he successfully lobbied for increased creative authority for directors.

[Walter Driver (2nd ed.)]

ALDROPHE, ALFRED-PHILIBERT (1834–1895), French architect. Born in Paris, Aldrophe designed the French buildings at the international exhibitions (1855, 1867). He designed the synagogues in the Rue de la Victoire and at Versailles. He also built private homes in Paris including that of Baron Gustave de *Rothschild. He erected several important monuments in the Père-Lachaise cemetery.

ALDUBI, ABRAHAM BEN MOSES BEN ISMAIL (14th century), Spanish talmudist. Aldubi studied under Solomon b. Abraham *Adret and was the teacher of *Jeroham b. Meshullam. The whole of his *Seder Avodah bi-Kezarah*, dealing with the Day of Atonement service in the Temple, was incorporated by Jeroham in his *Toledot Adam ve-Ḥavvah*. Aldubi's book *Ḥiddushim ve-Shitah* to *Bava Batra* is mentioned in the responsa of Moses b. Isaac Alashkar (1554), and one of his responsa is printed in the *Zikhron Yehudah* (1846) of Judah the son of *Asher b. Jehiel.

BIBLIOGRAPHY: Jeroham b. Meshullam, *Issur ve-Hetter* (1960), introd.; D. Cassel, in: *Zikhron Yehudah (b. Rosh)* (1846); Michael, Or, 15, no. 54; A. Freimann, in: JJLG, 12 (1918), 278, 284.

[Zvi Avneri]

ALECHINSKY, PIERRE (1927–), Belgian painter. Alechinsky was leader of the CoBrA group of artists, formed in Brussels, which fostered a spontaneous approach to painting and opposed social realism on the one hand and a calculated abstraction on the other. Alechinsky's works have been described as "explosive." They are characterized by a sense of perpetual movement and flux in which incomplete forms appear and dissolve. Alechinsky studied at the Ecole Nationale d'Architecture et des Arts Décoratifs in Brussels. In 1951 he moved to Paris, joining other members of the CoBrA group. Later he visited Japan, where he made a film on Japanese calligraphy. Alechinsky exhibited at the Venice and São Paulo Biennales.

BIBLIOGRAPHY: F.C. Legrand, in: *Quadrum*, 11 (Fr., 1961), 123–32; J. Putman, in: *L'Oeil*, (Nov., 1966), 36–42.

ʾALEF (Heb. אָלֶף ;א), first letter of the Hebrew alphabet; its numerical value is 1. It is a plosive laryngal consonant, pronounced according to the vowel it carries. The earliest clear representation of the *ʾalef* is to be found in the Proto-Sinaitic inscriptions of c. 1500 B.C.E. This acrophonic pictograph of an ox-head (*ʾalp*) [sign] develops through the Proto-Arabic [sign] and South Arabic [sign] into the Ethiopic [sign] on the one hand, and through the Proto-Canaanite [sign] and [sign] into the tenth–ninth centuries B.C.E. classical Phoenician *ʾalef* [sign] on the other hand. The Ugaritic consonantal cuneiform script of the 14th century B.C.E. has three ʾalef signs: [sign] (ʾa), [sign] (ʾi), and [sign] (ʾu). About 800 B.C.E. the Greeks borrowed the Phoenician *ʾalef* and used it as a vowel (*alpha*). They altered its stance and turned it into A, a shape which was adopted by Latin, among other scripts. While the Phoenician *ʾalef* underwent its own evolution ([sign] – fifth century B.C.E., [sign] – Punic, [sign] – Neo-Punic), the Hebrew and the Aramaic scripts, which derived from Phoenician, developed it as follows: in seventh century B.C.E. Hebrew, along with the cursive forms [sign] and [sign] there existed a formal one: [sign]. The latter survived in the Paleo-Hebrew Dead Sea Scrolls and its variations occur on Jewish coins as [sign], [sign] and in late Samaritan as [sign]. The development of the Aramaic cursive *ʾalef* in the seventh and sixth centuries B.C.E. was [sign] → [sign] → [sign] → [sign]; and in the fifth century B.C.E., it reached its classical form [sign]. The latter is the ancestor of the first letters of many alphabets which developed from the third century B.C.E. onward. They include: Nabatean: [sign] → [sign] → [sign] → [sign] → l. The last form, which occurs in the first century C.E. documents found near the Dead Sea, indicates the date when the Arabic *ʾalif* was fixed. The Palmyrene [sign] turned into the Syriac [sign] (Estrangela), but in other Syriac systems it is a vertical stroke resembling the Arabic. The Jewish (square Hebrew) *ʾalef* preserved the shape of its Aramaic ancestor. Although there is a tendency to curve the left leg – as in Nabatean and Palmyrene, e.g., the Nash Papyrus – the straight-legged *ʾalef* [sign] prevails. The Jewish cursive forms of the time of the Herodian dynasty [sign], [sign] disappeared apparently after the period of Bar Kokhba. The Jewish formal *ʾalef* did not change its basic shape during the following period. In the cursive styles of the various Jewish local systems the left leg became the main stroke – [sign]; so it is in the Ashkenazic cursive from which stems the modern cursive *ʾalef* [sign], [sign]. See *Alphabet, Hebrew.

[Joseph Naveh]

Alef in *Aggadah* and Folklore

The *alef* is more personified than any of the other Hebrew letters. Praised is its humility, which is reflected in the fact that it did not ask God to be the means of creation nor that the Bible be started with it (the Bible begins with the second letter of the alphabet *bet*). The *alef* was rewarded by starting the Decalogue (אָנֹכִי, *Anokhi*; "I") and by denoting the highest number, אֶלֶף (*elef*, "thousand"). The three letters (ף ,ל ,א) which constitute the *alef* have been interpreted according to different homiletic means such as the *notarikon אֶפְתַּח לְשׁוֹן פֶּה (*eftaḥ leshon peh;* "I shall open the tongue (and) mouth") which is the opening phrase of God's proclamation: "I shall open the tongue (and) mouth of all people to praise Me, or to study, and teach" (*Midrash Alfa Beta de-Rabbi Akiva* in A. Jellinek, *Beit ha-Midrash*, 3 (1938²), 12–14; cf. the use of the root אלף in Job 33:33). Since *alef* is the initial letter of God's name at the time of Creation (אֱלֹהִים, *Elohim* in Gen. 1:1) and of the three words alluding to His Ineffable Name (אֶהְיֶה אֲשֶׁר אֶהְיֶה in Ex. 3:14), it is fundamental in Hebrew inscriptions in *amulets and letter magic. Similarly, the letter "A" is to be found at the end of the European magic-formulistic inscriptions belonging to the "abracadabra" type. The expression "from *alef* to *tav*" (Shab. 55a and Av. Zar 4a) corresponding to that of "Alpha and Omega" (Rev. 1:8 and 22:13) denotes complete integration.

[Dov Noy]

BIBLIOGRAPHY: F. Dornseiff, *Das Alphabet in Mystik und Magic* (1925[2]); Ginzberg, Legends, 7 (1938), 24; D. Neuman, *Motif-index to the Talmudic-Midrashic Literature* (1954), 311, no. D 1273. 4; S. Thompson, *Index of Folk-Literature*, 2 (1956[2]), 162, no. D 1273. 6.

ALEGRE, ABRAHAM BEN SOLOMON (1560–1652), rabbi and scholar of Constantinople. Ḥayyim *Alfandari in his *Maggid me-Reshit* records Alegre's controversy on a halakhic issue (responsa 4, 5). His own responsa were published together with those of Jacob Shalem Ashkenazi (Sephardi emissary of Jerusalem), in Salonika in 1793. Alegre is more widely known by the title of his extensive commentary on Maimonides' *Sefer ha-Mitzvot, Lev Same'aḥ*, (Constantinople, 1652), printed in the Israeli edition of the *Mishneh Torah* (vol. 1, 1962). In this work, which took 40 years to complete, Alegre analyzes the 14 principles defined by Maimonides in the introduction to his *Sefer ha-Mitzvot* and those on which he based the enumeration and classification of the *mitzvot*. He particularly justifies Maimonides against the strictures of Naḥmanides on the *Sefer ha-Mitzvot*. His son-in-law, Levi Teglio, in a foreword to the *Lev Same'aḥ*. states that Alegre wrote a homiletical work and a book of responsa.

BIBLIOGRAPHY: Azulai, s.v. *Abraham Alegre;* Michael, Or, no. 238; Rosanes, Togarmah, 3 (1938), 128; Fuenn, Keneset, 10.

[Abraham Hirsch Rabinowitz]

ALEINU LE-SHABBE'AḤ (Heb. עָלֵינוּ לְשַׁבֵּחַ; "It is our duty to praise [the Lord of all things]"), prayer now recited at the conclusion of the statutory services. Originally it introduced the *Malkhuyyot* section of the Rosh Ha-Shanah additional service in which the kingship of God is proclaimed and where it is recited with great solemnity. Its theological importance secured for it, from the 12th century at least, a special place in the daily order of service (*Maḥzor Vitry*, p. 75); first at the conclusion of the morning service and later at the end of the other two daily services as well (*Kol Bo*, no. 16). As with some other prayers, it was taken over from the New Year liturgy into the additional service of the Day of Atonement.

The style of *Aleinu* is that of the early *piyyut*, composed of short lines, each comprising about four words, with a marked rhythm and parallelism. It is one of the most sublime of Jewish prayers, written in exalted language.

It is referred to as *Teki'ata de-Vei Rav* ("The *Shofar* Service of *Rav") and it has therefore been ascribed to this third-century Babylonian teacher (TJ RH 1:3, 57a; cf. Av. Zar. 1:2, 39c). But the *Aleinu* may be considerably older. According to one popular tradition, it was composed by Joshua (*Arugat ha-Bosem*, ed. by E.E. Urbach, 3 (1962), 468–71); according

'ALENU

Ex. 1 Three "Realizations" of the 19th Century.

to another, it was written by the Men of the Great Assembly during the period of the Second Temple (Manasseh Ben Israel, *Vindiciae*, vol. 4, p. 2). There are good reasons for placing it within that period, because there is no mention of the Temple restoration in the prayer while there is reference in it to the Temple practice of prostration. Prostration during *Aleinu* is still customary in the Ashkenazi rite in most communities on Rosh Ha-Shanah and on the Day of Atonement, while in the other services the congregants bow when reciting the words "we bend the knee…." The description of God as the "King of the kings of kings" may be due to Persian influence, since the Persians described their king as "the king of kings" (cf. Dan. 2:37). It has been suggested that the prayer has its origin in early *Merkabah mysticism; a version of *Aleinu* was recently found among hymns used by the early mystics (see bibliography).

Contents

The main theme of the prayer is the kingdom of God. In the first part, God is praised for having singled out the people of Israel from other nations, for Israel worships the One God while others worship idols. The second paragraph expresses the fervent hope for the coming of the kingdom of God, and the universal ideal of a united mankind which will recognize the only true God, and of "a world perfected under the kingship of the Almighty." The juxtaposition of the two paragraphs provides a coherent theology connecting the idea of a chosen people (Israel) with the challenge that such distinctiveness has for its purpose, religious union and the perfection of mankind under the kingdom of God.

Censorship

In the Middle Ages the prayer was censored by Christians as containing an implied insult to Christianity. They claimed that the verse "for they prostrate themselves before vanity and emptiness and pray to a God that saveth not" was a reference to Jesus. Pesaḥ Peter, a 14th-century Bohemian apostate, spitefully alleged a connection between the numerical value of the Hebrew word וָרִיק (*va-rik*; "and emptiness") and יֵשׁוּ (*Yeshu*; the name of Christ). The elder *Buxtorf (16th century) and *Eisenmenger (17th century) and others repeated the charge; and Jewish apologists from Lippmann Muelhausen (15th century) to Manasseh Ben Israel and Moses Mendelssohn were at pains to refute it. However, the 13th-century *Arugat ha-Bosem* by Abraham b. Azriel does mention a tradition that the numerical value of לָהֶבֶל וָרִיק (*la-hevel va-rik*; "vanity and emptiness") equals יֵשׁוּ וּמְחַמַּד (*Yeshu u-Muḥammad*; Jesus and Muhammad). Some ecclesiastical censors also deleted the previous passage: "Who did not make our portion like theirs, nor our lot like that of all their multitude." Eisenmenger refers to the custom of spitting at the offending word which he interprets as an additional insult to Christianity. This was, no doubt, a popular gesture suggested by the double meaning of *rik* ("emptiness" and "spittle"). In view of this accusation, rabbis such as Isaiah Horowitz discouraged the indecorous practice. (The popular Yiddish phrase, *er kummt tsum oysshpayen* ("he comes at the spitting") came, therefore, to describe someone who arrived at a service as late as the concluding *Aleinu*.) The censors remained adamant even when it was pointed out that the offending phrase is found in Isaiah (30:7; 45:20), that the *Aleinu* prayer is probably pre-Christian, and that if Rav was the author, it was composed in a non-Christian country. The line had to be removed from Ashkenazi prayer books. In 1703 its recital was prohibited in Prussia. The edict, which provided for police enforcement, was renewed in 1716 and 1750. Even earlier, some communities omitted or changed the offending lines as an act of self-censorship (e.g., by replacing *she-hem*, "for they [prostrate themselves before vanity]," with *she-hayu*, "for they used to…"). The Sephardim – especially in Oriental countries – retained the full text and it has now been restored to some prayer books of the Ashkenazi rite as well.

The Blois Tragedy

*Ephraim of Bonn tells how the Jews of *Blois, martyred in 1171, went to their death chanting *Aleinu* to a soul-stirring melody which "at the outset… was subdued, but at the close was mighty." The messianic theme of the second paragraph would have made it especially significant for the Jew in the tragic moments of his history, and it takes its place with the *Shema* as a declaration of faith. Its introduction into the daily service may have been an act of defiance when Christian pressure was on the increase.

Reform Usage

In the Reform liturgy the prayer, with some modifications, has retained its importance and is called the "Adoration." The Ark is opened and the congregation bows as the words "we bow and prostrate ourselves" are recited.

Music

The *Aleinu* of the **Musaf* prayer of the Penitential Feasts is notable, in Ashkenazi tradition, for its music; the Sephardi and eastern communities sing it to one of their regular prayer modes. A musical peculiarity was claimed for the Ashkenazi tune as early as 1171, when it was sung by the martyrs of Blois (Neubauer-Stern, p. 68, 202). Its written tradition, however, dates from the 18th and 19th centuries. The Ashkenazi *Aleinu* belongs to the class of unchangeable **Mi-Sinai* tunes. Thus, it cannot be traced back to a definite archetype, but only to a basic concept or musical idea which is executed differently in every performance.

The *Aleinu* tune consists of seven melodic sentences or "themes" (see Music Example), always produced in the same order. Four of them, nos. I, IV, V, and VI, are virtually invariable in outline; the others, especially the final themes III and VII, are frequently changed. The *Aleinu* has several themes in common with other *Mi-Sinai* tunes: IV, V, VI, and VII³ recur, in the same order, in the *Avot* Benediction; II, V, and VII² are known from the **Kol Nidrei*. Apart from mere ornamental elaboration and minor variants, three main patterns of melodic realization can be distinguished: (1) the predominant version (Examples IA and IB), known to both western and eastern Ashkenazi communities. This is well on the way to major tonality which gradually replaces the original mode (featuring a diminished seventh). Cantors from Russia often omitted some of the themes, except 1 and 5, replacing them by repetitions. This points to a western-Ashkenazi origin for the tune. (2) "Acculturated" versions (such as Example IC) came into being in the mid-19th century. They feature drastic reduction of coloraturas and decided major tonality. (3) A presently obsolete, expanded version was current in the 18th and early 19th century. It is excessively ornate, and may be regarded as a cantorial development of or a "fantasia" on the traditional tune. Many of its extended vocalizations and trumpet flourishes represent a musical illustration of certain mystical intentions (*kavvanot*) connected with the prayer. An old theory proposes a relationship between the tune of *Aleinu* and the Sanctus of the Roman Mass IX. Since the latter, however, is not dated earlier than the 14th century, no conclusions can be drawn from the slight similarity between the two tunes.

[Hanoch Avenary]

BIBLIOGRAPHY: Baer, S., Seder, 131–2, 397–8; *Siddur Oẓar ha-Tefillot* (Ashkenazi rite, 1923), fol. 217ff.; H. Brody and S. Wiener, *Mivḥar ha-Shirah ha-Ivrit* (1922), 9–10; Davidson, Oẓar, 3 (1930), 278, no. 676; Elbogen, Gottesdienst, 80; 143; Krauss, in: *Festschrift… A. Freimann* (1935), 127; G. Scholem, *Jewish Gnosticism* (1965²), 105; Heinemann, in: JJS, 5 (1960), 246ff.; idem, *Ha-Tefillah bi-Tekufat ha-Tanna'im…* (1966²), 173ff.; Liebreich, in: HUCA, 34 (1963), 162, 168; Abrahams, Companion, LXXXVIff.; Baron, Social², 4 (1957²), 138, 307, n. 60; 7 (1958²), 76, 89; Neusner, Babylonia, 2 (1966), 163ff.; J.R. Marcus, *Jew in the Medieval World* (1960³), 95, 116. MUSIC: Idelsohn, in: *Zeitschrift fuer Musikwissenschaft*, 8 (1926), 456ff.; Avenary, in: I. Adler (ed.), *Yuval* (1968), 65–85; W. Apel, *Gregorian Chant* (1958), 417–20; H. Anglés, in: *Journal of the International Folk Music Council*, 16 (1964), 56.

°**ALEKSANDER JAGIELLONCZYK** (1461–1506), grand duke of Lithuania 1492–1501, king of Poland 1501–06. In 1495 Aleksander expelled the Jews from Lithuania. The young prince may also have been indoctrinated by his rabidly anti-Jewish mentor Jan *Dlugosz. Aleksander would also have found it convenient to confiscate the property of the exiles to finance his wars against Russia. When elected king of Poland, however, Aleksander's attitude toward the Jews was more tolerant. In 1503 he allowed the exiled Lithuanian Jews to return. The Polish code, compiled by his chancellor Jan Laski (1506), includes the former grants of privileges accorded to Polish Jewry, but with the preamble that their incorporation is "to protect the citizenry from the Jews."

BIBLIOGRAPHY: Dubnow, Hist Russ, 1 (1916), 4–5; I. Halpern (ed.), *Beit Yisrael be-Folin*, 1 (1948), 14–16. **ADD. BIBLIOGRAPHY:** M. Balaban, *Historia i literatura zydowska*, 2 (1925), 350–53.

[Nathan Michael Gelber]

ALEKSANDRIYA, small town in Rovno district, Volhynia, Ukraine. The Jews settled there before the *Chmielnicki uprising (1648–50) and suffered at the hands of the Cossacks. Few Jews lived there until 1700, when they were obliged to pay a 350-zloty head tax. The community grew rapidly in the 19th century. In 1847 it numbered 728 and in 1897, 2,154 (out of a total population of 3,189). Jews built a sugar refinery, textile factories, and a sawmill, and rented flour mills from Count Lubomirski. The community maintained a school, a club, and a Hebrew library. The Zionist movement was very popular there. The Hebrew Tarbut school founded in 1917 served as a model for most of the towns of Volhynia. The Jewish population numbered 1,700 in 1939. During Soviet rule in 1939–41 all Jewish political parties, organizations, and cultural institutions were closed and the economy was nationalized. The Germans occupied Aleksandriya on June 29, 1941, and in the following days pillaged Jewish property and burned down the synagogues with the help of local peasants. On July 31, 85 Jews were executed. On September 22, 1942 about 1,000 Jews, including women, children, and the aged, were taken to the forest at Swiaty and murdered. Fifty Jews returned to the town after the war but soon left for Palestine.

BIBLIOGRAPHY: *Yalkut Volin*, 1 (1945), 15; 4 (1947), 24; Eisenstein-Keshev, in: *Fun Noentn Over*, 4 (1959), 191–231.

[Shmuel Spector (2nd ed.)]

ALEKSANDRIYA (originally **Becha**), town in Kirovograd district, Ukraine. The first Jews settled in Aleksandriya at the end of the 18th century. In 1864 they numbered 2,474, and in 1897, 3,735 (26% of the total population). In 1910 the community had five synagogues, a *talmud torah* and a communal school, and 11 *ḥadarim* with 230 pupils. The main occupation of the Jews in Aleksandriya was garment manufacturing. In a pogrom on April 23, 1882, Jewish shops and homes were pillaged. On the Day of Atonement of 1904 (September 6), three Jews were killed and several injured in a pogrom. During the civil war of 1919–20, the Jews in Aleksandriya endured great suffering, Aleksandriya being the headquarters of Ataman Grigoryev, leader of the Ukrainian pogrom bands. They were also attacked by Denikin's "White" army. In 1926 the Jewish population in Aleksandriya numbered 4,595 (23% of the total). During the Soviet period most of the Jews worked as artisans in cooperatives. The central Chabad synagogue was still operating in the early 1930s. The Jewish population declined to 1,420 persons in 1939 (total population 19,755). Aleksandriya was occupied by the Germans on August 6, 1941. They murdered 463 males on September 19, and over 300 on August 29. In all, 2,572 were murdered, including Jews from the surrounding area.

BIBLIOGRAPHY: E. Tcherikower, *Di Ukrainer Pogromen in 1919* (1965); B. West, *Naftulei Dor*, 1 (1947), 133–6. **ADD. BIBLIOGRAPHY:** PK Ukrainah, s.v.

[Shmuel Spector (2nd ed.)]

ALEKSANDROW (**Danziger**), influential dynasty of ḥasidic rabbis in Poland active from the second half of the 19th century (see *Ḥasidism). Their "court" was at *Aleksandrow Lodzki (Yid. Alexander), a small town near Lodz. In contrast to the Ḥasidim of Góra-Kalwaria (Yid. Ger), the Aleksandrow Ḥasidim generally did not take part in Jewish party politics in Poland.

The founder of the dynasty, SHRAGA FEIVEL DANZIGER (d. 1849) of Grójec (Yid. Gryce), was rabbi in the small towns of Sierpc, Gąbin, and Maków; Shraga succeeded his *rebbe*, R. Isaac of Warka. His son, JEHIEL, the disciple of Isaac of Warka, settled in Aleksandrow and made it the seat of the "court." Jehiel's son, JERAHMEEL ISRAEL ISAAC (1853–1910), was the outstanding member of the dynasty. He was learned in a wide variety of subjects and had a keen intellect, and was beloved by the Ḥasidim. A natural leader, Jerahmeel would question his followers about their circumstances and advise them accordingly, consoling, encouraging, and reproving. He had a small circle of learned disciples, but also provided moral guidance to all his followers. He wrote *Yismaḥ Yisrael* (1911). Jerahmeel's brother and his successor was SAMUEL ẒEVI (d. 1925). The last rabbi of the line, ISAAC MENAHEM (1880–1943), established a network of Aleksandrow yeshivot in various places. He perished in the concentration camp at *Treblinka. He wrote *Akedat Yiẓḥak* (1953). After the war, JUDAH MOSES TIEHBERG, Jehiel's grandson, head of a yeshivah in Bene-Berak, was declared "Aleksandrow Rabbi." He wrote *Kedushat Yiẓḥak* (1952) on the Aleksandrow dynasty.

BIBLIOGRAPHY: A.H. Zamlung, *Eser Zekhuyyot* (1931), 58f.; I.M. Bromberg, *Admorei Alexander* (1952); Aescoly, in: I. Halpern (ed.), *Beit Yisrael be-Polin*, 2 (1954), 131f.

[Zvi Meir Rabinowitz]

ALEKSANDROW LODZKI, town in central Poland, founded in 1818. The first Jewish residents were under the jurisdiction of the Lutomiersk *kahal*, but an independent community was established in 1830 by Jews who came from Lutomiersk. In 1826 the governor of the Polish Congress Kingdom granted the community a privilege permitting them to reside and acquire property in specified areas of the town. The Jewish population of Aleksandrow Lodzki numbered around 1,000 in the 1850s; 1,673 (27.9% of the total population) in 1879; 3,061 (24.1%) in 1909; and 2,635 (31.9%) in 1921.

Holocaust Period

In 1939 there were 3,500 Jews in Aleksandrow, comprising one-third of the total population. The German army occupied the town on Sept. 7, 1939, and on the following day set the main synagogue afire and forced the Jews to burn the Torah scrolls which were found in private homes. There were several cases of *kiddush ha-Shem* when Jews sacrificed their lives while trying to save the sacred books. Kidnapping of Jews in the streets, open robbery, and the imposition of ever higher ransoms continued until the end of 1939. In this period the famous "court" of the Aleksandrow zaddik (Danziger) was liquidated. All Jews of Aleksandrow were expelled to Glowno (in the Generalgouvernement) on Dec. 27, 1939. Some of them remained there and the others were deported to other towns of the Generalgouvernement. The Jewish cemetery of Aleksandrow was plowed up and turned into a park.

BIBLIOGRAPHY: *Aleksander (al-yad Lodz)* (1968), memorial book in Heb. and Yid.

ALEMÁN, MATEO (1547–c. 1615), Spanish novelist of "New Christian" descent. He studied medicine at Salamanca and Alcalá. Always poverty-stricken, he was several times imprisoned for debt. *Conversos were forbidden to leave Spain, but Alemán secured permission by means of a bribe and arrived in the New World in 1608. Alemán's fame rests on one great work, the *Guzman de Alfarache*, the first part of which was published in 1599, the second in 1604. This is a picaresque novel marked by a skillful fusion of narrative and didactic elements. The picaresque genre was introduced in 1554 with an anonymous work called *La vida de Lazarus de Tormes ....* The bitterness expressed in the novel has been ascribed to its author's position as a Converso, one of whose ancestors was burned in an auto-da-fé, while some have suggested that it may merely reflect Alemán's personal disillusionment. In the novel Alemán contrasts the nobility that has possessions and power with the "ignobility" that lacks lineage and respectability. He died in Mexico.

BIBLIOGRAPHY: A. Valbuena Prat, *La Novela Picaresca Española* (1946²), 46–59. **ADD. BIBLIOGRAPHY:** R. Bjornson, *The Picaresque Hero in European Fiction* (1977), 43–65; C.B. Johnson, *Inside Guzmán de Alfarache* (1978); B. Brancaforte, *Guzmán de Alfarache: Conversión o proceso de degradación?* (1980); M. Cavillac, *Gueux et marchands dans le Guzmán de Alfarache ...* (1983); M. Molho, in: REJ, 144 (1985), 71–80; C. Guillén, in: *El primer siglo de oro ....* (1988), 177–96.

[Kenneth R. Scholberg / Yom Tov Assis (2nd ed.)]

ALEMANNO, JOHANAN BEN ISAAC (1435/8–after 1504), philosopher, kabbalist and biblical exegete. A descendant of an Ashkenazi family expelled from France, his father married an Aragonese Jewess, and the family came to Italy because of his grandfather's (Elijah) mission to the Pope.

Alemanno himself was born in Mantua and was reared in Florence in the house of Jehiel of *Pisa, where he acquired a thorough education in several disciplines, especially philosophy. Later he taught in various cities in Italy. At the age of 35 he settled in Mantua where he was among the guests of Luigi III Gonzaga, and studied with R. Yehudah Messer Leon. In 1488 he returned to Florence, where he again stayed with the family of Jehiel of Pisa until they left Florence in 1497. In the house of this patron Alemanno spent some quiet years and was able to complete the works he had begun and to embark on new ones. The most important of these works are the following:

(1) *Ḥeshek Shelomo*, a philosophical commentary on the Song of Songs, which Alemanno began at the age of 30. In 1488 he read portions of his manuscript to Giovanni *Pico della Mirandola who urged him to complete it. The work, thus far never printed in its entirety, is extant in manuscripts (Bodle-

ian, 1535, British Museum 227, Ms. Moscow-Guensburg). A substantial part of Alemanno's introduction to it was published by Jacob Baruch under the title *Sha'ar ha-Heshek* (Leghorn, 1790) in a very imperfect edition, which was reprinted in Halberstadt (c. 1862) without change. In addition, some fragments of the work were published in various places. The introduction constitutes almost half of the book, and opens with a lengthy section, *Shir ha-Ma'alot li-Shelomo*, glorifying King Solomon, as a philosopher, Kabbalist and magician. Alemanno goes on to discuss the content, character, form, and significance of the Song of Songs. In his opinion, the book in its simple sense treats of earthly love, although allegorically Solomon sought to depict divine love.

(2) *Einei ha-'Edah* an unfinished philosophic-kabbalistic commentary on the Pentateuch still in manuscripts. The general line of thought resembles that of the *Ḥeshek Shelomo*.

(3) *Ḥei ha-Olamim* is Alemanno's chief work, on which he labored from 1470 until 1503. One manuscript is found in the library of the Jewish community of Mantua, and another in the Jewish Theological Seminary (Rab. 1586). The work deals with the problem of how man may attain eternal life and rise to communion with God. The introduction prescribes a twofold method of instruction to be followed by every teacher: for the masses, a simple method readily understandable to all; and for the learned and informed, a logical one calculated to remove doubt. In this work Alemanno makes use of both methods. He introduces two characters, the *Meliẓ Yosher al-Leshono* ("the felicitous interpreter") who presents each subject in succinct and simple words; and the *Dover Emet bi-Levavo* ("one who speaks the truth in his heart") who engages in elaborate proofs. The author charts the career of the ideal man; he describes man's physical life from conception to maturity and indicates the preparations one should undertake at every stage of his life to attain perfection. Then he discusses man's spiritual development through the perfection of his moral and intellectual capacities. The final goal is the attainment of the perfect love of God and union with Him. The work constitutes an encyclopedia of the knowledge of Alemanno's time.

(4) *Likkutim* are various notes and reflections, among them, those of the years 1478 and 1504, which Alemanno had intended to later incorporate into his other work. It is extant in manuscript (Bodleian 2234). The material preserved in this compilation reflects the wide scope of his reading and his acquaintance with philosophical, Kabbalistic, magical and astrological traditions of Spanish extraction, and they serve as the main source of inspiration for his later works.

Alemanno often mentions a work of his entitled *Ha-Me'assef*; perhaps the reference is to the *Likkutim*. (The name *Likkutim* was originally used by Abraham Joseph Solomon Graziano in the 17th century.) Alemanno presumably wrote annotations to the *Ḥai ben Yoktan* by Abu Bakr ibn Tufayl found in manuscript (Munich 59). Another work by Alemanno, *Zeh Kol ha-Adam*, is also occasionally mentioned; it is probably identical with *Ḥai ha-Olamim*. In addition, he probably wrote *Pekah Ko'ah*, which has been lost. The works *Melekhet Muskelet* – a book of magic translated from Greek into Latin and extant only in some Hebrew fragments from the circle of Alemanno – and *Peri Megadim* have been erroneously ascribed to him. Alemanno was well-versed in Greek and Arabic-Jewish philosophy and familiar with the Latin literature of antiquity and the Middle Ages. His erudition and writings were held in such high regard in his day that a scholar such as Pico della Mirandola wished to become his student in Hebrew literature. The hypothesis that Alemanno was the same person as Dattilo or Mithridates, both of whom moved in the circle of Pico della Mirandola, is unfounded. Alemanno's son Isaac was the teacher of Giovanni Francesco, the nephew of Pico della Mirandola. Alemanno influenced a series of Jewish Italian thinkers, more notably R. Isaac de Lattes and R. Abraham Yagel.

Alemanno was well-acquainted with Italian Jewish Kabbalah: mostly Abraham Abulafia's prophetic Kabbalah, and Menahem Recanati's writings, and he was part of a revival of interest in this lore evident among Jews and Christian in the Florentine Renaissance. He conceived magic as a high form of activity, even higher than Kabbalah, and described it as *Ḥokhmah ruḥanit*, "the spiritual lore". He studied a number of Jewish and other type of magical books, like *Sefer ha-Levanah* and a *Sefer Raziel* translated from Latin, and resorted to astro-magic views, under the impact of the tradition of Abraham ibn Ezra and his many commentators in 14th–early 15th century Spain, whose writings he often quotes. This synthesis between Kabbalah and magic is evident also in Pico della Mirandola's thought. The affinities between Alemanno's thought and that of his Florentine Christian contemporaries still waits for detailed investigations. It is possible that Alemanno arrived in Jerusalem in 1522.

BIBLIOGRAPHY: A. Altmann (ed.), *Jewish Medieval and Renaissance Studies* (1967), 190, 328; U. Cassuto, *Gli Ebrei a Firenze…* (1918), 301–17, 403f., 427f., Heb. trans.: *Ha-Yehudim be-Firenzi bi-Tekufat ha-Renaissance* (1967), index, s.v. *Yohanan Alemann*; Perles, in: REJ, 12 (1886), 244–57; H. Pflaum, *Die Idee der Liebe* (1926), 67–70; Reggio, in: *Kerem Hemed*, 2 (1836), 48–53; Vogelstein-Rieger, 2 (1896), 75–77. **ADD. BIBLIOGRAPHY:** M. Idel, "The Anthropology of Yohanan Alemanno: Sources and Influences," in: *Topoi*, 7 (1988), pp. 201–10; idem, "The Study Program of Rabbi Yohanan Alemanno," in: *Tarbiz*, 48 (1979), 303–30 (Heb.); idem, "The Concept of Sefirot as Essence and as Instruments in Kabbalah in the Renaissance," in: *Italia*, 3 (1982), 89–111 (Heb.); idem, "The Magical and Neoplatonic Interpretations of Kabbalah in the Renaissance," in: B.D. Cooperman (ed.), *Jewish Thought in the Sixteenth Century* (1983), 186–242; idem, "Magical Temples and Cities in the Middle Ages and Renaissance: A Passage of Masudi as a Possible Source for Yohanan Alemanno," in: *Jerusalem Studies in Arabic and Islam*, 3 (1981/82), 185–89; idem, "Astral Dreams in R. Yohanan Alemanno's Writings," in: *Accademia*, 1 (1999), 111–28; F. Lelli, *Yohanan Alemanno, Hai ha-Olamim (L'Immortale)* (1995); idem, "L'educazione ebraica nella seconda meta del '400, Poetica e scienze naturale nel '400, Poetica e scienze naturali nel *Hay Ha-'Olamim* di Yohanan Alemanno," *Rinascimento*, 36 (1996), 75–136; A. Lesley, "The 'Song of Solomon's Ascents', Love and Human Perfection according to a Jewish Associate of Giovanni Pico della Mirandola" (doctoral dissertation, Berkeley, 1976); A. Melamed,

"The Hebrew Encyclopedias of the Renaissance," in: *The Medieval Hebrew Encyclopedias of Science and Philosophy* (2000) 441–64; idem, "The Hebrew 'Laudatio' of Yohanan Alemanno in Praise of Lorenzo il Magnifico and the Florentine Constitution," in: *Jews in Italy* (1988) 1–34; idem, "Yohanan Alemanno and the Development of Human Society," in: *World Congress of Jewish Studies*, 8c (1982), 85–93 (Heb.); C. Novak, "Giovanni Pico della Mirandola and Jochanan Alemanno," in: *Journal of the Warburg and Courtauld Institutes*, 45 (1982), 125–47; E. Rosenthal, "Yohanan Alemanno and Occult Science," in: Y. Maeyama and W.G. Saltzer (eds.), *Prismata, Naturwissenschaftsgeschichtliche Studien, Festschrift fuer Willy Hartner* (1977), 349–61.

[Umberto (Moses David) Cassuto / Moshe Idel (2nd ed.)]

ALEPPO (Ar. **Ḥalab**; called by the Jews **Aram-Ẓoba** (**Aram Ẓova**)), second-largest city in Syria and the center of northern Syria. The Hebrew form of Aleppo (Ḥaleb) is, according to a legend quoted by the 12th-century traveler, *Pethahiah of Regensburg, derived from the tradition that Abraham pastured his sheep on the mountain of Aleppo and distributed their milk (*ḥalav*) to the poor on its slopes. According to Jewish tradition, mentioned by Rabbi Abraham Dayyan, the beginning of the community was in the era of Joab ben Ẓeruiah, the conqueror of the city in the time of King David, who also built the great synagogue. There are also other non-Jewish traditions which confirm the existence of the community in the Greek period. It would seem that the establishment of the Jewish community was in this period. Jewish settlement there has continued uninterruptedly since Roman times. The ancient section of the great synagogue was built in the form of a basilica with three stoae during the Byzantine period; an inscription on it dates from 834. The Jews lived in a separate quarter before the Muslim conquest in 636. They lived separately during the Muslim period in the northeastern area of the city. The most ancient synagogue, named Kanisat Mutakal, was built in the fourth century and was located in the Parafara quarter in the northeastern region of the city. It is the oldest Jewish building in the city. During the Muslim period the Jewish quarter was named Mahal al-Yahud. In the Seljuk period the Jewish quarter was spread over a large area of the walled city. On the south it bordered on the market street, on the west the castle, on the east the Dār Al-Bbatih food merchandise area, and on the north the wall and the Jewish gate (Bab al-Yahud). This latter gate was named from the end of the 12th century Bab al-Naṣr (Victory Gate). In the anarchic period (1023–79) it seems that there were also Jews who lived outside the Jewish quarter. A document from the 12th century deals with a Jewish building in the market street. There was also a synagogue located in a new suburb outside the walls.

*Saadiah Gaon was in Aleppo in 921 and it is said that he found Jewish scholars there. In the 11th century learned rabbis led a well-ordered community. R. Baruch b. Isaac was its leader at the end of the 11th century: fragments of his commentary on the *Gemara* as well as responsa have been found in the *genizah*. Apparently the *rosh kehillot* ("head of communities"), i.e., a leader common to the various communities of Jews (such as Babylonians, Palestinians, etc.), represented all Jews before the Muslim authorities. The leader of the community of Aleppo during the years 1015–29 was Jacob ben Joseph, who came to Aleppo from Fustat and served there as *dayyan*. He was also the *dayyan* responsible for the other communities in the region and received the title *rosh kala* from the Babylonian academy. He also had in Aleppo a *bet midrash* and had students from various countries. His successor in the 1030s was Jacob ben Isaac, who served as the *dayyan* of the Aleppo community. He died c. 1036. His successor as *dayyan* was Tamim ben Toviah. His grandson Tamim ben Toviah is known from another document dated 1189. A famous rabbi of the community, Barukh ben Isaac, served as *dayyan* in Aleppo from the 1180s. In the 1190s he headed a *bet midrash* and students gathered there around his son Joseph. Rabbi Barukh gave the proselyte Obadiah, who came to his *bet midrash*, a recommendation to the Jewish communities. Rabbi Barukh was known also as a significant halakhic *posek*, and as a Talmud *parshan*, too, and his commentaries were cited by scholars from Aleppo. He was busy also in public affairs.

The community seems to have had close contacts with Palestine, and heads of Palestinian yeshivot visited Aleppo. In the second half of the 12th century the great yeshivah of Baghdad was in contact with Aleppo. R. Zechariah b. Barachel, a disciple of the *gaon* *Samuel b. Ali of Baghdad, was appointed to head Aleppo's *bet din*. The scholars of Aleppo also exchanged letters with *Maimonides; R. *Joseph b. Aknin, Maimonides' disciple, lived in Aleppo at that time. We identify this scholar with the leader of the community in the 12th century, Joseph b. Judah Ibn Simeon. This scholar was a merchant who traveled to India and other lands and later returned to Aleppo, bought a big estate outside the city, and founded on it a *bet midrash*. He was also the court physician of Al-Malik Al-Tahir. Maimonides wrote that the Jews of Aleppo were very sociable, sat in taverns, and listened to music. In the castle of the city, ancient Jewish tombstones from the years 1148 and 1217–31 survived. With the inclusion of the town in Nūr al-Dīn's (Noureddin) kingdom in 1146, security improved. *Benjamin of Tudela estimated in 1173 the number of Jews in Aleppo as 5,000 (according to the best-preserved manuscript versions, but according to another manuscript the number was only 1,500). Community leaders such as R. Moses Alcostandini, R. Israel, and R. Shet appear in the letters of the Gaon *Samuel ben Ali. After *Saladin's death, Aleppo became the capital of an independent kingdom and until the middle of the 13th century the city enjoyed security and prosperity which the Jews shared. In 1217, Judah *Al-Ḥarizi visited Aleppo and reported that there were several Jewish scholars, physicians, and government officials active there at the time. He noted the names of R. Samuel, who was a scribe in the court, and the physician Eleazar. Among other persons cited by him were R. Azaryahu, a descendant of the exilarch; R Samuel b. Nissim (*ḥakham* Nasnot), who was the head of the local academy; R. Yeshuah; R. Yachun; Shemarya and his sons Muvkhar and Obadiah; R. Joseph, the son of Ḥisdai; R. Samuel, who was the king's scribe; and the physician Hananiah b. Bezalel. Al-

Ḥarizi died in Aleppo in December 1225. A famous scholar who lived in Aleppo during the 13th or 14th century was R. Judah *Al-Madari, who wrote commentaries on the *Gemara*. In 1014 Muslims plundered and destroyed Jewish and Christian houses. The great synagogue was under the authority of the Ereẓ Israel *gaon*, and the small synagogue was under the authority of Babylonian *geonim*. In the *Seljuk period only two synagogues survived in the city. In the *Ayyubid period the Muslim authorities converted synagogues into mosques. In the days of al-Malik al-Tahir the Jewish cemetery and the Jewish gate were destroyed. Muslims used Jewish tombstones to reconstruct the castle. Throughout the Muslim period the Jewish community in Aleppo had considerable autonomy and organized institutions.

The Mongol conquest (1260) led to the slaughter of Jews, but the central synagogue, untouched by the invaders, offered asylum to many. The same year, the Mamluks defeated the Mongols and ruled over Syria until the beginning of the 16th century. Aleppo, their stronghold in northern Syria, contained a large garrison which brought further prosperity to the community. There were several wealthy merchants, officials, craftsmen, and outstanding scholars among the Aleppo Jews. The rich community maintained educational institutions and scholars. The growth of Muslim intolerance under rulers from Cairo and Damascus and the periodical publication of discriminatory laws against non-Muslims had their effect on the life of the community. In 1327, the synagogue was turned into a mosque with the approval of the sultan of Cairo and its name became the Al-Hayyat ("Snake") mosque. In the 13th century a group of *Karaites lived in Aleppo, but they disappeared in the following centuries. The end of the 14th century saw a power struggle between opposing factions of the leaders of the Mamluks and heavy taxes were imposed on the civilian population. In 1400, Tamerlane captured Aleppo with much bloodshed and destruction. Many Jews were killed and enslaved. The community gradually overcame this disaster and in the second half of the 15th century Aleppo Jews again traded with India and scholars resumed their learned activities. In the Mamluk period (1260–1517) the Jews lived in the old quarter and were active as merchants. Between 1375 and 1399 R. David, the son of Joshua, the *nagid* of Egypt, settled in Aleppo. The *nasi* of the community c. 1471 was Joseph b. Zadka b. Yishai b. Yoshiyahu. R. Obadiah of *Bertinoro pointed out in 1488 that the Jews of Aleppo had a good income. According to a census, 233 Jewish families lived there during 1570–90, but the real number was probably higher.

At the beginning of the 16th century exiles from Spain started to arrive in Aleppo, among them outstanding rabbis. They established a separate community although sharing the general institutions with the *musta'arbim* (Orientals). The Jewish population increased markedly; the great synagogue (called, "the Yellow") could no longer accommodate all the congregation and in the second half of the 15th century an additional (eastern) wing was added where the Sephardim prayed. The leaders of the *Musta'arab* congregation were members of the Dayyan family until the 19th century – in the 16th century: Moses and Saadiah Dayyan; in the 17th: Mordecai, Nathan, and Joseph Dayyan; in the 18th: Nathan, Mordecai (d. 1733), Samuel (d. 1722), Joseph, and Mordecai (d. 1774) Dayyan. The communal leader of the *Musta'arab* congregation during the 16th century was the *sheikh al-yahud*. The spiritual and intellectual leadership of the community gradually passed to the Sephardim, and important rabbis include R. Solomon Atartoros in the middle of the 16th century and after him R. Abraham b. Asher of Safed, R. Moses Chalaz, R. Eliezer b. Yoḥai, and R. Moses Halevi Ibn Alkabaz, R. Samuel b. Abraham *Laniado, his son, R. Abraham (who officiated until 1623), and his grandson, R. Solomon. In the 16th century disputes broke out between the *Musta'arab* and the Sephardi congregations, but later the relations between them improved and they lived peacefully. The leader of the community in the beginning of the 18th century was Samuel Rigwan. Other famous rabbis in the 18th century were Joseph Abadi, Samuel Deweik Hacohen (d. 1732), Samuel Pinto (d. 1714), Mordecai Asban, Judah Kazin, Zadka Hutzin, Gabriel Hacohen, Yeshayah Dabah, Michael Harari, David Laniado, Ḥayyim Ataya, Elijah Laniado, Isaac Antibi, Yeshayah Ataya, Ezrz Zaig, and Isaac Beracha. Famous scholars in the city in the same time period were the brothers Joseph (d. 1736) and Yom Tov Safsaya. From the end of the 17th century an academy (yeshivah) operated in Aleppo. In 1730 R. Eliya Silvera founded a Midrash Silvera and the first head of this institution was R. Yeshayah Dabah (d. 1772). R. Samuel Pinto was head of a *bet midrash* in the first half of the 18th century. Many of the above scholars wrote books on rabbinic subjects, most of them printed in Italy. In the 17th century significant Jewish manuscripts from Aleppo were bought in France and Britain. After the Ottoman conquest in 1517, constant contacts were established with the great communities in Constantinople and the other towns in Turkey, as were trade links with them and with Persia and India. Contacts with the Jews of Palestine were also close, and the influence of the Safed kabbalists was marked. Shabbateanism found many adherents in Aleppo, especially R. Solomon Laniado and R. Nathan Dayyan, R. Moses Galante and Daniel Pinto, and after *Shabbetai's apostasy, *Nathan of Gaza went to Aleppo and continued his activities there. In 1684 R. Solomon Laniado wrote a letter as the rabbi of the two congregations.

The traveler Texieira estimated c. 1600 the Jewish population of the city at about 1,000 families, many of them wealthy. According to the census of 1672 there lived in the city 380 Jews who paid the *jizya*, most of them *musta'arabs* and 73 of Spanish origin. In 1695 there were 875 Jewish families. The Jews numbered about 5% of the city's population in the Ottoman period. In 1803 the traveler Taylor estimated that there were only 3,000 Jews in the city.

In 1700, R. Moses b. Raphael Harari of Salonika was rabbi of Aleppo. He died in 1729. At that time, European Jews from France and Italy also settled in Aleppo; they participated in the extensive trade between Persia and southern Europe in which Aleppo served as an important station. These merchants, called *Francos, enjoyed the protection of the consuls of the European powers and this created antagonism in the community. The Francos liberally supported communal institutions, but refused to pay the regular taxes and did not recognize the authority of the community. R. Samuel Laniado II, rabbi of Aleppo in the first half of the 18th century, strongly demanded that the Francos have the same obligations as all other Jews in Aleppo and that all the rules should bind them. In the second half of the 18th century the dispute flared up again when the chief rabbi, Raphael Solomon (b. Samuel) Laniado, tried to compel the Francos to accept the rules of the community and was opposed by R. Judah Kazin, who defended the Francos; the latter, in protest, ceased to take part in public prayers. The dispute had a social background, since the Francos were wealthy and learned and were attached to the ideas and customs they brought from Europe. At the end of the 18th century, with the decline of trade between Aleppo and Persia, the number of Francos dwindled. The prominent families among the Francos included Ergas, Altaretz, Almida, Ancona, Belilius, Lubergon, Lopez, Lucena, Marini, Sithon, Selviera, Sinioro, Faro, Piccotto, Caravaglli, Rodrigez, and Rivero. There were also Jewish translators employed by the European consuls. The Ottoman authorities attempted to extort money from the Jewish translators by putting pressure on the Jewish community. The Jewish community, however, refused to release these translators from paying their share of the communal taxes.

From the 1520s until the mid-17th century, Jews as well as Christians filled the post of *emini gümrük*, that is, the chief officer of the local customs house charged with the collection of receipts. Many Jews died in the plagues which occurred during the Ottoman period. Many scholars in the community created halakhic literature, especially responsa, codes, homiletics, exegesis of the Bible, and liturgy. There were also rabbis who created kabbalistic literature. Many of these scholars settled in Ereẓ Israel.

Between 1841 and 1860 three *blood libels occurred in Aleppo. In June 1853 the Greek-Catholic patriarch accused the Jews of Aleppo of kidnapping a Christian boy for ritual purposes. Despite the tension between Jews and Christians in the city, the Picciotto family helped the latter. Only a few Jewish students studied in the Christian schools. In 1854 the rabbis of Aleppo declared a *ḥerem* (boycott) on any relations with the Protestant missionaries who tried to proselytize Jews. From 1798 until the end of the 19th century several European states appointed European Jews who had settled in Aleppo as their consular representatives. The first was Raphael Picciotto, who was appointed in 1798 consul of Austria and Toscana, and other members of his family were later appointed consuls of other states. Another Raphael Picciotto was consul of Russia and Prussia between 1840 and 1880; the consul of Austria-Toscana was Elijah Picciotto and after his death in 1848 his son Moses inherited this office. The consul of Holland was Daniel Picciotto and of Belgium Hillel Picciotto. The consul of Persia was Joseph Picciotto and of Denmark Moses Picciotto, of Sweden and Norway Joseph Picciotto, and of the U.S. Hillel Picciotto. In the 18th century many local Jews acquired French or British citizenship. Until 1878 the French consul's attitude to Jews was negative, following the policy set by the consul Bertrand during his years in Aleppo (1862–78), but from 1878 the policy was changed by the consul Destree. British consuls protected the Jews of Aleppo throughout the century.

The *ḥakham bashi* in Aleppo was the supreme spiritual authority and from the 1870s there were two chief rabbis. The chief rabbi in 1858–69 was Hayyim Lebton, and after his death Saul Duwek (d. 1874), Mennaseh Sithon (1874–76), and Aaron Sheweika in the year 1880. The later rabbis were Moses Hacohen and Moses Sewid. The Francos established in the 18th century two schools for orphans and poor children. A great yeshivah was active. In 1862 the *vali* imprisoned R. Raphael Kazin, and freed him only under the order not to establish a Reform community in Aleppo. In 1865 a book by R. Elijah b. Amozeg of Leghorn, *Am le-Mikra*, was burned in Aleppo. In 1868 the first Jew was appointed to the *meclis* (city council) of Aleppo. From 1858 on Jews officiated in the mercantile court of law in Aleppo. In 1847, 3,500 Jews lived in the city, and in 1881, 10,200. During most of the Ottoman period Aleppo had the largest Jewish community in Syria. The majority of its Jews belonged to the middle class and were known as diligent merchants and agents. The local government, the European consuls who lived in the city, and the European agents of the trading companies recognized the economic power of Aleppo's Jews. A few Jews also had roles in the administration of the *Vilayet* of Aleppo, for the most part as tax collectors, custom officers, and **sarrafs*, some earning vast amounts from these positions in addition to their own businesses.

In the first half of the 19th century, the status of the community declined both economically and culturally. At the same time hostilities erupted between the various religious communities in Syria. The opening of the Suez Canal in 1869 greatly affected the international trade of the Jewish merchants of Aleppo. In 1875, a blood libel was spread about the Jews of Aleppo; however, the missing Armenian boy, whose absence had provided the charge, was found in a nearby village. In 1869 the *Alliance Israélite Universelle established a school for boys with 68 students from the wealthy families and 15 children from needy families, but most of the latter left the school. In 1873 the school was closed and in 1874 it was reopened. In 1872 the Alliance established a school for girls, with 20–30 students, utilizing European teaching methods. It was closed and reopened a few times and only in the 1890s did it operate at full capacity. In 1865 Abraham Sasson and his sons set up a printing house in Aleppo, one of the sons having learned the craft in Leghorn. In 1887 Isaiah Dayyan established another printing press with the help of H.P. Kohen from Jerusalem. Two years later they had to cease operation, not being able to obtain a government license. The license was obtained in 1896 and printing resumed and continued until World War I. Having learned the craft with Eliezer *Ben-Yehuda in Jerusalem,

Ezra Ḥayyim Jouegati of Damascus set up and operated a press from 1910 to 1933. Another printing press was founded by Ezra Bijo in 1924 and continued until 1925. Altogether, approximately 70 books were printed in Aleppo, mostly works by local scholars, ancient manuscripts found locally, and prayer books of the local rite. From the 1850s immigrants from Aleppo settled in Western cities like Manchester and opened firms there. The immigration of Jews from Aleppo to other countries and to Ereẓ Israel was limited until the 1870s and the majority of the immigrants settled in Egypt, but in the 1880s and 1890s it grew and became a flood as thousands traveled to North and South America. The immigrants wished to improve their socio-economic circumstances. Many Jews from Aleppo emigrated to Beirut as well from the middle of the 19th century until the 1940s. After World War I there were over 6,000 Jews in Aleppo. The wealthy moved from the Jewish quarter, which was surrounded by a wall, to new quarters. However, the link with Jewish culture was not severed; traditional learning was not neglected and a few hundred immigrated to Palestine. In 1931 there were 7,500 Jews in Aleppo, of whom 3,000–3,500 were poor laborers. In particular among the others were merchants and brokers, and some 20 Jews were wealthy and had big firms while five or six were bankers.

There are descriptions from the years 1931 and 1934 of the impoverishment of Aleppo Jewry. Most of the immigrants to Ereẓ Israel were needy. In the 1940s many Jews immigrated through *"illegal" immigration (*Aliyah Bet*). In the year 1944, in the wake of the deteriorating political and economic situation of the community, 510 emigrated from Aleppo to Ereẓ Israel. In 1945 many children and young men immigrated to Ereẓ Israel. The police accused the leader of the community of Aleppo, Rachmo Nechmad, of aiding the secret immigration to Ereẓ Israel. Among the scholars of the first half of the 20th century were R. Ezra Abadi, R. Abraham Salem, R. David Moses Sithon, R. Elijah Lopez, R. Judah Ataya, R. Abraham Isaac Dewik, and R. Isaac Shehibar.

[Eliyahu Ashtor / Leah Bornstein-Makovetsky (2nd ed.)]

In 1947, Aleppo had a Jewish community of about 10,000. In an outbreak of violence against the Jews in December 1947, all the synagogues were destroyed and about 6,000 Jews fled the city. Many of them secretly crossed the frontier into Turkey or Lebanon, where they settled, or continued to Israel, Europe, or America. On December 1, 1947, anti-Jewish riots broke out in the Jewish quarter of Aleppo. About 150 buildings, 50 shops and offices, ten synagogues and five schools were damaged; 160 old Torah scrolls from the Baḥsīta synagogue were burned. The leaders of the community preserved the famous *Keter Aram Ẓova*. Thanks to their efforts most of the scroll arrived in Israel. In November 1947 the Jewish Telegraph Agency reported that 22 Jews from Aleppo had been arrested when they tried to pass the frontier between Lebanon and Israel. There are other reports about many Jews from Aleppo who tried to escape to Israel. The Jews also suffered under the reign of Colonel Adib Shishakli (1949–54). The principal leaders of the community in 1953/1954 were Chief Rabbi Moses Mizrachi, who was 90 years old, R. Zaʿafrani, and Selim Duek. The latter was a wealthy merchant who had relations with the local authorities. According to a report by the president of the Beirut community in 1959, around 2,000 Jews lived in Aleppo then. The 1,000 Jews living in Aleppo in 1968 resided in two quarters: Baḥsīta, the old quarter; and Jamīliyya, founded after World War I. Muslims, who had moved into these quarters after the departure of the Jewish residents, occasionally assaulted their Jewish neighbors and several cases of murder were recorded. The four schools of the Alliance Israélite Universelle were closed by the government in 1950, and thereafter most of the children studied at a religious elementary school (*talmud torah*). As the community dwindled, this school was also closed, and some Jewish children studied at Christian schools. A special prayer-custom, the Aram-Ẓobah rite, existed in Aleppo (its prayer book was printed in Venice, 1523–27). In July 1967 Jewish teachers were dismissed and degrading regulations against the Jews were issued by the government. In that year only 1,500 Jews were living in Aleppo. The Jews of Aleppo in the last generation tried to maintain their Jewish identity. They published lectures by Edmond M. Cohen, which were distributed at great risk in the 1970s and 1980s. This was the last book produced by the remnants of the community.

Aleppo immigrants in Buenos Aires in the 1920s, under the leadership of R. Saul Sithon Dabbah, lived traditionally, as in Aleppo. During the 1930s, integration into the life of Argentina increased and with it came a decline in religious and ethnic identity. This trend reversed itself after one more generation, under the guidance of R. Isaac Shehebar.

[Hayyim J. Cohen / Leah Bornstein-Makovetsky (2nd ed.)]

Musical Tradition

Syrian Jewry and, particularly, the community of Aleppo long enjoyed a reputation as lovers of music and singing. In the course of eight centuries, they developed a characteristic style in their liturgical and related activities. As early as the 13th century, the Spanish Hebrew poet Judah *Al-Ḥarizi, referring to Syrian personalities, mentioned the cantor R. Daniel and said his performance conquered "the hearts of the holy people by his delightful song" (*Taḥkemoni*, 46). From about the same time we have evidence concerning the adoption and singing in Aleppo of the Arabic poetical strophic genre called *muwashshaḥ* (Hebrew *shir ezor*) invented in Andalusia by the beginning of the 10th century. This new genre, soon after its creation, gained great favor and knew wide circulation. One can infer from the question concerning its singing addressed by the Jews of Aleppo to Maimonides that it was already then popular among them and that it probably provoked the dissatisfaction of the rabbinical authorities. Their question was whether the singing of Arabic *muwashshaḥāt* (plur. of *muwashshaḥ*) with instrumental accompaniment was permitted. The question probably implied secular and/or paraliturgical singing.

Almost all the chants and hymns sung outside the formal religious service were the work of distinguished Aleppo rabbis such as Moses Laniado, Raphael Antebi, Jacob and Mordecai Abbadi, and Mordecai Levaton, who were poets as well as composers. Some of them may have modeled themselves on the poet Israel *Najara of Damascus who was highly esteemed by composers of the period. This encouragement of the art of singing by the rabbis found strong support in R. Mordecai Abbadi's introduction to a book of *bakkashot* (Sephardi hymns), *Mikra Kodesh*, published in 1873. The melodic style of Aleppo belongs to the Arabian-Turco-Persian musical family, but also shows other influences, mainly those of Sephardi Jews. Both in prayers and other songs, the **maqām* style (melodic pattern) and elaboration prevail. For each Sabbath or festival prayer there is an appropriate *maqām*, and the various *zemirot* (hymns) also conform to the *maqām* pattern.

The Aleppan musical tradition was instrumental in the evolution of the Sephardi-Jerusalemite style, which currently dominates the entire realm of the liturgical and paraliturgical in many Oriental communities in Israel. It probably started with the singing of *bakkashot* and its fascinating dissemination and wide adoption by many immigrant groups. The establishment of formal cantorial training seminaries in the last decades certainly was determinant in consolidating the style toward which most of the generation of the Israeli-born Oriental cantors inclined.

See also *Bakkashah.

[Amnon Shiloah (2nd ed.)]

BIBLIOGRAPHY: Ashtor, Toledot, 1 (1944), 267ff.; 2 (1951), 16ff., 117ff., 425ff.; Rosanes, Togarmah, 1 (1930), 182; 2 (1938), 146–7; E.N. Adler, *Jews in Many Lands* (1905), 159–68; Lutzki (Dotan), in: *Zion*, 6 (1940/41), 46–79; idem, in: *Sefunot*, 1 (1957), 25–61; A. Yaari, *Ha-Defus ha-Ivri be-Arẓot ha-Mizraḥ*, 1 (1936), 31–52; idem, in: KS, 24 (1947/48), 66–67; *Ha-Rofe ha-Ivri*, 10 (1937), 145–59; 27 (1954), 145–56; 28 (1955), 102–4 (bibliography); Idelsohn, Melodien, 4 (1923), introd.; Katz, in: *Acta Musicologica*, 40, no. 1 (1968), 65–85. **ADD. BIBLIOGRAPHY:** A. Ben-Yaacov, in: *Sefunot*, 9 (1965), 363–82; L.A. Frankl, *Yerushalayma* (1860), 106–21; Alḥarizi, *Taḥkemoni*, ed. by A. Kaminka (1899), index; N.A. Stillman, *The Jews of Arab Lands: A History and Source Book* (1979); A. Yaari, Iggerot, index; Lewis, in: *Studia Islamica*, 50 (1979), 109–24; M.A. Epstein, *The Ottoman Jewish Communities and their Role in the Fifteenth and Sixteenth Centuries* (1980); D. Laniado, *Li-Kedoshim Asher ba-Areẓ, le-Toledot Ḥakhmei ve-Rabbanei Aram Ẓova* (1980); J.M. Landau and M. Maoz, in: *Pe'amim*, 9 (1981), 4–13; T. Philipp and N. Zenner, in: *Pe'amim*, 3 (1979), 45–58; A. Marcus, in: IJMES, 18 (1986), 165–83; A. Shamosh, *Sippuro shel Keter Aram Ẓova* (1987); J. Hacker, in: *Zion*, 52 (1987), 25–44; J. Sutton, *Aleppo Chronicles: The Story of the Unique Sepharadeem of the Ancient Near East in Their Own Words* (1988); B. Masters, *The Origins of Western Economic Dominance in the Middle East: Mercantilism and the Islamic Economy in Aleppo, 1600–1750* (1988); J. Hacker, in: *Galut Aḥar Golah* (1988), 497–516; H. Abrahami, in: *Shorasim ba-Mizraḥ* (1989), 133–72; A. Marcus, *The Middle East on the Eve of Modernity: Aleppo in the Eighteenth Century* (1989); A. Rodrigue, *De L'instruction à l'émancipation* (1989), index; A. Rodrigue, *Ḥinukh, Ḥevrah ve-Historiya* (1991); Z. Zohar, *Massoret u-Temurah, Hitmodedut Ḥakhmei Yisrael be-Miẓrayim u-ve-Suriya im Etgarei ha-Modernizaẓiyah 1880–1920* (1993); Z. Zohar, in: *Pe'amim*, 44 (1990), 80–109; Frenkel, in: *Pe'amim*, 45–46 (1991), 284–70; M. Frenkel, in: *Pe'amim*, 61 (1995), 57–74; H. Talbi, in: *Pe'amim*, 67 (1996), 111–19; W.P. Zenner, in: W. P Zenner (ed.), *Jews among Muslim Communities in the Precolonial Middle East* (1996), 61–172, 173–86; Z. Zohar, in: *Pe'amim*, 66 (1996), 43–69; M. Frenkel, in: *Pe'amim*, 66 (1996), 20–42; E. Schlossberg, in: *Pe'amim*, 66 (1996), 128–37; M. Laskier, in: *Pe'amim*, 66 (1996), 70–127; Y. Harel, in: *Michael*, 14 (1997), 171–86; idem, *Ha-Sifrut ha-Toranit shel Ḥakhmei Aram Ẓova* (1997); M. Gil, *Be-Malkhut Ishma'el bi-Tekufat ha-Geonim*, 1–3 (1997), index; J. Hacker, in: *Zion*, 62 (1997), 327–68; E. Picciotto, *The Consular History of the Picciotto Family* (1998); Y. Harel, in: IJMES, 30 (1998), 77–96; idem, in: *Jewish History*, 13/1 (Spring 1999), 83–101; B. Masters, in: E. Eldem (ed.), *The Ottoman City between East and West* (1999), 17–78; S. Brauner Rodgers, in: *Pe'amim*, 80 (1999), 129–42; R. Lamdan, *A Separate People, Jewish Women in Palestine, Syria and Egypt in the 16th Century* (2000), index; Y. Harel, in: *Jewish Political Studies Review*, 12/3–4 (2000), 13–30; W.P. Zenner, *A Global Community, The Jews from Aleppo Syria* (2000); Y. Harel, *Bi-Sefinot shel Esh la-Ma'arav, Temurot be-Yahadut Surya bi-Tekufat ha-Reformot ha-Otmaniyot 1840–1880* (2003); L. Bornstein-Makovetsky, in: *Jewish Law Association Studies*, 14 (Jerusalem 2002 Conference Volume) (2004), 17–32. MUSIC: M. Kligman, "Modes of Prayer: Arabic *Maqāmāt* in the Sabbath Morning Liturgical Music" (Ph.D. dissertation, New York University, 1997); K. Shelemay, *Let Jasmin Rain Down: Song and Remembrance among Syrian Jews* (1998); K. Yayama, "The Singing of *Bakkashot* of the Aleppo Jewish Tradition in Jerusalem" (Ph.D. dissertation, Hebrew University of Jerusalem, 2003).

ALÈS (or **Alez**; until 1926, **Alais**; אליץ in Hebrew sources), town in Provence, S.E. France. There was a Jewish community there in the Middle Ages. Solomon b. Abraham *Adret refers in a responsum to a custom followed in the communities "between Narbonne and Alais." The text of the oath used by Alès Jewry is mentioned in the *Coutumes d'Alais*, the costumal of Alès, for 1216–92. In the mid-13th century Jacob b. Judah in the *migdal Aloz*, apparently the citadel of Alès, copied the Hebrew translation of Maimonides' Arabic epistle on astrology addressed to the sages of Montpellier. The physician Jacob ha-Levi, who wrote a medical treatise *Makkel Shaked* in 1300 (Bod. Ms. 2142), also lived in Alès. After their expulsion from the kingdom of France in 1306, the Jews of Alès took refuge in Provence and the Comtat Venaissin.

BIBLIOGRAPHY: Gross, Gal Jud., 59–60; G. Saige, *Juifs du Languedoc* (1881), 13, 33, 36, 41, 241.

[Bernhard Blumenkranz]

ALESSANDRIA, town in northern Italy. The first known Jewish settler in Alessandria was Abraham, son of Joseph Vitale de Sacerdoti (Cohen), who opened a loan bank in or about 1490. The subsequent history of the community, to modern times, continued to center around, and to a great degree consisted of, the record of his descendants, later known by the name Vitale. In 1550, it was proposed to expel the Jews from the Duchy of Milan, which since 1535 had been under Spanish rule. Simone (Samuel) Vitale thereupon went to Madrid and secured authorization for two families to reside in the city.

When the Jews were finally expelled from the Duchy of Milan in 1590, he again traveled to Spain and received permission to remain in Alessandria in consideration of the large sum owed him by the government. Thereafter, the community was concentrated around the Vitale family, whose approval had to be obtained by all newcomers before they could settle there. Of the 230 Jews living in Alessandria in 1684, 170 were members of the Vitale family; in 1761, out of 60 households, 36 bore this name. The wealthier members of the community were engaged in the manufacture of textiles and silks; their mills gave employment to many Christians. General conditions remained unchanged when Alessandria passed to the House of Savoy in 1708. The administration of the community remained distinct from that of Piedmont Jewry. The ghetto was established in 1724. In 1761, the Jewish population amounted to 420 persons, the Vitale family having lost the right to approve the newcomers. From the 18th century, the rabbinate became an almost hereditary office held by the family of Levi (de) Veali. The Jews of Alessandria, with the rest of Italian Jewry, enjoyed temporary civic emancipation during the period of French influence in Italy in 1796–1814. Subsequently, there was a sharp reaction. In 1837, Alessandria Jewry was again restricted to the ghetto, although its gates were not renewed. At a wedding celebration in 1835, an overcrowded house in the area collapsed, killing 42 persons, including 17 Christian guests and R. Matassia b. Moses Zacut Levi de Veali. Although from 1848 the Jews of Alessandria enjoyed complete emancipation, many of them were attracted to the larger cities. Between 1900 and 1938, the total of Jewish residents decreased from 868 to 101 according to Mussolini's census.

[Cecil Roth]

Holocaust Period

Starting in 1938, the Jews suffered under the regime's anti-Jewish laws, but the final phase of persecution began only at the end of November 1943, after Minister of the Interior Buffarini Guidi ordered all provincial chiefs to send all Jews to the "appropriate concentration camps." During the night of December 13, supporters of the German-imposed Italian Social Republic attacked the synagogue in the via Milano, destroying or stealing the silver objects. Books and precious manuscripts were burned in a great bonfire in Piazza Rattazzi that same evening. Also in December, 11 Jews from Alessandria were arrested and sent to Fossoli, from where they left for Auschwitz in February 1944; another six were seized by the Germans in the spring of 1944. The roundups continued in two other important old Jewish communities in the province of Alessandria. Twelve people were deported from Acqui, including the entire impoverished family of Arturo Bachi. Eighteen people were deported from Casale. In all, 48 Jews were deported from the entire province of Alessandria.

[Alberto Cavaglion (2nd ed.)]

After the war 168 Jews lived within the community, but their number decreased to 90 by 1969. At the turn of the 20th century Alessandria no longer operated a Jewish community and was under the jurisdiction of the community of Turin, as were all other nonfunctioning communities of Piedmont (Asti, Carmagnola, Cherasco, Cuneo, Mondovì, Saluzzo, and Ivrea).

[Manuela Consonni (2nd ed.)]

BIBLIOGRAPHY: Foa, in: RMI, 23–25 (1957–59); Roth, Italy, index; Milano, Italia, index. **ADD. BIBLIOGRAPHY:** G. Pipino, "La Questione ebraica e i commercianti di Alessandria nella seconda metà del '600'," in: *La Provincia di Alessandria. Rivista dell'amministrazione provinciale* (1991) 97–100; C. Manganelli and B. Mantelli, *Antifascisti, partigiani, ebrei: i deportati alessandrini nei campi di sterminio nazisti, 1943–1945* (1991); M. Dolermo, "Gli ebrei di Acqui tra emancipazione e leggi razziali," in: *Quaderno di storia contemporanea*, 27 (2000), 61–102; A. Villa, *Ebrei in fuga: Chiesa e leggi razziali el Basso Piemonte (1938–1945)* (2004); D. Sorani, "Ebrei in Piemonte, un'assidua presenza," in: *Scritti sull'ebraismo in memoria di Emanuele Menachem Artom* (1996), 304–13; F. Lattes, "Le sinagoghe: frammenti di storie ebraiche in Piemonte," in: *Musei ebraici in Europa* (1998), 103–11; M.D. Anfossi, *Gli Ebrei in Piemonte: loro condizioni giuridico-sociali dal 1430 all'emancipazione* (1914; reprinted 2001); A. Perosino, "La comunità ebraica di Alessandria dal 1842 a oggi, indagine stastica," in: *Rassegna Mensile di Israel* 68 (2002), 43–82; A. Perosino, *Gli ebrei di Alessandria: una storia di 500 anni* (2003); Y. Green, "*Sha'aruriat ha-Kiddushin be-Alessandria (1579)*," in: *Asufot*, 5 (1991), 267–309.

ALEXANDER (c. 36–7 B.C.E.), son of *Herod and *Mariamne. As Herod's heir presumptive, Alexander was educated in Rome with his younger brother Aristobulus from c. 23–17 B.C.E. On his return to Judea he married Glaphyra, the daughter of Archelaus, king of Cappadocia. His arrival aroused the fears of those members of Herod's retinue who had been responsible for the death of Mariamne, for they assumed Alexander would avenge his mother's death. *Salome – who had been chiefly to blame – incited the king against Alexander, insinuating that he and his brother intended to take revenge on him for their mother's death. Influenced by these slanders, Herod recalled *Antipater, his son by his first marriage, to support him. In 12 B.C.E. the king took both princes with him to Italy to arraign them before Augustus on charges of conspiracy. At their meeting in Aquileia, the emperor managed to effect a reconciliation between the father and the sons. However, the intrigues against the princes continued, and relations with their father deteriorated irrevocably. Alexander was put in irons and his life threatened. As a result of the intervention of Archelaus, Herod was pacified and Alexander released. The machinations against him continued, however. This time it was the Spartan Eurycles, a guest at Herod's court, who incited the king against him after accepting a bribe from Antipater. Herod then suspected two men of plotting with Alexander to kill him. Alexander was again imprisoned, to-

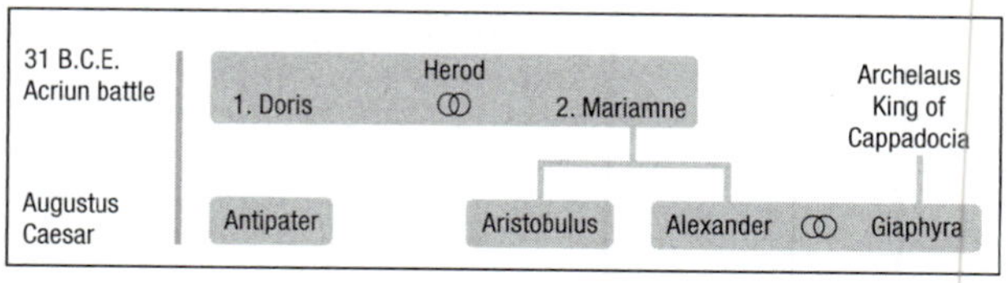

gether with his brother. After Alexander confessed that they wanted to escape to Italy to take refuge from their accusers, Herod again lodged a complaint about his sons' conduct to Augustus. The emperor granted Herod permission to judge them as he saw fit, but advised him to try them in a court composed of Roman well-wishers and officials. The trial took place in Berytus (Beirut). Alexander and his brother were sentenced to death and sent to Caesarea. There a commander of the garrison, Tiro, a veteran in Herod's service, attempted to gain them a reprieve. His plea that if the executions took place riots would erupt only served to incense Herod further. Tiro was put to death together with other friends of Alexander. The two brothers were brought to Sebaste (Samaria) where they were executed by strangling.

BIBLIOGRAPHY: Jos., Ant., 15:342; 16:78–129, 189 ff., 230 ff., 244 ff., 301 ff., 356 ff.; Klausner, Bayit Sheni, 4 (1950[2]), 153 ff.; A. Schalit, *Hordos ha-Melekh* (1964[3]), 286 ff.; Schuerer, Gesch, 1 (1901[4]), 369 ff., 407 ff.; Graetz, Hist, 2 (1893), 112–3.

[Abraham Schalit]

°**ALEXANDER**, name of seven popes. The following are the most significant for Jewish history:

ALEXANDER II, reigned 1061–73, consistently followed the policy set by Pope *Gregory the Great at the end of the sixth century of applying suasion rather than force to convert Jews. When the Christian reconquest of the Iberian peninsula began in earnest, he urged the bishops of Spain to continue defending the Jews against attack by native and foreign soldiers, especially the unruly bands of French knights who had joined the Christian armies against the Muslims. He wrote in the same vein to Berengar, viscount of Narbonne, and to Wifred, its bishop, in 1063. In 1065 Alexander issued a strong warning to the prince of Benevento, in southern Italy, who was using force to convert the Jews.

ALEXANDER III, reigned 1159–81, reissued the *bull *Sicut Judaeis* protecting Jews against physical injury and interference with their religious rites. He objected when the Jews in Bourges, France, erected a synagogue which was not only new, but also higher than a neighboring church. The Third Lateran Council, which met in 1179, prohibited Christians from serving in Jewish homes; urged the secular authorities not to confiscate the property of converts from Judaism lest, being impoverished, they reverted to their former faith; and requested the civil courts to admit the testimony of Christians in lawsuits involving Jews. The pope also objected to Jews having the right to cite a cleric before a secular court. Because of prevailing conditions in Europe, most of these restrictive measures were not enforced for a long time, but they eventually found their way into the *Corpus Iuris Canonici* of 1580, the official collection of church law. The possibility that the pope would urge the council to force the Jews to wear a distinguishing *badge was averted, perhaps through the influence of Jehiel, grandson of *Nathan b. Jehiel, the compiler of the *Arukh*, who held a high post in the papal household.

ALEXANDER IV, reigned 1254–61, reissued the bull *Sicut Judaeis* in 1255. During the bitter struggle of the papacy against the imperial Hohenstaufen family, he granted letters of protection to a number of Roman Jewish army suppliers, exempting them from having to pay extra tolls on the roads. That this did not represent a generally favorable attitude is evident from his other pronouncements. Alexander IV insistently enforced the wearing of the distinguishing Jewish badge and the confiscation of the Talmud. The pope commended Louis IX of France and Count Thibaut of Champagne (who was also king of Navarre) for having taken away from the Jews sums which had presumably been gained through usury. He granted them the right to use such money for "pious purposes" (1258). In a letter addressed to several churchmen, the pope expressed horror that certain clerics had left church articles with the Jews as pledges for their debts.

ALEXANDER V, reigned 1409–10, was elected by the Council of Pisa in a vain effort to end the schism within the church. He shared the superstitions of his day, blaming the division within the church on bad Christians and on Jewish magicians. The Jews, he asserted, corrupted the world by consulting the Talmud and practicing usury.

ALEXANDER VI (BORGIA), reigned 1492–1503, displayed an ambivalent attitude toward the Jews. Where personal gain or the exigencies of diplomacy made it desirable, he was harsh; but where he was free to use his good sense, he showed understanding and humanity. After the expulsion of the Jews from Spain and Portugal, he permitted *Marranos to continue residing in the environs of Rome. When, however, King Ferdinand of *Spain protested, alleging that the pope's leniency encouraged their flight from Spain, Alexander compelled the refugees publicly to reaffirm their Christian loyalty. Even so, he appears to have profited financially from his refusal to take more extreme measures. While the pope reduced the size, and therefore the prominence, of the distinguishing Jewish badge, he lengthened the distance of the disgraceful annual races in Rome in which Jewish participants had to run naked, so as to be able to watch them from his residence at Castle St. Angelo. He imposed on the Jews an additional tribute of 5% for three years, to help defray the expenses of the Turkish War. Alexander treated favorably the Jews he employed as his personal physicians; one of these Bonet *Lattes, dedicated to him his book on astronomy.

ALEXANDER VII, reigned 1651–67. His policy toward the Jews was primarily motivated by zeal for making converts. Though he did not apply force, he frequently applied indirect compulsion. Residence in the ghetto was strictly regulated, and the entire Jewish community was held responsible for the rental of an apartment vacated by a convert or through the death of its occupant in the recent plague, for Jews were not permitted to own property even within the ghetto (1658). Christian contact with Jews was assiduously discouraged. In 1659 Jews were prohibited from teaching or learning under Christians. To be the servant of a Jew was a punishable offense.

The one improvement in the Jewish situation under Alexander VII was the abolition, in the last year of his papacy, of the shameful annual races (cf. Alexander VI).

BIBLIOGRAPHY: Vogelstein-Rieger, index (incl. bibl.); E. Rodocanachi, *Le Saint-Siège et les Juifs* (1891); S. Grayzel, *Church and the Jews* (1966), index; E.A. Synan, *Popes and Jews in the Middle Ages* (1965).

[Solomon Grayzel]

°**ALEXANDER**, name of three Russian czars.

ALEXANDER I, czar of Russia 1801–25. Alexander I's character and actions were to a large extent shaped by the vicissitudes he experienced in his struggle against *Napoleon. His ties with Metternich and the Holy Alliance were a result of his reaction against the spirit of the French Revolution; Alexander activated and joined the Alliance as "the gendarme of Europe" after Napoleon's downfall. When Alexander ascended the throne, Russian policy toward the large Jewish population living in former Polish territory, constituting the so-called Jewish question, had already been under active consideration for some time in government circles. In November 1802 Alexander appointed a committee to consider all aspects of the Jewish question in Russia. Some of its members were his personal friends and, like Alexander at that stage, harbored liberal ideas. The committee's report was approved by Alexander and promulgated in 1804 as the Jewish Statute. It was the first comprehensive piece of Russian legislation to deal with Jewish affairs. The statute, as well as subsequent legislative and administrative measures concerning the Jews taken during Alexander's reign, was based upon the assumption that the Jews were a parasitic element, an undesired legacy bequeathed by the defunct Polish state. The policy underlying the statute, therefore, was that the Jews must be directed toward employment in productive occupations, such as agriculture and industry. On the other hand the native population, especially the peasants in areas that had formerly belonged to Poland, had to be protected from alleged Jewish exploitation and influence. At the same time measures should be taken to raise the Jews from what was considered their debased cultural condition by encouraging secular education and *assimilation into the Russian Christian social and cultural environment. A program of repression and restrictions was therefore embodied in the statute, which imposed limitations on Jewish residence, occupations, and land tenure. The full brunt of the legislation was partially averted during the Napoleonic Wars, when the Russian government was concerned that the Jewish population might be driven to help the French, but the measures were resumed with even greater force after the war. The efforts of the English missionary Lewis *Way to induce Alexander to grant the Jews emancipation had no practical results. Alexander, at this time inclining to pietism and mysticism, initiated a policy intended to promote the conversion of the Jews to Christianity. In 1817 a "Society of Israelitic Christians" was founded and placed under the czar's personal patronage.

ALEXANDER II, czar of Russia 1855–81. Developments in Russia under Alexander II and the measures he adopted were a result of the harsh legacy of the reign of his father *Nicholas I, the aftermath of the Crimean War, and his attitude toward the rising revolutionary movement in Russia. Alexander's accession raised great expectations among the Jewish as well as the Russian population. The Jews hoped for a change in the oppressive policies pursued by Nicholas I. The abolition in 1856 of the special system of recruiting Jews for the army (see *Cantonists) appeared as a good omen. Alexander, however, was firmly opposed to the abolition of the Pale of *Settlement restricting Jewish residence. The basic Russian policy toward the Jews, which aimed to "reeducate" them and make them "useful members" of the state (see Alexander I), underwent no change during his reign. Alexander II, however, attempted to promote their "improvement," and ultimate "fusion" with the Russian people, by extending the rights of certain groups within the Jewish population. These, by virtue of either their economic situation or education, were considered free of "Jewish fanaticism." His policy was also dictated by the demands of the Russian economy which could utilize Jewish capital and skill for its development. Alexander accordingly approved certain reforms to alleviate conditions for the Jews. In particular, the restrictions applying to rights of residence and entry into government service were eased for merchants of "the first guild" (i.e., wealthy merchants), university graduates, and artisans. All these partial and limited concessions were kept within the bounds personally prescribed by Alexander. In the last decade of his reign, when revolutionary tension mounted, the anti-Jewish oppressive policy again intensified. Nevertheless, Alexander was remembered by the Jews as a friendly and enlightened ruler. His assassination on March 13, 1881, brought this relatively liberal interlude to an end and initiated a period of violent reaction.

ALEXANDER III, czar of Russia 1881–94. The reign of Alexander III was dominated by the rising tide of the revolutionary movement in Russia, in which Jewish youth took an increasing part. Ascending the throne after his father Alexander II's assassination, Alexander III was determined to suppress all liberal tendencies and maintain an autocracy. The czar's teacher, Konstantin *Pobedonostsev, procurator-general of the Holy Synod (the supreme authority of the Russian Orthodox Church), a fanatic reactionary, became the most powerful figure in the state. The first organized *pogrom against Jews was perpetrated in Yelizavetgrad (today *Kirovograd), in southern Russia, in April 1881. It was followed by a series of similar outbreaks of anti-Jewish violence in the course of 1881–84. Alexander and his government accepted the theory that the pogroms stemmed from the inherent hatred of the indigenous population for the Jews because of their "economic domination." This led to the conclusion that the indigenous population must be shielded "against the harmful activity of the Jews."

The "Temporary Regulations" of May 3, 1882 (see *May Laws) followed. These prohibited Jews from resettling in the villages or from holding real estate outside the urban areas, and authorized the village communities to oust the Jews already settled among them. These measures were succeeded by partial expulsions of "illegal" Jewish settlers from the interior of Russia, and in 1891 by the eviction of about one-half of the Jewish population from Moscow. Admission of the Jews to the bar was temporarily halted in 1889, and their participation in local government was curbed in 1892. A *numerus clausus*, restricting the proportion of Jews allowed to enter secondary schools and universities to between 3% and 10% of the admission total, was imposed in 1887. This policy was adopted by Alexander in the face of the majority report of the governmental commission under the chairmanship of Count Pahlen, sitting between 1883 and 1888, which was opposed to a regressive policy and counseled "a graduated system of emancipatory and equalizing laws." Alexander was ready to support the planned Jewish emigration from Russia suggested to the Russian government by Baron Maurice de *Hirsch.

BIBLIOGRAPHY: Gessen, in: YE, 1 (c. 1910), 797–839; idem, *Istoriya Yevreyskogo Naroda v Rossii*, 1 (1925/26), 138–239; Dubnow, Hist Russ, 1 (1916), 335–413; 2 (1918), 154ff.; I. Levitats, *Jewish Community in Russia, 1772–1844* (1943); L. Greenberg, *Jews in Russia*, 2 vols. (1944–51), index; Weinryb, in: L. Finkelstein (ed.), *Jews, Their History, Culture and Religion*, 1 (1960³), 321–75 (incl. bibl.); Klausner, in: *He-Awar*, 7 (1960), 91–122; B-Z. Dinur, *ibid.*, 10 (1963), 5–82.

ALEXANDER, English family of printers.

ALEXANDER ALEXANDER (d. 1807?), pioneer of the Hebrew press in London with Benedict Meyers (Hebrew: Jost) of Halberstadt. In 1770 Alexander and Meyers produced an edition of the Ashkenazi prayer book with English translation; the list of subscribers included many non-Jews. This was followed by a *Haggadah* in two editions, Sephardi and Ashkenazi. Originally Alexander did not do the actual printing himself. He produced many liturgical works, including the complete liturgy according to the Sephardi and Ashkenazi rites with slovenly executed English translations (1773), as well as a Pentateuch with translation (1785). In 1772 he began to issue a series of annual pocket calendars. His son LEVY (JUDAH LEIB; 1754–1853) also printed Hebrew and English works for many years, reproducing several of his father's editions. Failing to secure for one of these the patronage of Chief Rabbi Solomon *Hirschel, he published a number of scurrilous attacks on him ("The Axe laid to the root, or, Ignorance and Superstition evident in the character of the Rev. S. Hirschel," 1808; "A Critique of the Hebrew Thanksgiving prayers … on Thursday the 7th of July … With an anecdote of the humorous sermon delivered by the High Priest the Rev. Solomon Hirschel… for the occasion," 1814). He continued the attack on the wrappings of his edition of the festival prayers issued in parts from 1808–15. His own writings include a reply to the proposals of J. *Van Oven on the problem of the Jewish poor (1802), and an English grammar in rhyme (1833). His *Memoirs of the Life and Commercial Connections of the Late Benjamin Goldsmid of Roehampton* (1808) contains piquant details of contemporary Jewish life in London.

BIBLIOGRAPHY: C. Roth, *History of the Great Synagogue* (1950), 147, 186–7; Roth, Mag Bibl, index. **ADD. BIBLIOGRAPHY:** D.S. Katz, *The Jews in the History of England, 1485–1850* (1994), 280, 302; T.M. Endelman, *The Jews of Georgian England, 1714–1830* (1999), 190–91, 234–35.

[Cecil Roth]

ALEXANDER, ABRAHAM (**Senior**; 1743–1816), Revolutionary War officer, U.S. Custom House auditor, and *ḥazzan* of Charleston's Beth Elohim Congregation (1764–84). Born and educated in London, Alexander, the son of Joseph Raphael Alexander, immigrated to Charleston, South Carolina, before the American Revolution. He served for many years as a volunteer lay minister (known then as *ḥazzan*). A Hebrew scholar and scribe, he wrote, in his own hand, a prayer book for the High Holy Days "according to the custom of the Sephardim" (1805). During the Revolution, when Charleston fell to the British in 1780, he surrendered at first, along with the rest of the population, but soon afterward left the city to join patriot forces in the backcountry. After he was commissioned a lieutenant of the dragoons, his regiment's guerilla fighting helped drive the British from the Carolinas. Alexander, a widower, in 1784 married Ann Sarah Huguenin Irby, a widow of French Huguenot affiliation. Intermarriage was unusual for the times, especially since he was a strict adherent to Orthodox Judaism. Yet before their marriage she became a devout Jewess, one of the earliest converts of American Jewish history; apparently, however, he resigned his position as *ḥazzan* of the congregation. Alexander entered the service of the new federal government at Charleston's U.S. Custom House, as clerk in 1802 and then as auditor until his retirement in 1813. An active Mason, he is notable in Masonic history as one of 11 founders and the first secretary-general of the Supreme Council, 33rd Degree, Scottish Rite Masonry ("mother council of the world"), which was founded in Charleston in 1801.

BIBLIOGRAPHY: H.A. Alexander, *Notes on the Alexander Family of South Carolina* (1954); C. Reznikoff and U.Z. Engelman, *Jews of Charleston* (1950), index; R.B. Harris, *History of the Supreme Council, 33rd Degree, Ancient and Accepted Scottish Rite of Freemasonry, Southern Jurisdiction, U.S.A. 1801–1861* (1964), 45–48.

[Thomas J. Tobias]

ALEXANDER, BEATRICE (1895–1990), founder of the Madame Alexander Doll Company and one of the best-known U.S. female entrepreneurs. Alexander was born in Brooklyn, N.Y., to Hannah Pepper, a widow. When Beatrice was a toddler, her mother married another Russian immigrant, Maurice Alexander; the couple went on to have three more daughters. Beatrice always considered Alexander, who established the first doll hospital in the United States, as her real father. She learned the craft of dollmaking in her father's shop where she observed both the fragility of the china dolls of that era and their importance to children. The contrast between the wealth of many of Maurice's customers and the poverty of the neighborhood made a deep impression on her and she became determined to achieve a better future. Alexander's early surroundings also accustomed her to seeing women contributing to the family economy; her mother worked with her husband in his shop, as well as having full responsibility for the home. In 1915, a few weeks after serving as high school valedictorian, Alexander married Philip Behrman, who later joined her in managing the Madame Alexander Doll Company. The couple had one daughter, Mildred, who grew up in the business, as did her son, William Alexander Birnbaum, company president until 1994.

"Madame Alexander" began her career during World War I when the decrease in imported dolls from Europe created a shortage. Her first project was the "Red Cross Nurse" rag doll. In the 1920s she formally created one of the largest doll manufacturing companies in the United States. The Madame Alexander Doll Company has created more than 5,000 different dolls, often based on literary figures and Disney characters, as well as real people. Madame Alexander dolls, known for their high quality and artistry, are on permanent display at a number of museums worldwide and have received numerous awards. In 1986, Beatrice Alexander was honored with the Doll of the Year Lifetime Achievement Award.

Alexander, who began to withdraw from the business in the 1970s, was a well-known philanthropist, supporting American and Zionist causes. A trustee of the Women's League for Israel, Alexander gave particular support to projects benefiting children.

BIBLIOGRAPHY: J. Altman, "Alexander, Beatrice," in: P.E. Hyman and D. Dash Moore (eds.), *Jewish Women in America*, 1 (1997), 34–35; Jewish Women's Archive, "JWA – Beatrice Alexander," at www.jwa.org.

[Judith R. Baskin (2nd ed.)]

ALEXANDER, BERNARD (1872–1935), South African lawyer and communal worker. Born in the province of Poznan (Poland), Alexander went to South Africa as a child. In 1903 he helped to establish the Jewish Board of Deputies of the Transvaal and Natal; he was its president when, in 1912, the South African Jewish Board of Deputies was founded, with the Transvaal Board as one of its constituents. He became vice president and from 1916 to 1927 was president of the South African Board. Alexander took a leading part in congregational activities and Jewish institutions in Johannesburg. During his chairmanship of the Jewish War Victims' Fund (1915–25), it raised more than £500,000 for Jewish war relief. Alexander was a member of the Johannesburg City Council and served on civic and educational bodies. As solicitor to the Paramount Chief of Swaziland, he headed (1929) a mission to the British government on behalf of its people.

BIBLIOGRAPHY: G. Saron and L. Hotz, *Jews in South Africa* (1955), index; *The South African Jewish Year Book* (1929), 295.

[Louis Hotz]

ALEXANDER, FRANZ (1891–1964), U.S. psychoanalyst, criminologist, and author. Alexander was born in Budapest and studied medicine there. During World War I, he served in the Austro-Hungarian Army at a bacteriological field laboratory. After the war he did postgraduate work at the psychiatric hospital of the University of Berlin. With the establishment of Berlin's Institute for Psychoanalysis in 1921, he became its first student and stayed on there for ten years as clinical associate and lecturer. During that period he formulated his ideas for his first book: *Die Psychoanalyse der Gesamtpersoenlichkeit* (1927). Early in his career as a psychiatrist Alexander became convinced that the vital approach of psychoanalysis should be the exploration of the human mind to lead men and women to more constructive and satisfying fulfillment in their lives. His research provided much understanding about "psychosomatic specificity" tracing such psychosomatic symptoms as peptic ulcer to their origin in childhood neurotic conflict, and "dream pairs" showing how dreams occur in complementary pairs to produce wish fulfillment. Alexander also made many attempts to shorten therapy through use of the patient's transference relationship with his or her therapist. His famous work *Der Verbrecher und seine Richter* (1929; *The Criminal, the Judge and the Public*, 1931), written with H. Staub, a lawyer, led to an invitation to teach at the University of Chicago. Here he established the world's first university chair in psychoanalysis. From 1931 to 1932, Alexander was research associate in criminology at the Judge Baker Foundation in Boston. He incorporated his findings in his book, *The Roots of Crime* (1935), written with William Healy. In 1932 he established and became director of the Chicago Institute for Psychoanalysis. From 1938 to 1956 he was also professor of psychiatry at the University of Illinois. In 1956 he was appointed head of the new psychiatric department of Mt. Sinai Hospital in Los Angeles and professor of psychiatry at the University of Southern California. Among the many high posts he occupied were president of the American Psychoanalytical Association, president of the American Society for Research in Psychosomatic Medicine, and president of the Academy of Psychoanalysis. He was one of the founding editors of the professional journal *Psychosomatic Medicine* (1939). His other books include *The Western Mind in Transition* (1960); *The Scope of Psychoanalysis* (1961); and *Psychosomatic Specificity* (1968).

BIBLIOGRAPHY: Pollock, in: *Archives of General Psychiatry*, 11 (1964), 229–34.

[Zvi Hermon]

ALEXANDER, HAIM (**Heinz**; 1915–), composer and pianist. Alexander was born in Berlin. In 1936, following the ascent of the Nazis to power, he settled in Jerusalem and studied with Stefan Wolpe and Joseph *Tal at the Palestine Conservatory. He was one of the founders of the Academy of Music in Jerusalem (later the Rubin Academy), where he was professor until his retirement. He also lectured at the musicology department of the Hebrew University of Jerusalem, at the

University of Pennsylvania, at the Jacques Dalcroze Institute, Geneva, and at NYU. A versatile musician and superb improviser, he taught piano, harpsichord, improvisation, theory, and composition. Like all other Jewish composers who emigrated from Central Europe in the 1930s, Alexander established his own personal response to the dialectics of the ideological pressure of the Zionist vision of the East and the internal pressure to retain and absorb the great European heritage. He was always alert and open to new ideas and influences. In the 1950s Alexander attended avant-garde seminars in Darmstadt and added the serial technique to his rich vocabulary, such as in *Patterns* (1965) for piano, while still retaining his penchant for lyrical, tuneful writing in the *Nature Songs* (1988). In 1971 Alexander undertook a large-scale project of transcribing traditional songs kept at the Jerusalem Sound Archives, many of which he later arranged for various ensembles. He published a textbook *Improvisation Am Clavier,* with two cassettes (Schott, 1987). His large output includes many choral works, songs for voice and chamber ensembles such as the cycle *Ba-Olam* ("In the World,"1976), orchestral works such as the Piano Concerto, chamber works, and many compositions for piano.

BIBLIOGRAPHY: Grove online.

[Jehoash Hirshberg (2nd ed.)]

ALEXANDER, JASON (1959–), U.S. actor and entertainer. Born in Newark, N.J., as Jay Scott Greenspan, Alexander starred in 180 episodes, over nine years, of the wildly popular situation comedy *Seinfeld,* starring Jerry *Seinfeld. Alexander portrayed the hapless George Costanza, a "schlepp" partly based on the show's co-creator, Larry *David. Costanza, neurotic, devious, and unscrupulous, was one of the more memorable characters in television series history.

Although he was short, chubby and began to grow bald at an early age, Alexander had such a commanding stage presence that he was invariably cast as the star in school plays, in roles ranging from romantic leads to elderly character parts. He won a scholarship to Boston University's drama department and at 20 was cast in the Stephen *Sondheim Broadway musical *Merrily We Roll Along,* but the show closed shortly after it opened. Alexander left college soon thereafter to pursue his acting career. He got his first film role in *The Burning,* produced by Harvey *Weinstein, in 1981 and three years later he played four roles in the Broadway musical *The Rink.* He created the role of Stanley Jerome in Neil *Simon's semi-autobiographical play *Broadway Bound* and then took on a starring role in *Jerome Robbins' Broadway,* for which he won the Tony, Drama Desk, and Outer Circle Critics awards as best actor in a musical.

Alexander's voice appeared in a number of animated features, including *Aladdin, The Return to Jafar,* and *The Hunchback of Notre Dame.* In 1997 he played an AIDS-afflicted drag queen who finds romance in the movie *Love! Valour! Compassion!* He also got a lead role in the Los Angeles stage version of *The Producers.*

After *Seinfeld,* for which he won six Emmy nominations, four Golden Globe nominations, and other honors, Alexander starred as a self-help guru in a television series, *Bob Patterson,* but it was quickly canceled. In 2004 he starred in another situation comedy, *Listen-Up,* based on the life of a sportswriter. He also made a quick, highly publicized trip to Israel to air his views about the Israeli-Palestinian conflict.

[Stewart Kampel (2nd ed.)]

ALEXANDER, KOBI (1952–), Israeli high-tech entrepreneur. Alexander was born in Tel Aviv. He served as an intelligence officer in the army. In 1977 he graduated in economics from the Hebrew University of Jerusalem and in 1980 he received an M.B.A. degree from New York University. In 1980–81 he worked as an economic consultant for several international corporations. In 1982 he and his two partners, Boaz Misholi and Yehiam Yemini, established Efrat Future Technology Inc. in 1984, after the development of the firm's first product, Tadiran joined the partnership and later on a group of American investors joined as well. In 1986 Comverse USA was established, the mother company of Efrat. In 1987 Efrat took big losses, its stock failed, and Yemini retired. In 1988 Alexander moved to New York and succeeded in stabilizing the firm and bringing it back to profitability. Efrat employed 1,500 workers with a turnover of $300 million dollars a year and is a leading firm in the field of software and systems enabling network-based multimedia enhanced communication services. Alexander is the chairman, president, and CEO of Efrat. In 1997 Comverse and Boston Technologies were merged, and Alexander became the head of a firm with revenues of over $1 billion a year He also served as a director of the venture fund established by Comverse and George Soros.

[Dan Gerstenfeld (2nd ed.)]

ALEXANDER, MICHAEL SOLOMON (1799–1845), the first Anglican bishop in Jerusalem. After an Orthodox Jewish upbringing, in 1820 Alexander left his native Germany for England, where as Michael Solomon Pollack he served as *ḥazzan* and *shoḥet* to the small communities in Norwich (1820–21), Nottingham (1821–23), and Plymouth (1823–25). Coming into contact with Christian missionaries, he was converted to Christianity in 1825. Alexander then moved to Dublin, where he taught Hebrew, was ordained, and where, in 1827, he was appointed to a curacy. Later he was sent as a missionary to Danzig by the London Society for the Promotion of Christianity among the Jews. In 1830 he returned to London in the service of the society. From 1832 to 1841 he was professor of Hebrew and rabbinics at King's College, London. He collaborated with Alexander McCaul in Hebrew translations of the New Testament and the Anglican liturgy. In August 1840 he, with other converts, signed a protest against the *Damascus blood libel. When, on the withdrawal of *Muhammad Ali from Palestine, it was decided to establish an Anglican and Lutheran bishopric in Jerusalem under the auspices of Great

Britain and Prussia, with missionary as well as political objectives, Alexander was appointed the first incumbent (November 1841). Although the British consul, on the instructions of the Foreign Office, did not support his missionary activities, Alexander zealously carried out the duties of his office as he conceived them, visiting Egypt, Syria, Iraq, and Abyssinia, which were included in his diocese. He died while on one of his visits to Egypt; his body was brought back to Jerusalem where he was buried in the Christian cemetery on Mt. Zion. His tombstone bears a long inscription in Hebrew, English, Greek, and German. His published works include *The Hope of Israel*, a lecture (1831); *The Glory of Mount Zion*, a sermon (1839); and *The Flower Fadeth* and *Memoir of Sarah Jane Isabella Wolff… eldest daughter of… M.S. Alexander* (1841).

BIBLIOGRAPHY: M.W.M. Corey, *From Rabbi to Bishop: The Biography of… M.S. Alexander…* (1956); A. Finn, *Reminiscences of Mrs. Finn* (1929), passim; H.J. Schonfield, *History of Jewish Christianity…* (1936), 216–19; A.M. Hyamson, *British Consulate in Jerusalem in Relation to the Jews of Palestine 1838–1861*, 1 (1939), 46–63; *Handbook of the Anglican Bishopric in Jerusalem and the East* (1941), 3–7.

[Cecil Roth]

ALEXANDER, MORRIS (1877–1946), South African lawyer and politician. Alexander went to South Africa from East Prussia as a child. He practiced law in Cape Town and soon became involved in politics and in Jewish communal affairs. He played a leading part in the formation of the Cape Jewish Board of Deputies (1904) and was its president and most active figure until its merger with the South African Board of Deputies (1912), thereafter serving as vice president of the United South African Board and chairman of its Cape Committee until 1933. As a Jewish spokesman in matters of immigration and naturalization, Alexander was largely instrumental in having Yiddish recognized as a European language in the immigrant's literacy test (1906). He was elected to Parliament in 1908 and for 35 years was known as a champion of the Indian and Colored communities against discriminatory laws. He was an active Zionist and was a lay preacher to the Cape Town New Congregation. His first wife, Ruth, was the daughter of Solomon *Schechter. His second wife, Enid, wrote his biography *Morris Alexander* (1957). The large collection of Alexander's papers – documents covering his entire life – are housed in the University of Cape Town.

BIBLIOGRAPHY: G. Saron and L. Hotz, *Jews in South Africa* (1955), index; G. Saron, *Morris Alexander* (1966).

ALEXANDER, MOSES (1853–1932), first Jewish governor of an American state. Alexander, who was born in Obrigheim, Germany, immigrated to America in 1867. He became mayor of Chillicothe, Missouri (1887), and moved to Idaho around 1891. A successful businessman, he was elected mayor of Boise in 1897 and served two terms. As the Democratic governor of Idaho, serving for two terms (1915–19), Alexander achieved great popularity in his own state and elsewhere, earning a reputation for wit, eloquence, and progressivism. He secured legislation on behalf of workmen's compensation, the state highway system, irrigation, reclamation and waterway systems, and prohibition. He also rallied Idaho around Woodrow Wilson's call to enter World War I, and he supported the women's suffrage movement.

He helped organize and lead the first synagogue in Idaho. The town of Alexander, Idaho, is named for him.

To commemorate his achievements, the Idaho State Historical Society in Boise installed the Moses Alexander Collection to highlight this American success story. The exhibition's 80 cubic feet of material, dating from 1876 to 1987, sheds light on the role Alexander played in shaping Idaho's business, political, and religious communities. The collection includes original and carbon copy correspondence, telegrams, newspaper clippings, speeches, videos, photographs, scrapbooks, fiscal records, and court proceedings, as well as assorted printed material such as blueprints, maps, and certificates that are supplementary to the correspondence.

BIBLIOGRAPHY: B. Postal and L. Koppman, *A Jewish Tourist's Guide to the U.S.* (1954), 133–7; *An Illustrated History of the State of Idaho* (1890), 594–5; AJA, 8 (Oct. 1956), 127–8.

[Robert E. Levinson / Ruth Beloff (2nd ed.)]

ALEXANDER, MURIEL (1884–1975), South African actress and producer. Born in Exeter, England, Muriel Alexander was a member in 1904 of the first class held at Tree's Academy, London, which later became the Royal Academy of Dramatic Art. She won a scholarship and acted in Sir Henry Tree's company at His Majesty's. Settling in South Africa after World War I, she founded the Johannesburg Repertory Players, which had a predominantly Jewish membership and directed them for many years. In 1960 they renamed their theater The Alexander.

ALEXANDER, SAMUEL (1859–1938), British philosopher. His family originated in Alsace and he was born in Australia. From 1882 to 1893 he taught at Oxford as a fellow of Lincoln College, being the first Jew appointed to a college fellowship in an English university. From 1894 to 1924 he was a professor of philosophy in Manchester. In 1930 he was made a member of the Order of Merit, the highest honor in British intellectual life. Alexander also participated in Anglo-Jewish communal life and was a member of the academic council of the Hebrew University. Alexander was the principal exponent of metaphysical realism in England. In his view, metaphysics is a descriptive science, which elucidates the most universal levels of reality. There are various levels in the unfolding of reality, each of which is rooted in the one preceding it and emerges from it. The most important of these emergent levels which have thus far manifested themselves are those of matter, the physical-chemical life, and mind. However, the creative potential of the cosmic order has not ceased – the next level to evolve will be that of "deity." The relationship of "deity" to mind will be of the same order as that of mind to matter and of matter to space-time. The impending advent of "deity" in the process of emergent evolution is evidenced by the existence of religious consciousness. Deity is the goal of the ever-advancing craving – perhaps asymptotic – for it. His doctrines have much in common with those held by Alexander's friends and contemporaries, A.N. Whitehead and Lloyd Morgan. In his later life, Alexander turned to the study of aesthetics in which he found much substantiation for his views on the cosmic order. The most original and characteristic portion of his work in metaphysics is the recognition of the reality of time, change, process, and the concept of "point-instants" as ultimate units of reality. The "pragmatic deduction" of the categories (i.e., categories of reality, not of thought) is found in the second part of his book *Space, Time and Deity* (2 vols., 1920). His most lasting contribution to epistemology is his elaborate distinction between "contemplation" of an experience and the "enjoyment" of it: the objective awareness of an "-ed" and the subjective "non-accusative" enjoying self-awareness of an "-ing." Many modern philosophers not otherwise in sympathy with Alexander's realistic metaphysics owe to him this celebrated distinction. His other major writings are *Moral Order and Progress* (1889); *Locke* (1908); *The Foundation of Realism* (1914); *Spinoza and Time* (1921); *Beauty and Other Forms of Value* (1933); *Philosophical and Literary Pieces* (edited 1939).

BIBLIOGRAPHY: B. Bosanquet, *The Meeting of Extremes in Contemporary Philosophy* (1924), index; P. Devaux, *Le systéme d'Alexander* (1929); R. Metz, *Hundred Years of British Philosophy* (1938), index; M.R. Konvits, *On the Nature of Value: The Philosophy of Samuel Alexander* (1946). **ADD. BIBLIOGRAPHY:** J. Laird (ed.), "Memoir," in: *Philosophical and Literary Pieces* (1939); J. Passmore, *A Hundred Years of Philosophy* (1978), index; M.A. Weinstein, *Unity and Variety in the Philosophy of Samuel Alexander* (1984); *The Collected Works of Samuel Alexander* (2000), a 1,988 page collection of his writings; ODNB online.

[Leon Roth]

°**ALEXANDER BALAS**, king of Syria, 150–146 B.C.E. According to Diodorus and Strabo, Balas was his original name before he assumed the cognomen Alexander. Many of his contemporaries state that Alexander Balas was a native of Smyrna, of lowly parentage, but he pretended to be the son of Antiochus IV Epiphanes and claimed the throne of his alleged father in opposition to Demetrius I Soter. Alexander was supported by Attalus II of Pergamum and was recognized by Ptolemy VI Philometor of Egypt. The Romans, inclined to encourage the disturbances in Syria, also allowed Alexander's adherents freedom of action. In 153 B.C.E., Alexander led an army of mercenaries against Demetrius. The pretender's first act was to win Jonathan the Hasmonean to his side by appointing him high priest and leader of the Jews. Demetrius fell in battle, and Alexander assumed the throne in 150. To strengthen his position in Syria he married Ptolemy's daughter. However, when he conspired against him, Ptolemy withdrew his support and allied himself with Demetrius II, son of the late king, who now laid claim to his father's throne. In the ensuing battle between Alexander and Ptolemy on the River Oenoparas near Antioch, Alexander was defeated and Ptolemy mortally wounded. Alexander took refuge with the Arab chieftain Zabeilus, who slew him and sent his head to Ptolemy who had not yet died from his wounds.

BIBLIOGRAPHY: I Macc. 10:1ff., 15ff.; 11:1ff.; Jos., Ant., 13:35ff., 58ff., 80ff., 103ff.; Klausner, Bayit Sheni, 3 (1950²), 54–59; A. Bouché-Leclercq, *Histoire des Séleucides*, 1 (1913), 338ff.; Schuerer, Gesch, 1 (1901⁴), 227ff.

[Abraham Schalit]

ALEXANDER THE FALSE, impostor who pretended to be the son of Herod and Mariamne. According to Josephus, after Herod's death in 4 B.C.E., there appeared "a young man, Jewish by birth but brought up in the city of Sidon by a Roman freedman" who "on the strength of a certain physical resemblance passed himself off as the Prince Alexander, whom Herod had put to death." He successfully deceived several Jewish communities on his way to Rome, but when he arrived there, he was unmasked by the emperor Augustus; Celadus, a freedman who had known the real Alexander, informed the emperor of the deception. The impostor's life was spared, however, and he became an oarsman in the imperial galleys.

BIBLIOGRAPHY: Jos., Wars, 2:101–10; Jos., Ant., 17:324–38; Klausner, Bayit Sheni, 4 (1950²), 177–8.

[Isaiah Gafni]

°**ALEXANDER THE GREAT** (356–323 B.C.E.), king of Macedonia who conquered most of the Near East and Asia. A legend preserved in Josephus (Ant., 11:329ff.) tells that when Alexander was besieging Tyre, Sanballat, the leader of the Samaritans, came to him at the head of 8,000 men. Alexander received him in a friendly manner and acceded to his request that he be allowed to build a temple on Mount Gerizim, where Sanballat's son-in-law Manasseh would serve as high priest. According to this legend, Alexander demanded of the high priest, Jaddus (Jaddua), the surrender of Jerusalem and of the Jewish people, and when the latter refused on the grounds that he had sworn loyalty to Darius, Alexander marched on Jerusalem at the head of his army to punish the panic-stricken Jews. However, Jaddus succeeded in calming the Jews by making it known that he had a revelation in a dream that no harm would befall the city and the Temple. On the following day Jaddus set out with the chief priests, the elders, and the leading citizens, and awaited Alexander's arrival at Ẓofim, to the north of Jerusalem. When Alexander saw the high priest he prostrated himself before him, telling his men that Jaddus had appeared to him in a dream and informed him that he would defeat the Persian king. Alexander then went up to the Temple, offered a sacrifice, and granted the Jews extensive privileges. When the Samaritans heard of the success of the Jews they invited Alexander to visit their temple on Mount Gerizim on his return from Egypt. Their efforts, however, proved unsuccessful.

A similar story, but with different names for the high priest and the meeting place, occurs in the Talmud: "The twenty-fifth [of Tevet] is the day of Mount Gerizim, on which no public mourning is permitted, it being the day on which the Cutheans [i.e., the Samaritans] requested the House of our God from Alexander of Macedonia in order to destroy it and he granted it to them. People came and informed Simeon the Just. What did he do? He put on his priestly garments, and he and some of the nobles of Israel who carried burning torches in their hands walked all night, some on one side, others on the other, until dawn. When dawn rose he [Alexander] said to them: 'Who are these?'

They answered: 'The Jews who rebelled against you.' When he reached Antipatris and the sun shone, they met. On seeing Simeon the Just, Alexander descended from his chariot and prostrated himself.

[They] said to him: 'Should a great king like you prostrate yourself before this Jew?'

He answered: 'The image of this man wins my battles for me.'

He said to the Jews: 'Why have you come?'

They replied: 'Is it possible that star-worshipers should mislead you into destroying the House in which prayers are said for you and your kingdom that it may never be destroyed!'

'To whom are you referring?'

'To the Cutheans who stand before you.'

'They are delivered into your hands.'

At once they pierced the heel of the Cutheans, tied them to the tails of their horses and dragged them over thorns and thistles, until they came to Mount Gerizim, which they plowed and sowed with vetch, even as the Cutheans had planned to do with the House of our God" (Yoma 69a).

The legend in Josephus ascribes to Alexander things which are highly improbable. After the battle at Issus, Alexander set out hurriedly for Egypt in order to dislodge the Persians from the Mediterranean coast. The siege of Tyre was protracted and Alexander had no time to turn aside from his main route in order to visit a city as unimportant as Jerusalem was then, or the Jews, who were a small nation. It is obvious that Alexander advanced with his army along the coast and did not then visit the interior of the country, although undoubtedly he did so in the spring of 331 B.C.E. The Roman writer Curtius Rufus relates that when Alexander was in Egypt the news reached him that the Samaritans had rebelled and had consigned Andromachus, the Macedonian governor of Samaria, to the flames. Alexander hurried to Samaria, reestablished order with an iron hand, and stationed Macedonians there. On this occasion Alexander probably visited the Samaritan temple on Mount Gerizim, a visit which would not have been friendly (as is evidenced by the discoveries of the remains of Samaritan fugitives in the caves of Wadi Daliyeh (see F.R. Cross in bibl.). The Jews in Jerusalem presumably rejoiced at the reversal of the Samaritans and tried to appear before Alexander as a people loyal to him and to his rule, in which purpose they doubtlessly succeeded. An intimation of this success may be gleaned from the legendary account that Alexander granted to the Jews special privileges not only in Jerusalem but in the Diaspora as well. Nonetheless, there is no basis for assuming that he visited the Temple in Jerusalem, for had he done so, such an important event would assuredly have been referred to in the Talmud, which contains many stories about Alexander of Macedonia (Tam. 31b–32b). It may be reasonably assumed, however, that the Jews approached Alexander before his journey to Samaria to correct any false impression he may have had, fearing that he might confuse them with the Samaritans and include them in their punishment. This is clearly reflected in the above-mentioned *aggadah*, which gives the place of the meeting as Antipatris. Although this name does not fit in with the time of Alexander, the Talmud is most probably preserving an authentic popular tradition (Antipatris was on the main route along which an army had to pass when marching from north to south). The *aggadah*, however, is not precise in naming Simeon the Just as the officiating high priest at that time. As for the Jews' destroying Samaria on that occasion, the allusion is probably to its destruction by the Jews in the days of John Hyrcanus.

[Abraham Schalit]

In the *Aggadah*

The legends about Alexander of Macedonia do not so much portray his historical image, as describe the Greeks as a whole, as they were known to the peoples of the East, including the Jews. According to Plato (*Republic*, 435–6), the love of knowledge is characteristic of the Greeks and the love of money and possessions, mainly of the Phoenicians and the Egyptians. According to the *aggadah*, however, the heart of the Greek is torn by two conflicting desires: a craving for money and a hankering after knowledge; for while the Greek loves gold, he also longs to observe people and their customs, to become acquainted with new countries and new manners, thus increasing his knowledge. He delights in proclaiming the latter desire, and he attempts to conceal the former. He is deeply humiliated when he finds that he has failed to do so, as was the lot of Alexander upon his visit to King Kaẓya for the assumed purpose of observing his administration of justice (TJ BM 2:5, 8c). The disdain of the people of the East for the rapacious Greek conquerors is a conspicuous feature of the *aggadah*, which describes Alexander's visit to the country of the Amazons (Tam. 32a). The aggadic account of Alexander's wish to enter the Holy of Holies and of the sage who dissuaded him from doing so (Gen. R. 61:7) was intended to demonstrate to the Jews that the sword is not always the most effective weapon against enemies like Alexander; moderation and discretion, guarded compromise and the exploitation of an enemy's weakness, courage and strength of spirit, often accomplish what the sword cannot. One *aggadah* in which the personality of the Macedonian king bears a close resemblance to the historical Alexander, reports a discussion between him and the elders of the south country (Tam. 31b–32a). Here he is featured as a typical Greek philosopher, bent upon learning from every man and from every nation, inquiring into every purpose, seeking precise definitions of concepts.

[Elimelech Epstein Halevy]

In Medieval Hebrew Literature

Stories about Alexander were included in Hebrew literature throughout the Middle Ages. They may be divided into two categories: (1) Stories describing his wisdom and high moral standards, reflecting the belief that as a pupil of Aristotle he had to be a philosopher. As early as the 11th century, Solomon ibn *Gabirol included such a story in his ethical work, *Tikkun Middot ha-Nefesh*. This practice was imitated by most medieval Hebrew moralists. Stories about him and epigrams attributed to him are found in Arabic works translated into Hebrew, e.g., *Musrei ha-Filosofim* by Ḥunain ibn Isḥaq and the pseudo-Aristotelian *Sod ha-Sodot.* (2) The medieval romance, the *Gests of Alexander,* was known in Hebrew, and published in many versions. This work, which originated in Hellenistic literature, is known in Greek as the *Pseudo-Callisthenes*; it was written around 300 C.E. by an anonymous Alexandrian author. According to W. van Bekkum, one of the recensions of the Greek text was believed to have been done by a Jew who added new elements taken from Josephus and the rabbinic literature, but Trumpf has proven that it was written by a Christian author who used the Septuagint. Some of the Hebrew versions seem to draw upon the *Pseudo-Callisthenes*, but most of them are based on the Latin version, the *Historia de proeliis Alexandri Magni*, a recension of the Latin translation by Archpresbyter Leo of Naples (mid-10th century). It seems that at least one version was translated into Hebrew from the Arabic, itself a translation of the Latin version. There are five printed versions of the Hebrew text of the *Gests of Alexander* (and others in manuscript):

(a) In the 12th century a version of this work was included in the *Josippon (written 200 years earlier) and became in this way part of Hebrew historical literature.

(b) Israel Lévi printed a version from an Arabic translation attributed to Samuel ibn Tibbon, based on the Latin *Historia de proeliis.* It was a deficient edition of the Ms. Héb. 671.5 in the Bibliothèque Nationale, Paris, of the *Sefer Toledot Alexander* (*Kovez al Jad*, 2 (1886), 1–82). A critical edition of the same manuscript was published, with English translation, by Wout Jac. van Bekkum: *A Hebrew Alexander Romance according to Ms. Héb. 671,5 Paris, Bibliothèque Nationale* (Groningen, Styx Publications, 1994). According to the editor, there is a tendency to cleanse the Hebrew text of mention of paganism and idolatry in the Latin text, although some of the pagan names still remain.

(c) Wout Jac. van Bekkum also published the first critical edition of the Alexander Romance according to another London Ms.: *A Hebrew Alexander Romance according to Ms. London Jews' College no. 145* (Leuven, Uitgeverij Peeters en Departement Oriëntalistik, 1992). This manuscript is also based on the Latin translation by Leo of Naples, but it represents a different version of the Hebrew translation, with its own characteristics.

(d) I.J. Kazis printed a Hebrew version (1962) based on the Paris manuscript Ms. Héb. 750.3, translated by Immanuel b. Jacob *Bonfils (mid-14th century) from the same Latin text of the *Historia de proeliis*, which was compiled from other sources as well.

(e) Another version, printed also by I. Lévi (in: *Festschrift... Steinschneider* (1896), 142–63), based on the Ms. 53 of the Estense Library in Modena, seems to be unrelated to the Latin text; Lévi conjectured that this version may be derived directly from the Greek *Pseudo-Callisthenes.* Its story is more imaginative and fanciful than that of the other versions, and has sometimes parallels with texts in the Talmud and Midrash. Two more manuscripts have, according to W. van Bekkum, a similar nature: Ms. Héb. D.11 from the Bodleian Library, Oxford, and another one from Damascus.

Besides being popular as a novel, the *Gests of Alexander,* constructed from hundreds of stories which can exist independently, was also used in Hebrew literature as a source for short stories. The name of the hero, Alexander, is often omitted and only the plot proves its origin in this romance (e.g., *Sefer Ḥasidim*, 379).

[Joseph Dan / Angel Saenz-Badillos (2nd ed.)]

BIBLIOGRAPHY: Lévi, in: REJ, 2 (1881), 293–300; 3 (1881), 238–65; 7 (1883), 78–93; 12 (1886), 117–8; 28 (1894), 147–8; J. Spak, *Der Bericht des Josephus ueber Alexander den Grossen* (1911); Guttmann, Mafte'aḥ, 3, pt. 1 (1924), 67–69; idem, in: *Tarbiz*, 11 (1939/40), 271–94; I. Abrahams, *Campaigns in Palestine from Alexander the Great...* (1927); Klausner, Bayit Sheni, 2 (1951^2), 85–107; V. Tcherikover, *Hellenistic Civilization and the Jews* (1959), 1–5, 40–48; E.E. Halevy, *Sha'arei ha-Aggadah* (1963), 115–37; D. Flusser, in: *Tarbiz*, 26 (1956/57), 165–84; I.J. Kazis (ed.), *The Book of the Gests of Alexander of Macedon* (1962), 223–7 (bibliography); F.R. Cross, in: Freedman and Greenfield (eds.), *New Directions in Biblical Archaeology* (1969), 41–62.

ALEXANDER LYSIMACHUS (Gr. Ἀλέξανδρος Λυσίμαχος), a leader of the Jewish community in Alexandria, Egypt, in the first century C.E., and a member of one of the most illustrious and wealthy Alexandrian Jewish families. Alexander was the brother of *Philo of Alexandria and the father of *Tiberius Julius Alexander and Marcus Julius Alexander. He served as *alabarch during the reigns of Tiberius and Claudius. He was imprisoned by Caligula, but Claudius released him and restored him to office. Alexander also served the younger Antonia, Claudius' mother, as procurator of her large estates in Egypt. When Marcus Julius Agrippa was on his way to Rome, he visited Alexandria and asked Alexander for a loan; Alexander lent the sum to Agrippa's wife *Cypros. He made a gift to the Temple, plating its gates with gold and silver.

BIBLIOGRAPHY: Jos., Ant., 18:159–60; 19:276; 20:100; Jos., Wars, 5:205; A. Fuks, in: *Zion*, 13 (1948), 15–17; Schuerer, Gesch, 1 (1904^4), 567; 2 (1907^4), 64; 3 (1909^4), 64, 132, 134; V. Burr, *Tiberius Julius Alexander* (Ger., 1955).

[Abraham Schalit]

°**ALEXANDER OF APHRODISIAS** (end of second century–beginning of third century C.E.), Greek philosopher, commentator on the writings of *Aristotle, and author of independent works. Alexander was important for his systematization of Aristotle's thought and for the formulation of a number of distinct doctrines, especially in psychology. A number of his commentaries and independent works were translated into Arabic, and the views contained in them became an important part of medieval Islamic and Jewish Aristotelianism. The first book of Alexander's *On the Soul* was translated into Hebrew by Samuel ben Judah of Marseilles from the Arabic translation made by Ḥunain ibn Isḥaq. This translation, which contains brief annotations, was completed in 1323 in Murça and a revised version of it was finished in 1339–40 in Montùlimar.

Alexander, it was commonly thought, wrote a second book in psychology, called *Treatise on the Intellect*, and it circulated in Arabic translation. Averroes wrote a commentary to this work that was translated into Hebrew and is extant in manuscript only with the supercommentaries of *Moses b. Joshua of Narbonne (1344) and Joseph b. Shem Tov *Ibn Shem Tov (1454). H.A. Davidson edited the Averroean portions of the commentary themselves, without these supercommentaries, in 1988.

*Maimonides' estimation of Alexander may be gathered from a famous letter which he wrote to Samuel ibn *Tibbon. Evaluating the philosophical literature of the day, Maimonides advises his translator that for a correct understanding of Aristotle's teachings he should read, beside the commentaries of *Themistius and Averroes, also those of Alexander (A. Marx, in JQR, 25 (1934/35), 378). Maimonides used works by Alexander in the composition of his *Guide*, and Alexander's views formed part of Maimonides' own brand of Aristotelianism (for details see S. Pines, "Translator's Introduction," *Guide of the Perplexed* (1963), lxiv–lxxv). Maimonides cites Alexander as his source for his discussion of the factors which prevent man from discovering the truth (Guide 1:31), for his account of the celestial motions and intelligences (2:3), for his knowledge of the views of certain Greek philosophers (2:13), and for his discussion of God's knowledge (3:16). Alexander may also have influenced Maimonides' views on religion and political history, particularly the view that God used "wily graciousness" in bringing man from inferior forms of worship to more adequate ones (3:32).

Of special importance for Jewish philosophers was Alexander's doctrine of the intellect, discussed in detail particularly by *Gersonides (*Wars of the Lord*, Book 1). Aristotle's views (especially *De Anima* 3:5) were rather enigmatic. Central to Aristotle's discussion was the distinction between the agent intellect (*nous poietikos*) and the passive intellect (*nous pathetikos*). Interpreting Aristotle's views, Alexander held that the agent intellect did not form part of the individual human soul, but was identical with the intellect of God; while the passive intellect belonged to the soul as a mere predisposition or ability for thought. The passive intellect was also called material or hylic intellect (*nous hylikos*), and when actualized by the agent intellect became the acquired intellect (*nous epiktetos*) or intellect in habit (*nous kath'hexin*). The passive intellect, according to Alexander, being part of the individual human soul, is, like it, mortal; only the acquired intellect is immortal, insofar as the objects of its thought are the immaterial beings, in particular, God. While Alexander's doctrine of the intellect was more precise than that of Aristotle, it contained enough ambiguities to give rise to further refinements on the part of Islamic and Jewish philosophers.

Jewish, as Islamic, philosophers accepted Alexander's notion of the agent intellect, but instead of identifying it with God, they identified it with the lowest of the celestial intelligences, which, on the one hand, governs the sublunar world, and, on the other, is a causal agent in the production of human knowledge (see also *cosmology). The agent intellect is also important to Jewish Aristotelians for its roles in the production of prophecy. While there was general agreement about the nature of the agent intellect, there was disagreement about the nature of the passive one. Alexander's acquired intellect became a commonplace in Jewish philosophy, though the medievals refined this notion by distinguishing between the intellect in actuality, and the acquired intellect. Medieval philosophers disagreed about the exact nature of the acquired intellect, but it became important for their doctrine of the immortality of the *soul and the world to come (for details see *Intellect, Doctrines of).

BIBLIOGRAPHY: P. Moraux, *Alexandre d'Aphrodises, exégète de la noétique d'Aristote* (1942); R. Walzer, *Greek into Arabic* (1962), index; Steinschneider, Uebersetzungen, index; idem, *Die arabischen Uebersetzungen aus dem Griechischen* (1893), 93–97; J. Finnegan, in: *Mélanges de l'Université St. Joseph*, 33 (1956), 159–62; E.I. Freudenthal, *Die durch Averroes erhaltenen Fragmente Alexanders zur Metaphysik des Aristoteles* (1885); A. Guensz, *Die Abhandlung Alexanders von Aphrodisias ueber den Intellekt* (1886). **ADD. BIBLIOGRAPHY:** A.P. Fotinis, *The De Anima of Alexander of Aphrodisias* (1979); A.H. Armstrong, *The Cambridge History of Later Greek and Early Medieval Philosophy* (1967), 117–23; H.A, Davidson, *Alfarabi, Avicenna, and Averroes, on Intellect* (1992), 20–24; idem, "Averroes' Commentary on the *De Intellectu* Attributed to Alexander," in: *Shlomo Pines Jubilee Volume* (1988), 205–17.

[Julius Guttmann / Alfred L. Ivry (2nd ed.)]

°**ALEXANDER OF HALES** (d. 1245), English scholastic philosopher and theologian. Alexander joined the Franciscan order after 1230, while teaching at the Faculty of Divinity in Paris. Since he did not complete his comprehensive work, *Summa universae theologiae* (4 vols., 1481–82; 1924–48), which was first edited by his pupils, the extent of his responsibility for the attitudes and opinions expressed in it, and according to which his personal character has been traced, remains controversial. The section on Jews in Christian society confirms the ecclesiastical tradition of restricted toleration. The existence of the Jewish people serves as lasting witness to the origins of Christianity; their conversion at the end of days, according to the teaching of St. Paul, will mean the conclusion of mankind's salvation. Therefore, a definite distinction is drawn between the believers in the Old Testament and the Saracens, who then occupied the Holy Land. Obviously, this remark had a topical relevance in the period when Louis IX was preparing another Crusade. Jewish blasphemies against Christ must be severely punished, if made in public, but not more severely than those committed by Christians. Books containing such utterances must be burned.

Alexander's *Summa* originated at a time when the Talmud and post-biblical Jewish literature were under attack. Thus, although the *Summa* uses *Maimonides' *Dux neutrorum (Guide of the Perplexed)* as a source of philosophical doctrine, especially in the discussion of cosmological questions, the author was reticent in identifying the source of his doctrines. Jacob Guttmann found Maimonides mentioned only twice, although soon afterward his name became a household word among the masters of the schools. Most striking is the use of Maimonides' reflections on the meaning of biblical commandments, intended to affirm the Old Testament's character as divine revelation, in opposition to the dualistic theories of contemporary heretics. In this context "Rabbi Moyses Judaeus" is mentioned by name with his differentiation of *judicia* and *caerimonialia*. This interest in the teachings of the third book of the *Dux (Guide)* prepared the way for *Aquinas' interpretation of Deuteronomy as the model of his social theory. Alexander was also influenced by Ibn *Gabirol (Avicebron), although he does not mention this philosopher by name.

BIBLIOGRAPHY: J. Guttmann, *Die Scholastik des XIII. Jahrhunderts in ihren Beziehungen zum Judenthum und zur juedischen Literatur* (1902), 32–46; idem, in: REJ, 19 (1889), 224–34.

[Hans Liebeschutz]

°ALEXANDER POLYHISTOR (first century B.C.E.), Greek scholar. Alexander was born in Miletus in Asia Minor. He was taken prisoner by the Romans, but was later freed, and continued to live in Italy as a Roman citizen until his death (c. 35 B.C.E.). He was called Polyhistor (very learned) because of the wide variety of subjects on which he wrote. His works included three volumes on Egypt, one on Rome, and a work entitled "Concerning the Jews." This last work reflects the growing Roman interest in the Jewish people at the time of Pompey's conquest of Judea. Lengthy fragments from this work have been preserved by *Eusebius (*Praeparatio evangelica*, 9), and by Clement of Alexandria. From these it seems apparent that he combined relevant excerpts from Jewish, Samaritan, and gentile writers and reproduced them in indirect speech. Thus, valuable fragments of the writings of Hellenistic-Jewish authors have been preserved of which nothing would otherwise be known. Alexander cites the historians *Aristeas, *Demetrius, *Eupolemus, and *Artapanus, the tragic poet *Ezekiel, the epic poets *Theodotus and *Philo the Elder, as well as non-Jewish writers such as the historian Timochares, author of "The History of Antiochus," and *Apollonius Molon.

It seems that Alexander made little original contribution to the subject. In his works he made indiscriminate use of traditions both favorable and hostile to the Jews. He also dealt with the Jews in other works. In his book on Rome he states that a Jewish woman named Moso wrote the Law of the Hebrews, i.e., the Torah (see Suidas, s.v. Ἀλέξανδρος ὁ Μιλήσιος). Although Alexander was fully aware of the Jewish tradition concerning Moses, he appears to have seen nothing wrong in quoting a conflicting tradition from a non-Jewish source. His explanation that Judea was named after one of Semirasis' sons must have been taken from a similar source (quoted in Stephanus Byzantinus' exposition on Judea).

BIBLIOGRAPHY: J. Freudenthal, *Hellenistische Studien: Alexander Polyhistor* (1874); A.V. Gutschmid, *Kleine Schriften*, 2 (1890), 180ff.; Schuerer, Gesch, 3 (1909^4), 469ff.; F. Jacoby, *Die Fragmente der griechischen Historiker*, 3A (Texts; 1940), 96–126; 3a (Commentary; 1943), 248–313; Reinach, *Textes*, 65–66.

[Menahem Stern]

ALEXANDER SON OF ARISTOBULUS II (d. 49 B.C.E.), one of the last of the *Hasmoneans. Alexander, eldest son of Aristobulus II, was the son-in-law of *Hyrcanus II. His wife, *Alexandra, was the mother of *Mariamne, wife of *Herod the Great. As a result of the struggle between Aristobulus II and Hyrcanus II for the throne of Judea, Alexander was sent by Pompey in 63 B.C.E. as a captive to Rome – with his father and the rest of his family. He escaped on the way and returned to Judea, where he succeeded in mustering an army of 10,000 infantry and 1,500 cavalry, and in occupying the strongholds of Alexandreion, Hyrcania, and Machaerus. *Gabinius, recently arrived in Syria as proconsul, collected a force to oppose him and sent his adjutant Mark Anthony ahead. Anthony equipped an additional Jewish contingent under the Jewish commanders Peitholaus and Malichus. Gabinius defeated Alexander's army in the vicinity of Jerusalem, and the remnant fled to Alexandreion. Besieging the fortress, Gabinius promised Alexander his freedom and an amnesty for his troops if he surrendered. His mother also pleaded with Alexander to accept this condition and he left Alexandreion which was then razed to the ground by Gabinius. Gabinius thereupon introduced a much more stringent administrative system than was in force earlier.

Alexander rebelled a second time in 55 B.C.E., when Gabinius was in Egypt. He again mustered a large force and began to drive the Romans from Judea. Gabinius returned and immediately advanced to meet Alexander. He employed *Antipater to persuade Alexander's army to desert to Hyrcanus. Alexander, however, still had thirty thousand men left and he met in battle the armies of Gabinius and Hyrcanus at

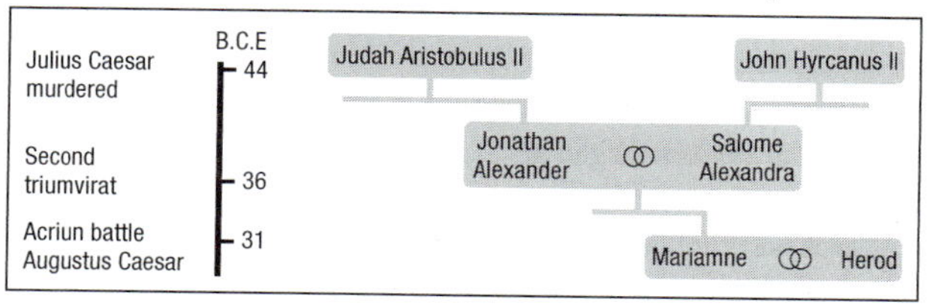

Mt. Tabor and was defeated. The defeat shattered Alexander's resources. Antipater, however, succeeded in effecting a reconciliation between Alexander and Hyrcanus, by arranging a marriage between Alexander and Hyrcanus' daughter Alexandra, which might eventually enable Alexander to become high priest. When civil war broke out in Rome between Julius Caesar and Pompey in 49 B.C.E., Pompey ordered his father-in-law Q. Caecilius Metellus Scipio, then proconsul in Syria, to put Alexander to death in Antiochia.

BIBLIOGRAPHY: Jos., Ant., 14:80–125; Jos., Wars, 1:160–85; A.H.M. Jones, *The Herods of Judaea* (1938); Klausner, Bayit Sheni, 3 (1950^2), 236ff.; Schuerer, Gesch, 1 (1901^4), 338ff.; Graetz, Gesch, 3 (1905^5), 166–7, 171ff.; A.Schalit, *Hordos ha-Melekh* (1964^3), 26ff.

[Abraham Schalit]

ALEXANDER SUSLIN HA-KOHEN OF FRANKFURT (d. 1349), German talmudic scholar. Alexander was born in Erfurt and taught there as well as in Worms, Cologne, and Frankfurt. Although he was apparently still in Frankfurt in 1345 he sometime toward the end of his life resettled in Erfurt where he died a martyr's death. He is the last of the early German halakhic authorities. Alexander's fame rests upon his *Aguddah* (Cracow, 1571; photostatic copy 1958; critical annotated edition, Jerusalem, 1966–), a collection of halakhic decisions derived from talmudic discussions and arranged in the order of the tractates of the Talmud. It includes novellae (his own as well as those of some of his predecessors), and a commentary and collection of *halakhot* to the minor tractates and to the Mishnayot of the orders *Zera'im* and *Tohorot*. The language is very concise and it can be seen that he wrote it in great haste, under the stress of the expulsions and persecutions of his time. Indeed the purpose of the book is to give halakhic rulings in a concise form, ignoring differences of opinion, for a generation which was harassed and persecuted. His sources are *Mordecai b. Hillel ha-Kohen and *Aher b. Jehiel, and they often have to be consulted in order to understand him. The *Aguddah* was published in 1571 from a defective and faulty manuscript by Joseph ha-Kohen, brother-in-law of Moses *Isserles, who attempted to correct the text, but with only partial success. A digest, called *Ḥiddushei Aguddah*, compiled by Jacob Weil, was published as an appendix to his responsa (Venice, 1523), and has been frequently reprinted. *Aguddah* on the order of *Nezikin*, with notes by J.H. Sonnenfeld, came out in Jerusalem, 1899. The later halakhic authorities attached great value to his works; Jacob ha-Levi Moellin and Moses Isserles (in his glosses to the Shulḥan Arukh) in particular regarded his decisions as authoritative, and quote from him, although they were aware of his sources. He was eulogized in a dirge *Ẓiyyon Arayyavekh Bekhi* (published in the addenda to Landshut's *Ammudei ha-Avodah* (p. III–IV)).

BIBLIOGRAPHY: Abramson, in: *Sinai*, 58 (1956), 188–91; M. Horovitz, *Frankfurter Rabbinen*, 1 (1892), vii, 9.

ALEXANDER SUSSKIND BEN MOSES OF GRODNO (d. 1793), Lithuanian kabbalist. Alexander lived a secluded life in Grodno, never engaging in light conversation so as not to be deterred from study and prayer. Many stories were told about him. According to a well-substantiated one, several days before Passover in 1790, a Jewish victim of a blood libel was sentenced to death unless he agreed to convert. Alexander, afraid the condemned man would be unable to withstand the ordeal, obtained permission to visit him in prison, and persuaded him to choose martyrdom. The execution was scheduled for the second day of Shavuot; on that day Alexander left the synagogue in the middle of the service for the place of execution, heard the condemned man recite the prayer of martyrdom, said "Amen," and returned to the synagogue, reciting the memorial prayer for the martyr's soul. The second incident relates that Alexander was imprisoned in a German town for soliciting money for the Jews of Ereẓ Israel, as it was illegal to send money out of Germany. On being freed, he immediately resumed collecting, ignoring the danger involved.

Alexander's most important work, *Yesod ve-Shoresh ha-Avodah* (Novy Dvor, 1782; corrected edition, Jerusalem, 1959), a book of ethics, touches upon many aspects of Jewish life. It is divided into 12 sections, the final section *Sha'ar ha-Kolel*, concluding with an account of the coming of the Messiah. According to the author, the basis of divine worship is love of God and love of the Jewish people. Alexander emphasizes that a Jew must be grieved at the contempt in which the God of Israel and the people of Israel are held among the Gentiles, who persecute the chosen people and then ask mockingly, "Where is your God?" He speaks often and with great sorrow of the desolation of the holy city of Jerusalem and of Ereẓ Israel and extols "the greatness of the virtue of living in the Land of Israel." In Alexander's view, the essence of observance is intent (*kavvanah*); the deed alone, without intention, is meaningless. For this reason, he insisted on clear and meticulous enunciation of each word in prayer, giving many examples of how words are distorted in the course of praying. He also laid down a specific order of study: Talmud, *musar*, literature, and then Kabbalah. He emphasizes the need for study of the geography of the Bible.

Alexander was rigid in the matter of religious observance, threatening violators with severe retribution in the hereafter. He asked every Jew to resign himself to "the four forms of capital punishment of the *bet din*" and in his will he ordered that upon his death his body be subjected to stoning. Yet the central theme of his work is "worship the Lord in joy." His ideas make Alexander's writings closely akin to the basic tenets of Ḥasidism and *Naḥman of Bratslav said of him, "he was a Ḥasid even before there was Ḥasidism." In annotated prayer books, especially in those of the Sephardi rite, his *Kavvanot ha-Pashtiyyut*, the "intent" of the text of the prayers as set forth in the *Yesod ve-Shoresh ha-Avodah*, is appended to most of the prayers. He was deeply revered and as long as there was a Jewish community in Grodno, men and women went to pray at his grave. Descendants of his family who originally went by the name of Braz (initials for Benei Rabbi Alexander Zusskind) later assumed the name Braudes.

BIBLIOGRAPHY: S.A. Friedenstein, *Ir Gibborim* (1880), 62–63; A. Susskind b. Moses, *Ẓavva'ah*, ed. by A.L. Miller (1927), 5–8 (introd.); J. Klausner, *Darki Likrat ha-Ge'ullah ve-ha-Teḥiyyah* (1945), 9–10, 84; Klausner, Sifrut, 5 (1955²), 347; idem, in: *Sefer Assaf* (1953), 427–32; Benjacob, Oẓar, 226, no. 319, 506, no. 40.

[Joseph Gedaliah Klausner]

ALEXANDER THE ZEALOT, joint leader, with *Eleazar b. Dinai, of an armed band of Jews during the administration of the Roman procurator Ventidius *Cumanus (48–52 C.E.). They led a punitive expedition after a group of Galilean Jewish pilgrims had been murdered while passing through Samaria on their way to Jerusalem to celebrate one of the festivals. Cumanus, bribed by the Samaritans, took no steps to punish the guilty parties. The Jews thereupon abandoned the celebration of the festival and, under the leadership of Alexander and Eleazar, attacked several Samaritan villages, "massacred the inhabitants without distinction of age and burnt the villages." After a show of force by Cumanus and entreaties by the Jewish leaders of Jerusalem the armed bands dispersed, the zealots returning to their former strongholds in Judea.

BIBLIOGRAPHY: Jos., Wars, 2:232ff.; Jos., Ant., 20:118–24, Schuerer, Gesch, 1 (1901⁴), 569ff.

[Isaiah Gafni]

ALEXANDRA, Hasmonean princess, daughter of *Aristobulus II, king of Judea. Captured by Pompey, Alexandra was brought to Rome in 63 B.C.E. together with her father, her two sisters, and her brother *Antigonus II. The family was released in 56 B.C.E. and returned to Jerusalem. After the death of her father in 49 B.C.E., Alexandra was sent with Antigonus and her two sisters to Chalcis in Lebanon at the invitation of its ruler, Ptolemy, the son of Mennaeus. Alexandra married Ptolemy's son, Philippion. But Ptolemy, jealous of his son, executed him, and then married Alexandra himself. Nothing more is known of her.

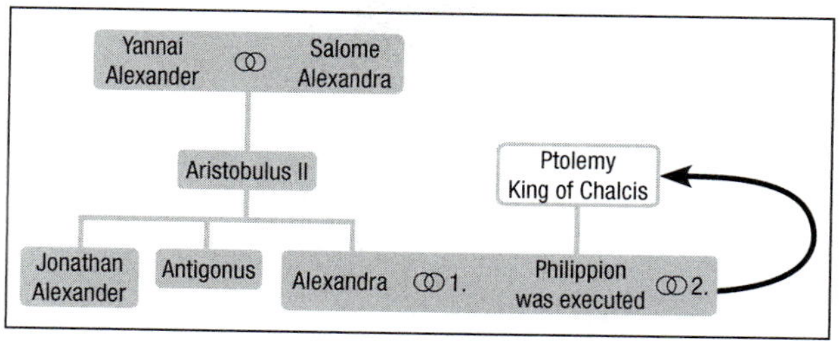

BIBLIOGRAPHY: Jos., Ant., 14:79, 126; A. Schalit, *Hordos ha-Melekh* (1964³), 29; Klausner, Bayit Sheni, 3 (1950²), 226; Schuerer, Gesch, 1 (1901⁴), 300.

[Abraham Schalit]

ALEXANDRA (d. 28 B.C.E.), daughter of *Hyrcanus II; wife of *Alexander, the son of Aristobulus II; and mother of Aristobulus III and of *Mariamne, Herod's wife. Alexandra regarded Herod's appointment of the Babylonian (or Egyptian) Ananel (Hananel) to the high priesthood as a violation of the

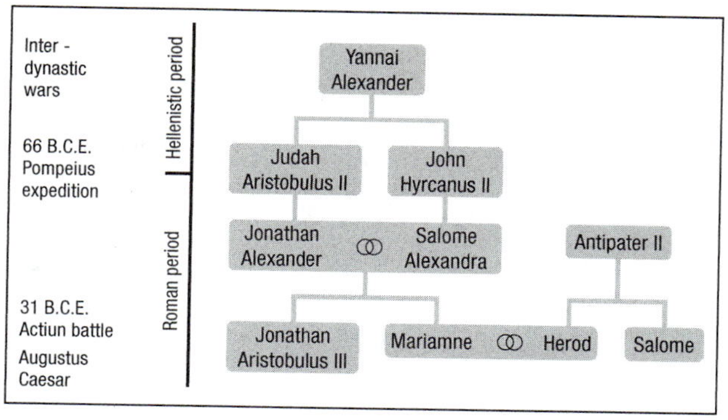

Hasmonean family's right of succession to the office and attempted to secure it for her son Aristobulus. Though Herod acceded to her request, he was unable to forgive her, and did not allow her to leave the palace. When Alexandra tried to escape with her son, Herod foiled the attempt. He then affected a reconciliation. When, however, her son was drowned in a swimming pool, Alexandra accused Herod before Cleopatra of engineering his death and asked her to have Mark Antony charge Herod with the murder. Herod was summoned to Laodicea, but cleared himself by bribery.

After the battle of Actium (31 B.C.E.), it seemed certain that Herod could not escape punishment, since he had sided with Antony against Octavian (Augustus). When Herod returned from a meeting with Octavian with added honors, Herod's sister Salome, Queen Mariamne's implacable enemy, slandered her and Alexandra to her brother, and Mariamne was condemned to death for treason. According to Josephus' biased account, Alexandra escaped the same fate by dishonorably accusing her condemned daughter of disloyalty to her husband. Her own fate was not long delayed. After Mariamne's death Herod fell ill and appeared likely to die. Alexandra, thinking that her opportunity had now come, attempted to obtain control of the two fortresses in Jerusalem. When this was reported to Herod, he ordered her immediate execution. With Alexandra's death, the last member of the Hasmonean dynasty to play an active role in history disappeared. Alexandra cannot be considered exceptionally sagacious or gifted with insight into Herod's character. In all, she seemed to resemble her grandfather Alexander Yannai; she was courageous, but lacked flexibility and guile, and hence was no match for Herod.

BIBLIOGRAPHY: Jos., Ant., 15:23, 80, 232ff., 247ff.; Klausner, Bayit Sheni, 4 (1950²), 12ff.; Graetz, Gesch, 3 (1905⁵), 186, 199ff., 216ff.; Schuerer, Gesch, 1 (1901), 378ff., 386; H. Willrich, *Das Haus des Herodes* (1929), 48ff.; A.H.M. Jones, *The Herods of Judaea* (1938), 52ff., 58, 61; A. Schalit, *Hordos ha-Melekh* (1964³), index; Pauly-Wissowa, suppl. 3 (1918), 79.

[Abraham Schalit]

ALEXANDRI (Alexandrah, Alexandrai, Alexandros; third century), Palestinian *amora*. He was a leading aggadist of his day. Many of the scholars who quote Alexandri belong to the *amoraim* who centered around the academy at Lydda. It is therefore probable that Alexandri came from Lydda. It is related that he used to go about the streets of the town urging people to perform good deeds. He once entered the marketplace and called out: "Who wants life?" When the people answered him affirmatively he responded by quoting the verse: "Who is the man that desireth life … Keep thy tongue from evil, and thy lips from speaking guile. Depart from evil and do good; Seek peace and pursue it" (Ps. 34:13–15; Av. Zar. 19b). Many of Alexandri's homiletical dissertations are based on the book of Psalms. "Break Thou the arm of the wicked" (Ps. 10:15) is quoted by him as an indictment of profiteering. From Psalms 16:10 he derived that whoever hears himself reviled and does not resent it deserves to be called pious (*ḥasid*). He also said: "When man uses a broken vessel he is ashamed of it, but not so God. All the instruments of His service are broken vessels, as it is said: 'The Lord is nigh unto them that are of a broken heart' (Ps. 34:19); or 'Who healeth the broken in heart'" (Ps. 147:3, PR 25:158b).

He customarily concluded his daily prayers: "Sovereign of the Universe, it is known full well to Thee that it is our desire to perform Thy will, and what prevents us? The yeast in the dough (i.e., the evil inclination which acts as a fermenting and corrupting agent) and subjection to foreign rule. May it be Thy will to deliver us from their hand, so that we may be enabled to perform the statutes of Thy will with a perfect heart" (Ber. 17a).

No details of his life are known, except that his statement "The world is darkened for him whose wife has died in his days" (Sanh. 22a) may have had a personal application. Scholars by the name of Alexandri b. Haggai (b. Ḥagra, b. Ḥadrin), Alexandri "Kerovah" ("the hymnologist"), and Alexandri de-Zaddika ("the Just"), are mentioned in isolated talmudic passages and one of these may be identical with this Alexandri.

BIBLIOGRAPHY: Hyman, Toledot, s.v.; Bacher, Pal Amor, index.

[Yitzhak Dov Gilat]

ALEXANDRIA, city in northern *Egypt.

Ancient Period

Jews settled in Alexandria at the beginning of the third century B.C.E. (according to Josephus, already in the time of Alexander the Great). At first they dwelt in the eastern sector of the city, near the sea; but during the Roman era, two of its five quarters (particularly the fourth (= "Delta") quarter) were inhabited by Jews, and synagogues existed in every part of the city. The Jews of Alexandria engaged in various crafts and in commerce. They included some who were extremely wealthy (moneylenders, merchants, *alabarchs), but the majority were artisans. From the legal aspect, the Jews formed an autonomous community at whose head stood at first its respected leaders, afterward – the ethnarchs, and from the days of Augustus, a council of 71 elders. According to Strabo, the ethnarch was responsible for the general conduct of Jewish affairs in the city, particularly in legal matters and the drawing up of documents. Among the communal institutions worthy of mention were the *bet din* and the "archion" (i.e., the office for drawing up documents). The central synagogue, famous for its size and splendor, may have been the "double colonnade" (*diopelostion*) of Alexandria mentioned in the Talmud (Suk. 51b; Tosef. 4:6), though some think it was merely a large meeting place for artisans. During the Ptolemaic period relations between the Jews and the government were, in general, good. Only twice, in 145 and in 88 B.C.E., did insignificant clashes occur, seemingly with a political background. Many of the Jews even acquired citizenship in the city. The position of the Jews deteriorated at the beginning of the Roman era. Rome sought to distinguish between the Greeks, the citizens of the city to whom all rights were granted, and the Egyptians, upon whom a poll tax was imposed and who were considered a subject people. The Jews energetically began to seek citizenship rights, for only thus could they attain the status of the privileged Greeks. Meanwhile, however, *antisemitism had taken deep root. The Alexandrians vehemently opposed the entry of Jews into the ranks of the citizens. In 38 C.E., during the reign of *Caligula, serious riots broke out against the Jews. Although antisemitic propaganda had paved the way for them, the riots themselves became possible as a result of the attitude of the Roman governor, Flaccus. Many Jews were murdered, their notables were publicly scourged, synagogues were defiled and closed, and all the Jews were confined to one quarter of the city. On Caligula's death, the Jews armed themselves and after receiving support from their fellow Jews in Egypt and Ereẓ Israel fell upon the Greeks. The revolt was suppressed by the Romans. The emperor Claudius restored to the Jews of Alexandria the religious and national rights of which they had been deprived at the time of the riots, but forbade them to claim any extension of their citizenship rights. In 66 C.E., influenced by the outbreak of the war in Ereẓ Israel, the Jews of Alexandria rebelled against Rome. The revolt was crushed by *Tiberius Julius Alexander and 50,000 Jews were killed (Jos., Wars, 2:497). During the widespread rebellion of Jews in the Roman Empire in 115–117 C.E. the Jews of Alexandria again suffered, the great synagogue going up in flames. As a consequence of these revolts, the economic situation of the community was undermined and its population diminished. See also *Diaspora.

[Avigdor (Victor) Tcherikover]

Alexandrians in Jerusalem

During the period of the Second Temple the Jews of Alexandria were represented in Jerusalem by a sizable community. References to this community, while not numerous, can be divided into two distinct categories: (1) The Alexandrian community as a separate congregation. According to Acts 6:9, the apostles in Jerusalem were opposed by "certain of the synagogue, which is called the synagogue of the Libertines and Cyrenians and Alexandrians, and of them of Cilicia and of Asia." The Alexandrian synagogue and congregation are mentioned in talmudic sources as well: "Eleazar b. Zadok bought a synagogue of the Alexandrians in Jerusalem" (Tosef. Meg. 3:6;

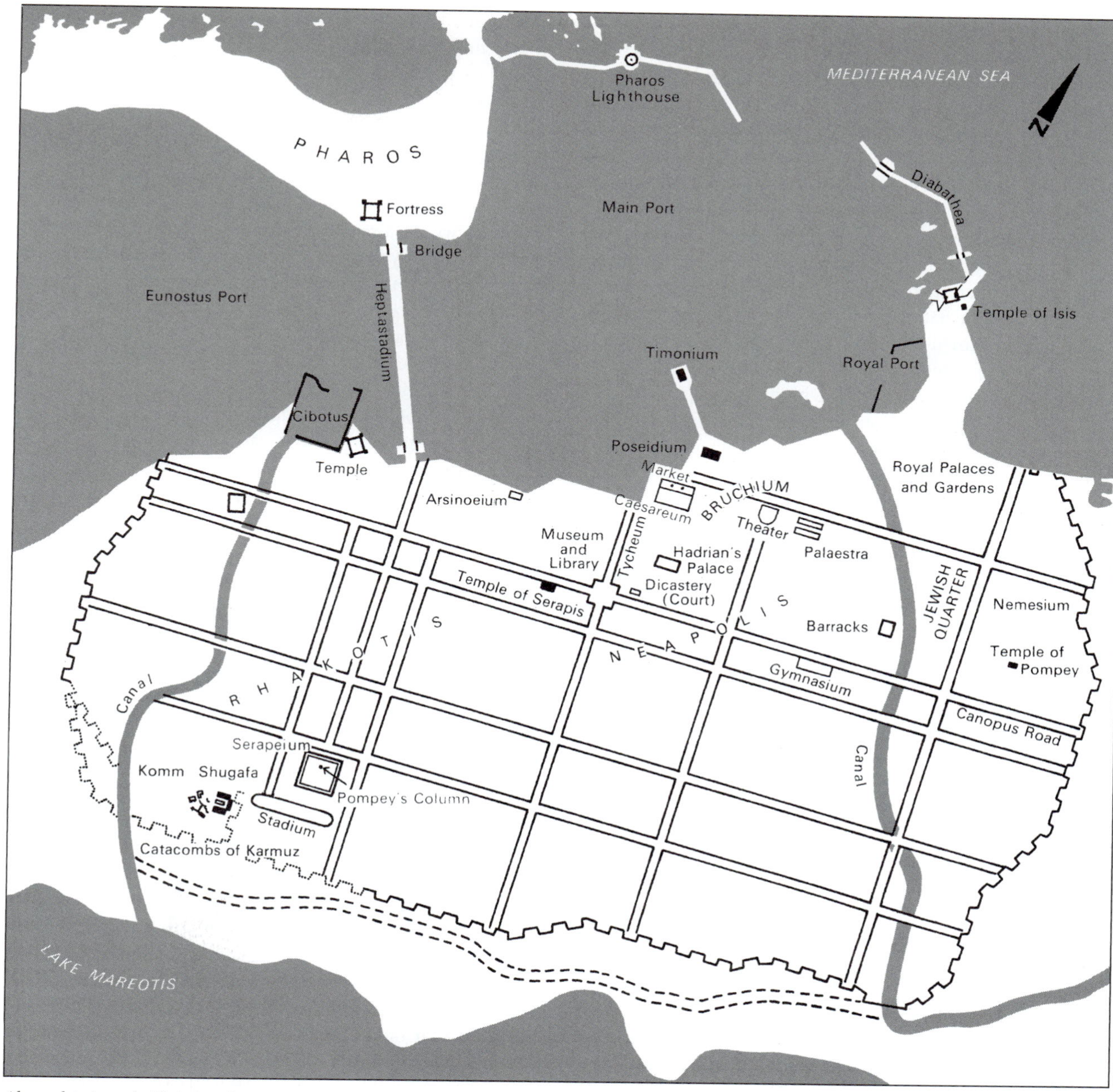

Alexandria in early Christian times.

cf. TJ Meg. 3:1, 73d). (2) References to particular Alexandrians. During Herod's reign several prominent Alexandrian Jewish families lived in Jerusalem. One was that of the priest Boethus whose son Simeon was appointed high priest by Herod. Another family of high priests, the "House of Phabi," was likewise of Jewish-Egyptian origin, although it is not certain whether they came from Alexandria. According to *Parah* 3:5, Ḥanamel the high priest, who had been appointed by Herod in place of Aristobulus the Hasmonean, was an Egyptian, also probably from Alexandria. "*Nicanor's Gate" in the Temple was named after another famous Alexandrian Jew. Rabbinic sources describe at length the miracles surrounding him and the gates he brought from Alexandria (Mid. 1:4; 2:3; Yoma 3:10; Yoma 38a). In 1902 the family tomb of Nicanor was discovered in a cave just north of Jerusalem. The inscription found there reads: "The bones of the sons of Nicanor the Alexandrian who built the gates. Nicanor Alexa."

[Isaiah Gafni]

Jewish Culture

The Greek-speaking Jews of Alexandria were familiar with the works of the ancient Greek poets and philosophers and acknowledged their universal appeal. They would not, however, give up their own religion, nor could they accept the prevailing Hellenistic culture with its polytheistic foundations and pagan practice. Thus they came to create their own version of Hellenistic culture. They contended that Greek philosophy had derived its concepts from Jewish sources and that there was no contradiction between the two systems of thought. On the other hand, they also gave Judaism an interpretation of their own, turning the Jewish concept of God into an abstraction and His relationship to the world into a subject of metaphysical speculation. Alexandrine Jewish philosophers stressed the universal aspects of Jewish law and the prophets, de-emphasized the national Jewish aspects of Jewish religion, and sought to provide rational motives for Jewish religious practice. In this manner they sought not only to defend themselves against the onslaught of the prevailing pagan culture, but also to spread monotheism and respect for the high moral and ethical values of Judaism. The basis of Jewish-Hellenistic literature was the Septuagint, the Greek translation of the Bible, which was to become the cornerstone of a new world culture (see *Bible: Greek translations). The apologetic tendency of Jewish-Hellenistic culture is clearly discernible in the Septuagint. Alexandrine Jewish literature sought to express the concepts of the Jewish-Hellenistic culture and to propagate these concepts among Jews and Gentiles. Among these Jewish writers there were poets, playwrights, and historians; but it was the philosophers who made a lasting contribution. *Philo of Alexandria was the greatest among them, but also the last of any significance. After him, Alexandrine Jewish culture declined. See also *Hellenism.

Byzantine Period

By the beginning of the Byzantine era, the Jewish population had again increased, but suffered from the persecutions of the Christian Church. In 414, in the days of the patriarch Cyril, the Jews were expelled from the city but appear to have returned after some time since it contained an appreciable Jewish population when it was conquered by the Muslims.

Arab Period

According to Arabic sources, there were about 400,000 Jews in Alexandria at the time of its conquest by the Arabs (642), but 70,000 had left during the siege. These figures are greatly exaggerated, but they indicate that in the seventh century there was still a large Jewish community. Under the rule of the caliphs the community declined, both demographically and culturally. J. *Mann concluded from a *genizah* document of the 11th century that there were 300 Jewish families in Alexandria, but this seems improbable. The same is true for the statement of *Benjamin of Tudela, who visited the town in about 1170 and speaks of 3,000 Jews living there. In any case, throughout the Middle Ages there was a well-organized Jewish community there with rabbis and scholars. Various documents of the Cairo *Genizah* mention the name of Mauhub ha-Ḥazzan b. Aaron ha-Ḥazzan, a *dayyan* of the community in about 1070–80. In the middle of the 12th century Aaron He-Ḥaver Ben Yeshuʿah *Alamani, physician and composer of *piyyutim*, was the spiritual head of the Alexandrian Jews. Contemporary with *Maimonides (late 12th century) were the *dayyanim* Phinehas b. Meshullam, originally from Byzantium, and *Anatoli b. Joseph from southern France, and contemporary with Abraham the son of *Maimonides was the *dayyan* Joseph b. Gershom, also a French Jew. In this period the community of Alexandria maintained close relations with the Jews of Cairo and other cities of Egypt, to whom they applied frequently for help in ransoming Jews captured by pirates. A letter of 1028 mentions this situation; it also praises Nethanel b. Eleazar ha-Kohen, who had been helpful in the building of a synagogue, apparently the synagogue of the congregation of Palestinians that may have been destroyed during the persecution of the non-Muslims by the Fatimid caliph al-Ḥākim (c. 996–1021). In addition to this synagogue there was a smaller one, attested to in various medieval sources that mention two synagogues of Alexandria, one of them called "small." The Jews of Alexandria were engaged in the international trade centered in their city, and some of them held government posts.

Mamluk and Ottoman Periods

Under the rule of the Mamluk sultans (1250–1517), the Jewish population of Alexandria declined further, as did the general population. *Meshullam of Volterra, who visited it in 1481, found 60 Jewish families, but reported that the old men remembered the time when the community numbered 4,000. Although this figure is doubtless an exaggeration, it nevertheless testifies to the numerical decrease of the community in the later Middle Ages. In 1488 Obadiah of Bertinoro found 25 Jewish families in Alexandria. Many Spanish exiles, including merchants, scholars, and rabbis settled there in the 14th–15th centuries. The historian *Sambari (17th century) mentions among the rabbis of Alexandria at the end of the 16th century Moses b. Sason, Joseph Sagish, and Baruch b. Ḥabib. With the spread of the plague in 1602 most of the Jews left and did not return. After the Cossack persecutions of 1648–49 (see *Chmielnicki) some refugees from the Ukraine settled in Alexandria. During the 1660s the rabbi of the city was Joshua of Mantua, who became an ardent follower of *Shabbetai Ẓevi. In 1700 Jewish fishermen from *Rosetta (Rashīd) moved to Alexandria and formed a Jewish quarter near the seashore, and in the second half of the 18th century more groups of fishermen from Rosetta, *Damietta, and Cairo joined them; this Jewish quarter was destroyed by an earthquake. At the end of the 18th century the community was very small and it suffered greatly during the French conquest. Napoleon imposed heavy fines on the Jews and ordered the ancient synagogue, associated with the prophet Elijah, to be destroyed. In the first half of the 19th century under the rule of Muhammad ʿAli there was a new period of prosperity. The development of commerce brought great wealth to the Jews, as to the other merchants in the town; the community was reorganized and established schools, hospitals, and various associations. From 1871 to 1878 the Jewry of Alexandria was divided and existed as two separate communities. Among the rabbis of Alexandria in modern times were the descendants of the Israel family from Rhodes: Elijah, Moses, and Jedidiah Israel (served 1802–30), and Solomon Ḥazzan (1830–56), Moses Israel Ḥazzan (1856–63), and Bekhor Elijah Ḥazzan (1888–1908). As a result of immigration from Italy, particularly from Leghorn, the upper class of the community became to some extent Italianized. Rabbis from Italy included Raphael della Pergola (1910–23), formerly of Gorizia, and David *Prato (1926–37). Later rabbis were M. *Ventura and Aharon Angel. During World War I many Jews from Palestine who were not Ottoman citizens were exiled to Alexandria. In 1915 their leaders decided, under the influence of *Jabotinsky and *Trumpeldor, to form Jewish battalions to fight on the side of the Allies; the Zion Mule Corps was also organized in Alexandria.

[Eliyahu Ashtor]

Modern Times

In 1937, 24,690 Jews were living in Alexandria and in 1947, 21,128. The latter figure included 243 Karaites, who, unlike those of Cairo, were members of the Jewish community council. Ashkenazi Jews were also members of the council. According to the 1947 census, 59.1% of Alexandrian Jews were merchants, and 18.5% were artisans. Upon the outbreak of the Israeli War of Independence in 1948, several Jews were placed in detention camps, such as that at Abukir. Most of the detainees were released before 1950. There were several assaults on the Jewish community by the local population, including the throwing of a bomb into a synagogue in July 1951. With *Nasser's accession to power in February 1954, many Jews were arrested on charges of *Zionism, communism, and currency smuggling. After the *Sinai Campaign (1956), thousands of Jews were banished from the city, while others left voluntarily when the Alexandrian stock exchange ceased to function. The 1960 census showed that only 2,760 Jews remained. After the *Six-Day War of June 1967, about 350 Jews, including Chief Rabbi Nafusi, were interned in the Abu Za'bal detention camp, known for its severe conditions. Some of them were released before the end of 1967. The numbers dwindled rapidly; by 1970 very few remained and in 2005 just a few dozen, mostly elderly people.

[Haim J. Cohen]

Hebrew Press

The first Hebrew press of Alexandria was founded in 1862 by Solomon Ottolenghi from Leghorn. In its first year, it printed three books. A second attempt to found a Hebrew press in Alexandria was made in 1865. Nathan *Amram, chief rabbi of Alexandria, brought two printers from Jerusalem, Michael Cohen and Joel Moses Salomon, to print his own works. However, these printers only produced two books, returning to Jerusalem when the second was only half finished. A more successful Hebrew press was established in 1873 by Faraj Ḥayyim Mizraḥi, who came from Persia; his press continued to operate until his death in 1913, and his sons maintained it until 1916. Altogether, over 40 books were printed. In 1907 Jacob b. Attar from Meknés, Morocco, founded another press, which produced several dozen books. Apart from these main printing houses, from 1920 on the city had several small presses, each producing one or two books. A total of over 100 books for Jews were printed in Alexandria, most of them in Hebrew, the others in Judeo-Arabic and Ladino. Most of them were works by eminent Egyptian rabbis, prayer books, and textbooks.

[Avraham Yaari]

BIBLIOGRAPHY: ANCIENT TIMES: V.A. Tcherikover, *Hellenistic Civilization and the Jews* (1959), index; idem, *Corpus papyrorum… judaicarum*, 1 (1957), index; Klausner, Bayit Sheni, 4 (1950^2), 267–86; A. Bludau, *Juden und Judenverfolgungen im alten Alexandrien* (1906); H.I. Bell, *Jews and Christians in Egypt* (1924); idem, *Juden und Griechen im roemischen Alexandreia* (1926). ALEXANDRIANS IN JERUSALEM: PEFQS (1903), 125–31, 326–32; E.L. Sukenik, in: *Sefer Zikkaron… Gulak ve-Klein* (1942), 134–7; Schuerer, Gesch, 2 (1907^4), 87 n. 247, 502, 524 n. 77; S. Lieberman, *Tosefta ki-Feshutah*, 5 (1962), 1162; Stern, in: *Tarbiz*, 25 (1965/66), 246. ARAB PERIOD: Mann, Egypt, 1 (1920), 88; Ashtor, Toledot, 1 (1944), 247–8; 2 (1950), 111–2; 3 (1970); idem, in: JJS, 19 (1968), 8ff.; B. Taragan, *Les communautés israélites d'Alexandrie* (1932). OTTOMAN PERIOD: J.M. Landau (ed.), *Toledot ha-Yedudim be Miẓrayim ha-Otmanit* (1988), index; idem, *Jews in Nineteenth-Century Egypt* (1969), index; Tcherikover, Corpus, index; idem, *Hellenistic Civilization and the Jews* (1959), 541–9 (bibliography), and index; Toledano, in: HUCA, 12–13 (1937–38), 701–14. HEBREW PRINTING: A. Yaari, *Ha-Defus ha-Ivri be-Arẓot ha-Mizraḥ*, 1 (1937), 53–56, 67–85; idem, in: KS, 24 (1947/48), 69–70.

ALEXANDRIAN MARTYRS, ACTS OF, genre of patriotic Alexandrian literature containing heavy overtones of antisemitism. This is known also as the "Acts of the Pagan Martyrs" (mistakenly, since the martyrdom has nothing to do with religion). Fragments of this literature were first published at the end of the 19th century. At that time the fragments were understood to be of a strictly official nature, in effect the protocols of numerous trials of Alexandrian representatives before the Roman Caesars. These missions would inevitably end in the execution of the delegates, thus arousing further the Alexandrians' hatred both of the emperor and his presumed allies, the Jews, although a number of specimens make no mention of their part in the proceedings. With the publication of additional fragments, this view was modified, and it is now accepted that "this genre has nothing to do with official documents, and the protocol form… is merely a literary disguise" (Tcherikover, Corpus, 2 (1960), 56).

The background for the various trials covers a period of 150 years. The earliest embassy is associated with *Caligula (37–41), the latest (*Acta Appiani*) probably refers to the emperor Commodus (180–192). However, the most widely discussed fragments are those belonging to the *Acta Isidori et Lamponis* (for literature see *ibid.*, 66–67). Isidoros, the head of the gymnasium of Alexandria, launched a vigorous attack against the Jewish king *Agrippa I, and summoned him before the court of Claudius. The dialogue between the emperor and Isidoros is heated. At one point Claudius refers to Isidoros as "the son of a girl-musician" (i.e., a woman of loose morals) whereupon the latter immediately rebuts: "I am neither a slave nor a girl-musician's son, but gymnasiarch of the glorious city of Alexandria. But you are the cast-off son of the Jewess Salome!" (*ibid.*, 80f.). Isidoros and his colleague Lampon were immediately sentenced to death. The trial probably took place in 41 C.E. (although many scholars favor 53), for in that year a series of debates on Jewish civic rights came before Claudius. It would be mistaken, however, to conclude from this document that all the Acts were aimed solely at arousing anti-Jewish sentiment. Tcherikover has shown clearly that antisemitism in the Acts "plays a secondary part only, the major theme of the work being the clash between the Alexandrians and Rome." The author's main purpose was to ridicule the Roman emperors, and for this purpose it was often sufficient to allude to the alleged cordial understanding between the emperors and the Jews.

BIBLIOGRAPHY: H.A. Musurillo, *The Acts of the Pagan Martyrs* (1954); Tcherikover, Corpus, 2 (1960), 55–107 nos. 154–9.

[Isaiah Gafni]

ALEXAS, friend of Herod the Great (37–4 B.C.E.) and husband of Herod's sister, Salome. Herod forced Salome to marry Alexas, after threatening her with open enmity if she refused. Apparently Alexas was among the dignitaries who became powerful under the patronage of the new Judean dynasty. According to Josephus, Herod gave Alexas instructions about the procedure to be followed after his death. Alexas seems to have wielded sufficient authority to secure the release of the prisoners whom Herod had ordered to be executed on the news of his death to insure that the nation would mourn. But the whole story is probably a malevolent legend without foundation. Alexas had a son named after him, but with the surname Helcias. This son, known as Helcias the "Elder" or "Great" (ὁ μέγας), was apparently among the important members of the house of Herod. He is also referred to as "Helcias the Prefect" (Ant., 19:353). By the third generation, the house of Alexas had already obtained Roman citizenship, for Helcias' son was named *Julius Archelaus. Josephus states that he was "well versed in Greek learning," and Archelaus was therefore among the first to receive the historian's works (Apion, 1:51).

BIBLIOGRAPHY: Jos., Wars, 1:566, 660, 666; Jos., Ant., 17:10, 175, 193–4; 18:138; Stern, in: *Tarbiz*, 35 (1965/66), 243–5.

[Isaiah Gafni]

ALEXEYEV, ALEXANDER (1820–after 1886), apostate and Christian propagandist. He was born Wolf Nachlas into a ḥasidic family in Nezarinetz, Podolia, and became a Christian after his impressment into the Russian army. During his army service Alexeyev was made a noncommissioned officer for his zeal in persuading Jewish child conscripts to convert to Christianity. Later he became paralyzed and was discharged. Alexeyev was subsequently appointed to attend the *Saratov blood libel case (1853) as an expert. He wrote a pamphlet entitled "Do Jews Use Christian Blood for Religious Purposes?" (1886), which boldly defends the Jews against this particular accusation. Other writings, however, aimed at winning Jewish converts, attacked the Talmud and the rabbis in crude terms which made an impact at the time.

BIBLIOGRAPHY: S.A. Venegerov, *Kritichesko-Biograficheskiy Slovar*, 1 (1889), 375–6; S.L. Zitron, *Meshumodim* (Yid., 1921), 91.

ALFALAS, MOSES (late 16th century), preacher, lived in Tetuan, Spanish Morocco. Alfalas, in common with R. *Judah Loew of Prague, employed philosophical terms in his preaching, without retaining their accepted meaning. Many of his sermons were delivered in Salonika, and he probably lived there some time. His printed works are *Ho'il Moshe* (1597), 13 chapters of homiletic treatment of the midrashic sayings that refer to the meaning of the Torah and the relationship between Israel and the Torah; *Ba Gad* (printed together with the above), which contains seven chapters of homilies explaining the significance of the *milah* ("circumcision"); *Va-Yakhel Moshe* (1597), 25 homilies which he had preached in Venice, Salonika, Tetuan and other towns, including some homilies written by his students under his supervision. All three books include an index of contents and sources, compiled by Samuel ibn Dysoss.

BIBLIOGRAPHY: Steinschneider, Cat Bod, 1769 no. 6428.

ALFANDARI, family originating in Andalusia, Spain, and claiming descent from the family of Bezalel of the tribe of Judah. After the Expulsion (1492) the family spread throughout the Turkish Empire and France. For many generations they were among the major scholars and communal leaders of Constantinople, Brusa (Bursa), Smyrna, Egypt, and Ereẓ Israel. The first member of the family of whom there is knowledge is ISAAC B. JUDAH, who died in Toledo (1241). JACOB B. SOLOMON of Valencia and Solomon Zarẓah translated *Sefer ha-Aẓamim*, attributed to Abraham *Ibn Ezra, from Arabic into Hebrew. The name "Alfandery" was known in 1506 both in Paris and in Avignon, and, in 1558, in Lyons. Variants are "Alfandaric" and "Alfandrec." Members of the family lived in Egypt immediately after the Expulsion from Spain at the end of the 15th century; they were primarily merchants. A 1515 document from Cairo mentions the merchant DAVID ALFANDARI. ISAAC, who traveled to Yemen on business, also lived there. Later, several members of this family immigrated to Egypt from Portugal, while some Marrano members of the family remained in Portugal. OBADIAH (mid-17th century), apparently a member of the Egyptian branch of the family, was the last marketer for the woolen industry in Safed, where he was known as "chief of the artisans." His business failed as a result of the exorbitant demands made upon him by the authorities in Safed, he left for Egypt, and it was on a journey from Egypt that he was robbed and murdered (c. 1661). JACOB (second half of 16th century), a noted scholar of the Turkish branch, was the father of two well-known rabbis, Ḥayyim and Shabbetai. ḤAYYIM (the Elder; 1588–1640) was a noted scholar, communal leader, and *dayyan* in Constantinople, his birthplace. He wrote a great number of responsa, four of which were in the possession of his grandson, Ḥayyim b. Isaac. Among his correspondents was Jacob di Trani. He also wrote commentaries to most of the talmudic tractates, as well as novellae on the Tur of Jacob b. Asher, but these have not survived. SHABBETAI, born c. 1590, achieved fame as a scholar in his youth, and corresponded with two of Safed's great scholars, *Ḥiyya Rofe and Yom Tov *Ẓahalon, with whom he developed close ties upon their visit to Constantinople. Ḥayyim the Elder's son JACOB *ALFANDARI was one of the leading scholars of Constantinople. Ḥayyim's other son, ISAAC RAPHAEL (c. 1622–c. 1687), studied under Joseph Trani and about 1665 was appointed rabbi of one of the congregations in Brusa, a position he held until his death. Isaac Raphael, whom A.M. Cardoso met in Brusa in 1681, is purported by the latter to have expressed his belief in Shabbetai Ẓevi to him, but this testimony is spurious. Isaac Raphael wrote many responsa and corresponded with Ḥayyim *Benveniste, who lauded him highly. His son Ḥayyim b. Issac *Alfandari was a noted scholar. ELIJAH B. JACOB ALFANDARI (1670?–1717), rabbi and halakhic authority, was *av bet din* in Constantinople, where he was born and died. He fought Shabbateanism. His works include *Seder Eliyahu Rabbah ve-Zuta* (1719) on the laws of *agunah* and *Mikhtav me-Eliyahu* (1723), on the laws of divorce. Approximately at the same time there were in Salonika two scholars, both among the most distinguished of Solomon b. Isaac ha-Levi's pupils: MOSES ALFANDARI, scholar and pietist, and his brother ISAAC.

ḤAYYIM ALFANDARI, known as "Rabbenu" to distinguish him from the Elder, was a rabbi in Jerusalem. In 1758 he was included among the members of Judah Navon's *bet midrash*, "Damesek Eliezer." He was also one of a delegation of the seven rabbis including Ḥ.J.D. *Azulai sent on a special mission to Constantinople (but getting no farther than Egypt) to oust the official representative of Jerusalem's "*Va'ad Pekidei Ereẓ Israel.*" JOSEPH ALFANDARI (d. 1867), a *dayyan* and preacher in Constantinople, studied under Isaac *Attia, author of *Rov Dagan.* He wrote *Porat Yosef* (1868), responsa to which he appended his teacher's responsa, and talmudic novellae, and *Va-Yikra Yosef* (1877), homilies with some responsa.

SOLOMON B. ḤAYYIM ALFANDARY (d. 1773), rabbi and *dayyan* in Constantinople, signed documents and halakhic decisions along with the other rabbis of the community from 1746 to 1764. He later became chief rabbi. His two sons, who also served as rabbis in Constantinople, were RAPHAEL HEZEKIAH ḤAYYIM and ABRAHAM.

FERNAND ALFANDARY (1837–1910), a judge, was appointed to the Court de Cassation in Paris (1894).

BIBLIOGRAPHY: Ashtor, Toledot, 2 (1951), 486–7; S. Aviẓur, in: *Sefunot*, 6 (1962), 69; M. Benayahu, in: *Aresheth*, 2 (1960), 111–2; idem, *Rabbi Ḥ.Y.D. Azulai* (Heb., 1959), 380–1; Conforte, Kore, 46b; A. Galanté, *Histoire des Juifs d'Istanbul*, 1 (1941), 127.

ALFANDARI, AARON BEN MOSES (1690?–1774), rabbi and author. He taught at the yeshivah of Smyrna, where he served as *dayyan.* About 1757 he settled in Hebron where he was appointed chief rabbi. He wrote *Yad Aharon*, an attempt to bring Ḥayyim *Benveniste's *Keneset ha-Gedolah* up to date by including later decisions as well as sources not available to Benveniste. He also added his own decisions, as well as a work on the methodology of the Talmud. The volume on *Oraḥ Ḥayyim* was published in Smyrna in 1735; on *Even ha-Ezer* in two volumes in 1756–66. The one to *Yoreh De'ah* and the uncompleted manuscript on *Ḥoshen Mishpat* were destroyed in the great Smyrna fire of 1743. He also wrote *Mirkevet ha-Mishneh*, a commentary on Maimonides' *Yad Ḥazakah;* most of it was destroyed in the same fire and only the first part was published (1755).

BIBLIOGRAPHY: Azulai, 1 (1852), 16 no. 119, s.v. *Aharon Alfandari;* M. Benayahu, *Rabbi Ḥ.Y.D. Azulai* (Heb., 1959), 355; Michael, Or, no. 302.

ALFANDARI, ḤAYYIM BEN ISAAC RAPHAEL (c. 1660–1733), kabbalist and rabbi. He lived at Brusa, Turkey, where in 1681 he met Abraham Miguel *Cardozo [Cardoso]. According to the latter's testimony, Alfandari later came to him in Constantinople for esoteric study and believed in Cardoso's concept of the Divinity. For this reason Alfandari quarreled with Samuel *Primo, the rabbi of the Adrianople community. He was summoned before the scholars of Constantinople (c. 1683) and warned to disassociate himself from Cardoso's circle. On this occasion he denied belonging to Cardoso's circle and accused the latter of belief in the Trinity. Later Alfandari became an extreme Shabbatean. He signed his name "Ḥayyim Ẓevi," called himself "Messiah," and gathered a group of followers in Constantinople. Cardoso accused them of desecrating the Sabbath and eating forbidden food. In 1696 Alfandari settled in Jerusalem as head of the community *(resh mata).* He was active in public affairs and presided over a yeshivah. At one time he resided in Egypt, where he studied Isaac *Luria's writings which were in the possession of Moses Vital, grandson of Ḥayyim *Vital. He also lived in Safed, where he wrote a booklet called *Kedusha de-Vei Shimshei* (printed in J. Kasabi's *Rav Yosef*). By 1710 he had returned to Constantinople where, in 1714, he was a signatory to the excommunication of Nehemiah *Ḥayon during the controversy on *Oz le-Elohim* (1713). In 1717, however, Alfandari was Ḥayon's envoy and delivered letters of the scholars of Hebron and Salonika to the rabbis of Constantinople, and in 1718 he tried to reconcile Ḥayon with Naphtali *Katz. In 1722 his name appeared first on the list of the Safed scholars confirming Daniel Kapsuto's credentials as emissary. He returned to Constantinople, and died there. He wrote *Esh Dat* (1718), homilies on the Torah, and at the end of that work, *Muẓẓal me-Esh* by his uncle Jacob; and *Maggid me-Reshit*, a collection of responsa by his grandfather Ḥayyim the Elder, which closes with *Derekh ha-Kodesh* (1710). Alfandari's kabbalistic works have not survived.

BIBLIOGRAPHY: N.Ḥ. Ḥayon, *Ha-Kolot Yeḥdalun* (Amsterdam, 1725), 6a; *Leḥishat Saraf* (letters against Ḥayon, 1726), 11b, 14b; Rosanes, Togarmah, 4 (1935), 195–7; I. Ben-Zvi, in: *Reshumot*, 5 (1953), 56; I. Molcho and A. Amarilio, in: *Sefunot*, 3–4 (1959–60), 222–5, 227; Y. Nadav, *ibid.*, 325; R. Shatz, *ibid.*, 429, 431.

ALFANDARI, JACOB (c. 1620–1695), halakhic writer and preacher, the oldest son of Ḥayyim Alfandari the Elder, one of the leading scholars of Constantinople. Alfandari, who studied under his father, taught at a yeshivah. His disciples included Jacob Sasson. According to Abraham Miguel Cardoso, he urged his devotees not to accept the teaching of Shabbetai Ẓevi. He wrote many responsa, but most of his writings were destroyed in a fire in Constantinople. Some were rescued and published by his nephew Ḥayyim b. Isaac Alfandari, under the title *Muẓẓal me-Esh* ("Saved from Fire"; appended to his *Esh Dat*, Constantinople, 1718). Another portion, also published under the same title, was incorporated in Joseph Kasabi's responsa *Rav Yosef* (Constantinople, 1736), which was edited by Kasabi's pupil Jacob b. Judah Alfandari, grandson of the author. The responsa that he sent in reply to his brother Isaac Raphael's inquiries were published in *Maggid me-Reshit* (1660–74). A book of his sermons was in the possession of his nephew, Ḥayyim b. Isaac Raphael, who, in his *Esh Dat*, frequently cites homiletical expositions in his uncle's name. His rhetorical style, which is replete with rabbinical sayings, caused Ḥayyim Joseph David Azulai to call him "the father of rhetoric." His grandson Jacob was a prominent disciple of Ḥayyim b. Isaac Alfandari, and wrote an introduction to *Mikhtav me-Eliyahu* by Elijah Alfandari (1723).

BIBLIOGRAPHY: Ghirondi-Neppi, 180 (but the mention of a book on the Torah in manuscript may refer to a work by another scholar of the same name).

ALFANDARI, SOLOMON ELIEZER BEN JACOB, known as **Mercado** or **Maharsha** (**M**oreinu **ha-R**av **Sh**elomo **E**liezer; 1826 or 1829–1930), rabbinic authority. Alfandari was born in Constantinople. When he was about 25, he headed the yeshivah founded by a certain Foa, a wealthy resident of Constantinople, and among his pupils were many who subsequently became important rabbis. At the age of 30, he was elected a member of the general religious council (*Majlis*) of Constantinople. During the sultanate of Abdul Ḥamid, Alfandari opposed the conscription of Jews into the Turkish army, on the grounds that such conscription constituted interference with their religious practice, in violation of an agreement made by the Spanish exiles with the Turkish authorities as a condition for their settling in Turkey in the late 15th century. The order of conscription was finally rescinded. Alfandari was later appointed chief rabbi of Damascus, and from 1904 to 1918 served as chief rabbi of Safed. In 1926 he settled in Jerusalem.

Regarded as one of the great scholars of his time, Alfandari was accepted by both Sephardim and Ashkenazim and despite his exceptional firmness, his responsa and rulings were honored without demur. During the last years of his life, he was visited by Ḥayyim Eleazar Shapira, rabbi of the Munkacs Ḥasidim, who was deeply impressed by his personality. After his death, the Ḥasidim of Munkacs dedicated to his memory *Masot Yerushalayim* (1931), a hymn in his praise. Some of Alfandari's responsa were published in the periodical *Torah mi-Ẓiyyon*, in the *Kanah Avraham* of Abraham Ḥai Amozag, and in the works of his contemporaries. A few of his responsa were published by Isaac *Nissim, under the title *She'elot u-Teshuvot Maharsha* (1932). His remaining works are still in manuscript.

BIBLIOGRAPHY: M.D. Gaon, *Yehudei ha-Mizraḥ be-Ereẓ Yisrael*, 2 (1937), 85f.; Ben-Jacob, in: *Hed ha-Mizraḥ*, 4 (1945), 7f. no. 6; Ben-Zvi, in: *Oẓar Yehudei Sefarad*, 6 (1963), 8–11, 14; idem, *Ketavim*, 3 (1966), 91f., 99.

[Abraham David]

ALFASI, family of Tunisian rabbis that originated in Fez, Morocco. MASʿUD RAPHAEL ALFASI (1700?–1774), halakhist and kabbalist. Born in Fez or Tunis, he studied in the latter under Ẓemaḥ Ẓarefati, Abraham Tayyib, and Isaac Lumbroso. He established a great yeshivah in Tunis that has continued to bear his name to this day, and served as chief rabbi there from 1741 until his death. His writings included a large work on Maimonides' *Yad* patterned on Judah *Rosanes' *Mishneh la-Melekh* (1731), and a commentary to the Talmud. *Mishḥa de-Ravevata* (2 vols., Leghorn, 1805) is a commentary on the Shulḥan Arukh and includes responsa. His homilies on the Pentateuch and for Sabbath and holy days are extant in manuscript (Ben-Zvi Institute, no. 713); his grandchildren came into possession of a work on the Zohar, the *Idrot*, and Isaac *Luria's kabbalistic works (see edition of *Zohar*, Leghorn, 1872). SOLOMON BEN MASʿUD RAPHAEL ALFASI (1721–1801), his son, succeeded his father as rabbi of Tunis. His work on the Shulḥan Arukh as well as his responsa are included in the second volume of his father's *Mishḥa de-Ravevata. Keruv Mimeshaḥ* (Leghorn, 1858) includes novellae on the Talmud and on Maimonides' Yad as well as a talmudic methodology. Alfasi was renowned as a pietist and a wonderworker; many miraculous tales were told about him. His brother ḤAYYIM BEN MASʿUD RAPHAEL (1756–1783) wrote novellae on the Shulḥan Arukh – entitled *Ḥiddushei Maharḥa* – which were included in his father's *Mishḥa de-Ravevata* (1805) and in his brother's *Keruv Mimeshaḥ*.

BIBLIOGRAPHY: D. Cazès, *Notes bibliographiques sur la littérature juive-tunisienne* (1893), 157–68; Arditti, in: *Revue Tunisienne*, 2 (1931), 115–6.

ALFASI, DAVID BEN ABRAHAM (Ar. **Abu Suleiman Dā'ūd ibn Ibrahim Al-Fāsī**; tenth century), Karaite grammarian and commentator. Alfasi, who came from Fez, Morocco, spent a number of years in Ereẓ Israel where he composed a Hebrew-Arabic lexicon of the Bible (*Kitāb Jāmiʿ al-Alfāẓ*). The dictionary is extant in both a long and a short version, which was published in a critical edition by Skoss (see bibl.). The exact relationship between the two is not clear yet and needs further investigation. The dictionary consists of 22 chapters, one for each letter of the Hebrew alphabet. The entries are arranged according to the principle of bi-literal roots. He cites the translations of Onkelos and Jonathan b. Uzziel by name or refers to them as *al-Targum, al-Suryānī*, or *al-Mutarjim*. He also quotes the Mishnah and the Talmud, the masorah and the Rabbanite *siddur*. Alfasi mentions *Saadiah twice as "*al-Fayyūmī*," but he frequently uses and criticizes his commentaries without mentioning his name. He often designates the Bible *al-Qur'ān* or *al-Kitāb* (the Scriptures) and the Jewish scholars, *al-Rabbānīn* or *al-Rabbūnīn*, as was customary among Karaite authors. Alfasi's dictionary is one of the earliest and most important for the investigation of the history of Hebrew philology. The author reveals a fine sense for language and a profound, and, for his time, comprehensive, knowledge of ancient Hebrew linguistics. One of the important aspects of the dictionary is the comparative one: He quotes numerous parallels between biblical Hebrew and Aramaic, Arabic (both literary and spoken), and mishnaic Hebrew, many of which tally with those found in the *Risāla* of Judah b. Quraysh (whom the author does not mention), and many which have been accepted by present-day philologists. Alfasi explains many roots by metathesis or permutation of letters. He follows the Tiberian systems and the Palestinian grammarians as to the masoretic text, vocalization, and accents. The dictionary contains a wealth of information pertaining to early Karaite Bible exegesis as well as historical and material conditions in Ereẓ Israel in Alfasi's time. Compendia of the short version were compiled successively by *Levi b. Japheth, Eli b. Israel, and *Ali b. Suleiman (and were incorporated by Skoss in the apparatus of his edition). Alfasi's commentaries on the Psalms and the Song of Songs have not been preserved.

BIBLIOGRAPHY: S. Pinsker, *Likkutei Kadmoniyyot*, 1 (1860), 117ff., 223ff.; S.L. Skoss, *Hebrew-Arabic Dictionary of the Bible of David Abraham al-Fasi*, 1 (1936), introd.; 2 (1945); EJ, 3 (1929), 273–5 (includes detailed bibliography). **ADD. BIBLIOGRAPHY:** A. Maman, *Comparative Semitic Philology in the Middle Ages: From Sa'adiah Gaon to Ibn Barun (10th–12th c.)* (2004), passim, esp. 182–275; G. Khan, in: M. Polliack (ed.), *Karaite Judaism: A Guide to Its History and Literary Sources* (2003), 291–318.

[Solomon Leon Skoss]

ALFASI, ISAAC BEN JACOB (known as **Rif**; 1013–1103), author of the most important code prior to the *Mishneh Torah* of Maimonides. In a sense, Alfasi brought the geonic period to a close. The last of the Babylonian *geonim*, Hai Gaon, died when Alfasi was 25 years old. Alfasi himself was called "gaon" by several early halakhic authorities. *Judah b. Barzillai al-Bargeloni sometimes refers to him simply as "the Gaon." Alfasi was a native of Qal'at Ḥammad near Constantine, in Algeria, and is therefore sometimes called "ha-Kala'i." According to Abraham ibn David, Alfasi studied in Kairouan under both *Nissim ben Jacob and *Hananel b. Ḥushi'el, but nowhere does Alfasi mention them as his teachers.

After a period of study in Kairouan, Alfasi settled in Fez (hence his surname "Alfasi" or Rif, initials of **R**. **I**saac **F**asi). He remained there until 1088, when, in his 75th year, he was denounced to the government by enemies and was forced to flee to Spain. After a few months in Cordova he moved to Lucena, where he remained until his death. Shortly after his arrival in Lucena, he became head of the yeshivah (1089), following the death of Isaac b. Judah ibn Ghayyat. The most famous of his many students were Joseph *Ibn Migash, *Judah Halevi, Ephraim of Qal'at Ḥammad, and Baruch b. Isaac ibn *Albalia. Before his death, Alfasi designated Ibn Migash as his successor, even though his own son, Jacob, was a distinguished scholar. His death was mourned in dirges by various poets, among them Moses Ibn Ezra. Another, hitherto regarded as by Judah Halevi, is now attributed by Abramson to Joseph ibn Sahl. In his *Shirat Yisrael*, Moses Ibn Ezra praised Alfasi, describing him as a man unsurpassed in keenness of intellect, whose wisdom was deep beyond compare, whose pen was swift, outdistancing that of any rival, and whose equal in intensity of religious feeling could scarcely be found. Alfasi dedicated his life to the study of the Talmud and its dissemination among the masses. Long before he came to Spain, his intellectual stand was decided and he was not influenced by the cultural life of Spain.

Hundreds of Alfasi's responsa have survived. Many of them were written while he was still in Fez, the majority in Arabic. In character and in style, Alfasi's responsa are still close to those of the Babylonian *geonim*. Alfasi's fame however rests on his great work *Sefer ha-Halakhot* (or *Halakhot Rabbati*). In the composition of this work Alfasi had a two fold purpose: (1) extracting all the halakhic material from the Talmud, ascertaining the decision, and providing a comprehensive compendium for ready reference; (2) preparing an essential summary of the Talmud, thereby facilitating its study. Concerning the first purpose Alfasi confined himself to those portions of the Talmud which were still operative and practiced, and excluded those of only academic importance. His code, therefore, covers the three orders, *Mo'ed, Nashim*, and *Nezikin* and the individual tractates *Berakhot* and *Ḥullin*. Even here Alfasi omitted entire chapters, such as the laws of the Paschal sacrifice (in the tractate *Pesaḥim*) and all that portion of the tractate *Yoma* which deals with the Temple Service on the Day of Atonement. Alfasi arranged laws scattered throughout the orders *Kodashim* and *Tohorot* which retain their relevance such as the laws of the Torah scroll, *mezuzah*, and *tefillin*, under the special title of *Halakhot Ketannot*. *Sefer ha-Halakhot* deals with 24 tractates of the Talmud.

Alfasi's quotations from the Talmud are often longer than necessary for the mere determination of a decision; often he explains the cited passage. For the most part, his explanations are brief, and in several instances discernible only when compared with the talmudic text. He comments at some length on instances where the *geonim* differed in their interpretations, discussing the different views and giving his own interpretation. Such treatment at times mars the structure. Alfasi himself apologized for it in several places. On the other hand these extended comments greatly enhanced the value of the book.

To a certain extent Alfasi models himself on the *Halakhot Gedolot*, but Alfasi's book is much superior. The halakhic material is three or four times that in the *Halakhot Gedolot*; the aggadic material is even more. Alfasi exercises greater freedom in the handling of his material, and in the placement of certain discussions, often assembling into one place statements dealing with a specific subject but scattered throughout the Talmud. For example, he assembles all discussions on the scope and definition of censure and reproof at the end of chapter two of tractate *Shabbat*. Similarly he arranges the discussions of the *Gemara* relevant to many Mishnayot. He first quotes the discussions which bear directly on the Mishnah, then those which have a loose bearing on it, and finally those which have some association with it in terms of subject matter. Alfasi cites all the material from the Talmud necessary to establish the argument for each law and for every opinion, whereas the *Halakhot Gedolot*, for the most part, quotes only the law itself. Alfasi's sources are varied, but usually he does not identify them. In addition to the Babylonian Talmud and the geonic literature, he uses especially the *She'iltot* of *Aḥa of Shabḥa, *Halakhot Pesukot, Halakhot Gedolot*, Hai Gaon's responsa and commentary, and Hananel b. Ḥushi'el, upon whom most of his book is based and which he mostly copies. Other sources are an anonymous *Sefer Metivot*, Nissim Gaon's works, the *Hilkheta Gavrata* of Samuel ha-Nagid, and *Ḥefeẓ b. Yaẓli'aḥ. Nevertheless, Alfasi only dealt with those laws which originated in the Talmud. Alfasi also dealt with the *aggadah* in the Talmud which had been almost completely ignored by all the codifiers before him. He included those *aggadot* which taught good conduct and moral behavior, paving the way for all later codifiers. Alfasi's book is thus a source of considerable value for the *aggadah* also, and justly deserves the name "*Talmud Katan*" ("Little Talmud") given to it.

The *Sefer ha-Halakhot* was first published in Constantinople (1509), and this edition is now very rare (it was published in Jerusalem in 1969). The second edition (which was published in Venice, 1521) has many addenda from various glosses, thus altering the form of the book. All the later editions up to the Vilna Romm edition (1880–86) were based upon the Venice edition. The Vilna edition was compared with the first edition but is an eclectic version and so only enhanced the confusion. A complete and scientific edition – based on ancient prints, manuscripts, and **genizah* fragments – is still lacking. The Pressburg edition (1836) includes pseudo-Alfasi on *Nedarim*. An important aspect of the *Halakhot* is Alfasi's numerous revisions of what he had already written "and ordered to be corrected." These corrections were partly due to criticism, especially from his pupil Ephraim. This is attested to by various *rishonim* (e.g., *Ba'al ha-Ma'or* by Zerahiah ha-Levi to Sanh. 28b): "It seems that because of this Alfasi changed his opinion and ordered the erasure of what he had written on the subject… and the substitution of the corrected form… as you can find in some of the copies," and as Alfasi himself comments (A.A. Harkavy (ed.), *Koveẓ Teshuvot ha-Ge'onim* (1887), p. 327). His corrections have not always been included in the different manuscripts, and this accounts for the many variants in the versions of his book.

Jewish scholars of later generations were unstinting in their admiration of Alfasi and his book. Maimonides wrote "The *Halakhot* of the great rabbi, our teacher Isaac, of blessed memory, has superseded all these works (geonic codes)…for it contains all the decisions and laws which we need in our day… and, except for a few *halakhot*, not exceeding ten, his decisions are unassailable." Nevertheless, in one of his responsa Maimonides wrote that he differed from Alfasi in about 30 instances. In a letter to his disciple Joseph b. Judah, he advised him to make Alfasi's *Halakhot* his major study; and Maimonides himself taught it to his students. *Isaac b. Samuel ha-Zaken said of him: "A man will toil in vain to produce such a work, unless the spirit of God rest upon him" (introduction to *Menahem b. Aaron ibn Zerah's *Ẓeidah la-Derekh*, Ferrara, 1554). *Abraham b. David of Posquières, who tended to be severely critical of other authors, wrote of him: "I would rely on the words of Alfasi even if he should say that right is left." Even Alfasi's critics, and those who commented upon or supplemented his writings, never set out to find flaws in his work, but merely to correct whenever they deemed necessary; for they recognized the great usefulness of the book and wanted to see it used more widely. It was recounted that Jacob of Marvège, a tosafist, inquired in a dream whether the law concerning a certain case was according to the *geonim* or according to Alfasi; he received an answer from heaven: "And I shall establish my covenant with Isaac" (Gen. 17:21). Menahem ha-*Meiri always referred to Alfasi as "the greatest of codifiers." Joseph *Caro regarded Alfasi as the first among the three pillars of learning upon whom the house of Israel rests (Alfasi, Maimonides, and Asher b. Jehiel), and upon whose authority he determined the laws in his Shulḥan Arukh. Thus Alfasi's influence pervades Jewish code-literature up to modern times. At the close of the Middle Ages, when the Talmud was banned in Italy, Alfasi's work was expressly exempted, so that between the 16th and 19th centuries it was a principal subject of study among Italian Jews.

There is an extensive literature of commentary on Alfasi, some in amplification, others in condensation of his works. Among his critics and commentators were some of the greatest talmudic scholars, such as Ephraim his pupil, Zerahiah ha-Levi, *Abraham b. David, *Jonathan b. David ha-Kohen of Lunel, *Naḥmanides, *Meshullam b. Moses of Beziers, Aaron ha-Levi of Barcelona (see *Ha-Ḥinnukh), *Samuel b. Meir, Jacob *Tam, *Nissim b. Reuben Gerondi, and Joseph ibn Ḥaviva, author of *Nimmukei Yosef*. Almost all of them were scholars of Spain and Southern France, for in these countries, especially the former, the *Halakhot* was studied even more than the Talmud itself. More often than not, these commentators amplified, updated, and extended the discussion of Alfasi's themes rather than actually commenting on his text. A commentary on Alfasi to *Ḥullin* by an anonymous Yemenite scholar of the 12th century (1960), attests to the wide popularity of this work. The vast literature that was produced about Alfasi further testifies to the high regard in which he was held by subsequent generations.

In addition to the critics and commentators to Alfasi there is a ramified literature including works not really dependent upon Alfasi, but which follow his method of arrangement rather than that of the Talmud. The most eminent are those of Asher b. Jehiel and Mordecai b. Hillel, though the latter does not mention Alfasi at all. There are other books which include the whole of Alfasi and which expand his work with parallels and references to his sources and responsa. The most important of these is *Sefer ha-Ittim* of Judah al-Bargeloni.

Over 300 of his responsa, translated into Hebrew, have been collected and published (first edition Leghorn, 1781). Over 150 were published in their original Arabic with a Hebrew translation by A.A. Harkavy in *Kovez Teshuvot ha-Ge'onim* (1887), most of them having previously been included in the Leghorn edition. Another edition (*Ginzei Kedem*, 4 vols. (1930), 38–49), based upon the Oxford manuscript, was published by B.M. Lewin. Most of these responsa too are included in the Leghorn edition with some changes (cf. also *Kohelet Moshe* of S.A. Wertheimer, 1899). Another collection of Alfasi's responsa was edited by Z. Byednowitz (1934). Most of these are included in the previous editions. All these responsa were republished by Z. Leiter (1954). Many of Alfasi's responsa are still extant in manuscript. Variae lectiones based upon manuscripts were published by A. Sofer in his *Teshuvot Ḥakhmei Provinzyah* (1967). Many of Alfasi's responsa are scattered throughout the works of the early halakhic scholars, such as Judah al-Bargeloni, in the books of those who used his works, including *Isaac b. Abba Mari, Baruch b. Isaac, and Judah *Almadari's commentary on Alfasi's *Sefer ha-Halakhot*. Several of Alfasi's responsa are to be found in the famous collection of Maimonides' responsa, *Pe'er ha-Dor*, Leipzig, 1859, nos. 182–208.

BIBLIOGRAPHY: B. Cohen, in: JQR, 19 (1928/29), 335–410; Lewin, in: *Alummah*, 1 (1936), 105–13; H. Tchernowitz, *Toledot ha-Posekim*, 2 (1947), passim; Benedikt, in: KS, 25 (1948/49), 164–76; 26 (1949/50), 322–38; 27 (1950/51), 119f.; 28 (1952/53), 210–32; N.N. Rabinowitz, *Ma'amar al Hadpasat ha-Talmud* (1952), 256–7; A.N.Z. Roth, in: *Sura*, 3 (1957/58), 143–50; Habermann, in: *Tarbiz*, 19 (1959/60), 190f.; Sh. Abramson, *Rav Nissim Ga'on* (1965), 214–22 and index, s.v. *Yizḥak b. Ya'akov Alfasi*; idem, *Bi-Leshon Kodemim* (1965), 64–71; Sh. Shefer, *Ha-Rif u-Mishnato* (1967). **ADD. BIBLIOGRAPHY:** E.D. Shevet, "*Meḥkerei Mavo be-Mefarshei ha-Rif*," diss., Bar-Ilan Univ. (1995).

[Simha Assaf / Israel Moses Ta-Shma]

ALFEI MENASHEH (Heb. אַלְפֵי מְנַשֶּׁה), urban community in western Samaria, close to central Israel. The settlement is located on a hill, 1,082 ft. (330 m.) above sea level, and has an area of 1.8 sq. mi (4.6 sq. km.). In 1981 Ezer *Weizman, then secretary of defense, and Ariel *Sharon, secretary of agriculture, initiated the "seven star" plan to establish seven settlements at strategic points near the borders of Judea and Samaria. In 1983 the first settlers arrived at Alfei Menasheh. At the beginning, the community was part of the regional council of Samaria. In 1985 it received municipal council status. In the following years it came under terrorist attack. In 1987, in one such attack, the Moses family was decimated: the mother and one of the children were killed and the father and two other children severely injured. Between 1987 and 1989, three additional terror incidents rocked the community. The precarious security situation served to curtail the settlement's development, but in the 1990s it recovered and new neighborhoods were built. In 2002 its population was 5,250. The name of the settlement derives from Deuteronomy 33:17, which speaks of "the thousands of Manasseh."

[Shaked Gilboa (2nd ed.)]

ALFEROV, ZHORES I. (1930–), Russian Nobel laureate in physics. Alferov was born in Vitebsk, U.S.S.R. (now Vitsyebsk, Belarus), and graduated with a degree in physics (1952) from the Lenin Electrotechnical Institute in Leningrad (now St. Petersburg). From 1953 he was a staff member of the Ioffe Physico-Technical Institute in St. Petersburg, where he obtained his D.Sc. in physics and mathematics (1970) and which he directed from 1987. His academic appointments included dean of the Faculty of Physics and Technology at St. Petersburg Technical University. His main research interests concerned the theory and practical applications of semiconductors. He was awarded the Nobel Prize for physics (2000) jointly with Herbert Kroemer and Jack S. Kilby for his contributions to the double heterostructure concept. His research is of fundamental importance to the development of electronics, lasers, solar power usage, and communication technology. His honors include membership in the Russian (formerly U.S.S.R.) Academy of Sciences (1972), of which he was vice president from 1989, and the Lenin Prize of the U.S.S.R. (1972).

[Michael Denman (2nd ed.)]

ALFES (Alfas), BENZION (1850–1940), Yiddish and Hebrew writer. Born in Vilna, Alfes settled in Palestine in 1924; his earlier attempt to do so in 1871 had failed for family reasons. In Vilna he worked as a proofreader and for many years managed his wife's stocking factory. Alfes devoted his life to religious education, and was one of the few writers of his time who attempted to stem the secularizing drift of the Haskalah and its successor ideologies by writing religious literary works in Yiddish and Hebrew in a modern, popular style. He reacted to the late-19th-century proliferation of secular novels with his Yiddish *Ma'aseh Alfes* ("Alfes' Story"), published serially starting in 1900. The work consists of ethical and moralistic love tales in which he cast traditional allegorical and didactic elements in epistolary form. The work went through 12 editions and became a household name. Alfes also translated many religious Hebrew works into Yiddish (e.g., Gerondi's *Sha'arei Teshuvah* and Maimonides' *Ẓavva'at ha-Rambam*), and edited several works of other authors. Many of Alfes' commentaries were included in liturgical texts. At the age of 90, he wrote his autobiography, *Toledot ve-Zikhronot* (published posthumously in 1941).

BIBLIOGRAPHY: Rejzen, Leksikon, 1 (1928), 107–11; LNYL, 1 (1956), 118–20; Kressel, Leksikon, 1 (1965), 117.

[Leonard Prager]

°ALFONSO, name of many Spanish sovereigns. Of special significance in Jewish history were the following:

Kings of Aragon

ALFONSO I (1104–34; "the Battler"). After capturing Tudela from the Moors in 1114, he permitted Jews who had fled during the fighting to return to the city. ALFONSO II (1162–96). He employed a number of Jews as stewards or physicians. ALFONSO V (1416–58). In 1414, as infante, he intervened on behalf of the *Saragossa community, which had been ordered to send a delegation of representatives to the papal court at the time of the disputation of *Tortosa. Alfonso asked the pope for a postponement until the Jewish leaders could complete their seasonal duties in the community. As king, in 1424, Alfonso confirmed a ban prohibiting the establishment of a Jewish community in Barcelona.

Kings of Castile and Leon

Alfonso VI (1072–1109). After the capture of *Toledo from the Muslims in 1085, Alfonso permitted the Jews to remain in their quarter (*judería*), and granted residence rights to Jews seeking refuge there. He also appointed Jews to important state posts. Thus, Joseph b. *Ferrizuel (Cidellus), became royal physician. ALFONSO VII (1126–57). Like his father, Alfonso VI, he also appointed Jews to high positions; Judah ibn Ezra was his *almoxarife* ("collector of revenues") and in 1147 was in charge of *Calatrava, a stronghold on the Muslim border, where Jewish refugees from the *Almohad persecutions were welcomed. ALFONSO VIII (1158–1214), had a number of Jewish courtiers. He also settled Jews in frontier garrison towns, with complete autonomy within their fortified quarters. ALFONSO X (1252–84; "the Wise"). He was a patron of scholarship, and several Jewish translators and scientists, such as Isaac ibn Sid (Don Çaf) and Judah b. Moses ha-Kohen, worked under his auspices. Notable among their productions were the Alfonsine Tables *Libros del saber de astronomía*, one of the important scientific achievements of the reign. The code known as the *Siete Partidas* was produced under Alfonso's auspices, though not enforced until the following century. While this guaranteed the Jews physical security and rights of worship, it ordered the enforcement under the severest penalties of the conventional restrictions on the Jews, like the wearing of the Jewish *badge, and authorized judicial prosecution of the Jews for ritual murder (see *Blood Libel). Toward the end of his reign, Alfonso's attitude to the Jews changed for the worse. In 1279 he had all the Jewish tax-farmers imprisoned. In January 1281, he ordered the wholesale arrest of the Jews while they were attending synagogue on the Sabbath and demanded a ransom of 4,380,000 gold *maravedis* for their release. ALFONSO XI (1312–50). Although Jewish officials, such as Don Yuçaf (Joseph) de *Ecija, attended his court, his policy toward the Jews was often influenced or directed by the church or by anti-Jewish courtiers, such as Gonzalo Martinez de Oviedo. In 1348 Alfonso prohibited moneylending by Jews, but the Cortes revoked the decree in 1351.

BIBLIOGRAPHY: Baer, Spain, index; Neuman, Spain, index; M. Kayserling, *Juden in Navarra* (1961), index s.v. *Alphons*; REJ, index to vols. 51–100 (1936); *Sefarad*, index to vols. 1–15 (1957), 381–2.

°ALFONSO DE ESPINA (or **de Spina**, **D'espina**; second half of 15th century), principal originator of the Spanish Inquisition and its ideological and methodological program. Few details are known about his life. A Franciscan friar, possibly of Jewish birth or descent, he became rector of the University of Salamanca, and was confessor of the powerful Alvaro de Luna. Espina's most important work is *Fortalitium fidei contra Judeos, Saracenos et alios Christianae fidei inimicos*, written in 1458–59 and circulated in 1460. It was frequently printed (Nuremberg [1485–98], Lyons [1511]). The title, "Fortress of the Faith to give comfort to believers and defend the holy faith," indicates his object. The *Fortalitium fidei* consists of five sections, divided into chapters (*Considerationes*) and subdivided into *Haereses* ("heresies"); the second and third sections, *De bello hereticorum* and *De bello Judeorum*, contain his original views. The second section furnishes minute particulars of the sins committed by Jewish converts to Christianity (see *Conversos) and the means they adopted to continue observance of Mosaic Law. This seems for the most part to be based on accurate observation and is supported by various historical sources, including the Inquisitional records. Espina derived his knowledge of Jewish matters from his predecessors, such as Raymond *Martini and *Abner of Burgos, as well as from first-hand information. He recommends the establishment of an Inquisition in Spain and a detailed program. In the third section, tales about the *blood libel are revived. Here Espina explicitly suggests expelling the Jews from Spain, on the lines of the expulsion from England in 1290, implying that since England had managed to exist without the Jews, Spain could do likewise. The only way in which Spain can be converted into a truly Christian state, Espina states in this hate-obsessed work, is by extirpating the "Jewish heresy," expelling the Jews, and conquering the Muslims remaining on its soil.

BIBLIOGRAPHY: T. de Azcona, *Isabel la Católica* (1964), 377ff.; Baer, Spain, index; A.A. Sicroff, *Les Controverses des statuts de "pureté de sang"*... (1960), 74–76; H. Beinart, *Anusim be-Din Ha-Inkvizizyah* (1965), index; H. Kamen, *Spanish Inquisition* (1965), 30f., 42.

[Haim Beinart]

ALFONSO DE OROPESA (d. 1468), head of the Geronimite Order in Spain, said to have been of Jewish descent. In the early 1460s clashes took place in the cities of Castile between the ex-Jews who had adopted Catholicism (*Conversos) and their opponents among the Old Christian population. Alfonso now advised King Henry IV to take measures to supervise the Conversos and punish backsliders to Judaism. The king authorized him to execute his relatively moderate program, and Alfonso then conducted the investigation in Toledo and its environs for an entire year, imposing what he considered were adequate penalties. In 1465 Alfonso completed his *Lumen ad Revelationem Gentium* ("to prove the unity of all the faithful"), in which he explained his plan for the solution of the problem of both the Conversos and the Jews.

BIBLIOGRAPHY: Baer, Spain, 2 (1966), 289ff., 302; H.C. Lea, *History of the Inquisition of Spain*, 1 (1906), 127, 153; A.A. Sicroff, *Les controverses des statuts de "Pureté de Sang" en Espagne du XVe au XVIIe siècle* (1960), 67ff. M. Orfali, *"Ha-She'elah ha-Yehudit bi-Tfisato shel Frey Alonso de Oropesa,"* in: *Zion*, 51:4 (1986), 411–33.

[Zvi Avneri]

ALFONSO OF ZAMORA (c. 1474–1544), Spanish scholar. He was the son of Juan de Zamora, apparently one of the exiles of 1492 who subsequently returned to Spain, father and son being baptized together in 1506. Alfonso, who had received an adequate Jewish education before baptism, became professor of Hebrew at Salamanca, one of the European universities where Hebrew studies had been established by a decree of the Council of Vienna in 1311–12. He published in Latin an introduction to Hebrew grammar, dictionaries, and contributions to Bible study as well as a conversionist letter to the Jews of Rome (Alcalá de Henares, 1526). Alfonso is mainly remembered for his participation in the pioneering Complutensian Polyglot edition of the Bible, in the preparation of which he worked for some 15 years.

BIBLIOGRAPHY: F. Perez Castro, *El manuscrito apologetico de Alfonso Zamora* (1950); *Sefarad*, Index Volume (1957), s.v. *Zamora*.

[Cecil Roth]

°**ALFONSUS BONIHOMINIS** (**Buenhombre**; d. 1353), Spanish Dominican, born in Cuenca or Toledo. From a stay in Morocco, where he had been imprisoned, Alfonsus claimed to have brought back the Arabic original of the *De adventu Messiae*, an anti-Jewish epistle allegedly written by one Samuel of Fez. He said that he had translated this text in Paris in 1339. Known as the "Epistola Samuelis Maroccani," it was later translated into several languages and widely circulated in Europe. In fact, it seems that he himself was the author, drawing largely from another tract in Arabic written by a Jewish convert to Islam, *Samau'al b. Judah ibn Abbas, probably with the intent of presenting it as a Christian rather than a Muslim polemic. Alfonsus also translated another Arabic treatise by Samuel (or possibly wrote it himself): *Disputatio Abutalib Saraceni et Samuelis Judaei quae fides praecellat: christianorum, an iudeorum, an saracenorum* (Ms. Madrid Nac. 4402, fol. 103–10), a disputation between a Saracen and a Jew.

BIBLIOGRAPHY: A.L. Williams, *Adversus Judaeos* (Eng., 1935), 228–32; Loeb, in: RHR, 17 (1888), 311; M. Steinschneider, *Polemische und apologetische Literatur in arabischer Sprache...* (1877), 27, 187, 408; Moersseman, in: *Archivum Fratrum Praedicatorum* 10 (1940), 77ff.; Blumenkranz, in: JJS, 15 (1964), 125.

[Bernhard Blumenkranz]

ALGAZI, family which flourished between the 16th and 19th centuries in Turkey, Crete, Ereẓ Israel, and Egypt, and produced a large number of rabbis, kabbalists, and authors. Its members include (1) ABRAHAM BEN MOSES (1560?–before 1640), born in Constantinople, son-in-law of Joseph Benveniste de *Segovia, a pupil of Isaac Luria. A renowned talmudic scholar, he corresponded with the greatest of his contemporaries. After 1600, he resided on the island of *Chios and in Brusa (now *Bursa), Turkey, where he headed the community until his death. (NISSIM) SOLOMON *ALGAZI, Ḥayyim, Moses, and Joseph were his sons. (2) ḤAYYIM BEN ABRAHAM (?) (1614–before 1668), a Turkish scholar who studied under Joseph di *Trani and Abraham *Shalom in Constantinople, where he later headed his own yeshivah. He was the son-in-law of Judah ibn Ya'ish. His uncompleted commentary, *Netivot Mishpat*, to the *Meisharim* of Jehoram b. *Meshullam was published in Constantinople in 1669. His manuscript responsa and homilies were lost. (3) MOSES BEN ABRAHAM (d. before 1671) was one of the scholars of Bursa. Some of his novellae were published in his grandfather Joseph de Segovia's work, *Dovev Siftei Yeshenim* (Smyrna, 1671) to which was appended his booklet, *Sefat Emet*. (4) YOM TOV BEN (NISSIM) SOLOMON (d. 1727), a poet, lived in Constantinople. Letters and poems from his correspondence with the rabbi-poet Aaron de Toledo are extant. ISRAEL JACOB B. YOM TOV *ALGAZI was his son. (5) ABRAHAM BEN (NISSIM) SOLOMON (d. 1700), one of the scholars of Smyrna, edited his father's *Shema Shelomo* (Smyrna, 1659). (6) ḤAYYIM BEN MENAHEM (1640?–1710?), grandson of R. Ḥayyim Alfandari the Elder, was born in Smyrna. He studied under (Nissim) Solomon and Aaron *Lapapa. He served as rabbi of Rhodes and, after his son Abraham's death, returned to Smyrna. One of his students, Meir Danon, edited and published his *Ba'ei Ḥayyei* (Constantinople, 1712), novellae on Jacob b. Asher's *Turim*, on the Talmud, and on problems in Maimonides' *Mishneh Torah*. His manuscript homilies were lost. (7) NISSIM JACOB BEN ḤAYYIM SOLOMON, one of the scholars of Constantinople, settled in Safed. He visited Salonika in 1731 as emissary for Safed, returning by 1736. He is the author of responsa and novellae on Maimonides' *Mishneh Torah* (Ms. in Benayahu Collection). (8) SOLOMON BEN ABRAHAM *ALGAZI (1673–1762) was rabbi and codifier. (9) ISAAC BEN ABRAHAM (17th century), rabbi of Chios, studied under Ḥayyim *Benveniste, author of the *Keneset ha-Gedolah*, and (Nissim) Solomon Algazi. At the age of 17, he wrote *Doresh Tov*, a book of homilies. His manuscript responsa are in the Guenzburg collection in Moscow (no. 400). Some of his responsa were published with those of Ḥayyim Benveniste, *Ba'ei Ḥayyei*. (10) YOM TOV B. JACOB *ALGAZI (1727–1802) was a kabbalist and master of *halakhah*. (11) ḤAYYIM ISAAC (d. 1814) was chief rabbi of Smyrna in the late 18th century. (12) JUDAH, a rabbi in Smyrna, visited Ereẓ Israel. His commentary to Maimonides' *Mishneh Torah*, explanations of talmudic discussions, and homilies were published together as *Sha'ar Yehudah* (Salonika, 1805). Some of his manuscript works were lost. (13) MOSES BEN JOSEPH (1764–1840), a grandson of Solomon b. Abraham (8), was born and died in Cairo; in 1830, he was appointed chief rabbi of Egypt. That same year, with Adolphe *Crémieux's aid, he founded a modern school to which he also admitted Karaites. In 1840, he helped liberate the victims of the *Damascus blood libel. He was succeeded by his son Joseph.

BIBLIOGRAPHY: Azulai, 1 (1852), 163, no. 23; M. Benayahu, *Rabbi Ḥ.Y.D. Azulai* (Heb., 1959), 571, no. 39 (on Solomon II b. Abraham).

ALGAZI, ISAAC BEN SOLOMON (1882–1964), Turkish Sephardi *ḥazzan* and composer. Algazi, who was born in Izmir, at an early age joined the "Maftirim Choir" led by his father, himself a noted *ḥazzan* and author of religious poetry. He served as a teacher at the *talmud torah* and later as *ḥazzan* in his native town. He also became proficient in Turkish art music and for many years arranged special courses for the members of his community; A. Hemsi and other musicians were among his pupils. Algazi was a noted performer of classical Turkish music and adapted some to Hebrew texts which he himself translated. In 1923 he was appointed *ḥazzan* and music instructor at the "Italian" synagogue at Galata (Istanbul), which had a long tradition of musical activity. In 1930 Algazi became associated with the Jewish newspaper *La voz de Oriente*. In 1933 he went to Paris, but settled finally in Montevideo (Uruguay) where he was prominent in Sephardi congregation activities. Algazi's abilities as a composer and adapter were combined with a pleasant, flexible voice and a highly distinguished performing style. He imparted a Turkish influence to Eastern synagogue song. The sole printed work ("adaptation") of Algazi connects five *piyyutim* to form a Turkish "Fassil" (Suite), with each piece following a different rhythmical pattern ("uzul"). This work was published as *Extrait du Fassil Husseini des chants juifs orientaux… adapté sous le contrôle de M. Isaac Algazi* (1924–25).

As is usual with Eastern music, most of Algazi's compositions and arrangements were transmitted orally, but several have been recorded (collection of Israel Broadcasting Authority, Jerusalem). Some of his outstanding works which survive in oral tradition are: *The Song of Deborah*; *Ha-Ben Yakkir Li Efrayim*; *Kiddush*; *Seliḥot*; two "*Peshrev*" for choir, to Hebrew texts; songs of the Ladino Folklore. A selection of Isaac Algazi's poetry has been published in: *Shirei Yisrael be-Ereẓ ha-Kedem* (1921).

In addition to his main interest in Sephardi music, Algazi also devoted himself to the dissemination of Judaism and wrote two works in Spanish, *El judaismo, religion de amor* (Buenos Aires, 1945) and *La Sabiduría Hebrea* (Montevideo, 1949).

BIBLIOGRAPHY: M.D. Gaon, *Yehudei ha-Mizraḥ be-Ereẓ Yisrael*, 2 (1938), 43; Morguez-Algranti, in: *El Tiempo* (Tel Aviv, Oct. 20, 1964), 3–4.

[Hanoch Avenary]

ALGAZI, ISRAEL JACOB BEN YOM TOV (1680–1756), halakhic scholar and kabbalist, grandson of both (Nissim) Solomon *Algazi and Joseph *Ḥazzan. Probably born in Smyrna, Algazi lived in Safed, and for a few years, prior to 1730, in Smyrna. He was a member of a closed circle of kabbalists headed by Jacob Vilna. Algazi copied and published *Ḥemdat Yamim* (Smyrna, 1731–32), with many of his own glosses. By 1737 he was in Jerusalem and, a year later, dedicated "Neveh Shalom Berit Avraham," a yeshivah founded there for him. Algazi became head of Bet El, a *bet midrash* for pietists, and was consequently known as "the pietist rabbi." His was the first signature on the constitution of the kabbalistic group Ahavat Shalom. Algazi was appointed chief rabbi upon the death of his colleague, Isaac ha-Kohen (1755), but he died the following year. One of the most productive scholars of his time, he wrote many halakhic and homiletic works including *Emet le-Ya'akov* (Constantinople, 1764) on the laws of Torah scrolls; *Ara de-Rabbanan* (*ibid*., 1745), reprinted with Judah Ayyash's commentary; *Afra de-Ara* (Leghorn, 1783), a methodology for Talmud and codes; *Ḥug ha-Areẓ* (Jerusalem, 1910; with addenda, 1927), on the laws of Purim; *Ne'ot Ya'akov* (Smyrna, 1767); *Kehillat Ya'akov* (Salonika, 1786), a methodology; *Shalmei Ẓibbur* and *Shalmei Ḥagigah* (Salonika, 1790), on the laws of prayer and blessings; sermons Part 1, *Shema Ya'akov* (Constantinople, 1745); and Part 2; *She'erit Ya'akov* (*ibid*., 1751). Some of his works still survive in manuscript form. Ḥ.J.D. *Azulai, an acquaintance, condensed and completed Algazi's work, *Emet le-Ya'akov*, which he published under the title *Le-David Emet* (1786).

BIBLIOGRAPHY: M. Benayahu, *Rabbi Ḥ.Y.D. Azulai* (Heb., 1959), 351ff.

ALGAZI, LEON (**Yehudah**; 1890–1971), conductor, composer, and collector of Jewish music. Algazi, who was born in Romania, studied music in Vienna and Paris, and graduated from the Ecole Rabbinique de France. From his early studies with Abraham *Idelsohn, he acquired an interest in Jewish folklore and tradition. For many years, he taught at the Ecole de Liturgie et de Pédagogie in Paris. From 1929 he presented a weekly program of Jewish music on the French radio, and in 1937 became conductor at the Rue de la Victoire Synagogue. He helped to establish the "Mizmor" section of the Salabert publishing house, taught Jewish music at the Schola Cantorum (1936–40), and in 1961 was elected director of music for the temples of the Paris Consistoire. Among Algazi's many compositions of liturgical and folkloristic character are *Service sacré pour le samedi matin et pour le vendredi soir* (New

York, 1955), orchestral suites, psalms, harmonizations of traditional songs, and incidental music for the cinema and the theater. He published one extemely valuable collection, *Chants séphardis* (London, 1958). He also wrote essays on Jewish music in many scholarly publications.

BIBLIOGRAPHY: Sendrey, Music, nos. 488, 2901, 6275, 9121.

[Hanoch Avenary]

ALGAZI, (Nissim) SOLOMON BEN ABRAHAM (1610?–c. 1683), rabbi. Algazi, the grandson of Joseph de Segovia *Benveniste, was born in Borsa. He studied under his father and the poet Joseph Ganso, as well as Joseph Sasson and Meir de *Boton at their yeshivah in Gallipoli. Algazi settled in Jerusalem in 1635, but was in Smyrna in 1646 – apparently in order to publish some of his works. Here he remained and was considered one of the city's outstanding scholars. He founded a *bet midrash* whose students included his son-in-law, Aaron *Lapapa, and Ḥayyim b. Menahem Algazi, later rabbi of Rhodes. Algazi opposed *Shabbetai Ẓevi and his followers; together with his son-in-law and other scholars, he excommunicated Shabbetai Ẓevi and stated that he deserved the death penalty. Compelled to flee and hide outside the city, when Shabbetai Ẓevi's apostasy became known (1666) he returned to Smyrna and resumed his position. Algazi assumed the additional name Nissim on recovering from a serious illness contracted during his travels. He returned to Jerusalem about 1670, and by 1673 was head of the local *bet din*. Algazi achieved a reputation for his saintliness and was reputed as a miracle worker.

Among his many works are *Yavin Shemu'ah* (Venice, 1639), a commentary to the *Halikhot Olam* of *Jeshua b. Joseph and to *Sefer Kelalei ha-Talmud* of Joseph *Caro with additions entitled *Halikhot Eli* (Smyrna, 1663); *Gufei Halakhot* (*ibid.*, 1675); *Ahavat Olam* (Constantinople, 1642), the first of four volumes of homiletics; *Razuf Ahavah* and *Appiryon Shelomo* (Verona, 1649), a commentary to the homiletical passages of the tosafists; *Ta'avah la-Einayim* (Salonika, 1655), an elucidation of difficult talmudic passages in the *Ein Ya'akov* of Jacob *Ibn Ḥabib, with the addition of passages omitted by him; and *Leḥem Setarim*, on the tractate *Avodah Zarah* (Venice, 1664); his *Ziknat Shelomo*, a commentary on the *Ittur* of *Isaac b. Abba Mari, was never published.

BIBLIOGRAPHY: M. Benayahu, in: *Sinai*, 17 (1945), 304–9; Scholem, Shabbetai Ẓevi, index; Mifal ha-Bibliografyah ha-Ivrit, *Ḥoveret le-Dugmah* (1964), 28–31.

[Abraham David]

ALGAZI, SOLOMON BEN ABRAHAM (1673–1762), rabbi and halakhist. Algazi, who was apparently born in Jerusalem, was the half brother of Ḥayyim b. Moses *Abulafia, who restored the Jewish settlement in Tiberias.

Algazi was a pupil of Hezekiah da Silva. He served in the *bet din* of Abraham Yiẓḥaki, and taught in his yeshivah. One of his outstanding pupils was Judah Navon, author of *Kiryat Melekh Rav*. In 1728 Algazi immigrated to Cairo, where he also served in the *bet din* and c. 1740 was elected chief rabbi of Egypt. Algazi rescinded the resolution of the Egyptian rabbis not to study the *Peri Hadash* of da Silva which was made on the ground that he differed in several instances from Maimonides and other leading halakhists; all Algazi's decisions were based on da Silva. He also wrote responsa and a book on Maimonides, now lost but which was seen by Ḥayyim Joseph David *Azulai in 1753.

BIBLIOGRAPHY: Azulai, 1 (1852), no. 23; M. Benayahu, *Rabbi Ḥ.Y.D. Azulai* (Heb., 1959), 571.

ALGAZI, YOM TOV BEN ISRAEL JACOB (1727–1802), kabbalist and halakhist. He studied with his father and was a close friend of Ḥ.J.D. *Azulai. Both studied under R. Jonah *Navon and R. Shalom *Sharabi. Algazi was a member of the Ahavat Shalom group of kabbalists and signed its articles of association in 1754, 1758, and 1759. He was a member of *bet ha-midrash* Neveh Shalom and of Bet El. R. Shalom Sharabi succeeded Algazi's father as head of the kabbalists' yeshivah, but Yom Tov Algazi administered it. Following R. Sharabi's death in 1782 he was elected rabbi and *dayyan* and in c. 1777 he became *rishon le-Zion*. The period of his office was a difficult one for the Jews of Jerusalem who were vexed by the authorities. Algazi's leadership, influence, and fame in the Diaspora were of help to the community. In 1764 he accompanied R. Abraham b. Asher and Ḥ.J.D. Azulai on a mission, on behalf of the Pekidei Ereẓ Israel be-Kushta ("Agents for Ereẓ Israel in Constantinople"). From 1770 to 1775 he was sent on other missions from Jerusalem to Constantinople, Adrianople, and Belgrade. He traveled in Italy, France, Holland, Germany, and Poland and returned to Jerusalem (1777) via Italy and Smyrna. He appointed his son Jacob a *parnas* of the Hebron community (1787). As the debts of the Hebron community increased, Algazi and his son endured a most difficult period (1793–95). Both father and son were in danger of imprisonment. Creditors became violent and Jacob Algazi was badly beaten up. In the month of Elul 1795, Algazi went to Constantinople and within three months collected a large sum of money for Hebron; he also conducted a large collection in Smyrna and Salonika. However, before he returned to Jerusalem, his son died (1796) from the blows which he had received. His works are distinguished by their sharpness and depth. They are *Hilkhot Yom Tov*, printed with the Vilna Talmud, on *Ḥilkhot Bekhorot ve-Ḥallah* by *Naḥmanides, which he found in a manuscript in Italy (1795); *Simḥat Yom Tov*, responsa (1794); *Kedushat Yom Tov*, responsa and sermons (1843); *Get Mekushar,* studies on the marriage contract, in *Ne'ot Ya'akov* (1767), 24–79.

BIBLIOGRAPHY: A. Rivlin, in: *Zion*, 5 (1933), 131–40, supplement; Ya'ari, Sheluḥei, 535–40; M. Benayahu, *Rabbi Ḥ.Y.D. Azulai* (Heb., 1959), 353–4.

ALGERIA (Central Maghreb; Ar. **al-Jazā'ir**), modern designation for the central part of North Africa, bordered by *Morocco on the west and *Tunisia on the east. Resistance

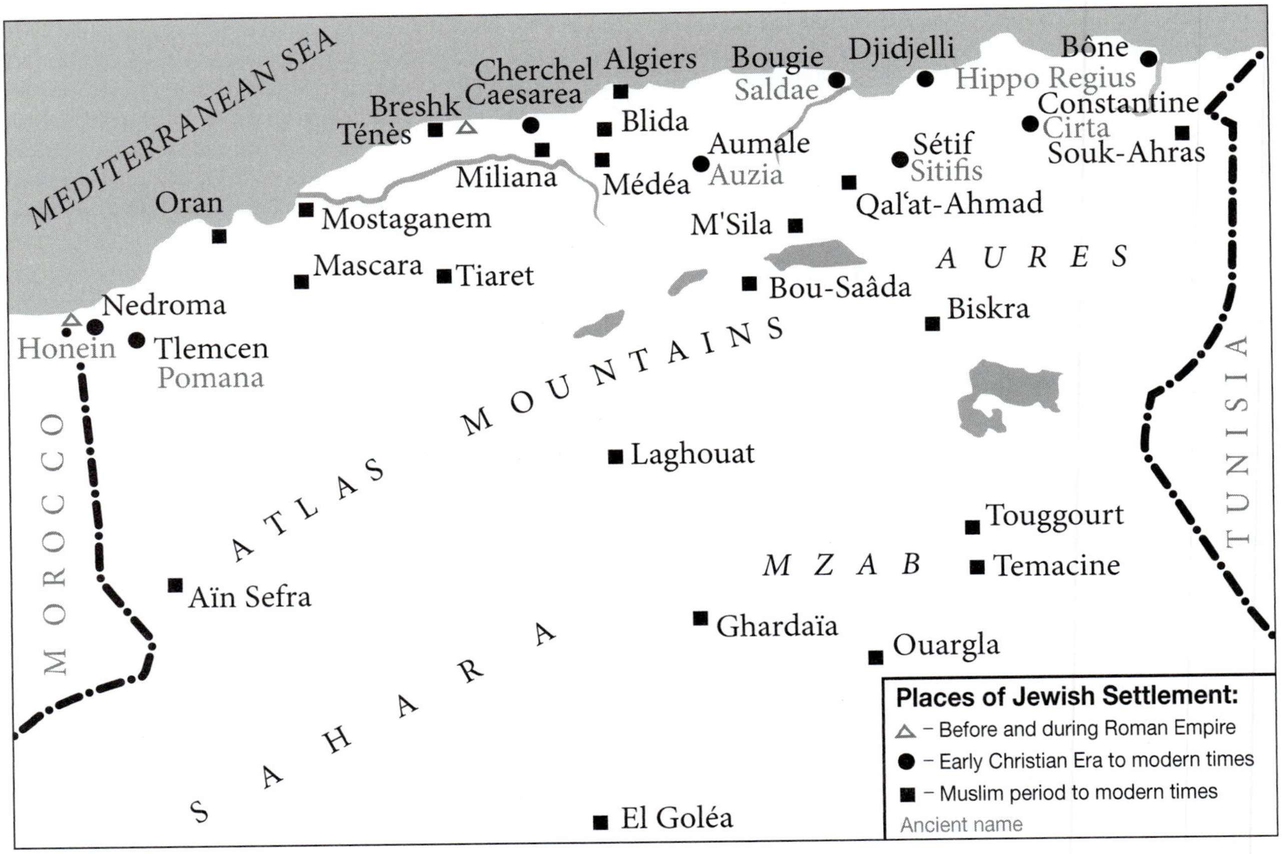

Places of Jewish settlement in Algeria.

against the Arab invasion in the seventh century was organized first near Biskra and later in the Aurès mountains, where the **kāhina* (an epithet meaning priestess), the "queen" of the Judeo-Berber tribe Jarawa, won brilliant victories. With the death of the *kāhina* in 693 came the collapse of *Berber independence. Most of the Jarawa adopted Islam, others escaped to the west and south reinforcing the Jewish elements there. Oriental Jews, who followed in the wake of the Arab armies in large numbers, rebuilt the old destroyed communities of Algeria. The Jews in the urban centers, such as Mejana or Mesila, were Rabbanites; so also were the Jews in the capitals of the various Berber kingdoms – Ashir, Tahert (Tiaret), where the philologist R. *Judah ibn Quraysh lived, *Tlemcen, and *Qalʿat Ḥammād, where R. Isaac *Alfasi was probably born. These communities were in contact with the communities of *Fez in the west and *Kairouan in the east, and even with the *geonim* of Babylonia and Palestine. It is partly through them that the teachings of the academies of *Sura and *Pumbedita, and later of Kairouan, spread to Morocco, and from there to Spain. Thus, the influence of these communities on the intellectual and religious development of the Jews of Spain can be seen. The teachings of the sages were spread to the area north of the Sahara Desert from Gabès, Tunisia, to Sijilmassa (in the Ziz Valley), Morocco, by traveling merchants. The Jewish tribes of the region of Wargha were *Karaites. They were nomad warriors. Their descendants were called "Bahusim" and remained in the eastern part of Algeria up to modern times. In the tenth century, a Jew named Abu al-Faraj instigated an important revolt against the Zirid sovereigns of the Berber tribes in the Setif region. Defeated, he was tortured to death in 989.

Apart from the fact that the community of *Tlemcen was destroyed, almost nothing is known about Algerian Jews during the rule of the Almohads in the 12th and 13th centuries. In any case, after that period of disorder the Jewish population of Algeria was considerably diminished. In the 13th and 14th centuries some Jewish merchants residing in Algeria had regular contacts with other countries, particularly with Catalonia, and these ties served to keep open channels of communication with the more developed Jewish communities. Jews of Languedoc and even Marseilles lived in Bougie, the Algerian harbor town, from 1248. Tlemcen, gate to the Mediterranean and a final station on the Sudanese gold route, known as the "Jewish Road," had a small but lively community, which was sustained by the rich Jewish merchants of Barcelona, Valencia, Tortosa, and Majorca. Most of these merchants were actually natives of the Maghreb and particularly favored by the kings of Aragon, who relied on them as essential to their prosperity. Their relatives had remained in the Maghreb, settling at *Algiers, Cherchel, Tenes, Mostaganem, and Tlemcen. At that time there was a continuous emigration of Muslims from the Christian kingdoms of Spain to Africa and they were assisted by the Jews in Spain. This was the very remunerative business of the great Jewish African-Spanish family Alatzar (also al-ʿAzār), in particular. The Jewish merchants of the central Maghreb had many trade activities, including the slave trade, so important at the time. However, they traded chiefly in Sudanese gold. Many traded with the Balearic Islands using their own ships.

The Christian kings of Spain appointed many Jews as their ambassadors to the Muslim courts. In that capacity Abraham and Samuel *Bengalil, Judas "Abenhatens," and the *alfaquim* ("physician") *Bondavin made their first visit to Tlemcen in 1286. In 1305 Solomon b. Zequi of Majorca was chosen to settle a dispute with the town of Breshk. These experts in North African diplomacy, as well as the wealthy merchants in the country, were exceptions among the mass of Algerian Jewry, whose level of culture was very low. Largely because of them and the possibility of communication with the important economic centers which they represented, many Spanish refugees of 1391 chose Algeria as their haven. They emigrated in continuous groups from Catalonia and the Balearic Islands. They were favorably received by the Muslim authorities, in particular by the Ziyanid princes. In contrast, their relations with the local Jews, who had at first received them fraternally, later became tense. Their numbers gave rise to fear of competition in their professions. Differences in ritual, language, customs, and above all social conceptions, caused conflicts between the two communities. The Sephardi Jews asserted themselves by their intellectual superiority, financial means, and skills. The older community resisted the attempt of the newcomers to dominate communal life. However, there were refugee leaders who were able to mitigate the conflicts between the two groups. The learning and dedication of the new immigrants renewed the moral and religious life of Algerian Jewry. Their talent in organizational activities strengthened the Jewish institutions of Algeria.

R. Ephraim Ankawa reestablished the community of Tlemcen; the eminent talmudic authorities R. *Isaac b. Sheshet Perfet (*Ribash*), R. Simeon b. Ẓemaḥ *Duran (*Rashbaẓ*), and the latter's descendants were mainly responsible for Algiers becoming a religious and intellectual center. The communities of *Honein, *Oran, Mostaganem, Miliana, Médéa, Tenès, Breshk, *Bougie, *Bône, and *Constantine, although dependent on Algiers, also became centers of Jewish learning under the leadership of the rabbis Amram Merovas Ephrati, Samuel Ḥalawa, the brothers Najjār, and others.

Very few of the Spanish exiles of 1492 came to Algeria. The only city that attracted them was Tlemcen, which they reached by way of Oran. It has been said, however, that the loss of Granada, Spain, in 1492 by the Muslims had grave repercussions for the Jews in Algeria. In cases such as that of the Muslim preacher al-Maghillī, resentment was expressed in violent tirades against the Jews. The prosperous and powerful communities of Tlemcen and, in particular, Tuat were destroyed some years later as a result of such agitation. Just after these events, the Spanish occupation of Oran (1509–1708) and Bougie (1509–55), resulted in Jewish property being pillaged and the Jews themselves sold as slaves. Finally, however, some influential families such as Jacob *Cansino, Jacob b. Aaron, and *Sasportas convinced the Spaniards in Oran that their Arab policy would best be served by accepting a Jewish community in Oran. In the 17th and 18th centuries, descendants of Marranos and Jews from Leghorn, Italy, settled in Algeria, especially Algiers. Among the first who arrived were the Lousada, Alvarenga, Zacuto, Molco, and dela Rosa families; among the later ones were the Soliman, *Busnach, *Bouchara, *Bacri, Lealtad, and *Delmar families. They played an important role in ransoming Christian captives for European governments, and their commercial activities enriched the country.

The "refugees of 1391" had stimulated Algerian trade and brought prosperity to remote communities. They exported ostrich feathers from Mzab and African gold from Tuat, as well as burnooses, rugs, cereals, wool, and pelts to Europe, while European products were in turn sold in Africa by the same merchants. At that time the Jews owned estates, slaves, and flocks. In the regions subject to a central power, the Jews paid the **jizya*, the tax levied on all non-Muslims. Their rabbis were exempted from it, as were the merchants, mainly descendants of *megorashim*, because they paid customs on their imports. The native Jews were thus in an inferior position. Moreover, the *megorashim* had a separate quarter, synagogue, and even cemetery. Their dress was also different from that of the native Jews; they continued this distinction by wearing berets or hoods. Thus, they were called *baʿalei ha-kappus* or *kabbusiyyin*, in contrast to the *baʿalei ha-miẓnefet*, native Jews who wore turbans.

The organization of the communities that was established in the 14th century was in effect until 1830. At the head of each community was a *Sheikh al-Yahūd*, or *Zaken ha-Yehudim*, called also **muqaddam*, who was appointed by the Muslim authorities. His powers were discretionary, tempered only by protests of the rabbis. A prison and the police were at his disposal for punishing and carrying out the sentences of the *bet din*. He also named the officers (*gedolei ha-kahal, ziknei ha-kahal*) who were charged with the collection and administration of charity funds, and the management of the synagogue and charitable institutions. The Judeo-Spanish groups chose their officers (*neʾemanim*) themselves. The rabbinical courts were composed of three judges chosen and paid by the community. Only civil disputes were brought to them; they had no jurisdiction in criminal matters.

Although the rabbinical courts were available to Algerian Jews, they tended more and more to turn to Muslim civil courts. To discourage this practice the rabbis were able to threaten, and indeed put into effect, decrees of excommunication. On questions of *minhag*, however, the rabbis were often compelled to approve the local custom followed by African Jews. Some later practices originated in *takkanot*. The *haskamot*, agreements over administrative regulations, also legalized local practices. The particular regulations of each community gave it a certain individuality that it jealously preserved for future generations. This resulted in collections of *minhagim*, prayers, and liturgy (*piyyutim*), the work of local rabbis, written either in Hebrew or Judeo-Arabic. The communities of Tlemcen, Oran, and Algiers each had its own *maḥzor*. Sometimes the synagogues of the same town even had different liturgies. Thus, in the 18th century the community of Algiers was convulsed by disputes over liturgy.

Jewish-Muslim relations were, on the whole, good. It was only occasionally that outbursts of fanaticism gave rise to local persecutions. In certain towns it was accepted that at such times the mosques, although forbidden to infidels, should serve as a refuge to the Jews. The religious Muslim leaders sometimes helped them; for example, the *marabout* (Muslim holy man) of Blida, southwest of Algiers, stopped a pogrom and forced the plunderers to return their booty.

Generally, from the 16th century the situation of the southern Jews was better than that of their coreligionists in the centers under Turkish domination. The Turks were the ruling class who had come to exploit the country, and they treated the natives, both Muslims and Jews, roughly. Most Jews, living in separate quarters, were at their mercy. They increased the restrictions imposed on Jews in Islamic countries more through greed than fanaticism. On the other hand, the "sovereign" days, chosen by the Janissaries, and the beys, governors of provinces, humored the upper-class Jews, from among whom they chose their counselors, physicians, financiers, and diplomats. The Muslim rulers charged these diplomats with the difficult assignment of maintaining relations with European Powers, a task that was complicated by the pirate raids on European ships, condoned by the Algerian rulers. It was usually the wealthy and influential Jews originally from Leghorn, the *Gorenim* who received these assignments. Their high positions could not, however, protect them against the violence of the Janissaries who resented the favors the Jews received from the bey. The assassination in 1805 of the bey's chief aide, the powerful Naphtali Busnach, was followed by the only massacre of Jews to take place in Algiers.

The French government had accumulated enormous debts to the Bacri and Busnach families, relatives and partners, who had been delivering grain to France for them since the end of the 18th century. These unpaid debts were the cause of diplomatic incidents that resulted in the French conquest of Algiers in 1830. The French conquest opened a new era for the 30,000 Jews of Algeria. In the beginning the communities were allowed to continue their self-government, and the rabbis continued to administer justice. But this autonomous structure was soon overturned. Rabbinical justice was deprecated and jurisdiction of the Jews passed to the French tribunals. The *muqaddam*, who had previously headed each Jewish community, was replaced by a deputy mayor. These reforms did not give rise to any protests on the part of the Jewish population, as they retained their previous legal status. However, the changes caused some to leave: many European Jews returned to Leghorn, and the middle class, small tradesmen, and craftsmen emigrated to Morocco and Tunisia. On the other hand, Moroccan and Tunisian Jews, attracted by new conditions, immigrated into Algeria. There was also a movement of Jews from the south toward the centers and the port towns.

The Jews under French Rule

French colonialism lasted from 1830 to 1962. The duration of colonialism, the presence of French settlers, the involvement of French Jewry, and the impact of the changes in the country, its people, and its Jews shaped Jewish community history during this period. The cornerstones of the period were the establishment of the consistorial organization in 1845, the naturalization of the Jews in 1870, World War II and its impact (1939–45), and the decolonization processes from 1954 to 1962. The modernization process of Algerian Jewry was the most complete in the Muslim world; Jews became French citizens and dissociated themselves from Muslim society. It is not surprising that at the end of the colonial area most Algerian Jews continued their life in France, like all the French settlers.

Under the French each municipal council and chamber of commerce had one or two Jewish members. In 1858 a Jewish general counselor was elected for each province. In 1845, after a long mission of two French Jews, Jacques-Isaac Alters and Josef Cohen, consistories, on the model of those of France, were created in Algiers, Oran, and Constantine. Chief rabbis, brought from France, were appointed and paid by the government, and presided over all other religious functionaries. One of the tasks of these chief rabbis was to promote the emancipation of their followers, although they were not yet French citizens. Cultural assimilation was so rapid that it provoked a break with the old Jewish world. Some attempted to fight the trend toward total assimilation in such undertakings as the establishment of Hebrew printing houses in Algiers in 1853 and Oran in 1856 and 1880. French education, despite its advantages, led many Jews who were unprepared for it to leave Judaism. To counteract this trend *talmud torah* schools were opened in many cities. Several highly influential families formed a Jewish intelligentsia, capable of assimilating French civilization yet maintaining their own traditions. Members of these families were the first to enter the liberal professions, becoming magistrates, physicians, lawyers, engineers, high-ranking officers in the army, and, later, university professors. Both they and the French Jews favored the naturalization of Algerian Jews as did also French liberals.

Algerian Jews were granted the right of individual naturalization in 1865, and on October 24, 1870, by the *Crémieux Decree all Algerian Jews were forced to become French citizens, with the exception of those in the south, whose legal situation remained uncertain. This was the first instance in the Muslim world in which the Jew's legal status changed so radically. The naturalization of some 35,000 Jews resulted in a wave of antisemitism. Jews were attacked and in Tlemcen in 1881, in Algiers in 1882, 1897, and 1898, in Oran and Sétif in 1883, and in Mostaganem in 1897, where the violence reached its peak. Up to 1900 there were in all towns and villages cases of looting and killing, and numerous cases of synagogues being sacked and the Holy Scrolls desecrated and used as banners by the rioters. The *Dreyfus affair in France inflamed the anti-Jewish campaign even more. An antisemitic party came to power: Edouard *Drumont was elected the representative of Algiers and Max Regis became its mayor. Extraordinary measures were taken against the Jews. In Constantine, by decision of the deputy mayor Emile Morinaud, Jewish patients were not admitted to hospitals. The illegality of such steps, together with the fact that the Muslims failed to support the movement, brought about the defeat of the antisemitic party; in 1902 it ceased to exist altogether.

It should be emphasized that the wave of antisemitism came only from the French colonial settlers. It was a modern form of antisemitism deriving from the fear of a breakdown of the colonial hierarchy in which "inferior" elements might become part of the ruling class.

The heroic participation of Jews in World War I caused an improvement of relations, although in 1921 there was a renewed outburst of hatred in Oran. Hitler's rise to power, greeted with rejoicing by the antisemites, caused a new wave of antisemitic campaigns, which resulted in a massacre in Constantine in 1934.

The crisis was renewed in 1936, when Léon *Blum, a Jew, became premier of France. The Jewish Algerian Committee for Social Studies, directed by Henri Abulker, André Lévi-Valensi, Elie *Gozlan, and others, undertook intensive activities aimed at curbing the racial unrest. Subsequently, the Union of Monotheistic Believers (Union des Croyants Monothéistes) was formed; during World War II it was responsible for the Muslims declining to identify themselves with the antisemitism of the Vichy government.

Holocaust Period

Despite the bravery shown by the Jews on the front during World War II, one of the first measures taken after the French defeat in 1940 was to abrogate the Crémieux Decree. The 117,646 Jews of Algeria became the object of daily suffering: they were cast outside the pale of society, impoverished, and humiliated. The Algerian administration applied the racial laws of Vichy with excessive severity. After Jewish children were banned from attending schools and restrictive clauses were applied in institutions of higher learning, Robert *Brunschwig organized private courses and schools. The expenses of these private schools were met by the communities jointly, although the financial burden was heavy. Some time later, the government totally forbade Jewish higher education and put the Jewish schools under strict, malevolent supervision without, however, contributing toward their upkeep. Only the rabbis were granted the right to represent the community before the authorities.

Algerian Jewry, in danger of total destruction, was saved only by its own determination. The Algerian resistance movement was the work of Jews, and consisted almost entirely of Jews. Among its leaders were Raphael and Stéphane Abulker, Roger and Pierre Carcassone, Jean Dreyfus, Jean Gozlan, and Roger Jais. Their activity led to the insurrection of Algiers led by Jose Abulker on November 8, 1942, which neutralized the capital while the Americans landed in the country as part of Operation Torch. Paradoxically, after this victory of the allies in Algeria, General Giraud, Admiral Darlan, and Governor Yves Câtel, with the complicity of the local diplomatic representative of the U.S.A., Robert Murphy, took new measures against the Jews, including the establishment of detention camps. The protests of Jewish international and Algerian organizations and the French Committee of National Liberation in London, the intervention of highly placed Jews, Muslims, and Christians against this injustice, and a world-wide campaign were all of no avail against the will of the antisemites. Finally after the personal intervention of President Roosevelt, the Crémieux Decree was again put into force on October 20, 1943. However, it was only in 1947 that equality for all was proclaimed.

[David Corcos / Haim Saadoun (2nd ed.)]

Contemporary Period

During the postwar period a number of Jewish organizations were formed in Algeria. The Fédération des Communautés Israélites d'Algérie was established in April 1947 for the purpose of defending Algerian Jewry and safeguarding its religious institutions. *ORT was founded in 1946 in Algiers and Constantine; the Ecole Rabbinique d'Algérie, established in 1947, began its activities in 1948; the Comité Juif Algérien d'Etudes Sociales, formed after World War I, resumed its activities in 1948 and published a monthly, *Information Juive*, from 1948 to April 1962 in Algiers and from September 1963 in Paris.

Although the formal structure of the Algerian community resembled the French pattern centering around legally sanctioned "religious associations," in practice each *kehillah* functioned autonomously. Until 1961 the Fédération united 60 different communities. Thereafter the communal structure underwent a gradual disintegration and communal life became primarily a function of local customs and traditions.

The fate of the community was fundamentally determined by the Algerian nationalist struggle for independence. Tragically caught between two violently opposed forces the marginal position of the Jews in Algerian society exposed them to constant danger.

The conflict had already become clear in August 1956 when the FLN (Front de Libération Nationale – the Algerian National Liberation Front, an organization dedicated to achieving Algerian independence) appealed to the "Algerians of Jewish origin" who "have not yet overcome their troubled consciences, or have not decided which side they will choose" to opt for Algerian nationality. Jewish fears increased when, on February 18, 1958, two emissaries of the Jewish Agency were kidnapped and assassinated by the FLN. In December 1960 the Great Synagogue of Algiers was desecrated and the Jewish cemetery in Oran was defiled. The son of William Levy, a Jewish socialist leader was killed by the FLN and subsequently Levy also was assassinated by the OAS (Organisation Armée Secrète – a counter-terror organization opposed to an independent Algeria). In May 1956 the Mossad, the Israeli secret service, which had begun to work in North Africa and created networks of Algerian Jews from Constantine, attacked the Muslims of Constantine in response to continuous attacks against Jews. About 20 Muslims were killed as a warning to Algerian Muslims not to involve the Jews in their struggle with the French.

Until 1961 the majority of Algerian Jews had hoped that partition or a system of dual nationality would obviate the conflict. As the struggle developed, however, they increasingly feared that popular reaction would be directed against them not only as Europeans but as Jews and Zionists. Consequently, although the community never adopted an official anti-independence position, in March 1961 a delegation from the Comité Juif Algérien d'Etudes Sociales urged that the negotiations then in prospect should obtain official recognition of the French nature of the Algerian Jewish community. (Later it was agreed in Evian to treat Jewish Algerians as "Europeans.")

By the 1960s the "Gallicization" of the large mass of Algerian Jews had developed to the point where both their emotional allegiances and cultural predispositions were largely French. The resulting diminution of Jewish observances did not, however, reflect a positive integration into the Algerian French community which was less a community than a settlement of colons. Fundamentally, however, the separate identity of the community was maintained by the system of status inherent in Islamic society where religion and family and not formal nationality and cultural behavior were the determinative factors. The term "Frenchman" in Algeria did not apply to either Arab or Jew. The FLN and OAS reign of terror and counter-terror in 1961 and 1962 had catastrophic consequences for the Jewish community. As elsewhere in North Africa the Jewish quarters often straddled the European and Arab sections. These quarters often sustained the first and sometimes only Muslim reprisals after attacks by European terrorists on the Muslim quarters. These often degenerated into pitched battles between the two communities, especially their youth.

Throughout this period there was a steady flow of emigration of Jews from Algeria. The rate of emigration rose steeply in mid-1962 when, as a result of OAS violence, the community feared that the proclamation of independence would precipitate a Muslim outburst. By the end of July 1962, 70,000 Jews had left for France and another 5,000 for Israel. France treated the Algerian Jews on an equal footing with the non-Jewish repatriates. The United Jewish Social Fund made extraordinary efforts to help the refugees. In the course of a few months, no fewer than 32,000 refugees arrived in Paris and the nearby communities. Many Jewish refugees from southern Algeria found a haven in Strasbourg and its vicinity and were gradually integrated with the aid of the existing Jewish community. It is estimated that some 80% of Algerian Jews settled in France.

After Algeria had achieved its independence, all its Jews who held French citizenship retained it, except for a few iso-

Algerian towns and corresponding Jewish population figures, 1838–1968.

Year	1838	1861	1881	1901	1921	1941	1955	1968
Algiers	6,065		5,372	10,822	17,053	25,591	30,000	400
Aumale			270	29	145	221		
Biskra			38	112	28		500	
Blida	113		395	1,077	962	1,269	2,500	
Bône	283	607	625	1,387	1,733	3,147	4,000	
Bougle	10	216	482	561	132	625		
Bou-Saâda			343	433	682			
Constantine		4,093	5,213	7,196	9,889	13,037	16,000	
Ghardaïa						1,642	1,100	
Laghoust						443		
Mascara			696	384	81	1,958		
Médés			1,460	1,398	1,005	529		
Miliana			850	827	649	557	450	
Mostaganem	698		1,230	766	152	1,828	2,300	
Nedroma			267	386	529	560		
Oran	5,637		3,549	10,651	15,943	26,671	30,000	400
Sétif		736	936	1,601	3,015	2,050		
Souk-Ahras		198		416	516	624	750	
Tiaret			342	416	92	1,586	2,000	
Tlemcen			3,745	4,910	5,150	4,907	5,000	
Total		21,048	47,500	50,000	73,967	120,000	140,000	3,000

lated cases. The regime of Ben-Bella maintained a correct relationship with the Jews. During the years 1963–65, the minister of culture addressed the Jewish congregation at the synagogue of Algiers on the Day of Atonement.

In February 1964 a General Assembly was held at Oran by the Jewish communities of Algeria, which elected Charles Hababou as its president. After Houari Boumédienne rose to power in 1965 the situation rapidly deteriorated. Heavy taxes were imposed on the Jews, and discrimination of various kinds betrayed the anti-Jewish tendencies of the government. The rabbis no longer received their salaries from the state. This was explained by the fact that they had not become Algerian nationals. The Supreme Court of Justice declared that the Jews were no longer under the protection of the law, and an intensive economic boycott was instituted against Jewish merchants. The police engineered a libel suit against Hababou on the grounds that he had had connections with Zionism. In September 1966, as the result of a case brought before the Economic Court, Désiré Drai was condemned to death together with two non-Jews; but whereas he was executed on the day of Rosh Ha-Shanah, the two others were pardoned. On June 5, 1967, the Algerian press launched a violent attack against Israel and the Jews. The walls of the synagogues of Algiers and other Jewish communities were defaced. With one exception, all the synagogues in the country were taken over and converted into mosques, and the Jewish cemeteries of the country fell into decay. By 1969 fewer than one thousand Jews remained in Algeria. Most of the young men and women left, and thus there were hardly any marriages. The property of the Jewish communities was abandoned. (See Table: Algerian towns and corresponding Jewish population figures, 1838–1968.)

[Robert Attal]

The Jews who remained in the 1970s were mostly of advanced in age, unwilling to leave their assets behind and emigrate with the rest of the Jewish community to France. Only 50 Jews remained in Algeria in the 1990s, nearly all in Algiers, but there were individual Jews in Oran and Blida. A synagogue functioned in Algiers but had no rabbi. All the other synagogues were taken over for use as mosques.

Relations with Israel

On gaining independence, Algeria joined the *Arab League and fully participated in its conferences against Israel. On June 5, 1967, Algeria along with other Arab states declared war on Israel, sending military assistance to Egypt. Even the Egyptian acceptance of ceasefire was denounced by Algerian mobs. Consequently, President Boumedienne pressed the U.S.S.R. to adopt a firmer anti-Israel policy, "a firm commitment to wipe out traces of the aggression" as well as to give military aid, some of which was subsequently channeled to Egypt. On July 23, 1968, the PFLP ("Popular Front for the Liberation of Palestine,") hijacked an El Al plane to Algeria. The plane, the crew, and its male Israel passengers were kept under detention for several weeks and only released in return for terrorists being held by Israel. Algeria adopted an extreme attitude among the anti-Israel Arab factions, and gave full support to the Palestinian terrorists. It repeatedly expressed its official reservations regarding the Israeli-Palestinian peace process.

[Robert Attal]

BIBLIOGRAPHY: General. A. Cahen, *Les Juifs dans l'Afrique septentrionale* (1867), passim; I. Bloch, *Inscriptions Tumulaires des Anciens Cimetières d'Alger* (1888); N. Slouschz, *Travels in North Africa* (1927), 295–343; M. Ansky, *Les Juifs d'Algérie* (1950); A. Chouraqui, *Between East and West* (1968); R. Attal, *Les Juifs d'Afrique du Nord – Bibliographie* (rev. 1993); H.Y. Cohen, *Asian and African Jews in the Middle East – 1860–1971; Annotated Bibliography* (1976); R. Attal, in: *Bi-Tefuẓot ha-Golah* (1961), 14–20; idem, in: *Sefunot*, 5 (1961), 465–508; Hirschberg, Afrikah; idem, in: *Journal of African History* (1963), 313–9. BERBER-ARAB RULE (680–1516). I. Epstein (ed.), *Responsa of Rabbi Simon b. Ẓemaḥ Duran* (1930); R. Brunschvig, *La Berbérie Orientale sous les Ḥafṣides*, 1 (1940), 396–430; A.M. Hershman, *Rabbi Isaac ben Sheshet Perfet and his Times* (1943); Hirschberg, in: *Tarbiẓ*, 26 (1956/57), 370–83; Corcos, in: JQR, 54 (1963/64), 275–9; 55 (1964/65), 67–78; idem, in: *Zion*, 32 (1967), 135–60; C.E. Dufourcq, *L'Espagne Catalane et le Magrib aux XIIIe et XIVe siècles* (1965), passim. TURKISH RULE (1516–1830). J.M. Haddey, *Le Livre d'or des Israélites Algériens* (1872); R.L. Playfair, *The Scourge of Christendom* (1884), passim; M. Eisenbeth, in: *Revue Africaine* (1952), 112–87, 343–84; Mainz, in: JA, 240 (1952), 197–217; Rosenstock, in: JSOS, 14 (1952), 343–64; HJ, 18 (1956), 3–26. FRENCH RULE UP TO 1948. C. Frégier, *Les Israélites Algériens* (1865); Féraud, in: *Revue Africaine* (1874), 30ff.; J. Cohen, *Les Israélites de l'Algerie et le Décret Crémieux* (1900); J. Hanoune, *Aperçu sur les Israélites Algériens* (1922); C. Martin, *Les Israélites Algériens de 1830 à 1902* (1936); M. Abulker, *Alger et ses Complots* (1945); Mainz, in: PAAJR, 21 (1952), 63–73; HJ, 18 (1956), 27–40. ANTISEMITISM: J.F. Aumerot, *L'Antisémitisme à Alger* (1885); E. Drumont, *La France Juive*, 2 (1886), 4ff.; G. Meyné, *L'Algérie Juive* (1887); G.R. Rouanet, *L'Antisémitisme Algérien* (1900); L. Durieu, *Les Juifs Algériens*, 1870–1901 (1902); Brunschvig, in: *Revue d'Alger*, 1 no. 2 (1944), 57–79; M. Eisenbeth, *Pages Vécues*, 1940–1943 (1945); Szajkowski, in: JSOS, 10 (1948), 257–80. CONTEMPORARY PERIOD. JC (Oct. 19, 1962, June 12, 1964, Aug. 30, 1968); *Congress bi-Weekly*, vol. 35, no. 15 (1964), 9–11; *L'Arche*, no. 40 (1960), 24; *Information Juive*, 139 (Sept. 1963), 3; 151 (Dec.–Jan. 1965), 6; 185 (Aug.–Sept. 1968), 7; Mandel, in: AJYB, 64 (1963), 403–11; 65 (1964) 326–30; 66 (1965) 478–83; 67 (1966) 441–4; idem. in: *Commentary*, 35 (June 1963), 475–82; *In the Dispersion*, 5–6 (1966), 318–20 (list of articles). **ADD. BIBLIOGRAPHY:** M. Heoxter, "*Ha-Edah ha-Yehudit be-Algeria u-Mekomah be-Ma'arekhet ha-Shilton ha-Turki*," in: *Sefunot*, New Series, Book 2, 17 (1983), 133–63; A. Ben-Haim, "*Mivtzah Zebbu, Algeria 1947–1948*," in: *Shorashim ba-Mizraḥ*, Book 3, (1991), 213–31; A. Attal, "*Ha-Itton ha-Yehudi ha-Rishon ba-Magreb* L'Israélite Algérien (*hadziri*) *1870*," in: *Pe'amim*, 17 (1984), 88–95; idem, "*Ha-Defus ha-Ivri be-Woharran*," in: *Kiryat Sefer* anthology, suppl. to vol. 68 (1990), 85–92; D. Cohen, "*Megoiasim Yehudim me-Algeria bi-Shenot 1875–1878, Hebetim Kalkaliyyim ve Ḥevratiyyim*," in: *Pe'amim*, 15 (1983), 96–111; E. Sivan, "*Sin'at Yehudim be-Algeria ke-Tolada shel Matzav Koloniali*," in: *Pe'amim*, 2 (1979), 92–108; G. Amipaz-Zilber, *Maḥteret Yehudit be-Algeria 1940–1942* (1983); M. Abitbol, *Mi-Kremieux le-Peten; ha-Antishemiut be-Algeria ha-Kolonialit 1870–1940* (1984); M. Laskier, "*'Ha-Mossad' ve-ha-Du-Kiyyum ha-Muslemi-ha-Yehudi be-Algeria ha-Kolonialit, Parashat Constantin 12–13 1956*," in: *Pe'amim*, 75 (1984), 129–143; J. Allouche-Benayoun, D. Bensimon: *Les Juifs d'Algérie. Mémoires et identités plurielles* (1998); R. Attal, *Regards sur les Juifs d'Algérie* (1996); A. Chouraqui, *Chronique de Baba; lettres* *d'Abraham Meyer, mon grand-père, à ses fils (1914–1918)* (2000); D. Cohen, "Le Comité juif algérien d'études sociales dans le débat idéologique pendant la guerre d'Algérie (1954–1961)," in: *Archives Juives*, 29:1 (le semestre 1996), 30–50; idem, "Les circonstances de la fondation du Comité Algérien d'Édudes sociales ou la prise de conscience d'une élite intellectuelle juive face au phénomène antisémite en Algérie (1915–1921)," in: *Revue des Etudes Juives*, 161 (2002), 179–225; idem, "Algeria," in: R. Simon, M. Laskier, S. Reguer (eds.), *The Jews of the Middle East and North Africa in Modern Times* (2003), 458–470; G. Dugas, "La guerre d'Algérie comme métaphore obsédante; 'Les Bagnoulis' d'Albert Bensoussan," in: *Archives Juives*, 29 (1996), 82–86; E. Marciano, *Les Sages d'Algérie; dictionnaire encyclopédique des sages et rabbins d'Algérie, du haut moyen âge à nos jours*. Adaptation et iconographie de Jacques Assouline (2002).

AL-GHARĪḌ AL-YAHŪDĪ (early seventh century), poet, singer, and composer from *Medina in Arabia. Al-Gharīḍ al-Yahūdī is not to be confused with al-Gharīḍ (nickname meaning the fresh voice), one of the four great singers in the early Islamic era (d. 716). The biographical account of al-Gharīḍ the Jew is reported by the 10th-century author al-Iṣfahānī in his monumental *Kitāb al-Aghānī* ("Book of Songs"), which contains a collection of poems from the pre-Islamic period to the ninth century, all of which had been set to music. Al-Gharīḍ the Jew is described in this book as a Kohen descended from Aaron ben Amram and a member of the Jewish group living in Yathrib (i.e., Medina, the city of the Prophet *Muhammad). Al-Iṣfahānī mentions in the same context other Jewish poets belonging to the same group, but the very fact that he dedicated a special entry to al-Gharīḍ points to his artistic ability and reputation. Al-Iṣfahānī even reports that Muhammad was pleased with one of al-Gharīḍ's songs.

BIBLIOGRAPHY: Al-Iṣfahānī, *Kitāb al-Aghānī al Kabīr*, 3 (Cairo, c. 1929), 116–117; al-Salawī, *Idrāk al-ma'ānī*, ms. 2706 of the Moroccan Royal Library, v. 21, f. 136–138; H.G. Farmer, *A History of Arabian Music to the 13th Century* (1929), 80–81.

[Amnon Shiloah (2nd ed.)]

ALGHERO, Sardinian port. The Jewish community developed there in the second half of the 14th century after Sardinia was acquired by the crown of Aragon. In 1354 Jews supplied the conquering army of Peter IV of Aragon and took part in the siege of Alghero. Among them were Jews from Castile, Sicily, Catalonia, and Majorca. Several are listed as soldiers. Following the conquest, many remained in Alghero. The first group of immigrants was joined in 1370 by families coming from Catalonia and southern France. Around 1400, new waves of immigrants came to Alghero, mainly from Provence. In 1360 King Peter IV conceded the Jews of Cagliari the privilege of erecting a tower in Alghero and permitted them to affix a commemorative stone to the wall to mark its foundation. The synagogue, built in 1381, was enlarged in 1438. The cemetery was established in 1383 and extended in 1435. As long as the attitude of the Aragonese authorities toward the Jews remained favorable, they were prominent in Alghero's economic life. A Jew, Vidal de Santa Pau, advanced money to the authorities for restoring the city walls in 1423. In 1454 Samuel de Carcassona and Jacob Cohen, secretaries of the Jewish community of Alghero, obtained the right to emblazon the royal coat of arms on the wall of the synagogue. The wealthy Carcassona family loaned money to the Aragonese kings throughout the 15th century. In 1481 the brothers Samuel and Nino Carcassona were victualers for the royal galleys and military paymasters. Maimon Carcassona gave hospitality to the viceroy on his visits to Alghero. Moses, the richest property owner in the Jewish quarter, was the official collector of taxes and duties. Several celebrated physicians, including Bonjudes *Bondavin of Marseille, lived in Alghero. The friendly attitude of the Aragonese authorities toward the Jews found expression in the regulations of 1451 exempting them from wearing the Jewish *badge and from having to listen to missionary sermons. They were also granted judicial autonomy and exemption from taxation. Conditions for Alghero Jewry began to deteriorate in 1481 when they shared the treatment meted out to the Jews of Spain. They were expelled in 1492 after the general edict of expulsion from the Spanish dominions. The Carcassona family, who became Christians, remained. Antonio Angelo Carcassona (born in 1515) studied law at the universities of Bologna and Rome, graduating as a doctor of both civil and canon law. In 1533 and in 1586 members of the Carcassona family were tried by the Spanish Inquisition for inviting foreign Jews as guests in their house in Alghero.

BIBLIOGRAPHY: G. Spano, in: *Rivista Sarda*, 1 (1875), 23–52; L. Falchi, *Gli Ebrei nella storia e nella poesia popolare dei Sardi* (1935), 23–28; A. Boscolo, in: *Annali della Facoltà delle Lettere e di Filosofia dell'Università di Cagliari*, 19, pt. 2 (1952), 12; R. Latardi, in: RMI, 33 (1967), 207–10; Milano, Italia, index; Roth, Italy, 263ff. **ADD. BIBLIOGRAPHY:** M. Perani, *Italia*, 5 (1985), 104–44; C. Tasca, *Gli ebrei in Sardegna,Cagliari* (1992), 98–114, 127–34; A. Rudine, *Inquisizione spagnola censura e libri proibiti in Sardegna nel '500 e '600* (1995), 61–76; D. Abulafia, "Gli ebrei di Sardegna," in: C. Vivanti (ed.), *Storia d'Italia. Annali 11, Gli ebrei in Italia. Dall'alto Medioevo all'età dei ghetti* (1996), 83–94.

[Attilio Milano / Nadia Zeldes (2nd ed.)]

ALGIERS (Al-Jazair), capital of *Algeria. The small Jewish community in the late Middle Ages was enlarged after 1248 by Jews from the Languedoc and about 1287 by Jews from Majorca. The population of Majorcan Jews increased between 1296 and 1313, when the town enjoyed a short-lived independence. The Majorcan Jews were arms suppliers. Before 1325 the port was visited regularly by Catalans and Genoese, as well as by Jewish shipowners and merchants.

The first Jewish refugees from Spain were warmly welcomed in 1391, but their increasing numbers caused anxiety among the Muslims and the native Jews, who feared their competition. One individual (whose identity cannot be ascertained), himself an immigrant, used his influence to prevent the landing of 45 newcomers and advised that all the fugitives be sent back, as they were accused of being Marranos. The *qadi* (Muslim religious judge) intervened in their favor.

The Spanish Jews prospered greatly and finally became the majority; they separated themselves from the native Jewish community by acquiring a cemetery and synagogue of their own and moving into a separate quarter. The leader of these Jews at first was R. Saul Ha-Kohen *Astruc, a scholar and philanthropist, who served as judge for the whole community. His successors were the famous R. Isaac *Bonastruc, R. *Isaac b. Sheshet (Ribash), and R. Simeon b. Ẓemaḥ *Duran; they instituted the so-called *takkanot* of Algiers which governed the religious life of Algerian and Tunisian Jews. Because of the school of Isaac b. Sheshet and the Durans, Algiers became a major religious and intellectual center in the 15th century. Many Marranos moved there in order to practice Judaism openly. The large-scale maritime trade of the Spanish Jews at the end of the 14th century gave economic impetus to the city and prepared it somewhat for its future role.

From early in the 16th century, the Turks ruled in Algiers. In order to develop trade, they encouraged the creation of a privileged class. They employed Jews as advisers and physicians; Jews were also responsible for the coining of money and the accounts of the treasury. The mass of the people, Moors and Jews, suffered periodically from the whims of the Janissaries and the cruelty of the militia. In 1706 an outbreak of the plague and a terrible famine reduced many Jewish families to indigence. Then, influenced by false accusations, the bey imposed an exorbitant fine on the community and ordered the destruction of the synagogues, which were saved only by the payment of a further sum. This ruined the majority of the Jews. They commemorated the failure of the Spanish who attacked Algiers in 1541 and 1775 by instituting two "Purims" of Algiers, which were celebrated every year by the whole community. From the 17th century onward, former Portuguese Marranos and many Dutch, Moroccan, and Leghorn Jewish families went to settle there. Proficient in business, many owning their own ships, they gained control of Algerian commerce and extended the system of letters of exchange, and that of concessions and agencies in Europe and the East. These new immigrants intermarried with the older families of the town and settled on the Street of the Livornese, completely separated from the *Ḥara* ("quarter"). These "Juifs Francs" ("Francos," i.e., free from the obligations of other Jews), or "Christian Jews" (because they wore European garments), were employed by all European countries to ransom Christian prisoners. Many were able diplomats who negotiated or signed various peace and trade treaties. Among these diplomats in the second half of the 17th century were Jacob de Paz, Isaac Sasportas, David Torres, Judah Cohen (d. early 18th century), and Soliman Jaquete (d. 1724). Their families became the aristocracy of the community and were active in promoting its welfare.

Internal strife in the Jewish community appeared only when the kabbalists R. Joshua Sidun, R. Joseph Abulker, R. Aaron Moatti, and above all R. Abraham Tubiana (d. 1792) introduced new rituals in their synagogues in accordance with the theories of R. Isaac *Luria. Members of other synagogues considered this sacrilegious and accused the innovators of promoting a schism. Until the mid-20th century two different rituals were followed in the synagogues of Algiers, that of the *mekubbalim*, or kabbalists, and that of the *pashtanim*, or those who followed the original customs of the refugees from Barcelona and Majorca. The intense religious life of the community was stimulated later in the 16th century by eminent scholars such as R. Abraham Tawa, R. Moses Meshash, R. Abraham *Gavison, physician to the famous "beylerbey" (Ottoman governor) Euldj Ali (1568–87), R. Solomon Duran II and his disciple R. Judah Khallas II (d. 1620), R. Solomon Ṣeror (d. 1664) and his grandson Raphael-Jedidiah Ṣeror (d. 1737), the philosopher R. Mas'ud Guenoun (d. 1694), the poet R. Nehorai Azubib (d. 1785), and R. Judah *Ayash, one of the most venerated rabbis of Algiers. Their works, however, were neglected by the new generations, which turned toward other forms of culture.

In the late 18th–early 19th centuries the wealth of certain families added to the enormous influence of Naphtali *Busnach; this aroused the jealousy of the Janissaries, who assassinated Busnach. The day after Busnach's assassination (June 29, 1805), they sacked Algiers killing between 200 and 500 Jews. Despite this catastrophe, the great families would not forgo their internal disputes nor their fierce competition for power. David Bacri succeeded his partner and relative Naphtali Busnach as head of the community. He was beheaded in 1811 by the dey and replaced by David Duran who represented the opposing families. The latter was in his turn put to death by the dey during the same year, and Joseph Bacri assumed the title of **muqaddam* (head of the community). Involved against his will in disputes between the Jewish families, the rabbi of Algiers, R. Isaac Abulker, was dragged to the stake with seven other notables of the town (1815). After the landing of the French in 1830, Jacob Bacri was named "Chef de la Nation Israélite"; he was replaced by Aaron Moatti whose appointment was terminated in 1834.

In 1870 Algerian Jews became French citizens; subsequently antisemitism spread throughout the country manifesting itself in serious pogroms, particularly in Algiers (1884–87, 1897–98). After World War I a Zionist conference, the first in Algeria, was organized at Algiers. Although the Jewish élite was always active in the defense of Judaism, they were loyal French citizens.

The Algiers community was deeply affected by the nationalist struggle for independence. Much of the communal structure ceased to exist. The Great Synagogue in the ancient quarter, ravaged in the Christmas Eve riots of 1960 was only temporarily restored. The Maimonides rabbinical college was closed. During the French army's search of Bab-el-Oued in 1962, in reprisal for the machine-gunning of French soldiers by the local OAS, the synagogue of that quarter was ravaged.

Population Statistics

During the last four centuries the Jewish population of Algiers declined and increased according to the economic and political situation of the capital. In the 16th century it declined from 2,000 to 750 persons, because of the Spanish assaults. In the 17th and 18th centuries the number of Jews rose to 15,000, but then decreased to 7,000 and later, to 5,000. About the same number was found there by the French in 1830. Eight years later there were over 6,000 Jews, but after the antisemitic persecutions of the last decades of the 19th century only 5,000 remained. After 1900, with the defeat of the anti-Jewish party, the Jewish population increased continuously: 10,822 in 1901, 17,053 in 1921, 23,550 in 1931, and 25,591 in 1941. During World War II Algiers received over 1,000 Jewish refugees from Europe; after the uprising against the French in 1954 a large number of Jews from the interior settled in Algiers. Over 95% of this population, numbering about 34,000, left the capital when the declaration of independence was proclaimed in 1962. The vast majority immigrated to France, some went to America, and others to Israel. By 1963 only 2,500 Jews remained in Algiers. In 1969 their number was reduced to a few hundred and at the turn of the century to a few dozen.

For bibliography see *Algeria.

[David Corcos]

ALGUADES (Alguadez), MEIR (d. 1410), personal physician to successive kings of Castile, chief rabbi, and chief justice of Castilian Jewry. After the massacres of 1391, Alguades devoted his energies to rehabilitating the stricken Spanish communities, despite his personal misfortunes (his son-in-law had accepted baptism during the persecutions). Alguades' activities extended beyond the frontiers of Castile into Aragon and Navarre. He was a friend and patron of Solomon ha-Levi of Burgos (later *Pablo de Santa Maria), Benveniste de la *Cavalleria, and Ḥasdai *Crescas, the learned apologist and satirist Profiat *Duran, and the poet Solomon da Piera, who composed an elegy on Alguades' death. Alguades translated into Hebrew Aristotle's *Ethics* (ed. by Satanow, Berlin, 1790) and in his foreword speaks of the obstacles which he encountered in his work, while leading the life of a courtier bound to accompany the monarch on his travels. A number of medical prescriptions written by Alguades in Spanish have been preserved in Hebrew translation. Beside his activities as court physician, Alguades was apparently a tax-farmer. The statutes of the Castilian communities issued at *Valladolid in 1432 confirm that Alguades' widow and daughter were to be exempted from taxes because of the services rendered by him to the Jewish communities. The local legend associating Alguades with the *host desecration charge which entailed disaster for the community of *Segovia in 1410 seems to have no basis other than the improbable account of *Alfonso de Espina in his *Fortalitium Fidei*.

BIBLIOGRAPHY: Baer, Spain, index, s.v. *Meir Alguadex*; S. Usque, *Consolation for the Tribulations of Israel*, ed. by G.I. Gelbart (1962), 325–33; I. Rodríguez y Fernández, *Segovia-Corpus* (1902); *Boletín de la Real Academia de la Historia, Madrid*, 7 (1885), 397ff.

ALGUM, a tree which cannot be definitely identified. Mentioned among the trees of Lebanon which Hiram, king of Tyre, sent to Solomon for the building of the Temple and the palace (II Chron. 2:7), it is referred to elsewhere as having been imported from tropical Ophir (II Chron. 9:10–11; I Kings 10:11, where it is called *almog*). The Septuagint identifies the tree brought from Lebanon as a species of pine and that from Ophir as apparently a species of Tuja, while the Jerusalem Talmud and the Midrash identify it with *alvos*, i.e., *Aquilaria agallocha*, which is a tropical tree of high quality used in the making of furniture. It has also been identified with the biblical aloe (Num. 24:6; Ps. 45:9; Prov. 7:17; Song 4:14) used in incense and for perfume. In modern Hebrew *almog* is used for coral, which is also the meaning given to it in the Talmud (RH 23a).

BIBLIOGRAPHY: J. Feliks, *Olam ha-Ẓome'aḥ ha-Mikra'i* (1968²), 124–5.

[Jehuda Feliks]

ALḤADIB (al-Aḥdab), ISAAC BEN SOLOMON BEN ẒADDIK (mid-14th century–after 1429), Hebrew poet and astronomer. Of Spanish origin (very likely from Castile), after the events of 1391, Alḥadib went to Sicily in 1396. He lived first in Syracuse and then (1426) in Palermo. He applied his scientific interests to biblical interpretation, and also wrote secular and liturgical poetry. O. Ra'anan published in 1988 a critical edition of almost 90 of his poems, most of them secular, including monorhymed and strophic compositions and some rhymed prose. His poetry, with popular tendencies, is sometimes didactic, ethic, or sapiential, but sometimes also humorous or satiric, including some riddles, proverbs, and polemics, and introductions to prose works. Two interesting poems, alluding to the 13 principles of Maimonides, were written on the occasion of the wedding of his two sons. Like other late Hebrew poets, he wrote in a mannered style (for instance, a poem has one thousand words starting with the letter *nun*), imitating the octosyllabic structure of Romance poetry in many of his Hebrew verses. He wrote a hymn on Esther giving his name in acrostic, and an addition to the poem with which Moses Handali opened his commentary on the Hebrew translation of Al-Fergani's astronomy.

Only one of his works in prose has been published in full, *Leshon ha-Zahav*, on weights and measures mentioned in the Bible (Venice, undated). His writings (in manuscript) include *Oraḥ Selulah*, on calculations; *Iggeret Kelei Ḥemdah*, describing an astronomical apparatus wich he invented in Sicily; *Keli ha-Memuẓa* or *Keli ha-Emẓa'i*, also on astronomy; and *Ma'amar be-Gidrei ha-Devarim*, on theological terminology.

BIBLIOGRAPHY: Steinschneider, Uebersetzungen, 7 (1864), 112; M. Rabinowitz, in: *Mizraḥ u-Ma'arav*, 3 (1929), 219–23; Davidson, Oẓar, 4 (1933), 417; Roth, in: JQR, 47 (1956/57), 324. **ADD. BIBLIOGRAPHY:** *Shirei Yitzḥak Ben Shelomoh Al-Aḥdab*, ed. O. Ra'anan (1988); Schirmann-Fleischer (1997), 618–24.

[Abraham Meir Habermann / Angel Saenz-Badillos (2nd ed.)]

AL HA-MISHMAR (Heb. עַל הַמִּשְׁמָר), Hebrew daily newspaper of the Israeli left-wing *Mapam Party, its affiliated Ha-Shomer ha-Ẓa'ir youth movement, and the Kibbutz Arẓi network of agricultural settlements. Established in Tel Aviv in 1943 under the editorship of Mordekhai *Bentov as *Ha-Shomer*, it became *Al ha-Mishmar* five years later after Ha-Shomer ha-Ẓa'ir merged with Aḥdut ha-Avodah into Mapam. The newspaper was both a voice of the strident left-wing of the Zionist movement and the more inward-looking network of agricultural settlements. A quality newspaper, it covered national and international developments as well as local kibbutz news. In its earlier days its journalistic style was of a party organ. Yet its literary pages in particular were open to non-party voices. Its journalistic workforce consisted of members of kibbutzim on loan to work on the newspaper. After Bentov was elected a Mapam member of the Knesset, he was replaced as editor by Ya'akov Amit. Other editors of the paper were Marek Geffen, Ḥayyim Shaw, Sever Plotzkur, and Zvi Timor. In later years the paper's style was characterized by less ideological rigidity. Its staff included not only kibbutz members but also professional journalists. Its readership reached 15,000–18,000, but 10,000 of these were kibbutz subscriptions. Its circulation declined to 8,000 in the 1990s after kibbutz members were no longer required to read the paper. Their preference for the non-party commercial press, and for television over neswspapers, together the financial problems which struck the kibbutz movement, caused the paper to close in March 2005.

BIBLIOGRAPHY: Y. Tzafati, "*Al ha-Mishmar – Anatomiyah shel Iton Miflagti*," in: *Kesher*, 27 (May 2000).

[Yoel Cohen (2nd ed.)]

ALHANATI, DAVID (1908–1990), Greek attorney and community activist. Alhanati was born in Athens to a mixed Romaniote/Sephardi family from Ioannina and Larisa. He studied law at the University of Athens and from 1935 until 1942 he was legal advisor to the Jewish Communities of Greece and served on its board. During World War II, he fought in the Greek army on the Albanian front in 1940–41, was arrested by the Italians in 1942 as a prominent member of the Athenian Jewish community, and during the German occupation from September 24, 1943, went into hiding in the mountains and found refuge with a Greek friend in Pirgos until the liberation. Previously, he had assisted Rabbi Barzilai when he was pressed to hand over community lists to the Germans, and burned the Athenian community Jewish archives.

In 1945, he founded the Board of Jewish Communities of Greece (KIS) and served as its first chairman. He also founded the OPAIE Organization of Rehabilitation of Jews in Greece and was its vice president from 1945 until 1952. He represented the Jewish community of Greece in war trials held in the late 1940s and 1950s in Greece against Jewish and German Nazi collaborators. In 1945–46, together with the Mosad le-Aliyah Bet, he helped organize the voyage of four boats of illegal immigrants from Greece and Northern Europe departing from the Sounion coast, southeast of Athens, to Ereẓ Israel. He established two *hakhsharah* (training) farms in 1945, which housed *ma'pilim* ("illegal" immigrants), as they waited for their departure to Ereẓ Israel.

Alhanati was president of the Union of Greek Zionists (1965–84), was Greek delegate to the 26th and 27th World Zionist Congresses, and was president of the Jewish National Fund in Greece from 1965 until his later years. He also was secretary-general of the HELLAS-Israel organization and a lifetime member of B'nai B'rith.

In Athens, Alhanati also represented the legal interests of the Jewish National Fund and the Jewish Agency, and worked together with the Joint Distribution Committee to rebuild the lives of Greek Holocaust survivors and help Jewish refugees from Arab Middle Eastern countries and the former Eastern Bloc of the Soviet Union reach the West for relocation.

[Yitzchak Kerem (2nd ed.)]

AL HA-NISSIM (Heb. עַל הַנִּסִּים; "for the miracles"), thanksgiving prayer added to the penultimate benediction of the *Amidah* and to the Grace after Meals on Ḥanukkah and Purim. The prayer starts with a general introduction: "For the miracles, the redemption, the mighty deeds, the saving acts, and the (victorious) wars, which Thou didst for our fathers in former times at this season." On Ḥanukkah a condensed account of the Hasmonean Revolt is added. The opening words of this section "In the days of Mattathias, the Hasmonean, son of Johanan the high priest…" present some difficulties owing to an apparent confusion between Jonathan, the high priest, and Johanan, father of Mattathias the Hasmonean. The additional recitation for Purim briefly retells the story of Purim. This prayer dates back to talmudic times (Shab. 24a). Several ancient sources also have the addition "as Thou hast done for them, thus perform for us, Lord our God, miracles and wonders, in our days" (Sof. 20:8, also *Siddur R. Amram Ga'on, Seder Ḥanukkah*, and *Siddur R. Sa'adyah Ga'on*, 256), but the prayer books omit this phrase on the halakhic principle that petitions and thanksgivings should be kept separate (Sh. Ar., OḤ 682:1). An imitative form of *Al ha-Nissim* was inserted into the *Amidah* and the Grace after Meals on the local Purims (see Special *Purims), and an attempt has been made to establish the recitation of such a prayer on Independence Day in Israel.

BIBLIOGRAPHY: Elbogen, Gottesdienst, 130ff.

AL-ḤARIZI, JUDAH BEN SOLOMON (1165–1225), Hebrew poet and translator. He was born in Spain, very likely in Christian Toledo, a city that at this time preserved Arabic culture and that he describes with particular detail; however, there are no conclusive proofs of it, and other places have also been suggested. His education in this cultural atmosphere made him familiar with Arabic and Hebrew language and literature. Al-Ḥarizi was a member of a wealthy family which became impoverished, and was therefore dependent on patrons.

He spent some years in Provence, where he translated several Arabic works into Hebrew for the non-Arabic speaking Jews and participated in the ideological disputes of the time, returning to Spain in 1190; in 1205 he was in Toledo and wrote a poem on the death of Joseph ben Shoshan. During discussions of the work of Maimonides he defended the Master against the anti-rationalist rabbis from Toledo. Some time later he left Spain to travel to the Orient. He first went to Marseilles, and from there he sailed to Egypt; in 1215 he arrived in Alexandria and from there he visited Cairo, later continuing to Palestine, Syria, and Iraq. According to the information that he gives us in one of his works, in 1218 he was in Jerusalem. Damascus, Aleppo, Mosul, and Baghdad were among the cities visited. He mentions seeing the tombs of the prophet Ezekiel and of Ezra in Susa. The ten last years of his life, until his death in Aleppo in 1225, are now much better known thanks to important documents discovered and published in recent years. J. Sadan published in 1996 an Arabic biography written by Ibn al-Sha'ar al-Mawṣilī in a work on the poets of his time (the first half of the 13th century). There are also many details about his travels in his *Taḥkemoni* as well as in an Arabic description, *Al-rawḍah al-anīqah* ("The Pleasant Garden"), written by Al-Ḥarizi himself in his last years, which has been published and annotated by Y. Yahalom and Y. Blau (2002).

We do not know exactly the reasons for Al-Ḥarizi's travels. Scholars usually allude to his curiosity, to spiritual motifs, like the love for Zion, to the search for rich patrons in the Orient, etc. Al-Ḥarizi's visits to these countries helped to acquaint the Jewish communities there with Spanish-Hebrew culture. Most of his compositions were written during his travels and contain reflections on his experiences. He wrote many poems in honor of the prominent Jewish men of these communities, both satirizing their defects and praising their virtues, and used to revise what he had previously written, sometimes leaving different versions of his writings.

Al-Ḥarizi's most important literary translation is his Hebrew rendering of the *maqamat* of the Arabic poet Al-Ḥariri (Bosra, d. 1121), which he entitled *Maḥbarot Iti'el* ("Notebooks of Ithiel"), completed before 1218. His translation of the *maqama*, an Arabic literary form in rhyming prose, attains the quality of an original composition, and imparts a Hebrew flavor to Al-Ḥariri's typically Arabic art; it reproduces the elusive word play and ornate style of the original. Al-Ḥarizi's translation contained 50 *maqamat* of which only a portion of the first and 26 of the subsequent *maqamat* have been preserved. The *Maḥbarot Iti'el* were published by Th. Chenery (1872), and more recently by Y. Peretz (1951).

Al-Ḥarizi himself used this form for his major work *Sefer Taḥkemoni* ("The Wise One"?), completed after 1220; he was among the first to use this genre in Hebrew literature. Its 50 *maqamat* show Al-Ḥariri's influence, being at the same time his way of showing the possibilities of the Hebrew language and of defending its usage. The language, rhymed prose with some poems intermingled in the text, is taken from the Bible and is often a mosaic of biblical quotations. The different addressees of the work that appear in the manuscripts are not surprisingly Oriental Jews, as Al-Ḥarizi composed this book in his travels through the Orient, from one country to the other, or, as he says, from Egypt to Babylon.

The *maqamat* of the *Taḥkemoni* begin with a narrative frame introduced by the narrator, Heman the Ezrahite, who represents in many cases the opinion of the writer. The main character, Ḥeber the Kenite, resembles the heroes of the Arabic *maqama* in his nature, a roguish polymath and rhymester. He appears in many different forms and is only recognized at the end of the narratives, after having shown his abilities and wisdom. The book includes love ditties, fables, proverbs, riddles, disputes, and satirical sketches, such as the descriptions of a flea and a defense by a rooster about to be slaughtered.

Apart from its literary merit and brilliant, incisive style, the *Taḥkemoni* also throws valuable light on the state of Hebrew culture of the period, and describes the scholars and leaders of the communities visited by the author. Al-Ḥarizi gives vivid descriptions of the worthies of Toledo, the poets of Thebes, a debate between a *Rabbanite and a *Karaite, and conditions in Jerusalem. The *Taḥkemoni* also contains critical evaluations of earlier and contemporary poets, although Al-Ḥarizi's appraisal of his contemporaries is not always reliable and occasionally misses their most essential features.

In spite of the existence of many manuscripts, and of the edition of *Sefer Taḥkemoni* by Obadia Sabak (Constantinople, 1578) and the more modern ones by de Lagarde (1883; 1925); by A. Kaminka (1899); by Y. Toporowsky (1952), etc., no critical edition of the *Taḥkemoni* has been published. Several of the *maqamāt* were translated into Latin, English, French, German, and Hungarian. There is an English translation by V.E. Reichert, *The Tahkemoni of Judah al-Harizi, an English translation*, 2 vols. (Jerusalem, R.H. Cohen's Press, 1965); and a new one by David S. Segal, *The Book of Tahkemoni: Jewish Tales from Medieval Spain* (Portland, Oregon, Littman Library of Jewish Civilization, 2001), with a long section dedicated to the analyses of each *maqama* and a detailed bibliography. A Spanish translation, with introduction and notes, appeared in 1988: *Las asambleas de los sabios (Tahkemoní)*, by C. del Valle (Murcia: Univ. de Murcia).

Al-Ḥarizi also wrote the *Sefer ha-Anak* ("The Necklace"), a collection of 257 short poems on moral and pious themes, mainly composed in two stanzas with rhyming puns (like the book of the same name by Moshe Ibn Ezra). It was published by H. Brody, *Sefer ha-Anak*, in *Festschrift Harkavy* (1908); and by A. Avronim (Tel Aviv, 1945).

In one of the last *maqamāt* of the *Taḥkemoni* Al-Ḥarizi includes more than 170 Hebrew poems according to the Andalusian tradition. In his stay in the Orient he wrote also poems in Arabic and sometimes, in Hebrew and Arabic. A number of his poems not included in the *Taḥkemoni* and *Sefer ha-Anak* are extant in manuscript. Yahalom and Blau have published an autographic letter found in the *Genizah*.

Al-Ḥarizi was notably active as translator of philosophical, halakhic, and medical works from Arabic to Hebrew. Under the Hebrew title *Muserei ha-Filosofim* he translated for the sages of Lunel the *Adāb al-Falāsifa* ("Dicta of the Philosophers") of Ḥunain ibn Isḥak, a collection of proverbs synthesizing Greek and Arabic wisdom literature. This translation was published by Loewenthal in Frankfurt/Main in 1896.

The most important of his prose translations is that of *Maimonides' *Moreh Nevukhim* (*Guide of the Perplexed*, published by A.L. Schlossberg, London 1851–79; reprint Tel Aviv, 1952). Al-Ḥarizi, who translated the book after Samuel ibn *Tibbon for some Jews of Marseille, intended to render it simply and clearly, employing biblical Hebrew. In spite of two chapters added by him explaining difficult words and describing the contents of the chapters, the translation was considered of literary value but failing in accuracy. For this reason it was received with much criticism, and Ibn Tibbon's translation is generally preferred (Y. Shiffman, *Journal of Semitic Studies*, 44/1 (1999), 47–61). It was, however, through Al-Ḥarizi's translation that Maimonides' ideas were propagated in the Christian world. An anonymous Latin translation of the *Guide*, published in Paris by Agostino *Giustiniani in 1520, is based on Al-Ḥarizi's translation and was used by the English schoolmen. Al-Ḥarizi's version also served as the basis for Pedro de Toledo's Spanish translation (published by M. Lazar according to the Ms. 10289, B.N. Madrid, in 1989, Culver City, Calif: Labyrinthos).

Al-Ḥarizi translated in Lunel, for Jonathan ha-Kohen, Maimonides' introduction to the Mishnah and his commentary on the first five tractates of the Mishnah order *Zera'im*. He also translated other minor works, like the *Medicine of the Body* (Ferrara, 1552) and a few short works attributed to Aristotle or Galen.

Al-Ḥarizi's prominence in medieval letters is due both to his light, entertaining, and allusive style, and to the variety of his subject matter. In consonance with the tendencies of the time in Romance literature, his descriptions of nature are more realistic than those generally found in other Spanish Hebrew poets, with a feeling for the rural life and the animal world. He described storms at sea and, with the exception of *Samuel b. Joseph ha-Nagid, was the only medieval Hebrew poet to describe battle scenes.

[Aharon Mirsky and Avrum Stroll / Angel Saenz-Badillos (2nd ed.)]

As a Musical Writer

Al-Ḥarizi's Hebrew translation of Ḥunain's *Adāb al-Falāsifa* contains, in its first part, three chapters (18–20) on music. As usual in *adāb*-literature, the text consists of sayings and aphorisms uttered by ancient Greek philosophers or other famous men. They deal with the miraculous power of music, its influence on soul, temperament and even animal life, its therapeutic value, and the like. Al-Ḥarizi was the first to introduce these ideas of late Hellenism, which had been transmitted by Ḥunain to Arab philosophy, into Jewish philosophical and musical thought. Circulating in many manuscripts and a print of 1562, they were continually perused and quoted as a source of musical knowledge, and even as late as 1680 by Shabbetai *Bass.

As the original Arabic text has not yet been published from the manuscripts, Al-Ḥarizi's Hebrew version and its modern (though inadequate) translations serve as sole source to students of musical history up to now. The chapters on music in Arabic were edited by A. Shiloaḥ (1958), who showed that Al-Ḥarizi's text is governed by a deep understanding of this intricate subject.

[Hanoch Avenary]

BIBLIOGRAPHY: J. Schirmann, in: *Moznayim*, 11 (1940), 101–15; S.J. Kaempf, *Die ersten Makamen aus dem Tachkemoni oder Divan des Charisi* (1845); idem, *Nichtandalusische Poesie andalusischer Dichter* (1858); Steinschneider, Uebersetzungen, 251, 355, 428–32, 851f., 857f.; J. Schirmann, *Die hebraeische Uebersetzung der Maqamen des Hariri* (1930), 113–6; A. Percikowitsch, *Al-Harizi als Uebersetzer der Makamen Al-Hariris* (1932), 1–5; A.M. Habermann, in: *Sinai*, 31 (1952), 112–27; Davidson, Oẓar, 4 (1933), 388–90; S.M. Stern, in: JQR, 50 (1959/60), 269–76, 346–64; idem, in: *Papers of the Institute of Jewish Studies, London*, 1 (1964), 186–210; V.E. Reichert, *The Fourteenth Gate of Judah Al-Harizi's Tahkemoni* (1963). **ADD. BIBLIOGRAPHY:** Y. Sadan, in: *Pe'amim*, 68 (1996), 16–67; *Harizi, Judah ben Solomon. Ma'ase Yehudah: Ḥamishah Pirkei Masa Meḥorazim*, ed. J. Yahalom, Joseph and J. Blau (2002); Schirmann-Fleischer, 2, 145–221; A. Sáenz-Badillos, in: *Miscelánea de Estudios Arabes y Hebraicos*, 34/2 (1985), 61–70; R. Brann, in: *Princeton Papers in Near Eastern Studies*, 1 (1992), 1–22; R. Scheindlin, in: *Studies in Muslim-Jewish Relations*, 1 (1993), 165–75. MUSIC: M. Plessner, in: *Tarbiz*, 24 (1954/55), 60–72; A. Shiloaḥ, *Pirkei ha-Muzikah ba-Kitāb adāb al-falāsifa* (Thesis, Jerusalem, 1958); E. Werner and J. Sonne, in: HUCA, 17 (1942–43), 513–32, 558–63; H.G. Farmer, *A History of Arabian Music to the 13th Century* (1929), 126–7.

ALḤAYK, UZZIEL BEN MORDECAI (1740?–1820?), Tunisian rabbi. Alḥayk was born in Tunis where his father was a *dayyan* and communal leader. He studied in the yeshivah of Nathan b. Abraham *Bordjel, the greatest scholar of Tunis, and under David b. Moses Najar. He was appointed rabbi of the Portuguese community in Tunis. Most of his rulings deal with financial problems and testify to his great juristic ability. Alḥayk was very familiar with business and economic problems, and it is possible that he himself engaged in business. His responsa are an important source for the history of the Jews of Tunis of his time. He became friendly with Ḥayyim Joseph David *Azulai during the visit of the latter to Tunis in 1774. He collected the *takkanot* of Tunis which he published in his *Mishkenot ha-Ro'im* (102aff.; Leghorn, 1860), his most important work, comprising alphabetically arranged articles on the Shulḥan Arukh. It deals primarily with civil law and, to a lesser extent, with laws of marriage. Many of the articles consist of his own responsa and rulings. He wrote *Ḥayyim va-Ḥesed* (Leghorn, 1865), sermons delivered between 1767 and 1810, including eulogies on Tunisian sages and other contemporaries.

BIBLIOGRAPHY: E. Cazès, *Notes bibliographiques sur la littérature juive tunisienne* (1893), 169–73.

AL ḤET (Heb. עַל חֵטְא; "for the sin"), first words of a formula of confession of sins (and of each line in the formula) recited on the *Day of Atonement. The confession of sins during the afternoon *Amidah* on the eve of the Day of Atonement and in every *Amidah* (and repetition of the *Amidah*) on the day itself, with the exception of that of the **Ne'ilah* service, is required according to a *baraita* (Yoma 87b). In talmudic times, apparently, any expression admitting sinfulness sufficed, but in time a set form of confession evolved. There are two such forms: **Ashamnu*, known as the "Shorter Confession," and *Al Ḥet*, the "Great Confession" (so called in the **Maḥzor Vitry*, 374; *Siddur Rashi*, 96; and *Ha-Manhig*, 60a).

Al Ḥet contains a list of sins in alphabetical order, two sins being allotted to every letter. Each line begins: "For the sin we have sinned before Thee." After the 44 sins in alphabetical order, another nine lines are added enumerating sins according to their prescribed punishments. The recitation is divided into four parts. After each, the formula, "And for all these, O God of forgiveness, forgive us, pardon us, grant us atonement, is chanted during the reader's repetition. The list of sins embraces the specific (e.g., unchastity) and the general (e.g., those committed "unwittingly"), but sins of a ritual nature are not included. The whole confession is in the first person plural, perhaps as an expression of the doctrine of collective responsibility.

The authorship of the *Al Ḥet* is unknown. It is first mentioned in the *She'iltot* of Aḥai Gaon (eighth century) and an abbreviated and probably more original form is found in the *Seder Rav Amram*. The Christian *Didache* (second century) also contains traces of an earlier Jewish alphabetical confession suggesting that this arrangement is very ancient. In the Sephardi rite the alphabetical arrangement is only one letter for each sin, but in some this is followed by a reverse-order alphabetical arrangement. The Yemenites use a shortened version. There are many textual variants of *Al Ḥet* according to different rites; an interesting example of the confession apparently used in pre-expulsion England is contained in the *Ez Ḥayyim* (ed. I. Brodie, 1 (1962), 102ff.). It is customary to recite *Al Ḥet* while standing with the head bowed, and to beat one's breast at the mention of each sin. In Reform usage the *Al Ḥet* has been considerably shortened.

BIBLIOGRAPHY: Baer S., Siddur, 416ff.; Elbogen, Gottesdienst, 150; Idelsohn, Liturgy, 229; Hertz, Prayer, 910–8; Abrahams, Companion, cc; Adler-Davis, 2 (1915), 79; E. Levi, *Yesodot ha-Tefillah* (1961^5), 262.

ALI (Ben David; 12th–13th century), physician and poet. Ali, who lived in the Near East, probably in Syria, influenced poets in his time and exchanged verses with them. The ten poems which he wrote to his friend Aaron ha-Kohen (possibly Aaron ha-Kohen b. Marion of Acre), and Aaron's ten poems for Ali, are preserved in the Cairo *Genizah*, the former apparently in Ali's handwriting. These metrical poems express mutual praise and longing and reflect the influence of Spanish poetry. Several poems, written when the two friends were separated, express sorrow at the unfortunate fate of kindred souls. Some of the poems found in the *Genizah* which are signed "Ali," are presumably by him.

BIBLIOGRAPHY: M. Zulay, in: *Sinai*, 23 (1948), 217–28.

[Abraham Meir Habermann]

ALIAV (Kluger), RUTH (1914–1980), the only female member of Mosad Le-Aliyah Bet, the organization which saved Jews from the Holocaust by smuggling them into Ereẓ Israel, in defiance of the restrictions on immigration imposed by the Mandatory Government (see "Illegal" *Immigration). The name Aliav, given to her by David Ben-Gurion, is an anagram of *Aliyah Bet*.

Aliav was born in Kiev; her family later settled in Czernowitz, Romania. She immigrated to Ereẓ Israel in 1934 and settled with her husband on a kibbutz. She was one of the founding members of the Mosad and in 1939 returned to Romania to organize the escape of Jews and their illegal immigration to Ereẓ Israel. In 1941, when further rescue work became impossible, she fled to Turkey from which she proceeded to Egypt to continue her rescue activities in bringing Jews from Arab countries.

From 1942 to 1945 she worked closely with the French and Dutch Resistance movements in Europe, became a colonel in the *Haganah, and was appointed by David Ben-Gurion as the only official Israeli representative in Europe. She was the first woman to enter the concentration camps upon their liberation. She continued her activities until 1947, serving directly under Ben-Gurion.

In 1947 she was awarded the Croix de la Lorraine by General de Gaulle, and the Legion d'Honneur of France. After the establishment of the State of Israel she headed the public relations and press department of Zim, the Israeli Navigation Company which evolved out of the "Illegal Immigration" ships of the Haganah; was the Israeli president of the International Federation of Business and Professional Women; and was honorary life president of the International Public Relations Associations. Her book, *The Last Escape*, is a dramatic account of her two years' activity in Romania.

ALIBAG, Indian town on the Konkan Coast, south of Bombay; formerly the leading settlement of the *Bene Israel community. Its synagogue, "Magen Avot," was founded in 1840 (rebuilt in 1910) on the initiative of the *ḥakham* Shalom Shurrabi, author and sponsor of liturgical works for the Bene Israel community. Alibag was the favorite resort of retired military personnel of the Bene Israel group and the center of Hebrew instruction for youth from neighboring Bene Israel settlements. The historian of the community, Ḥayyim Samuel *Kehimkar, was born in Alibag. The synagogue in Alibag was still functioning in the beginning of the 21st century.

BIBLIOGRAPHY: H.S. Kehimkar, *History of the Bene Israel of India* (1937); S. Samuel, *Treatise on the Origin and Early History of the Bene Israel of the Maharashtra State* (1963). **ADD. BIBLIOGRAPHY:** J. Roland, *The Jewish Communities of India* (1998).

[Walter Joseph Fischel]

ALI BEN AMRAM (second half of the 11th century), religious head of the Palestinian community in Fostat (Old Cairo), Egypt. Ali was the colleague and eventually successor of R. *Ephraim b. Shemariah, who bore the honorary title of *he-ḥaver ha-me'ulleh* ("most excellent scholar"). In a letter, written about 1060, that was found in the Cairo *Genizah*, Ali addressed the court physician Abraham b. Isaac ha-Kohen b. Furat, informing him that on Sabbaths and holidays he would receive public recognition in the synagogue for his virtuous acts. Two letters addressed to Ali from Palestine concerning the Jews in Tiberias and one intro-ducing Moses b. Joseph, a Spanish scholar on diplomatic assignment, were also discovered in the *Genizah*. Ali was the author of a lengthy poem, extant in manuscript, dedicated to one Ali b. Mevasser. Two letters from the *gaon* Daniel b. Azariah to Ali have been preserved: in one, the *gaon* expresses his great confidence in Ali and gratitude for his kindnesses; in the other, the *gaon* asks Ali to hand over to the bearer contributions that had been collected in Fustat, probably for the yeshivah in Jerusalem. Ali was also in close touch with *Samuel ha-Nagid and his sons Jehoseph and Eliasaph in Granada.

BIBLIOGRAPHY: Mann, Egypt, 2 (1922), index; idem, in: HUCA, 3 (1926), 279, 283–8; Mann, Texts, 2 (1935), index; Ashtor, Korot, 2 (1966), 82–83.

[Moshe Nahum Zobel]

ALI (or **Eli**) **BEN ZECHARIAH** (13th century), *gaon* and head of the Pumbedita academy. Ali was born in the town of Erbil (now Iraq), and lived in Baghdad. From Arab sources it appears that while *Daniel b. Samuel ha-Kohen ibn Abi-Rabīa was the *gaon* of the academy, Ali made a claim for the post. The dispute came before the vizier, who in 1250 decided in favor of Ali and appointed him *gaon* (chief judge, as the office is designated in Arab sources). The poet *Eleazar b. Jacob ha-Bavli composed a poem in Ali's honor. Although Baghdad was captured by the Mongols in 1258, during Ali's gaonate, the office continued to exist. Of Ali's sons, two are known: Zechariah, who was deputy head of the academy, and Isaac, referred to as "prince."

BIBLIOGRAPHY: Mann, Texts, 1 (1931), 225–7, 299, 301–2; Fischel, Islam, 131–3; idem, in: MGWJ, 79 (1935), 315–8; A. Ben-Jacob, *Yehudei Bavel* (1965), 33–34; Eleazar b. Jacob ha-Bavli, *Divan*, ed. by H. Brody (1935), nos. 55, 182, 221; S. Poznański, *Babylonische Geonim im nachgaonischen Zeitalter* (1914), 49–52. **ADD. BIBLIOGRAPHY:** M. Gil, *Be-Malkhut Ishmael*, 1 (1997), 463–64, 511.

[Abraham David]

ALIENS ACT, measure enacted by the British parliament in 1905 which restricted immigration into Britain from areas outside the British Empire; it is generally believed to have been chiefly a response to heavy East European Jewish immigration into Britain after 1880. (In British law, the age-old term "alien" is used to designate someone who is not a citizen of Britain or its Empire; it has no derogatory connotations.) Agitation to restrict Jewish immigration began in the 1880s and became more outspoken through the actions of a number of right-wing groups and activists. In 1902, a Royal Commission was held into this question which recommended that there should be no general restriction on immigration but that "undesirable" migrants should be excluded. By the Act of 1905, would-be immigrants had to disembark only at a designated port, where officials could deny entry to "undesirable" immigrants, especially those without means of support. Historians have generally believed that the Aliens Act reduced East European Jewish immigration to Britain by about one-third in the years 1905–14. Recent research, however, has suggested that the Act had only limited effects, and that immigration declined because of perceptions of much greater economic opportunity in America. As Britain had *no* immigration restrictions prior to the 1905 Act, plainly something like it was inevitable. In 1919, following World War I, the 1905 Act was replaced by a much more stringent one which virtually ended Jewish immigration to Britain until the 1930s.

BIBLIOGRAPHY: V.D. Lipman, *Social History of the Jews in England, 1850–1950* (1954); B. Garner, *The Alien Invasion: The Origins of the Aliens Act of 1905* (1972); G. Alderman, *Modern British Jewry* (1992), 132–37; W.D. Rubinstein, *Jews in Great Britain*, 153–58; A. Godley, *Jewish Immigrant Entrepreneurship in New York and London, 1880–1914: Enterprise and Culture* (2001).

[William D. Rubinstein (2nd ed.)]

ALIGER, MARGARITA YOSIFOVNA (1915–1992), Russian poet. Aliger was born in Odessa and began to publish verse in 1933. Her prewar collections, *God rozhdeniya* ("Year of Birth," 1938) and *Kamni i travy* ("Stones and Herbs," 1940) although somewhat imitative and conventional, showed an unusual lyrical gift. She achieved fame in 1942 with her long poem *Zoya* (Stalin Prize, 1943) based on newspaper accounts of the life and death of a Moscow schoolgirl who fought behind the German lines during the defense of Moscow. In her long poem, "*Tvoya pobeda*" ("Your Victory"), Aliger, for the first time, turned to a Jewish theme and, while declaring unreserved love for her Russian homeland, bitterly complained about the historical injustice of German and Russian antisemitism. Expunged from subsequent editions of the poem, the passage in question widely circulated in manuscript during the 1940s and the 1950s. The poem reflected the ideological and emotional crisis of the Communist Jewish intelligentsia, brought about by the Holocaust and the upsurge of overt antisemitism in the U.S.S.R. during World War II. A number of her poems were translated into English by Elaine Feinstein (*Collected Poems and Translations*, 2002).

BIBLIOGRAPHY: *Kratkaya Literaturnaya Entsiklopediya*, 1, 154.

[Omri Ronen]

ALI IBN SAHL IBN RABBĀN AL-ṬABARĪ (ninth century), physician and medical writer in Iraq. He was born in Tabaristan, south of the Caspian Sea, son of a well-known Jewish astronomer and mathematician, Sahl ibn Rabbān, whose greatest astronomical feat was his translation into Arabic of the *Almagest* of Ptolemy around 800. Because of civil disturbances Ali moved to Raiy, in the vicinity of Teheran, and became the teacher of Muhammad al-Rāzī, the Muslim medieval scholar and mystic. He then took the post of secretary to Māzyār ibn Qārin, prince of his native Tabaristan, and became a Muslim and a leading figure at the courts of the caliphs al-Mu'taṣim and al-Mutawakkil. His medical writings, especially the *Firdaws al-Ḥikma* ("Garden of Wisdom"), a medical compendium in seven parts (edited by Max Meyerhof), introduced Indian medical lore to Arab readers and to contemporary Western medicine. His other works include treatises on diet, on the proper care of health, on amulets and magic, on cupping and similar subjects. He also wrote a book in praise of Islam called *Kitāb al-Dīn wa al-Dawla* ("The Book of Religion and Empire").

BIBLIOGRAPHY: H. Friedenwald, *Jews and Medicine*, 1 (1967), 173; Brockelmann, Arab Lit, 1 (1898), 231.

[Moshe Rosen]

ALI IBN SULEIMAN (c. 1200), Karaite exegete and philosopher. It is conjectured that he was a member of the Karaite academy in Jerusalem. Ali's literary activity was mainly confined to publishing older Karaite works in abridged form. These include (1) an Arabic commentary on the Torah (parts on Num. and Deut., preserved in manuscript in the British Museum and in Leningrad); (2) a compilation in Arabic of the compendium of *Abu al-Faraj Harun on he Torah (Ms. Sulzberger, in the Jewish Theological Seminary in New York; another part in the second Firkowitsch Collection in Leningrad); (3) the *Agron*, a dictionary of Hebrew rootwords in Arabic, based on the work of David *Alfasi, but incorporating several Hebrew roots and derivatives omitted by Alfasi, and explaining biblical terms by reference to the Mishnah, Talmud, and Targums (Ms. Leningrad); and (4) a philosophical treatise (manuscript in British Museum).

BIBLIOGRAPHY: S. Pinsker, *Likkute Kadmoniyyot*, 1 (1860), 175–216; Steinschneider, Arab Lit. (1902), no. 180; S. Poznański, *Karaite Literary Opponents of Saadiah Gaon* (1908), 54; S.L. Skoss, *The Arabic Commentary of 'Ali ben Suleiman the Karaite on the Book of Genesis* (1928); idem, in: *Tarbiz*, 2 (1930/31), 510–13; Mann, Texts, 2 (1935), 41–42, 98; L. Nemoy, *Karaite Anthology* (1952), 235, 377.

ALISTÁL (Slov. **Dolny Stal**, today **Hrobonovo**; Heb. **אלישטאבא, העלישטאבא**), village in Slovakia, near Bratislava. A community was established at Alistál in the 14th century by Jews from Bohemia and Moravia, who exported horses from the nearby royal stables. A synagogue was built in 1579. A community is mentioned again in records of 1780. Jews without residential rights in Pressburg (Bratislava) were enabled to live in Alistál under royal protection. In 1929 the Jewish population in Alistál and environs numbered 259; approximately half were occupied in agriculture. The community came to an end during World War II.

BIBLIOGRAPHY: *Magyar Zsidó Lexikon* (1929), 26. **ADD. BIBLIOGRAPHY:** E. Bárkány and L. Dojč, *Židovské náboženské obce na Slovensku* (1991), 163–64.

ALITURUS or **ALITYROS** (first century), Roman actor; *Josephus, in his autobiography, describes him as a special favorite of the emperor Nero and of Jewish origin. He relates how, going to intercede for three priests who had been sent to Rome in bonds by Felix, procurator of Judea, on a "trifling charge," he won the friendship of the actor, who introduced him to the empress Poppaea. With her aid he secured a pardon for the priests. The Polish novelist Sienkiewicz introduced "the actor Aliturus" in his *Quo Vadis* as Nero's instructor in the use of gesture in oratory.

BIBLIOGRAPHY: Jos, Life, 3:16.

ALIYAH (Heb. עֲלִיָּה; "ascent"), (1) the coming of Jews to the Land of Israel as *olim* (fem.: *olot*; sing.: *oleh, olah*) for permanent residence; (2) Jews coming from a particular country or region, or during a particular period, for this purpose, e.g., the Polish *aliyah*, the First Aliyah. *Aliyah* means more than immigration: it is a major ideal of *Zionism and the primary means for its realization. It implies personal participation in the rebuilding of the Jewish homeland and the elevation of the individual to a higher plane of self-fulfillment as a member of the renascent nation.

In earlier years the majority of *olim* were inspired by idealistic motives and even during the period of mass *aliyah*, when the main driving force was persecution and distress, many were motivated by messianic yearnings and there was always an infusion of idealists. *Aliyah* has been an almost uninterrupted process ever since the crushing of Jewish resistance by the Romans, but the term has been used particularly in connection with the modern Jewish return to the Land of Israel. Five major waves have been distinguished during the period of Zionist resettlement, each of which played its part in molding the *yishuv*, the Jewish community which constituted the Jewish state in embryo.

The First Aliyah, 1882–1903, consisted of individuals and small groups, mainly under the inspiration of *Ḥibbat Zion and the *Bilu movement, who established the early moshavot (see *moshavah). Some 25,000 – mostly from Eastern Europe – arrived during this period. There were two main influxes: in 1882–84 and 1890–91.

The Second Aliyah, 1904–14, which laid the foundation for the labor movement, consisted mainly of pioneers from Eastern Europe, who generally worked as hired laborers in the moshavot or the cities. They established the first Jewish labor parties and self-help institutions, the *Ha-Shomer watchmen's association, and the first *kevuẓot* (see *kibbutz), and laid the foundations for a new Hebrew press and literature. The influx, which totaled about 40,000, was interrupted by the outbreak of World War I.

The Third Aliyah, 1919–23, which started immediately after World War I, contained many young pioneers (*ḥalutzim*) belonging to the *He-Ḥalutz and *Ha-Shomer ha-Ẓa'ir movements. Together with the veterans of the Second Aliyah, they established the *Histadrut and *Gedud ha-Avodah, worked on road-building, set up more *kevuẓot* and kibbutzim, and founded the first *moshavim. Over 35,000 arrived during this period.

The Fourth Aliyah, 1924–28, which totaled some 67,000, contained many middle-class *olim*, over half of them from Poland. Some four-fifths settled in the main cities, considerably increasing the urban population, building new quarters, and setting up workshops and small factories. Development was halted by an unemployment crisis in 1926–28.

The Fifth Aliyah, 1929–39, accounted for an influx of over 250,000 Jews and transformed the character of the *yishuv*. A prominent part was played by refugees from Nazi Germany, over a quarter of the total, who transferred large amounts of capital and contributed valuable skills and business experience.

Aliyah continued during and after World War II, totaling about 100,000 in 1940–48 (sometimes referred to as the Sixth and Seventh Aliyot). Under British rule (1918–48) *aliyah* was regulated by the Government of Palestine. The official criterion for the numbers admitted was, in normal periods, the country's "economic absorptive capacity," on which the British authorities and Jewish leaders did not agree, but in periods of crisis *aliyah* was often halted or severely restricted on political grounds. Between 1934 and 1948, some 115,000 *olim* were brought into the country in defiance of British restrictions, while another 51,500 were interned by the authorities in Cyprus and admitted only after the achievement of independence. This influx was described by the British as "illegal" *immigration and by the Jews as Aliyah Bet or *ha'palah*.

Independent Israel immediately removed all restrictions on *aliyah* and enacted the *Law of Return (1950), which guaranteed every Jew the right to immigrate to Israel as an *oleh*, unless he or she was a danger to public health or security, and to become a citizen immediately on arrival. The mass *aliyah* that followed the establishment of the State assumed the character of *kibbuẓ galuyyot* ("the *ingathering of the exiles"), almost entire Jewish communities, such as those of Bulgaria, Yemen, and lraq, being transferred to Israel. The resources of the State, as well as massive contributions from world Jewry through the Jewish *Agency, were mobilized for the transportation, reception, and integration of the *olim*. Mass *aliyah* – mainly from Eastern and Central Europe, North Africa, and the Middle East – resulted in the immigration of over a million and a quarter Jews in Israel's first two decades, the influx rising to its greatest heights in 1948–51 (684,000), 1955–57 (161,000), and 1961–64 (220,000). After the Six-Day War of 1967 there was a considerable increase in "voluntary" *aliyah* from Western Europe and the Americas. In the 1970s, as a result of pressure from Israel and other Western countries, the U.S.S.R. opened its gates, enabling more than 150,000 Jews to make *aliyah*. The majority arrived until 1973, and later on many of them left Israel and moved to other Western countries. The next massive *aliyah* from the U.S.S.R. began in 1989 when it reestablished relations with Israel. In 1990–91, 350,000 Russian immigrants arrived in Israel, and by 2003, over a million had emigrated from the former Soviet Union, making them the country's largest immigrant group. The majority were motivated by economic and social factors rather than Zionist ideology. Many were professionals – physicians, engineers, musicians, etc. – and by the end of the 1990s over 30% were non-Jews (as opposed to 10% in the 1990–95 period), benefiting from Israel's liberal Law of Return, which accords the right to immigrate to non-Jewish descendants of Jews. Though their absorption in the country was often difficult, they became a highly visible and influential population group in the course of the years.

During the same period Israel also faced *aliyah* from Ethiopia. The first *olim* arrived at the end of the 1970s, after R. Ovadiah *Yosef acknowledged their Jewishness. About 5,000 arrived independently at refugee camps in Sudan and were brought from there to Israel. As many of them lost their lives on the way, the Israeli government initiated Operation Moses at the end of 1984, in which 8,000 were airlifted to Israel in a 45-day period. In 1985, Sudan closed its borders and the Ethiopian *aliyah* ceased. In May 1991, it was renewed, with another 14,000 arriving in a dramatic 36-hour airlift (Operation Solomon). Since then, more have arrived in small groups, bringing the total of Ethiopian Jewry to 80,000 in 2002. Their integration into the country's life, socially and economically, has been extremely problematic, though the younger generation is being steadily "Israelified."

In the early years of the 21st century, *aliyah* consisted of small groups of *olim*, mainly from Argentina and France.

See also State of *Israel: Aliyah, Absorption and Settlement, where a bibliography is given.

For *Aliyah le-Torah*, see *Torah Reading.

[Misha Louvish/Fred Skolnik (2nd ed.)]

ALJAMA (derived from the Arabic *al-Jamāʿa*, an assembly or congregation), self-governing Jewish or Moorish community in medieval Spain. In the Iberian Peninsula the term refers to the legal institutional framework in which the Jews lived in a locality. It was the *kehillah* as perceived in Jewish jurisdiction and recognized by the authorities. The appellation also denotes the quarter inhabited by Jews or Moors. Other forms of the word are *aliama* and *alcama*; in Aragonese documents it sometimes appears as *yema* while in Portuguese the word is *Alfama*. The term was also used regularly in Sicily, and sometimes in south Italy, to designate the Jewish community. It was declined as a Latin noun, and still appears in Spanish dictionaries.

BIBLIOGRAPHY: I. de las Cacigas, in: *Sefarad*, 6 (1946), 91–93. **ADD. BIBLIOGRAPHY:** D. Romano, in: *Sefarad*, 39 (1979), 347–54; Y. Assis, *The Golden Age of Aragonese Jewry* (1997), 67–73.

ALKABEẒ, SOLOMON BEN MOSES HA-LEVI (c. 1505–1584), kabbalist and mystical poet, composer of the Sabbath hymn "**Lekhah Dodi*" ("Come, my Beloved"). In 1529 he decided to settle in Ereẓ Israel. In the course of his trip he stayed briefly in Adrianople. Here, a group of kabbalist ascetics asked him to instruct them in the spiritual life and in his methods of worship of God. At Nikopolis, he was probably in contact with Joseph *Caro, who greatly appreciated Alkabeẓ' knowledge of Kabbalah. Alkabeẓ states that while they were both studying the Torah on the night of Shavuot, the **maggid* appeared to Caro. They therefore established the custom of staying awake on the night of Shavuot to study the Torah. The custom, which became widespread, is known as "*Tikkun Leil Shavu'ot.*" Alkabeẓ preached wherever he went, and Samuel b. Israel de Uceda, Eleazer *Azikri, Abraham *Galante, Elisha Galileo, and Isaac Gershon were among those who listened to his preaching and quoted from his sermons. Alkabeẓ probably arrived in Safed in 1535. Very little is known of his life there. His signature on rulings and documents is rarer than that of any other important Safed scholar. Nothing is known about his attitude to Isaac *Luria. It seems that he was head of the Meron yeshivah and it is almost certain that he was an officiating rabbi in Safed. A prolific author, he wrote some works on the Bible, and others of a kabbalistic nature. Many of his manuscripts were stolen when he died. It is not clear whether this was done during persecutions, or by other authors. None of his purely kabbalistic works was printed or preserved in manuscript.

Alkabeẓ, in order to understand the secrets of the Zohar, used to go out with his students to pray and meditate on the graves of *ẓaddikim*. This practice was called *gerushin* ("banishment"). During these *gerushin*-peregrinations, they concentrated on rousing their contemplative powers spontaneously and without any previous preparation. Alkabeẓ had a powerful gift for stimulating spiritual revivals and mystical life. His best-known disciple was Moses *Cordovero (who married Alkabeẓ' sister). It seems, however, that the teacher became student. This is mainly apparent from Alkabeẓ' *Likkutei Hakdamot le-Ḥokhmat ha-Kabbalah* ("Collection of Introductions to the Doctrine of Kabbalah," Oxford Ms. 40). The structure of this work is analogous to that of Cordovero's first important book, *Pardes Rimmonim*, and the opinions expressed in both works are generally the same. In one matter of principle, however, Alkabeẓ took a more extreme view. According to him, the *Sefirot* ("Divine Emanations") are the essence of God, and he moved toward the conception of God as immanent in the world. His kabbalistic doctrine emphasized the theoretical element and attempted to endow these symbols reflecting an inner, hidden world, with a conceptual character.

As a kabbalistic commentator on the Bible, his system generally follows that of his teacher, Joseph *Taitaẓak. His manner of developing an argument by first raising a series of difficulties as a basis for the understanding of his text, is similar to that of the Sephardi commentators and homiletic authors of his time. In his opinion, the sayings of the talmudic sages were the true Kabbalah, because they possessed authentic traditions which were handed down from generation to generation and their commentaries were not homiletical interpretations of the text. He believed that the *aggadot* of the sages were reliable, and that one should not be given preference over the other. His writings show that in addition to expressing purely kabbalistic opinions in unique style, he was one of the first to bring full-length quotations from the Zohar and to explain them. The work also includes esoteric aspects of the Torah which are interpreted in brief (*Shoresh Yishai* (1561), 77). More than any other scholar in Safed and in Turkey, he made extensive use of the kabbalistic writings of *Eleazar b. Judah of Worms, particularly *Sha'arei Binah* and *Ma'aseh Roke'aḥ*. His attitude toward the sciences was negative. He often quoted commentaries of latter-day authors, some of whom lived close to his own times, as well as his older contemporaries. Among these were the treatises on the Bible by Joseph Gakon and Joseph Jabeẓ he-Ḥasid. He also quoted from his father Moses Alkabeẓ, his uncle Joshua, Joseph Taitaẓak, and the great halakhist Jacob *Berab (c. 1474–1541).

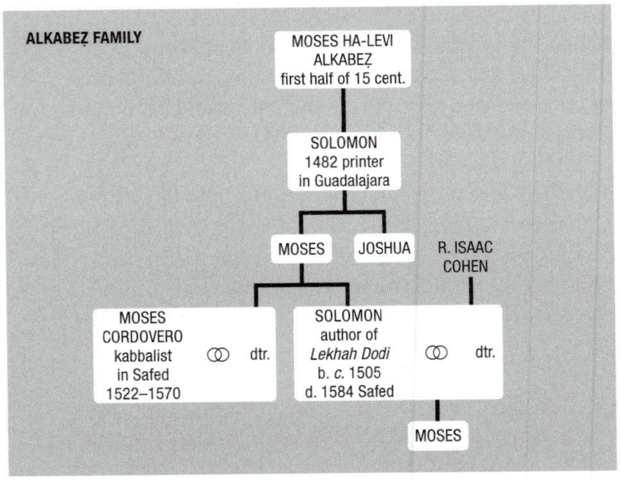

A collection of Alkabeẓ's prayers has been preserved (Moscow, Ms. Guenzburg 694, and Paris Ms. 198). They contain supplications, confessions, admonitions, and songs of praise, both in the form of hymns and of meditations in the style of Gabirol's "*Keter Malkhut*." Alkabeẓ probably initiated the custom practiced by the kabbalists of Safed of going out to the fields to welcome the Sabbath with a recital of his hymns. His "*Lekhah Dodi*" achieved unparalleled popularity, and is sung in Jewish communities at **Kabbalat Shabbat*. "*Lekhah Dodi*" was accepted soon after it was written and was introduced into the prayer book in 1584 (Sephardi version, Venice). The meaning of this hymn, which is permeated by a longing for redemption and the regeneration of the **Shekhinah* ("Divine Presence"), was changed by the Shabbateans who contended that the Messiah had already arrived, and they adapted it to conform to their views.

His works include *Ayyelet Ahavim* (1552, on the Song of Songs), *Shoresh Yishai* (1561 or 1566 on Ruth), *Manot ha-Levi*

(1585, two commentaries on the Scroll of Esther), *Divrei Shelomo* on the Minor Prophets, *Ne'im Zemirot* on Psalms, and *Piẓei Ohev* on Job. The titles of his other works on the Bible are not known. His sermons are also found in the book *Or Ẓaddikim*. His other writings are all kabbalistic: *Oẓar Neḥmad, Amarot Tehorot*, on the *Sefirot* and some sayings of the Zohar; *Appiryon Shelomo, Beit Adohai, Beit Tefillah* constitute "a comprehensive interpretation of all the prayers of the year"; *Berit ha-Levi*, a commentary on the Passover *Haggadah* in both the literal and the kabbalistic manner; *Leḥem Shelomo*, the devotional rules of the meals, in the kabbalistic manner; *Mittato shel Shelomo* on the mystical significance of sexual union; *Sukkat Shalom, Avotot Ahavah, Shomer Emunim*, prayers and litanies (Ms. 8° 1008, Jerusalem).

BIBLIOGRAPHY: S.A. Horodezky, in: *Sefer ha-Shanah shel Ereẓ Yisrael* (1935); R.J.Z. Werblowsky, in: *Sefunot*, 6 (1962), 135–82; idem, *Joseph Karo, Lawyer and Mystic* (1962), 19–20, 51, 99–111, 119, 142; M. Benayahu, in: *Sefunot*, 6 (1962), 14–17.

ALKAḤI, MORDEKHAI (1925–1947), Jew executed by the British in Palestine. Alkaḥi was born in Petaḥ Tikvah and grew up under difficult circumstances. He joined I.Ẓ.L. in 1943 and gained a reputation for his courage and initiative. He was captured together with Yeḥiel *Drezner and Eliezer *Kashani on Dec. 29, 1946, while attempting to kidnap some British officers, and with his companions was hanged in Acre.

BIBLIOGRAPHY: Y. Nedava, *Olei-ha-Gardom* (1966); Y. Gurion, *Ha-Niẓẓaḥon Olei Gardom* (1971).

ALKALAI, ABRAHAM BEN SAMUEL (1750?–1811), Bulgarian rabbi and codifier. Alkalai, who was apparently born in Salonika, studied under his uncle Reuben b. Jacob, whose novellae he sometimes quotes in his works. He served as rabbi of Dupnitsa, where he also headed a yeshivah (1781). He visited Salonika in 1798, and Adrianople on his way to Constantinople (1802), as emissary of his community, which was suffering great hardships. Later he settled in Safed. His best-known work is *Zekhor le-Avraham*, in which he arranged alphabetically the laws of the Shulḥan Arukh (2 vols., Salonika, 1798; vol. 3, addenda, 1815). A second edition of the first two volumes, published by his nephew Judah Ḥayyim Alkalai, included an abridgment of vol. 3 with his own additions (1818). He also wrote responsa, *Ḥesed le-Avraham* (2 vols., 1813–14). A manuscript volume of his sermons is in the Jewish Theological Seminary library in New York (no. 9425).

BIBLIOGRAPHY: Rosanes, Togarmah, 5 (1938), 160; 6 (1945), 135–8.

ALKALAI, DAVID (1862–1933), founder and leader of the Zionist movement in Serbia and Yugoslavia. Alkalai, who was born in Belgrade, was a grandnephew of Judah *Alkalai, whose granddaughter he married. He studied law in Vienna, where he joined the Zionist students' association *Kadimah, and was active in the group centered in the first Zionist periodical **Selbstemanzipation*. Alkalai continued his studies in Vienna and Tübingen, then returned to Belgrade, where he practiced law. He represented Belgrade at the First Zionist Congress in Basle (1897), was elected to the Zionist General Council (the Actions Committee), and from then on was the moving spirit in the Zionist movement in Belgrade and in Serbia. In 1924 he became president of the Zionist Organization in Yugoslavia, and was, for many years, president of the Belgrade Jewish community. He was instrumental in winning Yugoslav statesmen over to Zionism. Alkalai was a pioneer in the publication of Zionist literature in Serbian. He appears as Aladin, a Sephardi, the Jew heading the Land Acquisition Department in Herzl's novel *Altneuland*.

BIBLIOGRAPHY: N. Agmon (Bistritzkij) (ed.), *Megillat ha-Adamah*, 2 (1951), 233–4; A.L. Jaffe (ed.), *Sefer ha-Congress* (1950^2), 89–90, 292–3; *Ha-Olam* (Feb. 16, 1933).

[Getzel Kressel]

ALKALAI, JUDAH BEN SOLOMON ḤAI (1798–1878), Sephardi rabbi and precursor of modern Zionism. Alkalai was born in Sarajevo (then Bosnia) and brought up in Jerusalem, where he was strongly influenced by Sarajevo-born R. Eliezer Papo. From 1825 until he again moved to Jerusalem in 1874, Alkalai was rabbi of Semlin (Zemun), near Belgrade. He taught Hebrew to the young men of the congregation, whose mother tongue was Ladino. As a young man, Alkalai was introduced to the concept of the Jewish nation by the rabbi of Corfu, Judah b. Samuel *Bibas, one of the originators of the idea of Ḥibbat Zion and settlement in Ereẓ Israel. The struggle of three nations – Turkey, Austria, and Serbia – for the domination of the town of Semlin also directed his thoughts to a modern political conception of the destiny and aspirations of the Jewish people.

His first two books were written in Ladino; the rest in Hebrew. In his first book, *Darkhei No'am* (1839), a Ladino-Hebrew textbook, the outstanding feature is his revolutionary attitude toward redemption as opposed to the traditional religious interpretations. *Teshuvah* ("repentance"), which, according to the Talmud (Sanh. 97b), is the precondition for redemption, is interpreted by Alkalai in its literal sense, i.e., *shivah*, return (to Ereẓ Israel). This approach, which was first expressed by R. Bibas and was later developed in Alkalai's writings, is the foundation of his preaching for a Return to Zion within the framework of traditional religious thought. He interpreted the traditional meaning of *teshuvah* as *peratit* ("personal"), i.e., "that each man shall return from the path of evil according to the definitions of repentance given by the early sages," whereas the new meaning refers to *teshuvah kelalit* ("general return"), i.e., "that all of Israel should return to the land of our fathers."

Alkalai's second book was a rebuttal to the scornful criticism that was heaped upon these interpretations. Entitled *Shelom Yerushalayim* (1840), it contained the first reaction to the *Damascus Affair and hints of a Return to Zion. The united stand of world Jewry during the Damascus Affair, as well as the struggle of the Serbs for their independence, led him to publish his first Hebrew work *Minḥat Yehudah* (1843). In this work he interprets the year of the Damascus Affair, 1840, as a fateful and symbolic year for the Jewish nation on its road to redemption. The libeling and suffering of Damascus Jewry occurred in order to arouse the Jewish people to their plight in exile and "to the remoteness of Jerusalem." "Complacent dwellers in foreign lands" should learn the lesson of the Damascus Affair.

In all his writings, Alkalai cites passages from the Talmud, the Midrash, and the Kabbalah, to which he adds his own mystical interpretations. His own views, however, which he repeated both verbally and in writing, are clear, namely that redemption is primarily in the hands of man himself, of the people, and redemption through a miracle can only come at a later stage. This introduction of a natural voluntaristic factor into the yearnings for redemption was a daring concept for his period.

Alkalai aroused strong opposition in Orthodox circles, which rejected the modern concept of redemption. However, he continued to publish pamphlet after pamphlet, stressing that the settlement of Ereẓ Israel was the primary solution to the Jewish problem in Europe. In these pamphlets he quoted the early and later sages, also using *gematria. From these pamphlets, a far-reaching plan for the realization of the return to Ereẓ Israel emerged. Alkalai called for the introduction of the tithe for financing settlement, for the achievement of international recognition of Jewish Ereẓ Israel, for the restoration of the assembly of elders as a Jewish parliament, for the revival of Hebrew (particularly spoken Hebrew), for Jewish agriculture, and for a Jewish army. He expressed the hope that Great Britain would supervise the execution of the program. He opposed a plan, discussed in the early 1860s, to erect houses for the Jews in Jerusalem (*battei maḥaseh*) as being merely of temporary benefit, whereas agricultural settlement would prove of permanent value.

In 1852 Alkalai visited England in order to propagate his idea for a return to Ereẓ Israel. He subsequently traveled to several other West European countries seeking support for his plan. In each locality that he visited he founded a Society for the Settlement of Ereẓ Israel. He corresponded with prominent rabbis in Germany and Austria who gave their imprimatur to his pamphlets. Alkalai also called for the establishment of an international Jewish association, which was realized only in 1860 with the founding of the *Alliance Israélite Universelle. He requested of this organization to help him carry out his plans. However, when, in 1870 the Alliance established the *Mikveh Israel agricultural school in Ereẓ Israel, he opposed the project, arguing that, despite the usefulness of the school in training future Jewish farmers, the only worthwhile activity was the large-scale acquisition of land for settlement purposes. Alkalai opposed the religious Reform Movement in Germany which omitted the references to Zion and Jerusalem from its prayers. He also had no faith in the Emancipation movement, which he regarded as an unwanted diversion from migration and settlement in Ereẓ Israel. For this reason, he also opposed Jewish emigration to the U.S. and elsewhere.

His efforts brought few results. He encouraged the Society for the Settlement of Ereẓ Israel, founded by Ḥayyim *Lorje, but it achieved nothing. Alkalai eventually lost faith in his own society and those founded by others. He went to Ereẓ Israel in 1871 and founded the Kol Israel Ḥaverim society for the settlement of Ereẓ Israel, giving it the same name as the Hebrew translation of Alliance Israélite Universelle, as if to establish an Alliance branch in Ereẓ Israel. However, when Alkalai returned to Serbia, the organization failed as a result of the opposition of the Jerusalem zealots and the Amsterdam center for the distribution of **ḥalukkah* funds. Alkalai violently attacked the Jerusalem zealots and all other opponents of the settlement of Ereẓ Israel, from leading Orthodox rabbis to the heads of the Reform movement.

He published 18 pamphlets and many articles in Hebrew newspapers. One of his pamphlets, *Mevasser Tov*, also appeared in English translation entitled *Harbinger of Good Tidings: An Address to the Jewish Nation on the Propriety of Organizing an Association to Promote the Regaining of Their Fatherland* (1852). A selection of his writings, with a bibliography and an introduction by G. Kressel, was published in 1943. A complete edition of his works, with an introduction by Y. Werfel (Raphael), appeared in 1944. Alkalai is the hero of a novel by Yehudah Burla, entitled *Ba-Ofek* ("On the Horizon," 1943–47).

BIBLIOGRAPHY: A. Herzberg, *Zionist Idea* (1960), 32–36, 103–7; Kressel, Leksikon, 1 (1965), 119–20 (incl. bibl.). **ADD. BIBLIOGRAPHY:** M. Penkower, in: Judaism, 33:3 (1984), 289-95; Y. Rephael, *Kitvei ha-Rav Yehudah Alkalai*, 2 vols. (1974); Z. Loker, "Le Rabbin Juda ben Salomon Hay Alacalay et l`Alliance Israélite Universelle à propos de ses letters inédites," in: *Revue des Etudes juives*, 144 (janvier–septembre 1985), fasc. 1–3, 127–44; J. Lebl, "*Ḥoleh Ahavat Yerushalayim*," in: *Peʿamim*, no. 46 (1989), 21–48.

[Getzel Kressel]

ALKALAJ, ARON (1880–1973), author and communal leader. Alkalaj, the son of a cantor, was born in Belgrade, where he became a bank director and Jewish communal and cultural leader. Apart from works on finance and economics, he published a biography of Moses (1938); a work about Josephus and the fall of Judea, *Josif Flavije i pad Judeje* (1965; orig. in *Jevrejski almanah*, 1963–64); a study of Jewish life in Belgrade; a monograph on Moses and a book about Israel (1960).

ALKAN, ALPHONSE (1809–1889), French printer and author. Born in Paris, Alkan worked as a printer, but also wrote for printing and bibliographical magazines. He later became secretary to the comte de Clarac, keeper of the Museum of Antiquities in the Louvre. There he was also able to exercise his knowledge of printing by acting as a proofreader. Alkan wrote several books on printing and its history, including *Les Etiquettes et leurs Inscriptions des Boîtes – Volumes de Pierre Jannet, Fondateur de la Bibliothèque Elzévirienne* (1883), *Un Fondeur en Caractères, Membre de l'Institut* (1886), and *Les Quatre Doyens de la Typographie Parisienne* (1889). Other significant books by Alkan dealt with bibliography.

[John M. Shaftesley]

ALKAN (real name **Morhange**), **CHARLES HENRI-VALENTIN** (1813–1888), French pianist and composer. The son of a school director, Alkan, a child prodigy, became a concert pianist but retired in 1839. He spent the rest of his life almost in seclusion, teaching, composing, and studying literature, especially the Talmud. Alkan wrote almost exclusively for the piano. His music fell into neglect, perhaps because of its tremendous technical difficulties, but in recent years concert pianists have rediscovered him. Alkan liked the grotesque and the macabre, and his melody is somewhat dry and unexpressive. Searching for orchestral sound on the piano, he achieved interesting effects of color and harmony through surprisingly modern-sounding chords by adding foreign tones and by unusual pedal effects. His brother NAPOLEON (1826–1888) was also a pianist and composed some salon pieces.

BIBLIOGRAPHY: Grove, Diet, and Supplement; Riemann-Gurlitt, Sendrey, Music, no. 4569.

[Claude Abravanel]

ALLEGORY, a narrative in which the agents and the action, and sometimes the setting as well, are contrived not only to make sense in themselves, but also to signify a second correlated order of things, concepts, or events (Abrams).

In the Bible

A pure parable differs from a pure allegory in two respects: (1) it is simple and credible in itself; it begins by saying that case A is like case B. The parables in the Midrash and Gospels are of this sort (e.g., prodigal son: Luke 15:11–32; fatherless steward: *ibid.* 16; the 11th hour: Matt. 20:1–16). There are, however, some parables which tell a tale simple and credible in itself but do not begin by saying case A is like case B, but rather leave the hearer wondering, or – at first – deliberately mislead him (e.g., Nathan's parable, I Sam. 12:1–7; the "story" told by the anonymous prophet in I Kings 20:39). The latter might be called quasi-allegories or crypto-allegories. These stories are not as contrived as Ezekiel 17:1ff., which only makes sense as a "riddle" (*ḥidah*; Ezek. 17:2). This is not an allegorically applied parable but an allegory pure and simple. A similar quasi-allegory is the "Song of the Vineyard" in Isaiah 5:1–6, which, however, has an allegorical element (cf. verse 6 b) in the story as well as being allegorically interpreted in verse 7. The fact is that biblical Hebrew was hardly aware of a distinction between simile, metaphor, parable, and allegory. Thus, in Ezekiel 24:3 the word *mashal* designates a metaphor, whereas in 17:2 it introduces, together with the word *ḥidah*, a typical allegory (Ezek. 17:3–24). In fact, both these words cover the gamut of figurative language, including not only parable and allegory, but fable, tale, enigma, maxim, and proverb.

Beside allegorical figures, such as kindness (grace; *ḥesed*), faithfulness (*emet*), righteousness (*ẓedek*), integrity (*shalem*) in Psalms 85:11–12, 14 and 89:15, wisdom (*ḥokhmah, ḥokhmot*) in Proverbs 1:20; 8:1, 12;9:1; 14:1, and folly (*kesilut, ivvelet*) in Proverbs 9:13, 14:1, maiden Israel, fair (lit. daughter) Zion, fair Jerusalem, and similar expressions in various poetical books, there are two principal kinds of allegory in the Bible. The first occurs when the narrative is based upon an image that suggests the intended subject. Allegories of this kind are often found in Ezekiel, perhaps the first Hebrew poet to make an extensive use of the metaphor. Thus, in Ezekiel, 16:3–63, Jerusalem appears as an adulteress, and in Ezekiel 23:2–45, the two adulterous sisters Oholah and Oholibah represent Samaria and Jerusalem. In Ezekiel 19:2–14, there is a twin allegory, in which the lioness and the vine stock symbolize the people of Israel. This allegory is perhaps partially inspired by an originally Sumerian lyric, *The Message of Lú-dingir-ra to His Mother* (see M. Civil, in: JNES, 23 (1964), 1–11; J. Nougayrol and E. Laroche, in *Ugaritica*, 5 (1968), 310–19, 444–5, 773–9). Another allegory of the vine stock is found in Psalms 80:9–17. In Ezekiel 31:3–18, the fate of the Cedar of Lebanon symbolizes the destiny of Pharaoh, while the allegory of the shepherds and the flock in Ezekiel 34:2–16, 17–22, alludes to the kings of Israel. Ezekiel's allegorical descriptions are sometimes followed by an interpretation of all the figurative elements, a method found later in apocalyptic literature; symbolic visions are explained by a heavenly being or a man of God. This occurs first in Ezekiel 17:3–24, one of the finest pieces of allegorical imagery, which represents the king of Babylon as an eagle and the house of David as a cedar. The same proceeding is found in Ezekiel's vision of the resurrection of the dry bones (37:1–14), an allegory of Israel's restoration. The description of the invaders' army in Joel 2:1–11 portrays in reality the invasion of locusts, which the poet considered a sign of the Lord's anger. The shepherd's allegory in Zechariah 11:4–14 is a kind of apology of the divine Providence toward Israel. Some visions of apocalyptic literature, such as Daniel 4:7–24 or 7:2–27, are akin to allegory inasmuch as the details have an assigned meaning. The allegory of old age in Ecclesiastes 12:1–7 is, in its individual figures, somewhat akin to a riddle.

The second kind of allegory occurs when the literary composition has a complete meaning contained within itself, independently of the moral or spiritual framework that lies beyond it. There is perhaps one sustained allegory of this type in the Bible, namely the Song of Songs, which is an artistically elaborate anthology of love lyrics. Some scholars have nevertheless attempted to see it as an allegorical narrative about the relations between God and His people. An allegorical interpretation may be imposed by others on a work whose author did not intend it to have any meaning on other than the literal level. The allegorical exegesis of the Song of Songs may reflect such a creative approach to a work, which originally had no allegorical meaning at all. In fact, allegorizing interpretations made their way into Judaism in the first centuries B.C.E. and C.E.

[Edward Lipinski]

In Talmudic and Medieval Literature

Allegory was used in the talmudic period, and especially in the medieval period, in three types of literature, each using allegory in its own, different way: (a) homiletical literature used allegory in trying to translate facts and ideas known to the public, into ethical teaching, by discovering the hidden meaning behind the well-known phenomena; allegorical interpretation of Scripture was frequently used in this literary type; (b) fiction, both poetry and prose, used allegory in order to develop a multi-level story or poem; (c) theological literature, especially medieval philosophy and Kabbalah, used allegory as a means to express the idea that the phenomena which are revealed to the senses are but a superficial and sometimes false part of the divine truth, whereas allegory can penetrate to deeper and truer levels.

The preachers of the talmudic and midrashic literature seldom used complete and systematic allegorical constructions. An attempt has been made to prove that two schools of allegorists existed in talmudic times, the *doreshei reshumot* and *doreshei ḥamurot*, both of which were frowned upon by the leading talmudic scholars. This may well be, and the result was that allegory is found in a scattered, unorganized way in this vast literature. One of the clearest examples of the use of allegory is to be found in the homiletical discussions of Ecclesiastes 9:15, 16 (Eccles. R., ch. 9). Here the characters in the biblical verse are interpreted in several allegorical ways, but each is complete, and explains every detail in the source, whether it is historical allegory, finding in the verse the story of Israel in Egypt, or ethical allegory, describing the relationship between the good and the evil (inclinations) in man. The midrashic preachers in this case, as in a few others, had no doubt whatsoever that the biblical verse is allegorical in nature; they discussed various possibilities of unveiling this allegorical meaning. This is a completely different situation from that found in the interpretations of the Song of Songs as allegory, for in that case the meaning (e.g., the relationship between God and Israel) preceded the detailed allegorical interpretations.

Later homiletical literature, in the medieval and early modern periods, revealed allegorical meanings not only in biblical verses, but in talmudic and midrashic passages. Obscure sayings of talmudic scholars, strange stories told by them (e.g., the stories of *Rabbah b. Bar Ḥana, allegorically interpreted by R. *Naḥman of Bratzlav in the first years of the 19th century), all served as material for allegorical interpretation, usually within an ethical, moralistic framework. However, here also systematic, allegorical structure is very rare.

The clearest examples of the use of allegory in fiction is to be found in the **maqama* of the 12th–14th centuries, especially in Spain. Characters in these works are sometimes allegorical entities, usually with some hidden philosophical meaning. Usually it is difficult to distinguish between a well-developed fable and allegorical elements in these works, but some allegorical tendencies are evident. Most of the writers of this school followed examples, or even definite works, by their Arab predecessors or contemporaries. In Hebrew poetry of the period, especially sacred poetry but sometimes also in the secular, allegorical elements may be found. However, it is difficult to point out a separate allegorical school. Abraham *Ibn Ezra's *Ḥai ben Makiẓ* is one of the best examples of allegorical works of this period.

It is not surprising that theological allegory is to be found more in the homiletical and exegetical works of medieval Hebrew philosophers and mystics than in the "straight" theological works. Allegory was used mainly to reconcile ancient lore with contemporary theology, and homiletics and exegetical literature are usually the meeting place of the old and the new. However, some use of allegory is to be found in stories and fables incorporated in theological works, e.g., in *Baḥya ibn Paquda's *Ḥovot ha-Levavot*," in the writings of R. Shem Tov ibn *Falaquera, or even in Maimonides' famous "parable of the Palace" (Guide, 3:51).

The philosophers used allegory not only to explain away the physical attributes of God in the Bible and the talmudic literature. They interpreted whole biblical stories as allegory. This tendency is less evident in the early development of Jewish medieval philosophy; it came into its own only in the 13th century, in the writings of Maimonists like R. Zerahiah Ḥen (see *Gracian), in his polemical letters and his exegesis of the book of Job, or R. Jacob *Anatoli, in his homiletical work, *Malmad ha-Talmidim*. In works like these, one plot is substituted for another: the story of Abraham and Sarah, for example, becomes a parable of the relationship between matter and form, and Noah's three sons represent the three Platonic social classes.

[Joseph Dan]

In Kabbalah

Allegory does not occupy a prominent place in kabbalistic thought and insofar as kabbalists used it, they were influenced by philosophical exegesis. The specific domain of kabbalistic thought is the aspect of *sod* ("mystery"), that is, viewing the processes of the world or interpreting the Scriptures in a manner which refers them to the mystery of the Godhead and its hidden life. However, opposed to *sod* is *remez* ("allusion"), which is allegory. Philosophical commentaries did not talk of processes within the divine world revealing themselves through symbols; but of parallelism between biblical data, e.g., the stories of the Bible, and philosophical views derived from Greek and Arab tradition. Such commentaries recur in certain parts of the Zohar, especially in the *Midrash ha-Ne'lam* concerning the stories of the patriarchs and Ruth, where these stories were interpreted as allegories of the fate of the soul in its descent from above into the human body, its vicissitudes inside the body, and the future allotted to it after death and in the world to come. Here and there such commentaries are also found in the main body of the Zohar. In kabbalistic literature this type of allegorical interpretation is prominent among those kabbalists who tended (especially in the 13th and 14th centuries) to seek a compromise between philosophy and Kabbalah, and to develop mystical views beyond the specific theosophical system of **Sefirot*. The main representative of this conception is *Isaac b. Latif. In the wide-ranging commentary on the Pentateuch of *Baḥya b. Asher the allegorical parts ("rational exegesis") were separated from the kabbalistic parts ("exegesis in the manner of the Kabbalah"). Allegorical interpretations are also found in the writings of kabbalists like Joseph *Ibn Waqar and Samuel *Ibn Motot. Allegory of the type which interprets the words of the Scriptures as referring to the history of man and his fate is found in abundance in the ḥasidic literature which combines the manner of the allegoristic and aggadic interpreters with the style of the kabbalists.

[Gershom Scholem]

One of the major kabbalists who systematically used philosophical allegories, especially Maimonidean ones, was Abraham *Abulafia. He describes this exegetical method as the fourth in his sevenfold system and applies it widely to the biblical texts in his Commentary on the Torah entitled *Sefer ha-Maftehot*. Moreover, unlike most of the other kabbalists and philosophers who allegorized the sacred scriptures, Abulafia composed some of his prophetic writings as allegories, inventing dramas whose specific meaning he himself interpreted by resorting to Maimonidean psychology or metaphysics.

The impact of his allegoristic approach is evident in Johanan *Alemanno, and in some instances of Ḥayyim *Vital's exegesis.

[Moshe Idel (2nd ed.)]

Modern Literature

Influenced by kabbalistic symbolism modern Hebrew (and later also Yiddish) literature developed the allegorical drama, of which the most outstanding examples are the moralistic dramas of Moses Ḥayyim *Luzzatto (e.g., *La-Yesharim Tehillah*). As to prose writings, while it is probable that the stories of R. Naḥman of Bratslav are of an allegorical nature, as they were later interpreted, there is no distinct allegory until the appearance of *Di Kliatshe* (Heb., *Susati*) of Sholem Yankev *Abramovitsh (Mendele Mokher Seforim). Also some of the writings of I.L. *Peretz and S.Y. *Agnon (e.g., *Pat Shelemah, Shevu'at Emunim*) were interpreted as allegories. Note should also be made of many political allegories which flourished during the years of Jewish underground activities in Ereẓ Israel in times when writers had to disguise their message for fear of the censors. Further examples may be found in the early stories of Abraham B. *Yehoshua (e.g., *Mot ha-Zaken*, 1962) and in some prose works of Yitzḥak *Orpaz, as both writers seek to explain the tensions within the personal and collective subconscious. The allegorical names given to some opf the characters are interwoven with realistic features (e.g., in Orpaz's novel *Or be-ad Or*, 1962). In his novella *Nemalim* ("Ants," 1968), Orpaz describes how a horde of mysterious, demonic ants invade an apartment, threatening to destroy the home of a couple on the verge of a divorce. The menace of the ants has been interpreted as an allegorical story about the horror of the modern family as well as the destructive forces among the Arabs. Benjamin Tammuz's novella *Ha-Pardes* ("The Orange Grove," 1971) is likewise an allegory about the relations between Jews and Arabs, set against the background of pre-State Israel.

[Anat Feinberg (2nd ed.)]

BIBLIOGRAPHY: E.W. Bullinger, *Figures of Speech Used in the Bible* (1898), 748–54; A.M.J. Lagrange, in: RB, 6 (1909), 198–212, 342–67 (esp. 347–55); C.G. Montefiore, in: JQR, 3 (1912/13), 623–4; O. Eissfeldt, *Der Maschal im Alten Testament* (1913), esp. 14–16; H. Gunkel and H. Gressmann, in RGG², 1 (1927), 219–20; A. Bentzen, *Introduction to the Old Testament*, 1 (19584), 179–80; F. Hauck, in: G. Friedrich (ed.), *Theologisches Woerterbuch zum Neuen Testament*, 5 (1954), 741–59 (esp. 744–6). **ADD. BIBLIOGRAPHY:** M. Abrams, *A Glossary of Literary Terms* (1971), 4; J. Fraenkel, *Darkhei ha-Aggadah ve-ha-Midrash* (Heb., 1996), 197–232; idem, *Midrash ve-Aggadah* (1996), 181–99; M. Idel, *Language, Torah and Hermeneutics in Abraham Abulafia*, tr. M. Kallus (1989).

ALLEN, ISAAC (1875–1973), U.S. Zionist pioneer and talmudic scholar. Born in Russia, Allen immigrated to the United States in 1891. He graduated from the Law School of New York University in 1901, and while still a student won the right for Jews not to be required to take examinations on the Sabbath. A devoted Zionist, as early as 1897 Allen helped establish the Federation of American Zionists and the New York Zionist Council, of which he became president in 1898, and was a founder of the Mizrachi Organization of America in 1912. He was also a founder of the American Jewish Committee and the American Jewish Congress. He was a delegate to the Ninth Zionist Congress in Hamburg in 1909 and to many subsequent ones. He wrote regularly in the Yiddish press on American law, history, civics, customs, and policies for the benefit of new immigrants and also lectured publicly on these subjects. For 20 years, until failing health and eyesight forced him to retire at the age of 93, Allen conducted classes in Talmud at no fewer than four synagogues in New York.

ALLEN, MEL (**Melvin Israel**; 1913–1996), U.S. sportscaster, member of the Baseball Hall of Fame. Allen was born in Birmingham, Alabama, to Julius, a traveling shirt salesman, and Anna, scion of a rabbinical family and related to Simon *Dubnow and Shmarya *Levin. Allen's Russian-born grandfather arranged for a *shoḥet* to come to Birmingham for the Bibb County Jewish community and built a synagogue next to his house. Julius and Anna kept a kosher home, celebrated all the Jewish holidays, and the family attended an Orthodox synagogue regularly. When Allen was working for the Yankees and would have the ballplayers out to his house for a cookout, Allen's mother brought out a separate set of dishes from the basement and would fry oysters and cook shrimps for the players.

The eldest of three children, Allen was bar mitzvah in 1926 in Greensboro, North Carolina, where his family had moved, giving his bar mitzvah speech in Hebrew. At age 15 he enrolled at the University of Alabama, where he received his undergraduate degree in 1932 and a law school degree in 1936.

He got his start in broadcasting while still a law student, when the Alabama football coach asked him to replace the team's announcer for $5 a game.

During a Christmas vacation in New York with friends, in 1936, Allen stopped at CBS for an audition on a lark and was shortly hired as a $45-a-week announcer, understudying Ted Husing, CBS's top sports announcer, and Robert Trout in news. Allen's father thought his son was wasting a good education, and was less pleased when Mel explained that CBS wanted him to change his name. "They said, 'Not that we have any objection to the name Israel, but we just think it's a little too all-inclusive.' So I dropped the last name and kept my father's middle name, which was Allen, so that I still felt at least I had part of my father's name." Thus Melvin Israel became Mel Allen.

His broadcasting for CBS included interrupting Kate Smith's afternoon program with a news bulletin reporting the crash of the German zeppelin *Hindenburg*. The first baseball game Allen ever broadcast was the 1938 World Series for CBS, and in June 1939 he was hired to call New York Yankees and New York Giants home games.

Allen's garrulous, infectious style made him one of the first prominent American sportscasters, and the icon voice of baseball as television replaced radio as the primary form of mass entertainment. This occurred at the same time that the Yankees were playing in 15 of 18 World Series beginning in 1947. The "Voice of the New York Yankees" broadcast from 1939 to 1964, and was present for many major Yankees' events during that time, including introducing Lou Gehrig at Yankee Stadium on July 4, 1939, when Gehrig made his famous "Today, I am the luckiest man" speech; introducing a dying Babe Ruth at his sad farewell in 1948; and Roger Maris' record-breaking 61 home runs in 1961. Allen saw Gehrig in the dugout one day in 1940, when the Yankee captain was dying of amyotrophic lateral sclerosis. "Lou patted me on the thigh and said, 'Kid, I never listened to the broadcasts when I was playing, but now they're what keep me going,'" said Allen, who was then 27. "I went down the steps and bawled like a baby."

It was Allen who gave the nicknames "Joltin' Joe" to DiMaggio, "Old Reliable" to Tommy Henrich, and "The Scooter" to Phil Rizzuto. His endearing signature phrases on the air were his sign-on, "Hello, everybody, this is Mel Allen," his exclamation at high points in a game, "How about that!" and his home run call, "That ball is going, going … gone!" His home run pronouncements were punctuated with reference to the team's sponsors, calling them "Ballantine Blasts" after the beer sponsor and "White Owl Wallops" for the cigar sponsor. Allen was abruptly fired after the 1964 season for reasons that have remained a mystery.

Allen broadcast Cleveland Indians games in 1968, and returned to call Yankees games on cable from 1978 to 1986. From 1977 he was the host of the long-running weekly television show, "This Week in Baseball," which continued to introduce the show with his voice even after his death. Allen also broadcast New York Giants baseball games from 1939 to 1943, 20 World Series, 24 All-Star baseball games, as well as 14 Rose Bowl games, five Orange Bowls, and two Sugar Bowls. He was the sports voice of Movietone newsreels and hosted boxing matches.

In 1978 he and sportscaster Red Barber were the first broadcasters awarded the National Baseball Hall of Fame's Ford C. Frick Award for "major contributions to baseball." Allen was the fourth person elected to the National (USA) Sportswriters and Broadcasters Hall of Fame in March 1972, was inducted into the American Sportscasters Hall of Fame in 1985, and was inducted into the Radio Hall of Fame in 1988. In 1959 he wrote *It Takes Heart* with Frank Graham Jr.

[Elli Wohlgelernter (2nd ed.)]

ALLEN, PAUL G. (1953–), U.S. entrepreneur. As the co-founder of the Microsoft Corporation, Allen became one of the wealthiest (third-richest) men in the world. He also became one of the world's most active philanthropists, supporting the Survivors of the Shoah Visual History Foundation, among other projects. In 2004 he gave away more than $500 million.

As a child, Allen attended Lakeside, a private school in Seattle known as a breeding ground for the city's future leaders. There he met Bill Gates and the two became fast friends. In 1975 someone brought to Lakeside a clunky Teletype-like computer and Allen convinced Gates that they should not miss out on the technology revolution. They set about developing an operating system for the computer, the Altair 8800, and succeeded.

Allen dropped out of Washington State University to work for Honeywell in Boston. There he again linked up with Gates, who was attending Harvard. They founded Microsoft in 1975. Allen had the programming expertise, Gates the financial acumen. In 1977 Allen said he expected the personal computer to become as much a part of everyday life as a telephone, and he envisioned innovations like E-mail and suggested the name Microsoft. He talked about a "wired world," a phrase he claims to have originated.

In 1982 Allen contracted Hodgkin's disease and endured months of radiation therapy. The following year, against Gates' wishes, Allen left Microsoft. The company did not go public for three years, but when it did, Allen's shares were worth $134 million. He invested $170 million in Ticketmaster, the computer-ticket service, and collected $568 million when he sold the stock in 2002. He then started Starwave, one of the first Internet content sites and in 1992 the first home to ESPN's sports coverage on the Web. Five years later he sold it to Walt Disney for $200 million. An early investor in Priceline.com, the online travel business, he invested $30 million in 1998 and collected $125 million when he sold his shares two years later. He was also a major investor in Dreamworks SKG, the film and entertainment studio headed by Steven *Spielberg, Jeffrey *Katzenberg, and David *Geffen. For an investment of $675 million, Allen was given 18 percent of the company and a seat on the board. Not all of his investments were successful. In 2003 and 2004 Allen pared his portfolio from 100 to 40 companies. In 1999, according to *Forbes* magazine, Allen was worth $40 billion. By 2003 his fortune was "down" to $21 billion, *Forbes* estimated. Allen's grants to outside organizations and individuals have varied. Asked whether he had philanthropic role models, he pointed to the Stroum family, a prominent Jewish family in Seattle which supported the University of Washington, the Seattle Symphony, and local Jewish institutions. Allen had "a broad and diverse range of interests," according to Laura Rich, author of *The Accidental Zillionaire: Demystifying Paul Allen*. One of Allen's strongest interests was music. He played the guitar and collected memorabilia about Jimi Hendrix, the rock and blues guitarist and, like Allen, a Seattle native. Allen played with the Butcher Shop Boys (known for butchering songs, he said). He owned a recording studio and taught himself to play "Purple Haze," a Hendrix signature number.

Passionate about the arts, Allen hired Frank *Gehry to create an interactive rock 'n' roll museum, the Experience Music Project, in 2000 at a cost of $240 million. He was also involved in a documentary on blues music for public television and organized benefit concerts to raise money for music education and blues artists. He also supported efforts to increase public understanding of science. In 2001 his documentary company produced a seven-part television series on evolution and helped fund another documentary on global public health. In 2004 Allen provided the British entrepreneur Richard Branson with the funds to build an aircraft for manned commercial space flight.

Allen was keenly devoted to sports. He owned the Portland Trail Blazers, a professional basketball team, and paid $46 million of the $262 million cost of the Rose Garden, a 21,500-seat arena in which the team plays. He also bought the Seattle Seahawks, a professional football team. Allen lived alone – and well – on Mercer Island, an enclave of old Seattle wealth and new millionaires. In 2004 Allen's wealth was estimated at $18 billion, including $3.8 billion of Microsoft stock, enough to afford a 413-foot Octopus yacht, the world's largest and, at $200 million, the most expensive.

[Stewart Kampel (2nd ed.)]

ALLEN, WOODY (originally **Allen Stewart Konigsberg**; 1935–), U.S. comedian, filmmaker. Born in Brooklyn, New York, Allen started selling one-liners to gossip columns at the age of 15. He began his career writing jokes for television comedians, such as Garry Moore and Steve Allen. He then appeared as a stand-up comedian and in comedy sequences based on the theme of failure. Short, slight of build, and wearing heavy glasses, he developed what he called "formless farce," exemplified by his film scripts for *What's New, Pussycat?* and *What's Up, Tiger Lily?* His play *Don't Drink the Water* opened on Broadway in 1966. He played the lead in the film *Take the Money and Run* in 1969. Allen soon emerged as one of the most notable figures in the film industry. From 1969, he directed and scripted an average of one film per year. His most successful was *Annie Hall* (1977), which won an Oscar for the best picture of the year; in addition, he took two other prizes for best director and best screenwriter. In 1978 he produced his first serious drama, *Interiors*. It has been compared in style and tone to the films of Swedish director Ingmar Bergman, whose work has influenced Allen greatly. In 1987 Allen won the best screenplay Oscar for *Hannah and Her Sisters*, as well as the American Comedy Award for Funniest Lead Actor. That year the American Comedy Awards also presented him with a Lifetime Achievement Award in Comedy.

Allen's other films include *Bananas* (1971), *Play It Again, Sam* (1972), *Everything You Always Wanted to Know about Sex but Were Afraid to Ask* (1972), *Sleeper* (1973), *Love and Death* (1975), *Manhattan* (1979), *Stardust Memories* (1980), *Midsummer Night's Sex Comedy* (1982), *Zelig* (1983), *Broadway Danny Rose* (1984), *The Purple Rose of Cairo* (1985), *Radio Days* (1987), *September* (1987), *Another Woman* (1988), *New York Stories* (1989), *Crimes and Misdemeanors* (1989), *Alice* (1990), *Shadows and Fog* (1992), *Husbands and Wives* (1992), *Manhattan Murder Mystery* (1993), *Bullets over Broadway* (1994), *Mighty Aphrodite* (1995), *Everyone Says I Love You* (1996), *Deconstructing Harry* (1997), *Celebrity* (1998), *Sweet and Lowdown* (1999), *Small Time Crooks* (2000), *Curse of the Jade Scorpion* (2001), *Hollywood Ending* (2002), *Anything Else* (2002), and *Melinda and Melinda* (2004).

In 1990, along with such fellow filmmakers as Stanley Kubrick and Martin Scorsese, Allen helped establish the Film Foundation, a group dedicated to preserving the heritage of American films.

In 1992 Allen caused a stir when it was discovered that he had been having a relationship with Soon-Yi Previn, the adopted daughter of his long-time girlfriend, actress Mia Farrow. In 1997 Allen, who was 62, and Soon-Yi, 27, were married in Venice.

Allen caused another stir in 1998, this time among the Jewish community, when he wrote an op-ed article in the *New York Times* (January 28) saying that he was appalled by Israel's treatment of the rioting Palestinians (during the first Intifada). He expressed incredulity at what he understood from the media to be "state-sanctioned brutality and even torture." Stressed Allen, "I can't believe it, and I don't know exactly what is to be done, but I'm sure pulling out my movies is again not the answer … to bring this wrongheaded approach to a halt."

As the perennial onscreen personification of angst and neurosis, Allen projects a love-hate relationship with himself and with his fellow Jews. Taking more of an amiable swipe than a nasty jibe, he peoples his films and peppers his dialogues with more Jewish wiseacres and wisecracks than most American directors or screenwriters ever have. A New Yorker to the core, Allen bases most of his films in his beloved hometown.

His dour, deadpan humor is just as funny off-screen as it is in his films. He is quoted as saying, "Most of the time I don't have much fun. The rest of the time I don't have any fun at all." And "If my film makes one more person miserable, I'll feel I've done my job."

Capturing that humor in print, Allen has written a number of books and plays as well. They include his short story collections *Getting Even* (1971) and *Without Feathers* (1975); his essays *Side Effects* (1980); and in addition to his theatrical fare *Don't Drink the Water*, such plays as *Death Knocks* (1971), *Death: A Comedy in One Act* (1975), *God: A Comedy in One Act* (1975), *The Floating Light Bulb* (1982), and *Three One-Act Plays: Riverside Drive, Old Saybrook, and Central Park West.* He also published *Woody Allen on Woody Allen: In Conversation with Stig Björkman* (1995).

Another of Allen's creative talents, his clarinet playing, is highlighted in the 1997 documentary film *Wild Man Blues*, directed by Barbara Koppel. The film follows Allen and his New Orleans jazz band on their European tour. A serious jazz musician, Allen has been performing for more than 25 years at a downtown club in New York.

ADD. BIBLIOGRAPHY: E. Lax, *Woody Allen: A Biography* (1991); S.B. Girgus, *The Films of Woody Allen* (2002^2); S. Lee, *Woody Allen's Angst* (1997); R. Blake, *Woody Allen: Profane and Sacred* (1995); F. Hirsh, *Love, Sex, Death and the Meaning of Life in the Films of Woody Allen* (1992); M.P. Nichols, *Reconstructing Woody: Art, Love and Life in the Films of Woody Allen* (1982).

[Jonathan Licht and Ruth Beloff (2nd ed.)]

°ALLENBY, EDMUND HENRY HYNMAN, VISCOUNT (1861–1936), British soldier. Allenby commanded the Egyptian Expeditionary Forces which, in 1917–18, defeated the Turks in Palestine. In June 1917 he was sent to Cairo to succeed Sir Archibald Murray as commander of the British forces in Egypt and Palestine. British troops were then held up at Gaza after two unsuccessful battles. Deceiving the enemy into thinking he would launch a third frontal attack, he took Beersheba instead (October 31), thus forcing the Turks to withdraw from Gaza, and leading to the capture of Jaffa and of Jerusalem (December 9, 1917). By the autumn of 1918, troops transferred from Mesopotamia and India to Palestine were ready for forays across the Jordan, in which the *Jewish Legion (38th and 39th Battalions of the Royal Fusiliers) took part. Allenby again deceived the Turks into thinking that he would attack once more with his right wing, but, having secretly transferred the bulk of his forces (some 35,000 men) to the orange groves north of Jaffa, he broke through on the night of September 18–19 and reached Nazareth via the Megiddo Pass before the Turks realized what was happening. Their escape routes blocked, tens of thousands of Turkish troops were taken prisoner in a decisive victory. Pressing on to Damascus and Aleppo, Allenby forced Turkey out of the war on October 31. For his achievements he was named Viscount Allenby of Megiddo and Felixstowe, and received a parliamentary grant of £50,000. Of massive build and forceful personality (known to his troops as "The Bull"), Allenby later became British high commissioner in Egypt (1919–1925). In 1918 he was present at the laying of the foundation stone of the Hebrew University on Mount Scopus. Though as a commander of the British Expeditionary Forces he was noncommittal toward Zionist aspirations, doubting the wisdom of British policy concerning a Jewish National Home, he later expressed an understanding of Zionism in a speech delivered at the inaugural banquet of the Hebrew University in 1925. One of the main streets in Tel Aviv is named in his honor.

BIBLIOGRAPHY: B. Gardner, *Allenby* (Eng., 1965); Great Britain, Army, *Brief Record of the Advance of the Egyptian Expeditionary Force, 1917–1918* (1919); T.L. Jackson, *With Allenby in the Holy Land* (1938); A. Wavell, *Allenby, a Study in Greatness*, 2 vols. (1940–43); Hebrew University of Jerusalem, *Banquet Speeches* (1925), 50–51. **ADD. BIBLIOGRAPHY:** M. Hughes and F. Cass, *Allenby and British Strategy in the Middle East, 1917–1919* (1999); D.L. Bullock, *Allenby's War: The Palestine-Arabian Campaign 1916–1918* (1988); L. James, *Imperial Warrior: The Life and Times of Field-Marshall Viscount Allenby, 1861–1936* (1994).

[Edwin Samuel, Second Viscount Samuel]

ALLGEMEINE ZEITUNG DES JUDENTUMS (AZJ, "General Journal of Judaism"), one of the first modern and certainly the most important of German Jewish periodicals of the 19th century. The AZJ was published in Leipzig and later in Berlin between 1837 and 1922. In 1860, the journal had a circulation of about 1,500 copies. It was read not only in Germany, Austria, and Holland, but also in Eastern Europe. Its success enabled it to be independent of subsidies from public bodies as well as to publish monographs by scholars such as I.M. Jost, S.D. Luzzatto, L. Zunz, A. Geiger, A. Jellinek, and Franz Delitzsch. The founder, Ludwig *Philippson, edited the paper from 1837 to 1889. During the first two years the AZJ was published thrice weekly, in 1839 twice weekly, then weekly, and finally only once every two weeks.

The AZJ advocated moderate religious reform and closer relations with non-Jews. It prompted the convention of the Rabbinical Conferences of 1844–46, the Reform Synod at Leipzig in 1869, and the establishment of the Lehranstalt fuer die Wissenschaft des Judentums in Berlin. However, its columns were open to varying views. After the adherents of other ideological trends in Central European Jewry established their own periodicals from the middle of the 19th century, the AZJ ceased to reflect the moderate view. A most important contribution to Jewish life in Central Europe was made through the journal's efforts to foster and spread "Jewish" belle-lettres. While ignoring the more realistic genre of "village and ghetto tales" (e.g., by Berthold *Auerbach), Philippson focused on historic and heroic texts to stress the "ideal" aspects of Jewish life. The journal was instrumental in the establishment and support of the Institut zur Foerderung der Israelitischen Literatur in the late 1850s. In 1866, Philippson's *Juedisches Familienblatt* with its literary content was integrated into the feuilleton of the AZJ.

Following Gabriel Riesser's paper *Der Jude* (1832–35), the AZJ understood itself as the main organ of the Jewish emancipation movement in the 19th century. Despite the political reaction after the 1848 revolution, it continued the battle. After the foundation of the German Reich, when full legal rights were achieved, the fight against antisemitism became the main focus of the AZJ. With the rise of Zionism, the journal declined in importance. Under the editorship of Gustav *Karpeles (1890–1909), its interests shifted towards the Jews of Eastern Europe and their situation. When Ludwig *Geiger took over (1910–1919), the journal assumed an anti-Zionist and anti-Orthodox position. Albert Katz (1858–1923), initially in charge of the supplement for communal affairs, became editor in 1919. In 1922, the AZJ finally merged with the *C. V.-Zeitung.*

The AZJ is available at http://www.compactmemory.de. **ADD. BIBLIOGRAPHY:** *C. V.-Zeitung* 16, No. 18 (May 6, 1937); J. Philippson, "The Philippsons, a German-Jewish Family 1775–1933," in: LBIYB 7 (1962), 95–118; ibid., "Ludwig Philippson und die Allgemeine Zeitung des Judentums," in: H. Liebeschütz and A. Paucker (eds.), *Das Judentum in der Deutschen Umwelt, 1800–1850* (1977), 243–91; M. Eliav, "Philippsons Allgemeine Zeitung des Judentums und Erez Israel," in: Bull LBI 46–47 (1969), 155–82; H.O. Horch, *Auf der Suche nach der juedischen Erzaehlliteratur* (1985); idem, "Auf der Zinne der Zeit," in: Bull LBI 86 (1990), 5–21.

[Ezriel Carlebach and Robert Weltsch / Marcus Pyka and Johannes Valentin Schwarz (2nd ed.)]

ALLIANCE ISRAELITE UNIVERSELLE (Heb. כָּל יִשְׂרָאֵל חֲבֵרִים כָּי״חַ "All Israel are comrades"), first modern international Jewish organization, founded in 1860, centered in Paris. The foundation of the Alliance expressed the renewal of Jewish cohesiveness after a short period of weakening in the second half of the 18th and up to the forties of the 19th century. Its inception was stimulated by ideological trends and political events in the national and international spheres in the second half of the 19th century.

Origins and Structure

From the outset the Alliance labored under a built-in tension; it was conceived to be a world organization of "fortunate" Jews, who had achieved emancipation and assimilation in their own countries, to help their fellow-Jews, wherever they were suffering for or discriminated against because of their religion.

The *Damascus Affair in 1840 renewed the urge toward Jewish solidarity and cooperation. Opinions were subsequently voiced, especially in Germany and France, that a regular body should be established to defend Jews everywhere, whenever discriminated against on religious grounds. The idea was discussed by various authors (Z. *Frankel; J. *Carvallo). The 1848 European revolutionary climate, however, worked against Jewish cohesion. On the other hand, the political constellation in Europe of the 1850–60s, and the hegemony of France under Napoleon III, was propitious for the establishment of a Jewish organization under French leadership for international Jewish work.

The *Mortara case in 1858 accentuated the urge for world-Jewish self-help, while the French hegemony in Europe pointed to French Jews as the natural leaders. Inter-European tensions in the Catholic Church also emphasized the international character of religious problems, and the need for international solutions. The same year, Isidor *Cahen declared in his *Archives Israélites* that the Jews should mainly rely on themselves for their own defense, and suggested the establishment of an intercommunal organization to be named "Alliance Israélite Universelle" to defend the interests of Jews throughout the world. In February 1860 Simon Bloch, the French writer and later secretary of the Alliance, repeated this proposal. The Alliance was launched in May 1860, the founder-members – J. Carvallo; I. Cahen; N. *Leven, the secretary of Adolphe *Crémieux; A. *Astruc, and the poet, E. Manuel – meeting in the house of Charles *Netter. In June 1860 they published their manifesto which stressed the need for solidarity on Jewish matters, and stated that the Alliance would "serve as a most important stimulus to Jewish regeneration."

The aims of the Alliance, as formulated by Carvallo and Netter were three: "to work everywhere for the emancipation and moral progress of the Jews; to offer effective assistance to Jews suffering from antisemitism; and to encourage all publications calculated to promote this aim."

The statutes of the Alliance stipulated a typically French centralism. It was to be administered by a central committee of 30 members, located in Paris, elected by the general assembly of all members of the organization. Two-thirds of the central committee had to be Paris residents. Seven formed a quorum. The central committee had to report annually to the general assembly. Regional and local committees everywhere had to transfer their funds to the central committee, or to use part of them locally, with permission of the central committee. All Alliance presidents have been French Jews with the exception of the German S.H. Goldschmidt (president 1881–98). Adolphe Crémieux (president 1863–80) did much for the development of the Alliance. Other presidents have included Solomon *Munk, Narcisse Leven, Sylvain *Lévi, and René *Cassin.

Aims and Activity

Its aims, as expressed in its statutes, have been implemented under changing historical conditions. These, ever since its establishment, have influenced the scale and direction of its activities, conducted mainly in the diplomatic, social, and educational spheres.

Diplomatic Activity

The Alliance soon became the address to which persecuted Jewish communities turned to for help throughout the world. From the 1880s its main diplomatic activities were conducted on behalf of Near-Eastern Jewish communities. Political intervention was secured by various means and the Alliance may be considered the pioneer of Jewish diplomatic methods in modern times. During and after the 1860s the Alliance made repeated appeals to obtain improvement of the legal status of the Jews of Serbia and Romania basing its case on paragraph 46 of the 1858 Paris Convention, which declared the principle of equal rights for the Jews. The Alliance interceded on behalf of the Jews of Belgium and of Russia, and for civil rights of the Jews of Switzerland. After Adolphe Crémieux became president, the French Foreign Office and French authorities in the colonies and protectorates frequently cooperated with the Alliance.

The peak period of Alliance diplomatic activity was during the Congress of Berlin (1878; see *Berlin, Congress of), when, in conjunction with the Joint Foreign Committee of the Anglo-Jewish Association, and the Board of Deputies it took steps to protect the interests of the Jews in the Balkan countries, obtaining the inclusion of a paragraph in the treaties with these states stipulating civil rights for all Jews. The Alliance interceded with the sultan of Morocco during the Madrid Congress of 1880, and obtained promises for the improvement of the status of Moroccan Jews. At the peace conference of Versailles, after World War I, the Alliance was active on behalf of the Jews of Poland, Hungary, Romania, and other countries affected by the peace treaties. It acted independently of the *Comité des Délégations Juives, since the Alliance opposed both the concepts of national *minority rights and of *Zionism; the Alliance then cooperated with those Anglo-Jewish organizations holding similar views.

ASSISTANCE TO EMIGRANTS. The Alliance began to provide assistance to Jews who wished to leave countries where they suffered from disabilities in 1869, mainly on behalf of Jews from Russia and Romania. It contacted both institutions and individuals in the U.S. to ascertain whether Jewish emigration there was desirable, the numbers that could be absorbed, and the most suitable qualifications. The Jewish migration was regulated by the committee for Jewish refugees in Koenigsberg, established and operated in collaboration with other Jewish organizations. The Koenigsberg committee also cared for the placement of starving Jewish orphans with German Jewish families for possible adoption. With the commencement of mass emigration from Russia after the pogroms of 1881, the Alliance again shared relief activities with other Jewish organizations.

When the first wave of 4,000 refugees arrived in Brody, Galicia, that year, Charles Netter went there on behalf of the Alliance. He failed, however, to cope with the unprecedented stream of emigrants. Subsequently the Alliance participated in several conferences of Jewish organizations and at that held in 1882, was charged to find opportunities for Jewish immigration outside the United States. It participated in two such conferences after 1891, although by then it had decided that it would not support the refugees in order to discourage further emigration. In matters of migration, the Alliance also cooperated with the *Jewish Colonization Association (ICA).

EDUCATION. In the 1890s the Alliance began to concentrate its efforts (in conjunction with ICA) on aiding Jewish education, especially in the Balkans (until after World War I) and the Middle Eastern countries. The educational activity of the Alliance was concerted with its diplomatic efforts, since it aimed at the betterment of the social and legal status of the Jews through their "cultural and moral elevation." It was also an expression of the French patriotism of the Alliance and its pride in French language and culture which it intended to disseminate among the Jews. The work encountered difficulties since certain communities viewed the propagation of French culture in the schools established by the Alliance as a danger to the traditional framework of Jewish life. The French character of Alliance education was also to prove its undoing as it became inconsistent with the new nationalist spirit in these countries following World War I.

The important network of schools established by the Alliance made rapid progress with the help of large donations by Baron Maurice de Hirsch "to improve the position of the Jews in the Turkish Empire by instruction and education." These amounted to one million gold francs in 1874 and ten million gold francs in 1889. In Greece ten schools were opened at intervals, but progress there was arrested in the period between the two world wars; only four remained open by 1939 and there were none by the 1960s. In Bulgaria, the Alliance established ten schools between 1870 and 1885; these gradually disappeared soon after World War I. A similar process took place in Turkey where in 1912, the Alliance possessed 71 boys' schools and 44 girls' schools, of which 52 were in European Turkey (including the Balkans) and 63 in Asian Turkey (including Iraq, etc.). From 1932 the Alliance gradually handed over its schools to the local communities. The few schools of the Alliance in Serbia and Romania similarly closed. The Alliance increasingly concentrated its educational activities in North Africa and the Near East, including Iran. In Morocco, the schools in Tetuan (founded 1862) and Tangiers (1869) were followed by schools in five major cities (1873–1902). In 1912 almost 5,500 pupils attended 14 schools. At that time, the French administration began to take an interest in these activities and an agreement was concluded between the local government and the Alliance in 1928, whereby Alliance schools were placed under the strict control of the Public Education Department, and were also assured of effective material support. The network of the Alliance henceforth became an integral part of the social and educational activities conducted in the protectorate. The Alliance social relief activities combined with the educational movement to improve the living conditions of the pupils from the mellah. In 1939, 45 schools in Morocco had 15,761 pupils. The support of the local authorities enabled the Alliance to continue its work even during World War II. It received a new impetus in 1945. From 14,000 pupils in 1945, the total rose to 28,000 in 1952, the increase in attendance being mainly in the large urban centers of Marrakesh, Fez, Rabat, and Casablanca.

The Ecole Normale Hébraïque of Casablanca fulfilled the local need for Jewish teachers. The Alliance also increased its activities in the small communities, and a school was established for every Jewish community numbering 300 to 400 persons. In Casablanca, the Alliance also established a school for sufferers from trachoma, as well as an institute for the deaf and dumb, in collaboration with *ORT and the *American Jewish Joint Distribution Committee. In Tunisia, the Alliance opened its first school in 1878; by 1960, there were 2,150 pupils in elementary schools, 700 in secondary schools, and 76 in commercial classes run by the Alliance. An attempt to open a school in Beirut in 1869 was unsuccessful, but later several schools were established.

Alliance schools in Beirut were destroyed by explosives in 1950, but were immediately rebuilt. In 1960 the schools of Saida and Beirut had 1,295 pupils. Several Alliance schools functioned in Syria, mainly in Damascus and Aleppo. In Iraq, where the Alliance opened a school in Baghdad in 1865, there were 6,000 pupils in its ten schools in 1947. In Iran, the Alliance inaugurated its first school in Teheran in 1898, not without encountering difficulties from the local Jewish community. In 1960, the school network of the Alliance in Iran had 15 schools with a total of 6,200 pupils, the greatest concentration being in Teheran; in the provinces all Jewish children attended Alliance schools. In Ereẓ Israel, the Alliance agricultural school at *Mikveh Israel was opened by Charles Netter in 1870; in 1882, an elementary school was opened in Jerusalem. Other schools followed in the important towns. In Egypt the local communities carried out the educational work on behalf of the Alliance by gradually taking upon themselves the responsibility for the local schools.

World War II marks a watershed in Alliance activities. All branches of its activities were cut off from the head office which in turn had to take refuge from Paris in the non-occupied zone. From November 1942 the isolation was complete (see *France). The Free French government interested itself in the fate of the Alliance, and General de Gaulle entrusted responsibility for it to René Cassin. After the liberation, the Alliance – with assistance from American Jewry – resumed its normal activities again in Paris, and immediately had to deal with the upheavals following the war. Its central problem involved the struggle for a Jewish state, in Israel and the upsurge of nationalism in the Arab countries, their fight against colonialism and their refusal to recognize the national existence of the Jews in Israel. The Alliance found itself in a delicate position in regard to the many schools which it maintained in the Middle East, particularly in Syria and Iraq. Redefining its policy and its *raison d'être*, the Alliance published a programmatic declaration in 1945, in which it reaffirmed its universal character, its attachment to educational work, and its determination to "demand for the Jews who so desired the right of entry into Palestine, under the auspices of the United Nations and on the responsibility of the Jewish Agency in Palestine."

The consequences of the Israel-Arab war of 1947–48 made themselves felt immediately by persecution of the Jews living in Arab countries and the mass exodus of Jews from these lands. After the departure of thousands of Jews from Iraq, all the schools of the Alliance there closed down. The same happened almost without exception in Syria and Egypt. In Morocco and Tunisia also, the success of the nationalist revolt, and the gradual achievement of independence from France, resulted in an exodus from North Africa to France as well as to Israel in the 1960s and upset the foundations of the educational project of the Alliance. In Israel, the Alliance had to relinquish the French orientation of its schools; its elementary schools were closed down or taken over by the Israel education system. These, however, combined to give preference to the teaching of French as the first foreign language. The Alliance concentrated on development of secondary education, opening schools in Jerusalem, Tel Aviv, and Haifa.

In Morocco, the number of pupils in the schools of the Alliance fell from 30,123 in 1959 to 13,527 in 1963. In 1960, the Moroccan government decided to integrate part of the Alliance schools into its own school system. The Alliance retained its remaining schools under the name of Ittihad-Maroc, but they steadily lost their character. The same debilitation process, due to the same causes, could be observed in Tunisia and in Iran.

Educational network of the Alliance Israélite Universelle in 1968.

Country	Number of Schools	Numbers of Pupils
Morocco (Ittihad)	31	8,054
Iran (Ettehad)	13	5,158
Israel	13	4,828
Lebanon	3	1,109
Tunisia	3	1,366
Syria	1	431
Total	64	20,946

In addition to schools, the Alliance had established in Paris, in 1867, the Ecole Normale Israélite Orientale to supply the necessary directors and teachers for its schools and to give their teaching staff a certain homogeneity. The Ecole numbered 120 pupils in 1968. The Alliance had also opened (1897) a rabbinical school in Istanbul for the Oriental communities, which functioned for about ten years. A valuable library on Jewish subjects was founded at the Alliance offices in Paris, at the instance of its secretary-general, the historian Isidore *Loeb; it also issued many publications (see Bibliography). The Alliance organized expeditions for the purpose of helping *Beta Israel in 1868, and the Jews in *Yemen in 1908.

In the 1960s, the Alliance intensified its educational activities in France, where many former pupils from North Africa now lived. The Ecole Normale Israélite Orientale ceased to be exclusively a professional school, and admitted students who did not necessarily intend to become teachers. Secondary schools were opened in Nice and in Pavilions-sous-Bois near Paris. The diplomatic activity of the Alliance were mainly carried on through the Consultative Council of Jewish Organizations (New York) founded in 1946.

In the course of its long career, the Alliance has not always been immune from controversy. In the eyes of antisemites, it became the embodiment of the Jewish international "octopus" strangling civilization. The nefarious myth of the *Elders of Zion crystallized around a falsified image of the Alliance. It was criticized for being too French and not sufficiently universal. Much criticism was directed after World War I against Sylvain Lévi who took a sharp anti-Zionist stand on behalf of the Alliance at the Versailles peace conference. In 1945, however, the Alliance took up a pro-Zionist stand.

In September 1989 the AIU inaugurated a new library which became the largest Jewish library in Europe, possessing over 120,000 items. Available at the library are the Alliance archives which have now been catalogued and offer a wealth of information on Jewish communities in the Mediterranean Basin as well as on French Jewry from the end of the 19th century through the first half of the 20th. The library also now houses specialized archives on Jewish medicine and Jewish education. It regularly organizes special exhibitions such as that on the Dreyfus Affair in 1995.

Publications of the Alliance Israelite Universelle have included: *Paix et Droit*, 1–20 (1921–40); *Cahiers* (1945–); *Maḥberet* (1952–); *The Alliance Israélite Universelle 1860–1895* (1895); *La question juive devant la conférence de la paix…* (1919); N. Leven, *Cinquante ans d'histoire… 1860–1910*, 2 vols. (1919–22). For other titles see Hebrew Union College Library, *Dictionary Catalog of the Kalu Library*, 1 (1964), 408–11.

Les Nouveaux Cahiers (1965–) is a quarterly publication offering a forum for topics in Jewish Studies as well as for current issues of note among French Jewry. The journal regularly devotes space to interfaith relations, a subject of great concern to AIU Day-long seminars are held once or twice a year under the auspices of the journal and are devoted to a historical, political, philosophical, or literary topic. A special annual appears with the papers of these seminars.

The AIU also has a College of Jewish Studies focusing its activities, under the direction of Shmuel Trigano, on in-depth study of Jewish thought in its various expressions. In addition to its regular courses, it organizes an annual symposium on a theme concerning the basic issues of Jewish existence and attracts French scholars as well as others from elsewhere.

In additions to its own widespread network of schools, the AIU has a growing number of affiliated institutions in France, Belgium, Spain, Canada, and Israel.

The Didactic Creativity department at the Paris headquarters places its services at the disposal of teachers interested in producing school materials. One project supported by AIU was a Hebrew–French dictionary for young children and another was a large colorful fresco on the principal stages of Jewish history.

To make the most important texts in Jewish tradition available to the largest possible reading audience, AIU sponsors the works in the "Les Dix Paroles" collection of the Verdier publishing house.

In Israel, the AIU took an active role in receiving new immigrants and helping in their absorption, particularly those from the areas of the former U.S.S.R. and from Ethiopia, and also expended great effort in facilitating contacts between young Jews and Arabs towards promoting mutual understanding and tolerance.

Prof. Adolphe *Steg became president of AIU in 1985, succeeding Jules Braunschvig, honorary president who died in 1994.

[Simon R. Schwarzfuchs]

Women Teachers and Students

By 1872, women were also included in the Alliance teaching force. Since few French Jews were willing to serve as teachers in the villages and towns of North Africa and the Middle East, the Alliance sent the brightest students from its schools to be trained in Paris. While the Ecole Normale Israélite prepared all male Alliance teachers, young girls arriving in Paris were assigned either to the École Bischoffsheim, a vocational and normal school, or to the middle-class boarding schools of Madame Weill-Kahn and Madame Isaac. The Alliance opened its own normal school for girls in 1922.

The female teachers of the Alliance were a diverse group. Students in one class at Mme Isaac's, for example, came from Constantinople, Adrianople, the Dardanelles, Tangier, Monastir, Alsace, Aleppo, Damascus, Aden, Beirut, and Salonika. They also differed in background, language, and piety as well as in temperament and intellect. Their teaching experiences were equally diverse, for the positions they were assigned and the cities to which they were sent (almost never to their town of origin) rarely had much in common. Women Alliance teachers were permitted to marry; most chose to do so, generally marrying their male counterparts, and large families were the norm.

In addition to founding, teaching in, and directing Alliance schools, women teachers also established workshops, organized cottage industries, and oversaw the employment of their graduates. They negotiated, not always easily or successfully, for the support of local community leaders, and provided the Alliance with ethnographic information which became the basis of its decisions and policy making. They had the benefit of a network of support (sisters, cousins, friends, and husbands) which, in contrast to their female counterparts in France (*institutrices*), often freed them to act independently.

The Alliance's goals of westernization and modernization were demonstrated in its women teachers, who were models of autonomy and literacy. Their examples spoke not only to the Alliance's vision of forming female students into good mothers and intelligent companions for their future husbands, but also to the empowerment of young girls, intellectually, physically, professionally, and spiritually. Reframing the ideology of French Jewry to reflect more accurately the needs of Jewish girls, the women teachers of the Alliance, and their many thousands of students, played a central role in their own emancipation.

[Frances Malino (2nd ed.)]

BIBLIOGRAPHY: A. Chouraqui, *L'Alliance Israélite Universelle et la renaissance juive contemporaine (1860–1960)* (1965); B. Mevorah, in: *Zion*, 23–24 (1958–59), 46–65; 28 (1963), 125–64; G. Ollivier, *L'Alliance Israélite Universelle 1860–1960* (1959). **ADD. BIBLIOGRAPHY:** E. Benbassa and A. Rodrigue, *The Jews of the Balkans* (1995); M.M. Laskier, *The Alliance Israélite Universelle and the Jewish Communities* *of Morocco 1862–1962* (1983); F. Malino, "The Women Teachers of the Alliance Israélite Universelle 1872–1940," in: J.R. Baskin (ed.), *Jewish Women in Historical Perspective* (1998²), 248–69; idem, "Prophets in Their Own Land? Mothers and Daughters of the Alliance Israélite Universelle," in: *Nashim*, 3 (Spring–Summer 5760/2000), 56–73; A. Rodrigue, *French Jews, Turkish Jews: The Alliance Israélite Universelle and the Politics of Jewish Schooling in Turkey, 1860–1925* (1990); idem, *Images of Sephardi and Eastern Jewries in Transition: The Teachers of the Alliance Israélite Universelle, 1860–1939* (1993).

ALLIANZ, ISRAELITISCHE, ZU WIEN, Jewish society in Vienna, originally intended to operate as a branch of the *Alliance Israélite Universelle in Paris, with similar aims. Since the Austrian authorities opposed affiliation with the Alliance, the Vienna Allianz was established as an independent society in 1873. Its first president was Joseph von *Wertheimer. Initially, it concentrated on assisting Jews in *Romania and *Siberia. It aided Jewish victims of the Russo-Turkish War in 1877 and supported the Alliance in its efforts to obtain equal civil rights for the Jews in the Balkans. At the Congress of *Berlin in 1878 the Allianz took up the Balkan issue in cooperation with the special Jewish committee for liaison with the congress. With the outbreak of the pogroms in 1881–82, the Allianz participated in relief and migration activities. It organized and maintained a number of educational institutions in Galicia and Bukovina, later supported by the *Baron de Hirsch Fund. The Allianz combatted antisemitism, notably at the *Tisza-Eszlar (1883) and *Polna (1899) blood-libel trials. Relief and emigration projects were established in conjunction with the "Esra" Association of Berlin and the *Jewish Colonization Association (ICA) to benefit Romanian and Russian Jewry between 1897 and 1905. During World War I, the society chiefly aided Jewish war victims; after the war it helped Jewish refugees and emigrants in transit through Vienna. The Allianz was liquidated in 1938 after the *Anschluss*.

BIBLIOGRAPHY: *Jahresberichte der Israelitischen Allianz zu Wien* (1873–); N.M. Gelber, *Aus zwei Jahrhunderten* (1924), 131ff.; idem, in: BLBI, 3 (1960), 190–203; Z. Szajkowski, in: JSOS, 19 (1957), 36–38.

[Nathan Michael Gelber]

ALLON, GEDALYA (formerly **Rogoznizki**; 1901–1950), historian. Allon was born in Kobrin, Russia, and studied at the Slobodka yeshivah. In 1917 he returned to Kobrin, where he became active in the Zionist movement and established a religious Hebrew school, Ḥevrona. After a year's study in Berlin in 1924 he immigrated to Palestine. He was in 1931 one of the first graduates of the Hebrew University and then taught Talmud and Jewish history there. Allon clarified many problems in the development of *halakhah* and the evolution of the social history of the Jews. He argued that the period following the destruction of the Second Temple should not be viewed as the beginning of the Diaspora, but as a continuation of the period of autonomous existence in Palestine, retaining the basic elements of national independence (the lack of which is characteristic of the Diaspora). Allon's work, combining an exhaustive acquaintance with source material and an acute critical sense, placed the history of Palestinian Jewry in the first centuries of the Common Era upon a new basis. His *Toledot ha-Yehudim be-Ereẓ Yisrael bi-Tekufat ha-Mishnah ve-ha-Talmud* ("History of the Jews in Palestine in the Period of the Mishnah and the Talmud," 2 vols., 1953–56) was published posthumously, as were *Meḥkarim be-Toledot Yisrael bi-Yemei Bayit Sheni u-vi-Tekufat ha-Mishnah ve-ha-Talmud* (2 vols., 1957–58) and collected essays that had appeared in various scholarly journals.

BIBLIOGRAPHY: Z. Dimitrowsky and S. Safrai, in: KS, 26 (1950/51), 308–14; *Le-Zikhro shel G. Allon* (1953), tributes by members of the faculty of the Hebrew University; *Sefer Zikkaron li-Gedalyahu Allon* (1970); *Sefer Kobrin* (1951), 275–7.

[Shmuel Safrai]

ALLON (Paicovitch), YIGAL (1918–1980), Israeli statesman and military commander; member of the Third to Ninth Knessets. Allon was born in Mesha, which later changed its name to *Kefar Tavor, in the Lower Galilee. His father, Reuven Yosef Paicovitch, a member of Hovevei Zion in Grodno, Russia, had settled in Eretz Israel in 1882. Allon received his elementary schooling in his native village and graduated in 1937 from the Kadoorie Agricultural High School. In that year he became one of the founders of Kibbutz *Ginnosar, where he was to reside for the rest of his life.

As a boy Allon joined the *Haganah, and in 1936, at the age of 18, became a member of the newly created special units (*peluggot sadeh*) under Yiẓḥak *Sadeh, rapidly rising to officer rank. In 1941 Allon was among the founders of the *Palmaḥ, and in this capacity he fought with the British forces in Syria and Lebanon in the years 1941–42. In 1943 he became the deputy commander of the Palmaḥ, and after Sadeh became acting chief of staff of the Haganah in 1945, he replaced him as its commander. In this capacity he was responsible for planning the Palmaḥ's multifaceted training program, operations against Arab bands, and attacks on civilian and military installations of the British Administration during the last years of its presence in Palestine. He also played a major role in smuggling immigrants illegally into the country (*Aliyah Bet*), and establishing settlements in prohibited zones. During the *War of Independence Allon commanded in decisive battles for the liberation of the Upper Galilee and Safed in the north; Lydda, Ramleh, and the Jerusalem Corridor in the center of the country; and the Southern Coastal Plain and the Negev, including Beersheba and Eilat, in the south. He also commanded the forces that entered deep into Sinai, as far as El-Arish, but was ordered by David *Ben-Gurion, who was under American pressure, to withdraw. Ben-Gurion also blocked his plans to capture the West Bank from King Abdullah's Arab Legion, even though Allon believed he could accomplish the mission within three weeks.

In 1950, following the dissolution of the Palmaḥ on Ben-Gurion's orders, Allon left active military service, but in the eyes of many remained a war hero whose military career had wrongfully been cut short. Allon then entered active politics, joining the leadership of the Kibbutz Hame'uḥad kibbutz movement, and *Mapam within the framework of his own movement. However, he objected to Mapam's pro-Soviet leanings and supported the decision of his movement's four MKs in Mapam to break away from the combined parliamentary group in the summer of 1954. Allon then joined the leadership of the reinstated *Aḥdut ha-Avodah-Po'alei Zion. In 1955 he was elected to the Third Knesset, and was to serve in all the Knessets until his death in February 1980. He resigned from the Fourth Knesset in October 1960 in order to pursue his studies at Oxford but was forced to cut short his stay in Great Britain because of early elections for the Fifth Knesset. Nevertheless, during his stay in Oxford, Allon met many of the leaders of the British Labour Party, several of whom became his personal friends.

From 1961 to 1968 Allon served as minister of labor, in which capacity he promoted the improvement of the state-run employment service and manpower training, initiated extensive road works, and introduced new legislation on labor relations, including laws regulating strikes and lockouts and the establishment of labor courts. During his term of office, social insurance was extended. During the crisis leading up to the 1967 *Six-Day War, when Prime Minister Levi *Eshkol was advised to appoint a minister of defense in order to soothe the public, Eshkol preferred Allon, but due to Allon's absence abroad in the critical days, and pressure from other quarters, it was Moshe *Dayan, Allon's long-time rival from the days of the Palmaḥ, who was appointed. Eshkol compensated him by appointing him deputy prime minister and minister for immigrant absorption.

Allon had strongly supported the establishment of the Alignment between *Mapai and Aḥdut ha-Avodah in 1965, and in 1968 supported the union of Mapai, Aḥdut ha-Avodah, and *Rafi to form the *Israel Labor Party. Following the Six-Day War he developed a plan for a permanent settlement of the Palestinian problem, which came to be known as the "Allon Plan." The plan, which sought to maximize Israel's security while minimizing the number of Palestinians who would remain under Israeli rule, proposed that most of the West Bank and Gaza Strip be handed over to Jordan, which would turn into a Jordanian-Palestinian state. Israel would remain in united Jerusalem, the Jordan Valley (except for a corridor connecting the Kingdom of Jordan with the West Bank around Jericho), the first mountain ridge west of the Jordan River, *Gush Etzyon, and the Latrun area. The Allon Plan was never adopted by the Government, but until 1977 most of the Jewish settlements in the territories were established within its parameters. Following the elections to the Seventh Knesset, held in 1969 under Golda *Meir's leadership, Allon was appointed deputy prime minister and minister of education and culture, and he was given the same positions in the government that Meir formed after the election of the Eighth Knesset on December 31, 1973. After Meir's resignation, following the publication of the Interim Report of the Agranat Commission on the outbreak of the *Yom Kippur War, Yitzhak *Rabin, who was elected by the Labor Party as its new chairman and its candidate for prime minister, appointed Allon deputy prime minister and minister of foreign affairs, in which post he replaced Abba *Eban, who was not included in the new government. As foreign minister Allon was a member of the negotiating team that held talks with U.S. Secretary of State Henry *Kissinger on the Disengagement Agreements with Egypt and Syria in 1974, and the Interim Agreement with Egypt in 1975. In 1974 he also tried to promote his "Jericho Plan," under which Israel would hand over Jericho and an area around it to King Hussein of Jordan, as a first step towards implementing the Allon Plan, but the results of the Rabat Arab Summit Conference foiled his plans.

Serving under Yitzhak Rabin, who had been his subordinate in the Palmaḥ and five years his junior, was not easy for Allon, but the relations between the two remained friendly. Following the 1977 election upset that brought *Menaḥem Begin to power, he remained a member of the Knesset, and was appointed chairman of the World Labor Zionist Organization. Among the issues that Allon promoted in the Knesset was the Mediterranean-Dead Sea canal for the generation of electricity. In the vote on the Camp David Accords with Egypt of September 1978, Allon abstained for ideological reasons. Allon also supported the creation of a united kibbutz movement, in order to better confront the economic difficulties that the kibbutzim faced following the 1977 elections.

In the books he wrote between 1948 and 1967 Allon developed a defense doctrine, which included the concept of "anticipatory initiative." He wrote "The Making of the Israeli Army," in M. Howard, *Theory and Practice of War* (1965), 335–7, and his books include *Ma'arekhot Palmaḥ* ("Palmaḥ Campaigns," 1966), *Masakh shel Ḥol* ("Curtain of Sand," 1968), *Shield of David* (1970), and *My Father's House* (1976).

Even after his premature death, differences of opinion remained as to whether Yigal Allon had been deliberately denied his rightful place as leader of the Israel Labor Party, or whether he had lost something of his charisma and qualities of leadership after ending his military career. In the late 1970s British Labour Party leader Harold Wilson said of Allon that he would never assume the leadership of his party, since he was "incapable of going for the kill." Friends and foes alike, however, never denied his humanity and charm.

BIBLIOGRAPHY: *Sefer ha-Palmaḥ* ("The Book of the Palmah"), Z. Gilad and M. Meged, eds., 2 vols. (1953), index; Y. Cohen, *Toḥnit Allon* (1972); A. Busheiri, *Tefisat ha-Bitaḥon shel Yigal Allon el Mul Tefisato shel Ben-Gurion* (2003); A. Shapira, *Yigal Allon: Aviv Kheldo* (2004).

[Susan Hattis Rolef (2nd ed.)]

ALLONEI ABBA (Heb. אַלּוֹנֵי אַבָּא), moshav shittufi in northern Israel, in western Lower Galilee. Affiliated with Ha-Oved ha-Ẓiyyoni movement, Allonei Abba was founded on May 23, 1948, during the War of Independence. Many of the settlers were survivors of the Holocaust from Czechoslovakia, Romania, Germany, and other countries. The economy was based mainly on farming: poultry, dairy cattle, field crops, and vineyards. In the mid-1990s the population was approximately 200, increasing to 283 in 2002. The name refers to the natural Tabor oaks in the vicinity (*allon*, "oak") and also commemorates the *Haganah hero Abba Berdiczew who died during World War II after having been parachuted into Slovakia.

[Efraim Orni / Shaked Gilboa (2nd ed.)]

ALLONEI YIZḤAK (Heb. אַלּוֹנֵי יִצְחָק), youth village in central Israel. It was founded in 1948 within the confines of neighboring *Kefar Glickson, with which it continued to be closely linked. In 1949 it received its own land in the vicinity. Its establishment was aided by the *General Zionist and Progressive parties and by the *Hadassah Organization of America. Within the framework of *Youth Aliyah, Allonei Yizḥak trained immigrant children, principally in agriculture, and held courses for American high school students under the auspices of its American-Israel Secondary School Program. Subsequently it became a boarding school housing 75% of the village's students and still absorbing immigrant youth with special ulpan courses to learn Hebrew. The village included various farm branches, where students worked one day a week. In the mid-1990s the population was approximately 300, dropping to 223 from 20 different countries in 2002. The name ("oaks of Yizḥak") refers to the oak forest formerly in the vicinity and to the Zionist leader Yizḥak *Gruenbaum.

WEBSITE: www.knay.alona.k12.il.

[Efraim Orni / Shaked Gilboa (2nd ed.)]

ALLONIM (Heb. אַלּוֹנִים; "oaks"), kibbutz in northern Israel, on the Tivon hills of western Lower Galilee. Allonim was founded in 1938 as a "tower and stockade" settlement during the Arab riots. The original settlers were graduates of the first *Youth Aliyah group from Germany. In 1968 it had over 500 inhabitants, including immigrants from various countries and Israeli-born. In 2002 the population was 547. The kibbutz economy was based on intensive mixed farming (field crops, dairy cattle, sheep, poultry). It was also home to the Algat Company, specializing in aluminum finishing processes for the aircraft, military, and other high-technology industries.

[Efraim Orni / Shaked Gilboa (2nd ed.)]

ALLOUCHE, FELIX NISSIM S'AIDOU (1901–?), Tunisian editor. Born in Sfax, Allouche was editor of the local newspaper *Dépêche Sfaxienne*, formed a Zionist club in 1919, and in 1929 became associated with Vladimir *Jabotinsky. In 1924 he founded the Jewish weekly, *Le Réveil Juif*, and in 1934 became editor of *Tunis Soir*, which took a militant Zionist line; he also helped to found the Zionist weekly, *La Vie Juive*. During World War II, he joined the Resistance and later served as Tunis correspondent for newspapers in Europe and America. Attacked bitterly by the Tunisian national press, he emigrated to Israel in 1956.

ALLUF (Heb. אַלּוּף), honorary title conferred on scholars of the Babylonian academies who had the privilege of sitting in the first row. The word is of biblical origin: the tribal chiefs of Edom were called *allufim* (Gen. 35:15 ff.). (1) In the Bible, this word has two principal meanings: (a) "friend, companion, intimate" (cf. Jer. 3:4; 13:21; Micah 7:5; Ps. 55:14; Prov. 2:17; 16:28; 17:9); (b) according to the current interpretation, "chieftain," but more probably (and this also applies to the Ugaritic *alp*) "clan" (which is also a meaning of *alluf* in Gen. 36:15–43; Ex. 15:15; I Chron. 1:51–54). (2) In the geonic period *alluf* was synonymous with the title of the *resh kallah* which was already current in the Babylonian academies in the talmudic period. Originally the title was conferred on the seven heads of the *Kallah* who served in Sura and Pumbedita, but from the ninth century onward it was also bestowed upon prominent scholars and personalities residing in other countries. (3) Based upon Psalms 55:14 the term *allufi u-meyudda'i* was used in classical-style Hebrew as an address in letters to a friend or teacher. Similarly, prominent members of the Jewish community councils were often referred to among Ashkenazim as *allufim*. (4) Rank in the Defense Forces of the State of Israel, equivalent to major general (see *Israel, Defense Forces).

BIBLIOGRAPHY: Mann, Egypt 1 (1920), 144 ff.; 2 (1922), 58 ff.; S. Eppenstein, *Beitraege zur Geschichte und Literatur im geonaeischen Zeitalter* (1913), 11 ff.; Poznański, in: *Ha-Kedem*, 2 (1908), 91–96; I. Davidson, *Saadia's Polemic* (1915), 35; Lewin, in: *Ginzei Kedem*, 3 (1925), 14 ff.

AL-MADARI (Al-Mudari, Al-Mundari, El-Modari), JUDAH HA-KOHEN BEN ELEAZAR (Eliezer?) HE-HASID (13th–14th century), talmudic scholar of Aleppo. Al-Madari compiled a commentary to the code of Isaac *Alfasi, part of which is no longer extant. Though he was commenting on Alfasi, he based his book on Rashi's commentary and also cited Maimonides and other later scholars. It is probable that the novellae to the Talmud quoted in his name by various authorities are in reality quotations from his commentary on Alfasi and are not from separate compilations. His commentaries on tractates *Yevamot, Ketubbot, Gittin, Kiddushin, Sanhedrin*, and *Avodah Zarah* were printed in the 1962 edition of the Talmud published in Jerusalem (Pardess, El Hamekoroth). His commentaries to *Pesaḥim* and *Megillah* were seen by H.J.D. Azulai.

BIBLIOGRAPHY: Steinschneider, in: JQR, 11 (1898/99), 133, no. 314; S. Assaf, in: KS, 23 (1946/47), 233–38.

[Abraham Hirsch Rabinowitz]

ALMAGIÀ, ROBERTO (1884–1962), Italian geographer and historian of cartography. He was born in Florence and in 1911 became professor at the University of Padua, which he left in 1915 to become professor in Rome. His early interests lay in geology and oceanography, but he moved to the history of geographical science and finally to the history of cartography. His first published work was *Studi geografici sopra le frane in Italia* (2 vols., 1907 and 1910). His *Cristoforo Colombo* appeared in 1918, and in 1937, *Gli italiani primi esploratori dell'America*, in which he dealt in detail with the Italian contribution to the discovery of America. From 1920 he was co-editor of the *Rivista Geografica Italiana*, published by the Società di Studi Geografici, of which he became president in 1955. In 1922 he published *L' "Italia" di G.A. Magini e la cartografia dell'Italia nei sec. XVI e XVII*. He edited in 1929 *Monumenta Italiae Cartographica*, a volume of reproductions of early maps of Italy. During World War II he was granted refuge in the Vatican, where he prepared *Monumenta cartografica Vaticana* (4 vols., 1944–55). *Il mondo attuale* (3 vols., 1953–56) and *L'Italia* (2 vols., 1959) are his outstanding works on general and Italian geography. Almagià achieved an international reputation and was the recipient of many honors. His interest in a Jewish homeland is shown in his *La Questione della Palestina* (1918), *Una Escursione in Palestina* (1925), and *Palestina* (1930).

BIBLIOGRAPHY: *Geographical Journal*, 128 (1962), 367–8. **ADD. BIBLIOGRAPHY:** S. Boorsh, "The Case for Francesco Rosselli as the Engraver of Berlinghieri's *Geographia*," in: *Imago Mundi* 56:2 (2004), 152–69.

ALMAGOR (Heb. אַלְמָגוֹר; "No Fear"), moshav on the Corazim Plateau N. of Lake Kinneret. Almagor was founded in 1961 as a *Naḥal outpost on the Israeli-Syrian border (until 1967). A number of its soldier-settlers fell in Syrian ambushes in the vicinity and a monument was erected here in their memory. Its economy was based on out-of-season crops, vineyards, sheep, and poultry as well as mango and olive orchards. The moshav also operated a rest house, pub, and sailing facilities on the lake. In the mid-1990s the population was approximately 250, dropping to 207 in 2002.

[Efraim Orni / Shaked Gilboa (2nd ed.)]

ALMAGOR, GILA (1939–), first lady of Israeli stage and screen; also the author of several children's books. Born in Petaḥ Tikvah, Almagor wrote about her troubled childhood as the daughter of a widowed, mentally ill Holocaust survivor in her book, *The Summer of Aviya*, which was filmed in 1988. It starred Almagor herself in a role based on her mother. The prize-winning film was followed by another book, *Under the Domim Tree*, and another film adaptation starring Almagor. These two films are highlights in a career that began when she was 17 and appeared in the Habimah National Theater's production of *The Skin of Our Teeth*. Her stage credits include *Medea*, *The Crucible*, and *Three Sisters*. She has appeared in over 35 films, including *Sallah Shabbati* (1964), *The House on Chelouche Street* (1973), *Operation Thunderbolt* (1977), *Life According to Agfa* (1992), and *The Gospel According to God* (2004). She was awarded the Israel Prize in 2004. Almagor is married to Ya'akov Agmon, the former director of Habimah.

[Hannah Brown (2nd ed.)]

ALMAGRO, town in Castile, Spain, administrative center of the Order of *Calatrava. Jews probably settled there soon after the Christian reconquest (14th century). It was one of only four communities in the area of Ciudad Real that existed in the 14th and 15th centuries. The community developed during the 15th century, when cities in the crown domains offered little security to their Jewish population, but from the amount of tax paid it was a small one. During the 1460s it was able to construct a synagogue. There was also a sizeable *Converso group, and many Conversos from Ciudad Real took refuge there when they were attacked in 1449, 1469, and 1474. A number of the New Christians in Almagro were sentenced by the Inquisition in Ciudad Real and Toledo. The Jewish community was assessed to pay 800 *maravedis* in 1474 and 4,365 *maravedis* in 1485 to finance the war against Granada, and survived until the expulsion of the Jews from Spain in 1492. There is no information on the location of the Jewish quarter.

BIBLIOGRAPHY: H. Beinart, in: *Sefer Yovel... Y. Baer* (1960), 207–15; idem, *Anusim be-Din ha-Inkviziẓyah* (1965), index; Baer, Urkunden, pt. 2 (1936), 370; Suárez Fernández, Documentos, 65, 80.

[Haim Beinart]

ALMAH (Heb. עַלְמָה), Israeli moshav on a basaltic plateau N. of Safed. Almah is affiliated with Ha-Po'el ha-Mizrachi. It was founded in 1949. In 1953 the original settlers, who came from Libya, were joined by the proselytes of *San Nicandro, Italy, who later moved to other places in Israel. In 1968 Almah's inhabitants were from Libya and Tunisia. The economy was based on hill culture (vineyards, deciduous fruit, vegetables) and beef cattle. In 2002 the population was 732. The name Almah is historical, mentioned by *Benjamin of Tudela in the 12th century.

[Efraim Orni]

ALMAN, SAMUEL (1877–1947), composer of synagogue and secular music. Alman was born in Sobolevka, Podolia. From 1895 until 1903 he studied at the Odessa and Kishinev conservatories. While at Kishinev, he was strongly influenced by the cantor *Razumni. After the *Kishinev pogrom (1903) Alman went to London where he attended the Royal College of Music, and wrote a biblical opera *King Ahaz* (performed in 1912). He served as choirmaster of various London synagogues (notably at Humpstead) and Jewish choral groups. Alman's style was deeply rooted in the Southern Russian cantorial tradition, and he owed much to the choral technique of the *meshorerim* ("choristers"), as heard in the compositions of N. Spivak. He solved the problem of modern harmonization by following (especially in his instrumental works) the impressionistic style of Debussy. Alman succeeded in preserving the melodic features and deep sentiments of the Eastern European Ashkenazi chant, often creating a mystical atmosphere. Among his published works are *Shirei Beit ha-Knesset*, 2 vols. (1925, 1938), for cantor and choir; *Psalm 15* (1915) for chorus and organ, and *Psalm 133* (1934) for chorus and piano; *"Mi addir"* and *"Sheva berakhot"* (1930) for cantor and organ; *Ethics of the Fathers*

(1928); many arrangements of Yiddish folk songs; and compositions for strings including the quartet suite *Ebraica* (1932). In addition, he edited *Shirei Rozumni* (1930) and the supplement to F.L. Cohen's *Voice of Prayer and Praise* (1933).

BIBLIOGRAPHY: A. Holde, *Jews in Music* (1959), 25; Ephros, Cant, 4 (1959^2), 126–8, 180–1,224; Sendrey, Music, 185, index.

[Hanoch Avenary]

ALMANSI (**Almanzi**), Italian family, originally deriving from Almansa, near Murcia, Spain. About 1665 Abraham Almansi established himself in Scandiano in the duchy of Modena. The family continued to be associated with this little place until the 20th century. The synagogue there, long maintained in the house of Isaac Almansi, was rebuilt by his sons in 1740. Later the family became scattered throughout Italy. BARUCH ḤAYYIM of Padua (d. 1837) was a noted bibliophile who purchased in 1812 a great part of the important library of Ḥayyim Joseph David *Azulai. His eldest son was Joseph *Almanzi (1801–1860) the poet and book collector. EMILIO (1869–1948) of Florence was a distinguished physicist and mathematician, noted for his contribution in the field of mechanics of the theory of elasticity. DANTE (d. 1948), a magistrate who was a Fascist party member and deputy chief of police (*prefetto*) was forced into retirement when the Italian racial laws came into operation in 1938. He was designated president of the Union of Italian Jewish Communities and made responsible for securing government authority in 1939 to found, together with Lelio Vittori Valobra, the vice president of the Italian Jewish Communities, Delasem (Delegazione Assistenza Ebrei). He presided over the Union of Italian Jewish Communities with exceptional dignity during the period of racial persecution.

BIBLIOGRAPHY: L. Padoa, in: RMI, 33 (1967), 37; M. Wilensky, in: JQR, 38 (1947/48), 189–96. **ADD. BIBLIOGRAPHY:** R.J. Almansi, *Dante Almansi: President of the Union of Italian Jewish Communities, Nov. 1939 to Oct. 1944* (1971); R. Almansi, "Ancora su Dante Almansi," in: *Rassegna Mensile di Israel*, 42 (1976), 453–54; idem, "Mio padre Dante Almansi," in: *Rassegna Mensile di Israel*, 42 (1976) 234–55; S. Sorani, *Virtù contra furore: l'assistenza ai profughi in Italia, 1933–1947: contributo alla storia della "Delasem"* (1978); D. Almansi, "Attività svolta dal consiglio della Unione delle Comunità Israelitiche Italiane dal 13 novembre 1929 al 17 novembre 1944," in: *Rassegna Mensile di Israel*, 45 (1979), 507–24; S. Sorani, *L'assistenza ai profughi ebrei in Italia (1933–1941): contributo alla storia delle Delasem* (1983); D. Almansi, "Dante Almansi, President of the Union of Italian Jewish Communities," in: S. Pugliese (ed.), *The Most Ancient of Minorities* (2002), 345–52.

[Cecil Roth / Manuela Consonni (2nd ed.)]

AL-MANṢŪR AL-YAHŪDĪ (early ninth century), court musician of the Umayyad caliph al-Ḥakam I, in Córdoba, Spain. A written record of this author's contribution to music is reported in the book *Nafḥ al- ṭīb* of the historian and biographer al-Maqqarī (1591–1632), who relied on other source material of the Andalusian historian ibn Ḥayyan (987–1076). Al-Maqqarī refers to al-Manṣūr in the colorful story describing the arrival in Córdoba in 822 of a leading musician, Ziryāb. The story relates that al-Manṣūr was sent by caliph al-Ḥakam to meet him in Kairouan and escort him to Córdoba. When the two musicians met, the news reached them of the sudden death of the caliph (822). Al-Manṣūr then succeeded in persuading Ziryāb to offer his services to the new caliph, 'Abd al-Raḥmān II. Thus, al-Manṣūr helped bring about the splendid era of Arab music in Spain inaugurated by Ziryāb. It is assumed that al-Manṣūr continued his musical activity together with Ziryāb.

BIBLIOGRAPHY: Al-Maqqarī, *Analectes sur l'histoire et la littèrature des Arabes d'Espagne*, 2 (1861), 85ff.; H.G. Farmer, *History of Arabian Music to the 13th Century* (1929), 129, 131.

[Amnon Shiloah (2nd ed.)]

ALMANZI, JOSEPH (1801–1860), Italian Hebrew author and poet. He was born in Padua and received his instruction in Jewish studies mainly from R. Israel *Conegliano, who remained his teacher for 20 years. He also acquired a knowledge of Samaritan, Syriac, Arabic, Latin, Italian, French, and German. Almanzi never married and devoted his time (when not engaged in trade) to Hebrew literary works and the expansion of his library. This contained thousands of Hebrew books, among them rare and valuable prints and manuscripts, several coming from the collection of Ḥayyim Joseph David *Azulai. Almanzi's collection became widely known among Jewish scholars and many of them turned to him for their literary research; he responded willingly and thereby became friendly with the greatest scholars of his generation, such as S.D. Luzzatto, Zunz, Fuerst, and Steinschneider. Toward the end of his life he moved from Padua to Trieste. Most of his poems, which bear the signature "Yoel," are sonnets of moral-didactic content. He also wrote: *Me'il Kinah* (a lament on the death of his teacher, R. Israel Conegliano (Reggio, 1824)); *Toledot R. Moshe Ḥayyim Luzzatto* (first published in *Kerem Ḥemed* and several times thereafter as a preface to the books of R. Moses Ḥayyim *Luzzatto), a detailed and accurate biography of M. Ḥ. Luzzatto; *Higgayon be-Khinnor*, original and translated poems (Vienna, 1839); *Kinnim va-Hegeh va-Hi* on the death of Jacob Ḥay Vita Pardo, published in S.D. Luzzatto's work *Avnei Zikkaron* (Prague, 1841); and *Nezem Zahav* (97 sonnets, Padua, 1858; new edition, Tel Aviv, 1950). In addition Almanzi published poems in various periodicals; these included a translated fragment from Horace's "On the Art of Poetry" (in *Bikkurei ha-Ittim ha-Ḥadashim*, Vienna, 1845). After his death, his heirs published a catalogue of books of Jewish interest found in his library; the catalogue was edited by S.D. *Luzzatto and entitled *Yad Yosef* (Padua, 1864). It lists also Almanzi's published works. Almanzi's manuscripts were described by S.D. Luzzatto in Steinschneider's *Hebraeische Bibliographie*, 4–6 (1861–68). In 1865 the British Museum bought Almanzi's manuscript collection for a thousand pounds; the collection served as the foundation for the large Hebrew manuscript department of that institution.

BIBLIOGRAPHY: Zeitlin, Bibliotheca, 4.

[Gedalyah Elkoshi]

ALMERÍA, Spanish Mediterranean seaport. A Jewish community was formed in Almería at the end of the tenth century by refugees from the neighboring settlement of Pechina. The community became one of the most prosperous and important in Andalusia. The Jewish quarter was near the harbor. With the fall of the Caliphate many Jews of Córdoba moved to Almería. The Jews were engaged in maritime trade. Approximately 2000 Jews lived in Almería at the time. In the 11th century, the vizier of Almería, Ibn Abbas, published libelous tracts against *Samuel ha-Nagid, vizier to the king of Granada, and the Jews. His attitude led to war, in the course of which the king of Almería was killed and Ibn Abbas executed on Samuel's instructions. According to Abraham *Ibn Ezra's historical elegy (*Ahah Yarad*, line 4), no Jews in Almería survived the Almohade persecution of the mid-12th century, but the community revived subsequently. Later, the *Black Death resulted in much suffering. The treaty of surrender on the Christian Reconquest of Almería in 1489 afforded the Jews the same protection as the Moors. The conquerors found there some Conversos who had fled from Castile. After the edict of expulsion of the Jews from Spain in 1492 a number of exiles sailed from Almería for North Africa.

BIBLIOGRAPHY: Baer, Spain, index; M. Garrido Atienza, *Las capitulaciones para la entrega de Granada* (1910), 187. **ADD. BIBLIOGRAPHY:** E. Ashtor, *The Jews of Moslem Spain* (1979), 295–300; L. Torres Balbás, in: *Al-Andalus*, 22 (1957), 438.

[Haim Beinart / Eliyahu Ashtor]

ALMOG, RUTH (1936–), Israeli writer. Almog was born in Petaḥ Tikvah to an Orthodox family of German descent. "My parents emigrated from Germany in 1933. My mother insisted on it, she was a pessimist while my father was an idealist. As he could not find work as a physician, which was his profession, he decided to become a farmer, partly out of idealism. And so they bought beehives." Childhood memories, the atmosphere of the first Hebrew *moshavah, and the figure of the father are indeed recurring elements in Almog´s prose. Almog studied literature and philosophy at the Hebrew University and taught in schools as well as at Tel Aviv University, making her home in Tel Aviv and from 1967 serving on the editorial staff of the literary supplement of the newspaper *Haaretz*.

Almog is considered one of the seminal women-writers in contemporary Hebrew literature. Relationships within the family, love, passion and betrayal, romantic dreams, and disillusionment are some of the major concerns in her prose. Following a collection of stories entitled *Ḥasdei ha-Laylah shel Margarita* (1969), she published *Be-Erez Gezerah* ("The Exile," 1971), the story of a young woman´s journey to Germany in search of her family roots and her own identity. In her novel *Mavet ba-Geshem* (1982; "Death in the Rain," 1993), set against the Mediterranean landscapes of Israel and Greece, she depicts an intricate relationship between three men and two women. *Shorshei Avir* ("Roots of Light," 1987) is the story of Mira Gutman, who desparately tries to disentangle her roots in an attempt to free herself from the coils of her family´s fate. Unlike some of the other women-figures in Almog´s stories, Mira, a modern Antigone, refuses to be passive and submissive. The death of her lover Jan during the Russian invasion of Czechoslovakia prompts her to fight for the ideal of freedom. The collection of stories *Nashim* ("Women," 1986) depicts women coping with loneliness, physical handicaps, and haunting memories: In "Rachel Stern meets Fellini in Rome," Almog juxtaposes the longing for life and the painful awareness of immanent death; In "Henya Is No Longer Blue," she describes Henya´s physical deterioration and her last moments of grace. The collection entitled *Kol ha-Osher ha-Mufraz ha-Zeh* (2003) depicts, amongst other things, Holocaust survivors and immigrants who are trying to build a new life in Israel. This is also the theme of *Me'il Katon* (1993), the story of the boy Shaul-Paul who grows up amidst old and sickly immigrants from Europe and Oriental Jews. Almog´s other works include the epistolary novel *Be-Ahavah, Natalia* (2005), various collections of stories, books for children, and two novels which she wrote together with Esther Ettinger (*Me'ahev Mushlam*, 1995, and *Estelina Ahuvati*, 2002). Almog was awarded the Brenner Prize (1989), the Agnon Prize (2001), and the Yad Vashem Prize for children's literature for "My Journey with Alex" (1999).

Almog's story "Shrinking" is included in *Six Israeli Novellas* (edited by G. Shaked, 1999); "Dora's Secret" appeared in *The Oxford Book of Hebrew Short Stories* (edited by G. Abramson, 1996); and "A Good Spot" is included in *New Women's Writing from Israel* (edited by R. Domb, 1996).

BIBLIOGRAPHY: G. Shaked, *Ha-Sipporet ha-Ivrit*, 5 (1998), 340–66; idem, *Bein Bat la-Avotehah*, in: *Moznayim* 72, 6 (1998), 8–12; P. Shirav, *Ketivah lo Tamah* (1998); Y.S. Feldman, *No Room of their Own: Gender and Nation in Israeli Women Fiction* (1999). A. Zehavi, in: *Yedioth Ahronoth* (Dec. 12, 1980); M. Geldman, in: *Haaretz* (Jan. 2, 1981); P. Shirav, *Derekh ha-Em*, in: *Alei Si'aḥ* 34 (1994), 69–82; N. Tamir-Smilanski, *Zikaron shel Nashim be-Sippurei R. Almog*, in: *Ha-Ḥinukh u-Sevivo* 20 (1998), 103–8; N. Gertz, *Mitaḥat lifnei ha-Shetaḥ: Al ha-Sippur she- mitaḥat le-Sippurah shel R. Almog "Gamadim al ha-Pidgamah,"* in: *Sifrut ve-Ḥevrah ba-Tarbut ha-Ivrit ha-Ḥadashah* (2000), 316–27; E. Adivi-Shoshan, *Zo Yalduti ha-Sheniyah: Al Sippurei ha-Yaldut shel R. Almog*, in: *Ha-Ḥinukh u-Sevivo* 24 (2002), 287–306.

[Anat Feinberg (2nd ed.)]

ALMOG (Kopeliovitz), YEHUDA (1896–1972), leading figure of the Third *Aliyah. Almog, who was born near Vilna, joined Joseph *Trumpeldor in organizing *He-Ḥalutz. In 1919 he settled in Palestine, where he was a founder of *Gedud ha-Avodah. In 1923 he went to Soviet Russia as an emissary of He-Ḥalutz and later to Persia and other countries. He was a founder of the kibbutz Ramat Raḥel, near Jerusalem. From 1934 onward Almog devoted himself to the needs of the potash factory workers living in the difficult conditions of Sodom as well as to the settlement of the Dead Sea area and the development of *Masada as a national monument. His writings include *Ḥevel Sedom* ("Sodom Region," 1945), and *Ḥevel Yam ha-Melaḥ* ("Dead Sea Region," 1956).

BIBLIOGRAPHY: Tidhar, 4 (1950), 2005; Y. Ereẓ (ed.), *Sefer ha-Aliyah ha-Shelishit* (1964), index; H.M. Sachar, *Aliyah: the Peoples of Israel* (1961), 155–91.

[Benjamin Jaffe]

ALMOGI (Krelenboim), YOSEF AHARON (1910–1991), Israeli politician and labor leader, member of the Third to Eighth Knessets. Almogi was born in Hrubieszow, Poland. In 1924 he joined the Dror youth movement and in 1928 started to prepare for his immigration to Ereẓ Israel. For a number of years after arriving in Ereẓ Israel in 1930, he worked as a laborer in orange groves and in construction. He was a member of the Kefar Sava Labor Council and joined the *Haganah. In 1936 he was sent to organize the *Hapoel defense units within the *Histadrut in the Tel Aviv area, and in 1937 he organized the Hapoel defense units within the Histadrut in Haifa. In 1940 he enlisted in the British Army; he was taken prisoner by the Germans in Greece, remaining in a prison camp until the end of the war and organizing the Jewish prisoners of war from Ereẓ Israel. In the years 1947–51 Almogi was acting secretary of the Haifa Labor Council, and in 1948 organized a special labor brigade which took over the essential services of the city when the British evacuated it. In 1951–59 he served as secretary of the Council.

Almogi was elected to the Third Knesset in 1955 as a member of *Mapai. He served as secretary-general of Mapai in 1959–61 and as minister of housing and development in 1963–65. He was one of the members who broke away from Mapai in May 1965 together with David *Ben-Gurion to form *Rafi, and subsequently resigned from the government. Half a year after Rafi participated in the formation of the *Israel Labor Party in January 1968, he was appointed minister of labor. Almogi was reelected to the Eighth Knesset in 1973, but was not given a seat in the government, since he was elected mayor of Haifa, a position he held in 1974–75. In 1975–78 he served as president of the World Zionist Organization. His autobiography, *Be-Ovi ha-Korah* ("In the Thick of Things"), was published in 1980.

[Susan Hattis Rolef (2nd ed.)]

ALMOHADS (Arab. *Al-Muwaḥḥhidūn*; "Those who Advocate the Unity of Allah"), Moroccan Berbers from Tinmel in the Atlas Mountains. Like their predecessors, the *Almoravids (*al-Murabitūn*), who ruled major areas of the Maghreb and Muslim Spain, the Almohads comprised a confederation of local Berber tribes. The Almohads were influenced by puritanical notions of Islam to even a greater degree than the Almoravids. They had been essentially inspired by the religious teachings of Ibn Tūmart (d. 1130), whose doctrine was a mélange of a strict conception of the unity of Allah, with a program of moral reform based on the Koran and the Sunnah: the traditional social and legal practice of the early Muslim community.

In 1121, Ibn Tūmart proclaimed himself the *mahdī*, or spiritual-messianic leader, openly questioned the legitimacy of Almoravid rule, and waged a protracted war against them in the Maghreb. Ibn Tūmart's actions came in the aftermath of a series of military challenges posed to the Almoravids also by the Christians in Spain, who had previously carried out the early phases of their plan of "re-conquest" and de-Islamization.

Under Ibn Tūmart's successor, 'Abd al-Mu'min, the Almohads brought down the Almoravid state in 1147; they captured *Marrakesh and transformed it into their Maghrebi capital. On the other hand, Almoravid domains in Muslim Spain were left virtually intact until the caliph Abu Ya'qūb Yūsuf forced the surrender of Seville in 1172. The spread of Almohad rule over the rest of Islamic Spain soon followed. During the reign of Abū Yūsuf Ya'qūb al-Manṣūr (1184–99) serious Arab rebellions devastated the eastern provinces of the empire, whereas in Spain the Christian threat remained constant. At the battle of Las Navas de Tolosa (1212), the Almohads were dealt a devastating defeat by a Christian coalition from Leon, Castile, Navarre, and Aragon. They retreated to their Maghrebi provinces, where soon afterwards the Muslim Hafsids seized power in Tunis, the Abd al-Wadids took Tlimsan (*Tlemcen), and Marrakesh, the Almohad capital, fell to the Marinids in 1269.

The decline and eventual fall of the Almohad state was attributed to three main reasons. First, it shared power with no group outside its own hierarchy placing the center of power solely in the hands of the founders and descendants. Secondly, the puritanical orientation of Ibn Tūmart waned gradually among his many followers after his death. Under his successors, precedents had been set for the construction of costly and lavish "non-puritan" monuments. The famous Kutubiya mosque in Marrakesh and the older parts of the mosque of Taza attest to this policy. Neither did the movement for a return to traditional orthodox Islam survive; both the mystical movement of the Sufis and the philosophical school represented by Ibn Tufayl and Averroes (Ibn Rushd) flourished under the Almohad kings. Finally, the Almohads proved to be intolerant toward their Muslim opponents and the Maghrebi Jewish minority, thus alienating diverse segments of the population. In fact, in the pre-Almohad Maghreb the position of the Jews was apparently free of significant abuses. No factual complaints were registered prior to 1147 of excesses, coercion, or malice on the part of the authorities. After the ascendance of the Almohad ruler Abū Yūsuf Ya'qūb al-Manṣūr, however, the Jews began to encounter humiliations; many were forced to convert to Islam and had to wear the *qalansuwa*, a cap of strange and ugly shape, reaching down to their ears. The Jews, who officially had been converted to Islam but were suspected of secretly practicing their own religion, were compelled to wear special, and rather ridiculous, clothes so that the Muslims easily identified them. At the same time, Jews were not the only victims of Almohad cruelty; the Muslim *maliki* school of Sunni Islam was banned in Almohad North Africa and its leading works were burned in the public squares.

BIBLIOGRAPHY: J.M. Abun-Nasr, *A History of the Maghrib in the Islamic Period* (1987); H.Z. Hirschberg, *A History of the Jews in North Africa* (1974); C.-A. Julien, *History of North Africa: Tunisia, Algeria, Morocco* (ed. and rev. by R. Le Tourneau, 1970); M.M. Laskier, *The Alliance Israélite Universelle and the Jewish Communities of Morocco: 1862–1962* (1983); R. Le Tourneau, *The Almohad Movement in North Africa in the 12th and 13th Centuries* (1969).

[Michael M. Laskier (2nd ed.)]

ALMOLI (Almuli), SOLOMON BEN JACOB (before 1485–after 1542), grammarian, physician, philosopher, and kabbalist.

Biography and Basic Works

Probably born in Spain, Almoli passed his early years in Salonika, but before 1515 settled in Constantinople, where he spent the rest of his life, serving as a *dayyan* and rabbi of one of the congregations there. Almoli devoted himself to the study of science and medicine, earning his livelihood from the latter, and serving, as it seems, as physician to the sultan. Few biographical details are known of his life except that it was marked by want and poverty. Having conceived the idea of compiling a general encyclopedia, he launched his undertaking enthusiastically, though fully aware that the work would take many years to complete and that large sums of money would be required for an adequate reference library. He was encouraged by the hope that others would take up his work in the event of his failing to complete it, but the scholars of Constantinople reacted disparagingly and rejected the plan. Almoli was also unsuccessful in his attempt to recruit a group of trainees for his work. He did, however, publish a small pamphlet of 24 pages under the title *Me'assef le-Khol ha-Maḥanot* (Constantinople, c. 1531), a prospectus of the proposed encyclopedia which was to be in three parts: (1) *Maḥaneh Yisrael*, on what every Jew needs to know; (2) *Maḥaneh Leviyyah*, on general knowledge; and (3) *Maḥaneh Shekhinah*, on Hebrew, Aramaic, biblical exegesis, theology, Kabbalah, and the commandments of the Torah.

The fate of the project is unknown. Also included is his *Sha'ar ha-Shem he-Ḥadash* (Constantinople, 1533), which he describes as being "the first section of the large book which deals with all matters of faiths." In it he treats the existence of God, His attributes and essence, according to the Kabbalah and philosophy. He states that "wonderful secrets and explanations, hitherto unrevealed" (p. 13a) have been disclosed to him. With one exception, all Almoli's other works are mere prolegomena to larger works which he contemplated. The exception is the *Mefasher Ḥelmin* (Salonika, c. 1515) often republished under its Hebrew title *Pitron Ḥalomot* ("Interpretation of Dreams") and translated into Yiddish (Amsterdam, 1694). In it he classifies dreams by categories and gives rules for their interpretation.

Other Publications

(1) *Halikhot Sheva* (Constantinople, c. 1520), according to Almoli, the introduction to a larger projected work on the science of Hebrew grammar. This is an original study, including rules for the pointing of the vowel *e*, under differing circumstances. The first part begins with general comments on the relationship between the *sheva* and the other vowels, which are significant guidelines for the history of the science of the Hebrew language. In the second part, the *sheva* is classified by categories. The third part deals with the different forms of the noun. Almoli cites various opinions as to the alternate pronunciations of the *sheva na'* ("mobile") and gives his own analysis of it as a third type of vowel, having its place midway between the short vowels and the *sheva naḥ* ("quiescent"). A critical edition was published by Ḥ. Yallon. (2) *Iggeret ha-Purim* is mentioned in *Halikhot Sheva* and is probably a treatise on the Scroll of Esther. (3) *Sha'ar ha-Yesod* (Constantinople, 1536) deals with the roots of Hebrew words. This book is not extant, except for the title page. (4) Almoli was also instrumental in the publication of books on language and vocalization by other authors. These are the *Magen David* (Constantinople, 1517) of *Elisha b. Abraham, in the writing of which Almoli participated, replying to Profiat *Duran's and David *Ibn Yaḥya's criticism of David *Kimḥi; the *Yesod Mora* (Constantinople, 1530) and the *Safah Berurah* (Constantinople, 1530) of Abraham *Ibn Ezra; the *Leshon Limmudim* (Constantinople, 1526) of David ibn Yaḥya, together with the *Shekel ha-Kodesh* on prosody. For many years this last book was also thought to be the work of David Ibn Yaḥya, but Ḥ. Yallon has shown that it was written by Almoli, who included in it criticism of the *Leshon Limmudim* (critical edition by Ḥ. Yallon, 1965). Almoli also composed poems which were published in his own books and in those he edited.

BIBLIOGRAPHY: Aloni, in: KS, 18 (1941/42), 192–8; Ḥ. Yallon (ed.), *Shelomo Almoli Halikhot Sheva* (1944), 79–115; idem, in: *Sinai*, 32 (1952/53), 90–96; idem, in: *Aresheth*, 2 (1960), 96–108; idem, in: KS, 39 (1963/64), 105–8; Gruenbaum, in: *Aresheth*, 4 (1966), 180–201. **ADD. BIBLIOGRAPHY:** S. Morag, "Some Notes on Shelomo Alomoli's Contributions to the Linguistic Science of Hebrew," in: J.A. Emerton and S.C. Reif (eds.), *Interpreting the Hebrew Bible, Essays in Honor of E.I.J. Rosenthal* (1982), 157–69.

ALMON or **ALEMETH** (Heb. עַלְמוֹן, עָלֶמֶת), levitical city in the territory of Benjamin (Josh. 21:18; I Chron. 6:45). Alemeth appears in the genealogical lists of Benjamin beside *Anathoth and Azmaveth (I Chron. 7:8; 8:36; 9:42) but it is missing in the list of Benjaminite cities in Joshua 18:21–28. Alemeth is identified with Khirbet Almit, 1 mi. (c. 2 km.) northeast of Anathoth. It was erroneously identified with Ailamon (Aijalon) on the Madaba Map which was based on a reference of Eusebius (Onom. 18:14). In the Crusader period Amieth (Alemeth) is mentioned with Aneth (Anathoth) and Farafonte (Ayn Fara).

BIBLIOGRAPHY: AASOR, 4 (1924), 156; Abel, Geog, 2 (1938), 242; Press, Ereẓ, 4 (1955), 730; Aharoni, Land, index.

[Michael Avi-Yonah]

ALMOND (Heb. שָׁקֵד), one of the "choice fruits of the land" sent by Jacob to the ruler of Egypt (Gen 43:11). The tree blooms in Israel in January or February, while other fruit trees are still bare. Moreover, the almond blossoms before it is covered with leaves. Thus it symbolizes (Jer. 1:11–12) the speedy fulfillment of the prophecy of doom. It may also signify old age and the imminence of death. It is used, allegorically, in this sense in Ecclesiastes (12:5) to describe the short cycle of human life. Although the tree blossoms early, the fruit only ripens late in the summer. *Ahikar accordingly advised his son: "Be not like the almond tree, for it blossoms before all the trees, and produces its fruit after them." The almond can be regarded as having two periods of ripening. It is edible together with its rind a few weeks after the tree blooms, while the fruit is still green. Its second ripening is three months later, when the outer rind has shriveled and the inside cover has become a hard shell. In its exposition of Jeremiah's vision, the Talmud has the first ripening in mind: "Just as 21 days elapse from the time the almond sends forth its blossom until the fruit ripens, so 21 days passed from the time the city was breached until the Temple was destroyed" (TJ Ta'an. 4:8, 68c), the 21 days being the period between the Seventeenth of Tammuz and the Ninth of Av. Beth-El was originally called *Luz (Gen. 28:19) which is the less common word for almond or almond tree in Hebrew, but *loz* is the regular Arabic word for almond. Several localities in modern Israel bear the Arabic name Al-Luz. Two strains of almond grow in Israel: one, the *amygdalus communis* var. *dulcis*, usually producing pink blossoms and sweet fruit; the second, the *amygdalus communis* var. *amara* producing white blossoms and bitter fruit. The latter strain grows wild in mountain groves. It is edible only with the rind when it is young (Tosef. Ma'as. 1:3). Roasting, however, destroys the poisonous alkaloid, and makes this almond edible even in its later stages (cf. Ḥul. 25b). The almond played a part in the modern history of Ereẓ Israel. Grown extensively in the earlier part of the 20th century, it was attacked by the borer beetle and almost all the orchards were destroyed. In the 1960s, almond cultivation was revived especially in the Northern Negev and again became an important branch of agriculture.

BIBLIOGRAPHY: Loew, Flora, 3 (1924), 242ff.; J. Feliks, *Olam ha-Ẓome'aḥ ha-Mikra'i* (1968^2), 56–59. **ADD. BIBLIOGRAPHY:** Feliks, Ha-Ẓome'aḥ, 165.

[Jehuda Feliks]

ALMOND, GABRIEL ABRAHAM (1911–2002), U.S. political scientist, credited with inventing modern comparative political science. Born in Rock Island, Illinois, Almond was the son of Russian and Ukrainian immigrants. His father was a rabbi. A student at the University of Chicago, he went on to earn his doctorate in 1938; but his thesis, *Plutocracy and Politics in New York City,* was not published until 1998. The work contained psychoanalyses of several wealthy New Yorkers, including unflattering references to John D. Rockefeller, a principal benefactor of the university. Charles Merriam, chair of the political science department, refused to recommend the thesis for publication unless the offending material was removed. Almond refused. The thesis remained in the stacks of the University of Chicago library, where it became an underground classic among scholars. It was finally published by Westview Press.

Almond taught political science at Brooklyn College from 1939. During World War II he was head of the Enemy Information Section at the War Information Office (1942–44). After the war he was professor of political science at Princeton, Yale, and Stanford. He also taught at universities in England, Japan, Brazil, and the Ukraine. He was elected chairman of the Social Science Research Council's Committee on Comparative Politics and, in 1966, president of the American Political Science Association. Almond's *Appeals of Communism* (1954), an empirical study of the attractions and weaknesses of Communism, was significant for its treatment of the psycho-sociological background of political behavior. Almond's major contribution in this field was the recognition of a cultural dimension in politics, and its application in the first nationwide study of political culture (G. Almond and S. Verba, *The Civic Culture* (1963)). The book examines the differences in the political cultures of five countries and looks at how these influence each nation's stability and prospects for democracy.

Almond also developed the "functional approach" to comparative politics. Later he turned increasingly to problems concerned with the theory of political development as seen in "A Developmental Approach to Political Systems" (*World Politics*, 17 (1964–65), 183–214), and in G. Almond and G.B. Powell Jr., *Comparative Politics: A Developmental Approach* (1966).

Other books by Almond include *Political Development: Essays in Heuristic Theory* (1970); *The American People and Foreign Policy* (1977); *Comparative Politics: System, Process, and Policy* (1978); *Sects in Political Science* (1989); *The Civic Culture Revisited* (1992); *Comparative Politics Today: A World View* (1999); *European Politics Today* (1998, 2001); *Strong Religion: The Rise of Fundamentalisms around the World* (2002); *Discipline Divided: Schools & The Ventures in Political Science: Narratives & Reflections* (2002).

[Moshe M. Czudnowski / Ruth Beloff (2nd ed.)]

ALMON-DIBLATHAIM (Heb. עַלְמוֹן דִּבְלָתַיְמָה), city in the northern Moabite plain (the Mishor) between Dibon-Gad and the mountains of Abarim (Num. 33:46–47), along the route followed by the Israelites on their way to the plains of Moab (Arvot Mo'av). Khirbet Deleilat esh-Sherqiyeh, a site containing Iron Age I–II pottery, located about 10½ mi. (17 km.) north-northeast of Dibon (Dhiban), has been suggested for its identification. It is probably identical with Beth-Diblathaim, a Moabite city which is mentioned in the Mesha inscription between Madaba and Beth-Baal-Meon and in the prophecy of Jeremiah after Dibon and Nebo and before Kiriathaim (Jer. 48:22).

BIBLIOGRAPHY: Glueck, in: AASOR, 14 (1934), 32; Abel, Geog, 2 (1938), 269ff.; Press, Ereẓ 1 (1946), 78–79; 4 (1955), 731; Aharoni, Land, index.

[Yohanan Aharoni]

ALMORAVIDS (Arab. *Al-Murābiṭūn*; "Warrior-Monks"), confederation of Berber tribes of the Sanhajah group who lived in the Moroccan Sahara Desert. Their religious fervor and fighting capabilities enabled them to establish a formidable empire in the Maghreb and Muslim (Andalusian) Spain in the 11th and 12th centuries. Their theological Islamic zeal is attributed to Yahya ibn Ibrahim, their spiritual leader, as well as to the *ʿalim* (religious scholar) ʿAbd Allah ibn Yasin. Imbued with Islamic zeal, the Almoravids conquered Morocco and major sections of western Algeria between 1054 and 1092. In 1062 they turned *Marrakesh into their base of operations and religious capital. Thenceforth, their main leaders embraced the title of *Amir al-Muslimin* ("commander of the Muslims") but nevertheless continued to recognize the legitimacy of a still higher authority in Islam: the Abbasid caliph in Iraq upon whom the title *Amir al-Mu'minīn* ("commander of the faithful") had been bestowed. It was toward the end of the 11th century that the Castilian Christians who held on to parts of Spain began challenging the authority of the Almoravids and encroaching on their territories. The Almoravid leadership succeeded in temporarily repulsing the Christians and foiling their plans to conquer such key cities as Córdoba and Toledo.

With the exception of Valencia, Muslim Spain remained under Almoravid control. Notwithstanding, perhaps the weakest aspect of Almoravid rule in Spain and the Maghreb is the fact that they were a Muslim Berber minority in charge of a Spanish-Arab empire. With the passage of time, they found it increasingly difficult to protect all their territorial possessions from the Christian reconquest, especially in the aftermath of the fall of Saragossa in 1118. Moreover, in 1125 the *Almohads (those who advocated the "Unity of Allah"), a confederation of rival Berber tribes, began to rebel against them in the Atlas Mountains. Following a protracted struggle and relentless fighting, the Almohads defeated the Almoravids in 1147; they transformed Marrakesh into their own capital and extended their authority into Muslim Spain.

In addition to the powerful military force that they created at their zenith, the Almoravid period is also interesting for its art and architecture. What characterized Almoravid art was its puritanism. As Saharan military monks, the Almoravids rejected the lavish decoration that had dominated the late Umayyad architectural style, and they built on a practical rather than a monumental scale. Piety and asceticism prevented them from erecting elegant palaces and magnificent monuments. The most famous architectural site that remained from the time of the Almoravids is the Great Mosque at Tlemcen, Algeria, built in 1082 and reconstructed in 1136.

The position of the Jews under Almoravid domination was apparently free of major abuses. Unlike the problems encountered by the Jews during the rule of the *Almohads (the Almoravids' sucessor dynasty), there are no factual complaints of excesses, coercion, or malice on the part of the authorities toward the Jewish communities.

BIBLIOGRAPHY: J.M. Abun-Nasr, *A History of the Maghrib in the Islamic Period* (1987); J. Clancy-Smith (ed.), *North Africa, Islam and the Mediterranean World* (2001); A. Julien, *History of North Africa: Tunisia, Algeria, Morocco from the Arab Conquest to 1830* (ed. and rev. by R. Le Tourneau, 1970); C.R. Pennell, *Morocco since 1830: A History* (2000).

[Michael M. Laskier (2nd ed.)]

ALMOSNINO, Sephardi family, originating in Spain and prominent later in Morocco, Salonika, Gibraltar, and England. The family was established from the 13th century at Jaca in Aragon, where BARZILLAI was *baile* in 1277 and JOSEPH and JACOB (possibly his sons) were "*adelantados*" of the Jewish community in 1285 (Régné, Cat, nos. 1277, 1370). ABRAHAM, an outstanding member of the Jewish community of Huesca, helped in the readmission of the converso Juan de Ciudad to Judaism in 1465. A generation later he was condemned by the Inquisition for his complicity in this and burned alive on December 10, 1489. His family thereafter settled in Salonika and were among the founders of the Catalan community there and legal proprietors of its synagogue. His children included the physician, JOSEPH, author of an elegy on the destruction of Jerusalem (published in *Sefunot*, 8 (1964), 264–5); a son ḤAYYIM, an active member of the Catalan community; and a daughter, who married R. Abraham Cocumbriel, son of Asach (Isaac: not Abraham, as the name was remembered in family tradition). Cocumbriel had perished together with Abraham Almosnino. The two families continued to intermarry, their descendants including BARUCH (d. 1563), head of the Catalan community in Salonika in the mid-16th century, father of *MOSES. Another ABRAHAM, a physician of Toledo (perhaps a cousin of the martyr), settled in Fez after the expulsion from Spain where he assisted in organizing the community of the *megorashim* ("exiles"). His son JOSEPH was a physician as well as a poet, and so was his grandson ABRAHAM. The

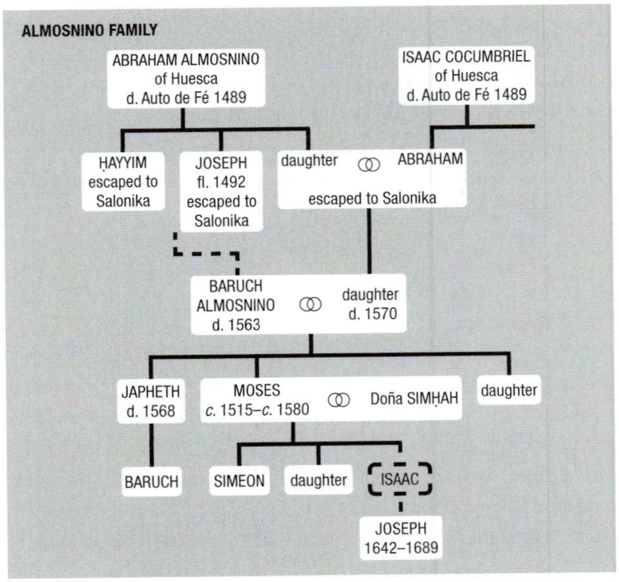

latter's nephew, ISAAC ḤASDAI (b. c. 1580), after many adventures, was arrested at Goa (India) on suspicion of being a New Christian physician from Oporto named Manuel Lopes and was sent to Lisbon for trial by the Inquisition. On successfully demonstrating that he was a Jew by birth, he was released and deported (Torre do Tombo Archives, Lisbon, *Inquisião de Lisbõa*, reg. 5393). In a later generation, ḤASDAI (c.1640–1727) was among the most prominent rabbis of Tetuán. He was probably the father of ISAAC (d. 1785), rabbi of Gibraltar, who went from there with other Jews to London during the siege of 1781. His son Hasdai became a member of the *bet din* of the London Sephardi community. Of the latter's sons, ISAAC (d. 1843), *ḥazzan* of the community, modernized the service, at the same time carrying on a protracted quarrel with the rabbi, Raphael *Meldola, over the pronunciation of Hebrew, and SOLOMON (1792–1877), was secretary of the community and exercised influence over it for many years.

BIBLIOGRAPHY: Baer, Urkunden, 1 (1926), 196; 2 (1936), 484ff.; E. Carmoly, in: *Univers Israélite* (Jan.–March 1850); A.M. Hyamson, *The Sephardim of England* (1951), 230–2.

[Cecil Roth]

ALMOSNINO, JOSEPH BEN ISAAC (1642–1689), rabbi, halakhic authority, and kabbalist. Almosnino was apparently born in Salonika, and studied under Hananiah Taitaẓak. He went to Jerusalem to study in Jacob Ḥagiz's *bet ha-midrash*, Bet Ya'akov, where he probably made the acquaintance of *Nathan of Gaza. About 1666 Almosnino was appointed a rabbi in Belgrade where he married the daughter of the rabbi of that city, Simḥah ha-Kohen, whom he succeeded c. 1668. He was won over to Shabbateanism and transcribed the writings of Nathan of Gaza which were sent to his community (Oxford Ms. no. 1777). The community suffered two serious blows during Almosnino's tenure of office: a great fire in which his library and part of his writings were burnt and, in 1688, the fall of Belgrade to the Turks, as a result of which the community was destroyed. Most of the Jews escaped, but some were taken captive. Almosnino afterward traveled to the German communities where he succeeded in raising funds to ransom the captives and reconstruct the community. He died in Nikolsburg, while on this mission.

Many communities turned to Almosnino with their problems. Moses *Ibn Ḥabib corresponded with him on halakhic matters and wrote an approbation to his responsa. Almosnino also corresponded with Ẓevi Hirsch *Ashkenazi. Many emissaries from Ereẓ Israel visited him, including Moses *Galante. Those of Almosnino's works which escaped the Belgrade conflagration were preserved by chance. They were sold to Arab dealers from whom they were acquired by a Jew. Two volumes of his responsa were published posthumously by his sons Simḥah and Isaac under the title *Edut bi-Yhosef* (Constantinople, 1711, 1713). Several of Almosnino's poems, though never published, are extant in the manuscripts of contemporary Turkish poets (Jewish Theological Seminary, Ms. no. 60, 353; Adler 358; Guenzburg 196). He wrote an autobiographical sketch that appears in the introduction to *Edut bi-Yhosef*.

BIBLIOGRAPHY: Rosanes, Togarmah, 4 (1935), 26ff.; Scholem, Shabbetai Ẓevi, 1 (1957), 189; 2 (1957), 535, 790; Attias, in: *Minḥah le-Avraham… Elmaleḥ* (1959), 135ff.

ALMOSNINO, MOSES BEN BARUCH (c. 1515–c. 1580), Salonika rabbi, scholar, and preacher. His numerous publications show his extensive knowledge of science, philosophy, history, and rhetoric. His rabbinic scholarship was widely respected. Although his responsa were never published in collected form, authorities such as Samuel de *Medina, Ḥayyim *Benveniste, Isaac *Adarbi, and Jacob di *Boton included some of them in their works. A gifted orator, he served in succession as preacher to the Salonika congregations Neveh Shalom and later the Livyat Ḥen, founded by Gracia *Nasi. A selection of his sermons, in Hebrew, is printed in his *Me'ammeẓ Ko'aḥ* (1582). In 1565 Almosnino was chosen as member of a delegation to Sultan Selim II to procure the confirmation of the privileges and exemptions granted by Suleiman the Magnificent to the Salonika community in 1537. The document had been destroyed in the great fire of 1545 and the local authorities again began to place crushing burdens on the community. The two other members of the delegation died en route. Almosnino, with the help of Joseph *Nasi, succeeded, after much heartbreaking effort, in obtaining a favorable decision (1568), and the Salonika community was given the status of a self-governing entity, which it enjoyed for many centuries. Almosnino's works in Hebrew include commentaries on the Five Scrolls (*Yedei Moshe*, 1582), a supercommentary on Abraham Ibn Ezra; a commentary on *Avot* (*Pirkei Moshe*, 1562); and comments on the Pentateuch and prayer book (*Tefillah le-Moshe*, 1563). While in Constantinople, Almosnino compiled in Ladino a description of Constantinople, published, with some rearrangement and omissions, in Spanish by Jacob *Cansino of Oran under the title *Extremos y Grandezas de Constantinopla*. It is one of the rarest works of Spanish Jewish literature and an important historical source. He published, also in Ladino, an ethical work, *Il Regimiento dela Vida* (Salonika, 1564; reprinted in Latin characters, Amsterdam, 1729), which enjoyed considerable popularity in its time. Appended to it is a lengthy treatise on dreams, "composed at the request of the most illustrious señor, Don Joseph Nasi" and giving a graphic description of the latter's luxurious way of life. He also published an exposition of Aristotle's *Ethics* and notes to Al-Ghazali.

BIBLIOGRAPHY: Kayserling, Bibl, 10–11; Molcho, in: *Sinai*, 6 (1942), 198–209; Ben Menahem, *ibid.*, 19 (1946), 136–171; C. Roth, *The Duke of Naxos* (1948), 165ff.

[Abraham Hirsch Rabinowitz]

ALNAKAR, ABRAHAM BEN JOSEPH (1740?–after 1803), Sephardi liturgical scholar. Alnakar was born and brought up in Fez. From there he went to Algiers but returned to Fez by 1783, in which year he began to travel extensively. He was in

Tlemcen in 1783, in Tunis in 1785, in Melian, in Tripoli the following year, and again in Tunis in 1788. From there he proceeded to Leghorn where he remained until his death. For a number of years he engaged in publishing. In 1789, he went into partnership with Jacob Benaim of Morocco and they published, at their own expense, *Tikkunei ha-Zohar*. They used the Constantinople edition of 1719 including the glosses of Jacob Vilna and Moses Zacuto. Alnakar added an introduction to the book, and songs of his own, which he printed in the book. The partnership was probably unsuccessful, since in 1791 his partner, together with Ḥayyim Abraham Israel Ze'evi, a Jerusalem emissary, published the Zohar with the glosses of Ḥ.J.D. *Azulai. Alnakar turned to the publication of prayer books. He became friendly with Azulai, receiving glosses to the festival prayers. In 1798 he published a prayer book for the New Year and the Day of Atonement, with his own commentary, *Zekhor le-Avraham*. This commentary appeared in almost every edition of the High Holy Day liturgy published in Leghorn, as well as in the Tripoli festival prayer book. In addition he published a small prayer book for the New Year and the Day of Atonement according to the rite of Argil (Leghorn, 1803). In the same year he published festival prayer books according to the rites of the Sephardim of Tunis and of Tlemcen. His *Afra de-Avraham* has remained in manuscript. He also drew a design of the Temple candelabrum with a kabbalistic commentary, of which he published a lithographic edition.

BIBLIOGRAPHY: J. Ben-Naim, *Malkhei Rabbanan* (1931), 18b; M. Benayahu, *Rabbi Ḥ.Y.D. Azulai* (Heb., 1959), 204–5.

AL-NAKAWA, ISRAEL BEN JOSEPH (d. 1391), ethical writer and poet. The Al-Nakawa family had lived from the 12th century in Toledo where a synagogue (Midrash Ben Al-Nakawa) had been established by Israel's uncle, Abraham b. Samuel (murdered in 1341). Israel studied with *Asher b. Jehiel and his son Jacob. During the attack on the Jewish community of Toledo in 1391, which claimed many victims and even more converts, the aged Israel was savagely attacked and dragged through the streets. He finally killed himself, an example followed by his brother Solomon. The harrowing details are described in a dirge by an otherwise unknown poet, Jacob ibn Albene. According to one interpretation of this poem, Israel was the *ḥazzan* of a Toledo congregation. His son Ephraim escaped to North Africa and became spiritual leader of the Tlemcen Jewish community. Israel is best known through his *Menorat ha-Ma'or*, a compilation of aggadic and halakhic material in 20 chapters. The author attributes the inspiration and name of his work to a vision (as other authors had before and after him) of the seven-branched holy candelabrum (cf. Zech. 4) and a scroll (cf. Ezek. 2:9–3:3), in which he was instructed to write a book with this title. Whatever the inspiration, the troubled times through which Spanish Jewry passed in the second half of the 14th century called for a handbook of ethical and ritual instruction such as the *Menorat ha-Ma'or*. After an introductory poem and an introduction in rhymed prose, the author describes the general need for a book such as his, in times of decline of religious knowledge and observance. The divisions of the book deal with the main themes of religious life: charity, prayer, repentance, humility, study of Torah, honor of parents, education of children, marriage, business morality, good manners, etc. Several supplements are appended to the work which, however, may not be by Al-Nakawa. The sources from which he drew his material include the whole range of rabbinic literature: the Talmud, the Midrashim, including some now lost, such as the *Midrash Hashkem*, the writings of the *geonim*, Maimonides, Naḥmanides, down to those of his teachers. Another work whose influence can be seen throughout the *Menorat ha-Ma'or* is that of *Mitzvot Zemanniyyot* by Israel b. Joseph. The Zohar is quoted under the otherwise unknown name of *Midrash Tehi Or* and in a Hebrew adaptation of the Aramaic original. It has been suggested that Israel was responsible for a Hebrew translation of the entire Zohar which was still current in the 16th century. The relationship between the *Menorat ha-Ma'or* and the *Midrash ha-Gadol* still needs investigation. In common with Isaac Aboab's *Menorat ha-Ma'or* (1514), Al-Nakawa's is of primary importance because of the texts, both extant and lost, quoted by the author. The originality of such a work lies in the arrangement of the material, in its emphases as well as in the "continuity" provided by the compiler. While Aboab's *Menorat ha-Ma'or* soon became one of the most studied and most often reprinted religious works, Al-Nakawa's remained relatively unknown. Though copies were current in Spain in the 14th and 15th centuries, only one complete manuscript has survived (Oxford, Bodleian Library, Ms. Opp. 146) which H.G. Enelow published in a monumental edition (4 vols., published 1929–32). The last chapter of the *Menorat ha-Ma'or* (on good manners) found its way into J.C. Wagenseil's *Belehrung der Juedisch-Teutschen Red- und Schreibart* (Koenigsberg, 1699), from a Judeo-German translation by Isaac b. Eliakim of Posen (Prague, 1620). Jacob Emden included the same chapter in the third part of his prayer book, *Migdal Oz* (Altona, 1748). The relations between Al-Nakawa's and Isaac Aboab's *Menorat ha-Ma'or* have been much discussed and it is generally assumed that Aboab used, adapted, and condensed Al-Nakawa. However, there can be no absolute certainty in the matter. The main differences are that Aboab's work is purely aggadic and more speculative, and that its structure is more logical; that it has practically no Zohar quotations and that many talmudic passages are quoted in the Aramaic original, whereas Al-Nakawa mostly translates them into Hebrew. Israel Al-Nakawa was renowned as a poet and as such is mourned by the writer of the elegy mentioned above. Davidson's *Oẓar ha-Shirah ve-ha-Piyyut* includes 16 of his compositions. Two *piyyutim*, with Al-Nakawa's acrostic, were published by Enelow (*Menorat ha-Ma'or*, 2:439–43) from a manuscript.

BIBLIOGRAPHY: Baer, Spain, 1 (1961), 374; Schechter, in: MGWJ, 34 (1885), 114–26, 234–40; Efros, in: JQR, 9 (1918/19), 337–57; Roth, in: JQR, 39 (1948/49), 123ff.; Waxman, Literature, 2 (1960²), 279–80.

[Moshe Nahum Zobel]

ALONI, NISSIM (1926–1998), Israeli writer and playwright. Aloni, who was born in Tel Aviv, served in the War of Independence, and studied in Jerusalem and Paris. In 1963 he established Te'atron ha-Onot ("The Theater of the Seasons"), serving as director and artistic manager. His first play, *Akhzar mi-Kol ha-Melekh* ("The King Is Cruelest of All," staged 1953) published in *Ha-Masakh*, 3 (1954), focuses upon the personality of Rehoboam, the king who revolted against Jeroboam in the name of freedom and justice, but who adopted his rival's evil ways upon assuming the monarchy. In *Bigdei ha-Melekh ha-Ḥadashim* ("The King's New Clothes," staged 1961) and *Ha-Nesikhah ha-Amerikait* ("The American Princess," staged 1963; Engl., 1980), the influence of the Theater of the Absurd is evident. In his plays Aloni constructed a highly original world. Its basic components are drawn from the earliest elements of the European theater: myth, mask, costume, stock characters, etc. Aloni eschewed any blatant philosophical or emotional expression that might have been conceived in a situation existing outside the clear-cut boundaries of theatrical action. His play is to be judged by the author's ability to marshal these various theatrical components to express this imagined universe. He employed various means, such as the tape recorder or the cinema, to emphasize the clear and unique connection of his characters with imaginary reality. Other plays by Aloni include "Eddy King" (French, 1985), "The Bride and the Butterfly Hunter," "Napoleon, Dead or Alive," "Aunt Lisa," and "The Gypsies of Jaffa." Similar thematic elements also appeared in the few stories which Aloni published. Their main subject is a "reconstruction" of the world of childhood as a world of imagination, which may have been created either in the imagination of the child protagonist or of the adult narrator. Aloni's published works include the prose collection *Ha-Yanshuf* (1957, 1996). *"Liheyot Ofeh"* appeared in English translation as "To Be a Baker," in S.Y. Penueli and A. Ukhmani (eds.), *Hebrew Short Stories*. Aloni was awarded the Israel Prize for theater in 1996.

BIBLIOGRAPHY: Nathan, in: *Keshet* (Summer 1966), 5–39. **ADD. BIBLIOGRAPHY:** G. Shaked, *Ha-Sipporet ha-Ivrit*, 5 (1998), 133–38; Ch. Shoham, in: L. Ben-Zvi (ed.), *Theater in Israel* (1996), 119–32; E. Rozik, in: L. Ben-Zvi (ed.), *Theater in Israel* (1996), 133–50.

[Matti Megged]

ALONI (Adler), SHULAMIT (1928–), Israeli politician and civil rights activist. She served in the Sixth and Eighth to Thirteenth Knessets. Shulamit Aloni was born in Tel Aviv. She served in the *Palmaḥ during the *War of Independence and was taken prisoner by the Jordanians in the Jewish Quarter of Jerusalem. After her release she worked with immigrant children. She received a law degree from the Hebrew University of Jerusalem and joined *Mapai in 1959. In 1961–65 she produced a radio program dealing with issues of legislation and legal procedures, establishing a reputation as a fighter for citizens' rights, and as a critic of the bureaucracy in Israel. It was largely due to her advocacy that the Commission for Public Complaints was established by Prime Minister Levi Eshkol in 1965. She was elected on the Mapai ticket to the Sixth Knesset in 1965. During this period she established the Consumers' Council and served as its chairperson until 1970. Her refusal to toe the party line, and personal animosity between herself and Prime Minister Golda *Meir, resulted in her exclusion from the Mapai list for the Seventh Knesset. As a result, in September 1973, before the elections to the Eighth Knesset, she established the Civil Rights Movement (Ratz), which managed to pick up some of the protest votes following the *Yom Kippur War, and received three Knesset seats. In the government formed by Yitzhak *Rabin, following Meir's resignation, Aloni was appointed minister without portfolio, but when the National Religious Party joined the government in October 1974, she resigned. In the Tenth Knesset, after receiving only one seat, Aloni joined the Labor-Mapam Alignment for the duration of the Knesset, for tactical reasons. In the course of the Twelfth Knesset Aloni was one of the advocates of the establishment of a new parliamentary group, made up of the ten members of the CRM, *Mapam, and Shinui. The new group called itself *Meretz and ran in the elections to the Thirteenth Knesset under Aloni's leadership. Meretz joined the government formed by Rabin in 1992, and Aloni was appointed minister of education, culture, and sport. However, she had frequent verbal clashes with the leaders of the *Shas religious party, which was also a member of the government, and in order to avoid a coalition crisis agreed, in May 1993, to hand the ministry of education over to Amnon *Rubinstein of Meretz, while she became minister of communications, science, and arts. Aloni decided not to run in the elections to the Fourteenth Knesset, but continued to fight for the issues she believed in from outside the Knesset.

Over the years Aloni helped numerous couples, unable to marry in Israel for halakhic reasons, to draw up marriage contracts, and participated in other activities designed to abolish or circumvent what she regarded as religious coercion. She was also active in helping establish shelters for battered women and stations to assist rape victims. In 1982 she was one of the founders of the International Center for Peace in the Middle East. In 2000 she was awarded the Israel Prize for her special contribution to Israeli society.

Among her books (all in Hebrew) are "Children's Rights in the Laws of the State of Israel" (1964); "Social Legislation" (1970); "The Arrangement: From a State of Law to a State of Halakhah" (1970); "Women as Human Beings" (1976); "Citizen and State: Basic Principles of the Doctrine of Citizenship" (1985); "Can't Do It Any Other Way" (1997).

[Susan Hattis Rolef (2nd ed.)]

ALOUF, YEHOSHUA (1900–1980), educator. Alouf was born in Slonim, Belorussia, but was sent to Ereẓ Israel at the age of 12 to study at the Herzliah Gymnasium in Tel Aviv. Returning for the holidays in 1914, he was caught up in World War I and continued his studies in Warsaw where he became a top gymnast with the local Maccabi. He returned to Tel Aviv in 1920 and was appointed teacher of physical education at the Gymnasium, later completing his studies at the Physical Education Institute in Copenhagen in 1925. From 1938 until his retirement in 1965 he served as national supervisor of physical education in Israeli schools. He was prominently associated with the Maccabi Sports Organization in a number of capacities, and was in charge of the first five *Maccabiahs. Alouf was responsible for the coining of modern Hebrew nomenclature in sport. He wrote many books on physical education. Alouf was awarded the Israel Prize for physical education in 1974.

ALPER, MICHAEL (1902–1955), U.S. rabbi and educator. Alper was born and educated in New York City, receiving his bachelor's, master's, and doctoral degrees from Columbia University as well as rabbinical ordination from the Jewish Institute of Religion. Early in his university career, Alper became the director of Jewish Education for the Hebrew Orphan Asylum. His tenure in this position coincided with a period of rapid growth and modernization in Jewish education in America. Advances in the field of general education were applied to Jewish schools and adult classes. Alper was a leading participant in this process of professionalization, writing textbooks and articles on educational topics, overseeing the publications of the American Association for Jewish Education and the Jewish Education Committee, and editing the journals *Jewish Education* and *Adult Jewish Leadership*. For the last nine years of his life, Alper taught at the Hebrew Union College–Jewish Institute of Religion, specializing in the training of teachers of religion. He was also involved in the nascent Reconstructionist movement, editing the *Reconstructionist* magazine for 15 years. Alper wrote *The Bible Retold* (1930), *Outline in Jewish Education* (1950), and *Reconstructionism and Jewish Education* (1954).

BIBLIOGRAPHY: *American Jewish Year Book*, 57 (1956); *New York Times* (Jan. 31, 1955); *Who's Who in American Jewry* (1938–39).

[Adam Mendelsohn (2nd ed.)]

ALPERSOHN, MARCOS (Mordecai; 1860–1947), Argentine farmer and Jewish writer. Alpersohn was born in Kamenets-Podolski, Russia. His father, Israel, was a *shoḥet* and *melamed*. In his youth Alpersohn was a *maskil*, writing Hebrew articles in the Jewish press. In 1891 he emigrated to Argentina and settled in Colonia Mauricio, the first agricultural colony founded by the *Jewish Colonization Association (ICA). From the very outset he wrote pamphlets in Yiddish under a pseudonym criticizing the ICA administration. After 43 years in Mauricio, he began to spend winters in Buenos Aires but remained on his farm during the summer.

Alpersohn was a prolific writer. In his three volumes of memoirs ("The ICA and Its 30 Years of Colonization in Argentina"), novels, plays, stories, and newspaper articles, he described with much color the life of the Jewish farmers in the ICA colonies. He is considered one of the outstanding Yiddish writers of Argentina.

BIBLIOGRAPHY: M. Alpersohn, *Colonia Mauricio* (n/d); H. Avni, *Argentina ha-Aretz ha-Ye'udah* (1973).

[Efraim Zadoff (2nd ed.)]

ALPERSTEIN, AVRAHAM ELIEZER BEN YESHAYA (1853–1917), rabbi. Born in Kobrin, Grodno Province, Alperstein studied under the direction of Rabbi Joseph Dov Halevi *Soloveitchik and Rabbi Jacob David *Willowski, who later became Alperstein's colleague in Chicago. He then studied at yeshivot in Kovno and Vilna and was granted rabbinical ordination from Rabbi Mordecai Meltzer, communal rabbi in Lida, and Rabbi Aryeh Leib Yellin of Bilsk, and then briefly served as rabbi of the Kaminetzer synagogue in Vilna before becoming the communal rabbi in nearby Novograd. A few years later, he accepted a position as rabbi of the Ẓevaḥ Ẓedek synagogue in the vibrant Jewish community of Slobodka near Kovno.

Alperstein came to New York in 1881 together with the first wave of immigrants. He served as rabbi of Congregation Adath Jeshurun in New York. Three years later he moved to Chicago, where he remained for 15 years, serving in several synagogues, Congregation Oheb Shalom Bnai Marienpol, Anshei Kovno, and the Suwalker shul. While in Chicago, Alperstein published his only book, a commentary on the Jerusalem Talmud, Tractate *Bikkurim*. After spending two years in St. Paul, Minnesota, Alperstein returned to New York in 1901 to become rabbi of the Yagustava shul on Rutgers Street, which enabled him to work together with Rabbis Moses *Matlin and Judah David Bernstein on the yeshiva named for Rabbi Isaac Elchanan Spektor of Kovno. Alperstein campaigned throughout the *shteiblach* of the Lower East Side, appealing for funds on behalf of RIETS, which began to grow and prosper. He arranged for the school to transfer its program to the Yagustava shul, where he served as rabbi and taught Talmud. By 1905, the year he became rabbi at Congregation Mishkan Israel, approximately 100 students were engaged in Torah study at RIETS. Alperstein was also active on behalf of the newly formed Agudat Harabbonim, the Orthodox rabbinical association.

Following his death, his wife founded in his memory the Beth Abraham Home for the Incurably Sick in the Bronx, which at present is the Beth Abraham Hospital, part of the Montefiore-Einstein complex.

BIBLIOGRAPHY: *Ha-Me'assef*, 8:2 (1903), 18; 8:4 (1903), 47; 8:5 (1903), 54; 8:11 (1903), 145; 9:3 (1903), 34; B.Z. Eisenstadt, *Chachmei Yisrael b'America* (1903), 14; idem, *Anshei ha-Shem be-Arẓot ha-Berit* (1933), 41.

[Moshe Sherman (2nd ed.)]

ALPERT, HERB (1935–), U.S. trumpeter, bandleader, composer, and producer. Born in Los Angeles, Alpert studied jazz and classical trumpet and served two years in the army as a trumpeter and bugler. His first success in the music industry was the writing and recording of the instrumental hit "The

Lonely Bull" (1962) with his backup group the Tijuana Brass. Alpert's style influenced a number of other groups, such as Diana Ross and the Supremes and the Beatles. In 1962 he used his royalty monies to purchase the old Charlie Chaplin studio and form A&M Records in partnership with Jerry Moss. Under Alpert's guidance, A&M signed many famous pop performers such as the Police, Cat Stevens, Joan Baez, and the Carpenters. In addition, Alpert himself recorded the number one hit single "This Guy's in Love" (1972). In 1990 he and Moss sold A&M and in 1994 started a new record label – Almo. His albums showed an eclectic style with influences from Africa, funk and disco, Big Band sounds, and hip-hop. Among his recordings are *Herb Alpert and Hugh Masekela* (1978); *Rise* (1979); *My Abstract Heart* (1989); *North on South Street* (1991); the jazz album *Midnight Sun* (1992); *Second Wind* (1996); and *Passion Dance* (1997).

BIBLIOGRAPHY: Grove online; MGG^2.

[Jonathan Licht / Israela Stein (2nd ed.)]

ALPHABET, HEBREW. The origin of alphabetic script has always been a subject of human curiosity. According to Greek mythology, script was brought to Greece from Phoenicia. This tradition was accepted by the Greek and Roman writers, some of whom developed it even further, and stated that the Phoenicians learned the art of writing from the Egyptians. In the 19th century there were scholars who subscribed to the theory of the Egyptian origin, while others believed that the Phoenician script developed from the Akkadian cuneiform, Cretan linear, Cypriote syllabic, and Hittite hieroglyphic scripts.

This entry is arranged according to the following outline

NORTH-WEST SEMITIC
CURSIVE SCRIPT
SQUARE SCRIPT
MASHAIT SCRIPT
LETTERS USED AS NUMBERS
BRAILLE
MANUAL (DEAF)
SHORTHAND

NORTH-WEST SEMITIC

The Proto-Canaanite and Cuneiform Canaanite Scripts

Modern investigation into the origin of the alphabet began in 1905 with the discovery of the Proto-Sinaitic inscriptions by Sir Flinders Petrie at Sarābīṭ al-Khādim in the Sinai Peninsula. These were short texts inscribed in an unknown pictographic script of approximately the middle of the second millennium B.C.E. The first steps toward decipherment of these texts were taken 12 years later by Sir Alan Gardiner, who noted a recurrent series – oxgoad (= Canaanite *lamd*); house (= *bayt*); eye (= *ʾayn*); oxgoad (= *lamd*); cross (= *taw*) – and realized that if the signs followed an acrophonic principle, their parallel Canaanite value (*lamd-bayt-aʿyn-lamd-taw*) would be *lbʿlt* – "for the lady" (goddess). Since then many attempts at decipherment have been made. The most eminent study is that of W.F. Albright, who believes that it is possible to identify 23 of the probable 27 letters occurring in these texts. Accepting Gardiner's Canaanite acrophonic theory and assuming that these texts are votive inscriptions written by West Semites who were employed by the Egyptians in the turquoise mines of Sarābīṭ al-Khādim, Albright bases his readings on the recent knowledge of the Canaanite dialects (mainly Ugaritic) in the second millennium B.C.E.

AN EARLY PALESTINIAN EPIGRAPHIC CORPUS. For several decades it was assumed that these West Semite workers (or slaves), while being in daily contact with the Egyptian hieroglyphs, invented the first alphabetic writing. However, at some sites in Palestine several similar pictographic inscriptions were found. Most of them are of a later date than the Proto-Sinaitic texts (mainly from Lachish, but also from Haṣī, el-Amarna, Beth Shemesh, Megiddo), but at least three are earlier than the Proto-Sinaitic inscriptions (from Shechem, Gezer, and Lachish). This early Palestinian epigraphic corpus consists mainly of inscribed shards and jar inscriptions (partly fragmentary), but there are also inscriptions on seals, a dagger, and javelin heads. The latest specimens (from the end of the Late Bronze period and from the very beginning of the Iron Age) display simplified linear letter forms which developed from the early pictographs. The script of these texts is called Proto-Canaanite (see figure 1).

The order of the early alphabetic texts is suggested by F.M. Cross, Jr. as follows:

I. The Proto-Canaanite Texts
  a. Old Palestinian (17th–12th century B.C.E.)
  b. Proto-Sinaitic (15th century B.C.E.)
II. Canaanite Cuneiform Texts
  a. Ugaritic (14th–13th century B.C.E.)
  b. Palestinian (13th–12th century B.C.E.)

PROTO-CANAANITE SCRIPT AS THE SOURCE OF LATER ALPHABETS. The Proto-Canaanite alphabet seems to copy some pictographic signs from the Egyptian hieroglyphs. Some Canaanite communities adapted the method of writing as in the Akkadian cuneiform syllabic script (i.e., clay tablet and stylus) to the new alphabetic system. Akkadian cuneiform was used in the latter half of the second millennium for international correspondence even between the Egyptian pharaoh and his vassals in Palestine (see *el-Amarna). The cuneiform alphabet was not limited to Ugarit in northern Canaan; specimens of this script were found at three sites in Palestine (Beth-Shemesh, Taanach, and Naḥal Tabor). However, whereas the cuneiform alphabet, as far as is known, ceased to exist with the beginning of the Iron Age (12th century B.C.E.), the Proto-Canaanite script was the source of all alphabetic scripts which later spread throughout the entire world. From this script the Proto-Arabic script branched off in the course of the 13th century B.C.E. (This is the parent script of the South Arabic monumental and the Ethiopic script, as well as the

Proto-Sinaitic, c. 1500 B.C.E.	Palestinian Proto-Canaanite inscriptions, 13–11ᵗʰ cent. B.C.E.				Phoenician c. 1000 B.C.E. (Ahiram Sarcophagus)	Modern Hebrew
𐤀	𐤀	A	ⵣ ⴿ	ⵣ ⴿ	K	א
⊓	ⴹ	ⵎ	ⴻ	𐤁	𐤁	ב
∟		⌃		ⵑ ⵔ	ⵔ	ג
⬦			▽ ◁	◁	△	ד
𐤄	[E/Ǝ]				Ⅎ	ה
φ				Y	Y	ו
=		H		I	I	ז
目		𐤇	I ⫫	目	𐤇	ח
ſ	ſ			ⵥ ⵥ	ⵥ	י
𐤊		ᴡ		ↆ	ↆ	כ
ⵏ	G	◉	? ? ? ⵏ	ⴹ ⵏ	ⵏ	ל
ⵎ	ⵥ	ⵎ		ⵥ	ⵥ	מ
ⵏ	ⵏ	ⵏ	ⵥ ⵥ ⵥ	ⵥ		נ
ⴰ		◉ ○	▽ ○ ○	○	○	ע
			ⵏ ⵏ Y	ⵥ ⵏ		צ
𐤓		Λ	ⵔ ⵔ	ⵔ	ⵔ	ר
ⵯ	ⵥ ⵎ	ⵯ	ⵯ	ⵯ ⵯ	ⵯ	ש
✝	✝		✝ ✝	✝	✝	ת

Figure 1. *Proto-Canaanite script, with its predecessor and main offshoot. From F.M. Cross, "The Origin and Early Evolution of the Alphabet,"* Eretz Israel, 8. Jerusalem, 1967.

Thamudic, Safaitic, and Lihyanic scripts.) The main offshoot of the Proto-Canaanite script, however, is the Phoenician, from which the (Ancient) Hebrew and Aramaic as well as the Greek alphabets evolved (figure 2).

THE TERM "ALPHABETIC SCRIPT." It has been alleged that the term "alphabetic" does not fit West Semitic writing. This script, using letters for consonantal phonemes (i.e., each sign represents a consonant plus any vowel (or "zero" vowel)) is, in I.J. Gelb's opinion, a system of syllabic writing. While it is true that the West Semitic system of writing is a less developed stage than the Greek, the term alphabet itself does not mean that each letter must stand for either a consonant or a vowel, or for a consonant plus any vowel. Alphabet means a number of letters (20 or 30 approximately) listed in a fixed order, notwithstanding their individual values. The first abecedary known until now, found in Ugarit, belongs to the 14th century B.C.E., and its order (after omitting some letters) generally fits that of the Hebrew alphabet (figure 3). The reduction of the symbols to represent consonantal phonemes was a revolutionary step toward spreading literacy, and the systematic insertion of the vowel signs into the script was only a further, though important, step in this process. Therefore there is no reason to restrict the term alphabet to Greek or Latin scripts.

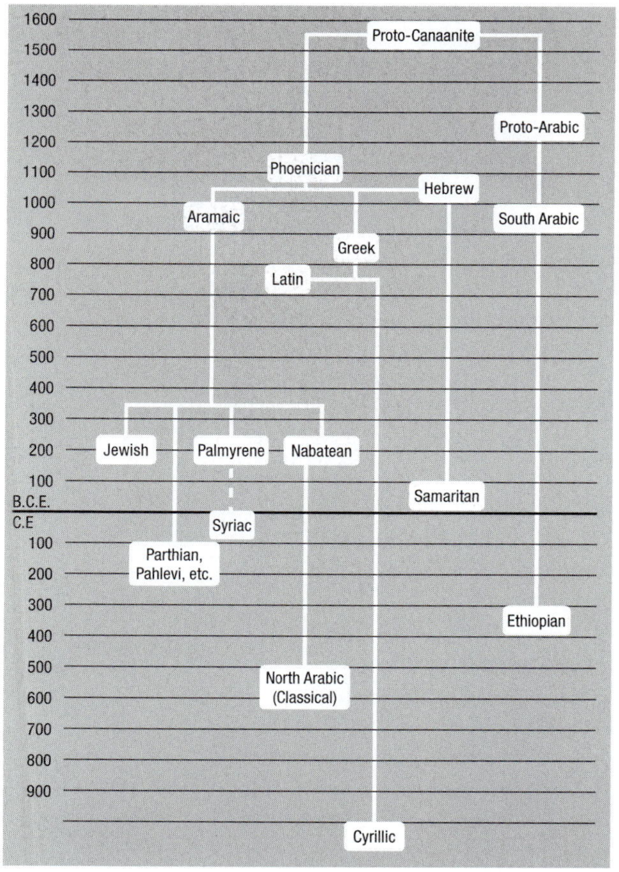

Figure 2. Offshoots of the Proto-Canaanite script. J. Naveh, Jerusalem.

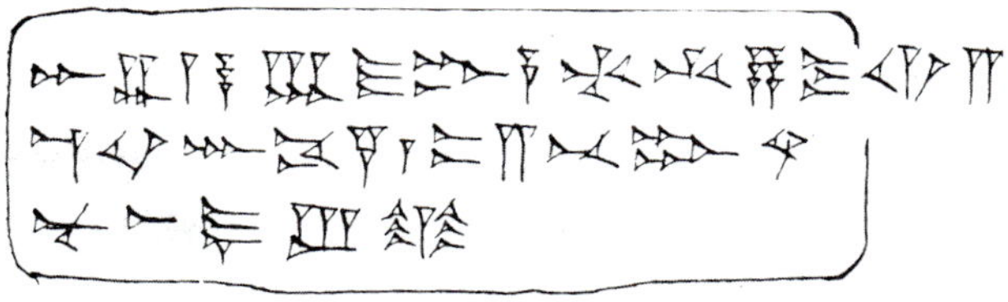

Figure 3. The Ugarit abecedary, 14th century B.C.E. After Virolleaud, Syria, *28, Paris, 195,22.*

The Phoenician Script

The Proto-Canaanite and the cuneiform alphabetic (as well as the South Arabic and the Classical, or North Arabic) scripts have 27–30 letters; the cuneiform also distinguishes between *ʾalef* – a, *ʾalef* – i, and *ʾalef* – u. The Proto-Canaanite inscriptions were written either in vertical columns, in horizontal lines or, quite frequently, in boustrophedon. In the 11th century B.C.E., with the development of the linear letter forms, the stabilization of the right-to-left direction, and the reduction of the number of letters to 22 consonants, the Proto-Canaanite developed into the Phoenician script. (The c. 1000 B.C.E. inscription on the Ahiram sarcophagus found at Byblos displays this stage of evolution.) It seems likely that the Phoenician phonemic system consisted of 22 consonants; but the phonemic systems of the Hebrew and Aramaic languages were richer than that of the Phoenician language. When the Hebrews and Arameans adopted the Phoenician script they could not express in writing these phonemes which did not occur in Phoenician. In Hebrew, for example, there exists *š* (*shin*) and *ś* (*sin*), but both phonemes are designated by the same letter ש; only in a relatively late period, with the invention of the diacritic signs, was it possible to distinguish between שׁ (*shin*) and שׂ (*sin*).

The Phoenician people traded throughout the ancient world, and Phoenician inscriptions have been found as far apart as at Ur in the Persian Gulf and in Spain (figure 4). Most of these inscriptions, however, originated in Phoenicia, Cyprus, and Carthage. The Carthaginian inscriptions and those which were found in the western Phoenician colonies are called Punic inscriptions. While it is possible to distinguish between the dialects which were spoken in Phoenicia proper, in Cyprus, and in the Punic colonies, no special local characteristics in the scripts of the various centers developed. This one-trend evolution seems to be reflected in the scarce ink-written cursive material, but it is especially obvious in the many monumental (mainly votive) inscriptions. Whereas the Phoenician inscriptions of eastern origin after the third century B.C.E. are rare, the number of the Punic inscriptions (mainly from Carthage) increases in the late third and early second centuries until the destruction of Carthage in 146 B.C.E. It seems likely that in this period there developed in the west an independent cursive, which was later adapted to monumental writing by the neo-Punic communities existing in North Africa after 146 B.C.E. This is the neo-Punic script.

6

8

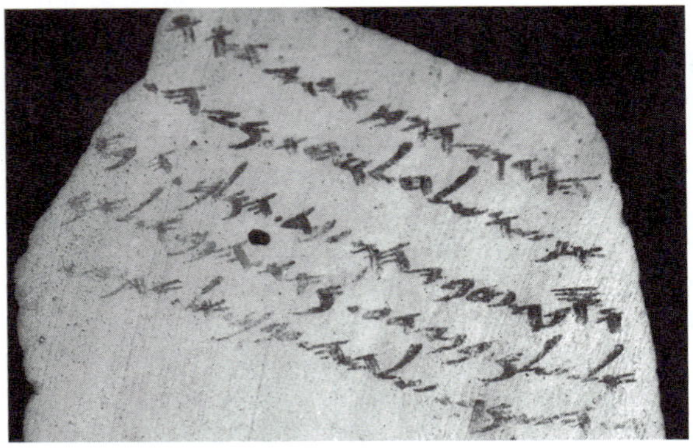

4

NORTH-WEST SEMITIC

Figure 4. Phoenician inscription of the sarcophagus of King Eshmun'ezor at Sidon, fifth century B.C.E. *Louvre.*

Figure 5. The earliest known Hebrew inscription: detail from the Gezer Calendar, c. 950–918 B.C.E. *Louvre.*

Figure 6. The Royal steward inscription from Siloam, Jerusalem (eighth century B.C.E.*) shows the developing cursive character of the Hebrew script. From a plaster cast of the original inscription in the British Museum.*

Figure 7. One of the Arad ostraca, c. 600 B.C.E. *Jerusalem, Israel Museum.*

Figure 8. One of the 18 Lachish ostraca, from the destruction level at Lachish, 587/6 B.C.E.*, reflecting the most developed cursive hand of this period. Jerusalem, Dept. of Antiquities and Museums.*

Figure 9. A 12th–13th century. C.E. *inscription from a Samaritan synagogue near Shechem shows the Samaritan script which was developed from the Paleo-Hebrew. Jerusalem, Israel Dept. of Antiquities and Museums.*

7

9

5

The Hebrew Script

The Hebrews adopted the alphabetic script together with other cultural values from the Canaanites in the 12th or 11th century B.C.E. They followed the current Phoenician script until the ninth century, when they began to develop their own national script.

EARLY INSCRIPTIONS. The *Gezer Calendar is considered to be the earliest Hebrew inscription known. Its script resembles the scripts of the tenth century Phoenician inscriptions from Byblos. The spelling of two words reflects the contraction of the diphthong *ay*, which is either a Phoenician or a North Hebrew (cf. Samaria ostraca) linguistic feature. On paleographical grounds, the Gezer Calendar should be dated in the late tenth century B.C.E. (i.e., in the time of Solomon) when Gezer was an Israelite city (I Kings 9:16), and thereby determined as a Hebrew inscription (figure 5).

As strange as it may seem, the earliest clear Hebrew features can be discerned in the scripts of the ninth-century Moabite inscriptions, namely the stele of *Mesha (the Moabite Stone) and in a recently found fragmentary stele where *kmšyt*, the name of Mesha's father, is mentioned (for the Moabite script, see below).

As the eighth-century Hebrew inscriptions exhibit many specific and exclusive traits, it is obvious that in the ninth century the Hebrew script was written by wide scribal circles. The fact that up to the present almost no Hebrew inscriptions have been found from the ninth century is accidental, but the quantity of the epigraphic material from the eighth century onward shows a gradual increase of the spread of the knowledge of writing among the people of Israel and Judah.

DEVELOPMENT OF THE INDEPENDENT HEBREW SCRIPT. The evolution of the independent Hebrew script is one of a specific cursive character: the further it diverges from the (Phoenician) mother script, the more it drops the lapidary features. This one-trend development is obvious in the eighth-century engraved inscriptions, namely the Siloam Inscription, the Royal Steward (figure 6), and other tomb inscriptions (all from Jerusalem), as well as from the fragmentary Hebrew inscription on an ivory which was taken as booty (probably from Samaria) to Nimrud, and the hundreds of the eighth- to the sixth-century Hebrew seals from various sites. These inscriptions on hard material were written in a cursive style, copying even the shading, which is a natural feature of pen-and-ink writing. This lack of lapidary script may indicate that the custom of erecting stelae by the kings and offering votive inscriptions to the deity was not widespread in Israel. Such an assumption would explain how the specific lapidary element could disappear from the Hebrew script.

HEBREW EPIGRAPHIC MATERIALS. There is some indication of the common use of papyrus. In addition to the seventh-century palimpsest papyrus, preserved in the dry climate of Wadi Murabbaʿat near the Dead Sea about 20 clay sealings of papyrus rolls have been found (mostly in Lachish).

The majority of the Hebrew epigraphic material which has been found is pottery. About 100 jar inscriptions are known today. Sixty jar handles, inscribed after firing, were found in Gibeon, and other jars bear inscriptions on their bodies. Some were incised or written in ink after firing, but others were inscribed before firing the vessels. These inscriptions are mainly the names of the owners or the names of those responsible for their capacity, and others indicate the measure of capacity (*bt lmlk*, "a royal *bat*"). Toward the end of the seventh century B.C.E. it became more usual to impress a seal on the jar handle rather than to write on the soft clay. Recently 80 "private" seal impressions of some 30 specimens and about 800 royal (*lmlk*) seals were listed (M.L. Heltzer, in: *Epigrafika Vostoka*, 17 (1965), 18–37).

The most important Hebrew epigraphic material consists, of course, of ostraca, some of which were incised (e.g., two dockets from Tell Qasile, a name-list, and a message-like short letter from Samaria), but most were written in ink. The majority of ostraca were found in Samaria, Lachish, and Arad. This corpus, together with the Siloam Inscription and an ostracon from Meẓad Ḥashavyahu, are the most important sources for the study of the Hebrew language in the period of the First Temple.

SOURCES FOR THE HEBREW LANGUAGE IN THE FIRST TEMPLE PERIOD. The Samaria ostraca consist of 63 dockets belonging to the eighth century B.C.E., probably to the time of Jeroboam II. They were found in the storage rooms of the royal palace and describe shipments of wine and oil brought in by farmers from various places, presumably as taxes. This material is the main source for the study of the Hebrew dialect spoken in the Northern Kingdom, while the other material reflects the Judahite, or Jerusalemite, dialect.

The Siloam Inscription describes the building of the tunnel through which the water of the Gihon was brought into the city of Jerusalem, presumably in the time of Hezekiah (II Kings 20:20; II Chron. 32:30).

The ostracon found at the seashore fortress called today Meẓad Ḥashavyahu, near Yavneh Yam (Mīnat Rūbīn), is a letter written by a reaper who worked in the royal estate of Josiah, king of Judah. The reaper complained to the local governor of the confiscation of his garment (cf. Ex. 22:25–27; Deut. 24:10–13).

The Arad ostraca, which have only been partly published, were found in various levels of the eighth and seventh centuries. The published material from about 600 B.C.E. consists mainly of short messages dealing with supplies for the mercenaries employed in guarding the southern border of Judah (figure 7).

The 18 Lachish ostraca are letters sent by an officer to the governor of Lachish, who was probably in charge of the defense of the area, on the eve of the Babylonian conquest of Judah just before the destruction of the First Temple in 586 B.C.E. These ostraca reflect the most developed cursive hand (figure 8).

Figure 10. (1) Aḥiram sarcophagus, c. 1000 B.C.E.*, Phoenician; (2) Gezer Calendar, late tenth century* B.C.E.*, Hebrew; (3) Mesha stele, mid-ninth century* B.C.E.*, Moabite; (4) Samaria ostraca, eighth century* B.C.E.*, Hebrew; (5) Bar-Rekub stele, late eighth century* B.C.E.*, Aramaic; (6) Siloam inscription, c. 700* B.C.E.*, Hebrew; (7) Meẓad Ḥashavyahu ostracon, late seventh century* B.C.E.*, Hebrew; (8) Saqqara papyrus, c. 600* B.C.E.*, Aramaic; (9) Hebrew seals, late seventh-early sixth century* B.C.E.*; (10) Lachish ostraca early sixth century* B.C.E.*, Hebrew; (11) Elephantine papyrus, late fifth century* B.C.E.*, Aramaic; (12) Eshmun'azor inscription, fifth century* B.C.E.*, Phoenician; (13) Exodus scroll fragment, second century* B.C.E.*, Paleo-Hebrew. Copyright Joseph Naveh, Jerusalem.*

The Paleo-Hebrew Script

The Hebrew script did not cease to exist after the Babylonian capture of Judah, when most of the nobles were taken into exile. It was used by the people who remained to work the fields; the sixth-century inscribed jar handles from Gibeon, on which the names of winegrowers are listed, are an example. However, from the fifth century onward, when the Aramaic language and script became an official means of communication, the Paleo-Hebrew script (i.e., the ancient Hebrew characters as used in the time of the Second Temple) was used for writing Hebrew both in Judah and Samaria. It was preserved mainly as a biblical book hand by a coterie of erudite scribes (presumably of the Zadokite priesthood; cf. the Paleo-Hebrew Pentateuch fragments found among the *Dead Sea Scrolls). The vast majority of the *Hasmonean coinage as well as the coins of the First and Second Jewish Revolts bears Paleo-Hebrew legends. Although this script is a relatively static, formal hand, it seems likely that the Hasmoneans did not revive a forgotten national script; they struck coins with legends of a known writing which survived – though in a narrow circle – in the period of the Second Temple.

Together with the discovery (in Wadi Daliʾyeh) of Aramaic deeds written on papyrus in Samaria in the fourth century B.C.E., two clay sealings with Hebrew texts written in the Paleo-Hebrew script were found there without any Samaritan peculiarities. It seems likely that the divergence of the Samaritan script began sometime in the last two centuries of the first millennium B.C.E. The Samaritans continued to use this script for writing both Hebrew and Aramaic texts, but the Jews ceased using it after 135 C.E. A comparison of the earliest Samaritan inscriptions and the medieval and modern Samaritan manuscripts clearly indicates that the Samaritan script is a static script which was used mainly as a book hand (figure 9).

The Rise of the Aramaic Script

The Arameans adopted the Phoenician script in the 11th or 10th century B.C.E. The first *Aramaic monumental inscriptions originating in the Aramean kingdoms in the ninth and eighth centuries (Damascus, Hamat, and Samaʾl) were written in the Phoenician script. The earliest clear Aramaic features are discernible in the cursive script of the mid-eighth century. In this period the Assyrians introduced the Aramaic language and script as a common means of communication among the various nations in the Assyrian Empire. Moreover, it became a *lingua franca* and was used from then on as a diplomatic and commercial language. For example, an Aramaic papyrus letter sent from Palestine about 600 B.C.E. was found at Saqqara in Egypt.

THE ARAMAIC SCRIPT COMPARED TO CONTEMPORARY PHOENICIAN AND HEBREW SCRIPTS. A comparison of the Aramaic script of the Saqqara letter and other Aramaic cursive material of the same time with the contemporary Phoenician and Hebrew cursives (e.g., the Arad and the Lachish ostraca) is most instructive. (It should be remembered that the independent development of the Aramaic script began 100 years after that of the Hebrew.) The Aramaic script, omitting various bars, looks like shorthand in comparison with the Phoenician and particularly the Hebrew script. This phenomenon can be explained by the differing geopolitical and cultural factors prevailing among the respective peoples using the various scripts. The Phoenician script was relatively widely used among this trading people but remained a national script. The conservative Hebrew script was developed by a nation tending to preserve its traditional values; from the late eighth century B.C.E. (the fall of Samaria) this script was more or less restricted to Judah and was written by a people dwelling in a mountainous land away from international highways. On the other hand the Aramaic script, written by many peoples, became a strictly practical means, stripped of all sentiment (figure 10).

The Moabite, Edomite, and Ammonite Scripts

The inscriptions found in various sites in Transjordan provide a quite clear picture of the scripts used by the peoples living there and reflect their cultures.

The scripts of the ninth-century Moabite stelae – namely the Mesha stele and the fragmentary *kmšyt* stele – display definite Hebrew characteristics, though their language is not Hebrew but Moabite (another Canaanite dialect, different in some aspects from Hebrew). Later Moabite inscriptions (mainly seals from the seventh and sixth centuries) show clear Aramaic letters written side by side with letters of Hebrew form or of specific local character. The inscriptions bearing Edomite theophoric names (e.g., *Qwsʿnl*) found in Elath and in Umm al-Biyāra near Petra, exhibit a similar state of affairs. The writing of the Moabites and the Edomites in the ninth century did not differ from that of the Hebrews, while in the late seventh and sixth centuries clear signs are to be found of the intrusion of Aramaic elements into these two scripts. This intrusion probably began in the last third of the eighth century B.C.E. when the political influence of Israel and Judah came to an end and the Assyrians appeared on the King's Highway south of Damascus.

The recently published ninth-century B.C.E. Amman citadel inscription shows that the Ammonites spoke in a Canaanite dialect (similar to Hebrew and Moabite) but adopted the Aramaic script from the Arameans who lived in Damascus. About a score of Ammonite seventh-century seals written in contemporary lapidary Aramaic indicate that the Ammonites followed the Aramaic scribal tradition common in the Assyrian Empire.

The Official Aramaic Script and Its Descendants

Aramaic, being an official language of the Assyrian, neo-Babylonian, and Persian empires, was spoken and written in a vast area. Aramaic inscriptions have been found in Egypt, North Arabia, Palestine, Syria, Asia Minor, Mesopotamia, Persia, Afghanistan, and Pakistan. The examination of all this epigraphic material has shown that until the end of the third century B.C.E. (i.e., about 100 years after the fall of the Persian Empire) no local script developed and the Official Aramaic script remained a uniform script.

Figure 11. Examples of the Jewish script. (1) Exodus fragment; (2) Bar Kokhba letter; (3) Bet Mashko letter; (3a) Signatures of witnesses to no. 3; (4) Aramaic deed; (4a) Signatures of witnesses on no. 4; (5) Dura-Europos fragment; (6, 7) Bet She'arim tomb inscriptions; 1–4a from Wadi Murabba'āt, i.e., before 135 C.E.*; 5–7 of the third century* C.E. *Copyright N. Avigad in* Scripta Hierosalymitana, *4, 1957.*

Many nations used Aramaic as a second language, and often it became the main spoken tongue. This was the situation in the fifth-century B.C.E. Jewish military colony in *Elephantine, where over 100 Aramaic papyri and ostraca were found. This corpus – which is a main source for knowledge of the Official Aramaic language and script – consists of legal documents and private and official letters, as well as two literary works. In the Persian period there existed an Aramaic lapidary script (cf. the fourth-century Judean jar-stamps), but the influence of the cursive hand was so strong that many inscriptions on hard material were written in the cursive style. The lapidary script died out in the late fourth century B.C.E., but the use of the standard Aramaic cursive went on for at least 100 years after the fall of the Persian Empire (330 B.C.E.). Aramaic was widely spoken and written and continued to flourish in various centers even in the Hellenistic period, when Greek became the official language.

THE DEVELOPMENT OF ARAMAIC LOCAL SCRIPTS. In the third and second centuries B.C.E. local scripts began to develop from the Aramaic. In the West two national scripts were born, the Jewish (square Hebrew) and the Nabatean, while the eastern offshoots are many: Palmyrene, Syriac, Mandaic, as well as the local scripts of Hatra (Mesopotamia), Nisa (Turkmenistan), Armazi (Georgia), and Elymais (Khuzistan). The Jewish book hand became stabilized in the Herodian period, and it did not undergo essential alterations until the present. From the Nabatean cursive hand the North Arabic script developed. The eastern branches and their relations to each other have not yet been studied thoroughly, but the developments of some trends are quite clear. The script of the ostraca of the first century B.C.E. found at Nisa (a Parthian capital) is a transitional stage between Official Aramaic on the one hand and Parthian (Pahlavik), Persian (Parsic), Book-Pahlavi, and other scripts which were invented for Middle Iranian languages on the other hand. This writing also employed a system of Aramaic ideograms. The script of the inscriptions and a coin-legend of the Elymeans is the ancestor of the Mandaic writing. The Mandeans are a religious sect living in Khuzistan near the Persian Gulf who preserved an eastern Aramaic dialect resembling that of the Babylonian Talmud.

The earliest Syriac inscriptions stem from the first and second centuries C.E. This script was employed by Christians in Syria-Mesopotamia. There are three main Syriac styles of writing: the Estrangelo, which resembles the script of the early inscriptions, is formal; the Serto, ordinarily used by the Jacobites, is a developed cursive; the Nestorian hand is another cursive variation. Syriac is an Eastern Aramaic dialect spoken by the Christian communities in Edessa (modern Urfa) and its vicinity. However, although the Palestinian Christians spoke in a Western Aramaic dialect, they adopted the Syriac script and wrote in a style similar to Estrangelo. The Manichaic script is an offshoot of Syriac; it was invented in the third century C.E. by Mani, the founder of the Manichean sect, as a book hand for writing religious manuscripts in a Middle Iranian dialect.

The Jewish Script

The talmudic tradition (Sanh. 21b) ascribes the adoption of the Aramaic ("Assyrian") script to Ezra, who brought it from the Babylonian captivity. However Aramaic arrived in Judea also through the Babylonian and mainly through the Persian administrations. At any rate it became the colloquial language, at first of the educated classes and then of wider circles. It seems likely that in the Persian period the Aramaic script was used for writing Aramaic texts only, but the earliest Hebrew manuscripts found in Qumran are fragments of Exodus and Samuel, probably written in the second half of the third century B.C.E. in the Proto-Jewish script, which displays the earliest Jewish national development of the Official Aramaic script. From this period on the Paleo-Hebrew script was restricted to Hebrew texts, but the Jewish script was used both for Hebrew and Aramaic. (The Samaritan script – a descendant of Paleo-Hebrew – was employed both for Hebrew and the Western Aramaic dialect spoken by the Samaritans.)

The most important material for the study of the early evolution of the Jewish script are the scrolls from the Qumran caves and the other documents found in the caves of Wadi Murabbaʿat and Naḥal Ḥever. The other material consists of tomb and ossuary inscriptions (mostly from Jerusalem) as well as some ostraca found mainly in *Masada (where a scroll of the apocryphal Book of Ben Sira was also discovered) and at *Herodium.

THE JEWISH CURSIVE HAND. As the development of the formal book hand will be dealt with below (see below, Square Script), the earliest Jewish cursive will be considered here. This cursive hand began to develop in the Late Hasmonean and Early Herodian periods (cf. the Jason Tomb inscription from Jerusalem), and flourished in the time of the Second Revolt (132–135 C.E.). As in other cursive scripts the letters are generally rounded, and there is a tendency to join the letters. However there was not sufficient time for the development of a fully ligatured writing (e.g., Syriac, Mandaic, and North Arabic; figure 11). Several minor cursive inscriptions are among the inscribed ossuaries and on the ostraca, but most of them are known from the papyri, messages of Bar Kokhba and his officers, found in Naḥal Ḥever and Wadi Murabaʿat. The influence of this hand was strong enough to affect the formal hand. Therefore some biblical manuscripts and mainly legal documents were written in semiformal or semicursive styles. It seems likely that the cursive style ceased to exist with Bar Kokhba's defeat or soon after it, while from the surviving Jewish book hand other cursive offshoots have been born.

See also entries on individual letters of the Hebrew alphabet.

[Joseph Naveh]

CURSIVE SCRIPT

It is only natural that letters, notes, business matters, legal documents, etc., should be written with less care and accuracy than books. The writer does not intend to reproduce exactly the letters of the formal script. His intent is to give the basic structure of the letters, that is, an approximation of the "ideal" forms. This is clearly illustrated by figure 1 (second century C.E.). In the course of time there is less and less approximation, i.e., changes take place. Unwittingly, to save time and effort, the writers omit certain details by linking individual strokes, which were formerly not linked, and by uniting or fusing certain strokes. The pace of such structural development is much faster than the changes in the square script,

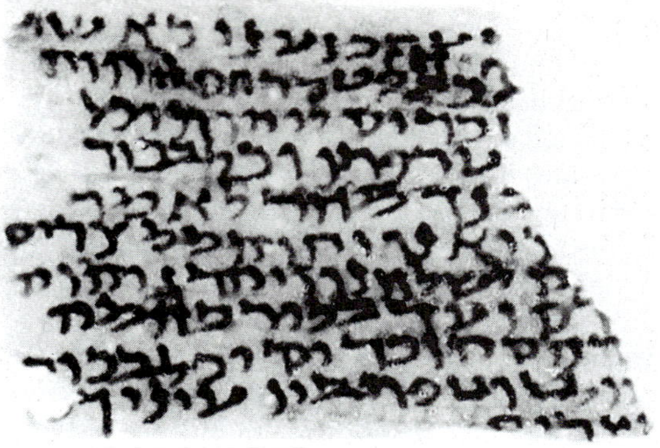

Figure 1. Fragment of Exodus 13 in Palestine cursive script, second century C.E. *Jerusalem, Hebrew University Dept. of Archaeology.*

which, by comparison with the cursive, hardly moves at all. The result is the rise of a full-fledged cursive style which can no longer, by any stretch of imagination, be called a simplified square. The changes that have taken place are so great that many letters have become utterly different from their counterparts in the square style. It should be mentioned that occasionally books are penned in cursive. Figure 2 (fifth–sixth centuries) is an early stage specimen. It contains a form that is decidedly cursive – the open *he*. This was not, at that time, a recent development; it had been in existence for centuries but it stayed outside formal writing until almost the end of the Middle Ages. The early cursive seems to have lasted until the eighth–tenth centuries, but further research and/or new material might change the present picture.

Figure 2. Mosaic inscription in the synagogue of Jericho, fifth–sixth century C.E. in situ.

PALESTINE-SYRIA TYPE. The 11th-century Palestine-Syria type is a fully developed cursive style, although the connection with the square script is quite clear. In figure 3 (12th century) the right strokes of the *alef* are high up, and the left one practically always joins the top of the middle stroke; *bet* and *kaf* differ greatly; *lamed* consists of two strokes only; final *nun* is regularly joined to the preceding letter; the middle stroke of *shin* is a small horizontal curve joined to the top of the left stroke. Whether the modern script of the Palestinian-Syrian

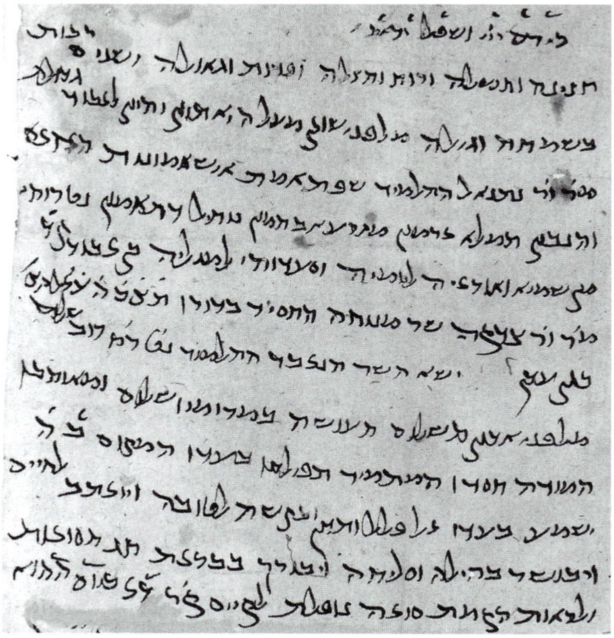

Figure 3. Palestine cursive script in a letter written in 1114 C.E. *Cambridge University Library, T-S 13-J. 13/3.*

region (figure 4) is a continuation of the style shown in figure 3 cannot presently be established.

One special group of cursive in ancient Palestine is characteristic of the Negev. This writing (figure 5; second century) appears, at first glance, to be undecipherable and its connection with the square script could only be established with difficulty. Documents of this type dating from the second half of the first century B.C.E. until the end of the Bar Kokhba War are extant. The fact that it disappeared without a trace shows that it was not the general Jewish cursive.

EGYPT TYPE. In Egypt the early stage of the cursive style seems to reach into the eighth century. The fully developed cursive style dates from the ninth to tenth centuries. Figure 6 belongs to the fifth century, figure 7 to the eighth, figure 8 to the 11th; in the latter, the *alef* appears in two forms at the same time – regular and cursive – and the final *nun* is written separately; generally the left downstroke of the *tav* is hardly severed from the top stroke. Four centuries later (figure 9) the *alef* is more cursive; final *he* is joined to the preceding letter and is a long inverted S-wave: the right and left downstrokes have been linked, in consequence of which the left one has been dragged down to a position below the line bottom; the same has happened, in most cases, to *tav* but there the linking stroke has not disappeared into the wavy line.

BABYLON TYPE. The early stage of the Babylonian cursive is represented by the fifth/sixth century incantation bowls (figure 10). The earliest available example of the fully developed cursive style (figure 11) belongs to the 11th century. *Alef* has the structure of K in the Roman alphabet. In the modern cursive (figure 12) many letters are very far removed from their original forms, e.g., *alef, gimmel, he, tet*, etc.; the original top and right strokes of *tav* have been merged into the top of the left stroke, which runs very far down and finally bends leftward, sweeping still further in that direction.

PARSIC TYPE. The earliest specimens of the Parsic type (figure 13; 11th century) show a fully developed cursive style. *Alef* has both the K- and the N-form; in *he* and *tav* there is no tendency toward a linking up of the two downstrokes, such as completed in the Babylonian type. In figure 14 (modern) the upper right stroke of *alef* has become the main stroke's top part; *gimmel* resembles *nun* but the upper stroke of the letter tends to be vertical, and the corner of the *gimmel* is an acute angle; at the lower end, *zayin* bends with a little rightward slant. These features are not of recent origin: they gradually came into being after the period of figure 13.

TEMANIC TYPE. The earliest available specimen of the Temanic cursive dates from the 12th century (figure 15) and later material of this type is also very scarce. Figure 15 contains no very specific cursive forms: *zayin* developed into the question mark type only some time between then and the 16th century; its usage has continued to the present day.

MAARAVIC TYPE. The available cursive documents of the Maaravic type begin in the 11th century, and then, for a considerable time, continue to be scarce. In figure 16 (11th century) *alef* has the K-form; the right stroke of *mem* does not turn leftward at the bottom and the left stroke is as long as the right one, being practically on the same level. Figure 17 (15th century) presents the most unusual appearance among all the cursives, and its highly developed aesthetic character does not make for easy reading. This difficulty is increased by the fact that those letters which end in a leftward movement touch those which follow them, that when *bet* or *kaf* or, sometimes, *dalet* precede a *vav*, this is linked up with it and thereby dragged down from the line, the *he* in final position is linked with a preceding *resh* and placed below it, and the *yod* is placed inside a preceding *bet* or *kaf*. *Alef* has two forms, one that is initial and medial, the other final. In the latter the original main stroke is high and short, and the right stroke sits on its right end; the former is even more contracted: the two right strokes have been merged into one small vertical, while the left stroke slants down to the left. *He* is a kind of inverted S-wave; final *mem* is more or less an oval; *samekh* has a long tail; the right stroke of *ẓadi* and final *ẓadi* is generally above the line ceiling, and is joined to the tip of the main stroke; the top bar and right downstroke of *tav* have been fused into a curve, and the left stroke is joined to its bottom end. The modern hand of figure 18 is a very careful one. *Alef* has become a shallow S-wave starting above the line ceiling (the "full" form which is often used in this specimen seems to be an unusual attempt at special clearness); the top stroke of *dalet* is above the line ceiling; *he* is an inverted shallow S-wave of line height; *mem* tallies with the Ashkenazic form; *resh* is a tall letter – when followed by *he* or *yod* it is linked with them, the *yod* being reduced to a dot; *tav* is a long, straight, oblique line.

SEPHARDIC TYPE. The available Sephardic material of fully developed cursive starts from the beginning of the 11th century. Figure 19 dates from the middle of the 11th century: *alef* has the K-form but in final – and, less often, in other positions – the two right strokes are high up, joined to the top of the left stroke; the *alef* part of the *alef-lamed* ligature is preserved in its angular form; the right part of *tet* is usually in the upper half of the line; the left stroke of *samekh* is generally not written with much care so that the letter is then identical with final *mem*, being of circular or oval outline. Figure 20 (15th century) illustrates a writing that forms a counterpart to the Maaravic hand of the same time (figure 17) but does not present the same extreme degree of parallelization. This kind of script is a book hand, but much plainer types are also used in books. Upon the introduction of the printing press it was not adopted as a type face and became very rare: it seems to have died out in the 18th century. The modern hand (figure 21) is not a continuation of it but of the plain sort, being clear and easily legible. *Alef* is a long letter, an S-wave beginning on top, at the right, with a narrow loop; *he* is a little inverted S-wave, mostly in horizontal position. The form of the *lamed* is identical with that of the present handwritten, but what appear to be the corresponding strokes are not really so. The main stroke of the Old Semitic form survives in the right stroke of the Hebrew cursive but the Western cursive in the left one. *Resh* is very often a tall letter; *yod* following *alef, dalet, samekh*, or *resh* is attached to them as a dot; a *he* which follows resh is linked to it.

YEVANIC TYPE. Figure 22, a dipinto from Magna Graecia (c. fourth century), shows the early cursive stage of the Yevanic type. Figure 23 (15th century), while resembling the Sephardic type in certain respects and Oriental types in others, is independent of either. The similarities are due to convergent developments, growing from the same original forms. The most characteristic letters are *alef, dalet, he, zayin, tav; he* and *tav* appear in double forms, one being more highly cursive than the other. A characteristic feature of this script is the rightward blob at the end of *dalet* and *zayin*.

ITALKIAN TYPE. The earliest available examples of the Italkian type also come from Magna Graecia. Their script is the same as that of the early Yevanic, from which it developed. Figure 24 (11th century or somewhat earlier) is a more developed cursive, written with great care and used as a book hand. Little is left of these forms by the 13th century, and even less by the 16th: the writing of figure 25 is not particularly legible. The two downstrokes of *he* are linked but the left one remains in its position, thus the letter differs very much from those hitherto met with, where the left stroke had been dragged downward. The lower stroke of *lamed* has become a cross stroke – a feature unknown in the other cursives. *Samekh* as a plain circle is very rare in other types. The *pe* is another unique form: it

CURSIVE SCRIPT

4

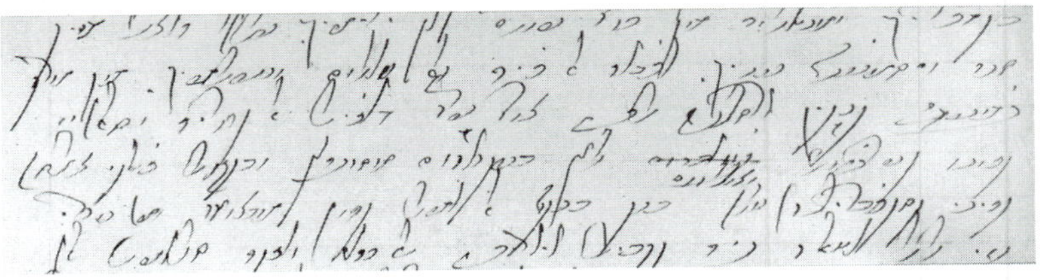

Figure 4. Palestine cursive script of the 20th century. London, S.A. Birnbaum Collection.

Figure 5. Fragment from a marriage deed in Palestine cursive Negev script, 117 C.E. Jerusalem, Dept. of Antiquities and Museums.

Figure 6. Egyptian cursive script of the fifth century C.E. London, British Museum, Ms. Or. 9180C.

Figure 7. Egyptian cursive script of the eighth century C.E. S.A. Birnbaum. The Hebrew Scripts, London, 1954–57, Fig 153.

Figure 8. Egyptian cursive script of the 11th century C.E. Oxford Bodleian Library, Ms. Heb. 6.3, fol. 1.

5

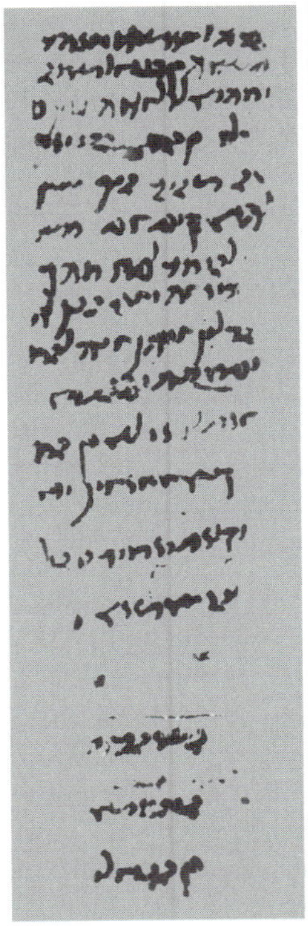

6

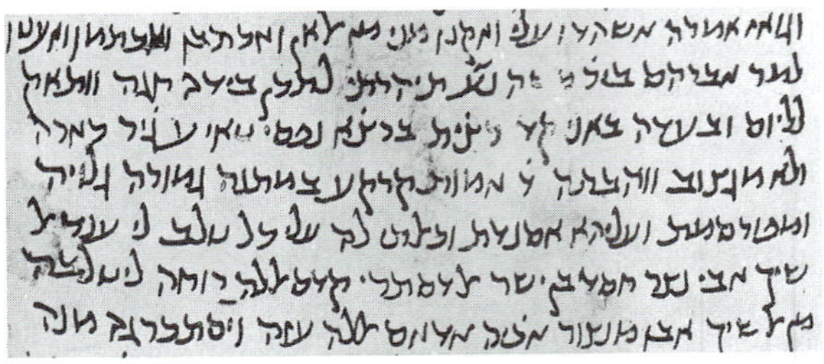

8

7

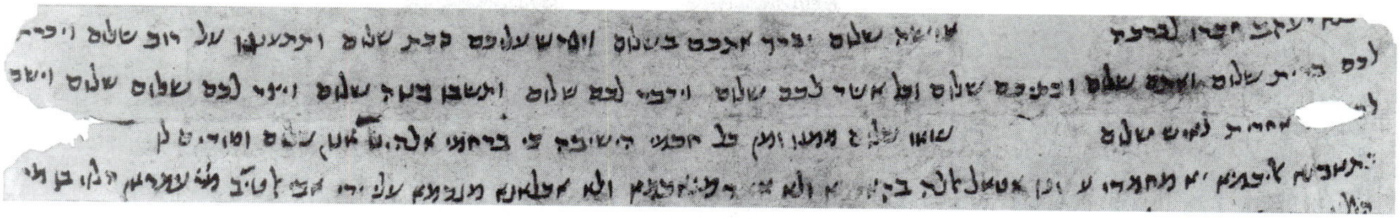

11

9

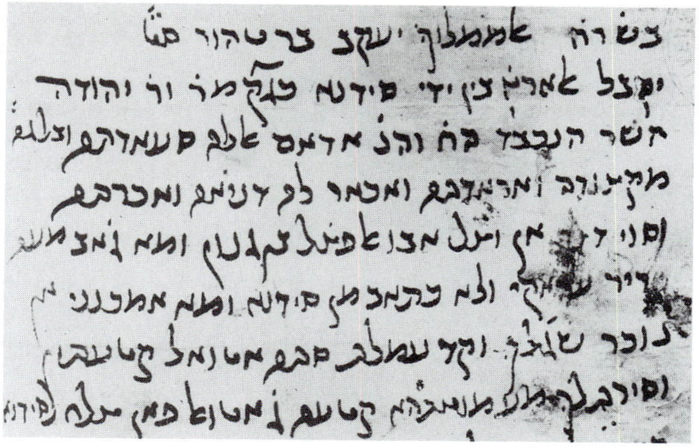

10

Figure 9. Letter in Egyptian cursive script, 1436 c.e. *Cambridge University Library, Ms. Add. 3415.*

Figure 10. Babylonian cursive script on an incantation bowl of the fifth–sixth century c.e. Ibid. *Figure 187.*

Figure 11. This letter written in 1007 c.e. *is the earliest example of the fully developed Babylonian cursive script. Cambridge University Library, T-S. 12.829.*

Figure 12. Babylonian cursive script of the 20th century. London, S.A. Birnbaum Collection.

12

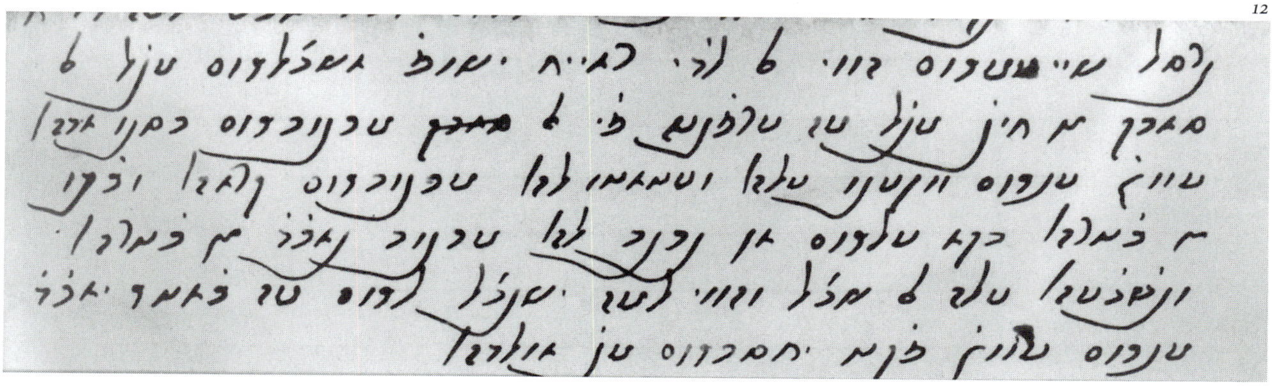

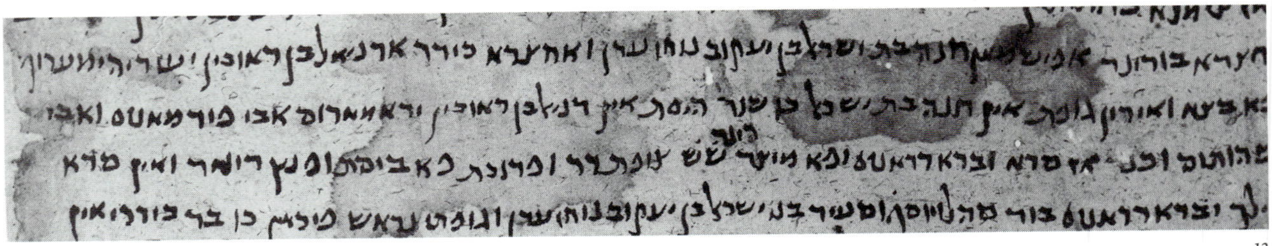

13

Figure 13. Legal document of 1021 C.E. *in Parsic cursive script. Oxford Bodleian Library, Ms. Heb. b. 12, fol. 24r.*

Figure 14. Parsic cursive script of the 20th *century. London, S.A. Birnbaum Collection.*

Figure 15. Temanic cursive script in a letter of 1133 C.E. *Cambridge University Library, T-S. 20.173.*

Figure 16. Maaravic cursive script in a letter of 1035 C.E. *Oxford Bodleian Library, Ms. Heb. d. 65, fol. 4r.*

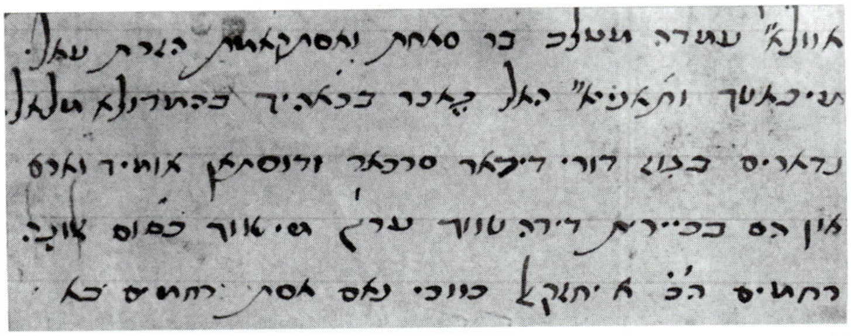

14

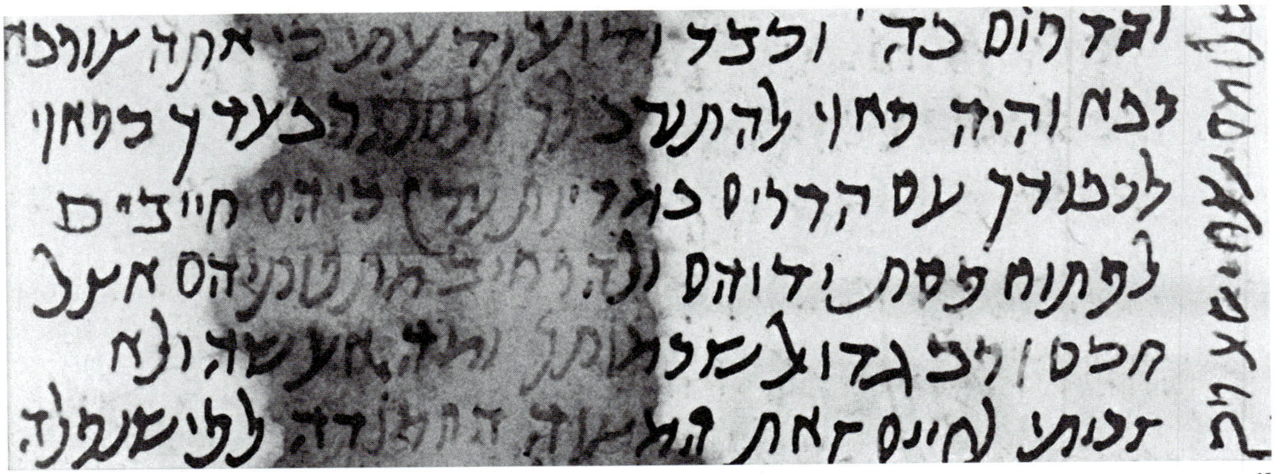

15

16

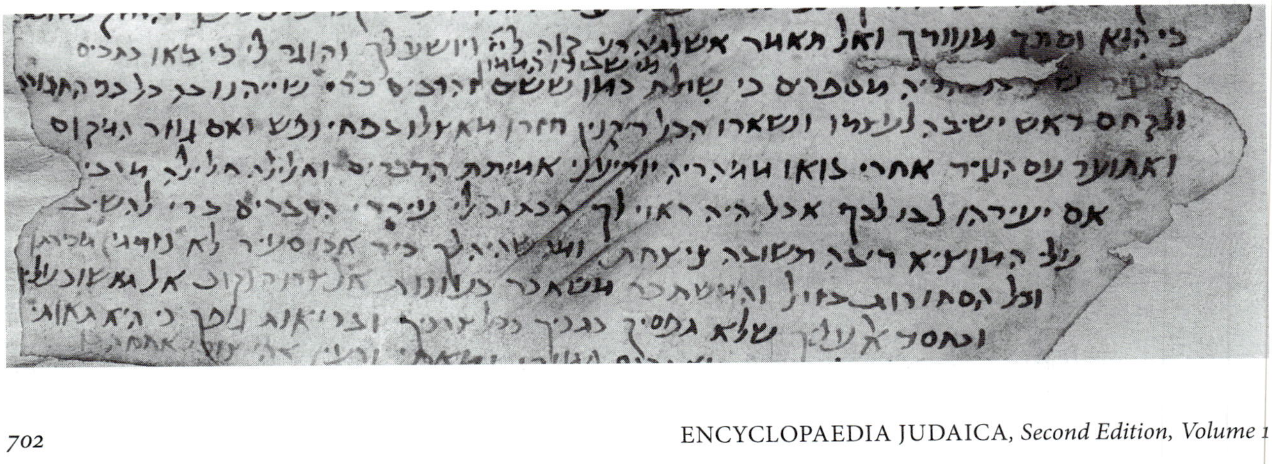

17

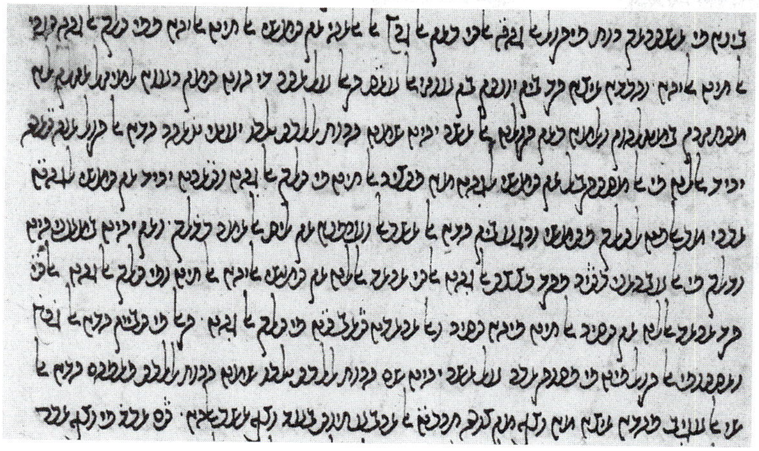

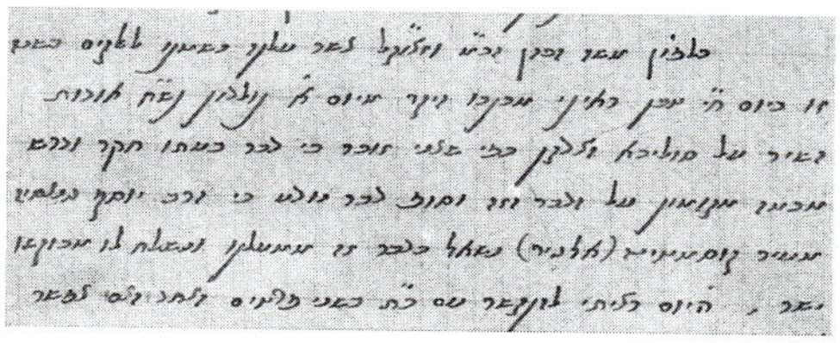

18

19

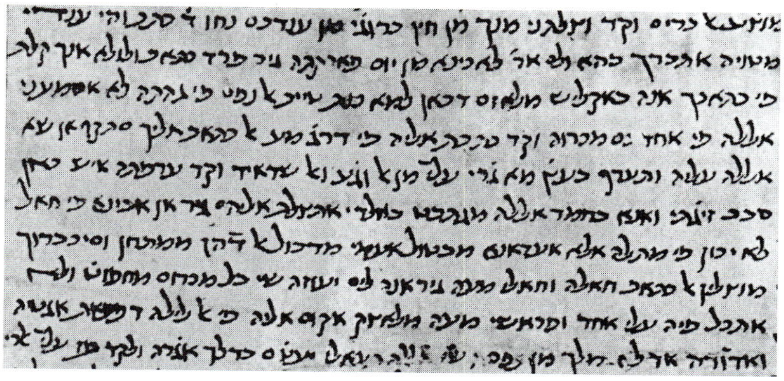

Figure 17. Fifteenth-century manuscript in Maaravic cursive script. Paris Bibliothèque Nationale, Ms. 2235, Heb. 758, fol. 17.

Figure 18. Maaravic cursive script of the 20th century. London, S.A. Birnbaum Collection.

Figure 19. Sephardic cursive letter of 1053 C.E. Cambridge University Library, T-S. 13. J.9.4.

Figure 20. Fifteenth-century medical work in Sephardic cursive script.

Figure 21. Modern Sephardic cursive script. London, S.A. Birnbaum Collection.

Figure 22. Yevanic cursive script on an epitaph from the catacombs at Magna Graecia, Italy (fourth century C.E.).

22

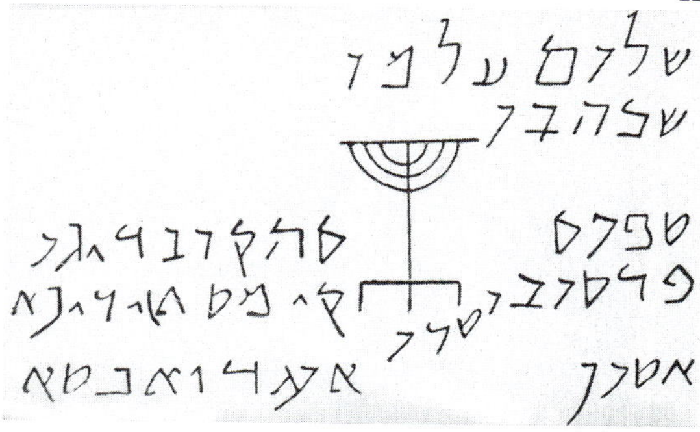

20

21

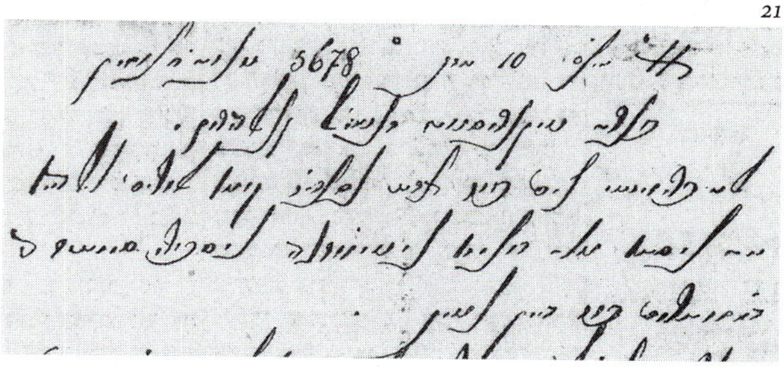

23

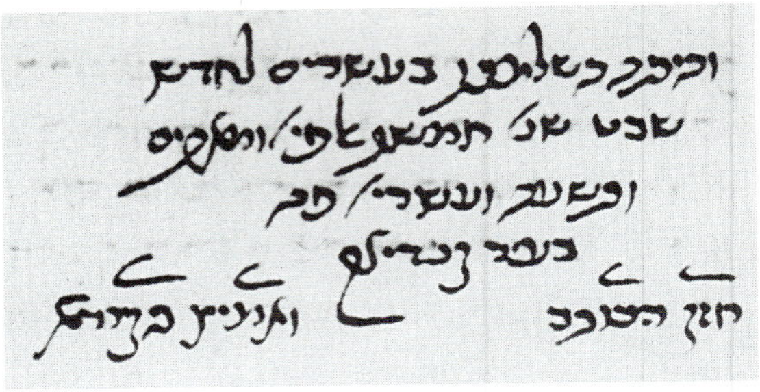

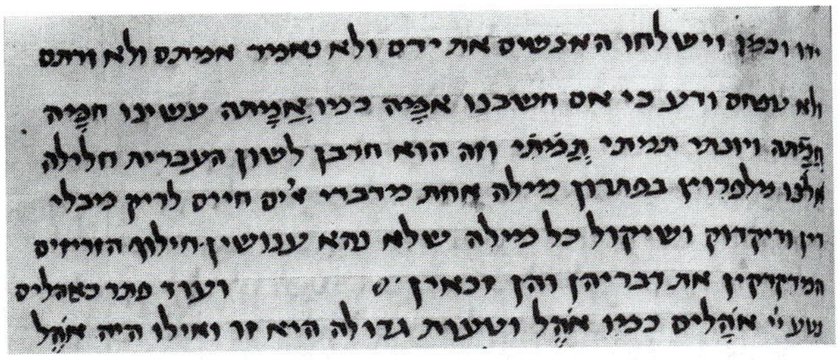

24

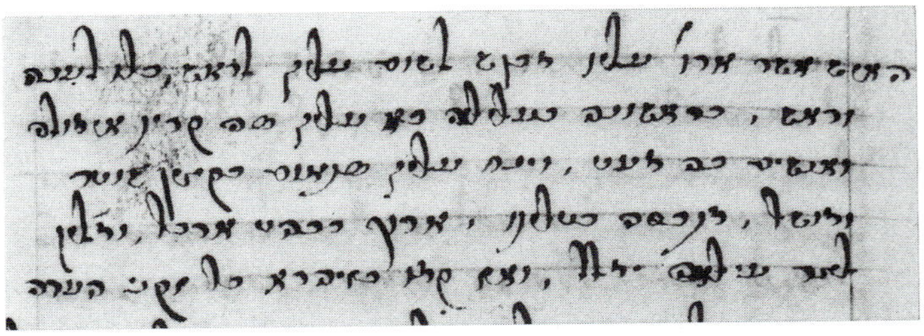

25

Figure 23 Yevanic cursive script used for a copy of Joseph Albo's Sefer ha-Ikkarim *made in 1469. Rome, Vatican Library, Ebr. 257, fol. 309b.*

Figure 24. The Italkian cursive script in a manuscript of the 10th or 11th century. London, British Museum, Ms. Add. 27214, fol. 202a.

Figure 25. Halakhic letter in Italkian cursive script written by Isaac of Morell in 1581. London, British Museum, Ms. Add. 27012, fol. 101a.

Figure 26. Italkian cursive script of 17th century. London, British Museum, Ms. Add. 27085, fol. 28b.

Figure 27. A receipt in Ẓarphatic cursive script written in 1182 with a quill. London, British Museum, Ms. Add. ch. 1250v.

Figure 28. A 14th-century businessman's notes in Ẓarphatic cursive script. Dijon, Archives du Département de la Côte d'Or, B. 10. 410.

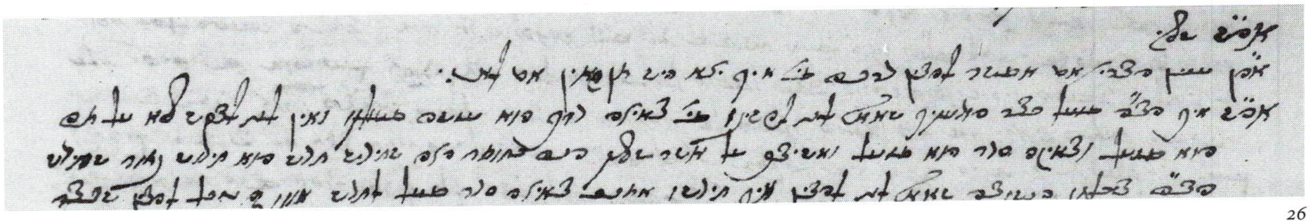

26

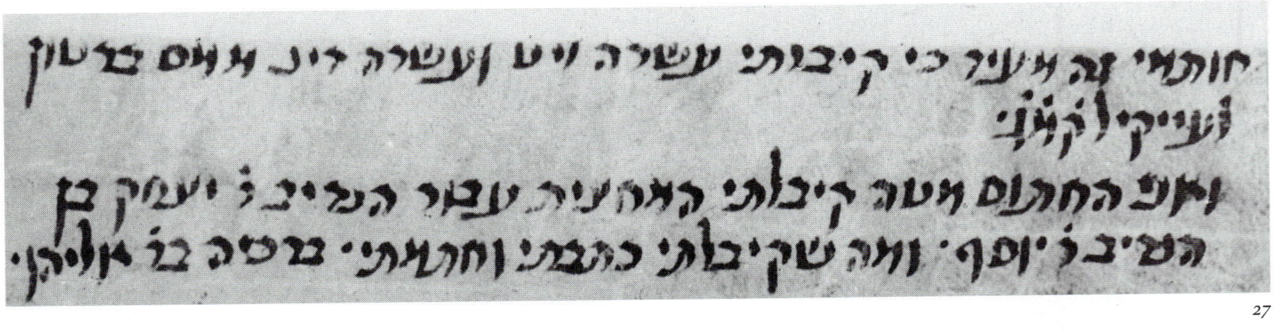

27

28

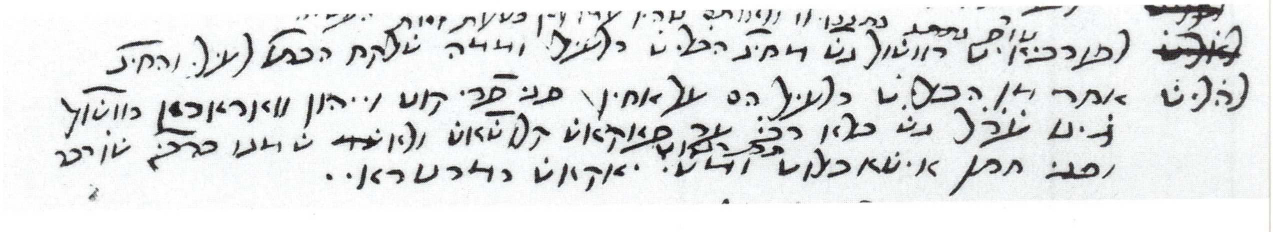

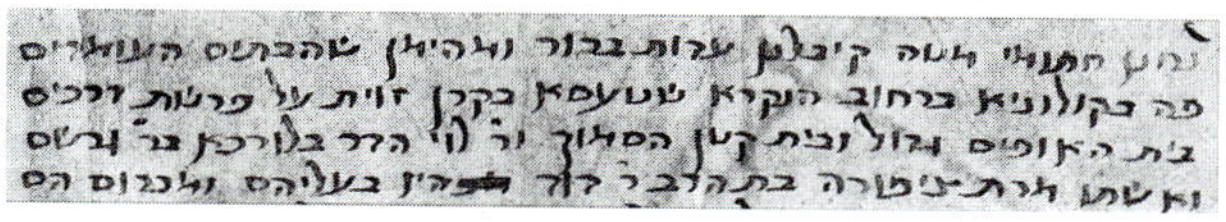

29

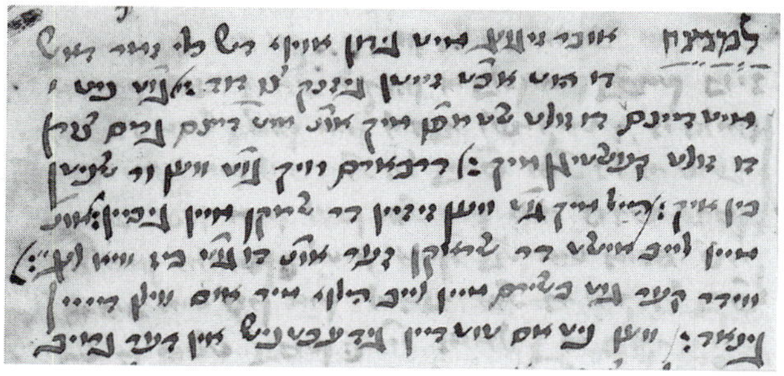

30

Figure 29. Diposition of a witness in Ashkenazic cursive script, 1266 C.E. *Cologne, Rheinisches Museum, Judenschreinsbuch, No. 87, fol.4b.*

Figure 30. Psalm 6 written in Yiddish in Ashkenazic cursive script, 1532. Hamburg, Staats- und Universitaetsbibliothek, Cod. hebr. 181, fol.3r.

Figure 31. Yiddish version of the Book of Esther in Ashkenazic cursive script, 1631. Hamburg, Staats- und Universitaetsbibliothek, Cod. hebr. 144, fol. 31v.

Figure 32. Yevano-Karaitic cursive script, 16th to 17th century C.E. *Paris, Bibliothéque Nationale, Ms. Héb. 1014.*

Figure 33. Yevano-Karaitic cursive script 1759. Cambridge University Library, Ms. Add. 2660, fol. 21b.

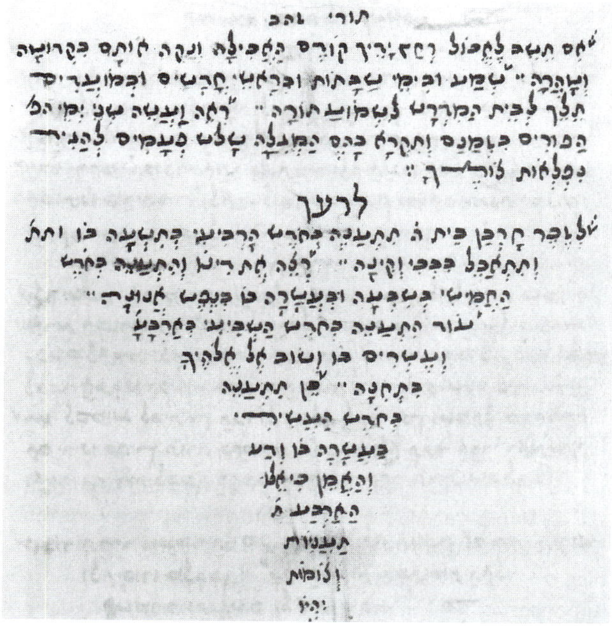

33

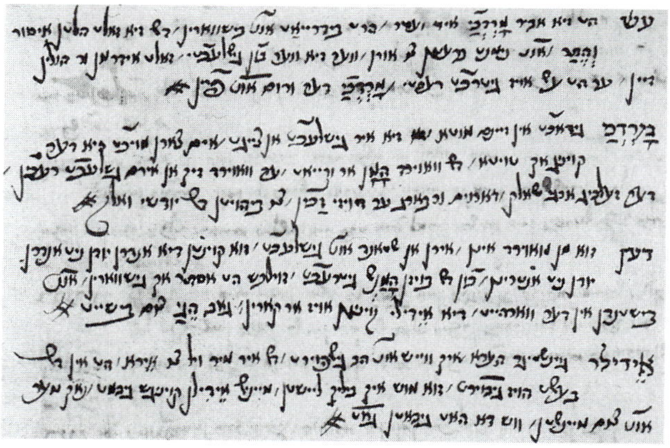

31

32

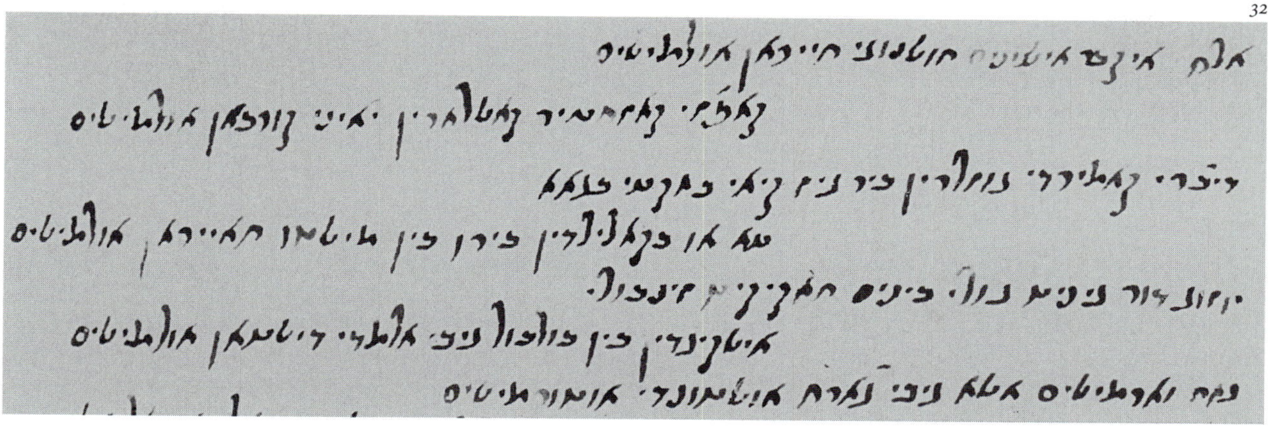

looks like horizontal figure 8 – the strokes increasingly curved until even the one on the left, originally a straight line, had become circular. In the centuries that followed there was some slight development. For instance, in *he* (figure 26) the left stroke and the link with the right stroke merged to form a dot; the result is that the letter is now virtually identical with modern Ashkenazic *pe*.

ẒARPHATIC TYPE. The Ẓarphatic writing of figure 27 (12th century) might appear at first glance to be related to the Italkian type. However, it is unmistakably of a different kind. Perhaps the similarity arises from their both having been written with the same sort of pen – a quill – while the other types from early centuries previously dealt with here, were produced by a reed pen. The forms in figure 27 are all in a properly developed cursive, although they do not differ greatly in their basic structure from the square letters. The most characteristic are the *alef, lamed, mem, final pe*, and *shin*. This document is written in a book hand. Figure 28 (14th century) is in a less careful hand of the same type.

ASHKENAZIC TYPE. The early Ashkenazic cursive is practically identical with that of the Ẓarphatic. Figure 29 (13th century) is not as carefully written as figure 26. It is not a book hand. During the next three centuries considerable changes took place (figures 30 and 31): the downstrokes of *dalet* and *zayin* end in a curve which is open to the left; *tet* has become a tick; the middle part of *lamed* has vanished, the letter being almost a straight line; in *mem* the left stroke is parallel with the right one and is generally of equal length – they are connected by a bridge, which is mostly horizontal.

KARAITIC TYPE. There are two extant specimens of Karaitic cursive. Figure 32 (16th–17th centuries) represents Yevano-Karaitic. The right strokes of *alef* are high up; *gimmel* resembles *nun* but its bottom stroke is straight and horizontal; the upper part of *tet* is in the upper half of the line; *lamed* has lost the middle stroke; the right stroke of *mem* is extremely short, the left stroke is very long, starting high above the line; final *mem* is circular; the same is true of *samekh* but it has a tail on the left; the inner stroke of *shin* is joined to the top of the left one, slanting down from above. The forms of Crimean Yevano-Karaitic (figure 33; 18th century) are more or less the same in structure as in figure 32 and yet the writing looks very dissimilar. There is a structural difference in the *dalet* and *zayin*, where the downstroke finally turns rightward.

[Solomon Asher Birnbaum]

SQUARE SCRIPT

Sixth Century B.C.E. to Second Century C.E.

The square script belongs to the Aramaic branch of Semitic writing. In the Babylonian-Assyrian and Persian empires the Aramaic language and its alphabet became the official language and script of the administration. They were also adopted by the Jews in Babylonia and elsewhere, and later penetrated Palestine. When the new script was officially adopted for the writing of Torah scrolls the change-over from the Paleo-Hebrew alphabet was complete although the old script was twice revived, centuries later, for legends on the coins under the Hasmoneans and under Bar Kokhba. The oldest dated document in the new script and language comes from Egypt (515 B.C.E.; figure 1). The script is highly stylized, with very thin downstrokes slanting to the left and very thick horizontals (or near-horizontals) dominating the picture. From this general Aramaic writing the Jews and the other peoples of the region – Palmyrene, Nabateans, etc. – in the course of the next few centuries developed types of their own. By the end of the fourth century B.C.E. the Jewish forms closely approached the full-fledged Jewish script (figure 2). Therefore it should properly be termed Jewish script rather than "Hebrew script," since it was used by Jews, not by Hebrews (nobody would apply the term Hebrews to the Jews of that period). In speaking of this writing the designation Hebrew script should therefore be dropped; it could then be employed to describe the alphabet of the Hebrews. This would, in addition, have the advantage of conforming to the usage in the ancient sources, where *ketav ivri* denotes the pre-Exilic script. So long as the name Hebrew script continues to be used for the Jewish script, the script of the Hebrews ought to be designated Paleo-Hebrew, the term introduced in *The Hebrew Scripts* (see bibliography). In the second half of the third century B.C.E. Hebrew writing was already on the threshold of the square script (figure 3). By the middle of the second century B.C.E. further development had noticeably taken place (figure 4) and during the first centuries B.C.E. and C.E. the final form had almost been reached (figure 5).

The evolution from the sixth century B.C.E. was considerable. Figure 6 illustrates this step by step, through the six stages of the final *mem*. The top of the first form is a cursive development of the original W-form (which has been preserved in the Roman M).

Appearance of the Letters

For the second century C.E. it is already possible to speak of the square script proper (figure 7). By the seventh century (figure 8) almost every letter of the alphabet had either a top bar or a head, while many had a base as well. The invisible frame within which a letter was written was a rectangular oblong standing on one of its shorter sides. Only rarely was this frame a square. Hence the name square script is really a misnomer. At certain periods in certain regions the frame was not rectangular, the downstrokes being oblique while the top and bottom strokes remained horizontal (see, for instance, figures 24, 29, 34). After the first few centuries the evolution proceeded at a very slow pace. The changes did not involve the structure of the letters but the style of the writing. Perhaps by the seventh century (figure 8) there was a tendency for the horizontals to be thick, while the downstrokes were thinner, or thin. The first dated manuscript (from 896 C.E.) of the fully developed calligraphic kind (figure 9) was written in a style which has remained virtually unchanged ever since (figure 10). While the horizontals had originally played a very minor role compared with the uprights, the opposite extreme had now been reached. The near-polarization of horizontal and upright strokes had not resulted in a dull geometrical pattern: some oblique strokes were left outside the system, some strokes extended above or below the line – the strokes themselves were not geometrically straight but slightly curved, wavy, or tapering. The great weight of the horizontals created a clear impression of continuity along the line. Half the letters rested on their bases, and the other half partly stood and were partly carried by their neighbors, in the manner of a suspension bridge. But, although strongly linked together, they did not lose their individuality. The evolution of the forms from the sixth century B.C.E. is here illustrated by the letters *he* and *samekh* (figure 11). It can be seen that the change in the first five centuries (see lines 1–5) was much greater than during the last eight (see lines 6–7).

One detail in the development of the forms – the rise of the *litterae dilatabiles* – requires special mention, because it falls outside the category of structural evolution, and is of a purely aesthetic nature. Certain letters, when they stood at the left end of a line but did not reach as far as the actual edge of the column, had their top bars extended to that edge so that the line might be of the same length as all the others. The effect was to make the left edge of the column neat and straight, and ensure that the general appearance of the page should be pleasing to the eye. This device – dilatation is the term introduced in *The Hebrew Scripts* – no doubt arose spontaneously and spread among the scribes because it combined the virtues of simplicity and effectiveness. These forms do not appear to antedate the sixth to seventh centuries C.E.

Although an increasing number of Jews lived outside Palestine after the Babylonian Exile, there must have been close contact between them and Palestinian Jewry. This is evidenced by the fact that for a long time no divergent development took place. But such a state of affairs could not continue beyond a point, as forms do not remain static forever and writing, like language, is subject to change. As the dispersion of the Jews increased, separate developments set in, and each distinct cultural branch which grew up had its own type of writing. In some cases differentiation was restricted within narrow limits but in others divergence went very far, even though the conscious aim of the scribes was to reproduce faithfully the traditional forms of the letters, especially in the copying of synagogue scrolls. Other than in scrolls, *tefillin*, and *mezuzot*, the square script was used in biblical, liturgical, and talmudical codices but hardly ever in any other books. Certain letter forms were reserved for the scroll script.

Basic Types

The main groups or types of writing which came into being in the various Jewries are Ashkenazic in Germany and in Ashkenazi settlements elsewhere, Babylonian, Egyptian, Italkian, Maaravic in the Maghreb, Palestinian-Syrian, Parsic in Persia and Parsi settlements, Sephardic in the Iberian Peninsula and Sephardi settlements, Temanic in the Yemen, Yevanic in the Balkans and Crimea, and Ẓarphatic in northern France. There were also some small groups, e.g., the scripts of the Jews in China or India. The Karaites developed three main types of their own (see below).

It is hardly ever possible to establish, with any measure of certainty, the genetic relation between the types, because the small amount of early material known was penned centuries after the group in question came into existence, and by then time had effaced any obvious clues. Sephardic appears to be an extension of Maaravic. Maaravic is presumably a continuation of the Palestinian-Babylonian-Egyptian complex. Parsic, though very individual, might be descended from Babylonian, and the same possibly holds good of the equally individual Temanic. There is, however, one exception where the relationship between two types is beyond doubt: the case of Ashkenazic and Ẓarphatic. Ashkenazic is definitely the continuation of Ẓarphatic.

Egypt Types

Outside Palestine only the Egyptian branch provides pre-square material (see above, figures 1 and 2). The oldest datable Bible manuscript, written in Egypt in a calligraphic hand, is of about the fifth century C.E. (figure 12). Although earlier than figure 8, it is in a more regular, formal style. A non-biblical manuscript dated three centuries later is written in an almost modern hand (figure 13).

The final stage of calligraphic development in Egypt was reached in the 10th and 11th centuries (figure 14), when horizontals were thick but not excessively so.

Babylon Type

The forms in figure 15, a non-biblical Babylonian manuscript of about the eighth century, are even less formal than those of the corresponding manuscript of the same time in Egypt but the forms in the biblical manuscript in figure 16 (written in 916 C.E.) are practically identical with those in the corresponding manuscript written in the Egyptian type; however, in figure 16 there is not much contrast between the thickness of the horizontals and verticals.

Parsic Type

The Parsic type, i.e., the script of the Persian Jews and their descendants outside Persia, is presumably derived from the Babylonian one, although there is too little early comparative material available to arrive at a paleographical decision. The earliest available documents already show a highly individual development. By the 16th century (figure 17, of 1571) the forms were so completely different from the Babylonian ones that the gulf must by then have been in existence for a very long time. The style was much less regular and formal, and there was an absence of monumentality. The horizontal strokes were very thick, the downstrokes thin. This contrast was already in evidence, though to a less marked degree, in the tenth century, when it is encountered in Palestine and Egypt – a striking example of how, in spite of geographical separation, new developments spread from group to group.

Temanic Type

Yemen was the southernmost early seat of Jewish writing. The available material begins approximately with the 12th century (figure 18). The contrast in thickness between horizontals and downstrokes was by then in full force. The term for this type as used in *The Hebrew Scripts* is Temanic. Like the Parsic type it is not regular and formal, and thus contrasts sharply with the Palestinian-Syrian, Egyptian, and Babylonian types. However, Temanic does not otherwise resemble Parsic, as a comparison of a manuscript of 1468 (figure 19) with the Parsic one of 1571 (figure 17) will show.

Maaravic Type

The northwestern shore of Africa – the Maghreb – was the home of the Maaravic type of the Jewish script, which had presumably followed the line of migration from Egypt westward, its forms being closely related to those of the Palestinian-Syrian/Egyptian/Babylonian complex. The general impression given by the script of the earliest available dated Maaravic Bible manuscript of 946 C.E. seems to point to a closer relationship with the Palestinian than with the Egyptian and Babylonian types. The contrast between thick and thin strokes is clear but not so great as in some of the above-mentioned types. In the non-biblical fragment of 978 C.E. (figure 21) the writing is slightly less formal. But Maaravic is connected not only with the east; there is also a close link with Europe, i.e., with the Sephardic type of the Iberian Peninsula.

Sephardic Type

This type is practically identical with Maaravic. It is to be assumed that Sephardic was introduced from Africa. However, available material of both types, which is of rather late origin, provides no definite proof. An epitaph which is of an unusually earlier date (sixth century, figure 22), and contains some rather archaic forms, also provides no proof in this respect. The possibly oldest pen-written Sephardic manuscript available comes from the ninth-tenth century (figure 23). Here the contrast between thick horizontals and thin down strokes is great. The writing is considerably less formalized than that of the Palestinian-Syrian-Egyptian-Babylonian complex. That stage was reached, and surpassed, by the 12th century.

The biblical manuscript of 1207, illustrated in figure 24, shows forms which are harmonious and regular without being rigid. The next three centuries saw hardly any change at all, and, upon the introduction of the printing press, the typeface was designed on the basis of contemporary manuscript forms. Through a historical accident only this typeface has survived to the present day, while the two other early typefaces (see below) disappeared. In the course of the centuries it deteriorated very much aesthetically, as a comparison between figure 24 and printed books from various ages will show.

The Sephardic type was not restricted to the Iberian Peninsula. It spread to the north of it; it was also employed in Provence, Languedoc, and Comtat Venaissin. When contact with Spain ceased, upon the expulsion of the Jews in 1492, the script north of the Pyrenees and that of the exiled Sephardim started developing on divergent lines. In the new settlements, too, differentiation arose. The form used in the largest and most important of these – that in Turkey – is the main representative of the Sephardic type.

Yevanic Types

With Sephardic the Jewish alphabet entered Europe from the southwest. But its southeastern entry was perhaps of even greater consequence. Hardly any material has survived from Greek-speaking Jewry in Asia Minor and Greece during the Hellenistic period. However, slightly more material, the oldest available documents of the Yevanic type in Europe, has survived from Magna Graecia. These documents are also the earliest extant written in the Jewish script in Europe (see above, the section Cursive Script, figure 22). The oldest available example of the square style comes from Asia Minor (figure 25). It clearly belongs to the neighborhood of figure 5. No early biblical manuscript is available from this group but to judge by the conditions in other types the tenth-century fragment shown in figure 26 might indicate that there was a calligraphic biblical square style then in existence.

Italkian Types

The next stage was in Italy. Is the Jewry of this country descended mainly from the Jews who lived there in antiquity, or is the main source perhaps the settlement in Magna Graecia? If the latter, the Italkian type would have its roots not in the Palestinian but in the Yevanic type. The documents (inscriptions) start about 300 C.E. (figure 27). The earliest square manuscript, a biblical one, is of 979 C.E., the oldest from Europe that is dated (figure 28). The contrast between thick and thin strokes is strong. The style of the writing is quite unlike that of the contemporary western Oriental groups or that of Maaravic and Sephardic. Comparing the forms with those of figure 10, it would be most difficult, at first glance, to say exactly what makes them appear so different although the corresponding letters are constructed identically. In the 15th century the thick/thin feature was – perhaps under Ashkenazic influence – so pronounced that the script looked as if it consisted only of horizontals (figure 29, of 1466). When, not much later, the typeface was designed, this kind of writing was not chosen as a model (figure 30).

Ẓarphatic Types

In central and northern France the Sephardic type that was encountered in southern France was not found, a result of the southern provinces coming only very late to the French Crown. It is therefore misleading to use, in this context, the word French, with its wide connotation. The traditional Hebrew name for the northern and central region, Ẓarefat, is the source of the term Ẓarphatic, introduced in *The Hebrew Scripts*. In the earliest manuscripts certain similarities with the Italkian type can be noted. Was there perhaps a genetic

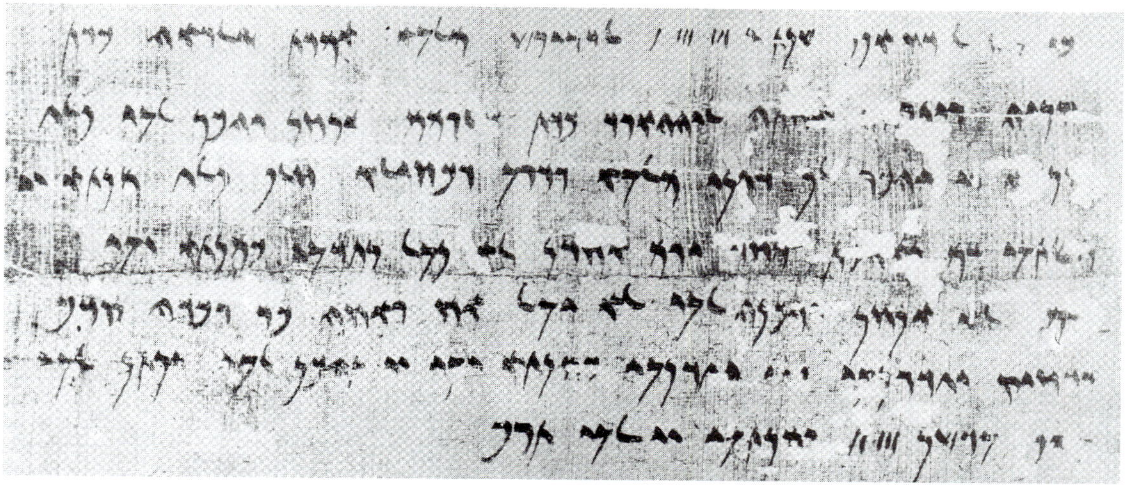

Figure 1. The oldest known example of Aramaic square script, a papyrus deed of 515 B.C.E.

Figure 2. The transition to Jewish square script is shown in this document of c. 300 B.C.E. *Berlin, Staatliche Museum, Papyrus 10678.*

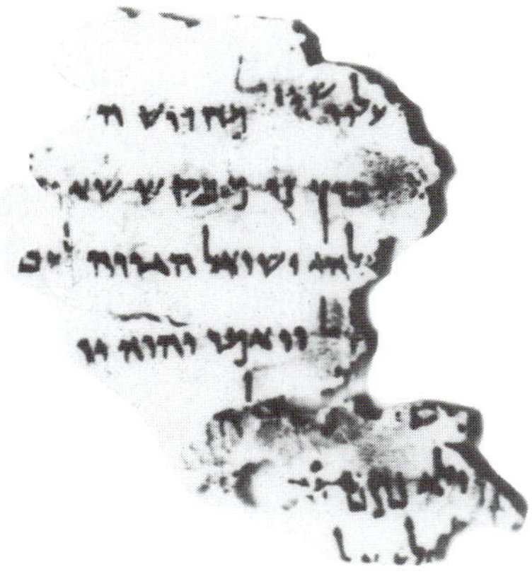

Figure 3. The earliest example of Jewish square script: a passage from I Sam., c. 230 B.C.E. *Jerusalem, Israel Museum, IV Q Sam. b.*

SQUARE SCRIPT

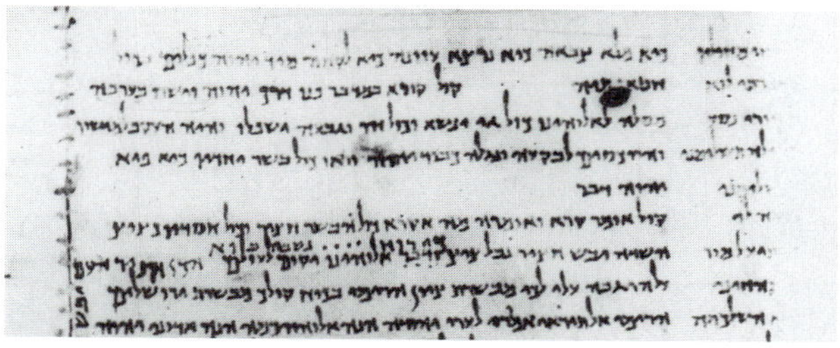

Figure 4. Square script of the mid-second century B.C.E. *in one of the Dead Sea Scrolls. Jerusalem, Israel Museum, Shrine of the Book, Isaiah Scroll A.*

Figure 5. Tablet recording reburial of the remains of King Uzziah between first century B.C.E. *and first century* C.E. *Jerusalem, Israel Museum.*

Figure 6. Evolution of square script illustrated in the final mem.

Figure 7. Passage from Exodus in Jewish square script, first half of the second century C.E *Jerusalem, Israel Dept. of Antiquities and Museums.*

Figure 8. Excerpt from Palestinian Targum, c. seventh century C.E. *in Jewish square script. Cambridge University Library, T-S. 20. 155.*

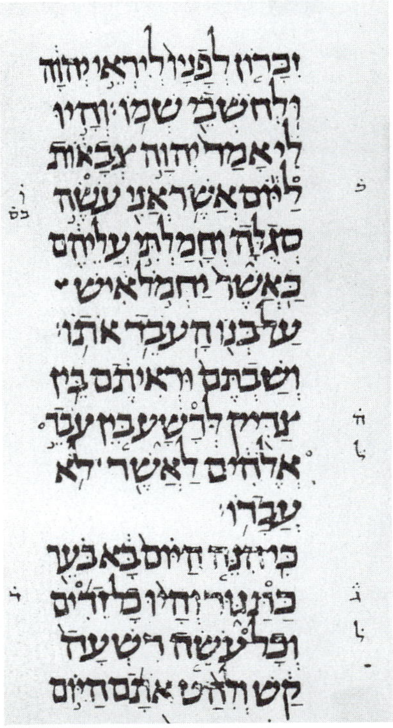

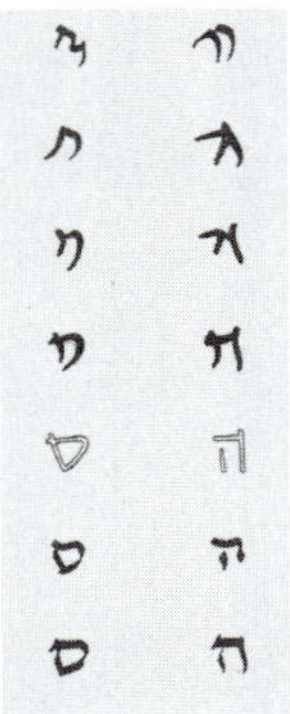

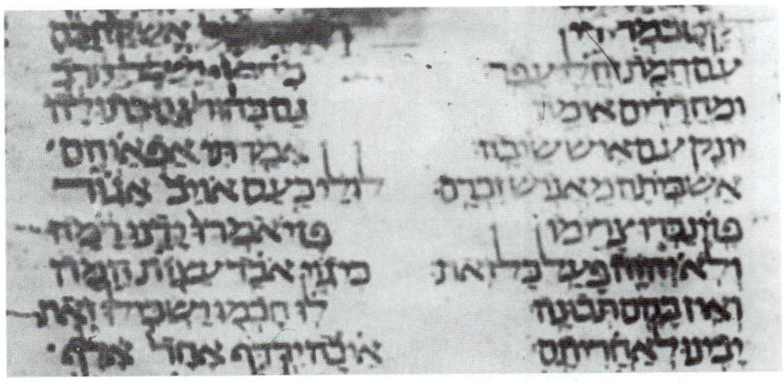

Figure 10. Passage from Deuteronomy in Jewish square script 930 C.E. *Leningrad, Public Library, II Firkovitch.*

Figure 11. Evolution of the letters he *and* samekh *between the sixth century* B.C.E. *and the seventh century* C.E.

Figure 9. Earliest extant example of the fully developed Jewish square script, 896 C.E. Ibid., *Fig. 92.*

Figure 12. The oldest datable Bible in Egyptian square script, c. fifth century C.E. *London, Egypt Exploration Society, Antinoöpolis Fragment No. 47.*

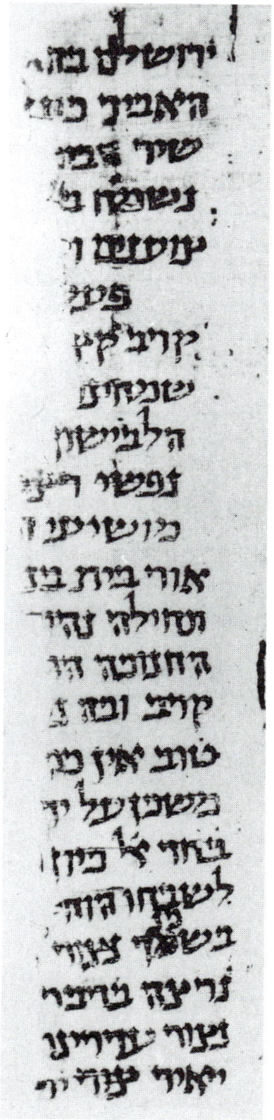

Figure 13. Piyyut by Eleazar Kallir in Egyptian square script c. eighth century C.E. *Cambridge University Library, T-S. 6. H. 13.*

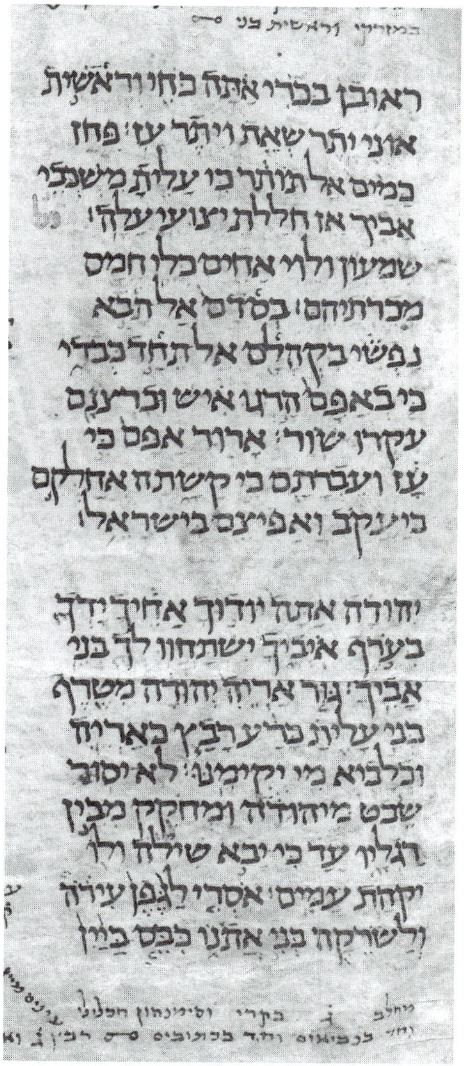

Figure 14. Final development of Egyptian square script: manuscript of Genesis c. tenth century C.E. *Ann Arbor, University of Michigan Library, Ms. Heb. 88, fol. 39a.*

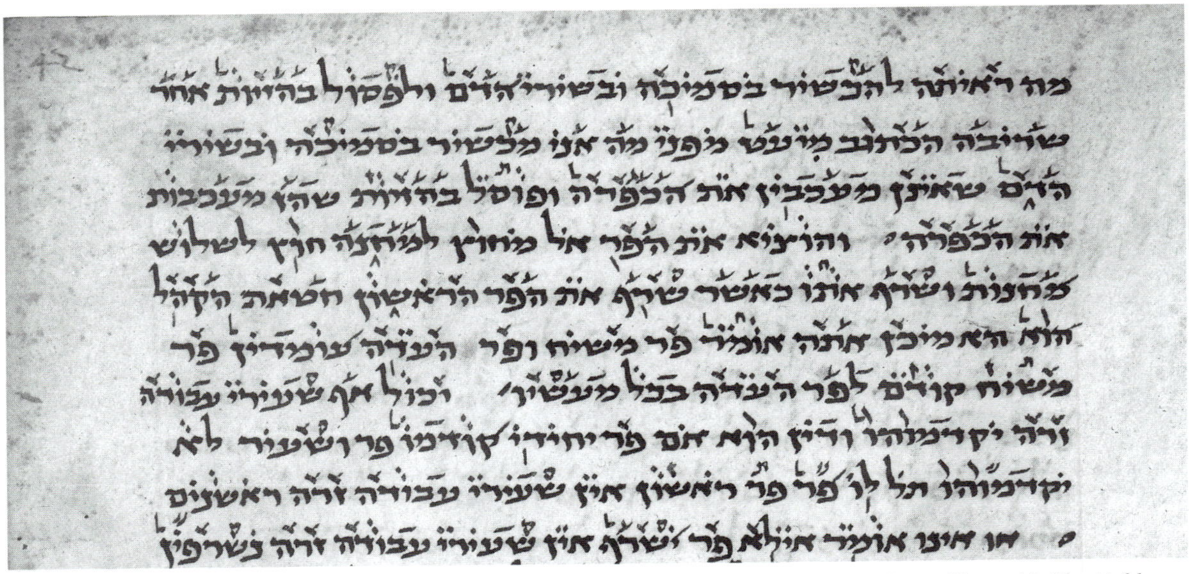

Figure 15. Babylonian square script used for a halakhic Midrash to Leviticus, c. eighth century C.E. *Rome, Vatican Library, Ms. Ebr. 66, fol. 42a.*

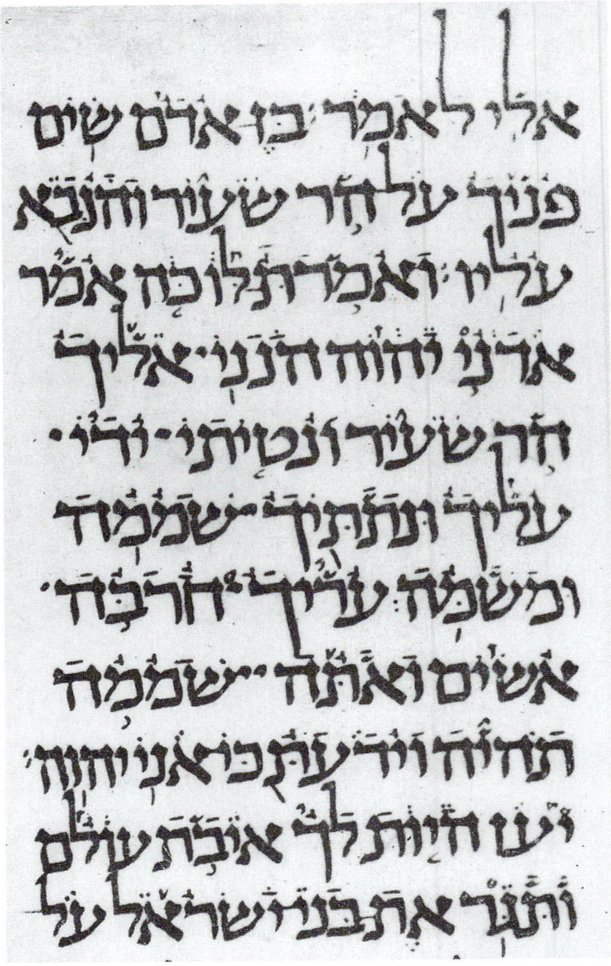

Figure 16. Excerpt from Book of Ezekiel in Babylonian square script, 916 C.E. *Leningrad, Public Library, Firkovitch Ms. B.3.*

Figure 17. Passage from Leviticus in Parsic square script 1571 C.E. *New York, Jewish Theological Seminary of America, Ms. Adler 313.*

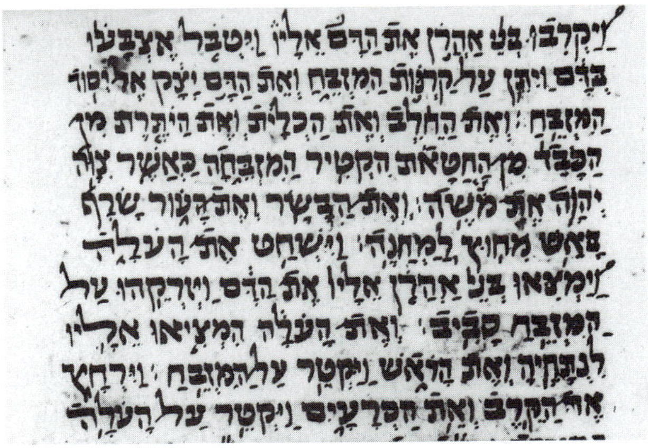

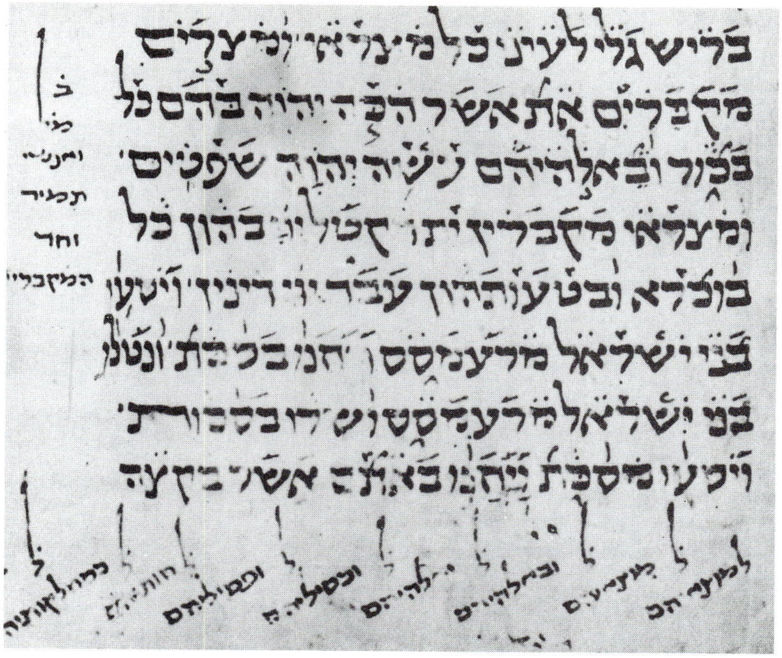

Figure 18. Temanic square script, 11th–12th century C.E. *A Yemenite manuscript of Numbers with Targum. London, British Museum, Ms. Or. 1407.*

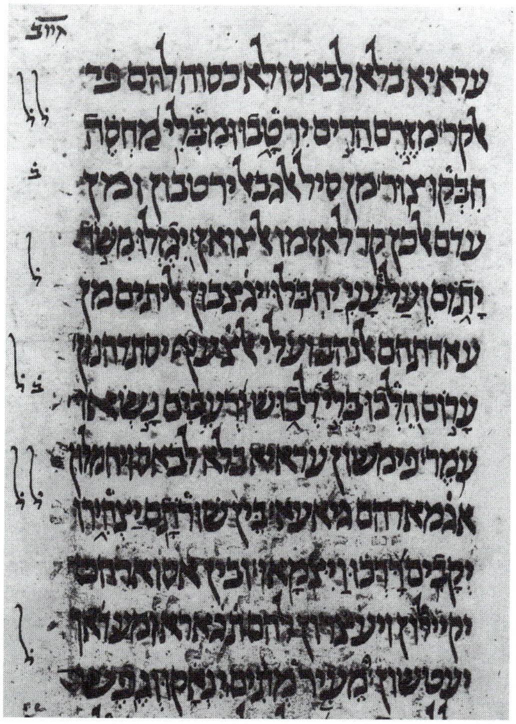

Figure 19. Passage from Job in Temanic square script, with Arvic translation, 1468. London, British Museum, Ms. Or. 2375, fol. 105a.

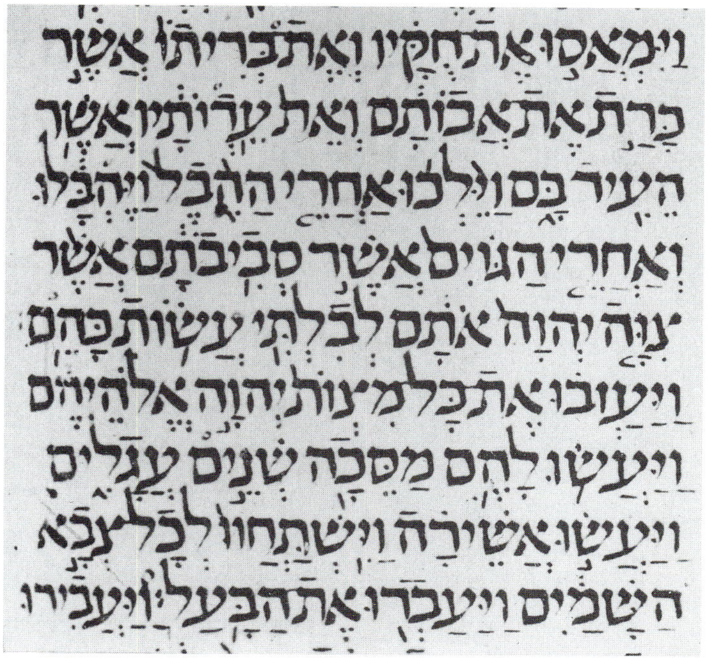

Figure 20. Earliest dated Bible manuscript in Maaravic square script, 946 C.E.

Figure 21. Fragment of legal deposition in Maaravic square script, 978 C.E. *Cambridge University Library, T-S. 12,468.*

Figure 22. Epitaph in Sephardic square script from Tortosa Cathedral, Spain. Sixth century C.E.

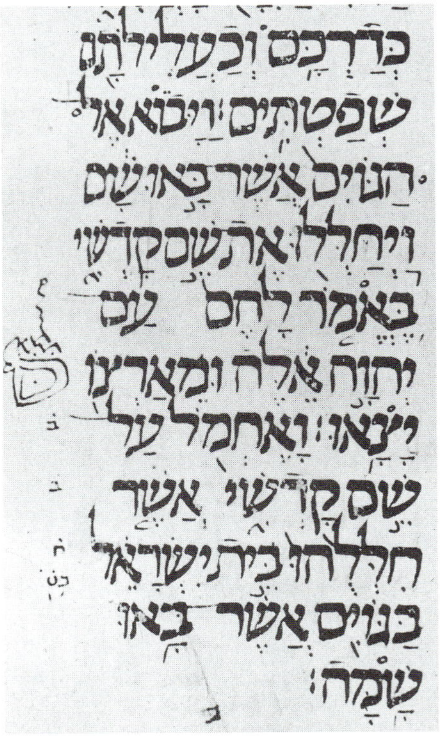

Figure 23. Sephardic square script ninth–tenth century C.E.

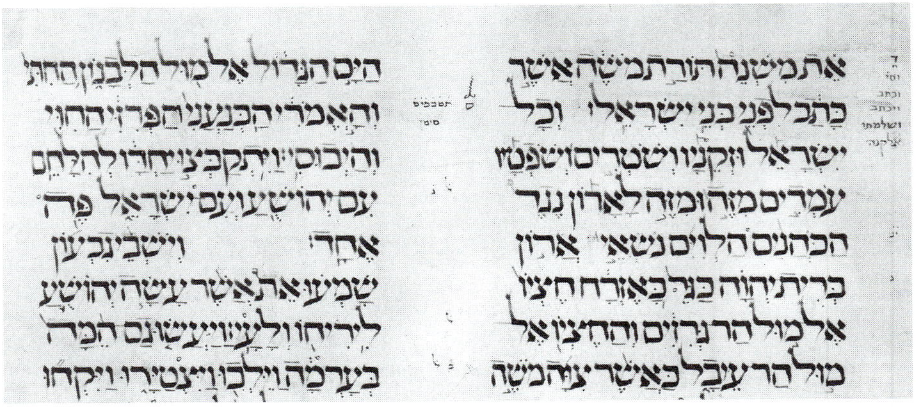

Figure 24. Passage from Joshua in Sephardic square script, 1207. Paris Bibliothèque Nationale, Ms. 2235, Heb. 82, fol. 10.

Figure 25. Epitaph in Yevanic square script, early second century C.E. *Turkey, Afyon Museum.*

Figure 26. Yevanic square script in a Hebrew-Greek glossary of the tenth century C.E. *Leningrad Public Library, Antonin Evr. III B.*

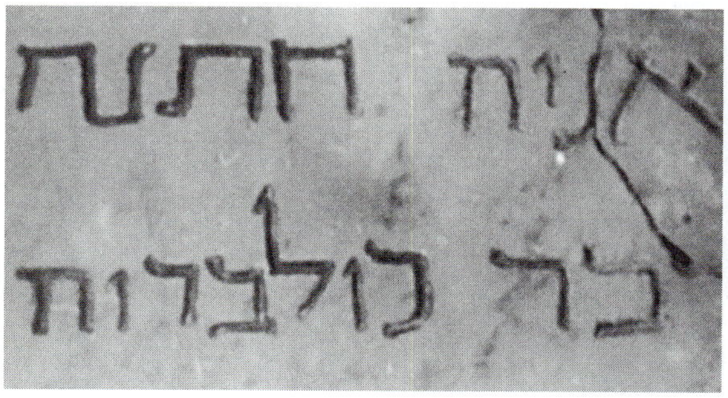

Figure 27. Epitaph in the Monteverde Catacomb, Rome, in Italkian square script, c. 300 C.E.

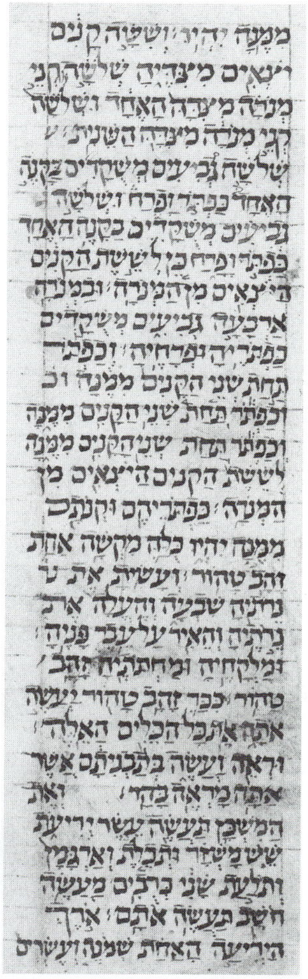

Figure 28. The oldest European Ms. in Italkian square script. Bible dated 979 C.E. *Rome, Vat. Lib., Ms. Urb. Ebr. 2, fol. 41a.*

Figure 29. Extract from a prayer book in Italkian square script, 1466. London, British Museum, Ms. Harl. 5656, fol. 273a.

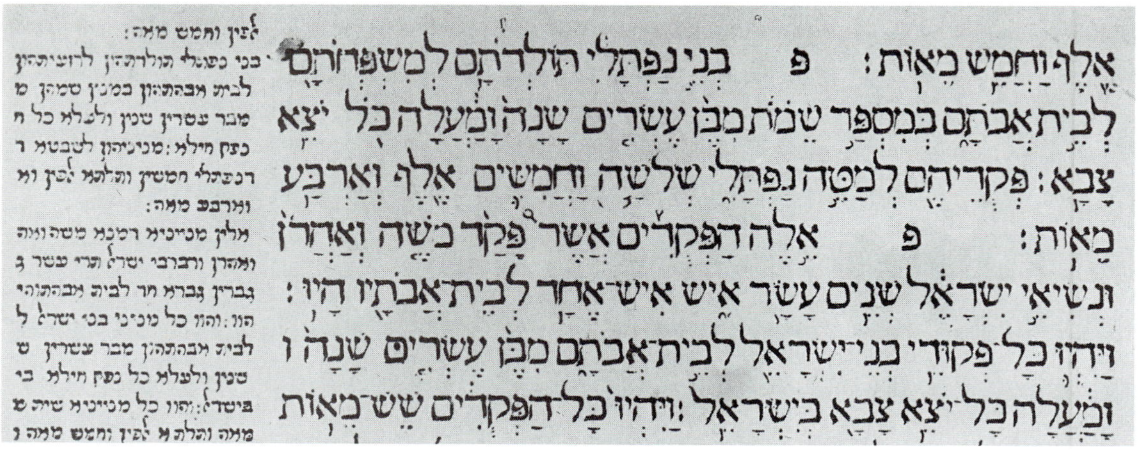

Figure 30. Early printed Bible in Italian square script, 1482.

Figure 32. Epitaph from Mainz, Germany, in Ashkenazic square script, 1082 C.E.

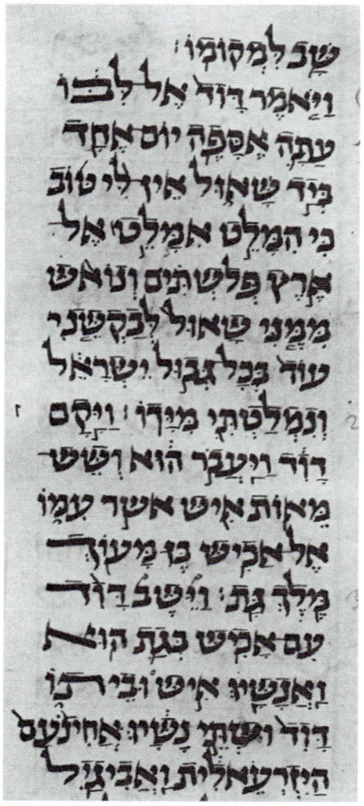

Figure 31. A 12th-century Bible Ms. in Ẓarphatic square script, London, B.M., Ms. Add. 21161, fol. 6a.

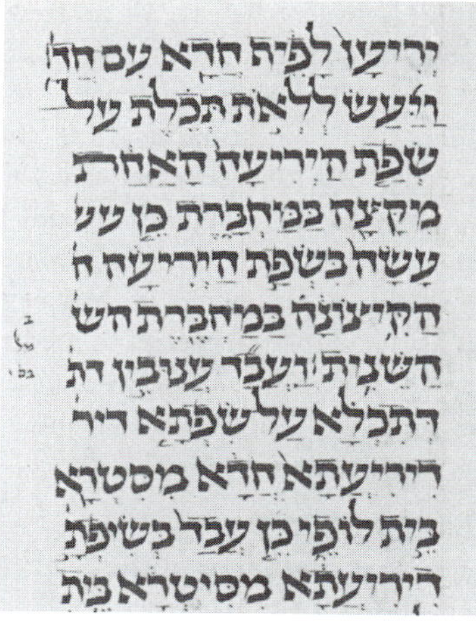

Figure 33. Extract from Bible of 1236 in Ashkenazic square script. Milan Biblioteca Ambrosiana, B. 30 inf., fol. 96r.

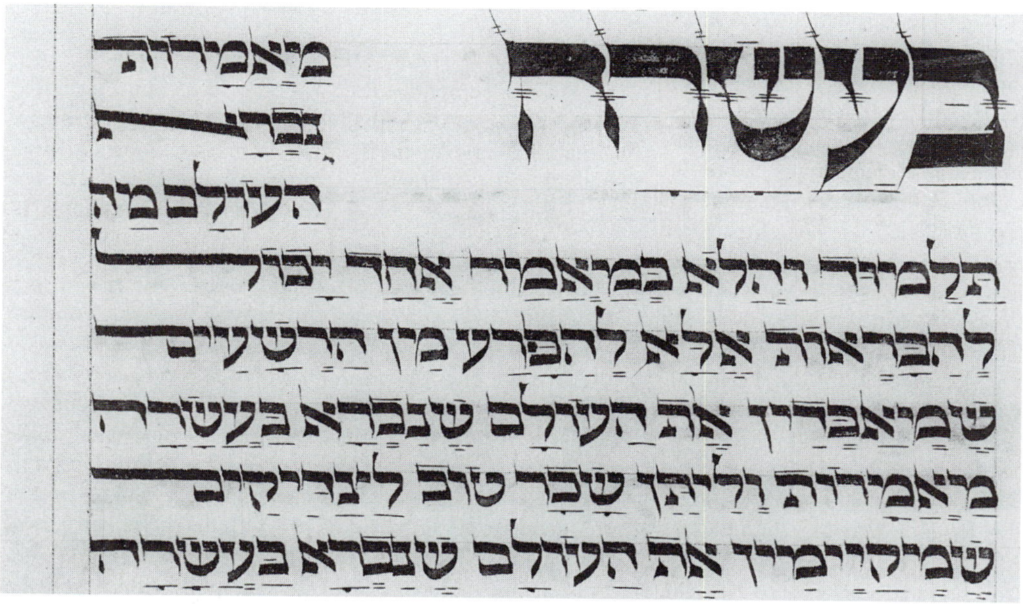

Figure 34. Extract from the tractate Avot *in Ashkenazic square script, 1432. Karlsruhe, Badische Landesbibliothek, Ms. Reuchlin 4, fol. 239r.*

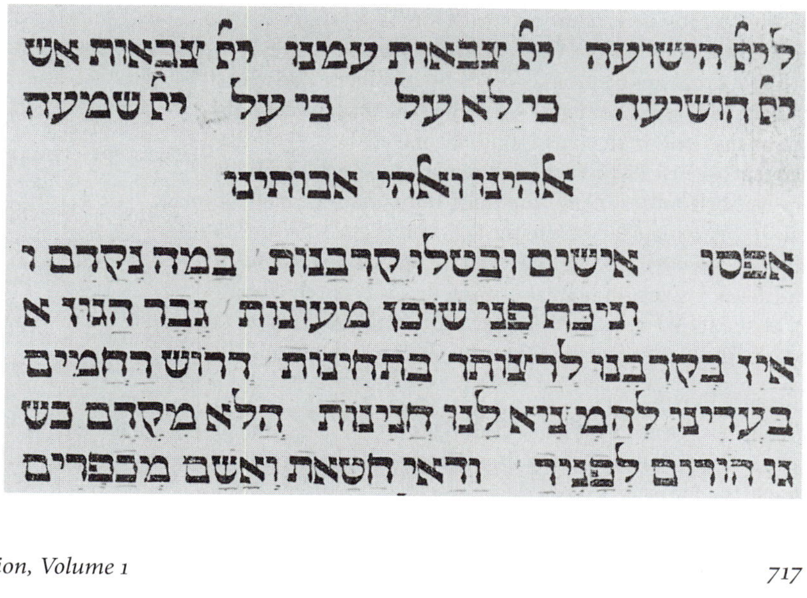

Figure 35. Fifteenth-century typeface in Ashkenazic square script.

relation between the two, or do they represent separate, independent developments going back to Roman times? Current information is insufficient to answer the question, as no available Ẓarphatic manuscripts antedate the 12th century (figure 31). The difference between thick and thin strokes was strongly marked. Ẓarphatic did not long survive the expulsion of the Jews from France (1394) because the refugees were absorbed into the Jewries of their new homes. The Ẓarphatic type also included the script of medieval England, where the Ẓarphatim had settled in Norman times. It came to an end after only two centuries, when the Jews were expelled from England in 1290.

Ashkenazic Types

The earliest specimens of the Ashkenazic type (Ashkenaz is the traditional Hebrew name for Germany) show identity of script with Ẓarphatic. It therefore may be concluded that the Ashkenazic group is descended from Ẓarphati Jewry – which confirms the existing tradition to that effect, and corroborates the evidence provided by the Romance element in the Yiddish language. Available Ashkenazic material dates from the first half of the 11th century, consisting of epitaphs, the first dated one being of 1034, while the earliest manuscripts can be ascribed to the 12th century; of these, the first dated manuscript in square script is from 1236. Ashkenazic is one of the three richest sources of codices, the others being Sephardic and Italkian. The early epitaphs showed well-proportioned, pleasing lettering (figure 32, of 1082). Here there was no difference between the thickness of horizontals and verticals, while the Bible manuscripts of even earlier dates in the other types already had that feature fully developed. The earliest dated Ashkenazic Bible manuscript had the thick/thin contrast (figure 33, of 1236). By the 15th century the domination of the horizontal strokes had reached its climax (figure 34, of 1432): the horizontals were longer, i.e., the letters were wider. In addition, the letters had a characteristic stance. In all groups and during all periods the downstrokes slanted somewhat to the right, so that the letters leaned slightly to the left. But now the slant had become considerably more pronounced (compare figure 34 with, for instance, figure 29, which was otherwise written in the same kind of script). Curves and undulating elements decreased, the forms became slightly rigid, though less so than in the printers' typeface (figure 35): When the typecutters transferred the handwritten forms onto the metal, they regularized them geometrically. They also diminished the preponderance of the horizontal strokes. The thick horizontals began to be taken over for lapidary use in the 13th century; they became the rule toward its end. Detailed research might establish whether the development of the thick/thin feature was purely a matter of aesthetics, or whether there was a special reason, or a partial one, perhaps the transition from the reed pen to the quill.

Karaitic Types

Finally, there was the script of the Karaites. They had cut themselves off from rabbinical Judaism in early times but continued to use the Jewish script, as they considered themselves to be the real Jews. In their hands it underwent a distinctive development, which is not surprising as there is an intimate connection between religion and script throughout history and in all cultures. No single Karaite type existed; in various regions different Karaitic types developed from the Rabbanite types. Material dated from the 11th century onward is available, but on the whole is sparse. There was a southern Karaitic type in Egypt and Palestine, Yevano-Karaitic in the Byzantine regions, Parso-Karaitic in Persia.

From the above review of the square script it may be seen that there are many unsolved problems. An answer to some might be found by further research. For the fact is that the study of the Hebrew, i.e., the Jewish script, is, after all, still only at its beginnings. And the field is vast – stretching over more than two thousand years and many regions of the Old World.

[Solomon Asher Birnbaum]

MASHAIT SCRIPT

Cursive was sometimes used as a book hand when, of course, more care was taken with the writing. But this did not involve an approximation to the square; it led to elaboration and ornamentality of a different kind, and thus to the shaping of a new style, the mashait script (incorrectly designated "rabbinic").

The Palestine-Syria Type

This development took place independently in the various types and differed in degree from type to type. Evolution away from the cursive was greatest in the European types; in the Oriental ones there was little of it. A good example is in a specimen of the Palestine-Syria type (figure 1; 11th century). *Alef* has the pure K-structure; in *lamed* the horizontal stroke is omitted; *mem* has no base; final *nun* starts with a curve at the line bottom and is thus rather short; the inner stroke of *shin* tends to be slightly curved and joins the upper part of the left stroke. The forms in figure 2 (15th century) show very little change in detail but the general impression is one of a regular, pleasing hand. *Alef* has the square construction; *zayin* is a wavy line of the question mark type; the *alef* part of the *alef-lamed* ligature is a flattish parabola; final *nun* is a shallow S-wave, starting from the line ceiling; the inner stroke of *shin* is a little curve in horizontal position, joined to the top of the left stroke.

Egypt Type

This type, like Palestine-Syria, is the basic kind of mashait (figure 3; 13th century). The two right strokes of the K-form of *alef* are joined high up to the top of the left stroke; the left stroke of *tet* is of double height but does not extend below the line bottom; *lamed* has the two-stroke form; *mem* has no base; final *nun* starts slightly below the line ceiling; *samekh* is a circle; the middle stroke of *shin* is a horizontal curve joined to the top of the left stroke. Figure 4 (1326) shows a somewhat more formal hand. The two right strokes of *alef* are high up but, in contrast with that in figure 3, the letter is based on the square construction, except that the right stroke joins the outer end of the middle stroke; generally the left stroke does not extend beyond the line ceiling; the *alef* part of the *alef-lamed* ligature is a shallow oblique S-wave, or even a straight line; the left stroke of *samekh* is short and only starts at the line bottom so that the letter is open on the left.

Babylonia Type

Figure 5, a Babylonian specimen (tenth century), also represents the basic kind. The *alef* part of the *alef-lamed* ligature is the unchanged right-hand part of *alef*; *mem* has a short base which is often curved; the inner stroke of *shin* is joined to the middle of the left stroke. The modern hand is shown in figure 6. The right stroke of *alef* is above the line ceiling, joining the top of the left one – it often looks as if it were its top part; the original middle stroke is strongly curved and situated in the upper half of the line height; *gimmel* has the form of what, in most types, is a *nun; he* has the question mark shape; *lamed* has the two-stroke form; the right stroke of *mem* has shrunken to a tiny stroke at the line ceiling – it is now nothing but the beginning of the inner stroke, changing it into a shallow S-wave; the left stroke has become long, filling the whole line height, without, however, extending above the line ceiling; final *mem* is a circle; *ẓadi* is a tall S-wave; the inner stroke of *shin* has become a dot at the top of the left one; the left downstroke of *tav* is severed from the top stroke, beginning at the line bottom and running rather far down.

Parsic Type

Although the individual letter forms of the Parsic type (figure 7; 14th century) present nothing unusual, the general picture is very distinctive. The main reason is the thickness of the horizontal strokes, which has the effect of reducing the distance between the top bar and base to a very narrow gap. *Alef* looks like a Roman N with the two right strokes half up the line height; *zayin* is a flattened Roman Z – it has thus almost returned to the Old Semitic form; the middle stroke of *lamed* has become the top part of the curve which is the lower half of the letter; *mem* has no base; the inner stroke of *shin* is a small curve in horizontal position. The top stroke of *gimmel* in figure 8 (18th century) slants down rightward, and is continued on the line bottom by a horizontal piece, which then slants down leftward below the line bottom. The *zayin* of figure 8 (18th century) has become unsymmetrical: the top stroke is much smaller than the bottom stroke, and sometimes disappears altogether; *mem* has no base; the inner stroke of *shin* has become a small curve, joined to the top of the left one. The modern forms (figure 9) do not differ from those of figure 8, or, for that matter, from modern cursive. The form of the *alef* here is an extremely rare one; what distinguishes *gimmel* from *nun* is that it is an acute angle, whereas *nun* has a rounded corner; the downstroke of *dalet* ends by turning right; *zayin* is of the question mark type; final *mem* is circular but the stroke often ends outside the letter with an upward movement; *samekh* is written in the same way, but when the top is reached a downstroke is added. In the somewhat cursive writing of figures 8 and 9, the thickness of the horizontals is less pronounced. The tall forms of *dalet* and *resh* are very rare, and have obviously been adopted from outside – they were used in the neighboring Babylonian type at least from the late 15th century.

Temanic Type

This type shares with Parsic the thick horizontals and the consequent narrowing down of the space between the top bar and the base (figure 10; 13th century). The main stroke of *alef* has become horizontal, resting on the line ceiling; the *alef* part of the *alef-lamed* ligature is, on the whole, rather angular, as in *alef*; *zayin* is a small – sometimes very small – downstroke, crossed by a short horizontal; *tet* is like the Ashkenazic cursive form but preserves the inner stroke; the middle stroke of *lamed* is straight and horizontal; the right stroke of *mem* very occasionally ends in a short base; final *mem* differs from *samekh* in not having a downstroke on the left; *samekh* is generally less wide, and the downstroke has sometimes become a mere tail, resulting in an open letter. All downstrokes slant rightward. Three centuries later (figure 11; 15th century) the style is rather different, although very little change has taken place in the forms themselves. The horizontals are much less thick. The middle stroke of *alef* begins by being straight and horizontal, and then curves downward but does not reach the line bottom; the *alef* part of the *alef-lamed* ligature generally corresponds to the form in figure 10, but two other types are occasionally to be met with – one is identical with the right part of the square form, and the other is a shallow S-curve, running from the top right to the bottom left; the top of *zayin* is a tick, and the end of the downstroke turns rightward. The general style of figure 11 continues unchanged for two more centuries (figure 12; 17th century). The lower right stroke of *alef* now reaches the line bottom, unless prevented by the preceding letter; the *alef* part of the *alef-lamed* ligature corresponds to the square form; *zayin* is unchanged.

Maaravic Type

The forms of the Maaravic type (figure 13; 14th century) are cursive but written with care and regularity. The same applies to the specimen from the next century (figure 14). Here the parallelism of the downstrokes is developed to an extreme degree. Its impact is intensified by the high and narrow look of the letters, arising from the shortness of the horizontals. The right part of *alef* is high up and very small; *gimmel* is a right angle; final *mem* is an oval in the upper half of the line; *samekh* is triangular. The style of extreme parallelism seems to have been characteristic of one particular region and period, and is not met with again subsequently (see, for instance, figure 15; 18th century). An interesting detail in this specimen is that the *alef* of the big display script used for two initial words, is written in cursive, while the text itself is in mashait.

Sephardic Type

This type (figure 16; 11th century) corresponds to the cursive of the same period (figure 19, Cursive Script). It is clearly well advanced toward a fully developed mashait, although, in many letters – e.g, in *he, mem, shin* – formality is achieved by features from the square. *Alef* is of the K-type; the middle stroke of *lamed* is fused with the downstroke to form a semi-circle in vertical position; final *mem* is more or less round; *samekh* is quadrangular; *shin* consists of a base and three parallel downstrokes, the inner one of which often does not reach the base. In the 15th century Sephardic mashait (figure 17) reached its climax, being a beautiful book of a high order. Legibility, however, is not good, the letters are narrow and very close to each other, and any downstrokes that end leftward touch the next letter. When the right downstroke of a letter does not turn leftward at the line bottom, it stops midway down the line height. Starting from the tip of the left stroke the lower right stroke of *alef* begins horizontally on the line ceiling and ends by curving clown to the middle of the line height; the right top stroke is very thin and short, above the line ceiling; final *mem* consists of two more or less rounded halves, top right and left bottom; the bar of final *pe* has a little stroke at its left end, which represents the original top of the left stroke; the right stroke of *ẓadi* and final *ẓadi* is an extremely short horizontal which joins the top of the left stroke; the same applies to the inner stroke of *shin*. Transferred to the typeface of the printing press, this script, like the square, lost much of its beauty (figure 18; 18th century). Although only a shadow of its former self, it is still a pleasing hand. The usual, but incorrect, designation for it is "Rashi script," obviously because *Rashi's commentaries on the Bible and Talmud – the books which everybody was constantly handling from boyhood to old age – were printed in (Sephardic) mashait. Rashi himself, naturally, wrote in Ẓarphatic (see below).

Provencal Sephardic Type

For a long time this type did not differ from the Iberian type. Figure 19 (13th century) is a very plain hand. *Alef*, more often than not, has the cursive form. Figure 20 (15th century) is a beautiful hand. Figure 21 (18th century) is far inferior, but its mashait character is more pronounced than in the Sephardic type of figure 18.

Yevanic Type

The 13th century Yevanic mashait is a very plain hand (figure 22). *Alef* consists of a lower main part and an upper one, the lower combines the lower halves of the former left stroke with the former main stroke, resulting in a circumflex; the former right stroke and the upper part of the former left stroke remain separate; the downstroke, both of *dalet* and *he*, finally turns rightward. Figure 23 (15th century) is a more formal script but much less elaborate than contemporaneous Sephardic. In contrast with the latter, the horizontals play a very big role. *Dalet* and *zayin* have the same characteristics as in figure 22; the inner stroke of *shin* is short and joined to the middle of the left one.

Italkian Type

The first specimen of Italkian mashait (figure 24; c. 11th century) shows a very regular and pleasing hand, which, however, is not yet calligraphically developed. The left downstroke of *he* still issues from the top bar; *shin* is practically triangular, and the middle stroke is short and does not reach the line bottom; the frequent expression "he said" is always rendered by an abbreviation; the left stroke of *alef* and the left top stroke of the *mem* are omitted. In the 14th century a highly calligraphic style was reached. The horizontals dominate the picture in the way they do in the square, and a number of letters have the same structure, although their appearance is very different indeed – cf., for instance, the *mems* or *nuns* of the two styles occurring in the specimen (figure 25). There are practically no straight strokes; everything is curved. About a century later (figure 26) the difference between the thick horizontals and thin downstrokes is even greater. The latter have become thinner, longer, and straighter, and all the letters have a strong leftward slant. The downstrokes of the long letters are shallow S-curves, rather thick in the middle. Figure 27 shows the contemporaneous typeface. The designer evidently wished to avoid extremes.

Ẓarphatic Type

The Ẓarphatic forms of 12th-century mashait (figure 28) are clearly distinct from those of the contemporaneous cursive: not only are they very carefully written but they differ in many details. The right part of *alef* is at the line ceiling; the top part of *kof* is a horizontal line – only the merest trace of the downstroke is left. The fully developed calligraphic hand begins in the 13th century. Most downstrokes are shallow S-waves, thickened in the middle (figure 29; 14th century). Neither horizontals nor verticals dominate the picture. The distance between the letters is reduced to a minimum; very often they actually touch. *Shin* has a wide horizontal base. By the 15th century, only traces of this calligraphic style (figure 30) survived.

Ashkenazic Type

The differences between the 13th-century Ashkenazic mashait of figure 31 and the almost contemporaneous Ẓarphatic of figure 28 appear to be due only to the individualities of the scribes. Further research is needed to establish when the divergence between the two types became pronounced. It seems that the full development of the calligraphic style was reached in Ashkenazic very slightly later than in Ẓarphatic and that, like there, it was soon simplified (figure 32), surviving only as a display script (figure 32, top and bottom). The plain style is the basis of the typeface (figure 33).

Southern Karaitic Type

The 16th-century Southern Karaitic type of figure 34 is pleasant to the eye. There is not much difference between the thick and the thin strokes. The opposite may be said of the Yevano-Karaitic specimen (figure 35; 16th century).

[Solomon Asher Birnbaum]

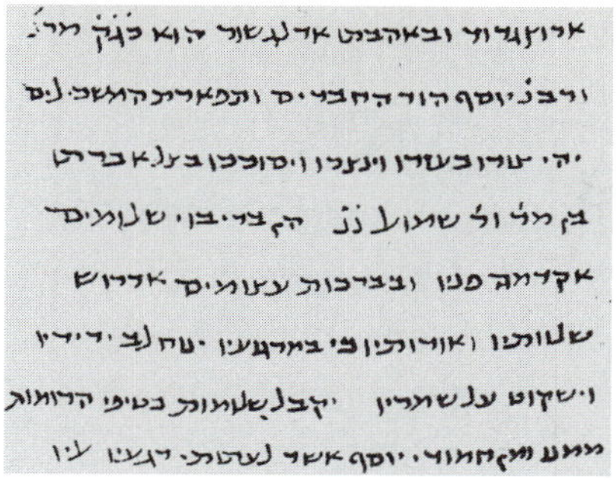

1

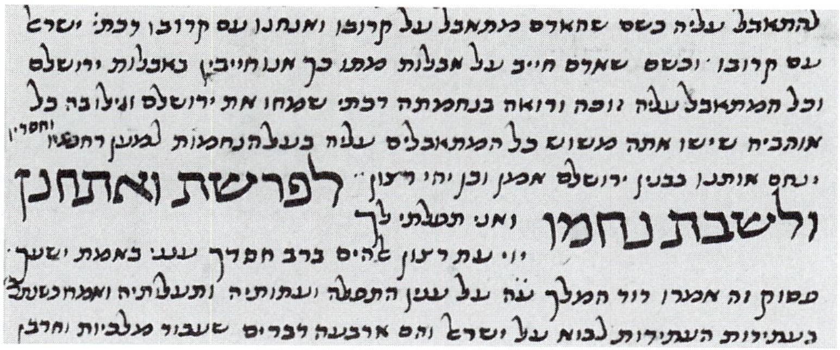

2

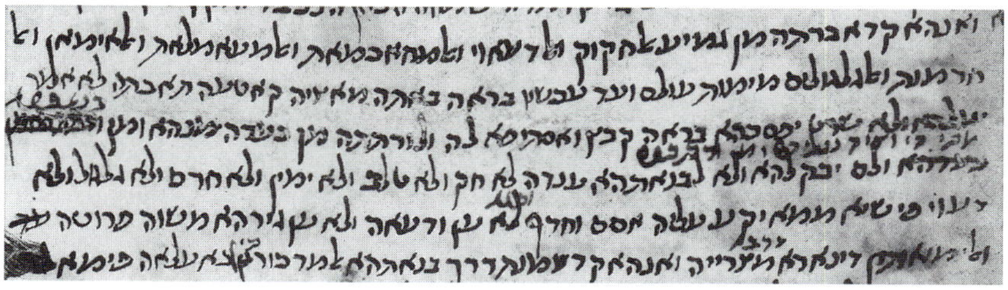

3

MASHAIT SCRIPT

Figure 1. Excerpt from letter in Palestine-Syria mashait script, 1094 C.E. Cambridge University Library, T-S. 20, 141.

Figure 2. Palestine-Syria mashait script, 1443. Hamburg, Staatsund Universitaetsbibliothek, Cod. heb. 56, fol. 32v.

Figure 3. Deposition by a witness in Egyptian mashait script, 1218. Cambridge University Library, T-S. 13. J. 3. 27b.

Figure 4. Part of Tanḥum Yerushalmi's commentary on Ecclesiastes in Egyptian mashait script, 1326. London, British Museum, Ms. Or. 5063, fol. 142a.

Figure 5. Babylonian mashait script, end of tenth century C.E. Cambridge University Library, T-S. 13. J. 25/5.

Figure 6. Modern Babylonian mashait script. London, S.A. Birnbaum Collection.

Figure 7. Grammatical treatise in Parsic mashait script, 1312 C.E. Letchworth, Sassoon Collection, 1065, p. 72.

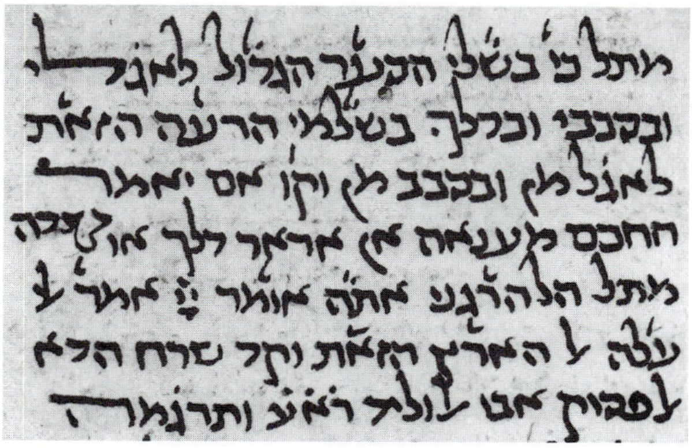

4

7

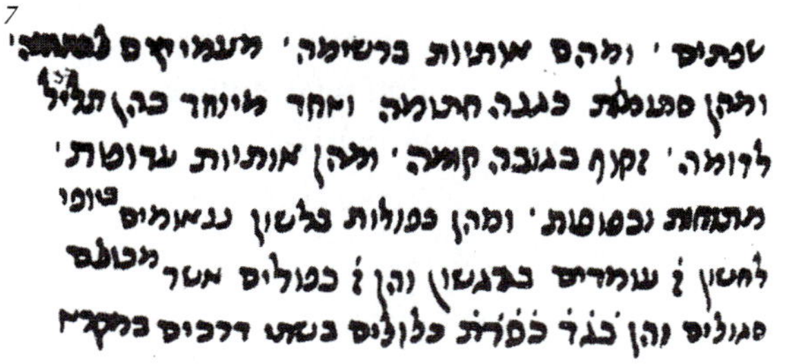

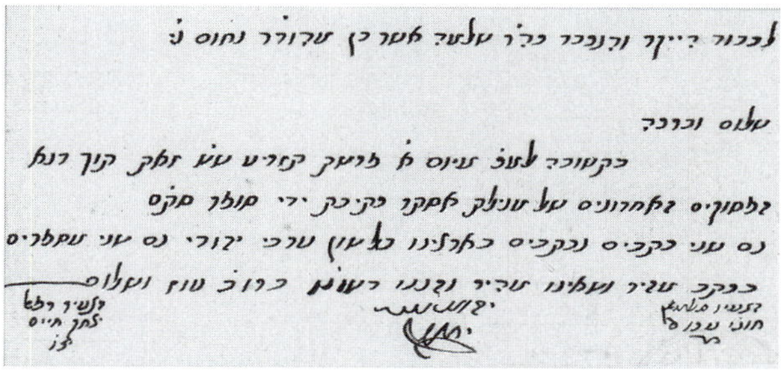

6

5

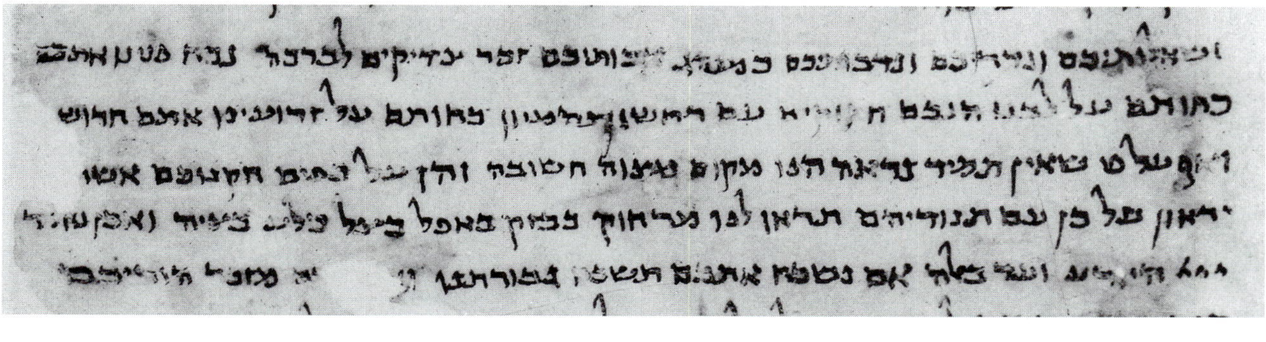

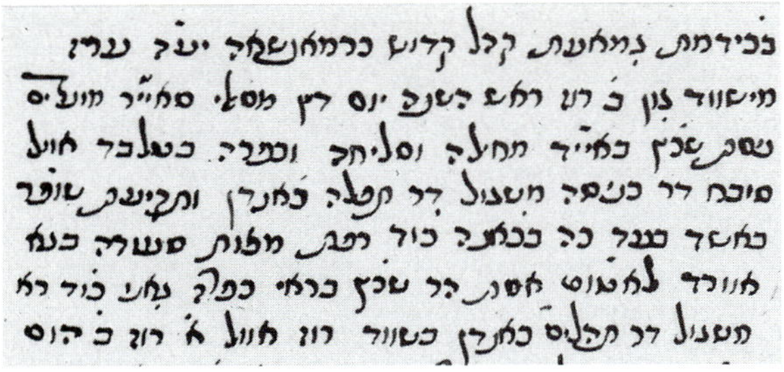

9

Figure 8. Excerpt from Shahin Shirazi's Judeo-Persian paraphrase of the Pentateuch in Parsic mashait script, 1702. London, British Museum, Ms. Or. 4742, fol. 342b.

Figure 9. The Parsic mashait script of today. London, S.A. Birnbaum Collection.

Figure 10. Temanic mashait script used in a copy of Maimonides' commentary on the Mishnah, 1222 C.E.

Figure 11. Temanic mashait script as used in the Maḥberet attijan*, 1490. London, British Museum, Ms. Or. 2349.*

Figure 12. A maḥzor *of 1674 in Temanic mashait script. London, British Museum, Ms. Or. 1479, fol. 72b.*

Figure 13. Colophon in Maaravic mashait script, 1364 C.E. Cambridge University Library, Ms. D.d. 11. 22, fol. 80b.

Figure 14. Extract from a maḥzor *in Maaravic mashait script, 1401. Paris Bibliothèque Nationale, Ms. héb. 657, fol. 81b.*

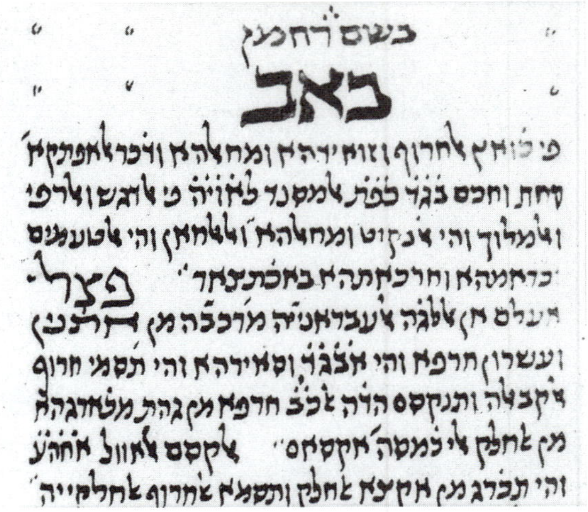

11

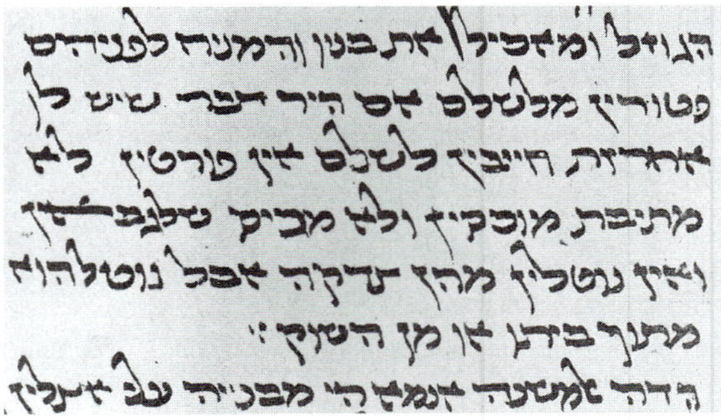

10

14

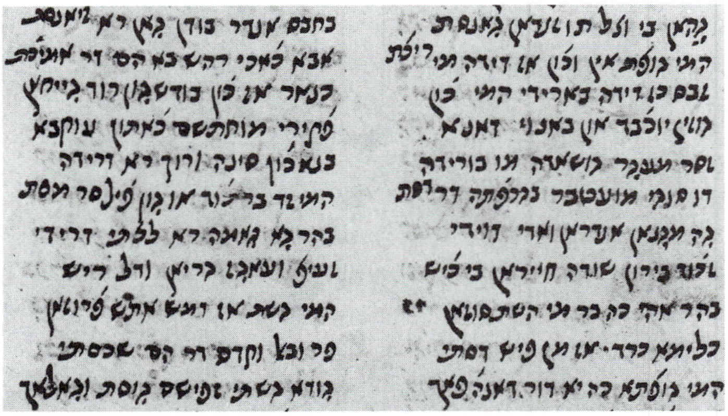

8

12

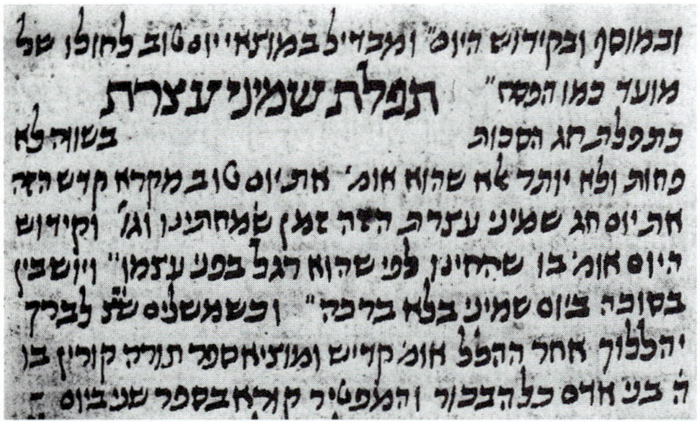

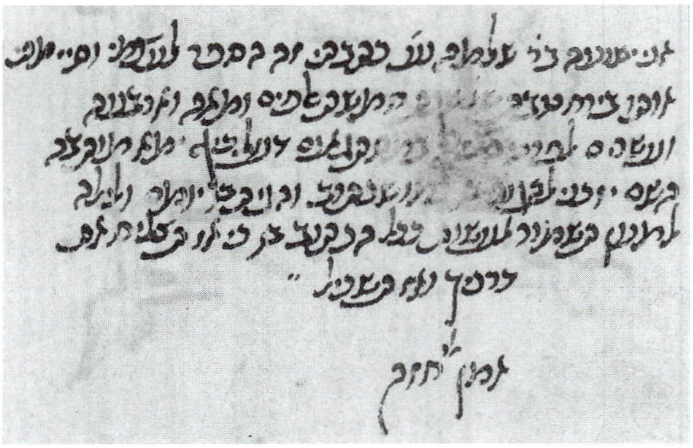

13

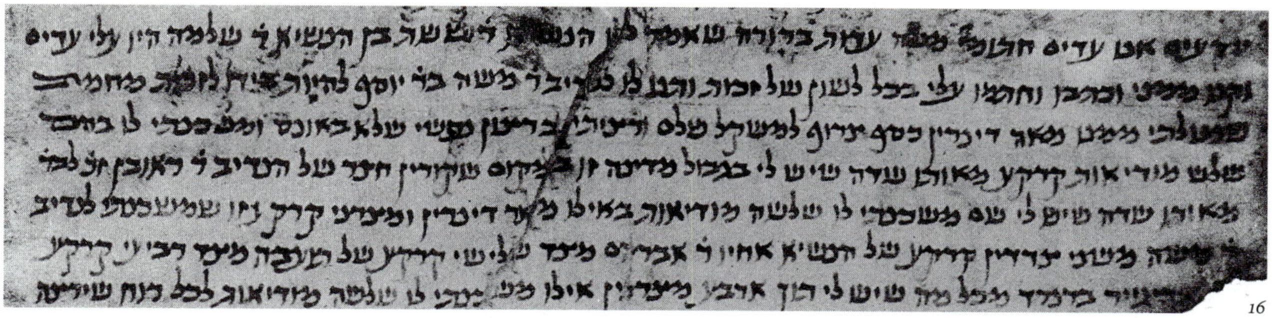

16

17

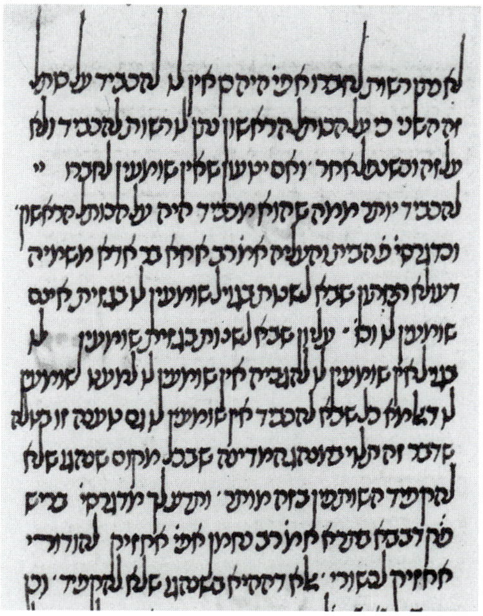

20

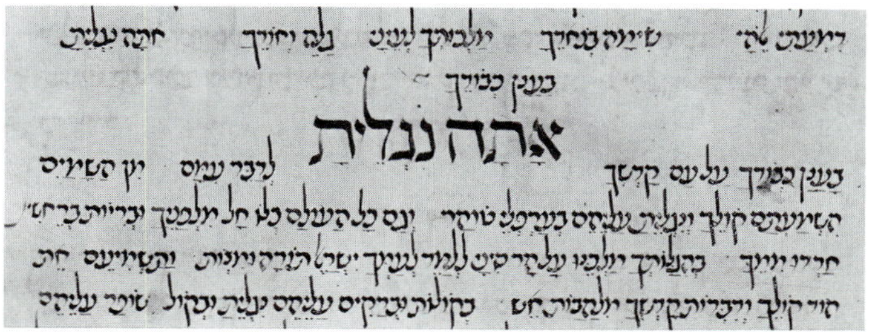

Figure 15. Maaravic mashait script from a maḥzor *of 1769. New York, Jewish Theological Seminary, Adler 2306, fol. 99a.*

Figure 16. Deposition by a witness in Sephardic mashait script, 1096 C.E. Barcelona Cathedral Library.

Figure 17. Responsa of 1417 in Sephardic mashait script. Cambridge University Library, Ms. Add. 499, fol. 324v.

Figure 18. Marriage deed printed in Sephardic mashait script, London, British Museum, Ms. Or. 7951.

Figure 19. Grammatical treatise in Provençal Sephardic mashait script, 1264 c.e. Madrid, Biblioteca Nacional, Ms. 5660, fol. 195a.

Figure 20. Maḥzor *of 1453 in Provençal Sephardic mashait script. Paris, Bibliothèque Nationale, Ms. 2235, héb. 735, fol. 13r.*

19

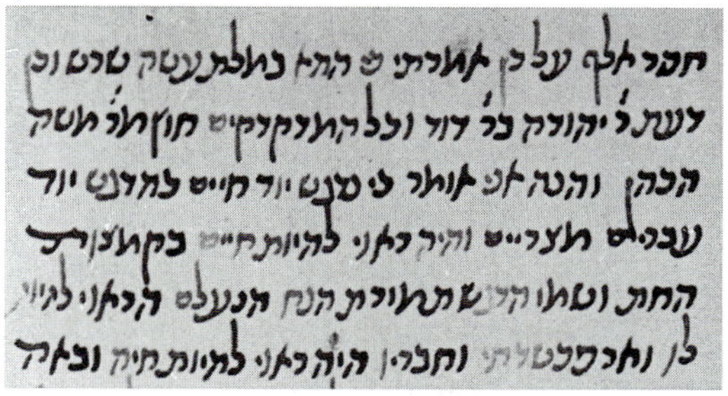

18

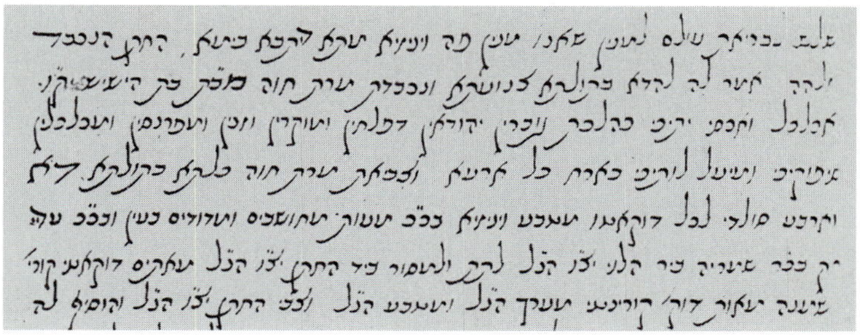

15

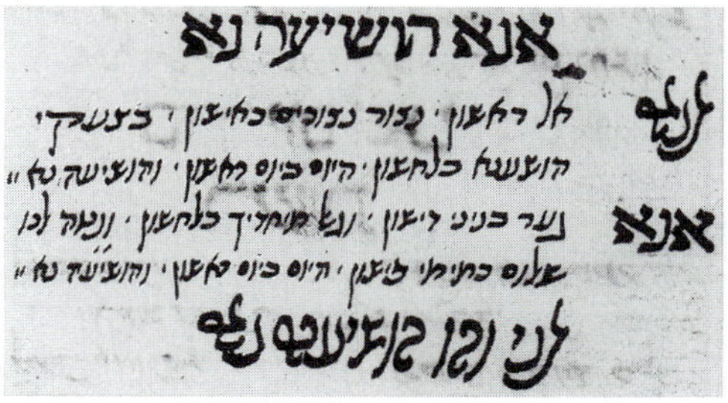

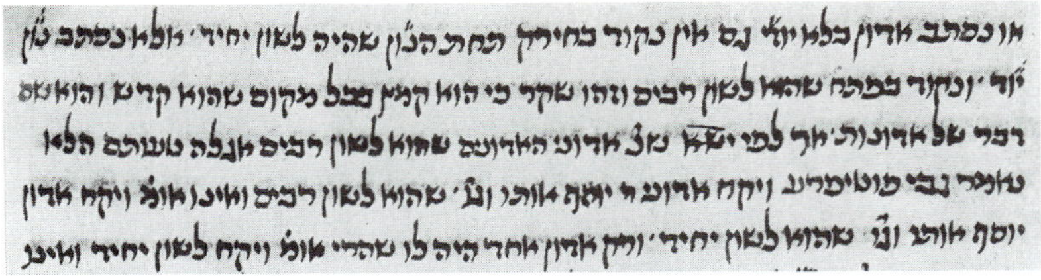

23

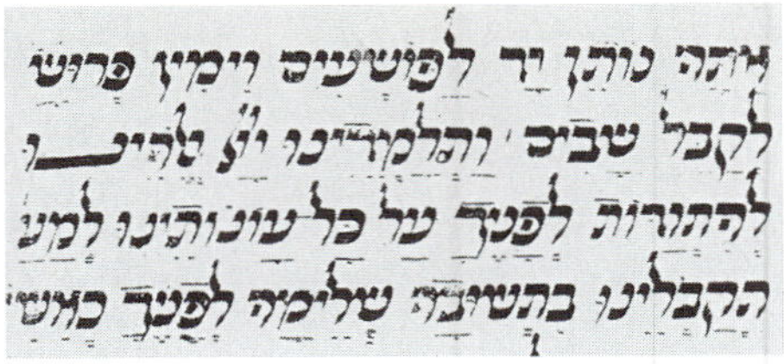

26

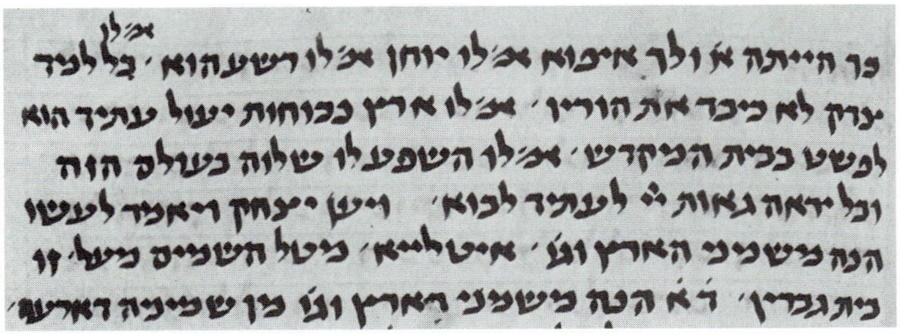

24

Figure 21. Maḥzor *of 1713 in Provençal Sephardic mashait script. New York, Jewish Theological Seminary, Ms. Adler 1938, fol. 72a.*

Figure 22. Excerpt from Abraham Ibn Ezra's astrological treatise, Reshit Ḥokhmah, *in Yevanic mashait script, 1267. Oxford Bodleian Library, Ms. Opp. Add 40. 160, fol. 37r.*

Figure 23. Excerpt from Yom Tov Lipmann Muelhausen's Sefer Niẓẓaḥon *in Yevanic mashait script, 1459. Bibliothèque Nationale, Ms. 2235, héb. 735, fol. 13r.*

Figure 24. An 11th-century copy of the Midrash Genesis Rabbah *in Italkian mashait script. London, British Museum, Ms. Add. 27169, fol. 184a.*

Figure 25. Italian translation of a hymn, written in Hebrew Italkian mashait script, 1383. London, British Museum, Ms. Or. 2433, fol. 78b.

Figure 26. Maḥzor *in Italkian mashait script, 1466. London, British Museum, Ms. Harl. 5686, fol. 177a.*

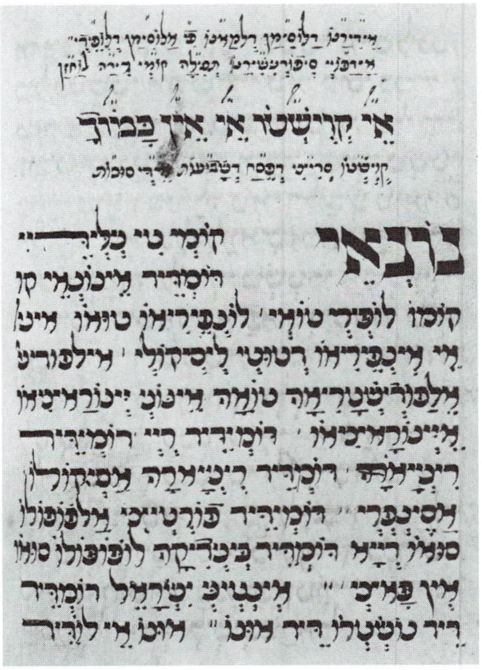

25

21

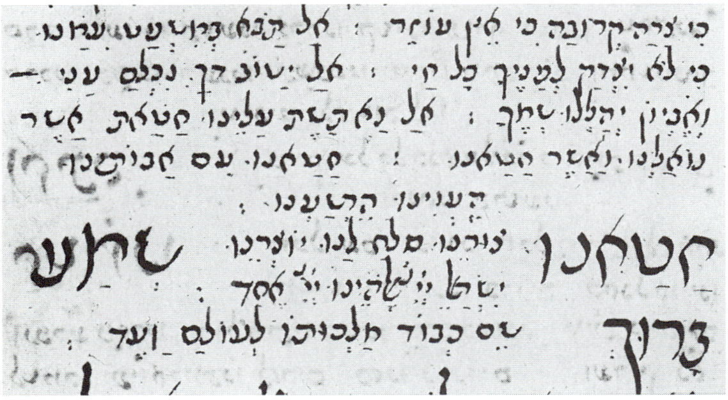

22

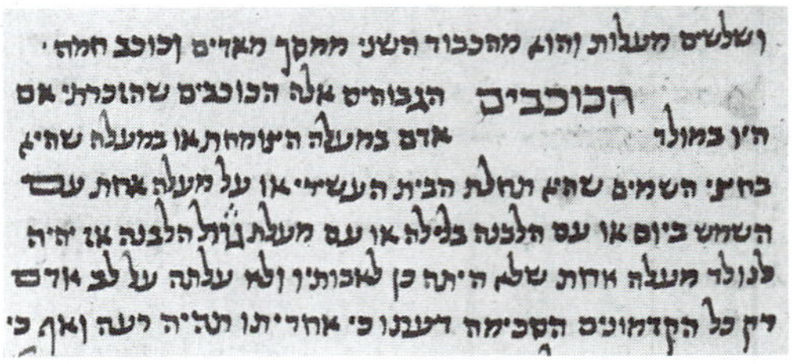

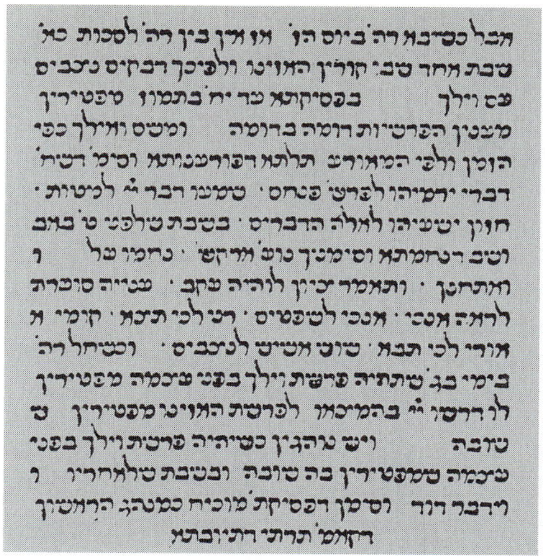

27

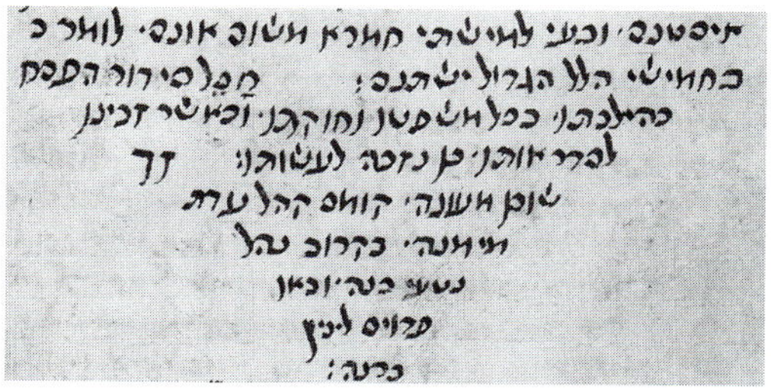

28

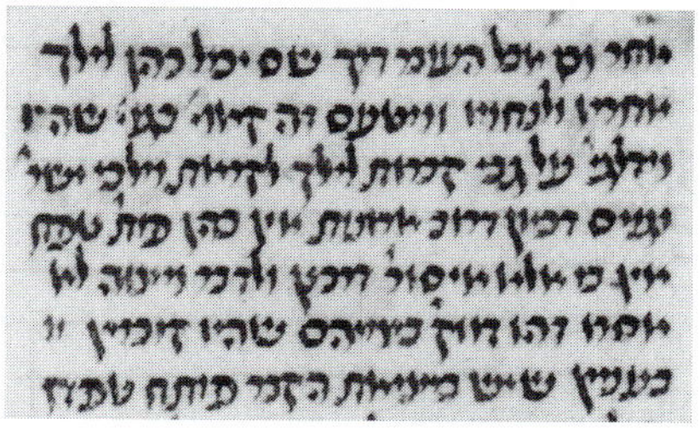

30

Figure 27. Excerpts from a book printed in Italkian mashait script, 1476.

Figure 28. A liturgical poem in Ẓarphatic mashait script, c. late 12th century. Paris Bibliothèque Nationale, Ms. 2235, héb. 635, fol. 12v.

Figure 29. Commentary on the Rosh Ha-Shanah liturgy in Ẓarphatic mashait script. 1301 C.E.

Figure 30. Ẓarphatic mashait script, 1429. Hamburg, Staats- und Universitaetsbibliothek, Cod. hebr. 244, fol.111v.

Figure 31. Ashkenazic mashait script, 1220. Cambridge University Library, Ms. Add. 667.1, fol. 24a.

Figure 32. Extract from Isaac Dueren's Issur ve-Hetter *in Ashkenazic mashait script, 1477, Hamburg, Staats- und Universitaetsbibliothek, Cod. Scrin. 132, fol. 63a.*

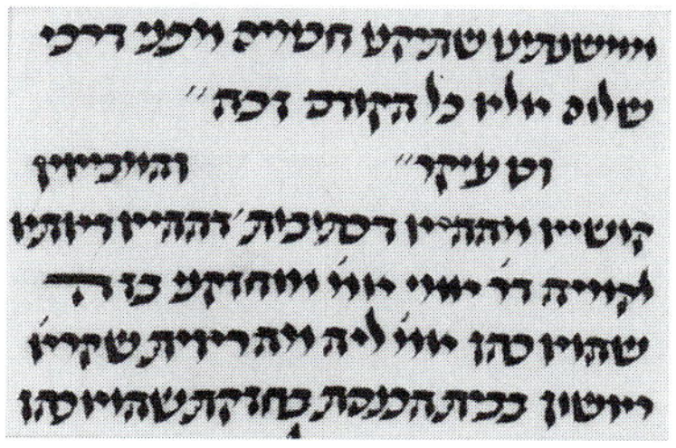

31

29

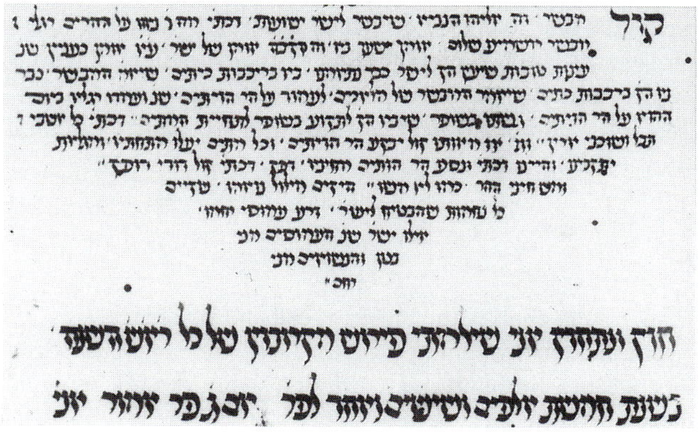

32

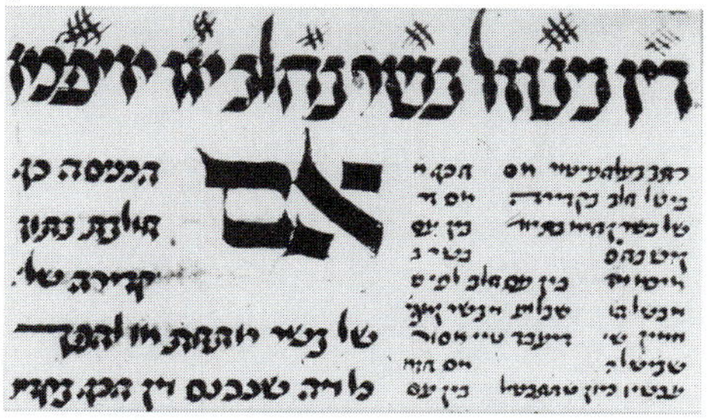

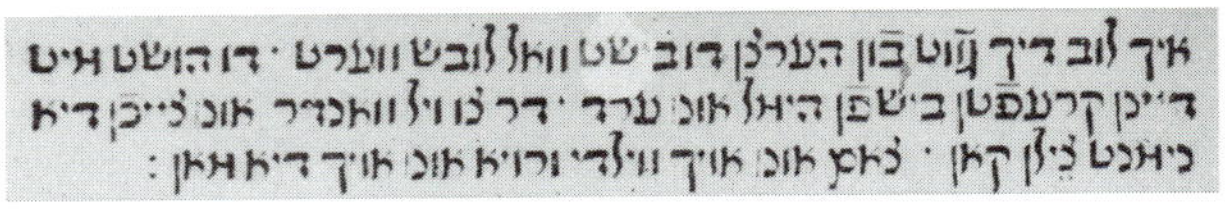

Figure 33. Ashkenazic mashait script in a book printed in Yiddish, 1543.

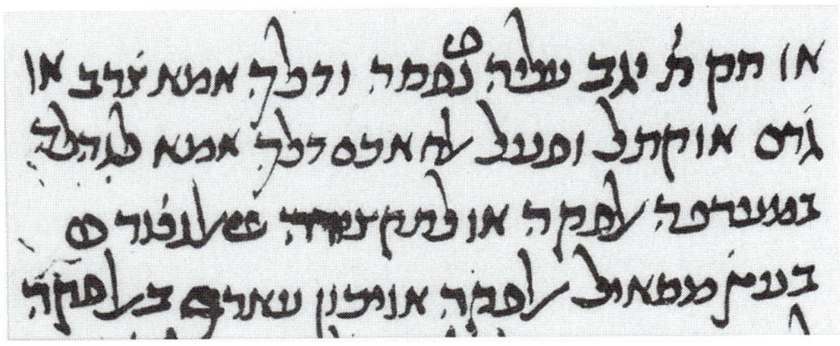

Figure 34. A manuscript of 1520 in Southern Karaitic mashait script. London, British Museum, Ms. Or. 2406.

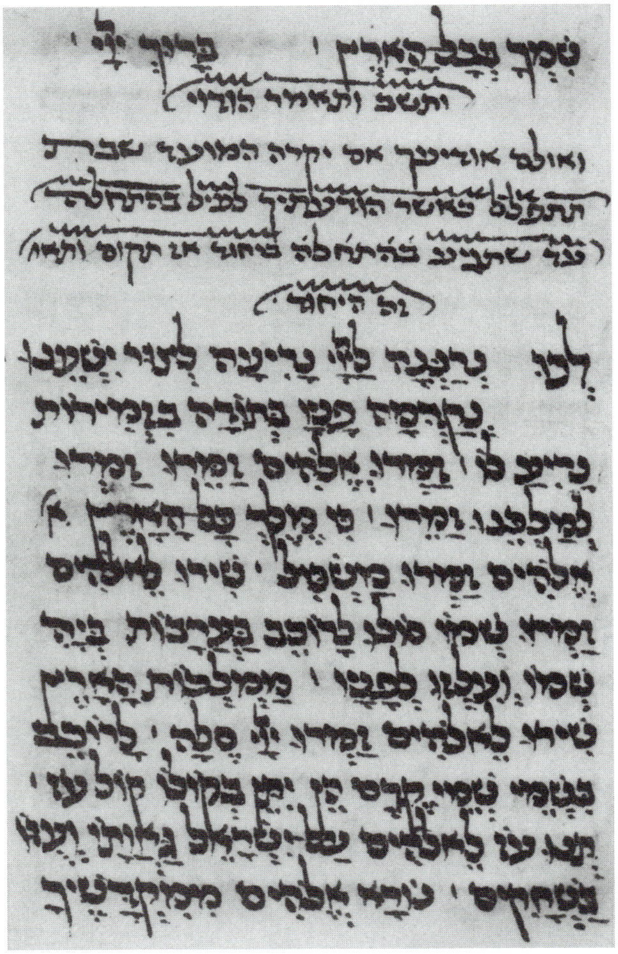

Figure 35. Extract from a prayer book in Yevano-Karaitic mashait script, 1525. London, British Museum, Ms. Or. 1104, fol. 60a.

LETTERS USED AS NUMBERS

Although in some early Hebrew inscriptions (such as the Samarian ostraca) there appear certain symbols which may be taken as numerals, in general letters of the alphabet were used as numerical signs. This usage is not biblical. It may have been an imitation of the Greek custom; the first traces of it are found on Hasmonean coins (c. 135 B.C.E.) The letters from *alef* to *tet* stand for the units in succession; *yod* to *ẓadi* for the tens, and *kof* to *tav* for hundreds (that is, up to 400). In the Talmud the numbers above 400 are formed by compositions (500 = 400 + 100 (ת"ק); 900 = 400 + 400 + 100 (תת"ק), and so on; in later times the final forms of the letters *kaf* ך,

100	ק	19	י"ט	10	י	1	א
200	ר	20	כ	11	י"א	2	ב
300	ש	30	ל	12	י"ב	3	ג
400	ת	40	מ	13	י"ג	4	ד
500	ת"ק / ך	50	נ	14	י"ד	5	ה
600	ת"ר / ם	60	ס	15	ט"ו	6	ו
700	ת"ש / ן	70	ע	16	ט"ז	7	ז
800	ת"ת / ף	80	פ	17	י"ז	8	ח
900	תת"ק / ץ	90	צ	18	י"ח	9	ט

mem ם, *nun* ן, *pe* ף, and *ẓadi* ץ were not infrequently used for 500, 600, 700, 800, 900). The thousands are represented by the same letters as the units, but are generally followed by a kind of apostrophe (or two dots are placed above them: 5727 = ה' תשכ"ז). Numbers above ten are expressed by a combination of letters, those denoting the higher numbers being placed toward the right (e.g., 182 = קפ"ב). In an indication of the date of the year, the letter representing the thousands is generally omitted (5727 = תשכ"ז). The numbers 15 and 16 are not denoted by the letter י"ה and י"ו (since these combinations represent the abbreviated form of the Tetragrammaton): instead, the combinations ט"ו ("nine and six") and ט"ז ("nine and seven") are used.

[David Diringer]

BRAILLE

This system enables the blind to read and write Hebrew with speed and relative facility. Until the 1930s, each school engaged in educating the blind and in printing Hebrew works in Braille developed its own system of Braille signs. There was no standard system of pointing Hebrew letters and a pupil graduating from a given Jewish school for the blind was unable to read the literature published by another. In 1936, an agreement was concluded among all the institutions engaged in the publication of the Bible, the translation and copying of books into Hebrew, and the writing and editing of material in Hebrew Braille. The agreement called for a uniform method of Hebrew Braille pointing to be adopted by all educational institutions concerned with the needs of blind children, as well as by the cultural centers providing Braille literature in Hebrew for the blind all over the world.

The problem and lack of uniformity in Braille writing existed in all languages and in schools for the blind all over the world. As a result of a UNESCO agreement in 1950, on the occasion of the international meeting on Braille uniformity, and upon the recommendation of the International Hebrew Braille Committee 1936–44, it was decided to adopt a uniform Hebrew alphabet in all countries and languages. According to this system, there are signs for the following characters: (1) all the Hebrew letters (with the exception of the end forms); (2) punctuation signs; (3) mathematical signs (numbers and notation); (4) all the Hebrew vocalization signs (the signs always follow the letter to which they belong); (5) signs for chemistry and physics; (6) signs for musical notes. Errors can be erased by straightening the embossed dots with the aid of a special implement or by passing six consecutive dots over the error. There are four institutions in the world engaged in the printing and publication of the Bible and books in Hebrew Braille: (1) the Jewish Braille Institute of America, New York; (2) the Israel Ministry of Education and Culture, Department of Special Education; (3) the Central Library for the Blind, Netanyah, Israel; and (4) the Jewish Institute for the Blind, Jerusalem.

[Zvi Hermann Federbush]

MANUAL (DEAF)

In Europe and America finger spelling as a means of communication between the deaf has been accepted for decades. Latin finger spelling is not identical for all languages which use the Latin alphabet. In all systems of Latin finger spelling one principle determines the position of the fingers: the similarity of the position to the shape of the written letter. This principle aids in learning and memorizing finger spelling. This is also the reason that the finger spelling of many letters is identical in the systems used for the different languages written in the Latin alphabet. The need for finger spelling depends directly on the cultural needs of the deaf in his society. Hebrew finger spelling probably was not developed sooner because the intellectual level of the deaf in Israel, now average, was low 35 years ago. During the second decade of the existence of the State of Israel, educational and instructional activities for children and adults in the community of the deaf were greatly expanded. Even though only a small percentage of the members of the Association of the Deaf and Mute in Israel draws its information from reading, this group continues to grow. They express a readiness to learn writing and finger spelling in the clubs for the deaf which exist in several centers in the country. This is especially true of Helen Keller House in Tel Aviv, the national center for the deaf.

Hebrew Finger Spelling

In 1968 a system of Hebrew finger spelling was published by Jonathan Shunary, a teacher of the deaf. The system was developed according to the following principles.

(1) Thirteen of the 22 letters in the Hebrew alphabet are expressed by accepted positions for the Latin alphabet as established by the World Federation of the Deaf (the International Manual Alphabet). However, almost all of the positions adapted for Hebrew finger spelling represent sounds different from those used in the International Manual Alphabet. This was done to keep to the principle of making the position of the hand as similar as possible to the intended letter. This was important to make it easier to learn the system and to spread its use quickly among the deaf in Israel. The letters *y*, *l*, *m*, and *n*, are expressed as in the International Alphabet, since it is possible to associate these to the Hebrew letters. The letter *a* was given the numerical value of one, and the letter *b* the numerical value of two. For several letters the position suggests a word beginning with that letter (Heb. דֶּבֶק, *devek*, "*glue*"; Heb. קַרְנַיִים, *karnayim*, "horns"), or symbolizes the position of the mouth during the articulation of the letter: for *h* the mouth is opened wide so the sign is a scratching palm, *s* is pronounced with a strong burst of air and so the fist is closed.

(2) Three letters representing consonants not used in the Hebrew language are included in the Hebrew system. This is necessary for foreign names, place names, names of people active in international politics, science, sport, cinema, etc. The sign for *ğ* (pronounced like the *g* in English "gin") is a reversed *g* with the fingers pointing down; the sign for *ž* (pronounced like the *j* in the French word "*jour*," or *s* in the English word "leisure") is a reversed *z*; and that for *c* (pronounced like the *ch* in the word "church") is a reversed *c*.

(3) The system makes it possible to represent vowels which are not written in Hebrew as letters. (a) Every consonant followed by an *a* vowel can be expressed by moving the palm being used to the right. (b) *e* vowels are expressed by moving the palm being used downward. (c) *i* vowels are expressed by a slight twist of the palm being used. The letter *vav* thus serves to indicate two vowels, *o* and *u*, just as it does in written Hebrew. (d) *o* vowels are expressed by pointing the thumb up.

(e) the *u* vowel is expressed by pointing the thumb to the left and moving it in that direction.

Just as many signs are expressed while simultaneously employing the mouth or without sound, so there are those who use a combination of finger spelling and this type of speech. In this case the lips are used to express the vowels and the finger spelling is made simpler.

[Jonathan Shunary]

SHORTHAND

The first attempts at evolving shorthand were made in the 19th century. In 1866, for example, Max Gondos adapted the Gebelsberger German method to Hebrew. Other attempts were made by Wilhelm Lerfler, Dr. Hedrich, and L. Kutz. In 1918 Lenis tried to evolve a system of Hebrew shorthand. The reason for the late appearance of Hebrew shorthand ties into the fact that Hebrew was not utilized as a living language until the 1880s. The need became pressing after World War I when Hebrew was recognized as one of the official languages of Palestine and began to be used in courts of law and for administrative purposes. Although it was widely believed that there was no need for Hebrew shorthand, since the Hebrew spelling omits a considerable number of vowels, this view proved unfounded and it was discovered that ordinary writing could not keep up with the speed of speech. Methods were invented after World War I by (1) Ben Yisrael Zulman (1919); (2) D. Tames (1921); (3) Mrs. P. Shargorodska (1926); and (4) J. Maimon (1929).

Of all these methods, Maimon's proved the most successful and popular among Hebrew shorthand writers. He began to evolve his method in 1924, basing it on the international shorthand system invented by General Felix von Konovsky. However, he also took into consideration the sounds and grammatical problems peculiar to the Hebrew language. He accordingly introduced amendments into the shortening of syllables and vowels and also invented special ideographs for Hebrew words. After working for several years on improvements, he published his first textbook of Hebrew shorthand in 1929; in 1932 he produced a guide called *Elef Kizzurei Millim* ("One Thousand Ideographs"). Maimon decided that Hebrew shorthand must be liberated from the traditions of the normal Hebrew lettering and be independent of it. He therefore established that Hebrew shorthand should be written from left to right, unlike the square Hebrew lettering, since this movement is easier for the right hand, as in Latin characters, and that Hebrew shorthand should also represent the vowels, as in Latin characters, and not omit them, as in previous methods. He explained that in Hebrew, vowels often serve as important aids to recognition of a word, and that if the vowel of the first syllable is represented it would be possible, in many cases, to shorten the word without reducing the possibility of deciphering it. Furthermore, according to his method (and in accordance with international practice) the vowel signs in shorthand can serve as links between the consonant signs. Other systems have also been propounded: e.g., by Ḥ. Bar-Kama and H. and R. Shtadlan, who trained a considerable number of students and won a certain amount of popularity among Hebrew shorthand writers.

[Jacob Maimon]

BIBLIOGRAPHY: NORTH-WEST SEMITIC: S.A. Birnbaum, *The Hebrew Scripts*, 2 vols. (1954–57); G.R. Driver, *Semitic Writing, from Pictograph to Alphabet* (1954²); Avigad, in: *Scripta Hierosolymitana*, 4 (1958), 56–87; Cross, in: *The Bible and the Ancient Near East, Essays in Honor of W.F. Albright* (1961), 133–202; Cross, in: BASOR, 165 (1962), 34–42; 168 (1962), 18–23; I.J. Gelb, *A Study of Writing* (1965²); W.F. Albright, *The Proto-Sinaitic Inscriptions and their Decipherment* (1966); Cross, in: *Eretz-Israel*, 8 (1967), 8*–24*; D. Diringer, *The Alphabet, a Key to the History of Mankind*, 2 vols. (1968³); J.B. Peskham, *The Development of the Late Phoenician Scripts* (1968); J.D. Purvis, *The Samaritan Pentateuch and the Origin of the Samaritan Sect* (1968). MASHAIT SCRIPT: W. Wright, *Facsimiles of Manuscripts and Inscriptions* (*Oriental Series*; 1875–83); C.D. Ginsburg, *A Series of 15 Facsimiles…* (1897); P. Kahle, *Masoreten des Ostens* (1913); E. Tisserant, *Specimina Codicum Orientalium* (1914); C. Bernheimer, *Catalogue des manuscrits et livres rares hébraïques de la Bibliothèque du Talmud Tora de Livourne* (1914); idem, *Paleografia Ebraica* (It., 1924), 1–34; *Catalogue of Hebrew Manuscripts… of E.N. Adler* (1921); A.Z. Schwarz, *Die hebraeischen Handschriften der Nationalbibliothek in Wien* (1925); P. Kahle, *Masoreten des Westens* (1927); idem, *Die hebraeischen Bibelhandschriften aus Babylonien* (1928) = ZAW, 46 (1928), 113–37 and tables; D.S. Sassoon, *Ohel Dawid*, 2 vols. (Eng., 1932); S.A. Birnbaum, *The Qumrân (Dead Sea) Scrolls and Palaeography* (1952). BRAILLE: C.N. Mackenzie, *World Braille Usage* (1954), 109–12; G. Kronfeld, *Braille Ivri* (1956); E. Katz, *Ha-Braille ha-Ivri* (1957).

ALPHABET, HEBREW, IN MIDRASH, TALMUD, AND KABBALAH. The rabbis ascribed special sanctity to the letters of the Hebrew *alphabet. The Psalmist's declaration that "By the word of God were the heavens made" (Ps. 33:6) was taken to indicate the power of the letters, which form the "Word" of God. Bezalel succeeded in the construction of the tabernacle because he "knew how to combine the letters by which the heavens and earth were created" (Ber. 55a). These divine letters cannot be destroyed, and even when the material tablets were broken by Moses, the letters flew upward (Pes. 87b). Similarly when R. Ḥananiah b. Teradyon was wrapped in the Scroll of the Law and burnt by the Romans, he exclaimed, "the parchment is burning but the letters are soaring on high" (Av. Zar. 18a). The alphabet played a role in the creation of the world. *Bet* was chosen as the proper letter with which to begin the creation since it is also the initial letter of the word *berakhah* ("blessing"). Furthermore, the letter *bet* had other desirable features. "Just as the *bet* is closed on all sides and open in front, so we have no right to inquire what is below, what is above, what is back, but only from the day that the world was created and thereafter" (Gen. R. 1:10). The claim of the letter *alef* was also acted upon favorably. It was finally placed at the beginning of the Ten Commandments. Another reason given for creation with a *bet* was to "teach that there are two worlds since *bet* has the numerical value of two" (*ibid.*). The Talmud related that this world was created with the letter *he* and the future world with the letter *yod*, both letters forming one of the names of God (Men. 29b). Every letter in the alphabet is granted symbolic meaning by the Talmud. Thus, for example, "*alef bet* means to learn wisdom (*alef binah*) while *gimmel dalet* means to show kindness to the poor (*gemal dallim*)" (Shab. 104a). Even the way the letters are written has significance. R. Ashi declares, "I have observed that scribes who are most particular add a vertical stroke to the roof of the letter *ḥet*." This stroke signifies that "He lives in the height of the world" since the *ḥet* is the initial letter of the word *Ḥai*, "He lives." The stroke above the letter indicates that the abode of the living God is on high. The addition of a letter from God's name to a person's name is indicative of Divine guidance and protection. Thus God placed a letter from his name, the *vav*, on Cain's forehead (Gen. 4:15; PdRE 21). Abram's name was changed to Abraham by the addition of the letter *he* (Gen. 17:5; Gen. R. 39:11). The *yod* which the Lord took from Sarai when her name was changed to Sarah complained to the Almighty that, "Because I am the smallest of all letters, Thou hast withdrawn me from the name of the righteous woman." God finally appeased the *yod* by utilizing it when Hoshea's name was changed to Joshua by addition of this letter (Gen. 17:15; Num. 13:16; Gen. R. 47:1). The total number of letters in the alphabet, 22, is also given significance. The wicked King Ahab merited royalty for 22 years "because he honored the Torah which was given in 22 letters," by refusing to surrender it to Ben-Hadad, king of Aram (Sanh. 102b). Great significance is given to those psalms which are alphabetically arranged (in 119 and 145), as are the first four chapters of Lamentations. Of the latter, R. Johanan declares that they were smitten by this alphabetical dirge, "because they violated the Torah, which was given by means of the alphabet" (Sanh. 103b). Halakhic exegesis also derives important laws from superfluous or missing letters in the bible and even from the flourishes and other graphic peculiarities.

[Aaron Rothkoff]

In Jewish Mysticism

The early mystical literature of the Jews, composed soon after the Talmud was concluded, dealt extensively with the symbolism and secret meaning of the alphabet. Apart from the special mystical alphabets such as the *Otiyyot de-Rabbi Akiva* (c. 700) and the alphabet of *Ben Sira (*Alphabetum Siracidis*, c. 700), attention was devoted to the secret meaning of the letters. The most noteworthy works are the *Sefer *Yeẓirah*, the *Heikhalot* writings, the *Pirkei de-Rabbi Eliezer*, the *Sefer Temunah, *Shi'ur Komah, Ḥarba de-Moshe, Sefer ha-Yashar*, the *Book of *Razi'el* and the *Book of *Bahir*. The important role that mystical symbolism of letters plays in these writings is already partly evident from their alphabetical structure and shape. The belief that the alphabet has mystical significance is based on the idea that the 22 letters of the alphabet are spiritual essences which came into being as emanations from God. The Talmud had already stated that God created heaven and earth with the help of the alphabet (Ber. 55a), and the idea that the 22 letters as spiritual states were the basis of creation recurs throughout mystical literature (*Sefer Yeẓirah*, 2:2; 5:22; *Zohar*, 1:3; 2:152; *Zohar Ḥadash*, Ruth; Moses Cordovero, *Shi'ur Komah*, 8; *Yal. Reub.*, Gen., and elsewhere).

The Letters As Spiritual and Material Structures

The letters, as written in the Torah, are reflections of the heavenly letters. Their relation to each other is like that of the male and female which attain fulfillment only in union (*Zohar*, 2:228; cf. 3:220). This characteristic is also expressed in the shape of the letters: *alef* is male, *bet* female, *gimmel* is again male, *dalet* female, and so forth (*Zohar Ḥadash*, Ruth). The form of the letters is not accidental; they are "spiritual essences whose external shape corresponds to their internal essence." The spiritual counterpart of each letter derives from the individual **Sefirot*; thus, for instance, *alef* comes from *Keter* ("Crown"), *bet* from *Ḥokhmah* ("Wisdom"), *gimmel* from *Binah* ("understanding") and so on (M. Cordovero, *Pardes Rimmonim*, 27:2; *Sefer ha-Temunah*, the end of *alef*). When a person pronounces or uses letters of the alphabet, it awakens the spiritual essence contained in them and "sacred forms" come into being which rise and unite with their origins, the heavenly letters, "which are the sources of emanation"; there they become subtle and incorporeal, similar to what they were before they took on a definite material shape in man's mouth (Cordovero, op. cit., 27:2; 9:3; 15:3; idem, *Shi'ur Komah*, 53; idem, *Elimah* (Ms.), 132; *Sefer ha-*Kanah*, 24; *Dov Baer of Mezhirech, *Or ha-Emet*, 12; idem, *Maggid Devarav le-Ya'akov*, 28). The whole doctrine of the spiritual, supernatural character of the letters seems to have originated under the influence of the Pythagorean theory of numbers.

The Letters of the Torah and Prayers

The letters "are the apparel of the Torah, woven from all the colors of the light, white, red, green, and black" (foreword to *Tikkunei Zohar*). An individual section of the Torah, composed of verses, is as "the soul for its physical members [the verses]" and in the same manner as the words draw their vitality from the verses so do the letters from the words: the one is the soul of the other and the apparel of the one is that of the other (*Pardes Rimmonim*, 21:5). This explains the particular sanctity of the scroll of the Torah and of the act of writing it (*ibid.*, 27:2; 20:1). The writing of a letter constitutes the material stage, its pronunciation, the spiritual stage, and its transition from oral pronunciation to thought is the third stage. Hence the special sanctity of prayer performed with purity and fervor, for it transforms the letters of the prayer into spiritual substances which rise, toward their heavenly origins (Cordovero, *Shi'ur Komah*, 19).

The Sequence of the Alphabet

Alef as the first letter encompasses all the others: "*Alef* is their primary source and they all draw from it." The remaining letters are organized in three groups, each consisting of seven letters: *bet, gimmel, dalet, he, vav, zayin, ḥet* "are the mystery of the rule of Grace," *tet, yod, kaf, lamed, mem, nun, samekh* "that of the rule of Mercy," and *ayin, pe, ẓaddik, kof, resh, shin, tav* "that of the rule of Strict Justice" (*Pardes Rimmonim*, 27:21).

Final Letters

The five final letters, which in the Talmud were stated to have been instituted by the Prophets (Shab. 104a), according to the Zohar were originally preserved by God, together with the "primordial light," for a better future; only Adam knew them. After the Fall they were hidden from him too, until Abraham through inspiration came to know them. Abraham bestowed the knowledge of the final letters on Isaac, he, on Jacob, and the latter, on Joseph. After Joseph's death, during the period of servitude in Egypt, they were eventually forgotten. The knowledge was regained when Israel received the Torah "and apprehended them in their essence," but after the worship of the golden calf they were lost to the people. Only Moses, Joshua, and the 70 elders still knew them. They brought the knowledge with them to Ereẓ Israel and there they were again revealed in the Song of Songs to the whole people and added to the other 22 letters of the alphabet (*Zohar Ḥadash*, Ruth). When Moses ascended Mount Sinai he found God designing crowns for the individual letters (Shab. 89a). These are the crown-shaped flourishes which point to the ten *Sefirot* (*Sefer ha-Peli'ah*, 73) and represent the life-principle (*nefesh*) of the letters (Vital, *Eẓ Ḥayyim*, 1:5, 9). The vowels are the *neshamah* ("soul") and *ru'aḥ* ("spirit") of the letters, which emanated from the *Sefirah Ḥokhmah* ("Wisdom"; *Pardes Rimmonim*, 9:5; 28:6; *Tikkunei ha-Zohar*, 5). The cantillation accents evolved from the *Sefirah Keter* ("Crown") (otherwise *ibid*., = Tikkunei Zohar *Pardes Rimmonim* 29:5). Each *ẓeruf* ("combination of letters") has its special purpose, and is based on a particular mystical idea. The doctrine of the combination of letters is already found in talmudic literature. In esoteric literature this doctrine is further elaborated, first in *Sefer Yeẓirah* and subsequently in numerous commentaries on it, in particular that of Shabbetai *Donnolo (tenth century). Through the linking together of letters it is possible "to call into existence new creatures" and the *amora* Rava tried to create a man in this manner (*Pardes Rimmonim*, 8:4; *David b. Solomon ibn Abi Zimra, *Magen David*, introduction; Rashi to Sanh. 65b). The doctrine of combination of letters regarding the Divine name was derived from the doctrine of *ẓeruf* (Abraham Abulafia in his letter to R. Solomon; cf. *Sefer ha-Bahir*). The entire kabbalistic literature abounds in speculations about the alphabet, but the following writings deal particularly with this subject: *Sefer Barukh she-Amar* (1804); N. Bachrach, *Emek ha-Melekh* (1648), chapter *Sha'ashu'ei ha-Melekh*; Elijah ha-Kohen, *Midrash Talpiyyot* (1736), s.v. *Otiyyot; Isaac ha-Levi, Otiyyot de-Rabbi Yiẓḥak* (1801).

[Samuel Abba Horodezky]

BIBLIOGRAPHY: Judah Leib b. Joseph Ozer, *Einei Ari* (1900); S.A. Horodezky, *Kivshono shel Olam* (1950), 29–47; E. Lipiner, *Geshikhte fun a Fargetert Ksav* (1956); idem, *Oysyes Dertseylen…* (1941).

°ALPHONSE OF POITIERS (1220–1271), brother of Louis IX (Saint Louis) of France. His jurisdiction extended over *Poitou, Saintonge, and Auvergne, and areas including Agenais, Quercy, and the *Comtat-Venaissin, i.e., almost one-third of present-day France. Alphonse treated the Jewish inhabitants in his domains with arbitrary harshness. In July 1249, he decreed the expulsion of the Jews of Poitou. The order was apparently not implemented, unless for a short period. In October 1268 he ordered the wholesale arrest of the Jews in his territories, and seizure of their movable property to finance his departure on a crusade. He subsequently fixed the tax liability of the Jews in his domain at 8,000 livres for the communities in Poitou, 6,000 for Saintonge, 2,000 for Auvergne, and 3,500 for Toulouse. In July 1269 Alphonse compelled the Jews to wear the Jewish *badge; those who failed to comply had to pay the heavy fine of ten livres. In July 1271, during Alphonse's absence, his "vice administrators" (*vices gerentes*), claiming his authorization, expelled the Jews of Moissac.

BIBLIOGRAPHY: A. Molinier (ed.), *Alfonse de Poitiers, Correspondance Administrative*, 2 vols. (1894–1900); P.F. Fournier and P. Guébin (eds.), *Alfonse de Poitiers, Enquêtes Administratives* (1959), includes bibliography; Nahon, in: REJ, 125 (1966), 167–211.

[Bernhard Blumenkranz]